FILM REVIEW ANNUAL

2000

Films of 1999

FILM

REVIEW

ANNUAL

2000

Films of 1999

Film Review Publications
JEROME S. OZER, PUBLISHER

Editor: Jerome S. Ozer
Associate Editor: Richard Zlotowitz

ISBN 0-89198-154-3
ISSN 0737-9080

Manufactured in the United States of America

Jerome S. Ozer, Publisher
340 Tenafly Road
Englewood, NJ 07631

TABLE OF CONTENTS

PREFACE

FILM REVIEWS   1

CONTENTS   iii

PREFACE

The FILM REVIEW ANNUAL provides, in a convenient format, a single reference volume covering important reviews—*in their entirety*—of full-length films released in major markets in the United States during the course of the year.

The format of the FILM REVIEW ANNUAL has been kept as clear and simple as possible. Films are reviewed in alphabetical order by title. Following each film title, we provide production information, cast and crew listings, the running time, and the MPAA rating. The reviews for each film are arranged alphabetically by publication. Each review is identified by the name of the publication, the date of the review, the page number, and the name of the reviewer. After the last review of a film, there is an *Also reviewed* section which lists other publications in which the film was reviewed. Because of restrictions in obtaining permission, we were unable to include reviews from certain publications. However, we felt that users of the FILM REVIEW ANNUAL should have help in gaining access to those reviews. Therefore, we included the *Also reviewed* section.

At the end of the FILM REVIEW ANNUAL, we provided full listings of the major film awards, including the nominees as well as the winners.

There are eight Indexes in the FILM REVIEW ANNUAL: Cast, Producers, Directors, Screenwriters, Cinematographers, Editors, Music, and Production Crew.

We have not attempted to force a single editorial style upon the reviews for the sake of achieving consistency. The reader will readily recognize that some reviews were written under deadline pressure and that others were prepared in a more leisurely and reflective style. Some reviews were written to help the moviegoer determine whether or not to see the film. Other reviews assumed the reader had already seen the film and was interested in getting another point of view. We believe this diversity of purposes and styles is one of the major strengths of the FILM REVIEW ANNUAL.

Because of our respect for the integrity of the writers' styles, we made changes from the original only where absolutely necessary. These changes were confined to typographical errors in the original review and errors in the spelling of names. When the reviewer made a reference to another film, we inserted the name of that film. Otherwise the reviews remain as written. British spelling used in English publications has been kept.

We have tried to make the FILM REVIEW ANNUAL pleasurable to read as well as useful for scholars and students of film, communications, social and cultural history, sociology, and also for film enthusiasts. We, the editors, would appreciate your suggestions about how we might make subsequent editions of the FILM REVIEW ANNUAL even more useful.

FILM REVIEWS

ACID HOUSE, THE

A Zeitgeist Films release of a FilmFour presentation of a Picture Palace North/Umbrella Productions in association with the Scottish Arts Council National Lottery Fund, the Glasgow Film Fund and the Yorkshire Media Production Agency. *Producer:* David Muir and Alex Usborne. *Director:* Paul McGuigan. *Screenplay (based on short stories from his book "The Acid House"; in Scottish dialect with English subtitles):* Irvine Welsh. *Director of Photography:* Alasdair Walker. *Editor:* Andrew Hulme. *Sound:* Alan Brereton and Brian Howell. *Production Designer:* Richard Bridgland and Mike Gunn. *Art Director:* Rohan Banyard and Jean Kerr. *Costumes:* Tait and Lynn Aitken. *Make-up:* Marilyn MacDonald and Sarah Fidelo. *Running time:* 112 minutes. *MPAA Rating:* Not Rated.

CAST: THE GRANTON STAR CAUSE: Stephen McCole (Boab); Maurice Roeves (God); Garry Sweeney (Kev); Jenny McCrindle (Evelyn); Simon Weir (Tambo); Iain Andrew (Grant); Irvine Welsh (Parkie); Pat Stanton (Barman); Alex Howden (Boab Sr.); Ann Louise Ross (Doreen); Dennis O'Connor (PC Cochrane); John Gardner (Sgt. Morrison); William Blair, Gary McCormack, and Malcolm Shields (Workmates); Stewart Preston (Rafferty); A SOFT TOUCH: Kevin McKidd (Johnny); Michelle Gomez (Catriona); Tam Dean Burn (Alec); Gary McCormack (Larry); Scott Imrie (Pool Player); Niall Greig Fulton (Alan); William Blair (Deek); Cas Harkins (Skanko); Maurice Roëves (Drunk); Morgan Simpson (Chantel, Baby); Marnie Kidd (Chantel, Toddler); Alison Peebles (Mother); Joanne Riley (Diana); Srah Gudgeon (New Girl); Katie Echlin (Wendy); William "Giggs" McGuigan (Pub Singer); THE ACID HOUSE: Ewen Bremner (Coco); Martin Clunes (Rory); Jemma Redgrave (Jenny); Arlene Cockburn (Kirsty); Jane Stabler (Emma); Maurice Roëves (Priest); Doug Eadie (Coco's Father); Andrea McKenna (Coco's Mother); Billy McElhaney (Felix the Paramedic); Ricky Callan (Tam the Driver); Barbara Rafferty (Dr. Callaghan); Stephen Docherty (Nurse Boyd); Ronnie McCann (Andy); Cas Harkins (Skanko).

LOS ANGELES TIMES, 8/13/99, Calendar/p. 16, John Anderson

[*The following review by John Anderson appeared in a slightly different form in* **NEWSDAY, 8/6/99, Part II/p. B12.**]

This month's issue of an insistently hip downtown New York publication includes a story on Scots novelist Irvine Welsh, suggesting that after the success of "Trainspotting" he had a decision to make: Embrace popular culture, or make his work more hard-core.

All you can say is: Hello?

What else—after the junkies, baby death and general squalor of "Trainspotting"—was Welsh going to do? Do a punk version of "Mary Poppins"? Naturally, he had to step it up. It's not an artistic decision—well, it could be. But it's certainly good business as well.

The most recent result of this "maverick" move by author-screenwriter Welsh is "The Acid House," a virulent but thoroughly entertaining trilogy of tales about the besieged lower classes of Edinburgh, ripe with vulgarity, self-loathing, violence and economic disorder. Subtitled—mercifully—in English, its frankness is alarming, its stories are brutal, its humor is purely from the gallows.

The first story, "The Granton Star Cause," examines the sundry woes of Boab (Stephen McCole), who, on the same day he's kicked off the Granton Star football team, fired from his job, ditched by his girlfriend for sexual incompetence and asked by his parents to move out, meets God (Maurice Roeves). In a bar. "You're just like me," the disgusted deity tells him. "A dirty, lazy, slovenly expletive." He turns into a fly, by which Boab gets his revenge on the world.

The second, "A Soft Touch," has as its title character Johnny (Kevin McKidd), who marries a woman of questionable character, raises their baby single-handedly (well, maybe it's theirs), gets beaten up by the wife (Michelle Gomez) and her boyfriend (Gary McCormack) and by the end of the story hasn't learned a thing at all.

The third is "The Acid House," which proves that while LSD might not have enlightened the masses, it gave filmmakers an excuse to ham it up. Summoning up all the technique of his music video days (he's done work for Britain's Channel 4), debuting feature director Paul McGuigan tells the story of Coco Bryce (Ewen Bremner of "Trainspotting"), who during a particularly harrowing acid trip switches brains with a newborn baby—a grotesque little tyke who finds joys in breast-feeding most infants have never known. Meanwhile, the adult-size Coco, now with a baby brain, lolls about a hospital, as his girlfriend (Arlene Cockburn) still tries to rope him into marriage.

"The Acid House" easily the funniest of the three stories, probably the sickest and, despite what they write in certain magazine articles, the wisest career choice in the bunch.

NEW YORK POST, 8/6/99, p. 50, Jonathan Foreman

A derivative, would-be rock'n' roll romp that trips over its own skanky hipness, "The Acid House" is a three-part film adapted by "Trainspotting" author Irvine Welsh from his own short stories.

It depicts a similarly scuzzy, druggy world inhabited by lumpen, thuggish Scot project dwellers, but it lacks the humanity and consistently humorous tone—and the top-notch acting—that made the movie of "Trainspotting" so enjoyable.

All three stories are noisy, obscenity-filled tales of bleak degradation, intermittently leavened with dark humor, but lacking a single sympathetic character.

In the first story, lazy 23-year-old Boab (Stephen McCole) is dropped from his soccer team, kicked out by his parents, fired from his job, dumped by his girlfriend and beaten up by the cops for vandalizing a telephone booth—all in the space of a few hours. Nursing his wounds, he goes to a pub and meets God (Maurice Roeves), who tells him that Nietzsche was wrong: "I'm not dead. I just don't give a f---" before turning Boab into a fly.

As an insect, Boab proceeds to take revenge on the people who've wronged him by poisoning their food until he's killed by his mother in the midst of an (explicit) S&M sex session.

In the second story, "The Soft Touch," Johnny (Kevin McKidd) marries vicious slut Catriona (Michelle Gomez), who is pregnant by one of her other lovers. Once they move in together, she abandons the baby, turns tricks and then takes up with Larry (Garry McCormack), the thieving bully who lives upstairs. This is the only story without a supernatural or surreal element; it also goes nowhere.

The third story is a basically a knockoff of "Big," except that this time an LSD-dropping soccer hooligan (Ewen Bremner) switches bodies with the newborn baby of an earnest middle-class couple (Martin Clunes and Jemma Redgrave).

As a foul-mouthed animatronic infant, the hooligan soon undermines the marriage of the tots' parents, while the real baby, reduced to a semi-vegetable by an apparent overdose, gets manipulated into an engagement by the ruffian's girlfriend Kirsty (Arlene Cockburn).

Documentary director Paul McGuigan's MTV-style visual tricks, while recalling "Trainspotting" and "Lock Stock & Two Smoking Barrels," have a stale, trying-too-hard quality.

SIGHT AND SOUND, 1/99, p. 40, Xan Brooks

A portmanteau film of three tales from present-day Scotland.

"The Granton Star Cause" finds lad-about-town Boab dropped from his local football team, dumped by girlfriend Evelyn, sacked from his job and thrown out of home by his long-suffering parents. After vandalising a phone box, Boab is held in a police cell and beaten up by the cops. Drinking at a local pub, he is confronted by God in the guise of a hard drinker. God accuses him of wasting his life and turns him into a fly. In his new guise he gets revenge on all those who rejected him until he is swatted dead by his mother.

"A Soft Touch" focuses on the trials of pliant Johnny, whose wife Catriona takes to cheating on him with Larry, the boorish lout who lives upstairs. Larry uses the electricity from Johnny's flat and beats him up when he protests. When Catriona becomes pregnant, Larry dumps her. Johnny takes her back.

In the last tale, "The Acid House", rave-kid Coco drops acid and switches personalities with Tom, a new baby born to middle-class Rory and Jenny. Coco is thus regarded as brain-damaged, and Tom as a precocious, if foul-mouthed, wonderkid. Coco and Tom finally encounter each other in the pub and swap back to their rightful identities.

By the simple law of averages you're bound to like at least some portion of a portmanteau or multi-story film. If one tale doesn't interest you, rest assured there's another one on the way. You can appreciate them in isolation or speculate on their possibly interrelated nature.

What links the three stories of *The Acid House* is Irvine Welsh. The *Trainspotting* author's scabrous wit, rave aesthetic and skewed world view run through each tale. For added familiarity, *Trainspotting* graduates (the actors Kevin McKidd and Ewen Bremner) crop up in parts two and three respectively.

The sniffy line on Welsh is that he is a one-book wonder, yet the three stories here (culled from his short-story collection of the same name) at least display a semi-fresh diversity. "The Granton Star Cause" is Kafka's *Metamorphosis* set on a Scottish housing scheme while 'A Soft Touch' is a kind of social-realist Special Brew opera. 'The Acid House', the concluding part of the triptych, is both the most ambitious and the least satisfying. Tilting at a kind of record-deck aesthetic, this loops and scratches its dialogue like a dance remix set in celluloid. In it, Welsh audaciously marries the revelations of an LSD trip to the trauma of birth, and sex (Coco entering his girlfriend) with labour (Tom exiting his mother). But its fascinating strands are finally too undigested. In the event, 'The Acid House' ends up wallowing for way too long in its central hallucination segment. It is also too close to *Look Who's Talking* for comfort.

Debut director Paul McGuigan has gone from stills photography to television documentary work (on programmes as varied as *Walk on the Wild Side* and *The Dani Behr Show)* and this multi-discipline pedigree serves him well. Originally the producers envisioned their film helmed by three different directors, yet (at least until that garbled final chapter) McGuigan moves beautifully with the shifting landscape of Welsh's tales.

On the absurdist, flight-of-fancy first part his style is jaggedly cartoonish, switching into grainy camcorder footage for the insect's point of view. For the next tale he adopts a more formal, less showy approach in keeping with the subtle, naturalistic mood and one that effectively hands the floor to McKidd's startlingly strong performance as the emasculated Johnny. Although McGuigan claims never to have seen *Trainspotting,* occasionally sequences seem like direct allusions. The grotesque baby puppet from 'The Acid House' calls to mind the ceiling-crawling sprog in Renton's bedroom, while the opening sequence of 'The Granton Star Cause' (characters introduced in freeze frame at a football match) looks like a copy of the first moments of Danny Boyle's picture.

It should be stressed, though, that *The Acid House* is not another *Trainspotting*. It lacks its pin-up inhabitants, its easy dash, its mainstream handling of charged material. McGuigan's fractured film is altogether smaller, edgier, darker and more in tune with the grimy, hit-and-miss panache of Welsh's prose. It chooses a life that is all its own.

VILLAGE VOICE, 8/10/99, p. 68, Jessica Winter

In Irvine Welsh's "The Granton Star Cause," one of three short stories from his collection *The Acid House* adapted for this film trilogy, a laddie loses his job after his boss takes a training course called "Positively Managing the Redundancy Scenario." The movie itself faces this challenge: like Welsh's more celebrated novel *Trainspotting,* it focuses on the static, dissipated lives of the Scottish bottom-rung classes, where despair is numbed by drugs, petty crime, and "fitba." But *Trainspotting* didn't wallow in its native misery; an air of bemused detachment enabled the movie to see how the impotent rage borne of class barriers and squandered potential begets not only violence and self-medication but also fierce humor and—sometimes—decisive, life-altering action.

In *The Acid House* (subtitled for American release), misery only begets more misery: meandering lives don't stray from their crooked circular path, and nobody changes. There's so little leavening humor here, and so much physical and emotional violence visited upon the already abject, that the film seems as pointless as the wasted lives it purports to examine. In "The Granton Star Cause," a lazy yob loses everything he has and then meets God, who turns him into a fly. The title story's football hooligan (Ewen Bremner, who played Spud in *Trainspotting*) takes too much LSD and switches bodies with an infant. "A Soft Touch" is the only installment unencumbered by fatuous supernatural devices: a sap marries his pregnant girlfriend, who then leaves him with the baby while she screws the neighbor upstairs. (The gull is played by Kevin McKidd, also from *Trainspotting;* these familiar faces inspire more unflattering comparisons to the earlier film.)

A major problem may be that Welsh wrote the screenplay for *The Acid House* himself. For all his scatological realism and contempt for sentimentality, Welsh has a tendency toward moralism in the exacting way he hands out comeuppances. The film of *Trainspotting* avoided this pitfall through ironic distance and sheer speed, but *The Acid House* never escapes its own redundancy scenario. Like its characters, it's defeated by sloth and precedent, and going nowhere slowly.

Also reviewed in:
NEW YORK TIMES, 8/6/99, p. E14, Stephen Holden
VARIETY, 6/15-21/98, p. 102, Brendan Kelly

ADVENTURES OF ELMO IN GROUCHLAND, THE

A Columbia Pictures release of a Jim Henson presentation of a Children's Television Workshop production. *Executive Producer:* Brian Henson, Stephanie Allain, and Martin G. Baker. *Producer:* Alex Rockwell and Marjorie Kalins. *Director:* Gary Halvorson. *Screenplay:* Mitchell Kriegman and Joseph Mazzarino. *Story:* Michael Kriegman. *Director of Photography:* Alan Caso. *Editor:* Alan Baumgarten. *Music:* John Debney. *Music Editor:* George E. Martin. *Choreographer:* Miranda Garrison. *Sound:* Carl S. Rudisill and (music) John Kurlander. *Sound Editor:* Louis L. Edemann. *Production Designer:* Alan Cassie. *Art Director:* William G. Davis. *Set Designer:* Christopher Scott Baker, Helen Williams, and Alan Hook. *Set Decorator:* James E. Ferrell, Jr. *Special Effects:* Michael A. Schorr. *Costumes:* Polly Smith. *Make-up:* Cecelia M. Veradi. *Muppet Stunt Coordinator:* Fred Buchholz. *Running time:* 90 minutes. *MPAA Rating:* G.

CAST: Mandy Patinkin (Huxley); Vanessa Williams (Queen of Trash); Sonia Manzano (Maria); Roscoe Orman (Gordon); Alison Bartlet-O'Reilly (Gina); Ruth Buzzi (Ruthie); Emilio Delgado (Luis); Loretta Long (Susan); Bob McGrath (Bob); *VOICES:* Kevin Clash (Elmo/ Pestie/Grouch Jailer/Grouch Cab Driver); Fran Brill (Zoe/Pestie/Prairie Dawn); Stephanie D'Abruzzo (Grizzy/Pestie); Dave Goelz (Humongous Chicken); Joseph Mazzarino (Bug); Jerry Nelson (Count/Pestie/Grouch Mayor/Grouch Cop); Carmen Osbahr (Rosita); Martin P. Robinson (Tellie/Pestie); David Rudman (Baby Bear/Caterpillar/Pestie/Collander Stenchman/Ice Cream Customer); Carroll Spinney (Big Bird/Oscar); Steve Whitmire (Ernie/Stuckweed/Football Stenchman/Ice Cream Vendor/Parrot); Frank Oz (Bert/Grover/Cookie Monster).

LOS ANGELES TIMES, 10/1/99, Calendar/p. 16, Gene Seymour

[The following review by Gene Seymour appeared in a slightly different form in
NEWSDAY, 10/1/99, Part II/p. B6.]

When Elmo, by far the cuddliest of "Sesame Street's" monsters, first appears on the big screen, something alarming happens. He becomes, well ... monstrous! On television, you don't mind it when he leaps in your face like a puppy who's glad you finally came home. But when he does the same in this feature-length setting, your first impulse is to duck and cover before you get a face full of red hairball.

Mind you, this is subjective. For everyone who reacts in this fashion, there are dozens of others for whom Elmo can do no wrong. And because of his widespread and, in toy-marketing terms, lucrative, appeal to small children, Elmo gets to carry the ball for the 30-year-old "Sesame Street" franchise. (It would be worth checking the gossip Web sites to find out whether veteran monsters like Grover or Cookie Monster had any resentment over being reduced to background players.)

Whatever the flaws of "The Adventures of Elmo in Grouchland," it would be an indictable offense to prevent the toddler-to-kindergartner closest to you from seeing it. Because this movie likely will for many children be their first, much care has been taken to ensure that the experience will be as painless and as interactive as possible. Old reliables Bert and Ernie have been pressed into service to make those in the audience "help out" with the action and, most important, get them through the scarier moments.

What, after all, could be scarier than losing your best friend? In this case, Elmo's blanket—named, of course, Blanket—somehow slips out of his grasp and flies onto Sesame Street where, after being tugged and torn by Elmo and his almost-best friend Zoe, ends up in Oscar the Grouch's trash can.

If you ever wondered what it was like in that sorry-looking disposal unit, wonder no more. It has a vortex that takes Elmo and Blanket into Grouchland, USA, whose ill-tempered populace writhes under the clammy, greedy thumb of one Mister Huxley (Mandy Patinkin, sporting thick eyebrows and an ingratiatingly campy sneer).

If Huxley sees it, it's his. And that includes Blanket, which (who?) is spirited away to Huxley's far-away hovel. Does that stop Elmo? Does the letter E come before the letter F? Not even the sinister, voluptuous Queen of Trash (Vanessa Williams) can stop our hero from retrieving his buddy.

The movie doesn't entirely forget there are grown-ups in the audience. These are the Muppets, after all. Which means you can count on a smattering of groaner puns and inside jokes related to Broadway shows and blockbuster movies.

Still, if the monsters who run movie studios are going to the trouble of giving "Sesame Street" a big-screen close-up, they could have done much more than make it louder and longer than the average TV episode. There's something threadbare and ramshackle about the design of "Elmo." It looks as if no one bothered to deliver more than the minimum requirement of magic or artistry.

NEW YORK POST, 10/1/99, p. 62, p. 62, Lou Lumenick

The "Adventures of Elmo in Grouchland" won't tickle anyone much above the age of 6. The first full-fledged "Sesame Street" movie in 15 years is a by-the-numbers musical targeted almost entirely at the very young, who turned Elmo into the hottest toy on the market a couple of years ago, and the parents who eventually will buy it for them on video.

In fact, whenever the story gets intense (and it does to a surprising extent for a film aimed at young children), the action is literally paused for some reassuring words from Bert and Ernie, who remind young viewers that with the notable exception of "Titanic," people don't pay to see movies with sad endings.

The story is a variation on "The Wizard of Oz," with Elmo transported to Grouchland via a sort of time-space warp at the hitherto-unseen bottom of Oscar the Grouch's garbage can. nyHe ends up there as the result of a tug-of-war in which he refuses to share his beloved blanket with his friend Zoe.

Of course, the denizens of the trash-strewn Grouchland are utterly uninterested in helping little red Elmo (performed by Muppeteer Kevin Clash) get back his blanket, which has fallen into the clutches of an overly aquisitive bully named Huxley (a broad but amusing Mandy Patinkin), who stamps all his belongings "Mine."

Boasting huge eyebrows, Patinkin gets to sing the best of the movie's unmemorable songs with rhymes of "Atari," "Ferrari" and "Safari"—and to quip that "I fancy myself a singer ... I almost performed in a bus-and-truck tour of 'West Side Story,' but they didn't see me as Maria."

He fares better than Vanessa Williams, who plays the Queen of Trash and looks like a character out of a bus-and-truck tour of "The Wiz," turning up just long enough to sing one number.

An appearance by Kermit the Frog and Miss Piggy would have helped immensely. But Big Bird, Cookie Monster, Count von Count and the others are all on hand—as are "Sesame Street" stalwarts Roscoe Orman, Sonia Manzano and, if you look very quickly, Bob McGrath and Ruth Buzzi.

Adults will find nothing here that hasn't been done better, but "The Adventures of Elmo in Grouchland" should entertain less jaded youngsters.

SIGHT AND SOUND, 7/00, p. 38, Heather Puttock

Sesame Street. Elmo refuses to let his friend Zoe stroke his blanket. They fight over it and it accidentally ends up in Oscar the Grouch's trash can. Elmo goes after it and is taken, by way of a magic funnel, to Grouchland, a country where trash is held in high regard. Huxley, a villain who steals children's toys, snatches Elmo's blanket. Elmo asks the native Grouches for help but they refuse. Secretly, a Grouch called Grizzy tells him that Huxley lives on Mount Pickanose.

The Sesame Street team—Oscar, Big Bird, Zoe, Prairie Dawn, Gina, Bob and Luis—arrive in Grouchland only to be put in prison. After escaping from a cave, Elmo meets Huxley's chief henchman Bug who misdirects him to the Queen of Trash's kingdom. Huxley releases a huge chicken which tries to eat Elmo. Meanwhile, the Sesame Street team persuade their guards to release them.

Elmo bursts into Huxley's castle and grabs his blanket but Huxley traps him in a basket. The Sesame Street team arrive, followed by the Grouches. In the ensuing fracas Elmo is freed from the basket which in turn traps Huxley. The blanket is retrieved by Bug. Huxley asks Bug to return the blanket to him and promises to give back every toy he stole. Bug isn't convinced and gives it to Elmo. Back on Sesame Street Elmo tells Zoe she can borrow his blanket any time.

Produced by the non-profitmaking educational Organisation the Children's Television Workshop, the US television series *Sesame Street* features a cast of humans and puppets who give their preschool viewers lessons in the alphabet and counting. Their second venture into film (the first was *Sesame Street Presents Follow that Bird*), *The Adventures of Elmo in Grouchland* broadens the pedagogical scope by teaching its intended audience of toddlers basic lessons in developing their social skills. To this end, during his travels in the altogether strange Grouchland, the child-like Elmo learns to be more self-aware (at one point, he has a flashback to a time when his selfish behaviour was just as bad as the villain Huxley's) and begins to recognise the importance of such concepts as friendship (his Sesame Street pals rescue him) and sharing (at the film's close, Elmo is happy to lend his blanket to his friend Zoe). The astute script, by Mitchell Kriegman and Joseph Mazzarino, also sticks to the worldview of its pre-school viewers by turning their everyday fears—of the dark, of losing a favourite blanket—into major dramatic events.

The film's relentless lessons in self-affirmation—there seems to be an unstoppable parade of woodland creatures who bolster Elmo's morale through the power of song—may grate with accompanying adult viewers. But the rickety sets and creaky animation are likely to evoke a nostalgic twinge in those who grew up with the show. Although sharing the television series' commitment to pre-school education, *Elmo in Grouchland* sadly lacks the gentle, hippy-like sense of irony which pervaded *Sesame Street* in its 70s heyday. There are a few moments when the spirit of the late Jim Henson (who created *Sesame Streets* muppet residents) winks slyly at the older members of the audience: when Elmo first arrives in Grouchland, he is greeted with a sign declaring "Unwelcome to Grouchland" and soon discovers an Ugly Parlour and best of all—a cinema ad for Sharon Groan in *It Basically Stinks*. Ultimately though, *The Adventures of Elmo in Grouchland* is just like its toddler hero: all wide eyed and innocent and longing to be praised.

Also reviewed in:
CHICAGO TRIBUNE, 10/1/99, Friday/p. N, Monica Eng
NEW YORK TIMES, 10/1/99, p. E24, Anita Gates
VARIETY, 10/4-10/99, p. 85, Joe Leydon
WASHINGTON POST, 10/1/99, p. C5, Rita Kempley

ADVENTURES OF SEBASTIAN COLE, THE

A Paramount Classics release of a Culpan Productions production. *Producer:* Karen Barber and Jasmine Kosovic. *Director:* Tod Williams. *Screenplay:* Tod Williams. *Director of Photography:* John Foster. *Editor:* Affonso Goncalves. *Music:* Lynn Geller. *Sound:* Tom Varga, Tom Efinger, and Robert Fernandez. *Costumes:* Eric Daman. *Running time:* 99 minutes. *MPAA Rating:* R.

CAST: Adrian Grenier (Sebastian); Clark Gregg (Hank/Henrietta); Aleksa Palladino (Mary); Margaret Colin (Joan); John Shea (Hartley); Marni Lustig (Jessica); Joan Copeland (Grandmother); Tom Lacy (Grandfather); Gabriel Macht (Troy); Russel Harper (Wayne); Greg Haberny (Jimmy); Peter McRobbie (Principal).

LOS ANGELES TIMES, 8/6/99, Calendar/p. 20, Kevin Thomas

With quirky charm "The Adventures of Sebastian Cole" chronicles the senior year of high school of an upstate New York youth with many telling moments that don't quite add up to a satisfying whole. Writer-director Tod Williams nonetheless displays considerable promise, and its title role shows newcomer Adrian Grenier to fine advantage.

In an old farmhouse dining room, decorated with a burnished homespun elegance Martha Stewart might envy, an upscale family gathers to celebrate the 1983 high school graduation of its Stanford-bound patrician daughter, Jessica (Marni Lustig). The lively mood of the occasion is swiftly shattered by the announcement of Jessica's stepfather, Hank (Clark Gregg), that he is about to embark upon a sex change that will transform him into Henrietta. Its seismic impact prompts Jessica to dash to Palo Alto, while her mother, Joan (Margaret Colin), heads back to her native England with her 17-year-old son, Sebastian (Grenier), in tow, leaving behind a filing for divorce and a for-sale sign on the house.

Yet, after an apparently desultory summer abroad, Sebastian returns for his senior year, which means moving in with Henrietta as she prepares for surgery. It would seem that when all is said and done, the only relative who ever had time for Sebastian was Hank, including his actual father (John Shea), a hard-working, intensely focused architect with whom Sebastian has had little connection. Sebastian is a cool kid and accepts Hank's ongoing gender transformation, as does the community, to a greater extent than you might imagine. Production notes assert breezily that the film is "just another story of a boy and his dad."

Unfortunately, that's precisely what it's not. When action refocuses on Hank/Henrietta to give some poignancy at the film's climax, the tactic backfires. Emotional impact has to be built up and earned, yet the picture has concentrated primarily on the usual advent of romance and buddy-buddy shenanigans, albeit from a fresher perspective than countless other coming-of-age tales. In short, an opportunity has been lost to grapple with a youth maturing just as his parent is changing gender, an atypical situation, to say the least, for the movies.

The treatment of Hank as a pre-operative transsexual is, in fact, superficial in the utmost. Whereas John Lithgow's Roberta Muldoon in "The World According to Garp" was a completely convincing transsexual, an individual at once brave and humorous, Gregg's Henrietta is merely a granite-jawed macho male in a dress who can pack a mean punch at any detractor. While Gregg's underplayed approach is preferable to easy camp, we have no sense of what's going on inside this individual who, after all, has embarked on a uniquely challenging journey. The only moment of genuine interaction between Sebastian and Henrietta occurs when the teenager finally vents his anger over the timing of his stepparent's announcement, which so effectively blasted the family apart. One does wonder why Hank couldn't have waited just another year or so, when both Sebastian and Jessica would be settled into college. In any event there's scant development in Hank/Henrietta, hormonal or otherwise.

If Williams comes up short as a screenwriter he displays an easy, casual style and a bemused point of view as a director, and apart from the problematic Gregg, he certainly knows how to get the best out of his cast, which includes Aleksa Palladino as Sebastian's down-to-earth yet vulnerable girlfriend. Grenier is impressive in the way he is able to make Sebastian mature before our eyes in a natural, unstudied manner. If "Adventures" leaves you wanting more, it also leaves you wanting to see more of Williams in the future.

NEW YORK POST, 8/6/99, p. 51, Rod Dreher

By simply standing there looking horny and available, newcomer Adrian Grenier is easily the most interesting thing about the subpar and totally forgettable "The Adventures of Sebastian Cole."

In the title role of a bored, vaguely delinquent teenager, Grenier parlays his pouty, pre-Raphaelite looks to maximum advantage, suggesting the smoldering vagabond sensuality of a young Travolta.

He's all sexed up with nowhere to go in Tod Williams' downbeat, early 1980s coming-of-age film. In rural Dutchess County, where the drama is set, they have an extraordinarily liberal standard for what constitutes "adventure."

The most exciting thing that happens is what kicks the movie off. Sebastian's stepfather Hank (Clark Gregg) announces his intention to become a woman.

Sebastian's shattered mother (Margaret Colin) flies home to England with the boy, who, bored and unhappy, returns to New York for his senior year. He moves in with Hank, an extremely ugly transsexual now calling himself Henrietta.

What next? Sebastian has a sexual affair with a girl (Aleksa Palladino). He gets in trouble at school. He smokes a little pot. He gets a lot drunk. He goes to Manhattan one night. He clashes with Henrietta, who tells him to do better in class. And life goes on.

No big whoop. Neither is this slack, aimless movie.

NEWSDAY, 8/6/99, Part II/p. B7, Gene Seymour

It seems like a millennium ago that people were talking about movies replacing novels as vehicles for personal expression. Even novelists themselves strenuously claimed that film was where the next Saul Bellows and Toni Morrison would make their presence felt.

Because it attempts to fulfill such now-quixotic hopes, "The Adventures of Sebastian Cole" merits serious attention. This is personal moviemaking with a vengeance and its ambitions are, so impressive you wish you could give writer-director Tod Williams the benefit of the doubt when, as frequently happens, you're ready to either punch out the film's eponymous hero or throttle him loose of his lethargy.

As played by Adrian Grenier, Sebastian is a prototype of the 1980s "blank generation." His parents are divorced. But despite Sebastian's persistent underachieving in school, his life is still basically tolerable in upstate New York with his emotionally shaky British-born mom (Margaret Colin) and tough-but-tender ex-Marine stepdad, Hank (Clark Gregg).

Then the bottom falls. Big time. Hank announces to the family that he's decided to become a woman. Mom runs back to England with Sebastian in tow. He drifts back home to stay with Hank/Henrietta, who vainly tries to instill some discipline in Sebastian's life. The kid wants none of it, figuring that education is a waste of time for someone like him who wants to be a writer and therefore needs "adventures" more than classes.

These "adventures" turn out to be depressingly mundane. He has a fling with a nice, cute fellow student (Aleksa Palladino), but zones out when she says "I love you." Just for the experience, he drinks himself to within an inch of death-by-poisoning. He makes a nuisance out of himself by riding his bicycle through the high school corridors and bluffing his way through senior year.

All these aimless mishaps are intended to give picaresque heft to this story in the tradition of Huck Finn, Augie March and Jack Kerouac. Yet they end up making the movie feel as emotionally weightless as Sebastian, who is made only barely interesting by Grenier's seedy devilishness. The only moments when the story achieves definition are in the scenes with Sebastian and his stepdad, who, largely through Gregg's grace and warmth, is elevated from quirky plot device to complex hero/heroine.

VILLAGE VOICE, 8/10/99, p. 64, Gary Dauphin

Looking like a bad boy Donny Osmond, the eponymous hero of *The Adventures of Sebastian Cole* is no loser geek, just a boozing teenage underachiever with dreams of being a writer. Set in '80s upstate New York, the movie follows Sebastian through an ambling group of randomly quirky set pieces, and although first time writer-director Tod Williams could have trimmed some self-indulgent, adolescent fat, he does manage to say a few interesting things about growing up smart but affectless.

Sebastian (played with no small measure of blank charm by Adrian Grenier) is already a child of divorce, but his life goes seriously haywire when his aggressively decent stepdad, Hank (Clark

Gregg), announces out of nowhere that he's going in for sex reassignment surgery. Sebastian is freaked out but typically contained ("So. You're gonna have your dick cut off," he mutters into a soda) and when Mom flees to her native England, she leaves Sebastian in the care of the recently rechristened Henrietta. From there Sebastian doesn't fall apart so much as he gets a newfound sense of—and appreciation for—all the ways he doesn't fit in. He wings it through senior year, meets a girl, and takes trips down to punk shows in New York City, alternately testing his own mettle and engaging in an unexpectedly credible emotional staring match with Henrietta. Just like its hero, *The Adventures of Sebastian Cole* has the feel of a promising work in progress, but the beginner's missteps fade before the high points, as when Henrietta, the ex-marine transsexual, takes cuts with his stepson in a batting cage and gives him that most familiar of pep talks about his grades.

Also reviewed in:
CHICAGO TRIBUNE, 8/20/99, Friday/p. M, John Petrakis
NEW YORK TIMES, 8/6/99, p. E32, Stephen Holden
VARIETY, 9/21-27/98, p. 109, Joe Leydon
WASHINGTON POST, 8/20/99, p. C5, Stephen Hunter
WASHINGTON POST, 8/20/99, Weekend/p. 43, Desson Howe

AFTER LIFE

An Artistic License Films release of a TV Man Union Inc./Engine Film Inc. production. *Executive Producer:* Yutaka Shigenobu and Masahiro Yasuda. *Producer:* Shiho Sato and Masayuki Akieda. *Director:* Hirokazu Kore-eda. *Screenplay (Japanese with English subtitles):* Hirokazu Kore-eda. *Director of Photography:* Yutaka Yamazaki and Masayoshi Sukita. *Editor:* Hirokazu Kore-eda. *Music:* Yasuhiro Kasamatsu. *Sound:* Osamu Takizawa. *Art Director:* Toshihiro Isomi and Hideo Gunji. *Costumes:* Shigeru Aoki. *Make-up:* Mutsuki Sakai. *Running time:* 118 minutes. *MPAA Rating:* Not Rated.

CAST: Arata (Takashi Mochizuki); Erika Oda (Shiori Satonaka); Susumu Terajima (Satoru Kawashima); Taketoshi Naito (Ichiro Watanabe); Kyoko Kagawa (Kyoko Watanabe); Kei Tani (Ken-nosuke Nakamura); Takashi Naito (Takuro Sugie); Sadao Abe (Ichiro Watanabe, Student Days); Toru Yuri (Kisuke Shoda); Kazuko Shirakawa (Nobuko Amano); Yusuke Iseya (Himself); Hisako Hara (Kiyo Nishimura); Sayaka Yoshino (Kana Yoshimoto); Kotaro Shiga (Kenji Yamamoto); Natsuo Ishido (Kyoko Tsukamoto, Student Days); Akio Yokoyama (Doorkeeper); Tomomi Hiraiwa (Announcer); Yasuhiro Kasamatsu (Composer).

LOS ANGELES TIMES, 7/9/99, Calendar/p. 8, Kenneth Turan

You could spend eternity watching movies and not see one with the qualities of "After Life." That's how special, how original this intimate Japanese film is.

Written and directed by Hirokazu Kore-eda (whose first feature, "Maborosi," was a success on the festival circuit), "After Life" is simple in structure but poignant almost beyond words in effect. A meditation on the randomness of pleasure, of memory, of life itself, "After Life's" story of a week spent at an unusual facility starts slowly and simply yet ends up as close to transcendent as cinema gets.

It begins on a Monday, the first day of the week, and employees are doing the usual grousing about their jobs as they report to an unprepossessing institutional building, a former school perhaps. They complain about the chill in the air as their supervisor advises them that this week's workload is heavier than usual.

Out of a blinding white fog, other people walk up a few stairs and sit expectantly in the building's waiting room, old and young chatting politely with one another. Then each person is called individually to a room, where the following information is imparted:

"As you know, you died yesterday. You will stay here for a week, and there is one thing you must do. You must select one memory, the one most meaningful and precious to you. We will re-create it for you on film, so you can relive it, and you will take only that memory with you into eternity."

There is something innately appealing about this concept, as there is about the simplicity and everydayness of a ramshackle halfway house between Earth and the next life. But again, the magic in "After Life" is in more than the simplicity of the concept, it's in the subtle and perceptive way it's executed.

Though he uses it to very different effect, writer-director Kore-eda shares with Belgium's Dardennes brothers ("La Promesse" and the Cannes prize-winning "Rosetta") a background in documentary work that is both considerable and essential. That experience adds grace to the straightforward interview shooting of the 22 people who must choose memories this particular week, all of whom face the camera in classic neo-documentary poses. In developing the script Kore-eda interviewed more than 500 subjects about the memory they would choose, and those on screen include actors working from a script, as well as actors and nonprofessionals recounting their own experiences.

Possibly because we're told that these are dead men and women talking, there is something intrinsically moving about the ways, ranging from wistful to matter-of-fact, that these people provide exquisite snapshots of what has mattered to them in their lives.

A 78-year-old woman, for instance, talks about a new dress bought for a childhood dance recital. A prostitute remembers a client who was kind; a potential suicide recalls what made him pull back from the brink; a pilot thinks about clouds; an old man remembers the breeze on his face when he rode a trolley to school; and a wild-haired 21-year-old wearing leather pants refuses point-blank to choose anything at all.

Some of "After Life's" most moving moments are its smallest. A man who claims all his memories are bad feelingly says, "You can forget? That really is heaven." A pretty, vivacious girl is going to put down a trip to Disneyland until convinced otherwise. And a tiny, bird-like woman (Hisako Hara) quietly scavenges treasures from nature and hardly talks at all.

"After Life" spends different amounts of time with different people, gradually concentrating most on retired steel executive Ichiro Watanabe (Taketoshi Naito), a man whose ordinariness seems a barrier at first, and staff member Takashi Mochizuki (Arata) who's been assigned to help him.

As involving as the newly dead, it turns out, are the adventures of the staff, who though no longer living are not immune from the pleasures of tea, the excesses of fits of temper or the frustrations of having crushes on co-workers like the one young Shiori Satonaka (Erika Oda) has on Mochizuki. When he offers to lend her his mystery novel, she replies that she's currently reading something else: a multivolume world encyclopedia. "Time," she says artlessly, "I've got plenty of."

Once a memory is chosen, the staff also aids in filming it, using simple special effects that couldn't be further from state-of-the-art. The role of movies, even the most primitive, in molding, enhancing and even changing our memories is one of this film's recurring themes, and one of its most telling.

All this is accomplished with a level of delicacy and restraint that is rare and welcome. In its examination of what is fleeting and what remains, "After Life" is not only perceptive, it leavens everything it touches with a surprisingly sly sense of humor. Few films about death, or about life for that matter, leave you feeling so affirmative about existence.

NEW STATESMAN, 9/27/99, p. 71, Jonathan Romney

In cinema, the ideas of heaven and the afterlife have long been associated with bureaucracy. Powell and Pressburger's *A Matter of Life and Death* made celestial judgement seem as jovially parochial a business as a rainy afternoon at the county court. In *It's a Wonderful Life*, James Stewart was saved by an angel whose success would determine whether he qualified for wings, as if seraphic status were the equivalent of a Boy Scout badge. Such conceits are a belated reaction to the 19th century's sentimental, hyperbolic picture of a sugarcandy celestial city—a picture that, just last year, Hollywood unexpectedly tried to sneak back into play with the wretched Robin Williams farrago *What Dreams May Come*.

This, at any rate, is the western tradition. Whether there's any equivalent in the cast is hard to say. I can't remember any Asian images of heaven, but I've seen a few of hell notably the manic Hong Kong swashbuckler *A Chinese Ghost Story,* where hell is home to a tree-wraith with a hundred-foot tongue. But, as far as I know, the Japanese film *After Life* is the only example of Asian cinema to follow the tradition of the bureaucratic beyond. Here, however, we get not the usual domesticating gag but a philosophical conceit to be taken seriously, a metaphor for the way our minds work and our lives shape themselves.

Written and directed by Hirokazu Kore-eda, who made the exquisitely melancholic *Maborosi, After Life* is set in heaven, or perhaps purgatory—a drab, functional welcomingly station where the newly dead report for duty. At the start, the week's new intake of dead arrive in the lobby of a crumbling official building, like a school or a tax office. Each is assigned to a counsellor, who interviews them about their memories, and each is given three days to identify the single moment that he or she wants to remember for eternity.

After Life feels less like a celestial fantasy than a documentary in which a cross-section of ordinary people confess their intimate memories in long takes, talking-head style. Some of the interviewees are professional actors, others are non-professionals who appear to be talking about themselves; you can't easily tell which are which. It goes without saying that the selected moments range from the sublime to the ridiculous. One man remembers the flash of light that saved him from suicide; an elderly roué bangs on about his talent for finding prostitutes at bargain prices. A young girl waxes ecstatic about Disneyland, and her counsellor discreetly informs her that she is her 30th client to make this choice.

There are the harder cases, too: a punky young smart-arse who refuses to play ball, and a sullen old gent who needs to review his entire life on video before he can find a moment he's happy with. We learn just as much about the counsellors—overworked, well-meaning types who clock in every week to learn that their workload has increased. In their time off, they chat in spartan living quarters or rehearse the establishment's marching band. They're regular working stiffs (as it were—they are dead, too) but conscientious and devoted to their work.

The central idea is so satisfying that Kore-eda could have got by with that alone, but he adds a couple of complex strokes that intensify the insight enormously. One is to make two people's lifetime memories, a client's and a counsellor's, cross over unexpectedly. The other is to introduce the self-reflexive business of film. When old Mr Watanabe reviews his life, he's given 72 cassettes, one for each year; he watches them all, apparently without fast-forwarding, but manages to get through the lot in a couple of days. At the end of the week, each chosen memory is recreated on film for the clients to take away into the empyrean. The counsellors function as a sort of public-access film company, working on minimal budgets. If a man remembers an incident on a bus, they have to find a bus. If it's a plane, they'll have to make do with a section of the wing, in the interests of time and economy, and cotton wool for clouds.

Comic as this is, it's also an eloquent profession or faith in cinema as a means of understanding life; and it suggests that memory is itself a kind of artificial cinema, as if we retained key moments by artificially filming them in our imaginations, like "clips" that stand for the whole six-reeler of the overall life. *After Life* is an indirect contemplation of the problems of portraiture—of how you represent someone's whole being in a single image, and how that image might help people to know themselves. It reminded me of that exuberant sequence in Mike Leigh's *Secrets and Lies,* where Timothy Spall's jobbing photographer enhances the lives of a random bunch of customers by breathing some impromptu life into their posed studio portraits.

Kore-eda does something equally compassionate in his film, which, in its austere, restrained way, is richly comic and heart-warming. *After Life* is as humanist as any feel-good Hollywood film, but with a philosophical underpinning that endlessly repays thought. I wouldn't be surprised if it ends up being one of those films that people choose to take to their desert island—or to Cloud Nine.

NEW YORK POST, 5/12/99, p. 56, Jonathan Foreman

"After Life" is a strange but thought-provoking Japanese film that tackles big issues of love, memory and death with remarkable (non-denominational) lightness and a gently comic sense of humor—without recourse to fancy special effects.

At first, it seems stagy and slow and even to verge on the pretentious, but the film steadily accumulates dramatic power as its carefully sketched characters reveal their internal lives. By its end, "After Life" has developed into one of those haunting movies whose scenes can pop back into your consciousness hours or days after you have seen it.

In what looks like a dingy, abandoned school, a group of mostly young men and women are "processing" a newly arrived batch of mostly elderly people.

This odd setting turns out to be a bureaucratic way station between heaven and earth. It is here that the recently deceased decide on the one memory they may take with them to eternity, with the help of the polite, respectful people who live and work at the center.

You have a week to choose, and if you like you can watch videos of your life to jog your memory of the good or significant times. At the end of that week, the folks working at the school will go into a studio and film that one memory for you. Your final moments in a human body are spent in a screening room, watching that scene.

The movie follows one particular batch of the dead, including a teen-aged girl, a prostitute in her 40s, a middle-aged man who lived for flying, and an old man (Taketoshi Naito) who cannot think of a single worthwhile moment in a long but mediocre life.

But it is really about the souls doing the interviewing—especially Mochizuki (Arata), and Shiori (Erika Oda), the young assistant who loves him—and the way they are affected by talking with their clients about love and memory.

Only at the end does the film reveal what happens if you refuse to choose a memory to take with you, and just who the interviewers are.

Former documentary filmmaker Hirokazu Kore-Eda (whose feature "Maborosi" screened here a few years back) cleverly contrasts the security-camera style videotapes of the clients' lives with the filmed memories they get to take with them.

And his own spare, elegant camera work (especially the shots of snow falling on park benches) gives the whole production a very Japanese, bittersweet tone that goes well with the subject matter.

NEWSDAY, 6/18/99, Part II/p. B16, John Anderson

The first feature by Japanese director Kore-eda Hirakazu was the haunting, elegaic "Maborosi," a powerfully visual meditation on how death and grief affect the living. So perhaps it makes sense that Kore-eda's "After Life" should be a funny, rough-hewn, off-kilter comedy about the dead, coming to grips with having lived.

The hereafter of "After Life" is not exactly paradise. Through the mist-lit doorway of what looks like a rundown public school (paint peeling, fuses blowing), the recently departed check in with a group of grief counselors ("I'm very sorry for your loss ..."), who will help them select a single memory from their life. That memory will be made into a short film (filmmaking-after-death being one of Kore-eda's droner ideas) and then accompany them on the next step of eternity—a step never quite defined, but from which no one apparently ever returns.

The jokes are multiple, devastatingly subtle, even movie-happy: the lowbudget afterlife, for instance, with the mise-en-scene of each favorite moment being patched together with spare parts and found props. Kore-eda, who began as a documentarian, uses a lot of his old, non-slick technique—talking-head interviews, scratchy handheld camera work and the use of nonactors, who deliver some of the film's more endearing performances. The result is a pre-Eden that feels like a community theater that just lost its NEA grant. But as dryly funny as it is, one never quite escapes the undertone of melancholia that stems from the characters' near-impossible task: distilling one's life to one memory, or finding the one that defines your existence.

I say "your existence" for a reason. There are movies that resonate the way "After Life" does, but usually not until they're over. Kore-eda, however, has us assessing our own lives while his film has barely begun, so that our own ruminations are engaged with those of the characters—all fully fleshed out, not to make a pun. There is the old man who talks incessantly about his sex life, with unconvincing bravado; the retired executive, Watanabe (Naito Taketoshi), who resists choosing a memory because of unresolved issues with his late wife; the young girl who for her memory picks her trip to Disney World, a moment of stunning cultural-cognitive dissonance ("You've just died!! Whattya gonna do now ... ??!!).

Much of the beauty of "After Life" is in its small, subtly revealing moments. Shiori (Oda Erika), one of the counselors, talks the young girl out of Disney World—and then we see her, briefly, walking alone and unhappy, showing all the symptoms of grief over her life's lack of substance and its brevity.   Shiori's feelings for her colleague Mochizuki (Arata), a mix of petulance and adoration, are revealed in small, glimpsed moments of diamond clarity. Conversely, the history of someone like Kawashima (Terajima Susumu) is revealed only over the course of the film: He died when his daughter was 3. And when a conversation turns to people's earliest memories, which it's suggested can begin as early as 3, it's as if Kawashima's world has collapsed. Ours, too.

"After Life" is a mystery.   Who are the people and why are they here?   The answers are revelatory.   And so is the movie.

SIGHT AND SOUND, 10/99, p. 36, Tony Rayns

Limbo, a way-station where the newly dead are invited to select their single happiest memory. Recreated on film by the Limbo staff, this memory will erase all their other memories. *Monday.* Section chief Nakamura assigns new arrivals to his three clerks for processing: eight to Kawashima, seven to Sugie and seven to Mochizuki, who is assisted by Shiori and seems oblivious to her crush on him. They begin interviewing the dead, helping each to select a defining memory. *Tuesday.* The interviews continue and the clerks report their problems to Nakamura. Mochizuki has difficulty with Ichiro Watanabe, a retired steel-company executive, who insists that his life was entirely average and uneventful; Mochizuki orders up celestial-surveillance videotapes of his life to help him decide.

Wednesday. Most of the dead succeed in choosing memories. Watching tapes with Watanabe, Mochizuki is amazed to discover that his wife Kyoko was the fiancée he himself lost when he died of a war wound in 1945. *Thursday.* Preparations are made for recreating the memories on film; the young punk Iseya refuses to choose. *Friday.* The memories are mocked up and filmed. Watanabe, revaluing his marriage, chooses the moment when he promised to take Kyoko regularly to the movies.

Saturday. Snow falls. The dead disappear from Limbo as they relive their memories in the cinema. Mochizuki finds a note left for him by Watanabe, who realised that he was Kyoko's former fiancé. Shiori finds Kyoko's filmed memory in the archive: it shows her last meeting with Mochizuki. The emotionally frozen Mochizuki (who works in limbo because he couldn't choose a memory for himself) is shocked and moved to discover he was part of her happiness.

Sunday. Mochizuki tells Nakamura he has finally chosen a memory and is given exceptional permission to film and relive it so that he can move on from Limbo. He is filmed alone on the park bench seen in Kyoko's memory, but his memory includes Shiori and other colleagues in the act of filming him. *Monday.* Another consignment of the dead arrives for processing. Iseya, still in limbo, is assigned work as Kawashima's assistant, and Shiori is promoted to take Mochizuki's place. She nervously prepares to conduct her first interview.

One of the visual motifs which runs through *After Life* turns out in retrospect to be a kind of running gag. Limbo staff-members passing through the corridor on the upper floor of the institution (evidently a former schoolhouse) look up at a skylight and see, variously, the full moon, daylight, falling snow or a crescent moon. But the 'moons' are revealed to be illusions: just shapes formed by a hole in the skylight's cover. This chimes neatly with the wry exposé of film-studio artifice in the Friday chapter, but it also relates to something that section chief Nakamura says to Shiori after she has had a row with Kawashima. The moon is fascinating, he says, because our perception of it changes with the available light, whereas the moon itself never changes.

Separately, both points are easily grasped: simple illusions can generate potent images and reactions; everything depends on how you see it. Together, though, they offer a philosophical conundrum with clear relevance to the ways films are made and seen. Exactly the same can be said of Kore-eda's film itself, which deals directly and straightforwardly with all kinds of human issues—the psychological processes of constructing and editing memories, emotional exchange versus dependency, the elusive line between solitude and loneliness—but somehow also adds up to a meditation on cinema as a medium.

The film's genius—and, no doubt, a reason for its popular success in Japan, the US and elsewhere—lies in the way it integrates very disparate materials in an organic whole. The fictional premise that a civil-service bureaucracy awaits us when we die is not original (the film's title in Japan, *Wonderful Life,* acknowledges that Frank Capra, amongst others, got there first) but Kore-eda uses it in a way that no film-maker has done before: to interweave fiction and non-fiction so that each invigorates the other. Documentary material of purely anecdotal interest (for example, a 78-year-old woman's memories of dancing for her supper in the cafés of Aoyama in the 20s) is far more resonant in this fictional context than it would be otherwise; and fictional material (for example, a boring 70-year-old man's belated realisation that his "average" marriage meant the world to him) gains strength and credibility from being intercut with real-life testimonies.

At the same time, the film's fiction/nonfiction interface reflects the premise that memories can be recreated in a film studio with results so 'real' that those remembering can be transported to another plane. Limbo's sound-stage is decidedly low-tech, and the film has a lot of fun watching technicians simulate a solo flight in a Cessna with cotton-wool clouds or a tram ride on a hot, breezy day with off-screen manpower providing the rocking motion. Much effort goes into fabricating images which will connote the senses beyond film's reach: touch, smell, taste. By playing with the ontology of images, Kore-eda also blurs the distinction between life and cinema.

Much of this must be very personal to Kore-eda, who came to fiction films from a decade making television documentaries, several of which reflect the impossibility of remaining objective and detached when filming prickly human subjects. The film expresses the awkward tension between detachment and engagement in metaphorical terms as Mochizuki's struggle to maintain his virginal cool when brought face to face with the realisation that he represented 'happiness' to someone else. This realisation prompts him to choose his own memory (something he has been unable or unwilling to do for the 50-odd years since his physical death), but it's a memory which bucks the system: Mochizuki chooses to go out remembering not only his earthly engagement to a woman who married someone else after he died but also the team camaraderie and work from his time in Limbo, not to mention the young woman who adored him there. The tangle of emotional and cinematic issues here is almost mystical, but the film's simplicity and transparent sincerity make it easy to accept. Kore-eda's unique achievement is that he has turned a deeply personal and private problematic into a mirror for every viewer's own fears, desires and memories. 'Masterpiece' seems not too strong a word.

VILLAGE VOICE, 5/18/99, p. 121, J. Hoberman

Touched by an angel: seraphim spotting is said to have surpassed UFO sightings, not to mention Elvis alerts, in the annals of American supernaturalism, but *After Life*—the new film by Japanese director Kore-eda Hirokazu—is predicated on an otherworldly conceit so off-putting in its whimsy that it might daunt Steven Spielberg. To even describe it risks alienating those viewers who would most appreciate this surprisingly resonant movie.

Briefly put, Kore-eda's second feature concerns a week in the lives of several celestial caseworkers whose collective task it is to re-create the memories of the newly dead. In the *After Life* cosmology, the deceased are required to select their most precious memory, which, with the help of the caseworkers, shall then become the single recollection of earthly existence that will stay with them through eternity.

Imagining the divine plan as a celestial bureaucracy, *After Life* belongs to the World War II "film blanc" tradition that includes both inspirationals *(A Guy Named Joe)* and comedies *(The Horn Blows at Midnight)* and was revived a decade ago in movies like Wim Wenders's *Wings of Desire,* Albert Brooks's *Defending Your Life,* and Spielberg's *Always.* (To put you in the mood, Film Forum is also screening Chris Wedge's Oscar-winning animated short, *Bunny,* in which an elderly rabbit ascends from her lonely kitchen to a luminous paradise.) But where wartime Hollywood favored misty, art deco heavens, *After Life* is considerably more grounded. The dead are housed in a dormitory on what might be a slightly shabby college campus; the caseworkers are as overburdened and harried as their mortal counterparts.

After Life's premise may be sitcom-cute, but the movie is shot documentary-style with much handheld camera and direct address. The clients' fairly detailed memories of World War II, their childhood experiences, love lives, or, in one case, day in Disneyland are delivered across a desk straight into the camera. A veteran TV documentarian, Kore-eda began by videotaping interviews with a range of individuals, incorporating some of the material into the film. (Ten of the 22 subjects who are processed over the course of the week are played by nonactors.) The tone is always matter-of-fact-leaving it to the viewer to be saddened or not by the presence of a few relatively young clients.

In the course of their interviews, the caseworkers struggle to get exact details. The mood is overwhelmingly practical. One modified punk wants to know if he can spend eternity with a dream; another problem client, older and more depressed, sits in a room reliving his entire boring life on the videotapes that have been produced over the years, unbeknownst to him, as a sort of monstrous camcorder total surveillance. As the deadline for choosing the memory approaches, the staff become filmmakers—scouting locations, doing research, holding story conferences, studying rushes. The scenes are eventually restaged in a studio complete with sets and archaic special effects.

Like Kore-eda's earlier, much acclaimed *Maborosi* (a film that paid tribute to the restrained style and hyper-precise mise-en-scéne of Hou Hsiao-hsien), *After Life* is essentially concerned with the power and fragility of human recollection. Reenacting the memories of the dead is one more way of making the ephemeral real. But although equally oblique in making its points, *After Life* is far less studied—and even less precious—than the earlier film, which, released here briefly in 1996, was the story of a young woman unable to reconcile herself to her husband's inexplicable suicide.

Like *Maborosi, After Life* is unexpectedly very touching—a meditation on abandonment, solitude, the solace of memory. Are the underlying metaphysics Buddhist, Taoist, or Shinto? Suffice to say that the scenario, which ultimately turns on the relationships between the various caseworkers and their back stories, seems extremely Japanese in its discretion. (One can only imagine the hell of a Hollywood remake directed by Nora Ephron as a vehicle for Meg Ryan and John Travolta, or, if Miramaxed, for Gwyneth Paltrow and Matt Damon.) But the *After Life* premise is not exactly a metaphor. The film's essential dialectic has less to do with life and death than it does with the relationship between documentary and fiction.

Although it would be unwise to subject Kore-eda's fantasy to logical analysis, some might well wonder just how this particular bureaucracy managed to re-create memories before the invention of motion picture technology—or, at least, the development of photography. That, of course, is a question implicitly posed by this sweetly self-reflexive film, and I've no doubt that Kore-eda wonders how as well.

Also reviewed in:
NATION, 5/24/99, p. 33, Stuart Klawans
CHICAGO TRIBUNE, 8/6/99, Friday/p. P, Michael Wilmington
NEW YORK TIMES, 5/12/99, p. E5, Stephen Holden
VARIETY, 9/21-27/98, p. 108, Derek Elley
WASHINGTON POST, 9/8/99, p. C9, Stephen Hunter

AGNES BROWNE

A USA Films/October Films release of a Hell's Kitchen production. Produced with the support of investment incentives for the Irish Film Industry provided by the Government of Ireland. Produced with the assistance of Bord Scannán na Héireann/The Irish Film Board. *Executive Producer:* Morgan O'Sullivan, Tom Palmieri, Laurie Mansfield, and Gerry Browne. *Producer:* Jim Sheridan, Arthur Lappin, Angelica Huston, and Greg Smith. *Director:* Anjelica Huston. *Screenplay:* John Goldsmith and Brendan O'Carroll. *Based on the novel "The Mammy" by:* Brendan O'Carroll. *Director of Photography:* Anthony B. Richmond. *Editor:* Eva Gardos. *Music:* Paddy Moloney. *Music Editor:* Alex Gibson and George A. Martin. *Sound:* Peter Sutton. *Sound Editor:* Peter Austin. *Casting:* Maureen Hughes. *Production Designer:* David Brockhurst. *Special Effects:* Jim Brady. *Costumes:* Joan Bergin. *Make-up:* Melissa Lackersteen.

Make-up (Angelica Huston): Morag Ross. *Stunt Coordinator:* Donal O'Farrell. *Running time:* 92 minutes. *MPAA Rating:* R.

CAST: Anjelica Huston (Agnes Browne); Marion O'Dwyer (Marion Monks); Niall O'Shea (Mark Browne); Ciaran Owens (Frankie Browne); Roxanna Williams (Cathy Browne); Carl Power (Simon Browne); Mark Power (Dermot Browne); Gareth O'Connor (Rory Browne); James Lappin (Trevor Browne); Ray Winstone (Mr. Billy); Arno Chevrier (Pierre); Gerard McSorley (Mr. Aherne); Tom Jones (Himself); Fionnuala Murphy (Girl at Social Security Office); June Rodgers (Fat Annie); Jennifer Gibney (Winnie the Mackerel); Gavin Kelty (Micko); Richie Walker (Jacko the Box); Brendan O'Carroll (Seamus the Drunk); Malachy Connolly (Buddha); Katriona Boland (Splish); Bernadette Lattimore (Splash); Sean Fox (Liam the Sweeper); Pauline McCreery and Chrissie McCreery (Women in Market); Virginia Cole (Woman with Jumpers); Steve Blount (Tommo Monks); Noirin Ni Riain (Church Soprano); Arthur Lappin (Priest); Paddy McCarney (Hearse Driver); Terry Byrne (Carmichael); Joe Hanley (Rooney); Joanne Sloane (The Widow Clarke); Cristen Kauffman (Woman Buying Fish); Joe Gallagher (Post Office Clerk); Frank Melia (Shopkeeper); Keith Murtagh (Market Spiv); Clodagh Long (Mary Dowdall); Aedin Moloney (Shop Assistant); Eamonn Hunt (Mr. Foley); Jim Smith (Butcher); Olivia Tracey (Posh Customer with Dog); Tara Van Zyl (Shop Assistant); Tallis Music Service (Band on Seaside Pavilion); Peter Dix (Man in Pub); Anna Megan (Woman in Pub); Anne Bushnell (Singer in Restaurant); Pat Fitzpatrick, Patrick Collins, and Michael Flynn (Restaurant Band); Frank McCusker (Tom O'Toole); Doreen Keogh (Nun in Mortuary); Sandra Corbally (Nurse in Mortuary); Joe Pigott (Wally the Ticket Tout); Maria Hayden (Receptionist at The Shelbourne Hotel); Cecil Bell (Mr. O'Dwyer); Don Archell (Tom Jones' Minder).

LOS ANGELES TIMES, 12/3/99, Calendar/p. 9, Jan Stuart

[The following review by Jan Stuart appeared in a slightly different form in **NEWSDAY, 12/3/99, Part II/p. B6.]**

If Cinderella lived in Dublin, reared seven children and found her Prince Charming in the guise of a doughy French baker, she might resemble Agnes Browne.

There is a lovely Cinderella moment in "Agnes Browne," Anjelica Huston's unabashedly moist film adaptation of an Irish bestseller by Brendan O'Carroll. A frumpy and nurturing produce vendor with a life-devouring smile, Agnes (Huston) is going out on her first date since the untimely death of her husband. Beautified by her girlfriends and bedecked in a glamorous blue gown financed by her seven devoted children, she steps into the living room to show off the results. As the family oohs and aahs, we purr our approval in silence. You go, girl.

It's high corn, and "Agnes Browne" boasts a bumper crop of such moments. A working-class fairy tale with a little "Beaches" and Dickens thrown in for seasoning, "Agnes Browne" wears its ebullient heart on its sleeve, bandanna, mohair scarf and just about everything else in sight.

Stoically marching down the crowded market streets the day her husband dies, Agnes is greeted with condolences by what seems to be half of Dublin. It's 1967 and life is tight, between the funeral, the kid's communion and the heavy interest payments for the smarmy neighborhood loan shark. But Agnes gets by with the unstinting support of the neighborhood; her kids; her chum Marion (Marion O'Dwyer), who is secretly dying of breast cancer; and the courtly attentions of a French baker with Gerard Depardieu hunk appeal (Arno Chevrier).

After an irritatingly artificial opening scene in which Agnes is rebuffed by a nasty pension clerk, "Agnes Browne" settles in for a warming succession of tableaux that celebrate the virtues of family, friendship and community. The humor is whimsical to a fault (Agnes and Marion commiserate over their sex lives and what it feels like to have an "organism") and the plot points are thuddingly predictable: This is the kind of movie in which fiends will be foiled and all modest dreams will come true, whether they be a blue evening gown or tickets to a Tom Jones concert.

But Huston radiates an irresistible earth-mother glow that all but spills off the screen during a bawdy pub sing-along. She has such an unbridled affection for Agnes and her milieu that one is inclined to gloss over the flat-footed choices in her directing. Huston is a sucker for sentiment, and "Agnes Browne" is a sap's holiday. Those averse to easy tears should stay home and rent a Peter Greenaway movie.

NEW YORK POST, 12/3/99, p. 50, Lou Lumenick

The movie version of "Angela's Ashes" is still three weeks away, but a more lighthearted view of Irish poverty is on view in "Agnes Browne," starring Anjelica Huston (who also directed) as a struggling mother of seven in 1967 Dublin.

"We're the Brownes—we stick together!" Agnes tells her brood, ranging in age from 2 to 14, after their father is abruptly killed in a car accident.

Facing endless red tape when she tries to collect death benefits, Agnes is forced to turn to Mr. Billy (Ray Winstone), the ruthless local loan shark, to pay for her husband's burial—which turns into a farce when three funerals arrive at the cemetery simultaneously.

Agnes supports herself by running an outdoor fruit stand. She becomes fast friends with a neighboring vendor, Marion (Marion O'Dwyer), who encourages her to date a hunky French baker (Arno Chevrier) and buys tickets to a concert by Agnes' idol, singer Tom Jones (who appears as himself).

Meanwhile, the Browne children are having their own seriocomic adventures, including puberty and their problems with Mr. Billy. But "Agnes Browne" is the sort of film in which every adversity—including the death of a major character—is rather easily overcome.

This unpretentious little movie is based on "The Mammy," a highly sentimental novel by Irish comedian Brendan O'Carroll, who earlier invented the characters of Agnes and her foul-mouthed brood for radio soap opera.

At 48, Huston is pushing it as a 34-year-old, but she gives a very funny, touching performance as the beleaguered and earthy Agnes, who survives largely on charity from her friends. She remarks at one point, "Seven children—and not an orgasm to show for it."

As a director (she previously helmed "Bastard Out of Carolina," which aired on Showtime), Huston stages scenes effectively and gets solid supporting performances from all, including the kids.

O'Dwyer is outstanding as Marion, who helps Agnes get over her loss with her bawdy sense of humor. "Agnes Browne" is a satisfying Irish stew made from very familiar ingredients.

SIGHT AND SOUND, 3/00, p. 38, Kevin Maher

Dublin, 1967. Newly widowed Agnes Browne, the mother of seven children, borrows money from the local moneylender Mr Billy to pay for her husband's funeral. One month later, Mr Billy accosts Agnes and takes her children's allowance book as security against repayments. Agnes' best friend Marion discovers a lump in her breast and goes for tests while Pierre, a French baker, asks Agnes out. A pension cheque allows Agnes to pay off Mr Billy, but he secretly loans more cash to her son Mark. Agnes discovers Marion is dying, and the two women go on a day trip on which Marion buys tickets to a Tom Jones concert.

Agnes buys Marion a driving lesson, but she collapses while having it and dies later in hospital. Mr Billy tells Agnes that thanks to Mark, she now has until Christmas week to pay back £10. Agnes receives a letter from her husband's old union saying she has £25 to collect from the hotel where he worked.

The Browne children run down to the hotel where they meet Tom Jones. They tell him their story. He visits Agnes and helps her pay off Mr Billy. That night at his concert, he dedicates a song to Agnes Browne.

With her directorial debut *Bastard out Of Carolina*, actor-turned-director Anjelica Huston essayed the domestic violence and sexual abuse that defined the dysfunctional family in Dorothy Allison's source novel. With her second film *Agnes Browne* Huston swings in the opposite direction. Despite the similar set-up—it's also adapted from a novel, *The Mammy* by Brendan O'Carroll, about working-class family hardships—this is mawkish fantasy, wrapped up in jaded Irish cultural clichés.

The very first crane shot dipping into Dublin's Market Street, where Agnes (Huston) has her fruit-and-vegetable stall, says much about Huston's over-reliance on misty-eyed *Quiet Manner-*

isms for her portrait. Here a traditional music group plays while a young colleen dances a jig along the footpath (no, seriously). Meanwhile pub sing-alongs break out as the Market Street sellers take afternoon breaks for streetside porter drinking sessions. The characters too, living up to expectations, are devout God-fearing churchgoers and borderline alcoholics. They call sex 'the quare thing' and have never heard of orgasms, French kissing or breast cancer. When Agnes' best friend Marion announces, with a bland halfsmile playing across her lips, "I'm after getting a lump on me diddy," the movie unwittingly verges on crude self-parody.

Agnes' predicament of being a single mother of seven living in debt is rarely squeezed for its dramatic potential (these are the most contented, peaceful and loving seven starving children you've ever seen). Instead, taking her cue from *The Commitments, The Snapper* and *The General*, Huston prefers to play urban Irish poverty for its humour—"Mark, get out a tha' fuckin toilet now!" she bellows in her best Dublin accent, only minutes before her husband's funeral.

Much of this grandstanding originates in O'Carroll's novel and screenplay (adapted with television writer John Goldsmith) which is in thrall to the idea of the Dublin 'character'—a literary archetype passed down from James Joyce to Sean O'Casey to Brendan Behan—the garrulous working class individual who's never short of a well-constructed witticism. So many of *Agnes Brownes* scenes are set up solely for the comic pay-off. "Seven children and not one organism to show for it!" she says, milking the malapropism.

Dramatic and narrative logic are equally neglected. Agnes' burgeoning relationship with Pierre the French-national-stereotype baker simply fizzles out once all the French-kissing jokes are used up. Similarly, Agnes' best friend Marion is plucked out half way through the movie (she's given a pain-free cancer that knocks her out and kills her on the same day) with no effect on Agnes or the movie's storyline.

Generally the narrative is episodic, rambling from mildly distracting set piece to set piece until an uncomfortable-looking Tom Jones arrives to cauterise this endless tale with a feel-good concert finale. Unfortunately the presence of a clearly 1999 Tom Jones in a 1967 period tale destroys what thin veil of illusion *Agnes Browne* was trying to cast. Nonetheless, it seems an appropriate, whimsical ending to an extremely slight movie experience.

VILLAGE VOICE, 3/7/00, p. 128, Michael Atkinson

One would hope that Anjelica Huston, who grew up in the remote fields of County Galway, would have the bitter reality of Irish proles in her blood, but *Agnes Browne* is soft-boiled blarney so sluttish with Hollywood clichés it could've been made in Burbank. Huston's heroine is a piss-poor city widow/fruit vendor with seven children who, you get the sense, are raising themselves while their mum is out having middle-aged romances and pubbing with her blowsy buddy Marion (Marion O'Dwyer). She's trying her noble best, of course, to keep things together (though with her ubiquitous fag, hair kerchief, and too-small cardigan, she helplessly evokes Terry Jones in drag), but her bashful liaison with a Depardieu-esque French store owner (Arno Chevrier) is sodden by Marion's inevitable cancer and her nine-year-old son's not-so-inevitable trouble with a local loan shark (a preposterously villainous Ray Winstone).

Not entirely charmless, *Agnes Browne* is most amusing when Agnes and Marion are chortling about sex: "Seven children and no organism to show for it," Agnes burbles, not long before insisting on seeing Marion's pre-op crotch shave job. But rather than tell a story, Huston's film teeters between beery melodrama and overscored *Moonstruck*-ness, and, given the opportunity, Huston always goes for the dirt-cheap laughs and choke-ups. When the final, cheesy transcendent moment comes, it belongs to the likes of Tom Jones, arriving in a black limo to solve all of Agnes's problems and croon "She's a Lady" one more time. Ireland was never like this.

Also reviewed in:
CHICAGO TRIBUNE, 3/3/00, Friday/p. A, Michael Wilmington
NEW YORK TIMES, 12/3/99, p. E25, Stephen Holden
VARIETY, 5/31-6/6/99, p. 32, Emanuel Levy
WASHINGTON POST, 3/3/00, p. C5, Stephen Hunter
WASHINGTON POST, 3/3/00, Weekend/p. 46, Michael O'Sullivan

ALL ABOUT MY MOTHER

A Sony Pictures Classics release of an El Deseo S.A., Renn Productions, and France 2 Cinema co-production. *Executive Producer:* Agustin Almodóvar. *Producer:* Agustín Almodóvar. *Director:* Pedro Almodóvar. *Screenplay (Spanish with English subtitles):* Pedro Almodóvar. *Director of Photography:* Affonso Beato. *Editor:* José Salcedo. *Music:* Alberto Iglesias. *Sound:* Miguel Rejas and (music) José Luis Crespo. *Casting:* Sara Bilbatua. *Art Director:* Antxón Gómez. *Set Decorator:* Federico Garcia Cambero. *Costumes:* Jose Maria De Cossio and Sabine Daigeler. *Make-up:* Juan Pedro Hernandez. *Stunt Coordinator:* Antonio Lemos. *Running time:* 100 minutes. *MPAA Rating:* R.

CAST: Cecilia Roth (Manuela); Marisa Paredes (Huma Rojo); Candela Peña (Nina); Antonia San Juan (Agrado); Penélope Cruz (Sister Rosa); Rosa Maria Sardá (Rosa's Mother); Fernando Fernán Gómez (Rosa's Father); Toni Cantó (Lola); Eloy Azorin (Esteban); Carlos Lozano (Mario); Fernando Guillén (Doctor in "Streetcar Named Desire"); WITH: Manuel Morón; Jose Luis Torrijo; Juan José Otegui; Carmen Balague; Malena Gutierrez; Yael Barnatán; Carmen Fortuny; Patxi Freytez; Juan Márquez; Michel Ruben; Daniel Lanchas; Rosa Manaut; Carlos G Cambero; Paz Sufrategui; Lola Garcia; Lluis Pascual.

LOS ANGELES TIMES, 11/24/99, Calendar/p. 1, Kenneth Turan

Spain's Pedro Almodovar understands that true drama can be found in the heart of outrageous melodrama, and he underlines the point with his most accessible film to date, "All About My Mother."

The most universally popular entry among both audiences and critics at Cannes, where Almodovar won the best director prize, "All About My Mother" is a surprisingly satisfying combination of bawdy sexual humor, genuine emotion and a plot with mechanics so excessive that Almodovar himself calls it "a screwball drama."

One of Spain's most celebrated writer-directors since the mid-1980s, Almodovar and his films (the Oscar-nominated "Women on the Verge of a Nervous Breakdown" is his best known over here) have always been celebrated for their wacky shenanigans, and this is no exception. Who else but he could combine in one picture a pregnant nun, a heroin-addicted lesbian actress and a transvestite father with AIDS? All this in a film typically dedicated, in part, "To all women who act, to men who act, to men who act and become women, to all the people who want to be mothers, to my mother."

While the earlier Almodovar enjoyed creating excessive creatures for satiric purposes, "All About My Mother" (the title is a homage to "All About Eve") demonstrates a new world view. The director, paralleling the great 1940s Hollywood melodramas he so admires, has made his characters more fully human, in effect using melodrama as a vehicle for creating emotion that is deeper than we may be expecting.

Helping him is an ensemble of Spanish-speaking actresses—Cecilia Roth, Marisa Paredes, Penelope Cruz, Antonia San Juan and Candela Pena—whose cumulative impact is the film's greatest strength. Clearly enjoying both the characters they're playing as well as the experience of sharing the screen with one another, these women make the melodrama real, simply by playing it that way.

Since matters of life and death are a key part of any melodrama, it's fitting that "All About My Mother" starts in a Madrid hospital where Manuela (Roth) works as the coordinator of organ transplants. An actress in her youth, Manuela now performs only in videos used to help potential donors with their decision.

The heart of Manuela's life is her teenage son Esteban (Eloy Azorin), a precocious writer who is desperate to know more about the one person Manuela refuses to talk about: his father. As a 17th birthday present, she takes the young man to a performance of "A Streetcar Named Desire" starring the grand diva Huma Rojo (Paredes) as Blanche and a surly young actress named Nina (Pena) as Stella.

Desperate to get Huma's autograph, Esteban runs blindly into the street on a rainy night and (did anyone mention melodrama?) dies almost before viewers will have settled into their seats.

Ravaged by grief, Manuela decides she has to go to Barcelona, the city she left nearly 18 years ago when she was pregnant and alone. Once running from Esteban's father, she's now going in search of him.

In Spain's second city, gradually and almost without knowing it, Manuela in effect constructs a second family for herself, an all-female cocoon of caring outsiders who amuse and support one another.

She first runs into an old friend named Agrado (San Juan), a tart-tongued transvestite who says, "All I have that is real are my feelings and silicone." Through Agrado she meets Sister Rosa (Cruz), a true innocent who always tells the truth. And, wouldn't you know it, that fatal production of "Streetcar" rolls into town, and Huma and Nina become part of Manuela's life as well.

Truly, coincidence is this film's lifeblood, but Almodovar, understanding this, has said he compensated by deciding during the rehearsal period that "the performances should be as sober as possible." As a result, "All About My Mother's" continual stream of hugs, tears and crises, its mix of the serious and the sendup played out against the director's love for the brightest possible colors, ends up the director's most completely realized film. If, as Almodovar comments archly in the press notes, "the word 'maturity' doesn't have a good reputation," this film should help in the restoration process.

NEW STATESMAN, 8/30/99, p. 31, Jonathan Romney

The first thing we see in Pedro Almodóvar's new film is a fluid drip in a hospital, and some might think that's an appropriate image: it's often said that Almodóvar's cinema has been needing a transfusion of fresh spirit. From the start, with his recurring themes and family of repertory players, Almodóvar's cinema has been self-enclosed, each new feature prefaced with the words "An Almodóvar film", like a brand name telling us more or less what to expect. Indeed there have been times (*High Heels* and *Kika* in particular) when he simply wasn't able to surprise any more, no matter how freakish or transgressive the films seemed to be.

Occasionally Almodóvar has announced projects that promised to take him in a new direction—but then, even if he had made his western or his Marlene Dietrich biopic, it's a dead cert that they would have been Almodóvar to the hilt. His last film, however, saw him taking on new and unlikely sustenance—an adaptation of Ruth Rendell's novel *Live Flesh* that was, as it happened, pure Pedro, with Rendell present only as a teasing trace element.

All About My Mother, though, is probably his freshest and most complete film, which is all the stranger in that it barely departs from what we might think of as the Almodóvar model. In fact it's pretty much an archetype of the director's work—at times, you even feel you're watching all his previous films rolled into one. The cast, for example, includes not only Marisa Paredes, a regular in his recent films, but the Argentinian actress Cecilia Roth, who appeared in some of his early ones. And the story and imagery are riddled with echoes. The several transsexuals recall Carmen Maura's career-making turn in *The Law of Desire*. When one of them gets up on stage to announce, "I'm authentic!", it's practically a verbatim echo of a speech in *Kika*. There's even a hospital scene repeated from *The Flower of My Secret*.

What's going on here—self-vampirism as admission of exhaustion? Rather, it's the other way round—Almodóvar gives himself, and his repetitions, a new surge of life by making such grafting a theme in itself. This is, after all, a film about borrowed identities and acquired body parts, about surgically transformed identities and about people's life force and body fluids suffused into each other for better or for worse.

The plot, in which nearly all the characters are women (including those who may once have been men), involves Manuela (Roth), a nurse whose teenage son is killed while trying to get the autograph of Huma (Paredes), a theatrical *grande dame* starring in *A Streetcar Named Desire* (or, in Spanish, named Deseo—which is also the name of Almodóvar's production company). The stricken Manuela travels to Barcelona—an old haunt for her, a radically new one for the Madrid-based director—to search for the boy's father.

What follows is an extended demonstration of the efficacy of female bonding. Manuela befriends Huma and rescues the transsexual prostitute Agrado (Antonia San Juan), who introduces her to the young nun-in-distress Sister Rosa (Penelope Cruz), and before long all of them are having a jolly, boozy evening on the sofa—"Just like *How to Marry a Millionaire,*" they exclaim. Digging through his own back repertoire, Almodóvar has made his most Freudian film to date, a search for origins that concludes that identity is never as fixed as we imagine and that, although the past can't be undone, it can always be re-rehearsed, redramatised. The theatrical metaphor, as usual, is foremost—the film begins with Tennessee Williams performed in a style you'd more readily associate with Lorca and ends with Lorca himself.

Everyone is performing, wearing a costume of sorts, whether they're a nun, a nurse or a transsexual hustler. Agrado, performed with swaggering, rough-edged panache by the newcomer San Juan, goes from demi-monde PVC to natty Chanel to the more casual look she wears on stage when she tells a rapt audience about the cost of her authenticity, all accounted for in surgeon's bills. Even Barcelona itself is defined by its look, its dressiness—whether in Gaudi's architecture or the chaotically mosaicked interiors.

The film's title revolves around an observation made by Manuel's son when they're watching Bette Davis in a dubbed *All About Eve* on television: its Spanish title ought not to be *Eva Desnuda* (literally, "Eve stripped bare") but *Todo Sobre Eva*—hence Almodóvar's title *Todo Sobre Mi Madre*. The point is that, sexually and socially, people are rarely stripped bare but take on disguises of various sorts, which become their real selves. The only nakedness here turns out to be facial, as the film movingly contrasts theatrical make-up with the unadorned, often haggard faces of its stars—Roth, lined and drained by grief, or San Juan after taking a beating, black-eyed and with the faintest hint of stubble.

Somehow the effect of highlighting all the masks and self-reference is quite the opposite to what you'd expect—this proves to be Almodóvar's most emotionally direct film. But it may also be his most thematically complex and intellectually rich one. And there's undoubtedly one subtext missing—Williams, Lorca and *All About Eve* certainly, but as cinema's great celebrator of performance and masquerade, Almodóvar has surely become the Oscar Wilde of the age.

NEW YORK, 11/29/99, p. 128, Peter Rainer

Manuela (Cecilia Roth) is only eighteen years older than her teenage son, Esteban (Eloy Azorin), but she seems magnificently world-weary.

She's one of those women whom the ravages of life have made more ravishing—the kind of woman who by right inhabits the center of great drama, and great weepies too. That makes her the ideal heroine for Pedro Almodóvar's *All About My Mother*, which, even more so than most of his movies aspires to both greatness and teariness. For Almodóvar, the distinction between the two may not be necessary.

Shortly after the film begins, Manuela reads from the preface of a book she has given Esteban for his 17th birthday, Truman Capote's *Music for Chameleons:* "When God hands you a gift, he also hands you a whip; and the whip is intended solely for self-flagellation." This seems odd coming from Capote—whose whip often snapped outward—and it doesn't always apply to the best of Almodóvar, either, though it does to his worst. What's truly original in his movies, especially *Women on the Verge of a Nervous Breakdown* and *What Have I Done to Deserve This?!*, isn't the hothouse masochism but, instead, the fun-house mix of machismo and kitsch and melodrama and froufrou, all done up in bright florid Pop. The instability of this mix stabilizes Almodóvar, for whom only the "unnatural" is natural. The changeability of sex roles calls forth a farrago of confusions. Men turn out to be women or, as in the case of *All About My Mother,* men *and* women, while women are life's essence: In his press notes for his new film, Almodóvar writes, "Three or four women talking represent for me the origin of life, but also the origin of fiction, and of narration."

This is a lot to lay on the gender. (I wonder if Almodóvar has ever watched *The View.*) But one can, I suppose, accept it as a poetic conceit, the way one might accept it in Tennessee Williams, whose presence permeates *All About My Mother.* Manuela once played Stella in an amateur production of *A Streetcar Named Desire* opposite Esteban's father (also named Esteban), whom she ran away from without ever telling him he had a son. When Manuela and her boy attend a performance *Streetcar* in Madrid, the theatrics onstage have the same temperature as the action offstage. The flamboyance of the drama is merely an extension of the lives of its players.

Huma Rojo (Marisa Paredes), who stars as Blanche in the production, is a damaged diva in love with Nina (Candela Peña), the actress playing Stella, about whom she says, "She's hooked on junk, but I'm hooked on her." (The line is a sex-switched homage to the wronged-woman melodramatics of Hollywood's Golden Age.) When Esteban runs after Huma for an autograph in the pouring rain after the show, he's hit by a car and killed; his heart is transplanted into the chest of another man, and Manuela, whose job it is to oversee donor-organ transplants for a Madrid hospital, lives out for real the scenario she once only acted in medical-training films playing a donor's widow. Because it was her son's wish to know his father, she returns to Barcelona after eighteen years to find him—now a he-she named Lola whom Manuela describes as "the worst of a man and the worst of a woman."

The title, *All About My Mother,* is a takeoff on *All About Eve*—which we see Manuela and her son watching on television when the film begins—but the movie is not about female-against-female connivance, as the Bette Davis movie was. It's about Woman, specifically Manuela, as divine caregiver. For Almodóvar, the glory of women, and also the source of their tragedy, is their horror of being alone, and what they do to avoid it. In Barcelona, Manuela takes up the care of the nun Sister Rosa (Penélope Cruz), who is pregnant and HIV-positive from an encounter with Lola; the sorrowing mother resumes a connection from the old days with the hooker Algrado, whom she knew before Algrado acquired breasts. Played by the Spanish nightclub performer Antonia San Juan, Algrado's a pansexual imp in *faux*-Chanel couture whose finest hour comes when she stands before an audience of theater patrons after a canceled performance of *Streetcar* and announces, with an impromptu flourish, that "a woman is more authentic the more she looks like what she has dreamed for herself."

Algrado is the comic spirit of *All About My Mother,* and Almodóvar periodically gives the film over to her camp antics. It's a good thing, too—the director's swoony and serioso vision of femalehood is otherwise a bit much, even though excessiveness here is obviously the point. Almodóvar isn't merely playing around with kitsch, which he clearly adores; he's also buying into its most sentimental attitudes. The women in *All About My Mother* are all Blanches looking for the kindness of strangers. Those strangers, of course, are other women, or men who want to be women, and therefore no strangers at all.

This is Almodóvar's best film in a long while. Cecilia Roth and Antonia San Juan are great, emblematic opposites. Their performances are both stunners. But I don't think we should unqualifiedly hail the director for growing out of the Pop playfulness of a movie like *Women on the Verge of a Nervous Breakdown* in favor of the supposedly ripening maturity of this film. For Almodóvar, females are the life force because they must be actresses in their own lives to survive; beneath the frazzled histrionics, his women's spirits rage to be free. May I suggest that kitsch is kitsch, whether it's served up with the brazen lyricism of an Almodóvar or the deluxeness of a Ross Hunter?

NEW YORK POST, 9/24/99, p. 44, Thelma Adams

Blanche Dubois and sister Stella, Margo Channing and Eve Harrington, Truman Capote and Tennessee Williams all make themselves heard in Pedro Almodovar's "All About My Mother".

The poignant comedy is the most engaging film to open the New York Film Festival since "Pulp Fiction" five years ago.

The film takes its title from the 1950 Bette Davis classic "All About Eve."

Almodovar garnered best director honors at this year's Cannes Film Fest for his playful and at times painful—homage to maternity and actresses, to men who dress like women and women in dresses who exercise power in everyday life through the dramatic art of lying.

Despite many high-flown literary and cinematic references, the latest from the "Live Flesh" director is equally indebted to the overheated plots and long-suffering heroines of Hispanic telenovelas.

These same sudsy stories of passion and transformation, of characters trapped in identities not of their choosing, fascinated Manuel Puig and his idealized transvestite in "Kiss of the Spider Woman," the Argentinean novel that later wove its web over Broadway and Hollywood.

The central mother in Almodovar's 13th film is Manuela (Cecilia Roth). A Madrid organ transplant nurse, the single mom celebrates her son Esteban's 17th birthday by treating him to a Spanish-language production of Williams' "A Streetcar Named Desire."

While waiting to catch sight of the play's stars at the stage door, Manuela recalls playing Stella in an amateur production of "Streetcar," opposite Esteban's father as Stanley Kowalski. Manuela is finally ready to reveal the secret of Esteban's paternity to her son, but not before the aspiring writer and autograph hound dies while chasing after "Streetcar" star Huma (Marisa Paredes).

Manuela confronts her profession's supreme test: Can she donate her son's heart to save another's life? The more central question: Does Esteban survive in a stranger's body or his mother's heart?

With minor exceptions, Almodovar manipulates the baroque plot with a magician's flourish.

"All About My Mother" is an adoration, a story of family reunion and family re-creation. The film echoes Blanche Dubois' famous line: "I've always depended on the kindness of strangers."

As Almodovar, whose mother died this month, told a crunch of press at the Walter Reade Theater: "When faced with the great problems facing us in the world, the only way to cope is the kindness of those around us."

NEW YORK POST, 11/19/99, p. 59, Lou Lumenick

Life has rarely imitated art as beautifully or entertainingly as in Pedro Almodovar's intricately structured "All About My Mother," which showcases no fewer than six of the year's best female performances.

When the great Spanish director describes his latest film as a "screwball drama," that doesn't begin to hint at the wild and heartbreaking events that envelop Manuela (the incandescent Cecilia Roth), an earth mother who works as an organ transplant coordinator in Madrid.

She lives with her son Esteban (Eloy Azorin), and the two are first seen watching "All About Eve," Joseph Mankiewicz's classic about an aging diva upstaged by her assistant. It's a film that inspires Almodovar's latest work well beyond its title.

For Esteban's 17th birthday, he asks to see Manuela at work—where she plays an accident victim's mother in an organ-donor training film that eerily foreshadows events to come.

That night, mother and son attend a performance of "A Streetcar Named Desire" and Manuela makes a rare confession about Esteban's father, whom the boy has never seen, not even in a photograph.

Years ago, the two of them appeared as Stanley Kowalski and Stella in an amateur production of "A Streetcar Named Desire." Manuela reluctantly agrees to tell Esteban more about his father, whom she has always refused to discuss.

But it never happens; in a homage to John Cassavetes' "Opening Night," Esteban is cut down by a speeding car while pursuing an autograph from Huma Rojo (Marisa Paredes), the show's flamboyant Blanche Dubois.

After she's caught spying on the man who receives a transplant of Esteban's heart, the devastated Manuela flees to Barcelona to track down Esteban's father—a transsexual prostitute with a drug problem who goes by the name Lola.

But it isn't long before Manuela's mothering instincts come to the fore and she's taking care of Agrado (Antonia San Cruz, who's hilarious), another transsexual prostitute who was ripped off by Lola; Rosa (Penelope Cruz), a young nun with her own surprising connection to Lola; and the nun's neurotic mother (Rosa Maria Sarda), who's overwhelmed by taking care of her senile husband.

Manuela also links up with Huma Rojo, who's romantically hooked on Nina (Candela Pena), the drug-addicted ingenue who plays Stella in the show, which has moved to Barcelona.

Manuela takes a job with Huma Rojo, and in another nod to "All About Eve," ends up going on in Nina's place.

The plot makes several other astonishing twists as the six women's lives become entangled, with hilarious and heartbreaking complications. They're all forced, in one way or another, to play roles that would challenge the most experience actress.

"All About My Mother," Almodovar's most mature and assured film, ties all these strands together in a wonderfully generous, life-affirming climax that make the year's best foreign-language movie an absolute must-see.

NEWSDAY, 11/19/99, Part II/p. B9, John Anderson

Flipping the classic mother-whore dichotomy on its (her?) head, Spanish director Pedro Almodóvar's "All About My Mother" gives us transsexuals, transvestites, prostitutes, actresses, actresses who are lesbians, transsexuals who are prostitutes and a nun who's pregnant and HIV positive. Oh yes, and mothers.

But whose mother is the mother of the title? Most obviously, Manuela (Cecilia Roth), whose son Esteban (Eloy Azorin) is hit by a car in the movie's first few minutes. This sends Manuela on a pilgrimage of pain from Madrid to Barcelona and into the milieu she'd fled some years before—one inhabited by her ex-husband (the one with the enormous breasts) and Adrado (Antonia San Juan), a wisecracking trannie/hooker with a heart of gold and a mouth like the carburetor on a '47 Buick.

Less obviously, but obviously, Almodóvar is also paying tribute to "Bette Davis, Gena Rowlands, Romy Schneider... to all actresses who have played actresses" while saluting all women, who are actresses by nature of their sex—and who, in Almodóvar's affectionately hilarious movie, include men who want to be women, men who become women and then become prostitutes and anyone who wants to be a mother.

"All About My Mother," which takes several cues from "All About Eve," certainly takes a walk on the wild side—if you contrast the film's characters with standard film characters. Not, necessarily, if you contrast it with life. Almodóvar's palette is hot, his humor is tart, but the humanity of the film is rich to the point of pain—without ever actually spilling over into mawkishness or mush.

The acting by all four lead performers is first rate—in addition to Roth and San Juan, Spanish starlet Penelope Cruz is Rosa the outreaching nun; Marisa Paredes is Huma, the actress playing Blanche Dubois (yet another actress). And their talent fine-tunes Almodóvar's instinct for the killer joke, or the heartbreaking moment: Although it's been done thousands of times, thousands of ways, there's never been a better example of maternal wretchedness than when the doctors tending Esteban approach Manuela, utter the word "Unfortunately... " and she breaks down in utter sorrow. The economy of words is pure eloquence.

And, in contrast, there's Adrado's stand-up routine, in which she catalogs her generous physical attributes—and all the pesos it took to buy them. Anyone familiar with Almodóvar's earlier dozen features—including "Women on the Verge of a Nervous Breakdown," "Kika," "High Heels" "The Flower of My Secret," "Live Flesh" and "Tie Me Up! Tie Me Down!"—knows how effortlessly he can marry real feeling with outrageous wit. He's just never done it better than in "All About My Mother."

NEWSWEEK, 11/22/99, p. 91, David Ansen

Pedro Almodovar, *enfant terrible* whose gaudy, hilarious, gender-bending melodramas helped reinvent post-Franco Spain, has stopped pretending to be 21 anymore. With "All About My Mother," he gives us the most moving film of his career—a heartfelt tribute to women, actresses, art and "the kindness of strangers." Almodóvar may have mellowed with middle age, but his characters are still more outrageous than most. His protagonist, Manuela (Cecilia Roth), is a single mother whose life is devastated when her teenage son, Esteban, is run over by a car. To restore her shattered equilibrium, she goes to Barcelona in search of the boy's father. What her son never knew is that his dad is now a woman named Lola.

On her journey, she links up with three women who will become her new family—a chatty - transvestite hooker (Antonia San Juan); a naive, pregnant nun (Penélope Cruz), and the theatrical diva (Marisa Paredes) whose autograph Esteban was rushing to get when he was killed. Both funny and deeply felt, the movie traces the ways these wounded, resilient women save each other's lives. This is humanism in drag: Almodóvar's passionate redefinition of family values.

SIGHT AND SOUND, 9/99, p. 40, José Arroyo

Manuela is a single mother living in Madrid. She takes her son Esteban on his seventeenth birthday to see a production of *A Streetcar Named Desire* starring Huma Rojo. Moved by the performances, they wait for autographs. Manuela, who has told Esteban nothing about his father except that he died before Esteban was born, confesses she once played Stella to his father's Stanley. She promises she will tell him more once they return home. Huma and her co-star Niña appear and board a taxi. Running after Esteban is hit by a car. He dies and Manuela donates his organs. Later, she decides to honour Esteban's last wish by going to Barcelona to find his father and tell him about his son.

While looking for Esteban's father at a pick-up place, Manuela helps a transvestite being beaten up by a punter. The transvestite turns out to be La Agrado, who 20 years ago had lived with Manuela and Esteban's father—also called Esteban before he had a sex-change to become Lola the Pioneer. La Agrado tells Manuela she took in the sick Lola only for her to run off with La Agrado's belongings. While Manuela finds a job as Rojo's assistant, La Agrado decides to change her life and goes to see a nun, Sister Rosa, for counselling. Sister Rosa was impregnated and infected with HIV by Lola. Manuela nurses Sister Rosa through her pregnancy, the birth and eventually her death. Lola finally appears, ravaged by Aids. The child is born HIV+. Manuela decides to bring up the child, who is named Esteban. Before Lola dies, Manuela presents her with the newborn Esteban and tells her about the dead one. Later, the third Esteban has neutralised the virus naturally.

The title of Almodóvar's latest film is inspired by *All About Eve*. Like *Eve, All About My Mother* is about actresses and relationships between women, but its focus is on mothers. Here mothers are like actresses in that they can symbolise, embody, educate, improvise and bring characters to life. At the beginning of *My Mother* Manuela reads to her son the opening lines of Truman Capote's *Music for Chameleons*. "When God hands you a gift, he also hands you a whip; and the whip is intended solely for self-flagellation." Manuela was a good actress but her greatest act of creation was giving birth to and bringing up her son.

Almodóvar's talent has always been acknowledged as unique, but *All About My Mother* demonstrates how great it is as well. The storytelling is complex but not confusing; the large number of characters who anchor, explain and propel the story are individuated and fleshed out to such a degree that, without distracting from Manuela's adventures, we get a sense of their lives beyond their relation to her. The decor and music are as effective as ever but less obtrusive (the decorating tips one usually expects from Almodóvar are not the first thing you notice). His trademark mixture of humour and emotion is still evident here but with a greater accent on emotion, evoked with insight and delicacy.

Almodóvar is also a great director of actors (each gets a chance to shine and all do, Marisa Paredes and especially Cecilia Roth with particular brilliance) and a master of *mise en scène*. But the complexity of his most recent work seems to come from a better understanding of human behaviour, accompanied—tempered some might say—by greater compassion, generosity and even optimism. In the hands of a lesser director *All about My Mother* might have poked fun at La Agrado's condition, pitied Huma for being hooked on a junkie or blamed Lola for the havoc she's wreaked. But although he holds his characters duly responsible for their actions, Almodóvar enables his audiences to understand, forgive and even like them. As precisely pitched, variegated and intense as the film's depiction of loss, mourning and pain is, nevertheless it is wittily optimistic. While acknowledging that even when parents are there for their children, they can't always protect them, the film posits mothers who not only love but take the care to care afterwards.

Almodóvar's detractors will also find ammunition here. The two good mothers have no active sex lives and work in traditionally feminine and caring occupations (Manuela is a nurse, Rosa a nun—significantly Rosa's more selfish mother is a forger; she doesn't create, she merely reproduces). Fathers (so noticeably missing in Almodóvar's oeuvre) are absent. Esteban was erased from his first son's life when he chose to become Lola; he will die before his second son learns to say 'papa'. Sister Rosa's senile father can't even recognise his daughter, much less help her.

All about My Mother explores vividly the universal theme of motherhood and its performance in and through a particular, and appropriate, matrix of references from a broad range of queer cultures: twentieth-century classics (Truman Capote, Federico Garcia Lorca, Tennessee Williams), a tradition of queer interpretative communities (the use of the clip from *All about Eve* with particular reference to Davis as a queer icon) and the combination of low camp and high melodrama. That a paean to motherhood should be so queer might be a commonplace. That such a queer film dramatises a general condition with formal elegance, nuanced observations and emotional resonance is rare indeed.

TIME, 11/15/99, p. 100, Richard Corliss

The word for life in Spanish ought to be Almodovar. As in Pedro, the writer-director and all-round vital force in two decades of mostly terrific movies. He loves to tell stories, whether in his 13 features or across a restaurant table.

This enchanting chatterbox, with the round face and electrified hair of a Madrid muppet, makes you believe the oldest myth of cinema: that the magic is real, that movie people in person are as delightful, as bigger-than-life, as they are on the giant screen. Thus the truest compliment to pay his movies—those tangy, nourishing stews of bent men and brave women, of comedy and melodrama, passion and grief—is to say they are every bit as beguiling as he is. And the only thing to say about his new film, *All About My Mother*, is that it is even better: the most mature and satisfying work in a glittering, consistently surprising career. "Pedro is a great dancer," says Marisa Paredes, one of six superb actresses in *Mother*, "and this is his tango."

Hollywood likes his movies too. In a U.S. market where foreign-language films are hard to find even in art houses, Almodovar, 48, is a reliable moneymaker. He also makes the kind of bright, saucy films Hollywood wishes it could. So the studios have courted him ever since his 1988 hit *Women on the Verge of a Nervous Breakdown*. They bought remake rights for Jane Fonda, then for Whoopi Goldberg (though the film wasn't made), then they asked him to direct *Sister Act, First Wives Club, Runaway Bride* and, he says, "anything with drag queens." But though he hopes to make a film soon in Florida, based on Pete Dexter's novel *The Paperboy*, Almodovar's roots are deep in the Iberian psyche. He has never filmed outside Spain. Indeed, he hadn't shot outside Madrid until he made *All About My Mother*, set mostly in Barcelona.

The trip was a tonic for him; this film, for all its verbal and emotional buoyancy, touches a depth his earlier work danced around, like revelers on a volcano's edge. *Mother* begins by painting an idyll: of Manuela (Cecilia Roth), a nurse who works in her hospital's organ-transplant unit, and her darling son Esteban (Eloy Azorin). Manuela is the mom every gay, or simply sensitive, son would adore. She watches *All About Eve* with him, gives him a Truman Capote book for his birthday, takes him to a production of *A Streetcar Named Desire*. He is a sweet, giving lad with a lot of promise. Almodovar is careful and caring in setting up this lovely couple—one could build a fine movie around them—and then he is ruthless in tearing them apart. With Esteban gone, Manuela has a mission: to grieve heroically and heal the wounds of other desperate souls. She is the ultimate organ donor. Now that her heart has been broken, she gives pieces of it to everyone.

She goes to Barcelona, hoping to find Esteban's father, whom the boy never knew. There, by chance or fate, she meets her flock: Sister Rosa (Penelope Cruz), a nun who deserves many fretful prayers, and her bitter mom (Rosa Maria Sarda); Huma Rojo (Paredes), an actress who is playing Blanche in the touring production of *Streetcar* that Manuela and her son had seen in Madrid; Huma's druggie lover Nina (Candela Pena); and Agrado (Antonia San Juan), a transsexual prostitute who has raised artifice to a philosophy. "You are more authentic," this dear creature says, "the more you resemble what you dreamed you are." Manuela helps all these women resemble their dreams on their way to transcendence, accommodation or early death. By the end, Manuela—whose son is gone and whose dreadful ex-husband poisons all he touches—has knitted her *de facto* sorority into a family.

There is another family in this briskly cathartic film: the brilliant acting ensemble. Almodovar cherishes the notion of a family of actors—the gypsies who, for a few months, become as close as siblings under the maternal eye of their director. So with each new project he plans reunions, forming the tightest stock company in movies. Nearly a dozen actors have appeared in three or more of his films. One, Antonio Banderas, segued into American stardom. The others are all actresses, including Paredes, Carmen Maura and Victoria Abril. Almodovar is the man who loves women, who understands them, who writes women's roles that any actress would die or kill for.

"Sometimes my main characters are men," he says, "and the script is written from their masculinity—a very testicular movie. But I do prefer to work with women. Maybe that's because when I was young, I was surrounded by strong women, real fighters. This was in La Mancha, a very machista and conservative region. There, the man is a king sitting on his throne. And the women are like the prime minister; they are the ones who govern the house, resolve the problems."

In his new film, when Manuela discovers her son's fate, she lets out a hoarse wail of sorrow, chilling in its nakedness. Much later she is onstage, filling in for Nina as Stella in *Streetcar*, and she emits precisely the same cry; she has remembered and transformed her mourning into art, and the audience applauds fervently. It is a lovely clue to one of the movie's themes, as Almodovar describes it: "the capacity of women to act without being professional actresses: to lie, to fake, to perform. Men and women both have loneliness, pain, the same kind of suffering. But the way women react to these things is much more spectacular, much more cinematic. It does seem that men are made up of fewer pieces than women."

Almodovar can wax eloquently and congenially on any subject. But if you want to get this bachelor auteur steamed, try asking snoopy questions about his private life. "I don't want to be rude talking about America," he says, "because you treat me very well, and I have to say thank you every day. But in Spain nobody would dare ask artists about their sexuality during an interview." (P.S.: we didn't ask, not really.) To Almodovar, aside from its indelicacy, such a question is limiting; it suggests, for instance, that gay directors can make only gay films. "I know there's a difference in gay and heterosexual sensibilities, but I don't divide things, and above all I don't divide films in terms of their directors' sexual orientation. It's like saying Orson Welles could only make fat movies. It's a joke; it doesn't matter. What am I? I'm what you see."

But he is also, as Agrado, the transsexual in *Mother*, would say, what he dreams. Almodovar dreams of humanity as a band of madwomen looking for good men and great women looking to do without. When he dreams a film as rich and wrenching as his *Mother*, the world's movie dreams can come true.

VILLAGE VOICE, 11/23/99, p. 135, J. Hoberman

Almodóvar's *All About My Mother* is as straightforward and plot-driven as any movie about life imitating art imitating life could possibly be. While Almodóvar has never lacked for international attention—in America, he's surely been the most widely distributed foreign-language filmmaker of the past 15 years—with his 13th feature, the 48-year-old writer-director has received the best notices of his career, and not without reason.

Erupting out of the Super-8 underground, Almodóvar started wild and then, after the superb one-two punch of *Matador* and *Law of Desire*, turned wildly uneven. Hot fluff like *Women on the Verge of a Nervous Breakdown* and *High Heels* gave way to the sour s/m of *Tie Me Up! Tie Me Down!* and *Kika*, and the less-than-successful attempts to break into something more sober with *The Flower of My Secret* and *Live Flesh*. *All About My Mother* is the achieved synthesis of the whole Almodóvariety show, a new genre—part farce, part weepie, low camp and high melodrama, caustic yet heartwarming, humanist and programmatically gender-blurring.

Opening with a close-up pan down an IV drip, *All About My Mother* is concerned with scripting its own mortality. Almodóvar evokes sacred texts only to rewrite them. The nurse Manuela (Cecilia Roth) and her teenage son Esteban watch *All About Eve* on TV, then, to celebrate his birthday, take in a performance of *A Streetcar Named Desire*. The play already has talismanic significance for Manuela—she met her long-vanished husband in an amateur production wherein she played Stella to his Stanley. It acquires even greater weight when, after the performance, Esteban dies in an attempt to secure an autograph from the diva Huma Rojo (Marisa Paredes), who plays Blanche DuBois.

More screwball tragedy: After arranging for Esteban's heart to be transplanted, devastated Manuela goes to Barcelona in search of the boy's father, once Esteban but now Lola. Cruising the local meat market in an absurdly lyrical sequence, she finds instead Lola's transsexual friend La Agrado (Antonia San Juan), who gets most of the movie's best lines: "All I have that's real are my feelings and those pints of silicone that weigh a ton." Manuela also encounters a beautiful young nun (Penelope Cruz) who happens to be pregnant. As God is everywhere, so *A Streetcar*

Named Desire is playing here too. Manuela goes backstage, like (but unlike) Eve Harrington, and winds up as Huma's personal assistant.

All About My Mother is a movie in which wallpaper patterns border on the lysergic, women typically wear red, and characters are prone to compare any given situation to something out of *How to Marry a Millionaire*. It is also a movie in which forms of motherhood proliferate—as does the kindness of strangers—and fathers are generally worse than useless. Although Manuela never gets over her son's death (throughout, she is compelled to repeat the story of his fatal accident), Almodóvar does contrive to crown her maternal sorrow with a climactic miracle.

The filmmaker dedicates *All About My Mother* to "all actresses who have played actresses, to all women who act, to men who act and become women, to all the people who want to be mothers," and to his own mother. Pagan as Almodóvar's exuberance may be, his cult of the Madonna, his meditation on the notion of a virgin birth, and his insistence on martyrdom all seem profoundly Catholic. In any case, I'd very much like to have our mayor (no mean cross-dresser himself) see the movie and explain how it's not.

Also reviewed in:
NATION, 10/18/99, p. 34, Stuart Klawans
NEW REPUBLIC, 1/31/00, p. 30, Stanley Kauffmann
NEW YORK TIMES, 11/19/99, p. E14, Janet Maslin
NEW YORKER, 11/22/99, p. 204, David Denby
VARIETY, 4/19-25/99, p. 47, Jonathan Holland
WASHINGTON POST, 12/22/99, p. C2, Rita Kempley
WASHINGTON POST, 12/24/99, Weekend/p. 32, Michael O'Sullivan

ALL THE LITTLE ANIMALS

A Lions Gate Films release of a Recorded Picture Company presentation in association with British Screen/J & M Entertainment Isle of Man Commission BBC Films and Entertainment Film Distributors. *Executive Producer:* Chris Auty. *Producer:* Jeremy Thomas. *Director:* Jeremy Thomas. *Screenplay:* Eski Thomas. Based on the novel by: Walker Hamilton. *Director of Photography:* Mike Molloy. *Editor:* John Victor Smith. *Music:* Richard Hartley. *Casting:* Celestia Fox. *Production Designer:* Andrew Sanders. *Costumes:* Louise Stjernsward. *Running time:* 90 minutes. *MPAA Rating:* R.

CAST: John Hurt (Mr. Summers); Christian Bale (Bobby); Daniel Benzali (De Winter); James Faulkner (Mr. Whiteside); John O'Toole (Lorry Driver); Amanda Boyle (Des); Amy Robbins (Bobby's Mother); John Higgins (Dean); Kaye Griffiths (Lepidopterist); Sevilla Delofski (Janet); Helen Kluger (Ice Cream Vendor); Shane Barks (Young Bobby); Sjoerd Broeks (Mark); Elizabeth Earl (Child in Van); Andy Dixon (Philip); Michael Lewis (Vicar); Ruth Wright (Sandra).

LOS ANGELES TIMES, 9/3/99, Calendar/p. 10, Gene Seymour

[*The following review by John Anderson appeared in a slightly different form in* **NEWSDAY, 9/3/99, Part II/p. B7.**]

So many movies require their 20-something heroes to be super-aggressive that it seems churlish to jump all over "All the Little Animals," whose protagonist is a brain-damaged 24-year-old man-child whose soft, sweet personality makes Forrest Gump seem like Rambo by comparison.

We meet Bobby (Christian Bale, who inhabits this man-child role with impressive, engaging thoroughness) on the day of his mother's funeral. Despite his age, he's got the sensibility of a gifted, overly sensitive 8-year-old. He was "never right again" after a childhood head injury.

He's not so dim, however, as to be unaware of the cruelty and greed of the stepfather he calls "the Fat." (Is poor Daniel Benzali doomed to play these scary roles for the rest of his life?) Fat presses Bobby to sign over the family department store, threatening to institutionalize the reluctant lad if he doesn't. For good measure, this monster-in-a-suit murders Bobby's pet mouse.

Bobby leaves his gated suburban London mansion and literally heads for the hills, where he encounters a strange man (John Hurt, natch) who wanders the roads looking for dead animals killed by motorists. He doesn't eat them. He gives them proper burials. Bobby, enchanted, has found both a home and a calling. Somehow, though, you just know he hasn't seen the last of the Fat.

Veteran producer (of films by Bernardo Bertolucci and David Cronenberg, among others), Jeremy Thomas makes his directing debut with this adaptation of a novel by the late Walker Hamilton, which became a cult favorite among ecologists and, presumably, young readers of the Aquarian age who found its fairy-tale trappings irresistible. The picturesque Cornwall countryside provides some magic. But there's something plodding and uncomfortably strident about "Little Animals" that keeps the audience from sharing, much less understanding, Bobby's enchantment.

There's also something bizarre, at the very least, about the story's moral center—Hurt's Mr. Summers—who finds critters more worthy of preservation than people. (Reasons for which are eventually submitted in tortuous detail.) Still, Hurt, adding yet another eccentric to his impressive gallery of idiosyncratic portrayals, manages to make Summers' itchy misanthropy seem somewhat rational.

NEW YORK POST, 9/3/99, p. 43, Jonathan Foreman

"All the Little Animals" is a surprisingly nasty fable about a particularly silly, very English brand of animal-nights extremism. It's the kind favored by upper-middle-class eco-nuts who associate "nature" only with cute, cuddly, furry animals that don't eat other animals.

The villain is a fat, besuited, physically violent Goldfinger-esque capitalist who drives a Rolls-Royce and could have come straight out of a 1930s propaganda cartoon.

The main good guy is a noble murderer, on the run from the law, who makes burying road kill his life's work.

"All the Little Animals" is so self-righteous and morally inverted in its combination of misanthropy and anthropomorphic sentimentality about animals that I couldn't help remembering halfway through that Hitler, too, was a vegetarian who preferred animals to human beings.

Christian Bale plays Bobby, a mentally and emotionally retarded young man left in the custody of his sinister stepfather De Winter (Daniel Benzali) after his mother's death.

De Winter pressures Bobby to sign over to him the family department store, threatening to institutionalize him. The stepfather backs up the threat by killing Bobby's pet mouse.

Bobby runs away. Wandering along the highway on the outskirts of London, he is picked up by neo-hippie travelers who take him to England's rural West Country.

Then he gets a lift from an Irish truck driver, who deliberately aims his vehicle at a fox standing in the middle of the road. Bobby grabs the wheel and the truck crashes.

When Bobby crawls from the wreckage he meets Mr. Summers (John Hurt), a supposedly charming crank devoted to a supposedly noble cause. He picks up road kill and rather than eating it—or leaving it for other animals to eat—buries it.

"People. They're no use. That kind can bury their own," says Mr. Summers as he walks past the dying trucker.

First-time director Jeremy Thomas, an Oscar-winning producer, does come up with some pretty views of the English countryside.

But these are not enough to distract from Eski Thomas' earnest, crude script with its heavy-handed symbolism. It's certainly not worth the price of admission.

VILLAGE VOICE , 9/14/99, p. 146, Michael Atkinson

Smooth genre entry that it is, *Stir of Echoes* demonstrates there's something to be said for a firm control of storytelling convention, a principle that evades veteran producer Jeremy Thomas with his directing debut, *All the Little Animals*. Quite the off-kilter, half-baked eco-sermon to begin with, Thomas's movie crumbles in its last quarter or so like a stack of supermarket cans. Christian Bale plays the dim-witted scion of a wealthy chain-store-owning Brit family, Daniel Benzali is the menacing stepfather looking to squeeze the heir out of the business, John Hurt is a homeless vagabond dedicated to burying roadkill whom Bale joins up with after running away. There's no accounting for the strange foolhardiness of the film's story (based on a novel by Walker Hamilton), and little excuse for the blistering incoherence of the film's climactic scenes, which dispense with plausibility altogether.

Also reviewed in:
CHICAGO TRIBUNE, 9/3/99, Friday/p. A, Michael Wilmington
NEW YORK TIMES, 9/3/99, p. E23, Stephen Holden
VARIETY, 6/1-7/98, p. 38, Todd McCarthy

AMERICAN BEAUTY

A Dreamworks Pictures release of a Jinks/Cohen Company release. *Producer:* Bruce Cohen and Dan Jinks. *Director:* Sam Mendes. *Screenplay:* Alan Ball. *Director of Photography:* Conrad L. Hall. *Editor:* Tariq Anwar and Chris Greenbury. *Music:* Thomas Newman. *Music Editor:* Bill Bernstein and Joanie Diener. *Choreographer:* Paula Abdul. *Sound:* Richard Van Dyke and (music) Dennis Sands. *Sound Editor:* Scott Martin Gershin. *Casting:* Debra Zane. *Production Designer:* Naomi Shohan. *Art Director:* David S. Lazan. *Set Designer:* Andrea Dopaso and Suzan Wexler. *Set Decorator:* Jan K. Bergstrom. *Special Effects:* John C. Hartigan. *Costumes:* Julie Weiss. *Make-up:* Tania McComas. *Make-up (Annette Bening):* Julie Hewett. *Stunt Coordinator:* Ben Scott. *Running time:* 115 minutes. *MPAA Rating:* R.

CAST: Kevin Spacey (Lester Burnham); Annette Bening (Carolyn Burnham); Thora Birch (Jane Burnham); Wes Bentley (Ricky Fitts); Mena Suvari (Angela Hayes); Peter Gallagher (Buddy Kane); Allison Janney (Barbara Fitts); Chris Cooper (Colonel Fitts); Scott Bakula (Jim #1); Sam Robards (Jim #2); Barry Del Sherman (Brad); Ara Celi (Sale House Woman #1); John Cho (Sale House Man #1); Fort Atkinson (Sale House Man #2); Sue Casey (Sale House Woman #2); Kent Faulcon (Sale House Man #3); Brenda Wehle and Lisa Cloud (Sale House Women #4); Alison Faulk (Spartanette #1); Krista Goodsitt (Spartanette #2); Lily Houtkin (Spartanette #3); Carolina Lancaster (Spartanette #4); Romana Leah (Spartanette #5); Chekesa Van Putten (Spartanette #6); Emily Zachary (Spartanette #7); Nancy Anderson (Spartanette #8); Reshma Gajjar (Spartanette #9); Stephanie Rizzo (Spartanette #10); Heather Joy Sher (Teenage Girl #1); Chelsea Hertford (Teenage Girl #2); Amber Smith (Christy Kane); Joel McCrary (Catering Boss); Marissa Jaret Winokur (Mrs. Smiley's Counter Girl, Janine); Dennis Anderson (Mr. Smiley's Manager); Matthew Kimbrough (Firing Range Attendant); Erin Cathryn Strubbe (Young Jane Burnham).

CINEASTE, Vol. XXV No.2, p. 51, Paul Arthur

By the time you read this, the unctuous afterlife of *American Beauty*'s deceased hero and voiceover narrator—"My name is Lester Burnham. This is my neighborhood ... In less than a year, I'll be dead"—has likely drifted from stifling suburb to the commercial nirvana of Oscarland. This transmigration is, perhaps, not unfitting given the film's heated emphasis on redemption and just rewards. In the homespun philosophy of its white middle-class male-in-crisis, as shaped by writer Alan Ball and director Sam Mendes, the story of Les is inherently More: more than slick satire, cautionary tale, or critique of bourgeois values. It is, or purports to be, an authentic Life Lesson, a spiritual world view grounded in the discovery of beauty in mundane existence. Despite confirmation of such lofty self-judgment by the film-critical establishment, sumptuous imagery and a wily structure cannot disguise what is only more of the same: a postmodern pastiche bristling with cynical manipulations of the viewer's sympathies, undergirded by rank misogyny and a familiar parade of social evasions.

In our giddy climate of public gloating about limitless economic prosperity, there is no denying the surface appeal of movies aiming to skewer vulgar manifestations of status and rampant materialism (undoubtedly trickier targets in periods of economic downturn). Of course, rather than directly attack the gospel according to Dow Jones, Hollywood and its indie franchises summon the shopworn ancillary proxies of suburban ennui, the success myth, and heedless consumerism, spiked with trendier evils of oppressive gender roles and sexual dysfunction. Adopting what might be called an 'anti.com' party line, *American Beauty* shares not only core ideological assumptions but also similar dramatic situations, character types, and allegorical yearnings with films as otherwise disparate as *Fight Club, Being John Malkovich, Happiness, In the Company of Men* and, in an un-ironic register, *Bringing Out the Dead*. In each case, an outrageously depersonalizing, meaningless, and/or coercive job triggers or merely augments an extreme acting out of individual pathologies related to confusingly repressive demands of masculine performance. Regardless of how crazy, damaging, or counterproductive these forms of 'rebellion' might seem, the discourse in each film situates socially obnoxious behavior as a necessary, if not unequivocally liberatory, strategy by which to confront authority and thereby achieve a measure of self-cognizance and personal renewal.

The sense of everyday frustration, indeed rage, issuing from these films is a variation on what Carol Clover, referring to Joel Schumacher's *Falling Down,* dubbed "white noise," albeit with the bullying thrust of high-caliber mayhem refracted through the prism of satirical humor. In this light, novelist Brett Easton Ellis could champion *Fight Club* as "a horror film about consumerist discontent. It's about what happens when a world defines you by a nothing job." For Alan Ball, *American Beauty* was structured as a "wake-up call" to jettison encrusted social routines, "about how it's becoming harder and harder to live an authentic life when we live in a world that seems to focus on appearance." Leaving aside disparities in genre expectations, it is still significant that the spectacle of workday revenge set in motion by Lester Burnham, or his fellow malcontents, has a different tone and trajectory from the blood-soaked trek of *Falling Down's* fired defense worker—a narrative pattern with queasy echoes in recent real-life 'occupational' murders in Atlanta, Seattle, Honolulu, and Orlando. Nonetheless, there is little in the transposition of xenophobic gun-toting nerd to introspective, sexually unbuttoned homebody that justifies claims of a progressive social agenda. Lester may embody any number of dicey midlife fantasies but principled resistance isn't one of them (cf. *The Insider* for a passable version).

American Beauty contains far too much plot to be rehearsed here. Suffice it to say that poor Lester (Kevin Spacey, boasting his trademark smirk and sexually ambivalent body language) labors to no ostensible purpose for an advertising trade magazine whose imminent threat of downsizing signals the first step in an agonized fall into grace. His affluent home, haunted by aggressively withholding wife Carolyn (Annette Bening), with real estate on the brain, and surly teenage daughter Jane (Thora Birch), is flanked by gay neighbors—the film's most extravagantly well-adjusted characters—and an extravagantly deranged family: paranoid tyrant Colonel Fitts (Chris Cooper), his near-catatonic wife (Allison Janney), and their drug-dealing minicam-voyeur son Ricky (Wes Bentley). From beyond the grave, Lester annotates scenes from his former life in a litany of complaint: "In a way, I'm dead already"; "I have lost something. I'm not exactly sure what it was." Lo and behold, he discovers what it was during halftime of a high-school basketball game in an instant flash of erotic fascination with Jane's cheerleader friend Angela (Mena Suvari). Prompted by Angela's coy intimations of mutual attraction, Lester proceeds to blackmail his boss into a year of severance pay, take up body building, dope smoking, and "classic rock"—infallible indicators of the hippest sort of regression—which in turn fuel feeble attempts at reasserting an Alpha-male posture within the domestic regime.

Meanwhile, Carolyn initiates a duly businesslike affair with a local real-estate guru, Jane becomes romantically entangled with Ricky despite Angela's ceaseless put-downs, and Colonel Fitts is beating the crap out of his Un-American progeny for the slightest deviation in discipline. Will Lester consummate his lust for Angela? Will Ricky and Jane escape the velvet shackles of suburbia? Will the Colonel flip out and whack the entire neighborhood? Will Mrs. Fitts ever smile? Deploying a swarm of melodramatic quandaries, the enunciative voice of *Beauty,* hovers above the fray, trying to have it both ways as it solicits emotional involvement in the characters' journeys of self-discovery while reminding us not to take them too seriously because, after all, this is a comic fable, not a realistic portrait of contemporary malaise. The constant push-pull of identification creates a passive yet titillating affect that is virtually the opposite of what Fassbinder, or even Sirk, extracted from comparable dramatic material.

One thing we know for certain: Lester is going to die, there are three potential suspects, and as the film approaches its inevitable climax, it toys with the killer's identity in a set of visual maneuvers calculated to deflect the obvious choice; and, more to the point, it implicates the viewer in making a false moral judgment. Make that two things we know: appearances are deceiving, an axiom of *Beauty* that is propounded verbally, enhanced by formal means, and glibly abstracted as a symptom of denial on the part of characters and viewers alike ("Never underestimate the power of denial," remarks truth-teller Ricky). Although we are encouraged to imagine the worst possible scenario for every narrative dilemma, it turns out that Lester is a decent guy, redeemed by his refusal to deflower a willing Angela. Ricky and Jane bravely flaunt the myopic biases of conformism. Angela is absolved of jaundiced dick-teasing by confronting the reality of her frightened innocence. Even benighted Colonel Fitts, living a lie of compulsory heterosexuality while seeing homos behind every window, is granted a glimpse into the terrifying abyss of his own sexual repression. The real sin here is failure to take the intrapsychic plunge, thus risking the security of bourgeois ideals for the goal of self-knowledge. Thus it must be Fate, or a less thematized brand of 'denial,' that two characters are excluded from the orgy of redemption, Carolyn and Mrs. Fitts, the only adult women in the film, neither of whom has a clue about the path to enlightenment (unless you count Carolyn's repeated mantra, "I refuse to be a victim," as she checks the clip on her handgun).

It's true, appearances are deceiving, and at several levels. Ricky, dedicated to finding beauty and meaning concealed in everyday experience—with the aid of his trusty video camera—speaks for the film in an epiphany involving a windblown plastic bag: "I realized that there was this entire life behind things, and this incredibly benevolent force that wanted me to know there was no reason to be afraid." At the very end Lester picks up the thread of a vaguely Buddhist notion of acceptance: "... then I remember to relax, and stop trying to hold on to it, and then it flows through me like rain and I can't feel anything but gratitude for every single moment in my stupid little life." If the world sucks, get over it; or rather, to cite *Beauty's* tag line, "look closer."

Assigned the task of making us appreciate every single (estheticized) moment of suburban angst, veteran cinematographer Conrad L. Hall delivers images of such eye-popping sensuality that we are sorely tempted to believe the film's visionary prattle. Of course it's a lesson in seeing we've learned before, especially at the hands of avantgarde masters like Stan Brakhage and Bruce Baillie, but not often enough. Unfortunately, most of what passes here for visual—or dramatic or thematic—grace is not forged by original discovery but borrowed from the warehouse of movie history. Although it never foregrounds an indebtedness to, or critical dialog with, our common image culture, the web of intertextual connection is as thick as any in recent memory. A partial list would include *Sunset Boulevard, Peeping Tom, Blue Velvet* (bloody roses in the opening sequence), *Pulp Fiction* (perspectival looping for the murder scene), Tarantino in general (a gloppy selection of pop music), *The Babysitter, In the Company of Men* (Kubrickian frontality and symmetry in Lester's workplace), *Psycho* (Ricky, referred to as "psycho-boy," bears an uncanny resemblance to Norman Bates). As for the dancing bag, it is a virtual copy of a shot from avantgardist Nathaniel Dorsky's little-known *Variations* (a film that DreamWorks executives are rumored to have screened during production). The point is not that *American Beauty* lacks imagination but that it undercuts its own deeply professed esthetic and moral imperatives in a wave of fashionable appropriation. From this perspective, *Beauty's* only skin deep and, like the visage of Dorian Gray, it gets old really fast.

LOS ANGELES TIMES, 9/15/99, Calendar/p. 1, Kenneth Turan

Unsettling, unnerving, undefinable, "American Beauty" avoids quick and easy categorization. A quirky and disturbing take on modern American life energized by bravura performances from Kevin Spacey and Annette Bening, "Beauty" is a blood-chilling dark comedy with unexpected moments of both fury and warmth, a strange, brooding and very accomplished film that sets us back on our heels from its opening frames.

"This is my neighborhood, this is my street, this is my life," Lester Burnham (Spacey) says in neutral voice-over as the camera narrows in from an aerial perspective to his red suburban front door as he delivers shock No. 1: "I'm 42 years old. In less than a year, I'll be dead. Of course, I don't know that yet. In a way, I'm dead already."

To inform us that, as in "Sunset Boulevard," we're watching a film narrated by a corpse is a quick way to get everyone's attention, but "Beauty," the provocative debut for director Sam

Mendes, goes further. Layered with surprises, at home in unfamiliar territory, this film more than doesn't let on what it's thinking or where it's going; it intentionally misleads with dramatic dodges and feints calculated to throw everyone off balance and keep them there.

Whenever a film is this distinctive, it invariably starts with the writing. "Beauty" is the first feature by veteran TV writer Alan Ball ("Cybill" and the upcoming "Oh Grow Up"), and in its ability to make us uncomfortable by changing emotional colors as subtly and gradually as a kaleidoscope, it bears the hallmarks of someone pouring everything he felt constrained from doing in one medium into an extremely personal piece of work in another.

"American Beauty's" subject is the hollow space behind the American dream, the frustrations that hide under the perfectly mannered surfaces of our lives. "Never underestimate the power of denial," one character says, but in some ways what we're shown is not the power but the price of denial, how a world without moorings, without honesty, without human connections turns everyone into a lost soul on the verge of a self-centered psychotic breakdown.

Lester certainly fits that description when he takes us on a voice-over tour of his life. The first stop (and, he coolly informs us, the high point of his day) is Lester masturbating in his morning shower before putting in his time at a trade magazine called *Media Monthly*. His wife and daughter, Lester says, consider him "this gigantic loser," and, not really disagreeing, he tells people who've forgotten they've met him, "I wouldn't remember me either."

Lester is equally savage about the other family members. Stepford Wife Carolyn (Bening) is a residential broker locked into a perennially losing battle with Buddy Kane, the self-proclaimed King of Real Estate (Peter Gallagher). She prefers elevator music during dinner and spends her spare time worrying about her furniture and growing roses. "See the way the handle on those pruning shears matches her gardening clogs?" Lester asks witheringly. "That's not an accident."

Then there's 16-year-old daughter Jane (Thora Birch). Unsmiling, insecure and ferociously unhappy, her sullen anger is as constant and unwavering as an eternal flame. "I wish I could tell her that's all going to pass," is Lester's cold-blooded assessment, "but I don't want to lie to her."

These kinds of acerbic comments, while striking in their drop-dead glibness, are deceptive because they make "Beauty" seem more familiar than it is. We've all seen this kind of highly stylized verbal farce, complete with sarcastic line readings, but director Mendes has something more complex and more subversive in mind.

Though he's only 34, the English director has already established himself in the theater, directing the Nicole Kidman-starring "The Blue Room" and a celebrated revival of "Cabaret." His accomplishment here is to capture and enhance the unlooked-for duality that is at the core of Ball's discomforting screenplay. For in addition to being stylized, "Beauty's" characters have an unmistakable sincerity about them; they manage to appear simultaneously as caricatured sendups and painfully real individuals. As their emotional valence fluctuates, so does our understanding of what is going on with them. Several different events unsettle the bitter and resentful lassitude into which the Burnham family has sunk, happenings that threaten to collapse the emotional walls the members have painstakingly created around themselves.

Goaded by his wife to take an interest in their daughter's life, Lester accompanies Carolyn to a Rockwell High basketball game, where Jane is a member of a cheerleading squad called the Dancing Spartanettes. Desultorily watching their routine, Lester suddenly has a vision and, not unlike Paul on the road to Damascus, is instantly transformed. He sees Angela Hayes (Mena Suvari) and nothing is the same.

A fellow Spartanette and friend of Jane's, Angela is such a classic all-American blond (think angel) that Lester has erotic visions of her unclothed under layers of deep red rose petals. He immediately contrives to meet her, and his midlife fantasy of seducing Angela becomes so strong it galvanizes him to completely change his life.

While wife Carolyn is too focused, in more ways than one, on real estate king Kane to notice what's going on, daughter Jane is horrified at her father's lust. "Could he be any more pathetic?" she disgustedly asks, but Angela seems to enjoy entertaining the idea. Used to guys drooling over her, she fears nothing in life more than being ordinary, and Lester's interest in her is proof of her special qualities.

Meanwhile, a different kind of dysfunctional family has moved in next door to the Burnhams, headed by a just-retired career military man who always introduces himself as "Col. Frank Fitts, U.S. Marine Corps" (Chris Cooper). But before we meet the colonel, his catatonic wife, Barbara

(Allison Janney), and their mysterious teenage son Ricky (Wes Bentley), we are aware of their presence when the film's point of view suddenly changes and Lester and his daughter are viewed through the lens of a digital camera.

Ricky Fitts, it turns out, is a fanatic for video; it's his way of interfacing with a world and a father that have not come close to understanding him. He records everything; his room is lined with the discs he's filled with images, and right now there's nothing he wants to record more than Jane. He finds her interesting, he tells her, and despite Angela's horror and Ricky's Bible salesman way of dressing, Jane finds herself drawn to the one quality he has that she lacks: quiet but complete self-confidence.

If there is any constant in "American Beauty's" story of how this island of lost souls resolves itself, it's that things rarely go where you think they will. Scenes ambush us out of nowhere, revealing both flash-floods of fury and frustration too powerful to contain, and moments of sadness, wistfulness, even hope that are both convincing and able to catch us completely unawares.

With a film so delicately balanced, the quality of the acting is especially crucial, and it's hard to overstate how difficult these duality-laden roles are and how faultlessly the actors handle them. Bening's image-obsessed and frustrated wife, Birch's despairing daughter, Suvari's conniving proto-Lolita, these characters are all inhabited completely and convincingly.

Equally effective are "Beauty's" two key males. Bentley, in a haunting role numerous young actors were after, brings a commanding but low-key intensity and intimacy to Ricky Fitts that never promises more than it can deliver. And Spacey's power is finally the energy that drives this film. It's not that we're always on his side—far from it—but that we can't help being involved in his quest to recover the ideals and enthusiasm that once animated his life.

There is also a sense about "American Beauty" that it has paradoxically benefited from director Mendes' debut status, an anything's possible daring that was fortuitously married to his great experience with drama that enabled him to try for original emotional effects that might have daunted more experienced hands.

Mendes was also shrewd in his choice of supporting staff, including highly regarded composer Thomas Newman and one of the great names of cinematography, the eight-time Oscar-nominated Conrad Hall, who gives the film a dreamlike quality set off by the right touch of cool, composed reality.

It's also Hall, in a dialogue with fellow director of photography Haskell Wexler in a recent issue of *American Cinematographer*, who provides a key insight into this unusual film. Hall relates going to Mendes and saying, "'I love this story and the project, but my God, how can you like these characters?' He told me, 'Well, Conrad, you have to like them. If you don't like them, we don't have a picture here.'" Against considerable odds, we do like them, and there definitely is a hell of a picture here.

NEW STATESMAN, 1/31/00, p. 46, Jonathan Romney

Do white picket fences really exist in the American suburbs, or are they simply an invention of cinema? Over the past two decades, the picket fence has become shorthand for the bland American exteriors that conceal unimaginable strangeness. It's invariably accompanied by—is almost interchangeable with—the words "dark underbelly".

From *Blue Velvet* on, suburban madness has been such a well-mined scam that you can't help wondering whether *American Beauty* is just a little late off the blocks, or whether it's so old that it's new, a fresh spin on a strictly generic topic. In the US, no one seems to have objected much to the familiarity of its themes: Sam Mendes's film has been hailed as a triumph for all concerned and a multiple Oscar shoo-in.

American Beauty, is indeed a class act, yet it's oddly run-of-the-mill. The story is hardly a departure: middle-aged suburbanite Lester (Kevin Spacey) is tired of his job, tired of domestic life with discontented teenage daughter (Thora Birch) and neurotic estate agent wife (Annette Bening). But his life is transformed: first by conceiving a passion for vacuous teenage sexpot Angela (Mena Suvari), then discovering that Ricky, the weird, sullen kid next door (Wes Bentley) is a supplier of grade-A hash. Lester decides to get in trim for teenage lust, ditching his job and devoting himself to what made him happy in his youth—slinging burgers, smoking dope and driving his dream car with seventies rock at full blast.

It all seems screamingly formulaic: a ready-made mid-life-crisis story spelt out in broad strokes—and, where Bening's character is concerned, starkly misogynistic ones. But we're told to expect something more beneath the surface—"Look closer," the poster tag line urges—and people, predictably, prove to be not what they seem. Lester's rebellion turns the world inside out, right up to a multiple-twist ending dripping with manipulative suspense, when he delivers on his opening voice-over promise to explain his premature death.

Theatre *Wunderkind* Mendes, best known as guiding spirit of the Donmar Warehouse theatre in London, is in no way a dilettante slumming on screen: he takes to his new medium with flair and confidence. He gets terrific performances from his cast, although some (notably Bening) are required to breathe show-stopping fire into entirely hollow characters. Mena Suvari makes Angela that abrasive bit more than the *Clueless* valley girl; Chris Cooper makes savage capital out of the bullet-headed marine next door.

Spacey's is such a rich, finely judged turn that no one could begrudge him the inevitable Oscar. Yet his Lester feels like a commentary on a part that Spacey doesn't entirely inhabit. Faintly camp and full of subliminal winks to our cultural knowledge, Spacey wants us to recognise that his Lester is more of a wise ironist than the script's Lester: the actor is indeed "looking closer"—more closely, perhaps, than the character allows for. Such a spectacular show of insightfulness seems curiously counterproductive.

The film's look is broadly realistic but larger than life quite literally so, given Conrad Hall's composed, immaculately sheened widescreen photography. But the contrast makes the story look all the more slender; the script, by the former sitcom writer Alan Ball, might have stood up better to a rougher, more modest treatment (see Alexander Payne's recent, not dissimilar, comedy *Election*). Mendes isn't averse to the theatrical, using the image like a proscenium, showing the family dinner side-on and symmetrically, or positioning Carolyn against a screen of louvre windows. He also pulls some showy coups—a cheer leader routine stopped dead by Lester's lustful reverie, or showers of rose petals tumbling from Angela's naked body (but, oh, how he overworks those red, red roses).

There are some worrying cultural anomalies, although I couldn't tell whether Mendes was playing them for incongruity. Would a couple in their mid-forties eat dinner every night to tunes from *South Pacific*? Conceivably they share an ironic taste for kitsch, but I think it's clumsily contrived to make their life look vapid. (And if "Bali Hai" is understood to be such an abomination, how does DreamWorks have the gall to include it on the soundtrack CD?)

The film ends with Lester confiding that he has known beauty after all: we're left with Ricky's cloyingly poetic video of a bag blowing in the wind. The grace note in Lester's farewell message so glibly ties up the film's argument that it suddenly makes perfect sense that *American Beauty*, is a DreamWorks release: its sweetly acidic, sanitised homily all too easily fits Steven Spielberg's idea of risk and adventure.

Mendes has insisted that *American Beauty* is a fable, rather than a satire. But, whether you call them satires or not, it compares badly with other recent suburban stories: Todd Solondz's genuinely risky *Happiness;* Ang Lee's socially acute *The Ice Storm;* and Paul Thomas Anderson's forthcoming *Magnolia*, a film that has the courage to let its curiosity and narrative appetite run riot.

Mendes's suave, virtuoso number—which actually does feature white picket fences—is just too neat a package. Look closer, by all means, but there's not much more than meets the eye.

NEW YORK, 9/20/99, p. 68, Peter Rainer

Lester Burnham (Kevin Spacey) in *American Beauty* is a big zero with a boring desk job whose highlight of the day is masturbating in the shower. Then he goes through a life change and is supposedly reborn. I say "supposedly" because the new Lester, apart from being more buff and gruff and wide-eyed, isn't a big improvement on the old Lester—he's zero and a half. This is not, however, how we are meant to respond to him: *American Beauty* is a movie in which not only Lester but practically all the other characters are designed to confound our preconceptions and unfold their secret selves. In most cases, though, this two-step agenda comes across as simply one kind of shallowness giving way to another.

The tag line to the film's title is "Look closer," and we're pressed by Sam Mendes, the celebrated theater director *(Cabaret, The Blue Room)* making his movie-directing debut, and his screenwriter Alan Ball, a TV-comedy writer who was co-executive producer of *Cybill*, to look closer at the archetypes of Anytown Americana.   Lester's real-estate-agent wife, Carolyn (Annette Bening), for example, with her pasted-on smiles and cast-iron coif, has the veneer of a perfect suburban wifey-wife, but she holds Lester in deep contempt.   So does their teenage daughter, Jane (Thora Birch), who undergoes a transformation of her own when she falls for Ricky (Wes Bentley), the mental-case video-voyeur classmate next door, who, of course, turns out to be not so much nuts as "mad"—the way romantic poets are mad. He sees beauty where you would least expect to find it, and that's what *American Beauty* wants to do, too.

But why should we trust this simplistic film's notions of the ineffable? Mendes has been quoted in the *New York Times* as saying that *American Beauty* "sounds like some dreadful sitcom on speed," adding that "it's not [that] at all. It's so filled with loneliness and beneath the surface it's very funny." The sitcom connection is apt, though—and, by now, overfamiliar. *The Truman Show* and *Pleasantville* have already raked over much of this turf, and some of us didn't buy it then either.   These movies express outrage that the Ozzie-and-Harriet lives we never really believed in anyway are false. Maybe some sort of Hollywood-boomer midlife crisis explains why we're now getting all these films in a row. Moviemakers who feel betrayed by the cheery sitcoms of their adolescence can now take it out on all the rest of us and, as a bonus, get points for profundity too.

There's something else afoot in *American Beauty*. Lester is not only the anti-Ozzie Nelson, he's also a counterculture washout who smoked dope and partied in the sixties and now has nothing to show for it. Why should we care about him? What ideals did he leave behind? We're never really told. The filmmakers apparently don't feel the need to fill out Lester's character; it's as if he were fated to become a drone by the country's straitjacket culture. Carolyn is also a casualty of the culture. She says that "my job is selling an image, and part of my job is living that image," but real life keeps getting in the way. When she can't sell a house, she goes into a screaming fit, bawling and slapping herself and smearing her makeup. She's in awe of the local real-estate king (Peter Gallagher), who has florid, soap-opera good looks and seduces her with his success talk. Their roll in the hay emboldens her, giving credence to the enlightened notion that all she needed was to get laid.

Unlike Lester or Jane, Carolyn is never really brought into the realm of our sympathy; she's a façade selling façades. When Lester, swigging a beer, tries to get amorous with her and calls upon their fun-loving past, she warms a bit and then pushes him away, fearing the beer will spill onto her expensive couch. We're supposed to understand, of course, that what Carolyn really fears is closeness, but she's too villainized in our eyes for that to sink in. Although both actors pull out the stops—Spacey alternates fey snideness with moist wistfulness while Bening does a contortionist's number on her smile muscles—there is hardly anything in either of their performances to indicate even a faded blush of marital longing.

The filmmakers want us to know that we can't choose what will liberate us; we have to be prepared for transcendence to come from the unlikeliest sources—like, for example, from the weirdo Ricky, whose video of a white plastic bag swirling around in the wind he describes to a rapt Jane as "the most beautiful thing I've ever filmed." Because of the prominence Mendes gives this clip, we're supposed to agree. Ricky, who deals dope to fund his video habit, is the son of a brutally repressive Marine ex-colonel (Chris Cooper)—is there any other kind?—and a catatonic mother (the wonderful Allison Janney, underused), and so, in the best sentimental juvenile-delinquent tradition, his troubles are bought off, justified. Ricky the new-style hippie is balanced out by the rejuvenated, superannuated hippie Lester, who buys the kid's weed, drops out of the rat race, and finds his own measure of transcendence in the person of a stuck-up cheerleader pal of Jane's, Angela (Mena Suvari), whom he repeatedly fantasizes festooned in rose petals. In these moments he gets a lulling look of complete repose; he looks postcoital without ever having had the coitus.

It's difficult for us to know how to take Lester's rebirth: His yearning for his daughter's friend has incestuous overtones that are never developed; and in a movie about the tyranny of façades, it doesn't help Lester's credibility that, long before he gets to really know her, he's enamored by Angela's all-American, blonde-haired, blue-eyed cheerleader looks. Because this middle-aged guy is so dimensionless, his supposed entrancement comes across more like plain old chickie lust. Angela looks like every Hollywood movie producer's second wife.

American Beauty plugs into a widespread boomer paranoia that, like Rip Van Winkle Lester here, we've wasted away our past twenty years in a kind of coma and now it's too late to change. What gives the movie its air of seriousness is the attempt to spiritualize this emptiness; Mendes really loves his floating plastic bags and rose petals. The film is like a sportier, homegrown version of all those Antonioni-ish movies about the depleted upper-middle classes zombified by regret. It flatters its audience by turning burnout and midlife itch into tragic states, but a zero in torment is still a zero.

NEWSDAY, 9/15/99, Part II/p. B3, John Anderson

There have been countless ordinary movies about extraordinary people, far fewer extra ordinary movies about ordinary people. "American Beauty" is nothing if not extraordinary—its satirical take on boomer suburbia qualifies as both caustic comedy and Greek-level tragedy and couldn't be more timely in its portrait of amorphous American mores: The title alone, suggesting the possibility that we might all share some perception of grace, at the same time mocks the very idea.

But the characters, their unhappy situations and their calamitous fates are the result of such unspectacular causes—a lapse in timing, a lapse in taste—that you can't help but love them. Or suspect, perversely enough, that there must be a guiding intelligence behind so many lives going so profoundly astray.

The spiritual aspects of the story are hardly derailed by the fact that Kevin Spacey—who rides this particular vehicle the way Slim Pickens rode Strangelove's H-bomb—is introduced as the woeful Lester Burnham via a "Sunset Boulevard"-ian voice-over: He will, he assures us, be dead within a year. ("I may," he adds wearily, "be dead already.") You could call Lester henpecked, if wife Carolyn (a perfectly pitched Annette Bening) actually thought that much about him. His job is killing him psychically, his wife is starving him sexually, daughter Jane (Thora Birch) is dissing him daily. We've even seen the disgruntled Jane discussing on videotape—videotape being the endocrine gland of "American Beauty"—what appears to be the assassination of her father.

The plot has not just thickened, it seems to have congealed. But director Sam Mendes—making his feature film debut following the Broadway successes of "The Blue Room" and "Cabaret"—has miles to go before Lester sleeps. Working within the multiple layers of meaning in Alan Ball's screenplay, he gives us such a precisely constructed introduction to the Burnham family that within the film's first 10 minutes we know them intimately. Their life is manicured and thoroughly miserable.

Carolyn sells houses—she worships local mogul Buddy Kane (Peter Gallagher), the "King of Real Estate"—and dotes on her roses ("Eggshells and Miracle Gro," Carolyn tells their two gay neighbors, both named Jim and played by Scott Bakula and Sam Robards). "We used to be happy," Lester tells Carolyn, although one can't imagine how. Jane, meanwhile, is busy comparing herself to her empty blond schoolmate Angela (Mena Suvari) and wondering what's up with her strange new neighbor, Ricky (Wes Bentley), who seems to have her in the viewfinder of his digital camera night and day.

"American Beauty's" wide-screen format and Conrad Hall's cinematography alternately flash-freeze the characters into a kind of moral Siberia or exalt them to icon status. The result is a dreamy quality that makes "American Beauty" into allegory—as does Ball's script, which includes a succession of banalities somehow inflated to proverbial status ("There's nothing worse in life than being ordinary"; "In order to be successful one must present an image of being successful at all times"; "I rule!!!"). It's a devious twist. But so is Lester, who starts to remake himself on the slim chance he might ever sleep with Angela and is completely sympathetic, to a large extent because Spacey makes him so funny.

But Lester is, by every existing standard, a moral bankruptcy. He buys high-grade pot from the teenage Ricky, right under the nose of his Marine colonel father, Frank (a transfixing Chris Cooper). He lusts after his daughter's 16-year-old best friend. And, although it's done in self-defense, he negotiates a severance package by threatening to tell the magazine he works for that his boss put hookers on his company MasterCharge.

The thrust of "American Beauty"—which can refer, if you wish, to the vacuous Angela, or the far more interesting Jane, or the roses Carolyn grows, or the depth of aesthetics and meaning Ricky finds in a dead bird, or a plastic bag turning circles in the wind—is whether there is an existing standard about anything. Carolyn, for whom cliches have become gospel, is a lost soul (and her portrayal as shrew is probably unfair). Ricky, caught between his father and a set of ideas his father would never understand, is in a kind of intellectual limbo.

And while Col. Frank—whom Cooper gives the face of pure betrayal when he considers the world around him—may be an abusive, homophobic cliche of American manhood and military discipline, Mendes and Ball also have the insight and humanity to ask whether anyone else has anything better to say. Or think. Or feel. Or whether believing in something, even if you're deluding yourself, isn't better than leading the kind of life that Lester can finally admit he loves with all his heart, but only after he's dead.

NEWSWEEK, 9/27/99, p. 68, David Ansen

There is a very special alchemy at work in "American Beauty" a movie composed of familiar parts which manages to feel strikingly new. Moviemakers have been busy exposing the hollow heart at the suburban supermarket for a good five decades. Now along comes a gifted screenwriter, Alan Ball; a remarkable first-time movie director from England, Sam Mendes, and a superlative cast to make those old tropes feel frisky, and potent again.

Borrowing a page from "Sunset Boulevard," this dreamy black comedy is narrated by a corpse: Lester Burnham (Kevin Spacey), a going-nowhere-writer for Media Monthly who already considers himself among the walking dead. His Realtor wife (Annette Bening) is chilly and compulsive, his daughter (Thora Birch) loathes him and his boss is about to fire him. What brings him back to life is a glimpse of his daughter's high-school classmate Angela (Mena Suvari), seductively strutting her cheerleader's stuff on a basketball court. Emboldened by mad desire, he quits his job, starts pumping iron, smoking pot and generally behaving like a man "with nothing to lose. Lester is in a state of reckless, deluded grace, and Spacey, whose comic timing is as dry as a perfect martini, manages to make him both snakily dangerous and strangely endearing.

"American Beauty" is a very funny film that packs an unexpected emotional wallop. It seems to condescend to its characters, but just when you think it will turn sour, these cardboard cutouts turn flesh and blood. Bening, a wonderful comedian, zigzags dazzlingly between parody and pathos. The film's most mysterious character is the strange, pot-selling teenager, Ricky Fitts (Wes Bentley), who falls for Lester's daughter. He's the son of a homophobic ex-Marine colonel (Chris Cooper) who's just moved next door. It's typical of the movie's sleight of hand that the eeriest character just might be the film's moral center.

Mendes, who directed the acclaimed stage revival of "Cabaret," uses the screen like a born filmmaker. He and cinematographer Conrad Hall create bold, spare images suspended somewhere between Caravaggio and comic strip. His film examines a malaise that's been plaguing the affluent, deracinated middle class since the suburbs were invented. It's about the power of the images we have in our heads, and the painful gulf between those fantasies and the reality we can't seem to grasp. The beauty of "American Beauty" is how wickedly entertaining it makes this bleak diagnosis.

SIGHT AND SOUND, 2/00, p. 40, Kevin Jackson

Connecticut, the present. Lester Burnham's life is cracking up: his wife Carolyn, an estate agent, and his daughter Jane both despise him; his new boss is threatening to fire him. Lester becomes obsessed with his daughter's schoolmate, the sexually precocious Angela, after seeing her perform a cheerleading routine. Meanwhile, Ricky—the son of the Burnhams' new nextdoor neighbour, a violent and reactionary retired marine colonel named Frank Fitts—makes videos of Jane.

Pursuing his lost youth, Lester quits work and takes a job in a fast-food restaurant. He also starts to work out and indulge in recreational drugs supplied by Ricky. Carolyn begins an affair with her commercial rival Buddy Kane, and Jane and Ricky begin to fall in love. Disgusted by her father's infatuation with Angela, Jane asks Ricky to kill him. Lester finds out about

Carolyn's affair when she and Buddy drive by his new workplace for burgers. Buddy breaks off the affair.

One night, Frank spies on Ricky and Lester. Because of the angle from which he sees them rolling and smoking a joint, Frank mistakenly concludes Lester is forcing the boy to fellate him. Frank beats up his son, so Ricky prepares to leave town with Jane. Distraught, Carolyn drives through the night with a loaded gun. Frank confronts Lester, apparently with violence in mind, but instead makes a homosexual advance which Lester refuses. Lester finally gets a chance to have sex with Angela, but on finding she's actually a virgin, grows paternal instead. Frank enters the house and shoots Lester. At the moment of his death, Lester sees his life pass before him.

The raw material of *American Beauty* does not, let's be frank, sound very promising. A satirical portrait of suburban conformity? My dear, how terribly bold. A comic study of an *homme moyen sensuel* in the throes of a midlife crisis? How fearsomely original.

This just goes to show how misleading mere synopses can be. If there's hardly anything in the film's plot which isn't a cliché, there's hardly anything in its execution which doesn't seem effortlessly, indeed brilliantly, to transcend cliché. It's a wonderfully resourceful and sombre comedy and, like the greatest examples of the form, is as much about the perennial themes of self-delusion, conceit and madness as it is about the ephemeral idiocies of the day. To compare the story of Lester Burnham's midlife crisis with other comedies about ageing guys with the hots for a nubile girl *(Blame It on Rio,* say) would be as misconceived as bracketing *The Alchemist* with *Are You Being Served?* Even when *American Beauty*'s comedy is at its broadest and most grotesque—and there are moments which are every bit as brazenly laugh-seeking and laugh-getting as a good episode of *Frasier* or *The Simpsons*—the proceedings are given some unexpected nuance.

Take the scene in which Lester's wife Carolyn and her ghastly lover Buddy drive by the fast food joint and are served by Lester in his adopted role as a born-again proletarian. It plays well enough as a farcical agony of embarrassment, but what really tells in the scene is the note of steely aplomb in Lester's voice as he asks them if they'd like special sauce with their order. If only for a second or two, he's made himself top dog by glorying in the position of bottom dog, and the sense of power tastes more delicious to him than any fancy ketchup.

Kevin Spacey has had so many raves over the past few years that it seems almost redundant to point out what a superbly accomplished actor he is. *American Beauty* allows him to shine in certain ways we've not seen before. What renders his performance as Lester so satisfying is partly his ability to make the man seem both sap and hero (a man who should be acting his age, for God's sake and is absolutely right not to act his age) and partly his evocation of a soul managing to grow, or be refound, out of banal misery. If I had to pick a single simple moment from the whole film to demonstrate to sceptics quite how remarkable he is, it would probably be the one when he tells Frank he's not up for gay sex. Spacey delivers it with unimpeachable gentleness: it's the actorly equivalent of a note hit by a singer with perfect pitch.

With a central performance of this calibre, probably the most remarkable thing about *American Beauty* is that Spacey doesn't upset the film's dramatic balance. Sam Mendes, as you might expect of a director with a hefty track record in the theatre (he directed *The Rise and Fall of Little Voice* on stage), has made Alan Ball's intricate script play fluently as an ensemble piece, deftly serving every change of tone from goofy knockabout to beady observation.

You'd never guess Mendes was new to the cinema, though you might infer his knowledge of the stage from his penchant for head-on tableau compositions and the occasional touch of heightened reality in the performances, as with Annette Bening's sado-masochistic pep talk to herself about selling houses. Time and again, you fear Mendes won't be able to sustain such a confident shuffling of his pack, but somehow he does, and for once the result is a genuine surprise. At the end of the press screening I saw, a total stranger came up to me and said, in tones of disbelief, "That was a *gem*!" Politeness obliged me to agree; so did honesty.

TIME, 9/20/99, p. 79, Richard Schickel

Lester Burnham (Kevin Spacey) hates his job and the cubicle to which it confines him. He has also come to despise his tense and frigid wife Carolyn (Annette Bening), to mourn the sullen silence that has descended between him and his teenage daughter Jane (Thora Birch), to loathe

the sterile suburbia where they all try to make emotional ends meet. Lester masturbates a lot, especially when he gets to thinking about his daughter's friend Angela (Mena Suvari), the *American Beauty* of the title.

Oh, God, not that again. Not another midlife crisis, with its subcurrents of suppressed violence and repressed sexual longing. Not another tale in which we wait patiently or impatiently—depending on our tolerance for cultural clichés—for the cathartic, concluding burst of morally instructive gunfire.

But wait. Sometimes there is salvation in parentheses, especially when they surround the name of Kevin Spacey, giving a truly great performance. He's cynical. He's funny. He's angry. He's rueful. He's a mean truth teller and sometimes a curiously tender one. Best of all, he makes the transitions between these and a dozen other emotions heedlessly, without warning or visible preparation. You never know where he's coming from, or where he's going to end up in a scene. Yet boldly challenging our sympathies, he somehow wins them because, to borrow a phrase, he's a man in full.

He also has a dark and problematical double, the weird, smart boy next door. His name is Ricky (Wes Bentley). He deals drugs underneath the crazy nose of his abusive father (Chris Cooper), a retired Marine colonel of the neo-fascist persuasion, and creepily stalks Lester's daughter with his everpresent camcorder, eventually winning her because of the purity of his subversive nature. He is, perhaps, everything Lester might have been, if he had not long ago compromised himself. This also, perhaps, explains why Jane falls in love with him.

Ricky is a disturbing presence. Prior to Littleton, he might have been dismissed as an improbable one. But that tragedy—created by kids held in contempt by their peers and able to conduct a criminal life free of parental interference—gives him a peculiar, if entirely coincidental, resonance. He is not, in the end, tragedy's primary victim, but he is its precipitator, and the instructor of the complacency that it is the business of this movie to shatter.

Shatter stylishly, one must add. The writing by Alan Ball, whose first produced screenplay this is, consistently surprises—not so much in what it says, but in how it says it. He even risks having his story narrated by Lester from beyond the grave and makes Billy Wilder's old trick seem fresh. And the stage's Sam Mendes, also making his first film, dares a touch of expressionism, which we happily indulge, partly because he knows when to stop, mostly because the energy and conviction he and his cast bring to this movie do not permit second thoughts—at least until you are outside the theater, trying to shake off its mysterious spell.

VILLAGE VOICE, 9/21/99, p. 155, J. Hoberman

Talkin' 'bout that generation, September brings two richly metaphoric songs of male Boomer pathos: the midlife-crisis dark comedy *American Beauty,* and the sanctimonious baseball-veteran weepie, *For Love of the Game.*

The story is the same—dude, do your thing and regain your youth—but the attitudes are a bit different. Looking for some instant edge, *American Beauty* opens with a home video of an unhappy teenager whining that she needs a father "who's a role model, not some horny geek boy" drooling over her friends. The girl considers her dad "too embarrassing to live" and, in fact, he doesn't, narrating *American Beauty* from beyond the grave. Altogether more reverential, *For Love of the Game*'s precredit home movies show a cute Little Leaguer and his pop. No geek boys here, and the supernaturalism is far more natural—the images are rendered in slo-mo and accompanied by the sort of Americana religioso music sure to go into heavy rotation the day Ronald Reagan dies.

Bland and nasty, *American Beauty* has the slightly stale feel of a family sitcom conceived under the spell of *Married ... With Children.*   The location is generic suburbia; the houses are showroom stage sets. Lester, Carolyn, and Jane Burnham are a hapless bunch of middle Americans—a loser (Kevin Spacey), a bitch (Annette Bening), and their teenage brat (Thora Birch), all bound together in collective loathing and individual failure. Lester is an adman whose job hangs by a thread. Carolyn's a realtor who can't sell a house. Jane, the most sympathetic of the trio, is merely suffused in the sullen self-hatred characteristic of her class.

Directed by theatrical wunderkind Sam Mendes *(The Blue Room, Cabaret)* from Alan Ball's script, *American Beauty* has aspects of movie-industry allegory. It's predicated on middle-aged

Lester's life-changing lust for his daughter's lush-lipped, ultrablond best friend (Mena Suvari). Gotta get a slice of that American Pie. Although the fear-and-loathing-drenched conversations between the two girls provide the film's most resonant moments, this is hardly Catherine Breillat territory. The most perverse thing about Lester's *l'amour fou* is its liberating self-actualization.

Spacey underplays his role to appealingly hangdog affect. The same cannot be said for Bening but then, once his character lets go, Spacey has the better material. This is a man's world, or at least a boy's. Jerking off in the marital bed (rather than the shower), smoking pot with the neighbor kid Ricky (wooden Wes Bentley), revisiting the classic rock of his adolescence as he bench-presses in the garage, chucking his office job to get one flipping burgers, Lester is triumphantly regressive. His wife, meanwhile, can only reenact a tired, grown-up scenario of tawdry motel-room adultery and fantasy vengeance. Her form of self-actualization is learning to shoot a .44 Magnum.

Spacey's scenes have a slyly provocative slacker quality that nothing else in the movie achieves. The rest of the cast, including Peter Gallagher's holographic real-estate agent and the grim American Gothic family next door, serve largely as props. There's too much dead air around the dialogue and the comic pacing is nonexistent. For his first feature, Mendes seems to be striving for a tricksy, overstylized naturalism without much concern for visual coherence. Bouncing from one quick fix to another, the director shifts to video-surveillance mode or cuts to an overhead angle, strews one scene with symbolic rose petals and lights another in ostentatious chiaroscuro, then, when all else fails, sneaks outside to shoot the action softcore-porn style through a rain-streaked bedroom window.

Mendes's harsh and hyperbolic, if not particularly funny, satire of suburban angst makes *The Ice Storm* seem a nuanced masterpiece of engaged cine-humanism and wiseguy Todd Solondz look like a Swiftian genius. Bleak as it is, *American Beauty* has a certain car-wreck fascination but, with all the rubbernecking, there's no narrative flow. As studied as its title would suggest, this is one cold movie. All elements do laboriously come together as the action finally congeals into drama and, amid moments of sexual truth, goes glacially over the top.

Although its mood is as wintry as Ingmar Bergman, *American Beauty* has a backbeat of New Age mysticism. In keeping with the generational schema, this wisdom is imparted to Lester by young Ricky (an avant-garde video artist as well as a pothead): "It's hard to stay mad when there is so much beauty in the world." Easy for him to say. It's not even a lesson Mendes applies to his own film.

In a last bit of '60s feedback, *American Beauty* drafts a late Beatles dirge for its title crawl. Still, as misplaced nostalgia, few things are worse than the spectacle of Kevin Costner in a Detroit Tigers uniform, bucking the odds and pitching toward a comeback, alone on the mound with Bob Seger singing "Against the Wind."

In *For Love of the Game*, Costner plays 40-year-old Billy Chaplin, who, as we're more than once told, is a future hall-of-famer, as well as the Tigers' "heart and soul." Costner himself is the doggedly humorless heart and soul (and brains?) of this monumentally maudlin picture, directed by Sam Raimi from a script by Dana Stevens, the woman responsible for transforming *Wings of Desire* into *City of Angels*. Cocooned in self-congratulation, Costner's is the resident male ego who gets pumped up hearing his lady Jane (Kelly Preston, in a part, clothes, and coiffure seemingly designed for Meg Ryan) say things like "You are *such* a guy—you're the *ultimate* guy."

Nothing if not a structural film, *For Love of the Game* unfolds as sore-armed Billy is pitching a perfect game against the Yankees in New York while pondering the unhappy trajectory of his five-year-long affair with headstrong Jane. Flashbacks alternate with strikeouts. (Although the movie is a daunting two hours and 24 minutes long, the key scene is less than 30 seconds. Preston, smoothing Costner's hair as she cradles his head in her lap: "Do you believe in God?" Costner, after a slight pause: "Yes." And cut! God has got to be relieved.)

Costner must feel like he invented baseball in *Bull Durham* and brought down its commandments in *Field of Dreams*. I don't mind *For Love of the Game*'s ragging on obnoxious Yankee fans but it is pretty churlish that, in all the hubbub over Billy's fictional accomplishment—scarcely more amazing, if you think about it, than the idea of Kevin Spacey's fortysomething zhlub nailing Mena Suvari on his living-room couch—none of the real-life color commentators have the good grace to evoke the Yankees' own recent perfectos, David Cone or

David Wells. Instead we get Vince Scully going all incantatory: "He's pitching against time, he's pitching against the future, he's pitching against his own mortality." Yeah, yeah, he's pitching you a screenplay.

Sam Raimi made his bones with *Evil Dead* just about the time Billy supposedly reached stardom with the Tigers, but this sentimental epic is a new sort of horror film. *For Love of the Game* is designed to put a baseball-sized lump in your throat. Well before that, however, you may feel like putting a lump on Kevin Costner's head.

Also reviewed in:
CHICAGO TRIBUNE, 9/24/99, Friday/p. A, Michael Wilmington
NATION, 10/11/99, p. 34, Stuart Klawans
NEW REPUBLIC, 10/11/99, p. 36, Stanley Kauffmann
NEW YORK TIMES, 9/15/99, p. E1, Janet Maslin
NEW YORKER, 9/20/99, p. 133, David Denby
VARIETY, 9/13-19/99, p. 40, Todd McCarthy
WASHINGTON POST, 9/24/99, p. C1, Rita Kempley
WASHINGTON POST, 9/24/99, Weekend/p. 45, Desson Howe

AMERICAN HOLLOW

Executive Producer: Sheila Nevins. *Producer:* Rory Kennedy. *Director:* Rory Kennedy. *Director of Photography:* Nick Doob. *Editor:* Adam Zucker. *Music:* Bill Frissell. *Running time:* 90 minutes. *MPAA Rating:* Not Rated.

WITH: Iree Bowling; Bass Bowling; Edgar Bowling; Clint Bowling; Shirley Couch; Samantha Canada; Jody Canada; Lanzo Bowling.

NEW YORK, 5/31/99, p. 98, Peter Rainer

Documentary filmmaker Rory Kennedy followed a dirt-poor family clan in eastern Kentucky for an entire year, and the result is *American Hollow*. The Bowlings have lived more than a century between two mountains, and very few of them have ever made it out. Some of them work the land—what little there is to work—but most rely on government assistance. Kennedy doesn't attempt to poeticize these people or put them on display. The harrowing aspects of their lives are presented matter-of-factly: the endemic alcoholism, the legacy of wife abuse, the casual outlawry (the nearest police station is two hours away by car). Iree, the family matriarch, who's in her sixties and looks mid eighties, is proud of her brood. In the midst of much misery, she makes the most beautiful quilts.

NEW YORK POST, 5/26/99, p. 52, Rod Dreher

The largely forgotten rural poor of Appalachia are a natural subject for documentary filmmaker Rory Kennedy, whose late father, Bobby, made several visists to the hardscrabble region to draw attention to the residents' plight.

Her "American Hollow" is a clear-eyed and refreshingly unsentimentalized portrait of a Kentucky clan struggling to hold on to their increasingly untenable backwoods way of life.

The Bowling family has lived for more than a century in a remote ravine in eastern Kentucky. They live in what most Americans would think of as extreme poverty and deprivation, bunking in shacks and mobile homes, sustaining themselves by collecting herbs and welfare checks.

Though faced with enormous obstacles including geographical isolation, lack of education, joblessness, alcoholism, domestic violence—the prideful clan sticks fiercely together.

Aged matriarch Iree Bowling is the family's spiritual center. She's 68, but looks two decades older; the years of raising 13 children and overseeing a household in such primitive conditions having taken their toll on her scrawny body.

The film focuses most movingly on the long-suffering (but uncomplaining) women of the hollow, who keep the fragile society together.

Through three separate but skillfully edited narratives involving various members of the clan, we see that Iree's is a troubled family. The stories show the tangled skein of seemingly intractable problems that keep people like the Bowlings poor and miserable.

In many ways, the Bowlings live up to the classic hillbilly stereotype: They're violent, undisciplined, partial to moonshine, child brides and lawlessness. Though Kennedy clearly sympathizes with them, she doesn't make excuses for their folly.

Yet the director, who lived off and on with the Bowlings for the year it took to make "American Hollow," also uncovers the family's humanity.

They take pleasure in home-grown food and the company of kin, and don't whine about their lot. Their almost savage loyalty, both to their family and to their hollow, is a fascinating anachronism; all they have is their little scrap of land and each other.

These are people who don't expect to prevail, who seem happy enough just to endure.

VILLAGE VOICE, 6/1/99, p. 124, Gary Dauphin

The patch of rural Kentucky that *American Hollow* methodically turns is poor but fertile ground, growing big families and persistent problems that the locals confront with a particularly American combination of rural understatement and hot-blooded, often self-destructive intensity. Documentarian Rory Kennedy (yes, of those Kennedys, and the maker of several respected docs about women and children) worked her way into isolated Saul, Kentucky, and the over-40-strong Bowling clan, producing a rare problem-people doc that chooses complicated truth over simple message making.

Like the family it documents, *Hollow* flows from a single stream, the Bowlings' 67-year-old matriarch, Iree. One of those strong, ambulatory-oak-type grandmothers that no folksy family seems to be without, Iree shows off her family tree with a graceful unpretentiousness that has little use for face-saving white lies. She introduces her husband Bass and almost all of their 13 children with visible pride before turning to their various failings.

We meet Lanzo, Iree's Prozac-popping, root-gathering son, and his teenaged progeny Clint, a wiry Wu-Tang Clan fan who wants to marry his sweetheart Shirley despite not having a dime to his name. Lanzo beats his son down verbally while trying to suggest that the kids should wait a bit, and Clint hits back with the familiar fury of hard-luck adolescents everywhere. But when Clint sets a date, his family ponies up the money for the marriage license anyway, *Hollow* turning the collection of a mere $35 into moving, wrenching drama.

Then there's Iree's son Edgar, who is jailed and seems headed for more trouble despite having gotten a bum rap, and her granddaughter Samantha, who's shadowed by the husband who threatens to kill her on a daily basis. But just when it seems these people are irrevocably mired in bad luck, *Hollow* lights up with some bright, deeply human glow. Iree shows off the luminously beautiful quilts she makes; laughter and good food abound around a reunion table; and Iree's weekly trip to her Pentecostal Holiness church gives off preternatural, spirit-catching heat. *Hollow* takes both the good and bad with admirable openness, looking to slay not just *Deliverance* but also the faux-confessional, white-trash excesses of talk TV. To Kennedy's (and Iree's) credit, the Bowlings are never reduced to their hand-to-mouth, patchwork circumstances; their eager openness never erases any darker truths.

American Hollow was a hit at the last Sundance and the accolades it received feel justified while you're sitting there mutely fascinated by the trials and tribulations unfolding on screen. You come to see (or, more truthfully, imagine) certain symmetries to *Hollow*'s own existence in the world: the Bowling women's clear willingness to work with Kennedy becoming an extension of the gendered, generations-long work women put in nurturing hearth, home, and memory. *Hollow* does seem to upend stereotypes about poor white rural folks, but there is something easy about the upbeat, life-affirming angle, how it turns every glimmer of joy or inner life into the stock victory for the human spirit (replete with jangly banjos). It's no surprise that people in all kinds of fucked-up situations maintain enormous amounts of dignity, self-awareness, and humanity, making *American Hollow*'s larger tragedy all the ways those qualities can count for nothing, especially when you're poor and your husband's prone to drink and you've nothing to your name except the stories you tell.

Also reviewed in:
NEW YORK TIMES, 5/26/99, p. E5, Stephen Holden
VARIETY, 3/8-14/99, p. 66, Joe Leydon

AMERICAN LOVE STORY, AN

An American Playhouse/ITS/Zohe Film Productions release. *Executive Producer:* Lindsay Law and Barbara Ludlum. *Producer:* Jennifer Fox. *Director:* Jennifer Fox. *Director of Photography:* Jennifer Fox. *Editor:* Jay Freund. *Music:* Marcus Miller. *Sound:* Jennifer Fleming. *Running time:* 540 minutes. *MPAA Rating:* Not Rated.

WITH: Karen Wilson; Bill Sims; Cicily Wilson; Chaney Sims.

NEW YORK POST, 6/23/99, p. 44, Jonathan Foreman

Baggy, incoherent, grossly underedited, "An American Love Story" may be the most boring and unenlightening documentary ever made in this country.

Plowing through the nine hours of what the publicity notes misleadingly call "an epic, real-life drama of an interracial marriage" feels like the cinematic equivalent of a year in solitary confinement.

To begin with, you wonder if filmmaker Jennifer Fox became so involved with the Wilson-Sims family—which she followed with a camera for 18 months—that she lost the ability to distinguish between the interesting and the banal.

But as one unfocused hour piles on another, you begin to ask if all the tedium isn't deliberate—as if Fox wants to say, "Look how ordinary and dull this mixed-race family is!"

Either that, or Fox presumes total ignorance of black and interracial America on the part of the audience.

Black blues musician Bill Sims (who sounds like Barry White), his white wife, Karen, and their two good-humored children, Cicily, 19, and Chaney, 12, live in Queens. The parents come from Marion, Ohio.

They are good, if slightly overprotective, parents with a penchant for tradition, despite their peace-sign earrings and their having married long after their first daughter was born. They say they are still in love, and they seem to get along OK.

Potentially interesting things happen to the family during the year and a half that Fox was with them. Karen gets sick and has an operation. Bill has troubles getting gigs and has to go back to Marion, when his son from an earlier marriage is arrested for drug dealing.

Cicily has a falling out with her dad when he complains about her doing nothing to get a job after graduation from college, but unlike an episode of "The Real World," you don't actually see it—you just hear about it.

The images you see are mostly there to accompany voice-overs and rarely have any intrinsic visual interest. The camera lingers for an age on things like the family getting into a cab or Dad working in the kitchen.

You can only take so much cooking and dishwashing, all from the same angle, before it becomes like wallpaper. And by the third episode you find yourself checking out the family's changing haircuts over time, anything to stay awake while folks talk about how time just flies when you have kids.

The home-movie style camera work is shockingly bad. The only exception is in episode No. 3—the hour in which the camera is in the hands of Cicily and her pals during a semester in Nigeria.

This episode isn't just better photographed, it contains genuinely moving and shocking material. Her camera records the way Africa brings out the worst among the black students, who become increasingly hostile to both their white peers and the Nigerians.

Even as she falls in love with a Nigerian student who cannot understand the anti-white animus of the African-Americans, the young bigots from Colgate call Cicely a "half-breed." When she refuses to get "down" with their separatist program, one young man even threatens her physically. This is terrific stuff, and if it were a film by itself it would merit an excellent review.

VILLAGE VOICE, 6/29/99, p. 148, Amy Taubin

An American Love Story is a 10-hour television series directed by Jennifer Fox, who, in the early '90s, spent more than a year videotaping the daily life of the Sims-Wilson family: Bill Sims, Karen Wilson, and their daughters, Cicily and Chaney. For much of this time, Fox (who shot the series herself and Jennifer Fleming, her sound recordist, lived with the Sims-Wilsons in their far-from-spacious Queens apartment. I'm not sure why the family members allowed these two women such extraordinary access, but they seem motivated by an honest desire to share their beliefs, doubts, and ambivalences, rather than by gross exhibitionism. The result is unlike anything else in movies or television—*An American Family,* the groundbreaking 1972 series about the Loud family, seems trivial by comparison—and is surely among the most serious studies of American culture produced in a visual medium.

At the time the series begins, Bill, a blues and jazz musician who loves to cook, and Karen, who works in the human resources department of a large corporation, are in their late forties; Cicily, 20, is a student at Colgate—and Chaney, 12, is in junior high. Karen and Bill are both from Ohio, where they met in 1967. They were friends for quite a while before they became lovers, and lovers for years before they married, in 1979. ("I married Bill," says Karen, "thinking I could divorce him anytime.")

To say their relationship was difficult from the start is to laughably understate the case. Bill is black and Karen is white. When they met, he was already married with a child, and he also drank and drugged with abandon. Karen, one of the most popular girls in her high school class, was ostracized once she got involved with Bill. A male friend from that time says, with discernible relish, that she became "the scum of the town." Bill was hounded by the cops and thrown in jail more than once. The situation only became worse when Cicily was born and Karen refused to give her up for adoption.

The year the Supreme Court finally overturned state laws prohibiting interracial marriage, 1967 was also the year Bonnie and Clyde painted movie screens red and became emblematic outlaws and fashion statements. Pretty, fair-haired Karen, who says her rebel streak was encouraged by her father, seems to have incorporated Bonnie into her fantasy life. Getting involved with Bill was her way of becoming an outlaw. He also, she says, was simply the most interesting person to talk to that she'd ever met. Bill seems to have found a much-needed stability in the relationship, which worked, moreover, because Karen allowed him mostly to come and go as he pleased. All four family members agree that there are two Bills—the real Bill and the other Bill, who puts his music first and gets mean when he's drunk.

Karen and Bill moved to multiculti Flushing so that their daughters would not be subject to the same hostility as they'd been. And Bill realized that, as a black man, there was no future for him in Marion, Ohio, which his grown-up daughter from his first marriage describes as "the twilight zone." One of the underpinnings of the series is the contrast between big-city and small-town life. In a particularly painful episode, Bill goes back to Marion to see his son, who's about to go to jail for dealing coke. And the series concludes with Karen and Bill traveling together to Ohio for her 25th high school reunion.

There are also glimpses of Bill on the road with his band, and episode three is shot almost entirely by Cicily and her classmates in Nigeria during their semester abroad. But for the most part, the series takes place in the family's apartment, where, despite the presence of the camera, which they often acknowledge, occupants and visitors alike behave with a notable lack of self-consciousness. I could only pity, however, the 13-year-old boy who comes to take Chaney on her first date and finds himself being videotaped. At such moments, one wonders about the behind-the-scenes negotiations that made possible the seemingly free flow of daily life we see onscreen.

Although a number of extremely dramatic events occur during the course of the series (surgery, malaria, alcoholic bingeing, and full-scale depression), *An American Love Story* never seems like a soap opera. In part that's because Karen and Bill are both quite reserved, albeit in very different ways. And in part it's because Fox has organized the material to show how tensions gradually build and dissipate over the course of a long, largely successful relationship. It slowly becomes clear why Karen and Bill are well matched and how much more interesting their lives are because they've troubled to stay together. They are also extremely thoughtful, loving parents, and their daughters, as a result, are terrific young women.

Although the series will probably be described as cinema verité, it's hardly that. Fox uses a ton of voice-overs that function partly to fill in the back story and partly as interior monologues do in novels. Thus we interpret what we see on the screen in terms of what the family members say about their feelings, beliefs, and desires in audio interviews conducted at a different time during production. In other words, this documentary "reality" is more complicated in its construction than it might appear at first glance. And indeed, *An American Love Story* has a novelistic shape that becomes more engrossing the more we come to know the characters. Fox takes a big risk in the first two episodes by making race not only the major issue but the exclusive issue that seems to shape the Sims-Wilson family. And it is the delineation of race as a factor conditioning every moment of quotidian existence that makes the series so unique. But as our understanding of the characters deepens, race becomes only part of the picture—for a couple of stretches, we may lose track of it entirely.

An American Love Story is screening at the Film Forum in three separate programs, each comprising three 55-minute episodes. One episode is being withheld so that PBS can premiere the series in its entirety in September. Created as a television series, it is seen to best advantage on the small screen, where the intimacy of the viewing situation mirrors the intimacy of the narrative. On the other hand, there's something to be said for experiencing the volatile reactions the show evokes in the company of a larger audience.

Also reviewed in:
NEW YORK TIMES, 6/23/99, p. E1, Stephen Holden
VARIETY, 1/25-31/99, p. 74, Joe Leydon

AMERICAN MOVIE

A Sony Pictures Classics release of a C Hundred Film Corporation/Bluemark production. *Producer:* Sarah Price. *Director:* Chris Smith. *Director of Photography:* Chris Smith. *Editor:* Barry Poltermann, Jun Diaz, and Chris Smith. *Music:* Mike Schank. *Sound:* Sarah Price. *Running time:* 104 minutes. *MPAA Rating:* R.

WITH: Mark Borchardt (Filmmaker); Monica Borchardt (Mark's Mom); Cliff Borchardt (Mark's Dad); Chris Borchardt (Mark's Brother); Alex Borchardt (Mark's Brother); Ken Keen (Friend/Associate Producer); Joan Petrie (Mark's Girlfriend/Associate Producer); Bill Borchardt (Mark's Uncle/Executive Producer); Mike Schank (Friend/Musician).

LOS ANGELES TIMES, 11/12/99, Calendar/p. 18, Kevin Thomas

Chris Smith's "American Movie," which took the Grand Jury Prize for best documentary at Sundance this year, is sure to draw lots of laughs. Here's this small-town Wisconsin guy, Mark Borchardt, trying to make a movie on a shoestring with the help of some pals, in particular his spacey, shaggy musician friend Mike Schank, while coaxing money out of his frail, bleary 82-year-old uncle Bill Borchardt. These people say and do goofy things from time to time, and they all sound like the people in "Fargo."

Chroniclers of the independent filmmaking scene, however, may not be so easily amused. We know all too well that the world has an abundance of Mark Borchardts, and the likelihood of any of them getting anywhere is no better than winning the lottery.

Even so, although overly long at 107 minutes, "American Movie" is an incisive, largely absorbing work and a far more mature effort than Smith's "American Job," which sent the message, intentionally or otherwise, that menial jobs are beneath young white males.

Never condescending to Borchardt, a tall, lean 30-year-old with a goatee, long hair and outsize glasses, Smith assumes a detached stance at the start and sticks to it. In doing so, he invites us to see Borchardt as an archetypal all-American individualist determined to pursue the American Dream in an era of lowered expectations.

For years Borchardt has been working intermittently on "Northwestern," which he describes as about a bunch of guys "drinkin', drinkin', drinkin'"—and which sounds more than a little autobiographical. Early on in "American Movie," Borchardt is forced to abandon the project once again, for the usual reason, a lack of funds. Instead, he resumes work on a supernatural horror thriller, "Coven," shooting in 16 millimeter. Even if he succeeds in completing it, it will have taken him three years to do so. That Borchardt's hero is "Night of the Living Dead's" George Romero is evident in glimpses we get of "Coven."

To his credit, Borchardt, who began making movies at 14, is a resourceful, knowledgeable craftsman; he knows what he wants and how to get it. He's strong-willed, hard-working and focused. He's chronically deep in debt and in a precarious position in a looming custody struggle with his ex-girlfriend over their children. He supports himself delivering papers and working as a cemetery maintenance man. He's a motor-mouth who can be pretty wearying but has an open, affable quality that makes you hope he somehow miraculously beats the odds and enjoys some measure of success.

His Swedish-born mother is supportive, and her estranged husband, Mark's father, wishes his son well but is understandably dubious. Even more so is one of Mark's brothers, who says he thinks Mark would be better off working in a factory and wonders who would want to see "Coven" anyway.

At one point Mark pauses to consider that here he is, 30 years old, and having to clean up a filthy restroom at the cemetery. The question he needs to ask himself is how he would feel about still doing it at 40.

Note: "Coven," which runs about 38 minutes, stars Borchardt as a freelance writer who, facing a deadline, fortifies himself on such a combustible mixture of pills and booze that he winds up in an emergency room. Upon release, he's persuaded to join what sounds like Alcoholics Anonymous but turns out to be a sinister group indeed. "Coven" is too obvious and juvenile to hold much interest, but Borchardt, as a filmmaker, is energetic and personal, knowing how to protect what clearly are his own fears and frustrations. Clearly, filmmaking is for him a means of self-expression, but whether he has what it takes to make a feature-length film that audiences can connect with remains to be seen.

NEW STATESMAN, 7/3/00, p. 48, Jonathan Romney

I can't remember the last time I heard a film-maker invoke the American Dream, but it was most probably a fictional one—a a sleazy producer, perhaps, hoodwinking an innocent hopeful in some satire on Hollywood squalor. But in Chris Smith's documentary *American Movie*, it's the hopeful who takes the phrase as a mantra. "The American Dream stays with me each and every day," declares Mark Borchardt early on. By the end, he's swearing in desperation: "I will be goddamned if I don't get the American Dream."

Smith's film presents Borchardt as the ultimate American Dreamer, which is tantamount to saying the ultimate American Loser. He's a motormouth fantasist who spends his whole life dreaming of making movies, and even puts considerable effort into making them, although the results seem fated to calamity. Aged 30, Borchardt has three children from a failed relationship, lives with his mother in a Milwaukee suburb, is deep in debt and has been trying for years to make a thinly veiled autobiographic feature called *Northwestern*. But he seems chronically incapable of finishing anything he starts, and abandons *Northwestern* to complete his horror short, *Coven* (rhyme here with "cloven"). Although Smith's film is subtitled "the making of *Northwestern*", it is actually *Coven* that gets made.

Between fits of active self-doubt, Borchardt has infinite faith in himself and seems to have the gift of making friends and collaborators share this faith. His family just about tolerate him—his brothers feel Mark would have been more suited to life as a factory worker, or possibly a stalker. Borchardt's closest friend is Mike Schank, a gentle guitarist whose amiably sloth-like personality is explained by a rich fund of drug anecdotes.

It's hard not to see *American Movie* as a docu-sitcom—a real-life *Wayne's World* about suburban no-hopers and their ludicrous aspirations, with Borchardt as a cartoon creation who incidentally has an autonomous existence in the real world. We laugh at his grandiloquence, proverb-mangling and second-hand motivational movie-speak. And we marvel at the larger-than-life characters around him: the goatee'd luvvie who plays Bela Lugosi to Borchardt's Ed Wood, or the decrepit, trailer-dwelling "executive producer" Uncle Bill, kvetching away in his barely intelligible, doom-laden mumble.

But if we laugh at Borchardt's circle, is it the film's problem or ours? Admittedly, Smith editorialises, cutting for maximum comic effect so that scenes tend to end on a punchline of verbal pratfall. We feel we're invited to snigger at the hicks, to see Borchardt's world as an extended freak show. But Smith doesn't package that world's tragedy quite as obviously as he does the comedy. It's up to the viewer to look beyond the farce and see how serious Borchardt's existence is, how desperate and economically driven is his dream of a "second chance".

Borchardt's erratic grip on reality is explained by a turbulent family background, while his monomania is clearly endangering his own children's future. Mike, similarly, is not just a sweet-natured lunk, but apparently an irreparable drugs casualty, while cranky old Bill is a wealthy man who seems to have chosen an existence of decaying dementia. All this makes *American Movie* as much a horror story as Borchardt's own *The More the Scarier III*.

There's actually much to admire in Borchardt's obsessiveness, although that makes his propensity to fail all the more distressing. He doesn't just sit and talk about film, but gets on with it, displaying an impressive degree of technical know-how—he's fanatically hands-on, tirelessly acting, shooting, editing and recording. His ranting apart, Borchardt may well be no more incompetent or deluded than the armies of no-budget film-makers who regularly achieve moderate success in the US. It just happens that the *Blair Witch Project* crew beat Borchardt to the punch. But, had he been more astute at career-building, there's no reason why it might not have been him.

American Movie also conveys a delicate understanding of Borchardt's relations with others, which are tempered with real love. Mike Schank ceases to be a joke figure as we realise how much he holds Borchardt's universe together, simply by making him smile. We may laugh at the squalid anarchy of the scene in which Borchardt helps his Uncle Bill have a bath, but beneath the grim farce is some of the tenderness with which the British photographer Richard Billingham has documented his own chaotic family background.

Unlike Billingham, Smith is an outsider looking in. Whether or not we accept *American Movie* depends on how we perceive the pact between Smith and his subjects. Could Borchardt possibly have known, and accepted, that he would emerge as a larger-than-life comic creation? Or perhaps he realised that he would always be his own creation, and that Smith was offering him his big break, if not as film-maker then as a sort of novelty talk-show turn, an exemplary American Case History? Some critics have called Smith irresponsible in giving Borchardt the limelight, in encouraging him to take himself seriously. But attention is what Borchardt seems to crave more than anything, even more than achievement as a director. In this sense, everybody wins: Smith makes his documentary, while Borchardt becomes a genuine cult figure and gets to tour the world with in-person appearances and screenings of *Coven*. Horror buff's tell me that it's actually not too bad.

NEW YORK POST, 11/5/99, p. 60, Lou Lumenick

"American Movie" is a frequently hilarious, if overlong, documentary about a young Wisconsin man who struggles over three years make an ultra-cheap horror movie.

Mark Borchardt, who supports himself by delivering the Wall Street Journal and doing menial jobs at a cemetery, is a hard-drinking, dope-smoking 30-year-old slacker who's been making short films since he was 14.

As "American Movie" opens, Borchardt abandons plans to complete an autobiographical drama called "Northwestern" and decides instead to revive an abortive short slasher film called "Coven," which he plans to sell directly on video for $14.95 to fund a more ambitious project.

The motor-mouth Borchardt demonstrates a genius for talking people into contributing their time. But his drinking, lack of focus and his personal problems (including lack of money and arguments with the mother of his three young children) conspire to drag out shooting of the 35-minute, black-and-white feature.

"American Movie" director Chris Smith spent years following the movie in production and filmed extensive, sometimes remarkably frank interviews with Borchardt, members of his family, his friends, and members of the cast and crew of "Coven"—many of whom are highly skeptical of Borchardt's abilities as a filmmaker.

Excerpts from "Coven" suggest it's closer in quality to "Plan 9 From Outer Space" than "The Blair Witch Project," but Borchardt plows ahead, borrowing $3,000 from his 80-year-old—and possibly senile—uncle, who leaves his trailer-park home to appear in the opening scene of "Coven." The uncle requires more than 30 takes to re-record his one-line part.

Other major characters include Borchardt's best friend, another stoner named Mike Schrank whose contributions to the movie's soundtrack stop just short of plagiarism, and his long-suffering girlfriend Joan Petrie, who serves as the movie's executive producer.

The documentary follows Borchardt and company through crisis after crisis, up to the premiere of "Coven" in 1997—and it's hard to resist his often-misplaced enthusiasm.

"American Movie" director Smith and his producer, Sarah Price, have an obvious affection for their subject. But they clearly had difficulty cutting the 90 hours of footage they amassed, and their film starts outwearing its welcome just past the 60-minute mark.

NEWSDAY, 11/5/99, Part II/p. B6, Jan Stuart

You couldn't ask for a more perfect response to "The Blair Witch Project," a horror movie about a neophyte filmmaker shooting a documentary, than "American Movie," a documentary about a neophyte filmmaker shooting a horror movie.

There are those who would find "American Movie" to be the real horror story.

Chris Smith's frightening and funny chronicle of one man's efforts to see a low-budget movie to its conclusion would undoubtedly strike terror in the hearts of the families and friends of neophyte filmmakers everywhere, if not in the fledgling directors themselves.

At 30, Mark Borschardt of Wisconsin is still delivering newspapers and cleaning toilets to subsidize his efforts to be the next George Romero. An acolyte of such cult bloodbaths as "The Texas Chainsaw Massacre" and "Dawn of the Dead," he has cobbled together a modest list of his own credits with such titles as "The More the Scarier," "I Blow Up" and "The More the Scarier II & III." His next project, a stop-and-go labor of love called "Northwestern," has to be put on the shelf once again till he can raise the necessary financing by making a quickie thriller called "Coven." For Borschardt, who also supports three kids from a broken marriage and has a troublesome alcohol habit, the arrival of a new MasterCard in the mail is as close as life gets to promising. And everyone in Borschardt's local-call range gets collared to act, edit or, in the case of his irascible 82-year-old uncle, donate money: his mother, his girlfriend Joan, his ex-con buddy Ken and his musician friend Mike Schank.

A reformed pothead whose years of partying have reduced him to something out of "Night of the Living Dead," Mike shares with Uncle Bill duties as "American Movie's" unintended comic relief, as well as receptacle for our most fervent there-but-for-the-grace-of-God sighs. Our feelings for Borschardt are far more complex. His aging-slacker ambience is belied by a manic determination: While you can't help but sympathize with his brother Alex' skepticism at Borschardt's artistic agenda, you also have to admire Borschardt's all-American resilience and stick-to-itiveness.

"American Movie" won a Grand Jury Prize at Sundance, where the identification factor runs strong. For the rest of us, Borschardt's coterie of real folks wears out its welcome well before "Coven" has its premiere. Still, it is to the credit of his observer, Chris Smith, that we are left wondering whether we have just witnessed the American Dream in action or an American nightmare.

VILLAGE VOICE, 11/9/99, p. 140, Amy Taubin

A portrait of an aspiring film director, Chris Smith's *American Movie* has its share of disconcerting power relationships. Smith's minimalist first feature about overqualified wage slaves wasn't exactly a Hollywood calling card, but it certainly alerted people to his talent.

Rather than pursue the fiction feature route, Smith spent three years documenting obsessed Wisconsin filmmaker Mark Borchardt as he attempted to get his dream project, *Northwestern,* off the ground.

Though he's acquired basic film-school lingo, Borchardt's appreciation of cinematic form and expression is limited to the ghoulish ambience and gory specifics of the films that fascinated him as a prepubescent: *Night of the Living Dead, Dawn of the Dead,* and *Texas Chainsaw Massacre.* While there's no doubting his passion, as a filmmaker he's an uninteresting case of arrested development.

Smith films Borchardt on the set and in various home environments with his three kids, doting mom, skeptical dad, loyal girlfriend, and contemptuous ex-wife. His decrepit Uncle Bill is persuaded to provide completion funds for the 20-minute horror short, *Coven,* to which Borchardt returns when *Northwestern* proves overly ambitious. His brain permanently scrambled by bad acid, Borchardt's best friend Mike Schank makes an indelible impression, as does Mark's alarmingly affectless brother, who must be projecting when he opines, without a trace of humor, that he expected Mark to become a serial killer.

His honorable intentions notwithstanding, Smith has preempted Borchardt's cherished *Northwestern* by packaging it as *American Movie.* With a passive-aggressiveness worthy of Warhol, he has used the camera to exacerbate a relationship of unequal power. Borchardt has been accompanying Smith to one major festival after another. Although I don't begrudge Borchardt his year of fame, what he doesn't seem to understand about his exploitation creeps me out.

Also reviewed in:
CHICAGO TRIBUNE, 1/21/00, Friday/p. A, Michael Wilmington
NEW YORK TIMES, 11/5/99, p. E20, Janet Maslin
VARIETY, 2/8-14/99, p. 77, Glenn Lovell
WASHINGTON POST, 12/17/99, p. C4, Stephen Hunter
WASHINGTON POST, 12/17/99, Weekend/p. 45, Michael O'Sullivan

AMERICAN PIE

A Universal Pictures release of a Zide/Perry production. *Producer:* Chris Weitz, Warren Zide, Craig Perry, and Chris Moore. *Director:* Paul Weitz. *Screenplay:* Adam Herz. *Director of Photography:* Richard Crudo. *Editor:* Priscilla Nedd-Friendly. *Music:* David Lawrence. *Music Editor:* Charles Martin Inouye. *Sound:* Cameron Hamza and (music) Guy Defazio. *Sound Editor:* Richard Legrand, Jr. *Casting:* Joseph Middleton. *Production Designer:* Paul Peters. *Art Director:* Paul Peters. *Set Designer:* Joshua Lusby. *Set Decorator:* Amy Wells. *Set Dresser:* Jeffrey Snyder. *Special Effects:* Ron Trost. *Costumes:* Leesa Evans. *Make-up:* Rod Wilson. *Stunt Coordinator:* Russell Towery. *Running time:* 100 minutes. *MPAA Rating:* R.

CAST: Jason Biggs (Jim); Jennifer Coolidge (Stifler's Mom); Shannon Elizabeth (Nadia); Alyson Hannigan (Michelle); Chris Klein (Oz); Clyde Kusatsu (English Teacher); Eugene Levy (Jim's Dad); Natasha Lyonne (Jessica); Thomas Ian Nicholas (Kevin); Chris Owen (Sherman); Lawrence Pressman (Coach Marshall); Tara Reid (Vicky); Seann W. Scott (Stifler); Mena Suvari (Heather); Eddie Kaye Thomas (Finch); Molly Cheek (Jim's Mom); Christina Milian (Band Member); Woody Schultz (Party Guy); Casey Erklin (Drinking Buddy); Annika Hays (Party Girl); Eden Riegel (Sophomore Chick); Justin Isfeld and John Cho ("MILF" Guys); Alexandra Adi (Central Girl); Veronica Lauren and Monica McSwain (Vocal Jazz Girls); Akuyoe Graham (Vocal Jazz Teacher); Katie Lansdale (Enthralled Girl); Jay Rossi (Sushi Customer); Linda Gehringer (Vicky's Mom); Ashton Dane (Vicky's Dad); Sasha Barrese (Random Cute Girl); Eric Lively (Albert); Eli Marienthal (Stifler's Younger Brother); Travis Cody Aimer (Computer Nerd); Mark Hoppus, Thomas M. Delonge, and Scott Raynor (Garage Band); Danny Spink (Guy with Monkey); James DeBello (Enthusiastic Guy); Amber Phillips and Clementine Ford (Computer Girls); Hilary Salvatore (Girl Holding Out); Jasmine Stocken and Jillian Bach (Bathroom Girls); David Kuhn (Prom Band Singer); Markus Botnick (Assistant Lacrosse Coach); Casey Affleck (Kevin's Brother).

LOS ANGELES TIMES, 7/9/99, Calendar/p. 1, Kenneth Turan

"American Pie" is the damndest thing. Both warmhearted and foul-mouthed, this unlooked-for hybrid of "South Park" and Andy Hardy uses its surface crudeness as sucker bait to entice teenage audiences into the tent to see a movie that is as sweet and sincere at heart as anything Mickey Rooney and Judy Garland ever experienced.

As a card-carrying contemporary youth comedy, "American Pie" does have its gross-out credentials in what you might call apple pie order. Front and center are jokes about voyeurism, diarrhea, premature ejaculation, the drinking of beer with a semen chaser and, in the film's signature moment, masturbation with one of those homemade pies.

It all sounds as vulgar as the tolerant MPAA allows, but to see "American Pie" is to know that all this foolishness is only window-dressing for a film that at its core is surprisingly innocent and good-natured and even finds the time to promote decent values. If America's teenagers have a biological need to sneak into crass R-rated movies, and apparently they do, this is the one parents not only can feel safest about but might even enjoy themselves.

"American Pie" is the feature debut for screenwriter Adam Herz, who apparently used his own not-that-distant school years at Michigan's East Grand Rapids High as inspiration. Paul and Chris Weitz, the director and co-producer, respectively, collaborated on the writing of both "Antz" and "Madeline," and while that latter film's nuns might need a stretcher after exposure to some of the humor here, they'd find a lot to like as well.

For one thing, this has got to be one of the least mean-spirited of recent American comedies. Cast from top to bottom with extraordinarily likable young actors who we instinctively want to be happy, "American Pie" also benefits from screenwriter Herz's clever plotting and his exact sense of what is due to each character, even the most hostile and profane.

More than that, "American Pie" is unusual in its ability to mix bodily functions humor with a sincere and unlooked-for sense of decency. Though its characters obsess endlessly about sex, even to the point of wondering if Ariel in "Little Mermaid" would be an appropriate partner, the film finally comes down emphatically in favor of treating people with consideration and acting from the heart as the keys to happiness.

"American Pie" opens with the sounds of a woman moaning in sexual ecstasy in a teenager's room, but it's not a real woman, it's a scrambled broadcast on an adult channel, which is as close to actual sexual experience as Jim (Jason Biggs) and his friends have had, endless talk and fantasizing notwithstanding.

Kevin (Thomas Ian Nicholas) does have a steady girlfriend, the beautiful Vicky (Tara Reid), but they've yet to find the perfect moment to go all the way. Totally without female companionship are Chris "Oz" Ostreicher ("Election"'s marvelous Chris Klein), who devotes his life to lacrosse, and the dry, intellectual Finch (Eddie Kay Thomas), who enjoys using Latin to make jokes about the dog eating his homework.

Clustering around this core group are other archetypal high school characters. On the hip side are the crude party animal Stifler (Seann W. Scott), who calls his house "Stifler's Palace of Love," and the wise, sexually experienced Jessica (Natasha Lyonne of "Slums of Beverly Hills"). Further down the pecking order are braces-wearing Sherman (Chris Owens), a.k.a. "the Shenninator, a sophisticated sex robot sent back through time," and Michelle (a delightful Alyson Hannigan), a flute player who thinks of nothing but band, band, band.

Fearful of, God forbid, graduating high school as virgins, Jim, Kevin, Oz and Finch make the pact that drives "American Pie's" plot: They will motivate and support one another so that, by prom night, exactly three weeks away, they will no longer be sexual novices. "We will become," Kevin proclaims in a mock-passionate speech, "masters of our sexual destiny."

This vow, not surprisingly, becomes the basis for numerous moments of embarrassment and mortification; if there is a wrong or awkward thing to be said or done, one of these guys will say or do it. The most intriguing scenarios involve Oz, who meets the beautiful Heather (Mena Suvari) when he expands his sensitive side and tries out for jazz chorus, and woebegone Jim, who endures a father (Eugene Levy), whose attempts to help are tone-deaf, and what he fears is an unattainable crush on stunning Czech exchange student Nadia (Shannon Elizabeth).

Though wincing at what its characters go through is the main source of "American Pie's" laughs, the film manages to treat almost everyone with respect, even, for the most part, the women, rarely the case in films like this. Naturally, everything comes down to a post-prom party at Stifler's mom's (Jennifer Coolidge) lakeside vacation home where wacky plot turns culminate in the kind of unexpected good feelings that characterize this most surprising of teenage films.

NEW YORK POST, 7/9/99, p. 48, Jonathan Foreman

"American Pie" may be a tiny bit less obscene than "There's Something About Mary," but it deserves every bit of its "R" rating, and no one should even think of seeing it with their parents—or, for that matter, with their kids.

It is vulgar and lewd and raunchy like you wouldn't believe, and absolutely hilarious from beginning to end.

Sure, it shares plot elements and cast members with every high-school movie hit of the last three years. It's also the first comedy to use the Internet to excruciatingly funny effect. But it's really a throwback to lubricious teen sex comedies of the 1980s like "Porky's," "The Last American Virgin" and "Fast Times and Ridgemont High."

The main difference—and it's a big one—lies in "American Pie's" relatively authentic and well-written female characters. As befits the era of TV's "Felicity," "Buffy the Vampire Slayer" and "Party of Five," the girls in "American Pie" are much more than life-support systems for breasts.

The film also differs from recent teen flicks, not only by virtue of some superior performances, but also in its use of a high-school setting that is not just upper middle-class suburban but almost exclusively white.

Four ordinary high-school seniors resolve to lose their virginity by prom night, gored by the apparent sexual success of a dweeby pal. Kevin (Thomas Ian Nicholas) has already reached third base with his girlfriend Vicky (Tara Reid), but she wants to wait until things are perfect. Oz (Chris Klein, playing almost the same part he did in "Election"), is the handsome lacrosse star who is too trapped within a boorish jock culture to appeal to girls. Jim (Jason Biggs) cannot even talk to a girl without making a total fool of himself. And otherwise sophisticated Finch (Eddie Kay Thomas) is too uptight even to use the school bathrooms.

So Oz decides to develop his sensitive side by joining the choir, Finch pays a tough-talking female pal Jessica (Natasha Lyonne) to spread popularity-enhancing rumors about his hidden charms, Kevin studies a secret oral-sex manual handed down through the generations, and Jim stakes everything on a wild and gorgeous exchange student from the Czech Republic (Shannon Elizabeth).

When Jim's bid for sexual initiation fails in a spectacularly public way, he gives up and agrees to go to the prom with flautist Michelle (Alison Hannigan, playing a nerdier version of her role as Willow in TV's "Buffy"). Nothing goes as planned, and various lessons—some of them harsh, others sweet—are duly learned.

Klein could make a whole career out of playing sensitive but not-too-bright hunks. Biggs is a standout as a horny Everyman who suffers one excruciating embarrassment after another. Lyonne, from "Slums of Beverly Hills," and Owen, from "She's All That" and "October Sky," both steal the few scenes they're in.

And you wish that beautiful Mena Suvari, who plays Oz's love-interest, Heather, and looks like Christina Ricci crossed with Julia Stiles, had more time on screen.

NEWSDAY, 7/9/99, Part II/p. B7, John Anderson

It's a bit perplexing what to think of "American Pie"—a movie that, in a slightly earlier era, might have been used to blackmail most of the people in it. But we live in an enlightened age—an age in which a major motion picture studio can produce a movie in which a teenager has sex with an apple pie. Then, once this great moment in baked goods becomes the calling card of the film much like the permanent wave in "There's Something About Mary" or the "coffee" in "Austin Powers: The Spy Who Shagged Me."

God help the pie if it tries to find work. But most of the cast probably will. After all, they hardly started the current race for bad taste. And despite all the rutting and jumping that goes on in this puerile (and, we might add, ineptly made) movie, the film does come fully equipped with the message that sensitivity toward women is a good thing.

Of course, such conclusions are never allowed to preempt the fun: One young woman being transmitted nude on the Internet, for instance, or another making an oral deposit into a cup of beer (one movie's beer, as they say, is another's hair gel) or a third getting to explain her own personal woodwind variation on female sexual satisfaction. This is called having it both ways. Which in this film is saying a mouthful.

Oh, yes, the plot. As it were. Four high school friends—Jim (Jason Biggs), Oz (Chris Klein, kind of a pumped-up Keanu Reeves), Kevin (Thomas Ian Nicholas) and Finch (Eddie Kaye Thomas)—make a pact to lose their virginity on or about Prom Night. All have their respective obstacles to overcome, primarily a lack of willing accomplices. Kevin's longtime girlfriend, Victoria (Tara Reid), is waiting for things to be "perfect," which seems like a pipe dream as long as she's dating Kevin. Jim is just a mega-dork. Finch is a pseudo-intellectual, latte-sucking poseur. Oz is a lacrosse-playing choir member, so he may have other issues entirely.

In the course of their less-than-compelling journey toward "manhood" does the sexual dysfunction of people who've never had sex really qualify as dysfunction?—there are various teen antics: Slipping Finch a massive laxative (with no moment left to the imagination). The aforementioned Internet show involving a Romanian exchange student played by Shannon Elizabeth. (Want my advice? Go back to Romania.) And the excruciating father-son "chat" between Jim and his dad (a woeful Eugene Levy), during which Jim looks really embarrassed—suggesting, all things considered, that he's got a lot of nerve.

Alyson Hannigan, of TVs "Buffy, The Vampire Slayer," is quite good as the band-camp geek who hooks up with Jim. But like so many teen movies, the prom—half beatification, half abject humiliation—is missing the one guest who would have made it a night to remember: Carrie. As it is, you can only pray for your own death, not the mass carnage and scorched earth that would have made "American Pie" the family film it was meant to be.

NEWSWEEK, 7/12/99, p. 62, Jeff Giles

Is there anything a struggling young actor won't do? Consider Jason Biggs, 21. In the new high-school sex comedy *American Pie,* Biggs plays a horny, hapless teen who has an intimate encounter with—how to put this?—the title character. Biggs was only too eager. Later the ratings board told the makers of American Pie that if they wanted to avoid an NC-17, the actor couldn't thrust at the apple pie quite so many times. How many thrusts are seen in the finished movie? There's maybe two or three thrusts, says Biggs. How many were there originally—five? Maybe five. And how many thrusts seem right, you know, as an artist? Biggs laughs. I think we got our point across with two or three.

Now consider Heather Donahue, 24. In *The Blair Witch Project,* Donahue plays a student filmmaker who goes into the Maryland woods to shoot a documentary about a terrifying local legend—and never comes out. Prior to filming, the directors told Donahue that in the interest of realism, she and two other actors would have to trek into the forest alone and that they'd have to improvise all their own dialogue, as well as shoot the movie themselves on film and video. The more people I told about the movie, says Donahue, the more they said, "What, are you nuts? You can't possibly be considering it!" I mean, it was going to be me, two guys I didn't know and a video camera in the woods. When Gregg Hale, the producer, called and offered me the part, I said, "Look, is this a snuff film?"

It turns out that struggling young actors know best. *American Pie* and the *Blair Witch Project* have emerged as two of the most eagerly anticipated underdogs of the season, particularly among teens and twentysomethings. Both *Pie* and *Blair* were made by first-time directors. The former movie was a collaboration between Paul and Chris Weitz, sons of the fashion designer John Weitz. (They were previously co-writers on *Antz.*) The latter was directed by the Orlando-based duo Eduardo Sanchez and Daniel Myrick. Both *Pie* and *Witch* are full of new faces. And thanks to months of preview screenings, both have already launched careers and inspired fan sites on the Web.

Beyond all that, the films are different animals, one being a demented studio comedy, the other a supernaturally spooky independent movie. *Blair* cost so little to make that if it brings in $10 million it'll be a coup by art-house standards. *Pie* cost $11 million, and it's expected to be a solidly profitable sleeper making $75 million. Hollywood has such high hopes for *Pie* that Universal was taken to task in the press when it sold the foreign rights for a song. I can understand Universal thinking, 'Well, are French people really going to give a crap about these American teenagers?' says Chris Weitz, 29. But I think every male everywhere in the world would like to have sex as soon as possible.

American Pie is a funny movie, though hardly a great one, a shiny new machine built out of spare parts from *Porky's* and *Fast Times at Ridgemont High*. *Pie* centers on four hopelessly virginal high-school buddies in East Great Falls, Mich.: Jim (Biggs), Kevin (Thomas Ian Nicholas), Oz (Chris Klein) and Finch (Eddie Kaye Thomas). The guys make a pact to lose their virginity by prom night. Then they set about wooing and/or begging a choir girl (Mena Suvari), a lusty foreign-exchange student (Shannon Elizabeth), an earnest young woman looking for capital-L love (Tara Reid) and a hilariously boring band nerd (Alyson Hannigan). *Pie* is full of crude antics almost worthy of *There's Something About Mary*—there are set pieces devoted to four different involuntary bodily functions. Still, it turns out to be a surprisingly earnest and cautionary movie, careful to attract female viewers and not freak parents out too badly.

This latest high-school confidential is the brainchild of Adam Herz, 26, a jittery, likable first-time screenwriter who clearly modeled Biggs's shy character after himself. Did he date in school?, Um, no. Herz holds forth improbably about *Pie*'s predecessors (The thing that people forget about *Porkys*' is that it had some good issues—there was some truth in that movie, too), and waves off highbrow fare (You mean do I think *Citizen Kane* is the greatest movie of all time? I think it's boring. I had trouble staying awake through it). Herz was broke when he wrote *Pie*. To get by, he cashed savings bonds from his bar mitzvah. Herz called his screenplay *Untitled Sex Comedy Which Can Be Made for Under $ 10 Million That Studio Readers Will Most Likely Hate But I Think You Will Love*. Universal bid $750,000. Herz has since turned down more than 50 projects because, as he says flatly, most stuff in Hollywood sucks.

It usually does. Which makes the iconoclastic *Blair Witch* a welcome entry this summer. The premise is elegantly scary: an obsessive filmmaker named Heather (Donahue), her slacker cameraman (Joshua Leonard) and snarky sound guy (Michael Williams) vanish in the woods while on the trail of a supposedly mythical local figure, the Blair Witch. A year after they disappear, their footage is found. There are the black-and-white reels that were intended for the documentary, as well as Heather's behind-the-scenes video, which tells the crew's story as they find themselves lost in the woods, stalked by something they can hear but cannot see. Though *Blair* is a horror movie, it bears no relation to that Neve Campbell flick or its increasingly bad Xeroxes. In fact, there's absolutely no explicit violence on screen. *Blair* is about dread and isolation—it's a fairy tale reminding us that childhood fears are deep and tangled as tree roots. Heather's shaky video work can induce motion sickness—it looks like combat footage as she bolts through the woods—but just try turning away.

During the *Blair* shoot, the directors had little contact with the actors. For eight mornings they left them plot instructions, as well as a dwindling supply of food. At night the directors impersonated the Blair Witch and staged terrors near the actors' tent. The only time I felt guilty was when I could go home and sleep in my bed, and they were still out there, says director Sanchez, 30. But it was hard on us, too. They could sleep as late as they wanted. We had to be up in the middle of the night to go scare them.

Sanchez and Myrick spent about $40,000 on *Blair* before bringing it to Sundance, where Artisan Entertainment snapped it up for a reported $ 1.1 million. Donahue, who used to support herself as a temp, suddenly had an agent, a manager and a lawyer. When I first moved to L.A., I had shown people some footage from the film—casting directors and stuff, she says. And they were like, 'OK, whatever, buh-bye.' Now all of a sudden they're all calling me because I'm the 'Blair Witch' girl. It's the same stuff! So before Sundance no one recognized that the footage had, at the very least, a lot of indie cool? Oh, not at all, says Donahue. It looked like I got stoned with my roommates and went on a camping trip.

As *Pie* and *Blair Witch* head into theaters, their casts and crews seem slap-happy one moment, wistful the next. They're wistful because you only get one First Time. We're never going to be able to make a movie like this again, says *Blair* director Myrick, 35. There was so much serendipity involved. We had just the right actors. Nobody broke their ankle in the woods.

Nobody dropped the camera in the creek. They're elated because they know damn well their movies are better than most Gen-X and -Y fare. There's all this horrible, horrible stuff being made, says *Pie*'s Alyson Hannigan, 25. Before 'Scream,' these things would have been in the recycle bin. But now it's like, 'It's a teen movie? OK, we'll produce it! *American Pie* and *Blair* will turn heads. One tickles, the other terrifies. Both are truly a scream.

SIGHT AND SOUND, 10/99, p. 37, Kevin Maher

East Great Falls High, Michigan, the represent. Senior student Jim is caught masturbating by his parents. The next day the brash Stifler invites Jim and friends Oz, Kevin and Finch to a party. At the party, Kevin's girlfriend Vicky spits a mouthful of Kevin's semen into a glass of beer which Stifler accidentally drinks. Jim and his friends pledge to lose their virginity by Prom night—three weeks away. Jim's father lectures him about the female form; Oz, a talented lacrosse player, joins the school choir to get close to singer Heather; and rumours spread about Finch's sexual prowess.

Told that 'third base' feels like apple pie, Jim is caught having sex with an apple pie. Czech exchange student Nadia comes over to study with Jim. She changes in his room while Jim secretly watches her. He comes back into the room while she's masturbating; she forces him to strip for her. He has two premature ejaculations.

In school Jim's performance has made him a laughing stock. Shy band member Michelle invites him to the prom. Stifler discovers that Finch has been paying for his own rumours, and tricks him into drinking a laxative. Oz leaves the lacrosse team for Heather. At the prom Jim has sex with Michelle, Kevin with Vicky, and Finch with Stifler's mother.

That debut screenwriter Adam Herz has used Bob Clark's *Porky's* (1981) as a structural template for *American Pie* is obvious. From the opening erection gag through to the alternative penetration setpiece, this bawdy account of over excitable high-school teens who 'just gotta get laid' is surprisingly faithful to the crude episodic pay-offs of its predecessor. But, whereas *Porky's* crudely celebrated the scopophilic urge of its male leads to view women as strippers, prostitutes or virgin cheerleaders from the safety of hidden peepholes, the actual, naive engagement of *American Pie*'s young protagonists with their objects of desire lends the film an apologetic and often sweetly emasculated tone.

Herz and director Paul Weitz (co-writer of *Antz*) have dispensed with the usual hierarchy of teen-movie characters, where the smart students are socially maladjusted nerds and the athletes thuggish jocks. Instead, Jim, Kevin, Oz and Finch are a largely anonymous, banal, foursome. The characters are ciphers of adolescent trauma, easy targets that provide this slim tale with its comic centre. There are some overtly Oedipal obsessions—Stifler's mother represents the ultimate in sexual booty, Jim chooses to have sex with his mom's apple pie, and the gang even have a category of desirable women known by the acronym MILF ("Moms I'd Like to Fuck").

On a more conspicuous comedic level, there are inserts from the *Something About Mary* school of body horror, for instance Jim's two consecutive premature ejaculations and Kevin's accidentally imbibed semen. But surprisingly enough, given the film's reactionary antecedents, it is only in the presence of the female characters that *American Pie* offers genuine wit and sparkle.

An opening exchange between a nervous Oz and the college girl who announces that she's studying "Post Modernist Feminist Thought" sets the standard. The control exercised by Natasha Lyonne's cynical Jessica, Alyson Hannigan's introverted dominatrix Michelle, and Mena Suvari's virgin Heather over their ineffectual menfolk provides the film's narrative momentum. Jessica's tale-spinning leads to Finch's crisis; Heather's belief in virginity brings Oz off the sports field and into the school choir, even Shannon Elizabeth's thankless role as Nadia, the semi-naked exchange student, is given a pro-active twist when she forces Jim to perform a humiliating striptease.

On a technical level though, banal sitcom shooting style and generic teen performances often make *American Pie* indistinguishable from the likes of *She's All That* and *Varsity Blues*. And even Herz and Weitz's overhaul of the *Porky's* formula has its flaws—the bullying of an incontinent classmate, the introduction of a college heirloom of secret sexual technique, and the beginning of Nadia's bedroom frolics all seem to be lazily skewed towards a familiar teenage male demographic. An ending that sees our boys return from the sexual front rejoicing in bachelorhood also rings off on a conservative note: "This is the coolest!" says Kevin, as the boys drink shakes together safely beyond the grasp of female interference. For such a shameless re-invention of 80's smut, *American Pie* is better than we might expect, but in the end it's simply a noble addition to the lower ranks of thoughtful teen comedies.

VILLAGE VOICE, 7/13/99, p. 66, Dennis Lim

No less tunnel-visioned than *Arlington Road* [see Lim's review] but not nearly as, um, overbaked, *American Pie* returns the teen movie to the uncomplicated glory days of *Porky's* and *Losin' It*. Which, in the scheme of things, is preferable to the terminal blandness of *Varsity Blues* and *She's All That*. Four high-school seniors—shy jock, creepy geek, luckless schmuck, and another one I can't remember much about—resolve to be rid of their virginity by prom night. Epic, mostly public, humiliation ensues, some of it very funny, all of it very stupid and in terrible taste.

Director Paul Weitz (who cowrote *Antz)* never quite pulls off the balancing act of *There's Something About Mary,* in which the Farrellys managed to be goofy and sweet and gross all at once. *American Pie* is best when it's disgusting, which, admittedly, is a lot of the time. The target demographic of young, horny males (or those who empathize, whoever they may be) is guaranteed to lap this up, and I fear to think of the fate that now awaits various baked goods at fraternities around the country.

Also reviewed in:
CHICAGO TRIBUNE, 7/9/99, Friday/p. A, Mark Caro
NEW YORK TIMES, 7/9/99, p. E14, Stephen Holden
NEW YORKER, 7/12/99, p. 88, David Denby
VARIETY, 6/28-7/11/99, p. 69, Todd McCarthy
WASHINGTON POST, 7/9/99, p. C5, Stephen Hunter
WASHINGTON POST, Weekend/p. 43, Michael O'Sullivan

AMONG GIANTS

A Fox Searchlight Pictures and Capitol Films release with the participation of British Screen/The Arts Council of England/BBC Films/Yorkshire Media Production Agency of a Kudos production. *Executive Producer:* Jana Edelbaum. *Producer:* Stephen Garrett. *Director:* Sam Miller. *Screenplay:* Simon Beaufoy. *Director of Photography:* Witold Stok. *Editor:* Elen Pierce Lewis and Paul Green. *Music:* Tim Atack. *Sound:* Rosie Straker. *Sound Editor:* Tim Lewiston. *Casting:* Di Carling. *Production Designer:* Luana Hanson. *Art Director:* David Hindle. *Costumes:* Stephanie Collie. *Make-up:* Christina Baker. *Stunt Coordinator:* David Cronnelly. *Running time:* 93 minutes. *MPAA Rating:* R.

CAST: Pete Postlethwaite (Ray); Rachel Griffiths (Gerry); James Thornton (Steve); Lennie James (Shovel); Andy Serkis (Bob); Rob Jarvis (Weasel); Alan Williams (Frank); Emma Cunniffe (Barmaid); Steve Huison (Derek); Sharon Bower (Lyn); David Webber (Billy); Alvin Blossom (Steve's Dad); Sam Wilkinson (Ray's Son); Jo Wilkinson (Ray's Daughter).

NEW YORK, 4/5/99, p. 71, Peter Rainer

If you're going to make a movie about a subject as outlandish as wayfaring high-wire electric-tower painters, shouldn't the movie be outlandish, too? The British *Among Giants* manages the peculiar feat of reversing our curiosity: We start out by thinking we've never seen anything like its ragtag crew and end up believing we've seen it all before. Pete Postlethwaite plays Ray, the painters' foreman, who enlists an itinerant Australian mountain climber, Gerry (Rachel Griffiths), into his raffish all-male brigade. There's a good scene early on, in a bar, when Gerry tries to prove her mettle by catwalking around the confines without once touching the floor. But there's way too much metaphorical malarkey in this movie—starting with its title. Giants, indeed. The mavericks who work the electrified pylons are romanticized right out of their riggings. Meanwhile, a deeper issue is skimped on: the paradox of men who feel compelled to bludgeon the spirit of the fancy-free women to whom they are attracted.

NEW YORK POST, 3/26/99, p. 62, Rod Dreher

"Among Giants" is an engaging but slight English working-class melodrama about the search for love and a sense of place among free-lance electric-tower painters in the English countryside.

Quirky? Sort of, inasmuch as it's not every day the love lives of electric-tower painters seek to engage our attention at the movies.

But that's how it is with these postage-stamp English movies these days—films like "Brassed Off," for one, the megahit "The Full Monty" for another, and also the forthcoming "Metroland."

They explore everyday problems and human-scaled stories, depending more on the quality of storytelling than standard Hollywood fare.

That's all to the good, when the writing is strong. But that's not the case with "Among Giants," which raises more interesting questions than Simon Beaufoy's screenplay satisfactorily answers.

Beaufoy, who penned "Among Giants" before his worldwide triumph with "The Full Monty," explores similar territory: the blasted landscape of contemporary manhood, in a world where a man's ability to earn a living is uncertain, and post-'60s sexual freedom, combined with feminist notions of gender roles in the workplace, clashes confusingly with traditional masculine responsibilities.

Ray (Pete Postlethwaite) is an unemployed worker hired, with his crew, to paint electric towers (the "giants" of the title) in the damp English countryside over the course of a summer.

They're paid under the table, for reasons not quite clear, and told to have the job done by summer's end, at which time the juice will be turned back on.

Things get complicated from the first, when Gerry (Rachel Griffiths), a wiry Australian hitchhiker, shows up and asks to join the crew.

The men gripe, but Ray hires her. The two also fall in love, a bit improbably (Postlethwaite is old enough to be Griffiths' father), causing friction between Ray and his roommate, Steve (the Matthew McConaughey-esque James Thornton), who is more age-appropriate for Gerry, but lager-loutish and immature.

The best parts of "Among Giants" contrast Ray's love of Sheffield, where the film is set, with the almost desperate desire the younger characters have to escape.

Gerry has left her home to peregrinate around England, and fears settling down as much as she secretly wants to. Steve dreams of leaving dreary England for the sunny beaches of India.

Director Miller finds surprising beauty in the industrial wasteland where Ray lives, and has learned to love. But Beaufoy's screenplay hesitates to go below the surface of these underwritten characters' thoughts and feelings about their hopes and their homes.

If only the material were as strong as the performances.

NEWSDAY, 3/26/99, Part II/p. B7, John Anderson

Quiz question: How do you get your screenplay made into a film? Easy: Write a successful screenplay.

No, the answer's not as lame as it seems. It wasn't until the Simon Beaufoy-scripted "The Full Monty" became one of the great success stories of 1997 that Beaufoy got "Among Giants"—his very first screenplay—brought to the screen (the small screen initially, as this is a BBC & Associates production). As a career move, you can't beat it.

The milieu is more or less the same—Thatcherite casualties trying to make ends meet, marriages work and life make sense. No one resorts to public nudity to solve their problems (private nudity, yes), and neither is there anything close to the bruising hilarity of "Monty."

But what we see of modern England through Beaufoy's eyes is more or less the same scorched economic landscape, plus the cliffs of Sheffield, where unemployed pals Ray (Peter Postlethwaite) and Steve (James Thornton) spend their many off hours rock climbing. When Ray is approached with an under-the-table gig—painting 15 miles of high-tension electrical towers in only three months—it seems like the perfect cash-only job for them and their lager-pounding pals.

But onto the job and into their lives walks Gerry (Rachel Griffiths), an Australian nomad and rock-climber—and, as everyone knows, when an attractive woman enters a happily macho setting like this one, calamity is sure to follow. Sure enough, she hits it off with Ray, who puts her on the job, and there is consternation among the ranks—including Steve, who has a bit of thing for her himself.

The problem is, the conflicts within "Among Giants" never manage to leave Beaufoy's pages and take flight. There is some fairly nutty stuff going on—a nude walk in a teeming rain by Ray and Gerry is refreshingly frank but makes little sense otherwise; the aerial shots are plentiful and the countryside looks charming.

Under the debuting Sam Miller's direction, however, imminent romantic disaster can be indicated by an errant meeting of eyes, or a character's display of doomed self-assurance, but most of what happens happens just to move the plot along; little, in other words, feels inevitable. There seems no reason Ray and Gerry can't succeed together (Postlethwaite and Griffiths are, as always, terrific to watch) and no real reason to believe the sexual tension between Gerry and Steve. A story where things happen because other things happen, "Among Giants" isn't quite happening.

SIGHT AND SOUND, 6/99, p. 34, Philip Kemp

The Yorkshire moors, the present. Ray, a 52-year old unemployed labourer and keen amateur rock climber, is offered an unofficial, cash-in-hand job by Derek (who works for the local electricity company) to paint 15 miles of pylons in three months. With the help of his voting lodger and fellow climber Steve, Ray recruits a gang of painters: Bob, Frank, Weasel and Shovel. On the moors they meet Gerry, a young Australian woman, who's backpacking around the world. Despite Ray's misgivings, he lets her join the workgang. She proves to be an adept climber and worker and is accepted by the others.

After a tough day, Ray, who's separated from his wife Lyn, invites Gerry back for a shower. They become lovers, and go climbing together. Ray asks Gerry to marry him. Steve, embarrassed and jealous, moves back home, but the rest of the gang celebrate the engagement by painting a pylon pink overnight. Bad weather hampers the work. Frank, oldest of the gang, cracks under the pace. Gerry smothered by Ray's affection, breaks the engagement and moves out. She goes to Steve and they have sex, but he rejects her. Climbing without equipment, she falls and injures herself. The power in the lines is turned on ahead of time; Shovel narrowly escapes death. Visiting Gerry in hospital, Ray accepts they have no future together; once recovered, she travels on. Steve realises his dream of going to India.

"Don't go enjoying yourself," warns a character in *Among Giants*, "you'll only worry about it in years to come." There's a strong element of dour Yorkshire puritanism in Simon Beaufoy's script. Pleasure, sooner or later, has to be paid for in mental if not physical anguish, and nothing good lasts. Even Gerry, the happy-go-lucky, Aussie backpacker, is infected by this Calvinist miasma. To punish herself for her infidelity to Ray she goes climbing solo and unroped, courting the inevitable disaster. Unlike Beaufoy's acclaimed script for *The Full Monty* (written later, though filmed earlier), there's no final freeze frame triumph here, just a melancholy dying fall on the autumnal moors.

Still, it's not all unrelieved gloom. Moments of joy, if transient, are infectious and genuine: a rowdy line dance in a pub (throughout the film, the bitter-sweet tones of Country and Western pervade the soundtrack); a boozy evening under the stars when a truck driver mate shows up with a tankerload of whisky; Ray and Gerry stripping off for an impromptu shower in a disused cooling-tower. Above all, there's the heady exhilaration of high places, whether rock peaks or pylons. Making his feature debut as director, Sam Miller sheds the twitchy camera moves and relentless close ups that characterised his work on the television series *This Life*. Instead we get long, lyrical swoops along lines of pylons as they stride across the landscape.

Pete Postlethwaite, an unconventional but affecting choice as romantic lead, expresses all the wary delight of a man finding love long after he's ceased looking for it. He's well matched by Rachel Griffiths' quizzical, androgynous charm; their initial love scenes together feel convincingly tentative, neither one quite sure what they're getting into. As the third point of the triangle, James Thornton (from Jimmy McGovern's television drama series *The Lakes)* makes what he can of an underwritten role.

Among Giants is let down by the predictability of its storyline, and by a reluctance to confront the full dramatic consequences of its events. The antagonism between the devious Derek and the painters he's exploiting never comes to a head, and the rancour between Ray and his estranged wife is simply presented as a given, not fully explored. More than once we seem to be heading for a tragic catharsis: when the elderly Frank collapses under the pressure, when the gentle black worker Shovel is trapped on an unexpectedly repowered pylon, and when Gerry takes her quasi suicidal fall. Each time the film sidesteps any disastrous outcome. It's as if the affection Beaufoy feels for his up-against-it working-class characters (a sentiment also evident in *The Full Monty*) makes him over-protective, reluctant to let anything really bad happen to them. If so, it does his heart credit, but it crucially weakens the impact of the film.

VILLAGE VOICE, 3/30/99, p. 126, Jessica Winter

Simon Beaufoy's script for *Among Giants* follows a motley crew of laborers hired to paint miles of electrical columns lining the Yorkshire moors. Since the movie was written before Beaufoy's *The Full Monty*, it appears he has since improved on a formula. *Monty*'s misfit band dropped trou because stripping was the best-paying gig in town, but we can't be sure why anyone needs foreman Ray (Pete Postlethwaite) and his boys to slap a new coat on hundred-foot pylons in the middle of nowhere, and at such risk: they're on a rigid timetable, since the voltage is due to rev up again soon. Still, only sporadic attention is paid to any race-the-clock anxiety once enigmatic drifter Gerry (Rachel Griffiths) backpacks her way into a place on the crew and into Ray's bed. While Postlethwaite cuts a quick swath through Beaufoy's typically wry-and-whimsical, school-of-hard-knocks dialogue, Griffiths is just listless. What really draws our attention are those mammoth pylons, which seem less a hokey metaphor for the perils of love than a good excuse for director Sam Miller to take panoramic advantage of the drearily beautiful, rain-soaked Yorkshire countryside. *Among Giants* isn't much of a movie, but it makes a fine landscape painting.

Also reviewed in:
CHICAGO TRIBUNE, 4/9/99, Friday/p. D, Michael Wilmington
NEW REPUBLIC, 3/22/99, p. 30, Stanley Kauffmann
NEW YORK TIMES, 3/26/99, p. E24, Stephen Holden
VARIETY, 6/15-21/98, p. 103, David Stratton
WASHINGTON POST, 4/9/99, Weekend/p. 51, Desson Howe

ANALYZE THIS

A Warner Bros. release in association with Village Roadshow Pictures and NPV Entertainment of a Baltimore/Spring Creek Pictures/Face/Tribeca production. *Executive Producer:* Billy Crystal, Bruce Berman, and Chris Brigham. Producer: Paula Weinstein and Jane Rosenthal. *Director:* Harold Ramis. *Screenplay:* Peter Tolan, Harold Ramis and Kenneth Lonergan. *Story by:* Kenneth Lonergan and Peter Tolan. *Director of Photography:* Stuart Dryburgh. *Editor:* Christopher Tellefsen and Craig P. Herring. *Music:* Howard Shore. *Music Editor:* Jennifer L. Dunnington and Dan Evans Farkas. *Sound:* Les Lazarowitz and (music) John Kurlander. *Casting:* Ellen Chenoweth and Laura Rosenthal. *Production Designer:* Wynn Thomas. *Art Director:* Jefferson Sage. *Set Decorator:* Leslie E. Rollins. *Special Effects:* Steve Kirshoff. *Costumes:* Aude Bronson-Howard. *Make-up:* Michael Laudati. *Make-up (Billy Crystal):* Peter Montagna. *Make-up (Lisa Kudrow):* Collier Strong. *Make-up (Robert De Niro):* Ilona Herman. *Stunt Coordinator:* Daniel W. Barringer. *Running time:* 110 minutes. *MPAA Rating:* R.

CAST: Robert De Niro (Paul Vitti);   Billy Crystal (Ben Sobel);   Lisa Kudrow (Laura MacNamara);   Chazz Palminteri (Primo Sindone);   Kresimir Novakovic ('50s Gangster);   Bart Tangredi (Young Vitti);   Michael Straka (Young Manetta);   Joe Rigano (Manetta);   Joe Viterelli (Jelly);   Richard Castellano (Jimmy);   Molly Shannon (Caroline);   Max Casella (Nicky Shivers);

Frank Pietrangolare (Tuna); Kyle Sabihy (Michael Sobel); Bill Macy (Isaac Sobel); Rebecca Schull (Dorothy Sobel); Pat Cooper (Salvatore Masiello); Leo Rossi (Carlo Mangano); Aasif Mandvi (Dr. Shulman); Neil Pepe (Carl); Tony Darrow (Moony); R.M. Haley (Producer); Ian Marioles (Soundman); Donnamarie Recco (Sheila); Vince Cecere (Tino); Jimmie Ray Weeks (FBI Agent Steadman); Robert Cea (FBI Agent Ricci); William Hill (FBI Agent Provano); Ira Wheeler (Scott MacNamara); Luce Ennis (Belinda MacNamara); Elizabeth Bracco (Marie Vitti); Gina Gallagher (Theresa Vitti); Francesca Mari (Anna Vitti); Vincent Vella, Jr. (Anthony Vitti); Mickey Bruno (Miami Soldier); Dave Corey (Miami Hall Guard); Fred Workman (Justice of the Peace); Daniel W. Barringer and John J. Polce (Dream Sequence Gunmen); Drew Eliot (Priest); Grace DeSena (Tommy Angel's Widow); "New York Joe" Catalfumo (Exuberant Mourner); Michael Guarino, Jr. (Stevie Beef); Clem Caserta (Handsome Jack); Tony Ray Rossi (Potatoes); Judith Kahan (Elaine Felton); Ted Neustadt (Rabbi); Pasquale Cajano (Joe Baldassare); Gene Ruffini (Frank Zello); Alfred Sauchelli, Jr. (Mo-Mo); Tony DiBenedetto (Johnny "Bigs"); Frank Aquilino (Eddie "Cokes"); Tony Bennett (Himself).

LOS ANGELES TIMES, 3/5/99, Calendar/p. 1, Kenneth Turan

Paul Vitti, "Mr. V" to his intimates, is one of New York's most powerful gangsters. His shoes are polished, and so is his snarl; when he walks into a room, strong men panic. But, hey, being a Mafia don is stressful work, and underneath his expensive tailored suits, Vitti is a psychological mess.

Ben Sobol, Ben to his intimates, is one of New York's least celebrated psychiatrists. It's his father, Isaac, author of best-selling self-help books, who's the famous one. A divorced dad who's about to be remarried (his father has too many book signings to make the wedding), Ben spends his days dealing with suburban patients whose time-wasting problems are barely able to keep him awake.

The concept of a mobster who's enough of a mental health mess to seek professional help is a promising one, as HBO's superb new series "The Sopranos" is proving on TV. But despite having Robert De Niro as the don, Billy Crystal as the shrink and Harold Ramis as co-writer/director, the big-screen "Analyze This" sounds funnier than it plays. It does have laughs, but it's unable to capitalize sharply enough on its main idea.

Part of the problem may be that "Analyze This" isn't sure exactly what that main idea is. Three separate credited writers (Peter Tolan, Ramis and Kenneth Lonergan) took cracks at the story, and an inability to integrate different points of view is visible in the final product. "Analyze This" not only wants to make you laugh, it apparently wants you to think at least semi-serious thoughts about therapy and violence. A fine idea, perhaps, but the way it's developed feels played out and tired.

Even for a Mafia chieftain, Vitti is an unlikely candidate for stress problems. He was groomed by his father for a career in the mob, and he's prospered in the work. Until now, when he finds himself hyperventilating and suffering the classic symptoms of a panic attack. Except that no one is eager to use that word with Mr. V, who's already nervous because of an impending bloody clash with rival hoodlum Primo Sindone (Chazz Palminteri).

Sobol comes into Mr. V's life when his car accidentally rear-ends a mob vehicle being used to transport a bound-and-gagged hostage and the shrink gives his business card to Vitti's bodyguard and right hand Jelly (a consistently amusing Joe Viterelli).

To everyone's surprise, Mr. V. takes a shine to the buttoned-down therapist, even offering to personally clear Sobol's entire schedule, a gesture Sobol finds terrifying. "When I got into family therapy," he says, "this is not the kind of family I had in mind."

Unfortunately, Mr. V's interest in becoming a patient coincides with Sobol's pending wedding to neurotic Miami TV newswoman Laura MacNamara (Lisa Kudrow), who is unnerved by the way the mob starts infiltrating her fiance's life. The FBI is interested as well, as is Primo Sindone, who detects a new tone in his rival and demands to find out exactly what this thing called closure is all about.

All this can be made to sound amusing (and is in fact thoroughly entertaining on "The Sopranos") but "Analyze This" is hampered by too many people going through the motions. Kudrow has hardly anything of interest to do, Crystal's performance feels overly familiar, and De Niro falls back too readily on what can only be called Mafia shtick.

Co-writer/director Ramis, responsible for "Groundhog Day" and many other comedies, is a gifted man but "Analyze This" is both too unfocused and overly familiar. It has enough comic energy to generate some chuckles, but even when we laugh we're always wondering why the jokes aren't funnier.

NEW YORK, 3/15/99, p. 57, Peter Rainer

The dysfunctional family has been in the pop-psych pantheon for so long that it was only a matter of time before Hollywood came up with the bright idea of highlighting a dysfunctional Family—as in mafiosi. Actually, crime clans in the movies have always been clinical cases; it's just that until recently, nobody thought to put them on Prozac. The HBO series *The Sopranos* features James Gandolfini as an anxiety-choked New Jersey mob underboss who begins seeing a psychiatrist (played, fittingly, by Lorraine Bracco, from *GoodFellas*). Now there's the new Robert De Niro comedy *Analyze This*, which proceeds from the perfectly reasonable assumption that gangsters are human, too. They may even need some counseling in order to become happy, well-adjusted gangsters. Paul Vitti (De Niro), ascending to his role as crime-family capo, suddenly finds himself experiencing panic attacks. He backs down from whacking one of his rivals as his goons look on dumbfounded. Things get worse. He bawls uncontrollably; his mistress no longer turns him on. Vitti's bodyguard, Jelly (Joseph Viterelli), delivers his boss to a psychiatrist (an unduly dour Billy Crystal) with all the trepidation of feeding him to the fishes.

The spectacle of a Mafia boss crying his eyes out in therapy, or being asked to work out his rage by slamming a pillow, almost compensates for this comedy's many missed opportunities. Harold Ramis—who directed from a script he co-wrote with Peter Tolan and Kenneth Lonergan—doesn't get maximum laughs from the material because, on some level, he seems to think therapy might actually *work* for his crime capo. What should be a send-up of both mob movies and touchy-feely psychiatry ends up being more like a winsome buddy film about a pair of self-actualized commanders-in-chief with matching baggage: Vitti had a distant relationship with his crime-boss dad, and Ben Sobol, the psychiatrist, has his own Oedipal load. His pop-therapist father (Bill Macy), author of the best-seller *Tell Me What You Feel, Tell Me What You Want,* regards his son as a mope, and won't even guarantee an appearance at Ben's impending wedding to a TV newscaster (Lisa Kudrow). Ben and Vitti learn life lessons from each other. And what we learn—yet again—is that potentially terrific comedies are often whacked by filmmakers who feel the need to spread a little therapy themselves.

Nevertheless, it's still possible to have a good time at this movie, and the primary reason is De Niro. He turns himself into a great big crybaby goon: At times, Vitti is like a made-man version of Lou Costello. (Ben is his Bud Abbott.) He's a guy who's always on the lookout for enemies but is totally flummoxed in confronting the enemy within. He approaches his analytic sessions as if they were summit meetings. Usurping the doctor's armchair, he swigs a Scotch. Initially on guard, he begins to catch on to the ritual—he's a fast learner. With his crook's wiles, he sizes up Ben's weak points and turns the tables. It's like learning a new scam.

De Niro was reportedly wary of lampooning his trademark mafioso character, but the truth is, it's high time he lightened up. He's been coasting for a long time on his Greatest Living American Actor rep. When he plays a serious role now, mostly what we get are the tics and flourishes of a once formidable talent. There's a sameness to his presence, because this actor who used to set off depth charges chooses to keep things on the roiling surface. He's become a kind of brand name. You know what you're getting when you see him: a woozy wariness, a modicum of danger, world-weariness, a cracked smile.

But comedy—in its largest sense—brings De Niro back to life as an actor; it always has. Back in 1970, when he was first becoming recognized in the movies, he appeared in Brian De Palma's *Hi, Mom!* as a Vietnam vet guerrilla terrorist/porno-peep-show player, and he gave it a revue-sketch jive. In *Mean Streets* and *Taxi Driver* and, for some of the way, *Raging Bull* and *King of Comedy*, he brought out the comic horror in derangement as nobody had ever done before. He was unreachable in a new and ghastly groove that seemed peculiarly modern-both in-your-face and far gone—and his chill cackle carried no overtones. De Niro was the emblematic actor of his generation because he seemed to embody the country's furious contradictions. Later on in his career, after the heat burned off his performances, he could still refresh himself with a wonderful doodle of a comic turn, as he did in *Wag the Dog,* playing a presidential adviser with a poise so calculated it seemed like effrontery.

De Niro is having fun in *Analyze This* in the same way Brando did in *The Freshman* when he lampooned his Don Corleone. Brando was attacked for that movie as if he'd committed sacrilege, and yet he'd given a real performance. He twirled our memories of him in *The Godfather,* incorporating all the jokes and takeoffs that had built up around his portrayal over the years. De Niro's twirlmanship isn't as adept, but it recalls the improv-class looseness of his *Hi, Mom!* days. His presence here is such a whammy, that we may never be able to keep a straight face watching him play another deadly goombah. If we're lucky, maybe he won't want to play those roles anymore anyway.

NEW YORK POST, 3/5/99, p. 51, Rod Dreher

"Analyze This" is a one-joke comedy, but in the hands of Billy Crystal and the hilarious (!) Robert De Niro, it's a surprisingly enjoyable one.

In a thoroughly entertaining performance that recalls the sly self-mockery Marlon Brando pulled off in "The Freshman," De Niro plays a New York mob boss named Paul Vitti, a wiseguy in need of a shrink to rub out his neuroses. Vitti's facing a showdown with rival mobster Primo (Chazz Palminteri), but discovers to his horror that he's losing his nerve. He just can't whack 'em like he used to. "Slap a pair of t--- on me, and I'm a woman," he wails.

Enter Dr. Sobel (Crystal), a psychiatrist who one night rear-ends a limo driven by Vitti's henchmen. The trunk pops open to reveal a bound and gagged victim, but Vitti's beefy right-hand man Jelly (Joe Viterelli, with a head like a Brylcreemed meatball) slams the trunk down and warns him off. Ever the good citizen, Dr. Sobel gives Jelly his business card for insurance purposes—which enables Jelly to track poor Sobel down for his boss.

Dr. Sobel doesn't want to take the notorious gangster on as a patient, but—heey-yooo!—Vitti makes him an offer he can't refuse. Cracks Sobel, "When I got into family therapy, this wasn't the 'family' I had in mind."

The gags spark out of the culture clash between the crude Italian mobster from Bensonhurst and the upscale Jewish shrink from the suburbs. Dr. Sobel has to help Vitti become a more efficient mobster, while rough-guy Vitti struggles to adapt to the exigencies of psychotherapy. When Dr. Sobel explains the Oedipus complex to his patient, Vitti goes nuts, feeling that his mama has been insulted.

Later, when the doctor encourages Vitti to use therapeutic jargon to explain himself to his deadly rival, puzzled Primo commands his goon to "Get me a dictionary and find out what dis 'closure' is."

Vitti has a knack for invading squirrelly Sobel's life at all the wrong moments—at almost every moment, actually, much to the consternation of the shrink's fiancee (Lisa Kudrow), who has her wedding ruined by Mafia shenanigans.

Ultimately, "Analyze This" is pretty thin sauce, but De Niro and Crystal are a treat together, director Harold Ramis keeps things moving briskly and the screenplay was typed by schticky fingers adept at tapping more laughs out of a slight, sitcom-y premise than you'd expect.

NEWSDAY, 3/5/99, Part II/p. B3, John Anderson

What about Bob? No, what is it about Bob? There's this thing that Robert DeNiro does with his mouth that has always been the tip-off that baaaaaaaaad things were going to happen. He did it as Max Cady in "Cape Fear" before putting the bite on Illeanna Douglas. He did it as Al Capone in "The Untouchables" before stepping up to the plate, and he may have done it in "Mary Shelley's Frankenstein," although the stitches made it hard to tell.

In other words, when he does this thing, nothing that follows is going to be particularly funny.

And there he was, making this particular monster moue in the ads for "Analyze This" and you had to worry; past experience demanded it. Poor little Billy Crystal, you thought: He should have jumped into that grave he dug in Kenneth Branagh's "Hamlet."

Not, however, to worry. Although "The Sopranos" beat them to the couch, and despite a casting coup that seems so obvious it hurts—Crystal as a menschy Manhattan psychiatrist? DeNiro as virtual John Gotti?—the two of them are as funny as anybody has been since DeNiro and Charles Grodin in "Midnight Run." It's funny how funny DeNiro is, actually (especially when he makes that mouth), considering what a travesty this whole movie might have been.

Comedy is hard, as either Edmund Kean or Edmund Gwenn said on his deathbed, but it's also delicate. Audiences laugh a lot less easily than they cry and they laugh even less easily when the jokes are shoehorned into a format that doesn't fit.

Confirming the widely held theory that the best comedies are no more than 90 minutes long, "Analyze This" is precisely 15 minutes longer than it should be. But it works as well as it does because director Harold Ramis ("Caddyshack," "Groundhog Day") gives the jokes priority over the reputedly high-concept story line, lets the laughs come where they will, and—by acknowledging just how obvious the whole setup is through several very smart allusions to his star's filmography—makes his audience his co-conspirators. Let's face it, you laugh more easily with your friends than your enemies.

And Paul Vitti (DeNiro), a capo of the Nike-and-sharkskin-wearing variety, has enemies. There's a big meeting of the five families coming up and Vitti should be psyching himself up. Instead, he's having a breakdown—"panic attacks" as one unfortunate doctor diagnoses (in one of the movie's missteps)—and Vitti, his lofty position and Old World honor both at risk, decides to surreptitiously see a psychiatrist.

Which is bad news for Ben Sobol (Crystal), a divorced Manhattan analyst who daydreams about telling his patients to "stop whining" and has a nagging Oedipal headache about his father (Bill Macy), a more successful, self-promoting author-doctor. When Ben rear-ends a limo that contains both Vitti henchman Jelly (Joseph Viterelli) and a bound body in the trunk, it leads to Vitti demanding that Ben restore his confidence and his manhood and to do it before the big meeting two weeks away. ("When I went into family therapy," the besieged Ben says, "this wasn't the family I had in mind.")

The Ramis-Peter Tolan-Kenneth Lonergan script is rich in one-liners, and while a number of scenes are pretty inside baseball, they also help make the film friendly: The opening scene, set during the raid on the celebrated 1957 mob summit in Apalachin, N.Y., borrows the tone of the introductory sequences in "GoodFellas." The attempted assassination of Vitti at a Little Italy restaurant is a slow-motion shoot-up that aspires to operatic grandeur. A dream sequence in which Ben imagines his own rubout is a shot-by-shot homage to the street hit on Vito Corleone in "The Godfather." You begin to think that directors Scorsese and Coppola should have gotten some screen credit.

But this is all good-natured tribute to DeNiro, who's assisted by a terrific supporting performance by the very meaty, very funny Viterelli and a Crystal who's more understated—and thus more palatable—than he's probably ever been, outside of his Oscars duties (and if he were hosting this year, we'd say, whoopie). Lisa Kudrow is saddled with another whiny role that's beneath her and Palminteri, as Vitti's arch-foe Sindone, not only chews the scenery but bites off pieces and digests them. But "Analyze This" can handle the small stuff, because it takes very little seriously besides making us laugh.

SIGHT AND SOUND, 9/99, p. 40, Charles Taylor

New York, the present. Paul Vitti, head of a New York crime family, is stressed out. The first meeting in 40 years of all America's crime bosses is looming, a gathering that may set off a gang war and that reminds him of his father's murder soon after the last such meeting. Two weeks beforehand, Vitti survives a hit that leaves a friend dead and others suspicious that he ordered it. Jelly, Vitti's associate, is in a minor car accident with psychiatrist Dr Ben Sobol and gives Vitti the shrink's name. An initial meeting convinces Vitti Ben can help. Vitti soon has Ben at his beck and call, and even travels to Miami and disrupts Ben's wedding to his fiancée Laura.

Under surveillance by both the Feds and Primo Sindone, a rival boss, Vitti piques the curiosity of both parties about Ben. The Feds assume Ben is privy to information that can deliver Vitti to them. They pressure him to wear a wire by faking a tape to convince Ben Vitti intends to kill him. Vitti becomes convinced Ben is betraying him and accedes to his associates' demands that Ben be killed. But before Vitti can carry out the plan, Ben guides him to the psychological breakthrough that has eluded him. A relapse prevents Vitti from attending the meeting of the crime families, and Ben is plucked from his rescheduled wedding to act the role of consigliere. A recovered Vitti arrives to announce he's quitting the business. Before he can leave, Primo tries to kill him and wounds Ben instead, and the Feds arrive to arrest the gathering. Vitti is sentenced to 18 months in prison. He agrees to continue his sessions with Ben.

There are plenty of good Mafia jokes in *Analyze This,* but the best is the one that informs the whole movie: life has become so stressful that *everybody* feels their job is too much. When Robert De Niro's mobster Paul Vitti starts blubbering at a commercial showing a grown man hero-worshipping his elderly father, the joke isn't just the tough guy crying, it's the way society's demands have left us all vulnerable to the sappiest manipulations. *Analyze This* makes comedy out of the same subject that was swamped in melancholy in director Harold Ramis' last picture, the touching and bungled *Multiplicity*—the price we pay for the satisfactions of the good life.

Since *Groundhog Day* Ramis films have been rare. He's a director of popular comedies that are truly funny without being juvenile, sweet-tempered or softheaded. The laughs in his pictures grow out of character and situation. *Analyze This,* which was written by Ramis, Peter Tolan and Kenneth Lonergan, has a good, profane edge that's never abrasive. It's a near-flawlessly paced comedy in which Ramis pulls off a note-perfect, dream-sequence parody of the attempt on Don Corleone's life from *The Godfather,* as well as a subtler reference to the most affecting moment from *Once Upon a Time in America.*

Billy Crystal, underplaying nicely as straight man to De Niro, is rewarded with a sequence where, posing as Vitti's consigliere, he gets to cut loose with a version of Mafiaspeak that includes the gem "Badda-bing, badda-bang, Betty Boop". And De Niro is remarkable, giving an out-and-out comic performance that's still recognisably De Niro. He pushes moments like Vitti's crying jags as far as they'll go, and plays up to his ominously funny mood swings, such as the way his compliments to Crystal—"You have a gift, my friend. Yes, you do, *you DO.*"—wind up sounding like threats. Yet he also makes this tough guy temporarily reduced to sad sack a real character.

The stars are lucky to be supported by a bunch of gifted second bananas. If the force that can rattle Lisa Kudrow exists, she has yet to meet it. After her first attempts at matrimony fall prey to mob business, she tells De Niro off as if he were a caterer who screwed up the place settings. As Crystal's teenage son, round Kyle Sabihy isn't the usual brat or calculated charmer. You can imagine more experienced actors killing to deliver line readings as flabbergastingly dry. Best of all is tubby, bulbous nosed Joe Viterelli as Vitti's right-hand man Jelly. it would be impossible to say which affords Jelly greater protection—his impenetrable bulk or his impenetrable skull. Viterelli (he was the guy who, laying eyes on Arnold Schwarzenegger in *Eraser,* inquired, "Who's the tree trunk?") lifts the dumb mobster schtick to something approaching comic grace.

VILLAGE VOICE, 3/9/99, p. 113, J. Hoberman

Somewhat overoptimistic in its title, Harold Ramis's *Analyze This* is enjoyable but slight—an intermittently funny, one-joke vaudeville in which Robert De Niro's mafioso, seeking to cure the crying jags and panic attacks he suffers after narrowly avoiding a hit, goes into therapy with Billy Crystal's bemused psychoanalyst.

Two comic stereotypes, two modes of ethnic discourse: Mugging outrageously, De Niro tap-dances through the film, replaying his *Untouchables* Al Capone for laughs; Crystal, meanwhile, strokes his beard and brays, oscillating between quick wit and craven intimidation, storing up energy for the final switcheroo. The narrative is simple: Whenever the wiseguy has a problem, he hijacks the shrink. Shamelessly referencing *The Godfather* and cribbing from old Woody Allen, *Analyze This* might have seemed edgier 20 years ago. (Indeed, the idea of a mobster in analysis is central to HBO's current *The Sopranos.)* Still, however familiar, the gag does lend itself to amusing elaboration. Crystal introduces De Niro to the notion of the Oedipus complex and subsequently hears him complain that "after what you told me, I'm afraid to call my mother on the phone."

By making Crystal the son of a bestselling psychobabbler and the father of an overweight problem child, as well as introducing Lisa Kudrow in the Diane Keaton role as Crystal's neurotic WASP fiancée, *Analyze This* suggests a richer milieu than it delivers. Focusing so intently on the bonding potential of the two principal characters (as well as their attempts to heal their wounded inner children), the movie squanders its chances to be much more than the Odd Couple with guns.

Ultimately a therapeutic success story, *Analyze This* is closer to *City Slickers* than it is *Groundhog Day*. Whether or not this represents the triumph of the innocuously positivist Crystal Weltanschauung over Ramis's somewhat more cynical one, it subsumes all manner of promising developments into the spectacle of the two stars muscling in on the action and doing their thing.

Also reviewed in:
CHICAGO TRIBUNE, 3/5/99, Friday/p. A, Michael Wilmington
NEW REPUBLIC, 4/5/99, p. 28, Stanley Kauffmann
NEW YORK TIMES, 3/5/99, p. E12, Janet Maslin
VARIETY, 2/22-28/99, p. 40, Todd McCarthy
WASHINGTON POST, 3/5/99, p. C1, Rita Kempley
WASHINGTON POST, 3/5/99, Weekend/p. 41, Desson Howe

AND BABY MAKES TWO

A First Run Features release. *Producer:* Judy Katz and Oren Rudavsky. *Director:* Judy Katz and Oren Rudavsky. *Director of Photography:* Oren Rudavsky. *Editor:* Kate Taverna. *Sound:* Judy Katz. *Music:* Joel Goodman. *Sound:* Tom Paul and (music) Reilly Steele. *Sound Editor:* Sylvia Menno and Tony Martinez. *Running time:* 60 minutes. *MPAA Rating:* Not Rated.

NEW YORK POST, 6/25/99, p. 57, Rod Dreher

When Dan Quayle gave his infamous "Murphy Brown" speech complaining about pop culture's validation of single motherhood, he wasn't attacking unwed mothers generally, many of whom show great courage in choosing to bear their children after being abandoned by their male partners.

Rather, his target was those yuppie single women who consciously choose to conceive with no intention of giving the child a father—as if the only essential role men have in the lives of children is that of sperm donor.

If you believe the social science research, Dan Quayle was right. But the many problems faced by fatherless children and the moms struggling to raise them are not of much interest to the makers of "And Baby Makes Two," a hopelessly sentimental, one-sided and unrealistic celebration of a gaggle of would-be Murphy Browns who live in New York City.

The one-hour documentary follows these women, all in early middle age and single, as they pursue happiness by seeking pregnancy by any means necessary.

There's no denying the pain these childless career women suffer, but it's astonishing and more than a little sickening how they all seem to think of babies as accessories to personal fulfillment.

They won't take just any baby, either. One emotional woman tells a group that the amniocentesis test revealed her unborn child was a Down Syndrome child. So she aborted the baby at once.

"That's really brave of you, April," says her friend. No, April, that's sick. You chose to bring a child into existence, then ended her life because she didn't fit your idea of acceptable.

The babies here are adorable, and the new moms on display obviously love their kids. Fine. But "And Baby Makes Two" is all about feeling; any moral or practical thinking about this dubious, consciously anti-male project is largely absent from this film.

NEWSDAY, 6/25/99, Part II/p. B13, Gene Seymour

There's a lot of primal joy, heartbreak and intensity packed into the 60 minutes of "And Baby Makes Two," a documentary focusing on a Manhattan-based support group of single women who are or want to be mothers. Those who identify with these women will find commiseration or hope in this film, made by public TV vets Judy Katz and Oren Rudavsky. But you don't have to be a mom, would-be mom, mom-to-be—or even a woman—to be caught up in this emotional roller coaster.

At the center of this film are two 43-year-old women, identified only by their first names. Debbie is having her baby the old-fashioned way (only with the father stepping aside, by mutual agreement, after conception) while Jan is trying to conceive by artificial insemination with little success. After several heartbreaking disappointments, Jan decides to adopt, though she remains crestfallen about missing out on the experience of childbirth.

A response to the hoo-hah raised by Dan Quayle at decade's cusp over the decision by the title character of TV's "Murphy Brown" to have a baby and stay single, "And Baby Makes Two" makes it clear that the decision made by these mostly successful, mostly middle-aged women to pursue single-motherhood isn't done on a whim.

Leaving aside the risks of physical hardship and psychological trauma, there's also the disapproval or misunderstanding of parents and loved ones. The determination to stare down these grim prospects gives these women the kind of courage that even the stoniest Republican patriarch could (however grudgingly) admire.

VILLAGE VOICE, 6/29/99, p. 148, Abby McGanney Nolan

This short documentary about single motherhood follows eight women in a support group as they try to either get pregnant or adopt an infant. Conventionally assembled, it focuses on the women's ambivalence about raising children without partners. That the group is somewhat homogeneous—professional, heterosexual Manhattanites—makes the film less than comprehensive, but it's affecting nonetheless, particularly with a birth scene and the first glimpse of a much-longed-for adopted daughter. The issue of single motherhood as a societal hot button—seven years after Dan Quayle's *Murphy Brown* speech—is secondary to family dynamics. We see disappointment and disapproval from the parents of these women, then gradual acceptance. As one mother says about her daughter's efforts to adopt, "I feel like she's coming out of an adolescent phase."

Also reviewed in:
NEW YORK TIMES, 6/25/99, p. E13, Lawrence Van Gelder

ANGELA'S ASHES

A Paramount Pictures and Universal Pictures International release of a David Brown/Scott Rudin/Dirty Hands production. *Executive Producer:* Adam Schroeder and Eric Steel. *Producer:* Scott Rudin, David Brown, and Alan Parker. *Director:* Alan Parker. *Screenplay:* Laura Jones and Alan Parker. *Based on the book by:* Frank McCourt. *Director of Photography:* Michael Seresin. *Editor:* Gerry Hambling. *Music:* John Williams. *Music Editor:* Ken Wannberg. *Sound:* Ken Weston and (music) Simon Rhodes. *Sound Editor:* Eddy Joseph. *Casting:* John Hubbard, Ros Hubbard, and Juliet Taylor. *Production Designer:* Geoffrey Kirkland. *Art Director:* Malcolm Middleton. *Set Decorator:* Jennifer Williams. *Special Effects:* Yves de Bono. *Costumes:* Consolata Boyle. *Make-up:* Sarah Monzani. *Stunt Coordinator:* Martin Grace. *Running time:* 120 minutes. *MPAA Rating:* R.

CAST: Emily Watson (Angela McCourt); Robert Carlyle (Dad, Malachy McCourt); Joe Breen (Young Frank); Ciaran Owens (Middle Frank); Michael Legge (Older Frank); Ronnie Masterson (Grandma Sheehan); Pauline McLynn (Aunt Aggie); Liam Carney (Uncle Pa Keating); Eanna MacLain (Uncle Pat); Andrew Bennett (Narrator); Shane Murray Corcoran (Young Malachy); Devon Murray (Middle Malachy); Peter Halpin (Older Malachy); Aaron Geraghty (New Born Michael); Sean Carney Daly and Oisin Carney Daly (Baby Michael); Shane Smith (Middle Michael); Tim O'Brien (Old Michael); Blaithnaid Howe (Newborn Alphie); Klara O'Leary and Caroline O'Sullivan (Baby Alphie); Ryan Fielding (Older Alphie); Daire Lynam (Margaret Mary); Ben O'Gorman (Eugene); Sam O'Gorman (Oliver); Frank Lavery (Young Paddy Clohessy); James Mahon (Middle Paddy Clohessy); Laurence Kinlan (Older Pady Clohessy); Lucas Neville (Willie Harold); Walter Mansfield (Fintan Slattery); Des McAleer (Mr. Benson); Sean Kearns (Dotty O'Neill); Les Doherty (Mr. O'Dea); Brendan

Cauldwell (Mr. O'Halloran); Shay Gorman (Mr. Hannon); Johnny Murphy (Seamus); Jon Kenny (Lavatory Man); Susan Fitzgerald (Sister Rita); Brendan McNamara (Toby Mackey); Maria McDermottroe (Bridey Hannon); Oliver Maguire (Confession Priest); Daithi O'Suilleabhain (Young Priest); Eileen Pollock (Mrs. Finucane); Alvaro Lucchesi (Laman Griffin); Mark O'Regan (Dr. Troy); Moira Deady (Mrs. Purcell); Kerry Condon (Theresa); Gerard McSorley (Father Gregory); Garrett Keogh (Mr. Hegarty); Eamonn Owens (Quasimodo); John Anthony Murphy (Redemptionist Priest); Phelim Drew (Rent Man); Brendan O'Carroll (Funeral Carriage Driver); Maggie McCarthy (Miss Barry); Bairbre Ni Chaoimh (Mrs. O'Connell); Nuala Kelly (Dance Teacher); Brian Clifford (Telegram Boy); Edward Murphy (Young Mikey Molloy); Kieran Maher (Older Mikey Molloy); James McClatchie (Bishop); Patrick Bracken (Younger Question Quigley); Terry O'Donovan (Older Question Quigley); Danny O'Carroll (Clarke); David Ahern (Cyril Benson); Marcia Debonis (Mrs. Leibowitz); Helen Norton (Delia); Eileen Colgan (Philomena); Alan Parker (Dr. Campbell); Stephen Marcus (English Agent); Pauline Shanahan (Eye Nurse); Gerry Walsh (Farmer); Brendan Morrissey (Brother Murray); Daragh Neill (Heffernan); Sarah Pilkington (Minnie MacAdorey); Donncha Crowley (Sacristan); Veronica O'Reilly (Mrs. Carmody); Ann O'Neill (Mrs. Dooley); Phil Kelly (Father Gory); Jaz Pollock (Roden Lane Neighbor); Patrick David Nolan (Travel Agent); Gerard Lee (Carmody Priest); Martin Benson (Christian Brother); Birdy Sweeney (Old Priest); Owen O'Gorman (Sleeping Sailor); Pat McGrath (Butcher); Ray McBride (Mill Foreman); John Sheedy (Coal Yard Foreman); Sam Ryan and Donnacha Gleeson (Shaved Head Boys); Jim McIntyre and Richard Walker (Gravediggers); Mary Ann Spencer, Kathleen Lambe, and Jer O'Leary (Parents).

CINEASTE, Vol. XXV, No2, p. 56, Michael Gray

The astonishing success of *Angela's Ashes*, Frank McCourt's Pulitzer Prize-winning memoir of his dismal Irish childhood in the slums of Limerick—five million copies sold and counting, and still in the upper reaches of bestseller lists worldwide—made a cinematic adaptation of the book virtually inevitable. When the word went out in Ireland and beyond in early 1998 that Alan Parker would direct the film version, the versatile English director seemed the right choice to bring McCourt's text to life on screen. The resounding commercial and artistic success of Parker's previous Irish film, *The Commitments*, established beyond doubt his feel for the cadence of urban Irish slang and showed a ready understanding of inner-city Irish locales that eludes so many of his countrymen. Add to Parker's team two of the finest actors working in Britain today, Emily Watson from *Breaking the Waves*, to play the title character, Frank's mother Angela, and *The Full Monty* and *Trainspotting* star Robert Carlyle as Frank's drunken, feckless father, ignore the usual carping from disgruntled Irish people about the surfeit of native actors who might have filled those roles, and it seemed the filmmakers couldn't go wrong. All they needed to guarantee awards and a return to bumper box office for Parker after the mixed response to *Evita* and *The Road To Wellville* was a casting call to the schoolboys of Ireland to find a few cute moptops to draw freckles on for the juvenile roles. And find them they did, turning up three Frankies and three Malachys, after putting thousands of youngsters through their paces at auditions nationwide, to play the McCourt siblings at different ages.

But the plot went astray on them when it came to the one crucial component that made all those millions of readers bear with McCourt through hundreds of pages of misery, hunger, and deprivation: the narrative voice. The story that had rattled around in the author's head for decades before he finally committed it to paper was told in the voice of his younger self, starting as a near-infant in Brooklyn, progressing seamlesssy, and always in the present tense, to that of a Limerick primary schoolboy, then adolescent, and finally young adult. The maturing of the young mind was deftly handled by the author, and his ability to project himself into the mindset of the boy he once was, at seven, eleven, and sixteen—to recount his story with a child's bewilderment, humor and anger—is the book's greatest strength. McCourt was not actively involved in writing the screenplay, turning the task of adaptation over to Australian screenwriter Laura Jones.

Jones and cowriter Parker decided early on to tell Frank's tale in the well-modulated tones of an adult narrator, thus losing the child's immediacy of the original text. Children live in the present, care little about what has gone before and, despite the best efforts of adults to make them worry about it, couldn't be bothered pondering the future. An adult narrator looking back across half a century will inevitably lose all of the wonder and perplexity of the child Frankie as he tries to figure out what's going on in a grim world run by hapless adults, and it is very much to the detriment of the film that Parker decided to make this fundamental departure from the original work.

The heartrending episodes from McCourt's book are all there—the deaths of Frank's sister Margaret and his twin brothers Oliver and Eugene, his father's chronic failure to provide the basics of food, clothes, and shelter for his starving family, and the daily cruelties inflicted by the Catholic education system on the poor of Limerick. They're all vividly depicted, but recounted with a narrative distance that fails to engage the viewer. Carlyle's efforts as Frank's drunken father, the North of Ireland man with the funny manner who can't hold down a job, are negated by the fact that he's playing a character typified more by his absence than his presence; and the role of Angela, a paragon of passivity and resignation, wilting from hunger, despair, and poor health, leaves Emily Watson short on dialog and makes the McCourts' mother as inscrutable on screen as she was in the book.

While the film is impressively dressed by Ireland's top costume designer Consolata Boyle, and faithfully recreates the dank Limerick slums of Roden Lane in which the McCourts struggled to survive, it delivers too much rain-drenched deprivation and not enough of the book's emotional engagement and loquacious use of language. His tough childhood left McCourt with little room for sentimentality, but Parker has no qualms about trowelling it on in Spielbergian quantities. Towards the end of the film, he finally turns off the rain machines for a night scene to reveal a gigantic moon worthy of E.T., illuminating a tacky apparition of his younger selves to the near-adult Frank, before he takes the boat to America and salvation. This scene comes out of nowhere in an otherwise hard-realist film, and is both untypical of its director and at odds with its source material. Despite this unevenness, Parker can count on a sizable number of the five million who bought the book and have been eagerly awaiting the film to show up at the cinema turnstiles, but it's inevitable that they will find the screen version falls far short of the raconteurial highs of the original work.

Angela's Ashes has been doing brisk business in Ireland, where the film industry badly needs a sizable hit after years of lackluster commercial returns. The audience response from Irish viewers is as divided about the film as it had been three years earlier about the book. This suddenly modern island, sprouting satellite dishes and sporting cellphones in every household since the mid-Nineties, has prospered to a point where many natives are less sensitive than previously about harsh depictions of Irish poverty, as long as they are seen to belong firmly in the past. For the citizens of Limerick, however, McCourt and Parker are rinsing ragged and filthy laundry a little too publicly and much too close to home. Many locals objected to the film's depiction of the city as a cold, heartless place with scant charity for its poor. The Catholic archdiocese of Limerick, displeased at McCourt's unsympathetic depiction of its predecessors as sadists and hypocrites, refused Parker permission to film in Limerick churches, forcing the director to go to the Dublin archdiocese to shoot chapel interiors.

Actor and formidable Limerick native Richard Harris, a Jesuit-educated ex-rugby player from a fancier part of the Shannonside city than the McCourts, weighed in against Parker's film in a January opinion piece in the *London Sunday Times*. Harris took umbrage at all the moaning and groaning in Parker's depiction of the city, declaring that Limerick would be famous for its water polo rather than its rugby if it rained as much as Parker had shown in *Angela's Ashes*. Limerick is a tough town, known throughout Ireland as 'Stab City' for the manner in which local youths settle differences of opinion with knives, and Harris, good Limerick lad that he is, pledged to take a sword to anyone else who castigated the hometown he loves so much but rarely visits This controversy won't do the film any harm in Ireland. For every person who denounces *Angela's Ashes* for its relentless precipitation and its pitiless indictment of arrogant churchmen, half a dozen more will show up to see what all the fuss is about. In the U.S., Limerick and its prewar Dickensian slums are far enough away in space and time, that audiences can take the poverty tour without smelling the squalor or getting any of it on themselves. Irish-Americans, often prevailed upon by parents and grandparents to feel sentimental about a country they may never visit, will be glad their elders left such a fetid dump to come to America where it's usually warm and dry-even if they didn't all become multimillionaires like Frank McCourt.

McCourt took his sweet time about making a success of himself, fulfilling the American Dream that forms the punchline to Parker's dreary film forty-odd years after arriving in New York as a young adult. Alan Parker takes his time as well in getting to his clichéd conclusion. The Statue of Liberty looms over New York Harbor, promising salvation in the land of opportunity for tired, huddled Frank at the feel-good finale of the film. The ordeal is over for the aspiring author, and for the cinema audience too. Fans of *The Commitments, Mississippi Burning*, and *Angel Heart* will be left wondering how Alan Parker's usual facility for deft pacing could desert him in converting a compelling story like *Angela's Ashes*, making two and a half hours of grinding poverty feel like a lifetime.

LOS ANGELES TIMES, 12/24/99, Calendar/p. 2, Kenneth Turan

Primitive peoples, or so it's said, resist being photographed, believing that the creation of an image robs them of their souls. A quaint notion, perhaps, but how else can you explain what's happened to "Angela's Ashes"?

The film version of Frank McCourt's memoir of growing up in Ireland, the most literate of bestsellers, is not the usual case of a book being trashed on its way to the screen. Far from it.

Director Alan Parker and the screenwriter he shares credit with, Laura Jones, have treated "Angela's Ashes" with scrupulous respect and care. And working with his longtime production team, including cinematographer Michael Seresin, the director has compellingly re-created McCourt's city of Limerick in the 1930s and '40s.

More than that, Parker, a filmmaker ("Evita," "The Commitments," "Mississippi Burning") not always known for moderation, has done the most restrained and artful work of his career here, beautifully using both established professionals Emily Watson and Robert Carlyle to play McCourt's parents and a fine trio of neophyte actors (Joe Breen, Ciaran Owens and Michael Legge) to create the three ages of the youthful author.

But good as all this is, "Angela's Ashes" is missing something essential, something almost indefinable and perhaps inevitably lacking. Despite extensive use of voice-over (smoothly read by Andrew Bennett), the elegance and wit of McCourt's language, with you every step of the way in the book, is largely missing from the screen. That language made the misery of McCourt's impoverished childhood bearable and even infused it with humor and heart. Without it, the story, beautifully told though it is, feels as though it's lost its soul.

Part of the problem is that seeing grinding poverty on screen is quite different than reading about it on a page, anyone's page. Using muted, subdued colors, "Angela's Ashes" has quite correctly decided that making misery too pretty would be insupportable. But as a result the family's continual hunger and the ever-present squalor and pestilence of their surroundings grind at us just as they do the McCourts with a depressing relentlessness that the book miraculously avoids.

"Angela's Ashes" opens with the family living not in Ireland but in Brooklyn in 1935. But despairing situations, in this case the death of Frank McCourt's small sister, haunt them even here and soon the McCourts become, in Frank's droll words, "the only Irish family in history saying goodbye to the Statue of Liberty."

Back in Limerick, a city known for its piety and its numbing rains, Angela's Catholic family rains disdain on her husband, Malachy, a Protestant from the North. Both Angela's mother, the matriarchal Grandma Sheehan (Ronnie Masterson), and her censorious sister Aggie (Pauline McLynn) never miss an opportunity to say things like "It's the Northern Ireland in you that attracts the dirt" whenever Frank gets filthy, which is often.

While Watson as Angela is compelling as always, she's mainly called on to suffer and endure; Malachy, as played by Carlyle ("Trainspotting," "The Full Monty"), is a more troubling and complex character.

Malachy is a craven alcoholic, "a slave to the drink" who has "gone beyond the beyond." But the film, like the book, resists painting him as a villain. Rather Carlyle's haunted father and husband is an ill-starred, inept dreamer, a great spinner of tales who finds the dreariness of Irish reality more than he can manage.

Because Malachy is so feckless, unable to hold a job for more than a day and incapable of doing anything with money except spend it on the drink, the McCourt family is subject to all manner of depredations. And from flea-ridden mattresses to a waterlogged residence next to the only outhouse in the neighborhood, we get to see them all on screen.

Mostly what we see is McCourt growing up, embarrassed at his extreme poverty, joyous at sneaking into the Lyric Theater to watch Jimmy Cagney, discovering girls and the wonder of "the Shakespeare," a writer whose words he savors like "mashed potatoes, you can't get enough of them."

What impacted young McCourt most was his education at the hands of a series of Jesuit fathers. Not shy about opinions, they had no hesitation about blasting "the devil's henchmen in Hollywood" or saying the virtue of taking communion was "now you can die a martyr if you're murdered by Protestants."

But more eloquent thoughts were expressed as well, by the teacher who said, "Euclid is grace and beauty and "elegance," and the one who advised McCourt, "Stock your mind. It's your house of treasure, no one can interfere." It's advice the boy followed and if this beautifully made if flawed film sends people back to his book, it will have done good work for sure.

NEW YORK, 1/3/00, p. 85, Peter Rainer

Angela's Ashes, directed by Alan Parker, converts Frank McCourt's whimsical coming-of-age memoir into a sodden, drizzly thing. No blarney will be found here, but also no spirit, no humor, no depth.

NEW YORK POST, 12/24/99, p. 36, Jonathan Foreman

"Angela's Ashes" should have been more than rain, mud and a parade of babies arriving and dying soon after. But Alan Parker's adaptation of Frank McCourt's wonderful, best-selling memoir of his impoverished Irish childhood lacks the humor and charm that fills the book and makes it so much more than a catalog of suffering.

McCourt's wonderful mordant humor and his ruefully amused voice make the terrible tale of his early life both bearable and all the more effective in the book. Here, there are some funny lines and scenes, but they seem dropped in to provide light relief from all the carefully reproduced scenes of destitution, ignorance and drunkenness.

These scenes follow one another like items on a laundry list, and many of them are just too short to allow a fine cast to really strut its stuff.

The result is a film that takes an hour to warm up and make you start caring about the characters, and which too often feels like a documentary or an earnest TV history movie.

The film begins in Brooklyn in 1935, with the McCourt family living in dire poverty. The story is seen through the eyes of little Frank (played first by the terrific Joe Breen, then by Ciaran Owens and finally by Michael Legge).

Angela (Emily Watson) goes to pieces when her baby daughter suddenly dies, and the squalor in the household becomes so bad that it's decided it would be best for the family to move back to Ireland. So Angela, her unemployable, irresponsible husband, Malachy (Robert Carlyle), and their four sons sail back to the old country.

They don't get much of a welcome from Angela's family in Limerick; her kin have always disapproved of Malachy, a Northerner they believe to be a Protestant. Nor is there much work to be found. And when Malachy does get a job, he usually loses it quickly.

Worse still, he's in the habit of spending all of his wages on drink, even when his wife has a hungry new baby at home. Meanwhile, Frank and his surviving brother go to a school where most of the teachers are religious fanatics or nationalist nutcases or both.

Soon one infant dies of malnutrition, and then another. (Babies come and go so often in this movie it's almost comical.) Eventually, Malachy goes to England to find work, but he drinks his wages there, too, and finally abandons the family altogether. You're told that the boys find Malachy charming despite his grotesque irresponsibility, because he sings songs and tells stories, but you don't really see those qualities.

The family ends up moving in with a cousin who expects sexual favors from Angela in lieu of rent. It's only when the teenage Frank gets a job as a mailman that life begins to look up. He gets to have sex with a consumptive girl and then gains access to a source of money for the hoped-for escape to America.

Watson, the queen of suffering-female roles, is as good as ever. Her character is unattractively passive, but when you see her try to hold her head up high as she begs for charity, it grabs your heart.

Film can glamorize even the ugliest subject, and the grim Irish poverty of "Angela's Ashes" is no exception, thanks to Parker's penchant for bathing the rain-drenched slums of Limerick in blue light, so that the mud-choked alleyways seem almost as beautiful as the misty shots of the river Shannon.

NEWSDAY, 12/24/99, Part II/p. B6, John Anderson

There's a vague inevitability about memoirs—the protagonists usually have survived, after all. But there's a concrete certainty about best-selling memoirs: They will become movies, whether they belong onscreen or not.

Frank McCourt's enormously popular "Angela's Ashes" is one of those less-than-likely candidates for the Hollywood treatment. Its subject matter is the "miserable Irish Catholic childhood" (although, as McCourt has written, "the happy childhood is hardly worth your while"). Its milieu is the rain-slicked, slate-gray streets of '30s Limerick and the "haunted inkpots" (as Joyce described them) that housed the Irish poor. It has no narrative arc to speak of—just anecdotes, really, about surviving an alcoholic home, the church, your relatives, your life.

And yet there's a compelling momentum to "Angela's Ashes," Alan Parker's very faithful, if poetically subordinate, version of McCourt's book, which imposed elegance on squalor and intelligence on the indolence cultivated by poverty.

The McCourts were outcasts among outcasts. After a young daughter's death, Angela (Emily Watson) and Malachy (Robert Carlyle) took their children from New York back to Ireland at a time when everyone else was going the other way.

Angela's Catholic family resented Angela's marriage to the Protestant Malachy; that he was from the north, and sounded like it, gave him a stigma in the south that he couldn't escape. That he was addicted to drink made him virtually unemployable. Ignominious poverty was the lot of their brood.

Children die like untended livestock; Dad even uses one son's coffin as a table in the pub. It would be a relief to say that love conquered all, but as McCourt and Parker both know, love can only withstand so much misery—something Watson and Carlyle bring to the movie, this touch of emotional desolation and Catholic self-recrimination that flourishes despite all the loaded dice. It's the boys who save the day, the ones who play Frank from tiny to grown, in particular little Joe Breen, whose face peers out from all those ads and seems to embody both the tenacity and tenderness of his author.

NEWSWEEK, 12/20/99, p. 41, David Ansen

The movie that Alan Parker has made from Frank McCourt's astonishingly popular memoir of his miserable, poverty-stricken Limerick childhood will not offend any of the book's legions of fans. Neither will it replace the original in anyone's affections. Parker and fellow screenwriter Laura Jones obviously have respect for their source. They understand its mordant wit; they' not afraid of its pile-up of Irish woes—dead children; and irresponsible father (Robert Carlyle); a mother (Emily Watson forced to beg for leftovers from the priests' dinnertable; flooded floors and cruel teachers and a hunger so piercing it makes one eat an old newspaper that was used to wrap food in.

Parker's rainy, gray-blue images are artful and authentic looking, but still they can only be a pale reflection of McCourt's lilting, sardonic prose. Significantly, when we are moved—as in the moment when the adolescent Frank watches his defeated Da leave the family for America— it's the *narration* that generates the emotion, not the scene itself. Three young actors play Frank as he grow up, all of them fine. As well-crafted and sensitive as it is, the movie remains one step removed from inspiration.

SIGHT AND SOUND, 1/00, p. 42, Nick Roddick

Brooklyn, 1935. Five-year-old Frank McCourt lives in a tenement with his four-year-old brother Malachy, toddler twins Eugene and Oliver, father Malachy Sr and mother Angela. Delight at the birth of a new baby sister turns to despair when she dies. Angela is unable to cope, Malachy Sr goes on another drinking binge and Angela's mother sends money for a journey back to Limerick, where life is even harder.

Frank grows up against a background of desperate poverty. Malachy Sr drifts in and out of work and of the city's pubs, frittering away his wages on drink while the family starves. Angela pleads for charity. Oliver and Eugene fatally succumb to the damp and cold, but Frank gradually manages to find a place for himself in Limerick, progressing through school, his first communion, his first pint and first job as a coalman's assistant, a job which near blinds him with conjunctivitis. When World War II starts, Malachy Sr goes to England in search of work, returns fleetingly one Christmas and is never seen again. Evicted from their house, the McCourts move in with their cousin Laman, who treats them like slaves and expects sexual favours from Angela. Frank leaves school and home and gets a job as a telegram delivery boy through which he meets Theresa, a young girl with consumption, with whom Frank loses his virginity before she dies. Frank also makes extra money writing letters for the local moneylender. When she dies, he finds her hoard of cash and, after a final confrontation with his mother, leaves for the United States.

The television documentary *A Turnip Head's Guide to British Cinema* which Alan Parker made in 1986 has achieved a certain notoriety in British critical circles, mainly for its jibes at those critics whose agenda he felt to be more intellectual (or, as he would have it, pretentious) than artistic. Since critics don't like being criticised, it won him few friends. What made the attack interesting, though, was that Parker knew about this stuff. it's hard to imagine Ridley Scott or Adrian Lyne, the other two members of the triumvirate of British commercials directors who established a Hollywood foothold in the 70s, caring what the academic journal *Screen* said about them.

Parker has always been more sensitive to British criticism than he lets on, and his choice of projects has always been more driven by that illusory mainstream notion of 'quality' than that of the other two, resulting in some dead ends *(The Road to Wellville)* but some equally surprising renewals *(The Commitments)*. His latest film *Angela's Ashes* is certainly not a dead end, nor is it really a renewal, but it has 'quality' stamped all over it, from its subject matter (a Pulitzer Prize-winning quasi-autobiography by Limerick raised novelist Frank McCourt), to the cinematography by regular Parker collaborator Michael Seresin (who also shot Parker's *Bugsy Malone, Midnight Express, Fame, Shoot the Moon, Birdy, Angel Heart* and *Come See the Paradise*). Seresin's damp, green-tinged images come close to creating the cinematic equivalent of the very Irish idea of a 'soft day' (one on which it never stops raining)—particularly apt given Limerick's reputation as the wettest place on an already rain-sodden island.

Cinematic schooldays

It is easy to see what appealed to Parker about *Angela's Ashes*: another Irish group movie, albeit on a bigger and more serious scale than *The Commitments*; a portrayal of the struggle against poverty in keeping with the social conscience which, however it may be dramatised, has always infused his films; and, above all, the chance to work with kids. This last area is the only one in which the balance of the film tips away from McCourt's book, where the focus is far more on narrator Frank's family. At a guess, I'd say up to a quarter of *Angela's Ashes* the film takes place in Leamy's National School, which provides the movie with its most enjoyable scenes. Parker has lost none of his skill at directing children and none of his eye for making a selection from the performers placed in front of him by his casting directors. But the reason the school scenes work best also points to the problems involved in turning McCourt's novel into a film: they have a cinematic structure. Co-screenwriter of several Jane Campion films and veteran adapter of novels Laura Jones (who did the first draft) and Parker himself (who claims to have followed 'her template' in producing his version) never quite find a way to make the other three-quarters of the film equally cinematic.

Shell of irony

It is not a question of fidelity: *Angela's Ashes* is amazingly faithful to its source material. It is a question of the difference between literary and cinematic storytelling. A fantastic amount happens in McCourt's book. He moves from Brooklyn to Limerick and back again. He loses three brothers and a sister. His father leaves home. He grows up. But it is not a narrative in the cinematic sense. And above all, it is 'told' by McCourt with an ironic tone which, if not inimitable, is definitely more literary than cinematic. Take the second paragraph of the book, repeated at the start of the film. "When I look back on my childhood I wonder how I managed to survive at all. It was, of course, a miserable childhood: the happy childhood; the happy childhood is hardly worth your while. Worse than the ordinary miserable childhood is the miserable Irish childhood, and worse yet is the miserable Irish Catholic childhood.

These sentences encapsulate McCourt's approach: a hint of sentimental nostalgia wrapped in a solid shell of irony. And, as the words are spoken in the cinema, the audience laughs. McCourt uses the same technique to narrate the death of his twin brothers. Five paragraphs describe how the family band together after Oliver dies, and how their Dad says his Eugene is lucky to have his two big brothers to help him get over his twin's death.

Then comes a bombshell of a threeword paragraph: "He died anyway." Its message is tragic, but its delivery is essentially comic in structure, like the punchline to a joke. The words also appear in the film (in voiceover of course), but by then we have already seen Eugene's lifeless head on the pillow, and the effect is quite different: the information has already been conveyed, the punchline-structure loses its drama, and the irony vanishes.

It is a small but telling problems, which takes much of the impact away from this otherwise admirable and extremely beautiful film. The performances of the kids—especially Joe Breen, Ciaran Owens (younger brother of Eamonn, who was Neil Jordan's butcher boy) and Michael Legge as Frank at various ages—are all excellent. And Robert Carlyle and Emily Watson as Dad and Mam are solid screen presences despite the fact that they generally have little to do but react. But the delicate balancing act between Frank's love of his father and hatred of his drinking, and between his adoration of his mother and despair at the way she caves in to circumstances, does not entirely survive the transition from book to film. The remarkable thing, though, is that the sense of exhilaration which leads McCourt to conclude that "looking back on it all, I see what could have been, but am grateful for all that it was"—has survived, despite the depressing subject matter and the relentlessness of the hand fate deals Frank.

TIME, 12/27/99, p. 166, Richard Corliss

No one need bother mocking or pitying the Irish; they do such a good job of it themselves. Frank McCourt beautifully juggled contempt and sympathy in his memoir of growing up poor and wet in Limerick in the '30s and '40s, before squandering the goodwill he had accrued with the taint of *'Tis* (it'll be a while before that sour screed is filmed). Parker, who did right by the Irish in *The Commitments*, has a go at the impossible task of adapting *Angela's Ashes* and trying to satisfy all those who loved the book so much that McCourt's painful past miraculously became theirs.

The movie, unable to pack in the book's entire accumulation of incident, is necessarily anecdotal. Frank's mother (Watson) has been slightly sanctified, and Dad (Carlyle) given the lilt of Irish laughter to go with his wastrel ways. But the film has the vitality of remembered truth. Is Frank hungry? He licks a newspaper for the residual grease of the chips it held. Is he sopping? He steps in more puddles than Gene Kelly in *Singin' in the Rain*. (Ten years the family rented the same flooded ground floor, and no one thought to lay a plank from the doorway to the stairs.) The three boys playing Frank at 7, 11 and 15 are fine. They create a collective portrait of a child tough enough to survive a horrendous youth and a man brave enough to recall it.

VILLAGE VOICE, 12/28/99, p. 126, Amy Taubin

If Minghella ratchets up the Grand Guignol aspect of [*The Talented Mr.*] *Ripley* (by the end, it's like you're watching the Andrew Cunanan story), Alan Parker mutes Frank McCourt's riotous and extremely moving autobiographical account of a destitute childhood in Ireland. Parker is not a director to scant on body fluids, and his adaptation of *Angela's Ashes* is awash in chamber-pot overflows and outhouse leakages. But for all the grungy detail, the film is far too tidy and polite. I don't have the emotional attachment to McCourt's writing that I do to Highsmith's, but most readers will miss the irrepressible gallows humor of the original, not to mention its vivid real-life characters. As Frank's long-suffering mom and charming but irresponsible alcoholic dad, Emily Watson and Robert Carlyle do what they can with the sketchy script. Parker seems to feel obliged to visit as many of the novel's scenes as possible in a 145-minute movie (a modest length by Christmas 1999 standards) with the result that the film lacks development and dramatic coherence. Frank, who ages 12 years over the course of the film, is played by three young actors, none of them distinguished.

Also reviewed in:
CHICAGO TRIBUNE, 1/21/00, Friday, p. A, Michael Wilmington
NATION, 1/24/00, p. 35, Stuart Klawans
NEW YORK TIMES, 12/24/99, p. E1, Janet Maslin
VARIETY, 12/13-19/99, p. 106, Todd McCarthy
WASHINGTON POST, 1/21/00, p. C1, Rita Kempley
WASHINGTON POST, 1/21/00, Weekend/p. 43, Desson Howe

ANNA AND THE KING

A Fox 2000 Pictures release of a Lawrence Bender production. *Executive Producer:* Terence Chang. *Producer:* Lawrence Bender and Ed Elbert. *Director:* Andy Tennant. *Screenplay:* Steve Meerson and Peter Krikes. *Based on the diaries of:* Anna Leonowens. *Director of Photography:* Caleb Deschanel. *Editor:* Roger Bondelli. *Music:* George Fenton. *Music Editor:* Michael T. Ryan and Graham Sutton. *Sound:* Brian Simmons and (music) John Richards. *Sound Editor:* John A. Larsen. *Casting:* Priscilla John. *Production Designer:* Luciana Arrighi. *Art Director:* Tom Nursey, Marc Fisichella, and John Ralph. *Set Decorator:* Ian Whittaker. *Set Dresser:* Beverly Dunn. *Special Effects:* Steve Courtley. *Costumes:* Jenny Beavan. *Make-up:* Morag Ross. *Make-up (Jodie Foster):* Jean Luc Russier. *Stunt Coordinator:* Martin Grace. *Running time:* 140 minutes. *MPAA Rating:* PG-13.

CAST: Jodie Foster (Anna); Chow Yun-Fat (King Mongkut); Bai Ling (Tuptim); Tom Felton (Louis); Syed Alwi (The Kralahome); Randall Duk Kim (General Alak); Lim Kay Siu (Prince Chowfa); Melissa Campbell (Princess Fa-Ying); Keith Chin (Prince Chulalongkorn); Mano Maniam (Moonshee); Shanthini Venugopal (Beebe); Deanna Yusoff (Lady Thiang); Geoffrey Palmer (Lord John Bradley); Ann Firbank (Lady Bradley); Bill Stewart (Mycroft Kincaid); Sean Ghazi (Khun Phra Balat); K.K. Moggie (Phim); Dharma Harun Al-Rashid (Noi); Harith Iskander (Nikorn); Yusof B. Mohd Kassim (Pitak); Afdlin Shauki (Interpreter); Swee-Lin (Lady Jao Jom Manda Ung); Ramli Hassan (King Chulalongkorn); Robert Hands (Captain Blake); Lim Yu-Beng (Scarfaced Leader); Kenneth Tsang (Justice Phya Phrom); Kee Thuan Chye (Second Judge); Patrick Teoh (Third Judge); Aimi Aziz (Lady of Court No. 1); Ellie Suriaty Omar (Lady of Court 2); Tina Lee Siew Ting (Lady of Court 3); Wong Chui Ling (Lady of Court No. 4); Zaridah Abdul Malik (Lady of Court No. 5); Fariza Azlina (La-Ore); Ahmad Mazlan (Scout No. 1); Mohd Razib Saliman (Scout No. 2); Zaibo (Siamese Trader); Pak Ling (Shipping Dock Woman); Mahmud Ali Basah (Mercenary); Zulhaila Siregar (Distraught Villager).

CHRISTIAN SCIENCE MONITOR, 12/17/99, p. 15, David Sterritt

Holiday time is family time at the movies, and Hollywood never fails to notice box-office opportunities. Two of the season's most heavily promoted family films arrive this week, both offering a mixture of kid-friendly excitement and adult-oriented nostalgia. Each has its virtues, but it's unlikely that the mild-mannered exoticism of "Anna and the King" will capture as many hearts as the whimsical humor of "Stuart Little."

Anna and the King is based on the memoir by Anna Leonowens that also inspired "The King and I," the, classic 1956 musical. More than one moviemaker has been drawn to this story lately—an animated version was one of last summer's flops—and the latest version isn't short of star power. Jodie Foster plays the English schoolteacher who tutors a Siamese prince and enters a deliciously complex relationship with his regal father, played with aplomb by Chow Yun-Fat, an action specialist looking to diversify his career.

The makers of "Anna and the King" leaned over backwards to differentiate their movie from its 1956 predecessor. The musical numbers are gone, the subplot about a forbidden love affair is different, and perfunctory adventure scenes have been added. The result still seems like a half-hearted throwback to the '50s—neither modern enough to please young viewers nor persuasive enough to bring old-fashioned styles convincingly alive.

Most important, Chow's capable acting is no match for the memory of Yul Brynner's astonishing performance in the original movie. Since it's available on home video, this is one case where a trip to the rental outlet will pay larger dividends than a visit to the theater.

Stuart Little is more fun than "Anna and the King," turning E.B. White's lovely book into a romp as likable and amusing as its hero. He's a mouse with a human-sized vocabulary and a yen for family living, standing him in good stead when he's adopted by a mom and dad who want to give their son a little brother. Complications arise when a mouse couple arrive on the doorstep claiming to be his real parents. Things eventually work out fine, but Stuart and his household first pass though several hair-raising scrapes.

Told through a mixture of animation and live action, "Stuart Little" lacks the subtle sense of mystery that distinguished White's book, but nicely conveys its playful spirit and amiable tone.

LOS ANGELES TIMES, 12/17/99, Calendar/p. 2, Kenneth Turan

"Anna and the King" is stuffed with things: 19 costumed elephants, 500 gilded Buddhist statues, 4,000 square feet of marble polished with coconut oil and banana leaves, nearly 10 miles of Thai cloth used to dress the background players, not to mention the largest set built from scratch since "Cleopatra." But what it doesn't have is what viewers may miss most: songs.

Though the story of a love that dared not speak its name between widowed Victorian schoolteacher Anna Leonowens (Jodie Foster) and the autocratic King of Siam (Chow Yun-Fat) did not start life as a musical, it's best known as the inspiration for Rodgers and Hammerstein's "The King and I" and songs such as "I Whistle a Happy Tune," "Hello, Young Lovers," "Getting to Know You" and "Shall We Dance?"

Harking back to the story's cinematic roots (it was filmed straight in 1946 as "Anna and the King of Siam"), this "Anna and the King" has designs on being taken seriously as a drama. Which is why Chow's King Mongkut has to contend with things like death squads and corpses hanging from trees that would've defoliated Yul Brynner's head if it wasn't already bald.

More flat and disappointing in a wasted opportunity kind of way than anything truly bad, the problem with "Anna and the King" is that it's caught halfway between then and now. As written by Steve Meerson & Peter Krikes and directed by Andy Tennant (who did the similarly well-intentioned but vapid "Ever After"), the film tries to throw in notions of cultural relativism and big power imperialism, but can't do without corny shtick like a monkey stealing the king's spectacles and Anna's young son asking, "Mother, what's a concubine?" Alternating ancient jokes about elephants' rear ends with battles and explosions may seem like a path to a film for everybody, but what it really leads to is a film for nobody in particular.

What can't be second-guessed about "Anna and the King" is its ravishing look, the work of top-drawer talent like production designer Luciana Arrighi ("Howards End," "Remains of the Day") and costume designer Jenny Beavan ("A Room With a View," "Sense and Sensibility"), all expertly photographed by Caleb Deschanel ("The Black Stallion," "Fly Away Home"). The physical re-creation of 1862 Bangkok and the king's genuinely palatial palace compound is so appealing that we often wish we could abandon the film and wander around the compound on our own.

While having the gifted Foster as your star is usually a bonus, her effectiveness is hampered here by wrongheaded character development that results in the actress being too unlikable for too long. When Anna and her son arrive in Siam to tutor the children of the king, especially his eldest son and heir to the throne Prince Chowfa (Lim Kay Siu), in the English language, science and literature, she is an unregenerate chauvinist and testy know-it-all who believes "the ways of England are the ways of the world."

While this point of view is creditable and initially necessary for the film to develop its predictable "she learns from the East, the East learns from her" theme, problems develop because Foster embraces this attitude too intensely and for too long.

Headstrong to the point of foolhardiness, a busybody who is either pursing her lips or speaking through clenched teeth when she's not doing both, Anna is so singularly lacking in charm that the king, not the most easygoing of fellows, is moved to comment on her irritatingly superior attitude." Your husband, he tells her at another point, "must have been very understanding."

Of course, the king, being a king, is mostly bemused by Anna's insolence and actually takes pleasure in her forthrightness and spunk. Audiences may be less understanding, and though Anna eventually loosens up a bit, the film has pretty much lost us by that point.

Though he looks regal enough, Chow (still best known to Western audiences for his Hong Kong John Woo films despite U.S. ventures like "The Corruptor" and "The Replacement Killers") does not strike notable sparks with Foster, not even in the waltz they share together in an elaborate banquet scene that tries to be the film's emotional centerpiece.

Maybe that's because in "Anna and the King" the king has a whole lot to worry about besides a tutor who stomps around as if she owned the palace. There's his lovely new concubine Tuptim (Bai Ling), who's pining for the guy she left behind outside the palace. And then there are those pesky corpses up north. Are the British behind the outrage, the French, someone else? If only His Majesty could be taught to whistle a happy tune, he'd probably feel a whole lot better about everything. Even Anna.

NEW YORK POST, 12/17/99, p. 61, Lou Lumenick

"Anna and the King" is a politically correct update of the old chestnut about the Victorian governess—now played as a feminist by Jodie Foster—and the Siamese monarch, charismatically portrayed by Asian superstar Chow Yun-Fat.

Chow, regal and charming in the role that won a Tony and an Oscar for Yul Brynner—who offered a vastly different interpretation in the musical "The King and I"— is the best thing in this lush, beautifully shot, but quite draggy nonmusical version, directed by Andy Tennant ("Ever After").

King Mongkut—previously portrayed as an uncouth, semi-barbarian who is civilized by the governess Anna Leonowens—is now depicted as a highly educated, skilled diplomat who maintained Siam (now Thailand) as an independent nation in the colonial era.

Attitude aside, the much worked-over screenplay—attributed to Steve Meerson and Andrew Krikes ("Star Trek 4—the Voyage Home") and allegedly "inspired by" the (largely fictional) diaries of the real-life Leonowens—is actually very similar to the 1946 nonmusical version with Rex Harrison and Irene Dunne.

Anna arrives in Bangkok in 1862 with her young son, hired to teach English to the king's 58 children. After waiting three months for a royal audience, she immediately comes into conflict with the king. who isn't used to anyone—much less a woman—talking back to him.

The two develop a grudging respect that blossoms into romance when they dance together at a state dinner. But they have a falling out when Anna tries to stop the execution of Tuptim (Bai Ling of "Red Corner"), one of the king's concubines who is caught meeting with her ex-boyfriend.

The previous versions ended with Anna and the king reconciling on his deathbed, but this "Anna" instead invents a palace coup and a ridiculous action climax straight out of "The Bridge On the River Kwai."

Anna isn't a great role for Foster, who struggles with her English accent and the greatly softened dramatic conflict between her character and the king—who this time around is more bemused than angered by her Victorian attitudes.

Moreover, the movie isn't even presented from her point of view. It's weirdly framed by narration from the king's eldest son.

The movie is a treat for the eye, with lots of elephants and other animals, and beautifully shot (by Caleb Deschanel) pageantry—sequences that help prolong the proceedings to 2½ hours.

"Anna and the King" is the kind of unsophisticated family entertainment they supposedly don't make anymore—though parents should be warned this PG-13 rated feature fleetingly depicts one character being shot point-blank in the head.

NEWSDAY, 12/17/99, Part II/p. B8, Jan Stuart

Five million were used to build the Siamese palace sets of "Anna and the King," gloats the studio press kit. And, by golly, it looks it. Decorated and bejeweled within an inch of its wide-screen life, "Anna and the King" boasts the sort of storybook opulence that fires a young moviegoer's wanderlust and sets a travel agent's phone clanging with package tour reservations.

Those of us who remember Anna Leonowens' autobiographical tale of East meets West from either the Rex Harrison-Irene Dunne movie or the Rodgers and Hammerstein musical expect nothing less. The question that lingers on the tongue as one contemplates its current film go-around, however, is: Do we need this?

Directed by Andy Tennant with a sense of style as vague as his production is detailed, this fitfully entertaining rendition nevertheless answers in the affirmative on two important counts: the fascinating intrusion of global tensions and the sly, sensual and sanguinely Asian presence of Chow Yun-Fat as Siam's King Mongkut. But what are we to do with the chilly and flaccidly patrician Anna of Jodie Foster?

There are few indicators from the familiar opening panorama of a bustling Siamese seaport (Malaysia is the celluloid stand-in) that this "Anna and the King" is going to take us places we haven't been before. As Anna prepares her hyper-inquisitive son Louis (Tom Felton) for their arrival after a long boat ride from Bombay, it is all we can do to purge the opening bars of "Whistle a Happy Tune" from our brains.

Tennant's remake adds a new and sobering wrinkle to the exotic landscape, with the first sighting of dead peasants hanging from banyan trees, the victims of neighboring Burmese rebels. In Steve Meerson and Peter Krikes' erudite screenplay, the assimilation of a headstrong British schoolmarm into the former Thailand's royal household becomes a lightning rod for triangular tensions between Siam, Burma and England (Burma's then-colonial patriarch).

Exhibiting a political savvy unusual for this brand of family entertainment, the film examines the rock-and-a-hard place position of King Mongkut, trying to court the favor of the very British empire whose Burmese subjects are maneuvering to overthrow his government. The entanglements build to the sort of rip-snorting action climax that owes more than a small debt to Kipling and "The Bridge on the River Kwai."

Action film star Chow gives a splendidly regal performance, bringing an aristocratic intelligence, poise and naturalness to the King that escaped Yul Brynner's overgrown adolescent of a ruler. This King speaks English with the fluidity of a UN secretary general and doesn't need to be taught how to cut a rug. He conveys the worldliness of a man who would think to import a European schoolteacher for his 58 children and the refined machismo of a man who has 27 wives and 42 concubines to keep happy.

As Anna, Foster has one foot in Victoria's England and the other in Hillary Clinton's America, with all the starch and charmlessness that that implies. One can't fault either her English accent or her feminist moxie: If this was a docudrama about the British suffragette movement, she'd be entirely credible. But somewhere behind the 5 million nails, the 7,000 sheets of gilded plywood and the 4,000 square meters of marble, there is supposed to be a love story. This "Anna and the King" leaves the monarch stranded at the ball, holding the dance floor with a cold crumpet.

NEWSWEEK, 12/20/99, p. 41, David Ansen

It's no mean feat to play the King of Siam and effortlessly erase all memory of Yul Brynner. But that's just what Chow Yun-Fat quietly, wittily and charmingly accomplishes in this sumptuous, nonmusical version of the story of tutor Anna Leonowens and her encounter with the 19th-century monarch.

Political intrigue, deadly ambushes and the threat of war provide a welcome element of surprise for those who think they've heard this tale too often, though the additions reek of Hollywood artifice.

Jodie Foster takes on the role of Anna, but it's not a comfortable fit. She seems drawn and oddly inexpressive. It's not her fault that the character, revamped to conform to current political wisdom, seems more than a little schizoid—one minute acting like a confirmed colonialist, the next spouting stirring multi-culturalist speeches. Director Andy Tennant doesn't have much magic up his sleeve, but he moves things along at a pleasantly dawdling pace, giving the audience its money's worth of eye-popping sets, costumes and landscapes. Hollywood rarely mounts these lavish period epics anymore. It's nice to see them try, even if the result is somewhat less than heart-stopping.

SIGHT AND SOUND, 2/00, p. 41, Pamela Church Gibson

Bangkok, 1862. The recently widowed Englishwoman Anna Leonowens arrives from India, accompanied by her eight-year-old son Louis and two servants, to take up a post as tutor to King Mongkut of Siam's eldest son. She refuses to kneel before the king and generally defies conventions, impressing him with her strength of character. He orders her to teach all 58 of his royal children.

Her clashes with the Siamese way of life are set against a backdrop of escalating political conflict. The British protectorate of Burma is being used as a base for raids on Siamese villages. The king, anxious to keep Siam independent, arranges a diplomatic banquet for the British envoy. Anna organises it and they dance together, flushed with success and mutual sexual attraction. An expedition to stop the raids ends in the discovery that the seemingly loyal General Alak is behind the raids; he hopes to overthrow the king.

Meanwhile, royal concubine Tuptim flees to be with the man she loves. She is captured and executed with her lover for this 'treachery'. Appalled, Anna arranges to leave Siam, just as Alak's duplicity is revealed and the lives of the royal family are threatened. She stays to help the royal family escape to safety and saves the king's life en route during a confrontation with Alak. Order is restored and Anna leaves Siam.

Anna Leonowens' autobiographical novels (more fictional than most autobiographies) about her stint teaching English in the Siamese court spawned first the movie *Anna and the King of Siam* (1946, with Rex Harrison as the king and Irene Dunne), then the Broadway musical *The King and I*, filmed in 1956 with Yul Brynner and Deborah Kerr, and a cartoon based on the last two just last year. *Anna and the King* wants to be more than just another lavish remake of its source material. Although clearly part of a mainstream entertainment, the story seems to be reshaped, incorporating a feminist perspective for a post-colonial era, giving the film a liberal spin that marks it out as "quality" cinema. As spectacle, it's adequate but as an exercise in historical redress it won't fool many. Hoping to film in Thailand, the filmmakers allegedly rewrote the script five times to appease the authorities, only to have the end product—filmed in Malaysia—now banned in Thailand.

The attraction between the two leads can be treated very differently today than 30 years ago, when a more marked racism kept the relationship between Anna and the king strictly professional (and Chow Yun-Fat, although Chinese not Thai, is the first Asian to play the part on screen). As buttoned down and repressed in Jodie Foster's hands as in all the previous incarnations, this Anna is nonetheless clearly fascinated by the king's exotic otherness and blatant sexual appetites. (Concubine Tuptim, about to be deflowered, is assured he's a good lover.) An update on that old east-meets-west cliché, the film makes the confrontation between a woman brought up to accept the supremacy of the British empire and an eastern man who wields absolute power its central dramatic and romantic meat.

Director Andy Tennant, whose *Ever After* was a similarly revisionist take on the Cinderella story, cites as cinematic inspiration *Doctor Zhivago* and *Braveheart*. But his privileging of spectacle swamps any attempt to address seriously the problems of colonialism and cross-cultural confrontation. As with many heritage films, the radical thrust is stifled by sumptuous decor and costuming, while the epic-style visual effects overwhelm any potential subtleties in the drama. Politics and characters are similarly simplified.

The culture clash here functions principally as backdrop to the love story. Anna's feminist spirit and her fierce opposition to slavery—she lends the heir to the throne a copy of *Uncle Tom's Cabin* to read—are strong, but seem less important than her increasingly sexually-charged clashes with the king. She does, it is true, come to criticise colonialism, taking the British envoy to task and telling him she's ashamed to be British. (The closing intertitles explain that her pupil, the prince, grew up to abolish slavery, reform the judicial system and establish religious freedom, implicitly because of her.) Nonetheless, she gets to preach the 'western' beliefs of mercy and freedom, while the king must control an autocratic regime. The emphasis on the king's desire to protect his people from western rapacity and some humbling attempts to show us the complexities of Thai culture never restore any balance.

The apogee of the film's distinctive mix of spectacle and sentiment is achieved in the final denouement. The king is saved by Anna's ingenuity, deploying her son's bugle and some fireworks to persuade the rebels that help has arrived. Anna, with a soot-blackened face, the very epitome of the plucky Englishwoman abroad, tells him proudly, "I've already lost one man to the jungle—I wasn't going to lose another!"

TIME, 12/13/99, p. 97, Richard Schickel

Certain properties in popular culture fasten their fangs on our pants leg and never let go, no matter how we kick and yell. The story of Anna Leonowens, British tutor to the numerous progeny of testy King Mongkut, ruler of 19th century Siam, is perhaps the most persistent of these terriers.

It began life as a (possibly fictionalized) diary by its heroine and has since been a novel, a movie, a Broadway musical, a movie version of that musical and an animated feature. It is now back to being a straight movie—without songs, without the Small House of Uncle Thomas ballet (thank God), but with a lot of exotic spectacle and a rather murky colonial confrontation that gives Jodie Foster, playing Anna, a chance to behave like a slightly prissy but good-hearted 20th century liberal.

The basic titillation of the tale is intact in "Anna and the King": the grieving widow is, as usual, brought back to life by the affection (which dares not speak its name) that develops between her and the sexy King. Of course, since they started telling and retelling this story, miscegenation has become a nonstarter as a cause for sundering true love. Hence the thought that Anna and the monarch might logically repair to a quiet room in the palace to relieve their headaches keeps nagging as this movie unfolds.

That's especially true since he is played by the marvelous Chow Yun-Fat, who interprets the role as if the cranky volatility of Yul Brynner and Rex Harrison never existed. He has all his hair, doesn't comically fracture his English and, though he occasionally loses his temper, never loses his quiet wit. There is about him a sort of watchful wariness, a thoughtful, insinuating manliness that avoids macho strutting in favor of bemused calculation. He is, in short, an absolute monarch for our postfeminist time. Cutting through the epic gesturings of Andy Tennant's direction, he provides reason enough to return one last time to this otherwise weary romance.

VILLAGE VOICE, 12/21/99, p. 156, Dennis Lim

Flash-forward 2000-plus years to another visionary ruler and the no-bullshit woman he loves [The reference is to *The Emperor and the Assassin*; See Lim's review.] The century's most bizarrely enduring culture-clash fable gets dusted off for one more run-through, and for those who applauded Titanic's old-is-new ethos, the moth-eaten, barely breathing *Anna and the King* will serve as a slap in the face. In what counts as progress, King Mongkut of Siam—previously embodied by Rex Harrison and Yul Brynner—is here recognizably Asian, though not Thai. Hong Kong star Chow Yun-Fat, the best thing about this lumbering, mindlessly pretty movie, plays the monarch with sly poise and under-his-breath amusement. Jodie Foster, meanwhile, invests the role of the Victorian schoolteacher with misplaced nervous energy and a mild protofeminist charge, which is quickly smothered by the film's bland plushness.

Divested of Rodgers and Hammerstein saccharine, the tin-eared screenplay struggles to fill dead air, throwing in a treason subplot that culminates with an escape to the jungle and a bridge being blown up. Bursts of subtitled Thai represent a token stab at veracity, though for emotive monologues, Thai characters routinely break into English (the over-enunciated, article-free brand-"Man never tell woman he's sorry"—that used to denote "foreign tongue" in Old Hollywood). Anna and the King make eyes at each other throughout, but the movie hinges less on repressed attraction than on the comedy of East-meets-West confusion and the resulting process of mutual self-actualization—the pair don't so much converse as lob tough-love platitudes back and forth.

Also reviewed in:
CHICAGO TRIBUNE, 12/17/99, Friday/p. A, Mark Caro
NEW YORK TIMES, 12/17/99, p. E22, Stephen Holden
NEW YORKER, 12/27/99 & 1/3/00, p. 130, Anthony Lane
VARIETY, 12/6-12/99, p. 83, Emanuel Levy
WASHINGTON POST, 12/17/99, p. C1, Rita Kempley
WASHINGTON POST, 12/17/99, Weekend/p. 44, Desson Howe

ANOTHER DAY IN PARADISE

Trimark Pictures release of a Chinese Bookie Pictures production. *Producer:* Stephen Chin, Larry Clark, and James Woods. *Director:* Larry Clark. *Screenplay:* Christopher Landon and Stephen Chin. *Based on the book by:* Eddie Little. *Director of Photography:* Eric Edwards. *Editor:* Luis Colina. *Music:* Howard Paar and Robin Urdang. *Sound:* Arthur Rochester. *Sound Editor:* Lance Brown and Bruce Fortune. *Casting:* John Papsidera. *Production Designer:* Aaron Osborne. *Art Director:* Erin Cochran. *Set Designer:* Cara Hoepner. *Set Decorator:* Michelle Munoz. *Special Effects:* Darryl Pritchett. *Costume Designer:* Kathryn Morrison. *Make-up:* Elisabeth Dietrich Fry. *Special Effects Make-up:* Elisabeth Deitrich Fry. *Stunt Coordinator:* Steven Lambert. *Running time:* 101 minutes. *MPAA Rating:* R.

CAST: James Woods (Mel); Melanie Griffith (Sid); Vincent Kartheiser (Bobbie); Natasha Gregson Wagner (Rosie); James Otis (Reverend); Brandon Williams (Danny); Brent Briscoe (Clem); Peter Sarsgaard (Ty); Paul Hipp (Richard Johnson); Kim Flowers (Bonnie Johnson); John Gatins (Phil); Ryan Donahue (Barry); Christopher Doyle (Conan); Dick Hancock (Breather); Pamela Gordon (Waitress); Jay Leggett (Security Guard); Michael Jeffrey Woods (Big Man); Karen Lee Shepherd (Big Man's Wife); Mitchell Orr, Jr. (Big Man's Boy); Leo Fitzpatrick (Guard at Reverend's Gate); Simon Williams (Maitre d'); Steven Gererd Connell (Gas Station Attendant); Clarence Carter (Himself); Lou Diamond Phillips (Jewels).

LOS ANGELES TIMES, 12/30/98, Calendar/p. 2, Kevin Thomas

[The following review by Kevin Thomas appeared in a slightly different form in **NEWSDAY, 1/22/99, Part II/p. B3.]**

Larry Clark's "Another Day in Paradise" detonates the same compelling yet disturbing charge as his first film, "Kids," and his celebrated photo essays, in particular "Tulsa," documenting outlaw teens caught up in sex and drugs. Now Clark has drawn upon ex-convict Eddie Little's novel, astutely adapted for the screen by Christopher Landon and Stephen Chin, to express the yearning for family ties within a crime spree plot.

Not another bloody killers-on-the-run saga, you might well say. But such is the power of Clark and his colleagues that you're able to connect your own sense of ambivalence over the film to its central character, Mel, played by James Woods with ferocious wit, and to the film's profoundly ambivalent view of the American family as alternately nurturer and destroyer. The filmmakers are not about to let us get around the old truism that violence is as American as apple pie, but they do so in a complex way, juxtaposing it against a tenderness so raw and direct yet at times so ironic as to be darkly funny.

"Another Day in Paradise" is as mercurial and reckless in tone as are its junkie characters, and Clark catches all these quicksilver shifts with unstinting perception and even compassion. As contradictory as it is energetic, the film takes as many risks as its people do and as a result strikes a highly contemporary nerve.

"Another Day in Paradise" is "Bonnie and Clyde" for the '90s. Vincent Kartheiser's Bobbie and Natasha Gregson Wagner's Rosie are teen lovers, runaways from terrible families, holed up with other kids in an abandoned warehouse in an unnamed city. Bobbie survives by robbing vending machines with a screwdriver, and when he endures a savage beating from a security guard, his loft pal calls on his Uncle Mel, a career criminal, for help.

Mel treats Bobble's wounds and cases the pain with some of his best smack. Mel swiftly recruits Bobbie to help him on his next job, which propels Bobbie and Rosie on to the road with Mel and his lady Sid (Melanie Griffith).

Lean and intense with a gift of gab, Mel sells Bobbie and, to an extent, us as well, about what a savvy crook he is. He's a tough taskmaster, but Bobbie sparks a paternal warmth and concern in him. Still glamorous for all the shooting up she does, Sid is even more maternal toward Bobbie and especially Rosie.

Burgeoning emotional ties, the ruthless demands of high-risk thievery and the impact of drug-taking on judgment make for a volatile combination that leads to a finish that you think you can predict, but it plays out differently in its final moments of critical, character-defining choices.

Woods and Griffith, between whom there is much electricity, are the kind of go-for-broke actors who continually come up with all sorts of fresh shadings and nuances along with depth and passion. "Another Day" represents a high point for both, and Kartheiser and Wagner express a wrenching vulnerability and naivete. The awful irony is that Mel and Sid, who are not exactly Ozzie and Harriet, as the reflective Sid points out, give them more parental love and affection than either has ever known.

"Another Day" is like Todd Solondz's "Happiness" from earlier this year in its insistence on showing how closely intermingled our best and worst impulses can be. Clark presents it with an unnerving sense of absurdity that is embodied in the Reverend (James Otis), who is pure American Gothic, as fervent a preacher as he is an efficient gun supplier (and medic for wounded criminals). There's a zingy unbilled cameo by Lou Diamond Phillips as one of Mel's erstwhile partners, an outrageous but even more dangerous gay man.

Cinematographer Eric Edwards captures images as memorable as Clark's photographs, production designer Aaron Osborne and costume designer Kathryn Morrison give the film its enticingly seedy road movie look, and a lot of rhythm & blues songs—soul singer Clarence Carter appears in the film—enhance the movie's strong sense of mood and pace. The film is no more violent in actual content than countless other movies but deliberately makes its violence as disturbing as possible.

NEW YORK, 1/22/99, p. 47, Peter Rainer

With James Woods, the normal rules of overacting don't really apply because he often plays people who already overact in their own lives. The touchstone in his work is hysteria. His characters aren't larger than life, exactly; they're just more high-strung than life. And even though Woods projects a rapacious intelligence—which is why he was perfect for the lizardly wiles of Roy Cohn in the HBO movie *Citizen Cohn*—he's not a cerebral actor. His performances are sparked by flash points of feeling, and they have a present-tense immediacy.

Which is not to say that Woods is exonerated from all charges of overdoing it. Take Larry Clark's *Another Day in Paradise*, for example. As Mel, a journeyman crook in the Midwest looking for one last big score, he acts as if he's barefoot on a griddle. This is appropriate up to a point—it makes sense that this fast-patter junkie sociopath would be a jumping bean of neuroses. But around halfway through the movie, I muttered to myself, *actor's holiday*. It's more of a vacation for Woods than for us. He doesn't just chew the scenery; he practically strip-mines it. The outsizeness of the performance is entertaining but jarring: We're watching a show-off actor giving a show-off portrayal of a show-off character, and that's one too many levels of peacockery.

By contrast, Melanie Griffith, playing Mel's partner Sid, is a marvel of underplaying. Her dozy cuddliness can be a little creepy—infantilized yet carnal—and it works best in counterpoint. It needs the spectral, depraved context provided for her by a Jonathan Demme *(Something Wild)* or a Brian De Palma *(Body Double)*. In *Another Day in Paradise,* her snuggly babykins voice goes well with Woods's feral rat-a-tat. Part moll, part den mother, Sid is in the criminal life because it pay's off, and because there's sexiness in the danger. This may seem like a romanticized view typical of Clark—who perpetrated the egregious, hipper-than-thou grungefest *Kids* and the seventies photo album *Tulsa,* which canonized Midwest outlaws—but there's a level of truth in it. A crime movie that says crime's a thrill will no doubt be accused of irresponsibility; *Bonnie and Clyde,* an infinitely better movie and a model for this one, drew the same rap. But Clark isn't being irresponsible here. He's just being accurate.

If the film had stuck with Mel and Sid, it might have dipped into the duskier reaches of black comedy—Jiggs and Maggie on dope on the run. But they're only half the story. There's also Bobbie (Vincent Kartheiser), a young delinquent with vacant eyes who robs vending machines and falls under Mel's sleazo tutelage, and Bobbie's girlfriend Rosie (Natasha Gregson Wagner), a fresh-faced junkie. Between bloodbaths, this quartet lives high and lies low. We're meant to see Bobbie and Rosie as new-style babes-in-the-woods—babes gone bad; Mel and Sid, tooling around in their big black El Dorado, are the parents they never had.

It's all too neat and sentimental. Clark—working from a script by Christopher Landon and Stephen Chin based on a novel by ex-con Eddie Little—tries to introduce a newer, more neurasthenic level of creepiness into this crime world by portraying Mel and Bobbie as essentially conscienceless perpetrators. But he falls back on a plush cushion of pop-psych clichés: He's made a movie about the need to connect. There's lots of dewiness in the acrid air. When Rosie, for example, turns out to be pregnant, she tells Bobbie, "We can be the kind of parents our parents never were." You just know they're headed for a fall, in the same way you know Mel's last big score isn't going to be merry. Clark wants to get points for a higher realism while still attaching himself to the same old corn that was already getting popped around the time of *Little Caesar.* The final effect is disjointed: We appear to be watching an avant-garde antique.

NEW YORK POST, 1/22/99, p. 54, Rod Dreher

To say director Larry Clark loves to romanticize the low life is like saying Woody Allen has a fondness for Manhattan. In "Another Day in Paradise," his comparatively mild follow-up to the grotesque "Kids," Clark rolls in sleaze and squalor like a mangy dog on steaming roadkill.

"Another Day in Paradise" is the grit-crusted story of a patched-together crime family, a foursome of desperadoes who drive around doing drugs, having sex and committing crimes on the road to certain doom. The characters are all repulsive, having given themselves over to blank outlaw lives of dope, cruelty, sex and stupidity.

The pleasures to be taken from "Paradise" are almost all cheap and voyeuristic: you keep watching the movie to see how degraded these wastrels will become. But without a larger moral context framing their actions, or a sense that the characters are morally aware enough to seek redemption, the drama quickly becomes attenuated. We're left with a grim, clichéd portrait of wretched sickos, nothing more.

That said, James Woods plays one hell of a wretched sicko. Woods is so ferociously good here that he nearly saves the grim, greasy picture. He plays a bad, crazy junkie named Mel, who offers juvenile delinquent Bobbie (Vincent Kartheiser, a trailer-park Leonardo DiCaprio) a way out of the small-time larceny that gets him beaten to a pulp for chump change in the movie's opening sequence.

Bobbie and his bony girlfriend Rosie (a slack Natasha Gregson Wagner) hit the road with Mel and his old lady Sidney (Melanie Griffith) in a black Cadillac. The cigarettes-and-smack-fueled journey takes them through mainlining jags at sleazy motels, various robberies, revolting rap sessions, a raunchy gay bar (where a feral Lou Diamond Phillips turns up as the meanest queen since Bloody Mary), and sundry seediness.

Mel's outlaw vitality initially seduces the passive Bobbie, but it's his combustible menace that ultimately binds the others to him out of terror. No one else in this grifter quartet can match Mel for spirited malevolence, and if Woods' acting weren't enough to unbalance the picture, the dramaturgy itself turns "Another Day in Paradise" into a one-man show. Kartheiser and Wagner barely register. A puffy, ravaged Griffith is better than usual, and her woozy tenderness toward Bobbie and Rosie provides what little humanity and tragedy there is in the soulless "Paradise."

SIGHT AND SOUND, 8/99, p. 38, John Wrathall

Oklahoma, the 70s. After being beaten up, teenage junkie Bobbie is nursed back to health by Mel, a friend's uncle, who gives him heroin to kill the pain. Mel and his girlfriend Sid take Bobbie and his girlfriend Rosie under their wing. Bobbie helps Mel steal speed from a clinic, but they are double-crossed by the white-supremacist gang to whom they try to sell the pills. In the ensuing gunfight Mel is wounded and the four supremacists killed. On the run, the 'family' take refuge in the home of Reverend, a gun-dealing minister. When they have recovered, Mel contacts Jewels, a gangster who recruits him to rob a jeweller's shop, arranged by the jeweller himself as an insurance scam. Mel and Bobbie break into the jeweller's safe, but find it empty. Returning to the motel where they are staying, Bobbie finds Rosie dead from a heroin overdose.

Mel, Bobbie and Sid go to the home of the jeweller who double-crossed them. Bobbie finds Jewels torturing the jeweller; trying to make him stop, Bobbie accidentally shoots Jewels. The jeweller's wife pays Sid the money they're owed but as the jeweller and his wife are witnesses to Jewels' murder, Mel kills them. Stopping as they make their getaway, Mel tells Sid he is planning to kill Bobbie. Sid warns Bobbie, who runs away. When he finds out, Mel punches Sid. Then they drive off together, apparently reconciled.

Tulsa, Larry Clark's 1971 book of photographs of drug buddies in his Oklahoma hometown, was an acknowledged influence on Gus Van Sant's *Drugstore Cowboy,* a similarly nonjudgmental look at the outlaw lifestyle of a bunch of 70s junkies. Van Sant repaid the favour by executive-producing Clark's first feature, *kids.* And now Clark has returned the compliment with his second feature *Another Day in Paradise,* a film much closer in tone to *Drugstore Cowboy*'s breezy, happy-go-lucky take on 'shocking' subject matter than to the starker, grittier approach of Clark's previous work as photographer and film-maker. Like *Drugstore Cowboy, Another Day in Paradise* offers an intimate look at a surrogate family of drug-users drifting around 70s urban backwaters from one motel to the next, supporting themselves with low-rent heists until, inevitably, they get out of their depth. In contrast with the recent wave of slick 70s nostalgia (see *Boogie Nights),* Clark's film actually feels as if it could have been made at the time, complete with grainy, low-contrast photography and a boom microphone wandering intermittently into shot. (Clark's quest for a certain brand of scratchy 70s authenticity is symbolised by the name of the production company he co-runs, Chinese Bookie Pictures, presumably after Cassavetes' 1976 classic *The Killing of a Chinese Bookie.)*

Refreshingly, despite finding his original fame as a still photographer and for his meretricious *kids,* Clark here seems more interested in performances than look or style. James Woods is one of the film's producers and it's not difficult to see why he leapt at the role of Mel after a decade of colourful but hardly taxing supporting turns in such films as *Contact, Casino* and *Nixon.* With the ceaseless self-justifying patter that shrouds his world-weariness, his horror at the open spaces of the countryside, his sudden explosions of violence and equally frightening mirth, Mel is a Woods creation par excellence, in the manic tradition of *Salvador*'s Richard Boyle and *The Boost*'s Lenny Brown.

With Woods on this sort of form, perhaps all a director needs to do is wind him up and point him in the right direction. But Clark deserves credit for extracting an equally striking performance from Melanie Griffith as Sid. The prospect of Griffith injecting herself in the neck, or toting a pump-action shotgun in a tight polo neck might sound laughable. But, against the odds, Clark discovers in her a bruised, Jeanne Moreau-like dignity as Sid struggles to keep the family together. Lou Diamond Phillips contributes a similarly revelatory cameo as the sequinned gangster Jewels. Holding one's own in this company would be a tall order for any inexperienced young actor. But the young leads Vincent Kartheiser and Natasha Gregson Wagner are disappointingly blank, cast more for their skinny, bedraggled, very *Tulsa* looks than for any performing spark.

VILLAGE VOICE, 1/26/99, p. 59, J. Hoberman

Love it or hate it, Larry Clark's *Kids* was some sort of movie. Part exploitation flick, part cautionary shocker, the cult photographer's overhyped but skillfully made and undeniably disturbing debut feature gave definitive cinematic expression to the condition of being young, dumb, and horny. The use of nonactors and nonjudgmental—if voyeuristic—camera placement might even suggest a debased species of Bressonian cinema.

Kids was a world of sexual nihilism in the skateboard Sodom of a Christian Coalition nightmare, the *Los Olvidados* of the libido, as well as a visceral AIDS allegory. Clark's follow-up, *Another Day in Paradise,* is a lot more conventional and a lot less shocking—even if its particular milieu is closer to Clark's own notoriously drug-dependent past. A pair of veteran thieves, Mel (James Woods) and Sid (Melanie Griffith), team up with a couple of delinquent kids, Bobbie (Vincent Kartheiser) and Rose (Natasha Gregson Wagner), for a giddy ride toward oblivion.

Another Day in Paradise presents itself as a corrective of sorts to Gus Van Sant's *Drugstore Cowboy,* a movie Clark feels—with good reason—to have been inspired by, if not ripped off from, his photographs. Clark may know this world better than Van Sant but he lacks the filmmaking chops to reclaim it. *Another Day* is slackly directed and badly acted. Nor does Clark show any particular flair for mayhem. Despite a well-orchestrated deal gone wrong, the ensuing carnage is too clumsily staged and awkwardly contrived to carry any emotional weight. Barely enlivened by the presence of bluesman Clarence Carter or Lou Diamond Phillips's cameo as the meanest queen in East L.A., *Another Day* lurches in and out of credibility, slouching from contrived situations of horror to fake revelations of synthetic soul.

Four actors, four movies. The typically wired Woods is acting solo. Kartheiser manages to survive a lot of punishment and still look minty fresh. The only thing more embarrassing than Melanie Griffith's blowzy mother-hen is stoned kewpie doll Wagner's valley-girl whine of junkie need. *Kids* asked to be read as a cautionary movie about AIDS. *Another Day in Paradise* illustrates a lesser social problem—the danger that, for a photographer, everything is a pose.

Also reviewed in:
CHICAGO TRIBUNE, 2/26/99, Friday/p. M, Michael Wilmington
NEW REPUBLIC, 2/8/99, p. 24, Stanley Kauffmann
NEW YORK TIMES, 1/22/99, p. E1, Janet Maslin
NEW YORKER, 1/25/99, p. 95, David Denby
VARIETY, 9/21-27/98, p. 111, David Rooney

ANY GIVEN SUNDAY

A Warner Bros. release of an Ixtlan/The Donners' Company production. *Executive Producer:* Richard Donner and Oliver Stone. *Producer:* Lauren Shuler Donner, Dan Halsted, and Clayton Townsend. *Director:* Oliver Stone. *Screenplay:* John Logan and Oliver Stone. *Story:* Daniel Pyne and John Logan. *Director of Photography:* Salvatore Totino. *Editor:* Tom Nordberg, Keith Salmon, Stuart Waks, and Stuart Levy. *Music:* Robbie Robertson, Paul Kelly, and Richard Horowitz. *Music Editor:* Bill Abbott, Johnny Caruso and Denise Okimoto. *Sound:* Peter Devlin. *Sound Editor:* Wylie Stateman and Kelly Kabral. *Casting:* Billy Hopkins and Mary Vernieu. *Production Designer:* Victor Kempster. *Art Director:* Stella Vaccaro. *Set Designer:* Stephanie Girard, Jeff Adams, and Richard Fojo. *Set Decorator:* Ron Reiss and Fred Wheeler. *Special Effects:* Kevin Harris and Michael E. Doyle. *Costumes:* Mary Zophres. *Make-up:* John Blake. *Stunt Coordinator:* Allan Graf. *Running time:* 120 minutes. *MPAA Rating:* R.

CAST: Al Pacino (Tony D'Amato); Cameron Diaz (Christina Pagniacci); Dennis Quaid (Jack 'Cap' Rooney); James Woods (Dr. Harvey Mandrake); Jamie Foxx (Willie Beamen); LL Cool J (Julian Washington); Matthew Modine (Dr. Ollie Powers); Charlton Heston (AFFA Football Commissioner); Ann-Margret (Margaret Pagniacci); Aaron Eckhart (Nick Crozier); John C. McGinley (Jack Rose); Jim Brown (Montezuma Monroe); Lawrence Taylor (Luther "Shark" Lavay); Bill Bellamy (Jimmy Sanderson); Andrew Bryniarski (Patrick "Madman" Kelly); Lela Rochon (Vanessa Struthers); Lauren Holly (Cindy Rooney); Elizabeth Berkley (Mandy Murphy); James Karen and Gianni Russo (Christina's Advisors); Duane Martin (Willie's Agent); Clifton Davis (Mayor Tyrone Smalls); John Daniel (Suitor in Christina's Box); Patrick O'Hara (Tyler Cherubini); Jerry A. Sharp (McKenna); Marty Wright ("Beastman"); Mazio Royster and Todd

Smith (Wide Receivers); Jamie Williams, Craig Thompson, and Greg Orvis (Tight Ends); Rick Johnson (Dallas Quarterback); Bjorn Nittmo (Kicker); Matt Martinez (Shark Fullback); Pete Ohnegian (Shark Centre); John Clark and Brian O'Neal (Shark Linebackers); Steve Raulerson (Shark Chaplain); Oliver Stone (Tug Kowalski, TV Announcer 1); Phil Latzman (Kevin Branson, TV Announcer 2); Barry Switzer (Dallas Announcer); Mark Ellis (Quarterback Coach); Anthony L. Tanzi and Joseph A. Wilson (Shark Coaches); Margaret Betts (Mayor's Aide); Antares Davis (Mayor's PR Woman); Liz Petterson (Society Lady at Mayor's Party); Lester Speight (Shark's Security Guard); Daniel Marino, Alexandra L. Hellman, and Hunter White (Cap Rooney's Children); Micah West ("Madman's" Wife); Christy Trummond (Dr. Mandrake's Girlfriend); Eva Tamargo, Debbie Howard, and Tucker Brown (Tunnel Reporter's, Game 3); Bob St. Clair (Opposing Coach, Game 1); Y.A. Tittle and Pat Toomay (Opposing Coaches, Game 2); Dick Butkus (Opposing Coach, Game 3); Warren Moon (Opposing Coach, Game 4); Johnny Unitas (Opposing Coach, Game 5); Bruce C. Hardy (Dallas Knights Chaplain); Drew Rosenhaus (TV Announcer, Willie's Apartment); Hunter Reno (Reporter at Mayor's Party); Dorothy J. Morrison (Willie's Mom); Vincent DiFatta, Jim Gasser, and Allen Reidel ('Fan' Business Men at Mayor's Party); Luciano Armellino (Tony's Bartender).

LOS ANGELES TIMES, 12/22/99, Calendar/p. 1, Kenneth Turan

Think of the Oliver Stone-directed "Any Given Sunday" as a fan's notes. This energetic and diverting sports soap opera throws a few head fakes in the direction of an iconoclastic examination of the dark side of professional football, but at the end of the day it comes out squarely for, hold onto your hats, the rewards of teamwork and unselfish behavior.

Put this one on the shelf next to "Knute Rockne, All American." Flash, dazzle and full-frontal male nudity notwithstanding, it belongs there.

Who better than Stone, after all, to deal with the orgiastic frenzy of violence, hysteria and macho posturing that has given America's undying passion for professional football the feel of the last days of the Roman Empire? Big salaries, big egos, big pressure games, it's all ripe for the outlandish nothing-succeeds-like-excess treatment it gets here.

Who but Stone, for that matter, would think of intercutting clips from the chariot race in "Ben-Hur" with the on-field action, or using Native American burial chants on the soundtrack? Also for ears only are waves of amplified grunts and the thuds of bodies crunching against bodies that make the Sunday contests sound more bone-jarring than combat in Vietnam. If you can't be over the top, "Any Given Sunday" says, what's the point of playing?

When it comes to actually re-creating games, Stone pours on the razzle-dazzle, even putting cameras on players' helmets to get unusual angles. Working with cinematographer Salvatore Totino, whose career has been all in commercials and music videos, as well as a team of editors with extensive experience in those areas, Stone favors a nervous, jittery camera style that slices and dices the action footage in a way that will make even fans of ESPN's "Sports Center" dizzy. The downside of all this technique is that if you're not a football fan it's likely you'll be baffled by the on-field proceedings.

When it's not occupied by all these pyrotechnics, "Any Given Sunday" (written by John Logan and Stone from a screen story by Daniel Pyne and Logan) does nod in the direction of some of the game's problems familiar to readers of daily sports pages. Lightly touched on are the abuse of painkillers, the winking at serious medical conditions, the apparent omnipresence of willing women and wild parties, the pernicious influence of big TV playoff money on the nature of the game as well as the wheeling and dealing that go on when teams pit cities against cities in attempts to get newer, more profitable stadiums built.

Although in "JFK" Stone was willing to posit that the entire U.S. government was corrupt to the core, he apparently has more respect for the game of football. There's more mythologizing than idol-breaking going on in "Any Given Sunday"—it opens with a quote from legendary coach Vince Lombardi—a film driven by the belief that if everyone concentrated on winning and losing like men, problems would disappear. No one quite says, "There's no 'I' in 'team,'" but it's even money that the line was in an earlier draft.

The NFL, scared of its own shadow when it comes to the possibility of less than worshipful treatment, did not cooperate with "Any Given Sunday," so the film had to come up with its own league (Associated Football Franchises of America), its own Super Bowl (the Pantheon Cup), even its own teams, complete with wacky uniforms and names like the Rhinos, the Crusaders and the Sharks.

Those gritty Miami Sharks, whose black uniforms and "Whatever It Takes" motto bring the Oakland Raiders to mind, are the film's focus. The eye of the hurricane is Tony D'Amato (Al Pacino), the Sharks' veteran coach who is under pressure on and off the field.

Never mind that the coach has sacrificed family and friends to football, never mind that he truly believes "this game has got to be about more than winning." Christina Pagniacci (Cameron Diaz), who owns the team along with her alcoholic mother, Margaret (Ann-Margret), thinks he's lost a step. And his veteran quarterback, Jack "Cap" Rooney (Dennis Quaid), is out of action with a serious injury.

The only replacement he has is an untried kid named Willie Beamen (Jamie Foxx), who turns out to have a gift for the game but also a selfish arrogance and a weakness for the blandishments of fame. Can a coach from a different generation teach a youngster who "doesn't give a gee-whiz about anybody" what football is all about in time for the make-or-break big game? Yes, it's that kind of a movie, and if you know what you're getting into, it's unlikely you'll be bored.

Fleshing out the picture are lots of awfully familiar roles, like the craven sportswriter (John C. McGinley), the long-suffering girlfriend (Lela Rochon), the scheming wife (Lauren Holly), the running back in love with his own statistics (LL Cool J), the ruthless team orthopedist (James Woods) and the more idealistic internist (Matthew Modine). NFL veterans like Jim Brown playing defensive coordinator Montezuma Monroe and Lawrence Taylor as defensive captain Luther "Shark" Lavay also get in the act, and Stone has even given himself a cameo as a TV color commentator.

All acquit themselves well enough, and in any case memorable acting is not what this picture is all about. Still, "Any Given Sunday" does err in casting Pacino as the old school coach. Yes, he can yell when he has to, which is often. But Pacino is so self-centered an actor he has difficulty conveying a believable interest in other people, specifically the players, that great coaches, no matter how egomaniacal, must have. Stone and company are right, it is a jungle out there, and even warriors need someone who cares on their side.

NEW YORK, 1/3/00, p. 85, Peter Rainer

Typically, when a sports movie comes out, we're told by the filmmakers that what we're watching isn't really about sports at all; its about life. In the case of Oliver Stone's *Any Given Sunday*, I'm tempted to go along with the life-not-sports line because the film seems so transparently a playing-out of Stone's conflicted feelings about Hollywood. (This qualifies as life, doesn't it?) Al Pacino plays Tony D'Amato, the head coach of the Miami Sharks football team, now on a losing streak. The film ostensibly slams the country's win-at-all-costs culture, but I've rarely seen a movie that put such a premium on the thrill of victory. *Any Given Sunday* is a powermonger's fantasy about saying *screw you* to the front office while still winding up on top.

NEW YORK POST, 12/22/99, p. 53, Lou Lumenick

Oliver Stone tackles pro football in "Any Given Sunday," a testosterone- and cliché-fueled epic that will have some hoping for sudden death as it stumbles toward the three-hour mark.

This movie adds up to less than the sum of its parts, which include a huge, impressive cast headed by Al Pacino, Cameron Diaz, Jamie Foxx, Dennis Quaid and James Woods.

A restrained (for him) Pacino is very good indeed as Tony D'Amato, the coach of the fictional Miami Sharks, who is fighting a losing battle against time.

The teams ruthless owner, Christina Paniacci (a miscast Diaz) is losing patience with Tony's traditional style, which hasn't led to the championship she needs to make a killing by selling the team.

When the team's aging star quarter-back Cap Rooney (Quaid, not at his best,) is sidelined, Tony is forced to send in Willie Beamen (Foxx, who's excellent), a cocky third-stringer who couldn't care less about teamwork.

But Willie starts winning games, and Christina starts plotting to dump Cap, whom Tony regards as a son. Waiting in the wings to replace Tony is Nick Crosier (Aaron Eckhart), the team's offensive coordinator.

The unwieldy screenplay by Stone, John Logan and a platoon of uncredited writers) also pits the unscrupulous team doctor (Woods) against a more idealistic colleague (Matthew Modine), who fights to stop a linebacker (Giants legend Lawrence Taylor, astonishingly good) who's determined to risk his life by playing with injuries.

It's reasonably entertaining, but for all the split-screens, hair-trigger editing and fancy camera-work from Stone's dog-eared playbook, "Any Given Sunday", is probably the most predictable and blatantly commercial—movie he's ever directed.

It's the old chestnut about the young hotshot who learns how to be a team players dressed up with music-video clips and a few observations about alleged racism in the NFL. Stone even drags in Charlton Heston (also seen in inspirational clips from "Ben Hur") for a cameo as the league commissioner.

Ironically, the huge cast—John C. McGinley, as a snarky sportscaster: LL Cool J as a running back who detests Willie; and Jim Brown, as Tony's world-weary assistant, are standouts—never quite jells as a team. Even the inevitable confrontation between Pacino and Woods fizzles.

As usual, Stone's female characters are horrors: They include Christina, a one-note villain; her mother, a pathetic drunk (Ann-Margret): Cap's bitchy wife (Lauren Holly in one great scene); and Elizabeth Berkley as a whore.

"Any Given Sunday" (which buries a not-so-surprise ending in the closing credits) illustrates why so few major films about pro football have been made in more than two decades. It's a sport that works far better on TV (where the action is ideally seen from a distance) than on a movie screen (where close-ups make it hard to follow).

NEWSDAY, 12/22/99, Part II/p. B11, Gene Seymour.

The Miami Sharks are at a crossroads similar to one faced a year ago by another fabled pro-football dynasty, the San Francisco 49ers. Stumbling their way through a midseason losing streak, the once-mighty Sharks are showing the telltale signs of age and complacency that turn a powerhouse into a patsy.

And now the valuable collarbone of John "Cap" Rooney (Dennis Quaid), the team's 39-year-old Hall of Fame-caliber quarterback, has been shattered in the second quarter of another apparent loss. Head coach Tony D'Amato (Al Pacino) brings in the second-stringer—who himself gets rocked by the opposing defense.

So who's left? A restless 26-year-old bench jockey named Willie Beamen (Jamie Foxx), who is so taken aback by his sudden call to the huddle that he vomits on camera. "Well, that's different," says Coach D'Amato.

So, it turns out, is Beamen, who after a couple of games has revitalized the sagging Sharks with his swashbuckling play and improvisational leadership. Team owner Christina Pagniacci (Cameron Diaz) is excited—purely from a marketing standpoint—by Beamen's charisma and "suggests" as gracefully as modern-day management can that "Tony Dee" make the kid a permanent starter even after Rooney heals ...

If what you've just read sounds too much like the kind of stuff you hear in pregame football gab-fests, then consider it a backhanded tribute to the way Oliver Stone yanks you into the alternate big-sports universe he's established in "Any Given Sunday," a bombastic, overblown and—despite its many flaws—compelling entertainment.

Made without the cooperation of the National Football League, Stone nonetheless crams much of the mythos of pro football into his movie so he can spend its three-hour length gouging holes into it. He gooses his verisimilitude by populating his movie with real-life legends. Johnny Unitas and Dick Butkus play opposing coaches, and Lawrence Taylor enacts, with striking bravado, a role he was born to play: a mad-dog linebacker who is one concussion away from eternal numbness.

As always with big subjects, Stone bites off far more than he can chew, bringing in subplot after subplot intended to make points about corporate sterility, corrupt team doctors such as James Woods' sleazy Dr. Mandrake, the hypocrisy of racial politics in pro sports, the clash between teamwork and individualism. Clearly, Stone's research shows up in the product, from the on-field etiquette between coaches to the banter that goes on in boardrooms and at team parties.

To filter this unwieldy batch of raw material, Stone relies on his patented jump-cutting narrative style, marinated here with hip-hop rhythms that make it seem as if the movie is "sampling" its own plot line. For a while (especially in the early segments, which, thanks to some superb sound work, replicate as well as anything can the experience of being caught up in football's violent whirlwind), this approach seems as effective as anything Stone has done in his mercurial career.

But it doesn't take long (exactly two hours by my count) before "Any Given Sunday" begins to do what even the best of Stone's movies do: overwhelm you with its unceasing rhetorical excess. Moreover, Stone never quite reconciles his own skepticism toward his subject with what is clearly a fondness for its hoariest cliches about winning, losing and being a Real Player.

Yet, through these aforementioned excesses, an intensely personal theme can be perceived that accounts for what is genuine and moving about "Any Given Sunday." The clue is in Pacino's grizzled, surprisingly ruminative portrayal of D'Amato, who reminds you of precisely no other football coach, past or present, despite the Vince Lombardi photo in his office.

D'Amato's fumbling attempts to reach out to his young quarterback seem more emblematic of guys in Stone's postwar generation who have reached middle age, still feeling the same urges and drives as they did in their 20s, but realizing that the world keeps moving without them and that the real 20-somethings couldn't care less about your own crises.

So that's one good thing you can say about "Any Given Sunday." The other is that the performances, big and small, are superb. Foxx is terrific in what should be a star-making role, Diaz' cool blond shark is crisply played, and Ann-Margret is a hoot as her dipsomaniacal mom. The biggest surprise is that Jim Brown, after 34 years in the movies, gives his finest, most relaxed performance as, of all things, a defensive coach. If you're hip to the irony of that, then you might get a few thrills out of "Any Given Sunday" before the inevitable overkill settles in.

NEWSWEEK, 12/20/99, p. 40, David Ansen

The matchup of Oliver Stone and pro football makes a not-so-surprisingly good fit: afterall, Vince Lombardi often compared football to war, and war is Stone's favorite cinematic turf. Using all the weapons in his overflowing technical arsenal, Stone hurls the audience onto the field, surrounding us with the most bone-crunching, earth-shaking game of football ever put on film. The Miami Sharks—coached by veteran Tony D'Amato (Al Pacino)—lose two quarterbacks to injury, opening the way for third stringer Willie Beamen (Jamie Foxx) to take his shot at glory. But first, he pukes all over the field live on network TV.

D'Amato and Beamen are men of two opposing generations. D'Amato has sacrificed his family, even his self-esteem, in his devotion to the sport: it's the one pure thing in his life. Guys like Beamen, quick to cash in on their instant fame belong to a generation that puts self above teamwork—which makes him a liability as a QB, for all his talent. But even worse, in D'Amato/Stone's eyes (for the director clearly sees himself in this flawed but unbroken warrior), is the team's cutthroat owner, Christina Pagniacci (Cameron Diaz), for whom nothing matters but the bottom line.

If you pare "Any Given Sunday" down to its raw bones, it's the oldest sports story in the world—the one about the guy who has to learn to play for the good of the team. But Stone creates such a sizzling, raunchy, vital world that the clichés almost seem new. He gets the details right: the macho locker-room swagger, the parasitical media, the bartering of celebrity for sex, the spoken and unspoken issues of race. In pro football, Stone has found a metaphor for all he loves and hates in contemporary America, and it results in his most entertaining movie in years. As usual, he often turns up the gas too high and his view of women (bitches, whores) is as enlightened as ever. Well, as any football player can tell you, victory doesn't come clean.

SIGHT AND SOUND, 4/00, p. 38, 40, Mark Kermode

Florida, the present. The football team the Miami Sharks, under coach Tony D'Amato, lose their fourth game in a row, despite an impressive display by third-string reserve-quarterback Willie Beamen, brought in after star player Jack 'Cap' Rooney and his usual substitute are both injured off. The Sharks' president and co-owner Christina Pagniacci, whose father built the team with Tony, berate the coach and announces Cap will soon be farmed off. When Willie wins the game against the Rhinos, his stardom comes between him and his girlfriend Vanessa.

Playing against the Rhinos, rival between the heavily sponsored Julian Washington and rising star Willie (who now overrules the coach and claims sole credit for the victory) leads to tactical errors, allowing another key player to be injured. Despite the efforts of team orthopaedist Dr Harvey Mandrake, new medic Dr Ollie Powers detects a potentially fatal injury in Luther 'Shark' Lavay, whom Pagniacci insists should appear in the playoffs against Dallas. Tony agrees to include him in the line up if he signs a waiver, but against Christina's wishes enlists the recovering but battle-weary Cap to lead the team, as Beamen has lost his men's respect. At the game, Cap scores an inspiring touchdown before being replaced on field by the now reformed team-player Beamen who leads the Sharks to victory, while Lavay is stretchered off, hurt but not dead. At his retirement celebration, Tony announces that he has accepted a position coaching an upcoming team, for which he claims to have signed Beamen.

After the almost wilful uncertainty of *U Turn*, Hollywood's most belligerent auteur Oliver Stone returns to the terrain he knows best: the visceral depiction of the strange bonds between men at arms. Despite its recreational subject matter, *Any Given Sunday* attempts to do for American football what *Wall Street* did for the cut-throat world of high finance: turn it into a war zone as deadly as any portrayed in Stone's more overtly military movies. Owing less to the dewey-eyed philosophising which made the baseball movie *Field of Dreams* an international hit than to the meat-grinding menace which kept William Friedkin's basketball film *Blue Chips* out of UK theatres altogether, Stone's "homage to Robert Aldrich" (director of *The Dirty Dozen* 1967, and the football movie *The Longest Yard* (1974) is a tale of warriors at work. From starting gun to final whistle, we are dragged brusquely from the touchline to the huddle to the post-game shower, leaving us battered and bruised from our encounter with Oliver's army. What else would you expect?

Opening with a quotation from Vince Lombardi which exalts those lying "exhausted on the field of battle", the screenplay (by Stone and John Logan) harks right back to *Platoon,* with the footballers learning—much like those Vietnam GIs—that only when they rely on each other do they have any chance of survival. Centring the relationship between old-style coach Tony D'Amato (Al Pacino) and rising star Willie Beamen (Jamie Foxx), *Any Given Sunday* throws endless issues into the mix—race, gender, wealth—only to conclude that nothing is relevant except teamwork. As Pacino declares in one of his many rants, "We either heal now as a team, or we will die as individuals."

For D'Amato, of course, that message has been lost along with the rules of engagement which once determined fair play on the field. The culprit in his eyes (and presumably the director's) is the media, or more specifically television. Stone suggests this medium's omnipresence by filtering the film through a variety of formats, presenting a channel surfing assault on the eyes and ears. Just as *JFK* jittered between jumpy Zapruder-style Super-8, grainy black-and-white film and urgently colourful scope to represent the multiple versions of Kennedy's assassination, so *Any Given Sunday* vibrates with incessant montage, split-screen effects and freeze frames turning the game into an MTV-style meltdown. (However, nearly 10 minutes of football footage has been cut for the UK release.) From the opening seconds, the first voice we hear is not that of a player or a coach, but of a commentator (Stone himself joining the howling throng) whining that things do not look good. D'Amato—permanently wired for sound—struggles to be heard over the endless cacophony of television spin doctors and franchise contractors who buzz around the screen and the soundtrack, distracting attention from the final goal. "TV changed everything," mumbles Tony. "The first time they stopped the game to cut away to some fucking commercial, that was the end of it."

The fervour with which Stone sinks his teeth into his ancient enemy at times approaches quasi-religious devotion. While the bone-crunching moments of self-sacrifice on the field are often accompanied by slo-mo visions of the heroic past, the bite sized fragments of televised temptation gradually assume demonic stature as the players are dragged down into a hell of sponsored self-interest. "Speak of the devil," says Tony's comrade-in-arms as the record-selling, product pushing image of Beamen flickers on to the screen. Later, Beamen himself (whose mother thinks that Sunday is for church, not sport) tells his platoon of the demonic possession which turned him from team-player into solo-flyer. "It wasn't me," he says, "it was the devil," a confession delivered with none of the irony of *Natural Born Killers*. This time Stone really seems to mean it.

Underpinning all this angst is a more down-to-earth, father-son motif which runs alongside the military and media metaphors. Both Tony and Willie have lost their fathers: Tony's died on the battlefields of World War II; his own children have lost him on the football fields. "My daddy died because of this," says team president Christina Pagniacci (Cameron Diaz), surveying the legacy she has inherited from her own father. Later, in her only moment of emotional vulnerability, Christina overhears her mother (splendidly played from the bottom of a Martini glass by Ann-Margret) note that Christina's dad always wanted a son. In the end of course, she cannot be his son (or a good team president) because she doesn't really love football. It's a guy thing and she simply doesn't have the balls.

It's perhaps inevitable (if regrettable) that *Any Given Sunday* deals such a lousy hand to its female characters. Diaz often seems to be in a different, more glassy movie to the whirlpool-eyed Pacino, although it's tempting to attribute her fish-out-of-water quality to a screenplay which essentially casts her as an interloper throughout. Elsewhere, the shrill harpiness of the assembled team wives borders on caricature, as does Lauren Holly's tight-skinned bitch who refuses to allow her ailing husband Dennis Quaid to retire gracefully. Like Christina, she's more concerned with pay packets than with the game, and like her sister-in-crime she's vilified for not being one of the guys. It's locker-room stuff and if you don't like the smell of testosterone, then Stone's film may not be the perfect way to spend a Sunday.

As for the guys, however, they're a splendidly solid bunch throughout, from Pacino's permanently ruffle-headed coach who can make even a tuxedo look dishevelled, to Foxx's word-perfect TV hero, whose on-air interview style is unnaturally natural. But as ever with an Oliver Stone movie, it's the supporting players who win the game, from James Woods and Matthew Modine stealing home as the nice-and-nasty team medics, to LL Cool J as the preening former prize-winning player. Few directors could command such an impressive roster and Stone wisely ensures no one is wasted or left on the substitute bench without a chance to score.

There's a dazzling diversity too in the musical score. Revelling in the opportunity to push the ludicrous pageantry of the game beyond the touchline of taste, Stone serves up knights in armour charging around on horseback to the sounds of Black Sabbath's "Paranoid" and forward passes from Gary Glitter to Fatboy Slim like a celluloid jukebox on random select. Elsewhere, a shower room showdown between rap and Metallica plays out issues of black and white sporting rivalries as a Battle of the Bands. Similarly, the bone-crunching audio-effects turn every tackle into a medical trauma and there are near-subliminal cues which achieve a dreamy trippiness sadly lacking from most Hollywood fodder. This is what ultimately makes an Oliver Stone movie such fun: the unabashed enthusiasm for experimentation, the willingness to use jump cuts, side-steps and non-linear interruptions just because it might work, it just might add something. The fact that he may win only one game in three makes him all the more matchable, because even when he fails, he does so in spectacular fashion. *Any Given Sunday* may fall on its face a few times during the game, but wouldn't you rather watch a team going recklessly for the touchdown than playing safely for time?

TIME, 12/27/99, p. 172, Richard Schickel

Basically, it's your mean, very mean, standard sports story: an aging coach (Pacino) who is on a losing streak; a great veteran quarterback (Quaid) whose winning spirit has gone south; a cocky kid (Foxx) who needs some life lessons before he can step into the starter's shoes. The up-to-date spin on this tale is provided by the tough and scheming owner (Diaz), who has inherited the team, the Miami Sharks, from her more benign father and wreaks a certain amount of nontraditional havoc before she gets some sort of comeuppance.

Director Oliver Stone, who wrote *Any Given Sunday*'s screenplay with John Logan, may be momentarily in a nonpolitical mood, but that does not mean he has given up his preoccupations with paranoia, greed and the brutality of American life. He sees his warriors as innocent animals, the purity of their violent athletic endeavors under constant threat of corruption by people trying to make a buck off their pain. Or, in the case of a particularly noxious sports reporter (John C. McGinley), a know-nothing who thinks he knows it all, just trying to make a name for himself.

McGinley's relationship to the game is interesting. So is Lauren Holly's with the crippled quarterback, finally letting the inner bitch residing beneath her cool jock's-wife beauty savagely surface. The trouble with the movie is its style, all handheld shots and short, jagged cuts. They're supposed to represent the barely controlled anarchy of the sport (and to let Stone touch on far too many narrative points). But almost three hours of this jitter deteriorates from bravura filmmaking to annoying mannerism, and *Any Given Sunday* ends up less than the sum of its many, often interesting parts.

VILLAGE VOICE, 12/28/99, p. 121, J. Hoberman

This is the week of the new and improved: *Man on the Moon* resurrects Andy Kaufman in the form of superstar Jim Carrey, Julie Taymor turns Shakespeare's worst play into flashy Oscar fodder, and Oliver Stone tackles the great macho American metaphor.

Neither spectacle nor drama, Stone's 160-minute football saga *Any Given Sunday* is more like a visual concussion. The camera is moving, the actors are screaming—and those are just the locker-room scenes. Stone must've run five editors' ragged assembling the game footage. Rub-your-nose-in-the-dirt close-ups alternate with dirigible high-angle shots, and there's a great recurring effect where the ball spirals downfield toward the camera until—wham!—some tight end flies on-camera to snag it. But mostly, the on-field trials of the Miami Sharks are rendered in the filmmaker's patented LSD-laced-with-strychnine effect—power blurs, slo-mo double vision, kaleido fades, lightning bolts, and celestial superimpositions.

How can Stone's flawed hero, Sharks coach Al Pacino, blame TV for the degradation of the game when the soundtrack suggests a two-and-a-half-hour loop of the theme to *Sports Machine* punctuated with Indian chants and the sound of snapping bones? Even Pacino is subsumed in the bombast, as is corrupt team doctor James Woods, until he gets the hook—still screaming, "They ARE gladiators, they are WARRIORS!" The action itself is interspersed with cutaways to dishy cheerleaders and Stone himself in the broadcast booth: "Holy mackerel—that is football!" What makes him so sure? You might see the same thing if someone clamped your head between those paddles the guys in *Bringing Out the Dead* used to shock stilled hearts.

The movie is its own half-time show, complete with beer commercials when the Sharks play touch football with a beachful of bethonged beauties. *Any Given Sunday* doesn't look like any previous sports film—*He Got Game* is Ozu by comparison—but the narrative is somewhat less novel. When the Sharks' star quarterback (Dennis Quaid) is injured, the unknown third-stringer (Jamie Foxx) takes over. Brilliant but moody, Foxx's character has a trademark upchuck routine and harbors some attitudes— indeed, the militantly square Pacino, suffering through a film-length midlife crisis, discovers that the kid is a sort of hip-hop black nationalist philosopher. Pacino is getting old. The team's ruthless boss lady (Cameron Diaz) criticizes his lack of intensity—even if his idea of relaxing has something to do with blasting the chariot race from *Ben Hur* on a wall-sized TV.

For a mad minute, it seems as though Stone might be making a movie about how football wraps religion, business, sex, and violence in one superbly telegenic package. Later, he settles for the less ambitious notion that America is all about kicking ass. (The socially conscious director does include a scene alluding to athletes and domestic violence: Quaid is verbally and physically abused by his harridan wife.) Ultimately, everything turns out to be corrupt and also beautiful ... homosocially speaking of course.

Any Given Sunday slows to a crawl before the big game—a monstrous anthology of clichés, including the gimpy old quarterback's last hurrah, the young buck's coming of age, the coach fighting for his career, and the injured vet playing on bad debts and cortisone. The fate of the Free World hangs in the balance, and Stone is back in the booth warning that "this is where the famous rubber meets the famous road."

Everything from the goal-line stand to the 10-second Hail Mary happens more or less on schedule—although I did see one of the "screening extras" used to pad the press preview clap with excitement four plays before the game ended. Don't you make the mistake of bolting before the credits end. There's a last-minute zinger—although I'm pretty sure that in the real-life NFL it would be considered tampering.

Also reviewed in:
CHICAGO TRIBUNE, 12/22/99, Tempo/p. 1, Michael Wilmington
NATION, 1/24/00, p. 35, Stuart Klawans
NEW REPUBLIC, 1/17/00, p. 24, Stanley Kauffman
NEW YORK TIMES, 12/22/99, p. E1, Stephen Holden

NEW YORKER, 1/10/00, p. 90, David Denby
VARIETY, 12/20/99-1/2/00, p. 56, Todd McCarthy
WASHINGTON POST, 12/24/99, p. C1, Stephen Hunter
WASHINGTON POST, 12/24/99, Weekend/p. 32, Desson Howe

ANYWHERE BUT HERE

A Fox 2000 Pictures release of a Laurence Mark production. *Executive Producer:* Ginny Nugent. *Producer:* Laurence Mark. *Director:* Wayne Wang. *Screenplay:* Alvin Sargent. *Based upon the Book by:* Mona Simpson. *Director of Photography:* Roger Deakins. *Editor:* Nicholas C. Smith. *Music:* Danny Elfman. *Music Editor:* Ellen Segal. *Sound:* Joseph Geisinger. *Sound Editor:* Michael Silvers. *Casting:* Victoria Thomas. *Production Designer:* Donald Graham Burt. *Art Director:* Kevin Constant. *Set Designer:* Robert Harbour and Theodore Sharps. *Set Decorator:* Barbara Munch. *Set Dresser:* Nick Rymond and Chad Hagaman. *Special Effects:* R. Bruce Steinheimer. *Costumes:* Betsy Heimann. *Make-up:* Robert J. Mills. *Make-up (Susan Sarandon):* Marilyn Carbone. *Stunt Coordinator:* Glory Fioramonti. *Running time:* 113 minutes. *MPAA Rating:* PG-13.

CAST: Susan Sarandon (Adele August); Natalie Portman (Ann August); Eileen Ryan (Lillian); Ray Baker (Ted); John Diehl (Jimmy); Shawn Hatosy (Benny); Bonnie Bedelia (Carol); Faran Tahir (Hisham); Shishir Kurup (Voice of Hisham); Samantha Goldstein (4-Year Old Ann); Scott Burkholder (Man with Mercedes); Yvonna Kopacz (Assistant Hotel Manager); Eva Amurri, Kieren Van Den Blink, and Jennifer Castle (Girls on TV); Caroline Aaron (Gail Letterfine); Bebe Drake (Mrs. Rush); Paul Guilfoyle (George Franklin); Allison Sie (Teacher); Sharona Alperin (Real Estate Agent); Mary Ellen Trainor (Homeowner); Elisabeth Moss (Rachel); Ashley Johnson (Sarah); Heather DeLoach (Ellen); Corbin Allred (Peter); Stephanie Niznik (Waitress); Heather McComb (Janice); Lindley Harrison (Janice's Mother); Michael Milhoan (Cop); Bob Sattler (Bernie); Hart Bochner (Josh Spritzer); Nina Leichtling (Josh's Wife); Jay Harrington (Waiter); Andrew Bowles (Mourner); Rick Hurst (Reverend); Rachel Wilson (Sylvia); Stephen Berra (Hal); Nina Barry (Casting Assistant); Cricky Long (Casting Executive); Lillian Adams (Jack's Mother); John Carroll Lynch (Jack Irwin); Megan Mullally (Woman Buying Car); George Peck (Man with Luggage); Thora Birch (Mary Ann's Friend).

LOS ANGELES TIMES, 11/12/99, Calendar/p. 23, Kenneth Turan

It borders on the unforgivably glib to say "Anywhere but Here" is where you want to be while the Wayne Wang-directed version of Mona Simpson's novel is on the screen, but it's also close to the truth. While adapting accomplished fiction such as this is a lure Hollywood can never resist, some characters breathe better on the page, and that is the case here.

While it's a given that Simpson's subtly written, 500-plus-page novel about a complex and painful mother-daughter relationship can't be transferred to the screen in toto, it's unfortunate that what we are given is so standardized and generic. And while Natalie Portman's work as 14-year-old daughter Ann is keenly empathetic, Susan Sarandon and her character do not make a good fit.

Sarandon's Adele August is the latest in what seems to be an interminable line of live-for-the-moment, force-of-nature screen mothers who are so involved grabbing all the gusto and throwing themselves into life that they don't notice all the chaos they are causing for the people they nominally care the most about.

So it is with Adele, first glimpsed chomping unself-consciously on junk food and humming along with the Beach Boys as she drives an understandably sullen Ann from their home in Bay City, Wis., to what she firmly believes, based on very little hard evidence, is going to be a much better life in glamorous Beverly Hills. Scattered, selfish and self-absorbed, Adele is the kind of person who is so busy "trying to taste the entire world" that she can't remember to pay the electric bill. Bored by reality and intoxicated by her own fantasies, she is so full of pert and chipper energy and bogus happy-face homilies ("Be optimistic: smile, smile, smile!") you want to hide under the seat.

It's not just that a more irritating character is difficult to imagine, it's that Adele is so one-dimensional, so completely a movie construct, that any situation she's involved in automatically becomes bogus and unbearable. When daughter Ann snaps, "I hate you," or when a Los Angeles cop bawls Adele out, we want to rise in our seats and cheer.

Not surprisingly, Adele felt that small-town Bay City and second husband and ice-skating teacher Ted (Ray Baker) were just too limiting for her sublime designs. She tells everyone she's doing it for Ann, for her daughter's desire to be a child star, but in fact Ann is torn up to be leaving behind her cousin and best friend Benny (Shawn Hatosy), her aunt Carol (an under-utilized Bonnie Bedelia) and her grandmother Lillian (Eileen Ryan).

In Los Angeles, Adele does find employment as a school speech pathologist, and she and Ann move into a series of barely furnished apartments that enable Ann to attend Beverly Hills High, an institution and a locale that suit Adele's fantasy life.

While Adele hunts for a suitably wealthy boyfriend (Hart Bochner's hunky orthodontist is a candidate for a while), Ann focuses most of her energy on just trying to survive her mother and cope with the absence of her Egyptian-born father, now relocated to Las Vegas. (A phone conversation between father and daughter turns out to be the film's most emotionally affecting sequence.)

Brief moments notwithstanding, very little of interest happens in "Anywhere but Here," hampered as it is by a syrupy soft rock score and too dispirited overall to be anything more than a wannabe sentimental wallow. Both director Wang ("The Joy Luck Club") and screenwriter Alvin Sargent (an Oscar winner for "Ordinary People" and "Julia") have had better luck with other family situations.

Though Ann has to like Adele at least a little bit—she's her mother, after all—audiences are under no such compunction. "Even if you hate her," the daughter says about Adele at one point, "can't stand her, even if she's ruining your life, there's something about her, some romance, some power." Ann truly believes this, but nothing on the screen backs it up.

NEW YORK, 11/22/99, p. 88, Peter Rainer

Susan Sarandon is usually at her best playing in the normal range of human emotion. She *already* looks larger than life: it's a mistake for her to make even more florid what was florid to begin with, which is precisely what she does in *Anywhere But Here*. Wayne Wang's tepid movie based on Mona Simpson's celebrated 1986 novel. Sarandon's Adele August, with her unwilling daughter Ann (Natalie Portman) in tow, ditches her working-class family in Bay City, Wisconsin, for the promised land of Beverly Hills and keeps up a running pattern of hyperbolic jabber all the way. Adele is supposed to be one of those maddening, impossibly eccentric mamas who make their children's lives both miserable and worth living.

Ann, who is as levelheaded as her mother is flighty, wants to flee, and yet we're supposed to see that her days are richer for having been tethered to this human wind machine. In order for this material to work we have to feel a familial connection between these two, but Adele and Ann don't really seem like mother and daughter: their conflicts are more a matter of theatrical convenience than something born in the blood. In fairness to Natalie Portman, Sarandon's excessiveness would be difficult for any actress to match up with, but, in any event, she hasn't found the way to do it. She spends most of the movie looking clenched and glum. Maybe it was her way of setting herself apart from her co-star's antics—of being anywhere but there.

NEW YORK POST, 11/12/99, p. 50, Lou Lumenick

"Anywhere But Here" is a wonderful showcase for Natalie Portman, who gives an Oscar-caliber performance as a teenager suffering through life with her overbearing and flamboyant mom, acted with relish by Susan Sarandon.

They're vastly better than Wayne Wang's movie, a shapeless soap opera about their efforts to scrape by in Beverly Hills after the 40-something Adele August (Sarandon) walks out on her second husband, an ice-skating instructor, uprooting her 15-year-old daughter, Ann (Portman), from family and friends in Bay City, Wis.

Setting out in a gold Mercedes that Adele impulsively bought, they travel across the country (in sequences recalling "Thelma and Louise") and settle into a rundown apartment on the fringes of Beverly Hills.

Adele goes to work as a speech therapist at a slummy public school—then fantasizes about bagging a rich husband and an acting career for Ann.

Playing a role that might well have gone to Shirley MacLaine 15 years ago, Sarandon lights up the screen as the histrionic, utterly irresponsible Adele, who keeps forgetting to pay the electric bill and instead takes Anne out to fancy meals.

It's funny and more than a little pathetic when Adele, who spurns the attentions of nice guys her own age, mistakes a one-night stand with a hunky orthodontist (Hart Bochner) for the start of a relationship.

It's the kind of showy part that gets Oscar nominations, but it's Portman who burns a hole in your heart. She subtly and intelligently conveys Ann's pain at being trapped with a totally embarrassing Monster Mom, whom she alternately hates and loves.

Wang directs Portman with just enough of an edge to keep the screenplay, attributed to Alvin Sergeant (from a novel by Mona Simpson), from becoming sloppily sentimental.

"Anywhere But Here" covers very familiar territory—the down-and-out-in-Beverly Hills bit has been done before and better. But it's well worth seeing for the incandescent Portman.

NEWSDAY, 11/12/99, Part II/p. B3, Gene Seymour

"Anywhere But Here" wastes no time in proclaiming its chief assets: the faces of its two stars.

Susan Sarandon's tanned, vibrant features convey the overbearing avarice and childlike exuberance of Adele August, a dreamer from the Midwest aiming her Mercedes-Benz like a copper-colored arrow toward Southern California. At Adele's side, heat-ray eyes firing noiseless darts from beneath the rim of a baseball cap, is her daughter Ann, played by Natalie Portman with the implacability of a bill collector and the grace of a baby deer.

Anyone who has read Mona Simpson's best-selling novel about Adele and Ann's adventures between the "here" of their Wisconsin family home and the "anywhere" of their nomadic Los Angeles life couldn't have imagined better casting than Sarandon and Portman. And they don't disappoint, even if the movie does.

The billowy sprawl of Simpson's novel is neatly—perhaps too neatly—compacted by screenwriter Alvin Sargent into a tightly focused chronicle of Adele and Ann's ups and downs in the City of Angels. Ann, who is 14 when the movie begins, feels as if she is kidnaped when Adele decides on little more than a whim to clean her slate and head west.

"I wish," Adele says to Ann, "somebody had kidnaped me when I was your age."

"Me, too," Ann fires back, sullenly.

That exchange should give you some idea of the spiky tension between mother and daughter, who come across a little like a distaff Martin-and-Lewis comedy team, with Sarandon's Adele bouncing and skittering along the L.A. landscape like Jerry while Portman's Ann does her best, like Dean, to parry the wackiness.

The next couple years for Ann and Adele are a blur of apartments routinely darkened by unpaid electric bills. Adele chases her dreams, however vaguely defined, in a headlong, painfully earnest fashion. She sees sexual fulfillment and dollar signs in a fling with a hunky orthodontist (Hart Bochner). ("And he's writing a screenplay!" an impressed Adele proclaims to Ann.) When Adele is burned, here and elsewhere, Sarandon makes her heartbreak all the more palpable as she barely keeps her character from emotionally collapsing from the weight of crumpled illusions.

Portman's Ann is made of more complex, less demonstrative elements than Sarandon's Adele. The audience is encouraged to share her impatience with her flighty mother. Yet Ann is, in her way, as much of an impossible dreamer as Adele. She tries vainly to connect with her father, who abandoned them both.

She clings desperately to some of the people left at home, including her too-good-to-be-true cousin (Shawn Hatosy). And she pursues, with much of her mom's single-mindedness, a means of going to college as far away from the left coast as possible.

It takes subtlety on the part of writer, director and actor to make you aware of such irony without pounding it into your head. Sargent's lean script, Portman's brittle poise and the seamless direction of Wayne Wang ("The Joy Luck Club") conspire to make Ann's seeming placidness more mercurial. In the same fashion, Sarandon's Adele ultimately comes across as a hapless monster with mortifying wounds. Never are our sympathies with these characters given more of a stress test than the moment when Ann, auditioning for a sitcom role, gives a gross, yet devastatingly dead-on impression of her mother. The look on Adele's face as she inadvertently catches this act hits your chest like a spike.

With all these fine moments, you wonder just what it is about "Anywhere But Here" that keeps it from being great. Part of the problem may be that the focus on Ann and Adele is so intense that everyone around them is reduced to a state of unbaked shapelessness. The dynamism of the two leads can't help but subsume everything in its path. But such dynamism, as a result, ends up throwing off sparks in a relative vacuum.

Toward the end, the movie struggles to gather enough energy to force audiences to reach for their handkerchiefs. But the last-second drive for sentiment only makes plain that there's something missing in the core of "Anywhere But Here." Maybe it needed a wider angle of vision. Or, more pointedly, some of Adele's go-for-broke adventurism.

NEWSWEEK, 11/15/99, p. 88, Jeff Giles

When Ann August (Natalie Portman) was 4, her father left in the middle of the night. What's worse, her mother stayed. Adele August (Susan Sarandon) is colorful, blustery and a constant source of embarrassment to her 14-year-old daughter, whom she still calls Pooh Bear. In director Wayne Wang's "Anywhere But Here," Adele buys a gold Mercedes she can't afford, and tells Ann they're dumping Wisconsin and heading for Beverly Hills. Adele claims she doesn't want her daughter to wind up "a nothing girl in a nothing town." But even young Ann can tell that it's her own life Adele is trying to save.

"Anywhere"—adapted from the terrific Mona Simpson novel—is a touching but melancholy narration on a tune we've heard many times. It's about how a mother and daughter can love and hate each other in the same instant, about how often children end up raising their parents, about what a lousy place L.A. is to be poor. (In this, the movie recalls the far quirkier "The Slums of Beverly Hills.") Portman gives a superb, understated performance as a teen who gets whipplash from watching her mother's mood swings. Sarandon is convincing, but she's played mouthy, tough-but-tender broads too many times to be a revelation here.

As for the story line, it's too predictable. It's a litany of dreams deferred, whereas the novel was rich with life. Adele convinces herself that the pick-up artist she met on the beach is going to sweep her away. ("He's more than just a dentist." she gushes. "He's writing a *screenplay.*") Ann fantasizes about finding her father and living a "normal" life. A *normal* life? Not if Adele can help it.

SIGHT AND SOUND, 1/00, p. 42, Charlotte O'Sullivan

Tired of life in Wisconsin, Adele August decides she and her 14-year-old daughter Ann should move to Los Angeles. There, Adele gets a job but doesn't earn enough for the lifestyle she covets. Ann settles into school but still misses her favourite cousin Benny, and finds her mother's mood swings difficult to cope with. Benny visits. Josh, a handsome dentist, calls for a date and he and Adele sleep together. When he fails to ring again, Adele becomes obsessed with him. Benny is killed in a car accident. After a trip home for the funeral, Adele quits her job and spirals into depression.

Shortly afterwards, Adele sneaks into an audition she has strong-armed Ann into attending, only to see Ann mimicking her. The pair row. Ann contacts her father; he's mistrustful and unenthusiastic. Despite their precarious economic situation, Ann's relationship with a boy at her school begins to flourish. In the meantime, her mother has found a new job and acquired a new suitor. Ann is accepted by a college on the East Coast but doesn't have enough money to go. Adele sells her beloved car, and gives the money to Ann.

In-the-name-of-the-daughter movies form a genre all of their own. From such grimly fiendish *noirs* as *Stella Dallas* (1937) and *Mildred Pierce* (1945) to soupy, semi-comedic dramas like *Terms of Endearment* and *Postcards from the Edge*, all have at their centre a maniacally aspirational mother whose attempts to control her daughter create an emotional competition between them. The energy it requires to manage the daughter's economic and sexual well-being invariably endows the mother with a vitality that makes her seem socially vulgar, oversexed, but most important of all, alive. However virtuous or demonic, the daughter is destined to play second fiddle. *Smoke* director Wayne Wang is clearly familiar with this type of woman's picture (there's a direct reference to *Terms of Endearment*). Keeping the novel's first-person narration—encouraging us to believe the daughter Ann's version of events is the definitive one—he seems keen to redress the balance in her favour.

This version can be reduced to a simple formula: daughter capable and desirable, mother incompetent, dishonest, superficial, jealous, hysterical and pitiful. A few scenes surprise us such as the one where Ann's mother Adele admits she can't "cope" with going to the posh Christmas party she had previously angled an invite for. It's like a car alarm being switched off. In the horrible ensuing quiet Susan Sarandon's familiar beat up eyes and toffee-ice-cream voice appear too vulnerable for her suddenly small body and you long for the protective high volume to be restored. Most of the time you see her being knocked back; here we discover how she behaves when she's welcomed. You don't pity her, but for the first time you understand her. Such glimpses of Adele's hidden life are all-too rare. Like the gruff, paternal traffic cop whom mother and daughter meet on Christmas day, we're asked instead to chuckle and roll our eyes at Adele's eccentricities. There's nothing seriously wrong with her; she just needs to listen to more of the 'good' men in her life. When at the end of the film the cop tells Adele to do right by her daughter, she does.

Sarandon can't transform this kind of fluff into drama, but it's Natalie Portman you feel really sorry for. There's nothing for her to do here. Ann is your typical American success story—a naturally 'classy' individual who resists her mother's attempts to twist the truth. She also overcomes all obstacles in her path, inspiring admiration wherever she goes. Her one rejection—from her father—can be blamed on her mother. Prickly and suspicious when she rings him, dad is unable to separate the two women in his mind—something the film achieves all too easily. As the tag line says, this is a story about a mother who knows best, and a daughter who knows better.

The trouble with this kind of wish fulfillment is that it's excluding. The film wants us to love Ann but also to envy her and the two sit together uneasily. It's impossible to take Adele seriously, but that doesn't mean you identify with Ann. In fact, by the time she's being waved off at the airport to her brilliant future ("I love you", "I love you too, sweetie"), you may, like me, be praying for a plane crash.

Adele's sacrificing of her car is the last straw. Ann mentions dreams in which she cuts off her mother's feet. In giving up her car—her mobility—it's as if Adele cuts off her own feet. In *Stella Dallas* we're allowed to wonder at the world Barbara Stanwyck's daughter has been fed into. This film sheds no such ambiguous light on a privileged East Coast education. Adele's self-sacrifice, in other words, gets the full thumbs-up.

Mildred Pierce and *Stella Dallas'* camp melodrama can of course be improved upon, but Wang and his particular brand of schmaltz prove unequal to the task. As the credits roll, Ann says of Adele, "When she dies, the world will be flat." In its eagerness to give voice to the overshadowed daughter, the film never allows the mother to live. Flat is precisely the word one would use to describe this.

Also reviewed in:
NEW YORK TIMES, 11/12/99, p. E22, Janet Maslin
NEW YORKER, 11/15/99, p. 116, Anthony Lane
VARIETY, 9/20-26/99, p. 81, Emanuel Levy
WASHINGTON POST, 11/12/99, p. C1, Stephen Hunter
WASHINGTON POST, 11/12/99, Weekend/p. 47, Desson Howe

APPLE, THE

A New Yorker Films release of an MK2 Productions and Makhmalbaf Productions film. *Executive Producer:* Iraj Sarbaz. *Producer:* Marin Karmitz and Veronique Cayla. *Director:*

Samira Makhmalbaf. *Screenplay (Farsi with English subtitles):* Mohsen Makhmalbaf. *Director of Photography:* Ebrahim Ghafori and Mohamad Ahmadi. *Editor:* Mohsen Makhmalbaf. *Sound:* Behroz Shahamat. *Running time:* 85 minutes. *MPAA Rating:* Not Rated.

CAST: Massoumeh Naderi (Massoumeh); Zahra Naderi (Zahra); Ghorbanali Naderi (Father); Soghra Behrozi (Mother); Azizeh Mohamadi (Social Worker).

CHRISTIAN SCIENCE MONITOR, 2/19/99, p. 15, David Sterritt

As more international movies slide onto American screens during the current slack time for Hollywood pictures, it's noteworthy how many films from other lands are taking children as their main concern.

These portraits of youngsters aren't all rosy in their outlook, but they suggest that a healthy number of societies are taking an active cultural interest in the well-being of their smallest citizens.

None is more fascinating than *The Apple*, an Iranian drama that is itself the product of a teenage director, Samira Makhmalbaf, who started work on the project at age 17 and completed it a year later. It. was written by her father, filmmaker Mohsen Makhmalbaf, whose colorful "Gabbeh" attracted many American viewers in 1997.

"The Apple" was inspired by news reports about an aging couple in Tehran who kept their twin daughters literally imprisoned in their house for 12 years until neighbors realized the children's plight. Investigating this harrowing situation, Samira Makhmalbaf became acquainted with the parents, learning that they suffered from exaggerated fears of the outside world spurred by religious beliefs and their own physical infirmities and believed they were acting in their daughters' best interests.

Showing great initiative and creativity, Makhmalbaf persuaded the family to reenact their story for her camera. The result is an absorbing movie that treads the delicate line between documentary, since the facts and personalities are real, and fiction, since events have been arranged and condensed to form an orderly narrative line.

"The Apple" is a particularly good example of contemporary film in Iran, where the industry has learned to avoid censorship by focusing on young people's lives and on the process of filmmaking itself.

Both of these tendencies also can be seen in Jafar Panahi's comedy-drama "The Mirror," playing now in American theaters, and concern for kids surges through Majid Majidi's poignant "Children of Heaven," an Academy Award nominee for best foreign-language film.

"The Apple" and "Children of Heaven" have received criticism from some observers who feel American importers are overemphasizing Iranian pictures that happen to portray poverty and ignorance. Americans are well advised to keep a sense of proportion about such matters, but this doesn't cancel out the warm human properties of so many recent Iranian imports.

FILM QUARTERLY, Winter 1999-2000, p. 47, William Johnson

Few films these days are simple in a nonpejorative sense, relying on a straightforward narrative structure presented with economy of means. Of all the selections at the 1998 New York Film Festival, *The Apple* was by those standards the simplest; yet only a little probing will reveal underlying issues of considerable complexity.

The narrative derives from a real-life incident: An elderly man and his blind younger wife have kept their 11-year-old twin daughters, Massoumeh and Zahra, shut up in their house since birth. (The wife, too, rarely goes out.) Neighbors complain to the Social Services authorities, who bring the girls in to be examined and then let them go home on the condition that they be allowed out. When a visiting social worker finds the girls still kept inside, she releases them, and on the second occasion also locks the father in for a time. At first the girls are afraid of their freedom; they also have no knowledge of outside life, assuming (for example) that a street vendor is simply giving away his ice cream. But they begin to learn from other children they meet: a boy at an upstairs window teasing them with an apple on a string and then taking them to a fruit store; two girls playing hopscotch in a park. At the end the father appears to accept his daughters' freedom as he joins them for a walk outside, and the mother goes out far enough to encounter the boy with the apple.

The most general issue raised here is cultural: To what extent can a viewer understand a film in an unfamiliar language from an unfamiliar society? The problem becomes acute with a country that differs from ours in politics and religion as sharply as does Iran. (My own knowledge is based precariously on some 30 Iranian films and miscellaneous reading.) And with a film as simple as *The Apple,* non-Iranian viewers may believe they understand elements that in fact they are misinterpreting.

That cultural difficulty extends into another issue: How much "reality" is there in a film based on a real-life incident? Whereas Iranian viewers were likely to know both the facts of the case (which was covered in their media) and the plausibility of certain incidents, most of us start from scratch. Some internal evidence (notably the writing credit) suggests that incidents were changed or added—but which? It struck me, for example, that the social worker's locking in of the father was astonishingly interventionist, but I could not judge its plausibility. Only by interviewing Samira Makhmalbaf did I learn that it was fictional.

Fidelity to the facts, however, is not the heart of the issue. Can a fictional film based on a real situation ever offer more than a false promise of being "true to life," or can it retain some extrafictional value?

The Apple takes an unusual approach to its reconstruction. All of the main characters-father, mother, twins, and social worker—are "played" by their real-life counterparts. The only recent film I know of that uses the same strategy also comes from Iran: Kiarostami's *Close-Up,* about a movie buff who posed as Molisen Makhmalbaf (Samira's father). Yet in *The Apple* the strategy gains even more immediacy, partly because it enters deeply into a family's emotional life and partly because Samira Makhmalbaf began filming only four days after the twins were taken to the welfare center, at a time when the parents' resentment at the bad publicity was still burning and the twins had scarcely begun to taste their new freedom. The film was shot in sequence, Makhmalbaf told me, and as far as the twins were concerned, "This is documentary, not fiction. I didn't direct them to do anything they couldn't do. For example, people ask me, How could these girls play hopscotch so soon after coming out? Well, I shot for only eleven days, so it's a first time for nearly everything they do. Hopscotch was on the eighth day, and it was their first reaction to it."

The third issue concerns Makhmalbaf herself. Only 17 when she made the film, she lives in a society that generally considers youth and femaleness unsuitable for positions of responsibility and respect. True, she had already made two short films and served as an assistant on her father's full-length *The Silence.* On the other hand, not only did her father give her entree into the world of filmmaking but his credits on *The Apple* might suggest an even larger role in its making.

Ironically, it was Makhmalbaf's youth and gender that lay behind both the decision to make the film and the real-life family's willingness to take part in it. "When I saw the events on TV, I couldn't stop thinking about it," she said. "I could put myself in the girls' situation—I was a girl, and I was in that culture, it could have been me or my sister, and I wanted to help them. And another reason was I was interested in sociology, and I wanted to know what would happen to the two girls, how they would communicate with the outside world, what would be their reactions." As for persuading the family to take part, she knew that this meant persuading the father, whom she saw at the Social Services center after the twins were taken there. "I thought that it would be hard for him to communicate with a woman, a girl. So I just listened to him, I didn't judge him, I just wanted to know his reasons, instead of condemning him like everyone else. So I think he trusted me. And I never asked him, Let me come to your home, I want to make a film—he just took me there, and started telling me about his life. It was very simple. And I was fond of him."

Makhmalbaf was in sole charge of the filming. As for her father's script: "I didn't want to have a script before meeting the family, I wanted to keep my eyes and ears open before using my imagination about it. After the shooting started, every night, my father and I had some kind of conversation together, and had an idea. Then my father threw out some kind of note about it, not the details, not the dialogue; so the whole script wasn't finished until after the shooting. For example, on the first day of shooting I went to the Social Services and found the father and mother and the social worker all worrying about the girls' future, but the girls were enjoying their life there, they had some apples and were tasting them. So I talked with my father about it and he found this metaphor about Adam and Eve and the apple, so in the film the apple means the knowledge and enjoyment of life."

While that metaphor recurs openly with the boy dangling the apple, first over the twins and at the end over the mother, who finally grasps it, the idea that knowledge and freedom go together is absorbed into the film's entire fabric. *The Apple* consists of a progression (reinforced by shooting in sequence) front enclosure to open space, from restriction to tolerance, not just for the twins but also—as at the end the father walks out with them and the mother emerges more tentatively—with the implicit hope it will come for everyone.

Makhmalbaf sets that theme in the opening shot, a medium close-up of a potted plant against a sunlit wall. A hand holding a pot enters the frame above right and begins to tip water onto the plant. A pan and upward tilt reveals that the hand belongs to Massoumeh, who stands behind a locked metal gate with her arm stretched out and down between the bars. The plant lives in sunlight and open air; the girl does not.

The twins go through more than one stage toward freedom. The gated house door opens onto a small garden surrounded by high walls, and a locked door in the facing wall leads to an alley. Only beyond the alley does the wider world begin. When the social worker first opens the gate and the garden door, the twins stay in the garden. Then she ushers them out, but they stay close by in the alley. It is the boy with the apple who leads them father away. Then they discover the park—their first truly open space—and two girls who play with them and teach them hopscotch (which reflects their progressive "leaps" toward freedom).

When the social worker locks the father inside the house, she gives him a hacksaw and tells him he has to cut his way out. But the point is not just to make him experience what it's like to be locked in. Before he has gotten very far with his sawing, she returns with the twins and gives them the key. If they can unlock the door, she says, he will be free. After several attempts, Massoumeh turns the key. Her knowledge is his freedom.

Near the end of the film, the twins are fascinated by a street vendor's wares. They go home and ask their father to come back with them and buy them a watch. To their new knowledge of space they want to add knowledge of time.

The fictional elements in the film (notably the boy with the apple and the social worker's actions) intensify the implicit theme of progressive freedom and knowledge. By highlighting the symbolism, however, I have probably made it seem obtrusive, which in context it is not. In viewing the film, it is almost impossible to doubt that the twins are genuinely naive and barely able to speak. When they try to grab the dangled apple, they are clearly enjoying a game; when Massoumeh annoys one of the friends by suddenly tapping her on the forehead with an apple, and then makes up by giving it to her, the incident looks as unscripted as it actually was. With the adults, Makhmalbah simply explained the situation and let them find their own words. "For example," she told me, "I'd listened to the father—and I knew what would be his reaction to certain questions. I was waiting for the dialogue I wanted him to say but I didn't dictate it. Because I can't, even the best writer can't know what this real mother and father are going to say." Even the fictional elements had to reflect the temperaments and attitudes of the real-life participants. As Makhmalbaf said of the social worker's fictional locking up of the father, "It was something that suited her character, something she would like to do."

There is no fracture in *The Apple* between documentary and fiction. In one sense it is all fiction (except for the few scenes at the welfare center), since even the unscripted incidents were embedded in performances done for the camera. Yet in another and strong sense it is all documentary, since the filmmaking itself was an integral part of the family's response to the twins' temporary removal. With Makhmalbaf's prompt start on the film, everything in it, scripted or not, records the family's real-life experience. But *The Apple* does not flaunt these complexities; it remains a simple film: touching, sometimes amusing, always engrossing.

LOS ANGELES TIMES, 3/5/99, Calendar/p. 11, Kevin Thomas

Samira Makhmalbaf's "The Apple" is astonishing on at least three counts. First, it is a beguiling and tender film about an off-putting true-life incident: An impoverished 65-year-old Tehran man was discovered to have never allowed his 11-year-old twin daughters out of the house. Second, that it is the debut film of a 17-year-old filmmaker, daughter of major Iranian director Mohsen Makhmalbaf, known for such films as "A Moment of Innocence," "Once Upon a Time, Cinema" and "Gabbeh." And third, that Makhmalbaf was able to persuade the man and his family to play themselves in a work in which the line between fiction and documentary is blurred in a singularly effective, persuasive and responsible manner. "The Apple" is the latest in a series of Iranian films, including "The White Balloon" and the Oscar-nominated "The Children of Heaven," that deal with the lives of children to reveal a society whose cinema is heavily censored.

Drawing upon her father's writing and editing skills, Makhmalbaf wisely whisks past one of most unsettling aspects of the case: that the girls had never been bathed because their blind mother could not take them to the neighborhood public bath. Because they are hidden by their chadors, we don't get a good look at the girls until they're in the custody of a welfare worker (Azizeh Mohamadi, also playing herself), who has scrubbed them thoroughly and given them short haircuts. Massoumeh and Zahra walk and talk haltingly, but they're smiling, even happy youngsters. They are remarkably healthy physically, and clearly theirs is a loving family.

What Makhmalbaf discovers and explores so eloquently is a conjunction of circumstance and ultra-conservative tradition. Certainly, life would have been different for the twins had their mother, who speaks only Turkish, not been blind and their parents less impoverished and better educated. As it is, the family subsists on charity, and the father, Ghorbanali Naderi, is afraid to let them out of the house. The deeply religious Naderi is so conservative that he believes that should he allow his daughters to play in the tiny, walled yard in front of their small house, they might be dishonored if one of the neighborhood boys were to so much as touch them. Because the boys play in the narrow street in front of the house, they sometimes climb over the wall to retrieve a ball. "My girls are like flowers. They may wither in the sun," Naderi asserts. "A man's touch is like the sun."

Yet without contact with the outside world, deprived of education and exercise, the girls are withering away mentally and physically, hardly suitable for marriage, which custom dictates. Looking to be in failing health, the overwhelmed Naderi has not asked himself what would happen to his helpless, innocent daughters and his nearly as helpless wife should something happen to him.

Makhmalbaf got Naden's cooperation because when the plight of his daughters' life-long imprisonment became a media scandal, he believed he did not get his say and felt acutely dishonored when it was falsely reported that he had kept the girls chained hand and foot. Fixated on this inaccuracy, he's unable to comprehend the widespread outrage directed at him.

In depicting the girls' discovery of the outside world, Makhmalbaf sets up a series of situations and shows how the girls react—for example, a boy selling ice cream bars happens by, and the girls, who'd really rather have an apple, neither know what ice cream is nor that if you take a bar you have to pay for it. Amazingly, Makhmalbaf was able to start shooting only four days after the story broke in the press and shot her entire film in 11 days; her ability to get this particular family to behave naturally and without self-consciousness is quite an accomplishment.

At the heart of the matter, of course, is that the twins represent the extreme oppression of women in Iran, yet Makhmalbaf is careful to suggest that the angry reaction to their plight reveals that the status of women is improving within a patriarchal Islamic society. "The Apple," whose title takes on a subtly symbolic meaning, answers lots of the questions it raises with such deftness, but leaves to us to ponder why it took neighbors so many years to petition Tehran's welfare organization to investigate the twins' dire situation.

NEW STATESMAN, 12/18/98, p. 97, Jonathan Romney

Considering the recent surge in that hybrid TV form the docu-soap, you might think we'd be sceptical about the supposed separateness of filmed reality and fiction. Yet at heart we're still so convinced that drama is drama and documentary is unmediated reality that it hits us like a bomb when we learn that documentary may not be showing us the whole truth—as in the scandal over *The Connection*, the Carlton drug-running report recently exposed as riddled with deceptions.

In Iranian cinema, documentary and fiction have a much more equitable relationship; as some recent films suggest, they are just two different routes for getting to the truth. Reality may not necessarily be whatever is in front of the camera. It can also be what evades the camera, and therefore has to be reconstructed, evoked—for want of a better word, faked.

Abbas Kiarostami's 1989 film *Close-Up*, released here last year, was about a real-life case involving a fellow Iranian director, Mohsen Makhmalbaf. An unemployed man had passed himself off as Makhmalbaf and led a credulous family to believe that he would cast them in his next film. The case went to court where the accused was acquitted of fraud on the grounds that his imposture was motivated by a genuine, morally serious love of cinema. Kiarostami recreated the story as docufiction, in which the accused and the family re-enacted their own roles.

In a film about pretense and appearance, you were never entirely sure what, or who, was real, what was performed. But through this perplexing construction, Kiarostami at once interrogated the nature of cinematic truth and allowed accusers and accused to settle their differences through the reconciling medium of cinema. *Close-Up* represented something we can't quite imagine in the west—a sort of judicial cinema in which wrongs are publicly righted. Related, but diametrically opposed, to the hysterical pillorying on *The Jerry Springer Show*, it restores dignity to the public and to the medium.

In Makhmalbaf's own *A Moment of Innocence*, recently released here, the director himself is the subject for redemption, having stabbed a young policeman during the Shah's reign. Twenty years on, the policeman and Makhmalbaf unite to shoot an account of the incident, which is recreated, and transformed, in an eloquent closing freeze-frame—a device which is one of the defining rhetorical trademarks of new Iranian cinema.

The latest example of cinema as courtroom is *The Apple*, by Samira Makhmalbaf, the 18-year-old daughter of Mohsen, who wrote and edited it. *The Apple* is a true story (this term is used with caution) about two 11-year-old girls, Zahra and Massoumeh, living in poverty with their father and blind mother in Tehran. The parents have never let the girls set foot in the street, until their neighbours at last alert the welfare department, which intervenes to restore the children to the world.

A documentary sequence on video recounts the family's first encounter with the world and the camera—the children have reporters' microphones thrust into their faces and respond with inchoate mutters and inscrutable grins. We can't be sure that their video verite isn't as much a set-up as the rest of the film. But it marks the highly staged sequences that follow as a vivid fiction, and by contrast gives them the heightened quality of a public reckoning.

As the girls step into the world, the camera hovers over them like a solicitous nanny. Strangers both to words and to the freedom of body language, the girls hobble up and down the street with furious intent, grinning conspiratorially and homing in on the trouble they've always been kept away from—they immediately waylay a young ice-cream vendor and feed his wares to a goat. In a wonderful sequence, they meet a crisply bossy little girl who decides that the best way to socialise them is to take them shopping for watches.

It's impossible not to respond to Zahra and Massoumeh as screen naturals, vigorously anarchic spirits who seem to blossom as the film unravels. Rather than being exploitative, the film seems to be giving them their overdue day in the sun. But it's clear that their father is less comfortable, aware that he's being tried by both the camera and the daily press, which he scans with horror. Here the film's courtroom function is seen at its harshest, although he seems to submit to it willingly as a force of moral authority.

But what's also on trial, by extension, is Iranian society and women's role within it. The girls' prison has its parallel in the veil that their mother—invisible under her own chador—claps on them the minute they're reunited. The father quotes the dictum "A girl is like a flower—if the sun shines on her, she will fade", but *The Apple* proposes itself as a rescue operation for those who fade in darkness.

Another of the startling final freeze-frames suggests that another family member has been brought into the light. Iranian cinema is bold with symbolism that might seem heavy-handed in any other context. *The Apple* is not only one of the most entertaining films of the year, but also one of the most serious—a profession of faith that the intermingling of documentary and drama can produce something truer and more complex than straight reality, and can perhaps change the shape of the world, too.

NEW YORK POST, 2/19/99, p. 55, Rod Dreher

It's hard for us to imagine an act of social repression so heinous it would shock Iranian society under the Islamic regime. But the Iranian public was scandalized two years ago when it came to light that a poor, ignorant Teheran father had kept his twin daughters locked away with his blind wife in their squalid apartment for all 12 years of their life.

The Naderi family had no running water, and because the obsessively protective father refused to take his daughters outside their apartment to the public baths, the children had never been washed.

After neighbors complained on the girls' behalf, a social worker seized the pitiful pair, who were not mentally deficient but who could hardly talk or walk, owing to their extreme social isolation. The social worker returned the children to the family after Mr. Naderi promised to quit locking them away.

Samira Makhmalbaf, then 17 and the daughter of the great Iranian filmmaker Mohsen Makhmalbaf, instantly recognized the pathos and humanity in this story, and rushed out with her dad's camera to make a feature film about the Naderi family's plight.

Though she had fantastic material to work with and her famous father's help, "The Apple" is, unfortunately, about what you would expect when you put enormous filmmaking responsibility in the inexperienced hands of a high-school girl.

Which is to say, it's inept and monumentally boring, and would be rightly ignored were Miss Makhmalbaf not the daughter of a famous director. Iran now has its own Sofia Coppola.

"The Apple" follows a simple narrative line, in which we see the children set free by the social worker, who, in turn, locks Father (Ghorbanali Naderi) behind the bars of the family apartment, intent on teaching him a lesson.

Though "The Apple" is obviously an allegory for the plight of women in the Islamic republic, Makhmalbaf doesn't want to demonize the ultra-traditionalist father. He emerges as a victim of poverty and ignorance, and though the film doesn't excuse his misguided cruelty, it highlights the difficulty of raising the Great Unwashed from the mire of ignorance and meanness.

The film's title comes from the fruit's symbolism in Iranian culture. According to the press notes, Iranians are taught that all humanity came from Eve's taking the apple from Satan. The animal-like Naderi girls, once free to run the streets, look for apples to eat. The film suggests that authentic life can only be experienced if one is free to deal with the temptations that inevitably arise from interaction with others.

One can imagine what a more experienced director could have done with such captivating subjects and such a powerful theme. You can't fault Miss Makhmalbaf for trying, but this "Apple" is like the one the Wicked Witch gave Snow White. It puts you soundly to sleep.

NEWSDAY, 2/19/99, Part II/p. B10, John Anderson

The film is Iranian, it's titled "The Apple," it's vaguely concerned with cultural repression and its lead characters are children. So what to expect? Well, judging by all the "White Balloons," and "Children of Heaven," and tracing the pattern back to early Kiarostami masterpieces like "The Traveller" and "Homework," what we might expect is allegorical-Biblical-Koranic fable-making with a strong moral imperative and a shot of invective at the social order.

What we get via the first feature film made by then-17-year-old Samira Makhmalbaf, daughter of the Olympian Iranian director Mohsen Makhmalbaf, is something almost completely different, something that may even redefine what we mean by "cinema." And that's not a compliment. Makhmalbaf the younger comes dangerously close to pure voyeurism in this documentary hybrid—which means, of course, that it's totally engrossing even while being morally suspect.

Religious-cultural-political prohibitions make it difficult for Iranian filmmakers to make movies at all, but particularly about adult women—so children, especially female, have become a favored subject. Still, we've never seen children quite like these.

Massoumeh and Zahra Naderi, 12-year-old twins, have been locked up all their lives, kept in their home and deprived of social contact with anyone but their marginally employed/ultra-religious father and blind mother.

Their movements are spastic, their language skills stunted, their hygiene nonexistent. Only after neighbors alert the authorities to the plight of the girls (after 11 years) are they taken away, cleaned up and—of course—returned to their parents.

And did we mention this was a true story? It was the news coverage that attracted Samira Makhmalbaf to the case, where she found a genuine feminist cause celebre—boys, certainly, would never have been treated this way—and constructed a dubious conceit: Cast the movie about the family with the family and design situations in which, for instance, the father would become ashamed and infuriated and act out his story.

"The Apple" isn't being presented as a documentary, so perhaps no journalistic ethos need apply. But if there's something that differentiates Makhmalbaf's technique from that of the TV-caster sticking his/her mike in a face and waiting for the tears, well, it eludes me. There's an unsettling element of freakshow in "The Apple" which isn't ameliorated by the fact that no one seems to notice that the girls are irreparably damaged (or seem to be, since I hold no degree in behavioral science).

"They should get married," says the social worker (played by Zahra Saghrisa), and one thinks, "Yes, indeed, since they can barely walk down the street."

Allowing such statements to go unquestioned may be Makhmalbaf's slap at bureaucratic stupidity, but she certainly seems guilty of a comparable crime, the exploitation of her subjects. Since it played at last year's New York Film Festival, there's been a lot of critical praise for "The Apple," much of it citing Makhmalbaf's sense of place and pacing (her father edited the picture) and her artistic daring.

This is all fine, but one has to take exception when the conveniences of fiction are allowed to obscure the facts—which, after all, are the "hook" on which "The Apple" hangs. For example, do the girls seem developmentally challenged because they've been confined? Or were they confined because they were developmentally challenged? Or is that an unreasonable question? Maybe. But either way, it goes completely unanswered by "The Apple."

SIGHT AND SOUND, 1/99, p. 41, John Mount

Concerned families in a poor district of Teheran, Iran, petition the director of welfare about the Naderi family. The parents, a 65-year-old unemployed man and his blind wife, have virtually imprisoned Zahra and Massoumeh, their 12-year-old twin daughters. The girls are illiterate, unwashed and profoundly lacking in social skills. They are taken into care temporarily while their welfare is assessed.

The parents plead for custody of their children, promising to change their ways. The girls are returned with strict instructions on their upbringing from a woman social worker. The father initially makes an effort to teach housework to the girls, but locks them up again when he goes shopping. During a visit, the social worker finds the girls incarcerated. When their father returns, she sends the girls out to play and locks him behind his front door, handing him a saw and telling him to cut the door's bars if he wants freedom.

The girls steal ices from a young ice-cream vendor (a sympathetic neighbour pays for them). They encounter a small boy who jerks an apple on a string in front of them from his upstairs bedroom. They return to their father who reluctantly gives them money to buy apples. The girls meet and play with two sisters. After a trip to an old watch-seller they all return to their father's house and set him free. He leaves the house with the social worker's approval to buy the girls watches. Their blind mother stumbles out into the street and grasps the same apple the boy dangles before her.

Samirah Makhmalbaf's impeccable feature-film debut is a witty and precociously intelligent docudrama whose focus is fixed firmly on its subject rather than on its making. (Selfreflexiveness is becoming all-too common in contemporary Iranian films.) The 18-year-old director was fascinated by the media coverage of the Naderi family and their imprisoned children and contacted them immediately. This being film-friendly Iran, she was able to involve all members of the family, various neighbours and the authorities (as well as several members of her own family) in a fictional, semi-improvised recreation of the twins' experience that was shot in a couple of weeks while they were still in the process of acclimatising to the outside world. And although her father, director Mohsen Makhmalbaf, collaborated as editor and scriptwriter, the film is very much her own.

Perhaps because the writing of the script followed rather than preceded each day's filming, the performances are relaxed, natural and strikingly unaffected (especially the children), even when the characters—such as Ghorban Ali Naderi, the father—are dissembling. His overprotection of the girls never quite squares with their neglected state. But his simplistic, slightly self-serving devotion to the patriarchal Islamic codes he grew up with and his penurious dependence on handouts and small payments in return for prayers (he is jocularly referred to as "the Mullah" at one point) explain much. His blind wife, who resembles a shrouded rag doll coming apart at the seams, is an even sorrier sight—full of mistrust and quick to curse. As Ghorban says of his predicament: "I have hot bread in one hand and ice in the other."

But the film's main concern is the girls and their introduction to the neighbourhood. The sight of the twins stumbling from their courtyard like liberated battery hens, struggling to comprehend and communicate with the outside world, is especially resonant. The calm, assured persistence of the indefatigable social worker who is bold enough to lock the father in his own house until he sees sense points to the increasingly prominent role of women in Iran and the contribution the twins can offer society if given a chance. Nonetheless, this is a freedom for women that is to some degree at odds with western notions of women's empowerment. Still, this pragmatic determination is written into the film: Makhmalbaf shot her first scenes in video out of necessity and switched to film when she could lay her hands on stock.

Makhmalbaf is scrupulously non-judgemental and takes a carefully liberal line that skirts explicit criticism of any concerned parties. But beneath its superficially simple documentary appearance, this is a highly aestheticised film with remarkably assured direction. The mysterious chanting on the soundtrack, chosen in preference to a more traditional score, creates a subtle, uncertain atmosphere. And allegorical visual motifs are artfully arranged throughout like illustrative tiles to add a further layer of poetic ambiguity. The image of the hand of one twin watering a sickly pot plant through a barred door encapsulates their misfortune. Mirrors introduce the girls to themselves and the apple the twins cherish hints at sustenance and the getting of wisdom. In an almost cruelly funny final scene, this apple is dangled before the blind mother before she grasps it. It's interesting, given this scene's directorial ambivalence, that although the film seems to end on a positive note for the family, in reality the girls have been placed in a new home, presumably because the behaviour of their parents was too ingrained to change.

TIME, 3/15/99, p. 85, Richard Corliss

A child's arms stretches out, as far as it can, to pour water from a cup onto a scruffy potted plant. This, the first image in Samira Makhmalbaf's *The Apple*, introduces with poetic clarity the film's strange, true story: of 12-year-old twin girls imprisoned by their father in their Tehran home, away from sunlight, from the friendship of other kids, from the smallest ecstasies and exasperations of childhood. This wise, poignant film was made under unusual circumstances. The father and the girls were persuaded to play themselves, and Makhmalbaf was only 17 when she shot it. But extraordinary Iranian films have been almost ... ordinary. Savvy cinephiles know that Iran is the place where movie miracles happen all the time.

Iran is today's one great national cinema. Not since the Czech New Wave of the mid-'60s has a country made such a lovely noise at the big festivals and in Western capitals where the term foreign film doesn't evoke a yawn. Directors Abbas Kiarostami (*A Taste of Cherry*), Jafar Panahi (*The White Balloon*) and Samira's father Mohsen Makhmalbaf (*Gabbeh*) are as revered in the world film community as they are anonymous at American 'plexes.

To most Americans, the Islamic Republic of Iran is known for denouncing the Great Satan U.S., swearing out *fatwas* on any renegade soul and defining women's rights as the privilege of wearing a chador. For two decades, Iran has been, notoriously, fascism with a cleric's face. So it is a conundrum and a wonder that the republic has allowed the production of highly sophisticated films that are both touching, in the style of Italian postwar neorealism, and at least implicitly critical of aspects of the ruling theocracy. How do Iran's auteurs pull off this double feat? Frequently, by cloaking grownup stories in toddler raiment. For Iran is not only a leader in world film; it is the leader in children's films. This is Iran's cinema spirit: humanism with a kid's face.

Children's films—by which is meant movies about the young but not necessarily for them—have an honorable pedigree in Iran. The Shahrina sponsored a children's film festival for a dozen or so years before her husband was overthrown in 1979.   Under the Ayatullah, as in the Pahlavi regime, Iranian films proved a valuable cultural export.   Last month Majid Majidi's *Children of Heaven* became the first Iranian movie nominated for an Academy Award as best foreign film.

Children's stories are often tales of desperate travels through far-off lands.   In Iranian films, the terrain is typically the child's own hometown.   And the potential tragedy can be as simple as being left alone at school, as in Panahi's deliciously devious *The Mirror*.   Or, as in *Children of Heaven*, the loss of your sister's shoes.

Ali (Mir Farrokh Hashemian) leaves them outside a grocer's, where a blind trashman spirits them off.   Fearful of their father's wrath, the boy and his kid sister Zahra (Bahare Seddiqi) agree to share Ali's sneakers; Zahra will wear them to her school each morning, Ali to his in the afternoon.   Complications ensue, vitalized by the boy's heroic goodwill and the girl's frantic fretting—her petulance is comically magisterial.   When Ali enters a 4-km race, the film gets a case of slo-mo sentimentality; it becomes a sort of *Chariots of Farsi*.   But Majidi can show family love among the poor without finger wagging.   Ali and his clan have the affection of an ideal movie family.   American kids and their parents ought to love them.

The Naderi family, in *The Apple*, is far more troubling.   Neighbors petition the authorities about the girls' confinement; Zahra and Massoumeh are removed for haircuts and a good scrubbing, then sent home.   But the old father keeps them locked in.   His blind wife can't keep an eye on them, and there are boys living nearby. If anyone touched the girls, he says, "I'd be dishonored."

The girls yearn to see growing things; they make a painting of a flower by splatting two sooty handprints on a wall.   Finally they do get out and play with two other girls, in a meeting as sweet and spooky as the one between E.T. and little Drew Barrymore.   Massoumeh smacks an apple against one girl's face, then hands her the fruit.   Baffled but beguiled, the girl kisses Massoumeh—who, inferring that this was a reward for aggression, hits the girl again!

The Apple, like the best Iranian films, is full of such privileged moments.   But it is no simple fable of the Wild Child civilized.   For two girls and their blind mother thrust into the light, a cave has its security, and the world its perils.   The film can only wish the Naderi family the success that Iranian cinema had when it emerged from the shadow of the imams and into the glare of the world screen.

VILLAGE VOICE, 2/23/99, p. 109, J. Hoberman

The teenaged daughter of an internationally celebrated filmmaker makes a feature-length documentary about twin 11-year-old girls who have been locked up at home since birth by their blind mother and elderly, fundamentalist father. By its very existence, *The Apple* articulates, in a way no fiction could, the contradictions of Iran's Islamic Republic. Sometimes, it takes a global village. Samira Makhmalbaf, who captivated American journalists when she appeared with *The Apple* at the last New York Film Festival, says that she was inspired to make her first movie by a TV report on the residents of a poor Tehran neighborhood who had petitioned a state welfare agency to redress the twins' situation. Using film stock approved for a project to be directed by her father Mohsen Makhmalbaf (best known here for *Gabbeh*), the 17-year-old neophyte made *The Apple* in 11 days. According to the filmmaker, *The Apple* had no prepared script. After a brief introduction—shot on video, handheld verité-style—showing the parents reclaiming their girls from the welfare-agency offices, Makhmalbaf devised and filmed a series of situations that compelled the actual family to react. If the methodology is avant-garde and the directorial mode behavioral, it might be said that Makhmalbaf had been preparing for her own performance all her life, having appeared as a child actress in her father's 1988 feature *The Cyclist* and served as a production assistant on his latest film, *The Silence*. Initially, the two girls—Massoumeh and Zahra—can barely speak. Although well-behaved and good-natured, they are scarcely socialized; they appear infantile, if not mentally retarded, all the more so once their parents come to fetch them. But if the girls seem feebleminded, what is one to make of their pathetically wimpering father? Or of their fully veiled mother whose constant sotto voce muttering (in Turkish, the only language she understands) has more than a whisper of insanity. But who is crazy here, the family or society? As extreme as the particular situation may be, it is impossible not to treat this found metaphor as a cultural critique—particularly once Makhmalbaf switches to 35mm film and, with a surprising degree of delicacy and tact, allows her subjects to redramatize their life together.

The "group therapy" portion of the movie is signaled by Makhmalbaf's shift to a deliberate overhead angle as the father brings Massoumeh and Zahra back home and, ignoring the welfare agency's injunction, once more locks them in the house. Skinny and sweet, with big eyes and lolling tongues, the twins are as much mischievous pets as prepubescent children. They clown behind their gate—beating spoons on the bars—until the old man returns like the witch in a fairy tale, carrying their daily bread and ice. In a bit of mordant comedy doubtless staged for the benefit of the filmmaker, father treats the twins to a cooking lesson and (prompted by a newspaper clipping that Makhmalbaf evidently sprang on him) argues with a neighbor, bitterly complaining that he has been "slandered." Meanwhile, the twins are distracted by the presence outside their gate of a child ice-cream vendor, even younger than themselves. At length, the state power arrives in the person of a no-nonsense social worker, bringing an ultimatum for the father and little mirrors for the girls. The mirror is not just the movie's main special effect but the signifier of its intentions. But what exactly does *The Apple* reflect? In an inspired bit of forced role-playing, the social worker locks the old man in the house and, leaving him with a hacksaw to cut away the bars on his front door, shoos the shuffling, mugging children out into the street. *The Apple* is hardly straight documentary. Developing specific visual metaphors, Makhmalbaf has a bit of her father's hieroglyphic style. (*The Apple* doesn't fall far from the tree.) Massoumeh and Zahra enact little scenes—stealing ice cream, chasing the eponymous fruit that's dangled in front of them by a neighbor boy, heading off to the marketplace with two other little girls from their street. In the end, the twins head back to the market with their father, leaving their mother alone in the courtyard. Sightless and without language, she's the real prisoner and yet, even in her case, there is the possiblility of transformation. Makhmalbaf was the same age as the underground filmmaker Barbara Rubin was when she made her orgiastic, taboo-breaking *Christmas on Earth* and, although the two films could not be more different, there is a kindred purity in their desire for liberation. ("Barbara Rubin has no shame; angels have no shame; Barbara Rubin is an angel," Jonas Mekas wrote.) A font of excuses, the father compares his daughters to delicate blossoms. His house is their shelter. "They may wither and die in the sun." But we see them seek the light and bloom in the clear gaze of Makhmalbaf's camera. Experimental docudrama, open-ended essay, *The Apple* is a remarkable movie. Still, the question remains: Is Samira Makhmalbaf the real flower of the Islamic revolution or a hothouse orchid? Have Massoumeh and Zahra truly been set free? Or will they be shut in again two years hence?

Also reviewed in:
CHICAGO TRIBUNE, 5/14/99, Friday/p. G, John Petrakis
NATION, 3/8/99, p. 34, Stuart Klavans
NEW YORK TIMES, 2/19/99, p. E18, Lawrence Van Gelder's
VARIETY, 3/9-15/98, p. 46, Godfrey Cheshire
WASHINGTON POST, 6/11/99, Weekend/p. 41, Desson Howe

ARLINGTON ROAD

A Screen Gems release in association with Lakeshore Entertainment of a Gorai/Samuelson production. *Executive Producer:* Tom Rosenberg, Sigurjon Sighvatsson, and Ted Tannebaum. *Producer:* Peter Samuelson, Tom Gorai, and Marc Samuelson. *Director:* Mark Pellington. *Screenplay:* Ehren Kruger. *Director of Photography:* Bobby Bukowski. *Editor:* Conrad Buff. *Music:* Angelo Badalamenti. *Music Editor:* Mark Jan Wlodarkiewicz. *Sound:* Pud Cusack and (music) Michael Semanick. *Sound Editor:* Phil Benson. *Casting:* Ellen Chenoweth, Kathleen Chopin, and Tracy Kaplan. *Production Designer:* Therese DePrez. *Art Director:* David Stein. *Set Decorator:* Barbara Haberecht. *Set Dresser:* Darren Patnode. *Special Effects:* Randy Moore. *Visual Effects:* Gene Warren, Jr. *Costumes:* Jennifer Barrett-Pellington. *Make-up:* Bob Harper. *Make-up (Jeff Bridges):* Edouard Henriques. *Make-up Special Effects:* Phil Nichols, Melissa Nichols, and George W. Simpson III. *Stunt Coordinator:* Vince Deadrick, Jr. *Running time:* 117 minutes. *MPAA Rating:* R.

CAST: Jeff Bridges (Michael Faraday); Tim Robbins (Oliver Lang); Joan Cusack (Cheryl Lang); Hope Davis (Brooke Wolfe); Robert Gossett (FBI Agent Whit Carver); Mason Gamble (Brady Lang); Spencer Treat Clark (Grant Faraday); Stanley Anderson (Dr. Archer Scobee); Vivianne Vives (Nurse); Lee Stringer (Orderly); Darryl Cox (Troopmaster); Loyd Catlett (Delivery Man); Sid Hillman (Phone Technician); Auden Thornton (Hannah Lang); Mary Ashleigh Green (Daphne Lang); Jennie Tooley (Ponytail Girl); Grant Garrison (Student Kemp); Naya Castinado (Student O'Neill); Laura Poe (Leah Faraday); Chris Dahlberg (Buckley, FBI); Gabriel Folse (Merks, FBI); Hunter Burkes (Hutch Parsons); Diane Peterson (Ma Parsons); Josh Ridgway (18-Year-old Parsons); Hans Stroble (16-Year-old Parsons); Michelle Du Bois (Parsons Girl); Steve Ottesen (TV Reporter #2); Harris MacKenzie (TV Reporter #3); John Hussey (Accident Detective); Charles Sanders (Camp Official); Todd Terry (2nd Camp Official); Gina Santori (Party Girl/Student); Denver Williams (FBI Guard #1); Willie Dirden (FBI Guard #2); Paul Pender (FBI Van Agent); Charlie Webb (FBI Van Agent #2); Billy D. Washington (FBI Agent #3); Cindy Hom (TV Reporter #4); Dave Allen Clark (TV Reporter #5); Ken Manelis (Reporter Charles Bell); Deborah Swanson (Bomb Site Reporter); Homer Jon Young (Student); Robin Simpson and Doug Francis (Pilots).

CHRISTIAN SCIENCE MONITOR, 7/9/99, p. 15, David Sterritt

Americans used to think of terrorists as alien intruders, but events of recent years have focused attention on home-grown militants preaching the rhetoric of patriotism and tradition.

Do such ideologues really believe they're waging a just war for long-lost American values? Are there elements within the American experience that inadvertently nurture—or even cause—subversive movements whose paranoid ideas may erupt into awful violence?

The new thriller "Arlington Road" doesn't probe very deeply into these issues, but it raises them with a vividness that makes it one of the summer's most thought-provoking pictures.

Jeff Bridges plays Michael Faraday, a widowed professor who divides his time between raising a young son, wooing a former graduate student, and teaching a college course on American terrorism. He also broods over his wife's death in a pointless shootout between her FBI unit and a gunowning rural family.

He's not exactly a loner, but he's so preoccupied that it takes an odd accident in the neighborhood to get him acquainted with the new couple (played by Tim Robbins and Joan Cusack) who've moved in nearby. While they seem as nice and normal as anyone on their suburban block, Michael comes to think they're hiding a secret, and his knowledge of radical militancy leads his thoughts in ominous directions.

Could these churchgoing, family-loving folks be at the center of a terrorist plot? Or is his own history causing him to see violence and insanity where they simply don't exist?

Moviegoers looking for light summer entertainment might not want to travel down "Arlington Road," since it pursues these questions to grim and unsettling conclusions. But its remarkably well-acted, and director Mark Pellington keeps Ehren Kruger's screenplay moving so inexorably that you almost don't notice its occasional lapses into far-fetched coincidence.

In all, it's the closest thing to a truly Hitchcockian thriller that we've seen in a long time.

LOS ANGELES TIMES, 7/9/99, Calendar/p. 6, Kevin Thomas

"Arlington Road" belongs to that splendid Hollywood tradition of dealing with serious, timely issues in the form of a suspense thriller. It's a tradition too often neglected nowadays, but which has been revived with bristling imagination and urgency—and without compromise—by director Mark Pellington, writer Ehren Kruger and stars Jeff Bridges and Tim Robbins.

This Columbia-Screen Gems presentation (originally a Polygram film that was auctioned off when Seagram acquired the music conglomerate) could scarcely be more timely yet never exploits its concern with the seemingly inextricable and all-too-literally volatile relationship between contemporary terrorism and paranoia. It's a film that actually asks you to think at the same time it's bringing you to the edge of your seat, a refreshing change from so much mindless Hollywood fare.

When George Washington University history professor Michael Faraday (Bridges) rushes an unknown, injured 9-year-old (Mason Gamble) to the hospital, in effect saving the youngster's life, naturally Faraday becomes quickly acquainted with the boy's parents, Oliver (Robbins) and Cheryl Lang (Joan Cusack), who have recently moved in across the street from Faraday on Arlington Road, in an upscale suburban Washington, D.C., tract filled with spacious near-identical brick homes done in an ungainly though expensive watered-down Georgian style. Widower Faraday, his 10-year-old son (Spencer Treat Clark) and Faraday's girlfriend, Brooke Wolfe (Hope Davis), his former teaching assistant, soon become regulars at the Langs' backyard barbecues.

Yet for all their warm hospitality and down-to-earth manner, Faraday soon starts becoming suspicious of Oliver Lang, who has said he's a structural engineer currently working on a shopping mall parking structure addition. Very quickly Faraday has reason to feel that this doesn't sound quite right; nor do a number of other things about Lang.

As it happens, Faraday teaches a course in American terrorism that seems calculated to leave his students in a state of paranoia rather than to explore possible solutions. This becomes understandable when we learn that his wife, an FBI agent, had been killed in a misfired siege, clearly a variant of the 1992 Ruby Ridge standoff. Pretty soon Faraday is beginning to wonder if Lang isn't a terrorist of some sort, much to the chagrin of Wolfe, who criticizes him for beginning to invade Lang's privacy.

Kruger and Pellington are whizzes at leading us up the garden path: Just as you thought Faraday's classes were awfully preachy—and thereby the film itself—you learn about his wife. Just as you begin thinking that Wolfe is obtuse, and then Faraday a bit too paranoid, the plot really thickens as little by little, more is revealed.

In short, "Arlington Road" is diabolically clever in the way it creates impressions of individuals and events only to get you questioning their validity in the very next scene. But it is a cleverness that is not trying to be mystifying for its own sake or even to heighten suspense, but to raise the larger issue of how terrorism, which inevitably produces paranoia, can both spread in a society in which impersonal government bureaucracies, whether on a federal, state or local level, can devastate individual lives yet so often not be held accountable.

"Arlington Road" reveals the dangerously growing chasm between government and segments of its people at a time when technology makes the invasion of privacy so much easier than in the past. It reminds us similarly of the vast array of sophisticated lethal technical devices available to those groups that feel driven to protest monolithic government with the most extreme violence.

The makers of "Arlington Road" have, in sum, brought all the cinematic talent and craft—including, crucially, those of virtuoso cinematographer Bobby Bukowski and inspired composer Angelo Badalamenti—they could muster to lay bare a dark undertow in American life that, left unaddressed, will surely proliferate at increasing peril to everyone.

This is an awful lot of serious thought to have been generated by what is first and foremost so successfully an edgy, action-filled entertainment, sustained by Bridges' enduring ability to project thoughtful men of decency and courage and by Robbins' complementary gift in being able to seem alternately ambiguous and convincing. Davis maneuvers Wolfe's shifting responses effectively, and as for Cusack, she to the end deftly keeps us guessing: Is she her husband's ally in whatever it is he may or may not be up to, or is she a veritable Stepford Wife? What is not at question is the creation of a rightly disturbing vision of America in a manner that is as provocative as it is responsible.

NEW YORK, 7/19/99, p. 73, Peter Rainer

Arlington Road tries to give us the willies by stirring two creepy genres in the same Crock-Pot: The *Do You Know Who Your Neighbors Really Are?* movie and the increasingly popular *Do You Know You're Being Targeted by Terrorists?* flick. Jeff Bridges plays Michael Faraday, a suburban Washington, D.C., college history professor whose FBI-agent wife was offed in a Ruby Ridge-style face-off, and who now is obsessed with paramilitary conspiracies. His new neighbors, played by Tim Robbins and Joan Cusack, are so clean-cut and accommodating that it's not long before Michael is suspicious. Is he paranoid or is he right? Or both? If you've seen the trailer for this film, you already know the answer: Like most trailers these days, it blithely gives the whole show away in a scant few minutes. Not that there's any doubt what's going on: If the bad guys in the real world were all this obvious, life would be a whole lot easier.

NEW YORK POST, 7/9/99, p. 48, Jonathan Foreman

"Arlington Road," like "The Siege," is a dumb, overheated thriller pretending to be a smart, topical one.

While Ehren Kruger's half-witted screenplay makes knowing references to the Oklahoma City bombing and neo-Nazi militias, it's really a rip-off of the Red-scare flicks of the 1950s. The hysterical message is that your normal-looking neighbor and his Stepford wife might well be crazy, ultra-secretive neo-Nazi bombers.

And the Cub Scout-like group they sponsor, with its emphasis on honor and the family, is nothing but a sinister front organization, designed to brainwash your children.

The movie's unlikely and unlikable everyman is Michael Faraday (Jeff Bridges), a bitter, paranoid history professor who teaches a conspiracy-obsessed current-events course. His late wife, an FBI agent, was recently killed in a botched, Ruby Ridge-type raid, and Faraday likes to bring his students to the spot where she was shot.

One day, Faraday notices that his nice neighbor Oliver Lang (Tim Robbins) is receiving alumni mail from the University of Pennsylvania, even though Lang told him he went to Kansas State. Immediately, Faraday starts snooping around the Langs like a deranged but none-too-bright secret policeman.

His girlfriend (Hope Davis) and his late wife's partner think Faraday's off the wall. But the idea that Lang, whose son is now Faraday's son's best friend, is some kind of terrorist, sends an increasingly crazed Faraday into a yelling, ranting sweat.

Every event in the chain set off by Faraday's obsession is signaled a mile off, except for a final plot twist that is ridiculously implausible even for a paranoid thriller.

For suspense, the film relies on music and cheap-shot visual effects. It's not just that no one ever turns on a light when they go home at night or work late in the office. To give you that feeling of dislocation, things are always going out of focus or into super close-up.

Still, there are some exciting and some creepy moments, including one that makes good use of Joan Cusack's usual ditz-with-something-going-on-below-the-surface shtick.

Director Mark Pellington also does a fine job with the movie's car chases: for once, they actually look and feel dangerous. But Pellington also manages to elicit subpar performances from two of movieland's best male leads.

Robbins is all staring eyes and robotic calm, while Bridges spends the entire movie shouting. Given that his character is so unattractive to begin with, there are times when you wish the bad guys would just finish him off.

But the worst thing about "Arlington Road" isn't the performances or the uneven pacing, it's the way it gets American terrorists and militias so totally and ignorantly wrong.

Unlike the real Oklahoma City bombers, these chaps are professional, suburban types (the only giveaway is their short haircuts), smart enough never to manifest any of their extremist beliefs. Even more absurdly, when they blow up buildings they don't do it to send a message like real-life terrorists—indeed, they try to make it look like the work of a crazed loner. They do it just because.

And in the warped universe of "Arlington Road," the feds actually want everyone to believe that these atrocities are the work of lone crazies rather than terrorist conspirators, because that way the public will somehow feel more secure.

This isn't just stupid, it's the kind of nonsense you have to come up with to achieve the shrill, almost fascistic scare-mongering that makes "Arlington Road" such an ugly piece of work.

NEWSDAY, 7/9/99, Part II/p. B3, John Anderson

Mark Pellington's domestic-terrorism thriller "Arlington Road" may star Jeff Bridges and Tim Robbins, but it also has an uncredited list of spiritual advisers that includes Randy Weaver, David Koresh and whoever you think shot down TWA Flight 800. Mostly, it seems to have been in-spired by the Oklahoma bombing, but has the kind of immediacy one hopes won't be prescient: One is reminded of 1962's "The Manchurian Candidate," which, because it seemed to eerily foreshadow the Kennedy assassination, disappeared for about 25 years.

But the last thing "Arlington Road" suffers from is bad timing. Far from it: It may be the movie of its time. More "Parallax View" than "Manchurian Candidate," it biopsies, in a ruthlessly surgical style, our well-founded national paranoia about the madmen among us. And it's a first-rate suspense film because what it purports to be true might easily be.

An almost unbearably tense sequence sets off the story, full of hallucinogenic halftones and smeary, stuttering images, Hitchcockian dread and Bunuelian irony. College professor Michael Faraday (Bridges) driving through his own shiny suburb, comes up behind a young boy stumbling down the center of the street (the last middle-of-the-road image we'll get). He has maimed himself with a homemade bomb. As the boy's blood drips slowly onto his sneakers, Faraday's mind soaks it all in.

The movie is, to this point, pure perpetual motion. Screaming, traumatized, Faraday rushes the near-comatose kid to the nearest emergency room, with the kind of vehicular abandon usually reserved for movie climaxes, or the Daytona 500. If Bridges is our best leading man and he is—it's largely because he's both reluctant sex-symbol and eager Everyman (that Gary Cooper thing). But it's also because, as an actor, he's capable of convincing us that as sickened as Faraday is by the kid's horrific condition, he's equally ashamed at not knowing his name—even though Brady Lane (Mason Gamble) and his parents Oliver (Robbins) and Cheryl (Joan Cusack), live just across the street from Faraday and his own son (Spencer Treat Clark).

No otherworldly coincidence this; no calculated agenda. Is it? Regardless, the neighborhood situation is obviously something Faraday, the college professor, must have thought about—this suburban anonymity, this proximity without community. He's glad to have saved the kid's life, but chagrined by his own lack of neighborliness. So he makes an effort; the boys become friends. Oliver, in his Bill Gates haircut and baby-blue pullovers, Cheryl with that smile that could out-creep the Addams Family, become the nicest of neighbors, consoling as they can be as Michael struggles to get by the central tragedy of his life: the death of his wife, Leah, an FBI agent (Laura Poe, in flashback) killed during a botched raid on the home of a gun-collecting survivalist.

The Lanes listen. They understand. Partly in penance, partly in vengeance, Faraday has created a class in Domestic Terrorism at his university, where he delivers too-passionate lectures on the incompetence of a government that's made itself the target of ultra-right terrorists. And on the blinkered nature of law-enforcement philosophies. And on the importance of identifying someone, anyone, when an act of terror occurs—because "we feel safe because we know his name."

It's the nameless Other that's the nightmare entity of "Arlington Road," an Other that Faraday gradually begins to believe lives directly across the street.

Mark Pellington—who may become the first great director/ graduate of the music-video school of cinematic arts—doesn't just deliver a thriller that exploits the news. He takes us inside the paranoia—not of the wellscrubbed Lanes, necessarily, whom Faraday pursues with a humiliating degree of zealotry, but of Faraday himself.

"Arlington Road" is Faraday's fever dream, everything filtered through the bile-clogged artery of his perception. His internal combustion is illuminated brilliantly by Pellington and director of photography Bobby Bukowski's haunting use of focused light, which emphasizes both the roiling suspicions within Faraday's mind and his inevitable isolation. Because no one—not his girlfriend Brooke (Hope Davis) or his FBI pal Whit (Robert Gossett)—really wants to believe the things Faraday believes. His demons are too outlandish to be entertained, the culmination of the movie too traumatizing to be digested, at least not at once.

And this is why, weeks after you see the film, you may be puzzling over its plausibility, looking for an explanation, a flaw—in other words, a way out. Because we don't really want to know these things can happen, even though we know full well they can. And have. And will.

SIGHT AND SOUND, 4/99, p. 36, Ken Hollings

History professor Michael Faraday lives with his son Grant in a suburban street near Washington DC. Their new neighbours from St Louis are Oliver Lang, his wife Cheryl and their three children. Following an accident Michael rushes Lang's son to hospital, and the two households become friends. While Grant is slow to accept Michael's new girlfriend Brooke, Michael's university course on urban terrorism reawakens painful memories of his FBI agent wife's death. Odd lies lead Michael to suspect Lang is connected to a bomb attack in St Louis, but no one believes him. He suspects Lang is planning a similar outrage in DC. Even when he reveals Lang tried to bomb a government office before, Lang shames Michael, accusing him of invading his privacy.

After witnessing Lang visiting the Liberty Delivery Service, Brooke is suddenly killed in a car crash. Michael uncovers evidence linking Lang to the St Louis bombing but is prevented from using it when Lang kidnaps Grant. Lang admits to murdering Brooke and discloses his new target: the FBI's DC headquarters. Michael intercepts a Liberty Delivery Service van, believing it contains both Grant and the explosives. Having pursued the van into the FBI's underground garage, Michael realises too late he is carrying the bomb in his own car and is killed in the explosion. The media describes Michael as a terrorist. The Langs wonder where their next home will be.

Reverberations from the Oklahoma and World Trade Center bombings continue to run slow and deep in the US. Following *The Siege* and *The X Files* movie, this is at least the third major US release to feature the FBI losing a prime piece of real estate to terrorists. From its opening sequence, in which Lang's young son Brady staggers down the middle of the street unaware his hand has been mutilated, *Arlington Road* establishes itself as a psychological thriller more concerned with questions of perception than motivation. "We don't know why he did this," history professor Michael Faraday says of the lone bomber thought to be responsible for killing 63 people in St Louis, "and we'll never know. And still we feel safe because we know his name." Michael's argument is not with the facts but their interpretation: "We wanted one name and we wanted it fast." This neatly lays the ground for the film's final irony, concerning the identity of who it is that blows up the FBI's Washington headquarters, killing 184 people.

As the liberal academic Faraday, Jeff Bridges gives a finely graded portrayal of a decent man struggling to conceal feelings of resentment against the establishment. Ultimately his struggle blinds him to how much he resembles the terrorist Lang. From the moment a hospital orderly mistakenly assumes Faraday to be Brady's father, the sinister parallels and similarities begin to multiply. Faraday and Lang both feel betrayed by their government and share the same belief in family values. A perfect match for Faraday's closeted liberalism, Lang articulates right-wing notions of self-reliance with candour. Claiming to be a structural engineer, he refers earnestly to "the buildings I leave behind". But it's Faraday whose workroom is plastered with anti-federal, white-supremacist posters while Lang's study is neatly hung with framed prints of Thomas Jefferson's Montecello, New York's Woolworth Building and the St Louis Arch. Even Lang's real name, Michael Fenimore, echoes Faraday's.

After Faraday's son is kidnapped, the film takes on an increasingly hallucinatory quality. Scenes end in slow fades to deep black. A 70s disco party at which Lang reveals that Brooke has been murdered is bathed in subterranean greens and blues. White light bleaches out a harsh close-up on Faraday's sweating face as he begins to comprehend his entrapment.

During the final chase, Bobby Bukowski's deliberately erratic photography suggests an ever-more skewed sense of perspective. The editing contrasts asphalt-level shots of road surfaces with detailed crane shots of the Washington Mall, tidily laid out as if part of some architectural model or designer's plan. Long-term David Lynch collaborator Angelo Badalamenti, whose moody score gives the film's earlier scenes of neighbourly peace and good order an edge, supplies a pommelling, bass-heavy charge to the final descent into the FBI's underground car park. Perhaps the most unsettling aspect of *Arlington Road,* however, is not the sight of smoke rising over the Capitol, nor even the media's distorted speculations concerning the final bomber's 'motive', but that Lang's reasons for acting as he does remain as mysterious as ever.

TIME, 7/12/99, p. 68, Richard Schickel

The thinly fictionalized references to recent bloody events—Ruby Ridge, the bombing of the federal building in Oklahoma City, even kids playing with explosives—are transparent. (Release of the movie was delayed to separate it from the Columbine tragedy.) But *Arlington Road* is not a cheesy exploitation film. Nor is it a routine paranoid thriller featuring drooling perps of the easy-to-deny sort. It wants to be seen as a sober, thoughtful contemplation of domestic terrorism. It also wants us to think there is more of it around, and hiding in fairly plain sight, than we would like to believe.

How far one wants to go along its chosen path probably depends on the state of one's mental health. That of professor Michael Faraday (Jeff Bridges) is pretty shaky when we encounter him.

He has recently lost his wife, an FBI agent, in a shoot-out that should never have happened. He's also not exactly a model of scholarly dispassion as he teaches a course in the politics of terror, while more than half convinced that there are more and larger conspiracies at work in our world than anyone is admitting. The movie is, indeed, rather good on the erratic way officialdom sometimes overestimates, sometimes underestimates the threat of organized terror in modern life and how that poses a threat to civil comity.

What Ehren Kruger's script doesn't do so well is suspensefully build Faraday's suspicions about his new neighbors, Oliver and Cheryl Lang (Tim Robbins and Joan Cusack), and their creepy kids. There's always something eerie about Robbins' geniality—in his screen persona he's never been a guy from whom a sensible person would buy a used car—and almost from the outset you agree with Faraday that he and his kin are surely up to something distinctly antisocial. One-two-three, Faraday acquires the evidence suggesting that Oliver has taken over another man's identity and is almost certainly a quietly mad bomber. The cautionary notes struck by Faraday's new girlfriend (Hope Davis) and old FBI friend (Robert Gossett) seem purely conventional and very likely a signal that they're not going to survive to the end of the movie.

Mark Pellington's jittery direction is not much help in establishing the false calm out of which true suspense might be built. He's one of those music-video refugees for whom you want to take up a collection so he can add a tripod and an editing machine with a functioning Pause button to his filmmaking arsenal.

But despite its mannerisms and one of those where-are-the-cops-when-you-need-them car chases through downtown Washington, *Arlington Road* comes to a conclusion as lugubrious as it is surprising. It really doesn't earn its messy, crudely ironic ending, however. The ability of terrorism to rend cruelly the vulnerable skin of our civility is its most commonly remarked-upon quality. But that does not mean it is as pervasive, intricately organized and irresistible as this breathlessly striving movie makes it out to be.

VILLAGE VOICE, 7/13/99, p. 66, Dennis Lim

A shrill, underhanded, neighbor-from-hell thriller, *Arlington Road* seems genuinely unable to distinguish between topicality and exploitation. The Unabomber and Oklahoma City are distinctly felt presences, but primal fears have no other purpose here than to fuel generic paranoia, which MTV-reared director Mark Pellington methodically strips of meaning, cranking it up to a pitch at which morality, ideology, and logic become irrelevant.

Slicker and more suspect than *The Siege*, last year's bombs-away opportunist, *Arlington Road* is both single-minded and thoughtless in its scaremongering. Jeff Bridges plays Michael Faraday, a professor of American history with a specialization in domestic terrorism. Faraday is something of a conspiracy nut (his lectures take the form of loopy, free-associative theories) and an embittered, paranoid head case, largely due to the recent death of his FBI-agent wife in a shoot-out.

Faraday really starts to lose it with the arrival of his new neighbors, the Langs (Tim Robbins and Joan Cusack), whose haircuts, wardrobe, and cheery demeanor signify a profound dislocation from reality and (probably) latent homicidal impulses. Going to great lengths to confirm that Oliver Lang has been white-lying about his past, Faraday stumbles upon potentially devastating news. Of course, no one believes him; Hope Davis plays Faraday's girlfriend, a role that consists exclusively of being skeptical and whiny.

The mode is hysteric-Hitchcockian, the result mostly devoid of suspense. The is-he/isn't-he game never gets off the ground—the filmmakers briefly entertain the notion that it's all in Faraday's head, but they're more intent on overdrawing Lang as a psycho. You wonder if this might be a double bluff, then promptly dismiss it as too sophisticated a ploy—this is, after all, a film whose favorite scare tactic involves sneaking up on people and going boo.

As you'd expect, *Arlington Road* has been directed and edited with sweaty palms and an attention deficit, but the real culprit is Ehren Kreuger's screenplay, which won some fancy fellowship and is a steaming pile of nonsense. Kreuger's model is *The Parallax View*, down to the sucker-punch ending, which in this case hinges on an outrageous series of coincidences; worse, he clutters the narrative with crude, expository passages—most absurdly, a scene in which a distraught Faraday takes his students on a field trip *to the scene of his wife's death*. Boxed into one credibility-defying situation after another, the actors somehow keep pace, scaling new, ugly heights of hysteria—paradoxically, their commitment to the material may be what hurts the film most.

Also reviewed in:
CHICAGO TRIBUNE, 7/9/99, Friday/p. A, Michael Wilmington
NEW YORK TIMES, 7/9/99, p. E14, Janet Maslin
NEW YORKER, 7/19/99, p. 98, Anthony Lane
VARIETY, 3/22-28/99, p. 35, Todd McCarthy
WASHINGTON POST, 7/9/99, p. C1, Rita Kempley
WASHINGTON POST, 7/9/99, Weekend/p. 43, Desson Howe

ASTRONAUT'S WIFE, THE

A New Line Cinema release of a Mad Chance production. *Executive Producer:* Mark Johnson, Brian Whitten, and Donna Langley. *Producer:* Andrew Lazar. *Director:* Rand Ravich. *Screenplay:* Rand Ravich. *Director of Photography:* Allen Daviau. *Editor:* Steve Mirkovich and Tim Alverson. *Music:* Paul Broucek and George S. Clinton. *Music Editor:* Mike Flicker. *Choreographer:* JoAnne Fregalette Jansen. *Sound:* Paul Ledford and (music) John Whynot. *Sound Editor:* Blake Leyh. *Casting:* Rick Pagano and Debi Manwiller. *Production Designer:* Jan Roelfs. *Art Director:* Sarah Knowles. *Set Designer:* Randall Wilkins. *Set Decorator:* Leslie A. Pope. *Special Effects:* Michael Lantieri. *Costumes:* Isis Mussenden. *Make-up:* Deborah K. Larsen. *Stunt Coordinator:* Tim Davison. *Running time:* 100 minutes. *MPAA Rating:* R.

CAST: Johnny Depp (Spencer Armacost); Charlize Theron (Jillian Armacost); Joe Morton (Sherman Reese); Clea DuVall (Nan); Samantha Eggar (Doctor); Donna Murphy (Natalie Streck); Nick Cassavetes (Alex Streck); Gary Grubbs (NASA Director); Blair Brown (Shelly McLaren); Tom Noonan (Jackson McLaren); Tom O'Brien (Allen Dodge); Lucy Lin (Shelly Carter); Michael Crider (Pat Elliot); Jacob Stein (Calvin); Timothy Wicker (Wide-eyed Kid 1); Brian Johnson (Excited Fourth Grader); Sarah Dampf (Paula); Charles Lanyer (Spencer's Doctor); Carlos Cervantes (Doctor); Conrad Bachman (Reporter); Rondi Reed (Dr. Conlin); Seth Barrish (Yuppie Shark); Ellen Lancaster (Dried Up Socialite); Julian Barnes (Waiter); Priscilla Shanks (Woman); Jennifer Burry (Second Woman); Susan Cella (Third Woman); Linda Powell (Fourth Woman); Lyndsey Danielle Bonomolo (Screaming Girl); Elston Ridgle (Security Guard); Robert Sella (Maitre d'); Smantha Carpel (Reporter, Video); Lahai Fahnbulleh (Taxi Driver); Stephen Berger (Doorman); Michael Luceri (Waiter at Party); Ben Van bergen (Storage Facility Client); Edward Kerr (Pilot); Cole Mitchell Sprouse and Dylan Thomas Sprouse (Twins).

LOS ANGELES TIMES, 8/30/99, Calendar/p. 3, Kevin Thomas

Rand Ravich's "The Astronaut's Wife" is a moderately diverting thriller that builds suspense and entertains effectively—but don't ask any more of this sleek, costly production, whose strongest selling point is Charlize Theron.

Since her debut in "2 Days in the Valley" she's appeared in a string of major features, but it's surprising that so early on in her career she's able to carry so big a picture with ease and finesse. The other surprise is that she is in fact the star, billing aside, with Johnny Depp her leading man in a role that places minimal demands on his protean talent. You can understand why Theron would be attracted to this project, but not how as adventuresome an actor as Depp would go for what is clearly a subordinate role.

In any event, Theron's Jillian is a beautiful young Florida grade school teacher happily married to an astronaut, Spencer (Depp). While on a space shuttle mission with his fellow astronaut Alex (Nick Cassavetes), NASA loses contact with the men while they seemingly have lost consciousness themselves. They return safely, but Alex's heart has been so severely strained by the mysterious mishap that he eventually succumbs to a violent seizure, with his benumbed wife (Donna Murphy) committing suicide soon afterward.

Spencer, however, has been pronounced perfectly healthy, and leaves NASA with a hero's status for a cushy rocket-designing job at a major company in Manhattan, which allows the couple to move up to a lavish lifestyle. Jillian is less than thrilled with the move and its fancy trappings, but she's game. However, she continues experiencing nightmares and senses that something may not be quite night with Spencer. Her worst suspicions are confirmed soon enough by the sudden appearance of Spencer's distraught former colleague (Joe Morton) at NASA, which in effect has gotten rid of him because he's voiced suspicions about Spencer, who may in fact be an alien on some sort of takeover mission.

Very quickly Theron finds herself in the classic lady-in-distress predicament of realizing nobody could be expected to believe her, which means she must try to confront a mysterious, evil, destructive force all by herself. Theron makes Jillian and her predicament quite convincing while Depp moves from good ol' boy to an increasingly cool and controlling presence.

In his feature debut, Ravich demonstrates some sense of how to build tension gradually. What "The Astronaut's Wife" needed to lift it above the ordinary, however, is another layer of meaning. The film might have achieved that extra dimension if we were truly kept guessing whether the film would turn out to be a psychological thriller or a thriller of the supernatural. While we're given to understand that Jillian experienced a breakdown after the death of her parents, Ravich makes it all too clear that Jillian isn't crazy while Spencer truly is sinister. This handsome-looking film, which has a notable supporting cast that includes Samantha Eggar as Jillian's patrician doctor, works up to a reasonably edgy if unsurprising finish.

"The Astronaut's Wife" is not nearly as special as you suspect New Line was hoping it would be, but by no means is it as terrible as you expect most films opening sans previews to be.

NEW YORK POST, 8/28/99, p. 21, Jonathan Foreman

"The Astronaut's Wife" is a good-looking film that could have been written by a computer programmed to cannibalize previous sci-fi films—with particular attention paid to the impregnated-by-an-alien subgenre.

In his feature debut, writer-director Rand Ravich draws on "Aliens 3," "Demon Seed," both versions of "Village of the Damned," "I Married a Monster From Outer Space" and various "X-Files" episodes. (He also owes debts to "Invasion of the Body Snatchers" and "The Thing.")

Unfortunately, his is not an inspired or imaginative rip-off—apart from some really great sets. And a deadly combination of pedestrian dialogue, underwritten characters and poor pacing defeats the talents of a fine cast.

Johnny Depp plays Spencer, an astronaut with a Southern accent. Charlize Theron is his mournful wife, Jillian, the world's hottest second-grade teacher.

Something goes wrong on Spencer's mission to repair a satellite, and he and his partner, Streck (Nick Cassavetes), are out of contact with NASA for two minutes (apparently a big deal).

Back on Earth, neither astronaut remembers what happened, but soon Streck is dead. His wife (Donna Murphy) commits suicide at his wake, after mumbling something about her husband "hiding inside me."

Jillian is upset; Spencer is not. They move to New York, where he takes a job in the private sector, and they get a stunning duplex apartment.

Following a bout of strangely cold, brutal sex, Jillian discovers that she's pregnant with twins. She also finds out that Spencer's not just a corporate figurehead, but is actually helping to design a revolutionary warplane.

Suffering from nightmares and suspicious of her husband's strangeness, Jillian thinks she's having a breakdown. Then she's visited by Reese (the always excellent Joe Morton), an apparently paranoid and clearly doomed former NASA exec who is convinced that aliens somehow entered the astronauts during their two minutes alone in space.

Just as Jillian realizes that she is being used as an incubator by whatever being possesses Spencer, she also finds out that there's a periodic psychic connection between husband and wife (although the line in the trailer about his knowing exactly what she's thinking seems to have been cut from the final print).

The aliens' plot is never clear, and several gross violations of common sense undermine the drama, along with some odd continuity problems: Depp's blond highlights suddenly spread all over his head, and Theron gets on the subway in the middle of the night and gets off a few minutes later in broad daylight.

Depp is appropriately sinister but doesn't have enough time on screen. His gorgeous co-star, on the other hand, has too much time to cry and mope. The combination of her weepiness and her cropped haircut are enough to make you wonder if she's still playing the role of Keanu Reeve's wife in "The Devil's Advocate."

Still, both leads look terrific, and when Theron does a little solo salsa in the apartment you can see that (unlike Rene Russo and Pierce Brosnan in "The Thomas Crown Affair"), this babe can dance.

There's also one great line that cannot be repeated in a family paper.

SIGHT AND SOUND, 12/99, p. 36, Ken Hollings

The US, the present. Having survived a two-minute blackout while repairing a satellite in orbit, space-shuttle pilot Spencer Armacost decides to retire from NASA. He moves with his wife Jillian to New York and becomes an executive in an aeronautics company. However, Armacost refuses to discuss what happened in space, even when his commanding officer Alex Streck dies and Streck's widow commits suicide at the funeral by electrocuting herself with the radio set Streck obsessively listened to after his return to Earth. Soon Armacost also is listening constantly to the radio.

Discovering she's pregnant with twins, Jillian encounters ex-NASA employee Sherman Reese, who reveals that Armacost and Streck were taken over by a mysterious entity in space and that Streck's wife was also carrying twins when she killed herself. Jillian begins to doubt whether Armacost or the unborn twins are human. Armacost prevents Jillian from inducing a miscarriage and has her hospitalised. Realising he's communicating with the foetuses inside her, Jillian lures Armacost to their apartment where she electrocutes him with the radio. A transluscent organism escapes from Armacost's dead body and enters Jillian. Later, Jillian is seen living next to an air base and married to a pilot, raising identical twin boys who obsessively listen to the radio.

It doesn't take long to see why Charlize Theron kept the close blond crop she sported in *Mighty Joe Young:* any similarity with Mia Farrow's hairstyle for *Rosemary's Baby* (1968) is not entirely coincidental. Substituting weird alien science for Satanism, Rand Ravich's ambitious directorial debut is an attempt to make a Polanski film in the US without Polanski. Fortunately, Ravich has just the right blend of objectivity, malice and cinematic smarts to pull it off.

More concerned with demonstrating the disorienting effect of the familiar on our expectations than with playing space invaders, *The Astronaut's Wife* scrambles established notions of human scale and perspective. Jillian and Spencer Armacost are constantly seen either in extreme close-up, their proximity to each other emphasised by the beating of her heart on the soundtrack, or as isolated figures set within vast spaces overlaid with a restraining lattice of vertical and horizontal bars. At a NASA press conference, Jillian and Armacost are dwarfed by gigantic US flags. Their New York City apartment block may not be as dark and brooding as the Dakota Building, made famous in *Rosemary's Baby,* but it contains a similar warren of corridors, passageways and doorways, which Spielberg alumni Allen Daviau's camerawork explores with restless invention. In fact, the whole of Manhattan becomes a gigantic extension of Jillian's mental space, right down to the chicken wire-covered windows at the special ante-natal classes she attends for women expecting twins.

Ravich's script keeps all alien elements to an elegant minimum: no reason is ever given for the mysterious entity's presence on Earth. There is little in Johnny Depp's brilliantly guarded portrayal of Armacost that hints at a game plan much beyond a very human biological need to reproduce. Building on his character's former attributes as an astronaut, Depp offers an acidic, unsettling study of the Right Stuff going horribly wrong. His sexual playfulness becomes brutally urgent; his bravado in the face of danger a dead-eyed indifference to the sufferings of others. The biggest irony of his performance is that Armacost retains his masculinity long after losing all trace of humanity. Accused by Jillian of having killed her husband, the creature callously retorts that it also 'fucked his wife,' as if it were settling some old score with the man whose identity it has usurped. It's a genuinely chilling moment, suggesting that little more than a change of perspective separated the NASA space hero from the marauding alien life-form. Polanski would undoubtedly approve.

Also reviewed in:
NEW YORK TIMES, 8/28/99, P. B14, Janet Maslin
VARIETY, 8/30-9/5/99, p. 51, Joe Leydon

AT FIRST SIGHT

A Metro-Goldwyn-Mayer Pictures release. *Producer:* Irwin Winkler and Rob Cowan. *Director:* Irwin Winkler. *Screenplay:* Steve Levitt. *Based on the story "To See and Not See" by:* Oliver Sacks, M.D. *Director of Photography:* John Seale. *Editor:* Julie Monroe. *Music:* Mark Isham. *Music Editor:* Tom Carlson. *Sound:* James Sabat and (music) Stephen Krause. *Sound Editor:* Michael O'Farrell. *Casting:* Billy Hopkins, Suzanne Smith, and Kerry Barden. *Production Designer:* Jane Musky. *Art Director:* Robert Guerra. *Set Decorator:* Susan Bode. *Special Effects:* Connie Brink. *Costumes:* John Dunn. *Make-up:* Rosemarie Zurlo. *Make-up (Val Kilmer):* Leonard Engleman. *Make-up (Mira Sorvino):* Kathy Jeung. *Stunt Coordinator:* Frank Ferrara. *Running time:* 128 minutes. *MPAA Rating:* PG-13.

CAST: Val Kilmer (Virgil Adamson); Mira Sorvino (Amy Benic); Kelly McGillis (Jennie Adamson); Steven Weber (Duncan Allanbrook); Bruce Davison (Dr. Charles Aaron); Nathan Lane (Phil Webster); Ken Howard (Virgil's Father); Laura Kirk (Betsy Ernst); Margo Winkler (Nancy Bender); Diana Krall (Singer); Brett Robbins (Ethan); Willie Carpenter (Jack Falk); Charles Winkler (Health Instructor); Drena De Niro (Caroline); Kelly Chapman Meyer (Susan); Jack Dodick (Dr. Goldman); Nina Griscom (Christie Evans); Mortimer B. Zuckerman (Homeless Man); Gene Kirkwood (Marshall); Richard Euell (Carl Kipling); Carl Matusovich (Tommy); John W. Guidera (Virgil's Co-worker); Jack Cooper (Overweight Man); Jennifer Wachtell (Eva); Marty Davey (School Mother); Ben Wolfe (Bass Player); Casey W. Harris (Casey); Ricky Trammell (Loft D.J.); J.P. Patterson (Waiter); Bonnie Deutsch (Worker).

LOS ANGELES TIMES, 1/15/99, Calendar/p. 4, Kevin Thomas

"At First Sight," an exceptionally touching and provocative love story, gets underway swiftly. Mira Sorvino's stressed-out Manhattan architect Amy Benic heads for an Adirondacks resort and signs up for a massage from Val Kilmer's Virgil, whose touch is so relaxing and tender it reduces her to tears. Since Virgil is also handsome, the lovely Amy is not surprisingly attracted to him. But she is shocked to discover that he's blind.

A romance blossoms, but when Amy comes across an article about an eminent Manhattan ophthalmologist (Bruce Davison) and his breakthrough treatment of blindness tucked away in Virgil's scrapbook she takes matters in her own hands. Soon Davison's Dr. Aaron has restored Virgil's sight, which had faded by the time he was 3 from a combination of severe cataracts and retinitis pigmentosa.

Director Irwin Winkler and writer Steve Levitt, in adapting Oliver Sacks' New Yorker story "To See or Not to See"—Sacks' work also provided the basis for the 1990 film "Awakenings"— have now reached the heart of the matter: Virgil now has sight but he has to learn to see. The psychological and emotional validity with which Virgil's predicament is imagined and developed is wrenchingly persuasive.

(Those of us who have had the parallel experience of a parent who acquired near-normal hearing through surgery in middle age know that the capacity to hear does not automatically confer the ability to listen. You learn that a suddenly acquired sense, if it is not developed consciously, can perversely seem to have the potential to do more harm than good in various and unanticipated ways, as incredible as that may seem.)

To its credit "At First Sight" deals with all these challenges and more that face Virgil, who moves in with Amy and hopes to continue his work as a masseur. The magnitude of the learning Virgil has to acquire is exemplified by the fact that he must associate all his knowledge of the physical world with his actual seeing of it—he must connect the taste and feel of an apple with what an apple looks like. He must learn to read people's faces with the same care with which he has listened to their voices all his life. He must learn to read and then remember what he's read, a task that threatens to overwhelm him.

What Virgil is experiencing of course impacts upon his relationship with Amy, its special dimension of sensitivity threatened by the reality that they are becoming increasingly a normal couple coping with the usual pressures of everyday life. Yet "At First Sight" digs even deeper as it progresses, raising the question of whether Amy ever dealt with the possibility of loving Virgil, of staying in a permanent relationship with him, had his surgery not succeeded.

"At First Sight," enveloped as it is in a most appealing love story, is about taking chances and responsibility, questioning values and priorities, and even more crucially, about acceptance and perception. Embodying the film's complex view of behavior is Virgil's older sister Jenny (Kelly McGillis), who has quietly sacrificed her life to caring for her brother in such a manner as to give him as much independence as he can handle.

Jenny, who remembers how at the age of eight Virgil was subjected to one doctor, healer and futile treatment after another, now feels threatened by the possibility of losing him. The strength of the film is that we get to know its key people in stages, the same way they get to know one another and themselves.

Inspired by a true story, "At First Sight" is a handsome, expertly crafted film with an understated Mark Isham score and an appropriate end title song, "Love Is Where You Are," with lyrics by Alan and Marilyn Bergman. There are a couple of glitches in the script: For example, how did that article on Dr. Aaron turn up in Virgil's scrapbook? Was it passed on to him by his solicitous town librarian (Margo Winkler)? The whole character of Dr. Aaron, as well-played as he is by Davison, is somewhat problematical. Not only is he dizzyingly swift in having his institution underwrite the expenses of Virgil's surgery but also he seems oddly negligent in not having had Nathan Lane's dedicated and unorthodox visual therapist enlisted to help Virgil adjust from the start. There's a streak of opportunism in the doctor that might have been brought out to give an edge to a film determined to have no villains beyond Virgil's irresponsible father (Ken Howard).

"At First Sight," which marks 30 years of Winkler's work in Hollywood as a consistently creative filmmaker, is more than strong enough to overcome such quibbles, and it leaves you moved and impressed by the completeness of Kilmer's, Sorvino's and McGillis' portrayals. The way in which Virgil has been written, directed and portrayed is a singularly impressive feat of imagination and illumination.

NEWSDAY, 1/15/99, Part II/p. B3, Jack Mathews

Virgil Adamson (Val Kilmer) is a blind masseur with the best hands and bedside manner at Bear Mountain Inn, a resort spa about an hour up the Hudson from New York City. For a woman to lie naked on his table and turn her tense muscles over to his kneading hands is an act of almost spiritual self-gratification.

Ask Amy Benic (Mira Sorvino). On the first morning of her much-needed holiday, during the opening moments of Irwin Winkler's "At First Sight," the workaholic Manhattan architect is getting the massage of her life from Virgil, and showing her gratitude with a series of involuntary low moans and deep sobs.

"Do you make all the girls cry?" she asks.

He's making me cry. I want his job, I want to be him! I want to raise my voice two octaves, and have words fall from my lips like silk marinated in rum. I want to have my hands named as corespondents in a messy divorce case. I want to inspire temples and statues and songs.

What I could do without is a sappy movie based on my experiences, especially one inspired by the work of M.D. cum author Oliver Sacks, the man partially responsible for Penny Marshall's "Awakenings." That dreadful 1990 film mythologized the true story of a doctor's pioneering work with comatose patients. It starred Robin Williams as the earnest doctor and Robert De Niro as Leonard Lowe, a patient who awakes from a 30-year nap, fit as a fiddle, and says, "Let's dance!"

"At First Sight" is essentially a replay of "Awakenings," with congenital blindness subbing for post-encephalitic sleeping sickness, but with the same biblical arc: The Lord giveth, the Lord taketh away. Like Lowe, whose cure is short-lived, Virgil Adamson's nascent vision, a result of his romance with Amy and her insistence that he undergo cataract surgery, lasts only long enough for him to assess the world around him, and to decide he hasn't missed much.

Steve Levitt's script includes a lot of disease-of-the-week exposition about Virgil's condition, and his status as one of only 200 documented cases of recovered sight. And there are, we're assured, real people supporting the movie's events. But rarely does "At First Sight" rise above Hollywood melodrama, let alone create a sense of reportage.

As a movie-movie, it's just so-so. Sorvino and Kilmer make an attractive couple, but the Amy-Virgil relationship is a screenwriter's sham. OK, a good massage may feel like good sex, and a lady may like to follow those hands wherever they lead her. But, as far as we know, Amy develops an undying love for him then and there, where his fingers plumb her trapezius, and she never looks back.

Sorvino has an awkward presence. It's as if she's emotionally cut off by Kilmer's mannerisms, and the loss of eye contact. Kilmer does a good job of miming a man blind since early childhood. Before he regains his sight, Virgil wears a kind of goofy-amiable smile; it's the facial posture of someone who can't visualize honest expression.

Later, when he does begin to see, and adapt not only to the physical world but to the emotional expression of other people, Virgil's body language changes dramatically. "Sight" is at its best depicting Virgil's reactions to his new environment, and Kilmer nicely captures the emotional and physical tug-of-war.

But Winkler, the producer ("Rocky") turned director ("The Net"), doesn't have the skill to overcome Levitt's mundane script, which works in such loose ends as a jealously protective sister (Kelly McGillis), a long-lost dad (Ken Howard) and a metaphorical unfinished sculpture. The story's real drama is the light show playing inside Virgil's head, but we barely get a glimpse of what he sees.

Looking back at the film's sensuous opening, we might wish the filmmakers had abandoned Sacks' case study altogether and focused instead on Virgil's magic fingers. Call it "At First Touch," and watch for an enrollment boom at Massage U.

SIGHT AND SOUND, 6/99, p. 36, Geoffrey Macnab

New York-based architect Amy Benic heads out of town to rest and relax at a rural hotel where she meets Virgil Adamson, the hotel masseur. Amy strikes up a friendship with Virgil, only belatedly realising he is blind. They become lovers. Virgil's protective older sister Jennie is deeply suspicious of Amy, and worries Amy will abandon Virgil. Amy discovers there could be a way of restoring Virgil's sight but he is reluctant to put himself through an operation which might fail. However, he eventually agrees and his sight is restored. At first, he finds vision deeply disorienting and continues to rely more on his sense of touch as he learns to use his eyes. He moves to New York with Amy, but struggles to adjust to his new life, and their relationship is put under strain. Virgil's father, who abandoned him and his sister many years before, now wants to make amends, but Virgil refuses to meet him.

It transpires the operation has not been a complete success; Virgil will soon lose his eyesight. He finally confronts his father and breaks up with Amy. She realises she was pushing him too hard. Blind again, Virgil takes a job with a visual therapist, Phil Webster. Amy tracks Virgil down in the park—it is clear that they still love each other.

In W.C.Fields' *It's a Gift* a blind man leaves a trail of chaos in his wake and confounds everybody who tries to treat him with kid gloves. Fields may have been motivated by misanthropy, but at least he didn't patronise or pity his subject. *At First Sight* does both. Based on a true story by Dr Oliver Sacks, this is one of those self-righteous, sermonising melodramas which Hollywood occasionally makes about the afflicted.

Mark Isham's score, full of tinkly little piano bits which rekindle memories of Richard Clayderman, signals from the outset that the film will be very slushy indeed. Much of the dialogue chimes in perfectly with the music: "I can feel everything when it rains," Virgil rhapsodises when he is caught in a storm. He is the strong, sensual, poetic type who relies on his senses of smell and touch to judge character. His being a masseur also enables the filmmakers to include several scenes of him rubbing oil on Amy's shapely back.

Although Val Kilmer's Virgil has a well-nigh permanent smirk on his face, he's supposed to be naive and gentle, instinctively understanding of what Amy feels, unlike the yuppies in her architectural firm. After the supremely novelettish beginning, the film briefly turns into a medical drama hinging on whether Virgil's sight can be restored. Jargon is lobbed to and fro by vaguely sinister-looking men in white coats as he prepares for the operation. Then, in a powerful and disquieting scene, the bandages are removed and Virgil is confronted by a blur of terrifying imagery.

To do justice to Virgil's burgeoning alarm and wonder at the world he's seeing for the first time would take a far more imaginative film maker than Irwin Winkler, a producer turned director who conspicuously lacks visual flair. Here, despite the efforts of cinematographer John Seale *(The English Patient, City of Angels)*, we're offered stock images of the New York skyline or shots of Virgil staring in confusion at his own mirror image. At least, when his sight is restored, Virgil stops grinning and gets truculent and bad tempered. As he puts it, 'seeing sucks,' and it's during these scenes that Kilmer's performance briefly flickers into life.

This may be adapted from a true story, but it follows the contours of the most manipulative tearjerker. The fact that Virgil is an ardent ice-hockey fan rekindles memories of the equally maudlin *Love Story,* in which Ryan O'Neal was similarly enthusiastic about the sport. There are also echoes of *Good Will Hunting,* with Kilmer as the outsider who needs guidance from a cuddly and eccentric therapist (Nathan Lane here, Robin Williams in *Good Will Hunting)* to quell his inner demons.

Unfortunately, catharsis does not come quickly enough. The film drags on for more than two hours before Winkler signs off with yet another of the film's endless crane shots—the camera soars into the air as the couple walk away into the distance, an appropriately cornball ending for a film which feels contrived and phoney from start to finish.

VILLAGE VOICE, 1/26/99, p. 106, Dennis Lim

From the *Patch Adams* and *Stepmom* school of audience manipulation comes *At First Sight,* a romantic melodrama cynically constructed around disability and a highly dubious representation of medical science (not to mention human nature). Irwin Winkler's weepie is every bit as fatuous as its current competitors, though not quite as abhorrent, for no other reason than its sheer listlessness: the film slips into a coma early on and never awakens.

Winkler wastes a soapy eternity establishing the central relationship, and takes even longer to subject it to the routine romance-under-pressure trials. An obviously strained Mira Sorvino plays Amy, a workaholic architect who's so tightly wound that a simple massage from kindly, hunky spa worker Virgil (Val Kilmer) sets her off on a weeping jag. Blind since early childhood, Virgil projects a naive, big-lug charm that Amy finds captivating. Go-getting Manhattan career woman that she is, she convinces him to try restorative, experimental eye surgery.

At First Sight, like *Awakenings,* is based on an Oliver Sacks case history, and it follows the same narrative arc: miracle recovery, traumatic adjustment, cruelly brief period of soft-focus wellness, inevitable relapse, last-minute coming-to-terms uplift. Winkler proceeds through this checklist with catatonic gracelessness, weighing scenes down with lead-ballast epiphanies (there's a difference between seeing and looking; you don't always see with your eyes; even the sighted sometimes live in darkness).   John Seale's humdrum cinematography and the earnest, embarrassing performances only compound the constipated TV-movie tone.

Also reviewed in:
CHICAGO TRIBUNE, 1/15/99, Friday/p. B, Michael Wilmington
NEW REPUBLIC, 2/15/99, p. 26, Stanley Kauffmann
NEW YORK TIMES, 1/15/99, p. E10, Janet Maslin
VARIETY, 1/11-17/99, p. 114, Lael Loewenstein
WASHINGTON POST, 1/15/99, p. C5, Rita Kempley
WASHINGTON POST, 1/15/99, Weekend/p. 33, Michael O'Sullivan

AUSTIN POWERS: THE SPY WHO SHAGGED ME

A New Line Cinema release of an Eric's Boy, Moving Pictures & Team Todd production. *Executive Producer:* Erwin Stoff, Michael De Luca, and Donna Langley. *Producer:* Suzanne Todd, Jennifer Todd, Demi Moore, Eric McLeod, John Lyons, and Mike Myers. *Director:* Jay Roach. *Screenplay:* Mike Myers and Michael McCullers. *Based on characters created by:* Mike Meyers. *Director of Photography:* Ueli Steiger. *Editor:* John Poll and Debra Neil-Fisher. *Music:* George S. Clinton. *Music Editor:* Mike Flicker. *Choreographer:* Marguerite Derricks. *Swimming Choreographer:* Becky Dyroen-Lancer. *Sound:* Kenneth McLaughlin and (music) John Whynot. *Sound Editor:* Frederick Howard. *Casting:* Juel Bestrop and Jeanne McCarthy. *Production Designer:* Rusty Smith. *Art Director:* Alexander Hammond. *Set Designer:* John Jeffries, Stephen Cooper, and Andrew Reeder. *Set Decorator:* Sara Andrews-Ingrassia. *Set Dresser:* Maya S. Grafmuller, Jeannine Fenton, Peter Emshwiller, Mike Malone, and Alan K. Harrison. *Special Effects:* Mike Meinardus. *Costumes:* Deena Appel. *Make-up:* Patty York. *Make-up (Heather Graham):* Steve Artmont. *Stunt Coordinator:* Bud Davis. *Running time:* 95 minutes. *MPAA Rating:* PG-13.

CAST: Mike Myers (Austin Powers/Dr. Evil/Fat Bastard); Heather Graham (Felicity Shagwell); Michael York (Basil Exposition); Robert Wagner (Number Two); Rob Lowe (Young Number Two); Seth Green (Scott Evil); Mindy Sterling (Frau Farbissina); Verne J. Troyer (Mini-Me); Elizabeth Hurley (Vanessa); Gia Carides (Robin Swallows); Oliver Muirhead (British Colonel); George Kee Cheung (Chinese Teacher); Jeffrey Meng (Chinese Student); Muse Watson (Klansman); Scott Cooper (Klansman's Son, Bobby); Douglas Fisher (Man, Pecker); Kevin Cooney (Norad Colonel); Brian Hooks (Pilot); David Koechner (Co-Pilot); Frank Clem (Guitarist with Willie Nelson); Herb Mitchell (Sargeant); Steve Eastin (Umpire); Jane Carr (Woman, Pecker); Kevin Durand (Assassin); Melissa Justin (Chick #1 at Party); Nicholas Walker (Captain of the Guard); Steve Hibbert (Guard at Jail Cell); Eric Winzenried (Private Army Soldier); Tim Bagley (Friendly Dad); Colton James (Friendly Son); Mike Hagerty (Peanut Vendor); Jack Kehler (Circus Barker); Kirk Ward (Soldier); Jeff Garlin (Cyclops); Rachel Wilson (Fan); Jennifer Coolidge (Woman at Football Game); John Mahon (NATO Colonel); Michael McDonald (NATO Soldier); Jeannette Miller (Teacher); Mary Jo Smith (Unibrau); Carrie Ann Inaba (Felicity's Dancer #1); Jennifer Hamilton (Felicity's Dancer #2); Ayesha Orange (Felicity's Dancer #3); Natalie Willes (Felicity's Dancer #4); John Corella (Party Dancer #1); Alison Faulk (Party Dancer #2); Michelle Elkin (Party Dancer #3); Shealan Spencer (Party Dancer #4); Tovaris Wilson (Party Dancer #5); Bree Turner (Dancer #1); Marisa Gilliam (Dancer #2); Mark Meismer (Dancer #3); Sal Vassallo (Dancer #4); Jason Yribar (Dancer #5); Chekesha Van Putten (Go-Go Dancer #1); Tara Mouri (Go-Go Dancer #2); Gigi Yazicioglu (Go-Go Dancer #3); Sarah Smith, Faune A. Chambers, and Gabriel Paige (Scene Break Dancers); Jim Boensch (Queen's Guard); Ron Ulstad (Chief of Staff); Tim Watters (Bill Clinton Look-Alike); Todd M. Schultz (Jerry Springer's Bodyguard #1); Steve Wilkos (Jerry Springer's Bodyguard #2); Scott Patton (Puppeteer); Burt Bacharach (Himself); Elvis Costello (Himself); Will Ferrell (Mustafa); Woody Harrelson (Himself); Kristen Johnston (Ivana Humpalot); Charles Napier (General Hawk); Willie Nelson (Himself); Tim Robbins (The President); Rebecca Romijn Stamos (Herself); Jerry Springer (Himself); Fred Willard (Mission Commander).

CHRISTIAN SCIENCE MONITOR, 6/11/99, p 15, David Sterritt

"Austin Powers: The Spy Who Shagged Me" wasn't shown at this year's Cannes filmfest, but its producers made sure it was among the most noisily hyped movies on the festival's sidelines.

That's not because the original "Austin Powers: International Man of Mystery" (1997) was a walloping hit. Just the opposite: It did disappointing business overseas, and even its American grosses were lower than expected (it earned less than $10 million its first weekend). It gained new energy on video, though, reawakening hope that Austin's goofy adventures might become a comedy series. Hence the decision to pitch the sequel with as much oomph as Hollywood can muster.

Mike Myers returns as the title character, a '60s-style secret agent who struts and womanizes like a James Bond run amok. Again his nemesis is Dr. Evil, whose goals include that old standby, world domination. Also on hand are an Evil clone named Mini-Me and an Austin ally named Felicity, played by Heather Graham with her usual charm.

Myers plays everyone else important, including Dr. Evil and another "heavy" who barges through the movie like a literal bull in a china shop. He also sets the tone for the constant sexual and scatological humor. Some may find this Rabelaisian and refreshing, while others may detect the end of civilization as we know it. In any case, the screenplay—reportedly improvised to some extent—is coarse and crude enough to throw the PG-13 rating's credibility into permanent disarray.

It's wildly inconsistent, too, careening from hilarious wordplay to fatuous gross-out jokes in the blink of an eye. Look up "scattershot" in next year's dictionary, and you'll find a photo of Austin Powers grinning back at you.

LOS ANGELES TIMES, 6/11/99, Calendar/p. 1, Kenneth Turan

There's no searching for coherence in the raucous and rowdy "Austin Powers: The Spy Who Shagged Me," no plot worth revealing, no attempt to make any sense. Laughs are all this film cares about, and it's wickedly unconcerned about how it gets them.

More energetic and funnier than its predecessor, the considerable video hit "Austin Powers: International Man of Mystery," this edition of Austinania is an "Airplane!"—type cornucopia of spoof humor that takes gleeful potshots at a wide range of pop culture targets. It doesn't connect every time—there's no way it could—but its batting average is gratifyingly high.

Once again directed by Jay Roach and written by star Mike Myers (helped this time by co-writer Michael McCullers), "The Spy Who Shagged Me" relates the further adventures of the delusional secret agent and his equally incompetent nemesis, the shiny-suited, bald master of mayhem, Dr. Evil.

Both men were cryogenically frozen in the swinging 1960s only to be thawed out in the go-go '90s to face off in "International Man of Mystery." In this latest chapter of what will no doubt be a continuing saga, the two men go back in time to duke it out once more in those wild and crazy '60s.

The thin reed of a plot on which considerable madness is balanced is that Dr. Evil has concocted a plan to steal Austin's libido, known as his mojo. Waiting in the '60s to help the doctor is Young Number Two (Rob Lowe, doing a good imitation of Robert Wagner, the original Number Two) and waiting to bewitch Austin is agent Felicity Shagwell (don't ask), played with the correct amount of bemusement and attractiveness by Heather Graham.

Also new to Austin's world is the tiny, one-eighth-sized miniature clone of Dr. Evil (played by 2-foot, 8-inch Verne Troyer) that the great man dubs Mini-Me and immediately involves in all manner of surreal shenanigans.

"The Spy Who Shagged Me" throws so many kinds of things at you so fast, watching it can be pleasantly disorienting. If the film wants to have Burt Bacharach and Elvis Costello appear out of nowhere to sing "I'll Never Fall in Love Again" on the streets of London, they're there. For those who've never experienced an Austin movie, here are some other ideas of what to expect:

* Inane sexual humor. This includes a character named Ivana Humpalot (she's Russian, if you must know), an elaborately edited sequence invoking nicknames for the male sexual organ that features both Willie Nelson and Woody Harrelson, and lines of dialogue like a woman asking Austin if he smoked after sex and the rascal responding, "I don't know, baby, I've never looked."

* Toilet humor. Literally and a lot of it. With key sequences involving bowel movements and an odoriferous stool sample, anyone old enough to get into an R-rated movie will be hard-pressed to find this amusing.

* Yiddish-tinged humor. As in the first film, there's a country named Kreplachistan and a key character named Frau Farbissina (Yiddish for embittered), making clear that Myers' heart is in the Catskills, not the Highlands.

* Movie references and spoofs. Given that Austin himself is a spoof of James Bond, it's not surprising that numerous other films get parodied, including "Star Wars," "The Exorcist," "Jerry Maguire" and "The Island of Dr. Moreau." The references are dead-on but so fleeting it's possible to miss them if you're not paying attention.

Hard to miss is "The Spy Who Shagged Me's" infatuation with "The Jerry Springer Show." In a mock episode titled "My Father Is Evil and Wants to Take Over the World," Dr. Evil's disaffected son Scott (Seth Green) confronts the old man and gets to hear himself dissed as "the mayonnaise, the Diet Coke of evil."

With humor like this all over the place, "The Spy Who Shagged Me" couldn't succeed without a unifying force, and that has to be the protean Myers, who in addition to playing both Austin and Dr. Evil spent nearly five hours per session climbing into a Stan Winston-designed latex suit to play a heavyweight villain with a 70-inch waistline subtly named Fat Bastard.

As these films and his earlier "Wayne's World" demonstrate, Myers has a singular talent for skit humor. Seeing him play both the sniggering, snaggle toothed Austin, "the man who put the grr in swinger," and the fussy, pinky-waving Dr. Evil is to see a gifted performer who knows his strengths and is not afraid of playing to them. You can get away with an awful lot of gross, juvenile humor if you've got that to fall back on.

NEW YORK, 6/21/99, p. 60, Peter Rainer

The opening crawl for *Austin Powers: The Spy Who Shagged Me* is a takeoff on the one from the *Star Wars* movies, and other Lucas-aimed jokes keep popping up. The film builds its *Phantom Menace* counterprogramming status right into the material, which may make it something of a marketing first. It also loads up the usual commercial tie-ins: not only for Heineken and Bob's Big Boy and Virgin Atlantic Airways, which features Austin Powers in its billboards, but, conspicuously, for Starbucks, which functions in the movie as a cash cow for Powers's nemesis, Dr. Evil, who once again plans to take over the world. In this much ballyhooed sequel to *Austin Powers: International Man of Mystery,* there's a lot more flogging than shagging going on.

The original 1997 film did only moderately well in theaters but has turned out to be a continuing smash on the video circuit, largely because kids are tickled by Mike Myers's fur-ball, snaggletoothed kookiness in the same way they might be with a favorite daytime cartoon character—except Austin's a little lewder than a Smurf. Although *Austin Powers,* with its suave spies and flower-power psychedelia, sent up swinging-sixties camp, the spoofing in the new movie is far more self-referential. *The Spy Who Shagged Me* is less about the Bond movies and *In Like Flint* and Carnaby Street and more about all the Austin Powers crotchets and catchwords. We're treated to a dazzling array of doo-doo jokes, some of which are quite funny and all of which are exceptionally tasteless, as well as lots of obesity gags and cleavage comedy. The British music hall, of course, has a tradition of this sort of thing, and Mike Myers has never been given enough credit (or blame) for revamping that tradition. Still, a closer heritage here would be *Mad* magazine and junior-high-school bathroom graffiti.

Myers is pretty consistently hilarious as Austin Powers—he's one of those characters, like Peter Sellers's Inspector Clouseau—who makes you laugh before he even opens his mouth, and then tops that laugh when he does. (For kids, Powers's instant-recognition factor might be a form of pop-cult connoisseurship.) But there's too much Dr. Evil this time, and there's also a third Myers creation, a behemoth Scots spy, who didn't do much for me, and a mini Dr. Evil (Verne Troyer), who would seem more at home in a David Lynch movie. Heather Graham is decorative but disappointingly bland as CIA agent Felicity Shagwell. On the other hand, you won't want to miss Rob Lowe, as a younger version of Dr. Evil's second-in-command, doing a letter-perfect imitation of Robert Wagner. Who'd have thought that bland-on-bland could have this many levels?

NEW YORK POST, 6/11/99, p. 41, Rod Dreher

Crikey! Like teen-age sex and Rolling Stones tours, it turns out that anticipating the new "Austin Powers" movie is a lot more fun than actually experiencing it.

Mike Myers' swinging, sex-mad spook returns in this often amusing but ultimately disappointing sequel to the 1997 surprise smash "Austin Powers: International Man of Mystery," which uproariously sent up the early James Bond films and the cheesy, gleefully sleazy trappings of fin-de-'60s English pop culture.

As brilliant a comic conception as Austin Powers and his Day-Glo, madly mod world are, "Austin Powers: The Spy Who Shagged Me" reveals the whole thing to have been a clever joke, but a one-note one all the same. Myers is just coasting here.

It plays like a classic overlong "Saturday Night Live" skit in which all concerned hit on a cracking good premise, then proceed to beat all the life out of it for lack of knowing what to do next.

The new "Austin Powers" finds our shagadelic hero on his honeymoon in the '90s with a nice new set of Martin Amis-sed choppers and lovely bride Vanessa (Elizabeth Hurley) lingering from the first movie. Alas, Vanessa's uncovered as a deadly fembot in disguise, sent by the vicious Dr. Evil (Myers, in a dual role) to do Austin in.

What's more, Dr. Evil, who has amassed a latter-day corporate empire as the chief of Starbucks (nice jibe!), time-travels to the past with the mission of stealing Austin's "mojo"—that is, his ultragroovy sex drive.

A grotesquely obese Scottish secret agent, Fat Bastard (Myers, yet again), has been planted in the British defense ministry, where he extracts Austin's mojo from his cryonically preserved body. The Mr. Creosote-like Fat B. delivers the go-go goods to Dr. Evil's lair, and after making a disgusting but hilarious potty joke or two (toilet humor is big here), hands the precious fluid over.

Our hero has to limp, har-har, back in time to track down Dr. Evil, who is also planning to destroy Washington, D.C., from a Death Star-like moon base, and save the U.S. capital while rescuing his libido.

Happily, the journey gives Austin back his atrocious teeth, which deserve a special chapter in the horror classic "The Big Book of British Dentistry." He's assisted by the lovely Felicity Shagwell (Heather Graham), an indescribably comely CIA agent who's only job is to appear staggeringly shaggable in every possible scene. Memo to Heather Graham: mission accomplished, baby!

The new movie puts more emphasis on Dr. Evil's satanic shenanigans, which are pretty consistently funny. He reproduces himself in a pint-sized clone called Mini-Me (Verne Troyer), has a giggly interlude with Frau Farbissina (Mindy Sterling), his Teutonic lesbian henchwoman, and continues his running argument with his pathetically needy son Scott (Seth Green), who never tires of pointing out how ridiculous his chrome-domed daddy is.

But it all gets repetitive, and after about the halfway point, you get the feeling that Myers and Co. don't know where to go next, and are making it up as they go along.

Austin's Carnaby Street crash pad and the wild threads he and his associates wear are the last word in retro cheek, but we've seen it before. Truth be told, the first "Austin Powers" was not a sustained piece of comedy writing, but Myers was able to generate hysterical laughs by merely suggesting these outrageous characters and places.

The novelty has by now worn off—thanks in part to the deluge of hype—and the lack of inventive plotting or developing the concept gives a whiff of staleness to "The Spy Who Shagged Me."

And this movie gives dismaying evidence of the creeping Ewok-ization of Austin Powers: he's becoming less a movie character and more a cute marketing device. There are so many gratuitous product endorsements here it seems that Myers is trying to ensure he makes as much money from licensing as he will at the box office.

That said, "Austin Powers" groupies will still want to see the sublimely silly movie, which will suffice, if only just, until the next, better-written (we hope) sequel comes along. "The Spy Who Shagged Me" leaves us with a real cliffhanger: will Mike Myers figure out how to make irrepressible Austin swing as hard as he did two summers ago, or will he too lose his mojo?

NEWSDAY, 6/11/99 Part II/p. B2, John Anderson

Students of Swinging' 60s superspy/fashion photographer Austin Powers—dashing, dentally challenged International Man of Mystery—will be shocked to learn in "Austin Powers: The Spy Who Shagged Me" that his stolen mojo looks like a lava lamp.

Shocking, yes. But true. When heisted and bottled by the fiendish Dr. Evil, Austin's life force-cum-libido—the soul of these particular '60s—resembles the representative icon of all things '70s.

Decades from now, when Myers has begun to morph into William Shatner and they hold "Austin Powers" conventions at the nearly rebuilt Nassau Veterans Memorial Coliseum, Powers Studies professors from the Adam Sandler School of Comparative Comedy will pore over this seemingly innocuous thread of information as if it were a Dead Sea Scroll or Fermat's Theorem.

How could it have happened? When during Austin's travels—from the '90s, where he learns his bride, Vanessa (Elizabeth Hurley), has actually been a murderous "fembot", to the '60s, where he meets the luscious Felicity Shagwell (Heather Graham) and saves the world from Evil (Myers)—did he have the time or opportunity to influence home decor in the era of gas lines and leisure suits?

Clues will be sought. Wormholes explored. Papers presented. Degrees awarded.

This scenario—as well as any third Austin Powers movie, or the eventual "prequel" trilogy—depends on the stock market never crashing, communism never bouncing back from embarrassment and fin de siecle navel-gazing never ending. It depends on popular culture continuing its inconsequential but oh-so-profitable course toward an inward focus so terrifyingly telescoped that the recycling of cultural matter will continue until all that's left is vapor.

That said, it should surprise no one that the funniest bit in the vaporous "Austin Powers: TSWSM" is beaten to death twice before the movie is over (it involves Evil's phallic spaceship). Or that the funniest bit in the original "Austin Powers"—a "classic" among more discerning middle-schoolers—would be the first and most prolonged bit in Myers' new comedy (the strategic obscuring of his genitalia as he dances through the opening credits). That most people will find at least some of the movie funny seems pretty likely. That they'll find it desperate seems inevitable.

But then, the very ethos of "Austin Powers" is, to put it nicely, overkill and homage: first, to all those '60s spy shows and espionage comedies that were spoofs of cool to begin with; now, to the original "Austin Powers" itself. One has to presume that its young target audience has not a clue about the references in the film. The Shirley Bassey-ized theme song, the faux "Bond girl" Ivana Humpalot (Kristen Johnson), the erotized "Thomas Crown" chess game—they're not just obscure, they're fossilized. As is anyone who doesn't think this bag of spare parts and bad timing is the funniest movie ever made.

That it's not is almost beside the point. Lame jokes, like the relentless product placement that riddles this wildly uneven movie, are part of its aesthetic; bad taste, in other words, is not just timeless, it's intentional. When Fat Bastard, Myers' bagpipe-playing, Buick-sized bad guy, rolls around in bed—nude, save for the congealing chicken fat smeared around his face—the cringe one feels is a tribute to his creator. When Austin and Felicity deliver the archly facetious and sophomorically suggestive dialogue ("You're very good on your feet." "I'm even better off my feet."), the moan you suppress is a sign of love. When Austin, after several false starts, finally does drink the stool sample he's mistaken for coffee, your gag reflex is testimony to the cultural acuity of Myers and Co., who know their audience and what it wants.

The movie doesn't miss much in the way of targets. A Scottish villain. A murderous Arab (Will Ferrell). A Nazi-fied lesbian (Mindy Sterling). Dr. Evil's disgruntled Gen-X son (Seth Green), who goes gay by the end of the film. Dr. Evil's clone, Mini-Me (Verne Troyer), whose dwarfism is a constant visual joke (and whose piano duet with Evil is a grotesque ref to the Brando-Frankenheimer "Island of Dr. Moreau"). And, of course, Austin himself, the vaguely effeminate Brit, whose insistent sexuality is obviously masking a psyche in the closet (with the fat character as id and Evil as superego).

Austin exemplifies how English vulgarity is so much more genteel than ours—genteel enough that a euphemism for sex is not just the title of an ostensibly mainstream film, but the basis of an ad campaign for a major British airline. In the end, it's tough to criticize "Austin Powers" for sinking to new lows, because the rush to get down there with him looks like a stampede.

NEWSWEEK, 6/14/99, p. 66, Kendall Hamilton

The second coming of Austin Powers isn't exactly the return of "Star Wars"—thank heavens. Yes, "Austin Powers: The Spy Who Shagged Me," has been awaited by legions of panting devotees. Hollywood projections have Mike Myers's swinging spy sequel, finishing second only to Lucas's latest in the summer box-office sweepstakes. And, yes, store shelves this summer will be jammed with merchandise spinoffs from both movies—though here, we begin to sense a distinction. "Star Wars" fans will want one of those neat double-bladed lightsabers. Fans of the International Man of Mystery, on the other hand, will have to weigh the pros and cons of approaching the cash register clutching a genuine Austin Powers Swedish Penis Enlarger. But the most important difference is this: "The Spy Who Shagged Me" is mostly the goofy, jubilant fun it ought to be.

The sequel picks up where the original "Austin Powers" left off, go-going its way through another decade-straddling, Ian Fleming-on-Ecstasy plot. We start off in the present day, where oversexed agent Powers (Myers) is relaxing between the sheets until his chrome-domed nemesis Dr. Evil (Myers again) spoils the mood. This time Evil's gunning for Washington, D.C., with a giant laser cannon stationed on the moon. But in the meantime, he's got something else up the sleeve of his beloved Nehru jacket.

Dr. Evil and his new pride and joy, a pint-size clone he dubs Mini-Me (Verne Troyer), time-travel back to the '60s to put Powers out of commission retroactively. With the aid of an obese, baby-eating Scotsman named Fat Bastard (Myers, yet again), Dr. Evil steals Powers's "mojo," the vague but vital life force that puts the lead in our hero's pencil. Powers is right behind, natch, with the CIA's Felicity Shagwell (Heather Graham) in tow, seeking to recover his mojo, save the planet and, of course, shag the girl. If it all seems a bit dizzying, it is. When Powers himself begins ruminating on the logical loopholes that all this time travel presents, his boss cautions, "I suggest you don't worry about this sort of thing and just enjoy yourself." He then addresses the audience. "That goes for you all, too."

Take his advice—there's plenty to enjoy. Like the 1997 original, "The Spy Who Shagged Me" spits out snappy double entendres, killer sight gags and outright absurdity thicker than the thatch on our hero's oft-bared chest. "Do you smoke after sex?" asks comely Vanessa (a cameo by proto Powers girl Elizabeth Hurley). Powers: "I don't know, baby. I've never looked." One priceless gag from the original, in which various objects—vases, coconuts, etc.—strategically pop up to interfere with the audience's view of bared body parts, is repeated here during the film's opening credits. Later, the same concept gets a clever verbal spin, as rapid-fire context-shifting prevents characters from directly describing a distinctly phallic spaceship. Radar operator: "It looks like a giant ..." Cut to fighter pilot: "Dick! Dick, look out to starboard!"

These days, of course, lowbrow comedy is king, and "The Spy Who Shagged Me" doesn't buck the trend. Toilets and their contents get a starring role in several scenes, and the unspeakably hideous Fat Bastard—who figures in a love scene with Heather Graham—provides fodder for some of the grossest gross-out humor this side of Monty Python's exploding Mr. Creosote. No matter. More likely to offend is the shameless parade of product promotions. Virgin Atlantic, Volkswagen, Starbucks, Heineken and AOL all intrude.

Myers juggles his roles admirably, though his Powers seems a lighter shade of paisley this time round. Since he spends most of the movie inhabiting his native '60s, the fish-out-of-water humor that worked well last time is missing. The Powers-centered plot lines also tend to bog down in a dull romance and in music-video-like interludes that bleed air out of the film's tires. As Dr. Evil, though, Myers is shinier than his own shaved pate. His awkwardly autocratic bad guy steals the show, particularly as we follow the continuing Freudian psychodrama between the doctor and his son, Scott (Seth Green). The old man, it seems, has taken to Mini-Me. When Scott makes overtures toward a reconciliation, he's rebuffed. "You had your chance," Dr. Evil says. "I already have someone created in my image. He's evil, he wants to take over the world and he fits easily into most overhead storage bins." Graham is suitably gorgeous, but doesn't display the easy way with an absurd line that Hurley mustered in the original. One caveat: this film was reviewed from a videocassette, so we can't say much about its visual impact. But we don't think the humor shrank in the translation. In the film's last line, Dr. Evil promises, "We'll be back." Count on it.

SIGHT AND SOUND, 8/99, p. 39, Xan Brooks

London, 1999. Ensconced in his honeymoon suite, British agent Austin Powers discovers new bride Vanessa is actually an exploding robot sent from his arch-enemy Doctor Evil. Meanwhile, Evil squabbles with his truculent son Scott and reveals his new miniature clone of himself, which he calls Mini-Me. Evil's other innovation is a time machine with which he travels back to 1969. There, Evil hires a Scottish security guard called Fat Bastard to steal Austin Powers "Mojo", and so thwart his enemy's powers in the 90s. Austin himself heads back to 1969 where he teams up with lissom CIA-operative Felicity Shagwell but, Mojoless, is unable to consummate their relationship. Doctor Evil has no such problems. He drinks from Powers' Mojo and subsequently fathers for henchwoman Frau Farbissina the child who will grow into the sulky Scott. Evil moves his gang to a base on the moon and threatens to blow up Washington DC with a giant laser. Austin and Felicity travel to the moon where they defeat Evil, Fat Bastard and Mini-Me. The elusive Mojo smashes on the floor, but Austin discovers he can cope just as well without it. Triumphant, Austin Powers spirits Felicity back to his pad in 90s London.

The opening scene in *Austin Powers The Spy Who Shagged Me* finds Mike Myers' wacky British agent lounging in bed watching the 1967 spy comedy *In Like Flint*. "My favourite movie," boasts Powers, and with that one line he jams the guns of a thousand film critics by acknowledging that, yes, the *Austin Powers* concept is old hat, dated, done to death. In the first place, *In Like Flint* was actually a sequel to *Our Man Flint* (1965), just as *The Spy Who Shagged Me* is a sequel to 1997's *International Man of Mystery*. And second, *Flint*'s patented line of comedy is already over 30 years distant. Let's face it—spoofs on the espionage genre are almost as old as the genre itself. The golden age of *007* was paralleled by a host of spoofs, from *Flint* and the *Pink Panther* series to *Carry On Spying* (1964) and *Casino Royale* (1967, featuring Woody Allen as little Jimmy Bond). And perhaps even these parodies were missing the point. Check out Sean Connery's line in selfmocking machismo, or Roger Moore's sense of being in on the joke, and another possibility comes to mind: that the James Bond series was nothing more than a thinly veiled spoof itself.

All of which ought to make *The Spy Who Shagged Me* utterly redundant. What we have here is a film out of time; a loop of self-referentialism; a spoof of a spoof of a genre that was already two-parts spoof to begin with. And yet in the end, its very second-hand nature proves the film's greatest asset, its staleness what makes it so exotic. As a film, *Austin Powers* is simple to the point of idiocy (Austin travels back in time to retrieve his 'Mojo', a liquified libido, after it has been stolen by his arch nemesis Doctor Evil, also played by Myers). As a concept it is strange, garbled and elusive.

The original *Austin Powers* was released to little fanfare and faired middling-well at the box office before blooming into a best-seller on video (its turnabout triggered by the same word-of-mouth that helped Myers' previous incarnation, the dweebish compere of *Wayne's World*). *Powers 2*, by contrast, rides in on the back of a reputed $40 million promotion budget, its coffers swollen by lucrative product placement and advertising tie-ins (Starbucks, Heineken and Virgin Atlantic have all hopped into bed with Powers). The big-money approach seems to have paid off. Incredibly, *The Spy Who Shagged Me* equalled the entire box-office run of its predecessor in the first three days of its US release and knocked *The Phantom Menace* off the number-one slot in the chart.

But what initially strikes you about *Powers 2* is how little of this production muscle seems to have been exerted on the film itself. If anything, *The Spy Who Shagged Me* is even more amateurish than *Man of Mystery,* the latter a loosely set of skits, sketches and pooh jokes that doesn't even attempt to cohere into a bonafide narrative. *Powers 2* makes a great show of its slapdash stupidity and plundered ingredients, and pretends its budget is smaller than it actually is. So the British setting is explicitly southern California dressed up with a red phone box and a sign that reads "English Countryside", and its cinematic allusions (Doctor Evil calls his moon-base the Death Star) are constantly held up to ridicule. Meanwhile, Austin's panic over the yarn's scrambled grasp of time-travel is sweetly glossed over by his superior. (Michael York). "I suggest you don't about this sort of thing and just enjoy youself," York says, then turns to camera: "That goes for you all, too."

Austin Powers, then, is not only cheap candy that admits it's cheap candy; it advertises itself as cheap candy. Pruned of plot, logic or rhythm, the picture's elements sit in their own separate pockets like gaudily wrapped chocolates in a selection box. We have a pretty piece of decoration in Heather Graham's knee-booted CIA agent ("one groovy baby"). We have some punning names (Ivana Humpalot, Robin Swallows, whose maiden name was Spitz), some indulgent cameos (Jerry Springer, Woody Harrelson) and a running penis gag which—at the risk of jumping on the film's double entendre bandwagon—feels worryingly over-extended.

Some continuity is provided by Myers in a breathless trio of roles when he should really have stuck at two. Credit where it's due: Myers' title hero is undeniably a sprightly comic creation, a ludicrous conflation of David Bailey the Monkees' Davey Jones who comes over all dewy-eyed when confronted by the murderous Mini-Me ("poor little bugger—like a little doll or something"). And his Doctor Evil proves a likable foil with his boiled-egg head and wafer-thin ego. But Fat Bastard (a scatological Scotsman given to leaving unflushed turds in toilets) really is a bad mistake, a crumb thrown to the dumbest juvenile in the house. Even when he's sending up British culture, it seems Myers is not averse to borrowing from the worst aspects of home-grown comedy. Still, such hit-and-miss humour is the natural result of a picture so reliant on the talents of one man. The film's supporting cast (Graham, Robert Wagner, Rob Lowe) is just ballast; its nominal director Jay Roach, director of the first *Powers* film) simply there to frame the star.

The Spy Who Shagged Me lives or dies on the lively, cartoonish antics of its chief creator. But inevitably the *Powers* phenomenon is more complicated than that. Look at it closely and this slight slip of a summer comedy turns out to be a truly devilish contraption. *The Spy Who Shagged Me* sends up British culture at a time when Cool Britannia is still a buzz term in the US; pokes fun at the concept while simultaneously luxuriating in its stylistic trappings. So the film's retro setting offers what Roach calls "a theme-park version of the 60s" not far removed from the view of contemporary London peddled by lazier sections of the world's media—a ludicrous yet nostalgia-stuffed Eden where double-deckers come emblazoned with Union Jacks and Elvis Costello and Burt Bacharach can be found busking outside the Tube. This, then, is a film which has it both ways: a spoof so affectionate as to buttress effectively that which it sets out to ridicule, a studio product which poses as amateur-night entertainment, an anti-blockbuster with a blockbuster's publicity budget. Ultimately, *The Spy Who Shagged Me* is a thing of Machiavellian genius. $50-odd million on its opening weekend. For cheap candy. For tatty, so-stupid-it's-funny, throwaway fun. Doctor Evil would kill for so brilliant, so fiendish a scheme.

VILLAGE VOICE, 6/22/99, p. 149, J. Hoberman

Austin Powers: The Spy Who Shagged Me would be a neo-new wave movie if only for existing largely in a realm of movie references—mostly taken from *Austin Powers: International Man of Mystery*, the 1997 movie which first defrosted Mike Myers's Carnaby Street relic. But it has additional relevance for its burlesque of Richard Lestees Swinging London commercialization of Godardian cinema.

Essentially the same '60s/'90s joke as the original *Austin Powers, The Spy Who Shagged Me*—also directed by Jay Roach from Myers's script—is no less funny, being similarly founded on groovy, pop-op set design and James Bond-parody parody, and enlivened by a now familiar mix of lewd anatomy jokes, bad puns, Mel Brooks character names (Ivana Humpalot) and Yiddishisms (Kreplachistan, Frau Farbissina), free-floating scatology, prancing go-go girls, and tacky psychedelic effects. (Myers's other persona Dr. Evil isn't kidding when he cries "send in the clones!") Certain bits of business are simply repeated, with Burt Bacharach grinning zombielike through his requisite cameo as though being rediscovered for the first time.

In short, the sequel attempts to place the original within quotation marks embellishing, rather than extending, the original premise. Well before the opening credits end, *The Spy Who Shagged Me* has demolished its predecessors happy ending while reestablishing Myers's exhibitionist credentials. Austin's new bride turns out to be a fembot with machine-gun jumblies—giving him license to dance naked through the hotel lobby looking for birds. His replacement love interest (Heather Graham) is a luscious CIA operative who aspires to be the female Austin Powers.

But although Austin's shag-pad includes his own pseudo-Warhol portrait and the plot contrives for him to be joined by his 10-minutes-future self, the nominal hero is overshadowed by his various alter-egos. The epicene Dr. Evil gets at least as much screen time as Austin, plus the theme song ("Evil is his one and only name"). There's also a scaled-down Dr. Evil replica (32-inch Verne Troyer), complete with a bald kitten to cuddle, whom the original dubs "Mini-Me." Myers further enhances the Peter Sellers effect and ups the gross-out quotient by appearing as Dr. Evil's most disgusting henchman, the F/X-padded, kilt-wearing, slobbering Scotsman accurately known as Fat Bastard.

Although not as brilliantly scored as the original, *Austin* redux is even more a musical. While the obligatory polka-dot swirl disco scene, in which Graham dances down from the balcony to "American Woman," prompts the unhappy—and accurate-suspicion that we'll never again get to watch her frug, Dr. Evil has a memorable Marvin Gaye pas de deux with Frau Farbissina. Even better, when he sings "Just the Two of Us" to Mini-Me, he turns Will Smith's rap ballad into the perfect anthem for a movie narcissistically encrusted with its own mythology.

Also reviewed in:
CHICAGO TRIBUNE, 6/11/99, Friday/p. A, Michael Wilmington
NATION, 7/5/99, p. 35, Stuart Klawans
NEW YORK TIMES, 6/11/99, p. E1, Janet Maslin
NEW YORKER, 7/5/99, p. 90, David Denby
VARIETY, 6/14-20/99, p. 32, Dennis Harvey
WASHINGTON POST, 6/11/99, p. C1, Rita Kempley
WASHINGTON POST, 6/11/99, Weekend/p. 40, Desson Howe

AUTUMN TALE

An October Films release of a Les Films du Losange, La Sept Cinéma with the participation of Canal+, Sofilmka and Rhône-Alpes Cinéma. *Producer:* Françoise Etchegary, Margaret Menegoz, and Eric Rohmer. *Director:* Eric Rohmer. *Screenplay (French with English subtitles):* Eric Rohmer. *Director of Photography:* Diane Baratier. *Editor:* Mary Stephen. *Music:* Claude Marti. *Sound:* Pascal Ribier. *Running time:* 110 minutes. *MPAA Rating:* Not Rated.

CAST: Marie Rivière (Isabelle); Béatrice Romand (Magali); Alain Libolt (Gérald); Didier Sandre (Étienne); Alexia Portal (Rosine); Stéphane Darmon (Léo); Aurélia Alcaïs (Émilia); Matthieu Davette (Grégoire); Yves Alcaïs (Jean-Jacques).

LOS ANGELES TIMES, 7/23/99, Calendar/p. 4, Kenneth Turan

Though you wouldn't know it from Hollywood's kids 'r us obsessions, directors actually can improve as they advance in age. The droll and delicious "Autumn Tale" is the 22nd feature in 79-year-old writer-director Eric Rohmer's four-decade career, and besides being one of his wisest and most enjoyable films, it also has the light-fingered vigor and panache more chronologically youthful directors are not always able to muster.

Rohmer, along with Jean-Luc Godard, Francois Truffaut and Claude Chabrol, is one of the New Wave directors who revolutionized French film starting in the late 1950s. Over the years, he's made such favorites as "My Night at Maud's," "Claire's Knee," "Chloe in the Afternoon" and "Pauline at the Beach," all marked, as "Autumn Tale" is, by elegant, character-driven plots as carefully worked out as intricate mathematical proofs.

Mostly, as those films indicate, Rohmer's work has focused on the male fascination with (invariably) younger women. Recently, however, not only have Rohmer's titles gotten simpler ("Autumn Tale" was preceded by "Summer's Tale," "Winter's Tale" and "Tale of Springtime," all part of his decade-long "Tales of the Four Seasons" series), but he has tended to see things more from the female point of view.

"Autumn Tale" is also unusual for Rohmer because it's involved with women "of a certain age," focusing on the romantic difficulties of a 45-year-old widow and the increasingly frenetic efforts of the well-intentioned but misguided friends who try to help her.

Rohmer has retained not only the assurance that comes with great experience, but also his marvelous sense of character. It's a pleasure to have a writer-director who understands people so well; his sense of how the combination of good intentions and faulty judgment can land us in a terrible mess is both compassionate and exact.

More than anything, Rohmer's people love to talk. Passionate about their own thoughts and ideas (though not necessarily anyone else's), these formidably articulate individuals analyze, reflect on and consider everything they do—not once but several times—all to magnificent effect.

The main talkers are two longtime friends living in the Cote du Rhone region of southern France: Magali (Beatrice Romand, who debuted in 1970's "Claire's Knee") and her closest confident, Isabelle (Man'e Riviere, also in Rohmer's acting stable). Happily married Isabelle is dealing with her daughter's impending wedding, while Magali, a bit estranged from both her grown children, devotes herself to the winery left her by her parents.

An early scene of these two women walking and talking among Magali's plantings illustrates the subtlety of Rohmer's approach. Nominally nothing of substance is discussed as the two women wander aimlessly amid the vines, but, in fact, everything we need to know about both of them, about Magali's forthrightness and stubborn candor as well as Isabelle's flighty, not quite practical nature, is gracefully revealed, as is the intimacy they share.

Chatting later in the farmhouse, Magali reveals that while she would like to have a man in her life, she's all but given up on the idea as impossible. "It's the hardest thing of all," she explains. "At my age, it's easier to find buried treasure!" Prospects are even more unlikely in her case because, as Magali is the first to admit, "I need to meet a man but I refuse to do anything about it."

Undaunted, Isabelle, who owns a bookstore, forms a plan to help her friend out. Not only does she place a misleading personal ad ("Fun-loving, lively, sociable") in Magali's name in the local newspaper, she also decides, in an excess of comradely zeal combined with a desire to bring a little flirtation into her own life, to impersonate her friend and test-date Gerald (Alain Libolt), the most likely of the candidates, herself.

Also for personal reasons, someone else is simultaneously trying to act as matchmaker for Magali. The beautiful young Rosine (Alexia Portal) is nominally the girlfriend of Magali's son Leo, but her strongest emotional attachment is to Magali.

Young though she is, Rosine has romantic complications of her own. She's trying to get over a love affair with her insufferable college philosophy professor Etienne (Didier Sandre). Ignoring his obsession with young women, she thinks that if she's successful in hooking him up with Magali, she'll have succeeded in killing two birds with the same stone.

These romantic shenanigans are all the more appealing because Rohmer understands that when adults are involved with affairs of the heart, their nominal maturity often disappears, leaving them as shy, awkward and accident-prone as the most love-struck teenager. When you're going out on a first date, it's always high school in your mind.

With his characters hatching more and more complicated schemes, Rohmer delights in revealing how we inevitably complicate our lives simply by being human. When Isabelle writes in her personal ad that what's wanted is a man "interested in moral as well as physical beauty," she could be describing this consummate filmmaker just as easily as Magali's imaginary dream date.

NEW YORK, 7/19/99, p. 72, Peter Rainer

The emotional nuances in Eric Rohmer's movies are so carefully calibrated that at times we seem to be watching the enactment of a theorem. What rescues his best films from desiccation is the playfulness behind the theorizing—he's a genial *philosophe*. It may be a little maddening, on occasion, watching his people act out their moral comedies within such a circumscribed radius; the greatest art isn't so finicky, so tamped-down. But Rohmer, although he's made movies touched with greatness such as *Claire's Knee* and the uncharacteristically free-form *Le Rayon Vert*, is best understood for the modesty of his designs. He's not out to jostle our complacencies but only to give them a little nudge. He's a moralist of a particularly comfy and bourgeois sort—he massages the notions his art-house patrons already have about people and life and the sexes. There are no shocks of recognition in Rohmer's movies, just little *frissons* of feeling.

Autumn Tale is the last of a four-season cycle. (The previous entry, *A Summer's Tale*, made in 1996, has gone undistributed in this country.) Rohmer is fond of cycles and series—his most celebrated lineup is the *Six Moral Tales*, including *My Night at Maud*'s and *Claire's Knee*, which he followed with six *Comedies and Proverbs*—but the link-up of titles is essentially a high-toned marketing device; the thematic conjunction between films is what one would expect anyway from a filmmaker with such a controlling sensibility. His latest has a plot that, if we're all so unlucky, will end up transposed to Hollywood: Isabelle (Marie Riviere), a married bookstore owner, wants to reconnect Magali (Béatrice Romand), her widowed best friend, with the world of men. Magali lives in the country, where she works the vineyard she inherited from her parents; she wouldn't mind having a man, but she doesn't want to go through the rituals and the turndowns. So Isabelle decides to secretly place an ad on Magali's behalf in the personals and then impersonate her friend on dates in order to pre-screen the candidates. Meanwhile, Rosine (Alexia Portal), the girlfriend of Magali's son, decides her college professor and lover Etienne (Didier Sandre) would go best with Magali.

For a long time, Isabelle's ruse is like a private joke she uses to titillate herself. Her first respondent, Gerald, a divorced salesman and the son of a vintner (well played by Alain Libolt), falls for her on their first encounter. Isabelle makes jokes at her own expense—she puts herself down for being too tall—but she's also preening before a man she knows she'll never have. She regards her subterfuge as "a game that amuses me, even though it's dangerous," and that sums up the movie's effect on us as well. It's always on the verge of breaking into something unruly and troubling, but Rohmer keeps things tidy. Isabelle is not tempted by Gerald; her friendship with Magali is never seriously strained, even when the jig is up. There's an element of cruelty in what Isabelle perpetrates with Gerald, but it's treated as a confectionery whim. "I want all men to love me," she tells him with a smile. "Especially the ones I *don't* love."

All this might seem too diagrammatic and coy except for the presence of Béatrice Romand, whose Magali makes all ruses worthwhile. Her big blur of wiry hair rests lightly on her head; her face is both cherubic and weathered. Magali is a self-described peasant woman, but she's not earthy, or if she is, some blue sky got mixed in with the portrait. There's something cloud-borne about this woman; her encounters with both Gerald and Etienne, which take place during a wedding party for Isabelle's daughter, bring out the cuckoo in her. She's reliving the throes of adolescent-style awkwardness. Between bouts, she looks out at the Rhone Valley in the far distance and sulks. She's not used to feeling love-struck, or lovelorn either, and her bewilderment only makes her more fetching. The joke in *Autumn Tale* is that it doesn't matter how old you are; the entanglements of romance end up juvenilizing you. Rohmer, who is 79, has often worked out his moralizings with a younger cast of characters. Here, with an older set, he retains the youthful blush.

Rohmer sees men as being at a disadvantage in the mating game. Flummoxed by feminine conspiracies they're always the last to know about, they have no choice but to open up. In the male-female universe of *Autumn Tale,* it is the women who are canny and sphinxlike while the men, desperate to be understood, spill their souls out and are no wiser for it. (Gerald, smitten, does practically all the talking when he's with Isabelle, and the pattern is later repeated with Magali.) There's a form of poetic justice in all this, and it gives the film, otherwise straitlaced, its jagged wit: Women on the lookout for love may be fools, but they make sure to turn the men who romance them into even bigger ones.

NEW YORK POST, 7/9/99, p. 58, Rod Dreher

"Autumn Tale" is the newest film from the venerable Eric Rohmer, but there's never anything new about a Rohmer film. You know what you're going to get: a literate, talky, character-driven story about the private lives of the French middle class.

Some people find this sort of thing comforting; others, like me, tend to agree with Gene Hackman's famous observation (in "Night Moves") in which he describes watching a Rohmer film as "like watching paint dry."

Ditto for the somnolent, draggy but occasionally warm-hearted "Autumn Tale," the fourth installment of Rohmer's "Tales of the Four Seasons." Still, what a lovely texture the paint in this movie has, and it really is a wee bit newish, at least for Rohmer.

The 79-year-old director usually focuses on the romantic foibles of young adults. This time he writes about middle-aged characters looking for love in the autumn of their lives.

Widowed Magali (Beatrice Romand) presides over a vineyard in France's Rhone Valley, and pines for male companionship, though her admirable pride keeps her isolated. "I need to meet a man," she says, "but I refuse to do anything about it."

Her son's girlfriend, Rosine (Alexia Portal), contrives to fix Magali up with a middle-aged former lover of hers, a professor named Etienne (Didier Sandre). Meanwhile, Magali's lifelong best friend, Isabelle (Marie Riviere), places a personals ad on Magali's behalf. Though happily married, Isabelle pretends to be Magali for several dates with Gerald (Alain Libolt), the accomplished but lonely middle-aged gentleman who responds to the ad.

The wacky idea is to check Gerald out to make sure he'd be right for Magali, and to maneuver them into a meet-cute situation. Eventually the truth comes out, in a series of gently comic misunderstandings, at a wedding party in Isabelle's garden.

It's somewhat amusing to see these aging grown-ups fidget like teenagers, but there's never a chance of things ending badly.

The story is mellow to the point of slackness, but the characters are likable, and the beautifully shot film is perfumed with the slyly intoxicating atmosphere of the southern French countryside.

"Autumn Tale" may be no more narratively interesting than Olivier Assayas' similarly conversational "Late August, Early September," which opened this week, but it's vastly preferable as an aesthetic experience.

NEWSDAY, 7/9/99, Part II/p. B7, Gene Seymour

At quicker tempos and noisier pitches, Eric Rohmer's movies could be mistaken for the kind of comedies that slid off the Hollywood assembly line in bunches from the 1930s through the early 1960s.

Amorous intentions, missed signals, the assurances of intelligent men and women punctured by events beyond their control or understanding; these have all figured somehow into Rohmer's movies. Unlike Hollywood comedies, Rohmer's people speak at length in complete sentences and take time to reflect on their actions. This doesn't stop them from tying themselves in knots at inappropriate times.

"Autumn Tale," the last installment in the director's "Tales of the Four Seasons" cycle, is in many ways a consummate expression of Rohmer's graceful, humane and reflective art. Its main characters are strong, self-possessed women, both played by actresses who have appeared in other Rohmer films.

The film also engages, within a hyper-realistic context, the many ways people view love in both the abstract and literal sense. And it is paced in a measured manner that, in a celebrated cheap shot from Arthur Penn's "Night Moves" (1975), compared viewing a Rohmer film to watching paint dry.

If paint was as lush and beautiful as "Autumn Tale's" Rhone Valley setting in the south of France, what's the problem? It is here that Magali (Beatrice Romand) tends to a vineyard. She is a 40-something widow whose children, including son Leo (Stephane Darmon) have all grown and left.

Magali, still attractive and very lonely, is timid about looking for new love. So, unbeknownst to her, two friends conspire to fix her up in separately devised scenarios. Leo's headstrong girlfriend Rosine (Alexia Portal), a philosophy student, is certain that Magali's just the woman to get her loose from the unwanted advances of a philandering professor (Didier Sandre) twice her age.

Isabelle (Marie Riviere), a happily married bookstore owner who's known Magali from childhood, has another elaborate, but seemingly more rational plan in mind. She places a personal ad in the paper in Magali's name and begins "dating" one of the respondents, a shy, sweet middle-aged guy named Gerald (Alain Libolt). He likes Isabelle well enough, but is somewhat thrown when she tells him she's not the one looking for a suitor.

All these scenarios come to a head at the wedding of Isabelle's daughter, and Magali's just about the only one who ends up not being bemused or enchanted by the efforts on her behalf. Whether you are depends on how much you enjoy the elegant design and ruminative pace of Rohmer's movies. He isn't to everyone's taste. But when you're 79 years old and can still tell well-shaped stories with as much attention to beauty and detail, you've earned the right to make the movies you want. Think of "Autumn Tale" as a leisurely summer afternoon well spent.

SIGHT AND SOUND, 4/99, p. 37, Ginette Vincendeau

The southern Rhône valley, in the autumn. Isabelle, the owner of a bookshop, and her husband are planning the wedding of their daughter Emilia. Isabelle worries about the isolation of her best friend Magali (a widowed wine grower), now that Magali's grown-up children have left home. Rosine, the girlfriend of Magali's son Leo, is also concerned about Magali's loneliness. She plots to introduce Magali to Etienne, Rosine's former philosophy teacher and lover.

Meanwhile, Isabelle secretly writes a lonely-heart advertisement on Magali's behalf. Isabelle meets Gérald through the ad and lets him think she's her friend. After having lunch with him three times, she reveals her deception. At Emile's wedding, Magali is introduced to both Etienne (whom she dislikes) and Gérald (whom she likes). When the lonely-heart scheme is revealed to her, Magali is initially mortified and furious with Isabelle. Nevertheless, she's smitten by Gérald, who is also attracted to her, and she invites him to come and visit her.

The genius of Eric Rohmer has always been to make so much out of so little. Throughout his long and productive career he has worked on what could be described as small canvases, with faithful teams of actors and technicians and meagre budgets, with his production company Les Films du Losange. He shoots on location from his own scripts and eschews mainstream stars. *An Autumn Tale* which completes Rohmer's *Contes des quatres saisons/Tales of the Four Seasons* quartet, is a beautiful, witty and serene film. It also vindicates the aesthetic and production ethos that's guided his career since his beginnings in the new wave.

Despite Rohmer's reputation (especially in the UK) as a cerebral and literary film-maker, his work has a concrete, documentary quality that suggests *cinéma vérité*. The first thing we see in *An Autumn Tale* is a road sign telling us where we are: Saint Paul Trois Chateaux, a small town in the Rhône valley. The glowing autumn light and the old buildings' and narrow streets' warm tones sketch out an idyllic backdrop. Water gurgles from a fountain in the middle of a square, an archetypal motif of Provençal iconography—*Alfresco* lunches are served under rustling trees. Isabelle's house and Magali's kitchen wouldn't be out of place in the pages of lifestyle magazines.

Yet Rohmer's Rhône valley is made up of working—albeit middle-class—people: bookshop keepers, wine growers, salesmen, students, teachers. They love their region and admire its landscape, but they also take stock (as does the camera) of its modernisation. Magali's defence of biological wine growing against intensive farming and her work on the ageing of Rhône wines (based on Rohmer's research in the area) suggest this underlying tension.

This tangible social background serves as the bedrock of the characters' dissection of life and love, in the manner of a French analytical novel. But the film never falls into the talking-heads trap. Encounters in cars, cafés, gardens and restaurants are visually dramatised, allowing the characters' philosophies (the action of the film, as it were) to be expressed dynamically. And this literary emphasis on language, something of a cliché with Rohmer, and the simplicity of the *mise en scène* rest on tight plotting in the tradition of Rohmer's master, Hitchcock.

As with its predecessors in the *Contes des quatre saisons* and the earlier *Comedies and Proverbs, An Autumn Tale* hinges on the plotting of Rosine and Isabelle, both engaged in parallel attempts at matchmaking Magali with a man. If this is reminiscent of Jane Austen's *Emma*, the emphasis on vision, impersonation and misrecognition reinforces the Hitchcock references. Rosine's two photographs of Etienne and Magali are key props. Isabelle and Rosine spot each other with a man across a square, a sighting from which each constructs a fiction about the scenario. And in a moment reminiscent of many other Rohmer films (such as *Pauline a la plage, La Femme de L'aviatieur, Les Nuits de la pleine lune, L'Ami de mon amie*) Magali opens a door on what looks like, but is not, an amorous embrace between Isabelle and Gérald. Misunderstanding will arise from this, though it will be cleared up in the films 'happy end'.

An Autumn Tale is the last in the *Contes des quatre saisons* and the work of a 78-year-old director, so it's tempting to read it as some kind of concluding point and reflection on Rohmer's career. All the more so because Rohmer has said he has no current film project, and because the two leads, Marie Rivière (Isabelle) and Béatrice Romand (Magali) are habituées of his work. Romand appeared notably in *Le Genou de Claire* (1970) and *Le Beau Mariage* (1981), and Rivière in *La Femme de L'aviatieur* (1980) and *LeRayon vert* (1986). More specifically, Rivière in *Le Rayon vert* and Romand in *Le Beau Mariage* are women in search of a man. The time gap between these films and *An Autumn Tale*, however, signals a maturing of perspective matching that of the heroines. Rohmer's cinema has always favoured women. Even in the Morla tales of the 60s and early 70s, structured around a man who hesitates between two women, the main female character (see *Ma nuit chez Maud)* was far more lively and interesting than the man. In the *Comedies and Proverbs* of the 80s and the 90s films, female characters were constructed in a way which allows for the expression of their own desires, sometimes in ways close to obsession.

Rohmer, like Jacques Rivette, is known for involving his actresses in the construction of the story, as well as in their performances. This is unusual enough in French cinema. But Romand and Rivière in *An Autumn Tale* offer something even more unusual: fortysomething women who are both 'good mothers' and sexual beings, who eclipse the women of the younger generation, and whose relationship with each other is at least as important as their relationship to men. Even Rosine says at one point that it's Magali she really "fell in love with" rather than Léo. Indeed, in the uncovering of Isabelle's plot, Magali is more upset about her friend's deception than she is by how it might affect her possible relationship with Gérald.

Rohmer has said recently, "I've never wanted for my films to be great commercial successes, but I still think that art should serve audiences. I therefore try hard each time to give something new to my spectators." A fitting comment on both this film and his career as a whole.

VILLAGE VOICE, 7/13/99, p. 57, J. Hoberman

Will the current craze for filmed Shakespeare and the ongoing one for genteel adaptations of 19th-century novels vault the great miniaturist Eric Rohmer beyond his own long-established niche? Here is an auteur whose movies are as richly verbal as any stage play, as steeped in romantic complication as Edith Wharton, and, albeit less obviously so, as purely cinematic as those of his model, Alfred Hitchcock.

Autumn Tale, the latest and perhaps the last Rohmer opus, is set somewhere in the Rhone valley in the south of France. Summer may be ending, but meals are still taken alfresco and talk of marriage is in the air. The film's opening scene has the fortysomething Isabelle (Marie Rivière) discussing daughter Emilia's wedding, then musing on the lonely situation of her best friend, Magali (Béatrice Romand), a widow with a small vineyard and an empty nest.

Hoping to find the diffident Magali an appropriate suitor, Isabelle, who owns a bookstore in town (proof of her business acumen and romantic imagination), places a discreet personal ad in a local paper. Then, posing as Magali—who, of course, knows nothing of this scheme—Isabelle dates the most promising prospective swain, a *pied-noir* salesman named Gerald (played with smooth eligibility by Alain Libolt), before comically disorienting him with the explanation that she is only a surrogate.

Nor is Isabelle the only one to ponder the seemingly self-sufficient Magali's romantic situation. Adding to the confusion, the precocious student Rosine (Alexia Portal), girlfriend to Magali's son Leo but even more devoted to Magali, is hatching her own plot to fix up the older woman. Even more ambitious than Isabelle, Rosine hopes to kill two birds with a single stone by matching Magali with her own older lover (and former philosophy professor) Etienne and thus force an end to their relationship.

Headstrong and self-possessed, Rosine is full of youthful arrogance, playing at being Jane Austen's Emma even while staging, behind her own back, some sort of oedipal scenario. She's the callowest of the principals—as Rohmer's vineyard metaphor none too subtly suggests, aging is to be desired. As the obscure and unknowing object of desire, Romand—wide-eyed and pouty, with a great corona of frizzy hair—becomes an increasingly interesting character as the action proceeds. Indeed, for those of a certain age, *Autumn Tale* derives considerable subtext from her presence along with Rivière, another Rohmer veteran; both first appeared in his movies when they were gamines.

"What's got into you all?" Magali asks at one point, as well she might. Like any number of previous Rohmer films, *Autumn Tale* is a comedy predicated on two rival strategies. The sullen Leo, who doesn't seem to like his mother much, is appalled by Rosine's "monstrous" attempt to match Magali and Étienne (whom he fails to recognize as a rival). "Kids shouldn't mess in their parents' lives," he explains, to which Rosine responds that Étienne is not her father. This sort of elaborate minor-key argument is the essence of cinema Rohmer.

It is one of the director's paradoxes that, compared to those in most other movies, his "naturalistic" actors give performances that seem as stylized as those found in the silent cinema. Typically sharing the screen with another avid conversationalist (rather than appearing in shot-countershot), Rohmer's creatures express themselves as much by "talking" (and listening) as by what they actually say. Speech has a material character—in addition to constant chatter, the soundtrack is rich with the sound of rustling leaves and barking dogs.

Its season notwithstanding, *Autumn Tale* has more of a summertime indolence than the brisk pace of fall. But if the carefully planted romantic intrigue is serenely slow to ripen, the process is never less than intriguing. Events finally reach fruition at Émilia's wedding. This lengthy set piece is staged with Rohmer's mathematical plot construction and shot with an analytical eye—as well as the droll recognition that anything can happen at the marriage carnival.

Autumn Tale is not one of Rohmer's series of "moral tales," but it does suggest a few pop-song truisms: to wit, "to everything there is a season" because "you can't hurry love." The he-said, she-said shenanigans suggest that high school may be eternal but autumn has its wisdom. In the last scene, the 78-year-old filmmaker brings his favorite conspirator back for a last dance—it's a vintage performance that invites applause.

Also reviewed in:
CHICAGO TRIBUNE, 8/20/99, Friday/p. F, Michael Wilmington
NATION, 8/9 & 16/99, p. 44, Stuart Klawans
NEW REPUBLIC, 8/2/99, p. 30, Stanley Kauffmann
NEW YORK TIMES, 7/9/99, p. E8, Stephen Holden
VARIETY, 9/7-13/98, p. 74, Lisa Nesselson
WASHINGTON POST, 8/13/99, p. C1, Stephen Hunter
WASHINGTON POST, 8/13/99, Weekend/p. 43, Desson Howe

B. MONKEY

A Miramax Films release of a Miramax Films and Scala presentation of a Scala/Synchronistic Pictures/Stephen Woolley production. *Executive Producer:* Nik Powell, Bob Weinstein, and Harvey Weinstein. *Producers:* Stephen Woolley and Colin Vaines. *Director:* Michael Radford. *Screenplay:* Chloe King and Michael Thomas. *Based on the novel by:* Andrew Davies. *Director of Photography:* Ashley Rowe. *Editor:* Joëlle Hache. *Music:* Jennie Muskett. *Music Editor:* Gerard McCann. *Sound:* Peter Lindsay and (music) Geoff Foster. *Sound Editor:* Rodney Glenn. *Casting:* Sharon Howard-Field and Karen Lindsay-Stewart. *Production Designer:* Sophie Becher. *Art Director:* David Hindle. *Costumes:* Valentine Breton Des Loys. *Make-up:* Beverly Pond-Jones. *Stunt Coordinator:* Andreas Petrides. *Running time:* 91 minutes. *MPAA Rating:* R.

CAST: Asia Argento (B. Monkey); Jared Harris (Alan); Rupert Everett (Paul); Jonathan Rhys Meyers (Bruno); Juliet Wallace (Mrs. Sturge); Ian Hart (Steve Davis); Tim Woodward (Frank Rice); Bryan Pringle (Goodchild); Clare Higgins (Cherry); Simone Bowkett (Angie); Michael Fitzgerald (Magnus); Marc Warren (Terence); Camilo Gallardo (Barman, Conrans); Michael Carlin (Carlo); Paul Ireland (Barman, Kings Head); Elisabeth Ash (Nurse); Catherine Carter (Joy); Kate McGeever (Judith); Jason Rose (Rudy); Amanda Boxer (Tory Lady); Vincent Regan (Johnny Hart); Kerry Shale (Texan); Serretta Wilson (Texan Wife); Eddie Marsan (Young Thug); Garry Gatlin (Jim Arkwright); Jason Howard (Ricky Sturge); Tony Cyrus (Algerian Man); Paul Angelis (Gangster); Robin Lermitte (Manager); Dick Brannick (Mr. Gibson).

LOS ANGELES TIMES, 9/10/99, Calendar/p. 4, Kevin Thomas

"B. Monkey" takes its title from the nickname of its heroine, a beautiful, fearless Italian-born jewel thief (Asia Argento) who swoops down on posh London jewelry stores and scoops up the goodies with the greatest of ease. She works with an equally nervy young guy, Bruno (Jonathan

Rhys Meyers), and they in turn work for and live with Paul (Rupert Everett, ever the charming wastrel), an aristocrat who's made a career of supplying drugs to celebrities only to devour his profits, not to mention his inheritance, by becoming his own best customer.

Bruno and Paul are lovers, Paul and B. share a deep platonic love, and all three live in the messy grandeur of Paul's venerable Chelsea apartment. To celebrate Bruno's birthday, they head for a pub, where Paul announces he's throwing Bruno out for stealing. Fireworks ensue, and among the observers in the pub is Alan (Jared Harris), a rangy, attractive grade-school teacher who moonlights as a DJ on a hospital radio station. His sedate life is about to change abruptly, for he is transfixed by the dark beauty and magnetic presence of B. When they cross paths at the pub some months later, Alan, who has never stopped thinking about her, approaches her. As it happens, he connects with her at the very moment that her thrill with living on the edge is beginning to ebb and her survival instincts are telling her she'd better quit while she's ahead.

They click, they take off for a weekend in Paris, and the question quickly becomes: Can a jewel thief settle down and find happiness with a teacher who's great with kids and loves his work? "B. Monkey" sounds like vintage Claude Lelouch, and he might well have made a more convincing movie of Michael Thomas and Chloe King's script from a novel by Andrew Davies than "Il Postino" director Michael Radford has. That's not to say "B. Monkey" isn't fun in its delirious way, but Lelouch has an absolute belief in his material and in the dictates of fate, coupled with an insight into criminal mentality and, when he's in top form, a deftness in playing moments of documentary-like realism against sweeping, swoony romantic flourishes. In short, the veteran French director at his go-for-broke best can be amazingly persuasive in creating a seductive suspension of disbelief, a goal that here tends to elude Radford more often than not.

In the time-honored fashion of movie crooks trying to go straight, B. has a tougher time putting her past behind her than she had imagined. The occasional rush of a heist proves hard to resist, and then there's the tug of her loyal feelings for Paul, who's deeply in debt to East End gangster Frank (Tim Woodward), who also wouldn't mind making use of B.'s formidable skills. As B.'s resolve begins to waver, Alan becomes increasingly determined to take her away from it all, for a rural existence in Yorkshire. Without going into detail, you know very well that's not going to be the end of it.

The chemistry between Argento, who has a stylish presence as compelling as her father Dario Argento's horror pictures, and Harris is instantaneous and palpable. As skilled, resourceful actors, they make B. and Alan a more believable couple than you would have thought possible. If only "B. Monkey," as sleek as it is, were as easy to believe in as its two lovers.

NEW YORK POST, 9/10/99, p. 57, Rod Dreher

When a movie has been sitting on a shelf for years, you have to assume it's so bad its distributors are stalling for time while they figure out how to market the unmarketable.

What a surprise, then, to discover that the long-unreleased "B. Monkey" isn't bad at all.

In fact, this story about a mild-mannered primary schoolteacher (Jared Harris) who falls in love with a punkish bank robber (Asia Argento) is almost good. It's got strong performances, particularly by the ever-fascinating Rupert Everett in a supporting role, and director Michael Radford is accomplished at conjuring a mood of sexy melancholy (the gloomy-gray English clouds hover like a Chet Baker trumpet solo).

Yet that insinuating, sublime atmosphere is consistently being intruded upon by the distractingly silly plot, which isn't credible for a second.

The film's title comes from the nom de crime of Beatrice (Argento), a scrappy Italian "femme Nikita" type known in the London underworld for her burgling skills. She lives with teen gay hustler Bruno (Jonathan Rhys Myers) and Paul (Everett), a decadent aristocrat fashionably decaying from drugs and drink.

One night in a pub, B.'s eyes meet those of Alan (Harris), a lonely teacher who is instantly smitten with her. He's a tender romantic who spins jazz records for sick patients in a hospital.

They begin dating, and good Alan offers B. a way out of the low life. But can the wiry adrenaline junkie really give up the dangerous thrills of street life and her dismal friends?

Argento is jolting as the unstable B., bringing to mind Beatrice Dalle's sex-bomb wacko in "Betty Blue." Harris limns the nuances of his sensitive jazz guy character effectively, but the duo have no chemistry together. And, absent that, it's hard to understand what he sees in her.

The best part of "B. Monkey" is Everett, an actor who seems incapable of an uninteresting performance. His posh Paul character is pure "Brideshead Revisited" stuff, a gripping portrait of burnt-out Sebastian at the end of his life.

Everett gives every scene he's in—and there are too few of them—more dramatic texture and moral weight than anything else in this entertaining but forgettable little film.

VILLAGE VOICE, 9/21/99, p. 170, Michael Radford

Playing the mild, schlumpy schoolteacher who falls for the beautiful, eponymous thief in *B. Monkey*, Jared Harris puts on the self-deprecating air of someone who can never make his words come out quite the way he wants, whose full intelligence and humor is always halted by self-consciousness. None of these nuances exist in the script, which finds Harris chasing his raven-haired fashion plate down a dark, rain-slick London avenue on second sight; rather, Harris devises means for edging around the histrionics of the film, which seems awfully humorless for such a rote retreading of the one-last-fix-and-then-I'm-going-straight hoodlum plot.

In fact, all of the principal players escape unscathed. As B. Monkey herself, or Beatrice as she's known at her desk job, Asia Argento emanates cool, confident sexuality. Rupert Everett portrays an old-money, layabout starfucker whose debts to loan sharks detain his pal Beatrice in her life of crime; as in *An Ideal Husband,* Everett murmurs all his lines with melancholic absentmindedness. On the other end of the spectrum is Jonathan Rhys Meyers, flinging himself headlong into his role as Beatrice's getaway driver and Everett's mercurial boy toy, screaming and thrashing and flapping those lips like *She's the Boss*-era Mick Jagger. Director Michael Radford (*Il Postino*) doesn't give anyone enough to do—Harris broods, Argento pouts, Meyers plays Mr. Furious, Everett smokes an assload of pot—but the cast tries their darndest anyway, even once Beatrice follows her man to the Yorkshire countryside (of course, every time she thinks she's out, they keep pulling her back in); indeed, when Beatrice says, "I couldn't be happier," the movie has finally found a suitable key of bittersweet resignation. *B. Monkey* is crawling with smart actors saying things they don't quite mean, and while that's not enough, it's a good time watching them extricate themselves from one sticky situation after another without tripping any wires. A new conceit: acting as cat burglary.

Also reviewed in:
NEW YORK TIMES, 9/10/99, p. E16, Anita Gates
VARIETY, 9/16-22/98, p. 36, Derek Elley

BABY GENIUSES

A TriStar Pictures release of a Steven Paul/Crystal Sky production. *Executive Producer:* David Saunders. *Producer:* Steven Paul. *Director:* Bob Clark. *Screenplay:* Bob Clark and Greg Michael. *Story:* Steven Paul, Francisca Matos, and Robert Grasmere. *Director of Photography:* Stephen M. Katz. *Editor:* Stan Cole. *Music:* Paul Zaza. *Sound:* Brian Bidder. *Casting:* Dorothy Koster-Paul. *Production Designer:* Francis J. Pezza. *Art Director:* Michael Roth. *Set Designer:* Deren Paul Abram, Martin Roy Marvel, and Ben Ball. *Set Decorator:* Josh Newman and Robert L. Zilliox. *Costumes:* Betty Pecha Madden. *Make-up:* Shauna Giesbrecht. *Stunt Coordinator:* Michael R. Long. *Running time:* 94 minutes. *MPAA Rating:* PG.

CAST: Kathleen Turner (Elena); Christopher Lloyd (Heep); Kim Cattrall (Robin); Peter MacNicol (Dan); Dom DeLuise (Lenny); Ruby Dee (Margo); Kyle Howard (Dickie); Kaye Ballard (Mayor); Leo Fitzgerald (Sly & Whit); Myles Fitzgerald, Gerry Fitzgerald, and Connor Leggett (Sly); Griffin Leggett (Sly & Whit); Megan Robbins and Gabrielle Robbins (Carrie); Breanna McConnell and Brittany McConnell (Lexi); Jacob Daniel Handy and Zackery Handy (Duby); Amanda Fein and Caitlin Fein (Teddie); Jim Hanks (Goon Ray); Sam McMurray (Goon Bob); Bill Wiley (Wino); Randy Travis (Control Room Technician); Judith Drake (911 Lady); Melissa Bickerton (Diaper Cart Nurse); Chip Heller (Baby Bunting); Dan Monahan (Reporter); Robin Klein and Russell Milton (Babyco Executives); Luis Esmenjaud (Santa Claus);

Christopher Broughton (Clown);   Mark Graciale and Thomas Crawford (Hypnotized Guards); Hank Garrett (Guard);   Ariel Clark (Alien);   Allyssa Herrmann (Wendy);   Adam Koster (Male Nurse);   Shepard Koster (Technician);   Daniel Coulter Longcope (Habitat Guard);   Eugene Osment (Cop on Hailer);   Bonnie Paul (Headquarters Nurse);   Randall Hall Senter (Security Guard);   Michael R. Long (Diaper Truck Driver).

LOS ANGELES TIMES, 3/12/99, Calendar/p. 8, John Anderson

[The following review by John Anderson appeared in a slightly different form in **NEWSDAY, 3/12/99, Part II/p. B11.]**

There are several ways to describe "Baby Geniuses," an alleged comedy about alleged babies. One, it's a shameless recycling of "Look Who's Talking." Two, it's a charmless rip-off of "Rugrats." Three, it's a Christmastime movie being opened in March. Be particularly frightened by No. 3.

The premise in this lackluster comedy from Bob Clark—who directed the annual holiday present "A Christmas Story" as well as the celebrated smut-fest "Porky's"—is that "infant pre-language" contains all the secrets of life. Adults need only crack the linguistic code to discover the genetically imprinted wisdom of the ages. But they have to do it quickly: Once babies "cross over" to adult speech, according to the Tibetans—hey, don't the Tibetans have enough problems?—they lose their status as sophisticated savants.

Of course, the movie's idea of a sophisticated savant would be Rodney Dangerfield in a diaper. Wisecracking, pun-hurling enfants obnoxious, the kids engage in exhaustingly trite repartee and are computer-manipulated to the point of demonic possession. If they're more charming than the adults, it is merely a symptom of our child-crazed culture. And that's if it's true at all: With all the groin-injury jokes popping up in "Baby Geniuses," at least half the audience should be predisposed to hate them.

The movie's researchers-in-hot-pursuit are Dr. Elena Kinder (Kathleen Turner), president of the multinational BABYCO and the personification of evil, and her nephew-in-law Dr. Dan Bobbins (Peter MacNicol) who, with his wife Robin (Kim Cattrall), runs a nursery staffed by a couple of old hippies played by Dom DeLuise and Ruby Dee (call your agents).

Dan is close to decoding the baby talk, but what he and Robin don't know is that their adopted son Whit is the twin brother of baby Sly, the centerpiece of Elena's self-aggrandizing study of the infant mind. And when Sly breaks out of stir—throwing kung fu moves on a gang of security goons—hilarity and comical child endangerment are expected to ensue. They don't, largely because the movie seems to have been knocked off between Similacs at the local baby bar.

But the film also has a problem keeping its own premise in order. One gets the feeling sometimes that the babies are speaking regular English when they think no one's watching; Dickie (Kyle Howard), the nursery gofer, eavesdrops on them, but what is he hearing?

Later, during the climactic face-off between Sly and Elena, he speaks out loud to her and she seems to understand. There may have been a plot point I missed en route to the finale that explained all this. But I have to confess to drifting off a bit, daydreaming about the relative golden age of John Hughes' "Baby's Day Out" or the virtual Noel Cowardisms of Bruce Willis in "Look Who's Talking" and wondering if babies can be brought up on charges of adult abuse.

NEW YORK POST, 3/12/99, p. 46, Rod Dreher

The advent of a baby has a way of separating even the crankiest reviewer from his inner Fran Lebowitz. Since my wife and I discovered we were expecting, I have been amazed to find myself stopping on the sidewalk to coo at adorable infants and cute baby clothes. It happens to the worst of us.

So, folks like me are exactly the sort of chronic cooers the film "Baby Geniuses" is aimed at. Aimed like a sawed-off shotgun loaded with double-ought blasts of stupidity, that is.

The movie begins with Sylvester, a crafty 2-year-old, escaping from the high-tech underground lab of Babyco, an evil corporation trying to whelp and nurture a superior breed of young 'un. It's run by Dr. Kinder, a Cruella de Vil-like scientist played by the unfortunate Kathleen Turner, who chews scenery like a great white pie-eyed on fresh chum.

The big idea here is that babies are born knowing all the secrets of the universe, and their goo-goo baby talk is really an ultra-sophisticated language. Hollywood's idea of sophisticated baby repartee involves describing feces as "diaper gravy," and putting the following kiss-off in a tiny mouth:

"Listen, Doc, if you're going to talk out of your a-- all the time, maybe you should wear a bow tie on your butt!" Charming.

Nazoid Dr. Kinder's kind-hearted rival, Dan Bobbins (Peter MacNicol), who runs a comfy orphanage with his wife (Kim Cattrall), is on the verge of decoding the babies' language. But his research is interrupted when fugitive Sylvester inadvertently trades places with Whit, their adopted son and Sly's separated twin (both roles are played by the Fitzgerald triplets). Sylvester organizes the Bobbins brood into a toddler SWAT team that sets out to rescue Whit and bring down Dr. Kinder's evil corporate empire.

"Baby Geniuses" is schmaltzy, ghastly and unendurable—but not entirely without merit. Check out the Bobbins' lovable handyman. It's nice to know there's still work in Hollywood for former sandwich-bag pitchman and Burt Reynolds tummler Dom DeLuise.

Also reviewed in:
CHICAGO TRIBUNE, 3/12/99, p. N, John Petrakis
NEW YORK TIMES, 3/12/99, p. E28, Janet Maslin
VARIETY, 3/8-14/99, p. 59, Lael Loewenstein

BACHELOR, THE

A New Line Cinema release of a Lloyd Segan Company production in association with George Street Pictures. *Executive Producer:* Michael De Luca, Chris O'Donnell, and Donna Langley. *Producer:* Lloyd Segan and Bing Howenstein. *Director:* Gary Sinyor. *Screenplay:* Steve Cohen. *Based on the play "Seven Chances" by:* Roi Cooper Megrue and the *screenplay by:* Clyde Bruckman, Jean Havez and Joseph Mitchell *for the film starring and directed by:* Buster Keaton. *Director of Photography:* Simon Archer. *Editor:* Robert Reitano. *Music:* David A. Hughes and John Murphy. *Music Editor:* J.J. George. *Sound:* Richard Bryce Goodman and (music) Rick Riccio. *Sound Editor:* Nils Jensen, Douglas Jackson, and David Kern. *Casting:* Valerie McCaffrey. *Production Designer:* Craig Stearns. *Art Director:* Randy Moore. *Set Designer:* Eric P. Sundahl and Barbara Mesney. *Set Decorator:* Ellen Totleben. *Set Dresser:* Chris Fielding, Jeff Halvorsen, Karen Weinstock, and Rosemary Tupta. *Special Effects:* David Kelsey. *Costumes:* Terry Dresbach. *Make-up:* Gary Liddiard. *Make-up (Chris O'Donnell):* Leonard Engleman. *Make-up (Renée Zellweger):* Sharon Ilson. *Stunt Coordinator:* Rocky Capella. *Running time:* 90 minutes. *MPAA Rating:* PG-13.

CAST: Chris O'Donnell (Jimmy); Renée Zellweger (Anne); Artie Lange (Marco); Edward Asner (Gluckman); Hal Holbrook (O'Dell); James Cromwell (Priest); Marley Shelton (Natalie); Peter Ustinov (Grandad); Katharine Towne (Monique); Rebecca Cross (Stacey); Stacy Edwards (Zoe); Mariah Carey (Ilana); Sarah Silverman (Carolyn); Jennifer Esposito (Daphne); Brooke Shields (Buckley); Lydell M. Cheshier (Sanzel); Robert Kotecki (Hodgman); Pat Finn (Bolt); Timothy Paul Perez (Stone); Romy Rosemont (Rita); Kelly Jean Peters (Waitress); Jane L. Powell (Straight Room Singer); Jim Jackman (Nervous Guy); Christopher Carroll (Mairte d'); Kevin Jones (Florist); Michael Deeg, Erik Kever Ryle, and Brian Leonard (Customers); Mary J. White (Florist Assistant); Edith Fields (Edith); Joe Meek and Michael Lee Merrins (Traders); Lisa Nalen ("Anne" on the Street); Brantley Bush (Stagehand); Nichols Pryor (Dale); Maree Cheatham (Mona); Mark Norby (Suspect); Ken Baldwin and Gustavo Vargas (Salsa Dancers); Natalie Bartlett (O'Dell's Daughter); Cheri Rae Russell (Biker Bride); Jodi Taylor (Older Bride); Jenni Pulos (Big Hair Bride); Rebecca Gray and Kiva Dawson (Punk Brides); Anastasia Horne (Preppy Bride); Niecy Nash (African-American Bride); T.L. Brooke (Big Bride); Marnie Alexenberg (Brunette Bride); Lea Moon Llovio (Latina Bride); Robin Lyon, Elizabeth Guber, and Nancy O'Dell (Questioning Brides); Marnie Schneider (Muslim Bride); Louis Ganapoler (Baker).

LOS ANGELES TIMES, 11/5/99, Calendar/p. 12, Eric Harrison

For the first 60 seconds or so, "The Bachelor" comports itself like a movie with quirky yet real potential. A herd of wild horses stampedes across sun-blasted plains, while David Byrne bleats out the words to "Don't Fence Me In" on the soundtrack. In voice-over, Chris O'Donnell testifies to this truth: Men treasure freedom, he tells us. "In his heart, every man is a wild, untamed mustang."

It's a fleet-footed start for a flat-footed film. The movie could go anywhere from here but chooses to take us to a parallel world—or at least it might as well be for all the similarity it bears to life as we know it. The city announces itself as San Francisco, but it is San Francisco as imagined by Ozzie and Harriet Nelson. Folks are neighborly. The sun is always shining. And streets are free of traffic until the plot calls for a car.

O'Donnell plays Jimmy Shannon, a clean-cut guy's guy who stands to inherit $100 million, but only if he gets married by 6:05 p.m. on his 30th birthday. Unfortunately, his birthday is tomorrow, and he's already proposed and been turned down by his girlfriend Anne (Renee Zellweger). She could tell he didn't really want to get married. The tip-off was the way he sat the ring on the table and said, "You win."

Now Jimmy is eager to get hitched, money his incentive. Thinking that Anne is out of the country, he sets out on a mission to find a bride.

The movie is an update of a 1925 Buster Keaton film, "Seven Chances." Three-quarters of a century ago, no doubt, there was humor in seeing a man flee a thousand brides. In 1999, our responses are a bit more complicated. No matter how lightweight the movie, we wonder why these women are so desperate to wed a stranger. It can't just be that they live in San Francisco. And we're a bit uneasy at the way the movie makes fun of them.

Because his friend (Artie Lange) runs a newspaper ad, Jimmy goes from being a man who can't get any of his ex-girlfriends to marry him to the city's most eligible bachelor. Through it all, though, he comes to realize that it's Anne he really wants. Guess who he winds up with at the end?

This is meant to be a romantic comedy told from the guy's perspective, so Jimmy is surrounded by male friends and advisors, all with their own views on marriage. In addition to the obnoxious, loudmouthed Lange, they include Edward Asner and Hal Holbrook as the family attorney and stockbroker, who seem to have nothing better to do than hang out with Jimmy. These actors all emote too much, playing their characters as broadly as possible. When they are on screen, the movie feels like a bad TV sitcom.

At other times, but never for very long, it's reminiscent of more gentle (and far better) comedies like "When Harry Met Sally." It never comes close to working at that level, though, in part because we never understand the main characters' attraction for each other.

In voice-over, Jimmy tells us in the beginning that he likes Anne because she's not clingy. But then the movie is so eager to get to the big dilemma that it rushes through the evolution of their relationship. O'Donnell and Zellweger are easy on the eyes, but we're asked to take it on faith that they have other qualities that would make a person care for them. The movie never shows what those qualities might be. And not long after those first 60 seconds, we stop even wondering.

NEW YORK POST, 11/5/99, p. 61, Lou Lumenick

"The Bachelor," the latest and most unfortunate manifestation of Hollywood's millennial obsession with weddings, is so unremittingly vulgar and inept it makes "The Best Man" and "Runaway Bride" look like masterpieces by comparison.

This update of Buster Keaton's 1925 "Seven Chances" focuses on the frantic matrimonial efforts of Jimmie Shannon (Chris O'Donnell), a pool-table-company heir whose grandfather's will leaves him $100 million—but only if he gets married by 6:05 p.m. the next day, his 30th birthday.

Keaton's film isn't remembered for this creaky plot gimmick but for one of the greatest sight gags in movie history—the Great Stone Face being pursued by 1,000 would-be brides in gowns after a pal tips off a newspaper to his plight.

Three-quarters of a century later, the sight of O'Donnell being chased by throngs of women through San Francisco is still good for a chuckle. But almost nothing else here works.

There's an utter lack of chemistry between O'Donnell and his long-suffering girlfriend (an annoyingly twitchy Renee Zellweger). When she turns down his insulting marriage proposal ("You win," he tells her), Jimmy approaches (and is turned down by) a series of ever-more - hideously caricatured ex-girlfriends, including a feminist who dismisses his proffered roses as "symbolic vaginas."

That not-great gag is repeated at least twice, along with every other joke in the movie— especially references to wild mustangs made by Jimmy, whose commitment problems are conveniently solved by a priest (James Cromwell) recruited to perform the quickie wedding.

Director Gary Sinyor drags out every scene and encourages all hands—including such pros as Peter Ustinov (sporting a horrible Southern accent), Ed Asner and Hal Holbrook—to overact with abandon.

The most excruciating moments in "The Bachelor" belong to Brooke Shields, transcendently awful as a financially distressed socialite who contemplates marrying Jimmy for money. She's lit, photographed and costumed so badly that she—along with Mariah Carey, who turns up briefly as an opera singer—bears an unfortunate resemblance to a drag queen.

NEWSDAY, 11/5/99, Part II/p. B6, Gene Seymour

Just this minute, I remembered what "The Bachelor" reminded me of. And no, it's not the Buster Keaton silent comedy "Seven Chances," which did, in fact, inspire Steve Cohen's script. I was thinking more of a Three Stooges short from the late 1940s in which Shemp (aka "the noir stooge") had only seven hours to find someone to marry or lose a half-million-dollar inheritance.

Fifty years inflates things. In this movie, it's more like $100 million left to a billiard-table manufacturer from San Francisco named Jimmie Shannon (Chris O'Donnell) by his unpleasantly eccentric grandfather (Peter Ustinov). The catch: Jimmie has until nightfall of his 30th birthday to tie the knot or he doesn't see a proverbial red cent. And his birthday is the following day.

Jimmie, who's allergic to the notion of romantic commitment, has just blown his second attempt at proposing marriage to Anne (Renee Zellweger), a sweet, no-nonsense photographer. She leaves the Bay Area just when Jimmie realizes that losing the money means losing his company.

So with help—loosely speaking—from his best friend, Marco (Artie Lange), his lawyer (Ed Asner) and his broker (Hal Holbrook), Jimmie scrambles through his myriad ex-girlfriends to find a bride, any bride. This motley group includes an opera singer (Mariah Carey), a cop (Jennifer Esposito), a cold-blooded rich witch (Brooke Shields) and a host of others who for various reasons disqualify themselves from certain wealth. Eventually, the whole city of San Francisco finds out about Jimmie's impending legacy and soon every hilly street is overrun by women-in-white in pursuit.

One would have hoped that director Gary Sniyor, whose facility with knockabout farce was demonstrated in "Leon the Pig Farmer" and "Stiff Upper Lips," would have tapped "The Bachelor's" potential for antic mayhem. Instead, the thing plods like a hopeless, awkward suitor up until the climactic chase scene, which comes across as overblown. Also—and this is crucial—none of the guys in this movie (except for Holbrook in a couple of dotty moments) is as funny as Larry, Moe or Shemp.

But there's one thing the Stooges didn't have and that's Zellweger, who for once gets to play a light-comic role and brings enough emotional range and spirited intelligence to the project without weighing things down. Jimmie isn't worthy of Anne and "The Bachelor" isn't worthy of Zellweger.

SIGHT AND SOUND, 4/00, p. 41, Danny Leigh

San Francisco, the present. Bachelor Jimmy Shannon cherishes his girlfriend Anne, but remains terrified of marriage. Visiting his grandfather whose business he runs, Jimmy is instructed to wed as a matter of urgency. Reluctantly, he proposes to Anne. However, his wording is so inept she dumps him. Jimmy's grandfather dies: the will bequeaths $100 million and control of the company to Jimmy on condition he marries before his thirtieth birthday—which will be 6:05pm the following day. With a priest in tow, Jimmy again proposes to Anne. Unaware of his grandfather's will, she refuses and leaves town. Jimmy embarks on a manic nocturnal mission to find a bride, approaching all his ex-girlfriends. By morning, each has rejected him.

Jimmy's friend Marco guarantees him a wife, and disappears. In the meantime, the priest convinces Jimmy to wed Anne. Jimmy enters the church, where he is besieged by the city's single women; Marco got the story of Jimmy's inheritance on to the front page of the local newspaper. Jimmy learns Anne is back in town. Fleeing the church, he tells her about the will and convinces her he is ready to commit. The pair are separated as Jimmy is pursued through the city by a mob of women, but in the nick of time Jimmy and Anne wed at exactly 6:05pm.

Besides its appeal (or otherwise) as a generic romantic comedy, *The Bachelor* holds a particular interest for those who cherish Buster Keaton since it is (at least ostensibly) a remake of the great man's *Seven Chances* (1925). It may be worth noting, however, that the resemblance is entirely fleeting. Once the premise of a confirmed singleton needing to marry fast to inherit millions has been appropriated, *The Bachelor* only invokes the spirit of its source material for its climactic chase sequence.

Needless to say, this is the best moment *The Bachelor* has to offer. *Seven Chances* is, after all, a masterclass in the on-screen hunt (with almost half its running time devoted to Keaton's blank-faced flight), and—even stripped of Keaton's cascading boulders—the spectacle of a thousand angry brides in vexed pursuit of their prey, wedding dresses careening in the wind, remains astoundingly funny. In the workmanlike context of its surroundings here, the effect is rather like seeing a band struggle through a set of lacklustre originals, only to raise the roof with a timeless cover as their closing number.

Equally, you can't help feeling the chase is something of a high point for director Gary Sinyor himself, whose inspired debut *Leon the Pig Farmer* (and subsequent hit-and miss CV) demonstrated his strengths lie firmly in the deadpan. Time and again, Sinyor seems happiest when dabbling in impassive, Keatonesque absurdity. There's a similar glee in Jimmy's first proposal to his girlfriend Anne at San Francisco's famously romantic Starlight Rooms, accompanied by countless identical males going through exactly the same ritual at exactly the same time, right down to the synchronous popping of questions and champagne corks at every table.

It's only when he has to deal with the formulaic stodge between the set-pieces that Sinyor and *The Bachelor* come unstuck. For a start, the film never reveals exactly what it is Jimmy and Anne see in one another. She begins proceedings as an independent minded match for her capricious beau, only to dissolve into the kind of woman who literally sits by the phone waiting for him to call. Jimmy, meanwhile, veers between egotistical corporate goon and selfless philanthropist with disconcerting regularity.

That said, the situation isn't helped by the leads' performances. Renée Zellweger (Anne) appears to be acting from the nose, wrinkling it one way to denote pleasure, another to indicate melancholy; Chris O'Donnell (Jimmy) finds himself in the unenviable position of inviting comparison with his predecessor and, whatever else he may be, he's no Buster Keaton. The result, intermittently cute though it may be, ultimately fails to rise above the level of innocuous fodder (albeit with an exceptional pedigree).

Also reviewed in:
CHICAGO TRIBUNE, 11/5/99, Friday/p. A, Mark Caro
NEW YORK TIMES, 11/5/99, p. E28, Stephen Holden
VARIETY, 11/8-14/99, p. 37, Todd McCarthy
WASHINGTON POST, 11/5/99, Weekend/p. 49, Desson Howe

BANDITS

A Stratosphere Entertainment release in association with Bavaria Film International of an Olga Film production in co-production with Vela X in association with ProSieben and Flach Film/Jean-François Lepetit. *Producer:* Harry Kügler, Molly von Fürstenberg, and Elvira Senft. *Director:* Katja von Garnier. *Screenplay (German with English subtitles):* Uwe Wilhelm and Katja von Garnier. *Based on an idea by:* Ben Taylor and Katja von Garnier. *Director of Photography:* Torsten Breuer. *Editor:* Hans Funck. *Music:* Bandits. *Sound:* Michael Hinreier. *Casting:* Sabine Schroth. *Production Designer:* Susann Bieling. *Costumes:* Claudia Bobsin. *Running time:* 109 minutes. *MPAA Rating:* R.

CAST: Katja Riemann (Emma); Jasmin Tabatabai (Luna); Nicolette Krebitz (Angel); Jutta Hoffmann (Marie); Hannes Jaenicke (Schwartz); Werner Schreyer (West); Peter Sattman (Gold); Andrea Sawatski (Ludwig); Oliver Hasenfratz (Schneider); Barbara Ahren (Roth).

LOS ANGELES TIMES, 10/1/99, Kevin Thomas

The spirit of "Thelma & Louise" hovers over the rock'n'roll adventure "Bandits." Dynamic German director Katja von Garnier has made a movie that's as fun and exuberant as the best Hollywood entertainments yet has still come up with an emotion-charged tale that's also an edgy commentary on women's destinies and how they're still so largely affected by men.

In her Oscar-winning student film "Making Up!" (1993), Von Garnier showed that she was a sharp, stylish observer of the challenge modern women face in squaring away their longing for freedom and independence with their attraction to the opposite sex and in their longing for love—concerns that very much underlie the go-for-broke "Bandits."

Katja Riemann, a major German star of beauty and versatility who appeared in "Making Up!," plays Emma, one of four inmates in a women's prison who form a scorching rock band. When they escape they more than live up to the name they've given their group, Bandits, who become folk heroes as they elude the police while their clandestine recordings zoom to the top of the charts. There's a strong element of action-comedy fantasy in their escapades, but Von Garnier is adept at playing against her escapees-on-the-run plot with strong characterizations of a group of highly diverse women who we come to feel have been more sinned against than sinning.

So convinced is Emma, who claims she killed her brutal lover in self-defense, that she will win an appeal that in prison she remains uptight and withdrawn. When she loses it, Emma reveals what a sensational drummer she is, joining forces with the gifted but hot-tempered and headstrong singer-guitarist Luna (Jasmin Tabatabai), the pretty guitarist Angel (Nicolette Krebitz) and the older, vulnerable Marie (Jutta Hoffinann), their keyboardist. Von Garnier has given her actresses plenty to work with and inspires them to pull out all the stops, Barbara Stanwyck-style, but without going over the top.

The Bandits captivate us—both as individual women and as musicians; in fact the super-charged songs, most of which are sung in English, by the way, were written by Krebitz and Tabatabai. There's a good mix of humor and pathos in this most vital and passionate of movies, and Von Garnier, working with a crackerjack cameraman, Torsten Breuer, brings it an unflagging panache and scope.

NEW YORK POST, 9/24/99, p. 51, Lou Lumenick

"Bandits" is basically a feature-length rock video from Germany with appealing performers, decently written characters, a killer score, and an interesting premise.

It never bores, even when it turns into a mishmash of melodrama, farce and frantically edited musical numbers. The film's breakdown is a pity, because director Katja von Garnier etches her protagonists well in the opening scenes.

They're four hard-bitten, mad-at-the-world female criminals in jail who yearn for freedom while wrapping airline utensils in plastic. They reluctantly bond together as a prison band called Bandits.

They get their break—in more ways than one—when a liberal cop invites them to be the featured attraction at a policeman's ball.

Luna (Jasmin Tabatabai), the most psychotic of the quartet, blows her stack at a crude proposition from a guard accompanying them to the ball, triggering a brutal assault and their escape.

The Bandits follow up their jailbreak with a TV interview—prompting a record company to dig up a previously rejected demo tape by the group and promote it to take advantage of the publicity windfall. Before long, the Bandits are national celebrities—and public enemies Nos. 1 through 4.

While the girls know they should lie low until their planned departure for Guyana, they just can't resist the limelight—and the repeated opportunities it offers to mock the authorities by turning up before an adoring public.

Tabatai, who also wrote the songs, is a powerful presence as the short-fused Luna, as is Katja Riemann as Emma, a grave-looking redhead doing time for murdering her abusive boyfriend. The quartet is rounded out by Marie (Jutta Hoffman), affecting as an older woman who poisoned her lover, and Angel (Nicolette Krebitz), a sex-kittenish bank robber. All do their own singing on the soundtrack.

The film's male characters are buffoons or worse who seem to have wandered in from a completely different movie. Hannes Janenicke is particularly annoying as the bumbling police inspector on the Bandits' trail, and Werner Schreyer is little more than eye candy as their not-so-reluctant American hostage.

"Bandits" is ultimately exasperating, but von Garnier is a director to watch.

NEWSDAY, 9/24/99, Part II/p. B9, Jan Stuart

And now, for the I-know-I've-seen-this-somewhere-before-but-I-can't-quite-put-my-finger-on-it moment of the week.

It's been a stressful couple of days for the escaped convicts. They've managed to elude the cops time and again (movie cops are dumb). They've switched vehicles, taken a hostage, donned wigs and sunglasses (movie cops are blind).

The longer they stay on the lam, the more the public adores them (movie publics are suckers). Taking five from the chase to smoke a cigarette, they daydream about drinking cocktails on a sandy beach after they hop the boat to South America.

Do they get to South America? Lips are sealed. What matters here is that the convicts are women and that they've got a hit CD. The Spice Girls Escape From Alcatraz? The German-imported "Bandits" is better than that. A popular success in Europe where the sound-track album went through the roof, Katja von Garnier's engaging cat-and-mouse drama reinvigorates the women-behind-bars cliches for the MTV generation.

The Bandits' lead singer is Luna (Jasmin Tabatabai). The drummer is Emma (Katja Riemann). The guitarists are Angel (Nicolette Krebitz) and Marie (Jutta Hoffmann). The four women meet in prison, where they are doing time for a gamut of crimes from bigamy to armed robbery. When a gig at a policemen's ball offers an opportunity for a spontaneous breakout, they flee into the clamoring arms of the media and the recording industry. Contracts are signed. News exclusives are televised. Fame happens.

Those of us not accustomed to breaking out of prison every day might foolishly think that anonymity was the name of the game, but not the Bandits. If there is a stage, they're on it. If there isn't, they invent one. For all the grit and debasement of the early prison scenes, it soon becomes clear that this is a wish fulfillment fantasy. Stylishly synthesizing the female-bonding esprit of "Thelma and Louise" with the thumb-nosing cheek of "Pump Up the Volume," "Bandits" appeals to the rebel spirit in us.

The songs, a mixture of folky ballad and hard-driving rock that is well-performed in English, are captured with a flashfire cross-cutting of performance shots and fantasy imagery that has become de rigueur in this age of the music video. Director von Garnier's kinetic approach seems fresher in the nonmusical sequences, when it breathes life into the more pedestrian turns of the story.

As with the Spice Girls, everyone will have a favorite Bandit. Mine is Emma, thanks to the surly, intellectual intensity of Riemann. None of the actresses, however, ever for a moment convinces you that these gals are really from the wrong side of the tracks.

When they take a cigarette break to daydream about the beaches of South America, you can't help but feel they'll be flying there in the first class cabins of Lufthansa.

VILLAGE VOICE, 9/28/99, p. 128, Jessica Winter

If *Dog Park* (see Winter's review) is a series of moments that don't quite add up to a movie, then the German release *Bandits*—a confusingly edited music-video hodgepodge concerning a gang of female convicts who form a rock band in jail and later break out, driving across country while their demo tape becomes a radio sensation—is a movie embodying a single, indelible moment. Think of that scene from *Light of Day* that VH-1 uses to promote *Rock 'n' Roll Picture Show*, the one where Joan Jett turns to Michael J. Fox, her lips jutting and sneering, and intones, "Music is all that matters." Mike stares at her quizzically, shaking his Flock of Seagulls mane but still willing to Believe. Rest assured that the runaways in *Bandits* retain a firm hold on their faith, as well as—it would seem—a prison hairdresser (perhaps the stylist employed in *Brokedown Palace*) and a wardrobe consultant once they hit the road. Joan Jett wouldn't have had to tell these girls anything, but she might have hit them up for some cash.

Also reviewed in:
CHICAGO TRIBUNE, 11/5/99, Friday/p. B, John Petrakis
NEW YORK TIMES, 9/24/99, p. E18, Lawrence Van Gelder
VARIETY, 10/13-19/97, p. 100, Derek Elley

BATS

A Destination Films release. *Executive Producer:* Steve Stabler, Brent Baum, John Logan, and Dale Pollock. *Producer:* Brad Jenkel and Louise Rosner. *Director:* Louis Morneau. *Screenplay:* John Logan. *Director of Photography:* George Mooradian. *Editor:* Glenn Garland. *Music:* Graeme Revell. *Music Editor:* Ashley Revell. *Sound:* Stephen A. Tibbo and (music) Mark Curry. *Sound Editor:* Andrew DeCristofaro. *Casting:* Laura Schiff. *Production Designer:* Philip J.C. Duffin. *Set Decorator:* Cynthia Epping. *Special Effects:* Eric Allard. *Costumes:* Alexis Scott. *Make-up:* Gina Homan. *Stunt Coordinator:* Kurt Bryant. *Running time:* 91 minutes. *MPAA Rating:* PG-13.

CAST: Lou Diamond Phillips (Emmett Kimsey); Dina Meyer (Dr. Sheila Casper); Leon (Jimmy Sands); Carlos Jacott (Dr. Tobe Hodge); Bob Gunton (Dr. Alexander McCabe); David Shawn McConnell (Deputy Munn); Marcia Dangerfield (Mayor Branson); Oscar Rowland (Dr. Swanbeck); Tim Whitaker (Quint); Juliana Johnson (Emma); James Sie (Sergeant James); Ned Bellamy (Major Reid); George Gerdes (Cheswick); Kurt Woodruff (Second Major); Joel Farar (Bartender).

LOS ANGELES TIMES, 10/22/99, Calendar/p. 18, Kevin Thomas

[*The following review by Kevin Thomas appeared in a slightly different form in*
NEWSDAY, 10/22/99, Part II/p. B17.]

"Bats" is an ecological disaster movie so formulaic that there's scarcely an ounce of life in it. A wildlife zoologist (Dina Meyer), her assistant (Leon) and local sheriff (Lou Diamond Phillips) wind up single-handedly having to combat an attack upon a small Texas town by genetically altered, virus-infected Indonesian bats, ominously referred to as "flying foxes."

It's an instance of Gallup, Texas, today, tomorrow the world on the part of the killer bats, which have been lethally modified by a local scientist (Bob Gunton). It doesn't come as a complete shock that Gunton is in the employ of the U.S. government or that when the military does show up, they're such idiots that they increase the danger posed by the bats infinitely rather than combat it. In short, it looks like the bad, old military-government complex is at it again.

Still, John Logan's script is nothing if not efficient, and it allows director Louis Morneau to bring it to the screen with bravura dispatch—furious whooshes of the camera and virtuoso editing do a terrific job of creating the impression of massive, repeated assaults by these outsize, demonic-looking creatures. (Those whooshes help offset the fact that the bats are so large and evil-looking as to be laughable when the camera lights upon them for more than an instant.)

Unfortunately, this frenetic effect is showy rather than scary, and Logan does the film no favors by allowing us to wonder why the clearly crazed scientist is not swiftly placed under some kind of custody by the sheriff. You guessed it: Once he has the opportunity, as he tags along with the trio on its final showdown with the bats, he's going to do something loony and lethal.

Phillips brings to the picture a welcome solid presence and Leon some equally appreciated comic relief. But the admirably game but exceedingly earnest Meyer is stuck with playing a huffy, righteously indignant type who becomes rapidly tedious and doesn't display enough personality to overcome such a hapless role.

"Bats" is one of those films of which it can be said that it's all up there on the screen; you have the feeling that every cent of a modest budget has been spent to make the picture look as big and impressive as possible. The trouble is that "Bats" is so uninvolving it scarcely matters what it looks like.

NEW YORK POST, 10/22/99, p. 57, Lou Lumenick

"Bats" sucks. And I don't mean blood. Not especially scary or funny, this lame comedy-thriller wastes a decent cast in a plodding tale about giant, genetically engineered bats that wreak havoc on a small Texas town.

Dina Meyer ("Dragonheart") plays Dr. Shiela Caspar, a zoologist brought in to help by the Centers for Disease Control when a specially bred pair of Indonesia flying fox bats escape. They've begun leading the local bats in attacks on humans.

"This sort of thing is not supposed to happen," she says, examining the corpse of a dead teenager.

"It's a damned shame," says sheriff Kimsey (Lou Diamond Phillips). "What we need to do is avoid any sort of panic."

It turns out the killer bats were a Department of Defense project.

"Now, why would you do that?" Dr. Caspar asks a government researcher, played with eyeball-rolling glee by Bob Gunton.

"Because I'm a scientist," he replies. "We try to make everything better!"

"Bats" tries to combine the laughs of, say, "Gremlins" (the critters tend toward the anthropomorphic, and Leon, as Dr. Caspar's assistant, desperately tries to provide comic relief) and the suspense of "The Birds"—but director Louis Morneau's efforts fall flat.

He isn't helped by laughable special effects, sloppy editing or by a wildly illogical script that merely recites horror-movie cliches.

When the Army proposes bombing the bats from the air, our heroes race to freeze the bats instead—and then seal the entrance to the mine where the winged critters have gathered.

"Bats" is the kind of movie in which you have plenty of time to wonder why they don't simply seal the entrance. But that would eliminate a sequence that mires Dr. Caspar and the sheriff shoulder-deep in bat guano—which is pretty much how the audience may feel by then.

SIGHT AND SOUND, 8/00, Kim Newman

Gallup, Texas, the present. A young couple are killed by a swarm of bats. Dr Tobe Hodge of the Center for Disease Control puts together a bat-fighting team comprising expert Dr Sheila Casper and her assistant Jimmy, military researcher Dr Alexander McCabe and Gallup's sheriff Emmett Kimsey. McCabe reveals that he has experimented with a pair of Asian flying foxes. Having escaped from his laboratory, these foxes are infecting other bats with a viral agent that makes them intelligent and vicious.

After Sheila and Kimsey survive an encounter with the bats, Jimmy works out that the new species could overrun the world. The bats mount a mass attack on the town, during which Hodge is killed. The military considers carpet-bombing the county, although Sheila believes this will be useless. She is given a short amount of time to put into action her own plan, which involves locating the bats' lair and using a freezing device to force them into hibernation. The bats attack again. The pair of flying foxes that infected the other bats kill McCabe, but not before the scientist has admitted he deliberately let them loose from his laboratory. The military bungle an attempt to deploy the freezing device in the bats' lair, an abandoned mine. Though an air strike is imminent, Sheila and Kimsey venture into the mine, turn on the freezer, kill one of the flying foxes and seal the lair. The bombing is called off, but the surviving flying fox makes it to the surface only to be run over by the departing bat-fighters.

The Southwestern United States was last threatened by bats in *Nightwing* (1979), a minor revolt-of-nature horror movie adapted from a novel by Martin Cruz Smith. The model for this lively film, though, would seem to be Joe Dante's *Piranha* (1978), in which ravaging monsters were blamed on a military programme designed to mutate vermin into "perfect killing machines". Like the recent killer crocodile film *Lake Placid, Bats* sticks to the ground rules of its genre—the opening sequence has a pair of young lovers torn apart by creatures that dart out of the sky—and gets through a story at once predictable and preposterous with an ingratiating absence of pretension.

Lacking the knowing edge which made *Piranah* and *Lake Placid* such enjoyable crossover successes, *Bats* will probably play best to horror devotees. A little-known cast cope with sketchy roles to the best of their ability. As star scientist Sheila, Dina Meyer has a well crafted speech about how she overcame her childhood fear of bats by becoming an expert on the species. Lou Diamond Phillips is relaxed as a Texan lawman whose darkest secret is that he's a covert opera buff (he plays *Lucia di Lammermoor*—presumably there wasn't a copy of *Die Fledermaus* to hand—while the library is being equipped with an electric fence). Revitalising that stock horror cliché, the figure of the mad scientist, Bob Gunton lurks nicely—feigning guilt at first, then becoming increasingly strange in a role that brings to mind the villainous character Bela Lugosi played in *The Devil Bat* (1941) who created an enlarged bat trained to kill when exposed to a particular scent.

Director Louis Morneau has a track record in ambitious titles, notably his time-travel thriller *Retroactive,* that have gone straight to video in the UK. Given a modest budgetary leg up, he makes good use of his desert locations, flashes of distorted bat point of view vision and tricksy editing devices that compensate for the sometimes creaky special effects. The bat attacks are mostly satisfactory: Sheila is at one point trapped in the ticket booth of a movie theatre (just as Tippi Hedren is confined to a phone booth in *The Birds,* 1963). *Bats* also recalls *Gremlins*—where a small town was attacked by similarly deadly furry creatures—during the scenes where Gallup's complacent residents discover their cherished guns are of little use to them when the bats descend. After a decade awash with CGI monsters, the rubbery look of the special effects that went into creating the lead bats almost gives rise to a twinge of nostalgia. Unfortunately, the bats don't quite deliver the fearsome charge the script requires of them, which means that subplots involving perilous mines and an imminent air strike are needed to heighten the tension. Full marks, though, for the film's closing moments which see the literal squashing of that horror cliché—the appearance of a lone striving monster intent on launching one final shock attack—under the wheels of a departing vehicle.

Also reviewed in:
CHICAGO TRIBUNE, 10/22/99, Friday/p. M, John Petrakis
NEW YORK TIMES, 10/22/99, p. E28, Lawrence Van Gelder
VARIETY, 10/25-31/99, p. 38, Joe Leydon

BEDROOMS AND HALLWAYS

A First Run Features release of a Pandora Cinema presentation in association with ARP/Pandora Film/BBC Films of a Berwin and Dempsey production. *Director:* Rose Troche. *Screenwriter:* Robert Farrar. *Director of Photography:* Ashley Rowe. *Editor:* Chris Blunden. *Music:* Alfredo

D. Troche and Ian MacPherson. *Sound:* Ian Voigt and (music) Cameron McBride. *Sound Editor:* Colin Chapman. *Casting:* Gail Stevens. *Production Designer:* Richard Bridgland. *Art Director:* Steve Carter. *Set Decorator:* Penny Crawford. *Costumes:* Annie Symons. *Make-up:* Annie Buchanan. *Running time:* 96 minutes. *MPAA Rating:* Not Rated.

CAST: Kevin McKidd (Leo); Hugo Weaving (Jeremy); Jennifer Ehle (Sally); Simon Callow (Keith); Harriet Walter (Sybil); Tom Hollander (Darren); Julie Graham (Angie); Christopher Fulford (Adam); James Purefoy (Brendan); Paul Higgins (John); Con O'Neill; (Terry); Merelina Kendall (Lady Homeowner 1); Victoria Williams (Lady Homeowner 2); Simon Green (Gentleman Homeowner 2); Nicola McAuliffe (Lady Homeowner 3); Rowland Ogden (Gentleman Homeowner 3); Jane Garioni and Joe Geary (Estate Agents); Sophie Ashton and Staley Ashton (Homeowner 2's Children); Paul Augarde and Joe Geary ('Jane Austen' Scene Movers); Bruce Wang (Chinese Takeaway Waiter); Max Keene (Burglar); Robert Farrar (Man at Bus Stop); Gavin Hale and Tatiana Hale (Couple in Park).

LOS ANGELES TIMES, 11/4/99, Calendar/p. 19, Kevin Thomas

Rose Troche, whose "Go Fish" five years ago was a breakthrough lesbian romantic comedy, returns with "Bedrooms & Hallways," which was shown at Outfest '99. It's a jaunty British romantic comedy written by Robert Farrar and starring Kevin McKidd and James Purefroy as a gay man and a straight man discovering sexual fluidity as they become involved not only with each other but also, unwittingly, the same woman (Jennifer Ehle). There's also an amusing spoof of the men's self-esteem movement embodied by Simon Callow's unctuous New Age guru.

NEW YORK POST, 9/3/99, p. 50, Rod Dreher

The splashy, effervescent sex comedy "Bedrooms & Hallways" offers so much fizzy fun, you almost—but not quite—forget how shallow and unsatisfying the screenplay is, even by the undemanding standards of the genre.

"Friends" meets early Almodovar in this London-set romp, directed with great flair by Brooklyn filmmaker Rose Troche ("Go Fish").

She's got an irresistible style, a jaunty cast and interior production design (by Richard Bridgland) so lush it suggests a spin-off subgenre: home-decor porn. Swell packaging indeed for Robert Farrar's subpar script.

Leo (Kevin McKidd) is gay and single, and dreading turning 30 because he doesn't have a boyfriend. His arch, mincing flatmate, Darren (Tom Hollander), thinks Leo should forget true love and concentrate on good sex.

Darren certainly does, meeting his real-estate-agent lover (Hugo Weaving) in various houses for kinky assignations. Eager to be comforted, Leo is talked into joining a heterosexual men's encounter group, headed by Keith (Simon Callow).

The movie pokes gentle fun at the group's New Age touchy-feeliness, but things turn more serious when Leo, encouraged to be honest, tells the circle he's turned on by Brendan (James Purefoy).

Brendan is the group's tall, dark and handsome Irishman, and he's straight as a board. But he's just coming out of a bad breakup, and Leo's confession makes him curious.

Soon enough, they're a twosome. Leo, though, can't shake the fear that he's losing his heart to an essentially straight man who will abandon him.

Further complicating matters, Leo discovers that Brendan's ex is Sally (Jennifer Ehle), who was Leo's teenage flame before he burst out of the closet. Surprising himself, Leo finds he still has feelings for her, prompting disapproving Darren to squeal, "If he wants to be heterosexual, fine; just don't drag me into it."

"Bedrooms & Hallways" has all the ingredients for a hysterical farce, but the screenplay is too flat-footed and conventional, despite its icky polymorphous perversity, to keep up with the buoyant cast and Troche's deft visuals.

You don't go to slight, silly movies like this looking for deep insight into human relations, but there's less here than meets the eye.

Last week's "The Very Thought of You" is a similarly plotted (and similarly frothy) comedy of manners, but it boasts pluckier writing and livelier characters. And the liveliest character in both movies is played by exciting newcomer Tom Hollander.

He's a scream as the randy record exec in "Very Thought," and his puckish take on slutty sprite Darren in "Bedrooms & Hallways" is the best thing in a fresh, funky but ultimately underwhelming movie.

SIGHT AND SOUND, 5/99, p. 38, Liese Spencer

London, the present. At his birthday party, Leo remembers the chain of events linking his guests together.

Some months earlier: gay Leo is looking for a new relationship. His flatmate Darren and neighbour Angie encourage him to meet more people, so when his friend Adam suggests he come to a men's group, Leo agrees. There, Leo confesses he fancies Brendan, a fellow member. Darren is conducting an affair with Jeremy, an estate agent who likes to have sex in the properties he's selling. Leo embarks on an affair with Brendan, who is splitting up with his partner Sally. But Sally traces one of Brendan's calls, rings the number and speaks to Angie. Assuming Brendan is sleeping with her, Sally goes to the flat to confront Angie but meets her childhood sweetheart—Leo. After helping Sally move out of the flat she and Brendan are selling, Leo kisses her, then leaves confused. Leo goes to the café where Brendan and Sally work to confront Brendan. He tells Sally about the affair. She leaves, pursued by Brendan.

Back at the party. Leo talks to Sally and says he is over Brendan. Jeremy and Darren leave to have sex at Angie's. The rest of the party pair off, leaving Leo and Sally alone. When Darren returns he finds Leo and Sally asleep together on the sofa.

Five years after making a splash with her $15,000-budget black and white debut Go Fish US-born director Rose Troche returns with a colourful sex comedy set in London. A more expensive and technically accomplished movie, Bedrooms and Hallways shares with Go Fish a glib good humour, though it may lack some of the latter's unaffected emotional power. If Go Fish offered an audaciously angst free lesbian love story, Bedrooms goes one step further, escaping the ghetto of 80s identity politics to investigate the mutability of sexual identity. So while Leo's romance with Brendan initially appears to be at the heart of Robert Farrar's screenplay, Troche's multi-stranded narrative smoothly develops into a pansexual ronde which blurs the boundaries between gay and straight. And as with Go Fish Troche avoids the pitfalls of political correctness by approaching polymorphous perversity not as an ideal but as a given. Characters here may agonise about jumping into bed with one another, but they are defined not so much by whom they sleep with as by what they feel about it. The implicit ethos seems to be that everyone is entitled to life, liberty and the pursuit of happiness, wherever one happens to find it.

Played with endearing earnestness by Kevin McKidd, Leo does not conform to the usual a 'clone' stereotype. Dressed in chunky-knit jumpers and jeans, Leo just wants to find a nice man and settle down. But by the end of the film, even that nesting goal has shifted, as Leo cuddles up chastely with his childhood sweetheart Sally on the couch. Thanks to Troche's fluid direction and the a ensemble cast's warm, layered performances, it is only when you see this heterosexual ending dismissed by Darren as a 'passing phase' that you realise how effortlessly 'queer' the film really is.

For all that, this is a fun-loving rather than a profound film. And it's certainly not flawless. Robert Farrar apparently wrote the script in 1993, and despite the relish with which Harriet Walter and Simon Callow play their Hampstead gurus (arguing about who gets to the "truth stone" and so on), the gags about New Age self-discovery groups feel decidedly dated. Moreover, in the time its taken to shoot the movie in 1997 and procure its UK release, such multi-charactered, interlocking-narrative films as This Year's Love and Playing by Heart have come along. After Leo and Brendan's romance ends the film loses momentum, but it remains a pleasure to watch thanks to its zippy visual style. Tactically placed dream sequences punctuate the narrative and in one scene Troche has fun lampooning Jane Austen costume dramas. Intercutting Darren and Jeremy's torrid affair with the rest of the narrative, Troche puts titles across the bottom of the screen to spell out the name, address and price of the properties they're defiling. Much of the film's humour is sparked by this pair. At one point the camera cranes down to focus on a swimming pool in which Darren is floating face down, naked but for a pair of pink waterwings. When Jeremy slaps his bottom and swims away, he asks plaintively: "Do you think our relationship has too much emphasis on the physical?" As Darren, Tom Hollander steals the picture. Whether gamely flouncing about in platform trainers and a leopard-skin hat, or being caught handcuffed on a stranger's bed and pretending to be an "S&M-ogram", Hollander is hilarious, displaying fantastic comic timing and a truly camp understanding that too much is never enough.

VILLAGE VOICE, 9/7/99, p. 113, Amy Taubin

Just as sweet, but somewhat more sophisticated [The reference is to *Outside Providence*.] Rose Troche's *Bedrooms and Hallways* is a romantic comedy about twentysomething Londoners looking for love.

Leo (Kevin McKidd) and Darren (Tom Hollander) are gay flatmates whose sexual fantasies run in opposite directions. Darren's current flame is a buttoned-up real-estate agent (Hugo Weaving) who enjoys using the homes to which he has professional access as he would his own. It's cheaper than doing it in hotels and twice as kinky. The more serious Leo scandalizes the men's group he's been attending by confessing that he has a crush on one of the members, a smoldering Irish hunk named Brendan. Much to Leo's surprise, Brendan, who's in the throes of breaking up with his girlfriend (the wonderful Jennifer Ehle), proves more than amenable to a new and different adventure. The problem for Leo is that Brendan may not be able to stop at one adventure.

Smartly written by Robert Farrar and performed with considerable panache, *Bedrooms and Hallways* could be the pilot for a television series (a gay-friendly *Friends*) except that it's more chaste than some of what's on British TV (the BBC series *This Life,* for example). Troche, who directed the no-budget lesbian romantic comedy *Go Fish,* shows that she's capable of a conventional style when the occasion warrants. But *Bedrooms and Hallways* doesn't play by the rules when it comes to identity politics, which may be what drew Troche to the material. Like *Go Fish,* it suggests that there's nothing as anarchic as sexual desire, and that when it comes to love affairs, nothing is as compelling as breaking a taboo, whether cultural or personal. *Bedrooms and Hallways* goes a step further by proposing that the common ground between gay and straight identities is that both are mutable. Doctrinaire gays may not approve, but, honestly, c'est la vie.

Also reviewed in:
CHICAGO TRIBUNE, 12/10/99, Friday/p. I, John Petrakis
NATION, 9/20/99, p. 68, Stuart Klawans
NEW YORK TIMES, 9/3/99, p. E18, Stephen Holden
VARIETY, 6/1-7/99, p. 41, David Rooney

BEEFCAKE

A Strand Film release of an Emotion Picture Independent/Alliance Films/Channel Four/Odeon Films/Mikado Films/La Sept Arte production in association with Telefilm Canada and Nova Scotia Film Development Corp. *Producer:* Shandi Mitchell and Thom Fitzgerald. *Director:* Thom Fitzgerald. *Screenplay:* Thom Fitzgerald. *Director of Photography:* Thomas M. Harting. *Editor:* Susan Shanks and Michael Weir. *Music:* John Roby. *Casting:* Michael Weir. *Production Designer:* D'Arcy Poultney. *Costumes:* James A. Worthen. *Running time:* 93 minutes. *MPAA Rating:* Not Rated.

CAST: Daniel MacIvor (Bob Mizer); Josh Peace (Neil O'Hara); Carroll Godsman (Mrs. Mizer); Jack LaLanne (Himself); Russ Warner (Himself); Dave Martin (Himself); Jim Lassiter (Himself); Joe Lietel (Himself); Joe D'Allesandro (Himself); Valentine Hooven (Himself).

LOS ANGELES TIMES, 10/29/99, Calendar/p. 18, Kevin Thomas

Thom Fitzgerald's "Beefcake" is an illuminating and engrossing look at the life and times of pioneer Los Angeles physique photographer Bob Mizer (1922-1992) that combines clips from Mizer's films, a fictional story and interviews with people who knew or worked with Mizer. Inspired by Valentin Hooven's book of the same name, Fitzgerald has succeeded in making his ambitious film work on several levels.

First, there's an exploration of the relationship between Mizer (Daniel MacIvor, who actually resembles the large, unprepossessing Mizer) and his mother (Carroll Godsman), who is depicted as disapproving of her son's work but was supportive of him to the end of her life. MacIvor's Mizer was a shy, secretive gay man who loved photographing beautiful young men and in 1945 formed the Athletic Model Agency, which soon became a cottage industry, with Mizer's brother handling the books and working as a handyman, his mother making the posing straps worn by her son's models—they were also sold via mail order, as were AMG photos and films.

Mother and son lived for decades in a large Edwardian house on 11th Street near Alvarado, to which had been added a studio and an outdoor roof pool, the site of a zillion photo shoots and kitschy short movies involving near-naked Roman soldiers, wrestlers, sailors and cowboys.

Fitzgerald's take on Mizer is that he was a romantic who could be vulnerable to the overtures of the young men who passed through his portals, but who was not a pimp. Unfortunately, Mizer's era coincided with that of Joseph McCarthy with its intense, witch-hunting homophobia. It was perhaps inevitable that in those repressive times Mizer would run afoul of the law, accused of being a pornographer and of being involved in prostitution. Sometimes, it seems, Mizer referred his models to other photographers, who sometimes had sex with them; there may have been more to it than that, for Mizer could be a shadowy man.

In any event, Mizer was always at risk because so many of the young men who posed for him were also hustlers or had criminal records.

Mizer did away with posing straps when frontal nudity became legal but never made hard-core films. Seen today, his work seems innocent, a celebration of young male beauty. (Back in the '50s Mizer would have had to defend his work as art and not admit, at least publicly, that such art could also be homoerotic in impact.) As Hooven remarks, those who bought his long-running magazine/catalog Physique Pictorial knew what they were buying and why. He adds that purchasing such a magazine was an "adventure, an act of courage in 1955," especially for a teenage boy confronting his homosexuality, as Hooven was at the time.

In order to tie the film together Fitzgerald has come up with the fictional story of a young man, Neil O'Hara (Josh Peace), who ditches Nova Scotia farm life for the bright lights of 1950s Hollywood and dreams of movie stardom. Neil is the archetypal boy-next-door Mizer model, nice-looking and well-built, but not so handsome and buffed out that, as Mizer puts it, his customers couldn't "imagine themselves in your shoes." Naive and well-mannered, Neil surely must have been like many of Mizer's models, who are seen in the many clips from Mizer films that Fitzgerald deftly integrates into "Beefcake."

Among the interviewees are Mizer contemporaries and fellow physique photographers Russ Warner (a bodybuilder himself) and Dave Martin, who relate their own run-ins with the law. There are also reminiscences from Mizer models Joe Leitel (who went on to an acting career), Jim Lassiter and most famously, Joe Dallesandro, who is quite candid about mixing in hustling with modeling and who became one of the most famous of the Andy Warhol stars. Nowadays, a beefy, middle-aged character actor, Dallesandro says that he never thought much about the photos he posed for or the films he appeared in but today appreciates them as a record of his youth.

The most unexpected participant in the film is none other than fitness legend Jack Lalanne, who apparently never posed for Mizer but did so frequently for Warner, whose work was a staple of the bodybuilding magazines of the era. Philosophical about Mizer's life and career, Lalanne says of hustling, "I would never do that," but mischievously asks the off-screen Fitzgerald, "Why are you asking? You want a date?"

Without a doubt there could be a deeper, more polished film about Mizer than "Beefcake," but who could say for certain that it would ever get made? In the meantime Fitzgerald, whose autobiographical debut feature was "The Hanging Garden," has actually covered all the key bases in Mizer's life and done so with insight, compassion and humor. Culminating as a courtroom drama, the well-researched "Beefcake" gives younger audiences a clear idea of just how hypocritical and unjust institutionalized homophobla could be back in the '50s.

NEW YORK POST, 10/13/99, p. 67, Jonathan Foreman

"Beefcake," a campy docu-drama about the secretly gay world of 1950's muscle magazines, is not much more than an excuse to show a lot of young muscular men naked or wearing thongs.

It focuses on the career of Bob Mizer, a repressed gay man who created Physique Pictorial magazine and ran the Athletic Model Guild—an agency for muscle models—out of his house in L.A.

Many of the models, both gay and straight, moonlighted as hustlers, and Mizer was eventually charged with running a prostitution ring.

Filmmaker Thom Fitzgerald discovered Mizer's vast archive of still photographs and muscle movies. You see this material now—endless, lovingly photographed shots of near-naked young men wrestling or pretending to be sailors or prison inmates—and it's hard to believe that anyone ever bought the notion that it was all innocent stuff about health and fitness.

The movie, opening today at Film Forum, also contains some interesting interviews with photographers and models who worked with Mizer, including actor Joe D'Alessandro and the always entertaining exercise guru Jack La Lanne.

But the rest of the film is taken up with the amateurishly written, directed and acted story of fictional Nova Scotian youth Neil O'Hara (Josh Peace), who gets discovered by Mizer (Daniel MacIvor), joins his extended family of muscle boys and witnesses his trial.

The mixture of original footage and dramatic re-enactment is an uneasy one, and Fitzgerald seems more interested in soft-core gay-porn imagery than in the history of this strange subculture.

He also tends to treat the exploitation and prostitution of good-looking kids who turned up in Hollywood looking for stardom as something kinky and cute rather than sad and ugly.

It's not an attitude that everyone will share.

NEWSDAY, 10/13/99, Part II/p. B11, Jan Stuart

The comely young man rips off his shirt for the photographer, who quickly admonishes his subject to slow down. "We want the viewer to be able to examine your definition," he patiently explains, "before being confronted with another muscle group." Perhaps the only thing more unlikely than a movie about the male pinup culture of the 1950s is that someone should fashion something wry and sweet-spirited around that pre-porn milieu. But that is exactly what Thom Fitzgerald has fashioned with "Beefcake," a flaky, disarming and, yes, titillating trip down one memory lane that may be alien to the street map of your own life experience.

An odd-duck blend of talking heads commentary, dramatized history and archival photos and movies, "Beefcake" zeroes in on the self-styled "physical culture photography" of Bob Mizer, who celebrated his ardor for the male physique in a body-building rag called "Pictorial Physique." With the often bemused support of his mother, (who sewed the jock-strappy "posing pouches" that satisfied the no-full-frontal-nudity rules of the '50s), Mizer turned his home into a kind of winterized Muscle Beach-and-photo studio.

Interspersed with interviews with such erstwhile beefcake models as Jack LaLanne and Warhol superstar Joe Dellasandro is a camped-up biography of Mizer (played here by Daniel MacIvor) by way of one of his subjects, Neil O'Hara (Josh Peace), a wide-eyed Nova Scotia farmboy who becomes a "Pictorial Physique" star and enters a strange new world of sex, drugs and rock and roll.

The repressiveness of the era comes to full light when it is revealed how the gentlemanly Mizer chronicled each of his models with a secret code. His observations would be translated into poker-faced magazine copy ("This problem child tends to be a bit of a late riser") that reads like Playboy bunny travesties.

What begins as camped-up mockumentary becomes a sober plea for tolerance, as Mizer is eventually arrested on obscenity charges. Coming off the ineffable coming-of-age drama "The Hanging Garden," director Thom Fitzgerald certainly cannot be accused of repeating himself.

VILLAGE VOICE, 10/19/99, p. 144, Vince Aletti

Beefcake, Thom Fitzgerald's fizzy pastiche of talking heads, camped-up docudrama, courtroom theatrics, and vintage film clips, is, we're told, "inspired by a true story." The story, stranger than fiction, centers on queer cult photographer-entrepreneur Robert Henry Mizer and his Athletic Model Guild, the physique photo studio that he ran out of his L.A. home. Beginning in the late '40s and ending only with his death in 1992, Mizer photographed thousands of young men—from pro muscle builders to high-school jocks—in as little clothing as the law would allow. For much of AMG's history, that meant nylon G-strings sewn by Mizer's mother, who also lived on the studio compound, along with an aunt, a brother who kept the books, and a menagerie of animal props.

Mizer's studio, which also served as a crash pad for homeless models, is *Beefcake's* prime setting, and AMG's photos and films are used throughout. But *Beefcake* is a kaleidoscope, and it shifts focus constantly. To animate AMG's cottage industry as gay idyll, Fitzgerald introduces a clean-cut ingenue named Neil O'Hara (Josh Pearce in the Patty Duke role) who is soon stripped down, oiled up, and smoking pot with one of the studio's most cunning rascals. During an exchange of vintage slang, this fox clues the improbably innocent Neil into the seamier side of the physique world, including the occasional "one-on-one rumble with some gassy stud." Though the fatherly, fastidious Mizer (Daniel MacIvor) prefers not to think about that part of his stable's income, he can't ignore it when a new model is arrested, and the police, always ready to pounce on physique photographers, accuse him of running a prostitution ring.

Mizer's trial, re-created from court transcripts, grounds the film in the grim reality of homophobic persecution but doesn't ignore the cast of sleazy creeps on the margins of the physique biz. To put all this into perspective, Fitzgerald weaves in vivid testimony from a group of former models and retired photographers. The models, including former Warhol beauty Joe Dallesandro and the perennially pumped-up Jack LaLanne, provide *Beefcake* with its most soulful and honest moments. "You had to sleep where you could and with who you could," one faded hunk says. "There was no pick or choose or else you went hungry." Though all these pieces don't exactly mesh into a coherent movie, Beefcake's messiness has real charm, and its tribute to Mizer is both appropriately complicated and poignantly sexy.

Also reviewed in:
NEW YORK TIMES, 10/13/99, p. E5, Stephen Holden
VARIETY, 3/8-14/99, p. 63, Dennis Harvey

BEING JOHN MALKOVICH

A USA Films release of a Gramercy Pictures presentation of a Propaganda Films/Single Cell Pictures production. *Executive Producer:* Charlie Kaufman and Michael Kuhn. *Producer:* Michael Stipe, Sandy Stern, Steve Golin, and Vincent Landay. *Director:* Spike Jonze. *Screenplay:* Charlie Kaufman. *Director of Photography:* Lance Acord. *Editor:* Eric Zumbrunnen. *Music:* Carter Burwell. *Music Editor:* Adam Smalley. *Choreographer:* Tony Maxwell. *Sound:* Forrest Brakeman and (music) Michael Farrow. *Sound Editor:* Richard Anderson and Elliott Koretz. *Production Designer:* K.K. Barrett. *Art Director:* Peter Andrus. *Set Designer:* Fanee Aaron, Sloane U'ren, and Elisa Bussetti. *Set Decorator:* Gene Serdena. *Set Dresser:* Grant D. Samson, James A. Fleming, Allan Davis, Brian Derfer, Robert Anderson, Bobby Pollard, and Rick Staves. *Special Effects:* John Gray. *Visual Effects:* Daniel Radford. *Costumes:* Casey Storm. *Make-up:* Gucci Westman. *Special Make-up Effects:* John Vulich. *Stunt Coordinator:* Dan Bradley. *Running time:* 112 minutes. *MPAA Rating:* Not Rated.

CAST: John Cusack (Craig Schwartz); Cameron Diaz (Lotte Schwartz); Ned Bellamy (Derek Mantini); Eric Weinstein (Father at Puppet Show); Madison Lanc (Daughter at Puppet Show); Octavia L. Spencer (Woman in Elevator); Mary Kay Place (Floris); Orson Bean (Dr. Lester);

Catherine Keener (Maxine); K.K. Dodds (Wendy); Reggie Hayes (Don); Byrne Piven (Captain Mertin); Judith Wetzell (Tiny Woman); John Malkovich (John Horatio Malkovich); Kevin Carroll (Cab Driver); Willie Garson (Guy in Restaurant); W. Earl Brown (First J.M. Inc. Customer); Charlie Sheen (Charlie); Gerald Emerick (Sad Man in Line); Bill M. Ryusaki (Mr. Hiroshi); Carlos Jacott (Larry the Agent); James Murray (Student Puppeteer); Richard Fancy (Johnson Heyward); Patti Tippo (Malkovich's Mother); Daniel Hansen (Boy Malkovich); Mariah O'Brien (Girl Creeped Out by Malkovich); Gregory Sporleder (Drunk at Bar); Kelly Teacher (Emily).

CHRISTIAN SCIENCE MONITOR, 10/29/99, p. 15, David Starritt

Send in the clowns! While most movies fall into well-worn patterns, this season a handful of comic talents are cooking up inventive new approaches.

Making us laugh may be their main agenda, but in the process they're shaking up old formulas and giving us some of the most surprising cinema we've had in ages.

The most uproarious example is *Being John Malkovich*, which pitches so many curveballs that even its title is a joke. Seeing those words on a theater marquee, unwary moviegoers might expect a documentary about the respected actor whose credits range from "In the Line of Fire" to "Death of a Salesman."

The picture bearing his name is anything but a documentary, though, and Malkovich isn't even the main character. The hero is an unemployed puppeteer (John Cusack) who takes a filing clerk job with an obscure Manhattan company.

Prowling the murky corners of his new office, he finds a secret passageway that whisks him to a strange destination: For exactly 15 minutes, he finds himself peering through the eyes of John Malkovich as the actor goes about his daily life. When the quarter-hour is up, the bewildered visitor flies out of Malkovich's mind and into a ditch alongside the New Jersey Turnpike, where he dusts himself off and makes his way home.

What's going on here? Our hero has no idea, but he and his new girlfriend see moneymaking potential in his discovery. They place an ad in the paper, and soon the office is filled with stargazers happy to pay for 15 minutes in Malkovich's mind.

Still unresolved are several key questions. What accounts for this bizarre phenomenon? What will happen if Malkovich finds out about the mental trespassers trooping through his brain? And weirdest of all, what would happen if he walked through the passageway and entered his own consciousness as a visitor?

As if this weren't enough material, "Being John Malkovich" has a number of subplots that spin in various directions—including some explicit sexual content—before dovetailing in time for the final credits. One focuses on the hero's girlfriend, a coldhearted co-worker who's not averse to disrupting his 10-year marriage. Another deals with his wife, who cultivates a passion for pets while waiting to have a real family.

And then there's that odd little company where the story jumps into action: Why is it located in an architectural twilight zone between the buildings seventh and eighth floors, and just what business is it in, anyway?

"Being John Malkovich" is directed by Spike Jonze, coming to feature films after a music-video career, and written by Charlie Kaufman, also a newcomer to theatrical movies. Their work is so bold, funny, and original that it's hard to believe they aren't wide-screen veterans.

At a time when many filmmakers pride themselves on directing their own screenplays, it's worth noting that another of this year's most brilliant comedies "Election"—is also the work of a writer-director duo. Perhaps the movie world is returning to the bygone era when well-teamed collaborators rather than do-it-all auteurs set Hollywood's highest standards.

"Being John Malkovich" has enough gender-bending sexual twists to earn an R rating even if it didn't have a large four-letter word vocabulary, so it certainly isn't for everyone.

Audiences at various film festivals have embraced it warmly, though, and it's easy to imagine all kinds of Oscars for its ingenious makers as well as the superbly chosen cast including Catherine Keener as the hero's partner, Cameron Diaz as his long-suffering wife, and Orson Bean as an eccentric old man. Not to mention Cusack and Malkovich, who fill the screen with comic energy.

LOS ANGELES TIMES, 10/29/99, Calendar/p. 1, Kenneth Turan

"Being John Malkovich" is a clever and outrageous piece of whimsical fantasy that is unique, unpredictable and more than a little strange. You could see a lot of movies over a lot of years and not hear a line of dialogue as playful and bizarre as "I'll see you in Malkovich in one hour." What the heck is going on here?

The debut film for both director Spike Jonze and writer Charlie Kaufman, "Being John Malkovich" takes a genuinely surreal premise and manages to make it more plausible than "Armageddon." It's an Alice in Wonderland film that slyly raises all sorts of philosophical questions about the nature of reality, identity and self, and deals with them in a genially unhinged way.

Before we meet the film's namesake we are introduced to the life and work of New York hunger artist Craig Schwartz (John Cusack). Craig is not starving by choice, it's just that there's a limited amount of demand for a puppeteer whose racy street-corner version of the story of Heloise and Abelard gets him regularly beaten up by irate pedestrians.

Craig's wife, Lotte (Cameron Diaz), works in a pet store and it's difficult to tell where her job ends and her life begins. There's a bird that awakens Craig with a chirpy "Time to get up" and a monkey that needs therapy for an ulcer brought on by suppressed childhood trauma.

Understandably anxious to get out of the house and needing the money, Craig's fast hands get him a job as a file clerk at LesterCorp, run by a 105-year-old fool for carrot juice named Dr. Lester (Orson Bean). LesterCorp is located on the Mini-me-sized 7 1/2th floor of the Mertin-Flemmer Building, a space so small Craig spends his entire time there bent in half just to fit in.

Craig hardly notices this discomfort, because on his first day on the job he gets infatuated with cold and conniving co-worker Maxine (Catherine Keener), a Ming the Merciless type who couldn't care less about him. "If you ever got me," she tells him in a rare moment of compassion, "you wouldn't have a clue what to do with me."

Then comes that pivotal moment when Craig discovers a tunnel hidden behind a file cabinet in the deep storage room. Curiosity leads him inside, and suddenly he's whoosed out of sight only to find himself looking out at the world through the eyes of (yes, it's really him) actor John Malkovich. For a brief period of time—which invariably ends with him being inexplicably dumped out somewhere on the New Jersey Turnpike—Craig has found a way to literally be in someone else's skin.

Though this experience, as one character puts it, "opens a metaphysical can of worms," for a puppeteer like Craig it's a dream come true. It also proves powerfully addictive, not only for him but later on for wife Lotte and even Maxine.

For Craig's discovery of this strange portal makes him immediately more interesting to the clever Maxine. Ever entrepreneurial, she dreams of letting the rest of the world in on the Malkovich experience. For a price, of course, with an ad line perfectly suited to these celebrity-addicted times: "Be all that someone else can be."

In addition to doing a capital job of impersonating his haughty and distant public persona, the real John Malkovich deserves thanks for allowing this goofy charade to go on: The filmmakers say they couldn't imagine any other actor in this pivotal spot. And co-stars Cusack, Diaz (both of whom look different than they ever have on screen) and Keener enter into the spirit of the piece with energy, daring and a zest for the unusual.

That's even more true for director Jonze, who displays the same kind of unexpected delight in playing with reality that he used in music videos and celebrated commercials for Nike and Nissan trucks. His gift here is being able to treat a highly unusual scenario as if it were the most normal of situations, guiding audiences who have no idea where they're going because no one's ever been there before.

Credit for thinking up this delirious and delicious situation goes to writer Kaufman, who has a truly singular imagination. Kaufman says he wrote the script "without an outline, blindly, with no sense of direction," and if this film has a flaw it's the way that technique ultimately catches up with him.

For once "Being John Malkovich" determines it has to explain itself, what it comes up with is not only flimsy but barely understandable and harder to credit than what we've experienced with our own eyes. That throws a bit of a wrench into the proceedings, but finally we side with the character who says, "Art always tells the truth even when it's lying." It may not be clear just what that means, but like the rest of the "Malkovich" experience it's a lot of fun going down.

NEW YORK, 11/8/99, p. 63, Peter Rainer

Being John Malkovich is the most comically strange and original movie of the year. Like most one-of-a-kind films, it exists almost entirely within its own wiggy frame of reference, and yet, by touching on so many aesthetic conundrums, it's the art film of the moment—or the moment just ahead. Dazzlingly singular movies aren't often this much fun. The director Spike Jonze and his screenwriter Charlie Kaufman, both making their feature-film debuts, transform their notions about the nature of celebrity and time and inspiration into a kind of metaphysical vaudeville. Imagine Pynchon or Nabokov or Borges with a neo-slacker's absurdist spin, and add to it something far more mysterious, a feeling for the crawl spaces in our pop-cult consciousness. There's more going on inside this movie's brainpan than in many a pretentious European import, or stateside equivalent, and yet, in the best American tradition, it wears its intelligence lightly. Only after the film is over do you realize the passion and melancholy that also went into it. *Being John Malkovich* may turn out to be the latest word in cutting-edge hip, but it's just about the least *cynical* hip movie ever made.

The filmmakers at once parody and dignify the earnestness of the self-conscious artist, personified here by Craig Schwartz (John Cusack), a dejected puppeteer who believes himself unemployable because he "raises issues." He does, but that's probably not the only reason he's unemployable: He's also one ornery prima donna. He creates a mini-ballet called *Dance of Despair and Disillusionment,* featuring a puppet with a painted-on face identical to Craig's, which, incidentally, resembles Jesus'; he stages on the streets of New York a lyrical marionette play featuring Abélard and Héloïse, concluding with the two medieval lovebirds, separated by a cell wall, simulating sex. (A father, watching his young daughter gape at the sight, punches out the puppetmaster.) Craig has the ratty, blasted look of a street person who could be bonkers or some kind of visionary (or both). His idea of existence is simple and self-pitying: *I think, I feel, I suffer*. He's a poseur but also highly gifted. Enthralled by his own expressiveness, he's the master of his play-act domain. Craig's wife, Lotte (Cameron Diaz), works in a pet store and crowds their cramped apartment with its denizens, including a brash parrot and a chimp named Elijah. (She's been taking him to a chimp shrink.) Wearing no makeup, frumpily dressed, with wide, blank eyes and big frizzed hair, Lotte has a vaguely tropical, gone-native look. Just as Craig is more intensely connected to his puppet world than to the people world, Lotte is emotionally of-a-piece with her pets: She brings Elijah into their bed for consoling.

Up until this point we've been witnessing a fractured romantic farce in which both romancers are essentially wooing themselves. But Jonze and Kaufman move way beyond the formalities of genre; the film progresses in a series of riffs and spirals, each one wilder than the one before, and yet it's all highly controlled, deadpan. The 29-year-old Jonze (whose real name is Adam Spiegel, of the Spiegel catalogue family) is perhaps the best of the music-video and TV-commercial directors, but he doesn't go in for a lot of whiz-bang gyrations here; he understands how the film's transcendent strangeness is best served straight up.

What follows is a daisy chain of loopy linkages. Here's a taste: Craig takes a job as an entry-level filing clerk on floor seven and a half of a Manhattan office building, with ceilings so low that employees walk beneath them crookbacked. Craig's boss (Orson Bean) is a hale-looking 105-year-old who survives on carrot juice; Maxine (Catherine Keener), a snappish fellow employee, draws out Craig's lust and throws it back at him, unrequited. Then Craig discovers behind a filing cabinet in his office a portal which leads him, with a whoosh through its oozy dampness, straight into the head of John Malkovich; for precisely fifteen minutes he sees the world through the unsuspecting actor's eyes—reading his *Wall Street Journal,* munching his morning toast—before dropping rudely down to earth in a ditch beside the New Jersey Turnpike. Craig and Maxine seize the entrepreneurial moment: After hours they charge people $200 to "be" John Malkovich for fifteen minutes. Lotte gets in on the ride, too—she finds herself inside Malkovich as he makes love to Maxine, and falls for her, and she for Lotte, but only when Lotte is looking back at her through the eyes of the actor. All of which brings on Craig's jealousy; he decides he must inhabit Malkovich and dominate him the way he does his puppets.

The grandest joke in the movie is that, for the people who inhabit Malkovich, it's enough that they are inside him: It makes no difference if he's simply picking at some Chinese takeout from the fridge or ordering up bathroom mats from a catalogue. Celebrity is all—even if, as with most of the people who are in for the ride, the specifics of the celebrity are fuzzy. (No one seems to know the exact nature of Malkovich's credits).   The vicariousness of life lived through another—which is the hallmark of our celebrity-obsessed age—is here rendered literally; even mundaneness is made to seem special when viewed through the eyes of a star. The famous are our portals into an enhanced nothingness, and we gladly go for it.

John Malkovich is the ideal actor to play, well, John Malkovich. His air of wayward distraction is aggressively creepy; his big, baldish head here has a puppetlike blockiness, and he looks like he might indeed have another pair of eyes inside his own. In fact, every actor in this movie, and they are all marvelous, appears to be inhabited. They contain a multitude of selves, like those Russian dolls-within-dolls. And yet, this flurry of inner identities—transgendered, transfixed, evanescent—feels right; it's how we see ourselves now, not as a single character but as a gallery of characters butting up against each other.

And the gallery is always up for grabs. When Malkovich, upon discovering what's going on, yells at Craig to seal up the portal because *It's my head*, Craig responds, *It's my livelihood*. Here, in a nutshell, is the postmodern condition: You no longer own your mind. And yet the movie doesn't stop there, for what is acting—what is all art—but a form of vicarious byplay? The audience sees through the eyes of the artist and, whether it be for fifteen minutes or fifteen hours, co-opts the artist's way of seeing. The metaphor of the movie ultimately collapses in upon itself: Jonze and Kaufman condemn the way the culture invades our heads, but their film is itself a portal into their own minds. For the artist, for the audience, there is no way to escape being a voyeur.

I hope I'm not making *Being John Malkovich* out to be some kind of philosophy seminar in camouflage, but, like Craig, it "raises issues," and I don't see why they should be downplayed just because the movie is such an abracadabra joyride. It couldn't come at a better time, both in terms of the Zeitgeist it's lancing and in terms of the film industry, which needs all the replenishing it can get. It's the most impressive debut movie I've seen in years.

NEW YORK POST, 10/29/99, p. 37, Lou Lumenick

There's a temptation to describe "Being John Malkovich" as the best episode of "The Twilight Zone" never made—but that doesn't begin to do justice to the year's smartest, most stunningly original movie.

In an era when most movies are depressingly alike and can be summarized in one sentence, "Being John Malkovich" defies such easy description. The best advice I can give you is to stop reading now, get yourself to a theater and revel in the nonstop surprises director Spike Jonze and screenwriter Charlie Kaufman have up their sleeves.

John Cusack plays Craig Schwartz, an unemployed street puppeteer who's ready to hang up his strings after being punched out during a suggestive performance of "Tristan and Isolde."

He takes a job filing records downtown on the 7½th floor of the Mertin-Flemmer building, where the ceilings and overhead are very low (as explained in one of two hysterically funny mock documentaries within the film).

Craig's boss, the Mysterious Dr. Lester (Orson Bean) claims to be 105 years old and mistakenly thinks he has a speech impediment—though the problem is with his ditzy secretary (Mary Kay Place).

One day Craig moves a filing cabinet and discovers an old door behind it—and gets sucked through a portal into the mind of the distinguished actor John Malkovich. Craig experiences life as Malkovich, eating toast, reading the Wall Street Journal—and correcting a taxi driver who knows Malkovich is a famous actor but doesn't remember why.

Then, after his Andy Warhol-predicted 15 minutes of fame, Craig gets ejected onto the side of the New Jersey Turnpike.

Craig is wowed by this "metaphysical can of worm," as he calls it, but when he confides the details of his wild ride to Maxine (Catherine Keener), a sarcastic co-worker on whom he has a crush, she has more practical ideas.

Maxine, who previously wouldn't give Craig the time of day, sees Malkovich's fame as a money-making attraction—and places newspaper ads asking, "Did You Ever Want to Be Someone Famous?"

Soon people are lining up outside the Mertin-Flemmer building and forking over $200 a pop for the thrill of experiencing Malkovich ordering hand towels from catalogues and foraging in his refrigerator for leftover Chinese food.

But the most avid tourists turn out to be Craig and his frumpy, animal-loving wife Lotte (an unrecognizable Cameron Diaz)—who develops her own sexual obsession with Maxine after her first trip through Malkovich.

Soon Lotte and Maxine are vying to manipulate Malkovich (and Maxine) toward their own romantic ends—with increasingly hilarious complications.

Malkovich gives an extraordinary performance as a highly stylized version of himself—a vain lecher with no compunctions about meeting a strange woman for a middle-of-the-night assignation, even when she insists on calling him "Lotte."

And when Malkovich finally gets around to exploring his own portal, the results are literally mind-blowing.

It's hard to imagine any other actor in this razor-sharp satire on contemporary celebrity. Malkovich fearlessly dons a variety of comical hairpieces, gives a near-nude performance as a life-size marionette and even has a fictional friendship with Charlie Sheen (who also plays himself).

Malkovich's bravura work is nicely offset by the low-key performances of Cusack and Diaz, who help Jonze, a leading music-video director, keep the increasingly Kafkaesque proceedings grounded in a sort of alternative reality.

Keener is sharp and funny as the grasping Maxine, and Bean (a TV fixture in the 1950s and 1960s) is appropriately creepy as Dr. Lester, who has his own plans for Malkovich.

"Being John Malkovich," which contains not a frame of extraneous footage, is more than a must-see movie: It's a must-see-more-than-once event. The lightning-fast tour of Malkovich's subconscious alone will keep future video watchers occupied for days.

NEWSDAY, 10/29/99, Part II/p. B3, John Anderson

Audacity is almost unheard-of at the movies, where the product passes through so many hands, and is poked and probed by so many stubby corporate fingers, that any trace of the outrageous evaporates faster than spilt Veuve Clicquot on the hood of a '00 Mercedes SL. "Whaaaa?" in other words, may be provoked by your phone bill or the Brooklyn Museum of Art, but certainly not by the local movie house.

"Being John Malkovich," however, the better-than-audacious comedy written by the clearly twisted Charlie Kaufman and directed by hotter-than-tomorrow director Spike Jonze, will prompt not just a spontaneous "whaaa?" but maybe even a "huh?" and possibly a "How did it ever get made?" A movie whose premise intrudes into the very cerebral cortex of actor John Malkovich pretty much necessitates the presence of John Malkovich; once you've seen the film, it's hard to imagine anyone else at the center of this particular demented fantasy. And much of the movie's nervy charm can be credited to the fact that Malkovich is here.

In retrospect, of course, why wouldn't he be? "Being John Malkovich" not only venerates the idea of John Malkovich, it provides the actor an opportunity to show how good-natured he is, as well as to star in a movie where the star is cruelly used by the masses: When Craig Schwartz (John Cusack), an impoverished but gifted street puppeteer, takes a job as a filing clerk, he finds behind a cabinet a tunnel/portal that delivers him inside the actor's brain. There, he sees the world through Malkovich-colored lenses, lives the life of an actor (and becomes an actor, too!). After 15 minutes, he's deposited on the shoulder of the New Jersey Turnpike. Nothing could be riper for commercial exploitation.

The movie is rather devious in the way it reviews itself. The Malkovich experience, Craig tells his chimp-keeping wife, Lotte (a virtually unrecognizable Cameron Diaz), is about "the nature of self, the existence of the soul." Jonze and Kaufman are clearly out to torpedo any attempts at brow-knitting or hand-wringing; to paraphrase Mark Twain, any person attempting to find a moral here will be shot.

Anyone laughing hysterically, however, will be forgiven. Craig's employer, Lestercorp—situated on the 7½ floor of Manhattan's "Mertin-Flemmer" building—is owned by the seemingly deranged old Dr. Lester (a terrific Orson Bean) assisted by Floris (Mary Kay Place). Craig's more personal plight is summed up when he surreptitiously meets his disarmingly candid co-worker Maxine (Catherine Keener) after work for an illicit drink. "I'm a puppeteer," he says.

"CHECK!!!" she says.

Although he and Maxine eventually turn the portal into a thriving, $200-a-shot reality vacation for the self-loathing, Craig's no competition for Malkovich (the actor eventually becomes a one-word phenomenon, such as when Maxine asks Lotte, "Have you done Malkovich yet?"). Nor can Craig hold his own against Maxine: While she may be immune to Craig's erotic obsession, she is pretty taken with Lotte, especially when Maxine makes love to Malkovich while Lotte is inside his brain.

Everybody's good in "Being John Malkovich," not excluding Malkovich. Keener, who's finally gotten a break from playing betrayed wives and best friends, shows what kind of heat she can stir up as a femme fatale. Cusack and Diaz are adorable schlumps. But the nature of self? The existence of the soul? How about the absurdity of sex? Where "Malkovich" deposits us is not some sarcastic terrain of celebrity or mortality (Dr. Lester has his own secrets about portals and souls) or even the New Jersey Turnpike. It's about the Lotte-Maxine romance, which thrives because a female mind has taken up residence inside a male body. "Being John Malkovich" may be a self-reflective hoot, but a lot of men are going to think it very apt that it's opening Halloween weekend.

NEWSWEEK, 11/1/99, p. 85, Jack Kroll

There being little work for a puppeteer who stages risque versions of "Heloise and Abelard" on the streets of New York, the bearded, angst-ridden artiste Craig Schwartz (John Cusack) takes a job as a filing clerk at Lester Corp. This odd company is on the 7½th floor of a Manhattan office building, where the ceilings are so low the employees have to stoop over and the boss is an affable 105-year-old (Orson Bean) who apologizes for a speech impediment he doesn't have. Craig, unhappily married to a pet-obsessed wife (Cameron Diaz, almost unrecognizable), falls hard for his foxy new co-worker Maxine (Catherine Keener), who couldn't care less about a guy who plays with puppets.

It's at this point in the already bizarre "Being John Malkovich" that we really go down the rabbit hole. Behind a filing cabinet at work Craig discovers a door that leads to a tunnel that leads ... inside John Malkovich's brain. For 15 glorious minutes, Craig experiences the thrill of being someone he is not—and for once knowing exactly who he is. At the end of 15 minutes, he is dumped out on the side of the New Jersey Turnpike. Quick to see the possibilities, Maxine turns this magical portal into a business: for $200 a pop, anyone can briefly be John Malkovich.

Working from a teemingly imaginative screenplay by newcomer Charlie Kaufman, ex-music-video director Spike Jonze has made a deliciously one-of-a-kind surrealist farce. The smartest decision Jonze makes is to underplay everything. Instead of trying to match the script's lunacy with an equally flamboyant style Jonze goes for a rough-hewn almost-realism.

Kaufman's tale keeps spinning with ever more baroque twists. We watch with a mounting sense of glee: *where next?* Well, for one thing, Maxine meets and seduces the famous actor in his apartment, which sends Craig rushing to get back inside Malkovich so he can be the one who's actually making love to her. But what happens when Craig's wife, Lotte, gains possession of Malkovich—and the romantic sparks start to fly between *her* and Maxine? And when Malkovich himself—after discovering that he has become a kind of public thrill ride—gets sucked down the tunnel into his own brain?

Kaufman and Jonze are riffing on all sorts of notions about identity and celebrity and sexual displacement. "Being John Malkovich" plays Ping-Pong with our heads, but the beauty of it is how lightly it tosses its ideas around. It aims to please, not lecture. Malkovich himself must have sensed the film's essentially benign spirit when he sportingly agreed to play this fictitious, and none too flattering, version of "himself." "Shall we to the boudoir?" the "real" J.M. leers to Maxine with that epicene affectlessness that has made him one of the most enigmatic and unlikely of movie stars. This may be the role he was born to play, and he plays it brilliantly. Keener is smashing as the cynical and sensual Maxine, Bean is dottily inspired and Cusack captures the mopey self-importance of the puppeteer with perfect pitch. I don't know how a movie this original got made today, but thank God for wonderful aberrations.

SIGHT AND SOUND, 3/00, p. 40, Jonathan Romney

Manhattan, the present. Under pressure from his wife Lotte, street-puppeteer Craig Schwartz takes a job as a clerk with LesterCorp, run by Doctor Lester, a company located on the low-ceilinged seventh-and a-half floor of an office tower. He falls in love with his co-worker Maxine. Craig discovers a hidden door leading to a passage which sucks him into the head of actor John Malkovich, whose life he experiences for 15 minutes before being ejected on to the side of the New Jersey Turnpike. Craig introduces Lotte to being John Malkovich, and while she is inside him, she/Malkovich makes love to Maxine; the two women fall in love, but can only enjoy each other physically when Lotte is in Malkovich.

Craig and Maxine start a business charging people to be Malkovich. Eventually Malkovich rumbles their scam and enters his portal himself, discovering a world where everyone is him. Craig and Lotte struggle for possession of Maxine. Eventually, Craig uses his puppeteering skills to enter Malkovich permanently and turns Malkovich into a world-famous puppeteer; Maxine becomes his lover. Lester explains to Lotte that Malkovich is the latest in a line of conduits used by a secret society to enjoy eternal life in new bodies. Craig is tricked out of Malkovich; Lester and the channellers take over the body. Years later, Lotte and Maxine are a happy couple with a daughter; Craig is inside their daughter, still in love with Maxine, now his mother.

There's a current running joke about *Being John Malkovich* that speculates on what the film might have been if its star and ostensible subject hadn't agreed to play along: what, in other words, if Spike Jonze had to settle for *Being Jeremy Irons? Charles Dance? Julian Sands?* You can only imagine that Malkovich agreed out of a sort of inverse vanity: "Be mean to Malkovich," he apparently urged the film-makers. It's not unusual for actors to dismantle their own image on screen, but in most cases, they have the safety net of fiction. What's remarkable here is that Malkovich agreed to supply his name, face and presence, and then to have all three subverted in a manner that is anything but gently well-meaning. The film makes rich capital out of Malkovich's peculiar public image, yet this is just the tip of the iceberg. The most eccentric US debut feature in recent memory—for both Jonze and screenwriter Charlie Kaufman—is at once a Dada screwball comedy; an inquiry into the nature of personality; a metaphysical conspiracy story; and a comment on the way we invest our own desires into public figures, hollowing them out into blank receptacles.

The film's jibing at Malkovich is certainly its most approachable aspect. In recent years, his career choices have been far stranger than anything the film imagines, from high art foreign language roles for Raul Ruiz and Manoel de Oliveira, to the barmy and often lazy overplaying in commercial fare such as *Rounders*. But here Malkovich may have found his greatest role, playing himself, or a vain, lasciviously suave caricature of himself, lounging in his penthouse with a copy of Chekhov, or attempting to lure a lover with a murmured, "Shall we to the boudoir?" Malkovich's air of narcissism is such that it comes as no surprise when, as the film puts it, he goes "up his own portal"—into a screen actor's poetic-justice nightmare world in which everyone has the face of Malkovich.

The film is partly about the empty nature of modern fame: people know your face and name, but not what you've done. No one can think of a Malkovich film, except the one in which he played a jewel thief (but there's no such film, he protests). He becomes literally a locus for other people's dreams. People inhabit him for a while: one man learns what it is like to be Malkovich ordering towels by phone. Lotte and Maxine use him as a sort of prosthetic love attachment, an animated trysting place; Craig sees him as "a really expensive suit that I enjoy wearing." In this sense, the film is an extended joke about the contemporary dreams of vicariousness and virtuality: the actor's body becomes a living version of the *eXistenZ* computer game devised by David Cronenberg. (Alternatively, you could see the film as a rewrite of the sci-fi topos of dimension travel: a celebrity-culture *Stargate.*) But the process works both ways: Craig gets to inhabit the actor and achieve his dreams, by making Malkovich the star puppeteer he could never be. They're made for each other, the actor's pretensions easily matched by Craig's delusions of profundity. But it's Malkovich who reaps the rewards of fame and a new existence, while Craig remains anonymous and in the cold.

But the film constantly shifts too much for us to pin it down: it can't easily be tagged as screwball or surreal, as a paranoid fantasy or a media satire. It's forever slipping into sideshows and diversions, from a lunatic corporate video to a hallucinatory sequence inside a chimp's memory. Nor is it in any way a typical video-maker's movie (Jonze won his spurs directing for the Beastie Boys and Björk *et al*), but a visually low-key, formally sober film that above all values shifts of tone and a very concrete sense of space, playing claustrophobia against spatial fluidity (the film begins in the enclosure of a puppet theatre and ends underwater, in a swimming pool). There's extraordinary use of sound, too, as if the world turns inside out when we're in Malkovich's head: we actually hear a hand brushing roughly across his scalp.

Finally, the film is a triumph of casting in which no one is what we expect them to be. John Cusack's face is barely visible behind the shaggy hair, Cameron Diaz barely recognisable under baggy tracksuits, fluffy wig and a scowl of discontent. The biggest revelation is Catherine Keener, usually cast as an ingenue doofus. Here she's a sleek, impeccably cruel vamp who sets the film's initial sexual certainties spinning wildly out of control, seducing both Malkovich himself and Lotte, who hides out inside the actor's body. *Being John Malkovich* is an incredibly rich and entertaining (not to say, laudably malevolent) film that far transcends its already way-out title premise: not just a *Larry Sanders* self-reflexive swipe at stardom, but, as Craig puts it, "a metaphysical can of worms."

VILLAGE VOICE, 11/2/99, p. 133, J. Hoberman

Directed by MTV whiz Spike Jonze from Charlie Kaufman's highly original script, *Being John Malkovich* is the sort of prize head-scratcher that invites analogy-seekers to cast their nets wide. The most offbeat studio comedy since *Rushmore,* it drafts the brain-twisting conundrums of Jorge Luis Borges, the grotesque humor of Czech animator Jan Svankmajer, and the narrative extravagance of *Celine and Julie Go Boating* in the service of a pop, Warholian riff on celebrity—which is to say, this droll, uncanny, live-action puppet show is actually something new.

Being John Malkovich opens with a thrashing marionette doing a dance of despair. The protagonist, Craig Schwartz (John Cusack), is a lank-haired puppeteer prematurely gone to seed, sharing a dump with his wooden creatures as well as the menagerie belonging to his frumpy frau, Lotte (Cameron Diaz as you've never seen her). Domestic baggage made tangible, his dolls and her pets are the least of the movie's metaphors. Like their characters, the filmmakers are at play in the house of fiction; once Craig spots a rival showing his 60-foot-tall Emily Dickinson puppet on TV, it's clear this is a jape in which anything is possible.

Craig gets a suitably grubby job as a file clerk on the 7 1/2th floor of a midtown office building. (The cramped spaces occasion much crouching and many repeated jokes about low overhead.) Among his coworkers is a self-assured gal of mystery, Maxine (a fabulously sarcastic Catherine Keener). Craig doggedly pursues her—making a Maxine puppet to talk to—but the movie truly goes through the looking glass when he discovers a little door behind a filing cabinet, opening on a slide that sends him zipping through time and space and ... into the brain of John Malkovich (John Malkovich).

Craig first experiences Malkovich reading *The Wall Street Journal* over breakfast—just like a real celeb. Then, after the proverbial 15 minutes of fame, the puppeteer is ingloriously dumped out in Palookaville, somewhere by the New Jersey Turnpike. This brief experience of subjective Malko-vision offers a new twist to Bazin's myth of total cinema even as it deranges any sense of a psychologically coherent human subject. Craig shows both Maxine and Lotte the portal. Maxine sees it as a merchandisable thrill ride; Lotte, who inhabits Malkovich taking a shower, undergoes a personality change. "I was John Malkovich, I was John fucking Malkovich."

Fascinated by Malkovich's "vaginal" portal, Lotte thinks she might be a transsexual, particularly after she gets to be Malkovich during his dinner with the seductive Maxine, who is playing both sides of the equation. Keener—an actress whose presence has improved every movie she's been in from *Johnny Suede* to *Your Friends and Neighbors*—here plays "beautiful." Malkovich may be the unlikely babe magnet, but caustic Maxine is the universal object of desire, leading to a romantic triangle in three dimensions. Maxine prefers Lotte to Craig but only when Lotte is inside Malkovich. (This creates a new language of trysts: "OK, I'll see you in Malkovich in one hour.")

Thanks partly to Maxine's inadvertent cry of passion ("Fuck me Lotte!"), Malkovich comes to the post-Freudian realization that there's someone else inhabiting his brain. "Maybe she's using you to channel some dead lesbian lover," his pal Charlie Sheen (Charlie Sheen) sagely suggests. As Malkovich grows paranoid, the premise pretzels around, at one point allowing Malkovich the narcissistic pleasure of passing through his own portal and at another affording a chase through the Malkovich unconscious.

Kaufman has described the creation of his script in terms that recall those Buñuel and Dali used to characterize the automatic writing of *Un chienandalou*. (And Jonze has, knowingly or not, followed the precedent of the seminal surrealist masterpiece by employing a surprisingly classical editing style.) But what obscure urge prompted John Malkovich to agree to make this movie? The premise could only work with an actor so peculiar—that is, with an actor so actorly. How does Malkovich "be" John Malkovich? The movie presents him as famous for being famous. (It's a running gag that, while everybody knows his face, hardly anyone remembers his movies.) There is, however, ample emphasis on his craft, as well as on the exhibitionism necessary to follow it.

The fantasy of ultimate fan invasion, *Being John Malkovich* initially suggests a parable of fame and desire. Later, it seems a metaphysical riff on immortality. But once "Malkovich" becomes Craig's puppet (and Malkovich starts to play Cusack), it's clear that *Being John Malkovich* is a movie about acting—or rather, a movie about acting in reverse. This is a theme park for theorists. Where is the identification? Who inhabits which role?

Also reviewed in:
CHICAGO TRIBUNE, 10/29/99, Friday/p. A, Michael Wilmington
NATION, 11/22/99, p. 34, Stuart Klawans
NEW YORK TIMES, 10/1/99, p. E10, Janet Maslin
NEW YORKER, 11/22/99, p. 208, David Denby
VARIETY, 9/6-12/99, p. 61, David Rooney
WASHINGTON POST, 10/29/99, p. C1, Stephen Hunter
WASHINGTON POST, 10/29/99, Weekend/p. 41, Desson Howe

BESHKEMPIR

A Fox Lorber Associates release of Kirgizfilm/Noe Productions production. Producer: Irizaï Alybaev, Cedomir Kolar, Marc Bashet, and Frederique Dumas. *Director:* Aktan Abdykalykov. *Screenplay (Kyrgyzstani with English subtitles):* Aktan Abdykalykov, Avtandil Adikulov, and Marat Sarulu. *Director of Photography:* Hassan Kidirialev. *Editor:* Tilck Mambetova. *Music:* Nurlan Nishanov. *Art Director:* Emil Tilelov. *Sound:* Bakyt Niyaraliev. *Running time:* 81 minutes. *MPAA Rating:* Not Rated.

CAST: Mirlan Abdykalyko; Albina Imasheva; Adir Abilkassimov; Bakit Dzhylkychiev; Mirlan Cinkozoev; Talai Mederov.

CHRISTIAN SCIENCE MONITOR, 2/19/99, p. 15, David Sterritt

Iran doesn't have a monopoly on children's issues, of course, [the reference is to The Apple; see Sterritt's review.] and similar concerns are woven through *Beshkempir—The Adopted Son*, the first feature-length production from Kyrgyzstan, a former Soviet republic.

Arriving in the US with film-festival prizes to its credit, it centers on a boy whose life is shaken when he learns that he was born into a large family and then adopted by a childless couple, in accordance with an old Asian custom.

As directed by Aktan Abdykalykov, a promising newcomer, "The Adopted Son" is amusing in its views of adolescent mischief and candid in its recognition of developing sexual interests.

Most impressive of all is its eye-catching blend of color and black-and-white cinematography, lending it a visual beauty as internationally appealing as its simple but compelling story.

NEW YORK POST, 2/17/99, p. 41, Jonathan Foreman

Filmgoers with a pronounced taste for the exotic may find that "Beshkempir—The Adopted Son," the first feature film to come from the former Soviet republic of Kyrgyzstan, is hard to beat.

But this elegantly photographed slice of Central Asian life is mighty slow going—especially during the first half—and even those who go for this sort of thing are best advised to enjoy its sumptuous images on a good night's sleep or a strong cup of coffee.

Beshkempir is one of a small gang of kids on the cusp of adolescence who hang out on the land around their village. One day he learns from a playmate, jealous of the attention Beshkempir is getting from a local girl, that he is adopted.

This causes a painful rift with his friends and then between his mother and the other women in the village, and worsens an already difficult relationship with his father. It will take the death of his grandmother and the elaborate communal funeral that follows to make his life whole again.

It may be that this film's stately pace is intended to reflect the pace of life in a village where farming is done without benefit of any machinery more modern than a bicycle. And certainly you get a very complete picture of the way Kyrgyz women, most of them prematurely aged by a grueling rural existence, shape dung into cakes and make bricks from mud and straw.

The acting is for the most part minimalist, although the fights among the teen-age boys are remarkably realistic. And the film switches from black-and-white to sepia to color for no apparent reason.

Still, it's a fascinating film, and we are likely to hear more from director Aktan Abdykalykov and his country.

NEWSDAY, 2/17/99, Part II/p. B9, John Anderson

It may not be quite enough to call "The Adopted Son" the best Kyrgyzstani movie of the year. It certainly wouldn't do justice to the film. So let's not mention it at all.

We might say that in constructing his tale of cruel adolescence and cultural identity, first-time Kyrgyzstani feature-maker Aktan Abdykalykov walks a thin line between making a movie about a village outsider and making an outsider's film. Amid all the stunning images— predominantly of silky black and white, with the occasional, logical spasm of color—he seems to have assumed an alien's view of what happens to his alienated foundling. The characteristics of village life—from the various forms of food collection, to the outdoor movie theater to the obese woman bleeding herself with leeches—are as strange to the director as they are to us ("us" being all readers not raised in the remote regions of Eurasian Kyrgyzstan). Around this lack of familiarity swirls a vague suggestion of contempt.

At the same time, "The Adopted Son" or "Beshkempir" (which means five grandmothers, because that's who adopts the boy in the movie's opening ritual) is a gorgeous visual achievement, a large-hearted film—and as good a portrait of adolescent maleness and its attendant peculiarities as any movie since "Stand By Me."

Beshkempir, not the most attractive boy but certainly no wimp, is vaguely ostracized by the other kids in what has got to be the only clique in town. Why? The suggestion is that they have an innate sense of the outsider, or have picked up a whiff of prejudice from their parents, because none of the kids including Beshkempir knows the truth—that he was a foundling and an orphan.

There are certainly clues: Verbally abused by his adoptive father, treated with indifference by his adoptive mother, Beshkempir gets real love only from his doting grandmother, whose death—together with the revelation of his unorthodox origins—spark the crisis of his life. And this is where "The Adopted Son" really sets itself apart—by making joy and liberation out of the triumph of truth. As he discovers the truth about himself, Beshkempir discovers himself. It's not the discovery of his real story that causes pain—it was the lie that caused the pain all along! What a simple, wonderful idea. And how contrary to the simplified narrative conceits we're so used to. It's enough to make you head for the next Kyrgyzstani film festival, even if you have to fly American.

VILLAGE VOICE, 2/23/99, p. 109, J. Hoberman

A no-less-exotic Central Asian neorealist child-centered family drama, [The reference is to *The Apple*, see Hoberman's review.] *Beshkempir—The Adopted Son* arrives here from the former Soviet republic of Kyrgyzstan, the first feature by 42-year-old Aktan Abdykalykov. *Beshkempir* is set in a Kyrgyzstani village and predicated on the still-existing ancient custom by which the parents of a large family offer a baby, generically known as Beshkempir, to a childless couple. The movie has been compared to Mohsen Makhmalbaf's ethno-poetic *Gabbeh* but it is less fancifully folkloric and more polished—an understated, idealized, and fastidiously crafted movie in the manner fostered by the no-longer-extant Soviet film schools. Modest as it is, *Beshkempir* is less concerned with the specificity of rural Kyrgyzstan than with a kind of natural kid culture. Instinctual creatures, five pre-adolescent boys splash in the mud, run from bees, steal eggs, and spy on village women before sculpting one out of dirt, prone and spread-eagle, as the arena for their sexual games. (This last activity is amusingly interrupted by a herd of cattle.) Ultimately the pack behavior turns on the adopted son who, teased as an orphan, is driven to fisticuffs with his former friends. One unforgettable line, directed at Beshkempir by another boy's angry mother: "He's not your wife to beat up like that." As in *The Apple,* a mirror is the movie's most important special effect, but Abdykalykov has no particular overview on gender, or social relations. Life in his Kyrgyz village is traditionally ordered, although seemingly unencumbered by government or religion. The only sign of state power is a brief glimpse of paper money, and the most elaborate local ritual (an eloquently simple funeral notwithstanding) is the outdoor projection of a Hindi musical, shown to the appreciative villagers one reel at a time. Abdykalykov is most drawn to vivid detail. *Beshkempir* begins with a lateral pan along a boldly patterned rug as if to preview the movie's patchwork assemblage of tightly framed incidents. The black-and-white narrative is interspersed with brief color epiphanies. The deliberate, busy soundtrack of birdcalls, dog barks, sheep baas, wind, and water sounds contribute to the sense of a vast landscape on which only the sketchiest human notations are inscribed.

Also reviewed in:
CHICAGO TRIBUNE, 4/2/99, Friday/p. D, Michael Wilmington
NEW YORK TIMES, 2/17/99, p. E5, Stephen Holden
VARIETY, 8/31-9/6/98, p. 99, Derek Elley

BESIEGED

A Fine Line Features release of a Fiction and Navart/Mediaset production in association with BBC Films. *Producer:* Massimo Cortesi. *Director:* Bernardo Bertolucci. *Screenplay:* Bernardo Bertolucci and Clare Peploe. *Based on a story by:* James Lasdun. *Director of Photography:* Fabio Cianchetti. *Editor:* Jacopo Quadri. *Music:* Alessio Vlad and Strefano Arnaldi. *Sound:* Maurizio Argentieri. *Sound Editor:* Sandro Peticca. *Casting:* Lucy Boulting, Fabiola Banzi, and Lenny Juma. *Production Designer:* Gianni Silvestri. *Set Dresser:* Cinzia Sleiter. *Costumes:* Metka Kosak. *Make-up:* Roberta Petrini. *Running time:* 92 minutes. *MPAA Rating:* R.

CAST: Thandie Newton (Shandurai); David Thewlis (Mr. Kinsky); Claudio Santamaria (Agostino); John C. Ojwang (Singer); Massimo De rossi (Patient); Cyril Nri (Priest); Andrea Quercia (Child Pianist at Concert).

LOS ANGELES TIMES, 5/21/99, Calendar/p. F10, Kevin Thomas

From the start of the enchanting "Besieged," a film that combines a stunning sensuality with a rigorous economy, you know that you're in the hands of a filmmaker who trusts in the storytelling power of the camera. And since the filmmaker happens to be Bernardo Bertolucci, you can count on his images to be ravishingly beautiful.

It begins this way: Bertolucci cinematographer Fabio Cianchetti's gracefully fluid camera picks out a beautiful young woman (Thandie Newton) caring for a large group of disabled children at a rural clinic in an unnamed African nation. A series of shots of posters of a military leader being pasted up everywhere in the area follows. Then cut to a man in a schoolroom asking his pupils if they know the difference between the words "boss" and "leader."

In a rapid montage we see a group of soldiers brutally take the schoolteacher into custody as the young woman, Shandurai, is bicycling home. Next, we see Shandurai awaken from her troubled sleep in a room so humble and nondescript that we don't know that we've moved from Africa to Rome, where Shandurai has fled from her homeland, which clearly has been taken over by a military dictatorship. Her room is on the ground floor of an ancient Roman villa, where she works as a housekeeper while pursuing her medical studies.

The owner of the villa is a Mr. Kinsky (David Thewlis), a young English pianist-composer who spends most of his time at the piano. He also gives lessons to a number of clearly gifted children. He is a tall, thin man, not conventionally handsome but attractive, absorbed in his music and a shy loner of exceptional intelligence yet possessed of warmth and kindness.

Shandurai is so zealous a housekeeper that you wonder when she finds time to devote to her studies—and how and when she became so fluent in Italian; so seductive is this film that you just take it on faith that she can handle the load. You also begin to suspect that all that intense scrubbing and dusting is a kind of exorcism for her, a way of dealing with survivor's guilt and her worry about the now-imprisoned schoolteacher, who happens to be her husband.

As caught up in his work as he is, Kinsky, who inherited the villa from an aunt, can't help but notice Shandurai's diligence and, more important, cannot help but notice her striking looks and be stirred by the grace with which she performs household tasks. She is an alluring woman, all the more so for being so completely natural and spontaneous.

One day Kinsky, who has no idea that Shandurai is married, places on a dumbwaiter a large diamond ring, which had been his aunt's, and sends it down to Shandurai's room. Perplexed and upset, Shandurai tells him she can't accept such a gift. He blurts out that he loves her and wants to know how he can prove it to her. Now thoroughly upset, she retorts in exasperation that he can do so by getting her husband out of prison.

Working from a script he adapted with his longtime co-writer Clare Peploe, from a short story by James Lasdun, Bertolucci spins a tale with the assurance, fascination and subtlety of an Isak Dinesen novella. When he's in top form, as he is here, Bertolucci displays an innate sense of proportion, as at home with the epic scale as with the intimate. In keeping with his strong appreciation of the visual, Bertolucci keeps dialogue to a minimum, which means Newton must be as expressive as a silent-era actress. He makes the same demands upon Thewlis, and both his stars glow under his direction.

He has also understood that with this particular material the setting is crucial and the villa in fact becomes almost a third character. An irresistibly charming structure of shabby elegance, it is dominated by a dramatic circular staircase that allows Bertolucci to suggest the levels and shifts within the relationship—the spiraling emotions—between Shandurai and Kinsky.

"Besieged" is heady stuff, and Bertolucci has always been an impassioned filmmaker, starting with the bravura "Before the Revolution," which made his international reputation 35 years ago. With "Besieged," as with all his best work, Bertolucci confronts tempestuous circumstances with complete control of his material. Such discipline only intensifies the impact of "Besieged's" hard-to-predict finish.

NEW YORK POST, 5/21/99, p. 53, Rod Dreher

Smaller and tighter is better for Bernardo Bertolucci, the Italian director of such gassy epics as "Little Buddha" and the languorous Tuscan indulgence "Stealing Beauty." Coming in at just over 90 minutes, "Besieged" is the sharpest and most focused work he's done in years.

It's also the most formally audacious. Made originally for Italian television, "Besieged" will be more cherished by art-film enthusiasts than by the general public. That's because Bertolucci tells the story primarily with deeply poetic images (alluringly photographed by Fabio Cianchetti), using a bare minimum of dialogue.

It is not another of Bertolucci's lushly detailed visual banquets. Indeed, "Besieged" is lovely but downright austere compared with "Stealing Beauty." It's that the delicate emotional complexities in the narrative are conveyed almost entirely with pictures. "Besieged" is unusually demanding, but also surprisingly rewarding.

The story begins in an unnamed African country, with a dissident schoolteacher being hauled away by soldiers as his wife, Shandurai (Thandie Newton), watches in stark terror.

Jump to Rome, where Shandurai has come to enter medical school. She pays her rent by serving as housekeeper in the luxurious town house of Mr. Kinsky (David Thewlis), a rarefied English aesthete who lives on the top floor.

While Shandurai scrubs in the shadows of this desolate dwelling, the aristocratic loner plays classical music on his piano. Wasting away in his aerie, he hears the Afro-pop beats coming from her tiny first-floor apartment and is mesmerized.

Kinsky sends her gifts, which she refuses. One day, overcome with passion, he declares himself in a mad clutch.

"If you love me," she spits, tearing away, "then get my husband out of prison."

Poor Kinsky had no idea she was married, and he withdraws. Slowly, however, art objects begin disappearing from his apartment. A wary Shandurai can only guess what he's up to. Their story spirals upward to a powerhouse, O. Henry-like conclusion, abruptly showcasing the terrible beauty of sacrificial love.

A film like this, with very few spoken words, puts enormous responsibilities on its actors. Newton and Thewlis are up to the task. While a more conventional storytelling style would likely have given the viewer more emotional satisfaction (Newton and Thewlis are so fascinating they make us want to know more about them), Bertolucci shows us how elegantly expressive silence can be.

NEWSDAY, 5/21/99, p B7, Gene Seymour

Love stories, as we've come to know them in the movies, are a dime a dozen. It's the rare movie that dares to take an oblique angle towards love as a way of exploring its possibilities, terrors and limits.

Bernardo Bertolucci has made at least two such films. "Before the Revolution," his breakthrough feature from 1964, followed a romantic young poet through his rhapsodic love affair with his young aunt while the notorious, still provocative "Last Tango in Paris" from 1972 focused on a burned-out romantic's all-or-nothing sexual tryst with a young woman whose name he insists on not knowing.

The male protagonists of both these masterworks were blatant, albeit fascinating, narcissists. Love is all about them with everything else blurred or subsumed by their own desires.

"Besieged," the latest of Bertolucci's inquiries into the nature of desire, shares with the others an obsessive pursuit of romantic satisfaction as a central theme. The difference—one that makes "Besieged" the most emotionally demanding Bertolucci film since "Last Tango"—is that the male lover, a reclusive British composer-pianist named Kinsky (David Thewlis) is compelled to look beyond his own needs to engage those of the woman he loves, an African medical student named Shandurai (Thandie Newton).

Kinsky and Shandurai are the sole occupants of a house overlooking Rome's Spanish Steps. She is in exile from her unnamed country, whose military dictatorship has imprisoned her husband. He is in retreat from the public, zealously shielding his art, playing only mostly for himself and for Shandurai, who lives in an apartment below his and comes up only to do his housekeeping in exchange for her lodging.

Along with his laundry, Kinsky sends cryptic messages to Shandurai—a sheet of composition paper with a question mark, soaring classical melodies filtering through an open door, a diamond ring—intended to lure her to his apartment where, one night, he professes his love. She tells him she cannot understand his music or accept his gift. He asks what he can do to win her love. She demands that he get her husband out of jail, knowing as she does so that she's probably asking the impossible.

Days pass. Nothing more is said about the matter for the rest of the movie. Yet Shandurai begins to notice some things as she goes to and from class and conducts her housekeeping duties. For instance, Kinsky's apartment seems to be losing its expensive artwork and decor by degrees. One day, while vacuuming Kinsky's apartment, she hears him to play music deeply inflected with seductive African rhythms.

More days pass. She sees Kinsky agree to sell his piano. Why? She sees him talking with an African priest. Why? Then she gets a letter telling her that her husband is about to receive a civil trial. She concludes that Kinsky had something to do with it. As thrilled as Shandurai is, both her conscious and subconscious minds share apprehension, even fear aroused by Kinsky's selflessness. In each tentative gaze, each hesitant sentence, Newton delivers the full spectrum of her character's conflicting emotions. Is this strange man giving up all he owns so he can "own" her? Or is this merely a communion between two lonely people struggling to remain true to themselves along the margins of society?

Bertolucci leaves such questions open. He tells his story in an allusive, intensely lyrical style, much like the music Kinsky plays. Indeed, the director orchestrates this delicate story in the same manner that a composer resolves a bittersweet melody. With so many movies around that insult your intelligence and spell things out in big block letters, you owe yourself a rare chance to see a master filmmaker bring you into the storytelling process and give both your mind and heart a workout.

SIGHT AND SOUND, 5/99, p. 40, Sally Chatsworth

In Kenya, Shandurai's husband Winston is arrested for opposing the military government. Shandurai moves to Rome to study medicine; she cleans the house of an English composer and pianist named Kinsky in exchange for lodgings and befriends a gay fellow-student named Agostino. One evening Kinsky gives Shandurai a diamond ring and declares his love. She tells him she cannot understand his music or accept the ring. When he offers to do anything to win her love, she asks him to get her husband out of jail. Kinsky listens intently to the music at an African church service.

Passing an antiques shop, Shandurai sees Kinsky's statuettes on sale; the paintings have disappeared from the walls of the house. She vacuums Kinsky's piano-room while he plays music infused with black rhythms, at which she smiles and almost dances. She sees him meeting an African priest. Later, she receives a letter saying that Winston is to receive a civil trial, and catches Kinsky bargaining for the sale of his piano. He invites her to a private recital at his house, where she receives a telegram saying that Winston, now freed, will arrive in Rome the next morning. She asks Kinsky if Winston can stay at the house and he agrees. That evening, after covering whole pages with "Thank you", Shandurai writes, "Dear Mr Kinsky, I love you," on a note and goes to bed. She awakens, takes her note upstairs and lies down beside a drunken Kinsky in his bed. The next morning, Winston rings the bell repeatedly while Shandurai lies beside Kinsky. Finally she gets up.

Bertolucci's favoured genre has always been melodrama in which feelings are vehicles for meanings. *Besieged* establishes a triangle between Shandurai, Winston and Kinsky which develops throughout the film: Shandurai moves from one man to the other. One might wonder whether she loves Kinsky because he gets Winston freed from jail. But what makes Kinsky so lovable is that he expresses his love for Shandurai by restoring her husband to her.

The main characters are all cultural outsiders. Kinsky's world is made up of music, art and love. His love for Shandurai makes him interact with others, but his love for music is too great to let him play in public. Shandurai is a foreign student, an outsider within Roman culture, as is her gay friend Agostino. Winston is opposed to his government, and consequently in jail. After his release he arrives to be with his wife—at that moment in bed with Kinsky. The film ends with Winston's attempts to gain entry to what has become a "community" of outsiders.

Shandurai and Kinsky also change in cultural terms. To seduce Shandurai, Kinsky transforms his music, bringing it closer to African composition. We do not see the genesis of his infatuation with her—it is there at the outset of the film, which delicately portrays Shandurai's growing sympathy and affection for him. She inhabits two worlds: on the purely material level Rome, on the emotional level Kenya, kept apart from others by something inside her. In her case, we know what that is; in Kinsky's case, it seems to be art. For both of them, love breaks down this sense of "being elsewhere". The film uses sound, framing and montage rhetorically. The music (diegetic music as opposed to background, non-diegetic music) comes from within the story so forcefully it seems stronger than the images. The same is true of the noise of Kinsky's dumb waiter. Both we and Shandurai are besieged by two sets of sounds: those of Kenya, and those of Kinsky, so that sound, rather than the camera, creates a perspective for the viewer.

Much use is made of a handheld camera, filming close up and cutting very swiftly on movement, a style of cinematography Bertolucci once eschewed. A long and beautiful pull up the stairwell away from Shandurai washing the floor is broken up by cut aways to other shots. We are no longer at an observer's distance from what is photographed, and the slow-motion, stop-action cinematography is part of the attempt to communicate feeling. Bertolucci has always used montage to manipulate time, to convey what is inside his characters and the presence of the past in the present. Shandurai lives in a present Rome through a Kenyan past, an "elsewhere" both cultural and geographical. Bertolucci is constructing what he calls "a dramaturgy without conflicts, one that is held up by feeling". Unlike characters in his films from *Prima della rivoluzione* to *The Last Emperor*, these characters do not struggle for a social identity—they are resigned to not belonging.

Besieged is an intimist film—an intimate chamber work—but it is not shot with the restraint customary of intimist films. It rides current Italian bandwagons—third-world immigrants, gayness, art—yet it is not essentially 'Italian'. With its mostly English dialogue, it is an Italian product projected at the international market. The production companies, however, are based in Italy (Silvio Berlusconi's Mediaset, and therein lies a tale), so this is no Jeremy Thomas-produced international blockbuster.

Does this allusive, delicate story work? The answer is yes, provided you are sympathetic with what Bertolucci is trying to do.

VILLAGE VOICE, 6/1/99, p. 119, J. Hoberman

Like *Eternity and a Day*, Bernardo Bertolucci's *Besieged* should come with the disclaimer "Danger: Artiste at Work." Still, however clueless and condescending, *Besieged* is less intolerable than *Eternity*, mainly for being shorter and more sybaritic in its rescue fantasy. Bertolucci's we-are-the-world love story may be schematic but it's also showy. The movie is a little textbook of svelte, sub-Scorsese, New Wave filmmaking—a farrago of jump-, match-, and audio shock-cuts, camera spins, odd angles, and dropped narrative transitions.

Besieged, which had its world premiere last September at the Toronto Film Festival, was regarded by many of the director's devotees as a return to form. But, lacking the overblown, camp absurdity of *Little Buddha* or *Stealing Beauty*, it's still a prime example of cinema *National Geographic*. It opens in West Africa—land of strolling bards and military thugs—with a rural schoolteacher's arrest by the minions of the local dictator. Helpless witness to this outrage, the teacher's young wife, Shandurai (Thandie Newton), next appears in Rome, where she studies medicine while supporting herself as the live-in housecleaner for an eccentric pianist she calls Mr. Kinsky (played, with excruciating archness, by David Thewlis).

Do you believe in magic? The reclusive Mr. Kinsky is understandably fascinated by this mysterious willowy creature—timorous yet steely—as she tidies up his objets d'art—crammed palazzo before rushing off to her class in human anatomy. Nor can Bertolucci's camera resist feasting on Shandurai's lissome vulnerability. Much of the movie is a prolonged, spastic flirtation in which Shandurai is drawn to Mr. Kinsky's music (supposedly the very essence of European culture) but repelled when he jumps her with a gulping, snuffling proposal of marriage.

Thus, in a distended short story with a modified 0. Henry twist, audience sympathies are reversed. The displaced and persecuted Shandurai appears as haughtily withholding as a fashion model—and has enough outfits to prove it—while kinky Mr. Kinsky turns out to have a soul as big as Little Buddha. The viewer may well question the nature of Kinsky's sacrifice—particularly after hearing his ambitious attempt to fuse Edvard Grieg with Papa Wemba. Suffice to say that his alter ego Bertolucci is not giving up anything—he's far too generous to withhold that which he's been dangling before our eyes.

Bertolucci's fantasy of New Age bwana-dom is not the first Euro art film to contemplate the spectacle of a beautiful African woman alone in the metropolis—just the most fatuous. Distributor New Line should be compelled to show it on a double bill with the Dardenne brothers' 1997 illegal-alien drama *La Promesse* or, better yet, Ousmene Sembene's 1965 *Black Girl*—a clear-eyed (no less New Wave) account of misplaced love and neocolonial objectification. Shandurai may speak three or four languages and be an A medical student but, dazzled by the white man's voodoo, she's a tongue-tied, barefoot child of nature at heart.

Also reviewed in:
CHICAGO TRIBUNE, 6/11/99, Friday/p. A, Michael Wilmington
NEW REPUBLIC, 6/21/99, p. 30, Stanley Kauffmann
NEW YORK TIMES, 5/21/99, p. E1, Stephen Holden
VARIETY, 9/21-27/98, p. 107, Derek Elley
WASHINGTON POST, 6/11/99, p. C1, Stephen Hunter
WASHINGTON POST, 6/11/99, Weekend/p. 40, Desson Howe

BEST LAID PLANS

A Fox Searchlight Pictures release of a Fox 2000 Pictures presentation of a Dogstar Films production. *Executive Producer:* Mike Newell. *Producer:* Alan Greenspan, Betsy Beers, Chris Moore, and Sean Bailey. *Director:* Mike Barker. *Screenplay:* Ted Griffin. *Director of Photography:* Ken Seresin. *Editor:* Sloane Klevin. *Music:* Craig Armstrong. *Music Editor:* Graham Sutton. *Sound:* Reinhard Stergar and (music) Rupert Coulson. *Sound Editor:* Ross Adams. *Casting:* Mali Finn. *Production Designer:* Sophie Becher. *Art Director:* John Zachary. *Set Designer:* Sloane U'ren. *Set Decorator:* Nicki Roberts. *Special Effects:* Gary D'Amico. *Costumes:* Susan Matheson. *Make-up:* Brad Wilder. *Running time:* 90 minutes. *MPAA Rating:* R.

CAST: Alessandro Nivola (Nick); Reese Witherspoon (Lissa); Josh Brolin (Bryce); Rocky Carroll (Bad Ass Dude); Michael G. Hagerty (Charlie the Proprietor); Terence Howard (Jimmy); Jamie Marsh (Barry); Gene Wolande (Lawyer); Jonathan McMurty (Vet); Terrance Sweeney (Priest); Rebecca Klingler (Diner Waitress); Kate Hendrickson (Bar Waitress); Owen Bush (Vagrant); Jess Woodrow (Roach Coach Clerk); Jamie Marsh (Barry); Michael McCleery (Recycling Owner); Sean Nepita (Freddie); Jody Wood (Brushfire Cop); Teddy Vincent (Lawyer Secretary); José Mendoza (Renaldo); Jane Morris (Realtor); David Mandel (Evangelist); Alec Berg and Jeff Schaffer (Phone Guys).

LOS ANGELES TIMES, 9/10/99, Calendar/p. 12, Kevin Thomas

"Best Laid Plans" is a sharp contemporary noir thriller that may be a tad too clever for its own good at the finish, but getting there is sufficiently tense and intriguing that you may not mind too much that the overly abrupt ending is somewhat of a letdown. First-time director Mike Barker and second-time writer Ted Griffin, as neophytes, seem to have set the stakes a little too high.

In any event, "Best Laid Plans" is a fine mood piece with lots of atmosphere and boasts terrific performances from its stars. Alessandro Nivola's Nick has dropped out of college to return to his seedy hometown to care for his dying father. He has taken a job at a recycling plant and has the feeling he is going nowhere when he runs into Bryce (Josh Brolin), a friend from school who has just landed a job teaching English at a small college. Bryce is a big, handsome man, more than a little oafish yet grateful for his new gig, having been cut off by his rich parents.

The guys hit a bar, have more than a few rounds, but Nick calls it a night when Bryce starts zeroing in on a pretty girl (Reese Witherspoon) who comes in alone and sits down at the bar. She makes her interest in Bryce crystal-clear.

Hours later Nick is awakened by a frantic call from Bryce, who insists he immediately come up to the lavish modern home that Bryce is house-sitting for its owners. The girl has accused Bryce of rape and threatens to go to the police; in desperation Bryce has bound and gagged her, securing her to a pool table. Bryce is verging on hysteria, not believing he actually raped the girl yet was too drunk to be absolutely sure of himself. He sees his life destroyed in an instant and begs Nick to come to the rescue—somehow.

At this point the film pulls back to reveal the first of its surprises. You don't have to give away the plot to reveal that "Best Laid Plans" is a classic cautionary tale about how a person, not just Bryce but anyone, can take a single misstep in crisis and see his or her life start to come apart.

Nick is lots more mature than Bryce, yet he's just as vulnerable to drastic error. Witherspoon's character proves lots more resilient and sensible in the crunch than either of the men.

"Best Laid Plans" is not as individualistic and well-thought-out as the recent, somewhat similar "Dead Dogs," which draws more from life than from old movies, but it has its share of compelling moments. The look of the film, shot in Bakersfield and Ventura County, is seductive in its garish aridity, reminiscent of the bleak urban landscapes of "Paris, Texas."

Until its denouement "Best Laid Plans" maintains a sure sense of pace, but then its timing and rhythm go haywire. The final revelation, which is tricky and treacherous, unfortunately smacks of contrivance and awkward construction. In a sense, "Best Laid Plans" messes up—just like its characters do.

NEW YORK POST, 9/10/99, p. 56, Jonathan Foreman

"Best Laid Plans" is a pretentious and amateurish noir thriller, based on a fairly inventive con-within-a-con-within-a-con plot.

It's the kind of atmospheric film in which the protagonist always has a two-day growth of beard, everything looks bathed in neon light, and the camera whirls around pointlessly.

But the stylistic clichés wouldn't really matter if the screenplay weren't such a dog's dinner of unwieldy flashbacks and unbelievable dialogue—and if the whole movie didn't seem so pleased with its supposed cleverness.

It opens with Nick (Alessandro Nivola) and Bryce (Josh Brolin), two former college buds, getting together for drinks in a small-town bar. Nick is bitter and sullen; Bryce is noisy and obnoxious.

They have a tedious conversation, during which Lissa (Reese Witherspoon) walks into the bar and catches Bryce's eye.

Later that night, Nick gets a panicked phone call from Bryce and goes over to the swanky home where Bryce is house sitting. It turns out that Lissa went home with Bryce, they had sex, and afterward she accused him of rape.

Fearful for his career, Bryce has dragged her to the basement, where she's now gagged and tied up to a pool table. Nick is shocked at first, then tells Bryce he knows exactly what to do.

Nick goes down to the basement alone and it becomes clear that he and Lissa are somehow in cahoots—but that a plan of some kind has gone wrong.

You then see a long flashback that explains how the two of them met four months before, how Nick didn't get the inheritance he expected when his father died, how he got involved in a disastrous burglary, and why Nick and Lissa are trying to pull a scam on Bryce.

Director Mike Barker, in his first U.S. feature, mostly does OK by a cast almost talented enough to distract you from Ted Griffin's gimmicky screenplay.

Most movie scripts are designed to tell a story, but Griffin's seems to be an effort to show off the fact that he went to college. He wants you to know that he knows who Adam Smith was and Abraham Lincoln, too.

Josh Brolin gives a terrible, shouting, over-the-top performance. Reese Witherspoon doesn't have much to say, but she at least gets to be cute and appealing again, after convincingly playing a frightening young politician in "Election."

SIGHT AND SOUND, 6/99, p.38, Liese Spencer

Tropico, the US. After the death of his father, Nick hopes to leave his job and move away. He meets Lissa and they begin a romance. Debts swallow Nick's inheritance, so he decides to be the getaway driver for a robbery planned by a colleague. The heist goes according to plan, but the drug dealer they steal from discovers the money is missing.

Abducting Nick, the dealer takes him to a warehouse where people are being tortured. He releases Nick but demands $15,000, sending a picture of the now-dead colleague as persuasion. Nick convinces Lissa to help him in an elaborate sting on his friend Bryce which involves framing him for the rape of an underage girl. Lissa—armed with a fake, underage ID—picks up Bryce in a bar and they subsequently have sex. Lissa claims to have been raped but instead of letting her go and paying the money, Bryce phones Nick in panic. Arriving on the scene, Nick finds Lissa handcuffed in the basement. He persuades Bryce their only option is to kill Lissa. He pretends to murder her, puts her in the car boot hoping to drive her home. But Bryce insists on coming with him.

On the way, the car is hijacked by the drug dealer and his gang. Abducted and taken to the warehouse where Lissa is being held hostage, Nick stumbles into an adjacent room where he discovers the robbery was an elaborate hoax to extort his non-existent inheritance: his colleague is alive and well; the drug dealer is really a finance major. Back in town, Nick and Lissa bump into Bryce and confess their scam. Traumatised by Bryce's rape of her, Lissa leaves but Nick runs after her and the pair are reconciled.

Like its anti-hero, *Best Laid Plans* is an educated underachiever. Scripted by 26-year-old screenwriter Ted Griffin and directed by British director Mike Barker *(The James Gang)*, this over-plotted, over-long potboiler flashes with intellect and style before collapsing into a silly charade. It opens explosively enough with Nick answering a late-night call from his friend Bryce. Driving through a brush fire, Nick arrives after picking up a girl in a bar his is now being accused of rape. Nick offers to threaten her into silence, and descends to the basement where she is being held. "We're fucked," he tells her. "You're telling me," she replies.

The film cuts to four months earlier, and Barker's *faux* first act seems to augur a murky *noir* tale of rape, murder and extortion. Setting his convoluted story in a fictional space somewhere between *The Postman Always Rings Twice* and *Red Rock West* and shooting it using a poisonous palette of liverish reds, livid greens and toxic yellows, Barker successfully suggests the sinister claustrophobia of Nick's home town. Stuck recycling rubbish at the local dump, he stares out at a desert landscape full of human litter: dim-witted workmates he despises, one-time buddies who patronise and bore him. When his late father's will fails to provide the money he needs to escape, crime is the next desperate step. Thanks to Alessandro Nivola's naturalistic performance, it's possible to swallow the unlikely scheme Nick and Lissa subsequently hatch to blackmail Bryce. Unfortunately, from then on the film falls apart.

Ethical questions and motivations raised by the action are ignored in a hectic rush to dazzle us with verbal and visual tricks. For instance, the relationship between Nick and his late father goes undeveloped while the amorality of the films central players is awarded only improbably erudite lip-service. College-educated he may be, but would Nick really persuade Bryce into murdering Lissa by arguing it would achieve "the greatest good for the greatest number of people"? And how many psychopathic drug dealers would ask you if you had read Adam Smith?

A generous viewer might read the friction between Griffin's gritty, blue-collar thrills and college-boy banter as a deliberate inconsistency designed to prepare for the final twist. But if such absurd speechifying makes more sense in the light of the film's trick ending, Griffin's anti climactic resolution only raises more problems. Like a sour surprise birthday party, Griffin's bathetic *coup de théâtre* shows the various, apparently unconnected players in Nick's nightmarish drama all plotting against him behind the walls of a hastily constructed set. Perhaps it's meant to add another layer to Griffin's role-playing game of self-serving deception, or perhaps it's meant to critique the luridly theatrical earlier events, but either way the bald conclusion merely seems an easy, cheating way out.

Developed from a short story Griffin wrote at college, *Best Laid Plans* has a callow cleverness which never gets to grips with the weighty subjects it summons. Setting itself up as a self-conscious study of greed, lust and survival, it succeeds only in sending a group of ciphers through a maze of moral dilemmas. While the best *noir* has an ambiguity that keeps us questioning everything we see and hear, *Best Laid Plans* is just implausible, its muscular performances undermined by literate but ludicrous dialogue.

VILLAGE VOICE, 9/14/99, p. 144, Dennis Lim

By all means bring a dumb date to *Best Laid Plans,* a creakily mechanical B-noir that leaves scheming lovers Alessandro Nivola and Reese Witherspoon and blowhard-chump Josh Brolin entangled in a *Red Rock West*-ish series of double-bluffs. (There's also an Indecent Proposal of sorts involved.) British director Mike Barker plays up the showiness of Ted Griffin's script. The film opens with a cliffhanger, then flashes back four months, fills in the details, and builds to the opening sequence, which is then replayed with the benefit of perspective. Encompassing as it does a catalogue of Amerindie bad habits, the movie works as a kind of reverse primer, a how-not-to (or a please-don't).   A shortlist of offenses: said gimmicky structure, wacky cinematography (circular dolly shots especially), a villain who quotes Adam Smith's *The Wealth of Nations,* and, worst of all, a deflationary, *Usual Suspects*-style punch line.

Also reviewed in:
CHICAGO TRIBUNE, 9/24/99, Friday/p. K, John Petrakis
NEW YORK TIMES, 9/10/99, p. E22, Janet Maslin
VARIETY, 6/14-20/99, p. 33, Derek Elley

BEST MAN, THE

A Universal Pictures release of a 40 Acres and a Mule Filmworks production. *Producer:* Spike Lee, Sam Kitt, and Bill Carraro. *Director:* Malcolm D. Lee. *Screenplay:* Malcolm D. Lee. *Director of Photography:* Frank Prinzi. *Editor:* Cara Silverman. *Music:* Stanley Clarke. *Music Editor:* E. Gedney Webb. *Choreographer:* Michelle Robinson. *Sound:* Bill Daly and (music) Steve Miller. *Sound Editor:* Paul Urmson. *Casting:* Robi Reed-Humes. *Production Designer:* Kalina Ivanov. *Art Director:* Wing Lee. *Set Decorator:* Christina K. Tonkin and Paul Weathered. *Set Dresser:* Kathy Fundis, Natalie N. Dorset, Joe Vilchock, Jr., Gerard Engrassia and Joe Tagliariano. *Costumes:* Danielle Hollowell. *Make-up:* Toy Van Lierop. *Stunt Coordinator:* David Lomax. *Running time:* 118 minutes. *MPAA Rating:* R.

CAST: Taye Diggs (Harper); Nia Long (Jordan); Morris Chestnut (Lance); Harold Perrineau (Murch); Terrence Howard (Quentin); Sanaa Lathan (Robin); Monica Calhoun (Mia); Melissa De Sousa (Shelby); Victoria Dillard (Anita); Regina Hall (Candy); Jim Moody (Uncle Skeeter); Jarrod Bunch (Wayne); Stu "Large" Riley (Fandango); Liris Crosse and Lady Madonna (Strippers); Linda Powell (Wedding Coordinator); Willie Carpenter (Pastor); Malcolm D. Lee (Emcee); Doug Banks (Himself); DeDe McGuire (Herself); Renton Kirk and Patrick Malcolm (Groomsmen); Linda Murrell and Willie Gaskins (Lance's Parents); Emilie Gaskins and Don Clark Williams (Mia's Parents); Charltina "Chasha" Banks and Aleisha Allen (Flower Girls); Vance Allen (Broom Bearer).

LOS ANGELES TIMES, 10/22/99, Calendar/p. 12, Eric Harrison

Taye Diggs acts in movies as if he has a sign dangling from his neck that reads "Future Major Star." With his sculpted torso and a face that looks stunning in profile, he shortly may well become one.

But the effort of projecting all of that star charisma surely takes a toll. Maybe it siphons off energy he'd ordinarily use for acting, because Diggs, who made his debut as Angela Bassett's boy toy in "How Stella Got Her Groove Back," doesn't really create fully fleshed-out characters. He is a Presence for Hire. This causes problems for his new movie, "The Best Man," because we never know what we are to make of his Harper Stewart.

Malcolm D. Lee, the film's first-time writer and director, seems to want us to like the character, this even though he is, at heart, not very nice. Harper (Diggs) is to be the best man at the wedding of a former college classmate Lance (Morris Chestnut) and his sweet, almost innocent fiancee (Monica Calhoun). As a varied cast of friends gather in New York for the wedding, it turns out that an advance copy of Harper's first novel is making the rounds. The book is a poorly veiled autobiography, and in it he reveals that sometime after he introduced the couple, Harper slept with Lance's future bride.

The movie centers on Harper's efforts to keep his friend—a hulking, hot-headed professional football player—from finding out. At the same time, the commitment-shy Harper has broken the heart of his lover (a very appealing Sanaa Lathan) and left her at home in Chicago. He's entertaining notions of picking up where he left off with former almost-girlfriend Jordan (Nia Long), who still wants him badly.

"The Best Man" is Lee's attempt at making a romantic comedy that black audiences can enjoy without having to reimagine themselves as Hugh Grant and Julia Roberts. Turnabout is fair play, so Lee talks in interviews about the story's universality, which is his way of inviting white folk to the party.

For large stretches of this nicely mounted production it looks as if the filmmaker (Spike Lee's cousin) has what it takes to pull off his crossover dream. Somehow, though, those stretches all got bunched up near the end. The first half of the movie, however, lies there like an overturned bus—you wonder how it'll ever get uprighted, but you don't really want to stick around to find out.

Lee spends what feels like an inordinate amount of time moving his chess pieces into place. All the while, the characters can't stop talking—a lot of back story has to get filled in. Trouble is everyone's having the same conversation. The characters and locations may change—men try on tuxedos or play cards or Harper and Jordan buy a wedding gift together—but all of this is overlaid with a running dialogue about the book, the past and man-woman relations. It might as well be radio—what they're doing hardly matters. Lee, nevertheless, is a talented filmmaker, and one whose sensibility and approach are totally different from that of his older, politically minded and aesthetically daring cousin (who's one of the producers of "The Best Man").

Once the story gets underway, the movie is quite funny, and except for Diggs' blurry characterization, the actors all shine in sharply defined roles. Lee has a gift for snappy, character-revealing dialogue. He makes a misstep, though, in allowing his males to overindulge in profanity and frequent uses of a certain racial epithet. His defense doubtless would be that he's "keeping it real." But such language is jarring in a romantic comedy, especially when spoken by educated, supposedly sophisticated professionals in a movie that aims for "universal" appeal.

"The Best Man" has a decidedly male focus—Lee seems to think that having Diggs and Chestnut take off their shirts a lot will get women into seats. Some of the language and sexist attitudes keep you from feeling too warmly about the two main male characters, though. For all of Harper's sins, Lance is worse. He is an unrepentant chauvinist who wears his religion on his sleeve. When he gets upset, which is often, he hits first and prays later.

Long, Harold Perrineau and Terrence Howard shine in supporting roles. Perrineau ("The Edge," HBO's "Oz") plays a meek buddy who comes into his own over the course of the film. The standout character, though, is Howard's Quentin, a ne'er-do-well friend who initially comes off as the least likable of the bunch. The character is a triumph of both writing and acting. Howard's sly, devilish charm helps transform him into the movie's unlikely voice of wisdom and moral conscience.

Howard plays him in a low-key fashion. He never shouts "Look at me," but you do anyway because he's the most interesting person on the screen. Diggs may well succeed in becoming the next Denzel Washington, but for now, in this movie, Howard's off-kilter radiance blows him off the screen.

NEW YORK POST, 10/22/99, p. 56, Lou Lumenick

Take "The Big Chill," replace the characters with black professionals and drop out the politics and Motown score, and you've more or less got the frequently hilarious "The Best Man."

What draws these six friends together for a reunion seven years after their college graduation isn't a funeral—it's the wedding of Lance (Morris Chestnut) a professional football running back, and his longtime love, Mia (Monica Calhoun).

Lance's best man is Harper (Taye Diggs), an ambitious Chicagoan whose autobiographical first novel has just been chosen as a selection for Oprah's book club.

But an advance copy has begun circulating among his old classmates in New York City. And Jordan (Nia Long), an equally ambitious TV producer who's angling to get a scoop on the wedding for her network, has figured out that Harper has more or less admitted sleeping with the bride-to-be during their college days.

When the troublemaking Quentin (Terrence Howard) jokingly suggests to Lance that Mia might not have been strictly faithful during his promiscuous college days, Lance explodes in a jealous fury—a fury that makes Harper very nervous, since he knows Lance is slowly making his way through Harper's book.

"The Best Man" climaxes with a wild and bawdy bachelor party, during which the truth gradually dawns on Lance—with near-lethal results for Harper.

Malcolm D. Lee (his cousin Spike produced) makes an auspicious debut as a writer-director with "The Best Man." But he's more assured as a writer than he is behind the camera.

But the performances by the attractive ensemble cast are uniformly solid, especially when it comes to the romantic chemistry between Diggs ("Go") and Long ("Stigmata") as two careerists whose egos tend to get in the way of their happiness.

"The Best Man," which should please a more mainstream audience than most movies with predominately black casts, builds to a side-splitting, and ultra-romantic climax.

Stick around when the credits roll; one of the biggest laughs comes in the middle of them.

NEWSDAY, 10/22/99, Part II/p. B9, Jan Stuart

You don't have to drop a small pile on subscriptions to Vogue and GQ to realize just how ugly and unkempt you really are. A couple of hours among the sensationally svelte and soigné cast of "The Best Man" should send you skulking off to the land of the cosmetically challenged for the rest of your born days.

If you don't mind feeling insecure about your appearance, chances are you will snuggle right up to "The Best Man," a smart-looking and smart-talking buppie comedy from writer-director Malcolm D. Lee. The buzzmakers have been likening it to "The Big Chill" for its circle-of-friends ensemble format, but it's really more like a sophisticated Stanley Donen romantic comedy with the genetic selectivity of "Brave New World."

Setting the glamorous tone is Taye Diggs, a rising romantic star who looks so dashing in glasses he could prompt a lull in laser eye surgery appointments for the next month. Diggs plays Harper, an on-the-brink novelist whose two-year relationship with his girlfriend Robin (Sanaa Lathan) begins to strain as he goes off to be the best man at the wedding of old friends, football star Lance Sullivan (Morris Chestnut) and his fiancee Mia (Monica Calhoun).

Lance and Mia are not the only unwitting participants in Harper's first novel, a roman à clef with a cast of characters heavily borrowed from his old college chums. And they are all at the wedding to applaud and jeer Harper's literary larceny: TV producer and would-be girlfriend Jordan (Nia Long), for whom he still carries a torch; musician and rebel spirit Quentin (Terrence Howard); henpecked schoolteacher Murch (Harold Perrineau) and his manipulating girlfriend Shelby (Melissa De Sousa).

Writer Lee (cousin of Spike, who co-produced the film) shows a flair for the sort of tart, grown-up repartee once favored by Cary Grant and Audrey Hepburn, reinvigorated with a knowing, '90s New York edge. His directing rhythm is relaxed and unhurried to a fault: He keeps a dozen balls in the air and trusts his audience will stay with him even as a couple of the balls drop, as they do in the protracted second half.

"The Best Man" peaks halfway in with one genuinely terrific scene, a late-night poker game in which Harper, Lance and their chums trade friendly insults. Abetted by Stanley Clarke's propulsive scoring, the scene has a bristling energy the rest the movie never quite matches. The film's unwavering spark plug is Terrence Howard, whose naughty-boy grin and towel-snapping comic timing are a joy to watch. He's the real thing, a refreshing blast of rudeness amid perfectly bleached smiles.

SIGHT AND SOUND, 11/00, p. 44, Kay Dickinson

US, the present. Harper, a successful novelist, is about to publish a semi-autobiographical account of his student years. Leaving girlfriend Robin at home, he joins friends whom he met at university in New York for a weekend reunion which is to culminate with the wedding of Mia and Lance (for whom he is best man). Harper discovers Jordan, a television producer whom he nearly slept with at college, has circulated his book among their friends.

It becomes clear that the novel describes a sexual encounter between characters similar to Harper and Mia. During the stag night, Lance realises this, attacks Harper and declares the wedding cancelled. Harper retreats to Jordan's house. They argue and he sleeps on the sofa. Oblivious to all this, Mia and guests gather at the church the next day and await Lance's arrival. Harper convinces Lance to go through with the wedding; he then decides that he and Jordan are unsuited and proposes to Robin.

With *The Best Man* debut director Malcolm Lee shows recognisable links with the work of his film making colleague and cousin Spike (acting, in this instance, as co-producer). But while this new-Lee-on-the block shares Spike's political approach to film-making in his insistence on interrogating Hollywood's gallery of African-American stereotypes, his film lacks his relative's comedic irreverence.

Set during a weekend reunion for friends who met at college. *The Best Man* is let down by Lee's well-intended attempt to fill the film with positive African-American role models. The movie's world of yuppie characters, rose-petal baths and constant references to university does at least mark a shift from US cinema's tendency to associate African-American culture with inner-city violence and deprivation. The trouble with *The Best Man*, however, is that its eager to please tone is almost as predictable and limiting as the ghetto haunts of, say, *Juice and Menace II Society*. in his earnestness Lee forgets that we need engagingly defective objects of mockery for comedy to work and instead falls back on characters who exhibit no demeaning flaws. Most perplexingly there's a lack of logic about the proposed respectability of the main character Harper, a novelist who very publicly dishes the dirt on his friends via a book that is due for heavy promotion on Oprah Winfrey's television show.

With political tip-toeing so high on *The Best Man*'s agenda it becomes difficult to stop oneself from asking why Jordan, the film's ambitious career girl, is left resigned to a single life at the end of the movie, while Robin, the lackadaisical caterer who wants babies, wins the marriage proposal from the leading man. Stereotypes from beyond the domain of racial identity rear their heads after all, notably Murch, the henpecked boyfriend who ditches his nit picking paramour for a tart-with-a-heart. While harmless enough, these buffoons make us aware of the main characters' lack of comic bite.

Thankfully, the film's double bind relying on caricatures to raise a laugh, but not wanting to denigrate any African Americans in the process is eluded by pleasingly acerbic dialogue. An early boys-only poker game zips through the conversational gamut of infidelity with jagged comments ricocheting across the card table until the scene cuts off on an ambiguous note with two of the friends nearly coming to blows. Their motives are left unresolved and such curious, unexplained currents, along with regular comic relief in the form of genuinely sharp one-liners, make for some lively moments. But the film's overarching problem remains that the yuppie lifestyle, regardless of colour, is hardly the stuff of riveting entertainment.

VILLAGE VOICE, 10/26/99, p. 162, Amy Taubin

The Best Man is an unabashedly mainstream romantic comedy about an upwardly mobile group of twentysomethings who are making choices about love and work that will determine the next 40 years of their lives. Everything about the film is familiar except that the twentysomethings are all African American (no bows to the "crossover audience" here), and that alone breathes a bit of new life into the genre.

On the other hand, this is not a film about race or racism. Race is even less an issue in Malcolm D. Lee's debut feature than Jewishness is in Woody Allen films. Woody Allen always has a couple of WASPs around to tickle his neuroses. In *The Best Man,* there are no white people and hence no racism. Nor are there any poor African Americans, and hence, no African American bourgeois guilt. Maybe *The Best Man* is escapist entertainment plain and simple, or maybe it's a subtle act of revenge on a century of American movies that painted the world as white, or maybe it's an accurate depiction of the self-protective mindset of a generation. One thing is sure: although *The Best Man* was coproduced by the director's cousin, Spike Lee, he has never directed a film that goes down as easily as this one does.

Harper Stewart (Taye Diggs) is a young writer whose soon-to-be-published first novel, *Unfinished Business,* is favored by Oprah. Like many first-time novelists, Harper has written about what he knows best—himself and his friends. Two of these friends are getting married and the groom has chosen Harper as his best man. The problem is that an advance copy of *Unfinished Business* has been circulating among the wedding party. Harper's friends, who have some quibbles about the way they're portrayed, are also worried that the groom, despite his busy schedule, might get far enough into the book to discover that if fiction mirrors fact, his bride isn't as perfect as he fantasizes and that he was betrayed by his best man.

Harper's profession is crucial for the plot but insignificant in terms of the film's milieu. *The Best Man* eschews the black bohemian edge of *Hav Plenty* or *Love Jones*. And Diggs, despite his wire-rimmed glasses, hardly seems a writerly type. The best man is not only the film's leading man but also the straight man for most of its comedy. Diggs is a terrific-looking guy, but he's easily upstaged by some of the quirkier actors who have less screen time but more showy roles. Among the standouts: Morris Chestnut as the groom, a football superstar who can't square his jealousy and sexual double standard with his religious beliefs; Harold Perrineau as a dreadlocked social worker who's under the thumb of his nouveau riche girlfriend; and Terrence Howard as the group's put-down artist who hasn't a clue what to do with his own life.

Lee manages to juggle several plot lines while fleshing out a half-dozen characters, although the women are mostly clichés. The dialogue is fast, funny, and based in character. Adroitly directed, the film moves briskly once Lee gets past the awkward lovers-quarrel-in-a-bathtub opening. (And where have we seen those rose-petal-covered bodies before?)

One of the problems of the romantic comedy genre is that it's based on the assumption that 100 movie minutes is all that's needed to change two imperfectly matched humans into ideal mates for life. *Bringing Up Baby*'s Cary Grant probably returned to being a stick in the mud as soon as he married Katharine Hepburn. And I suspect that it won't be long before *The Best Man*'s groom gets into a jealous rage at his new wife. I got a bit teary during the wedding, but I doubt that the marriage will survive the century's end.

Also reviewed in:
CHICAGO TRIBUNE, 10/22/99, Friday/p. E, Barbara Shulgasser
NEW YORK TIMES, 10/22/99, p. E26, Janet Maslin
VARIETY, 9/20-26/99, p. 83, Emanuel Levy

BETTER THAN CHOCOLATE

A Trimark Pictures release of a Rave Film production supported by Telefilm Canada and British Columbia Film. *Producer:* Sharon McGowan and Peggy Thomson. *Director:* Anne Wheeler. *Screenplay:* Peggy Thomson. *Director of Photography:* Gregory Middleton. *Editor:* Alison Grace. *Music:* Graeme Coleman. *Sound:* Gael McLean. *Production Designer:* David Roberts. *Art Director:* Kate King. *Set Decorator:* Penny Chalmers. *Costumes:* Brad Gough. *Casting:* Lynne Carrow. *Running time:* 103 minutes. *MPAA Rating:* Not Rated.

CAST: Wendy Crewson (Lila); Karyn Dwyer (Maggie); Christina Cox (Kim); Anne-Marie MacDonald (Frances); Peter Outerbridge (Judy/Jeremy); Marya Delver (Carla); Kevin Mundy (Paul); Tony Nappo (Tony); Jay Brazeau (Mr. Marcus).

LOS ANGELES TIMES, 8/13/99, Calendar/p. 10, Kevin Thomas

"Better Than Chocolate" is a breezy romantic comedy that finds a vivacious Vancouver 19-year-old, Maggie (Karyn Dwyer), dropping out of college to take a job at a lesbian bookstore, figuring that since she wants to be a writer she needs to do some learning from life itself. As it happens, a cool, stunning blond, Kim (Christina Cox), an itinerant artist, has set up her easel nearby. The attraction between the two is instantaneous and mutual, and with Kim's van parked nearby, swiftly consummated. Maggie couldn't be more delighted.

Then she gets the wholly unexpected phone call from her mother, Lila (Wendy Crewson), saying that her husband, Maggie's stepfather, has left her and that she and Maggie's younger brother Paul (Kevin Mundy), who live some distance away, are on their way to move in with her. Maggie hasn't exactly been leveling with her mother, who doesn't know that she's dropped out of school, sleeping at the bookstore, dancing nights at a lesbian nightclub—or even that she's a lesbian.

Caught completely off-base, Maggie's not ready to be candid with her mother. She scrambles to find suitable living quarters, landing a loft that she is able to rent only on a short-term basis. You can tell that Maggie has too open and sunny a personality not to come out to her mother eventually, and you sense that she simply would like to be able to pick and choose the circumstances. Of course, you don't always have such luxury of choice, but that's just one of life's lessons that Maggie is about to learn.

Writer Peggy Thomson and director Anne Wheeler are intent upon striking a blithe, upbeat note, but that doesn't keep them from taking note of some of the harsher realities. The bookstore is beginning to be targeted by the puritanically minded for carrying a line of sex toys; Maggie and Kim are thrown out of a local cafe for kissing in public; and Maggie's transsexual friend Judy (Peter Outerbridge) is vulnerable to harassment at its most hateful.

While she feels understandably crushed by the breakup of her marriage, Lila seems well-meaning, though ripe for revitalizing her own life and expanding her horizons. However, as the film wears on, she seems increasingly obtuse in regard to her daughter's sexual orientation, which has the effect of undermining the movie's credibility. What's more, you don't get the feeling that she could possibly be so rigidly homophobic that she would actually reject her daughter for being a lesbian.

Even though you could wish that "Better Than Chocolate" was a little more substantially developed, it nonetheless brims over with good humor and high spirits and has some moments of stunning yet tasteful eroticism. Dwyer and Cox are charmers, and that's also the case with "Better Than Chocolate."

NEW YORK POST, 8/13/99, p. 62, Jonathan Foreman

"Better Than Chocolate" boasts a fresh collection of characters whose world is centered on a lesbian bookshop in Vancouver and some sex scenes during the first act that are genuinely hot stuff.

So it's a shame that this romantic comedy from Canada gradually degenerates into a cliché-ridden mess at once syrupy and cheesy.

By the end, you wonder if the filmmakers weren't following the instructions laid down in some Big Book of Gay Movie Clichés—late '80s edition. And it's not just the compulsory climactic gay-bashing scene or the predictable Lilith Fair score (the title comes from the Sarah McLachlan song "ice cream").

College dropout Maggie (Karyn Dwyer), who is supposed to be only 19 and has great curly, red hair, works at Ten Per Cent Books and sleeps on a couch in the back.

The imminent arrival in town of her mother and brother prompts Maggie to get a huge sublet, but the night before moving in, she hooks up with Kim (Christina Cox), a tough, nomadic artist who saves her from some skinheads.

Kim has already moved in, and the two women are enjoying a shower together when mother and 17-year-old brother turn up.

By the next morning, brother Paul (Kevin Mundy) has figured out what's going on. But Maggie's mom, Lila (Wendy Crewson, overacting wildly), is too grotesquely stupid to figure it out.

Maggie's unexplained reluctance to confess her orientation to Lila (even though everyone else in town, including the local skinheads, know that she's "out") then becomes the dilemma that is supposed to drive the plot.

The problem is that Maggie has no reason not to tell Lila the truth. And in any case, Lila is so unbelievably, irritatingly clueless that there's no chance she'll ever put two and two together by herself. In fact, mom seems to have wandered in from another movie and another time. She becomes friends with tall, deep-voiced male-to-female transsexual Judy, and it just doesn't occur to her that Judy (Peter Outerbridge) might once have been a man.

Perhaps this ludicrous portrayal of an ultra-straight "straight" plays OK in a small, Canadian gay community, but in New York it—and the movie—comes off as embarrassingly provincial. It's a shame because there's real chemistry between the two leads (you have to take it on trust that they share true love rather than mere horniness). And there are also some promising subplots, including a possible romance between uptight bookstore owner Frances and Judy, an affair between pansexual bookstore worker Carla (Marya Delver) and Paul, and a conflict with the Canadian customs over the importation of lesbian porn from the United States.

"Better Than Chocolate" is well-filmed and for the most part well-acted. But its technical professionalism only serves to make the amateurishly crude patches of Maggie Thomson's script more obvious.

NEWSDAY, 8/13/99, Part II/p. B7, John Anderson

Like fireworks on the 5th of July, "Better Than Chocolate" triumphs and exults and probably would have been infectious if it had just arrived on time. A comedy, a romance and a lesbian film—it more or less insists on the nomenclature—it's hardly the only selection on its particular menu. Gay film festivals are breaking out all over. "Ellen," lest we forget, took a gay heroine to prime-time TV—a kicking and screaming prime-time TV, but TV nonetheless. And The Advocate reports that Salma Hayak has agreed to do same-sex scenes in order to play artist Frida Kahlo. "Chocolate," however, seems to think it's on the ramparts and that the ramparts are on fire.

What do we have? Like "Trick," which is more or less its male counterpart, "Better Than Chocolate" is about true love stymied by circumstance, about the logistical problems of sex and is a likable enough film, if only because of its likable actors. Karyn Dwyer, whose Maggie is a college dropout, bookstore clerk and aspiring nightclub performer, is adorable. So is Wendy Crewson, who plays her suddenly single, totally clueless mother Lila, who announces that she and son are moving in with Maggie just as the younger woman makes the romance connection with Kim (Christina Cox), Brad Pitt-lookalike and nomadic street artist.

But in addition to all the narrative wheel-spinning that keeps her movie from ever getting anywhere, director Anne Wheeler seems to want to create a catalog of types, a time capsule of lesbian cinema. There's Judy/Jeremy (Peter Outerbridge), the delicate pre-op transsexual who's in love with Frances (Ann-Marie MacDonald), the uptight, can't-deal-with-her-sexuality book-store owner; Tony (Tony Nappo), the not-so-raging bull of a coffee shop owner, who's not averse to lesbians but won't let them kiss in his cafe. And Carla (Marya Delver), a sort of comedy implant whose bisexuality equals promiscuity-something the movie clearly finds amusingly untoward and the moral equivalent of political fence-sitting.

To its credit, "Better Than Chocolate" acknowledges the homophobic outside world—skinheads are an irregular threat in the characters' latte-and-lipsynching world, so we don't get the sociological terrarium effect imposed by directors or writers who operate solely on wishful thinking.

But there's enough that's familiar here: Crewson, who steals the picture in Lila's pearls and sweater sets, is presumed tragic because she left a promising (we assume) music career to marry and raise a family and can't quite get her mind around the fact that the world's changed—or, for that matter, that her daughter is sleeping in the next room with another woman. What's confusing to us is Lila's age. She can't be more than 40, so what does she represent? Not the prefeminist 1950s. She's too young to symbolize the traditional thinking Wheeler wants to critique.

The various blowups by the various characters that set up the dramatic resolutions are totally contrived, as is the blowing up of Tony's cafe—anyone stupid enough to hook up their gas range with the gas running deserves immolation. Far more irritating, though, is the fact that every time two people go into a clinch, another alt-rock selection is cued up. Even Wheeler seems to acknowledge it—when Judy and the neurotic object of her affection, Frances, break after an awkward embrace, the music stops abruptly. If there'd been a little more such self-awareness on the movie's part, it would have been better for all of us.

VILLAGE VOICE, 8/17/99, p. 68, Jessica Winter

Better Than Chocolate: as in "Your love is...," as in the Quik-secreting Sarah McLachlan ballad. The namesake film is an amiable, scatterbrained tale that emits enough patchouli-tinged sisterly warmth to aromatize several Lilith Fairs, but all the sapphic good vibrations may induce nausea even in attendees familiar with such sticky, syrupy coming-out herstories.

Nineteen-year-old Maggie (Karyn Dwyer) has just dropped out of college and fallen into love with portrait artist Kim (Christina Cox) when Mom, freshly dumped by her second husband, announces she's moving into her daughter's flat with Maggie's doofus brother in tow. Not just clueless about her little girl's sexuality, Mom (Wendy Crewson) also seems unclear on what year it is, and the movie's level of subtlety can be gauged by its illustration of her bondage in housewifedom: though the setting is present-day Vancouver, she sports sweater sets, pearls, and a coiffure petrified halfway between Donna Reed and a B-52. Mom, a puritanical chocoholic, cluelessly bonds with male-to-female transgendered lesbian Judy (Peter Outerbridge), who's smitten with Frances (Ann-Marie MacDonald), Maggie's high-strung boss at Ten Percent Books (Mom: "So you're working at a discount bookstore?"). Meanwhile, Maggie tries mustering the gumption to tell her mother about her relationship with Kim (we know the couple's love is true, since another gauzy acoustic ditty pops up on the soundtrack every time the girls come near each other).

These voyages of self-discovery wouldn't be complete without a few narrative landmines contrived for maximum melodrama. Judy gets bashed at a dyke bar (with a handbag, no less) for, um, using the wrong bathroom (no justice, no peace!) while skinheads firebomb the bookstore, with a naked Maggie inside. Love and understanding is readily found among the ruins—there's nothing like a well-timed disaster to smooth over any rough edges, especially in a movie that can only open its eyes enough to see the good in everything.

Also reviewed in:
CHICAGO TRIBUNE, 8/27/99, Friday/p. I, John Petrakis
NEW YORK TIMES, 8/13/99, p. E26, Stephen Holden
VARIETY, 2/22-28/99, p. 58, David Stratton
WASHINGTON POST, 9/3/99, p. C1, Rita Kempley

BEYOND THE CLOUDS

A Sunshine/Cine B/France 3 Cinema/Cecchi-Gori Group Tiger Cinematografica/Road Movies Zweite Produktionen GMBH coproduction. *Executive Producer:* Danielle Gegauff Rosencrantz, Brigitte Faure, and Pierre Reutfeld. *Producer:* Stephane Tchalgadjieff and Philippe Carcassonne. *Director:* Michelangelo Antonioni and Wim Wenders. *Screenplay (English, Italian and French with English subtitles):* Tonino Guerra, Michelangelo Antonioni, and Wim Wenders. *Based on his collection of short stories "Quel Bowling sul Tevere.":* Michelangelo Antonioni. *Director of Photography (for Antonioni):* Alfio Contini. *Director of Photography (for Wim Wenders):* Robby Muller. *Editor (for Antonioni):* Cladio Di Mauro. *Editor (for Wenders):* Peter Przygodda and Luciano Segura. *Production Designer:* Thierry Flamand. *Costumes:* Esther Walz. *Running time:* 104 minutes. *MPAA Rating:* Not Rated.

CAST: John Malkovich (The Director); Kim Rossi-Stuart (Silvano); Ines Sastre (Carmen); Sophie Marceau (Girl); Fanny Ardant (Patricia); Peter Weller (Husband); Chiara Caselli (Mistress); Irene Jacob (Girl); Vincent Perez (Boy); Jean Reno (Carlo); Marcello Mastroianni (Painter); Jeanne Moreau (Friend).

LOS ANGELES TIMES, 12/3/99, Calendar/p. 20, Kevin Thomas

In recent years, Italy's grand master, Michelangelo Antonioni, has been largely silenced by a 1985 stroke that has left his speech impaired but from which he otherwise recovered. In 1995, he returned to feature filmmaking after a 13-year absence with the assistance of Germany's protean Wim Wenders for "Beyond the Clouds," a shimmeringly beautiful and wise reverie on love and desire, which arrives at last in a regular run.

"Beyond the Clouds" is a homage to passion recollected in tranquillity. Antonioni's usual preoccupation with alienation in modern life remains but is supplemented with an aura of warmth and gratitude on the part of the filmmaker for having lived and loved, coupled with an acceptance of the transient and the elusive that marks so many human encounters.

It is composed of four vignettes drawn from a collection of short stories by Antonioni and adapted to the screen by him with Wenders and the distinguished veteran Tonino Guerra. They are linked by Antonioni's alter ego, the Director (John Malkovich), whom we meet on a plane bound for Antonioni's hometown, Ferrara.

The Director tells us that although he's tired from just completing a film, he nevertheless feels compelled to start searching for ideas for the next one.

"Beyond the Clouds" therefore unfolds as a journey that takes the Director from Ferrara to Portofino to Paris and finally to Aix-en-Provence.

The framing story, directed by Wenders, is rich in Antonioni's feelings about cinema and what it has meant to him.

Each of the film's settings is of surpassing beauty and grandeur, captured gloriously by cinematographer Alfio Contini; Antonioni's style remains inimitable.

Visually, every nuance of feeling and thought is expressed cinematically in the boldest, most distinctive and imaginative use of camera movement and placement.

What counts here, and what gives this film its power, is the intense yet bemused compassion that Antonioni is able to convey about his people and their romantic predicaments.

Matching Memories to Specific Places

Antonioni always has been a master of moods, and his lyrical imagery and pacing have been complemented by Lucio Dalla and Laurent Petitgrand's poignant score, which deftly includes selections from Brian Eno with U2 and from Van Morrison.

"Beyond the Clouds" unfolds as a series of memories rekindled and shared with the audience as the Director visits each place.

In short, he becomes a compelling storyteller as we first meet, in Ferrara, a handsome young man, Silvano (Kim Rossi-Stuart) and a beautiful young woman, Carmen (Ines Sastre), guests at the same hotel.

Their attraction is mutual and immediate. This first episode leaves you feeling that Antonioni is drawing from a personal experience never to be forgotten.

Moving on to Portofino, the Director himself is drawn to a lovely young woman (Sophie Marceau) who works in a clothing boutique and is in turn drawn to him. She tells him that she had murdered her father, stabbing him 12 times, but was subsequently acquitted. The Director proceeds to have a romantic rendezvous with her, but the artist in him, ever in search of perfection, realizes that for him 12 times is excessive—any more than three stabbings offends his artistic sensibilities!

In a Paris bistro, a lovely young woman (Chiara Caselli) enchants an American (Peter Weller) with her story of a group of scientists on an expedition in South America whose native guides refuse to take another step. Three years into Weller and Caselli's affair, the American's elegant French wife (Fanny Ardant) has finally had it with her husband and moves out of their posh apartment.

Entering the swanky new apartment she has just rented, with her furniture soon to follow, she encounters a man (Jean Reno) standing in stunned silence.

His wife has just done to him what Ardant has done to Weller: abruptly departed with most of their possessions. As Ardant and Reno lock into a gaze, we're left to wonder whether he'll have to move after all.

As the Director proceeds to Aix-en-Provence, Wenders digresses briefly for an interlude reuniting the stars of Antonioni's landmark 1961 "La Notte," Marcello Mastroianni and Jeanne Moreau.

Mastroianni is a painter, contentedly at work on a landscape in what his friend (Moreau) recognizes as an emulation of Cezanne.

She laments a society that insists on copying everything from master paintings to suitcases, while Mastroianni's artist explains that for him the thrill is in attempting to recapture the gesture of a genius—which seems a clear homage from Wenders to Antonioni, whose style he and his cameraman, Robby Muller, emulate lovingly in their linking episodes.

In Antonioni's climactic sequence, the radiant Irene Jacob is resisting ever so politely the overtures of the young man (Vincent Perez) who is beguiled by her at first sight.

It's enchanting as these two young people discover that while she may be scared of life, he may in turn be afraid of death.

"Beyond the Clouds," in all ways an enthrallingly exquisite film, leaves us feeling that Antonioni may well see himself in both characters.

NEW YORK POST, 12/1/99, p. 58, Lou Lumenick

Legendary director Michelangelo Antonioni, sidelined by a stroke in 1985, returned to filmmaking a decade later with "Beyond the Clouds," a beautifully photographed film that he completed with considerable help from German director Wim Wenders.

Sadly, only one of the four episodes devised by the director of such masterpieces as "L'Adventurra," "The Passenger" and "Blow-Up," is involving—a Paris-set triangle involving an American (Peter Weller), his wife (Fanny Ardant) and his mistress (Chiara Caselli), and a second man (Jean Reno) who provides an 0. Henry-like twist.

Despite an intriguing cast, the four stories are linked by pretentious narrative sequences (credited to Wenders) featuring John Malkovich as a film director who tries to explain what we've seen.

His character also appears in one of the stories, stalking a Portofino shopgirl (Sophie Marceau) who admits to stabbing her father 12 times.

That story is about as slight as another episode, in which a young man (Kim Rossi-Stewart) is unable to consummate his relationship with a woman he's sought for years, and the final story, wherein a footloose young man (Vincent Perez) falls for a young woman (Irene Jacob) who's about to enter a convent.

"Beyond the Clouds," a multilingual mishmash that also includes brief goodwill cameos by Jeanne Moreau and the late Marcello Mastroianni, is most notable for its exquisitely composed, painterly images, photographed by Alfio Contini and Robby Muller.

VILLAGE VOICE, 12/7/99, p. 148, Michael Atkinson

Part of the price we have to pay, it seems, for the international art-film mardi gras of the '60s and '70s is the discomfiting experience of watching the giants inch into their dotage, refusing against better judgment to retire. While some have maintained a degree of grace (Kurosawa's *Madadayo*, premiered this September on TCM, was lovely and adroit), some, like the ailing Michelangelo Antonioni, are encouraged by habit, ambition, or desperation to press on. A full decade after being hit with a massive stroke in 1985, Antonioni assembled *Beyond the Clouds* from a selection of his own short fiction, with Wim Wenders contracted as backup for insurance purposes and to direct a series of connective "interludes" following "the Director" (John Malkovich) as he dallies around Italy.

It's not easy to endure, despite—or due to the embarrassment of—an all-star cast (Fanny Ardant, Sophie Marceau, Jean Reno, etc.). Antonioni's dreamy, pretentious fickle-finger-of-fate mini-tales struggle to wrestle with love and desire, but truck in adolescent ideas and delight in nothing so much as undressing their many young actresses. The good deal of preposterously casual (but lifeless) sex in the movie seems only to invoke an itch the 83-year-old filmmaker can perhaps no longer scratch. The dialogue, backgrounded by actors standing around lovely Mediterranean byways, is witheringly silly—"Nobody watches sunsets anymore," somebody opines apropos of little; "Love is an illusion," someone else shamefacedly utters. The thing is, at least in parts, *Beyond the Clouds* doesn't feel all that different from many other Antonioni films; a reevaluation of the man's oeuvre, after one undergoes the "story" in which "the Director" ("Malkovich, Malkovich!") stares down the peachy Marceau until she non-sequitur-ily tells him she murdered her father, doesn't seem very promising. Was he just fashion?

Also reviewed in:
NEW YORK TIMES, 12/1/99, p. E3, Stephen Holden

BICENTENNIAL MAN

A Touchstone Pictures and Columbia Pictures release of a 1492 production in association with Laurence Marks Productions and Radiant Productions. *Executive Producer:* Dan Kolsrud. *Producer:* Wolfgang Petersen, Gail Katz, Laurence Mark, Neal Miller, Chris Columbus, Mark Radcliffe, and Michael Barnathan. *Director:* Chris Columbus. *Screenplay:* Nicholas Kazan. *Based on the short story by:* Isaac Asimov *and the novel "The Positronic Man" by:* Isaac Asimov and Robert Silverberg. *Director of Photography:* Phil Meheux. *Editor:* Neil Travis. *Music:* James Horner. *Music Editor:* Jim Henrikson. *Sound:* Nelson Stoll and (music) Simon Rhodes. *Sound Editor:* Robert Shoup. *Casting:* Janet Hirshenson and Jane Jenkins. *Production Designer:* Norman Reynolds. *Art Director:* Mark Mansbridge, William Hiney, and Bruton E. Jones, Jr. *Set Decorator:* Anne Kuljian. *Set Designer:* William A. Taliaferro, Geoff Hubbard, Darrell L. Wight, and James E. Tocci. *Set Dresser:* Ruby Guidara. *Special Effects:* John McLeod. *Visual Effects:* James E. Price. *Costumes:* Joseph G. Aulisi. *Robotic Effects:* Steve Johnson. *Make-up (Old Age):* Greg Cannom and Keith Vanderlaan. *Make-up:* Brad Wilder. *Make-up (Robin Williams):* Cheri Minns. *Stunt Coordinator:* Mike Mitchell. *Running time:* 132 minutes. *MPAA Rating:* PG.

CAST: Robin Williams (Andrew); Embeth Davidtz (Little Miss/Portia); Sam Neill (Sir); Oliver Platt (Rupert Burns); Kiersten Warren (Galatea Robotic/Human); Wendy Crewson (Ma'am); Hallie Kate Eisenberg (Little Miss, 7 Years Old); Lindze Letherman (Miss, 9 Years Old); Angela Landis (Miss); John Michael Higgins (Bill Feingold); Bradley Whitford (Lloyd); Igor Hiller (Lloyd, 10 Years Old); Joe Bellan and Brett Wagner (Robot Delivery Men); Stephen Root (Dennis Mansky); Scott Waugh (Motorcycle Punk); Quinn Smith (Frank); Kristy Connelly (Monica); Jay Johnston (Charles); George D. Wallace (Male President); Lynne Thigpen (Female President); Ples Griffin (Zimbabwe Representative); Marcia Pizzo (Lloyd's Wife); Paula Dupre' Pesmen (Feingold's Assistant); Clarke Devereux (Priest); Bruce Kenneth Wagner (Engagement Party Guest); Paula West (Singer); Kevin "Tiny" Ancell (Restoration Worker #1); Richard Cross (Restoration Worker #2); Adam Bryant (Humanoid Head).

LOS ANGELES TIMES, 12/17/99, Calendar/p. 14, Kevin Thomas

"Bicentennial Man" is a mainstream holiday movie, complete with stupendous special effects, amazing make-up artistry and sumptuous production design that takes us from the years 2005 to 2205. It stars Robin Williams, persuasive as both a robot and a man.

There's no denying that the film is affecting or that it delivers the goods for those hungering for the glossiest possible escapist fantasy. But you wish that the film unfolded on a more modest scale and in the real world rather than in an unblemished earthly paradise, one that seems almost laughably gaudy, whether by design or not. And parents of younger children should know that in its concerns with mortality—and to a lesser degree, sexuality—"Bicentennial Man" becomes increasingly adult.

It figures that a man (Sam Neill) wealthy enough to afford a vintage English cottage-style mansion—in reality a William Randolph Hearst estate in Northern California, no less—could afford to buy a robot to do household chores. He in fact isn't even the first in his suburban Bay Area community to acquire an NDR-114 robot; his is named Andrew by Amanda (Hallie Kate Eisenberg, the dimpled young girl from those popular Pepsi ads), the younger daughter of Neill's Richard Martin.

His older daughter, Grace (Lindze Letherman), finds Andrew's (Williams) presence so intrusive she tries to get him to self-destruct; for this she is soon banished from the story line. Meanwhile, Richard and his wife (Wendy Crewson) take pains to program Andrew properly, with Richard becoming fascinated with the entire phenomenon of artificial intelligence and its remarkable capacity for development.

One day when Amanda hands Andrew her treasured crystal unicorn, he drops it, and it shatters into a million pieces. Comprehending that Amanda is devastated, Andrew starts researching ways in which to replace it and soon presents her with a replica, which he carved from wood. The

Martin family is at once stunned and delighted, and at this moment both Richard and Amanda instinctively begin treating Andrew more like a man than a machine.

Working from Nicholas Kazan's screenplay from a short story by Isaac Asimov and its subsequent expansion into a novel written with Robert Silverberg, director Chris Columbus—who directed Williams in "Mrs. Doubtfire"—and Williams do a masterful job of imagining Andrew's transformation. They convincingly depict Andrew's gradual comprehension of the world and of self, of the concept of humanity, encouraged always by Richard and Amanda.

In the first half of the film, Andrew is the perfect servant in his shiny robot armor, and Richard and Amanda become known to us by how Andrew addresses them: Sir and Little Miss—even after Amanda grows up and is played by the lovely Embeth Davidz. In his crisp formality and tact, and especially his speech, Andrew sounds and acts so much like Roddy McDowall you could believe Williams intended an homage to the late actor.

As time goes by, we're told that robots start losing favor with the public because they represent a threat to the human work force. This means that research in their development grinds to a halt—but not before Andrew's metallic face is given rudimentary expression. Once Andrew dons a tux for the wedding of Little Miss, he wants to wear clothes from then on.

He later encounters Rupert Burns (Oliver Platt), the grandson of the scientist who invented him. In a quaint workshop, Rupert continues his grandfather's work. He gives Andrew a human appearance—at this point Williams is able to shuck the robot suit. He also gives him a central nervous system, a digestive tract and even functional sexuality. For all intents and purposes, Andrew has become a human being—except that he never ages.

As Andrew's evolution takes place, he inevitably comes to see himself as a slave and demands his freedom. Ultimately he falls in love with Little Miss' granddaughter Portia (also played by Davidz). Thus "Bicentennial Man" emerges as above all a romantic sci-fi fable that ponders the nature of humanity, the right of individuals to transform themselves into whatever it is possible for them to be, and mortality as the ultimate defining trait of humanity. Throughout, James Horner's score sustains a mood of wonderment and stirred emotions.

While it's true that Little Miss makes a bad marriage (because she's really in love with Andrew) and that the Martins are subject to the natural cycle of life and death, the family and its descendants lead an otherwise problem-free 200 years during which time San Francisco acquires an ever-more futuristic skyline.

"Bicentennial Man" takes place entirely in luxurious or spectacular interiors or natural locales as perfect as calendar art. Indeed, on a design level "Bicentennial Man" is a nouveau riche dream world come true, in which luxury and grandeur banish all notions of taste or restraint. This gorgeous Las Vegas vision of the future is amusing—and possibly unintentional.

The film's vulgar aura of conspicuous consumption does not take away from the remarkable artistry of Keith Vanderlaan's make-up creations or Greg Cannom's design and application of them. Neither does it take away from the notable performances by Neill as a man of refined sensibility; Platt as a warm whimsical scientific genius; or above all by the tenderness of Williams and Davidz as lovers caught up in a most unusual romance. The damn-the-expense look and feel of "Bicentennial Man" does inject a valuable note of irony, intended or otherwise, leaving us to ponder a materialistic future, with Andrew as the ultimate inflatable boy toy in a gleaming, shiny world in which money can literally buy everything but the desire to live forever.

NEW YORK POST, 12/17/99, p. 60, Lou Lumenick

The once-funny Robin Williams is still stuck in his excruciating touchy-feely mode for "Bicentennial Man," a tinny fantasy about a softhearted robot that spans 200 years.

This failed family entertainment feels almost that long, with no fewer than three deathbed scenes and more speeches than Oscar night.

Williams spends most of this singularly cheerless movie encased in heavy robot makeup—the same mistake that destroyed Andy Kaufman's movie career. (In Kaufman's case the vehicle was "Heartbeeps," a mercifully forgotten Christmas-season bomb of 18 years ago.)

Like the unfortunate Kaufman, Williams plays a household robot in the-not-too-distant future who yearns for human-style love. His feelings—attributed to mechanical malfunction—are encouraged by his owner known simply as Sir (Sam Neill), who lives on a massive Marin County estate with his chardonnay sipping wife (Wendy Crewson) and two young daughters.

After an early episode in which the robot, named Andrew, jumps out a window at one of the girl's command, the laughs are few and far between.

When Andrew, having given years of faithful service, proclaims that "millions have died for one idea—freedom." Sir (who's supposed to be a clockmaker but acts more like a movie producer) agrees to set Andrew free. Andrew builds himself a beachfront home and supports himself by making clocks.

Andrew eventually develops a crush on the younger of the girls (Embeth Davidtz), whom he persists on calling Little Miss, even after she grows to adulthood—and is heartbroken when she marries.

Decades later, Andrew meets up with Rupert Burns (Oliver Platt), a brilliant engineer who gives Andrew an "upgrade" that makes him look like a human being—specifically, Williams with a deep tan and dyed chestnut hair.

The improved Andrew sets about wooing Little Miss' granddaughter Portia (also played by Embeth Davidtz)—and pleading with a world court to be recognized as a human.

"Bicentenial Man," which advocates vegetarianism, euthanasia and mixed-species marriages, follows such Williams clunkers as "Jakob the Liar" and "What Dreams May Come." My personal idea of hell is being forced to watch all three on a daily basis.

NEWSDAY, 12/17/99, Part II/p. B17, Jan Stuart

The American movie industry has produced a cascade of films of startling freshness and edge in 1999. And Robin Williams has appeared in none of them. Instead, he has persisted in his dreary lifelong makeover from funnyman to feeling man, plunking himself atop groaningly heavy pedestals that showcase him as Hollywood's god of sensitivity and good will.

Williams achieves a more literal makeover in "Bicentennial Man," in which he plays a defective robot named Andrew who exhibits more emotion than the family he serves. The wealthy couple who give him his marching orders, Sir (Sam Neill) and Ma'am (Wendy Crewson), live on a sprawling estate and lord over successive generations of children so obnoxiously spoiled that one begins to think communism wasn't such a bad idea.

The youngest of their girls, Little Miss, survives her brat years to grow into Embeth Davidtz, who is so sweet-natured that Andrew calls her Little Miss even when she becomes wrinkled and cuddly like Helen Hayes. As the calendar years drop away and Andrew submits himself to a doctor/mechanic (Oliver Platt) to upgrade his human faculties, he falls in love with Little Miss' grown granddaughter Portia, who looks exactly like Embeth Davidtz.

In a more innocent time, "Bicentennial Man" would play itself out in 80 minutes on a B-movie budget. Now that Hollywood and its stars have descended into a new age of self-importance, this adaptation of an Isaac Asimov short story has been inflated to a portentous 133 minutes. What this means is that much more time passes between the narcissistic moments in which the characters laugh adoringly at Robin Williams' jokes. "Bicentennial Man" has much more cosmic things on its mind, and no less than three deathbed scenes to prove it.

Directed with absurd solemnity by Chris Columbus, "Bicentennial Man" oozes forward like mercury through a thermometer. The story spans five generations and then some, but long before the fadeout we feel as if we've witnessed the complete procreative cycles of the Book of Genesis. By the end, airborne automobiles are whizzing by the Brooklyn Bridge in Manhattan, the Presidio in San Francisco and the Capitol in Washington D.C., progress and tradition serenely co-existing. We can safely presume that when the Jetson family comes of age, there will still be entertainments like this, dumb little movies that long to be monuments.

NEWSWEEK, 12/20/99, p. 43, David Ansen

One could describe this movie as the story of a woman (Embeth Davidtz) who falls in love with a household appliance (Robin Williams). But that would make it sound funny. While there are a few good jokes scattered about, this is, alas, yet another of Williams's earnest attempts to make us all Better, More Sensitive People. Cast as an android with unusually human proclivities (he listens wistfully to opera), the actor has made the first touchy-feely robot movie. The tone of director Chris Columbus's moist, disjointed film is hushed and reverent, as we follow Andrew the android's 200-year quest to achieve full humanity. Many homilies follow. Eventually our hero sheds his metallic mug, starts looking a lot like Robin Williams with a good tan, and has sex with the great-granddaughter of the woman who first owned him. Kids will be bored, the rest of us baffled.

SIGHT AND SOUND, 3/00, p. 41, Mike Higgins

The US, the present. Richard Martin and his young family acquire an NDR 114 domestic android (nicknamed Andrew) which quickly exhibits an uncannily human personality. As the years pass, Andrew cultivates his 'humanity' under the tutelage of Richard and his youngest daughter, the by-now adult 'Little Miss'. Andrew then requests and is reluctantly granted his freedom by Richard. Andrew comes across Rupert Burns, the son of the man who designed him, and funds Burns to complete his transformation, physiologically at least, into a human being.

He returns to Little Miss and, following her death from old age, falls in love with and proposes to her granddaughter Portia. However, the World Congress states Andrew's effective immortality prevents Congress from recognising him as a human being so his marriage attempt is rejected. Burns enables Andrew to age and die. Years later, he and Portia die together as the World Congress finally declares Andrew 'human'.

In a film which shows the passage of 200 years with such blandness, perhaps it's understandable director Chris Columbus turns a blind eye to the history of cinema—a mere century, after all. Almost wilfully, Columbus ignores the long film heritage of the mechanical man—and the fundamental issues raised by that walking, talking oxymoron—in this risibly uninspired adaptation of Isaac Asimov's and Robert Silverberg's writings. So Andrew the android (aka NDR 114) has none of the disarming peevishness of *Star Wars* C3PO nor any of the simple pathos of the Tin Man in *The Wizard of Oz* (1939). Instead his appeal rests largely on the fact that he's a positronic analogue of Robin Williams. That stocky frame, those restless eyebrows, the characteristic simper set in a metallic rictus—Andrew's very specific anthropomorphism even extends to a faltering approximation of the star's trademark manic wisecracking.

Irritating with the cloying sentiment Williams' presence has long guaranteed in any film of his, Columbus is unable even to draw out the dramatic or intellectual implications of Andrew's personal development. One need look no further than Hal in *2001: A Space Odyssey)* (1968), the replicants of *Blade Runner,* or even *RoboCop* to see the dramatic potential of Frankensteinian machines exercising apparent human consciousness. Instead Columbus refers mainly to his own egregious body of work after all, comparable issues of unasked for freedom crop up in his earlier *Home Alone* films so Andrew ends up being a techno version of a small boy left to his own mischievous devices in a big house.

As it is, Andrew's growth into a human being is brought about by the most objectionably conservative means: a series of fireside chats with the paternalistic Richard Martin, the love of a good woman and a lot of plastic surgery, all laced together with clumsy biblical overtones (he is expelled from the Edenic Martin household and makes a prodigal's return decades later). A similar lack of imagination is at work in the film's woefully anachronistic *mise en scène*. Dismayingly, the Martins inhabit an insipid future world reminiscent more of post-war science expo films than any of the compellingly grubby dystopias envisaged by science-fiction cinema over the last 25 years.

Were there some consistency to this banal vision of the near future, *Bicentennial Man* might hope to have conveyed some of its literary sources' epic time scales. But the film swiftly settles into an unevenly paced, episodic structure, unsure whether it's a family saga, a sci-fi drama or a children's comedy. The interminable passage of succeeding generations of the Martin family is punctuated only by several protracted death-bed scenes. Indeed, the one distinguishing feature in this narrative desert— Little Miss' unrequited love for Andrew and his eventual marriage to her granddaughter—leaves a nasty taste in the mouth precisely because we're asked to consider as straightforwardly romantic a cross-generational, quasi-incestuous relationship between a 150-year old robot and a young woman. It makes you imagine what *Bicentennial Man* could have been like in the hands of David Cronenberg.

TIME, 12/27/99, p. 186, Richard Corliss

To love your mechanical playmate is an agreeable, G-rated notion; that's *Toy Story*. To want to have sex with it: that's the premise of Robin Williams' latest foray into ickiness. As Andrew, the robot with a heart, he beguiles the family that buys him in the year 2005. Beneath the metal casing, he is really a middle-aged gentleman, sweet of disposition, wryly amusing, sympathetic to women—hey is this guy gay? Not at all: Andrew wants the love of a good woman. Davidtz plays his first keeper-girlfriend and her granddaughter. "I would rather die a man than live for all eternity as a machine," he says in one of the many fortune-cookie aphorisms in Nicholas Kazan's script. And she is eager to live and die with him.

The result isn't quite as awful as you'd expect from the star of *Patch Adams* and the director of *Stepmom*, 1998's most tasteless glops of Christmas treacle. Williams restrained is a tad more endurable than Williams rampant. And it's always nice to see Hollywood recognize that old people can love and letch. But the tone is cloying, the running time bloated. Will someone in the near future please invent a Robin Williams movie worth sitting through? Puh-*leeze*?

VILLAGE VOICE, 12/28/99, p. 130, Jessica Winter

The robotics guys working on Chris Columbus's latest minivan—his usual rich-suburban, vaguely fascistic dramedy guaranteed by Satan's henchmen in Glendale to pull off a triumph of the till—have encased Robin Williams from head to toe in a silicone-and-plastic robot suit so that he can portray the positronic, immortal title character of *Bicentennial Man*. This remote-controlled contraption reproduces Williams's facial tics with minimalist precision, amounting to a fine unwitting joke on his beatific love-me shtick. But laughter turns to tears when Williams goes in search of robots produced in the same assembly line and they all look like—Robin Williams! Dear God, they're multiplying!

We're supposed to be weeping because Williams's compatriots have all been "deleted" or "reprogrammed" by their manufacturer, since a systems glitch invested them with emotions and an inkling of free will: scary stuff for the suits who created them. "It is a household appliance and yet you act like it was a man," The Man says nervously to Williams's sympathetic owner (Sam Neill, playing a disposable income in a Polo sweater and penny loafers). The film, spanning 200 years with the same set design, wants to draw an analogy between the robot technology of "the not-too-distant future" and bigotry; Williams vomits up half-digested molasses like "Millions have died for one idea: freedom" and "How does one obtain freedom?" and the robot's human paramour (Embeth Davidtz) worries that "if we're together, we'll never be accepted—we're different." Amid the complacent self-congratulation (the film's sole black character is the president of the World Congress) is a bizarre reactionary bent: An underfunded inventor makes enough snide asides about "relentlessly unfashionable android technology" that you half expect Williams to start speechifying about the merits of cloning. After all, clones are people too. He should know.

Also reviewed in:
CHICAGO TRIBUNE, 12/17/99, Friday/p. A, Michael Wilmington
NEW YORK TIMES, 12/17/99, p. E10, Stephen Holden
VARIETY, 12/13-19/99, p. 108, Todd McCarthy
WASHINGTON POST, 12/17/99, p. C12, Rita Kempley
WASHINGTON POST, 12/17/99, Weekend/p. 44, Desson Howe

BIG DADDY

A Columbia Pictures release of an Out of the Blue Entertainment/Jack Giarraputo production. *Executive Producer:* Adam Sandler, Robert Simonds, and Joseph M. Caracciolo. *Producer:* Sid Ganis, and Jack Giarraputo. *Director:* Dennis Dudgan. *Screenplay:* Steve Franks, Tim Herlihy, and Adam Sandler. *Story:* Steve Franks. *Director of Photography:* Theo Van de Sande. *Editor:* Jeff Gourson. *Music:* Teddy Castellucci. *Music Editor:* Stephen Lotwis. *Sound:* Tod Maitland

and (music): Gabe Veltri. *Sound Editor:* Mike Wilhoit. *Casting:* Roger Mussenden. *Production Designer:* Perry Andelin Blake. *Art Director:* Rick Butler. *Set Decorator:* Leslie Bloom. *Set Dresser:* Gary Aharoni. *Visual Effects:* Sheena Duggal. *Costumes:* Ellen Lutter. *Make-up:* Carla White. *Make-up (Adam Sandler):* Ann Pala. *Stunt Coordinator:* Roy Farfel and George Aguilar. *Running time:* 95 minutes. *MPAA Rating:* PG-13.

CAST: Adam Sandler (Sonny); Joey Lauren Adams (Layla); Jon Stewart (Kevin); Cole Sprouse and Dylan Sprouse (Julian); Josh Mostel (Mr. Brooks); Leslie Mann (Corinne); Allen Covert (Phil); Rob Schneider (Delivery Guy); Kristy Swanson (Vanessa); Joe Bologna (Mr. Koufax); Peter Dante (Tommy); Jonathan Loughran (Mike); Steve Buscemi (Homeless Guy); Tim Herlihy (Singing Kangaroo); Edmund Lyndeck (Old Man); Larkin Malloy (Restaurant Owner); Samantha Brown (Employee); Neal Huff (Customer); Geoffrey Horn (Sid); Greg Haberny (NYU Student); Jacqueline Titone (Waitress); George Hall (Elderly Driver); Peggy Shay (Lady at Tollbooth); Alfonso Ramirez (George); Salvatore Cavaliere (Angry Motorist); Kelly Dugan (Kelly); Jared Sandler (Jared); Jillian Sandler (Jillian); Helen Lloyd Breed (Ms. Foote); Chloé Hult (Schoolteacher); Carmen deLavallade (Judge); Steve Brill (Castellucci); Glen Trotiner (Bailiff); Jorge Buccio (Himself); Cat Jagar (Receptionist); Deborah S. Craig (Paralegal); Nicholas Taylor (Older Kid); Cole Hawkins (Cole); Gabriel Jacobs (Jeff); Michael Arcate (Broken Arm Kid); Gaetano Lisi (Hot Dog Vendor); Michael Giarraputo (Hoboken Motorist); Steve Glenn (Guy at Party); Al Cerullo (Helicopter Pilot).

LOS ANGELES TIMES, 6/25/99, Calendar, p. 1, Kenneth Turan

Ever since he made a surprising success of "The Wedding Singer" last year, the media has been beside itself about the presence of not one but two Adam Sandlers: the sweet-natured, gentle romantic of that film and the more, shall we say, juvenile comic of "Happy Gilmore," "Billy Madison" and "The Waterboy."

"Big Daddy," Sandler's latest film, reconfirms the existence of those two Adams. It also shows that, commercial considerations aside, inviting them to share a film is a miscalculation, the equivalent of asking Jerry Springer and Charlie Rose to co-chair the same charity ball.

"Big Daddy" started life as a script by Steve Franks about a single guy who suddenly has to cope with a child in his life. When that notion was transmogrified into a vehicle for a major star, the comic and his writing partner Tim Herlihy completely Sandlerized the premise to the point where many of the things that take place on screen make sense for Sandler's super-popular persona but not for the film.

Sandler plays 32-year-old Sonny Koufax, once a promising lawyer but now a prototypal Manhattan slacker and a drag on everyone's reality who has a job taking tolls at a bridge but really lives off a settlement he got as the result of a minor traffic accident.

Sonny's girlfriend Vanessa (Kristy Swanson), who's put up with him for quite awhile, is getting tired of our hero's aimless life. She precipitates a crisis by leaving the city for a few days and letting Sonny know that she's seriously considering leaving him as well.

Even before a sad-eyed child appears on Sonny's doorstep, there is a major disconnect between what the film, directed by "Happy Gilmore's" Dennis Dugan, tells us this man is like and the evidence of our own eyes.

Yes, "Big Daddy" admits, Sonny may be a bit irresponsible, but he's really just a fun-loving big kid, someone who's never ever too busy to stop and smell the beer while his careerist friends plunge ahead in a search for worldly success.

The Sonny we see, however, is nothing of the kind. He's whiny, obnoxious and insulting in both passive-aggressive and old-fashioned aggressive ways. Nothing pleases Sonny more, for instance, than the mean-spirited teasing he rains on Corinne (Leslie Mann), the fiancee of his roommate and best friend Kevin (Jon Stewart). Now a doctor, Corinne once worked as a waitress at Hooters, and Sonny would sooner die than miss an opportunity to relentlessly taunt her about her anatomy. All in good fun, you understand, all in good fun.

While Kevin's away on business, that small child with the most woebegone face in the Empire State is delivered to the apartment. This is 5-year-old Julian (played by twins Cole and Dylan Sprouse), sent to live with Kevin, the father who doesn't even know he exists.

Having no choice but to look after the boy until his roommate returns, Sonny doesn't know what to do with Julian except treat him as an equal. That means turning the lad into a kind of Austin Powers-ish Mini-Me, a junior version of Sonny's antisocial persona.

So off the two of them go to Central Park, where Sonny teaches Julian to trip in-line skaters because they look funny when they fall down. Sonny also teaches Julian to urinate on the walls of snooty restaurants (an image that's been plastered across America) and when the youngster wets his bed, Sonny just puts some newspapers over the damp sheets. Who knew child-raising could be so simple and so much fun?

At some point in all of this, Sonny gets the crack-brained idea of pretending to be Julian's father so he can adopt the tyke and make a favorable impression on Vanessa. Sonny's censorious father (Joe Bologna) thinks the boy would be "better off living in a dumpster," and it's an open question whether he's right or not.

It is the iffy premise of "Big Daddy" that this experience with care-giving suddenly and miraculously turns Sonny into a better human being. This is dubious even in theory, and in practice Sonny's conversion is more simplistic and pro forma than it sounds. "Big Daddy" is so bound and determined to have a sensitive Sandler it doesn't notice that the changeover couldn't be less believable.

The same goes for the love affair that improbably flourishes between Sonny and Corinne's attorney sister Layla, played by "Chasing Amy's" Joey Lauren Adams like even she can't believe what she's getting into. No, no, no, you want to yell at the screen, no way this is the man of your dreams.

Sandler, if press reports are to be believed, all but micromanages his films, worrying over them to the smallest degree. A good thing, but in this case it led to a not-seeing-the-forest-for-the-trees scenario that contributes to "Big Daddy's" problems.

For if this film's underdeveloped script and dubious premise are to work, you have to unconditionally love the actor no matter what he's doing. You have to take his good humor, his miraculous conversion, everything good about him, completely on faith, just because he's Adam and you love him. There's no doubt Sandler is talented, but if he persists in believing that, like Elvis, his presence alone covers a multitude of omissions and inconsistencies, he will squander his gift and make a series of forgettable films in the process.

NEW YORK, 7/12/99, p. 49, Peter Rainer

Adam Sandler's new comedy is being touted as a step forward for him, which I find funnier than anything in the movie. A step forward from *what? Big Daddy* is more like a step backward—into sappiness. This melange of *The Kid* and *The Champ* plus all the previous Sandler comedies continues the date-movie-friendly tone of *The Wedding Singer* and *The Waterboy.* Instead of appealing only to goony male adolescents, Sandler is broadening his base to include goony couples. He's playing Sonny, a law-school graduate living off the hefty damages he received when a car ran over his toe. (It's basically a sham disability.) Loafing in his New York loft when he isn't working part-time as a toll collector, Sonny ends up adopting a 5-year-old boy mistakenly sent to him for custody. Thinking the adoption will show off his sensitive-man side and reclaim his errant girlfriend, or attract a new one, he ends up as a funky single papa: The film's ubiquitous ads, which are representative of the entire movie, show him and the boy urinating against the side of a building. (I prefer the Dr. Evil-Mini-Me knockoff of this ad for *The Spy Who Shagged Me.)* In a way, Sandler is trying to do to the audience what Sonny is attempting with his girlfriend: He's pimping pathos to win our hearts. But Sandler being Chaplinesque isn't pretty; he's just doing his smart-aleck slacker shtick with a moister eye.

NEW YORK POST, 6/25/99, p. 48, Rod Dreher

In the instance of Adam Sandler and his curiously lucrative career, has anybody parlayed so little into so much since Hillary Clinton deigned to trade commodities for a day?

He's a minimally talented comic actor who has found one thing he's good at—playing sweet, dumb and puppy-dog cute—and turned it into fame and fortune.

So what? His movies are often amazingly stupid, but there's a good-naturedness about them that appeals to kids, and to the kid in many adults.

Sandler's not to everyone's taste, but unlike many critics, I've not been able to muster much interest in loathing the guy. Heaven help us if we can't enjoy a good booger joke every now and then.

All the same, "Big Daddy" is easily the laziest, most slapdash and altogether crummy picture Sandler's done to date. The writing—by Sandler, Tim Herlihy and Steve Franks—is so cornball and comically feeble it makes "The Waterboy" play like a lost masterpiece of Shavian wit.

And the way this film treats children is contemptible.

Sandler plays Sonny Koufax, a man-child layabout who works one day a week collecting tolls on the Jersey Turnpike and spends the other six goofing around his SoHo loft, living off the proceeds of a lawsuit. Sonny's girlfriend, Vanessa (Kristy Swanson), threatens to leave him unless he gets his act together.

Just as his roommate, Kevin (Jon Stewart), goes overseas on business, a 5-year-old orphan named Julian (played by twins Cole and Dylan Sprouse) turns up on their doorstep. Kevin is thought to be the kid's real dad, but Sonny acts as a reluctant father figure until Kevin returns, hoping to impress Vanessa with his willingness to take on grown-up responsibilities.

Sonny, an overgrown kid himself, lets Julian behave like an animal. He feeds him ketchup for dinner. He teaches him to pee in public. He lets him dress like a ninny and rename himself "Frankenstein" (or "Fwankenstein," as pronounced by the Sprouse twins, the cutest movie tots since that bucket-headed scamp in "Jerry Maguire").

All this is mildly, and very occasionally, amusing, but when "Big Daddy" attempts to leaven the gross jokes with Sandler's ingratiating, aw-shucks smarm, it loses what little appeal it has.

A perfunctory love interest for Sonny pops up in the person of a lawyer, played by Joey Lauren Adams. It all ends up before a judge, of course, with Sandler delivering a maudlin courtroom soliloquy that's impressive only in that grown-ups get paid big bucks to write dialogue this lame.

If boring, insipid writing were the only thing wrong with "Big Daddy," it would be merely a disappointment. But there's something infuriating about the way the Sandler character abuses the innocence of this kid—and, indeed, of the child actors who play Julian/Fwankenstein.

Sonny uses filthy language in front of the little boy, and teaches him to do the same. We're supposed to find it funny that a child learns to swear and comment on adult sexual situations. Sandler uses the kid to take a swipe at his detractors, having him say in the courtroom that "critics are cynical a -------."

Later, the lad makes a crack about an old man's testicles. The real cynical a ------ is the kind of man who would go for a cheap laugh by putting words like that in the mouth of a 5-year-old.

NEWSDAY, 6/25/99, Part II/p. B3, John Anderson

Some people anticipate Adam Sandler movies the way they anticipate a trip to Motor Vehicles. It can't possibly be pleasant, of course. But it doesn't have to be excruciating. Just find your center. Zen out. The entire experience—like a difficult labor or a speech by Fidel Castro—eventually has to end.

Others, of course, seek in Sandler's movies a rich, rewarding tapestry of turgid sentimentality and toilet humor. And that they will certainly find in "Big Daddy," Sandler's latest and one in which the more or less unalterable Sandler Character—here named Sonny Koufax—comes into possession of a small boy. If nothing else, this should prompt an immediate suspension of the gun-control debate in favor of a demand for three-day waiting periods on movie characters wanting to adopt children.

Like a wedding on a sitcom, the addition of a child into the Sandler formula suggests the ship has run aground on the shoals of low box office. In fact, nothing of the kind has occurred. The breakdown on the last four Sandler features is as follows. Take note of any disturbing trends:

"Billy Madison," $25.4 million;

"Happy Gilmore," $38.6 million;

"The Wedding Singer," $80.2 million;

"The Waterboy," $161.4 million ($100 million by its third week).

Given that each movie seemed to cost about $2.25 to produce, that seems like a reasonable return.

Still, Sandler's anti-movie ethos—manifesting itself in purposefully stilted acting, hoary scatology and the most banal of plotlines—suggests rebelliousness. Anarchy, even. Which is odd, given how he and his audience always manage to have it both ways: The sentimentality is so overripe you could gag, but the star reads his lines with such obvious sarcasm that you couldn't possibly take any of it seriously.

And "any" includes the abject stupidity. Sandler's Sonny Koufax, a law-school graduate living (in SoHo!) off the settlement he got in a cab accident, is loath to take the marriage route, so his girlfriend, Vanessa (Kristy Swanson), checks out. When the love child of Sonny's best friend, Kevin (a strangely inert Jon Stewart), arrives on the doorstep—a delivery sure to be misunderstood by Kevin's less-than-understanding fiancee, Corinne (Leslie Mann) Sonny takes the kid, thinking it will show Vanessa what a stand-up, mature guy he is. What she thinks is, he's a nut.

Sandler's characters never act their age. Why should the kid? Julian (played by twins Cole and Dylan Sprouse) is supposed to be 5 but acts like 3. Lisping. Whining. Wetting the bed. When Sonny says something about the boy's metabolism and Julian wistfully asks, "Metalobism?" you'll pwobabwy want to fwow up.

Sonny and Julian have fun around Manhattan, bonding, watching pro wrestling, sabotaging in-line skaters with strategically placed tree limbs and breaking into houses. For some reason, Layla (Joey Lauren Adams), a go-get-'em activist attorney, decides it would be a good idea to hook up with Sonny. It's all so warm and fuzzy. It's also science fiction. But with its several moments of genuine humor, "Big Daddy" really points out the utter poverty of comedic writing throughout the movie industry, as well as the selectivity of memory. A couple of laughs. Eighty-five minutes of dead air. What do people remember? Check the receipts Monday morning.

NEWSWEEK, 7/5/99, p. 58, David Ansen

After "The Wedding Singer," which reinvented Adam Sandler as a sensitive sweetie with an uncanny resemblence to the young Bob Dylan, and his megahit "The Waterboy," which reverted him to anarchic-moronic adolescent form, you have to wonder which Adam Sandler will show up in "Big Daddy." Well, Sonny Koufax, the upper-middle-class slacker who reluctantly discovers the joys of parenting when a 5-year-old tyke is deposited on his doorstep, is a kind of Every-Adam, designed to ring every demographic bell in the land. Sweet and sour, Sonny is like a shotgun-wedding between his subversive W. C. Fields/Jerry Lewis side and his sentimental Wallace Beery/Tom Hanks Mr. Softie.

Amiable, schizoid and disposable, "Big Daddy" is just as formulaic as you might imagine: any story in which an irresponsible slob decides to adopt an orphan can be headed in only one uplifting direction. But there are enough rudely funny surprises along the way to hold your attention. Just because Sandler's Sonny makes little sense as an actual human being doesn't mean he won't make you laugh. This improbable father figure is a big kid himself, living off insurance money from a car accident. One day a week he works in a freeway tollbooth (sure, whatever), yet he's actually a law-school grad whose friends are mostly Yuppies. Woefully unprepared for the arrival of little Julian (twins Cole and Dylan Sprouse), he treats the kid like an unruly puppy: when the boy wets his bed, or throws up on the floor, he simply puts down newspapers. The same guy who can pass the bar exam pees on the sides of restaurants, insults old people and taunts his buddy's fianceé for once working at Hooters.

That's the old Adam. The new Adam, of course, is redeemed by the love of a good lawyer (strangle-voiced Joey Lauren Adams from "Chasing Amy") and his Julian-inspired awakening to Responsibility. (Where the kid ends up is the movie's biggest cop-out.) Who would have thought Billy Madison would grow up to be Mr. Family Values? Will Sandler's young male fans sit still for his bourgeois transformation? This may be the acid test for the '90s' most unexpected superstar.

SIGHT AND SOUND, 10/99, p. 38, Kevin Maher

In his Manhattan apartment, law-school graduate Sonny Koufax is dumped by his girlfriend Vanessa. That night, before leaving for China his flatmate Kevin announces his engagement to girlfriend Corinne. The next day a five-year old boy, Julian, dropped at Sonny's apartment, claims to be Kevin's son. Sonny spends a day with Julian and decides to adopt him in order to impress Vanessa. Believing Sonny to be Kevin, social services agree with the decision. Sonny calls at Vanessa's apartment with Julian, where she reveals that she's having an affair.

Sonny allows Julian to do whatever he likes. He meets Corinne's sister Layla and invites her out on a date. After being told by Julian's headmistress that Julian is falling behind in class, Sonny begins to keep Julian neat and tidy, and improve his school work. Social services realise their mistake, take Julian into care and prosecute Sonny. In court Layla acts as Sonny's defence lawyer but his negative character witnesses hamper his case. At the last minute Kevin refuses to press charges against Sonny. Kevin decides to take over the parenting of Julian. Some time later, Sonny is a lawyer married to Layla with a child of their own.

Not since the breakthrough movies of Jerry Lewis—*The Bellboy* (1960), *The Errand Boy* (1961) and *The Patsy* (1964)—has there been a performer with as strict an authorial control over his comic persona as Adam Sandler. Like Lewis, Sandler has been heavily involved in the production of his films to create a man-child character, unchanging from movie to movie, of unerring stupidity but displaying charming flashes of self-effacing naivety. With *Big Daddy* Sandler, as co-writer and executive producer, remains loyal to his previous films *Billy Madison, Happy Gilmore* and *The Waterboy*, presenting us with another maladjusted outsider, Sonny Koufax. Only this time Sonny, a law-school prodigy living off a compensation claim, is a slacker by choice and not necessity.

The movie opens on familiar Sandler ground. First Sonny's father warns him that he needs to grow up (pace *Billy Madison),* and then, in a dialogue exchange lifted practically verbatim from *Happy Gilmore,* Sonny's girlfriend Vanessa announces that she's leaving him because "You refuse to move out of the second phase of your life!" But whereas in *Gilmore* Sandler had to prove his worth by growing up and finding money for his homeless granny, here he demonstrates that juvenile knows best by parenting homeless five-year-old Julian (twins Cole and Dylan Sprouse). And so begins a lazy retread of that sentimental Hollywood tale, seen in such films as *Little Miss Marker* (1934) and *40 Pounds of Trouble* (1962), where a disreputable adult (usually a bookie, or a casino manager) is purified by the love of abandoned child.

Unfortunately, *Big Daddy*'s biggest draw, the Sandler persona, is also its biggest flaw. Sandler has made Sonny almost embarrassingly invincible. He can solve complex legal cases in seconds, he can be goofy and attractive with new girlfriend Layla, or he can be authoritative and intimidating to total strangers. Surrounded by people who either fear him or worship him, Sonny ultimately comes across as a flat, unappealing bully. In what surely must be the film's comic nadir, Sonny even breaks into the flat of an elderly Upper East Sider when the unfortunate man refuses to comply with Julian's trick-or-treat demands.

The simplistic shooting structure which slavishly separates comic set-pieces and plot exposition with musical montages doesn't help things. That the court battle itself turns out to be risible is hardly a surprise. The film's real shock comes in its final moments. After hinting at Sonny's future as a househusband ("I'm in love with a young girl who makes plenty of money!" he exults), the film suddenly shows its true conservative colours. The closing shot reveals former power-dresser Layla in dowdy maternal prints holding onto her very own baby, while husband Sonny breezes into the bar in a corporate suit, flush with victory, and straight off the latest hot court case. Big Daddy? Sure, but for how long?

VILLAGE VOICE, 6/29/99, p. 152, Michael Atkinson

American male culture fluctuates like a bobbing cocktail stork between being self-satisfied with its progressively earned enlightenment and believing that stone knives and hickory clubs work just fine, thank you. Here we are in just such a Paleolithic phase, in which Man finds pride not merely in salaries or learnedness or good works, but also in beer bellies and living-room Jets shrines. Adam Sandler, who doesn't glorify contented dim-wittedness so much as telethon for it, is the moment's Will Rogers, a Today's Man ideal as unchallenging as a broken-in recliner.

That Sandler can often be brilliantly funny, at least outside of his movies, is hardly unusual or of consequence to *Waterboy* fans, for whom *Big Daddy* has been brought to the table with hopeful studio hearts. But is it another profit cow? Maybe not, because someone had the bright idea of pairing Sandler with a five-year-old (Cole and Dylan Sprouse) and running the star through a *Little Miss Marker* scenario, thereby imposing a paternal dynamic where only incorrigible immaturity is expected. (You'd think they'd have Sandler relive the Jerry Lewis experience and maybe remake *The Bellboy*, but that is perhaps where SNL alumni fear to tread.) There are even tearful moments of orphan anxiety, with swelling score peaks you'd swear belong to the Julia Roberts movie playing next door.

As a slacking (but talented!) law-school grad with the rough idea of adopting his roommate's illegit son in order to win back an errant girlfriend, Sandler is less goofy than spitefully self-absorbed, and most of the comedy feels like child abuse. Sandler embodies the ultimate nightmare sports dad, bellowing at a preschooler when he cries, taking him to the Blarney Stone, and letting him sleep in spilled food rather than interrupt the Rangers game.

It doesn't last, of course: Sandler straightens up, everybody admires his tenderness, Joey Lauren Adams does career time as his obscure object, Kristy Swanson and Lesley Mann both radiate career helplessness as blond bitches with ridiculous cleavage, and the whole megillah ends up in custody court. There are laughs (for instance, Sandler grilling innocent kindergartners on substance abuse), and also bids for a wider audience—this is, after all, the only film guaranteed to be seen by every football player in Wisconsin that prominently features an openly endorsed, tongue-kissing gay couple. If nothing else, *Big Daddy* is an acknowledgment that cave dwelling ain't what it used to be, despite the Chief Jay Strongbow wrestling moves and Hooters product placement.

Also reviewed in:
CHICAGO TRIBUNE, 6/25/99, Friday/p. A, Mark Caro
NEW YORK TIMES, 6/25/99, p. E13, Janet Maslin
VARIETY, 6/21-27/99, p. 76, Robert Koehler
WASHINGTON POST, 6/25/99, p. C1, Rita Kempley
WASHINGTON POST, 6/25/99, Weekend/p. 47, Desson Howe

BLACK CAT, WHITE CAT

An October Films release of a CIBY 2000/Pandora Film/Komuna Film coproduction. *Executive Producer:* Maksa C'atovic'. *Producer:* Karl Baumgartner. *Director:* Emir Kusturica. *Screenplay (Serbo-Croatian and Romany with English subtitles):* Gordan Mihic and Emir Kusturica. *Director of Photography:* Thierry Arbogast. *Editor:* Svetolik Mica Zajc. *Music:* Nelle Karajlic, Voja Aralica, Dejan Sparavalo, and Emir Kusturica. *Sound:* Vojislav Aralica and Ivan Kljsic. *Casting:* Slobodan Dedcic. *Production Designer:* Milenko Jeremic. *Art Director:* Rade Mihajlovic. *Set Designer:* Zivan Todorovic and Dobrica Milosevic. *Set Decorator:* Fragan Vracar. *Special Effects:* Petar Zivkovic. *Costumes:* Nebojs'a Lipanovic'. *Make-up:* Mirjana Stevovic. *Running time:* 135 minutes. *MPAA Rating:* Not Rated.

CAST: Bajram Severdzan (Matko Destanov); Florijan Ajdini (Zare Destanov); Jas'ar Destani (Grga Vellki); Zabit Mehmedovski (Zarije Destanov); Sabri Sulejmani (Grga Pitic'); Adnan Bekir (Little Grga); Srdan Todorovic (Dadan); Salija Ibraimova (Afrodita); Branka Katic' (Ida); Stojan Sotirov (Bulgarian Customs Officer); Ljubica Adzovic' (Uncle Sujka); Predrag Pepi Lakovic' (The Priest); Zdena Hurtecakova ('Black Oblelisk'); Jelena Jovicic, Vesna Ristanovic and Natalija Bibic (Dadan's Girls); Zeljko Stefanovic and Dejan Sparavalo (Violin Players); Desauka Kostic (Ida's Friend); Minaza Alijevic, Javorka Asanovic, and Nena Kostic (Dadan's Sisters); Rifat Sulejman (Disco Dancer); Predrag Miki Manojlovic' (Registry Officer).

CHRISTIAN SCIENCE MONITOR, 8/27/99, p. 15, David Sterritt

Yugoslavia has a long history of substantial filmmaking, ranging from the movies of world-class auteurs Emir Kusturica and Dusan Makavejev to the work of the Zagreb Animation Studio, which set an international standard for cartooning. Now that the once-unified nation has broken apart, many of its screen artists continue to labor hard and creatively despite the hardships they often face.

The vicissitudes of Kusturica's career have led him far from his native Bosnia—as the title of his "Arizona Dream," starring Johnny Depp and Jerry Lewis, attests—but he has always retained a keen interest in his roots and in the Gypsy culture that flourishes there. Gypsies are the chief inhabitants of his best movie, "Time of the Gypsies," and they make an aggressive comeback in *Black Cat, White Cat*, his first release since the grandiose "Underground" won the top prize at the Cannes filmfest four years ago.

The complicated web of relationships at the heart of "Black Cat, White Cat" is woven around a Gypsy community that dwells alongside the Danube River, better known for inspiring graceful Strauss waltzes than for the shenanigans that go on in this movie.

The plot involves a bungled train robbery, an arranged marriage, and sundry double-crosses and triple-crosses spanning at least three generations. Most of the characters are rogues and rascals, but enough of them have decent spirits to make them mildly interesting company for the length of a feature film.

As in Kusturica's other recent work, the story is stronger on sound and fury than clarity and coherence. It provides a glimpse of lives and loves we don't often see at the movies, though, and proves that his country's hard times haven't dimmed his cinematic zest.

LOS ANGELES TIMES, 9/17/99, Calendar/p. 17, Kevin Thomas

It's not surprising that master director Emir Kusturica, from a former Yugoslav republic, would seek a change of pace after his 1995 Cannes prizewinner, "Underground," a controversial, bleakly absurdist epic take on half a century of Balkan turmoil. He's followed it up with a raucous, knockabout comedy, "Black Cat, White Cat," a paean to love, freedom and friendship, which won Kusturica a Silver Lion at Venice for his direction.

Screenwriter Gordan Mihic, who co-wrote Kusturica's memorable "Time of the Gypsies" a decade ago, persuaded Kusturica to do a documentary on musicians inspired by those they had worked with in "Gypsies."

The idea was to follow band members as they played at a wedding, but luckily for us, Kusturica and Mihic couldn't resist cooking up a story instead. "Black Cat, White Cat" has all the Gypsy music you could possibly want plus a dizzyingly inspired comic plot that does in fact culminate in a wedding, an event struck with mayhem.

Along the Danube in a beautiful, wide-open countryside, a feckless petty crook named Matko (Bajram Severdzan, also known as Doctor Kolja) lives in a picturesque houseboat in a Gypsy community with his father, Zarije (Zabit Mehmedovski), and 17-year-old son Zare (Florijan Ajdini). The mournful-looking Matko's latest scheme involves stealing a trainload of gasoline that's being shipped from Jordan.

Sure enough, Matko is double-crossed, which puts him at the mercy of his backer, the exuberant gangster Dadan (Srdan Todorovic), a good-looking guy who dresses '70s Vegas-style—sideburns, open shirt, miles of gold chain—including one from which is suspended a thick cross containing the cocaine he sniffs so frequently. Dadan favors stretch limousines and at least four sexy ladies to do his bidding at the snap of his fingers; he lives with his four unmarried sisters in an old palace he's remodeling.

Matko can clear his debt by marrying off Zare to one of Dadan's sisters. But Zare has just fallen for blond, free-spirited Ida (Branka Katic), the granddaughter of a hearty riverside cafe proprietor (who's eager to sell Ida to Dadan).

Also getting into the act is Zarije's old pal Grga Pitic (Sabri Sulejmani), a rich and shady entrepreneur who gets around in Rube Goldberg-like vehicles and who loves to play his "Casablanca" video over and over. (There's also a nod to Billy Wilder, when Ida orders Zare: "Kiss me, stupid.") All of this offers Kusturica plenty of opportunity to indulge in his near-surreal sense of humor, which here has the lightheartedness of his "Arizona Dream."

Two hours and nine minutes is an awfully long running time for a comedy, but because "Black Cat, White Cat" has such a beguiling rambling shaggy dog-story quality, it gets away with it better than most over-long movies.

Kusturica works marvels with his endlessly amusing cast, and his film has an appealingly free and easy tone. "Black Cat, White Cat," by the way, takes its title from a pair of amorous felines whose antics have a fateful consequence.

NEW STATESMAN, 5/10/99, p. 34, Jonathan Romney

Emir Kusturica is currently the bogeyman of European cinema—only in part because of his larger-than-life reputation for brawling, name-calling and profligate movie-making. His last film, *Underground*, which won the Palme d'Or at Cannes, was undoubtedly an "event movie", even though its box-office performance was unimpressive. But its broadly allegorical, cartoon-folktale depiction of postwar Yugoslavia led to the Bosnian director—born in Sarajevo of mixed Serb and Muslim origins being attacked as an apologist for Serbian militarism. The debate around the film was particularly heated in France, with the philosopher Bernard-Henri Levy launching a heated polemic against Kusturica, resulting in the director's declaration that he would never make another film.

Underground was set and shot in Belgrade, but aside from that it was hard to see quite how the accusations would stick. The only clear point, in a confused magic-realist history of the Belgrade community, was that the film was at once nostalgic for the old unified Yugoslavia and a satire on the mystifications by which the Tito regime claimed to unite it. The story of a community tricked into hiding for years literally underground, Kusturica explained, depicted the "metaphorical cellar" that Tito had created. Meanwhile, Kusturica himself, now based in France, continues to refer to himself as Yugoslavian and to speak of the old days in unambiguously nostalgic terms.

Having quickly broken his vow to retire, Kusturica has now made what seems a deliberate attempt to evade further controversy. *Black Cat White Cat*—again filmed around Belgrade—is a knockabout farce that presents itself as pure entertainment in an entirely facetious vein. Made under the twin influences of Fellini and Garcia Marquez, it's set in a rural gypsy milieu, among rival clans of Romany gangsters. The gangling, rubbery Bajram Severzdan plays Matko, an amiable chancer who lives in a crumbling encampment by the Danube and who strikes a deal with the gypsy mob godfather Grga Pitic (Sabri Sulejmani, the skeletal owner of the most terrifying dental work ever seen on screen). Grga sponsors Matko's attempted petrol heist, but the whole business ends with Matko's son obliged to marry "Ladybird", a gangster's daughter. In the explosive climax, the calamities pile up, as do the extraordinarily naff wedding gifts.

The plot makes some degree of sense, but you don't follow it too closely, dazzled as you are by the sheer grotesqueness of the cast, an endless parade of bizarre phantasms. There's a Scarface-style mobster with a coke-stuffed crucifix; a techno theme song ("Pitbull! Terrier!") and two molls to provide backing vocals; a green-haired henchman; an ailing grandfather supplying the film's keynote when he yells out for "Music! Aggression!". There are also limitless supplies of farm life: a vast pig idly feasting on a rusty car; the cats of the title who skitter throughout as an anarchic leitmotiv; and armies of geese, ceaselessly bustling across the screen, just to keep things moving.

Kusturica might not seem the most discerning of comic directors—whenever things flag, just throw a goat at someone, especially if they're riding a motorbike. What's extraordinary is the concertedness of the juggling act—the sense of the world as perpetual circus. Everything comes down to acrobatics: stunts with sidecars, a brass band strung up on a tree trunk, a grisly routine with a railway level crossing. This sort of humour, owing as much to Tex Avery as to Fellini, makes more sense in a strictly farcical milieu than in the overtly allegorical *Underground*. Here, it becomes peculiarly a self-referential form of comedy that does not actually require you to find it funny—the point is not so much to laugh as to marvel at it.

The film is an expression of faith in universal confusion; Kusturica proposes a cosmology of chaos, in which all things are bound to collide, endlessly and permanently. Whether this worldview is open to political interpretation is another question. In the film's gypsy universe, set outside and in opposition to the overground world, everything is up for grabs, everything is run by crazed brigands: you'd be within your rights to read it as another cartoon of Yugoslavia, if not specifically of Serbia. Even the way Kusturica orchestrates his comedy routines is open to such interpretation. It's never simply a question of several things happening at once—iceblocks tumbling downstairs, while a bystander juggles with grenades—but of things happening in different directions. All objects, people and animals have their own agendas here, and are all shoehorned into the same space only by the most tenuous and precarious accord.

This may be the worst possible time to release a Kusturica film in Britain—even *Underground*, with its obvious headline appeal, found scant audience, and a screwball, Serbian-shot farce may strike many people as not altogether appropriate viewing during the Kosovo crisis. But *Black Cat White Cat* deserves an audience, arguably more than the confused *Underground*: though he's rather less ambitious here, Kusturica is actually on top of his game. Think of the film as *The Beverly Hillbillies* fuelled by slivovitz, and its appeal quickly becomes apparent.

NEW YORK POST, 9/10/99, p. 56, Rod Dreher

Returning from self-imposed artistic exile in the wake of controversy over his last film, wildly inventive Bosnian filmmaker Emir Kusturica revisits the tin-cup baroque world of Balkan Gypsies in this rollicking farce.

Set in a Gypsy community on the banks of the Danube River, the tangled plot follows the misadventures of a hapless ne'er-do-well, Matko (Bajram Severdzan), and the schemes he falls into with the prosperous gangster Dadan (Srdan Todorovic).

Kusturica's love and respect for Gypsy culture is obvious, but he doesn't romanticize the Romany culture. Rather, he celebrates its gaudy humanity in a joyous picture that is his most lighthearted and amusing work to date.

His kitchen-sink style is not to everyone's taste, but you can be sure you'll not see anything else like "Black Cat, White Cat" all year.

SIGHT AND SOUND, 5/99, p. 41, John Wrathall

Yugoslavia, the present. Planning the theft of a trainload of petrol, Matko Destanov secures financial backing from gypsy godfather Grga Pitic, and enlists the help of gangster Dadan Karambolo. But when the train arrives, Dadan drugs Matko and steals the money and petrol for himself. Unaware it was Dadan who ripped him off, Matko must agree to the gangster's demand for compensation: an arranged marriage between Matko's son Zare and Dadan's unmarriageable sister Afrodita, nicknamed Bubamara (Ladybird) on account of her tiny stature. This is a disaster for Zare, who is in love with Ida, a local waitress. Meanwhile, the equally unwilling Bubamara dreams of falling in love with a tall stranger.

Just before the wedding, Matko's father Zarije dies but Dadan refuses to delay the wedding for the funeral. Instead, he persuades Matko to hide Zarije's corpse in the attic. During the party after the wedding, Zare helps Bubamara escape. While fleeing through a wood Bubamara meets and instantly falls in love with Grga Pitic's grandson Grga Veliki, who is bringing his grandfather to pay his respects to his old friend Zarije. Grga Pitic makes peace, arranging for Grga Veliki to marry Bubamara, leaving Zare free to marry Ida. But before the joint wedding takes place, Grga Pitic dies. He too is hidden in the attic so the ceremony can go ahead. Just before the wedding, the two old men come back to life. Zare sabotages the outdoor lavatory so that Dadan falls into a cesspit. Zare and Ida kidnap the registrar and set off down the danube. They are married on the boat.

In 1995, worn down by the controversy surrounding his last film *Underground*, which was widely (and unfairly) pilloried for its allegedly pro-Serbian take on Yugoslavia's descent into chaos, Emir Kusturica announced his retirement from film-making. For his comeback—hardly unexpected, given that he was only 41 when he threw in the towel—the Sarajevo-born director has chosen to make a comedy deliberately designed to steer clear of the internecine politics of his divided homeland. Described by Kusturica as his first movie in a major key, *Black Cat White Cat* returns to the milieu of his best-loved film *Time of the Gypsies,* and uses the same sreenwriter, Gordan Mihic, and several cast members from that film. Once again a young innocent, here Florijan Ajdini's Zare, falls foul of the dodgy deals of a roguish gypsy godfather against a backdrop teeming with all the director's hallmarks: wandering bands, flocks of geese, Heath Robinson-type contraptions and chaotic weddings.

At one point the gangster Dadan is jokingly referred to as a war criminal. But beyond the implication that Serbia is now run by men like him, there's nothing else in *Black Cat White Cat* to suggest the turmoil of Yugoslavia's recent history. This was clearly Kusturica's intention. But the refusal to countenance anything but 'fun' has resulted in a marked coarsening of his style, giving the film a mood of forced jollity. If his previous work thrived on the tension between the contrasting styles of his three avowed idols—Tarkovsky, Fellini and Leone—it's Tarkovsky who has been sacrificed here. (The absence of Goran Bregovic's haunting music, following a feud between the director and his regular composer over credits on the soundtrack CD of *Underground*, is another factor.) Without the sudden flights into lyricism and tragedy which made his earlier work so extraordinary, *Black Cat White Cat* risks turning into *Carry On Kusturica*—not least in the long, relentlessly raucous interlude involving a diva who extracts nails from blocks of wood with her arse as she sings.

That's not to say the film is ever dull. Shot on the banks of the Danube by ace French cinematographer Thierry Arbogast (best known for his work with Luc Besson), it has a breezy, open-air feel, especially in the rapturous scene where Zare and Ida make love in a field of sunflowers. Kusturica gets wonderfully vivid performances out of his largely non-professional cast. And the grotesque Serb techno concocted by Nelle Karajlic, the director's former colleague in the pop group Zabranjeno Pusenje, is a hoot.

However, the film's most memorable images all seem to be either irrelevant diversions (like the pig eating car) or reruns of previous greatest hits. For instance Bubamara's escape through the woods, concealed under a mobile tree stump, is a repeat of a running gag involving a cardboard box in *Time of the Gypsies*. The final scene, meanwhile, in which the lovers Zare and Ida float off down the Danube, recalls *Underground*, with its suggestion that escape is the only happy ending possible in Yugoslavia.

VILLAGE VOICE, 9/14/99, p. 133, J. Hoberman

Rollicking ensemble comedies both, the Yugoslav *Black Cat, White Cat* and the Japanese *Welcome Back, Mr. McDonald* partake of the carnival spirit that, in current American movies, is pretty much a teenage thing. The anarchy, however, is controlled from the top. Writer-directors Emir Kusturica and Koki Mitani are tyrannical masters of fun, orchestrating revels that suggest some sort of hoochie-koochie striptease—the ultimate revelation being an amiable contempt for the audience.

The, word "manic" is barely adequate to characterize Kusturica's *Black Cat, White Cat* (which was first shown here at the last New York Film Festival). Bravura moviemaking by any objective standard, this vehicle for the director's lowdown magic-realist fantasies about Romany gangsters has a velocity that belies its jerry-built mise-en-scène. Kusturica's extravagantly coarse burlesque is a careening contraption fueled by a high-octane combination of Balkan craziness, blatant stereotyping, and disco-thump hysteria. (No previous Kusturica film has made the 45-year-old filmmaker's rock 'n' roll yearnings more apparent.)

Personnel oscillates between *A Thousand Clowns* and *Ten Thousand Maniacs* as a throng of volatile hustlers, smugglers, and schemers plot, strut, and zorba their way toward the grand climax of the world's most mondo gypsy wedding. Coming after Kusturica's controversial Serbian allegory *Underground, Black Cat, White Cat* is actually something of a light romantic comedy. It's also a bit of a menagerie. The title creatures are much in evidence while, over the course of the movie, a pig devours a derelict car and flocks of geese storm across the screen at every opportunity. Nor does Kusturica neglect his humanoids.

While the younger performers are largely experienced actors, many of the most colorful roles are filled by grinning local personalities—most notably the wizened godfather Uncle Grga (Sabri Sulejmani, the retired proprietor of a "shoeshine salon," with no previous acting experience). Tattooed, with a mouth full of gold teeth and a matching Mogen David moon-and-star pendant, Grga is "elegant as a vampire," in the words of his long-lost buddy, Zarije (Zabit Memedov, a goofball veteran of Kusturica's *Time of the Gypsies*). Grga is also sentimental; he watches the end of *Casablanca* over and over, and like all of the movie's more sympathetic characters wears his heart on his sleeve.

This is a film without a single quiet moment. A gypsy band squeezes itself into a hospital ward to escort the ailing Zarije. ("Music! Aggression!" he cries, at least according to the subtitles, as he dances out.) Set mainly in a Dogpatch resort on the banks of the Danube, *Black Cat, White Cat* is largely a succession of stunts. In the most exuberantly grotesque of these, a Wagnerian tango singer with a lacquered pompadour demonstrates the strength and precision of her sphincter muscles by parking her ample posterior against a wooden plank and extracting a nail.

The narrative is otherwise predicated on an obscure double cross involving Zarije's feckless son, Matko, and the coked-up "war criminal" Dadan. (As played by Srdan Todorovic, this fiercely glazed character not only steals a trainload of Bulgarian oil but the movie as well—punctuating each of his brainstorms with a frantic burst of pumped-up shadowboxing.) Matko is further tricked into marrying his teenaged son to Dadan's diminutive sister—a "horrible grouchy midget" as one character unsympathetically puts it. The boy, meanwhile, is smitten with an obstreperous, long-limbed barmaid (Branka Katic).

Black Cat, White Cat's raucous first hour is a buildup to the mismatched wedding. But then the narrative trips over an accumulation of unquiet corpses and runaway brides to land, literally, in the shit. Lacking the emotionally charged metaphors that made *Underground* something more than a virtuoso Saint Vitus dance, *Black Cat, White Cat* is determined to twist every character into an ideogram for vulgar humanity. Perhaps these gypsies are a screen on which the Bosnian-born director can project his own feelings of ostracism and homelessness. In any case, the scatological closer rebounds unpleasantly on him.

Also reviewed in:
CHICAGO TRIBUNE, 10/22/99, Friday/p. A, Michael Wilmington
NATION, 9/27/99, p. 35, Stuart Klawans
NEW YORK TIMES, 9/10/99, p. E10, Janet Maslin
VARIETY, 9/21-27/98, p. 110, David Stratton

BLACK MASK

An Artisan Entertainment release. *Executive Producer:* Tsui Hark. Producer: Charles Heung. *Director:* Daniel Lee. *Screenplay:* Tsui Hark, Koan Hui, Teddy Chen, and Joe Ma. *Director of Photography:* Cheung Tung Leung. *Editor:* Cheung Ka Tai. *Music:* Teddy Robin. *Art Director:* Eddie Ma and Bill Lui. *Visual Effects:* Stephen Ma. *Costumes:* William Fung and Mabel Kwan. *Running time:* 90 minutes. *MPAA Rating:* R.

CAST: Jet Li (Tsui); Karen Mok (Tracy); Lau Ching Wan (Rock); Françoise Yip (Yeuk-lan); Patrick Lung Kang (Commander Hung); Anthony Wong (King Kau).

LOS ANGELES TIMES, 5/17/99, Calendar/p. 5, Eric Harrison

You know you're living in a global village when a martial arts movie from Hong Kong comes laced with gangsta rap and when every other gloomily lit, elliptically cut shot reminds you of a) a mainstream Hollywood action flick, b) an American superhero comic book, c) bad '60s TV or d) an incomprehensible if stunning-to-watch rock video.

The motion picture in question, the frenetic "Black Mask," stars Jet Li, the Chinese wushu (martial arts) star who made his American debut as the bantamweight heavy in "Lethal Weapon 4." First released in Hong Kong in 1996, "Black Mask" opened here Friday without previews, which is just as well because this is a critic-proof movie if there ever was one.

The reason it's similar to American action movies, of course, is that so many Hollywood films these days are themselves the result of cultural miscegenation, borrowing liberally from a Hong Kong cinema that has long excelled at this sort of "B" action picture.

"Black Mask" is sprinkled with references to "The Green Hornet" and "Batman," yet it feels unadulterated. Excess plot and texture have been burned away. What's left may not be pure, but even the impurities have been stripped to their essence.

These kinds of movies don't exactly aspire to the Aristotelian ideal. What counts is the frequency and audaciousness of the stunts, the inventiveness with which people get maimed or killed. (This is not the movie to show Congress given the current anti-movie-violence mood).

The whoa! quotient of "Black Mask" is very high and at times it's quite funny. And like those aforementioned rock videos, it has its share of evocative shots (a flying white dove here, a visual quote from Sergie Eisenstein there) that look cool but signify nothing.

That said, be aware that much of "Black Mask's" plot and a good deal of its rapidly cut action sequences are mystifying. Characters show up without cause or plausibility whenever the screenwriters need them. People behave illogically, which perhaps is a given, but even the movie's own internal logic is peculiar.

If you think about what you're watching, you'll find yourself asking over and over why did this character do this or how does that one know that?

The secret, of course, is not to think. Just go with it. Either you can hang or you can't. If you can't, well, you shouldn't be here.

The plot, such as it is: Li is a former member of an elite military force, now leading the peaceful life of a librarian. The squad was abandoned by the government after it learned that the chemicals that gave members their super powers would eventually kill them. But the remnants of the squad turn up and disrupt Li's quiet routine. They're murdering the drug lords of Hong Kong and taking over their business. World domination is their aim.

Li was All-Around National Wushu Champion in China for four years running before becoming a popular action star. He is a magnetic presence—and his balletic stunts are amazing. Lau Ching Wan is equally powerful as Rock, a hardheaded police detective who thinks he's invincible. And Francoise Yip, as a kung fu-fighting femme fatale, could teach Carrie-Anne Moss from "The Matrix" a thing or two about high kicking. (She will be familiar to American audiences as Jackie Chan's co-star in "Rumble in the Bronx.")

Most of the humor is supplied by Karen Mok, who plays the equivalent of Lois Lane. She's new to U.S. audiences but whenever she's on screen, her rubbery face and comic timing give the movie the familiar feel of an American TV sitcom.

NEW YORK POST, 5/15/99, p. 21, Rod Dreher

Artisan opened the Hong Kong chop-socky extravaganza "Black Mask" yesterday without screening it in advance for critics. Surprise, surprise. Aside from some furious martial-arts combat sequences stylishly choreographed by Yuen Wo Ping, there's nothing of interest here to those who aren't serious fans of the genre. And even then, some may be put off by the bloody monsoon of gun violence and graphic savagery.

Originally released overseas in 1996, "Black Mask," now well-dubbed into English, is coming out stateside to take advantage of the splash its star, Jet Li, made in "Lethal Weapon 4." In this film, Li plays Michael, a bio-engineered superkiller who has left the violent life behind, and is trying to live as a shy, pacifist librarian.

But when Hong Kong's leading drug lords begin turning up savagely murdered by death squads, Michael knows the masters of mayhem are none other than his former superkiller comrades. Knowing the police don't have a chance against them, the mild-mannered librarian by day turns into the vigilante Black Mask at night. To protect his identity, Michael dons a black leather fedora and a ridiculous Lone Ranger-type mask made of corrugated rubber. Whoa.

Michael must also face down the temptation to give in to the dark side of the force, and rejoin the evil legion, which hopes to rule Hong Kong. They probably could do so, too: Director Daniel Lee loads the film with enough firepower and explosives to fight a war. Where's the fun in seeing kung-fu fighting when everybody's mowing each other down with submachine guns? At least Jackie Chan movies have a sporting sense of humor.

The plot is idiotic, the acting mediocre and the lurid sadism extremely hard to stomach. Nothing like watching a dominatrix banshee slit a man's throat with a razor blade concealed in her mouth to ruin your day.

NEWSDAY, 5/18/99, Part II/p. B11, Bob Heisler

Here's the question: Why didn't Simon, aka retro hero *Black Mask*, die when the Commander put a sonic destroyer blast through his chest? The ray went through a concrete pillar, then cleanly through his body. And surely the Commander, head of the bio-engineered good-guys-gone-bad-except-for-Simon, wouldn't have used the sonic shotgun unless he knew it would be deadly.

Wouldn't he? And come to think of it, since Simon and the Commander each possessed superhuman strength and were impervious to pain, why were they whaling on each other in the first place? So much blood. So few answers. Welcome to Hong Kong, 1996, home of the nonstop killing game called the action movie. On your behalf, I tried to count the bodies. After about 20 minutes, having run out of ink at number 47, I settled for keeping track of the ways to dispatch my enemies, should I ever find myself as Simon did—running from his past, hiding his awesome, mysterious power as a librarian whose only friend is the police detective assigned to discover who is killing the crowned drug kings of the territory.

In "Black Mask," people are killed by machine guns, of course, and by fist, foot, head-butt and fall from lofty perch. Also by cell phone bomb, concussion bomb, plain old time bomb, fire, tractor crushing, grenade, impaling, razor blade, electric cord, scalpel and flying CD.

"It's always the quiet guys who get the most done," Simon reminds an erstwhile girl companion. "They don't waste time talking." There's a plot and Jet Li is a likeable hero trapped in his destiny. There is high-speed extreme martial arts of the bouncing-off-walls, cartoon variety, some very funny lines courtesy of the dubbed dialog and the usual last-second escapes from fates even worse than death.

But there is also a fleet of bad guys in long, black trenchcoats and four limb severings (none delaying the fighting), which suggests that the real message of "Black Mask" can be found in its rating: R—Persons under 17 must be accompanied by a parent or guardian. Let your kids see this without you and forfeit your right to deny responsibility for their actions.

Also reviewed in:
NEW YORK TIMES, 5/15/99, p. B15, Lawrence Van Gelder
WASHINGTON POST, 5/15/99, p. C5, Stephen Hunter
VARIETY, 1/20-26/97, p. 48, Derek Elley

BLACK AND WHITE IN COLOR

A Czech Television and Arcimboldo release. *Producer:* David Charap and Cestmir Kopecky. *Director:* Mira Erdevicki-Charap. *Screenplay (Czech with English subtitles):* Katerina Ondrejkova. *Director of Photography:* Marek Jicha. *Editor:* David Charap. *Music:* Vera Bila and Kale. *Running time:* 58 minutes. *MPAA Rating:* Not Rated.

WITH: Vera Bila; Kale Band.

NEW YORK POST, 12/15/99, p. 56, Hannah Brown

Gypsies on film usually fit into one of two stereotypes: The gold-toothed, ruthless con man or the tragic nomad, wailing plaintive tunes.

But Vera Bila, the subject of the documentary "Black and White in Colour," is neither of these clichés.

The lead singer of Kale, a Gypsy band based in Prague, Bila looks like a fat lady out of a nightmare in a Fellini film, but she sings with a rare and haunting purity.

Crude and voracious (she cooks and eats huge meals, chain-smokes and plays slot machines), she's almost cartoonish as she declares her devotion to her husband: "I trim his toenails with my teeth."

Although her band is beginning to catch on (it's funny to see the slender black-and-denim-clad Czechs applauding her music), Bila isn't very interested in her growing fame.

Rather than trying to promote herself, she frets that she may lose her welfare payments, since the authorities will think she's rich.

She tries to find a suitable Gypsy bride for her son, who is soon to be released from prison, where he's serving time for burglary.

The most moving parts of the film show her visiting impoverished Gypsy villages in her search for a daughter-in-law.

Director Mira Erdevicki-Charap stages a mock music video in one village as Bila lip-syncs to a playback while Gypsy children dance around her.

The sequence satirizes all those videos and fashion layouts that use Gypsies and Third World poverty merely as exotic backgrounds.

"Black and White in Colour" presents a lively, charming portrait of a woman who is the opposite of all things politically correct (I will never lose weight. I don't even want to," says Bila, eating and puffing on a cigarette) and loves herself for it.

VILLAGE VOICE, 12/21/99, p. 152, Richard Gehr

There have been few less likely singing sensations than Vera Bila, the Nusrat Fateh Ali Kahn of gypsy music. The subject of this intimate documentary about an artist trapped between her Romany roots and artistic potential, Bila is a golden-voiced and fascinatingly unhealthy-looking Slovakian Gypsy. She shares a modest flat in the Bohemian village of Rokycany with her beloved yet cranky invalid husband ("I trim his toenails with my teeth," she admits adoringly) and an adopted son jailed for robbery. The film's title works on two levels: Bila is Czech for "white," while her band's name, Kale, means "black"; a repeated song bemoans the "black-haired woman" rejected by the white world.

Contradictions abound. Celebrated in Paris and Prague, where we see her perform, Bila complains constantly about press that makes it appear as though she's rich when she clearly is not—not if scenes of her haggling over secondhand clothes or pawning her stereo for what she claims is the 18th time are any indication. (The end of the film finds her indicted for illegally receiving state support, a charge that was eventually dropped.) Likewise, Bila wants to remain true to her Slovakian heritage but is appalled by the poverty she encounters upon returning to her native village to purchase a wife for her son. Her associates lead double lives, too: Her exasperated manager sells sausage on the side, and her drummer appears white but takes pride in being "100 percent Romany."

"I just sing about the troubles I have," states Bila, whose utterly blues-worthy life is remarkable to behold. And the same goes for the wildly kinetic Bulgarian Gypsy wedding band seen in *Ziganska Musica*. Where *Black and White* depicts one poignant scene after another, the short film accompanying it captures a single highly emotional wedding and the feverish music that drives it.

Also reviewed in:
NEW YORK TIMES, 12/15/99, p. E5, Lawrence Van Gelder
VARIETY, 11/8-14/99, p. 42, Lael Loewenstein

BLAIR WITCH PROJECT, THE

An Artisan Entertainment release of a Haxan Films production. *Executive Producer:* Bob Eick and Kevin J. Foxe. *Producer:* Gregg Hale and Robin Cowie. *Director:* Daniel Myrick and Eduardo Sanchez. *Screenplay:* Daniel Myrick and Eduardo Sanchez. *Director of Photography:* Neal Fredericks. *Editor:* Daniel Myrick and Eduardo Sanchez. *Music:* Tony Cora. *Sound:* Dana Meeks. *Production Designer:* Ben Rock. *Art Director:* Ricardo R. Moreno. *Running time:* 87 minutes. *MPAA Rating:* R.

CAST: Heather Donahue (Herself, Cameraperson/Narrator); Michael Williams (Himself, Sound Recordist); Joshua Leonard (Himself, Cameraman); Bob Griffith, Jim King, Sandra Sánchez, Ed Swanson, and Patricia Decou (Interviewees).

LOS ANGELES TIMES, 7/16/99, Calendar/p. 12, Kevin Thomas

"The Blair Witch Project" has received so much advance press that you probably already know that it is a "mockumentary" that's received rave reviews on the festival circuit. And that's too bad since all that attention ultimately does a disservice to the audience.

Those who go into the film cold are of course more likely to experience thrills and chills than those who know what they're getting into—the second group, however, can expect an unsettling experience, capped by a couple of jolts at the finish, as the film's twists and turns are impossible to predict and do generate low-key suspense. Some rave quotes suggest that you're in for a scare of "Exorcist" proportions, whereas "Blair Witch" is essentially an exceedingly ingenious diversion.

In short, the film is a clever, entertaining stunt, no more, no less, and a terrific calling card for its fledgling filmmakers, Daniel Myrick and Eduardo Sanchez.

An opening statement tells us that on Oct. 21, 1994, Heather Donahue, Joshua Leonard and Michael Williams hiked into Maryland's Black Hills Forest to shoot a documentary on a local legend of the so-called Blair Witch, a woman named Elly Kedward who was supposed to have caused half the youngsters of Blair village to vanish more than 200 years ago. In 1824, the town of Burkittsville was founded on the site of Blair; between November 1940 and May 1941, the town was rocked by the ritualistic slayings of seven children by a local hermit named Rustin Parr, who, after giving himself up, tells authorities that he did it for "an old woman ghost."

Once we're informed that the student filmmakers disappeared without a trace but that we will be looking at the footage they shot—found a year later—we are abruptly thrust into the quickly menacing world of that footage. The filmmakers have taken tremendous pains to bring to it enough coherence so that we can be involved in the students' plight as it unfolds yet maintain enough jaggedness so that "Blair Project's" fakery is utterly convincing.

Leonard serves as cinematographer, shooting in 16 millimeter, while Williams is the project's sound man. In the meantime Heather records the group's growing rifts on High-8 video and her comments on those rifts; this is an unobtrusive and persuasive device that provides a crucial narrative flow in a completely natural way.

Heather, whose project it is, comes off as headstrong and determined to maintain control of her shoot at all costs. She's strong on using all the correct terms for the shoot-from-the-hip kind of documentary she's trying to make. There's something highhanded, a little condescending and insensitive about Heather as she goes about interviewing locals before she and her crew enter the forest, where they quickly get lost and soon become subjected to a series of mysterious and malevolent incidents.

The men become outraged at Heather for the predicament she got them into, but all three young people are smart enough to know that if they are to have a hope of making it out of the forest they've got to pull together.

All three are playing roles, although they use their actual names, and the way in which Myrick and Sanchez make improvisation work within their outline, keeping their cast in the dark and off balance as much as possible, is nothing less than amazing. You can, if you want, buy into the possibility of supernatural forces acting as the prime mover or believe the trio has fallen victim to some unseen person or people who simply are in the grip of madness. Donahue, Leonard and Williams are as absolutely believable as everything else about the film.

If you're willing to look beyond the fright tactics in "Blair Witch," you can enjoy it as a kind of mordant commentary on the presumptuousness of brash and inexperienced documentary filmmakers who, in this extreme instance, plunge into a forest wilderness with woefully inadequate preparation and who actually think they will somehow be able to record supernatural manifestations on film. In the final analysis, "Blair Witch" is perhaps more amusing and satisfying as a cautionary tale deflating a certain kind of filmmaking arrogance than it is as an offbeat horror show.

NEW YORK, 8/2/99, p. 59, Peter Rainer

As an antidote to the strong-arm pseudo-horrifics of *The Haunting*, you might want to check out the zero-budget *Blair Witch Project*, written, directed, and edited by Daniel Myrick and Eduardo Sanchez, with the actors themselves (Heather Donahue, Michael Williams, Joshua Leonard) shooting and improvising for eight days as filmmakers who hiked into the Black Hills Forest in Maryland to make a documentary about the local Blair Witch legend. Since we're told from the start that the footage we're seeing was found a year after the trio disappeared, the cold creeps set in early. The improvisations sometimes sound too much like improvisations, the handheld camerawork should probably not be viewed on a full stomach, and there's enough nattering and bickering to make you wish the legend would become a reality a lot faster. Despite all this, the dread is palpable. You don't need buckets of moolah and a zillion computer-generated effects to get a rise out of an audience. Just a little imagination, a little suggestive terror, will do quite nicely.

NEW YORK POST, 7/14/99, p. 47, Jonathan Foreman

Despite the absence of scary music, sudden jolts and flashing knives, "The Blair Witch Project" may be the creepiest and most original horror film since John Carpenter's classic "Halloween."

In a brilliant and original update of a traditional horror device, the "found" diary—it's the form Brain Stoker used when he wrote "Dracula"—the movie purports to be an edited version of film and tape recordings discovered in the Maryland woods after a documentary team disappeared there in 1994.

The team is led by Heather Donahue (played by an actress named Heather Donahue), who is making a documentary about the 200-year-old legend of the Blair witch for a college project.

She's also narrating and keeping a videotape record of the filming on her camcorder. The filming is being done by Joshua Donahue, who operates the black-and-white 16mm camera, and Michael Williams, the sound man.

Through the footage shot on her camcorder we see the trio load up, drive to Burkittsville, Md., and talk to the locals. They film one interview with a mad old lady who claims to have seen the Blair witch, in the form of a fur-covered woman, and then another one with two fisherman who direct the filmmakers to a logging trail that leads to an old murder site known as Coffin Rock.

Then they drive up to the woods, park the car and hike into the interior with the equipment on their backs.

The first night passes quietly enough. But during the day they see strange piles of rocks, like grave markers. The second night they hear strange noises, and in the morning they come upon bundles of twigs tied together to resemble a human being with arms outstretched.

And then they get lost.

The recordings account for three more days and nights, as hunger, exhaustion and fear take their toll. The woods aren't even particularly dark or creepy ones. But as the three kids run out of food, water and confidence, the forest seems ever more hostile and alien.

You never see who or what is harassing and finally attacking them. But very cleverly you see the way the group loses its cohesion, thanks to teen-age acting-out and the onset of panic.

There isn't a single moment when the footage, dialogue and group dynamics don't ring true. The actors look and act just like real people, and the tension builds up slowly—just like it does in real life.

And because you see everything through the characters' eyes—in particular, those of the redoubtable, tough-talking Heather—the whole nightmare is that much more intense.

For some people "The Blair Witch Project" could do for overnight hiking what "Jaws" did for midnight skinny-dipping.

For others it may just be a strong argument for making use of the right to bear arms.

NEWSDAY, 7/14/99, Part II/p. B9, Bob Heisler

You know what's going to happen to the three film students who walk into the Maryland woods on Oct. 21, 1994, to make a documentary about a local legend called the Blair Witch. It's a classic horror-movie variation. To be successful, the movie must have the how, when and where fall into place like the tumblers of a bank safe, locking you into the journey. Low-tech, special-effects-free and largely ad-libbed, the film and its young cast pull off this year's oddest, creepiest and most effective stumble into fear.

Co-directors and writers Eduardo Sanchez and Dan Myrick have used the Internet to create a complete universe—a record of the Blair Witch myth dating from 1785, when Elly Kedward is found guilty of witchcraft and takes her revenge on the children of Blair, Md., to 1941, when the bodies of seven children are found in a hermit's cabin.

Sanchez and Myrick also have found three capable young actors to shoot the film.

When the students—team leader Heather Donahue and camera operators Michael Williams and Joshua Leonard—fail to return from their weekend in the woods, we're told at the start of the movie, police search for them unsuccessfully. A year later, a team of University of Maryland anthropology students discover a duffel bag containing film cases and camera buried under the foundation of a secluded cabin. "The Blair Witch Project" is the editing together of the raw documentary footage along with a videotape taken by Donahue of the "making of" the film.

The result begins as a mix of formal black-and-white scripted material shot by Leonard with Donahue doing stand-up reporting, and color from a hand-held camera.   The effect is disorienting. Like an amusement park ride, you keep your arms inside your car and hang on.

As the students move deeper into the woods, losing their bearings, their film-school cool and their grasp on reality, the quality of the images they record deteriorates, too. The screen goes black on occasion, focus is forgotten and the camera bounces along through the brush. It's a little like your vacation video, if you vacation with Wes Craven.

Donahue, the boss, can't admit she's lost. Her crew can't believe she has put their lives at risk; that wasn't part of the weekend assignment. Donahue can't let go of the project. Her crew can't control their anger at her incompetence or their need for her leadership. They'll find their way out in the morning, they hope, but then there's a noise outside their tent and a pile of twigs left at their campsite.

The dialogue, mostly improvised, is not the stuff of measured discussion of Early American superstition and its impact on the development of racial intolerance. In fact, its reliance on one four-letter word to express anger, frustration and anxiety becomes a little tiring. It does, however force your attention to the visuals.

And by the time the running, spinning, squinting visuals drag you to the edge of panic, it doesn't matter whether "The Blair Witch Project" is real. Your heartbeat is.

NEWSWEEK, 7/12/99, p. 62, Jeff Giles

[*The Blair Witch Project* was reviewed jointly with *American Pie*; see Giles' review of that film.]

SIGHT AND SOUND, 11/99, p. 38, Charles Taylor

Titles inform us that the footage we are about to see was shot by three student film-makers who went into the woods surrounding the town of Burkittsville, Maryland, and were never heard from again. The footage was discovered by a search party a year later.

Burkittsville, 1994. Heather, a director, josh, a cameraman, and Mike, a soundman, head for the woods to investigate the local legend of the Blair Witch, a spirit blamed for various disappearances and the murders of several children many years before. After stocking up on provisions for a three-day trip and interviewing locals for their stories about the Blair Witch, the three set out. Things immediately start to unravel. The map Heather relies on leads the three in circles, and her insistence on filming everything, including the trio's arguments, exacerbates the tension. Soon they're awoken in the middle of the night by the sounds of children screaming. Strange piles of rocks and stick figures made out of branches are left outside their tent.

Shortly after josh finds his belongings strewn over their campsite, he disappears. A few days later Heather finds a bundle made of torn strips of Josh's shirt with an unidentified piece of bloody viscera inside. With food and hope gone, Heather and Mike stumble on a house in the woods ...

Glee is understandable when a small-budget ($25,000) independent film not only rivals Hollywood's summer blockbusters at the box office (*The Blair Witch Project* has taken more than $100 million and counting) but also captures the public's imagination in a way no Hollywood release of the season has managed. There's some poetic justice in the idea that a film made by unknowns and shot on video with no stars and no special effects could trounce its prepackaged competition. The ways 'entertainment reporting' has elevated the business side of movies over discussion of their quality have resulted in moviegoers who are cynically knowing about deals and grosses but conditioned to accept the junk shovelled at them. So it's not surprising that audiences respond to the zero-style of *Blair Witch*. With special effects announcing nothing so much as their own price tag, this picture's flat replication of reality, achieved using handheld video, and its ability to scare audiences witless with nothing more than shots of rocks and twigs are genuinely jolting. Because the film is so deliberately lacking in 'art' in much the same way *Night of the Living Dead* (1968) was, you can be lulled into thinking what you're seeing is actually happening.

This has been encouraged by the filmmakers Daniel Myrick and Eduardo Sanchez presenting the film as a documentary, assigning their characters the same names as the actors who play them, and their now-notorious filming method. Given camcorders, the three actors were sent into the woods for a week (the provisions we see them buying are what they actually lived on). Each morning they picked up written directions from the film-makers on what to shoot that day. The finished product is edited from the footage shot by the actors. In the interviews that accompanied the US release, Sanchez and Myrick boasted about how they induced real fright by waking their actors in the middle of the night with tapes of children screaming or, in the climactic scene, having camouflaged crew members leap out of the darkness to grab Heather Donahue. "We wanted this thing to be 100 per cent real," Sanchez told *Spin*. "We didn't want any of that movie shit."

But as the megalomaniacal director played by Peter O'Toole in *The Stunt Man* (1979) asked, "How tall is King Kong?" Don't Myrick and Sanchez know that movies *are* fake? Apart from the sadism of keeping your (non-union) cast hungry, cold and terrified for a week, there's the question of why you hire actors if you don't trust them to act? Certainly the unmediated hysteria we see the actors sliding into is part of what makes the film so terrifying. It's also what makes it so unpleasant. The method makes nonsense of the implied criticism of Heather's inability to put down her camera and deal with the reality in front of her. How can you take that criticism seriously from a film designed to eke every ounce of real misery and terror from its cast?

Myrick and Sanchez's method may be the opposite of Hollywood's, but by banishing psychology, characterisation and finally humanity from their film, by excluding anything but sensation, the effect is ultimately not that much different from that of, say, *Armageddon*. The most persistent *Blair Witch* myth is that the film eschewed the usual methods of marketing. In fact, no film in recent memory has been as shrewdly pre-sold as this one. The buzz it generated at the Sundance Film Festival earlier this year was sustained via a website, an hour-long 'documentary' on the history of the Blair Witch (shown on US primetime television three nights before the film opened) and pre-release displays of 'artefacts' in the lobbies of theatres. Currently you can purchase a *Blair Witch* comic, a film companion book, t-shirts and a soundtrack. Now comes word that a sequel is on the way. The most amusing thing about Hollywood's hottest new 'directors' is that they haven't actually directed anything. The producer who takes credit while doing no work has long been a staple of Hollywood satire. Myrick and Sanchez have gone that stock figure one better, as they told one interviewer, sitting in a burger joint laughing about the actors—hungry, cold and scared in the woods—who shot the movie Myrick and Sanchez have taken credit for. Somewhere, P.T. Barnum is smiling.

VILLAGE VOICE, 7/20/99, p. 135, J. Hoberman

Most horror films are spectacles of excess, based on special effects and gross-out gore. An anachronistic few subscribe to the countertradition of psychological suggestion, identified with the cycle of literate low-budget thrillers produced by Val Lewton in the 1940s. *The Blair Witch Project* has been strenuously promoted over cyberspace and cable but this clever, creepy indie is a throwback—inexpensively produced and suffused with the subtle Lewtonian atmospherics of B movies like *Return of the Cat People* or *I Walked With a Zombie*.

Written and directed by Florida-based neophytes Daniel Myrick and Eduardo Sanchez, *The Blair Witch Project* is a priori conceptual. It purports to be a sort of found actuality—the raw footage shot by a trio of Maryland film students who, making a documentary on a spooky local legend, ventured into the Black Hills Forest in October 1994 and were never seen again. The opening title explains that the students' stock and equipment were recovered a year after their disappearance; thus, however immediate, the material is shadowed with foreboding—cast as the artifact of a lost expedition to the South Pole, or worse.

Although the movie's complicated back story—vastly elaborated upon on its Web site—concerns an instance of colonial witchcraft and a century of intermittent child disappearances and gruesome murders, *Blair Witch* is shot first-person and in artless "vérité" that seems beyond handheld. (Apparently some who saw *Blair Witch* at Sundance were convinced that they were watching the real thing.) By way of introduction, the project's director, Heather (Heather Donahue), and her crew, the high-strung camera operator Josh (Joshua Leonard) and doofus soundman Mike (Michael Williams), playfully document themselves clowning around their motel room and visiting a supermarket to squeeze the Halloween marshmallows. They shoot an introduction in a graveyard, interview a few locals, and then plunge into the autumn woods.

Blair Witch makes much of its innocent larkiness. True Americans, the protagonists have no sense of an implacable past or a dreadful fate. They spook one another with recollections of *Deliverance* and campfire accounts of weird noises in the night. "What killed this dead mouse? Was it witchcraft?" Heather asks her Hi-8 video camera. (A true obsessive, she's making a documentary of her own documentary.) "Witches in days gone by were roasted—just like my Vienna sausage." Brash, nervous, constantly rapping, Heather is a type familiar to anyone who has served time in film school. Before long, however, the jokes are wearing thin. Searching for an abandoned cemetery in the woods, the trio find instead sinister rock cairns surrounding their tent and realize that they are no longer hunting but hunted.

A decade ago, Patrick Duncan's Vietnam War indie, *84 Charlie MoPic,* used a similar first-person camera—held in that case by a combat newsreel photographer—to tell the tale of a lost patrol. The strategy was intriguing but problematic. The viewer spent too much time wondering why the cameraman never had to change the magazine or just how many rolls of film he was carrying. *The Blair Witch Project* may not push its own formal conceit as far as it might—it doesn't get into how the footage was supposedly assembled—but it's a more successful tour de force. Unlike *Charlie MoPic* (or Hollywood's once-famous experiment in subjectivity *The Lady in the Lake,* where the camera represented the detective-hero's point of view), *Blair Witch* manages to involve the spectator in its protagonists' psychology.

As the filmmakers venture deeper into the woods, they lose first their map and then their minds —wandering in circles and stumbling upon a voodoo grove with strange-fruit fetishes dangling from the trees. ("This is no redneck," one yelps. "No redneck is this creative.") The acting is as impeccable as the nightmare is compelling—in fact, most of the dialogue was improvised and all of the movie was shot by the performers. Personality disintegration notwithstanding, *The Blair Witch Project* is made without F/X although, of course, the movie apparatus is itself the greatest special-effects generator of all. The movie casts its spell through the most economical means while leaving the sly suggestion that the project's real witch might be the driven director, Heather.

"I don't want to go cheesy," the bossy auteur announces at the onset and, although the real filmmakers, Myrick and Sanchez, are sometimes obliged to stretch for ways to insure that their increasingly terrorized characters keep filming, *Blair Witch* never does betray Heather's aesthetic. Paranoid, hysterical, and programmatically subjective, the movie is in every sense a psychological thriller. Although the payoff is ambiguous, the experience remains in the mind. It's an absolutely restrained and truly frightening movie. As Heather puts it, "I'm scared to open my eyes and I'm scared to close them."

Also reviewed in:
CHICAGO TRIBUNE, 7/14/99, Tempo/p. 1, Mark Caro
NATION, 9/6 & 13/99, p. 34, Stuart Klawans
NEW YORK TIMES, 7/14/99, P. E1, Janet Maslin
NEW YORKER, 7/26/99, p. 86, David Denby
VARIETY, 2/8-14/99, p. 79, Todd McCarthy
WASHINGTON POST, 7/16/99, p. C1, Lloyd Rose
WASHINGTON POST, 7/16/99, Weekend/p. 43, Desson Howe

BLAST FROM THE PAST

A New Line Cinema release of a Midnight Sun Pictures production. *Executive Producer:* Amanda Stern, Sunil Perkash, and Claire Rudnick Polstein. *Producer:* Renny Harlin and Hugh Wilson. *Director:* Hugh Wilson. *Screenplay:* Bill Kelly and Hugh Wilson. *Story:* Bill Kelly. *Director of Photography:* Jose Luis Alcaine. *Editor:* Don Brochu. *Music:* Steve Dorff. *Music Editor:* Chris Ledesma. *Choreographer:* Adam Shankman. *Sound:* Mark McNabb and (music) Rick Riccio. *Sound Editor:* Bruce Stambler. *Casting:* Denise Chamian. *Production Designer:* Robert Ziembicki. *Art Director:* Ted Berner. *Set Designer:* Colin DeRouin. *Set Decorator:* Michael Taylor. *Set Dresser:* Ed Martin, Kinney Booker, Philip Calhoun, Chris Fielding, Tony

Pillar, and John Krueger. *Special Effects:* David Waine. *Visual Effects:* David Waine. *Costumes:* Mark Bridges. *Make-up:* Heidi Seeholzer. *Make-up (Alicia Silverstone):* Ronnie Spector. *Stunt Coordinator:* Aj Nay. *Running time:* 105 minutes. *MPAA Rating:* PG-13.

CAST: Brendan Fraser (Adam); Alicia Silverstone (Eve); Christopher Walken (Calvin); Sissy Spacek (Helen); Dave Foley (Troy); Joey Slotnick (Soda Jerk); Dale Raoul (Mom); Hayden Tank (Adam, Age 3 1/2); Douglas Smith (Adam, Age 11); Ryan Sparks (Adam, Age 8); Don Yesso (Jerry); Scott Thomson (Young Psycho); Ted Kairys (Navy Pilot); Rex Linn (Dave); Cynthia Mace (Betty); Harry S. Murphy (Bob); Wendel Meldurm (Ruth); Richard Gilbert Hill (Guest); Steve Bean (Harold); Ann Ryerson (Woman Guest #1); Donovan Scott (Ron); Hugh Wilson (Levy); John Roselius (Atkinson); Bill Gratton (Boss); Bill Duffy (Workman #1); Bill Stevenson (Workman #2); J. Bruce Eckert (Realtor); Karen Geraghty (Woman Buyer); Christopher Holloway (Man Buyer); Harrison Young (Bum); Jazzmun (Streetwalker); Hannah Kozak (Drunken Hag); Dori Mizrahi (Pakistani); Fred Pierce (Bystander #1); Annie O'Donnell (Woman); Caroline Wilson (Child); Julie Zelman (Mother); Monty Ash (Old Jewish Man); Sheila Shaw (Bakery Clerk); Michael Hagiwara (Japanese Produce Clerk); Todd Susman (Butcher); Rosalee Mayeux (Hotel Registration Clerk); Danny Zorn (Bellboy); Rod Britt (Hotel Desk Clerk); Robb Skyler (Marine Manager); Nathan Fillion (Cliff); Todd Robert Anderson (Jason); Michael Gallagher (Jonathan); Carmen Moré (Sophie); Deborah Kellner (Miss Sweet); Mary Ann Hermanson (Heather); Jenifer Lewis (Dr. Aron); Jonathan Stockwell Baker (Broker); Brian Blondell (Mr. Brown); Sonya Eddy (Postal Worker); Mary Portser (Woman Guest #2); Hubert Hodgin (Bystander #2); Gary Cruz (Low Rider); Robert Sacchi (Bogart DJ); Eddie Moore (Startled Pervert).

LOS ANGELES TIMES, 2/12/99, Calendar/p. 10, Kenneth Turan

If you do something often enough, you're likely to get better at it. Even if it's playing the fool.

Brendan Fraser has done well by acting dumb. As the title character in the successful "George of the Jungle," he was regularly outsmarted by his animal friends, and in "Gods and Monsters" he's a bear of little brain outmaneuvered by Ian McKellen's canny James Whale.

With "Blast From the Past," his latest film, Fraser is getting more assured and sophisticated about his innocence. As Adam Webber, a naif raised under unusual circumstances to be the perfect gentleman, he gives an engaging and endearing performance. It's so good, in fact, it throws into relief what's lacking in the rest of the film.

Fraser co-stars in "Blast From the Past" (with Alicia Silverstone) as a hunk and a half who's been raised in total ignorance of present-day life; he's more or less the physical embodiment of the title. But while Fraser's good humor is contagious, it doesn't infect enough of the film to make a major difference.

As directed by Hugh Wilson ("The First Wives Club" and TV's "WKRP in Cincinnati") from a script he co-wrote with Bill Kelly, "Blast" begins in 1962 with the happily married Southern California couple of Calvin and Helen Webber (Christopher Walken and Sissy Spacek).

While the pregnant Helen is occupied fine-tuning the perfect pot roast, Calvin, once a Caltech professor, toils as a self-employed inventor, "a bona fide genius but a borderline nut case," someone says, who spends a lot of his time drinking hot Dr Pepper and worrying about the Red menace.

Calvin is so fearful about the communist threat that he's built an enormous bomb shelter under his house, as well-stocked as any Safeway. When a misunderstanding on the night of John Kennedy's Cuban missile crisis speech causes Calvin to think a nuclear war has started, he hustles his wife underground and sets the shelter's time locks for 35 years, the half-life of the atomic radiation he thinks is covering the Earth.

Both Walken and Spacek, though unconventional choices for comedy, give adept performances as the happily obsessed couple. Still, even with the amusing rifts about the changes a malt shop built above the shelter undergoes in 35 years, the first half-hour of "Blast" has a pokey, half-formed feeling, like it sounded funnier in the pitch meeting than it ends up playing on screen.

Once Fraser makes an appearance as Calvin and Helen's grown son, the film's energy level shoots up. Raised to be an earnest "yes, ma'am" kind of guy, a lover of Perry Como whose strongest expression is "hot diggity dog," Adam can hardly wait to venture forth into L.A. in search of a potential bride, who, his father advises, "doesn't glow in the dark."

In Fraser's hands, Adam's bottomless, puppy-like demeanor is a pleasure to experience. Whether it's encountering the sky, the ocean or any number of new phenomena, Fraser makes Adam's enthusiasm so funny and so palpable we almost rediscover the world along with him.

The appropriately named Eve Rostokov is the first potential mate Adam sees, and he is immediately smitten. It must be love, or else why would such a sweet guy fall for such a sour young woman?

Silverstone rose to almost immediate stardom on the strength of her fresh and cheerful performance in "Clueless," and it's unfortunate that "Blast" is unable to utilize her to her best advantage. Her character's complete cynicism and whiny, pouting ways do not wear as well as Adam's cheerfulness, and even the addition of a pro forma gay best friend (Dave Foley) does not make Eve any less strident. It's hard not to feel that Adam deserves better than this, and, so does this intermittently appealing movie romance.

NEW YORK POST, 2/12/99, p. 45, Jonathan Foreman

Thanks to a clever script, tight direction, a first-rate cast and the dynamite combination of Brendan Fraser and Alicia Silverstone, "Blast from the Past" blows away the recent crop of romantic comedies. And it deftly makes a resounding point about the very real cost to society of the baby boom generation's standards of manners and civility.

Calvin Webber (Christopher Walken) is a brilliant but paranoid scientist who—as the 1962 Cuban missile crisis reaches its diciest point—takes his pregnant wife Helen (Sissy Spacek) down into the oversized bomb shelter he has constructed below the basement.

Almost immediately, a plane crashes on the house above them. Hearing the impact. Calvin assumes that atom bombs are falling and seals the shelter for 30 years, by which time the radiation should have cleared.

Helen gives birth to Adam (Brendan Fraser) and, over the next decades, the Webbers do their best to educate their son for the future they will face in the late '90s. His mother teaches him how to dance, his father teaches him how to box and both teach him how to behave.

When Adam does emerge into the L.A. of 1998 and meets the jaded, cynical Eve (Alicia Silverstone), he is as comically naive as you would expect. But although he's a freak, he's also oddly well-prepared for life in the '90s—and not just because he owns extremely valuable vintage baseball cards.

This easygoing date movie shows what lies beneath the '90s taste for martinis, Rat Pack slang, sharp clothes and sharper dance-floor moves. It encapsulates the swing subculture's rebellion against slovenly, selfish, boomer ways, and its yearning for an era when parents not only stuck together but were more grown-up than their children.

While this film (unlike last year's "Pleasantville") doesn't toe the usual Hollywood line about how cool and liberated we all are today and how stupid and uptight everyone was in the past, it's also far too smart to imply that everything was wonderful back in 1962. Spacek's Helen is a frustrated, bored housewife whose ennui is intensified by her imprisonment underground.

In "Blast from the Past," the delicious Ms. Silverstone proves wrong anyone who gave up on her because of her ill-fated turn in the awful "Batman and Robin." She's quite believable as a tough chick who's seen enough of life to give up on romance. Fraser, who seems to be making a career of movies in which he plays a lunky but sweet fish out of water ("Encino Man," "George of the Jungle," the forthcoming "Dudley Do-Right") is perfect as a gentle but upright epitome of old-fashioned masculinity and innocence. The two of them together have something of the glamour of old-fashioned moviestar couples.

NEWSDAY, 2/12/99, Part II/p. B7, Jack Mathews

Since he was dug up, thawed out, washed, dressed, coiffed and named Link in the 1992 caveman comedy "Encino Man," tall, dark and vaguely simian Brendan Fraser has been condemned to playing innocent, lovable hunks on a learning curve in a strange world.

He does this well: Witness his engaging turns as a klutzy Tarzan in the family movie "George of the Jungle" and his lovestruck puppeteer in love with a conwoman in the romantic drama "Still

Breathing." Even in the current "Gods and Monsters," his character—a heterosexual gardener being inspired, if not aroused, by a gay filmmaker whose lawn he tends—is a variant of the missing link.

But with his latest role in Hugh Wilson's "Blast From the Past," the story of a 35-year-old man who enters society after having spent his entire life in a bomb shelter, Fraser has pretty much worn out the act. In fact, "Blast's" Adam Webber may be seen as the second coming of "Encino Man."

There's a better premise to this story, which begins in 1962, when Adam's father, Calvin (Christopher Walken), a paranoid engineer and pioneer survivalist, herds his pregnant wife, Helen (Sissy Spacek), into his elaborate shelter at the height of the Cuban Missile Crisis, and sets the door's timer 35 years ahead, when the half-life of radiation will have expired and it will be safe to come out.

For the next 3½ decades, the family—newborn Adam makes three—is suspended in time, with film reruns of "The Honeymooners," a lifetime supply of Perry Como albums and just enough cooking sherry to keep Mom's anxieties calmed until the end of the millennium.

"Blast From the Past" divides itself between below and above-ground sections, with intermittent success at both levels. Walken, whose gift for light comedy has been underused, is very funny as the nerd scientist, convinced that he's raising a son for a post-apocalyptic world that he'll have to help rebuild, and Calvin's shelter is an ingenious space, with hydroponic farms and fish tanks.

But Wilson ("The First Wives Club") devotes more time to their sheltered life than the claustrophobic setting and Calvin's eccentricities can support. When they finally do begin to emerge, the time-warp contrast is never as imaginative or as magical as you would hope. The script, by Wilson and story creator Bill Kelly, is awash in the obvious and void of any genuine insight or irony.

In ways, "Blast" is the obverse of "Pleasantville." Here, the holy innocent is beamed forward in time, where he encounters an incomprehensibly jaded environment. Adam is a three-way virgin—soul, mind and body—and there's nothing like him on earth. Naturally, he's viewed as either a bumpkin or a mental case by the people he encounters, including Eve (Alicia Silverstone), a young woman who rescues him from a fleecing and then, while trying to shake him, begins to fall for his otherworldly gentleness and charm.

There are some clever conceits along the way. Among Adam's possessions are his father's baseball card collection, worth thousands, and his IBM and AT&T stocks, worth millions. But there are some real harebrained concoctions, as well, notably the presence of a drug-addled ex-hippie who builds a cult religion around the exit hole of the Webber bomb shelter.

Once Adam is out among 'em, searching for supplies to restock the shelter, "Blast" adopts the rhythm of situation comedy. Watch Adam react to tough guys, see him cut a rug at a '40s swing club (Fraser actually shows some deft footwork), see him try to drive a car (he parks like O.J. Simpson).

Fraser and Silverstone do manage a spark of chemistry, and it's hard not to root for a guy who offers a valuable baseball card for a ride home and a girl who's too principled to accept it. But "Blast" is finally a squandered opportunity, a lot of situation with very little comedy.

SIGHT AND SOUND, 4/99, p. 38, Robin Dougherty

Los Angeles, 1962. After learning that Russian missiles have been sighted in Cuba, former college professor Calvin rushes his pregnant wife Helen into an elaborate bomb shelter under their garage. Calvin has stocked the shelter with every possible amenity, making it an underground twin of their ranch house. When a plane inadvertently crashes into the house, Calvin thinks the impact is a nuclear explosion. Fearing radiation fallout, he sets the shelter locks to stay shut for 35 years.

Within days, Helen gives birth to Adam, who grows up without ever living above ground or meeting anyone outside the family. The bomb shelter preserves Calvin and Helen's favourite aspects of a pre-rock'n'roll US. Adam never learns about the Vietnam war, premarital sex or the urbanisation of the San Fernando Valley. After 35 years pass, the locks open and Adam goes above ground to find a wife. He meets Eve, who at first mistakes him for a rube. They fall in love and eventually build Adam's parents a new house above ground. Adam becomes a millionaire when he cashes in his father's IBM stocks.

Blast from the Past puts a fresh twist on the fish-out-of-water comedy formula by throwing 35-year-old Adam who has grown up in a bomb shelter into the modern-day US which has, of course, changed drastically since 1962. Unfamiliar with such commonplace developments as urban poverty, credit cards and adult-video stores, Adam is able to see our world with fresh eyes. He can't believe people have computers in their homes. His guilelessness and honesty are unappreciated by the characters around him, but they make for comic scenarios. For instance, after emerging from his bomb shelter, he's mistaken for a god by the squatters hanging out in the hovel where his parents' house once stood.

Brendan Fraser played another time-travelling innocent in *Encino Man* where he was a caveman defrosted in modern L.A. Less prone to grunting this time round, he brings a puppy-dog charm to his character, virtually following Alicia Silverstone's Eve home before they fall in love. She saves him from selling off his father's vintage baseball-card collection for chump change, but remains suspicious of him because he's so nice. Naturally, they don't see that they're made for each other until the requisite complications bite in, but unfortunately, the screenplay strains at forestalling the final union, throwing synthetic obstacles in the couple's path. It is neither believable nor helpful that Eve embraces Adam's naiveté one day and tries to have him committed the next.

For that reason, the first half of the film, in which we watch Adam grow up in a bizarre parallel universe stuck in 1962, is the most compelling sequence. Here, director Hugh Wilson *(The First Wives Club)* punctuates the action with a deftness that eludes him once Adam goes above ground. He reveals details sparingly, showing us that Calvin has equipped the refuge with its own grocery store as well as a tank of fresh fish. The production design lovingly preserves every delicious period element, from the family's turquoise kitchen appliances to their swank *moderne* lighting fixtures.

It's this unabashed nostalgia for an earlier era that *Blast from the Past* is selling. (A childhood of dancing to his parents' records has conveniently prepared Adam for the swing-music craze of the 90s.) A running joke—in which Helen is shown to be slowly going mad from the stifling limits of a housewife's existence—is the one bit of subtlety the story allows itself. The film embraces the view that the wholesomeness we now associate with the early 60s was more than superficial. Anyone looking for a more sceptical reading of the time will be disappointed.

VILLAGE VOICE, 2/23/99, p. 114, Gary Dauphin

Like the isotopes that provide the plot's organizing principle, *Blast From the Past* is half-gone halfway through, a darkly promising gambit decaying into a rote, soft-focus romantic comedy. *Blast* starts in the wild days of the Cuban Missile Crisis, imagining not the eradication of an L.A. nuclear family but its accidental encasement in concrete: A twitchy scientist (Christopher Walken, puffing at a pipe as if he were perpetually smoke-signaling DAD) mistakes a plane crash for the Big One and seals himself and his family into a backyard shelter with a three-decade time lock on the door. Dad laments the lost upper world but as the years grind on, you get the feeling he knows he's not only avoided atomic annihilation but the fall of Saigon, the Panthers, Women's Lib, and Watergate. He's clearly pleased as punch, but isolation forces his wife (an appropriately scattered Sissy Spacek) to self-medicate on the dwindling hooch while son Adam grows into the perfect, albeit chastely horny, progeny (effectively played by that master technician of blandness, Brendan Fraser).

When the 30-year timer on the shelter pings, Adam is sent up top for supplies and finds L.A. a bewildering wonderland. "The amount of reconstruction is amazing," Adam quips earnestly about the skyline (folks think he's referring to earthquakes), and he about falls over when he sees his first real-life black person (she just thinks he's white). But Adam is no dope and realizes there has been no apocalypse; his situation is complicated by a love interest unfortunately named Eve (Alicia Silverstone), as well as by the good son's impulse to protect daddy's fragile, outmoded worldview. The film's first half does an unexpectedly energetic dance in which retro-Americana worship is paired with a knowing wink. But about the time Adam and Eve get down to re-creating their own personal Eden, *Blast* loses its way, settling for the standard coupling two-step. Things pick up slightly during the last reel (Adam's talk about his parents living in the ground starts causing problems), but oddly enough father does end up knowing best here, *Blast From the Past* most fun when it's locked up with daddy.

Also reviewed in:
CHICAGO TRIBUNE, 2/12/99, Friday/p. A, Mark Caro
NEW REPUBLIC, 3/15/99, p. 26, Stanley Kauffmann
NEW YORK TIMES, 2/12/99, p. E10, Janet Maslin
VARIETY, 2/15-21/99, p. 65, Dennis Harvey
WASHINGTON POST, 2/12/99, p. C1, Rita Kempley
WASHINGTON POST, 2/12/99, Weekend/p. 49, Desson Howe

BLIND FAITH

A Roxie Releasing release of a Neufield/Rehme Productions/Showtime Entertainment production. *Executive Producer:* Mace Neufield and Robert Rehme. *Producer:* Nick Grillo. *Director:* Ernest Dickerson. *Screenplay:* Frank Military. *Director of Photography:* Rodney Charters. *Editor:* Stephen Lovejoy. *Music:* Ron Carter. *Sound:* Stephen Barden. *Casting:* Beth Klein, Alysa Wishingrad, and Ross Clydesdale. *Production Designer:* Jeff Ginn. *Art Director:* Brandt Gordon. *Set Decorator:* Brendan Smith. *Set Dresser:* John Mainwaring, Jesse O'Connor, and Arlind Vicente. *Costumes:* Martha Mann. *Make-up:* Lynda McCormack. *Stunt Coordinator:* John Stoneham, Jr. *Running time:* 118 minutes. *MPAA Rating:* Not Rated.

CAST: Charles S. Dutton (Charles Williams); Courtney B. Vance (John Wiliams); Kadeem Hardison (Eddie Williams); Lonette McKee (Carol Williams); Garland Whitt (Charles Williams Jr.); Karen Glave (Anna Huggins); Jeff Clarke (Timothy); Nancy Herard (Rose); Jim Jones (Philip); Alex Karzis (Frank); Dan Lett (Frank Minor); Aron Tiger (Judge Aker); Birdie M. Hale (Mrs. Barry).

NEW YORK POST, 2/26/99, p. 58, Rod Dreher

"Blind Faith," a so-so potboiler that originally aired on the cable-TV channel Showtime, starts off reasonably strong, but it can't rise above the schematic plotting and shrill message-movie piety often found in the made-for-TV genre.

In telling the story of a racially charged murder in 1950s New York, director Ernest Dickerson (Spike Lee's frequent cinematographer) and writer Frank Military set out to discredit bourgeois morality, as embodied by ex-Marine Charles Williams (Charles S. Dutton), a strict, religious family man who aspires to become the first black police sergeant in The Bronx. He believes that if he works hard within the system, he and his family will be rewarded with social progress.

But as far as this movie is concerned, he's a chump. The cat who knows what it's all about is Charles' brother Eddie (Kadeem Hardison), a Greenwich Village jazz musician thrown out of Charles' house for smoking reefer. Caught between the two is their brother John (Courtney B. Vance), a lawyer whose services to his family become vital when Charles Jr. (Garland Whitt) is arrested for murdering a white kid in Van Cortlandt Park.

Charles Jr. has confessed to the crime, but he's always been a good kid, and his Uncle John knows he's lying even though the boy faces the death penalty if convicted. Charles Sr. is of little help. He's a Great Santini-type brute so obsessed with his social position that he can't talk through the veil of his anger and shame.

John puts together a team of law students to investigate the case, and they discover the crime involves police corruption, racism and homophobia.

The courtroom theatrics of "Blind Faith" are fairly routine, and the more compelling story—the cracking of the fault lines within a family—is left underdeveloped. "Blind Faith" is preoccupied with scoring ideological points off the cardboard-villainous Charles Sr. rather than with exploring his anger and anguish. It's also a waste of Dutton, one of the finest actors around.

Though "Blind Faith" is fairly entertaining, and its performances good, one is troubled by the film's glib justification of perjury on the grounds that the legal system is fraught with racism.

Twice, lawyer John elicits lies under oath from defense witnesses to help his case. The moral implications of this violation are given no consideration by the screenwriter. Equally facile are his conclusions that the civil rights movement for blacks is the same as the gay rights movement.

Righteousness and the craving for a pat moralizing may have short-circuited Military's attention to detail. Though the film is set in 1957, John sarcastically asks an inattentive law student, "Would you like to work on Brown vs. Board of Education?" That case had been decided by the U.S. Supreme Court three years earlier.

VILLAGE VOICE, 3/2/99, p. 150, Gary Dauphin

When you're introduced to the Williamses, the black middle-class clan about to be cut to pieces in *Blind Faith,* they're so stolid and familiar you imagine you understand the calamity that's about to befall them. The year is 1957 and burly patriarch Charles (Charles Dutton) is a hardworking, go-along-to-get-along cop. His brother, John (Courtney B. Vance), is a small-time lawyer looking to move up to "contracts and real estate," while Charles's son, Charlie Jr. (Garland Whitt), is too good either to be true or to survive. When Charles Sr.'s precinct calls with the news that his son has been arrested for the murder of an Irish boy in Van Cortlandt Park, the charge is as outrageous as it is sadly expected. These are black people with hopes, means, and dreams; it's no surprise their luck has run out.

The prosecutors quickly put together an open-and-shut case: Charlie Jr. just walked up to seven white boys in order to rob and strangle the largest. Despite the huge gaps in logic, at first Charles Sr. seems angriest at his son, who almost insists upon his own execution by corroborating the half-baked police chronology. John starts an impassioned defense of his nephew, but his biggest obstacle isn't the racism of judges and hooligan witnesses; it's his own brother's unwillingness to dig too deeply into what Charlie Jr. was doing in the park that night.

Director Ernest Dickerson, previously director of photography for six Spike Lee joints, handles the proceedings with impressive agility, balancing the appropriately raw performances of his able cast with blue-drenched period visuals that ache as much as they soothe. Few audience members will be surprised by the film's final turns, but credit *Blind Faith* for investing them with unexpected power nonetheless.

Also reviewed in:
NEW YORK TIMES, 2/26/99, p. E11, Janet Maslin
VARIETY, 1/26-2/1/98, p. 69, Dennis Harvey

BLOOD, GUTS, BULLETS & OCTANE

A Lions Gate Films release of a Short Fuse Films production in association with Next Wave Films. *Executive Producer:* Peter Broderick and Charles Leis. *Producer:* Leon Corcos, Patrick M. Lynn, Dan Leis, and Joe Carnahan. *Director:* Joe Carnahan. *Screenplay:* Joe Carnahan. *Director of Photography:* John A. Jimenez. *Editor:* Joe Carnahan. *Music:* Mark Priolo and Martin Birke. *Sound:* Spencer Mulcahy. *Sound Editor:* John Flanagan. *Art Director:* Eric Lutes. *Costumes:* Mooshie. *Make-up:* Eric Lutes. *Stunt Coordinator:* Rockne Carnahan. *Running time:* 87 minutes. *MPAA Rating:* R.

CAST: Mike Maas (Victor Drub); Nick Fenske (Mechanic); Mark Priolo (Frank Priolo); Joe Carnahan (Sid French); Andrew Fowler (Mike Carbuyer); Gloria Gomez (Julie Carbuyer); Dan Leis (Bob Melba); Josephine Arreola (Elda); Dave Booth (Jerry); Kevin Hale (Pinto Guy); Max Ancar (Frank Manzano); Leah Carnahan (Ginger); Scott Tayler (Dick Dupree, Sr.); Eric Lutes (Dick Dupree, Jr.); Carlos Hernandez (Diaz Carbajal); Dan Harlan (Danny Woo); Karla Cave (Dottie Woo); Karen Olsen (Attendant); Matt Carnahan (Mitchell Wayne Richter); James Salter (Raymond Phelps); Ken Rudulph (FBI Agent Jared); Jerry Rainbolt (Jerry Goldman); Carol Curry (Stripper); Rick Reinaldo (Inmate 1); Dave Collagan (Inmate 2); Michael Saumure (Vernon Cash); Kurt Johnson (Hillbilly Sniper); Hugh McChord (Mr. Reich); Tanja Anguay (Woo Cowgirl 1); Priya Patel (Woo Cowgirl 2); Chuck Leis (Pete the Bartender); Mike Mass

(Dumpster Bum); Kellee Benedict (FBI Agent Little); Mark S. Allen (FBI Agent Franks); Shad Shelby (Paramedic); Spencer Mulcahy (Hick in Overalls); Dave Pierini (Bill the Mechanic).

LOS ANGELES TIMES, 4/9/99, Calendar/p. 6, Kevin Thomas

"Blood, Guts, Bullets & Octane" is a hilarious black comedy in which a pair of luckless, 30ish, small-town car salesmen, driven to desperation, agree to take 48-hour custody of a burgundy 1963 Pontiac Le Mans convertible—in exchange for $250,000.

Blond and beefy Sid (Joe Carnahan, also the film's writer, director and editor) and Bob (Dan Leis), a handsome Dapper-Dan type, know full well the car's trunk holds more than a spare tire. But with an eviction notice staring them in the face, not to mention a meager inventory, they allow their seedy, decidedly sinister car broker (James Salter) to talk them into agreeing to the obviously shady deal. What we know and they don't is that an awful lot of people who've been connected with that mysterious Le Mans have already bitten the dust.

Carnahan deftly juggles considerable action, humor and irony to a genuinely unexpected finish with a surprise twist. He and Leis display terrific rapport, having fun with every wretched excess of every slick used-car dealer anyone ever encountered, and Carnahan just as skillfully enfolds the comedy within a bloody thriller plot.

Carnahan has a splendid ear for dialogue and a broad and outrageous sense of humor. There's an inspired comic debate about just what Johnny Cash experienced in prison, and he gets lots of mileage out of Ken Rudolph, cast as a super-smart and ultra-efficient FBI agent whose lengthy and meticulous reports handle large chunks of exposition in a dryly amusing manner. How Carnahan managed to direct as well as co-star in this gutsy little movie with its restless, urgent hand-held camera style is downright confounding, but surely the sharp skills and flexibility of cinematographer John A. Jimenez has lots to do with it. The film, which was shot in Sacramento, has a sizable cast that is uniformly effective, with a special nod to Dan Harlan as Bob and Sid's fast-talking, shameless former boss, a used-car king with a remarkably profound devotion to his ailing wife.

Fast-paced, edgy and imaginative, "Blood, Guts, Bullets & Octane" is more than a film industry calling card for Carnahan and his colleagues; it's a highly diverting and fully realized entertainment.

NEW YORK POST, 4/9/99, p. 59, Jonathan Foreman

"Blood, Guts, Bullets & Octane" sounds like the title an eighth-grader might give to his home version of a Tarantino flick. Which is more or less what first-time filmmaker Joe Carnahan has made, except he's thrown chunks of Mamet-style dialogue into the mix.

Here we meet Sid (Joe Carnahan) and Bob (Dan Leis) two used-car dealers on the brink of bankruptcy. They are offered $250,000 to keep a red '63 Pontiac convertible on their lot for two days. The car is the key to a complicated plot. But long before a talky, misfiring climax, Sid 'n' Bob's conversations have become a bore. There are some funny lines here and there, but this low-budget rehash of tough-guy scenes from other movies comes out half-baked rather than hard-boiled.

NEWSDAY, 4/9/99, Part II/p. B11, John Anderson.

The convenient tag on "Blood Guts Bullets & Octane"—director Joe Carnahan's debut and a motor-mouthed caper film of invention and carnage—is Mamet-meets-Tarantino: The testosterone-fueled verbosity of the used-car game mated with the out-of-control mayhem of an 18-car pile-up.

Cross-breeding jumpy, hand-held camerawork with stenciled supertitles and black-and-white flashback/ hallucinations, Carnahan creates a convincingly erratic milieu in which Bob (Dan Leis) and Sid (Carnahan himself) are driving their foundering car business into the ground. Having left the highly successful, highly self-promoting Danny Woo (Dan Harlan) to strike out on their own, they're merely striking out. They can't even foist a bum car on a kid—not when his father comes back with a baseball bat and then leaves with a better deal.

Somewhere in the middle of nowhere, a Vegas hustler is shot dead after paying $5,000 for a Pontiac convertible. Shortly thereafter, said '63 LeMans arrives at Sid and Bob's along with an offer: Leave it on the lot for two days without trying to sell it, drive it or open its trunk, and you'll get $250,000. Break the contract and ... well, God knows what'll happen.

Naturally—or there wouldn't be a movie—Sid and Bob decide they're being set up, and despite the sniper who's been posted outside their office as contract insurance, they get the car off the lot, find out it has been wired with plastic explosives and try to ransom it back to whomever it belongs to. With each figurative border they cross, another ugly murder ensues. A plot involving wholesale murder in a South American jungle begins to leach into a movie that we thought was about used-car dealers. And if Carnahan's intent was to suggest that something has replaced our sense of control over modern existence, he makes a pretty convincing argument for total chaos.

But for all the high tension, "Blood Guts Bullets & Octane" is mostly—and despite a penchant for at least narrative gore—a brisk, exciting ride with a script that's colorfully vulgar and rich. And it is delivered by the two principals with a realistic sense of the machismo ethos of small-time car salesmen, who compensate (as did David Mamet's real estate drones in "Glengarry Glen Ross") for their daily dose of groveling before a demanding and demented general public.

Once they make the psychological break with order, it's a small step into uncontrolled mayhem. And you root for them. Too bad they're as adept at handling small-arms fire as they are at foisting off late-model lemons.

SIGHT AND SOUND, 9/99, p. 42, Jamie Graham

Needles, California. Bob and Sid run an auto emporium, overshadowed by rival Danny Woo's far bigger car dealership. Heavily in debt, they take up an offer to babysit a 1963 Pontiac Le Mans for two days in return for $250,000. What Bob and Sid don't know is that an FBI search has linked the Pontiac to 34 roadside murders, as well as the ritual slaying of an entire South American tribe. The FBI speculate that the Pontiac's trunk contains a shipment of narcotics with which the tribe interfered.

The Pontiac and $125,000 are dropped off at Sid and Bob's garage. After a mix up during which Sid is shot, the pair decide to steal the car and demand $500,000 for its return. They arrange a meeting point on a highway. Crimelord Mr Reich arrives and refuses to pay. Sid shoots at him but misses and is killed in return. Danny Woo then steps out of Mr Reich's car. Woo explains that his wife is very ill and the only cure comes in the form of the 'blessed' blood of a particular South American tribe. Having been refused blood for a transfusion, Woo hired Reich to slaughter the tribe and drain their blood, which is now kept in the Pontiac. Woo kills Reich and gives Bob the remaining $125,000 and the keys to Reich's unregistered car, his way of returning a favour Sid and Bob did for him when they lied to auditors checking up on Woo. Bob heads for Mexico.

Blood Guts Bullets & Octane is a maverick debut in a long line of maverick debuts where the story behind the film is as important as the film itself. Its director Joe Carnahan failed to finish film school and, deprived of an official qualification, set out to shoot this calculated calling card of a movie. Armed with a video camera, $7,300 and friends willing to work for beer and Doritos, Carnahan aped Robert Rodriguez' guerrilla tactics and wrote, directed and edited his very own *El Mariachi*.

Like its production history, the movie also echoes Rodriguez' debut with its fetishistic use of weapons and Western overtones. A final confrontation on a highway is shot like a high-noon showdown, all looming close-ups and long establishing shots. The overexposed stock also gives the film a burnished quality that perfectly complements its dusty, sun-drenched locations. Like Rodriguez, Carnahan turns his limitations into strengths: the action plays out in a loose style, the handheld camera is eager to view events from unexpected angles. A succession of whip pans, white-flash edits and black-and-white flashbacks lend the film a frantic, wired energy, and 'mistakes' are left in.

Such aggressively freestyle tactics—partly wilful, partly enforced by budgetary constraints—have long been a feature of independent film-making. Likewise, it is impossible to ignore the Tarantino influence that seeps into so many movies of the last few years. This is, after all, a convoluted, time-fractured tale of two black-suited car salesmen who become embroiled with all manner of criminal lowlifes. The macho leads fire off forever quotable lines of expletive-ridden dialogue, quibble over the merits of folk singer Johnny Cash and hold women, who aren't featured in the film at all, in bitter contempt. The "what's in the car boot?" hook, meanwhile, recalls at the very least the briefcase macguffin of *Pulp Fiction* (itself stolen front *Kiss Me Deadly*, 1955). Yet despite his liberal borrowing and, for some tastes at least, over-eagerness to prove what he can do, Carnahan emerges from his debut as a genuine talent. The fact that he also found time to turn in a fine performance as Sid makes the feat doubly impressive.

VILLAGE VOICE, 4/13/99, p. 154, Gary Dauphin

Bob (Dan Leis) and Sid (Joe Carnahan), the hapless heroes of *Blood, Guts, Bullets and Octane*, are fast-talking used-car salesmen who at film's opening find themselves an inch away from both the poorhouse and the jailhouse. Moving their clunker wares with one part gift of gab and two parts upbeat deceit, they're introduced impressively enough by a gassy series of hard sells, but having fallen behind the financial eight ball (and clearly buzzing on their own fumes) they make a shady deal to hold a car on their lot in exchange for a quarter of a million dollars. Since no parking space is worth that much, the pair soon find themselves trapped in a grungy netherworld of hit men, drug dealers, and mysterious South American mass murders; their only option is to talk their way back the way they came in.

Writer, director, and star Carnahan comes up with some very funny yacking set pieces but his ear is ultimately much better than his eye, this indie directorial debut looking like an awkward jumble of ill-fitting stand-up skits. Since 90 percent of everything the characters say is a bald-faced lie, *Blood, Guts* rolls along in a fogged but energetic rush, but after the umpteenth outburst of pointless verbal pyrotechnics it's hard to remember what any of the fuss is about and harder to sit through any more of it.

Also reviewed in:
CHICAGO TRIBUNE, 4/9/99, Friday/p. H, John Petrakis
NEW YORK TIMES, 4/9/99, p. E26, Stephen Holden
VARIETY, 2/9-15/98, p. 74, Dennis Harvey

BLUE STREAK

A Columbia Pictures release of an Indieprod/Neal H. Moritz/Jaffe production. *Executive Producer:* Daniel Melnick and Allen Shapiro. *Producer:* Toby Jaffe and Neal H. Moritz. *Director:* Les Mayfield. *Screenplay:* Michael Berry, John Blumenthal, and Steve Carpenter. *Director of Photography:* David Eggby. *Editor:* Michael Tronick. *Music:* Edward Shearmur. *Music Editor:* Amanda Goodpaster and Tom Kramer. *Sound:* Kim Ornitz. *Sound Editor:* John Morris. *Casting:* Lynn Kressel. *Production Designer:* Bill Brzeski. *Art Director:* Philip Toolin. *Set Designer:* A. Todd Holland. *Set Decorator:* Brana Michelle Roenfeld. *Special Effects:* Clayton W. Pinney. *Costumes:* Denise Wingate. *Make-up:* Melanie Hughes. *Stunt Coordinator:* R.A. Rondell and Alan Oliney. *Running time:* 93 minutes. *MPAA Rating:* PG-13.

CAST: Martin Lawrence (Miles Logan); Luke Wilson (Detective Carlson); Dave Chappelle (Tulley); Peter Greene (Deacon); Nicole Ari Parker (Melissa Green); Graham Beckel (Captain Rizzo); Robert Miranda (Glenfiddish); Olek Krupa (LaFleur); Saverio Guerra (Benny); Richard C. Safarian (Uncle Lou); Tamala Jones (Janice); Lulio Oscar Mechoso (Diaz); Steve Rankin (Agent Gray); Carmon Argenziano (Captain Penelli); John Kawkes (Eddie); William Forsythe (Detective Hardcastle); Frank Medrano (Frank); Octavia L. Spencer (Shawna); Timothy Dale Agee (Cop in Alley); Bayani Ison (Uniform Outside Station); Scott Sowers (Prison Guard #37); Christopher Stapleton (K-9 Cop); Eddy Donno and Troy Gilbert (Guards); Kenny Endoso (Clerk); Googy Gress (Desk Sergeant); Robert LaSardo (Twitchy Suspect); Bill Ferrell (Cop in Elevator); Billy Williams (Cop in Gem Store Elevator); Greg Montgomery (Cop in Precinct); Jason Kravits (Customs Guy); Henry Hayashi (FBI Tech); James Gavin (Helicopter Pilot); Anne Marie Howard (Female Officer); Jane Carr (Museum Official); Brandon Michael DePaul (Little Friend); Amy Oberer (Terrified Woman); Ash Winfield

(Briefing Room Detective); Erik Rondell (François); J. Kenneth Campbell (Peterson, FBI Section Commander); John Hurt Jones (Tipsy Cop); Darryl Brunson (Office Porter); Shawn Elaine Brown Chiquette (Friendly Officer); Christian J. Christienson (SWAT Team); Michael A. Grasso (SWAT Team); John McCarthy (SWAT Team); Jeff Xander and Damian Foster (Thugs); Yetta Ginsberg (Repelled Passer-by); Daniel Rogerson (Chinese Delivery Man).

LOS ANGELES TIMES, 9/17/99, Calendar/p. 2, Gene Seymour

[The following review by Gene Seymour appeared in a slightly different form in **NEWSDAY, 9/17/99, Part II/p. B11.]**

Committees make movies like "Blue Streak" and the finished product looks as if this particular panel still hasn't reached a quorum, much less a consensus.

It starts out like a caper flick that shifts, almost by accident, into an episode from the old "Martin" TV series. Eventually, it settles for being a bleached, cluttered photostat of "Beverly Hills Cop," if only a bit more clever than the original.

What makes this confusion troubling is that "Blue Streak" represents Martin Lawrence's first real chance to distinguish himself as a movie lead, unencumbered by charismatic sidekicks like Will Smith ("Bad Boys") or Eddie Murphy ("Life") sharing top billing.

Even more than those aforementioned stars, Lawrence's manic teddy-bear persona is capable of making you laugh at him the moment he appears on screen. If we lived in smarter, better times, someone would have thought long ago about giving Lawrence's penchant for outrageous comic transformation the kind of cinematic framework Peter Sellers was routinely given in his early years.

Instead, critics and producers alike pegged Lawrence as being little more than a Murphy clone. This is the same stupid thinking that puts Chris Rock and Chris Tucker as equals because they're black, funny and have the same first names. Still, if I were Lawrence, the last (or next-to-last) thing I'd want for my own vehicle is the kind of action-comedy that made Murphy a box-office powerhouse.

Nonetheless, here is Lawrence, going for the gold as Miles Logan, a clever, quick-on-his-feet jewel thief whose plans to steal a $20-million diamond are waylaid by a treacherous partner. Just before he's caught, Miles stashes the rock in the air duct of a half-finished building in downtown Los Angeles. Two years later, he's paroled and ready to collect his prize. Instead, he gets the surprise of his life: The finished building houses the police department's 37th precinct.

All he has to do is find the air duct, pick up the diamond and split. To do this he has to pretend to be one of the police department's finest. Trouble is, Miles is so convincing—and effective—as a faux robbery cop that he can't get his buddies in blue to leave him alone long enough to get his prize.

The premise is clever enough, but the movie weighs it down with so many digressions (the obligatory foreign drug kingpin, Dave Chappelle as Miles' street-punk confederate) that its 90-plus minutes seem more like 180.

Still, Lawrence handles both the comic and action sides of his role with surprising ease. The odds of pulling this off are just as formidable as those Lawrence recently faced in real life after collapsing into a coma while jogging in extreme heat. If and when he fully recovers, he has every right to be proud of carrying this rickety film on his stooped shoulders. But, as Murphy himself eventually did, he also should ponder more challenging vehicles to drive.

NEW YORK POST, 9/17/99, p. 51, Jonathan Foreman

"Blue Streak" is a lowbrow action-comedy vehicle for Martin Lawrence aimed at the teenage market. As you might expect, it isn't particularly subtle or original. But it's a good-natured late-summer romp fueled by Lawrence's manic shtick.

Lawrence has often been upstaged by his co-star, whether it was Will Smith in "Bad Boys" or Eddie Murphy in "Life." Here the star, who recently emerged from a coma after collapsing while running, finally gets a chance to show off his considerable comic talent. But he also reveals the flaws that have held him back from Murphyesque stardom.

Lawrence has a pronounced tendency to grandstand just a little too long, and there are moments when he shows an angry-clown edge that makes him less lovable than Murphy.

You first meet jewel thief Miles Logan (Lawrence) in the midst of an improbably high-tech heist, as he and his crew slide down a skyscraper's elevator shaft in pursuit of a fist-sized diamond. Logan has just penetrated the security system and grabbed the jewel when his partner Deacon (Peter Greene) pulls a double cross, killing a member of the team and accidentally alerting the police.

Logan briefly escapes onto a nearby building under construction and is able to hide the rock in air duct before being arrested.

Two years later, Logan gets out of jail and makes his way to the building where he hid the diamond. To his horror, it has become an LAPD precinct house.

Logan tries to get into the building disguised as a buck-toothed pizza-delivery boy. The attempt fails, but Logan is able to steal a swipe card from Carlson, a rookie detective (Luke Wilson).

Equipped with the swipe card and a fake LAPD badge provided by a forger, Logan gets into the station. He's just about to climb into an air vent in the ladies' room when he bumps into an escaping criminal suspect. Logan is immediately credited with foiling the guy's escape.

Forced to play along with his bogus identity as "Detective Malone," Logan is assigned to the burglary detail with the greenhorn Carlson. He cannot help applying his experience as a thief to his new role and quickly becomes a star of the department.

While impressing everyone with his insight into the criminal mind—and with his cheerfully violent approach when it comes to interrogating suspects—"Malone" keeps searching for the diamond in the air ducts. But his thieving past begins to catch up with him.

Director Les Mayfield ("Encino Man") gets competent performances despite the thinness of the characters. The always excellent character actor William Forsythe stands out as a tough, cynical detective.

Like last year's "Rush Hour," this is a formula picture that never rises above the generic but entertains nevertheless.

SIGHT AND SOUND, 1/00, p. 44, Danny Leigh

LA, two years ago. From the rooftop of a museum, jewel thief Miles Logan steals a diamond worth $17m. About to make his getaway, he is betrayed by his lieutenant Deacon. Trapped, Logan hides the diamond in a nearby derelict building before giving himself up to the police.

Two years later, Logan returns on parole to retrieve his prize, only to discover the building is now a police station. Logan acquires a forged police ID to gain entry. However, once inside he inadvertently foils a suspect's escape and is mistaken for a cop. Sent out on patrol with rookie detective Carlson, Logan becomes the toast of the force after apprehending an armed robber who is a former criminal cohort of Logan's named Tulley. Logan finally locates the diamond, only to lose it in a stash of heroin intended for a sting operation against a gang of drug dealers on the Mexican border. Accompanying Carlson and another detective, Hardcastle, to the sting, Logan is confronted by Deacon, who has pursued him in the hope of appropriating the diamond. In the subsequent shoot-out Deacon is killed, while the dealers are all arrested. Logan recovers the diamond. Carlson and Hardcastle inform him they have been aware of his true identity for some time, but as he is over the border, they are powerless to act. Thanking them, he flees.

Brimming with such cop-movie clichés as irascible chiefs, odd-couple partnerships and jokes about doughnuts, *Blue Streak* is not a film in danger of out thinking its audience. Many of the script's comic set pieces, even its central cop-robber role-reversal conceit, could have serviced star Martin Lawrence's occasional mentor Eddie Murphy at any point over the last two decades. The only surprising thing about it is how frequently it abandons even vague plausibility.

Such is the lot of the contemporary comedy-star vehicle, still reliant on the all too-basic template of the Murphy showcase *Beverly Hills Cop* (an obvious antecedent here). And while it would be unfair not to give *Blue Streaks* director Les Mayfield credit for a competence belied by a CV featuring *Flubber* and *Encino Man* his direction is riddled with stolid pans across the LA skyline and unnecessary, intrusive reaction shots which act as visual exclamation marks at the climax of almost every scene. It's no small testament to Lawrence that he manages to elevate such an essentially prosaic project beyond the mediocrity it would otherwise be destined for. Given the limitations of the form, it's the star's performance on which the vehicle stands or falls, and here Lawrence displays a manic charm which outstrips both the tiresome lachrymosity of, say, Adam Sandler, and the curmudgeonly delivery of his own sidekick roles in *Bad Boys, Nothing to Lose* and *Life*.

Lawrence brings an engaging sardonic quality to routines which could potentially appear unpleasant, such as his reprisal of Martin Luther King's 'free at last' speech for the benefit of a busload of new inmates. At the same time, he manages not to capsize his character's essential amiability. Midway through being dumped by his girlfriend after she discovers his criminal activities, for example, Lawrence pleads, "but I didn't rob *you*," with an estimable lack of the pat roguish disingenuousness Murphy (for all his talent) would surely have been unable to resist. That said, Lawrence's efforts are bolstered by the supporting cast, particularly Luke Wilson's off-kilter turn as the quintessential hapless white guy Carlson. Lending this profoundly hackneyed part an air of wide eyed neurosis, Wilson even manages to enliven the predictable moment when he's taught to appreciate "the funk" by his savvy black partner. You only hope that in their next outings, neither he nor Lawrence have to contend with such ordinary screenwriting.

VILLAGE VOICE, 9/21/99, p. 170, Jessica Winter

Searching for means of extrication is recent heatstroke victim Martin Lawrence, who'd surely like to divorce himself from an ongoing string of public mishaps. In *Blue Streak*, Lawrence also plays a jewel thief, albeit one who impersonates a cop in order to locate a diamond lost in a botched heist. Lawrence's gun-toting safecracker is just a nice guy earning honest pay (Dave Chappelle, in the Jonathan Rhys Meyers role as Lawrence's hothead driver, sums it up during a cartoonish convenience store shootout: "Hey! I'm workin' here!"). The contortional physical shtick familiar from Lawrence's sitcom, laden with a dollop of Three Stooges violence, should keep the boys happy, and Lawrence's deft byplay with Chappelle (who benefits from smashing lines like "I'll rip ya lips off and kiss my ass with them shits") showcases a comedian still somehow on his game.

Also reviewed in:
CHICAGO TRIBUNE, 9/17/99, Tempo/p. 5, Barbara Shulgasser
NEW YORK TIMES, 9/18/99, p. B15, Lawrence Van Gelder
VARIETY, 9/13-19/99, p. 41, Robert Koehler
WASHINGTON POST, 9/17/99, p. C5, Rita Kempley

BODY SHOTS

A New Line Cinema release of a Colomby/Keaton production. *Executive Producer:* Michael Keaton, Guy Riedel, Michael De Luca, and Lynn Harris. *Producer:* Jennifer Keohane and Harry Colomby. *Director:* Michael Cristofer. *Screenplay:* David McKenna. *Director of Photography:* Rodrigo Garcia. *Editor:* Eric Sears. *Music:* Paul Broucek. *Music Editor:* Marvin Morris. *Choreographer:* Mary Ann Kellogg. *Sound:* Jose Garcia and (music) Stephen Krause. *Sound Editor:* Dave McMoyler. *Casting:* Junie Lowry Johnson and Libby Goldstein. *Production Designer:* David J. Bomba. *Art Director:* John R. Jensen. *Set Designer:* Daniel Bradford. *Set Decorator:* Kathy Lucas. *Set Dresser:* Chadler Vinar, Jennifer LaGara, Richard Lambert, Erin Gould, Russell Bobbitt, Cheryl Gould, Bart Barbuscia, and Jimmy Meehan. *Special Effects:* Dan Sudick. *Costumes:* Carolyn Leigh Greco. *Make-up:* Nena Smarz. *Stunt Coordinator:* Rob King. *Running time:* 115 minutes. *MPAA Rating:* R.

CAST: Joe Basile (Bartender); Scott Burkholder (Man in Bar); Liz Coke (Girl #2); Allison Dunbar (Girl #3); Sean Patrick Flanery (Rick Hamilton); Edmond Genest (Sara's Dad); Adam Gordon (Burger Joint Cop); Mark Hicks (Bodyguard); Larry Joshua (Detective Richards); Elizabeth Liebel (Mrs. Drofsky); Ron Livingston (Trent); Marc Lynn (Disco Bartender); Jerry O'Connell (Michael Penorisi); Lou Paget (Oral Sex Instructor); Amanda Peet (Jane Bannister); Adina Porter (Detective Thompson); Emily Procter (Whitney Bryant); Benny Quan (Burger Joint

Manager); Tara Reid (Sara Olswang); Brad Rowe (Shawn Denigan); Wendy Schenker (Doctor);
Nick Spano (Jeff the Doorman); Sybil Temchen (Emma Cooper).

LOS ANGELES TIMES, 10/22/99, Calendar/p. 9, Kevin Thomas

[The following review by Kevin Thomas appeared in a slightly different form in
NEWSDAY, 10/22/99, Part II/p. B8.]

"Body Shots" offers the lurid tale of a night out gone drastically wrong. It's set in a trendy
slice of L.A. and features lots of sex, miles of raw dialogue and an ensemble cast of eight
attractive and talented young actors. What may come as a surprise is where "American History
X" writer David McKenna and director Michael Cristofer, the Pulitzer- and Tony Award-winning
playwright and screenwriter, take us.

Ultra-stylish, "Body Shots" opens with Sean Patrick Flanery's Rick and Amanda Peet's Jane
in a bed, so wasted from heavy drinking they really are not sure what they have or haven't done,
unsure even of each other's names, with Rick at first uncertain whether they're in Jane's bed or
his own. All of a sudden Jane's roommate, Sara (Tara Reid), staggers in, bedraggled and
bleeding and in a state of hysteria.

Before Sara can capture our attention fully, the filmmakers flash back to introduce us to all eight
of the 20-somethings who converge one evening at a large club, clearly the venue du jour and
jam-packed with people, all under 30. As we meet these young men and women, most of whom
are securely positioned on the corporate ladder, they all address us on the only topic that seems
to concern them: sex.

They discuss it crassly, clinically, endlessly. They seem to possess scant individuality, and you
soon get the feeling that they live such insulated lives that they don't really have to think about
anything but sex.

This is just how the film's makers want us to feel about their people, because when they get
back to Sara and what may—or may not—have happened to her, it leaves her friends and
acquaintances so shaken that they gradually become individuals to whom we start paying attention.

What is most disturbing and pervasive about this group portrait is its collective compulsion to
numb feelings with such large quantities of alcohol that it becomes impossible for anyone to
remember exactly what happens, good or bad. You're given the feeling that this boozy rite of
passage, familiar to so many generations, has grown only more extreme, more common and more
dangerous than ever.

The "Body Shots"' cast delivers well. Rick and Jane emerge as more intelligent and mature
than the others. But before moving back to them, the focus shifts to Sara, a pretty blond
determined to get drunk quicker and more thoroughly than any one else, and Jerry O'Connell's
Michael, an imposing and fearless ex-football star used to having women throw themselves at
him—and also used to assuming that they could be interested only in his body rather than his
mind.

In more subsidiary roles are Brad Rowe as Shawn, who would like to think that he needs to get
to know a woman before making any moves toward her—until he comes across Sybil Temchen's
sex-starved Emma. Shawn's roommate Trent (Ron Livingston, star of the hilarious "Office
Space") is the group's smart mouth, and Emily Procter's Whitney is a statuesque blond who's into
kinky games of bondage and domination.

Structure is everything in making "Body Shots" play as well as it does. Its constant shifts
between past and present and between individual stories creates varying perspectives that add
dimension and insight to material that might play tritely if presented in straightforward narrative
form. This approach is key to creating empathy, to making us aware that even the coarsest types
might, in different contexts, prove to have something going for them. "Body Shots" is too
shrewd to ask us to like these people much and, instead, opts to leave us feeling that the lonely
crowd seems to be getting lonelier than ever.

NEW YORK POST, 10/22/99, p. 56, Jonathan Foreman

"Body Shots" is a slick, lurid and pretentious movie that pretends to say something important
and sophisticated about sex and love among 20-somethings in contemporary L.A.

But the vulgar, tone-deaf screenplay by David McKenna Just isn't up to the task, and the end result is an ultra-stylized, empty mess.

It's a shame, because the movie boasts an attractive and capable cast, including the lovely Amanda Peet from TV's "Jack and Jill."

She plays a lawyer named Jane, who is lying on the bed in her apartment with (fully dressed) fellow lawyer Rick (Sean Patrick Flanery) when the film opens. The doorbell rings and a bedraggled, bleeding girl comes in and announces that she's just been raped by the guy she was fooling around with earlier.

The movie then flashes back to the evening before. We see a quartet of unusually good-looking girls (Peet, Tara Reid, Emily Procter and Sybil Temchen) and four boys (Flanery, Jerry O'Connell, Ron Livingston and Brad Rowe) as they dress, drink and go out to a huge club.

There is then a series of flashes forward and back as we learn who hooked up with whom and how. In between, each of the eight characters turns to the camera and tells us his or her philosophy of sex. There's also a nasty, bloody fight between the football player played by O'Connell and a bodyguard who rudely bumps him in the club.

Shawn (Rowe) the group's token romantic, says he believes that "sex without love equals violence." And the rape of Sara (Reid) by Mike (O'Connell) is presumably supposed to demonstrate the truth of this, even though he might not have actually raped her.

We see the incident from two perspectives, "Rashomon"-style, and neither character really remembers what happened. And they each have to be coached by their lawyer friends when the law gets involved.

Director Michael Cristofer uses lots of fashionable stylistic tricks: The action slows down or speeds up around two characters as they kiss; you hear people talking before you see them speak, etc.

But these flourishes only underline the film's essential vapidity.

SIGHT AND SOUND, 4/00, p. 42, Kevin Maher

Los Angeles, the present, late Friday night. Rick and Jane, both in their twenties, lie on a bed talking. Jane's friend Sara enters and claims she has just been raped by Rick's friend Mike. Flashbacks reveal earlier events. That same night, Rick, Mike and their friends Trent and Shawn prepare for a night out. They discuss their sexual techniques and moral attitudes. Meanwhile, Jane and Sara and their friends Emma and Whitney do the same. After getting drunk in separate bars, the girls and boys meet up in a nightclub. Rick and Jane kiss. Shawn, shy and withdrawn, is attracted to Sara, but Mike, loud and abrasive, tries to seduce her. Sara is especially drunk.

Outside the club, Mike beats up a security guard, then leaves in a taxi with Sara. A dejected Shawn has sex with Emma; Trent has sex with Whitney. Later on, Sara arrives at jane's apartment in tears. She describes how Mike came back to her place and raped her. Mike gives a very different account of the same events to Rick, who is also his lawyer: he says they had consensual sex. Jane advises Sara not to go to court because she was so drunk. She proceeds with the case, but the result is a hung jury. Rick and Jane meet up afterwards. They go back to Jane's apartment and lie on the bed.

Body Shots tries so hard. It wants to be an attractive post-teen romantic-comedy ensemble, a quirky satire of vapid millennial dating habits and a shocking exposé of sexual hypocrisy all at once, but ends up being merely banal and confused. The handiwork of director Michael Cristofer (whose screenwriting credits include *Less than Zero* and *The Bonfire of the Vanities*), working from a script by David McKenna (*American History X*), *Body Shots* initially invites comparisons with such archetypal Brat Pack movies as *"About Last Night ..."* and *St Elmo's Fire* with its attractive, upwardly-mobile cast (four boys, four girls) fretting over the pitfalls of modern relationships. Lifting a narrative conceit from *He Said, She Said* (and before that *Rashomon,* 1950, among other films) the characters relate conflicting his and her versions of past events, such as Trent and Sara's contradictory takes on his liaison with an older woman and, more centrally, Sara and Mike's different accounts of their sexual encounter: she calls it rape, he describes it as a one-night stand.

With the introduction of this theme, the film is left nervously scrambling to find the right tone, unable to fall back on the light gender-based comedy of its early part. Ultimately it ends up glossing over the rape itself to focus moral opprobrium on the group's alcoholic tendencies—both

Sara and Mike are censured by the gang for "blacking out". In a final inexplicable coda, the characters—all shallow narcissists up until this point suddenly become wise philosophers on the nature of love, announcing sagely that, "It's love that makes you vulnerable." McKenna's script is peppered with many of these fortune-cookie aphorisms, often delivered with ill-disguised incredulity by the cast.

Cristofer is certainly enthusiastic with his camera, and together with cinematographer Rodrigo Garcia *(Mi vida loca),* he uses a visual arsenal of tricks to convey the feel of a hyper-kinetic night of debauchery, firing off extreme close-ups, smudge motion and frenzied handheld club shots. But most of all, Cristofer loves filming his designer clad, beautiful cast. This is a film enthralled to youth, beauty, bodies, breasts and glistening limbs which makes its depiction of rape hugely problematic.

Despite the early attempts to destabilise the narrational point of view making us wonder if we're seeing a man's or woman's version of particular events—it quickly becomes clear that the spectatorial point of view is resolutely male. Sara and Mike's "contradictory" versions of the rape story are illustrated by two voyeuristic soft-porn segments, and in both actress Tara Reid is stripped, objectified and fetishised for the camera's gaze. This context makes the movie's final plea for a new Puritanism, free from alcohol and casual sex, particularly nauseating.

VILLAGE VOICE, 11/2/99, p. 140, Jessica Winter

Zoot-suited gym boys and anorexic bleach blonds frugging in a cavernous club out of *Miami Vice,* tracked by a camera that alternately seizures and passes out in a slo-mo stupor (that's what you get for mixing cocaine and alcohol), while Jerry O'Connell barks into a cell phone, "If there's pussy on the menu, I'm there": This is the state of being single, white, rich, and plastic-fantastic in the '90s, according to *Body Shots.* Tara Reid gets a few gruesome scenes as an alleged date-rape victim (the film's most vomitous aspect is in positing this bloodied, terrified girl as one half of a he-said-she-said scenario), but more moving is the sight of sad-eyed Brad Rowe, now on *Wasteland* and fondly remembered as the cute intern on *NewsRadio*—he might as well be stranded on the hillside with Rupert and Samantha, wondering what in God's name he's doing here.

Also reviewed in:
CHICAGO TRIBUNE, 10/22/99, Friday/p. M, Michael Wilmington
NEW YORK TIMES, 10/22/99, p. E31, Lawrence Van Gelder
VARIETY, 10/11-17/99, p. 43, Robert Koehler
WASHINGTON POST, 10/22/99, p. C5, Stephen Hunter

BOILING POINT

A Winstar Cinema release. *Producer:* Okuyama Kazuyoshi. *Director:* Takeshi Kitano. *Screenplay (Japanese with English subtitles):* Takeshi Kitano. *Director of Photography:* Yanagishima Katsumi. *Editor:* Taniguchi Toshio. *Special Effects:* Kikuo Notomi. *Costumes:* Kenji Kawasaki. *Make-up:* Yoshie Hamada. *Running time:* 98 minutes. *MPAA Rating:* Not Rated.

CAST: Masahiko Ono (Masaki); Takeshi Kitano (Uehara); Minoru Iizuka (Kazuo); Hisashi Igawa (Otomo, the Gang Boss); Koichi Akiyama (Gas Pump Attendant); Takahiko Aoki (Saburo); Makoto Ashikawa (Akira); Yuriko Ishida (Sayaka); Takahito Iguchi (Takashi Iguchi); Hitoshi Ozawa (Kanai); Shinobu Tsuruta (Gas Station Boss); Hiroshi Suzuki (Takuya); Tsuneo Serizawa (Makoto); Katsuo Torashiki (Tamagi); Jennifer Baer (Woman on the Beach); Bengal (Muto); Eri Fuse (Fumiyo); Naotaka Hanai (Rich Kid on Motorcycle); Hiroshi Ide (Hajime); Kenzo Matsuo (Naoya); Johnny Okura (Minamizaka); Ronny Santana (GI in Okinawa).

NEW YORK POST, 11/19/99, p. 59, Lou Lumenick

"Boiling Point" is a slow-paced thriller with a baseball background, written and directed in 1990 by Japanese TV-personality-turned-filmmaker Takeshi "Beat" Kitano, who later gained a following with such films as "Fireworks" and "Kikujiro."

Masaki (Masahiko Ono) is a minor-league baseball player who stupidly punches out a *yakuza* mobster who hassles him at the gas station where he works. He turns for help to Uehara (Kitano), a polysexual *ex-yakuza* who has some scores of his own to settle with his former colleagues.

Directed with an indifference for narrative drive reminiscent of Jean-Luc Godard, "Boiling Point" crawls until its final 15 minutes, a symphony of graphic (but not terribly convincing) violence, including a gasoline truck driven through a plate-glass window.

Also reviewed in:
NEW YORK TIMES, 11/19/99, p. E22, Lawrence Van Gelder

BONE COLLECTOR, THE

A Universal Pictures and Columbia Pictures release of a Bregman production. *Executive Producer:* Michael Klawitter and Dan Jinks. *Producer:* Martin Bregman, Louis A. Stroller, and Michael Bregman. *Director:* Phillip Noyce. *Screenplay:* Jeremy Iacone. *Based on the novel by:* Jeffery Deaver. *Director of Photography:* Dean Semler. *Editor:* William Hoy. *Music:* Craig Armstrong. *Music Editor:* Joe E. Rand. *Sound:* Simon Kaye, Allan Byer and (music) Geoff Foster. *Sound Editor:* Bruce Stambler and Martin Cantwell. *Casting:* Bernard Telsey, William Cantler, and David Vaccari. *Production Designer:* Nigel Phelps. *Art Director:* Claude Paré and Jeff Sage. *Set Decorator:* Marie-Claude Gosselin and Harriet Zucker. *Set Dresser:* Eve Boulonne and Susan C. MacQuarrie. *Costumes:* Odette Gadoury. *Make-up:* Kathryn Casault. *Make-up (Denzel Washington):* Carl Fullerton. *Make-up (Angelina Jolie):* Janeen Schreyer. *Stunt Coordinator:* Jery Hewitt, Michael Scherer, Jean Frenette, and Mike Russo. *Running time:* 118 minutes. *MPAA Rating:* R.

CAST: Denzel Washington (Lincoln Rhyme); Angelina Jolie (Amelia Donaghy); Queen Latifah (Thelma); Michael Rooker (Captain Howard Cheney); Mike McGlone (Detective Kenny Solomon); Luis Guzman (Eddie Ortiz); Leland Orser (Richard Thompson); John Benjamin Hickey (Dr. Barry Lehman); Bobby Cannavale (Steve); Ed O'Neill (Detective Paulie Sellitto); Richard Zeman (Lt. Carl Hanson); Olivia Birkelund (Lindsay Rubin); Gary Swanson (Alan Rubin); Jim Bulleit (Train Engineer); Frank Fontaine (Grandfather); Zena Grey (Granddaughter); Daniel C. Brochu (N.Y.U. Student); Desmond Campbell (Taxi Inspector); Christian Veliz (Young Boy); Mercedes Gomez (Ortiz's Mother); Mary Hammett (Girlfriend in Nightclub); Amanda Gay (Girl in Nightclub); Steve Adams and Larry Day (Gas Workers); Burke Lawrence (Police Instructor); Terry Simpson and Eric Davis (Cops in Apartment); Arthur Holden (Bookstore Clerk); Yashmin Daviault (Rhyme's Sister); Keenan MacWilliam (Rhyme's Niece); David Warshofsky (Amelia's Partner); Mateo Gomez (Hot Dog Vendor); Ted Whittall (Oritz's Assistant); Peter Michael Dillon (Homicide Detective); Jonathan Stark (Male Detective); Fulvio Cecere (Forensics Expert); Hal Sherman (Fingerprint Cop); Russell Yuen (Forensics Worker); Andy Bradshaw (Uniform Cop); Jean Marc Bisson and Christopher Bregman (Rescue Workers); Sonya Biddle (Nurse).

LOS ANGELES TIMES, 11/5/99, Calendar/p. 1, Kenneth Turan

"The Bone Collector" remembers what thrillers often forget. A tribute to old-fashioned craftsmanship and skill both on and off the screen, it's as crisp and efficient as its law enforcement protagonists, able to make the best of its traditional genre elements.

Although his name won't bring many people into the theater, Australian filmmaker Philip Noyce is perhaps the key player. His breakthrough as a director was the Nicole Kidman-starring thriller

"Dead Calm," and he did excellent work on "Clear and Present Danger" and "Patriot Games." Confident and very much at home with this kind of familiar material, Noyce has the skill to keep the plot percolating and overcome its occasional missteps.

The elements Noyce has to work with are all strong, starting with Jeremy Iacone's capable adaptation of Jeffery Deaver's successful novel about an unusual detecting team, unwilling partners well played by Denzel Washington and Angelina Jolie.

Washington's role is especially challenging because his character, New York police detective Lincoln Rhyme, is a quadriplegic, injured in the line of duty and unable to use his arms or legs. "One finger, two shoulders and a brain is all I have," Rhyme says, and he is not happy about it.

Rhyme is a world-renowned expert in forensics, the science of criminal investigation, and the author of the classic textbook "Scene of the Crime." But after four years on his back, with the possibility of a seizure that could mentally incapacitate him looming larger, not even the ministrations of feisty private care nurse Thelma (Queen Latifah) can keep him from taking steps toward a physician-assisted suicide.

An actor with enormous presence, Washington uses all of it to make the immobile Rhyme into someone who dominates every scene while flat on his back. And as Amelia Donaghy, the partner who reluctantly enters his life, Jolie ("Gia," "Pushing Tin") displays the confidence, charisma and New York accent needed for her forceful and strong-minded character. When Rhyme tells her, "Stubbornness is something we both share," it's clearly the truth.

A rookie street cop trying to get a transfer into youth services, Amelia has the moxie to stand in front of and stop a huge Amtrak train because it threatens to disturb the crime scene around a corpse she's come across. "If you were any more wound up," a colleague says, "you'd be a Timex."

The clues she discovers intrigue the otherwise disconnected and phlegmatic Rhyme, and he agrees to help the police, who include Capt. Howard Cheney (Michael Rooker), his successor at the department, and old colleagues Paulle Sellitto (Ed O'Neill) and Eddie Ortiz (Luis Guzman). Impressed with Amelia's "natural instinct for forensics," he also wants her on the team.

Vaguely contemptuous of Rhyme as "the textbook guy" and with her own secret reasons for wanting out of the grinding parts of police work, Amelia is very believable as someone sullenly resistant to the blandishments of a taskmaster known, not always affectionately, as "the world's most cranky criminologist."

Unable to resist the call of destiny, Amelia agrees to be on the team, to be a fresh pair of hands and eyes at gruesome crime scenes with her only lifeline being a headset connected to Rhyme, who promises that "I'll be with you every step of the way." Together, they take on a serial killer who seems to be taunting the police, leaving clues and daring them to find him and stop him.

This is not exactly uncharted territory, but director Noyce, cinematographer Dean Semler, production designer Nigel Phelps and editor William Hoy manage to bring visual variety to a kind of Sherlock Holmes setup, where the great thinker sits in his apartment surrounded by banks of computers and tries to connect the dots and solve the puzzle.

Though it mostly stays the course, there are moments when "The Bone Collector" is too pro forma, when the plotting is overly familiar and the murder situations a bit too gruesome. Most clunky are the film's romantic elements and a final coda that is so unreal it seems to have come from another picture. But if Noyce (visible in an unbilled cameo as a bookstore patron) can't turn some of this dross into untarnished gold, his work is never less than professional, and that counts for a lot.

NEW YORK, 11/15/99, p. 69, Peter Rainer

[*The Bone Collector* was reviewed jointly with *Rosetta*; see Rainer's review of that film.]

NEW YORK POST, 11/5/99, p. 52, Lou Lumenick

Entertaining but terminally dopey, "The Bone Collector" is yet another grisly movie about a devious serial killer—pursued in this case by a brilliant quadriplegic criminologist working with the NYPD's most beautiful officer.

Denzel Washington plays Lincoln Rhyme, an overbearing grouch confined to a bed in his SoHo loft after his spinal cord is severed in a nasty crime-scene accident. He can move one finger, which he uses to operate an impressive array of computers to track down a homicidal taxi driver who, in the film's opening and scariest sequence, abducts a middle-aged couple from an airport.

When the husband's mutilated body turns up at an underpass, Rhyme is impressed with the young patrolwoman who stops a speeding Amtrak train to collect evidence—just like Rhyme suggests in the NYPD training manual he wrote.

"I'd say you have a natural instinct for forensics," Rhyme tells police Officer Amelia Donaghy (a horribly miscast Angelina Jolie), a former fashion model who he's decided is the only member of the 38,000-member NYPD who can do his legwork. When she resists ("Do you think your condition gives you the right to push people around?" she asks Rhyme), she's strong-armed into working the case under threat of dismissal.

It turns out the killer—a la "Seven"—is deliberately leaving obscure clues leading to his victims and challenging Rhyme to save them. Through a mind-boggling series of deductions, Rhyme is somehow able to figure out the woman abducted from the airport has been placed in a steampipe at a Wall Street intersection that will erupt at precisely 4 p.m.

Director Phillip Noyce generates considerable suspense, expertly using camera angles and some interesting locations, including an abandoned, turn-of-the-century slaughterhouse in Greenwich Village and a closed subway station near the Battery.

But for every smart scene, there's something as ridiculous as the killer cabbie speeding away from Grand Central Station—at the height of the rush hour. Jeremy Iacone's script is riddled with plot holes you could drive a train through. And it's filled with risible dialogue, as when Rhyme instructs Donaghy about a freshly killed victim, "You've got to saw her hands off at the wrist line! I've got to have those [hand]cuffs for [finger]prints!"

Truth is, the Rhyme-and-Donaghy story (her father, an NYPD officer, committed suicide; Rhyme wants to kill himself before his seizures turn him into a vegetable) is basically tangential to this matchable, yet fairly hokey, mystery. Washington does what he can with his paper-thin character, who's such a genius he can recognize a logo from a 100-year-old book and send his unlikely partner off to an antiquarian bookstore when the solution (no kidding) hits her over the head.

Jolie, who perpetuates one of the phoniest-looking crying scenes ever, is thoroughly unconvincing as a cop. She's consistently upstaged by Queen Latifah, whose sassy presence turns what might have been a thankless role as Rhyme's nurse into a minor triumph. Everyone else—including Michael Rooker as a bad cop and Mike McGlone and Ed O'Neill as good cops—are reduced to an exposition-spouting stereotype.

"The Bone Collector" boasts a truly ridiculous, out-of-left-field ending. Suffice to say it's a lot closer to an episode of "Ironside" than to "Rear Window," much less "The Silence of the Lambs."

NEWSDAY, 11/5/99, Part II/p. B6, John Anderson

Flashback: NYPD crime-scene expert Lincoln Rhyme (Denzel Washington) crawling through a claustrophobe's nightmare of subway tunnel and being nearly cut in two by a falling beam.

Cut to: His bedroom, four years later, where the quadriplegic Rhyme, increasingly susceptible to seizures that may eventually leave him vegetative, has decided to make his "final transition" out of this life and into the next.

Cut to: A metro airport, where a couple off the red-eye from Los Angeles gets into a cab whose on-duty light should read "Destination: Hell." Cut to: A Brooklyn apartment with a great Manhattan view, a cop's regalia strewn about the floor, a male body in the bed and a pensive Amelia Donaghy (Angelina Jolie), who happens to be the cop, wondering what's next in her unhappy life.

Well, she's about to find out.

"The Bone Collector," Philip Noyce's very slick, frequently disturbing and generally entertaining adaptation of the Jeffery Deaver novel, is—like "Seven" (1995), probably its closest progenitor—a movie that sinks its teeth into us not by what we see but what we know: namely, the methods of the maniacal serial killer who's terrorizing Manhattan and leaving behind obscure clues that are obviously the work of a criminal genius, but which, Rhyme eventually realizes, are intended specifically for him.

The first of these fetishized clues is discovered at an Amtrak railyard where a hand—one finger having been pared to the bone—is found sticking out of the track bed. Amelia, scheduled for transfer to the relative boredom of Youth Services, performs so intrepidly at the crime scene—she actually stops a train with her flashlight to preserve the evidence—that it brings her to Rhyme's attention. He'd like her to be his legs as they track down the killer. She'd rather not.

She loses the argument.

Like the split atmospherics of Noyce's New York—the antiseptic environment of Rhyme's SoHo apartment vs. the hellishness of the crime scene and the abomination of the crimes (one victim is chained before an open steam pipe; another is devoured by rats)—"The Bone Collector" balances its assets delicately. There are the physical aspects of the stars, of course—whose faces Noyce obviously loves, and dwells on—and a ripe cast of supporting players, including Queen Latifah as Rhyme's nurse, Ed O'Neill as the cop who brings Rhyme into the case, and the ubiquitous Luis Guzman as a police researcher who has all the funniest lines, or makes them that way.   Conversely, there is a nightmarish trip into a nocturnal Manhattan of abandoned slaughterhouses, subterranean squalor and our own fearful imaginations. The combo is pretty irresistible.

Throughout literature's better detective fiction, the hero is not a figure of action but of intellect. Seldom has one had so limited a sphere of action as Lincoln Rhyme, but Washington makes him both believable and complex and a great matchup for the up-and-coming Jolie, who can act. One wishes "The Bone Collector" didn't have an ending that was simultaneously crowd-pleasing and intellectually unsatisfying. One wishes the story made more of its ostensible connection with old New York history. But while "The Bone Collector" may not quite be "The Silence of the Lambs," it's the best thriller we've seen in some long time.

SIGHT AND SOUND, 3/00, p. 42, Jason Drake

The present. Manhattan police detective Lincoln Rhyme, an expert on serial killers, is injured in a freak accident while attending a crime scene. Left a quadriplegic as a result, he is confined to his apartment bed where he relies heavily on his nurse Thelma and lifesupport machines. Depressed by his condition, Rhyme arranges for his doctor to assist him in taking his own life. Meanwhile, beat-patrol cop Amelia Donaghy discovers the body of a man who was abducted with his wife. Her quick thinking preserves some key evidence at the crime scene. Rhyme's boss brings the evidence to him and asks for his help in catching the killer. Initially he refuses, but after seeing the evidence Rhyme becomes interested and asks to see Donaghy. Rhyme persuades her to work the case with him, but they fail to stop the dead man's wife being killed.

After a third victim is found the case is taken out of Rhyme and Donaghy's hands, but the investigation fails to locate the killer. Frustrated, the pair review the evidence which leads them to another murder at the river side. At the crime scene Donaghy realises the killer is now targeting Rhyme. Rushing back to his apartment she saves Rhyme by shooting the killer, who a is cardiac-unit technician. Later, a more positive Rhyme welcomes visitors to a Christmas party at his apartment.

Having made the disastrous high-octane action-movie version of *The Saint*, mainstream journeyman Phillip Noyce returns to the thriller genre with *The Bone Collector*, a film as mediocre as his earlier *Sliver*. The story of a quadriplegic detective called Lincoln Rhyme who co-ordinates the hunt for a serial killer, it owes an obvious debt to *Se7en* and *Copycat*. And after so many recent films on the same subject it's difficult to see *The Bone Collector* as anything more than an undistinguished addition to a slightly jaded genre.   We've seen the rain-soaked, claustrophobic city before. We understand a number of victims have to be grimly dispatched by the killer before he (always a he) is caught. We know it's only a matter of time before the killer turns his attention to the detective, and so on. The film halfheartedly reconfigures a few of the traditional elements, but not in an interesting or original way. For instance, the role of the detective is split in two, with Amelia Donaghy acting as Rhyme's pupil and surrogate legs. But still the film is more focused on the chase than on the pursuers.

There is a slackness to the film's narrative structure. Why the killer collects bones or why he even bothers to murder his victims when his target all along is actually Rhyme is never explained. And the ending—where two hours of grim bleakness and grinding pessimism are suddenly replaced by a short, would-be uplifting scene as everyone gathers at Rhyme's apartment, accompanied by Peter Gabriel's 'Don't Give Up' is particularly unconvincing.

Denzel Washington is an actor of enormous grace, glowing with sexual charisma, so the physically immobile Rhyme marks a noticeable departure from his previous roles. His restriction might have been used more effectively to overturn the convention of an athletic, physically powerful hero. But again the film chooses an easier path, preferring instead to make a banal point about the possibility for optimism when faced with a personal handicap.

Another case of the film running scared from its own shadow is the way it sets up a possible relationship between white Donaghy and black Rhyme and then sidesteps it completely. Although the pair do begin to show a degree of affection (in one scene where he surreptitiously smells her hair and in another where she strokes Rhyme's only moveable finger while he is unconscious), at the end it's not even clear whether they are just close professionally or if a romance is in place.

The film is often overly grim just to gain attention. Noyce concentrates on the murders in greater detail than usual, so that we get to see or experience more than we expect or want of the terror and pain of the victims as they are killed in increasingly distressing ways. But there is also an underlying sense of melancholy running through the film. Both Rhyme and Donaghy are introduced as depressed people: Rhyme wants to kill himself rather than be left in a persistent vegetative state by one of his increasingly frequent seizures, Donaghy is unable to commit to a relationship and is disenchanted with her work.

Ultimately, the film fails to come up with anything approaching a new take on the standard serial-killer thriller (of which we've seen so many examples of late) other than a few shock effects. In one scene a handful of street manhole covers are blown into the air by an underground explosion, a scene that Noyce obviously took a liking to since he repeats it a second time, a pointless use of intense volume and physical impact typical of the film as a whole.

VILLAGE VOICE, 11/16/99, p. 136, Amy Taubin

A glossy package that carries the banner of two studios, *The Bone Collector* borrows liberally from both *Silence of the Lambs* and *Seven*. The result is so formulaic and predictable that you're bored even when you're scared.

Amelia Donaghy (Angelina Jolie) is an NYPD rookie whose talent for detection brings her to the attention of forensic genius Lincoln Rhyme (Denzel Washington). Rhyme's spine was crushed in a job-related accident, leaving him paralyzed below the neck except for his right index finger. His will to live is revitalized when he gets involved in the investigation of a grisly murder, one of many by a killer who seems to have spent too much time watching *Seven*. Donaghy discovered the first murder, her photos of the corpse and the arcane clues left by the killer convince Lincoln to make her his eyes, ears, hands, and feet. While she does the walking, he directs her via cell phone. They examine the evidence using the elaborate voice-activated computer system that turns his loft into an editing suite. This allows director Phillip Noyce to display hideously mutilated corpses and to fetishize the details-skin carved, burnt, or bitten down to the bone—in giant digitalized close-up. We've come a long way-technologically speaking-since *Blow-Up*.

Washington is more personable than the film deserves, and it's outrageous that he's only allowed to have a romance with a white woman when he's been virtually castrated (although that index finger should not be underestimated). Given the circumstances, Jolie takes herself a bit too seriously, but Queen Latifah and Luis Guzman are breezy comic relief. Noyce, who directed the truly terrifying *Dead Calm,* does this one strictly by the numbers. A measure of how not scary *The Bone Collector* is: Although the killer uses a yellow cab to kidnap his victims, I leapt into the first one I saw outside the theater.

Also reviewed in:
CHICAGO TRIBUNE, 11/5/99, Friday/p. A, Michael Wilmington
NEW YORK TIMES, 11/5/99, p. E20, Stephen Holden
VARIETY, 9/6-12/99, p. 66, Dennis Harvey
WASHINGTON POST, 11/5/99, p. C5, Stephen Hunter
WASHINGTON POST, 11/5/99, Weekend/p. 47, Michael O'Sullivan

BOWFINGER

A Universal Pictures and Imagine Entertainment release of a Brian Grazer production. *Executive Producer:* Karen Kehela and Bernie Williams. *Producer:* Brian Grazer. *Director:* Frank Oz. *Screenplay:* Steve Martin. *Director of Photography:* Ueli Steiger. *Editor:* Richard Pearson. *Music:* David Newman. *Music Editor:* J.J. George. *Sound:* Martin Raymond Bolger and (music) John Kurlander. *Sound Editor:* Ron Bochar. *Casting:* Margery Simkin. *Production Designer:* Jackson DeGovia. *Art Director:* Tom Reta. *Set Designer:* Karl Martin, Les Gobruegge, and Dawn Snyder. *Set Decorator:* K.C. Fox. *Set Dresser:* David E. Saltzman, Gary S. Isbell, Scott Garrett, Jack Forwalter, and Oscar X. Delgadillo. *Special Effects:* Philip Cory. *Costumes:* Joseph G. Aulisi. *Make-up:* Steve Artmont. *Make-up (Steve Martin):* Frank Griffin; *Make-up (Eddie Murphy):* Toy R. Van Lierop. *Make-up (Special Effects):* Matthew W. Mungle. *Stunt Coordinator:* Bud Davis. *Running time:* 97 minutes. *MPAA Rating:* PG-13.

CAST: Steve Martin (Bobby Bowfinger); Eddie Murphy (Kit Ramsey/Jiff Ramsey); Heather Graham (Daisy); Christine Baranski (Carol); Jamie Kennedy (Dave); Barry Newman (Kit's Agent); Adam Alexi-Malle (Afrim); Kohl Sudduth (Slater); Terence Stamp (Terry Stricter); Robert Downey, Jr. (Jeffrey Renfro); Alejandro Patino (Sanchez); Alfred De Contreras (Martinez); Ramiro Fabian (Hector); Johnny Sanchez (Luis); Claude Brooks (Freddy); Kevin Scannell (LA Cop); John Prosky (MindHead Executive); Michael Dempsey (Camera Security Guard); Walter Powell (Federal Express Man); Phill Lewis (Actor at Audition); Marisol Nichols (Young Actress at Audition); Nathan Anderson (Clothing Sales Clerk); Brogan Roche (Renfro's Executive); John Cho (Nightclub Cleaner); Lloyd Berman (Camera Store Clerk); Zaid Farid (Kit's Limo Driver); Aaron Brumfield and Kevin Grevioux (Kit's Bodyguards); Kimble Jemison (Kit's Assistant); Alex Craig Mann (Studio Executive); Laura Grady (E Channel Interviewer); Reamy Hall (Farrah).

CHRISTIAN SCIENCE MONITOR, 8/13/99, p. 17, David Sterritt

Mediocre movies can be irksome, tedious, and very hard to sit through. But bad movies—really bad ones, made so incompetently that you can't imagine how they ever made it from the drawing board to the theater—have a fascination that can't be denied.

Take a picture like "Plan 9 From Outer Space" directed in 1958 by Edward D. Wood Jr., who would be a completely obscure figure if the sheer goofiness of his haphazard techniques hadn't caught the public's fancy. Far from forgotten, he's the main character of Tim Burton's 1994 bio-pic "Ed Wood," and an unproduced screenplay Wood wrote ("I Woke Up Early the Day I Died,") is coming to the screen next month courtesy of Hollywood star Billy Zane.

Other examples abound. Steve Martin's new comedy, "Bowfinger," plunges into these eccentric waters with gusto. The hero, Bobby Bowfinger, is a would-be movie director whose ambitions far exceed his abilities. A master of self-delusion, if little else, he convinces himself that a powerful producer will support his science-fiction project, "Chubby Rain," if he can land international superstar Kit Ramsey for the lead.

Kit won't even talk to him, much less sign on the bottom line, but Bobby is undeterred. He'll simply film Kit on the sly, using hidden cameras, while he shoots the rest of the story with a regular cast and crew. Who cares if the result is an incomprehensible mess? It'll have action, aliens, special effects, and Kit Ramsey's handsome face—all the ingredients for a sure-fire hit.

Viewed through Bobby's eyes, this plot recalls "Ed Wood," which is also about a talent-free director who never heard of quality control. Viewed through Kit's eyes, it's another twist on "The Truman Show" and "EDtv," with predatory cameras stalking a reluctant star. What gives "Bowfinger" its own personality is a subplot about Kit's unique blend of egomania and paranoia. Bobby's movie crew keeps harassing him with horror-movie gizmos, not realizing that Kit—already a believer in alien conspiracies and outer-space invasions—sees their science-fiction fantasies as proof of his own worst nightmares.

"Bowfinger" would be a better entertainment if it were more firmly separated from the bad-movie scene it satirizes. It has hilarious moments, especially when Bobby and company start experimenting with fantasy-film effects, which they see as a matter of gooey liquids and breakaway body parts. But too much of "Bowfinger" relies on the sort of frantic bad taste that the onscreen filmmakers like to indulge in. In the end, "Bowfinger" is mediocre whereas "Chubby Rain" would be absolutely awful if it really existed, and probably more fun to watch.

The cast of "Bowfinger" is solid, headed by Martin as the title character and Eddie Murphy as both the unwitting superstar and his addleheaded brother. Frank Oz directed Martin's screenplay, providing almost enough chuckles to keep you from noticing how wildly uneven the picture is.

LOS ANGELES TIMES, 8/13/99, Calendar/p. 1, Kenneth Turan

People bring out the best in Eddie Murphy: the more of them he plays on screen, the drop-dead funnier he becomes.

While Murphy doesn't turn into an entire family in "Bowfinger" as he did in "The Nutty Professor," he is able, with the help of writer and co-star Steve Martin, to create two completely different characters whose cumulative comic impact is overwhelming.

It was Martin who came up with the idea for this likable albeit hit-and-miss farce, directed by Frank Oz, which deals with low-rent dreamers on the fringes of the movie business determined to make it big in Hollywood.

Martin has the right touch for Bobby Bowfinger, the alpha and omega of Bowfinger International Pictures, a company so threadbare even schlockmeister Ed Wood would've looked down on it. But it's Murphy who has the showier and funnier part, or parts, and he makes the most of it, or them.

Murphy is first met as Kit Ramsey, a.k.a. "the hottest, sexiest action star in the world." But though the man has the requisite mansion, fancy cars and entourage, success has not brought him mental stability. Far from it.

Murphy takes special and biting glee in delivering Ramsey's delusional tirades—his fury at getting scripts that make extensive use of the letter "K" (they remind him of the KKK) and his disgust that while white actors get all the good punch lines black actors only win Oscars when they play slaves. It's no wonder that he seeks the help of MindHead (a clever spoof of Scientology-type organizations), where cool Terry Stricter (Terence Stamp) is in charge and believers walk around with triangles on their heads.

Ordinarily, someone like Bobby Bowfinger would never cross Kit Ramsey's path. A producer-director so impoverished he shoplifts his wardrobe and can't pay a $ 5.43 phone bill, Bowfinger's past credits include the Glendale Tent Players' production of "Once Upon a Mattress" and a film called "The Yugo Story" (it's about the car, not the country). But dreams die hard, and Bowfinger's latest is a script called "Chubby Rain."

Written by his accountant (Adam Alexi-Malle), "Chubby Rain's" story of aliens disguised as raindrops sounds like a winner to Bowfinger. When top executive Jerry Renfro (a Robert Downey Jr. cameo) tells him he might go for it with Kit Ramsey attached, Bowfinger tells his crack team of dimwits ("the most promising group of young professionals I've ever worked with") to get ready to go.

These include a star-struck ingenue from Ohio (Heather Graham), a handsome if limited actor (Kohl Sudduth), an overly dramatic leading lady (Christine Baranski) and a studio gofer-cameraman (Jamie Kennedy) who knows how to walk off the lot with any piece of equipment that's not tied down.

What the group doesn't include is Kit Ramsey, who, not surprisingly, wants nothing to do with "Chubby Rain." Fueled by desperation and feeling his last chance slipping away, Bowfinger comes up with a lunatic idea: He'll follow Ramsey around town and secretly film him interacting with the cast members. "Kit doesn't want to see the camera," he tells his own gullible actors. "It breaks his concentration."

Murphy is especially funny in the scenes of panicky befuddlement that result when these strangers come up to him talking "some secret white language I can't decode." His confusion eventually leads to chaos, which is where Jiff, a look-alike for Ramsey that Bowfinger hires when his unknowing star proves temporarily unavailable, enters the picture.

As the innocent, glasses-and-braces-wearing Jiff, someone whose show business experience is limited to being "an active renter at Blockbuster" and who would consider a career running errands to be a major break, Murphy has even more fun than he does with Ramsey. And it's his zeal for creating such disparate comic characters that gives "Bowfinger" its particular zest.

For Murphy has the ability, not shared by all comics or even all actors, to convincingly become different people with different voices and even different physical auras. Playing multiple characters seems to liberate a kind of energy in him, as it did in Peter Sellers, an energy that heats up Martin's cool, cerebral humor and helps it ignite.

"Bowfinger" has its share of down time, proves better at its set pieces than in the continuity between them, and also misses Murphy when he's not on the screen. But given how many people he plays, it's not long before someone shows up to make us laugh.

NEW STATESMAN, 10/25/99, p. 45, Jonathan Romney

The new Steve Martin film begins with the picture of a broken man. Bobby Bowfinger, a failed Hollywood director, sits in his apartment surrounded by the detritus of faded hopes—from the posters of the summer stock shows he once acted in, to trophies of his time as a commercials hack. As a blues song moans on the soundtrack, he looks for encouragement to his dog, but even she slopes off in embarrassment. We'd almost be ready to weep for the man, if he didn't at the very last moment lower his head, revealing the ultimate sign of Tinseltown abjection—a nasty little ponytail dangling over his neck.

This is a remarkably downbeat start for a Hollywood comedy, and you wonder if Martin is telling us something. As the recent BBC documentary about him revealed, his output of the past few years (the nadir being a *Sgt Bilko* movie) finally made him feel enough was enough. He has spent recent years revitalising himself by writing a play and assorted off-the-wall squibs for the *New Yorker*. His comeback film *Bowfinger*, which Martin has written himself, is almost this self-portrait—and looking at Bobby Bowfinger's cheery cabaret posters, you can't help thinking of Martin's own early years as a trouper on the stages of Disneyland.

You have to be pretty confident to make a comedy about irredeemable wretchedness, and in Bowfinger, Martin really is as bullishly inventive as he's been since his early anarchic goofball stuff. Directed by Frank Oz, *Bowfinger* may be a throwaway showbiz farce, yet it's rather more trenchant about film-world folly than the supposedly lethal insights of satires such as *The Player* or *Get Shorty*. The crushed but crazily ebullient Bowfinger is convinced there's always one more stab at success, and his last hope is a sci-fi script entitled *Chubby Rain* (why "chubby"? Because it contains aliens, of course). As far as we know, it has nothing going for it except its closing line—"Gotcha, suckers!" And indeed, up in Beverly Hills, action star Kit Ramsey (Eddie Murphy, doing a cruel parody both of his own hot-shot persona and of Will Smith) is after just such a career-capping catchphrase: "Where's my *'Hasta la vista*, baby'?".

Bowfinger's ploy is to film Ramsey without him realising—it—a sort of sampled-vérité approach or, as he prefers to call it, "Cinéma Nouveau". It's a brilliant, preposterous idea, although not as unlikely as all that. After all, Roger Corman gave Peter Bogdanovich his first break by letting him recycle spare footage from an unfinished Boris Karloff vechicle, then splice in the real Karloff. And the notorious hack savant Edward D Wood made his legendary farrago *Plan 9 from Outer Space* with Bela Lugosi in a starring role, even though Lugosi died halfway through shooting.

Bowfinger offers a pretty extensive panorama of Hollywood High and Low—from Bowfinger's shoddy pseudo-hacienda to the plush eateries where it doesn't matter who you know, but whom you eavesdrop on. There's a wonderful bit of tomfoolery in one such place, when Bowfinger—hastily whipping of his passé ponytail, which was Velcro all along—riffs of Robert Downey Jr's conversation in the next cubicle. The film has a sharp eye for upwards-and-downwards career traffic. While Christine Baranski's no hope *grande-dame* plummets with glory, Heather Graham's schoolmarm hick (sweetly parodying her role as the ingénue porn queen in *Boogie Nights)* determinedly climbs the fame ladder by screwing every appreciative dope in sight.

Considering it's so much his film, Martin is remarkably generous in encouraging Murphy to steal the show relentlessly in not one but two roles. As Kit Ramsey, he's a hard man teetering on the edge of gibbering paranoia—detecting covert KKK presence in an action script, and looking for salvation in a barmy self-enhancement cult, where he frenetically chants his personal mantra: "Keep It Together—keepittogetherkeepittogetherkeepittogether!"Murphy also plays Kit's idiot twin, a nerdy delivery man who'd rather fetch coffee than play stunt double in murderous traffic sequences. Even though they don't really play off each other (which is in the nature of the film), Murphy is the best foil Martin has had since he shared a body with Lily Tomlin in *All of Me.*

When Hollywood stars do this sort of fond salute to the humbling "little guys", the results often smack of condescension, especially when a huge budget has manifestly been ploughed into an authentically scuzzy look. It's one thing to be nostalgic for Z-grade ineptitude when you're in the audience: you're bucking the system, however infinitesimally, when you opt to watch an Edward D Wood film instead of *Independence Day*. But when it's the Studios celebrating beautiful losers, that's something else again—and for a successful bizarro auteur such as Tim Burton to hail a Poverty Row buffoon as a founding father, as he did in *Ed Wood*, looks like bad faith. There's a fond fantasy at work in *Bowfinger*, too, namely the secret wisdom of Hollywood that every movie really costs $2,184. Unlike Burton's Wood, however, Bobby Bowfinger is no more visionary or exalted than the rest of Hollywood—he's just capable of being a bigger crook on a smaller scale. And it's clear that if he ever gets his big chance, he'll be quite capable of making a multi-million-dollar movie look as if it cost $2,184. You'd be surprised how many of them do.

NEW YORK, 8/23/99, p. 51, Peter Rainer

Producer-director Bobby Bowfinger (Steve Martin), the head of near-bankrupt Bowfinger International Pictures, is an impostor in big-time Hollywood, which is another way of saying he's a low-rent con man trying to make it as a high-rent con man. He wants into the game—he wants to do power lunches and wear trendy threads and go about yelling *Action!* and *Cut!* In Hollywood, monomania is often mistaken for artistic temperament, and, even though Bowfinger's methods and imagination aren't on a much higher level than Ed Wood's—in fact, Wood may have the edge—Bowfinger has a passion for the process. He's a very specific Hollywood type—a driven schlockmeister—and his wiles and gumption grow on you. You want to see him make it.

Written by Steve Martin and directed by Frank Oz, *Bowfinger* is somewhat uneven, which may be unavoidable at a time when probably no studio comedy can get financing unless its smarts are leavened with teen-friendly yocks for the multiplex masses. There are sequences, such as a ninja-movie takeoff at the end, that jangle the prevailing tone of inspired silliness. (That ninja scene is uninspired silliness.) Fortunately, the movie's good stuff is so rampant that you easily forgive the flubs. It's been quite awhile since Steve Martin, who is perhaps Hollywood's greatest physical comic since Buster Keaton, looked like he was enjoying himself in a comedy. Encased in formulaic family entertainments like *Mixed Nuts; Father of the Bride, Part II; Sgt. Bilko;* and *The Out-of-Towners*, he seemed dutifully dithery. But Bobby Bowfinger is a crackerjack role for him because it fuses the two warring sides in his artist's nature: the rhapsodic screw-loose dreamer, who reached his pinnacle in *Roxanne* and *L.A. Story*, both written by Martin; and the larcenous huckster, whom he played with a chilling gravity in movies like the underrated *Leap of Faith* and, more recently, David Mamet's *The Spanish Prisoner*. (It's as if, with those latter two films, he could only once again find gratification in acting if he first cleared away any pretense of comedy.) *Bowfinger* is both petty and large-spirited. He's carried away by his own contrivances, and you can't believe he's on the level about anything with anybody. Yet his drive for success is dead serious. Beneath his inauthenticity lurks an authentic wannabe.

Bowfinger's grand scheme for glory involves getting Hollywood's biggest action star, Kit Ramsey (Eddie Murphy), to star in Bowfinger International's zilch-budget sci-fi thriller *Chubby Rain*—without even knowing he's in it. Assembling a crew of Mexican-border illegals and a cameraman (Jamie Kennedy) who "borrows" equipment from the studio where he works as a gofer, Bowfinger leads them, along with his actors, on commando-style raids where they intersect with the startled, freaked-out Ramsey as he's caught eating in trendy restaurants, leaving home in his limo, walking alone in an underground parking garage. Bowfinger has already lied to his cast that Ramsey is a fully aware, if reclusive, participant in the production; when the actors ambush him and spout scripted dialogue about alien takeovers, he runs away shrieking, and they think he's playing his part. Bowfinger touts his hit-and-run tactics as a new filmmaking style—"cinema nouveau"—and as the ruse is played out he begins to actually fancy himself an auteur. Caught up in the spirit, the Mexican crew takes to poring over *Cahiers du Cinema*. The film's leading lady, played by Christine Baranski as a faded stage diva festooned in scarves and jewelry, professes to "respect" Ramsey's way of working. (The ingenue, played by Heather Graham, is a more sensible sort: She sleeps her way into a juicier piece of the action.) The dissonance between the group's inflated pretensions and the cheesiness of their enterprise is deeply satirical and also, given the nature of Hollywood, deeply realistic: Pretentious and cheesy are never far apart out there.

Like Steve Martin, Eddie Murphy gets to show off his split-level personas in *Bowfinger:* He plays not only the ego-charged Kit Ramsey but also his grinning, cretinous brother Jiff, who winds up as the star's double in *Chubby Rain.* Murphy has cleaved himself in two before, in *The Nutty Professor,* and the gambit once again does wonders for him. Freed up from the need to unify his dual instincts as a performer into a single character, he goes all the way with each: action-hero jokester with an attitude and goofball innocent. His Kit Ramsey isn't just a smart-ass megastar, he's a turbocharged nutcase who believes racist messages are encoded in his scripts and that aliens really *are* after him. (He's ministered to by a New Age guru played by Terence Stamp—a far sleeker con man than Bowfinger.) What's funny about Ramsey is that, with all his behind-the-scenes looniness, he's a major star anyway. His status is a commentary on the looniness of the movie industry, and a kind of tribute too. For what comes through in the film, finally, is a great affection for a business that can accommodate so many cuckoos and connivers. In *Bowfinger*'s Hollywood world, you have to be crazed to make it—you have to be crazed to even want to make it. And then you have to stay crazy to stay a success. But the small-timer has his recompense, too. When Bowfinger, at the premiere for *Chubby Rain,* gazes up at the screen, he's not registering the same dud we are. He's watching his masterpiece. He doesn't look beady-eyed anymore. He looks moonstruck.

NEW YORK POST, 8/13/99, p. 54, Jonathan Foreman

Playing two fresh, very un-"Beverly Hills Cop" roles, Eddie Murphy is even better in "Bowfinger" than he was in "The Nutty Professor." The movie as a whole doesn't always pull off its mixture of low farce and sharp satire—though it does contain some side-splitting scenes—but it assures Murphy's comeback as one of our most brilliant comic talents.

It also shows off co-star Steve Martin's chops as a writer: In a deceptively genial way, "Bowfinger" is Hollywood satire as cutting and accurate as "The Player." And it takes on an impressively wide range of targets within the industry. There's even an implicit dig at Martin's ex-girlfriend Anne Heche.

Martin plays Bobby Bowfinger, a sleazy, failed film producer who runs Bowfinger International out of the living room of his L.A. shack. Desperate to become a somebody after years on the bottom, he seizes on a sci-fi script penned by Afrim, his Iranian accountant-cum-receptionist (Adam Alexi-Malle) as a last, best hope for glory.

Making the most of a "borrowed" car, clothes and a cell phone, he engineers an encounter with a powerful studio executive (the recently jailed Robert Downey Jr.) who agrees to get behind the film if Bowfinger can deliver action star Kit Ramsey (Murphy) as the lead.

Ramsey happens to be desperate for a film that ends with a quotable tag line like "Hasta la vista, baby." And Bowfinger's dreadful script about aliens coming to Earth in oversized raindrops contains just such a line.

The problem is that Ramsey is a racist nut case surrounded by hangers-on who feed his conspiracy theories about white people and alien invasions.

When Bowfinger can't get Ramsey to sign on, he decides he'll make the movie (for just under $3,000) by filming the star without him knowing it (after all, he reasons, "Tom Cruise had no idea he was in that vampire movie until two years later") and by hiring a cast and crew willing to work for nothing.

They include: Daisy (Heather Graham), an apparently clueless babe fresh off the bus from Ohio who turns out to be a ruthless sexual manipulator; Carol (Christine Baranski), a never-made-it theatrical grande dame; and an ultra-dorky delivery boy, Jiff, who powerfully resembles Ramsey and turns out to be his brother.

Bowfinger also gets the help of a friendly studio gofer (Jamie Kennedy), who's able to "borrow" everything from cameras to props to expensive cars for Bowfinger's meetings.

Wherever Ramsey goes, he finds himself confronted by strange people babbling about aliens—all while the hidden cameras roll. The encounters feed his hilarious paranoia (he thinks that Bowfinger's actors are speaking "some secret white language"), which forces him into ever greater reliance on the sinister boss (Terence Stamp), who leads a New Age, pseudo-scientific spiritual cult called MindHead.

"Bowfinger's" terrific set-pieces—like the scene in which Jiff is forced to run across a freeway, and the one in which the filmmakers set out to terrify Ramsey in an underground garage—more than make up for the odd weak moment or thin performance (Graham is surprisingly insubstantial as Daisy).

And there's something gutsy about the end joke being on the audience: You cannot help but root for these losers and their dream to make a movie, even though their film is bound to be atrocious, cliche-ridden crap.

NEWSDAY, 8/13/99, Part II/p. B3, John Anderson

The pairing of such Olympian comedians as Eddie Murphy and Steve Martin might have been a recipe for disaster, but the mechanics of "Bowfinger" sort of suss things out. Martin plays the main character, but Murphy plays two. While Murphy's primary role is never seen on screen with Martin's, Murphy's alter ego—one of those substrata characters that seem to make him so happy—is the funniest thing in the picture.

Everything else being equal, though, it's Martin that makes this Frank Oz comedy tick, and not just because Martin wrote the movie. Murphy can be funny just standing there—and so can Martin. Murphy can mug shamelessly—and so can Martin. But while Murphy almost always maintains his dignity, Martin's is in constant danger. The implicit running gag of his career has been the depths one has to reach if one wants to make people laugh for a living. Back in the '70s, when he was the host-of-choice on "Saturday Night Live," he always wore a suit—and an arrow through his head. Ever since, he's been the affronted clown of American comedy.

Which makes "Bowfinger" ideal. Hollywood survivalist Robert Bowfinger—head of Bowfinger International Pictures, whose major work seems to have been "The Yugo Story"—has everything you need in Hollywood, except the money. He's ruthless—he asks someone for a favor and then hangs up. He's insincere—"Love what you do," he says, pointing at someone he doesn't know, but knows is influential. He can bluff his way to a prime table near one of Hollywood's prime movers (Robert Downey Jr.) armed with a "cell phone" (the cord is hanging off the end). And he can get Downey to green-light his picture—as long as he gets action icon Kit Ramsey (Murphy) to star.

Downey's character is kidding, of course. But the movie's bittersweet element—the thing Martin handles so well—is Bowfinger's desperation to believe, to get a movie made, an impulse that easily overrides his otherwise native intelligence.

The "con," as the ads are calling it, is to make a space invader movie called "Chubby Rain" based on a script by Bowfinger's accountant (Adam Alexi-Malle) and starring Kit Ramsey—who won't know he's in it. There are only six scenes in most action movies, Bowfinger says. If he can manipulate Kit and his cast into the right situations, he can pull it off.

His cohorts include all the friends he's been failing and lying to for years—including his ultra-theatrical girlfriend (Christine Baranski), who is told Kit won't talk to her because of his "method." The cast also comes to include a seemingly naive Ohio girl played by Heather Graham, who has given herself a week to become a star, sleeps her way through most of the cast and crew and finally beds the director himself—who salvages his dignity by stealing her credit card.

The setup, the gags, the various wild swings—the subcontinental accountant with the hundreds of relatives, the crew that consists of illegal Mexican immigrants—are only mildly funny. "Bowfinger's" soul may be Martin, but its stroke of brilliance is Murphy's Kit, who unbeknownst to Bowfinger is a raging paranoid and a member of MindHead, a Scientology parody headed by a vaguely malevolent guru wearing one of Martin's old white suits (Terrence Stamp).

Kit, for instance, counts the times the letter K appears in a given script and when it turns out to be divisible by three (i.e., KKK) he assumes it's a subliminal racist message. In addition to his obsession with the Laker Girls, he thinks aliens are really out there—so that when Bowfinger's cast acts out its Troma-esque street scenes, he believes it's actually happening. Ignorance and psychosis make beautiful music together.

For sheer laughs and goofiness, though, it's Murphy's turn as Jiff—a semi-intelligent Kit look-alike hired for the back of his head—who's very happy picking up coffee orders at Starbucks and has an insight worth more than all the space goo the movie has to offer. "It's weird to get credit for looking like somebody," he says, and you can hear Martin saying, yeah, even if, occasionally, that someone is you.

SIGHT AND SOUND, 11/99, p. 39, Charles Taylor

Would-be film-maker Bobby Bowfinger is forever scrounging on the fringes of the Hollywood system. When his accountant writes *Chubby Rain* an alien-invasion script, Bowfinger shows it to studio executive Jerry Renfro who becomes interested in the project—but only if Bowfinger can guarantee the involvement of action-movie superstar Kit Ramsey.

Bowfinger contrives to make Kit the unknowing star of *Chubby Rain* by shooting him surreptitiously as his actors approach him and say their lines. Kit, who has sought the help of a cult to cure his paranoid delusions about extraterrestrials, falls prey to those delusions once again as he is confronted by strangers spouting gibberish about aliens. Needing some way for Kit to participate in dialogue scenes, Bowfinger stumbles upon the movie buff Jeff who bears a strinking resemblance to Kit, and who turns out to be his brother. Filming proceeds, ultimately with Kit's knowing involvement, and *Chubby Rain* becomes a hit.

For satire to work it has to focus on its target with laser-guided precision, or take pot-shots so wild that sheer audacity keeps it bowling along. But *Bowfinger*'s director Frank Oz has never been known for his finesse, and Steve Martin, who wrote the screenplay and also plays the title role, hasn't decided whether this take on the movie business is satire, farce or twisted wish-fulfilment fantasy. There was an element of wish fulfilment in Martin's screenplays for both *Roxanne* (1987) and *L.A. Story* (1999). The latter was savvy to the plastic unreality of Los Angeles but what came through most strongly was Martin's pixilated affection for the city. The more fanciful elements, such as the digital freeway sign that flashed private messages, came to seem like natural phenomena in a town where the inhabitants have remade reality itself.

In *Bowfinger* that affection has been replaced by contempt. Oz trains the camera on the decaying brown walls of Bowfinger's Spanish-style bungalow and sees none of the seedy vitality found, say, in *The Late Show* (1977), Robert Benton's noir-ish take on movieland's shabby fringes. *Bowfinger* looks at its namesake with the same disdain with which studio honchos regard him when he tries to crash a power lunch. Neither Oz's shoddy staging nor the undeveloped tone of Martin's script is as bad as the film's self-congratulatory cynicism. The particular hypocrisy of *Bowfinger* is that the movie is so clearly a product of the big-budget mainstream it invites the audience to feel superior to. (It has been sold in the US as the meeting of two big comic stars with an ad campaign that ingnores Eddie Murphy's role as Kit.)

The treatment of Murphy and Heather Graham is particularly problematic. Murphy brings some satirical juice to the rantings of a pampered black star about the racism that pervades the industry. But the laughs these lines might get stick in your throat when you see he has been shot in sputtering, eye-rolling close-ups, uncomfortable traces of Hollywood's racist stereotyping of black performers. Graham's role as an opportunist whose talent is for sleeping her way to the top and who winds up a lesbian is simply vile, Martin's caddish and transparent jibe at his ex Anne Heche. Given the quality of Martin's recent work *(Father of the Bride, Sgt Bilko)* and the quality of Heche's in *Donnie Brasco* and *Psycho*, you'd hardly think he's in a position to comment on her talent.

Often it's impossible to tell how Bowfinger wants us to react. It's a film that wants us to laugh knowingly at the dealmaking that takes place over a power lunch, but also to accept that a starry eyed Midwestern girl getting off a Greyhound and asking, "Where do I go to become an actress?" can make it. It wants us, in the age of *The Matrix*, to believe that Bobby Bowfinger's Ed Wood-style epic would be a smash. The only real accuracy and sting come in Robert Downey Jr's brilliant cameo as the essence of all the young execs who take pleasure in being so mindless. Satire that doesn't draw blood risks stroking the targets it claims to skewer, affirming the status quo it means to upset. Bowfinger should please the big stars and studio execs who can laugh at their on-screen representations and thus display their own hipness, and it should please audiences who can pretend that swallowing the crap Hollywood shovels out is fine as long as you're hip enough to know it's crap. *Bowfinger* bears the same relation to satire as reports of the weekend grosses do to journalism.

TIME. 8/16/99, p. 65, Richard Schickel

Hollywood, as we all know, runs on high hopes and impossible dreams, which just often enough—about once in a thousand times come true. But at a certain level, it also runs on cold pizza, unpaid phone bills and scripts by people for whom English is a second language. It's at this latter level that Bobby Bowfinger (Steve Martin), who operates Bowfinger International Pictures out of his ratty bungalow, scrounges along.

Far above him, seemingly safe behind the walls of his estate, his entourage and his raging paranoia, lives the world's greatest action star, Kit Ramsey (Eddie Murphy), his sanity tenuously secured by devotion to a group that bears a passing resemblance to Scientology.

Bowfinger, perhaps the funniest movie for grownups so far this year, recounts the attempt of the desperate former to feature the fame-addled latter in his absurd project. Basically, this involves making Kit the star of a movie without telling him he's in it. That in turn requires Bobby and his crew to stalk and provoke the star into photographable action. Since Kit is at least half convinced that he is being plagued by space aliens, these intrusions add fuel to the flame of his pathology.

Preposterous, you say. It would never work. But part of the weird genius of *Bowfinger* is that its central conceit never falls into total implausibility. At some point in the picture, you begin to see that this mad scheme is working. Or maybe it's just that you succumb to the enthusiasm with which Bobby and his associates perpetrate their con.

They are a wonderfully rum lot and include an ingenue fresh off the bus from Ohio (Heather Graham) who doesn't know much about Hollywood except that a girl is supposed to sleep her way to the top, which she's up for; a failed leading lady (Christine Baranski), boldly living out her frustrated dreams of Method acting in all the wrong places; and a production crew composed of illegal aliens who start out not knowing one end of the camera from the other and end up in learned discussions of how Fellini or Orson Welles might have shot the scene.

That's all good stuff, but the best thing about *Bowfinger* is the way the script by Steve Martin is tooled to his own and Murphy's comic strengths. At its best, Martin's screen character is a dislocating combination of yearning and take-no-prisoners opportunism. He's like a premoral child—appalling yet somehow charming. Murphy has the comic nerve to play stardom as a form of flat-out psychosis. His sweet side surfaces in the second character he plays, Kit's brother Jiff, whom Bobby hires as a part-time gofer, part-time stunt double, full-time victim of everyone's heedlessness.

The movie satirizes everything from the cell-phone culture to celebrity fawning, but its director, Frank Oz, knows that satire—especially show-biz satire—is what closes on Saturday night. So his style is casually naturalistic. He makes you believe this goofiness might really be happening. You know what? Somewhere, not necessarily in the movies, not necessarily so merrily, it probably is.

VILLAGE VOICE, 8/17/99, p. 59, J. Hoberman

Bowfinger, the character Steve Martin plays in the new comedy of the same name, is a particularly contemporary figure—the ridiculously persistent independent filmmaker. Like the overreaching Heather of *The Blair Witch Project* and the dogged subject of the upcoming doc *American Movie,* untalented Bobby Bowfinger hustles his way towards Sundance like a vine spiralling to catch the sun.

Bowfinger opens with its crackbrained hero hunkered down in his dank Hollywood bungalow, surrounded by tacky memorabilia, dodging bill collectors and plotting how to produce *Chubby Rain,* the moronic extraterrestrial-invasion script written by his even more dim-witted accountant. Pretending that action icon Kit Ramsey (Eddie Murphy) has signed onto the project, Bowfinger rallies his usual collection of losers and holds a paid audition that yields an ambitious would-be starlet, Daisy (Heather Graham). Then he sneaks across the border to round up an illegal-alien crew and begins stalking Ramsey—his scheme is to incorporate secretly filmed footage of the star unwittingly interacting with the Bowfinger stock company.

A group of young Soviet filmmakers had a similar idea in the mid 1920s, using newreels taken of the American superstars Douglas Fairbanks and Mary Pickford on a visit to Moscow to make them unwitting characters in their own movie. But *Bowfinger,* which Martin wrote, is clearly inspired by the legendary bargain-basement bad movie auteur Edward D. Wood Jr., particularly as he was projected in Tim Burton's 1994 biopic. A true believer in movie magic, Wood completed his preposterous *Plan 9 From Outer Space* without the presence of his leading man Bela Lugosi by mismatching a few old shots of the recently deceased star with a highly unsuitable body double.

No less optimistic, *Bowfinger* inhabits Ed Wood territory with a sub-Woodian gang of dopey starstruck sidekicks. The difference is that Wood was some sort of skid-row visionary while *Bowfinger* has no more conviction than the power of Martin's trademark fake sincerity. Alternately innocent and sly, either demonstrating inane faith or conning his way with vague directorial doubletalk, *Bowfinger* is a plot device whose mentality shifts as the scene or joke requires. When one of his more credulous associates wonders how Ramsey could be starring in *Chubby Rain* but be seemingly unaware of it, Bowfinger explains that "Tom Cruise had no idea he was in that vampire movie until two years later."

Indeed, *Bowfinger* is less intriguing as filmmaker fantasy than celebrity nightmare. The tightly wrapped, compulsively exhibitionist, already paranoid Ramsey—who is controlled by a high-powered therapeutic cult-freaks when Bowfinger's looniest actress (Christine Baranski) approaches him on Rodeo Drive, babbling about aliens from outer space in what he later describes to his cult controller (Terence Stamp) as "some secret white language." Crazy and getting crazier, Ramsey is driven to imagine that he is living inside Bowfinger's cheap remake of *Invasion of the Body Snatchers*. When he is secreted away into cult seclusion, Murphy gets to play a second role as the nerdy stand-in recruited by the ever-pragmatic Bowfinger.

Toward the end, director Frank Oz moves the show up to Griffith Observatory for the manic *Chubby Rain* climax, but *Bowfinger* itself never hits a note of high hilarity. The genially mediocre direction blunts whatever bite the script might have had. Oz and Martin are mischievous in sending up Scientology but, as a Hollywood satire, *Bowfinger* doesn't begin to approach Albert Brooks's *The Muse,* which opens in two weeks.

Bowfinger sustains a level of mild amusement throughout. It's no small thing but no big deal either. The best routine may be the extended punchline—an elaborate bit of fake kung fu that underlines the movie's vaudeville dependence on ethnic stereotypes, even as it allows Martin to revisit his past with a bit of physical comedy at once nostalgic and mean-spirited.

Also reviewed in:
CHICAGO TRIBUNE, 8/13/99, Friday/p. A, Michael Wilmington
NATION, 9/6 & 13/99, p. 34, Stuart Klawans
NEW YORK TIMES, 8/13/99, p. E18, Janet Maslin
NEW YORKER, 8/16/99, p. 90, Anthony Lane
VARIETY, 8/9-15/99, p. 39, Todd McCarthy
WASHINGTON POST, 8/13/99, p. C1, Rita Kempley
WASHINGTON POST, 8/13/99, Weekend/p. 43, Desson Howe

BOYS, THE

A Stratosphere Entertainment release of an Arena Film production in association with the Australian Film Commission, Premium Movie Partnership for Showtime, SBS Independent, Axiom, Screen Partners, New South Wales Film & TV Office. *Executive Producer:* Douglas Cummins. *Producer:* Robert Connolly and John Maynard. *Director:* Rowan Woods. *Screenplay:* Stephen Sewell. *Based on the play by:* Gordon Graham. *Director of Photography:* Tristan Milani. *Editor:* Nick Meyers. *Music:* The Necks and Sean O'Brien. *Sound:* Sam Petty, Phil Judd, and (music) Ross A'Hern. *Casting:* Lesley Burgess. *Production Designer:* Luigi Pittorino. *Costumes:* Annie Marshall. *Make-up:* Jan Zeigenbein. *Stunt Coordinator:* Lawrence Woodward. *Running time:* 86 minutes. *MPAA Rating:* R.

CAST: David Wenham (Brett Sprague); Toni Collette (Michelle); Lynette Curran (Sandra Sprague); John Polson (Glenn Sprague); Jeanette Cronin (Jackie); Anthony Hayes (Stevie Sprague); Anna Lise (Nola); Pete Smith (George 'Abo'); Sal Sharah (Nick); Lawrence Woodward (Prison Officer); Peter Hehir (Graham Newman); Andrew Heys (Sparrow); Teo Gebert (Constable Zammit);   Anthony Kierann (Constable Maguire);   Stephen Leeder (Supervising Detective); Veronica Neave (Girl at Bus Stop).

NEW YORK POST, 10/15/99, p. 58, Jonathan Foreman

"The Boys" is yet another Australian film that has the self-consciously grubby feel of the so-called British kitchen-sink plays of the 1960s.

It's about a sociopathically vicious bloke (David Wenham) from the criminal class and how he manipulates his pathetic brothers and violently mistreats his doting mom and girlfriend.

You find out from flash-forwards that the three brothers eventually commit a terrible crime.

Though stagy—it's based on an award-winning 1991 play (which was itself based on a true story)—and shot with an excess of close-ups, it's very well-acted and filled with bullying menace.

Both Toni Collette and David Wenham are terrific. The problem is that you've seen this claustrophobic world and these dangerous, rage-filled men many, many times before.

NEWSDAY, 10/15/99, Part II/p. B6, Jan Stuart

The prison population has been soaring at the movies in recent weeks, with characters buzzing in and out of jail and back in again at a rate that would seem to belie the general downturn in crime.

In Australia, a land founded on a tradition of incarceration, it would appear to be business as usual. At least as evidenced by "The Boys," a moody and disturbing new drama from Oz.

Brett Sprague (David Wenham), the prickly young anti-hero at the film's center, is singing the recidivist blues. Not a single family member visited him during his year's sentence on an assault charge. And when he returns to his simmering cauldron of a home, everything seems to be egging him to go back to prison.

Love is at a premium at the Spragues. The household is barely held together by Brett's struggling mother, Sandra (Lynette Curran), who gazes blankly at a coffee table that Brett built for her in prison shop and presides cluelessly over his lay-about brothers, Glenn (John Polson) and Stevie (Anthony Hayes).

It quickly becomes clear that misogyny rules and the brothers' tight-knit fraternity suffocates any liberty and equality. Within moments of his homecoming, Brett is fomenting strife between his brothers and their women: Glenn's yuppie wife, Jackie (Jeanette Cronin), Steve's pregnant waif of a girlfriend, Nola (Anna Lise), and Brett's hard-bitten steady, Michelle (Toni Collette of "The Sixth Sense"). Sandra's diffident Maori lover, George (Pete Smith), is no match for the brothers Sprague, who send the women packing one by one as they move toward an inevitable explosion of violence.

Tristan Milani's poetic photography and The Necks' jazzy score heighten the smoldering, Pinter-esque mood to the max. The fly in an otherwise seductive ointment is the confounding time frame. In adapting "The Boys" from a play by Gordon Graham, screenwriter Stephen Sewell and director Rowan Woods muddy the waters with an exasperating stream of flash-forwards and flashbacks that throw the viewer needlessly off track.

The lengths film directors will go to rid any trace of staginess—God forbid—from their work! The itinerant storytelling fortunately doesn't rob from the crackling performances all around and the vicarious allure of watching other families self-destruct with a fury that makes us count our blessings.

SIGHT AND SOUND, 11/98, p. 43, Richard Falcon

Sydney, Australia. Brett Sprague is released from prison after serving 12 months for assault. His brother Stevie drives him back to his mother Sandra's suburban house, where Brett alienates his girlfriend Michelle by accusing her of sleeping around. Brett discovers that his drugs stash has been taken and accuses his other brother Glenn. Intermittent flashforwards reveal Brett burning his clothes, being arrested, being beaten up in prison and Sandra receiving an anonymous obscene phone call on the day of his sentencing.

In the present, Brett and the brothers taunt the man Brett assaulted. Brett rounds on Glenn's partner Jackie and she leaves. Later she offers Glenn a chance at reconciliation which he rejects in favour of his brothers. Brett beats up George, Sandra's lover. Brett's failed attempts to have sex with Michelle lead to violence. Nola, Stevie's pregnant girlfriend, calls the police. Sandra attacks Brett when she realises he has hurt Michelle. A flashforward shows Sandra visiting Brett in prison. High on drugs, the brothers drive off into the night and Brett decides to attack a young woman at a bus stop.

Rowan Woods' first feature adapts the 1991 stage play *The Boys* which was controversial for taking inspiration from a notorious Sydney murder case. Chief among the series of utterly convincing performances on which the film turns is David Wenham's riveting Brett, distinguished from his dissolute siblings by his misdirected willpower, finally revealed as pathological. Leaving prison into a drab landscape of industrial estates and surveillance cameras, Brett arrives home with a coffee table he has made and his mother Sandra (an essay in careworn hopelessness by Lynette Curran) stands looking at it in silent suffering. This could be a cue for sympathy or pathos, but the Spragues are already too far gone for home improvement. The table joins the cluster of decayed domestic furnishings, shown in close-up at the film's start, intercut with saturated video images of a road at night. Brett's bedroom too is a time-warped space for lost boys' dreams, kitted out with a padlocked locker with pin-ups and wallpaper decorated with World War Two bombers. Woods' framing accentuates the claustrophobia, while the grungy, unobtrusive set is quietly articulate of the depressive shift from standard-issue boys' fantasies to an untenable adulthood. The surveillance camera slow-motion tracking shots (often accompanied by impressively unsettling sound design) add to the film's discomforting intensity, loading with menace such incidents as the brothers' glimpse of Nola hitching a nocturnal lift on a bleak road.

The Boys examines the details of its desperate familial and sexual relationships during Brett's homecoming day by juxtaposing them with flashforwards. The first, "8 hours later", shows Brett burning his clothes in the garden, soon followed by glimpses of the aftermath of an unspecified brutal crime. The flashforwards raise the stakes on the confrontations punctuating the brothers' reunion. Will upwardly mobile Jackie or agonisingly passive Glenn be the victim? Or Brett's girlfriend Michelle, who mocks him for his sudden impotence? Or the pregnant, browbeaten Nola to whom Brett is queasily solicitous and who informs the police when she hears Brett and Michelle's fight?

The kindly George, or the macho bottle-shop owner seem less likely candidates since it's dysfunction between the sexes that is remorselessly stressed, from the opening dialogue between Brett and Stevie to the harrowing sequence in which Brett vents his frustration on Michelle. Escape seems the only option here and the closure involves a visit from Sandra to an unrepentant Brett which also makes it clear that Michelle has left him. It is a badly needed moment of comfort, as is George's kindness to Sandra after she has received an obscene phone call.

Ultimately, *The Boys* avoids giving us any answers to the question of why crimes like this are committed by grounding its banal evil in a casebook full of contributory factors— unemployment, drugs, boredom, regressive fraternal bonding, a dysfunctional maternal relationship, prison as a violent training ground, even the trash existentialist power fantasies of Brett's sci-fi paperbacks. ("These are the worlds we have made," he quotes from one before the violent attack of the last scene.) But it leaves us with Brett's obdurately opaque psychopathy. This makes for powerful drama, but the film allows us to escape at the very point our own mounting horror makes us desperate to do so. The suspicion arises that by vividly depicting a detailed day in the life of the so called underclass, dramatically destined to end in random viciousness, *The Boys* leaves itself open to an interpretation that aligns it with reactionary tabloid views.

VILLAGE VOICE, 10/19/99, p. 140, Michael Atkinson

A scalding, groggy poison-pen portrait of criminal working-class dead-endism, Rowan Woods's *The Boys* is built to impress—what it judiciously avoids doing is the primary source of its bad-boy electricity. Based on what must've been a helluva-night-out play by Gordon Graham, the movie assumes pathologies are unknowable, and judgment beside the point. A true story, about three good-for-little Aussie brothers descending into capital crime, is in there somewhere, but the thrust is universal—we've all witnessed the blown fuses of uneducated masculine aggro. Shot in gritty neo-Cassavettes and unstructured as a commingled series of beery blackouts, *The Boys* leaves whole tragedies up to our imagination. Only the knowledge of very bad things to come is for certain.

At first blush, a page might seem to be taken out of the *Mean Streets/Laws of Gravity* hornbook here, but the dynamic is much scarier: instead of just one Johnny Boy, there are three, Brett (David Wenham), Glenn (John Polson), and Stevie (Anthony Hayes). The movie is one long living-room laze with beer, but with the brotherly feed-and-bite at full cry, there's always blood in the water. The authentic sociopath, Brett, is just home from a year in stir for assault, and his wary homecoming is a quiet nightmare of avoided eye contact and predation; as his blowsy mom (Lynette Curran) prepares endless meals and excuses, Brett is trying to discover who stole his drug stash and how much his bleached hood-groupie Michelle (a sharp-eyed Toni Collette) dicked around on him while he was away. The family house is, of course, a purgatory for women: tough as artificial nails, Michelle barely gets out alive, while Nola (Anna Lise), Stevie's terrified, pregnant girlfriend whose baby is nowhere to be seen after a "Six Months Later" title, has roadkill written all over her.

The Boys is a bolero of tension, and Wenham's rip through the part of a boneheaded menace is largely why. Still, efforts to regain the paradisiacally grainy '70s seem like frustrated nostalgia, and *The Boys* smacks of study—its realism is several steps short of chaos. Executed with remarkable restraint and spatial wisdom, Woods's movie boils but doesn't burn.

Also reviewed in:
CHICAGO TRIBUNE, 2/4/00, Friday/p. I, John Petracks
NEW YORK TIMES, 10/15/99, p. E24, Anita Gates
VARIETY, 2/23-3/1/98, p. 78, David Stratton

BOYS DON'T CRY

A Fox Searchlight Pictures release in association with the Independent Film Channel of a Killer Films/Hart-Sharp Entertainment production. *Executive Producer:* Pamela Koffler, Jonathan Sehring, Caroline Kaplan, and John Sloss. *Producer:* Jeffrey Sharp, John Hart, Eva Kolodner, and Christine Vachon. *Director:* Kimberly Peirce. *Screenplay:* Kimberly Peirce and Andy Bienen. *Director of Photography:* Jim Denault. *Editor:* Lee Percy and Tracy Granger. *Music:* Nathan Larsen. *Music Editor:* Allan Zaleski. *Sound:* Mark Melson and (music) Robert Fernandez. *Sound Editor:* Lewis Goldstein. *Casting:* Billy Hopkins, Suzanne Smith, Kerry Barden, and Jennifer McNamara. *Production Designer:* Michael Shaw. *Art Director:* Shawn Carroll. *Special Effects:* Jack Bennett. *Costumes:* Victoria Farrell. *Make-up:* Renée Lecuyer. *Stunt Coordinator:* Russell Towery and Ben Loggins. *Running time:* 114 minutes. *MPAA Rating:* Not Rated.

CAST: Hilary Swank (Brandon Teena); Chloë Sevigny (Lana); Peter Sarsgaard (John); Brendan Sexton, III (Tom); Alison Folland (Kate); Alicia Goranson (Candace); Matt McGrath (Lonny); Rob Campbell (Brian); Jeannetta Arnette (Lana's Mom); Cheynne Rushing (Nicole); Robert Prentiss (Trucker); Josh Ridgway (Kwik Stop Cashier); Craig Erickson (Trucker in Kwik Stop); Stephanie Sechrist (April); Jerry Haynes (Judge); Lou Perryman (Sheriff); Lisa Wilson (Pam); Jackson Kane (Sam Phillips); Joseph Gibson (Tom); Michael Tripp (Nerdy Teen); Shana McClendon (Girl in Car); Libby Villari (Nurse); Paige Carl Griggs (Dave, Deputy); Gail Cronauer (Clerk).

CHRISTIAN SCIENCE MONITOR, 10/8/99, p. 15, David Sterritt

Boys Don't Cry, coming to US theaters from the Toronto and New York filmfests, tells a fact-based story that illuminates many sad headlines about hate crimes. It gives a partly fictionalized account of Brandon Teena, a young Midwesterner who felt uncomfortable as a woman and decided to pass as a man.

Directed by Kimberly Peirce from a screenplay she wrote with Andy Bienen, the movie paints a candid portrait of Teena's sexual confusion, troubled relationships, and tragic death. Hilary Swank, a talented film and TV actress, gives one of the year's most devastating performances as the profoundly troubled protagonist.

CINEASTE, Vol. XXV, No. 2, p. 54, Melissa Anderson

[See a review of this film in *Film Review Annual 1999.*]

LOS ANGELES TIMES, 10/22/99, Calendar/p. 2, Kenneth Turan

"I hate my name, I'm thinking of changing it," gawky, awkward Candace confesses to the dishy young man who takes the seat next to her at a rowdy Midwestern bar. Handsome, buoyant Brandon Teena knows just what she means. "Sometimes," he says, all casual confidence, "it helps."

Sometimes, too, a life not like our own can shine a clear and discomforting light on the hidden recesses of the human heart, and it's hard to think of a life more different, or more illuminating, than the one lived by Brandon Teena, the charming youthful Lothario of Lincoln, Neb., a young man for whom changing names had been just the beginning.

Terribly unhappy as a woman named Teena Brandon, Brandon Teena was someone who'd cut her hair boyishly short and took to wearing loose-fitting flannel shirts. She became adept at "strapping and packing," flattening her breasts and stuffing socks down her pants—someone who so succeeded in gender disguise that it's difficult to talk about her without feeling that "him" is the more appropriate pronoun.

Based on the agonizing true story of a fatally deceptive life, "Boys Don't Cry" is an exceptional—and exceptionally disturbing—film from a first-time director and writer (with Andy Bienen) named Kimberly Peirce. Unflinching, uncompromising, made with complete conviction and rare skill, this Middle American "M. Butterfly" is a passionate story about the price of dreams, a story that goes into a world few of us know and comes out with a drama we all can find a place in.

For who has not fantasized about being somehow different than we are, thinner, more glamorous, more appealing. But, as minorities of all stripes have always known, being different can cut two ways. And because Brandon Teena's fantasy involved transsexualism—not just seducing women but actually being a man—she put herself in the zone where difference is dangerous, where departure from the norm can inspire fear and revulsion.

It's because of this gift for taking a very specific story and giving it universal resonances that the savage but sometimes wistful "Boys Don't Cry" is as powerful, and as wrenching, as it is. And without Hilary Swank's astonishing performance as Brandon Teena, the film's success would not be possible.

What Swank, a young actress previously seen in "Buffy the Vampire Slayer" and "The Next Karate Kid," accomplishes is nothing like the "Victor/Victoria"-type stunt it may appear to be. Just as Brandon Teena took her deception further than anyone could have anticipated, so Swank, in a piercing performance, makes us complicit in the agony and glee of Brandon's days and nights, letting us share in the strangeness, the bravado and the yearning desire to connect of this secret life on the edge. It's a bravura piece of work that not only lets us see how the real Brandon convinced so many people she was a man, it just about convinces us of the same thing even though we know the truth from the outset.

"Boys Don't Cry" starts out in 1993 in Lincoln, Neb., Brandon's hometown. There, he persists in going out on dates with impressionable young women even though some local men are riled up enough about his methods to attack the trailer he crashes in with his cousin Lonny (Matt McGrath).

"You're not a boy," Lonny screams, but Brandon, impervious to harsh logic, just grins and says, "Then how come they say I'm the best boyfriend they ever had?" Soft-spoken, thoughtful, considerate, quick with compliments and small gifts, Brandon certainly seems like the kind of dreamy guy not often found in those parts.

That's certainly what Candace (Alicia Goranson) thinks when she chats up Brandon in that Lincoln bar, and her grungy pals John (Peter Sarsgaard) and Tom ("Welcome to the Dollhouse's" Brendan Sexton III) initially share her good opinion as they watch Candace's new friend, never at a loss for nerve, throw himself into a fight with a much larger man.

These folks live in Falls City, a hamlet that makes Lincoln seem like Manhattan. They invite Brandon to hang out there and he agrees because the absence of people who know him makes it easier to do the one thing that lends a measure of pure ecstasy to life's most ordinary events, and that is acting out the pretense of maleness.

If there is a key element to Swank's characterization, it's the quick and ready hypnotic grin she uses to convey the sheer mind-bending joy Brandon felt when the deception was going well and everyone was fooled. Getting people, men as well as women, to treat him like a guy makes Brandon so pleased with himself he can barely stand it. He's in fact so heedlessly jazzed by what he's pulling off that he can't be bothered to see how much he's in over his head, to recognize the frightening position his fantasy life has placed him in.

Upping the ante is Brandon's love-at-first-sight crush on Lana (played with haunting immediacy by the versatile Chloe Sevigny), a teenager with a sick-of-it-all attitude who is romantically connected to John but whom Brandon immediately covets. Swank and director Peirce are especially good at creating empathy for Brandon, even when he acts with such utter foolishness he doesn't deserve it, and that concern for character, that refusal to typecast, refreshingly extends to John and Tom, who turn out to be an increasing unstable and violent pair of ex-cons.

All this is harder to accomplish because, as one character says and anyone who's seen the documentary "The Brandon Teena Story" can testify, Brandon's crowd in Falls City is part of a white trash world, where people mutilate themselves out of boredom, drink themselves into unconsciousness and genuinely believe there is good money to be made in singing karaoke.

Helped by Jim Denault's truth-captured-on-the-fly neo-documentary cinematography, director Peirce and Bienen and the expert cast engage us in the actuality of these rootless, hopeless, stoned-out lives without sentimentalizing or romanticizing them. The actors are especially adept at adding enough of their own innate inner lights to bring a level of interest to characters who in reality might not have had much at all.

One thing "Boys Don't Cry" doesn't do is soft-pedal the painful and horrifying aspects of Brendan's story; we share his lacerating journey night to its dark end. Unlike scenarios that play at disturbance, this film, especially in its graphic and devastating rape scene, is genuinely hard to take. Yet with an ability to metaphorically transform harsh aspects of existence, to show us reflections of our shared humanity in difficult, unlikely places, it enlarges our consciousness and reminds us of the truth of the often-quoted aphorism of the Roman playwright Terence. "I am a man," he wrote. "Nothing human is alien to me."

NEW YORK, 10/18/99, p. 56, Peter Rainer

Boys Don't Cry, directed by first timer Kimberly Peirce, is based on the real-life story of Teena Brandon, who, calling herself Brandon Teena, passed as a boy, romanced the girls, and was murdered for her deceptions in Falls City, Nebraska in 1993 by a pair of ex-cons (Peter Sarsgaard and Brendan Sexton III) she'd befriended. As Brandon, the talented Hilary Swank has a delicateness and a fine-cut androgyny that seem supremely out of place in the film's trailer-trash milieu. When Brandon is smitten by Lana (Chloë Sevigny) at a local bar, her pursuit becomes a kind of mad love with no way out. Peirce doesn't attempt a psychological explanation of Brandon, which is probably all for the best, since she was perhaps unexplainable. But the film could have used a tougher and more exploratory spirit; for Peirce, there was no cruelty, no derangement in Brandon's impostures toward the unsuspecting. The film is framed, too unquestioningly, as a transgender *Rebel Without a Cause,* with Brandon the martyred innocent who dies for her infatuations. To quote from the ad, *Boys Don't Cry* is about "finding the courage to be yourself," but Teena Brandon's life was too complex to be employed as an anthem for self-actualization.

NEW YORK POST, 10/11/99, p. 44, Jonathan Foreman

"Boys Don't Cry" is a haunting, superbly made film. But it's also an unrelentingly sad and depressing experience, being the true story of a young Nebraskan woman who successfully masqueraded as an attractive young man before being raped and murdered in 1993.

It takes the lost trailer-park world that inspires endless episodes of the Jerry Springer TV show and uses it as a source of tragedy rather than farce. It's a grim, squalid tale of pathetic people who inhabit a grim, squalid stretch of the country, and you know from the start that it will end in horror.

When you first meet Brandon Teena (Hilary Swank) she's already reversed her given name—Teena Brandon—had her hair cut and started dressing like a guy. When she goes out to a Lincoln, Neb., disco she's thrilled to discover that she's not just convincing as a man but attractive enough to pick up a pretty girl. She even kisses her on the way home.

But the pretty girl's brothers are furious when they realize their sister has been seduced by a "dyke"—and they attack the trailer where Brandon lives with a gay male friend.

So Brandon, who's in trouble with the law and is an incorrigible liar, goes on the road—as a guy. (She doesn't consider herself a lesbian, but rather a boy in a girl's body, and hopes to have a sex-change operation one day.)

After a bar fight near the small town of Falls City, she finds herself adopted by a "family" of white-trash misfits. They include mercurial ex-con John (Peter Sarsgaard); his single-mom sister, Candace (Alicia Gorenson); his ex-girlfriend Lana (Chloe Sevigny); Lana's drunk mom (Jeannetta Arnette), and John's pal and fellow ex-con Tom (Brendan Sexton III).

They're all charmed by Brandon's enthusiasm and pretty-boy looks. But Brandon falls for Lana and Lana falls for him/her.

Somehow (shades of "M. Butterfly") they manage to make love without Lana figuring out Brandon's secret. But it's only a matter of time until the volatile folk who've adopted Brandon realize that she's been deceiving them, and none of them are what you would call open-minded.

First-time director Kimberly Peirce maintains a steady if not especially swift pace and successfully evokes a number of other films, such as "The Executioner's Song," that deal with violence in the heartland.

More impressive is the way she inspires powerful, convincing performances from the whole cast.

Swank, best known for her work on TV's "Beverly Hills 90210," does Oscar-caliber work as Brandon, and Sevigny shows once again what a terrific actress she is.

If there's a major problem with this tale of quintessentially American self-reinvention gone horribly wrong, it's not that all the male characters are repulsive—although they are—but that the film presents the violence of Teena's story with what feels like gratuitous relish.

The rape scene is the most sickeningly graphic one since 1988's "The Accused" with Jodie Foster. The filmmakers want to teach us some kind of lesson about tolerance and gender roles, but the scene is so unbearably explicit that you just know it will be replayed again and again by past and future sex-criminals, and you wonder if it was really necessary.

NEWSDAY, 10/8/99, Part II/p. B8, John Anderson

The landscape of Kimberly Peirce's "Boys Don't Cry" is the Charles Starkweather-Perry Smith-inhabited grassy flat killing floor of a near-mythic Midwest; its time is perpetual nightfall, the hour of the predator. Its climax is rape and multiple murder. Its screaming tabloid story is a chilling account of sexual transgression, aggression and death.

That the film's lingering sentiment turns out to be love seems close to miraculous. But so is much of Peirce's sensational and sensationally moving debut film, beginning with Hillary Swank's performance as Brandon Teena—the young heartbreaker who, back in 1993, knocked the young women of dusty Falls City, Neb., off their feet. And then turned out to be a woman.

Although its basic story has been recounted in the Village Voice, The New Yorker and a recent documentary ("The Brandon Teena Story"), "Boys Don't Cry" is a testament to the power of fiction to find the truth—no straight story, after all, could possibly be as moving or as deeply troubling as Peirce's film, at whose center is the romance between Brandon and Lana Tisdel (a fabulous Chloe Sevigny) and the consistent sense of sexual disequilibrium that makes the movie so compelling.

It would be easy to say that Swank makes a convincing man, and she does, but the effect of the movie's Brandon Teena (originally name, Teena Brandon) is all about the actress' performance, rather than the actress. (It would be hard to call Swank even remotely androgynous.) Part of what director Peirce is about with "Boys Don't Cry" is the more-than-willing suspension of disbelief among the young women of Falls City, because they find in Brandon what they want to find in a man—someone who knows how a woman wants to be treated.

That sense of disequilibrium, by the way, may be three-fourths embarrassment, at least among heterosexual men—just as the rage that Brandon's ruse eventually sparks among his Falls City friends is about a lot more than a sense of mere betrayal.

The Falls City crew, which includes the vicious and slightly crazy ex-cons John Lotter (Peter Sarsgaard) and Thomas Nissen (Brendan Sexton III), aren't the most sophisticated bunch; Lana, for one, aspires to be a professional karaoke singer. But as they say in the restaurant business, presentation is everything, and Brandon—Ace-bandaged and sock-stuffed—knows how to put on an act.

But even while Swank gives a technically adept performance-within-a-performance, what makes it so touching is the near-visceral understanding she gives us of Brandon's need, this need to be who and what he wants to be—and Lana's need as well. One of the more astounding bits in the film comes after Brandon, who in addition to being a chameleon is also a scofflaw and a thief, is busted for an outstanding ticket (and his masquerade begins to unravel). Brandon's feeble, fumbling attempts to explain to Lana why he's in the women's section of the jail when she comes to bail him out couldn't be more pointless—she simply doesn't want to know. (It's easily Sevigny's finest moment in the film.) Her "blindness," if you will, continues well past the scenes when Brandon is literally exposed and abused by Lotter, Nissen and—not physically, but brutally—Lana's mother (the very scary Jeannetta Arnette).

The perception among critics might be to withhold praise for a director's first film; where, after all, can Peirce possibly go from here? On the other hand, a film that plays so adeptly with perception deserves all the praise it can get.

SIGHT AND SOUND, 4/00, p. 43, Xan Brooks

The US Midwest, the early 90s. Teena Brandon, a petty thief from Lincoln, Nebraska, cuts her hair, binds her breasts and reinvents herself as a boy named Brandon Teena. Alighting in the depressed Nebraskan township of Falls City, Brandon befriends young single mother Candace and her dropout buddies: ex-cons John and Tom and vixenish teenager Lana. John lives at the home of Lana's mother and is fiercely protective of Lana, who is herself attracted to Brandon. Lana and Brandon begin a relationship.

However, when Brandon's warrant sheet catches up with him, the authorities realise he is actually a girl and place him in the women's cell. Brandon tells Lana he is a hermaphrodite and she arranges his bail. Back at Lana's house, a disgusted John and Tom strip Brandon naked to prove he is actually a girl. Later that night, John and Tom drive Brandon to a remote part of the country where they rape and beat him. Brandon presses charges and hides out at Candace's home where he plans to escape Falls City with Lana. Informed of his whereabouts by Lana's mother, John and Tom drive over and kill Brandon and Candace. End credits reveal they are both serving time for murder. Lana left town but later returned to Falls City.

Fledgling film-maker Kimberly Peirce first learned of the murder of Teena Brandon from a 1994 article in that oracle of New York hipness, the *Village Voice*. She developed it as a feature in tandem with quintessential East Coast indie-producer Christine Vachon, of *Safe*, *Kids* and *Happiness* fame. As a result, this glue-fume drama of disaffected American youth boasts an exotic, mongrel pedigree. Just as the charismatic, shape-shifting Brandon Teena arrives in Falls City, Nebraska, from "someplace beautiful", so *Boys Don't Cry* frames its big sky, flat land backdrop with a decidedly East Coast sensibility. Peirce's film casts Manhattan icon Chloë Sevigny as a small town factory girl and filters its true crime material through the prism of New Queer Cinema. A missive from the American Midwest, it is, paradoxically, very New York, very *Village Voice*.

Strange to note, then, that *Boys Don't Cry*'s gender bending concerns fit with a surprising snugness into its stolid heartland setting. After all, the American West has always trumpeted itself as a place of renewal and reinvention, a land where pioneers could throw off the shackles of the past and live the life they always dreamed of. And what is Teena Brandon if not a contemporary update of the 19th-century frontiersman, asexual pioneer who sheds her old skin in Lincoln to become a plaid-shirted lad about town in Falls City?

Peirce elects to keep her protagonist's unhappy Lincoln experiences abbreviated, but the implication is clear. Teena Brandon is more successful as a man than she was as a woman. Rebranded as Brandon Teena, this lonesome petty thief becomes an admired confidant of the local toughs and an object of desire for both single mum Candace and town temptress Lana. By playing Brandon this way, Peirce effectively turns the whole macho West on its Stetsoned head. In contrast with the self-possessed Candace and Lana, the film's two main male characters, John and Tom, are an insecure, emasculated ex-con and a subordinated self-abuser respectively. Both find themselves decisively out-boyed by the handsome, sexually adept newcomer Brandon Teena who knows exactly how to please women, both carnally and emotionally.

Not that *Boys Don't Cry* is ever so obvious, so explicit in its gender politics. On the contrary, Peirce's picture is marked throughout by a lovely, lyrical ambiguity. Despite the sheer gut-churning horror of its central rape scene, the perpetrators are never demonised as brutish monsters, and while Peirce stacks the cards substantially in Brandon's favour (the director has admitted she "fell in love" with the character during the making of the film), Hilary Swank's wary, edgy interpretation saves him from becoming a simple martyr. Most impressive of all is Sevigny's perfectly weighted *tour de force* as Lana. For a start, the actress hits the right note physically: her heavy-jawed beauty contrasts nicely with Swank's more refined, aquiline looks and further blurs the tale's gender roles.

More importantly, Sevigny manages to conjure Lana into an astonishingly subtle and unreadable creature. We peg her for a dupe—a naive white-trash vixen who's in for a big surprise—only to realise that she is actually two steps ahead of everyone else. The enigmatic Brandon offers Lana a way out of her rut and the possibility of a real and lasting love. To quote the title of a Flannery O'Connor story, this girl understands a good man is hard to find. *(Boys Don't Cry*'s atmosphere of surrealism and inarticulacy recalls O'Connor's similarly strange and depressed fictional worlds.)

Lana knows what she knows, trusts in her lover and is reluctant to dig any deeper. In the end, the relationship between Brandon and Lana turns out to be the crowning glory of *Boys Don't Cry*.

On a stylistic level, of course, this poetic slice of trailer park blues also takes its lead from the true-crime prose of *In Cold Blood* and *The Executioners Song* or Terrence Malick's lovers on the-run classic *Badlands* (1973, similarly based on a true story). But in its themes, implications, and its haunting emotional resonance, Peirce's film stands alone. *Boys Don't Cry* is a crime story, a queer Western, a boy-meets-girl romance. It runs throughout on an almost unbearable sexual tension. In doing so, it shows the strange—and yes, beautiful ways that love can go.

VILLAGE VOICE, 10/5/99, p. 201, J. Hoberman

Good-looking stranger moves to a small town, changing lives while harboring a secret past. *Mumford* [see Hoberman's review] and *Boys Don't Cry*—two hits at the recent Toronto Film Festival—are tales from the heartland, accounts of second chances taken and personal reinventions tried. Though equally all-American, they might be set on different planets. One is an amiable, Capra-esque fairy tale, the other a violent nightmare of tabloid truth.

Boys Don't Cry, recounts the lurid, shocking fate of 21-year-old drag king Brandon Teena—a narrative that, since it was first reported in the *Voice* five years ago, has served as the basis for numerous daytime TV shows, a 19-page *New Yorker* piece, and videomaker Shu Lea Cheang's interactive artwork, as well as a documentary shown at Film Forum last fall.

As directed by Kimberly Peirce, who cowrote the impressively lean script with fellow Columbia alum Andy Bienen, the Brandon Teena story has the awe-inspiring horror of Greek tragedy and the flaming trajectory of a Roman candle. The movie is both thoughtful and visceral. Teena Brandon of Lincoln, Nebraska, changes her gender and moves to nearby Falls City. Successfully romancing several girls until found out, s/he is brutally raped and consequently executed, along with two others, by a pair of local thugs, Thomas Nissen and John Lotter.

Peirce sets this taboo-breaking, gender-confounding tale in a near-magical realm of rich, saturated colors and velvet honky-tonk nights. Drifting around, Brandon (Hilary Swank) connects with a clan of dissolute bad-boys and their dissatisfied girlfriends, some with babies and most working the late shift. A happy, polite, androgynous little bantam who pals with the guys, appreciates the girls, and is inexplicably drawn to their kids, Brandon is living in low-rent wonderland. The film is almost entirely nocturnal and, thanks to Jim Denault's exemplary cinematography, unfolds in a shadowy, glamorous void of disappearing roads and illuminated refineries.

The world is presented through Brandon's reborn eyes. Viewed with a mixture of desire and empathy, the girls are lush, soft, and delightfully clueless. Brandon is smitten by the gangly, diffident Lana (Chloë Sevigny), whom he recognizes and successfully pursues as a potential partner in fantasy—her ambition is to become a professional karaoke singer. The guys, John (Peter Sarsgaard) and Tom (Brendan Sexton III), are scarcely less fascinating but far more dangerous. These are the irrational others whose horsing around and violent, self-mutilating ways Brandon must learn to keep from being branded a hopeless pussy. Mimicking the mimicry of manhood, Swank gives a fascinating double performance—although *Boys Don't Cry* is rich with skillful characterizations (Alicia Goranson as Lana's sweetly bovine friend, Jeannetta Arnette as her defeated, alcoholic mother).

From Lana's perspective, the hot but solicitous Brandon is a new sort of man. *Boys Don't Cry* strongly (and reasonably) suggests that, on some barely unconscious level, Lana knows that her dream lover is female and doesn't care. Don't ask, don't tell. Brandon has had to solve many technical problems—tampon consumption not the least—but there's an undeniable grandeur to Lana's absolute denial. The reality principle finally intrudes when Brandon is busted as a result of an old speeding ticket. The scene in which Lana bails him out of jail—ignoring his feeble explanation for having been locked up in the women's cell—is one of the movie's few daytime occurrences.

For Lana, the true Brandon lives by night. He has not only reconfigured gender but reinvented the sex act *just for them* . The night the couple subsequently spend together in a turquoise sedan is shot as science fiction—the parked pleasure dome lit from within, as though temporarily sheltering E.T. In this sense, *Boys Don't Cry* is far more convulsively romantic than David Cronenberg's dour adaptation of the similarly gender-bent *M. Butterfly*. Even when Brandon is visibly exposed, Lana fights to preserve the enchantment, screaming for John and Tom to "leave him alone."

Coproduced by the tireless Christine Vachon, *Boys Don't Cry* has a family resemblance to *I Shot Andy Warhol,* which she produced in 1996. Like the Warhol film, *Boys Don't Cry* is a polished first feature, ripped from the headlines and constructed around a stellar stunt performance. More crucially, both movies are intelligently glamorous evocations of sexual insurrection. But where Valerie Solanas the antiheroine of *I Shot Andy Warhol* was her own ideologue, the surreal being at the heart of *Boys Don't Cry* left no text beyond a dreadful martyrdom. Hence, the temptation to temper the tragedy with tendentiousness.

The scene in which totally accepting Lana and finally exposed Brandon make love as themselves is so transcendently sentimental it should have been set in the Garden of Eden or accompanied by a celestial choir. Still, the writing on the whole is so adroit, the performances so nuanced, and the material so compelling one barely notices this nod toward sexual correctness. *Boys Don't Cry* scorches the screen like a prairie fire, as "Brandon" is consumed by desire and consigned to oblivion.

Also reviewed in:
CHICAGO TRIBUNE, 10/22/99, Friday/p. L, Mark Caro
NATION, 11/8/99, p. 35, Stuart Klawans
NEW YORK TIMES, 10/1/99, p. E10, Janet Maslin
NEW YORKER, 10/18 & 25/99, p. 252, David Denby
VARIETY, 9/6-12/99, p. 61, Emanuel Levy

WASHINGTON POST, 10/22/99, p. C1, Stephen Hunter
WASHINGTON POST, 10/22/99, Weekend/p. 47, Desson Howe

BREAKFAST OF CHAMPIONS

A Hollywood Pictures and Flying Heart Films release. *Producer:* David Blocker and David Willis. *Director:* Alan Rudolph. *Screenplay:* Alan Rudolph. *Based on the novel by:* Kurt Vonnegut, Jr. *Director of Photography:* Elliot Davis. *Editor:* Suzy Elmiger. *Music:* Mark Isham. *Music Editor:* Steve Borne. *Sound:* Susumu Tokunow. *Sound Editor:* Paul P. Soucek and Eliza A. Paley. *Casting:* Pam Dixon Mickelson. *Production Designer:* Nina Ruscio. *Art Director:* Randy Eriksen. *Set Decorator:* K.C. Fox and Bob Fox. *Set Dresser:* Mike Vojvoda, Mara Massey, Max Brehme, and John Garrett. *Special Effects:* Bobby Riggs. *Animator:* Ingin Kim. *Costumes:* Rudy Dillon. *Make-up:* Gerald Quist. *Stunt Coordinator:* Greg Walker. *Running time:* 110 minutes. *MPAA Rating:* R.

CAST: Bruce Willis (Dwayne Hoover); Albert Finney (Kilgore Trout); Nick Nolte (Harry Le Sabre); Barbara Hershey (Celia Hoover); Glenne Headly (Francine Pefko); Lukas Haas (Bunny Hoover); Omar Epps (Wayne Hoobler); Buck Henry (Fred T. Barry); Vicki Lewis (Grace Le Sabre); Ken Campbell (Eliot Rosewater); Jake Johannsen (Bill Bailey); Will Patton (Moe); Chip Zien (Andy Wojeckowzski); Ken Campbell (Gilbert); Owen Wilson (Monte Rapid); Alison Eastwood (Maria Maritmo); Shawnee Smith (Bonnie MacMahon); Michael Jai White (Howell); Keith Joe Dick (Vernon Garr); Diane Dick (Rosemary Garr); Michael Duncan (Eli); Lahmard Tate (Elmore); Kurt Vonnegut, Jr. (Commercial Director); Dawn Didawick (Lottie); Bill Nagel (EPA Lawyer); Karl Wiedergott (Homer); Patti Allison (Blossom); Alexa Robbins (Art Hostess "Kaye"); Debra Dusay (Art Hostess "Faye"); Tom Robbins (Pesky Webber); Raymond O'Connor (Rabo Karebekian); Tisha Sterling (Beatrice Keedsler); Matt Callahan (Zeke the Gas Station Attendant); Tracey Lee Mapstone (Mailwoman); Mary Kennedy (Waitress); Greg Walker (Highway Patrolman); David Blampied (Prison Guard); Greg Moore (Porn Store Patron); Doug Hamblin (Mugger); David Blampied (NY Policeman); Patrice Thomas (NY Policewoman); Nancy Volle (Marlo); Danielle Kennedy (Motel Clerk); Scout Willis (Young Girl); Nicolas Small (Young Boy); Denise Simone ("Blue Monday" Housewife); Russell Wilson ("Blue Monday" Doctor); Scott Beauchemin ("Trypepton" Husband); Kassandra Kay ("Trypepton" Wife); Ken Odom ("Prodigal Life" Husband); Erica Evans ("Prodigal Life" Wife); David Kyle ("Prodigal Life" Child); Richard Sheehan (Voice-Over).

LOS ANGELES TIMES, 9/17/99, Calendar/p. 12, Kevin Thomas

For years, writer-director Alan Rudolph had wanted to film Kurt Vonnegut Jr.'s "Breakfast of Champions," a dark, satirical comedy of middle-aged, Middle American angst, and Bruce Willis finally made his dream come true by signing on both as star and, in an uncredited role, executive producer. With Willis in place as Dwayne Hoover, the most successful car dealer in the Four Corners region of the U.S. and the most trusted citizen of Midland City, Albert Finney, Nick Nolte, Barbara Hershey, Glenne Headly, Lukas Haas and Omar Epps came aboard.

This starry ensemble dazzles, but the film never comes fully alive until its climactic 20 minutes, which are deeply moving. That's a lot to ask of audiences, but those who value the big attempt over the easy success—and especially those who know and cherish the novel—may well feel rewarded for their patience.

Dwayne is becoming unglued. His ultra-square suits, the combed-over hair, the prissy round-lens glasses have become as much a straitjacket as the TV commercials he delivers with such gusto, which have made him such a local celebrity that he's a veritable deity. He's a modern-day Babbitt who has played by the rules and won big, only to find himself lonely and isolated and feeling increasingly at odds with the image and values he has projected so successfully.

His wife, Celia (Hershey), has become a TV addict who never leaves the bedroom and who can no longer know whether to trust the man who is her husband or the man she sees constantly on TV. Their only son (Haas) is pursuing a career as a lounge singer at a local club, where he bills himself "Bunny Hoover" and seems to be taking his sartorial tips from Liberace. Epps plays a convict named Wayne Hoobler, who has become so obsessed with the similarity between his name and that of the car dealer he's come to know on TV that, once free, he heads to Midland City.

Dwayne no longer gets comfort from his affair with his secretary Francine (Headly), who is terrifically sexy but is a cliche-spouting airhead with whom it is impossible to have any kind of genuine relationship. She does, however, come up with an idea that Dwayne grabs at as possible salvation: She thinks he should seek out writer Kilgore Trout (Finney), so obscure and unsuccessful that his work is published only in porn magazines and in paperbacks with lurid sexploitation covers. Trout, a scruffy mountain man with only a parrot for companionship, is hitchhiking to Midland City to be honored at its first arts festival, sponsored by a rich local eccentric and rabid Trout fan (Ken Campbell).

Francine thinks maybe Trout will have some answers for Dwayne.

Meanwhile, Dwayne's lifelong pal and crack sales manager, Harry Le Sabre (Nolte), is himself in an increasingly bad way, convinced that it's going to come out that he wears women's lacy red lingerie under his somber suits and when making love with his accepting wife, Grace (Vicki Lewis). Grace, who's the only liberated individual we meet, assures him confidently that "we're the only people in this town who have any kind of sex life—you should be proud." But he's not hearing her, and when Dwayne calls him into his office, he's convinced his boss has found out his secret; in fact, Dwayne is actually looking for moral support.

The men rant and rave, never really hearing each other at all. Willis and Nolte are amazing in this sequence, at once very funny and very sad in their total lack of communication. As the film progresses, Trout, the reclusive reprobate, seems increasingly wise and sane—but if and when they should meet, will he be able to get Dwayne to find any consolation in the classic philosopher's stance: It's the questions you pose, not answers you find, that are important?

In short, there's a lot going on in "Breakfast of Champions," which takes its title from an expression invariably used by a cheery cocktail waitress when she's presenting a martini to a customer early in the day.

Rudolph keeps things going briskly, but his entire approach to "Breakfast of Champions" is highly problematic.

The film has a deliberately garish look and features a lot of cartoonish Pop Art fantasy touches that create an aura of overwhelming artificiality. The effect is to make everything and everyone seem unreal, a feeling heightened by the fact that it's impossible to believe that in contemporary America, when the film is set, a small-city car dealer could attain such status in the era of cable and every sort of media blitz. When TV was new in Los Angeles, for example, colorful hucksters such as Fletcher Jones, the Yeakel Brothers and Madman Muntz did become figures of local folklore—but that was nearly half a century ago.

Rudolph might well have profitably set "Breakfast of Champions" that far back—or at the very least the early '70s, when the book came out and when the Vietnam War was raging—to give a contrasting edge to Vonnegut's concern with raging consumerism, a by-now-familiar target. (That gifted composer Mark Isham incorporates a clutch of exotic Martin Denny standards from the '50s is inspired and adds to the feeling that the further back in the past, the better for this material.)

As it is, "Breakfast of Champions" is too in-your-face, too heavily satirical in its look, and its ideas not as fresh as they should be. For the film to have grabbed us from the start, Rudolph needed to make a sharper differentiation between the everyday world his people live in and the vivid world of their tormented imaginations. You wish that Dwayne and Harry, so brilliantly played by Willis and Nolte in all their pain and ludicrousness, could have seemed more real and less caricatured. Ironically, "Breakfast of Champions" was filmed largely in Twin Falls, Ida., which is the name of a current venturesome film about conjoined brothers—and one which handles feelings of longing and desperation in a more believable universe than the one depicted here.

NEW YORK POST, 9/17/99, p. 42, Jonathan Foreman

"Breakfast of Champions" is an adaptation of Kurt Vonnegut's 1972 book of the same name, and it doesn't work.

The novel was very much an artifact of its time, a clever post—'60s attack on America's out-of-control consumerist culture, which took the form of a faux-naif fable. It was the kind of book that had an enormous appeal for teenagers—myself included.

Writer-director Alan Rudolph has reset the story in the present day, but hasn't updated Vonnegut's hippie-ish take on America. The result is a crude, manic and embarrassingly unfunny satire that feels off from beginning to end.

Car dealer Dwayne Hoover (Bruce Willis), the richest and most beloved man in Midland City, is beginning to go nuts. His wife (Barbara Hershey) is already nuts. His son, Bunny, is a military-school student turned gay lounge singer.

Everyone loves and trusts Dwayne, but even those closest to him—such as his mistress, Francine (Glenne Headly), and his right-hand man Harry Le Sabre (Nick Nolte)—don't really understand that he is losing his mind.

Meanwhile, impoverished science-fiction writer Kilgore Trout (Albert Finney) is making his way to Midland City to be the guest of honor at the town's first arts festival. When Hoover and Trout meet, their conversation will send Hoover over the edge into violent madness—but also point him toward redemption.

It's not an easy book to adapt for the screen. But Alan Rudolph's attempts to update the story are almost all pointless or crass. He takes one of the book's smaller side plots—the fact that Le Sabre likes to dress up in women's clothes—and makes it a centerpiece of the movie.

And the dialogue he has retained from the novel reveals an extraordinary deafness to the book's tone.

The saddest thing about "Breakfast of Champions" is that a really good cast works so hard to breathe life into it. Nolte and Omar Epps are particularly good. Unfortunately, Rudolph has Willis play Hoover with a broadness reminiscent of his equally unbelievable role in "Death Becomes Her."

The best thing about "Breakfast of Champions" is a terrific lounge music score.

NEWSDAY, 9/17/99, Part II/p. B3, Gene Seymour

When Alan Rudolph gets in a goofy mood, he's like no other filmmaker in America. This, in no way, implies that what results from Rudolph's highbrow eccentricity is always a good thing. But even those who disliked such over-the-top films as "Choose Me" (1984), "Trouble in Mind" (1985), "Equinox" (1993) or "Afterglow" (1997) couldn't mistake them for any other movie sanctioned by Hollywood. As the masses get less tolerant of sustained quirkiness, those who like having Rudolph around feel the need to protect his movies from harm the way you save ugly, abandoned puppies from blizzards.

The latest endangered-mutant product of Rudolph's exotic mind is "Breakfast of Champions," a hyperbolic adaptation of Kurt Vonnegut's surreal 1973 novel of middle-American angst that has "Too Weird to Live" tattooed across every frame.

You just know it's going to get kicked and jumped on from all sides of the cultural mainstream. At times, you can even understand their point.

Yet, so help me, this crazy thing held me in its tight, clammy grip from the time Dwayne Hoover (a baby-smooth and jittery Bruce Willis) is shown shoving the barrel of a revolver in his mouth. Hoover, a car dealer whose round-the-clock TV ads have made him one of Midland City's most famous men, is losing his mind in chunks. His wife (Barbara Hershey) has all but checked out of the known universe. His son (Lukas Haas) has become a fey crooner at the local motel lounge.

Dwayne has picked a heck of a week to wonder what the meaning of life is. Harry Le Sabre (Nick Nolte), Dwayne's sales manager, is wound just as tightly over worries that the boss knows about his habit of wearing women's clothes. A mentally challenged ex-con named Wayne Hoobler (Omar Epps) follows what he thinks is his destiny by moving into Hoover's car lot. True destiny, meanwhile, staggers to Midland City—and Dwayne's spiraling life—in the form of a grizzled science-fiction hack writer named Kilgore Trout (Albert Finney).

Though Rudolph's adaptation shaves off some of the darker edges of Vonnegut's book, he keeps this story in frenzy's red zone. If you can stand the tumult, you may find yourself feeling giddy as you watch old pros like Nolte, Willis, Hershey and, especially, Finney play at such a high pitch. Epps' perpetually smiling visage may put off some people. Yet his character's mismatched, shabby wardrobe and inappropriate optimism embody the whole enterprise. Don't be surprised if, at the end, you're also grinning for no good reason.

SIGHT AND SOUND, 9/00, p. 38, Edward Lawrenson

Midland City, the US, the present. Having failed to go through with a suicide attempt, Pontiac car salesman Dwayne Hoover bids goodbye to his depressed wife Celia and leaves for work. Pulp science fiction writer Kilgore Trout, meanwhile, has been invited by millionaire admirer Eliot Rosewater to an art festival he's bank-rolling in the city. Curious, the writer begins to hitchhike there from Detroit.

At Hoover's showroom, car salesman and secret cross dresser Harry Le Sabre mistakenly thinks that Hoover, his boss, knows he's a transvestite. Later, Hoover slips away with his employee Francine and has sex with her in a hotel.

Afterwards, he runs into his son, cocktail pianist Bunny, whom he's disowned for being gay. Wayne Hoobler, who has been obsessed with Hoover while serving time at Shepardstown Adult Correctional Centre, a nearby prison, is released and camps out at Hoover's showroom; Le Sabre, meanwhile, reveals his penchant for wearing women's clothes live on television while advertising Hoover's showroom. Trout makes it to the festival hotel as Hoover—in the throes of a mental breakdown—checks in. At the festival, Hoover meets Trout, attacks Bunny and runs off. On the outskirts of the city, Hoover is reconciled with Bunny and Celia.

In the preface to his 1973 novel *Breakfast Of Champions,* Kurt Vonnegut admits writing the book was a way to clear his head of "all the junk in there". This authorial aside is typical Vonnegut: chatty, confessional and self-deprecatory. And it's this sprightly tone which makes his rather dated satire on consumerism worth reading. Interspersing his tale of car salesman Dwayne Hoover's breakdown with frivolous illustrations and his alter-ego novelist Kilgore Trout's darkly comic observations on life—at one point, Kilgore tells us he wants his epitaph to read, "He tried"—Vonnegut at least makes a pretty display of all the junk he disgorges.

Sadly, director Alan Rudolph's adaptation has none of this assured lightness of touch. Structurally, the film is a mess: on screen, the novel's digressive, anecdotal narrative seems directionless and muddled. Trout's long trek, for instance, across the US for an arts festival in Midland City is ponderously done; and when he finally gets there, his brief scenes with Hoover are curiously throwaway, their dialogue heavy on allusive aphorisms ("It's all life, so make use of it"). For most of the film, Albert Finney's performance as Trout is one long monologue: muffled by a thick coat and fur hat, the writer's wheezy pronouncements can be enjoyable, but Finney has none of the old-man insouciance of the novel's Trout. There, Trout talked to his pet bird because he wanted to and didn't care if it seemed weird; in the film, he also talks to his bird, but this time it feels like a handy way for Rudolph to impart crucial plot points.

But the film is at its most disappointing depicting Hoover's mental breakdown. When we first see the successful car salesman, he's quivering in his bathroom, with a gun jammed in his mouth. And that's about the sanest he gets; from then on, it's all unhinged histrionics, maudlin asides and uncalled-for assaults on his mild-mannered employees. Bruce Willis attacks the part at full throttle. But while the partly self-financed film is no vanity project—at one point, after sex with his secretary in a cheap hotel, Hoover's brush-over hairstyle peels away from his bald patch and falls limply to one side—Willis' performance, all madness, no method, soon feels embarrassingly indulgent. Rudolph—best known for such romantic dramas as *Afterglow*—has a reputation as an actor's director, but here his impressive cast, including Nick Nolte as a cross-dressing car salesman and Omar Epps as Hoover's harmless stalker, are allowed to over-act wildly. Despite a few rather forced visual flourishes—feet sinking into a CGI pavement as if it's made of treacle—Rudolph relies largely on crudely overblown acting styles to convey Hoover's increasingly skewed world view. At times, the result leaves you thinking of an actors' improvisation session gone badly wrong. Judging from the film's perfunctory UK release, it seems the distributors are quietly burying *Breakfast of Champions.* And in the end, the kindest comment you can make about Rudolph is the very thing Kilgore Trout wanted on his tombstone: he tried.

VILLAGE VOICE, 9/28/99, p. 126, Amy Taubman

Alan Rudolph's *Breakfast of Champions,* an adaptation of Kurt Vonnegut Jr.'s surreal comic novel about the routine madness of American life, suffers from a saccharine ending, but that's hardly its worst problem. Another middle-aged male-crisis opus, it begins on a note of total migraine-inducing hysteria, which continues unabated throughout.

Bruce Willis plays Dwayne Hoover, owner of a used-car franchise, whose TV commercials have made him the biggest celebrity and most trusted man in his prefab, strip-malled Midwestern town. In wire-framed glasses and a plastered-down rug that dips discreetly onto his forehead, Willis looks exactly like Buck Henry, which would be weird enough were Henry not also in the film (looking, of course, nothing like himself because he's 25 years older than he was when he became an American comic icon).

How we've substituted icons and tacky television commercials for real life is part of the horror that *Breakfast of Champions* tries to deal with. I guess it's also part of what drives poor Dwayne, his pill-popping wife (Barbara Hershey), and his sales manager (Nick Nolte) over the edge, although the film is too frantic to allow one enough mental space to make connections. Like all the actors, Nolte is too one-note, but it's a hoot to see him in red-lace undies—the sales manager is a closeted cross-dresser who can't resist dropping his trousers for the omnipresent television cameras. Albert Finney has the most thankless role and gives the most eye-rolling, jaw-waggling performance as an unrecognized great writer who hitchhikes cross-country and wades through the bubbling blue industrial-waste swamp behind Dwayne's car lot to deliver the message that saves the day. And high time he got there, I thought, fleeing the theater, feeling as if I'd been beaten head to toe with a bag full of tennis balls.

Also reviewed in:
NEW REPUBLIC, 10/18/99, p. 28, Stanley Kauffmann
NEW YORK TIMES, 9/17/99, p. E14, Stephen Holden
VARIETY, 2/22-28/99, p. 58, Derek Elley

BRINGING OUT THE DEAD

A Paramount Pictures and Touchstone Pictures release of a Scott Rudin-Cappa/De Fina production. *Executive Producer:* Adam Schroeder and Bruce S. Pustin. *Producer:* Scott Rudin and Barbara De Fina. *Director:* Martin Scorsese. *Screenplay:* Paul Schrader. *Based on the novel by:* Joe Connelly. *Director of Photography:* Robert Richardson. *Editor:* Thelma Schoonmaker. *Music:* Elmer Bernstein. *Music Editor:* Kathy Durning and Bobby Mackston. *Sound:* James J. Sabat and (music) Dan Wallin. *Sound Editor:* Philip Stockton. *Casting:* Ellen Lewis. *Production Designer:* Dante Ferretti. *Art Director:* Robert Guerra. *Set Decorator:* William F. Reynolds. *Costumes:* Rita Ryack. *Make-up:* Linda A. Grimes. *Make-up (Special Effects):* Manlio Rocchetti. *Stunt Coordinator:* G.A. Aguilar. *Running time:* 115 minutes. *MPAA Rating:* R.

CAST: Nicolas Cage (Frank Pierce); Patricia Arquette (Mary Burke); John Goodman (Larry); Ving Rhames (Marcus); Tom Sizemore (Tom Walls); Marc Anthony (Noel); Mary Beth Hurt (Nurse Constance); Cliff Curtis (Cy Coates); Nestor Serrano (Doctor Hazmat); Aida Turturro (Nurse Crupp); Sonja Sohn (Kanita); Cynthia Roman (Rose); Afemo Omilami (Griss); Cullen Oliver Johnson (Mr. Burke); Arthur Nascarella (Captain Barney); Martin Scorsese (Dispatcher); Julyana Soelistyo (Sister Fetus); Graciela Lecube and Marylouise Burke (Neighbor Women); Phyllis Somerville (Mrs. Burke); Mary Diveny (Neighbor Woman); Tom Riis Farrell (John Burke); Aleks Shaklin and Leonid Citer (Arguing Russians); Jesus A. Del Rosario, Jr. (Man with Bloody Foot); Larry Fessenden (Cokehead); Bernie Friedman (Big Feet); Theo Kogan and Fuschia Walker (Prostitutes); John Heffernan (Mr. Oh); Matthew Maher, Bronson Dudley, and Marilyn McDonald (Mr. Oh's Friends); Ed Jupp, Jr. and J. Stanford Hoffman (Homeless Men in Waiting Room); Rita Norona Schrager (Concerned Hispanic Aunt); Don Berry (Naked Man); Mtume Gant (Street Punk); Michael A. Noto (Grunt); Omar Sharif Scroggins (Bystander);

Mums (Voice in Crowd); Michael Kenneth Williams (Drug Dealer); Andrew Davoli (Stanley); Charlene Hunter (Miss Williams); Jesse Malin (Club Doorman); Harper Simon (I.B. Bangin'); Joseph Monroe Webb (Drummer); Jon Abrahams (Club Bystander); Charis Michelson (I.B.'s Girlfriend); Lia Yang (Doctor Milagros); Antone Pagán (Arrested Man); Melissa Marsala (Bridge & Tunnel Girl); Betty Miller (Weeping Woman); Rosemary Gomez (Pregnant Maria); Luis Rodriguez (Carlos); Sylva Kelegian (Crackhead); Frank Ciornei (Doctor Mishra); Catrina Ganey (Nurse Odette); Jennifer Lane Newman (Nurse Advisor); John Bal and Raymond Cassar (Police in Hospital); Tom Cappadona, Jack O'Connell, and Randy Foster (Drunks); Richard Spore (Homeless Suicidal); James Hanlon and Chris Edwards (Firemen); Mark Giordano (Police Sergeant); Michael Mulheren and David Zayas (Cops in Elevator); Terry Serpico, Brian Smyl, and Floyd Resnick (Cops); Megan Leigh (Surgeon); David Vasquez (Screaming Man); Judy Reyes and Joseph Reidy (ICU Nurses); Queen Latifah (Voice of Dispatcher Love).

CHRISTIAN SCIENCE MONITOR, 10/22/99, p. 15, David Sterritt

"Cause or effect?" asked a headline in Variety, the entertainment trade paper, over a recent article on whether movie violence produces social ills or simply reflects them.

"Clear answers were scarce," the report continued, noting that a Hollywood panel on the problem found it too complex for easy solutions.

Whichever answer comes closest to the truth, Hollywood shows few signs of moderating its violent habits. Current movies like Martin Scorsese's disturbing "Bringing Out the Dead" and David Fincher's sadistic "Fight Club" serve up megadoses of bone-crunching images enhanced by high-energy cinematography and eardrum-quivering sound.

These put both pictures beyond the limits of acceptability for moviegoers craving a warmer, more uplifting vision of life. In addition, both pictures show early signs of polarizing the audiences they're primarily aimed at.

Each has enough star power and promotional clout to guarantee a strong start at the box office. But some feel "Bringing Out the Dead" dilutes Scorsese's stylistic brilliance with too much of the ambiguous philosophizing of screenwriter Paul Schrader ("Taxi Driver," "Raging Bull," "Affliction"). And rumblings are being heard from Fincher fans who think "Fight Club" substitutes action-fantasy clichés for the sardonic originality of his earlier "Seven" and "The Game."

Whatever their financial destinies ("Fight Club" was No. 1 at the box office last weekend), what's most interesting about these pictures is not the violence they flaunt but the twists they bring to the "cause or effect" question. In different ways, Scorsese and Fincher both suggest that misery and malaise are running rampant in American society, creating a dehumanized environment in which suffering and brutality are taken as natural parts of life.

Viewed from this angle, "Bringing Out the Dead" and "Fight Club" are noisy wake-up calls that may jolt complacent attitudes even as they capitalize on the less-appealing aspects of current taste.

Taking a cue from TVs popular police and hospital dramas, Bringing Out the Dead focuses on an ambulance driver (Nicolas Cage) whose working hours are filled with one awful emergency after another. On one level, the movie—set in central Manhattan, not a slum or ghetto—is a catalog of how many horrors can erupt (drugs, crime, exploitation) in a modern city. Deeper down, it's a heartfelt cry of rage against these evils, as experienced by a protagonist who's literally haunted by the people he's tried and failed to save during his harrowing career.

While the story is underscored by Scorsese's trademark bursts of visual expressionism, its driving force is the murky but sincere humanism of Schrader's screenplay, which sees every new affliction as an opportunity for self-sacrifice and perhaps redemption.

Being an all-too-ordinary human who never asked to be a hero, Cage's character bungles these opportunities with amazing regularity. But their presence is a sign that "Bringing Out the Dead" has more on its mind than the depictions of decay and despair that provide much of its content.

Fight Club begins with the fashionable pop-culture message that middle-class life is too boring and brainless for a truly cool person to put up with. Freed from this tedium when an explosion destroys his earthly goods, a young man (Edward Norton) teams up with an alienated friend named Tyler (Brad Pitt) to start a new kind of secret society, dedicated to the proposition that feeling a punch in the nose is better than feeling nothing at all.

Their masochistic clique spreads far and wide, and soon Tyler starts planning the next logical step: escalating from personal pain to terrorist violence that will inflict maximum punishment on the society he despises so much.

Sliding from ersatz sociology to sadistic comedy to apocalyptic hallucination, "Fight Club" undermines any seriousness it might have harbored with an avalanche of smirky cynicism designed to flatter the hipper-than-thou fantasies of adolescent moviegoers.

This said, it must be added that the picture offers an implicit critique of its own unpleasant agenda, since the spectacle it provides—full of rage, hate, and aggression—is an obvious equivalent of the fight club itself, which merely adds the extra ingredient of bodily sensation.

Fincher's movie joins "Bringing Out the Dead" in suggesting that social dysfunction breeds a tragic heritage of human pain and suffering. The irony of "Fight Club" is that it embodies the very symptoms it calls attention to.

LOS ANGELES TIMES, 10/22/99, Calendar/p. 1, Kenneth Turan

Like many another Martin Scorsese protagonist, Frank Pierce is looking for salvation. The difference in the gritty, hallucinatory "Bringing Out the Dead" is that he's doing it while simultaneously trying to save other people.

Based on a novel by Joe Connelly, who spent nearly a decade as an Emergency Medical Services paramedic on the surreal and (yes) mean streets of Manhattan, "Bringing Out the Dead" is at its best capturing the crazed cacophony of lives sustained by adrenaline and coffee, as feckless ambulance personnel fling themselves into the maw of the city at night in a whirl of sirens, anxiety and blinking lights.

This, as the film's notes take pains to point out, is the pre-Mayor Rudy Giuliani early 1990s New York, when all the circles of hell seemed to be concentrated on one small island. As the hour grows later, each person encountered is crazier, more desperate, more dangerous than the last, and working the late shift into the wee hours is like living in a permanent dark night of the soul.

It's not surprising that director Scorsese and frequent screenwriting collaborator Paul Schrader were drawn to this material: One early review of the book even claimed "it does for ambulances what the movie 'Taxi Driver' did for Yellow Cabs." And, in everything from shots of emergency vehicles moving through clouds of steam to its fascination with violence and lives lived on the edge, "Bringing Out the Dead" provides a quarter-century-later bookend to that early effort.

Working with virtuoso cinematographer Robert Richardson (an Oscar winner for "JFK") and longtime editing collaborator Thelma Schoonmaker, Scorsese turns this project into an impressive exercise in visual style that compensates, up to a point, for the film's parallel deficiency, a kind of emotional coldness that may simply go with the territory. Though there's no denying that this is beautiful filmmaking, "Bringing Out the Dead" is a film you admire more than warm up to.

Obviously jazzed by the rush inherent in the subject matter, Scorsese and company have produced an effortless variety of visual looks and inventive camera placements, all played against an eclectic soundtrack that finds room for 10,000 Maniacs, the Marvelettes and the Melodians.

Pierce (a spaced-out Nicolas Cage) has, after five years with EMS, simply been on the job too long. A walking Nineteenth Nervous Breakdown, he tells everyone who will listen that he can't take the carnage anymore. But he's got no sick time left and, in a Catch-22 situation, the more desperate he is to get fired the more his bosses adamantly refuse to dismiss him.

Frank also fails to get sympathy from the three partners he works with in the 56 consecutive hours—two days and three nights—we spend in his company. Larry (John Goodman) is just marking time, Marcus (a delightful Ving Rhames) has embraced Jesus, and Tom Walls (Tom Sizemore) lives only to inflict punishment. These options for dissociation have varying degrees of validity, but none of them work for Frank.

It's no shock that Frank's feeling more like "a grief mop" than a valued member of society: Given the hellacious living nightmare world he works in, it's amazing it didn't happen sooner. Night after night, the dispatchers (the unseen voices of director Scorsese and Queen Latifah) relay the bizarre, dispiriting news: Woman reports roach in her ear, man sets his pants on fire, elderly woman abducted by her cat. And that's on a slow night.

Frank's motto used to be "Help others and you help yourself," but lately that's not been working for him. It's partially because he hasn't saved anyone's life in months, and saving lives is the grail of paramedic work, "like falling in love, the greatest day in the world." Instead he's burdened by dealing with the likes of Mr. Oh, the malodorous homeless man who is the EMS' most frequent flier.

But more than that, Frank, who grew up in the same Hell's Kitchen neighborhood he now drives in, is haunted by the ghosts of the people who died on his watch. He's especially shadowed by the spirit of Rose, an 18-year-old asthmatic whose death he feels particularly responsible for and whose presence he sees everywhere.

Maybe that's why Frank is attracted to Mary Burke (Patricia Arquette, Cage's real-life wife), the estranged daughter of a heart attack victim he transports to the overflowing Our Lady of Mercy (a.k.a. Our Lady of Misery) emergency room, a chaotic snake pit where unflappable Nurse Constance (Mary Beth Hurt) tells drug users desperate to be helped, "I can't see why we should. If I'm mistaken here, correct me, OK? Did we sell you the cocaine? Did we push that cocaine up your nose?"

As Frank fitfully attempts to connect with Mary, she worries about not only her father but also Noel (singer Marc Anthony), a kid from the neighborhood who's turned into a deranged street person. Meanwhile, the specter of Red Death, a new and potent kind of crack, haunts the neighborhood both Frank and Mary still call home.

Despite the virtuosity with which it's made and the way it's enlivened by periodic use of black humor, "Bringing Out the Dead" has the same kind of difficulty connecting with the audience that Frank has with Mary. Though the argument could be made that poignancy or even warmth is not on its agenda, without something for us to hang onto, this film dances on the edge of flat-lining Just like the DOAs that are Frank's stock-in-trade.

NEW STATESMAN, 1/10/00, p. 47, Jonathan Romney

Downbeat though it is, there's a curious air of nostalgia hovering around Martin Scorsese's new film *Bringing Out the Dead* rather as if your favourite '70s rockband had reformed. For years, Scorsese has been making films that either didn't feel entirely like Scorsese (his contemplative Buddhist epic *Kundun*, the fragrant costumer *The Age of Innocence*) or felt too much like Scorsese, as if he were pastiching himself *(GoodFellas,* the maligned masterpiece *Casino).* But now he has returned to an early stamping ground, the festering, violent New York of *Mean Streets* and *Taxi Driver.* He has also reunited with *Taxi Driver*'s writer Paul Schrader, a man recently lost in the wilderness of his own erratic directing career. Everyone, then, ought to be happy; but *Bring Out the Dead*—adapted from Joe Connelly's novel—doesn't feel entirely like a decisive event. It seems more like one of those sign post films that major directors make, providing tantalising clues while you speculate about their next move. That's the downside to being taken as seriously, watched as closely as Scorsese is: you get far less critical leeway than most directors.

The *déjà vu* begins at the start: vintage Van Morrison blasting out and a title telling we're in New York in the early 90s, before Giuliani and Disney wielded their brooms. The streets are wet with neon, and an ambulance cruises along, close-ups of its horns making them seem heavenly trumpets come to summon dying souls. The driver is Frank Pierce (Nicolas Cage), a man at the end of his tether, battered and punchdrunk from a life of urgency, sleep deprivation and failure. He's part of an absurd machine: condemned for ever to arrive too late to save lives, but repeatedly providing reprieves for the self-destructive crazies who strain the resources of Our Lady of Mercy (or"Misery") Hospital. Frank's personal cross is a young woman named Rose, whom he couldn't save: in a striking digitally achieved dream sequence, he sees her accusing features in every face he passes.

Because of the setting, the writer and the story of a lonely desperado on wheels, *Bringing Out the Dead* has widely been received as a variant on *Taxi Driver.* Like that film's Travis Bickle, Frank fixates on a fallen-angel figure: the significantly named Mary, daughter of a man he has revived from a heart attack. Mary is the film's weak link. This is partly because Patricia Arquette's performance rarely registers more than a bloodless, fatigued void, but largely because the character is so overstated as a spiritual redeemer and redeemee: she could have been a nun, but was a junkie instead, and the film won't be over till she and Frank huddle together in a glow of radiant white. I attribute this to Schrader, who has long been committed to Bresson-style redemptive endings. *Bringing Out the Dead* seems as much like a Schrader film as a Scorsese one: not so much an echo of *Taxi Driver* as of Schrader's own tale of urban angst and insomnia, *Light Sleeper*.

What really interests Scorsese in this story, I think, is less the linear path to daylight and salvation than the business of keeping a chaotic, infernal nightworld spinning with teeming wildlife and sudden explosions of calamity. There are extraordinary turns and moments: Ving Rhames's ebulliently religious orderly persuading a club full of sullen goths to join hands for an OD'd friend; the Cerberus-like ward guard whose perennial threat is to remove his mirror shades; Cliff Curtis as a suave pusher who presides over the Oasis, a narcotic refuge from the city hell and the very heart of that hell. In the film's most memorable, nightmarish scenes, Frank visits the Oasis and undergoes a drugged temptation akin to the one that Scorsese once controversially staged for Christ. When Scorsese perceives grace, it's above all in visual terms: a shower of blowtorch sparks suddenly becomes a full-blown firework display over Manhattan.

Despite the pacing and intense visual urgency (the photography is by Oliver Stone's regular, Robert Richardson), *Bring Out the Dead* feels oddly narcotised, sluggish—although that's entirely in keeping with the state of Frank's soul, caught between the buzz and the void. But what drags the film down are niggling errors of judgement, such as the confused pop soundtrack: Van Morrison and Johnny Thunders are perfect, the Clash, UB40 and REM seriously misplaced. And the serious casting problem is that Nicolas Cage no longer supplies any surprises: we expect from him the brittle rage of a disintegrating soul, but imagine what a revelation Tom Hanks, say, might have provided in that role.

One side effect of the film's oddly narcoleptic all-nighter quality is that I emerged from it feeling washed-out, woozy, not entirely able to take stock of what I'd seen. I suspect this is one of those films that, on release, disappoints everyone, but with time is remembered as having been entirely underrated; it's odd how many Scorsese films fall into this category. *Bringing Out the Dead* may be a noble failure, but it's an urgent, fevered failure. Through the 1990s, Scorsese tended to play the confident, august Visconti-esque maestro, something he does well; but it's a fascinating, if frustrating, shock to get a glimpse again of the nervy, omnivorous hustler.

NEW YORK, 11/1/99, p. 119, Peter Rainer

Martin Scorsese's *Bringing Out the Dead*, scripted by Paul Schrader from the 1998 Joe Connelly novel about paramedics in Hell's Kitchen, is set in the early nineties—the pre-Giuliani years, before the renovations in Times Square and 42nd Street and at the height of the crack epidemic. Only a troll could feel nostalgia for all the sleaze and misery on display here, and yet there's a sense in which Scorsese—who also collaborated with Schrader on *Taxi Driver*—is goosed by the grunge. Once again, this carnival of lost souls gives him the stylistic equivalent of an adrenaline boost; intellectually, Scorsese may not pine for the early nineties, but they're custom-fit for his perpetual theme of redemption through suffering, and the vistas—the steam heat rising like hellfire from the streets, the phalanx of hookers and dopers, the whole vast detritus of the human comedy—leave him rapt. Scorsese used to make movies about this world when it was right on top of him; in *Bringing Out the Dead*, he's serving up what amounts to livid pictographs from the cave of an earlier era. Not too much earlier, though. His point may be that there's still a lot of Then in Now.

Scorsese has the ability to make you look at anything he puts on the screen, and he brings to this movie an aliveness that's doubly remarkable considering how much of it was filmed in the cramped interiors of an ambulance, or in hospital emergency wards, so overly familiar to us from ER and its clones. But ultimately, Scorsese's visual tropes and pirouettes, as well as the themes he plays out once again on these mean streets, are overfamiliar, too. *Bringing Out the Dead* is at once galvanizing and rote.

Nicolas Cage plays paramedic Frank Pierce, who has been working the graveyard shift for Our Lady of Perpetual Mercy hospital for about five years. Over the course of three nights and two days, we see Frank live out the horrors and occasional highs of his job while in a state of almost trancelike sleep deprivation. He sees all around him the specters of the dead he couldn't raise, especially Rose, a homeless teenager he believes he killed while trying to save and whose accusatory gaze bears witness for all who have been lost. When he's not feeling the godlike power of life-giving, Frank is racked with guilt, wanting only to quit his work—to close his eyes and drift off forever. His paramedic partners, one for each night, include the burbly Larry (John Goodman), who regards Frank as a liability; Tom (Tom Sizemore), whose sadistic streak complements Frank's role as ruined angel; and Marcus (Ving Rhames, a real shot in the arm), a lascivious Christian revivalist who sweet-talks his favorite lady dispatcher as if he were Barry White and resuscitates a strung-out doper with ringing prayer.

The only person in the movie with whom Frank can carry on a near-normal conversation is Mary Burke (Patricia Arquette), the estranged daughter of a man he has brought back to life, if not sentience. Mary was going to be a nun once, before she turned to junk. Frank is from roughly the same urban Catholic background as she is; his mother used to tell him he looked like a priest. For those in the audience with an eye for Scorsese's brand of religioso freneticism, it should come as no surprise that this Mary will cradle Frank *Pietà*-style—asleep at last.

When Scorsese and Schrader first read the novel by Joe Connelly, who worked for nine years as a paramedic in New York City, they must have recognized a soul brother. No wonder: The book was influenced by *Taxi Driver* and also *Raging Bull,* which Schrader co-wrote—not so much in its prose, which is less racy than straight-ahead, as in its religious-symbolic textures. The book shares the filmmakers' predilection for what Schrader describes, in the film's press notes, as "occupational metaphors," and it's been rather too faithfully adapted. Frank is saddled with enough metaphorical baggage to sink a tanker. No wonder Nicolas Cage seems slugged most of the time, only occasionally breaking into an inspired scat lunacy.

Frank is a doctor of the streets, an angel of mercy, a giver of life, a priest defrocked by his own suffering, a sinner. New York stands in for a lot, too: This Hell's Kitchen is just that. (Imagine how different the film would be if Frank's beat instead covered, say, the Upper East Side.) The city's skankier nabes undoubtedly have a lot to answer for, but maybe it's time to declare a moratorium on New York's rep as ground zero of all sacrilege: The religio-metaphorical haze in *Bringing Out the Dead* gussies up the horrors. The filmmakers don't recognize, as they did when they made *Taxi Driver,* that the true surrealism of the streets, the true black comedy, is best captured realistically—in the scrupulous, scarily unadorned detail. When Frank aids a drug lord impaled on a spike, and blowtorch-bearing police rescuers shower sparks into the air, the Fourth of July-meets-the Crucifixion tableau is too florid, too fake. And this is the movie's big set piece, no less.

Scorsese doesn't trust the power of simplicity to rock us. He's not looking at hellfire, or anything else, with fresh eyes, and, coming after his last film, the Dalai Lama drama *Kundun,* that's a letdown. Somewhat inert as narrative, *Kundun* was nevertheless an extraordinary stretch: With its ritualism and its patterned palette and its stillnesses, it represented a whole new way of seeing for Scorsese. And a new way of feeling too—a kind of contemplative delirium. *Kundun* was a heroic achievement for a filmmaker so far along in his career, and its commercial failure may have pushed Scorsese back into the safety zone of *Bringing Out the Dead.* His new film is worth seeing, and it's delirious, all right, but it's a delirious recap.

NEW YORK POST, 10/22/99, p. 49, Jonathan Foreman

Downbeat and at times strangely slow-moving despite all its beautifully shot high-speed ambulance rides, "Bringing Out the Dead" is as technically brilliant as you would expect from a film directed by Martin Scorsese.

But thanks to a story that goes nowhere and a shortage of fully drawn characters, it's also a film that leaves your heart untouched. Sure, it's compellingly surreal, and there are bursts of cruelly funny graveyard humor. But in the end there's something cold and alienating about it, as if it were a mere exercise in style.

And the movie's many deliberate echoes of "Taxi Driver," including a Travis Bickle-esque narration over eerie music, only underline the film's relative plotlessness: This is a movie that depicts a man beset by a spiritual crisis without resolving that crisis.

Nicolas Cage is Frank, a paramedic on the edge of collapse. The city he works in is New York, but it looks and feels nothing like contemporary Gotham. This New York—most of the film is set in the West 40s—is a hellish, apocalyptically chaotic place with a degraded, doomed populace. The filthy, graffiti-splattered streets are crawling with junkies, hookers, criminals and an army of ragged homeless people.

The production notes (though not the film itself) take pains to explain that the action is set in the early 1990s. And no Giuliani campaign commercial could ever paint such a powerful picture of the sheer grossness of New York before the current renaissance. You can all but smell the trash spilling over onto the sidewalks.

Frank travels through this infernal city over three nights with three different partners: detached, food-obsessed Larry (John Goodman), fatalistic, religious Marcus (Ving Rhames) and angry, violent Tom (Tom Sizemore).

They have all found ways to deal with the horrors of the job. But Frank has had a long run of not saving any lives and he's falling apart. He survives on booze, caffeine and the ride—but everywhere he goes he sees the ghost of a patient he lost.

One night, he and Larry revive a heart-attack victim (Cullen Oliver Johnson) and bring him to the hospital. The man's good-hearted ex-junkie daughter Mary (Patricia Arquette) strikes a chord in Frank.

She, like Frank, is desperate to find some kind of redemption, but in the course of their strange, delicate relationship she leads Frank instead to the lair of seductive drug dealer Cy Coates (Cliff Curtis).

Cage does a reasonable burned-out Travis Bickle imitation, despite his monotonous voice, but his performance is limited by a storyline that doesn't allow his character to change or grow in any way. Arquette, drab, dowdy and unimpressive, offers little relief. After a while you wish that the film would let you spend more time with the subsidiary characters, all of whom are enlivened with bravura performances.

Goodman, Sizemore (playing a nut case again) and Rhames are all terrific. Mary Beth Hurt and Arthur Nascarella also do fine work as a tough ER doctor and the EMS captain who refuses to fire Frank. And Marc Anthony has real presence as Noel, a dreadlocked crazy homeless man.

NEWSDAY, 10/22/99, Part II/p. B3, John Anderson

Is that the sickly sweet smell of nostalgia coming off "Bringing Out the Dead"? You wouldn't think so. Martin Scorsese's latest, a giddy/somber roller-coaster ride with burnt-out Hell's Kitchen paramedics, is based on the novel by Joe Connelly—which in turn was based on his decade as a city EMS worker when Manhattan was knee-deep in crack vials and slumbering homeless. The movie takes such pains, in fact, to establish itself in pre-Giuliani time—"New York City in the early '90s" reads an introductory title, emphasis on "early"—that it's hard not to read all the subsequent Dickensian squalor and gaga Gotham as a form of GOP fund raiser.

If that's the case, the movie could also serve as a big fat plug for Disney (parent of the movie's co-distributor, Touchstone Pictures), which always gets co-billing in the Rebirth of Manhattan story anyway. But by the end of the film—scripted by longtime Scorsese collaborator Paul Schrader ("Raging Bull," "Taxi Driver," "The Last Temptation of Christ") and thus subject to a certain perverse perspective—one wonders whether "Bringing Out the Dead," as a work of cinema, is really about the price of sociocultural pasteurization. And the essential passion to be lost along the queue for Splash Mountain.

The movie is, after all, a Passion play, a hybrid partially attributable to Schrader's Calvinism and Scorsese's Catholicism. Set over a sweltering "full-moons" weekend, it tours various circles of urban perdition that include emergency rooms, underground tramp communities, dope dens, squatters' digs and the well-scorched mindscape of veteran paramedic Frank Pierce (Nicolas Cage).

Frank's worked too many hours, seen too many deaths—he's particularly haunted by the ripe face of Rose (Cynthia Roman), a young girl he lost when she collapsed on the street and who materializes before him with increasing frequency as he makes his way through the weekend. Gaunt, gray-pallored and frazzled, Frank is taking the ills of the world unto himself like some alcoholic Christ, in an urge to purge himself and his city of its sins.

"Bringing Out the Dead" is about bringing back the dead. Although Frank is trying to get fired, he also needs to save a life—he's gone too long without giving God an assist. But when he finally does—resuscitating the already expired father of his amour-to-be, Mary Burke (Patricia

Arquette)—it doesn't redeem him. The comatose man really wants to die—as he tells Frank, from beyond his air tubes and heart monitor, every time Frank comes into his vicinity.

This a young man's movie; Scorsese is fearless about turning the city into a Tex Avery cartoon or sending Looney Tunes ambulances down melting-neon streets. But the young man often turns out to be himself "Taxi Driver" (1976), the great Schrader-Scorsese collaboration, is evoked with regularity, from its rearview mirror view of the world, to its meditative voice-overs, to its offhanded snapshots of city weirdness—Sister Fetus (Julyana Soelistyo), for instance, a pint-sized nun with a handheld mike exhorting Times Square crowds to a God-fearing existence. In "Taxi Driver," however, Scorsese imposed lyricism onto madness. In "Dead," he lets chaos speak for itself. And the results are just as often numbing as they are eloquent.

"Bringing Out the Dead" is a movie that lives by its supporting players and dies by its leads. Cage, who seems to have sacrificed whatever edge he had to whatever gods were responsible for "Con Air" and "8MM," is adequate; acting isn't really required, since Frank is so erratic and never develops over the course of the film. Arquette is close to awful. When the couple have the screen to themselves, the movie loses its pulse entirely.

But as his various partners—John Goodman, Ving Rhames and, especially, a crazed Tom Sizemore—pick up the film and run with it; Mary Beth Hurt, confined to the movie's "ER"-style ER, is hilarious as a cynical, junkie-baiting nurse. As the deranged Noel, Marc Anthony (of Paul Simon's "Capeman") is thoroughly believable—as is Cliff Curtis, as a pseudo-benevolent drug dealer whose pyrotechnical rescue from a towering Manhattan apartment building leaps from reality to fantasy with breathtaking ease.

One expects that Scorsese could easily have made a more conventionally accessible movie. What one sees in "Dead" is a filmmaker who continues to push, with perhaps mixed but admirable results. In his last feature, "Kundun" (1997), Scorsese sought, and succeeded, in making the spiritual aspirations of the Dalai Lama integral not just to the story but to the process of the film. "Bringing Out the Dead" possesses the irregular heartbeat of its characters, whose lives are a discombobulating mix of adrenaline, boredom, black humor and sobering reality. If that's what the director intended with this unwieldy movie, then you'd have to say he's succeeded.

SIGHT AND SOUND, 1/00, p. 45, Kevin Jackson

New York City, the early 90s. Frank Pierce, an ambulance driver who works the graveyard shift, is close to cracking up. On one mission he revives Mr Burke from a heart attack and rushes him back to the ER at Our Lady of Mercy hospital where he is put on life support. Nonetheless, Frank still feels guilt about the death of Rose, a young woman whose ghostly face he sees everywhere. Like his fellow-drivers—Larry, Marcus and Tom—with whom he works on three successive nights, Frank is enraged by those who use and abuse the service. Frank begins to fall for former drug-user Mary, the daughter of Mr Burke. Frank declares his intention to quit one night after his ambulance crashes. He tries unsuccessfully to get himself fired.

Accompanying Mary to the apartment of Cy, a drug dealer who gives her a powerful drug, Frank follows suit and experiences macabre hallucinations. Back at the ER, Frank seems to hear the disembodied voice of Mr Burke begging Frank to let him die. On another mission, Frank is called to help Cy, who has been impaled on a spiked railing after a rival gang's attack. Later, Frank almost succumbs to the temptation of helping Tom beat up Noel, a local drug casualty, but repents at the last minute. He returns to the ER and, giving in to the ghostly voice, allows Mr Burke to die peacefully. He goes to tell Mary the sad news; she invites him in and cradles him as he drifts towards sleep.

Why, this is hell; we've been here before. The sulphurous visions of nocturnal streets splashed with garish neon and prowled by "whores, skunk pussies, buggers" and other oiks, sneaks and cads; the speed-driven loner who stares at it all with enthralled horror from his roving vehicle as he nurses chronic insomnia and a hypertrophied craving for redemption; the enigmatic young woman, the Beatrice figure, who may both save and be saved—similarities between *Taxi Driver* (1976) and *Bringing Out the Dead* are clear beyond reasonable dispute. The only shouting match worth having just now is whether the new film amounts to director Martin Scorsese and screenwriter Paul Schrader offering us a rich reworking of their original tragic material from the chastened perspective of maturity, something along the lines of, say, *Othello* and *A Winter's Tale*, or sad self-plagiarism.

I'm inclined to agree broadly with David Thompson's contention (S&S December 1999) that the old team's return to familiar turf has produced a very different and, in many respects, very impressive film. Talent aside, much of *Taxi Driver*'s thrilling originality came from the (relative) youthfulness of its makers, and many of its qualities are those found in gifted adolescents: morbidity, introspection, rage, a sense of the world's endemic rottenness and a stubborn refusal of compromise. (A quarter of a century on, the movie still casts a spell on teenagers and on the teenager in grown-ups who should know better.) *Taxi Driver* also made delicious mock of its otherwise dangerously appealing protagonist, since Travis Bickle, "God's lonely man", is not just a psychopath but a goon: Homer Simpson as imagined by Robert Bresson.

Frank Pierce, the driven driver of *Bringing Out the Dead,* just isn't like that. Yes, he's a profoundly troubled man, worn raw by the violence and stress of his job, but he's a good man. And that simple fact may be the very thing that will disappoint some viewers, since one of the most telling differences between the two films is that *Bringing Out the Dead* is far less smitten than its precursor with the glamour of being a misunderstood outsider. "No one asked you to suffer," Mary gently rebukes Frank as she cradles him, pieta-fashion, at the end of his dark working nights of the soul. "That was your idea." Her words, which sound less sententious in Patricia Arquette's quiet, bone weary delivery than in cold print, strike just the right cautionary note of perspective. Frank's martyrdom is at least partly self-elected, as any decent grown-up could have told him.

For all its frequent bloodiness and immaculately crafted frenzies—and some of the film's sequences of ambulances hurtling down the streets are terrifically exciting, all berserk camera angles, cranked-up Clash anthems and spasms of accelerated motion—*Bringing Out the Dead* is unwontedly tender at the core, closer in some ways to Scorsese's overtly religious films such as *The Last Temptation of Christ* or even *Kundun* than to his contemporary thrillers. Nicolas Cage even looks like Christ (like a distressed El Greco painting of Christ that is, not like Willem Dafoe). When the camera dotes intently on his increasingly wan, drawn and bestubbled features on the rare occasions when he laughs or smiles, it's as if his face is quoting somebody else's.

Oddly enough, Frank does have a fair bit to laugh about since *Dead* is heavily interlarded with chunks of fast-talking gallows humour, some of it provided by the ambulance men's radio banter with their off-screen controllers (spoken by Scorsese himself and Queen Latifah), some of it by the tasteless antics they dream up to sweeten their chores. Ving Rhames (a pure joy every time he's on screen as Marcus, one of Frank's partners) has a wonderful scene in which he coerces a bunch of gawky goths to join hands and pray for their overdosed pal. But all the scenes of medics and drivers at work are finely done—pacey, witty and a sight more convincing than ER.

If Scorsese and Schrader hadn't brought humour and authenticity to bear on this loaded material, it would have been a lot closer to *Taxi Driver* and so a lot weaker. Their film firmly places Frank's hyperbolic view of Manhattan/hell (every prostitute's face a dead girl's, every underlit alley or stairwell an out-take from *The Fisher King)* as the distorted vision of stress and drugs and shock and soul-searching. At heart, it seems conceived more in sorrow than in anger, with a hero struggling confusedly towards health rather than towards a convulsive and gratifyingly apocalyptic expression of his sickness. If we persist in finding Scorsese's avenging angels more irresistible than his angels of mercy, that may well be a sign of our unregenerate appetites, not the director's allegedly waning powers. Or, more simply: the devil has all the best goons.

TIME, 10/25/99, p. 118, Richard Schickel

Frank Pierce's life is basically a high-speed pursuit of a state of grace that keeps eluding him. Frank, who in Martin Scorsese's new film *Bringing Out the Dead* is played in a sort of stunned frenzy by Nicolas Cage, is a New York City paramedic working Hell's Kitchen on the aptly named graveyard shift. He's been on the job too long, and lately its only compensation—the rush, the high of saving a life—has eluded him. He's famished, but he can't eat. He's exhausted, but his sleep is haunted, particularly by the vision of a young woman who died as he tried to bring her back from death.

Frank's desperation will remind some people of *Taxi Driver*—and, indeed, the movies share the same director, the same screenwriter (Paul Schrader) and the same ambiance (New York's night streets, teeming with hookers and junkies, quickened with the threat of sudden, pointless death).

There is also, of course, the same sort of harsh yet slightly fantastical realism and the same sort of antisocial protagonist, who thinks his life might be justified if he could just leave these hellish streets behind. The fact that Frank's vantage point is, like Travis Bickle's, a moving vehicle (in Frank's case, an ambulance), from which one's perspective is hasty and incomplete, is another significant parallel.

But there's a key difference between the two characters. Travis was, at the least, a sociopath; Frank, no less than the people he tries to help, is a victim. The movie is powered by his yearning not just for usefulness but also for transcendence. He hungers for peace, meaningful contact and someplace he can rest and heal from the nightly horrors he sees on the job.

His best hope for that is Mary Burke (Patricia Arquette), daughter of a heart-attack victim Frank has brought into the hospital, where the man lingers between life and death and where Mary hangs out, awaiting his fate. In her repressed way, she's as strung out as the medic, and perhaps not good news for him. But she's the only hopeful news in sight, and their tentative flirtation keeps getting interrupted—by cardiac arrests in nightclubs, by the allegedly virgin birth of twins, by the running violence of an often half-naked street person (well played by the singer Marc Anthony, who sports dreadlocks for the role).

Even when nothing is doing, something is doing, for Frank's driver partners are all loony in different ways. John Goodman's false reasonableness, Ving Rhames' born-again religiosity, Tom Sizemore's addiction to violence—nothing about any of them can help Frank. The film is full of casual dark humor, but what's best about it is its resistance to the conventional three-act movie structure. Its string of incident is relentless, virtually undifferentiated, like life, and contains no promise of uplifting resolution. *Bringing Out the Dead* is like its title—blunt, truthful, uncompromising. It is hard on an audience, even harrowing. But that's exactly what Martin Scorsese was put on earth to do.

VILLAGE VOICE, 11/2/99, p. 133, J. Hoberman

Bringing Out the Dead, directed by Martin Scorsese from Paul Schrader's adaptation of Joe Connelly's first-person novel, opens with its paramedic hero's brashly tormented voice-over, as he pilots his EMS vehicle through the rain-slicked, hooker-clogged, neon-reflective, night-scum mean streets of his old neighborhood while the director himself is heard as a hectoring dispatcher. Is this *Being Travis Bickle?*

Actually, *Bringing Out the Dead* is a sort of *Pilgrim's Progress* allegory in which angel of mercy Frank Pierce (Nicolas Cage) shuttles between the blasted nightmare of crack-crazed Hell's Kitchen and the gruesome "heaven" of the emergency-room madhouse at Our Lady of Mercy Hospital. While nothing here matches the cynicism of the ER-set musical ad Spike Jonze produced for Levi's jeans, Frank, who is given to high-flown musings (when not reading Shelley, Calvino, and Céline), has lost his faith. He's burned-out. He yearns to be fired, but his God-like boss won't let him go, so he drinks and rants and, in the course of this monstrous 56-hour shift, keeps running into Mary (Patricia Arquette), an ex-junkie whose brain-dead father is on life support.

Frank rescues Mary from a faux Caribbean underworld presided over by a diabolical smoothie (Cliff Curtis), but *Bringing Out the Dead* is more dependent for drama on the hero's ambulance rapport with his showboat partners—crazy John Goodman, crazier Ving Rhames, and craziest Tom Sizemore. The Rhames character is the most entertaining sidekick—an ebullient con man with an outrageous tent-revivalist style. Performances, however, are secondary. Much of *Bringing Out the Dead* is the equivalent of digging an ambulance siren while grooving on the flashing light. The mood is less angst-ridden than hypercaffeinated, as Scorsese keeps cranking the velocity-bloodbath in the reggae inferno, exploding skyline pietà, climactic white light of redemption.

"Every day is Judgment Day," the novel's narrator maintains. Scorsese's sin-drenched fallen world is again yoked to Schrader's agonized spiritual quest, though this time there's a bit of Buddhism in the bouillabaisse-karma, telepathy, the transmigration of souls (including the sense of Scorsese doing Spike Lee doing Scorsese). Weirdly, the movie sets its racially coded action in the early '90s. Is this a concession to the Giuliani juggernaut? Get thee behind me, Dinkins. Hail Rudy full of grace.

Also reviewed in:
CHICAGO TRIBUNE, 10/22/99, Friday/p. A, Michael Wilmington
NATION, 11/15/99, p. 30, Stuart Klawans
NEW REPUBLIC, 11/22/99, p. 26, Stanley Kauffmann
NEW YORK TIMES, 10/22/99, p. E1, Janet Maslin
NEW YORKER, 11/1/99, p. 123, Anthony Lane
VARIETY, 10/18-24/99, p. 35, Emanuel Levy
WASHINGTON POST, 10/22/99, p. C5, Rita Kempley
WASHINGTON POST, 10/22/99, Weekend/p. 46, Desson Howe

BROKEDOWN PALACE

A Fox 2000 Pictures release of an Adam Fields production. *Executive Producer:* A. Kitman Ho. *Producer:* Adam Fields. *Director:* Jonathan Kaplan. *Screenplay:* David Arata. *Story:* Adam Fields and David Arata. *Director of Photography:* Newton Thomas Sigel. *Editor:* Curtiss Clayton. *Music:* David Newman. *Music Editor:* Tom Villano. *Sound:* John Midgley and (music): John Kurlander. *Sound Editor:* Sandy Berman and John A. Larsen. *Casting:* Julie Selzer. *Production Designer:* James Newport. *Art Director:* Neil Lamont. *Set Designer:* Roger A. Bowles, Peter Francis, and Daniel Fernandez. *Set Decorator:* Peter Walpole. *Set Dresser:* Gilbert Garantuza, Alexander Dipon, Rolando Ramos, Renato Ignacio, Greg Lipit, Saluz "Sammy" Maestro, Rodel Villar, and Ronnie Jacosalem. *Costumes:* April Ferry. *Make-up:* Felicity Browning. *Make-up (Claire Danes):* Erica Rosenast. *Stunt Coordinator:* Kerrie Cullen and Tim A. Davison. *Running time:* 100 minutes. *MPAA Rating:* PG-13.

CAST: Claire Danes (Alice Marano); Kate Beckinsale (Darlene Davis); Bill Pullman (Hank Greene); Jacqueline Kim (Yon Greene); Lou Diamond Phillips (Roy Knox); Daniel Lapaine (Nick Parks); Tom Amandes (Doug Davis); Aimee Graham (Beth Ann Gardener); John Doe (Bill Marano); Kay Tong Lim (Chief Detective Jagkrit); Beulah Quo (Guard Velie); Henry O (Emissary to Crown); Bahni Turpin (Jamaican Prisoner); Amanda De Cadenet (English Prisoner); Indhira Charoenpura (Prisoner Shub); Lilia Cuntapay (Old Prisoner); Somsuda Chotikasupa (Glasses Guard); Maya Elise Goodwin (Mary); Chad Todhunter (Ferg); Lori Lethin (Lori Davis); Hayley Palmer (Heidi Davis); Rhency Padilla (Pool Boy); Victor Neri (Bellhop); Ermie M. Concepcion (Paku); Nopachai Israngkur Na Ayudhya (Cabbie #1); Ayutthaya A. Payakkapong (Cabbie #2); Kawee Sirikhanaerut (Shouting Soldier); Sahajak Boonthanakit (Sgt. Choy); Mario Valentino Victa (Lt. Tung); Joonee Gamboa (Attorney Montree); Phikun M. Sabino (Guard Sorhirun); Toun Tolentino (Old Dorm Guard); Tawewan Promgontha (Young Dorm Guard); Sawan Edo (Guard Sawalee); Sudarat L. Gaoat (Guard Mangman); Tawatchai Teeranusoon (Thai Judge #1); M. Tom Visvachat (Thai Judge #2); Tony Carney (Doug's Translator); Pichada De Jesus (Darlene's Translator); Sutagorn Jaiman (Prosecutor); Pathompong Supalert (Defense Attorney); Achavasak Phitak (Officer Deesom); Songkran Somboon (Officer Changjarung); Harry E. Northup (Leon Smith); Johnny Ray McGhee (DEA Agent); Phanom Promguntha (Customs Supervisor); Jake De Asis (Royal Thai Guard); Olympio D. Franco (Sick Prisoner); Ronnie Lazaro (Security); Parinya Pattamadilok (Shop Owner); Yuthana Kaewdaeng (Thai Vendor).

LOS ANGELES TIMES, 8/13/99, Calendar/p. 2, Kevin Thomas

The first 20 minutes of "Brokedown Palace" promises an exciting and suspenseful adventure. Two lifelong friends, Alice (Claire Danes) and Darlene (Kate Beckinsale), in a small Midwestern town, are graduating from high school and will be headed in separate directions. Why not, then, have a last fling—let's say, a two-week Hawaii vacation? But Alice, the more venturesome and resilient of the two, has noticed the label on a bottle of imported beer at a graduation eve blast and persuades Darlene that they should go to the more exotic Thailand—but in the event of parental disapproval, they'll let everyone believe that Honolulu rather than Bangkok is their destination.

Bangkok lives up to their expectations, and in their state of elation they decide to take drinks by the side of a pool at a posh hotel. In her larky mood, Alice charges their tab to a room number she picks at random. Just as a meticulous waiter is catching her in the act of deception, a personable, good-looking young Australian businessman, Nick (Daniel Lapaine), comes to her rescue, pretending to know her and saying that she must have forgotten their room number.

When Nick continues on his way out of the hotel, Alice insists he let her and Darlene treat him to drinks to repay him for his face-saving gesture. Nick swiftly sweeps Darlene off her feet and proposes the girls join him on a quick trip to Hong Kong. Feeling left out in the face of her friend's unexpected budding romance but finally wanting to be a good sport, Alice reluctantly agrees. No sooner do the girls arrive at the airport than they are surrounded by Thai police and DEA officers, who discover substantial amounts of heroin packed in their luggage.

Facing 33-year sentences, they wind up in a vast, primitive prison, referred to as the Brokedown Palace by its inmates. At this point, it's the movie that breaks down, spiraling from bad to worse. As written by David Arata from a story he wrote with the film's producer, Adam Fields, this Fox 2000 presentation is just another lurid, contrived, xenophobic tale about Americans trapped in hideous foreign prisons. Very soon you wish you were watching one of those deliberately delirious vintage made-in-the-Philippines Roger Corman women's prison pictures that were so much less pretentious and so much more fun than this nonsense. (Not helping matters is that this picture was, in fact, filmed largely in the Philippines, too, which is pretty clear in the prison sequences.)

All but one of the Thai people depicted are either corrupt or venal, or at the very least, harshly unjust. Darlene's father (Tom Amandes) proves to be a jerk, an Ugly American of the first magnitude, whereas Alice's widowed father (John Doe) is hopelessly ineffectual; in short, the dice are loaded at every turn. The girls' only hope is a local expatriate attorney, married to a native lawyer, and Bill Pullman and Jacqueline Kim try to bring wry humor and compassion to their roles.

Danes and Beckinsale are exceptionally talented young actresses, and you can see how they would have been tempted by the opportunity to play big, dramatic roles; unfortunately, the script's seriously underdeveloped context defeats their considerable efforts at every turn, culminating in a climactic sequence that can only be described as ludicrous.

Jonathan Kaplan is a fine action-suspense director, and he did excellent work with Jodie Foster in "The Accused," Michelle Pfeiffer in "Love Field" and Bonnie Bedelia in "Heart Like a Wheel." But there's not much he can do when weighed down under an avalanche of contrivances. Like Danes and Beckinsale, he is worth far better than "Brokedown Palace."

NEW YORK POST, 8/13/99, p. 63, Jonathan Foreman

Startlingly grown-up by this season's standards, "Brokedown Palace" is a movie about teenagers and teenage friendship that takes you far away from the world of high school proms.

In the tradition of "Midnight Express" and more recently "Return to Paradise," it's a story of young Americans who fall prey to lush temptations abroad—in this case, Thailand and who pay a hefty price for their mistakes.

Alice (Claire Danes) is the wild child, Darlene (Kate Beckinsale) is the good girl. They decide to celebrate their graduation from high school in Ohio by taking a two-week trip to Bangkok, telling their parents that they're going to Hawaii.

After a few hectic days exploring the splendors of the city, they take a break from budget-traveler squalor by sneaking into a fancy hotel, where they order food by the pool. Just as they get in trouble for pretending to be guests, a handsome young Aussie businessman comes to their rescue.

Nick Parks (Daniel Paines) wines and dines them, and both girls are smitten. So when he suggests that they join him for a weekend in Hong Kong on his dime, they immediately agree. He'll be going out there a day early.

But when Alice and Darlene get to the airport, they're immediately arrested by heavily armed police who proceed to find heroin in their luggage. They are quickly convicted and given 33 - year prison sentences.

Thailand is a country that severely punishes drug smugglers—despite the easy availability of drugs and the complicity of government officials in the narcotics business "Brokedown Palace" is the nickname of the prison the girls are sent to. And while it's not particularly brutal, it certainly isn't college. The girls' only hope of getting out, say some fellow foreign inmates, is a sleazy expatriate American lawyer called Yankee Hank (Bill Pullman), although prisoners with enough cash to bribe the right guards have been known to escape.

Hank and his Thai lawyer wife, Yon (Jacqueline Kim), work on an appeal. They find that police have been less than honest and have made no effort to find Nick Parks.

But as a cynical U.S. DEA agent played by Lou Diamond Philips points out, even if the girls didn't get an entirely fair deal at trial, they were guilty of carrying heroin. And although both Alice and Darlene insist they didn't know how it got into their luggage, Hank is sure that one of them is lying.

Director Jonathan Kaplan ("The Accused," "Unlawful Entry") gets strong performances from a fine cast. Danes is more confident than ever. Beckinsale, who was so good as a cynical, twentysomething New York publishing chick in "The Last Days of Disco," is equally convincing as a naive Midwestern teen. (With her flawless accent, she puts to shame her British contemporaries who have tried to talk like Amurrikans.)

"Brokedown Palace" also has going for it unusual authenticity—with the obvious exception of the girls' absurdly healthy, coiffed appearance after a year in a Third World jail. (All Hollywood prison movies presume you can get a great haircut in the slammer.)

It's not a great movie but it tells a moving, believable story set in the real world.

NEWSDAY, 8/13/99, Part II/p. 7, Gene Seymour

Claire Danes is a gymnast of angst. She may well be the Olga Korbut of expressing wounded, fractured emotion. Her star has risen over the past few years through her ability to dive into a deep stare and somersault through jolting mood swings. But Danes had better watch it. There's only so much that can be mined from a soulful gaze and mercurial temperament before people start wondering if there's anything else she can do.

As Alice, one of two white-bread teenage girls from Ohio thrown into a dank Thai prison on drug-smuggling charges in "Brokedown Palace," Danes is once again compelled to lay her guts on the ground while maintaining an icy and, at times, bratty patina. It's an impressive balancing act. But you're aware throughout the movie that you've seen it before. As a result, Danes' raw, contemplative methods only add to the ballast dragging this sour tale through one leaden complication after another.

"Brokedown Palace" starts out like a "Gidget" movie on downers and turns into a slicker, air-brushed version of "Midnight Express" before borrowing, at the end, from "A Tale of Two Cities," to the point of practically paraphrasing Sydney Carton's "far, far better thing ... " tagline.

Danes' Alice is supposed to be the naughty, insurgent contrast to the doelike vulnerability of Kate Beckinsale's Darlene. It's Alice who decides, after their high-school graduation, to tell their parents and friends they're heading to Hawaii while sneaking off to Bangkok. Why? "Too many tourists" in Hawaii, Alice explains with an insouciance that's sure to win her sympathy from those in the audience who must make do with day-trips to Jones Beach.

After shopping, sightseeing and sweltering, the girls are given a stress-test on their friendship through their encounter with a blonde Australian rogue (Daniel Lapaine), who flirts with Alice, but seduces Darlene. Things may be settled when they go with him to Hong Kong for a day. But before they can get on the plane, Alice and Darlene are stopped at the gate by police who find tin cans stuffed with heroin in their carry-on bags.

Their subsequent stay in prison, slated to last at least 33 years, is marred by old-school corporal punishment and swarms of cockroaches whose sadism knows no bounds. (One crawls inside Darlene's ear. Gross!) Worse, no one believes in their innocence until an expatriate American lawyer with the unfortunate nickname "Yankee Hank" (nice to see Bill Pullman playing a normal good guy) takes their case.

Jonathan Kaplan ("Heart Like a Wheel," "Over the Edge") directs this inchoate story with workmanlike panache. And Beckinsale holds her own in what is the more thankless of the two leading roles. As for Danes, you hope for her sake that she takes a vacation from Sturm und Drang and lightens up before her on-screen suffering becomes merely insufferable.

SIGHT AND SOUND, 12/99, p. 37, Philip Kemp

Childhood friends Alice Marano and Darlene Davis graduate from their Ohio high school. To celebrate, they take a trip to Bangkok where they meet young Australian Nick Parks. Darlene sleeps with him, arousing Alice's jealousy. Nick invites them to Hong Kong. They accept but are arrested before boarding the plane; heroin is found in their luggage. Chief Detective Jagkrit tricks Darlene into signing a confession. The girls protest their innocence, but are found guilty and sentenced to 33 years in jail.

The girls hear of an American expat lawyer, Henry Greene, who with his Thai wife Yon helps US prisoners for a price. Darlene's parents and Alice's father put up $15,000 to pay for an appeal and a new hearing, but the sentence is confirmed. Henry continues his investigation unpaid, discovering that Nick, a professional drug smuggler, had other couriers on the same flight and used Alice and Darlene as sacrificial decoys. The girls try to escape but are caught and sentenced to 15 more years each. Henry traces a link between Nick and Jagkrit, and puts pressure on the cop to allow a pardon. Jagkrit agrees, but goes back on his word. At the pardon hearing, Alice confesses to the crime and begs for Darlene's freedom. Darlene is pardoned and takes a tearful leave of Alice, promising to work for her release.

The name of Thailand in Thai, tearaway teenager Alice Marano tells her staider friend Darlene, means 'freedom', and Bangkok offers the enticing prospect of "Las Vegas without parents or laws". But the absence of parents and laws that these girls can comprehend means danger no less than opportunity. "We're from Ohio, for God's sake!" protests Alice once she and Darlene are arrested, but the cosy small-town values of the Midwest carry little weight in the Piranesian labyrinth of the Thai penal system. The girls' light-hearted larceny, conning themselves free drinks by the pool of a posh hotel, incurs a terrible price. *Brokedown Palace* often comes across as an old-fashioned morality tale about the perils of dishonesty, lying to your parents and swarming off to foreign countries.

Altogether, there's a disquieting flavour of xenophobia about Kaplan's film. Thais, for the most part, are treacherous and corrupt, while Americans are straightforward if naive. Even Bill Pullman's expat lawyer, though ostensibly venal, comes good in the end. Thailand itself is shown as intrinsically deceptive: behind the tourist facade of smiling dancers and delicate temples lie dirt and squalor, rivers choked with effluent and cruddy hotels infested with cockroaches. Initially charmed to find one can gain virtue by buying songbirds in the market and letting them fly free, Alice and Darlene later learn that the birds are trained to wing straight back to their cages. But by the time they find out about the scam, the girls themselves are trapped and caged—in a jail in whose filth and privations we're invited to see mirrored the underlying reality of Thailand itself. No wonder the shoot had to be relocated to the Philippines.

Throughout the film, echoes abound of *Midnight Express* (1978), another innocent-abroad saga that used a squalid jail as metaphor for a whole country. But *Brokedown Palace* thankfully lacks the bludgeoning intensity of Alan Parker's film, substituting a lighter, more feminised tone. The jail, though filthy and restrictive, is far from the brutal Turkish hellhole of the earlier film and the Thai prison regime more uncaring than sadistic. This is reflected in the overall look of the two films: Parker's dank, gloomy dungeon gives way to air and sunlight for Kaplan. After their escape attempt the girls are thrown into solitary, but the episode isn't dwelt on. And surprisingly given Kaplan's earlier hit, the rape-drama *The Accused* (1988) and Bangkok's reputation as sex-tourism Mecca—there's no hint of sexual threat.

Claire Danes and Kate Beckinsale, each cast interestingly against type, bring warmth and urgency to the central relationship, though there's a feeling that both they and Bill Pullman are striving to bring out ambiguities absent from David Arata's underwritten script. Given greater psychological depth in the writing, the last-reel resolution might have seemed less sentimental and tacked on. But at least it leaves intact the mystery of which girl, if either, stashed the heroin in the luggage; a nudgingly long-held shot just before the airport scene hints that the guilty party may in fact have been yet another duplicitous Thai.

VILLAGE VOICE, 8/24/99, p. 122, Amy Taubin

As if more proof were needed that there are almost no good roles for women in Hollywood, we have the very talented Claire Danes—who seemed on a fast track, after *My So-Called Life* , to becoming a star—reduced to being just about the only thing worth watching in two of the year's biggest duds: first *Mod Squad*, now *Brokedown Palace*. About two years ago, Kathryn Bigelow was courting Danes to play Joan of Arc, a project she'd been trying to get off the ground for about 10 years. Someone in Danes's camp decided that it was a bad idea for her to follow *Romeo and Juliet* with another costume picture (or at least that's what was reported in the trades). Why they thought the ankle-length saffron-colored sack that she wears throughout almost all of *Brokedown Palace* would be less of a costume than Joan's suit of armor is anyone's guess. But the result was that Bigelow's deal fell apart, Leelee Sobieski (Danes's closest competitor in the milky-skinned, intelligent-ingenue category) won a bunch of prizes for her portrayal of Joan in a European TV version, and poor Danes is in the absurd position of trying to make a movie about a Thai prison into a feel-good experience for the American youth market.

In *Brokedown Palace*, Danes plays Alice, an impulsive, adventurous teenager who, with her best friend, Darlene (Kate Beckinsale), celebrates high school graduation with a trip to Thailand. (Their parents think they've gone to Hawaii.) They meet Nick (Daniel Lapaine), a dashing Australian who surprises both girls by putting the make on the shy Darlene, turning Alice into a third wheel. It's the first time anyone has come between the two, but Nick turns out to be more trouble than either of them could have imagined. A well-connected heroin dealer, he makes Alice and Darlene unwitting decoys, and they wind up with 33-year jail sentences. Their only hope is a Bangkok-based American lawyer, "Yankee Hank" (Bill Pullman), who's known to have a soft heart and occasional success with the corrupt Thai justice system.

Part cautionary tale, part moral-uplift saga, *Brokedown Palace* is as dull as it's absurd. Given the target audience, any semblance of realism in the depiction of daily life in a Thai prison must have been ruled off-limits. Yes, Alice is beaten when she takes an apple without permission, and Darlene freaks at the sight of a bug-covered latrine and later is sent to the infirmary because a roach has crawled into her inner ear. However, most of the time the girls hang out in the prison courtyard looking slightly haggard and dirty, but never less than glamorous, as they devise various schemes to regain their freedom. Newton Thomas Sigel's cinematography is gorgeously golden; the omnipresent pop music soundtrack is unfailingly upbeat (even P.J. Harvey seems too bright for the circumstances).

On the other hand, we have to be grateful that director Jonathan Kaplan has refrained from the images of female degradation that are a sadist's delight. But he's in as hobbled a position as his two lead actors. Beckinsale, admirably, makes Darlene not only shy but mealymouthed and even untrustworthy. Danes, who always seems true to the moment no matter how ridiculous the film is, pulls off a kind of Joan of Arc transformation at the climax. Still, it would be best if she fired whoever got her involved with this two-bit travelogue.

Also reviewed in:
CHICAGO TRIBUNE, 8/13/99, Friday/p. A, Barbara Shulgasser
NEW YORK TIMES, 8/13/99, p. E18, Stephen Holden
VARIETY, 8/16-22/99, p. 29, Todd McCarthy
WASHINGTON POST, 8/13/99, Weekend/p. 44, Desson Howe

BROKEN GIANT, THE

A Blue Guitar Films release. *Producer:* Jeffrey Clifford and Jonathan Cohen. *Director:* Estep Nagy. *Screenplay:* Estep Nagy. *Director of Photography:* Garrett Fisher. *Editor:* David Leonard. *Music:* Will Oldham. *Casting:* Carder Stout. *Production Designer:* Michael Krantz. *Set Decorator:* Daniel Soder. *Costumes:* Stephanie Maslansky. *Running time:* 83 minutes. *MPAA Rating:* Not Rated.

CAST: Brooke Smith (Rosemary Smith);   John Glover (Bennett Hale);   George Dickerson (Thomas Smith); Missy Yager (Clio Hale); Will Arnett (Ezra Caton); Chris Noth (Jack Frey).

NEW YORK POST, 6/25/99, p. 56, Rod Dreher

"The Broken Giant," filmmaker Estep Nagy's beautifully lighted but insufferably sluggish debut, is a dreary hybrid of Woody Allen's "Interiors" and the late, unlamented TV series "Nothing Sacred."

It focuses on a hunky but troubled cleric, Ezra (Will Arnett), who is not liked by folks in the gloom-shrouded New England village where he pastors a church (St. John's Wort parish, it would seem).

He broods with English grad-student poesy, like John-Boy Walton on an Ingmar Bergman bender. The congregation hates his depressing sermons, and he has a thing for banging out secret notes to his dead grandfather, then burning them immediately.

When he's not smoldering with affected seriousness, Pastor Ezra is shagging Rosemary (Brooke Smith), the waitress at the coffee shop. Trouble falls off the turnip truck when a hottie vagrant named Clio (Missy Yager) turns up at the church door looking distraught and seeking sanctuary. Ezra asks nothing of the comely weirdo, but lets her crash in the parsonage—because without that, there's no movie.

Clio's greaseball papa (John Glover) comes looking for her, but because everybody in this exasperatingly low-key drama mumbles monotonously, as if talking through a hangover, it's not certain what he wants, other than his grown daughter back.

Pop does offer this oblique mot: "Only time is a circle, because if it's a straight line, that's terrifying, because then you're only a mile marker to the future."

Thanks, Deepak! This being a stolid exercise in Yankee Gothic, you can bet your last Prozac pill that something grotesque and violent is bound to happen.

When it at long last does, you're so grateful for a sign of life from these narcoleptics that you willingly overlook the event's preposterousness. Blanche, honey, I do believe these Yankees are a *embalmed.*

VILLAGE VOICE, 6/29/99, p. 150, Jessica Winter

Twenty-seven-year-old Estep Nagy's debut film does no hand-holding of either the expositional or moral sort in telling the tangled, ugly story of Ezra Caton, a young church minister in a back-roads burg. One day a distraught woman, Clio, appears on his doorstep, having fled from a nearby town. The presence of Ezra's beautiful, nearly speechless new housemate angers many, including Ezra's girlfriend and Clio's menacing father. Even at 83 minutes, *The Broken Giant* is glacially paced; essential details are teased out as the camera inches from one starkly lit interior to another. The film's mournful air, its fearlessness of silence, its sudden explosions of violence—all these recall Malick's best moments (Clio's hometown, incidentally, is called Terrence), culminating in a finale that stuns with its chilling inevitability and resolute moral ambivalence. There are flaws here, no doubt: every performance is affectless, while the movie's speech is needlessly stilted; despite its biblical underpinnings—the film opens with a Book of Job quotation—the story is not a parable, the characters not abstractions. One hopes for a future project whose script will match Nagy's sense of atmospherics.

Also reviewed in:
NEW YORK TIMES, 6/25/99, p. E18, Lawrence Van Gelder
VARIETY, 12/28/96, p. 69, Dennis Harvey

BROKEN VESSELS

A Unapix Films/Zeitgeist Films release of a Ziehl & Zal production. *Producer:* Roxana Zal and Scott Ziehl. *Director:* Scott Ziehl. *Screenplay:* David Baer, John McMahon, and Scott Ziehl. *Director of Photography:* Antonio Calvache. *Editor:* David Moritz and Chris Figler. *Sound:*

Vince Garcia. *Sound Editor:* Lydian Tone and Barry Key. *Casting:* Robyn Knoll. *Production Designer:* Rodrigo Castillo. *Art Director:* Kristen Gilmartin. *Costumes:* Roseanne Fiedler. *Make-up:* Myles O'Reilly. *Running time:* 90 minutes. *MPAA Rating:* R.

CAST: Todd Field (Jimmy Warzniak); Jason London (Tom Meyer); Roxana Zal (Elizabeth Capalino); Susan Traylor (Susy); James Hong (Mr. Chen); Patrick Cranshaw (Gramps); Brent David Fraser (Jed); Stephanie Feury (Jill); Dave Nelson (Rick); William Smith (Bo); Charley Spradling London (Ginger); Ashley Rhey (Karen); Rodrigo Castillo (Oscar); David Baer (Bob); Al Isreal (Detective McMahon); Bobby Harwell (Detective Baer); Shashawnee Hall (Crazy Sword Man/Ricky); Rose Marie (Mr. Chen's Secretary); Rose Powell (Earl's Wife); Rita Solomon (Waitress); Herman Solomon (Gambler); Robert Kropt (Earl); Justin Herwick (Mick); Gerald Lee (Lance); Vidette Schine (Lawyer); John McMahon (Scotty); Ron Jeremy and Marcia Gray (Porn Stars); Christopher Gallivan and Jenny White Buffalo Clay (Ravers); Dolores Anderson (Mother of Crazy Man); Lisa Davis (Hooker); Eugene Pagano and Alfred Pagano (Bartenders); Kevin O'Connell (Fire Captain); Barbara Volz and Joseph Oritz (Firefighters); Evelyn Jensen and Jeff Rogers (Medics); Kevin Brown (Drug Dealer); George Gunderson (Chester); Ben Liou (Drowning Victim); Juan Morales (Best Man); Fernando Manzanilla (Groom); Shawna L. Brown (Bride); Frank Bustamante (Groomsman); Valeria Hernandez (Bridesmaid); Porfirio Cordova (Father); Jim Zarneski (Bob's Friend); Gelene Collings (Accident Victim #1); David Ziehl (Accident Victim #2); Jack Kerrigan (Drunk Driver).

LOS ANGELES TIMES, 7/30/99, Calendar/p. 11, Kevin Thomas

Movies don't get much more corrosive or gripping than Scott Ziehl's high-energy first feature, "Broken Vessels," which finds a young man (Jason London) from a small town running from a dark secret and landing a job in L.A. as a paramedic. London's naive Tom, seeking redemption in helping others, could not have made a worse choice, for his excitable, profit-minded new boss (James Hong) teams him with star ambulance driver Jimmy (Todd Field), a crackerjack paramedic on crack—and just about every other illegal drug known to man.

When we meet Jimmy he's riding high, in all senses of the word. Drugs at once give Jimmy an edge and numb him from the pain he's witnessed the last five years. They also shield him from the knowledge that he's stuck in a low-paying yet highly demanding job and never going to make it into the Los Angeles Police Department; cops, in his view, have all the power and prestige. Jimmy easily seduces Tom into his danger-embracing lifestyle, for in the well-meaning Tom, hidden guilt outweighs his urge to stick to the straight and narrow, making him vulnerable to all the horrors he witnesses on the job and the drugs that obliterate those horrors and the past along with it.

Jimmy exudes self-confidence and self-control; he's a fast but skilled driver, a drug user who knows when to quit and who has become as addicted to his job as to drugs. Tom, on the other hand, proceeds swiftly into a downward spiral, but as he goes plummeting you have to start wondering just how long Jimmy will be able to maintain any semblance of balance in his frenetic life.

Ziehl and his co-writers make a screen full of people come alive, not just Jimmy and Tom and their money-grubbing boss. Tom soon learns since the age of 13 Jimmy has lived off and on with his longtime heroin-addicted grandfather (Patrick Cranshaw), whom he keeps supplied now that the old man is living in a retirement home. Susan Traylor is Jimmy's speed-freak neighbor, alternately amusing and pathetic in her manic behavior, and Roxana Zal is the gentle, caring nurse Tom attracts but all too easily loses. The actors, including the ever-reliable William Smith in a cameo, are all on the money in their portrayals in exceptionally well-drawn roles, crackling with pungent dialogue. In major, demanding roles London and Field are especially impressive.

Field has a deceptive facade of all-American clean-cut looks that allows him to suggest a wide range of emotions and thoughts behind such a regular-guy appearance; in "Ruby in Paradise" he expressed such uncommon decency and intelligence you had to wonder how Ashley Judd's hardscrabble Ruby could ever have considered letting him get away. In "Eyes Wide Shut" he's the likable med school dropout turned saloon piano player, and here he's an increasingly raging sociopath. In all these roles Field has the precious gift of being able to surprise you and to command your attention on screen.

"Broken Vessels" could take Ziehl far. It has that kind of kinetic energy that fuses style and theme, as Tom and Jimmy careen through L.A. streets both in answer to emergency calls and in pursuit of a fix. In Antonio Calvache, Ziehl has an ace cinematographer who can generate visceral impact with panache yet switch mood and tempo with ease; he captures a fresh slice of lowdown L.A. that is always visually enticing. The scorching sound of the score composed by Field and others plus music chosen by music supervisor Tracy McKnight complement the film throughout. No wonder "Broken Vessels" walked off with the audience prize at the 1998 Los Angeles Independent Film Festival.

NEW YORK POST, 7/2/99, p. 48, Hannah Brown

Watching a dope fiend get through his days is boring and icky. The fact that the addicts in the film "Broken Vessels," happen to be working paramedics adds little originality or interest to this tale of alienated L.A. junkies.

The early scenes hold some promise of a gritty, behind-the-scenes look at the lives of stressed-out paramedics, but the film quickly turns into a cliché-ridden drug movie, complete with lots of shooting up and vomiting.

The naive Tom (Jason London), a recent college graduate, forsakes academia to ride the streets of Los Angeles with veteran ambulance driver Jimmy (Todd Field).

Tom looks up to the tightly wound Jimmy, who knows how to handle even the most chaotic accidents but drinks on duty, robs and molests patients and takes all kinds of drugs.

Tom resists at first, but soon joins Jimmy in the kind of binging that is often referred to as a "downward spiral," although that makes it sound more exciting than it really is.

Tom, it turns out, suffers deeply because of a dark secret, revealed in hazy flashbacks, the revelation of which will not surprise anyone who has ever seen a TV "Movie of the Week."

In spite of the characters' action-packed jobs, "Broken Vessels" lacks the energy and black humor that enlivens the best drug movies, like "Drugstore Cowboy" and "Trainspotting."

London gives such a wooden performance it's hard to tell when he's in a drug haze and when he's agonizing from guilt over his irresponsibility.

The one saving grace is Field as Jimmy. The actor, who also has a part in "Eyes Wide Shut," gives a scary and compelling performance as a self-justifying sociopath. He bears an uncanny resemblance to the young Martin Sheen, circa "Badlands."

But even he cannot repair "Broken Vessels," which is so grim it makes the recent drug flick "Permanent Midnight" look like "The Little Mermaid."

NEWSDAY, 7/2/99, Part II/p. B6, John Anderson

The idea that the EMS technician attending to your wounds could be a crack-smoking alcoholic is just one of those recessed anxieties—somewhere between the dread of having food on your teeth and the fear of being buried alive that helps give modern life its frisson of peril. And it's what helps give "Broken Vessels" its generally creepy feel.

More specifically, however, this first feature by Scott Ziehl is, like the ambulance that barrels through it, more or less a character unto itself. As Tom (Jason London) and his tour-guide-to-oblivion Jimmy (Todd Fields) make their way from relative respectability to utter degradation, the film swings along with them, gradually growing darker and more infected as the slope gets slipperier.

Fields, soon to be seen as Tom Cruise's best friend in Stanley Kubrick's "Eyes Wide Shut" (and probably best known for playing Ashley Judd's sensitive squeeze in Victor Nunez' "Ruby in Paradise") makes Jimmy a paradigm of seductive corruption, exhibiting both licentiousness and control as he leads the neophyte Tom down the road to vehicular mayhem and personal destruction.

"Jimmy's had a lot of partners," says Mr. Chen (the ubiquitous James Hong) when he hires Tom as his newest paramedic—and sends him off with the EMS equivalent of Hunter S. Thompson.

"Broken Vessels" turns darkly funny—very darkly—right away: Jimmy uses their defibrillator to turn unruly patients catatonic; smuggles Valium to his heroin-addict grandfather (Patrick Cranshaw); picks up coke-snorting women with the drugs he and Tom pick up under the L.A. freeway. Then they start robbing jewelry off unconscious women, pawing them a little, and stealing VCRs from elderly angina victims.

Fields is particularly good, but so is Susan Traylor as Susy, the boys' speed-freak-nextdoor, a manic, maddening drug casualty and comic/pathetic chatterbox. She's got all the month and all the motions of a disintegrating meth-head, but there's also a certain degree of pathos that keeps Suzie off cinematic skid row.

"Broken Vessels" does, unfortunately, suffer from a score that tends toward the cloying and an epilogue that sounds as tacked on as it does insincere. What the movie is about is motion—the ambulance, the pulse of Los Angeles and the all-too-rapid descent into a hell that Tom and Jimmy enter with blind abandon. Most of the film is good enough to forgive a preachy ending, but everyone should really recognize that we got the point, well before the onset of sanctimony.

SIGHT AND SOUND, 4/00, p. 44, Philip Kemp

The present. Tom Meyer, a young man from Pennsylvania, arrives in Los Angeles and starts work with LA City Rescue, an ambulance service run by Mr Chen. Chen teams him with a more experienced paramedic, Jimmy Warzniak. At first impressed by Jimmy's cool demeanor Tom realises that his partner is doing drugs and stealing Valium for his elderly grandfather. Initially outraged, Tom gradually finds himself adopting Jimmy's skewed values. Finding a camcorder in the ambulance, he starts filming the more traumatic events that take place on their shifts. After he accidentally kills his flatmate's tropical fish, Tom moves in with Jimmy. There, he meets his junkie neighbour Susy.

Susy takes in a lodger, Elizabeth, who soon moves out but not before she and Tom have begun seeing each other. Increasingly hooked on heroin, Tom stands her up. When Jimmy steals from an elderly couple, Tom is disgusted and resolves to kick the habit, but following a crash caused by a drunk driver he goes back on drugs. Jimmy's grandfather dies; Jimmy starts peddling the dope made by Susy's friend Jed in her garden shed. Susy blows up the shed, killing Jed and herself. Tom tries to cheat one of their dealers, who pulls a gun; as Tom and Jimmy make a frantic getaway they crash the ambulance. Jimmy is killed. Tom, threatened with prosecution, gets off thanks to a tape he shot earlier revealing police brutality.

It's *Broken Vessels'* misfortune to be following Scorsese's *Bringing Out the Dead* so closely into UK cinemas—not only because Scott Ziehl's low-budget indie was in fact shot first, but because the two films have rather less in common than their coincidence of plot and subject matter (ambulance drivers cracking up) might suggest. Where Scorsese and Paul Schrader's film is ultimately a quest for redemption, Ziehl gives us something far bleaker: a manic downward spiral into perdition. Tom Meyer arrives in LA haunted by a fatal event in his past that he hopes to expiate by taking on a paramedic job, saving lives to make up for those he took only to find he can save nobody, not even himself. If there is a Scorsese parallel, it's more with the earlier *GoodFellas,* whose hero likewise emerges from a paroxysm of drug-fuelled hysteria to find himself left with nothing but a devalued freedom.

If this sounds off-puttingly grim, it's worth emphasising that *Broken Vessels* is powered by a contagious headlong energy and is often outrageously funny. Most of the best moments of black humour stem from Tom's anti-mentor Jimmy, a *tour deforce* performance of deranged truculence from Todd Field (last seen as Tom Cruise's pianist friend in *Eyes Wide Shut).* At one point, transporting an obstreperous patient, Jimmy casually swings round, slams heart stimulators on each side of the guy's head and jolts him out cold. It's inevitable that the impressionable Tom should be drawn to the older man's amoral cool, ignoring the warning signs: early on Jimmy confides his ambition to become a cop because "they make their own rules". Tom's own morality is precarious: after Jimmy robs an old couple, Tom's brief attempt to kick both the drugs and his partner's influence stems as much from their brush with the law as from disgust at the theft.

Jimmy's self-justifying credo stems from a sense of his own devaluation, of being obliged to deal with the dregs of society while he's treated as little better. "We make the difference between life and death—and some guy flipping burgers earns more than you," he tells Tom. In ways that parallel the relationship between Brad Pitt's Tyler Durden and Edward Norton's narrator in *Fight Club,* Jimmy is Tom's dangerous, charismatic alter ego, saying and doing the things the younger man doesn't quite dare to. But as they sink deeper and faster into the morass of subcultural LA, their paths, and their characters, converge until at the end the dead Jimmy seems to have taken Tom over. Ziehl, directing, co-producing and co-scripting, powers this blackly comic drive to the abyss with reckless gusto, much aided by some richly off-the-wall performances (Susan Traylor's is a standout) and Antonio Calvache's frenetic camera movements and murky, subaqueous lighting. The occasional roughness of the production values does nothing to detract from the film's impact. In fact, it enhances the sense of a world careering out of control and leaking vital fluids at every orifice.

VILLAGE VOICE, 7/6/99, p. 65, Dennis Lim

A particularly softhearted specimen of the just-say-no morality tale, *Broken Vessels* is a tawdry, flashy portrait of addiction whose main reference points seem to be other junkie movies. The stultifying setup leaves little room to maneuver: fresh-faced Tom (Jason London) flees his native Pennsylvania for L.A. (stylized hallucinatory sequences denote a dark back story) and, upon finding work as a paramedic, is partnered with weaselly destructive influence Jimmy (Todd Field). Presumably worn down by their high-stress, low-pay jobs, the pair relieve tensions by transforming their ambulance into some sort of debauched bachelor pad—they steal dope, get high, molest unconscious patients, and, to cover their asses, even take time out to videotape violent cops in action. Director Scott Ziehl, who collaborated on the screenplay with David Baer and John McMahon, plays some of this as mild, men-behaving-badly comedy, most of it as finger-wagging before-the-fall ugliness.

Constrictingly drawn though the two protagonists may be, the peripheral roles are even more ludicrous. There's an angelic love-interest nurse (Roxana Zal, the movie's coproducer), who offers Tom solace and advice ("You have to stop with the drugs") that he shuns, and a speed freak next door (Susan Traynor, doing a sporadically compelling whacked-out upspeak thing). Also for purported comic relief, Tom is stuck at one point with a swishy roommate, who throws a womanish hissy fit when Tom pukes into his aquarium.

In both style and content, *Broken Vessels* indulges one drug-movie cliché after another. It plays for the most part like bad television—it's not just the glibly episodic structure, pat psychology, or simplistic morality, but the way the situations and dialogue strain for snappiness. Ziehl (who's set to direct an action thriller for Miramax) works overtime to evoke Drug Hell—woozy slow motion, oblique camera angles, and blaring electronics. Music of choice to shoot up to: the Chemical Brothers, apparently.

Also reviewed in:
CHICAGO TRIBUNE, 7/2/99, Friday/p. B, John Petrakis
NEW YORK TIMES, 7/2/99, p. E13, Stephen Holden
VARIETY, 4/27-5/3/98, p. 60, Leonard Klady

BUENA VISTA SOCIAL CLUB

An Artisan Entertainment release of a Road Movies production in association with Kintop Pictures and Arte, Channel 4. *Executive Producer:* Ulrich Felsberg. *Producer:* Ulrich Felsberg and Deepak Nayar. *Director:* Wim Wenders. *Director of Photography (Amsterdam Crew):* Robby Müller, *(New York Crew):* Lisa Rinzler, and *(Cuban Crew):* Jörg Widmer. *Editor:* Brian Johnson. *Music:* Sigfredo Ariel. *Sound:* E. Benjamin Posnack and (music) Rail Rogut and Ry Cooder. *Running time:* 106 minutes. *MPAA Rating:* Not Rated.

WITH: Joachim Cooder; Ry Cooder; Ibrahim Ferrer; Juan de Marcos González; Rubén González; Pio Leyva; Manuel "Puntillita" Licea; Orlando "Cachaito" López; Manuel "Guajiro" Mirabal; Eliades Ochoa; Omara Portuondo; Compay Segundo; Barbarito Torres; Amadito Valdés.

FILM QUARTERLY, Summer 2000, p. 47, Cary Hentzi

Cuban music is in the air again, wafting into the North American consciousness as it has at regular intervals since the end of the last century, when the rhythm of the *habanera* first made its way to these shores and influenced New Orleans musicians like Jelly Roll Morton. What Morton called "the Spanish tinge"—an essential component of real jazz, according to him—was thus originally a Cuban import, albeit an unacknowledged one, as has so often been the case with things Cuban in this country. In recent years, however, we have seen some notable efforts to correct our vagueness about Cuba's cultural heritage and to remind us of what we perhaps once knew and have forgotten about its relationship to our own. Among the best of them are these two fine documentaries, both of which are closely related to important recording projects and concerts. At the same time, and from very different perspectives, these films succeed in making complex statements that surpass their apparent goal of providing a cinematic record of some notable musical events.

Of the two, Andy Garciá's portrait of Israel López ("Cachao") comes closest to being a traditional concert film, drawing the bulk of its footage from rehearsals and from a 1992 concert held in Miami in honor of the great bassist and composer, who is, for all of his humility, one of the most important living figures in Cuban music. A former child prodigy who hails from a family that includes over 40 bass players (it is a poignant commentary on the divisiveness of Cuban history that his counterpart in *Buena Vista Social Club* is his own nephew, "Cachaíto," a highly respected bassist on the island), he made his first significant contribution in the late 1930s as a member of the celebrated *danzón* orchestra *Antonio Arcaño y Sus Maravillas,* when he added driving, syncopated figures to the relatively sedate, European-influenced form of the *danzón,* anticipating the mambo and actually authoring a piece by that name with his brother Orestes. In the late 50s, he was responsible for another outstanding innovation when he gathered together some of the leading musicians in Havana to record several albums of jam sessions known as *descargas* (literally "discharges," with the sense of unloading or unburdening oneself), which established a uniquely Cuban brand of improvised music comparable to North American jazz. The twofold nature of Cachao's personal legacy was emphasized in the concert and is echoed by Andy García's film, which captures many beautifully executed performances of *danzones* and *descargas,* featuring some of the most gifted exponents of Latin music in the United States. More generally, the film—and even more so, the two albums that came out of the project *(Master Sessions,* volumes I and II)—offers a splendidly instructive panorama of Cuban musical genres, from the elegant *danzas* of Ignacio Cervantes and Ernesto Lecuona to the major African-influenced forms like the *son,* the *conga,* the *guaracha,* and the type of traditional *rumba* known as the *yambú.*

Yet the motives for this effort of instruction are profound and carry the film beyond the usual territory of a music documentary. As Cachao says more than once onscreen and even in the lyrics of his music ("El Son No Ha Muerto"), the important thing is to maintain the tradition. This is, of course, not just simple aesthetic conservatism. In this case music, and cultural tradition generally, is a bulwark against the indignities and ironies of exile, which, on the one hand, have forced this extraordinary musician to earn his living for many years by playing weddings and christenings and, on the other, have seen the film's director become a famous actor in the English-speaking world. Rich or poor, Cuban-Americans are beset by the problem of identity and the desire to preserve some sense of imaginative connection to a country from which they have been absent for so long, and it is one of the strengths of Andy García's film that it communicates the force of this desire without falling into strident political posturing. Indeed, one of the few overtly political gestures that the filmmaker allows himself takes the form of a reading of García Lorca's great poem "Son de Negros en Cuba" ("When the full moon rises/ I'll go to Santiago") against a swelling musical accompaniment, as if to affirm that here politics will speak only in the voice of art (although his reading of the poem on *Master Sessions,* volume 1, is given a more aggressively personal turn when he substitutes the name of his family's hometown, Bejucal, for Santiago de Cuba).

More subtle but even more suggestive are the discussion sequences, a number of which include the wellknown Cuban writer Guillermo Cabrera Infante, whose knowledge of music and trademark puns are also on display in his liner notes for the two albums. These fragments of conversation are occasionally accompanied by a discreet, carefully edited soundtrack of musical allusions, the audio equivalent of scholarly footnotes, illustrating, for example, a passage in George Gershwin's *Cuban Overture* and then comparing the famous *son,* "Echale Salsita," that it quotes—all by way of enriching an anecdote from Cabrera Infante about how the author of the piece, Ignacio Piñeiro, was once surprised to hear fragments of his own melody in Gershwin's work. While the detailed presentation aims to set the record straight and to recover a piece of the Cuban past, which is always in danger of being lost or absorbed into the North American context, the opposite experience is on record here as well. In another discussion, the brilliant clarinetist and alto saxophonist Paquito D'Rivera explains that he became fully aware of the accomplishments of Cuban musicians only *after* he came to the United States; as he puts it, he "discovered the greatness of Cuban music on the banks of the Hudson River." Such a moment conveys, with fine understatement, the exile's peculiarly intense passion for the culture of his homeland and the especially lustrous beauty that it acquires in foreign surroundings.

Whereas the emphasis of *Cachao ... Como Su Ritmo No Hay Dos* is on the role of traditional Cuban culture in the experience of exile, the underlying subject of Wim Wenders' *Buena Vista Social Club* is the continuing fascination that Cuba and the United States have for each other even after decades of political strife, a fascination that is experienced as equal parts dream and memory on both sides. The ostensible concern of the film is the unexpected success enjoyed by a group of Cuban musicians, most of them in their seventies and eighties, in a recording project initiated by the British producer Nick Gold together with the American guitarist and folk music specialist Ry Cooder. That project now includes more than half a dozen albums, beginning with the Grammy-winning disk from which the film takes its title, and is largely responsible for the current wave of interest in Cuban music. As in Andy García's film, there are interviews with all of the major players in this unlikely drama, and concert footage from their appearances in Amsterdam and New York is intercut with studio scenes shot during the recording of a solo album by Ibrahim Ferrer, the extraordinary 71-year-old *sonero* and *bolerista* who had been slicing shoes for a living when he was invited to join the group.

To an even greater extent than in *Cachao,* however, the director's aims exceed the mere documentation of musical activities. This larger ambition is apparent first of all in the visual texture of the film, which is the result of its having been shot in high-definition video rather than directly on film stock. Wenders has experimented with video technology before, notably in *Until the End of the World* (1991), where it was employed in the sequences involving a machine that records people's dreams so that they can be watched on television. As William Hurt's character explains in that film, "The camera records what you see, but it also records how your brain reacts in response to what your eyes see." For Wenders, the pixilated, slightly hazy quality of video, with its blurred movements and images running off into large fields of light or dark, is associated with the inevitably subjective quality of experience, and his use of video in *Buena Vista Social Club* helps to suggest that our impressions of a foreign country are necessarily a kind of dream or imaginative construction made up of sound and image as well as our own desires. And since a film about subjectivity must have a perceiving subject, that role is assigned to the American visitors, Ry Cooder and his son Joachim, as they drive along the Malecón among ancient Chevys and Buicks and through the weathered but still grand streets of Old Havana, with their windowless windows, pitted facades, and shadowy archways. But the most evocative element in this tropical dreamscape is, of course, the music, and above all the old-fashioned boleros like the startlingly beautiful "Silencio," here sung in a haunting, smoky-romantic arrangement by Ibrahim Ferrer and the regal Omara Portuondo.

It would, however, be a mistake to overemphasize the purely dream-like quality of the film, for Wenders also shows us something else, beyond the layers of imagination and desire. Revising a famous piece of ignorance by J.A. Froude, one might say simply, There are people there. The story of Ry Cooder's acquaintance with Cuban music is emblematic. He was first drawn to Havana over twenty years ago by a tape that seemed to promise untapped musical fiches in the form of some astonishing playing by an anonymous performer on an unidentifiable stringed instrument. Then, during the recording of the *Buena Vista Social Club* album, Cooder discovered that one of the participating musicians was the very man whose playing had beguiled him so many years before, and we are duly introduced to the mustachioed virtuoso himself, Barbarito Torres, who is the country's leading performer on a small, lute-like instrument of Arabic origin called the laoud. This pattern is repeated several times over the course of the film. For example, in the very opening sequence, we ride in a vintage convertible with the 90-year-old patriarch of the group, Compay Segundo, in search of the original Buena Vista Social Club, a black-only hotspot in pre-revolutionary Havana. , The location is not obvious; it becomes necessary to ask the old people of the neighborhood for help. "Where are the *viejos?*" asks Compay; and for a brief, wistful moment it appears that his search may end unsuccessfully for lack of any living witnesses from the older generation. A moment later, however, he is besieged by *viejos* with long memories squabbling over who gets to deliver the information. He enters into discussion with them about, among other things, hangover remedies.

Thus, we come to understand that, in spite of various losses and imminent departures, much remains of the way of life from which this music grew. Behind the famous songs, behind the romantic images and legends are people, with dreams, memories, and desires of their own. One such fantasy that is hinted at from time to time throughout the film (as when Ibrahim Ferrer sings a few bars of "Chattanooga Choo-Choo") and then emerges movingly in the final segment is the Cubans' own dream of the United States, which is realized in the form of a visit to New York and a wildly popular concert in Carnegie Hall. (Tickets to this show sold out in three days without advertisement.) As one of the revolutionary slogans on a Havana billboard declares, "Dreams Do Come True." Perhaps the most scandalous aspect of *Buena Vista Social Club,* at least for anyone who feels that a documentary about contemporary Cuba is required to present a grim indictment of the government, is the extent to which this is a film about happiness and acceptance of the ups and downs of life. To be sure, the extraordinary good fortune documented by the film comes late, but not too late to be enjoyed if one knows how, as Ibrahim Ferrer implies when he remarks (unexpectedly, in view of his humble surroundings), "We Cubans are very lucky"; and the viewer is treated to the satisfying spectacle of a man who prefers to savor what he has been given rather than bemoan what he has been denied. To have put such a rich mixture of human dreams and human reality on film is a remarkable achievement on the part of the director. And for that we are the ones who are lucky.

LOS ANGELES TIMES, Calendar/p. 10, Kenneth Turan

It's the incongruity that strikes you first, the contrast between the considerable ages of the musicians in "Buena Vista Social Club," the marvelous new documentary on Cuban music produced by Ry Cooder, and the vibrant, irrepressible sounds they turn out.

But soon enough it becomes clear that it's precisely the music's rejuvenating qualities, the seductive, melodic rhythms and the simple but indelible beauty of these songs that has kept its players, now known in Cuba as "los superabuelos," the super grandfathers, as forever young as they seem to be.

Named after a long-gone nightspot in Havana where this music was nurtured, "Buena Vista" the movie is an offshoot of the hugely successful, Grammy-winning CD of Cuban music that guitarist Cooder, who has always embraced and promoted a variety of world music styles, produced in 1996.

That disc's success led to Cooder's return trip to the island in 1998 to record a solo album with 70-year-old vocalist Ibrahim Ferrer, Cuba's Nat King Cole, who literally wandered in off the street to participate in the first CD. German director Wim Wenders, who initially worked with Cooder on 1984's "Paris, Texas," asked to come along, and this film is the serendipitous result.

Though Wenders' work is usually much heavier in theme and execution, these intoxicating sounds mandated a different spirit and style. "In Cuba the music flows like a river," the director reports. "I want to make a film that'll just float on this river. Not interfere with it, just drift along."

Under Wenders' direction, "Buena Vista Social Club" has a trio of focuses: the people who make the music, the city and country that nurtured them, and, most gloriously, the music itself.

In addition to Ferrer, who credits much of his success to the Santeria deity Saint Lazarus, we spend time with Cuban diva Omara Portuondo as she walks around her old neighborhood; hear 92-year-old paterfamilias Compay Segundo recall lighting cigars for his grandmother as a 5-year-old; and listen to legendary 80-year-old pianist Ruben Gonzalez, who had stopped playing for a decade, reminisce about how he began.

Besides allowing these sharply dressed, stylish veterans to tell their stories, "Buena Vista" provides a tour of beautiful but crumbling Havana, routing us along the sea-swept boulevard called the Malecon and revealing the sad states of disrepair the city's elegant buildings have fallen into. That this caliber of music comes out of these melancholy and romantic streets is no surprise at all.

Finally, of course, it is the music that is everything in this film. Evocatively photographed in rehearsals in Havana and concerts in Amsterdam and New York's Carnegie Hall by Robby Muller and Lisa Rinzler in addition to director of photography Jorg Widmer (all using a Sony DigiBeta Cam and a Handycam), "Buena Vista" creates a completely relaxed, welcoming feeling that couldn't be more inclusive.

Trading riffs and smiles, these players delight one another as well as audiences with the breathtaking casualness of their musicianship as they play songs they've known for decades. As percussionist Joaquim Cooder, who plays on the sessions along with his father, says, "It's so subtle and quiet, so powerful at the same time."

Cooder senior, who counts the CD as the biggest success of his 35-year career, says that the rediscovery and unexpected success of this vibrant musical subculture, long forgotten but alive and well, is something that "might just happen to you once in your lifetime." Being able to hear this kind of playing is a special moment in time, one we don't want to end and one that we're privileged to experience.

NEW STATESMAN, 8/9/99, p. 31, Jonathan Romney

In 1978 Martin Scorsese made *The Last Waltz*, a film about the farewell concert of the Band. In it, the group came across like ageless veterans who'd been trawling up and down life's highway since time began. In fact they'd been in the public eye for just over a decade. But then rock has a remarkably short memory compared with other musical forms. With Wim Wenders' new film, *Buena Vista Social Club*, things go back a bit further. The oldest musician is over 90 and wrote his first song in 1922. Overall *The Last Waltz* is probably the closest comparison to *Buena Vista Social Club*, in that there aren't many instances where major filmmakers drop their usual *auteur* preoccupations and stand back admiringly while the musicians bask in the documentary limelight. Wenders' film is the result of a singularly bizarre musical phenomenon: somehow a group of aged Cuban musicians playing traditional acoustic music ended up making a million-selling, internationally acclaimed record. It's even stranger that Wenders, who has spent recent years agonising about "the crisis of the image", should be the one to film them.

In the field of music documentary, directors tend either to overegg the mixture with technology or to go for extreme functional simplicity, as Jonathan Demme did in his Talking Heads concert film, *Stop Making Sense*. Wenders, however, is content simply to hang around, catch the highlights of recording sessions and concerts, throw in the odd interview or street scene and let a loose shape emerge. The one thing he does to give the film a distinctive signature is to shoot on digital cameras: Havana streets take on an odd pink-grey candy colour; vivid abstract impressionist images emerge from the distressed paint on cars.

The film was largely shot when Wenders' frequent collaborator Ry Cooder, who first recorded the Social Club in 1996, returned to Havana to produce a solo record for the singer, Ibrahim Ferrer. Cooder turns up with his guitar and his drummer son, Joachim, takes a back seat and watches approvingly as the veterans let rip. They gobble up the attention, as well they might—they're show-stoppingly charismatic. The pianist, Ruben Gonzalez, whose style Cooder describes as "a cross between Thelonious Monk and Felix the Cat", is a benign, white-haired gent of studious demeanour, with a beautifully tangential mathematician's touch. Ibrahim Ferrer is heard airing his light, lilting tones to spectacular effect on the haunting "Silencio" and seen proudly displaying his good-luck totem. His singing partner, Omara Portuondo, wanders down the street, trading verses with passing women. The most flamboyant of the lot is the guitarist, Compay Segundo, a more than dapper nonagenarian, who professes his undying passion for women and outsize cigars.

The film could have been cosily poignant—all these stately old geezers getting a belated stab at the big time, finding their lifetime's fulfilment on the stage of the Carnegie Hall. But the music is nothing like a living fossil—more like a coelacanth that's been unfrozen after decades and proves friskier than a fresh salmon. For many listeners, these songs evoke a past known only from Hollywood pastiches of the music: some of them could easily have been recorded in the 1950s, and you could imagine these musicians playing behind Lauren Bacall in a Howard Hawks adventure.

By all accounts, some younger Cuban musicians are more than sceptical and have even accused Cooder of being a CIA plant, determined to undermine the new salsa scene. Unfortunately the film doesn't do much to put the Social Club phenomenon in context. It doesn't tell us much about life in Cuba either today or before Castro and, although it doesn't indulge in postcard clichés, Wenders tends to go for the lightly amusing detail—the lugubrious dog on the corner, the old lady chomping a cigar that would have felled Lew Grade.

As for the musicians, we know they're hardy survivors, many of whom have been out of action for years. But we have only hints of what they've been doing with themselves (in Ferrer's case, shining shoes for years) or how the revolution affected musicians' lives. (Elsewhere, Ferrer has said it did wonders for them, because they could play for Cubans instead of tourists; one wonders whether that's still the case.)

Hugely enjoyable as the film is, you rather miss the pushy, worried style Wenders displayed in other documentaries: here, it feels as if he's taking a sunshine leisure break. At one point we see a slogan on a wall reading, *"Esta Revolucion es Eterna"*—this revolution is eternal. You feel we're meant to take this as meaning: the music is the revolution, man. But from the viewpoint of our own youth-fixated culture, there is something rather subversive about these venerables, looking fragile but feisty as they blaze away at their variously louche and sultry repertoire. Put it this way, it's a damn sight livelier than *Last of the Summer Wine*.

NEW YORK, 6/14/99, p. 53, Peter Rainer

Many of the marvelous Cuban musicians and singers in Wim Wenders's wonderful documentary *Buena Vista Social Club* are well beyond 60, but they don't see themselves as aged. Onstage, jamming together, or in smaller recording sessions, they have an aliveness that obliterates any concerns we might have about their frailty. It's not simply that music keeps these artists vital. It's as if they never grew old at all. I've never seen another movie that so clearly expresses the sensual sustenance that great folk culture provides its practitioners.

The film grew out of sessions with the artists in 1996 organized by the guitarist, composer, and record producer Ry Cooder; the album that resulted, called *Buena Vista Social Club* in honor of one of East Havana's long-gone music-and-dance emporiums, became a surprise best-seller worldwide, revitalizing many careers. In 1998, Wim Wenders, returning with Cooder to Havana, filmed the musicians as they recorded an album showcasing bolero singer Ibrahim Ferrer. During their days off, Wenders filmed them talking, informally, about their pasts.

The 92-year-old guitar and *tres* player Compay Segundo, with his wide, lewd smile, and Ruben Gonzalez, the 80-year-old jazz-and-mambo pianist whom Cooder once described as a Cuban cross between Thelonious Monk and Felix the Cat, seem to exist totally within the realm of their music. As with most folk artists, their sounds are inextricable from the anecdotage of their lives. Their stories, their histories, are all of a piece with the words they sing and the notes they play—with their lilt and whoop and glide. The performers are ecstatically comfortable in the spotlight and equally at ease away from it. The way they carry themselves offstage is gently stylized, as if, in sauntering down the streets or roaming about their cramped apartments, they were shimmying up to the fates. The graceful slow-motion swing of their movements is a kind of offering—a way of acknowledging the blessing that has been bestowed upon them by a life of music.

Ibrahim Ferrer, whom Cooder brought out of oblivion, says at one point, "We Cubans are very fortunate—we have learned to resist the good and the bad." This lyrical evenness of temperament shows up in his vocalizing, which seems beyond the injuries of infirmity or society's neglect. In his white jacket and white cap, the 72-year-old Ferrer, with his soft speaking voice and beautiful, becalmed face, is a radiant icon of elegance. The implicit assumption behind his singing—it was the same with Nat "King" Cole—is that there is silk to be found in the rumble of the world. Ferrer's voice draws out a clean, silky line; it's so pure it doesn't seem to be born of experience—it's just there, floating and seraphic. His sounds represent a dream of how we wish our drudgeries and defeats could be recomposed, transcended.

Wenders filmed the Cuban artists along with Cooder and Cooder's drummer son Joachim performing not only in Havana but also in concert in Amsterdam and, triumphantly, in Carnegie Hall. (It was the first time most of the Cubans had been to New York.) The best group number in the movie, Compay Segundo's "Chan Chan," is also its first; it has the slow stealth of a leopard's lope, and it seems to tune your entire body as you listen to it.   Segundo—born Francisco Repilado and raised in Santiago—has a deep-down gladness, almost a mirth, when he plays guitar and sings. He's immensely tickled by the provocativeness—the presence of the carnal—in his tone. He's a great old bawd: His seductions are embracing, but there's some heavy fondling in the embrace.

The irony reflected by this movie is that, on the one hand, everybody who listens to the traditionally acoustic Afro-Cuban music is turned on by it: not just the musicians and recording engineers and audiences but the people in the street. (At one point, the terrific bolero singer Omara Portuondo, the only female in the group, starts wailing, and a passerby, a middle-aged woman, joins in as if to do so were the most natural thing in the world.) And yet this is a minority music in Cuba, in the same way that jazz is in America. The neglect that these musicians fell into parallels what happened to many of our jazz and blues legends. Even before Communism's full flowering, many of their careers were on the wane, and Wenders is wise not to politicize their plight. Swooning right along with the rest of us, he's too carried away by the music for that.

We understand completely what Ry Cooder is talking about when he says he prepared his whole life to produce these artists; he first heard tapes of Cuban musicians back in the seventies and made a trip to Havana to hear more, but it wasn't until 1996 that he was able to return and make recordings. The music is a siren call for Cooder; when he joins in on the Buena Vista sessions, he's not being a bwana but insinuating himself into the music as an act of devotion. (His son Joachim, the drummer, in the course of just moving about the streets, seems to boogie with a perpetual beat, as if Cuba itself were one big jam session.)

Cooder is an exemplary artist-producer. He's mixed in the celebrated older Cuban musicians with some younger members of the group, such as the astonishing *laud* player Barbarito Torres, and, on bongos, Julienne Oviedo Sanchez, who also plays with the new-style big band N G La Banda. The result, although you would never think of it in such academic terms, is an anthology of Cuban musical styles. The mesh is perfect; it all goes together, and the beaming faces of the performers conferring joy on one another is itself a piece of music. "I'm under the spell of this," Ibrahim Ferrer says with poignant simplicity as he walks down Fifth Avenue before his Carnegie Hall appearance. Watching this movie, we're spellbound, too. We're in a state of rapt, sexy, swinging awe.

NEW YORK POST, 6/4/99, p. 49, Rod Dreher

In the splendid "Buena Vista Social Club," director Wim Wenders documents a musical miracle: the virtual resurrection of aged and forgotten Cuban son musicians, brought together two years ago in Havana to make the glorious (and bestselling) record that shares a title with Wenders' film.

The miracle-workers were guitarist Ry Cooder and record producer Nick Gold, who re-discovered the elderly all-stars of Cuban music, many of whom had fallen on hard times (the magnificent vocalist Ibrahim Ferrer, for example, had been shining shoes to pay the rent). The joyous album they recorded went on to sell millions of copies internationally, win a Grammy award, and revive the careers of these living monuments of world music.

In "Buena Vista Social Club"—the movie—Wenders returns with Cooder to Havana for a studio reunion of the band members, and he also shows them in concert in Amsterdam and New York. The filmmaker introduces us to the leading lights of the group and has them talk about how their early lives, and introduction to music.

This is sheer delight. Snowy-haired pianist Ruben Gonzalez muses gently under the banyan tree in a Havana park, while the courtly old rascal Compay Segundo, 92, puffs a stogie and brags about his virility. The film shows us extensive Havana street scenes, showcasing the crumbling beauty of the Spanish colonial city and drawing a moving contrast between the material poverty of the people's lives and the richness of their music.

The one flaw in Wenders' approach is the inexplicable absence of any detailed discussion of Cuban musical traditions and how they developed. Cuban son music's distinct sound comes from a tempestuous marriage of African rhythm with Latin melodies and, like the blues in this country, largely springs from the lives and experiences of downtrodden Afro-Cubans. This is left dismayingly unexplored.

That aside, if you're one of the millions who fell in love with the "Buena Vista Social Club" record, this film is without question a must-see. It concludes with the group's final performance, at Carnegie Hall. We see these old Cuban gentlemen, who live so meagerly, and in such isolation from the rest of the world, walk the streets of Manhattan as if they were in heaven itself. That final concert is both a remarkable triumph of the spirit and a hell of a good show.

SIGHT AND SOUND, 10/99, p. 40, Peter Curran

A documentary featuring the 'lost' Cuban musicians who were brought together by guitarist Ry Cooder to record the million-selling album *Buena Vista Social Club*. The 90-year old musician Compay Segundo revisits a Havana neighbourhood looking for the eponymous club. Cooder explains his passion for this music. At a studio, the band records their next album, a showcase for singer Ibrahim Ferrer. Each of the main players—singers Ferrer and Omara Portuondo, pianist Ruben González, Segundo and others recount their lives and personal philosophies. This is intercut with concert footage shot in Amsterdam and the studio sessions from Ferrer's solo album. The band travels to New York where the impressions of those who have never been outside Cuba are mixed with songs from their climactic performance at Carnegie Hall.

Making the film of an album that was perhaps the last, eloquent atmospheric word on the spirit of Cuba, director Wim Wenders finds himself in the middle of the dance floor, shifting awkwardly from foot to foot. Despite his felicity as the director of such documentaries as *Notebook on Cities and Clothes* and *Tokyo-Ga*, here Wenders elbows his way into the extraordinary musical performances with cutaways to interviews, exteriors and queasy steadicam shots. There are moments when the music is so badly out of synch with the pictures that it might be two different performances stuck together. At other times, with its numerous voiceovers from the Buena Vista Social Club artists describing their lives, the film seems to be revising Wenders' superb motif from *Wings of Desire* in which the soundtrack gave us access to solitary characters' thoughts. The more extrovert members of the band sound wise and engaging; the quieter ones like they're giving a statement to the police.

Despite the clumsy execution, the film is a valid celebration of musical sophistication and ageless optimism. This is no slap-down for the running dogs of Yankee imperialism; there's a *Cocoon*-like aura about all the participants—their musical gift has thrown up a force field against cynicism during hard times. The visual evidence of Cuba's decline is beautifully caught with overexposed film to create a sunbleached effect that goes with the now anaemic Cadillacs and Buicks that were once part of the sumptuous pre-revolutionary Cuban experience of the 50s.

The musicians are rightly the stars of the film. The singer Ibrahim Ferrer was reduced to shining shoes before being rediscovered and offers rum and biscuits to a small deity in his home, thankful that Cuba's lack of consumerism has protected the human spirit. The elegant 80-year-old pianist Rubén González successfully eludes documentary inquisition by affecting a Ralph Richardson-like air of bemusement. By contrast, the incorrigible Compay Segundo—a combination of Dean Martin and Sid James—brandishes his cigar as he assures us that years of toil in the tobacco fields have had little effect on his sexual potency. The one woman featured is wreathed in old school glamour: Omara Portuondo wafts through her childhood streets singing to curious bystanders. As she nears the end of the road, you expect her to cry, "I'm ready for my close up now, Mr DeMille!" On stage she delivers words loaded with raw experience and you feel guilty for thinking her a sentimental old diva.

The concert sections are the most expansive and entertaining parts of the movie. Scorsese's *The Last Waltz* (1978) apart, few music films ever transmit the immediacy and emotional thrill of live performance. This one does. The musical dynamic fluctuates between strutting, sensual urgency and delicate pathos, and throughout the band smile easily at each other as if they have no real control over this extraordinary rush of dexterity and power. This transcendence is what their musical lives have been about. The performers are physically divided into two tiers. Cooder, dressed in black, positions himself towards the back of the stage, leaving the frontline and the spotlight to the Cubans. Yet because the director repeatedly cuts to him, in his discreet gloom he begins to resemble a brooding gorilla whose continuing approval of the music going on in front of him must be constantly monitored.

When the band prepares for their final concert at Carnegie Hall, there is an opportunity for most of these aged players to see New York for the first time. it's a moving moment when the anti-consumerist Ferrer presses himself against a wall amid the high-rise, traffic-clogged intestine of American capitalism, exclaiming, "It's so beautiful!" Two band members fail to recognise a bust of JFK in a novelty-shop window. The film-maker's lingering reliance on observing these innocents abroad raises an impatience for the final rush of concert footage. The band suddenly look their age as they strike up amid the vastness of Carnegie Hall and are visibly affected by this unexpected gift of noisy acclaim near the end of their lives. The playing is as exuberant as ever and the indestructible tautness of their technique leaves you in awe of the superannuated cool of the Buena Vista Social Club, reaching the summit of their career after only half a century of hard climbing.

VILLAGE VOICE, 6/8/99, p. 66, Richard Gehr

Like the vintage hand-tinted postcards it resembles, Wim Wenders's film about the Buena Vista Social Club—the dozen or so aging Cuban singers and musicians who recorded the mellifluous million-selling album of the same name—feels like a timeless blast from the past. Assembled in 1997 by guitarist Ry Cooder for Havana recording sessions, the Buena Vista Social Club is a stylish, distressed signifier for the nostalgic glories of prerevolutionary Cuban culture.

Life before Castro "wasn't what it is now," says 72-year-old singer Ibrahim Ferrer, the famously rediscovered son and bolero singer who shined shoes for a living prior to hooking up with Cooder. "It was harder." Aside from Ferrer's comment, however, and some revolutionary graffiti, the film maintains an apolitical distance from the strained Cuba-U.S. relationship. As it happens, the Club has skirted the U.S. government's cultural embargo more successfully than any other Cuban musicians to date.

In making their case for a naive *campesino* music that transcends ideology, Wenders and producer Cooder film the Club's key members in isolation as they reminisce in fabulously dilapidated art-deco bars. Since nobody seems to know where the original Buena Vista Social Club was located (92-year-old, cigar-puffing string player Compay Segundo pokes around a Havana neighborhood for it in one amusing sequence), the film serves as a sentimental journey back into its heyday. Emotions run thick when Ferrer sings the bolero "Silencio" in a recording studio with 69-year-old Omara Portuondo, and then thicker when Wenders cuts directly to the group's first public performance of the song, in Amsterdam.

Self-effacing to a fault (apart from his signature slide-guitar accents), Cooder is known as much for his film scores (such as Wenders's *Paris, Texas)* as for his collaborations with such musicians as Mali's Ali Farka Toure and India's Vishwa Mohan Bhatt. But the film sheds little light on the crosscultural creative process—it could have included more informal studio give-and-take.

Buena Vista Social Club makes a sharp turn when the band visits New York for a final proud and exciting concert at Carnegie Hall (I vividly recall 77-year-old pianist Ruben Gonzalez basking as long as possible in well-deserved adulation). Wenders follows three of the musicians as they wander down Seventh Avenue after the concert, chatting about "the good life" they find reflected in tacky souvenir statues of American presidents. "If we'd followed the way of possessions," Ferrer had said back in Havana, "we would have been gone a long time ago." Possibly. Having followed the directions to Carnegie Hall so well, they only really seem lost after they've played there.

Also reviewed in:
CHICAGO TRIBUNE, 6/25/99, Friday/p. A, Alejandro Riera
NATION, 7/12/99, p. 36, Stuart Klawans
NEW YORK TIMES, 6/4/99, p. E24, Stephen Holden
VARIETY, 2/22-28/99, p. 56, Eddie Cockrell
WASHINGTON POST, 6/18/99, p. C1, Richard Harrington
WASHINGTON POST, 6/18/99, Weekend/p.45, Desson Howe

CABARET BALKAN

A Paramount Classics release of a MACT Productions/Ticket Productions/Stefi 2/Mine Film/Vans/Gradski Kina-Skopje production with the participation of Canel + and the support of Eurimages. *Producer:* Antoine de-Clermont-Tonnerre and Goran Paskaljevic. *Director:* Goran Paskaljevic. *Screenplay (Serbo-Croatian with English subtitles):* Dejan Dukovski, Goran Paskaljevic, Filip David, and Zoran Andric. *Based on his play "Bure Baruta":* Dejan Dukovski. *Director of Photography:* Milan Spasic. *Editor:* Petar Putnikovic. *Music:* Zoran Simjanovic. Sound: Nick Despotidis and (music) Vladan Korac. *Sound Editor:* Branko Neskov. *Art Director:* Milenko Jeremic. *Set Decorator:* Zivojin Savic. *Costumes:* Zora Mojsilovic. *Make-up:* Isabelle Goulliart and Marinela Spasenovic. *Stunt Coordinator:* Miomir Radevic. *Running time:* 100 minutes. *MPAA Rating:* Not Rated.

CAST: Nikola Ristanovski (Boris); Nebojsa Glogovac (Taxi Driver); Lazar Ristovski (Sparring Partner); Ana Sofrenovic (Woman on a Train); Ivan Bekjarev (Bus Hijacker); Mirjana Jokovic (Ana); Miki Manojlovic (Michael); Toni Mihajovoksi (George); Vojislav Brajovic (Topi); Mirjana Karanovic (Natalia); Marko Urosevic (Alex); Bogdan Diklic (Jovan); Danil Bata Stojkovic (Viktor); Dragan Nikolic (Boxer); Aleksandar Bercer (Dimitri).

CINEASTE, Vol. XXV, No 1, 1999, p. 44, Andrew Horton

"Why do you laugh at me? Do you think I'm funny?," asks the campy, Dracula-like stage performer/narrator in the Cabaret Balkan nightclub in the opening of Goran Paskaljevic's provocative black comedy, *Powder Keg* (retitled *Cabaret Balkan* for its U.S. release). For the next hundred minutes the audience is trapped inside Belgrade on a winter's night several years ago—after the Bosnian War and more than a year before the Kosovo War—as a series of interlocking stories and interwoven characters act out explosive relationships.

The film was the leading box-office hit in 1998 in the former Yugoslavia and has received festival awards and wide attention abroad, as its release has coincided with the public's desire to learn more about the Balkans than CNN and the daily newspapers have provided. What audiences learn almost immediately is that nothing depicted in the film is lightheartedly comic, even though there is much laughter. Based on a stage play by the coscreenwriter Dejan Dukovski, a twenty-six-year-old playwright from the Former Yugoslav Republic of Macedonia, Paskaljevic's film is a searing look at contemporary Belgrade (Skopje in the stage play) during a twenty-four-hour period in 1995, as the Dayton Peace Accord regarding Bosnia is being settled 'off camera' in the background. What we experience is a slice of Serbian society caught between war and peace, basically cut off from Western Europe by NATO sanctions, and with no clear future or solutions in view.

The American title *Cabaret Balkan* emphasizes the theatrical framing of the film, which bookends and intersperses the 'real-life' stories with a sense of performance, reminiscent of films such as Bob Fosse's *Cabaret* (1972), based on Christopher Isherwood's book, *Goodbye to Berlin,* about life in pre-WWII Berlin as the Nazi party was coming to power. That Paskaljevic's narrator speaks directly to us establishes the performance basis of the entire film. The narrator ends the film in the same mode. But this time he is 'off duty,' seated at the bar, repeating the "good health" wish that has brought nothing but disaster to characters throughout the film who have uttered the same words, and then he passes out. Halfway through the film another cabaret interlude connects the narrator to one of the tales. He is the brother of the former wife of one character who has returned to Yugoslavia to win back her love. Theater and life become, finally, not a 'powder keg' but unconsciousness, as Belgrade and the cinema fade to black.

Such a frame to this Balkan tale invites us and, in fact, demands that we look at the 'real' stories as performances, too, or at least as variations on a theme of what happens when the slightest incident can cause people to explode into excesses of speech, action, and violence toward themselves and those around them. The Balkan wink to the audience that all is 'performance' and that the narrator is alive at the film's end suggests survival despite all, and that is a form of triumph, the basis of a wider definition of comedy. As Croatian director Rajko Grlic recently said,

"For us in the ex-Yugoslavia, laughter is a way of survival but there is no comedy without suffering."

Despite the film's sense of performance, it candidly confronts the social and political brutality which has engulfed Yugoslav society. In one confrontation after another, escalating to the climactic stoning and torching of a young Bosnian refugee boy who is wrongfully accused of stealing gasoline, the 'powder keg' theme of Serbian society on the edge is explored with riveting performances by an impressive ensemble of Serbian actors. Much like Robert Altman's *Short Cuts* or even Max Ophul's *la Ronde*, based on Arthur Schnitzler's sarcastic and stylish play, *Cabaret Balkan* interweaves the stories of characters who are not directly connected but who cross paths in ironic, brutal, and often darkly comic ways, coming full circle to an 'explosive' ending. A middle-aged man and his friend trash the respectable old apartment of a family whose seventeen-year-old boy accidentally damaged the man's car in a traffic collision. A young cab driver follows a badly crippled police officer into a bar and roughs him up, explaining that it was indeed he himself who crippled the officer in the first place, when the officer attacked him for parking with his girlfriend, an act of police brutality which has left the cabbie sterile. Two old friends trade insults about screwing each other's wives and girlfriends, escalating to the point where one murders the other. A man, angered that a city bus is fifteen minutes late, hijacks the bus for a joyride through town, terrorizing the riders until the Bosnian University professor—now turned bus driver—catches up with him and beats him unconscious. This is but a partial list of horrors that become even more disturbing because, as Paskaljavic has explained, he consciously wanted the film to have almost no reference to 'the war' or scenes on the battlefield. All these stories unfold with hatred and violence on the streets, within homes, and in public places of today's Belgrade.

Key to the film's theme is the question of guilt or blame. Who is guilty or responsible for the 'situation' that has turned every citizen into a miniature powder keg? What the film accomplishes so intensely is a feeling that all are guilty of something but that no one is taking responsibility for anything. A middle-aged gentleman in a suit urges the man whose car is damaged by a teen in another car to smash the windshield and pull the boy out through the window. Passengers on the hijacked bus show some signs of fear but even more of enjoyment of this illegal action. The overall feeling, therefore, is of complete hopelessness.

Cabaret Balkan has been important for the audience Paskaljevic originally targeted: Serbs and former Yugoslavs everywhere. Yugoslav cinema of the past twenty years has been one of the most vibrant, imaginative, and provocative cinemas anywhere, with filmmakers such as Emir Kusturica, Rajko Grlic, Goran Markovic, Srdjan Karanovic, Slobodan Sijan, Milcho Manchevski, and Goran Paskaljevic achieving commercial success and winning numerous international awards (see my article, "Satire and Sympathy: A New Wave of Yugoslavian Filmmakers," in *Cineaste,* Vol. XI, No. 2). That generation, which came into prominence in the late Seventies, was building on the ground-breaking innovations of the so-called "black cinema" filmmakers of the Sixties such as Dusan Makavejev, Zika Pavlovic, and Aleksandar Pekovic.

If one could identify a major trend among these filmmakers, it would be their ability to mix social satire embracing or bordering on surrealism with playfully imaginative tales of individuals attempting to find personal happiness against all odds. Paskaljevic's film and Dukovski's play derive from Serbia's rich tradition of theatrical social comedy, especially as seen in the works of Branislav Nusic in the early decades of the century. Nusic's plays balance caricature with character satire, farce with a comedy of manners, and almost always depicted patriarchal traditional society under siege from peasant culture, on one hand, and from 'modern' hedonistic trends on the other. One senses something of an echo of Nusic's sarcastic and biting wit in many of the exchanges throughout *Cabaret Balkan,* especially as spoken by our cabaret narrator. Belgrade audiences expect such cutting wit and timely references in their films. The narrator's volcanic flow of language halfway through the film sounds almost like some form of a Balkan rap song, half-mad and half-playful, anarchistic, absurdist, and definitely excessive:

All the politicians
Europe's undertakers
The worms, ideas, chaos,
ghettos of paranoia

hermetic circles
esoteric circles
dickomantics, schizomantics,
necromantics, metamantics.
Fuck it all
It's so boring, children.
Ethnic tension civil war
brother killing brother
If you have an open wound
Don't wait for somebody to help you.
Cauterize it.
Don't pity anybody.
If you pity anybody
Fuck him till he's dead.
Because death is beautiful
and the world is absurd.
Politics is madness
and I'm full of shit.

The lines both amuse and frustrate us, for, like the film itself, Paskaljevic's cabaret narrator becomes an absurd nihilist who sarcastically undermines his own position so that we cannot criticize him, for he is "full of shit."

The arresting premise at the center of the script is the frighteningly, honest perception that the real 'powder keg' in the former Yugoslavia does not have to do with Muslim against Orthodox Nationalists but, ultimately, Serb against Serb, as the 'situation' appears to leave drained away all aspects of humanity and civility. Paskaljevic also leaves us with no doubt that these problems appear almost entirely male-centered, with women forced to react to and/or accept the excessive and immature behavior of the men around them. This diminished sense of Balkan women at the end of the century has been well-described recently by Sabrina Ramet in *(Gender Politics in the Western Balkans,* when she writes, "In the age of politicized nationalism, the self-proclaimed defenders of 'the Nation' reinterpret the community in folk-mythological terms, reducing women to 'womenfolk' who need men's protection and construing feminists who dare to challenge the patriarchal agenda of the nationalists as witches."

Yet for all of this brilliance, *Cabaret Balkan* gives in too easily to its own despair. Ultimately we are shuttled so swiftly among so many characters that most become little more than stereotypes with no chance or time for development beyond a kind of 'performance' theme that the 'Cabaret' establishes. Even given the 'life on the edge' premise, it is difficult to imagine some ten stories from one city with barely a single trace of redeeming humanity. *Cabaret Balkan* creates its own 'performance' and judges its world as 'hopeless' and "full of shit." It collapses, like its narrator, in its own bleak nihilism. Many Serbian filmmakers and intellectuals admire the film for just such glorious pessimism. A common refrain has been, 'Yes. We are excessive and self indulgent and abusive of women, but, after all, we are Balkans. That's the way we are.' When one tries to suggest that even such a concept is a 'performance' they've adopted, the topic often changes swiftly, with a refusal to take the challenge seriously.

The confusion many American and other foreign audiences feel about these 'ghettos of paranoia' enacted in *Cabaret Balkan* is understandable. Earlier Serb 'comedies' left no such confusion. Slobodan Sijan's *Who's That Singing Over There?* (1980), for instance, frames a tale about Yugoslav culture on the eve of Germany's bombing of Belgrade in 1941 with two gypsies facing the camera and singing a song to us about their life. Because they sing to us directly throughout the film, as if this were a performance, we come to accept the whole film as a 'song' they are joyfully singing, despite the sadness within the words. At film's end, everyone on a bus they have been riding is apparently killed in the bombing. The two gypsies nevertheless climb out of the rubble, dust themselves off, face us, and start singing the same song they began the film with, this time adding some new lyrics. We can't help but smile. We 'get' the comic sense of triumph.

Even Paskaljevic's earlier films have managed a less self-indulgent blend of dark comedy and social observation than seen in his latest effort. *Special Treatment* (1980) is, like *Cabaret Balkan,* an ensemble piece, one which tracks the inmates of an alcoholic ward of a hospital under the tyrannical rule of a totalitarian Dr. Ilich who wishes to use them for an experiment in psychodrama outside the hospital. This thinly veiled satiric send-up of communism turns into a carnival of failure but, much like *One Flew Over the Cuckoo's Nest,* to which it bears similarities in shape and style, Paskaljevic's film of almost twenty years ago leaves us with a thoughtful smile rather than a confused pessimism.

Cabaret Balkan succeeds in conveying the sense that all its characters are guilty to one degree or another. Surely the explosive despair depicted in the film reflects many of the unresolved hostilities within Serbian culture. Its over-the-top quality, however, leaves one feeling numb rather than enlightened about the darkening pages in Serbia's dangerous situation. In Paskaljevic's latest and darkest work—unlike the gypsies at the end of *Who Is Singing Over There?*—no one climbs out of the wreckage to face us with wide grins, as they begin once more to sing their troubles away. *Cabaret Balkan* is a brilliantly acted message-in-a-bottle film, but the bottle seems to be exploding before it reaches the shore.

LOS ANGELES TIMES, 8/27/99, Calendar/p. 18, Kevin Thomas

Goran Paskaljevic's corrosive "Cabaret Balkan" deftly lifts Dejan Dukovski's prizewinning play off the stage and out into the streets of Belgrade to reveal in the everyday encounters between people a society rapidly disintegrating. The very fabric of civilization is in such tatters that everyone seems vulnerable to regressing to the most savage displays of anger and ruthless survival-of-the-fittest behavior. At the same time, the filmmakers manage to find an exceedingly bleak humor in the absurdity of their country's predicament, which is characteristic not only of the present-day Balkan cinema but also of that of long-beleaguered Eastern Europe.

Much like the effete emcee in "Cabaret," this film's decadent-looking Belgrade nightclub entertainer, Boris (Nikola Ristanovski), opens the film with his pithy, cynical comments on the current state of affairs in the former Yugoslavia. A chain-smoking taxi driver (Nebojsa Glogovac) drops off Michael (Miki Manojlovic) at that club. (That driver will reappear, as do many others, as vignettes interconnect.) Michael fled the country five years earlier without so much as leaving a note behind and has now returned, much better off financially and eager to make amends to his abandoned fiancee, Natalia (Midana Karanovic), who happens to be Boris' sister.

Meanwhile, a young unlicensed driver, Alex (Marko Urosevic), has collided with a vintage VW belonging to the irate Jovan (Bogdan Diklic), who has owned it for decades without getting so much as a scratch. Alex expresses a desire to resolve the matter amicably, but like many others, Jovan vents upon whoever's handy his displaced rage over what's happening in his country, in this case the hapless Alex and even Alex's father, Viktor (Danil Bata Stojkovic), wrecking the family apartment in the process.

Jovan has brought along his boxer buddy (Dragan Nikolic) who, in turn, later gets into a deadly match in the ring with an old friend (Lazar Ristovski); they launch into such a lengthy confession of mutual betrayals that you know it won't end well.

One encounter leads to another until almost all the film's 22 key characters either give way to anger or become its victims. As unflinching as it is, "Cabaret Balkan" is an edgy entertainment that is as zesty as it is mordantly outrageous. Miki Manojlovic, who has appeared in an array of films in Western Europe and even the U.S., is perhaps the film's dominant figure, a character who naively thinks you can go home again, even when your homeland is falling dangerously apart. Everyone involved, however, contributes strongly to making "Cabaret Balkan" a bristling, furious valentine to the former Yugoslavia.

NEW YORK POST, 7/23/99, p. 61, Rod Dreher

Ferocious, thrilling, arch and ultimately humane, "Cabaret Balkan" is not only one of the best films of the year, but one of the timeliest.

Though it says little directly about the bloody Balkan wars, this gripping, Serbian-made black comedy offers more insight into the cultural roots of that barbaric mess than six months' worth of "Nightline." Of course, nobody goes to the movies for geopolitical seminars, and "Cabaret Balkan" wisely doesn't offer any. It is a powerfully written and acted series of sketches on the related themes of fear, rage and power, structured as a "Blue Room"-style roundelay taking place one fateful night in Belgrade.

But its political point could hardly be sharper: that the Serb people, possessed by bitter pride and vengefulness, are destroying their nation and themselves.

The film, directed by the anti-Milosevic Serbian filmmaker Goran Paskaljevic, was called "The Powder Keg" in Europe, a title referring not only to the traditional metaphor for the Balkans, but also the combustibility of every citizen in a Serbia under duress from war, economic ruin and a corrupt authoritarian government.

What gives the film such power and immediacy is the way normal people come entirely unhinged at the slightest provocation. These lunatic Belgraders seem a lot like us. To wit: An early scene shows a perky teen-ager (Marko Urosevic) crashing his car into a well-dressed older man's prized Volkswagen.

The older man (Bogdan Diklic) is furious, and kicks in the kid's windshield. That's taking it a bit far, but you understand how the VW man feels, and you hope he catches the punk. But there's more.

The man's road rage takes him to the kid's father's apartment, where VW man and a thuggish friend tear the place apart, seeking payback. The scene has a terrible giddiness: You don't know how far it will go, and you desperately wish it would stop, but there's something primal and satisfying in the destructive act.

Different versions of this fevered drama play out over the course of the long, spite-filled Belgrade night. A drunken man with nothing to lose considers raping a girl on a train. A woman sexually harassed by a cocky hijacker finds her insanely jealous boyfriend blaming her for infidelity.

Friends turn on each other, fathers betray sons, the strong bully the weak, and we are mesmerized by the actions and reactions of these characters, pitiless and pitiable, all too human.

The decadent emcee who introduces the film (in an obvious nod to "Cabaret") promises to screw with the audience's head. He does.

Coming out of the screening tied in knots, exhausted but exhilarated, I was surprised to realize how little graphic violence there is in the film.

But Paskaljevic and his immensely talented cast keep the tension level near the bursting point constantly, as if each celluloid frame were bathed in adrenaline.

The riveting "Cabaret Balkan" demonstrates the cathartic attraction of violence while exposing its pathos and futility. You can see why Paskaljevic and his movie are banned in Slobbo's Belgrade. But if this movie were only about Serbs, it wouldn't be nearly so powerful.

NEWSDAY, 7/23/99, Part II/p. B12, John Anderson

Some movies you leave dancing, some you leave singing. "Cabaret Balkan" you exit with a case of nervous exhaustion. "Smoke kills," mutters the Cab Driver (Nebojsa Glogovac). "Everything here kills." By the time the arm rest has come loose from your seat, you're pretty well convinced.

Directed by Goran Paskaljevic—whose bittersweet "Someone Else's America" should be rented immediately if you haven't seen it—the movie is an attempt to mine the psyche of Yugoslavia postwar, midwar and, by every indication, prewar. It declares that a ceaseless engine of anger fuels erstwhile Yugoslav society, act of violence begetting act of violence, and that the misdirected passions of its people would be comic, save for those bodies strewn across the countryside.

Bookended, a la "Cabaret" (another play that turns on the fulcrum of war) by a draggy nightclub emcee (Nikola Ristanovski), "Cabaret Balkan" takes the "La Ronde" route (with a hint of "Slackers"): An eclectic cast of characters, representing different aspects of the Yugoslav experience, who intersect in a fashion so graceful it approaches irony.

There's a returning expatriate (Miki Manojlovic) being driven by the Cab Driver, who just misses hitting Alex (Marko Urosevic), who, while harassing a young woman on the sidewalk, broadsides the vintage VW driven by Jovan (Bogdan Diklic). His fury at the fleeing Alex leads him and a boxer friend (Dragan Nikolic) to Alex' home, where they intimidate his father (Danil Bata Stojkovic) and wreck the joint.

The falling glass hits the roof of the shanty where a Bosnian bus driver and his family gives us a quick intro to the perils of ethnic intermarriage, the toll of the black market and traditional values torn asunder. Two boxers, lifelong friends, tell each other secrets that lead to murder. In a train car, the man who's killed his friend and a woman carrying the knapsack of her dead soldier find release via hand grenade. An impatient bus rider takes mass transit for a ride until a wrench meets his forehead. One of the passengers and her jealous boyfriend find themselves at the mercy of coke-snorting cigarette smugglers. A case of mistaken identity—and isn't that a running Yugoslav joke—ends with an enormous explosion and white-out crucifixion.

Paskaljevic uses three leads from Emir Kusturica's "Underground" (the ubiquitous Manojlovic, Mira Jokovic and Lazar Ristovski) and what might be its raucous brass band as well; "Cabaret Balkan" looks like the all-star game of Balkan cinema. Rich in character, structurally sound, powerfully acted and unendingly tense, the film (formerly "The Powder Keg") was made by a Serb who spent most of the war years in Paris. But a certain distance might have helped Paskaljevic portray what he clearly feels is the endemic violence that's the legacy of Yugoslavia. "Cabaret Balkan"—a French-Greek-Macedonian-Turkish-Yugoslav co-production—doesn't quite tie up all its tangents and its digressions are occasionally a puzzle. But even on a strictly visceral level, its dynamics are hair-raising.

VILLAGE VOICE, 7/27/99, p. 64, Amy Taubin

Cabaret Balkan begins with an incident of road rage. A hapless teenage tough, weaving through the dark streets of Belgrade in an unlicensed yellow cab acquired from who knows where, is so intent on terrorizing a pretty young woman out walking by herself that he slams into a parked car. The car's owner, outraged by this assault on his most prized possession, single-handedly demolishes the cab and then pursues the driver to his father's apartment where he proceeds to smash a lifetime accumulation of furniture and chotchkes. That his attention is diverted just when he's about to strangle a pair of twittering songbirds is such a relief that the scene tips toward comedy, albeit of the darkest variety.

It's a canny opening gambit by director Goran Paskaljevic, since road rage is the closest experience we in the so-called civilized world have to the roiling anger that is a way of life in the former Yugoslavia. Having been reminded of our own irrational outbursts and disproportionate desire for revenge on anyone who slows us down or steals a parking place we assumed was ours for the taking, we cannot regard the characters in Paskaljevic's film, no matter how badly they treat one another, as less human than we.

And they do treat one another very badly indeed. *Cabaret Balkan* is shaped as a series of vaudeville blackout sketches; but the punch line in almost all of them is an explosive act of violence. Set in Belgrade in 1995, the film involves about 20 characters who cross paths during the course of a single night. With nerves frayed by a decade of civil war and by the poverty caused by the economic embargo imposed on the Milosevic regime, they respond to every encounter in full fight or flight mode. The film's original title, *The Powder Keg,* is a longstanding metaphor for the Balkans, but here it also seems to describe how under such pressure, every person is potentially a walking time bomb and how individual acts of violence fuel the giant conflagration at the end of the film.

But the new, sexier title, *Cabaret Balkan,* is apt in another way, making the connection between Belgrade today and Berlin in the '30s. It also underscores the film's gallows humor, the vivacity of Paskaljevic's filmmaking, and the panache of the ensemble cast. By constructing the film as a theatrical entertainment—even when the events it depicts are most dire—and giving us front-row seats, Paskaljevic puts us on the side of these Belgradians. I wouldn't want to be the young woman trapped in a railroad compartment with the drunken boxer who has just finished carving up his best friend with a broken bottle and now wants to top off the night with a rape; but the position Paskaljevic places the viewer in—watching from the outside—allows her to feel awed by the life force raging within him, or, to put it another way, to feel that cathartic, Aristotelian blend of pity and terror.

The boxer is played by the great Lazar Ristovski who takes over the screen the way Depardieu used to and, occasionally, still does. Ristovski played Blacky, the leading character in Emir Kusturica's *Underground,* and his galvanic presence is one of the reasons that one can't help but compare the two films. Admirable for its sustained, feverish intensity and epic sweep,

Underground is also a mess, and the attack on it for being pro-Serbian (though Kusturica is a Bosnian Muslim) somewhat justified. *Cabaret Balkan* is a tougher and politically sharper film. Paskaljevic, a Serb who lives in Paris, is an opponent of both the Milosevic regime and the NATO bombing of Kosovo. *Cabaret Balkan* is not a didactic film, but its political message is clear. In every scene, Paskaljevic shows that by taking out their anger and guilt and frustration on one other, or even worse, hoping they can avoid trouble by keeping quiet, these people are engaged in collective suicide.

Also reviewed in:
CHICAGO TRIBUNE, 8/6/99, Friday/p. P, John Petrakis
NEW YORK TIMES, 7/23/99, p. E13, Stephen Holden
VARIETY, 9/14-20/98, p. 38, David Stratton
WASHINGTON POST, 9/10/99, p. C5, Stephen Hunter

CARTOON NOIR

A Cinema Village Features release of a compilation of six international animated shorts: Pedro Serrazina's "Story of the Cat and Moon"; Jiri Barta's "Club of the Discarded"; Julie Zammarchi's "Ape"; Piotr Dumala's "Gentle Spirit"; Paul Vester's "Abductees"; Suzan Pitt's "Joy Street". *Running time:* 83 minutes. *MPAA Rating:* Not Rated.

NEW YORK POST, 12/3/99, p. 50, Lou Lumenick

Animation fans looking for something more challenging than "Toy Story 2" may want to check out "Cartoon Noir," a collection of six sophisticated cartoons on such themes as suicide, incest and cannibalism.

From the Czech Republic, there's Jiri Barta's 25-minute "Club of the Discarded," about the conflict between the Cold War generation and Western-influenced youth culture—enacted by animated mannequins in an abandoned warehouse.

Suzan Pitt's "Joy Street" depicts a suicidal woman who's rescued by a cartoon mouse, while Piotr Dumala's "Gentle Spirit" evokes incest with stunning images of paint on plaster.

VILLAGE VOICE, 12/7/99, p. 144, Richard Gehr

Countless forgettable examples of East European animation later, cartooning remains devoted to the timeless art of kid pacification. Especially in America, animators tend to play it far too safe and keep it far too light. The best works in this six-film grab bag of darker-than-usual animation, however, avoid yuks in favor of a refreshing experimentalism. Five years in the making, Suzan Pitt's *Joy Street* reaches back into '30s cartoon archetypes to make a squeaky reanimated ashtray mouse the shamanic savior of a suicidal woman via a hallucinogenic rainforest trip. The music—Jazz Passenger Roy Nathanson's updated swing arrangements—is as fascinating as the images, which express an impressively wide range of emotions. The program's other highlight, Paul Vester's *Abductees*, combines hypnotic regression tapes with captivating animated accounts of degrading encounters with big-eyed extraterrestrials. Two other shorts are outright grim. With its dusty middle-aged mannequins besieged by a posse of rebellious younger counterparts, Jiri Barta's *Club of the Discarded* seems straight out of the Twilight Zone. And Piotr Dumala's paint-on-plaster piece *Gentle Spirit* is a disturbing Dostoyevsky story rendered on what looks like a redwood's ancient ring work. Although none of these films possess the bomb-throwing zeal of John Kricfalusi's *Boo Boo Runs Wild* (currently in rotation on the Cartoon Network), they make a modest collective case for an animation of cruelty.

Also reviewed in:
NEW YORK TIMES, 12/3/99, p. E21, Anita Gates

CASTLE, THE

A Miramax Films release in association with Village Roadshow Pictures and Working Dog. *Executive Producer:* Michael Hirsh. *Producer:* Debra Choate. *Director:* Rob Sitch. *Screenplay:* Santo Cilauro, Tom Gleisner, Jane Kennedy, and Rob Sitch. *Director of Photography:* Miriana Marusic. *Editor:* Wayne Hyett. *Music:* Craig Harnath and Jane Kennedy. *Sound:* Chris Izzard and (music) Ross Cockle. *Sound Editor:* Peter Graham. *Casting:* Jane Kennedy. *Production Designer:* Carrie Kennedy. *Art Director:* Ben Morieson. *Special Effects:* Aaron Beaucaire. *Costumes:* Kitty Stuckey. *Make-up:* Steven Clode. *Running time:* 85 minutes. *MPAA Rating:* R.

CAST: Michael Caton (Darryl Kerrigan); Anne Tenney (Sal Kerrigan); Stephen Curry (Dale Kerrigan); Anthony Simcoe (Steve Kerrigan); Sophie Lee (Tracey Kerrigan); Wayne Hope (Wayne Kerrigan); Tiriel Mora (Dennis Denuto); Eric Bana (Con Petropoulous); Charles 'Bud' Tingwell (Lawrence Hammill); Robyn Nevin (Federal Court Judge); Costas Kilias (Farouk); Bryan Dawe (Ron Graham); Monty Maizels (Jack); Lynda Gibson (Evonne); John Benton (Mr. Lyle); Laurie Dobson (John Clifton); John Lee (Chairman); Stephanie Daniel (Council Officer); John Flaus (Sergeant Mick Kennedy); Les Toth (Heavy at Door); Erik Donnison (Barlow Representative); Roger Neave, Tony Evans and Robin Miller (High Court Judges); Julie Kulpinski (Kerry); Sam Gleisner (Steve & Kerry's Child); Sebastiano Liotta (Mr. Petropoulos); Josie Noviello (Mrs. Petropoulos); Linda Keane (Federal Court Lawyer); Marilyn Chestnut (High Court Stenographer); Julian Scarff (High Court Clerk of Courts); Marie-Therese Byrne (Assistant to Chairman); Clare O'Sullivan, Warwick Begg, and Michael Roland (High Court Lawyers); Maria Theodorakis (Federal Court Stenographer); John Evans (Federal Court Clerk of Courts); Matthew Giordanella (Con & Tracey's Son); Larry Emdur (Himself); Ian Ross (Himself); Tony Martin (Adam Hammill).

LOS ANGELES TIMES, 5/7/99, Calendar/p. 10, Bob Heisler

[The following review by Bob Heisler appeared in a slightly different form in **NEWSDAY, 5/7/99, Part II/p. B7.]**

A quartet of TV comedy writers spent two weeks writing "The Castle" and 11 days shooting it with one camera, and there's a great temptation to quote my mother who, I believe, coined the phrase, "You only get out of a project as much as you put into it."

And yet ...

Despite half-baked nods to Monty Python, Rowan Atkinson, the lower-class half of "Keeping Up Appearances" and—in its oh-so-cutesy use of narration—Jay Ward's "Fractured Fairy Tales," "The Castle" has the ultra-slow pace, ultra-thick characters and ultra-slim plot of a PBS sitcom pilot. Hardly worth a night at the movies.

And yet...

If a man like Darryl Kerrigan of Cooloroo, Australia, is thankful to the point of tears that he has a pool room for his trophies, who are we to point out that his trophies are junk, his pool table tilts and his house is a hovel hard by the runway of Melbourne's airport with a toxic waste-filled backyard and an unfinished addition that even duct tape couldn't heal?

If a man like Darryl Kerrigan is happy with his lot in life, who are we to suggest that he take the money and run when the mega-conglomo-airport company condemns his house and tells him to move?

Yes, it's a little guy versus big guy movie. You know the story. You know the outcome. You know you have to root for the little guy.

The Kerrigans, on the other hand, don't know much. Mum's a home-decorating maniac who can't leave a surface unfrilled or unfringed, badly. Son Wayne is in jail for theft. Son Steve fills the house with items bought through the newspaper—overhead projector, anyone? Son Dale serves as the narrator and keeper of the family's umbrella smile, though his narration is usually immediately repeated as dialogue. Daughter Tracey, a certified hairdresser who marries a kick-boxer, is the only Kerrigan who has actually made use of the airport.

As Daryl, Aussie sitcom vet Michael Caton presides over his Love Boat ship of fools with such genuineness, such certainty that his is a world without end, you have no option but to say amen. His cup overflows with praise for the smallest accomplishment, finding pleasure in meatloaf, pride in an overhead power line and giving encouragement to the hapless lawyer who defended his son into prison to take his case to the highest court on the continent.

Like a solemnly presented, "Home Sweat Home" sampler sewn for Father's Day in second-grade art class, "The Castle" is charming and, yes, uplifting. A man's house is a commodity easily bought and sold; his home is something to which no one else can set a price.

NEW YORK POST, 5/7/99, p. 52, Rod Dreher

Like "Analyze This," the scruffy, offbeat Aussie comedy "The Castle" proves yet again that a simple, unoriginal premise worked over by talented gag writers can yield surprisingly satisfying results.

The budget on this charming little picture wouldn't have paid half a day of De Niro's "Analyze This" salary, but the audience rakes in just as many terrific lowbrow laughs.

The Kerrigan family is a sad-sack lot, pasty-skinned simpletons who live in Cooloroo, a cruddy Melbourne suburb, under power lines and at the edge of an airport. It ain't much, but it's home.

Dad Darryl (Michael Caton, in an uproariously good performance) is a hale and hearty tow-truck driver bursting with democratic optimism and robust, unaffected pride in his homely family and modest holdings.

He kvells over wife Sal's (Anne Tenney) meatloaf as if it were a delectation from Julia Child's own kitchen. Darryl's sons haven't got the sense God gave gravel, but to him, they're gems. His dink-brained daughter Tracey's certificate from a beauty academy means as much to this proud papa as a Harvard Ph.D. In short, Darryl is a good ol'boy in the best sense of the phrase.

But the Kerrigans failed to get the message that they're white trash who ought to roll over at the command of their social betters. When the government tries to force the family off their land so the airport can be expanded, Darryl won't stand for it; he can't be bought out, and he can't be pushed off. "It's not a house, it's a home!" he fumes.

He takes his quixotic fight through the courts, convinced, in a "Winslow Boy" sort of way, that right will be done. Not a chance—until a sophisticated retired lawyer (Charles "Bud" Tingwell) takes up Darryl's crusade.

There's never a moment's doubt as to how this crowd-pleaser will end, so all its pleasures lie in the baroquely detailed, wickedly observational humor. It's like an affectionate social anthropology lesson on the lower middle class, almost all of which translates just fine from its Australian setting.

Hearing Tracey Kerrigan (Sophie Lee), just back from her Thailand honeymoon, raving about the wonders of airline food, reminded me of my own granny's "stately pleasure dome" recollection of the shiny bathrooms at Shoji Tabuchi's theater in Branson, Mo.

"The Castle's" four writers know what they're talking about.

Not everything works. The jokes become a bit too obvious, and attempts at socially aware commentary ("I'm beginning to understand how the Aboriginals feel") seem belabored.

Even so, "The Castle" was a massive hit in Australia, and it's easy to see why. It's a relentless sendup of working-class suburban tastes and attitudes, but one that gives its audience permission to laugh at its unfashionable targets by championing their underdog status and celebrating their essential decency.

The Kerrigans are holy fools, and "The Castle's" foolishness is irresistible.

NEWSWEEK, 5/10/99, p. 85, David Ansen

The insanely happy Kerrigan family finds delight where others would find horror. This lovey-dovey Australian crew lives in a house perched atop a toxic landfill, situated next to a deafening airport runway overseen by looming electrical-power poles. The proud patriarch, Darryl (Michael Caton), a tow-truck driver, waxes enthusiastic about his fake chimney, his pet greyhounds and his hairdresser daughter's horrid hairdo. In his incurably optimistic eyes, he is living a charmed life in the perfect abode, and nobody is going to take it away from him. Not even the government, which orders him to sell his home to make way for an expanded airport.

"The Castle" is further proof that the Aussies love to make affectionate fun of the tackiest aspects of their culture. (Remember "Strictly Ballroom"?) This modest little comedy, tossed off in 11 days by director Rob Sitch, became the country's biggest-grossing film of 1997. While it obviously struck a deep chord in its homeland, here it's not much more than a light tap on the funny bone. The irrepressibly tacky Kerrigans make an amusing first impression, but the movie essentially has only one joke to offer: the family's beaming pride in every appalling detail of their lives.

SIGHT AND SOUND, 8/98, p. 34, Jamie Graham

The outskirts of Melbourne, Australia. Darryl Kerrigan and his family live, quite contentedly, in the shadow of the airport. They are "the happiest family in the world"—until a letter arrives informing them that the airport is expanding; the Kerrigans' house is to be compulsorily acquired for $75,000. With the aid of Dennis Denuto, an incompetent lawyer friend with no relevant experience, Darryl decides to contest the decision. The case is lost and the Kerrigans begin to pack.

However, new hope arrives in the form of Lawrence Hammill, an elderly gentleman whom Darryl briefly met at the courthouse. It transpires that Hammill is a retired QC who specialised in constitutional law. He offers to represent the Kerrigans free of charge. At the High Court in Canberra Hammill points out that the constitution states that the government has the right to acquire property on just terms, which is not the case in this instance. Drawing on past trials and Darryl's persuasive testimony, Hammill wins the case.

The Castle—like several antipodean hits of recent years—is a modern-day David and Goliath parable. *Muriel's Wedding, Shine* and *Mr Reliable A True Story* all share the same narrative arc in which an ordinary individual confronts, battles with and wins out against tremendous odds, emerging as a hero. QC Lawrence Hammill's inspired court summation—"a home is built not of bricks and mortar but love and memories" would certainly meet with the approval of Jimmy Stewart in *Mr. Smith Goes to Washington* (1939) and Gary Cooper in *Mr. Deeds Goes to Town* (1936). But this, as youngest son Dale Kerrigan's closing voice-over notes, is the story of Darryl versus Goliath—and Darryl Kerrigan, for all his honesty, integrity and perseverance, owes as much to Forrest Gump as to Frank Capra.

Taking inspiration from the recent trend in US comedy to revel in the moronic (*Dumb & Dumber, Kingpin, BAPS*), Darryl is stupid, plain and simple and it is these qualities that provide most of the film's laughs. This type of burnout can translate as patronising, especially when applied to such working-class characters as the Kerrigans. Such was the case in Woody Allen's *Mighty Aphrodite*, with its constant mocking of Mira Sorvino's dim-witted prostitute, and it is a problem that threatens to undermine much of Mike Leigh's work. *The Castle*, written and directed by the same team that satirised current-affairs journalism in the television series *Frontline*, circumvents this pitfall by treating the Kerrigans with affection. And, as in Mike Leigh's *Secrets Lies*, the generosity pays dividends.

Yet funny as the movie certainly is, writer/director Rob Sitch scores bonus points for successfully interweaving social comment with humour. Obvious class frictions and hypocrisies are brought to the fore through Darryl's occasional rants and the contrasting pair of lawyers Dennis Denuto and Lawrence Hammill, but there is also the frequent citing of the 'Mabo case'. A 1992 litigation brought by Koiki Mabo and two fellow Murray Islands plaintiffs, this case resulted in the recognition that native title could exist, and overhauled the previous belief that Australia's indigenous groups were unsettled, with no social or political organisation. Though never fully explored or explained in the film (the 'Mabo case' will mean little to most overseas viewers), the point is made often enough to invite the link: the story of the Kerrigans and their home parallels that of the Aborigines and their land, which was also compulsorily acquired.

These undercurrents are further invited to the surface by *The Castle*'s rhythm and *mise en scène*, which consciously distance the film from the frantic, glossy world of much contemporary comedy. Sitch shoots in long, static takes comprised largely of medium two-shots and relies on deliciously deadpan deliveries and unobtrusive edits to supply a gentle but congenial cadence. Miriana Marusic's photography also ignores the conventional cosmetic sheen, instead favouring muddy browns and muted greens. Even the occasional blue fails to provide relief, being so washed out as to resemble the faded sweater worn by Darryl's wife Sal. It would be easy to overlook *The Castle*'s mordant subtexts; the film may play dumb but don't be fooled for a second.

VILLAGE VOICE, 5/11/99, p. 116, Dennis Lim

The Kerrigans are simple folk who reside on the outskirts of Melbourne. How simple? They live right next to an airport runway—and they like it! Not just simple, but kooky too. Every family member is a shtick figure: narrator Dale is deadpan and dopey; brother Steve scours classified ads for bargains; sister Tracey is a hairdresser with bad hair; another brother, Wayne, is doing time for armed robbery and not much of a talker; Mom smiles, makes hideous craft objects, and cooks bland food; Dad, a home-improvement nut, raises greyhounds, likes speedboats, and is consistently bowled over by Mom's bland food.

The Ealing/Disney/Capra plot is set in motion by an eviction notice (the airport is expanding). And so, the everyman against the Man, a man's home is his et cetera, geddit? Miramax coughed up $6 million for this bit of nonsense, which, incredibly, took four people (director Rob Sitch included) to write. The screenplay's favorite comic strategy is repetition—every gag, however feeble, boomerangs right back at you. Beneath the snide-but-jolly veneer, there are larger problems. The movie's attitude toward the working class stops just short of contempt, its idea of social comment is pathetic ("I'm starting to understand how the Aborigines feel"), and it's not above racist gibes (a Lebanese neighbor refers to bombs—twice, naturally). Like too many Aussie kitschfests, *The Castle* is transparently opportunistic—the tone starts out more mocking than affectionate, but an avalanche of gooey sentiment arrives on cue to make sure you end up rooting for the poor fools. Sorry, not an option.

Also reviewed in:
CHICAGO TRIBUNE, 5/14/99, Friday/p. I, John Petrakis
NEW YORK TIMES, 5/7/99, p. E20, Stephen Holden
VARIETY, 4/21-27/97, p. 65, David Stratton
WASHINGTON POST, 5/14/99, Weekend/p. 50, Desson Howe

CHERRY

A Cypress Films release. *Producer:* Joseph Pierson and Jon Glascoe. *Director:* Jon Glascoe and Joseph Pierson. *Screenplay:* Terry Reed. *Director of Photography:* Phil Abraham. *Editor:* Susan Graef. *Music:* Joel Goodman. *Sound:* Noah Vivekanand Timan. *Casting:* Ellen Parks. *Production Designer:* Sherri Adler. *Set Decorator:* Allyn Howard. *Costumes:* Mary Ann McAlpin. *Running time:* 90 minutes. *MPAA Rating:* Not Rated.

CAST: Shalom Harlow (Leila Sweet); Jake Weber (Dr. Beverly Kirk); Isaach de Bankole (Menu Man); Laurel Holloman (Evy Sweet); Donovan Leitch (Eddie the Clown); Gil Rogers (Uncle Ernest); David McCallum (Mammy); Aleksa Palladino (Darcy); Heather Matarazzo (Dottie).

NEW YORK POST, 12/10/99, p. 54, Hannah Brown

Model Shalom Harlow could have chosen a better vehicle for her first big movie role than "Cherry." This sweet-natured, occasionally amusing little comedy suffers from slack pacing and a hackneyed script that feels like something expanded from a reject episode of "Sex in the City."

Leila (Harlow) is a 29-year-old virgin who was left at the altar at the age of 18 and resolved never to love anyone again. This resolution seems to have precluded fooling around of any kind, because there's a suggestion that this gorgeous woman hardly even knows how to kiss.

Ivy League-educated but so naive she seems half-witted, Leila runs a muffin shop that makes no money and has a dog named Paxil. Her parents were killed in an accident when she and her less-screwed up sister (Laurel Holloman) were kids, and she was brought up by her gay uncle Ernest (Gil Rogers) and his partner Mammy (David McCallum). Now she wants a baby.

For some unexplained reason, artificial insemination is out of the question, so Leila advertises for a genetically suitable man to impregnate her in a night of love-free sex. None of the hundreds who respond seems right.

Instead, two unlikely candidates emerge, a clown (Donovan Leitch) she met because they had easily confusable phone numbers, and Leila's gynecologist, Dr. Kirk (Jake Weber). Though written by a woman, this is one of those movies that attribute sexiness to a pelvic exam in the stirrups.

It isn't just the central dilemma that seems fake. The movie is supposed to take place in New York, but the city Leila lives in has the feel of a provincial town like, say, Seattle.

It's hard not to feel embarrassed for David McCallum: It's a long way from Ilya in "The Man From U.N.C.L.E." to this crude imitation of a good-hearted queen.

On the other hand, Harlow (who played a strung-out mannequin in "In and Out") shows both that she can act and that she has a charming, slightly goofy screen presence.

And Heather Matarazzo steals several scenes as a slacker waitress.

Also reviewed in:
NEW YORK TIMES, 12/10/99, p. E37, Janet Maslin
VARIETY, 5/17-23/99, p. 59, Lael Loewenstein

CHILDREN OF HEAVEN, THE

A Miramax Films release of an Institute for the Intellectual Development of Children and Young Adults production. *Producer:* Amir Esfandiari and Mohammad Esfandiari. *Director:* Majid Majidi. *Screenplay (Farsi with English subtitles):* Majid Majidi. *Director of Photography:* Parviz Malek-zadeh. *Editor:* Hassan Hassan-doost. *Music:* Keivan Jahan-shahi. *Sound:* Yadollah Najafi. *Sound Editor:* Mohammad Reza Delpak. *Running time:* 88 minutes. *MPAA Rating:* Not Rated.

CAST: Mohammad Amir Naji (Ali's Father); Amir Farrokh Hashemian (Ali); Bahare Seddiqi (Zahra); Nafise Jafar-Mohammadi (Roya); Fereshte Sarabandi (Ali's Mother); Kamal Mirkarimi (Assistant); Behzad Rafi (Trainer); Dariush Mokhtari (Ali's Teacher); Mohammad-Hasan Hosseinian (Roya's Father); Masume Dair (Roya's Mother); Kambiz Peykarnegar (Race Organizer); Hasan Roohparvari (Race Photographer); Abbas-Ali Roomandi (Shoemaker); Jafar Seyfollahi (Green Grocer); Qolamreza Maleki (Salt Seller); Zahra Mirzai (Zahra's Teacher); Sara Zamani (Trainer); Mohammad Haj-Hosseini (Mosque Servant); Kazem Asqarpoor (Grand Father); Mohammad Hossein Shahidi (Alireza); Seyd-Ali Hosseini (Ali's Friend); Haj-Ali Salimi (Old Man); Ahmad Mokhber (Mash Ramezan); Golnaz Tariqat (Ms. Koubab); Mash-Ebrahim Safari (Ali's Father's Friend); Davud Shams (Shoe Seller); Azade Qale Noi (Video Camerman); Faramarz Safarizadeh (Video Camerman); Hossein Ahamdloo, Siamak Haj-Amini, and Soheil Haj-Amini (Photographers); Rahman Kharazchi, Jamshid Yusefi, and Javad Kazemi (Referees); Mohammad Oskooi, Reza Dehghan, and Ali Chaharian (Award Presenters); Amir-Ali Kazemi (First Runner); Navid Feyzabadi (Second Runner/Third Runner); Pasha Shoja Zadeh (Fourth Runner).

LOS ANGELES TIMES, 1/22/99, Calendar/p. 8, Kevin Thomas

Majid Majidi's "Children of Heaven" is so similar to "The "White Balloon" (1995)—surely the Iranian film most familiar to American audiences—that this resemblance must be dealt with right off in order to judge the newer film on its own considerable merits.

In "White Balloon," an adorable little girl meets disaster when she is given precious coins from her mother to buy a goldfish to celebrate the New Year; in "Children of Heaven," a sad-faced 9-year-old boy (Mir Farrokh Hashemian) goes to pick up his adorable younger sister's shoes at the shoemaker's, only to find they've been somehow lost. In both films, youngsters go to extremes to try to solve the problems themselves and thereby prevent, at all costs, their impoverished parents from learning the truth. This means embarking on odysseys that bring them into contact with a cross-section of humanity.

"The White Balloon" has a stunning simplicity and unity, leavened with a wry humor, whereas "Children of Heaven" is wider-ranging and bleaker. In any event, the children in "Heaven," who go to school (in Teheran) at different shifts, agree to swap footwear. Zahra (Bahareh Seddiqi) must rush home so that she can exchange her older brother's sneakers for her own sandals. The film is enormously touching in its depiction of steadfast devotion between siblings, a devotion constantly being put to the test by fate and youthful human nature.

The children are terrified of their father (Amir Naji) yet understand the pressures on him to provide for them, especially since their mother is suffering from a debilitating back condition. The brother and sister's various adventures culminate in the brother's brave decision about how to get his sister a decent pair of shoes.

"Children of Heaven" has a glowing look and takes us into a world of ancient narrow alleys in which homes look like fortresses to the street, but within contain charming courtyards with fish ponds in the center. Majidi is not trying for social criticism as much as paying tribute to the potential for the noble, self-sacrificing gesture within the human spirit. Hashemian and Seddiqi are as irresistible as the tiny heroine of "The White Balloon," and this film leaves you moved—but also wishing it didn't seem so derivative.

NEW YORK POST, 1/22/99, p. 54, Jonathan Foreman

One wonderful movie after another comes out of Iran despite, or perhaps because of, the restrictions placed on artistic expression by the ruling Mullahs.

Very often these films are about children—with the opportunities for subtle but powerful social comment. "Children of Heaven," an utterly delightful, moving story about a little boy and his sister who live in one of Teheran's poorest quarters, is no exception.

"Children," directed by Majid Majidi, contains obvious echoes of Vittorio De Sica's neo-realist classic "The Bicycle Thief" and Bille August's "Pelle the Conqueror."

But despite its effective depiction of the humiliations of poverty, it is never depressing—or predictable.

Much of the plot centers on a pair of shoes—a possession that prosperous folk take for granted but the truly poor do not.

One day, little Ali (Mir Farrokh Hashemian) picks up his sister Zahra's (Bahareh Seddiqi) only pair from the cobbler but proceeds to lose them while doing some errands for their ailing mother.

Zahra now has no shoes to wear to school. The children cannot tell their parents because Ali is sure that his Turkish immigrant father (Amir Naji), who pours tea at the local mosque, cannot afford to buy her new ones.

So the children work out a scheme whereby Zahra wears Ali's sneakers to her classes in the morning, then runs back to meet him so he can wear them to his school in the afternoon.

But the shoes don't really fit Zahra, and the changeover means that Ali is late for class.

Then Zahra sees another girl wearing her lost shoes. She resolves to get them back until she discovers that this girl is the daughter of an even-poorer blind peddler.

A solution seems at hand when Ali's father tries to make some extra money as a gardener in the far-off rich neighborhoods of North Tehran.

This and other episodes in "Children of Heaven" allow Majidi to explore some fascinating aspects of Iranian society: from the regimentation of Zahra's school to the huge gulf between the Westernized rich and the deferential poor.

There are a few overdone moments in "Children of Heaven" and some minor technical flaws including points when the dialogue is obviously dubbed.

But it never ceases to be a real story about real people, told with skill, humor and delicacy. It's also acted with remarkable authority by both children and adult players.

"Children of Heaven" is likely to receive an Oscar nomination for best foreign-language film, an honor its creator deserves.

NEWSDAY, 1/22/99, Part II/p. B6, Gene Seymour

A writing teacher I once had was exasperated by the number of Beckett-Pinter-life-is-absurd pastiches that kept finding their way onto his desk. "If you want to write about life," he told us, "don't write about life-with-a-capital-L. Write about a carrot. Or a lost shoe."

The wisdom of this advice has been backed by a handful of recent Iranian films in which children's seemingly simple travails assume epic levels of emotional intensity and social observation that most "adult dramas" made in this country rarely approach. The work of Abbas Kiarostami ("Where is My Friend's House?") and Jafar Panahi ("The White Balloon," "The Mirror") have become landmarks of this emergent tradition.

Majid Majidi's "Children of Heaven" is so reminiscent of such films that it comes dangerously close to mere imitation. Still, it's difficult to resist the charm in this tale of a pair of poor Tehran siblings Ali (Mir Farrokh Hashemian) and Zahra (Bahareh Seddiqi) who must share the same woebegone pair of sneakers because Zahra's faded pink shoes, the only pair she owns, were accidentally picked up by a blind peddler while Ali was bringing them home from the cobbler's.

Wishing neither to make their invalid mother (Fereshteh Sarabandi) sicker than she is nor incur the wrath of their blustery, overworked father (Amir Naji), the pair work out a scheme in which Zahra wears Ali's sneakers to school for the first part of the day and then gives them back to Ali so he can wear them to his afternoon classes.

The plan and the sneakers themselves go through several near-death experiences. One of the shoes, too big for Zahra's feet, falls into a sewage drain and in the anxious moments that follow, you're almost embarrassed to be rooting for this dumb, sodden sneaker to find its way out. Which it does.

Meanwhile, Ali and his father take a bike trip "uptown" in search of gardening jobs from the city's tonier classes. Maybe if they get extra money, the kids can get new shoes and their problems will be moot. Then again, their bike could lose its brakes and the accident could keep papa out of work, putting them right back where they started.

The wide class disparities depicted in this sequence may surprise American filmgoers unfamiliar with the nuances of Middle East society. But even here, Majidi can't resist adding sweetener in the form of an encounter between Ali and a rich boy looking for someone to play with.

Majidi's absorption in the children's universe may leave the grownups in the film somewhat blurred and broadly drawn. But he knows that's how grownups look to kids, especially when they're seriously engrossed in making the best of a bad situation. However awkward or static it moves, "Children of Heaven" shares with its Iranian counterparts an engrossing focus on the perils, hurts and furtive pleasures of being a kid with hard problems to solve.

VILLAGE VOICE, 1/26/99, p. 59, Michael Atkinson

As if Harvey Weinstein himself sat down to make his own *Il Postino*-ish version of a Kiarostami scenario, Majid Majidi's ham-handed Iranian minidrama practically remakes *Where Is the Friend's House?* and *The White Balloon* by way of test-screening cards. ("Did you like/dislike those sweet, opal-eyed Persian kids?" Loved 'em.) Unquestioning and patronizing, *The Children of Heaven* is, relative to Kiarostami's ambiguous elegance, a crying clown on black velvet. We look down at Majidi's kids as sympathetic grown-ups, while in Kiarostami we're with those kids, and their single-minded missions, from the git-go. Removed from its daunting Kiarostamian context, it's just another imported open-heart massage movie with adorable tots, difficult trials, and slow-motion triumph.

In a by-now familiar north Iranian setting, a young boy (Mir Farrokh Hashemian) loses his sister's shoes, and so secretly arranges to swap his own threadbare sneakers with her as they come and go to school. For the sister (the peach-cheeked Bahareh Seddiqi), the world suddenly becomes filled with opulent footwear, but her brother is perennially late for school despite his mad dashing, which could get him expelled. When a regionwide marathon race is held, the little urchin hopes to win not first but third prize, which includes a pair of sneakers he could give to his sister.

You can't miss the dis of Western consumer culture any more than you can miss the film's final endorsement of same. Clumsily staged (a bike accident any 15-year-old Super-8 maven could've cut better), lit like a soap opera, and acted with all the bribed relish of an opera, and acted with all the bribed relish of a peanut butter commercial, Majidi's movie is merely the simplistic bid being made by every national industry impatient for mass audience attention. Gallingly, it may succeed.

Also reviewed in:
CHICAGO TRIBUNE, 2/5/99, Friday/p. J, Michael Wilmington
NEW REPUBLIC, 2/22/99, p. 30 Stanley Kauffmann
NEW YORK TIMES, 1/22/99, p. E20, Janet Maslin

CHILL FACTOR

A Warner Bros. release of a James G. Robinson presentation of a Morgan Creek production. *Executive Producer:* Jonathan A. Zimbert and Bill Bannerman. *Producer:* James G. Robinson. *Director:* Hugh Johnson. *Screenplay:* Drew Gitlin and Mike Cheda. *Director of Photography:* David Gribble. *Editor:* Pamela Power. *Music:* Hans Zimmer and John Powell. *Music Editor:* Adam Smalley. *Sound:* Peter J. Devlin and (music) Malcolm Luker. *Sound Editor:* Terry Rodman. *Casting:* Pam Dixon Mickelson. *Production Designer:* Jeremy Conway. *Art Director:* Freddy Slavin. *Set Designer:* Colleen Balance, Kevin Hardison, Glenn Rivers, and Michael Ward. *Set Decorator:* Claudette Didul-Mann. *Set Dresser:* Eric Luling, Michael A. Shapiro, Jeffrey Barrows, Andrea "Drew" Sywanyk, Bennett Silver, Patrick Fuhrma, Lance Totten, and Justin Hill. *Special Effects:* Michael Vezina. *Visual Effects:* Jay Riddle. *Costumes:* Deborah Everton. *Make-up:* Rick Pour. *Make-up (Cuba Gooding, Jr.):* Stacye Branch. *Stunt Coordinator:* Gary Hymes. *Running time:* 110 minutes. *MPAA Rating:* R.

CAST: Cuba Gooding, Jr. (Arlo); Skeet Ulrich (Tim Mason); Peter Firth (Captain Andrew Brynner); David Paymer (Doctor Richard Long); Hudson Leick (Vaughn); Daniel Hugh Kelly (Colonel Leo Vitelli); Kevin J. O'Connor (Telstar); Judson Mills (Dennis); Jordan Mott (Carl); Dwayne Macopson (Burke); Jim Grimshaw (Deputy Pappas); Richard Todd Aguayo (Gomez); K. Addison Young (Ranger at Dam); James Van Harper (Ranger in Chopper); Tommy Smeltzer (Deputy Art Lewis); Geoff Palmer (Vitelli's Helicopter Pilot); Rhoda Griffis (Pregnant Woman); Johnny Cenicola (Little Boy); Larry Black (Fat Man in Tunnel); David Sharp Fralick (Blond Biker); Garrett Warren (Bearded Biker); Ron Clinton Smith (Hemmings); Stephen Robert (Vitelli's Lieutenant); Quint Von Canon (Crew Member #1); Bart Hansard (Crew Member #2); Howard Carroll (Volvo Driver); Lonnie Smith (Pumper); Johnell Gainy (Ranger Sergeant at Tech Site); Martin Valinsky (Big Ranger at Tech Site); Terry Loughlin (Courtroom General); Bob Penny (Motel Manager); Richie Dye (Ice Cream Andy); Mike Davis (Technician); Afemo Omilami (Courtroom Colonel); Steve Coulter (Sweeney); Phillip Devona (Young Guard); Suzi Bass (Darlene); Gordon A. Johnson (Hardware Store Owner); Tim Dabbs (Gomez's Pilot); Camden Dixon (Mailman); Peter MacKenzie (Technician); Wanda Acuna (Medic #1); Erin Daniels (Medic #2); Jason Cairns (Male Medic).

LOS ANGELES TIMES, 9/1/99, Calendar/p. 4, Kevin Thomas

"Chill Factor" melts swiftly. As the theme-park-ride movie of the week, it jolts over Montana highways like a roller coaster loaded with thrills and spills, but don't expect a shred of credibility. If you find yourself unable to go along for this ride, it's going to seem as yet another silly, bloody and bloated Hollywood behemoth. Alongside this Warners release, "Speed," the high end of the genre, plays like a work of uncompromising realism.

In a prologue set in 1987, Dr. Richard Long (David Paymer) is about to launch a chemical warfare experiment, code name "Elvis," on a remote South Seas island that the officer in charge, Capt. Andrew Brynner (Peter Firth), believes is both immoral and dangerous. Long at once reminds him that he does not answer to Brynner and assures him everything is safe; seconds later, the whole test goes drastically wrong, with 18 soldiers—whom Brynner had wanted to evacuate—dying hideous deaths from a substance that consumes their bodies like fire. The rap is laid on Brynner rather than Long, and 10 years in Ft. Leavenworth turns Brynner into a madman consumed with revenge.

Segue to Jerome, Mont., where Long, still working away at "Elvis" for the Army, has found a fishing companion in Tim Mason (Skeet Ulrich), a young drifter haunted by a past tragedy who works at a local diner. After Capt. Brynner and his gang of thugs catch up with Long, the dying scientist entrusts his "Elvis" capsule with Tim, explaining that he must keep "Elvis" on ice and take it to Ft. Magruder 90 miles away. If its temperature climbs above 50 degrees it will detonate, killing all forms of life for hundreds of miles around.

Just at this turn of events, Cuba Gooding Jr.'s Arlo, a high-spirited ice cream delivery man based in Missoula, has the misfortune to arrive and wind up being pressed by Tim into providing the transportation for "Elvis." Feature-debuting director Hugh Johnson and a clutch of writers finally get the show on the road, which sets Brynner ruthlessly pursuing Tim and Arlo, who are making do with Arlo's rickety truck.

"Chill Factor" is a typical rambunctious action comedy, although you may have difficulty in seeing the humor in a madman intent on getting hold of an ultra-lethal chemical agent to sell to the highest bidder—Brynner expects to clear a cool $100 million.

The actors already mentioned, and numerous others, are capable, but the characters they play, heroes or villains, are too unevenly written to care about.

Technical credits are superior, the scenery is gorgeous, but "Chill Factor," for all its virtuoso calamities, is just another demolition derby.

NEW YORK POST, 9/1/99, p. 53, Rod Dreher

"Chill Factor" is a ho-hummer of a "Speed" knockoff that will leave most audiences cold.

It's a waste of time and talent for Skeet Ulrich and Cuba Gooding Jr., miscast as a salt-and-pepper buddy team (think Lawrence Fishburne and Stephen Baldwin in the crummy "Fled"). Then again, not even Gibson and Glover could redeem a screenplay as hackneyed as this one.

The action begins on a South Pacific atoll, where a secret military chemical-weapon experiment, code named "Elvis," goes horribly wrong, killing 18 soldiers.

The only survivors: Dr. Richard Long (David Paymer), the weapon's inventor, and Capt. Andrew Brynner (Peter Firth), who is sent to prison as the fall guy for Dr. Long's screw-up.

Ten years later, Brynner shows up at a Montana research lab with a high-tech goon squad to kill Long and steal Elvis, hoping to sell the weapon to the highest bidder. Dying from gunshots and fleeing Brynner, Long hands Elvis off to store clerk Tim Mason (Ulrich), begging him to deliver the death device to nearby Fort Magruder before Brynner gets it.

Long also warns Mason to keep the cylinder temperature below 50 degrees, otherwise the bomb will go off and kill millions, melting them like Fudgsicles on a sizzling summer sidewalk.

Conveniently, a jumpy ice-cream truck driver named Arlo (Gooding) happens to be making a delivery to Mason's store. Mason carjacks Arlo and the truck, and off they go on a hazardous journey across Montana, with heavily armed paramilitaries in hot pursuit.

Arlo and Mason squabble comically while helping each other out of lethal scrapes with Brynner's bunch.

"Chill Factor" tosses up the usual chase-movie scenarios, few of which have any energy or impact. The action is competently directed by first-time helmer Hugh Johnson and always matchable—but nothing more special than a "Starsky & Hutch" rerun.

The script, by Drew Gitlin and Mike Cheda, has holes big enough for a fleet of Mr. Softee vans to drive through. This is the kind of movie in which the save-the-world plot hinges on a cell-phone working in an underground tunnel. Even more unbelievable, this is the kind of movie that has a black guy named Arlo.

Ulrich and Gooding (now there's a law firm for you) may have a chemical weapon hidden in the Nutty Buddies, but they have no chemistry between them. Ulrich is too dour, Gooding way, way over the top. His overcaffeinated shtick was hilarious in "Jerry Maguire," but can't he do anything else?

Throughout "Chill Factor," he's two tics away from grabbing his face and letting fly a Curly-like woop-woop-woop-woop!

If this Academy Award-winner's career ever tanks—and with more movies like "Chill Factor," it surely will—Gooding's got a great future entertaining children at birthday parties.

SIGHT AND SOUND, 8/00, p. 42, Kim Newman

Horn Island, 1987. Working for the US military, Dr Richard Long tests an experimental defoliant which proves more powerful than he first thought when it kills 18 men. An inquiry unjustly blames Captain Andrew Brynner, who is sentenced to 10 years in prison. Once released, Brynner recruits a crew of mercenaries and plots to steal the defoliant, code-named Elvis, from Long's laboratory in Jerome, Montana.

Long is fatally wounded during the raid but escapes with Elvis, which he passes on to his fishing partner Tim Mason, an employee in a local diner. Long tells Mason the defoliant will combust to devastating effect if its temperature rises above 50 degrees. Tim coerces the ice-cream delivery man Arlo to store Elvis in his refrigerated truck. Together, they travel across the state, pursued by Brynner. Brynner makes contact with Tim via mobile phone and tries to talk the young man into handing over Elvis, which he plans to sell to the highest bidder. Tim and Arlo refuse. Brynner captures Arlo and tries to force Tim to hand over Elvis; Tim instead delivers a mock-up of the defoliant in exchange for Arlo. Having escaped from Brynner, Tim and Arlo are cornered in a road tunnel by Deputy Pappas, a policeman who thinks Tim is responsible for Long's murder. They are sealed inside the tunnel by Colonel Vitelli, who's responsible for retrieving the stolen defoliant. Tim persuades Pappas of his innocence; Arlo helps the deputy get the trapped motorists to safety while Brynner makes a last bid for Elvis. Arlo and Tim escape as Elvis detonates, killing Brynner.

Following *Broken Arrow* and *Hard Rain*, *Chill Factor* belongs to the one-damn-thing-after-another genre of action movies. Taking elements from earlier suspense films and tossing them together like a salad, *Chill Factor* seems to have been pitched as an answer to such questions as 'what would *Speed* have been like if the bomb were hooked up to a thermometer' or 'how would *The Wages of Fear* (1953) have played out had the nitro-laden trucks trundling over dangerous roads been pursued by a crew of ninja mercenaries?' The problem with these hybrid concepts is that great suspense usually comes from the simplest of premises. Such advice is lost on the makers of *Chill Factor*, as they pile up yet more unlikely dilemmas for the film's two heroes, the terror we're supposed to be anticipating established by a fairly impressive defoliant explosion in the prologue—gets lost in the mix. Given the dramatic potential of a doomsday device that has to be kept cold, *Chill Factor* fails even to make much of the blazing Montana sun and loses all credibility as the defoliant, named Elvis (cue the inevitable 'Elvis has left the building' line), is thrown all over the place by heroes and villains alike.

Debut director Hugh Johnson, previously a cinematographer for Ridley Scott *(White Squall, G.I. Jane)*, is bloodied with the required ridiculous set pieces: a stolen boat tobogganing down a thickly wooded hillside, a wide truck edging along a crumbling mountain road. Unfortunately the production—with its protracted cross-state car chase sequence—feels somewhat cramped, evoking 70s television series *The Dukes of Hazzard* rather than the work of action supremos James Cameron and Jan De Bont. *Chill Factor* is further burdened with a script that hammers home all its points with crushing obviousness (an early monologue on fly-fishing gives Tim, determined to prevent the defoliant from falling into the hands of the villain, the idea of mocking up a bogus Elvis).

Most dramatic weight falls on Peter Firth, an English actor cast as an American villain. His character Brynner is at least unusual in that his army career has been compromised by his unwillingness to condone the murders of civilians in Vietnam and his 'moral objections' to ambitious scientist Long's research. Having been turned into a regulation mercenary mastermind during years spent unjustly in prison, Brynner carries on like a fanatical fiend to get his hands on Elvis, though Tim and sidekick Arlo's public-spirited actions cause the odd challenge to his cynicism ("So, a pair of average citizens have decided to risk their lives for their country. I almost remember what that feels like"). Since it is impossible for a young Hollywood actor to get ahead without an action movie on the CV, one can't blame Cuba Gooding Jr and Skeet Ulrich for accepting such a ropy vehicle. This said, neither Ulrich's brooding intensity nor Gooding's funky panic act (he whines throughout the stunt work) add much to the enterprise.

Also reviewed in:
CHICAGO TRIBUNE, 9/1/99, Tempo/p. 1, Michael Wilmington

NEW YORK TIMES, 9/1/99, p. E3, Stephen Holden
VARIETY, 8/30-9/5/99, p. 52, Robert Koehler
WASHINGTON POST, 9/3/99, Weekend/p. 43, Desson Howe

CIDER HOUSE RULES, THE

A Miramax Films release of a FilmColony production. *Executive Producer:* Bob Weinstein, Harvey Weinstein, Bobby Cohen, and Meryl Poster. *Producer:* Richard N. Gladstein. *Director:* Lasse Hallström. *Screenplay (based on his novel):* John Irving. *Director of Photography:* Oliver Stapleton. *Editor:* Lisa Zeno Churgin. *Music:* Rachel Portman. *Music Editor:* David Carbonara. *Sound:* Petur Hliddal and (music) Chris Dibble. *Sound Editor:* Maurice Schell. *Casting:* Billy Hopkins. *Production Designer:* David Gropman. *Art Director:* Karen Schulz-Gropman. *Set Decorator:* Beth Rubino. *Set Dresser:* Tyris Smith, Chris Fousek, Richard Oeser, and Phyllis Penfold. *Special Effects:* Ron Bolanowski. *Costumes:* Renée Ehlrich Kalfus. *Make-up:* Ellie Winslow. *Make-up (Charlize Theron):* Deborah Larsen. *Stunt Coordinator:* Charlie Croughwell. *Running time:* 125 minutes. *MPAA Rating:* PG-13.

CAST: Tobey Maguire (Homer Wells); Charlize Theron (Candy Kendall); Delroy Lindo (Mr. Rose); Paul Rudd (Wally Worthington); Michael Caine (Dr. Wilbur Larch); Jane Alexander (Nurse Edna); Kathy Baker (Nurse Angela); Erykah Badu (Rose Rose); Kieran Culkin (Buster); Kate Nelligan (Olive Worthington); Heavy D (Peaches); K. Todd Freeman (Muddy); Paz De La Huerta (Mary Agnes); J. K. Simmons (Ray Kendall); Evan Dexter Parke (Jack); Jimmy Flynn (Vernon); Lonnie R. Farmer (Hero); Erik Per Sullivan (Fuzzy); Spencer Diamond (Curly); Sean Andrew (Copperfield); John Albano (Steerforth); Sky McCole-Bartusiak (Hazel); Clare Daly (Clara); Colin Irving (Major Winslow); Annie Corley (Carla); Patrick Donnelly (Adopting Father); Edie Schechter (Adopting Mother); Kasey Berry (12-Year-Old Girl); Mary Bogue (Big Dot); Victoria Stankiewcz (Debra); Christine Stevens (Florence); Earle C. Batchelder (Dr. Holtz); Norma Fine (Mrs. Goodhall); Daniel Walsh (Adopted Child); Kathleen E. Broadhurst (Little Girl); John Irving (Station Master).

CHRISTIAN SCIENCE MONITOR, 12/10/99, p. 15, David Sterritt

[The *Cider House Rules* was reviewed jointly with *The Green Mile*; see Sterritt's review of that film.]

LOS ANGELES TIMES, 12/10/99, Calendar/p. 1, Kevin Thomas

"The Cider House Rules," Lasse Hallstrom's superb film adaptation of the acclaimed John Irving novel of the same name, takes its title from a short, typed list posted on the wall of an old building on a New England apple farm. The barn-like structure serves as a dormitory for migrant workers, and the list is composed of simple requests, such as not climbing on the roof of the Cider House to take a sun bath.

Self-evidently sensible, the rules nonetheless take on huge symbolic value in the course of the film, as its people keep discovering the chasm between the ideal, represented by that roster of arbitrary regulations, and the real, a distance they must navigate the best they can.

"Cider House," however, does not begin at the apple farm but at St. Cloud's Orphanage, a vast, shabby but magnificent Victorian structure in the Maine countryside. If St. Cloud's might be a tad forbidding at first sight, it proves to be a haven of warmth, love and security, presided over for decades by sagacious, witty, loving and independent-thinking Dr. Wilbur Larch (Michael Caine in a career-crowning portrayal).

Dr. Larch early on decided that the point of living is "to be of use." In the years 1943-45, in which "Cider House" mainly takes place, Dr. Larch, aided by the dedicated nurses Edna (Jane Alexander) and Angela (Kathy Baker), run the institution harmoniously, as they have for years. One of their charges, Homer Wells (Tobey Maguire), who never found a suitable adoptive family, became special to Dr. Larch and has grown up to be his assistant. Dr. Larch's concept of being useful extends beyond delivering unwanted babies to performing abortions.

Homer is a serene, boyish-looking young man, educated entirely on the premises, who has never really been anywhere. It's not that he doubts that the outside world is as harsh as Dr. Larch says it is; it's that he has a healthy impulse to discover that for himself. When a young Air Force lieutenant, Wally Worthington (Paul Rudd), about to be dispatched to the Pacific theater, and his girlfriend Candy Kendall (Charlize Theron), two months pregnant, seek out Dr. Larch's services, Homer departs with them, to take a job as an apple picker at Wally's family farm, run by his mother (Kate Nelligan).

Armed with the rock-ribbed New England character of his upbringing at St. Cloud's and a native intelligence, Homer has a family physician's experience and knowledge, but is otherwise an innocent. Mrs. Worthington's black laborers, headed by the patriarchal Mr. Rose (Delroy Lindo), are wary of a young white man sharing decidedly primitive quarters with them—remember that even the U.S. Armed Forces were still segregated at the time.

But Homer is so self-possessed, so direct in his gaze and manner, and so unpretentious as well, he is soon accepted by Mr. Rose and his small crew, which includes his pretty daughter Rose (Erykah Badu).

The Worthington farm is an easy train ride away from St. Cloud's, but Homer has in fact entered that big outside world where people and their fates are a mass of contradictions. Homer is soon to learn that good and evil can reside within the same individual, that people's lives can be altered in an instant through no fault of their own and that ultimately only individuals can make decisions as to what is the best course—for their lives. It's not that Homer hasn't seen a lot at St. Cloud's, starting with death, whether it's that of a sickly child or a young girl who's come to Dr. Larch suffering from a horribly botched abortion; it's that he's experienced it within the sheltering love and security of St. Cloud.

That Irving adapted his novel to the screen himself and, even more, that Hallstrom directed it, makes "Cider House" a far better film than other film adaptations of Irving's work— "The Hotel New Hampshire" and "The World According to Garp." In those films the characters seemed literary conceits instead of actual people—with the exception of John Lithgow's unforgettable transsexual in "Garp." Having Hallstrom direct is perfect casting. His "My Life as a Dog" revealed his astute way with children and their lives, and "What's Eating Gilbert Grape" showed he could handle the tragicomic with assurance, and he puts both these strengths to splendid use in "Cider House."

The opening sequences at St. Cloud's, with its raft of adorable youngsters and their heart-tugging predicaments, presents a huge potential for sentimentality, just as Wally's going off to war inevitably draws Homer and Candy closer. But Irving and Hallstrom move way beyond the seemingly predictable to ponder the way in which everyone must make his or her way through life's constant interplay of choice and fate.

They've been aided immeasurably by a large cast in which everyone seems so well-suited that you don't even want to think about anyone else in the roles. Maguire's combination of ordinary, clean-cut looks and inner resources is just what Homer requires. And if you're old enough to have been in grammar school during World War II, Theron strikes you as the archetypal pretty young woman of the era, the girl whom just about every young serviceman dreams of coming home to. Lindo suggests the full range of human behavior in his eloquent Mr. Rose, and Rudd is the handsome yet likable and responsible beau ideal.

Caine, in his understated yet towering portrayal, reveals in Dr. Larch the vulnerability that lurks within—and, indeed, informs—individuals of formidable resolve and strength of character. Sterling key support comes from the always notable Alexander, Baker and Nelligan and from newcomer Badu. Kieran Culkin, Heavy D, K. Todd Freeman and Paz de la Huerta head a long list of staunch featured players.

Ventfort Hall, the decaying 1893 Massachusetts summer cottage of J.P. Morgan's sister Sarah, served as St. Cloud's exterior and entry hall; its interiors were filmed in an abandoned state hospital. Production designer David Gropman took inspiration from Andrew Wyeth paintings of the era; cinematographer Oliver Stapleton created mellow, burnished images.

Renee Ehrlich Kalfus' costumes are spot-on for time and place, and Rachel Portman's soaring score supports but never overwhelms the story's sweeping, ever-shifting emotional tides. "The Cider House Rules" looks to achieve that prized goal of combining prestige with popularity.

NEW YORK POST, 12/10/99, p. 55, Lou Lumenick

Novelist John Irving has no one but himself to blame for the stillborn screen version of "The Cider House Rules," his great 1985 novel about a Maine orphan's struggle with the abortion issue.

Irving himself wrote the screenplay and handpicked Swedish director Lasse Hallstrom, who displayed a flair for offbeat storytelling in films like "My Life as a Dog" and "What's Eating Gilbert Grape."

The mystery is how these two could produce a movie so bland and conventional that Irving's novel is brought to life only fleetingly.

The best parts are set at the rambling orphanage in remote St. Cloud's, Maine, presided over by Wilbur Larch (Michael Caine), an ether-addicted obstetrician who has devoted his life to delivering babies, performing abortions and raising orphans.

Larch's favorite is Homer Wells (Tobey Maguire), who after several failed adoptions is trained to be a doctor by Larch, who hopes one day that Homer will succeed him at St. Cloud's.

Homer loves Larch like a son, but the young man doesn't believe in abortion. When the beautiful Candy Kendall (Charlize Theron) arrives for a "procedure" with her wealthy boyfriend Wally Worthington (Paul Rudd), Homer sees a way out of his moral dilemma.

He goes to live on an apple farm owned by Wally's family and promptly falls in love with Candy—an attraction Homer isn't seriously tempted to act on until Wally, an Army pilot during World War II, is shot down over Burma and goes missing.

Homer, who lives in the farm's cider house (where the rules of the title are displayed and routinely flouted), is also drawn to Rose Rose (singer Erykah Badu), a teenager whose father, Mr. Rose (Delroy Lindo), the foreman of the orchard's pickers, is hiding a terrible secret that will force Homer into a crisis of conscience.

Irving's novel is an eloquent, 700-page debate between the pro-choice Larch and Homer, who refuses to assist in the taking of what he considers human life.

In condensing action that runs from the turn of the century to the mid-1950s into a two-year period ending in 1945, Irving has thrown out the first 100 pages or so, eliminated several key characters—and greatly weakened his (often gory) arguments for legalized abortion as an alternative to back-alley butchers.

What's mostly left is a fairly routine coming-of-age love triangle with the kind of painstakingly re-created period setting common to almost every other movie this season.

Except for an over-the-top Lindo, the cast is excellent—including Jane Alexander and Kathy Baker, seen too briefly as Larch's nurses.

Caine, attempting an (eccentric) American accent for the first time since "Hurry Sundown" three decades ago, is particularly effective as the flinty Larch. But he has little rapport with Maguire; and neither Maguire nor Rudd has any sexual chemistry with Theron.

A major disappointment, "The Cider House Rules" pales by comparison with the gutsier, more full-bodied adaptation of Irving's "The World According to Garp."

NEWSDAY, 12/10/99, Part II/p. B3, Jan Stuart

The orphanage and baby clinic at the extravagant heart of "The Cider House Rules" houses some of the most captivating waifs to cajole a moviegoer's tears. Director Lasse Hallström, who first nuzzled America with "My Life as a Dog," knows a thing or two about young actors. And novelist-screenwriter John Irving, who sensitively filters anti-abortion sentiments into this marvelous coming-of-age tale, understands instinctively that the way to argue on behalf of children is through children.

Recent efforts to adapt Irving's 1985 novel for Off-Broadway by playwright Peter Parnell resulted in a two-part marathon that tried audiences' patience and producers' purse strings. For the movies, Irving has condensed his sprawling work with an artisan's economy and a novelist's affection for his own characters. There are many, and they are eminently worth caring for.

Set in 1943, the quietly magnetic center of "The Cider House Rules" is Homer Wells (Tobey Maguire), an even-tempered teenager who has stayed on at St. Cloud's orphanage in Maine to become the elder statesman among its small tenants. Mentored by the clinic's compassionate, if ether-addicted, head, Dr. Larch (Michael Caine, in one of the most poignant performances of his career), Homer has been thoroughly schooled in the skills of pediatric medicine and child nurturing. He confidently delivers babies, but draws the line at performing abortions, despite Dr. Larch's humane arguments in favor.

After a lifetime sequestered at St. Cloud's, Homer is struck by wanderlust when a comely young woman named Candy Kendall (Charlize Theron, a thinking man's Sandra Dee) arrives for an abortion accompanied by her pilot fiance Wally Worthington (Paul Rudd). To Dr. Larch's despair, Homer flees with the couple and takes a job picking apples on the Worthington family farm, where he is supervised by the diligent but kindly Mr. Rose (an award-worthy turn by Delroy Lindo). Once Wally goes off to war, Homer's personal ethics are put to the test by the flirtations of Candy and the shocking plight of Mr. Rose's daughter Rose, played by recording artist Erykah Badu. (Hers is the plaintive film debut that reaffirms one's sense that the really good torch singers are but a grace note away from the rigors of dramatic performance.)

Oiled by Rachel Portman's elegiac scoring and Oliver Stapleton's lyrical photography, "The Cider House Rules" is a voluptuous page-turner of a movie, old-fashioned storytelling with unmistakably contemporary resonances. Irving makes his points about family planning elegantly and nondidactically, underscoring the emotional toll that unwanted children take on all parties, regardless of the choices made by their would-be parents.

Hallström suspends the entire film in a delicate state of wistfulness that could easily spill into monotony or bathos in the wrong hands. Fortunately, he's marshalled a commanding ensemble. Among those who make bold impressions with swift strokes are Kathy Baker as a sweet-natured nurse, hip-hop star Heavy D as an easygoing apple picker and Spencer Diamond as the frailest of orphans. Among the kids, Sean Andrew is so rapturously lovable one only wonders why he wasn't snatched up for adoption a long time ago.

But "The Cider House Rules" may well be remembered as the career coming-of-age of Tobey Maguire, a handsome young actor of such laconic grace and serenity that it is easy to underestimate the power of his work here. Watch how he confronts Delroy Lindo in a moment of crisis with an awkward smile that belies his inner agitation, or the big-brother empathy with which he comforts an orphan rejected by prospective parents. Charisma is a mysterious gift, and Maguire is proof positive that understatement can be its best ally.

SIGHT AND SOUND, 2/00, p. 42, Peter Matthews

Maine, 1943. Abandoned by his parents in infancy, Homer Wells grows up at St Clouds orphanage. Unofficially trained in obstetrics by resident doctor Wilbur Larch, Homer helps deliver unwanted babies, but refuses to assist at the illegal abortions Larch does at St Clouds.

One day, fighter pilot Wally Worthington and his pregnant girlfriend Candy Kendall show up for a termination. After the operation, Homer impulsively decides to leave with the couple. He is hired as an apple picker at the orchard run by Wally's mother in a nearby coastal town. Wally ships off to war, and Homer gets acquainted with the farm's migrant workers, including crew boss Mr Rose and his daughter Rose Rose. In Wally's absence, Homer and Candy fall in love. The governors of St Clouds want to replace Larch with a more orthodox physician. Hoping Homer will succeed him, Larch trumps up a phoney medical career for him, but Homer declines the post to stay with Candy.

Rose Rose confesses to Candy she's pregnant by her own father. Homer performs an abortion assisted by Mr Rose, who later kills himself. News arrives that Wally was shot down over Burma and is now paralysed. Candy elects to take care of him and ends the affair with Homer. Larch dies from an overdose of ether. Homer returns to St Clouds, where he is joyfully greeted by the orphans.

If you never quite got over *Annie* and long for another batch of whimsically forlorn muppets, make haste to *The Cider House Rules*. It's true the orphans here don't sing or dance, but they compensate by occasioning more syrupy bathos than the screen has witnessed in decades. Just for starters, there's an irresistible tyke named Curly, who delivers the plaintive refrain "I'm the best!" whenever browsers drop round the asylum. Then there's Fuzzy, confined to an oxygen tent and gasping his last with a heart tugging blatancy that would have embarrassed Little Nell. Clearly John Irving, who adapted the script from his mammoth 1985 novel, intends a cunning pastiche of Victorian sentimentality—he wants to kid the clichés and reactivate them at the same time. The shamelessness works to the extent that you can't help choking up a little even while you're giggling. But such are the twists of the author's baroque imagination that the orphanage doubles as an undercover abortion clinic—and what's bizarre about the movie is how it grafts greeting-card schmaltz on to a muckraking liberal agenda.

The fusion is broadly reminiscent of Dickens, and there are scattered hints that Irving fancies himself the heir apparent. Every night before bedtime, embattled pro-choicer Dr Wilbur Larch reads to the enraptured tots another instalment from *David Copperfield.* Pretty soon, Homer Wells, who decides against performing abortions himself, is caught up in his own thrilling *Bildungsroman.* Eventually required to perform an illegal abortion on an incest victim, our priggish hero learns abstract moral codes don't answer to the messiness of human reality.

At least I guess that's what the story is about, since once Homer enters the big wide world, the film becomes a masterpiece of dithering. Crammed with picaresque incident, quirky caricature, conceits and philosophising, the book is an unwieldy juggernaut that rolls along on pure pop energy. It must have been a bitch to condense, and Irving strains to locate a functional dramatic arc somewhere inside his loose, baggy monster. The screen version devolves into a parade of amorphous scenes that drift by without gathering emotional weight. Practically Teflon-coated, the movie raises a raft of momentous issues that refuse to stick. Not just abortion, but sexual abuse, race relations and women's independence get floated at sundry times, each theme limping off apologetically in turn. Even the titular rules are so hazily signposted their ultimate defiance holds scarcely any symbolic resonance.

There may be an additional reason for the curious lack of focus. As he proved in *My Life as a Dog* and *What's Eating Gilbert Grape*, Lasse Hallström has a wry, delicate touch—and that's exactly wrong for a hard-sell contraption like *The Cider House Rules.* The director's sensitivity here serves merely to undercut the book's aggressive showmanship, leaving little more than a texture of undifferentiated blandness. What's probably needed is the *outré* stylisation that Tony Richardson brought to Irving's *The Hotel New Hampshire* or the commercial zing of George Roy Hill's approach to *The World According to Garp.* As it stands, the unholy marriage of two disparate sensibilities ends up cancelling out the movie.

VILLAGE VOICE, 12/14/99, p. 180, Amy Taubin

The subject of *The Cider House Rules* is also sex and the family, and director Lasse Hallstrom brings a somewhat arty European approach to the material, but the comparison to *The War Zone* ends there. This adaptation of John Irving's novel about an orphan boy coming of age on the home front during World War II is as paternalistic, puffed-up, and dull as a congressional debate about abortion rights.

Homer Wells (Tobey Maguire) is the favorite child of Dr. Larch (Michael Caine), an orphanage director and obstetrician rolled into one. He not only delivers babies, he takes them off the hands of mothers who don't want or can't care for them, and he unquestioningly performs abortions if that's what a woman chooses. Dr. Larch is something of a saint but his addiction to sniffing ether makes him less than a perfect prochoice advocate.

Larch wants Homer to follow in his footsteps, but Homer refuses to assist with abortions. To avoid a confrontation (and also because he's fallen in love), Homer goes out into the wide world in search of knowledge and independence. He learns that human relations are messy and complicated, and that one must take responsibility for one's actions based on a moral code that's not necessarily in tune with prescribed social rules posted on the cider house wall. He performs an abortion on an incest victim and in doing so becomes a man.

The Cider House Rules is being passed off as a film in support of a woman's right to choose, but its implicit position is that abortion is wrong except in cases of rape or incest. Worse still, it makes men the arbiters of what happens to a woman's body and the abortion debate a defining factor of manhood. The mind boggles at the plethora of patriarchal assumptions. Hallstrom's direction signals every turn of the plot five minutes before it occurs, and the actors are all dreadfully earnest, none more so than Maguire, who seems to be channeling Forrest Gump.

Also reviewed in:
CHICAGO TRIBUNE, 12/17/99, Friday/p. A, Michael Wilmington
NEW YORK TIMES, 12/10/99, p. E28, Stephen Holden
NEW YORKER, 12/13/99, p. 113, Anthony Lane
VARIETY, 9/13-19/99, p. 48, David Rooney
WASHINGTON POST, 12/17/99, p. C5, Stephen Hunter
WASHINGTON POST, 12/17/99, Weekend/p. 44, Michael O'Sullivan

CITY, THE (LA CIUDAD)

A Zeitgeist Films release of a North Star Films production. *Executive Producer:* Doug Mankoff, Robin Alper and Andrew Hurwitz. *Producer:* David Riker and Paul S. Mezey. *Director:* David Riker. *Screenplay (Spanish and English with English subtitles):* David Riker. *Director of Photography:* Harlan Bosmajian. *Editor:* David Riker. *Music:* Tony Adzinikolov. *Sound:* Richard Fleming and Alex Wolfe. *Production Designer:* Ariane Burgess and Roshelle Berliner. *Running time:* 88 minutes. *MPAA Rating:* Not Rated.

CAST: BRICKS: Ricardo Cuevas, Moises Garcia, Marcos Martinez Garcia, Mateo Gomez, Cesar Monzon, Harsh Nayyar, Fernando Reyes, Victor Sierra, and Carlos Torrentes (The Men); Anthony Rivera (The Boy); Joe Rigano (Contractor); Miguel Maldonado (Organizer); Maite Bonilla (Voiceover); HOME: Cipriano Garcia (Young Man); Leticia Herrera (Young Woman); THE PUPPETEER: Jose Rabelo (Father); Stephanie Viruet (The Daughter); Gene Ruffini (City Worker); Eileen Vega (Health Worker); Denia Brache (Friend); Marta De La Cruz (School Registrar); SEAMSTRESS: Silvia Goiz (Seamstress); Hyoung Taek Limb and Jawon Kim (Sweatshop Managers); Maria Galante (The Designer); Monica Cano and Ernesto Lopez (Workers in Hallway); Galo Rodin Schneider (The Cousin); Jaime Sanchez (Dress Store Manager); THE PHOTO STUDIO: Antonio Peralta (Photographer).

LOS ANGELES TIMES, 11/5/99, Calendar/p. 15, Kevin Thomas

David Riker's "The City" ("La Ciudad") is one of the most memorable movies in last year's Latino Film Festival. This sensitive, beautifully expressive film is composed of four vignettes mostly involving the bitter struggle for survival among the most vulnerable of New York City's wave of Latin American immigrants.

Each segment opens with one of its principal figures having his or her picture taken at the same photo studio, the old-fashioned kind that offers a selection of kitschy roll-down idyllic backdrops, settings at ironic odds with the customers' harsh circumstances.

The first, "Bricks," tells of a young laborer—scavenging for bricks with other workers—severely injured when an old factory wall collapses on him and speedy aid proves impossible; the second, "Home," finds a young man (Cipriano Garcia) newly arrived from Puebla, Mexico, meeting a young woman (Leticia Herrera), coincidentally from his neighborhood back home, only to lose track of her.

The third, "The Puppeteer," deals with a homeless puppeteer (Jose Rabelo) who has contracted tuberculosis from staying in a shelter; he tries to enroll his beloved little daughter (Stephanie Viruet) in school only to be refused because he cannot produce either a phone bill or a rent receipt. The final, and strongest, sequence, "Seamstress," chronicles a sweatshop seamstress (Silvia Goiz) who hasn't been paid in weeks; she's struggling to get $400 to pay for her daughter's hospitalization in her native country.

Shot in black and white, "The City" has a poetic, flowing quality combined with superbly composed images that attest to Riker's training as a photographer. Actually, Riker began this film while a student at NYU's graduate film school. One day Riker came upon a man sitting in a station wagon listening to the radio while a little girl in the back seat seemed to be daydreaming, rocking back and forth. As they both seemed to be somehow suspended in time, Riker wondered what they were waiting for; from that wondering he was inspired to make "The Puppeteer."

Once it was completed he was able to show it by way of inducement to the nonactors he wanted to appear in the other three segments. Eventually he came up with a feature-length film.

Inevitably, "The City" recalls the films of Italian Neo-Realism not only in style but also in Riker's ability to elicit the most natural portrayals from nonprofessionals. "The City" is a most-affecting experience, an impressive accomplishment in all its aspects.

NEW YORK POST, 10/22/99, p. 67, Lou Lumenick

"La Ciudad ("The City") is writer-director David Riker's documentary-style collection of four short stories about struggling Latino immigrants in New York City.

One is a student film Riker made at New York University in 1992, about a tubercular, homeless puppeteer who tries to enroll his daughter in a school. Others revolve around a worker hired to gather bricks in an abandoned lot for a pittance in New Jersey, with tragic results, and a sweatshop seamstress' frantic efforts to earn money to care for her sick daughter back home.

The best of the lot is a bittersweet love story about a young Mexican immigrant, lost in the city, who meets a girl of his dreams at a Sweet 16 party, then loses her in a housing project.

Filming in gritty, black-and-white 16mm, Riker gets terrifically natural, often moving performances from his mostly non-professional cast.

NEWSDAY, 10/22/99, Part II/p. B15, John Anderson

That one immigrant group oppresses (or just dismisses) the next is the great irony of New York City history. Or U.S. history in toto, for that matter. Yes, we're a theoretical melting pot. But first you have to pass through the crucible of blood that's just to the left and back of that big green woman in the harbor.

With that in mind, the great irony of David Riker's "The City (La Ciudad)" is that it meets all the standard requirements for a foreign film—subtitles, spartan aesthetics, black and white cinematography, foreigners—while actually being the most American movie of this or any other recent year. While owing much of its emotional immediacy to Riker's Italian neo-realist approach and the haunting score of Tony Adzinikolov, it gradually touches something much deeper: the idea that every immigrant American experience is founded in loss—of country, customs and often kin. And that the various peoples called Hispanics are just one more test case in our ongoing experiment in human tolerance.

A virtually silent movie—the often mute faces are eloquent enough—"The City" is composed of four singular stories, linked by a photo studio in Brooklyn, where the various characters come to have their portraits taken. Those characters—some of whom are played by professionals, but many of whom were cast from among New York's Ecuadoran, Mexican, Cuban, Peruvian, Nicaraguan and Colombian enclaves—include a seamstress (Silvia Goiz), exploited by a Manhattan sweatshop and desperate to send money home to her sick daughter. The stories include "Home," an achingly bittersweet tale of love found and lost between two Mexican teenagers, and "The Puppeteer" (which began as Riker's award-winning NYU thesis film), in which a homeless, tubercular street entertainer (Jose Rabelo) is confounded in his attempts to get his daughter (Stephanie Viruet) enrolled in school.

The first installment, "Bricks," owes the most to the de Sica-Rossellini school, with its documentary take on day laborers, clamoring for work on an early morning Brooklyn street. That they eventually find themselves on some unknown moonscape of ruined walls and piles of bricks, with no phone, car or map, takes Riker's theme of dislocation to an extreme place. Everything he wants to say in "The City," in fact, he essentially says in "Bricks." Although sobering, spare and possessed of an archetypal simplicity one usually finds only in Iranian movies, "The City" is not a cynic's film. Riker wears his heart on his sleeve, but then his stories and subjects are intended for the generous, tolerant and open-minded. Just like America.

VILLAGE VOICE, 10/26/99, p. 157, J. Hoberman

David Riker's *The City* is a movie no one will ever accuse of irresponsibility. Six years in the making, developed in community workshops, cast largely with nonactors who are photographed for maximum aesthetic gravitas in astonishingly crisp black and white, Riker's updated, episodic

How the Other Half Lives represents New York as a city of lost and exploited Latino immigrants. (Virtually all the dialogue is in Spanish. This is one U.S. indie without a part for Parker Posey.)

The City is heroically somber and unfashionably social-realist. Riker alternates tragic, ennobling compositions with recurring shots of his bereft, discarded protagonists—living in abandoned cars, scavenging old bricks for pennies—as they are dwarfed by an unfeeling environment. However loaded, these images can be heartbreaking in their eloquence. Still, Riker doesn't completely trust their power. His mini-narratives—each predicated on an instance of innocence betrayed— invariably call attention to their own contrivances, even as the obtrusive dirge of Tony Adzinikolov's score pushes them to the verge of neorealist bathos.

Despite (and ultimately because of) its heavy-handedness, *The City* is an old-fashioned monument to immigrant courage, and as such, it succeeds in making the invisible evident. The sweatshop where much of the final episode is set is a location more horrific than any of the various rubble-strewn lots. Riker links his four stories with scenes in a Queens photo studio where immigrants come for ID pictures or portraits to send home. Nothing in *The City* is more haunting than the rapt close-ups of these stoical faces.

Also reviewed in:
CHICAGO TRIBUNE, 1/7/00, p. O, John Petrakis
NATION, 11/8/99, p. 36, Stuart Klawans
NEW YORK TIMES, 10/22/99, p. E12, Stephen Holden
VARIETY, 9/28-10/4/98, p. 36, Glenn Lovell

CLOSE-UP

A Zeitgeist Films release of an Institute for the Intellectual Development of Children and Young Adults production. *Executive Producer:* Ali Reza Zarrin. *Director:* Abbas Kiarostami. *Screenplay (Farsi with English subtitles):* Abbas Kiarostami. *Director of Photography:* Ali Reza Zarrin-Dast. *Editor:* Abbas Kiarostami. *Sound:* Mohammad Haghighi and Ahmad Asgart. *Sound Editor:* Changiz Sayyad. *Production Designer:* Hassan Agha-Karimi. *Make-up:* Farima Zand-Pour. *Running time:* 90 minutes. *MPAA Rating:* Not Rated.

CAST: Hossain Sabzian (Himself); Mohsen Makhmalbaf (Himself); Abolfazl Ahankhah (Father of the Family); Mehrdad Ahankhah and Manoochehr Ahankhah (Family Sons); Mahrokh Ahankhah and Nayer Mohseni Zonoozi (Family Daughters); Ahmed Reza Moayed Mohseni (Family Friend); Hossain Farazmand (Reporter); Hooshang Shamaei (Taxi Driver); Mohammad Ali Barrati (Soldier); Davood Goodarzi (Sergeant); Haji Ali Reza Ahmadi (Judge); Hassan Komaili and Davood Mohabbat (Court Reporters); Abbas Kiarostami (Himself).

NEW YORK POST, 12/31/99, p. 38, Hannah Brown

Years before "Being John Malkovich," Iranian director Abbas Kiarostami examined the question of stealing identity and of the public's fascination with movies and celebrity in his film, "Close-Up."

It follows the true story of a man who posed as the well-known film director Mohsen Makhmalbaf ("Gabbeh") and the impostor's subsequent capture and trial for defrauding a well-to-do Tehran family out of money under the pretense that he would use them as stars in a movie.

Oddly, the impostor, Hossain Sabzian, plays himself, as do the members of the Ahankhah family whom he duped. It's not clear from the film, which is a kind of quasi-documentary, whether the trial is real or staged, though scenes in which Sabzian meets the mother of the family on a bus and visits the Ahankhahs at home are obviously re-created.

As the story unfolds, it becomes clear that there are no real victims or villains here. Everyone wants to be in show business; everyone is fighting for center stage.

The nerdy, Mehrdad Ahankhah, a screenplay-writing unemployed engineer, is the most wounded by the scam, and it is he who argues the family's case in court.

Unlike his brother, also an engineer by profession who now works as the director of a bakery, Mehrdad has refused to compromise, and he describes his choice dramatically: "Instead of bread, I chose art."

But it is Sabzlan himself who is the most compelling figure, yet he remains a mystery throughout. He seems to have decided to impersonate the director on impulse, and then simply went on with the scam as long as he could.

But he does idolize the director and has impersonated him before. "By acting like a famous person, I made them all obey me," he explains to the judge, with some satisfaction.

"Close-up" was made in 1990, long before Kiarostami won the Palme D'Or at Cannes for "Taste of Cherry." In the intervening years, "Close-Up" has acquired a cult reputation as a masterpiece.

However, for all its wit and intricacy, the film is often ponderous. Serious film buffs will want to see "Close-Up," but they shouldn't go in with unrealistic expectations.

SIGHT AND SOUND, 12/97, p. 40, Jonathan Romney

In present-day Tehran, Hossain Farazmand, a journalist, goes to cover the arrest of Hossain Sabzian, a young man accused of fraud. Earlier, Sabzian had persuaded the Ahankhah family that he was the well-known film director Mohsen Makhmalbaf, then borrowed money from them. Sabzian was arrested. Farazmand attempts to borrow a tape recorder. Director Abbas Kiarostami begins a documentary investigation of the case. He interviews the police, the Ahankhahs, and finally Sabzian himself, an unemployed print-worker who is eager for Kiarostami to make a film of his suffering. Kiarostami visits the judge and asks permission to film the trial.

The trial begins with an account of Mrs Ahankhah's meeting with Sabzian. Seeing him reading a book of Makhmalbaf's film *The Cyclist,* she initiated a conversation and he told her he was Makhmalbaf. In court, Sabzian says that he acted as he did from his love of art, and because playing Makhmalbaf gave him self-respect. In a flashback to the day of the arrest, Sabzian talks *about* his love of nature before Farazmand and the police arrive.

Sabzian tells the court he regrets playing with the family's feelings, but says he really would have shot his film if he had the money. The Ahankhah family's son Mehrdad believes Sabzian is still playing a part, but the family at last withdraw their complaint. After the trial, Kiarostami films Sabzian's meeting with the real Makhmalbaf, who takes Sabzian by scooter to visit the Ahankhahs.

The jigsaw structure of *Close-Up* makes it seem an obvious candidate for inclusion in that diverse and hard-to-define category, the fake documentary. But on closer inspection, it proves to be more of a fake fiction, in which what at first appears to be a piece of tale-spinning—a story about a pathological teller of tales—turns out to contain more truth than we expected. Its subject is an apparent no-hoper who briefly mistakes himself for a film-maker; but Abbas Kiarostami's generous undertaking is to demonstrate that Hossain Sabzian is a filmmaker of sorts, or at the very least, has the soul of one. *Close-Up* allows Sabzian to become the subject of the sort of film he dreams of, an honest chronicle of his travails; and in the final sequence, it lets him realise his total identification with his idol Mohsen Makhmalbaf (Best known in Britain for *Gabbeh,* Makhmalbaf has long been admired in Iran for such socially involved dramas as *The Cyclist,* Sabzian's favourite in *Close-Up.)*

Sabzian's adventure recalls John Guare's play *Six Degrees of Separation* (filmed by Fred Schepisi), in which a wealthy family is gulled by a man claiming to be Sidney Poitier's son. But if, in the West, fame invariably stands for hollow seduction, the basis of Sabzian's imposture is completely different. For the Ahankhah family, the name 'Makhmalbaf' represents not self-referring glamour but a morally commanding set of values: art and social compassion. The family cannot entirely be blamed for wanting to participate in Sabzian's imaginary project, for it offers the chance to appear in a Makhmalbaf film. Indeed, their real fault consists of suspecting Sabzian, of breaking a contract they had freely entered into.

Where the family reneges, Kiarostami steps in with a deal of his own, promising Sabzian that his camera will allow him to make his own testimony to the world, in exchange for his services as an actor playing himself. Both Sabzian and Kiarostami are fortunate in having the trial presided over by a judge who is unusually sensitive to dramatic paradox. "What part would you have liked to play?" he asks Sabzian. "My own," replies the defendant. "You are playing your own part," the judge replies.

Kiarostami similarly reminds us that he too is playing a film-maker's role: he flashes a clapperboard at us and, with breathtaking cheekiness, asks the judge to move the trial date to suit his own shooting schedule. Such interventions oblige us to reach our own understanding of the distinction between imposture and reliable appearance. As far as one can tell, the only reliable documentary footage in the film appears to be of the trial itself, and some of the interviews; more equivocal are those apparently unstaged sections of the coda with Makhmalbaf, in which authenticity is questionably signalled by the apparent technical hitch of the sound cutting in and out.

But for much of the film, Kiarostami persuades his subjects to play themselves, reconstructing their original conversations. This gives a particularly fictional feel in the opening with the journalist Farazmand which leads us to expect an investigation story. The blatantly contrived exposition puts the subsequent trial sequences in relief, they derive a particular weight from extended close-ups of Sabzian explaining his motivations: a passion for art in general and Makhmalbaf's films in particular, and a new sense of self-respect gained from impersonating his hero.

Bringing us progressively closer to Sabzian in the court scenes, Kiarostami finally takes a step back, sabotaging his own soundtrack so as to acknowledge how indiscreet it would be to give us the full exchange of confidences between Sabzian and the real Makhmalbaf when they meet at last. For Kiarostami's structural gaming is not mere philosophical formalism, but very much an ethical matter. Questions of intrusion, respect, contractual trust are bound up in the camera's distance from or proximity to its subjects. (Kiarostami investigated these implications at length in the *mise en abime* of his rural trilogy initiated by *Where is My Friend's House*).

Close-Up is specifically a moral enquiry into the possible benefits and benevolent motives of imposture, and works overall as a process of redemption: Sabzian is given a chance to vindicate himself by fully acting out his investment in the dream of film-making. Such a process is perhaps no longer imaginable in Western cinema, where the very terms 'fiction' and 'dream' bear inherent connotations of moral compromise.

But the film comes across as a generous gesture on Kiarostami's part since everyone gets what they want: Farazmand catches a local anecdote that really does turn into a big story; the Ahankhahs get their dose of cinema; and Sabzian gets at once to be 'Makhmalbaf' and to be himself in a way he was not otherwise able to be. In what may be a specifically Islamic inflexion on the idea of world as stage, Kiarostami proposes that all living is acting, and that actors have the right to be seen giving the best and truest performance they possibly can, even if truth has to pass through the detour of imposture.

VILLAGE VOICE, 1/4/00, p. 108, Michael Atkinson

A full decade after its making, Abbas Kiarostami's *Close-Up* emerges from the closed country of Rumored Masterpieces to no doubt pass through our cultural pipes as effectlessly as pork fat through a goose. (Zeitgeist displays admirable holiday spirit distributing it.) The must-see Iranian Godardian knot a movie, *Close-Up* is no crowd-pleaser, but neither is it less breathtaking than Godard in his salad days. Most of this year's best releases—*Les Amants du Pont Neuf, Boiling Point, A Moment of Innocence* included—have spent lonely years on the market, but Kiarostami's film has artichoke-like layers which, once peeled, are forever resonant. How simple yet inexhaustible can a film text get? Here you have in vitro the ruminative spiral-evolution of Kiarostami's Quoker "earthquake" trilogy and the mysterian subtractions and realist ellipses of *Taste of Cherry* and *The Wind Will Carry Us*. Seemingly bottomless Kiarostami's reflexivity never obscures his deep, aching concern for people. Nobody makes or has ever made movies with such mundane majesty.

Kiarostami began the movie by filming the court case against Hossein Sabzian, an out-of-work Iranian man who, posing as controversial director-celebrity Mohsen Makhmalbaf, insinuates himself into an upper-class Teherani family's life under the pretense of casting them in a film. Ironically, Kiarostami does cast them here: entire segments of Sabzian's strange little history with the family are reenacted for the camera, and we're never clear exactly how much of what we see is true and how much is fiction. The courtroom footage is authentically "real," but that means little as the cameras emerge as important forces in how Sabzian's fate is handled by the court and his accusers. Of course, eventually Makhmalbaf himself enters the reenactment fray, as himself.

The hall of mirrors is deep, but it all reflects, humanely, on both Sabzian and his prey's intoxication with movie-world fame and respect. If Godard was on the giddy Chuck Berry of self-reflexive movie-movie-ness, Kiarostami is the Dylan, moving past the bop and onto the straight goods. Indeed, his unpredictable, and unpredictably moving, investigation into the silent collision between genuine experience and cinema isn't only about the viewer's perspective, but Kiarostami's own. But, like nearly every other Kiarostami film, *Close-Up* takes questions about movies and makes them feel like questions of life, death, and meaning. He makes movies as if they were the manifest vapor trails of human need, hanging in the air even as we search. Once upon a time, one year or two was all it took for great films to surface; that *Pokemon* took months, and *Close-Up* 10 years, is cut-and-dried proof of our craven descent into irrelevance as an educated consumer culture. Any arguments?

Also reviewed in:
NEW YORK TIMES, 1/31/99, p. E24, Stephen Holden
VARIETY, 3/7/90, p. 32

CONCEIVING ADA

A Fox Lorber release of a ZDF/Arte/Hotwire Productions/Complex Corporation coproduction. *Producer:* Henry S. Rosenthal and Lynn Hershman Leeson. *Director:* Lynn Hershman Leeson. *Screenplay:* Lynn Hershman Leeson and Eileen Jones. *Director of Photography:* Hiro Narita and Bill Zarchy. *Editor:* Robert Dalva. *Music:* The Residents. *Music Editor:* Jake Tornatzky. *Sound:* Tone Sanchez. *Sound Editor:* Dave Nelson. *Production Manager:* Debbie Brubaker. *Art Director:* Laura F. Haynes. *Costumes:* Lea Ditson. *Make-up:* Marine Macerot. *Running time:* 85 minutes. *MPAA Rating:* Not Rated.

CAST: Tilda Swinton (Ada Byron King, Countess of Lovelace); Timothy Leary (Sims); Karen Black (Lady Byron/Mother Coer); Francesca Faridany (Emmy Coer); John O'Keefe (Charles Babbage); J.D. Wolfe (Nicholas Clayton); John Perry Barlow (John Crosse); John Perry Barlow (William Lovelace); Esther Mulligan (Mary Shelley); R.U. Sirius (Barlow); Owen Murphy (Dr. Fury); Mark Capri (Dr. Locock); David Eppel (Simon); Pollyanna Jacobs (Cocktail Server); Lillian L. Malmberg (Anne Isabelle Byron); Cyrus Mare (Ralph Byron); David Brooks (Children's Tutor); Michael Oosterom (Lord Byron); Kashka Peck (Teenage Ada); Rose Lockwood (Child Ada/Claire); Charles Pinion (CD-ROM Byron); Jesse Talman Boss (Baby Ada); Chris Von Sneidern (Musician in the Elevator); Joe Wemple (Priest/Talk Show Host); Roger Shaw (Voice of Priest); Lavay Smith (Lead Singer, Club Band); Bing Nathan (Upright Bass, Club Band); Chris Siebert (Piano, Club Band); Bill Stewart (Alto Sax, Club Band).

NEW YORK POST, 2/26/99, p. 48, Hannah Brown

Feminist geeks, take heart: Now there's a film just for you. Web girls will flock to "Conceiving Ada," while the rest of the moviegoing public will be confused and annoyed by this esoteric and pretentious film.

"Conceiving Ada" is the story of Emmy (Francesca Faridany), a cool computer genius, and her quest to make contact with the Victorian-era mathematician Ada Byron King (Tilda Swinton, of "Orlando").

Ada, a daughter of Lord Byron, is credited with developing the prototype for today's computer programs.

She was, by all accounts, an amazing woman. Married to a nobleman, she carried on affairs openly, bore three children, worked on her mathematical theories and was a compulsive gambler.

Using DNA code, computer programs and an "agent," a digitally created bird that can fly through centuries of cyberspace, Emmy finally reaches Ada.

Basically, it's the old "Time Machine" scenario, updated with computer jargon.

Lynn Hershman Leeson, director and co-author of the screenplay, aims high in her first feature and occasionally achieves the haunting mix of technology and drama that she was reaching for.

In a footnote to cyberdelic history, Timothy Leary makes an appearance (taped days before he died) as Emmy's enigmatic cyber guru.

And Karen Black plays a dual role as the mother of both Ada and Emmy.

If "Hackers" crossed with "Interiors" is your idea of the perfect movie, then put your computer into "sleep" mode and head for this film. If not, wait for a less gimmicky, more dramatic version of Ada Byron King's life.

NEWSDAY, 2/26/99, Part II/p. B13, Gene Seymour

The idea of time travel through computer to retrieve the genetic code of a long-dead Victorian mathematician carries so many delicious possibilities for Nabokovian wit and Borgesian mischief that you're tempted to give writer-director Lynn Hershman Leeson credit for even coming up with the conceit behind "Conceiving Ada." That such possibilites are nowhere near realized makes you want to throw the nearest piece of obsolescent software at the screen.

Despite the casual drop of Nabokov's name, this is not the "Ada" of the master's own time-spanning epic, but Ada Byron King (Tilda Swinton), Countess of Lovelace, who was as much an audacious libertine as her father, Lord Byron and, given her skill at mathematics and codes, just as gifted. The countess is an unsung heroine among today's cyber-crowd for being the first to predict the computer's impact on culture as well as science.

Ada becomes an obsession for Emmy Coer (Francesca Faridany), a modern-day computer genius who is herself something of a misunderstood visionary, plagued by a disapproving mother (Karen Black) and dull-witted lover (J.D. Wolfe). She is also pregnant and warned that she should, for the baby's sake, hold back on her research into genetic-memory retrieval. The only one egging her on is the mysterious Mr. Sims (a haggard Timothy Leary, weeks from his death, who can barely get his lines out). He suggests that Emmy use her own genetic code to gain access to Ada's 1840s era ... and to her soul.

Leeson's film boasts all kinds of high-tech tricks, including the use of actual photographs of Victorian-era rooms as digitalized backgrounds for Ada's scenes. Indeed, it seems as if most of the film's imagination went into these effects, which, in the end, don't look much more compelling than a grade-school diorama.

The awkwardly designed dramatic conflict, meanwhile, is shortchanged by the film's equally clumsy stretch into the realm of ideas. It's only in Swinton's performance, especially in Ada's testament just before her death, that any real magic can be found.

VILLAGE VOICE, 3/2/99, p. 150, Dennis Lim

Ambitious but confused, *Conceiving Ada* is a noble attempt at retracing the life of Ada Lovelace—the daughter of Lord Byron and, more importantly, the Victorian mathematician credited with writing the first computer program. In her first feature, Lynn Hershman Leeson deploys virtual sets (inserting actors into digitally tweaked photos) and an old chestnut of a framing device, connecting Ada (Tilda Swinton) with a present-day kindred soul, computer "genius" Emmy (Francesca Faridany). Beguiling in fits and starts, the result is mostly airless and awkward—avowedly highbrow, decidedly low-impact.

Balanced on a far-fetched premise that it doesn't bother to flesh out (or treat as suitably metaphysical), *Conceiving Ada* features Emmy and Ada bonding across time and space. Information waves, DNA strands, and artificial life have something to do with it. (Oh, and so does Timothy Leary, in a game cameo filmed a week before his death.) This incoherence would be beside the point had Leeson approached her subject with some degree of playfulness, but the film's straight-faced single-mindedness is stultifying.

With the help of a "live agent" (a metal bird that flies through computer screens), Emmy gains access to Ada, the latter's life—as a compulsive gambler, highly sexed lover, and all-around fascinating creature—coming into focus on Emmy's monitor. Both women have domineering mothers (played in both instances by a monstrous Karen Black) and experience man trouble (though Ada's are more bothersome). Emmy is also pregnant, facilitating a genetic miracle that the title gives away. Pretentious and nonsensical as it can be, *Conceiving Ada* does occasionally exert a curious magnetism. The iconic Swinton is compelling almost by default, as is Lovelace, whose life clearly deserved a more viscerally imaginative interpreter.

Also reviewed in:
CHICAGO TRIBUNE, 3/12/99, p. M, Michael Wilmington
NEW YORK TIMES, 2/26/99, p. E11, Stephen Holden
VARIETY, 12/15-21/97, p. 63, Leonard Klady

COOKIE'S FORTUNE

An October Films release of a Sandcastle 5 and Elysian Dreams production. *Executive Producer:* William Baer. *Producer:* Robert Altman and Etchie Stroh. *Director:* Robert Altman. *Screenplay:* Anne Rapp. *Director of Photography:* Toyomichi Kurita. *Editor:* Abraham Lim. *Music:* David A. Stewart. *Music Editor:* Helena Lea. *Choreographer:* Jennifer M. Mizenko. *Sound:* Mark Weingarten and (music) Lee Manning.. *Sound Editor:* Frederick Howard. *Casting:* Pam Dixon Mickelson. *Production Designer:* Stephen Altman. *Art Director:* Richard Johnson. *Set Decorator:* Susan J. Emshwiller. *Set Dresser:* Phillip Thoman. *Costumes:* Dona Granata. *Make-up:* Manlio Rocchetti. *Running time:* 118 minutes. *MPAA Rating:* PG-13.

CAST: Glenn Close (Camille Dixon); Julianne Moore (Cora Duvall); Liv Tyler (Emma Duvall); Chris O'Donnell (Jason Brown); Charles S. Dutton (Willis Richland); Patricia Neal (Jewel Mae "Cookie" Orcutt); Ned Beatty (Lester Boyle); Courtney B. Vance (Otis Tucker); Donald Moffat (Jack Palmer); Lyle Lovett (Manny Hood); Danny Darst (Billy Cox); Matt Malloy (Eddie "The Expert" Pitts); Randle Mell (Patrick Freeman); Niecy Nash (Wanda Carter); Rufus Thomas (Theo Johnson); Ruby Wilson (Josie Martin); Preston Strobel (Ronnie Freeman); Ann Whitfield (Mrs. Henderson/Herodias); Hank Worsham (Tigellinus); Kenny Pillow and Derek Guyer (Soldiers); Emily Sindelar (Marlene); Heath Lail (Prop Boy); Shari Schneider (Mrs. Tippett); John Sullivan (Mr. Tippett); Red West (Mr. Henderson); Ferguson Reid and Chris Coulson (Deputies); Cheryl Cole (Picnic Lady); Fred Sanders (Guitarist); Jimmy Ellis (Drummer); Solomon McDaniel (Keyboardist); Terris Tate (Bass Guitarist).

LOS ANGELES TIMES, 4/2/99, Calendar/p. 1, Kevin Thomas

Robert Altman's "Cookie's Fortune" is a gem among the fabled director's ensemble movies, a Southern charmer—full of good humor and mature wisdom—that views human foibles with the bemused compassion of a Jean Renoir. This beautiful, beguiling film marks the feature debut of its writer, Anne Rapp, who, as a veteran script supervisor, clearly has developed a sense of the importance of structure and characterization, but the vision she has provided Altman goes way beyond craft. This is a film filled with a patient and loving understanding and a knowledge of the value of subtlety and ease.

Its setting, the actual Mississippi town of Holly Springs, is so full of period charm, captured glowingly by ace cinematographer Toyomichi Kurita, that you feel like taking off and visiting the place. Living in the decayed grandeur of a splendid antebellum house is Patricia Neal's hearty, uninhibited Jewel Mae Orcutt, known by one and all as Cookie, including her longtime family retainer Willis (Charles S. Dutton, a warm and powerful presence). Cookie remains full of spirit, but she's becoming forgetful, and that worries the devoted Willis as much as the fact that it's only a matter of time before she can no longer climb the stairs to her bedroom. For her part, Cookie, played with such resonance and gusto by Neal, is increasingly overcome with longing for her beloved late husband, Buck, so much so that she decides it's time to end it all.

As luck would have it, Cookie, having gone to her reward, is discovered by her ferociously proper and pretentious spinster niece Camille (Glenn Close), who's in the midst of directing a church Easter pageant derived from Oscar Wilde's "Salome," with her younger sister Cora

(Julianne Moore) in the title role. (Camille's revisions of Wilde lead her to claim a co-writing credit!) Suicide is too scandalous for Camille to stomach, so, drawing on her self-proclaimed theatrical expertise, she makes her aunt's death look like a murder without giving a thought to the consequences. Indeed, so self-involved is Camille that it never occurs to her that when the police tape off Cookie's house to protect the crime scene that it's meant to be off-limits to her as well. Bossy, obtuse, dominating Cora totally, Camille is labeled by her independent niece Emma (Liv Tyler), who's returned to town just before Cookie's death, as a "stupid, insensitive bitch."

Calamity compounds calamity, and a Shakespearean sense of the human comedy surfaces as the convoluted plot, propelled by the urges of human nature, both noble and otherwise, plays itself out under Altman's affectionate, never condescending, gaze.

In this film, the characters really are "characters," and with what relish Altman's actors play them. For all the trouble Camille unleashes, she's too unintentionally funny to hate, and you can't wish upon her a villain's fate, so clueless and pathetic is she, and played with a wonderfully focused daffiness by Close. Moore's lovely Cora proves to be unexpectedly far from docile. Tyler's Emma is smart, headstrong, living in the here and now, attracted to her old boyfriend, a wet-behind-the-ears policeman (Chris O'Donnell), and attracting to her wistful new boss (Lyle Lovett). Ned Beatty is the wise local cop who has to sort out the mess Camille has created, and seemingly not helping matters are a pair of comically zealous out-of-town investigators (Courtney B. Vance and Matt Malloy). Equally wise, however, is the leading local attorney (Donald Moffat).

This is a glorious cast, and it makes "Cookie's Fortune" an unalloyed pleasure as deep dark secrets start tumbling out, one after another. "Cookie's Fortune," which knows how to treat serious matters with humor, is to be treasured as an utterly distinctive work by one of America's finest filmmakers.

NEW YORK, 4/12/99, p. 81, Peter Rainer

Robert Altman, at 74, keeps turning them out. You never know what he's going to give you, and sometimes after you've seen one of his films, you *still* don't know. His latest, *Cookie's Fortune,* set in smalltown Mississippi, is pleasingly shaggy. You keep expecting it to drop a few octaves, but it never does; it's Delta pop that never becomes Delta blues. Still, this may not be such a bad thing. Altman's folkloric feints and throwaways are very easy on the eyes; he shows off his townspeople with such affection that after a while they begin to glow. The movie is a jaunty little jape.

The Cookie of the title is Jewel Mae Orcutt (Patricia Neal), a pipe-smoking crone who lives alone and so laments the loss of her late husband, Buck, that shortly into the movie she writes a farewell note and then ceremoniously puts a pillow over her head and shoots into it. Cookie's niece Camille (Glenn Close) stumbles in on the splatter, swallows the note, and, for the sake of southern family pride, tries to make the leavetaking look like murder—that is to say, something *respectable.* Willis (Charles S. Dutton), Cookie's caretaker and best friend, gets blamed, but nobody in town is convinced. The local policeman (Ned Beatty) knows Willis couldn't do such a thing, because he's a fishing buddy. It's that kind of film.

Southern gothic has often swung down from the branches of gnarled family trees. Altman and his screenwriter, Anne Rapp, parody the twistedness of southern family genealogy; our confusion about who means what to whom becomes part of the fun. So does the way the smallness of this town prevents anything from being a secret for long. The more you try to cover up the more you reveal.

Camille, the impresario of the Easter play—Oscar Wilde's *Salome,* no less—is a wannabe aristocrat who keeps getting brought up short by her community's common ways. She sees herself as an antebellum lady of quality, but in the overwrought way in which Close portrays her, she's more like Cruella DeVil or Norma Desmond (both of whom Close has already played).

The rest of the cast is more congenial to Altman's low-key wigginess—especially, and surprisingly, Liv Tyler and Chris O'Donnell, as moonstruck lovers addicted to impromptu sessions of heavy petting. Julianne Moore, as Camille's sister, is a lyric cuckoo. Playing Wilde, she takes her role so seriously that offstage, after rehearsals, she works Salome-like phrasings into her already addled patter. (As she also demonstrated in *Boogie Nights,* Moore is incomparable at playing terrible actresses.) Best is Dutton, who gives Willis such an easygoing comic grace that he seems to be dancing the part. No one should live out this year without watching Willis waddle his way home with a whiskey bottle tucked in his pants. It's a thing of beauty.

NEW YORK POST, 4/2/99, p. 47, Rod Dreher

Robert Altman gets all magnolia-mouthed in "Cookie's Fortune," a genteel ramble through the manners and mores of a small Mississippi town. It promises to be a rich, closely observed character piece about a peculiar but genial town and its eccentric social customs, but turns into a conventional screwball swimming in Southern Gothic gravy. Too many kooks spoil the broth.

Charles S. Dutton is almost always the best part of anything he's in, and that's true here as well. He plays Willis, a kindly handyman working for Miss Cookie Orcutt (Patricia Neal), a widow who smokes a pipe and misses her late husband Buck something fierce. When sad old Cookie crumbles, committing suicide in her bed, Willis gets the blame.

His accuser is Cookie's hideous niece, Camille (Glenn Close). Having discovered Cookie's body, Camille eats the farewell note and instructs her painfully shy and pliant sister Cora (Julianne Moore) to shush up about it.

"Only crazy people commit suicide!" warns snobbish Camille, all too happy to see poor Willis go to jail to keep the neighbors from thinking ill of the Orcutts.

What makes this comedy, not tragic drama, is that nobody else in town believes Willis did it. The sheriff (Ned Beatty) is Willis' fishing buddy, and puts him in jail as a matter of irritating duty, but doesn't lock the cell. He even lets Cora's daughter Emma (Liv Tyler) move in out of solidarity with her pal Willis—which puts her closer to a hapless deputy and would-be suitor (Chris O'Donnell).

Working from a screenplay by Anne Rapp, Altman gives these characters space to breathe. Yet this lack of focus compromises both the script and the picture as a whole. There are subplots and subplots of subplots, and too many characters going every which way.

Unfortunately, Close's over-the-top Camille sets the shrill and not very believable tone for the film.

She's a cornpone Cruella de Vil, an over-the-top schemer and would-be aristo who busies herself directing the local Presbyterian church play (a revival of Wilde's "Salome"). Could've been a hoot, if "Cookie's Fortune" didn't strive to make serious points about justice, intermarriage and racial identity. Half these people belong in a laid-back "To Kill a Mockingbird," while the other half seem to have wandered in from a madcap "Steel Magnolias." It plays like a shotgun wedding: There's fun to be had, but the whole thing feels forced and fraudulent.

NEWSDAY, 4/2/99, Part II/p. B7, John Anderson

The good news is, there's a kinder, gentler Robert Altman behind "Cookie's Fortune." The bad news is, there's a kinder, gentler Robert Altman.

That he's abandoned, or perhaps even lost, the virulent misanthropy that had been marring such '90s efforts as "Short Cuts," "Pret-a-Porter" and even "Kansas City" is not a bad thing. Altman has always had a susceptibility to his subjects' point of view—if he's filming star-worshiping Hollywood types, a la "The Player," for instance, he becomes one himself. But that also means that a sweetly goofy southern parable like "Cookie's Fortune" can make him a little sweet. Also goofy.

And it means that a small-town, small-time drama like this—in which local life and its principals are illuminated by a solitary tragedy—isn't going to inspire Altman to reach out and touch the horizon. (There is a phenomenal lack of heredity between this movie and one like, let's say, "McCabe and Mrs. Miller." They really don't seem to be by the same person.)

"Cookie" is a play, essentially, an ultra-stagy construct in a static world; there are virtually no people inhabiting the movie besides the main characters (a few scenes include crowd shots, but very few). And while this does give a Faulknerian torpor to the streets of Holly Spring, where everyone but those main characters seems to have fled indoors to escape the sun, it also heightens your suspicion that those characters are a bunch of Hollywood actors who don't know enough about the native customs to come in out of the heat.

They include the stalwart Willis (Charles S. Dutton), who keeps a pint of Wild Turkey on his hip and looks after the aged Cookie (Patricia Neal). He's also fond of Cookie's wild grandniece, Emma (Liv Tyler), who's straining her luck with the cops and with her coveralls while cleaning catfish for Manny (Lyle Lovett) and living in her van since returning home. She's back because of a run-in with her aunt Camille (Glenn Close) and mother Cora (Julianne Moore)—a couple of fading southern belles who keep stark raving madness at bay with a delicate dabbing of Eau de Blanche Dubois.

The only other people in town seem to be police, including Jason (Chris O'Donnell), who's mad about Emma, and Lester (Ned Beatty), who's mad about fish.

Even if he's made an airless movie, Altman's a prankster. At the center of the action, as it were, is dotty Camille's staging of an Easter play at the local church—the obvious choice, Oscar Wilde's "Salome." With its wooden acting and Biblical gestures, the deadly "Salome" is a daring choice to counterpose with Altman's movie and with the highly theatrical personality of Anne Rapp's script—little that we need to know needs be communicated through motion or expression, because it's all there in the dialogue. Neal tells us—with her face everything about Cookie in the film's first five minutes—that she misses her dead husband, Buck, and has decided to join him. But then she tells us so anyway. When Willis heads out to the store and Cookie tells him "goodbye," no one but Willis is unaware that Cookie's about to go upstairs with Buck's pistol, put a pillow over her head and blow her brains out.

This does not sit well with Camille, who is appalled by a suicide in the family but keeps her wits about her long enough to pocket Cookie's jewels and make the whole thing look like a robbery. It's Willis who takes the rap, and clearing him preoccupies the second half of the film.

Close has given some wonderful performances ("Dangerous Liaisons") and may have certain things to atone for—"Sunset Boulevard," "Paradise Road" but she breathes life and lunacy into "Cookie's Fortune." Camille is a powder keg of presumably old-line southern nuttiness, and Close keeps her on the edge, simultaneously the arbiter of taste in Holly Springs and its loosest cannon.

"Cookie's Fortune" is a tidy little drama, and we must assume Altman was drawn to it because he got to work small with a lot of people he likes and has worked with before (notably Lovett, whose character is charmingly useless). Dutton is very low-key, but it works nicely for him; Moore plays Cora as dumb but not too dumb; Tyler is as subtle as a day-old catfish but she has a definite presence, and Rapp has made Emma and the rest all distinctly novel entities—every character, in other words, is a character in "Cookie's Fortune," and they're played so broadly and against a mortified backdrop that, while graceful and even fun, it's really not a lot of movie.

SIGHT AND SOUND, 9/99, p. 44, Geoffrey Macnab

Jewel Mae 'Cookie' Orcutt is an elderly woman who lives alone in a Deep South mansion house, pining for Buck, her dead husband. Her only friend is Willis, a middle-aged black man who does odd jobs around the house. She is at loggerheads with her two nieces, Camille Dixon and Cora Duvall, who are scandalised by her unconventional behaviour. Cookie's favourite relative Emma (Cora's daughter) is back in town and working for the local catfish supplier. Willis tracks her down and tells her that Cookie would like to see her. Desperate to be reunited with Buck, Cookie shoots herself. Not long after her death, Camille and Cora arrive at the house fresh from rehearsal of the Easter pageant, a reworking of Oscar Wilde's *Salomé*. When Camille discovers Cookie's body, to avoid a scandal she eats the suicide note and tampers with the evidence so it looks as if her aunt has been murdered.

Willis is arrested and charged with the killing. He is put in the local jail (where he is joined by Emma) while the police mount an investigation. Eventually, blood marks are discovered which incriminate Camille, who cut her finger on the site of the crime. Camille is arrested. To everybody's amazement, Cookie's will names Willis as her closest living relative. Cora, the only one who can establish Camille's innocence, sticks to the 'murder' story. Emma learns that Camille, not Cora, is her mother. Camille goes to prison where she has a mental breakdown. Willis is released.

Cookie's Fortune, Altman's second film on the trot to be set in the Deep South, is in a far more relaxed groove than its predecessor *The Gingerbread Man*. It takes the widow Cookie an eternity to walk up and down the staircase of her southern mansion and Altman is determined to show every last step. Likewise, her companion Willis may be falsely accused of her murder, but that doesn't mean he is going to move in anything other than his usual shuffling gait. Altman and his actors take their tempo from the slow, mournful blues which fills the soundtrack, and it's only when Ruby Wilson belts out the opening song that the pace picks up.

One character who isn't in the slightest laid-back is Camille, the arch conspirator and busybody who directs the townsfolk in a truly atrocious Easter-pageant production of *Salomé*. Camille's cast declaim their lines with a dreary solemnity while Camille's sister Cora hoofs her way through her own clumsy version of the Dance of the Seven Veils. There is something perverse about watching highly accomplished actors pretending to be bungling amateurs, but Camille's directorial approach doesn't seem markedly different from that of Altman himself. She shares his morbidity ("that needs more blood around the neck," she complains about the severed head of John the Baptist) and, like Altman, she seems to enjoy working with a large ensemble cast. If her production of *Salomé* is mannered and a little absurd, so too is *Cookie's Fortune*.

Anne Rapp's screenplay tries—not entirely successfully—to undercut its own prevailing mood of whimsy by hinting at the dark events which cloud the protagonists' lives. This is a tale about a dysfunctional family which could easily have slipped over into Flannery O'Connor-style Southern Gothic. Most of the menfolk seem to be absent—either dead or fled—and those who remain are either vaguely sinister, like Lyle Lovett's voyeuristic catfish supplier, or downright goofy, like the sheriff's infatuated deputy.

But Rapp can't resist poking gentle fun at the foibles of the small-town folk: Cookie smokes a pipe; Willis is obsessed with fishing. The mood is closer to that of Garrison Keillor's *Lake Woebegone* than to the pessimism of Raymond Carver (whose stories Altman adapted with such skill and perception in *Short Cuts*). Mild eccentricity reigns. "She's a kinder soul, and has a rare ability to find in these characters an authentic, truthful quirkiness," the director has observed of Rapp. In trying to be faithful to her screenplay, he risks acting against his own nature: woolly-minded benevolence is not what you expect from the soured old magus. Just as Camille has a neat way of sweeping anything disagreeable under the carpet, Altman chooses not to make too much of an issue out of Camille's racism or Cookie's suicide—the latter's death turns out to be little more than the macguffin that sets the plot rolling.

Still, there are neat touches. Altman makes the most of the creaky gun cupboard door which never stays closed, and marks Cookie's death in mordantly funny fashion with an explosion of feathers. (She shoots herself through a pillow.) Liv Tyler, as the coltish, long-limbed, dulcet-toned Emma, and Charles Dutton as Willis have an easy comic rapport. Their scenes together yield the film's warmest and most likable moments. Unlike *The Gingerbread Man*, which could have been directed by anybody, *Cookie's Fortune* does bear Altman's imprimatur. The old energy and bite may be lacking, but at least this lazy, amiable shaggy dog story was made in the same freewheeling, idiosyncratic way as Altman's best work.

VILLAGE VOICE, 4/6/99, p. 121, J. Hoberman

Self-consciously nestling into the richest, most fashionable and comforting of American regional cultures, *Cookie's Fortune* received an enthusiastic reception when it opened the most recent Sundance Film Festival. This new Robert Altman film might wish to be a languorous spring afternoon in a sun-dappled, magnolia-scented garden. But, long before it ends, its leisurely immersion in the Mississippi Delta has turned downright lukewarm and even chilly.

Holly Springs, Mississippi—never to be confused with Hollywood, California—is a laid-back town where the local cops can talk fishing with a mystical sense of awe, where the cheerful, if entropic, juke joint is run by Rufus "Walkin' the Dog" Thomas, where one lawyer represents everybody's interests, and where (in an audio tic reminiscent of Jerry Seinfeld's imaginary—and scarcely less cozy—Upper West Side) every other scene reverberates with a single bent note from a slide guitar. That mournful, gut-bucket quaver is there to alert you that *Cookie's Fortune* will be a movie about roots.

As organized by Anne Rapp's script, the Holly Springs social order is an extended matriarchy. Perched atop in a decrepit antebellum home is the grand-dame wacko Cookie (Patricia Neal). Beneath are her nieces, the disapproving fussbudget Camille (Glenn Close) and the mush-brained Cora (Julianne Moore). Below them is Cora's "bad girl" daughter Emma (inertly embodied by ex-indie queen Liv Tyler), newly returned to town after some unspecified scandal. Shuttling between them all is Cookie's live-in handyman, Willis Richland (Charles S. Dutton), who functions as the clan's fairy godfather.

Willis shuffles through town, a portly presence with a bluesman's gold tooth and dapper stingy-brimmed panama—his considerable reservoir of good humor supplemented by the pint of Wild Turkey tucked in his back pocket. In contrast to the unassuming, homey juke joint where Willis borrows his booze is the local white-folks church. No gospelizing here. Instead, control freak Camille rehearses her pathetic sister Cora in a seasonal pageant that ludicrously revises Oscar Wilde's *Salome*.

Altman has rather too much fun with Camille's genteel playhouse of the ridiculous—not to mention her diva posturing and autocratic orchestration of her amateur cast. Bad acting is endemic to Holly Springs. If diva Neal appears to be having the time of her life as a pipe-smoking kook installed in a complementarily creaking old house, she doesn't overstay her welcome. Indeed, she rises splendidly to the occasion of her departure—effectively burying the movie's discomfiting echoes of *Driving Miss Daisy*, albeit raising the specter of *To Kill a Mockingbird* lite.

Even more than Woody Allen, Altman is a filmmaker who aspires to the choreographed and socially astute ensemble humanism epitomized by Jean Renoir's *The Rules of the Game*. But unlike Renoir, he has a saturnine temperament—he cannot help but condescend to half of his characters and ridicule the rest. In the Renoir film, it is famously said that everyone has their reasons; in *Cookie's Fortune*, it's more like everybody has their shtick, from the imperious red-hot mama Josie (Ruby Wilson) to the hapless catfish wholesaler (Lyle Lovett).

It's fitting, I suppose, that the ever-enthusiastic Close shoulders the film's burden of nastiness and self-delusion—she is after all playing a director. Still, the absurd church thespians notwithstanding, the proceedings are pretty amiable until the screeching Camille installs herself at the center of the movie's various plots. Thereafter, the characters get dumber and the writing more cutesy—at one point the goodies huddle together for warmth in the town jail under the benign eye of Ned Beatty's nice cop. The pace slows down even as the narrative grows more antic—with Tyler hurling herself at regular intervals at rookie lawman Chris O'Donnell.

Not that *Cookie's Fortune* ever takes itself too seriously. Once Camille's plot comes unraveled, we're left with Altman and Rapp's schematic, half-cracked exposition. The movie climaxes with a weird *Sunset Boulevard*-style arrest (as, in another echo of *Rules of the Game*, the church actors shuffle through Holly Springs in their Salome outfits) and then a series of family revelations. One well-telegraphed disclosure is heartwarmingly self-congratulatory, the other genealogical bombshell totally inconsequential. It's been nearly a quarter of a century since the *Nashville* apocalypse and Robert Altman has decreed that America is a peaceable kingdom after all.

Also reviewed in:
CHICAGO TRIBUNE, 4/9/99, Friday/p. A, Michael Wilmington
NEW REPUBLIC, 4/19/99, p. 28, Stanley Kauffmann
NEW YORK TIMES, 4/2/99, p. E13, Janet Maslin
NEW YORKER, 4/12/99, p. 109, David Denby
VARIETY, 1/25-31/99, p. 74, Todd McCarthy
WASHINGTON POST, 4/9/99, p. C5, Stephen Hunter
WASHINGTON POST, 4/9/99, Weekend/p. 50, Desson Howe

CORRUPTOR, THE

A New Line Cinema release of an Illusion Entertainment Group production. *Executive Producer:* Oliver Stone, Terence Chang, Bill Carraro, and Jay Stern. *Producer:* Dan Halsted. *Director:* James Foley. *Screenplay:* Robert Pucci. *Director of Photography:* Juan Ruiz-Anchia. *Editor:* Howard E. Smith. *Music:* Carter Burwell. *Music Editor:* Adam Smalley. *Sound:* Douglas Ganton and (music) Eric Flickinger. *Sound Editor:* Michael Wilhoit. *Casting:* Mary Vernieu and Anne McCarthy. *Production Designer:* David Brisbin. *Art Director:* Paul Denham Austerberry and Scott P. Murphy. *Set Designer:* Thomas Carnegie and Tom Warren. *Set Decorator:* Jaro

Dick and George Detitta, Jr. *Set Dresser:* David Orin Charles, Paul S. Gaily, and Steve R. Kreiger. *Special Effects:* Kaz Kobielski and Steve Kirshoff. *Costumes:* Doug Hall. *Make-up:* Donald J. Mowat. *Make-up (Special Effects):* John Caglione, Jr., Francois Dagenais, and Paul Jones. *Stunt Coordinator:* Philip Neilson. *Running time:* 111 minutes. *MPAA Rating:* R.

CAST: Chow Yun-Fat (Nick Chen); Mark Wahlberg (Danny Wallace); Ric Young (Henry Lee); Paul Ben-Victor (Schabacker); Jon Kit Lee (Jack); Andrew Pang (Willy Ung); Elizabeth Lindsey (Louise Deng); Brian Cox (Sean Wallace); Byron Mann (Bobby Vu); Kim Chan (Benny Wong); Bill MacDonald (Vince Kirkpatrick); Susie Trinh (Amy San); Ho Chow (Black Eyes); Olivia Yap (Tai); Lynda Chiu (Kim); Marie Matiko (May); Pak-Kong Ho (Phan Ho); Tim Progosh (Lackey); Beau Starr (Captain Stan Klein); LeRoy Allen (Guard One); Simon B. Cotter (Lawyer); Frank Pellegrino (Large Agent); Tovah Feldshuh (U.S. Attorney Margaret Wheeler); Tig Fong (Sumo Guard); Chuck Scarborough (Himself); Karen Huie (Woman in Brothel); Mike Jung (Doctor); Howard Hoover (Smaller Agent); Lucille Soong (Elderly Immigrant); Mark Williams (Co. Captain); Alice Poon (Masseuse); Jason Ting (Young Boy); Arthur Lo (Man on Street); Alice Lee Chun (Frightened Women).

LOS ANGELES TIMES, 3/12/99, Calendar/p. 2, Gene Seymour

[The following review by Gene Seymour appeared in a slightly different form in **NEWSDAY, 3/12/99, Part II/p. B7.**]

Forget "The Replacement Killers." Pretend it never happened. If America really wants to know what made Chow Yun-Fat a superstar of Chinese cinema, "The Corruptor" is the place to start.

As Lt. Nick Chen, the lethally effective, if ethically challenged, head of the NYPD's Asian Gang Unit, Yun-Fat holds your attention span as if it were a kitten he likes to tease. He may be the only action star in the world who still knows how to make walking into a room seem like an existential act. His broad face is a road map of hard-won wisdom and sardonic glee. Even with all the gunplay and explosions as distractions, you miss Yun-Fat whenever he's not on screen.

Giving a badge to Yun-Fat's internationally renowned bad/good guy persona is a smart move on somebody's part. Pairing him with Mark Wahlberg, as Chen's laconic, idealistic partner Danny Wallace, likewise turns out better than one might have expected. Between these two enigmas, "The Corruptor" manages to make a meat-and-potatoes action flick into a cunning little meditation on personal loyalty and situational morality.

Chen and his fellow Asian strike force commandos find it peculiar, to say the least, that a callow-looking white guy like Wallace is assigned to their basement office, just as Chinatown is literally exploding in a turf war between the ruling Triads and a brutal, well-armed gang of young insurgents called the Fukinese Dragons.

To keep the lid on, Chen has for years maintained a Faustian bargain with the Triads, with whom he has made shady deals in exchange for high-profile busts. Chen tries to shield Wallace from such greasy dealings. But, with the heat on, Henry Lee (Ric Young), the sybaritic serpent who controls the Triads, pulls Wallace in for some of the action. Wallace finds this process dicey to say the least, but the spoils come in handy, especially with an ex-cop dad (Brian Cox), addicted to booze and gambling, who's in deep trouble with loan sharks.

This might have been a routine police story, except that stories this deep and dark aren't told as routinely as they once were. Car chases are all that audiences today seem to want from these movies, and "The Corruptor" delivers an extravagantly vicious example.

But director James Foley, who has shown a tightly wound affinity for such tales of mundane corruption as "After Dark, My Sweet" (1990) and "Glengarry Glen Ross" (1992), keeps the action firmly anchored to the story. And the story does get complicated, selling out your own expectations just as the characters keep selling each other out.

It's hardly the pinnacle of such detective thrillers, but compared with, say, the last couple of "Lethal Weapons," it's damned close to the platinum standard.

In fact, with all due respect to Mel Gibson in his Martin Riggs mode, Yun-Fat's Nick Chen comes across as the kind of guy Riggs imagines himself to be on his best days, but falls a few meters short. It's taken some time for the news to get here, but with "The Corruptor,"

Hollywood seems to have finally figured out what other continents already knew: Yun-Fat is a movie star of the first magnitude.

NEW YORK POST, 3/12/99, p. 38, Jonathan Foreman

Those of you who remember "Year of the Dragon," the intense Mickey Rourke thriller, along with "The Replacement Killers," starring Chow Yun-Fat, may have excessively high expectations for this dark cop thriller.

It's nowhere near as good as Michael Cimino's "Dragon," and Chow doesn't get to strut all of his athletic stuff. Yet "The Corruptor" is still an enjoyable ride and superior in every way to recent thrillers such as Mel Gibson's "Payback."

Chow plays Lt. Nick Chen, a brutally effective Chinatown cop whose corrupt accommodation with one of the local tongs—the semi-legal associations that control organized crime in the area—becomes problematic when its rivalry with a gang of immigrants from the Fukien region of China explodes into a bloody war.

As the bodies start to pile up, a young white cop, Danny Wallace (Mark Wahlberg), is assigned to Chen's Asian Gang Unit. Wallace knows more about Chinatown and Chinese ways than Chen and his Chinese-American cops expect. But Wallace doesn't know as much as he thinks he does, and when one of the local bigs, Henry Lee (Ric Young), starts giving him some tips and then some favors, he, too, gets in a tangled web of tainted loyalties.

This is one of those movies where no one is what he seems. Everyone lies, and corruption may well be a necessary evil. With casual cynicism, the film assumes that sometimes the best cops may be the most corrupt. And there's no question that snatching on someone who's watched your back in a gunfight is a far worse crime than taking money and favors from a pimp ...

Chow, as always, has amazing screen presence, exuding charm and ruthless menace—and his English is now more than adequate.

He usually plays morally compromised, dark heroes, and Nick Chen is no exception. You almost don't want him to become a father figure to Wahlberg's Wallace, especially once you meet Wallace's real father, Sean (an excellent Brian Cox), a disgraced ex-cop in hock to the Mafia. But if Wallace has to choose between Chen and Henry Lee—or, for that matter, the ruthless investigators from the FBI ...

The strength of "The Corruptor" is its meditation on different kinds of loyalty to different kinds of family: blood relations, partners, the police department, criminal organization or ethnic group. Its weaknesses lie primarily in a lack of pace; this is the first action movie directed by James Foley ("At Close Range"). There are also some departures from believability that might be hard to take, especially for New Yorkers.

This is not just a matter of the usual unrealistic police-movie conventions, like the hero going into a dark alley without backup, or one cop with a pistol being more than a match for several gangsters with submachine guns. Nor is it the strangeness of a massive body count in a New York where the murder rate has dropped below 700 corpses a year.

The Chinatown in this movie is so miraculously free of traffic that you can have a long, bloody car chase through it. It's a place so underpoliced that there are still no cops on the street even after dozens of passersby have been cut down. Worse still, it's a Chinatown without atmosphere: You get no sense at all of the crowds, noise and bustle that make it such a fascinating place.

But if anyone in Hollywood had doubts that Chow Yun-Fat could make it as a real movie star in the West as well the East, this movie should lay them aside.

SIGHT AND SOUND, 6/99, p. 41, Jamie Graham

Chinatown, New York, the present. A turf war has erupted between the Fukienese Dragons, led by Bobby Vu, and the Tongs, a Triad family fronted by Benny Wong and Henry Lee. Keeping the peace is the Asian Gang Unit led by Nick Chen, a detective with close ties to the Tongs. Chen's mistrust of new squad arrival Danny Wallace is cemented when Wallace busts some drug pedlars only to discover that one of them is an undercover FBI agent. Benny Wong and Henry Lee decide they want to work with Wallace as well as Chen. Lee gains Wallace's favour by leading him to a lair of illegal immigrants. Chen asks Lee to leave Wallace alone, telling him about the FBI informer as a trade. The FBI blame Chen for their agent's subsequent death. Taped evidence incriminating Benny Wong is rendered worthless by Wong's execution, a hit orchestrated by Henry Lee and Bobby Vu, covertly in league.

Chen visits one of Bobby Vu's minions, Jack, and forces him to set up Vu. Jack tapes a meeting between Lee and Vu. Lee discovers Wallace is actually working for Internal Affairs on a case against Chen. He warns Chen and tells him of a shipment of illegal immigrants due that night, demanding that Chen should greet it and kill both Vu and Wallace. A shoot-out then ensues with the Fukienese Dragons. Vu and his gang are killed but not before Chen is fatally wounded. Wallace files a clean report about Chen's conduct before arresting Henry Lee, helped by Jack's tape.

Perhaps having learnt from last year's *The Replacement Killers* that working for a John Woo-imitator is no substitute for the real thing, Chow Yun-Fat has this time attached his talents to a proven American director, working within a proven US format: the buddy-cop movie. That said, *The Corruptor* opens with a high-tempo gun battle that calls for Chow to adopt his trademark pose gliding through the air with a gun in each fist. Add the exhilaratingly photographed Chinatown backdrop, echoing Chris Doyle's work for Wong Kar-Wai, and it would seem that director James Foley *(Glengarry Glen Ross, Fear)* is diligently Xeroxing the Hong Kong action flick.

When Danny Wallace arrives, however, the focus begins to shift. Assigned to Chen's Asian Gang Unit as much to lend ethnic diversity as to bolster their attempts to end a Triad turf war, his appearance causes Chen to complain, "He's not just white, he's green." Here, we're introduced to two cop-movie clichés—the pairing of the world-weary detective with the naive partner, and a clash of races examined, however glibly, within the microcosm of the squad car.

Content to work from such standard foundations, Robert Pucci's script adheres steadfastly to formula. Wallace wins Chen's respect and friendship, racial hurdles are neatly vaulted and the by-the-book rookie soon learns that sometimes the job can only be done by getting your hands dirty. Yet, despite a lack of originality, further emphasised by the routine car chases that punctuate the action, *The Corruptor* is efficient enough to invite viewer leniency. James Foley's eagerness to draw attention to the Emperor's new clothes cloaking his genre film also begs forgiveness. The exotic eastern score often gives way to rap and snippets of US-made source music, and the frequent bird's-eye shots of New York are forever placing Chinatown within its wider context.

Indeed, with his plot revolving around illegal immigration, dog-eat-dog greed and territorial battles, Foley even seems to be using Chinatown to study the dark side of the American Dream. It is not by accident that a fleeting shot of the Statue of Liberty appears in the final minutes and, when Chen remarks on Triad leader Henry Lee's avarice, he replies, "What do you expect? I'm American."

VILLAGE VOICE, 3/23/99, p. 130, Amy Taubin

James Foley's *The Corruptor*, is the kind of film that gives exploitation a bad name. An imitation John Woo *policier*, it stars Chow Yun-Fat, the Jean Gabin of Hong Kong cinema, as a pragmatic New York cop and Mark Wahlberg as his new partner. The Chinatown they patrol is a teeming cesspool where dumpsters are the last resting place of murdered prostitutes and nightly gang warfare leaves streets littered with corpses. If Giuliani's figures are to be believed, then more people are murdered in Chinatown in the course of this movie than in all of New York during 1998.

The time may be right for a movie that's about a cop who's not a pillar of virtue, but when that cop is Asian, and his white buddy is the one who's pure as the driven snow, I'd say we have a bit of a problem. The *Corruptor* is as racist a movie as I've seen in years. But as unforgivable as Foley's depiction of Chinatown society is, it's nothing compared to what he does to Chow Yun-Fat, turning his best moves to shtick by depriving them of any context. That in such a miserable film I could still care whether his character lived or died is, perhaps, the greatest proof that he's a movie star.

Also reviewed in:
CHICAGO TRIBUNE, 3/12/99, Friday/p. A, John Petrakis
NEW YORK TIMES, 3/12/99, p. E12, Stephen Holden

VARIETY, 3/15-21/99, p. 38, Emanuel Levy
WASHINGTON POST, 3/12/99, p. C5, Stephen Hunter
WASHINGTON POST, 3/12/99, Weekend/p. 42, Desson Howe

CRADLE WILL ROCK

A Touchstone Pictures release of a Havoc production in association with Krakower/Beacham productions. *Executive Producer:* Louise Krakower, Frank Beacham, and Allan Nicholls. Producer: Jon Kilik, Lydia Dean Pilcher, and Tim Robbins. *Director:* Tim Robbins. *Screenplay:* Tim Robbins. *Director of Photography:* Jean Yves Escoffier. *Editor:* Geraldine Peroni. *Music:* David Robbins and Marc Blitzstein. *Music Editor:* Daniel Lieberstein. *Choreographer:* Rob Marshall. *Sound:* Tod A. Maitland and (music) Gary Chester. *Sound Editor:* Eliza Paley. *Casting:* Douglas Aibel. *Production Designer:* Richard Hoover. *Art Director:* Troy Sizemore. *Set Decorator:* Debra Schutt. *Set Dresser:* Jo Ann Atwood, Rebecca Meis, Joan Finlay, Philip Canfield, Ruth De Leon, Jeffrey Brink, Deborah Canfield, Mark Newell, James Archer, Kevin Blake, Conrad Brink, Kelly Canfield, Patrice Longo, and Sarah Fredericks. *Special Effects:* J.C. Brotherhood. *Costumes:* Ruth Myers. *Make-up:* Linda Grimes and Michael Bigger. *Stunt Coordinator:* Jery Hewitt. *Running time:* 132 minutes. *MPAA Rating:* R.

CAST: Hank Azaria (Marc Blitzstein); Ruben Blades (Diego Rivera); Joan Cusack (Hazel Huffman); John Cusack (Nelson Rockefeller); Cary Elwes (John Houseman); Philip Baker Hall (Gray Mathers); Cherry Jones (Hallie Flanagan); Angus MacFadyen (Orson Welles); Bill Murray (Tommy Crickshaw); Vanessa Redgrave (Countless La Grange); Susan Sarandon (Margherita Sarfatti); Jamey Sheridan (John Adair); John Turturro (Aldo Silvano); Emily Watson (Olive Stanton); Bob Balaban (Harry Hopkins); Jack Black (Sid); Kyle Gass (Larry); Paul Giamatti (Carlo); Barnard Hughes (Frank Marvel); Barbara Sukowa (Sophie Silvano); MAXINE ELLIOT'S: Victoria Clark (Dulce Fox); Erin Hill (Sandra Mescal); Daniel Jenkins (Will Geer); Timothy Jerome (Bert Weston); Chris McKinney (Canada Lee); Henry Stram (Hiram Sherman); Adele Robbins (Augusta Weissberger); Lee Arenberg (Abe Feder); Allan Nicholls (George Zorn); Rob Carlson (National Guardsman); Alison Tatlock (Reporter); Dina Platias (Lucille Schly); Pamela D. Henry (Alma Dixon); Emma Smith Stevens (Stagehand); Steven Tyler (Lehman Engel); Charles Giordano (Accordion); Jeffrey Kievit (Trumpet); Kenneth Finn (Trombone); Kenneth Hitchcock (Clarinet); David D'Angelo (Alto Saxophone); David Ratajczak (Percussion); FEDERAL THEATRE: Stephen Spinella (Donald O'Hara); Brenda Pressley (Rose); Brian Brophy (Pierre De Rohan); David Costabile (Beaver Man); Marla Schaffel (Beaver Woman); Dominic Cortese (Beaver Accordion Accompanist); POWER: John Carpenter (William Randolph Hearst); Gretchen Mol (Marion Davies); Gil Robbins (Congressman Starnes); Harris Yulin (Chairman Martin Dies); Ned Bellamy (Paul Edwards); V.J. Foster (James); William Duell (Butler); Albert Macklin (Tailor); Scott Sowers and Bobby Amore (Reporters); SILVANO: Lynn Cohen (Mama); Dominic Chianese (Papa); Peter Jacobson (Uncle); Evan Katz (Joey); Alysia Zucker (Chance); Sarah Hyland (Giovanna); Stephanie Roth (Marta); VAUDEVILLE: Spanky McHugh (Melvin); Todd Stockman (Puppeteer); Patrick Husted (Vaudeville Theatre Manager); Jay Green (Plate Twirler); Carolyn West (Assistant Plate Twirler); BLITZSTEIN: Steven Skybell (Bertolt Brecht); Susan Heimbinder (Eva Blitzstein); Audra McDonald ("Joe Worker" Singer); Robert Ari (Liberty Committee #1); Michele Pawk (Liberty Committee #2); Gregg Edelman (Dream Larry Foreman); Matthew Bennett (Dream Cop); ROCKEFELLER CENTER: Brian Powell (Aide); Jack Willis (Lawyer); Gilbert Cruz (Mendez); Robert Hirschfeld (Sol); P.J. Brown (Guard); Michael Rivkin and Keira Naughton (Protesters); Taylor Stanley (Claire); Tommy Allen (Pete); Jeff Butcher (Mendez Double); Sandy Hamilton (Sol Double); DIEGO: Corina Katt (Frida Kahlo); Josie Whisttlesey, Sandra Lindquist, and Tamika Lamison (Models); OPENING: Edward James Hyland (Worker in Theatre); Boris McGiver (Man on Street); WPA: Chris Bauer (Carpenter); Leonardo Cimino (Man in Line); Patti Tippo (Clerk); Carrie Preston (Administrator); RIOT: Tony Amendola (Carl Jasper).

CHRISTIAN SCIENCE MONITOR, 12/10/99, p. 15, David Sterritt

[*Cradle Will Rock* was reviewed jointly with *The Green Mile*; see Sterritt's review of that film.]

LOS ANGELES TIMES, 12/8/99, Calendar/p. 1, Kenneth Turan

"Those who cannot remember the past," philosopher George Santayana wrote, "are condemned to repeat it," and writer-director Tim Robbins has no intention of letting anyone forget. His smart and pleasingly ambitious "Cradle Will Rock" is not only a lively and fittingly chaotic look at a time of unprecedented social and political change, it has made the excitement and ferment of America in the volcanic 1930s its own.

Calling itself "a (mostly) true story," "Cradle" uses its impressive ensemble cast to confidently intercut characters playing out a fistful of stories over an eight-month period from the fall of 1936 through a legendary performance of the Marc Blitzstein musical on June 16, 1937, that gives the film its name.

As a Robert Altman-influenced kaleidoscope of interlocking scenarios—some true, some exaggerated, some completely made up—"Cradle" has more energy than sense at times, and its passion for screwball farce is not always welcome. But its fidelity to the tenor of the times as well as its nervy decision to cut as wide a swath as possible through one of the most exciting and meaningful periods of our history have created something that's impossible not to both applaud and enjoy.

This is Robbins' third film as a writer-director (after "Bob Roberts" and "Dead Man Walking") and as a group they reveal a rare gift for making serious material completely accessible. What Robbins has been understandably attracted to here is a moment in time when artists were socially conscious and they were proud their work was known as committed and political.

Blitzstein's play (full title "The Cradle Will Rock"), described as the first American musical about serious issues, fits that scenario snugly. Set in the mythical Steeltown, it follows a union struggling against the power of ruling capitalist Mr. Mister. We see Blitzstein (Hank Azaria) composing the musical under the spell of both his dead wife and a still-living Bertolt Brecht, who tells the writer not to forget to include "an artist or two. They are the biggest whores."

Blitzstein's is only one of the many stories "Cradle" follows, almost too many to even list. Here's young Nelson Rockefeller (John Cusack), sparring with Mexican artist Diego Rivera (Ruben Blades) over a mural commissioned for Rockefeller Center. And there's the real-life Margherita Sarfatti (Susan Sarandon), described by Rivera as "the publicity queen for the new Roman Empire," trying to get industrialists like fictional steel magnate Gray Mathers (Philip Baker Hall) to offer tangible financial support to the Mussolini regime.

Most of "Cradle's" drama involves the Federal Theater Project (an offshoot of the New Deal's Works Progress Administration), an enterprise that reached 25% of the American population and was as close as this country ever came to having a genuine national theater.

Cherry Jones, a superb Tony-winning stage actress, gives her most impressive screen performance to date as Hallie Flanagan, the woman who ran the Federal Theater Project. Jones' controlled energy and charisma simultaneously drive the film and ground it in a reality it needs, and her's is the one performance that stands out in a very accomplished crowd.

Flanagan's most high-profile producing/directing team are John Houseman (Cary Elwes) and Orson Welles (Angus Macfadyen), already old hands at the bickering collaboration that would end up animating the Mercury Theater. They are putting on Blitzstein's "Cradle," a production that also employs fictional actor Aldo Silvano (John Turturro), having trouble with his proto-fascist family, and the real-life would-be actress Olive Stanton (Emily Watson), down on her luck and hoping for a chance at a real job.

All this is happening under the malignant shadow of the Dies Committee, a congressional precursor to the House Un-American Activities Committee that is preparing to hold hearings about the presence of communists in the Federal Theater Project.

Cheering the committee along is the humorless Hazel Huffman (Joan Cusack), a worrywart vigilante who fears the Red Menace. And cheering her on is Tommy Crickshaw (Bill Murray), a proud but sour ventriloquist whose main beef about communists is that they're just not funny.

Though Murray is brilliant as always and convincingly antediluvian, "Cradle's" more obvious attempts at humor do not come off. Especially irritating is Vanessa Redgrave as madcap social butterfly Countess La Grange, the wife of steelman Mathers, whose protege Carlo (Paul Giamatti) is nowhere near as amusing as the Preston Sturges character he seems a knockoff of.

Willing to move mountains to make its points, "Cradle" squeezes together into its eight months events that were years apart: the Rivera-Rockefeller conflict goes back to 1933, and Hallie Flanagan's Dies Committee testimony didn't happen until 1938. More troubling than this minor date switching is the way poor Marion Davies, in reality one of the true talents of the silent screen, is yet again (this time played by Gretchen Mol) maligned as no more than the dumbbell mistress of William Randolph Hearst.

But quibbling with a film this enterprising is really beside the point. As a mixture of drama, humor and history, a melange of seriousness and slapstick, real people and imagined characters, it definitely stands out. This is our history, and it's good to have it back again.

NEW YORK, 12/20-27/99, p. 60, Peter Rainer

Topsy-Turvy could also serve as the title of writer-director Tim Robbins's *Cradle Will Rock*, which is spiritedly obsessed with the follies and pizzazz of the gypsy theatrical life and with moneyed society. (By a happy coincidence, it's practically a companion piece to Leigh's film.) Robbins is almost insanely ambitious in attempting a full-scale, tumultuous portrait of art, theater, and politics in thirties New York. The film's focal point is the politically motivated cancellation by the Works Progress Administration of Marc Blitzstein's leftist opera *The Cradle Will Rock*, a Federal Theater Project presentation produced by John Houseman and staged by Orson Welles, and the subsequent raucous, impromptu restaging of its premiere twenty blocks uptown.

As a director, Robbins doesn't really have the chops to bring most of it off, but he's made the right decision to frame this story as a comedy; at its best, the film suggests what Preston Sturges might have come up with if he suddenly turned Altmanesque. The cast is varied and wildly uneven: Angus Macfadyen's Orson Welles is mostly a blur of bellowing and bad manners, but Rubén Blades's Diego Rivera, who clashes with John Cusack's Nelson Rockefeller, is a roaring success, and Bill Murray, who plays a scarily despondent vaudeville ventriloquist, demonstrates yet again, after *Rushmore*, that he's a major actor who can disturb us as resoundingly as he once made us laugh.

NEW YORK POST, 12/8/99, p. 53, Jonathan Foreman

"Cradle Will Rock" is an attempt to do for the ideological and artistic battles of the Depression years what Milos Forman's excellent "Ragtime" did for the early 1900s.

But despite a contingent of Hollywood's most talented actors, there is hardly a moment during this overlong, stunningly smug exercise in moral selfsatisfaction when you actually care about a character, real or invented.

It's almost as if director Tim Robbins and his cast were so thrilled with their impersonations of genuinely brave, smart and interesting leftists of the 1930s that they forgot to make the movie entertaining.

The result is a confused, unrefined agitprop movie about an agitprop musical: a Baby Boomer cartoon of popular-front politics that actually demeans the memory of the pre-war left.

Crudely written, this is the sort of film in which the rich dance in 18th-century dress while fist-waving actors in cloth caps march through the streets: There's no real feeling or conviction, just posturing.

Several subplots interlock, in "Ragtime" fashion, in a story that centers on the first production of Mark Blitzstein's fabled operetta "The Cradle Will Rock," about a strike in a steel town.

The militantly pro-labor play was developed by the Federal Theater Project, a part of the New Deal's Works Project Administration that brought live, inexpensive theater to millions of people across America.

Directed by the young Orson Welles (Angus Macfadyen), and produced by John Houseman (Cary Elwes), the show was about to open when the Federal Theater Project closed the theater after the organization was attacked by Red-baiters in Congress.

After Houseman—unfairly portrayed here as an effeminate, foolish fop—managed to find an empty theater, the cast—and audience—moved (in real life by cars and bus, in the movie by foot) 20 blocks uptown, to the Venice Theater.

There, union restrictions forced the cast to perform from the orchestra floor while the playwright sat on stage at a battered, borrowed piano. You might not realize it from the corny way it's staged by Robbins, but it was one of the most exciting moments in American theatrical history.

As Blitzstein, Hank Azaria is shown as being visited by phantoms of his dead wife and Bertolt Brecht. Emily Watson (playing yet another suffering, wide-eyed waif) is a destitute girl who gets a break from the project and a part in the play.

Bill Murray, funny as always, is an alcoholic ventriloquist who has decided that Reds "just aren't funny" and resents his teaching work for the WPA.

In a subplot that is supposed to raise more interesting questions about art, patronage and censorship, Ruben Blades plays the Mexican artist Diego Rivera—whose pro-Lenin mural for Nelson Rockefeller (John Cusack) was destroyed on the billionaire's orders—and Susan Sarandon is Madame Sarfatti, a former mistress of Mussolini and enthusiast for artistic modernism. (The film isn't sure if modernism is a good or bad thing.)

The best performances come from Cherry Jones, who is superb as Hallie Flanagan, the chief of the Federal Theater, and Vanessa Redgrave, who is absolutely delightful as the Countess La Grange, a society wife and enthusiast for the arts.

NEWSDAY, 12/8/99, Part II/p. B2, John Anderson

It's an aspect of New York theater that's been grievously overlooked by historians, but according to director Tim Robbins, Depression-era Broadway actually served as a kind of pilot for "The Jerry Springer Show." Take Orson Welles, for instance. Most contemporary observers say that by fall of 1936—when he'd begun staging composer Mark Blitzstein's "The Cradle Will Rock" for the WPA's Federal Theater Project—he'd already achieved immortality with his all-black "Macbeth" and a revolutionary production of "Doctor Faustus." But no, Robbins tells us, Welles (Angus MacFadyen) was actually a bellicose drunk of no discernible talent, engaged in an ongoing hissy fit with his producer, a mincing, foppish prig named John Houseman (Cary Elwes).

Blitzstein (Hank Azaria), meanwhile, saw visions of Bertolt Brecht (and of Blitzstein's dead wife in a wedding gown). Across town, Mexican muralist Diego Rivera (Ruben Blades) was suffering under the delusion that he could paint Lenin in the lobby of Rockefeller Center without compromising his communism. And William Randolph Hearst (John Carpenter)—dressed for a ball in the robes of Cardinal Richelieu—plotted the creation of noncontextual, apolitical modern art.

In "Cradle Will Rock," a movie whose sense of smugness rivals its disregard of truth, Robbins mounts a pageant—a high school pageant, but a pageant nonetheless—around one of the really thrilling chapters in the chronicle of New York theater: the defiant performance of Blitzstein's "Cradle," which was torpedoed by attacks from the right, union fiats from the left and was closed before it opened. When the soon-to-be-unemployed actors and musicians, forbidden to perform on stage, rise from their seats to sing Blitzstein's proletariat operetta in a hurriedly borrowed Manhattan theater house, it's a moment not even "Cradle Will Rock" can totally defuse.

But most of Robbins' film—hampered as it is by his script, a warped synthesis of pure exposition and political presumption—is a cartoon. "A (Mostly) True Story" may be how it announces itself, but the fictionalized elements prompt one to ask why he made the film at all. The actors—Cherry Jones, for instance, who plays besieged Federal Theater Project director Hallie Flanagan, and John Turturro, as antifascist Italian actor Aldo Silvano—never stop playing to the cheap seats.

Although Robbins has, on paper, assembled one of the more impressive casts of any movie in years, he allows them (or instructs them) to play so broadly that the tone becomes farce. Vanessa Redgrave is nearly hysterical as the dilettante-lefty wife of Gray Mathers (Philip Baker Hall), himself a composite of period industrialists. Susan Sarandon, as Mussolini's art-dealing fund-raiser Margherita Sarfatti, gives the unintentionally comic performance of the year.

There are two explanations for what's happening in "Cradle Will Rock." One, Robbins is so convinced of his movie's political correctness that he couldn't see its lack of dramatic cohesion or luster. Two, he wanted to re-create the kind of Odetsian agitprop that the original "Cradle" embodied—theater as political pamphleteering.

But why he sabotages the real heroes of the piece is a mystery—Welles, for instance, whom Blitzstein always said was behind the "spontaneous" performance of "The Cradle Will Rock," but in Robbins' account is totally surprised by it.

You also have to wonder about the simply mean-spirited portrayal of someone like Hearst's mistress, Marion Davies (Gretchen Mol), who is remembered not just as a gifted comedienne, but as a genuine human being (and who sold her jewels to prop up Hearst when his newspaper empire went south). Robbins sticks her in the movie without any lines and has her swill champagne like a well-kept fish, showing a strange disregard for history, to say nothing of generosity.

Oddly enough, the two characters with the most substance are fictional: Tommy Crickshaw (Bill Murray), an embittered ventriloquist, and Hazel Huffman (Joan Cusack), a Theater Project employee who testifies about the Red Menace before Congress and finds a kindred spirit in Tommy—while being ostracized by everyone else. Such people are consigned to the dustbin of history, Robbins wants us to know. But then, when the historian is Robbins, the dustbin is a relatively safe place to be.

NEWSWEEK, 12/13/99, p. 87, David Ansen

It's always a shock to run into a Hollywood movie with a sense of history, much less one as ambitious as Tim Robbins's "Cradle Will Rock." Perhaps inspired by the mural Nelson Rockefeller (John Cusack) commissioned from Diego Rivera (Rubén Blades) for Rockefeller Center, Robbins has mounted a swirling mural of his own, attempting to capture the political and artistic fever of New York in the mid '30s. Here are Orson Welles (Angus MacFadyen), producer John Houseman (Cary Elwes) and composer Marc Blitzstein (Hank Azaria) mounting their Federal Theatre production of the political musical "The Cradle Will Rock," when it is suddenly shut down by the government on the eve of production. Here are socialist Rivera and millionaire Rockefeller fighting over control of that doomed mural (never mind that this took place three years earlier). Here are a Jewish Mussolini sympathizer (Susan Sarandon) trying to raise money for Il Duce from rich industrialists, a fake countess with bohemian urges (Vanessa Redgrave) and a self-righteous informant (Joan Cusack) betraying her co-workers to the committee investigating anti-American activities in the WPA.

Mixing fictional characters (a bitter ventriloquist played by Bill Murray) with broad, controversial portraits of real people (Welles is a drunken blowhard here), Robbins eschews leftist diatribes for a bold cartoon version of history. It's as crowed and energetic as a big parade—and just about as subtle.

SIGHT AND SOUND, 5/00, p. 45, Philip Strick

New York City, 1936. Devised as a programme of recovery from the Great Depression, the WPA (Works Progress Administration) has funded the Federal Theater Project, subsidising low-cost theatre and thousands of backstage jobs throughout the US. But the project is under attack from congressmen out to discredit the WPA. As project-head Hallie Flanagan prepares to defend its achievements to the hostile Dies Committee in Washington, composer Marc Blitzstein completes his "play with music" *The Cradle Will Rock* for presentation at the Maxine Elliott theater on Broadway by Local 891, a drama company headed by John Houseman and Orson Welles. With a cast including the recently homeless Olive Stanton and Aldo Silvano, an Italian immigrant, the *Cradle* rehearsals are cheered on by arts fan Countess La Grange. Like his friends William Randolph Hearst and Nelson Rockefeller, the Countess' husband Gray Mathers secures invaluable classic paintings in return for donations to Margherita Sarfatti, an agent for Mussolini. Rockefeller also commissions Mexican painter Diego Rivera to create a mural for the Rockefeller Center.

A Federal Theater employee, Hazel Huffman, tells the committee about her fears of Communist infiltration. She finds a kindred spirit in ventriloquist Tommy Crickshaw, who blames the project for the decline of his own failing career. After Hallie testifies to the committee, funds for Federal Theater productions are cut. Soldiers cordon off the Maxine Elliott and the performers' unions insist on strike action, but Houseman and Welles find a substitute theatre. *The Cradle Will Rock* is performed without sets, costumes or orchestra, the cast (led by Olive and Aldo) performing their parts from their seats, risking expulsion from the union. The play is a riotous success. Rivera's mural, featuring a portrait of Lenin, is destroyed by order of its sponsor, while out on Broadway a funeral cortège marks the demise of Federal Theater.

Introducing itself as "a (mostly) true story", *Cradle Will Rock* depicts the events and characters surrounding the 1936 stage production of composer Marc Blitzstein's "play with music" *Cradle Will Rock* directed by Orson Welles and financed by the left-wing Federal Theater Project. The story is passingly familiar to Orson Welles admirers but otherwise so long overlooked several of director Tim Robbins' own production unit for this film assumed he was making it all up. Authentication of the key events can be found in John Houseman's autobiography *Unfinished Business* with its wry, admiring account of the theatrical coup achieved by boy-wonder Welles between making an all-black theatre production of *Macbeth* and his first film *Citizen Kane* (1941). But Welles plays only a small part in Robbins' complex reconstruction, assembled with the generosity of an anthologist reluctant to bypass good colourful material, particularly when it substantiates his main purpose. Given, for instance, that Blitzstein first showed his dramatic sketch for the play to Bertold Brecht (to whom *Cradle Will Rock* was dedicated), Robbins writes a 'ghost' Brecht into the film's action, creating another of the alternative realities which have haunted his previous films.

The unreliable senatorial campaigner in *Bob Roberts* and the self-deluding killer in *Dead Man Walking* neatly prepare the trail for Robbins' latest anti-authoritarian venture. Both characters have their deadly charm and illustrate a bigotry Robbins would find more amusing if it weren't so universal and sinister. In chilling anticipation of the McCarthy era, here a blustering congressman demands to know whether Christopher Marlowe (1564-93) is known to have Communist sympathies. And this clumsy phobia is equally apparent in desk-clerk Hazel Huffman (Joan Cusack) who suspects a pro-Russian agenda in the Federal Theater's affairs, the office staff who turn against *her*, and the people who misinterpret the daft children's pantomime *The Eager Beaver* as an allegory about workers versus capitalists. Even the best intentions of Nelson Rockefeller (John Cusack) turn repressive in a subplot after artist Diego Rivera (Rubén Blades) proves intransigent over the subject of his mural for the Rockefeller Center. "Nothing in art is inappropriate," growls Rivera, a sentiment heartily endorsed by Robbins' screenplay which freely appropriates whatever it pleases.

The stifling of such freedom is naturally Robbins' major concern, and his films are fashioned from constraints and barriers, perpetual gulfs in communication. *Dead Man Walking* is a long succession of faces framed by prison bars, reappearing in *Cradle* with Blitzstein's imaginary private prison. A key victim in this society where free speech can spell ruin is the ventriloquist Tommy Crickshaw (Bill Murray), so dumbfounded by his collapsing world and the students who steal his routine he can barely talk except through an ungainly puppet. The agonising interdependence between the magician and the torments he has devised for himself afflicts all the puppetmasters in *Cradle Will Rock,* from William Randolph Hearst and Rockefeller to Blitzstein (Hank Azaria) and Rivera. In each case, the puppets finally speak up for themselves. And Crickshaw's alter ego remains alone on stage singing 'L'Internationale' to a bewildered audience until it is carried away in a coffin down Broadway.

The many parallel productions within *Cradle Will Rock* all conclude with a similar uncertainty, rather like the series of concerts in *Bob Roberts* where the refrains are so extreme ("Hang'em high," he sings of drug dealers) that the voting public could hardly be expected to take them seriously. Crickshaw's act, Rivera's mural, the Eager Beavers, even the rehearsal for Welles' production of *Doctor Faustus* (in which the Seven Deadly Sins were portrayed by a "sinister puppet troupe"), are all brought to an untimely end, foreshadowing the disintegration of the Federal Theater Project itself. Less prominent performances—the fancy-dress ball, Carlo's diabolical piano concert or the behind-the-scenes steering of the Dies Committee radio-show witch hunt—also echo the ardous shaping of Blitzstein's composition, destined only for cancellation.

"I've always wanted to observe the process of art-making!" chirps art patron Countess La Grange (Vanessa Redgrave) in part apology, one suspects, for Robbins himself who, floating his camera above a phalanx of spinning plates on the vaudeville stage, clearly regards art-making as a balancing act. From the title onwards, his film concerns itself with stability, as much in romance as in politics, as much in post-Depression recovery as in the symmetry of a single mural, as much in the Welles-Houseman unit (an alliance of opposites) as in the juggling task Robbins has set himself. It makes for quite a display of dexterity.

Striving to maintain the film's range of checks and balances is an impressive army of female activists, rebels with whole-hearted causes. With an appealing precision, each is challenged by a partner/opponent. The vulnerable Olive (Emily Watson) finds and loses an urbane union leader; the Italian fundraiser Margherita Sarfatti (Susan Sarandon) finds her match in Rivera; the redoubtable Hallie (Cherry Jones) does battle with the icy congressman; and the Countess skirmishes with her wearily wealthy husband (Philip Baker Hall). Even as would be actor Aldo (John Turturro) is being warned by his wife (Barbara Sukowa) that *Cradle Will Rock* is a risky venture, Blitzstein is being warned from beyond the grave by *his* wife (Susan Heimbinder) he hasn't had enough sleep.

From his serpentine opening shot, Robbins would have us believe Olive is at his story's centre. Certainly her enterprise is what rescues the performance from being just a solo recital, but she is quickly absorbed by the collective participation of the entire cast. The cunning of Robbins' Wellesian dialogue lies in the amount of information it contrives to share about Roosevelt's New Deal and the rise of Mussolini, while linking Olive's plight with the song being composed in Blitzstein's studio at that very moment, a song she will eventually sing. At the same time, the booming newsreel commentary speaks of "hope for the future", exactly the theme proposed by Rockefeller for Rivera's mural.

As the story closes, all that remains of the mural is a fragment, reminding us that the near future for the *Cradle* generation is in fact painfully short of hope. But Robbins is disinclined towards gloom and turns the climactic *Cradle* performance (a touch misleadingly shown through a collection of passionate extracts) into a welter of praise and euphoria, as if by sheer force of goodwill the political tide could have been reversed. Houseman reported that apart from Blitzstein's piano only one other instrument, an accordion, accompanied the show, but the film adds several extras and the soundtrack knows no limits. While sharing Blitzstein's affection for sung drama (apparently inspired by a combination of *The Threepenny Opera* and Gilbert and Sullivan), Robbins concentrates on celebrating his cast and design team. With its sudden explosions of visual energy—the fancy-dress ball, the wild dance at Rivera's studio, the street parade—and its cascade of fine performances (the verbal sparring between Cary Elwes as Houseman and Angus MacFadyen as Welles provides particular enjoyment), *Cradle Will Rock* may not be all true but provides a concert of admirable variations.

TIME, 12/27/99, p. 179, Richard Corliss

No age was so towering that a cynic looking back could not have contempt for it. To re-create the bustling, politically contentious '30s, when a young Orson Welles tried to stage the socialist musical *The Cradle Will Rock* with federal funding, Robbins has splashed a couple of dozen real people onto a garish movie mural, Diego Rivera-style. While Welles (MacFadyen) and producer John Houseman (Elwes) try to persuade their government patron (Jones) not to cancel the show, Nelson Rockefeller (Cusack) romances Rivera (Blades), then literally trashes his work. There's also a young actress (Watson), a jaded ventriloquist (Murray), a swank saleswoman for fascism (Sarandon)—anyone who was alive then, and dabbling in the arts, is in this too-much of a movie.

How could it have failed? With a smugness that smothers the actors' energy and obliterates the historical reality. Welles is a pompous oaf here, and Houseman his toady. The rich are scheming, the poor artists clichés of do-gooder striving. These are caricatures drawn so violently that one sees blotches of ink instead of quick, deft lines.

Perhaps, in the long run, we are all idiots. But we don't need a 60-year perspective to see Robbins' attitude revealed in all its meanness of spirit. If he hated these folks so, why did he waste his time and ours putting them on film?

VILLAGE VOICE, 12/14/99, p. 173, J. Hoberman

There's a rush-hour sense of history to Tim Robbins's *Cradle Will Rock*. Historical forces and famous ghosts jostle past each other in this evocation of mid-1930s New York like harried commuters at Grand Central Station.

Robbins's frantic period-pageant is named for and centered on the Federal Theater production of Marc Blitzstein's leftist musical drama, first staged in June 1937 by then 22-year-old "boy wonder" Orson Welles. Defunded by the government at the last minute, perhaps because of its radical politics, the show went on in the street—a mythic moment in Popular Front culture, as well as Welles's career. (Indeed, Welles's last project was a script about this particular adventure.)

Himself a brash writer-director (but not, here, actor), Robbins acknowledges Wellesian theatrics with his opening scene, in which homeless waif Emily Watson wakes up behind a movie screen upon which a newsreel is being projected. But Robbins's real artist-hero is bland Blitzstein (Hank Azaria), introduced with a showboat dolly-shot in the throes of creation and thereafter shown wandering through Manhattan, composing his play whilst communing with the spirit of the still-living Bertolt Brecht.

Opening titles call *Cradle Will Rock* "a (mostly) true story" and Robbins turns the period between late 1936 and the following summer into an essence of the era by importing a few events -mainly the 1933 scandal over Diego Rivera's Rockefeller Center mural, which included the image of Lenin, and the December 1938 congressional hearings on the Federal Theater. Leaping from one situation to another, *Cradle Will Rock* is a hubbub of historical confluence: "May I present Mr. Nelson Rockefeller?" "Mr. Hearst, always a pleasure." Although the jazzy cocktail-party atmosphere suggests certain Robert Altman movies, Robbins's mix of fiction and history can be derived from John Dos Passos's U.S.A. trilogy—itself a Pop Front sacred text.

Blitzstein, who is far more serious here than Welles (Angus Macfadyen, always stridently on and yet barely present), pitches his project to Federal Theater head Hallie Flanagan (Cherry Jones as a paradigm of sunny virtue), as Rockefeller (played by John Cusack as an exuberant young idiot) pays a studio visit to Rivera (Ruben Blades, who has the look). After commissioning him to decorate his family's corporate headquarters, Rocky winds up dancing with the portly artist and his half-naked models to a song Billie Holiday would not record for several years. Meanwhile, various magnates are busy swapping embargoed steel for smuggled-in old masters with Mussolini agent Margherita Sarfatti (Susan Sarandon, having a bit of fun with her role as a glamorous Jewish fascist).

The two art projects evolve in tandem. Meanwhile, the plutocrat antics of a fictional steel magnate (Philip Baker Hall) and his dizzy aristo wife (Vanessa Redgrave) entwine with stories of the invented little people—abused but plucky natural talent (Watson) and struggling Italian American antifascist actor (John Turturro)—who realize themselves in Blitzstein's play. Everyone is true to their social role. The most interesting of Robbins's imagined characters is Bill Murray's Federal Theater-employed ventriloquist, a depressed anti-Communist who argues politics with his dummy and attempts to seduce priggish bureaucrat Joan Cusack by coaching her to inform on subversive superiors.

Robbins can be quite ingenious at excavating '30s New York (although the period design isn't as clever as that other Depression fantasy, *Sweet and Lowdown*). Still, loath to wax nostalgic for an America that no longer exists, he emphasizes the most contemporary aspects of this New Deal *kulturkampf,* making much of the battle over state-funded art and equating red-baiting with homophobia. Burned by the radical Rivera, Rocky has a vision of the Abstract Expressionism to come: "Colors and form, not politics." His education is furthered by an even wiser patron: "Artists are whores like the rest of us ... We control the future of art because we pay for the future of art."

Win some, lose some: Blitzstein's play comes to life even as Rivera's mural is pulverized (and pulverized—the Rockefellers could rape Venezuela in the time it takes here to destroy one little wall). Something of a public mural itself, *Cradle Will Rock* is a lofty, well-intentioned, and flat history lesson. Moving quickly, if not without signs of exertion, the movie never pauses for breath or suggests an inner life. The effect is willfully superficial. Robbins may be less smug and more politically attuned than Alan Rudolph, but—thoughtful as it is—*Cradle Will Rock* can't help seeming as full of winking poseurs as Rudolph's kindred period, pieces, *The Moderns* and *Mrs. Parker and the Vicious Circle.*

Cradle Will Rock is ultimately too exhausted to fulfill the promise of its title—although the finale is stirring in a dopey way. Robbins, like Blitzstein, is basically preaching to the choir (and that choir is a lot smaller than 60 years ago). Still, his parting shot is well-taken. The final leap onto the crass Broadway of *Miss Saigon* and Robbins's studio, Disney, reinforces the notion that, once upon a time, for a short time, middlebrow culture was oppositional—or so it seemed.

Also reviewed in:
CHICAGO TRIBUNE, 12/24/99, Friday/p. A, Michael Wilmington
NATION, 12/27/99, p. 34, Stuart Klawans
NEW REPUBLIC, 1/10/00, p. 26, Stanley Kauffmann
NEW YORK TIMES, 12/8/99, p. E1, Janet Maslin
NEW YORKER, 12/13/99, p. 111, Anthony Lane
VARIETY, 5/24-30/99, p. 36, Todd McCarthy
WASHINGTON POST, 12/24/99, Weekend/p. 38, Desson Howe
WASHINGTON POST, 12/25/99, p. C1, Stephen Hunter

CRAZY IN ALABAMA

A Columbia Pictures release of a Green Moon production in association with a Meir Teper production. *Executive Producer:* James R. Dyer. *Producer:* Meir Teper, Linda Goldstein Knowlton, Debra Hill, and Diane Sillan Isaacs. *Director:* Antonio Banderas. *Screenplay (based on his novel):* Mark Childress. *Director of Photography:* Julio Macat. *Editor:* Maysie Hoy and Robert C. Jones. *Music:* Mark Snow. *Music Editor:* Jeff Charbonneau. *Sound:* Doug Arnold and (music) Larold Rebhun. *Sound Editor:* Tim Chau. *Casting:* Mindy Marin. *Production Designer:* Cecilia Montiel. *Art Director:* Michael Atwell. *Set Decorator:* Robert Greenfield. *Set Dresser:* David Erwin. *Special Effects:* Joe Ramsey. *Costumes:* Graciela Mazon. *Make-up:* Elisabeth Fry. *Make-up (Melanie Griffith):* Valli O'Reilly. *Stunt Coordinator:* Jeff Imada. *Running time:* 104 minutes. *MPAA Rating:* PG-13.

CAST: Melanie Griffith (Lucille); David Morse (Dove); Lucas Black (Peejoe); Cathy Moriarty (Earlene); Meat Loaf Aday (Sheriff John Doggett); Rod Steiger (Judge Mead); Richard Schiff (Norman); John Beasley (Nehemiah); Robert Wagner (Harry Hall); Noah Emmerich (Sheriff Raymond); Sandra Seacat (Meemaw); Paul Ben-Victor (Mackie); Brad Beyer (Jack); Fannie Flagg (Sally); Elizabeth Perkins (Joan Blake); Linda Hart (Madelyn); Paul Mazursky (Walter Schwegmann); Holmes Osborne (Larry Russell); William Converse Roberts (Murphy); David Speck (Wiley); Philip Carter (Deputy Tyrone); Carl Le Blanc III (David Jackson); Louis Miller (Taylor Jackson); Marion Zinser (Saleswoman); John Fleck (Jake); Jack Stephens (Conventioneer); Mark Whitman Johnson (Pool Manager); Tom McCleister (Croupier); J.R. Dyer (Gambling Man); Tony Amendola (Casino Boss); Milly Ericson (Cashier); Jim Antonio (Dr. Ward); Thurn Hoffman (Bellhop Ted); Michael Arata (Photographer); Lance Spellerberg (Interviewer); Elizabeth Perkins (Joan Blake); Madison Mason (Alexander Powell); Amanda Aday (Assistant at Bewitched); Randal Kleiser (Bob); Charlie Dell (Darrin's Stand-in); Oliver Clark (Endora's Stand-in); Tracy Griffith (Samantha's Stand-in); Dudley F. Craig, II (Reverend); Barbara Tasker (Organizer); Brent Briscoe (Jury Foreman/Chester's Voice); Sidney J. Lodrigue and Urisino Frank Lourino (Hecklers on Balcony); Kirk Fox (Patrolman); Wayne Ferrara, Jerry Lee Leighton, and Don Thomas (Reporters); Marva Wright (Singer at Pool); Dane Le Blanc (Marlon); Dexter Le Blanc (Farley); Emily Guidry (Judy); Jess Bryan (Cary); Dakota Johnson (Sondra); Stella Banderas (Marilyn); Jackson Isaacs (Rock); Lia Chapman (Woman on Phone).

LOS ANGELES TIMES, 10/22/99, Calendar/p. 20, Kevin Thomas

"Crazy in Alabama" gives you two movies for the price of one, but it's no bargain.

One picture is about a boy, Peejoe (Lucas Black), who is 12 years old and living in rural Alabama in the summer of 1965, when the civil rights movement reaches the community, revealing racism at its ugliest. The other is about Peejoe's Aunt Lucille (Melanie Griffith), who, fed up with her terrible husband, murders him, dumps her seven children on her mother and takes off for Hollywood in a red 1964 Ford Galaxie to pursue her long-deferred dream of movie stardom.

In bringing Mark Childress' adaptation of his own novel to the screen, debuting director Antonio Banderas intercuts between the worsening situation in Alabama and Lucille's madcap adventures on the road, but the juxtaposition of grim reality and pure fantasy doesn't work. Instead of yielding a sense of absurdity over life's endless injustices, cruelties and quirks of fate, it makes the entire film seem artificial and contrived. You know that the two stories will eventually connect, and while they provide the indestructible Griffith some terrific scenes, it's not enough to make "Crazy" convincing. In her big self-justifying moment Lucille reveals a sensibility, the vocabulary even, of a woman of the '90s rather than the '60s.

You can see how Banderas, whose mentor, Pedro Almodovar, is the master of dark, outrageous comedy, would be drawn to a story that has the stuff of slapstick tragedy, but even Almodovar might have found "Crazy" daunting to transpose to the screen. In short, Banderas, whose ambition is certainly admirable, has taken on too much for a first-time director. The film might have worked—or worked better—had it stuck to the film's narrator, Peejoe, since the story unfolds from his point of view. But Banderas strays so far and so frequently from Peejoe that Lucille in effect becomes the film's principal figure, which throws the film off balance and keeps it there.

"Crazy in Alabama" needs to have been unified by a strong vision and style, and a shrewd, distinctive sense of humor. Maybe John Huston or Robert Altman might have pulled it off.

Lucille winds up wowing a Hollywood agent (Robert Wagner) and a producer (Paul Mazursky) and lands a recurring role in "Bewitched" (where she is directed by director Randal Kleiser). Meanwhile Peejoe's Uncle Dove (David Morse), a man of conscience, is coping with a local sheriff (Meat Loaf Aday), a hysterical racist, on a lethal rampage all because some black youths decide they have the right to swim in the local municipal pool. What ensues is terrifyingly credible but presented with a righteous and heavy hand while Lucille's cross-country escapades are presented as broadly as possible. (By the time we inevitably end up in a courtroom, it seems entirely appropriate that Rod Steiger do a bit of grandstanding as the colorful presiding judge.)

Even though stuck with unflattering dark hair, Griffith remains endearing and persuasive playing a woman about a decade younger than she actually is. Morse and Black and several others in a huge cast seem true to life whereas the sheriff and Uncle Dove's flashy wife (Cathy Moriarty) come across as caricatures. But you can't really fault actors in a film that lacks the very quality it needs most: an assured mastery of drastically shifting tones. "Crazy in Alabama" wants badly to use humor in the war against ignorant and evil oppressors, whether they're racists or abusive husbands and fathers, but instead misfires—badly.

NEW YORK POST, 10/22/99, p. 57, Lou Lumenick

No one can accuse Antonio Banderas of playing it safe with his movie directing debut, "Crazy in Alabama," which showcases his wife, Melanie Griffith, as a mad husband-murderer against the background of the civil rights struggle in the South.

This seriously demented hybrid of "Thelma & Louise" and "To Kill a Mockingbird," adapted by Mark Childress from his 1993 novel, contains some dizzying transitions between farce and drama. But it's quite entertaining on its own wacky terms.

The more prominent of the two widely divergent stories is pure Southern Gothic farce. As the film opens, it's 1965 and Lucille is saying goodbye to her seven children and setting out for Hollywood, having just done in her abusive husband, Chester, with rat poison.

She's cut off his head with an electric knife and placed it in a Tupperware container on the front seat of her Mustang convertible.

No one is more confused about this turn of events than her adoring young nephew Peejoe (Lucas Black), an orphan in whom she's confided her show-biz aspirations. He's entrusted to the care of Lucille's brother Dove (David Morse), a mild-mannered undertaker, after Sheriff Doggett (Meat Loaf) starts pressing the youngster for details of his aunt's whereabouts.

Peejoe gets involved with his own drama when a group of black kids tries to integrate the municipal pool. Peejoe is the only witness as Dogget pulls down a youth climbing a fence, leading to his death.

Meanwhile, Aunt Lucille, who has already robbed a New Orleans bar and seduced a sheriff, her agent and a TV producer, among others, nabs a supporting character opposite Dick York on "Bewitched," But she's also carried her husband's head to a Hollywood party, where things unravel hilariously. Will Lucille become the second woman in a movie this fall (after "Double Jeopardy") to get away with murdering her husband?

Banderas gets wonderful performances from his cast (including Robert Wagner, Paul Mazursky and Rod Steiger) but has no ear at all for Southern accents. The sweetly endearing craziness of Griffith is an effective contrast to the quiet intensity of Black, who was so wonderful in "Sling Blade."

"Crazy in Alabama" risks trivializing history and pandering to feminist fantasies, but it may be the year's most fearless movie.

NEWSDAY, 10/22/99, Part II/p. B8, Jan Stuart

Watching "Crazy in Alabama" is like dating someone with a split personality, each side of which is competing jealously for your attention. One of them is sincere and well-meaning, the other is simply embarrassing and refuses to go away.

Scripted by Mark Childress from his novel, "Crazy in Alabama" begins as a dippy-lyrical slice of Southern Gothic as seen through the eyes of a plain-spoken orphan named Peejoe ("Sling Blade's" Lucas Black, a young actor of compelling gravity).

The year is 1965, when Peejoe's Aunt Lucille (Melanie Griffith) has just poisoned her husband, cut his head off and set off to Hollywood in search of fame and fortune. "Aunt Lucille blew into town," says the literary voiceover, "and nothing was ever the same."

It is not the last time that Childress will short-sheet his alternative concern, the civil rights struggle in the Deep South. In truth, the real life-changing event for Peejoe is meeting a black youngster named Taylor Jackson (Louis Miller Jr.), who inspires a wave of civil disobedience when he decides to go swimming in a whites-only pool. Peejoe witnesses Taylor's murder at the hands of Sheriff Doggert (played with Snidely Whiplash malevolence by Meat Loaf Aday), a local Simon Legree who is also hell-bent on seeing Aunt Lucille fry.

With the schematic pulse of a metronome, Childress and first-time director Antonio Banderas swing between Aunt Lucille's cross-country trek and the deepening tide of racial unrest that results from Taylor's death. It is conceivable that Childress found an elegant solution in his book for alternating Aunt Lucille's daffy exploits—robbing bars, raking in a fortune in Las Vegas, taking Hollywood by storm in just one week—with the grim realities of racial prejudice. On screen, the juxtaposition is discomforting at best.

Possibly not since Scarlett O'Hara fiddle-dee-deed while Atlanta burned has Hollywood trivialized Jim Crow with such giddy abandon. Childress fully intends to justify his odd strategy with a big, grandstanding courtroom monologue for Lucille, who speaks out for abused housewives everywhere. It's supposed to be a plea for human freedom in all its aspects, but the real moral is: If you're going to kill your husband, be sure you get a full Hollywood makeover before the cops get you.

Griffith continues her pursuit of Judy Holliday's screwball throne with mixed results. So goes director Banderas, who is more comfortable handling the civil rights scenario than the awkward magic realism of Lucille's journey. (She carries on tete-a-tetes with her dead husband's head.) The only big winner here is Rod Steiger who pulls off a delicious 11th-hour cameo as a judge with a weakness for French phrases and sultry housewives in distress.

Also reviewed in:
CHICAGO TRIBUNE, 10/22/99, Friday/p. A, Michael Wilmington
NEW YORK TIMES, 10/22/99, p. E26, Janet Maslin
VARIETY, 9/13-19/99, p. 45, Todd McCarthy
WASHINGTON POST, 10/22/99, p. C5, Rita Kempley

CREMASTER 2

A Glacier Field release of a Glacier Field production. *Producer:* Barbara Gladstone. *Director:* Matthew Barney. *Screenplay:* Matthew Barney. *Director of Photography:* Peter Strietmann. *Music:* Jonathan Bepler. *Production Designer:* Matthew D. Ryle. *Costumes:* Laurence Esnault and Linda LaBelle. *Make-up Effects:* Alan Tuskes. *Running time:* 79 minutes. *MPAA Rating:* Not Rated.

CAST: Norman Mailer (Harry Houdini); Matthew Barney (Gary Gilmore); Anonymous (Baby Fay La Foe); Lauren Pine (Bessie Gilmore); Scott Ewalt (Frank Gilmore); Patty Griffin (Nicole Baker); Michael Thomson (Max Jensen).

NEW YORK POST, 10/14/99, p. 51, Lou Lumenick

"Cremaster 2," the fourth in a series of bizarre (and eccentrically numbered) films by Matthew Barney, is a visually striking but inscrutable and lethally slow-moving deconstruction of Norman Mailer's "The Executioner's Song."

Barney—recently anointed "the most import American artist of his generation" by the New York Times—himself plays Gary Gilmore, the Utah murderer whose 1977 execution by a firing squad was the subject of Norman Mailer's book.

Mailer himself turns up briefly as magician Harry Houdini who, Gilmore family legend has it, was Gilmore's grandfather by way of a chance encounter with his grandmother Fay (played by an anonymous, wasp-waisted fetish model) at the Colombian Exposition of 1893.

None of which is readily ascertainable from viewing "Cremaster 2," which takes its name from the muscle that controls the elevation of the testicles.

Barney doesn't concern himself with conventional narrative as such, and the movie contains barely a page of dialogue throughout.

As an artist, Barney is more concerned with arresting images, including bees, blood, flags, Mounties and a remarkable simulation of the Mormon Tabernacle Choir.

His camera dwells endlessly. The movie opens with a five-minute shot of what is later revealed to be a mirrored saddle, and Barney's surrealistic re-creation of Gilmore's murder of a gas station attendant takes up what feels like half the movie's 79-minute running time.

"Cremaster 2," reaches a climax of sorts with a rodeo staged on Utah's Salt Flats, but what it all means I don't even want to guess.

NEWSDAY, 10/15/99, Part II/p. B12, John Anderson

In "Cremaster 2"—the fourth Cremaster film and the penultimate in his now celebrated series —artist Matthew Barney doesn't exactly break new ground. Not theoretically. Yes, he makes implicit connections between images, cultural associations and historical ephemera; he knows that the movie camera can make the pedestrian fabulous and the extraordinary mundane. But these are matters that have been explored by experimental filmmakers for years.

Barney's status in the art world—as one of his generation's hotter youngish talents—has allowed him production values unheard of in the cut-and-splice world of experimental film and the freedom to impose his visual whims in fantastic ways. Where much "art" film is about found materials, Barney's manufactured constructs make him the F.W. Murnau of the'90s avant-garde.

"Cremaster 2" would seem to be numbered out of order, but the two of the title seems to refer—and nothing here is written in stone—to the symmetrical compositions that run through the film, and the historical reflections it contains involving Harry Houdini (Norman Mailer), Gary Gilmore (Barney), the movie's ever-present honeycomb imagery (references to both Gilmore's home of Utah, the Beehive State and its resident Mormon Church) and the twinned images to be found in the movie's themes of fertility, reproduction and sex. (The cremaster, not coincidentally, is the muscle that raises and lowers the testicles.)

Barney's mix of illusory visuals and historical fact and fiction allows the viewer a wide range of associations. Some are more obvious than others. The Mailer-Gilmore connection is most evident in the author's "The Executioner's Song," which chronicled Gilmore's crimes and execution; more obscurely, Gilmore's grandmother Faye (played here by the wasp-waisted Anonymous) once claimed to have had an illegitimate son by Houdini (and even more obscurely, Mailer made one of his more famous film appearances playing architect Stanford White, who knew something about symmetry, in the film version of "Ragtime," a story that concerned itself largely with Harry Houdini).

One of the extended sequences in "Cremaster 2" involves a pair of Ford Mustangs connected by a kind of fabric tunnel; inside is Gilmore, outside is Max Jensen (Michael Thomson), the man he kills. What the tunnel represents is Gilmore's birth canal—in which he stalls his own birth, probably because he's already in the coveralls of the Utah Department of Corrections, which can only mean that Barney sees Gilmore's fate as having been decided before he was born and thus beyond the redemption of the Mormon Church. Barney may be renowned as a visual artist, but he's a storyteller, too. Or should we make that 2?

VILLAGE VOICE, 10/19/99, p. 140, Amy Taubin

Matthew Barney's *Cremaster 2* is glossier and less surprising than the three previous films in his *Cremaster* series, numbers 4, 1, and 5. Like everything else in the oeuvre of this perverse and occasionally exciting visual artist, the out-of-order numbering is an invitation to exercise the hermeneutic impulse. What you see on the screen is far less involving than what you might make of it after the fact.

The cremaster is a small muscle that, when activated by cold or fear, lifts the testicles so that they are in a more protected position. The first male characteristic to appear in a developing fetus, the cremaster is a symbol of maleness and also a departure point for all kinds of binary oppositions (men have it, women don't).

Cremaster 2 revolves around Gary Gilmore, played by Barney, and Harry Houdini, played by Norman Mailer (although "played" is far too active a term for such minimalist performances). Mailer wrote *The Executioner's Song* about Gilmore, who, according to family legend, is related to Houdini through an act of sexual indiscretion on the part of his grandmother. Gilmore lived and was executed in the state of Utah; bees are the Utah state symbol, which could be why there are several images of bees in *Cremaster 2*. Had I not read about such associations in the program notes, I never would have gleaned them from what transpires on the screen. One could observe a similar gap between, say, the films of Stan Brakhage and the notes that accompany his screenings. The difference is that Brakhage's films are aesthetically and intellectually satisfying because of what's on the screen.

Although shot in such awesome locations as Jasper's glacial ice fields and Utah's salt flats (a favorite of Bill Viola), *Cremaster 2* is more like a Robert Wilson theater spectacle than a film. The film also lacks the oozing biomorphic imagery that made the first two *Cremasters,* at the least, a visceral experience. Barney has little sense of rhythm or movement in terms of camerawork or editing, and the bits of sync-sound dialogue introduced here are just one more filmic element that he does not deign to explore.

Also reviewed in:
NEW YORK TIMES, 10/13/99, p. E1, Stephen Holden
VARIETY, 10/25-31/99, p. 39, Oliver Jones

CRUEL INTENTIONS

A Columbia Pictures release in association with Original Film and Newmarket Capital Group of a Neal H. Moritz production. *Executive Producer:* Michael Fottrell. *Producer:* Neal H. Moritz. *Director:* Roger Kumble. *Screenplay:* Roger Kumble. *Suggested by the novel "Les Liasons Dangereuses":* Choderlos De Laclos. *Director of Photography:* Theo Van de Sande. *Editor:* Jeff Freeman. *Music:* Edward Shearmur. *Music Editor:* Amanda Goodpaster. *Sound:* Kim H. Ornitz and Rosa Howell-Thornhill. *Sound Editor:* Bob Newlan and John Morris. *Casting:* Mary Vernieru and Anne McCarthy. *Production Designer:* Jon Gary Steele. *Art Director:* David S. Lazan. *Set Decorator:* Tessa Posnansky. *Set Dresser:* Josh Ian Elliott and Robert Currie.

Special Effects: Matthew Pope. *Costumes:* Denise Wingate. *Make-up:* Bradley Wilder. *Stunt Coordinator:* Peter Bucossi and Shane Dixon. *Running time:* 97 minutes. *MPAA Rating:* R.

CAST: Sarah Michelle Gellar (Kathryn Merteuil); Ryan Phillippe (Sebastian Valmont); Reese Witherspoon (Annette Hargrove); Selma Blair (Cecile Caldwell); Louise Fletcher (Helen Rosemond); Joshua Jackson (Blaine Tuttle); Eric Mabius (Greg McConnell); Sean Patrick Thomas (Ronald Clifford); Swoosie Kurtz (Dr. Greenbaum); Christine Baranski (Bunny Caldwell); Alaina Reed Hall (Nurse); Deborah Offner (Mrs. Michalak); Tara Reid (Marci Greenbaum); Herta Ware (Mrs. Sugarman); Hiep Thi Le (Mai-Lee); Charlie O'Connell (Court Reynolds); Fred Norris (Meter Maid); Ginger Williams (Clorissa); Drew Snyder (Headmaster Hargrove).

LOS ANGELES TIMES, 3/5/99, Calendar/p. 6, Kevin Thomas

The question: Can producer Neal H. Moritz take a couple of his stars from his teen horror hit "I Know What You Did Last Summer" and successfully transport them to yet another screen version of "Les Liaisons Dangereuses"? The answer: an unequivocal "yes."

In his feature film debut, writer-director Roger Kumble honors the spirit of the 1782 Choderlos de Laclos novel with admirable fidelity. In doing so he's asking young audiences to identify with the eternal dark side of human nature in contemporary yet ultra-aristocratic settings instead of with mainly decent, middle-class kids caught up in scary situations that are the staple of the youth market. And in place of thrills and chills there is quite a bit of blunt language and sexuality, both appropriate, however, to the milieu.

"Cruel Intentions" is a stretch for all concerned, including the targeted audience, one that pays off handsomely—and works for older moviegoers as well. Actually, simply setting De Laclos' cautionary tale in a younger generation arguably enhances its impact, for young people are less likely than their elders to realize that vulnerability can turn out to be the obverse side of cynicism.

No two young people could be more cynical than step-siblings Kathryn Merteuil (Sarah Michelle Gellar), whose mother has married the father of Sebastian Valmont (Ryan Phillippe). Rich, bored and clearly neglected by their parents—for whom they have nothing but contempt—Kathryn and Sebastian, who live alone in a vast Upper East Side apartment, have no real interests outside playing games with other people's emotions. The unthinkable has happened to Kathryn: Her boyfriend has dumped her for the innocent, klutzy Cecile (Selma Blair). Sebastian, who already has a reputation as a lady-killer, readily agrees to deflower the virginal Cecile in revenge.

But higher stakes loom: Sebastian reads in Seventeen a column by Annette Hargrove (Reese Witherspoon), daughter of the new headmaster of the posh Manhattan prep school Kathryn and Sebastian attend; in it Annette asserts that she intends to save herself for marriage. That does it: If he succeeds in seducing her, Kathryn will give herself—"the only woman you can't have"—to him. If he fails, he has to give Kathryn his 1956 red Jaguar.

Many more machinations ensue, involving many others, all of which bring Kathryn and Sebastian into confrontations with themselves. They are glib, ruthless, glamorous—and unknowing of their own hearts.

Beneath her chic wardrobe and patina of sophistication, Kathryn, played with cold confidence by Gellar, is no different from the campus queens of many another teen movie. Sebastian has a tad more conscience, not to mention hidden emotional depths, than Kathryn and is more interesting for it. The filmmakers have deliberately echoed the atmosphere of the De Laclos novel, and in fact the French interiors of many a luxury 1920s Manhattan apartment or great country estate of earlier eras have 18th century French-style interiors, some of them lifted from actual chateaux and Paris townhouses. In these Louis XV-XVI settings, Phillippe fits right in; his golden good looks are like those of the lovers in the Fragonards and Bouchers at the Frick Museum. More important, as an actor Phillippe is engaging and equal to the range that Sebastian affords him.

Witherspoon's Annette is chaste without being a prude, religious without being puritanical, a thoroughly likable young woman who ultimately is less naive than either Kathryn or Sebastian. Blair is a delicious scene-stealer, and her Cecile is the amusingly thickheaded type who always thinks she's got it when she's utterly clueless.

There are especially sharp portrayals from Christine Baranski as Cecile's social-climbing, racist mother; Swoosie Kurtz as a slick, mercenary therapist; and Sean Patrick Thomas as Cecile's amorous music teacher. Jon Gary Steele's production design is knowing, detailed and crucial to this handsome film set entirely in the world of the privileged, and Edward Shearmur's score echoes the film's shifting moods elegantly but with a jaunty driving insistence that underlines the film's witty, satirical tone and relentless sense of inevitability.

Given a rich, burnished look by cinematographer Theo Van de Sande, "Cruel Intentions" is a very grown-up picture for kids.

NEW YORK POST, 3/5/99, p. 50, Rod Dreher

"Cruel Intentions" demonstrates the difference between good trash and bad.

Writer-director Roger Kumble transposes the French novel "Les Liaisons Dangereuses" into the posh, amoral world of Manhattan private school kids. But don't expect the panache and psychological intrigue of the 1988 movie "Dangerous Liaisons," the best of the four film versions made of the 18th-century saga about vicious upper-class jealousies.

"Cruel Intentions" is like a potty-mouthed "Melrose Place" unspooling on "Dynasty" sets—except those Aaron Spelling trashterpieces have a brash cheesiness that delivers honest cheap thrills. The misbegotten "Cruel Intentions" serves up great glittering gobs of cheap, without the thrills.

Blank-staring pretty boy Ryan Phillippe takes the Valmont role as Sebastian, a cruel, callow, insanely rich seductor who prides himself on the number of high school honeys he's bonked. The Marquise de Merteuil shows up as Kathryn (Sarah Michelle Gellar), Sebastian's wicked, scheming stepsister. Sebastian wagers that he can swipe the virginity of the new girl in town, virtuous Annette (Reese Witherspoon).

If Sebastian fails, he relinquishes his vintage Jaguar convertible to Kathryn. If he wins, Sebastian gets to have sex with his stepsister. The movie frequently indulges in groping, gross flirtations with the incest taboo, culminating in Kathryn's blunt demand to Sebastian, offering up her every orifice as a potential receptacle, and bitchily declaiming: "I want to [expletive] now!"

That's what passes for wit and daring in this picture, alas. There's a bit of ham-handed humor in Kathryn's attempts to educate the dopey naif Cecile (Selma Blair) in the ways of the world. But a tongue-kissing lesbian interlude in Central Park is, well, icky and dumb. There's little seductive allure in this corruption.

Witherspoon's is the only believable character and credible performance. Annette may be a virgin, but she's worldly wise and far more intelligent than one-note Sebastian—which makes her falling for his underwear-model charms ludicrously forced, and his discovery of a soul before film's end implausible.

What's so unappealing about the film's setup is the eagerness with which Kumble cynically throws his teen characters into the sleazy sexual situations. Their insouciant amorality is both incredible and depressing as hell.

When, in "Dangerous Liaisons," John Malkovich and Glenn Close manipulate their friends and destroy lives for the sake of cheap thrills, their actions have moral weight and dramatic power. That's in part because they are sophisticated grown-ups behaving like vicious children, with all that implies about human nature.

Watching spoiled little brats do the same is rather less compelling. As my wife said while watching selfish twit Monica Lewinsky's TV confessions this week: "Hearing a rich, middle-aged, Upper East Side broad say these things would have been interesting. But she's just a ditz acting on instinct."

NEWSDAY, 3/5/99, p. B7, John Anderson

"Cruel Intentions" stars teenthrobs Sarah Michelle Gellar (TV's "Buffy"), Reese Witherspoon, late of "Pleasantville," and Ryan Phillippe, whose star appears to be on the rise despite appearing in "54." Relocated to the Upper East Side—where spoiled children re-enact the sexual cruelties of 18th-Century French aristrocrats—"Cruel Intentions" works fairly well, as long as everything is played for maximum tongue-in-cheek (and everywhere else, for that matter). Once it starts expecting its audience to actually care for these woefully self-impressed characters (and actors) it falls quickly apart, seemingly oblivious to the fact that their insignificance was keeping the film afloat to begin with.

More irritating is the sexual license of the film, as hypocritically chaste as much of it is. High schooler Kathryn (Gellar), her flagrant bust seemingly steel-reinforced and hollow crucifix full of coke around her neck, asks her unctuous stepbrother Sebastian (Phillippe) for a favor: Deflower and abandon the innocent Cecile (Selma Blair), for whom Kathryn's boyfriend has thrown her over. He obliges, but they also make a wager: that he can do the same to Annette (Witherspoon), the headmaster's daughter and the author of a Seventeen magazine article titled "Why I Plan to Wait." The stakes are Sebastian's 56 Jaguar vs. Kathryn's, shall we say, booty.

For those familiar with the Frears film, the player roster is thus: Gellar is Glenn Close, Blair is Uma Thurman, Witherspoon is Michelle Pfeiffer and Phillippe, of course, is John Malkovich, all of which should have suggested to director Roger Kumble that he keep things light and campy. But no. Sebastian falls deeply in love with Annette (the part Annette Bening played in "Valmont" by the way) and this sets Kathryn on a vengeful path. We don't care.

"Cruel Intentions" is offensive for the truly bad acting that lurches through it, but also for a sexual explicitness that seems at least irresponsible if not downright evil. The audience for a movie cast with Gellar, Witherspoon and Phillippe is, obviously, a teenage one, possibly a very young teenage one, and the casual promiscuity—bordering-on-nymphomania that Kumble makes seem so acceptable simply isn't. Without belaboring the obvious—pregnancy, AIDS, etc.—it's a degraded humanity the movie portrays. The message in every other version of "Les Liaisons Dangereuses" has been that the politicking of seduction has its soul-shriveling cost. "Cruel Intentions" can't pull that much off. And as a result, it's corrupt.

SIGHT AND SOUND, 6/99, p. 42, Edward Lawrenson

New York. On a school break, Kathryn Merteuil tries to persuade her stepbrother Sebastian Valmont to deflower Cecile because she is now dating Kathryn's ex-boyfriend Court. Sebastian prefers to pursue the virginal Annette Hargrove. Kathryn bets him he can't sleep with her before school convenes.

Sebastian meets Annette, but she's wary of his libertine reputation. Cecile falls in love with her music teacher Blaine, but the two are parted when Cecile's mother Bunny finds out about the relationship. Sebastian seduces Cecile when he discovers it was Bunny who tipped off Annette about him. But he and Annette are falling in love and eventually have sex. Taunted by Kathryn for falling for Annette, Sebastian breaks up with her but regrets it. Denied access to her, he sends her his journal which details the bet he made with Kathryn and begs for forgiveness. Kathryn falsely tells Blaine, her new lover, that Sebastian beat her up. Infuriated, Blaine attacks Sebastian in the street; Annette, having read the journal, turns up. Sebastian is killed pushing her out of the path of a passing car. At his funeral, Cecile hands out copies of his journal which exposes Kathryn's wicked ways.

"E-mail is for geeks and paedophiles"—so the incorrigible young Lothario Valmont tells us in writer-director Roger Kumble's debut film *Cruel Intentions*. This typically sharp line allows the movie to retain the narrative logic behind Choderlos de Laclos' *Les Liaisons dangereuses*, the 1782 epistolary novel on which it is based. Motivating journeys to drop-off points, acting as incriminatory evidence, letters here have a far more important function than, say, the drippy e-mails exchanged in *You've Got Mail*.

But there's another reason why Kumble's updating of Laclos' eighteenth-century classic to the world of rich New York teenagers works so well. Familiar from many a teen-pic, the milieu of *Cruel Intentions* is almost as preoccupied with social standing—with jocks and preppy model students at the top of the pile, geeks at the bottom—as the society Laclos was writing about. The film draws out these parallels without straining for effect. Valmont's opulent apartment is decorated with Louis XIV-style furniture while the dialogue echoes lines from the novel. The young cast display a flair for Kumble's very specific comedy of manners, memorably demonstrated, for instance, by the disgust that flickers on Kathryn's face as Cecile suggests they have a girly "sleepover". Newcomer Selma Blair as Cecile is a particular revelation, changing under Valmont's generous tutelage from gauche schoolkid to sexually experienced young woman.

A clever reworking of a literary classic, *Cruel Intentions'* brand of intertextuality is closer to *Clueless* and a bit more upmarket than the knowing references to horror schlock that pepper Kevin Williamson's teen-pics. But despite the air of cynicism exuded by its coolly uncaring characters, it also turns out to be a rather wholesome and morally upright movie, though not quite as trite or dispiritingly bland as Williamson's television series *Dawson's Creek*.

So while the film contains a few swipes at high-school conformity (gay football star Greg's fear of being outed) there's none of the mischievous anger found in, for example, *Heathers*. Kathryn may complain about having to behave like "Marsha fucking Brady" but she's such a wilfully unscrupulous character it's difficult to take anything she says at face value. Valmont, meanwhile, ultimately renounces his libertine ways; he dies saving Annette, only to be fondly remembered by her as she drives off in his car in an unusually sentimental montage sequence. Here, Kumble preserves the book's moralistic suggestion that Annette's virtue can redeem even a sinner such as Valmont. Unlike Laclos, who dispatches her counterpart to a convent where she dies, Kumble rewards Annette for her virtue. Speeding off in Valmont's Jaguar, she's sent out into the world, enriched by her experiences.

TIME, 3/15/99, p. 84, Richard Schickel

Adolescents are, by their nature, heartless, randy and, as all the books inform their frantic parents, eager to test authority's limits. In other words, they have an affinity for *Les Liaisons Dangereuses*. Now that a young writer-director named Roger Kumble has turned Pierre Laclos's malevolent, much adapted minor masterpiece into a nastily assured teen flick, one has to wonder why it took so long for somebody to age-down its louche protagonists and update its setting.

In place of Laclos's 18th century decadents, *Cruel Intentions* offers us a modern prep-school Lothario (Ryan Phillippe, who looks a little like Leonardo DiCaprio on mean pills) and his half-sister (Sarah Michelle Gellar, deploying her TV vampire-slaying smarts in a lesser cause). But what they do on their summer vacation (misspent in upper-crust Manhattan and Long Island) is the same old story—an elaborate scheme to deflower a couple of virgins (Reese Witherspoon and Selma Blair) whose virtue irritates and challenges them. As in all the other versions of this story, they succeed, but eventually receive a morally satisfying comeuppance.

As if we cared. Our fascination with this tale has always derived from its cool portrayal of utter amorality, which Kumble and his cast nicely energize with their heedless, youthful intensity. This may not go over with the kid audience, which prefers to view itself onscreen as victims or heroes. But their weary parents may just get a kick out of seeing the little monsters presented as, well, the little monsters they so often are.

VILLAGE VOICE, 3/9/99, p. 122, Dennis Lim

The premise of *Cruel Intentions*—a retread of *Les Liaisons Dangereuses* with high-school kids—can be distilled to a single joke: 18th-century French aristocrats and spoiled 20th-century Manhattan teens have more in common than you'd think. Both inhabit social realms distinguished by fragile reputations, highly developed carnal appetites, and petty, savage head games. Though writer-director Roger Kumble doesn't fully exploit this conceit, *Cruel Intentions* is still briskly enjoyable, what people might call a "guilty pleasure"—only it's the sort of film that would mock anyone who felt guilt in pleasure.

The source material (a novel by Choderlos de Laclos) has already spawned three movies— Roger Vadim's moody 1959 update, Milos Forman's frisky *Valmont,* and Stephen Frears's robust adaptation of Christopher Hampton's play. Next to these, *Cruel Intentions* doesn't come off badly. Kumble deftly negotiates the plot convolutions, preserving the story's headlong momentum, if not its psychological complexity.

The two protagonists—who coldly fuck and mindfuck their way through high society before they're thwarted by unexpectedly genuine romantic pangs—are former lovers in the original; Kumble heightens the erotic charge between them and renders it vaguely taboo by making them step-siblings, played by Sarah Michelle Gellar and Ryan Phillippe.

The corruption of a pure maiden (Reese Witherspoon) is still central to their schemes, though here the victim's chastity is public knowledge thanks to her "Virgin's Manifesto" in *Seventeen*.

Cruel Intentions is as eager to provoke as it is to please—Gellar has some vicious one-liners ("You're moving at the speed of a Special Olympics hurdler"); black and gay characters are trotted out for some knowing stereotype tinkering—and it's a questionable strategy. A more fundamental problem, though, is that Kumble's screenplay isn't sufficiently liberating. His characters are nominally high-schoolers, but the action unfolds in Upper East Side townhouses and Long Island mansions (over summer break). There's a residual drawing-room archness to the dialogue, which is more outright filthy than actually funny. *Cruel Intentions* isn't entirely even in tone, either, flirting with camp, anti-p.c. comedy, teensploitation, and earnest romance; as such, the final tragedy doesn't resonate as it should (though, always ready with a smirk, Kumble may not want it to).

In the end, the principals are what make the film. Gellar is unflappable (and, to her credit, doesn't merely do a Glenn Close or, God forbid, a Shannen Doherty). It's the Valmont role that's the litmus test, though—would all these women fall for this shit? The question has come up in every previous version, but Phillippe's supremely cocksure performance dismisses it out of hand. The movie itself has a similarly irresistible confidence—it knows it's basically a cheap thrill, and sees no shame in that.

Also reviewed in:
CHICAGO TRIBUNE, 3/5/99, Friday/p. A, Mark Caro
NEW YORK TIMES, 3/5/99, p. E28, Stephen Holden
NEW REPUBLIC, 4/5/99, p. 28, Stanley Kauffmann
VARIETY, 3/1-7/99, p. 77, Emanuel Levy
WASHINGTON POST, 3/5/99, p. C1, Stephen Hunter
WASHINGTON POST, 3/5/99, Weekend/p. 41, Desson Howe

DANCEMAKER

An Artistic License release of a Walter Scheuer production in association with The Four Oaks Foundation. *Executive Producer:* Walter Scheuer. *Producer:* Jerry Kupfer and Matthew Diamond. *Director:* Matthew Diamond. *Director of Photography:* Tom Hurwitz. *Editor:* Pam Wise. *Sound:* Peter Miller. *Sound Editor:* Margaret Crimmins and Paul D. Hsu. *Running time:* 98 minutes. *MPAA Rating:* Not Rated.

WITH: Paul Taylor (Artistic Director); Bettie De Jong (Rehearsal Director); Ross Kramberg (Executive Director); DANCERS: Francie Huber; Andrew Asnes; Thomas Patrick; Caryn Heilman; Patrick Corbin; Rachel Berman; Lisa Viola; Richard Chen See; Kristi Egtvedt; Silvia Nevjinsky; Andrew LeBeau; Takehiro Ueyama; Ted Thomas; Heather Berest; Maureen Mansfield; Michael Trusnovec.

LOS ANGELES TIMES, 3/12/99, Calendar/p. 14, Kenneth Turan

A burst of dance energy jump-starts "Dancemaker" as lithe performers, alive with the joy of movement, throw themselves across the stage in the Paul Taylor-choreographed "Esplanade." To watch that piece unfold on film is to wonder where it all comes from, the ideas, the energy, the passion. "Dancemaker" lets you in on that, and more.

Nominated for both a Directors Guild Award and an Oscar for best documentary, "Dancemaker" is not content with furnishing a remarkable look at the world of modern dance. Directed by Matthew Diamond, himself a former dancer, it's also an insightful portrait of creativity itself, a chance to see the highs and lows, the ins and outs of that celebrated process.

"Dancemaker" is the word Taylor uses to describe himself A former dancer with Martha Graham, he has evolved into a man Newsweek called the world's greatest living choreographer, a major force in American dance who takes pride in his company's having been one of the first to offer his dancers enough work to qualify them to collect unemployment.

Genial but autocratic, a gracious gentleman who can be ruthless when need be, Taylor is an ideal subject. His articulate comments go from the humorous (he tells and then debunks a story of being inspired by a record he found in the trash) to the pointed, and he clearly respects Diamond (who previously worked with him on a pair of PBS "Dance in America" programs).

The choreographer granted the director unrestricted access, and the glimpses we get of the first and succeeding rehearsals (plus the eventual New York debut) of a new work set to Astor Piazolla's music and called "Piazolla Caldera" are compelling. We see Taylor using his dancers as building blocks in an intense and very human trial-and-error process. "I'm not seeing the dance in my mind," he admits. "I'm fooling around and trying things."

Diamond and cinematographer Tom Hurwitz, whose extensive previous work includes documentaries on Bill T. Jones and Suzanne Farrell, beautifully capture segments of numerous Taylor dances (including "Musical Offering," "Polaris," "Cloven Kingdom" and "Last Look") on film, a range that is accurately described by a critic as "beautiful dances and those that scare the daylights out of you."

Perhaps most poignantly, vintage clips of Taylor fluidly dancing one of his signature roles, "Aureole," are smoothly intercut with the work of Patrick Corbin, the Taylor dancer who does it with today's troupe.

But dance is not a one-person operation; as critic Deborah Jowett says onscreen, "the process of creation is an extraordinarily social event, both exciting and debilitating." Diamond has as much rapport with the Taylor dancers as with the choreographer, and the heart of the film is the push-pull relationship, both agonizing and ecstatic, between the man and those who execute his vision.

"Dancemaker," to its credit, does not neglect the more troubling aspects of the dance world. Touched on are the relentless rehearsal process, the pain of working through serious injury, the plague of AIDS-related deaths, the intense competition and the agony the whole company goes through when a dancer is fired in a 30-second phone call.

Also examined are the kinds of mind games that occur between dancer and choreographer; dancers relate how Taylor would tell them on the eve of a performance that the piece wasn't working because of them. Dancers talk about their worries of not being good enough, of when to speak up and when to remain silent, the bite of manipulative comments. The process, says a former Taylor dancer, "is so intimate, so revealing of yourself, and it can be turned against you."

But, with viewers as well as the dancers, it's the memory of the glorious side of dance that makes the most lasting impact. Dancers talk about the joy of "falling in love for six minutes" during a Taylor duet, of the choreographer's gift for "allowing the creative person in you to come out and merge with his."

"Dancemaker" also gives an almost thrilling sense of how emotionally sustaining this kind of work can be. When a Taylor dancer says, "I wouldn't trade anything in the world for being in the studio making something with Paul," you feel that if the choice were yours, you wouldn't make the trade either.

NEW YORK POST, 3/3/99, p. 47, Rod Dreher

"Dancemaker" is an affectionate and accomplished documentary portrait of legendary modern-dance choreographer Paul Taylor and his esteemed company of dancers. Filmmaker Matthew Diamond, himself a former dancer, combines extensive performance footage with interviews and demanding rehearsal scenes.

The result is more satisfying for showing the world-class dance troupe at work than in illuminating either Taylor's character or the nature of his genius. Ultimately, "Dancemaker," whose two-week run coincides with the Paul Taylor Dance Company's 1999 season at City Center, has far more appeal to balletomanes than to general documentary audiences.

Taylor, now in his 60s, was one of Martha Graham's star proteges, a tall, broad-shouldered, exceptionally imposing dancer, as demonstrated in black-and-white archival film uncovered by Diamond. Taylor's own avant-garde choreography has not always been well-received by critics, but the entire body of his work has distinguished Taylor as one of the true geniuses of 20th-century dance.

Diamond reveals Taylor primarily through his choreography, which is deeply expressive and supremely graceful. Yet the viewer who is as equally interested in Taylor the man as Taylor the artist will wish for more than "Dancemaker" provides. The Post's own Clive Barnes appears in the film to note that much of Taylor's choreography was accomplished "to annoy Martha Graham."

It's a great line, but Diamond doesn't follow up on it. The film ought to have explained why Taylor fell out personally and artistically with the grande dame of modern dance, and how, and to what extent, his work is a response to Graham's.

Furthermore, the film pays insufficient attention to Taylor's personal history. We learn that he was abandoned by his parents and raised by a farm family, and that young Paul was shocked to discover the family had been paid to take care of him. Those who know Taylor characterize his choreography as based in his essential loneliness, but Diamond only glosses over these discomfiting aspects of the deceptively mild-mannered Taylor's private life. It could be that Diamond, who now heads video projects for Taylor's company, was too close to his subject to pry past respectful boundaries.

Nevertheless, "Dancemaker," which has been nominated for an Academy Award for documentary filmmaking, is filled with marvelous dancing. The film's shortcomings as biography are exceeded by the sheer beauty of Taylor's art.

NEWSDAY, 3/3/99, Part II/p. B2, John Anderson

During this month's Academy Awards program, we'll be told frequently how film is a "collaborative medium"—usually by individuals taking home single statuettes. If one of them is Matthew Diamond, the director of the Oscar-nominated "Paul Taylor: Dancemaker," the honor certainly won't be undeserved. Or surprising. In fact, let's recite his acceptance speech right now.

First, he'd like to thank cinematographer Tom Hurwitz, who in shooting the work of the Paul Taylor Dancer Company captures their heroically modernist movement with crispness, fluidity and a compositional eye that enhances the experience of Taylor's choreography. And editor Pam Wise, who made it possible for a dancer to do a rolling hurtle out of the wings on one camera and come to her feet in the frame of another, without ever disturbing the rhythm. And Diamond's sound engineers, who gave the entire film a tactile quality and a vicarious athleticism, especially when their gorgeous and often pain-ridden bodies bounced against the stage and back.

Diamond, a former dancer, starts his film with dance, ends his film with dance and along the way tells a story of Paul Taylor, the not-so-little boy who was raised by foster parents, was mentored by and then purged himself of Martha Graham and has become what Newsweek called "the world's greatest living choreographer." This comes early, as documentaries need to establish right away that they're not about the world's second-greatest anything, but Diamond makes a pretty good case for Taylor, even while exposing some of the bunions on his professional sole.

Not to be a philistine, but while the ostensible mission of "Dancemaker" is to document Taylor's creative process, the real payoff is the dancing itself. Hurwitz, whether shooting in black and white (rehearsals) or color (performances) doesn't really open up dance as much as create a whole new medium. Careening past faces and around body parts, the viewer's eye is taken on a genuine trip: No one gets to watch modern dance this way—not the people in the patron's seats, not even the dancers themselves.

Diamond does put the biographical stuff in an illuminating context. He takes, for instance, Taylor's upbringing—his parents divorced when he was young, and he lived with a foster family for much of his boyhood—and finds in it a root cause of Taylor's resistance to and resentment of dancers demands for money (drawing a quite reasonable line between parents who were paid for affection and dancers who can't work for love). He then takes this a step further, finding in one Taylor work, with its yearning gestures and lack of contact, a choreographed symptom of Taylor's unresolved childhood. Such critical thinking isn't always in evidence, however.

A good deal of "Dancemaker" is about the Sisyphean efforts to keep a modern dance troupe alive and kicking (sorry) in a country where arts funding is held in low esteem. Although beautifully composed, the fact that the film is shot in TV screen proportion (aspect ratio 1:33, if you're keeping score at home)—while nearly screaming for a wide-angle look at Taylor's work—says something about the realities of arts-based cinema.

But the movie directs its anger at an easy target. When the company's two-week season at Manhattan's City Center, which is critical to its annual funding efforts, is threatened with protests by the musicians' union, we get Taylor's executive director Ross Kramberg venting about the greed of the musicians, the injustice of it all, the impossibility of working New York—thus demonizing another group of artists trying to survive in a culture that doesn't value them. To Diamond's discredit, there's no response for the musicians, or any indication that they refused to comment.

VILLAGE VOICE, 3/9/99, p. 118, Elizabeth Zimmer

The most interesting thing about Matthew Diamond's Oscar-nominated documentary on choreographer Paul Taylor is not its incisive portrait of backstage life—though it certainly offers one—or the compelling biographical information it shares about a major figure in American dance. Its triumph is the way it renders the dance world as a complicated place full of dramatic conflict between opposing forces. Art and money, workers and management, passion and practicality: all square off in this 98-minute trip through a year in the life of one of the world's best modern companies. No buildings explode, but emotions hit the boiling point, and when the sound system suddenly fails at a crucial point during a command performance in India, the backstage drama keeps you on the edge of your seat.

Taylor himself is a piece of work, an almost Mephistophelean figure in a big, square body who for more than 40 years has been exacting from dancers amazingly articulate performances. His choreography veers between the lyrically luminous and the depraved, sometimes in the same work. He let Diamond, a former dancer and choreographer who's spent years directing sitcoms and TV specials while getting to know his artful quarry, follow his process from the first day of rehearsal on a new piece (the sultry *Piazzola Caldera)*. The dancers welcomed the filmmaker into their private conversations (and in one case even into the shower).

"I get my energy from being afraid," Taylor confesses early on. "Afraid to fail."

Colleagues who've been watching him for years—his manager, his rehearsal assistant, critics like Deborah Jowitt and Anna Kisselgoff—talk to the camera about his genius and his accomplishments. Former company members reflect on his difficult personality.

Editor Pam Wise's cutting—fast, precise, rhythmical—keeps us riveted even in the casual, conversational sections. She brilliantly interweaves shots of the young Taylor dancing in his early works with images of the patriarch, visibly moved, as he watches artists who could be his grandchildren perform them. The current dancers are beautiful, smart, and astonishingly diverse, especially the men. When this company holds auditions, hundreds of hopefuls compete for a single spot, despite grueling tour schedules and the emotional roller coaster of life with an insecure genius.

"I'm a hick, basically, and proud of it," says the choreographer, who looks these days like an aging adman trying, and failing, to quit smoking. "I'm a terrible spy. I watch people. I have no moral attitude, really," he tells a listener. "I'm a reporter, I report things as I see them." And Diamond, with great wit and clarity, does that too.

Also reviewed in:
CHICAGO TRIBUNE, 4/23/99, Friday/p. N, Sid Smith
NATION, 3/29/99, p. 35, Stuart Klawans
NEW YORK TIMES, 3/3/99, p. E1, Janet Maslin
VARIETY, 7/27-8/2/98, p. 54, Ken Eisner
WASHINGTON POST, 3/19/99, p. C1, Sarah Kaufman

DAY OF THE BEAST, THE

A Trimark Pictures release of a Sogetel/Iberoamericana Films Produccion/M.G. SRL co-production in association with Canal +. *Executive Producer:* Andrés Vicente Gómez. *Producer:* Antonio Saura and Claudio Gaeta. *Director:* Alex de la Iglesia. *Screenplay (Spanish with*

English subtitles): Jorge Guerricaechevarria and Alex de la Iglesia. *Director of Photography:* Flavio Martínez Labiano. *Editor:* Teresa Font. *Music:* Batitista Lena. *Sound:* José Antonio Bermúdez, Carlos Garrido and (music) Paolo Venditti. *Production Designer:* José Luis Arrizabilaga. *Special Effects:* Reyes Abades. *Costumes:* Estibaliz Markiegui. *Make-up:* José Quetglas. *Make-up (Special Effects):* José Antonio Sanchez. *Stunt Coordinator:* Ignacio Carreño. *Running time:* 104 minutes. *MPAA Rating:* R.

CAST: Alex Angulo (Angel Berriartúa, Professor of Theology); Armando de Razza (Ennio Lombardi, 'Professor Cavan'); Santiago Segura (José María); Terele Pávez (Rosario); Nathalie Seseña (Mina); María Grazia Cucinotta (Susana); Jaime Blanch (Toyota 1); Gianni Ippoliti (TV Producer); El Gran Wyoming (New Cavan); David Pinilla, Antonio Dechent, and Ignacio Carreño (Toyotas); Saturnino Garcia (Old Priest); Pololo (Dying Man); Higinio Barbara (Satan); Daniel Cicare (Argentinian Lecturer); Javier Manrique (Distributor); Aitor Fernandez, David Gil, and Carro Summers (Editors); Carlos Lucas (Alderman); Enrique Villen (Security Officer); Def Con Dos (Satannica band); Rosa Campillo (TV News Reader); Manuel Tallafe (Friendly Guard); Aquilino Gamazo (Guy); Paloma Montero (Virgin/Gypsy); José Colomina (San José Gypsy); Paco Maestre (Huge Guy); Ramón Churruca (Ugly Guy); Teresa Enric (Warehouse Saleswoman); Antonio de la Torre (Salesman); Juan Ymedio (Cop); Ramón Aguirre (Car Guy); Antonio Chamorro (Father); Ignacio Ruiz and José Sainz (Slaughtered Cops); Jamie Barnatan (Little Gordo); Lourdes Bartolome (Little Gordo's Mother); Mario Ayuso (Little Gordo's Father); Otilia Laiz (Mother); José Alias (Conference Security Guard); Ricardo Ingles (Dying Conductor); Trinidad Corredor (Man with Megaphone); Bigarren (Cop at Big Warehouse); Arri (Ugly Thief); Carmen Martinez (Secretary at Big Warehouse); Paco Aragúetes (Bartender); Maria Bardem (Interviewee); Salvador Pons (Old Man); José Maria González-Sinde (Organist).

LOS ANGELES TIMES, 12/23/98, Calendar/p. 3, Kevin Thomas

Alex de la Iglesia's "The Day of the Beast" takes place as Christmas Eve swiftly approaches, but it abounds in gore rather than conventional holiday cheer. For horror fans, however, it's a welcome present, a blisteringly audacious, headlong nonstop thriller of unflagging inventiveness and outrageous dark humor.

A priest, Father Angel (Alex Angulo), a professor of theology, is talking intensely in a church with one of his superiors, saying anxiously that he's got to go out and do all the evil he can. Further explanations are muffled by the tolling of the church's bell, and not long after, the older priest meets a shocking fate.

Father Angel believes his study of scripture has yielded the terrifying warning that the anti-Christ will be born in Madrid before Dec. 25 dawns. He sees no way but to connect with Satan himself if he is to stave off the apocalypse. Fate brings him into contact with a record store clerk, Jose Maria (Santiago Segura), a sweet, courageous guy who looks like a member of the Hells Angels, and then with an immensely popular TV guru, the self-styled psychic, Professor Cavan (Armando de Razza), a rakish type in black leather with a wicked-looking goatee.

The way in which de la Iglesia brings this highly unlikely trio together and propels them into increasingly dangerous and mind-boggling adventures is never less than awesome and amusing, its moments of savagery fast and furious, undercut by humor. And if de la Iglesia has lots of fun sending up TV shamans he also evokes a strong sense of the eternal struggle of good and evil; as scabrous as it gets, this film could only come from someone rooted in ancient Roman Catholic culture.

De la Iglesia puts his cast through some exceedingly rigorous paces, and all his actors come through with panache. Its hard-rock soundtrack is just right, as are the sooty hues of Flavio Martinez Labiano's terrific color camera work, including many complicated and venturesome sequences shot in the heart of Madrid, decked out in holiday decorations and thronged with last-minute shoppers. Horror pictures rarely win prestigious prizes, but "The Day of the Beast" managed to walk off with six Goyas, Spain's Oscars.

NEW YORK POST, 6/18/99, p. 56, Jonathan Foreman

A big hit in Spain that has taken nearly five years to cross the Atlantic, "The Day of the Beast" is a jokey shlock-horror take on the "Omen" movies.

While director Alex de la Iglesia lacks the slickness of fellow Spaniard Pedro Almodovar, he has a similar darkly comic sensibility and a fondness for pop-culture trash.

Brilliant but naive priest/theologian Father Angel (Alex Angulo) computes the actual date of the Antichrist's birth, and it's the next day.

He also deduces that the Antichrist will be born in Madrid (why else would there be so many horrible unexplained crimes taking place in the city?) and resolves to join Satan's followers.

That way he can ensure his presence at the Evil One's birth and then save humanity by killing the Devil's spawn.

Not knowing where to start, the gentle priest goes to the city and starts sinning as much as he can, stealing money from beggars and pushing a mime down subway stairs.

But it's only when Father Angel turns up in a record store specializing in "death metal" and the friendly rocker salesman Jose Maria (Santiago Segura) recommends a tape by "Satannica" that he starts to narrow down the likely whereabouts of the event.

The unlikely duo obtain by force the aid of one "Professor Cavan" (Armando de Razza), a cynical TV fortuneteller who specializes in forecasting bad news to the folk who call his show ("your husband will never get a job and you will contract a terrible illness"). But the three of them find that the Devil is no easy opponent.

Like most films in the religious-horror genre, "The Day of the Beast" takes the notions of sin and evil seriously, and de la Iglesia struggles to balance that seriousness with the movie's comic tone and relatively crude special effects.

SIGHT AND SOUND, 12/96, p. 42, Paul Julian Smith

Spain, December 1995. After 25 years of study a humble priest, a professor of theology at the University of Deusto in the Basque Country, has discovered the secret of the Apocalypse of St John. After he has communicated his discovery to an older colleague, the latter is crushed by a giant crucifix which falls on him in the chapel. The younger priest arrives in Madrid, determined to make contact with the devil by committing wicked deeds. Fetching up in a heavy metal record shop, he is given the address of a *pensión* by the shop assistant: hairy but harmless drug abuser José Maria. The priest has no time to settle in at the hostel, run by José Maria's formidable mother Rosario and virginal assistant Mina: he believes that the Anti-Christ will be born that night (Christmas Eve) in Madrid.

After seeing the lurid television show of the Italian 'Professor Cavan', a charismatic but fraudulent Satanist, the priest and José Maria track him down to his luxurious flat on the Gran Via in central Madrid. They hold him and his buxom girlfriend Susana hostage until Cavan has revealed the ritual for calling up the devil. When the Beast duly appears (in the form of a grinning ram), the unholy trio set out with renewed desperation to discover the birthplace of the Anti-Christ and thus save the world. After a series of action set-pieces—a perilous descent from a tall building; a brawl in an infernal nightclub; the slaughter of the Magi outside a department store—Cavan identifies the devil's sign, which leads the three men to the site of an unfinished skyscraper. Here they encounter the Holy Family (in the form of homeless destitutes) and Fascist vigilantes in the devil's pay. When the Beast appears, José Maria is dropped to his death from the top floor and Cavan is set alight by the vigilantes. A coda, however, shows the priest and the scarred Cavan on a park bench nine months later: they have saved the world from the Anti-Christ, but can tell no one what they have done.

In the slyly comic credit sequence of this, Alex de la Iglesia's second feature, there is a brief shot of raggle-taggle beggars complete with goat in front of the twin towers of the skyscrapers known as the 'Gate to Europe'. It is a typically resonant image of what will prove to be a major theme of the film: the conflict between tradition and modernity. But as the mild-mannered priest goes about his unholy mission (stealing alms from a blind beggar, taking the wallet from the pocket of a dying man), the swift pace of the action makes any such reflection impossible. *The Day of the Beast* may share with its predecessor, the Almodóvar-produced *Acción mutante*, a unique art design and an admirably perverse 'high concept' ('Priest saves the world by doing evil'); but whereas *Acción* fell to pieces after 20 minutes, *Beast* achieves that holy grail of Spanish cinema: a compelling narrative which builds, sustains, and resolves in the best Hollywood tradition.

This parodic plot is deftly built around multiple references, lightly underscored: thus the three unlikely friends (priest, heavy metal fan, and pseudo-Satanist) are the new Three Kings, unwilling celebrants at a diabolical birth. More cheekily, a shot of de Palma look-alike Nathalie Seseña earnestly ironing in front of the television is a quote from *Kika*, a previous parody of Spanish television by de la Iglesia's erstwhile mentor Almodóvar. The humour is equally assured. *Beast* is packed with glorious sight gags (the naked, acid-tripping grandfather in the hostel); and cartoon-like farce, which owes much to its director's background in comics (the bouncing breasts of Susana, pursued down a staircase by the heavily armed priest). But the verbal humour is as precisely pitched as the visual: amongst all the mayhem, the characters address each other in precisely formal tones; and the script makes energetic use of the blasphemous profanity that is ubiquitous in spoken Spanish, but is here cunningly transformed by the apocalyptic context. So while the choice of iconography and central character might suggest Buñuel, there is no simple anti-clericalism here. Rather like the Devil who (we are told) imitates God in order to make fun of him, de la Iglesia, himself a graduate of the priest's University of Deusto, offers a fond and faithful parody of Basque Catholicism.

This subtle take on tradition recurs in the casting. Nathalie Seseña is a regular on those same television channels to which her character, the virginal Mina, is addicted: or again, Terele Pávez, the gun-toting, urban mama, is known as the long suffering matriarch in such impeccably tasteful exercises in ruralism as Mario Camus' *The Holy Innocents (Los santos inocentes)*. Performances are uniformly excellent: Pávez vigorously dissects a rabbit for dinner as she discusses blowing away the assorted scum on the streets, and the unassuming Angulo plays the priest quite straight, lending dignity to absurdity and thus increasing immeasurably the comic effect. De la Iglesia's policy of upgrading supporting actors to principals comes up trumps here, especially in the context of a Spanish cinema which normally works to death the three or four stars of the moment. Production credits are also uniformly excellent, from the sulphurous night photography of Flavio Martinez Labiano to Battista Lena's original music, which mixes Bernard Herrmann and Black Sabbath. The art design is blackly witty and stylish and the sound design matches it in subtlety: as the characters watch an exorcism on television we can just make out the jolly jingles of Spanish slot machines in the background. Few European films can boast the quality of optical and prosthetic effects in such sequences as the climactic confrontation with the Beast on top of the skyscraper. The financial backing of Spain's most powerful producer, Andrés Vicente Gómez, has clearly paid off in spades.

The Devil warns his supplicants, "This is not a game,": and in the great tradition of dystopia, de la Iglesia's final twist is that the funniest Spanish film of the decade is also one of the most serious. The unfinished and ironically named Gate to Europe (the most spectacular real-life landmark of the film) is as clear a symbol to Spaniards as Canary Wharf is to Britons of the avarice and corruption of recent times and the incomplete modernization of a struggling state. In spite of its grotesque humour and fantasy, then, *Beast* communicates the seedy splendour of the Spanish capital more convincingly than any of the so-called 'Madrid comedies' of old hands Fernando Colomo (*Allegro ma non troppo*) or Fernando Trueba *(Belle epoque)*. More particularly, it exploits to spectacular effect the faded charms of Madrid's Broadway, the Gran Via, built in the 20s and 30s as a would-be rival to Chicago and Manhattan. De la Iglesia's remedy for such a decline is ecumenical: clearly he has as much affection for the seedy *pensiones* of the past as he does for the equally tawdry heavy metal clubs of the present. Alluding ever so lightly to street crime, drug-related violence, and the rise of the Right, he makes his own devilishly accurate prediction: since the film was made, the Spanish government has passed from the exhausted Socialists to the untried People's Party, raising for older Spaniards unwonted memories of a diabolical past. Cavan warns his audience: "While you're at home watching television, the Anti-Christ is on the loose outside." De la Iglesia's brilliant mockery, like that of the devil, is thus not simply a game; and as the camera lingers pointedly on a poster of Silvio Berlusconi (a major player on the Spanish media scene), the devil seems truly to be knocking at the door.

VILLAGE VOICE, 6/22/99, p. 154, Gary Dauphin

Imported from Spain, where it was one of 1995's highest homegrown grossers, *The Day of the Beast* is an unexpectedly wry and fresh little horror flick. Opening on the well-trod turf of a Catholic priest's battle against forces secular and demonic, *Beast* follows the darkly comic misadventures of Father Ángel (Álex Angulo), a bookish theologian who discovers that Saint John's Revelation is actually a code containing the coming birth date of the Antichrist. Wise in the ways of the Word but not the world, Father Ángel sallies forth from his academic cocoon into the violent underbelly of Madrid, where he desperately tries to join the ranks of the damned (as a double agent, of course) before the beginning of the end of the world.

Despite a thick veneer of solemn, biblical exegesis, *Beast* has a distinct, uptempo charm thanks to the slapstick-like distance director and coscreenwriter Álex de la Iglesia keeps from his apocalyptic premise. Father Ángel's vague plan to cozy up to Satan by learning "to do evil" unfolds with a wacky but sinister earnestness that's as comfortable with the possibility that he's a fruitcake as with the more standard proposition that he's a legit, albeit overmatched, seer. From his early, baby-step crimes (the padre pushes a mime down a flight of stairs) to his haphazard pursuit of virgin's blood (it's needed to invoke the devil), Ángel is more sympathetic bumbler than hardcore spiritual warrior, theoretically astute but lacking in practical know-how. He does get help, first in the form of a burly, gun-toting record store clerk, then in the incredulous company of a fraudulent TV psychic, but it's a typical with-friends-like-these setup, with the trio adding up to less than half a Hollywood exorcist. *Beast* is laden with wisecracks and concisely drawn, comic bit players, but you're never sure exactly who the joke is on. Even the money shot that should push the proceedings firmly into the camp of the supernatural thriller has a jokily ambiguous quality—the unexpected appearance of a low-budget goat-devil sends Father Angel and his assistants screaming like Stooges, but only after they've dropped a few tabs of acid.

On the F/X front *Beast* lacks digital polish, but that's no loss; the kitschy stop-motion demons manage to come off as thematic choices as opposed to financial necessities. Reminiscent of the nasty fun of *Evil Dead*-era Sam Raimi, *Beast* is hardly a genre buster but de la Iglesia clearly understood the particular strengths of his story, working overtime to make his various aesthetic ends meet while serving up familiar yuks and frights in consistently inventive ways.

Also reviewed in:
NEW YORK TIMES, 6/18/99, p. E18, Lawrence Van Gelder
VARIETY, 10/2-8/95, p. 61, David Rooney

DEEP BLUE SEA

A Warner Bros. release in association with Village Roadshow Pictures/Groucho III Film Partnership of an Alan Riche/Tony Ludwig/Akiva Goldsman production. *Executive Producer:* Duncan Henderson and Bruce Berman. *Producer:* Akiva Goldsman, Tony Ludwig, and Alan Riche. *Director:* Renny Harlin. *Screenplay:* Duncan Kennedy, Donna Powers, and Wayne Powers. *Director of Photography:* Stephen Windon. *Editor:* Frank J. Urioste, Derek G. Brechin, and Dallas S. Puett. *Music:* Trevor Rabin. *Music Editor:* Will Kaplan. *Sound:* Tim Cooney and (music) Steve Kempster. *Sound Editor:* J. Paul Huntsman and Robb Wilson. *Casting:* Christine Sheaks. *Production Designer:* William Sandell and Joseph Bennett. *Art Director:* Mark W. Mansbridge. *Set Designer:* Bill Taliaferro and Javier Nava. *Set Decorator:* Debra Echard. *Special Effects:* John Richardson. *Costumes:* Mark Bridges. *Make-up:* Jeff Dawn. *Make-up (Special Prosthetics):* Matthew W. Mungle, Clinton Wayne, and Chad Atkinson. *Stunt Coordinator:* R.A. Rondell. *Running time:* 100 minutes. *MPAA Rating:* R.

CAST: Saffron Burrows (Dr. Susan McAlester); Thomas Jane (Carter Blake); LL Cool J (Sherman "Preacher" Dudley); Jacqueline McKenzie (Janice Higgins); Michael Rapaport (Tom "Scog" Scoggins); Stellan Skarsgård (Jim Whitlock); Aida Turturro (Brenda Kerns); Samuel

L. Jackson (Russell Franklin);   Cristos (Boat Captain);   Daniel Bahimo Rey and Valente Rodriguez (Helicopter Pilots);   Brent Roam (Helicopter Winch Operator);   Eyal Podell (Boy 1); Erinn Bartlett (Girl 1); Dan Thiel (Boy 2); Sabrina Geerinckx (Girl 2); Tajsha Thomas (Janice's Friend); Frank W. Welker (Parrot Sounds); Ronny Cox (Franklin's Boss).

CHRISTIAN SCIENCE MONITOR, 7/30/99, p. 15, David Sterritt

[*Deep Blue Sea* was reviewed jointly with *Runaway Bride*; see Sterritt's review of that film.]

LOS ANGELES TIMES, 7/28/99, Calendar/p. 1, Kenneth Turan

A liquid to rely on, water is right there when we're hot, when we're thirsty, when we want things to grow. But who speaks up for water's dark side, for its implacable force, the terrifying power of its raging torrents? "Deep Blue Sea" does, that's who.

A rousing adventure yarn that's paced to kill, "Deep Blue Sea" is an example of how expert action filmmaking and up-to-the-minute visual effects can transcend a workmanlike script and bring excitement to conventional genre material. There's little in this man-versus-shark story we haven't seen before, but we haven't seen it quite like this.

"Deep Blue Sea" is also a return to form for action director Renny Harlin. Considered one of Hollywood's top shooters after "Die Hard 2" and "Cliffhanger," Harlin lost his way for a while in the great dismal swamps of "Cutthroat Island" and "The Long Kiss Goodnight."

Here, helped by a trio of veteran editors (Frank J. Urioste, Derek G. Brechin, Dallas S. Puett), cinematographer Stephen Windon and top-of-the-line animatronic and computer-generated image people, Harlin has energetically pounced on this classic Don't Mess With Mother Nature premise.

In addition to reinvigorating Harlin, "Deep Blue Sea" also brings the shark back to a place of prominence in the menace hierarchy. While this film doesn't approach the elan of the brilliant "Jaws," that picture never did manage a completely workable shark. Here, the combination of animatronic and digitally created beasts, plus footage of the real thing, gives us a 25-foot mako and two smaller companions that are the epitome of destruction.

Yet, even though we get enough close-ups of nasty-looking teeth to delight a convention of orthodontists (no one has to tell these behemoths to open wide), it is the water as much as the shark that terrifies us here. The nightmarish vision of liquid torrents roaring out of control in a confined space is every bit as scary, if not more so, than creatures that bite for a living.

That space would be Aquatica's floating oceanic research station, an elaborate compound that's situated almost entirely below the surface. Here the all-business Dr. Susan McAlester (Saffron Burrows) heads up a team that includes hunky shark wrangler Carter Blake (Thomas Jane), comic-relief chef Preacher Dudley (LL Cool J), deep thinker Jim Whitlock (Stellan Skarsgard), a marine biologist (Jacqueline McKenzie) and an engineer (Michael Rapaport).

Working from the curious premise that sharks might produce a protein that would regenerate human brain cells and thus prevent Alzheimer's disease, Dr. McAlester and company have been breeding bigger and smarter sharks in the hopes of harvesting a potent version of that substance.

Some bad publicity leads money man Russell Franklin (Samuel L. Jackson) to consider pulling the plug on the whole project, but before he does, Dr. McAlester convinces him to take a flying visit to the facility to see the research for himself. Definitely not a good idea.

For what Franklin and the research team simultaneously discover is that these sharks, including a giant 8,000-pound beast with a brain the size of a V-8 engine, have gotten too darn big and too darn smart for anyone's good but their own. It's uh-oh time in a big way as the scientists realize "We've taken God's oldest killing machine and given it will and desire." Dear me.

While "Deep Blue Sea's" script (by Duncan Kennedy and Donna Powers & Wayne Powers) is not going to win any Writers Guild awards, its savvy enough to efficiently set the scene for the physical madness that follows and then get out of the way.

Yes, there are the expected moments such as doors that are closed just in time and a fetching female who has to strip down to bikini underwear to save her life (don't ask), but the film does manage several twists that are surprising. And the casting of actors who for the most part are unknown to action audiences helps the scenario get closer to plausibility than films like this usually manage.

The thrills begin, classically, on a dark and stormy night, and once the mayhem commences, with raging waters, dangerous fires and out-of-control sharks attacking every human in sight, there is no rest for the weary. Harlin, orchestrating on-screen hysteria and menace as adroitly as he combined the work of the eight effects houses that contributed to the film's verisimilitude, is completely in his element making sense out of the chaos. This is one summer action film that really knows how to move.

NEW YORK POST, 7/28/99, p. 75, Hannah Brown

Just when you thought it was safe to go back to the floating medical research lab, those pesky genetically enhanced sharks get loose.

That's the premise of "Deep Blue Sea," the latest attempt at a mindless summer-fun flick. But, as it turns out, mindless fun requires a lighter touch and more suspense than director Renny Harlin can deliver.

In the classic "Jaws," Steven Spielberg scared thousands out of the water with just one shark off an ordinary beach. But in "Deep Blue Sea," which features millions of dollars in special effects and three killer super-sharks on the loose in a confined area, there isn't a moment that evokes the fear of the midnight swim in the opening of "Jaws."

Given the claustrophobic setting, an ocean-based lab called Aquatica (doesn't it sound like a theme park?), "Deep Blue Sea" is far from the updated "Jaws" with cutting-edge special effects that the movie's posters promise.

Instead, it's more like a cross between "Jaws 3-D" and "Waterworld."

The plot concerns a drug company project headed by anorexic-looking Saffron Burrows as the driven researcher who will stop at nothing to find a cure for Alzheimer's, including performing illegal genetic tampering to increase the size of sharks' brains.

Looking as if she'd be more at home in a fashion layout than a lab, she's certainly the skinniest marine biologist since Charlotte Rampling played one in the ghastly killer-whale flick "Orca."

A very stiff Samuel L. Jackson plays a venture capitalist who has invested $200 million in Burrows' project.

He stands around looking awestruck by the smart sharks and gets stuck with some of the movie's worst lines, such as, "Nature can be lethal, but it doesn't hold a candle to man."

That's right, this is another man-shouldn't-mess-with-nature movie, and the script hammers that home relentlessly.

"She screwed with the sharks, and now the sharks are screwing with us," says Michael Rapaport, playing one of the crew members, case anyone didn't get it.

The movie's saving grace is LL Cool J as the Bible-quoting cook who keeps the one-liners flowing even when it looks as if he's about to become a shark snack. And his rap song on the closing credits is wittier than anything in the rest of the movie.

Still, in spite of all its flaws, there are some good action scenes. And for those people who wait all year for "Shark Week" to play on the Discovery Channel, it's a must-see, if only so they can find out how far animatronic sharks have come in the last 20 years.

The film also mixes in computer-generated sharks (which swim like lightning, but aren't that scary) and some footage of real sharks.

One thing's for sure: Seeing "Deep Blue Sea" won't make anyone afraid to go for a swim.

NEWSDAY, 7/28/99, Part II/p. B2, John Anderson

Like the sand and the surf, the sun and the sky, the lobster and the butter, "Deep Blue Sea" is a marriage of elements that belong together: Blood-thirsty, man-eating beasts. And director Renny Harlin ("Cliffhanger," "Cutthroat Island," "Die Hard II"), who's never created a character you'd miss.

So while you can't quite sit back and relax during Harlin's techno-giddy, gadget-happy, humans-into-chum story—it's hard not to be startled when sharks are jumping like trout and cutting people in half—you don't really have to worry about losing anyone you care about, because there's hardly anyone here to care about.

That even includes—no, that specifically includes—Dr. Susan McAlester (Saffron Burrows), the head of an offshore, subsurface research facility, where she's violated every scientific ethic in her obsessive hunt for a shark-based cure for Alzheimer's disease. "Have you ever known anyone with Alzheimer's?" she asks pleadingly of money man Russell Franklin (Samuel L. Jackson). Instead of the obvious answer ("I can't remember"), Franklin the financier is seduced by McAlester's tearful tale of family woes and goes off with her and her team to a place where horrible things are going to happen. And not a minute too soon.

"Deep Blue Sea" is one of those man-playing-God movies—or, in this quite progressive case, woman-playing-God movies—that indulges in all sorts of impressive-sounding scientific jargon and then throws physics out the window.

The beasts in question—which, thanks to McAlester, have become smarter than the average shark—also seem able to change size at will: Depending on what the situation calls for, they're either as big as two Flippers or half the Queen Mary ("Deep Blues Sea," by the way, was filmed on that celebrated Rosarita, Mexico, water tank built by James Cameron for "Titanic.") But size hardly matters, because when water rushes into the facility under 10 tons of pressure, it moves in slow motion. And when McAlester needs to electrocute Sharkenstein, she merely pulls an electrical cable off the wall, stands atop her folded wet suit (providing Harlin the bonus opportunity of posing Burrows in her underwear) and zaps him. Or was it her? As unappealing as the McAlester character is, she runs only a distant second to Carter Blake (Thomas Jane) in terms of general repugnance. The research group's shark wrangler—he can mount a rushing mako without a scratch to his pecs, abs or sleeveless Armani wetsuit—is smugness personified. Which, in Renny Harlin World, means he has a lot better chance of making it to the end credits than Stellan Skarsgard, the respected Swedish actor relegated here to fish food, or the sassy Jacqueline McKenzie, who plays Janice (what's her job? I don't remember) or, best of all LL Cool J, whose Preacher is the real hero of the movie—as well as a welcome antidote to all the chewing, swallowing, fussing and preening that make "Deep Blue Sea" the undigestible summer dish it is.

NEWSWEEK, 8/9/99, p. 68. David Ansen

It doesn't really matter if you think Renny Harlin's "Deep Blue Sea" is totally preposterous. It will scare you any way. It makes surprisingly little difference if the laughter it provokes means the audience is laughing at it, with it, or simply because it needs relief from the tension. This highly unlikely story about genetically enhanced sharks that terrorize the scientists who created them is one summer movie that deliver exactly what it promises: nonstop popcorn thrills. In the season of "Lake Placid" and "The Haunting," that's nothing to sneeze at.

The setting is a floating lab somewhere in the Atlantic that is quickly destroyed by a timely tropical storm. The unlucky team researchers (including Saffron Burrows as a chilly British scientist, Samuel L. Jackson the project's CEO, Thomas Jane as a "shark wrangler" and LL Cool J as an intrepid chef) is trapped in submerged, flooding chambers. If the ocean doesn't swallow them á la "Titanic," the brainy mako sharks will have them for lunch.

Harlin ("Die Hard 2;"'Cliffhanger") has some wicked fun undermining our expectations. In the movie's most startling moment one of the main characters is suddenly, unexpectedly swallowed whole. This drew applause from the preview audience not because they hated the victim, but because the were happy to be so expertly faked out. "Deep Blue Sea" gives good *rush*—earning its stripes as one terrific junk movie.

SIGHT AND SOUND, 11/99, p. 40, Jamie Graham

An underwater research centre off the coast of Mexico. Searching for a cure for Alzheimer's disease, a team of scientists, led by Dr Susan McAlester, attempt to reactivate degenerate human brain cells by injecting them into sharks' brains. As a result of their experiments, three mako sharks grow to 40 feet and demonstrate intelligent behaviour.

Russell Franklin, president of a pharmaceuticals company, arrives with a view to funding the research. An anaesthetised shark—injected with human cells—awakens and bites off scientist Jim Whitlock's arm. The helicopter transporting Whitlock to surgery crashes into the side of the research laboratory causing its computer system safeguarding the workers from the sharks to crash. The shark breaks the complex's viewing window; the centre floods and the three makos enter. The remaining scientists, accompanied by shark handler Carter Blake, cook 'Preacher'

Dudley and Franklin attempt to fight their way to the surface. Dudley kills one of the makos by igniting a gas cooker, while McAlester electrocutes another. Franklin and scientist Tom Scoggins are killed. McAlester, Blake and Dudley reach the surface. McAlester jumps back into the water to act as bait before the last shark can escape the compound. She is killed, but Blake and Dudley destroy the mako.

It is inevitable that any film featuring giant man-eating sharks will be compared to *Jaws,* but Renny Harlin's underwater thriller shares little with Spielberg's 1975 *magnum opus. Jaws* worked very much in the tradition of Val Lewton's masterly horror flicks of the 40s, wringing suspense from unseen terrors and, for the most part, keeping its monster off screen, barring the occasional dorsal fin. *Deep Blue Sea,* on the other hand, is a product of our CGI-dominated age and is eager to show off its digital wares. So we're treated to shot after shot of jerky, frequently risible sharks zipping across the frame or barrelling towards the camera. There's even one moment—designed, perhaps, to mimic the dual T-Rex attack in *The Lost World: Jurassic Park*—when two mako sharks converge on a hapless victim and tear him asunder as they exit from either end of the screen.

Deep Blue Sea has inherited more of its genes from the *Jaws* sequels than from the original. Set in and around an underwater research facility which is eventually breached by marauding sharks, its basic premise and set construction invite comparison to the Sea World aquarium of *Jaws 3-D.* And, just as the tag line to *Jaws: the Revenge* would have it, this time it's personal, with super-intelligent sharks breaking down steel doors and weeding out the nasty scientists who played God by experimenting on them.

However, *Deep Blue Sea* is ultimately more of a disaster movie teetering on 'B'-movie legs than a *Jaws* rip-off or bizarre slasher film hybrid. To his credit, Harlin (*Cliffhanger*) recognises and embraces this. The characters spend much of the film ascending through the compound's submerged levels to surface safety, a single-minded quest that echoes that of the rag-tag ensemble who struggled through *The Poseidon Adventure* (1972). It is a strong concept which, when fleshed out by the shark element, should have made for gripping viewing. Instead, as the characters grapple with locked doors, their perilous under-takings often resembling an episode of the quiz show *Crystal Maze,* the result is a soggy effort. Thankfully, however, there are some surprises: the cast diminishes in a quite unexpected order, Stephen Windon's underwater photography is luminous and there's even the occasional inspired flourish, such as a spilt glass of red wine more disturbing than any of the graphic bloodletting.

VILLAGE VOICE, 8/10/99, p. 70, Michael Atkinson

Back at the underwater lab full of genetically smartened mako sharks, we can't rely on much of anything to keep us awake. *Deep Blue Sea* is one of those hellishly predictable digital-monster gauntlets that makes you pity the actors, particularly Saffron Burrows (this is her first Hollywood lead) and LL Cool J, who, in the tradition of Mantan Moreland, plays a terrified chef given to chugging cooking wine and talking to God in moments of panic. Of course, the sharks are bigger (unexplained), smarter (explained via anti-Alzheimer's drug research), and ridiculously faster (animation wonks will be boys) than real makos. Go to the aquarium instead.

Also reviewed in:
CHICAGO TRIBUNE, 7/28/99, Tempo/p. 5, Barbara Shulgasser
NEW YORK TIMES, 7/28/99, p. E3, Stephen Holden
VARIETY, 8/2-8/99, p. 33, Robert Koehler
WASHINGTON POST, 7/28/99, p. C1, Stephen Hunter
WASHINGTON POST, 7/30/99, Weekend/p. 45, Desson Howe

DEEP END OF THE OCEAN, THE

A Columbia Pictures release of a Mandalay Entertainment presentation of Via Rosa production. *Executive Producer:* Frank Capra, III. *Producer:* Kate Guinzberg and Steve Nicolaides.

Director: Ulu Grosbard. *Screenplay:* Stephen Schiff. *Based on the book by:* Jacquelyn Mitchard. *Director of Photography:* Stephen Goldblatt. *Editor:* John Bloom. *Music:* Elmer Bernstein. *Music Editor:* Kathy Durning. *Sound:* Petur Hliddal and (music) Dan Wallin. *Sound Editor:* Ron Bochar. *Casting:* Lora Kennedy. *Production Designer:* Dan Davis. *Art Director:* Bill Hiney. *Set Designer:* Barbara Mesney, Mark Poll, and Carl Stensel. *Set Decorator:* Bill Cimino. *Set Dresser:* Joshian Elliott. *Special Effects:* Joe Ramsey. *Costumes:* Susie DeSanto. *Make-up:* Rick Sharp. *Make-up (Michelle Pfeiffer):* Ronnie Specter. *Stunt Coordinator:* Allan Graf and Mickey Giacomazzi. *Running time:* 108 minutes. *MPAA Rating:* PG-13.

CAST: Michelle Pfeiffer (Beth); Treat Williams (Pat); Whoopi Goldberg (Candy); Jonathan Jackson (Vincent, Age 16); Cory Buck (Vincent, Age 7); Ryan Merriman (Sam); Alexa Vega (Kerry, Age 9); Michael McGrady (Jimmy Daugherty); Brenda Strong (Ellen); Michael McElroy (Ben); Tony Musante (Angelo); Rose Gregorio (Rosie); John Kapelos (George); Lucinda Jenney (Laurie); John Roselius (Bastokovich); K.K. Dodds (Theresa); Joey Simmrin (Schaffer); Holly Towne (Martha); Mary Anne Summers (Cecil Lockhart); Susie Spear and Lisa Maris (Cheerleaders); Daniel Hagen (Hotel Manager); McNally Sagal (Woman Cop); Robert Cicchini (Joey); Frank Marocco (Bandleader); Aison McMillian (Desk Clerk); Stephanie Feury (Waitress); Wayne Duvall (McGuire); Gerald McSorley (Father Cleary); Mickey Swenson (Cop Tommy/Cop #1); Todd Jeffries (Cop Ricky); Ken Magee (Cop #2); Van Epperson (Guard); Jennifer Reznikoff (Waitress); Ron Von Gober (Police Officer); Steve Blalock and Mike Watson (ND Cops); Robert "Bobbyz" Zajonc (Helicopter Pilot); Jim James, Emidio Antonio, and Patricia M. Leahy (Zoo Employees); Pete Sutton (Community Center Volunteer).

CHRISTIAN SCIENCE MONITOR, 3/12/99, p. 15, David Sterritt

"The Deep End of the Ocean" begins on a deceptively calm note, as a mother heads for a high-school reunion with her two little boys in tow.

In a crowded lobby she leaves them alone for a moment, and when she returns one of them has vanished, destroying her tranquillity in an instant.

Her first reaction is panic, then anguish, and then as days turn into weeks and months enduring grief and guilt. Life goes on, but her pain goes so deep that she hardly dares trust her senses when she realizes she may have discovered the child a decade after his disappearance.

The experiences this woman goes through are so poignant, unsettling, and suspenseful that it's surprising how little the movie manages to do with them.

On the plus side, Michelle Pfeiffer and Treat Williams are convincing as the parents. Ryan Merriman and Jonathan Jackson are even better in the main adolescent parts. Whoopi Goldberg adds flash as a sympathetic detective, and John Kapelos is best of all in the underwritten role of a neighbor who holds a key to the mystery.

On the minus side, the filmmakers fall short of their own high standards. The director, Ulu Grosbard, falls to elicit the heartfelt acting that made pictures like "Straight Time" and "Georgia" so memorable. The screenwriter, Stephen Schiff, loses the atmospheric depth that distinguished his recent "Lolita" adaptation. And few would guess that Elmer Bernstein is one of the screen's greatest composers from the cloying set of tunes he turns in here.

Fans of Jacquelyn Mitchard's novel may find enough echoes of the book to justify the price of admission. But others can see this sort of thinly crafted melodrama in TV movies every week. For free.

LOS ANGELES TIMES, 3/12/99, Calendar/p. 1, Kenneth Turan

The bottomless dread of having a child disappear or die is a parent's most consuming nightmare. Those who have experienced that kind of loss say that when it happens, your life takes a sharp turn and you sense at once that things are never going to get back to normal again.

For Beth Cappadora (Michelle Pfeiffer), that loss happens quite literally. In Chicago for her 15th high school reunion in "The Deep End of the Ocean's" opening 1988 sequences, Beth momentarily leaves her 3-year-old middle child, Ben, in the charge of his 7-year-old brother,

Vincent. When she returns, Ben is gone and no one, not even experienced police detective Candy Bliss (Whoopi Goldberg), can find him.

Taken from Jacquelyn Mitchard's best-selling novel (the first selection of Oprah's Book Club), "Deep End" takes a stab at telling both this wrenching tale and its surprising aftermath set nine years later.

Under Ulu Grosbard's careful, measured direction, the film is ambitious to be a truly heartbreaking story. But though a lot of complex psychological issues about the nature of family are raised, "Deep End" ends up insisting on pat and overly tidy resolutions that are at variance with the emotional chaos it's nominally attempting to convey.

Even the film's partial success wouldn't be possible without an exceptional performance by Pfeiffer, one of her best ever. The actress is that rare great beauty who is as empathetic as she is attractive, one who can convey pain, hysteria and misery and make us believe them.

Reaching into herself, Pfeiffer produces a scream of chilling agony when Beth finally acknowledges that her child is gone, and when someone tries to reassure her by saying they know how she feels, she answers with a devastating, "You don't know, I don't even know." It's a performance so strong and true that at times it seems as if it were intended for a different film.

Before Ben was lost—or so the glimpse we're afforded of that life tells us—Beth was living in Madison, Wis., contentedly married to restaurateur Pat Cappadora (Treat Williams). She worked as a freelance photographer while taking care of her family, which included a new baby girl, but all of that, even her ability to care for her remaining children, is destroyed by her grief.

The depiction of the near-madness Beth descends into is the film's most affecting section. Looking drawn and cadaverous, Pfeiffer brings a compelling desperation to the brittle, almost completely shattered Beth. Well-directed by the rigorously unsentimental Grosbard ("Straight Time," "True Confessions"), the actress carries us with her even when her character is at its most driven, obsessive and unappealing.

But when we jump forward nine years, "Deep End" seems to run aground and lose focus. Unexpected developments flowing from a chance neighborhood encounter put the family's troubles into a different perspective, and Beth and her entire family learn that having what you dream of is not always exactly what you'd wish for.

It's difficult to pinpoint why "Deep End of the Ocean" is not as compelling in its second half. Partly there seems to be a retreat in Stephen Schiff's underdeveloped script from the complete honesty, the willingness to embrace the messiness of life, that marked the first part of this film as well as Grosbard's excellent last feature, "Georgia."

While "Georgia" was an independently made film that in fact had difficulty finding distribution, "Deep End" is a studio project and that status seems to have naturally emphasized and heightened the schematic qualities of the book. Nothing too raw, nothing too unresolved, is allowed here, and while that makes the proceedings more palatable, it also robs them of a kind of intensity that the situation dealt with ought to have, the intensity that Pfeiffer's performance lends it at critical junctures.

Also a drawback is a performance by Treat Williams as long-suffering husband Pat that never seems as sure of itself or as compelling as Pfeiffer's. The only actor who comes close to matching her is, of all people, young Jonathan Jackson (a daytime TV Emmy winner for a recurring role on "General Hospital"), who plays Vincent at 17 with just the right touch of the unfathomable. It's a performance that reminds us, as this film alternately does and does not, how perplexing and exasperating relationships between people who love each other can be.

NEW YORK, 3/22/99, p. 99, Peter Rainer

When we first see Beth Cappadora (Michelle Pfeiffer) in the uneven but affecting *Deep End of the Ocean*, she's bundling up her three young children for a trip to Chicago for her fifteenth high-school reunion. Her happiness with her brood is palpable—it's close to exultation. Her husband, Pat (Treat Williams), who runs an Italian restaurant in Madison, Wisconsin, basks in the warmth. If Beth represents the maternal ideal, Pat is its masculine counterpart—the provider as patriarch. Though the film starts out in 1988, the Cappadoras seem right out of a spiffy fifties-era sitcom. Their radiance is practically a manifesto. It's telling us there is no better way to live.

The retro mood is a setup for the shock that soon follows, as Beth's 3-year-old son Ben, left alone for three minutes with his 7-year-old brother Vincent, vanishes in the bustling lobby of the reunion hotel. It's as if at this moment the real world—the howling world blocked out by the Cappadoras' bliss—suddenly breaks through. The setup is reminiscent of those horror films where you just know something bad is going to happen because everything is looking *too* good. And yet there's a stark realism in the way Beth is jolted into terror; this, too, is the way life can be.

Nothing else in *The Deep End of the Ocean* matches the extended sequence in which Beth—disbelieving at first, then stunned, then raving—comes apart. It's like watching a slow-motion explosion. Ulu Grosbard, directing from a script by Stephen Schiff based on the Jacquelyn Mitchard best-seller, keeps the focus squarely on Beth, as her friends, the police, and, finally, Pat crowd the scene. Her brimming, aghast eyes seem to fill the frame. The reassurances she is given about Ben's return are weightless. Dread has already taken her beyond all that.

What eventually becomes clear is that Ben—despite community-action volunteers and an intense police search and a cover story in *People*—is gone, kidnapped. But the movie isn't about how a family copes with its baffling loss. That's just the beginning. Nine years later, after the Cappadoras have picked up the pieces and moved to Chicago, Ben re-enters their life, innocently, as a neighborhood kid who offers to cut their lawn. Beth, who had been a professional photographer, stares at the boy, now called Sam (Ryan Merriman), and it's as if she's looking at a phantasm. While he mows, she clicks away in secret, and when she develops the pictures, you don't expect his image to emerge. He's a mirage. It's only when his fingerprints check out that this mirage is made flesh.

The Deep End of the Ocean is a very scrupulous piece of work. I'm tempted to call it a superior TV movie-of-the-week, except some of it, notably the performances of Pfeiffer and Jonathan Jackson, who plays the 16-year-old Vincent, resonates in a way unfamiliar to that tamped-down genre. Still, as the film begins to expand on the Big Issues—the meaning of family and all that—it loses its withering power. Sam has been raised by a kind man (John Kapelos) who doesn't suspect the boy's history; it is he whom Sam considers his true father even when, somewhat against his will, he moves back with the Cappadoras. Vincent resents Sam's presence, while to Beth and Pat he's regarded as the dauphin. Everything in the film plays out with textbookish intent; each scene makes its clinical point. Beth feels guilty for what happened to little Ben; so does Vincent. Pat wants his harmonious homestead back; Beth realizes that's a pipe dream. Meanwhile, Sam, at worst, just seems bummed out. The filmmakers have idealized even his pain.

The emotional resolutions aren't pat, exactly. But they're not messy either, and for material this inherently volatile, that seems like a cheat. We see Beth go from being the most devoted of mothers to becoming a selfless archangel willing to lose her son again for his own well-being. She wants Pat to know that the storybook family he has in his head doesn't exist. The film would have been strengthened if Beth also realized that her family even before the kidnapping didn't fully exist, either; that all that lovey-dovey sitcom sweetness was a bit hysterical. Beth is sanctified for our benefit. She's a role model of how to cope in a crisis.

Pfeiffer's performance is best in the early scenes, before she's required to be valiant. Watching her come apart is doubly harrowing because at first she seems so vibrant. Convinced Ben is lost forever, she takes to her bed for days; sorrow makes her a zombie. It's one of the most harrowing portraits of heavy depression I've ever seen in a movie. Pfeiffer may be a delicate, fine-boned beauty, but she's one of the least fragile actresses on the planet. When she takes you into a character, into a mood, you're pulled in all the way, whether she's slithering across a piano top and singing "Makin' Whoopee," in *The Fabulous Baker Boys,* or shimmering with frail virtue as Madame de Tourvel in *Dangerous Liaisons.* She can make the loss of innocence tragic; she can make seductiveness seethe. I've always wished she would play Chekhov—*Uncle Vanya,* to be precise. What a Yelena she'd make! (Julianne Moore, who has something of Pfeiffer's range and resplendence, played her in Louis Malle's great *Vanya on 42nd Street.)* Pfeiffer is rare among great beauties in that she doesn't act as if the spotlight was invented solely for her. In her scenes with other actors, she confers her glow, and the inspiration is often returned.

Pfeiffer must have inspired Jonathan Jackson. Near the end, when Vincent has made himself an outcast, Beth visits him in jail, and the alternating current of hurt and adoration and shared remorse between mother and son makes the screen crackle. Vincent is never more his mother's child than in this moment. They even begin to *look* alike. The *Deep End of the Ocean* stays mostly in the shallows, but in scenes like this, it's full fathom five.

NEW YORK POST, 3/12/99, p. 39, Rod Dreher

"The Deep End of the Ocean" is about what happens to a family when a kidnapped child returns years later as an adolescent—as the millions who read the Jacquelyn Mitchard novel puffed by Oprah's Book Club or saw the movie version's revealing trailer know. Awareness that a child-snatching is the film's catalyst makes the opening scenes, in which distracted mom Beth Cappadora (Michelle Pfeiffer) wanders unaware with her children into a trap, breathlessly tense and terrifying—and all but unbearable for parents.

The riveting setup, which takes place in a crowded hotel lobby where Beth and her little ones are attending her class reunion, is by far the best part of this middling domestic melodrama. It clamps like a snapping turtle on the nerve cabled to a parent's greatest fear: that through a moment's negligence, their child will fall victim to calamity. An exceptionally good Pfeiffer shows us the searing effects of a mother's guilt and rage, fear and despair, which all but annihilate the Cappadora family bonds.

Pity, then, that the rest of the picture never comes close to the intensity of the kidnapping and its immediate aftermath. "Deep End" starts to go slack as the family descends into unfathomable grief, and by the time it jumps into the future for its second half, the picture has thoroughly collapsed into the TV-movie mold. The characters don't command much emotional investment, and the excruciating traumas they confront carry little more dramatic resonance than a disease of the week.

Unlike Mel Gibson's kidnapping thriller "Ransom," this film focuses not on the hunt for Ben, the stolen child (conducted by a police detective played by Whoopi Goldberg), but the impact the event has on the middle-class suburban Cappadora family. As the film's title implies, Ben's kidnapping has effectively cast the Cappadoras into the abyss and forced them to learn how to swim.

As stolid husband Pat, who harbors secret resentment toward Beth for losing his son—a factor Stephen Schiff's screenplay adaptation leaves bafflingly underdeveloped—the usually solid Treat Williams gives a performance susceptible to termites. The fault, though, is the screenplay, which doesn't give him much to work with. Pfeiffer, so effective in the first half, is similarly handcuffed in the second.

And the second part should be the most interesting portion, because gentle Ben (played as an older child by Ryan Merriman) is discovered after nearly a decade and reunited with the Cappadoras. But he has grown up as "Sam" in the care of an innocent father (John Kapelos), and understandably rankles at having to leave the family he knows for these strangers with whom he has only a biological affinity. What is a family, after all? "Deep End" raises the question King Solomon strained to answer.

But you rarely feel the pain of the asking. "Deep End" treats the chaos and dread inherent in this horrifying situation with frustrating patness. It fails to connect with the electrifying emotions that convulse Pfeiffer (and us) at first, closing the characters off behind a wall of bland dialogue, and keeping the emotionally brutal mess at a safe distance. Which is exactly the wrong place.

NEWSDAY, 3/12/99, Part II/p. B3, John Anderson

Since this is the time of year when movies are cast out to fend for themselves like unwanted orphans, why not one about an abducted child?

Even coming as it does during the movie industry's equivalent of garbage time, "The Deep End of the Ocean" is one strange bird. Based on a best-selling novel, adapted by the up-and-coming ex-New Yorker writer Stephen Schiff, directed by the estimable Ulu Grosbard and starring the equally estimable Michelle Pfeiffer, the film seems to have all the makings of a Major Movie. And yet, everything about it screams disaffection and abandonment.

Yes, the subject matter is difficult—a family loses its 3-year-old son, whose miraculous reappearance nine years later totally reorders the roles of birth parent and abductor. Someone apparently thought it so difficult that the posters for the movie not only are devoid of information about the movie's plot, they carry a photo of Pfeiffer that's so distractingly airbrushed that people have been breaking into conversation about it at bus stops.

But Pfeiffer the face is fine, as is Pfeiffer the actress. As Beth Cappadora, whose son Ben is stolen at her Milwaukee high-school reunion, Pfeiffer is believable when she's distraught, believable when she's maintaining control, and believable when she tells her in-laws that they shouldn't have bought Ben Christmas presents because he isn't coming home. She's an instigator of nail-biting and a very modulated font of self-pity.

Grosbard begins the film with an atmosphere that can best be described as chirpy: Elmer Bernstein's music suggests suburban complacency of the species Sitcom; yet the entire mood suggests a world poised for disaster (which would be fine if, once disaster arrives, the movie shook off the chirpiness).

But while Grosbard gets a good performance from Pfeiffer and a decent performance from Treat Williams as her near-saintly husband, Pat, the movie has been edited within an inch of its life. Much time and film is devoted to scenes that create atmosphere and embellish character, but little is done about creating a narrative fabric that will hold together. We leapfrog from episode to episode, from Beth's encounter with Milwaukee detective Candy Bliss (Whoopi Goldberg), to several inexplicable encounters with friends, to her return to a photography career, to the family's move to Chicago, to the appearance one day of a neighbor (Ryan Merriman), who happens to be her long-lost son.

Time is a confusing quantity in "The Deep End of the Ocean." Scenes that make no sense are included; scenes that logically should be there aren't. It's hard to believe that Grosbard or Schiff would move with such abruptness through a story that cries out for exposition in so many instances, or that so many useless aerial shots would be in the movie if someone weren't trying to justify their cost by including them.

However, "Deep End of the Ocean" is, if nothing else, educational. You realize while you're watching just what it is that makes a movie fluid and moving, what makes a story cohere and make sense. And you realize that this isn't it.

SIGHT AND SOUND, 8/99, p. 41, Charlotte O'Sullivan

Contented wife, mother and career woman Beth Cappadora takes her three children—baby Kerry, toddler Ben and six-year-old Vincent—to an out-of town high-school reunion. Arriving at the hotel, she goes to reception, leaving Ben in Vincent's care. When she returns, Ben has disappeared. The police investigate but Ben is nowhere to be found. The family returns home. Beth becomes depressed, losing interest in her career as a photographer and arguing incessantly with her husband Pat.

Nine years pass and the Cappadoras move to Chicago. One day a boy comes to mow their lawn, calling himself Sam. Beth is sure it's Ben and begins photographing him. Using the pictures as evidence, she convinces the police of his identity. Beth confronts Sam's adoptive father. It turns out Beth's barren, mentally unstable schoolfriend Cecil Lockhart stole Ben at the reunion and later killed herself. Vincent is hostile to Sam. After a few nights with the Cappadoras, a miserable Sam runs back home. Vincent becomes increasingly rebellious and ends up in prison. Sam pays a visit and the brothers bond. A few days later, Sam returns to the Cappadoras.

Compare and contrast Todd Haynes' *Safe* with *The Deep End of the Ocean* directed by Ulu Grosbard (last film *Georgia*). The titles alone are instructive—the one concise and resonant, the other ungainly and presumptuous. Both are concerned with miserable suburban women unable to cope with 'normal' life. But where *Safe* is a pastiche of the crisis-of-the-week television movie, *Deep End* is an inflated version of it.

Critics have dubbed Michelle Pfeiffer's performance here "unvain," but as in *A Thousand Acres,* her grim ordinariness comes vacuum packed, somehow more plastic than her glamorous turns in other films. But it's the script (based on Jacquelyn Mitchard's bestseller) which is most disappointing. We spend forever gazing at Beth's beautiful drawn face, but never crawl beneath its skin. At one point we learn that Beth has no family—an enticing discovery, given that this is a film all about the importance of family but this goes unexplored.

Beth's emotional present is as inscrutable as her past. Husband Pat wants a perfect, golden family and to be envied (and what is the kidnapping, but the ultimate compliment: I want what you have). But why does Beth take all her kids to the reunion if not to show them off? Unfortunately, her insecurities are not what this film is interested in. Beth's reactions are always understandable (in other words uncontroversial). She's impeccably behaved, never once suspecting any of her schoolfriends of the crime. Her relationship with her best friend consists simply of supportive hugs, ditto her friendship with gratuitously wacky policewoman Candy. This is blandness as a virtue. When Beth begins to take furtive photographs of Sam (who may be her lost son) you wonder in vain if finally a little *Don't Look Now* weirdness is going to be allowed to seep in.

Beth is a woman in a plastic panic bubble, but the film doesn't make us feel that panic so we also can't tell the difference when she emerges from it. Sam tries to escape his 'real' family and Beth supports him, unlike rigid, patriarchal Pat. We're supposed to realise Beth has learned selflessness through her ordeal, but she just seems more of a Stepford wife than ever, the family's blank conscience and anchor. Presenting itself as a feminist, 90s critique of the sunny 50s ideal, *Deep End* merely rams the old messages home: mom, put those kids first; dad, when it comes to the domestic sphere, mom knows best. Meanwhile, to the soupiest of scores, characters meet emotional hurdles with such lines as: "You don't get to be ready for this."

Luckily, this is a film of two halves. The clue comes early on, when we see little Vincent rushing to pinch his baby sister, knowing that her squeal will interrupt his parents' row. Such diagonal abuse blossoms when Ben eventually returns to the family home, with sibling rivalry at last providing a form of envy we can believe in and, more to the point, care about. Ryan Merriman is marvellous as Sam, the golden toddler now tarnished a dull bronze by age. Stolid, diffident, he has none of the charisma of long-limbed Vincent.

What the film captures so well, however is that their roles remain the same—Sam effortlessly (unwillingly) drifting centre stage. You dread the brothers' inevitable bonding scene, but when it comes—with Vincent revealing that at the hotel he told his brother to "get lost"—you can smell the musty grief. We know that Sam is going to forgive him, but thanks to Jonathan Jackson's fine acting, it's not clear that Vincent does. As he receives his absolution, years tumble off his face. Sam, though, looks more wizened than ever. Sam's loss isn't smoothed away. He talks repeatedly of his love for his 'mad' adoptive mother and you can feel her memory winding its way through his bloodstream. Before it all ends in a mushy game of basketball, you can almost believe in the danger of these lives. Todd Haynes, I'm sure, would approve.

TIME, 3/15/99, p. 84, Richard Corliss

Life is a stern professor: It teaches us how to say goodbye. We lose—or simply misplace—our youth, many of our dreams, the bounce in our step, the dewy dependence of our children. We grow, then decay; our kids grow up and grow away. For most of us the process is so gradual that we take it for granted. We accommodate ourselves to loss, as a rehearsal for the ultimate accommodation of dying. But what if you have this good life—the sweet husband, the three kids—and then it disappears from under you, like a magic carpet yanked by a prankster? What if your three-year-old son were kidnapped?

That happens to Beth Cappadora (Michelle Pfeiffer) in *The Deep End of the Ocean*, adapted by Stephen Schiff from Jacquelyn Mitchard's novel. In a crowded hotel lobby, she leaves little Ben in the care of his seven-year-old brother for a few minutes, and when she returns he has wandered off—or fallen off the end of the earth. A kidnapping scenario has the makings of melodrama or piety, but this carefully complex movie, directed by Ulu Grosbard, finds urgency in more ambiguous family vectors.

Beth's husband Pat (Treat Williams) and remaining son Vincent (Cory Buck at seven, Jonathan Jackson at 16) dare to pretend that life goes on. But Beth makes a career of her guilt and grief; she builds a mausoleum for her lost child and moves into it. She sleeps all day and leaves the tending of her infant daughter to the two males in the house. In a nice vignette, young Vincent comes home, sees that his sister is being ignored, picks up her rattles and puts them in the playpen, then walks through the foyer, knocking over a vase that smashes on the floor as he passes. The heart's violence has rarely been dramatized with such telling nonchalance.

This is a ghost story where the ghost comes back to life. For Ben is found, nine years later, and his name is Sam. O.K., he's back—now what? For Sam (Ryan Merriman) was happy with the folks he thought were his parents. And now that he's back "home," getting bear-hugged by strangers, he wants to return to the loving man who adopted him; the boy feels he's been kidnapped twice. But really it's Beth who vanished, from herself and her family. She was the ghost, sleepwalking for years, reminding everyone that the odor of catastrophe can't be Lysoled away. Now she has her boy back. Can she give him away again?

Deep End may remind you of a "quality" TV play of the '50s: it is conscientious, delicately acted, lacking in visual flair. It is so generous to all the characters that it tends to meander. Now it's Beth's story, now Vincent's, now Sam's. It has little interest in villainy: the backstory of the kidnapping takes just moments. But in a time when there are few serious family dramas—and when those few, like *Stepmom*, play it shrill and sticky—the old limitations can look like cardinal virtues.

The entire cast does fine work, but Pfeiffer is a treasure. She calibrates each nuance of loss without seeming calculating. She makes Beth sensible and alive, as understandable as that nice woman next door whose sobs wake you in the night to remind you that we are all one vagrant step from heartbreak.

Also reviewed in:
CHICAGO TRIBUNE, 3/12/99, Friday/p. A, Michael Wilmington
NEW YORK TIMES, 3/12/99, p. E24, Janet Maslin
VARIETY, 3/1-7/99, p. 77, Emanuel Levy
WASHINGTON POST, 3/12/99, p. C1, Stephen Hunter
WASHINGTON POST, 3/12/99, Weekend/p. 42, Desson Howe

DEFYING GRAVITY

A Jour de Fete and Boom Pictures release of a Boom Pictures production. *Producer:* David Clayton Miller and Jack Koll. *Director:* John Keitel. *Screenplay:* John Keitel. *Director of Photography:* Thomas M. Harting. *Editor:* Matthew Yagle. *Music:* Jon T. Howard and Tim Westergren. *Sound:* Darryl Patterson. *Casting:* Patrick Baca. *Production Designer:* Scott McPhail. *Art Director:* Bob Peterson. *Costumes:* Billy R. Miller. *Running time:* 100 minutes. *MPAA Rating:* Not Rated.

CAST: Daniel Chilson (John Griffith); Niklaus Lange (Todd Bentley); Don Handfield (Pete Bradley); Linna Carter (Denetra Washington); Seabass Diamond (Matthew McDougal); Lesley Tesh (Heather); Ryan Tucker (Gary Buchanan); Nicki Lynn (Gretchen); Laura Fox (Mrs. Bradley); Kevin P. Wright (Mr. Bradley).

LOS ANGELES TIMES, 10/15/99, Calendar/p. 16, Kevin Thomas

John Keitel's aptly titled "Defying Gravity" opens with a young man, Griff, waking up and rushing out of an old private home to a nearby fraternity house in an attempt to get into his bed before anybody realizes he hasn't been sleeping there all night. We quickly learn that this happens fairly frequently with Griff and that the bed in that old house belongs not to a coed but a fraternity brother with whom he has been having the most secret of affairs.

Griff (Daniel Chilson) wants it both ways: to pass as straight but also to enjoy a sexual relationship with Pete (Don Handfield). You can understand why readily enough: Griff fits right in with his fraternity brothers, all of whom are good-looking and athletic. Besides, Griff hasn't really accepted that he is gay and falls back on that oldest of consolations: "Maybe it's just a phase."

Pete, however, has progressed considerably further than Griff although he could also pass as straight. He hasn't come out to their fraternity brothers yet but moving out of the frat house is for him a crucial first step in accepting and exploring his sexual orientation. Pete has started frequenting a local gay hangout whereas Griff is singularly uncomfortable about meeting Pete there for coffee.

Despite their mutual attraction and feelings for each other they become increasingly tense with each other, and just when you're wondering how much tension their relationship can sustain Pete becomes the target of a gay bashing so severe that he's been left in a coma from which he might not emerge.

Griff therefore is hit hard himself—by reality. All at once he's got to deal with whether or not to tell the police what he knows of Pete's whereabouts prior to the attack. He's confronted with having to deal with how he really feels about Pete and their relationship, and he's got to face the fact that if he is to be a responsible citizen, that if he cares at all about Pete as a human being, let alone as a lover, he is almost certain to have to come out of the closet in the process.

"Defying Gravity" is a straightforward drama done with a maturity and conviction impressive for a first film. Keitel, who earned his master's degree in cinema at USC (the locale for his film), is especially adept at the key task of depicting Griff, so selflessly portrayed by Chilson, going through the painful process of growing up fast out of necessity. Keitel is also skilled at suggesting fraternity house homophobia as largely—but by no means entirely—a reflexive, unthinking reaction and not necessarily deriving from deeply held anti-gay beliefs. In short, even a severe gay bashing can be a chillingly casual, even random act, and not a carefully planned attack fueled by conscious hate. You could even imagine Pete's attackers considering gay bashing a kind of sport.

Chilson and Bradley are capable and focused as are their colleagues, which include Niklaus Lange, an actor of strong presence who plays Todd, Griffs best friend, a young man who has no trouble accepting Griff. Linna Carter is also impressive as a young black lesbian with whom Griff forms a bond, reaching across race when they discover that they are exactly in the same place, both in need of self-acceptance and overwhelmed with the prospect of coming out.

As traditional in style as "Defying Gravity" is, it can be subtle, as when Todd tells Griff he is so in love with his girlfriend he now sees her instead of himself when he looks in the mirror. When Griff looks in the mirror and still sees himself rather than Pete he tries to tell himself, in a desperate act of self-deception, that this means he's not truly gay. A touch like this lifts "Defying Gravity" above the conventional.

NEW YORK POST, 7/9/99, p. 58, Rod Dreher

The surprisingly sexless gay frat boy melodrama "Defying Gravity" can be summed up in one wonderfully hoot-worthy line from its script: "Are you, like, in love with him, dude?"

Call me naive, but how is it possible that a gay man (writer-director John Keitel) can pen such lame, literal dialogue? The whole picture plays this way, as if it were a Very Special Episode of some barfly TV series. As a gay friend of mine reassures me, "Bad writers come in all colors of the rainbow."

So do bad actors, which brings us to the handsome but extremely limited lead, Daniel Chilson, who is stiff in all the wrong ways. He's cast as Griff, the film's All-American, sexually conflicted protagonist, who is secretly exploring his Greek identity with Pete (Don Handfield), a frat brother who came out of the closet and left the animal house.

Pete wants Griff to be more honest about himself and their romantic relationship. Griff just wants to have sex while leading an outwardly heterosexual life on campus. When Pete is brutally gay-bashed, Griff confronts the emotional consequences of lying to himself and everybody else.

There's never the slightest doubt as to how Griff will resolve his dilemma in this tension-free pic ("Defying Gravity" is very much in favor of uplift). Diversity raises its gratuitous head when whitebread Griff becomes pals with a lesbian-ish African-American woman (Linna Carter), who exists just to show how sensitive the frat lug is becoming.

The material is potentially rich with psychological turmoil, which Keitel has no idea how to dramatize. Griff is trying to figure out what it means to be masculine, and to count the cost of believing one thing but living another. He's coming to terms with the prospect of exile from his fraternity tribe if he follows his heart, and facing his fear that identifying as gay will press him into a dismaying conformity.

Interesting stuff, but Keitel can't, or won't, write thoughtful dialogue exploring these areas and revealing character.

Instead, he gives us long stretches of the Griffster staring soulfully and pensively into space, while sensitive music mewls in the background.

You know he's just sitting there thinking, like "South Park's" Kyle and Cartman, "What would Brian Boitano do?"—but this is a movie, not a novel, so the least the hunky dolt could do is favor us with a song.

VILLAGE VOICE, 7/13/99, p. 60, Dennis Lim

Denying Reality, more like. John Keitel's first feature is impossibly naive, even as smoothed-over coming-out tales go, and its sole, cursory twist—a frat-house setting—registers mainly as an autobiographical indulgence. Frat boy Griff has the hots for Pete, who has recently left the house for a more liberating lifestyle off campus. But Pete, newly sensitive homosexual, wants a relationship, while Griff, big-time closet case, just wants to fuck. When Pete is gay-bashed into a coma, Griff, a possible witness, risks outing himself if he comes forward. This half-assed melodramatic contrivance is the crux of the film, which stalls periodically even though its foregone conclusion is never less than in plain sight.

The actors—blow-dried, blandly attractive, barely distinguishable—deliver their starchy lines with vacant earnestness, and the overall effect is strongly evocative of porn with the sex edited out. Keitel's screenplay is certainly thinly plotted enough to qualify. Griff, it turns out, has little cause for worry. He finds a confidante in a female classmate who also happens to be sexually confused, and just about everyone, including his superstraight-jock best friend, is in the end fabulously supportive—not, I suspect, to demonstrate that these are indeed enlightened times we live in but because any serious signs of conflict or emotional distress would prove too much of a strain on the pitifully two-dimensional script and actors.

Also reviewed in:
NEW YORK TIMES, 7/9/99, p. E8, Lawrence Van Gelder
VARIETY, 6/23-29/97, p. 97, Emanuel Levy

DESERT BLUE

A Samuel Goldwyn Films release of an Ignite Entertainment production. *Executive Producer:* Leanna Creel, Marc Butan, and Kip Hagopian. *Producer:* Andrea Sperling, Nadia Leonelli, and Michael Burns. *Director:* Morgan J. Freeman. *Screenplay:* Morgan J. Freeman. *Director of Photography:* Enrique Chediak. *Editor:* Sabine Hoffman. *Music:* Vytas Nagisetty. *Sound:* Margaret Crimmins and Paul D. Hsu. *Casting:* Susan Shopmaker. *Production Designer:* David Doernberg. *Art Director:* Amy Beth Silver. *Costumes:* Trish Summerville. *Running time:* 87 minutes. *MPAA Rating:* R.

CAST: Casey Affleck (Pete); Sara Gilbert (Sandy); Ethan Suplee (Cale); Lucinda Jenney (Caroline); Brendan Sexton III (Blue); Kate Hudson (Skye); John Heard (Lance); Christina Ricci (Ely); Peter Sarsgaard (Billy); Sara Gilbert (Sandy); Isidra Vega (Haley); Renee Rivera (Dr. Gordon); Lee Holmes (Deputy Keeler); Jerry Agee (Insurance Agent); Daniel von Bargen (Sheriff Jackson); Richmond Arquette (Truck Driver); Michael Ironside (Agent Bellows); Nate Moore (Agent Red); Ntare Mwine (Agent Green); Aunjanue Ellis (Agent Summers).

LOS ANGELES TIMES, 6/18/99, Calendar/p. 8, John Anderson

[The following review by John Anderson appeared in a slightly different form in **NEWSDAY, 6/4/99, Part II/p. B6.]**

Like "Peanuts" with hormones, the shipwrecked slackers of "Desert Blue" are a universe unto themselves. There are genuine adults in the general vicinity, but their influence is as marginal as everything else in a town where the main attractions are a 60-foot ice cream cone and an unfinished water park waiting for the water.

The follow-up to his 1997 festival favorite, "Hurricane Streets," "Blue" marks a leap forward for director Morgan J. Freeman. He may not have had much of a budget, but he has a terrific young cast and an apparent gift for letting them relax and do their best work.

Brendan Sexton III, who played the pre-pubescent would-be rapist in "Welcome to the Dollhouse," is a convincing lost boy as Blue, whose father's death has left him at loose ends; Christina Ricci has seldom been better than she is as Ely, who breaks up the boredom of Baxter, Calif., (alleged population: 89) by blowing things up with mail-order explosives. Casey Affleck has the easy role as wise guy Pete, but both Isidra Vega ("Hurricane") and Ethan Suplee (the hulking neo-Nazi of "American History X") are very genuine, real without being cloying, and this in a story that sneers at reality every chance it gets.

What's so seductive about "Desert Blue" is just how casually and economically Freeman: (a) establishes his back story and his characters and (b) passes off the most absurdist elements of his plot without our even noticing we're being had.

His convergence of events is a miracle of suspended disbelief. At the moment that haughty sitcom actress Skye (the estimable Kate Hudson) is pulling through town with her father, Lance (John Heard)—a professor of cultural studies and roadside attractions who specifically wants to see the ice cream cone—a truck carrying the secret ingredient for the villainous Empire Cola (which stole the water from Baxter's water park) crashes outside of town. When the driver unexpectedly dies, the spill becomes a possible environmental disaster and everyone in town is quarantined.

What Alfred Hitchcock used to call the MacGuffin, the ultimately inconsequential thing that jump-starts a story, runs fairly amok in "Desert Blue," which has as many MacGuffins as Baxter has people. Would Skye even be with her father, starlet that she is? Probably not, but we buy it anyway. Would Empire Cola need to receive or send a truckload of Secret Ingredient when its major plant is right there in Baxter? Unlikely. Who cares?

And would the closing off of the town really matter to anyone, when no one's ever felt the need to leave before? Nah. But then, Freeman isn't making one of those blockbuster sci-fi movies where everything is supposed to make sense. Instead, he's really depicting a kind of teenage terrarium in which his well-defined kids are bored (as they are everywhere) and looking for love (ditto) and struggling to adjust (you get the point).

Unlike "Notting Hill's" faux celebrity romance, you can believe the Skye-Blue match (that no one in Baxter has cable, of course, diminishes Skye's wattage a bit) as well as the eventual bonding that takes place between her and the other kids, because Freeman has written it with real humans in mind.

It's a small story, perhaps even an ephemeral movie, but "Desert Blue" also has a novelistic capacity for character and setting, without either the maudlin sentimentality or gratuitous vulgarity of most teen-oriented movies. It's got heart, in other words, although if you called it a fairy tale, it would probably be embarrassed.

NEW YORK POST, 6/4/99, p. 48, Jonathan Foreman

"Desert Blue" is a sweet-natured, low-budget ensemble romance blessed by a fine young cast but cursed with a terrible, boring beginning.

Fortunately, just when you've given up on it as another self-indulgent hipster comedy set in an oh-so-wacky small desert town (populated by the usual quirky folk with secrets), it turns into a genuinely charming and engaging little movie.

Into Baxter, Calif, pop. 87 (though it seems less), drives a shaggy professor of small-town kitsch (John Heard) and his gorgeous but snotty TV-star daughter, Skye (Kate Hudson).

She hates everything about Baxter; dad loves the place for its giant ice-cream cone and abandoned waterpark.

They encounter the local group of all-terrain-vehicle-driving teen-agers at the town's otherwise empty diner. There is: sweet Blue (Sexton), who immediately takes a shine to Skye; tiresome Pete (Casey Affleck); Ely (Christina Ricci), who is obsessed with explosives; fat boy Cale (Ethan Suplee), who dreams of being a deputy sheriff and is attracted to Haley (Isidra Vega), the daughter of the Indian 7-11 owner; and ice-cream salesgirl Sandy (Sarah Gilbert).

Almost immediately, a tanker carrying the foul-smelling secret ingredient of a locally produced cola overturns on the highway and the driver dies after being contaminated by the contents. The FBI and the EPA quarantine the town, so Skye and her dad are stuck until the all-clear is given.

Skye ends up hanging out with the bored teens in the waterless ocean park. And while she learns to get over herself, her presence—combined with impending doom—rekindles everyone's romantic urges.

It may be hard to go wrong with this cast, but Freeman gets good performances from almost everyone. Ricci (in trademark gothic eye makeup) redeems herself after the awful "200 Cigarettes." And lovely Hudson, who had the misfortune to debut in the same disaster, is a star in the making.

It's a shame that despite a facility for snappy one-liners and genuinely appealing characters, director Morgan J. Freeman's writing is so uneven. The movie staggers under chunks of exposition and trips over some grotesque improbabilities.

Some of the wackiness, such as the game of baseball with oranges, is just too cutesy. And when Freeman moves from the personal to the political, you get what might just pass for wit and wisdom in junior high: stuff like Skye's tired "shoot a cop; save a donut" joke about the LAPD. And Ely's enthusiasm for making pipe-bombs may strike post-Littleton audiences as less than hilarious.

"Desert Blue" ends too suddenly—as if it were the pilot for a cool new series on the WB Network. But by then you really do want to know what happens to the characters next, and that's all too rare in this genre.

VILLAGE VOICE, 6/15/99, p. 150, Justine Elias

Baxter, California, population 89, is a desert town with only one landmark: a giant ice cream cone. When a truck carrying possibly hazardous materials is wrecked on the highway, and the town is sealed off by federal officials, residents seem almost relieved to have something to talk about. For once, the town appears poised to become a hotbed of activity, but it never happens. *Desert Blue,* the second feature from *Hurricane Streets* writer-director Morgan J. Freeman, is as sleepy as its lonely setting. Everyone in the film is smothered by the local ennui: one FBI agent barely raises an eyebrow when Christina Ricci's Unabomber-in-training blows up some government property. There are a few sharply observed scenes involving the local kids, played by Brendan Sexton III, Casey Affleck, Isidra Vega, and Ethan Suplee. When one gets into an accident, his friends gather at his bedside to console him—and to sample his prescription painkillers. By and large, though, *Desert Blue* is done in by its too-accurate portrayal of listlessness, and the movie doesn't invite much interest beyond its indie all-star cast.

Also reviewed in:
CHICAGO TRIBUNE, 9/10/99, Friday/p. B, Monica Eng
NEW YORK TIMES, 6/4/99, p. E19, Lawrence Van Gelder
VARIETY, 9/21-27/98, p. 109, Glenn Lovell

DETROIT ROCK CITY

A New Line Cinema release of a Takoma Entertainment/Base-12 Productions/KissNation production. *Executive Producer:* Michael De Luca and Brian Witten. *Producer:* Gene Simmons, Barry Levine, and Kathleen Haase. *Director:* Adam Rifkin. *Screenplay:* Carl V. Dupré. *Director of Photgraphy:* John R. Leonetti. *Editor:* Mark Goldblatt and Peter Schink. *Music:* J. Peter Robinson. *Music Editor:* Lisé Richardson. *Sound:* Steve Aaron and (music) Robert Fernandez. *Sound Editor:* Frank Gaete. *Casting:* Valerie McCaffrey. *Production Designer:* Steve Hardie. *Art Director:* Lucinda Zak. *Set Decorator:* Cal Loucks. *Set Dresser:* Greg Pelchat. *Special Effects:* Michael Kavanagh. *Costumes:* Rosanna Norton. *Make-up:* Geralyn Wraith. *Stunt Coordinator:* Alison Reid. *Running time:* 100 minutes. *MPAA Rating:* R.

CAST: Giuseppe Andrews (Lex); James De Bello (Trip); Edward Furlong (Hawk); Sam Huntington (Jam); Lin Shaye (Mrs. Bruce); Melanie Lynskey (Beth); Natasha Lyonne (Christine); Miles Dougal (Elvis); Nick Scotti (Kenny); Emmanuelle Chriqui (Barbara); David Quane (Bobby); Rodger Barton (Mr. Bumsteen); Kathryn Haggis (Mrs. Bumsteen); David Gardner (Priest); Shannon Tweed (Amanda Finch); Kristin Booth (Cashier); Joe Flaherty (Father McNulty); Cody Jones (Little Kid); Matt Taylor (Chongo); Joan Heney (Study Hall Teacher); Rob Smith (Simple Simon); Aaron Berg (Bartender); Paul Brogren (Roadie #1); Allan Clow (Man with Coat); Chris Benson (Mr. Johansen); Colleen Williams (Nun); Richard Hillman (Scalper); Stephen Joffe (Six Year Old #1); Ryan Letriard (Six Year Old #2); Joseph Haase (Security Guard); Ron Jeremy Hyatt (MC); Kevin Corrigan (Beefy Jerk #1); Steve Schirripa (Beefy Jerk #2); Lindy Booth (Girl #1); Christina Sicoli (Foxy Girl); Michael Barry (Nerd); Vic Rigler (Pizza Boy); Eileen Flood (Female Parishioner); Pamela Bowen (Matmok Lieutenant); Johnie Chase (Cop #1); Julian Richings (Ticket Taker); Gene Simmons, Paul Stanley, Ace Frehley, and Peter Criss (Kiss); Shane Daly and Noah Danby (Chongo's Friend); Christopher Lee Clements (Stripper #1); Jonathan Cuthill (Stripper #2); Neno Vojic (Stripper #3); Rich Coulson (Stripper #4); Michael Kremko (Stripper #5); Derek De Luis (Stripper #6); Tara Elliot (Babe #2); Elissa Bradley (Babe #3); Cherry Flatley (Babe #4); Leilene Onrade (Babe #5); Hazel K. Anderson (Babe #6); Jessica Kleiner (Babe #7); Nadia Dalchand (Babe #8); Kerri Michalica (Babe #9); Kerry Robinson (Babe #10); Dino M. Sicoli (Really Lucky Hot Tub Dude).

LOS ANGELES TIMES, 8/13/99, Calendar/p. 6, Kenneth Turan

[*The following review by Kenneth Turan appeared in a slightly different form in*
NEWSDAY, 8/13/99, Part II/p. B11.]

It would be a comfort of sorts to say that "Detroit Rock City" is a new low in the current spate of gross-out teen comedies, but even that meager satisfaction is denied us. Rather the depressing truth is that this aggressively stupid film is merely business as usual, a compendium of all the current obsessions and fixations that make so many of these films such unhappy experiences.

The story of four hormonally challenged Cleveland teenagers who more or less worship KISS and would do anything to get to that rock group's 1978 concert in nearby Detroit's Cobo Hall, "Detroit Rock City" is chock-a-block with crude, humiliating sex and bodily function jokes. If "American Pie" is an example of how to do a raunchy coming-of-age story right, this contemptuous, mean-spirited piece of business—which finds humor in using someone's head to clean a pizza off a car windshield—shows how to do it wrong.

The four guys are high school seniors who play in a KISS knockoff group called Mystery and call each other by their band nicknames: Hawk (Edward Furlong), Lex (Giuseppe Andrews), Trip (James DeBello) and Jam (Sam Huntington).

As much as these guys idolize KISS, that's how much Jam's mother, Mrs. Bruce ("Something About Mary's" Lin Shaye), can't abide the group. Horribly caricatured as a devout Catholic who reads Erma Bombeck and listens to the Carpenters, Mrs. Bruce considers KISS (no kidding) "the devil's music" and says the letters stand for Knights In Satan's Service.

Mrs. Bruce's objections are only one of the obstacles the guys have to face in their quest to get to Detroit. Tickets to the event appear and then disappear like mirages in the desert during the course of the film, part of which deals with the extreme lengths the gang will go to get inside the arena.

In fact, one of the most tiresome things about "Detroit Rock City" (produced by KISSer Gene Simmons and featuring a cameo by the band) is having to listen to an endless stream of pro-KISS propaganda that lauds this group as the most awesome band ever, even though most serious rock people didn't pay any more attention to them than, well, the Carpenters.

And that's not even the most tiresome part of Carl V. Dupre's unendingly banal script. In fact, it's hard to pinpoint its worst aspect: its trite dialogue, its opportunities for thuddingly dull physical humor, its penchant for brainless coincidences or its occasional embarrassing attempts at serious speeches. Let's call it a dead heat.

First-time director Adam Rifkin (he previously wrote "Mouse Hunt" and "Small Soldiers") is energetic enough but nothing can make us care the slightest bit about these guys, accurately described by someone else in the film as "total morons" and not any more appealing or intelligent than the film's nominal villains.

As if to prove the point, the quartet actually spends some time physically beating each other up. They've been such bone-headed irritants, both individually and as a group, it actually feels like poetic justice to see them flail away at one another. It's just too bad they couldn't have done it earlier and knocked themselves and this film into well-deserved states of complete unconsciousness.

NEW YORK POST, 8/13/99, p. 63, Rod Dreher

We need a great movie about the sheer brainless joy of being a teenager so in love with a rock band you'd do anything to see them. After "Detroit Rock City," we still need that movie.

It's another lousy entry in this summer's moron-a-thon celebrating teenage-male cloddishness. And this tribute to the devotion KISS fans have to the massively untalented rock band doesn't even have the wit to offer guilty pleasure, however crude. It's loud, lame and painfully obvious, so at least it's true to KISS's music.

"Detroit Rock City" is about four pimple-popping mouth-breathers from Cleveland—Hawk (Edward Furlong), Trip (James DeBello), Lex (Giuseppe Andrews) and Jam (Sam Huntington)—who play in a KISS tribute band. The year is 1978, and getting to the upcoming KISS concert in Detroit is a grail quest for these guys.

The fire-breathing dragon out to thwart them? Mrs. Bruce (Lin Shaye), Jam's mom, a hysterically devout Roman Catholic and bug-eyed enemy of KISS. Propagating an urban legend of the era, Mrs. Bruce swears the group's name is an acronym for "Knights in Satan's Service."

Lord knows we don't lack for religious nuts who see the devil behind every minor chord banged out on a Stratocaster. But this movie's extreme caricature of Catholicism is hateful.

The film suggests that Mrs. Bruce—who chain-smokes, so you know she's evil—is a hypocrite whose real problem is that she's dying to get laid by a priest. Jam's triumphal moment of rebellion is preceded by resisting a pervert priest and losing his virginity to a female classmate in the confessional.

If Judaism or Islam were treated this way, "Detroit Rock City" would be condemned for bigotry.

As it is, the movie should be condemned for idiocy. The boys stop at nothing to get to the KISS show and drag us through a series of badly written (by Carl V. Dupre) scenario involving farting, vomiting, vulgar sex jokes and dopey attempts at physical humor.

The film reaches its comic nadir when a drunk Furlong is cajoled into doing a striptease on stage, culminating in a festival you might call Upchuckapalooza. Ha.

"Detroit Rock City" is alternately feeble and appalling, an inadvertent parody of teen rebellion (though a tribute to how ingeniously KISS has exploited it). But the picture turns truly pathetic in the grand finale, when the actual members of KISS give a performance as their 1978 selves.

News flash: They're old and flabby, and no amount of ridiculous stage makeup and strategically chosen camera angles can hide that unfortunate fact. Let's just say that "Detroit Rock City" is the movie KISS fans deserve.

SIGHT AND SOUND, 11/99, p. 42, Paul Elliott

1978. Four Midwestern high-school students—Lex, Trip, Hawk and Jam have tickets to see their favourite band Kiss in concert in Detroit. The boys' excitement turns to horror when Jam's mother burns the tickets in the belief that Kiss' music is inspiring delinquency in her son. Jam is sent to a church school, but his friends steal Lex's mother's car and effect Lam's escape by feeding a drug-laced pizza to the school's principal. Trip, meanwhile, wins four more tickets in a radio phone-in, but on arrival in Detroit discovers the tickets have been awarded to another caller because Trip hung up before leaving his name.

The quartet separate to try their luck at finding yet more tickets. Their ensuing adventures lead both Hawk and Jam to lose their virginity, the latter in a church confessional box, the former to an older woman whom Jam meets in a bar after trying to win a strip contest. After a fruitless quest, the four friends resort to beating one another up in order to trick concert stewards into believing they have been mugged and had their tickets stolen.

As they arrive at the venue, four hoodlums who have extorted money from Trip also turn up. Trip convinces the stewards that these are his attackers. The thugs are ejected and their tickets given to Trip and his buddies. At last, they see Kiss live on stage.

Combining the 70s period detail of Paul Thomas Anderson *Boogie Nights* with the timeless appeal of a teenage-gang adventure tale, *Detroit Rock City* is a rock-'n-roll comedy high on energy, yet—strangely for a film centred on teenage friendship—low on warmth. Director Adam Rifkin (who wrote *Mousehunt*) likens his film to classic teen dramas *American Graffiti* (1973) and *Rock 'N' Roll High School* (1979), but at its most childish *Detroit Rock City* is more akin to the low farce of the notorious Porky's series, albeit with a vintage rock soundtrack.

Detroit Rock City benefits from a painstaking attention to detail. Rifkin himself was a Kiss fan growing up in 70s Midwestern America, and with Kiss bassist Gene Simmons acting as co-producer, the era's celebratory rock culture is expertly recreated, with lots of knowing in-jokes. Veteran Kiss fans will smile, for instance, when the boys assure a disco fan: "One thing Kiss will never do is make a bullshit disco record." In fact, they made just such a record in 1979, just a year after this film's date.

Rifkin also puts his rock soundtrack to good use. Alongside a slew of classic Kiss songs are period pieces from other rock giants of the late 70s. Many of the tracks are used to comedic effect, if a little literally: when Jam is busted out of reform school, Thin Lizzy's "jailbreak" accompanies the escape; later, Jam tells his pious mother to go to hell to the strains of Van Halen's "Running with the Devil".

But *Detroit Rock City* comes apart when it comes to creating characters with anything more than the emotional depth of their 90s cartoon counterparts Beavis and Butt-head. There's also an unpleasantly cruel streak underlying much of the teenagers' behaviour in Detroit. Trip, the token pot enthusiast, might end the film as an accidental hero, having foiled a convenience-store heist, but earlier he threatens to beat up a prepubescent Kiss fan if the kid refuses to hand over his ticket. Later the four friends beat a lone aggressor with belts and chains in a vicious revenge attack before attempting to coerce their victim's date into performing sex acts in return for a ride into Detroit.

Kiss themselves appear towards the end of the film. They give a spirited, fittingly climactic performance in an otherwise predictable coming-of-age teen movie (during the course of their night in Detroit Hawk and Jam both lose their virginity, the latter to school sweetheart Beth—also the name of Kiss' biggest love song).

It's essentially a guest appearance by the veteran rockers—no amount of make-up or stage pyrotechnics can hide their ages—and a far cry from their more substantial film effort, *Kiss Meets the Phantom of the Park* (1978). That exercise in high kitsch, in which the group battled a mad scientist in a fairground to hugely comic effect, much of it unintentional, has now acquired a cult status among Kiss fans. Little more than another hard sell for the most astutely marketed rock band of the past 30 years, *Detroit Rock City* is neither good nor bad enough to make such a lasting impression.

VILLAGE VOICE, 8/17/99, p. 59, Gary Dauphin

There's an awful lot of rocking out going on in *Detroit Rock City*, but then rocking out is this occasionally clever but lifeless movie's reason for being. Set in the Carter-era flatlands of Michigan, *City* follows four buds (Edward Furlong, Sam Huntington, James DeBello, and Giuseppe Andrews) on a borderline-epic quest to (finally) attend their grail-like show of shows, a Kiss concert in Detroit. Their obstacles: Mom, their own stupidity (or at least the stupidity of requisite stoner DeBello), and the inevitable calamities that befall those under 18 who borrow their parents' Volvo.

Things go awry for the quartet when one of their hyper-Catholic mothers discovers the tickets and sets them ablaze. The boys are bummed, but after the deus ex machina of a call-in radio promotion, they're back on course, hightailing it for Detroit in the aforementioned Volvo. Along the way they meet a saucily game disco diva (Natasha Lyonne, who, typically, has a real mouth on her) and lose the car and the second set of tickets. They eventually sneak into the show, but first they get laid, foil a convenience store robbery, and, in the case of nominal leader Furlong, dance in a Chippendales-style amateur revue. (His is by far the most random of the guys' solo adventures, but it's also the most engaging by virtue of being so damned bananas.)

Cheerfully bombastic, *City* has its share of smart-stupid jokes and an unexpectedly wry texture, from the ongoing disco vs. rock squabbles to the lightly malevolent twists Carl Dupre's script takes as the ticket situation becomes increasingly dire. Still, there's something tiring about watching the boys jump through hoops that are clearly destined to evaporate exactly five minutes before show time. It wouldn't have been very fair to keep the kids out of the arena of their dreams, but it would have definitely made *Detroit Rock City* a better movie.

Also reviewed in:
CHICAGO TRIBUNE, 8/13/99, Friday/p. A, Mark Caro
NEW YORK TIMES, 8/13/99, p. E24, Janet Maslin
VARIETY, 8/9-15/99, p. 39, Dennis Harvey

DEUCE BIGALOW: MALE GIGOLO

A Touchstone Pictures release of a Happy Madison production in association with Out of the Blue Entertainment. *Executive Producer:* Adam Sandler and Jack Giarraputo. *Producer:* Sid Ganis and Barry Bernardi. *Director:* Mike Mitchell. *Screenplay:* Harris Goldberg and Rob Schneider. *Director of Photography:* Peter Lyons Collister. *Editor:* George Bowers and Lawrence Jordan. *Music:* Teddy Castellucci. *Music Editor:* Steve Lotwis and Stuart Grusin. *Choreographer:* Adam M. Shankman. *Sound:* David Kelson. *Sound Editor:* Elmo Weber and Gary S. Gerlich. *Casting:* Marcia Ross, Donna Morong, and Gail Goldberg. *Production Designer:* Alan Au. *Art Director:* Domenic Silvestri. *Set Decorator:* F. Beauchamp Hebb. *Special Effects:* David Blitstein. *Visual Effects:* John Van Vliet. *Costumes:* Molly Maginnis. *Make-up:* Jackie Dobbie. *Stunt Coordinator:* Gregg Smrz. *Running time:* 84 minutes. *MPAA Rating:* R.

CAST: Rob Schneider (Deuce Bigalow); William Forsythe (Detective Chuck Fowler); Eddie Griffin (T.J. Hicks); Arija Bareikis (Kate); Oded Fehr (Antoine Laconte); Gail O'Grady (Claire); Richard Riehle (Bob Bigalow); Jacqueline Obradors (Elaine Fowler); Big Boy (Jabba Lady); Amy Poehler (Ruth); Dina Platias (Bergita); Torsten Voges (Tina); Deborah Lemen (Carol); Bree Turner (Allison); Andrew Shaifer (Neil); Allen Covert (Restaurant Manager); Elle Tanner Schneider (Girl of America); Barry Cutler (Dr. Rosenblatt); Jacqueline Titone (Sally); Karlee Holden (Megan); Chloé Hult (Amber); Natalie Garner (Natalie); Robb Skyler (District Attorney); Jason Wall (Bailiff); John Harrington Bland (Patient); Caroline Ambrose (Mother); Louise Rapport (Old Woman in Line); Pilar Schneider (Old Lady at Restaurant); Shain Holden (Waiter at Pool); Gabrielle Tuite (Beautiful Porsche Woman); Charlie Curtis (Half Dressed Girl); Thomas Bellin (Elderly Man in Car); Flora Burke (Elderly Woman in Car).

LOS ANGELES TIMES, 12/10/99, Calendar/p. 10, Gene Seymour

[The following review by Gene Seymour appeared in a slightly different form in **NEWSDAY, 12/10/99, Part II/p. B8.]**

Only the innate sweetness of both its lead character and its base premise keeps you from wanting to slap "Deuce Bigalow: Male Gigolo" upside its mangy, empty head.

As "doofus comedies" go, it falls short of the Farrelly brothers' "Dumb & Dumber" and (even!) "Kingpin," but it's several notches above such woeful misfires as "Lost and Found." At least some of the giggles in "Deuce" are honestly earned—even if it takes a while for you to remember what, exactly, you found funny. And why.

From the time Deuce Bigalow (Rob Schneider) is shown cleaning an aquarium tank in the buff in front of startled visitors, you know you're in for the obvious as far as funny stuff goes. Bigalow is an amiable jerk with no girlfriend, no prospects and no hope of any life beyond scraping algae off glass surfaces and rescuing goldfish from toilet bowls.

Then one extraordinary day, Deuce is asked to house-sit for a dark and dangerous-looking male prostitute named Antoine (Oded Fehr), whose expensive fish need some medical care. How bad could living on the Malibu beach be? Not bad at all, until Deuce accidentally busts Antoine's fish tank and turns his fabulous digs into a science project.

Now, Deuce has three weeks to make everything right before Antoine comes home. Where's he going to get the scratch to fix the tank? A phone call from one of Antoine's clients provides a way out and before you can sing along with the first line of Blondie's "Call Me," Deuce's professional life makes an emergency turn toward the gigolo's trade.

From here, the plot takes on a handful of semipredictable set pieces as T.J. Hicks (Eddie Griffin, who does well in the kind of role you'd always hoped he'd avoid), Antoine's pimp, sets Deuce up with women who are too tall, too heavy, carry sleep disorders or are given to venomous outbursts. Yet, despite the suspicions of a crazed LAPD detective (William Forsythe), Deuce doesn't actually do anything with them except tend to their insecurities the way he tends to sick fish. Only Kate (Arija Bareikis), who seems perfectly normal, makes him want to do more than "just talk."

Though the limits of "bathroom humor" are redefined to excessive degrees in "Deuce Bigalow," you can't be too salty with a movie targeted for the adolescent mind that encourages adolescents to respect the dignity of all persons, even the height- and weight-challenged. And Schneider does befuddlement so well that you almost wish he were in a better movie. But if "Deuce" were a better movie, would its, um, lessons be lost on the doofuses it means to reach? There's a dilemma worth chewing your cud over.

NEW YORK POST, 12/10/99, p. 54, Jonathan Foreman

Why they called this movie "Deuce Bigalow: Male Gigolo" is slightly mysterious. After all, there's no such thing as a *female* gigolo (and the term preferred by the script is "man-whore.")

But it's the kind of carelessness you'd expect from an inconsistently funny film that draws heavily and obviously on recent successful low-brow comedies like "There's Something About Mary" and "Austin Powers."

There are poop jokes, penis jokes and some daring new variations on the cripple jokes pioneered by the Farrelley brothers' "Mary" masterpiece.

It's not to say that the adolescent humor isn't funny; some of it is hilarious. It's just that this movie lacks the overarching comic sensibility that made "Mary" and even Adam Sandler comedies like "Happy Gilmore" and "The Waterboy" so satisfying.

For example, there are two visual jokes that spoof "The Matrix." They work just fine, but they don't sit well amid all the gross-out humor.

Deuce Bigalow (Rob Schneider) is a slobbish but decent fish-tank cleaner whose life is transformed when he's asked by one of his clients, a sinister male escort named Antoine (Oded Fehr) to look after his huge Malibu bachelor pad while he goes off to Europe for three weeks.

When Deuce accidentally smashes a $6,000 fish tank, he remembers that Antoine promised to kill him if anything went wrong. He's at a loss as to what to do about the tank when one of Antoine's clients calls to arrange an appointment.

In desperation, Deuce decides to substitute for his employer and is soon attempting to parlay his extremely limited charms into a new career. He's helped by T.J. (Eddie Griffin), a pimp with odd notions of Jacuzzi hygiene and a knack for inventing fresh slang for a new kind of prostitution.

Deuce discovers an odd ability to please a variety of freakishly afflicted clients, just as he comes to the attention of a demented, sexually insecure vice cop (William Forsythe) and meets the truly lovable Kate (Arija Barekis).

"Saturday Night Live", alumnus Schneider has no problem playing this kind of lovable doofus, and it's easy to foresee him making a lucrative career out it.

SIGHT AND SOUND, 6/00, p. 38, Keith Perry

California, the present. Aquarium-cleaner Deuce Bigalow is fired from his regular job and starts working for gigolo Antoine Laconte. When Antoine goes away on business, Deuce accidentally wrecks the house. Desperate for money, Deuce reluctantly becomes a gigolo. His pimp, T.J., gives him the most difficult clients and warns against falling in love. Deuce does not have sex with any of the women, but does fall for Kate, who believes Deuce to be a blind date. Deuce refrains from telling Kate his profession.

Detective Fowler, who is pursuing Antoine, threatens Deuce with prison. Fowler confesses to Deuce that his wife is one of Antoine's clients. Deuce saves the couple's marriage and quits prostitution. When Kate learns the truth about their initial meeting, she leaves him. Deuce is arrested, but his clients testify no sex occurred. Deuce and Kate reunite. With his new friends, Deuce repairs Antoine's flat; when Antoine discovers what went on he becomes violent. A fight ensues and Fowler arrests Antoine.

Hollywood's fascination with the oldest profession continues apace. *Deuce Bigalow: Male Gigolo,* produced by Disney's Touchstone studios, must be one of the first to feature no transactional sex whatsoever. The film perversely uses the milieu of hookers and pimps to press home the standard Disney message that everyone has their own special place in the world. When Deuce becomes a low-rent gigolo, his pimp T.J. gives him the most troublesome clients, including an obese woman, a giantess with a glandular disorder and a narcoleptic. These women may repel Deuce, but he offers them all compassionately happy alternatives to loveless sex. For example, provided with the shy Ruth who has Tourette's Syndrome, Deuce takes her to a baseball game, where her insults become a rallying cry for the crowd.

As if to answer the question of why the disabled should not be entitled to sexual satisfaction, the film-makers give Deuce's girlfriend Kate a false leg, revealed in a scene that lampoons *The Crying Game.* Given Hollywood's regrettable tendency for patronising minorities, it's almost refreshing to see Kate's blind flatmate, Bergita, be such an incompetent. She seems a sop to all those resourceful blind loners served up over the decades to undermine assumed audience prejudice. Ultimately, everyone in this film has problems with their body, except Antoine and a woman who works in Deuce's local pet shop—both of whom are depicted as beyond the reach of ordinary mortals. Physical perfection, the film maintains, goes hand in hand with unavailability.

Deuce is content to be an amalgam of its superior predecessors. The prostitution-being-used-to-pay-for-damaged-property set-up is lifted from *Risky Business,* while there is a twist along the lines of *Midnight Cowboy* (1969) in making the naive male lead a hooker rather than the pimp. (The burst of Blondie's 'Call Me' on the soundtrack refers directly to *American Gigolo,* and is used to underscore how Deuce's feeble posing falls short of Richard Gere's narcissistic routines in that film.)

Rob Schneider has a face doomed to sit atop a dirty vest and baggy shorts; he's perfect as Deuce, the unshaven cherub. It is a shame, however, to see William Forsythe—one of the best character actors around—slumming it in the role of Detective Fowler, whose main concern is the girth of his member. Debut-feature director Mike Mitchell keeps the proceedings mercifully brisk. With comedian Adam Sandler as executive producer, there's a slew of scatological jokes, but these don't conceal the script's moments of insight when it comes to money, sex and work. Deuce is feminised by his transformation into a male prostitute—a process reflected in his coiffure and depilatiod at a beauty salon. Expanding on a theme *The Full Monty* touched on, *Deuce* portrays how a disenfranchised man's attempt to reassert himself through commodified sex leads to further emasculation. T.J.'s jargon picks up on this: Deuce has become a "he-bitch", and his penis is now a "mangina" or a "he-pussy", while T.J. himself is a "male madam". Following such lamentable homegrown films as *Love, Honour and Obey, Deuce Bigalow* is another reminder that, despite its crassness and questionable taste, a bad US comedy is still preferable to a bad British one.

Also reviewed in:
CHICAGO TRIBUNE, 12/10/99, Friday/p. F, John Petrakis
NEW YORK TIMES, 12/10/99, p. E36, Lawrence Van Gelder
VARIETY, 12/13-19/99, p. 110, Robert Koehler
WASHINGTON POST, 12/10/99, Weekend/p. 45, Michael O'Sullivan

DEVIL'S ISLAND

An Artistic License Films release of an Icelandic Film Corporation/Peter Rommel Filmproduktion/Filmhuset/Zentropa Entertainment co-production. *Producer:* Fridrik Thor Fridriksson, Egil Ödegaard, and Peter Rommel. *Director:* Fridrik Thor Fridriksson. *Screenplay (Icelandic with English subtitles):* Einar Kárason. *Director of Photography:* Ari Kristinsson. *Editor:* Steingrímur Karlsson and Skule Eriksen. *Music:* Hilmar Örn Hilmarsson. *Sound:* Kjartan Kartansson. *Production Designer:* Arni Páll Jóhansson. *Costumes:* Karl Aspelund. *Make-up:* Ragna Fossberg. *Running time:* 103 minutes. *MPAA Rating:* Not Rated.

CAST: Baltasar Kormákur (Baddi Tomasson); Gísli Halldórsson (Tommi Tomasson); Sigurveig Jónsdóttir (Karolína Tomasson); Halldóra Geirhardsdóttir (Dollí); Sveinn Geirsson (Danni Tomasson); Gudmundur Olafsson (Grettir); Ingvar E. Sigurdsson (Grjóni); Magnús Olafsson (Hreggvidur); Pálína Jónsdóttir (Hveragerdur); Saga Jónsdóttir (Gógó); Arnljótur Sigurdsson (Older Bóbó); Gylfi Sigurdsson (Younger Bóbó); Valgedur Sigurdardóttir (Gíslína); Óskar Jónasson (Lúí Lúí); Aevar Orn Jósepsson (Maggi); Helga Braga Jónsdóttir (Gréta); Margrét Ákadóttir (Fía); Sigurdur Sigurjónsson (Tóti); Gudrún Gísladóttir (Thórgunnur); Atli Vidar Hafsteinsson (Diddi); Árni Tryggvason (Afi); Gudbrandur Valdimarsson (Priest); Gunnar Eyjólfsson (Flight School Manager); Björgvin Halldórsson (Bóddi Billó); Darren A. Foreman (Soldier at Gate); Jón Júlfusson (Singing Old Man); Björn Ingi Hilmarsson (Young Man in Vetragardi); Harald G. Haraldsson (Workman); Jóhannes B. Gudmundsson (Postman); Geo von Krogh (Norwegian); Örvar Jens Arnarsson (Manni); Fridrik Steinn Fridriksson (Gosi); Greg Alldredge (Charlie Brown); John O'Neill (Tom); Matt Perkins (Dick); Samuel LeFever (Harry); Jón Ólafsson (Priest); Valdimar Örnólfsson (Acquaintance with Horn); Fridur Hannesdóttir (Well-to-do Woman); Helgi Valdimarsson (Factory Worker); Viggó Valdimarsson (Taxi Driver); Bjarni Geir Bjarnason (Hotel Borg Doorman); BÖDDA BILLÓ SEXTET: Thórir Baldursson (Keyboards); Vilhjálmur Gudjónsson (Guitar); Tómas R. Einarsson (Contrabass); Einar V. Scheving (Drums); Árni Scheving (Vibraphone); Rúnar Georgsson (Saxaphone).

NEW YORK POST, 3/12/99, p. 46, Jonathan Foreman

Partly about the subversive effects of American pop culture on a small community, partly a family saga, the sometimes charming Icelandic film "Devil's Island" suffers from a scattershot plot, sloppy direction and an eccentricity that feels increasingly contrived as the story lurches along.

It takes place during the 1950s on an abandoned U.S. Army base that has been handed over to poor, homeless Icelanders. The film mostly follows the fortunes of a single extended family. You first meet middle-aged Go Go and her American husband—but they soon go off to Kansas. They bring one young adult son—Baddi (Baltasar Kormakur)—with them and leave behind the other Danni (Sveinn Geirsson)—with Grandpa Tomas (Gisli Halldorsson) and crazy Grandma Karolina (Sigurveig Jonsdottir).

Baddi comes back with a leather jacket, a pompadour, a collection of American wisecracks and a bad attitude. He's now a selfish, obnoxious, greedy punk who extorts cash from his oddly cowed family. He's also a drunk, but then so is almost everyone who lives in the camp. Meanwhile shy Danni takes flying lessons.

There are some funny and moving moments here. And although you only get to see some of Iceland's extraordinary scenery at the end, there are some lovely sunsets along the way.

NEWSDAY, 3/12/99, Part II/p. B6, John Anderson

No movie is an atoll, per se, and Fridik Thor Fridriksson's "Devil's Island" situates its director in a sort of Ironic Triangle whose lonely points are Helsinki (home of the filmmaking Kaurismaki brothers), New York (Jim Jarmusch), and of course, Reykjavik. There, the Icelandic director is practicing a kindred brand of observation that's assuredly self-deprecating, but never loses sight of the true source of tragedy.

In the case of "Devil's Island" that source is the 1950s United States, which after debauching a host of Icelandic women and treating their men like cattle, has finally ended its World War II occupation and left its abandoned army barracks for homeless housing. The barracks outcasts, held in about the same contempt by their countrymen as the Americans had for Iceland, live in a wind-scraped squalor saturated with mud and alcohol. For grandfatherly Tommi (Gisli Halldorsson), life is a series of long work days, small humiliations and the screech-owl rantings of his Old Testament wife Karolina (Sigurveig Jonsdottir). The blackness of the comedy is matched by the bleakness of the terrain.

Among the villagefull of idiosyncratic hut-dwellers, grandsons Danni (Sveinn Gersson) and Baddi (Baltasar Kormakur) are shiftless louts. But when their mother marries a U.S. soldier, Baddi follows her to America and returns with a shark-finned Plymouth, a mouthful of English song lyrics and the leather and sneer of Elvis Presley. Barracks life will never be the same.

Fridriksson—whose first feature, "Children of Nature" was nominated for an Academy Award in 1992—has now made a film that's in many ways the flip side of his droll and moving 1995 movie "Cold Fever." In that one, a Japanese executive—in Iceland to perform a traditional funeral rite for his parents in the place where they died—provided the outsider's perspective on Iceland, exalting the national temperament through his uptight persona. In "Devil's Island," the national character is sent reeling by Baddi's manifestation of Elvis-rebel posturing, which is dangerous, decadent, corrupt and irresistible (especially as embodied by the talented Kormakur).

What differentiates Fridriksson from many contemporary filmmakers (but binds him to those mentioned above) is his willingness—and ability—to accommodate both real humor and real tragedy within the same movie. There's nothing prankish about a child killing itself with a soldier's stolen gun, or in the changes a hard life inflicts on Fridriksson's characters, or in the cultural inferiority complex imposed on the rest of the world by the glandular hysteria of American culture. These are real and they're treated as such.

But there's also a spacey kind of absurdist whimsy that emanates from Fridriksson's work, one that may be as singular as the Icelandic landscape but isn't really all that unfamiliar.

SIGHT AND SOUND, 1/98, p. 39, Geoffrey Macnab

Reykjavik, Iceland, the 50s. Poor families eke out an existence in Camp Thule, a set of abandoned US military barracks. Divorcee Gógó marries an American GI and emigrates to the US. Her son Baddi joins her there, but returns after a little while, with an Elvis-style quiff and an American car. His superstitious grandmother Karolína dotes on him. But the rest of the family—including his hard working grandfather Tommi, his shy brother Danni, and his sister Dollí and her husband—resent his laziness and noisy, all-night parties with his dissolute friends. One of Baddi's drinking partners is next-door neighbour Hreggvidur who breaks the world shot-putt record at the local games but is promptly disqualified for cheating. Baddi marries Hreggvidur's pretty daughter, Hveragerdur. She becomes pregnant. Baddi and Hreggvidur interrupt their brawling and drinking to attend the birth.

Meanwhile, Danni has been secretly having flying lessons. He gets his pilot's licence and carries out a daring airborne rescue. He becomes the shining light of the family while Baddi, for so long the favourite, turns into an alcoholic wreck. Karolína is distraught when Baddi announces his plan to return to the US. She has foreseen that somebody in the family will die in a plane crash. However, Danni is the one who dies. For the funeral, Gógó comes back from the US, separated from her American husband. She immediately takes up with a new man. The family prepare to move out of Camp Thule, into more modern housing.

Devil's Island Fridrik Thor Fridriksson's sprawling, muddy family epic, presents a stark contrast to its predecessor, the tidily plotted *Cold Fever*. In that earlier film, a Japanese businessman set out on a quest across the frozen plains of Iceland, but this film is almost entirely set within a single, claustrophobic location. From the drunken wedding which opens the action to the end, we're barely allowed out of Camp Thule (the slum nicknamed 'Devil's Island'). As if to emphasise how confined his characters' lives are, Fridriksson repeatedly uses the establishing shots of the Camp, a disused US army barracks which has been squatted by poor families. The flimsy buildings with their iron roofs sit on the barren landscape like ugly toy houses.

These so-called "barrack people" are social outcasts living in abject poverty and spurned by the rest of Reykjavik. Fridriksson celebrates their resilience and eccentricity. Einar Kárason's script portrays the slum dwellers as flamboyant, larger-than-life characters. Thus, most of the performances are wilfully exaggerated, with the actors aiming for pantomime-style caricature rather than psychological realism. Even seemingly banal incidents, such as the delivery of a car from the US, are invested with an unlikely comic grandeur.

In its attempt to transform dour, provincial life into something magical, *Devil's Island* rekindles memories of Bruno Schulz's short stories, collected under the title *The Street of Crocodiles*. As in Schulz's work, the characters here live under the shadow of consumer culture. The flickering, black-and white images on bad-son Baddi's television screen provide tantalising hints of a world of brightness and plenty. Fridriksson effectively conveys their hankering for a better life while also showing how drink, superstition and poverty dampen the barrack people's dreams.

At times, though, the film itself risks becoming as surly and bogged-down as its characters as we lurch from set-piece to set-piece. There is some spirited slapstick humour—for instance, gawky brother Danni's disastrous first driving lesson or the wedding party cabaret at which the light-fingered Grjóni picks the pockets of various guests—but scenes often taper off into a drunken melancholy while the narrative grinds to a halt. After a while, *Devil's Island* seems more like a series of soap-opera episodes strung together than a feature in its own right.

Fridriksson avoids preaching, but his knockabout approach to the material risks trivialising the slum dwellers' problems. Dysfunctional family life—the often abusive relationships between husbands and wives, fathers and daughters—is played for laughs. Magnús Ólafsson is very funny as the obese, drunken patriarch Hreggvidur who cheats his way to a shot-putt world record, but the fact that he terrorises his household is overlooked. Even when Fridriksson hints at the bad feeling between the various neighbours, he does so tongue-in-cheek. (In one scene, we see a family traipse from door to door with Christmas presents. The gifts are snatched, but none of the recipients shows any gratitude or warmth in return.)

The idea of an impoverished community in thrall to US culture is hardly original. (John Byrne's recent film version of *The Slab Boys* also featured provincial adolescents with quiffs, sideburns and leather jackets trying to escape from their oppressive backgrounds.) Here, Baltasar Kormákur's rebel-without-a-cause routine is more laboured than charismatic. He mutters his smattering of English words (Wipe the window! Check the oil!) as if they are magical mantras, but he's a type we've seen countless times before. As he becomes more and more surly, his brother Danni emerges into the limelight. His transformation into a Tintin-like flying ace is handled with plenty of wry charm. The scenes in which he soars over the mountains in his little plane provide a welcome antidote to the ground-eye view presented by the rest of the film.

Despite the rambunctious energy of the actors and Fridriksson's facility for knockabout comedy, *Devil's Island*'s random narrative is not easy to watch. The film, a huge box-office hit in Iceland, clearly has resonances for local audiences which outsiders struggle to grasp. But compared to, say, a similarly picaresque Scandinavian saga Lars von Trier's hospital-based *The Kingdom*, it can't help but seem lumbering and unfocused.

VILLAGE VOICE, 3/16/99, p. 130, Gary Dauphin

Ghosting the cramped homes of a metallic ghetto outside of Reykjavik, *Devil's Island* is on off-kilter and conflicted tale about family and change in '50s Iceland. Directed by Fridrik Thor Fridriksson with the same eye for stark landscapes and human quirks he brought to his road movie, *Cold Fever*, *Island* ambles about a smaller patch of frozen Icelandic turf, lensing a disappearing world throughout the cracked glasses of two very different brothers.

Baddi (Baltasar Kormakur) is the loud and indulgent son, Danni (Sveinn Geirsson) the sensitive, awkward one. The pair have been left with their cackling grandmother (Sigurveig Jonsdottir) and wise but timid grandfather (Gisli Halldorsson) since their floozy mom married an American soldier and moved to the television-lit pastures of Kansas. After a visit to Mom, Baddi returns with a mouthful of nonsense JD-movie comebacks, a new muscle car, and a severely worsened attitude. Quoting Elvis songs, he quickly degenerates into a beer swilling couch potato in pompadour, hustling his pliant grandparents for kronur while Danni watches a little shocked from the edges of the frame.

Island is too knowing just to be the tale of a small-town boy ruined by American movies and rock and roll, Fridricksson patiently moving Baddi and the surrounding cast of ecccentrics through well-wrought episodic changes. (Danni of course gets to flower while his brother wilts.) Unfortunately, once the director's done complicating *Island*'s basic binaries of family   and culture, he settles for a fimiliar way-north brand of tragicomedy, dragging his helpless characters through increasingly forced turns. *Devil's Island*'s rich vein of deadpan humor makes for a wry visit, but much like Baddi and Danni, no one in the audience would want to linger here very long.

Also reviewed in:
NEW REPUBLIC, 4/12/99, p. 28, Stanley Kauffmann
NEW YORK TIMES, 3/12/99, p. E30, Lawrence Van Gelder
VARIETY, 3/3-9/97, p. 70, David Stratton

DIAMONDS

A Miramax Films release of a Total Film Group and Cinerenta presentation. *Executive Producer:* Gerald Green. *Producer:* Patricia T. Green. *Director:* John Asher. *Screenplay:* Allan Aaron Katz. *Director of Photography:* Paul Elliott. *Editor:* C. Timothy O'Meara. *Music:* Joel Goldsmith. *Music Editor:* Rick Chadock. *Sound:* Kelly Rush. *Sound Editor:* Marc Innocenti. *Casting:* Dan Parada. *Production Designer:* Vance Lorenzini. *Art Director:* Steve Aikens. *Visual Effects:* Reid Burns. *Costumes:* Vicki Sanchez. *Make-up:* Juliet Loveland. *Make-up (Lauren Bacall):* Wayne Massarelli. *Running time:* 90 minutes. *MPAA Rating:* PG-13.

CAST: Kirk Douglas (Harry); Dan Aykroyd (Lance); Corbin Allred (Michael); Lauren Bacall (Sin-Dee); Kurt Fuller (Moses); Jenny McCarthy (Sugar); Mariah O'Brien (Tiffany); June Chadwick (Roseanne); Lee Tergesen (Border Guard); Val Bisiglio (Tarzan); Allan Aaron Katz (Mugger); Roy Conrad (Pit Boss); John Landis (Gambler); Joyce Bulifant (June/Waitress); Liz Gandara (Roxanne); Rebecca Thorpe (Glory); Pamela Coleman (Penelope); Kamla Greer (Kim); Jacqueline Collen (Ellie); Karen Mal (Bev).

LOS ANGELES TIMES, 12/10/99, Calendar/p. 14, Kevin Thomas

[The following review by Kevin Thomas appeared in a slightly different form in **NEWSDAY, 12/10/99, Part II/p. B7.]**

Kirk Douglas is still the champ. Nearly four years ago, he was knocked to the mat with a stroke but immediately picked himself up, began rehabilitation, resumed his successful second career as a writer and a busy public life. Now he's back where he belongs, on the big screen, his name above the title, in "Diamonds," a heart-tugging comedy-adventure that's in the spirit of the holiday season.

Douglas plays Harry Agensky, who half a century earlier was known as the "Polish Prince," the welterweight boxing champion of the world. Since Douglas played a boxer in the 1949 "Champion," the film that consolidated his stardom, "Diamonds" opens with a montage of clips from that film showing Douglas in the ring, dissolving to the present, which finds his Harry peering into a mirror, perhaps remembering his younger self but good-naturedly concentrating on the business at hand, which is running through his facial and vocal exercises to improve his speech, slurred from a stroke suffered five years earlier, not long after the death of his beloved wife of 45 years.

Her death hit Harry harder than the stroke, but while understandably overcome by grief at her loss from time to time, Harry is a feisty, hearty guy with a wild, independent streak and is an irrepressible, fearless showoff. Still, he is 83 and has been living with his dutiful son (Kurt Fuller) and daughter-in-law in their home by a lake in the Canadian wilderness—and driving them crazy. Harry himself would rather live elsewhere, with a live-in companion. The hitch is the expense, but Harry's got the answer for that: Head for Reno and retrieve a cache of diamonds a mobster named Duff the Muff promised him for throwing a long-ago fight.

Harry's other son, Lance (Dan Aykroyd), a divorced San Jose Mercury-News sports writer, thinks it's a pipe dream but is willing to go along for the ride in an attempt to improve relations with the father he had little in common with and who seemed to have so little time for him when he was a boy. Also coming along on the trip is Lance's own son, Michael (Corbin Allred), who promptly tells him his soon-to-be stepfather is "twice the man" his father is. You have to feel for Lance, clearly a decent guy but perceived as a hopeless square by both his father and his son—Harry and Michael have a warm rapport.

Directed affectionately by John Asher and written by Allan Aaron Katz, "Diamonds" mixes humor, shameless sentimentality, the fanciful and the contrived with no small amount of bravery, wisdom and underlying seriousness. The result is a sturdy, though occasionally rambling, vehicle for Douglas, who seems to be having a helluva good time, surrounded by a sterling cast with the perfect leading lady, Lauren Bacall. Bacall last teamed with Douglas in 1950's "Young Man With a Horn," inspired by the life of jazz trumpeter Bix Beiderbecke.

Shrewdly, Katz suggests implicitly that Lance's biggest problem with both his father and his son is that he hasn't spent enough time with either to get to know them properly. By the time they arrive in Reno, they're in pretty good spirits collectively but not really interested in gambling. Therefore, they suddenly find themselves with that other item that's usually on the minds of any three men out on the town, especially in a resort city: sex.

The way in which the film handles this generation-spanning topic is amusing and, best of all, brings Bacall into the picture as the madam of the fanciest, frilliest bordello in the state of Nevada, if not all of the U.S. Bacall's Sin-Dee, thankfully, eschews the frills and furbelows of her Victorian maison de joie's decor in favor of dark, smart pantsuits that Bacall might wear in real life. Sin-Dee has seen it all, natch, and she and Harry have a real rapport: Both were born dirt poor but ambitious, both used their bodies to get ahead in life, and neither has regrets nor apologies. The unexpected pleasure of seeing Douglas on the screen again is doubled when he's playing opposite Bacall, a star as enduring as himself Sin-Dee's key ladies are played with humor by Jenny McCarthy and Mariah O'Brien.

Harry, as Douglas has himself, treats his slurred speech with humor, but just by appearing before the cameras once more, the vigorous Douglas becomes an inspiration, striking a blow against that real crippler, ageism, and showing the remarkable degree to which it is possible to overcome the ravages of a stroke. Douglas is at all times perfectly intelligible and in some passages his slurring seems to vanish entirely.

You can't come away from "Diamonds" without being aware that Douglas, while among the first wave of post-World War II stars that included Burt Lancaster, is virtually the last remaining actor to become a major star before TV came along to rob screen stars of that magical larger-than-life quality that Douglas has never lost.

NEW YORK POST, 12/10/99, p. 55, Lou Lumenick

"Diamonds" boasts a gem of a performance by Kirk Douglas as a stroke victim trying to stay out of a nursing home, but this hokey and contrived multi-generational comic drama is otherwise deeply flawed.

Douglas, in his first acting role since he suffered a real-life stroke a few years ago, shines as Harry Agensky, a former welterweight boxing champ once known as the "Polish Prince."

Harry has been living in Canada with his older son's family and they've just about had it with the cantankerous old man, who is given to saying things like "a stroke is God's way to make me shut up."

When his younger son Lance (Dan Aykroyd), a divorced middle-aged sportswriter, arrives for a visit with his 15-year-old son Michael (Corbin Allred), Harry tells Michael he wants to hunt down a cache of "magic diamonds" he was once promised by a Reno gangster named Duff the Muff. The idea is to use the proceeds to buy himself a ranch where he can live out his years.

Michael talks his father Lance—whose relationship with Michael is as strained as Lance's is with Harry—into taking the old man to Nevada to hunt for the gems. They also gamble and visit a brothel presided over by Sin-Dee (Lauren Bacall), a madam with a proverbial heart of gold who reluctantly agrees to the underaged Michael's sexual initiation at the hands of Sugar (Jenny McCarthy), while the older Agenskys are otherwise sexually occupied.

There isn't anything original in Allan Aaron Katz's screenplay or the direction by John Asher (Aykroyd's performance as the sad-sack Lance is particularly strained). But this little movie is clearly a labor of love for Asher—whose father, "Bewitched" and "Beach Party" auteur William Asher, also suffered a stroke—and all involved.

Douglas, always one of Hollywood's most vigorous actors, still commands the screen as Harry. Thanks to him, "Diamonds" is quite affecting—even if it's not a particularly good movie.

VILLAGE VOICE, 12/14/99, p. 184, Joe McGovern

Following Christopher Reeve in TV's busted *Rear Window,* post-stroke Kirk Douglas stars as a muttering geriatric in the fake-paste *Diamonds,* his first non-talk show, non-awards show, return-to-acting role. Douglas plays an erstwhile prizefighter (cue inserts of his 1949 boxing flick *Champion),* who, following a debilitating stroke of his own, takes his son (Dan Aykroyd) and grandson (Corbin Allred) on a whimsical diamond hunt through Reno, Nevada. Bursting with dialogue that's as feebleminded as its protagonist ("Live each day as if it were your last, and never give up"), *Diamonds* does pick up momentarily when the threesome visit a deluxe bordello where, unable to perform and fresh out of Viagra, Kirk is tenderly held by the sympathizing madam Sin-dee (Lauren Bacall). Douglas seems to be playing himself, and the film's most repugnant aspect is its false flattery—masking pity in the form of his costars' recurrent backslapping and awkward laughter. Worse still, Douglas will not go gently into that opening night; last month he publicly raged against the MPAA, demanding they replace *Diamonds'* R-rating with a PG-13. For the sake of his relatively untarnished legacy, won't he accept that—with its superficial script, toneless direction, and unadmirable intentions—*Diamonds* is inappropriate for audiences of all ages?

Also reviewed in:
CHICAGO TRIBUNE, 2/18/00, Friday/p. J, Michael Wilmington
NEW YORK TIMES, 12/10/99, p. E28, Stephen Holden
VARIETY, 9/27-10/3/99, p. 44, Lisa Nesselson
WASHINGTON POST, 2/18/00, p. C5, Stephen Hunter

DICK

A Columbia Pictures release of a Phoenix Pictures presentation of a Pacific Western production. *Executive Producer:* David Coatsworth. *Producer:* Gale Anne Hurd. *Director:* Andrew Fleming. *Screenplay:* Andrew Fleming and Sheryl Longin. *Director of Photography:* Alexander Gruszynski. *Editor:* Mia Goldman. *Music:* John Debney. *Music Editor:* Chuck Martin Inouye and Terry Wilson. *Sound:* David Husby. *Sound Editor:* Steve Williams. *Casting:* Pam Dixon Mickelson. *Production Designer:* Barbara Dunphy. *Art Director:* Lucinda Zak. *Set Designer:* Nancy Pankiw. *Set Decorator:* Donald Elmblad. *Set Dresser:* Mary Arthurs and Angelo Stea. *Special Effects:* Martin Malivoire. *Costumes:* Deborah Everton. *Make-up:* Ann Brodie. *Stunt Coordinator:* Branko Racki. *Running time:* 90 minutes. *MPAA Rating:* PG-13.

CAST: Kirsten Dunst (Betsy Jobs); Michelle Williams (Arlene Lorenzo); Dan Hedaya (Dick); Will Ferrell (Bob Woodward); Bruce McCulloch (Carl Bernstein); Teri Garr (Helen Lorenzo); Dave Foley (Bob Halderman); Jim Breuer (John Dean); Ana Gasteyer (Rose Mary Woods); Harry Shearer (G. Gordon Liddy); Saul Rubinek (Henry Kissinger); Devon Gummersall (Larry Jobs); Ted McGinley (Roderick); Ryan Reynolds (Chip); G.D. Spradlin (Ben Bradlee); Shannon Lawson (Kay Jobs); Karl Pruner (Frank Jobs); Brenda Devine (Mrs. Spinnler); Jonathan Ranells (First G-Man); Paulino Nunes (Second G-Man); Michael Dyson (Burglar #1); Jerry Schaefer (Burgler #2); Jack Mosshammer (Fat Freddy); Karen Waddell (White House Secretary); Richard Fitzpatrick (John Erlichman); Cole Barrington (Student #1); Scott Wickware (White House Guard); Mark Lutz (Hunky Secret Service Man); Kedar Brown (Mr. Samovar); Paul Wildbaum (Shredder Man); Kerry Dorey (Payola Man); Len Doncheff (Leonid Brezhnev); Igor Portnoi (Russian Translator); Jennifer Wigmore (Washington Post Receptionist); Jane Moffat (Kissing Secretary); Rob Nickerson (1st Police Officer); Bernard Browne (2nd

Police Officer); Rummy Bishop (Newsstand Guy); Deborah Grover (Pat Nixon); Stephen Robert (FBI Agent); Michael Kramer (TV News Reporter); Mike Anscombe (TV News Anchor); French Stewart (The Interviewer).

LOS ANGELES TIMES, 8/4/99, Calendar/p. 5, Kevin Thomas

Blame it on Bobby Sherman. What are two 15-year-old girls to do? They've just got to make that midnight deadline for posting an entry into the "Win a Date With Bobby Sherman Contest"—he's their singing idol—so what to do but sneak out, for it already is pretty late in the evening. This means going out the back stairs by the garage under the apartment house where Arlene (Michelle Williams) lives with her mother (Teri Garr), and taping over the lock in the rear door so that she and her friend Betsy (Kirsten Dunst) can get back in the building.

Alas, Arlene's apartment just happens to be in the posh Watergate complex in Washington, D.C., where, you guessed it, an alert security guard, noticing the tape, calls the cops, who come upon the White House "plumbers" intent upon bugging the Democratic National Committee headquarters housed in the building. And this is just the beginning of how two innocent girls in the early '70s come to change the course of history as hilariously outlined in the satirical comedy "Dick."

Give credit to director Andrew Fleming, who made his name with that nifty teen horror flick "The Craft," and his co-writer Sheryl Longin for their touching faith that today's teens have had sufficient education to know what the terms "Deep Throat" and "18 1/2 minutes" or even "Watergate" itself refer to; the core audience they're most likely hoping to connect with are Betsy and Arlene's contemporaries, who today would be hitting 40. Actually, "Dick" is so sharp and funny it should appeal to all ages.

As it happens, Betsy and Arlene are to go on a school tour of the White House, where they recognize G. Gordon Liddy (Harry Shearer) as the same man they encountered briefly as they were making their back-door exit at the Watergate. This chance meeting escalates complications that land them in the presence of President "Dick" Nixon (Dan Hedaya) himself. In his awkward way he charms the girls, making them official White House dog-walkers and later on, his secret youth advisors. They're now unwittingly poised to effect all manner of events, all of which are too inspired and amusing to be revealed here.

At the heart of the film is the transformation of two perfectly normal teenagers, who intuitively sense that the Vietnam War is wrong but who are momentarily charmed by their president, who assures them that he is laying the groundwork for peace as he speaks. Their inadvertent firsthand experiences, however, leave them as disillusioned with Nixon and his administration as the American public would soon be.

Dunst and Williams are a constant delight, making clear that the girls' naivete does not mean that they are in any way stupid. Hedaya is a wonderful Nixon, and while he's spoofing here, this fine, versatile actor arguably would have made a better serious Tricky Dick than Anthony Hopkins did in the Oliver Stone film biography. Fleming's actors have a field day sending up Nixon loyalists, although only the ever-admirable Saul Rubinek actually resembles the man he is playing, Henry Kissinger. Will Ferrell and especially Bruce McCulloch bear little resemblance to the Washington Post's Bob Woodward and Carl Bernstein, respectively, but they have so much fun sending up the investigative reporters' ferocious ambition it scarcely matters.

Wisely, the filmmakers waste no opportunity to find humor in the fads and styles of the early '70s since younger audiences may find them especially amusing. In any event, production designer Barbara Dunphy and costume designer Deborah Everton have the look of the era nailed down squarely without, thankfully, being heavy-handed or condescending about it—the very qualities Fleming himself avoids. "Dick" leaves you hoping it finds the audience it clearly deserves.

NEW YORK, 8/16/99, p. 56, Peter Rainer

Dick, co-written and directed by Andrew Fleming, is a cross between *All the President's Men* and *Romy and Michele's High School Reunion*, and as far as it goes, which isn't far enough, it's enjoyable. It wants to draw in the dumdums in the audience, but it also wants to have a brain; sharp satire alternates with cloddish comedy. Two ditsy 15-year-old best friends, Betsy (Kirsten

Dunst) and Arlene (Michelle Williams), accidentally implicate themselves in the Watergate break-in and end up playing Deep Throat to Woodward and Bernstein—played hilariously by Will Ferrell and Bruce McCulloch as a pair of flustered, uncomradely back-stabbers. Dan Hedaya plays Nixon to jowly perfection, and Harry Shearer's Gordon Liddy and Saul Rubinek's Henry Kissinger are so sharply drawn that you wonder: Will the core audience for this film, which at best is only vaguely aware of Watergate, appreciate the joke?

NEW YORK POST, 8/4/99, p. 43, Jonathan Foreman

"Dick" is a gleefully cunning comedy based on the conceit that Deep Throat was not a highly placed political operative inside the Nixon administration but rather a pair of utterly clueless teenage dog-walkers.

It's a very, very funny film. But it may well be hobbled at the box office by the fact that much of its hilarity (apart from the inevitable but still amusing double-entendre jokes on Richard Nixon's nickname) requires a basic knowledge of the Watergate scandal.

The year is, of course, 1972. Arlene (Michele Williams), who lives in the Watergate, and her marginally less ditzy best friend Betsy (Kirsten Dunst) are wandering around when who should they bump into on the stairs but G. Gordon Liddy (Harry Shearer) running the burglary that changed America.

On a school field trip to the White House a few days later, Arlene and Betsy see Liddy again and are really freaked out. Chief of Staff Bob Halderman (a terrific Dave Foley) quickly pulls them into an office to find out how much they know. But it's the president himself (Dan Hedaya) who conceives a brilliant damage-control strategy: He hires the two airheads as official White House dog-walkers.

Before long, Betsy and Arlene are coming over every day to walk Checkers (who actually died in 1964 and was replaced by King Timahoe in 1969) and to chat to Dick, who'd rather talk to them than to Henry Kissinger (Saul Rubinek). They give him simpletonic advice about ending the Vietnam War, and he makes them his "secret youth advisers."

Everyone in the White House falls in love with the cookies the two bring with them, which are baked with Betsy's brother's special leafy ingredient. And Arlene falls in love with Dick himself.

But it's inevitable that even dingbats like Arlene and Betsy will twig to the president's nasty side. And their response to Nixon's meanness and bad language is to start making crank calls to two reporters at the Washington Post.

Williams and Dunst are just right. As Nixon, Dan Hedaya is funny and weirdly sympathetic. Director Andrew Fleming, who co-wrote the screenplay with Sheryl Longin, adeptly weaves in cleverly chosen details from the historical Watergate. But even more impressive is his control of the film's delicately satirical tone.

"Dick" doesn't demonize Nixon and his henchmen, though Fleming does make it clear these are the kind of guys who wouldn't think twice about sending agents to tail and harass some ridiculous schoolgirls.

On the other hand, the film is merciless in its depiction of Woodward and Bernstein as a pair of whiny, self-righteous creeps. There are a couple of scenes featuring the preening pair, played by Will Farrell and Bruce McCulloch, that may make it impossible to see "All the President's Men" again with a straight face.

VILLAGE VOICE, 8/10/99, p. 59, J. Hoberman

History lodges itself in popular memory as mythic saga; myth becomes moralizing as compact fairy tale. The Kennedy administration morphs into Camelot and then the story of a doomed Tribeca prince. This process is virtually a movie industry mandate and its demonstrated equally by the family-oriented animation *The Iron Giant* and the teen comedy *Dick*—two very successful entertainments that attempt to make particular aspects of the recent American past comprehensible to those too young to have lived them.

In *The Iron Giant* (a movie that finally gives Warner Bros.'s animation unit a reason for being), a nine-year-old boy, a childlike robot from outer space, and a sympathetic beatnik confound the full might of what used to be called America's military-industrial complex to save New England from nuclear obliteration. In *Dick,* most conveniently synopsized as Romy and Michelle's

Watergate Adventure, a pair of ecstatically simpering 15-year-old ninnies effectively destroy the Nixon presidency. There's even a reconciliatory generational agenda: In both cases, the kids are all right *and* Boomerism rules.

Even funnier than it is puerile, *Dick* is only minutes old when bubbly Betsy (Kirsten Dunst) and her nerdy friend Arlene (Michelle Williams) unknowingly create the conditions by which a group of Republican ops get caught burgling Democratic headquarters. Having blundered upon the mission's menacing leader, G. Gordon Liddy (Harry Shearer), while they were sneaking back home through the Watergate stairwell, the girls reencounter him days later on a class visit to the White House and then meet Richard Nixon himself. Its no more improbable than the premise of *The American President* and, in some ways, a lot less fanciful. Nixon (Dan Hedaya) is first seen compulsively grousing that his new dog—which he persists in calling "Checkers"—doesn't really like him. One thing leads to another and Nixon offers the jumping, screaming girls the job of official White House dog walkers.

As demonstrated by actors ranging from Jason Robards to Rip Torn to Rich Little, playing Nixon is a ham bone's dream. (The only really bad impersonation was, of course, Anthony Hopkins's.) For look-a-like Hedaya, it's the role for which he was born. Wide-eyed and mirthless, shaking his blue jowls and squeezed into an ill-fitting suit with an American flag in the lapel, this sonorous, gloomy Nixon is a joke that never stops giving. Rather than surround him with digitally resurrected playmates, as Oliver Stone did in *Nixon*, writer-director Andrew Fleming recruits a suitable cast of trolls to play the president's men—with Saul Rubinek (elevated from a functionary in the Stone film) a particularly gruesome Kissinger.

High lowbrow, *Dick* is a mass of pop-culture detritus—teen comedy, conspiracy caper, political satire, nostalgia flick. The movie is built on the shards of old commercials and ancient TV shows and fueled by a constant infusion of '70s pop. Andrew Fleming's script, cowritten with Sheryl Longin, is designed to get maximum mileage out of the title pun, and his direction is aggressively cheesy. Famous news-photo tableaux are reenacted in the manner of cruddy wax museum displays. (The referenced images include a few scenes from *All the President's Men,* which is, after all, one of the prime Watergate myths.) The White House is less a crime scene than a virtual garage sale.

Once the girls inadvertently bake cannabis cookies and innocently feed them to the president, they're promoted to "secret youth advisers." Impressionable Arlene rips down her Bobby Sherman pictures and replaces them with images of R.N. Betsy and Arlene are nonplussed by the growing investigation—asking Dick, "Whats the deal with this Watergate thing?"—but when they blunder on a suitably clunky tape recorder and evidence of their hero's Oval Office rantings, they are actively disillusioned: "You kicked Checkers and you're prejudiced and you have a potty mouth!"

Myth reduced to fairy tale, *Dick* purports to reveal the true identity of Deep Throat and the actual cause of the 18-and-a-half-minute gap in the White House tapes. Desecration that it is, the movie also takes pains to travesty the heroes of *All the President's Men.* Bob Woodward suffers the indignity of being played by resident SNL nitwit Will Ferrell, although the preview audience with whom I saw the movie laughed even harder at Bruce McCulloch's portrayal of fellow reporter Carl Bernstein as a maniacal leprechaun, flipping his hair for the camera as he muscles in on Woodward's scoops. The only idiot missing in this bubblegum *JFK* is Forrest Gump.

In the end, the republic is saved by a couple of prank phone calls and a judicious burst of Olivia Newton-John so that, 24 years later, another young woman could all but bring it down. As always, the past is drafted to serve present needs.

Also reviewed in:
CHICAGO TRIBUNE, 8/4/99, Tempo/p. 1, Barbara Shulgasser
NATION, 9/6-13/99, p. 35, Stuart Klawans
NEW YORK TIMES, 8/4/99, p. E1, Stephen Holden
NEW YORKER, 8/16 & 23/99, p. 202, David Denby
VARIETY, 8/2-8/99, p. 32, Todd McCarthy
WASHINGTON POST, 8/4/99, p. C1, Rita Kempley
WASHINGTON POST, 8/6/99, Weekend/p. 42, Michael O'Sullivan

DINNER GAME, THE

A Lions Gate Films release of a Gaumont International production. *Producer:* Alaine Poiré. *Director:* Francis Veber. *Screenplay (French with English subtitles):* Francis Veber. *Director of Photography:* Luciano Tovoli. *Editor:* Georges Klotz. *Music:* Vladimir Cosma. *Sound:* Bernard Bats. *Sound Editor:* Jean Gargonne. *Casting:* Françoise Menidrey. *Art Director:* Hugues Tissandier. *Set Decorator:* Alain Pitrel. *Special Effects:* Jean-Louis Trinquier. *Animator:* Christophe Vallaux. *Costumes:* Jacqueline Bouchard. *Make-up:* Gill Robillard. *Running time:* 82 minutes. *MPAA Rating:* Not Rated.

CAST: Jacques Villeret (François Pignon); Thierry Lhermitte (Pierre Brochant); Francis Huster (Leblanc); Alexandra Vandernoot (Christine); Daniel Prévost (Cheval); Catherine Frot (Marlène); Edgar Givry (Cordier); Christian Pereira (Sorbier); Pétronille Moss (Mlle Blond); Daniel Martin (Messignac); Elvire Mellère (Gisèle); Philippe Brigaud (Tanner); Michel Caccia, Laurent Gendron, and Candide Sanchez (Guests); Benoît Bellal, Mykhaël Georges-Schar, and Jacques Bleu (Hosts); Pierre-Arnaud Juin (Boissonade); Rémy Roubakha (Carlier).

LOS ANGELES TIMES, 7/16/99, Calendar/p. 4, Kenneth Turan

Americans have never heard of him and even the French don't always respect the considerable talent of Francis Veber. As a writer and director, he's had a hand in some of his country's most popular films, including "La Cage aux Folles," "La Chevre," "Les Comperes" and "Les Fugitifs" (all of which were remade, often indifferently, by Hollywood), but high-end approval has been lacking at home and abroad. His latest film, "The Dinner Game," turned things around in France, and is bound to do the same over here.

Perhaps Veber's best work as a writer-director, "The Dinner Game" was not only the lone domestic film to seriously challenge "Titanic" at the French box office, it was also, and this was a first for him, nominated for six Cesars, the French Oscar, winning three awards, including one for Veber for best script.

Expertly acted by Jacques Villeret, Daniel Prevost (both of whom won Cesars) and Thierry Lhermitte, "The Dinner Game" is a classic French verbal farce, in which, inch by imperceptible inch, things get beautifully and hysterically out of control. No one in France orchestrates farce with quite the skill of Veber, who without visible effort creates structures as delicate and elaborate as, say, a scale-model Eiffel Tower built completely out of matchsticks.

Francois Pignon (Villeret) happens to be passionate about such matchstick models. A low-level functionary at the Tax Ministry, he spends nights and weekends working on them and is all too eager to let perfect strangers know it took 37 tubes of glue and 346,472 individual sticks to construct his tower. "And the angle of the matches," he says, his voice rising in excitement, "can't be even a 10th of a degree off." You don't say.

In the ordinary course of events, Pignon would never socialize with an upper-crust type like publisher Pierre Brochant (Lhermitte, who's made a career of these kinds of narcissistic roles). But Brochant, arrogant yuppie creep that he is, is involved in a snobbish scheme that causes their paths to cross.

Brochant is the moving force behind an idiots dinner ("Le Diner de Cons" is the film's French title), at which heartless co-conspirators are charged with bringing complete fools to the table so that everyone else can laugh at them behind their backs. Brochant's wife, Christine (Alexandra Vandernoot), thinks the scheme is vicious, but Brochant insists otherwise and feels supremely lucky when "an A-1 idiot" like Pignon crosses his path.

Luck, however, is soon to desert the disdainful publisher. He badly wrenches his back playing golf on the day of the dinner and so irritates his wife that she decides to leave him. It's in this state, unwillingly chained to his apartment, that the oblivious Pignon finds his patron.

Short, chubby, with frizzy hair and a hangdog face that easily gets crestfallen only to irrepressibly bounce back again, Pignon is the most well-meaning of individuals. He'd love to help Brochant, he really would, but this timid man turns out to be a world-class blunderer, someone with a gift for doing the worst possible thing at any given moment. The more he tries to assist his new friend, the more devastating, and funnier, the results turn out to be.

Is Brochant's wife gone? Pignon can fix that. Or at least he thinks he can. Is the publisher's mistress (Catherine Frot of "Un Air de Famille") also giving him some trouble? Pas de problem. One would-be good deed follows another, and soon enough the putative tormentor's life is in so complete a shambles that "Idiots Revenge" would be an appropriate title for what transpires.

Putting the situation even more out of control is the appearance of Pignon's great and good friend Cheval (Daniel Prevost, the film's other Cesar winner), who just happens to be the most feared and ferocious tax inspector in France. "He'd audit his own mother," Pignon says admiringly, a sentiment that the horrified and tax-evasive Brochant does not share.

To watch "The Dinner Game's" principals handle the film's delicious lines and situations with the aplomb of expert jugglers is like watching a master class in farce. This is a delicate style of acting that doesn't get called on much in this country, and though DreamWorks wisely owns the film's remake rights, it's doubtful that anyone anywhere can do this story better justice than is done right here.

NEW YORK POST, 7/9/99, p. 59, Rod Dreher

In this summer of smutty, gross-out film comedies, it's startling to realize how deeply hilarious a film as archaic as "The Dinner Game" can be. You can keep your cynical f-word shock-a-paloozas; in its virtuoso craftsmanship and jocose humanity, veteran writer-director Francis Veber's uproarious farce is the most audacious and outre comedy of the summer.

It's a comedy of errors as simple, old-fashioned and French as steak frites and Bordeaux, and just as delicious and satisfying. The short, zippy picture is radiantly suffused with wit, lightness and charm rarely encountered in Gallic imports these days.

The original French title of the film is "Le Diner de cons," which means, roughly, "The Schmuck's Dinner." A group of rich, smarty-pants Parisian men amuse themselves by hosting a weekly dinner in which each fellow invites an idiot to the table.

Those in on the joke laugh privately as the poor schmucks, who are never clued in, humiliate themselves with banal conversation and stupid observations. The man who brings the most idiotic guest wins.

Book publisher Pierre Brochant (Thierry Lhermitte) thinks he's struck gold when he meets Francois Pignon (Jacques Villeret), a dumpy functionary who takes inordinate pride in constructing replicas of famous buildings out of matchsticks.

On the night of the dinner, Brochant injures his back, and his wife (Alexandra Vandernoot) leaves him, sick of his meanness. Brochant tries to call Pignon to call things off, but it's too late.

Once the guest arrives at his door, the tables are inadvertently turned on the cruel host as poor dumb Pignon, trying to do the right thing ("I'm with you, Monsieur Brochant!" he unhelpfully asserts), makes a rollicking shambles of the rich jerk's life.

Nearly all the action takes place inside Brochant's apartment over the course of one evening, which gives the film a slightly stagy air. Yet there is so much screwball coming and going (friends, lovers, wives, even the taxman) that the story never feels house-bound.

Lhermitte makes a splendidly arrogant straight man, but the movie belongs to the deliriously funny Villeret, who has impeccable timing and the ability to make us adore Pignon's big, well-meaning heart while never losing sight of the fact that he's a pluperfect numbskull.

"The Dinner Game" will reportedly be remade here by DreamWorks. Risky business, this, considering how badly Veber's "Les Comperes" fared when translated as the godawful "Father's Day."

Let's hope somebody at the studio has the good sense to cast Steve Martin and Danny DeVito as Brochant and Pignon, and let Martin write the adaptation. But you'd be crazy to wait for Hollywood to muck up a movie as pitch-perfect and brilliantly structured as this one.

Reserve your table at the Paris tout de suite.

NEWSDAY, 7/10/99, Part II, p. B9, Bob Heisler

The menu for "The Dinner Game," a light, bright and very funny French comedy by writer/director Francis Veber, is crow. Large quantities of crow, followed by small dishes of skewered snob, in a fragrant stew of his own making.

Served with a side of popcorn, it makes a satisfying summer repast.

Veber, the wit, behind "La Cage aux Folles" (1978) and "The Tall Blond Man With One Black Shoe" (1972), has whipped up a most clever, theatrical, adult comedy in which every ingredient is ripe and cooked to a turn.

Pierre Brochant (Thierry Lhermitte) is a member of a weekly dinner club. Each member is responsible for bringing to the table an idiot for the amusement of the group, someone who is so serious about his hobby or behavior that he doesn't realize he is being mocked. An example: the man who throws boomerangs each morning before work.

Tipped by a friend, Brochant, a publisher smug and abusive enough to have been written by Neil LaBute, finds an intriguing case study: Francois Pignon (Jacques Villeret), a pudgy, balding government tax accountant who builds models from matches. His Eiffel Tower uses more than 350,000 matches! He's the kind of lonely, clumsy, emotionally damaged but good-natured soul most of us would smile at and move away from on the train. In short, a perfect target.

Pignon arrives for predinner drinks, lured by the prospect of creating a book of his models. In short order, doing his best to nurture his new friendship, he pushes Madame Brochant onto the threshold of adultery and Mr. Brochant's girlfriend to the brink of suicide and his host into the waiting arms of a major tax audit.

The meltdown takes place in the Brochants' apartment, mostly through Pignon's good intentions and Brochant's continued desire to put his idiot on display.

Villeret instantly commands sympathy; his need for friendship can't be derailed by simple insult. As Brochant's life unravels at warp speed, Lhermitte makes his loss of superiority a distasteful but necessary choice.

The humor is more head shaking than knee slapping. The odd couple finds, for instance, that the addition of a little vinegar to a vintage red—the better to fool the bulldog tax auditor—adds depth and complexity, but overpour and it makes you sick. In the wrong hands—LaBute's, for instance—"The Dinner Game" could have become a dark mishmash of unlikable stereotypes in search of a victim. Veber, a master, keeps the pace engaging, the people human, and the result a winner.

SIGHT AND SOUND, 7/99, p. 40, Philip Kemp

Pierre Brochant, a successful publisher, is one of a group of friends who organise an "idiots' dinner" every Wednesday. Each member has to invite an idiot as his guest; whoever brings the biggest idiot wins. Pierre's latest unwitting victim is François Pignon, a finance Ministry accountant. Playing golf, Pierre ricks his back. When François shows up at his apartment for a pre-dinner drink, Pierre tells him they must miss the dinner. Attempting to help, François makes the injury worse.

Pierre's wife Christine, who earlier walked out in disgust over the idiots' dinner, phones to say she's leaving him. Full of sympathy, François insists on sticking around and tries to phone Pierre's doctor. By mistake he contacts Pierre's ex-mistress, Marlène; to Pierre's horror, Marlène announces she's coming round. Suspecting Christine may be with her ex-husband, his former friend Leblanc, Pierre gets François to phone him on a pretext but Leblanc sees through the ruse and selflessly comes round to help.

Sent to head Marlène off, François encounters Christine, who has had a change of heart. Taking her for Marlène, he gives the game away. She storms off. Dismayed, Pierre concludes she's gone to Meneaux, a notorious womaniser. François contacts his tax-inspector colleague Cheval who's investigating Meneaux, and who reluctantly brings round the dossier revealing the whereabouts of Meneaux's love-nest. But Meneaux, when phoned, proves to be occupied with another woman altogether. Cheval leaves, threatening to investigate Pierre's finances.

News comes that Christine has been in a car crash; she's injured, but refuses to see Pierre. From Marlène, François learns the truth about his dinner invitation. Though deeply hurt, he phones Christine and persuades her how much Pierre needs her. Pierre, remorseful, is overcome with gratitude. But at the last moment François screws up again.

Francis Veber, one of France's most successful writer-directors, forms part of that long tradition of vernacular French comedy that has never quite made it across the English Channel; earlier outcroppings include Louis de Funès vehicles and the films of Philippe de Broca. In Britain, such movies fall between two stools: the audience for French films tends to go for the subtler humour of Eric Rohmer, while lovers of energetic farce mostly won't wear subtitles.

Veber probably remains best known over here for the 1973 *L'Emmerdeur* (poorly remade by Billy Wilder in 1981 as *Buddy, Buddy*), which he scripted from his own stage play for Edouard Molinaro.

In *L'Emmerdeur* the plans of Lino Ventura's taciturn hitman were constantly disrupted by a well-meaning dolt played by Jacques Brel. *Le Dîner de cons*, adapted by Veber from another of his stage hits, replays much the same relationship, with Thierry Lhermitte's supercilious publisher having his well-ordered life dismantled by the disastrously eager-to-please Jacques Villeret. (The characters played by Brel and Villeret in the films even share the same surname, Pignon.)

The key dynamic in this kind of comic pairing isn't the gravitation of the idiot to the straight guy, which is understandable enough, but the reverse: the fatal delusion on the part of a logical individual, operating on cool self-interest, that even the most unpromising human material can, with a little coaching, be co-opted into the same well-ordered system. Rather than recognising Pignon as a walking disaster area, to be shot of as rapidly as possible, Brochant treats him as a challenge to be overcome—a dire miscalculation.

As Brochant, Thierry Lhermitte's chiselled good looks and incredulous blue-eyed stare make him the ideal foil and Daniel Prévost contributes a pungent cameo (crowned with the best left-field gag in the movie) as a predatory tax inspector. But the film is stolen, as it must be if it's to work, by Villeret as Pignon. With his balding, spherical head, bug eyes and pudgy little mouth, Villeret seems like a cross between a giant baby and a less aggressive Zero Mostel. His comic persona also shares something of a baby's abrupt, discontinuous mood swings, and in the film's funniest moments the camera focuses delightedly on his mobile moon-face as it slumps from inane self-satisfaction to lip-quivering dismay.

Le Dîner de cons clocked up over 900 performances on the Paris stage before being filmed, so not surprisingly the pacing and mechanics of the comedy run with dovetailed precision. The only queasy moment comes towards the end, when Veber turns briefly sanctimonious and tries to make us, in the person of our surrogate Brochant, feel guilty for having treated Pignon as an idiot. Since the plot's entire comic *raison d'être*, up to this point, has lain in doing just that, this attempt to claim the moral high ground seems rather less than justified.

That apart, Veber's film offers all the undemanding, solidly old-fashioned pleasures of a traditionally well-crafted French farce. Old-fashioned enough, at times, to be positively nostalgic: how many British films these days would dare to depict football fans as trivia-obsessed buffoons?

TIME, 7/26/99, p. 74, Richard Schickel

Writer-director Francis Veber has repeatedly insisted that *The Dinner Game* is founded in reality: at some point in the fairly recent past, Parisian sophisticates took to hunting down idiots, issuing straight-faced dinner invitations to them and then awarding a prize to the swell who brought the most excruciating bore to the party.

All Veber imagined was a situation where one of the smart set is obliged to deal with one of his victims, one on one, man to man. That is simply arranged: Pierre (Thierry Lhermitte), a publisher, is suddenly immobilized by a backache on the very night he has asked François (Jacques Villeret), an accountant who makes matchstick models of things like the Eiffel Tower and the Concorde, over for a drink before the fools' parade. François is more than eager to divert Pierre from his pain.

Before the night is out, he has managed to estrange Pierre from both his wife and his mistress and to bring the tax collector (played with wonderful avidity by Daniel Prévost) down on him. But in the end, for all his clumsiness, François proves himself the better man—warmhearted and unworthy of the contempt that has been so richly visited upon him.

Veber, the author of the much adapted *La Cage aux Folles* as well as other farces, is a veteran of this sort of thing. His movies are slick, simple and irresistibly funny. Like all boulevard comedians, he understands that it is sex that drives everyone crazy. But of course not so much as a top button gets undone in *The Dinner Game*, despite the amount of libidinal energy running loose in Pierre's apartment and leaking down the telephone lines to a world just itching to compound the confusion.

What's good about the movie—and what sets it apart from American comedy at the moment—is the way it refuses to fall across the line into vulgarity, let alone grossness. One's enjoyment of it may very well derive from the way it contrasts with the climate in which it is released. There's something delightfully old-fashioned about its archness and its solid architecture.

VILLAGE VOICE, 7/13/99, p. 57, Jessica Winter

In the Annals of Idiocy—there with Dan Quayle, Charles Bovary, and Debbie Matenopoulos—surely a place is reserved for Pignon (Jacques Villeret), a portly, hapless French civil servant who spends his spare time constructing matchstick models of famous buildings. Just moments after meeting him, Brochant (Thierry Lhermitte), a smugly well-to-do publisher, knows he's found a diamond in the rough—he and his pals like to hold "idiot dinners," where they compete to bring the stupidest guest. When the unwitting Pignon arrives at Brochant's fab pad, however, the contender is down for the count: Brochant can't make it to the party, as he's thrown out his back and his wife, Christine, has just left him. Pignon resolves to stay and help his new "friend," in the process botching attempts to find Christine, inviting a tax collector into Brochants apartment, and even preventing Christine's return to her home.

The script for *The Dinner Game*—courtesy of director Francis Veber, a Frenchman whose films have provided the springboard for dozens of lousy Hollywood remakes (most recently *Father's Day*)—is at once blithe and meticulous about the tidy comeuppance it arranges for Brochants everyday cruelty, a tone that matches the jovial yet concentrated approach to humilation that he and his friends pursue. But the movie, thankfully, is not so conceited as that smarmy bunch. Clever, snappy, and inconsequential, it's essentially a two-character sketch, and one that never strains for a laugh (Lhermitte's subtle air of bemused fatalism toward the end of the film is funny in itself. True to its simple premise, *The Dinner Game* aspires to be not more nor less than an airy confection, as lightweight and briefly diverting as one of Pignon's matchstick towers.

Also reviewed in:
CHICAGO TRIBUNE, 8/27/99, Friday/p. F, John Petrakis
NEW REPUBLIC, 8/2/99, p. 30, Stanley Kauffman
NEW YORK TIMES, 7/9/99, p. E22, Janet Maslin
VARIETY, 5/4-10/98, p. 85, Lisa Nesselson
WASHINGTON POST, 8/27/99, p. C5, Stephen Hunter
WASHINGTON POST, 8/27/99, Weekend/p. 39, Desson Howe

DR. AKAGI

A Kino International release of an Imamura Productions/ToeiCo. Ltd/Imamura Productions, Toei Co. Ltd Tohoku Shinsha Kadokawa Shoten/Comme des Cinémas/Catherine Dusssart Productions/Le Studio Canal+ production. *Producer:* Hisa Ino and Koji Matsuda. *Director:* Shohei Imamura. *Screenplay (Japanese with English subtitles):* Shohei Imamura and Daisuke Tengan. *Based on the book "Doctor Liver":* Ango Sakaguchi. *Director of Photography:* Shigeru Komatsubara. *Music:* Yosuke Yamashita. *Sound:* Kenichi Benitani. *Casting:* Takefumi Yoshikawa. *Art Director:* Hisao Inagaki. *Costumes:* Keisuke Chiyoda and Ikuko Kozu. *Running time:* 120 minutes. *MPAA Rating:* Not Rated.

CAST: Akira Emoto (Dr. Akagi); Kumiko Aso (Sonoko); Jyuro Kara (Umemoto); Masanori Sera (Toriumi); Jacques Gamblin (Piet); Keiko Matsuzaka (Tomiko); Misa Shimizu (Gin); Yukiya Kitamura (Sankichi); Masa Yamada (Masuyo); Tomoro Taniguchi (Nosaka); Masato Ibu (Ikeda).

LOS ANGELES TIMES, 4/9/99, Calendar/p. 16, Kevin Thomas

Shohei Imamura's masterful, deceptively mellow "Dr. Akagi" takes its title from a physician whose dedication reminded Imamura of his own father. Based on a novel by the late Ango Sakaguchi, the film is set in a seaside island village in the spring of 1945. As the end of the war draws near, Dr. Akagi (Akira Emoto) grows evermore concerned with the spread of hepatitis, which he thinks has reached epidemic proportions. However, the army doctor at the nearby base is in as deep denial about the disease as the military is over Japan's imminent defeat.

In this manner, Imamura sets off the two contradictory impulses deeply embedded in Japanese—indeed, world—history and culture: humanism and militarism. As hardships increase and chaos looms, Akagi becomes obsessed with finding the cause and cure for hepatitis.

Under the circumstances, there is something absurd yet noble in his endeavor, and Imamura celebrates the human comedy in all its earthiness and idiosyncrasies against the mounting hysteria of the armed forces. "Dr. Akagi" is as funny as it is serious, and its shifting tones and moods are echoed in Yosuke Yamashita's venturesome modern jazz score.

The doctor, a middle-aged widower with a physician son serving in Manchuria, is a local character, sporting a straw hat and bow tie and dressed in summer whites as he hurries about his rounds; he's a man who never walks when he can run. Imamura takes his time revealing the life of the town, acquainting us with those close to the doctor: the exuberantly libertine monk Umemoto (Jyuro Kara); the disillusioned, morphine-addicted surgeon Toriumi (Masanori Sera); and the attractive, gracious madam of a local brothel, Tomiko (Keiko Matsuzaka). In one way or another they will find themselves caught up in Akagi's obsession, joined by Sonoko (Kumiko Aso), an orphaned fisherman's daughter who matter-of-factly turns to prostitution to help support her flock of younger siblings—even after she becomes Akagi's loyal and loving assistant. A wounded, escaped Dutch prisoner of war (Jacques Gamblin) will become part of Akagi's colorful ragtag research team.

"Dr. Akagi" has something of the warmth, sentiment, humor and expansiveness of Marcel Pagnol's Marseilles trilogy, coupled with Imamura's characteristic interplay of raw, primitive emotions and beliefs and modern, science-minded thought. Sonoko is an Imamura archetype, uninhibited as she is loving. She can take pleasure in discovering how happy she feels, even as she awaits for customers in Tomiko's brothel, dandling her 4-year-old sister on her knee as she lectures the uncomprehending child on not giving away "freebies" when it comes to sex.

Accomplished at expressing the complexities of human nature and emotions, Imamura has captured a sense of timelessness to the extent that we all but forget the time and place. Inevitably, there will be a moment of reckoning for Akagi and his grand project—and it will involve tragedy, but it will also give way to a larger perspective as the doctor himself comes to realize that he inadvertently has started sacrificing the immediate needs of his patients for his research.

Imamura continues deepening his vision, invoking feelings of love and destiny as his film builds to a final image at once as ominous, ironic and darkly amusing as a scene out of "Dr. Strangelove." At 72, Shohei Imamura continues growing as an artist, his status as one of the greatest figures in world cinema long ago secured.

NEW YORK, 1/25/99, p. 48, Peter Rainer

Set in the waning days of world War II, Shohei Imamura's *Dr. Akagi* is a gracefully perverse black comedy about a local physician (Akira Emoto) obsessed with eradicating hepatitis. Scampering through his seaside village in his straw boater and white coat, he's on perpetual house call to his patients; his fanaticism attracts oddball cohorts, including a morphine-addicted doctor, a Dutch POW escapee, a mad monk, and an enraptured hooker, who complains to Akagi: "You think only of your patients and at night you think only of bacteria." When, in the end, Akagi sees an A-bomb cloud in the far horizon, his only thought is that it resembles a hypertrophied liver. He's right, of course.

NEW YORK POST, 1/15/99, p. 46, Thelma Adams

With the success of last year's "The Eel," which landed on a number of top-10 lists, veteran Japanese director Shohei Imamura has become a critics' darling—and for good reason.

Imamura's "Dr. Akagi" opens today at the Lincoln Plaza after a successful premiere at last fall's New York Film Festival. It shares with its predecessor a take on life brimming with humanity and humor riding on a darker, violent, sexually kinky undercurrent.

Based on Ango Sakaguchi's novel about the so-called "Dr. Liver," Imamura's 25th film is set near Hiroshima in 1945 on the eve on the Japanese surrender. The seriocomedy focuses on the daily routine of a rural doctor (Akira Emoto) who believes hepatitis lurks behind each new fever or bellyache. Is this Asian Marcus Welby a quack or a genius?

With historical hindsight, we know what the varied and eccentric characters surrounding Akagi only suspect: that the A-bomb is about to drop and the village so teeming with life will be altered forever. As one man lying atop a prostitute tells the woman: "The war is over. We're all going to die." Unimpressed, she pushes him away, ready for her next trick.

Imamura's brilliant stroke is showing how much life, contradictory and exultant, sexual and violent, existed in the moment before the mushroom cloud. As Akagi, Emoto resembles an Asian Rex Reed; he brings an idiosyncratic charm and obsession to a memorable character.

NEWSDAY, 1/15/99, Part II/p. B11, John Anderson

Shohei Imamura, the grand old man of Japanese cinema, tickles the underbelly of Japanese society, but whatever laughter erupts is always couched in melancholia. Finding humanity in flaws, rather than flaws in humanity, is a serious business, one Imamura takes seriously.

But like his recent "The Eel," there's plenty to chuckle over in "Dr. Akagi," an absurdist romp set in the last days of World War II in a seaside village where the local factory is worked by Allied POWs (hence, no bombings), the skies are blue and the hillsides verdant. Here, Akagi (Akira Emoto) runs—literally—from patient to patient, pausing perhaps to unearth a tuber for sustenance but then resuming his unending race against bad health. "Being a family doctor is all legs," he sighs.

He's dubbed "Dr. Liver" (the title of Ango Sakaguchi's novel) because of his obsession with hepatitis. Akagi cuts a comic figure to the people of his village. But his mission is in earnest. In his haste, his passion and the way he's mocked by his community, Dr. Akagi has all the markings of a prophet. In fact, given his coterie—including the Magdelene-like Sonoko (Kumiko Aso), an incorrigible prostitute in love with the doctor—he may as well be Jesus.

But this is a Christ fable in which evil comes from without (the threat of U.S. airplanes) and within (Japanese soldiers, knowing that defeat is imminent, turning savage in that knowledge). Akagi's disciples are all misfits and outcasts—a morphine-addicted surgeon (Masanori Sera), an alcoholic (Jyuro Kara), an embezzling accountant (Yukiya Kitamura)—but within Imamura's critique of Japanese society they all serve a function, their faults being part of the fabric of the community. (Sonoko, for instance, is constantly harassed for charity sex.) It is, in fact, the soldiers and the solid citizens who cause the most havoc, while Akagi seeks his cure for hepatitis.

Magical realism and radical mood swings mark "Dr. Akagi," which more or less ignores the war—and then brings it back in a stunning coda that reorders all that has come before it. Akagi's eccentric saintliness is ultimately less divine than existential, a Sisyphean slap at insurmountable evil. Which is not to say that Imamura's film isn't funny, only that neither he nor you will exit laughing.

VILLAGE VOICE, 1/19/99, p. 66, J. Hoberman

Shohei Imamura has served notice that the long-germinating *Dr. Akagi* is his last movie. If so, Japan's 71-year-old master of bawdy black humor and enigmatic raunch has chosen to sign off with a thorough and characteristically wild recapitulation of his favorite themes.

Dr. Akagi, which had its local premiere at the last New York Film Festival and follows on the successful release of Imamura's *The Eel*, is a film about a Japanese country doctor and his patients scrambling to survive the final days of their disastrous Pacific War. As lively, irreverent, and bizarrely cheerful as any of Imamura's previous low-life sagas, *Dr. Akagi* is based on several stories by Ango Sakaguchi, a substance-abusing prodigy of the postwar period. But it may have an autobiographical backbeat: Imamura is the son of a country doctor (to whom the movie is dedicated) and was himself a teenager when World War II ended.

Shifting tone from shot to shot, *Dr. Akagi*'s opening is pure Imamura: American B-29s soar among the clouds while, on the ground below, a teenage sometime-hooker named Sonoko is squirming in the embrace of her hapless trick. Just then the couple is distracted by the heroic, heedless Dr. Akagi's boater and bow tie—as he dashes madly down the beach and through the town, accompanied by a burst of cocktail jazz that suggests Lalo Schifrin on pep pills.

Nicknamed "Dr. Liver" because he diagnoses everyone in this fishing village with hepatitis, Akagi (played by Akira Emoto, the lead in *The Eel)* is a crusader who is fighting his own war, conducting his own experiments, setting his own agenda: "Up there bombs, down here hepatitis." But Akagi is only one of the movie's raucous gallery of driven obsessives—embezzlers, drunken monks, morphine-addicted surgeons, and assorted sex fetishists. *Incorrigible* is an oft-used Imamura word, and it describes his sense of human nature. The army is busy teaching old people the basics of civil defense. Superstition competes with science—and usually wins. Sonoko goes to work for Akagi despite the pleas of her orphaned siblings. ("Dear Sis—We're starving. Go back to whoring, please.") Imamura has compassion for just about everyone in this absurd universe, except maybe the race-crazed soldier who beats a Dutch P.O.W. to death.

Before the movie's end, Akagi has turned well-meaning mad scientist—digging up corpses and cutting out their livers, rigging up a giant microscope that seems suspiciously like a movie projector. One critic of the movie wondered why the audience never gets a subjective shot through Akagi's microscope—perhaps it is because a close-up of swarming bacteria would be too close to Imamura's own view of humanity's frenzied flux. If, at just over two hours, *Dr. Akagi* feels a bit sprawling, that is at least partially a function of its considerable vitality. "I like to make messy films," Imamura has said.

As a filmmaker, Imamura is capable of knocking out passages of polished formal beauty. But he is also usefully untidy—as idiosyncratic as any of his characters and as true to his own instincts. Whatever it is, *Dr. Akagi* is never predictable. For his final statement, the director has concocted an ending of unsurpassed weirdness and apocalyptic poetry involving a whale, a water nymph, and a mushroom cloud.

Also reviewed in:
CHICAGO TRIBUNE, 5/7/99, Friday/p. H, Michael Wilmington
NATION, 2/1/99, p. 35, Stuart Klawans
NEW REPUBLIC, 2/8/99, p.24, Stanley Kauffmann
NEW YORK TIMES, 1/15/99, p. E14, Janet Maslin
VARIETY, 6/1-7/98, p. 37, Leonard Klady

DOG OF FLANDERS, A

A Warner Bros release of a Woodbridge Films presentation. *Executive Producer:* Martin J. Barab, Larry Mortoff, and Mark Damon. *Producer:* Frank Yablans. *Director:* Kevin Brodie. *Screenplay:* Kevin Brodie and Robert Singer. *Based on the book by:* Marie Louise de la Ramee. *Director of Photography:* Walther van den Ende. *Editor:* Annamaria Szanto. *Music:* Richard Friedman. *Sound:* Jacob Goldstein. *Production Designer:* Hubert Pouille and Attila F. Kovacs. *Art Director:* Stephan Rubens. *Set Decorator:* Gie Cantraine. *Costumes:* Beatrix Aruna Pasztor. *Running time:* 90 minutes. *MPAA Rating:* PG.

CAST: Jack Warden (Jehan Daas); Jeremy James Kissner (Nello); Jesse James (Young Nello); Jon Voight (Michel La Grande); Cheryl Ladd (Anna Cogez); Steven Hartley (Carl Cogez); Bruce McGill (William the Blacksmith); Andrew Bicknell (Stephens); Farren Monet (Aloise); Antje De Boeck (Millie); Madyline Sweeten (Young Aloise); Deborah Polit (Mary Daas); Dirk Lavrysen (Peter Paul Rubens).

LOS ANGELES TIMES, 8/27/99, Calendar/p. 16, John Anderson

[The following review by John Anderson appeared in a slightly different form in **NEWSDAY, 8/27/97, Part II/p. B6.]**

That director Kevin Brad can breathe any energy at all into "A Dog of Flanders" is something of a shaggy miracle. Its plot devices—noble orphaned boy, unknown father, faithful pet, injustice born of ignorance—may have been fresh when they appeared in the novel written by Ouida (a.k.a. Marie Louise de la Ramee) back in 1872, but since then they've been lifted quite often.

Not that there's a lot of effort expended. Set in early 19th century Flanders (Dutch-speaking Belgium), "A Dog of Flanders" is a clunky film about Nello (played by Jesse James young, Jeremy James Kissner older), whose mother dies shortly after dropping him at the home of her father (Jack Warden)—in a blinding snowstorm, naturally—and who grows up with his mother's artistic talent and no idea who fathered him.

His best friend—after the neighbor girl, Aloise (Madyline Sweeten young, Farren Monet older)—is Patrasche, a big, black, fluffy Bouvier des Flanders whom Nello finds nearly beaten to death. Boy and dog become constant companions.

This is a movie for younger children—they won't know the conventions of the story, they won't notice that only adults have accents, and they won't notice that the children deliver their lines with all the conviction of an airline flight boarding announcement.

There are few enough movies with younger kids in mind, so it's also forgivable that Jon Voight, as Nello's mentor, Michel La Grande, looks like he feels ridiculous (his wig makes him look like one of the Moody Blues), because he gives a reasonably heartfelt performance.

Younger children also will get a brief education into the life and work of the painter Rubens, Nello's idol, who, in a vision, even makes a brief appearance (and whose "Descent From the Cross" becomes not only a dramatic high point but also a cinematic one).

Those familiar with the book will be interested to know that the ending has been changed, into one much happier. The trade-off for this loss of profundity—even invigorating tragedy—is a gain in user-friendliness. Everyone can see "Dog of Flanders." Even French poodles.

NEW YORK POST, 8/27/99, p. 57, Rod Dreher

There are so few kids' movies today that when one comes along that children may enjoy, critics are loath to warn parents off, even if the film is flawed.

Hence my problem with "A Dog of Flanders," a film that parents can confidently and with pleasure take their little ones to see—but which is not quite a good movie.

Director Kevin Brodie's handsome-looking but timid update of the classic Belgian tale suffers from schmaltziness and a revised happy ending that robs the original story of its tragic (if melodramatic) power.

"A Dog of Flanders," based on a famous 19th-century children's book, tells the story of the orphan Nello, an impoverished peasant child of early 19th-century Flanders. He lives in a renter's shack with his twinkly grandfather (Jack Warden).

One day, Grampa and Nello (Jesse James as a little boy, Jeremy James Kissner as an older lad) find a dying Bouvier hound on the side of the road, beaten and left for dead by its mean owner, and they nurse the dog back to health.

"Patrasche," as Nello names the dog, becomes the boy's constant companion—and, weirdly, entirely extraneous to the drama.

Nello is also close to Aloise (Madyline Sweeten as a wee girl, Farren Monet as an adolescent), the daughter of the miller. Aloise's father (Steven Hartley), though, doesn't want his daughter risking attachment to a poor boy with a dismal future.

But Michel La Grande (Jon Voight), a great local painter with a kind soul and an eye for talent, hopes to change Nello's life by sponsoring his artistic career. Alas, heartless men and cruel fate conspire on several fronts to keep the winsome prodigy from receiving his due.

"A Dog of Flanders" is beautifully filmed, and no one can quibble with the story's moral exhortation to judge people not by materialistic criteria, but by the content of their character.

But the script is not especially interesting, and Brad can't resist piping in honeyed music to guide viewers' reactions at every turn. This oversweet film goes into sugar shock in a life-after-death scene in which Nello's disembodied spirit meets the ghost of his idol, the artist Peter Paul Rubens (Dirk Lavrysen).

Not to worry, the kid doesn't really die, unlike in the book. This "Dog of Flanders" has been neutered to protect the sensibilities of American children. The fake Hollywood happy ending wins out over artistic and emotional integrity. Again.

Also reviewed in:
NEW YORK TIMES, 8/27/99, p. E20, Stephen Holden
VARIETY, 8/30-9/5/99, p. 54, Joe Leydon
WASHINGTON POST, 8/27/99, Weekend/p. 38, Jane Horwitz

DOG PARK

A Lions Gate Films release of an Accent Entertainment production. *Executive Producer:* Jeff Sackman. *Producer:* Susan Cavan. *Director:* Bruce McCulloch. *Screenplay:* Bruce McCulloch. *Director of Photography:* David Makin. *Editor:* Christopher Cooper. *Music:* Craig Northey. *Music Editor:* Jane Tattersall and Trevor Ambrose. *Sound:* Henry Embry and (music) Mike Jones. *Sound Editor:* Jane Tattersall. *Production Designer:* Marian Wihak. *Art Director:* Arvinder Grewal. *Set Decorator:* Ane Christensen. *Set Dresser:* Andreas "Andy" Loew, Avril Dishaw, and Terry McGauran. *Costumes:* Linda Muir. *Make-up:* Geralyn Wraith. *Stunt Coordinator:* A. Tyukodi. *Running time:* 90 minutes. *MPAA Rating:* R.

CAST: Natasha Henstridge (Lorna); Luke Wilson (Andy); Kathleen Robertson (Cheryl); Janeane Garofalo (Jeri); Bruce McCulloch (Jeff); Kristin Lehman (Keiran); Amie Carey (Rachel); Gordon Currie (Trevor); Harland Williams (Callum); Mark McKinney (Dog Psychologist); Jerry Schaefer (Norm); Zachary Bennett (Dougie); Peter MacNeill (Old Neighbour); Ron James (Male Dog Owner); Albert Schultz (Male Dog Owner #2); Diane Flacks (Chirpy Dog Owner); Earl Pastko (Bartender); Nick Johne (Video Cashier); Jennifer Irwin (Woman); Myrna Sun (Hostess); Michael McManus (Derrick the Waiter); Tracy Wright (Dog Psychologist's Wife); Leisha Morais and Jason Arnott (Dog Psycologist's Children); Terri Hawkes (Announcer); Boyd Banks ("Go Away Stain" Host).

LOS ANGELES TIMES, 9/24/99, Calendar/p. 14, Robin Rauzi

[The following review by Robin Rauzi appeared in a slightly different form in
NEWSDAY, 9/25/99, Part II/p. B15.]

If the film "Dog Park" were the only guide to Toronto, one might easily conclude that only 10 people live there and that most of them tend toward obtuse.

Written and directed by one-time Kid in the Hall Bruce McCulloch, "Dog Park" has the outward appearance of a by-the-book romantic comedy. Peel away the layers of contrivances, however, and the leftover plot barely fills a doggy bag.

From the start, the ensemble orbits around Andy (Luke Wilson, also in the recent release "Blue Streak"), who mopes about after his girlfriend left him—and took the dog. The four women in his life are his ex, Cheryl (Kathleen Robertson); his best friend Jeri (Janeane Garofalo); a sexually aggressive nutritionist (Kristin Lehman); and the oh-so-lovely Lorna (Natasha Henstridge).

The idea here is that these characters' dogs reflect what is happening in their owners' lives. The reality, however, is that the people are hardly more complex than their four-legged friends. Defined solely by their dating lives—wary, intrusive, too-quick-to-commit—the characters are so uninteresting, it's difficult to believe they're interested in each other.

Wilson has a certain aw-shucks, nice-guy appeal, while Henstridge ("Species") is undeniably attractive to anybody who can get one eye open. Yet neither has the charm to create a whole character who can transcend stilted scenes and awkward dialogue such as "I liked holding your hair." (Huh?) McCulloch saves the best rant for himself as Jeff, Jeri's long-term boyfriend. Another Kids in the Hall alum, Mark McKinney, steals his few scenes as the dog psychologist unable to deal with humans.

Garofalo, in a smallish part, pretty much walks through the film, yet somehow infuses Jeri with a modicum of personality. Wilson's rising star, plus the combination of Garofalo and the word "Dog" in the title, must have been enough to interest New Line, which is distributing the movie in the United States. But this is no "The Truth About Cats and Dogs," which handled human insecurities with style and humor.

"Dog Park," rather than conflict, has coincidence: Lorna's ex is dating Andy's ex, etc. Their world gets smaller and smaller until, by the end, there are zero degrees of separation between any of the characters. The connections are supposed to be clever, but the result is claustrophobic. And baffling. How can this handful of people move in a circle so small, yet never realize how they are linked?

The too-small-world feel is made more disconcerting by the lack of extras in the bars, restaurant and park, compounded by the absence of ambient noise. Despite otherwise high production values, the story looks—and sounds—as if it takes place in an unpopulated alternate universe.

If that's what Canada is like, it sure would ease the minds of the Film and Television Action Committee that spearheaded the anti-Canada "Bring Hollywood Home" campaign. No worries, guys—there aren't any Canadians to take your jobs.

NEW YORK POST, 9/25/99, p. 21, Jonathan Foreman

"Dog Park" is a romantic comedy based on the promising (and probably true) premise that dog ownership is good for your love life.

Unfortunately, this film by Canadian funnyman Bruce McCulloch turns out to be a slack-paced, surprisingly bland affair, filled with jokes that sound like they should be funny but aren't.

Andy (Luke Wilson), a reticent, rather charmless journalist, has just been dropped by his girlfriend Cheryl (Kathleen Robertson), who took their dog Mogley with her when she moved into her new boyfriend's house.

A few days later, gorgeous Lorna (Natasha Henstridge) picks him up in a bar and goes home with him, but the evening ends prematurely when she throws up.

Lorna herself has just been dropped by her boyfriend—who we later discover is the same guy who has taken up with Cheryl—and she's so sorry for herself that when Andy tries to follow up on their abortive evening she blows him off.

Andy is then "bought" for the night at a charity auction by Keiran (Kristin Lehman), a sexually aggressive nutritionist. She seduces him, but he still pines for Lorna.

There are more strands to the story, but almost all the characters either have a dog enrolled at an obedience school run by dog psychiatrist Dr. Cavan (Mark McKinney) or are sleeping with someone else who does.

Everything comes to a head at the obedience school's graduation day in the park.

Wilson plays Andy as such a sad sack, you cannot believe that three such hot women would be interested in him. And he has absolutely no chemistry at all with Henstridge.

The best, and only notable performance in the movie comes from Janeane Garofalo as Andy's friend Jeri.

She has a strange knack for choosing lame projects, but she becomes more impressive and more appealing with every film she does.

VILLAGE VOICE, 9/28/99, p. 128, Jessica Winter

Even as light romantic comedies go, *Dog Park* takes one bland, maundering stroll. The film does have a thesis, though, and a sweet, earnestly presented thesis to boot—that the love missing or fraught in the average single thirtysomething's life can find ready, partial compensation in the unconditional dumb love of your dog. And, as it turns out, Taylor Dayne was wrong—it's not love that leads you back, but Fido, since you'll meet Mr./Ms. Right at the puppy run in the park, or reconcile with an ex at the dog psychiatrist after you've decided that your co-custody, Sparky, has absorbed your shared angst.

Cute, but *Dog Park*—a cluttered ensemble piece that pivots on Luke Wilson's beleaguered serial monogamist and his circle of romantically challenged, dog-owner friends—stays pinned to the grass by its contrived whimsy. The throwaway one-liners ("Love is not your scuba buddy") sound as if they should be funny, but never amount to anything more than tossed-off absurdity; the performances are similarly offhand (the invaluable Janeane Garofalo is an exception as a deludedly blithe, betrayed girlfriend, but must she martyr herself in every movie?). Writer, director, and supporting player Bruce McCulloch cut his teeth on sketch comedy with *Kids in the Hall,* and *Dog Park* has the feel of skits scrawled out on bar napkins and tacked together (he even regurgitates two old *Kids* bits). Isolated triumphs of wordplay emerge—the dog shrink delivers an impassioned soliloquy on his craft; a couple engages in a reasoned, circular discussion about whether they should go out to dinner or have sex first—but the rest looks like landfill. McCulloch, last seen in *Dick,* seems like a pretty clever guy; since flogging Carl Bernstein used to be Nora Ephron's job, one hopes that McCulloch isn't doomed to deliver formulaic, slapdash Comedy Lite for the rest of his days, but right now the odds look long.

Also reviewed in:
CHICAGO TRIBUNE, 9/28/99, Tempo/p. 2, Barbara Shulgasser
NEW YORK TIMES, 9/25/99, p. B12, Anita Gates
VARIETY, 9/28-10/4/98, p. 40, Brendan Kelly

DOGMA

A Lions Gate Films release of a View Askew production. *Producer:* Scott Mosier. *Director:* Kevin Smith. *Screenplay:* Kevin Smith. *Director of Photography:* Robert Yeoman. *Editor:* Kevin Smith and Scott Mosier. *Music:* Howard Shore. *Music Editor:* Shari Schwartz-Johanson. *Choreographer:* J. Thorstein. *Sound:* Whit Norris and (music) Howard Shore and Robert Cotnoir. *Sound Editor:* Ethan Van Der Ryn. *Casting:* Donna Belajac. *Production Designer:* Robert Holtzman. *Art Director:* Elise G. Viola. *Set Designer:* Larry M. Gruber. *Set Decorator:* Diana Stoughton. *Set Dresser:* Bill Franko, Ray Pivirotto, Charles Whatton, Jr., Greg Jones, Mary M. O'Brien, Fredo Donatelli, Steve Fabian, Elaheh Ferrari, and Jeffrey Hussett. *Special Effects:* Charles Bellardinelli. *Visual Effects:* Richard "Dickie" Payne. *Costumes:* Abigail Murray. *Make-up:* Jeannee Josefczyk. *Make-up (Linda Fiorentino):* Anita Gibson. *Make-up (Special Effects):* Vincent Guastini. *Stunt Coordinator:* Gary Jensen. *Running time:* 125 minutes. *MPAA Rating:* Not Rated.

CAST: Bud Cort (John Doe Jersey); Barrett Hackney, Jared Pfennigwerth, and Kitao Sakurai (Stygian Triplets); George Carlin (Cardinal Glick); Brian Christopher O'Halloran (Reporter); Betty Aberlin (Nun); Matt Damon (Loki); Ben Affleck (Bartleby); Dan Etheridge (Priest, St. Stephens); Linda Fiorentino (Bethany); Janeane Garofalo and Marie Elena O'Brien (Clinic Girls); Bryan Johnson (Protestor #1); Walter Flanagan (Protestor #2); Jason Lee (Azrael); Nancy Bach (Mrs. Reynolds); Alan Rickman (Metatron); Armando Rodriguez (Waiter); Jason Mewes (Jay); Jeff Anderson (Gun Salesman); Kevin Smith (Silent Bob); Scott Mosier (Married Man); Chris Rock (Rufus); Salma Hayek (Serendipity); Dwight Ewell (Kane); Benjamin Cain (Gangster #1); Richard Baderinwa (Gangster #2); Javon Johnson (Gangster #3); Derrick Sanders (Gangster #4); Mark Joy (Whitland); Ethan Suplee (Voice of No Man); Guinevere Turner (Bus Station Attendant); Jon Gordon (Blanket Boy on Train); Matthew Maher (Bartender); Robert Holtzman (Officer McGee); Alanis Morisette (God); Derek Milosavljevic and Lesley Braden (Kissing Couple); Monica Hampton (Seaman Smoocher); Linda Levine (Woman in Boardroom); Nancy Mosser Bailey (Governor Elizabeth Dalton).

CHRISTIAN SCIENCE MONITOR, 11/12/99, p. 15, David Sterritt

[*Dogma* was reviewed jointly with *The Messenger*; see Sterritt's review of that film.

LOS ANGELES TIMES, 11/12/99, Calendar/p. 1, Kenneth Turan

Only someone serious about religion in general and Catholicism in particular could have made "Dogma," but those expecting a modern version of "The Song of Bernadette" or "King of Kings" are going to find themselves dazed and confused.

For though the writer-director of this film is a practicing Catholic with a monk's fascination with concepts like transubstantiation, plenary indulgences and choirs of angels, Kevin Smith is also the man who brought the racy and irreverent "Clerks," "Mallrats" and "Chasing Amy" into the world. "Dogma" may be a believer's film, but that doesn't mean it's in any way conservative or conventional.

Instead, "Dogma" is a raucous, profane but surprisingly endearing piece of work, a funny and lively film of ideas that combines a breezy save-the-world fantasy with Smith's trademark adolescent sense of humor and a sincere exploration of questions of faith. If you can imagine intense doses of theology and religious doctrine alternating with juvenile sex jokes and a monster that emerges from a toilet, you've got "Dogma" pegged.

Not only does "Dogma" match the unmixable in terms of story, it does the same thing with its eclectic cast. To find polished British actor Alan Rickman, Smith's childhood buddy and alter ego Jason Mewes, comic tornado Chris Rock, cult items George Carlin and Bud Cort, heartthrobs Matt Damon and Ben Affleck—not to mention singer Alanis Morissette as God—together in one film is close to a unique experience.

What does link "Dogma" to much more mannerly religious vehicles is that it takes belief in God as a given. An early scene has Loki (Damon), one of a pair of renegade angels, ragging on his pal Bartleby (Affleck) for trying to talk a nun out of her religion. "You know for a fact there is a God, you've been in her presence," he says, and both Bartleby and the film agree that it's so.

Thrown out of heaven eons ago, Loki and Bartleby have been stuck in Wisconsin for almost all of recorded time. But now news comes to them that if they arrive at a certain church in Red Bank, N.J., on the day of its rededication, they'll be granted plenary indulgences and, through a loophole in Catholic dogma, they'll be able to get back into heaven.

The rededication and the indulgences are the idea of the forward-thinking Cardinal Glick (Carlin), whose mission it is to bring his religion up to date. "Christ didn't come to Earth to give us the willies," he says, announcing that the old gloomy image of the crucifixion will be replaced by statues of a smiling Jesus giving the thumbs-up sign, a.k.a. "the Buddy Christ."

What the cardinal doesn't know is that if Loki and Bartleby are granted those indulgences, that will, in effect, prove God wrong and fallible and, thus, undo reality and reduce existence to nothingness. Not a good idea, top angels agree, and so the high-ranking Seraphim Metatron, the Voice of God (Rickman), is dispatched in a cloud of fire to recruit Bethany (Linda Fiorentino), a conflicted Catholic who works in an abortion clinic, to lead a holy crusade to stop Loki and Bartleby.

A modern, skeptical woman, Bethany douses the flaming messenger with a fire extinguisher and is noticeably suspicious about her mission. What she doesn't know is that she's going to get help from the most ragtag bunch of spiritual pranksters.

These include a pair of prophets, talkative Jay (Mewes) and Silent Bob (Smith himself); Rufus, the hitherto unknown Thirteenth Apostle (Rock) who's irked at being left out of the Bible; and a muse named Serendipity (Salma Hayek) currently working as a stripper. Fighting on the other side are a slick demon named Azrael (Jason Lee), a trio of skating hit boys and a foul-smelling monster called Golgothan.

Complicated as this sounds, it doesn't capture a lot of the wackier elements in this densely plotted, off-the-wall film, everything from angels offering proof that they're sexually neutral to a bloody attack by Loki and Bartleby on the Mooby Corp., an empire based on an animated duck the way Disney's is based on a mouse.

And in between the bad jokes about bodily functions and sexual availability, "Dogma" offers a fair number of unexpectedly thoughtful moments. "I have issues with anyone who treats God as a burden, not a blessing," one character says. And then there is the notion that the world would be better off if there were more ideas than beliefs, because ideas can be changed if necessary.

While notions like God as a woman ("The whole book is gender-biased" is "Dogma's" verdict on the Bible) are certain to give religious conservatives pause, "Dogma's" pee-wee sense of humor will have their more liberal brethren occasionally tearing their hair out as well.

A film that knows that everything it does isn't going to work, "Dogma" is rescued again and again by its refreshing high energy level and the quirky preoccupations of its quick-witted, unabashed writer-director. To say no one but Kevin Smith could have made this film is, finally, to have said it all.

NEW YORK, 11/22/99, p. 88, Peter Rainer

Kevin Smith's *Dogma*, which is about fallen angels (Ben Affleck and Matt Damon) trying to connive their way back into Heaven, has a fair amount of notoriety going for it: Its distribution shifted from the Disney-owned Miramax to the more independent Lions Gate, and it's been attacked by the New York-based Catholic League for Religious and Civil Rights. For a film that ought to singe the sensibilities (isn't it time we had our very own Buñuel?) *Dogma,* however, turns out to be a rather street bit of blasphemy—if that's what indeed it is—committed by a director who sees the world not through a glass darkly, but through the eyes of a comic-book maven.

The characters in *Dogma*—including a seraph who speaks with the voice of God (Alan Rickman), a stripper Muse (Salina Havek), the thirteenth apostle (Chris Rock), and a woman who works for Planned Parenthood and tithes part of her salary to the church (Linda Fiorentino) all have the squiggly eccentricities of cartoons. And yet Smith's professed Catholic piety, or at least his irreverently reverent version of piety informs the film: Periodically, his characters come out with scrunched sermonettes about faith and reason and what all, and the effect is like listening to the socially conscious bits in message movies. Smith is a spirited jester, and parts of *Dogma* are bright, icon-busting fun, but most of it is a god-awful mess. And shouldn't a movie about transcendence have more transcendent imagery?

NEW YORK POST, 11/12/99, p. 50, Jonathan Foreman

An ambitious failure, "Dogma" is neither a savage attack on religion nor a hysterically funny spoof—unlike, say Monty Python's "The Life of Brian."

It takes belief seriously—in an intellectual rather than a heartfelt way—but filmmaker Kevin Smith's attempt to combine sketchy low comedy with long-winded theological speculation results in a mostly unfunny and occasionally tedious mess.

Smith was responsible for two remarkable independent films: the bold and, at times, brilliant "Clerks," and "Chasing Amy." In the publicity drive for this movie, he has made much of his being a believing (if unorthodox) Catholic and of his readings in theology.

With "Dogma," he's apparently attempting something reminiscent of the bawdy Catholic humanism of the 16th-century French satirist Francois Rabelais. But the experiment comes out half-baked, and the theology too often swamps the humor—all too much of which is reminiscent of Mel Brooks at his least inspired.

Two fallen angels, Loki (Matt Damon) and Bartleby (Ben Affleck), who have been exiled to Wisconsin for all eternity, are sent a newspaper clipping about a Church re-dedication. It says that the first people to go through an arch in the church will receive a plenary indulgence: All their sins will be forgiven. The two angels figure that they can go through the arch and then get back into heaven.

The problem with this, according to the good angel Metatron (Alan Rickman), is that if they do get back into heaven against God's will, then all of creation will be undone.

So Metatron contacts Bethany (Linda Fiorentino), a lapsed Catholic living in Illinois who happens to be a descendant of Jesus, and persuades her to help frustrate the plan hatched by Loki and Bartleby.

It's typical of Smith's lead-pipe irony that the woman who is God's best hope should work an abortion clinic.

Bethany travels to New Jersey, accompanied at times by a muse (Salma Hayek) and two teenage prophets: desperately horny Jay (Jason Mewes) and Silent Bob (Kevin Smith). A demon (Jason Lee) and his minions try to stop her.

Fiorentino is the stooge who gets to ask dumb religious questions that are then answered in jokey, faux-colloquial fashion by the various supernatural beings. The exposition drags on and on, but the ragged quality of the writing makes even non-Catholics wonder how accurate Smith's religious musings are.

It's not just that he has Chris Rock play the "13th apostle" when he more likely means the "13th disciple." Smith uses "obtuse" when he means "obscure." This kind of carelessness would matter less in a film with less serious aims.

The joke of having serious religious figures talk like late 20th-century Americans is only funny for the first 20 minutes or so, and the film trundles along for more than two hours.

Smith's grand notion of a modernized, humane Catholicism turns out just to be New Agey religion lite—not very different from the commercial E-Z piety that the film mocks George

Carlin's bishop for peddling (see Tom Lehrer's "Vatican Rag" for a superior version of Carlin's shtick).

As one character says after one of the many theological arguments, "It doesn't matter what you believe, as long as you have faith in something." In other words, the film espouses the usual cheap 'n' cheerful spiritualism beloved of sentimental Hollywood, and serves it up with a heavy gravy of predictable PC pseudo-daring. Not only is God a woman (Alanis Morissette) but Jesus was, of course, black.

In the end, "Dogma" is an oddly soulless, visually unimpressive waste of a fine cast and expensive special effects. The Spanish movie "Day of the Beast," released here last June, is a far better religious joke about the apocalypse.

NEWSDAY, 11/12/99, Part II/p. B7, John Anderson

"If he be an unbeliever," wrote the 19th-Century theologian John Cardinal Newman, "he will be too profound and large-minded to ridicule religion or act against it; he is too wise to be a dogmatist or fanatic in his infidelity ..." What would his eminence have thought of "Dogma," Kevin Smith's much-talked-about, railed-against comedy about God, church and the unsinkable accessories of faith? In all likelihood, that it was made by someone fanatic in his fidelity. Smith's movie may suffer from his own lack of visual style, unwillingness or inability to direct his actors and a proclivity for writing long-winded speeches; as has been evident since "Clerks," Smith was born for the golden age of radio. But while "Dogma" is a very funny, very sloppy movie, there's never any doubt that the director is dead serious about his faith.

That such a gleefully sophomoric, devoutly vulgar comedy should become the hotpoint of religious protests is rather funny—at least considering that the people protesting it may be among the few who will really understand it. As someone has already said, theaters should hand out catechisms, lest Smith's rococo applications of Catholic doctrine leave audiences slack jawed (or, worse, leave them with nothing but the film's mall-movie humor or the shimmy-shimmy-koko-bop of Salma Hayek as a table-dancing divinity). That the movie spins on the arcane doctrinal point of "plenary indulgences"—by which the homicidal-maniac angels Loki (Matt Damon) and Bartelby (Ben Affleck) plan to re-enter heaven and thus end life as we know it is an example of Smith's arcane way with religion. Who's even in the same pew, other than people so devoted to their faith they can't distinguish free will from blasphemy? Smith, like any parochial school kid too smart for his own good, is clearly out to offend despite the wimpy disclaimer that opens the film by using the church's teachings against it. Take Bethany (Linda Fiorentino), who's having a crisis of faith and is selected to save the world: Her profile makes her dangerously akin to a certain virgin (alert Rudolph Giuliani!). She's assisted on her pilgrimage to New Jersey by Rufus (Chris Rock), the previously undocumented 13th Apostle and confidant of Jesus ("Know him? The --- owed me 12 bucks"), the disembodied Voice of God (Alan Rickman), Hayek's aforementioned muse and those ubiquitous hormonal potheads, Smith-movie regulars Jay and Silent Bob (Jason Mewes and Smith himself). The lineup alone is apoplectic.

Our heroes' task is to stop Loki and Bartlelby and find God who has taken one of her periodic constitutionals and has disappeared near the Jersey shore.

Irreverent, certainly, but to what? Disney, for one thing. Loki and Bartelby execute en masse the "idolators" at the head of the Mooby Corp., whose trademark is a goofy looking cow in big-buttoned pants. There are a lot of harmless potshots at golfing priests and the less than revelatory news that Jesus was probably black. And then Smith throws a curve: "You don't celebrate your faith," a character says, "you mourn it." Now that's the kind of line that could really get us Catholics ticked off—if they went to see the movie.

NEW STATESMAN, 12/13/99, p. 47, Jonathan Romney

[*Dogma* was reviewed jointly with *End of Days*; see Romney's review of that film.]

NEWSWEEK, 11/15/99, p. 88, Jeff Giles

Loki (Matt Damon) and Bartleby (Ben Affleck) are angels with a bad employment history. Thousands of years ago, when God was in his act-of-vengeance mode, they did most of the heavy lifting: choreographing Noah's flood, slaughtering the first born in Egypt and bickering all the while. ("You got to just stand there and *read* at Sodom and Gomorrah," Loki complains. "I had to do all the work.") Then they decided that murdering, even in the name of God, was wrong. Loki got drunk and gave their boss the finger—and he and his celestial buddy were banished from heaven forever.

As Kevin Smith's manic comedy "Dogma" opens—in present-day New Jersey—the angels are scheming to sneak back in. If Loki and Bartleby make it, God will be proved fallible, and all existence will be obliterated. So a team of angelic superheroes bands together to stop them. There's a grumpy messenger (Alan Rickman), a muse who's now working as a stripper (Salma Hayek), an apostle named Rufus (Chris Rock) who claims he was left out of the Bible because he is black and an abortion-clinic worker (Linda Fiorentino) who's been chosen as the human who must save humanity. What follows is a movie about heaven that makes no earthly sense. To further complicate things, our superheroes are being followed by a satanic street-hockey team.

Director Smith ("Clerks," "Chasing Amy") attempts something ambitious with "Dogma"—an antic mix of the sacred and the very profane, of organized-religion bashing and sex jokes. And the movie is gutsy, too, at least in the sense that it will infuriate some devout Roman Catholics. (The movie was controversial before anyone even saw it. So the powers that be at Miramax, which is owned by Disney, decided to release it through another company, Lions Gate Films.) The real trouble here, however, isn't sacrilege: Smith clearly believes in God and fears hell and so on. The real problem is that "Dogma" isn't as funny as it thinks it is. The speechifying about religion is dull to a surreal degree—anybody want to hear from the noted theologian Salma Hayek?—and ultimately makes pedestrian points. Faith is good. The rigidity of the church is bad, etc.

For some reason, though, you never stop rooting for "Dogma." That's partly because the actors are mostly welcome faces. Rock is, as always, a furnace-blast of acerbic energy. Damon's Loki has some similarly edgy moments—he hates sinners so much that he wants to go on one last killing spree for old time's sake. (Loki is brilliant and homicidal—he's Will Hunting on speed.) And George Carlin turns up as a New Jersey cardinal who practices putting into a golden chalice and tries to rejuvenate his religion with an inane PR campaign called "Catholicism—Wow!" One of the cardinal's brainstorms is junking the old crucifix, which he regards as too dreary: "Christ didn't come down to Earth to give us the willies!"

Another reason you root for "Dogma" is that—as preposterous as the movie gets—it's clearly reveling in its own hokiness. The ending is a cheesy, operatic showdown between good and evil outside a cathedral. God herself (Alanis Morissette) makes a beguiling appearance. She never utters a word—but then "Dogma" would leave anybody speechless.

SIGHT AND SOUND, 1/00, p. 47, Kevin Maher

New Jersey, the present. An old man is badly beaten and sent into a coma. At Red Bank cathedral, Cardinal Glick reveals that the Pope has granted a plenary indulgence for anyone who enters the cathedral during its rededication ceremony in four days' time. In Wisconsin, fallen angels Bartleby and Loki decide to gain this indulgence to re-enter heaven. In Illinois, the seraph Metatron orders abortion-clinic worker Bethany Sloane—who's angry with God because of her own diseased womb—to protect the cathedral from the angels. Although initially reluctant, Bethany agrees. Drug dealers Jay and Silent Bob save her from a mugging and the three head for NJ. On the way they meet Rufus, the thirteenth apostle. They encounter Serendipity, a Muse, along the way and are attacked by the Golgothon, a 'Shit Monster', but Silent Bob destroys him.

Bartleby and Loki visit the offices of a giant cartoon franchise, and massacre the board of management for breaking the first commandment. On the train to New Jersey they confront Bethany, but Silent Bob throws them off. Metatron appears to Bethany and tells her she's the last descendant of Christ and that God is missing from Heaven. Arriving in Red Bank, Bethany and the others are trapped in a bar by the demon Azrael, while Bartleby slaughters those assembled at the cathedral. Having escaped the bar, Bethany realises God is trapped inside the comatose old man. Bethany runs to the hospital and kills him, thereby freeing God who undoes the slaughter and forgives Bartleby. Bethany discovers she's miraculously pregnant.

Despite the now notorious antiblasphemy campaign waged against *Dogma* in the US, the most controversial element in writer-director Kevin Smith's new 'religious satire' is not its alleged sacrilege, but its heavy-handed piety. This sporadically charming but pedagogical tale of abortion-clinic worker Bethany and her spiritual road trip is aggressively pro-faith. Bethany's journey to New Jersey is marked by several encounters with quasi-religious figures, such as Chris Rock's Rufus and Alan Rickman's Metatron, whose theology is part John Milton, part Christian mythology but all devotion. As Rufus declares, "It doesn't matter what you believe in, as long as you have faith!" And even though Smith's occasionally erudite script suggests the hardly groundbreaking notions that Christ was black and that Mary wasn't a virgin, this is still a movie whose narrative kernel is contingent on the infallibility of the Catholic Church.

Smith's structure here is an obvious departure from the films in his so-called New Jersey trilogy *(Clerks, Mallrats* and *Chasing Amy).* Instead of the usual simple three-act drama of the latter, he has embraced the episodic structure of road movies, making *The Wizard Of Oz* (1939) a key text. Accompanied by an *Oz*-like motley crew comprised of Rufus and the trilogy's recurring characters Jay and Silent Bob, Bethany's Dorothy figure is guided through an adolescence of theological confusion and sent home pregnant. Smith exchanges his crude but effective two-shots of people in strip malls and video stores for an array of crane shots, tracks and effects befitting a fantastical travelogue. DP Robert Yeoman (*Drugstore Cowboy*), replacing Smith regular David Klein, has added some elegant widescreen framing to the mix.

The unfortunate result of this bravura rejection of his trademark minimalism is that *Dogma* merely highlights Smith's weaknesses as a visual director. He overuses reaction shots when such scenes as the final scuffle with fallen angel Bartleby are virtually crying out for action, leaves jarring location changes unexplained, and subordinates action to dialogue. And while the dialogue displays Smith's canny gift for mellifluous everyday speech, the loftier-than-usual subject matter forces him into a defensive and all-too-regular use of comic relief. The appearance of the Golgothon 'Shit Monster' and the 'zany' boardroom massacre are both glaring comedy misfires, while Jay's overuse of sexual innuendo soon becomes tiresome and repetitious, as do the constant references to *Star Wars, Indiana Jones* films and *The Incredible Hulk*.

Yet there's a sporadic nonsensical energy to *Dogma* that's appealing, mainly due to the cast's camp showboating. Matt Damon and Ben Affleck as the fallen angels in particular seem to be poking fun at their media image. Linda Fiorentino's Bethany, though required to do a lot of blank-faced listening, is compelling in the unusual position of an autonomous heroine who's having a spiritual crisis rather than predictable boyfriend troubles. But, ultimately, *Dogma* is less than the sum of its components. It's clearly not a religious satire since its conclusion merely reinstates the theocratic hegemony it pretended to challenge in the first place. Nor does it quite work as a road movie. Not quite sure whether it's about Bethany's spiritual quest or Bartleby's redemption, the film splits our attentions and affections. As an ambitious and overreaching break with Smith's provincial milieu *Dogma* is a failed experiment, but a noble failure.

TIME, 11/15/99, p. 103, Richard Corliss

In September, the chunky young auteur faced a packed house at the Toronto Film Festival and smiled. "We're here tonight," Kevin Smith said, "and lightning has not struck the building. So I guess it's O.K. with the Lord." Smith, 29, had endured a rough six months, ever since the Catholic League, a lay group with 350,000 members and an intimidating letterhead, had pressured the Walt Disney Co. and its subsidiary Miramax Films to drop *Dogma*, Smith's rambunctious comedy about God, faith and a monster made of poop. Smith was able to make his movie freely, but if the protesters had had their way, he couldn't show it. To twist the famous bumper-sticker phrase, their karma ran over his *Dogma*.

Like the Synoptic Gospels, *Dogma* has a happy ending. Two, in fact. In the movie, God comes to earth, sets things right, then does a handstand. In the drama behind the film, Lions Gate, an independent distributor, opens *Dogma* this week after successful screenings at festivals in Cannes, Toronto and New York City. "Now we can put the rest of the stuff behind us and start fretting about the box office," Smith says. "I'm hoping that when people see the film, they'll say, 'Oh, it's not the movie that flips the bird at the church. It's actually kind of devout.'"

For all the fun it pokes at Catholic doctrine—that God is a woman (Alanis Morissette), that the last descendant of Jesus (Linda Fiorentino) works in an abortion clinic, that there was a 13th Apostle who was black (Chris Rock)—*Dogma* is a tortured testament from a true believer. In an age when not only belief in God but belief itself brings a smirk to hip, jaded faces, this is a film out of time, the most devout movie in a modern setting since Robert Bresson's *Diary of a Country Priest* (1951), and a worthy successor to *The Last Temptation of Christ*, Martin Scorsese's 1988 parable of doubt purified into faith. Love *Dogma* or dismiss it, but don't condemn the film for what it isn't. As Ben Affleck, one of the zillion-dollar stars in this $10 million film, says, "It's a rumination on faith. With dick jokes."

Every good Bible story needs a heavenly visitation. Bethany (Fiorentino) gets hers from the angel Metatron (Alan Rickman), who tells her she is Jesus' distant descendant and it is her destiny to save the world. Two fallen angels, Loki (Matt Damon) and Bartleby (Affleck), have found a doctrinal loophole that will allow them to return to Heaven by walking through a parish door in New Jersey. "It will undo the world," Bethany is told—unless she can stop the renegades from defying God.

So a skeptical Bethany travels from Illinois to Jersey, occasionally accompanied by a hot-wired demon (Jason Lee), a celestial muse (Salma Hayek), the 13th Apostle—and a pair of unlikely prophets, motormouthing Jay (Jason Mewes) and Silent Bob (Smith), the cynical chorus from the writer-director's previous films *Clerks, Mallrats* and *Chasing Amy*.

Smith calls the film "a bizarre mix of lowbrow jokes and highbrow concepts and then vice versa." Ain't it, though? He mixes poop and prophecy, scatology and eschatology; he crams his script with enough belly laughs for six Adam Sandler movies and enough citations of angelology and the Gnostic gospels to make a Jesuit's head split. This is a Shavian debate—Don Juan in New Jersey—with potty mouth. *Dogma*, recall, comes from the Greek word meaning "to think." And that's what Smith wants the viewer to do.

Smith gets steamed when he thinks about the *Dogma* protests. "Every week I go to church, and sooner or later the priest makes a joke! How come a priest can mix religion and jokes, but if I do it, I'm anti-Catholic? That just burns my ass, because I'm out there trying to get people to think about God. I am working the good cause—and I'm anti-Catholic? I tithe! I don't bend down and tie my shoe when the basket comes around!"

His life can now return to bustling normality. He will continue with his comic-book writing, scripts for Miramax and Warner Bros. (a Superman draft didn't work out) and a prime-time cartoon version of *Clerks* for, of course, Disney. "It's just rife with irony, isn't it?" he says. "Let's see if we can deliver the PG my mother was always lookin' for." But his biggest project is to enjoy time with his new wife Jennifer Schwalbach, a former writer for USA Today, and their newborn daughter Harley Quinn. "I want to take the next year off and raise my child," he says. "Do something noble."

Smith has already done that by raising profound issues in a pop context, bringing God to the mallrats, making a good movie. That should be O.K. with the Lord.

VILLAGE VOICE, 11/16/99, p. 129, J. Hoberman

Dogma, as you may have heard, is an Armageddon caper with a cast of characters that includes a pro-choice world savior, a divine messenger who complains of being "as anatomicall impaired as a Ken doll," a supreme deity who takes the form of Alanis Morrisette, and a 13th apostle named Rufus who, when asked if he knew Jesus Christ replies, "Nigger owes me 12 bucks!"

The Catholic League has been pursuing Kevin Smith's cheerfully vulgar, humorously violent, devoutly naughty mix of low comedy and high concept ever since it had its world premiere at Cannes back in May. Thanks to the ruckus over the "Sensation" show, the New York Film Festival dodged a bullet when *Dogma* screened last month. (Still, despite an elaborate special effect called a "Golgotha shit demon," the Holy Virgin Mary doesn't even have a cameo.) Catholicism, for Smith, seems less a source of awe than potentially awesome superhero antics and arcane japery.

Pitched somewhere between *Wings of Desire* and *Mystery Men, Dogma* elaborates the filmmakers parochial school musings into a cooler cosmology than the faux theological fantasies *Phantom Menace* and *Matrix* combined. Prompted by one of Satan's li'l devils (Jason Lee), a pair of yo-dude fallen angels (Matt Damon and Ben Affleck), exiled to Wisconsin for all eternity discover that the feel-good Catholicism promoted by a wacky New Jersey cardinal (George Carlin) has provided them with a loophole to redemption.   As it would confound God's infallibility, their salvation thus threatens to nullify existence. Sounds paradoxical, and the hunky angels dispute the finer points of this cosmic snafu at some length—one can only imagine the laddish shouts and high-fives that followed each take.

To save the universe, God's messenger (embittered-acting Alan Rickman) summons the Chosen One (played, with too much whining sarcasm, by seemingly depressed Linda Fiorentino) to journey out of a Midwestern abortion clinic to New Jersey, accompanied on her mission by Smith's recurring characters, the stoners Silent Bob (the filmmaker) and yammering Jay (Jason Mewes).   To add to the *Wizard of Oz* flavor, they're joined along the way by the apostle Rufus (Chris Rock) and a muse (Salma Hayek, whom Smith gets to prance and grind in her underwear).

Less than a struggle between good and evil (or being and nothingness), *Dogma* seems predicated on a cosmic sibling rivalry.   The firstborn angels are jealous of human free will, as well as the deity's seeming indulgence for human sin.   Damon's former angel of death has a particular propensity for freelance "smiting," which is visited most spectacularly on the corporate idolators who market the cartoon creature Mooby the Golden Calf—a blatantly Mickey Mouse? like fount of movies, videos, theme parks, and other ancillary items. (Some consider the desecration of this sacred cash cow to be the real reason Disney ordered its subsidiary Miramax to ditch *Dogma.)*

To its credit, *Dogma* has a Boschean element.   No less than the early Renaissance church painters, Smith is trying to make Christian mythology contemporary—although, unlike these precursors, he has no feel for composition, landscape, or character.   An opening disclaimer warns critics that "passing judgment is reserved for God and God alone"—perhaps it's a good thing then that, Salma Hayek notwithstanding, *Dogma* doesn't provide much to look at.   Indeed, Smith's desultory film sense seems all the more peculiar considering *Dogma's* insistence on cinema as the ultimate consciousness modifier.   A few abstruse points of dogmatic law aside, movies are virtually Smith's only cultural referent.   "If there isn't a movie about it, it's not worth knowing," the Heavenly Messenger complains.   "Mention something out of a Charlton Heston movie and everybody's a theology scholar."

Basically, Smith enjoys exegesis. Like *Clerks* and *Chasing Amy*, *Dogma* is a stand-up comedy. Once the ball is put in play, the viewer must endure a flat second half, indulging torturously static explanations delivered by characters so garrulous they make those of Eric Rohmer seem as tight-lipped as Silent Bob. (One reason why the eye-rolling Rock stands out is because he's a comic who can deliver one-liners—perhaps Smith should have done more with Carlin.) After slogging through a morass of exposition, the action picks up—but by then it is too late.   Whatever visionary potential Smith's saga once had has devolved to the level of doodling in church.

On one hand, *Dogma* exhibits a touchingly childlike faith.   On the other, it's a tediously childish exhibition. (The real disclaimer should warn against seeing the movie a second time.) For all its profane language and scatology, *Dogma* has nowhere near the anticlerical wit of Luis Buñuel's *Nazarin* or *Vindiana*—let alone his *L'Age d'Or,* an act of blasphemy that drove the 1932 Paris equivalent of the Catholic League to trash the theater and the pope to threaten its producer with excommunication.

Also reviewed in:
NATION, 11/29/99, p. 52, Stuart Klawans
NEW YORKER, 11/15/99, p. 115, Anthony Lane
NEW YORK TIMES, 11/12/99, p. E20, Janet Maslin
VARIETY, 5/24-30/99, p. 73, Todd McCarthy
WASHINGTON POST, 11/12/99, p. C1, Rita Kempley
WASHINGTON POST, 11/12/99, Weekend/p. 49, Desson Howe

DOUBLE JEOPARDY

A Paramount Pictures release of a Leonard Goldberg production. *Producer:* Leonard Goldberg. *Director:* Bruce Beresford. *Screenplay:* David Weisberg and Douglas S. Cook. *Director of Photography:* Peter James. *Editor:* Mark Warner. *Music:* Normand Corbeil. *Music Editor:* Craig Pettigrew. *Sound:* Rob Young and (music) Dennis Sands. *Sound Editor:* Sandy Berman and Michael Szakmeister. *Casting:* Deborah Aquila and Sarah Halley Finn. *Production Designer:* Howard Cummings. *Art Director:* Andrew Neskoromny. *Set Designer:* John Marcynuk, Allan Galajda, and Roxanne Methot. *Set Decorator:* Elizabeth Wilcox. *Special Effects:* Lars Lenander. *Costumes:* Rudy Dillon and Linda Bass. *Make-up:* Norma Hill-Patton. *Stunt Coordinator:* Glenn Randall. *Running time:* 106 minutes. *MPAA Rating:* R.

CAST: Tommy Lee Jones (Travis Lehman); Ashley Judd (Libby Parsons); Bruce Greenwood (Nick Parsons); Annabeth Gish (Angie); Benjamin Weir (Matty, Aged 4); Jay Brazeau (Bobby); John MacLaren (Rudy); Edward Evanko (Warren); Bruce Campbell (Bartender at Party); Brennan Elliott (Yuppie Man); Angela Schneider (Yuppie Girl); Michael Gaston (Cutter); Gillian Barber (Rebecca Tingely); Tom McBeath (Coast Guard Officer); David Jacox (Deputy Ben); Betsy Brantley (Prosecutor); Woody Jeffreys (Watch Stander); French Tickner (Judge); Roma Maffia (Margaret Skolowski); Davenia McFadden (Evelyn Lake); Maria Bitamba (Prisoner at Phone); Ben Bodé (Karl Carruthers); Robin J. Kelley (Parole Board Member); Dana Owen Still (Drug Counsellor); Gabrielle Rose (Georgia); Daniel LaPaine (Handsome Internet Expert); Maria R. Herrera (Libby's Roommate); Babz Chula (Ruby); Enuka Okuma (Parolee); Peter Kimmerly (Ferry Captain); George Gordon (Emergency Room Doctor); David Fredericks (Trucker); Anna Hagan (Libby's Mother); Fulvio Cecere (BMW Salesman); Tracy Vilar (Orbe); Addison Ridge (Boy at Door); Crystal Verge (Housewife); Joy Coghill (Neighbor in Garden); Bernard Cuffling (Gallery Owner); Ingrid Torrence (Maison Beau Coeur Clerk); Roger R. Cross (Hotel Manager); Pamela Perry (Mrs. Kritch); Tim McDermott (Bell Hop); Keegan Tracy (Boutique Saleswoman); Dave Hager (Mangold); Jason Douglas (Detective); Jeannie Grelier Church (Scarf Woman); Austin B. Church (Scarf Woman's Husband); Michael Shannon Jenkins (Doorman); Joe Simon (Singer at Auction); Charlie Detraz (Auctioneer); Susan Lecourt-Barbe, Ramona Tyler,m and C. Barrett Downing (Bidders); Michelle Stafford (Suzanne Monroe); Greg Di Leo and Lance Spellerberg (Bachelors at Auction); George Touliatos (New Orleans Bartender); Deryl Hayes (New Orleans Cop); Brent Woolsey (Mounted Cop); Eliza Murbach (Co-ed with Umbrella); Roland 'Bob' Harris (Preacher); Lossen Chambers (Lucy); Harold Evans (New Orleans Cabbie); Thomas M. Matthews and Gordon Starling, Jr. (Coaches); Spencer Treat Clark (Matty, Aged 11); George Montgomery, II (Matty Pretender).

LOS ANGELES TIMES, 9/24/99, Calendar/p. 2, Gene Seymour

[The following review by Gene Seymour appeared in a slightly different form in **NEWSDAY, 9/24/99, Part II/p. B7.]**

Now the "wrong man" crime story is so established in our folklore that it's practically a ritual. And while "Double Jeopardy" applies a couple of different spins on the formula (notably that there's a "wronged woman" involved here), many of the same conventions are intact.

Wouldn't you just know, for instance, that the minute poor Libby Parsons (Ashley Judd) picks up a blood-stained knife on the deck of a yacht that belonged to her now missing-and-presumed-dead husband (Bruce Greenwood), a passing Coast Guard cutter happens to shine a searchlight on her distraught, bedraggled form?

It won't take you long to figure out that Libby is hot-buttered toast, even with the sparsest of circumstantial evidence. Arrest. Trial. Conviction. Prison. And the requisite lingering agony over her estranged child, now adopted by a family friend (Annabeth Gish). Then one day, while trying to phone her son from prison, she hears the kid call out, "Daddy." And the phone goes dead.

Now she knows her husband is alive. She also knows, thanks to one of her prison pals, that she can legally kill the guy again and not have to face trial because of "double jeopardy" that allegedly protects her from getting convicted for the same crime twice. (In the real world that would offer no protection at all, according to a prominent legal scholar quoted in Entertainment Weekly, but this is, after all, the movies.)

Inspired, Libby trains like a kick-boxer for her release, which arrives in a swiftly moving six years, after which she comes out still looking like a million dollars.

Zipping right along, she checks into a halfway house run by a no-nonsense parole officer (Tommy Lee Jones), who warns her to stick close to home. But Libby wanders off to track down her ex-friend, husband and child. Thus begins a chase that moves from the waters of Washington state to Colorado to New Orleans for—you guessed it—the Climactic Confrontation. And you thought last year's Leslie Nielsen parody, "Wrongfully Accused," would stop anyone from ever again taking this subgenre seriously?

Still, for all its familiar conventions and hoary improbabilities, "Double Jeopardy" is a relatively efficient model of its kind. Director Bruce Beresford ("Tender Mercies" and "Driving Miss Daisy") moves things along at a brisk clip, never milking a scene for gratuitous thrills as is routinely done in big-budget chase movies.

Jones once again is compelled to chase a fugitive with his trademark hip bombast. He looks very, very tired of running. Judd, meanwhile, is cast in a higher-profile version of her role in "Kiss the Girls" (1997): the victim who fights back. She rides this old pony like a champ, giving enough energy and magnetism to the project to make you think that, as with "Kiss the Girls," she could have another hit on her hands. If so, it'd be nice if the next time she gets a crime story to do, she gets to be the detective for a change.

NEW YORK POST, 9/24/99, p. 50, Jonathan Foreman

As formula thrillers go, "Double Jeopardy" is an exceptionally pretty movie. But this visual lushness is almost the only indication that the movie was directed by the same Bruce Beresford who made "Breaker Morant" and "Driving Miss Daisy."

There are a few ingenious zig zags in its otherwise by-the-numbers plot, (as well as some hefty implausibilities), but what keeps you interested in this story of a framed mom out for vengeance and the parole officer who pursues her is the sheer movie-star presence of the actors in the lead roles.

Libby Parsons (Ashley Judd) is leading a wonderful life near Seattle with her financier husband Nick (Bruce Greenwood) and their towheaded little boy Mattie (Benjamin Weir).

One romantic weekend Libby and Nick go sailing. After an idyllic night of lovemaking Libby wakes up covered in blood. Nick is nowhere to be found, and when Libby goes on deck she sees a bloody knife.

Just as she picks it up a Coast Guard launch comes out of the fog.

Convicted of murder, Libby is sent to prison. She hands her son to her best friend Angie (Annabeth Gish) and persuades her to adopt the boy, who is now the beneficiary of Nick's life insurance policy.

But after a few months Angie stops bringing Mattie to visit her and then disappears completely. Libby is panicked, but her prison pals Margaret (Roma Maffia) and Evelyn (Davenia McFadden) tell her that no one really disappears.

Libby uses the phone to track Angie down in San Francisco, where she is living with Mattie and with Nick, who has resurfaced under another name.

They disappear again, but now Libby is determined to find them, get her son back, and get revenge. After all, once she's out of jail she'll be able to kill Nick with impunity: The legal doctrine of double jeopardy means that you cannot be tried twice for the same crime.

Libby's opportunity comes after six years of imprisonment, when she is paroled and sent to a halfway house run by tough, cynical Travis Lehman (Tommy Lee Jones).

After committing a burglary to find information about Angie's whereabouts, Libby breaks parole and goes looking for her son. Travis sets out after her, following her across country and morphing into a clone of the character Jones played in "The Fugitive" and "U.S. Marshals"—he's relentless but increasingly convinced of his quarry's innocence.

Still, it's just a pleasure to watch Jones inject life into tired material. And in this movie he makes particularly good use of his uncanny knack for giving an interesting, unpredictable reading to leaden dialogue.

SIGHT AND SOUND, 2/00, p. 44, Jamie Graham

Washington, the present. While sailing on the yacht Libby Parsons' husband Nick bought her as a present, Libby awakes in the night to find Nick missing. On deck, she picks up a blood-splattered knife just as the coast guards show up. An inquest declares Nick officially dead and Libby, due a $2M life-insurance payoff, is found guilty of his murder. Facing a six-year sentence, Libby signs the money and custody of her young son Matty over to her friend Angie, who suddenly disappears with the boy. Libby tracks Angie down, calls her from prison and is shocked when Matty is overheard greeting his father. Convinced Nick has faked his own death, Libby waits out her sentence: the 'double jeopardy' legal clause means she can kill him after her release and, having already done time for the crime, not be touched for it.

On release, Libby is placed under the supervision of parole officer Travis Lehman. But she jumps parole to pursue Angie (whom Nick has killed), Matty and Nick. Her search leads her to New Orleans, with Lehman in pursuit. Libby confronts Nick and demands Matty back. At the cemetery handover point, Nick tricks Libby and buries her alive in a mausoleum. She escapes and with the help of Lehman (who now believes her story) lures Nick into a taped confession. A shootout ensues, during which Lehman is wounded and Nick is killed. Libby is reunited with Matty.

Playing out like an amalgam of *The Fugitive* and the 'feminist' revenge dramas that spattered the horror genre at the end of the 70s (*I Spit on Your Grave*, 1978, *Angel of Vengeance*, 1980), *Double Jeopardy* is quick to establish its wronged-woman premise and to cut quite literally to the chase. Libby, however, is subjugated to a different form of humiliation than that of the revenge dramas in the opening reel, as her husband frames her for his own faked death and scarpers, leaving her to spend six years in prison. During her incarceration (and via a clumsy piece of exposition) Libby learns of the legal loophole which prevents anyone from being tried twice for the same crime, leaving her free to track down her mendacious husband and kill him with impunity after her release.

For an action-movie heroine, Libby is a slightly more multifaceted character than usual, maternal as well as murderous. Director Bruce Beresford has a well-established track record in such woman-centred dramas as *Tender Mercies* and *Driving Miss Daisy* and his sombre instincts anchor *Double Jeopardy* in character and motivation, keeping it from devolving into the string of affectless images endemic to this genre. Granted, he permits Tommy Lee Jones' parole officer, in frantic pursuit of Libby, to run and chase and bark and snap in a lazy reprise of his Oscar-winning turn in *The Fugitive,* but there's a steady current of quality amid the sea of mediocrity.

Particular highlights include a seamless match cut that transports Libby from her bed at home to the cot of her prison ward, a surreal underwater shot of Libby and her parole officer escaping a sinking car, and a marvellous pursuit through New Orleans' teeming streets, the action weaving through various blasts of discordant source sound. Elsewhere, it's thrill-ride business as usual, with overly tortuous plot twists, Hollywood clichés—Libby buffing up in prison *á la* Linda Hamilton in *Terminator 2*, the baddie leaving her an overlooked escape route instead of just killing—her and a distended finale, part of which steals shamelessly from *The Vanishing*.

Also reviewed in:
CHICAGO TRIBUNE, 9/24/99, Friday/p. D, Mark Caro
NEW REPUBLIC, 10/25/99, p. 32, Stanley Kauffmann
NEW YORK TIMES, 9/24/99, p. E12, Janet Maslin
VARIETY, 9/20-26/99, p. 81, Robert Koehler
WASHINGTON POST, 9/24/99, p. C5, Stephen Hunter

DOUG'S FIRST MOVIE

A Walt Disney Pictures release of a Jumbo Pictures production. *Producer:* Jim Jinkins, David Campbell, Melanie Grisanti, and Jack Spillum. *Director:* Maurice Joyce. *Screenplay:* Ken Scarborough. *Editor:* Alysha Nadine Cohen and Christopher K. Gee. *Music:* Mark Watters. *Music Editor:* Dominick Certo. *Sound:* Neal Porter and (music) John Richards. *Sound Editor:* Ron Eng and Louis L. Edemann. *Animator:* Kieran Dowling. Running time: 87 minutes. MPAA Rating: G.

VOICES: Thomas McHugh (Doug Funnie/Lincoln);   Fred Newman (Skeeter/Mr. Dink/Porkchop/Ned);   Chris Phillips (Roger Klotz/Boomer/Larry/Mr. Chiminy);   Constance Shulman (Patti Mayonnaise);   Frank Welker (Herman Melville);   Doug Preis (Mr. Funnie/Mr. Bluff/Willie/Chalky/Bluff Agent #1);   Guy Hadley (Guy Graham);   Alice Playten (Beebe Bluff/Elmo);   Eddie Korbich (Al & Moo Sleech/RoboCrusher);   David O'Brien (Stentorian/Quailman/Announcer);   Doris Belack (Mayor Tippi Dink);   Becca Lish (Judy Funnie/Mrs. Funnie/Connie);   Greg Lee (Principal White);   Bob Bottone (Bluff Assistant);   Bruce Bayley Johnson (Mr. Swirley);   Fran Brill (Mrs. Perigrew);   Melissa Greenspan (Briar Langolier).

LOS ANGELES TIMES, 3/26/99, Calendar/p. 8, Gene Seymour

[The following review by Gene Seymour appeared in a slightly different form in **NEWSDAY, 3/26/99, Part II/p. B11.]**

I have to tell you right off: I liked the Christmas special better.

That episode of "Doug" was about a half-hour long. And a half-hour of "Doug" is about as much "Doug" as anyone, of any age, can reasonably be expected to withstand at a time. The "Doug" universe is too sweet and too light to travel into the big, wide, often indelicate territory of feature films.

But the success of "The Rugrats Movie" has apparently convinced those who should know better that "Doug," originally another Nickelodeon cable network franchise that made good (and now is a Saturday morning fixture on ABC), is ready for its multiplex close-up, and so we get, naturally, "Doug's 1st Movie." This is the same "Doug" that, according to his creator, Jim Jinkins, started out as a doodle. Surely Jinkins must know that bad things happen when you give doodles a close-up.

For the benefit of quizzical readers who are not or do not have young children, Doug Funnie (voiced by Thomas McHugh) is a wispy-haired, 12-year-old—sorry, I've been informed by a young child in our office that he's a 12 ½-year-old—with a good heart and an overactive imagination. He lives in the town of Bluffington, "Bumper Sticker Capital of the World," with his squarer-than-square parents; hipper-than-hip older sister, Judy (Becca Lish, who, alas, is seen and heard only fleetingly here); and faithful Renaissance dog Porkchop.

Most of the stories on the "Doug" series are mini-sitcoms that generally speak to their young audience's secret hopes/fears of being perceived as either "cool" or "uncool" by their peers. The movie inflates this concept by showing the myriad consequences of Doug and his green-colored best friend Skeeter's (Fred Newman) discovery of the legendary "monster" of Lucky Duck Lake.

Doug thinks this find will impress his longtime crush, Patti Mayonnaise (Connie Shulman), who already seems fairly impressed with Doug, despite the best efforts of oily upperclassman Guy Graham (Guy Hadley) to have Patti all to himself as they plan the sixth-graders' Valentine's Day dance.

And speaking of oily, the big blue monster, which, of course, turns out to be anything but scary, is sought by sinister forces led by the town's richest man, Bob Bluff (Doug Preis), who fears that the beast's discovery will prove that his company fills the lake with pollutants. All this is supposed to be somehow resolved at the dance, but you're so loaded down with extra complications that you don't care how it's resolved.

NEW YORK POST, 3/26/99, p. 63, Rod Dreher

Entertainment for kids is so cynical and crappy these days that when a sweet but insubstantial little animated picture like "Doug's 1st Movie" comes along, it bears recommending for what it's not: smart-alecky, rude, insulting of adult authority figures and crassly exploitative of children-as-consumers.

Which is not quite the same thing as saying it's "good". Frankly, I was bored with the thing, but unlike Disney's "A Bug's Life," say, 'Doug's 1st Movie" has no interest in appealing to grown-ups. I get the feeling those tots who have made friendly Doug Funnie (voice of Thomas McHugh) and his pals such a big hit on Nickelodeon and ABC will get exactly what they expect to out of the ambitiously titled "Doug's 1st Movie." And mom and dad will find it eminently sit-throughable, which will just have to do; God knows parents usually suffer worse.

Twelve-year-old Doug is the Tintin of Suburbia, a likable middle-schooler who ambles around Bluffington, his non-threatening town, with his faithful dog Porkchop (voice of Fred Newman), flirting with his seventh-grade sweetie Patti Mayonnaise (voice of Constance Shulman), and knocking about with best bud Skeeter (Newman). Unlike Tintin, Doug's adventures don't take him much past the mall or the woods behind the subdivision, and the nastiest villains he faces are a meanie named Roger (voice of Chris Phillips) and a smarmy upperclassman named Guy Graham (voice of Guy Hadley), who covets the creamy Miss Mayonnaise's affections.

"Doug's 1st Movie" plays off plot points introduced in the animated TV series. Doug and Skeeter have long believed there's a monster lurking in the polluted lake behind the town, and in the movie, said beast emerges from the slithy toves. Turns out he's a genial reptile, eager to befriend Doug and Skeeter. They name him Herman Melville, and plan to introduce him to the world.

But to do so would mean revealing that Bill Bluff, led by the town's filthy-rich industrialist, is polluting the lake with his factory. Mr. Bluff, who talks like Foghorn Leghorn, conspires to kill Herman during the school's big Valentine's Day dance—unless Doug and Skeeter can stop him.

Whew! On the whole, this is pretty thin stuff, but harmless fun for wee ones. I do object to the movie's preachiness about pollution, and its demonizing of businessmen—what are they teaching kids on Earth Day, anyway?—but then again, I hope "Simpsons" mogul Monty Burns gets the Republican presidential nomination in 2000. The animation is plain and doodly, kind of Richard Scarry-ish, in keeping with the simple moral truths (e.g., Do the right thing, no matter what anybody else says) the screenplay conveys.

SIGHT AND SOUND, 8/99, p. 42, Leslie Felperin

Bluffington, a suburban town in the US. Seventh-graders Doug Funnie, his friend Skeeter and Doug's dog Porkchop discover a friendly mutant monster living in Lucky Duck Lake, created by pollution dumped by local industrialist Mr Bluff. The monster follows them home and they name it Herman Melville after it licks a copy of *Moby Dick*. While the friends try to figure out what to do with the monster, Doug pines for Patti Mayonnaise and tries to screw up enough courage to ask her to the school dance at the Funkytown disco.

Meanwhile Bluff and his cohorts, having learned of Herman's existence, plot to kill it to save face. Doug almost reveals the monster at a press conference but stops when he realises it's a trap set by Bluff. His attempts to woo Patti are thwarted by a rival, glamorous eighth grader Guy Graham. To impress Patti, Doug announces he will reveal Herman at the dance, but Bluff also plots to kill it that night. At the dance, Doug and his friends use a decoy robot to fool the baddies and disguise Herman as a foreign exchange student. The ruse works and they manage to smuggle Herman to the safety of an unpolluted lake and set him free. Doug wins Patti's heart, and they dance the night away together.

Having fared rather poorly at the US box office and being unlikely to catch on in Europe where the television series it's based on is hardly known, *Doug's 1st Movie* is likely to be his last. To be fair, it's just a slightly dull rather than a bad film. Adequately though not strikingly animated (movements are limited but it's strong on design), occasionally witty but never hilarious, its tale of junior-high school hijinks involving monsters and unrequited love is too anodyne to appeal to an older audience (unlike its more successful Nickelodeon-farmed stablemate *The Rugrats* series and film) and too drab to ignite the fantasies of the very young.

There are a few feints at self-reflexive wit, a seemingly mandatory component of cartoons aimed at a young demographic. At one point, Doug slips into a daydream about Patti, the orange skinned woman he loves, and the transition is marked by a waviness in the image, mimicking the opticals used in live action films to denote fantasy sequences. Doug's friend Skeeter remarks that he knows Doug is thinking of Patti because he's "got that blurry look". Another gag that works has Doug slipping on a virtual reality headset, only to see an exact recreation of the living room he's actually in. "It's exactly like reality except more expensive," is the comment. Elsewhere there's a spiky dig at Michael Flatley with Doug briefly becoming Lord of the Polka, and a just-for-the-grown-ups-dragged-along bit which alludes to the wrong-house crosscutting scene in *The Silence of the Lambs*.

Unfortunately, the blandly prosocial messages lack such humour or even imagination: after realising that he was exploiting the monster he found to impress Patti, Doug pronounces at the end that "it's important to do the right thing." ("Duh!" as any seven year old might say.) One could also interpret the hot-pastel palette of skin tones—making some characters green, lavender and turquoise as well as pink—as a politically correct conceit, a literalisation of the 'everyone is a different colour so labels like "black" and "white" don't mean anything' line. But all the characters are so homogeneously middle or upper middle class here that tolerance becomes a necessity only when encountering monsters and therefore merely theoretical. We also learn that reading is cool (*Moby Dick* serves an important plot point) and snobbery bad, and parents and other advocates of safety will be pleased to see the film endorses wearing helmets while cycling and not swimming in polluted lakes.

Also reviewed in:
CHICAGO TRIBUNE, 3/26/99, Friday/p. A, Mark Caro
NEW YORK TIMES, 3/26/99, p. E28, Anita Gates
VARIETY, 3/29-4/4/99, p. 68, Joe Leydon

DREAMING OF JOSEPH LEES

A Fox Searchlight Pictures release of a Christopher Milburn production in association with the Isle of Man Film Commission. *Executive Producer:* Mark Thomas. *Producer:* Christopher Milburn. *Director:* Eric Styles. *Screenplay:* Catherine Linstrum. *Director of Photography:* Jimmy Dibling. *Editor:* Caroline Limmer. *Music:* Zbigniew Preisner. *Music Editor:* Andrew Glen. *Choreographer:* Mary Mitchell. *Sound:* Phil Edward. *Sound Editor:* Paul Davies. *Casting:* Liora Reich and Carrie Hilton. *Production Designer:* Humphrey Jaeger. *Art Director:* Lucy Nias. *Set Decorator:* Richard Tongé and Colin Ellis. *Special Effects:* Tony Auger. *Costumes:* Tina Hackett-James. *Make-up:* Julie Van Praag. *Stunt Coordinator:* Richard Hammatt and Rod Woodruff. *Running time:* 92 minutes. *MPAA Rating:* R.

CAST: Rupert Graves (Joseph Lees); Samantha Morton (Eva); Nick Woodeson (Mr. Dian); Lee Ross (Harry); Felix Billson (Robert); Lauren Richardson (Janie); Frank Finlay (Father); Vernon Dobtcheff (Italian Doctor); Miriam Margolyes (Signora Caldoni); Holly Aird (Maria); Freddie Douglas (Danny); Richie Tonge (Nude Model); Harry Selby (First Boxer); Juan Thomas (Referee); Emma Cunniffe (Red-Haired Girl); Siân James (Singer); Dyfan Jones (Double Bass Player); Doug Davidson (Saxophone Player); Terry Quayle (Trombonist); Don Elliott (Trumpet Player); Jim Caine (Pianist); Peter Gardner (Guitarist); Ken Ingham (Drummer); Anthony Hannan (Wedding Guest); Margaret John (Aunt Margaret); Julian Symmonds (Second Boxer).

LOS ANGELES TIMES, 10/29/99, Calendar/p. 6, Kevin Thomas

"Dreaming of Joseph Lees" paints a portrait of a young woman who must at last assert herself if she is to have any hope of happiness. The beauty of this English picture is that until its very last seconds we don't know if she will or not, for her story could just as credibly go either way. However, by then we've long since become caught up in her psychological struggle.

Her name is Eva (Samantha Morton), and when we meet her we're surprised to discover that the year is 1958 and not 1938, so out of date is her attire. Eva is the pretty and proper young secretary at a sawmill in Somerset, England, where she lives in a striking-looking but austere old house with her widowed father (Frank Finlay), whose poor hearing is symbolic of his obtuseness.

She has an ally in her bright adolescent sister Janie (Lauren Richardson), who is more perceptive and aware than Eva realizes. Director Eric Styles and writer Catherine Linstrum swiftly suggest that ancient and picturesque Somerset might be a nice place to visit, but you wouldn't want to live there; it's dull to its core. Eva's existence is so drab it's no wonder she dreams constantly of her handsome second cousin Joseph Lees (Rupert Graves), a geologist who recently lost his right leg in a quarry explosion in Italy.

In the meantime, Eva has attracted the interest of a pig farmer, Harry (Lee Ross), a sturdy, plain-looking young man of great intensity who hovers over her clumsily. Harry's constant, persistent attentions, coupled with her sexual and emotional longing, eventually cause Eva to decide to stop daydreaming about Joseph and settle for Harry, though she will live with but not marry him. Eva's decision is clearly daring for her time and place, and it predictably precipitates an avalanche of passion on the part of Harry, whose love for her is all-consuming. Who should then show up but Joseph, and the attraction between the second cousins is emphatically mutual.

"Dreaming of Joseph Lees" is in the long tradition of English movies about repressed emotions and their calamitous consequences. (The sisters Bronte would have appreciated this story.) Without being preachy about it the filmmakers make it clear that Eva is in a situation where little consideration is given to a woman's right to happiness, which makes it all the more difficult for her to cope with her predicament. What's more, as her feelings for Joseph intensify, Harry starts unraveling. Torn between love and duty, Eva feels her spirit being crushed to pieces.

Filmed entirely on the Isle of Man, "Dreaming of Joseph Lees" is a beautifully articulated and acutely perceptive work with impeccable, carefully shaded performances. You can feel the lives of its people weighing them down, yet the filmmakers surprise us with how effectively they can involve us so deeply in so bleak a picture.

NEW YORK, 11/1/99, p. 120, Peter Rainer

In *Dreaming of Joseph Lees*, set in 1958, Samantha Morton plays Eva, a withdrawn clerk in the rural English county of Somerset. Living at home with her doting, doddering father (Frank Finlay) and precocious younger sister (Lauren Richardson), she takes the brash step of moving in with Harry (Lee Ross), her working-class admirer, who tends pigs and looks at her with devotional eyes. Her real passion, though, is for her second cousin Joseph Lees (Rupert Graves), who disappeared into Italy years ago after losing a leg in a quarry accident and suddenly re-enters her life. The film is about how Eva, who wants only to do right by everybody, is destroyed by her own goodness. Too staid and classical, the film is nevertheless greatly enhanced by its actors, especially Morton, who has a luminous fragility, like the young Lillian Gish. She would have been wonderful in silent films.

NEW YORK POST, 10/29/99, p. 44, Jonathan Foreman

"Dreaming of Joseph Lees" is a strange romantic tragedy set in rural England in the 1950s. Evocative at times of Thomas Hardy's novels, it's beautifully shot and often moving.

Twenty-year-old Eva (Samantha Morton) has been secretly in love with her second cousin Joseph Lees since she was a child, though she hasn't seen him since he lost a leg in a quarry accident in Italy.

But when Harry Flyte (Lee Ross), an odd but ardent young pig farmer, starts to court her—successfully awakening her sensual side—she leaves her grumpy father (Frank Finlay) and smart little sister (Lauren Richardson), and moves in with him.

Then she sees Joseph Lees at a family wedding, and the two of them start a correspondence. (She's an artist, and he sends her books about Italy.) Harry becomes jealous and cheats on her. Eva leaves him, moving in with Lees.

Meanwhile, Harry starts to fall apart. Eva comes back—just to help him get back on his feet—but Harry then does something truly crazy that will affect all of them forever.

The main problem with "Dreaming"—besides an ending that leaves too much in the air—are the questions that screenwriter Catherine Linstrum never answers.

Why is Eva's much older sister Maria (Holly Aird) alone? And why can't she read? How does Eva get away with living with two different men in the late '50s? For that matter, how does she avoid conceiving a child? What was the great mistake that her mother made in life? And why would her father be opposed to a liaison with Joseph Lees?

Even more of concern is that you don't really have any idea of what is going on in Lees' mind.

But first-time feature director Eric Styles is a master of atmosphere, and he gets excellent performances from an able cast.

Morton in particular makes her underwritten role seem much more substantial and believable than it should be. Ross is impressive as the damaged Harry, and Lauren Richardson puts most child actors to shame as the precocious younger sister Janie.

NEWSDAY, 10/29/99, Part II/p. B6, Jan Stuart

The awful territory of the heart between a rock and a hard place is achingly mapped out in "Dreaming of Joseph Lees," a lush, romantic wallow of a film from first-time English director Eric Styles.

Inhabiting that no-win land is a willowy young sawmill clerk named Eva (Samantha Morton), whose latent artist's soul keeps her from succumbing entirely to the double repressiveness that is rural England in the late 1950s.

While Eva burns in silence with love for her itinerant cousin Joseph Lees (Rupert Graves), a geologist who lost a leg in a digging accident, she gives herself over to the puppy-dog ardor of an uncomplicated local lad named Harry (Lee Ross).

Big mistake. Surrounded by sweaty, testosterone-heavy male energy on the job and off, Eva defies all convention and propriety by moving in with Harry. She is barely settled in before passions belatedly explode between her and Joseph.

Faced with losing Eva, Harry reveals himself to be an emotionally crippled boy who goes to frightening extremes to prove his love. Ross is superb as he carefully delineates Harry's decline from a sweetly infatuated romantic to a man on the brink.

Derived from an original screenplay by Catherine Linstrum, "Dreaming of Joseph Lees" boasts all the pulp appeal of a Victorian romance, with an overlay of D.H. Lawrence-ian symbolism and simmering 1950s sexuality. While it is ostensibly Eva's story, Linstrum and director Styles cleverly position us to identify with Eva's younger sister Janie (the excellent Lauren Richardson), who is old enough to recognize love when she sees it but not old enough to understand why people can't do what makes them happy.

Styles doesn't always trust the material to deliver its wallop. Absorbing and deeply felt, "Dreaming of Joseph Lees" is souped up with more plangent scoring than any movie should have to bear and a few too many lovingly photographed rustic tableaux. The biggest debit may be Morton, a subtle, plain-Jane actress of the Sarah Miles-Emily Watson school who fails to convey whatever it is that two men get bent out of shape over.

SIGHT AND SOUND, 12/99, p. 42, Kieron Corless

Somerset, 1958. Unaware that his cousin Eva has been in love with him since they were teenagers, Joseph left England to pursue his geological career. He is now a recluse since an accident left him with an artificial leg. Local farmer Harry attempts to seduce Eva but she still dreams of Joseph and resists his advances. Eva is distraught when her father refuses to let her travel to a relative's funeral which Joseph will attend. She is increasingly attracted to Harry despite herself. After two months of courtship, she refuses marriage but moves in with him at his farm, with her father's blessing.

Eva finally meets Joseph at a family wedding where they discover a strong mutual attraction. Harry realises Joseph has supplanted him in Eva's affections. As his grasp on sanity becomes more precarious, Harry threatens suicide. He has sex with a local woman which drives Eva into Joseph's arms. Eva rejoins Harry when she hears his condition has worsened. Harry tries to saw one of his legs off, while he recuperates, Joseph arrives and implores Eva to go to Italy with him. Her final decision remains ambiguous.

"Follow your heart," counsels Eva's father when she declares her intention to move in with boyfriend Harry. Typical advice in the context of a romantic psychodrama, if a shade implausible from a 50s patriarch. Ironic too that Eva, unbeknownst to him, is acting on it in such a roundabout fashion. Her decision to live in sin is partly for expediency's sake, leaving her options open should her true love Joseph return. Eva's combination of sly opportunism and strategic romanticism seems calculated to resonate with modern audiences, but Eric Styles' debut feature is a timid, undercooked affair.

Dreaming of Joseph Lees unfolds at a brisk pace but its unwillingness to loiter means we never really explore the implications of the unfolding events or, more frustratingly, get a chance to probe the characters' motivations. Eva's love for her cousin, for instance, is presented as a given and we never really explore the reasons behind her prolonged obsession. Rupert Graves in the underwritten role of Joseph sleepwalks through the film looking understandably bemused by it all.

Harry's plunge into madness effectively kills off any chance of a full-blooded triangular drama, leaving Eva merely to resolve her conflict between duty and passion, and reducing him from a charismatic seducer to a rustic simpleton. And if the dramatic tone of the film varies wildly, its laboured visual style remains honey-coated throughout, with Styles demonstrating a particular fondness for light snaking through windows, drenching everything in an amber glow. The dreams of the title are principally figured as softly lit mood pieces lifted from Athena posters (aptly enough for a film so astonishingly coy about Eva's sexuality and unconscious life), while the overwrought score puffs and pants unremittingly towards emotional overkill.

Apart from Frank Finlay's enjoyably acerbic turn as Eva's father, Samantha Morton provides the film's sole interest. Morton's debut in *Under the Skin* revealed a brave, edgy talent, and in the penultimate scene here she pulls off a minor miracle. Joseph's arrival at the farmhouse finally confronts Eva with the stark choice of leaving with him or staying to tend Harry. She turns Joseph away initially, and for once the camera fixes at length on Eva as she collapses in the hallway alone, her face a riot of incomprehension and anguished conflict. Despite our total disengagement hitherto, the raw self-exposure and tensile force in Morton's performance here is credible and moving. The film stumbles on to a bizarre, snatched ending, but the prospect of this extraordinary actress returning to more challenging material in the future is a genuinely tantalising one.

VILLAGE VOICE, 11/2/99, p. 140, Jessica Winter

Much in *Dreaming of Joseph Lees* pivots on pathological jealousy, and the film casts a jaundiced eye indeed—interiors and exteriors alike emanate a strange yellow aura at all hours. One might suspect radioactivity, but despite the late-1950s Somerset backdrop, this isn't a Cold War allegory; we're left to infer the twilight glow of doomed romance, though the effect is less *Days of Heaven* than the incandescence of the tanning booth. A shy, bookish girl, Eva (Samantha Morton) takes care of her father and sister and secretly yearns after a second cousin, said Mr. Lees. Played by the suitably dreamy Rupert Graves, Lees is a geologist who has lost a leg in a quarry accident, which only enhances his tragic allure. Having established Eva's sense of duty to both her family and her fantasies, *Dreaming* then requires the girl to throw it all over and move in with a dim, clingy pig farmer named Harry (Lee Ross), though she refuses to marry him.

The fitful script ignores the social stigma of such an arrangement for its time as well as any character nuance that could explain it. Morton must vacillate between scenes of solitary pining for Joe and weary appeasement of her increasingly unhinged pigboy, whose deranged idea of guilt-tripping his lover mutates into a voyage of the damned. A third-act plot twist worthy of a V.C. Andrews paperback hurls the film off a high ledge, and the last scene reads like an admission of defeat: the bleak, beautiful English countryside, furnished with Morton and Graves, a lovely pair looking befuddled and awfully sorry.

Also reviewed in:
NEW YORK TIMES, 10/29/99, p. E13, Janet Maslin
VARIETY, 8/30-9/5/99, p. 56, Derek Elley

DREAMLIFE OF ANGELS, THE

A Sony Pictures Classics release of a Bagheera/Diaphana/France 3 Cinema production in association with Canal+ and the support of Conseil of Régional du Centre/Fondation GAN pour le cinéma/Procirep. With the suppport of Région Nord/Pas de-Calair/Atelier de Production Centre Val de Loire Associate producer Le Centre Régional des Resources Audiovisuelle du Nord-Pas de Calais Script development supported by Consell Régional du Centre. *Producer:* François Marquis. *Director:* Erick Zonca. *Screenplay (French with English subtitles):* Erick Zonca and Roger Bohbot. *Director of Photography:* Agnès Godard. *Editor:* Yannick Kergoat. *Sound:* Jean-Luc Audy and (music) Stéphane Thiébaut. *Sound Editor:* Muriel Moreau. *Casting:* Antoine Carrard. *Art Director:* Jimmy Vansteenkiste. *Costumes:* François Clavel. *Make-up:* Laurence Grosjean. *Running time:* 113 minutes. *MPAA Rating:* Not Rated.

CAST: Elodie Bouchez (Isa); Natacha Régnier (Marie); Grégoire Colin (Chriss); Jo Prestia (Fredo); Patrick Mercado (Charly); Francine Massenhave (Attendant); Zivko Niklevski (Yugoslav Patron); Murielle Colvez (Shop Foreperson); Lyazid Queldhadj (Ticket Seller); Frédérique Hazard (Marie's Mother); Jean-Michel Lemayeux (Intern); Louise Motte (Sandrine); Rosa Maria (1st Nurse); Corinne Masiero (Hollywood Woman); Xavier Denamur (Man with Skates); Juliette Richevaux (Solène); Stéphanie Delerue (Léa); Mireille Bidon (2nd Nurse); Christian Cailleret (Monsieur Val); Gérard Beyrand (Foreman).

LOS ANGELES TIMES, 4/2/99, Calendar/p. 20, Kenneth Turan

Frank, intimate, touching, with an emotional immediacy that is killing, Erick Zonca's "The Dreamlife of Angels" draws its intensity and feeling from a pair of actresses whose portrait of a troubled friendship is as moving a collaboration as the year has seen.

Since the film's Cannes debut, young stars Elodie Bouchez and Natacha Regnier have been showered with honors. They shared the best actress award at the festival, Bouchez won the Cesar (the French version of the Oscar) for best actress, Regnier the Cesar for best newcomer, and the film itself was named France's best of the year.

All this from the assured feature debut of a 42-year-old director who has fashioned an empathetic portrait of the kind of aimless outsiders we perhaps pass every day, dispossessed young women living on the fringe of society, trying to construct a life out of the most flimsy material.

Bouchez (already a Cesar winner for Andre Techine's "Wild Reeds" and an actress with the most open, enchanting smile) is Isa, a 21-year-old vagabond waif who arrives in the northern French city of Lille with her whole life in a knapsack. Resilient and game for anything, Isa has managed to retain her basically sweet nature despite having to cope with the perils of being on the road.

A chance encounter enables Isa to bluff her way into a job as a sewing machine operator in a clothing factory where Marie (Regnier), a sullen young wildcat with an attitude about everything, already works. Marie is house-sitting a large apartment belonging to a mother and daughter hospitalized after an auto accident, and soon Isa is sharing it with her.

These young women may be the angels of the title, but Zonca, careful not to idealize, doesn't hesitate to portray them as unconcerned instigators and frequent troublemakers who are more pleased with themselves than they have objective reason to be.

Despite the wide difference between Marie's furious stance and Isa's gamin-like simplicity, Zonca prefers, at least at first, to concentrate on what these two have in common. In addition to their shared smug looks, neither young woman is as in control of her life as she imagines, and though they don't realize it, fragility is as much a part of their makeup as toughness.

Marie and Isa also share an unspoken and unacknowledged longing to establish connections, and not necessarily romantic ones, to people outside themselves. The wary, gradual way in which these two become friends is one of "Dreamlife's" many pleasures, and the astonishment Marie displays at actually having a soul mate is subtly but unmistakably conveyed.

With less of a chip on her shoulder, Isa relaxes completely into her new life. When she finds the journal of the hospitalized young person in whose room she's staying, Isa's search for connection leads her to visit the comatose girl and get tentatively involved in her rehabilitation.

Marie, on the other hand, is less accepting of what life offers her. Unlike Isa, she won't think of applying for work as a waitress or walking around with an advertising sandwich board. She enters into a lethargic romance with an overweight but gentle club doorman named Charly (Patrick Mercado), but there is the sense that she is simply marking time, waiting for a prince to rescue her from her self-destructive fury.

Then Marie meets Chriss (Gregoire Colin), the self-satisfied son of one of the town's most successful restaurateurs. Marie, who like many untrusting people risks falling too hard when she lets her guard down, simultaneously resists Chris and wants him desperately. Her furtive vulnerability turns out, finally, to be more frightening than her hardest edge.

"The Dreamlife of Angels" focuses on how these outside connections affect Isa and Marie individually and impact their relationship with each other. It's an exceptional rendition of a friendship that holds us by the grace and skill with which it re-creates the very shape and texture of reality.

Zonca, a former actor who co-wrote "Dreamlife's" script with Roger Bohbot, has an impeccable sense of what's natural and unaffected on screen, so much so that it never seems that what's seen and heard began as words on a page. When Bouchez's and Regnier's honest and unguarded performances, captured in hand-held moments by cinematographer Agnes Godard, are added in, getting drawn into these unfocused, precariously balanced and heartbreaking lives is all but inevitable.

NEW YORK, 4/12/99, p. 80, Peter Rainer

Isa (Elodie Bouchez), in the marvelous French film *The Dreamlife of Angels*, is a 21-year-old vagabond with close-cropped black hair and saucer eyes. Her chunky backpack seems the most substantial part of her. We first see Isa trying to make a go of it in the streets selling handmade postcards, then working in a garment factory in Lille, in northern France, where her stitching is so inept she's fired. Taken in by a co-worker, Marie (Natacha Régnier), who is apartment-sitting for a teenage girl hospitalized after a devastating car accident, she's buoyant. Isa experiences life as a series of choice happenstances. She delights in seeing how things play out.

If Isa has the nascent look of a gamine, Marie, with her tight-drawn prettiness, seems prematurely hard-bitten. At first, these two hit it off: They prowl the malls and pull pranks and try to crash nightclubs: they smoke in bed together and razz men. But Marie is temperamentally Isa's opposite: she looks upon life not as a lark but as a minefield. Her hurts are deep, too deep for someone as blissfully naive as Isa to really comprehend. Ultimately, Marie can't comprehend them, either. Isa lives in a world in which suffering is just a station en route to some new Oz, while for Marie it's her first-and final-destination. The tragedy of their friendship is that they damage each other without meaning to. Isa's dawning realization that Marie is dangerously off-kilter suggests the way children are spooked by the depredations of adults. For Isa, Marie's raging woe becomes a kind of violation. and yet she doesn't condemn her friend. Isa is a rarity among movie heroines—she's believably beneficent. If she wants her dream life and her real life to match up, who can blame her? This ardent sprite deserves to exist in a state of grace.

The 42-year-old first-time feature director Erick Zonca, working from a script he co-wrote with Roger Bohbot, captures the whims and hesitancies of friendship, the way a simple shared excursion can turn into a delicious conspiracy. When Isa and Marie are denied entrance to a rock club, they mock the beefcake bouncers, Fredo (Jo Prestia) and the mutton-chopped Charly (Patrick Mercado), and the girls' taunts turn into street theater. They get high on their own verve, and the guys are charmed. (They end up good friends.) In *Masculin-Féminin* (1966), Jean-Luc Godard caught the rhythms of the mating dance of Parisian youth. Zonca has a similar affection for the ways the sexes pivot and preen for effect. *The Dreamlife of Angels* isn't just a movie about what it's like to be young: it has a rapturously rejuvenating spirit, which is what the early Godard movies had, too.

Zonca features Isa and Marie contrapuntally, as the yin and yang of feminine experience. Isa doesn't really form any sexual attachments, but her whole being is sensualized. She wants life to astonish her in the most pleasurable ways, and her little gambols are like come-ons to fate.

She forms deep attachments all at once, not only with Marie but with the comatose young girl whose apartment she occupies. Isa discovers the girl's diary and starts writing entries for her to read when she recovers; she visits her in the hospital, telling the nurse she's her friend—which, in a real sense, she is. Isa revels in the sheer *connectedness* of life; she wants to commiserate with everybody's mood.

Marie's mood is perpetually clouded. The vagaries of life—of men—bring her down. Sex is a subjugation she can't abide and can't do without. When she's caught shoplifting a leather jacket, a slick playboy club owner, Chriss (Gregoire Colin), gets her off the hook, and although she resists his moves, they end up entangled. In a rented-by-the-hour hotel room, she and Chriss go at it, as the camera rests on her desolate, implacable face. In a scene like this, Marie has gone beyond masochism into martyrdom. She's a sacrificial lamb offering herself up to the wolves. But she's smitten; she wants this wolf to love her. Marie is kin to Isabelle Adjani's Adele H., who was also destroyed by unrequited obsession. Adele's folly, however, had a romantic fullness; Marie's is deeply pathetic. She's contemptuous of rapture, and yet it enthralls her—it's the only thing that can knock her out.

Zonca doesn't moralize about any of this. His openness to experience is so all-encompassing that we accept Marie's calamities as unconditionally as we embrace Isa's revels. Both ring true. So does the way the girls' friendship not only comes apart but coheres, so that at times they seem like a pair of ragamuffin *pierrettes*. There's a lovely scene where both girls audition for a job requiring them to mimic celebrities; Isa impersonates Madonna doing "Like a Virgin" and then Marie, reluctantly, does Lauren Bacall. It's a perfect commingling of guises—the waifish tease and the sultry enigma. But this audition is only a passing fancy for the girls. Godard's brainy, romantic youths saw themselves as the seraphim of pop culture; they transformed fandom into lyric poetry. Zonca's young people are essentially post-pop; they have to fend for themselves, and their fantasy lives are shorn of cultural accoutrements. Isa and Marie are originals, though their predicament will no doubt resonate for a great many women, and men, in the audience.

The film gets into the quicksilver, inchoate areas of sexual byplay that most films avoid—especially the current ho-hum French crop obsessed with the adulterous bourgeoisie. And the performances are startling (the two women shared Best Actress honors last year at Cannes). Natacha Régnier seems to have imagined her role in one great arc: Everything she sets up in her early scenes pays off. When Marie first tells Isa that she "doesn't get stuck on guys," we can already hear the waver in her voice. Régnier's performing style is a marvel of conceptual acting. Elodie Bouchez's style is an intuitive triumph: She's working out her character in front of our eyes, amazing herself right along with us. Bouchez has been acting in the movies since 1991—most memorably in André Téchiné's *Wild Reeds*—but this film should send her into orbit. She expresses what Jean Renoir, who would have loved her, also held dear: a passion for the voluptuousness of the everyday. And that's what Zonca, at his best, expresses, too. The film wends its way into sadness, but it feels restorative by the end because the director hasn't been false to experience.

NEW YORK POST, 4/2/99, p. 46, Jonathan Foreman

"The Dreamlife of Angels" takes time to get going, but at last becomes an affecting story of doomed friendship between two young working-class women.

It's worth watching for Elodie Bouchez, one of those fascinating, jolie-laide French actresses whose charm grows on you the longer you see her on screen. And this Euro-paced film gives you plenty of time to appreciate her.

Isa (Bouchez) is a spike-haired, 21-year-old gamine drifting around France. Initially, she seems rather unattractive. She makes money for food by cutting pictures out of library books and making them into postcards to sell in the street.

In Lille, a grim French city, a prospective customer tells her about a job in a garment sweatshop. There she meets the difficult and sour Marie (Natacha Regnier), who agrees to put Isa up for the night.

Isa and Marie go out on the town and argue with some biker-bouncers outside a club. The next day Isa gets fired for incompetence, and the two young women become fast friends. Something about having a nice place to stay and a roommate starts to affect Isa in a positive way.

Later, the two women have a surprisingly gentle and friendly encounter with the biker-bouncers, and the four of them start hanging out together.   But just as Isa softens and blossoms—she enthusiastically looks for work and even makes the most of a ridiculous job that requires her to wear a costume and ride around town on roller skates—Maria's self-pity curdles into something that will poison their relationship.

Regnier and Bouchez are slightly hamstrung by the occasional incoherence of the script, but they both give fine, charismatic performances.   Jo Prestia and Patrick Mercado are convincing and affecting as the biker-bouncers.

So it's unfortunate that the ending of the film is so rushed and unsatisfying, especially given an overlong beginning that could easily have been excised without loss to the plot.

NEWSDAY, 4/2/99, Part II/p. B7, John Anderson

In his recent Nation review of Erick Zonca's "The Dreamlife of Angels," critic Stuart Klawans pointed to the fresh white scar over actress Elodie Bouchez' eye: It was characteristic of this *tres* confident film, he said, that we never get an explanation for it—that Isa, Bouchez' cheery hustler-gamine, remained at least a partial enigma, much like the movie itself.

It was an amusing testament to Klawans' point about malleability that when this critic saw the same scar, he interpreted it as a bankrupt body piercing: The jewelry pawned, no doubt, somwhere along Isa's route to Lille, where she had hoped to crash with a friend who's long since moved.

It turns out, according to "sources close to the film," that the scar was Bouchez' idea: Presumably caught up in Zonca mode, she just thought it would add one more element of unrevealed history to a character with plenty of it, and little but her good nature to see her through.

Perception and nature—the human variety, in Zonca's view intractable and inevitable—is the heartbeat of "The Dreamlife of Angels," which treads the familiar turf of young down-and-outs on the prowl for love and direction.   But where you expect flimsy glibness, rage against patriarchy and recycled *la vie de boheme*, you get a sort of timeless statement about the incurable course of personality and individual destiny.   Are these quaint ideas?   Yes, and beneath the hipster melodrama, they rumble and roar.

Isa, with no place to stay and no money, has resorted to what is clearly one of her standard survival tactics: Making greeting cards out of construction paper and magazine ads and "selling" them on the street; it's beggary, essentially, but her guilelessness is a marketing tool.   One potential customer, however, offers her a job in a sweatshop sewing pants, and Isa, with no experience at all, goes to work beside Marie (Natacha Regnier), who's a whiz with the machines and as angry as Isa is sunny.

Their life together takes some predictable routes through unpredictable people—a pair of biker-bouncers, for instance (Jo Prestia and Patrick Mercado), who turn out to be rather sensitive lugs, and an arrogant club owner (Gregoire Colin), in whom Marie sees a way out of poverty and into the life she thinks she deserves.

Isa, meanwhile, becomes obsesssed with Sandrine—the girl who used to live in their apartment, and who's on life support after the auto accident that killed her mother Isa has found Sandrine's journal and read it; she begins visiting her in the hospital, reading to her, in the hopes that her voice might bring the girl out of her coma.   Her empathy is such that Isa begins adding to the journal, inserting herself into Sandrine's life.   Marie, meanwhile, preoccupied with her ugly love affair, is concerned that if the girl dies—or even if she improves—they're going to lose their fine apartment.

So, for all its streetwise ambience, it's a fable Zonca's telling, one whose lesson is about the fatedness of character: Marie's problems are as shady as Isa's history, but there never seems to be a question that the past has a thing to do with how the two women conduct their lives.   It's all about soul and angels, one who falls and one who flies, in a duet of motion that's as old as time.

SIGHT AND SOUND, 11/98, p. 64, Gavin Smith

Isa (Isabelle), a drifter in her twenties, arrives in Lille, northern France. Taking a job in a dressmaking factory, Isa befriends fellow-employee Marie. She moves into the flat Marie is housesitting for Mrs Val and her teenage daughter Sandrine, who are in hospital in comas after a car accident. When Isa is fired from her job, Marie quits as well.

Trying to gain entry to Le Blue, a local nightclub, they meet bouncers Charly and Fredo. After reading Sandrine's diary, Isa visits her in hospital and learns that Mrs Val has died. Marie is extricated from a shoplifting incident by Chriss, the young owner of Le Blue, Chriss and Marie become sexually involved and Marie ends her relationship with Charly. Marie becomes obsessed with Chriss. Isa disapproves of Marie's surrender of self-respect and the two women's relationship unravels.

They learn the flat is to be sold; they must move out. Chriss asks Isa to inform Marie that he has broken up with her and Marie sinks into a deep depression. Isa resumes her vigil at the hospital when Sandrine's condition worsens. After a night in the hospital chapel, Isa learns that Sandrine has regained consciousness and is expected to recover, but decides not to make herself known to her. At the flat, Isa writes a farewell note reaffirming her friendship and wishing Marie well—only to see her commit suicide by leaping from a window. Isa begins a new job on an electronics factory's assembly line.

In this impressive first feature, director Erick Zonca sets up a carefully circumscribed dramatic framework: Isa's brief, intense and less-than-reciprocal relationships with Marie and Sandrine. Within these limits he achieves a well nigh flawless, subtly affecting narrative of emotional give and take. As with much of the best contemporary French cinema, Zonca's film pulls off a seemingly effortless tonal and stylistic balancing act between an unsentimental, authentic naturalism, a concise sense of social context, and intimate, nuanced character observation. The disarming narrative transparency of *La Vie rêvée des anges* distinguishes it from its ostensible precursor, Agnès Varda's formidable 1985 film about a female drifter, *Sans toit ni loi/ Vagabonde*. Its values and naturalism also suggest some affinity with Sandrine Veysset's *Will It Snow For Christmas?* and the films of Claire Denis *(Nenette et Boni, J'ai pas sommeil, S'en fout la mort)* which also deal with young people on the fringes of an exploitative, economically precarious social order. But where Denis and Varda honour their characters' opacity and unknowable otherness, Zonca precisely and unemphatically elucidates familiar characters and situations, using a skillfully edited succession of acutely observed moments.

Avoiding being too schematic, the film suggests intriguing but purposefully underdeveloped or blocked links and correspondences. The obliquely sketched circumstances that underwrite Marie and Isa's domestic arrangements—the flat's occupants, a single mother and her daughter Sandrine, are in hospital in comas after a car accident—seem to promise a metaphoric overlay that never arrives. Similarly, the narrative never yields an association between Marie, Isa or for that matter the comatose Sandrine and the angelic dreamlife of the title. Zonca ingeniously shortcircuits the doubling of Isa and Sandrine, and Isa's emotional investment in Sandrine's condition. Sandrine's diary entries ("I feel things inside, overwhelming things ... on the edge of an abyss I feel this crazy urge to jump") are far more reminiscent of Marie's instability than Isa's anything but-neurotic self-sufficiency and principled empathy. In fact, it is Isa's ready assumption of responsibility—for Sandrine, then for Marie and even for Chriss—that makes her at once exceptional and at a disadvantage.

Ultimately, the film's central concern is with capturing the processes by which the steady accumulation of experience shapes an individual's interior life and social negotiations. In Zonca's characteristic formal trope, the handheld camera holds on Isa at the end of a scene for several moments as she digests each new development or setback. Amid the hard knocks of Isa's world there seems little room for dreamlife. If it's manifested anywhere, perhaps it's in the childlike freedom of her creativity, whether purposeful (making Christmas cards to sell on the street) or for its own sake (we see her painting in later scenes); or in a fearless, game spirit that enables her to pull off a winning impersonation of Madonna during an audition for a waitressing job. (Marie's impression of Lauren Bacall carries far less conviction.)

Though everything suggests the resilience and endurance of Isa's spirit despite the disillusioning disintegration of her friendship with Marie, the film's last scene invites itself to be read as a final capitulation to conformity after the abrupt trauma of a tragedy that effectively negates the "miracle" in the hospital. The closure of the final camera move through the electronics plant perhaps represents a definitive enactment of Isa's absorption into the anonymity of soul-destroying, alienated labour—but as it pauses at each female assembly-line worker, it suggests the potential for new friendships (and similar women's stories) just around the corner.

VILLAGE VOICE, 4/6/99, p 126, Amy Taupin

Isa (Elodie Bouchez) and Marie (Natacha Régnier) are two young French women without a franc to their names Isa is a classic gamine—a forthright, impulsive, self-reliant tomboy with short cropped dark hair and pert features. She's something of a free spirit, but she's also well grounded Bold in asking for what she needs, she can shrug off rejection, but she won't allow anyone to treat her like shit.

Marie is in almost every way Isa's opposite a classic, fine-boned, blond beauty with an explosive rage simmering beneath her guarded, diffident facade. Masochistic and withholding Marie is so reminiscent of the heroine of Robert Bresson's *A Gentle Creature* that there's no doubt director Erick Zonca had that film in mind when he cast Régnier, a Dominique Sanda lookalike, in the role.

This is Zonca's first film, and it's so graceful and intelligent and complicated in its depiction of human interaction that it takes the notion of a remarkably assured directorial debut to a new level. There's a rare sense of collaboration—between the actors, between the director and the actors, between the director and the camerawoman (Agnes Godard), between the camerawoman and the actors—that makes the film seem lively and unpredictable even when, narratively speaking, not much seems to be going on.

Our two heroines meet in a sweatshop in the provincial town of Lille, where the gray blue light is as soft as the weather is hard. Within 24 hours, Isa is fired and Marie quits. Marie is taking care of an apartment whose occupants—a mother and her teenage daughter—have been in a car accident; Isa, who has been sleeping on the streets, asks Marie if she can stay there too. They form a fragile bond, although Isa is clearly more involved with Marie than Marie is with her. They exchange life stories, hang out in clubs and shopping malls, and pal around with two bouncers, Charlie (Patrick Mercado) and Fredo (Jo Prestia), burly guys with tender hearts.

Though Isa has no problem living from hand to mouth, Marie hates being poor. She gets involved with Chriss (Grégoire Colin), a spoiled playboy who rescues her when she's caught stealing a leather jacket. Marie envies Chriss's money and the freedom it buys him, and she convinces herself that he's her ticket to a better life. Chriss is turned on by her anger and resistance, but he's not serious about the affair. The imbalance of power makes for hot sadomasochistic sex and also feeds Marie's self-loathing.

Isa knows that Chriss is a scumbag but she can't stop Marie from pursuing him and humiliating herself. When Marie rejects her, Isa turns her attention to the girl who used to live in the apartment and has been in a coma since the car accident. Isa visits her daily in the hospital and tries to will her back to consciousness by reading to her from the diary that she's found in the apartment. By helping the girl find her way back to life, Isa finds new strength and desire in herself.

Thus, while one heroine is tumbling down, the other is rising up. But *The Dreamlife of Angels* never feels contrived. There's an emotional vibrancy and compassion in Zonca's filmmaking that makes us care about these two women and the moment-to-moment choices they make, even when those choices are overdetermined. One senses that Zonca is more on the side of Isa, who finds her strength through solidarity with others of her class and sex, than with Marie, who wants to deny and escape her own identity. But Zonca also gives us a glimpse of who Marie could have become, had she not succumbed to the self-hatred taught to her since birth.

Shot with a handheld camera and lots of natural light, the film has a sensuous, radiant surface that does justice to its title. The *Dreamlife of Angels* is both an unusually well-observed piece of realism and a subjective vision that's filtered through the fantasies, desires, and adrenaline rushes of two young women. Godard, who has shot most of Claire Denis's films, is a perfect cinematographer for Zonca. The fluidity of her framing and her ability to capture urban landscapes meld with his understanding that people, no matter how alienated they are, never exist in isolation. Isa and Marie define themselves and live out their dreams through interaction with others and with their environment.

Zonca is so adroit at conveying this sense of connection that Bouchez and Régnier were jointly named Best Actress at the 1998 Cannes Film Festival. *The Dreamlife of Angels* is ultimately an actor's movie, and while Bouchez and Régnier carry the film, Colin, Mercado, and Prestia, as the men who, in various ways, desire them, are just as fine. Mercado gives Charlie a surprising degree of tenderness and wisdom, particularly at the moment when he tells Marie that she should go for her dream even though she's breaking his heart in the process. Colin, on the other hand, doesn't flinch from making Chriss a complete cad When Chriss, who's too cowardly to jilt Marie in person, asks Isa to tell her that it's over, Isa belts him in the mouth. It's what we've been longing to do through the entire picture.

Also reviewed in:
CHICAGO TRIBUNE, 4/30/99, Tempo/p. 5, Michael Wilmington
NATION, 3/22/99, p. 34, Stuart Klawans
NEW REPUBLIC, 3/22/99, p. 28, Stanley Kauffman
NEW YORK TIMES, 4/2/99, p. E13, Janet Maslin
NEW YORKER, 4/5/99, p. 91, Anthony Lane
VARIETY, 5/25-31/98, p. 57, Brendan Kelly
WASHINGTON POST, 5/7/99, Weekend/p. 47, Desson Howe

DRIVE ME CRAZY

A Twentieth Century Fox release of an Amy Robinson production *Producer:* Amy Robinson *Director:* John Schultz. *Screenplay:* Rob Thomas. *Based on the novel "How I Created My Perfect Prom Date" by:* Todd Strasser. *Director of Photography:* Kees Van Oostrum. *Editor:* John Pace. *Music:* Greg Kendall. *Music Editor:* Glenn Auchinachie. *Sound:* Jonathan Earl Stein and (music) Malcolm Luker. *Sound Editor:* Andrew DeCristofaro. *Casting:* Sheila Jaffe and Georgianne Walken. *Production Designer:* Aaron Osborne. *Art Director:* Erin Cochran. *Set Designer:* Carl Stensel. and John R Uibel. *Set Decorator:* Melissa Levander. *Set Dresser:* Konnor Sawyer Jenson, Cole Broberg, Spencer Cope, Johnny Harris, and L.S. Prickett. *Special Effects:* Rick H. Josephsen. *Costumes:* Genevieve Tyrrell. *Make-up:* Greg T. Moon. *Stunt Coordinator:* Bill McIntosh. *Running time:* 93 minutes. *MPAA Rating:* PG-13.

CAST: Melissa Joan Hart (Nicole Maris); Adrian Grenier (Chase Hammond); Stephen Collins (Mr. Maris); Mark Metcalf (Mr. Rope); William Converse-Roberts (Mr. Hammond); Faye Grant (Mrs. Maris); Susan May Pratt (Alicia); Kris Park (Ray Neeley); Ali Larter (Dulcie); Mark Webber (Dave); Gabriel Carpenter (Brad); Lourdes Benedicto (Chloe Frost); Keri Lynn Pratt (Dee Vine); Natasha Pearce (Sue); Derrick Shore (Tom); Jordan Bridges (Eddie Lampell); Keram Malicki-Sanchez (Rupert); Andrew Roach (Big Fred); Joey Lopez (Student TV Director); Jessica Frandsen (Drena); Kristy Wu (Liz); Lee Holmes (Joshua); Jacque Gray (Kathy); Ivey Lloyd (Pretty Girl); Terry Cain (Diner Waitress); Lauren Renée Boyer (Vixen #1); Elizabeth Hart (Vixen #2); Doug MacMillan (Mr. Webb); Mary A. Daniels (Faculty Sponsor); Holly Swain (Nordic Blonde); Maya Ford (Electrocutes Bass); Torrance Castellano (Electrocutes Drums); Allison Robertson (Electrocutes Guitar); Brett Anderson (Electrocutes Vox); Marc Valasquez (Pit Band Lead Singer); Brendon Te (Pit Band Guitar); Tone Te (Pit Band Drums); Darby Bailey (Pit Band Bass).

LOS ANGELES TIMES, 10/1/99, Calendar/p 14, Robin Rauzi

[The following review by Robin Rauzi appeared in a slightly different form in
NEWSDAY, 10/1/99, Part II/p B15.]

Regard with suspicion any movie named after a song. It suggests there's not much to latch on to about the film in question, so its handlers have tried to co-opt the persona of a popular tune. "Can't Buy Me Love" and "Something to Talk About" both leap to mind.

In the case of "Drive Me Crazy," anyone eligible to vote might not get the reference to the Britney Spears song—and that's likely intentional. The movie, which stars Melissa Joan Hart of TV's "Sabrina, the Teenage Witch," will fall completely beneath grown-up radar—and that's no great loss. Like the song, the movie is bouncy and catchy but disposable pop material.

Hart stars as Nicole Maris, a campus booster nonpareil. In with the popular crowd, but still remarkably wholesome, Nicole is organizing a sort of massive homecoming dance to celebrate the centennial of Timothy Zonin High School (aka Time Zone High). Her next-door neighbor, Chase Hammond (Adrian Grenier) is the kind of guy who pulls pranks on people like her and views high school as nothing worth celebrating.

Nicole gets jilted by her dream date, and Chase gets dumped by his tres political girlfriend. Guess what Nicole and Chase do? Go ahead.

Guess. OK, OK ... they pretend they're dating to make the other people jealous. And guess what happens? Go ahead. Guess.

But there's no point in being mean-spirited about a film like this. Slickly directed (though full of TV-style close-ups) and tightly cut, it is perfectly entertaining for 91 minutes. Like "She's All That," "Can't Hardly Wait" and others before it, "Drive Me Crazy" projects from the very beginning that nothing bad is going to happen in this movie. "Relax, it says. "It's all good here."

Adapted by TV writer Rob Thomas from the book "How I Created My Perfect Prom Date" by Todd Strasser, "Drive Me Crazy" is set in Utah, where somehow it is basketball season but also swim-in-the-river weather. Other aspects of Time Zone High, however, feel as real as home video, such as the drill squad and the morning student news show.

Whatever charisma Hart has on TV, the big screen dilutes it tenfold. Director John Schultz, formerly a documentarian, does her no favors by relying on the close-up. It's not that she's unattractive—it's more that she's inexpressive. Grenier, whose floppy curls and loping stride suggest high school, even if his five o'clock shadow does not, has far more charisma.

Not surprisingly, the movie is hyper-aware of its own soundtrack, even beyond the cut from Spears' absurdly platinum-selling " ... Baby One More Time" album. Don Philip, Steps and the Backstreet Boys—all notably on Jive Records—make musical appearances. Music supervisors Tom Wolfe and Manish Raval appear to hijack the movie for a short music video to the Backstreet Boys' "I Want It That Way."

"Drive Me Crazy" earns social points for giving the unpopular characters far more personality than most of the in-crowd. Mark Webber is Designated Dave, who volunteers to drive kids home from parties—kids who don't even know his last name. Kris Park plays Ray, a budding filmmaker who videotapes everything around him.

The cool kids—with one or two exceptions—aren't cruel. The film wants to side with the underdog geeks, but can't then criticize their desires to be popular. If the movie wants to have it both ways, that's easy to forgive. Remember, it's all good here.

If teens somehow get excited about "Drive Me Crazy," no harm done. But unlike, say, "Sixteen Candles," this won't be a picture today's teens and preteens look back to later with even campy nostalgia. It'll drop from memory as quickly as Britney Spears drops from the pop charts. That's got to happen soon, right?

NEW YORK POST, 10/1/99, p. 63, Jonathan Foreman

"Drive Me Crazy" recycles the teen romantic comedies of the last few years, from "Clueless" to "She's All That," and it's easily the worst of the lot.

This isn't because the story is predictable—that's true of most movies in the genre—but because it feels and looks like a lame imitation of a high-school flick made by people who don't get what makes the genre fun.

If concerned parents and teachers got together with Hollywood marketing folk to make a hip—but nice and responsible—film about the dangers of conformism, the need to be yourself and all that, it would likely result in something as bland, implicitly preachy and clueless about teen subcultures as "Drive Me Crazy."

Nicole (Melissa Joan Hart) is chief organizer of her high school's centennial party and an anchor on its TV station (!). She wants basketball star Brad (Gabriel Carpenter) to be her date for the party.

He asks her to go with him, but then he changes his mind and asks another girl. Partly to win him back and partly just to have a respectable date, she asks her next-door neighbor Chase (Adrian Grenier) to take her.

Chase has just been given the kiss-off by his hipster girlfriend, Dulcie (Ali Larter), so he agrees to pretend to be Nicole's boyfriend on the theory that jealousy will bring Dulcie back. The only problem is that good-looking but hippie-ish Chase doesn't have the right image for Nicole's crowd. So she takes him to the mall for a makeover.

Hanging out with Nicole, Chase begins to realize that the popular athletic kids aren't so bad after all, and that all the school spirit stuff at basketball games is actually quite fun. He also begins to fall for Nicole, and she for him.

But Chase's uncool friends think that he's betrayed them, even though most of them would do anything to be included in his new crowd. And things get more complicated in the course of this cluttered, badly organized tale when both Nicole's friend Alicia and Dulcie make plays for Chase's affections.

Hart, who plays "Sabrina the Teenage Witch" on TV—and who is currently embroiled in a controversy about some semi-nude poses she was photographed in for a men's magazine—was much better as an irritating goody-goody in last year's "Can't Hardly Wait." Here she's perky and bland to the extent that you almost wish one of Nicole's mean rivals would win Chase's heart.

SIGHT AND SOUND, 7/00, p. 42, Mike Higgins

US, the present. High-school senior Chase Hammond has just been dumped by his girlfriend. His neighbour Nicole Maris is failing to impress the school's star basketball player. In order to make their quarries jealous, they decide to pretend they are dating one another. The introspective Chase changes his image to suit the pert Nicole, thereby earning the suspicion of his two friends. With Chase at her side, Nicole realises that being one of the school's in crowd isn't as rewarding as it once was. The pair grow closer.

Chase is unhappy with the contempt his new acquaintances have for his old friends; Nicole is devastated when she spies Chase kissing her best friend. Days before the school prom, the pair split up. At the prom Nicole is reconciled with Chase and her too often-absent father. Arriving home, the children discover that Chase's father has spent the night with Nicole's mother. Pity the jobbing director, for whom the high-school feature was once bread-and-butter work to be churned out well away from the glare of publicity. Since Amy Heckerling's smart Jane Austen adaptation *Clueless*, US high schools—at least those portrayed in a crop of recent movies—have played host to Shakespeare *(10 Things I Hate about You)*, Choderlos de Laclos *(Cruel Intentions)*, entrepreneurial skulduggery *(Rushmore)*, and real-politik allegory *(Election)*. This is not to suggest that all of the new intake have thrived in their new surroundings; but enough have succeeded to raise our expectations of whatever next the genre has to offer. All of which is bad news for John Schultz's instantly forgettable film.

Given that his past credits include the popular teen television serial *Dawsons Creek* it is perhaps no surprise that screenwriter Rob Thomas paints an irredeemably bland portrait of contemporary American youth culture. His characterisation of Chase's loose group of geek buddies and the clean-cut preppies to whom Nicole pledges allegiance is dismally formulaic. Tensions between these two camps proceed along the most conventional of narrative routes: boy meets girl, with some soapy to-and-froing merely delaying the saccharine conclusion.

Whereas the more matchable of the recent US high-school comedies play selfconsciously to their pop-culture literate audiences, *Drive Me Crazy* feels like a throwback to a far less sophisticated breed of teen picture. (The title of the novel on which this film is based—*How I Created My Perfect Prom Date*—neatly evokes the juvenile tone of *Drive Me Crazy*.) Eschewing the smart intertextuality of such films as *Clueless*, *Drive Me Crazy* introduces into its vapid milieu various moments of apparent sociological topicality. At one point Chase's unpopular friend hijacks the school's television station to broadcast a short film satirising the herd instincts and pep-rally culture of his classmates. But while this scene might signal a sympathy on behalf of Schultz for the adolescent outsiders of teen society, *Drive Me Crazy* ends with a celebration of that bastion of high school conformity, the prom. As if to underline its socially cohesive function the prom even boasts the meek attendance of all the school's nerds. Another perfunctory touch—the single-parent status of Chase's father and Nicole's mother—does however provide the film its most memorable moment: Nicole's reconciliation with her often-absent father. Such reunions are, of course, staples of American youth movies; this one, however, must be the first to be staged in a hot-air balloon.

Also reviewed in:
NEW YORK TIMES, 10/1/99, p. E18, Lawrence Van Gelder
VARIETY, 10/4-10/99, p. 86, Robert Koehler

DROP DEAD GORGEOUS

A New Line Cinema release in association with Capella/KC Medien of a Hofflund/Palone production. *Executive Producer:* Claire Rudnick Polstein, Donna Langley, and Lona Williams. *Producer:* Gavin Palone and Judy Hofflund. *Director:* Michael Patrick Jann. *Screenplay:* Lona Williams. *Director of Photography:* Michael Spiller. *Editor:* David Codron and Janice Hampton. *Music:* Mark Mothersbaugh. *Choreographer:* Jerry Mitchell. *Sound:* Mack Melson and (music) Steve Kohler. *Sound Editor:* Cormac Funge and Frederick Howard. *Casting:* John Papsidera. *Production Designer:* Ruth Ammon. *Art Director:* Maria Baker. *Set Decorator:* Helen Britten. *Set Dresser:* Scott L. Nordhausen, John A. Champion, Warren Barrows, Jim Kindt, Trisha M. Herrman, and Chris Freeman. *Special Effects:* Paul Murphy. *Costumes:* Mimi Melgaard. *Make-up:* Mary K. Flaa and Desne Holland. *Make-up (Special Effects):* Crist Ballas. *Stunt Coordinator:* Eric D. Howell. *Running time:* 97 minutes. *MPAA Rating:* PG-13.

CAST: Kirsten Dunst (Amber Atkins); Ellen Barkin (Annette Atkins); Allison Janney (Loretta); Denise Richards (Becky Leeman); Kirstie Alley (Gladys Leeman); Sam McMurray (Lester Leeman); Mindy Sterling (Iris Clark); Brittany Murphy (Lisa Swenson); Amy Adams (Leslie Miller); Laurie Sinclair (Michelle Johnson); Shannon Nelson (Tess Weinhaus); Tara Redepenning (Molly Howard); Sarah Stewart (Jenelle Betz); Alexandra Holden (Mary Johanson); Brooke Bushman (Tammy Curry); Matt Malloy (John Dough); Michael McShane (Harold Vilmes); Will Sasso (Hank Vilmes); Lona Williams (Jean Kangas); Jon T. Olson (Pat); Casey Tyler Garven (Brett); Ashley Dylan Bullard (Fry Girl); Jacy Dumermuth (Pregnant Fry Girl); Nora Dunn (Colleen); Mo Gaffney (Terry); Adam West (Himself); Mary Gillis (Chloris Klinghagen); Richard Narita (Mr. Howard); Patti Yasutake (Mrs. Howard); Seiko Matsuda (Tina/Seiko Howard); Allyson Kearns (Candy Striper); Tom Gilshannon (Lars Larson); Claudia Wilkens (Iona Hildebrandt); Dale Dunham (Mayor); Amanda Detmer (Miss Minneapolis); Thomas Lennon (Voice of Documentarian); Eric D. Howell (Sound Recordist); Matthew G. Park (Crew Guy); Terry Hempleman (Cop #1); Christopher Carlson (Cop #2); James Cada (Lisa Swenson's Father); Kristin Rudrüd (Pork Products Lady); Luke Ingles (Rocker Kid #1); Nick Ingles (Rocker Kid #2); Jimmie D. Wright (Doctor); Peter Aitchison (Male News Anchor); Mary Rehbein (Female Reporter #1); Jeany Park (Female Reporter #2); Richard Ooms (Pastor); Robert-Bruce Brake (Mr. Melchoir); Bruce Linser (Ed); Tiffany Engen (Tap Dancer); Jennifer Baldwin Peden (Opera Singer); Annalise Nelson (Violinist); Samantha Harris (Miss Burnsville); Kari Ann Shiff (Miss Delluth); Mark Dahlen (Cops Crew Guy); Jeff Tatum (Fireman).

LOS ANGELES TIMES, 7/23/99, Calendar/p. 10, Kevin Thomas

The following review by Kevin Thomas appeared in a slightly different form in
NEWSDAY, 7/23/99, Part II/p. B10.]

Satirizing beauty contests is hardly new—Michael Ritchie's "Smile" did it brilliantly back in 1975—but since they're still around they remain ripe targets, as demonstrated with dark hilarity in "Drop Dead Gorgeous." Occasionally heavy-handed and overdone—and scarcely free from a self-congratulatory tone—this latest spoof is nonetheless lots of fun, clever and fearless, and loaded with wicked lines and touches.

Writer/executive producer Lona Williams, herself a former Minnesota beauty contestant, and first-time director Michael Patrick Jann unfold their film from the point of view of a crew of documentary filmmakers who have come to the fictional Minnesota town of Mount Rose, about to hold its annual American Teen Princess contest.

The winner will receive a $500 scholarship; more important, she will go on to participate in the state competition in Minneapolis and may even make it to the national pageant. The whole shebang has been sponsored for the last 50 years by the Sarah Rose Teen Cosmetics company of Atlanta—a fictional outfit, one must hastily add.

It's David and Goliath time. The local competition is run with an iron hand by a former winner, Gladys Leeman (Kirstie Alley), and this is the year her own daughter Becky (Denise Richards) is competing. Gladys is not about to have anybody but Becky win. Since her husband (Sam McMurray), a crass furniture store owner, is pretty clearly the town's leading merchant—he even puts up that $500 scholarship—and that Gladys is in the position to hand-pick a jury of village weirdos (including her husband's mousy secretary), Becky is pretty much a shoo-in.

Still, there is that pretty and sweet-natured Amber Atkins (Kirsten Dunst), a tap-dancing whiz who washes dishes in the school cafeteria and makes up corpses at the local mortuary to make ends meet.

Amber, peppy and naive, is also intelligent and ambitious; she takes Diane Sawyer as her role model. She lives in a trailer park with her salty single mom, Annette (Ellen Barkin), a hairdresser who is determined that her daughter escape Mount Rose for a better life. Against overwhelming odds, Amber and a host of other girls enter the contest.

As the day of reckoning draws near, a series of dire events commences. A hearty outdoors girl, the unlikeliest contestant, winds up dead—but then she did beat out Becky in the Lutheran Sisterhood Gun Club shooting competition. Amber opens her school locker to find a snapshot of the dead girl inscribed on the back with "You're next." And that's just the beginning.

Williams neither identifies the culprit right off nor makes it a matter of suspense and instead treats such deadly violence with a matter-of-factness that is all too timely. And the knockabout pacing Jann maintains is exactly right for a picture in which plot is way secondary to characterization and especially sharp observations.

"Drop Dead Gorgeous" is chock-full of zingers: In one especially stupefying turn, the contestants come out in hats of their own creations, intended to express a Proud-to-Be-American theme. Becky's depicts Mt. Rushmore, another girl perches a Statue of Liberty on her head, but best of all, a white girl, adopted by Japanese immigrant parents, sports a mushroom cloud representing atomic power—not exactly the most tasteful choice, considering her parents' native land.

There are all sorts of throwaway lines, such as Gladys' declaration that her husband's "furniture is as phony as my orgasms." And then there's the local reigning Teen Queen (Alexandra Holden) now hospitalized for anorexia—which is what you get when you jog 18 miles a day on 400 calories.

No small-town gaucherie is left unskewered, everyone talks like they're straight out of "Fargo," but the filmmakers retain plenty of affection for the hard-scrabble Atkinses and their hearty neighbor Loretta, a down-to-earth, fortysomething gal with a sense of humor who is made so real and wise by Allison Janney that she practically steals the film. Dunst and Barkin couldn't be better, Richards is as rightly nasty as she is pretty.

It's always a pleasure to watch the ever-venturesome Alley have fun with the monstrous Gladys. Adam West has a nifty Bert Parks-like turn as the national pageant emcee.

NEW YORK POST, 7/23/99, p. 61, Jonathan Foreman

It takes a special kind of talent to aim your satire at a target as big and easy as beauty pageants and miss it by a mile, especially when you've got an able, attractive cast and are using the mock-documentary format that worked so well in "This is Spinal Tap" and "Waiting for Guffman."

But "Drop Dead Gorgeous" is so crude and witless that, to the extent you feel anything at all, you end up feeling sorry for the small-town Minnesotans who are the main objects of the film's condescending cheap shots.

The faux documentarists introduce you to the eight contestants as they prepare for the competition. Among them there's a tramp, a dork, an athlete—who dies in a suspicious tractor accident—and the two girls who then become the favorites: Amber (Kirsten Dunst), a sweet blonde who worships Diane Sawyer and works in a mortuary, and scheming brunette Becky (Denise Richards), whose father sponsors the contest and whose evil mother (Kirstie Alley) runs it.

One contestant after another is somehow put out of action by someone determined that Becky—who happens to be a fine hand with both pistol and rifle—will win. The unknown villain even blows up the trailer where Amber lives with her white-trash mom, Annette (Ellen Barkin). But Amber has the support of Mom and Mom's slutty, hard-drinkin' friend Loretta (Allison Janney), and there's no way she'll give up.

Everyone sports an exaggerated "Fargo" accent. It's supposed to be hilarious when local rubes refer to themselves as "God-fearin' folk" and when Amber gets all excited about staying at an airport Howard Johnson's. Halfway through, director Michael Patrick Jann seems to forget that it's supposed to be a documentary and starts shooting it like a regular feature.

What saves "Drop Dead Gorgeous" from unwatchability are performances by Janney and Dunst that rise above screenwriter Lona Williams' amateurish material. Their deftness makes a wildly overacting Alley (and, to a lesser extent, Barkin) all the more embarrassing. Richards essentially reprises her spoiled-vixen role from last year's enjoyably trashy "Wild Things," but without exposing as much skin.

There are a few good jokes scattered about: One of the contestants chooses a monologue from the '70s sci-fi flick "Soylent Green" for the talent contest. But for the most part there's something desperate and creepy about all of the film's obvious cracks at the expense of small-town hicks, as if the writer, confusing snide snobbery with sophistication, were trying too hard to establish that she's not one herself.

The filmmakers try to push the envelope of acceptable comedy subjects—in the fashion of "There's Something About Mary"—by making fun of a fat, retarded man, a hospitalized anorexic and Japanese-Americans trying too hard to assimilate.

It's the kind of thing that only a really skilled filmmaker can pull off. Here, the effort feels uncertain and unconvinced—as if writer, director and actors were slightly embarrassed and the result is a series of sour misfires.

SIGHT AND SOUND, 10/99, p. 42, Charlotte O'Sullivan

In a Minnesota small town a documentary crew arrives to cover a beauty pageant. The event is organised by wealthy Gladys Leeman, whose own daughter Becky is in the competition. The crew are more interested in Amber Atkins, a hardworking urchin whose heroine is NBC anchorwoman Diane Sawyer. Amber is determined to win but Becky (with a little help from her mother) will stop at nothing to secure the prize for herself. As contestants die in mysterious circumstances, Amber remains unbowed. Even when her trailer-park home is blown into the sky (and her mother almost killed), a few supportive words from a friend give her the strength to go on.

On the day of the contest, the corrupt judges award Amber second prize while Becky wins the crown. But during the victory parade a freak accident burns Becky to a crisp. Amber becomes "teen princess" and is whisked off to the county finals, where this time she succeeds because the rest of the contestants fall ill with food poisoning. The national finals are cancelled due to problems with the IRS. Meanwhile, Becky's vengeful mother turns a gun on the crowd and in the process a female television reporter is killed. Taking instant advantage of this, Amber catapults herself into a plum anchorwoman job.

There's much about *Drop Dead Gorgeous*—a satire on all things smalltown and ultra-feminine—to shock and tickle us. The reigning 'teen princess' of the town beauty pageant, for example, is expertly cast: Mary Johanson is an anorexic who really looks like an anorexic. And her two scenes possess an eerie cynicism reminiscent of Michael Ritchie's neglected pageant-drama *Smile*. Early on, a two-faced Becky, desperate to demonstrate her femininity, brushes Mary's long, blond mermaid hair, which is falling out. It sticks to the brush like wool to a barbed wire fence. If Becky is a wolf in sheep's clothing, Mary is a sheep being led to the slaughter.

Later, on the point of handing over her crown, Mary appears in a wheelchair attached to a drip, with a wig—lip synching to weepy pop hit 'Don't Cry Out Loud' (the perfect song for the repressed crowd-pleaser). She looks like all those beauty queens, both the real ones (JonBenet Ramsey), and the metaphorical (Karen Carpenter), and she's beautiful too (a dead ringer for model James King). She's sex and death, skull and scented skin, in one flailing, dogged little package, and sadism (your own) snaps through the air like a whip.

Unfortunately, young scriptwriter Lona Williams chooses to play safe more often than not. Most crucially, she keeps Amber and her white-trash family uncontaminated by the town's corruption, which is a big mistake. From Cinderella on down, tales of poor girls battling with bitchy rich ones are two a penny and your heart sinks as you realise you're supposed to find Amber genuinely more attractive and more talented. Amber's routine at the talent contest is jazzily shot (even though this is meant to be a documentary) and edited like a pop promo. So why is maniacal tap dancing in a top hat any better than singing 'Can't Take My Eyes off You' with a crucifix strapped to your back (Becky's choice)? Can't they risk us thinking Amber's routine is tacky?

It's the old American dream nonsense. The film-makers don't trust us to urge on a heroine who's actually pretty much like the rest. We've got to believe in her plucky, self-reliant specialness. The irony is that having set her up as a trouper, she comes across finally as pampered, the film's own darling who's going to be made to look good whatever the cost. We're expected to laugh at cartoonishly ambitious Gladys Leeman but her principles are shared by the film itself. The danger is that it risks triggering a reaction: you end up begrudging Amber her success and wanting Becky (lent a mad sort of glow by Denise Richards) to win.

A little more effort in the script might have distracted us from this weakness. But where you expect to find sticky darkness, there's a vacuum. The mockumentary device, for instance, is never fully exploited. We never know why this particular bunch of slacker guys chose this subject nor what they're getting out of it. Only once are they tested by the central narrative: when one of the judges, realising they think he's a pervert, says, "Well, you guys have got a camera and no one's accusing you of anything." You assume this is the start of something postmodern and wily, but as with so many threads in this film, the crew just hang there, cluttering up the scenery.

Towards the end, Williams attempts to complicate things too late by pointing up Amber's ruthless side. But we can't tell if Amber's been hiding this side all along (the only one who really knew how to manipulate the cameras) or has been hardened by the contest itself. The film has no answers, so the twist offers no satisfaction (in any case, *To Die For* has been there, done that). All in all, the acknowledgement of Amber's dark underbelly feels like an opportunity missed, which just about sums up *Drop Dead Gorgeous* itself.

TIME, 7/26/99, p. 75, Richard Corliss

What should be put in a time capsule, the best of an age or the most brazenly typical? A Chuck Close painting or Drew Barrymore's gluteal tattoo? If you're looking for low familiar in a 1999 film, some concoction in which archetype meets stereotype, you might consider *Drop Dead Gorgeous*, a film that contains multitudes of better films in one disposable package. The other benefit of putting this instructively annoying dark comedy in a time capsule is that then no one would have to watch it.

A film team has come to Mount Rose, Minn., to document its annual Sara Rose Cosmetics Miss Teen Princess America Pageant. And this time it's personal. The local doyen (Kirstie Alley) is ready to kill, really, to ensure that her daughter Becky (Denise Richards) will win over trailer-park cutie Amber Atkins (Kirsten Dunst). Got all the movie references? Here is a mockumentary (*Waiting for Guffman, The Blair Witch Project*) about a high school contest (*Smile, Election*) set among the funny-talking rubes of rural Minnesota (*Fargo* or every third episode of *Mystery Science Theater 3000*).

Lona Williams' script has more lute-fisk and Lutheran gags than a year of *A Prairie Home Companion*. Williams and director Michael Patrick Jann are as eager to deride Middle America, with its oppressively cheerful whiteness, as they were to exploit the area's hospitality; the film was shot in half a dozen Minnesota towns. As Amber says, "The whole thing's kinda sad and lame at the same time."

Emerging valiantly from the debris are the two young stars. Dunst, 17, has grown up smartly before the camera; she has poise, wit and great dimples. Richards, 27 but plausibly teenish, uses her huge doll eyes (somehow calculating and dazed) and her brilliant teeth (all 50 or 60 of them, lined up like chorines ready to please the sugar daddies) to make Becky both the apotheosis and the parody of a precocious beauty-contestant pro. These are actresses worth watching, performances worth saving.

And when you pop *Drop Dead* into the time capsule, toss a reel of *American Pie* in with it. The guys from that movie and the girls from this one could tear one another apart.

VILLAGE VOICE, 8/3/99. p. 59, J.Hoberman

Even sillier than it is cynical, *Drop Dead Gorgeous* is a tiresome tale of a small-town competition that makes *Election's* blunderbuss satire seem masterful in its subtlety. Michael Patrick Jann's mock-documentary about a teen beauty pageant, set in a Minnesota community hitherto distinguished as the home of the Oldest Living Lutheran, is directed for maximum derision. Drifting in and out of concept, even as it strands a promising cast on a tundra of cheerily chirped *you betchas,* the movie focuses on the class conflict between two contestants—smug rich girl Denise Richards, daughter of past winner and current promoter Kirstie Alley, and Kirsten Dunst, a trailer-park rose who idolizes Diane Sawyer and works after school in the local morgue.

Lona Williams's ham-fisted script insures that the fix is in, in more ways than one. Like Michael Ritchie's *Smile*—the 1975 Altman wannabe that more or less invented this particular subgenre—*Drop Dead Gorgeous* feasts on the spectacle of the contestants' mealymouthed interviews and idiotic dance rehearsals. Will you appreciate a ballerina who signs inspirational lyrics as she dances. Or laugh at the grotesque joke of an anorexic in a wheelchair lip-synching "Don't Cry Out Loud"? Although the big goof is Richards singing "Can't Take My Eyes Off of You" to a crucified Jesus, the most appropriate number would have something to do with shooting ducks in a barrel.

Also reviewed in:
CHICAGO TRIBUNE, 7/23/99, Friday/p. A, Barbara Shulgasser
NEW YORK TIMES, 7/23/99, p. E8, Janet Maslin
VARIETY, 7/19-25/99, p. 26, Dennis Harvey
WASHINGTON POST, 7/23/99, p. C5, Rita Kempley
WASHINGTON POST, 7/23/99, Weekend/p. 37, Desson Howe

DRY CLEANING

A Strand releasing release of a coproduction Franco Espangnol: Cinea—Film Alain Sarde—Maestranza Films with the participation of CNC—Canal+—Region de Franche Comte—Sofinergie 4—Sofigram. *Director:* Anne Fontaine. *Screenplay (French with English subtitles):* Gilles Taurand and Anne Fontaine. *Based on original idea of:* Anne Fontaine and Claude Arnaud. *Director of Photography:* Caroline Champetier. *Choreographer:* Blanca Li. *Sound:* Cecile Ranc and Marie-Christine Ratel. *Casting:* Frederique Moidon. *Set Designer:* Antoine Platteau. *Costumes:* Elisabeth Tavernier. *Make-up:* Joel Lavau. *Running time:* 97 minutes. *MPAA Rating:* Not Rated.

CAST: Miou-Miou (Nicole Kunstler); Charles Berling (Jean-Marie Kunstler); Stanislas Merhar (Loic); Mathilde Seigner (Marylin); Nanou Meister (Yvette); Noe Pflieger (Pierre); Michel Bompoil (Robert); Christopher King (Steve); Gerard Blanc (Bertrand); Betty Petristy (Madame Bertrand); Bobby Pacha (Patron Ranch); Corinne Nejman (Josiane); Therese Gehin (Maryse); Joelle Gregorie (Travesti Banane); Pascal Allio, Caroline Galiani and Thomas Seiler (Dancers).

LOS ANGELES TIMES, 3/29/99, Kenneth Turan

The thickets of human desire are staples of the movie experience, but "Dry Cleaning," an exceptional new French film, explores them with unusual insight, empathy and daring. A dark and troubling film that investigates what we accept, what we encourage, and what we finally can't tolerate in our emotional and sexual relationships, "Dry Cleaning" mesmerizes with its ability to be both explicit and ambiguous, candid and restrained.

"Dry Cleaning" ("Nettoyage a sec" in French) is the second film for co-writer (with Gilles Taurand) and director Anne Fontaine, and on the surface it couldn't be more different than her debut, the bright and eccentric comedy "Augustin."

But like that film, "Dry Cleaning" displays a keen sympathy for people who live outside the norm and the ability to deal with extreme situations not with predictable cinematic exaggerations but rather with considerable sensitivity and tact.

Fontaine is helped enormously by a cast that includes Charles Berling ("Ridicule"), newcomer Stanislas Merhar and the luminous Miou-Miou (Bertrand Blier's "Going Places" and Diane Kurys' "Entre Nous" among others). Perfectly in tune with the director's intentions, these actors, especially Miou-Miou in perhaps the best work of her career, give off a believability that convinces us to follow them down a psychologically winding road.

Berling and Miou-Miou play Jean-Marie and Nicole Kunstler, a hard-working French couple who run a dry-cleaning establishment in the provincial town of Belfort. Living above the store with their young son and Jean-Marie's mother, the Kunstlers seem a contented pair whose labor-intensive work rarely allows them the luxury of time off.

On a rare night out, the couple visit a gay nightclub where they enjoy an intoxicating drag number by a two-person ensemble called the Queens of the Night. The next day, handsome young Loic (Merhar, who won a Cesar—the French Oscar—for best new actor for his performance) brings his unmistakable Queens costume into their shop for cleaning. "I've heard," he says, almost reflexively flirting with both husband and wife, "you do miracles."

Loic and his sister Marilyn (Mathilde Seigner) are the two halves of the Queens, and the first sign that their presence in the lives of Jean-Marie and Nicole will have an invigorating effect on the married couple's sex life is when Jean-Marie surprises his wife by trying on Loic's costume, which leads to a bout of passionate lovemaking.

Sexually active and a bit mercenary, Loic and his sister try to loosen their new friends up but in addition to attraction, there is also resistance. Still, when the Queens move on to another city, the husband and wife feel compelled, without ever acknowledging why, to take a rare vacation to catch their show.

That visit leads to an intensifying and increasingly complicated relationship between the angelic, androgynous-looking young man and both husband and wife, a tripartite relationship that is far more complex and unexpected than conventional plotting would have you imagine.

Initially, of course, there is the frisson, the whiff of excitement that clings to the danger of crossing the boundaries that separate the conventional from the forbidden, and "Dry Cleaning" manages to adroitly tantalize the audience as much as its characters.

But passions aroused can have a darker side, and the more intimately the couple get involved with Loic, the more the relationship reveals fissures in their marriage and in their lives. The question becomes not only can they go back to square one, but do they even want to.

As an intimate examination of the consequences of first exposing and then attempting to gratify longings that have remained well-hidden, this film is a knockout. As it builds toward an almost unbearable climax, "Dry Cleaning" reminds us that sometimes getting what we want or even what we need is only the beginning of the story.

NEW YORK, 2/15/99, p. 56, Peter Rainer

For such a supposedly sophisticated race, the French sure make a big deal about the transgressions of the flesh. Their film artists are too easily shocked: Adultery among the bourgeoisie is still Topic A in many of the Gallic exports. It's time this great national cinema got hip to a few new sins. What is the world coming to when even an American geekster like Todd Solondz *(Happiness)* can outshock the children of De Sade and Baudelaire?

Dry Cleaning is the latest French film to demonstrate that making whoopee has its downside. Jean-Marie (Charles Berling) and his wife, Nicole (Miou-Miou), run a cleaning shop in a provincial industrial town outside Paris. Their idea of a night out is grousing over dinner with the other merchants, but on one particular evening they attend a drag show at a local nightclub, La Nuit des Temps, and become unsettlingly enamored of one of the acts—a brother-sister combo. When Loic (Stanislas Merhar), the brother, shows up the next day at the couple's shop to get his sequined dress dry-cleaned, he recognizes his wide-eyed patrons. Before long, they're all back at La Nuit des Temps en route to a motel tryst where sister (Mathilde Seigner) pairs off with Jean-Marie and brother beds Nicole. Jean-Marie short-circuits the situation before the panting gets out of hand, but these prim bourgeoisie are goners: Pretty soon, Loic, now on his own, insinuates himself into their lives, even their home—and it's not just Nicole he's after but Jean-Marie as well.

Anne Fontaine, who co-wrote and directed, has a fine-cut humorlessness. Everything that she shows us is tinctured with double meaning. Even the laundry's rinse cycle is symbolic—whirling clothes equal whirling lives. It's all too patterned: The couple that spends its days cleaning other people's dirty laundry ends up swamped in its own. Something of grave consequence is supposedly being imparted, but the effect is lackluster—it's like a Pinter play that's been given a snide-ectomy. With his languid punk androgyny, Loic holds the screen, but Jean-Marie and Nicole don't have much charge. They're in the movie to be tossed and transgressed. Even when they're being perverse—even when it's clear Jean-Marie is savoring Nicole's infidelities as if they were his own—they're dullards. This is the kind of movie where the husband displays his terror at the interloper's advances by taking up smoking again.

Fontaine is an anti-hedonist. Her movie isn't about the virtues of freeing yourself up: it's about how letting go shuts you down. Watching Miou-Miou, we can choose to recognize in the tranced-out Nicole the gamine gleam of the actress from *Going Places* and *Jonah Who Will Be 25 in the Year 2000*. (It's the only way to make sense of the character.) But the gleam is faint. Nicole is a beautiful blank, and blankness has been Miou-Miou's façade for a while now. Offscreen, in her comportment and outspokenness, she still represents for the French the friskiness of common folk—the movie star as one-of-us. Onscreen, however, she exudes a wan respectability, and *Dry Cleaning,* despite its subject, changes none of that.

NEW YORK POST, 2/5/99, p. 62, Hannah Brown

"Dry Cleaning" is a movie that asks the question: Do dry cleaners ever wish they could make a few stains instead of just remove them?

Director and co-screenwriter Anne Fontaine gives it some serious consideration. Her answer: Yes, with a passion.

She has managed to make a compelling movie about a married couple who own a dry-cleaning shop in a small French city and get involved with a bisexual, cross-dressing nightclub performer.

It's a plot that sounds like a parody, but it's saved from silliness by a clever script and skillful performances from all three leads.

Nicole (Miou-Miou, who is so beautiful, she should be giving American actresses lessons on aging gracefully) and Jean-Marie (Charles Berling) work like dogs for every franc's worth of bourgeois comfort they enjoy.

But their orderly existence starts to fall apart when they go to a nightclub and see a kinky act by brother-and-sister cross-dressers. They are both charmed and drawn to the performers without knowing why.

Their connection to the siblings grows when the brother, Loic (Stanislas Merhar), has a stain removed from a glittery gown. Then his sister deserts him and he's adrift.

The movie makes it seem perfectly plausible that this straight-laced couple would take him in. Where this subtle film differs from so many other rough-loner-shakes-up-family movies is that Loic isn't stereotypically charismatic, but sweet and self-effacing.

Another witty touch is that while Nicole and Jean-Marie are attracted to Loic's sensuality, he is equally drawn to their stability and middle-class lifestyle. The young drag performer actually turns out to have a knack for the dry-cleaning business.

NEWSDAY, 2/5/99, Part II/p. B11, Jack Mathews

Managing sexual repression is a lot like managing a dry cleaning business. So much dirty laundry, so little time, and every day, another load.

At least, that's the metaphor being strained in French director Anne Fontaine's "Dry Cleaning," an offbeat drama about a bored middle-class couple—the owners of a dry cleaning business in a small industrial town—and their flirtation with a touring drag queen whom they befriend and bring into their home, where he attempts to seduce them both.

It all begins with a rare night out for Jean-Marie (Charles Berling) and Nicole (Miou-Miou), who leave their young son and Jean-Marie's mother at home and visit a nightclub with friends. There, they catch the erotic brother-sister drag act of Loic (Stanislas Merhar) and Marylin (Mathilde Seigner), and find themselves aroused.

Later, when Loic comes by their shop to have his dress cleaned, a personal connection is made between him and the couple, and soon Jean-Marie and Nicole are taking in a second show. That night ends with the two couples mixed and matched for some earnest groping, and though Jean-Marie cuts the evening short, it's clear both he and Nicole want some more.

At this point, "Dry Cleaning" smacks of French sex farce, and the audience will feel a step ahead of the filmmaker, confident that whatever dalliances and crises follow, the relationship between Jean-Marie and Nicole will be reinvigorated and strengthened. The audience will be surprised.

To save those surprises, we'll say only this much more about the plot. Loic's sister drops out early on and he ends up adopting Jean-Marie and Nicole as his new family. He goes to work as a cleaner apprentice, and the stage is set for a series of sexual awakenings, reawakenings, and reconsiderations.

Ultimately, the psychology seems as muddled as the dry cleaning metaphor. It's one thing for Nicole to be game for some funky extracurriculars; given her early reactions to Loic and Jean-Marie's nonchalance about it, no explanation is really necessary. But much of the story hangs on Jean-Marie's attraction to their androgynous lodger, and neither the film nor Berling's performance provides a plausible basis for that.

VILLAGE VOICE, 2/9/99, p. 65, J. Hoberman

A sexy stranger lands in the midst of a settled, community-sanctioned relationship with convulsive results. It's the story of *Picnic*, *Titanic*, and just about half the films noir ever made, but so intrinsic to the promise of the movies that it will never grow stale.

However else they may differ, Anne Fontaine's *Dry Cleaning* and Edoardo Winspeare's *Pizzicata*—two new European movies following that recipe and opening this week—could both take their epigram from Freud's *Civilization and Its Discontents*. "The feeling of happiness derived from the satisfaction of a wild instinctual impulse untamed by the ego is incomparably more intense than that derived from sating an instinct that has been tamed." Which is not to say that it is easier to watch someone else change their life on the screen than to think about your own.

In Fontaine's feature, the ego-tamed instincts belong to a hardworking married couple, Nicole (Miou-Miou) and Jean-Marie (Charles Berling), who operate a dry-cleaning establishment in the drab provincial town of Belfort, France. The movie shows something, if only a bit, of the oppressive heat, chemical fumes, and unending obligations of the dry-cleaning life. As professional enemies of dirt, sweat, and accidental spills, the couple could be seen as veritable instinct police. Indeed, Jean-Marie's emphasis on the importance of ironing a sharp pants crease suggests that the family business is less a matter of pressing than repressing.

As the dry cleaners never take vacations or, except for Sunday mass, even a day off, wild instinctual impulse arrives from without in the form of a suggestively incestuous brother-sister act called the "Queens of the Night." Improbably booked at a local bar, it's a tasteful show: the pair engage in sensuously synchronous grinding in matching lamé gowns, feathered boas, veiled hats while perched upon a rotating divan. The dry cleaners are turned on and tempted to change their lives, up to a point, especially after the act's flirtatious, omnisexual male member, Loïc (newcomer Stanislas Merhar), appears in the shop to get a stain removed from his gown.

The physical stain is erased; a psychic one takes its place. Nicole and Jean-Marie return to catch Loïc and his sister, Marylin, cross-dressed and posed on a motorcycle, lip-synching a duet by Franco-pop retro-icons Johnny Halliday and Sylvie Vartan. The ensuing elaborate approach-avoidance dance grows more intense after the Drones of the Day follow the Queens of the Night to Basel (otherwise known as the Sodom of the Alps) and the gay disco where Loïc and Marylin are cavorting in the guise of two Bavarian maidens. Marylin takes off, apparently setting the stage for a petit-bourgeois *Teorema*.

Dry Cleaning, which attracted much favorable attention when shown here last spring at the Walter Reade's French series, is a movie about sexual obsession that, at least for its first half, has a sunny, zipless feel. With the exception of the dry cleaners' sullen, sad-sack child (unusual in a French film), the principals are all thin, well-dressed, and *très-très* cute—Miou-Miou in particular. Working-class heroine that she is, this always-engaging actress is never too tired to twinkle for the camera. Less delightfully, the dry-cleaning household includes a loquacious grandmother who needs no encouragement to serenade all with an old cabaret song.

Grandma is soon dispensed with, but the tongues of Belfort really start to wag once Loïc moves in with Nicole and Jean-Marie and enters their employ. Although the kid shows a remarkable affinity (or perhaps we should say instinct) for the dry-cleaning operation, the house is even steamier than the shop. Actually, the whole setup—upstairs living quarters, first-floor business, basement storeroom—corresponds roughly with the paradigm of superego-ego-id. But who exactly is domesticating whom?

More contrived than structured, better written than directed, *Dry Cleaning* ultimately abandons its initial sense of humor. If the movie lacks the ferocity to really bore in on the peculiar ménage established between the drag artist and the dry cleaners, it's never less than a compelling spectacle of tortured ambivalence.

Also reviewed in:
CHICAGO TRIBUNE, 6/4/99, Friday/p. G, Michael Wilmington
NEW REPUBLIC, 2/15/99, p. 26, Stanley Kauffmann
NEW YORK TIMES, 2/5/99, p. E14, Stephen Holden
VARIETY, 10/13-19/97, p. 90, David Stratton

DUDLEY DO-RIGHT

A Universal Pictures release of a Davis Entertainment/Joseph Singer Entertainment/Todd Harris production. *Executive Producer:* Hugh Wilson. *Producer:* John Davis, Joseph M. Singer, and J. Todd Harris. *Director:* Hugh Wilson. *Screenplay:* Hugh Wilson. *Based on characters developed by:* Jay Ward. *Director of Photography:* Donald E. Thorin. *Editor:* Don Brochu. *Music:* Steve Dorff. *Music Editor:* Chris Ledesma. *Choreographer:* Adam Shankman. *Sound:* Martin Fossum and (music) Rick Riccio. *Sound Editor:* Alan Robert Murray. *Casting:* Denise Chamian. *Production Designer:* Bob Ziembicki. *Art Director:* Helen Jarvis. *Set Designer:* Richard Cook and Dan Hermansen. *Set Decorator:* Shirley Inget. *Set Dresser:* John Bayntun, Jesse Hanen, Bruno Coupe, and Kevin Griffin-Park. *Costumes:* Lisa Jensen. *Make-up:* L. Taylor Roberts. *Make-up (Brendan Fraser):* Ben Nye. *Make-up (Sarah Jessica Parker):* Richard Ogden. *Stunt Coordinator:* Brent Woolsey and Marny Eng. *Running time:* 90 minutes. *MPAA Rating:* PG.

CAST: Brendan Fraser (Dudley Do-Right); Sarah Jessica Parker (Nell Fenwick); Alfred Molina (Snidley Whiplash); Erid Idle (Prospector); Robert Prosky (Inspector Fenwick); Alex Rocco (Chief); Corey Burton (Voice of the Announcer): Jack Kehler (Howard); Louis Mustillo (Standing Room Only); Don Yesso (Kenneth); Jed Rees (Lavar); Brant Von Hoffmann (Barry); P. Adrien Dorval and Mark Acheson (Locals); Richard Side (Barber); L. Harvey Gold (Baker); Susan Astley (Baker's Wife); Douglas Newell (Bank President); Haig Sutherland (Teller); Jake T. Roberts and Scott Nicholson (Mounties); Kevin Griffin-Park (Bartender); Michael McCarty (Local Banker); Nicole Robert (Mother); Rondel Reynoldson, Rick Poltaruk, and Kevin Blatch

(Townspeople); Regis Philbin (Himself); Kathie Lee Gifford (Herself); Ernie Grunwald and Jennifer Clement (Customs Officers); Brian Arnold (Anchor); Joanna Piros (Fernandez); Paul Barsanti (Caitlin); Forbes Angus (Leader); Eddie Moore (Lefty); Eric Breker (Husband); Jennifer Rockett (Wife); Robert C. Saunders (Another Guy); C. Ernst Harth (Shane); Betty Linde (Secretary); Gerard Plunkett (Spinworthy); Greg Rogers and Bob Dawson (FBI Types); William Samples, Nick Misura, and Alex Diakun (Gentlemen); Michal Suchanek (Ten Year Old Boy); Brent Butt (A Bad Guy in Back); John Destrey (Another Bad Guy); David Fredericks (Yet Another Bad Guy); William MacDonald (In the Back); Robin Mossley (In The Way Back); Oscar Goncalves (Indian); Emmanuelle Vaugier (Indian Maiden); Jessica Schreier (Mrs. Darling); Kevin Mundy (Jim Darling); Justen Harcourt (Chad Darling); Nathan Bennett and Isis Johnson (Mother's Kids); Daniel Bacon and Jayme Knox (Miners); Art Irizawa (Asian Golfer).

LOS ANGELES TIMES, 8/27/99, Calendar/p. 8, Kenneth Turan

Who better, or so you might think, to play the lead in "Dudley Do-Right" than Brendan Fraser, an actor whose persona contains so much of the straight-arrow Canadian Mountie that you could run a retrospective of his career and call it a Dudley Do-Right celebration and no one would object.

But though it hurts to think unkind thoughts about the square-shooting Royal Canadian Mounted Policeman who is passionate about right and wrong, in reality casting Fraser as Dudley turns out to be too much of a good thing, a case of Blank Look Overkill.

But worse news is yet to come, because as uninspiring as Fraser is, the likable actor is still the best thing about this tiresome, inept farce that's not even a fraction as clever or entertaining as it likes to imagine it is.

Even viewers with fond memories of Dudley, his sweetheart Nell Fenwick and his nemesis Snidely Whiplash (all developed by Jay Ward as part of his Rocky Squirrel and Bullwinkle Moose stable of TV characters) should steer clear of this complete waste of time, which even at 72 minutes plays bloated and overlong.

Written, directed and executive produced by Hugh Wilson ("Blast From the Past," "Police Academy," TV's "WKRP in Cincinnati"), "Dudley" disappoints in every way possible, forcing its failed tongue-in-cheek humor and proving one more time that not all successful cartoons cry out for live-action treatment.

"Dudley" introduces its trio of protagonists as children, with Snidely set on a course of evil because bad guys have the most fun, Dudley sure it's his destiny to be a Mountie and Nell unwilling or unable to choose between them.

Nothing much has changed when these three are reconfigured as adults, except that Dudley is noticeably clumsier, liable to set his hat on fire and likely to cause floorboards to crash into his skull. As for Nell (Sarah Jessica Parker, a long way from "Sex and the City") and Snidely (a tiresome Alfred Molina), they pretty much play to expectations.

Snidely's pet project of the moment is to scare the residents of Semi-Happy Valley into deserting their quiet town (which he renames Whiplash City) so he can incite a fake gold rush and then make a fortune servicing the hordes who show up expecting to get rich quick.

Dudley would like to stop this from happening, but he's not quite up to the task, at least at first. However, with the help of a woebegone prospector (Eric Idle, who's at least close to funny), Dudley manages to get in touch with his dark side and fight Snidely (or "Whip," as his minions call him) on just about equal terms.

Either times have changed or the writing this time around is especially feeble (probably the latter), but many of the original Jay Ward techniques, such as having an omniscient narrator (the voice is Corey Burton's) making sarcastic comments, are tedious here. It is amusing to have Nell and Dudley sing the "Indian Love Call" that Jeanette MacDonald and Nelson Eddy popularized in 1936's "Rose-Marie," but in general, making these characters flesh and blood has simply made them less funny across the board.

Short though it is, "Dudley Do-Right" is rife with out-and-out padding, such as the "Riverdance"-type production numbers the local Canarsie Kumquat tribe is passing off as its authentic native rites. It's a mark of how enervating the film's line of chat is that we actually come to look forward to these dialogue-free moments when we don't have to put up with a stream of torpid repartee. Dumber than Dudley (no mean feat), dumber than most cartoons, this film will be forgotten well before it's gone.

NEW YORK POST, 8/27/99, p. 57, Hannah Brown

"Dudley Do-Right" is a kinder, gentler comedy that's perfect for children and parents to see together.

A live-action feature based on the TV cartoon about the brave Canadian Mountie (which was part of the "Adventures of Rocky & Bullwinkle" show), "Dudley" features enough sarcastic jokes (which 5- to 10-year-olds will consider the height of sophistication) and slapstick humor to make kids happy.

Unlike most movies for kids, though, it's not mean-spirited or filled with gross-out humor.

Fortunately, the kid stuff is interspersed with enough clever asides to keep parents from nodding off.

Adult fans of the TV series who plan to see this film on their own may be disappointed, however, since this is a movie designed mainly for the younger viewers.

The plot, which, like everything else in this film, is not meant to be taken seriously, follows Do-Right (Brendan Fraser) as he tries to foil a scheme concocted by evil Snidely Whiplash (Alfred Molina).

Whiplash sprays enough gold around an abandoned mineshaft in Semi-Happy Valley to convince people that the town is filled with gold.

Then he goes wild, overcharging gullible tourists for food, lodging and cheesy souvenirs.

In the middle of all this, Nell Fenwick (Sarah Jessica Parker) returns to town. A cute prologue featuring the three as children establishes that Do-Right and Whiplash have been fighting for Fenwick's hand for years.

Whiplash, who makes the point that it's always more fun to be the bad guy "until the ending," seems to be winning at first as he gets Do-Right fired.

The courageous but dim Mountie gets to don a motorcycle jacket (which looks great on him) and try to out-scheme the villain.

Some of the funniest jokes (at least for the over-10 set) include a string quartet of hoodlums playing "Born to Be Wild" and an appearance by a spaced-out gold prospector (Eric Idle) on "Live with Regis and Kathie Lee."

No one plays cute and dumb these days as well as Fraser. With his firm jaw and beefy physique, he manages to give the impression that he believes in himself as a hero, no matter how many stupid mistakes he makes.

He never steps outside the role to wink and mug just so everyone will know he's in on the joke, which makes him even funnier.

Molina has a great time hamming it up as Whiplash, and obviously should do more comedy.

It's showing with a new "Fractured Fairy Tales" cartoon short that won't make anyone forget the original TV series.

NEWSDAY, 8/27/99, Part II/p. B7, John Anderson

Relentlessly silly, less consistently funny, "Dudley Do-Right" continues the trend of remaking old TV series—in this case, the Jay Ward cartoon about the off-kilter Canadian Mountie. It also continues the trend of Brendan Fraser starring in remakes of Jay Ward cartoons— "George of the Jungle" having been his very successful foray into the, shall we say, genre back in 1997.

Whether "Dudley" is as successful as "George" will depend on a couple of things. There's far less of Fraser on display in the Hugh Wilson production; mounties wear red wool and jodhpurs, not loincloths. And "Dudley" may be even less restrained than "George"; the level of inanity, especially at the beginning, borders on the insane.

Dudley falls out of his chair four times, wears a Moosehead that falls off the wall, does a Nelson Eddy-Jeanette MacDonald routine with girlfriend Nell Fenwick (Sarah Jessica Parker) and has, as anyone familiar with the cartoon knows, an unnatural attraction to his horse (named Horse).

But once "Dudley Do-Right" gets into the swing of things—there's actually a terrific swing dance sequence right in the middle of the movie—it gets a lot better.

And writer/director Wilson imbues it with a real idea: That the bad guy has all the fun. "The bad guy has all the fun," says young villain-to-be Snidely Whiplash as he mashes an ice cream cone into Dudley's hair and steals a kiss from Nell.

And for most of the film, he's right.

In fact, the mature Snidely (Alfred Molina), who instigates a fake gold rush in the sleepy town of Semi-Happy Valley so he can take advantage of all his foreclosures and evictions, becomes the local hero: Everyone's thriving, so why question the morality of Snidely's behavior? (You have to wonder about Wilson's politics.)

Dudley, meanwhile, trying to be good, gets drummed out of the Mounties by Nell's dad, Inspector Fenwick (Robert Prosky), and winds up hapless and homeless, living with a reformed drunk-turned-guru (Eric Idle).

With nothing to lose, Dudley gets dangerous.

And the more dangerous he gets, the more attractive he becomes (to us as well as Nell). Granted, his wild and crazy behavior is limited to strewing toilet paper around Snidely's miniature golf course, or cruelly attacking a rhododendron with a chainsaw and turning it into topiary.

But there's certainly something going on beneath the flannel shirts and goofy jokes.

As with most remakes of old TV shows, "Dudley Do-Right" has a target audience too young to remember the series.

But, in this case at least, there's a real idea at work.

Besides, all the slapstick and action probably transcend any need for pop-cultural associations.

As an added bonus, a "Fractured Fairy Tale" titled "The Phox, the Box and the Lox" also by Jay Ward ("Rocky & Bullwinkle") plays before "Dudley Do-Right"and features a narrator who sounds just like original "Fairytale" narrator Edward Everett Horton.

Also reviewed in:
CHICAGO TRIBUNE, 8/27/99, Friday/p. A, Mark Caro
NEW YORK TIMES, 8/27/99, p. E14, Janet Maslin
VARIETY, 8/30-9/5/99, p. 49, Joe Leydon
WASHINGTON POST, 8/27/99, Weekend/p. 37, Desson Howe

EARTH

A Zeitgeist Films release of a Cracking the Earth Films production. *Executive Producer:* David Hamilton and Jhamu Sughand. *Producer:* Anne Masson and Deepa Mehta. *Director:* Deepa Mehta. *Screenplay (Hindi, Urdu, Parsi and Punjabi with English subtitles):* Deepa Mehta. *Based on the novel "Cracking India" by:* Bapsi Sidhwa. *Director of Photography:* Giles Nuttgens. *Editor:* Barry Farrell. *Music:* A.R. Rahman. *Sound:* Graham Ross. *Sound Editor:* Jim Hopkins. *Casting:* Uma Du Cunha. *Production Designer:* Aradhana Seth. *Special Effects:* Anthony Fernandez and Babu Meckwan. *Costumes:* Dolly Ahluwalia Tewari. *Make-up:* Nicole Demers. *Stunt Coordinator:* Alan Amin. *Running time:* 99 minutes. *MPAA Rating:* Not Rated.

CAST: Aamir Khan (Dil Navaz, The Ice Candy Man); Nandita Das (Shanta, the Ayah); Rahul Khanna (Hasan, The Masseur); Maia Sethna (Lenny Sethna); Kitu Gidwani (Bunty Sethna); Kulbushan Kharbanda (Imam Din); Gulshan Grover (Mr. Singh); Arif Zakaria (Rustom Sethna); Pavan Malhotra (Butcher); Sunil Mehra (Toto Ramji); Navtej Singh Johar (Sher Singh); Raghuvir Yadav (Hari); Gulshan Grover (Mr. Singh); Bobby Singh (Yousaf); Kabir Chowdhry (Cousin Adi); Lauren Walker (Mrs. Rogers); Cinia Jain (Mrs. Singh); Roshan Banu (Papoo); Radhika Singh (Muchoo); Varun Mehta (Boy at Bioscope); Mahosh Gahalot (Muslim Father); Gitanjili Chopra (Muslim Mother); Sahiba Chopra, Sia Chopra, and Annabelle (Daughters); Sandeep Singh (Little Sick Boy); Rahul Ram (Young Sikh Man); Ravinder Kumar (Young Muslim Man); Veer Prakash Nayar (Papoo's Groom); Bablu (Chotay); Kumar Rajendra and Ashok Jain (Refugee Police); Pradeep Kapoor (Station Master); Jaaved Jaaferi (Radio

Announcer); Hussain (Muslim Man Quartered); Malani Ramani (Cousin Adi's Mother); Arif (Refugee Boy); Mohni Mathur (Sher Singh's Mother); Mayura Baweja (Sher Singh's Sister); Madhavendra (Mob Leader); Bapsi Sidhwa (Older Lenny); Shabana Azmi (Older Lenny's Voice).

LOS ANGELES TIMES, 9/10/99, Calendar/p. 10, Kenneth Turan

The best thing about "Earth," the new film by Indian-born writer-director Deepa Mehta, is its ambition. A filmmaker without fear of large subjects—she called her last film "Fire" and has one called "Water" coming up—Mehta here takes on the broadest possible canvas, the agonizing 1947 partition that turned the subcontinent into two nations divided by religion, Hindu and Sikh India and Muslim Pakistan.

Far from being a dead issue, the wounds between the two countries have festered over the years, until now each nation is threatening the other with nuclear catastrophe. How could it be otherwise, when, as an on-screen text informs us, 1 million people died and some 12 million others were uprooted from their homes in what has to be the largest exchange of populations on record?

"Earth" is adapted from an autobiographical novel called "Cracking India" by Bapsi Sidhwa, the story of what a young polio-afflicted girl named Lenny Sethna (Maia Sethna) experiences as an 8-year-old living in Lahore in the fateful spring of the partition.

Lenny's parents are well-to-do Parsees, a neutral sect that has always tried to be, her mother tells her, the invisible yet sweet sugar in India's coffee. But, as an opening scene of a British administrator and a patriotic Sikh literally coming to blows at a Sethna dinner party illustrates, the days when Parsees could retreat to the tranquillity of their privileged lives is over.

Filmmaker Mehta, whose 1997 "Fire" successfully focused on the personal story of two married women who develop a sexual attraction for each other, works with cinematographer Giles Nuttgens and production designer Aradhana Seth to re-create vivid snapshots of a country in turmoil.

The striking visuals include the flowing green banners of a pro-Pakistan demonstration, the horror of discovering the evidence of a massacre on a train, and street battles that include Muslim firemen apparently spraying gasoline on fires set in Hindu tenements.

All this is well and good, but "Earth" also has several personal stories to tell, and these are not as satisfactorily realized as the historical re-creations.

The personal part of the story, as observed by Lenny, involves the romantic life of her nanny or ayah, the warmly beautiful Shanta ("Fire's" Nandita Das). Though she is Hindu, Shanta's attractiveness is such that suitors of all religious persuasions flock around her "like moths around a flame"—just one of the script's typical pieces of dead-on writing.

The two key suitors are both Muslims. One, ice candy seller Dil Navaz (Indian superstar Aamir Khan), is a suave and supercilious rascal, which may be the reason Lenny hopes Shanta will fancy him. Also very much in the running is masseur Hasan (Rahul Khanna, MTV Asia's first video deejay), whose soulful eyes and sincere demeanor are hard to argue against.

The problem with this aspect of "Earth" is twofold. One is that telling things through the eyes of a spoiled, precocious, troublemaking 8-year-old narrator is both an overdone device and not a particularly engaging one. Also, writer-director Mehta's dramatic taste tends to run to the strongly melodramatic, making a lot of what happens between these people both overly obvious and a cause of a fair amount of impatience.

When things get worse for India, when religious groups who have lived together for centuries start demanding their own land at any cost, things get better for "Earth." No one knows which country Lahore will be made part of and, in the interim, as one person says: "Fear is making people do crazy things."

So "Earth" shows us friends at one another's throats, people changing religion under duress, even one family marrying its 10-year-old-daughter to an aging dwarf whose only virtue is his neutral Christianity. "The apocalypse is here," someone says, and the world of Lenny and her chameleon-like parents, who believe "ballroom dancing is the best invention of the English," is fated to disappear almost without a trace.

NEW YORK POST, 9/10/99, p. 42, Jonathan Foreman

"Earth" is a remarkable accomplishment. It takes one of the century's vast tragedies—the mass slaughter in the Punjab after the hasty departure of the British from India in August 1947—and makes it heart-rendingly real and intimate.

As the province was partitioned between the new states of Muslim Pakistan and Hindu-dominated India, at least a million people died in religious pogroms so bloody and cruel that they beggar the imagination. Millions more became refugees.

"Earth" brings the horror home by showing it through the eyes of an 8-year-old girl, Lenny (Maia Sethna), who happens to be a member of the privileged, anglicized Parsee minority, and thus a neutral in the conflict between Muslims on one side and Hindus and Sikhs on the other.

You meet her sitting with Shanta (Nandita Das), her beautiful Hindu nanny, in a Lahore park on an idyllic pre-independence afternoon, surrounded by Shanta's male friends and admirers, who come from all of the city's religious communities.

The child's favorite among Shanta's suitors is the roguish Ice Candy Man (Bollywood star Aamir Khan) although the nanny prefers handsome Hasan (Rahul Khanna).

As independence draws near, these men who have been friends for years fall out. Riots spread through the city and little Lenny witnesses a grotesque murder.

As Pakistan comes into being, Sikhs and Hindus flee Lahore for their lives, and the city fills up with bloodied Muslim refugees from India. Still the inter-religious romance between Hasan and Shanta blossoms. But when Ice Candy Man (a Muslim) goes to meet his sisters' train and finds cars crammed with mutilated corpses, events are set in motion that will change Lenny's world forever.

Indian-Canadian writer-director Deepa Mehta makes the most of a strong cast. Das (who also starred in Mehta's "Fire"), whose character's fate is at the center of the film, gives a particularly poignant performance.

Beautifully photographed and accompanied by A.R. Rahman's haunting score, the film is a stylistic hybrid. It's no Bombay "masala" musical, but it's pacing, use of music and descents into sentimentality feel much more Indian than Western.

And although "Earth" strains to be fair to all parties, it is not what you would call a subtle film. There are more than a few moments (whenever the characters talk politics) when the dialogue is almost laughably crude and unrealistic—even if what we're seeing are the memories of a girl.

There is also a sex scene that is gratuitous even by Western standards. But in the end these flaws don't matter; "Earth" isn't about politics—it's a powerful, moving tale about real people caught in a historical nightmare.

NEWSDAY, 9/10/99, Part II/p. B11, Gene Seymour

It is the inalienable right of any culture to make kitsch out of a national trauma and, as such efforts go, "Earth" isn't as bad as one might expect. Actually, Deepa Mehta, who has turned Bapsi Sidhwa's novel, "Cracking India," into the second installment of a planned trilogy that began three years ago with the controversial "Fire," shows herself to be quite adroit with heart-clutching, deep-focus melodrama. Whether such entertaining maneuvers belong in a movie about mass murder and ethnic upheaval is another matter.

It is 1947, the summer that India will no longer be a British colony and take its place among independent democracies. So much for the good news. The bad news is that the unrest between Hindus, Muslims and Sikhs, once united in their opposition to the British, is festering as Muslims move into the newly created state of Pakistan and Hindus and Sikhs move to India. The upheaval is especially bloody. (An estimated 1 million people were killed in sectarian violence and families living in the "wrong" side of the divide were forced to leave.)

In the pre-partition state of Lahore, Lenny (Maia Sethna), a polio-stricken 8-year-old girl, lives in what seems like idyllic isolation from such tumult because her family is Parsee and, thus, a neutral party to the upheaval. Everything in her world seems perfect. Her beautiful Hindu nanny Ayah (Nandita Das from "Fire") takes her to the park. There, Ayah is pursued by men of all ethnic persuasions, notably two Muslim men: Dil Navaz (Aamir Khan), whom Lenny knows only as "the ice candy man" and Hasan (Rahul Khanna), a masseur.

As independence approaches and political rifts swell, the relative ease with which Muslims, Sikhs and Hindus deal with each other in Lahore deteriorates into rage and dread. Lenny's large eyes take in more than a child should have to bear: Sikhs torturing Muslims, Hindus killing Muslims and Hindus torching Muslims alive. Friendships end, nice men become bloodthirsty vigilantes and romance between Ayah and one of her suitors is too delicate to withstand history's harsh blows.

Those who have read Sidhwa's novel—and, for that matter, Salman Rushdie's "Midnight Children"—will be familiar with the historical and emotional territory covered here. Those who haven't will find some enlightenment and much entertainment in "Earth." Mehta is obviously a gifted storyteller. No amount of craft and style, however, can entirely cloak the suspicion that maybe this story is a little too slick for its own good.

SIGHT AND SOUND, 6/00, p. 40, Philip Kemp

Lahore, 1947. Eight-year old Lenny Sethna lives with her Parsee parents in a household staffed by Hindus, Muslims and Sikhs. She adores her ayah, Shanta, a Hindu whose admirers include the Sikh Sher Singh, and Dil Nawaz and Hasan, both Muslims. As independence approaches, rumours arise that the British will separate India into Hindu and Islamic states.

Unrest in Lahore escalates after it's announced that the city will fall within the Islamic state of Pakistan. As Parsees the Sethnas remain neutral, but several of their servants convert. Shanta urges her suitors to remain friends. On the eve of Partition a train arrives from Gurdaspur. The Muslims on board, including Dil Nawaz's sisters, have been slaughtered.

Dil Nawaz urges Shanta to convert and marry him. She refuses, turning instead to Hasan, who has hidden Sher Singh in his house. Hasan proposes they flee to Gurdaspur, where he will convert to Hinduism. They become lovers, observed by Dil Nawaz. The next day Lenny finds Hasan's murdered body. Dil Nawaz leads a Muslim mob to the Sethna house and tricks Lenny into revealing Shanta's whereabouts. The ayah is dragged away by the mob.

Enchanted, a young Parsee girl watches a nocturnal wedding, held beneath a canopy of coloured lights. The bride is a newly converted Christian only ten years old, and the guests are of all faiths an idyllic scene of tolerance and harmony. The groom is of a height with his bride; a boy of similar age, the girl assumes. But when he unveils, he proves to be a fat, elderly dwarf, the only available Christian husband the bride's panicked parents could find.

The scene forms the turning point of *Earth* Deepa Mehta's account of the cataclysm of Partition. Events are refracted to us through eight-year-old Lenny's eyes; hitherto, cocooned in her Parsee household, she's watched the portents of tragedy with incomprehension, never imagining they can touch her closely. True, this travesty of a wedding is mild enough compared to what's coming; but the child bride is her playmate, and for the first time it's brought home to her, as her ayah Shanta tells her, that "Fear is making people do crazy things." Alone in her room, trying to make sense of the destructive forces around her, she rips open one of her dolls: what does it feel like to commit violence? But even so, she still preserves enough of her sheltered innocence to let Dil Nawaz trick her into her final, fatal betrayal.

Earth is the second film in Deepa Mehta's trilogy that began with *Fire,* exploring the forces that have moulded (and distorted) modern India. Both films share a specifically female regard, but *Earth* widens the focus from a domestic to a national perspective, taking in both the particular and the general. In its scope and historical sweep it's at once a more ambitious and a more assured achievement, with none of the spasmodic uncertainties of tone that marred its predecessor. The choice of language helps a lot. *Fire* was shot almost entirely in English, which often made the dialogue feel stilted and unconvincing; almost all of *Earth*'s characters converse mainly in Hindi, and the gain in authenticity is palpable, in script as in acting. As Shanta, Nandita Das even surpasses her touching performance as Sita, the unhappy wife in *Fire*.

Most of the film was shot in New Delhi (standing in for Lahore), and Mehta makes shrewd use of her locations to enhance the sense of a rich, fragile world on the brink of destruction. The first tentative embrace between Shanta and Hasan takes place amid the ruins of an palace haunted by the desolate cries of peacocks, and the last moment of unalloyed happiness occurs at the Festival of Kites, with the delicate multi-coloured toys, flown by all city's residents, swooping in the sunlit air. Lenny watches the ceremony from Dil Nawaz's roof, from where she'll later look down in terror at a rampaging Muslim mob, and there's a visual echo of the fluttering kite-tails in the mob's elegant green banners.

Here as throughout the film, the impact of the mounting horror is all the greater for taking place in such beautiful surroundings, with Giles Nuttgens' camera caressing the warm soft reds of buildings, costumes and earth. In this, *Earth* recalls Satyajit Ray's *Distant Thunder/Ashani Sanket* (1973), which dealt with the 1943 Bengali famine, another Indian disaster triggered by the ineptitude of the Raj. There too, as Ray put it, "People died and suffered in surroundings of great beauty." in his film, as in Mehta's, the quiet restraint of the treatment, never indulging in hysteria, only underlines the grief and anger behind it.

Once or twice *Earth* overplays its symbolism. The caged lion guarded by zookeeper Sher Singh is mentioned a little too often, and the careful balance of sects in the Sethna household and among Shanta's admirers seems a touch schematic. But such considerations count for little beside the immediacy of the storytelling and the agonised sense of waste and loss. In a present day coda the adult Lenny (played by Bapsi Sidhwa, author of the source book) muses on the lasting effects of the nation's tragedy. With ethnic cleansing still rampant in the world, and India and Pakistan strutting their nuclear stuff at each other it's a moral that's all too horribly apt.

VILLAGE VOICE, 9/14/99, p. 146, Jessica Winter

A few minutes into Deepa Mehta's *Earth,* when a little girl drops a plate and it shatters to the ground, the child asks her mother, "Can one break a country?" The year is 1947, when a newly independent India split into Hindu and Muslim states. The divide between India and Pakistan forced one of the worst population upheavals in recorded history: 7 million Muslims and 5 million Hindus were driven from their homes, while 1 million people were killed in sectarian violence. It boggles the mind, therefore, when historical fact alone speaks so strongly, that Mehta feels compelled to twist the screw, shamelessly plying her audience with mawkish tropes wearing the garb of "innocence."

The polio-hobbled girl, Lenny, belongs to a well-off family of Parsis, a group whose close ties to the British government and steadfast neutrality mostly spared them from the Partition massacres. Lenny's gorgeous Hindu nanny, Shanta (Nandita Das), is courted by Hindus, Muslims, and Sikhs; daily outings to the park result in multireligious gatherings of suitors. As the political situation escalates, so does the tension within this loose-knit, aphorism-spewing group, culminating in a horrible betrayal.

Das bestows on Shanta the same grace and reserve that she brought to Mehta's previous film, *Fire* (the first of a planned trilogy of films on India), which spurred controversy in India with its depiction of a lesbian romance. Fire was a clumsy effort burdened by easy symbolism, but Mehta's camerawork was admirably restrained, her script taciturn. The same control is simply not present in *Earth,* right down to its oversaturated cinematography: from the lurid reds and purples coloring a tableau of bloodied bodies on a train car, to the warm yellow glow suffusing every household scene, Mehta has made a film at once exploitative and nostalgic. When Lenny encounters an impoverished Muslim boy who tells her that his parents were killed and his sister was raped, he asks her in the same breath, "Want to play marbles?" One audience member in the screening room responded to this scene with a tittering sound—somewhere between a giggle and an "Aww." Nothing in *Earth* suggests that Mehta would find this an inappropriate reaction to her film.

Also reviewed in:
CHICAGO TRIBUNE, 10/15/99, Friday/p. G, John Petrakis
NEW YORK TIMES, 9/10/99, p. E20, Stephen Holden
VARIETY, 10/12-18/98, p. 44, Leonard Klady
WASHINGTON POST, 11/5/99, p. C5, Stephen Hunter

EDGE OF 17

A Strand Releasing release of a Blue Streak Films & Luna Pictures presentation. *Producer:* David Moreton and Todd Stephens. *Director:* David Moreton. *Screenplay:* Todd Stephens. *Director of Photography:* Gina DeGirolamo. *Editor:* Tal Ben-David. *Music:* Tom Bailey. *Casting:* Tim Kaltenecker and Richard Whobrey. *Production Designer:* Ivor Stillen. *Costumes:* Ane Crabtree. *Running time:* 100 minutes. *MPAA Rating:* Not Rated.

CAST: Chris Stafford (Eric); Tina Holmes (Maggie); Anderson Gabrych (Rod); Stephanie McVay (Mom); Lea DeLaria (Angie); John Eby (Dad); Antonio Carriero (Andy); Jason Sheingross (Steve); Tony Maietta (Gregg); Jeff Fryer (Jonathan); Kevin J. Kelley (Chuckie); Mark Gates (Foodtown); Stevie Reese Desmond (Ruby Rogers); Barbie Marie (Frieda); Craig Shepherd (Irate Customer); Doug Millon (Security Guard); Clay Van Sickle (Ed); Jason Griffiths (Scott); Jimmy Mack (Bartender); Justin Leach (Tall Blond Guy); Jeff Abramson (Dan McAllister); Don Mitri (Teacher); Mike Roth (Wrestling Jock); Adam Penton (Joe Plonsky, Jr.); Tal Ben-David (Waitress); Dina Anderson, Karen Brooks, and Shannon Constantine (Bitchy Girls); Edd Martin (Drag Queen); Gregg Long (Mr. Johnson); Ryan Florio (Randy); Twiggy (Marlene Dicktrick); Dominic Carrion (Miss Anita Mann); Jesse Adams (Drag Atrocity); Joshua Elrod (Rod's Roommate); Diva (Herself).

LOS ANGELES TIMES, 6/11/99, Calendar/p. 10, Kevin Thomas

"Edge of Seventeen" is set in 1984, but it is a timeless and perceptive evocation of a Midwestern gay youth's coming of age. It was voted the audience favorite film at Outfest last year and, seen a second time, it seems even more resonant. With both compassion and detachment, writer Todd Stephens, drawing upon his own experience, and director David Moreton, backed by a dedicated cast and crew, have created a beautiful and touching film, made with love, wisdom and good humor.

Chris Stafford's Eric is a tall, thin youth with delicately handsome features who lives with his loving parents (Stephanie McVay and John Eby) and two younger brothers in a spacious turn-of-the-century home on a tree-lined street in Sandusky, Ohio (Stephens' actual hometown). You can't get much more Norman Rockwell than this.

Yet when Eric and Maggie (Tina Holmes), his lifelong friend and classmate who lives nearby, take summer jobs at an amusement park restaurant, Eric becomes self-conscious and awkward as he explains to Rod (Andersen Gabrych), who's also signed up for the summer, that Maggie is his best friend rather than his girlfriend. The sexy, bottle-blond Rod, who attends Ohio State, is an upfront gay. Rod backs off when Eric retreats, but fast-forwarding to the season's close, he comes on strong and Eric, attracted to him from the start, responds. (Later, we learn why Rod had not bothered to pursue Eric all summer.)

What Eric swiftly learns is that sex and love do not automatically go together and that one-night stands are routine for some gays. (Visually the film is discreet, but the dialogue is, at times, decidedly blunt.) This is just the beginning of Eric's odyssey of self-discovery, with his struggle to clarify and accept his sexual orientation accompanied by a growing need to be open about it.

"Coming of age" is an all but universally difficult phase, but "Edge of Seventeen," more than most films, suggests how much more difficult it is for gays and lesbians, particularly in small communities, where many people either consciously or unconsciously tend to deny that homosexuality even exists. Stephens and Moreton are very clear that, while it's worth it, there can be a price to be paid for being yourself when that means being gay and open about it. And that price can be exacted not only in your own hurt feelings and worse but also from those you love and who love you in return.

Eric starts asserting his emerging identity through his attire, his modish look and his advanced, for his community, tastes in music. He has the great fortune to have found a staunch and wise friend in Angie (Lea DeLaria, the one and only), his boss at the restaurant who, he later discovers, operates a local gay bar. Angie is a hearty lesbian, her robust, bracing sense of humor balancing the inevitable anguish of Eric's predicament.

She is strong and supportive without being pushy; she knows well that Eric is going to have to go through his rite of passage by himself but assures him that she will be there if he needs her. DeLaria has established herself as a powerhouse talent, but she understands the effectiveness of holding back, of how a knowing glance can convey that she's got the picture without saying a word. (One bothersome detail about Angie: How is it that she so easily serves minors? Or are those nonalcoholic beverages Eric is consuming?)

The pains that Stephens took in writing his script pays off not only in a dynamite part for an established actor like DeLaria but also for Stafford, Holmes, McVay and Gabrych, all making their screen debuts. That they also give selfless, comprehensive portrayals under the direction of Moreton, in his own feature debut, attests to the measure of commitment on the part of one and all in the making of this film.

Much is demanded of Stafford in taking us through all of Eric's changes, but arguably even more of Holmes, whose Maggie is in love with the understandably self-absorbed Eric without him realizing it. In his lack of awareness, Eric makes tremendous demands of her capacity for understanding and loyalty, and Holmes makes Maggie, an intelligent but young and unworldly woman, quite moving in her losing battle to be equal to the challenge. McVay is also quietly powerful in her portrayal of a forthright mother disturbed by her increasingly evasive and absent son.

Considering the scope and depth of the film's roles, it is all the more impressive that "Edge of Seventeen," resourcefully photographed by Gina DeGirolamo, is not at all theatrical in style or tone. You know that the film had to have been made on a tight budget, but there's never a sense of corners being cut. Strand Releasing, which is distributing "Edge of Seventeen" and is currently celebrating its 10th anniversary, confirms co-founder Marcus Hu's philosophy: "I've always felt you could make films on a shoestring budget and still convey a great story."

NEW YORK POST, 5/14/99, p. 48, Rod Dreher

"Edge of Seventeen" is a fairly decent gay coming-of-age film that will resonate with anyone, gay or straight, who served time as a small-town teen-ager in the 1980s.

Not only does autobiographical screenwriter Todd Stephens get the pop-culture details exactly right (the allure of Polo cologne, that weird way of fastening belts, etc.), he also treats the gay teen's coming-out with refreshing honesty, and those whose hearts are broken by it with surprising generosity.

Eric (Chris Stafford) begins the summer of 1984 working at a Sandusky, Ohio, amusement park. His best friend Maggie (Tina Holmes) carries on an ambiguous friendship with Eric, who also catches the eye of Rod (Anderson Gabrych), an openly gay college student with a Pepsodent smile.

Before Rod heads back to Ohio State for the fall, and Eric returns for his senior year of high school, the older teen sexually initiates the younger one.

Next thing you know, Eric, a Rust Belt Rupert Everett, is frosting his hair, buying Bronski Beat albums and sneaking off to a gay disco on the outskirts of town.

The hilarious club owner (lesbian comic Lea DeLaria) plays a protective materfamilias who stage-manages sweet, naive Eric's transformation from shy small-town boy to confident gay man.

It's not a great movie, though. The writing and editing is at times abrupt, some of the characters flat, and the brief, frank talk of gay sexual practices cringe-making.

Still, "Edge of Seventeen" excels at showing how an alienated teen-ager turned to New Wave music to comfort him and help him find his identity in a world of REO Speedwagon-listening jocks.

Even truer to life, the film refuses to pretend that life is perfect after coming out. Eric is hurt by the empty, predatory nature of gay male courting, and misuses Maggie in his efforts to resist his homosexuality.

The cast, aside from DeLaria all relative unknowns, is likable. Lead actor Stafford makes this summer's most appealing teen-age queen this side of Natalie Portman.

NEWSDAY, 5/18/99, Part II/p. B11, Bob Heisler

Honesty isn't always the best policy, Sandusky Ohio High School senior Eric learns when he tries to come out in "Edge of Seventeen," especially if you're not sure what you're being honest about.

It's not that Eric (Chris Stafford) believes he's straight. After all, he likes The Eurythmics, his best friend is a girl, he has no other friends, and until he is seduced by Ohio State University hotel management major Rod during a summer of slinging beans and pie at a local amusement park restaurant, he wants to move to New York City with his Moog synthesizer and become a musician.

To be a musician, Eric needs Manhattan. To be gay, he needs a disco and gay bar, conveniently provided by Angle (Lea DeLaria as the local mother hen/confidante/validator) and populated by one each of the usual stereotypes, plus a dorm-full of OSU men who find him cute.

So we follow Eric's coming-out-of-age story from giggling first touch to his mascara-and-lipstick debut as a card-carrying Culture Club Kid, from his on-the-rebound last grasp at heterosexuality with the loyal-till-it-hurts Maggie (Tina Holmes) to his where-did-we-go-wrong confrontation with the mother who gave up her own music career to have a family.

This is not new ground, of course, and the descent into cliche at the disco may have been avoidable, but where "Edge of Seventeen" scores is in its re-creation of 1984 in the life of a kid who is different. He dresses differently, listens to different music and has different friends than his high school peers. His parents are blissfully unaware that there are few places for "different" teenagers to go in Sandusky but all the way.

Screenwriter Todd Stephens, recalling events in his own life, and director David Moreton choose to focus on how the expectations of other people pull and tug at Eric's overwhelming need at 17 to find love at all costs.

This leaves the movie's real strength—its artful weaving of music and cultural artifacts (Polo cologne, for instance, and remember albums) into the stuff from which Eric tries to make a life—relatively unexplored. We never ask Eric why.

VILLAGE VOICE, 5/25/99, p. 132, Mark J. Huisman

With a sophisticated script by Todd Stephens, this tender film by David Moreton tells the story of Eric (Chris Stafford), a gangly teen in Sandusky, Ohio, with a sort-of girlfriend named Maggie (Tina Holmes). But when Eric develops a taste for mixed-pattern outfits, spiky hair, and a college freshman named Rod (Anderson Gabrych), our hero starts lying—to Maggie, Mom (Stephanie McVay), and, especially, himself—and finds it difficult stop.

Set in the early '80s, *Edge of Seventeen* is pure revelation, from Eric's burgeoning sexuality (perfectly played by Stafford, with simultaneous innocence and confusion) to the pained, angry reactions of Mom and Maggie. Seldom have stock female characters like "the mom" and "the girl" been created or performed with such complexity. Lea DeLaria is both funny and moving as Angie, the bar manager who moonlights as Eric's liquor-swilling, one-dyke support system.

Also reviewed in:
NEW YORK TIMES, 5/14/99, p. E12, Stephen Holden
VARIETY, 7/13-19/98, p. 57, Dennis Harvey

EDtv

A Universal Pictures and Imagine Entertainment release of a Brian Grazer production. *Executive Producer:* Todd Hallowell, Michel Roy, and Richard Sadler. *Producer:* Brian Glazer and Ron Howard. *Director:* Ron Howard. *Screenplay:* Lowell Ganz and Babaloo Mandel. *Based on the motion picture "Louis XIX: Roi des Ondes"* written by: Emile Gaudreault and Sylvie Bouchard and directed by Michel Poulette. *Director of Photography:* John Schwartzman. *Editor:* Mike Hill and Dan Hanley. *Music:* Randy Edelman. *Music Editor:* John LaSalandra. *Sound:* David MacMillan and (music) Elton Ahi. *Sound Editor:* Chic Ciccolini, III. *Casting:* Jane Jenkins and

Janet Hirshenson. *Production Designer:* Michael Corenblith. *Art Director:* Dan Webster. *Set Designer:* Kevin Cross, Al Hobbs, and Lauren Polizzi. *Set Decorator:* Merideth Boswell. *Set Dresser:* James R. Barrows, Charles T. Gray, Ryan T. Mennealy, and Mark Palmer. *Special Effects:* Robbie Knott. *Visual Effects:* Eric Nash. *Costumes:* Rita Ryack. *Make-up:* Fred C. Blau. *Make-up (Woody Harrelson):* Kimberly Greene. *Make-up (Jenna Elfman):* Ann Lee Masterson. *Make-up (Ellen DeGeneres):* Elaine Offers. *Stunt Coordinator:* Rocky Capella. *Running time:* 120 minutes. *MPAA Rating:* PG-13.

CAST: Geoffrey Blake (Keith); Gail Boggs (Wife); Jenna Byrne (Felicia); Merrin Dungey (Ms. Seaver); Ian Gomez (McIlvaine); Gavin Grazer (Cliff); Chris Hogan (Paul); Arianna Huffington (Panel Member); Larry Jenkins (Husband); Wendle Josepher (Rita); Scott LaRose (Desipio); John Livingston (Terry); Mitzi McCall (Fig Lady); Jim Meskimen (Dr. Geller); Don Most (Benson); Rick Overton (Barry); James Ritz (Tad); RuPaul (Himself); Rusty Schwimmer (Alice); Steven Shenbaum (Jack); Gedde Watanabe (Greg); Matthew McConaughey (Ed); Jenna Elfman (Shari); Woody Harrelson (Ray); Sally Kirkland (Jeanette); Martin Landau (Al); Viveka Davis (Marcia); Adam Goldberg (John); Ellen DeGeneres (Cynthia); Rob Reiner (Whitaker); Dennis Hopper (Hank); Elizabeth Hurley (Jill); Steve Kehela and Googy Gress (Reporters); Jo McGinley (Tracy); John Pirruccello (Kevin); Charles Berg and Anthony Jensen (Party Goers); Joe Bellan (Lou); Brian Michael Erlich and Marcus J. Oliver (Video Store Clerks); Sam Rubin (Entertainment Reporter); Mark Thompson (Anchor); Barry Wiggins (Sports Anchor); Michael Parsons (Kid); Zidu Chen (Dental Patient); Clint Howard (Ken); Eric Shinn (Camera Truck Tech Driver); Robert Pastoriza (Carlos); Jeffrey Schecter (Utility—1st Team); Michael Esposito (Camera Operator—1st Team); Connie Campbell-Gott and Louie Mejia (Camera Operators—2nd Team); Crystall Carmen (Utility—2nd Team); Matty Morrissey (Director—2nd Team); Marilyn Pittman (Woman in Window); Sommer Saqr, Jennifer Elise Cox, and Alexandra Holden (College Girls); Mark Wheeler (Bartender); Kathleen Marshall (Hygienist); Harry Shearer (Moderator); Michael Moore, Merrill Markoe, and George Plimpton (Panel Members); Geoff Bolt (Drunk Guy); Azalea Stanley and Ezra Stanley (Teenagers); Anna Karin (Snapple Girl); Todd Hallowell (Interviewer); Cyndi Pass (Cassie); Jen Moe and Velina Brown (Girls); Rod Tate (Moe); Todd Krainin (Younger Man); Zeidy Martinez, Azura Skye, and Daisy Clarke (Interview Teenagers); Lombardo Boyar, Rainbow Borden, and David Quane (New York Guys); Christian Kane (P.A.); Gina Hecht, Cheryl Howard, and Louisa Marie (Party Girls); Mike Grief (Repairman); Laurel Moglen (Underwear Woman); Wade J. Robson, Sy Hearn, and Nathan Paul (Teenage Boys); Bill Maher (Host); Anita Morales (Nurse); Lowell Ganz (Lawyer); Bob Sarlatte (Motorcycle Cop); Ashley Clark (Girl); William M. Connor (Toilet Man); Roberta Callahan (Cat Advocate); William Bagnell (Presidential Aide); Jay Leno (Himself); Julie Rose Stevens and Brigitte Jacoby-Baker (Ken Groupies); Joe Mazza (Vet); Mel Berger (Confused Man); Diane Amos (Autograph Mom); James Brooks (Delivery Man); Luke Esterkyn (Band Member); Mark Marking and Tom Turpel (Ed's Fans); Sun St. Pierre (Female Well-Wisher); Roger L. Jackson (Mama's Boy); Julie Donatt (Reporter); Thomas Barg (Boom Box Boy); Glenn E. Schuldt (Paramedic); Curtis Davis (Whoop Boy); William Dance (Beauty Salon Owner); Sonia Bhalla (Ticket Taker); Todd P. McCormick (P.I. Guest); Jordan Harrelson (Audition Guy); Tony Harras, Vince Lozano, and Rolando Molina (Warehouse Workers); Alberto Vazquez (Grave Digger); Lydee Walsh (College Girl); Veronica Moody (College Dorm Girl); Peter Starr (Motorcycle Driver); Alan D. Purwin (Helicopter Pilot).

LOS ANGELES TIMES, 3/26/99, Calendar/p. 1, Kenneth Turan

Like the television medium it genially satirizes, "EDtv" is a grab bag that's both amusing and frustrating. Simultaneously inspired and contrived, clever and crude, it's an eye-candy riff on a substantial topic, ambitious for Hollywood but only an inch deep—and like most junk food it satisfies for a moment but leaves you hungry almost as soon as it's done.

"EDtv" starts with a cable network called True TV ("We've taken you there, you've laughed, you've cried, you've almost died") that's in trouble. "We're getting our butt kicked by the

Gardening Channel," moans program director Cynthia Topping (Ellen DeGeneres).   "People would rather watch soil."

Hoping to gain market share and impress the network's head (Rob Reiner), what Topping sets out to do is find "one person, one normal person, and put his life on TV all day long." That fortunate individual turns out to be Ed Pekurny (Matthew McConaughey), a San Francisco video store clerk who becomes so popular that "EDtv," as in "All Ed All the Time," is inflated into a national mania.

If this sounds familiar, it's not because "EDtv," written by Lowell Ganz and Babaloo Mandel, was based on an obscure French-Canadian film called "Louis XIX: Roi des Ondes." Rather it's that many of the themes and issues it deals with were raised in a more interesting and adventurous way by the Jim Carrey-starring "The Truman Show."

The differences in the two films go beyond the basic one that Ed is aware of the cameras and Truman is not.   Directed by Ron Howard, "EDtv" is successfully intent on being safe, cheerful and middle of the road.   It knows how to entertain, how to make itself pleasing, but, more calculating than Fed Chairman Alan Greenspan, it is careful not to attempt anything that might challenge an audience.   Laughing freely at sections of "EDtv" is assured, and that is no small thing, but there is a pat quality to other parts that give it an inescapable "Truman Lite" quality.

"EDtv's" smartest move was casting McConaughey as Ed, a beer-drinking Pamela Anderson-T-shirt wearing 31-year-old with no life plan and nothing to look forward to, as his knuckleheaded brother Ray (Woody Harrelson) pointedly puts it, but a lifetime of rearranging "Ernest" tapes.

As no film since his starring role in "A Time to Kill" has, "EDtv" showcases McConaughey's powerful Texas charisma and shows how effective he can be in the right parts.   The actor exudes charm and casual sexual attractiveness as the easy-going cable star, and McConaughey's own brushes with the ups and downs of celebrity, one of "EDtv's" themes, no doubt gave the role a special resonance for him.

Ed is in fact so laid-back he doesn't even want to try out for the job that's going to change his life.   He gets physically pulled into an audition by careerist brother Ray, who repairs video equipment but considers himself in show business, and, much to Ray's chagrin, gets offered the slot.

Even after he accepts the job at Ray's urging ("How many chances do you and I get?"), Ed is a long time in realizing the ways he's being manipulated and how much chaos being followed around by a camera can cause in his life and the lives of his family and friends.

Soon enough, however, the EDtv camera crew wreaks havoc between Ed and Ray and does extensive damage to the marriage between Ed's mother, Jeanette (Sally Kirkland), and his stepfather, Al (Martin Landau).   It also leads to Ed's increasing attraction to Ray's nominal girlfriend and UPS driver Shari ("Dharma & Greg's" Jenna Elfman).

Howard, as always, has a nice touch with actors, and Elfman is especially effective in a role that calls for her to be so potentially unattractive that even RuPaul disses her charms.   Unexpected comic moments like the two brothers doing down-home chicken dances are irresistible, and so is Elizabeth Hurley, who deftly satirizes herself in a delicious role as femme fatale Jill, a "model and sometime actress" out to give Ed the romance of his life.

But for every smart move "EDtv" makes there are awkward or just plain ordinary ones on the order of Ed getting hit on the head by a football.   It's nice to see a film that understands, as Ed himself eventually does, that TV will eat you alive if you let it, that we live in a culture where celebrity has become, as one character puts it, "a moral good, its own virtue."   It's just hard to resist wishing "EDtv" was consistently smarter about making that case.

NEW STATESMAN, 11/22/99, p. 54, Jonathan Romney

There's an infallible way to tell if a media phenomenon has come of age—it's when you see it satirised on film and you realise that the film-makers are about a decade out of step with the world.   In Ron Howard's *EDtv*, video store clerk Ed (Matthew McConaughey) wakes up to find his bed surrounded by a TV crew recording his every move.   If the film were remotely on the ball, they'd be buzzing round him like fireflies with an arsenal of hand-held camcorders.   Instead, they tote huge shoulder-held machines, with boom mike bobbing obtrusively in everyone's face.

EDtv is the worst case of bad timing in recent Hollywood history.   Its premise—a man's everyday life becomes a nonstop real-time TV soap—is a pretty good idea, or was a few years ago, when some Canadian filmmakers first thought of it (they are duly acknowledged in *EDtv*'s credits). But an even better idea was had by the makers of *The Truman Show,* which pipped Howard's film to release by several months, and which spun the *vérité* premise into a paranoid fantasy about an innocent whose entire life turns out to be a lavishly constructed production.

EDtv, takes a strictly realist tack—its idea is that there's reality and then there's TV and never the twain should mix. But the genre of real-life docu-soap is all too familiar: it long ago became the British disease, and we're more than used to the sight of ostentatiously "ordinary" people, airline workers or cruise-line crooners, becoming larger-than-life quasi-celebrities. In fact *EDtv* acknowledges that its idea is not entirely new. There's a reference to the American 1970s documentary series that was a precursor to the BBC's own ground-breaking *The Family:* the first time that audiences realised how much a fly on the wall could affect what went on within the walls. Yet it seems to think that nothing has happened since. What supposedly makes the Ed show different is that it will be unedited, uncut and screened 24 hours a day.

Ambitions but well-meaning exec Ellen DeGeneres finds a likely subject in Ed, an easy-going, unambitious guy whom the camera simply loves. And the film's revelation, and complaint, is that if the camera doesn't love you, you're screwed. Ed's girlfriend Shari (Jenna Elfman) proves too real—not "hot" enough—for the public, which takes an implausibly extreme dislike to her. They root for a rival in the shape of "model and sort of actress" Jill (Elizabeth Hurley), who has the network's backing. The film is halfway to making a smart comment by casting Hurley, who has made a career out of being perceived as a hollow, camera-hungry dilettante. But, once again, the film is trumped by reality: the crowd that gathers for Jill and Ed's tryst isn't that much odder than the brouhaha around the supposed liaison of Chris Evans and Geri Halliwell (two people whose ordinariness parleyed into celebrity beats anything here).

Besides, the use of Hurley as an in-joke is diluted by the hackneyed use of real personalities to provide tut-tutting commentary and to show how everyone has become obsessed with Ed, from chat-show farceurs like Jay Leno to supposed heavyweights such as loudmouth provocateur Michael Moore, who pleads, "Let's get back to the way TV used to be". Used to be? Used to be? Presumably, as in the time of the feeble sitcom *Happy Days*, on which Ron Howard was a teenage star (and judging by *EDtv,* how he must have loathed his audience).

Too bad if *EDtv* is out-dated, but I doubt it would have been any better had it acknowledged that unedited *vérité* portraits actually screen all the time on the Internet, with subjects taking responsibility for presenting their own lives. The film is too committed to the dichotomy of real people versus parasitic media, and is unwilling to tackle the confident ways in which private individuals are now beginning to use media attention (how come Ed never thinks of getting his own Max Clifford?). *EDtv* belongs to a long trend of Hollywood cinema—bankrolled by the same companies that own the TV networks—sneering at TV viewers' passivity, while pretending that people who pay £7 to go out and watch trash are somehow smarter than those who watch trash, or turn it off, in the comfort of their own homes. *EDtv*, is joylessly sniffy about people who watch TV and people who make it, but still has the nerve to call in TV pundits such as George Plimpton as moral arbiters. Profoundly condescending in its attitude to its characters, especially to Ed's squabbling, KFC-guzzling family, the film makes it clear that blue-collar types just aren't smart or tough enough to withstand the debilitating glare of the cameras. Ultimately though, they are obliged to play TV's game if they're to escape it—the drama demands that Ed and Shari finally triumph by kissing on screen.

If they really wanted to know about the fluid, complex intersections of individual lives and television exposure, Howard and his screenwriters, Lowell Ganz and Babaloo Mandel, would have done well to brush up on *Paddington Green* or *The Real Holiday Show* or *Blind Date.* Or if they wanted a glimpse of how scathing media satire can be, they could have stayed at home and checked out re-runs of *Larry Sanders.* What's wrong with these people—don't they ever watch television?

NEW YORK, 4/5/99, p. 70, Peter Rainer

Couldn't we please have a moratorium on movies about the soul-sapping and celebrity-mongering ways of television? *The Truman Show* was bad enough, but then *Pleasantville* came along, and now here's the new Ron Howard comedy *EDtv.* I've never been sold on this anti-TV thesis. It's snooty. It assumes we in the audience have seen the light denied the lower orders. Invariably, the people in these movies who are rendered blotto by the tube are dingbat common folk. *EDtv* takes this notion to a new low by introducing as its hero a good ol'boy, Ed Pekurny (a livelier-than-usual Matthew McConaughey). Ed isn't just the ideal audience for TV pap; he turns out to be the ideal TV celebrity too. His life is transformed into a 24-hour television show by a cable network, and viewers can't get enough of it. Even when he's on the potty. His parents (Sally Kirkland and Martin Landau) and everyone else in his orbit get pulled into the media vortex. No one ends up looking good.

The big difference between *EDtv* and *The Truman Show* is that Ed *knows* he's being filmed and Truman, at least at first, doesn't. But the net result is the same: These guys want out of the celebrity circus. At first, Ed wants in. His story begins when the program director (Ellen DeGeneres) for the San Francisco-based cable-television documentary channel True TV offers to make him its round-the-clock star after viewing his audition tape. Puttering away at his video-store job, Ed doesn't have much going on; he accepts the offer and, for a while, can't get enough of the adulation. He equates the success of the show with a successful life.

It's part of the film's game plan that Ed is portrayed as slow on the uptake. For a long time, he doesn't realize he's trapped, while we, of course, see it at once. Either way, it's not remotely believable that Ed's soap-opera world becomes a national obsession. The makers of *EDtv*— Howard and screenwriters Lowell Ganz and Babaloo Mandel—are behind the times: "Reality-based" television isn't where it's at anymore. What piques the public isn't "real" people doing real things. Rather, it's big shots like, say, the President of the United States, acting real—i.e., screwing up just like us regular folks. And even this is getting old fast.

And so is the notion that in America, we all want to become celebrities. Someone in *EDtv* is overheard saying, "Nobody wants to be a nobody in America." This showbiz conceit is the propulsion behind the movie's moralizings. Only in Hollywood. *EDtv* gets huffy about stardom, but the high cost of fame is not an issue that burns brightly for most people, many of whom are probably more content than the stars they're supposed to idolize. The appeal of celebrity-gazing is, after all, essentially vicarious. It delivers the pleasures of being a big cheese without incurring the big-time hassles. Its satisfactions are pretty straightforward. *EDtv* turns the relationship between audience and celebrity into a compulsive contest between exhibitionist and voyeur. Howard and his writing team began their movie partnership on a pair of terrific comedies, *Night Shift* and *Splash*, both eminently un-messagey. But then came *Parenthood*, a "personal" comedy that was about as personal as a polished sitcom. *EDtv* has flashes of the trio's erstwhile knockabout silliness—especially in Landau's deftly addled performance and some of McConaughey's pluck—but it strains to be bigger than its preshrunk britches.

Even though the filmmakers are locked into a showbiz worldview, they still sentimentalize Ed's need to break free from showbiz. In *EDtv,* you can choose fame, or you can choose heart. Ed loves the limelight until it drives away the amour he was too dense to appreciate. Shari (Jenna Elfman), his sweetie, was initially paired with Ed's hoot-and-holler brother Ray (Woody Harrelson). Her switch to Ed is seen as a step up in class, but the media hoopla is too much for her—70 percent of the public polled thinks she's not good enough for him—and she flees. Coaxed by the network honchos into a fling with a British sexpot (Elizabeth Hurley), Ed begins to hanker for normality, especially when the network's pitiless CEO, Whitaker (Rob Reiner), makes it clear Ed's contract is unbreakable. Our TV hero longs to melt into the crowd and into Shari's embrace. And so *EDtv* becomes another testament to the powers of true love—even though, if truth be told, Shari is pretty drab.

Love can even quell the siren lure of a Jay Leno or a RuPaul—both of whom appear in the movie. George Plimpton also shows up as himself on a televised roundtable as he rails against Ed's extravaganza. "It's a joyous celebration of boobery," he sniffs, and we're meant to howl at his snobbery. The film plays it every which way: It makes fun of doofuses but also gets all populist about them. Whitaker refers to his star contemptuously as "Gomer." Ed shoots back that "we're not as dumb as you think we are." Meanwhile, an average-Joe viewer faced with the cancellation of Ed's show moans, "What do you expect me to do now?"

Even when the film tries to glorify Ed, it ends up belittling him. Here we have a guy who is moving in some pretty fast circles; his world expands beyond the confines of the video store and his ratty apartment. And yet the film doesn't perceive any upside to fame; ultimately, Ed doesn't use his newfound clout for anything except undoing his eminence. We're supposed to see this as heroic—this man of the people walks away from *People*—but instead he just seems stunted. The best Ed can do with his opportunities is manipulate his way back to boringness. Some victory.

NEW YORK POST, 3/26/99, p. 55, Jonathan Foreman

"Edtv" finally establishes Matthew McConaughey as a genuine movie star. It's also a funny, smart and satisfying film that is only superficially similar to "The Truman Show." Yes, it's about someone whose life is televised, but he knows and accepts it.

Less ambitious than "Truman," "EDtv" is also more enjoyable and, in a way, more relevant. It's not trying to say anything big and vague about the sinister ability of television to remake the world in a way pleasing to advertisers; it's about instant celebrity and the way it changes people's lives—a subject of particular interest in the Age of Monica.

A San Francisco-based cable channel decides that the way to win back its audience is to have cameramen follow an ordinary person 24 hours a day, seven days a week—excluding only the bathroom and the bedroom when the person is having sex. Of course, it's a set-up: producer Cynthia (Ellen DeGeneres) is out for a "train wreck," hoping for as much embarrassing footage as possible.

The candidate her team chooses is an amiable video store guy called Ed (Matthew McConaughey). Ed has an overbearing brother (Woody Harrelson) who sees gold in his brother's fame; a Texan mother (Sally Kirkland) with some skeletons in the closet; and a wisecracking, wheelchair-bound stepfather (Martin Landau).

He also has a real connection with his brother's girlfriend, Shari (Jenna Elfman), that very quickly turns into something more just as the cameras start to roll.

Cleverly, director Ron Howard and top comedy screenwriters Lowell Ganz and Babaloo Mandel never try to sell the audience on the notion that behind all the cameras and tabloid articles, celebrity just blows. On the contrary, it's clearly great fun—not least because babes like Elizabeth Hurley throw themselves at you.

"EDtv" says that celebrity is great as long as it's on your own terms—as long as you can turn it off. The problem is that you can't. (Unless, like the Tom Cruises of the world, you have the money and clout to ensure that the media and public are kept at a distance and satisfied by the occasional controlled, sanitized morsel of information.)

One of the things that "EDtv" does much better than "The Truman Show" is to give a sense of the way people respond to a dramatic TV spectacle and how media exposure can create the strange, one-sided intimacy that prompts total strangers to treat celebrities like family.

In a series of hilarious scenes, you get to know an amusingly diverse variety of "EDtv" fans and to see how the show affects them—sometimes dividing couples. As a result, by the time Ed ends up on his big date with Hurley, you really buy the notion that interest in whether he can "close the deal" has reached Super Bowl proportions.

With "EDtv," McConaughey comes into his own as an actor rather than a pretty face. It is by far his most accomplished performance, and he carries the movie with surprising ease and with a charm and confidence reminiscent of Paul Newman.

The rest of the cast is uniformly excellent. DeGeneres does a particularly effective, acerbic turn as the cynical program director who develops a conscience. It's unfortunate that the surprisingly effective Elfman spends most of the picture with her eyes puffy from crying—there are times it becomes hard not to agree with the audience surveys that she's too plain and to much of a drag to be Ed's girlfriend, and you almost but not quite find yourself rooting for Hurley's model-on-the-make as his new squeeze.

NEWSDAY, 3/26/99, Part II/p. B3, Gene Seymour

The typical Ron Howard movie is a people-pleasing machine that can tap seamlessly into an audience's dreams, give them a good shaking and send everybody home happy. Perhaps it's because he's spent so much of his professional life in Sitcom City that Howard has often seemed, maybe, too agile at containing the darkness of even his most harrowing movies, such as "Backdraft" (1992), "Apollo 13" (1996) and "Ransom" (1997). His polished craftsmanship, deft handling of actors and showman's savvy have made Howard a brand-name success as a producer-director. But you often wonder why he hasn't felt protected enough by that success to take more risks.

"EDtv" carries so many of Howard's virtues as an entertainer that you can't quite believe it to be the breakthrough that it is. But for the first time in his directoral career, Howard is merging everything he's learned as a filmmaker with everything he knows about fame, television and even the mass audience that has loved him for decades. The result is Howard's most accomplished movie yet; a satire of the media age that manages to be warm, funny and humane without concealing its weaponry.

The set-up is quickly, cleanly articulated. A wickedly imaginative producer (Ellen DeGeneres) for a San Francisco-based cable network comes up with the ne plus ultra in high-concept programming: a 24-hour program devoted to the daily life of an average person. Cameras would actually live with this person from dawn to dusk to dawn; nothing would be out-of-bounds. Her boss (Rob Reiner) is skeptical. After all, who would be crazy enough to submit to such scrutiny?

As it happens, there are lines of people queuing up in front of cameras all over town for informal auditions. Elbowing his way to the front of one rowdy mob is Ray (Woody Harrelson), a small-time gymnasium operator who is about to be married to Shari (Jenna Elfman), a willowy, demure UPS carrier.

But when the network honchos look at the video, they focus on Ray's nicer brother Ed (Matthew McConaughey), whose drawling, sloe-eyed charm bursts through the screen. Ed, who works in a video store, isn't as gung-ho about the gig as his brother. His stepfather (Martin Landau) and mother (Sally Kirkland) are even more skeptical. But Ed gradually warms to the idea—and to the prospect of more walking-around money.

He gets the money—and much more. When the cameras catch Ed's brother cheating on his fiancee, she literally falls into Ed's arms, thus turning what began as a banal TV show into a "real-life" soap opera. Within weeks, a nation is transfixed by the slow-motion riot that is Ed's day-to-day existence. His real father (Dennis Hopper) comes back from the (presumed) dead, throwing his family into chaos. Shari comes to despise being Ed's putative co-star—especially when the audience, even the network head, thinks she's "boring." Ed himself can't walk across the street without crowds following him and his ever-present camera crew.

Worse, after Ed and Shari break up, the network sets him up with a sexy model (who else but Elizabeth Hurley?). When it looks as if they're about to have sex, it becomes a public event on a par with the Super Bowl. Through it all, Ed can't seem to decide whether he's in control of the situation enough to enjoy his newfound fame or be buried by it.

NEWSWEEK, 3/29/99, p. 77, David Ansen

Since "EDtv" is about a guy whose life is played out in front of TV cameras, comparisons will be made to "The Truman Show." The similarities are obvious, with the crucial difference that Ed Pekurny (Matthew McConaughey), the 31-year-old video-store clerk in San Francisco who's catapulted to media stardom, is an entirely willing participant. The truth is that director Ron Howard's lively, Zeitgeist-surfing comedy is so topical it will call to mind everything from Larry Flynt's offer to pay for dirt exposing Republicans to Barbara Walters's Neilsen-busting Monica interview, a squirm-inducing two hours that, like "EDtv," shows us the ghastly repercussions of turning our private lives public.

Ed is a likable east Texas slob plucked out of the crowd by producer Cynthia Topping (a wryly funny Ellen DeGeneres) in a desperate effort to rescue her ailing True TV network. His vain brother, Ray (Woody Harrelson in full cracker mode), wanted the gig to promote his gym. Instead, good ole boy Ray settles for a supporting role that proves disastrous when the camera catches him betraying his girlfriend Shari (Jenna Elfman). The ratings soar when Shari, who always had eyes for little brother, falls hard for Ed. Can Ed and Shari's love survive the prying eye of the camera—and a USA Today poll that thinks she's not good enough to be his girlfriend? Will Ed succumb to the temptations of celebrity—which take the form of a knockout British model (Elizabeth Hurley) whose lusty seduction of our country-boy hunk provides Super Bowl-size ratings?

The omnivorous TV camera wreaks havoc on the lives of all it touches—including Ed's attention-craving mom (Sally Kirkland), his wheelchair-bound stepdad (a hilarious Martin Landau) and Ed's long-lost father (Dennis Hopper), who pops up to cash in on his son's newfound fame. While the nation watches transfixed, the pundits (from George Plimpton to Arianna Huffington) weigh in on the dire meaning of Ed-mania, and Jay Leno cracks wise.

Written by Lowell Ganz and Babaloo Mandel (inspired by an obscure 1994 French Canadian satire), "EDtv" isn't exactly breaking new ground. Albert Brooks's "Real Life" sent up the absurdity of turning private reality into mass spectacle nearly 20 years ago. Ron Howard's version is—no surprise—a funny audience-friendly entertainment that's ultimately less scathing satire than conventional Hollywood romantic comedy outfitted in trendy new clothes.

Elfman gives Shari poignance and some emotional heft—like Renée Zellweger, her emotions seem to overtake her like nasal congestion. But it's McConaughey's show, and he turns on an impressive display of charm. This role is just what the actor's stumbling career needed. After being badly miscast in "Contact" and "Amistad" he should never wear scarves or granny glasses), he's found redemption returning to his down-home roots. Indeed, if McConaughey weren't so likable we would be utterly appalled by the cavalier way Ed draws everyone around him into his ego trip.

Howard and his writers pull off a neat sleight-of-hand by turning the two characters who logically should be the movie's villains—the exhibitionist Ed and the cynical Cynthia, who dreamt up the idea—into its heroes. But their late-in-the-game change of heart is strictly by the numbers. There's something disingenuous about the way the film completely lets them off the hook—they take no personal responsibility for the mess they've created. Instead, Rob Reiner as the heartless network boss becomes the stock, easy-to-hate villain. Everything gets tied up in a neat and satisfying bow, and all the disturbing undercurrents are swept under the rug.

You'll have a good time watching "EDtv"- Howard is always at his best in comic mode ("Splash," the best parts of "Parenthood") and he gives the film a cleverly cluttered look that suggests the experience of watching reality on multiple monitors. Perhaps one reason his movie feels oddly tame is that reality, lately, has been far more outrageous than Hollywood's imaginings. As a sardonic comment on our media-twisted, confession-for-cash times it can't hold a candle to the Walters/Lewinsky interview (though it's certainly more fun). Great, if unwitting, satire is Barbara's pretending not to know what phone sex is, and Monica's apologizing for the pain she's caused Hillary and Chelsea, then heaping two more hours of unalloyed misery upon them. Even Ed Pekurny has a *little* shame.

SIGHT AND SOUND, 12/99, p. 44, Leslie Felperin

San Francisco, the present. Cable-station producer Cynthia Topping thinks up a new format to boost ratings: pick an ordinary person and broadcast his activities 24 hours a day. People all over the city send in audition tapes, including boorish Ray Pekurny. Cynthia and her colleagues choose Ray's brother Ed, spotted in Ray's tape. Transmission begins, and Ed's life—working in a video store, hanging out with his friends and working-class family—at first seems prosaic and uneventful. But when a romance unfolds on camera between Ed and Ray's girlfriend Shari (causing a rift between the brothers), ratings pick up and the show is networked across the country.

However, viewers don't warm to Shari and she soon splits up with Ed after humiliating media pressure. Ed starts dating an ambitious starlet Jill, who only wants the exposure. They eventually split up as Ed still hankers for Shari. His long-lost father Hank resurfaces after years of absence, much to the distress of Ed's mother Jeanette and his stepfather Al. Ed begins to tire of life in the limelight and tries to quit the show (with Cynthia's covert support) but television executive Whitaker holds Ed to his contract. Finally Ed appeals to viewers to send in embarrassing material about the stations executives. The blackmail works, and Ed is left alone to reunite with Shari.

With its Joe Schmo-protagonist the star of a 24-hour cable show that trades for its appeal on the very banality of his life, *EDtv* inevitably suffered on its US release through comparisons with the similarly plotted and critically acclaimed *The Truman Show*. Despite being a self contained feature in its own right, *EDtv* ended up looking like a pilot for a cheap, sunnily lit sitcom spun off from Peter Weir's film, an impression aggravated by the fact that both its screenwriters (Lowell Ganz and Babaloo Mandel) and director (Ron Howard) cut their teeth on such sitcoms as *Happy Days* (itself a sitcom cloned from the more bleak and brooding *American Graffiti*). In fact, *EDtv* is a remake of a little-known Canadian film, *Louis XIX. roi des ondes,* while *The Truman Show* itself garnered accusations of plagiarism.

In a way, these extra-textual debates about originality are superfluous since both *EDtv* and *The Truman Show* set up their stories' events as springing out of televisions ever-increasing problem with format exhaustion. Both Ed and Truman are hailed by their producers as antidotes to the authenticity anaemia of regular programming. The major difference between the two characters is their degree of complicity with their stardom. Ed's willing collusion means *EDtv* is at leisure to make light entertainment from his predicament and turn out a more specifically focused if disposable satire on television.

What you get from *EDtv,* apart from its mild romance, some well-timed comic performances and the debatable charms of Matthew McConaughey on constant display, is more of an insiders' spoof on small-screen shenanigans and a fuller examination of what role television plays in viewers' lives—we see far more of the reactions and opinions of Ed's fans, ranging from Hispanic security guards to camp boys debating the merits of gold-digger Jill's Versace dress. And there's a nice acidity in the portrait of the cable executives' meetings as they worry about their ratings (beaten by a gardening channel, one despairs that, "people would rather watch soil") and ruthlessly dissect their stars' performances. Like the filmmakers themselves, a goodly portion of the cast—from Woody Harrelson to Ellen DeGeneres—got their breaks on television, and there's a sense of scores being settled while they also affectionately salute the medium that made them stars.

TIME, 3/29/99, p. 215, Richard Corliss

All right, after three years of hype, hokum and ho-hum, we finally get it: Matthew McConaughey has star quality. We weren't so sure back when McConaughey was in every other film and on every other magazine cover. His summer-of-'96 double whammy, *A Time to Kill* and *Lone Star,* gave evidence of a gritty, ingratiating talent. But he looked lost amid the more seasoned actors in *Amistad,* and no one could have brought to sensible life the woozy guru he played in *Contact.* It seemed as if McConaughey might lapse into ex-hunk obscurity, like those slightly too-good-looking fellows spotted behind a counter at a California video store.

That's where Ed Pekurny, the guy McConaughey plays in the new Ron Howard comedy *EDtv,* works when he isn't tossing one back with his rakehell brother Ray (Woody Harrelson) or refereeing battles at home in a blue-collar section of San Francisco. Ed is apparently at ease in a bizarre family and unthinkingly content with a go-nowhere job. He doesn't even want what Ray has a quick itch for: to be on a TV show that will feature his real life 24 hours a day.

To figure out what happens next, Ed, or you, might look in a video store, under Jim Carrey. The ghost of *The Truman Show* stalks *EDtv,* and it can't be shaken, as—guess what—Ed is chosen to be in the show. Ray gets jealous, Ray's girlfriend Shari (Jenna Elfman) gets the warms for Ed, instant celebrity makes Ed antsy, and the network's Mephistophelian boss (Rob Reiner) tries to shape the story line of his new star's life, almost as Ed Harris' TV mogul did for Carrey's Truman Burbank.

Note: *EDtv* isn't copycat filmmaking, exactly. The Howard film—written, with their usual comic clarity, by Lowell Ganz and Babaloo Mandel—is a version of the 1994 Quebec farce *Louis 19, le roi des ondes.* But Hollywood, temporarily bereft of original ideas, has become fascinated by its power to create and corrupt. It looks at O.J., Monica, the rubes and rhubarbs on Jerry Springer and asks, with a mixture of self-accusation and self-awe, What have we done?

It's a bit disingenuous for rich and famous moviemakers to tell us how awful it is to be rich and famous on television. As it happens, the moral of *EDtv* is of less import than its tone—which seems loosey-goosey but is carefully land-mined with gags—and its characters, who are unremarkable but worth getting to know. Shari, for instance, is a woman at profound discomfort in her bountiful body. Ray treats Shari as a gaudy accessory, and she accepts his evaluation. Elfman paints a nice portrait of a woman fighting for esteem. *(Psst:* she gets it from Ed.)

But McConaughey is the news here, dimples showing through the chin scruff, drawling out punch lines so you don't hear the rim shot, anchoring a film with enough weirdos to populate a Preston Sturges comedy. It's odd that this movie, not a star vehicle, should allow him to radiate star quality, and that's due in part to Howard's gift with actors. But it's more about this actor's sure connection with the character and the camera, and through them, the mass of moviegoers. Here he plays a man with the resources to handle unearned fame. Now McConaughey has earned his own fame.

VILLAGE VOICE, 3/30/99, p. 130, Amy Taubin

Hollywood has been knocking TV since its inception, viewing it as a force no less malevolent than the Communist conspiracy—it came from outer space to steal the hearts, minds, souls, and dollars of formerly loyal picture-goers. With the two mediums now so intertwined that it's impossible to tell which is ancillary to which, you'd think the time had come to stop all the TV bashing. No way. Within nine months, we've had *The Truman Show, Pleasantville,* and now, *EDtv,* the slightest but most inadvertently revealing of them all.

Directed by Ron Howard (himself a former sitcom star), *EDtv* is the story of an affable, 31-year-old underachiever named Ed (Matthew McConaughey) who is chosen to be the star of a national cable-network program. The program, which is the brainchild of a San Francisco documentary television producer (Ellen DeGeneres, another sitcom refugee), is cablecast 24/7 and shows every minute of Ed's waking and sleeping life. There seems to be some arrangement that allows Ed time out to perform certain bodily functions but since Ed is a natural exhibitionist, in addition to being from a Texas white-trash family, he doesn't always close the door even when he's allowed. *EDtv* (the program, not the movie) opens with a shot of Ed, half awake, toying under the covers with his morning boner.

Viewers immediately are addicted, not only to the comely Ed, but to his family and romantic life, which plays out like a veritable soap opera. Ed's older brother (Woody Harrelson, and we know where he appeared) is pissed off that he wasn't chosen for TV fame and glory and he gets angrier still when he discovers that Ed has poached his girlfriend (Jenna Elfman of *Dharma and Greg).* Ed's father (Dennis Hopper), who deserted the family when Ed was a kid, shows up on his doorstep and reveals a not very interesting secret about Ed's mom (Sally Kirkland) and her second husband (Martin Landau). Then Ed's girlfriend splits because she's sick of the TV cameras and the network finds him a new supermodel girlfriend (Elizabeth Hurley) who turns on viewers, but not Ed.

It's a lot of plot but none of it is particularly funny or compelling. What keeps the film chugging along and also gives it a depressive aftertaste is a middle-aged male sexual anxiety subtext that intermittently sputters to the surface. It begins with that shot of the TV suits ogling McConaughey's morning hard-on, takes form when Ed's brother hauls a former one-night stand on camera to testify to his sexual prowess (she grudgingly gives him a four), and shows its true colors when it's revealed that the network's top suit (Rob Reiner) uses an "erectile device" to compensate for his "erectile dysfunction." Ergo *EDtv*—although I haven't a clue whether the actual creative team behind the film is consciously aware that the title stands for something more than the name of the main character.

Stranger still is the fact that director-producer Howard, producer Brian Grazer, and writers Lowell Ganz and Babaloo Mandel—the Imagine Entertainment team that created some of the biggest box office hits of the '80s and '90s—focus their fears exclusively around TV with nary a mention of the Internet, home to Jennicam and its spawn. But it's the Internet, the name they dare not speak, that makes the guys who run the film industry feel as if they're already in decline and anatomy is only part of the picture.

Also reviewed in:
CHICAGO TRIBUNE, 3/26/99, Friday/p. A, Michael Wilmington
NATION, 4/19/99, p. 42, Stuart Klawans
NEW REPUBLIC, 4/26 & 5/3/99, p. 74, Stanley Kauffmann
NEW YORKER, 3/29/99, p. 115, David Denby
NEW YORK TIMES, 3/26/99, p. E1, Janet Maslin
VARIETY, 3/15-21/99, p. 37, Todd McCarthy
WASHINGTON POST, 3/26/99, p. C1, Stephen Hunter
WASHINGTON POST, 3/26/99, Weekend/p. 65, Desson Howe

8 MM: EIGHT MILLIMETER

A Columbia Pictures release of a Hofflund/Polone production. *Executive Producer:* Joseph M. Caracciolo. *Producer:* Gavin Polone, Judy Hofflund, and Joel Schumacher. *Director:* Joel Schumacher. *Screenplay:* Andrew Kevin Walker. *Director of Photography:* Robert Elswit. *Editor:* Mark Stevens. *Music:* Mychael Danna. *Music Editor:* Thomas Milano. *Sound:* Willie Burton and (music) Brad Haehnel. *Sound Editor:* John Leveque. *Casting:* Mali Finn. *Production Designer:* Gary Wissner. *Art Director:* Gershon F. Ginsburg. *Set Designer:* Masako Masuda, Colin De Rouin, and Luis Russo. *Set Decorator:* Gary Fettis. *Special Effects:* Richard S. Wood. *Costumes:* Mona May. *Make-up:* Michael Mills. *Make-up (Nicholas Cage):* Allen Weisinger. *Stunt Coordinator:* Eddie Yansick. *Running time:* 120 minutes. *MPAA Rating:* R.

CAST: Nicolas Cage (Tom Welles); Joaquin Phoenix (Max California); James Gandolfini (Eddie Poole); Peter Stormare (Dino Velvet); Anthony Heald (Longdale); Chris Bauer (Machine); Catherine Keener (Amy Welles); Myra Carter (Mrs. Christian); Amy Morton (Mrs. Mathews); Jenny Powell (Mary Anne Mathews); Anne Gee Byrd (Senator); Jack Betts (Butler); Luis Oropeza (Archive Director); Rachel Singer (Neighbor); Don Creech (Mr. Anderson); Norman Reedus (Warren Anderson); Fran Bennett and Wilma Bonet (Nuns); Luis Saguar (Manny); Walter K. Jordan, Norm Compton, and Brian Keith Russell (Thugs); John Robb (Porn Dealer); Devan Brown (Flea Market Woman); Doris Brent (Machine's Mother); Robert Amico (Casting Director); Kiva Dawson, Eva Minemar, and Rachel Dara Wolfe (Girls in Hall); Suzy Nakamura (Computer Wizard); Torsten Voges (Stick); Tahitia Dean (Hollywood Prostitute); Terri Laird (Dino's Redhead); Vernon Guichard (Porn Guy); Emily Patrick (Porn Girl); Nancy Lynn Vaughn (Porno Make-up Artist); Lisa Vanasco (Topless Ticket Taker); Bridgett Vera (Ticket Taker); Jennifer Harris, Burton Richards, and Jovanna Vitiello (Strip Club Dancers); David U. Hodges (Surveillance Man); William Lawrence Mack (Bouncer); Lorena Martinez (Prostitute); Connie Mercurio (Nurse); William Buck (Mr. Christian); Kerry Corcoran (Cheating Son-in-Law); Mario Ernesto Sanchez (Taxi Driver); Claudia Aros (Miami Girlfriend).

CHRISTIAN SCIENCE MONITOR, 2/20/99, p. 15, David Sterritt

Just when we thought Mel Gibson had plumbed the lowest depths of big-studio nastiness in "Payback," along comes Nicolas Cage to do him one better. "8MM," named after a reel of ultrapornographic film, takes us into what Hollywood publicists like to call the "dark underbelly" of urban life.

That's legitimate terrain for storytellers to explore, but this particular excursion is so pointless and meandering that you can't help wondering why major players like Cage and his collaborators signed onto it.

Cage plays Tom Welles, a smooth-talking private eye who's hired by a wealthy widow to solve a mystery. Among the belongings left by her late husband is what appears to be a "snuff" film, showing the murder of a helpless teenage girl. The widow believes it's a fake—the porno equivalent of a special-effects fantasy—but she can't rest easily until she's certain. So she employs Welles to track down the young "actress" and establish that she's alive and well. If that's indeed the case.

Although it's hardly a complicated movie, "8MM" draws on different kinds of filmmaking for its techniques. It often looks like a horror picture, complete with monstrous characters and exaggerated violence. At other times it toys with devices used in low-grade documentaries—mannered lighting, odd-sounding music—to tantalize viewers with spookily "foreign" and "exotic" material.

And all too often it bears a creepy resemblance to the kind of movie its hero supposedly deplores. To be sure, it stays far enough short of true bottom-feeding pornography to not push beyond an R rating. But in the context of a heavily promoted mainstream entertainment, its titillating glimpses of sexual degradation seem almost as coarse, crass, and cynical as the real thing.

Throughout the nightmarish story, director Joel Schumacher plays the old sin-and-spectacle game of pairing salacious material with a main character who's shocked, shocked by the awful stuff the plot keeps surrounding him with.

At the end we're supposed to think Welles has passed through Purgatory and earned a measure of redemption from the horrors he's endured. But this doesn't counteract the movie's basically regressive message, which suggests that evil is not a condition to be conquered through its opposite, but a force to be battered with its own ugly weapons. "8MM" revels in that ugliness, making its patina of morality seem as false as it is superficial.

LOS ANGELES TIMES, 2/26/99, Calendar/p. 1, Kenneth Turan

Those foolhardy enough to place themselves at the mercy of "8MM" can expect the following emotions: disgust and revulsion, then anger, followed by a profound and disheartening sadness. There are some films whose existence makes the world a worse place to live, and this is one of them.

Disgust and revulsion because what director Joel Schumacher and company have created is a torture chamber of a film that mercilessly drags us through expensively re-created worlds of vivid sadomasochism, extreme bondage and worse as private eye Tom Welles (Nicolas Cage) tries to determine if a snuff film in his possession really shows a young woman being brutalized and killed. The truth is, after watching repeated glimpses of that stomach-turning horror show shot on 8-millimeter stock, as well as several other equally revolting items Welles turns up, it's hard to care. What's more to the point is why this film, which features women being graphically abused and tormented, that demeans the humanity in everyone in hopes of titillating an audience and earning a healthy return on investment, was ever made. During a sequence in Manhattan's meat-packing district, where sides of beef are trundled through the streets, the thought is inescapable that while government standards exist even for carcasses, there are apparently no limits to the degrading things women—and men, for that matter—can be put through on screen.

That's where the anger comes in, anger against Sony, which inexplicably put tens of millions of dollars into an unapologetically sleazy ordeal that delights in twisting the knife, a tawdry piece of work whose only raison d'etre is making the skin crawl in the name of box-office profit. If interviews are to be believed, Schumacher, Cage et al. consider this wretched business to be some kind of demented public service, a cautionary tale/wake-up call for a presumably somnolent America. A theory, no surprise, that the film in question in no way supports.

Just as much anger is directed toward a bankrupt MPAA rating system that gave "8MM" an R, a system that's gotten used to making deals and changing ratings for a cut here and a cut there. The ratings board has become so compliant with the major studios that it can't see the forest for the trees; it no longer has the stomach to insist that a film that graphically investigates the dehumanizing ultra-violent world of snuff films ought to have an NC-17 placed on it no matter what nips and tucks the studio coyly agrees to make.

The sadness comes from the realization that we are now imprisoned in a thoughtlessly amoral movie culture that considers films like this to be just swell, a culture that lionizes "8MM" screenwriter Andrew Kevin Walker, who made his career with the equally off-putting "Seven." Shamelessly pushing the envelope for what's acceptable on screen, celebrating every opportunity to creep audiences out more than they've ever been creeped out before, today's cutting-edge movies are well on their way to cutting their own throats.

Because it knows where it's headed, "8MM" makes a point of establishing Welles as a four-square family man who lives in rural Harrisburg, Penn., with his wife, Amy (Catherine Keener, wasted in a whiny part), and a baby daughter he adores. At least the film attempts to do this, but creating convincing normalcy is not something these folks are particularly good at.

As he dutifully follows the usual private eye routine of documenting adultery, Welles acts like a respectful zombie, polite and well-spoken. That attitude doesn't change when he gets called to an enormous estate where the recently widowed Mrs. Christian (Myra Carter), a wealthy woman with the demeanor of Eleanor Roosevelt, and her attorney Longdale (Anthony Heald), are in need of his assistance.

It seems that a tin of 8mm footage was found in the late Mr. Christian's private safe, a tin containing what appears to be an actual murder on film. Welles pooh-poohs this in theory, talking as knowledgeably as any critic about fake blood and special effects, but one glance at the footage, which begins with a petrified girl and a menacing man in a leather hood fondly examining a wide selection of terrifying knives, starts to change his mind.

Mrs. Christian wants to know if this film is real or not, and Welles, intrigued, takes the case, telling her he will treat it like any other missing person's investigation. And, in two shakes of a dominatrix's whip, he's discovered that the girl in question is a teenage runaway who's left behind a grieving mother (Amy Morton) in a naive quest for movie stardom.

Next stop is that well-known sinkhole and moral graveyard, Hollywood, where Welles connects with Max California (Joaquin Phoenix), an adult-bookstore clerk who reveals himself to be a cut above the rest because he's reading Truman Capote's "In Cold Blood" instead of your run-of-the-mill dirty book.

With Max as his guide, Welles descends into all the circles of porno hell, visiting outre bondage clubs, watching S&M films, hearing discussions of child pornography, observing rooms full of masturbating men. "There's things you're going to see that you can't unsee, that you can't get out of your head," Max tells him. "If you dance with the devil, the devil doesn't change, the devil changes you."

This kind of bleak voyeurism not only alienates an audience, it also distances Welles from his grumpy wife back home in Pennsylvania. Eventually the trail leads to pornmeisters Eddie Poole (James Gandolfini) and Dino Velvet (Peter Stormare), inanely described by Max as "the Jim Jarmusch of porn." There's also a human killing machine charmingly known as Machine (Chris Bauer), whose arrival signals the addition of excessive beatings and physical violence to the film's attractions.

Given that Schumacher and his cohorts have reasons of their own for wanting to make this film, they may be the only people who end up liking it. Even the most powerful microscope couldn't discover what's in this demeaning ordeal for anyone else.

NEW YORK, 3/8/99, p. 96, Peter Rainer

Set in the porno underworld, *8 MM* is an exploitation movie about an exploitation movie. Nicolas Cage plays Tom Welles, a surveillance expert known for his discretion who is hired by a rich widow when she discovers in her late husband's safe an 8-mm. snuff film. Welles is charged with finding out whether the terrified, stringy-haired girl in it was actually murdered. Meanwhile, the film *we're* watching wallows in its own muck.

Movies about the sex industry are always ripe for attack from both the right and the left. It would be unfortunate if the inevitable salvos aimed at *8 MM* boosted the film's credibility. Its crimes are aesthetic, not political. It's a movie about pornography that has virtually no feeling for what is being desecrated; the film's true obscenity is how out of touch it is with the most basic human sympathies. The gruesomeness—the torchings and throat-slittings and what all—is florid in the manner of a Hollywood fantasia. Director Joel Schumacher is still in his *Batman* mode. He turns degradation into couture.

And yet, at the same time, the film has the brass to palm itself off as deep, Dostoevsky-deep. Screenwriter Andrew Kevin Walker was the fun guy behind *Seven,* and he's up to his old tricks again: He drags in sleazo horror and then tries to exalt its significance. We're supposed to recognize in Welles our own compulsion to root out the dark side.

It doesn't work. Welles is a regular Roto-Rooter man, but there's nothing going on behind his wolfishness and dagger eyes. He's a blank, retreating not into temptation but further into blankness. His descent carries no horror because we never get to see him before the fall. He has a storybook family arrangement—woodsy suburban sprawl; doting, concerned wife (Catherine Keener); and baby daughter—but he's too spooked to appreciate any of it. On the road, pursuing the snuffmeisters, he calls home from dingy motel rooms, and the worry in his voice is palpable. "Is it getting to you?" his wife asks him in one of her more sympathetic moments. At other times, she's less kind. She resents him for keeping her in the dark about his mission; he's just trying to protect her, but she sees it as more of a connubial communication problem. "You better start talking if you want to stay married," she warns him, when it's all he can do just to stay alive. (To shut her up, maybe Welles *should* have fessed up to her. He could have said, "Honey, you just won't *believe* the nipple clamps I saw today.") The wife comes across almost as villainous as the porn purveyors, and yet, in what looks like an afterthought, she's also around to offer up her balm when Tom finally blasts his way out of the gunk.

When a director like Scorsese or De Palma or even Paul Thomas Anderson moves in on the sex-and-grunge subculture, you can feel the hot breath of hellfire on your face. These directors have a highly developed sense of sin—probably the first prerequisite for making a good film about porn (or a good porn film). Schumacher has a highly developed sense of box office. Sure, he and Walker cram in a bit of Christian symbolism near the end—a character is crucified with a crossbow, for example—but it's just stained-glass-window dressing. There isn't all that much difference between this film and a *Nightmare on Elm Street* flick, except that at least the *Nightmare* movies are honest about what they're up to: cheap thrills.

In *8 MM,* the bogeymen are high and low. The depraved ultrarich indulge their snuff thrills because they can afford to; the back-alley porn marauders wield their crossbows because they like it. The only character with any depth is the street-smart adult-bookstore clerk Max (Joaquin Phoenix), who acts as Welles's guide through the porno hades of L.A. and New York. Max is one of those lost souls who tried to make it as an underground musician and got sidetracked by Hollyweird. With his arm-length geisha tattoos and pierced eyebrows, he's like a depraved satyr needling Welles's weaknesses. "Do you get turned on?" he rasps as they make their way through a flea market of slime. Through sheer force of talent, Phoenix makes Max the star of the movie. He's atrocious but also recognizably human, pathetic. You'd hate to see *him* snuffed. As for everybody else connected to this sorry spectacle, how about banishment?

NEW YORK POST, 2/26/99, p. 41, Jonathan Foreman

"8mm" is a somber, often portentous but mostly gripping movie about a decent man's journey into the horrifying imaginary underworld of 'snuff' movies.

It takes evil as seriously as any recent Hollywood film. But unlike the even nastier "Seven" and many movies involving Dantesque trips into the minds of serial killers and Nazi sadists, "8mm" mostly resists the temptation to enjoy viciousness even as it condemns it.

This relative restraint is extraordinary, given that the movie was directed by Joel Schumacher, who put Batman and his sidekick into anatomically exaggerated rubber suits in his awful, campy "Batman and Robin." In fact, "8mm" exudes unambiguous loathing for the leather-bound, S & M porno subculture that it depicts in blue-hued semidarkness.

Nicolas Cage plays Tom Welles, a private investigator engaged by a rich widow to investigate an 8mm film found in her late husband's safe. It shows the apparent murder of a teen-age girl by a man wearing a leather mask.

Welles points out that "snuff" films are an urban myth. But it is obvious from the start that this reel is the real thing and that his assignment will take him down through the murkiest circles of the porn industry until he reaches a hell of pure perversion.

As soon as he meets porn-store clerk Max (the excellent Joaquin Phoenix), you know that he will be Welles' guide to the underworld. Equally predictable is the shadowy presence of someone who wants Welles' mission to fail, and the bloody battle that must take place at the end of his quest.

Two questions dominate: Will Welles' journey to Hades bring out the dark urges that lurk in us all, and will he be irredeemably corrupted by his exposure to all this slime?

None of this is original. Even the way Cage winces as he watches the snuff movie is taken straight from George C. Scott in 1979's "Hardcore." And the suggestion that the evil decadence of the very rich has no limits (presumably Mr. Schumacher would know) has been standard stuff since "Chinatown."

Besides some glaring implausibilities, including a sociology lecture by a murderer with a gun in his face, the most obvious weakness of "8mm" lies in its undeveloped characters. While an unusually subdued Cage makes a convincing private eye/family man, his fury at what he sees is unconvincingly superficial. Not for one second do you sense the kind of deep, vengeful anger that moved, say, Charles Bronson in "Death Wish," or even Mel Gibson in "Ransom."

Catherine Keener, so good in "Out of Sight," plays Welles' cardboard wife, who he keeps in total ignorance of his job. All she gets to do is to wait with the baby for her husband to come home (thus, of course, standing for purity and goodness).

The actors playing the lowlifes have a better deal. James Gandolfini (of "The Sopranos") makes particularly fine use of his role as a vicious sleazebag.

Part of the film is set in an imaginary red-light district in L.A., and in the end there is something depressingly cynical and manufactured about the outrage "8mm" evokes. What turns Welles into an avenging angel is, after all, an invented evil as if the real world of kiddie porn isn't ugly enough.

You almost wonder if Schumacher and scriptwriter Andrew Kevin Walker were guiltily taking pains to emphasize the moral difference between snuff films and Hollywood movies in which torture and murder are only simulated.

NEWSDAY, 2/26/99, Part II/p. B7, John Anderson.

A Hollywood movie decrying the evils of the porn industry is sort of like a Third World dictator complaining about voting irregularities in a Chicago alderman's race. But then, slippery moral footing is what *8MM*—aka Joel Schumacher's *Blow-Up*—is all about.

Following a trail that leads from Paul Schrader's *Hardcore* (with George C. Scott), to William Friedkin's *Cruising* (with Al Pacino) to Richard Tuggle's *Tightrope* (with Clint Eastwood), *8MM* gives us action-star presumptive Nicolas Cage as a good man who lies down with dogs and—surprise—gets fleas. Investigating the identity of a young runaway—whose apparent murder on film shows up in the personal effects of a recently deceased rich guy—Cage's private eye Tom Welles finds himself knee-deep in the septic tank of extreme voyeurism, S&M and murder for kicks. Can he extract himself? And when?

Not for at least two hours. By then, the mystery of Welles descent into hell has become far less psychological than visceral. Is there something on the dark side pulling Welles, Vader-like, into the maw of moral evil? Not really. His mission, identify a young girl whose fate is unknown, is hardly equivocal. His anger at the merchants of sleaze is never ambiguous, or unshared by us. The revulsion we presumably feel as the porn-clerk Max (a very funny Joaquin Phoenix) leads Tom, Virgil-to-Dante, into the third circle of L.A. erotica—and, ultimately, into the realm of the satanic Dino Velvet (Peter Stormare)—seems to be shared by our hero. Amid the sallow swirl of humanity with which Schumacher surrounds him, Welles seems perpetually safe from eternal damnation.

His temporal existence is plagued by locusts, however. Along with his suburban house, yard, SUV and baby daughter (whose existence spurs Tom's feminist anger), he has a wife—the usually glorious Catherine Keener—whose purpose is to nag him for all the traveling that comes with the job that pays for everything around her. This isn't anti-woman, necessarily—although given the abuses that punctuate *8MM*, the implication is that she's supposed to me more grateful. But it's certainly a lazy cliche, like several that pop up throughout what is basically an exploitation film with a nagging conscience.

There's a considerable amount of suspense in *8MM*, essentially of the there's someone coming up behind you variety. There's something strange about Mychael Danna's score, whose Middle Eastern flavor seems to imply some Northern African white-slaver motif.

If someone wants to find any parallels between Tom Welles odyssey and that of Nick Cage, who has moved from singularly eccentric acting to films like *Con Air* and *Snake Eyes* and all the extroverted eyebrow wielding that goes with them, be our guest. Like the kid who gets a 70 and the medal for most improved, however, director Schumacher should be commended for at least (on the heels of *Batman and Robin*) coming up with something thought-provoking, even if some of the thoughts are less about good vs. evil than about what distinguishes so-called smut from the respectable output of studio movies.

SIGHT AND SOUND, 5/99, p. 45, Mark Kermode

Private detective Tom Welles lives in Pennsylvania with his wife Amy and their baby daughter. Contacted by the wealthy and recently widowed Mrs Christian, Welles views an 8mm film found in her dead husband's safe which appears to depict a young girl's murder. She hires Welles to find out if the film is real. Identifying the girl as Mary Anne Mathews through federal missing person files, Welles visits her mother Janet and discovers Mary Anne left for Hollywood.

In Los Angeles, Welles meets porn-mogul Eddie Poole who put Mary Anne in hardcore movies. At a pornographic bookstore, Welles encounters young clerk Max California who offers to help him explore the underground world of porn. Searching for snuff movies, Welles and Max uncover only fakes, but a distinctive tattoo on the hand of masked-sadist Machine in a film directed by Dino Velvet matches one visible in Christian's 8mm movie. The pair visit Velvet in New York where Welles poses as a rich buyer wishing to commission a new snuff movie.

Dismissing Max, Welles proceeds with his plan to trap Velvet with evidence. But he is discovered by Velvet, who catches and kills Max after being tipped off both by Poole and Mrs Christian's lawyer (who originally commissioned the snuff film for Mr Christian). In a shootout, Velvet and the lawyer die but Machine escapes. Welles later corners and kills Poole. On learning the truth about the film, Mrs Christian commits suicide. Welles tracks Machine down and kills him. Returning home, he forwards his payment to Janet Mathews, who finally understands how her daughter died.

"Dance with the devil and the devil don't change; the devil changes you." This is the entire wit and wisdom of *8mm* summed up in one pithy line, an insight well known to any sixth former who has just stumbled on a volume of Nietzsche for the first time, read the sleevenotes to a Joy Division album, or just stayed up late with a six-pack wondering what Darth Vader was like before being drawn to the dark side. Here, however, we are treated to over two hours of bad acting, clumsy writing, cheesy lighting and moral posturing in order to learn some people are bad because they see so many bad things, others are just bad for the hell of it, and if you spend enough time around their badness, some of it will rub off. Probably. All this might be just about acceptable were it the work of a 16-year-old with a video camera preoccupied with the dangers of excessive masturbation. But it is entirely unforgivable when served up by arch rubber-fetishist and codpiece-waving campmeister Joel Schumacher, a man whose career is built on teenage titillation, and who is generally more concerned with his characters' hairstyles than their heads.

Clearly stung by the critical opprobrium heaped on his most visually coherent film *Batman & Robin* (a delightful romp with a target audience of six- to ten-year-olds), Schumacher has tried to make a movie with adult credentials. Although his first cut of *8mm* was trimmed in order to obtain an R rating in the US (a far from unusual event), and despite the MPAA's description of the finished film as still containing "strong perverse sexuality", Schumacher's vision of porno hell spends most of its time telling us filth is afoot while showing us nothing more than a few out-takes from a sub-Sisters of Mercy video. Worse still, Schumacher imagines that involving Andrew Kevin Walker, screenwriter of *Se7en* puts this project on an artistic par with David Fincher's masterpiece. He attempts cack-handedly to recreate *Se7en*'s visual style by desaturating Robert Elswit's cinematography, while retaining the trademark over-designed set dressing which is his own forte. The result is both ugly and silly.

A former costume-designer, Schumacher has always been at his best when dishing up tarts in eye-catching frocks (when was Val Kilmer better than in *Batman Forever?*) and at his worst when attempting to deal with serious issues such as death (*Flatliners*), racism *(A Time to Kill),* and cancer *(Dying Young).* Only in the relatively restrained *Falling Down* has Schumacher ever demonstrated an ability to tackle weightier issues with anything more than eye-popping prurience.

Despite all its pretensions, *8mm* is clearly aimed at viewers too young to know its central premise was considered hackneyed by straight-to-video filmmakers in the late 80s. As the millennium approaches, Schumacher's attempts to update Paul Schrader's *Hardcore* (1978) merely demonstrate that 70s sex-industry sensationalism has become laughable now that Larry Flynt is opening Hustler coffee shops and porno-chic is *de rigeur* among artistes as unthreatening as Lars von Trier. The porn industry just doesn't look scary any more.

For the record (as *8mm* grudgingly admits), snuff movies have long been recognised as nothing more than a media scare, whipped up in the late 70s by the likes of exploitation-film producer Allan Shackleton, who cleverly used unsubstantiated tabloid rumours to turn *Snuff* into a lucrative cash-cow. Shackleton's film was investigated by the New York district attorney's office, who simply produced the 'dead' girl, thus killing the film at the box office. Faced with widespread knowledge of such hoaxing, Walker has one of *8mm*'s villains commission a snuff movie precisely because he can't find a real one to buy. It's a neat twist, except that this snuff movie looks more like a hilariously botched showreel at which even Shackleton would have been embarrassed. In a movie which turns on the blurred line between what is and isn't real on film, such howlingly inept artifice instantly deflates any sense of tension or threat present in the original screenplay.

The characters are a carnival of caricatures, from Nicolas Cage's earnestly worried detective who ploughs through a ton-and-a-half of porno without ever apparently getting an erection (he tells us it's getting to him, but there is no hard evidence); to Peter Stormare's preposterous Dino Velvet, presumably meant to be a homicidal version of Greg Dark or Michael Ninn but more like Doctor Who's nemesis The Master. In the midst of all this silliness, poor Joaquin Phoenix tries his damnedest to inject some youthful punkiness, but is upstaged throughout by Catherine Keener who lights up the screen every moment she's on, even when reduced to playing the mumsy wife.

In a movie which allegedly confronts the issue of men taking pleasure in humiliating women, it seems particularly ironic that Schumacher should give Keener nothing to do except sit at home and look anxious while Cage, Phoenix, Stormare and James Gandolfini strut around like preening cocks. Then again, as the only genuinely mature element in this otherwise infantile venture, her presence could perhaps most accurately be read as that of a weary matriarch, waiting for her noisy children to stop showing off in the street and come in and have their tea.

VILLAGE VOICE, 3/9/99, p. 118, Dennis Lim

8MM pretends to be about evil—the enormity of evil, why it exists, how it contaminates, deep stuff like that. In case you don't pick up on this, someone in the film says, more than once, "You dance with the devil, the devil changes you." When it's not delivering knockout moral insights, *8MM* operates mostly as a plodding, doggedly tawdry thriller. Nicolas Cage, confusing lack of modulation with restraint, plays Tom Welles, a PI summoned by a rich old lady to determine the authenticity of a snuff film found among her late husband's possessions. The assignment takes him first to Ohio, where he establishes the identity of the girl knifed to death on film (white-trash runaway-aspiring actress), then to the L.A. porn netherworld (his tour guide is a wiseass porn-store clerk played by Joaquin Phoenix), and eventually to Manhattan's meatpacking district, where he must face down an eccentric auteur mystifyingly described as the "Jim Jarmusch of porn" (Peter Stormare, out of control) and a masked, leather-clad actor known only as "Machine."

Screenwriter Andrew Kevin Walker was also responsible for *Seven,* and he is, if nothing else, consistent. *8MM* shares *Seven*'s sadistic streak and reactionary bent. But filtered through director Joel Schumacher's myopic flash (as opposed to David Fincher's dystopic paranoia), it has absolutely none of the earlier film's grimy seductiveness. *8MM* is a nasty piece of work, and it's nasty in a particularly ostentatious and sophomoric way. This is most obvious in the final scenes, where vigilante hysteria masquerades as moral hand-wringing. (Schumacher's an old pro at rough justice, of course, having also directed *Falling Down* and the contemptible *A Time to Kill.)* Welles's eventual thirst for revenge is an illogical, out-there ploy that topples the narrative over into terrain the filmmakers evidently consider risky and profound. Cage doesn't pull it off, but then, I can't think of an actor who could. As his wife, Catherine Keener struggles fruitlessly with the worst-written female role since Gretchen Mol's in *Rounders.* She appears periodically at the end of a phone line to pledge devotion and express concern for her absent husband. (Cradling their baby daughter, she's also used to signal a potential threat to Welles's beloved family.) You can't fault filmmakers for wanting to wax philosophical on the nature of good and evil, but with this mindlessly sordid low blow, Walker and Schumacher aren't exactly staring into the void; they *are* the void.

Also reviewed in:
CHICAGO TRIBUNE, 2/26/99, Friday/p. A, Michael Wilmington
NATION, 3/29/99, p. 34, Stuart Klawans
NEW YORK TIMES, 2/26/99, p. E11, Janet Maslin
NEW YORKER, 3/8/99, p. 94, Anthony Lane
VARIETY, 2/22-28/99, p. 49, Derek Elley
WASHINGTON POST, 2/26/99, Weekend/p. 39, Desson Howe

ELECTION

A Paramount Pictures release of an MTV Films production in association with Bona Fide Productions. *Executive Producer:* Van Toffler. *Producers:* Albert Berger, Ron Yerxa, David Gale, and Keith Samples. *Director:* Alexander Payne. *Screenplay:* Alexander Payne and Jim Taylor. *Based on the novel by:* Tom Perrotta. *Director of Photography:* James Glennon. *Editor:* Kevin Tent. *Music:* Rolfe Kent. *Music Editor:* Richard Ford. *Sound:* Jon Ailetcher. *Sound Editor:* Frank Gaeta and Scott Wolf. *Production Designer:* Jane Ann Stewart. *Casting:* Lisa Beach. *Art Director:* Tim Kirkpatrick. *Set Decorator:* Renee Davenport. *Costumes:* Wendy Chuck. *Make-up:* James Ryder. *Stunt Coordinator:* Gary Wayton. *Running time:* 105 minutes. *MPAA Rating:* R.

CAST: Matthew Broderick (Jim McAllister); Reese Witherspoon (Tracy Flick); Chris Klein (Paul Metzler); Jessica Campbell (Tammy Metzler); Mark Harelik (Dave Novotny); Delaney Driscoll (Linda Novotny); Molly Hagan (Diane McAllister); Colleen Camp (Judith R. Flick); Frankie Ingrassia (Lisa Flanagan); Phil Reeves (Principal Walt Hendricks); Matt Malloy (Vice-Principal Ron Bell); Jeanine Jackson (Jo Metzler); Holmes Osborne (Dick Metzler); Loren Nelson (Custodian); Emily Martin (Girl in Crisis); Jonathan Marion and Amy Falcone (Classroom Students); Matt Justesen ("Eat Me" Boy); Nick Kenny ("Eat Me" Boy's Buddy); Brian Tobin and Christa Young (Adult Video Actors); David Wenzel (Tracy's Friend Eric); Joel Parks (Jerry Slavin); Larry Kaiser (Chemistry Teacher); Marilyn Tipp (Carver Office Lady); Jeannie Brayman (Faculty Ballot-Giver); Nick D'Agosto (Larry Fouch); James Devney (Motel Clerk); L. Carmen Novoa (Spanish Teacher); Jason Paige, Matt Golden, and Heather Koenig (Kids in Georgetown Hall); Jillian Crane (Jillian).

CINEASTE, Vol. XXIV, No. 4, 1999, p. 36, Thomas Doherty

Site of teasing, trauma, and tumescence, the American high school first began going steady with Hollywood cinema when *Blackboard Jungle* (1955) and *Rebel Without a Cause* (1955) incited a pioneer generation of teenagers to flex their demographic muscle at the motion picture box office. Since then, successive cadres of bluejeaned delinquents, breakfast clubs, and clueless kids have rushed up the down staircase for fast times, low comedy, and mawkish angst. Increasingly, as market forces and educators alike conspired to standardize and isolate teenage experience, the high school has become an enclosed social orb, a sealed, self-sufficient subculture whose rites are less a preparation for the great outside world than a microcosm of its pressures, hierarchies, and mind games. Why aspire to life after high school when life is high school? So shrugs the current grade of teen-targeted but adult-minded motion pictures, an exceptionally gifted class for 1998-1999 that already includes *Pleasantville, Varsity Blues, The Faculty, She's All That, Rushmore, Never Been Kissed, Cruel Intentions, Ten Things I Hate About You, Jawbreaker,* and, the most schematic recital of postgraduation realpolitik, *Election.*

Based on the election-year novel by Tom Perrotta and directed by Alexander Payne, *Election* prowls through the lily-white corridors of George Washington Carver High School in Omaha, Nebraska, during a ferocious contest for president of the Student Government Association. The upbeat voiceover of popular civics teacher Mr. Jim McAllister (Matthew Broderick)—all the kids call him "Mister M."—insists that things are just swell, but his purgatory of a home life belies his school spirit ("Fill me up!," demands his ovulating wife). No wonder he looks on a dynamo of extracurricular activities named Tracy Flick (Reese Witherspoon) with a mixture of envy, desire, and resentment. She has what he doesn't: a promising future. Chirpy, clipped, coiled like a rattlesnake, Tracy is that most-likely-to-succeed-and-piss-off-her-peer-group overachiever issued one-per-graduating class, the girl with complete homework, perfect hair, and sensible clothes who always thrusts her hand into the air like a Hitler salute when teacher asks a question. Foreseeing Tracy's political ascendancy as ever upward and more sinister, Mister M. determines to stop her in her patent-leather shoes. He recruits the sidelined jock Paul (Chris Klein), a likeable lug who has scored more points on the football field than his SATS, to oppose Tracy's plans for world domination. A wild card in the two-party system emerges when Paul's quirky sister, the lovelorn lesbian Tammy (Jessica Campbell), enters the race in a fit of romantic pique after her girlfriend defects to heterosexuality, dumping Tammy to take up oral sex and hot tubbing with Paul.

Perrotta and Payne's allegorical satire of American politics makes for an open-book test of connect the dots: corruption, sex, dirty tricks, media manipulation, voter fraud—just like the grownups. During the candidates' forum in the Carver High gymnasium, democracy in action is not a pretty sight. Speaking first is the unopposed candidate for the cipher position of SGA Vice President, a paraplegic student who joshes that although he cannot stand up, he will stand up for the student body. Self-packaged and self-possessed, Tracy is as earnest as a freshman congressman making her first C-SPAN floor speech, inaptly quoting Thoreau and making a cynical pitch for the Hispanic and African American homeroom vote. Befuddled Paul avoids eye contact and reads a rote declamation in a dull monotone that leaves even his cheering section speechless. Against expectations, the dark-horse candidate Tammy proves a natural demagogue. She faces down hecklers to deliver a Perotista rant capped with a campaign pledge to disband the student government and abolish forever these stupid assemblies! The kids go wild.

All the familiar teenage types sign the *Election* yearbook—the suck-up, the dumb jock, the arty misfit. To a man and woman, boy and girl, from first frame to last image, the roll call is incessantly one-note. The best note is the shrillest. As Flick, the nose-crunching and jut-jawed Reese Witherspoon is hypnotically neurotic: whether in the mode of whiny brat or she devil, she spits out her dialog in a staccato, high-pitched squeal that is harder to take than chalk screeching down a blackboard. Playing the dimbulb football player, with nary a mean bone in his body nor a deep thought in his head, Chris Klein (a pumped-up version of Keanu Reeves) is guileless enough to thank God for his larger than average penis and generous enough not to vote for himself. (Tracy knows immediately that Mister M. is behind Paul's sudden political ambitions: "Didn't bother me at all!," she fumes in voice-over.) A worn-out schlump whose private life unravels just as the election heats up, Mister M. is in worse shape than any of his young charges. When a symbolic bee sting swells up his eye, his failed moral vision causes him to make a serious ethical—or is it moral?—lapse. Of course, percolating underneath all the high-school hijinks is the creepy intertextual aura around Matthew Broderick, with flecks of gray hair, never getting a day off from his own plague of Ferris Buellers. ("Anyone?")

In such teen-colored flashbacks, the path of the plot is less interesting than the capacity to capture the atmosphere and regurgitate the emotional residue of high school life—the cheesy SGA posters and slogans ("Pick Flick!"), the choral moan of a classroom when a pop quiz is announced, and the strident posturing of teenagers as premature adults. In visual backdrop, set design, and costuming, *Election* can be terrifyingly evocative of the institutional psychosis roaming the hallways of American public education. The student assembly is held in a gymnasium of such eerie verisimilitude (scruffy floors, a feedback-prone PA system, truculent kids packed on bleachers screaming "Eat me!") that it may induce flop sweat in susceptible viewers.

A one-letter change in the film's title highlights another tension rising up as an *Election* issue: student-teacher sex. Like many adult-oriented teenpics, the film depicts high school kids as more sophisticated and predatory than their hapless elders. When the affair between Tracy and her dorky math teacher comes to light, the teacher is disgraced and consigned to a future in the retail trade while Miss Flick never breaks stride. McAllister looks appalled when his colleague describes the atmospheric conditions of Tracy's sexual apparatus, but during the enforced baby-making sessions at home the image of Tracy's face slips over his wife's. Later, during a real face-off, Tracy is emotionally controlled and sexually confident, Mister M. is flustered and outmaneuvered. If her lover hadn't gotten "all mushy" and written incriminating love notes, their affair would have remained secret, and, don't forget Mister M., my mother works as a paralegal.

The serene self-command in the reversal of student-teacher power signals that, despite the setting and situation, *Election* is not truly of the teenpic clique. The key to its generational allegiance lies neither in the allegorical plotline nor the sharp dialog, but in the individualistic temper of the student body. The adolescents here are autonomous units, loners whose relations are outward and goal oriented, when teenagers are creatures of their cliques, peer oriented and present minded. Being popular and well-liked is the focus of their emotional life. In bridging the teen/adult sensibility gap, *Romy and Michele's High School Reunion* and *Never Been Kissed* assume that the pangs of peergroup rejection linger long after graduation. Tracy doesn't want to be school president to validate her popularity, but to gain power and get her ticket punched for college.

Director Payne deploys an array of technical distancing devices for laugh lines and short-cut exposition. Freeze-framed snapshots put the film on pause for voice-over ruminations, interior monologues, and cartoonish vignettes. Supers, maps, cheapo archival footage, musical interludes ("Gonna Get Along without You Now" and "Jennifer Juniper" waft over the rose-colored bliss of Tammy's lesbian puppy love), and a loopy fantasy sequence in rear-screen projection (a faux Continental Mister M. cruises in a convertible as Marcello Mastroianni) punctuate and interrupt the narrative flow. Besides yuks, the devices are meant to reflect the patchwork quality of 60s-era yearbook design and 16mm educational films-though, in a deft act of Stalinist-style revisionism, Tracy uses computer graphics to wipe out the face of her disgraced teacher from a group yearbook picture.

The most notable distancing device in *Election* is the director's own attitude. As in *Citizen Ruth,* which snarled at both sides of the abortion debate, the student body and faculty of George Washington Carver High School warrant bemused condescension, as if to be shunned in the halls, walked past in the lunchroom, and put down with snide comments. A terrifying montage shows the quiet desperation of Mister M.'s cyclical vocation, explaining the Constitutional "separation of powers" clause to class after class, year after year, with the same executive-legislative-judicial triangle sketched on the blackboard. Only the lesbian Tammy—wise enough to see through the game, devious enough to play it to achieve her own ends—deserves a measure of sympathetic respect. Perhaps this is only due compensation for a century of ugly film stereotypes, but on the American screen today a gay character gets treated with the kind of reverence that classical Hollywood once reserved for Catholic priests.

The coda—a now obligatory device that is a legacy of that classic high-school road movie, *American Graffiti* (1973)—finds the Carver High alum graduating to predictable fates. The disgraced Mister M. lands a new job at the American Museum of Natural History, Tracy annoys a new set of classmates at Georgetown University, Paul throws a bitching senior-year party, and Tammy gets sent for "punishment" to lesbian heaven—an all-girls parochial school. One day, in Washington, D.C., Mister M. spots a power-suited Tracy getting cozy with a real life congressman. "What is she doing in that limousine?," he yelps in frustration, in impotence. Poor Mister M. still hasn't learned the cynical life lesson of *Election:* those who can, do.

LOS ANGELES TIMES, 4/23/99, Calendar/p. 1, Kenneth Turan

They get all the movies—or at least it seems that way. They control an impressive share of America's free time and disposable income. And most everyone covets their youthful good looks. You've always suspected it and "Election," a sharp and merciless comedy, tells you it's true: Teenagers rule.

The best and brightest high school adventure since the groundbreaking "Heathers" (1989), "Election" posits a devastatingly funny world where fumbling adults are powerless when confronted by determined young people motivated by the devil of self-interest. Co-written and directed by Alexander Payne ("Citizen Ruth") and powered by expert performances by Reese Witherspoon and Matthew Broderick, this is a fierce teen satire that adults will have no difficulty cherishing.

One reason high school has proved to be such an effective incubator of blackly humorous films is that it's the adult world writ small. Anyone looking, as Payne surely is, to skewer the ways self-centered behavior is camouflaged and rationalized by ambitious minds couldn't feel more at home than among the mainstream kids at Omaha's mythical George Washington Carver High.

Adapted from a novel by Tom Perrotta by Payne and his "Ruth" co-writer, Jim Taylor, "Election" is both funnier than that debut and subtler in its choice of targets. Helped by being adroitly cast down to its tiniest roles (Lisa Beach was the casting director), this is a nearly flawless little film, a cheerful nightmare that knows just where it wants to go and uses precisely calibrated comic effects to get there.

Payne and Taylor get some of their best results by employing multiple voice-overs. Each of the film's major characters has his or her shot at providing after-the-fact commentary on events as they unfold, competing in very much an adversarial way to get their personal version of what we see happening onto the official record.

In an alternate universe, Jim McCallister and Tracy Flick could have been allies, even friends. Both care enormously, almost unreasonably, about what happens at Carver High. But destiny pulls them apart, and as Tracy puts it with typical off-kilter bluntness, "you can't interfere with destiny. That's why it's destiny."

Broderick, in a role that is a near-perfect fit, plays the slightly lost, slightly woebegone but awfully sincere McCallister, the kind of educator everyone calls Mr. M. He's been named teacher of the year three times at Carver, a school record. Mr. M means it when he says, "I got involved, I made a difference."

Tracy (a completely delightful Witherspoon) also got involved, and with a vengeance. Bright-eyed, chipper and determined, she's everywhere at Carver, playing Hodel in "Fiddler on the Roof," working on the yearbook, and thinking nothing of customizing 480 cupcakes should the need arise. Mr. M views Tracy as the most ambitious student he's ever seen. And, for a variety of reasons, he can't stand her.

So when Tracy decides to run for student council president, Mr. M encourages star athlete Paul Metzler (a telling debut for Chris Klein) to run against her. The most popular as well as the densest man on campus, Paul is the kind of guy who seeks serious spiritual guidance from "The Celestine Prophecy" and then falls asleep trying to read it.

Naturally, Tracy takes competition as a personal affront; "the weak," she squeaks in her purposeful little voice, "are always trying to sabotage the strong." The battle that ensues, which eventually involves Tammy Metzler (Jessica Campbell), Paul's sexually confused sister ("I'm not a lesbian but I'm only attracted to women"), and even Mr. M's wife Diane (Molly Hagan), leaves few people or institutions unscathed.

"Election's" humor comes not just from its farcical situations but its dead-on, deeply tongue-in-cheek dialogue. And Payne, who enjoys periodically jolting the audience with either a bit of particularly raw sexual dialogue or an unexpected visual point of view, directs it with a great sense of dark comic style.

"Election" takes particular glee in demonstrating the obtuseness of adults like gee-whiz principal Walt Hendricks (Phil Reeves) and showing how conniving students can be when they're consumed by their jealousies, rivalries and relationships. "Election" enjoys making the audience complicit in all these wicked schemes; making us feel good about people being bad is one of this film's most satisfying triumphs.

NEW YORK, 5/3/99, p. 114, Peter Rainer

Election is a facetious, smarty-pants satire about a popular Midwest-high-school history teacher and student-government adviser, Jim McAllister (Matthew Broderick), who acquires as his nemesis the school's No. 1 student overachiever, Tracy Flick (Reese Witherspoon). Director Alexander Payne and his screenwriter Jim Taylor—who worked together on Payne's first feature, the abortion-rights comedy *Citizen Ruth*—should be commended for making a high-school movie that, for a change, isn't aimed only at high-schoolers. *Election* is an anti-high-school high-school movie, and it captures the drear institutional climate: the ugly green hallways and generic auditoriums and the way the principal says "People, *please*" and all the other memento mori of those years.

But *Election* could stand to be a bit less satisfied with its smarts. After a while, you begin to wonder what makes Payne and Taylor so all-fired special: Like brainy adolescents, they mock just about everybody in sight—not just two-faced teachers or the go-getter Tracy, with her predatory wiles, but the school's lunkhead football star, Paul (Chris Klein), whom Jim coaxes into running against Tracy for class president, thereby incurring her everlasting wrath. Paul's lesbian sister Tammy (Jessica Campbell), who stumps for president on an abolish-student-government platform and (intentionally) gets herself thrown into an all-girls parochial school, comes closest to being the movie's hero. Her snideness is a relief from Tracy's cast-iron twinkles. What is it about high-school overachievers that gets the goat of movie directors these days? Jason Schwartzman's turbocharged Max in Wes Anderson's' *Rushmore* is kin to Tracy; he's more personable than she is, but you still get the feeling, as you do in *Election,* that the filmmakers are settling an old score. Film directors tend to be overachievers, too. Maybe the score being settled is with themselves.

NEW YORK POST, 4/23/99, p. 50, Jonathan Foreman

Smart, funny and tough, "Election" is one of the best movies to come out this year. It's a terrific work of political and social satire set in a Nebraska high school that has the intelligence of (the less coherent) "Rushmore," while painting a much darker picture of politics and human relationships.

Tracy Flick (Reese Witherspoon) is a steel-willed goody-goody, running unopposed for president of the student government of Carver High. Part Bill Clinton, part Richard Nixon, she's not evil, but she's a ruthless overachiever, with a hefty chip on her shoulder.

Popular history teacher Jim McAllister (Matthew Broderick) is so alarmed by the progress of this ambitious little monster that he persuades Paul, a gentle but dumb football hero (Chris Klein), to run against her. It's the first of several ethical lapses that will lead an essentially decent man down a disastrous path.

But the battle between Jim and Tracy becomes more complicated when a third candidate joins the fray: Paul's sophomore sister Tammy (Jessica Campbell). Unlike the other candidates, she promises to do nothing as student president and to abolish the whole nonsense of student government. It's a platform that hits a nerve with the student body.

Deeply cynical about the democratic process, "Election" suggests that the problem with the system is that only a morally deformed person would have the combination of ambition and ruthlessness necessary to win office. But it is the combination of this suggestion with a profoundly bleak view of love, sex and marriage that enables "Election" to pack a nasty punch amid the laughs.

Cleverly written by Alexander Payne and Jim Taylor, and deftly directed by Payne, "Election" benefits from perfect casting. A surprisingly overweight Broderick and the ultra-chipper Witherspoon both give nuanced, believable performances. Witherspoon in particular is the ultimate incarnation of an intensely irritating type that everyone has encountered, but whose essence has seldom if ever been caught on screen.

Newcomers Campbell and Klein, as the sibling rivals who challenge Tracy, also do a fine job, and they both make the most of the zingers in their voice-over recollections of the movie's central incident.

Although not a "high school movie" of the sort that has recently overwhelmed the nation's cinemas, "Election" happens to present a much more realistic vision of the place than any of those films. The kids look like teen-agers. Some even had bad skin like teen-agers.

NEWSDAY, 4/23/99, Part II/p. B3, John Anderson

Those flaring nostrils and resolutely ungenerous lips of young Reese Witherspoon are not exactly the assets of choice for the ripely '90s ingenue. They didn't help when she tried playing sweetly virginal in the abysmal "Cruel Intentions"; they weren't particularly convincing when she played retro-slutty in "Pleasantville."

But they make fabulous accessories for Tracy Flick, the pathologically ambitious teen achiever of Alexander Payne's "Election," a just-this-side-of-plausible parable about a high school election that mirrors all the bilious cupidity of the political system at large. And a lot more.

Friendless and essentially joyless—despite her 100-watt and hair-trigger smile—Tracy has been stage-mothered (by a virtually unseen Colleen Camp) into a pubescent Liddy Dole. She's the girl whose hand is always raised highest in class, who's popular virtually by force of will and who's fated to become president of George Washington Carver High School's student government body. Not by virtue of democracy, exactly. More like divine right.

Tracy's counterweight-cum-nemesis is Jim McAllister (Matthew Broderick), Carver High's three-time Teacher of the Year, a man who wears crummy clothes while driving his crummy car to a school where the kids drive Miatas and wear Tommy Hilfiger and have allowances higher than his retirement package. He devotes himself to his students, though, enthusiastically working extracurricular activities, watching the occasional porn tape when his wife (Molly Hagan) is asleep, and engaging his students' minds—almost. When he pursues a discussion of ethics vs. morals, he never quite gets them to the point he seems to be trying to make—that ethics are the rules of a game, and morals are the reasons you play. Or don't.

Tracy is in the game, of course, and for keeps, but because for her the game is all there is. In fact, the only thing between Tracy Flick and a future investigation by an independent prosecutor is Jim McAllister.

If Tracy were just a character and not a symptom, Payne's movie wouldn't be as funny—or as cutting—as it is, but she's so repellent she's iconic. When Jim proposes to the sweetly dopey Paul Metzler (Chris Klein)—a popular football star who has demolished both leg and sports career in a skiing accident—that he oppose the unopposed Tracy, it unleashes the fumes of high school hell. Adding to the merriment is Paul's lesbian sister Tammy (Jessica Campbell), who decides to run, too, when her girlfriend dumps her for Paul. Tammy's revenge-inspired platform is pure anarchy—she promises, if elected, to dismantle the student government, which just serves to unleash more hair spray on the fire.

A movie posing a cynical teenager against an idealistic teacher is itself sardonic; the unsavory point of "Election" is that America's Children, whom the politicians are so fond of invoking ("our kids!!!!") are far more attuned to the world those very politicians have created than any high school civics teacher—whose influence over his adolescent charges seems minuscule compared with what they're fed by MSNBC or MTV (which co-produced this movie, ironically enough). The audience has the advantage of Payne's he-says-she-says set up, through which we get to know the guileless hero and Machiavellian heroine, and through which a great deal of crackling tension permeates the movie—even though the real thrill is seeing blackhearted cultural paradigms coming to life.

SIGHT AND SOUND, 10/99, p. 43, Geoffrey Macnab

The US Midwest, the present, Tracy Flick, star pupil at George Washington Carver High, is standing unopposed for president of the student government. Civics teacher Jim McAllister has a grudge against Tracy because of her part in a sex scandal which saw fellow teacher Dave Novotny sacked. McAllister encourages high school football hero Paul Metzler to stand against her. Paul's sister Tammy also joins the race after being dumped by her girlfriend (who, to spite Tammy, has become Paul's girlfriend and campaign manager). One weekend, Tracy loses her temper putting up posters in the school corridor and tears down the election banners. There is a school inquiry. Tammy takes the blame—even though she knows Tracy was responsible—and is suspended. Her parents decide to enrol her in a strict, all-girl convent school instead. As the election draws nearer, Jim has a brief fling with Dave Novotny's estranged wife Linda. Although he thinks he's in love, she dismisses the affair as a mistake and tells Jim's wife about it.

Jim oversees the election count; Tracy has won by one vote. Jim surreptitiously throws two votes for Tracy into a wastepaper basket and declares Paul the winner. Tracy is devastated. The school janitor finds the missing votes. The election result is overturned. Jim resigns in disgrace. His marriage breaks up. He heads to New York, where he gets a job working in a museum. While visiting Washington DC he sees Tracy climbing into a car with a Republican politician whose assistant she has become. He throws his drink at the car and runs off.

"It's like my mom said: the weak are always trying to sabotage the strong," proclaims Tracy Flick, the footstamping, cupcake-baking overachiever whose battle to become class president forms the backdrop to *Election*. As demure as Pippi Longstocking and as sanctimonious as Tipper Gore, Tracy works her heart out. She's also the only one in class who can explain the difference between morality and ethics, but that doesn't change the fact that she's a little monster. If Billy Wilder had been assigned to make a teen comedy, he might well have come up with a film as witty and sour as this. Alexander Payne's second feature (after *Citizen Ruth*), *Election* is a wonderfully acidulous satire which uses its high-school setting to make some barbed points about US politics and culture in general. We're offered a presidential campaign in microcosm, complete with dirty tricks, smears, a hint of a sex scandal, and even some unseemly vandalism.

Payne manages to make us see Tracy through the eyes of the one person who detests her—her teacher, Jim McAllister. Not that it is immediately apparent that the film is biased against her. The screenplay (co-written by Payne and Jim Taylor) seems scrupulously even-handed. In voiceovers running throughout the film, all the candidates are given the chance to reflect on the events surrounding the fateful election campaign. The mainstream is represented by high-school football hero Paul Metzler, a genial, simple-minded oaf with (so he's told) a big penis, who doesn't think it's right to vote for himself. We hear from the counterculture in the form of

Paul's sister Tammy, a nihilistic lesbian whose slogans "Who cares?" and "What does it matter anyway?" appeal infinitely more to the voters than Tracy's pious homilies. Tracy, for her part, represents ambition, self-help and "the American way". (Sure enough, she turns out to be a Republican.) The most compelling voice, though, belongs not to the candidates but to the teacher overseeing the campaign.

At GWC High, McAllister is all that stands between Tracy and absolute power. His hackles rise every time she shoots up her arm in class. US politics is about checks and balances, he tells his class, and checking Tracy's career becomes his fulltime obsession. After his experiences as a squeaky-clean juvenile lead in such films as *Ferris Bueller's Day Off* and *Project X*, it must surely have been liberating for Matthew Broderick to play a character as crumpled and seedy as McAllister, a man who keeps porn films in the basement. He suffers every manner of indignity. He is spat at. His car is bespattered with mud. He's stung in the eye by a bee. When he cheats on his wife, Payne makes him look all the more absurd by showing him groping with Linda Novotny from the baby's point of view. Still, he's as close as *Election* gets to a hero. He's the one who upholds democratic values—even if it means cheating. "Do you want an apple or an orange? That's democracy," he explains to a bewildered-looking Paul as he tries to ensure Tracy isn't elected unopposed.

Election turns the usual conventions of the high-school comedy on their head. There's no prom night. Payne doesn't labour the tension between the jocks and the nerds, or try to show school life from the rebel's perspective. The film may have been made by MTV, but its fairground-style music (by Rolfe Kent) sounds as if it were borrowed from some old Mack Sennett comedy. Just occasionally, we feel flickers of sympathy for Tracy. Nobody likes her much and her all-consuming ambition means she is never satisfied. Witherspoon, last seen as the goodie two-shoes in *Cruel Intentions,* plays her brilliantly, screwing up her features and scowling when things go against her and smiling insincerely at all other times. The funniest moments are often the cruellest. When gawky teacher Dave Novotny bursts into tears as he realises his affair with Tracy has ruined his career, the scene is played for laughs. (Perhaps Novotny deserves his punishment for using Lionel Richie's 'Three Times a Lady' as a seduction theme.) Jim's humiliations are also milked for comedy. The humour may be vicious, but there's also a strong vein of pathos running through the film. Payne's sympathies are with the underdog. Ultimately, it is success—at least in the way it is achieved by Tracy—which seems shabby.

VILLAGE VOICE, 4/27/99, p. 140, Dennis Lim

Director Alexander Payne follows up *Citizen Ruth,* his sharp, almost Sturges-like abortion-wars satire, with *Election,* a less ambitious film with a lower success rate. Nominally a high school comedy, *Election* is idiosyncratic enough to avoid the teensploitation trap but not sufficiently single-minded to wind up anywhere especially interesting.

Reference points abound when you're flirting with a genre as rampant as the teen movie, and for most people *Election* will simply be, for better or worse, *Ferris Bueller's Midlife Crisis.* Matthew Broderick, looking somewhat pudgy and a little the worse for wear, plays Jim McAllister, a teacher on the brink of burnout. Stuck in a fossilized marriage and a career holding pattern, he becomes consumed with hatred for one of his students, Tracy Flick (Reese Witherspoon), a monstrously perky overachiever who's running unopposed for student council president. Hell-bent on Tracy's downfall, Jim ropes in his own candidate, lovable dumb jock Paul (Keanu clone Chris Klein). A further complication arises when, as a by-product of a love-triangle subplot, Paul's lesbian sister (Jessica Campbell) enters the fray.

Transposing Tom Perrotta's novel from small-town New Jersey to his native Omaha (where *Citizen Ruth* was also set), Payne, with the help of Broderick's sly performance, evokes the sense of disquiet rippling beneath the surface of a go-nowhere life. Perrotta structured his book as a series of snappy first-person accounts, and Payne preserves this device, dividing narrating duties among Jim and the three candidates. Though he doesn't have, say, Wes Anderson's singular comic sensibility, Payne is adept at both low-key absurdity and broad caricature. Making liberal use of freeze-frames, he catches characters in unflattering facial contortions, while a narrator rips into them—it's cheap and silly, but you laugh regardless.

Perrotta says the three-candidate scenario was inspired by the '92 presidential race (his book opens with a quote by William Trevor: "The world is the School gone mad"). But the similarities are superficial, and *Election* buries its high-school-as-a-microcosm allegorical potential under a straight morality tale—one with a fairly stale aftertaste at that. With its sad yet almost uniformly unsympathetic characters, the film never finds a confident tone: it's pitched as a satire, but seems to have no real targets.

Also reviewed in:
CHICAGO TRIBUNE, 4/30/99, Friday/p. A, Mark Caro
NATION, 6/28/99, p. 31, Stuart Klawans
NEW YORK TIMES, 4/23/99, p. E21, Janet Maslin
NEW YORKER, 4/26-5/3/99, p. 192, David Denby
VARIETY, 4/19-25/99, p. 64, Todd McCarthy
WASHINGTON POST, 5/7/99, Weekend/p. 47, Desson Howe

EMPEROR AND THE ASSASSIN, THE

A Sony Pictures Classics release of a Shin Corporation and Le Studio Canal+ presentation of a New Wave Co. and Beijing Film Studio production in association with NDF/China Film Coproduction Corp. *Executive Producer:* Chen Kaige, Tsuguhiko Kadokawa, and Hiromitsu Furukawa. *Producer:* Han Sanping, Shirley Kao, and Satoru Iseki. *Director:* Chen Kaige. *Screenplay (Chinese with English subtitles):* Wang Peigong and Chen Kaige. *Director of Photography:* Zhao Fei. *Editor:* Zhao Xinxia. *Music:* Zhao Jiping. *Sound:* Tao Jing. *Production Designer:* Tu Juhua. *Special Effects:* Liu Shaochun. *Costumes:* Mo Xiaomin. *Running time:* 161 minutes. *MPAA Rating:* R.

CAST: Gong Li (Lady Zhao); Zhang Fengyi (Jing Ke); Li Xuejian (Ying Zheng, King of Qin); Sun Zhou (Dan, Prince of Yan); Lu Xiaohe (General Fan Yuqi); Wang Zhiwen (Marquis Changxin); Chen Kaige (Lu Buwei); Gu Yongfei (Queen Mother); Zhao Benshan (Gao Jianli); Ding Haifeng (Qin Wuyang); Pan Changjiang (Prison Official); Zhou Xun (Blind Girl).

LOS ANGELES TIMES, 12/17/99, Calendar/p. 24, Kevin Thomas

By 221 BC, after centuries of civil war, seven kingdoms became dominant in China. But the ruler of Qin, Ying Zheng, had been raised to believe he had an ancestral duty to unify all of China, and that was the year of his brutal conquest. He, in fact, succeeded, but what concerns Chen Kaige, in his magnificent and contemplative "The Emperor and the Assassin," is the enormous cost in terms of human suffering, even for Ying Zheng himself.

Chen's stunning film has the scope and grandeur of the traditional historical epic, yet the filmmaker plays against the expectations of the genre at every turn. He may show us thousands of troops massing for an assault—but not the assault itself. He repeatedly depicts the aftermath of bloodshed rather than dwelling on the blood being shed. This resolutely non-exploitative approach better allows Ying Zheng's reign of terror to sink in and to allow its implications to emerge, especially for the monolithic, totalitarian Communist regime that has ruled China for the last half century.

What, in essence, Chen has done is to endow Ying Zheng (Li Xuejian) and the other principals in his fate with Shakespearean dimensions. They are individuals of stature with the capacity for reflection and self-knowledge who may proceed with ruthlessness or naivete—or both—but ultimately come to realize the full motivation—and magnitude of their deeds and their awesome consequences. In short, Ying Zheng emerges as a genuinely tragic hero, not just another of history's many monsters. It may be a cliché to say so, but Chen has given history a human face, just as he did with mid-20th century China, the turbulent background for his masterful "Farewell, My Concubine."

No court in a Shakespearean tragedy could have more complicated relationships than that of Ying Zheng. The key factor in the ruler's life is that he was born in exile, in 259 BC, in the kingdom of Zhao, where his father was being held hostage until his death, at which time his son, at age 13, was allowed to ascend the throne of the kingdom of Qin.

Ying Zheng would look upon his childhood as a period of humiliation, although he knew many kindnesses from the Zhao people. His mother (Gu Yongfei) was, in fact, a Zhao princess and, even more significantly, he grew up with a Zhao servant girl who, as Lady Zhao (Gong Li), was to become the great love of his life. And the pivotal figure in his fate. Deceived by Ying Zheng as to his intentions for the Zhao people, Lady Zhao shifts her political and romantic allegiances to Jing Ke (Zhang Fengyi), of the kingdom of Yan, whose fate it is to attempt to assassinate the man who would be the first emperor of China. A subplot finds the Queen Mother, abetted by her lover (Wang Zhiwen), the effete, audacious Marquis Changxin, secretly opposing her son's rise to power, fearing that her own status would vanish along with her native kingdom. In the midst of all this growing turmoil is Ying Zheng's wise and humane prime minister, Lu Buwei (played by Chen Kaige himself), the one man with the strength of character to disapprove publicly of his ruler's rampant imperialist ambitions.

The fates of these individuals and, by extension, China itself, is played out more as a chamber drama than as a war movie, with, Chen, as already stated, suggesting the enormity of the resulting carnage without wallowing in it. Chen places the utmost demands on his actors, with Li showing the hysteria, fear and uncertainty that fueled Ying Zheng's ferocious campaign. His Ying Zheng is as emotionally extravagant as Gong's Lady Zhao is self-controlled, strong, outspoken but giving way to emotional display only under the most extreme prevarication. Zhang's assassin is a man who craves to live in peace and simplicity, a man who would like to put all killing behind him, but philosophically, if ruefully, accepts the inevitability of his destiny. Chen's three stars, all of them previous collaborators with the director, rise to the towering occasion, as do the supporting players.

"The Emperor and the Assassin" is a stirring, thought-provoking feat of filmmaking, accomplished in every facet. Throughout the film, Chen sustains a disturbing undertow, suggesting that the ultimate unification of nations is inevitable and, given human nature, inevitably tragic as well. In suggesting what we might be, Chen Kaige never loses sight of what we are.

NEW YORK POST, 12/17/99, p. 60, Jonathan Foreman

Like last year's "The Emperor's Shadow" "The Emperor and the Assassin" is a film about Ying Zheng, the warlord who bloodily unified the seven kingdoms of ancient China.

And like the earlier film, this one features large armies, fiery battle scenes and a beautiful woman being branded on the face.

But where last year's epic combined spectacular images with crude but vital storytelling, "The Emperor and the Assassin," by celebrated "Fifth Generation" writer-director Chen Kaige, meanders along in a confused, confusing way for what feels like hours.

Even the presence of actress Gong Li, one of the most beautiful women ever to appear on a movie screen, isn't enough to keep your attention off your watch.

Like most big-budget Chinese films, it's nicely photographed (by Zhao Fei), but the cinematography doesn't compare to Zhao Fei's own spectacular work on display in "Raise the Red Lantern."

Ying Zheng (Li Xuejian) is steadily conquering the other kingdoms of China, but he needs a pretext to invade the powerful state of Yan. Lady Zhao (Gong Li), his lover from childhood, comes up with a complex plan that involves her running off to Yan and persuading its king to send an assassin to make an attempt on Ying Zheng's life.

But while she's staying in Yan, Ying Zheng breaks a promise to her by invading Zhao, the country of her own birth, and slaughtering its women and children. Now she genuinely wants him dead.

Conveniently, she falls in love with Jing Ke (Zhang Fengyi), the Clint Eastwood-esque master assassin chosen to kill Ying Zheng. For some reason, Chen Kaige has his actors give performances in this film that are much more mannered and stilted to the Western eye than anything in his previous work.

Chen Kaige seems to be using the theme of unification by conquest to say something about modern Chinese politics—perhaps something about Taiwan or Tibet—only its not clear what.

NEWSDAY, 12/17/99, Part II/p. B17, John Anderson

That there exists an insoluble link between power and corruption has been a pet theme of Chen Kaige's, whether he's approached it obliquely ("King of the Children") or like a guided missile ("Farewell, My Concubine"). What distinguishes this not-so-remarkable worldview, however, is the director's conclusion that politics is inseparable from personality. That the abuse of power is ultimately personal.

Chen's latest, "The Emperor and the Assassin" certainly achieves monumental moments and possesses an epic sweep; Zhao Fei's gold-dusted cinematography and the great plains of Inner Mongolia imbue it with eye-popping grandeur. But in telling the story of Ying Zheng (Li Xuejian)—who, during the Third Century B.C., united the seven dominant kingdoms into the first unified China—the director again examines the magnificent through a telescoping lens of human foible, lust and egomania.

Under the mandate of his Qin ancestors, the king has set out to defeat and absorb the various states of China, including Zhao, where he and his wife-to-be, the beautiful Lady Zhao (Gong Li), spent their childhood. Although the emperor is a fearless warrior, one of his more effective weapons is persuasion; his speech about the rightness and inevitability of his crusade is a cross between Prince Hal's St. Crispin's Day speech and the turnip-eating oratory of Scarlett O'Hara.

The real Scarlett, however, is Gong Li, whose Lady Zhao will traverse the slaughter as if on roller skates and is no small-time Machiavelli herself. In order to get the neighboring kingdom of Yan to attempt an assassination of the king—thus giving him the provocation he needs to invade—Lady Zhao has her face branded (in a scene played for laughs), so she can then accompany home the freed Yan prince (Sun Zhou) and get his people to believe her tales of an imminent onslaught.

The plot thickens, occasionally to the point of obscurity: Once or twice, "The Emperor and the Assassin" seems to leap the tracks entirely, or at least jump a couple of connecting narrative threads. One is when Lady Zhao first joins her king, and immediately talks of leaving (huh?). The other involves the assassin chosen to execute the plot—who, of course, will be killed before pulling it off.

Having massacred an entire family of swordmakers, the assassin, Jing Ke (Zhang Fengyi) then watches as the lone surviving child—a blind girl—kills herself. Remorseful, he becomes a rather Christ-like ex-assassin, impoverished, barefoot and jeered when he tries to save a child thief from being steamed over a baker's cauldron. When he accidentally kills the child's tormenter and is jailed, he's found by Lady Zhao, who enlists Jing Ke in her plot only by making him love her, and hate the man who (he thinks) branded her.

What dictates the course of the emperor's actions are revelations at court—Chen Kaige himself playing the ousted prime minister Lu Buwei—that re-order all the emperor's assumptions about his ancestors, their mandate and his bloodline to the throne. That he's only spurred on—and made more ruthless—by these disclosures seems the height of irony to the director, who knows that the only thing propelling a prototypical butcher like Ying is an insatiable appetite for power—not ancestral mandates, royal obligation or the kind of common good achieved by killing the common people.

SIGHT AND SOUND, 8/00, p. 43, Richard Falcon

229 BC. King Ying Zheng of Qin wants to unify the seven warring Chinese states under his own rule as emperor. He captures the capital of the state of Han, defying his prime minister Lu Buwei. The main obstacle to unification is the powerful kingdom of Yan which Ying needs a pretext to invade. Lady Zhao, Ying's concubine whom he met during captivity in her home kingdom of Zhao, proposes to travel to Yan and contract an assassin to kill Ying Zheng. The attempt on his life by a Yan citizen will thus give Ying the excuse he needs for all-out war.

In Yan, Lady Zhao entrusts retired assassin Jing Ke with the job. Ying discovers from the Marquis Xhangxin, the queen mother's jester and lover, that he is the son of Lu Buwei, a revelation which endangers his right to the throne. Ying has the marquis killed and marches on

Zhao. In an attack on the Zhao capital, the city's children leap to their deaths rather than submit to Qin rule. Lady Zhao renounces Ying Zheng's cruelty and falls in love with Jing Ke. The assassin fails in his attempt to murder Ying and is killed. Ying Zheng succeeds in becoming the first emperor of China, but rules alone.

Along with fellow Fifth-Generation film maker Zhang Yimou, director Chen Kaige is best known among international arthouse audiences for his opulent visual style. But while delivering the exotic spectacle expected of Asian cinema by western audiences, Chen's films have also presented an oblique critique of the Communist authorities at home. (His 1993 epic *Farewell My Concubine*, for instance, with its bitter scenes set during the Cultural Revolution, was banned soon after opening in China.) In interviews about *The Emperor and the Assassin*, Chen has hinted at a connection between the quest for a united China pursued by Ying, the ambitious, murderous ruler of Qin, and the Chinese government's possible designs on Taiwan. But his latest film is weighted towards historical spectacle to such an extent that it's almost impossible to detect any contemporary subtext. Indeed, the involvement of the Chinese military in the films' battle scenes—unlike the CGI armies in *Gladiator,* the extras here are of the flesh-and-blood variety— suggests Chen has found favour at home with this account of the unification of China in the third century BC.

What remains in the mind are *The Emperor*'s expertly staged battle scenes reminiscent of Akira Kurosawa's *Ran* or even, in the film's most powerful sequence where the children of the Qin occupied Zhao leap to their deaths from the castle walls, the second of Fritz Lang's *Nibelungen* films *Kriemhild's Revenge* (1924). But in its more intimate scenes, the film falls short of the emotional peaks of Chen's past work and fails to gain our understanding of or empathy for such complex characters as Ying (whose motives for unifying China remain cloudy; you're never sure if they're noble or corrupt). In setting in train the intricate Shakespearean-like plot, Chen introduces a range of potentially fascinating figures, from the Prince of Yan, who plans to murder Ying Zheng, to the powerful general Fan Yuqi, whose loyalty is strained by Ying's escalating brutality. But as with the scant backstory provided about Ying's childhood spent captive in Zhao, Chen seems reluctant to yield much in the way of telling character details. Barely developed, the enigmatic figures who inhabit Chen's richly detailed *mise en scéne* make for a film whose key scenes, notably the climactic assassination attempt on Ying, lack any sense of tension or emotional resonance. The result recalls such stodgy Hollywood epics as *Demetrius and the Gladiators* (1954).

Chen punctuates the sumptuous spectacle with moments of uncomfortable cruelty: the samurai- like Jing Ke, for instance, is haunted by the suicide of a blind girl whose family he slaughtered and Lady Zhao (played by Gong Li) submits herself to a facial brand. But the film's failure to engage us reduces these moments to historical curiosities. Despite the entrancing Gong Li's subtle performance, her discreet, aestheticised facial scar only reminds us of her recent gig advertising cosmetics for L'Oréal.

TIME, 12/27/99, p. 186, Richard Corliss

In Hollywood these days, a spectacle is what some randy star makes of himself at 3 a.m. on Sunset Boulevard. American movies have lost the love of grandeur, of finding the heroic scale of historical figures. Chen Kaige to the rescue! China's longest-reigning angry young filmmaker has an eye for rapturous compositions on a huge and telling tapestry. His new film mixes DeMille and Dostoyevsky: the cast-of-thousands splendor of a biblical epic and the gnarled psychology of Chen's own *Farewell My Concubine*. And all in less time than a Stephen King prison drama.

The Emperor and the Assassin, set in the 3rd century B.C., relates the struggle of Ying Zheng (Li) to unify China and become its first emperor. His aims are honorable, his methods increasingly brutal; he might be the prototype for Lenin or Mao. Ying sends his lover Lady Zhao (Gong) to her Han homeland. Her mission is to find a professional killer (Zhang, in a potent turn) to fake an assassination attempt, whose "failure" will make Ying seem invincible to his adversaries. But Ying grows more ruthless, and the lady and the killer fall in love. Now they will try to put an end to the emperor's dynasty before it begins.

The film may confuse those unfamiliar with Chinese history, but never mind. Just pay heed to the glorious moviemaking. There is one scene that haunts the heart: an ethereally beautiful blind girl (Xun Zhou) kills herself after the assassin has eradicated the rest of her family. Few directors can create such indelible imagery; Chen does it in nearly every frame.

VILLAGE VOICE, 12/21/99, p. 156, Dennis Lim

China's Fifth Generation continues to work through its midlife crisis. Zhang Yimou retreats further from art house opulence (his modest inspirational tale, *Not One Less,* won him the Golden Lion at Venice this year); Chen Kaige, who came to international prominence with the exotic soap-operatics of *Farewell My Concubine,* presses on with hyperdesigned historical melodrama. While Chen's previous film, the ravishing opium hallucination *Temptress Moon,* was a boldly decadent pose, *The Emperor and the Assassin* is solid middlebrow entertainment, a vast period epic with an almost DeMillean taste for excess.

Like last year's *Emperor's Shadow,* the movie is set in the third century B.C. and concerns the power-crazed first emperor of China, Ying Zheng (Li Xuejian), a man obsessed with unifying the seven Chinese kingdoms under his rule (he considered it a mandate from ancestral gods). To justify the invasion of a neighboring state, the king and his lover, Lady Zhao (Gong Li), decide to engineer a fake attempt on his life. The plan is complicated by a revelation about his parentage that turns the king into a bloodthirsty maniac, and later by the dismayed Lady Zhao's increasingly close relationship with the brooding would-be killer (Zhang Fengyi). *The Emperor and the Assassin* alternates between thunderous, bloody set pieces and dense expository exchanges in lavish interiors—the elaborate imperial intrigue and incestuous backstories are outlined so methodically that they're not only easy to follow but tiresome. Chen is plainly in it for the spectacle. Aided by ever agile cinematographer Zhao Fei (who also shot *Sweet and Lowdown),* the director pulls off one dazzling combat scene after another, choreographing his cast of thousands with numbly impressive old-school pomp.

Also reviewed in:
CHICAGO TRIBUNE, 12/17/99, Friday/p. I, Michael Wilmington
NEW YORK TIMES, 12/17/99, p. E35, Stephen Holden
VARIETY, 5/17-23/99, p. 55, Derek Elley
WASHINGTON POST, 2/25/00, p. C1, Stephen Hunter

EMPTY MIRROR, THE

A Lions Gate Films release in association with Walden Woods Film Co., Ltd. *Producer:* David D. Johnson, M. Jay Roach, and William Dance. *Director:* Barry J. Hershey. *Screenplay:* Barry J. Hershey and R. Buckingham. *Story:* Barry J. Hershey. *Director of Photography:* Frederick Elmes. *Editor:* Marc Grossman. *Music:* John Frizzell. *Sound:* David Knuepper and Glenn T. Morgan. *Casting:* Judy Courtney. *Production Designer:* Tim Colohan. *Visual Effects:* David D. Johnson. *Costumes:* Melinda Eshelman. *Running time:* 119 minutes. *MPAA Rating:* Not Rated.

CAST: Norman Rodway (Adolf Hitler); Camilla Soeberg (Eva Braun); Peter Michael Goetz (Sigmund Freud); Doug McKeon (Typist); Glenn Shadix (Hermann Goehring); Joel Grey (Josef Goebbels).

LOS ANGELES TIMES, 5/7/99, Calendar/p. 8, Kevin Thomas

Barry J. Hershey's pretentious and boring "The Empty Mirror" imagines that Adolf Hitler did not commit suicide, at least not right away, but hung on in that bunker long enough to rant and rave as he reviews his life while he watches archival footage on a giant screen behind him.

Extracts from Leni Riefenstahl's "Triumph of the Will" and newsreels presenting Hitler exalting the masses amid pomp and ceremony are interspersed with Eva Braun's home movies, but as time marches on such glorifying imagery gives way to footage of German defeats on the battlefield and finally the inevitable concentration camp horrors. In the process Hitler (Norman Rodway) moves from arrogant leader exulting in his immeasurable Machiavellian evil to a defeated, pathetic old man.

To judge from this film, you would think that Hitler's psyche had never been probed before on the screen. But if you look at "Triumph of the Will" in its entirety, not just in the clips presented here, it will show you how effectively Hitler was able to sway vast numbers of people. Then watch Hans-Jurgen Syberberg's nine-hours-plus "Our Hitler: A Film From Germany," which insists on viewing Hitler as a product of German culture, history and mythology rather than as a crazed aberration, and finally Claude Lanzmann's Holocaust documentary "Shoah," also clocking in at more than nine hours, and you will get an idea of the magnitude of the man's evil, which also has been explored in countless other documentaries, night up to this year's Oscar-winning "The Last Days." It is hardly surprising therefore that Hershey's highly theatrical venture offers no new insights, even in Hitter's imaginary debate with Sigmund Freud.

As it progresses, however, the film becomes increasingly troubling and even offensive. That's because as conceived by Hershey and played by Rodway, a veteran member of the Royal Shakespeare Company, this film's remarkably eloquent and introspective Hitler becomes more and more Lear-like, in short a tragic figure. Hitler may have been complex, but he was above all evil and hardly deserving of the stature that tragedy confers. He triggered rather than embodied tragedy; the Holocaust, not Hitler, was tragic.

Rodway, whose resemblance to Hitler is slight at best, has stamina and passion—and not a little stolidity—but is not at all mesmerizing, which is what intimates like Albert Speer insisted over and over was so potent, so irresistible, about Hitler. In a much smaller role Joel Grey brings wit and a gleam of madness to his apt portrayal of Hitler's minister of propaganda, Joseph Goebbels. In mute, brief appearances Camilla Soeberg is too glamorous and beautiful as Eva Braun, and Peter Michael Goetz and Glenn Shadix have little opportunity to make much of an impression as Freud and Hermann Goering, respectively, and bare scant resemblance to them.

There's lots of flashy visuals as punctuation, but they simply serve to underline the theatricality of this entire endeavor, which belongs on a stage, if anywhere at all, rather than a screen in the first place. For a film that exalts the power of film, "The Empty Mirror" is far from cinematic.

NEW YORK POST, 5/7/99, p. 52, Rod Dreher

"Some will condemn me morally, but they cannot escape the power of my image!" fumes the protagonist of "The Empty Mirror."

Sadly, this is not the Pamela Anderson Lee biopic we've been lusting after, but just another movie about unbosomy mass murderer Adolf Hitler.

Norman Rodway is surely a fine actor, but he's plain ridiculous stomping around in a Fuhrer get-up, mouthing pretentious dialogue and pseudo-philosophical gasbaggery written for him by Barry J. Hershey, the film's director, and R. Buckingham.

"I am the Superman, the Teutonic knight on the quest for the Holy Grail!" says Hitler.

"Compared to you, Wagner was a minimalist!" says Goebbels (Joel Grey).

That sort of thing.

"The Empty Mirror" is a dark fantasia imagining a besieged Hitler, in his bunker after the war, ruminating on the failure of his project while dictating his memoir to his secretary (Doug McKeon).

He also presides over a hallucinatory salon, carrying on lengthy conversations with phantom images of Goebbels, Goehring (Glenn Shadix), Eva Braun (Camilla Soeberg) and, whaddaya know, Sigmund Freud (Peter Michael Goetz).

He's a talker, that Adolf. He thinks of himself as a composer, and Germany the symphony, except when he thinks of himself as a seducer, and Germany his lover. Oy.

Hershey ambitiously attempts to get into the mind of history's most fascinating villain, but the result is tedious, futile, even embarrassing. Great production design (chillingly effective, screening "Triumph of the Will" and Eva Braun's home movies in the background), but no movie that has Hitler sweetly dismissing blond children with, "Run along, my little golden Nordic nuggets" deserves to be taken seriously.

NEWSDAY, 5/7/99, Part II/p. B6, John Anderson

Could the timing be worse? Could the timing be better? We're in the midst of a high-brow Hitlerian renaissance—books, either biographical or philosophical, are coming out in bundles—his birthday was recently commemorated in Colorado with the murders of 15 people. We can't escape him, it seems. And we can't explain him.

But we keep trying, even if the excavation of Hitler's mind is usually a way of explaining ourselves. Do we need to know him? Should we try? Is silence the proper response to Hitler and his crimes? Should we take the Mel Brooks approach and assume that by laughing at Nazis we remove their power? Or, like Barry J. Hershey and his new film "The Empty Mirror," do we give Hitler a platform and debunk him on his own rhetorical turf?

Royal Shakespeare Company actor Norman Rodway looks so little like Hitler that when we first meet him in his bunker-like chamber—watching films of the real specimen addressing the multitudes at Nuremberg—we're not sure if what we're watching is some Aryan Nation maniac lost in obsessive fascination or a "real" Hitler remembering his triumphs. Or, perhaps, that we're in some territory in between. The uncertainty is engrossing. And the movie is as mad as its subject.

Along with Hitler in his subterranean quarters—the ante-chamber to hell, perhaps—is Josef Goebbels (Joel Grey), Hermann Goering (Glenn Shadix), Eva Braun (Camilla Soeberg), Sigmund Freud (Peter Michael Goetz) and a small crowd of Aryan children, all of whom create idealized caricatures of their real-life counterparts and act as a interchangeable Greek chorus to Hitler's seething reassessments of what went right and then went wrong. Basically, "Empty Mirror" is the interior monologue of a man progressively unhinged, even though Hershey allows Hitler enough lucidity to make his arguments.

The director is caught between making Hitler ridiculous—Rodway and Shadix, for instance, play their shared scenes very broadly—and wanting to let him excuse himself in the kind of truly appalling perversion of logic that marked the Thousand-Year Reich. As a result, the movie shifts and sways and each approach dilutes the other. In trying to capture visually the disintegration of Hitler's mind, Hershey also integrates some alarming effects among Rodway's performance and historic footage with the most affecting, as usual, being the photographic evidence of Hitler's atrocities.

Exploring Hitler's sexual anxieties and his frustrations as an artist ("Compared to you," Goebbel's says, "Wagner was a minimalist") come dangerously close to providing an alibi for his actions—or at least trying to provide an alibi. And that's where Hershey goes wildly astray, even while providing a kind of mirror for the audience to assess its own relationship with Adolf Hitler, the man who wouldn't go away.

VILLAGE VOICE, 5/11/99, p. 116, Jessica Winter

Press materials shriek that *The Empty Mirror* "defies the Hitler taboo" by camping out in what's apparently Hitler's bunker while the delusional Führer chats with ghosts from his past life. He lolls about in bed with Eva, talks shop with Goebbels (Joel Grey, looking like a bewildered kidnappee), and takes time out to watch a little *Triumph of the Will*. Those who stumble upon this monstrosity might recall the old *Kids in the Hall* bit "Censored Sketches," in which two members defend their suppressed skit "Hitler Fucks a Donkey" by arguing that, with the rise of neo-Nazism, such a sketch would present Hitler as "one bad customer." One can assert with all conviction that *The Empty Mirror* pulls off this feat.

Also reviewed in:
CHICAGO TRIBUNE, 5/14/99, Friday/p. K, Monica Eng
NEW REPUBLIC, 3/15/99, p. 26, Stanley Kauffmann
NEW YORK TIMES, 5/7/99, p. E23, Lawrence Van Gelder
VARIETY, 5/20-26/96, p. 33, Todd McCarthy

ENCOUNTERS IN THE THIRD DIMENSION

An N Wave Pictures release of an Iwerks Entertainment, Luminair and Movida presentation. *Executive Producer:* Ben Stassen. *Producer:* Charlotte Clay Huggins. *Director:* Ben Stassen. *Screenplay:* Kurt Frey and Ben Stassen. *Director of Photography:* Sean MacLeod Phillips. *Editor:* Sean MacLeod Phillips. *Music:* Louis Vyncke. *Casting:* Judy Taylor. *Production Designer:* Anthony Huerta. *Animation:* Jeremie Degruson and Sylvain Delaine. *Running time:* 45 minutes. *MPAA Rating:* Not Rated.

CAST: Stuart Pankin (Professor/Voice of MAX); Elvira (Herself); Harry Shearer (Narrator); Andrea Thompson (Ruth in the Booth).

LOS ANGELES TIMES, 2/26/99, Calendar/p. 20, Kathleen Craughwell

A large-format 3-D movie about the history of 3-D images on film sure sounds like a good idea, but ultimately "Encounter in the Third Dimension" is more a test of endurance than a history lesson or anything resembling entertainment.

The film begins in the make-believe Institute of 3-D Technology, a digitally created laboratory complete with the requisite absent-minded professor (played by Stuart Pankin) and plucky sidekick, in this case a wisecracking flying robot named Max.

The professor intends to educate the audience about the magic of 3-D technology with his latest invention, the Real-O-Vision, a gadget whose sole purpose seems to be to conjure up the outrageous television personality Elvira, Mistress of the Dark.

Things go awry with the Real-O-Vision, and while the professor tinkers behind the scenes, Max presents a more straightforward account of how 3-D images are created on film. Included in this segment is a re-creation of the Lumiere brothers' 1903 "L'Arrivee du Train" which literally scared turn-of-the-century audiences out of the theater, and a slew of fun clips from campy 3-D movie classics from Hollywood's 3-D heyday, the early 1950s.

Then it's back to the dreary, cavernous lab and what should be the highlight of "Encounter"—sneak peeks at the very latest applications of cutting-edge 3-D technologies, including a fleeting clip of the new theme park film "Terminator 2: 3-D." Unfortunately, it is this portion of the film that is the most tedious.

To be fair, much of the 3-D is impressive. But the filmmakers have chosen to use the technology to jolt and pummel the audience rather than dazzle and amaze. On a roller-coaster-like simulated trip to the center of the Earth, the film's effects are real enough to make you imagine that you are really moving (including a potential dose of motion sickness), but there's no real fun involved or any sense of where you're going on this ride.

The filmmakers have ballyhooed the fact that this is the first large-format film to open in both an institutional theater (the California Science Center) and commercial venues (two Edwards theaters) on the same day. The California Science Center has high standards about which films it will accept for exhibition—they have to be both entertaining and educational. Recently the center sparked controversy for turning away the 3-D romp "T-Rex: Back to the Cretaceous," which has been playing at commercial theaters for months but was deemed not learned enough.

But if "T-Rex" isn't scholarly, at least it's entertaining. "Encounter" strikes out on both counts. The entertainment value is almost nil—most of the jokes fall flat, and the entire plot line involving Elvira seems pointless—and what little information is offered is hardly worth the exercise. What it all amounts to in the end is a high-tech mess.

It takes more than effects to sustain any type of film, even one in which the star, in this case 3-D, is itself a novelty.

NEW YORK POST, 3/31/99, p. 72, Rod Dreher

Nobody goes to 3-D IMAX films looking for a great yarn, but "Encounter in the Third Dimension" offers a narrative that's paltry even by the minimal standards of the genre. Fans who go in for the awesome 3-D IMAX visual effects can expect the usual cornucopia of cool flying objects and queasy-making illusions, but the storytelling is beside the point at best, and frequently annoying.

In this 40-minute feature, Stuart Pankin plays a goofy professor who claims to have a perfect 3-D system called "Real-O-Vision." We visit him in his lab, where he prepares to test the gizmo by having it create a virtual-reality version of the Halloween beer shill Elvira, Mistress of the Dark (as herself).

Real-O-Vision goes kaflooey, and while the slapsticky professor works on it, he enjoins his cutesy robot assistant M.A.X. to entertain the audience with a history of 3-D filmmaking.

M.A.X. (voiced by Pankin) gives a diverting tour through 19th-century stereoscopy, through the 1950s heyday of 3-D goofy-glasses creature features, on to the present. The film uses clips from old movies, as well as several eye-popping segments from contemporary 3-D flicks like James Cameron's "Terminator 2: 3-D."

A roller-coaster ride through "the center of the earth" is pretty amazing, though I had to take my 3-D bandeau—specs off several times to keep my dinner down.

"Encounter in the Third Dimension" is little more than a special-effects show reel that plays like an amusement-park ride. This wacky whirligig approach may be enough for kids, but 3-D IMAX technology has been employed with much more interesting results in, for example, nature documentaries and the narrative feature "Across the Sea of Time."

The hyped-up finale of "Encounter in the Third Dimension" features pop-Goth thrush Elvira warbling a bland pop tune about a haunted house. It's disappointing in any dimension.

Also reviewed in:
CHICAGO TRIBUNE, 3/31/99, Tempo/p.1, Mark Caro
NEW YORK TIMES, 3/31/99, p. E5, Janet Maslin
VARIETY, 3/1-7/99, p. 80, Lael Loewenstein

END OF THE AFFAIR, THE

A Columbia Pictures release of a Stephen Woolley production. *Producer:* Stephen Wooley and Neil Jordan. *Director:* Neil Jordan. *Screenplay:* Neil Jordan. *Based on the novel by:* Graham Greene. *Director of Photography:* Roger Pratt. *Editor:* Tony Lawson. *Music:* Michael Nyman. *Music Editor:* Michael Connell. *Sound:* David Stephenson. *Sound Editor:* Mark Auguste. *Casting:* Susie Figgis. *Production Designer:* Anthony Pratt. *Art Director:* Chris Seagers. *Set Decorator:* Joanne Woollard and John Bush. *Special Effects:* Yves de Bono. *Costumes:* Sandy Powell. *Make-up:* Christine Beveridge. *Stunt Coordinator:* Greg Powell. *Running time:* 105 minutes. *MPAA Rating:* R.

CAST: Ralph Fiennes (Maurice Bendrix); Stephen Rea (Henry Miles); Julianne Moore (Sarah Miles); Heather Jay Jones (Henry's Maid); James Bolam (Mr. Savage); Ian Hart (Mr. Parkis); Samuel Bould (Lance Parkis); Cyril Shaps (Waiter); Penny Morrell (Bendrix' Landlady); Simon Turner (Doctor Gilbert); Jason Isaacs (Father Smythe); Deborah Findlay (Miss Smythe); Nicholas Hewetson (Chief Warden); Jack McKenzie (Chief Engineer).

CHRISTIAN SCIENCE MONITOR, 12/3/99, p. 15, David Sterritt

The *End of the Affair* comes from Neil Jordan, who established himself as a master of screen surprises with "The Crying Game" seven years ago. His new movie is adapted from a respected novel by Graham Greene, retaining the book's mixture of sensuality and spirituality while making various changes to condense, and streamline the story. The result is an unconventional drama that begins as a sexually explicit love story and ends as a sober reflection on the power of faith.

Ralph Fiennes plays an English author who hires a detective to investigate the life of a married woman (Julianne Moore) he had an affair with during the World War II era. Expecting to learn the sordid details of a subsequent romance she's had, he instead discovers why she abruptly stopped their own relationship years earlier. The answer hinges on a time when he was almost killed in a London air raid, leading her to promise God she'd sacrifice her love in return for his safety. Although she wasn't a religious person until the moment she made this vow, her leap of faith has gathered momentum and become a guiding force in her life—which her former lover finds impossible to understand until much later, when he witnesses a healing that even his skeptical sensibility finds impossible to deny.

Jordan hasn't been a religious filmmaker in the past, so the spiritual interests of "The End of the Affair" mark an unexpected turn in his career. It's hard to question his sincerity, though, or his apparent desire to prompt serious thought with this movie. Excellent acting by Fiennes and Moore further enhance the picture, ably assisted by Stephen Rea as the heroine's colorless husband.

Some viewers may question Jordan's decision to make parts of the film sexually graphic enough to deserve a hard R rating, but others will find this outweighed by the celebration of religious faith that closes the story.

LOS ANGELES TIMES, 12/3/99, Calendar/p. 4, Kenneth Turan

Handsomely mounted, literate, emotionally sophisticated, "The End of the Affair" has everything a period romance should have, including a score by Michael Nyman and passionate performances by stars Ralph Fiennes and Julianne Moore. But to call this brooding, complex film simply a romance is to miss a good bit of the point.

"Affair" comes by its troubling qualities honestly, both from the 1951 Graham Greene novel it's based on and the moody sensibility of writer-director Neil Jordan, whose previous films include "The Butcher Boy," "Interview With the Vampire," "Mona Lisa" and "The Crying Game." Jordan has adroitly pruned and revised the original, in ways both substantial and specific—for instance, switching a key facial blemish from one character to another—to make it fit smoothly on screen.

Though love motivates its principals, "The End of the Affair" is more concerned with the corrosive power of jealousy and other dark, torturous byways of romantic attachment, as well as how destructive it can be when, as one character admits, your desire is nearer hatred than love and you measure the strength of passion by how far jealousy extends.

Yet even saying that doesn't completely describe "Affair," for a good part of the story, as was frequently the case with the Roman Catholic Greene's more serious works, deals with matters of the spirit, with questions of faith and belief that play an increasingly crucial role as events unfold.

And because protagonist Maurice Bendrix (Fiennes) is himself a novelist, and because this is said to be one of Greene's most personal books (he dedicated it "To C.," code for Catherine Walston, a married American with whom he had what biographer Norman Sherry called "the greatest literary affair of this century"), the film also deals from the inside with what it means to be a writer. "Greene said that there was a splinter of ice in the heart of every novelist," Jordan said in a recent interview, and that aspect of creativity is very much on the screen.

"The End of the Affair" introduces Bendrix at his typewriter, a glass of whiskey near at hand, writing and remembering. "This is a diary of hate," he begins, but knowing whom he truly hates and why is a piece of knowledge that is revealed only gradually and within the context of a carefully worked out chain of events.

Bendrix flashes back to 1946 when, on a rainy night in London, he runs into a distraught and soaked acquaintance named Henry Miles (a wonderfully restrained and subdued Stephen Rea). In a rare act of charity, Bendrix helps the man home, where Miles tells him he's worried about his wife, Sarah (Moore). Perhaps she's having an affair.

It has been two years since Bendrix has heard Sarah's name, but for the five years before that, he and Sarah had been engaged in the most all-consuming of liaisons, one that she suddenly broke off without giving a reason. "Love doesn't end just because we don't see each other" is what she told him in one of the story's signature lines, but for someone like Bendrix, that was hardly enough.

Bendrix, as written by both Greene and Jordan and marvelously played by Fiennes (who seems almost born to the part), is a man adept at self-torture, self-pity and self-absorption. His love for Sarah is genuine and touching, but instead of elevating him it makes Bendrix almost monstrous in his heedless obsession, in his willingness, even eagerness to make life as miserable for everyone else as it is for him.

Latching on to Miles' despair, Bendrix offers to pose as Sarah's disaffected lover (which in fact he is) and hire a private detective to shadow her movements. Miles is offended by the idea, but, without telling the husband, Bendrix puts it into action anyway.

This brings the hangdog Parkis (excellently portrayed by Ian Hart) and his 12-year-old son Lance (Samuel Bould) onto the case, watching Sarah and reporting to Bendrix, who, far from having forgotten her, uses this situation as a reason to reestablish contact with the woman he is still desperately in love with.

"The End of the Affair" goes back and forth between the now of the detective's investigation and the then of heedless passion, when the dangers of wartime London added a frisson of excitement to the already torrid encounters between Sarah and Bendrix (evocatively shot by Roger Pratt with enough nudity to make them convincing). Both the events that triggered the breakup and their strange aftermath are revealed in the film's own good time.

Fiennes and Moore are two of the most impressive screen actors, and they have excellent chemistry together, as his fatalistic personality interacts splendidly with her warmer, more human but in some ways even more complex and unknowable persona.

Collaborating again with cinematographer Pratt, editor Tony Lawson, production designer Anthony Pratt and costume designer Sandy Powell, Jordan, a sometime novelist himself, has beautifully crafted this film with the cool novelist's sensibility he so admires in Greene. Both adult and melodramatic, a bit of a weepie alongside its sharp insights, it shows what Greene called "ordinary corrupt human love" in a clear and unapologetic light.

NEW STATESMAN, 2/14/00, p. 43, Jonathan Romney

How true to the text does a literary adaptation need to be? If the original is a novel about infidelity, then surely it's quite proper that a film should cheat on its source. Yet perhaps it takes a certain sort of cheating, a thoroughgoing formal boldness. If, on the other hand, you aim for a realistic evocation of a book's imaginative world yet make wilful narrative changes, as Neil Jordan does in his version of Graham Greene's *The End of the Affair,* then you might be justly accused of cheating not so much the book as the A-level students who may be using your film as a revision crib.

Jordan's film is a dutiful, honest rendering of Greene's 1951 novel—up to a point. It renders the place and period, wartime London, atmospherically but concretely; it honours its characters and gives them a plausible inner life and dignity; it even attempts to preserve the novel's complex structure of flashbacks and repetitions. It's serious, solid Greene—until Jordan decides to make the story fit the requirements of upmarket art-house romance.

Both novel and film are narrated by the novelist Bendrix (Ralph Fiennes), who recalls his affair with Sarah Miles (Julianne Moore), the wife of a stolid civil servant (Stephen Rea, giving his usual melancholy a rich new inflection of staid English gravitas). Obsessively angry at the affair's abrupt termination, Bendrix contrives to put a detective on Sarah's case; he assumes that she left him for another man, but discovers that the truth, a matter of sacrifice and religious faith, is more complex and ultimately more painful.

If it's the job of a literary adaptation to make you think that's exactly how you imagined it, then the film's first half is very good. Jordan avoids the gorblimey Blitz clichés and makes Greene's theatre of amorous war, centred around Clapham Common, drably unpopulated, the workaday place where literary passions would brew. Some critics have found Fiennes bloodless as Bendrix, but you can believe in his self-consumed, cerebral dandy in bookish solid fabrics. Moore is less convincing, doing a Meryl Streep routine with her vampishly sensual Home Counties accent. The grist of her performance is in the lascivious intelligence of her looks during the affair: the film capitalises fully on the fact that it is obliged to communicate through looks and carefully posed gestures, where the novel can simply imply passion and its movements.

You also believe in these poised, articulate people having hot, urgent sex: reckless screwing as the bombs drop, a tussle on the floor while a husband is walking up the stairs. The book must have seemed shocking, as well as truthful, in its time; today we may be even more alarmed to imagine that sex, let alone adultery, went on in 1940s Britain at all. No wonder the censors gave the film an 18 certificate: not for the sexual content itself, one imagines, but because the flesh is framed by sensible ration stockings and trouser braces.

The film is good on the hypocritical seediness that Greene limns around English sexuality: a meeting with James Bolan's horribly delicate detective agency head is a grim evocation of our culture of "discretion". But when Jordan, in the film's second half, attempts to recast the story for contemporary sensibility, then things go wrong. The couple, foiled by providence in the book, here gets a second chance in the form of a romantic sojourn in Brighton, as if today's audiences could only countenance an affair with a fully romantic pay-off to offset the Catholic anguish.

But, for Greene, the point is that Bendrix and Sarah always have to reckon with a jealous God, with whom she makes a pact of sacrifice after Bendrix is caught in a bomb blast (the blast is Jordan's show-stopper, a slow-motion routine that too literally plays up the notion of fall from grace). Jordan ruinously irons out the kinks in Greene's religious thematics. In the novel, Sarah has a sort of confessor in reverse: Smythe, a committed atheist who she hopes will offer instruction in rejecting God. But Jordan's Smythe is a personable young priest, while the facial blemish that torments Smythe in the novel is here transferred to a schoolboy, leading to a payoff that is conventionally sentimental, to say the least. Greene ends with an agonised Bendrix entertaining the possibility that he may yet come to believe in the possibility of miracles; Jordan ends by suggesting the possibility of a miracle, quite simply.

It's a subtle difference, but a crucial one, and it inflects our understanding of what the whole story is about. The novel is about how faith affects, even tarnishes, earthly love. The film is simply about love, and the theological underpinning is reduced to religiose flavouring. Sarah ends as an elegantly ailing tragic muse bathed in ennobling light. (And doesn't Jordan just know how lightning suits Moore's profile?) Bendrix may feel agonised straitened emotion (Michael Nyman's score is sharply suggestive of passions surging against the straitjackets of Englishness and intelligence), but he is never allowed the more complex fury and intellectual contradictoriness that make up Greene's Bendrix. In fact, you suspect, he's probably not half the writer.

NEW YORK, 12/13/99, p. 72, Peter Rainer

Neil Jordan's *The End of the Affair* has a hushed, spectral atmosphere more appropriate to a horror film than to a period British romance, but the mood is not unsuited to its source, Graham Greene's 1951 sin-and-redemption novel about an acidulous novelist and the wife of a meek civil servant with whom he has a soulful, crazy-making affair. The result is a bit like *Brief Encounter* meets *Tales From the Crypt;* the film has an impressive, and oppressive, weightiness. Ralph Fiennes, as the novelist, seems more animated than usual, maybe because, for a change, he's playing someone who doesn't look drip-dried. Venom becomes him. Julianne Moore, her skin alarmingly alabaster, works up a full repertoire of impassioned sidelong glances; as her poor-soul husband, who spends a fair amount of his time standing umbrellaless in the rain, Stephen Rea wilts impressively.

NEW YORK POST, 12/3/99, p. 51, Jonathan Foreman

"The End of the Affair" is an attempt to make an old-fashioned romantic weepie out of Graham Greene's novel of the same name.

But the characters are so unsympathetic, the adulterous love affair at the heart of the story so joyless, and the three main performances so mannered that it's hard to feel anything but disappointment and boredom by the time the picture grinds to a mystical ending.

It doesn't help that the flashback-filled structure is so confusing, and that it never stops raining.

But the main problem with the film is that writer-director Neil Jordan seems to think that upper-middle class English people in the 1940s were miserable all of the time, even when they made love. As a result, none of his main characters evince even a tiny amount of the life that animated Celia Johnson and Trevor Howard in "Brief Encounter."

Instead, they walk around looking as though the director's cramped notion of period atmosphere has forced them to don underwear several sizes too small.

Indeed, there are moments, thanks to Jordan's excessively spare dialogue and the actors' expressionless delivery, when this film could almost be a spoof of 1940s films like "Encounter," the David Lean classic. Dreadful, overwrought music by Michael Nyman that telegraphs every emotionally significant moment doesn't help.

The film opens in 1949 with the novelist Maurice Bendrix (Ralph Fiennes) telling us, as he types, that "this is a diary of hate." Then it flashes back to a wet night in 1946 when he sees Henry Miles (Stephen Rea) walking in the rain.

Miles is a civil servant, whose wife Sarah (Julianne Moore) had an affair with Bendrix during World War II.

Miles confides to Bendrix that he suspects his wife of having a lover, which inspires Bendrix to hire Parkis (Ian Hart), a private detective, to follow her around. Bendrix also starts seeing Sarah again, though he's still bitter about the way she ended their affair.

There follow a series of flashbacks to the beginning of their relationship in 1939, and flash-forwards to Sarah's death in 1946. In none of them do you get any sense of what drew the lovers to each other, although it's supposed to be more than mere sexual chemistry.

The key scene—and it's a brilliantly executed piece of filmmaking—is a wartime incident in which a German flying bomb explodes at Bendrix's house just after he and Sarah have made love.

The blast leaves Bendrix apparently dead on the staircase and prompts Sarah's turn to a mystical Catholicism.

Fiennes is believable as the obsessive lover who never, ever smiles. Moore, speaking with an unusually decent English accent, is less morose than he is—at least her character seems to get some physical pleasure out of their couplings—but there's something so hardworking about her performance that Sarah's story doesn't move you.

And Stephen Rea plays Henry Miles as a stereotypically dull civil servant in a shockingly one-note performance from such an accomplished actor.

NEWSDAY, 12/3/99, Part II/p. B7, Gene Seymour

It's the rain that comes down in three-ply unrelenting sheets over the principal male characters in "The End of the Affair" that makes you wonder whether Neil Jordan is kidding or not.

Audiences familiar with Jordan's previous films, notably "The Crying Game" (1992) and "The Butcher Boy" (1997), know him to be a writer-director compelled to mess with their conventional expectations of a feature film. And yet, here is Jordan making what seems to be the most conventional of British melodramas—the World War II romance—with the most conventional trappings imaginable. To wit: swirling string music, stiff-upper-lip dialogue and, as noted, London monsoons that all but swamp those moments when Something Significant is about to happen.

It's just such a downpour that comes early in this adaptation of Graham Greene's 1951 novel. Novelist Maurice Bendrix (Ralph Fiennes) happens to be taking a stroll in this wet weather (go figure), when he comes upon Henry Miles (Stephen Rea), a government bureaucrat whose wife, Sarah (Julianne Moore), has been late in getting home.

Unbeknownst to dour, prim Henry, dour, passionate Maurice is still recovering from the psychic wounds suffered a few years before during the war, when Sarah, suddenly and unaccountably, broke off their adulterous affair. It's only now that Henry suspects Sarah of cheating. Yet he stops short of hiring a private detective to follow her around.

Bendix, however, has no such qualms. On his own and for his own obsessive reasons, he hires a sleuth (Ian Hart in a neat, polished turn of a familiar archetype) to shadow Sarah. The findings lead Bendix to somewhat outrageous conclusions, including the possibility that her Other Man is a Catholic priest.

Sarah herself tries to explain things to Maurice, who is too petulantly hurt to listen.

But he does notice, as do we, that she's got a pretty bad cough. When a major character coughs like that in the first reel, it doesn't take a great imaginative leap to figure that she won't make it to the last reel. Jordan must know this. Once again, you ask: Is he kidding? Because it's Neil Jordan we're talking about, let's give him the benefit of the doubt and assume that he is goosing these melodramatic conventions on purpose.

When the whole story of Maurice and Sarah's affair is pieced together through flashbacks, Greene's vision of the mysteries of religious faith and its ambiguous, sometimes harsh effect on others comes into focus as it rarely does in other adaptations of his work.

Maybe Jordan believed such immersion in stylized mood and overheated plot would give his film the texture of a fever dream; perhaps even semi-rapture. If so, I don't think he quite pulls it off. Melodrama trumps vision here, as it tends to do in movies. Still, it's not the fault of the actors. Fiennes' hooded melancholy and simmering intensity perfectly capture the Greene patina. (Yes, he gets on your nerves with his whining and petulance. But he's supposed to.) Moore and Rea are likewise effective in modulating their respective characters' emotional levels.

Though not Jordan's best, "The End of the Affair" is cozy and absorbing in its own right to make it—well, a good rainy-day movie. I also figure that if and when I get my own repertory movie house, I'm using this baby as a lead-in to "Dogma."

SIGHT AND SOUND, 2/00, p. 46, Philip Kemp

London, 1946. Writer Maurice Bendrix encounters civil servant Henry Miles on Clapham Common. Maurice recalls how in 1939, just before the outbreak of war, he had begun a passionate affair with Henry's wife Sarah. It lasted until 1944. One day, when the lovers were in Maurice's flat, a bomb hit the house and knocked him unconscious. Immediately afterwards Sarah ended the affair without explanation. Now, hearing that Henry suspects Sarah of adultery, Maurice undertakes to investigate on his behalf. He visits a private detective who puts his operative Parkis on the case.

Sarah phones Maurice. They meet for lunch but his resentment drives her away. They're observed by Parkis and his young son Lance whose face is blemished by a strawberry birthmark. Parkis learns Sarah regularly visits a man called Smythe who later proves to be a Catholic priest. Parkis enters Sarah's house and steals her journal; from it Maurice learns that Sarah, a lapsed Catholic, had made a promise to God when the bomb fell. Thinking Maurice dead, she vowed never to see him again if his life was restored. She has been seeing Smythe for religious instruction.

Maurice rushes to see Sarah; she tries to evade him but her desire is too strong. They become lovers again and go away to Brighton together. Henry shows up and confronts them. He tells Maurice that Sarah is fatally ill, and invites him to move into their house. After a long illness, Sarah dies. At her funeral service, Maurice sees Parkis, who tells him Sarah kissed young Lance on his blemished cheek one day; since then his birthmark has vanished.

Should a film adapted from a novel (or play, or whatever) be judged purely on its merits as a film, without reference to its source material? Ideally, perhaps, yes. Yet when a film turns out as bland as Neil Jordan's The End of the Affair, despite its writer-director's evidently sincere admiration for Graham Greene's novel, it surely makes sense to invoke the original in trying to work out what went so wrong.

It's not just a matter of cinematic prettification, though that enters into it. In a crucial scene in the novel the two former adulterous lovers, Maurice Bendrix (played by Ralph Fiennes in the film) and Sarah Miles (Julianne Moore), meet in a church. It's cold and dark and comfortless. There's a "hideous statue of the virgin," writes Greene. In the film, the church has become spacious and opulent. The draperies are bright with blue and crimson, the rood screen a glowing expanse of gold. Hazy sunlight streams through the stained glass. This is symptomatic: an awkward, edgy, tormented novel has been upholstered for comfort. Unexpectedly, Edward Dmytryk's plodding 1954 black-and-white version, starring a badly miscast Van Johnson opposite Deborah Kerr, gets closer to the visual feel of it.

But the problem goes deeper than that. The key character in Greene's novel is a jealous, possessive lover. He's devious, underhand and calculating; he lies in wait, takes unfair advantage; he'll pull every trick in the book to prevent the woman he wants from succumbing to a rival. If necessary, he'll even kill her. This schemer isn't the writer Bendrix (a semi-autobiographical portrait by Greene), but Greene's personal and highly unorthodox version of the Roman Catholic God—a character who in Jordan's film has been marginalised, in places almost written out. Much of the power of the novel lies in the sense of God's trap closing inexorably, of every potential exit being quietly shut off as soon as glimpsed. In the film the trap is sprung open and the mice are out cavorting.

The central turning point, in the film as in the novel, is when Maurice reads Sarah's journal and discovers why she ended their affair so abruptly. He imagined she'd tired of him and, since her marriage to dull civil servant Henry (Stephen Rea) was a sexless shell, found herself another man. Instead it turns out she believed him killed by a flying bomb, and praying desperately, offered God a swap: bring him back to life and I'll give him up for ever. It's left ambiguous whether Maurice was really dead, or simply unconscious; but the vow is absolute. Greene's petty-minded version of the Deity sees to that. Each time either Maurice or Sarah tries to break the promise, God the supreme chessmaster moves deftly to block them. The lovers are kept apart until Sarah's death. Thereby, Greene implies, her soul is saved for the Church and she even becomes a miracle-working saint.

Whatever you think of this as theology—and many people, believers and non believers, have found it pretty repellent—it does at least give the story a consistent *raison d'être*. But Jordan's film blows it wide open. A few changes apart, he stays reasonably close to the original until the reading of the journal. He even preserves one of Greene's most Hardyesque ironies, when Maurice's own schemes are turned against him. Sarah, her resistance worn down, is packing to leave her husband at the very time when Maurice confronts Henry with (as he thinks) evidence of her affair with another man. Broken, Henry comes home and implores Sarah not to desert him, and she stays.

All this goes for nothing in the second half of the film. Having read the journal, Maurice rushes to Sarah. She resists briefly, then succumbs and they fall into bed together. Next we find them jaunting off for a dirty weekend in Brighton, where Henry bizarrely pops up to catch them together in the Pavilion. With this episode the whole fabric of the film coarsens: we even get a cliched shot of the grinning couple whirled around together at a fun fair. Perhaps Jordan fears modern audiences will find the concept of voluntary chastity incomprehensible, but these tinkerings make nonsense of everything that's gone before. What matters isn't that his film is not true to the book no reason why a film should have to be, after all—but that the film isn't true to itself.

One or two other changes seem ill thought-out. The facial strawberry birthmark that in the novel afflicts a different character is transferred to Lance, the son of the private detective Parkis (Ian Hart) Maurice hires to spy on Sarah. Since Parkis takes the boy (Samuel Bould) with him in his work, where his aim is to stay inconspicuous, this makes him not simply a pitiable figure but an incompetent fool. And it's scarcely credible that in 1946 an ultra-respectable senior civil servant like Henry would invite his wife's lover to join in a *ménage à trois*, even if the wife was dying. (In the novel Maurice move in after Sarah's death, which today might raise eyebrows for a different reason. Still, the love tangle from Greene's own life was bizarre enough by some accounts: Harry Walston, the husband of Greene's lover Catherine Walston, and Greene's wife Vivien both knew of and tacitly condoned the lovers' affair.)

It would be unjust to imply that *The End of the Affair* is some kind of write off. In the first half of the film Jordan skillfully sustains his three-way time scheme, switching from post-war to pre-war to wartime with deft visual economy and no loss of narrative clarity. At times, too, the performances all but carry it. Ralph Fiennes, fresh from *Onegin* has perhaps played too many guilt stricken lovers just recently; but Stephen Rea, with his doleful jowls, makes an ideal Henry, and Julianne Moore gives a vibrantly sensual performance, movingly convincing as a woman so selfless in her passion she would make the agonising bargain to have her lover alive even if forever unattainable.

But nothing can overcome the gap at the heart of the film. The story, Jordan has been quoted as saying, "is about the question of how far love goes between people. If somebody says, 'I will love you forever,' do you know how far they will carry that promise through?" At best, this is an oversimplification, at worst a total misreading. The story, at least as Greene conceived it, is about religion, seen not as a solace but as an affliction, presided over by a Deity who, for all Greene's Catholicism, has a lot in common with the grim Lutheran God of Ingmar Bergman: the malignant spider on the wall, watching and spinning his web. There's little place for such an implacable being in the comfortable, sunlit church of Jordan's film.

VILLAGE VOICE, 12/7/99, p. 139, J. Hoberman

The End of the Affair is Neil Jordan's technically accomplished adaptation of the time-shifting 1951 novel that put author Graham Greene on the cover of *Time* with the tantalizing headline "Adultery can lead to sainthood."

The End of the Affair is not exactly Bressonian, but it does open with its writer-hero, Maurice Bendrix (Ralph Fiennes), typing his "diary of hate." Brooding over his convoluted extramarital wartime affair with the mysterious Sarah (Julianne Moore), Bendrix is already on his road to

Damascus. In a flashback to a point some years after Sarah inexplicably left him, Bendrix meets her clueless husband Henry (Stephen Rea) to discover that, although unaware of the earlier affair, Henry now believes that Sarah is deceiving him with someone else. Madly jealous Bendrix hires his own detective (played with comic cockney tact by Ian Hart), and the action hopscotches through time to illuminate their relationship and his investigation.

Unlike the 1955 *End of the Affair*, which straightened out Greene's chronology (and starred Hollywood's adulteress of choice, Deborah Kerr), Jordan's remake is extraordinarily fluid in handling the narrative's temporal flights. But the erotic chemistry is tepid, despite Moore's characteristically bold performance. She gets the big lines and bravely held-back tears—although Jordan cancels out her restraint by contriving to set nearly every big scene in a seemingly tropical monsoon—while Fiennes is glumly downcast. No stranger to supernaturalism, Jordan is similarly lachrymose when he might have been sardonic. For all its obvious psychoanalytic implications, his wacky romantic triangle lost me long before it crawled to its spiritualist conclusion. (About halfway through I began to imagine it as it might have been directed by Douglas Sirk as a vehicle for Jane Wyman and Rock Hudson.)

The End of the Affair's protracted windup affords ample opportunity to ponder its unsubtle message. Greene's parable not only insists that faith is belief in the invisible but strenuously suggests that monotheism exists to police love—a notion common to cultural revolutionaries as otherwise disparate as Saint Paul and Wilhelm Reich, neither of whom clothed it in such sanctimonious kitsch.

Also reviewed in:
CHICAGO TRIBUNE, 12/24/99, Friday/p. A, Michael Wilmington
NEW REPUBLIC, 12/27/99, p. 24, Stanley Kauffmann
NEW YORK TIMES, 12/3/99, p. E1, Janet Maslin
NEW YORKER, 12/6/99, p. 173, David Denby
VARIETY, 11/22-28/99, p. 83, Emanuel Levy
WASHINGTON POST, 1/7/00, p. C5, Rita Kempley
WASHINGTON POST, 1/7/00, Weekend/p. 36, Desson Howe

END OF DAYS

A Universal Pictures and Beacon Pictures release. *Executive Producer:* Marc Abraham and Thomas A. Bliss. *Producer:* Armyan Bernstein and Bill Borden. *Director:* Peter Hyams. *Screenplay:* Andrew W. Marlowe. *Director of Photography:* Peter Hyams. *Editor:* Steven Kemper and Jeff Gullo. *Music:* John Debney. *Music Editor:* Tom Carlson. *Sound:* Gene S. Cantamessa and (music) Alan Myerson. *Sound Editor:* Mike Wihoit. *Production Designer:* Richard Holland. *Casting:* Jackie Burch. *Art Director:* Charlie Daboub. *Set Designer:* Al Hobbs, Mike Stassi, Julia Levine, Greg Berry, and Maya Shimoguchi. *Set Decorator:* Gary Fettis. *Special Effects:* Thomas L. Fisher. *Visual Effects:* Eric Durst. *Costumes:* Bobbie Mannix. *Make-up:* Jeff Dawn. *Creature Design:* Stan Winston and John Rosengrant. *Make-up Special Effects:* Shannon Shea. *Stunt Coordinator:* Steve M. Davison. *Running time:* 115 minutes. *MPAA Rating:* R.

CAST: Arnold Schwarzenegger (Jericho Cane); Gabriel Byrne (The Man); Kevin Pollak (Chicago); Robin Tunney (Christine York); C.C.H. Pounder (Detective Marge Francis); Rod Steiger (Father Kovak); Derrick O'Connor (Thomas Aquinas); Miriam Margolyes (Mabel); Udo Kier (Head Priest); Victor Varnado (Albino); Michael O'Hagan (Cardinal); Mark Margolis (Pope); David Weisenberg (OB/GYN); Rainer Judd (Christine's Mother); Luciano Miele (Pope's Advisor); Jack Shearer (Kellogg); Eve Sigall (Old Woman); Robert Lesser (Carson); Lloyd Garroway and Gary Anthony Williams (Utility Workers); John Nielson (Hospital Cop); Yannis Bogris (Skateborder); Elliot Goldwag (Thomas' Doctor); Elaine Corral Kendall (Anchor); Denice D. Lewis (Emily); Rebecca Renee Olstead (Amy); Matt Gallini (Monk 1/Intruder); Marc Lawrence (Old Man); Van Quattro (Satin Priest); Chuck Tamburro

(Helicopter Pilot); Lynn Marie Sager (Head Priest Wife); Linda Pine (Head Priest Daughter); David Franco (Assistant Priest); Steven Kramer (Businessman); Melissa Mascara (Businessman's Wife); John Timothy Botka (Cop at Thomas'); Walter von Huene (Motorman); Michael Rocha (Father Mike).

LOS ANGELES TIMES, 11/24/99, Calendar/p. 1, Eric Harrison

In Arnold Schwarzenegger's new loud, goofy, roller-coaster ride of a movie, Satan shows himself to be such an incompetent boob that, if these truly are the last days, we at least know the devil isn't to blame.

In "End of Days," Lucifer travels to Manhattan in search of his chosen bride but has a hard time finding her. (Neither he nor his minions think to check the phone book.) Then when he finally lays hands on her, he lets Schwarzenegger come and take her away.

The problem may be that he's spreading himself too thin. That was Satan cavorting in bed with Saddam Hussein in that "South Park" movie last summer. He took the form of a lascivious Al Pacino in "The Devil's Advocate" two years ago, and he reportedly makes an appearance in the upcoming "Lost Souls." And you didn't even know he had a SAG card.

Of the slew of movies that seek to capitalize on the millennial fascination with all things spiritual or apocalyptic, "End of Days" is the big-budget picture that tries to blow the rest away. Schwarzenegger vs. Satan on the streets of New York—how's that for high concept? It's an inherently silly—not to mention opportunistic—premise, and director Peter Hyams and writer Andrew W. Marlowe don't try to camouflage their story's vast gaps in logic. They're betting that if they keep it speeding along and throw in enough action and thrills, audiences won't care that it's all nonsense.

In "Days," Lucifer inhabits the body of a rich industrialist played by Gabriel Byrne so that he can find and impregnate the woman destined to bear his child (Robin Tunney). He has to do it in the last hour before the end of the century, but he's too cool to ever get in a hurry. He's a randy devil, too, that Satan. Got a roving eye. First thing he does after he gets his new hunky host body is boldly grope and kiss some woman in a restaurant. Second thing he does is he blows the place up after walking out. Maybe the soup was cold.

That tells you all you need to know about the way Ultimate Evil is characterized in this movie. He's walking the Earth to start the thousand-year reign of evil on Earth, or some such thing, but he spends most of his time either eyeing the babes or coming up with clever ways to cause mayhem. He's Satan as a 14-year-old boy might imagine him. (Catch the adolescently cool way he announces his arrival at the heavily guarded home of his intended.)

The net effect is that it makes Satan seem like a lot less fearsome foe than, say, Y2K. At least the trouble that may cause will be felt on more than just a few city blocks. The explosions and murders Satan commits in New York City barely get mentioned on the news.

Schwarzenegger plays a character with the unlikely biblical-sounding name of Jericho Cane, but it hardly matters because Schwarzenegger always plays Schwarzenegger. He's a high-tech bodyguard and former cop who stays a few steps ahead of the police in figuring out that a renegade band of Catholic priests (don't ask) is trying to kill the devil's intended bride. The bad priests, for their part, are a few steps ahead of the ineffectual good priests, who want to save her. Meanwhile, Satan and his band of zombie-like followers are also on her tail.

(So as not to rile the Catholic Church apparently, the pope is shown on several occasions in Rome, mouthing pieties and thinking good thoughts.)

The filmmakers knew that if they made their Satan any smarter and more powerful than, say, a T-1000 cyborg, then Schwarzenegger wouldn't stand a chance of beating him, and they wouldn't have a movie. (As it is, though, it won't spoil anything to say the 52-year-old muscle-bound former cardiac patient holds his own against the Evil One.)

That was an intentional reference to "Terminator 2: Judgment Day." Among the numerous movies from which this one draws inspiration ("Dracula" and "The Devil's Advocate" are among the others), the two "Terminator" movies rank at the top of the list. This isn't a criticism.

James Cameron doesn't make James Cameron movies anymore, so somebody's got to do it. Hyams has got most of the trappings right—the wall-to-wall action, the gripping chase, the loud explosions, eye-catching special effects—and he seems to know instinctively that an overgrown behemoth of a movie like this needs a strong beating heart to get it going and take it to another level. But, try as he might, he can't invest "End of Days" with one.

The movie is as bloodless as a cyborg, and it feels as if it has been assembled according to diagrams supplied by someone who studied every successful sci-fi action thriller and then multiplied the findings by 10. So, when the formula calls for an injection of soul, Hyams and Marlowe go into overdrive. They give us Schwarzenegger, the superhuman action hero, in mourning over the deaths of his wife and daughter. Schwarzenegger grappling with issues of faith. Schwarzenegger fighting the temptation to sell out to the devil for the chance to have his family back.

All of these moral crises provide a string of tiny set pieces in which the characters are asked to make choices, which makes this movie seem in some ways like an action-thriller version of "The Last Temptation of Christ," only without God (he or she stays strangely silent through all of this). But perhaps more important from a storytelling standpoint, it provides a half-baked reason why Satan doesn't just snap Arnie's neck or ram a crucifix into his skull, the way he dispatches a couple of the priests. Satan keeps him alive so that he can try to capture his soul. Otherwise, the movie would've lasted maybe 15 minutes.

Not until the very end, after Satan shows his true form does "End of Days" toss aside the contemporary action movie rule book and make an unexpected move. It's a good move, too—one true to the sketchy outlines of Schwarzenegger's character, and one meant to resound with the movie's implied themes of redemption and faith.

For it to work, though, the filmmakers needed to show that these issues meant something to them besides making nifty plot points. They don't, and so the ending resonates for maybe 10 seconds before it gets replaced in your mind by questions like: How did that statue of Jesus get back on its pedestal after you saw Satan knock it down?

NEW STATESMAN, 12/13/99, p. 47, Jonathan Romney

Last year, Hollywood forecasts predicted that the century's end would be marked if not by fiery portents in the sky then at least by a glut of millennial apocalypse movies. Like most prophecies of apocalypse, that one, too, has fallen flat: only a handful of such films have been made, and most of them are safely on their way to being forgotten come the 21st century—you do remember *Deep Impact*, don't you? We have only two more of them to go but, curiously, the religious aspects of apocalypse have been saved for last.

Once all the sci-fi fireworks are over, it's left to the stragglers to dust down the Book of Revelations and intone chapter and verse at us. In the States, this has happened literally in the shape of *The Omega Code*, a thriller that did respectably at the US box office and was produced by the evangelical Trinity Broadcasting Network. Michael York is a media mogul bent on world domination. I haven't seen the film, but I think it's safe to assume the good guys win.

The devil may have the best tunes, but his scripts are as ropy as anyone elses judging by *End of Days*. This infernal epic—no expense spared on digital fire and brimstone—sees the return from limbo of Arnold Schwarzenegger, as a suicidally depressed New York security man going *mano a mano* with Lucifer himself. Old Nick has come to town in the shape of Gabriel Byrne, snarling away like one of Brooklyn's suaver mafiosi. He's on the trail of his allotted bride, a gamine played by Robin Tunney: one roll for her in the satanic sack, and it's curtains for humanity.

The only interesting thing about Peter Hyams's inept extravaganza is the way it shoehorns together genres that simply don't fit—the satanic horror film and the heavy firepower action thriller. *End of Days* tries to have it all: highspeed subway chases and sombre priests (headed by Rod Steiger) mulling over ancient texts on their PCs. There's a ludicrous sequence where Arnie straps on the usual arsenal to defeat his foe. But Satan is Satan, after all, not just another Bond villain, and it rather diminishes the awe to see the Dark Prince fending off hails of bullets, or using his combustible pee to blow up trucks.

The film gets really crazy when it pitches the weary Schwarzenegger as a redeemer and martyr (St Arnie of the Bleeding Pecs). He not only gets crucified, he's beaten up by Miriam Margolyes and has his infernal temptation in visions of a family Christmas (Perry Como carols round the tree). He finally has his Passion facing down the fiend at midnight Mass. It's all balderdash, but not without curiosity value: after all, it's the nearest Schwarzenegger will ever come to one of those spiritual torment routines that Harvey Keitel used to do so heartily in Abel Ferrara films.

The year's final apocalypse is Kevin Smith's comedy *Dogma*, which Film 4 is releasing on Boxing Day. The latest from the wunderkind who made *Clerks* and *Chasing Amy*, *Dogma*'s combination of scatology and eschatology was vigorously condemned in the US by the Catholic League, but it offers a tame, heavy-handed kind of outrage. The plot—two fallen angels plan to return to heaven is an excuse for Smith to dramatise a number of whimsical theological fancies designed to put the wind up the well-starched cassock: God's chosen servant being a lapsed Catholic who works in an abortion clinic (Linda Fiorentino); a black 13th apostle (Chris Rock); two prophets in the form of foul-mouthed slacker cretins; and Alanis Morissette as the deity (silent, hallelujah).

The film's defenders have gone out of their way to stress that Smith is himself a devout Catholic, and somehow that's not surprising. Scabrously anti-religion but mawkishly pro-God, *Dogma* feels like a revue mounted by boisterous seminary students who want to prove that it's OK to read Marvel Comics and Thomas Aquinas. The best joke comes early: a cardinal introduces the new sect of Catholicism, Wow, which "retires" the crucifix and introduces a new, punter-friendly "buddy Christ". But *Dogma* feels at once puerile and pompous, beginning with the disclaimer: "Even God has a sense of humour." If so, I don't think he'll find much in *Dogma* to amuse him; *End of Days*, on the otherhand, will have him rolling in the aisles.

NEW YORK POST, 11/24/99, p. 58, Jonathan Foreman

"End of Days" starts off creepily enough, with dark hints that it will turn out to be an updated, high-testosterone version of a 1970s religious horror film like "The Omen" or "The Exorcist."

But while it moves along too swiftly ever to be boring, and there are some funny, dry lines along the way, "End of Days" soon degenerates into a hokey, overblown and deeply unsatisfying movie.

The devil has come to New York to find a breeding partner before the millennium. As the Vatican has long known from various biblical prophecies, if the Evil One has sex with a certain virgin between 11 p.m. and midnight on Dec. 31, that will bring about the End of Days.

At first, the devil takes the form of a blob of transparent goo—like the "Predator" monster in stealth mode. Then he takes over the body of a wealthy businessman played by Gabriel Byrne—who becomes super-attractive to women, superstrong and as resilient as the Terminator in "T2."

By coincidence, one of the machine-gun-toting, helicopter-flying security guards assigned to protect the businessman is Jericho Cane (Arnold Schwarzenegger), an alcoholic, widowed ex-cop with almost superhuman fighting abilities.

When a sniper tries to kill the businessman, Jericho is shot while foiling the assassination. Fortunately, he's wearing one of those movieland vests that can stop bullets from a high-powered rifle.

The would-be killer is a cellar-dwelling priest named Thomas Aquinas (not that anyone notices he has the same name as the great theologian) who has cut out his own tongue.

After he is murdered in the hospital (crucified against the ceiling) by Satan, Jericho and his wisecracking partner, Chicago (Kevin Pollak), conduct their own investigation, a few steps ahead of the NYPD's C.C.H. Pounder. Using deductive powers worthy of Sherlock Holmes they find their way to Christine York (Robin Tunney)—the chosen virgin.

She's a pretty, nubile young thing—you get to see her topless after a workout—living at the house of her stepmother, a wealthy former nurse and Satan-worshipper. When our heroes turn up, Christine is about to be killed by renegade priests desperate to avert the prophecy.

Having saved Christine for the Devil's delight, Jericho and Chicago soon encounter him in person. And it will be up to Jericho to prevent Satan from consummating the match by New Year's Eve.

Fortunately, the devil in human form can be slowed—though not killed—by machine-gun bullets and 40mm grenades in sufficient numbers.

The action takes place in a fake New York of alleys, abandoned train stations and graffiti-covered subway trains. In the strange, pagan-religious way of so many Hollywood movies, this one takes Evil and Satan seriously, but not God or Divine Love.   There's a crude nod to damnation but none at all to salvation.

For all its cheesiness. "The Devil's Advocate" with Al Pacino was vastly superior to this spiritually impoverished explosion-fest. At least that version of the path to hell included the traps of vanity and pride as well as lust. And it didn't take a grotesquely hypocritical approach to the sin of (violent) wrath.

Schwarzenegger is no better and no worse than ever—just visibly older. It's Gabriel Byrne who gives this production whatever class it has. And it's Kevin Pollak who gets to deliver with perfect timing—almost all the good jokes.

NEWSDAY, 11/24/99, Part II/p. B6, Jan Stuart

Arnold Schwarzenegger takes five from his latest carnival of destruction to whip up breakfast in a blender. Everything within reach goes into the mix: cartons of leftover Chinese food, a half-eaten piece of bread picked off the floor... waste not want not. Then click, whirr, down the hatch.

So goes "End of Days," a low-nutrient power drink thrown together from the leavings of just about every Schwarzenegger flick ever made, short of "Kindergarten Cop." For those who need to feel as if they are paying their $8.50 for something new, writer Andrew W. Marlowe also tosses in a Polish peasant woman who receives stigmata and raves in jibberish, a grinning albino man with nappy hair and a devil who slinks around Manhattan camouflaged as a sheet of Saran Wrap.

If the writers of the Book of Revelations knew that this would be the result of their handiwork 2,000 years down the line, they would have hung up their sheepskin notepads long before they finished. Revelations provides the barely recognizable basis for this apocalyptic tale, which has Schwarzenegger as a bodyguard for a powerful banker (Gabriel Byrne) whose body is inhabited by the Devil. Why? So that he can impregnate a chosen female named, so help us, Christine (Robin Tunney) and conceive a child who will grow up to wreak havoc upon the Earth.

Schwarzenegger must stop him. Why? He has nothing else to do: His wife and kid were slaughtered in a revenge killing and he has obviously not cracked a book since "Millennium for Meatheads." So, he and his wisecracking buddy Chicago (Kevin Pollak) charge into the fray, taking on a demonic policewoman (CCH Pounder) and a priest with cryptic doings in his crypt (Rod Steiger, who has plenty to atone for in the 45 years since "On the Waterfront").

Like most Schwarzenegger vehicles, "End of Days" is not a movie so much as a pileup of climaxes that enable the star to take punishment, give punishment and spray artillery while spouting smug rejoinders like "I could do this all day." No single line is more hilarious, however, than the spectacle of our hero finding God in the last two minutes, which is like an alcoholic chasing a 20-year bender with a thimble of soya milk.

In all fairness, there is something eerily amazing about an actor who so stubbornly refuses to grow up. At 52, Schwarzenegger is uncontestedly the oldest and beefiest Peter Pan to fly out of that Never Never Land otherwise known as Hollywood.

NEWSWEEK, 12/6/99, p. 82, David Ansen

Ever had the desire to see Arnold Schwarzenegger crucified? Hurled across a room by a pudgy middle-aged woman? Beaten and kicked by a gang of Satan-worshiping thugs? Engaged in a shoot-out with Roman Catholic priests? Undergo a religious conversion? It's not as cool as it sounds. Arnold's latest mayhemathon, "End of Days," is a flabbergasting amalgam of pseudoreligiosity and "Seven"-inspired sadism. This time the Big Guy takes on the Biggest Guy of all—Satan, who appears in New York on the eve of the millennium in the body of a wall Street bigwig (Gabriel Byrne). Satan's mission: to have carnal union with the chosen one (Robin Tunney), thus bringing about the dread "end of days."

Arnold, an alcoholic ex-cop whose wife and kid were murdered (there's a new one!), is for some reason the only guy who can stop this apocalyptic roll in the sack. But guns won't do the trick against the Devil (not that Arnold doesn't try—repeatedly). Only someone with purity in his heart can save the world. Cue the heavenly choirs. Peter Hyams's lurid, FX-happy thriller slams pieces of a dozen other movies into a noxious new compound. It has to be seen to be believed, but who'd want to?

SIGHT AND SOUND, 2/00, p. 45, Mark Kermode

New York, 1979. Christine York is born and secretly anointed by a satanic cult. December 1999, renegade priest Thomas Aquinas' assassination attempt on a Wall Street banker is foiled by bodyguard Jericho Cane. Aquinas rants about the "end of days" before he dies, but when his body is discovered to lack a tongue, Cane suspects he's gone mad himself. However, he learns of a Vatican conspiracy to prevent the birth of the Antichrist. Cane and his partner Chicago trace the now grown Christine York who is being pursued by both a priestly hit squad and by Cane's Wall Street client, who is possessed by Satan. The prince of darkness wishes to impregnate Christine with his child on the eve of the new millennium thereby bringing about the "end of days" foretold in the Book of Revelations.

Overcoming a horde of attackers, including Christine's nanny Mabel, Cane persuades Father Kovak and his band of priests not to kill Christine but to protect her in their church. Having failed to tempt Cane with the return of his deceased wife and child, Satan enters Kovak's church and attempts to deflower Christine while engaging in a violent battle with Cane. Satan is defeated finally by Cane, who sacrifices himself to save Christine. The world is saved.

"I've seen a lot," says Arnold Schwarzenegger in the middle of this abysmally lumpen cross between *The Omen* (1976) and *Lethal Weapon*, "but nothing that would make me cut out my tongue!" *End of Days* is dreadful enough to make most viewers consider gouging out their eyes in order to avoid seeing a second time the spectacle of the world's most wooden actor pretending to undergo a spiritual crisis. Idiotic beyond the point of redemption, this sinfully stupid farrago manages to insult audiences and critics, Christians and Satanists alike, reducing 2000 years of fertile mythology to the level of an incoherent pop video.

The problems with *End of Days* are legion. From Andrew W. Marlowe's stunningly illiterate script (which manages to make *The Omen*'s author David Seltzer's work read like the sublime visions of Pierre Teilhard de Chardin) to jobbing journeyman Peter Hyams' nuts and bolts direction (he was brought on board to join the dots when feature first timer Marcus Nispel was passed over), the entire film looks and feels like nothing more than a cynical salvaging exercise. The special effects are fabulously unspecial, the plot twists extravagantly straightforward, and the character development retarded beyond redemption. Worse still, the apocryphal source material, from which even the most talentless storyteller could spin a passable yarn, is made to sound boring.

The performances are also uniformly terrible. It's easy to laugh at Rod Steiger as the huffy priest who doesn't think there's anything funny about a man called Thomas Aquinas attempting to stop the devil getting laid, while boggle-eyed Udo Kier has never been anything less than hilarious. But we should expect more from Gabriel Byrne and Kevin Pollak, whose pairing constantly reminds us how good they both were in *The Usual Suspects*. Sadly, all we get here is a lazy turn from Pollak, and scenery chewing from Byrne, who outdoes his randy priest role in the equally abominable *Stigmata* and prances around like a man possessed by a fit of the vapours.

Bad acting honours, however, are reserved ultimately for Arnie himself, who moves like the ice-demon in the lowest ring of Dante's *Inferno*, with about as much human warmth and slightly less facial expression. Called upon to cry over the loss of his wife and child, he can do nothing more than wince like a constipated man with conjunctivitis. Equally, when asked to throw down his weapon before the altar and call upon God for help, Arnie's unique Austro-American lilt becomes more impenetrable than usual. Will God hear him? And if he does, will he be able to understand him? At the time of writing, *End of Days* had already flopped in the US, and by the time of publication, its dated millennial tag will doubtless have made it as appealing to punters as cold leftover turkey. All of which may prove that in the end Schwarzenegger was indeed a 20th-century phenomenon, and is now merely a man out of time.

VILLAGE VOICE, 12/7/99, p. 148, Michael Atkinson

Arnold Schwarzenegger certainly was, of a sort, and it seems as if the days when the popular culture rather generously made a home for this hydrant-headed dummkopf are coming to an end. Indeed, *End of Days* is Arnold's idea of stretching, playing a vodka-chugging security guard whose alcoholism hasn't interfered with his round-the-clock (and unreferenced, but c'mon) weight training, and who is called upon to stop Satan (inhabiting Gabriel Byrne's body and bank account) from making the beast of many backs with poor Robin Tunney and thereby fulfilling the Revelations. Making even the fibrillating sheepwash of *Stigmata* look sophisticated, *End of Days* is 85 percent explosions and editing idiocy (a window can't break without director Peter Hyams cutting between five different angles) and 15 percent Arnold trying to grow a third dimension. Seeing him try for "sad" is like watching a dog try to talk, but his climactic Christian epiphany, even preceded by Arnold's own crucifixion and Last Temptation, is more than I think remaining Arnold fans are ready to bear. The last-ditch eventuality of T3 notwithstanding, Arnold may be running out of options.

Also reviewed in:
CHICAGO TRIBUNE, 11/24/99, Tempo/p. 2, Michael Wilmington
NEW YORK TIMES, 11/24/99, p. E3, Janet Maslin
VARIETY, 11/29-12/5/99, p. 56, Todd McCarthy
WASHINGTON POST, 11/24/99, p. C1, Stephen Hunter
WASHINGTON POST, 11/26/99, Weekend/p. 47, Desson Howe

ENDURANCE

A Walt Disney Pictures release of a La Junta, LLC production in association with Film Four and Helkon Media Filmvertrieb. *Executive Producer:* Wallace Wolf. *Producer:* Edward R. Pressman, Terrence Malick, and Max Palevsky. *Director:* Leslie Woodhead. *Screenplay:* Leslie Woodhead. *Director of Photography:* Ivan Strasburg. *Editor:* Saar Klien and Oral Norrie Ottey. *Music:* John Powell. *Music Editor:* Adam Smalley and Brian Richards. *Sound:* Claude Letessier and (music) Alan Meyerson. *Sound Editor:* Claude Letessier. *Running time:* 83 minutes. MPAA *Rating:* G.

CAST: Haile Gebrselassie (Himself); Gebrselassie Bekele (Haile's Father); Assefa Gebrselassie (Haile's Brother); Alem Tellahun (Haile's Wife); Tizazu Mashresha (Haile's Police Trainer); YOUNG GEBRSELASSIE FAMILY: Yonas Zergaw (Haile); Shawanness Gebrselassie (Haile's Mother); Tedesse Haile (Haile's Father); Winishet Tesfaye (Shawanness); Abinet Tedesse (Assefa); Berhane Tesfaye (Ayralem); Bekele Negash (Tekeya); Berhane Taye (Zergaw); Endale Workineh (Adenew); Zinash Workineh (Ydarawerk); Mengistu Workineh (Belay); Bashamyelesh Workineh (Yeshye).

LOS ANGELES TIMES, 5/14/99, Calendar/p. 14, Gene Seymour

[The following review by Gene Seymour appeared in a slightly different form in **NEWSDAY, 5/14/97, Part II/p. B7.]**

In just about every country in the world except our own, Ethiopian gold medalist Haile Gebrselassie is a sports superstar of the first magnitude. The U.S. tends to prefer athletic heroes with more explosive, rapid-fire attributes than those, like Gebrselassie, who can merely run faster over longer distances than any human being on the planet.

For that reason and many others, "Endurance" seems as unlikely a candidate for domestic big-studio release as any film imaginable. Yet from the moment you hear the heart-stopping choral-and-symphony orchestra music following Gebrselassie as he flashes across the Ethiopian countryside, you understand why the folks at Disney believe you will be enraptured by this guy's story.

This stately hybrid of documentary and drama can be viewed as sort of a thinking-man's version of "The Jackie Robinson Story" (1950), which, like "Endurance," employed the real-life subject as a performer in the reenactment of his life.

Members of Gebrselassie's real-life family join him in acting out scenes from his life. The track star's nephew (Yonas Zergaw) plays him as a child, inspired enough by the 1980 gold medal run in the 10,000-meter race by fellow countryman Miruts Yifter to focus his dreams on someday matching that feat. The boy runs six miles to and from school every day with the prospect of punishment for lateness acting as an incentive for improving his time.

This daily regimen adds to the physical toil extracted from working on his family's farm. Neither the painful death of his mother nor his father's stern resistance stops him from going to Addis Ababa and training to be a part of his country's track team, world-renowned for producing such long-distance legends as Yifter and the late, great marathoner Abebe Bikila. All of which is interspersed with footage of Gebrselassie's dramatic run for the 10,000-meter gold medal in the 1996 Olympics, filmed by Mr. Olympic documentary himself, Bud Greenspan.

Writer-director Leslie Woodhead and cinematographer Ivan Strasburg collaborate on a view of the Ethiopian landscape that you would call sumptuous if you didn't already know how harsh it was.

(Somehow, you suspect co-producer Terrence Malick, whose "The Thin Red Line" overflowed with meditative pictures of remote land masses, had a hand in these shots.) The scenery's so stunning, it almost makes you forget how stilted and stiff some of the acting is by the largely amateur cast.

Ultimately, you can't label "Endurance" as anything more than an anthem to possibility, and as with most anthems, everything is orchestrated on an ascending curve with no dips or retreats. Even if you dismiss "Endurance" as a device for "psyching" yourself toward physical well-being, you'll be hard-pressed to find one that's more stirring.

NEW YORK POST, 5/14/99, p. 49, Jonathan Foreman

"Endurance" is one of the best-looking movies ever made about runners, running and the role that character plays in competitive sports. Part documentary, part re-enactment, it tells the story of Haile Gebrselassie, the modest Ethiopian farm boy who grew up to become a gold medalist at the Atlanta Olympics and arguably the greatest distance runner in the world.

Documentarist Leslie Woodhead, strongly influenced by Terence Malick—who is one of the film's producers—has crafted a long, slow feast of gorgeous photography and wonderful music. (The extraordinary score combines Ethiopian instruments and music with Western ones.)

It's also a fascinating piece of ethnography. "Endurance" takes you so deeply into the world of subsistence farmers living in the hills of southern Ethiopia that you can almost taste the flat bread cooking on the open fire and smell the farm animals sleeping next to the people in the Gebrselassie household.

With minimal dialogue, this "non-fiction feature" is composed of re-enacted scenes from Haile's boyhood (the six miles he ran to school, coming home to work on the farm) and his youth in Addis Ababa jogging through the slums at dawn). You get to see the re-enacted burial of Haile's mother, communal meals, and all sorts of traditional rites, such as the annual reading of entrails to predict the harvest.

There is also conflict within Haile's very large family. Haile's father opposed his devotion to running, for while thousands of Ethiopian men take part in the national sport, very few are lifted by it out of poverty to fame and fortune.

Haile introduces the film and plays himself as a young man. His nephew plays him as a boy. Haile's mother is played by his sister Shawanness and his father is played by his dad's first cousin. And for the most part, director Woodhead gets surprisingly convincing if low-key performances from this non-professional cast.

"Endurance" does sag in the middle under the weight of its long farm scenes. But it picks up again when Gebrselassie gets to Atlanta. You couldn't script a more dramatic race than the one in which Gebrselassie triumphed. Nor could it have been filmed more effectively.

VILLAGE VOICE, 5/18/99, p. 130, Gary Dauphin

In Leslie Woodhead's lengthy, understated docudrama, *Endurance,* Ethiopian distance superstar Haile Gebrselassie appears as himself, reenacting moments from his *Sports Illustrated*-ready biography, while his own homespun aphorisms ("If God doesn't help you, your work is nothing," he says, apropos of nothing) and thrill-of-victory footage unspool in the background. Woodhead brings an ethnographic take to the familiar runner's mythos of near mystical equanimity in the face of pain. The film was shot on location in Ethiopia and local actors (many of them real-life family members) re-create scenes from Gebrselassie's childhood. With nonactors playing themselves, *Endurance* is subject to occasional stiffness, but the subject's ability to, well, endure becomes the stuff of high drama in actual races shot by Olympic view-master Bud Greenspan. Asked about his discipline, Gebrselassie says all the right things, intoning about faith and God, but it's when he runs that those words take on their true meaning.

Also reviewed in:
CHICAGO TRIBUNE, 5/21/99, Friday/p. A, Barbara Shulgasser
NEW YORK TIMES, 5/14/99, p. E14, Stephen Holden
VARIETY, 9/14-20/98, p. 39, Todd McCarthy
WASHINGTON POST, 5/21/99, Weekend/p. 18, Desson Howe

ENTRAPMENT

A Twentieth Century Fox and Regency Enterprises release of a Fountainbridge Films and a Michael Hertzberg production in association with Taurus Film. *Executive Producer:* Iain Smith, Ron Bass, and Arnon Milchan. *Producer:* Sean Connery, Michael Hertzberg, and Rhonda Tollefson. *Director:* Jon Amiel. *Screenplay:* Ron Bass and William Broyles. *Story:* Ron Bass and Michael Hertzberg. *Director of Photography:* Phil Meheux. *Editor:* Terry Rawlings. *Music:* Christopher Young. *Music Editor:* Andrew Glen. *Choreographer:* Paul Harris. *Sound:* David John and (music) Geoff Foster. *Sound Editor:* Jim Shields. *Casting:* Michelle Guish and Donna Isaacson. *Production Designer:* Norman Garwood. *Art Director:* Jim Morahan. *Set Decorator:* Anna Pinnock. *Special Effects:* Neil Corbould. *Visual Effects:* Nick Davis. *Costumes:* Penny Rose. *Make-up:* Frances Hannon. *Make-up (Sean Connery):* Peter Robb King. *Stunt Coordinator:* Vic Armstrong and Jim Dowdall. *Running time:* 105 minutes. *MPAA Rating:* PG-13.

CAST: Sean Connery (Mac); Catherine Zeta-Jones (Gin); Ving Rhames (Thibadeaux); Will Patton (Cruz); Maury Chaykin (Conrad Greene); Kevin McNally (Haas); Terry O'Neill (Quinn); Madhav Sharma (Security Chief); David Yip (Chief of Police); Tim Potter (Millennium Man); Eric Meyers (Waverly Technician); Aaron Swartz (Cruz's Man); William Marsh (Computer Technician); Tony Xu (Banker); Rolf Saxon (Director); Tom Clarke-Hill (Operator); David Howard (Technician); Stuart Ong (Doctor); Ravin Ganatra (1st Security Guard); Rhydian Jai-Persad (2nd Security Guard); Hari Dhillon (3rd Security Guard).

LOS ANGELES TIMES, 4/30/99, Calendar/p. 1, Kenneth Turan

[The following review by Kenneth Turan appeared in a slightly different form in NEWSDAY, 4/30/99, Part II/p. B3.]

"Entrapment" is meant to be a glitzy bauble, but it hasn't been polished to a truly high sheen. While the film glistens a bit now and again, a closer look reveals you've been diverted not by a diamond but by a genuine synthetic zircon.

A glib caper thriller that echoes so many of its predecessors ("Rififi," "Topkapi," "To Catch a Thief," "The Thomas Crown Affair") that director Jon Amiel must have heard footsteps every time he approached the camera, "Entrapment" is both helped and hampered by a star pairing that looked ideal on paper but plays iffy on screen.

Yes, together again for the first time, it's Sean Connery, the man you've loved for, well, decades, and one of the most beautiful women of the moment, "The Mask of Zorro's" Catherine Zeta-Jones, who wasn't even alive when Connery first became a star. Strong cases can be made for each of them but put them together in a romantic scenario and their 40-year age difference leads to a situation that some people are calling "Grampy Kissing the Girl."

"Entrapment" opens, like the James Bond pictures Connery starred in long ago, with an elaborate physical stunt. It's the theft, by a single masked and daring cat burglar, of a multimillion-dollar Rembrandt from an elaborately guarded Manhattan office 70 stories off the ground.

Which is where Virginia "Gin" Baker (Zeta-Jones) comes in. An insurance investigator who specializes in high-end thefts, Gin tells boss Hector Cruz (Will Patton) that she's convinced the culprit is Robert "Mac" MacDougal (Connery), a legendary pilferer who may or may not be retired.

Offering herself and a priceless Chinese mask as bait, Gin poses as a thief and goes to Europe with the hope of trapping Mac. He and Gin connect and while they make elaborate plans to lift the object, there's talk of an even bigger score in the Malaysian capital of Kuala Lumpur that comes to involve shadowy henchpersons Thibadeaux (an underutilized Ving Rhames) and Conrad Greene (an out-of-control Maury Chaykin).

But the old man didn't get to be at the top of his game by being easily fooled, and duplicity turns out to be second nature to both of these folks. While they seem to find each other attractive, Mac's rule about nothing personal going on between partners keeps them warily apart, at least initially.

Director Amiel ("Sommersby") is reasonably good at the mechanics of the film's frequent action sequences. But satisfactorily modernizing traditional material is trickier than it seems, and "Entrapment" is not as much fun as, for instance, Martin Campbell's recent "The Mask of Zorro."

Part of the reason is that "Entrapment's" Ron Bass and William Broyles script, while it has designs on being clever and witty, is not as light on its feet as it imagines it is. The film does deliver some unexpected plot moves, but the repartee between Mac and Gin is uninspired, and the considerable stretch that Mac spends being a stern taskmaster to Gin is not particularly enthralling.

The film's acting is similarly haphazard. Connery has understandably been a major presence for forever and even when he's in a phoning-it-in mode, he has enough charm to create an acceptable amount of interest.

And while Zeta-Jones was used to better effect in "Zorro," she is inescapably radiant and that counts for something. When Gin answers in the negative when Mac inquires, "Has there been anyone you couldn't manipulate, beguile or seduce?," you know she's not just bragging.

But that pesky and persistent age difference makes it difficult to connect with Zeta-Jones and Connery as a putative romantic couple. As a result, "Entrapment" traps no one, and by the time some of the script's better twists kick in, we are well past caring.

NEW YORK, 5/10/99, p. 63, Peter Rainer

In the new caper *Entrapment*, Sean Connery plays Robert "Mac" MacDougal, the world's greatest art thief. The hollowest line of dialogue in the movie, which was directed by Jon Amiel from a script by Ron Bass and William Broyles, comes early on when an insurance investigator (Will Patton), scoffing at the notion that Mac could have pulled off a daring aerial abduction of a Rembrandt, says of him, "He's 60. He's not Spider-Man anymore." Actually, Connery is closer to 70, but with his silver-fox dashingness, he still outshines most actors a third his age. In *Entrapment,* he's more James Bond than Spider-Man. Not that he needs to be Bond, of course: I can't think of another performer famously identified with a role—with a franchise—who went on to so thoroughly re-create himself as an actor in the public imagination. The man who gave us the archetypal debonair stud—the pop prince 007—had it within himself to portray a fuller, more nuanced heroism. Connery's career—both as Bond and as the actor he became—represents perhaps the most satisfying expression of masculine force in the history of movies. Because of that force, almost any scene in which he appears with a woman becomes primal.

When he has a part worthy of him—as in *A Fine Madness, The Untouchables, The Russia House*, or *Robin and Marian*—he triumphs. To be fully realized, however, he needs to be grand-scale, and very few movies—the *Molly Maguires* and *The Man Who Would Be King*, perhaps—have filled out his epic presence. The Kipling adaptation was perfect for Connery: He doesn't, after all, need to be playing actual kings, only men with the emotions, the delusions of kings. Most of the time we learn to take Connery where we can—in junk like *The Rock* or mildly diverting knockoffs like *Entrapment*.

Amid the stunts and the fireworks and the ploddingly staged heists in cryptlike museums in London and gleaming computer banks in Kuala Lumpur, Connery actually gives a *performance*. So does Catherine Zeta-Jones, as Virginia Baker, an insurance investigator who is also Mac's partner in crime. Zeta-Jones, with her *Playboy After Hours* contours and her rueful expressiveness, is a female counterpart to Connery. Like him, she combines the hubba hubba of pop with an expansive, nuanced presence. Connery and Zeta-Jones not only look great together, they work well together, too. Connery can sometimes seem almost alarmingly hale, but Zeta-Jones's steady-state allure tempers him. Mac seems stunned—chastened—by her beauty; and for once in a movie featuring a May/December liaison, the age disparity isn't ignored. We watch Mac fall in love with Virginia, who returns the favor, but regret shrouds these two: Her youthful esprit leaves him misty-eyed. Still, I could have done with less melancholia and more whoopee. There's a perplexing scene in which Mac, about to have his way with Virginia, utters something gnomic and then backs off. You half expect Bob Dole to emerge from the shadows with a few words from Pfizer.

NEW YORK POST, 4/30/99, p. 54, Jonathan Foreman

"Entrapment" is a perfunctory imitation of "To Catch a Thief," and another soulless, by-the-numbers attempt to resurrect a genre that made money for the studios in the past.

It's a caper film, but it lacks the sophistication and humor of "To Catch a Thief" and "The Pink Panther"—not to mention any compelling or even believable human interaction.

Instead, it offers gleaming, high-tech burglary tools and drooling shots of Catherine Zeta-Jones doing gymnastics.

There is some real excitement to be had in the film's climactic raid on a computer vault in the world's tallest building—the Petronas Towers in Kuala Lumpur, Malaysia—but it's hardly worth the labored, predictable journey there.

The action begins with a daring art theft from a New York skyscraper, featuring bungee cords and night-vision devices—but designed by folk who know nothing about bungee cords or night-vision devices. It moves to London, a castle in Scotland, and finally to Kuala Lumpur, where the main characters try to pull off a millennium-eve caper that has something to do with Y2K testing and international money transfers.

The details of these immensely complicated heists are treated with such disregard that you almost expect the characters to finish each sentence with "whatever," as in "we're going to link the computers and steal some, you know, stock options, or whatever."

Gin (Catherine Zeta-Jones) works for an insurance company but may also be a high-tech cat burglar. She's sent to London to trap Mac (Sean Connery), the world's most successful art thief, by involving him in the theft of an ancient Chinese mask during a ball at a stately home.

She follows Mac around the city, but he makes contact with her first, turning up in her hotel room one night and proposing some kind of alliance. Of course, Gin and Mac aren't exactly what they seem, and the question is whether or not their growing mutual attraction will overwhelm any acts of betrayal they're planning against each other.

Thanks to Connery's grizzled sex appeal, the relationship between Connery and Zeta-Jones is less ludicrous than many recent older man/much-younger woman pairings. But Connery seems oddly absent behind his whiskers and wrinkles. Zeta-Jones, all lustrous hair, almond eyes and excessive makeup, gamely does her best with a character so underwritten you wonder why the filmmakers even bothered to give her a name.

The dialogue is credited to Ron Bass and William Broyles, but it might easily have been crafted by a clever computer program. It mainly features stuff like "It's 15 seconds ... Going hot!" And the movie is directed by Jon Amiel ("Sommersby") with brazen contempt for both the genre and the audience. (The long scenes in which Zeta-Jones practices undulating between laser beams are so obviously exploitative it's almost laughable.)

Ving Rhames, so good in "Pulp Fiction" and "Out of Sight," has a thankless, one-note cameo role as Mac's sinister partner, and Maury Chaykin gets to play a gay black-marketeer with a New York accent, living in decadent Asian exile.

SIGHT AND SOUND, 7/99, p. 41, José Arroyo

Sixteen days before the millennium. A thief slithers into a Manhattan high-rise building and steals a Rembrandt. Virginia 'Gin' Baker, an insurance investigator, notes that the theft has all the hallmarks of a job by Robert 'Mac' MacDougal, the world's greatest thief. She persuades her boss to let her entrap him. Gin contacts Mac with her bait a proposal to steal a Chinese mask worth $40 million. To test her, Mac asks her to steal a vase from an antique store. She passes and he whisks her off to his castle in Scotland where she is trained to avoid the laser security system protecting the mask.

Gin does her best to seduce Mac, but romantic involvement with a partner-in-theft goes against his professional code of conduct. Also, his mistrust of her is borne out when he taps her phone calls and learns of her intent to double-cross him. After the theft of the mask, Mac decides to drown her but she persuades him to let her live by suggesting an even larger theft of $8 billion. The sum could be siphoned off various bank accounts from the head office of a multinational in Kuala Lumpur during the several-seconds-long computer shutdowns for midnight, 1999. During the operation Gin and Mac are separated but meet later at a station where Mac reveals he's been double-crossing her all along. He allows her to escape but they reunite for a final clinch.

Entrapment luxuriates in the best Hollywood big bucks can buy: superb sets and cinematography, spectacular locations, expensive stars. During the opening credits the camera glides through a romanticised Manhattan skyline. The steel and chrome gleam, the lights of the skyscrapers are digital jewels and the frame of the screen is dynamically pierced at odd angles by a laser-like red beam. This sequence holds out a tantalising promise for the movie, particularly when the camera rests on a sinuous cat-burglar entering a high, tightly shut window with elegant ease. We expect an exciting, sleek and slick caper movie, something like *To Catch a Thief* (1954) or at least (let's not be *too* greedy) *Arabesque* (1966). It's not the stars' fault that *Entrapment* is disappointing. Sean Connery gets the Cary Grant treatment here, made the object of his costar's desire. Catherine Zeta-Jones chases him just as surely and shrewdly as Audrey Hepburn chased Grant in *Charade* (1963). Given the 40-year age gap between them, her instigation is presumably meant to make their romance less risible, but it's an unnecessary precaution. Close-ups reveal Connery's skin is losing the battle with time, but his appeal was never really based on youth.

Connery's stardom rests on his ability to represent a man completely at ease with his masculinity and his sexuality better than any other star of his generation. There was always something a bit suspect about prettier men like Paul Newman (cf. *Cat on a Hot Tin Roof* 1958) while tougher guys such as Clint Eastwood seemed too stiff to be turned on by anything but seaminess *(Tightrope,* 1984). Connery, however, deploys his physical size, gruff and commanding voice, a glance both sure and sly and a stillness that can pounce into graceful movement at any moment to project a sexuality so confident it can afford to be nonchalant and playful. We are easily convinced that what Zeta-Jones wants from him, give or take a couple of billion dollars, is delivery on the promise of a rough good time.

Zeta-Jones more than holds her own here. Connery may be the object of her desire, but Zeta-Jones is meant to be the object of ours. The sight of her leotard-clad figure practising gymnastics in order to avoid the burglar alarm's lasers is more spectacular and pleasurable than the action set pieces. She emerges from *Entrapment* a full-blown star, flirting with such intelligent sultriness not even a man of Connery's strength can resist. Good alone but even better together, the two have an undoubted chemistry.

Entrapment aspires to be nothing more than a bit of glamorous nonsense, but although it has done all right by the glamour, it has perhaps done too well by the nonsense. Very badly structured, the story begins to feel ripped off half way through, its maze of double-crossings never delivering a narrative payoff. At the unbelievable and tacked-on ending, even a cynic might feel a twinge of discomfort at the lack of even a half-hearted gesture towards a moral rationale for the action. We're meant to root for these thieves just because they look gorgeous, seem meant for each other and are good at their work.

The fact that the combination of sex and capital as spectacle is thought to need no other rationale says a lot about millennial culture, and would make a good subject for another movie. But this is by-numbers genre work which has forgotten a few sums. *Entrapment* fails as a caper film because it neglects that fundamental ingredient—a credible plot, evidently something even the biggest chequebooks in Hollywood can no longer guarantee.

VILLAGE VOICE, 5/4/99, p. 120, Gary Dauphin

Opening with a low-intensity but high-tech art heist, the new Sean Connery vehicle, *Entrapment*, tells the May-December crime capers of Virginia, an unusually limber insurance agent (the pretty but insubstantial Catherine Zeta-Jones), and Mac, a suave superthief (Connery). Initially cast as cat and mouse, the pair are quickly reenvisioned in the time-honored terms of amorous grad student and thesis adviser, Mac the walking repository of know-how, Virginia his eager receptacle. Posing as a budding thief herself, Virginia is whisked off to Mac's Scottish castle and heist boot camp (he barks orders at her while she crawls around on the floor -something to do with losers). Before you know it the pair are swiping 2000-year-old Chinese masks and hatching plans to rob a bank in Malaysia's Petronas Twin Towers (the real-life tallest buildings in the world), Virginia's loyalties as up for grabs as her frequently focused-upon bottom. (Ving Rhames makes his now standard appearance as millennial pusherman, slinging laptop computers and disks.)

Although the film's techno-fetishist set pieces and skyscraper-ledge freak-outs are the familiar subjects of the modern action flick, time is really what's on *Entrapment*'s mind or at least in Ron Bass's script. The Malaysian job hinges on a fantastical moment-stealing gimmick in which various clocks are confused on, you guessed it, New Year's Eve, 1999. On the human dial, *Entrapment* makes more nods than feints when it comes to the leading man's advancing age, dressing Connery like a sprightly retired tourist when he needs to blend into crowds, cutting sympathetically to his private cardiovascular distress when he takes Zeta-Jones jogging. *Entrapment* is rather honest about the fact that Mac is old enough to be Virginia's grandfather, but then why shouldn't it be? Connery's industrial balls are so well-ripened by now that *Entrapment*'s only kiss can hover cheekily between romance and parody, the slow drawing together of the stars interrupted not by the cops or an explosion but by a twinge in double-0-70's side. These acknowledgments of gerontological reality have a mildly refreshing quality to them, but Connery's innate timelessness makes them rather beside the point. If *Entrapment* stinks of the some old shit, that isn't the leading man you smell, just all the junk piled around him.

Also reviewed in:
CHICAGO TRIBUNE, 4/30/99, Tempo/p. 4, Michael Wilmington
NEW YORK TIMES, 4/30/99, p. E15, Janet Maslin
VARIETY, 4/26-5/2/99, p. 43, Todd McCarthy
WASHINGTON POST, 4/30/99, Weekend/p. 63, Desson Howe

ETERNITY AND A DAY

A Merchant Ivory Films release in association with Artistic License Films with the assistance of Canal+, Classic SRL, Istituto Luce, W.D.R. & Arte. *Executive Producer:* Phoebe Economopoulos. *Director:* Theo Angelopoulos. *Screenplay (Greek with English subtitles):* Theo Angelopoulos, Tonino Guerra, and Petros Markaris. *Director of Photography:* Girgos Arvanitis and Andreas Sinanos. *Editor:* Yannis Tsitsopoulos. *Music:* Eleni Karaindrou. *Sound:* Kostas Varybopiotis and (music) Giannis Smyrnaios. *Set Designer:* Giorgos Ziakas and Costas Dimitriadis. *Special Effects:* Manolis Sakadakis. *Costumes:* Giorgos Patsas. *Running time:* 132 minutes. *MPAA Rating:* Not Rated.

CAST: Bruno Ganz (Alexandre); Fabrizio Bentivoglio (The Poet); Isabelle Renauld (Anna); Achilleas Skevis (The Boy); Alexandra Ladikou (Anna's Mother); Despina Bebedeli (Alexandre's Mother); Eleni Gerassimidou (Urania); Iris Hatziantoniou (Alexandre's Daughter); Nikos Kouros (Anna's Uncle); Alekos Oudinotis (Anna's Father); Nikos Kolovos (The Doctor); Vassilis Seimenis (Son-in-Law); Petros Eyssoun (Voice of Alexandre); Pemi Zouni (Voice of Anna); K. Sahinidis and K. Chiamidis (Wedding Singers); Th. Papadimitriou, P. Pappas , and Th. Asteridis (Coach Singers).

LOS ANGELES TIMES, 5/28/99, Calendar/p. 6, Kevin Thomas

[The following review by Kevin Thomas appeared in a slightly different form in **NEWSDAY, 5/28/99, Part II/p. B6.**]

Theo Angelopoulos' towering, elegiac "Eternity and a Day" takes its title from the hero's late wife's answer to his question, "How long is tomorrow?" Facing death himself from cancer, Alexandre (Bruno Ganz), a middle-aged Greek writer and poet heralded as the conscience of his generation, is confronting the notion of eternity and longs to experience one final perfect day, to recapture the happiness of a day, some 30 years earlier, at the beach with his wife (Isabelle Renauld), their new-born daughter and their relatives. (Significantly, it occurred just before Greece fell under military rule.)

From his bedroom in his family's elegant 19th century seaside mansion in Thessaloniki, Alexandre has a view of that very beach. But as his pain grows unbearable, he must say farewell to his home and enter a hospital to die.

"Eternity and a Day," a shimmering, seductive reverie, begins with Alexandre overwhelmed with the feeling that, in his absorption in his work, he failed to express his love for his wife and others sufficiently.

This failure in turn is the reason he was never able to finish a cherished project, completing an unfinished poem by a 19th century Greek poet who had been so long in exile that upon his return home he had forgotten so much of his native language that he actually began buttonholing people in the street, offering to pay them for the words that eluded him. Alexandre sees in this poet his own emotional self-exile, his own inability to express his feelings.

There's no small irony in that Alexandre recalls in such detail that special day, Sept. 20, 1966, because of his discovery of a letter his wife wrote to him, expressing her love for him and her hope that, realizing that he lives alongside her and their baby daughter rather than with them, she'll be able "to capture him between books." When it comes time to drop by his daughter's apartment to give this treasured letter to her, we realize that, despite the clear affection between father and daughter, he has kept his distance, even hiding the state of his health.

Before he—or we—can get any notion of just how he's going to go about attaining that one last perfect day, he crosses paths with a boy (Achilleas Skevis), who looks to be around 9 and who squeegees the windshield of his car while he's waiting for a light to change. The boy repays Alexandre's tip with a radiant smile. When he encounters the boy again, under vastly different circumstances, he is caught up in a wholly unexpected adventure. The past continues to flood over him, but he realizes that what the boy, an Albanian refugee, needs more than anything is to feel loved; in short, Alexandre has unexpectedly stumbled upon a path of redemption. Skevis, who can express a capacity for reflection way beyond his years, and the ever-formidable Ganz, with his gift for plumbing the depths of his soul, are an unforgettable match.

All of Angelopoulos' films are odysseys—it is not too much to call him the modern Homer—and few artists in any medium use the journey as a metaphor for the eternal cycle of birth, life and death with such forceful eloquence and passion. No matter how natural an exchange between two people may be in a given moment, Angelopoulos will soon be affirming and reaffirming his vision of life as an endless procession, into which his characters and settings flow. And no matter how intimate a scene, Angelopoulos will return again and again to vistas of great depth; movement within his frames is echoed by endless tracking shots.

In this manner he is himself able to evoke a sense of the eternal and the immediate simultaneously, and thus at once cover terrain psychological, political and geographical. Most important, he is able to do this so compellingly, investing his images with such emotion and meaning, that his stylized, stately paced films catch you up completely and you find yourself surprised when they're over—they can seem a full hour shorter than they actually are.

Working with cinematographers Giorgos Arvanitis and Andreas Sinanos and composer Eleni Karaindrou, whose beautiful and stirring score greatly reinforces the film's impact, Angelopoulos has created another masterpiece, one that recalls such classics as Bergman's "Wild Strawberries" and Kurosawa's "Ikiru" (To Live).

NEW YORK POST, 5/28/99, p. 58, Rod Dreher

A European import as big, gassy, self-important—and unsuccessful—as Theo Angelopolous's pretentious "Eternity and a Day" hasn't hit New York since the Hindenburg last docked. Here is a maximo serioso movie that will give you a strange new appreciation for the oeuvre of Adam Sandler.

"Eternity and a Day"—a title that serves as a handy description of its running time—takes place in the final days of a famous Greek writer's life. Alexandre (the German actor Bruno Ganz, whose voice is dubbed into Greek) is suffering from a terminal disease and is closing out his affairs before heading to the hospital to die.

But when Alexandre goes to his yuppie daughter to turn over a cache of love letters his late wife once wrote to him, he discovers that the daughter and her husband plan to sell the family's ancestral villa. This makes him depressed, and he slinks off in a nostalgic reverie.

Then he sees street urchins being kidnapped by thugs, who arrange a clandestine meeting with wealthy Euro perverts interested in buying children. Alexandre buys the freedom of one boy (Achilleas Skevis), an 8-year-old Albanian refugee of Greek descent, and tries to return him to his home village.

Discovering that Albania will be like a concentration camp for the boy, whose name we never learn, Alexandre and the kid spend the rest of this long, long film on an excruciatingly slow and airless journey through the Land of Big Thoughts.

Angelopolous drags us through a series of glacial, embalmed set pieces in which we're forced to observe Alexandre grope toward stultifying epiphanies about art and life.

The director holds his shots so long he clearly intends for us to ponder this folderol with utmost gravity. Trouble is, Alexandre's speculations sound like a pseudo-philosophical blowhard in a bad Milan Kundera novel ("Why didn't we know how to love?"), and he is irrefutably a crashing, self-involved bore. And the kid's no Kolya, either.

None of this should be a surprise to anyone who has read about the vain, humor-impaired filmmaker pitching a public fit at Cannes four years ago when his "Ulysses' Gaze" failed to win the Golden Palm (which "Eternity and a Day" somehow landed in 1998, probably as a self-conscious poke in the eye to vulgar Hollywood). One thinks of Jon Lovitz's Master Thespian character on "Saturday Night Live" deciding that what he really wants to do is direct.

SIGHT AND SOUND, 6/99, p. 44, John Mount

Present-day Thessaloniki, Greece. Alexander is a terminally ill poet trying to put his affairs in order the day before he goes into a hospice. He visits his daughter and asks her to take his dog. She refuses and tells him that she and her husband have sold the family home by the sea. Memories of Alexander's beautiful wife Anna flood back from letters she wrote. While driving, Alexander helps a young Albanian child to escape arrest for illegally cleaning cars at traffic lights. Later he sees the boy abducted and rescues him from an illegal adoption ring.

Alexander decides to return the boy to Albania by driving him to the border. There he realises the boy has a better chance in exile and returns him to Thessaloniki. Alexander has abandoned his own writing in order to complete an unfinished poem by a great Greek poet who lived in Italy; on returning to Greece, the poet bought words from people in order to write his poems. The Albanian boy sells Alexander words to help him complete the poem. Alexander manages to find a home for his dog with his servant Urania during her son's wedding. The boy's best friend dies and Alexander attends a street kids' funeral for him. Alexander visits his mother in hospital. The boy arranges to sail from Greece. In the last hours before his departure the pair take a late-night bus trip around the town. Numerous mysterious characters, including the dead Greek poet, board and disembark the bus. The boy catches his boat and Alexander decides not to enter the hospice. Contemplating his life, he stares out to sea.

Theo Angelopoulos' favourite quotation by the modern Greek poet George Seferis is: "In the beginning was the journey." In his latest film he seems to be saying that at the end is the journey also. *Eternity and a Day* is an exquisitely poised film in which the narrative tension derives from a dying poet's decision to postpone his preparations for death in order to involve himself in the problems of an Albanian child refugee. Ironically, the poet's experiences of the grim realities of contemporary Europe and the friendship that grows between him and the child lead him to a better understanding of his own internal exile as a dislocated observer of Greece and his own life. At the same time, his semiarticulate communication with the boy brings him closer to the poem he is trying to complete.

The pairing of an elderly man and an uprooted child has been frequently used in recent European cinema *(Kolya* for example) to explore the troubles in the Balkans and the problems of formerly Communist Eastern Europe. In Angelopoulos' hands, the trope seems to represent a need to square the past with the future by looking at the fates of those on the receiving end of obdurate new nationalistic doctrines. Since the 80s Angelopoulos' films have shifted their focus from the examination of groups and the particularities of Greek history to the more universalised thematic approach of the chronicling of a single protagonist's travails in a wider, disintegrating Europe. Although Angelopoulos has expressed his disaffection with political activism, he still wishes to engage with what goes on around him.

In these later films he has used foreign actors such as Marcello Mastroianni and Harvey Keitel to play his troubled Greek artists. Bruno Ganz, whose past roles include detached witnesses in Alain Tanner's *In the White City* and Wim Wenders' *Wings of Desire,* is an inspired choice for *Eternity and a Day.* Slowly being sculpted by time into a beautiful older man, Ganz brings a tender, melancholy presence to the film, despite the fact his dialogue is dubbed. (Given Angelopoulos' preference for oblique angles and partially obscured profile shots—what David Bordwell calls "dorsality"—the dubbing remains discreet.)

Angelopoulos is a remarkably consistent director with a rigorous, modernist aesthetic. Made with such longtime creative partners as director of photography Giorgos Arvanitis, composer Eleni Karaindrou and script collaborator Tonino Guerra (also a writing partner of Antonioni), *Eternity* is permeated with Angelopoulos' socially committed and humane vision. For the most part the film is bathed in cool, opalescent light and muted colours which contrast sharply with warm, richly hued scenes from the writer's past that conjure up the nostalgic memory of his beautiful, beloved wife. The signature long shots and elaborate, fluid camera movements are also present. There are also some dramatic, flat-on compositions. Among the most memorable are a scene of Alexander and the child approaching a misty border crossing where living figures clenching the barbed-wire fence resemble a jagged paper chain, and a final scene of Ganz staring out to sea with his back to the camera. The sight of his crumpled ears and his tangle of damp, thinning hair produces a sublime expression of mortality and resignation. The seamless temporal shifts are also breathtaking in their simplicity and fluency as Ganz steps in and out of his past and relives moments of joy he had underestimated or simply forgotten.

Angelopoulos doggedly pursues an undervalued cinematic objective: to create time and space for an audience to think and ask themselves questions during his films. This is the antithesis of most contemporary mainstream cinema where the goal is to fill the audience with sensations and emotional excess, holding back reasoning at all costs. What's most fascinating about this beautiful and touching film is the way the protagonist's conundrum reflects Angelopoulos' own challenge as a film maker. By making art from life and living as an artist, the opportunity to experience the world in an unmediated manner and to participate unselfconsciously in it is lost. It's possible the rigorous formal system Angelopoulos imposes to express his concerns may, ultimately, cause the object of his attention to recede and become more elusive. For all that, the quiet, hypnotic intensity of the cinematic journey one experiences in *Eternity and a Day* is a rare and lasting pleasure.

VILLAGE VOICE, 6/1/99, p. 119, J. Hoberman

The Cannes Film Festival climaxed last week amid ritual hand-wringing over the decline of European art cinema. As if on cue, the home front's being treated to two recent examples of the mode by two vastly overrated, supremely solipsistic maestros.   To judge from Theo Angelopoulos's *Eternity and a Day* and Bernardo Bertolucci's *Besieged*, the Euro art film is not only deader than the dodo but dumber too.

Cannes's 1998 Palme d'Or laureate, the aptly named *Eternity and a Day,* is by far the weakest of the half-dozen or so Angelopoulos films I've sat through over the years, reveling as it does in its own intimations of mortality. The fun begins with a snatch of poetry, a burst of piano-doodling, the idyllic image of a child by the sea, and, preparing to check himself into the hospital, Euro-signifier Bruno Ganz as Alexandre—a great writer and an even greater cliché, who is now in late middle age and suffering from some unspecified terminal malady.

Call his illness delusions of grandeur. Angelopoulos insures that nothing Alexandre does will be without near world-historic import.   The writer begins his last day trying to park his immaculately groomed and hilariously silent labrador with his grown daughter—he winds up rescuing an Albanian street urchin who has been abducted and brought to an abandoned motel full of wealthy pederasts (or worse).   Thereafter, it's a glum and tedious recapitulation of Charlie Chaplin's *The Kid*—although, hunching through the movie in what might be Peter Falk's old gray raincoat, the Ganz character is much too enervated to do more than beam benignly down at his little charge.

This symbolic symbiotic relationship between the old and the young, the rich and the poor, the kindly and the cute, civilization and its discontents, is given pseudohistorical depth with the introduction of Albanian concentration camps and Alexandre's fey meditations on the exiled 19th-century Greek poet whom he has taken as his soulmate. What pushes the movie past the point of endurance, however, is the filmmaker's ponderous style.   Studied and humorless, the characteristic Angelopoulos movie is predicated on a series of somnolent takes, stately zooms, and slow white-outs. The effect is severely minimal, yet the mise-en-scéne absurdly glamorous. Every pad is lit as if for an *Architectural Digest* shoot, a hospital exudes the inviting atmosphere of a well-kept provincial museum; the city morgue has the stainless-steel chic of a trendy four-star restaurant.

Eternity and a Day is so ostentatiously self-regarding that when Alexandre repeatedly muses on his late wife's fawning love letters, it's easy to imagine they were written by Angelopoulos to himself. It's hard to know which is more ridiculous—the scene in which Alexandre interrupts the faux folk wedding of his faithful servant's son in order to leave his dog with her, or the one in which a group of street kids solemnly burn a dead comrade's pitiful belongings, reciting blank verse as the background oboe dirges and the camera inexorably moves in. A proponent of what might be termed abstract non-expressionism, Angelopoulos has no particular facility for imagining characters or directing actors. *Eternity and a Day* might have been more fluidly performed by a cast of statues—or even Wookies. Indeed, this is the art-house *Phantom Menace*—stilted, arid, pompous, at once enthralled by its own effects and burdened with bogus philosophizing.

Angelopoulos's flawed but memorable *Ulysses' Gaze* had a certain majestic indifference—or at least so it seemed as projected as a virtual installation on the big screen at the not-quite-bombed-out Anthology Film Archives, an almost empty theater on a derelict stretch of lower Second Avenue. Seeing it thus, one could almost believe that Angelopoulos had created the last European art film. *Eternity and a Day,* which is being released in the shadow of Lincoln Center and aggressively promoted by middlebrow overachievers Merchant and Ivory, is more like a grotesque précis of the mode.

Bluntly posing the eternal questions—"Why have I lived my life in exile?" "Why didn't we know how to love?" Angelopoulos dons the heavy mantle of Ingmar Bergman's dour despair, crowns himself with Andrei Tarkovsky's moral anguish, affects Miklós Jancsó's virtuoso formalism in search of Michelangelo Antonioni's allegorical landscapes only to wind up in the grand finale dancing by the sea like a stiff-jointed, tone-deaf Federico Fellini.

Also reviewed in:
CHICAGO TRIBUNE, 11/19/99, Friday/p. D, Michael Wilmington

NATION, 6/21/99, p. 32, Stuart Klawans
NEW REPUBLIC, 6/28/99, p. 34, Stanley Kauffmann
NEW YORK TIMES, 5/28/99, p. E10, Janet Maslin
VARIETY, 6/1-7/98, p. 33, David Stratton
WASHINGTON POST, 10/8/99, p. C5, Stephen Hunter

eXistenZ

A Dimension Films/Alliance Atlantis/Serendipity Point Films release in association with Natural Nylon Entertainment of a Robert Lantos production. *Producer:* Robert Lantos, Andras Hamori, and David Cronenberg. *Director:* David Cronenberg. *Screenplay:* David Cronenberg. *Director of Photography:* Peter Suschitzky. *Editor:* Ronald Sanders. *Music:* Howard Shore. *Music Editor:* Suzana Peric and Dan Evans Farkas. *Sound:* Glen Gauthier and (music) Howard Shore. *Casting:* Deirdre Bowen. *Production Designer:* Carol Spier. *Art Director:* Tamara Deverell. *Set Decorator:* Elinor Rose Galbraith. *Set Dresser:* Kevin Haeberlin and Dexter Bonaparte. *Special Effects:* Jim Isaac. *Visual Effects:* Jim Isaac. *Creature Effects:* Kelly Lepkowsky. *Costumes:* Denise Cronenberg. *Make-up:* Shonagh Jabour. *Make-up (Jennifer Jason Leigh):* Micheline Trepanier. *Special Make-up and Creature Design:* Stephan Dupuis. *Stunt Coordinator:* Alison Reid. *Running time:* 90 minutes. *MPAA Rating:* R.

CAST: Jennifer Jason Leigh (Allegra Geller); Jude Law (Ted Pikul); Ian Holm (Kiri Vinokur); Willem Dafoe (Gas); Don McKellar (Yevgeny Nourish); Callum Keith Rennie (Carlaw); Christopher Eccleston (Seminar Leader); Sarah Polley (Merle); Robert A. Silverman (D'Arcy Nader); Oscar Hsu (Chinese Waiter); Kris Lemche (Noel Dichter); Vik Sahay (Male Assistant); Kirsten Johnson (Female Assistant); James Kirchner (Landry); Balazs Koos (Male Volunteer); Stephanie Belding (Female Volunteer); Gerry Quigley (Trout Farm Worker).

LOS ANGELES TIMES, 4/23/99, Calendar/p. 18, Kevin Thomas

With "eXistenZ" David Cronenberg, Canada's master of the macabre, envisions a near-future in which virtual reality games will have become so perfected that their players may no longer be able to tell whether they're in a game or in real life. Cronenberg is not trying for a profound cautionary tale, but a provocative entertainment that allows him free range with his unique, darkly funny and disturbing vision. The Cronenberg trademarks are here in full force, including an outrageous sexual suggestiveness in his bizarre special effects.

The film opens in an old country church, where Allegra Geller (Jennifer Jason Leigh), the game designer supreme, is demonstrating her latest and most powerful games system, "eXistenZ". No sooner has she started than she is subject to an assassination attempt by forces apparently terrified at her skill at tapping into peoples' fears and desires.

She's swiftly on the run with a marketing trainee, Ted Pikul (Jude Law), who works for her employer, Antenna Research. They are thrust into a series of adventures in the countryside that reveal the spiraling paranoia that Cronenberg suggests virtual reality addiction generates.

(Allegra's predicament was inspired by an interview Cronenberg did with writer Salman Rushdie, who at the time was still under the Ayatollah's fatwa; could a games designer, an artist in her own right, be under a similar threat, he wondered? And then what if, in flight, such a designer could be caught up in a game of her own devising?)

There are key encounters with a service station owner (Willem Dafoe), who is enlisted by Allegra in inserting into Ted a Bioport, a spinal jack that allows her to plug in an UmbyCord attached to her MetaFlesh Game-Pod, a game module with roughly the shape of a human kidney in which she has stored "eXistenZ". Once Ted's central nervous system has been tapped, he is equipped to experience the wild ride with Allegra as they continue on the lam through the forest region, with a brief visit with Allegra's scientist mentor, Kiri Vinokur (Ian Holm), and a period of employment at a trout farm, now operating as a facility for harvesting creatures to be incorporated into the games in various ways.

Allegra and Ted encounter a tiny and whimsical yet sinister two-headed amphibian-mutation, which is another Cronenberg preoccupation. A favored weapon in this universe, all the more eerie for seeming so familiar, even homespun, is a gristle gun, created out of the body of a small mammal and designed to shoot teeth (!) instead of bullets and intended to slip by metal and synthetics detectors.

Of course, it must be kept in mind that all these incidents and more could be occurring within the game and not "reality"; the point that Cronenberg deftly makes is that fantasy can have dire real-life consequences. Caught up in your imagination you may kill for real an individual whom you see as a threat in your imagination.

These are the kind of thoughts you have after the fact, for to watch the film is like being caught up in a dream, or rather, a nightmare with its myriad menacing permutations.

Interestingly, "eXistenZ" is not heavy on action spectacle, but there is violence and gore, to be sure, and it has only a few key settings. Cronenberg instead skillfully generates an unsettling involvement and suspense by making us feel that he is playing with our minds, just as Allegra and Ted are doing that to others—and maybe themselves.

In any event, "eXistenZ" is a kind of ultimate nothing-is-as-it-seems movie and its stars contribute as much to sustaining mystery as Cronenberg himself. Jennifer Jason Leigh is an ideal Cronenberg heroine, projecting a personality that is smart, wary and capable of obsessiveness. Law, Dafoe and Holm are ideal foils for her, for they have wit and presence equal to hers.

Cronenberg films rely on exceptional contributions from his crew as well as his cast, and production designer Carol Spier has come up with one faultlessly seedy backwoods setting after another, while composer Howard Shore contributes a score that is as majestic as it is ominous, establishing the film's acute sense of mood and atmosphere right from the start. The eminent cinematographer Peter Suschitzky creates a series of images that are as beautiful as they are unnerving while Jim Isaac's visual and special effects are ingenious and magical.

Sci-fi fantasy/horror doesn't get more sophisticated than "eXistenZ," yet while the film invites speculation, it doesn't require it. As cerebral as "eXistenZ" is, it's nevertheless easy to go along for the ride, just for fun, as you would "Scream," and be rewarded with the stunning kind of payoff all thrillers should deliver regardless of their level of aspiration.

NEW YORK POST, 4/23/99, p. 51, Rod Dreher

Brilliant, subversive and flesh-crawlingly gruesome, David Cronenberg's virtual-reality stunner "eXistenZ" is one terrific movie. It's a "Matrix" for those who find the artsy execution of provocative ideas more thrilling than flashy special effects and virtuoso action sequences.

The question "eXistenZ" asks is: What happens when we give ourselves over to a technology that creates an illusion of life so absorbing we prefer it to the real thing? The consequences prove eerie, macabre and deliciously horrifying.

The film begins sometime in the near future, in a rural church setting. A group of virtual-reality fans are gathered to test the newest creation from the sorceress-like Allegra Gellar (Jennifer Jason Leigh). It's called "eXistenZ" because it envelops its players in a synthetic dream world so thoroughly absorbing it feels like existence itself. Players plug a cable that stretches like an umbilical cord from Allegra's fleshy, womblike game pod into their bodies and download the game directly into their nervous systems.

Just as the download begins, a teen-ager leaps up, brandishing a strange pistol that looks like it was constructed from stringy flesh and leftover bones. "Death to the demoness Allegra Gellar!" he shouts, firing teeth at her. Allegra flees with her p.r. flack, Ted Pikul (Jude Law), and they seek a place to hide after learning a shadowy terrorist group called the Realists has placed a bounty on Allegra's head.

With her game pod damaged by the shooting, sexy Allegra tells her companion the only way to test it is for the two of them to play "eXistenZ." But Pikul, a repressed control freak, doesn't have a bioport. In a bizarre, faintly hilarious psychosexual stunt, Pikul has one shot into the base of his spine by a grungy gas-station attendant (Willem Dafoe).

Cronenberg's not just being gross here. The film's idea is that people have become so addicted to the cyberthrills these games provide them that they've come to prefer the simulation of life to life itself. That's why he has come up with the indelible image of a fake uterus feeding artificial existence into a sphincterlike port. It's a grotesque simulacrum of fertile sexuality.

Allegra and Pikul hole up in a cheap motel and port into the trippy game world. The movie tracks the duo as they quest further and further into the game's universe, so spellbound by the imaginative stimulation it provides that they become increasingly abstracted from reality.

You can see how corruption sets in, and it's particularly dangerous because the game molds itself to the personality of its players. It adjusts to allow for their own fantasies and prejudices. How can you tell when the game stops?

The only problem with "eXistenZ"—aside from its entertainingly icky special effects that'll disturb many viewers—is that it is so idea-dense and intellectualized that it's difficult to make an emotional connection with its characters. The film makes marvelous watching, but it is even more fun to talk about and puzzle over for hours afterwards.

NEWSDAY, 4/23/99, Part II/p. B7, John Anderson

There's not a director whose work is more tactile or mischievously repulsive, whose intellectual challenges are as daring or whose erotic antennae are so attuned to end-of-spectrum transmissions than David Cronenberg. Nor is there one with as entertainingly depraved a sense of humor, especially about himself.

"eXistenZ," a trip into the only slightly futuristic world of virtual-reality game playing, is unmistakable Cronenberg—whose visually adventurous and potentially nauseating work has included "Naked Lunch," "The Fly" and "Dead Ringers." Its natural complement, however, would seem to be "Crash"—his last and perhaps most manifesto-like film, about fetishists, auto crashes and the erotic capacity of prosthetics and amputees.

In "Crash," crushed steel and chrome took on sexual potentialities. In "eXistenZ," hardware is made flesh—throbbing, fetuslike game pods, umbilical cables, weapons made from shards of spine that fire magazines full of molars. It's intriguingly ironic that the credits for "eXistenZ" should roll out over what looks like microscopic slides of slithering organisms, because although the slithering itself is perfectly fine, the abdication of biology is what "eXistenZ" is all about.

At what might be an AA meeting (and that's no coincidence), a group of highly sophisticated game enthusiasts assemble to meet the woman introduced by their host (Christopher Eccleston) as "the game pod goddess herself—Allegra Gellar" (Jennifer Jason Leigh). Gellar is greeted the way a high school chess club might welcome Bobby Fischer: A reclusive legend, she's the designer of the most intricate and involving variable-narrative virtual games—which are played through game pods "ported" into the spinal column of the game player. And her latest work, eXistenZ, is to be test-marketed on this very select audience tonight.

Almost immediately, however, an assassination attempt is made against Gellar, the act of a rebel movement opposed to techno-tyranny of corporate powers numbing minds with escapist entertainment (all analogies welcome and intended). She survives, but along with a young security trainee named Ted Pikul (Jude Law), Gellar flees, driving into a night full of weirdos, danger and games.

We're dealing with alternate and alternating realities here, and to even attempt explaining the plot complexities of "eXistenZ" would be like turning a blow-dryer on a soap bubble. Suffice to say that "eXistenZ" induced its own kind of virtual-reality experience in this reviewer: When its 90-odd minutes were over, it felt like 20 had gone by.

Performances are another matter. Law is fine, but Leigh is, essentially, a genius, who has insisted on making movies that suit her own artistic impulses rather than the needs of the marketplace or the fickle hearts of audiences. Even in a throwaway movie like "Miami Blues," she has given texture to the basest of characters—in that particular case, a woman whom we can see is basically a dimwit, fighting not to let the world know and thinking she's succeeded. In a far more ambitious film like "Washington Square," an underestimated entry on the Leigh resume, she again made real the character's internal, multi-layered performance and the rungs of truth and untruth that Henry James' heiress hung between herself and her world.

Part of the joke in "eXistenZ" is the parallel celebrity Leigh and Allegra Gellar share—a cultlike fervor among a few, general anonymity among the many. And a distancing intelligence. So what better director for Leigh than Cronenberg? If nothing else, they share a thundering lack of appreciation for the subtlety of their work and its deeper meaning. In "eXistenZ" the actress is easier, looser, more overtly sexy than she has ever been and, although it's not a quality usually associated with her, Leigh seems to be having fun.

As will the viewer, if not overwhelmed by Cronenberg's self-referential gross-outs. Is "eXistenZ" over the top? Perhaps. But consider, just for an example, Kim Novak's dual roles in Hitchcock's "Vertigo": Is the performance awful? Or is it a great portrayal of someone giving an awful performance?

The existence of "eXistenZ" is a vapor—nothing that happens can be objectively judged, which is Cronenberg's point. For all his perceived licentiousness—the gruesomeness of the imagery here is gratuitous even for him, but that's part of the send-up of "imagined worlds"—he's fairly bemoaning the state of a world in which so many intellectual escape hatches exist that a consensus reality is a virtual impossibility.

God help university English departments should Cronenberg decide to make a film about the postmodernist Jacques Derrida.

SIGHT AND SOUND, 5/99, p. 46, Kevin Jackson

North America, the near future. A group of players gather to try out eXistenZ, the latest brainchild of the games world's most notorious genius, Allegra Geller. eXistenZ is an elaborate game in which the players wire themselves up via a bioport—a plug inserted in the spinal column to a semi-organic game pod, to induce plotted hallucinations. However, as Allegra begins to download eXistenZ, an anti-games assassin opens fire on her.

Allegra is rescued by Ted Pikul, a junior company member. They set off on the run, pursued by bounty hunters, though Allegra is more concerned about her damaged game. She insists she and Ted must play eXistenZ to assess the damage. Initially fearful, Ted agrees finally to have a bootleg bioport shot into his spine by Gas, a roughneck garage man who turns out to be one of the enemy.

They flee to a ski resort where Allegra's colleague Kiri Vinokur replaces Ted's sabotaged bioport so the couple can finally plug in and play. Together, they enter a violent and frequently bloody set of narratives about spies, counterspies and assassins—a story which becomes increasingly confused with events in the outside world. Finally, it emerges that the entire action so far has itself been a game called transCendenZ; "Allegra", "Ted" and all the other men and women are merely players. "Allegra" and "Ted" are themselves the true anti-games terrorists. As the lethal couple corner transCendenZ's inventor Yevgeny Nourish, he asks them fearfully if this is only an episode in a still more inclusive game. They do not reply.

Fairly or otherwise, two of the critical terms least frequently applied to the Cronenberg oeuvre thus far have been "fun" and "cute": a regrettable state of affairs that *eXistenZ* should do much to remedy. First, the fun part: notwithstanding its showstopping metaphysical somersaults between Chinese-boxed levels of reality, *eXistenZ* is in many respects an unexpectedly conventional entertainment. Some of the conventionality is due, we must assume, to the imaginative tastes of Allegra Geller (or, more pedantically, of the transCendental inventor of "Allegra Geller"), who may be a whiz at bio-tech confections but seems to enjoy an essentially rather banal, if lurid, fantasy life. On the evidence of her taste in adventures, Allegra must have spent her childhood gorging on B movies, Bond films, *The Avengers* and such like, and she's plainly not averse to rescripting herself from a barely articulate wallflower in real life into a devastatingly sexy action babe in eXistenZ life. Somehow, Jennifer Jason Leigh manages to make Allegra into a sympathetic and very nearly plausible character, the single fleshed-out (if that is the apposite term) human being in a gallery of ciphers and caricatures. It's quite a feat.

Next, the cute part. At one point, Allegra notices and smiles at a frisky little two headed amphibian that wouldn't look out of place in a Disney confection. A few years ago, the *Independent* asked its readers to nominate the least likely combination of director and subject. The winning entry was: "David Cronenberg's *National Velvet*. Maybe that competition came to the director's notice, and gave him some ideas. Rest assured, the wee beastie meets a literally sticky end, for in most other respects *eXistenZ* is something of a resumé or, less kindly, a puree of just about every previous Cronenberg film, from the mournfully dignified score by Howard Shore to the sombre lighting and preposterous names. Among its equally familiar attractions are furtive visits to the House of Fiction (cf. *Naked Lunch),* a dangerously seductive new form of entertainment *(Videodrome,* the most obvious precursor of *eXistenZ),* crossings of the borderline between biology and technology (*Crash* and so on), lashings of erotic body modifications *(Rabid* and so on) and, of course, a generous portion of the old Cronenbergian red glop.

The red-glop factor is at its highest within the eXistenZ world particularly when the twists and turns of the games's plot land Allegra and Ted as labourers in a low-rent abattoir-cum-laboratory, where grubby workers hack up frogs and lizards for biotechnological ends, and take their lunch-breaks in a nightmarish Chinese restaurant. Here, Ted orders the daily special, chomps his way through the unidentifiable slippery, slimy horrors he's served, uses the leftover bone and gristle to construct a gun which fires teeth (the very weapon used on Allegra at the beginning) and murders the waiter with a well-aimed molar. At a guess, this is the point of Cronenberg's film at which a lot of younger viewers will find themselves thinking it might be worth saving up for a bioport implant.

But the same qualities which make *eXistenZ* potent for games-world addicts make *eXistenZ* inadequately satisfying for those of us who go in for less all-absorbing forms of diversion, like the cinema. As a thrill-ride in its own right, *eXistenZ* is fine—it's slick, swift and droll. But as an anxious entertainment, which is meant to nag and gnaw at our hunger for surrendering ourselves to surrogate thrills, especially of the disreputable kind that last about two hours (for what, the film keeps nudging us, is eXistenZ if not a hyper-real story, and what is Allegra but a *Künstler* with the *Gesamtkunstwerk* to trump them all?), it's more than a touch half-baked.

eXistenZ tries to make our flesh creep with the insinuation that many of us, if we weren't deterred by the prospect of spinal surgery, would cheerfully invest in bioports and drift away into other people's fantasies. It does its dutiful best to make that Huxleyan thought appear guilty and disquieting. But cheerfulness, or its nastier Cronenbergian equivalent, keeps breaking through the gloom, and the very qualities which make *eXistenZ* watchable also make eXistenZ seem like unthreatening fun. Cronenberg has said the film's point of departure was an interview he once did with Salman Rushdie, but as Kim Newman has pointed out elsewhere in these pages, its more compelling literary source is the haunted fiction of Philip K. Dick. Compared to Dick's writing at its ontologically insecure best, though, *eXistenZ* looks as trifling as it is diverting: a little too perky, a little too pat.

VILLAGE VOICE, 4/27/99, p. 131, J. Hoberman

David Cronenberg is body horror's acknowledged high muckety-muck, but his comic cyberthriller, *eXistenZ*, shows him in a relatively benign mind frame. Although scarcely unphilosophical in its implications, this assured riff on virtual-reality games or rather, that primitive precursor, the motion picture—is almost buoyant in its creepiness and positively bejeweled in its disgust.

Although hardcore Cronenbergians may find *eXistenZ* a disappointingly lite rehash of the superbly malignant *Videodrome* (his last original screenplay), the movie can be enjoyably considered as a self-conscious fiction in the convoluted tradition of Raul Ruiz or Brian De Palma's *Raising Cain*. Miramax is releasing *eXistenZ* through its "genre" division, but it's far more an art film than *Shakespeare in Love*—not to mention a wigglier trip than *The Matrix* (which it might almost be parodying *avant la lettre).*

Appropriate to a tale of total cinema, *eXistenZ* opens in a church, where a collection of company flacks are testing their new virtual-reality product, eXistenZ by Antenna, designed by the form's reigning "goddess," Allegra Geller (played with witchy gusto by Jennifer Jason Leigh). "Not just a game but an entirely new game system," she explains; *eXistenZ* is downloaded directly into its players through the special "bioports" they've had inserted at the base of their spines. You know you're inside Cronenberg's head when they're plugged in, via sinuous UmbyCords, to the appropriately nippled piece of pulsating protoplasm called the game pod.

Meanwhile, the so-called real world is being brutally contested. The shy but glamorous Allegra, it develops, is the subject of a fatwa ordered by "realist" fanatics perhaps in the employ of a rival game manufacturer. After one assassination attempt, she is forced to flee for her life in the company of Antenna PR nerd Ted Pikul (Jude Law). Allegra's straight man in more senses than one, Ted is barely cognizant of the games people play. (When the couple take refuge in a ski lodge, she reminds him that "nobody actually physically skis anymore.") In order to play eXistenZ with the imperious Allegra, who is seeking refuge inside her game, the apprehensive

Ted is subject to an illegal bioport insertion, performed in a back-road gas station by a grinning grease monkey (Willem Dafoe).

As this outrageous scene suggests, *eXistenZ* is unrelentingly blatant in its sexual entendres. It's also a virtual anthology of Cronenberg tropes—truly organic biotechnology, the creation and penetration of new bodily orifices, the horror of disease, and the fear of surgery. Outfitted with a fully developed slang, the movie also features several props more than worthy of the various gallery installations which have recently been devoted to Cronenbergiana, most impressively a bone-and-cartilage revolver that fires human teeth.

As in *The Matrix,* not to mention the novels of Stanislaw Lem and Philip K. Dick (to whom the movie tips its hat), virtual reality is presented as a sort of tawdry hallucinogenic drug. At once run-down and tarted-up, the world of *eXistenZ* is governed by an unknown conspiracy and populated by actors with heavy Hungarian accents, perhaps because theirs is the only way to pronounce the movie's title without sounding like a total fool. Some elements are heightened. Both Allegra and Ted start wearing their clothes as though auditioning for a road company of *Grease.* She gets sexier, he becomes more aggressive and slightly paranoid.

Indeed, Ted's initial mind-expanding experience occasions some of the funniest lysergic dialogue since Dennis Hopper guru'd Peter Fonda through the gaudy funnyhouse of *The Trip.* "That was beautiful. I feel just like me," Ted announces a bit too loudly, before wondering just exactly what might be happening to his real body back at the ski lodge. Allegra's injunctions against panic and her wonderfully schizoid advice ("It's your *character* who said it ... Don't fight it") culminate in an acid koan worthy of Timothy Leary: "You have to play the game to figure out why you're playing the game."

Where *Crash* was austere and metallic, *eXistenZ* is a creative compost of barnyard slaughterhouse yuck. The image of a cut UmbyCord spurting blood over Allegra's high-heeled pumps is only one of the images which have more to do with surrealism than science fiction. The movie's controlled splatter and inspired puppetry peak when Ted finds himself gutting mutant amphibians on a game-pod factory assembly line. This gloppy slime is echoed by the nearby, woodlands Chinese restaurant offering a squeamish child's worst nightmare of school-cafeteria chicken chow mein. "Free will is a fantasy in this little world of ours," Ted complains after ordering the special and then giving in to a "game-urge" so violent it might have been lifted from Camus's *The Stranger.* "It's like real life," Allegra explains. "There is just enough to make it interesting."

Like real life as well, Cronenberg's narrative doesn't completely add up—although one might wish to replay it to check. Nevertheless, the movie's mise-en-scéne never falters. (According to the filmmaker, the production design is based on video-game simplicity: God is in the details.) The final spiral of plot twists serves to reinforce the notion of aesthetic distance—a gloss on Oscar Wilde's dictum that only through art can we "shield ourselves from the sordid perils of actual existence."

Also reviewed in:
CHICAGO TRIBUNE, 4/23/99, Friday/p. A, Michael Wilmington
NATION, 5/10/99, p. 32, Stuart Klawans
NEW YORK TIMES, 4/23/99, p. E21, Janet Maslin
NEW YORKER, 5/10/99, p. 105, Anthony Lane
VARIETY, 2/22-28/99, p. 56 David Stratton
WASHINGTON POST, 4/23/99, Weekend/p. 49, Desson Howe

EXTREME

An Imax Corporation release of a Neils de Jong Franken production. *Producer:* Neils de Jong. *Director:* Jon Long. *Director of Photography:* Bill Reeve. *Editor:* Jon Long. *Music:* Soulfood and DJ Free. *Running time:* 44 minutes. *MPAA Rating:* Not Rated.

WITH: Francine Moreillon, Grant Moles, and Gordy Peifer (Skiers); Terje Haakonsen, Craig Kelly, Victoria Jealouse, and Brandon Ruff (Snowboarders); Ross Clarke-Jones and Ken Bradshaw (Surfers); Robby Naish, Bjorn Dunkerbeck, Jason Polakow, and Josh Stone (Windsurfers); Lynn Hill and Nancy Feagin (Rock Climbers); Barry Blanchard and Catherine Mulvihill (Ice Climbers).

NEW YORK POST, 6/4/99, p. 48, Hannah Brown

"Extreme," the two-dimensional IMAX movie opening today, is an excellent example of a new movie genre: adventure porn.

Like "Everest," perhaps the best adventure-porn flick, "Extreme" presents attractive people undertaking death-defying feats, as it thrills and teases with the possibility that the camera will record a sudden, violent death.

(Don't worry, though: Everyone in "Extreme" manages to stay alive—somehow.)

The stunning photography takes the audience on a thrilling ride and makes each sport so vivid and beautiful that "Extreme" will fascinate even the laziest couch potatoes.

And there's enough cheesecake and beefcake to keep everyone interested. Those thin, tan adventure babes look great in form-fitting Lycra.

While "Everest" followed the attempt of a group of climbers to ascend the Everest summit, "Extreme" cuts to the chase and shows only the most exciting—and hair-raising—moments as athletes take part in "extreme" sports.

The sports in question look like James Bond movie stunts: ice climbing (scaling frozen waterfalls hanging off mountains), surfing and windsurfing on what appear to be tidal waves, rock climbing, and skiing and snowboarding down sheer cliffs.

But if you're looking for insight into why people engage in such sports, "Extreme" won't help much.

"Fear is the thing that keeps you sane," intones one of the ice climbers solemnly (often, it's not clear exactly who is speaking, but since their ideas are so similar, it doesn't much matter).

Many of the athletes mumble about "respecting the ocean's power" or "being in harmony with the mountains."

But don't go to see "Extreme" for the athletes' deep thoughts.

See it because it's the perfect getaway on a rainy weekend. You can watch the waves crash into shore and imagine you're on a beach, or gaze upon the powdery slopes and dream that you're far, far away from the hot city.

NEWSDAY, 6/4/99, Part II/p. B7, Bob Heisler

The "X-Games" seems like silly made-for-TV fare compared with "Extreme," in which athletes do things your mother never warned you about because in her wildest dreams, she couldn't imagine another human being doing them.

Wait a minute; the "X-Games" is silly made-for-TV fare.

"Extreme," on the other hand, is nature sports taken to their logical conclusion by a group of adrenaline junkies—most world champions in their chosen fields—for whom there really ain't no mountain high enough to ski down or climb up.

Using the you-are-nearly-there IMAX format, director Jon Long takes you on a series of wild rides—skiing, snowboarding, surfing, windsurfing, rock climbing and ice climbing—linked by a narrative effort from the athletes to find spiritual meaning beyond a simple laugh-in-the-face-of-death wish.

Example: Snowboarding in Alaska where the thrill isn't just the drop, it's racing just ahead of the "snow wave" (some would call it an avalanche) you kick up on the way down.

It's a relationship movie of sorts, the relationship between extreme athletes and nature. You admire them, of course, but the lesson is: There's gotta be a calmer way to become "in tune" with nature, to forget your troubles, to find your center, to be at peace with the larger world, to carve out your place.

These are spiritual paths few of us can follow, so why worry about the higher level to which these folks have evolved thanks to their training, preparation, desire, inner strength and corporate sponsorship? The pictures are beautiful, though the panoramic "perspective" shots disturb the emotional rhythm and involvement. Perhaps the real heroes are the IMAX camera operators—remember, Ginger Rogers had to do everything Fred Astaire did, only backward.

At 44 minutes, "Extreme" is intense enough to raise your heartbeat, but not long enough to have lasting aerobic effect and, if you get butter on your popcorn, you could leave the theater in worse shape.

Also reviewed in:
NEW YORK TIMES, 6/4/99, p. E25, Lawrence Van Gelder

EYES WIDE SHUT

A Warner Bros. release of a Pole Star production. *Executive Producer:* Jan Harlan. *Producer:* Stanley Kubrick. *Director:* Stanley Kubrick. *Screenplay:* Stanley Kubrick and Frederick Raphael. *Inspired by "Traumnovelle" by:* Arthur Schnitzler. *Director of Photography:* Larry Smith. *Editor:* Nigel Galt. *Music:* Jocelyn Pook. *Choreographer:* Yolanda Snaith. *Sound:* Edward Tise. *Sound Editor:* Paul Conway. *Casting:* Denise Chamian and Leon Vitali. *Production Designer:* Les Tomkins and Roy Walker. *Art Director:* Kevin Phipps. *Set Decorator:* Terry Wells, Sr. and Lisa Leone. *Costumes:* Marit Allen. *Make-up:* Robert McCann. *Running time:* 145 minutes. *MPAA Rating:* R.

CAST: Tom Cruise (Dr. William Harford); Nicole Kidman (Alice Harford); Sydney Pollack (Victor Ziegler); Marie Richardson (Marion Nathanson); Rade Sherbedgia (Milich); Todd Field (Nick Nightingale); Vinessa Shaw (Domino); Alan Cumming (Desk Clerk); Sky Dumont (Sandor Szavost); Fay Masterson (Sally); LeeLee Sobieski (Milich's Daughter); Thomas Gibson (Carl); Madison Eginton (Helena Harford); Jackie Sawiris (Roz); Leslie Lowe (Illona); Peter Benson (Bandleader); Michael Doven (Ziegler's Secretary); Louise Taylor (Gayle); Stewart Thorndike (Nuala Windsor); Randall Paul (Harris); Julienne Davis (Mandy); Lisa Leone (Lisa, Receptionist); Kevin Connealy (Lou Nathanson); Mariana Hewett (Rosa); Gary Goba (Naval Officer); Florian Windorfer (Café Sonata Maitre d'); Togo Igawa (Japanese Man 1); Eiji Kusuhara (Japanese Man 2); Sam Douglas (Cab Driver); Angus MacInnes (Gateman 1); Abigail Good (Mysterious Woman); Brian W. Cook (Tall Butler); Leon Vitali (Red Cloak); Carmela Marner (Waitress at Gillespie's); Phil Davies (Stalker); Cindy Dolenc (Girl at Sharky's); Clark Hayes (Hospital Receptionist); Treva Etienne (Morgue Orderly).

CHRISTIAN SCIENCE MONITOR, 7/16/99, p. 16, David Sterritt

"Eyes Wide Shut," the last movie completed by Stanley Kubrick before his death last spring, is as difficult to pigeonhole as any movie of his career.

In some respects, it's a Hollywood marketer's dream, with sleek performances by two superstars and a sexually explicit plot about a married man facing bizarre temptations.

In other respects, it's a Kubrick film to its bones, using its seemingly lurid subject to spark a serious exploration of the human capacities for self-indulgence and self-delusion. It has raunchy moments, but in the end it sounds a cautionary note about unchecked sensuality, even hinting that the allurements of movies like this—promising the same sorts of forbidden thrills the hero encounters during his strange journey—contain implicit moral hazards we should all be alert to.

Tom Cruise and Nicole Kidman play Bill and Alice Harford, a couple with a beautiful home, a seven-year-old daughter, and a sophisticated Manhattan lifestyle. They're generally content with their achievements, but they're also nagged by the idea that their marriage carries a price tag, since it shuts the door to other close relationships they might desire, including sexual ones.

This restlessness reaches a crisis when Alice confesses a sexual fantasy she's had. Bill is called away from home before he's had time to assimilate this revelation, and finds himself wandering the streets with fantasies of his own. At once prodded by his imagination and restrained by his conscience, he falls into a series of events that lead him to a mysterious mansion full of illicit and perhaps deadly activities. He knows he doesn't belong here—and so do the proprietors of this weird place, who are outraged that a stranger has penetrated their hidden world.

Kubrick clearly intended "Eyes Wide Shut" to be as sexually bold as he could get away with, making one scene (an orgy in the mansion) so graphic that the film's distributor has added computer-generated "characters" to mask some of the action and ensure an R rating.

Yet it's equally clear that Kubrick was not engaging in mere titillation. The film's ultimate message, spelled out plainly in the final scene, is one many viewers will find responsible: that we must remain awake to the darker urges of human nature, and to the social influences that prey on those urges, relying on love and commitment to shield us from temptations that otherwise might wreck our lives.

"Eyes Wide Shut" may reach a large audience in the short run, thanks to its glamorous stars—both of whom give their most deeply felt performances to date—and exotic content. Its long-term popularity will probably be limited by its wordy screenplay and slow-moving story, designed less to build dramatic excitement than to enhance the effectiveness of Kubrick's ingenious visual concepts.

Even on the level of cinematic brilliance, however, the movie doesn't meet Kubrick's loftiest standard. While the immaculate framing, expressive camera movement, and neon-tinged lighting are close to visual perfection, these elements are hampered by the thinly fashioned narrative they have to serve. Zeroing in on crafty temptations that assault human nature from within and without, "Eyes Wide Shut" aims for the self-critical irony of "A Clockwork Orange" and "Full Metal Jacket," which tackled somewhat similar themes in very different ways. This is a subject Kubrick never quite conquered in those earlier films, however, and it eludes him again here. The greatest part of his legacy lies in other, richer works.

FILM QUARTERLY, Spring 2000, p. 41, Tim Kreider

Critical disappointment with *Eyes Wide Shut* was almost unanimous, and the complaint was always the same: not sexy. The reviewers of the national press sounded like a bunch of schoolkids who'd snuck in to see it and slouched out three hours later feeling frustrated, horny, and ripped off. Once again Stanley Kubrick flouted genre expectations, and once again, as throughout his career, critics and audiences could only see what wasn't there. Why exactly anyone who had seen his previous films believed the hype and expected his last one to be what *Entertainment Weekly,* breathlessly anticipated as "The Sexiest Movie Ever" is still not clear: the most erotic sex scenes Kubrick ever filmed were the bomber refueling in *Dr Strangelove* and the space docking in *2001*. He mocks any prurient expectations in the very first shot of this movie: without prelude, Nicole Kidman steps into the frame, her back to the camera. shrugs off her dress and kicks it away, standing matter-of-factly bare-assed before us for a moment before the screen goes black and the main title appears. It's as if to say, "You came to see a big-time movie star get naked? Here ya go. Show's over. Now let's get serious."

So okay, no, *Eyes Wide Shut* is not a sexy film. The story's sexual mores and taboos —jealousy over dreams and fantasies, guilt-ridden visits to prostitutes, a strained discussion of a positive HIV test that echoes the old social terror of syphilis—are all transplanted more or less intact straight out of Arthur Schnitzler's fin-de-siècle Vienna, seeming quaint and naive by the standards of the sordid year 1999. But *Eyes Wide Shut* is not about "sex." The real pornography in this film is in its lingering, overlit depiction of the shameless, naked wealth of end-of-the-millennium Manhattan, and of the obscene effect of that wealth on the human soul, and on society. National reviewers' myopic focus on sex and the shallow psychologies of the film's central couple, the Harfords, at the expense of every other element in the film—the trappings of stupendous wealth, the references to fin-de-siècle Europe and other imperial periods, the Christmastime setting, or even the sum spent by Dr. Harford on a single illicit night out—suggests more about the blindness of the elites to their own surroundings than it does about Stanley Kubrick's inadequacies as a pornographer. For those with their eyes open, there are plenty of money shots.

There is a moment in *Eyes Wide Shut,* as Dr. Bill Harford is lying to his wife over the phone from the apartment of a prostitute, when we see a textbook in the foreground called *Introducing Sociology*. The book's title serves as a sly, mirthless caption to the scene (like the slogan PEACE IS OUR PROFESSION in *Dr. Strangelove),* showing us prostitution as the basic and defining transaction of our society. It is also, more importantly, a key to reading the film, suggesting that we ought to interpret it *sociologically*—not, as most reviewers insisted on doing, psychologically.

"If Kubrick was going to make a movie about sexual obsession," wrote Stuart Klawans of *The Nation*, "he should have chosen characters with interesting individual psychologies." Michiko Kakutani of the *New York Times* pointed out that Kubrick "never paid much attention to the psychology of his characters, much less relationships between men and women," and has, in fact, "spent his career ignoring (or avoiding) ... the inner lives of people, their private dreams and frustrations." Unable to imagine what other subjects there could be, she, like so many reviewers over the years, shrugged Kubrick off as obsessed with pure sophistication of technique. These reactions recall the befuddlement of critics who complained that the astronauts in *2001* acted less human than the computer HAL, but could only attribute this (just four years after the performances of *Dr. Strangelove*) to bad direction. But Kubrick's films are never only about individuals. (Sometimes, as in the case of *2001*, they hardly even contain any.) They are always about civilization, about human history. Even *The Shining* is not just about a family, as Bill Blakemore has shown in his eye-opening article "The Family of Man," but about the massacre of the Native Americans and the recurrent murderousness of Western civilization.

Bill and Alice Harford's psyches do seem as naive and sexually sheltered as those of the Victorians in, say, Galsworthy's *Forsyte Saga* but to wish that the characters had been more complex or self-aware misses the point. To understand a film by this most thoughtful and painstaking of filmmakers, we should assume that this characterization is *deliberate*, the Harfords' shallowness and repression is the point. Think of Bill in the back of the cab, his face a sullen mask as he runs the same dirty black-and-white movie of Alice's imagined infidelity over and over in his head—a married man of nine years profoundly shaken by the revelation that his wife was once attracted to another man. (Anyone who doubts that it is the character, rather than the actor, who lacks depth and expressiveness should watch Cruise in *Magnolia*.) The intensely staged vacuity of the Harfords' inner lives tells us to look elsewhere for the film's real interests.

One place to look is not at the characters but around them, at the places where they live and the things they own. Most of the film's sets, even the New York street scenes, were constructed on sound stages and backlots, just like the Overlook Hotel, which was as central to *The Shining* as its actors. Precision of visual detail is as integral to the meaning of *Eyes Wide Shut* as is the use of famous, gorgeous faces familiar from the covers of supermarket magazines to play the conspicuously attractive high-society couple (like the casting of handsome, bland-faced Ryan O'Neal as the eighteenth-century social climber Remond Barry in *Barry Lyndon*). Even the street sets (criticized by the uniquely provincial New York press as inaccurate) are expressionistic in intent, with neon signs like "Pink Pussycat" and "EROS" foreshadowing and commenting on the action. In Kubrick's mature work, nothing is incidental: every detail of mise-en-scène should be assumed purposeful and significant.

Stephen Hunter of the *Washington Post* mentions, that the Harfords' apartment "must have cost $7 million," but only to mock Kubrick's apparent disconnection from contemporary America. But the meticulously rendered settings of the film, the luxurious apartments and sumptuous mansions, are *meant* to raise eyebrows. The Harfords' standard of living raises questions about their wealth and where it comes from. From Bill's sparsely scheduled private practice, or from his "house calls" and the sorts of under-the-table services we see him render at Ziegler's party? Bill Harford is on call to that class of person who can afford not to wait in emergency rooms or die in hospitals, people like Victor Ziegler. Although Bill condescendingly calls the prostitute Domino's apartment "cozy," his own place looks cramped and cluttered compared to Ziegler's, with its vast ballrooms and stairways reminiscent of the haunted Overlook Hotel, its cascades of glittering lights, its mirrors and gilt, its bedroom-sized bathrooms. And even Ziegler's house seems modest and sensible compared to the opulent Moorish palace of Somerton, where the secret orgy takes place (in Schnitzler's novella it is merely "a one-story villa in a modest Empire style"). To some extent, the fact that no reviewers recognized this as deliberate is forgivable; we've all learned to ignore the fantastic affluence of the sets and costumes in most movies and TV shows, just as black audiences have had, for decades, to filter out the whiteness of most characters in the media. But make no mistake: this is not a film about the "private dreams and frustrations" of what Ziegler calls "ordinary people": it is, very pointedly, about really *rich* people, that notorious one percent of the population that owns forty percent of the wealth.

The paintings that cover the Harfords' walls from floor to ceiling (most of them painted by Kubrick's wife Christine), almost without exception depict gardens, flowers, or food, making explicit the function of art in this environment as decor, art for consumption—a commodity. Helena, the Harfords' daughter, helps Alice Christmas-wrap a massive collection of reproductions by Van Gogh (the very icon of an artist who suffered pitiably for his work during his lifetime but whose reproductions on calendars, ties, and coffee mugs now produce quick multimillions for the canny profiteers of the museum industry). The apartment of Bill's patient Lou Nathanson is decorated with even more expensive objets d'art, tastefully placed in spotlit alcoves, and his bedroom is wallpapered with imperial blue and gold fleur-de-lis (just like the hallway outside the Harfords' own apartment). And Victor Ziegler has a famous art collection: corrections of antique china arrayed in glass cases, a soaring winged statue of Cupid and Psyche in his stairwell, and, reputedly, a collection of Renaissance bronzes upstairs. Like Clare Quilty's trashed mansion in *Lolita,* these houses are stocked with the plundered treasures of the world.

Sandor Szavost, Alice's would-be seducer at Ziegler's ball, inquires at one point whether she knows Ovid's *Art of Love,* a satiric guide to the niceties of seduction and intrigue, set among the elite classes of Augustus's imperial Rome, that includes valuable instruction on matters from buying gifts and bribing servants to not trusting your friends and keeping your mouth shut. Szavost, like Ovid, is urbane, witty and amoral, and his drinking, deliberately from Alice's glass is a move lifted straight out of Ovid's pick-up manual. The fact that Ovid was an exile from his own center of empire (Didn't he end up alone, crying his eyes out someplace with a very bad climate?" asks Alice) links him to the expatriate Hungarian Szavost, whose extraordinary skill at the defunct Viennese waltz allows him to guide Alice effortlessly around the ballroom, drunk though she is on champagne. (The presence of so many European expatriates in the film—Szavost, the models Gayle and Nuala, Mariane Nathanson, and Milich—reinforces the association of 1999 America with fin-de-siècle Europe, another corrupt and decadent high culture on the brink of disaster.) Szavost's invitation to Alice to come upstairs and see Ziegler's collection of bronze sculptures extends the instances of imperially sponsored high art from the Latin poetry of ancient Rome to the plastic arts of the Renaissance to ballroom dance of the Austro-Hungarian Empire and into contemporary New York's glittering, art-encrusted facade. America has absorbed and established continuity with all these earlier imperial periods.

Alice reluctantly resists Szavost's effort at seduction in the name of her marriage (though she later assures her husband that she knows he had only wanted to have sex with her). The theme of women being dangerously fucked at the epicenters of empire is meanwhile being established elsewhere. Behind the scenes at Victor's party, in an upstairs bathroom, Bill Harford finds the same thing that Jack Torrance finds in the Overlook's bathroom, and that Private Joker finds at the end of *Full Metal Jacket:* a woman's body. Banal dance music echoes hollowly from downstairs as we see Mandy sprawled naked in a narcotic stupor. Victor (an imperial name, like Alexander deLarge in *A Clockwork Orange)* is hurriedly pulling on his pants, his sexual use of the girl having been interrupted by her overdose. After Dr. Bill brings her around, Ziegler secures his compliance in keeping this near-scandal "just between us." But with reference to a broad sweep of imperial styles, and with eyes open to all of their exploitative associations (the painting on the wall behind Victor is a nude), our contemporary American artist-in-exile, Stanley Kubrick, in his own bitterly parodic *Art of Love,* tells all. Asked about Alex's fondness for Beethoven, Kubrick answered: "I think this suggests the failure of culture to have any morally refining effect on society. Many top Nazis were cultured and sophisticated men, but it didn't do them or anyone else, much good." The use of *Fidelio,* "an opera by Beethoven" as Nick Nightingale points out, as the password to the orgy is not just heavy-handed irony (fidelity) but a reiteration of this critique.

As omnipresent and unnoticed as the art in the film's backgrounds are its Christmas decorations. It's not incidental that the film is set at Christmastime, Schinitzler's book, which the script follows very closely in most other particulars, is not (it takes place "just before the end of carnival period"). Stanley Kubrick seems to have gotten seriously into the Yuletide spirit in this film: *Eyes Wide Shut* is *the* Christmas movie of 1999. Hardly an interior in the filter (except for the Satanic orgy) is without a gaudily baubled Christmas tree. Almost every set is suffused with the hazy glow of colored lights and tinsel. The film's denouement, the final conversation between the Harfords, takes place in a decidedly upscale department store where their daughter indulges herself "Christmas shopping," identifying items she wants exclusively for herself.

There is, in fact, a chain of allusions to the Judeo-Christian fall-and-redemption myth throughout the film; Alice's dream about being "naked and ashamed," and fucking "in a beautiful garden": the Harfords' Edenic apartment crammed with plants and paintings of gardenias; the picture of an apple with a single vaginal slice cut from it on the wall of Domino's kitchen; the self-sacrificial ritual at the orgy. But, compared to the subtler imagery in the rest of the film, these seem very clumsy and nineteenth-century and decidedly un-Kubrickian. (The only overtly Christian imagery in his film's are Alex's ceramic chorus line of dancing Christs and Biblical-epic daydream about being a centurion who gets to flog Him in A Clockwork Orange, in which film Christianity is clearly just another, less effective form of the sadistic Ludovico treatment.) In fact, these Biblical allusions only serve to show us how bankrupt the Christian ethic is in America at the turn of the millennium, how completely it has been coöpted and undermined by the culture of commerce. As Ziegler angrily tells Bill in their final confrontation. "That whole play-acted 'take me' phony sacrifice you've been jerking yourself off with had absolutely nothing to do with her [Mandy's] real death!" No—her real death had more to do with the cult of power and secrecy at the heart of wealth. In other words, just business.

In Eyes Wide Shut, as in the real world of the United States circa 1999, Christmas is less a religious observance than a frenzied, culminating orgy of consumerism, the climax of the retail year. MERRY CHRISTMAS banners hang in the backgrounds at places of business along with signs reading NO CHECKS ACCEPTED and THANK YOU FOR YOUR CUSTOM. Rows of Christmas cards are on display at Doctor Bill's office below a not particularly merry sign saying "Payment is expected at the time of treatment unless other arrangements have previously been made." These juxtapositions undercut the supposed significance of the holiday and reveal the real nature of the season, its ostensible warmth and sentimentality belied by the bottom line. Milich, the owner of Rainbow Costumes even calls holiday greetings after the two men who have just come to "another arrangement" concerning the use of his daughter. The whole movie is brimming over with the spirit of the season.

The Harfords themselves (like most of the film's reviewers) don't really see their surrounding mise-en-scène—their wealth, their art, the ubiquitous Christmas glitz. They're preoccupied instead with their own interior lives, the petty lusts and jealousies which they think of as distinct from their exterior world. But again and again Kubrick visually links his characters to their settings, indicting them as part of the rarefied world in which they live and move, through which his relentless Steadicam tracks them like an omniscient presence. At Ziegler's ball, the star-burst pattern of lights seen on the walls in the background is echoed in the lace edging of Alice Harford's gown and in the blue stelliform ribbon on Sandor Szavost's lapel. Domino first appears in a black-and-white striped fur coat, a pattern repeated in the zebra skin stool at her dresser and in the coat of a plush tiger on her bed. Like the art in the film, everything here is decor, commodity—everything can be bought.

And everyone. Alice Harford's status is subtly but unmistakably suggested: the wife as prostitute. She is associated with the streetwalker Domino by purple, the color of her sheets and of Domino's dress, and by their dressing-table mirrors. She's also associated with Mandy; we first see them both in bathrooms, they share a taste for numbing intoxicants, and Mandy's last night "being fucked by hundreds of men" is distortedly echoed in Alice's "nightmare." Mandy and Domino are connected, as in dream-associations, by the shared consonants of their names; Alice is similarly connected with Domino's roommate, Sally. These last two women are interchangeable; when Domino disappears, she is replaced by Sally the next day.

Although Alice is giggling in her "nightmare," clearly enjoying her betrayal and humiliation of her husband (just as she burst out laughing at him earlier), once she awakens her laughter turns to tears and she says "I had such a horrible dream." The repression is instantaneous. Her resentment of her husband, the malice that prompts her to tell him the story of the naval officer, may be motivated by her unconscious recognition that she is a kept woman. We know she is unemployed, her art gallery having gone broke. She tells Sandor Szavost she's "looking for a job," but we don't see her looking; mostly we see her being looked at. Her role as an object is defined by her first onscreen line: "How do I look?" Bill tells her she looks beautiful, as does everyone else; she's also complimented by such admirers of beauty as Victor Ziegler and Sandor Szavost.

Ziegler tells her she looks "absolutely stunning—and I don't say that to all the women." "Oh, yes, he does," says his wife—a joke that resonates unfunnily when we remember who "all the women" associated with Ziegler are. During the quotidian-life-of-the-Harfords montage in which her husband examines patients at the office, we only see Alice tending to her toilette: brushing her daughter's hair, regally hooking on a brassiere, applying deodorant in front of the bathroom mirror. Hers is the daytime life of a courtesan (or a movie star), devoted to the maintenance of her beauty. When we last see Alice in the film, in the department store, she is surrounded by shelves full of stuffed tigers identical to the one on Domino's bed, linking her again to the vanished prostitute. (Tiger- and leopard-print patterns are also used in *Lolita* to connote Charlotte Haze's predatory sexuality.)

Alice is also grooming her daughter Helena (named after the most beautiful woman in history) to become a high-priced thing of beauty like herself. During the Alice's-day-at-home montage, we see Helena alongside her in almost every shot, holding the hairbrush while her mother gathers her hair into a ponytail, brushing her teeth at the mirror while her mom applies deodorant, learning to attend to her appearance. When we overhear Helena doing word problems with her mother, she's learning to work out who has more money than whom. We hear her reading a bedtime story aloud, reciting the line, "… before me when I jump into my bed." In this film, a line about "jumping into bed" cannot be innocent. Her mother silently mouths it along with her, echoing and coaching her.

Like his wife, Bill is defined by his first line: "Honey, have you seen my wallet'?" Just as his wife is a possession, he is a buyer. ("Doctor Bill," as Domino calls him, is another of Kubrick's Swiftian puns, like Jack D. Ripper.) He flashes his credentials and hands out fifty and hundred-dollar bills to charm, bribe, or intimidate cabbies, clerks, and hookers all members of the vast compliant service economy upon whom the enormous disparities of American wealth are built, the sorts of people who just have to smile and take it if they're being paid. Bill is nothing if not a conspicuous consumer: including (unconsumated) prostitution, costume rental, and cab fare, his tab for a single night out totals over seven hundred dollars in cash. He does not seem fazed by the expenditure. His asking Domino "Should we talk about money?", his repeated insistence on paying her for services not rendered, his haggling with Milich over the cost of after-hours costume rental—these financial dialogues are too frequent, too conspicuous, and too drawn-out to be included only in the interest of mundane verisimilitude (they do not occur in the novel). Harford even tears a hundred dollar bill in half with a boyish, self-congratulatory grin, giving one half to his cab driver and keeping the other as insurance that the driver will wait for him. (You can't help but wonder whether it was a real Ben Franklin, and, if so, how many takes Kubrick required of this shot.)

Bill's nocturnal journey into illicit sexuality is, more significantly, a journey into invisible strata of wealth. Money is the subtext of sex from the very first temptation of Bill; the two models who flirtatiously draw him away from his wife at Ziegler's ball invite him, enigmatically, to follow them "where the rainbow ends." It's at that moment that he's called away, saying to them, "To be continued?" After he has gone, the two models exchange a cryptic, conspiratorial look. It's a moment, as Janet Maslin of the *New York Times* noted, that foreshadows Bill's finding himself at Rainbow Costume Rentals. "To be continued," indeed. We never find out exactly what the two models meant, but again every child knows what lies at the end of the rainbow.

The colorful arc of Bill's adventure does end at the pot of gold, the innermost sanctum of the ultra-wealthy where the secret orgy is held. The orgy scenes, in particular, were singled out by reviewers for disappointment, derision, and other disguised griping about critical blueballs. (David Denby, in *The New Yorker,* called it "The most pompous orgy in the history of film." "More ludicrous than provocative, more voyeuristic than scary." complained Michiko Kakutani. "Whose idea of an orgy is this," groaned Stephen Hunter, "the Catholic Church's?") But again reviewers mistake Kubrick's artistic choices, which are the opposite of the sensual. When Bill passes through the ornate portal past golden-masked doorman, we should know that we are entering the reality myth and nightmare. This sequence is the clearest condemnation, in archetypal dream-imagery, of elite society as corrupt, exploitative, and depraved—what they used to call, in a simpler time, evil. The pre-orgy rites are overtly Satanic, a Black Mass complete with a high priest gowned in crimson, droning organ, and backward-masked lyrics. The haunted ambiance recalls that of the film's other big exclusive party, Ziegler's, the opulent surroundings (including

492 FILM REVIEW ANNUAL

more appropriated historical styles, from Moorish to medieval to French imperial, floor-to-ceiling bookcases, tapestries, oil portraits of stern patriarchs), the mannered, leaden dialogue, the camera afloat like the disembodied point-of-view in a dream. A ballroom full of naked, masked couples dancing to "Strangers in the Night" again recalls the Overlook Hotel, whose ghosts also danced and coupled in costume. (Remember the single quick, surreal zoom shot in *The Shining* of some-one in a grotesque, bestial costume fellating the tuxedoed millionaire Horace Derwetit in an upstairs room.)

The scene makes the metaphor of sexual "objectification" visually literal. The ritual prostitutes, who are themselves objects purchased for sexual use, wear masks that make them identical and interchangeable. Their nude bodies are unnaturally perfect, smooth and immaculate as mannequins, photographed with the cold Kubrickian detachment that desaturates them of any eroticism. The sex we see consists of static tableaus of spectators (some of them digitally generated) posed around mechanically rutting participants. A man on all fours serves as a platform for a fornicating couple, a piece of furniture like the tables at the Korova Milk Bar in *A Clockwork Orange*. One might remember, with a shudder, the Lugosian-toned Szavost inviting Alice to have casual sex upstairs, among the Sculptures.

The Venetian masks worn by the revelers (Venice, center of another mercantile empire) serve a similar symbolic purpose, the transformation of the wearer into a soulless object. They certainly aren't expressive of ecstatic self-annihilation, as some critics have suggested, they're creepy as hell. We see a bird with a scythe-like beak, a cubist face fractured in half, contorted grimaces and leers, a frozen howl, painted tears, blindly gazing eyes. These revelers have "lost themselves" not in erotic abandon but in the same way that the recruits in *Full Metal Jacket* lose their selves, along with their hair and their names. The utterly still, silent shots of staring masks at Bill's "trial" are images of empty-eyed dehumanization, faces of death. Here, ironically, the guests at Ziegler's party are unmasked for what they really are.

Masks and mannequins are a recurring motif in Kubrick's work: the fight with mannequin limbs in *Killer's Kiss*, the erotic furniture at the Korova, the rubber masks worn by Johnny in *The Killing* and by Alex and his droogs. In *Eyes Wide Shut* they appear not just in the orgy but throughout the film, always as harbingers of death: a stone Greek mask stands by Lou Nathanson's deathbed, and African masks look down at the bed where Harford has his interrupted trick with the HIV-positive Domino like the marked spectators watching sex acts at Somerton. A "domino" is itself a kind of mask. Costumed mannequins surround Harford and Milich in the back room at Rainbow Costumes. "Like life, eh?" says Milich, just before he catches his daughter consorting with two men in lurid makeup and wigs. Milich's daughter, for all the coquettish depravity in her face, looks somehow as eerily inanimate as the Grady twins in *The Shining*—her skin is smooth and white as the mannequins' in the back room, her painted lips and glittering eyes perfect as a china doll's. "If Dr. Harford should need anything else," says Milich, hugging his daughter close like the little goldmine she is, "Anything at all ... it needn't be a costume." This line, obviously offering her for sale, reinforces the visual equation of the girl with the costumes which are the store's more legitimate merchandise. And the three times we see Mandy, the ex-beauty queen and hooker, her face is always a mask: in Ziegler's bathroom, as she's coming back from the brink of an overdose, her eyes are lit to appear as black, empty holes in her face; at the orgy, she's literally masked; and on the slab at the morgue her face is slack and white, her eyes wide open but sightless.

For all his flaunting of money and professional rank, and all his efforts to penetrate the inner circle of the elite, Bill Harford is ultimately put back in his place as a member of the serving class. Recall how he is summoned away from Ziegler's party in the same polite but perfunctory manner as is his friend, the pianist Nick; like Nick, Bill, too, is only hired help, the party physi-cian, called upon to repair (if possible) and cover up (if necessary) human messes like Mandy. When he goes to Lou Nathanson's, he is met at the door by a maid who approaches through a door from the other direction, mirroring his movement. They are both dressed in black with white collars, facing each other in a perfectly symmetrical foyer where every other object is in a matched pair. The shot doubles them, identifying them as equals. Bill is given away when he tries to infiltrate the orgy by telltale distinctions of his class status—he shows up in a taxi (not a limo) and has a costume rental slip in his coat pocket. When Ziegler calls him onto the carpet for his transgression, he chuckles at Bill's firm refusal of a case of 25-year-old Scotch (Bill's a

Bud man), not just because this extravagance would be a trifle to Ziegler, but because Bill's pretense of integrity is an empty gesture—he is already bought and paid for. Bill may own Alice, but Ziegler owns him.

When Bill persists in making inquiries, he is rebuked and intimidated into confession by his master. "You've been way out of your depth for the last 24 hours," Ziegler tells him, shaking his head in disgust. During the same conversation he says, "Who do you think those people were"? Those were not ordinary people there. If I told you their names—I'm not going to tell you their names, but if I did, you might not sleep so well." We can only assume they are politicians and moguls, the sorts of supremely wealthy and powerful men who can buy and sell "ordinary" men like Bill and Nick Nightingale, and fuck or kill women like Mandy and Domino.

Although Ziegler has a credible explanation for everything that's happened—Harford's harassment, Nick Nightingale's beating and coerced escort out of town, Mandy's death—we don't ever really know whether he's telling the truth or lying to cover up Mandy's execution and assuage Bill's unexpectedly activated conscience. Note how Ziegler introduces his explanation: "*Suppose* I were to tell you ..." giving Bill an escape, a believable story to buy. Ziegler does seem to have suspiciously privileged access to details of the case: "The door was locked from the inside, the police are satisfied, case closed! [dismissive fart noise]." And his last word on the subject—"Life goes on. It always does ... until it doesn't. But you know that, don't you, Bill?"—proffered with an avuncular, unpleasantly proprietary rub of the shoulders, is both a reassurance and a threat. In the end, Bill chooses to accept Ziegler's explanations not because there is any convincing evidence to confirm them, but because they are convenient, an excuse to back down from the dangers of further inquiry.

Of course, Bill hasn't actually killed anyone. But he is implicated in the exploitation and deaths of all the women he encounters. (As the sign over the bar at the Sonata Café says, "The Customer Is Always Wrong.") Bill didn't give Domino HIV, but he might as well have; she certainly contracted it servicing someone like him. Milich alternates with hilarious aplomb between berating the men he's caught with his daughter—"Will you please to be quiet! Can't you see I am trying to serve a customer?"—and unctuous apologies to Harford, conflating the two exchanges. (After all, Bill isn't playing just for a costume, but for the sexual opportunity he hopes it'll afford him.) And does it really make a difference whether Mandy was ceremonially executed by all evil cabal or only allowed, finally, to overdose after being gangbanged again? For the darkly humorous literalist in Kubrick ("Gentlemen, you can't fight in here: this is the War Room!", "Wendy. I'm not gonna hurt you ... I'm just gonna bash your brains in!"), when Ziegler explains that Mandy wasn't murdered, she just "got her brains fucked out," the contradiction is obvious. Bill learns of her death in a café whose walls are covered with antique portraits of women, while Mozart's *Requiem* plays in the background. The setting and the music make the moment timeless, universal: the requiem is not just for this one dead hooker—but for all the anonymous, expendable women who have been destroyed by men of Harford's class throughout the ages.

After Bill's confession to his wife, in the film's upbeat but dissonant denouement, the Harfords (like so many reviewers) are still wrapped up in the psychology of their own sexualities, missing the wider implications of what's onscreen. They've taken their daughter Helena Christmas shopping, but they respond to her wishes only politely, preoccupied as usual with their childish inner selves. Their dialogue, transcribed pretty much verbatim from *Traumnovelle,* is so allusive and disjointed that it's hard even to understand what they're supposed to be talking about. (If we believe that the mask was placed on Bill's pillow not by Alice but by Ziegler's cabal as a last warning and threat, then they're not just reconciling over Bill's indiscretions, they are agreeing to be accomplices after the fact to a homicide.) But, as in so much of Kubrick's work, the dialogue is misdirection: the real story is told visually. Ignored by her parents, poor Helena flits anxiously from one display to another, already an avid consumer, holding up one toy and then another. And every item she fondles associates her with the women who have been exploited by her father's circle: a baby carriage (recalling the stroller seen twice outside Domino's apartment, and placed next to a stuffed tiger just like the one on Domino's bed), an oversized teddy bear (next to a whole rack of those tigers), and a Barbie doll (recalling Milich's daughter) dressed in a diaphanous angel's costume like the one Helena wears at the beginning of the film. Another toy conspicuously displayed is called "The Magic Circle"; the name is an allusion to the ring of ritual prostitutes at the orgy, and the bright red color of the box recalls the carpet on which they genuflected to the cloaked high priest as well as the felt of the pool table over which Bill made his own bargain with the devil. The subplot with Milich and his daughter is clearly echoed here, in another place of business, as the Harfords, too, casually pimp their own little angel out to the world of commerce.

ALICE: And, you know, there is something very important we have to do as soon as possible.
BILL: What's that?
ALICE: Fuck.

As *Eyes Wide Shut* closes, this final exchange between Bill and Alice suggests that all the dark adventures they've confessed ("whether they were real or only dreams"), and all the crimes in which they are complicit, have occasioned nothing more than another kinky turn-on, no more enlightening than the dalliences at Ziegler's ball that inflamed their lovemaking when they got home. Bill and Alice have learned nothing; for all their incoherent talk about being "awake" now, their eyes are still wide shut. Reconciled, they plan to forget all this unpleasantness soon in the blissful oblivion of orgasm. (Try keeping your eyes open during orgasm.) Maybe, in the end, it *is* a film about sexual obsession after all; audiences and critics, like the Harfords, remain obsessed with sex to the end, oblivious to what's right before their eyes. Maybe the customer *is* always wrong.

Certainly a subtler psychological interpretation of the film than has been attempted would be possible. But to focus exclusively on the Harfords' unexamined inner lives is to remain blind to the profoundly visual filmic world that Kubrick devoted a career's labors to creating. The slice of that world he tried to show us in his last—and, he believed, his best work, the capital of the American Empire at the end of the millennium, is one in which the wealthy, powerful, and privileged use the rest of us like throwaway products, covering up their crimes with shiny surfaces and murder, ultimately dooming their own children to servitude and whoredom. The feel-good ending intimates, in Kubrick's last word on the subject, that the Harfords' daughter is—just as they have abandoned themselves to being—fucked.

LOS ANGELES TIMES, 7/16/99, Calendar/p. 1, Kenneth Turan

The combination of sex and death (have I got your attention yet?) has always tantalized artists, especially as they age, and, if "Eyes Wide Shut" is any indication, most especially Stanley Kubrick.

Far from the hot date-night movie the racy Warner Bros. campaign would have you expect, Kubrick's last film, completed just before his death and starring Tom Cruise and Nicole Kidman as a married couple who stumble onto the edge of a terrible moral abyss, is a strange, somber and troubling meditation on jealousy, obsession and (yes) sex and death. More European than Hollywood in tone, it's half brilliant, half banal, but always the work of a master director whose output has gotten increasingly distant and self-involved over the years—and not always to our benefit.

After turning out seven features in the first decade of his career, Kubrick directed only six more times in his final 35 years, and his last films, including costume drama "Barry Lyndon," horror film "The Shining" and war movie "Full Metal Jacket," have all been determinedly off the beat of genre expectations.

Written by Kubrick and veteran screenwriter Frederic Raphael ("Darling," "Two for the Road"), "Eyes Wide Shut" follows that pattern and, like those predecessors, makes its strongest impression not with dialogue but with virtuoso visual work. Despite all the time spent on the script (the numberless rewrites and rehearsals began three years ago), whenever the film has to depend on the written word for its effects the results tend to be unconvincing.

But when Kubrick, as in the dark and unnerving film-within-a-film orgy scene that is "Eyes Wide Shut's" centerpiece, cuts words to a minimum and uses pure cinematic technique to go to the core of his emotions, what results has the powerful, lacerating impact of inescapable nightmare. This is finally a film that is better at mood than substance, that has its strongest hold on you when it's making the least amount of sense.

"Eyes Wide Shut" is based on "Traumnovelle" (Dream Story), a 1926 novella by Arthur Schnitzler, a Viennese writer who was influenced by Sigmund Freud, his contemporary. Like

Clint Eastwood holding onto "Unforgiven" until the time was right, Kubrick has controlled the rights to the work for decades. And it's a mark of how much the novella touched him, how much of a soul mate he felt he'd found in Schnitzler (whose David Hare-adapted "The Blue Room" starred Kidman on the London and New York stage) that he's kept all "Traumnovelle's" major plot points intact and even been faithful in smaller areas, like the number of off-screen children a subsidiary character has.

What Kubrick must have connected with, aside from the novella's elusiveness, lack of structural rigor and a belief that "no dream is entirely a dream," was its air of sexual yearning and imminent death. He and Raphael moved the plot to contemporary Manhattan but kept the novella's sense of sexual experience that is just out of reach as well as the possibility that the happy life of Dr. William Harford (Cruise) and his wife, Alice (Kidman), is no more than a thin, "Matrix"-like veneer over a caldron of fear and desire.

Ever the showman, Kubrick starts "Eyes Wide Shut" with a startling shot of a completely nude Alice dropping her dress to the bathroom floor as she prepares for a black-tie holiday party given by one of her husband's patients, New York power broker Victor Ziegler (Sydney Pollack, who inherited the part when Harvey Keitel left the project).

At the ball itself (shot by Kubrick and his lighting cameraman Larry Smith in sweeping tracking shots), both Alice and her husband, married nine years with a 7-year-old daughter, engage in desultory flirtation. He chats with a pair of models (is no New York party complete without them?), she with Sandor Szavost (Sky Dumont), the most unctuous of Hungarian Lotharios, who tells her, oozing ersatz worldliness, "Don't you think one of the charms of marriage is that it makes deception a necessity for both parties."

Harford, meanwhile, has separate adventures. He reconnects with an old medical school classmate, Nick Nightingale (Todd Field of "Ruby in Paradise"), now a piano player for hire. And he's called upstairs to Ziegler's private apartment, where a beautiful nude woman has had a bad reaction to an unwise combination of drugs and nearly died.

Later, in a party postmortem held under the influence of marijuana, Alice and her husband get into an argument and she ends up relating something she experienced during a recent vacation taken together in Cape Cod. She saw a handsome naval officer in the lobby, and though they never so much as exchanged a word, Alice knew that if he'd wanted her she would have sacrificed everything, even her marriage if necessary, for those fleeting moments of passion.

That speech, one of a pair of affecting monologues the actress makes good use of, is close enough to Schnitzler to borrow phrases from the novella, and, as in the book, Alice's husband is shocked by his wife's bold candor about her sexual fantasies. He's almost immediately called out to make an appearance at the apartment of a wealthy patient who just died, but he's tormented by fantasies of the sexual encounter that never happened between his wife and the handsome naval officer, fantasies that Kubrick shoots in flickering black-and-white snippets that consciously call to mind old-fashioned stag movies.

Those moments point up the film's strangest aspect, its frankly voyeuristic quality. Given that Cruise and Kidman are married, its inevitable that we feel like we're eavesdropping on their lives, a feeling that is more disconcerting than pleasant, especially in the brief amorous embrace (to a marvelous phrase from Chris Isaak's "Baby Did a Bad Bad Thing") that has been featured in almost all the film's publicity. Other married couples have played married couples on screen (Elizabeth Taylor and Richard Burton coming most famously to mind) and it often is a dicey, disconcerting business, something Kubrick in his own odd way may have counted on.

Propositioned on an All-Night Ramble

Feeling his world is shattered, Harford embarks on a solitary journey, an all-night ramble through a dreamlike world of elusive sexual potential. The daughter of his dead patient (Marie Richardson, a favorite of Ingmar Bergman's and a late replacement for Jennifer Jason Leigh) propositions him, as does Domino (Vinessa Shaw), surely New York's most genteel and caring streetwalker.

These early sequences, frankly, all have a marking-time feeling about them, and the reason is not hard to discern. In "Eyes Wide Open," screenwriter Raphael's just-published memoir of working with Kubrick, he accurately notes that the director "seemed not very interested in words

... I slowly came to realize that ... he was not even eager that the characters should have any particular personality: He would as soon have types as individuals with specific histories."

While it's fascinating to speculate where this tendency toward the generic comes from (perhaps having made the emotional connections in his head Kubrick saw no need to put them on screen for the rest of us or else didn't realize he hadn't), its impact is clear: The script keeps everyone at an emotional remove, and empathetic connection with the characters happens much less often than you'd imagine.

Screenwriter Raphael has his own idea about why Kubrick did this and it is a shrewd one: "Film alone was his art form ... Kubrick wanted to show, not tell." And the director, who lit every scene in "Eyes Wide Shut" himself, is a brilliant visualizer with the skill to make New York City streets created on a British sound stage look like the real thing. He has pointed this entire film toward its orgy scene, and that's where his gifts show to their fullest advantage.

Harford hears about the orgy during his late-night wanderings when he runs into old friend Nick, who's scheduled to play piano at the event. Nick tells him where it is and how to get in, and after procuring (in one of the film's many unsettling and unsatisfying moments) the necessary mask and disguise from gruff costumer Milich (Rade Sherbedgia) and his sexually precocious and probably deranged daughter (Leelee Sobieski), the doctor takes a cab out to the secret site on Long Island.

Because Kubrick is working with the elements of film he loves best, including a brilliantly disturbing score by Jocelyn Pook and costumes topped by disconcerting Venetian carnival masks, the director is for once able to create exactly the nightmarish texture he's seeking. For though lascivious thoughts initially motivated Harford, once inside the secret doors the mood abruptly changes, in true nightmare fashion, to one of sheer, uncontrollable terror. It's an extended sequence that cuts so close to the bone it's hard not to feel that elements of the filmmaker's own secret terrors are finding their way on screen as well.

Scenes Obstructed for U.S. Viewers

Though this has to be one of the least erotic orgies ever filmed, there is enough strenuously simulated sex present for the MPAA to demand some changes. While the sex will remain in the European version, domestic viewers will have their views strategically obstructed by orgy-goers electronically dropped into the scene. Technology in the service of prudery is apparently no vice.

The orgy also features considerable full frontal female nudity, and in fact female (never male) nudity is a leitmotif of the entire production. Even at the orgy, however, that material is more wistful than lascivious in tone, the luxuriating of an older director in a fading dream that's reminiscent of the late paintings of artists like Rembrandt, Renoir and Picasso rather than the lecherous ogling of more priapic filmmakers.

Like a brutal, claustrophobic black cloud, the orgy sequence, which comes about midway in the film, casts its powerful shadow over the rest of "Eyes Wide Shut," making everything, including the other strong Kidman monologue, darker and more troubling than it otherwise would be. It's so strong, so strange, that when the filmmakers attempt to use the Ziegler character (the only major one not to appear in the novella) to explain what happened, to make that evening's events conform to everyday logic, you wish they hadn't even tried.

Though it's very different in numerous ways, "Eyes Wide Shut" strongly brings to mind Alfred Hitchcock's classic "Vertigo." In both films, the feeling is inescapable that a forceful, idiosyncratic director is using the resources of a major studio and the top stars of the day to in essence work out intensely personal preoccupations and obsessions, to explore his own fears, fantasies and midnight terrors. For better or worse, there's probably no other director working today who would want to—or could get away with—doing that on such a major scale.

Speaking of stars, both Kidman and Cruise are absorbing and acquit themselves quite well in their parts, but it's frankly not in the cards for any actor to figure prominently in discussions about "Eyes Wide Shut." Partly that's because of the script's purposefully generic nature, with one person being little more than the object of jealousy, the other the one who gets jealous. But more than that, when you work with Kubrick, it's always the director, never the actors, who is the real star. That can lead a film up or down or, as it does here, in both directions at the same time.

NEW STATESMAN, 9/13/99, p. 43, Jonathan Romney

You'll have read by now that Stanley Kubrick's final film *Eyes Wide Shut* is a terrible let-down—neither a definitive farewell statement nor the out-and-out art-bonkbuster promised by so many seasons of media gossip. Much of the talk even from those who haven't yet seen the film, is almost resentful: how dare Kubrick not deliver what everyone assumed he had promised?

The mood is akin to erotic disappointment, which is quite fitting, for that is essentially the film's subject. If *Eyes Wide Shut* leaves us frustrated, perplexed and a little chastened, then that's exactly how the hero feels by the end of it. Kubrick's swansong, unlike so many apparent "instant masterpieces", is no open-and-shut case.

Both mainstream and art cinema have struggled for years to find ways of dealing directly with sex, and reputed directors often confess an ambition to use the language of pornography to serious effect. The few who try do so at their cost: either they're branded as straightforward sleaze-mongers (as Bertolucci and Oshima have been) or they embarrass and alienate mainstream audiences who would love to see the occasional high-class skin-flick but recoil when the thornier dilemmas of desire are aired. *Eyes Wide Shut* addresses some traditional questions about what really goes between men and women in their beds and their heads, which makes it more unsettling than it would have been if Tom Cruise and Nicole Kidman had simply regaled us with a Jeff Koons and Cicciolina act for two hours.

Kubrick is in good company here. Catherine Breillat's soon-to-be-released *Romance,* which uses hard-porn conventions to ask what women really want, is lucid and awkward in equal measure, but it's a European art film and therefore perceived as having a licence to address the mind as well as the loins. No such permission was extended, however, to Roman Polanski's *Bitter Moon,* a black farce about the pitfalls of *amour fou.* I've rarely heard such derisive laughter from an audience, yet Polanski's film is largely about the excruciating incommunicability of other people's urges, and is seriously ripe for reappraisal.

Eyes Wide Shut is close to *Bitter Moon,* both in its sense of texual masquerade and in its unreal atmosphere. It was adapted by Kubrick and Frederick Raphael, from Arthur Schnitzler's brief *Dream Story* and is surprisingly faithful to it both in story and mood. Part of the film's fascination is the way that its ostensible New York setting melts into a *fin de siècle* Vienna of the imagination (Schnitzier's tale, though published in 1926, also seems to take place in an unspecified past). The story is a nocturnal odyssey of sexual non-event: made jealous by the confession of a secret desire by his wife Alice (Nicole Kidman), Dr Bill Harford (Tom Cruise) passes a night of perverse visions and failed encounters, culminating in a traumatic visit to a masked party.

Bewilderingly for viewers of 1990s mainstream cinema, in which sexual content is tossed in as randomly and routinely as product placement, Harford either refuses sex or finds it refused him. Viewers may wonder why sex or its absence is such a big deal, but that's precisely what the film wants to make us think about. The erotic appears in guises both disturbing and hackneyed, even kitsch. The private party is ludicrous, a quasi-masonic ritual that smacks equally of de Sade, Max Ernst and the Venice carnival at its tackiest. It's clearly a hollow charade—unless you choose to take it seriously, as the film dares us to.

At stake in this ambivalence is the individual's paranoia that sex is everywhere, hidden under the surface of the familiar world, and that everyone is conspiring to keep it inaccessible to him alone. Bill's ostensible fear is of exclusion from female desire, but it is also coloured by the heterosexual man's anxiety about exclusion from other shades of male sexuality.

In one scene, Bill has a run-in with students who call him a "faggot". In fact, the thrust of this moment in Schnitzler's story is that the students are anti-Semitic, which suggests that his hero Fridolin is excluded in another sense. The fact that Kubrick instructed Raphael to suppress any Jewish references in the script makes the theme all the more suggestive as a hidden subtext; one American critic has called this Kubrick's most Jewish film.

Eyes Wide Shut is uneven in many ways—there are some awkward character turns, and the last 20 minutes feel anti-climactic. But maybe we should suspend the reductive question, "Is it any good or not?" and acknowledge that it's a fascinating, tantalising film that will continue to be argued about. It's also a remarkable anomaly in look and feel: photographed with a strange Christmassy luminescence and on unusually grainy stock, it feels like a film from another time.

I'm tempted to see it as a follow-up to Kubrick's 1980 horror film *The Shining:* the opening party sequence could be another night at the Overlook Hotel. Like *The Shining*, *Eyes Wide Shut* is about the pressures within a marriage. It's also about the terror of what other people do for fun—and the fear of not being invited.

NEW YORK, 7/26/99, p. 49, Peter Rainer

Eyes Wide Shut is being billed as more than a movie, more than even a Tom Cruise-and-Nicole Kidman movie: It's a Stanley Kubrick movie, which means, if his rep holds, that it's supposed to somehow intuit what's going on in our innermost lives and divine a millennial mood we may not yet even be aware of. The film is poised to be an epochal pop-cultural event, an art blockbuster. And since it's Kubrick's last, the genius-visionary mystique machine has been turned on by the media full-blast. *Eyes Wide Shut* is going to be read or, more to the point, misread as some kind of valedictory. But Kubrick never intended for this film to be his last—he was, for example, famously caught up in preparations for a movie about artificial intelligence. Besides, for a director whose themes were as chumingly repetitive as Kubrick's, there can be no proper valedictory because the moment of serene repose never arrives.

It is this quality of personal obsession that makes *Eyes Wide Shut* such a hammerlock of an experience. It's a powerful movie without always, or often, being a very good one; watching it is a bit like being inside the twistings and conniptions of a control freak who longs to lose control, only to pull back tighter than ever. The oracular power often attributed to Kubrick's films from at least *A Clockwork Orange* on is keyed to the playing and replaying of a few themes and variations on paranoia and depravity. For all the vaunted bigness of his movies, they're not very symphonic—there are too few notes for that.

It's perhaps no coincidence that Kubrick punctuates the *Eyes Wide Shut* soundtrack with repeated earsplitting strikes of a single piano key whenever things get particularly deranged. The derangement starts early. Dr. William Harford (Cruise) and his wife, Alice (Kidman), segue from their swank Central Park West apartment to a pre-Christmas party at even swankier digs—an eerie aerie belonging to one of William's wealthy patients (Sydney Pollack) that resembles something out of *The Shining*. The coruscated moldings and gleaming amber interiors are internally luxurious; the Christmas-tree bulbs are like warning lights. Alice finds herself dancing with an aging Hungarian roué (Sky Dumont) who has a desiccated line of patter; he quotes Ovid to her and invites her to check out the sculpture garden with him. She demurs, waving her wedding ring as if it were a talisman. But the film's vampiric tone has been set—we're watching a movie about sex as the Other.

The tone is amplified when William, having been courted by two leggy models, is called upon to revive a nude woman who's OD'd in his host's private quarters. Her pristine body is photographed like carrion before the feast. At home afterward, Alice and William get stoned in their crimson-sheeted bed and the obligatory postcoital scene runs to jealousy. Alice accuses her doctor husband of party-time infidelity, he jokingly brings up the roué, and then she drops the bombshell: A reverie she had of being deeply smitten and willingly borne away forever from her husband and young daughter by a handsome naval officer she spied during the family's Cape Cod summer vacation. William listens to her rapt monologue with eyes wide open—Kidman gives a harrowing rendition—and the screen-filling close-up of him that Kubrick bestows is a doozy: This naïf looks positively poleaxed.

The Harfords, it would seem, are not the sort of couple who get turned on by one another's erotic indiscretions. That would make for a different movie. This one—written by Kubrick and Frederic Raphael and closely patterned on the 1926 Arthur Schnitzler Freudian fantasia novella *Dream Story*—is about the damning effect of carnal urges. William may be the shining prince of the Upper West Side who flashes his medical I.D. card as if it were a sheriff's badge; he may have women slavering all over him. No matter. Alice offers up her reverie and William looks into the chasm, where he imagines Alice and the officer locked in lust. (The couplings he fantasizes are rendered in a radioactive-looking black-and-white.) He moves into a night world that encompasses both the ratty Village apartment of a sweet-souled hooker (Vinessa Shaw) and, later, an elaborate masked ball in a forbidding upstate mansion: It's erotics high and low, and

Kubrick seems to be making the tired old point that upper-class sex is more decadent than the lower varieties.

Coming a little more than halfway through this two-and-a-half-hour movie, the masque is the film's centerpiece, and it's around this time that things start to get really, if unintentionally, silly. The way Kubrick stages the scene, it's like the Vanderbilt mansion meets Heff's place. People in gargoyle masks stride through echoey amphitheaters in caped costumes and monk duds, chanting and acting all incantatory while masked women mince about buck-naked and lead men away to some unspecified delectation. William glides goggle-eyed through the rutting tableaux, and who can blame him? (A few digitized figures were inserted into the scene to block the view and secure the film's R rating.) It's quite possible that Kubrick never saw a lot of the tony blue-movie schlock that this sequence conjures up, but he arrives at the same place anyway. Who would have believed Stanley Kubrick as a deluxe Radley Metzger?

Kubrick is perhaps the least sensual of all the major directors, and so, when it was announced, however sketchily, that he would be making a movie about carnal knowledge, skepticism yielded to curiosity: Maybe he could do for humping what he once did for nuclear proliferation and space travel? But Kubrick can't give us the pleasures of the illicit in *Eyes Wide Shut,* only the terrors; and without those pleasures, what is there for the good doctor to be drawn into or renounce? (In the movie's archetypal scene, William on a house call is lured by an amorous patient while a corpse rests in full view.) For all its supersophisticated stylistics, the film basically issues from a zone of bourgeois complacency. The message is: Play around, get in trouble.

But it goes deeper than that. Alice's indiscretions are reveries; William's are bona fide. The film is a male fantasy of how women's imagined urges can destroy you just as if they were real. ("No dream is just a dream," William says at the end.) Kubrick's view of females is double-edged: With their sexual capacity, their instinct for infidelity, their aphrodisiac they are the annihilators of male contentment. And yet there are women in *Eyes Wide Shut,* like that sweet-souled prostitute, who are a balm; at the masked ball, an enigmatic siren offers herself up to save William's life, sacrificing herself to redeem his transgressions. So men are a party to annihilation, too. *Eyes Wide Shut* just might be the most elaborate male mea culpa ever committed to film.

Still, none of the personal destructions on view resonate, because the movie seems to be populated by the soulless. The dead—the corpses and cadavers—are of a piece with the undead. The casting of Cruise and Kidman, movie stars who give off a chilly fortitude, is all too perfect. Kubrick brings out the alabaster whiteness in their skin; he bathes them in blue light. Their acting, except for Kidman's monologue and a few racked moments from Cruise, is overdeliberate; they seem not so much directed as commandeered.

Kubrick wasn't able to relinquish his customary iron grip over his material and move into more perilous and mellifluous realms of desire. William's dreamlike passage has the force of an obsession, but it's Kubrick's, not William's. Kubrick's passion, finally, is not for letting go but for holding on. It's an understandable response—a human response, especially as one gets older—and so there is a poignancy to it. But the only overwhelming emotion I felt from *Eyes Wide Shut* had nothing to do with the movie, really. What I experienced was a sadness that, with this last film of Kubrick's, there will be no others, and a vision, which certainly had its triumphs, has been taken away.

NEW YORK POST, 7/16/99, p. 38, Rod Dreher

"Eyes Wide Shut," is the classy art-house version of the overhyped but underwhelming "Phantom Menace"—quite good in parts and always dazzling to the eye but a letdown all the same.

It's shocking only in its banality, impotence and utter lack of heat—this, despite months of media blab about how daring and outrageous the last film by the late Stanley Kubrick would be. All that sturm und drang over a draggy, dated exercise in intellectualized softcore! "Eyes Wide Shut" is a sex-themed movie made by someone who hadn't left the house in 30 years.

Based on a 1926 novel by Arthur Schnitzler, "Eyes Wide Shut" surely would have been the last cinematic word in eros, fear and psychology had it come out prior to the sexual revolution. Watching it today makes one wonder: O sex, where is thy sting?

It begins at a luxurious Manhattan holiday party given by Ziegler (Sydney Pollack), a wealthy friend of Dr. Bill Harford (Tom Cruise) and his lovely wife Alice (Nicole Kidman). Giddy on champagne, Alice is chatted up by a dashing Hungarian (Sky Dumont), who propositions her with soapy lines one fears must have struck the out-of-touch Kubrick as ravishingly sexy.

She declines, but later that night a druggy and unguarded Alice confesses that several years earlier, while on vacation with Bill and their daughter, she spied a handsome stranger so hot that, in that moment, she would have given up everything she had for one night with him.

Bill, naturally, is shocked; we can tell this because Tom Cruise, not the subtlest of actors, stares straight ahead, like he's eyeballing a rattlesnake.

The phone rings, summoning the doctor downtown to the bedside of a just-dead patient. Thus begins jealousy-obsessed Bill's nocturnal odyssey through a mysterious shadow society in which the allure of complete sexual abandon and its concomitant deathly terror draws curious Bill further in.

And out to an isolated mansion on Long Island, where a clandestine cult of high-society decadents are holding a ritualized orgy. The mansion scene provides the film's only moment of palpable menace. Suitably costumed, Bill joins the cloaked-and-masked celebrants as they observe a scarlet-clad priest figure surrounded by nude statuesques, while sepulchral music (by Jocelyn Pook) sets a spine-tingling mood.

By the time Bill cruises voyeuristically through the mansion's orgiastic set pieces, we should be feeling the same fascination and horror we did when Dennis Hopper took Kyle McLachlan on the psychosexual highway to hell in "Blue Velvet." But Kubrick allows what suspense he's built to dissipate into histrionics more akin to Rod Serling's "Night Gallery."

Still, the orgy scene (which, despite all the female nudity, is as much a turn-on as a museum visit) displays Kubrick's pictorial talents at their most striking. What's particularly interesting is the way he uses lighting and stage design throughout the film to reinforce the idea that portals to the sexual underworld are present on almost every street. No matter how safe and solid one's world appears, its annihilation can be wrought by an unwisely spoken truth or by taking a few steps from the straight and narrow.

These aspects of "Eyes Wide Shut" will be slavered over by Kubrick aficionados and cineastes, but most people don't go to the movies to appreciate the formalistic qualities of composition and lighting. They go for a story, and they don't get much of one here.

Nor will they experience much emotional connection with the characters. Unfortunately, the film bears out the observation by Frederic Raphael, Kubrick's co-screenwriter, that the director was not interested in characters, only types.

Cruise is OK, if somewhat out of his depth, and Kidman does what may be the best work of her prominent but undistinguished career in what's essentially a supporting role.

But the narrative is not so much concerned with Bill and Alice as it is in exploring the thin veneer of civilization and how order is maintained by keeping lustful fantasies repressed.

But Kubrick, so far gone inside his own head, has abstracted this potentially combustible (if shopworn) material into chilly inertness.

NEW YORK POST, 7/16/99, p. 39 Jonathan Foreman

"Eyes Wide Shut" is Stanley Kubrick's Hindenburg.

It's not thrilling. It's not sexy. It combines all the flaws that marred his earlier work including a glacial pace, emotional coldness and the sudden eruption of scenes that seem to belong in a different movie.

But what makes "Eyes Wide Shut" actively bad is its combination of sheer silliness with a grotesque lack of authenticity.

As we have been told so often during the endless barrage of publicity for the film, the Master was obsessed with getting the details right. But there's scarcely a note here that isn't false—and the movie's so slow you can't help noticing the false notes.

For a start, Kubrick's notion of New York bears no physical or cultural resemblance at all to present day Gotham. It's a place where white ethnics still drive the cabs and Greenwich Village streets are prowled by gorgeous student hookers (who kiss their clients).

Here, young doctors live in vast $10 million apartments and the rich are so bored that they have to go to elaborate costume orgies held in an English castle on Long Island.

The orgy looks like a combination of the frat-house initiation scene in "Animal House" and Monty Python's version of the Spanish Inquisition—played straight.

Stanley Kubrick was a hermit in the English countryside for the past 35 years, and no one may have told him that things have changed since "Breakfast at Tiffany's." Indeed, the whole film seems to exist in a kind of early '60s time warp.

But there's a kind of deranged arrogance at work when, to make his London sets look like New York streets, the director merely substitutes blue square mailboxes for red round ones.

Not only does Tom Cruise look like a very recent graduate of the Top Gun medical school, he and his wife behave like gawping rubes when they attend a black tie party given by Sidney Pollack.

And when Kidman dances with a predatory Hungarian lothario out of central casting, her response to his flirtation is so slow and unsophisticated you wonder if she's supposed to be differently abled.

Kidman is dressed for "Sex and the City," but her demeanor is from another era.

So is this deeply disappointing movie.

NEWSDAY, 7/16/99, Part II/p. B3, John Anderson

You can no more ignore the fact that two stars named Tom Cruise and Nicole Kidman are in Stanley Kubrick's "Eyes Wide Shut" than you can write off to coincidence the fact that a movie director (Sydney Pollack) is playing its villain. After 30 or so years of chasing the dragon of an obscure, erotic Arthur Schnitzler novella—about the nature, pursuit and cost of pleasure—what Kubrick has made is a movie about sex that's as much about movies as it is about sex.

Cruise, as Dr. Bill Harford, and Kidman, his wife, Alice, add their considerable physical grace to a movie that's so zealously composed and visually potent it could only be Kubrick. Is it a posthumous masterpiece? On the basis of one viewing, and with the knowledge that it was a great director's final film, it seems more like the coda to a symphonic career, one in which many of the idiosyncrasies that marked his collected work coalesce and occasionally implode. It's a stunning film, provocative in the best sense, and thoroughly haunting.

Stardom, Jungian masks, the aesthetic bankruptcy that informed "A Clockwork Orange," the eroticism he couldn't explore fully in "Lolita," the obsessive-compulsion of most of his films—Kubrick imported real American trash to adorn his London set—it's all here. So is a great deal of nudity (more Kidman than Cruise, who surrenders only his upper torso to Kubrick's camera).

Much of the curiosity surrounding "Eyes Wide Shut"—which began shooting in November, 1996—was what drew Kubrick to Schnitzler's "Traumnovelle" in the first place. He'd optioned it in the early '70s, never quite got it made and now that he has, it seems perfectly clear.

Kubrick obviously found the sexual aspects of the story—about a doctor, his wife, the former's dangerous flirtation with a secret orgiastic society, the wife's own erotic dreams— irresistible. Likewise, the potential of cinema to re-create those dreams. "Eyes Wide Shut," ultimately, is a dream tale within a dream world. To make such a thing as richly ironic as possible, he needed the biggest stars in the world. When he got them the movie got made.

(Warner Bros., by the way, has taken steps to see that we don't see what Kubrick saw: Although the director had final cut, that doesn't mean that the studio hasn't obscured—in a laughably clumsy, most un-Kubrick fashion—much of the sex in the orgy scene. The "'Austin Powers' version," as Roger Ebert has reportedly dubbed it, will play America; Europe will get Kubrick's version. Perhaps we should all wait for the DVD, although Time Warner will own that, too.)

Meanwhile: Dr. Bill Harford and wife, Alice, live with their young daughter in Manhattan, leading what seems to be a perfectly Architectural Digest existence. When they attend a party thrown by Bill's friend Vic Ziegler (Pollack), however, Alice starts swallowing champagne in the manner not suitable to a woman whose life is a Central Park Western romance. Wooed on the dance floor by a Ricardo Montalban-ish Hungarian (Sky Dumont), Alice rebuffs him. But in a scene lit to a cottony softness, and in a film where some things or everything could be a hallucination, Alice seems to be acting the way she'd like to think she'd act. The theory of movie-as-dream is ahead by two lengths.

Bill? Elsewhere. Arm in arm with two stunning models who clearly have designs on the young doctor (if Cruise suggests Doogie Howser, there's not much he can do about it), he's suddenly called away to see his host, who has a leggy, naked, drugged-out, post-coital problem splayed out in an upstairs bathroom.

Bill brings the young woman around, but the incident becomes phase one in his journey to an erotic edge. Phase two: During a pot-smoking session, Alice tells Bill a story about another man, fleetingly glimpsed, but for whom she would have abandoned everything—husband, child—for one night of sex.

Granted, Bill and Alice are both high (pot, like dream sequences, allows characters to act oddly, and actors badly). But the effect on Bill is a kick to the head and/or groin. Gored on the horns of anger and eroticism, Bill slips into a vortex of sex—suddenly, it's everywhere. The first patient of Dr. Bill's we see (topless) looks like a Playboy centerfold. The affianced daughter of a just-deceased colleague throws herself at him while her father's body is cooling in its deathbed. Couples couple in doorways. His wife and another man grapple in his mind. Places like the Pink Pussycat Boutique suddenly dominate the thoroughfares of Greenwich Village as Bill stomps around its streets. An evidently gay hotel clerk (Alan Cummings) reacts to Bill the way a hotel clerk might react to, well, Tom Cruise.

Bill keeps telling people he's a doctor as if they don't believe him, including a hooker (Vinessa Shaw) he meets on the street who doesn't really want his money. We recall the models at the party. The smiling waitresses. A woman in a cafe. The artless performance Kubrick is getting out of Cruise. It becomes, all at once, hilarious: "Eyes Wide Shut" is about being Tom Cruise!

But how better to make the point about fantasy and desire? Kubrick's point is that stardom is a gross fiction, one linked to the Bill-Alice fantasies and ours as well: Instant gratification with no strings—but no effort either. It's the people who construct the machinery of their dreams—the members of that secret society whose orgy Bill crashes after a tipoff from his old pal Nick (Todd Field)—who have pushed the envelope into evil.

So the Kubrickian message is: If movies are fantasy and the active pursuit of fantasy is evil, then movie directors are evil. Sydney Pollack, call your agent.

Kubrick's New York—re-created, as per the wishes of a man who never left home, at London's Pinewood Studios and its Hatton Garden—is an anachronism. Knish shops. Jazz clubs with tuxedoed doormen. Bill gets out of his cab before he pays (who does that?). There are Manhattan streets that don't exist (Wren? Benton? Miller?), but, then, the city doesn't exist either. Kubrick lifted Schnitzler's story out of '20s Vienna (evoked mischievously in the recurring theme composed by Jocelyn Pook) and dropped it into a New York that's as quaint as his Bronx boyhood. But then, "Eyes Wide Shut" is all about memory and desire and, sadly, about what people don't want and how hard they'll work to get it.

NEWSWEEK, 7/19/99, p. 62, Jack Kroll

After three years of false rumors and a maddening mix of secretiveness and hype, Stanley Kubrick's "Eyes Wide Shut" is here. The 13th and last film of the legendary director, who died with shocking suddenness in March days after making the final cut, turns out to be his most personal work. After all, it deals with the most personal of subjects, sex. And by casting Tom Cruise and Nicole Kidman in the leading roles, Kubrick charged his cinematic batteries with maximum sexual voltage. He wastes no time in snapping the audience's eyes wide open. In the very first shot we see Kidman, her back to the camera, snake-hipping out of a black dress, to stand there nude in possibly the most beautiful human image ever to open a movie.

Female beauty is a subject that has been treated so crudely in movies for so long that it's almost shocking to see the care with which Kubrick handles this classical and potent theme of all art. The story deals with desire, an ineradicable appetite that threatens to breach the structures that society has built to contain it. Real-life spouses Cruise and Kidman play Dr. William and Alice Harford, married nine years with a little daughter and an affluent lifestyle. They find themselves going through an ordeal of sudden, inexplicable passion directed toward others, which puts a "sword in the bed" between them.

That phrase comes from the novella "Dream Story," by Arthur Schnitzler, that is the source of the screenplay by Frederic Raphael and Kubrick. Schnitzler is the Austrian writer whose psychological insight an astonished Freud compared "enviously" with his own. Kubrick had wanted to film Schnitzler's story for 25 years. In 1971 he told a French magazine that he'd been considering the possibility of making it into a hard-core pornographic film with big stars and a big budget. What he did do was make a remarkably faithful film version of Schnitzler's story, transferring it from fin de siècle Vienna to New York at the fin of this siècle. Bill and Alice go through an erotic odyssey that begins when they attend a fashionable Christmas party at which both are approached sexually. Bill is corralled by a pair of enticing predators, while a champagne-tipsy Alice fends off the moves of a Continental lounge lizard. The film, which began in mundane reality (while Bill dresses, Alice sits charmingly on the potty), melts into a dream ambience, the party lights blazing in blurry golden halos. As Alice and the slick seducer dance, the angles of their intertwined bodies are calibrated with a precise sensual tension that's pure Kubrickian choreography.

The tensions increase. Back home, Alice confesses a spasm of desire she once had for a naval officer she had only glimpsed, but for whom she was ready to give up everything, including her family, for just one night of passion. Both are shocked as the apparent solidity of their lives is undermined by fantasies that seem more powerful than reality. Later, Bill meets Nick Nightingale (Todd Field), a pianist who plays at masked orgies for the rich. Bill rents a costume from a dealer whose sideline is pimping for his 15-year-old daughter (Leelee Sobieski). Bill sneaks into the orgy, a kind of satanic ritual of mass sex, where he is discovered and is saved from death by a masked woman who volunteers to take his place and his fate. (It's this sequence that Kubrick had to alter to avoid an NC-17 rating. He inserted digitalized figures to obscure the sexual activity, which he had shot discreetly and distantly. The effect is, frankly, annoying and ludicrous. In one of the last "Friday the 13th" horrors, the monster Jason punches the head off one of his victims. With the censors it's decapitation yes, copulation no.)

After the orgy, events explode with the fierce softness of dreams. Mutual confessions by Bill and Alice lead to an emotional showdown. From the already famous "mirror" love scene, played with a carnal sweetness that's rare in the brittle, cynical sexuality of film today, to the anger, fear and pain of their final confrontation, Cruise and Kidman are open and touching. There's strong work from supporting players like Marie Richardson as a casual acquaintance who confounds Bill with a confession of love. The kaleidoscope of emotions on her face is one of the most powerful moments in the film. Under Kubrick's tight rein, the film devolves into a complex crescendo of feeling ranging from pure lust to loving tenderness. But there are ambiguous moments. Despite the surface modernization, the aura of Schnitzler's fin de siècle hangs heavily over the film. Much of the dialogue is straight from the English translation of the story, and some of it has a stilted quality that doesn't tally with contemporary rhythms. Oddly, this is most true in the extended scene that isn't in the original, an encounter between Bill and his rich friend Victor Ziegler (Sydney Pollack) in the latter's billiard room. The cadences, locutions and pauses in their conversation lend an artificiality to what's meant to be an exchange of great portent.

These lapses can be rationalized as part of the movie's dream atmosphere. The film clearly meant a great deal to Kubrick. After the apocalyptic satire of "Dr. Strangelove," the cosmic voids of "2001: A Space Odyssey," the sado-militarism of "Full Metal Jacket," Kubrick, approaching his 70s, came back to the ecstatic torments from which we struggle to create love. If some nagging sense of anachronism, a bit too much Freudian Vienna in his postmodern New York, prevents "Eyes Wide Shut" from the top of his list, it is Kubrick's most humane film. The final shots of a shaken Cruise and Kidman are moving, and suggest the courage that allowed them to spend nearly two years of their lives with the arch-controller Kubrick. The film ends with an unexpected last line, Alice's advice to her husband on how to start the process of reconciliation, advice that is at once practical, eloquent and obscene.

SIGHT AND SOUND, 9/99, p. 45, Charles Whitehouse

At a New York party, Dr William Harford is called upstairs by his host, Victor Ziegler, to treat a naked young woman who has OD'd. Meanwhile, a roué tries to seduce Alice, William's wife. Later, Alice tells William about a naval officer to whom she was once deeply attracted. Stunned, William visits the needy grieving daughter of a just-deceased patient and almost has sex with a prostitute, but stops when Alice calls him. William's old friend Nick tells him about a secret sex party where Nick plays piano blindfold, he gives William the password. Needing a costume for it, William gets one from Milich, a costumier, who turns out to pimp his own underage daughter.

A cloaked-and-masked William enters a mansion where a red-robed man is selecting naked masked women for various partners. One woman approaches William and warns him to leave, but he stays to observe the orgy. The red-robed man asks William for the second password. Rumbled, William unmasks, but 'his' masked girl says she will "redeem him". William is forcibly removed.

The next day, he tracks down Nick's hotel but finds he left in the night with two men. At Milich's, William returns his cloak but finds the mask is missing. William receives a note warning him not to enquire further about the orgy. He reads about the death of a model. Convinced she is his "redeemer", he visits the morgue and sees the body. Ziegler tells William it was the same girl, but she was just a junkie who OD'd. At home William finds his mask laid out on his pillow next to Alice. She tells him they should be grateful for what they have.

The dream interpreter is a kind of detective, and given the orgy of opinion about *Eyes Wide Shut* currently being enjoyed, let's use the detective's dictum and stick to the facts. The most shocking aspect of *Eyes Wide Shut* is not its long-anticipated sex scenes, but its fidelity to literature. No one expected such a faithful plot adaptation of Arthur Schnitzler's *Dream Story* (Schnitzler was a friend of Freud's).

Kubrick and screenwriter Frederic Raphael have changed the story's setting from *fin de siècle* Vienna to present-day New York and added two major scenes. The first, near the beginning, is at a blacktie party where Tom Cruise's Dr William Harford gets his pal Ziegler (Sydney Pollack) out of a sticky situation with a naked girl in a drug coma. The second is near the end, where a pool-playing Ziegler explains (or seems to) the fate of an anonymous woman who sacrificed herself for Harford when he was caught trespassing at a private orgy. Otherwise, the film strictly follows Schnitzler's curve. Harford is a man so jealous of a phantom—a naval officer his wife Alice (Nicole Kidman) confesses she was once passingly captivated by—that he can't go home again until he has committed some sort of sexual revenge.

But Cruise's Harford is an ineffective sexual adventurer. Presented with a queue of obliging fantasy women—a needy patient's daughter, a nice prostitute, an underage shopkeeper's daughter, a perfect-bodied masked orgygoer—he falters at consummation every time. While Alice mutters orgasmically to the pillowslips at home, Harford is cold and faithful: his revenge remains uneaten. Given that the new scenes stress his close male friendship with Ziegler, one wonders what became of Raphael's take on Kubrick's theme in his book *Eyes Wide Open*. "What he [Kubrick] wants is the naked woman at the refrigerator door as she remembers to put the chicken away before she goes to bed."

Eyes Wide Shut certainly starts with a bare-assed Kidman getting dressed, and the best example of what Raphael means comes shortly after, when Kidman's Alice is sitting on the toilet in her party frock. She flushes the toilet and asks Harford, "How do I look? "Great," he answers without turning round. The viewer is meant to enjoy the witty combination of female allure and domestic banality, though Harford does not. He will only see Alice sexualised as another's lover. That ironic split between Harford's viewpoint and ours also applies to the way we see the other women as they make themselves available to him.

So while Harford's moral probity (his ethical foreign policy) seems admirable, we the voyeurs are assumed not to be party to it. A couple of suspicions are aroused: is it that Kubrick's mordant humour can't resist a dig in the ribs every time we see a naked woman, or is he visiting implicit judgement on current inferior moral standards? Neither feels right. Kubrick's films are famed for their distanced-but-intimate point of view, but here the viewer's is set dead against the protagonist's from the start—something of a radical move, and one that eventually proves decisive.

The casting of Cruise and Kidman complicates matters. It helps the balance of the film that Kidman, rarely present on screen after the opening half hour, gives the more raw and powerful performance, while the permanently on-screen Cruise remains on 'cruise control', enhancing the films 'dream logic' with his passivity. But it is Cruise who has the burden of the dream. He tries to bring the intensity he won in *Born on the Fourth of July* to it—staring and shaking his head in awed disbelief a lot but too near the surface is the keen boy charmer just itching to show us his somersault, and there's no physical disability here to make that eagerness poignant. While the public face of this real life couple lends itself to the fictional New York marrieds and makes at least their routine togetherness feel natural, it likewise deepens the gulf between what we and Harford are supposed to be feeling when we see the same things.

As soon as Harford leaves home to visit a grieving girl—his first opportunity to cheat on Alice—Raphael's "eroticism of monogamy" theme is discarded. We are then forced to mimic Harford's fierce gaze as he surveys further heterosexual options to his sullied marriage. It's only then that Kubrick's strategy becomes clear: we the viewers experience Harford's will-he-won't-he dilemma as if we were wearing him as a mask. Our status as real spectators to Harford's pallid misfortune has no cathartic dimension.

In that sense, *Eyes Wide Shut* feels like a 70s Buñuel film, depending for its strangeness on enigmatic behaviour in formal surroundings. The film is resolutely old fashioned whenever illicit sexual contact begins: just as the deliberately clichéd dialogue between Alice and a Hungarian seducer at Ziegler's party reminds one irresistibly of the Ferrero Rochét adverts, so the mask-and-robe orgy, with its ponderous Gothic touches and echoes of *Histoire d'O,* feels like a stolid throwback to the more innocent times of Hammer horror or Roger Corman's Poe movies. The problem with setting such an orgy in modern New York is that contemporary audiences know what sexual extremes are really on offer there and how tame by comparison are the sculptural entanglements on offer here. Against this fact we have the commercial reality of a Cruise and Kidman movie needing an 'R' rating in the US, which has forced digital concealment of sexual thrusting on US release prints of a Stanley Kubrick movie.

Yet there's more to the dated feel of this movie than its crucifixion on the cross of movie-business double standards. Not only does it look visually modest in the age of *The Matrix* (a first for a Kubrick film), it's also dated in its fidelity to the mid-century ideal of the European art movie. Such a work, it assumes, should have a painstaking exposition that requires intellectual engagement by the audience—few people's idea of a Tom Cruise movie. The path through its philosophical maze concerns the destructive nature of truth telling between intimates. (My guess is that the phrase "Eyes Wide Shut" is shorthand for the most successful attitude a monogamous couple can adopt to viewing each other's inner life.) However, the trail keeps disappearing, lost to a more sweeping concern about the nature of our responsibility to all other humans for their safety—the doctor's dilemma, and Kubrick was of course a doctor's son.

Suppose, then, we presume that Stanley Kubrick was a little out of touch at the end of his life and that his need to shoot New York in England found him sleepifying the bustling metropolis, making it more fuzzily soft like *Dream Story's* Vienna? Perhaps he was dreaming of skating in Ophuls' dizzying *La Ronde* tracks (another Schnitzler tale) and didn't care so much where he was meant to be? Or perhaps Raphael is just too fusty a writer? Or is it that Kubrick knew that the fantasies of those who retire from the singles arena are often by their nature somewhat staid, that the very lack of imagination is what makes them both exciting and comforting? *Eyes Wide Shut* is no masterpiece, but it is endlessly fascinating.

TIME, 7/5/99, p. 67, Richard Schickel

History and horror, crime and war, Sci-fi and sexual transgression. He may have made only 13 feature films in the course of his 46-year career, but Stanley Kubrick covered a range that more prolific filmmakers might—and often did—envy. But whether the films were set in the deep past or the near future, whether their prevailing tone was comic or violent, sly or brutish, weary or idealistic, Kubric really made the same movie over and over again—vivid, brilliant, emotionally unforgiving, imagistically unforgettable variations on the theme that preoccupied him all his mature life.

That theme was at once simple and sophisticated: a man (or sometimes a group of men), without thinking very hard about it, places his faith either in his own rationality or in the rationality of the systems by which his world is governed, whereupon something goes awry, his illusions of order are stripped away, and he is left to fend with the sometimes deadly, always devastating consequences of that loss.

These occurrences need not be cataclysmic. They can be something as simple as the sight of a young girl practicing with her Hula Hoop (Lolita). Or a communications goof in the supposedly fail-safe nuclear-defense program (*Dr. Strangelove*). Or, as in the case of *Eyes Wide Shut*—which is due to open July 16 after years of wildly misguided speculation about its content—a confession of unconsummated sexual flirtation. Such incidents are usually not things most people notice much or worry about greatly. And often enough they're right. Normality generally reasserts itself after one of these blips.

The films that Kubrick cared about—there were three early ones he disowned—are all in one way or another explorations of how minor mishaps can grow into major disasters, with the one exception of *2001: A Space Odyssey,* in which miscalculation leads to redemption, rebirth, a radiant transcendence of ordinary expectations. But *Eyes Wide Shut,* though it is finally less bleak in its moral implications than most Kubrick movies, is in the more typical line of a man perpetually disappointed by the world's failure to abide by his standards of logic and civility.

Why, then, the avid interest in it, the reams of goofy gossip and scandalized speculation that have surrounded its lengthy creation? Maybe it had something to do with the very long time between Kubrick pictures—the last one, *Full Metal Jacket,* was released 12 years ago. Maybe the director's increasing elusiveness had its effect. He had quit talking to reporters years ago, and it seemed to the media's increasingly resentful minions that he got around in public even less than he formerly had, which was not very much. On the other hand, *Eyes Wide Shut* did encompass the three elements that legitimately capture the public's attention—story, stars, director—in a particularly piquant package.

When Warner Bros. (which is owned by Time Warner, the parent company of this magazine) announced the project in 1995, it merely stated that Kubrick was making "a story of sexual jealousy and obsession starring Tom Cruise and Nicole Kidman." Officially, no one has added anything substantive to that press release in the years since—which is, of course, why the rumor that Cruise and Kidman play psychiatrists drawn into a web of sexual intrigue with their patients got started. And the one about the mad genius Kubrick making an NC-17-rated blue movie. And the one that has Cruise wearing a dress in one sequence.

None of these are remotely true. Movies don't always follow the books on which they're based, but in this case anyone able to track down the novel from which the movie has been rather faithfully adapted by Kubrick and co-writer Frederic Raphael would have been more in the know. Titled *Traumnovelle* (Dream Story), it was first published in 1926 by Arthur Schnitzler, a Viennese playwright, physician and friend of Freud's, and has been available in paperback in the U.S. since 1995. Like a lot of the novels on which good movies are based, it is an entertaining, erotically charged fiction of the second rank, in need of the vivifying physicalization of the screen and the kind of narrative focus a good director can bring to imperfect but provocative life— especially when he has been thinking about it as long as Kubrick had.

Kubrick's widow Christiane remembers his asking her to read the book as far back as 1968, when he was looking for something to follow *2001.* She also remembers not caring greatly for it at the time, probably because she had become "allergic to psychiatric conversations." But Kubrick, she recalls, took the passion of their arguments about the "dream story," as evidence that material so stirring must be worth doing. In any case, using Jay Cocks, then a young film reporter for *TIME,* as a front, on the grounds that Cocks might acquire rights to the book more cheaply than a famous filmmaker could, Kubrick bought the property. For the next 2 ½ decades the book haunted him.

One could see, and somehow not quite see, the movie in this story of a fashionable yet conscientious physician and his wife whose nine-year marriage has produced an adored child, genuine mutual affection and a growing sexual restlessness. Everything depended on its realization. Cruise's character, Dr. William Harford, is in some ways a dim and passive fellow, self-victimized and hard to care for. His wife Alice would have been easy to play either ditsy or bitchy. But there is in Cruise a kind of passionate watchfulness and in Kidman a desperate and touching candor, and they keep drawing us past the narrative's improbabilities to its human heart. As for Kubrick, he is typically unsentimental and tough-minded, but his tracking shots are as unselfconscious as ever, gracefully enfolding us in his story.

Kubrick needed to be at his best, for the story turns on a very thin dime. The night after a grand party, at which both husband and wife indulge in potentially dangerous flirtations, she taunts him about his relationships with his female patients and insists on burdening him with a tale of an encounter she had at a seaside resort, where she and a young naval officer eyed each other erotically. Nothing more than that happened, but she tells her husband, in language that is almost identical in novel and screenplay, "Had he called me—I thought—I could not have resisted him ... and at the same time you were dearer to me than ever."

Cruise's William accepts this dubious reassurance but is haunted by powerfully lubricious visions of his wife making love to the officer as he goes about his night-time rounds in modern New York City, which Kubrick has substituted for Schnitzler's fin-de-siécle Vienna. The possibilities of relief—or should we call it revenge?—are everywhere: a newly dead patient's daughter comes on to William powerfully yet pathetically; a cheerful prostitute invites him to a casual coupling; and, finally, in the movie's central sequence, he succeeds in invading a secret orgy, where masked couples disport themselves sexually in a display that is more grim than wanton.

In all these encounters eros and thanatos are exquisitely mixed. The dead body of the first woman's father is clearly visible as she confesses her confused passion; the prostitute turns out to be under the threat of AIDS; the orgiasts, resenting William's intrusion on their saturnalia, threaten him with humiliation and death, and he is "redeemed" only by the intervention of a mysterious woman, who pays for his life with her own.

The orgy sequence, along with several others in the film, is full of naked (and mainly handsome) flesh. But as Christiane Kubrick says, "It has nothing to do with sex and everything to do with fear," and although this is the point Kubrick very obviously wanted to make, it may not be a point audiences want to take. Indeed, the deepest daring of *Eyes Wide Shut* lies in the way it keeps edging viewers toward a place they want very much to go (famous people making out before the camera, for example), then dashing those hopes. It is also a movie that, to put the matter bluntly, constantly edges right up to the thin line separating the emotionally persuasive from the risible, and one that at any moment in the process of (literally) fleshing out the novel's abstractions could dissolve into the unconsciously comical. That's the most obvious danger when your subject is not sex itself, where there are plenty of conventions to guide the filmmaker, but sex in the mind, for which there are very few precedents to guide him.

But Kubrick was used to that danger, even appeared in it. Most of his pictures, whatever their genre roots, disappointed genre expectations, not to mention critical anticipation and occasionally the studio's box-office ambitions. As *Eyes Wide Shut* seeks to avoid those perils, it has something besides its considerable intrinsic merits going for it.

That something is Cruise and Kidman. Kubrick was usually star shy, preferring ensemble casts of solid players to huge names. But when Terry Semel, who runs Warner Bros. in tandem with Robert Daly, gave the project its green light, he said, "What I would really love you to consider is a movie star in the lead role; you haven't done that since Jack Nicholson [in *The Shining*]." Kubrick was concerned that a movie star wouldn't share his tireless work ethic. Nevertheless, the Cruises were approached. The couple gave themselves over entirely to the project. It was, as both Cruise and Kidman agree, never a question of filling in the preordained blanks as efficiently as possible. Nor was it a matter of dithering over lining up or lighting a shot. All the technical side of moviemaking Kubrick had long since absorbed into his bones. It was always a question of getting the emotions right, bit by painful, exhilarating bit. Kubrick insisted on working as no one else in movies does, but as artists in the other forms—painting, music, literature—do: finding the piece as it goes along. That, of course, requires time, and with that he was profligate, ever willing to explore the possibly rewarding digression.

Sidney Pollack, the film director, who replaced Harvey Keitel as Victor Ziegler, the character who ties together all the evil that Cruise's character discovers and who is the most significant addition to the original story, observes that "Stanley had figured out a way to work in England for a fraction of what we pay here. "While the rest of us poor bastards are able to get 16 weeks of filming for $70 million with a $20 million star, Stanley could get 45 weeks of shooting for $65 million." in short, says Pollack, "he ensured himself the luxury of trying to work out something that's as complicated emotionally as this film was."

Cruise and Kidman, perhaps still caught up in their detailed work with Kubrick, prefer to see the movie rather indeterminately. "The movie is whatever the audience takes from it," says Cruise. "Wherever you are in life, you're going to take away something different." Kidman says, "I don't think its a morality tale. It's different for every person who watches it." But others draw distinct lessons from the film. Pollack says this "is the story of a man who journeys off the path and then finds his way back onto it, a man who almost loses himself because something awakens a darker part of him, and he follows it against his own better sense." When "he realizes that what he's lived through was about values so far below what he's lived his life for, he's devastated.

Anya Kubrick, one of the director's three daughters, goes further. She regards *Eyes Wide Shut* as "a very personal statement from my father. He felt very strongly about this subject and theme, and he honed down in it exactly the ideas, principles and moral philosophies he had lived by." Large among them, she says, was the idea that "we are all both good and evil, and if you think you have no evil in you, you're not looking hard enough." Her mother Christiane says the film reflects Kubrick's belief that "most of humanity is not quite bright enough to know what they want and plan how to get it." He did. But like everyone who knew Kubrick, she is at an angry loss to explain the public perception of him as a reclusive, obsessive misanthrope. John Calley, chairman of Sony Pictures and an old friend, spoke for many when he described Kubrick as a man true to an uncompromising vision who always "remained decent, with a family he loved, yet wise, fun, kind and not follow-the-leader."

That such a life revolved around the creation of dark visions of human nature and striving may be counted as an irony. In the end, people who really care about movies always knew, as Steven Spielberg put it, that when you saw one of Kubrick's movies, "you committed yourself to its being part of your life." When the dust of its release settles, it is a virtual certainty that we will be able to see *Eyes Wide Shut*, in all its challenging richness and strangeness, as Kubrick's haunting final masterpiece.

VILLAGE VOICE, 7/27/99, p. 59, J. Hoberman

The best thing about *Eyes Wide Shut* may be its title, but anyone planning to see Stanley Kubrick's long-awaited, posthumously released swan song is advised to go with their eyes open. Completed by Warner Bros. after the director's death last March (and shamelessly proclaimed a "brilliant," "haunting" "masterpiece" in the advance cover story provided by the studio's corporate sibling, *Time*), this two hour and 39 minute gloss on Arthur Schnitzler's fantasmagoric novella feels like a rough draft at best.

At worst, *Eyes Wide Shut* is ponderously (up)dated—as though Kubrick had finally gotten around to responding to Michelangelo Antonioni's druggy *Blow-Up*—if not weirdly anachronistic. (It's difficult to make a movie about a city you last set foot in 35 years ago.) Shot in London, *Eyes Wide Shut* opens in a fabulous Upper West Side apartment filled with florid paintings, Alice (Nicole Kidman) stripping down to dress up—and not for the last time. She and her doctor husband Bill (Tom Cruise) have been invited to the splendiferous Christmas bash hosted by a wealthy sleazebag of mystery (Sydney Pollack).

Lit like Bloomie's window and shot as though for *The Shining*, the party is charged with telegraphed sophistication and rich with significant meetings. Bill encounters an old med-school buddy playing piano; Alice is swept away by a predatory Hungarian for a foxtrot so torrid they're practically horizontal. Just as Bill is being waltzed off to pleasures unknown by a pair of flirtatious models, he is summoned, at the host's behest, to revive a very naked lovely who has inconveniently OD'd in the master bathroom. *Eyes Wide Shut*, as you may know, is about sex—albeit mainly in the head.

In one of the movie's two bravura scenes, Bill and Alice smoke weed and rehash their confusing Christmas party encounters. Irritated (or is it stimulated?) by Bill's smug denials, Alice launches into an impassioned riff on marriage, jealousy, and the alleged difference between the genders. Bill remains clueless: "Relax, Alice, this pot is making you aggressive." The scene demonstrates why Kubrick wanted a real-life couple—Cruise's evident discomfort is no less crucial than Kidman's ecstatic exhibitionism. The actress is not only a more assured performer than her husband but an incomparably greater showboat, almost absurdly comfortable acting without clothes. (A year spent shooting and reshooting this material must have propelled her into *The Blue Room*.)

The all-purpose conjugal argument, somewhat skewed by Kidman's stoned rantings and distracting dishabille, segues into a confession that she has only just finished making when the telephone rings. Summoned to his professional duties, the most boyish, least likely, doctor in New York City embarks on a stumbling sexual Cook's tour. Imagining his wife's imagined infidelity all the while, he is successively propositioned by a dead patient's neurotic daughter, gay-baited by six drunken teenagers, picked up by an exceedingly pretty hooker, made privy to a sordid instance of pedophilia, and ultimately transported to a masquerade orgy at a baronial estate somewhere in the richest, most Republican districts of Long Island.

The latter is the movie's set piece but, for all the bare breasts and velvet capes, black mass paraphernalia and strenuously implied in-and-out, it's less carnal cornucopia than a triumph of theatrical rustiness that effectively liquidates whatever mad oneiric momentum the movie has built up over the past hour. Hardly the sexual heart of darkness, this decorous gavotte is more studied than a fashion shoot and rather less explicit. The final shock: Two men dancing ... together!

The story of a guy who crashes out of his bourgeois existence into a nocturnal world of sexual gangsters and femmes fatales, *Eyes Wide Shut* is a kind of primal noir. The script, which Kubrick wrote with novelist Frederick Raphael, is, for much of its length, surprisingly faithful to the 1926 Schnitzler original—a fluid exploration of the marital magnetic field that, successfully blurring the boundaries of the real, keeps telling the same story again and again, charging it each time with additional psychosexual material. (Physician heal thyself: Schnitzler himself was a medical doctor and, like Kubrick, a doctor's son.)

While Bill's out exploring, Alice has been home in bed, dreaming. Far more cogent (and disturbingly erotic) than the vaunted orgy, Kidman's agonized recounting of her nocturnal adventure makes the movie's most compelling scene. Events staged are trumped by those imagined. *Eyes Wide Shut* is its own critique—no wonder Kubrick spent so many years pondering this project and so much time in production.

No small attention has been given to the digital figures that Warner Bros. introduced into Kubrick's footage, strategically positioned to block the action during the orgy scene. (The effect is not unlike the inscribed audience in *Mystery Science Theater 3000*.) Supposedly added to secure the movie's R rating, these computer-generated fig leaves may conceal something else.

Days after Kubrick's death, Warners' then co-chairman Terry Semel told *The New York Times* that *Eyes Wide Shut* was "totally finished." Save for "a couple of color corrections" and some unspecified "technical things," Kubrick had made "his final cut." From a semantic point of view, this last statement is undeniable—the director *had* made his last cut, at least on this earth. But *Eyes Wide Shut* may be scarcely more Kubrick's film than *Juneteenth* is Ralph Ellison's novel. Whether or not one believes the rumors that the *Eyes Wide Shut* release version was supervised by Steven Spielberg or Sydney Pollack or even Tom Cruise, the ponderous Temple of Doom orgy, crassly matched location inserts, overreliance on cross-cutting, and atrocious mixing (most obvious in the orgy's dreadful dubbing and oscillating hubbub level) all suggest the movie was quite far from completion when its notoriously perfectionist author passed away.

Eyes Wide Shut had more than a few problems for Kubrick to solve. Out of his depth playing out of his depth, Cruise is as blatantly miscast as his character is incoherent. (The role of this self-deluded society doc might have made more sense if Bill were unhappily Jewish, as Raphael wanted, or a closeted gay, as Kubrick sometimes hints.) The ridiculous orgy and the botched sense of place would have been difficult to repair, and I don't think there was any way to reconcile the cinematography's would-be grainy immediacy with the fastidious studio lighting and lavish New York street set. But although the sarcastic use of pop chestnuts like "Strangers in the Night" and "When I Fall in Love" sounds like Kubrick, it's difficult to find a precedent in his oeuvre for the embarrassingly insipid score.

Notwithstanding the misguided attempt in the movie's final half hour to rationalize Schnitzler's evocative material with a heavy-handed and ultimately nonsensical plot device, I'm not even convinced that this "haunting final masterpiece" has the tone that Kubrick intended. It requires but the barest familiarity with *Lolita* or *Dr. Strangelove* to see how *Eyes Wide Shut* might have been cut by 45 minutes and played for East European black comedy. (The movie is rife enough with broad performances—ranging from Sky Dumont's hokey Hungarian to the fey camping of Alan Cumming's desk clerk.)

There may be a scandal behind *Eyes Wide Shut*—which, even in this forlorn state, has enough stuff to suggest a Kubrick film—but it has nothing to do with explicit sex. Someday some dogged cine-archaeologist will get to the bottom of this corporate restoration and, figuring out just who did what to whom, sort the potential film from the apparent one. For most people, though, a single viewing will be more than enough.

Also reviewed in:
CHICAGO TRIBUNE, 7/16/99, Friday/p. A, Michael Wilmington
NATION, 8/9 & 16/99, p. 42, Stuart Klawans
NEW REPUBLIC, 8/16/99, p. 30, Stanley Kauffmann
NEW YORK TIMES, 9/16/99, p. E1, Janet Maslin
NEW YORKER, 7/26/99, p. 84, David Denby
VARIETY, 7/12-18/99, p. 37, Todd McCarthy
WASHINGTON POST, 7/16/99, p. C1, Stephen Hunter
WASHINGTON POST, 7/16/99, Weekend/p. 43, Desson Howe

FANTASIA/2000

A Walt Disney Pictures release. *Executive Producer:* Roy Edward Disney. *Producer:* Donald W. Ernst. SYMPHONY No. 5: *Director:* Pixote Hunt. *Music:* Ludwig Van Beethoven. *Art Director:* Pixote Hunt. PINES OF ROME: *Director:* Hendel Butoy. *Music:* Ottorino Respighi. *Art Director:* Dean Gordon and William Perkins. RHAPSODY IN BLUE: *Director:* Eric Goldberg. *Music:* George Gershwin. *Art Director:* Susan McKinsey Goldberg. PIANO CONCERTO No. 2, ALLEGRO, OPUS 102: *Director:* Hendel Butoy. *Music:* Dmitri Shostakovich. *Art Director:* Michael Humphries. CARNIVAL OF THE ANIMALS, FINALE: *Director:* Eric Goldberg. *Music:* Camille Saint-Saëns. *Art Director:* Susan McKinsey Goldberg. THE SORCERER'S APPRENTICE: *Director:* James Algar. *Music:* Paul Dukas. *Art Director:* Tom Codrick, Charles Philippi and Zack Schwartz. POMP AND CIRCUMSTANCE—MARCHES 1, 2, 3, and 4: *Director:* Francis Glebas. *Music:* Edward Elgar. *Art Director:* Daniel Cooper. FIREBIRD SUITE—1919 VERSION: *Director:* Gaëtan Brizzi and Paul Brizzi. *Music:* Igor Stravinsky. *Art Director:* Carl Jones. *Animation Director:* Hendel Butoy. *Editor:* Jessica Ambinder Rojas and Lois Freeman-Fox. HOST SEQUENCES: *Director:* Don Hahn. *Conductor:* James Levine and Leopold Stokowski. *Casting:* Ruth Lambert and Mary Hidalgo. *Running time:* 75 minutes. *MPAA Rating:* G.

HOSTS: Steve Martin (Symphony No. 5); Bette Midler (Piano Concerto No. 2); James Levine (Pomp and Circumstance); Itzhak Perlman (Pines of Rome); James Earl Jones (Carnival of the Animals); Angela Lansbury (Firebird Suite); Quincy Jones (Rhapsody in Blue); Penn & Teller (The Sorcerer's Apprentice).

CHRISTIAN SCIENCE MONITOR, 12/31/99, p. 16, David Sterritt

When the popular "Fantasia" had its premiere in 1940, the Walt Disney studio meant to introduce a new concept in filmmaking. Since the movie consisted of several different segments, each combining whimsical animation with appropriate music, Disney saw it as a sort of work-in-progress that could be continually changed. See it again in a year or two and its contents would be different!

"Fantasia" became a classic, but Disney didn't follow through on its idea of forever altering and revitalizing the material—until now. In superficial respects, "Fantasia/2000" is bigger and bolder than its predecessor, opening on huge IMAX screens, and its release date—Jan. 1—makes it the first major movie of 2000.

But in other ways, "Fantasia/2000" is mildly disappointing. Running just 75 minutes—about an hour shorter than its ancestor—it lacks the nonstop originality of the 1940 version. It's worth remembering that the dinosaur segment of the first "Fantasia" was set to Igor Stravinsky's ferocious "Rite of Spring," which had sparked a riot at its Paris premiere less than 30 years earlier. The new "Fantasia" avoids such feistiness.

This said, "Fantasia/2000" has plenty to offer, especially when it pairs Al Hirschfeld's drawing style with George Gershwin's tunes for a jazzy "Rhapsody in Blue," and when it juices up the stuffy "Pomp and Circumstance" marches by putting Donald Duck into Noah's ark. And then there's Mickey Mouse in "The Sorcerer's Apprentice," recycled from the original film. It's worth the price of admission by itself.

LOS ANGELES TIMES, 12/31/99, Calendar/p. 1, Kenneth Turan

Sixty years is quite a gap between an original and a sequel, but the 1940 "Fantasia" was never business as usual.

A melding of animation and classical music, it has been ignored (by audiences at its initial release), embraced (by succeeding generations), celebrated (for its "Sorcerer's Apprentice" sequence) and reviled (abstract filmmaker Oskar Fischinger called it "a conglomeration of tastelessness"). Whatever else may be said about its designated successor, "Fantasia/2000," it's unlikely to be that controversial.

Despite being trumpeted as the first feature-length animated movie to be released in large-screen Imax format, "Fantasia/2000" is more ephemeral than epochal. A pleasant enough diversion, with seven new sequences joining a reprise of "Sorcerer," it passes the time amiably enough (if you can get used to that overwhelming Imax screen) but doesn't leave much of a residue. Which may make it the paradigmatic entertainment, heaven help us, for the new millennium.

Many years in the making, "Fantasia/2000" follows the pattern of the original by having different animators linked to different pieces of classical music, some of which, like the three-minute version of Beethoven's Symphony No. 5, have been rather truncated. (The Chicago Symphony Orchestra, conducted by James Levine, provides the sounds.)

Perhaps because we've gotten used to all manner of animation as well as to classical music being used in a wide variety of contexts, this mixing of high and popular cultures doesn't raise the eyebrows it did in 1940. More than that, the system of live-action hosts used to introduce each segment seems quaint and old-fashioned; only Steve Martin and his "12 week home study course" for orchestra members survives with his sensibility intact.

One of the intriguing things about the "Fantasia" scenario is that it's the opposite of how music usually works for the movies. Typically, the composer comes in after the material has been shot and writes music to fit the images. Here, the composers are dead and gone and it's the filmmakers, in an adroit exercise in problem-solving, who have to fit their images to the music.

When this process works best, when the match is good, there is no sense that a match has even taken place. Sound and picture should enhance each other, creating a third entity that lives and breathes on its own. At its worst, the result is an odd hybrid, a forced illustration that allows neither element to stand on its own.

While all "Fantasia/2000" viewers will have their personal likes and dislikes—it's an anthology, after all—one of the places the synergy works well is the marriage of Hans Christian Andersen's "The Steadfast Tin Soldier" to Dmitri Shostakovich's Piano Concerto No. 2.

The concerto is a favorite of Roy Disney, executive producer of "Fantasia/2000," and he passed it on to director Hendel Butoy, who paradoxically uses computer-generated images to give a rich, old-fashioned look to the tale of a beautiful toy ballerina, a lascivious jack-in-the-box and a truly steadfast toy soldier.

Also making interesting use of CGI is the film's finale, directed by Gaetan and Paul Brizzi, Parisian-based animators who also worked on "The Hunchback of Notre Dame." They've not surprisingly turned Igor Stravinsky's "Firebird" Suite into an ecological fable of life, death and renewal that makes a fascinating counterpart to similar sections in Hayao Miyazaki's "Princess Mononoke."

Perhaps the most visually distinctive segment, directed by Eric Goldberg, uses an elegant visual style inspired by cartoonist Al Hirschfeld to choreograph a tribute to the hurly-burly of Manhattan in the 1930s to the music of George Gershwin's "Rhapsody in Blue."

Falling into the eye candy category are three abstract minutes of Beethoven's Fifth and the unexpected flying-whales motif Butoy used to accompany Respighi's "Pines of Rome." Among the other segments, the flamingos playing with a yo-yo sequence that goes with a fragment of Saint-Saens' "Carnival of the Animals" is too jokey, and Elgar's "Pomp and Circumstance" serves mainly to show us the caring side of a creature not previously known for his sensitivity, the dyspeptic Donald Duck.

Speaking of traditional Disney characters, the highlight of this "Fantasia," as of the first, remains the Mickey Mouse-starring version of Paul Dukas' "The Sorcerer's Apprentice" directed by the late James Algar. Grainy as it looks in its massive Imax blowup, Mickey's misadventures with water and a broom still have the kind of magic even modern technology can't always manage.

NEW YORK POST, 6/16/00, p. 53, Lou Lumenick

Walt Disney's nephew Roy E. Disney spent a decade producing this new edition of the 1940 animated classic, overseeing seven new high-quality segments set to classical music—a couple of them knockouts.

They accompany the original version of "The Sorcerer's Apprentice" with Mickey Mouse, which still looks great.

The very best of the newcomers is set to George Gershwin's "Rhapsody in Blue," under the direction of Eric Goldberg.

It's a witty, stunning evocation of New York City in the 1930s, done entirely in the style of legendary illustrator Al Hirschfeld, complete with his trademark use of his daughter Nina's name hidden in the drawings.

Less literal but no less spectacular is the closing segment, accompanied by Igor Stravinsky's "Firebird."

Using a combination of traditional animation and computer-generated effects, directors Gaetan Brizzi and Paul Brizzi enchant the eye with a volcano ravaging a forest—and the renewal that follows under the hand of a sprite.

Other segments are set to Ottorino Respighi's "Pines of Rome" (a pod of whales take flight when a star explodes over their Iceberg-laden habitat), Dimitri Shostakovich's "Piano Concerto No. 2, Allegro, Opus 102" (a beautifully drawn version of Hans Christian Andersen's "The Steadfast Tin Soldier") and Camille Saint-Saens' "Carnival of the Animals" (a pink flamingo playing with a yo-yo.)

The only segment that disappoints weirdly combines Sir Edward Elgar's "Pomp and Circumstance," a strangely mute Donald Duck (none of the animation has dialogue) and the story of Noah's ark.

Less highbrow and much shorter than its two-hour predecessor, this version has brief introductions by Steve Martin, Bette Midler, Itzhak Perlman, James Earl Jones, Angela Lansbury, Quincy Jones and Penn & Teller.

NEWSDAY, 12/31/99, Part II/p. B3, Jan Stuart

If you have somehow not heard "Rhapsody in Blue" in the months since your last oil change, you have a happy refresher waiting for you at Disney's souped-up new IMAX edition of "Fantasia."

Using the playful line-drawing style of illustrator Al Hirschfeld for inspiration, "Fantasia 2000" finds in the signature Gershwin piece a wonderfully droll day-in-the-life panorama of 1930s Manhattan. The artists evoke both the yearning and the bustle in the music: As city-dwellers burst from hotels and subway kiosks in mad, stampeding droves, a young black construction worker daydreams of cutting loose at a Harlem jazz club. Elsewhere, a down-and-out New Yorker pines simply for a job.

Admirably enough, this cityscape doesn't hide its eyes from Depression-era melancholy or current-day malaise. At one point, the black worker attempts in vain to get a taxicab uptown. This is about as blue as this "Rhapsody" gets, however. Honoring the film's title and status, it's a vintage burst of Disney animation and a buoyant fantasy spin on the Gotham of yore. The current mayor of New York will probably want to take credit for it.

"Rhapsody in Blue" is by far the best thing about this almost all-new edition of "Fantasia," which, but for its audience-devouring IMAX scale, is distinctly inferior to the one on which many of us were reared. Not that the 1940 original was by any means the Holy Grail of cartoon features: It was always a little tedious in its high-mindedness and warhorse menu of classical music. For provoking a childlike sense of wonderment, "Pinocchio" did it better. For sheer psychedelic trippiness, "Dumbo's" pink elephant sequence upstaged it. For introducing children to the joys of classical music, the Warner Bros.' Bugs Bunny cartoon shorts were far wittier and much less condescending.

What that first "Fantasia" had going for it was a provocative mix of the abstract with more literal visualizations of classical music. But for a phalanx of geometric butterflies propelled by Beethoven's Fifth Symphony, this new "Fantasia" drop-kicks the abstract in favor of pictorial illustrations, a la "Rhapsody in Blue." Aside from the Gershwin, the most satisfying results come from a dreamy setting for Respighi's "Pines of Rome," wherein a school of flying whales leaps toward the stratosphere. Abetted by the mammoth IMAX lens, the whales' cloud leaps are truly epic to behold.

The rest is a redundant and uninspired riff on music that needs no introduction because it will stalk you wherever you go till the day you die. I'm not sure what to make of this fetish Disney animators have for water. One too many of the sequences lean into people and things being swept by huge bodies of water, like a "Pomp and Circumstance"-led march of the animals to Noah's ark that climaxes with the Great Flood. The original waterlogged classic from which all of these segments ostensibly take their cue is "The Sorcerer's Apprentice," the only one of the original "Fantasia" sequences retrieved here.

In place of Dennis Taylor's windbag narration, a bevy of brand-name stars (Steve Martin, Bette Midler and James Earl Jones, for starters) provides introductory patter that succeeds only in breaking the music's spell and lending the film the vulgar edge of a bad TV variety special. The maestro successor to Leopold Stokowski is James Levine; who conducts a majestic-sounding Chicago Symphony Orchestra and occasionally confides in Mickey Mouse.

Messrs. Levine and Mouse, you'll be happy to know, are on a first-name basis. In the wake of "Stuart Little" and "The Green Mile," Disney's "Fantasia 2000" caps a banner year in the American cinema for tolerance and understanding of rodent equality.

SIGHT AND SOUND, 6/00, p. 41, Brian Sibley

Eight animated sequences illustrate classical music. Beethoven's 'Fifth Symphony' includes abstract butterfly shapes. Respighi's 'Pines of Rome' depicts a fantasy of flying whales. Gershwin's 'Rhapsody in Blue' plays out a saga of 30s New Yorkers. Shostakovich's 'Piano Concerto No. 2' dramatises Hans Christian Andersen's fairy tale 'The Steadfast Tin Soldier.' Saint-Saëns' 'Carnival of the Animals' features a yo-yoing flamingo causing mayhem. Dukas' 'The Sorcerer's Apprentice' has Mickey Mouse as a would-be magician who brings a broom to life and wreaks havoc. Elgar's 'Pomp and Circumstance' marches are set to the biblical story of the flood with Donald Duck as Mr Noah's assistant. Finally, Stravinsky's 'Firebird Suite' illustrates a woodland sprite facing the destructive fury of a volcanic eruption.

When Walt Disney released *Fantasia* in 1940, he described it as "an experiment in seeing music and hearing pictures". It was a revolutionary project for which he had big ambitions. He planned to revise the film regularly with new sequences, but for various reasons, this plan was never fulfilled. Now Walt's nephew, Roy E. Disney, and the Disney animators have dreamed up *Fantasia 2000*. But in revisiting the premise something vital has been overlooked: although the music and the accompanying visualisations in the first film were undoubtedly eclectic, the diverse sequences were held together by a continuity of style and an overarching vision, both of which are missing from *Fantasia 2000*. True, the film includes both the comic and the pastoral, just as its predecessor did; but the themes running through the old *Fantasia*—the struggle between light and dark, the war between chaos and order, the ultimate triumph of goodness—find only a pale equivalent in this new version. In fact, *Fantasia 2000* has less in common with the subtle structure of the original, than with the scrambled look of Disney's later compilation movies, *Make Mine Music* (1946) and *Melody Time* (1948), where anything and everything co-exist, rather like attractions at a theme park.

A vague attempt has been made to replicate certain aspects of the earlier version, such as beginning with the image of an orchestra, here assembled in a celestial Hollywood Bowl which creates itself in some distant spiral of the galaxy and recalls the heavenly courtroom in *A Matter of Life and Death*. The *Fantasia 2000* programme begins with a homage to its predecessor: an 'abstract' sequence—in the first film, Bach's 'Toccata and Fugue in D Minor', here the opening three minutes of Beethoven's 'Fifth Symphony'. But there is no challenge in these abstractions, which are little more than geometric shapes clearly intended to represent butterflies. The Beethoven is one of several computer-animated sequences which sit uneasily with those created in traditional line animation and which—particularly in the unappealing segment featuring a Shostakovich-scored version of Hans Andersen's 'The Steadfast Tin Soldier'—exhibit neither the personality nor the technical finesse found in the stunning *Toy Story* movies.

The film also suffers from a chronic unevenness of pace: Respighi's 'Pines Of Rome' opens breathtakingly with the explosion of a supenova over a shimmering Arctic sea. Towering icebergs are illuminated by the shifting rainbow light of the aurora borealis, as a family of whales breach the icy waters and fly. The viewer is then abandoned to a tediously slow section in which a cute baby whale gets separated from its parents in an ice-cave. By the time the child is finally liberated and the whales continue their flight to the stars, the magic has been overtaken by chronic boredom. In contrast, the frenetic finale of Saint-Saëns' 'Carnival of the Animals', accompanied by the irritating exploits of a yo-yo playing flamingo in a wishy-wash water-coloured pondscape, are so fast and furious they are over almost before they have begun.

Initially *Fantasia 2000* was to contain a number of sequences from the first film, however, after various changes of plan, the only item revived from *Fantasia 1940* is 'The Sorcerer's Apprentice', a sequence which began life as a short cartoon and from which the whole *Fantasia* project eventually sprang. While the screen quality of the 'Sorcerer' falls well short of today's standards (and particularly in the big-screen IMAX format the film was originally released on), the wit and invention are as fresh as ever.

Originally, at the end of this sequence, Mickey (speaking with the voice of Walt Disney) exchanged mutual congratulations with conductor Leopold Stokowski (correctly pronounced 'Stokoffski') before scampering off again. In *Fantasia 2000*, a re-dubbed Mickey now thanks a "Mr Sto-cow-ski" before joining James Levine to introduce the next sequence, a conglomeration of Elgar's 'Pomp and Circumstance Marches', illustrating the story of Noah's Ark with Donald Duck given the job of rounding up the animals. If it's odd to follow one musical joke with another, it's unwise to set such contrasting animation cheek-by-jowl, the confident, polished artwork from 1940 beside the shamefully sloppy animation with which the Elgar sequence opens—the animals processing to the ark, two by two, in an unimaginative reworking of the stunning opening to *The Lion King*. Fortunately the sequence is switly saved by a succession of great gags: Donald moving a reluctant hippo by whacking it with a porcupine and a group of mythical creatures laughing at the foolishness of the animals going aboard the ark.

Perhaps the two most successful sequences in the film are those which, ironically, hark back to earlier times. A brilliant evocation of 30s New York, set to Gershwin's 'Rhapsody in Blue', draws on the graphic style of the celebrated caricaturist Al Hirschfeld, and recreates the city's stoops, crowded subways, skyscraper building-sites and fashionable hotels with bustling crowds of Algonquin Round-Tablers rushing in and out of revolving doors. The interweaving dreams of a group of 'blue' city folk are told in strong lines and vivid, flat colours that are fashionably retro and recall the limited animation pioneered by UPA studios in the 50s in such films as 'Gerald McBoing Boing'.

The other sequence that securely links the two *Fantasias* is the concluding interpretation of Stravinsky's 'Firebird Suite' filled with classic Disneyesque effects. The spirit of the forest soars across a snowy landscape, bringing new life in the form of a spreading carpet of flowers and greenery, only to confront the explosive force of the volcanic Firebird in a sequence of exquisite beauty and raw natural violence, images of the kind which abounded in the first *Fantasia*. It is a reminder that, after all these years, memories of the first *Fantasia* can still conjure magic in the mind. And will the same be said of *Fantasia 2000* in 60 years' time? It's possible, but unlikely.

VILLAGE VOICE, 1/11/00, p. 108, Jessica Winter

A bundle of animated shorts set to famous classical music pieces, *Fantasia* hitched a supposedly lowborn art form to a high-hat soundtrack; Mickey Mouse shaking hands with Leopold Stokowski on the podium is a statement of intent. Uncle Walt's pricey experiment flopped upon release in 1940, but started turning a profit by the mid '50s; its stream-of-consciousness imagery and tone-poem rhythms also helped it join *2001* and *Yellow Submarine* in that rarefied realm of Great Films to Watch While You're Baked.

Budding young stoners have to hoof it to an Imax theater for the rehauled *Fantasia 2000*, which sports seven new shorts, keeping only "The Sorcerer's Apprentice" from the first version. The second new installment is the best: Mystic and austere, "Pines of Rome" lets Respighi's music color in the somber blues and grays of a young arctic whale's journey upwards through the icy surface to join his parents in some starry-skied cetacean Valhalla. The effect is hypnotic, oddly mournful, and vaguely unsettling, like a too-vivid dream. The rest is just a snooze: Al Hirschfeld's antiquated Gothamites shuttle about to the strains of "Rhapsody in Blue," emanating a musty whiff of Upper East Side gentility; a fretsome Donald Duck as Noah on the ark during "Pomp and Circumstance" is an unfunny bit of Disney nostalgia. Arriving just after the best year for animated film in recent memory, *Fantasia 2000* doesn't play like a celebration. In its sentimental yearning for a golden age when another one's upon us, it feels a little like a rebuke.

Also reviewed in:
CHICAGO TIMES, 12/31/99, Friday/p. A, Michael Wilmington
NEW YORK TIMES, 12/31/99, p. E1, Stephen Holden
VARIETY, 1/3-9/00, p. 79, Todd McCarthy
WASHINGTON POST, 6/16/00, p. C12, Stephen Hunter
WASHINGTON POST, 6/16/00, Weekend/p. 45, Desson Howe

FARE GAMES

An Edison Agami Film release of an Edison Agami Film production. *Producer:* Isaac Asami. *Director:* Brian O'Hara. *Screenplay:* Brian O'Hara. *Based on a story by:* Isaac Agami. *Director of Photography:* Larry Revene. *Editor:* Kevin O'Hara. *Music:* TAJ. *Running time:* 90 minutes. *MPAA Rating:* Not Rated.

CAST: Eddie Estefan (Jimmy); Russel Stewart (Martin); Elizabeth Curtain (Susie); Marina Morgan (Jennifer); Andre Leigh (Barbara).

NEW YORK POST, 5/7/99, p. 53, Hannah Brown

Watching "Fare Games" is like sitting through a 90-minute episode of the TV series "Taxi" with the good jokes edited out.

Producer and co-screenwriter Isaac Agami, who used to drive a cab himself, has devised a story about two cabbies who have affairs with their passengers.

Jimmy (Eddie Estefan), an unhappily married dad, has a fling with NYU co-ed Jennifer (Marina Morgan).

Jimmy's best friend, Martin (Russel Stewart), has a romance with Susie (Elizabeth Curtain), a stripper with a heart of gold.

Marina Morgan, who has a body worth displaying, seems notably more relaxed whenever she takes off her clothes.

The movie's saving grace is its postcard-pretty photography of the New York skyline and streets.

Perhaps there is a niche for "Fare Games" after all—as an R-rated tourist flick.

NEWSDAY, 5/7/99, Part II/p. B11, Gene Seymour

Jimmy (Eddie Estefan) is married, macho and can't control his libido. Martin (Russell Stewart) is divorced, gentle and apparently can't afford a confidence chromosome. All they have in common is that they're both in their 40s and they drive their own New York City cabs. This is the movies, so you know this is enough to make them the best of friends.

Through similarly serendipitous means, Jimmy and Martin find something else in common: a sexy fare who eventually becomes much more than a passenger. Each man gets the 20-something he deserves. For Jimmy, it's an oversexed NYU student (Marina Morgan) who takes him for rides he'd never imagined. Martin, meanwhile, befriends a dancer (Elizabeth Curtain), who finds herself jobless, scared and homeless after quitting her job at a topless bar.

Jimmy, who lives on the Island, finds himself coming home from his escapades so late that he has to devise elaborate excuses large enough for his skeptical wife (Andre Leigh) to swallow. His whoppers involve crippled dogs and marauding seagulls, prompting someone to observe to his wife that Jimmy "has worse luck with animals than Tarzan." I thought Tarzan got along better with animals than with people, but the script is so enamored with this lame joke, it repeats it.

"Fare Games" story is interspersed with the kind of random, unsurprising anecdotes of life as a New York cabbie. Angry bike messengers, mild-mannered sex freaks, drivers who cut in front and (always) miserly fares make guest appearances in writer-director Brian O'Hara's film. Doubtless most of these incidents came from the memory bank of producer Isaac Agami, who spent several years as a New York taxi driver.

Agami's film is hacking of a different sort. Cliched, predictable and plain, it sometimes seems, like Jimmy, too brash and satisfied with its limitations. Yet, like Martin, it also has an awkward sweetness that makes it bearable, even through a inexplicably ugly sequence at a Labor Day barbecue in Jimmy's backyard. In all, "Fare Games" plays the way a blind date is often sold: Not much in looks or class, but it's got personality.

Also reviewed in:
NEW YORK TIMES, 5/7/99, p. E19, Lawrence Van Gelder

FELICIA'S JOURNEY

An Artisan Entertainment release in association with Icon productions of an Icon production in association with Alliance Atlantis Pictures. *Executive Producer:* Paul Tucker and Ralph Kamp. *Producer:* Bruce Davey. *Director:* Atom Egoyan. *Screenplay:* Atom Egoyan. *Based on the novel by:* William Trevor. *Director of Photography:* Paul Sarossy. *Editor:* Susan Shipton. *Music:* Mychael Danna. *Sound:* Brian Simmons. *Casting:* Leo Davis. *Production Designer:* Jim Clay. *Art Director:* Chris Seagers and Jo Graysmark. *Costumes:* Sandy Powell. *Make-up:* Morag Ross. *Stunt Coordinator:* Colin Skeaping. *Running time:* 116 minutes. *MPAA Rating:* Not Rated.

CAST: Bob Hoskins (Hilditch); Elaine Cassidy (Felicia); Claire Benedict (Miss Calligary); Brid Brennan (Mrs. Lysaght); Peter McDonald (Johnny); Gerard McSorley (Felicia's Father); Arsineé Khanjian (Gala); Sheila Reid (Iris); Nizwar Karanj (Sidney); Ali Yassine (Customs Officer); Kriss Dosanjh (Salesman); Maire Stafford (Felicia's Great Grandmother); Gavin Kelty (Shay Mulroone); Mark Hadfield (Television Director); Danny Turner (Young Hilditch); Susan Parry (Salome); Jean Marlow (Old Woman); Sidney Cole (Ethiopian); Barry McGovern (Gatherer); Sandra Voe (Jumble Sale Woman); Leila Hoffman (Bag Lady); Bob Mason (Jimmy); Emma Powell (Clinic Receptionist); Julie Cox (Marcia Tibbits).

CINEASTE, Vol. XXV, No. 1, 1999, p. 42, Richard Porton

Neither a straightforward genre film nor a simple portrait of mental aberration, Atom Egoyan's *Felicia's Journey* brilliantly subverts the conventions of the standard Hollywood thriller as well as the clichés of the by-now hackneyed serial killer subgenre. While Egoyan's adaptation of William Trevor's novel possesses superficial affinities to the work of Hitchcock and Chabrol, the Canadian director's more meditative style prevents us—as audience members—from being pawns of an autocratic *auteur*. The emphasis in this film is less on individual psychosis than on the web of relationships (both social and implicitly political) that engender it.

Felicia's Journey promotes a distinctively contemplative form of suspense by recounting the commingled destinies of two mismatched protagonists: Felicia (Elaine Cassidy), an astonishingly naive teenager who yearns for a reconciliation with her unfaithful boyfriend, and Joseph Ambrose Hilditch (Bob Hoskins), a deceptively mild-mannered catering manager from the Birmingham suburbs with a penchant for befriending young women. When the newly pregnant Felicia, in flight from an almost premodern Irish adolescence, travels from her sheltered home to the Midlands' antiseptic industrial landscape (virtually a character in its own right), she has a fateful and nearfatal encounter with Hilditch. And, perhaps most tellingly, both characters are, to varying degrees, suspended in time. Felicia comes from an almost ludicrously verdant Irish village (in sharp contrast to contemporary Ireland's vibrant modernity) where her father treats the Easter 1916 rebellion as an event that might have happened yesterday and her great-grandmother invokes Eamon de Valera's memory in Gaelic. Hilditch, on the other hand, lives in a stodgy, commodious house where he recreates the supposedly more innocent 1950s with mementos from his childhood and syrupy recordings of obscure crooners.

Just as Trevor's novel marked the 'Chekhovian' humanist's newfound interest in the morbid terrain best personified by Patricia Highsmith's novels, Egoyan's film flirts with genre conventions that are, in the final analysis, skillfully deflected. Unlike charismatic killers such as Robert Walker's Bruno in *Strangers on a Train* or diabolically clever madmen like *The Silence of the Lambs'* Hannibal Lecter, Hilditch is an almost laughably banal psychotic. A man with exquisite manners who reveres the memory of his mother, a comically flamboyant TV chef, he fails to conform to the standard movie profile of a homicidal maniac. Despite recourse to violence that appears antithetical to this dullard's placid demeanor (the film itself is resolutely unviolent), his delusional reveries are not much different from the convoluted fantasies of garden variety neurotics in previous Egoyan psychodramas. The perverse alchemy that leads Hilditch to murder the objects of his affection, however, is (quite wisely) never clearly in focus. We only know that this pudgy, incurably lonely man, depicted (in vignettes that are equally farcical and macabre) cooking elaborate dinners for himself that could easily feed a dinner party for fifteen people or more, fancies himself a father figure to young women in need. In a key scene, Hilditch derides a salesman's pitch for an automated catering system, insisting that "food must be served by caring hands." Aptly enough, Hilditch—affable culinary expert—is close to being an automaton himself. Trevor's empathetic but ultimately unsparing portrait of this pathetically frustrated nurturer occasionally resembled a case study that verged on vulgar Freudianism. Egoyan's more detached portrayal of a colorless middle-class Everyman is, paradoxically, more frightening. Hilditch's fondness for kitsch pop music, especially the ultra-derivative ditty, "You Are My Special Angel," drives home the point that sentimentality can often conceal lethal delusions.

The film's boldest departure from its source material involves video interludes chronicling both Hilditch's eclectic gallery of female victims and his mother's zany cooking program. Egoyan once remarked that many of his protagonists were stymied by their "lack of self-awareness." Unable to emerge from a debilitating narcissism, these terminally alienated characters attempt to gain access to an identity that proves elusive by immersing themselves in hyper-real, although ultimately spectral, video images. Even though the source of Hilditch's madness cannot be fully explained, his mistaken belief that this repertoire of images, ritualistically played again and again in his womblike home, provides genuine solace unquestionably promotes his dissociation from reality. His video 'memory lane' only reinforces his mental deterioration: an eclectic assortment of young women (multiracial; innocent runaways as well as prostitutes—he is an equal opportunity killer) appear to him as an undifferentiated mass of wayward girls who have abandoned him. Similarly, his mother Gala's vaudevillian turns as a loopier version of Julia Child (played with brio and a wink to the audience by Arsinée Khanjian) hint at a deep-seated trauma that is never completely revealed. Undoubtedly a mamma's boy, Hilditch's is, nevertheless, far from a Norman Bates clone.

Egoyan's characteristically audacious editing and use of camera movement are also key components of his 'defamiliarization' of the suspense genre. For example, as Hilditch's anxiety reaches its apogee, a few well-chosen images economically pinpoint his festering masochism—a television set displaying a campy moment from Rita Hayworth's performance as Salomé is immediately juxtaposed with his memory of Strauss's "Salomé," which frightened him as a child. Traveling shots of water towers (adjacent to—but not glimpsed by—Felicia and Hilditch as they travel by car to pay a visit to the murderer's imaginary wife) are much more reminiscent of sequences from Antonioni's *Red Desert* than the shooting style embraced by most thriller directors. These unpeopled glimpses of ordinary industrial appurtenances, both ominous and lyrical, complement the central narrative's oscillation between sinister and poetic moments.

Although Hilditch's growing delirium at times threatens to subsume Felicia's own saga, her painful transition from innocence to hard-won experience constitutes a mini-*Bildungsroman*. In perhaps the film's cruelest scene, Hilditch accompanies Felicia to a pub where the object of her English quest—caddish boyfriend Johnny—strenuously ignores her. The fact that she is able to survive brutal rejection, as well as the more tangible threat to her life posed by Hilditch, imbues grisly material with cautious optimism. Like Nicole in *The Sweet Hereafter*, Felicia achieves a kind of secular redemption (totally unlike the hokey version of fundamentalist redemption touted by the film's Jamaican evangelist, Miss Calligary) because, against all odds, she is able to leave girlhood behind and become a free woman.

Felicia's self-liberation is far from treacly, but Egoyan is an ironist who eschews the smarminess of what currently passes for social satire in films. Avoiding the cartoonish characters who have become staples in recent facile attempts to unmask suburbia or the nuclear family, he evinces empathy for even his most repellent protagonists. In *Felicia's Journey*, he is greatly aided by the contributions of a gifted cast, particularly the brilliant Bob Hoskins. Known primarily for blustery, exuberant performances, he gives an astonishingly nuanced portrayal of Hilditch—even his tiniest gesture conveys this gentle monster's inner chaos.

LOS ANGELES TIMES, 11/19/99, Calendar/p. 22, Kevin Thomas

With "Felicia's Journey," Canada's masterful and ever-venturesome Atom Egoyan continues to explore the ways in which people are damaged by terrible loss and loneliness and how they strive to overcome them.

This wonderfully accomplished film, which Egoyan adapted from William Trevor's prize-winning 1994 novel, has the ingredients of a traditional-style psychological thriller, but what interests Egoyan is neither edge-of-the-seat suspense for its own sake nor the struggle between good and evil but instead the evocation of a tragic figure and beyond that, the hope of salvation and redemption. "Felicia's Journey" ranks up there with "The Sweet Hereafter" (1997) and "Exotica" (1994); the three form a kind of Egoyan trilogy, consolidating the Canadian filmmaker's status as a major director in contemporary world cinema.

The journey that Felicia (Elaine Cassidy) takes proves to cover a great deal more terrain than the merely geographical. She's a 17-year-old demure beauty from a rural Ireland village who has not heard from her lover who has gone to England, ostensibly to take a job in a lawn-mower factory in the Birmingham area. He had not sent his address as he had promised, and now that she has discovered that she is pregnant, she comes to England's Midlands industrial region in search of him.

In the meantime we meet Hilditch (Bob Hoskins), a fussy, middle-aged food services manager for an immense Birmingham factory. Hilditch is a perfectionist but is much appreciated, for he is quick to praise his staffers who meet his high standards and routinely seeks out workers to see if various dishes are as tasty as he thinks they should be. The result is that the workers where Hilditch is employed are most likely the best-fed in the entire city.

Egoyan backs into his story, letting us learn about Felicia and Hilditch bit by bit. Following Hilditch home, we discover that he lives in a large suburban residence in which nothing seems to have changed since the 1950s. In his out-sized kitchen Hilditch prepares elaborate formal meals for himself alone while watching flickering black-and-white videos of an old TV cooking show, featuring a glamorous, heavily French-accented chef named Gala (Arsinee Khanjian). In time we realize that Gala was Hilditch's mother, and that her shows were shot in the very home where her son continues to live.

Gala is a self-absorbed, highly theatrical personality, and when she sometimes lassos her pudgy adolescent son into appearing with her the experience for him is most likely unbearably humiliating. Gala's extravagant displays of affection for her son are betrayed by the ease with which she is able to dismiss him callously. (We know nothing of the boy's father.) Sometime in the past Gala apparently died, leaving her son permanently traumatized.

Felicia and Hilditch cross paths several times. As Felicia's plight goes from bad to worse, Hilditch's carefully measured remarks seem increasingly soothing. As time passes we detect a highly practiced quality in Hilditch's manner as he takes on an increasingly sinister cast.

In what is arguably Hoskins' finest performance, he gives us a man whose naturally kind and thoughtful impulses have been short-circuited, leaving him in a state of isolation from which his attempts to escape have taken on a dark, destructive form. It is a measure of the quality of the film's writing and directing and of Hoskins' talent that "Felicia's Journey" packs a real depth charge, for we are able to connect with Hilditch on a very deep level and see in him whatever traumatic losses we have ever experienced ourselves.

Hilditch is often amusing in the way his propensity for propriety and sentimentality assume bizarre proportions and grotesque expression, but ultimately he is to be taken very seriously. You could describe Hilditch as a twisted variation on the kindly driver Hoskins played so memorably in Neil Jordan's "Mona Lisa."

Cassidy, for her part, brings the sensitivity and radiance to Felicia needed to make her able to appeal to the humanity lingering in the monster Hilditch has become. Similarly, Claire Benedict also faces a formidable challenge in playing the very religious Miss Calligary, who must be genuinely sincere no matter how outrageously overbearing she becomes.

Clearly, Egoyan has inspired his actors to take risks while never losing his own perspective. It's evocatively photographed by Paul Sarossy and scored by Mychael Danna, whose ominous, edgy, sometimes outright jangly music plays such a large role in sustaining the film's portentous mood. "Felicia's Journey" is one of the year's riskiest yet most effective films.

NEW YORK, 11/22/99, p. 88, Peter Rainer

In *Felicia's Journey*, Bob Hoskins is playing Joseph Hilditch, a fastidious catering manager in England's industrial Midlands who also happens to be a serial killer. Hilditch may not be fully aware of the murders he's committed; the women that this painfully lonely man picks up and befriends, and secretly videotapes in his car, are a solace he ultimately can't abide. (The killings are never shown.) Felicia (Elaine Cassidy), who is taken up by him after arriving from Ireland pregnant and in search of her errant boyfriend, is the innocent who unknowingly risks her life and transforms him. Atom Egoyan's adaptation of the 1994 William Trevor novel is an attempt to make ghoulishness ethereal. Egoyan resists pulping the material, or maybe he's just no good at getting down and dirty. But pulp would have been preferable to all this sluggish, nondescript lyricism. Even Hoskins begins to fade into the high-toned haze after a while. He's described his character as being a cross between Jack the Ripper and Winnie the Pooh, but what we mostly get is Pooh. Hilditch is certainly in a state of massive denial, but Hoskins's performance denies him too much. This monster self-cancels as you watch him.

NEW YORK POST, 11/12/99, p. 59, Jonathan Foreman

"Felicia's Journey" is a typically stylish but shallow attempt by Canadian director Atom Egoyan to make an arty, David Lynch-style thriller out of William Trevor's celebrated novel about a naive young Irish girl who goes to England and is befriended by a sympathetic serial killer.

It isn't nearly as original, smart or genre-bending as the filmmaker thinks it is.

As you might expect from an Egoyan film, "Felicia's Journey" is elegantly photographed (though wide-screen Panavision is a strange choice for such a non-epic), well-acted and somber. Also as you might expect, it's marred by self-indulgence, though not to the same pretentious degree as "The Adjuster" or "Exotica."

Hilditch (Bob Hoskins) is the popular, middle-aged catering manager of a large factory and a man of exacting standards. He's a seemingly gentle, lonely man who lives in a house filled with antique appliances and who dresses in a formal, old-fashioned manner—behavior that in movieland immediately marks him out as pervert, murderer or both.

Every night, while listening to cheesy old ballads like "My Special Angel," Hilditch cooks enormous meals according to the instructions given by a videotaped TV cooking program hosted by his domineering late mother, Gala (Arsinee Khanjian) in the 1950s. (This is one of those films that wants us to understand serial killers as the inevitable creations of weird parents.)

Felicia, on the other hand, is a slightly simple-minded teen from rural Ireland. (It's the usual North American film version of that country: all green fields and crashing waves with breathy Enya-esque music on the soundtrack.)

She's pregnant by her boyfriend Johnny (Peter McDonald), who has gone to England to find work. Felicia's fanatical nationalist father (Gerard McSorley) has disowned her in the belief that Johnny is not working in a lawnmower factory but has, in fact, joined the British Army.

Felicia crosses the water to industrial Birmingham to look for him, using money she's stolen from her ailing grandmother. Without a passport, the name of the factory, an address for Johnny or a place to stay, Felicia is haplessly wandering the streets when Hilditch drives by in his strange old car and offers to help.

We later learn that Hilditch has "helped" many young, lost girls he's met on the street, and has videotaped his conversations with them in his little car. (There are no videotapes in the novel, but Egoyan films generally feature surreptitious videotaping, a twisted relationship between an older man and a young girl, and grief for the dead.)

But naive, good-hearted Felicia is different from the young prostitutes and runaways Hilditch has befriended before, and her presence in his life helps him understand the horror of what he has done.

By Egoyan standards, the storytelling is relatively straightforward, without too many loose ends or absurd coincidences. But given the potentially gripping subject matter, the film is fatally underedited: Every scene feels too-long. And the repetitive, often unnecessary flashbacks have the effect of leaching tension out of the picture.

As in "The Sweet Hereafter," Egoyan gets superb performances from his actors. The always terrific Bob Hoskins ("The Long Good Friday," "Who Framed Roger Rabbit") is restrained and utterly believable as Hilditch (although his Birmingham accent wavers), and young Irish newcomer Elaine Cassidy easily holds her own.

SIGHT AND SOUND, 10/99, p. 44, Jonathan Romney

Felicia, a young Irish girl, travels to England in search of Johnny Lysaght, the boy who has made her pregnant. In Birmingham, she encounters Mr Hilditch, a factory catering manager, who helps her search around the local industrial estates for the lawnmower factory where she believes Johnny works; in reality, however, Johnny has joined the British army, just as Felicia's disapproving father had told her. Hilditch lives alone, haunted by the memory of his mother Gala, a television cook of the 50s, whose programmes he watches obsessively on video; he is also a compulsive befriender of teenage girls, whose confessions he also has on tape. Felicia is given shelter by Miss Calligary, an evangelist, but is thrown out again when she reports the loss of her money, which Hilditch has stolen.

She turns to Hilditch, who pretends to have an ill wife in hospital. Felicia moves in only to find that Hilditch's wife has supposedly died. He persuades Felicia to have an abortion. On their return to the house, he drugs her; she realises that he has killed all the other girls in his life. While digging a grave in his back garden, Hilditch is interrupted by a visit from Miss Calligary. He allows Felicia to escape, and then hangs himself. Later, in London, Felicia embarks on a new life.

In a striking but perplexing moment in *Felicia's Journey*, caterer Hilditch (Bob Hoskins) walks up the stairs of his house carrying a mug of cocoa laced with pills, intending to poison his naive protégée Felicia (Elaine Cassidy). At the top of the stairs he pauses, then, in unsettling close-up, glares balefully straight at the viewer. Unmotivated by narrative logic, this moment of confrontation marks the point at which Hilditch's benign facade cracks to reveal the killer underneath. Unless, perhaps, this is Hilditch striking a pose, playing the killer he means to be. Or unless this is a self-conscious signal from director Atom Egoyan, underlining the fact that we are watching a pastiche of a famous scene from Hitchcock's *Suspicion* (1941), involving a similar deadly glass of milk.

Felicia's Journey seems Hitchcockian from the start. In the credit sequence, the camera prowls around the museumlike enclosure of Hilditch's house, frozen in the aspic of 50s English suburbia. This straightaway inclines us to see Hilditch as another Norman Bates, with his dominating mother embalmed in videotape. It's even tempting to think of the portly boy-man as himself a kind of Hitchcock; an avid voyeur feeding on female emotion, he 'casts' lead actresses, surreptitiously videoing a succession of teenage girls in the passenger seat of his car. The Hitchcock connection has been underlined by a side project: these sequences have become the basis of Egoyan's video installation *Evidence*, recently seen in the Hitchcock homage at Oxford's Museum of Modern Art. In fact, Egoyan has called *Felicia's Journey* 'antiHitchcockian', in that it's not really a matter of suspense. The Hitchcock references instead become a given, a familiar modern myth that structures the psychological narrative. Like his unexpectedly emotive adaptation of Russell Banks' *The Sweet Hereafter*, Egoyan's second literary dramatisation seems a far cry from the distanced, jigsawed psycho-dramas of his previous work. The story, from William Trevor's novel, seems simple: innocent leaves home, falls into bad company, survives at some cost to herself. The cost may be lesser in the film: Trevor's Felicia ends up a nameless, homeless wanderer. Here, she not only achieves freedom but also becomes the symbolic redeemer of Hilditch and his victims, finally intoning a voiceover memorial blessing.

But the film proves more fragmented and more flexible than it first seems. It strays from the book's path largely in the elaboration of Hilditch's mother, who here becomes Gala, a 50s television chef and professional Frenchwoman. Gala is exuberantly played in filmed flashbacks and on video by Egoyan's wife and regular star Arsinée Khanjian, and it's arguable that the couple overindulge each other. Gala's ooh-la-la flamboyance rather mitigates the film's sobriety, administering a grotesque comic jolt to Hilditch's stolid world. But the jolt also makes us question what we're really seeing: it's part of an excess that unsettles what might otherwise have been a straight psycho-thriller. Hilditch's life seems melodramatically overloaded with trauma, yet it's this gothic excess that gives the film its drive.

Felicia's Journey has as many flashbacks, ellipses and video inserts as any previous Egoyan film, even though the unity of the central narrative makes it seem perfectly coherent, if not linear. What makes it Egoyanesque is the way he shoehorns his trademark video material into a story where it might not obviously seem to fit. Along with flashbacks filmed in chemically unreal colour, Hilditch's childhood is captured on videos of Gala's television show, which he watches obsessively, copying her recipes step by step. But—to be pedantic—does he really have all her shows on video? And has he really filmed his victims on a tiny camera concealed in his Morris Minor? We see his tapes, but that's not necessarily any kind of evidence. It's possible to see all this documentation as metaphorical, a representation of fantasy and memory. (To stretch a point, there's no proof that Hilditch has actually murdered anyone, or that his digging of Felicia's grave is anything more than symbolic.)

To purists of literary adaptation, all this might seem unnecessarily disruptive. Yet Egoyan has made a film which is true to the spirit of Trevor's novel, especially in its exploration of a zone of life generally ignored in British film—the marginal landscapes of suburbia and industrial estates, photographed in stark panorama by Paul Sarossy. It's a truism to say that foreign directors bring a sharper, stranger look to British scenery, but Egoyan and Sarossy have captured this particular bleakness as effectively as, say, Jerzy Skolimowski, Bertrand Tavernier or Aki Kaurismäki in such films as *Deep End* (1970), *Deathwatch* (1979), and *I Hired Contract Killer* (1990). Egoyan also proves to have an ear for repressed English decorum in the case of Hilditch, whose arrested psychic growth seems to have affected his entire world: all his habitats, from factory to sitting room, seem frozen in a Light Programme past, orchestrated to the ersatz doo-wop of forgotten crooner Malcolm Vaughan.

In a compelling and heartening comeback from his ingratiating turns of recent years, Bob Hoskins incarnates Hilditch as a wonderful black-comic figure, evoking the fussy delicacy of a big man with small, precise gestures. Hilditch's compassion speaks the inappropriate language of *Songs of Praise* piety: his apocryphal wife's death was "a blessed release", a cliché suggesting the symbolic matricide behind the lie. At the most telling moments, Hoskins does it all with his eyes and mouth: following Gala's recipes, he displays a perfectionist's concern tempered with suppressed filial rage. Hilditch is so vivid that Felicia's story almost suffers by comparison. That it doesn't is partly due to the fragile but resilient portrayal by newcomer Cassidy. Even so, we're most aware of Felicia as a lost soul, a potential yet to blossom; her drives in seeking Johnny, the boy who impregnated her, remain less tangible. What does jar, however, is the Irish background: the disapproving father, the feckless swain and his hostile mother all inhabit a faint atmosphere of cliché compounded by the Celtic pastiche of Mychael Danna's score.

The Irish sections work best if seen in the context of a thematics of home: the film is not, despite appearances, a fairytale warning to innocents not to stray abroad, for Hilditch's problem is that he has never left home. Home, or surrogates thereof, prove to be hostile: Felicia finds succour in an evangelical hospice, but the ark turns out to be a madhouse. It's only after she's been through hell that she finds her own Eden. It's neither the Old Country, nor the celestial theme park promised by the evangelists, nor the degraded back garden of Hilditch's youth, but an ordinary municipal park where she works planting bulbs. The closing pan round it—at first sight, a bathetic, conventionally upbeat epilogue—allows sounding space for the resonances of a film that, satisfyingly, gives more complex signals than we might at first suspect.

VILLAGE VOICE, 11/16/99, p. 136, Amy Taubin

Serial killer films are a subspecies of the monster-movie genre, employing social criticism, psychodrama, police procedures, and the metaphysics of good and evil to get a handle on a terrifying being who is both more and less than what we consider human. The monster is a force of nature or a part of God's grand plan that society cannot eradicate or fully understand. If the social contract cannot be held entirely responsible for producing monsters, it certainly exacerbates their wrath.

Serial killers transcend the filmmaking class system. They erupt in art, studio, and exploitation movies. The classic serial killer films—*M, Pandora's Box, Peeping Tom, Psycho*—defy categorization. While not quite in their league, *Seven* and *Silence of the Lambs* gave blockbuster dimension to Baudelairean perversity. By comparison, the serial killer films of early November are empty clones.

Atom Egoyan's *Felicia's Journey,* adapted from the novel by William Trevor, has an exquisite surface. It brings together the sun-dappled green fields of County Cork, Ireland, the pollution-stained industialized landscape of Birmingham, England, and the varnished interior of a madman's clapboard cottage, filled with the relics—from Victorian birds' nests to '50s Mix Masters—of an agonizing childhood.

With sweeping camera moves and seamless editing, Egoyan unites past and present, country and city, Ireland and England, and the subjectivity and memories of two radically different characters. Every aspect of the filmmaking—particularly its symmetry and deliberate pace—suggests that Egoyan is taking the position of a higher power whose vision exceeds human understanding. Films made from an eye-of-God perspective, especially those with Bergman-esque overtones, inevitably excite the hermeneutic impulse in viewers. *Felicia's Journey* is so Bergman-esque that I was surprised its lead, scenery chewer Bob Hoskins, wasn't speaking Swedish, and I expect it will inspire many student papers on the nature of innocence or the question of fate vs. contingency. But one should bear in mind that God is not a filmmaker, and that the director of record is Egoyan, whose sophisticated eye is connected to a brain that seems, for the moment, to have gone dead. Perhaps it was chopped up in the Mix Master that is the film's unintended central metaphor. It may be Egoyan's saving grace that he can't control the leaks in his unconscious.

Felicia (Elaine Cassidy) is an Irish 17-year-old who comes to England in search of the boy she loves. This fellow, who carelessly took her virginity and got her pregnant, is a turncoat soldier in the British army. The proof of Felicia's innocence is that she enters England without a single piece of ID. It never occurred to her that she needed papers. The proof of her loss of innocence is the blood staining her nightgown after she's had an abortion.

I confess to having a particular aversion to films that make a bleeding uterus into symbol—even when the symbol is as muddled as it is here. I also lack sympathy for films that propose mothers as the source of all our discontent. In the course of her search Felicia meets Hilditch (Hoskins), a factory lunchroom caterer who goes home every night to his lonely house where he replays videotapes of his late mom (Arsinée Khanjian). Mom was a glamorous French cooking-show host who treated her pudgy son as a kitchen prop, stuffing his mouth with sausages and smothering him in her theatrical embrace. This seems to have caused him to confuse adoration and hatred, and pushed him over the edge into serial murder. Hilditch's m.o. is to befriend young prostitutes, secretly videotape them, a then killing them when they try to return to their own lives. But when Felicia crosses paths with this beast, both their lives take an unexpected turn.

The videotapes, which are not part of the novel, are a fetish that runs through all of Egoyan's films, functioning as the site of both memory and loss. Here, they also evoke *Peeping Tom,* just as the name Hilditch and some of the spooky props and camera moves evoke *Psycho.* In early films such as *Family Viewing,* Egoyan referenced the masters with a combination of cheek and obsession was all his own. That tone is absent in the grandiose *Felicia's Journey,* which sprouts enough hot air to carry its heroine home in a balloon.

Also reviewed in:
CHICAGO TRIBUNE, 11/19/99, Friday/p. A, Michael Wilmington
NATION, 12/6/99, p. 50, Stuart Klawans
NEW YORK TIMES, 11/12/99, p. E14, Stephen Holden's
VARIETY, 5/24-30/99, p. 65, Emanuel Levy
WASHINGTON POST, 11/19/99, p. C5, Stephen Hunter
WASHINGTON POST, 11/19/99, Weekend/p. 49, Desson Howe

FEVER PITCH

A Phaedra Cinema release of a Channel Four presentation of a Wildgaze Films production. *Executive Producer:* Stephen Woolley and Nik Powell. *Producer:* Amanda Posey. *Director:* David Evans. *Screenplay (based on his book):* Nick Hornby. *Director of Photography:* Chris Seager. *Editor:* Scott Thomas. *Music:* Neill MacColl and Boo Hewerdine. *Sound:* Jim Greenhorn and Aad Wirtz. *Sound Editor:* Pat O'Neill. *Casting:* Liora Reich. *Production Designer:* Michael Carlin. *Art Director:* Karen Wakefield. *Costumes:* Mary-Jane Reyner. *Make-up:* Penny Smith. *Running time:* 97 minutes. *MPAA Rating:* Not Rated.

CAST: Colin Firth (Paul); Ruth Gemmell (Sarah); Neil Pearson (Paul's Dad); Lorraine Ashbourne (Paul's Mother); Mark Strong (Steve); Holly Aird (Jo); Ken Stott (Ted the Headmaster); Stephen Rea (Ray the Governor); Luke Aikman (Young Paul); Richard Claxton (Robert); Bea Guard (Paul's Sister); Annette Ekblom (Robert's Mother); Peter Quince (Frank, Chip Shop); Charles Cork (Rex); Bob Curtiss (Stan); Philip Bond (Turnstile Operator); Scott Baker (Man Behind); Jackie Hyffes (Pupil's Parents); Graham Cull (Mr. Johnson); Mike Ingham (Radio Sports Commentator); Stam Dunbar Banks (Young Paul's Mate); Leigh Funnelle (Woman at Reading); David Hounslow (Hillsborough Man); Silas Carson (Indian Waiter); Geoffrey Drew (House Owner); Liam Stapleton (2nd Governor); Emily Conway (Sasha); Tony Longhurst (Taxi Driver); Shuli Morris-Evans (Party Baby).

NEW YORK POST, 10/15/99, p. 59, Jonathan Foreman

Essential viewing for anyone who has to live with a soccer fan or other sports-obsessive, "Fever Pitch" is also a contender for the best romantic comedy of the year.

It's almost everything you would hope for from an adaptation of a book by the best-selling English novelist Nick Hornby—even though it's based on a memoir rather than on one of his hilarious novels about commitment-phobic young men.

A satisfying combination of comedy and social realism, it's never less than smart, dryly funny and playfully observant about gender and parenthood, and the life-enhancing power of trivia.

Paul (Colin Firth), a teacher in his mid-30s, has been obsessed with soccer in general—and the Arsenal team in particular—since he was a boy.

It's an obsession that has kept him young and helps him bond with his students and colleagues. But Arsenal's disappointing record over the years has made him a confirmed pessimist. (As he asks at one point, "Is life s-- because Arsenal is s---, or is it the other way 'round?")

But when Paul hooks up with his single-minded colleague Sarah (Ruth Gemmell), his soccer obsession ensures that their relationship will be a stormy one at best.

Sarah makes a successful effort to understand the game and its appeal. But when Arsenal, for the first time in 18 years, has a chance to win the league championship, Paul just doesn't have the time or energy to balance his two loves.

Here Firth takes a break from upper-class roles (he played cuckolded husbands in both "The English Patient" and "Shakespeare in Love," and was a celebrated Darcy in the TV version of "Pride and Prejudice"). He shows himself to be a fine comic actor with a flair for the deadpan. Theater actress Ruth Gemmell is delightful in her first film role.

Vastly superior to the small and independent films that have come out during the last six months, this movie deserves a wider release than it's going to get.

SIGHT AND SOUND, 4/97, p. 41, Geoffrey Macnab

London, the late 80s. Paul Ashworth, an English teacher in his mid-30s at a North London comprehensive, is an obsessive fan of Arsenal football club. He has supported the team since early childhood, when his father used to take him to matches. A new teacher, Sarah Hughes, arrives at the school. A strict disciplinarian, she can't stand Paul's freewheeling approach to the job or his boorish behaviour in the staff common room. Despite their differences, they start seeing one another. She comes to realise just how obsessed he is with Arsenal, accompanies him to a game and develops a mild interest in the team herself.

But after Sarah becomes pregnant, the relationship comes unstuck. She is exasperated by Paul's childish attitude to fatherhood and they drift apart. Paul endures a rocky interview with the school governors when he applies to be head of year. The school football team, which he coaches, is narrowly defeated in the final of an inter-school competition. Even worse, it looks as if Arsenal have blown their chances of winning the League Championship. Having frittered away a substantial points lead, they need to defeat Liverpool by two goals away from home on the last day of the season—something which Paul doubts is possible.

Paul and his friend Steve watch the crucial match on television. Sarah, meanwhile, is at an end-of-term party. She leaves early and takes a cab to Paul's flat. He is too preoccupied with the football to answer the doorbell. Instead, not knowing who is there, he roars insults out of the window. She leaves. Into injury time, Arsenal score the goal which wins them the championship. Paul joins in the impromptu street party outside Arsenal's ground. He meets Sarah there, who is also celebrating the victory and now seems a die-hard Arsenal fan herself. Buoyed up by Arsenal's triumph, the two are reconciled.

In his autobiography, *Self-Consciousness,* John Updike recalls going to a cinema to see a film called *The Witches of Eastwick*; watching it with a strange fascination and wondering what relation, if any, it bore to his novel of the same name. Fans of Nick Hornby's *Fever Pitch* are liable to feel a similar bewilderment when confronted with the film version. Somehow Hornby's elliptical, witty confessional has turned into a screwball romantic comedy set in North London. Where the book used diary-style first-person narration and spanned more than 20 years of obsessive soccer fandom, the film is set almost exclusively during Arsenal's 1988-89 championship-winning season. The fluctuating fortunes of the hero Paul Ashworth's favourite football team are matched by the ups and downs in his relationship with fellow teacher, Ms Hughes (Ruth Gemmell).

Given that Hornby wrote the screenplay himself, the film can hardly be called a betrayal. It retains many of the original jokes and anecdotes, but attempts to graft them onto a conventional, linear narrative. Through evocative snapshots of lost afternoons at Highbury or Wembley, Hornby's book was able to rekindle memories of specific moments in his adolescence. In the film, this resonance is lost. As Hornby observes, there are never really any climactic points in an English football fan's life. With brief interruptions between May and August, the game rolls on from season to season. The same team which loses a Cup Final in May will be back in the competition the following January. Even what he refers to as The Greatest Moment Ever—the goal that Michael Thomas scored in injury time against Liverpool in the last match of the season to win Arsenal their first championship in 18 years—warrants only a chapter in the book, and it is immediately followed by an account of a game with Coventry the following season.

In the film, however, the Thomas goal is crucial. It is the moment towards which the entire narrative has been building, when the hero and his girlfriend are miraculously reunited, and VE Day-style street parties break out all over North London. (Not since the rioters took to the streets at the end of *Sammy and Rosie Get Laid* have there been less convincing crowd scenes in a British film.) This absurd finale is adolescent male wish-fulfillment fantasy at its most ludicrous. Thanks to Arsenal's moment of triumph, Paul (Colin Firth) is conveniently absolved of his responsibilities as a prospective father and would-be head of year (a job which, unsurprisingly, he fails to get). The film's earlier, fitful attempts at taking Sarah's point of view are shown to be little more than a distraction.

Visually *Fever Pitch* is stuck somewhere between *Grange Hill* and *Gregory's Girl*. Its low-key, unfussy naturalism is reminiscent of much recent television drama. (First-time feature director David Evans, whose television credits range from *Common as Muck* to *Band of Gold*, clearly has a small-screen sensibility.) There is something fetishistic about its attention to detail—there is an attempt in flashback to recreate its hero's childhood through sideburns, suede jackets, and old children's television shows such as *The Clangers*. The movie *Fever Pitch* is full of in-jokes and nostalgic allusions that may baffle anybody not steeped in the minutiae of 70s British popular culture. The blokeish tone soon begins to grate as do the occasional sociological asides—for instance the bathetic moment in which Paul watches footage of the Hillsborough disaster and pompously proclaims that football must "go on".

Unsurprisingly, the pleasures of *Fever Pitch* lie more in the incidental details than the overall structure. Colin Firth plays Paul with shambolic understatement. If he looks distracted, you know it is because he is thinking about his favourite football team. Whether attempting to teach his schoolboys to play an Arsenal-style offside trap or watching his friend Steve (Mark Strong) clowning behind a goal as somebody prepares to take a penalty, he offers an enjoyably deadpan caricature of the typical Arsenal fan—"dour, defensive, argumentative, repressed," as Hornby himself classifies the type.

The flashback scenes, in which Paul appears as an Adrian Mole-like youngster who can only establish a rapport with his divorced father (Neil Pearson) by watching football with him, are touching. There are also colourful cameos from Ken Stott as an irascible head teacher and from Stephen Rea as a football-fixated school governor. However, for all the film-makers' attempts to develop a little narrative momentum, *Fever Pitch* remains stubbornly intractable. As action switches from Paul and Steve's two 'men behaving badly', to Sarah and her flatmate Jo (Holly Aird), it begins to seem as inert and predictable as an extended sitcom pilot episode. Its self-deprecating irony and use of football as metaphor—the way it explores Paul's relationship with his father and his girlfriend through his obsession with Arsenal—mark it down as very different from more conventional boy's own football tales such as *Yesterday's Hero* or *When Saturday Comes*. But in its way, it is every bit as contrived. Drifting along nowhere in particular, it relies on a last-minute goal to knit matters together. The implication is clear: Paul will be a model father and teacher just as long as Arsenal keep on winning.

VILLAGE VOICE, 10/19/99, p. 140, Michael Atkinson

David Evans's film of Nick Hornby's *Fever Pitch* manages to capture the book's football-cult swoon (Hornby's a master at giving voice to going-nowhere subculture obsession) without being particularly funny or involving. Colin Firth is the lazy English teacher—cum—soccer hooligan; the lovely Ruth Gemmell is the uptight colleague he dates and knocks up. The entire matter of totemistic home-team dementia is roasted on a spit and then embraced for all its sorry pointlessness. (A flashback suite of crowd joy is scored to "Baba O'Reilly"; Pete Townsend's catalogue fire sale is making the world safe for soundtracks.) Hornby's script never tackles why Gemmell's acid-tongued beauty would endure so much braying sports-fan crap, but then, it's a common enough mystery.

Also reviewed in:
NEW YORK TIMES, 10/15/99, p. E18, Anita Gates
VARIETY, 3/31-4/6/97, p. 87, Derek Elley
WASHINGTON POST, 7/28/00, Weekend/p. 38, Desson Howe

FIGHT CLUB

A Fox 2000 Pictures and Regency Enterprises release of a Linson Films production. *Executive Producer:* Arnon Milchan. *Producer:* Art Linson, Cean Chaffin, and Ross Grayson Bell. *Director:* David Fincher. *Screenplay:* Jim Uhls. *Based on the novel by:* Chuck Palahniuk. *Director of Photography:* Jeff Cronenweth. *Editor:* James Haygood. *Music:* The Dust Brothers. *Music Editor:* Brian Richards. *Sound:* Jeff Wexler and (music) Michael Simpson and John King. *Sound Editor:* Malcolm Fife. *Casting:* Laray Mayfield. *Production Designer:* Alex McDowell. *Art Director:* S. Quinn. *Set Designer:* Luis G. Hoyos, Peter J. Kelly, Julia Levine, Hugo

Santiago, and Domenic H. Silvestri. *Set Decorator:* Jay R. Hart. *Set Dresser:* Gregory N. Rocco, Charles W. Belisle, Max E. Brehme, William Andrew John Grant, Chris Grantz, Tyler Patton, Doug Sieck, Tim Wiles, Adam Pearlman, and Kai Blomberg. *Special Effects:* Cliff Wenger. *Visual Effects:* Kevin Tod Haug. *Costumes:* Michael Kaplan. *Make-up:* Julie Pearce. *Make-up (Brad Pitt):* Jean A. Black. *Stunt Coordinator:* Michael Runyard. *Running time:* 135 minutes. *MPAA Rating:* R.

CAST: Edward Norton (Narrator); Brad Pitt (Tyler Durden); Meat Loaf Aday (Robert Paulsen); Zach Grenier (Richard Chesler, Regional Manager); Richmond Arquette (Intern at Hospital); David Andrews (Thomas at Remaining Men Together); George Maguire (Group Leader—Remaining Men Together); Eugenie Bondurant (Weeping Woman—Onward and Upward); Christina Cabot (Leader—Partners in Positivity); Helena Bonham Carter (Marla Singer); Sydney Colston (Speaker—Free and Clear); Rachel Singer (Chloe); Christie Cronenweth (Airline Check-In Attendant); Tim deZarn (Federated Motor Co. Inspector Bird); Ezra Buzzington (Federated Motor Co. Inspector Dent); Dierdre Downing-Jackson (Business Woman on Plane); Robert J. Stephenson (Airport Security Officer); Charlie Dell (Doorman at Pearson Towers); Rob Lanza (Man in Suit); David Lee Smith (Walter); Holt McCallany (Mechanic); Joel Bissonnette (Food Court Maitre d'); Eion Bailey (Ricky); Evan Mirand ("Steph"); Robby Robinson (Next Month's Opponent); Lou Beatty, Jr. (Cop at Marla's Building); Thom Gossom, Jr. (Detective Stern); Valerie Bickford (Cosmetics Buyer); Jared Leto (Angel Face); Peter Iacangelo (Lou); Carl N. Ciarfalio (Lou's Body Guard); Stuart Blumberg (Car Salesman); Todd Peirce (First Man at Auto Shop); Mark Fite (Second Man at Auto Shop); Matt Winston (Seminary Student); Joon B. Kim (Raymond K. Hessel); Bennie E. Moore, Jr. (Bus Driver with Broken Nose); W. Lauren Sanchez (Channel 4 Reporter); Pat McNamara (Commissioner Jacobs); Tyrone R. Livingston (Banquet Speaker); Owen Masterson (Airport Valet); David Jean-Thomas (Policeman); Paul Carafotes (Salvator—Winking Bartender); Christopher John Fields (Proprietor of Dry Cleaners); Anderson Bourell (Bruised Bar Patron #1); Scotch Ellis Loring (Bruised Bar Patron #2); Michael Shamus Wiles (Bartender in Halo); Andi Carnick (Hotel Desk Clerk); Edward Kowalczyk (Waiter at Clifton's); Leonard Termo (Desk Sergeant); Van Quattro (Detective Andrew); Markus Redmond (Detective Kevin); Michael Girardin (Detective Walker); Kevin Mack (Passenger Clutching Armrests).

CHRISTIAN SCIENCE MONITOR, 10/22/99, p. 15, David Sterritt

[*Fight Club* was reviewed jointly with *Bringing Out the Dead*; see Sterritt's review of that film.]

LOS ANGELES TIMES, 10/15/99, Calendar/p. 1, Kenneth Turan

"Fight Club," a film about men who like to fight, is an unsettling experience, but not the way anyone intended. What's most troubling about this witless mishmash of whiny, infantile philosophizing and bone-crunching violence is the increasing realization that it actually thinks it's saying something of significance. That is a scary notion indeed.

Director David Fincher, with "Alien 3," "The Game" and "Seven" in his past, is one of cinema's premier brutalizers, able to impale audiences on meat hooks and make them like it. So it's no surprise that "Fight Club's" level of visceral violence, its stomach-turning string of bloody and protracted bare-knuckles brawls, make it more than worthy of an NC-17 if the MPAA could ever work up the nerve (don't hold your breath) to give that rating to a major studio film.

What is a surprise is how much of "Fight Club" is simply tedious. It's not just the crack-brained nature of its core premise, that what every man wants, needs and appreciates in his heart of hearts is the chance to get kicked, gouged and severely beaten by another guy. It's also the windy attempts at pseudo-profundity in Jim Uhls' adaptation of Chuck Palahniuk's novel, the feeble dime-store nihilism on the order of "It's only after you've lost everything that you're free to do anything."

"Fight Club" opens with its two protagonists in a moment of crisis: Tyler Durden (Brad Pitt) has shoved a revolver down the throat of the nameless narrator the film sometimes calls Jack (Edward Norton) as both men occupy what Jack calls "front row seats for the theater of mass destruction."

An extensive flashback is clearly in order, and it begins with Jack's numbing life as a bland, robotic numbers-cruncher for a major auto maker whose job it is to determine how many deaths it takes to make it financially prudent to call for a product recall. (Protean actor Norton can disappear into anyone, but the spectacle of him disappearing into a barely-alive nobody is not particularly gratifying.)

Living in an apartment tower he characterizes as "a filing cabinet for widows and young professionals," Jack divides his time between two preoccupations. He compulsively shops for home furnishings ("We used to read pornography; now it's the Horchow Collection") and, unable to sleep, he attends touchy-feely support group sessions for people with life-threatening diseases. Here he meets Marla Singer (Helena Bonham Carter, as far as you can get from her Merchant Ivory past), a fellow faker with ratty hair and a rattier, cigarettes-and-cheap jewelery lifestyle who lives as if, yes, "we might die at any moment."

These initial parts of "Fight Club" are structured in part as satires on the modern mania for consumerism and the cult of New Age sensitivity. Certainly these areas are ripe for sending up, but this film is so contemptuous of anything human, so eager to employ know-it-all smugness, that the cure plays worse than the disease.

It's on an airplane that Jack runs into Durden, a primeval savant whose business is soap but whose wild red jacket and matching sunglasses mark him as a kind of walking id. Durden, we admiringly come to discover, spends his spare time splicing frames of pornography into family films (how brave! how iconoclastic!) and serving as "a guerrilla terrorist in the food service industry," fouling various foods with his own bodily fluids. Is it any wonder both the film and Jack view him as a truth-telling avatar of compelling frankness?

Soon the two men are living together in a dilapidated hovel (no consumerism for them) that looks like a slum the Addams family happily abandoned and Jack is absorbing Durden's bracing bons mots about the state of the American male, variously called "a generation of men raised by women" and "slaves with white collars." "Our great war," Durden all but preaches, "is a spiritual war, our Great Depression is our lives."

(In one of the more curious footnotes to modern culture, "Fight Club" plays at times like the bombast World Wrestling Federation version of Susan Faludi's "Stiffed," also a treatise on men who have "lost their compass in the world" and suffer from "the American masculinity crisis.")

Tyler's answer to this malaise is Fight Club, where strangers find that savagely beating each other is such a cathartic, practically religious experience that guys are, well, fighting to get in. While both Tyler ("I don't want to die without any scars") and Jack ("You weren't alive anywhere like you were there ... After fighting everything else in your life is like the volume turned down") are capable of extended neo-macho riffs on the virtues of Fight Club, that doesn't prevent the whole concept from playing like the delusional rantings of testosterone-addicted thugs.

Tyler keeps upping the ante for the men he recruits, turning Fight Club habitues into an organized mob of nihilistic bad boys wrecking havoc on our puny, emasculated civilization. Though the film employs dubious plot twists to quasi-distance itself from the weirder implications of a philosophy the Columbine gunmen would likely have found congenial, it's to little effect. Aside from the protracted beatings, this film is so vacuous and empty it's more depressing than provocative. If the first rule of Fight Club is "Nobody talks about Fight Club," a fitting subsection might be "Why would anyone want to?"

NEW STATESMAN, 11/15/99, p. 43, Jonathan Romney

David Fincher's grisly conceptual thriller *Seven* came as a shock; his new film *Fight Club* is nothing short of a scandal. That alone should make you want to see it—how many Hollywood films even dare to be contentious? Hollywood has had its *cause célèbre* follies in recent years—most notably and embarrassingly, Oliver Stone's *Natural Born Killers*—but it's rare for it to produce a film like this, that can startle, exhilarate, offend and keep you thinking long after you've left the cinema.

Fight Club is not the film you probably think it is. The prepublicity (shots of Brad Pitt's chest) suggested an extreme variant on the continuing strain of masculinity-in-crisis films: its story is of white-collar males venting their repressed rage by beating each other senseless in a bare-knuckle boxing cult. But that's only part of the story, and hardly enough to elicit the furious responses the film received at the Venice Festival, where, amid much excitement, it was also denounced as an implicitly fascistic glorification of violence.

Fight Club doesn't revel in brutality, but it is fascinated by the strangeness and perversity of male-on-male violence. It is less about violence to others than to oneself: in an extremely unsettling scene, Edward Norton's narrator-hero, ostentatiously beats *himself* to a pulp. The film's protagonists are men who choose to take body blows in order—as Pitt's charismatic fighter-philosopher Tyler explains—better to handle social blows. Just as Tyler takes his "no pain, no gain" ethos to parodic extremes, so Fincher and the screenwriter, Jim Uhls, use stylistic extremes to similar effect. Visually, emotionally and sonically, the film assaults us with an armoury of virtuoso devices, an informational overload. It's only when all certainties are thoroughly pulped that we can again start to piece the information together and make critical sense of what we're seeing.

The story, based on Chuck Palahniuk's novel, is narrated in dizzyingly prolix fashion by Norton's nameless (but let's call him "Jack") low-level executive. An insomniac plagued by a sleek, vapid existence, he realises he has become "a slave to the Ikea nesting instinct": in a brilliant sequence, the screen turns into a walk-through furniture catalogue. His doctor suggests he expose himself to real suffering and visit a cancer support group; the minute he does, he's hooked. At a testicular cancer meeting, he's hugged by bodybuilder Bob (Meat Loaf), whose treatment has left him with female breasts. It's the start of a new addiction—Jack becomes a tenderness junkie.

But there's another emotional tourist on the circuit, Marla (played in dead skin and inch-thick mascara, astonishingly out of character, by Helena Bonham-Carter), and the rivalrous pair are obliged to divvy up the groups: "I'll take the blood parasites"; "I want bowel cancer". The film then takes a sideways step, as Jack encounters the enigmatic Tyler, who embodies an MTV/Fashion Channel fantasy of bohemian rebellion. Played by Brad Pitt, parodying his own narcissistic image to perfection, Tyler lures Jack away from hugging, and into the more drastic, and overtly homoerotic, pleasures of flesh-and-bone catharsis. As one of Tyler's eminently quotable thought-bites goes, "Self-improvement is masturbation. Now, self-destruction ... " Setting up house together, the pair recruit disciples, and Tyler starts to issue hectoring slogans: "You are not," he yells at each acolyte, "a beautiful and unique snowflake."

Fight Club's narrative is daringly over-charged—there's a remarkable amount of event crammed into its 135 minutes, much of it intensely confusing. The film is also packed with a phenomenal density of pure *Zeitgeist*. If much of *Fight Club* seems familiar, it's not because we've been here before in any other film, but because no other film has taken in so many different sites of current cultural interest. First, *Fight Club* imagines a hysterical male response to the perceived emasculation in contemporary corporate society: it's bound to be quoted in endless articles, cross-referenced against Susan Faludi's recent book on the male condition, *Stiffed*. Concomitantly, it's a satiric response to compassion culture and the faith in emotional openness as an adequate response to tragedy. It's certainly the first film to make brutal, borderline callous (yet ultimately, morally serious) satiric use of support-group piety.

The film also addresses the corporate universe, its depersonalisation of the workforce (which is hardly a novel topic), and its complicity in murder (which is where the topic takes a novel turn). Jack's job is to quantify lethal accidents for a car manufacturer: a little chill of déjà vu sets in here, as the film pays all but explicit homage to J G Ballard's *Crash* and its thematic collision of death and eroticism, hard machines and fragile bodies. *Fight Club* is partly a 1990s response to Ballard's 1960s mechanical death-dreams, and a far more commanding response, in its vaulting, pumped-up hysteria, than the cool, detached glide of David Cronenberg's recent adaptation.

In its later stages, the film takes on a hue of conspiracy theory, to address cultism and underground fascism. Tyler's hardbody movement begins as an anti-therapy for beleaguered males; becomes an anarchist social cure-all, operating by means of radical pranksterism; and finally evolves into a scorched-earth nihilist faction. It's remarkable that anyone could read the film as fascist, as Tyler's hyper-cool charisma blossoms into a terrifying example of personality cult, his mottoes parroted by meat-headed recruits.

Here we're at the heart of late-1990s American *Zeitgeist:* starting with the ironic glamour of Generation X disenfranchisement, the film progresses to a picture of the resentment that fuels survivalists and lethal outsider enclaves like the trenchcoat Mafia of Littleton, Colorado. Yet this uncomfortably non-liberal film refuses to let us feel we're comfortably on the right side of things: it never lets us be sure exactly where we stand. Stylistically and thematically, we're shuttled from one angle to another—from ad-pastiche cool to pop-video frenzy, from sombre-toned realism to savage farce. Constantly breaking its own formal moulds, *Fight Club* is a relentless bad trip: the credit sequence sends us whizzing through Jack's brain, in and out of his synapses; the camera plummets several floors in a single shot. In Jack's paranoid warp-speed narration, words and thoughts become images instantaneously: if he dreams of a mid-air plane collision, it happens, boom.

Most audaciously of all, Fincher subverts film language to remind us that what we're watching is a satiric discourse, a fugue in celluloid: he actually makes the sprocket holes jump on the film. He even baits us with that supposedly apocryphal object of moral panic, the inserted subliminal, and then nudges us into realising what he's up to: Tyler, among his other terrorist guises, is a film projectionist of a very hands-on variety.

Just when you think the film has pushed it as far as things can go, it throws you with an 11th-hour twist that flouts its own outrageous impossibility, then caps that with the double whammy of an apocalypse and a throwaway punchline. *Fight Club* is an extraordinary gesture of provocation, both to the audience and to the Hollywood mainstream. Not so much a tossed gauntlet as a whack in the face, it demands to be seen and argued over. But any beautiful snowflakes among you, be warned.

NEW YORK, 10/25/99 p. 79, Peter Rainer

Cynical exercise in designer existentialism, *Fight Club* has that raw-sleek look that often shows up in fragrance or jeans commercials, and yet the film supposedly is all about how consumerism and the corporate culture destroy us—or, to be more specific, men. Intended as a great big howl of a movie, it comes closer to being a mammoth snit fit—a snit fit with pretensions (the worst kind).

Edward Norton plays the film's nameless narrator in a nameless city. (Beware of films set in nameless cities: they're out to sell you something.) Early in the movie, sodden with insomnia, he renews himself for a time by attending self-help groups for the terminally ill, embracing and weeping right along with his fellow twelve-steppers, who think he is one of them. This conceit has its black-comic possibilities, but the narrator is crying for himself before we've had much of a chance to find out who he is; and when we learn more, there's still not much there there. His condo is outfitted to the gills by Ikea, but the poor sap remains unfulfilled; his job as recall coordinator for a major auto company involves flying around the country checking on accidents to determine how cost-effective it would be for the company to lie low. He's the Organization Man as Everyman, and his little life is just waiting to be exploded.

The blandness of his days, played out in look-alike plane seats and hotel rooms, is interrupted when he meets Tyler (Brad Pitt), who wears loud print shirts and leather jackets and sunglasses indoors; Tyler sounds like a cross between a Bowery Boy and a Buddhist sage, and he's everything the poor sap apparently isn't. After the narrator's condo mysteriously blows up, he goes to live with Tyler in his condemned house near a toxic-waste site. This trickster makes ends meet working a projector at a movie house, where, for sport, he splices a few frames from a porno film—just enough to cause subliminal discomfort—into the evening's family-entertainment fare. He also makes soap, which, as we see from an escapade where he and his housemate raid the dumpsters of a liposuction clinic, derives from human fat. He gets a kick from selling the soap back to liposucked ladies.

The pair's greatest achievement, though, is the creation of Fight Club, where, in a hidden-away city basement, men congregate and pummel one another in order to experience the liberating effects of pain. We're treated to a succession of these head-splitting, blood-frothing spectacles, whose participants, led by Tyler, eventually form a cultlike terrorist militia aimed at taking out corporate America. The narrator, increasingly repulsed by Tyler's commando cruelties, tries to sabotage the sabotage.

In its muzzy mix of paleo-men's-movement musings and bone-crunch, *Fight Club* could be the god-awful offspring of the WWF's Vince McMahon and Lionel Tiger, or of the Susan Faludi of *Stiffed*. Clearly something deep and bellowing is going on here: These men, disenfranchised by franchise-mad America, are the rabid battalions Starbucks hath wrought; zonked by malaise, they can feel alive only when they hurt. Director David Fincher and screenwriter Jim Uhls, adapting the cult novel by Chuck Palahniuk, want us to know that like Tyler, we men are all living in a toxic dump, and it's called America. Even though Tyler turns into a scourge by the end, his rantings are meant to resonate: We've all been deluded by advertising, he says; we've had no great wars or Depressions to preoccupy our testosterone. What's a poor primal guy to do?

Fight Club rolls out its indictments and its Zen koans, but what it really resembles, perhaps unknowingly, is the squall of a whiny and essentially white-male generation that feels ruined by the privileges of women and a booming economy. (The underclass, which would feel excluded from this argument, isn't much of a factor in *Fight Club*—this is a well-to-do guys' whine.) Fear of castration is a running theme throughout: so is stigmata imagery for that holy, martyred effect. The male squadron in *Fight Club,* vaguely homo-erotic, is striking a blow for atavism, but it's the kind of tribal tom-tom atavism that doesn't allow for women who might also be enraged by the hollowness of corporate culture: the film doesn't even have the wit to recognize that that culture might itself just be a more lustrous and galvanized form of blood lust. (Haven't these filmmakers spent any time in Hollywood's corridors of power?) Except for an appearance by Helena Bonham Carter, playing a grungy vixen who moves in with the guys, the film is pretty much female-free in its front ranks—although serious sport is made of a twelve-stepper turned Fight Clubber (Meat Loaf Aday) whose steroids have given him D-cup dimensions. This is how pathetically low the men in *Fight Club* have sunk they've sprouted breasts! Even Marx could not have foreseen this baleful result of a capitalist free-market economy.

As part of the new growth industry in masculinist socio-pop fantasias. *Fight Club* at least has the distinction of being lively, like an acid-rock show. (Camille Paglia will want to take a look.) It's all hepped up about the vileness of materialism, and so, of course, David Fincher unleashes on us his vast array of TV-commercial-derived whammies: The film is a hard sell about no-sell. (Nothingness here looks awfully burnished.) Brad Pitt jangles like a lethal jitterbug, and Edward Norton, with his gift for making anonymity frightening, is perfectly cast. But I hope this film isn't going to be given the brink-of-the-millennium treatment by deep-think commentators. Ideawise, *Fight Club* has about as much going on in its head as an afternoon with Oprah. Actually, Oprah may have the edge.

NEW YORK POST, 10/15/99, p. 52, Lou Lumenick

"Fight Club" badly wants to be "A Clockwork Orange" for the millennium—and succeeds to a surprising extent until director David Fincher ends up sucker-punching the audience.

Edward Norton gives another extraordinary performance as this edgy, compulsively matchable film's nameless narrator, who joins with a charming psychotic (well-played by Brad Pitt in "Twelve Monkeys" mode) in founding a club where frustrated young men find release from their stifling lives by beating each other senseless.

The narrator is first seen with a gun in his mouth, warning—not unlike the narrator of the much better "American Beauty," some of whose concerns "Fight Club" addresses in an urban setting—that something awful is about to happen.

The narrator relates, in stunningly filmed flashbacks, how he suffered insomnia because of his soul-deadening job as a consultant for an automobile company—calculating whether to recall cars involved in grisly accidents or whether it would be cheaper to write off settlements as a cost of doing business.

Unable to sleep and without any family or close friends to turn to for help, the narrator tries to find temporary salvation, first in catalogue shopping, and then in the embrace of 12-stepping support groups by pretending to be dying of various maladies.

He embraces a testicular-cancer victim (the singer Meat Loaf, who's terrific). He cries. And he sleeps. But the fix doesn't last long. When another impostor—a goth princess named Marla (Helena Bonham Carter channeling Judy Davis, down to her walk)—crashes the party, the narrator needs another form of release.

He finds it during one of his endless cross-country business trips, when his fantasies about a midair crash (one of the movie's more alarming special-effects sequences) are interrupted by an encount with a soap-manufacturing anarchist named Tyler Durden (Pitt), who warns him of the evil's of consumerist society.

"Martha Stewart is polishing furniture on the Titanic," says Durden, whose personal solution to the Y2K problem eventually turns out to be blowing up the credit-card companies.

After his apartment mysteriously explodes, the narrator moves into Tyler's artfully ramshackle mansion—and he finds fulfillment in his new pal's arms, or at least his fists.

Before long, the narrator and his doppelganger Tyler are assembling throngs of misfits, who get their kicks by bashing each other in gory, bloody fights in basements, which again highlight the MPAA's double standard when it comes to sex and violence.

"Fight Club" is rated R, and what sex there is, though noisy and blatantly sadomasochistic, takes place mostly behind closed doors. When Tyler beds Marla, the narrator is jealous—even though it's rather unclear which one of them the narrator is really lusting after.

The film's homoeroticism comes out of the closet when Tyler casts the narrator aside for the younger and prettier Angel Face (Jared Leto), setting up the movie's second-most-harrowing sequence. (That scene and Tyler's demonstration of the effects of lye on exposed flesh, makes "Fight Club" a dubious date movie—unless you're trying to break up with someone.)

When Tyler starts setting up secretive fight clubs in other cities and raising a terrorist army, it's clear the movie has painted itself into a narrative corner. A "Sixth Sense"-style plot twist only makes you feel cheated and confused.

The screenplay by Jim Uhls (from Chuck Palahniuk's novel) seems to be suggesting that fascism (Tyler at one point makes soap from human fat, just like the Nazis did) is a natural by-product of a consumer-oriented society that denies men their primal, testosterone-laden urges.

But this Susan Faludi-esque argument ignores the fact that the narrator is much better off financially (and has more options) than Tyler's other nihilist poseurs—and treats terrorism as a form of benign "mischief." Does anyone buy that, even in a dark comedy, in post-Columbine America?

The more you think about them, the more annoying the contradictions are in "Fight Club." Tyler lectures the narrator that "self-improvement is masturbation"—but what a set of killer abs he's got!

With its studiously edgy sets, frenetic editing and dialogue, and nonstop violence pandering to its target audience of under-25 males, "Fight Club" is as carefully calculated a product as the ones it inveighs against.

NEWSDAY, 10/15/99, Part II/p. B3, John Anderson

Subversive, provocative and exhilaratingly brutal, "Fight Club"—The Film That Frightened Hollywood—is about a loose organization of men who bare-knuckle each other bloody for the sake of their humanity. They're trying to get in touch with their primal selves. The culture has stripped their lives of meaning.

So far, so good. But while the movie touches on a lot of genuine socio-sexual concerns (Susan Faludi should get co-writer credit), it never actually mentions middle-class white male rage, which is precisely what it's about. There's an unmistakable homoerotic impulse between the characters played by the film's costars—the reliably brilliant Edward Norton and a dynamic, swaggering Brad Pitt—even though cardboard "masculinity" is their Holy Grail. One of the movie's plaints is that modern existence has become one long sales pitch—so, naturally, director David Fincher ("Seven") cools his visual acrobatics once he's sucked us into the movie. And then the film takes the kind of plot turn almost guaranteed to turn audiences ugly.

"Fight Club," a bait-and-switch operation dressed up like a reformist movement, is full of inadvertent ironies, perhaps the least of which is the orgy of violence meant to demonstrate its characters' sensitivity. If, as a colleague suggested last week, "FC" is the Film Most Likely to Inspire Copycat Crimes, it may simply be because viewers feel they've been sold a bill of goods.

From the novel by Chuck Palahniuk, "Fight Club" erupts out of the anarcho-feminist presumption that modern life has left men useless and neutered; their female sides are killing them. "It used to be pornography," mourns the movie's narrator (Norton). "Now it's the Horchow's catalog."

Bemoaning his lust for IKEA furniture and coordinated decor, Narrator is a "recall coordinator" for an auto manufacturer who travels the country by air weighing the circumstances of a given smoldering car wreck against the limits of corporate liability. It's perfectly '90s Babbittry, and the job has turned Narrator into an insomniac addicted to 12-step meetings and support groups for habits and diseases he doesn't have (testicular cancer, to cite one glaringly metaphoric example).

"Every evening I died," he says, "and every evening I was born again." That is, until he meets a rival "tourist" on the support circuit—Marla Singer, a gaunt-but-beautiful street vamp played to the hilt by Helena Bonham Carter, who almost singlehandedly gives the film enough juice to keep it on its feet.

Marla does less for Narrator, at least at first. At one point, he's so low he prays for an air crash—the simulation of which is one of the more jarringly horrific special effects in a movie whose optics are frequently astounding. But instead of death, Narrator meets Tyler Durden (Pitt), swashbuckling homemade-soap sales man and iconoclast extraordinaire. When Narrator's apartment mysteriously explodes, destroying everything he owns, Tyler welcomes his new pal into his rotting nest, a falling-down wreck of a house on the outskirts of Nowhere, where the two become squatters/homesteaders on the frontier of New Maleness.

Tyler is the one who imagines Fight Club and articulates its purpose: Men have come to define themselves by what they own, what they wear. "We're a generation of men raised by women" he says, in one of the film's more insightful moments. Beating each other senseless, in the right spirit, becomes the ethos of the club, a thoroughly clandestine society that attracts more and more members in more and more cities until it takes on the proportions of a minor nation.

But formalizing Fight Club takes a lot of the sting out of "Fight Club"—as does the group's eventual metamorphosis into a neo-fascist paramilitary-terrorist claque and the Norton character's unconvincing epiphany that what they're doing might be wrong. Basically, "Fight Club"—dedicated to the proposition that men's lives have become routine—becomes a routine itself.

All the performances are good, especially Bonham Carter and erstwhile rocker Meat Loaf as a cancer-victim-turned-Fight-Clubber.

But the main ethic of Fight Club, as articulated by Tyler "It's only after we've lost everything that we're free to do anything"—sounds a lot like reheated Kris Kristofferson ("Freedom's just another word ... "). Or, as one suspects, both Palahniuk and Fincher were attracted by the idea of escorting F. Scott Fitzgerald (the desperation of the material class) up the aisle for a marriage to Ernest Hemingway (the cult of action) and creating, in other words, a movie that would have made a great undergraduate thesis.

NEWSWEEK, 10/18/99, 10/18/99, p. 77, David Ansen

Jack (Edward Norton), the narrator of David Fincher's seriously wacked-out "Fight Club," is an insomniac wage slave so alienated from his life he takes to frequenting support groups. He starts with Men's Testicular Cancer. Sobbing in the arms of men whose afflictions he pretends to share, he finds a temporary freedom by abandoning all hope. Soon he's become a recovery-group addict. Every night he finds a different group—sickle-cell therapy, bowel cancer—until his quest is spoiled by the presence of another "tourist" like himself, the ashen-faced, chain-smoking Maria (Helena Bonham Carter). How can he cry with another faker in the room?

So begins, promisingly and perversely, the darkest of dark satires from the director of the pitch-black "Seven" and the ultraparanoid "The Game." But Fincher's alternately amazing and annoying movie, written by Jim Uhls from a Chuck Palahniuk novel, has bolder provocations to come. On a business flight Jack meets the nihilist guru Tyler Durden (Brad Pitt), an anarchic Pied Piper in pimp's clothes who promises to lead this sorry Everyman to a higher Truth. Tyler sees through the facade of consumerist culture, with its meaningless devotion to materialism and self-improvement. He is given to grand pronouncements: "It's only after we've lost everything that we are free to do anything." "The things you own end up owning you." This charismatic prankster is the sort of fellow who, working briefly as a projectionist (in a bit stolen from Terry Southern's "The Magic Christian"), inserts subliminal frames of a penis into Hollywood family fare.

Taking Jack in when his apartment is destroyed by an explosion, Tyler initiates him into the ultrasecret male society called Fight Club. In parking lots and dark basement rooms, the members gleefully bash each other to a bloody pulp, and we are meant to understand that some deep atavistic warrior instinct's being satisfied. In the ecstatic blood rites of Fight Club, emasculated, feminized modern man can find the meaning corporate society denies him. (Susan Faludi should demand a percentage: did someone slip the screenwriter an advance copy of "Stiffed"?)

Already, however, strange subtexts are piling up. All these guys masochistically lining up to be beaten by Brad Pitt ... The homoeroticism is off the charts, but "Fight Club" can't bring itself to account for it. And when the movie, after satirizing the gym-enhanced bodies of men in Gucci subway ads ("Self-improvement is masturbation," Tyler pronounces), cuts to the impeccably lean and cut body of its leading man, it is in the grips of a style-content contradiction that this slick denunciation of surface values battles throughout.

We are clued in by the dankly hallucinatory style that "Fight Club" transpires somewhere to the left of the real world, like an emanation of the untrammeled male id. Reality becomes even more tenuous when Fight Club itself expands and transforms itself into Project Mayhem. Armies of black-clad urban terrorists take to the streets smashing car windows, trashing public art, building bombs. In the funniest outrage, members are urged to go out and pick a fight with the first person they come across: it plays like a satanic version of "Candid Camera."

What is the audience to make of Tyler Durden? Played with great bravado by Pitt, he's a kind of Nietzschean Robin Hood, using violence to restore dignity to the benighted American male. But when the real deaths start to pile up, even Jack begins to have qualms about where his bloodthirsty master is leading him.

By this point in Fincher's long fever dream of a movie, the audience's qualms may be mounting as well. Just as he let "The Game" fritter away its power in a preposterous conclusion, Fincher inflates "Fight Club" with apocalyptic mayhem that's positively Wagnerian in its pretension. There is a major plot twist a la "The Sixth Sense" that I won't divulge. It's clearly meant to spin the movie into a provocative new orbit of meaning, but it reads more as if the story has boxed itself into a corner and can't find a way out. The movie doesn't so much end as self-destruct. In the final frames, Fincher inserts the same porno images Tyler had subversively projected, and it's hard not to think of this as a gesture of contempt for the audience. No wonder we leave feeling more surly and exhausted than satisfied. Yet this is not a movie that can be easily dismissed—or forgotten. An outrageous mixture of brilliant technique, puerile philosophizing, trenchant satire and sensory overload, "Fight Club" is the most incendiary movie to come out of Hollywood in a long time. It's a mess, but one worth fighting about.

SIGHT AND SOUND, 12/99, p. 45, Charles Whitehouse

Warning: this synopsis gives away a crucial twist.

The present. The narrator, possibly named Jack, has a gun in his mouth in a building about to be blown up. Months before, Jack lives in an unnamed US city, has a good job and a trendy flat, but feels empty and can't sleep. Jack takes his doctor's flip suggestion he attend a testicular-cancer support group to find out "what real pain is" seriously. Moved to tears by the members' plight, Jack's insomnia is cured and he becomes hooked on group therapy. Soon he notices Marla, another "tourist", and his sleeplessness returns until they agree not to attend the same groups. On a plane, Jack meets Tyler Durden, who makes a living selling soap. When Jack's flat mysteriously blows up, Tyler offers him a place to stay, but only if Jack will hit him. Tyler and Jack beat each other up for fun. They start Fight Club, at which men can pummel each other with bare knuckles.

Marla calls Jack after taking an overdose; Tyler comes to her rescue and they begin a sexual relationship, much to Jack's disgust. Tyler reveals his soap is made from human fat stolen from liposuction clinics. Meanwhile, Fight Clubs spring up all over the country.

Tyler starts Project Mayhem, which involves acts of terrorism against corporations and big business. During one mission Mayhem-soldier Bob is killed. Jack is horrified; Tyler disappears. Jack crisscrosses the country in search of him, only to find everyone thinks he is Tyler. Realising they're right, Jack tries to foil Tyler's plan to blow up several highrise buildings (credit-card companies) at once, but is thwarted. At the primed-to-explode building seen in the opening sequence, Jack shoots himself in the head, only wounding his real body but 'killing' Tyler. Marla, whom he'd put on a bus to safety, is brought to him and they watch together as the bombs go off.

We know from *Se7en* and *The Game* that director David Fincher likes to evoke enclosed, solipsistic worlds which are also conundrums. *Se7en*'s world is an unnamed, sepulchral US city where it's always raining, and life runs inexorably to the countdown of seven murders. Each killing is a symbolic retribution for a deadly sin and a dreadful tease for the investigating detectives played by Morgan Freeman and Brad Pitt. In *The Game*, divorced financier Michael Douglas' insular life is upended when his younger brother signs him up for an exclusive new entertainment experience devoted to springing scary surprises on its clients. He soon finds himself in urban back lots, unable to distinguish real danger from the next 'surprise'. *Fight Club* not only fits the pattern of these predecessors like a bloodied rag glove, it also remakes them.

Just as Douglas' character suffers deep ennui at the consumer perfectionism of his existence, so Edward Norton's Jack, an accident investigator for an insurance company, is aghast at his own obsession with the Ikea catalogue. Just as Freeman and Pitt in *Se7en* are made to seem bent down by the weather and emasculated by propriety, so Jack the insomniac seems crushed by the lack of light, adventure and emotion in his life. Society in a Fincher film is an urban nightmare labyrinth disrupted by the seething, denatured and corralled male ego it was built to control. The difference with *Fight Club* is that nearly every other male in the film feels the same way as the protagonist. The Fight Clubs bring all men together, and what they seem to want to do is hit one another, hard, with bare knuckles, to get a sense of empowerment.

Long before we get to the on-screen hitting, though, the movie pummels the viewer with a furious attack of astonishing shots, body-slam cuts and Jack's chewable voiceover aphorisms: "I felt like putting a bullet in the eye of every panda that wouldn't screw to save its species." The plot starts with its end—Jack with a gun in his mouth—and shoots off back to the start of his insomnia. Even the sombre, night-time desolation that haunts Jack's first cure for sleeplessness—his slumming in victim-support groups (for Aids, alcoholism, drug abuse, testicular cancer and so on)—is a jagged affair of under-the-chin angles, eyeballing close-ups and shuddering sound effects. The arrival of Helena Bonham Carter as the slinky Marla, another group-therapy cuddle-junkie, ruining it for Jack, is announced with looks and sultry poses that jam into the corners of the frame. This is a movie that makes your skin crawl in a strangely delectable way.

But it's with the inception of Fight Club itself, which begins after Jack meets Tyler and right after Jack's apartment has inexplicably been blown up, that Fincher's most sophisticated conundrum yet hooks us. Tyler asks Jack to hit him in the face, hard. Jack hits him and gets hit back. As Jack and Tyler pound each other, men gather round intrigued and Jack is sure his sleeplessness has gone forever. Soon large groups of white- and blue-collar men file into bar basements and strip to the waist as Tyler expounds the rules: "The first rule about Fight Club is that you don't talk about Fight Club. The second rule about Fight Club is that you don't talk about Fight Club." The hitting makes a sly, seductive spectacle of lightweight masochism, homoerotic display and sardonic wit. Later, in one horrific scene of unhingement, it is brutally sadistic. But it remains a baffling, just-plausible compulsion.

Tyler seems to be completely free from any inhibition, able to acquire anything he wants through sheer force of will. Jack's exhilaration at meeting Tyler is undercut by Tyler's immediate sexual success with Marla and then dissipated when he fills their squatted house with Fight Club legions, organised to carry out terror missions. When Jack's grip on his self-control loosens, the film enacts a brilliant twist no caring reviewer ought to reveal. Inventive as it is, however, it also marks an escalation towards the fantastic which loses in conceptual momentum what it gains in dramatic thrills. So *Fight Club* is all of the following: a conspiracy thriller that never leaves the splashy imagination of a paranoid narrator; a value-free vessel that offers conflicting views on Nietzschean ideas about men and destruction; a dazzling entertainment that wants us to luxuriate in violence as we condemn it; a brilliant solution to depicting the divided self as a protagonist; and proof that Brad Pitt, as well as Edward Norton, can really act.

TIME, 10/11/99, p. 83, Richard Schickel

Let's say your life is so anonymous that the movie's credits list you only as "Narrator." Let's also say the symptoms of that condition include near terminal insomnia and an unsatisfiable urge for catalog shopping. Might you not then join a support group for the victims of TB or testicular cancer, just so you could hug, sob and generally surface some feelings, even if you don't actually have one of those diseases?

If your answer to that question is, "Are you kidding?" then Fight Club is not for you, though it must be said that early on, it funnily realizes the satirical possibilities of 12-stepping your way through life. The film remains strong when Edward Norton's Narrator meets Tyler Durden (Brad Pitt) on an airplane. He's everything Norton isn't—a bruising truth teller with a taste for urban anarchism. He's the kind of guy who splices pornographic flash cuts into family movies when he works as a projectionist, who pees in the soup when he works as a banquet waiter.

His big idea is, well, yes, a fight club—a basement he commandeers where ordinary guys can come and beat the crap out of each other in bareknuckle, no-holds-barred combat. This really puts them in touch with their feelings, which are incoherently rageful.

It also puts viewers in touch with director David Fincher's preferred mise-en-scène, which is almost always dark and, more important, damp—with rusty water, gushing blood and other bodily fluids of less determinable origins. It's definitely a style—see his *Seven* of a few years ago—and it enforces the contrast between the sterilities of his characters' aboveground life and their underground one. Water, even when it's polluted, is the source of life; blood, even when it's carelessly spilled, is the symbol of life being fully lived. To put his point simply: it's better to be wet than dry.

Before long, Tyler has a chain of fight clubs up and running all over the country and is molding their members into a paramilitary organization that aims, finally, to blow up all the credit-card companies and, just for good measure, TRW. It is along about here that *Fight Club*, which is Jim Uhls' adaptation of Chuck Palahniuk's novel, lurches from satire into fantasy. For we begin to realize that the hunky Pitt is the willowy Norton's doppelganger, a projection of fantasies about masculine mastery.

The movie manages this smoothly enough—both actors are excellent—but there's something conventionally gimmicky about the way it plays its reality/unreality game—of a lazy piece with its failure to do anything interesting with the woman in the story, Helena Bonham Carter's neurotically gnarly representation of feminism's failures to create a more sympathetic female.

Yet whatever its flaws—and they will, for some, include its brutal, off-putting imagery—*Fight Club* can't be ignored. It is working *American Beauty*—Susan Faludi territory, that illiberal, impious, inarticulate fringe that threatens the smug American center with an anger that cannot explain itself, can act out its frustrations only in inexplicable violence.

VILLAGE VOICE, 10/26/99, p. 157, J. Hoberman

Let us triangulate. David Fincher's *Fight Club* is not a brainless mosh pit. Nor is it a transgressive masterpiece. As provocations go, this malevolently gleeful satire (closely adapted from Chuck Palahniuk's confrontational first novel) is extremely funny, surprisingly well-acted, and boldly designed—at least until its steel-and-chrome soufflé falls apart.

Sometimes a skyscraper is only a skyscraper and a gun only a gun, but not here. Set amid the repressive trappings of ubiquitous phallocracy, *Fight Club* means to be one sustained psychosexual ejaculation. Edward Norton, who plays the nameless protagonist-narrator, is introduced sucking on a revolver. The rest of the movie flashes back to detail just why and how this conformist have not learned to stoke his testosterone levels and free his inner lad by playing body-slam with the primal horde. Meanwhile, Fincher flaunts his own mastery with a series of sleekly impossible, which is to say digitally contrived, camera moves.

Fight Club unfolds in the deadpan, five-minutes-into-the-future environment invented by J.G. Ballard. Ballardian, too, is the narrator's job as a corporate "recall coordinator"—an occupation that sends him flying all over the country studying car wrecks and imagining midair collisions. Living inside an Ikea catalog above the same generic city Fincher devised for *Seven*, this nerdy insomniac spends his evenings cruising support groups. His favorite, naturally, is the one for men with testicular cancer, where he develops a moist rapport with a hormonally whacked ex-wrestler (Meat Loaf) and a more ambivalent relationship with another "tourist," this one female.

A kohl-eyed, chain-smoking goth rag doll living in a hovel with a dildo on the dresser, Marla (Helena Bonham Carter, elaborating on her theatrical smolder in *Wings of the Dove*) is virtually the movie's only woman. *Fight Club* is boys' night out with a vengeance; the narrator's life really changes when he finds himself in a plane seat next to Tyler Durden, a vision of wildness played by Brad Pitt in red leather jacket, plaid shirt, checked pants, and orange shades. Pitt, as demonstrated in *12 Monkeys,* can be a highly charismatic maniac. After the narrator's condo explodes, he moves in with his volatile new ego-ideal, the two pals shacking up in a dank, decrepit Victorian that seems the natural efflorescence of the city's toxic waste dump.

Although Tyler's quaint job as a projectionist has bearing on the movie we are watching, the Norton character is even more captivated by his roommate's reckless taste for bare-knuckled violence. Soon the two are making a spectacle of themselves, staging nocturnal fist-fights in the parking lot outside their neighborhood bar. With its gurgling savoir faire and voluptuously decayed mise-en-scéne, *Fight Club* could be *Brazil* with bloody Chiclets. The narrator flails shirtless by night and shows up proudly battered at work the next morning. Then Marla takes up with Tyler. "She invaded my support groups, now she invaded my home," Norton's character whines. (In a clue to the narrator's fissured mind-set, this morning-after complaint provokes Tyler to wonder if he's back living with his parents.)

For all its sadomasochistic celebration of aggro fun and cosmetic bruises, *Fight Club's* gross-outs are mainly metaphysical. The narrator and Tyler steal fat from a liposuction clinic to make cosmetic soap. ("We were selling rich women their fat asses back to them.") Inevitably, Tyler's heavy-metal existentialism begins to attract followers. Soon, he's not only freaking out the local wiseguys with the bizarre Ramrod Club he's running down in their basement but pulling more extravagantly antisocial pranks—smashing cars, blowing up show windows, terrorizing 7-Eleven clerks.

Ultimately, *Fight Club* feels compelled to dramatize the lemming-like franchising of Tyler's avant-garde vision and, turning into a fashion-based critique of fascism, begins marching in lockstep toward oblivion. A plot twist anticipated by last winter's generally ignored independent *Six Ways to Sunday* notwithstanding, the last hour is gruelingly redundant—although the swank nihilism of the final, special-effects apocalypse is a climax worth waiting for. So, is this social metaphor or case history? Though *Fight Club* has been compared to David Cronenberg's *Crash,* it's more touchy-feely and less poignant in its posturing. There's no search for transcendence here.

Fight Club makes much of its tormented male characters' sense of abandonment: "We're a generation of men raised by women ... We are God's unwanted children." Unable to fight their fathers, they slug each other. In the movie's key scene, the narrator confronts his boss and proceeds to punch himself into a bloody pulp. As this self-administered beating suggests, *Fight Club* makes even the Nietzschean will-to-power a joke. Here's a question for daytime TV: Is it possible to play Oedipus in a world without Dad?

Also reviewed in:
CHICAGO TRIBUNE, 10/15/99, Friday/p. A, Michael Wilmington
NATION, 11/8/99, p. 32, Stuart Klawans
NEW REPUBLIC, 11/8/99, p. 64, Stanley Kauffmann
NEW YORK TIMES, 10/15/99, p. E14, Janet Maslin
NEW YORKER, 10/18 & 25/99, p. 252, David Denby
VARIETY, 9/13-19/99, p. 47, David Rooney
WASHINGTON POST, 10/15/99, p. C1, Stephen Hunter
WASHINGTON POST, 10/15/99, Weekend/p. 43, Desson Howe

FINDING NORTH

A Cowboy Booking release of a SoNo Pictures, Inc. production. *Executive Producer:* Hal "Corky" Kessler. *Producer:* Steven A. Jones and Stephen Dyer. *Director:* Tanya Wexler. *Screenplay:* Kim Powers. *Director of Photography:* Michael Barrett. *Editor:* Thom Zimny. *Music:* Café Noir. *Music Editor:* Brian Rund. *Sound:* Lance Hoffman. *Sound Editor:* Marshall Grupp and Pink Noise. *Casting:* Brett Goldstein. *Production Designer:* James B. Smythe. *Art*

Director: Terry Osburn. *Costumes:* Katelyn Burton. *Make-up:* Leah Rial. *Running time:* 95 minutes. *MPAA Rating:* Not Rated.

CAST: Wendy Makkena (Rhonda Portelli); John Benjamin Hickey (Travis Furlong); Anne Bobby (Debi); Rebecca Creskoff (Gina); Angela Pietropinto (Mama Portelli); Freddie Roman (Papa Portelli); Molly McClure (Aunt Bonnie Tucker); Jonathan Walker (Voice of Robert "Bobby" L. Sullivan); Yusef Bulos (Taxi Driver); Garrett Moran (Stripper); Steven Jones (Funeral Director); Lynn Metrik (Bank Manager); Phyllis Cicero (Janice); Spiro Malas (Waiter); Amy Zimmerman (Ticket Agent); Lisa Peterson (Car Rental Agent); Bo Barron (Counter Boy); Cherami Leigh Kuehn (Gretchen); Matt Whitton (Young Bobby); Jody Napolotano (Young Don Franklin); Gail Cronauer (Mrs. Penn); Jay Michaelson (Bud); Lou Ann Stephens (Ethel/Bethel); R. Bruce Elliot (TV Salesman); Kermit Key, Richard Rogers, and Russ Marker (Geezers); T.J. Morehouse (Drugstore Clerk); Mary Sheldon (Ellen); Westin Self (Younger "Devil" Bobby); Norman Bennett (Farmer McDonald); Marisa Perez (Baby Sitter); Harrison Lindley (Cowboy); Jesse Plemmons (Hobo); Sara Proctor (Princess).

NEW YORK POST, 6/4/99, p. 48, Rod Dreher

"Finding North" is a low-budget labor of love that's just plain labored. Good intentions never jell into anything of dramatic interest in Kim Powers' feeble screenplay, whose indefatigable striving toward the outer extremes of quirkiness gets old fast.

The unlikely—even for the movies—plot brings together lonely Rhonda Portelli (Wendy Makkena), a big-haired Brooklyn babe, with Travis Furlong (John Benjamin Hickey), a suicidal Manhattanite mourning the death of his longtime companion, Bobby.

Yappy Rhonda develops a crush on Travis, and attaches herself to him as he fulfills Bobby's last request: a road trip to north Texas, to see where Bobby came from.

The wacky setup makes little sense, and the plot goes even further out on a limb once they arrive in the Lone Star State. The duo keep encountering Texans so cliched and cornpone-cute you fear one of them might burst out with "Kiss my grits!" at the drop of a 10-gallon hat.

The characterization is apparently meant as a good-faith tribute to Texans, but it's cloying and condescending. Then again, Rhonda's zany Italian parents back home in Brooklyn are just as phony, like a cheap and unfunny imitation of Mr. and Mrs. Costanza from "Seinfeld."

There's an affecting scene near the end, when Travis meets Bobby's Aunt Bonnie (Molly McClure), a great old Texas broad with a stout heart and a magnificently weatherbeaten face.

It's the only moment in "Finding North" that feels true, and suggests what the film might have been had the script been better. There's no improving, though, on the jaunty, jazzy score by the combo Cafe Noir.

NEWSDAY, 6/4/99, Part II/p. B6, Gene Seymour

It's hard to imagine that there's anything new to be mined from the "Noo-Yawk-chick-with-big-hair" archetype. But darned if Wendy Makkena doesn't make the character of Rhonda Portelli seem like someone we've not only never met, but would like very much to know better.

Rhonda is a bank clerk from Brooklyn, hitting the big Three-Oh and still living at home with her parents. One night, riding across the Brooklyn Bridge with her girlfriends, she and they can't help but notice that a naked man is about to jump. She jumps into traffic to help, but he's changed his mind by the time she reaches him. All she has is a shoe.

Cinderella, you think. No. The guy she thinks is Prince Charming is Travis Furlong (John Benjamin Hickey), whose suicidal depression is brought about by the recent death of his lover, Bobby, from AIDS. The only thing getting in the way of his plans to do himself in is Bobby, who, from the grave, urges Travis to take his ashes to his Texas hometown and carry out a few tasks aimed at revealing the dead man's final request.

To do this, Travis needs to withdraw lots of money from a bank where Rhonda is clerking. Through circumstances too stupid to get into here, she is fired from her job and finds herself on the same plane as Travis, who takes an irritatingly long time to let her in on the fact that he is, by no means, Mr. Right. He doesn't even want to be friends.

And you know what? He's right. She's not worthy of him. Rhonda is kind, sensitive and tougher than she knows. Travis comes across as an insufferable prig despite Hickey's gallant attempt to make him sympathetic.

The trouble is that Travis' maudlin, self-absorbed spirit informs almost all of "Finding North." The movie comes across as patronizing toward "little people," whether they're from Flatbush or the Plains. Kim Powers' script and Tanya Wexler's direction spread themselves too thin and too wide in grasping for dry-witted profundity and easygoing whimsy. Somehow you've seen it all before and there's not enough reason to experience it again.

As noted, only Makkena brings something new to the party, though it's hard to put your finger on what that element is. Perhaps it's not a new spin so much as deeper shadows and sharper intelligence applied to what would otherwise be a predictable role. Her Rhonda deserved a better traveling companion. The performance deserved a better movie.

SIGHT AND SOUND, 6/99, p. 45, Melanie McGrath

After losing his lover Bobby to Aids, Travis Furlong finds himself on Brooklyn Bridge contemplating suicide. He is spotted by Rhonda, a friendless Bronx bankclerk looking for Mr Right. However, Travis doesn't kill himself. Instead, he turns up at her cashier's desk some time later and she decides they were meant to be together. Rhonda follows him to his apartment where he rebuffs her. Meanwhile, Travis has received a tape through the mail from Bobby instructing him to take his lover's ashes on a sentimental journey to Bobby's home turf in Texas. There he will find a series of clues leading him to his dead lover's last wish.

On the way to the airport he encounters Rhonda. Thinking she has at last found her Prince-charming, she follows Travis to Texas and the two embark on the journey of discovery, coming to an understanding of themselves and of each other and becoming firm Platonic friends. Having symbolically buried Bobby's ashes in the family plot, Travis and Rhonda head back north to begin their lives anew in New York City as was Bobby's last wish.

Film fashion being as starkly ephemeral as any other kind, it is hard to watch an Aids-issue film without feeling instantly transported back into the late 80s when Aids stood as much for American Independent Dreary Sob-story as it did for auto-immune deficiency syndrome. It's not that Aids is unimportant or unworthy of film narratives, it's just that it is no longer possible to represent it—as it was in so many American indies of the late 80s and early 90s—as a synonym for moral goodness. Over the intervening years Aids has become (quite rightly) integrated into the wider world of illness, its existence no more shocking than cancer or heart failure and its victims no more virtuous. We have, in other words, knocked Aids off its privileged perch. Its screen victims can no longer demand our sympathy; they must earn it.

Which is why, as a story of one man's redemption, first feature director Tanya Wexler's *Finding North* fails in all directions. Though we understand Aids has, ironically, become for the bereaved but HIV-negative Travis a psychological prophylactic, protecting him from the threat of true engagement with the world, he is just too narcissistic, too snobbish and too altogether humourless for us to be able to regard his neurasthenic withdrawal as the world's loss. John Benjamin Hickey gives a tight and sympathetic performance, but even he cannot save his character from coming over as a little shit. This is a man who announces "I'm going to floss" as though the free world depended on it. A man who with overtones of pygmalion thinks fit to advise his travelling companion to wear her hair small not big lest she appear too trashy.

And this is also a man who imagines that Texans don't know what cellphones are. Condescension pervades this film, not simply in the guise of Travis, but in the use of Texas as a liminal space peppered with freakish moteliers, meathead rednecks and noble-savage sensualists, designed for nothing so much as the psychic refurbishment of New Yorkers. This is the kind of Texas where the locals say, "down here we call that..." and everyone wanders about in chaps and Stetsons.

Wendy Makkena gets all the best lines and puts on a faultless show as the dry, kind, embittered Rhonda, turning 30 and battling with loneliness and a particularly nasty (and implausible) species of Jewish mother. But Rhonda, like Texas, is simply another device in Travis' sanctimonious conversion back to life. It's a pity, since Makkena is too good an actress and Rhonda too generous a character to be wasted like this. She may be necessary to redeem Travis but even she is not sufficient to redeem *Finding North*.

VILLAGE VOICE, 6/8/99, p. 64, Justine Elias

Finding North, the directing debut of Tanya Wexler (daughter of cinematographer Haskell Wexler), is a most paradoxical film: a road movie that feels almost entirely static. The first scene, at least, is a grabber: a naked man (John Benjamin Hickey) teeters on the railing of the Brooklyn Bridge, contemplating suicide. Instead of jumping, though, he hops a cab and heads home. (We later learn that he's just lost his longtime lover to AIDS, and intends to burn through their savings account before making his own final exit.) Through a series of unbelievable coincidences, Travis crosses paths with a bored bank teller named Rhonda, who witnessed his near-suicide and fell instantly in love with him.

Hickey has a certain Joel McCrea-like appeal, but here he seems to be conveying the idea that a man can go quite bland with grief. Wendy Makkena plays the big-haired, white-shoes-after-Labor Day heroine with a perplexing combination of moxie and confusion—it's hard to say if she's being true to the shtick-heavy, sitcomlike script, or trying to get out of its way.

Also reviewed in:
CHICAGO TRIBUNE, 9/10/99, Friday/p. B, Michael Wilmington
NEW YORK TIMES, 6/4/99, p. E14, Stephen Holden
VARIETY, 3/16-22/98, p. 68, Emanuel Levy

FIVE WIVES, THREE SECRETARIES AND ME

A Castle Hill Productions release. *Producer:* Jason Lyon. *Director:* Tessa Blake. *Running time:* 80 minutes. *MPAA Rating:* Not Rated.

WITH: Muffet Criner Adickes Blake; Sandra Tessman Blake; Betty (Boop) Blake; Sharon Simons; Harriet Leasey; Louise Turner; Barbara Tucker; Virginia Keasling; Chelo Maris.

NEW YORK POST, 10/11/99, p. 50, Lou Lumenick

"Five Wives, Three Secretaries and Me" is an engaging documentary made by a onetime debutante coming to terms with her crusty, womanizing father.

Tessa Blake doesn't hold back much about her dad, Houston oil billionaire Thomas Blake Jr., or his five spouses. Now in his 80s, Tommy admits that his current marriage to fifth wife Muffet has lasted 10 years because "we never ask where the other has been."

Tessa, raised largely by her Mexican nanny, presses him about his mistresses, but in the end reveals her dad to be a charming man who remains on good terms with most of his exes. "Five Wives" ends on a conciliatory note—and it's easy to see what all these woman love about Tommy.

VILLAGE VOICE, 10/19/99, p. 140, Gary Dauphin

Tessa Blake's portrait of her oilman father, *Five Wives, Three Secretaries and Me*, offers a case study in the possibilities and pitfalls of taking a documentary look at your own family—the film is as full of flickering warmth as it is bereft of larger insight. Returning in 1994 to the peroxide Texas high society of her birth, Blake (she's the "Me" on the marquee) puts her then 89-year-old father in front of the lens in hopes of capturing domestic fireworks, but Tommy Blake proves just another patriarch whose passage through twilight makes asking honest questions not just impossible but downright cruel.

It would take a more exacting (or more damaged) soul than Blake's to pin the old man to the wall, but *Five Wives* makes a half-hearted try anyway, rooting around Tommy's many marriages and demimonde for hard truth and, failing that, quirk. We meet current wife Muffet, the various "Texas Exes" (the director's flaky mother is #4), Daddy's three secretaries, and the Mexican nanny. The secretaries have been with Daddy longer than all the wives combined, and their wry memories of an often dictatorial, cheap, and aloof man counterbalance soft-focus images of Daddy stooped at a piano, crooning a lovelorn song.

Like any good liberal escapee from the heartland, Blake makes the standard feinting move toward matters racial, eliciting some bullshit commentary from her dad and trotting out her black boyfriend. The desire to move beyond family chitchat is admirable, but Blake loses her nerve when it comes to color, setting up a climactic encounter with Daddy about the boyfriend that goes nowhere. Tears stream down her face as she un-mics her father for the last time, and although you know she's crying for all the ways parents just don't understand, you also imagine she's crying for her own offspring, *Five Wives* not having turned out the way she'd hoped either.

Also reviewed in:
NEW YORK TIMES, 10/8/99, p. E15, Anita Gates

FLAWLESS

A Metro-Goldwyn-Mayer Pictures release of a Tribeca production. *Executive Producer:* Neil Machlis. *Producer:* Joel Schumacher and Jane Rosenthal. *Director:* Joel Schumacher. *Screenplay:* Joel Schumacher. *Director of Photography:* Declan Quinn. *Editor:* Mark Stevens. *Music:* Bruce Roberts. *Music Editor:* Daryl Kell. *Choreographer:* Keith Young. *Sound:* Chris Jenkins, Ron Bartlett, Mark Smith and (music) Bob Schaper. *Sound Editor:* John Leveque and Anthony R. Milch. *Casting:* Mali Finn. *Production Designer:* Jan Roelfs. *Art Director:* Sarah Knowles. *Set Decorator:* Leslie Pope. *Set Dresser:* Bruce Swanson, Deborah Prate-Panuccio, Denis Zack, Robert Klatt, John Cahill, John Basile, and Dennis Murray. *Special Effects:* Connie Brink and Matt Vogel. *Costumes:* Daniel Orlandi. *Make-up:* Margot Boccia. *Make-up (Robert De Niro):* Ilona Herman. *Stunt Coordinator:* Eddie Yansick. *Running time:* 110 minutes. *MPAA Rating:* R.

CAST: Robert De Niro (Walt Koontz); Philip Seymour Hoffman (Rusty); Barry Miller (Leonard Wilcox); Chris Bauer (Jacko); Skipp Sudduth (Tommy); Wilson Jermaine Heredia (Cha-Cha); Nashom Benjamin (Amazing Grace); Scott Allen Cooper (Ivana); Rory Cochrane (Pogo); Daphne Rubin-Vega (Tia); Vincent Laresca (Raymond Camacho); Karina Arroyave (Amber); John Enos (Sonny); Jude Ciccolella (Detective Noonan); Mina Bern (Mrs. Spivak); Wanda De Jesus (Karen); Madhur Jaffrey (Dr. Nirmala); Mark Margolis (Vinnie); Shiek Mahmud-Bey (Vance); Luis Saguar (Mr. Z); Kyle Rivers (LeShaun); Sammy Rhee (Mr. Pim); Hyunsoo Lee (Mrs. Pim); Richie LaMontagne (Carmine); Penny Balfour (Cristal); Winter B. Uhlarik (Tasha); Raven O (Notorious F.A.G.); Joey Arias (Stormy); Jackie Beat (Gypsy); Blake Willett and Ingrid Rivera (Cops); Craig Braun (Paulie); John Doumanian (Mr. Terzola); Melissa Osborn (Tourist); John Contratti (Customer); Stacy Highsmith (Denise); Rod Rodriguez and Alice Williams (Lesbians); Antonette Schwartzberg (Mrs. Terzola); Hamilton De Oliveira (Hotel Janitor); John Polce (Walt Stand-in); Logan McCall and John E. Mack (EMS Technicians); John R. Corcoran (Physical Therapist); Matt Merchant (Man in Crowd); Al Marz (Cristal's Boyfriend); Michelle Robinson and Nina Sonja Peterson (Dancers); Larry Marx (Bar Patron); Mitchell Lichtenstein (Gay Republican Spokesperson); John Fink (Gay Republican Lawyer); Bret Kropp (Drag Queen); Cooley (Cop); Constance Boardman (Reporter); Lucy Cerezo-Scully and Al Thompson (Paramedics).

LOS ANGELES TIMES, 11/24/99, Calendar/p. 2, Kevin Thomas

"Flawless" this Joel Schumacher film is not, but it plays so well that that scarcely matters. It was Schumacher's inspired idea to bring together a macho ex-security guard and a drag queen and see what would happen, and he had the good fortune to cast Robert De Niro, whose company also produced the film, and also the protean, fearless Philip Seymour Hoffman. De Niro and Hoffman are at once amusing and moving, and the result is a lively entertainment that manages some deft consciousness-raising.

In a dingy Beaux Arts apartment house on Manhattan's Lower East Side, De Niro's Walt Koontz prepares for a night out by covering up the gray creeping into his hair at the very moment his upstairs, across-a-light-well neighbor, Hoffman's Rusty Zimmerman, is putting the finishing touches on his makeup. The trim, rugged Walt is heading for a dance hall where he'll tango with his regular partner (Wanda De Jesus) before winding up in bed with her. Rusty is getting ready for a night's work as Busty Rusty, the Hostess With the Mostest, emcee and piano accompanist at a popular drag club.

Now retired, Walt is an authentic hero with the citations and trophies to prove it—a decade earlier he saved lives during a bank holdup. Long divorced, he leads a simple but contented life with a bunch of cronies who remain in awe of his bravery. Walt and Rusty don't really know each other, but their loathing is mutual. Rusty is constantly making gowns for his club colleagues and holding show rehearsals in his crowded, gaudy apartment, with Walt constantly complaining about the noise. Walt and Rusty and his pals yell back and forth, and you can well imagine the kind of language they use.

Meanwhile, Schumacher has been setting up the incident that will turn the enemies into friends. Not surprisingly, one of the other neighbors and her boyfriend are involved in drugs, with the boyfriend foolish enough to rip off the scary neighborhood drug dealer, Mr. Z (Luis Saguar), for a substantial sum of money. When the dealer's thugs come calling and the bullets start flying, the unwitting Walt goes into action, trying to save the girl's life—only to end up felled by a stroke that leaves his right side paralyzed and his speech substantially impaired.

Devastated, Walt becomes an instant recluse, too proud to leave his apartment except to limp out at night once a week for groceries. A dedicated doctor (the always-wonderful Madhur Jaffrey), however, seeks him out, arranges for a physical therapist (Kyle Rivers) to come to him and advises singing lessons as a way of improving his speech. Thus Walt unexpectedly needs Rusty, who could use the money.

Walt gets much more from Rusty than a gradual improvement in his speech. He discovers how gutsy Rusty, who has no time for pity, either for Walt or himself, has to be simply in being himself. Rusty is a transsexual who longs for the expensive surgery and treatments needed to match up with what he believes to be his true gender. Walt may see Rusty as caught up in a sexual fantasy, but it's Rusty who gives Walt constant reality checks. Ever so slowly they become friends, both loners longing for love and both possessed of much strength of character. Beneath wildly different exteriors Walt and Rusty at heart have more in common than either initially would like to acknowledge.

Meanwhile, Mr. Z and his henchmen are still searching for that missing money, and their frustration only heightens their savagery. While Schumacher does work the fate of that loot into his plot, you wish he could have played down the familiar brutal urban melodrama violence and put his screen time to better use in exploring Walt and Rusty's differing yet overlapping worlds even more completely. (There is, however, a gratifying confrontation between Rusty and his glittery friends and a group of conservatively dressed gay men, assimilationists who clearly wish the drags would disappear from the face of the Earth.)

In short, it would have been fun to spend more time with such barely glimpsed divas as Joey Arias and Jackie Beat than with thugs on a merciless rampage. In any event, no one can accuse Schumacher of stinting on action, even though what's of real interest here is his exploration of what it means to be a man.

De Niro underplays to the stocky Hoffman, so memorable in "Happiness," "Boogie Nights" and other films. Rusty may pin up glamour stills of Joan Crawford and other gay icons, but in his fluttery femininity—although not in his street survivor's vocabulary—he brings to mind Helen Morgan's plump, fading burlesque queen in "Applause."

Where "Flawless" is flawless is in Jan Roelfs' absolutely authentic production design, Daniel Orlandi's right-on costumes and in Declan Quinn's rich, noirish cinematography. You're not likely to forget Rusty—and Hoffman could well be remembered in the upcoming awards season.

NEW YORK POST, 11/24/99, p. 58, Lou Lumenick

"Flawless" is anything but, notwithstanding the presence of Robert De Niro as a conservative stroke victim who learns to communicate by taking singing lessons from a flamboyant drag queen.

De Niro plays Walt, a retired cop who's stricken while trying to rescue a neighbor in the rundown Lower East Side SRO where he lives. In his first screenplay since "St. Elmo's Fire," director Joel Schumacher, the man who put codpieces on Batman and Robin, contrives to have Walt turn to the flamboyant Rusty Zimmerman (Philip Seymour Hoffman) for help, though the two loathe each other.

It's tough to buy this premise—that Walt would put himself in the hands of someone he hates because he's too ashamed to leave the building. Still, De Niro gives a technically brilliant performance as Walt, struggling with a body that will no longer obey him.

But it's not much fun watching De Niro play a victim, a man whose girlfriend ditches him once he's no longer in a position to subsidize her living expenses.

Hoffman, who played the gay gofer in "Boogie Nights," is very good, though his part has been conceived as pure stereotype—complete with a drinking problem, a dying mother, an abusive married lover and a yearning for a sex-change operation.

"Flawless" is at its most tolerable when Schumacher concentrates on Walt and Rusty, and the scene in which they sing "The Name Game" has great charm, even if their relationship progresses in an entirely predictable fashion.

Guess who ends up saving whose life? Guess whose pals triumph in the big beauty contest at the gay and lesbian center?

"Flawless" offers few surprises.

NEWSDAY, 11/24/99, Part II/p. B9, Jan Stuart

Fans of such theatrical boxing matches as "Driving Miss Daisy" and "I'm Not Rappaport" have reason to sit up, if not rejoice. The two-character, one-set play beats in the old-fashioned heart of "Flawless," a pistol-packing variation on all those modest téte-a-tétes that were adapted from the stage from the '60s through the '80s.

There are many characters clattering about Joel Shumacher's original screenplay, but it still has the distinctly creaky feel of a two-hander that has been opened up for the screen. The modus operandi of such dramas is to throw an unlikely couple into a room (or a car, or onto a park bench) and have them go at each other until they discover their common humanity.

In "Flawless," which could also be titled "Teaching Miss Thing," we are asked to believe that a New York City drag performer (Philip Seymour Hoffman) would willfully consider the company of a neighboring cop (Robert De Niro) who is conceivably the most homophobic person on his Alphabet City block.

The excuse that Schumacher contrives is that Walt, the cop, has suffered a stroke while trying to bust up an assault and needs a speech therapist. Rusty, the performer, is down-and-out and needs the money. And as we learned from Greg Kinnear in "As Good as It Gets," homosexual men nurture superficial, fair-weather friendships and are thus obliged to depend upon the kindness of gay-bashing strangers.

If you can buy this premise, there are some antic pleasures to be derived from the bumpy getting-to-know-you dance between the nasty cop and the queen with a heart of lam. The credit owes less to De Niro, who squawks through pressed lips as if he'd just chomped down on a Duco Cement sandwich, than Hoffman.

Moviedom's male answer to Kathy Bates, Hoffman is a puffy, improbable chameleon of a character actor capable of multiple identities: a phone-sex maniac in "Happiness," a love-smitten production assistant in "Boogie Nights," a smarmy bookworm in "Patch Adams." Hoffman holds the center spotlight to bravura effect as he parries De Niro's insults with choice comebacks cultivated from years of facing down nightclub hecklers and neighborhood bigots. Gay moviegoers still reeling from "The Boys in the Band" will take exception to Rusty's self-pitying and dramatizing ("I'm a lonely, ugly drag queen"). For all his good intentions, Schumacher is hardly God's gift to gay enlightenment: He works up a sweat in the effort to give Rusty dimensionality, then paints all the other transvestites in the movie as bitchy, ruthless clowns.

There is a hyperbolic subplot having to do with hidden drug money, a nest of venomous gangsters and an unctuous desk clerk (Barry Miller). But the play's the thing here, as Walt and Rusty trade hard-knock stories of the lovers who do them wrong. Rusty's weakness is a rough-and-tumble married man who is pressuring him to have a sex-change operation. This particular theme is carried off with a grittier and far more credible hand in "Lola and Billy the Kid," a tautly spun German film which opened recently at Manhattan's Quad Cinema.

"Flawless" may not make any 10-best lists, but it's certainly the movie misnomer of the year.

SIGHT AND SOUND, 12/00. p. 47, David Jays

Walt, a retired security guard, lives in an apartment block on the Lower East Side in New York. When gangsters rampage through the building in search of stolen money, Walt tries to intervene but suffers a stroke. He is partially paralysed and his speech severely affected. In order to help his speech, he takes singing lessons with his neighbour Rusty, a drag queen and performer. Despite their mutual suspicion, their sessions go well, and Walt meets Dusty's fellow drag artists.

Rusty confides to Walt that he has hidden the gangsters' money in a dressmaker's dummy and can now afford a sex-change operation. Walt recovers sufficiently to dance at his regular bar with a hostess whom he had previously snubbed. That night, hearing Rusty being beaten by the thugs, who suspect him of having their money, he intervenes. He and Rusty fight off and shoot their attackers, but Walt is wounded. Rusty pays for the emergency treatment with the money earmarked for his operation.

Joel Shumacher's films are unsteady juggernauts. Brash liberalism hurtles alongside irresistible sentiment, precarious command of tone and flickering homoeroticism. *A Time to Kill*, his sweaty John Grisham adaptation, may be the most convincing of his films, but *Flawless* is enjoyable whenever the movie leaves its rails. A plot about stroke victim Walt learning song from drag queen Rusty conjures up such unpromisingly twinkling scenarios that it's good to see the characters resist togetherness. Ex-security guard Walt, played by Robert De Niro, proves resistant to campery, and bracing insult peppers the dialogue. Shumacher's screenplay cannily decoys its narrative of triumph-through-adversity when a dizzy queen assures Walt, "You have a *My Left Foot* thing going on, haven't you?" Rusty, played by Philip Seymour Hoffman, also maintains a wry commentary of movie references: during the final chase, he rallies by thinking of "Grace Kelly in *Rear Window*".

Shumacher insists on correspondences between his protagonists, especially in the sequence in which they prepare for a night out to the strut and swoon of a tango soundtrack. Each defines himself through paraphernalia—Walt lives among his dusty history, his medal for bravery and celebratory cuttings, while Rusty's apartment is cluttered with powder brushes and photos of screen divas. While Walt clears the floor with a slow-step at the Private Dancer bar, so Rusty, glittering in amber, teasingly comperes the cabaret at Femmes Fatales. More importantly, they share statuesque self-sufficiency, refusing pity and compromise. Neither bursts into "I Am What I Am", but you get the idea.

Flawless is a fractured picture, which is its most winning aspect. The apartment block is a heartbreak hotel for the elderly and the oddball. In an arresting stylistic tic, Walt's neighbour strums songs of abandonment through a half-open door. Jolts of inconsequentiality divert the films inspirational progress. An old dame greets Walt's accident with, "You think that's bad? I didn't sleep a wink last night!" The violence forcing the plot may be monochrome, but it's echoed in equally perfunctory clashes between rowdy drag gangs ("I need some dykes!" squawks a nervous peacekeeper).

Like other tales of New York—*Last Exit to Brooklyn* (1989), *Taxi Driver* (1976)—*Flawless* displays the freakshow of the lonely town. Walt's apartment sits in sullen puddles of blue grey light and director of photography Declan Quinn *(Leaving Las Vegas)* and production designer Jan Roelfs *(Orlando)* create the perfect environment for characters living separate lives in intrusive proximity. Even in their confessional cups, Rusty and Walt choose to sit alongside each other rather than face to face.

The leads perform interesting variations on their screen personae. De Niro is celebrated for the demands he has made on his body during his career (notably *Raging Bull),* and suits this role of reluctant transformation. Walt strains for fitness (as in the opening ball game), but grim lines tug at his mouth even before the stroke cruelly accentuates them, and his performance subsequently squeezes through vocal and physical constraints. Hoffman is similarly an artist of insistent, creative fleshiness. His characters have an uncomfortable relationship with clammy corporeality

(Happiness, Boogie Nights), or make their bulk an arrogant battering-ram *(The Talented Mr. Ripley)*. Rusty, planning a sex change, decorates but disdains his body. Hoffman also finds a terrific vocal register for the New Jersey queen, a husky plateau skating between sob and sass.

VILLAGE VOICE, 11/30/99, p. 142, Dennis Lim

Two Joel Schumacher movies in one year is more than the average human brain is built to withstand. Is this some sick cosmic joke? True, *Flawless* never approaches the rancid bluster of *8MM*, but it's an equally dishonest piece of manipulative hackwork. For his first screenplay since *St. Elmo's Fire*, Schumacher rehashes the feel-good improbable-bonding scenario of why-can't-we-all-get-along movies like *As Good As It Gets*, in which a comically antagonistic relationship turns lovey-dovey in the name of tolerance and self-improvement.

Robert De Niro plays Walt, a retired security guard who lives in an Avenue A flophouse. He's a guy's guy—plays handball with the neighborhood kids, treats women badly, yells at drag queens. After a stroke leaves him partially paralyzed, Walt's advised to take singing lessons as therapy, and—in one of many strikingly implausible plot points—decides to take them from Rusty (Philip Seymour Hoffman) the piano-playing drag queen upstairs whom he despises.

De Niro applies his brand of show-offy restraint to stroke-victim cadences. Hoffman brings occasional, unexpected nuance to a character written as equal parts hand-on-hip sassiness ("I'm more man than you'll ever be and more woman than you'll ever get") and tortured self-pity ("I'm lonely! I'm ugly!"). Schumacher's direction is less shrill than usual; the fatal flaws lie in his screenplay, which is bogged down with smug, unfunny one-liners and a dreary subplot about drug dealers and their missing loot. Schumacher—most offensive when feigning seriousness (see *A Time to Kill*)—takes pains to emphasize how alone and ironically alike the protagonists are, and the implicit equation of transgenderism with impairment leaves you sickened. Every non-*Batman* movie Schumacher makes is an argument for reviving the franchise.

Also reviewed in:
NEW YORK TIMES, 11/24/99, p. E5, Stephen Holden
VARIETY, 11/22-28/99, p. 84, Emanuel Levy
WASHINGTON POST, 11/24/99, p. C2, Rita Kempley

FOLLOWING

A Zeitgeist Films release of a Syncopy Films production. *Producer:* Christopher Nolan, Jeremy Theobald, and Emma Thomas. *Director:* Christopher Nolan. *Screenplay:* Christopher Nolan. *Director of Photography:* Christopher Nolan. *Editor:* Gareth Heal and Christopher Nolan. *Music:* David Julyan. *Fight Choreographer:* Darren Ormandy. *Sound:* Ivan Cornell, David Lloyd, David Julyan, and James Wheeler. *Art Director:* Tristan Martin. *Special Make-up:* Miranda Gunning. *Running time:* 69 minutes. *MPAA Rating:* Not Rated.

CAST: Jeremy Theobald (Young Man); Alex Haw (Cobb); Lucy Russell (Blonde); John Nolan (Policeman); Dick Bradsell (Bald Guy); Gillian El-Kadi (Home Owner); Jennifer Angel (Waitress); Nicolas Carlotti (Barman); Darren Ormandy (Accountant); Guy Greenway (Heavies); Tassos Stevens (Heavies); Tristan Martin (Man at Bar); Rebecca James (Woman at Bar); Paul Mason (Home Owner's Friend); David Bovill (Home Owner's Husband).

LOS ANGELES TIMES, 6/4/99, Calendar/p. 11, Kevin Thomas

"Following" is a taut, ingenious British neo noir in which its central character is a seedy young man (Jeremy Theobald) living a marginal existence so severe that he becomes obsessed with the act of following people. The intent is not to do them any harm, but simply to learn about their lives. He tells himself he's gathering material for the writing he plans to do, but what he's really doing is trying to fill up a remarkably empty life.

Inevitably, this young man is caught in the act—by another young man, Cobb (Alex Haw), who's well-dressed, confident and determined to confront his follower. Understandably defensive at first, the young man is astonished to discover in Cobb a man who convinces him that he too is a curiosity-filled follower.

But Cobb is soon taking the young man several steps further, introducing him to the thrills of breaking and entering. Cobb for sure has more sinister motives in mind, but writer-director-cinematographer Christopher Nolan keeps us guessing as to what they finally may be. He also makes you feel increasingly repelled by the duo's systematic, ultimately obscene-seeming invasion of other people's privacy.

Meanwhile, the young man meets a cool, well-dressed blond (Lucy Russell) who has a nicely furnished apartment. She seems to be a no-illusions dame looking out for No. 1—straight out of '40s Hollywood noir. Nolan plays mischievously with the plot he has so deftly set up, moving back and forth in time and mood, alternately revealing and concealing information, as if he were toying with a kaleidoscope. As tension builds steadily we begin to feel ever more keenly that the young man is getting in over his head. But into what and why?

"Following," which Nolan shot as well as wrote and directed, is a black-and-white B-movie made with an intricate, almost claustrophobic intensity. As a psychological mystery it plays persuasively if not profoundly. Nolan relishes the sheer nastiness he keeps stirred up, unabated for 70 minutes. You can, too, provided you don't ask more of it.

NEW STATESMAN, 11/8/99, p. 44, Jonathan Romney

To say that Christopher Nolan's *Following* is a quiet, discreet sort of pleasure is in no way to belittle it. I don't mean it's just a clever low-budget British independent thriller. I mean it's a film genuinely on the margins of things, a film that operates stealthily, deviously, along the lines of a covert mission.

It was shot on film for a remarkably low budget (reputedly for an initial £3,500), at weekends only, with a cast who had full-time jobs, and using ordinary, familiar London locations. It also seems to have circumvented the British media grapevine—for a considerable time before its release here, the film has been building a reputation on the international festival circuit. It's somehow appropriate for such an elusive venture that its place of origin should be the last place it's heard of.

Here's the pitch. A young man—no name, of course—is telling his story to some confessor or authority figure. He explains that he used to follow people at random in the street, just out of curiosity, having nothing better to do, and out of a vague ambition to be a writer. We watch this dishevelled, nervous would-be Bohemian (Jeremy Theobald) trail through the streets, and hear him tell his tale in voice-over, in a droning, uncertain um-er tone. We know things are bound to go wrong—and sure enough, we see him lying on the ground, hair trimmed, clean-shaven, wearing a suit, but with rubber gloves stuffed in his mouth. We make the connection—we've already seen gloved hands handling a box of objects at the start—but whose hands, and whose objects, and why the suit suddenly? We notch up the first set of unanswered questions and move on. The questions, naturally, accumulate.

The young man is caught out by the man he's been following, a confident sharp-suited smoothie (Alex Flaw) who announces himself as Cobb. He's a burglar. If our man really fancies himself as a writer, he should tag along and find out how it's done. So he gets involved. Then he meets a mysterious femme fatale, credited only as the Blonde: she's played with cool wryness by Lucy Russell, as the kind of platinum vamp who hasn't really haunted London since Ruth Ellis's day. She's involved with some sort of underworld heavy. And so the plot thickens—except that for every thickening, there's an unravelling, too, and we're caught in a constant to and fro, as Nolan keeps explaining a little more, and providing more narrative clues to make us backtrack and reconfigure our guesses so far.

Nolan's method is to cut disconcertingly from one narrative strand to another, flouting chronology in a trimmer, less impressionistic version of the Nicolas Roeg manner. The story is about following, remember—we're following the convoluted story of a man following his unwitting targets. In fact, his following ends early on, when he breaks the one rule—never follow the same person twice—that would have kept him out of these people's lives. But this is also a self-reflexive parable of reading and writing, as the best detective stories are. If we hope to follow this scrambled narrative, we have to rewrite it for ourselves from the diffuse scraps that Nolan provides. The hero tries to write his life into the shape of a thriller, but there's always the suspicion that he's being manipulated, that someone else is writing his story for him. And indeed, just when we think we've written the intrigue into some plausible cause -and-effect shape, Nolan pulls his final twists (thick and fast in the last ten minutes) and reveals that we've really been watching another story altogether.

Following is a genuine anomaly: a black and white London thriller that's very much of the moment with its no-budget aesthetic, yet oddly timeless. We know we're in the present, but the narrative harks back to film noir archetypes, while the edgy, seedy feel reminded me of some 1970s and 1980, British cinema—notably Chris Petit's half-forgotten but influential *Radio On* (1979), which similarly appropriated familiar locations to disorienting effect. Londoners will recognise most of the locations in *Following*, but Nolan shoots London as only foreign directors normally do—avoiding the landmarks, splicing in everyday locations and reassembling them into a maze as exotic and baffling as the story itself. It's not just a street-level maze, either, but delves into basements and ranges over rooftops. This London, says Cobb, is "full of dead spaces"—like the story itself, you're bound to conclude. But the way Nolan turns matter-of-fact urban geography into an ominous, evocative dream-space is right in the tradition of the early New Wave's Paris or the New York of Kubrick's *Killer's Kiss*.

The house-of-cards structure means that once you've reassembled the shuffled pack and the pay-off comes, the story is perilously close to resembling a mere *Tale of the Unexpected,* told with flagrantly generic elements—fall guy, villain, vamp. But that's partly the point: to confront avantgarde methods with the narrative certainties of the British crime tradition (there's a faint musty whiff of the two Edgars, Wallace and Lustgarten). The result is powerfully strange, all the more satisfying for the way it quietly delivers its punchline. Nolan and his cast are terrific finds: I wouldn't normally say this to struggling artists, but they might want to give up their day jobs.

NEW YORK POST, 4/2/99, p. 46, Thelma Adams

"Following" is destined for a big following. It's a fabulous poison pill, a sleek, taut, black-and-white mystery that's all lean, no fat.

English writer/director Christopher Nolan displays an uncanny sense of confidence for a feature debut. He stalks a shaggy, aspiring writer (Jeremy Theobald) with a peculiar hobby: following, or shadowing, strangers in the London streets.

What begins as a stark, Kafkaesque confession of a down-at-the-heels obsessive becomes an elegantly plotted puzzler that slinks forward and switches back on its trail like a fugitive shaking a police tail.

While the writer vows that he's only stalking random strangers to satisfy his curiosity, he soon tracks two regular targets: handsome, nattily dressed Cobb (Alex Haw) and a curvy gangster's dish known as the blonde (Lucy Russell).

From the icily confident Cobb the writer learns the delicious pleasures of breaking and entering, extending his voyeurism to new realms. The dame-in-distress offers the scribe a dangerous escape from his lonely little room into the chambers of her boudoir and the alleys of the criminal underworld.

The writer hardly realizes that as he pursues, so he is pursued. "Following" is more than a Hitchcockian meditation on voyeurism as the cineaste's obsession; it's about how easily we can be manipulated by greed, lust and loneliness into actions of which we never considered ourselves capable.

In the end, while we may never crack a safe or a stranger's skull, or slip a noose gently over our own heads, we understand how the writer without a single original story to his name would become enmeshed in Nolan's exquisite mess.

NEWSDAY, 4/2/99, Part II/p. B11, John Anderson

Picking people at random off the streets of London and following them wherever they lead, the footloose writer-to-be Bill (Jeremy Theobald) thinks he's researching characters and/or indulging a harmless hobby. But when he's confronted by Cobb (Alex Haw), one of his picks and an accomplished burglar, benign voyeurism takes on ominous overtones.

One of those films in which every element seems in sync, "Following," the debut by Christopher Nolan, qualifies as a state-of-the-art indie: dovetail plot lines, crisp handheld black-and-white cinematography, unknown actors, all of whom acquit themselves beautifully, and oblique allusions to filmmaking itself—the Cobb-Bill relationship symbolizes little if not the failure of art to equal life. There's also a sense of archness about it all, an acknowledgement that we're looking at familiar things with a slant—the fun-house mirror effect of the purposely warped perspective.

First, however, "Following" works as a thriller—a modulated thriller, but a thriller—whose structure is as engaging as its plot.

We keep seeing Bill in different guises—long-haired and goateed, short-haired and schoolboy-suited, or schoolboy-suited and badly bruised—the results of a beating he gets, or has gotten, or will get, from someone somewhere.

Whether it's from Cobb himself or the gangster boyfriend of his new blond girlfriend (Lucy Russell)—whose flat he and Cobb have robbed—or some other malcontent we've yet to meet is never clear until all the narrative pieces coalesce. And we're eager that they do.

What Bill definitely gets from Cobb is a tutorial in burglary technique and human nature. Bill wants to write about people? Cobb knows all about it—he's far less interested in monetary gain than in the human drama his break-ins incite, as he steals or upsets personal items, plants women's panties in a pair of husband's pants, or steals one earring while leaving the mate behind. His motivations are provocation and human response—he is, in other words, an artist.

"You take it away," he says of some victim's possession, "you show them what they had." He's also Bill's most interesting character, although Bill's not aware of it, or of anything else that's brewing about him.

Cobb, as played by Alex Haw, is also the best thing in the film—the way he surreptitiously shakes a beer can before handing it to Bill, for instance, is just a delicious bit of malicious mischief. But Jeremy Theobald is also fine in the less gratifying role of Bill. And Lucy Russell, who had never made a film before, is a gem and seems so familiar in her hard-shell sexiness that she might have been on screen forever. She is, however, according to her bio, the personnel assistant at an Austrian bank in the City of London. With "Following," apparently even the cast list has surprise endings and weird twists.

SIGHT AND SOUND, 12/99, p. 47, David Thompson

London, the present. Bill, a would-be writer, confesses to the police about his obsession with following complete strangers picked at random. Flashbacks reveal the following events.

When a suave young man called Cobb, whom Bill is following, confronts him, Bill is drawn into Cobb's obsession with casual burglary. Cobb's greatest thrill is uncovering victims' secrets. Bill visits a club and tries to chat up a blonde woman who warns him the manager is her jealous former lover. She tells him she was burgled the day before. Another day, Bill visits the blonde in her smart flat and they begin an affair. It was Bill and Cobb who burgled her flat, inspiring Bill to follow her. Unknown to Bill, Cobb is actually the blonde's current lover. Together they are framing Bill for the murder of an old lady during one of Cobb's burglaries.

While trying to retrieve some photographs the manager was using to blackmail the blonde, Bill kills a man with a hammer who interrupts him. Bill meets up with Cobb and tells him about the blonde, and Cobb responds with violence. The blonde tells Bill he's being framed by Cobb. Bill goes to the police. Later, Cobb tells her he's really working for the manager: his true plan is to frame Bill as her murderer by killing her with the hammer from the club. Bill learns from the police there was no old lady, the blonde has been found dead, and Cobb has removed all traces of his existence.

In a time long ago when a Wim Wenders film created a sense of anticipation, some may recall the subtle playfulness of *The American Friend* (1977), which celebrated within its Patricia Highsmith murder plot the cinematic *double entendres* of 'framing' and 'set up'. A comparable spirit of gamesmanship permeates Christopher Nolan's remarkable debut film which, like Wenders' movie, occupies a precarious no-man's land between popular thriller and art film. Nolan may have drawn inspiration from performance artist Sophie Calle's infamous shadowing of strangers, or even her fictive equivalent in Paul Auster's novel *Leviathan*. But it's just a starting point for his own exhilarating maze of games and deceptions which keeps the spectator guessing throughout *Following*'s relatively brief running time. Nolan keenly exploits cinema's narrative potential, busily flipping scenes so actions teasingly precede exposition in a way that hasn't been seen here since Nicolas Roeg's *Bad Timing* (1980).

Nolan's emotional aim may not be as high as Roeg's, but then his film doesn't pose the latter's painful, existential questions. Nor were Nolan's resources anything like as considerable. Shooting over weekends on 16mm black-and-white stock with what appears to be a minimum of lighting, Nolan shows a natural talent for a fluent handheld aesthetic. His unfamiliar cast acquit themselves well in a simple naturalistic style. Nothing distracts the viewer from the tantalising intrigue set up here, a precise justification of the lean (as opposed to Lean) quality of the film.

As such directors as Jacques Rivette (in *Celine and Julie Go Boating*, 1974) and James Toback (in *Fingers*, 1977) have demonstrated, there's a lot of mileage to be gained from having your main character follow a mysterious object of desire. But what they could accomplish in the irrepressibly cinematic Paris and New York, Nolan has managed to pull off in the usually intractable cityscape of London. Again, paucity of budget has presumably led him to reduce his locations to a series of sparsely populated café, clubs and flats, and from these Nolan has created a credible world of mysterious, disquieting corners with more than a tang of Godard's vision of Paris in *Alphaville* (1965).

To its credit, the film's gestures towards cerebral notions of narrative are not laboured. To continue the French references, *Following* echoes such Alain Robbe-Grillet films as *Trans-Europ-Express* (1966) in the way Bill's own writing constructs the plot in which he is enmeshed. If anything, the depiction of Bill's sweaty assaults on a Remington and his obsessive pursuit of material for stories parallels Mike Hodges and Paul Mayersberg's recent *Croupier*, another outsider film which took a similar delight in games and bluffs. Films like these, made in defiance of televisual and theatrical styles, occupy an awkward position in the prevailing consumer-led New British Cinema. Nolan has already gone on to make a film for HBO, apparently without compromising the storytelling dexterity displayed here. Will he be another talent allowed to wander far off the mean street of Wardour?

VILLAGE VOICE, 4/6/99, p. 130, Michael Atkinson

Perhaps the best you could say about Christopher Nolan's little-Brit-indie-that-could,*Following*, is that it trucks in ideas thick with tarnish (post-Hitch voyeurism, the romantic schmo caught between a bruised femme and a sadistic crime lord, the peeling of onionlike layers of double cross, etc.) and still comes off goosey with sweat and anxiety. Nolan's a first-timer, and his movie is half hand-held kitchen-sink realism (shot in moody black and white) and half curlicue plotline that, as subsequent layers of betrayal are exposed and its jigsawed time line begins to form a whole picture, cloys with archness. Moan as we might about ex-film students cranking out résumé movies, the Quentin Virus continues to spread. It's too bad we cannot somehow, mandate that young directors need to spend serious time with real criminals before being allowed to make a postnoir crime indie. You can bet the films would be very different, and far fewer. *Following* is modest and engaging, but in being strenuously clever, it surrenders any dibs it might have on being relevant or original.

Following starts with Bill (Jeremy Theobald, who also coproduced) confessing to what may be a shrink about his penchant for shadowing randomly selected people through their day, a pastime that evolved from wannabe-writer's research to a wasting compulsion. Taking the peeper paradigm to the streets, Nolan and his hero refreshingly shed the typical masturbating-in-the-dark-bedroom dynamic, and with it its familiar cinematic connections. But Nolan hasn't any other core ideas on hand and, at any rate, gives the scenario's psychosocial potential short shrift. Almost immediately into this thankfully brisk (70-minute) yarn, Theobald's shady creep trails after Cobb (Alex Haw), a polished professional burglar who turns the tables. The two fall in together and start robbing flats, less for the valuables than for a chance to invade and explore other people's lives. ("You take it away," Cobb says happily, "and you show them what they had.") The film's fashionable leaps back and forward in time have us understand that Bill gets involved with a gangster's bitter girlfriend (Lucy Russell), changes his appearance to match Cobb's, and eventually gets the crap kicked out of him.

Nothing, as they, say, is what it seems. Quaintly duping both the audience and his hero, Nolan misses his opportunity to explore the fusty emotional kinks in his story. Fittingly, Theobald reeks of unexplored neuroses, but Haw, looking like Rupert Everett's corporate lawyer twin and masticating his lines like George Sanders, camps it up in a role that's essentially a slick screenwriter's unlikely invention. *Following* asks to be take seriously, but it's just a riff.

Also reviewed in:
CHICAGO TRIBUNE, 8/6/99, Friday/p. Q, John Petrakis
NEW YORK TIMES, 4/2/99, p. E24, Janet Maslin
VARIETY, 5/11-17/98, p. 67, Dennis Harvey

FOOLISH

An Artisan Entertainment release of a No Limit Films presentation of a Shooting Star production. *Executive Producer:* Master P. *Producer:* Jonathan Heuer. *Director:* Dave Meyers. *Screenplay:* Master P. *Director of Photography:* Steve Gainer. *Editor:* Chris Davis. *Music:* Wendy Melvoin and Lisa Coleman. *Sound:* Jon Ailetcher. *Casting:* Megalarge. *Production Designer:* Chuck Conner. *Art Director:* Brian Livesay. *Set Designer:* Michelle Fornabi. *Set Decorator:* Tim Colohan. *Costumes:* Jhane Isaacs. *Running time:* 110 minutes. *MPAA Rating:* R.

CAST: Eddie Griffin (Miles "Foolish" Waise); Master P. (Quentin "Fifty Dollah" Waise); Amy Peterson (Desiree); Frank Sivero (Giovanni); Daphnee Lynn Duplaix (Charisse); Jonathan Banks (Numbers); Andrew Dice Clay (El Dorado Ron); Marla Gibbs (Odetta Waise); Sven-Ole Thorsen (Paris); Bill Nunn (Jimmy Beck); Bill Duke (Studio Producer); AJ Johnson (Himself).

LOS ANGELES TIMES, 4/12/99, Calendar/p. 4, Gene Seymour

When comedian Miles "Foolish" Waise (Eddie Griffin) gets on stage, no one wants him to leave. Even the most uptight-looking people in the house protest when he's forced by club management to curtail his nasty, fire-breathing routines so that other, lesser talents can get heckled.

That's the way you feel watching Griffin whenever he gets a head of steam going. Though he shares top billing with rapper-mogul Master P, "Foolish" is Griffin's vehicle. It's a rickety, misbegotten vehicle to be sure. But Griffin floors it, pushes it well beyond its capacity to cruise or stay on the road.

It's only when you don't see him performing or cutting up that you wonder just what "Foolish" is or why it was made. On the one hand, there's this plot involving Griffin and Master P as two siblings who are each chasing a Grail; Foolish in the comedy clubs, P's Fifth Dollah on the streets, doing business with such shady characters as Numbers (Jonathan Banks) and El Dorado Ron (a saturnine, surprisingly scary Andrew Dice Clay).

Then there's some conflict between the brothers over a woman named (honest!) Desiree (Amy Petersen), once Foolish's girlfriend, now romantically involved with Fifth and trying to get a showcase for Foolish that will make him a star on his terms. All of which is seasoned with anecdotes of family strife, bathos, threats of violence, etc. No need to detail all this stuff because, frankly, it's a mess.

It's Griffin who draws your attention, making everything around him hazy and inconsequential. He risks making himself look, well, foolish, especially when he loses his temper for reasons both good (defending himself against Hollywood sharpies who want him to compromise) and bad (smashing his own car to get back at his lover).

At times, he shows himself capable of big-league movie acting, especially when his character slides into the void following the death of his grandmother (Marla Gibbs). He can even be a little frightening when he shows Foolish straddling the edge of sanity. As anyone who's seen him live will tell you, the brother does have an insatiable appetite for nervous laughter.

Even "Foolish's" more dismal patches are redeemed toward the climax by a riveting autobiographical routine that has more poignancy, suspense and rich characterization in its 5 to 10 minutes than almost anything that came before it. You have to believe that Griffin's indomitable spirit will, sooner or later, push him toward far better movies than this one.

NEW YORK POST, 4/14/99, p. 21, Rod Dreher

"Foolish" is the name of the lead character in this sewer-mouthed comedy, but it's a good prediction of how you'll feel after having forked over good money to sit through the torrent of humor-free bilge erupting from the mouth of its star, comedian Eddie Griffin.

The movie is little more than a showcase for Griffin's stand-up act, which is as drearily unoriginal as it is repulsive.

Griffin plays stand-up comic Foolish Waise (get it, har har?), who cracks the room up night after night at a comedy club but can't seem to break big. He's offered a part playing a drag queen in a studio film, but rejects it as beneath his dignity.

You'd think it would be hard for a man whose entire routine consists of making racial and genital jokes in the crudest language imaginable to have much dignity. But doggone it, this potty mouth has pride.

Foolish is also bedeviled by a drinking problem, and a penchant for being cruel to his live-in girlfriend (he also chases her with a baseball bat).

In a weak subplot, his brother Fifty (rapper Master P, also credited with the screenplay) struggles to get free of his Mafia job.

Will Fifty trump the mob? Will Foolish become the next Martin Lawrence, and do so on his own terms? The more pressing question: Will this movie ever get funny?

The answer is yes, in the last five minutes, when Griffin at long last wisecracks about something other than sex. For example, here he is on white people's enthusiasm for dangerous pastimes: "Y'all pay to jump out of airplanes! You won't find a drunk n---- jumpin' off a porch!"

He also offers a theory of meteorological retribution for slavery that's pretty hilarious, and a riotous observation about racist space aliens. But that's about it.

Also reviewed in:
CHICAGO TRIBUNE, 4/15/99, Tempo/p. 2, Allan Johnson
NEW YORK TIMES, 4/10/99, p. B17, Anita Gates
VARIETY, 4/12-18/99, p. 65, Oliver Jones

FOR LOVE OF THE GAME

A Universal Pictures release of a Beacon Pictures/TIG Productions/Mirage Enterprises production. *Executive Producer:* Ron Bozman and Marc Abraham. *Producer:* Armyan Bernstein and Amy Robinson. *Director:* Sam Raimi. *Screenplay:* Dana Stevens. *Based on the novel by:* Michael Shaara. *Director of Photography:* John Bailey. *Editor:* Eric L. Beason and Arthur Coburn. *Music:* Basil Poledouris. *Music Editor:* Dick Bernstein and Curtis Roush. *Sound:* Ed Novick, Steve Maslow, Gregg Landaker and (music) Tim Boyle. *Sound Editor:* Kelly Cabral and Wylie Stateman. *Casting:* Lynn Kressel. *Production Designer:* Neil Spisak. *Art Director:* Jim Feng and Steve Arnold. *Set Designer:* Andrew Menzies and Sally Thornton. *Set Decorator:* Carolyn Cartwright and Karen O'Hara. *Set Dresser:* Joann Atwood, Donna Drinkwater, Gregory N. Rocco, Steven Emmett Adams, Bruce Bellamy, Nelson Bush, Debbie Canfield, Scott Canfield, T. Kelly Canfield, Ken Krammerer, Mark Little, Patrice Longo, Marco Martin Del Campo, Edward McCarthy, Ray Murphy, Michael S. O'Donnell, Mike Parmelee, Chris Pascuzzo, and Jennifer R. Raftery. *Special Effects:* Mark Bero and Al Di Sarro. *Visual Effects:* Peter Donen. *Costumes:* Judianna Makovsky. *Make-up:* Bernadette Mazur and Kris Evans. *Make-up (Kevin Costner):* F.X. Perez. *Make-up (Kelly Preston):* Joseph A. Campayno. *Stunt Coordinator:* Christopher Doyle. *Running time:* 140 minutes. *MPAA Rating:* PG-13.

CAST: Kevin Costner (Billy Chapel); Kelly Preston (Jane Aubrey); John C. Reilly (Gus Sinski); Jena Malone (Heather); Brian Cox (Gary Wheeler); J.K. Simmons (Frank Perry); Vin Skully (Himself); Steve Lyons (Himself); Carmine D. Giovinazzo (Ken Strout); Bill Rogers (Davis Birch); Hugh Ross (Mike Udall); Domenick Lombardozzi (Tow Truck Driver); Arnetia Walker (Airport Bartender); Larry Joshua (Yankee Fan in Bar); DETROIT TIGERS: Greer Barnes (Mickey Hart); Scott Bream (Brian Whitt); Jose Mota (Jose Garcia); Earl Johnson (Marcus Ransom); Chris Lemonis (Lee Giordano); Jesse Ibarra (Dennis Skinner); Pedro Swann (Juan Vasquez); Michael Rivera (Jimmy Pena); David Eiland (Releif Pitcher); Joe Lisi (Pete); Jim Colborn (3rd Base Coach); Michael Borzello (Catcher Double); Paul Bradshaw (Tiger Pitching Coach); Gene Kirley (Tiger Bench Coach); NEW YORK YANKEES: Michael Papajohn (Sam Tuttle); John Darjean, Jr. (Jonathan Warble); Donzell McDonald (Lenny Howell); Scott Pose (Matt Crane); Vick Brown (Jesus Cabrillo); Chris Ashby (Nardini); Bill Masse (Mike Robinson); Mike Buddie (Jack Spellman); Eric Knowles (Ted Franklin); Ricky Ledee (Ruiz); Juan Nieves (Francisco Delgado); Augie Garrido (Yankee Manager); Rick Reed (Home Plate Umpire); Rich Garcia (1st Base Umpire); Jerry Crawford (2nd Base Umpire); Robert Leo Shepard (Yankee Stadium Announcer); Eddie Layton (Yankee Stadium Organist); Robinson Frank Adu (Locker Room Attendant); T. Sean Ferguson, Victor Colicchio, and David Mucci (Hecklers); Jacob Reynolds (Wheeler's Nephew); Maurice Shrog (Yankee Stadium Usher); Karen Williams (Kisha Birch); Tracy Middendorf (Blonde Player's Wife); William Newman (Fitch); P.J. Barry (Waldorf Doorman); Frank Girardeau (Waldorf Bellhop); Caterina Zapponi (Waldorf Singer); Monty Alexander (Waldorf Pianist); Daniel Dae Kim (ER Doctor); Judith Drake (ER Nurse); Bill Vincent (X-Ray Technician); Billy V. Costner (Billy's Father); Sharon Rae Costner (Billy's Mother); Mark Thomason (Billy's Father, Early Years); Laura Cayouette (Masseuse); Christopher Cousins (Ian); Ted Raimi and Michael Emerson (Gallery Doormen); Shelly Desai (Taxi Driver); Lucinda Faraldo (Airline Ticket Agent); Ed Morgan (Man at Café); Brian Donald Hickey and Tracy Perry (Autograph Seekers).

CHRISTIAN SCIENCE MONITOR, 9/17/99, p. 15, David Sterritt

Many still think of Kevin Costner as the action hero of adventures—like "Waterworld" and westerns such as "Wyatt Earp," but lately the handsome star has been positioning himself as king of the male weepies. "Message in a Bottle" pulled out most of the sentimental stops, and "For Love of the Game" pulls out the rest. Moviegoers headed for this emotion-filled sports saga should stuff at least a dozen handkerchiefs into their baseball mitts.

Costner plays Billy Chapel, a 40-year-old pitcher with a passel of problems. His team is being sold, his throwing arm isn't what it used to be, and his girlfriend is pulling out of their relationship. The movie alternates between the ballfield, where Billy finds himself in the most amazing game of his life, and flashbacks to his love affair, which now appears to be in its last inning.

"For Love of the Game" is designed for baby-boom audiences, allowing them to shed empathetic tears over an aging sports star while enjoying the youthful virility of a movie star still in his prime. Like a contest between unequal teams, though, the story is wildly uneven. You needn't be a sports fan to get caught up in the ballpark scenes, which build a remarkable degree of suspense and sympathy. And you needn't be a hardhearted skeptic to find the romantic scenes badly overdone, from Kelly Preston's too-cute performance to the heavy-handed dialogue and syrupy music.

It's surprising to find so much schmaltz in a picture by Sam Raimi, who directed the "Evil Dead" thrillers as well as "A Simple Plan," one of last year's more subtle dramas. But the excesses of "For Love of the Game" probably won't stop Costner admirers, baseball fans, and romance buffs from storming the box office. It's a second-string film likely to become a first-string hit.

LOS ANGELES TIMES, 9/17/99, Calendar/p. 1, Kenneth Turan

Do you believe that the pitcher's mound is "the loneliest spot in the world"? Do you consider "The Kid From Tomkinsville" the greatest novel ever written? When an athlete says the only time his heart's been truly broken was when his team lost the pennant in 1987, do you nod your head in sympathy? "For Love of the Game" has your name on it.

Earnest enough to win the Gee Whiz triple crown, this reverential look at the game of baseball worships so passionately at the shrine of our National Pastime that it makes "The Natural" seem as dark and gritty as "8MM." Yet because it's been directed in an almost willfully old-fashioned way by the unlikely Sam ("The Evil Dead") Raimi, when "For Love of the Game" sticks close to the mound, those who have even a small soft spot for baseball's soothing rhythms will be hard-pressed to resist it.

Helping matters considerably was the decision to cast Kevin Costner as pitcher Billy Chapel, the Detroit Tigers' "great veteran right-hander" who has his whole life pass in front of him as he throws what may be the game of his career before a hostile Yankee Stadium crowd.

Of course, given his success in "Bull Durham" and "Field of Dreams," putting Costner in a baseball movie does not qualify as a major league risk. Yet even if the choice was obvious, the actor rewards it by giving one of his best performances. Laconic and iconic, able to lend a measure of credibility to the corniest dilemmas, Costner is intrinsically convincing as a star athlete, and it's pleasant to notice how he's been able to improve his work within his specific range.

Adapted from the Michael Shaara novella by Dana Stevens, "For Love of the Game" is at its best when it's on the field with Billy, listening to his mind work as he faces the Yankee lineup. Consulting with veteran catcher Gus Sinski (John C. Reilly) and carefully deciding what pitch will work for what batter in which circumstances, Billy artfully maneuvers himself into a shot at a perfect game.

Clearly a baseball fan, director Raimi (known for his "Evil Dead" horror trilogy and last year's "A Simple Plan" and, one would have erroneously thought, without a sentimental bone in his body) knows how to stage the on-field action so the hits and fielding chances have at least a whiff of reality about them.

If baseball is the most successful part of "For Love of the Game," romance is its least satisfying. For of the things that triggers Billy's Yankee Stadium reveries, aside from the news that the Tigers are being sold and he might be traded for the first time in his 19-year career, is a crisis with his longtime girlfriend Jane Aubrey (Kelly Preston).

She's a beautiful New York writer who's told him on the morning of the game that she's taking that job in London, leaving that very day in fact. "You don't need me," she tells him, flinging the words in his face romance-novel style, and he wonders, as the game progresses, if that could be true.

Sitting in the dugout inning after inning, Billy reflects back on his cute-meet with Jane, helping her with her broken car on a New York highway, and on the twists and turns of their five-year relationship, which starts as an oh-so-adult "don't ask, don't tell" kind of affair and ends in nothing but tears, tears, tears. "You are such a guy, you are the ultimate guy," Jane says at one point (truer words were never spoken) intimating that a guy of the regular variety would be enough for her.

Costner and Preston have an acceptable amount of chemistry, but these romantic shenanigans are not involving in the slightest. But while writer Stevens ("City of Angels" was her last credit) has an unfortunate fondness for "my heart leapt in my chest" dramaturgy, her script is actually a marked improvement over Shaara's paper-thin novella.

Though his brilliant Civil War novel "The Killer Angels" (glimpsed at one point as Billy's in-flight reading) was the deserved winner of the Pulitzer Prize, "For Love of the Game" was not published during the author's life and only discovered after his death by his son Jeff. It's clumsily written and so devoid of usable personal incident that if not for Stevens' shrewd addition of events and characters (like a daughter for Jane, well-played by Jena Malone) there would be no film to speak of.

But not even Stevens' plotting and the actors' efforts can hide the fact that all of this film's usable emotion is invested in its baseball sequences. The romance between people in "For Love of the Game" is awkwardly handled, playing like the afterthought Jane fears she's been in the pitcher's life. The only love that really matters here is the one between a man and the game he's played for a lot longer than five years.

Making the baseball sequences that much more effective is the constant voice-over presence of Vin Scully, the consensus pick for the best play-by-play announcer of our time. Scully's impeccable vocalizing, his innate sense of drama, adds a much-needed touch of classicism to the proceedings, reminding us, as this film is desperate to, what the sport's image was before umpires went on strike and agents controlled the game. Intended as a love note to baseball's old-fashioned aspects, "For Love of the Game" also ends up as an unintentional tribute to one of the greatest on-air voices the game has seen.

NEW YORK, 9/27/99, p. 80, Peter Rainer

When Kevin Costner starred as over-the-hill minor-league catcher Crash Davis in Ron Shelton's *Bull Durham*, he seemed to get it just right: the weariness and the regret and the prickly clubhouse jocksmanship. Crash was a romantic creation—an also-ran with the soul of a contender and an ever-ready ardor for the sport—but Costner didn't fuzzy up the iconography. He was playing a ballplayer, not a Lancelot or a Byron. It was, I believe, Roy Blount Jr. who said that one should never forget that baseball is a game played by guys who spend a lot of their time out in the field spitting and scratching their nuts. This startling insight is what's missing from most baseball movies—and from much baseball writing, too, which tends to wax lyrical over the Astroturf of yesteryear. It's certainly missing from the new Costner baseball movie *For Love of the Game*, which seems designed to undo all the good will he built up as Crash Davis. The film comes across like the un-*Bull Durham:* Every woozy cliché that Shelton and Costner refrained from has been given pride of place here.

Costner is playing Billy Chapel, a twenty-year pitching veteran of the lowly Detroit Tigers who is about to have his last hurrah hurling against the pennant-contending Yankees. Note the spelling of his last name. Couldn't the filmmakers at least have made it Chappell? Billy worships at the altar of baseball; the ballpark is his cathedral. Shortly before the big game, he's informed by the Tigers' departing owner (Brian Cox) that the team is to be sold to a corporate group intent on trading Billy to the Giants. For the owner, an old-fashioned type whose family held on to the team for generations, corporate muggery and big business have stunk up the sport, but Billy still thinks it's a great game, at least when his shoulder isn't hurting. A future Hall of Famer on the skids, he's got a lot on his mind on this day in Yankee Stadium, not the least of which is: Should he quit or go with the trade? The Yankees fans—who are portrayed, seemingly without exception, as a gaggle of hooligans—razz Billy as he stares up at the clouds and ponders his life.

The pondering gets pretty ponderous. Director Sam Raimi and his screenwriter, Dana Stevens, adapting the novel by Michael Shaara, go in for a creaky and confusing back-and-forth flashback structure that periodically retraces, mostly through photo stills and movie clips, Billy's ascension from tyke to Little Leaguer to major-league ace. Since many of the stills are actually of the young Costner, and since he uses his real-life parents, in at least one brief wordless flashback, to stand in for Billy's, the self-annunciatory tone gets a bit thick. (It would feel that way even if you didn't pick up on the personal connection.) Costner has a way of being both aw-shucks and holier-than-thou in the same pass; he canonizes his regular-guyness. *For Love of the Game* has the surfeit of saintly Costner close-ups we've come to expect from many of his films, even the ones he doesn't direct. (It must be a contractual thing.) The close-ups here say to us, *Feel his pain.*

Since *For Love of the Game* aspires to be more than just a baseball movie, the pain on view isn't really the kind where you stick your elbow in an ice bucket to make it feel better (though we see that too). Heartbreak is the film's reigning emotion, and the heartbreaker is Billy's on-and-off love interest, Jane Aubrey (Kelly Preston), a fashion-magazine writer and single mother of a teenage daughter (Jena Malone) who tells Billy before the Yankees game that she's taking a job in London because she realizes he doesn't *need* her the way she needs him. The filmmakers are in the business of hallowing baseball, but they also want us to know that winning doesn't mean much if you have no one to love. This is a crummy trick to play on the audience, or at least on the audience that isn't rustling for hankies. The whoop and holler of the sport, and even the prospect of a perfect game from Billy, get doused in weepiness.

The numerous flashback sequences between Billy and Jane replay their courtship and disaffection, creating a nimbus around this oddly solitary man figuring out the fundamentals of life away from the baseball diamond. He's a gentleman with Jane: Not only does he refrain from scratching his nuts and spitting, but he also keeps pretty quiet about the astronomical salary he must be pulling down and the groupies he's undoubtedly bagged. On the outs from his one true love, he stands forlornly in the rain looking up into her apartment window, like Barbara Stanwyck in *Stella Dallas*. He gives brisk inspirational talks to his error-prone teammates, and they repay his healing by performing miracles for him in Yankee Stadium.

I can't think of a modern-day Hollywood leading man who has more misjudged his true talents than Costner. After all these years, he's still trying to be the next Gary Cooper. What he may not acknowledge is that, like him, Cooper began his career with some mettle and sexual energy and then mythologized himself into blandness. Costner is trying to will himself into being a classic; his idea of a movie star is someone who projects a humorless, role-model rectitude. Why else would he keep starring in movies like *The Postman* and *Message in a Bottle* and, now, *For Love of the Game?* It's only when Costner's romantic looks are salted with moxie, with humor, that he shines. The self-ennobling Costner is not someone I care about: the New Age white man of *Dances With Wolves;* the sanctimonious savior of the People in *Robin Hood: Prince of Thieves* who sounded like the surfer dude of Sherwood Forest. I care about the Costner of *Silverado*, with his cackle and spunk; or the Crash Davis of *Bull Durham* romancing Susan Sarandon or throwing a tantrum on the field and kicking up dirt; or the escaped con in *A Perfect World* with wanness imprinted in his eyes. In *Tin Cup*, playing a has-been pro golfer, he had a slanginess and a spirit that kept the rue bouncy. Costner can be taken seriously when he doesn't take himself too seriously. That almost never happens in *For Love of the Game.*

NEW YORK POST, 9/17/99, p. 43, Rod Dreher

"For Love of the Game" is another two-hours-plus Kevin Costner strikeout, a gassy baseball elegy suffocating in Lite-Rock schmoopiness and Costnerian self-regard. It's "The Postman" on a pitcher's mound.

For love of the God, what is wrong with the once-likable Kevin Costner?

Costner's been in a slump the past few years, so it's not surprising that he would try to jump-start things with a third trip to the diamond ("Bull Durham" and "Field of Dreams" being career high points for the actor).

Unfortunately, the flabby "Game" script, adapted by Dana Stevens from Michael Shaara's novel, plays to Costner's worst instincts. Here he is, the epic hero once again, manfully bearing the weight of the world on his noble shoulders without the consolation of, say, a sense of humor. If you want an Ingmar Bergman-style yuppie baseball movie, look no further.

This time out, Costner is ace Detroit Tigers pitcher Billy Chapel, 40 years old and at the twilight of a brilliant career. His arm's giving out, he's about to be traded by the team's new corporate owners and his girlfriend Jane (Kelly Preston) has left him.

With all this hanging over his head, "Chappy" must take the mound at Yankee Stadium to throw what he knows may be the last game of his life.

"Billy, you've been the heart and soul of this team," someone says, in the first of the movie's many Metaphor Alerts. By the end, game announcer Vin Scully is klaxoning, "He's pitching against time, he's pitching against the future, he's pitching against his own mortality!"

"For Love of the Game" is structured as a series of flashbacks on Billy's five-year relationship with Jane. As the game progresses, we learn how the two met, how their relationship developed and how it went downhill.

Jane is a New York magazine journalist with a palpable wariness about men. They to-and-fro between crises and cuddling, but there's no drama or dynamism to their romance. Handsome Costner is gruff and inexpressive, and Meg Ryan wannabe Preston has the personality of flat Zima.

While struggling to keep an incredible no-hitter going, Billy reflects on what he's lost with Jane, who's headed to a new job and life in London, and why. Could it be that the love of a good woman is more important even than baseball? Given the thoroughgoing shmaltziness of Dana Stevens' screenplay, could it be anything else?

Costner, vain diva that he is, has whined publicly about the cuts Universal imposed on the 140-minute film—they even nipped out an image of Kevvo's wing-wang! Clearly, this was a mercy killing.

NEWSDAY, 9/17/99, Part II/p. B7, Jan Stuart

Top of the eighth. Billy Chapel has only six outs to go before pitching a perfect game for the Detroit Tigers.

Billy is 40, a Methuselah in baseball years. His shoulder is killing him. His personal life is down the drain. Can he pull it off? If he does, will this World Series hero let himself be traded away to another team, or will he throw in the towel after 19 years? The camera closes in. Billy shuts out the crowd noise. Billy winds back his arm. Billy throws.

Only five outs to go. Billy's shoulder is worse. His personal life is still down the drain. Can he pull it off? The camera closes in. Billy shuts out—Quick! Tape the windows. Grab the kitty. Hit the storm cellars. It's another endless Kevin Costner picture! As if we couldn't see it coming. The only sport more lead-footed than baseball, to a camera lens at least, is golf. The only romantic leading man more ham-handed than Kevin Costner is dead (Gary Cooper). Ergo, it makes a certain sense that Costner should spend what's left of his summer years making movies about baseball and golf.

To be fair, the troubles with "For Love of the Game" are not the game itself.

"It's a great game, Mr. Wheeler," says Billy (Costner), defending baseball to the cynical club owner who believes it's all gone to hell in a hand basket. We couldn't agree with Billy more. And cinematographer John Bailey captures all the big-stadium fever with a major-league virtuosity.

But there is the little matter of a love story. As in "Tin Cup" and his best sports flick, "Bull Durham" (sorry, "Field of Dreams" fans), Costner's character sets his sights on a smart, svelte and strong-willed career woman.

The object of Billy's affections is Jane Aubrey (Kelly Preston), a 30-ish divorcee who raises a nettlesome teenager and pays the rent on a fabulous Greenwich Village brownstone apartment by writing articles on lip gloss for Elle magazine. Add resourcefulness to Jane's list of assets.

The modest wrinkle that screenwriter Dana Stevens has added to the formula is that Billy has won Jane's heart at the top of the movie's first inning. No sooner does "For Love of the Game" telescope its hero's entire life behind the opening credits than Billy receives a triple punch: the Tigers owner (the redoubtable Brian Cox) is selling the team and trading Billy away. The salt on the wound: Jane is leaving him for a job in London.

That's as fast as director Sam Raimi operates, and those are the first 15 minutes. For the next two hours, we flashback leisurely through the dewy-eyed hills and dales of Billy and Jane's five-year romance.

Since there has to be an obstacle, we have Jane's reluctance to become just another Chapel groupie, an understandable sensitivity that is stretched to tiresome lengths. The film throws us a second curveball in the person of Jane's precocious daughter Heather (Jena Malone), who explains her mother's neuroses to Billy by saying, "She never had a love story, and now it's like she doesn't believe in it." As someone who has wallowed in "Somewhere in Time" with Christopher Reeve and Jane Seymour more times than I'd care to admit, I would be the first to concede that there is often nothing more satisfying than watching two pretty people romance to pretty music amid pretty surroundings. Period.

However.

The two leads here have prettiness to spare, and Preston (despite occasional attacks of the Meg Ryan giggles) has a tangy good humor to boot. But the push-pull of Jane's emotional frailties and Billy's physical deterioration is too slender a thread on which to hang this protracted and predictable dugout opera.

We may never survive the day the Motion Picture Academy rewarded Costner for his epic "Dances With Wolves" and Costner began to confuse size with significance.

At 135 minutes, "For Love of the Game" is shorter than "The Postman" (177) and "Wyatt Earp" (195) and on a par with "Tin Cup" and "Waterworld. " If this guy is getting paid by the minute, Sammy Sosa should consider renegotiating his contract.

SIGHT AND SOUND, 7/00, p. 44, Andy Richards

Detroit, the present. Billy Chapel is the star pitcher for the Detroit Tigers. The night before he's due to pitch the last game of the season (against the Yankees), Mr Wheeler, the owner of the Tigers, tells Billy that he's selling the team. Wheeler has an option of trading Billy to the Giants, but suggests that he might want to retire. Billy's girlfriend Jane tells him that she is leaving him for a job in London.

Next day, waiting his turn to pitch, Billy reminisces about his five-year relationship with Jane. They first met when he helped her with her broken-down car, and began dating soon after. She overcame her fears that she was perceived as a team groupie. When she came to visit him in Florida, Jane found him sleeping with his masseuse. Later, she asked him to help recover her runaway teenage daughter Heather. They spent more time together. Billy injured his hand, and took his anger out on Jane. Jane began dating her editor.

When pitching on the mound, Bill is ruthlessly focused. Jane, meanwhile, is bombarded with match coverage while waiting for her flight. Billy goes on to pitch a perfect game, before telling Wheeler that he is retiring. Billy goes to the airport, intending to fly to England, but Jane is still there waiting for him.

Baseball films have always been a favourite focus for explorations of American masculinity and they usually treat the game with quasi-mystical awe. The magic diamond is repeatedly envisioned in such films as *The Natural* and *Field Of Dreams* (Kevin Costner's breakthrough film) as a place where fallen men can be redeemed, where fathers and sons can bond in a shared tradition and where the American Dream can find its purest expression. *For Love of the Game,* however, leaves you feeling that the genre has perhaps already touched all its bases. So much so that, in the film's final act, you realise that 40-year-old Billy Chapel's mission to pitch the legendary "perfect game"—an entire line of zeroes on the board—to pitch, in the words of the commentator, "against time, against age, against ending," can only end by embracing well-worn clichés.

For the Love of the Game's complacency is revealed most clearly through its central romance, where the decks are stacked entirely in Chapel's favour. As Billy waits for his turn at the mound, he reflects on his relationship with Jane through a series of crudely cued flashbacks (he fingers a scar on his hand, or smells the leather of his glove). But any feelings he may have about his habitually selfish treatment of Jane are rigorously excluded on the pitch. Billy might be pitching his last game for the Tigers in the full knowledge that the club's owner wants to trade him to the Giants; but even here there's nothing at stake in the idea he should compromise his baseball career to concentrate on his relationship with Jane. Now in his forties, his decision to give up the game stems as much from a desire to retire gracefully and enshrine himself as one of the golden greats, as from a willingness to devote himself more fully to Jane.

Jane meanwhile is constantly asked by Billy to accept him as a baseball player before anything else; her own career ambitions are given short shrift (particularly in a scene which contrasts the pretensions of the New York arts scene with Billy's easy going naturalism). Their relationship is characterised by condescension on his part, and a nauseating deference on hers (she is shocked when he actually suggests spending time together with her and her teenage daughter).

Unsurprisingly, director Sam Raimi struggles to make much of such shallow material. Having made successful departures from the horror genre in which he made his name with the more mainstream films *The Quick and the Dead* and *A Simple Plan*, his involvement in this grating star vehicle is perhaps the most disappointing aspect of *For the Love of the Game:* the Evil Dead are, presumably, turning in their grave.

TIME, 9/20/99, p. 79, Richard Corliss

A perfect game in Yankee Stadium is no big deal these days; two have been pitched in the past 16 months.

But a good baseball movie, that's hard. Kevin Costner was in one of those (*Bull Durham*). In *For Love of the Game* he tries for two, as an aging Detroit Tigers pitcher in what may be his final game—a last shot at perfection.

Costner still twinkles and steams plausibly, but all else about the film is ludicrous. The nattering violins, orgasmic from the first moment, alert you that director Sam Raimi has either no control of the production or no belief in the material. And why should he believe? Dana Stevens' script buries the compelling story of an athlete's career crisis under a no-fun affair he has with a charmless woman (Kelly Preston—big mistake) and a daughter problem that adds 15 minutes of emotional lard. As domestic drama, it's down there with *Stepmom*. And much of the jock stuff will look loony to true fans. Costner has complained that his studio cut the film insensitively to get a softer rating, but what's left is nothing to brag about. If the filmmakers were ballplayers, they'd all be put on waivers.

There is a small, forlorn fraternity that thinks *The Postman*, Costner's widely reviled postapocalyptic romance, is a decent movie, acutely alert to the perils and pleasures of mythmaking. Maybe audiences will forgive Costner for making that noble flop and welcome him back to the baseball-weepie lode he mined in the sappy, canny *Field of Dreams*. (He even plays catch with his dead dad again.) Or perhaps, like this dogged Costner fan, you will simply want to shoot yourself by the third inning.

VILLAGE VOICE, 9/21/99, p. 155, J. Hoberman

[*For Love of the Game* was reviewed jointly with *American Beauty*; see Hoberman's review of that film.]

Also reviewed in:
CHICAGO TRIBUNE, 9/17/99, Friday/p. A, Michael Wilmington
NATION, 10/11/99, p. 36, Stuart Klawans
NEW REPUBLIC, 10/18/99, p. 28, Stanley Kauffmann
NEW YORK TIMES, 9/17/99, p. E14, Lawrence Van Gelder
VARIETY, 9/13-19/99, p. 41, Robert Koehler
WASHINGTON POST, 9/17/99, p. C1, Stephen Hunter
WASHINGTON POST, 9/17/99, Weekend/p. 52, Desson Howe

FORCE MORE POWERFUL, A

A Santa Monica Pictures release of a Peter Ackerman-York Zimmerman production. *Executive Producer:* Dalton Delan and Jack Du Vall. *Producer:* Steve York and Peter Ackerman. *Director:* Steve York. *Screenplay:* Steve York. *Director of Photography:* Giulio Biccari, Peter Pearce, and Dilip Varma. *Editor:* Joseph Wiedenmayer and Anny Lowery Meza. *Music:* John D. Keltonic. *Sound:* Ken Hahn. *Sound Editor:* Brian Cunneff. *Running time:* 110 minutes. *MPAA Rating:* Not Rated.

WITH: Ben Kingsley (Narrator); Devavrat Pathak; Alyque Padamsee; James Lawson; John Lewis; Diane Nash; Mkhuseli Jack; Janet Cherry; Tango Lamani.

NEW YORK POST, 11/19/99, p. 59, Lou Lumenick

"A Force More Powerful" means well, but it's a less-than-compelling documentary about the history of nonviolent resistance movements.

Writer-director Steve York, who has produced documentaries for NBC, PBS and various cable outlets, contrasts Gandhi's tactics in India in the 1930s with Martin Luther King Jr.'s efforts to integrate the South in the 1950s and the anti-apartheid struggle in South Africa.

Complete with soporific narration by Ben Kingsley, the film offers a familiar collection of film clips and talking heads, all too many of them pontificating college professors.

Also reviewed in:
NEW YORK TIMES, 11/19/99, p. E20, Anita Gates
VARIETY, 11/15-21/99, p. 90, Robert Koehler

FORCES OF NATURE

A Dreamworks Pictures release of a Roth/Arnold production. *Producer:* Susan Arnold, Donna Arkoff Roth, and Ian Bryce. *Director:* Bronwen Hughes. *Screenplay:* Marc Lawrence. *Director of Photography:* Elliot Davis. *Editor:* Craig Wood. *Music:* John Powell. *Music Editor:* Katherine Quittner. *Choreographer:* Adam Shankman. *Sound:* Geoffrey Patterson and (music) Alan Myerson. *Sound Editor:* David Hankins. *Casting:* Junie Lowry Johnson. *Production Designer:* Lester Cohen. *Art Director:* Christa Munro. *Set Decorator:* Leslie Morales. *Set Designer:* Jack Ballance. *Set Dresser:* Clifton T. Cooper, Scott A. Lawson, Larry Sauls, Stacy Weddington, and Todd Morris. *Special Effects:* John Frazier. *Costumes:* Donna Zakowska. *Make-up:* Cindy Jane Williams. *Make-up (Sandra Bullock):* Pamela Westmore. *Stunt Coordinator:* Cal Johnson. *Running time:* 102 minutes. *MPAA Rating:* PG-13.

CAST: Sandra Bullock (Sarah); Ben Affleck (Ben); Maura Tierney (Bridget); Steve Zahn (Alan); Blythe Danner (Virginia); Ronny Cox (Hadley); Michael Fairman (Richard); Janet Carroll (Barbara); Richard Schiff (Joe); David Strickland (Steve); Meredith Scott Lynn (Debbie); George D. Wallace (Max); Steve Hytner (Jack); John Doe (Carl); Jack Kehler (Vic); Anne Haney (Emma); Bert Remsen (Ned); Julie Ivey (Beth); Maia Lien (Sandy); Carter Reedy (Groomsman #1); Rafiki Smith (Groomsman #2); Franklin H.D. Ecker (Groomsman #3); Taylor Gilbert (Dr. Keller); Francisco De Ramirez (Bus Driver); Pat Crawford Brown (Florence); Bill Erwin (Murray); William Marquez (Herman); Michael Cudlitz (Bartender); Athena Bitzis (Juanita the Bull Tamer); Libby Whittemore (Car Rental Agent); Dan Albright (Officer McDonnell); Marshall Rosenblum (Ticket Vendor); Mike Pniewski (Conductor); Wes Kennemore (Thief); Brandon McLaughlin (Delivery Man); Marc McPherson (Hotel Manager); Justin Michael Benassi (Sarah's Son); Shelly DeSai (Cabbie); Cordell Nichols (Child on Train); Dan Biggers (Justice of the Peace); Lester Cohen (Port Authority Spokesman); Natalie Hendrix (Airport Reporter); Scott Pierce (News Anchor); Shannon Welles (Lady in Wheelchair).

LOS ANGELES TIMES, 3/19/99, Calendar/p. 1, Kenneth Turan

"Forces of Nature" fools you, and more than once. Everything about it, from its title to its casting (Sandra Bullock! Ben Affleck!) to its ad line ("He went from the eye of the storm into the arms of a hurricane") practically scream conventional romantic comedy. But this film has several surprises in its repertoire, and most—but not all—of them make this a most pleasant and diverting venture.

Smartly written by Marc Lawrence (whose remake of "The Out-of-Towners" is due out next month) and directed with a lively intelligence by Bronwen Hughes (who debuted with "Harriet the Spy"), "Forces of Nature" turns out to be an extremely likable vehicle with a genuine sense of fun.

So cleverly constructed it feels spontaneous, "Forces" does stumble in its one-twist-too-many resolution, but it's so consistently charming up to then that, like a favorite child we can't help cheering on, it's difficult to chastise it for its lapses.

"Forces of Nature" is one star vehicle that knows how to use its big names, starting with Affleck. He plays a young New Yorker named Ben (how convenient) who writes jacket copy for novels. When he's introduced at his bachelor party, being nonplused by exotic dancer Juanita the Bull Tamer, Ben is just days away from his marriage to the bright and lively Bridget (Maura Tierney, Jim Carrey's wife in "Liar, Liar").

As it turns out, Ben gets nonplused a lot. His best friend and best man Alan (the irresistible Steve Zahn) is on the wacky side, but Ben himself is a practical, reliable, buttoned-down kind of guy. Affleck is one of the few young actors who can make stuffiness appealing, and in his hands being square and sheepish looks like a heck of a life choice.

Circumstances too amusing to divulge dictate that Ben will be leaving New York for Savannah, the site of the wedding, a few days after Bridget. At the airport (disconcertingly shot at Washington Dulles), he catches a glimpse of kohl-eyed, tattooed Sarah, locked in a passionate embrace and oblivious to the world around her.

A person who naturally makes a public spectacle out of everything, Sarah is one of the forces of nature the title refers to. A former stewardess, exotic dancer, auto show hostess and wedding videographer, she's someone who just might kiss the floor of a Kmart if she finds it open 24 hours. Sarah is the last person Ben wants to meet—and the very one who sits next to him on the flight.

No one needs to be told that this kind of "I am the life force, hear me roar" woman is not exactly a character we haven't seen before. It is, however, a departure for the often demure Bullock. Her performance is both edgier and more relaxed than her standard fare, and the energy released via this act of self-liberation is visible on screen.

Naturally, these two excel at getting on each other's nerves. Even before they leave the airport, she peeks at his computer screen efforts at writing sincere wedding vows and deflatingly asks if he works for Hallmark. Later, she calls him a "blurbologist," and worse.

We all know, or at least we think we do, what's going to happen with these two. She's going to loosen him up and he's going to encourage her in a newly minted sense of responsibility. Yes, it's a tired concept, but several things make it hard to resist on screen, not the least of which is the ability of these actors, who have excellent chemistry together.

Also to be expected is that that flight to Savannah never quite leaves the airport. Determined to reach that city as soon as possible, Ben and Sarah embark on a makeshift car, train and bus trip South that might as well have been routed through the Bermuda Triangle. Meanwhile, fiancee Bridget is hanging out in Savannah, coping with troublesome parents (Blythe Danner and Ronny Cox) and an ex-beau (David Strickland) who thinks the romance isn't over.

What Lawrence and Hughes add to this is an exact eye for wonderful eccentrics met on the road (Junie Lowry Johnson did the fine casting) and a playful running gag about the dreadful perils of marriage. Everyone Ben talks to has a bad word to say about the institution, including his own grandfather, who dismisses sentimental thoughts about Ben's grandmother with a curt, "The woman looked like Tolstoy."

Lawrence's script is full of playful and unexpected lines that give the film a welcome personal feeling, as when someone who's been complaining about children is asked if he has any kids and replies, "Nah, but I see 'em all over." Though the resolution of "Forces of Nature" may leave you feeling swindled, there's comfort to be gained in knowing the deed was done by some extremely talented professionals.

NEW YORK POST, 3/19/99, p. 39, Jonathan Foreman

Although predictable, contrived and bespattered with annoying camera tricks, this road-trip comedy does have some funny moments that weren't in the trailer. Ben Affleck plays Ben, a solid, squarish, book-jacket-blurb writer on his way down to Savannah, Ga., to marry Bridget (Maura Tierney). He's nervous about the marriage and even more nervous about flying, so when his plane crashes on the runway, he takes it as a bad sign.

He decides to go south by road and rail with Sarah (Sandra Bullock), a fellow passenger on the ill-fated jet. She's one of those life-affirming free spirits beloved of such movies: She does wacky things like climbing onto a train roof and yelling like Tarzan.

The two have many misadventures on the way down: more signs that the marriage might be a mistake. And, of course, they begin to fall for each other.

As Sarah, Bullock makes a game effort to break away from her screen image as the sweet but sexless girl next door. Here she is supposed to be a slinky downtown wild-child, a combination of Melanie Griffith in "Something Wild" and Liza Minnelli in "Cabaret." She wears purple streaks in her hair, dark eye makeup, tank tops and a belly tattoo. And despite her skinny, boyish figure she actually succeeds in achieving a feline kind of sex appeal. Unfortunately there's no chemistry between her and Affleck—he seems vaguely interested in her, but she looks at him like he's a piece of furniture.

Affleck himself is affable but slightly stolid in a role which would have been perfect for Ben Stiller. A potentially terrific scene in which he has to strip in a gay bar is fumbled horribly by director Bronwen Hughes, who seems to be more interested in shooting raindrops in slow motion than in getting strong performances from her actors.

This would explain why the usually dependable Tierney plays Bridget as identical to her character in "NewsRadio" and keeps forgetting her Southern accent. Even Steve Zahn, who plays

Ben's pal Alan—an advocate of sleeping around as much as possible before marriage—seems oddly muted during his too-few moments on screen.

Despite Hughes' direction (and some serious believability problems with the story) cleverly written moments in Mark Lawrence's screenplay make for several good laughs. The best ones come during the first third of the movie, when everyone to whom Ben mentions his coming wedding launches into a rant about his or her own failed marriage, in an ironic inversion of the interviews that accompanied "When Harry Met Sally."

NEWSDAY, 3/19/99, Part II/p. B13, John Anderson

As our political leaders boldly straddle the middle of the road, network television programmers courageously champion the lowest common denominator and the state of the bagel is reaching crisis consistency, we find Ben Affleck and Sandra Bullock to be among our most popular film stars. One might say that, as a culture, we boast a reckless predictability.

And at the risk of sounding like a cranky old malcontent, they might not make movie stars like they used to, but they do make the movies. Remake them, that is. "Forces of Nature," which declares with utter conviction that people have second thoughts before their wedding(s) and that even the most improbable of lovers are fated to be together, has a structure that on the screen is as old as "Bringing up Baby" (1938) and that on the page is genetically linked to "Romeo and Juliet." Not that anyone is sheathing or unsheathing any daggers during this tiny comedy. But the audience might like to.

Affleck is Ben (yep) who, en route to his Savannah wedding to Bridget (the delightful and underused Maura Tierney), has his plane skid off the runway and his life slide into Sarah (Bullock), a punkish former erotic dancer among other things who is so different from the uptight Ben they just can't help becoming infatuated.

Their travels toward Savannah will involve any number of vehicles and weirdos and any number of coincidences that suggest a far fuller confidence in the movie's star caliber than its narrative logic.

No one, outside of the filmmakers obviously, needs to be told that the health and well-being of such an antiquated-bordering-on-condemnable structure—which will be built out of thoroughly contrived situations and characters—is totally reliant on chemistry. And while Bullock and Affleck are perfectly pleasant people to watch, their meandering trip southward has all the dynamic of a bus ride to Schenectady.

And do you want to pay the better part of 10 bucks to make the trip? That, young lovers, is the question. Bronwen Hughes, who directed the very palatable "Harriet the Spy" in 1996, knows what she has on her hands. She affects very arty dissolves and allows time-lapse storm clouds to rumble into view and allows Ben and Sarah to frolic in a Kmart while the soundtrack's eclectic and CD-friendly score rolls with them down the aisles.

You get the distinct feeling that Hughes was finding ways to amuse herself while making this movie, and that she should have shared it all with us.

NEWSWEEK, 3/22/99, p. 75, Yahlin Chang

Forces of Nature is made for anyone who's ever been caught cooing into the phone. The moment Ben (Ben Affleck) gets on the line with his fiancée, Bridget (Maura Tierney), the baby talk just pours out. Even in public, on a plane: "I love you more ... No, I love you more." A winsome little movie, "Forces" is unabashedly romantic: here is a man in love, making an idiot of himself for all the world to hear. "MmmOK, I have to go," he tells Bridget, "I just made another passenger nauseous."

Ben's on his way from New York to Savannah for the wedding when his plane skids off the runway, and a wild thing named Sarah (Sandra Bullock) literally falls into his straitlaced, button-downed life. Ben's afraid of flying anyway (hint, hint), so he and Sarah evacuate and embark on the old road-trip-from-hell. Everything seems to conspire to keep Ben from his nuptials. Everyone he meets has a sob story about a bad marriage. Fires, hurricanes and beautifully shot hailstorms intervene—and Ben and Sarah are falling for each other all the while.

It may sound formulaic, and you may think you know the ending—Sarah will save Ben from a life of drudgery, playing wild Jack to his repressed Rose. Thankfully, "Forces" gets messier than that, fast. Sarah's free spirit is weighed down with baggage like kids and do-nothing ex-husbands. And Bridget may be sweet, but she's not just a sap waiting for her man to come home. Director Bronwen Hughes wisely plays fair with all sides of the romantic triangle. Refreshingly, the movie doesn't treat you like a moron who needs to be told which woman to root for. If Ben has to choose, why shouldn't you?

Tierney's wholesome, down-to-earth quality makes Bridget extremely appealing even as she wails, "Where are you, Ben?" But Bullock is simply miscast. In one scene, she howls like Tarzan to show exactly how crazy spontaneous she can be, but all you see is an actress trying too hard. Still, Affleck manages to be entirely convincing in his awestruck pose toward her (though it could just be respect for her top billing). Ben's supposed to be a confused wreck anyway, asking the Big Question that looms over a generation of children of divorce. Why would anyone marry, when there are so many reasons not to and so many obstacles in the way?

Searching for the answer, Affleck gives a winning performance that in many ways reprises his role in "Chasing Amy"—he's always in top form playing a lovesick boyfriend. In fact, "Forces" may offer the best swooning opportunities in the Affleck canon. It may be cheesy, but it's cheese of the most satisfying kind—so warmhearted and fun that you don't even feel guilty for succumbing.

SIGHT AND SOUND, 5/99, p. 47, Philip Kemp

New York. Ben and Bridget are about to fly to her home in Savannah, Georgia, for their wedding. But at Ben's stag party his grandfather suffers a heart attack. Bridget goes on ahead, Ben, taking a later plane, is seated next to Sarah, an attractive, eccentric young woman. The plane skids off the runway; all flights are cancelled. Despite Ben's misgivings, he and Sarah beg a lift from a stranger named Vic who has secured a hire car.

On the road, Vic's pot smoking gets them run in by the local police. Released, Ben and Sarah catch a train, but wind up in the wrong section and have to get off. While they wait for a bus in the nearest town their money is stolen. Pretending she and Ben are newly-weds, Sarah cons them a lift with a busload of senior citizens, but they're unmasked when Alan (Ben's best man) and Debbie (Bridget's maid of honour) show up at the same hotel on their way to the wedding. Sarah coerces Ben into a striptease in a gay bar. It nets them enough cash to reach Savannah where a hurricane is brewing. Sarah is confronted by her husband, who accuses her of neglecting her son by her first marriage. Ben reaches the fast-disintegrating wedding, fends off both sets of parents and assures Bridget of his love. She accepts it and they fly off to get married in Hawaii. Sarah seeks out her son and reforges their bond.

"A lot of stuff's happening really fast," says Sarah, the would-be life-force heroine of *Forces of Nature,* "and you're not registering it." Unfortunately, she's wrong on both counts. By this stage of the film nothing is happening nearly fast enough, and what is happening registers all too clearly, with a series of dull, laborious thuds. *Forces of Nature* sets out to be a latterday screwball comedy, mixing in elements of *It Happened One Night* (1934), *Bringing Up Baby* (1938), *What's Up Doc?* (1972), *Something Wild, Planes, Trains & Automobiles,* and half-a-dozen other movies in which a nice, square citizen heading for a nice, square marriage is shaken out of his/her complacency by a wild, wacky character with no regard for convention. It's a serviceable if overused plotline, but if it's to work it needs two vital ingredients, both sadly lacking here: mutual chemistry and pace.

Things start promisingly enough. The opening stag-party sequence, where Ben's grandfather succumbs to a heart attack brought on by the ministrations of a stripper, gets up the right mood of black comedy, though already danger signals sound in the way the film backs off from having the old boy die. The plane crash is well handled too, and there are some diverting cameos along the way, with various characters sounding off on the pros and cons of wedlock. Especially amusing are the beaming elderly couple, seemingly long and happily married, who confide they're having an extramarital affair and enjoying the first good sex of their lives.

However, as the pace of the film bogs down, the string of disasters dogging the couple come across as increasingly mechanical and contrived. If Sandra Bullock and Ben Affleck had a good onscreen thing going, they might carry it, but there's no electricity between them. Bullock in particular seems over conscious of all her predecessors from Katharine Hepburn onwards, her kookiness unfocused and pasted on, while Affleck just looks stolid. A would-be zany episode in an all-night K-Mart falls woefully flat. And the besetting timidity doesn't help. Ben's gay-bar striptease scene lacks all sense of danger or even raunchiness, stopping far short of the full monty. The over flagged hurricane does little more than whisk a few leaves around in slow motion, and neither Ben and Sarah, nor Ben's fiancée Bridget and her importunate ex-boyfriend Steve, are allowed to get much further beyond a brief snog while horizontal.

This lack of consummation turns out to be deliberate, setting things up for the 'surprise' denouement in which Ben doesn't make the choice we've been led on to expect. But this peripeteia, evidently intended as heart warming, just feels like one more anti-climax—all the more so since it leads to a flaccid ending, with Ben's sententious voiceover reducing Sarah to a *Reader's Digest*-style Most Unforgettable Person I Ever Met. While he drones on, we see Sarah winning over her son, making up for ten years of absence with a lot of grinning and a $2 inflatable toy. One suspects such a victory would have needed a good deal more work, but then that goes for the whole film.

VILLAGE VOICE, 3/23/99, p. 125, Justine Elias

Trapped on the road to conformity, nice young men and women are happy to be waylaid by unmanageable forces. Or at least that's how it happens in the screwball comedies of the 1930s. More recently, in *Honeymoon in Vegas, In and Out,* and *Flirting With Disaster,* the weirdness began with the heroes: Nicolas Cage, Kevin Kline, and Ben Stiller, three actors who seem, even at the best of times, to be on the verge of becoming unhinged.

Now comes *Forces of Nature,* the story of a nervous groom-to-be who must contend with all manner of disasters on the way to his lavish Southern wedding and Hawaiian honeymoon. Unfortunately, the hero is played by the extremely unflighty Ben Affleck, who has no hinges to speak of. He is a solid wall of manhood. When he's cast as the go-to guy, as he was in *Good Will Hunting,* he's cool, tough, and reliable. Opposite a surprisingly raunchy Sandra Bullock, who plays the mysterious, moody woman he meets during his journey, Affleck never lets down his defenses. And why should he? He's got a rich, decent fiancée (Maura Tierney) waiting for him in Savannah. In short, he's too sturdy and sated. And you can't have screwball comedy if only one party desperately wants to screw.

The script, by Marc Lawrence, is a well-constructed, if chilly, road romance, with some great throwaway lines. Director Bronwen Hughes seems to favor the oddball minor characters, like the hero's tipsy, genteel future in-laws (Ronny Cox and Blythe Danner), and certain scenes—like Affleck's impromptu strip dance—don't go far enough. By the time a computer-generated storm arrives, throwing the wedding ceremony into disarray, *Forces of Nature* is less about the anarchic powers of love and sex than it is about the bond between a man, a woman, and two nonrefundable, first-class airline tickets.

Also reviewed in:
CHICAGO TRIBUNE, 3/19/99, Friday/p. A, Rick Kogan
NEW YORK TIMES, 3/19/99, p. E27, Janet Maslin
VARIETY, 3/15-21/99, p. 38, Joe Leydon
WASHINGTON POST, 3/19/99, p. C5, Rita Kempley
WASHINGTON POST, 3/19/99, Weekend/p. 43, Desson Howe

42 UP

A First Run Features release of a Granada Television production for the BBC. *Executive Producer:* Ruth Pitt and Stephen Lambert. *Producer:* Michael Apted. *Director:* Michael Apted. *Director of Photography:* George Jesse Turner. *Editor:* Kim Horton. *Sound:* Nick Steer. *Running time:* 130 minutes. *MPAA Rating:* Not Rated.

WITH: Nick, Symon, Andrew, Jackie, Lynn, Susan, Tony, Bruce, Paul and Neil.

LOS ANGELES TIMES, 12/10/99, Calendar/p. 18, Kevin Thomas

In 1963, filmmaker Michael Apted, then early in his career, assembled 14 7-year-olds representing a cross section of British society and interviewed them about their lives and their dreams. The British TV result was the internationally acclaimed "7 Up." Every seven years since, Apted has caught up with them to make another installment. The latest, "42 Up," opens a one-week run at the Nuart.

Time is truly on Apted's side because the passing of time not surprisingly brings a richer, deeper perspective with each new segment. The project allows Apted to dip into past segments to trace the growth of these individuals in a uniquely revealing and compelling manner—and at the same time making it unnecessary to have seen the earlier chapters to comprehend and enjoy the latest entry.

The big news is how encouraging "42 Up" is. Remarkably, all 14 are leading productive lives. Yes, most but not all are getting plump and paunchy, but the majority is happily married with children. By and large the upper-middle-class children knew early on what they wanted to do with their lives and proceeded to do it without undue obstacles. The working-class youngsters had decidedly fewer choices and opportunities, and some feel they settled for less while having worked very hard for whatever affluence and security they have accrued.

On the whole they are a likable, articulate group of staunch citizens, the bedrock of a solid society. Some find it quite enough to do the best they can for their families, but others are committed to helping others as well. On the whole the group seems to believe that there is more across-the-board opportunity in Britain now, but that the class system is still very much in place.

Although all are of interest, several individuals stand out. One is Lynn, who at 21 was a chain-smoking cynic but at twice that age has become an especially reflective woman, a dedicated wife and mother and parochial school librarian. She has learned to live with an inoperable but apparently benign brain tumor, accepting her doctor's opinion that she will probably die of something else when her time comes. She speaks out on the lack of values in modern life, "the lack of respect for anything." Both her two lifelong friends are divorcees: Jackie, a loving single mother of three young boys who is impoverished but far from defeated; and the very attractive Sue, who has raised two children largely on her own.

Of a group of three public school boys—which in Britain means private school—two no longer participate in the series. Even at 7, John, who in fact has become the highly successful barrister he intended to be, came across as a ferocious snob, while Charles, another series dropout, now produces science documentaries for British TV. Andrew, a solicitor also clearly programmed for success at 7, realizes that while his life, which includes a happy marriage, has unfolded according to plan, he nonetheless owes much to good fortune.

Still, like John and Charles, he regards the series as something of an intrusion, which, he says frankly, he wouldn't wish on his children. (The group collectively seems ambivalent about how participation in the series has affected their lives, though many note that it does force them to take stock of themselves every seven years, like it or not.)

Not surprisingly, Apted leaves the most atypical member of his group, Neil, to the last. Even as a child Neil radiated a special sensitivity that was soon manifesting itself in an increasingly intense temperament and personality. By 28 Neil was homeless, and, at 35, in retreat in the Shetland Islands. What he's doing with his life at 42 seems therefore astonishing, yet remarks he made earlier in his life actually pointed in the direction he has finally taken—one too dramatic to be revealed here. Very much a work in progress, Neil has strayed farthest but has emerged from a long odyssey as perhaps the wisest and most reflective of the group.

Apted has said that his initial impetus was to discover whether there was any truth to the old saying, "Give me the child at 7, and I will show you the man." Now that he has completed six installments, it would certainly seem that there is truth to that belief, for you can see a great deal of the children they were in these now-middle-aged men and women. This holds true even for Neil—perhaps especially so.

NEW YORK, 11/22/99, p. 88, Peter Painer

In 1964, Granada TV in England brought together fourteen children from multi-class backgrounds and made a documentary about them called *7 Up*. Subsequently Michael Apted, who began as a researcher on *7 Up,* has gone on to film the subjects at seven-year intervals (with only two of the original fourteen eventually dropping out). *42 Up,* the latest installment, finds most of its participants in the drear comfort zone of middle age. (Veteran viewers of the series will be glad to know that the troubled Neil is less troubled and living in London.) Apted works material from the five previous shows into this one, and the back-and-forth within each character —observed over a span of 35 years—is both highly emotional and wearying. The grand, class-society-embracing conception of this film has become too rich for its narrow stylistic confines.

NEW YORK POST, 11/17/99, p. 58, Jonathan Foreman

Documentaries don't get much better than the remarkable series that began with "7 Up" in 1964 and now offers a sixth installment, "42 Up."

The latest episode of this ongoing masterpiece of reality TV—which every seven years revisits a group of English people first interviewed as 7-year-olds in 1964—is every bit as enthralling as the earlier ones.

And, unexpectedly, it paints a more optimistic picture than either "35 Up" or "28 Up": You get the distinct sense that these people—all from radically different backgrounds—aren't facing midlife crises but instead have mostly found a sense of balance that once eluded them.

As before, the program deftly combines new interviews with quick clips and some unseen footage from the previous shows. The technique not only makes "42 Up" accessible to those who haven't seen any of the earlier installments, it also gives one an extraordinary picture of the way people experience their lives over time.

Eleven of the original 14 participants who were chosen by the English "World in Action" TV program in 1964 to talk about their expectations of life are still cooperating with director Michael Apted, who was a researcher on the original show.

At 7, almost all of the subjects were adorable little kids—whether they came from the working-class East End of London, a Yorkshire farm or a professional, middle-class home—which makes it all the more heartbreaking to see what happened when their childish optimism collided with life.

In the earlier programs, this was most true of Neil, a bright little boy from Liverpool who later suffered from mental illness, became homeless and actually disappeared in "28 Up". Amazingly, "42 Up" finds Neil back in London and involved in local politics.

Back in 1964, the politicized young filmmakers of "7 Up" wanted to take a snapshot of a class-ridden society. They were inspired by the traditional Jesuit maxim "Give me a child until he's 7 and I will show you the man." The main themes of this episode are marriage and divorce, the deaths of parents, and the sense of security and confidence that seems to have come to many of the interviewees since they were 35.

Then there's the effect that the series itself has had on its participants.

It's mostly benign, partly because this strange family that meets every seven years has worked its own spell on the filmmaker, ensuring that the program remains more respectful of participants' dignity than ordinary TV ever is.

VILLAGE VOICE, 11/23/99 p. 142, Amy Taubin

In 1963, the year that British rock began to transform the image of London from staid to swinging, Granada TV produced *7 Up,* one of the most visionary series in the history of televisions medium that is serial by definition. The goal was to offer a glimpse of what Britain would be like, particularly in respect to the class system, in the then almost unimaginable year 2000 and beyond. The method was to make documentary portraits of 14 seven-year-olds and to film follow-ups every seven years. Michael Apted, the eclectic director whose James Bond movie *The World Is Not Enough* opens this week, was a researcher on *7 Up* and has been at the helm ever since.

As the series and its participants grow older, the flashback material in the films has become at once more cumbersome and more fascinating. Like its subjects, *42 Up* is a bit slower and heavier, but its connection of past and present yields more subtle character twists and contradictions than ever before. Apted is very good at zeroing in on the expression of fears and desires that shape lives, albeit in unexpected ways.

There's nothing in *42 Up* as outrageous and naively revealing as the three upper-class boys in *7 Up* claiming that it's essential for their school to charge tuition because if it didn't "the poor people would come rushing in." But there's an enormous pleasure in discovering that Jackie (one of the three working-class girls), who at age seven was sure she wanted to become a mother—and who by age 35 had not only ended her long, intentionally childless marriage but also had had her first child as the result of a brief affair—now has three kids and is keeping her family together thanks in part to her loyal, second ex-mother-in-law.

Of the original 14 subjects, three have dropped out of the film (one dropout heads a documentary unit at Channel 4), but happily no one has died and no one's children have met with any catastrophes. There have been a fair number of divorces and almost everyone has lost one or both parents. The original choice of subjects now seems wildly revealing of the biases of the times. Only four were girls and only two were from what Thatcherism would come to define as the middle class. The other 12 were divided equally between the upper and lower classes.

If you've followed the series, you undoubtedly have worried about Neil, the endearing child who wanted to be an astronaut and who in adolescence was plagued with terrible feelings of inadequacy that made him borderline dysfunctional. In *35 Up,* Neil was living reclusively in the Shetland islands. He suspected that by the next film he would be homeless in London. Neil is back in the city, but what he's doing is so surprising (and yet so right in terms of the person we've come to know) that you'll have to see it to get the full impact. What's happened to Neil is in part due to the support of one of the other subjects—Bruce, the math teacher, who, incidentally, finally got married. Neil and Bruce struck up a lasting friendship at the cast party for *35 Up.* The *7 Up* series is thus one of the rare documentaries to have had a positive practical effect on the life of at least one of its subjects.

Also reviewed in:
NEW YORK TIMES, 11/17/99, p. E1, Janet Maslin
VARIETY, 11/1-7/99, p. 90, Eddie Cockrell

FREAKS UNCENSORED: A HUMAN SIDESHOW

A Bohemia Productions release. *Producer:* Vivian Forlander. *Director:* Ari Roussimoff. *Screenplay:* Ari Roussimoff and Vivian Forlander. *Editor:* Ari Roussimoff. *Music:* John Watts. *Running time:* 100 minutes. *MPAA Rating:* Not Rated.

CAST: Jeanie Tomaini (Half-Lady); Jack Dracula (Tattooed Man); Jennifer Miller (Bearded Female Performance Artist); James Taylor (Author of the Periodical "Shocked and Amazed"); Joe Petro, 3rd (Collector); David F. Friedman (Carnival Entrepreneur); Ari Roussimoff (The Jester).

VILLAGE VOICE, 3/2/99, p. 150, Gary Dauphin

In Ari Roussimoff's neatly jaunty documentary *Freaks Uncensored,* the barker's siren song leads to a world as fully fleshed as it is bizarre. A cornucopia of archival footage grounded by interviews with the survivors and modern-day descendants of sideshows, *Freaks* is an encyclopedic but breezy ride that shoots from the medieval origins of the carnival to P.T. Barnum to a veritable visual menagerie of pinheads, midgets, Siamese twins, giants, bearded ladies, dog-faced boys, and more.

Many of the images are unwatchable in a medical horror-show way, but *Freaks* never feels exploitative, Roussimoff always eager to point out how his ever-morphing cast of real-life and made-up characters were never quite what they seemed. *Freaks* isn't ever gushily life-affirming, but the misty and often wry recollections of the old-timers have a warmth that lingers long after the disturbing spectacle of their bodies has faded.

Also reviewed in:
NEW YORK TIMES, 2/26/99, p. E20, Lawrence Van Gelder

FREE ENTERPRISE

A Regent Entertainment release of a Mindfire Entertainment production in association with Triad Studios. *Executive Producer:* Mark Gottwald and Ellie Gottwald. *Producer:* Dan Bates, Allan Kaufman, and Mark A. Altman. *Director:* Robert Meyer Burnett. *Screenplay:* Mark A. Altman and Robert Meyer Burnett. *Editor:* Robert Meyer Burnett. *Director of Photography:* Charles L. Barbee. *Music:* Scott Spock. *Production Designer:* Cynthia Halligan. *Costumes:* Ann Lambert. *Running time:* 113 minutes. *MPAA Rating:* R.

CAST: Rafer Weigel (Robert); Eric McCormack (Mark); Audie England (Claire); Patrick Van Horn (Sean); Jonathan Slavin (Dan Vebber); Phil LaMarr (Eric Wallace); William Shatner (Bill).

LOS ANGELES TIMES, 6/4/99, Calendar/p. 12, Kevin Thomas

Director Robert Meyer Burnett and his co-writer Mark A. Altman breathe new life into the Hollywood-set romantic comedy genre with their funny, sharp and engaging "Free Enterprise," their debut feature; Regent Entertainment has selected it as its second film following its smash debut with "Gods and Monsters."

We at first think we've met their heroes before in many other movies, but they quickly prove to be idiosyncratic. Rafer Weigel's Robert and Eric McCormack's Mark, two super-bright, fiercely articulate industry wannabes, are about to hit 30. They are confronted with the inescapable fact that they're not where they had hoped to be in life.

While Robert is doing well enough financially as a writer of schlock horror pictures, he has cut himself off emotionally, interested only in shallow bimbo types. A film editor, Mark is a spendthrift romantic, always getting hurt. They both need badly to grow up, as many young American males do.

Mark spends most of what he makes on "Star Trek" collectibles and other movie-related memorabilia, videos and laser discs. Friends since childhood, Robert and Mark are serious Trekkers and cineastes extraordinaire. They can't conduct a conversation that's not loaded with movie references. Mark is beginning to wish that he could meet a woman who shares his passions instead of being told that being a Trekker is a "guy thing."

(You don't have to be a Trekker to enjoy this picture, but it couldn't hurt, just as familiarity with a slew of other pictures the guys revere, such as "Logan's Run," helps.)

Just as Mark meets Claire (Audie England), who could just be Ms. Right, he and Robert encounter their idol William Shatner at NoHo's Iliad Bookstore. They strike up an acquaintance with the actor, who tells him that he too is getting over a broken romance and like them wants to get his own project off the ground: a self-admitted "height of hubris" dream of turning "Julius Caesar" into a musical in which he would play all the roles except Calpurnia. (Shatner's thinking Sharon Stone, Heather Locklear or Julia Roberts for that part.)

Romance overtakes Mark and Claire, who is grounded enough to question the wisdom of Mark investing in a special edition laser disc of George Romero's "Dawn of the Dead" when he's unable to pay for the electricity he obviously will need to enjoy it. But "Free Enterprise" will ultimately emerge as a celebration of risk-taking in the spirit of the heroism of Captain Kirk.

"Free Enterprise" is in fact a most affectionate homage to Shatner, who plays himself, though not his actual self ("Free Enterprise" was shown at the Cannes Film Festival and Shatner showed up for some amusing promotional events.) The film respects Shatner's dignity and his status as an icon of popular culture but without stiff reverence or demeaning spoofery.

Burnett and Altman allow Shatner to suggest that he and Captain Kirk are not in fact one and the same, and that he's a man who may have more in common with Robert and Mark than they realize. In one of his most telling moments, he points out to Robert and Mark that they've programmed their lives to a 30-year-old TV show, adding gently that they might well consider adding" a little reality to their imaginations."

Burnett is a fine director of actors, and "Free Enterprise" is polished in all aspects. Weigel and McCormack (of TV's "Will and Grace") both make a strong impression, as does the supporting cast, which includes elegant Deborah Van Valkenberg, who understandably catches Shatner's eye.

Where "Free Enterprise" really scores is in its dialogue; Burnett and Altman's throwaway lines alone would brighten up 20 other modestly budgeted movies aimed at 30-something audiences.

NEW YORK POST, 8/6/99, p. 50, Jonathan Foreman

"Free Enterprise" is a strange but likable mixture: an apparently autobiographical Hollywood-insider comedy about low-level almost-players, and a vision of what happens to nerdy sci-fi fans when they turn into relatively attractive adults.

It's about two guys on the edge of Hollywood who have been best friends forever. Robert (Rafer Weigel) is an editor of B movies, while Mark (Eric McCormack from TV's "Will & Grace") runs a magazine but is pitching a flick called "Bradykiller" about a psycho who murders girls named Marsha, Jan or Cindy.

They are extreme movie buffs, obsessed in particular with science fiction—the kind of grown men who argue with 8-year-olds at Toys "R" Us on the proper pronunciation of Prince Xixor in one of the "Star Wars" spinoffs.

Emotionally immature to the extreme, Mark and Robert manage to bed (improbably) beautiful women but are terrified of commitment. Until this point they deal with their problems using episodes of the original "Star Trek" series—which they know by heart as a guide to life.

But things are changing. Mark is so panicky about his imminent 30th birthday, he dreams he's a fugitive in "Logan's Run." Robert's deepening financial irresponsibility—his power gets cut off when he spends the utility money on an action figure—is wrecking his personal life.

The end of childhood really begins to loom for the boys, however, when they befriend their idol William Shatner, whom they meet as he thumbs through skin mags in a bookstore.

Captain Kirk is now an alcoholic "Bill," who reveals his dream to do a one-man, six-hour musical version of Shakespeare's "Julius Caesar"—with a possible role for Sharon Stone.

Then Robert meets Claire (Audie England), the perfect sci-fi-obsessed woman in a comics store, and they fall in geek love. Will the relationship survive Robert's propensity to leave bills unpaid? And will the time he spends with Claire reading Stephen King novels in the bathtub end his friendship with Mark?

The film has inspired positive Internet buzz as a nerds' "Swingers." But while it has some very funny moments, it isn't as well-written or directed with nearly the same panache as "Swingers." The quality of the acting varies from scene to scene, and the whole movie would have benefited from stringent editing.

Shatner is sure to get kudos for lightly spoofing himself as a sad lush, but it's hard not to notice a rating self-consciousness and self-regard beneath the skin of his performance. Still, a final scene that features a duet between Shatner and the rapper Rated R is absolutely hilarious.

NEWSDAY, 8/6/99, Part II/p. B12, Gene Seymour

Robert (Rafer Weigel) and Mark (Eric McCormack) have known each other since grade school. They find themselves on the cusp of 30 as passionately devoted to pop culture as they were in their pre-adolescence. And what has it gotten them? Well, Mark edits a science-fiction fan mag called "Geek" and has been trying in vain to sell a slasher-movie script called "Brady Killer" about a psycho-killer who stalks women named Marcia, Jan and Cindy. Film editor Robert, meanwhile, keeps losing beautiful girlfriends as fast as he picks them up because none of them can understand why he spends the money he needs to pay his utilities bills on "Star Trek" collectibles.

Their favorite pastime is hanging out and complaining about their love lives. Which is what they're doing in a used bookstore when who should they see in front of them but "Star Trek's" James T. Kirk himself, William Shatner, idly making his way through a girlie magazine.

They can't help but introduce themselves to "Bill," who at first tries to shake them off but soon finds himself confessing to them his dream project: a musical version of Shakespeare's "Julius

Caesar" in which he plays every role except Calpurnia. ("Do you think Sharon Stone will do it?" "Bill" asks his new pals. "I ... *know* Heather Locklear. I can ask her.")

Finding out that their childhood hero is as awkward and insecure as they are prods Robert and Mark to do *something* to upgrade their fragile hold on maturity. The former manages to find a beautiful woman friend who loves genre junk as knowledgeably as he does, while the latter is struggling manfully to cope with his impending 30th birthday.

That "Free Enterprise" even exists should alarm those for whom the unapologetic-geek existence has no appeal whatsoever. But though, as with many movies these days, it's a little longer than it needs to be, Robert Meyer Burnett's film is carried along by its rueful, minty dialogue and its tender, knowing treatment of obsession, trivial and otherwise. And Shatner is a hoot. Good sportsmanship can't be the only rationale for assuming such a seedy, dorky role as "Bill." He must have been waiting his whole life—at least his life since, say, 1966, "Star Trek's" first season—to play this guy.

VILLAGE VOICE, 8/10/99, p. 64, Gary Dauphin

Imagining another kind of geek triumph entirely [the reference is to *Mystery Men*; see Dauphin's review], *Free Enterprise* is a reference-laden but emotionally thin relationship comedy set in the oddly intertwined worlds of *Star Trek* fandom and the straight-to-video industry. Following that age-old debut gambit where the frustrated film geek self-actualizes by making a movie, *Enterprise* tells the tale of Robert (Rafer Weigel) who, like director Robert Meyer Burnett, edits a sci-fi fan mag, and Mark (Eric McCormack, of TV's *Will and Grace*) a perpetually broke video editor.

The pair babble about laser disc re-masters of *The Planet of the Apes* and dreamt-of film projects while on a perpetual pussy hunt, Robert having "practice sex" with a shrewish ex-friend as Mark is serial-dumped over his tendency to buy memorabilia with the rent money. The winds of change blow into their lives in the form of a serious girlfriend for Mark (she's the only babe comics fan in California) and a chance meeting with their hero Bill, as in William "Kirk" Shatner. *Enterprise* doesn't know jack about love or making movies, but things do reach a point of high madness when Shatner confesses that his big ambition in life is to direct and star in a six-hour, one-man, musical adaptation of William Shakespeare's *Julius Caesar*. "I know it sounds ridiculous," he says in that famous stutter-step intonation, "but the thing is, I really think I can do it."

Also reviewed in:
CHICAGO TRIBUNE, 8/6/99, Friday/p. Q, John Petrakis
NEW YORK TIMES, 8/6/99, p. E21, Lawrence Van Gelder
VARIETY, 11/23-29/98, p. 50, Dennis Harvey

FRIENDS & LOVERS

A Lions Gate Films release of a C.E.O. Films presentation of a Josi W. Konski production in association with Laguna Entertainment. *Executive Producer:* Gregory Cascante and Eleanor Powell. *Producer:* Josi W. Konski. *Director:* George Haas. *Screenplay:* George Haas. *Story:* Neill Barry and George Haas. *Director of Photography:* Carlos Montaner. *Editor:* Barry Leirer. *Music:* Emilio Kauderer. *Casting:* Mike Fenton and Allison Cowitt. *Production Designer:* Ren Blanco. *Costumes:* Diane Kranz. *Running time:* 102 minutes. *MPAA Rating:* Not Rated.

CAST: Stephen Baldwin (Jon); Danny Nucci (David); George Newbern (Ian); Alison Eastwood (Lisa); Claudia Schiffer (Carla); Suzanne Cryer (Jane); David Rasche (Richard); Neill Barry (Keaton); Leon (Manny); Robert Downey, Jr. (Hans); Ann Magnuson (Katherine); Jamie Luner (Model); Courtney Bull (Little Girl); Ivo Lewis (Motel Clerk); Josi W. Konski (Tree Lot Owner).

LOS ANGELES TIMES, 4/16/99, Calendar/p. 12, Kevin Thomas

George Hass' "Friends & Lovers," a would-be romantic comedy, is inept in every aspect. In this trite, tasteless nonsense, a rich widower, Richard (David Rasche), invites his estranged son, Ian (George Newbern), and his L.A. pals to spend Christmas with him at his luxurious Park City chalet, where they'll be neatly, if mechanically, paired off by the time the film is over.

All arrive on time, except for Ian, who complains that his workaholic father never had time for him. In any event, when he gets there he finds himself attracted to the sister (Suzanne Cryer), pregnant and single, of his best friend, Keaton (Neill Barry). Keaton and an old friend Lisa (Alison Eastwood) suddenly discover each other. When another pal, David (Danny Nucci), admits he's a virgin, his friends conclude that he's gay and insist he pick up a handsome stranger (Leon).

Jon (Stephen Baldwin) arrives, expecting to score with Carla (Claudia Schiffer), a member of his group, but she's responding to the energetic advances of a local ski instructor (Robert Downey Jr.), who seems to impress her with his florid phony German accent. (Curiously, Schiffer is concentrating on eradicating any trace of her authentic German accent.) Meanwhile, Richard not only wants to make peace with Ian but also tell him that he's engaged to marry his secretary (Ann Magnuson), who's soon on her way to the chalet as well.

You would never know from this stale contrivance that Downey and Magnuson are performers of exceptional talent or that Nucci and Leon have done impressive work elsewhere. Eastwood manages to retain her poise; the circumstances are too dire to tell whether or not super-model Schiffer can act; and Newbern, Barry and Rasche are negligible.

Baldwin, playing a clod, and Cryer, cast as a garrulous know-it-all, are as lousy as their material. "Friends & Lovers" may have been shot largely in the Park City area, but you can be pretty sure that this loser could never make it to Sundance.

NEW YORK POST, 4/16/99, p. 56, Jonathan Foreman

"Friends & Lovers" is a leading contender for the worst movie of the spring, if not the year.

The terrible, tinny, disco ballad that accompanies the opening titles—and which sounds like something from those soft-core porn films they show on cable late at night serves as a warning for the stunning badness of what is to come.

"Friends & Lovers" is what TV's "Friends" would be if ripped off by a hopelessly untalented high-school theater group: a desperately unfunny orgy of bad writing, worse acting and tone-deaf direction.

It's the story of some longtime L.A. pals who go for a ski weekend in Utah at a house owned by the estranged dad of one of the guys.

There's Jon (Stephen Baldwin), an oafish, would-be Lothario who brings along spectacular German date Carla (Claudia Schiffer).

There's gay David (Danny Nucci), who's a virgin; there's Lisa (Alison Eastwood), who has a crush on Keaton (Neill Barry), and then there's Jane (Suzanne Cryer) Keaton's pregnant sister, who likes Ian (George Newbern).

But Ian might not come because he hates his father, Richard (David Rasche), who was never there when he was a kid.

On the way they meet Hans (Robert Downey Jr.), a crazy ski instructor with a ludicrous German accent. Hans fascinates Carla, who, being too dumb to test out his German, falls for his yoga seduction-shtick.

There's a kind of horrible car-accident fascination in the way joke after lame joke crashes to the floor. Richard is such a bad cook that he does things like put metal cans in the microwave, burns toast and puts coffee in the machine without first inserting a filter ...

With the exception of Downey, who is incapable of a bad performance, you can judge the quality of the acting by the fact that Claudia Schiffer is easily as good as the rest of the cast.

It's hard not to feel embarrassed for them as they giggle, mug and shout. And unlike Stephen Baldwin, Schiffer at least maintains some dignity. (This picture offers an interesting genetics lesson: It demonstrates that being a Baldwin makes you no more likely to possess acting ability than being a supermodel.)

Even the technical features of this film are lousy: The sound is terrible, and the condo and the snow on the slopes all look fake.

NEWSDAY, 4/16/99, Part II/p. B13, Gene Seymour

"Friends and Lovers" is one of those movies that looks as if it were a lot more fun to make than it is to watch. (Hey, if I'm a 20-something actor and somebody asked me to work for 21 days in a ski resort with people that are even prettier than I am, I should have something better to do?)

As easy as it is to imagine yourself with such a soft gig, it may be even easier to imagine a more original script for this pale attempt at old-fashioned "pairing off" comedy.

It's one of those weekend-in-the-boonies situations in which Ian (George Newbern) is invited to spend Christmas with his estranged dad (David Rasche) at the latter's house in Utah. Ian hates his dad, doesn't want to go. Unfortunately for him and for us, his friends do.

So off to the mountains go the following: Jon (Stephen Baldwin), a self-styled stud who's conned a model (Claudia Schiffer) into coming along; Jane (Suzanne Cryer), who's pregnant and knows the baby's gender but doesn't talk with the father; her brother Keaton (Neill Barry); shy, gay David (Danny Nucci), and Lisa (Alison Eastwood), who appears to be along for the ride because, as with everyone else in this group, there's little besides stock mannerisms and hairstyle to distinguish her from anyone else in the movie.

Even though you can tell almost from the beginning where and with whom everyone will end up, writer-director George Haas has spared no gratuitous contrivance, including the presence of a German ski instructor named Hans (Robert Downey Jr., wilding away with an accent broad enough to house a minivan) and an enigmatic snowboarder (Leon) for David to flirt with.

Haas even throws in running gags that don't work, like Dad's hopelessness in the kitchen. And just what are the odds on whether Ian and his pop will ever reconcile? If you don't know, check back after you've watched the next "Brady Bunch" marathon.

Wifty and bubble-brained as it is, "Friends and Lovers" may satisfy some abstract need you may have for a vicarious ski weekend. Hold out for better company.

VILLAGE VOICE, 4/27/99, p. 140, Dennis Lim

Just how bad is *Friends & Lovers*? Well, consider the movie's idea of a joke: "If I have sex with a pregnant woman, is it child abuse?" It's a measure of writer-director George Haas's subliterate, submoronic m.o. that he sees fit to follow that wisecrack with the riposte, "Depends on how big your penis is." Some combination of small penises, small brains, and big male egos must have gone into the making of *Friends & Lovers,* a movie that operates on a level of such staggering ineptitude that its very existence is offensive.

The film concerns a group of friends who, over one weekend at a ski lodge, have good sex and find true love. It's a sex farce derived from repellent attitudes toward sex (a hybrid of preadolescent and frat-boy). At one point, one of the actors (Neill Barry, who gets a story credit) flashes his dick at the women, who—evidently stunned by its dimensions—giggle, screech, and run away. Less a movie than a hate crime, *Friends & Lovers* has a contemptibly stupid view of humans and human interaction. Its misogyny and homophobia are particularly in-your-face. "You're not a *lesbo,* are you?" a woman asks her friend. Apparently not, but there *is* a gay male character, who's literally virginal. Robert Downey Jr., grotesque as a Bavarian ski instructor, does his best to elevate the movie to the level of train wreck, but the film, unbelievable as this sounds, is beneath him.

Also reviewed in:
CHICAGO TRIBUNE, 4/30/99, Friday/p. C, Mark Caro
NEW YORK TIMES, 4/16/99, p. E9, Stephen Holden
VARIETY, 4/19/-25/99, p. 47, Lael Lowenstein

FROGS FOR SNAKES

A Shooting Gallery release in association with Rain Films Inc. *Executive Producer:* Larry Meistrich and Daniel J. Victor. *Producer:* Phyllis Freed Kaufman. *Director:* Amos Poe. *Screenplay:* Amos Poe. *Director of Photography:* Enrique Chediak. *Editor:* Jeff Kushner. *Music:* Lazy Boy. *Casting:* Lina Todd. *Costumes:* Candice Donnelly. *Running time:* 92 minutes. *MPAA Rating:* R.

CAST: Nick Chinlund (Iggy); Robbie Coltrane (Al); David Deblinger (U.B.); Anthony Desando (Rilke); Harry Hamlin (Klench); Ian Hart (Quint); Barbara Hershey (Eva); John Leguizamo (Zip); Lisa Marie (Myrna); Debi Mazar (Simone); Ron Perlman (Gascone); Mike Starr (Crunch); Justin Theroux (Flav); Clarence Williams, III (Huck).

LOS ANGELES TIMES, 5/21/99, Calendar/p. 12, Kevin Thomas

"Frogs for Snakes" opens with Barbara Hershey tarted up in hot pants and a curly blond wig entering a Manhattan skyscraper and coolly pulling a gun on a guy who has only kinky sex on his mind. Sounding like Fran Drescher, she orders him to pay up and makes clear how serious she is by shooting him in the foot. She takes the money, heads home to her small apartment and sheds wig and accent for an enthusiastic night of love with her pal Zip (John Leguizamo).

We soon learn that Hershey's Eva and Zip are part of a large group of aspiring theater actors who make ends meet by working as illegal money collectors for Eva's ex-husband, Al (Robbie Coltrane), a ruthless loan shark with dreams of becoming a theatrical impresario. When he announces that he has decided he wants to stage David Mamet's "American Buffalo," the actors who work for him start meaning it when they say they would kill for a part.

This premise is not just a little contrived and farfetched, to say the least. But had writer-director Amos Poe played against it, taking his large and sparkling ensemble cast of well-known actors somewhere fresh and imaginative, "Frogs for Snakes" might have been fun in a darkly comic way.

Instead, it swiftly turns into a blood bath, with so many of Al's moonlighters killing each other off that you wonder how he can stay in business as a loan shark, let alone mount "American Buffalo" or, in time, even a one-character play.

The point of all this carnage is elusive, with Poe perhaps meaning to suggest that actors may confuse fantasy and reality in their quest for roles they crave. If so, it's scarcely enough to justify one increasingly wearying scene after another in which one actor wipes out another with escalating indifference. It's always hard to justify the depiction of nonchalant, affectless slaughter, and in the artificial, overly theatrical context of this picture—not to say recent events in Colorado—such incessant casual killing is especially repellent.

Among the other actors wasted here are Harry Hamlin, Debi Mazar, Ron Perlman and Clarence Williams III. Starting with Hershey, everyone registers effectively, but it matters not at all, because "Frogs for Snakes"—it's not worth explaining that title—is so swiftly a turnoff. If anything, matter-of-fact murder treated in a joking way in an arty picture with pretensions to sophistication is more disturbing than in your standard action picture, in which violence is a given.

NEW YORK POST, 5/21/99, p. 52, Jonathan Foreman

"Frogs for Snakes" starts out as yet another sub-Tarantino neo-noir film before turning into a feature-length joke about actors who literally kill for parts.

It's a clever, amusing joke, but one that would probably work better on the stage. Movies tend to favor relatively fast-paced, naturalistic storytelling. And in the end, the slowness, talkiness and studied jokiness of "Frogs for Snakes" (the title is from a 1957 blues song) make it hard to care about the plot or the characters.

For one thing, it's never entirely clear if the people we see shaking down debtors one minute and practicing their monologues for acting class the next, are theater folk obsessed with gangsterism or gangsters desperate to be actors.

Eva (Barbara Hershey) is the best enforcer for ex-husband Al (Robbie Coltrane), a loan shark/off-Broadway impresario. ("I don't kill, I maim," she tells a debtor who says that if she kills him, she won't get the money. She's also by far the best actor in her class.

She wants to get out of the business and move out to Long Island with her son. But the murder of her lover, Zip (John Leguizamo), by Al's driver—who wants Zip's role in a production of David Mamet's "American Buffalo"—changes everything.

Now Eva wants revenge as well as out, and she joins forces with her statuesque bad actress friend Myrna (Lisa Marie). But their plan coincides with the arrival in town of two tough jocks/actors/enforcers and the murderous breakdown of rival outerborough actress Simone (Debi Mazar).

It all takes place in the East Village. Everyone drives cars with fins and talks in creaky Noo Yawk accents—not surprising, given that half of the cast are actually Brits (Coltrane occasionally sounds sort of Russian). In between long monologues, some of which are played for chuckles, there is a lot of gratuitous, grisly violence, including a decapitation by shotgun blast.

The best thing about the film is Hershey. She looks terrific—and while movies featuring hot fortysomething actresses who sleep with younger men seem to be a Hollywood trend (see "The Love Letter"), it's no stretch to believe that Leguizamo would fall for her.

Director Amos Poe elicits smart, controlled and sometimes funny performances from the rest of a cast which includes Clarence Williams III (Linc from the original "Mod Squad") and Harry Hamlin. But in the end, Poe sinks the movie under his own hipsterism. You get the uncomfortable impression that it's all an indulgent in-joke for him and his friends.

NEWSDAY, 5/21/99, Part II/p. B7, Gene Seymour

Bad movies about bad actors give you the giggles whether they're supposed to or not. But the degree to which "Frogs for Snakes" isn't even unintentionally funny makes your hair itch. It may be that the talent summoned for Amos Poe's dark comedy is so formidable that you expect good things to happen.

One of "Frogs for Snakes" problems (its cool title, by the way, isn't one of them) is that it keeps you waiting too long for something, anything, to happen. The pacing problem is apparent from the start as Eva (Barbara Hershey) comes calling on a sleazy deadbeat with blonde wig, thick Noo Yawk accent and a pistol, whose contents she fires at his foot.

That takes a long time. So does the following scene when Eva, in bed with her lover (John Leguizamo), talk about their "real lives" as actors struggling for decent roles. OK, so they're shakedown artists and actors. After still more laggard development, Leguizamo's character is gunned down by a fellow shark-actor willing to "kill" for a role they're both up for.

OK, we get the joke, such as it is. The problem is that Poe uses all kinds of crude jolts and overblown dramaturgy to sustain the conceit.

Some of the performers are able to help carry the load, but Robbie Coltrane, as Eva's menacing ex-hubby who's both the loan-sharking kingpin and artistic director of a neighborhood theater, seems marooned as do tough-talking Debi Mazar, wifty Lisa Marie, dopey Justin Theroux and snarling Ron Perlman as other actors who literally threaten and main each other for a coveted roles. Ironically, its the TV vets Clarence Williams III and Harry Hamlin who, towards the end, show any real comic brio.

One can't blame Eva for wanting to get herself and her young son away from this smorgasbord of smoked hams. Hershey's role is so shallowly conceived that there's not much she can do with it except swerve between brittle sensuality and wounded desperation. It's almost enough. Hershey's smoldering presence makes you believe that Eva is the one class act of the motley bunch. As Eva heads off into the Long Island sunset, you also hope there's a better movie waiting somewhere for this resilient and luminous actress.

VILLAGE VOICE, 5/25/99, p. 132, Rob Davis

Screenwriting formulas dictate that for a movie to work, it needs to introduce the gist of its plot within the first 10 minutes. *Frogs for Snakes,* a particularly dreary rehash of everyone's favorite post-Tarantino indie-film standbys, snappy patter and gore, proves the point—even when it's over you can't tell what it was about. The film follows a few days in the life of a group of would-be

East Village actors who spend a lot more time shooting guns than acting. To make ends meet, they're all working for the local loan shark, whose business consists mostly of him hiring his own employees to kill each other. Unwieldy actor-criminal metaphors aside, writer-director Amos Poe (a local filmmaker you'd think would have more insight on the scene, or at least a better sense of the neighborhood geography) briefly captures some of the desperation and sycophancy innate to being a struggling artist, but quickly abandons any connection to reality in favor of potty-mouthed speechifying and gunfights passed off as punch lines. It's enough to make you wish *Pulp Fiction* had never existed.

Also reviewed in:
CHICAGO TRIBUNE, 5/21/99, Friday/p. B, Barbara Shulgasser
NEW YORK TIMES, 5/21/99, p. E16, 5/21/99, Lawrence Van Gelder
VARIETY, 3/23-29/98, p. 93, Derek Elley

GALAXY QUEST

A DreamWorks Pictures release of a Mark Johnson production. *Executive Producer:* Elizabeth Cantillon. *Producer:* Mark Johnson and Charles Newirth. *Director:* Dean Parisot. *Screenplay:* David Howard and Robert Gordon. *Story:* David Howard. *Director of Photography:* Jerry Zielinski. *Editor:* Don Zimmerman. *Music:* David Newman. *Music Editor:* Jeff Carson. *Sound:* Richard Beggs and (music) John Kurlander. *Sound Editor:* Tim Holland. *Casting:* Debra Zane. *Production Designer:* Linda DeScenna. *Art Director:* Jim Nedza. *Set Designer:* Robert Fechtman, Dianne Wager, Colin de Rouin, and Dawn Swiderski. *Set Decorator:* Ric McElvin. *Special Effects:* Matt Sweeney. *Visual Effects:* Bill George. *Animation:* Christopher Armstrong. *Costumes:* Albert Wolsky. *Make-up:* Hallie D'Amore Ve Neill. *Make-up (Alien/Creature):* Stan Winston. *Stunt Coordinator:* Andy Armstrong. *Running time:* 102 minutes. *MPAA Rating:* PG.

CAST: Tim Allen (Jason Nesmith); Sigourney Weaver (Gwen DeMarco); Alan Rickman (Alexander Dane); Tony Shalhoub (Fred Kwan); Sam Rockwell (Guy Fleegman); Daryl Mitchell (Tommy Webber); Enrico Colantoni (Mathesar); Robin Sachs (Sarris); Patrick Breen (Quellek); Missi Pyle (Laliari); Jed Rees (Teb); Justin Long (Brandon); Jeremy Howard (Kyle); Kaitlin Cullum (Katelyn); Jonathan Feyer (Hollister); Corbin Bleu (Tommy, Age 9); Wayne Péré (Lathe); Samuel Lloyd (Neru); Jennifer Manley (Shy Girl); John Patrick White and Todd Giebenhain (Teens in the Bathroom); Bill Chott (Fan #1); Morgan Rusler (Fan #2); Gregg Binkley (Fan #3); Brandon Michael Depaul (Fan #4); Paul G. Kubiak (Fan #5); Gregg Coldrook (Fan #6): John Patrick White (Teen in the Bathroom #1); Todd Giebenhain (Teen in the Bathroom #2); J.P. Manoux (Excited Alien); Dan Gunther (Navigator); Matt Winston and Brandon Keener (Technicians); Dian Bachar (Nervous Tech); Rainn Wilson (Lahnk); Susan Egan (Teek); Heidi Swedberg (Brandon's Mom); Isaac C. Singleton, Jr. (Sarris' Guard); Jerry Penacoli (Reporter); Joel McKinnon Miller (Warrior Alien); Kevin Hamilton McDonald (Announcer); Daniel T. Parker (Alien Fan); Dawn Hutchins (Inventory Clerk); Joe Frank (Voice of the Computor); Lawrence Richards and Mic Tomasi (Thermian Greeters).

LOS ANGELES TIMES, 12/24/99, Calendar/p. 2, Kevin Thomas

Imagine that during a "Star Trek" convention some actual aliens whisk off William Shatner, Leonard Nimoy and the rest of the crew, expecting them to help defeat a villainous monster in outer space.

That, roughly, is the premise that writers David Howard and Robert Gordon came up with, and under Dean Parisot's smart direction their script became "Galaxy Quest," a lively comedy action-adventure that also satirizes the "Star Trek" phenomenon with affection but with a pinch of tartness too. Fast, light and funny, "Galaxy Quest" has a wide, generation-spanning appeal—and you don't have to be a die-hard Trekkie to enjoy it.

The five stars of the movie's fictional "Galaxy Quest" series, which ran from 1979 to 1982, haven't been as fortunate as the Star Trekkers. No big-screen productions of the series have followed, and it would seem that the Questers' careers have pretty much been reduced to convention appearances and store openings. Tim Allen's Jason Nesmith plays Peter Quincy Taggart, commander of the Protector, and his key crew members are Sigourney Weaver's Gwen DeMarco as communications officer Lt. Tawny Madison; Alan Rickman's Alexander Dane as the half-human, half-reptilian Dr. Lazarus from the planet Tev' Meck; Tony Shalhoub's Fred Kwan as Tech Sgt. Chen and Daryl Mitchell's Tommy Webber, who was the starship's 10-year-old gunner-navigator.

While the Questers are less than thrilled with the state of their long-stalled careers, the live appearances are especially hard on Dane, who must don exoskeletal headgear and who feels that his identification with the short-lived series has wrecked his credibility as a Shakespearean actor. He is constantly reminding his colleagues that his Richard III drew five curtain calls.

But what really makes these reunions an ordeal is the obnoxious personality of the egomaniacal Nesmith, who demands special star treatment and cuts deals excluding the other Questers. Typically, he's outrageously late for group appearances, but as the film opens the other Questers are still managing to keep up the impression of mutual congeniality for the sake of the fans.

Their latest convention appearance is no different from countless ones before it. They're used to fans in full alien drag, and a group of nerdy-looking aliens seem no more persistent than others like them—at first. They are, however, for real: They're Thermians from the Klatu Nebula, and in a whoosh they sweep the Protector crew to outer space to help the beleaguered aliens defeat the fearsome monster Sarris (Robin Sachs).

It seems that the Thermians have been able to tap in to American TV, and they consider the old "Galaxy Quest" programs as "historical documents." Since the truth that the series is pure make-believe is beyond Thermian conception, the Questers have no choice but to try their best to really become the heroes they have heretofore only played.

On an action level, "Galaxy Quest" is a satisfying space adventure with fine special effects and an attractive overlaying of humor.

The "real-life" exploits become a form of potential redemption for the Questers, especially for Nesmith, who has the chance to display some authentic courage to become a true hero instead of the perpetual jerk he has long been. Similarly, Gwen at last has a chance to escape her statuesque blond bombshell stereotype as the durably glamorous Tawny. (It was apparently Weaver's inspired idea that Gwen be a blond.)

Parisot draws performances from his cast that are sharp-edged but bouyant. Everyone on both sides of the camera takes "Galaxy Quest" with just the right degree of seriousness needed to make it play effectively as a comedy.

In key support are Sam Rockwell as a pushy bit player in the series who ruefully winds up in outer space along with its stars and Enrico Colantoni as Mathesar the earnest Thermian leader.

NEW YORK, 2/7/00, p. 54, Peter Rainer

Galaxy Quest is still knocking about neighborhood theaters, and it's worth a look. Initially marketed as a space romp for the family, it's closer to being a satire of those films. A cast of TV actors in a *Star* Trek-style series ends up in a real interstellar shootout, and the drolleries take precedence over the special effects. The performers, including Sigourney Weaver, Tony Shalhoub, and Tim Allen, achieve a lilting tone of self-mockery and, as the Shakespearean actor reduced to playing an alien crew member with a crustaceoid forehead, Alan Rickman continues his unbroken string of stealing every movie he's in.

NEW YORK POST, 12/24/99, p. 37, Jonathan Foreman

An affectionate, often clever and unflaggingly funny satire of both the Trekkie phenomenon and "Star Trek" itself, "Galaxy Quest" goes a remarkable distance on a single conceit.

The idea is that the washed-up actors who once played an intrepid starship crew on a cult sci-fi series are assumed by TV-scanning aliens to be the real thing.

The extraterrestrials, who have naively mistaken the show for a historical document, want Commander Taggart and his team to save them from extermination.

The story starts at a "Questarian" convention, where costumed fans are pestering Jason Nesmith (Tim Allen), who used to play Commander Taggert, not just for autographs but for answers to ridiculous technical questions relating to the story lines of particular episodes.

Why, for example, did he use photon torpedoes instead of a laser cannon—when the torpedoes are so much more effective?

The egotistical Nesmith—Allen makes him sound suspiciously like William Shatner—actually enjoys these conventions.

But the other alumni of the series, Gwen De Marco (Sigourney Weaver), Alexander Dane (Alan Rickman) Fred Kwan (Tony Shalhoub) and Tommy Webber (Daryl Mitchell) resent what the show has done to their lives.

This is particularly true of Dane, a serious actor permanently associated in the public mind with his role as the half-reptile Dr. Lazarus.

When Nesmith is approached by uniform-clad "Thermians" he assumes that they're just more freaky Questarians who want him for another gig. But they take him aboard their starship, a craft they have reverse engineered from the Protector vessel of the TV series, and beg him to negotiate with the scaly alien Sarris (not the first movie villain to be named after a well-known movie critic).

The plot, dialogue and visual details abound with clever little jokes. My favorite is the way in which Sigourney Weaver, every time there's an explosion, has a little more of her cleavage exposed.

Director Dean Parisot ensures that the film never lags, and somewhat ironically, the special effects here are at least as good as those in the recent Star Trek movies.

Despite her work in "Dave," "Working Girl" and "Ghostbusters," most moviegoers don't associate Sigourney Weaver with humor, but here she shows again that she has a deft, self-deprecating talent for comedy.

Alan Rickman is perfect as the campy, resentful Dane, deftly underplaying a role that could all too easily have been wrecked.

And the always wonderful Tony Shalhoub steals scenes as the hapless, possibly stoned fellow who used to play the ship's chief engineer.

NEWSDAY, 12/24/99, Part II/p. B3, John Anderson

Imagine if the broadcast signals of "Star Trek," wandering through the refrigerated recesses of space, were picked up by an alien people. Would they think they were real? Would they build their society around the protocols of the Starship Enterprise? Would they make William Shatner a god? Would they click onto Priceline.com? "Galaxy Quest" isn't about "Star Trek"—not much. But its heroes are the cast of a canceled TV series whose fanatical devotees hold huge "Questerian" conventions and treat the show's scientific double talk as if it were the key to the Dead Sea Scrolls. The show's beleaguered cast—Jason Nesmith (Tim Allen), Gwen DeMarco (Sigourney Weaver), Alexander Dane (Alan Rickman), Fred Kwan (Tony Shaloub) and Tommy Webber (Daryl Mitchell)—are disgruntled has-beens who make personal appearances at the opening of appliance stores and are in disagreement about everything but their common contempt for Jason, who as "Galaxy Quest's" commander, is always the center of attention. And loves it.

Outside Galaxy Quest Convention 18 (meaning, among other things, that most of the attendees weren't even born when the show went off the air), Jason is approached by a foursome of costumed nerds—"from the Klatu Nebula"—who plead with Jason to help save their people from a evil warlord named Sarris (reportedly named for film critic Andrew Sarris, who once trashed "Galaxy Quest" producer Mark Johnson's "The Natural"). Jason, inured to the excesses of "Galaxy Quest" fans, thinks they're offering him a job. But he soon finds himself hurtling through space, wrapped in a gelatinous spacesuit and screaming incoherently.

There are a lot of terrific jokes in "Galaxy Quest"—many of which are tossed off so casually they might be missed—and an equal number of canny special effects. (Weaver, as the busty Gwen/Lt. Madison, is the beneficiary of two of them.) Director Dean Parisot ("Home Fries"), besides adopting the edits and rhythms of the old "Star Trek" series itself, also takes delicious advantage of the whole Trekkie phenomenon. The Thermians—many-tentacled beasts who assume human shape out of deference to the "GQ" crew—giggle, wobble, smile vacantly and are goofily adoring of their heroes. Since all Thermian technology is based on what was seen on

"Galaxy Quest," Jason and his crew have to call on the earthbound Brandon (Justin Long) and his crew of hard-core teenage Questerians to transmit instructions on how to navigate the ship and defeat Sarris. And Alan Rickman's droll performance as the nautilus-headed Alexander/Dr. Lazarus—a one-time Shakespearean actor turned unhappy cult figure—is a deft comment on the uneasy relationship between idol and idolator. (One recalls Shatner's "Saturday Night Live" skit in which he told Trekkies to "get a life.") Many of the giggles in "Galaxy Quest" arise from our common acquaintance with the conventions of sci-fi television-personified by Sam Rockwell's very funny Guy Fleegman, a supporting player who's afraid of dying, because on "GQ" that's precisely what supporting players did. Outside the theater where "GQ" was screened the other night, in fact, a critic said she'd never seen "Star Trek," and yet knew all the jokes. Culture, it seems, knows no bounds of time or space.

SIGHT AND SOUND, 5/00, p. 48, Kim Newman

The US, the present. Cancelled in 1983, the television show *Galaxy Quest* remains the subject of a fanatical cult following. The stars of the show—egotistical Jason Nesmith (Commander Peter Quincy Taggart), Gwen DeMarco (Tawny Madison), Alexander Dane (alien Dr Lazarus), Fred Kwan (Technical Sergeant Chen) and grown-up child-star Tommy Webber (Pilot Laredo)—are reunited at a Quest convention. Nesmith is approached by Mathesar, a real alien from the planet Thermia. Mathesar's civilisation has no concept of fiction and takes the television heroes for the real thing. Aboard a working replica of the spaceship *Protector,* Nesmith is asked to negotiate with alien tyrant Sarris and, thinking this is an acting job, orders an attack. Later, he persuades his fellow cast members, plus bit-player Guy Fleegman (once a nameless victim on the show), to join in the quest.

Escaping Sarris, the crew visit a desolate planet and secure a replacement for a damaged power source which enables the actors to approximate their on-screen heroics. Sarris catches up with the ship and Nesmith is forced to reveal to Mathesar he's only an actor, but using a comm-link to obsessive Quest fans on Earth for guidance—Nesmith is able to save the day. The Thermians take over the ship and the crew return to the convention, where Nesmith finishes off Sarris before an audience of Quest fans. A new series of *Galaxy Quest* goes into production, with Guy joining the crew.

Positing a fictional science-fiction series whose actors are suddenly whisked off by real aliens for an adventure, *Galaxy Quest* evokes the universe of *Star Trek* producer Gene Roddenberry with a keen awareness of such shows' potential absurdities and tackiness. Bit-part actor Guy worries he's the expendable crew member due a horrible early death until it's suggested he might be the 'plucky comic relief'; a trip through the starship is needlessly dangerous and complex, prompting Gwen to protest, 'This was a badly written episode.' It also embodies the ship-in-a-bottle utopia of *Star Trek* far more successfully than any of the pompous or camp feature films Paramount has spun out of its tattered franchise. While managing to satirise *Trek* its famously testy cast and its obsessive fans without real viciousness, it's still exactly the sort of picture which could be shown at a *Star Trek* convention.

It's an obvious ploy to have a character move from being a cynical-but-pathetic has-been to a gloryhound fantasist to a genuine hero, but Tim Allen's Nesmith/Taggart is a respectful evocation of the mix of bedrock decency and naughty boy rebellion that characterised William Shatner's Captain Kirk. This is one of Allen's more comfortable big-screen roles, even when he takes on such Shatner/Kirk staples as a shirtless scene and a mock punch-up with his alien best friend. Sigourney Weaver, always an underrated comedienne, finds a moment of real strength when she insists on doing her scripted job (repeating everything the ship's computer says) no matter how stupid it is, and goes along gamely with the adolescent premise by showing more and more cleavage as the perils increase.

The concept is not entirely original, having precedents in *The Last Star Fighter*, where a video-games champion was needed to win a space war, and the cable series *Adventures of Captain Zoom* in which the vain star of a 50s sci-fi show is asked to become a real hero by a race like *Quest's* Thermians. However, this is a far healthier production which flits easily between showing the lightly caricatured world of *Quest* fandom (nerds bombard actors with technical questions, dumpy women in unflattering uniforms stand around mooning over middle-aged matinee idols), the career afterlives of former stars and adventure. Aside from spaceship sets whose clean, television sci-fi look still feels like a 'real' environment, there are genuinely imaginative special effects which manage to be recognisably in the spirit of the cheesy originals.

The plot creates tension between the go-it-alone heroism of Allen's character and the grumbling of his often-overshadowed crew. But the film accords each cast member funny bits of business—after a space battle, a terrified Alan Rickman leaves the ship's bridge with the cry of, "I'm looking for a pub"—and there are amusing sub-plots. Tony Shalhoub's Kwan misses a crucial revelation and so is much more casual about dire peril than his teammates, while Sam Rockwell's Guy incredulously exclaims as the crew wander into danger, "Didn't you watch the show?" After finally impressing on the others he might really be endangered, Gwen makes the supremely unreassuring statement: "Let's get out of here before something eats Guy."

VILLAGE VOICE, 1/4/00, p. 108, Amy Taubin

As luck would have it, the last film I will have seen in a theater in the 20th century is *Galaxy Quest*. DreamWorks' *Star Trek* parody knocks off the characters and costumes of the familiar franchise and adds such Spielbergian touches as suburban science-prodigy teens and innocent aliens given to clapping their hands as if they believed in fairies, or more relevantly, as if they believed the *Galaxy Quest* TV series was a documentary about human space exploration.

The scientifically advanced but semiotically unsophisticated Thermians intercepted transmissions of *Galaxy Quest* and built their entire civilization around its technology and codes of comradeship. When their society is threatened by some very bad aliens who look rather like Maurice Sendak's Wild Things (courtesy of Stan Winston's creature-effects shop), they enlist the help of the *Galaxy Quest* cast (Tim Allen, Sigourney Weaver, Alan Rickman, Tony Shalhoub, and a particularly droll Sam Rockwell), who've spent the years since their show was canceled traipsing around to Trekkie-like conventions and presiding over cut-rate electronics-store openings. Believing that the aliens are merely enthusiastic fans, they allow themselves to be transported to another galaxy, where they're placed at the controls of a spaceship that looks exactly like the set of their TV show. They move the familiar levers and it flies. At this point the movie turns into an extremely elaborate video game featuring intergalactic flying mines and enemy spaceships. The many eight-to-11-year-olds in the audience seemed completely enthralled.

Also reviewed in:
CHICAGO TIMES, 12/24/99, Friday/p. 5, Mark Caro
NEW YORK TIMES, 12/24/99, p. E19, Lawrence Van Gelder
VARIETY, 12/20/99-1/2/00, p. 57, Joe Leydon
WASHINGTON POST, 12/24/99, Weekend/p. 37, Michael O'Sullivan
WASHINGTON POST, 12/25/99, p. C1, Rita Kempley

GAMBLER, THE

An Independent Artists release of a co-production of Channel Four Films and UGCDA International in association with Hungry Eye Pictures & KRO Drama presentation. *Producer:* Charles Cohen and Marc Vlessing. *Director:* Karoly Makk. *Screenplay:* Katharine Ogden, Charles Cohen, and Nick Dear. *Director of Photography:* Jules van den Steenhoven. *Editor:* Kevin Whelan. *Music:* Brian Lock. *Sound:* Wim Vonk and (music) John Pitt. *Sound Editor:* William Trent. *Production Designer:* Ben van Os. *Art Director:* Lórad Jávor and Tibor Lázár. *Set Decorator:* István Tóth. *Special Effects:* Ferenc Ormos. *Costumes:* Dien van Strazalen. *Make-up:* Károly B. Temesvári. *Stunt Coordinator:* Béla Unger. *Running time:* 97 minutes. *MPAA Rating:* Not Rated.

CAST: Michael Gambon (Fyodor Dostoyevsky); Jodhi May (Anna Snitkina); Tom Jansen (Stellovsky); Polly Walker (Polina); Dominic West (Aleksei); Angeline Ball (Mme. Blanche); Johan Leysen (De Grieux); Luise Rainer (Grandmother); John Wood (The General); Gijs

Scholten von Asschat (Maikov); Marjon Brandsma (Mme de Cominges); Ed de Bruin (Croupier 1); Vittoria de Bruin (Middle Aged Woman); Lucy Davis (Dunya); András Fekete (Potapych); Zoltán Gera (Creditor); Patrick Godfrey (Professor Ohlkin); Greet Groot (Ustinya); Lajos István Hadjú (Dwarf); William Houston (Pasha Isaev); Zoltán Kamondy (Man in Rags); János Koltay (Casino Manager); Antal Konrád (Creditor); Mark Lacey (Ivan); Nancy Manningham (Secretary); Károly Mécs (Hotel Manager); Peter Meikle (English Gentleman); Michael Mehllmann (Hangers on); András Mész (Young Aristocrat); Ferenc Németh (Doctor); Éva Papp (Grandmother's Maid); Géza Pártos (Pawnbroker); József Pilissy (Croupier 2); Miklós Törkenczey (Shorthand Professor); Vera Venczel (Anna's Mother); János Xantus (Karl).

LOS ANGELES TIMES, 8/13/99, Calendar/p. 18, Kevin Thomas

Some years ago American writer Charles Cohen came up with the idea that an interplay between the unfolding of the Fyodor Dostoevsky novel "The Gambler" and the fevered, dramatic circumstances under which it was written could make a compelling film.   When he saw a retrospective in New York of the films of the master Hungarian director Karoly Makk, he felt he had discovered the ideal director for the project.

Cohen was right on both counts, for "The Gambler" is a sweeping, romantic period film in the elegant European tradition, an intricately intertwined tale of grand passion and equally powerful obsession.   The deft intercutting between Dostoevsky's inventing his story and the telling of the story itself culminates in a graceful and provocative fusion of life and art.   Michael Gambon gives one of his typically splendid, multifaceted portrayals as Dostoevsky, surely one of his most demanding roles.   That Gambon was 56 when he made this film is no matter; Dostoevsky's hard existence would logically make him look older than his years.

When we meet Dostoevsky, in the fall of 1866, he could scarcely be in more dire straits.   At 45 he's an epileptic, given to bouts of hard drinking and is in such a desperate financial situation that in return for 3,000 rubles he signed away to his ruthless publisher Stellovsky (Tom Jansen) not only the right to publish a collected edition of his works but also the rights to all his works, past and future, should he fail to deliver a novel of no fewer than 160 pages.   A friend recommends that he hire a stenographer to help him meet his deadline, and that's how Anna Snitkina (Jodhi May), a 20-year-old whiz at this new profession, enters his life.

A lovely young woman of a good though impoverished family, Anna takes a stance of resolute independence and relentlessly efficient professionalism, but inevitably she becomes caught up in the maelstrom that is Dostoevsky's life.   In time she falls in love with him and becomes determined to be the mainstay of the novelist's life.

As Dostoevsky starts dictating his novel it comes alive on the screen, transporting us to the fictional spa of Roulettenberg, where an intricate tale of intrigue and desperation is being played out in its gambling halls and private suites.   We meet Dostoevsky's alter ego, the fiery young Alexei (Dominic West), enamored of the glamorous Paulina (Polly Walker), who in turn has become obsessed with an icy, phony French count, De Grieux (Johan Leysen), to whom her stepfather, the General (John Wood), a feckless gambler, has become deeply in debt.

As Dostoevsky, prone to compulsive gambling himself, teeters on the brink of disaster, so do his characters.   But there's a big difference: The devoted and steadfast presence of Anna's love may yet triumph over Dostoevsky's demons or at least hold them at bay enough for him to survive and to continue writing.

This film is remarkable in another way as well—the return to the screen of Luise Rainer after an absence of more than 50 years.   Rainer was the first person ever to win two Oscars in a row then quit after becoming swiftly disenchanted with Hollywood.   She deserves a grand entrance and that's exactly what Makk provides Rainer, whose Academy Awards were for her self-sacrificing wife in "The Good Earth" and as French star Anna Held in "The Great Ziegfeld," the first wife of the legendary showman who discarded her for actress Billie Burke.   As Grandmother, the mother of the General, Rainer arrives from Moscow, elegantly gowned and borne on a throne-like chair, determined to stop her son from further squandering the family fortune.   But in demanding to see the casino with her own eyes she soon succumbs to the thrill of the roulette wheel herself.

In a film steeped in emotional turmoil and despair Rainer brings a refreshing jolt of vitality.

Grandmother may be the oldest of the film's central characters, but she's the youngest at heart. Not for Rainer is the illusion of youth promised by cosmetic surgery. She wears the lines in her face honestly while her youthful spirit glows from within and lights up those large, dark, unchanged and unforgettable eyes. She was 87 at the time she filmed "The Gambler"; she is now 89 and busy promoting the film. Her presence recalls an earlier Makk coup: In 1970 he persuaded the great Hungarian actress Lili Darvas, widow of playwright Ferenc Molnar, to return home to play an aged aristocrat, lovingly sustained in her delusions by her daughter-in-law, in his most honored film, "Love."

Jules van den Steenhoven's glowing, luminous cinematography takes full advantage of "The Gambler's" many spectacular authentic locales. May's Anna, lovely, intelligent and centered, provides an effective contrast to so many stormy figures swirling about her. "The Gambler" was surely a gamble in itself, with its parallel stories, its combustible, larger-than-life hero and its unbridled romantic spirit, but it paid off handsomely.

NEW YORK POST, 8/4/99, p. 44, Rod Dreher

Writers looking for a subject are sometimes urged, "Write what you know." In the autumn of 1866, the great novelist Fyodor Dostoevski knew little more than misery and penury, brought on by his addiction to gambling.

Compounding his woe was a wicked bargain the desperate novelist struck with his unscrupulous publisher, Stellovsky. In exchange for Stellovsky paying his large gambling debts, Dostoevski signed an agreement to produce a novel of no less than 160 pages in a relatively short period of time.

If he failed, the rights to all Dostoevski's past and future works would pass to Stellovsky.

Hungarian director Karoly Makk's film "The Gambler" begins with a young stenographer named Anna Snitkina (Jodhi May) being sent to Dostoevski's apartment to help him, with only one month to go before the deadline.

The woebegone novelist, played here by the great Michael Gambon, is a mess: overweight testy, epileptic, chain-smoking, with not a single word committed to paper.

The film tracks Anna's deepening intellectual and emotional involvement with Dostoevski as she insistently coaxes the novel from him. She encourages him to explore the gambling obsession that has brought him to ruin, hoping the result will save the writer's career.

Fleshing out the connection between art and life, Makk's film jumps back and forth from the musty writer's apartment to the imaginary world of Roulettenberg, the fictional German gambling resort where the characters in Dostoevski's novel, "The Gambler," pursue their reckless passions.

Despite good performances by Gambon and May, "The Gambler"—the film, that is—feels stiff and stuffy, never urgent or involving. The Roulettenberg scenes, in which decadent Russian aristocrats risk their fortunes while slumming with rich, scheming Frenchmen, play like cheap TV costume drama, and they distract from the developing romance between the cautious, sensible Anna and her excess-driven employer.

One bright surprise: the return to the screen of Luise Rainer, who won the Best Actress Oscar in 1936 and 1937.

She plays the surprisingly feisty matriarch from the fictional story who arrives in Roulettenberg ready to gamble. The old gal—Luise, I mean—has still got it.

SIGHT AND SOUND, 11/97, p. 40, Julian Graffy

St Petersburg, 1866. Anna Snitkina, a young stenographer, is sent to take dictation from Fyodor Dostoyevsky of a novel he must complete within a month or he will lose the rights to all his future writings to his unscrupulous publisher Stellovsky. Dostoyevsky is tyrannical and difficult, but the story, a tale of gambling and passion in the German spa town of Roulettenberg, fascinates Anna. Its narrator, Alexei, young tutor to a general's children, tells of how the financially crippled general and his beautiful stepdaughter Polina fall victim to an adventuress, Mlle Blanche, and a predatory Frenchman, De Grieux. Their only hope lies in the death of the family's ancient grandmother, which will enable them to settle their debts. Polina sends Alexei to the casino to win the money that will free her from De Grieux, but he loses.

As the story develops, Anna is drawn under its spell, asking questions, even making suggestions. She becomes ever more important to Dostoyevsky, keeping his creditors and his sinister stepson Pasha at bay. In the story, the grandmother arrives, old but hale, and is herself swept up by the fatal charm of the roulette wheel. After initial wins she loses all her money. Polina succumbs to De Grieux and Blanche throws the general out.

Back in St Petersburg, Apollinaria (Polina) Suslova, Dostoyevsky's former mistress, arrives to take him off to Paris to "be [her] companion in hell", but Anna's spirited resistance defeats her. At the story's casino, Alexei breaks the bank, but Polina, discarded by De Grieux, refuses to take his money. Anna's commitment forces Dostoyevsky to complete his novel, her energy transcending his exhaustion and illness. As the novel reaches its doomed climax with Alexei an inveterate gambler, Anna and Dostoyevsky take the manuscript to Stellovsky within hours of the deadline. In a coda, Anna, now married to Dostoyevsky, comes with her child to reclaim him from a casino gambling table.

It is a commonplace of Dostoyevsky criticism that the author's personal addiction to forms of intensity—gambling, passion, hatred—fuelled the plots and characters of his novels. In particular, his affair with Apollinaria Suslova in the early 1860s inspired the "infernal women" of the late novels. Suslova is the antipode of the calm devout stenographer, Anna Snitkina, who took dictation of *The Gambler* in 1866 and became the writer's enduring second wife.

The veteran Hungarian director Károly Makk's *The Gambler* is both a version of the novel and, more centrally, the story of how conventional Anna is sucked into the passionate Dostoyevskian world. The unfortunate consequence of this insistent double vision is that both novel and biography are diminished. The film's reading of the novel is fragmented and opaque, with much of the plot and entire characters, sadly including the eccentric Englishman Mr Astley, jettisoned. The story of Anna is developed in a predictable way. She is given a tragic family and a dull clerkly suitor, and famous episodes from Dostoyevsky's biography (such as the arrest and mock execution, and the Siberian exile where he shared the fate of the Decembrists) are clumsily inserted by Dostoyevsky and members of his circle for the benefit of those members of the audience who might be cramming for 'A' levels.

But increasingly the film subsides into a mechanical succession of intercut scenes between the tale of passion and its passionate tellers, reducing art to sublimated autobiography, and downplaying the profound distinction between these two kinds of passion: the unthinking driven sensuality of the general's entourage and the inward intensity of Anna. Her passion is, though latent, just as importunate but considerably more mysterious, as suggested by the luminous performance of Jodhi May.

In general Károly Makk is well served by his actors, with Michael Gambon as the angular, irascible author, and Polly Walker as the voluptuous Polina. All too briefly, we're treated to the magnificent Luise Rainer as the grandmother, a part previously graced by Edith Evans, prey to the cultic thrall of a casino shot by Jules van den Steenhoven to look like a baleful cathedral.

In his long career Makk has been brilliant at suggesting the force of sometimes self-destructive passion. This was most powerfully evoked in his 1971 *Love*, the story of a family split by political repression in 1953 Budapest, while his 1982 *Another Way* sets a forbidden love affair against the compromises and evasions of Hungary after the failure of the 1956 Revolution. Both of these films draw much of their atmosphere front the ubiquitousness of prying eyes. The surveillance motif is pervasive in *The Gambler* too, and at least to this extent Makk stamps a personal signature on the film. Alexei and others watch the gambling, Anna records the story, Dostoyevsky's creditors and his reptilian publisher call constantly to monitor his progress, his malevolent stepson Pasha Isaev hovers voyeuristically around the flat, while outside a police spy keeps constant vigil and Anna's suitor, Ivan, peruses Dostoyevsky's file at the Ministry where he works. Gradually, observation and recording turn into enthralled participation and complicity, a transgression first anatomised in Russian literature by Pushkin with the sinister German in *The Queen of Spades*.

But the earlier films drew their specific intensity front Makk's immersion in the Hungarian political context. Making *The Gambler* he seems rudderless, reduced to addressing this quintessentially nineteenth-century story through the dull new conventions of "filming the classics". Too often the plot's developments are indicated through pathetic fallacy, in other words melodramatic signpost music accompanying melodramatic signpost weather (a sudden violent thunderstorm for crisis, followed by a blissful rural sunrise for its resolution). This stylistic anonymity leaves the enigmas of both Dostoyevsky's and Anna's personalities scarcely probed, and the sources and workings of his genius (as a postscript notes the 1860s was the decade of *Crime and Punishment* and *The Idiot*) insufficiently illuminated.

VILLAGE VOICE, 8/10/99, p. 59, Leslie Camhi

"The only true democracy in Europe" was how Fyodor Dostoyevsky described the casino in Wiesbaden, where submission to the laws of chance leveled many a class distinction. Whether radical politics, nihilist principles, or extreme masochism inspired the Russian writer to gamble, the roulette wheel consumed his fortunes repeatedly. *The Gambler,* Hungarian director Karoly Makk's carefully crafted and richly atmospheric adaptation of Dostoyevsky's eponymous novel, interweaves its story of gaming and erotic obsession with a period of 27 days in the writer's life, when his hopes for future solvency lay in that work's speedy completion.

At 45, the desperately debt-ridden author agreed to deliver a novel by a certain date, or his unscrupulous publisher would own everything he would ever write. In Makk's film, Dostoyevsky (Michael Gambon) is suffering from a nasty case of writer's block, when the frightfully efficient Anna Snitkina (Jodhi May), a student stenographer, appears at his door. After the requisite contest of wills, they get down to work, and the camera takes off into the swirling realms of fiction. There, in a sinister resort town, a young tutor (Dominic West) strives to win the love of a beautiful woman (Polly Walker) by earning large sums at roulette. Her stepfather, a general and closet gambler, is awaiting his mother's death to free himself from mounting debts. When the grande dame (screen legend Luise Rainer) turns up alive and kicking, all bets are off.

Skillfully flashing back and forth between the empires of the imagination and unnerving reality, Makk winds these parallel stories into reality, Makk winds these parallel stories into a thick coil of passion and disillusionment. Gambon is excellent as the snarling but tender, devout and messy, epileptic genius. The gradual growth of May's doglike devotion is initially grating but mirrors the facts of history, in which the enormous risks of love appear to have won, against all odds.

Also reviewed in:
NEW REPUBLIC, 8/23/99, p. 28, Stanley Kaufmann
NEW YORK TIMES, 8/4/99, p. E3, Stephen Holden
NEW YORKER, 8/16/99, p. 91, Anthony Lane
VARIETY, 11/10-16/97, p. 41, Lael Loewenstein

GENERAL'S DAUGHTER, THE

A Paramount Pictures release of a Mace Neufeld and Robert Rehme production and a Jonathan D. Krane production. *Executive Producer:* Jonathan D. Krane. *Producer:* Mace Neufeld. *Director:* Simon West. *Screenplay:* Christopher Bertolini and William Goldman. *Based on the novel by:* Nelson DeMille. *Director of Photography:* Peter Menzies, Jr. *Editor:* Glen Scantlebury. *Music:* Carter Burwell. *Music Editor:* Adam Smalley and Jim Henrikson. *Sound:* Tommy Lausey, Steve Maslow, Gregg Landaker, and (music) Michael Farrow. *Sound Editor:* Stephen Hunter Flick. *Casting:* Mindy Marin. *Production Designer:* Dennis Washington. *Art Director:* Tom Taylor and Ann Harris. *Set Designer:* Lorrie Campbell, Lynn Christopher, and Beverli Eagen. *Set Decorator:* Marvin March. *Special Effects:* George Paine, Chuck Stewart and Paul Lombardi. *Visual Effects:* Glenn Neufeld. *Costumes:* Erica Edell Phillips. *Make-up:* Toni G. *Stunt Coordinator:* Mark Riccardi. *Running time:* 118 minutes. *MPAA Rating:* R.

CAST: John Travolta (Paul Brenner); Madeleine Stowe (Sarah Sunhill); James Cromwell (General Joe Campbell); Timothy Hutton (Colonel Kent); Clarence Williams, III (Colonel Fowler); James Woods (Colonel Moore); Leslie Stefanson (Elisabeth Campbell); Daniel von Bargen (Chief Yardley); Peter Weireter (Belling); Mark Boone, Jr. (Elkins); John Beasley (Colonel Slesinger); Boyd Kestner (Captain Elby); Brad Beyer (Bransford); John Benjamin Hickey (Captain Goodson); Rick Dial (Cal Seiver); Ariyan Johnson (PFC Robbins); John

Frankenheimer (General Sonnenberg); Katrina vanden Heuvel (CNN Anchor); Chris Snyder (Deputy Yardley); Steve Danton and Rich Jackson (Bomb Van Soldiers); Joshua Stafford and Darius Montgomery (Soldiers Who Find Elizabeth); Mark Ivie (Fencing Loser); Michael Terry Swiney (Lockup Sergeant); Tait Ruppert (Young Tech); Lisa A. Tripp (Work Detail Leader); Steve Goyen (Honor Guard Commander); Pablo Espinosa (Color Guard Commander); Levin Handy, Jr. and Jason M. Luevano (Airborne soldiers); Gustavo A. Perdomo (Drill Team NCO); Rodney Mitchell and Ryan D. Kirkland (Ranger Instructors); Michael Gerald Jones, Jr. (Soldier in Locker Room); Matt Anderson (Firing Party Commander); Cooper Huckabee (Colonel Weems).

LOS ANGELES TIMES, 6/18/99, Calendar/p. 1, Kenneth Turan

Like a sinking fly ball that converging outfielders can't quite reach, "The General's Daughter" is what baseball announcers call a 'tweener. A middling, so-so thriller about a murder investigation on an Army base, it falls to Earth somewhere between failure and success, inconclusive to the end.

"The General's Daughter" stars John Travolta and Madeleine Stowe as the team doing the investigating and is based on a novel by best-selling author Nelson DeMille. Getting that book screen-ready was apparently not easy; two writers get actual credit (Christopher Bertolini and the veteran William Goldman), and press reports claim that a total of six were employed.

No matter who is responsible, the film's script is the nub of a problem. In the best whodunits, crackling direction and crisp acting combine to pull reluctant audiences over inevitable bumps in the exposition. Convoluted and occasionally far-fetched though it is, "General's" story line is salvageable, but it needs help from the rest of the talent if it's going to make the leap to plausibility—help that it doesn't get.

Simon West, an award-winning commercial director whose debut feature was the over-adrenalized "Con Air," apparently relished the chance to do something different, something in which words mattered more than the explosions. But even in a film like this, West's strength remains the visual.

"General's Daughter" is set in the vicinity of Ft. MacCallum, a fictitious Southern military base, and West and cinematographer Peter Menzies Jr. do such an effective job with the atmosphere that you can almost smell the swamp gas. And the credit sequence that introduces key character Gen. "Fighting Joe" Campbell (James Cromwell) is one of several that are smartly put together.

Army Criminal Investigations Division officer Paul Brenner (Travolta) has a soft spot in his heart for the fighting general, but Brenner's presence at Ft. MacCallum doesn't initially involve the great man, who is retiring from the Army and under consideration for a vice presidential nomination.

Similarly, when Brenner meets Capt. Elisabeth Campbell (Leslie Stefanson) who offers to change his tire, he doesn't connect her to the general. But once the captain is found dead on the base and the initial reports indicate torture and rape as well as murder, he understands soon enough just whose daughter she is.

This is such a big case that, at the strong urging of Col. William Kent (Timothy Hutton), the fort's provost marshal, Brenner is forced to work with another CID officer, rape investigator Sarah Sunhill (Stowe), a feisty operative who, as it happens, had a romantic fling with Brenner some time in the past.

Though the general asks Brenner as a good soldier to clear the case up in 36 hours—the better to keep the meddling FBI and the intrusive media out of the picture—the case soon becomes so complicated that it can barely be even understood in 36 hours.

Also, the deeper Brenner and Sunhill get into their work, the more threatening what they find becomes to people on and off the base. And Brenner's iconoclastic manner, likely to provoke an outraged, "Who, the hell do you think you are?" from those he questions, doesn't make things any easier.

Though we're inevitably curious about the identity of the murderer, seeing the investigation unfold on screen is less than compelling. West's visuals are effective, but there are a flatness and lack of subtlety in his direction of dialogue that make sequences irritating when they should be involving. Brenner's rivalry with the local sheriff, for instance, is so ponderous and pointless that it's hard to know why it's in the picture.

The film's acting also has a tendency to be unconvincing. The reliable Stowe is invariably solid, but Travolta never fully recovers from being forced to spend the film's first half hour as an undercover agent with a phony Southern accent that wouldn't fool Gomer Pyle.

Travolta's least tenable moments come in his verbal duel with Col. Robert Moore (James Woods), the dead woman's mentor at the base's psychological operations unit. Their dialogue is meant to be a display of sharp repartee, but the interchanges are listless and dispassionate, consistently off rather than on the beat.

Just as troubling is the graphic sexual violence toward women that is a key feature of "General's Daughter." Though the filmmakers probably feel they've been discreet and low-key in dealing with what is doubtless an important element in DeMille's novel, excessive shots of spread-eagled, tortured and raped victims are hard to stomach and in no way help this dramatically impoverished film gain the credibility it certainly needs.

NEW YORK, 6/28-7/5/99, p. 128, Peter Rainer

The best murder mysteries are usually the ones with the most red herrings. *The General's Daughter*, based on the novel by Nelson DeMille and starring John Travolta, certainly has its share of herrings, as well as sharks and whales and eels and blowfish. It's a regular Fulton Fish Market. But who cares about trying to puzzle out the day's catch? We never have the sense in this movie of being led willfully astray by the filmmakers. How can they pretend to be one step ahead of us when they're out of step themselves? The requisite Aha! moment when it all comes together turns out to be a ho-hum moment. Whodunit? Who cares?

As Paul Brenner, a top officer for the army's criminal investigation division, Travolta is investigating the murder at a Georgia military base of Captain Elisabeth Campbell (Leslie Stefanson), a psychological-warfare expert and the daughter of a retiring general (James Cromwell) short-listed for the vice-presidency. The pulp mix is all here—scandal, Washington, the military, S&M. But seaminess should be more redolent. Despite the anything-for-effect camera work—courtesy of director Simon *(Con Air)* West—the overriding tone is soggy. About the only thing that's crisp in this movie is the way everybody salutes.

Travolta has enough star presence to carry the picture—barely. Having been out of the limelight for so many years, he seems to be in every fourth movie now, and, marvelous as he often is, he could profit from acting less and choosing better. *The General's Daughter*, like last year's *A Civil Action*, plays into a dull streak of righteousness in Travolta; and like most actors, he's not at his best when he's bucking for sainthood, although these are often the roles that win awards. The rest of the cast, including Madeleine Stowe as Brenner's co-investigator and ex-fling, Timothy Hutton as the base's provost marshal, and James Woods as another psych-warfare expert—good casting!—seems primed for a script with better dialogue than the one they were handed. They all take turns overacting and underacting.

At the end of the movie, a message comes on telling us that there are now almost 200,000 women on active duty in the armed forces. This helpful tidbit is no doubt meant to take our minds off the movie's garish rape and near-rape scenes and convince us that what we've been watching actually has something to do with feminist travails in the military. Right—and *The Silence of the Lambs* was about the plight of the mad.

NEW YORK POST, 6/18/99, p. 57, Rod Dreher

On the way out of "The General's Daughter" screening, Paramount representatives handed critics cards asking them not to reveal the suspense thriller's "surprising twists and ending."

Even if we were authorized to reveal them, very few critics would be able to explain them. This movie's denouement is so nonsensical and asinine that it would take all 14,000 miles of cable holding up the Brooklyn Bridge to suspend your disbelief.

A real pity, that, because for most of its nearly two-hour running time, "The General's Daughter" is an entertaining and reasonably absorbing mystery. Cocky, thick-necked John Travolta, who manages to be both beefy and hammy here, plays Paul Brenner, an Army criminal investigator assigned an extremely sensitive case.

The daughter of a top general (James Cromwell) has been found naked, tied to the ground with tent stakes and murdered in the heat of a summer night down South. The catch: She doesn't appear to have been raped.

The Army wants to keep the investigation brief and top secret, for reasons both plain and obscure, and they believe they can count on Brenner's loyalty to the Army and to Gen. Campbell, under whom he served in Vietnam.

The dead woman, Capt. Elisabeth Campbell (Leslie Stephenson), was a hotshot officer on base but led a dark, sleazy double life.

"How she died seems to be related to how she lived," observes the shvitzing Sherlock (this is one of those Southern-set movies in which nobody has air-conditioning or the sense to open a window).

The deeper Brenner and his co-investigator, an old flame named Sarah Sunhill (Madeleine Stowe) go, the sicker the story gets. There's reason to suspect Capt. Campbell was helping the entire base get its kinks out as she knotted a tortuous (and torturous) web of deceit.

Fair warning: If depictions of violent, twisted sexuality turn your stomach, by all means go AWOL on this movie.

Though his character is little more than a stick figure, charismatic Travolta has fun with it, righteously pushing around uppity punk servicemen who get in his way like a pudgy Dirty Harry.

Cromwell cuts a dashing figure as the ramrod-straight general, but Stowe fades to nothing in her underwritten role (Paul and Sarah's past life together is a non-starter). The movie's freakiest performance comes from James Woods, natch, as Capt. Campbell's squirrelly superior in the Psychological Operations Unit.

The plotting of the movie, which is adapted from Nelson DeMille's novel by Christopher Bertolini and William Goldman, is paradoxically most predictable (this guy is obviously not the villain, that guy clearly has something to hide, and what's that straw-man Southern sheriff doing there?) and utterly daft.

"The General's Daughter" has a complicated, ironic point to make about family ties and women in the military—and yet it lacks the least credibility.

Those twists and turns we can't discuss make no sense, emotionally, politically, psychologically or dramatically, leaving you feeling like a chump for having bothered at all.

Forget the surreptitious off-base slap-and-tickle; the most perverse thing about "The General's Daughter" is the way it abuses the audience.

NEWSDAY, 6/18/99, Part II/p. B6, John Anderson

When a character is asked at the beginning of a film, "Are you a policeman or a soldier?" and he says, "A soldier, sir! " you're pretty confident that he's going to be a policeman in, oh, about 116 minutes.

But for most of "The General's Daughter," a damply steamy, barely structured thriller about the rape and murder of a female Army captain, you don't really care. As Paul Brenner, the Army investigator assigned to the case, John Travolta has a role that fits him like form-fitting fatigues: disheveled, rebellious and with enough patented goofiness to prevent the miscarriage of casting that plagued him in "A Civil Action."

As Sara Sunhill, Brenner's caustic partner in crime-busting (and former lover), Madeleine Stowe seems more relaxed than she's ever been. As a result, they achieve a biting, comic give-and-take that makes the film a very funny thriller indeed.

Unfortunately, "The General's Daughter," from the novel by pulp auteur Nelson DeMille, isn't a comedy, despite the witty script by Christopher Bertolini and the fabled William Goldman (or, for that matter, despite the laughs it may get out of its more surreal attempts at tragedy).

Travolta and Stowe can't do anything about the fact that "The General's Daughter" leapfrogs with dizzying disdain for narrative flow. Or that while bewailing the horror of sexual assault it virtually glorifies rape during a gratuitously lengthy re-enactment. Or—less distastefully but no less damaging—that the payoff of the film can't possibly meet the expectations of its setup.

The hypocrisy of honor is "Daughter's" big, billboard-size message: Brenner, a career military investigator, has to choose whether to bury the probe a la the suggestion of the distinguished Gen. Joe Campbell, who was Brenner's commander in Vietnam (one of the rare examples of a star making himself older than he is). Or, to pursue the case as far up the military ladder as it happens to go. Brenner, naturally, is unafraid of heights.

James Woods, who seems to be on a roll lately, is terrific as Moore, the psychiatrist/mentor of the beautiful Elisabeth Campbell (Leslie Stefanson), the ambitious but tortured Army captain who's found staked out, naked and dead on a patch of Army base. As her father, the rigid careerist Joe Campbell, James Cromwell ("Babe") is deliciously hateful. On the other hand, Clarence Williams III and Timothy Hutton, looking like he just graduated from "Taps," could have phoned the whole thing in. No, "General's Daughter" is the Travolta-Stowe Show, and they probably make the trip worthwhile, although I can't guarantee that when the murderer cries out, "She became my obsession... " you won't want to present arms and fire.

SIGHT AND SOUND, 10/99, p. 44, John Wrathall

Fort McCallum, the Deep South. When the naked corpse of Captain Elisabeth Campbell, daughter of General Joe Campbell, is discovered staked to the ground, Warrant Officer Paul Brenner of the Criminal Investigations Division has 36 hours to solve the case before the FBI is called in.

Brenner is teamed with his former girlfriend, army rape-counsellor Sarah Sunhill. Colonel Moore, Elisabeth's commander, is arrested when his fingerprints are found on the victim's dog tags. After Moore's apparent suicide, General Campbell's adjutant Colonel Fowler is anxious to pin the blame on Moore. But Brenner and Sunhill visit West Point, where they learn that Elisabeth, a few years back, was gang-raped on a training exercise, and left staked out on the ground. Her father persuaded her to hush the incident up.

From evidence provided by Colonel Moore's boyfriend, Brenner discovers that Elisabeth persuaded Moore to help her recreate the circumstances of her rape so that she could show her father what she had been through. But General Campbell, after discovering his daughter staked to the ground, decided to leave her there. Colonel Kent, who had an unrequited crush on Elisabeth, then killed her out of frustrated passion. Brenner races to the training ground to find that Kent has deliberately led Sunhill into a minefield. Brenner saves Sunhill before Kent kills himself by stepping on a mine. Instead of hushing up the case, Brenner threatens General Campbell with court martial for conspiracy to conceal a crime.

With *Con Air,* director Simon West demonstrated that he could deliver a pyrotechnic action thriller in the classic Jerry Bruckheimer mould by keeping the camera constantly on the move and cutting every few seconds. He applies the same approach to *The General's Daughter* with rather less success, because this salacious whodunit requires very little action, but an endless parade of dialogue scenes in which assorted suspects tell the investigating duo what happened, cueing thunderous flashbacks.

In a desperate bid to pump up the action quotient (and provide material for a trailer) West throws in a succession of ridiculous climaxes, as bombastic as they are irrelevant to the plot. For starters, there's death by motorboat propeller. Later, the discovery of Colonel Moore's corpse is orchestrated, preposterously, to *Carmina Burana* with baffling cut-aways to a fencing match in progress somewhere else on the base. Madeleine Stowe's role as Travolta's investigating sidekick, Sarah Sunhill, exists solely so that she can twice wander back to the crime scene at night there to be assaulted by different suspects in the murder (though, since only one of them was actually guilty, what was the other one playing at?).

Worst of all, however, are the grotesque flashbacks to Elisabeth Campbell's rape on a training exercise at West Point, recounted in gloating slow-motion. West belongs to the school of directors who believe that everything in a film should look glossy and beautiful, even if the event depicted is itself abhorrent He's a connoisseur of mist, low-angle tracking shots, helicopters and ejected cartridge cases cascading to the ground—but his ham-fisted deployment of these flashy clichés leaves one pining for the comparative subtlety of Tony Scott.

It's hard to see what else beyond money can have attracted John Travolta to the unrewarding role of Paul Brenner. In solving the murder, Brenner's sole act of detection is noticing a bin liner on a roof, an event which West, inevitably, tries to drum up into another action crescendo. The rest of the time, all Brenner is required to do is stare at suspects in that solid-jawed Travolta way until they tell him what they know, and launch us into another flashback. Brenner's character never develops, though he does mercifully drop his southern accent a few minutes into the film.

His past relationship with Sunhill (who, as someone actually points out in the film, has no real function in the investigation: why does the victim need a rape counsellor if she's already dead?) is a barefaced contrivance to give Brenner some substance.

The script is credited to Christopher Bertolini and William Goldman; the latter was presumably brought in for rewrites. Over the years, Goldman's two Oscars and his self-promoting handbook *Adventures in the Screen Trade* have given him an unassailable reputation as a script doctor, even now, nearly 30 years after *Butch Cassidy and the Sundance Kid*, he's one of the few screenwriters whose name the general public recognises. But his shoddy work on *The General's Daughter* is only the latest entry in a recent catalogue of trash: *Absolute Power*, *The Chamber* and *Maverick* among others. Take the characterisation of the only halfway interesting person in the film, James Woods' Colonel Moore: he has a funny way of holding a cigarette, listens to opera and is seen cooking his dinner with undue fastidiousness. Of course, he turns out to be gay! Nothing in West's overblown bag of tricks could hope to disguise such a thoroughly by-the-numbers piece of writing.

VILLAGE VOICE, 6/29/99, p. 143, Gary Dauphin

Mucking around the proving grounds and Big House residences of a Louisiana army base, *The General's Daughter* is a curiously primeval detective flick, one that unfolds in a mosquito-infested, Miranda Rights-free zone where a ballsy MP named Paul Brenner (John Travolta) gets his man mostly by cracking jokes and terrorizing suspects. ("You're in the army. You have no rights," Warrant Officer Brenner repeatedly and cheerfully explains.)

Plotwise, *Daughter* is an "aha!"-intensive but thoroughly random mystery beginning when a general's kid is found naked, spread-eagled, and strangled on her dad's bomb range. Poking his head where it doesn't belong and giving the secretive HQ stuffed shirts the what-for, Brenner discovers the general's daughter was into what you'd call a heavy scene, her life and murder comprising a psychosexual scandal that extends to the camp's highest levels, But Not the Way You Expect ... (That final twist is so random that there's actually no way to spoil it, its non sequitur specifics only materializing onscreen when—aha!—they occur to Brenner.)

Improbably diverting, *Daughter is* a displaced cop-versus-rapist flick, making the main action Travolta's winking, ends-justify-the-means antics; army investigator Madeleine Stowe comes along as side kick/banter-buddy. Equally adept at roughing up informants and spotting queer officers (before assuring everyone that what passes between consenting adults is nobody's business, of course), Brenner is more than just a cop; he's the perfect post-Cold War peace keeper, able to feel the under dog's pain even as he's kicking his ass.

Screenwriters Christopher Bertolini and William Goldman do deploy the military-crime saga's classic "truth vs. duty" conundrum in novel ways, but *The General's Daughter is* still pretty absurd, not the least for the way Travolta seems to be channeling a bizarro Bill Clinton throughout, his character as charming, cynical, and roguish as the original, but with a Bronze Star to boot.

Also reviewed in:
CHICAGO TRIBUNE, 6/18/99, Friday/p. A, Michael Wilmington
NEW YORK TIMES, 6/18/99, p. E1, Janet Maslin
VARIETY, 6/14-20/99, p. 32, Todd McCarthy
WASHINGTON POST, 6/18/99, p. C5, Rita Kempley
WASHINGTON POST, 6/18/99, Weekend/p. 45, Desson Howe

GENESIS

A Kino International release of a Kora Films/Balanzan/CNPC/Cinema Public Films coproduction. *Producer:* Jacques Atlan and Chantal Bagilishya. *Director:* Cheick Oumar Sissoko. *Screenplay (based on the "Book of Genesis 23-37") (French with English subtitles):* Jean-Louise

Sagot-Duvauroux. *Director of Photography:* Lionel Cousin. *Editor:* Alio Auguste. *Music:* Décor Sonore. *Running time:* 102 minutes. *MPAA Rating:* Not Rated.

CAST: Sotigui Kouyaté (Jacob); Salif Keita (Esau); Balla Moussa Keita (Hamor); Fatoumata Diawara (Dina); Maïmouna Hélène Diarra (Léa).

CHRISTIAN SCIENCE MONITOR, 12/3/99, p. 15, David Sterritt

Genesis, directed by Mali filmmaker Cheick Oumar Sissoko, retells the biblical story of Jacob and Esau with an eye toward illuminating today's widespread conflicts between clans, tribes, and nations that have differing visions of what constitutes a decent and constructive way of life. Combining its Old Testament story with vivid African imagery, the film may have confusing moments for moviegoers used to traditional Western treatments of this material. For those willing to meet it on its own terms, however, it offers rich new perspectives on a timeless subject.

NEW YORK POST, 12/3/99, p. 49, Lou Lumenick

Covering Chapters 23 to 37 of the Book of Genesis, Mali director Cheick Oumar Sissoko's "La Genese" ("Genesis") is an African-set rethinking of the story of Jacob and Esau.

It's set 300 years after the great flood, when Esau (singer Salif Keita), leader of the hunters, plots revenge against his younger brother Jacob (Sotigui Kouyate), the leader of the shepherds, who he believes has stolen his birthright.

Jacob, meanwhile, is mourning his son Joseph, whom he believes slain by wild beasts—and his daughter Dina is kidnapped and raped by Hamor, leader of the Canaanites.

At her brothers' demand, the Canaanites are all circumcised—the movie's most chilling scene—and then the Canaanites are attacked by the treacherous shepherds.

Not easily followed without a synopsis, the pageant-like "La Genese" concludes with a meeting of the warring tribes, whose elaborate costumes are one of the film's high points, along with stunning African vistas.

VILLAGE VOICE, 12/7/99, p. 144, Elliott Stein

The centerpiece of the recent African Diaspora Festival, *Genesis* audaciously transposes chapters 23 to 37 of the first book of the Bible to Mali, 300 years after the great flood. Cheick Oumar Sissoko's highly symbolic film centers on the war between clans led by two brothers, grizzled shepherd Jacob (Sotigui Kouyate, a veteran of Peter Brook's theater company) and Esau (singer Salif Keita), whose birthright was stolen by Jacob—he's first seen on a mountaintop, plotting revenge, surrounded by his fellow hunters. After a number of bloody deeds are committed on both sides, Jacob learns that his favorite son, Joseph, presumed dead and devoured by wild beasts, is in fact alive, well, and living in the land of the pharaohs. The two rival patriarchs finally make peace; then Jacob and his brothers descend into Egypt.

This French-Malian coproduction benefits from Lionel Cousin's first-rate cinematography. The action is dominated by the enormous Hombori Tondo rock formation in the Sahel desert—it has something of the magical, timeless presence of Monument Valley in John Ford's westerns. The script, by ex-theological student Jean-Louis Sagot Duvauroux, presents the Bible stories as a foreshadowing of ethnic clashes still prevalent today. Despite these interesting ambitions, *Genesis* doesn't work. With 10 features and docs to his credit, Sissoko is no novice, yet most of the film is static, staged like an outdoor school play and without the emotional surge its big theme demands. Principal characters remain archetypes, most of the key events are described rather than dramatized. This does give you plenty of time to admire the eye-popping array of costumes and headdresses.

Also reviewed in:
CHICAGO TRIBUNE, 3/24/00, Friday/p. C, John Petrakis
NATION, 12/20/99, p. 34, Stuart Klawans
NEW YORK TIMES, 12/3/99, p. E25, Stephen Holden
VARIETY, 5/31-6/6/99, p. 32, Deborah Young

GENGHIS BLUES

A Roxie Releasing release of a Wadi Rum presentation. *Producer:* Roko Belic and Adrian Belic. *Director:* Roko Belic. *Screenplay (English and Tuvan with English subtitles):* Roko Belic. *Original concept:* Jason Terrell. *Director of Photography:* Roko Belic and Adrian Belic. *Editor:* Roco Belic. *Sound:* Lemon DeGeorge. *Running time:* 88 minutes. *MPAA Rating:* Not Rated.

WITH: Paul Pena and Kongar-ol Ondar.

LOS ANGELES TIMES, 7/16/99, Calendar/p. 14, Kenneth Turan

It is a sound once heard, never forgotten. A sound with the power to rearrange your mind and transform your life. That's what it did for San Francisco-based blind blues singer Paul Pena, and "Genghis Blues," an enchanting documentary on a magnificent obsession, shows how it all went down.

The sound is that of throat singing, the ability to create two, even three distinct vocal tones simultaneously. The Washington Post calls the results "feats of harmonic acrobatics" and Pena describes it as sounding "just like Popeye singing the blues."

Throat singing is a national passion in Tuva, a North Dakota-sized Asian nation largely populated by nomadic herdsmen. Located north of Mongolia and now a part of the Russian Federation, Tuva was briefly independent from 1921 to 1944 (collectors have the vivid postage stamps to prove it) and takes pride in its association with Genghis Khan, whose top general, the conqueror of Europe, called Tuva home.

Tuva had also piqued the curiosity of celebrated physicist Richard Feynman, who believed that a nation with a capital city named Kyzyl had to be of interest. He and a friend, Ralph Leighton, formed Friends of Tuva, corresponded with Tuvans in their own language, and even got three Tuvans into a Rose Bowl parade.

Pena, not surprisingly, knew none of this back in 1984, when he picked up a random Radio Moscow broadcast while scanning his shortwave radio. A respected musician who'd played with John Lee Hooker, Muddy Waters and T-Bone Walker (and whose grandparents were from the Cape Verde Islands, home of world music star Cesara Evora), Pena heard throat singing for the first time and was transfixed. "That's for me, man," he remembers saying to himself "That's something I could get off doing."

It took Pena years to find anyone who even knew what he'd been listening to, further years to both learn some of the Tuvan language via English-Russian and Russian-Tuvan Braille dictionaries and to teach himself how to sing in kargyraa, one of the key throat-singing styles.

When virtuoso Tuvan throat singer Kongar-Ol Ondar (who's recorded with Frank Zappa, the Kronos Quartet and Mickey Hart) gave a concert in the Bay Area in 1993, Pena surprised him afterward by breaking into some impromptu vocalizing in the lobby. Greatly impressed, Ondar invited Pena to come to his country's next National Throat-Singing Symposium and Competition, scheduled for 1995.

With some financial help from Friends of Tuva ("One of our ideas is just to do crazy things," admits co-founder Leighton), an improbable, ragtag expedition to Tuva was put together. Besides Pena, members included friend and recording engineer Lemon DeGeorge; the late Mario Casetta, KPFK's irascible world music authority; and two young filmmakers, brothers Roko and Adrian Belic, who between the two of them wrote, directed, produced, edited and shot the film, their first.

Under the aegis of Ondar, whom the voice-over describes as "a combination of John F. Kennedy, Elvis and Michael Jordan" in his home country, the expedition went everywhere and met everyone, from the legends of throat singing to Ondar's mother. They also were guests at numerous celebrations at which the slaughter of sheep (shown in graphic detail in the film) was the main event.

Singing in the competition, Pena was a monster hit, living up to his nickname of "Earthquake" and astonishing the Tuvans with both his vocal work and his willingness to speak their obscure language. Despite being dogged by health and other problems, Pena and his companions clearly had the experience of their lives.

As culled by the Belic brothers from 150 hours of video, the 88-minute "Genghis Blues" (which won an audience award at Sundance) is nothing to write home about in terms of technique, but the story it tells couldn't be more charming. And the film's makeshift qualities echo the off-the-wall spirit of the trip itself. A more improbable and endearing yarn can't be imagined.

NEW YORK POST, 7/9/99, p. 59, Rod Dreher

Rookie documentarians Roko and Adrian Belic stumbled onto one hell of a story for their marvelous debut feature, "Genghis Blues."

It goes like this: Blind, impoverished and isolated San Francisco blues musician Paul Pena was up late one night listening to his short-wave, when a strange and captivating sound came over the airwaves, via Radio Moscow.

This is Pena's first encounter with "khoomei," the peculiar throat-singing style native to the isolated Tuva region of the former Soviet Union.

So Pena tracks down a rare recording of Tuvan throat-singing and spends 15 years teaching himself how to do it.

Meanwhile, he uses a Braille device to translate Tuvan into Russian, then Russian into English, so he can learn the language.

One day, a renowned Tuvan throat-singer gives a concert in San Francisco. Pena meets him after the show and belts out a few bars of khoomei.

Next thing you know, Pena's invited to come to faraway Tuva to compete in the country's triennial throat-singing contest. Off he goes, with a cheerful, motley entourage.

What they filmed is extraordinary. The Tuvans are awestruck, really knocked out, that Pena not only mastered their singing art (which sounds like you've swallowed a digiridoo), but even picked up some of their language.

They treat him like a king. Kongar-ol Ondar, the leading Tuvan throat-singer, becomes Pena's dear friend and boon companion, escorting him through the rugged Tuvan cowboy country.

"Genghis Blues" would be entertaining simply as a National Geographic travelogue, but the fact that the Tuvans are so unaffectedly welcoming to Pena makes it a compelling human-interest story.

Following the gravel-voiced hipster Pena on his journey, you can't help being moved by how a poor, suffering house-bound nobody is loved and adored by these foreigners.

"Back home I'm the alien," an incredulous Pena says. "Being blind is hard. I suffer from a lot of depression."

In turn, the Tuvans clearly appreciate the love this unlikely American shows for their culture. Though its production values aren't the best, the Belic brothers' highly entertaining documentary is rare and lovely, and a profoundly moving thing.

VILLAGE VOICE, 7/13/99, P. 60, Amy Taubin

Scruffy and ingenuous, Roko Belic's *Genghis Blues* is a documentary about Paul Pena, a blind San Francisco blues musician who trained himself in the art of Tuvan throat-singing after hearing a Tuvan recording on his shortwave radio. (Tuva is a tiny country on the border of Mongolia that enjoyed about 20 years of autonomy until it was taken over by China in the mid '40s.) In throat-singing, the vocal cords produce two or three different notes simultaneously—you harmonize with yourself without the aid of a multitrack mixer. Pena also taught himself the Tuvan language through a complicated process that involved two braille dictionaries—an English to Russian and a Russian to Tuvan—since no English to Tuvan one exists. When a group of Tuvan singers came to San Francisco on a concert tour, Pena was ready for them. They were so impressed by the way he sang their music and incorporated throat-singing into his own mix of blues and folk that they nicknamed him Earthquake (for the sound he made) and invited him to Tuva to participate in the annual throat-singing competition.

Largely a record of that trip, *Genghis Blues* is not only an ebullient music documentary but a fairly unsettling portrait of a tenacious artist who, aside from a brief success in the '60s, lived in poverty and isolation until he was discovered by a community of musicians in the most distant part of the world.

Genghis Blues is best when it sticks to straightforwardly recording Pena's onstage performances and his moving interactions with his Tuvan hosts. When Belic tries to liven things up with memory montages or even tiny cutaways, his inexperience as a filmmaker becomes painfully evident. But basically he's done right by Pena, and that's what matters. With a better camera, and some practice (Pena practiced throat-singing for 15 years and says he was still terrified when he took the stage in Tuva), have more to rely on than his natural empathy.

Also reviewed in:
CHICAGO TRIBUNE, 9/24/99, Friday/p. J, John Petrakis
NEW YORK TIMES, 7/9/99, p. E14, Stephen Holden
VARIETY, 5/10-16/99, p. 64, Dennis Harvey

GET BRUCE!

A Miramax Films release of an AJK production. *Executive Producer:* Gregory McClatchy and Susan B. Landau. *Producer:* Andrew J. Kuehn. *Director:* Andrew J. Kuehn. *Director of Photography:* Jose Luis Mignone. *Editor:* Gregory McClatchy and Maureen Nolan. *Music:* Michael Feinstein. *Music Editor:* Craig Pettigrew. *Sound:* Russ Simon, Bob Schuck, Keith Winner and Jim Mansen. *Make-up:* Donna Giffen, Charla Miller, Eugenia Weston, Roberto Ramos, Adam Heller and Francois Pelikan. *Running time:* 93 minutes. *MPAA Rating:* R.

WITH: Bruce Vilanch; Bette Midler; Billy Crystal; Robin Williams; Whoopi Goldberg; Lily Tomlin; Nathan Lane; Rosanne; Carol Burnett; Florence Henderson; Rosie O'Donnell; Raquel Welch; George Schlatter.

LOS ANGELES TIMES, 9/17/99, Calendar/p. 8, Kenneth Turan

It's too bad the title "Unzipped" is already spoken for: The fit would be perfect for the genial profile of writer Bruce Vilanch called "Get Bruce!"

That 1995 film, a portrait of designer Isaac Mizrahi, has a lot in common with "Get Bruce!" Both documentaries put a camera on smart, amusing, uninhibited individuals and their friends, then got out of the way. While "Unzipped" was set in the world of high fashion, the focus here is show business all the way.

While Vilanch's name probably registers only with that segment of the public that regularly watches "Hollywood Squares" (where he's chief writer and frequent player), it's something of a mantra to some of the biggest names in entertainment whose material he often ghosts when they appear at awards shows and charity events. "It's a very interesting, intricate kind of relationship," Shirley MacLaine says, "between a comedy writer and a person scared they're not going to be funny."

"Get Bruce!," produced and directed by Andrew J. Kuehn, opens with celebrities publicly singing his praises. Here's Rosie O'Donnell and Whoopi Goldberg dishing on Rosie's TV show and agreeing that "he's the guy you call when you want to say something funny." Adds Nathan Lane, "He's given more great lines to celebrities than a Hollywood coke dealer."

Prone to wearing distinctive eye wear and a daunting variety of T-shirts ("Will Work for Liposuction," "My Other Body Is in the Shop" and "Almost Famous" read a few), the bearded, elfin Vilanch (who actually played an elf on the TV movie "It Nearly Wasn't Christmas") is not just a sharp and funny writer.

Rather, he has both an exact knowledge of what the public personas of various celebrities are and how to write words that fit smoothly with their image. For Roseanne, known for her "gum-chewing dismissal of the world," he writes lines about the need for a "Trailer Court Barbie" and an "Eating Disorder Barbie," while he has an elaborately gowned Raquel Welch ask a crowd, "Do you like my dress? I borrowed it from Ru-Paul."

Though Vilanch has worked, in his own words, with everyone "from ABBA to Zadora," the biggest part of "Get Bruce!" are the segments devoted to the four people he's collaborated with the most and feels closest to.

The longest of Vilanch's creative relationships has been with Bette Midler, whom he met in the early 1970s when he was working as an entertainment columnist for the Chicago Tribune. They shared similar tastes (it was Vilanch who introduced Midler to the work of Sophie Tucker), and when she at one point asked him, "You got any lines?," it was, to quote Vilanch, "a phrase that has echoed through the corridors of time."

Another close collaborator, Goldberg, was responsible for Vilanch's most embarrassing moment. He apparently wrote, though at Goldberg's suggestion, the infamous blackface appearance of her then-boyfriend Ted Danson at a Manhattan Friars Club roast.

"Get Bruce!'s" most inside show-biz sequences involve Vilanch's work with Billy Crystal on Crystal's celebrated run as Oscar host. It's amusing to again see the clever sequences intercutting Crystal with nominated films like "Titanic" and "Jerry Maguire" and to hear about the playbook, "not unlike a football team's," potential material compiled by the writers. (Vilanch has written for nine Oscar shows, and on taking home an Emmy for one commented, "I'm very sorry I didn't have to sleep around to win this award.")

Another frequent collaborator is Robin Williams—though Vilanch says that writing for him is more a process of "holding on." Appearing here unbilled, Williams shows off the brilliant comic riffing he never gets to do in films anymore; his spontaneous routine about what "The X-Files" would be like if the two investigators were Jack Benny and Rochester is a pip.

Director Kuehn (in an earlier incarnation the founder of Kaleidoscope Films and one of the key figures in the evolution of the modern trailer) offers these laughs as well as an accurate sense of how today's Hollywood works by showing, for instance, how smoothly Vilanch accommodates tender egos like the one attached to action star Steven Seagal.

"Get Bruce!" offers only a few brief glimpses of Vilanch's more personal side, like his poignant comment that many of the people he works with are understandably too focused on themselves to be true pals. And even at his most vulnerable, crying after receiving an award at an AIDS benefit, Vilanch can't resist a quip. "I find myself breaking down for no reason," he says. "Like an old Buick."

NEW YORK POST, 9/17/99, p. 50, Rod Dreher

Bruce Vilanch is the roly-poly hairball who occupies the Paul Lynde Chair in Gay Wisenheimer Studies on the new syndicated version of "The Hollywood Squares." But as the awards-show gag writer for some of Hollywood's top stars, Vilanch's work is far better-known than his face is.

"He's given more great lines to celebrities than a Hollywood coke dealer," observes Nathan Lane in "Get Bruce!," an irresistible documentary tribute that's as yummy and insubstantial as a sackful of Twinkies.

You learn only a little bit about Vilanch's life and certainly nothing unflattering—but that's not why anybody's going to watch this movie.

You go to it to see Bruce make dishy asides about celebrity culture, and yuk it up in the company of people like Bette Midler, Billy Crystal, Whoopi Goldberg and Robin Williams. They are Vilanch's biggest clients and he has a fine, often racy, time with the them all.

The funniest parts have Crystal telling Vilanch jokes the censor cut from the Oscarcast, and Williams brilliantly making up an "X-Files" episode in which Jack Benny and Rochester meet aliens. Don't miss your chance to see the funny Robin Williams, who so rarely comes out to play anymore.

Vilanch says he developed his sense of humor as a protective shield against the grief he got in childhood for being fat and gay. He's always on, even when starting to sob when remembering dead friends onstage at an AIDS benefit.

"It's embarrassing to have a catharsis in front of all of you," Vilanch weeps. "But it never hurt Judy Garland."

NEWSWEEK, 9/27/99, p. 69, David Ansen

Bruce Vilanch, a portly gay man with a wild mane of unruly hair, is the Cyrano de Bergerac of the Hollywood comic community. Those hilarious one-liners Billy Crytal tosses off at the Oscars? Vilanch wrote them. That dirty-sweet Bette Midler Sophie Tucker persona? Vilanch created it. He's the guy Whoopi Goldberg turns to when she has to say something funny at

President Clinton's birthday bash. He can tailor a joke to fit Roseanne's "gum-chewing dismissal of the world" or Paul Reiser's style of "wry observation." As Nathan Lane quips, "He's given more great lines to celebrities than a Hollywood coke dealer." Could be Vilanch wrote that one, too.

This semipublic figure (he's on "Hollywood Squares") is the subject of the fond, frequently hilarious tribute "Get Bruce," made by Andrew J. Kuehn. It's worth the price of admission just to hear Vilanch bouncing ideas off of a revved Robin Williams, who shapeshifts into Jack Benny and Rochester before our eyes. Even Steven Segal hires Vilanch when he needs to be funny. Now that's called earning your money.

VILLAGE VOICE, 9/21/99, p. 166, Michael Atkinson

I'd take stakes driven right through my platform pumps over listening to Bruce Vilanch jokes, but that's me. As irrelevant as *Full Tilt Boogie,* another Miramax documentary about showbiz effluvia, *Get Bruce!* chronicles the life and times of Hollywood's most beloved gag writer. This is the man responsible for all of those award-ceremony routines, and no, Andrew J. Kuehn's film isn't the Claude Lanzmann-esque *j'accuse* it should've been. Being unfunny just skims it; Vilanch is a bloated, hirsute Mason Reese cabaret reject without whom our TVs would be less painful places to visit. Shouldn't we all hold a grudge? Billy Crystal, Bette Midler, Whoopi Goldberg, and other epochal figures disagree; in fact, if you believe them (and why shouldn't you?), they never utter a non-Bruce joke in public. They don't even seem ashamed to admit it.

Still, having invisible stakes hammered through your wrists and having Bruce Vilanch exhale old Redd Foxx jokes in your face is cake compared to watching Helen Mirren, John Gielgud, and Peter O'Toole struggle to retain their dignity in the pigpen that is *Caligula,* rereleased for reasons the Vatican is surely keeping secret. For sheer camp RBI, this Tinto Brass-Bob Guccione freak is the World Series played, won, and paraded. That is, if you remain conscious before the semi-*Satyricon* goonery, the somnambulistic sex, and Malcolm McDowell embarking in earnest upon his odyssey as his country's most reviled actor. For penance, you could do worse.

Also reviewed in:
CHICAGO TRIBUNE, 9/17/99, Friday/p. G, Michael Wilmington
NEW YORK TIMES, 9/17/99, p. E29, Stephen Holden
VARIETY, 3/8-14/99, p. 64, Dennis Harvey

GET REAL

A Paramount Classics release of a Graphite Films production in association with British Screen and the Arts Council of England. *Executive Producer:* Anant Singh and Helena Spring. *Producer:* Stephen Taylor. *Director:* Simon Shore. *Screenplay (based on his play "What's Wrong With Angry?"):* Patrick Wilde. *Director of Photography:* Alan Almond. *Editor:* Barrie Vince. *Music:* John Lunn. *Music Editor:* Graham Sutton. *Sound:* Bill Dodkin. *Sound Editor:* Steve Schwalbe. *Casting:* Di Carling. *Production Designer:* Bernd Lepel. *Art Director:* Terry Ackland-Snow and Roger Cain. *Set Decorator:* Simon Wakefield and Amanda Grenville. *Costumes:* Bernd Lepel. *Make-up:* Susan Parkinson. *Stunt Coordinator:* Mark Newman and Frank Henson. *Running time:* 110 minutes. *MPAA Rating:* R.

CAST: Ben Silverstone (Steven Carter); Brad Gorton (John Dixon); Charlotte Brittain (Linda); Stacy A. Hart (Jessica); Kate McEnery (Wendy); Patrick Nielsen (Mark); Tim Harris (Kevin); James D. White (Dave); James Perkins (Young Steven); Nicholas Hunter (Young Mark); Jacquetta May (Steven's Mother); David Lumsden (Steven's Father); David Elliot (Glen); Morgan Jones (Linda's Brother); Richard Hawley (English Teacher); Steven Mason (Cruising Man); Charlotte Hanson (Glen's Wife); Alina Hazeldine (Crying Baby); Louise J. Taylor (Christina Lindmann); Steven Elder (Bob, the Driving Instructor); Leonie Thomas (Aunt at Wedding); David Paul West (Bridegroom); Andy Rashleigh (Policeman); Ian Brimble (John's

Father);   Judy Buxton (John's Mother);   Dorothy Clark (Woman Driving Instructor);   Amy Redler (Julie);   Martin Milman (Headmaster);   Andy Tungate (Roger McGregor).

LOS ANGELES TIMES, 4/30/99, Calendar/p. 15, Kevin Thomas

It's safe to say that almost every gay teen fantasizes having a romance with the campus hero, inevitably a handsome star athlete and student leader, unattainable to all but the most beautiful and popular girls and surely the individual most out of bounds for a homosexual kid. But writer Patrick Wilde, in adapting his play "What's Wrong With Angry?" to the screen as "Get Real," asks what if that hero just happens to be gay himself?

"Get Real" illuminates with humor and compassion the plight of being 16, regardless of sexual orientation or gender, along with the added challenge of being gay. The setting is the attractive upper-middle-class suburb of Basingstoke, which is 40 miles southwest of London and visually identical to America's pricier neighborhoods. It is a conservative, utterly conventional community—"a dull commuter hub" is one description—that prefers not to acknowledge that gay people even exist, and when forced to, views them with reflexive disdain and disgust.

No wonder Steven (Ben Silverstone), a gangly youth who unfortunately for his circumstances combines a high IQ with an absolute lack of interest in sports, feels he must keep his homosexual feelings to himself, confiding only in his best friend, the girl next door, Linda (Charlotte Brittain), a beauty with a sharp wit and a plump figure, a combination that makes her an outsider as well.

Of course, Steven is a target for bullies, who taunt him as a sissy but don't seriously consider the unthinkable possibility that he may actually be gay. At home he's subject to constant pressure from his well-meaning father (David Lumsden) to be more like the other guys.

In short, everything that happens to Steven in his everyday existence conspires to reinforce his belief in his absolute necessity to stay in the closet in the interest of sheer survival, yet within him grow feelings of resentment and rebellion. He's taken to cruising the local park restroom, an activity Linda finds abhorrent and dangerous, while Steven points out that in their community there is no other place where he could hope to make contact with other gays. Apparently, his high school's track star John Dixon (Brad Gorton), the campus god, feels the same way, for that is where, much to Steven's understandable shock and John's initial deep chagrin, they meet.

Whereas Steven has never kidded himself that he is anything but gay, John strives mightily to deny he has homosexual feelings; the best he can muster is to admit to being "intrigued" on the basis of a single thwarted encounter he can't keep out of his mind. In short order the same young man who is loathe to acknowledge Steven's existence at school soon lunges at him with a passionate kiss, leaving Steven more startled than ever. He is also thrilled, excited and swiftly in love with John.

Soon, Steven and John are adding to the burden of keeping secret their sexual orientation the hiding of their blossoming romance. John is so happy yet so uptight in being with Steven that it is no small accomplishment that Steven finally succeeds in persuading John that it's only right that he publicly acknowledge Steven as a friend.

Wilde and his astute director, Simon Shore, have set up an increasingly tense predicament that is at once engaging and revealing. John, whose family lives in a mansion with a huge swimming pool, is in the tougher position; as the school's most envied student, he has much more to lose than Steven, for he confounds gay stereotypes. When he says to Steven, "You don't know what it's like being me," you can imagine Rock Hudson having said much the same thing.

Many people, including young inexperienced gays like Steven, can have a hard time comprehending that a man can be totally masculine, as Hudson was, and also be homosexual. Revelation of the truth about John would be considerably more earth-shaking than it would be for Steven.

Yet everything in "Get Real" builds to the point that coming out is the only course, no matter what the consequences. But will either Steven or John or both come out before they're found out? It's to the credit of the filmmakers, and to their talented young stars, that it is possible to care equally about what will happen to Steven and John.

Even when John's actions are far from admirable you feel his conflict, guilt and appreciation of the difference between right and wrong, although he may not always be able to live up to his best instincts. Silverstone, who made a memorable screen debut in Mike Figgis' "The Browning Version," and newcomers Gorton and Brittain set a solid standard of acting that the supporting players, which include Jacquetta May as Steven's staunch mother and Stacy A. Hart as a pretty student who comes to prefer the understanding Steven over her macho boyfriend (Tim Harris) and is hurt and puzzled when Steven doesn't respond to her romantic overtures.

Shore and Wilde have done an admirable job in re-imagining Wilde's play as a movie, and they've created a wrenching, thoughtful entertainment that incorporates considerable comic relief. But this enlightened—and enlightening—film absolutely lives up to its title, for "Get Real" is serious about getting real in the way we live our lives.

NEWSDAY, 4/30/99, Part II/p. B6, John Anderson

Given that schoolboy Steven Carter (Ben Silverstone) seems to spend half his time excelling at his suburban English prep school and the other half picking up men at park toilets, there's seems little question that he's both capable and incautious. Or that "Get Real" is going to be similarly schismatic and a dramatic structure in search of believable inhabitants.

Unless you're Robert Dornan, Gary Bauer or the Marquis of Queensbury, you'll probably want to like this film, the feature debut of British director Simon Shore, adapted by Patrick Wilde from his debut play. The sentiments are honest, the storyline is plausible, the hero is sympathetic and, in the wake of Littleton, he's a walking current-events class—a bullied high school outcast who wants to be honest about who he is.

Four or five minutes in, however, it's clear that the film is plummeting headlong into the recycling bin of gay-movie tropes and genre templates. Looking and often sounding like an Afterschool Special (do they still have Afterschool Specials? Long ago, they acted more or less as primers on social maladies and were as obvious as air freshener), "Get Real" doesn't get anywhere specific, since the characters are such bloodless replicas of actual human beings.

Still, it's not a movie without a lesson. Or, for that matter, a big boatload of conventions. Steven, pushed around at school by knuckle-draggers like Kevin (Tim Harris), has the requisite overweight gal-pal, Linda (Charlotte Brittain), the understanding mother (Jacquetta May), the clueless father (David Lumsden), and the equally clueless female schoolmate who falls for him (Stacy A. Hart). He's also part of the school-wide epidemic of unrequited lust for the statuesque track star John Dixon (Brad Gorton), who embodies all that's right with England, the flag and manhood itself

Until Steven's soulful, sexual rendezvous with John—surprise!—Steven's only romantic entanglements come via the men's room stalls at the local park, where he meets such prizes as Glen (David Elliott), who subsequently stand him up on dates. The only really cutting moment in "Get Real" comes when Glen arrives at Steven's father's photography studio, accompanied by cranky wife and screaming child. The lesson is obvious—it's the lesson of the entire movie in a nutshell—but one wishes that the nasty bite of that unhappy family portrait had lingered throughout the entire movie.

As it is, we get the valiant efforts of Steven to come clean about himself, combined with John's desperate attempts to keep his love for Steven under the covers and his thuggish pals like Kevin from finding out who he really is. There are moments of British dignity that were old when "The Browning Version" was young, a valiant speech before the parent-student body and a lot of pop music that serves to explain what it is we're supposed to be feeling. The problem is, nothing in "Get Real" needs explaining as much as it needs a little flesh and blood.

SIGHT AND SOUND, 5/99, p. 48, José Arroyo

Sixth former Steven Carter lives in Basingstoke and leads a double life. Only Linda, his best friend and neighbour, knows he's gay. A good student, he avoids the school rocks who are queer-baiting him without even knowing his sexual orientation. After school, he cottages in the park. Steven has sex with an older man named Glen who turns out to be married. Linda can't seem to pass her driver's test, partly because she has a crush on her married male instructor.

One of the men Steven cruises while cottaging turns out to be John Dixon, the class jock. They agree to forget about their encounter but John starts dropping by Steven's to bare his soul. Eventually they have sex and fall in love. While having sex in the park they're caught by the police. John escapes but Steven is brought home by the cops and his parents are lectured on what goes on in parks. Steven wants to come out but John is too scared. Steven wins an award for an essay on "Growing Up as We Approach the New Millennium", but anonymously submits another called "Get Real" on growing up gay. Just before the prize-giving ceremony, John and Steven are caught embracing and John beats Steven up so his mates won't think he's gay. A battered Steven publicly comes out at the prize-giving ceremony and earns the support of his family and classmates. While John stays in the closet, Linda and Steven, each having passed their own tests, throw their L-plates out the window as they drive off.

Get Real is the latest in a long line of coming-out films in which the protagonists keep getting younger and younger. At this rate, we'll have films where boys turn from crayons to perfume in kindergarten. This film's coming-of-age/coming-out story is similar to those of Beautiful Thing and the recent television series Queer as Folk. The comparisons are unavoidable and unfortunate: Get Real is occasionally charming but lacks the good nature, easy warmth and fairy-tale appeal of Beautiful Thing, while it hasn't got Queer as Folk's glossy look, relative glamour and knowing wit. Gay people have seemingly found a sense of enfranchisement from the increasing range of queer imagery across the media, but Get Real's good intentions don't quite seem sufficient.

Get Real benefits from a complex and compelling script, offering a range of rounded characters whose predicaments are admirably dramatised. The cottaging sequences, a scene in which teenagers Steven Carter and John Dixon can't help looking at each other while dancing with someone else, and the scene where John batters Steven are all memorably tense and compelling. However, there are elements that don't quite work. It's hard to believe that a sixth former is so queer acculturated as to make jokes about interior decoration and have a photo of Simone Signoret in Casque d'or (1952) posted above his bed. The ending might have benefited from more complexity: the celebration of Steven's coming out is arguably inevitable, but is it necessary to have it at John's expense? His completely understandable fear of coming out is first posited as cowardice and then given short-shrift as the spotlight is shone on the liberating powers of its young hero's moral virtue.

In spite of these reservations, the dialogue is generally very good, but the film could have been so much better. Fault must lie squarely with the direction. Filmed in widescreen, the individual shots are composed with self-conscious care, yet there is little to engage the eye, a visual paucity that widescreen magnifies. Likewise, the gifted cast, particularly the young players, seem over rehearsed, their line readings full of carefully considered inflections interspersed between numerous pauses. When John comes out to Steven—breaking down as he expresses his (beautifully written) fear, loneliness and desire—the extremely long take overstretches Brad Gorton, who despite his skill lacks the experience to sustain the scene. As it stands, director Simon Shore (who made the thriller The English Wife) leaves Gorton exposed and wastes an opportunity to show us more of Steven's reaction or the setting. Likewise, Steven's climactic coming out is filmed largely in profile, a type of shot which allows inspection without creating contact or offering intimacy. While it tries to be artful, Get Real ends up being merely likable and rather quaint. It's a petit-bourgeois Beautiful Thing—stolid, earnest and informed—and will no doubt find great favour with schoolteachers who want to get a discussion going but are afraid to expose their students to more challenging material.

VILLAGE VOICE, 5/4/99, p. 113, Dennis Lim

Eager to both please and educate, Get Real goes about its business with an earnest tunnel vision that's almost endearing. But it's mired in a fantasy that's become a regrettable staple of gay movies: sensitive, alienated boy falls for ostensibly straight hunk who—swoon—loves back. Beautiful Thing pulled off this wish-fulfilling premise thanks to its crazily romantic streak. Directed by Simon Shore and adapted by Patrick Wilde from his play, Get Real has broader coming-of-age issues on its mind, and clumsier ways of expressing them.

The setting—suburban Basingstoke—is significantly posher than the South London flats of Beautiful Thing, though arguably more stifling. The protagonist, gangly 16-year-old Steven Carter (Ben Silverstone), is smart, reflective, and reasonably self-possessed—he clearly knows his way around a public toilet. (Shore plays a cruising scene for maximum cutesiness, scoring it to the Troggs' "Love Is All Around.") Steven's only confidante is his neighbor, Linda (Charlotte Brittain), who is, predictably, overweight and a source of comic relief. The fun starts when drooled-over jock John (Brad Gorton) turns out to be sexually confused, and open to suggestion: as Steven's feelings intensify, so do his frustrations at having to keep them private. He writes an anonymous coming-out manifesto, which sets up a very public, cathartic burst of truth-telling —hence the title. Which, in retrospect, makes most sense as an injunction to the well-intentioned but hopelessly glib filmmakers.

Wilde's script, which has a weakness for mild, snickering double entendres, is notable for its near-total reliance on archetypes. But, to be fair, Steven's predicament, for all its clichéd trappings, *does* ultimately feel real, and it's all down to Silverstone, a talented young actor who can effectively and economically convey surges of overwhelming, paradoxical emotion. It's as thoughtful and complex a performance as the setup allows, and by far the main reason to see the film.

Also reviewed in:
CHICAGO TRIBUNE, 5/14/99, Friday/p. B, Michael Wilmington
NEW YORK TIMES, 4/30/99, p. E15, Stephen Holden
VARIETY, 9/21-27/98, p. 111, Derek Elley
WASHINGTON POST, 6/18/99, p. C5, Desson Howe

GIRL CALLED ROSEMARIE, A

A Castle Hill Productions and Hawkeye Entertainment release of a Constantin Film production. *Executive Producer:* Martin Moszkowicz. *Producer:* Bernd Eichinger and Uschi Reich. *Director:* Bernd Eichinger. *Screenplay (German with English subtitles):* Bernd Eichinger and Uwe Wilhelm. *Director of Photography:* Gernot Roll. *Editor:* Alex Berner. *Music:* Norbert Schneider. *Sound:* Michael Kranz. *Art Director:* Harald Turzer and Thomas Freudenthal. *Costumes:* Barbara Baum. *Running time:* 127 minutes. *MPAA Rating:* Not Rated.

CAST: Nina Hoss (Rosemarie); Heiner Lauterbach (Hartog); Mathieu Carrière (Fribert); Horst Krause (Bruster); Hannelore Elsner (Marga); Katja Flint (Christine); Til Schweiger (Nadler); Heinrich Schafmeister (Von Oelsen).

NEW YORK POST, 10/15/99, p. 58, Jonathan Foreman

Based on a real-life scandal and murder case that rocked a resurgent Germany in the mid-1950s, this well-made film follows the career of an orphaned hooker who becomes a rich man's mistress and then the key player in a high-stakes blackmail scam.

Fribert (Mathieu Carriere), a ruthless French businessman, teaches gorgeous Rosemarie (Nina Hoss) the social skills necessary to become a high-class call girl. But he uses her as a pawn in a corporate takeover.

Rosemarie, tough and trampy, has her own doomed agenda, however: She craves respectability and marriage to her upper-class lover Hartog (Heiner Lauterbach).

Overlong and accompanied by needlessly melodramatic music, "Rosemarie" is nevertheless entertaining, even moving.

VILLAGE VOICE, 10/19/99, p. 144, Jessica Winter

Sweet dreams to you who settle in for *A Girl Called Rosemarie,* the exertions of which mimic a good blow to the head—first you start, then you slump. In the first five minutes, our post-WW II German heroine pummels a prison warden who tries to confiscate her gold fuck-me pumps, screws a sweaty guard to secure her release, and claws her own face. You may think you're off to camp, but this autobahn heads straight for sleepy hollow, since once the tramp's on her own—she keeps busy as a prostitute-cum-spy—she's a walking, stalking Valium tab. Nina Hoss's Rosemarie clumsily suggests Barbara Stanwyck in *Baby Face*—both are career bed-hoppers who meet tragic ends, but Babs possessed humor and cool professionalism, and she never would have tolerated a weeping string section on her soundtrack, reminding us that, below the tough-broad exterior, the girl's an old softie inside.

Also reviewed in:
NEW YORK TIMES, 10/15/99, p. E18, Stephen Holden
VARIETY, 3/17-23/97, p. 54, Derek Elley

GIRL, INTERRUPTED

A Columbia pictures release of a Red Wagon production. *Executive Producer:* Carol Bodie and Winona Ryder. *Producer:* Douglas Wick and Cathy Konrad. *Director:* James Mangold. *Screenplay:* James Mangold, Lisa Loomer, and Anna Hamilton Phelan. *Based on the book by:* Susanna Kaysen. *Director of Photography:* Jack Green. *Editor:* Kevin Tent. *Music:* Mychael Danna. *Music Editor:* Thomas Milano. *Sound:* Jim Stuebe. *Sound Editor:* Howell Gibbens. *Casting:* Lisa Beach. *Production Designer:* Richard Hoover. *Art Director:* Jeff Knipp. *Set Designer:* Mary Finn and Patrick Sullivan. *Set Decorator:* Maggie Martin. *Set Dresser:* Josh Elliott. *Special Effects:* Ron Bolanowski. *Costumes:* Arianne Phillips. *Make-up:* Carol Schwartz and Jane Galli. *Make-up (Angelina Jolie):* Janeen Schreyer. *Stunt Coordinator:* Jennifer Lamb. *Running time:* 120 minutes. *MPAA Rating:* R.

CAST: Winona Ryder (Susanna); Angelina Jolie (Lisa); Clea Duvall (Georgina); Brittany Murphy (Daisy); Elisabeth Moss (Polly); Jared Leto (Tobias Jacobs); Jeffrey Tambor (Dr. Potts); Travis Fine (John); Jillian Armenante (Cynthia); Angela Bettis (Janet); Vanessa Redgrave (Dr. Wick); Whoopi Goldberg (Valerie); Drucie McDaniel (M.G.); Alison Claire (Gretta); Christina Myers (Margie); Joanna Kerns (Annette); Gloria Barnhart (Older Catatonic); Josie Gammell (Mrs. McWilley); Bruce Altman (Professor Gilcrest); Mary Kay Place (Mrs. Gilcrest); Ray Baker (Mr. Kaysen); KaDee Strickland (Bonnie Gilcrest); Christian Monroe (Ronny); Kurtwood Smith (Dr. Crumble); David Scott Taylor (Monty Hoover, the Cabby); Janet Pryce (ER Nurse); C. Scott Grimaldi (ER Resident); Ginny Graham (Arleen); Richard Domeier (Art Teacher); John Kirkman (Jack); Sally Bowman (Maureen); Misha Collins (Tony); John Lumia (Van Driver); Marilyn Brett (Italian Shop Keeper); Alex Rubin (Josh); Marilyn Spanier (Miss Plimack); Linda Gilvear (Miss Paisley); Allen Strange (Principal); Spencer Gates (British Teacher); Rebecca Derrick (Lillian); Anne Connors (Nurse); Steve Altes (Medic); Joe Gerrety (Cop); Anne Lewis (Dance Therapist); Donny Martino, Jr. (Naked Man); John Levin (ER Doctor); Irene Longshore (Connie); Katie Rimmer (Tiffany); Jonathan Martin Spirk (Tough Guy).

CINEASTE, Vol. XXV, No. 3, 2000, p. 48, Alice Cross

It is easy to see the appeal of *Girl, Interrupted* for young middle-class women, especially those who gravitate to the poetry of Sylvia Plath and Anne Sexton. The protagonist Susanna (Winona Ryder), a would-be writer, and her fellow inmates at Claymore Hospital in the early Seventies, find release in the 'parallel universe' of the madhouse. No longer expected to act as adults, they empower themselves by outsmarting the nurses and taking illicit nighttime jaunts through the bowels of the hospital. They smoke constantly, swear, bully and console each other, and do so without apology, without embarrassment. After all, they're crazy. They don't have to hide their aggressions, their anger, their wish to regress to childhood. Instead of directing their rage inward, as our society acculturates young women to do, or committing themselves politically in this volatile period, they act out, in the safety of the hospital, in fits of self-assertion and bravura wit.

The film, directed by James Mangold, with Ryder as executive producer, emphasizes again and again Susanna's control over what happens. She may have a "borderline personality disorder" now, but she can step over that border if she wants and become an "orderly" adult of her own creation. Both Valerie (Whoopi Goldberg), the self-contained head nurse on her ward, and Dr. Wick (Vanessa Redgrave), the genteel psychiatrist who treats her, assure Susanna that it is within her power to choose between madness and sanity, that she is "driving herself crazy." She may hide away in anger and confusion for awhile, but even the cabby who drives her to the hospital warns her, "Don't get too comfortable." (That Claymore is a renamed McLean's—home to various celebrity breakdowns, James Taylor's among them—adds an aura of 'privilege' to Susanna's madness.) The trick, then, is to find the balance between leaving the safety of "this 5-star hotel" too soon and giving way too fully to madness, lessons not internalized by Daisy (Britanny Murphy), who commits suicide after signing herself out, and Lisa (Angelina Jolie), the eight-year resident who, Susanna realizes at the end, need[s] this place to feel alive."

So, what kind of vision of madness is this? Although we see various characters taking medication, there is no mention of it as part of treatment; we see precious little therapy. In Susanna Kaysen's best-selling memoir of the same title, the author spends much time investigating what was wrong with her. The book begins or ends various chapters with pages from her medical file; she describes the drugged, heavy feeling that is depression; she speculates on the role of pharmaceuticals in treatment, on the difference between treating the brain and treating the mind.

None of this makes its way into the movie. Instead, what is emphasized is Susanna's deciding what kind of woman she will be, and in this arena there are indeed contradictory, maddening messages, though more for the viewer than the character.

The young women on the ward—there seems to be no patient over twenty-one—are a loosely bound, dysfunctional sorority. At first it seems that all they have is each other, so that by the time Susanna's boyfriend arrives and encourages her to run away to Canada with him—as if mental health were a woman's Vietnam—she is clear that this is her community and his dilemma is nothing in comparison to hers.

The queen of the ward is Lisa, whose madness is electrifying and whose fearlessness energizes Susanna. In this small, closed-off world, she becomes the group's Bernardine Dohrn, periodically breaking free of the hospital, then bearing the Isolation Ward lockup with proper hauteur. This cadre of women, however, is not really allied in opposition to anything and proves disloyal to its own. On one escapade Lisa and Susanna crash at Daisy's modest row house, a gift from her incestuous father upon her discharge from Claymore. Lisa torments Daisy—whose denial of her illness and her father's abuse Lisa cannot abide—until the fragile young woman hangs herself in despair. Lisa, in monstrous indifference, takes money from Daisy's purse and heads off for good times.

Later, back in the hospital, Lisa betrays Susanna by stealing her journal and showing other patients the 'objective' observations she had written about each. In the showdown between the two women, after the others have distanced themselves from her, Susanna realizes that she has "wasted a year of [her] life" and decides to follow treatment and take herself back into the world.

Once again, it is interesting to note the way in which screenwriter/director Mangold has altered the events in the memoir. There, Daisy commits suicide soon after leaving the hospital and in the absence of any contact with Susanna and Lisa. Also, near the end of the book, Susanna runs into Lisa and her small son in Harvard Square and discovers that she's acquired all the trappings of middle-class life: "I've got the kid. I take the kid to nursery school, I've got an apartment, I've got furniture."

Why demonize Lisa in the movie? Why can't Susanna's healing stem from these friendships, born of common confusion and vulnerability, instead of in rejection of them? Why pit one woman against another instead of showing how each must find her own way to survive and prosper?

Women in the movie seem to feel no solidarity. In fact, it is suggested that Susanna's "chasing a bottle of aspirin with a bottle of whiskey" is the fallout of a transgression against a friend of her mother's. Susanna slept with the woman's husband, and, overcome with the confusion of this affair, punishes herself with destructive behavior.

In a different kind of womanly betrayal, she is taken to the office of the psychiatrist who commits her to the "prison" of the mental hospital by her mother, who declines to tell Susanna where they are going, then leaves without saying goodbye or acknowledging what is happening. No wonder Susanna tells the admitting doctor that she does not want to be like her mother, though the alternate roles she sees do not appeal to her, either. "I'm not going to burn my bra."

Initially, *Girl, Interrupted* purports to be feminist, acknowledging Susanna's desire for independence of thought, as well as sexual independence, which partially translates into a desire for emotional independence from men. Yet her 'promiscuity' is cited by the male psychiatrist who commits her as one cause of her madness. The film neither attempts to explore the cultural implications of such a pronouncement nor the absence of solidarity among the women as possibly rooted within their disempowered status—not as mad women but simply as women.

There are staff members Susanna could choose as allies and role models, but, for the most part, they remain faceless, or insensitive to the longings of an artistic, imaginative young woman. Even the female panel who review her petition to leave the hospital, and whom we would imagine to be dedicated to instilling independence in their young charges, cast a disapproving eye when Susanna declares her intention to become a writer.

The only genuinely caring adult female with whom Susanna interacts is the nurse, Valerie. Whoopi Goldberg, in the caretaker mode she has played once too often, has her character bear up under the misbehavior of her coddled patients with weary, knowing dignity. One might, in fact, see Valerie as the antithesis of the volatile Lisa. Where Lisa is all id, Valerie is only Superego. Even when the young women hurl racial insults at her, she remains in control, acting as she ought, not as we would hope she might like.

That race is introduced at all is puzzling. The Valerie of the memoir is not African-American, but "looked a lot like Lisa." One could, of course, cast an actor of color into a role without altering her nature or function in the story, but to highlight race and class, as Mangold does in several scenes, is to change how the viewer perceives everything. The lost, troubled young woman suddenly turns ugly racist; her stay in the exclusive hospital becomes clear evidence of her privileged status and her remoteness from the struggles of women of less affluence. And the woman Susanna might see as a clear model and genuine friend becomes Other.

The film does not acknowledge any of these confusions. In fact, the superficial feminism displayed in Susanna's early voiceovers is echoed once again in her final reflections, as she pays tribute to Lisa, Daisy, and the others at Claymore. "They weren't perfect, but they were my friends."

Such shallow bonds, existing more in sentimental declaration than in action or thought, would be unlikely in a 'buddy' film, where events would bond the men irrevocably, no matter how much at odds they might find themselves at some point. In this film, it's every woman for herself.

LOS ANGELES TIMES, 12/21/99, Calendar/p. 1, Kenneth Turan

"Girl, Interrupted," Susanna Kaysen's exceptional memoir of the nearly two years she spent as a teenager in a mental institution, is about the porous line between sanity and madness. "People ask, How did you get in there?" the book begins. "What they really want to know is if they are likely to end up there as well. I can't answer the real question. All I can tell them is, It's easy."

"Girl, Interrupted," the James Mangold-directed, Winona Ryder-starring film made from Kaysen's book, walks a similarly delicate line, but this one is between Hollywood and reality, between the generic and the genuine.

The book, with its crystalline prose, is very much its own thing, episodic and without a high-powered story line. The film used three credited screenwriters (the director, Lisa Loomer and Anna Hamilton Phelan) to fill in the inevitable blanks, but in doing so it's had a hard time resisting manufacturing obvious, standard-issue drama of the "One Flew Over the Cuckoo's Nest" knockoff variety.

What helps the film stay as honest as it manages to sporadically be are the purity and grace of its lead performances by Ryder and Angelina Jolie. Both women have connected strongly to their parts, and they ensure their characters' reality even if the dramas they are involved with don't always rise to that standard.

It was Ryder's passion for the book (she's an executive producer) that got the film made, and she apparently identified with Kaysen's story so strongly that she took the less overtly dramatic role of the author for herself.

Kaysen was 18 years old in 1967 when, under pressure from her parents and at the insistence of a therapist who interviewed her only once, she admitted herself to a mental hospital the film calls Claymoore. (McClean in Belmont, Mass., was the real place, at different times home to Sylvia Plath, Robert Lowell, James Taylor and Ray Charles.)

When the cabdriver taking her to Claymoore asks what her problem is, Kaysen wistfully replies, "I'm sad."

There's more to it than that, of course, including the chasing of a bottle of aspirin with a bottle of vodka ("I had a headache" is her movie-glib explanation), but in truth this young woman seems more lost in space than genuinely mentally ill.

Playing someone who is acting sullen and betrayed when she's not dazed and confused is not the most promising of situations, but because Ryder has invested so much in Kaysen, we do as well. Not flashy or showy, Ryder's performance has an authenticity to it, and the actress knows how to make us care in the bargain.

Claymoore does have adults in supervisory positions, whether it be head nurse Valerie (Whoopy Goldberg) or psychiatrists Dr. Potts (Jeffrey Tambor) and Dr. Wick (Vanessa Redgrave). But they are marginal to both life at Claymoore and to the film. It's the girls that make the difference. There's roommate Georgina (Clea Duvall), in love with the "Wizard of Oz" books. There's gorge-and-purge Daisy (Brittany Murphy) and Polly (Elisabeth Moss), the cheerful burn victim. Most of all, there is Lisa.

It's hard to talk about Lisa, played by Jolie, without making her sound like a cliche, this film's version of Jack Nicholson's Randle P. McMurphy in "Cuckoo's Nest." Like him, Lisa is the ward's life force, a rebel who dominates everyone she comes into contact with and knows just how to bend the institution's rules.

Yet it's a mark of the strength of Jolie's performance that Lisa is in the most individual and believable character in "Girl, Interrupted." She has an enviably electric quality, and the roles she's had recently, from "Pushing Tin" to "The Bone Collector" show her to be an actress who can be convincing in a variety of guises.

But if these characters are real enough, the experiences they are burdened with often descend into pro forma stuff. The girls break into the hospital office, for instance, and read their records (enabling Kaysem to find out she's been diagnosed with the nebulous-sounding borderline personality disorder) though in reality this information isn't discovered until 25 years after her release.

You don't have to have read the book to know that this and a lot more of "Girl, Interrupted's" more obvious drama has been constructed just for the film. Fortunately, the girls on the ward pull us back time and again. We know they're only acting, but we also know they represent a reality that is all too believable.

NEW YORK POST, 12/21/99, p. 57, Jonathan Foreman

Thanks to some fine acting, particularly a terrific turn as a sexy sociopath by Angelina Jolie, "Girl, Interrupted" is more engaging than the Lifetime TV movies it often resembles.

There are several moving and amusing, scenes in James ("Copland") Mangold's overlong new film, but it's an odd mixture of an unsentimental, darkly humorous take on mental illness with the usual Hollywood loony-bin cliches.

Like Susanna Kaysen's best-selling memoir of the same title, the movie is set in the late 1960s. Yet apart from the clothing and the obligatory shots of mental patients and medical staff reacting with horror at the news of Martin Luther King's murder, you don't get much of a sense of the period.

Susanna (Winona Ryder) is upper middle class, spoiled and confused about life. Unlike the rest of her high school class, she hasn't applied to college. She has vague aspirations to become a writer, and you're supposed to see her as a free spirit more in tune with the times than her uptight parents.

After she sleeps with a married teacher and takes an overdose of aspirin, Susanna finds herself in a doctor's office agreeing to go to the local institution for a short "rest."

In her ward, Susanna meets Georgina, the pathological liar (Clea Duvall): Daisy (Brittany Murphy from "Clueless"), who's obsessed with laxatives and rotisserie chicken; Polly, who hideously burned herself as a child; and, finally, the seductive, cruel Lisa (Jolie).

It's a private hospital and relatively comfortable place that couldn't be further from a state "cuckoo's nest." As no-nonsense head nurse Valerie (Whoopi Goldberg) points out, Susanna may have been diagnosed with borderline personality disorder but her main problem seems to be that she's spoiled and self-indulgent.

It turns out that living with some truly ill people is what she needs before she can start sorting herself out. Not that it's all depressing: There are moments when the film could be a light high-school movie (one particularly funny sequence involves a supervised trip to the local ice cream shop).

Ryder gives an intelligent, nuanced performance, but there are times when she just doesn't seem troubled enough, and her character is clearly supposed to exude a kind of neurotic sexiness that is simply absent from Ryder's portrayal.

Still, it isn't Ryder's fault that her Susanna is overwhelmed by Jolie's Lisa—a wonderfully vivid and disturbing performance from an actress whose   career has been propelled more by her (extraordinary) looks than talent.

NEWSDAY, 12/21/99, Part II/p. B3, Gene Seymour

A pattern has emerged thus far in the work of James Mangold, whose two previous films focused on characters more acted upon than active in fulfilling their destinies. In "Heavy" (1995), it was Pruitt Taylor Vince's gentle, lovesick pizza chef, while in "Cop Land" (1997), it was Sylvester Stallone's dull-witted, hero-worshiping small-town sheriff.

It doesn't require too much of a stretch, then, to imagine what Mangold does with "Girl, Interrupted," Susanna Kaysen's journal of her 1967-68 season as a teen-age mental patient. He has smoothed over the spiky, edgy insights that made Kaysen's book something of a revelation and gives forth a Kaysen, portrayed here by Winona Ryder, who's not so much interrupted as seriously adrift. Even her affair with a married teacher and a suicide attempt seem to be things that just sort of happen to her.

The diagnosis for her condition is "borderline personality disorder," characterized as "uncertainty" about just about everything in her life: goals, self-image, values, friends. She is, in other words, the prototypical Mangold character.

These days, a stretch of weekly therapy is likely to be prescribed for such a "disorder." But, it being late 1967, Susanna is shipped off to Claymoore Hospital, outside of Boston, where she is placed in a ward with other girls her age. Soon, she forges a bond with such patients as Daisy (Brittany Murphy), who's got a serious eating disorder and a strange attachment to her rich father; Georgina (Clea Duvall), who's a compulsive liar, and Polly (Elisabeth Moss), badly scarred on the outside and the inside from a childhood mishap.

Last and not least, there's Lisa (Angelina Jolie), a swaggering, magnetic sociopath, who's been institutionalized for so long that her only way out is escape.

One has to resist the temptation to call this motley yet attractive crowd "Snake Pit 90210, " given some of their misadventures within and outside the ward. There's a cute bit in which the girls, on a field trip with their no-nonsense—is there any other kind?—chief nurse (Whoopi Goldberg), make barking sounds at the wife (Mary Kay Place) of the teacher with whom Susanna had an affair. But mostly, unrelenting grimness settles over the movie like a soupy fog, changing shape only to add unnecessary suspense to the more ominous—and obvious—plot turns.

Jolie livens things up, even—or especially—when Lisa's being very bad.

Alone among the cast, she seems to have emerged from a time-warp straight from the 1960s, oozing the sexy, scary recklessness of that era. Ryder is well-cast and keeps things anchored. Even at her best, she never makes you forget her star persona the way Jolie does.

Vanessa Redgrave's cameo turn as the head psychiatrist likewise takes the movie from beneath its ponderous cloud by shocking Ryder's Susanna and us with startling insights about her alleged malady. It's probably the only time the movie crackles with the same revelatory energy as its source material.

NEWSWEEK, 12/20/99, p. 41, David Ansen

In her acclaimed memoir, Susanna Kaysen wrote about her confinement in a mental institution when she was 17. The '60s were in full flower, and the line between what was crazy and what was sane was getting blurry for a lot of people, especially, a confused teenager—who had just attempted to take her own life. Director James Mangold and writers Lisa Loomer and Anna Hamilton Phelan have fleshed out and fictionalized Kaysen's episodic story. Barring one dreadfully trumped-up climactic scene, they've managed to avoid the usual asylum-movie clichés.

Curiously, "Girl, Interrupted" is being sold as if it were a '60s movie, pitting free-spirited crazies against uptight doctors. But what's good about it is precisely that it refuses to play those tired games. Here therapists (like Vanessa Redgrave's Dr. Wick) can actually help. The sulking Susanna (executive producer Winona Ryder) resists the hospital's efforts mightily, turning instead to the rebellious, ice-cold sociopath Lisa (Angelina Jolie) as a role model. But Susanna's instincts are often wrong, and it's to Ryder's credit that she shows us both the admirable and the brattish sides of Susanna's character. With a minimum of "Snake Pit" hysterics, Mangold's movie traces Susanna's long journey home.

SIGHT AND SOUND, 4/00, p. 47, Liese Spencer

New England, 1967. After washing down 50 aspirin with a bottle of vodka, 17-year-old Susanna is sent to Claymore psychiatric hospital. Diagnosed with a 'borderline personality disorder' Susanna seems saner than her new friends Lisa (a sociopath), Georgina (a compulsive liar), Daisy (a daddy's girl with an eating disorder) and burns-victim Polly. On the ward, Susanna remembers sleeping with her English teacher and a fellow-student, Tobias.

Tobias turns up one day and tells Susanna he's been drafted. The pair have sex but she turns down his offer to run away to Canada. That night Susanna sleeps with a male nurse and is sent to the head of the hospital the next day. Susanna and Lisa run away together and call in at Daisy's new flat. Lisa confronts Daisy about her father's sexual abuse. The next morning Susanna finds Daisy has hanged herself in the bathroom. Lisa is unrepentant but Susanna returns to the hospital where she recovers and is given a release date. Lisa is hauled back to Claymore. That night, she takes the girls down to the basement, where she reads them extracts from Susanna's diary. Lisa chases Susanna through the corridors taunting her. The next day Lisa is under restraint. Susanna says goodbye before leaving the hospital.

"So many buttons to press," screams Angelina Jolie's sociopath Lisa in *Girl, Interrupted*, "so why is nobody pressing mine?" Sedated by this sluggish screen adaptation of Susanna Kaysen's 1993 novel, it's easy to sympathise with Lisa's frustration. Perhaps the problem with James Mangold's movie is not that it fails to press the right buttons, it's just they've been worn out with overuse.

In publicity interviews for the film Mangold (director of *Heavy* and *CopLand*) admits Kaysen's episodic story "did not translate cinematically." Neither does its mordant wit, which has been compared to Sylvia Plath's *The Bell Jar*. Instead, it's a clumsy cross between an inspirational madness-as-personal-growth drama and a female coming-of-age movie. Attending her alternative "Ivy League", Susanna studies a group of colourfully mad mates who are, of course, more sane than those living in the crazy 60s outside. Patients are force-fed pills. Nurses preach tough love. Basically, it's *One Flew Over the Cuckoo's Nest* with less character development and more life lessons.

The odd wry observation survives, for instance in the scene where new-girl Susanna is given a rundown on the hospital and its patients by a roommate who ends her comprehensive brief by cheerfully confessing to being a pathological liar. However, for the most part, Mangold's direction is thuddingly conventional. Watching the film maker's blurred shots of Susanna's Valium vision and the *Wizard of Oz* imagery he uses to suggest Georgie's "parallel universe", it's easy to see how Hollywood, like Claymore, institutionalises its inmates.

As the film chronicles the day-to-day lives of Claymore's nutty dorm girls (including midnight trips to the underground bowling alley), it sags under the weight of its own inconsequence. Only some electric performances keep the flatlining narrative alive. All doe eyes and hunched shoulders, executive producer Winona Ryder is perfect as the fragile, solipsistic Susanna. Unfortunately, her bravely unsympathetic performance merely illuminates another problem in the shift from book to screen. On paper Susanna's borderline personality disorder may have offered a subtle exploration of the slim, socially determined line between sanity and madness. On screen she appears merely petulant. When nurse Whoopi Goldberg looks up from under her giant Afro and diagnoses Susanna as a "lazy, self-indulgent little girl driving herself crazy," it's hard not to agree and draw unfavourable comparisons with McMurphy's tragic fight against the system in *Cuckoo's Nest*.

In *Girl, Interrupted* it's Jolie who gets to sink her teeth into the Jack Nicholson role, her ferocious Lisa providing a much needed contrast with Ryder's understated sulking. Whether strutting across the screen in a blonde fright wig or waiting for an orderly to light her cigarette, she's a sociopath with star power. No less effective is the sad and spooky Brittany Murphy as Daisy, a blank-eyed abuse victim whose patina of pert domesticity disguises a raging appetite for laxatives and rotisserie chicken. But sadly, even Vanessa Redgrave's deliciously dry cameo as headmistressy shrink Dr Wick can't save the shapeless storyline. And Mangold is forced to bring his realist montage of dance lessons, therapy and definitive 60s television to a close with a contrived climax. As a spectral Jolie chases Ryder through the basement screaming "I'm playing the villain," *Girl, Interrupted* seems to have sunk into self-parody. All that's left is for Ryder's narrator to press the button marked 'trite' by saying at the end: "They were not perfect but they were my friends."

TIME, 12/27/99, p. 170, Richard Schickel

Sometime in the 60s, Susanna Kaysen was placed in an upscale psychiatric hospital. It appears from *Girl, Interrupted*, the book she wrote about the experience a couple of decades later, that she might have fared just as well as an outpatient. It appears from the movie version that we would have fared just as well if Hollywood had regarded the book as unadaptable.

It's not that director (and final-draft writer) James Mangold has botched the job. It's just that he made something rather conventional out of a memoir that was spare, terse and elliptically funny. And naturally, the film's attitude toward its patients is the only acceptable one these days: that they may be saner than their keepers—especially since this is the '60s, when the outside world is so crazy.

Call that the not-so-new sentimentality. But call Ryder's performance as Kaysen first rate. She moves very persuasively from puzzled, rather passive resentment over her incarceration to a lively awareness of her problems to, finally, edgy mental health. Jolie is more problematic as her best friend, an overt rebel whose assertiveness leads to the movie's most tragic—and heavily fictionalized—passage. There is something tiresome in her toughness. But that's emblematic of the whole movie, which misses what was most engaging about Kaysen's memoir—the unique sound of her voice, mostly drowned out here by too familiar attitudes and melodrama.

VILLAGE VOICE, 12/28/99, p. 130, Abby McGanney Nolan

Elliptical and mordantly witty, Susanna Kaysen's *Girl, Interrupted* recounts living as a teen in a mental hospital for a year and a half; it stands as one of the more evocative memoirs of '60s-era craziness. The new Winona Ryder vehicle, released now for Oscar contention, is a rather drab reworking that occasionally devolves into *Sorority Snake Pit*, particularly during a subterranean showdown (not in the book) with a charismatic sociopath. The heavy hand of director-cowriter James Mangold *(Copland)* is much apparent.

In 1967, when Kaysen entered the private McLean Hospital outside Boston, famous patients like Robert Lowell, Sylvia Plath, and James Taylor had mostly come and gone. But there was more than a whiff of privilege still hanging around her adolescent girls' ward—some of her fellow inmates had gotten sidetracked on their way to Seven Sisters schools. In a sense, McLean served as a shelter from the world, the TV a tightly closed window from which to view Vietnam, assassinations, and riots. Kaysen's book nimbly probes her ambivalence toward her confinement. On some level, she felt she belonged there (and she provides medical records and examples of her own delusional thinking); but she also recalls the time-killing, decidedly non-therapeutic routines with bitter irony. Ryder's Kaysen is less complicated, a wrongly imprisoned waif making the best of a bad situation, she tries to help other troubled girls (the fire-starter, the lesbian, the pathological liar) and seeks out a good-hearted nurse (a beaming Whoopi Goldberg). Ryder's is an earnest, well-meaning performance—and she also coproduced the movie—but the book's interesting tension and dark humor are pretty much absent. Instead, there's trumped-up drama—an escape, a suicide, the lurid basement confrontation—and a same-sex kiss.

Where Ryder seems to occupy as little space as possible, Angelina Jolie strides through the movie as Lisa, the resident nonconformist who challenges the others to disrupt the ward whenever possible. Not content with a larger-than-life performance, Mangold turns Lisa into an over-the-top monster in several invented episodes. *Girl, Interrupted* contains some nicely restrained turns, like Clea Duval as Kaysen's Oz-obsessed roommate, but mainly it's a showcase for Ryder's winsome victim.

Also reviewed in:
CHICAGO TRIBUNE, 1/14/00, Friday/p. A, Michael Wilmington
NEW YORK TIMES, 12/21/99, p. E1, Stephen Holden
VARIETY, 12/13-19/99, p. 108, Emanuel Levy
WASHINGTON POST, 1/14/00, p. C1, Rita Kempley
WASHINGTON POST, 1/14/00, Weekend/p. 35, Michael O'Sullivan

GLORIA

A Columbia Pictures release of a Mandalay Entertainment presentation of an Eagle Point production. *Executive Producer:* G. Mac Brown and Chuck Binder. *Producer:* Gary Foster and Lee Rich. *Director:* Sidney Lumet. *Screenplay:* Steven Antin. *Based on the screenplay by:* John Cassavetes. *Director of Photography:* David Watkin. *Editor:* Tom Swartwout. *Music:* Howard Shore. *Music Editor:* Dan Evans Farkas. *Sound:* Christopher Newman. *Casting:* Lou DiGiaimo. *Production Designer:* Mel Bourne. *Art Director:* Carlos A. Menéndez. *Set Decorator:* Laura Lambert. Set Dresser: Joseph M. Deluca. *Special Effects:* Steve Kirshoff. *Costumes:* Dona Granata. *Make-up:* Bernadette Mazur. *Make-up (Sharon Stone):* Michele Burke-Winter. *Make-up (Jeremy Northam):* Donald Mowat. *Stunt Coordinator:* Jack Gill. *Running time:* 115 minutes. *MPAA Rating:* R.

CAST: Sharon Stone (Gloria); Jeremy Northam (Kevin); Cathy Moriarty (Diane); Jean-Luke Figueroa (Nicky Nunez); Mike Starr (Sean); Sarita Choudhury (Angela Nunez); Miriam Colon (Maria); Bobby Cannavale (Jack); George C. Scott (Ruby); Barry McEvoy (Terry); Don Billett (Raymond); Jerry Dean (Mickey); Tony DiBenedetto (Zach); Teddy Atlas (Ian); Desiree F. Casado (Luz); Davenia McFadden (Female Guard); Chuck Cooper (Male Guard); Antonia Rey (Tenant); Sidney Armus (Pharmacist); John Heffernan (Hotel Clerk); James Lally (Freddie the Pawnbroker); Terry Alexander and Lillias White (Transit Cops); John Diresta (Radio Cop); Lou Cantres and José Rabelo (Dominican Men); Lisa Louise Langford (Waitress); Ray Garvey (Police Detective); Nicole Brier (Young Blonde 1); Laura Wachal (Other Young Woman); Elle Alexander (Blonde 3); Donald J. Lee, Jr. (Father Paul); Don Clark Williams (Video Reporter); Nick Oddo (Uncle Manny); Timothy K. Rail (Priest with Students); Martha Rentas (Bus Driver); Bonnie Bedelia (Brenda).

LOS ANGELES TIMES, 1/25/99, Calendar/p. 4, Jack Mathews

Sidney Lumet's new version of the late John Cassavetes' 1980 "Gloria" is not so much a remake of a film as it is a remake of an overcooked performance—a case of ham imitating ham. This is Sharon Stone doing Gena Rowlands' flamboyant impression of a middle-age moll on the run, with an orphaned boy, and being reborn as a nurturing mom. It's Damon Runyon in drag.

Why "Gloria" was remade is as much a mystery as why it was not shown to critics in advance. Lumet is too much of a craftsman to turn out the kind of stink bombs typically sneaked into theaters and his movie is exactly what you'd expect, given the source material and the casting.

Stone does Rowlands as well as she possibly could. She has Rowlands' voice inflections, her mannerisms, even her high-heeled, military stride. Sometimes, when she has her face screwed up to expectorate a phrase, she even looks like Rowlands—blond on blond.

It's not so much a bad performance as an unnecessary one. Anyone who has seen Cassavetes' film can imagine Lumet's and save eight bucks. Those who haven't can simply imagine Stone tramping around under a pile of unnaturally curly hair, in miniskirts that make police interrogators sweat, and piling on whenever a scene requires tearful emotion.

The friendliest of Cassavetes' critics considered "Gloria" a kind of slumming exercise, a post-feminist charade in which Rowlands plays a rogue moll. It's as if one of James Cagney's or Edward G. Robinson's girlfriends in a Warner Bros. gangster movie decided she was mad as hell and wasn't going to take it anymore.

In Lumet's film, adapted from Cassavetes' script by young actor Steven Antin (Det. Savino on "NYPD Blue"), "Gloria" is just out of prison, having done a three-year stretch for boyfriend/mob lieutenant Kevin (Jeremy Northam) and is determined to call in an old debt and go straight. But Kevin likes their old arrangement, where she is to him what dirt is to a fingernail, and when she balks, the lines are drawn.

It happens that when Gloria comes to collect from Kevin, he's holding hostage 7-year-old Nicky Nunez (Jean-Luke Figueroa), whose mother, father and older sister have just been murdered by one of Kevin's gang. Seems Nicky has a computer disc (it was a notebook in the earlier film) containing information that will unravel half of New York's two main industries, government and organized crime.

Gloria rescues Nicky from Kevin's clutches, and for the rest of the movie, she and the boy charge around Manhattan, trying to stay alive, and slowly, inevitably surrendering to the urge of co-dependence. Figueroa is a cute kid, and, if memory serves, his counterpart in Cassavetes' film wasn't. That's both good and bad.

For Gloria's transformation to be complete, there needs to be this great veil of coolness and antagonism between her and the child. Rowlands made Gloria as callous as a corn, and about as quick to soften. For this kind of two-character drama to carry a feature-length film, there has to be a lot of emotional ground to cover, and her change of heart has to be a genuine leap.

Stone, for all her arch vampiness in past roles, is really a softie. She looks comfortable with kids, and from the moment she makes off with Nicky, there's no question she'll protect him to the end.

There are shootings and car chases to break up the developing mother-son story, and an unusually restrained performance from George C. Scott as the old mob boss to whom Gloria pleads for help. But the movie exists as an acting exercise for Stone, which turns out—predictably—to be all sweat and no Gloria.

NEW YORK, 2/8/99, p. 58, Peter Rainer

It's bad enough when filmmakers remake good movies—case in point: the new *Psycho*—but do we really need remakes of mediocre ones too? The redo makes sense only if the original botched a marvelous opportunity. I've never detected any marvels in the 1980 John Cassavetes crime thriller *Gloria*, so its reworking by Sidney Lumet and screenwriter Steve Antin left me doubly cold.

The Cassavetes version was a gun-toting star vehicle for Gena Rowlands. Her replacement is Sharon Stone, brandishing an ultra-hokey Hell's Kitchen accent. Stone is best when she's a victimizer *(Basic Instinct)* and not a victim *(Sliver)*. This moll's heart of gold is pure tinsel.

Gloria discovers her maternal instincts while on the lam from the mob. In tow is 7-year-old Nicky (Jean-Luke Figueroa), a cuddlypoo charmer whose family was gunned down by henchmen of her ex-boyfriend (Jeremy Northam). No law mandates that an actress can't be sweet in one film and lethal in the next: Barbara Stanwyck, for example, had the range to play the blackest-hearted of vamps *(Double Indemnity)* and the most weepily sacrificial of mothers *(Stella Dallas)* and be equally amazing. But Stone dulls her intelligence, and her sass, when she gets all drizzly and heartfelt. Schmaltz doesn't become her.

Her allure has always been rather retro. Her hourglass curves and hyperprettiness fit into the glam era of Hollywood's Golden Age; even her emotionalism, when it pours out in *Casino* or *Last Dance* or *Gloria*, is the kind of bold Hollywood emotionalism we associate with iron butter-flies like Susan Hayward. It's probably no accident that Stone broke through with *Basic Instinct* at a time when Hollywood wasn't providing much in the way of compellingly contemporary roles expressing what women were actually going through in their lives. Her black-widow presence in that film at least filled a void. Her portrayal was a kicky, pre-feminist joke, although it wasn't played for laughs: When she uncrossed her legs for the cops during her interrogation scene, the gleam in her eye could have lasered through solid steel. Stone wasn't a camp vamp in *Basic Instinct;* she was more like a Joan Crawford bad girl for the scratch-and-sniff era.

Stone's stardom also coincided with the stepped-up globalization of Hollywood movies in the eighties. The stars who worked best overseas were the action-hero types—Stallone and Willis and Schwarzenegger (with whom Stone made her first impact with audiences in *Total*

Recall)—who could carry a movie with a minimum of dialogue. They represented a red-blooded archetype that fit a foreigner's movie-fantasy image of American maleness. The American woman had no such counterpart in the movies, but Stone's big-blondeness and cut-glass features came close. Her old-style glamour, her sheer celebrity-ness, gave her the sizzle of a dry-ice diva. She may have played characters who parted their legs, but she always seemed on-call for a Hurrell photo shoot. She *looked* like a movie star, and her image rivaled Monroe's in the shop windows of Paris and Tokyo.

Stone doesn't have quite the same cachet she had in her *Basic Instinct* period—perhaps because her retro quality is seeming a little retro itself these days. (Her remake of *Diabolique,* where she spent much of the movie in a cocktail dress, was de trop.) Her new film represents an attempt to once and for all cut through the femme fatale glam and get real, but it's just another species of movie hokum. Near the end, Nicky says to Gloria, "You're tough," and she shoots back, "It's all an act." That's the problem—it is all an act. Stone reads her lines as if every one were a zinger: not just the wisecracky stuff but the heartfelt stuff too. She tells a mob boss, "I'm not a mother; I've always been a broad," and it sounds like the lead-in to a number from *Guys and Dolls*. *Gloria* is such a sapfest that it accomplishes what Stone's slinkier movies never did: It turns her into a bimbo.

NEW YORK POST, 1/23/99, p. 23, Jonathan Foreman

When the studio decides to release a movie without critics' screenings, you know that they know that they've got a stinker on their hands. And the all-round awfulness of "Gloria" is such that reviewing it is akin to doing an autopsy on a rapidly decomposing body. Amidst all the mess, it's hard to tell what makes it such a tedious failure. Was it the lousy script, the absentee direction by Sidney Lumet or the noisy, empty and utterly unbelievable performance by Sharon Stone as a tough gangster's moll on the run?

It makes it worse that this is a remake of John Cassavetes' 1980 "Gloria," which itself wasn't all that good, but which looks like "Citizen Kane" in comparison. The new movie starts with Gloria (Miss Stone) being released from a Florida jail. You never find out what crime she committed, but she has the kind of artfully curled blonde hairdo that you can only get in movie prison.

But the real action begins in New York while Gloria is on a plane. A mob accountant—you can tell his profession because he's wearing an old-fashioned waistcoat—and his family in Washington Heights are shot by a mobster looking for a stolen computer disk. (In the original it was a notebook.) But before he's killed, the accountant gives the disk to his 7-year-old son. The boy, Nicky (Jean-Luke Figueroa), gets away down the fire escape but is caught by the gangsters and brought back to mob HQ—a ridiculously stylish, minimalist SoHo loft.

Just then Gloria arrives. She's the girlfriend of yuppie gangster Kevin (Jeremy Northam). Kevin doesn't seem particularly mean, but when Gloria realizes that his subordinates are planning to off the child, she rescues the boy. The next thing you know she's tottering around New York in her high heels with Nicky in one hand and a gun in another.

The basic plot was an old one even when John Cassavetes wrote the movie for his wife Gena Rowlands: the tough underworld denizen whose gruff decency is brought out when he or she is put in danger together with a little kid. It only works if you care about both characters, and in this remake there's no chance of that.

The problem is not in the small changes to the story: In the original the mobsters were Italian rather than Irish and Gloria was a next-door neighbor who gets the boy when she's looking for some sugar. The problem is that everything about Sharon Stone and most things about the rest of the cast are utterly unbelievable.

Unlike Gena Rowlands, who was terrific and natural as a tough middle-aged woman on the run, Stone overacts like crazy, emoting left, right and center with an agonizing deeze-dem-and-doze Noo Yawk accent.

At times she seems to have wandered onto the set of the wrong film, perhaps one in the 1940s, while everyone else especially the SoHo gangsters are clearly comfortable in the '90's. And gorgeous as she is, she looks at least 15 years older than her mobster boyfriend.

Stone is a genuine movie star, a beauty, and not a bad actress. But she clearly has a deluded notion of her own range, and terrible taste in parts. (Add this debacle to "Sliver," "Sphere," "Diabolique" and "Intersection.").

If only there had been some chemistry between Stone and Jean-Luke Figueroa, who plays the annoying orphan, there might have been some hope.

The fact that "Gloria" is barely directed at all is surely responsible for some of Stone's more embarassing moments on screen.   Sidney Lumet has copied one of Cassavetes' stylistic ties—multiple scenes in which people scream at each other at the same times—to no emotional effect.   And once again, the veteran director has made bizarre choices in casting.

Lumet's "Q&A" was all but ruined by the miscasting of his daughter Jenny as a Puerto Rican gangster's moll.   Here the mob accountant's Puerto Rican wife is played by the Indian-American actress Sarita Choudhury.

Hello?

SIGHT AND SOUND, 8/99, p. 44, Chris Darke

Gloria, a mob moll, is released from a Florida jail after serving three years.   In New York, the head of the family entrusts a computer disc that implicates the Mafia in corruption to seven-year-old son Nicky, who escapes moments before a hitman arrives and shoots the entire family.   Gloria arrives in New York and goes to her apartment where her mobster boyfriend Kevin and his crew are now staying.   They've caught Nicky and are planning to kill him.   Discovering Kevin has reneged on the deal he made to compensate her when she served time for him, Gloria flees with Nicky and the disc.   Ruby, the mob *capo* gives Kevin 48 hours to retrieve the disk.

Gloria takes Nicky back to his apartment only to witness bodies being extracted from the building.   Unaware family are dead, Nicky explains his father told him to go to his uncle Manny, but Gloria finds him killed as well.   They book into a hotel where Nicky hears on television that his family are dead.   Distraught, he flees, but Gloria catches up with him.   Gloria sees a priest who arranges to place Nicky in a school upstate, but the boy is immediately snatched by Kevin's henchmen.   Through Diane, a friend from her past, Gloria sets up a meeting with Ruby who agrees an exchange: the boy for the disc.   Gloria takes Nicky to the school but, having deposited him, has a change of heart.   She retrieves him and the couple fly off to Miami to together.

You wouldn't know it either from *Gloria*'s credits or its press material, but Sidney Lumet's Sharon Stone vehicle is a remake of John Cassavetes' 1980 film which starred Gena Rowlands as Gloria Swenson, the mob moll turned reluctant surrogate mother.   Cassavetes never considered Gloria as much more than a debt-paying exercise: "I wrote the story to sell, strictly to sell," he admitted. it was shot at the tail-end of the 70s, the decade in which Cassavetes had made his most groundbreaking features and cemented—with his wife and lead actress one of the key actress-director relationships in American cinema.

Cassavetes has been thoroughly airbrushed out of the remake's production history—there isn't even a reference to his having scripted the original, here reworked by Steve Antin.   But even with Stone in the lead, it's a little harder to work the same disappearing act on Gena Rowlands, this new film's other crucial haunting presence.   From the opening, where Stone exits the huge looming edifice of a Florida jail barely draped in a fabulously slinky dress, it's clear that she's more Ginger than Gena, playing a variation on her character in Scorsese's Casino. In this respect the film's condensed time scheme—Gloria has seven days to secure sanctuary for Nicky before she has to return to Miami to meet her parole officer—helps Stone draw on and develop that element of Ginger that was far more than simply a scene-stealing sulphurous blonde. In *Casino,* Stone played Ginger's appetites and opportunism with self-destructive vulnerability; her Gloria takes the actress into a new realm of harried resourcefulness.   But she has to work harder with the role than Rowlands did.   Cassavetes often found the compassionate, maternal element in Rowlands' performances—hardly surprising, given that so many of his films with her were about ideas of family.   But Stone is not an actress whose persona has anything near the skittish warmth that Rowlands exuded.   That said, she plays the sassy surrogate mother to Nicky—the would-be macho homunculus whose mantra is "I'm the Man"—in a gentle register of mocking comedy.

As for a director so thoroughly associated with New York, its streetlife and institutions, it's not hard to see why Lumet was attracted to the project.   Much of the film takes place at street level with the odd couple diving in and out of delicatessens, pawnshops and hotels pursued by mob hitmen run by Gloria's former boyfriend Kevin. The criminal backstory is actually the film's weakest element, despite the brutality with which Nicky's family are slayed. One can't help feeling it's precisely that brutality Lumet needs to make us fear for Gloria and Nicky. It's a gamble that doesn't pay off, though. The gang is never as fearsome as they should be, which probably accounts for George C. Scott's presence as Ruby, the local mob boss. It's a cameo, but performed with such a compelling combination of autumnal authority and slyness, Scott lazily steals all his scenes. Had Scott been given anything more than a cameo, he'd probably have stolen the film right from under Stone's satisfying interpretation of a well-chosen role.

Also reviewed in:
CHICAGO TRIBUNE, 1/25/99, Tempo/p. N, John Petrakis
NEW REPUBLIC, 2/22/99, p. 30, Stanley Kauffmann
NEW YORK TIMES, 1/23/99, p. B14, Lawrence Van Gelder
VARIETY, 1/25-31/99, p. 77, Godfrey Cheshire
WASHINGTON POST, 1/23/99, p. C1, Stephen Hunter
WASHINGTON POST, 1/29/99, Weekend/p. 42, Desson Howe

GO

A Columbia Pictures release of a Banner Entertainment production in association with Saratoga Entertainment. *Producer:* Paul Rosenberg, Mickey Liddell, and Matt Freeman. *Director:* Doug Liman. *Screenplay:* John August. *Editor:* Stephen Mirrione. *Music:* Christopher Sheldon and Dane A. Davis. *Music Editor:* Carl Kaller. *Choreographer:* Miranda Garrison. *Sound:* Jim Thornton. *Sound Editor:* Christopher Sheldon and Dane A. Davis. *Casting:* Joseph Middleton. *Production Designer:* Tom Wilkins. *Art Director:* Rebecca Young. *Set Decorator:* F. Beauchamp Hebb. *Set Designer:* Catherine Doherty. *Special Effects:* Martin Becker. *Costumes:* Genevieve Tyrrell. *Make-up:* James Ryder. *Stunt Coordinator:* Dennis Scott. *Running time:* 100 minutes. *MPAA Rating:* R.

CAST: Katie Holmes (Claire Montgomery); Sarah Polley (Ronna Martin); Suzanne Krull (Stringy Haired Woman); Desmond Askew (Simon Baines); Nathan Bexton (Mannie); Robert Peters (Switterman); Scott Wolf (Adam); Jay Mohr (Zack); Timothy Olyphant (Todd Gaines); Jodi Bianca Wise (Ballerina Girl); William Fichtner (Burke); Rita Bland (Dancing Register Woman); Tony Denman (Track Suit Guy); Scott Hass (Raver Dude); Natasha Melnick (Anorexic Girl); Manu Intiraymi (Skate Punk Guy); Josh Paddock (Spider Marine); Taye Diggs (Marcus); Breckin Meyer (Tiny); James Duval (Singh); Courtland Mead (Boy); Katharine Towne (Becky); Marisa Morell (Rebecca); Ken Kupstis (Sports Car Man); Nikki Fritz (Noelle); Tane McClure (Holly); Jimmy Shubert (Victor Jr.); J.E. Freeman (Victor Sr.); Jay Paulson (Loop); Jane Krakowski (Irene); Melissa McCarthy (Sandra); Shann Beeman (Jimmy); Willie Amakye (Waiter).

LOS ANGELES TIMES, 4/9/99, Calendar/p. 6, Kevin Thomas

If Ronna (Sarah Polley), an 18-year-old Von's cashier, weren't facing eviction and if her British co-worker Simon (Desmond Askew) hadn't gone off to Vegas, then we might have been cruelly deprived of all the inspired mayhem that makes "Go" such fun. "Swingers," which marked Doug Liman's much-noted 1996 directorial debut, does not prepare you for the heady rush or nonstop comic anarchy of his follow-up feature.

Whereas "Swingers" writer-star Jon Favreau provided Liman a sweet story of camaraderie among a group of guys not as cool as they think they are, "Go" writer John August creates a screenful of world-class risk-takers.

In place of the everyday reality in "Swingers," "Go" offers breathtaking comic-action fantasy. Yet both films seem to be taking place in the same world, that of young people living marginal lives and wishing they were lots closer to the center.

Since Simon, who has a sideline in drug dealing, is not around, Adam (Scott Wolf) and Zack (Jay Mohr), TV series co-stars, approach Ronna to see if she can supply them with 20 hits of Ecstasy to take to a Christmas season bash at a warehouse. With a coolness born of desperation, Ronna says yes, and she and her reluctant pal at the store, Claire (Katie Holmes), are off to Simon's supplier, Todd (Timothy Olyphant), a sexy but dangerous dude with Valentino sideburns. In a flash Ronna is in major trouble.

"Go" then cuts back to Simon, who is recklessness personified, with his pals, most notably level-headed Marcus (Taye Diggs), taking off for Vegas where they are plunged into ever-spiraling hair-raising adventures. In almost less time than it takes to report, Simon steals a car, shoots a lap-dance club bouncer and has sex with two women—simultaneously. (Never mind that they set a hotel room on fire in the process.)

Then we return to the moment Adam and Zack approach Ronna and follow their story, which includes a hilariously insinuating encounter with a rugged cop (William Fichtner) and his beautiful wife (Jane Krakowski)—and which eventually propels the clever resolution of all three episodes.

When all is said and done, "Go" is a film about people going too far, which works precisely because its makers know when to hold back. "Go" keeps us guessing, especially about Ronna's fate, but it never forgets it's a comedy; if it was too serious it would burst like a bubble.

So uniformly skilled and talented is the film's cast, which has 15 featured players, that it is impossible to single out any one. "Go" is perfectly titled: Exhilarating and sharp, it never stops for a second.

NEW YORK POST, 4/9/99, p. 49, Rod Dreher

Hipster filmmaker Doug Liman's breakneck, raucous and thoroughly exhilarating "Go" is flat-out the best thing I've seen all year.

It's pedal-to-the-metal mayhem and misadventure from the first flickering frames, shot in a rave club, and stops for a breath only when the colorful characters in this hit-and-run comedy careen fabulously into the wall.

"Go" gets off the mark in a dingy Los Angeles supermarket on Christmas Eve. Surly cashier Ronna (Sarah Polley) is subbing for colleague Simon (Desmond Askew), who has taken off with two pals for a night in Vegas.

A pair of pretty boys (Jay Mohr and Scott Wolf) drop Simon's name and ask Ronna if she can hook them up with the drug Ecstasy for a rave later that night.

In need of rent money, Ronna gutsily improvises a scheme to deal Ecstasy at substantial markup.

Leaving her shy friend Claire (Katie Holmes) as human collateral with sinister drug source Todd (snarly Timothy Olyphant), Ronna tumbles down a grungy rabbit hole.

The engagingly doltish Simon is simultaneously cavorting through the casinos with Marcus (Taye Diggs) and another pal. Simon just wants to have fun and is left doing clueless double takes at the trouble he gets into—hot monkey love, hotel fires, strip clubs, shotguns.

"Go"'s third story involves TV actors Adam (Wolf) and Zack (Mohr), who are trying to score drugs from Ronna. Like the others, Adam and Zack get dragged along by out-of-control circumstances like tin cans tied to a stock car's bumper.

Which is not quite the right simile, because the compelling characters often drive the plot by the impulsive choices they make. The cool, cutting dialogue and gonzo plot twists by first-time scripter John August are brought to thrilling life by "Swingers" director Liman's kinetic style.

The cast is something, too, starting with Canadian actress Sarah Polley, the Uma-in-waiting and uncrowned queen of Sundance for her work in "Go" and the forthcoming "Guinevere."

She's going to break big, as is Taye Diggs, who projects a sexy, authoritative cool as the straight man to Askew's chirrupy screwball. Other standouts include the feral dope dealer Timothy Olyphant, and William Fichtner as a kinky cop who tangles with Adam and Zack.

A herd of teen movies has galumphed through multiplexes lately, but none has felt so intensely young as this one. "Go" crystallizes something essential to youth: its crazy-making adrenalin rush, its reckless openness to experience, its bravado and idiot daring, its shoot-first, ask-questions-later fearlessness. "Go" is blithely amoral, but not dark and nasty. The filmmakers call it "optimistic," which is a stretch, but at least nobody dies, and everything that happens is in good, dirty fun.

NEWSDAY, 4/9/99, Part II/p. B3, John Anderson

There's this thing they call the sophomore jinx, which seems to plague second-time filmmakers coming off a successful first feature—directors like Doug Liman, whose debut, "Swingers," was a respectable if slightly cultish hit but who seems to have avoided the sophomore jinx entirely.

He has not just defied the odds, he has done it while waving a red flag in the face of Fortuna. "Go," his ferocious new comedy-slash-urban excavation of mores and morons, is as ungainly a project as he might have bitten off. A dozen characters, the choreographing of three intersecting narratives and a Los Angeles that's portrayed as a demented amusement park (to say nothing of Las Vegas, which we won't). It's impressive. Liman's "Go" is as tantalizing a film as we've seen thus far this year and not just because the whole thing is a house of cards.

Chief among his confident ensemble is Sarah Polley, who a seeming 15 minutes ago was playing a 14-year-old paraplegic folksinger in "The Sweet Hereafter" and suddenly has become Ronna, 18-year-old checkout person, delinquent rent-payer and field-commissioned scam artist. Hoping to make a killing in the absence of fellow checkout clerk and drug runner Simon (Desmond Askew), who's off to Las Vegas, she agrees to score some ecstacy from a semipsychotic dealer named Todd (Timothy Olyphant) and deliver them to Adam and Zack (Jay Mohr and Scott Wolf, stars of a television cop drama. Having left her worried friend, Claire (Katie Holmes), as "collateral" back at Todd's, she walks into the most obvious drug bust in the world, orchestrated by the heavyhanded cop named Burke (William Fichtner), whose mere presence prompts Ronna to hit the bathroom, flush the stash and get the heck out of Dodge.

What to do? Shoplift some cold medicine, sell it as ecstasy at an underground party on the outskirts of town and try to recoup the money she needs to get Claire away from Todd? What follows is the screeching of tires and the dull thud of flesh against sturdy Detroit hardware.

What's with Adam and Zack? Much, but before we get their story we get Simon's debauched trip to Vegas, where a sidetrip to a sex club ends in gunshots and mayhem and two very irritated heavies chasing the boys back to L.A.

And then, Adam and Zack. Ever since their own drug bust, Burke has been extorting the duo into enhancing his arrest record by acting as decoys—particularly for Ronna. Burke, however, is a man of many parts, some of them downright strange.

What Liman does with all this human drama—and does deftly—is structure the story in three overlapping chapters, all of which begin with Ronna in the supermarket and radiate out according to the subjects at hand. Aspects of each story illuminate the last, or the next, and in portraying an L.A. subculture that's wholly corrupt—but with characters who are wholly sympathetic (except maybe Burke) and who blend together despite their idiosyncratic quirks and troubles, he achieves a cohesive amalgamation that might even pass as community.

Mostly, "Go"—a phrase repeatedly used by characters fleeing cops, pushers, and other unpleasant situations—is a real joy to watch, fun, intelligent and seamlessly structured. It might indeed wind up among the better films of the entire year. And we do mean that as a compliment.

NEWSWEEK, 4/12/99, p. 72, David Ansen

Desperate for cash on Christmas Eve, an 18-year-old supermarket checkout clerk (Sarah Polley) takes it upon herself to score 20 hits of ecstasy for a couple of cute actors (Scott Wolf and Jay Mohr). In *Go*, Doug Liman, the director of the hip "Swingers," shows us the comically twisted fallout of her disastrous drug deal. It all takes place in 24 hours, but we see this day from three separate angles. In the first part, we get the checkout girl's story. Then we follow Simon (Desmond Askew), the young Brit who was supposed to do the deal but instead ends up in Las Vegas, setting fire to a hotel room and fleeing an armed stripclub owner. Finally, we watch the day from the point of view of the two actors, whose involvement in the drug transaction puts them at the mercy of a very peculiar cop (William Fichtner) who blackmails them into having dinner with his wife, where he makes an unexpected proposal.

John August's trickily structured script owes an all too obvious debt to "Pulp Fiction," but Liman's film is more like kiddie Tarantino. Guns are fired and shovels raised with murderous intent, but no one ever gets seriously harmed.

Like its naive protagonists, the movie flirts with danger, only to back off and announce "Just kidding!" As he showed in "Swingers," Liman has an ingratiating sensibility and an energetic

GO 611

style. "Go" is peppered with funny bits: kids talking themselves into a high on the cold medicine Polley passes off as ecstasy; Wolf and Mohr's bickering, showbiz relationship, and best of all Fichtner's insinuating lunacy as a drug cop with a screw loose.

Clever as the parts are, "Go" doesn't add up to much. It starts to go awry in the frenetic Vegas episode, when you realize that things happen because the screenplay wills them to happen, not from any internal logic. It's the *whatever* school of filmmaking. "Go" has its pleasures, but I didn't really believe a word of it.

SIGHT AND SOUND, 9/99, p. 46, John Wrathall

Los Angeles, Christmas Eve. Desperate to raise $400 to avert her eviction, supermarket-checkout girl Ronna agrees to work an extra shift to cover for Simon, who is going for a night out in Las Vegas. When Adam and Zack arrive, hoping to buy 20 Ecstasy tablets from Simon, Ronna offers to supply them. Ronna gets the drugs from Simon's source, Todd. At Adam and Zack's, she realises it's a set-up, and flushes the drugs down the toilet. She goes back to Todd and gives him 20 aspirins in place of the drugs, claiming the sale fell through. Then, with friends Claire and Mannie, she goes to the rave, where she sells more aspirin and makes the $400 she needs. Realising the drugs are fake, Todd follows Ronna to the rave. As he chases her through the car park she is run over.

Returning to the start again, we follow Simon to Las Vegas, where he accidentally shoots a strip club bouncer, Victor Jr, in the arm. Simon escapes, but he leaves Todd's borrowed credit card behind at the club. Returning to the start again, we follow Adam and Zack, an actor couple pressured by Burke, a cop, into setting up Ronna. After the sting goes wrong, they go to the rave, where they run over Ronna and leave her for dead, only to realise that Adam is still wearing the hidden microphone from the sting. Returning to dispose of Ronna's body, they find her still breathing and move her to ensure that someone else discovers her.

Looking for Ronna, Claire meets Todd and goes home with him for sex, but Victor Jr shows up, looking for Simon. When Simon arrives moments later, Victor plans to shoot him in the arm in revenge. Ronna wakes up in hospital and goes to the supermarket, where she meets Claire, and remembers she left Mannie passed out at the rave. They return to the deserted site and find him.

Like Doug Liman's first film *Swingers, Go* follows assorted young Los Angelenos around the city's nightspots—and in the central episode, to Las Vegas and back—in search of a good time. But there the similarity ends. While *Swingers* (scripted by Jon Favreau) was a gentle series of variations on a theme, John August's script for *Go* is frenetic, audaciously structured and plot-heavy, packed with enough incident for at least three films.

Structurally, *Go* is in the tradition of *Mystery Train* and *Pulp Fiction*, divided into three stories which happen over the same timespan (in this case, a single night) and which gradually inform each other. The way Ronna, after the near death experiences of her night out, ends up neatly back at work the following morning also echoes Scorsese's *After Hours*. Like these films, but unlike *Swingers, Go* isn't really concerned with character development. This isn't a coming-of-age story: the characters don't learn anything from the experiences of their big night. This is made clear at the end, when the wasted Mannie, who has spent most of Christmas Eve passed out under a pile of scrap metal, blithely asks, "What are we doing for New Year?" Next week, the implication seems to be, the cycle will start all over again. (It's tempting to perceive an allusion to Monopoly in the way the story keeps returning to the same initial scene, a narrative equivalent of passing "Go".)

The film's sense of frenetic activity purely for its own sake provides an apt reflection of the clubbing experience. Like a good DJ, Liman is skilled at varying the rhythm, building things up and then slowing them down. The first episode, 'Ronna', follows her attempts to obtain, then dispose of, then replace 20 tablets of Ecstasy. But within the film's simple, logical progression Liman finds room for two hilarious digressions exploring the drugs' effects on Mannie: an extravagant Latin dance fantasy in a supermarket and a deadpan conversation with drug-dealer Todd's cat, conducted entirely in subtitled 'thoughts'.

The second episode, 'Simon', picks up speed, hurtling through furious plot twists as Simon's night out in Las Vegas takes in gambling losses, a gatecrashed wedding, three-way sex, a hotel fire—and all before the story really starts. Then the third episode, 'Adam and Zack', slows right down again, straying into a bizarre shaggy-dog digression about a creepy Christmas dinner at the home of their police contact Burke before finally contriving an excuse for the pair to go to the rave, where their story collides with Ronna's.

As on *Swingers*, Liman functions as his own director of photography, giving him total control over the film's look, from grimy naturalism to drug-fuelled fantasy. He also elicits sprightly performances from his eclectic cast, ranging from committed indie kids (Sarah Polley from Atom Egoyan's films, Nathan Bexton and James Duval from Gregg Araki's) to US soap stars (Jane Krakowski of *Ally McBeal*, Scott Wolf of *Party of Five*) to British former child star Desmond Askew.

TIME, 4/12/99, p. 94, Richard Corliss

The one thing that's clear from the glut of contemporary teenpix is that a lot of young talent is being wasted in gonadal junk. If only these kids could find a smart script and a director who knew how to harness their coltish appeal, they might quickly turn promise into achievement. As it happens, the wait wasn't all that long. Here is a picture that has wit, a hairpin-turn narrative, high pizazz and ensemble star quality. Ready, set, *Go*.

To judge from the script by John August (a comer; no, an arriver), Ralph's Market in Hollywood is stocked with sirloin starlets. Katie Holmes, she of the angel-slut face, is there from *Dawson's Creek*. Sarah Polley—with Creature-from-the-Black-Lagoon eyes and a mouth born to pout (some clever director will cast her as Heather Graham's younger, savvier sister)—is a cashier. *Party of Five's* dreamboat Scott Wolf is in Polley's check-out line. The film isn't five minutes old and already you suspect you'll be entranced even if it stinks.

It doesn't stink. August and director Doug Liman, of that lovely L.A. fable *Swingers*, have many amusing tricks to play on you. Ronna (Polley) is substituting for Simon (Desmond Askew), now off to Vegas, who retails drugs on the side. Soap opera stars Adam (Wolf) and Zack (Jay Mohr) want to buy some from Ronna, who needs rent money. Claire (Holmes) thinks that's all very cool, until she is left as collateral with Simon's evil wholesaler Todd (Timothy Olyphant). The movie is rather too frolicsome about drug use, but it carries an internal message: if you're on dope, you won't be able to follow the plot.

It's worth following because it forks into a second story—Simon and his friend Marcus (Taye Diggs) go to a Vegas lap-dance parlor and play with gunfire—and a third, involving Adam, Zack and a narc (William Fichtner) who comes on to them like a Mark Fuhrman on Viagra. Though some of these folks shade into their 30s, all act like teenagers. The movie is set on Christmas Eve, but emotionally it's Mischief Night, when kids will do anything for the freewheeling hell of it. They fool around as if there were no tomorrow, not caring that tomorrow is ... Halloween.

Go is that kind of four-on-the-floor joyride, seemingly heedless of Hollywood story conventions as it spins from one attractive group of actors to the next. When Polley disappears after 40 minutes, you may feel no one can take her place; then Diggs (our choice for Afro-fab star of the future) assumes center screen and is just as beguiling. Wolf is delightfully disdainful of getting an ear kiss from the narc's free-love wife: "And that ear thing. I have Q-Tips, thank you."Olyphant is also an accomplished hunk. In fact, why not round up the entire cast for a sequel? Call it *Keep Going*.

O.K., the car chases and gunplay don't work as well as the character comedy does. The movie has so many different set pieces that it sometimes looks like Liman's demo reel. And all right, you've seen these elements before—but rarely so engagingly assembled. With its three-part structure framing a story of drugs and smart talk, but also with a heart so understanding that it lets nobody die, *Go* is a prime example of Tarantino cute: pup fiction.

VILLAGE VOICE, 4/13/99, p. 145, J. Hoberman.

Go, the bluntly titled action-comedy directed by Doug Liman in wide-screen pulsarama, is a disaster film with an exceedingly witty premise. Instead of a terrorist, volcano, or extraterrestrial invasion, catastrophe is precipitated by the madcap behavior of rash and reckless American youth.

If Liman's last feature, the indie smash *Swingers*, imagined a new sort of twentysomething lifestyle, *Go* provides that subculture's imagined slumming entertainment: the grunge *Speed*. So primed to party that the rave begins under its studio logo, the movie will probably never have a better screening than its midnight premiere at the last Sundance Film Festival—where the altitude enhanced the heady promise of demographic payoff.

Replaying the same Christmas Eve three times from as many perspectives, John August's script—his first—applies a fashionably cubist approach to the sex, drugs, and cheap-thrills antics of a few lumpen L.A. slackers. A hassled supermarket cashier named Ronna (Sarah Polley, the wan and calculating standout in a sparky young cast) takes over her colleague Simon's shift so that this carefree Brit (Desmond Askew) can spend his holiday in Vegas. She's about to be evicted, and so when two associates of Simon's show up looking to score some Ecstasy, she decides to orchestrate the deal herself, dropping in on Simon's supplier, Todd—menacingly bare-chested but crowned with a Santa's cap in the spirit of the season.

The deal has an appropriately ceremonial flavor—in general, Liman is good at elaborating youthful awkwardness and distinguishing between degrees of uncool. If Ronna's supermarket cohorts, including her more cautious friend Claire (Katie Holmes, the sweetheart of *Dawson's Creek)*, prove worse than useless in supporting her entrepreneurial spirit, the deal itself turns out to be a buy-and-bust setup—and that's just for starters. The night is still young when Ronna graduates from dealer to burn artist, although her place on the herb-to-carnivore food chain is by no means secure, particularly when vengeful Todd reenters the picture.

After Ronna has a run-in with a car and lands in a ditch, *Go* rewinds the action to pick up on blithe Simon driving to Las Vegas with a car full of wired idiots—including a belligerent white Negro and a tantric black man. Vegas is the capital of impulse behavior and that's certainly how Simon plays it—wandering into a wedding, falling into bed with two girls, inadvertently torching a hotel room, stealing a car, running amok in a raunchy lap-dance emporium. His escapades are certainly action-packed, but, less character-driven than those of the preceding section, they are also more predictable and ultimately tiresome.

Although the teenage Mack Sennett brutalism of bumper cars in the neon night threatens to capsize the entire project, *Go* regains its equilibrium and even a bit of spin in the final episode. The action backtracks once more to detail the surpassingly weird Christmas Eve spent by Adam *(Party of Five's* Scott Wolo and Zack (Jay Mohr), the two soap-opera actors who set the scenario in motion by coming to the supermarket to cop. Although the alert viewer may suspect that their path will likely recross Ronna's to tie the evening's adventures into a neat bow, the means by which it happens is fraught with surprises.

Go gets a lot nastier before delivering the last of its Christmas gifts. But remarkably the movie never becomes oppressive. There's a sense of detached problem solving, possibly arising from Liman's status as his own camera operator. A showy exercise in nervous grit, *Go* never strays too far from a sense of itself as stunt. Does Liman direct movies so that he can shoot them? It's that hired-gun brio that keeps *Go* from turning smugly bad-boy, a syndrome we might term *Very Very Bad Things*.

Also reviewed in:
CHICAGO TRIBUNE, 4/9/99, Friday/p. A, Mark Caro
NEW YORK TIMES, 4/9/99, p. E14, Janet Maslin
NEW YORKER, 4/19/99, p. 106, Anthony Lane
VARIETY, 2/8-14/99, p. 78, Todd McCarthy
WASHINGTON POST, 4/9/99, p. C1, Rita Kempley
WASHINGTON POST, 4/9/99, Weekend/p. 49, Michael O'Sullivan

GOD SAID, 'HA!'

A Miramax Films release of an Oh Brother production. *Executive Producer:* Quentin Tarantino. *Producer:* Rana Joy Glickman. *Director:* Julia Sweeney. *Screenplay:* Julia Sweeney. *Based on his stage production:* Greg Kachel. *Director of Photography:* John Hora. *Editor:* Fabienne Rawley. *Music:* Anthony Marinelli. *Music Editor:* Terry Wilson. *Sound:* Craig Woods and (music) Mark Curry. *Sound Editor:* Trevor Jolly. *Production Designer:* Gail Bennett. *Art

Director: Steve Joyner and Caylah Eddleblute. *Set Designer:* Thom Biggert. *Costumes:* Mary Zophres. *Make-up:* Patrice Ryan. *Running time:* 87 minutes. *MPAA Rating:* PG-13.

CAST: Julia Sweeney.

LOS ANGELES TIMES, 2/12/99, Calendar/p. 18, Kevin Thomas

By 1994, life was looking up for comedian Julia Sweeney. She had just completed a run on "Saturday Night Live" that brought her national acclaim and recognition (particularly for her androgynous character Pat), came to an amicable parting of ways with her husband and, best of all, bought her dream house, a small home in Hollywood.

That's when, to borrow the apt title of her heart-wrenching yet funny one-woman stage show, "God Said, 'Ha!'" It has now been preserved on film, thanks to Quentin Tarantino, who signed on as executive producer and brought the show to the attention of producer Rana Joy Glickman.

While no film of her show could probably equal the overall impact of its live performance (at the Coronet in Los Angeles, and then on to Broadway), this Miramax release comes close and does it justice; indeed, there are moments of Sweeney in close-up that bring an intimacy and power not possible across the footlights. In directing herself, she allows cinematographer John Hora to use effectively a fluid camera.

For some reason, the film also features joltingly abrupt cuts, yet the essence of the show comes across intact, punctuated discreetly by Anthony Marinelli's spare score. (Shooting took place principally on a sound stage rather than a theater, with production designer Gail Bennett replicating closely the living room furniture plus theater curtains Sweeney used as a setting on stage.)

Sweeney's annus horribilis began with her brother Mike being diagnosed as terminally ill with lymphoma and climaxed with the discovery that she was stricken with a rare form of cervical cancer. In between, her parents descended upon her from Spokane, Wash., for the duration, which meant, among countless other adjustments, that they took over her bedroom and her brother her guest room, while she slept in her backyard office.

Rocked by a sense of the absurdity of the cruel workings of fate, Sweeney, as a gifted comedian, began coping with them with humor by creating an act that she developed at Luna Park's "Uncabaret." This performance eventually grew into her one-woman show, whose title came from an old Yiddish saying: "If you want to make God laugh, make plans."

It's obviously no simple matter to transform personal catharsis into entertainment. Yet that is precisely what Sweeney accomplishes by playing the tragic deterioration of her brother (who gallantly proved pretty humorous himself in the face of grim fate) against the comic clashes of everyday life in a crowded household, where Sweeney began to feel like a teenager again instead of the independent woman in her mid-30s she had become. Her mother comes across as a sweetly obtuse sitcom parent, chagrined that her daughter would grate her own Parmesan cheese when she could buy it already grated; Sweeney says that early on she gave in to referring to pasta marinara as "macaroni with red sauce." (Sweeney, to her credit, is not above poking fun at her own yuppie strivings.)

She describes her father as something of a tippler with his Walkman constantly tuned to National Public Radio and forever covering the dining room table with picture puzzles. In the end, Sweeney sees her parents as heroes in their staunchness, infinitely more than "a source of comedy—or a reason for therapy." Sweeney's abundant gift of humor allows her unflinchingly to confront and report every harrowing detail of her brave brother's downward spiral. Consequently, against all odds, "God Said, 'Ha!'" manages to leave us with spirits uplifted.

NEW YORK POST, 2/12/99, p. 53, Rod Dreher

In 1995, comedian Julia Sweeney's "annus horribilis" was one for the record books.

Her marriage had recently ended (amicably, as it happened), and she was no longer on "Saturday Night Live." Her new film, "It's Pat!," based on Sweeney's SNL androgyne, revolted critics and turned cineplexes nationwide into Bikini atolls.

Career doldrums were more than exceeded by family traumas. Her uninsured brother Mike was diagnosed with advanced terminal cancer, and moved in to convalesce. Ma and Pa Sweeney also became lodgers to help care for gravely ill Mike. And if that weren't enough, Sweeney herself contracted a rare form of cervical cancer and underwent a hysterectomy.

And, indignity of indignities, she was recognized after having vigorously and inadvertently passed gas in a bookstore, while shopping secretly for the Pope's book.

That Sweeney can weave a confession of uncontrolled flatulence into a feature-length monologue about suffering and death shows you how jovial a Job she can be. "God Said, 'Ha!" is her wry, amusing and often touching account of that wretched year.

What began as Sweeney's working out her anxieties onstage at a Los Angeles comedy club was later refined into her popular one-woman New York stage show, and, thanks to production assistance from her pal Quentin Tarantino, is now a film.

At its best, "God Said, 'Ha!' is a chuckleworthy compendium of domestic anecdotes, as Sweeney struggles to deal with an NPR-addict father who thinks the sun rises and sets on Cokie Roberts, and a June-Cleaverish mom who thinks Sweeney an uppity sophisticate because she won't call pasta with marinara sauce by its proper name (noodles with red topping, natch).

The Sweeney siblings' saving grace is their sense of gallows humor. When Julia is diagnosed with the dread disease, Mike, himself at death's door, quips, "It must have been hard for you, being an actress with me in the cancer spotlight."

You like and admire this family for enduring prolonged trauma with morbid laughter, self-mockery and affectionate needling . But "God Said, 'Ha!'" is not much of a movie. If the laid-back Sweeney were a more kinetic teller of tales, like monologuist Spalding Gray, or if the narrative were more immediate and involving than this funny-sad ramble, "God Said, 'Ha!'" would be easier to recommend.

NEWSDAY, 2/12/99, Part II/p. B10, John Anderson

The facts of the matter are these: In 1994, Julia Sweeney, the former "Saturday Night Live" cast member and creator of the androgynous Pat, bought herself a little one-person house in Los Angeles, where she planned to assert her single personhood, buy furniture, have people over for dinner.

Then her brother got sick with cancer. And then he moved in. And then her parents moved in. And then she got cancer.

While these may be the facts of the matter, the resulting monological memoir "God Said, 'Ha!'"—which Sweeney originally performed as a one-woman stage show—is a lot more than just the facts of the matter. Which makes it a lot like life. Unlike her life, Sweeney can control what happens on stage, which of course automatically provides a schematic for the architecture of comedy, its relationship with pain and the mutual support system between the two.

Funny, sad and invariably human, "God Said, 'Ha!'"—inspired by the old Yiddish adage "If you want to make God laugh, make plans"—seldom turns angry or maudlin. Like Sweeney's personal pieces (such as the hilarious "Christmas letter" she did for National Public Radio's "This American Life" late last year), her recollections of her brother's illness and her parents' raging idiosyncrasies are buoyed by a gift for making self-delusion into a comedy device.

Sweeney is a bit of an old-fashioned performer in the way she relies on physical shtick to put herself across—the extreme posture, the grimaced delivery, the tongue between the teeth—and relies on us to be won over by it. Which we are, especially when the gestures accompany the oh-so-middle-class inflections she gives her wry observations of social or cosmic outrage, making us complicit in the absurdity she feels.

Despite the borderline blasphemous title, Sweeney doesn't blame, or pitch bile. Of course, distancing oneself from one's pain is the way art is attained. As has often been said, no one in the throes of love ever wrote a really great love poem. Likewise, few people in the throes of agony ever brought the house down. Sweeney is somewhere between recovery and perspective, but the results are therapeutic for all of us.

VILLAGE VOICE, 2/16/99, p. 143, McGanney Nolan

For those of us who get ornery when a head cold persists, the sight of Julia Sweeney wisecracking through the tale of her cancer-stricken household nearly rates as a medical miracle. *God Said "Ha!"*, a filmed version of Sweeney's acclaimed theatrical monologue, attests to the power of positive joking—not to zap away tumors, of course, but to get through horrendously difficult days and nights.

Sweeney cannily sets up her story by letting the audience in on her fantasy for what joys a post-divorce-and-*SNL* move to Los Angeles would bring—hosting rousing dinner parties at her cozy Hollywood bungalow, with days devoted to writing the screenplays just waiting to spring from her head. Instead, her brother Mike was diagnosed with lymph cancer and moved in, along with her parents, who are apparently possessed of enough quirks of behavior to fill a stand-up act. From the evidence here, Sweeney and her brother developed a keen sense of the absurd while growing up in their home. This is perhaps best illustrated by Mike's reaction to Julia's own subsequent diagnosis: "You couldn't stand it, could you? It must have been hard for you being an actress with me in the cancer spotlight."

Sweeney switches back and forth between her brother's illness and the problems with living with her parents again. (There's also the occasional perk—the titillation that arises when she and her new boyfriend are forced to sneak around.) Adept at impersonating others, Sweeney also makes fun of herself and others, Sweeney also makes fun of herself (and her famous "Pat" persona), perfectly capturing the moment when even modest coping mechanisms (smoking a cigarette and reading the pope's new book) backfire. In the end, though, *God Said "Ha!"* emerges as a tribute to Sweeney's brother, clearly one of the funnier men who have lately walked the earth.

Also reviewed in:
CHICAGO TRIBUNE, 2/26/99, Friday/p. M, Mark Caro
NEW YORK TIMES, 2/12/99, p. E16, Janet Maslin
VARIETY, 4/20-26/98, p. 43, Emanuel Levy
WASHINGTON POST, 4/2/99, p. C5, Jane Horwitz
WASHINGTON POST, 4/2/99, Weekend/p. 41, Desson Howe

GOING NOMAD

A Cinema Guild release of a Great Jones production. *Producer:* Art Jones. *Director:* Art Jones. *Screenplay:* Art Jones. *Director of Photography:* John Inwood. *Editor:* Jaces Cozza. *Sound:* Ron Richman. *Set Decorator:* Amy Portnoy. *Costumes:* Jennifer Crawford. *Running time:* 97 minutes. *MPAA Rating:* Not Rated.

CAST: Damian Young (El Cid Rivera); Victor Argo (Spiro); Jose Yenque (Jose); Tom Oppenheim (Eddie).

NEW YORK POST, 9/24/99, p. 50, Lou Lumenick

Watching "Going Nomad" is like meeting someone who won't shut up—and bores you to tears by telling you the same stories over and over.

It's extremely frustrating, because there is a decent little movie struggling to get out of this self-indulgent indie about first-time writer-director Art Jones' passion—cruising the streets of Manhattan late at night in vintage oversized cars.

The best parts of "Going Nomad" are the sequences of solitary drivers piloting their land yachts around the city to relieve their nocturnal yearnings, poetically shot by cinematographer John Inwood ("The Daytrippers"). Unfortunately, they're overlaid by plodding narration about driving LTDS, Lincoln Continentals, "the kind [of cars] that say, I may not know where I'm going but I'm on my way."

Which unfortunately sums up "Going Nomad," a movie that never shuts up long enough to decide what it's about.

The plot revolves around the tedious philosophizing of a group of underemployed barroom buddies, friends since grade school. El Cid Rivera (Damian Young, who deserves better), who would be the group's leader if it had one, is having a premature mid-life crisis as he approaches his 33rd birthday.

"I just want to feel like I'm something bigger than myself," he tells his buddies, who include a part-time wrestler, a defrocked priest-turned-toll-collector, a slum rental agent and a fellow whose sole preoccupation seems to be his hair.

El Cid struggles with the grandiose name foisted on him by his late mother and endless jokes about Charlton Heston (who played the original El Cid in a 1961 epic) foisted on him by Jones, who's clueless about staging scenes.

Redemption arrives for El Cid in the form of Officer Geraldine Fusco (Jourdan Zayles), another former classmate who becomes his take-charge girlfriend after years of mysteriously stalking him. The no-nonsense Zayles briefly breathes life into the movie, but it's soon back to barroom chats, monologues (including the dreadful talking-to-the-camera variety), imaginary talks with El Cid's dead mother—and yards of superfluous narration.

When El Cid and "Going Nomad" finally put the pedal to the metal, the audience is likely to have hit the road already.

NEWSDAY, 9/24/99, Part II/p. B9, Gene Seymour

His name's name's El Cid Rivera (Damien Young) because his late mother loved both Charlton Heston and the 1961 costume spectacular about the medieval Spanish warrior played by Heston.

But the strange joke—one of many in this movie—is that his madre made sure he never learned a lick of Spanish so as not to speak with an accent.

El Cid constantly hears his mother's ghost asking him if he's succeeding. Well, if you call hanging out with four losers every night in a corner bar and getting fired from every job one gets within days a successful way of life, Cid, as he's called for short, rules the universe.

The one time when Cid feels at ease with himself and the world is when he jumps in his oversized all-American gas guzzler and drives all over Manhattan between midnight and sunrise. He and his fellow "urban nomads" search for the perfect ride the way surfers pursue the perfect wave.

There's something of the all-or-nothing "poetry slam" in writer-director Art Jones' urban-picaresque tale, which is filled to bursting with headlong rhetorical flourishes rarely attempted in American movies. He's also lucky to have indie-movie vet Young playing El Cid with deadpan whimsy that offers a welcome contrast to the overamped emotional atmosphere.

Still, not even Young's ingratiating presence can negate the banal or aimless anecdotes of Cid's daylight existence; the best of which is a kinky short-lived romance with a tough-babe patrolwoman (Jourdan Zayles). The restlessness of Jones' enterprise is so overpowering that you'd be tempted to call it, "Going Nowhere," if it weren't for its streamlined look and robust goofiness.

VILLAGE VOICE, 9/28/99, p. 9/28/99, p. 128, Gary Dauphin

Going Nomad, writer-director Art Jones's low-budget ode to the nighttime streets of Manhattan, tries to get some mileage from one simple observation: people who have trouble sleeping often get in their cars and drive. While this isn't exactly a news flash (the Sunday *Times* City section did a typically overblown article on the subject last year, in which Jones figured prominently), the existential implications of a midnight driving habit obviously had dramatic possibilities. Unfortunately, few of them are realized in this pleasant but rather dull comedy.

Nomad follows the nocturnal nonadventures of one El Cid Rivera (Damian Young, who maintains a likable deadpan throughout), a thirtysomething slacker Latin-from-Manhattan whose basic deviation from amalgamated type is an inability to speak Spanish. (The outlandish moniker seems to exist only to prompt jokey Charlton Heston riffs.) Getting together every night with a band of one-note childhood buds for brews, El Cid finds his true (and only) joy while hitting quiet streets in his gas-guzzling, eight-cylinder "land boat," our hero brooding in voiceover while in search of the perfect ride, uninterrupted by stoplights.

There's a diverting love interest for El Cid, a borderline-dominatrix lady cop, and some purportedly life-altering suspense over his application to the Fire Department, but not much else happens; the plot tailgates the slow rides to nowhere that provide the film with its foundational conceit. Nomad does get some conceptual juice from a series of recurring monologues- poetic waxings from other asphalt junkies about the city, the road, the night, et cetera; the high-minded talk is eloquent, but it finds no reflection image-wise. Although El Cid's driving is presented as a kind of calling and art form, Nomad doesn't have much of an appreciation for physical space or automotive flow, first-time writer Jones penning car-centric dialogue and description that first-time director Jones can't convey visually beyond endless, static shots of El Cid behind the wheel. Ultimately, *Going Nomad* should provide Jones with an industry calling card, but that doesn't mean any paying customers will want to ride with him for very long.

Also reviewed in:
NEW YORK TIMES, 9/24/99, p. 37, Daniel Lorber
VARIETY, 8/3-9/98, p. 37, Daniel Lorber

GOODBYE LOVER

A Warner Bros. release of a Regency Enterprises presentation of an Arnon Milchan/Gotham Entertainment Group/Lightmotive production. *Executive Producer:* Arnon Milchan and Michael G. Nathanson. *Producer:* Alexandra Milchan, Patrick McDarrah, Joel Roodman, and Chris Daniel. *Director:* Roland Joffé. *Screenplay:* Ron Peer, Joel Cohen, and Alec Sokolow. *Story:* Ron Peer. *Director of Photography:* Dante Spinotti. *Editor:* William Steinkamp. *Music:* John Ottman. *Music Editor:* Amanda Goodpaster. *Sound:* Pawel Wdowczak. *Sound Editor:* Gregory M. Gerlich. *Casting:* Shari Rhodes and Joseph Middleton. *Production Designer:* Stewart Starkin. *Art Director:* Bruce Alan Miller. *Set Decorator:* Tessa Posnansky. *Set Designer:* Gae Buckley and Caroline Quinn. *Set Dresser:* Michael Johnson. *Special Effects:* Bruno Stempel. *Costumes:* Theadora Van Runkle. *Make-up:* Debbie Zoller. *Make-up (Mary-Louise Parker):* Jill Cady. *Make-up (Ellen DeGeneres):* Karen Kawahara. *Make-up (Special Effects):* James Robert MacKinnon. *Stunt Coordinator:* Rick Barker. *Running time:* 104 minutes. *MPAA Rating:* R.

CAST: Patricia Arquette (Sandra Dunmore); Dermot Mulroney (Jake Dunmore); Mary-Louise Parker (Peggy Blane); Ellen DeGeneres (Rita Pompano); Ray McKinnon (Rollins); Alex Rocco (Detective Crowley); Don Johnson (Ben Dunmore); Andre Gregory (Reverend Finlayson); John Neville (Bradley); Jo Nell Kennedy (Evelyn); Akane Nelson (Receptionist); Kevin Cooney (Company Man #1); Will Foster Stewart (Dennis); Nina Siemaszko (Newscaster); David Brisbin (Mr. Brodsky); Lisa Eichhorn (Mrs. Brodsky); George Furth (Mr. Merritt); Barry Newman (Senator Lassetter); Michael Krawic (Medical Examiner); Max Perlich (Will); Quincy Samuel Smith (Larry); Andi Chapman (Cop); John Prosky (Forensic Cop); Richard T. Jones (Detective One); Michael P. Byrne (Detective Two); Michael William James (Detective Three); Frances Bay (Old Woman); Pavel Cerny (Cabbie); Ernie Lively (Sheriff); Danny Goldring (Forensic Officer); Rob LaBelle (Minister); Leslie Jordan (Homer); Lou Myers (Police Captain); Doug Spinuzza (Gang-Banger); Lee Weaver (Old Codger); Newell Alexander (Minister #2); Molly Hager (Young Girl #2); Gerald T. Olson (Politician); Kenny Moskow (Commercial Guy); Bruce Rogers (Choir Conductor); Mary Lippman (Joan); Ken Lam (Coroner's Asst.); Darrick Lam (Police Officer #1); Marcus M. Shirey (Police Officer #2); Charles Gladney (Cop at College); Lisa Cohen (Battered Woman); Chic Daniel (Detective Daniel); Jay B. Yarnel (Detective Yarnell); Mike Singer (Company Man #2); Gary Sear (Company Man #3); Newell Alexander (Minister #2); Erin Keim (Young Girl #3).

LOS ANGELES TIMES, 4/16/99, Calendar/p. 6, John Anderson

[The following review by John Anderson appeared in a slightly different form in **NEWSDAY, 4/16/99, Part II/p. B11.**]

In spring, a studio's fancy turns to thoughts of unreleasable movies. And how to release them. In the case of "Goodbye Lover," the distributors/producers decided on attaching one of those enticing requests to the usual press notes: "Warner Bros. and New Regency would appreciate your not revealing to your readers and viewers who's doing what to whom."

Well, yeah, it's an old joke—but it's still better than any line in the film: What most of the characters in "Goodbye Lover" are doing to each other, Warner Bros. and New Regency are trying to do to you.

With only three writers credited, "Goodbye Lover" is one or two short of a totally unsalvageable disaster, but they come pretty close. What's in fact interesting about this depressed souffle a la Roland Joffe ("The Killing Fields") is watching the de-evolution of what may have been a decent story—not a particularly original story, but a story—being demolished by a surfeit of cooks doing unspeakable things to the broth.

Exhibit A is the treatment of the luscious and aptly named Sandra Dunmore (Patricia Arquette), who watches Martha Stewart on her TV, recites along with self-empowering Tony Robbins tapes in her car, passes the collection plate at her local church and listens obsessively to "The Sound of Music." This is like a remedial session in Set Up/Plot Twist 101: Yes, Sandra will turn out to be the nymphomaniacal-homicidal femme fatale of an elaborate insurance murder scheme. But it should be something of a shock—and might have been, if the opening scenes weren't of Sandra having enthusiastic phone sex with party or parties unknown.

But the entirety of "Goodbye Lover" is more or less the same, a string of red herrings, flopping around on dry land. Sandra's husband, Jake (Dermot Mulroney), is a substance-abusing problem child of a major public relations agency run by his suave brother Ben (Don Johnson), who is having a torrid affair with Sandra.

When Ben falls for another publicist, Peggy (Mary-Louise Parker), it seems to set Sandra off, which of course would be logical if the whole Ben affair wasn't a setup between Sandra and her husband to kill him and get the insurance payoff. "Goodbye Lover" could be indicted just for what it does to Ellen DeGeneres, who as the investigating officer is given easily the worst lines in an awful script. The best way to approach "Goodbye Lover," however, is to rent "Wild Things"—the Matt Dillon-Neve Campbell thriller that had all the sex, comedy and serpentine story line that "Goodbye Lover" aspires to and misses by a mile. To work another hoary joke into the ground and stay in the spirit of "Goodbye Lover," there's nothing like a smart, unpredictable, sophisticated thriller—and this is nothing like a smart, unpredictable, sophisticated thriller.

NEW YORK POST, 4/16/99, p. 57, Rod Dreher

Spring is fire-sale season at the studios, a period informally reserved for the unloading of rotten movies that have been moldering on the shelf and are approaching expiration date. Warner Bros. might have given Roland Joffe's stale neo-noir comedy "Goodbye Lover" a dignified, straight-to-video disposal, but it's going to let the public sniff the thing first for signs of spoilage.

Doesn't take much. Start with the opening sequence, in which platinum-blonde psycho-slut Sandra (Patricia Arquette) joins overripe lust monster Ben (Don Johnson, speaking in a mucousy Marlboro growl) for a cheesy-sleazy interlude in the organ perch at church. If the production values weren't so top-notch, you'd swear this was a USA Network movie.

Sandra puts the "kin" in "kink" all right: sex-crazed Ben is the brother of her husband, Jake (Dermot Mulroney), an out-of-control alcoholic executive at the sleek public-relations agency Ben helps run. If Jake finds out he's been cuckolded by his brother, Ben fears the unstable guy will off himself. Meanwhile, Ben abruptly begins an affair with secretary Peggy (Mary-Louise Parker), an office naif who becomes the No. 1 target for reckless, nympho Sandra.

To talk any further about the plot mechanics is to risk ruining one of the only pleasures "Goodbye Lover" has to offer: its double- and triple-crosses. Very few people are who they seem to be, of course, but when the nasty shocks come, they're strictly low-voltage. The script, which it took three writers to slap together, doesn't give us any reason to care about these characters, not even joy in hating their greedy guts. With no investment in them, it's no more than mildly diverting when titillation keeps turning to treachery.

The performances aren't bad, and Ellen DeGeneres even seems to be having a good time as Detective Rita Pompano, the gimlet-eyed cop who tangles with this brood of vipers when murder crops up among them. She gets the only funny lines in the film, and they're pretty lousy. But "Goodbye Lover" does have surface appeal, however thin; cinematographer Dante Spinotti, who shot "L.A. Confidential," creates a glitzy, tantalizing mood that's fun to loll in—and boy can that yummy Arquette sister loll. But there's a lot less to "Goodbye Lover" than meets the eye.

SIGHT AND SOUND, 10/99, p. 45, Mike Higgins

Los Angeles. Estate agent Sandra Dunmore wants her lover, PR guru Ben, to kill Jake, her husband and his brother. Instead Ben breaks off with her and starts seeing Peggy, his ambitious employee. Jake tells his brother he knows of the affair he had with Sandra, whereupon Jake and Sandra murder the heavily-insured Ben.

Detective Rita Pompano and her assistant Nathaniel Rollins begin an investigation. Peggy claims to have secretly wed Ben just before his death. Jake and Sandra hire an assassin to kill Peggy. It transpires Jake is seeing Peggy; Jake pays the assassin to kill his wife instead. Sandra learns of Jake and Peggy's romance and kills the couple. Pompano realises that Sandra, the sole beneficiary of an $8 million insurance pay-out, is responsible for the three killings. The detective blackmails her into splitting the money before killing the assassin as he is about to murder Sandra. One year later, Sandra and Pompano are seen shopping together in LA's expensive boutiques.

A convoluted reworking of Billy Wilder's 1944 classic *Double indemnity, Goodbye Lover* aspires to be a glossy, off-beat film noir. However, director Roland Joffe's film demonstrates neither the lightness of touch nor the generic discrimination necessary for such a precise exercise. In fact, Joffe's description of *Goodbye Lover* as *film gris* stands as an unwittingly acute comment on its muddled execution. *Goodbye Lover* has been languishing in the Warner vaults since its completion two years ago, a delay that afflicts it with more than the stigma of neglect. Moreover, its production roughly coincided with the outing of Ellen DeGeneres in 1997. One need hardly elucidate the overtones of DeGeneres' final, intimate interrogation of Sandra, bound, horizontal and bathed in red light, or their cosy departure together in the film's final scene. Had it achieved a more timely release, *Goodbye Lover* might just have got away with this coy allusion. As it is, Joffe's move from drama *(The Killing Fields, The Scarlet Letter)* to contemporary black comedy is culpable on other counts.

In the film's favour, cinematographer Dante Spinotti updates the baroque air of sleaze he brought to *L.A. Confidential,* lingering over the upwardly-mobile Sandra's stiletto heels and the harsh lines of her blonde page-boy bob. (The enthralling figure of Barbara Stanwyck in *Double Indemnity* comes to mind.) Costume designer Theadora Van Runkle adds a playful edge to this decadence, squeezing Arquette into some memorably vampish parodies of the outfits in which she clothed Faye Dunaway in *Bonnie and Clyde.* (1967).

It's a pity then that the tepid script (by first-time screenwriter Ron Peer, Joel Cohen and Alec Sokolaw) fails to echo this ripe visual wit, particularly in the character of Sandra. An unlikely church volunteer—her organ-loft seduction of Ben Dunmore during a choir practice is the film's most striking scene—Sandra belts out the hits of *The Sound of Music* to pep herself up. Handling such an ambiguous protagonist is new territory for Joffe, however, and he makes heavy work out of imbuing the murderous Sandra with an ironic, "can-do" irrepressiveness. With each double-cross itemised in prolix detail, she's promptly lost in a welter of immaterial plot exposition.

Furthermore, the knowing inclusion of clips from *Mildred Pierce* (1945) and *Pickup on South Street* (1953) serves only to expose what the film lacks in comparison: namely, any hint at the underlying cause of Sandra's relentless self-advancement and a palpable suspense surrounding the myriad betrayals.

Patricia Arquette struggles as Sandra, despite imbuing similar *femme fatale* roles in *Lost Highway* and *The Hi-Lo Country* with memorable intensity. Partner-in-crime Pompano is little more than a hard headed reprisal of DeGeneres's sitcom persona. The intended joke is that the dogged and unfashionable Pompano, a vision in plaid, eventually gets the better of the glamorous Sandra. Joffe even tries to suggest the pair's kinship by revealing a shared penchant for mirrors and cameras. However, much of the energy that could have been channelled into this potentially interesting subversion ends up in prurient speculation about Pompano and Sandra's developing relationship. The unfortunate consequence of this is to split up the most engaging partnership, that between the cynical Pompano and her naive Mormon partner Rollins (a winningly gormless turn from Ray McKinnon). As a misjudgement, it's minor compared to the catalogue that precedes it.

Also reviewed in:
CHICAGO TRIBUNE, 4/16/99, Friday/p. A, Mark Caro

NEW YORK TIMES, 4/16/99, p. E30, Stephen Holden
VARIETY, 5/25-31/98, p. 61, Todd McCarthy
WASHINGTON POST, 4/16/99, p. C5, Rita Kempley
WASHINGTON POST, 4/16/99, Weekend/p. 43, Desson Howe

GRANDFATHER, THE

A Miramax Films release of a Nickel Odeon production with the participation of Televisión Española. *Producer:* Luis María Delgado, Valentin Panero and Enrique Quintana. *Director:* José Luis Garci. *Screenplay (Spanish with English subtitles):* José Luis Garci and Horacio Valcárcel. *Based on the book by:* Benito Peréz-Galdós. *Director of Photography:* Raul Perez Cubero. *Editor:* Miguel Garcia Sinde. *Music:* Manuel Balboa. *Sound:* José Antonio Bermúdez and Antonio Garcia. *Art Director:* Gil Parrondo. *Set Decorator:* Julián Mateos. *Costumes:* Gumersindo Andrés. *Make-up:* Cristóbal Criado. *Running time:* 145 minutes. *MPAA Rating:* PG.

CAST: Fernando Fernán-Gómez (Rodrigo de Arista Potestad);   Rafael Alonso (Don Pío Coronado);   Cayetana Guillén-Cuervo (Dona Lucrecia Richmoni);   Agustín González (Sénen Corchado);   Cristina Cruz (Dolly);   Alicia Rozas (Nelly);   Fernando Guillén (Alcalde de Jerusa); Francisco Piquer (Prior de Zaratay);   María Massip (Gregoria);   José Caride (Venancio); Francisco Algora (Don Carmelo);   Emma Cohen (Vicenta);   Juan Calot (Medico);   Concha Gómez Conde (Doña Consuelito);   Nurla Rodríguez (Crisda);   José Luis Merino (Camarero Casino);   Antiono Valero (Don Jaime, Ministro).

LOS ANGELES TIMES, 10/8/99, Calendar/p. 18, Kevin Thomas

There's more than a whiff of "The Cherry Orchard" permeating Jose Luis Garci's "The Grandfather," a rueful, funny and deeply moving fable in which a curmudgeonly old aristocrat must choose between love and honor. An Oscar nominee for best foreign-language film of 1998, the period tale stars the formidable veteran Fernando Fernan-Gomez in a great role that crowns a long and distinguished career.

After a lengthy and foolish sojourn in Peru in a fruitless search for gold, Don Rodrigo, the count of Albrit (Fernan-Gomez), returns penniless to his magnificent ancestral lands in the province of Asturias.   A tall man with a mane of white hair and a flowing beard to match, Don Rodrigo, while given to delusions of grandeur, is not in denial over his penurious state, but this does not stop him from carrying on as if he were Louis XIV in high dudgeon.

With an eloquent command of language, the don is given to denunciations so withering as to be awe-inspiring.   During his absence of some seven or eight years, his son has died, and the don, taking his sources at face value, turns a verbal blowtorch on his beautiful and assured daughter-in-law Lucrecia (Cayetana Guillen Cuervo), an aristocratic woman with her own wealth. He blames her for his son's death, maintaining that she deserted him.   The couple were estranged, but you believe Lucrecia when she insists she married Don Rodrigo's son for love.

By contrast, it's mutual love at first sight between Don Rodrigo and his lovely granddaughters Dolly (Cristina Cruz) and her younger sister, Nelly (Alicia Rozas), who are in residence in the countryside at the Albrit manor house.   Quite quickly, too, Don Rodrigo forms a fast friendship with the girls' elderly tutor, Don Pio Coronado (Rafael Alonso), a woebegone intellectual weighed down by six un-married, termagant daughters.   Don Pio is as ineffectual as Don Rodrigo is forceful, but the teacher is so honest in his self-appraisal that the crusty nobleman cannot help but like him.   But Don Rodrigo's newfound happiness is imperiled by his penury and his foolhardy and unjust alienation of his daughter-in-law.

Indeed, Rodrigo is surrounded by those who loathe him for his stinging bluntness, overlooking the fact that the count of Albrit has always been the most generous and protective of patriarchs. These enemies, led by the shamelessly smarmy Senen (Agustin Gonzalez, in a delicious performance), are the same people who are toadying up to Lucrecia for favors.   Rodrigo and the film itself take a scathing view of the crass ambition of the nouveau riche yet recognize the inherent injustice of the class system.

But the big question that emerges is whether Don Rodrigo, beyond his Quixote-like blustering is merely a grandiose poseur or at heart a true gentleman, capable of genuine noblesse oblige in the crunch.

In between the don's amazing displays of bombast, there are scenes of tenderness between grandfather and granddaughters, and the granddaughters and their mother, and there's much amusement in Rodrigo and Pio's spirited and mutually affectionate conversations.

The late Alonso, in his final role, was as beloved a veteran as Fernan-Gomez, and it's a pleasure to watch the two actors play off each other with such delightful finesse. "The Grandfather" is a wise and beautiful film that, while acknowledging the inevitability of loss and change, bids a heartfelt and bemused farewell to the ancient regime.

NEW YORK POST, 10/11/99, p. 50, Lou Lumenick

"The Grandfather," Spain's nominee for this year's foreign-film Oscar, is a prettily shot soap opera that spends 2 hours telling a story that would be more effective in 90 minutes.

It's the turn of the century, and Count Rodrigo (Fernando Fernan-Gomez) has returned to his native Spain after losing his fortune in the American gold rush. The elderly widower comes back with a letter from his late son, revealing that one of the son's young daughters is illegitimate.

Rodrigo confronts his wealthy former daughter-in-law (Cayetana Guillen Cuervo), demanding to know which of his grandchildren is the result of her fling with an artist in Paris. She refuses to tell him, and, concerned about the growing bond between the count and the girls, packs him off to a monastery, from which he quickly escapes.

Director Jose Luis Garci gets uniformly fine performances from the cast, but the drama of "The Grandfather" is undercut by funereal pacing and an ending that seems more than a little contrived.

NEWSDAY, 10/8/99, Part II/p. B14, Jan Stuart

Fernando Fernan-Gomez is a commanding King Lear of a figure in the title role of "The Grandfather," the turn-of-the-past-century tale from Spanish director Jose Luis Garci. Peering out from behind probing blue eyes and a graying red beard of mythic proportions, the veteran actor squeezes every last drop from his role as an elderly noble who finds himself under the sway of his reviled daughter-in-law.

And a good thing, too. As the fulcrum of this ponderous drama of internecine family conflict, Fernan-Gomez is on screen for the better part of its 145 glossy minutes. You can't take your eyes off of him, whether you want to or not.

Fernan-Gomez' character, Don Rodrigo, Count of Albrit, has lost all of his fortune in Peru. He has returned to Spain to square off with his daughter-in-law Lucrecia (Cayetana Guillen Cuervo), whom he has learned through a letter was unfaithful to his late son. The letter also reveals that one of her two daughters was not fathered by his son, and the defeated grandfather is bent on determining which of them is the true heiress to his estate.

It is a humbling homecoming. Lucrecia returns his accusations with fiery invective of her own. His servants give him lip, and the town monks (at Lucrecia's behest) pressure him into moving into a monastery cell to spend his final days. His only support comes from his adoring granddaughters Dolly and Nelly, and his aging friend Don Pio Coronado (Rafael Alonso), a philosophical cipher determined to end his own life.

"The Grandfather" unspools at a stately pace from the opening credits, when the camera pans across an elegantly furnished house to the plangent and over-abused strains of Erik Satie music. The maudlin scoring is indicative of the unsubtle resolve with which Garci (who also directed the sappy Oscar-winner "To Begin Again") goes after our heartstrings. He all but mugs us with lovely, sun-washed shots of shorelines and countryside vistas.

Things pick up whenever the characters go for the jugular, but the acid is ultimately cut with a spoonful of sugar. "The Grandfather," nominated for Best Foreign Film in 1998, exemplifies the sort of sentimental, large-canvas corn from overseas that reduces Oscar voters to pod people.

VILLAGE VOICE, 10/12/99, p. 146, Michael Atkinson

Jose Luis Garci's *The Grandfather* is modest, sentimental lint whose every conversation runs on three times as long as necessary. The Miramax scouts are masters at plunging into international theaters and returning with undistinguished treacle, and Garci's film is duller than most. Here, a crotchety old aristocrat (Fernando Fernan-Gomez, resembling W.C. Fields with a Whitman beard) in turn-of-the-century Spain battles with his imperious (and widowed) daughter-in-law (Cayetana Guillen Cuervo) to uncover which of his young granddaughters is actually blood kin. Not only is the dialogue endless, it's horribly post-dubbed (creepily, the girls are voiced by mature-sounding women). Zamoran landscapes notwithstanding, it's like driving behind a 15 mph geezer on a one-way street.

Also reviewed in:
CHICAGO TRIBUNE, 10/29/99, Friday/p. E, Michael Wilmington
NEW YORK TIMES, 10/8/99, p. E22, Lawrence Van Gelder
VARIETY, 11/9-15/98, p. 33, Jonathan Holland

GREEN MILE, THE

A Castle Rock Entertainment release of a Darkwoods production. *Producer:* David Valdes and Frank Darabont. *Director:* Frank Darabont. *Screenplay:* Frank Darabont. *Based on the novel by:* Stephen King. *Director of Photography:* David Tattersall. *Editor:* Richard Francis-Bruce. *Music:* Thomas Newman. *Music Editor:* Bill Bernstein. *Sound:* Willie D. Burton and (music) Dennis Sands. *Sound Editor:* Mark Mangini. *Casting:* Mali Finn. *Production Designer:* Terence Marsh. *Art Director:* William Cruse. *Set Designer:* Donald Woodruff and Dianne Wager. *Set Decorator:* Michael Seirton. *Set Dresser:* Kurt T.V. Verbaarschott, Billy Baker, Melanie S. Cheetin, Chris F. Fielding and Jack Evans. *Special Effects:* Darrell D. Pritchett. *Visual Effects:* Charles Gibson. *Costumes:* Karyn Wagner. *Make-up:* Lois Burwell. *Make-up (Tom Hanks):* Daniel Striepeke. *Stunt Coordinator:* Jeff Imada. *Running time:* 180 minutes. *MPAA Rating:* R.

CAST: Tom Hanks (Paul Edgecomb); David Morse (Brutus 'Brutal' Howell); Bonnie Hunt (Jan Edgecomb); James Cromwell (Warden Hal Moores); Michael Clarke Duncan (John Coffey); Michael Jeter (Eduard 'Del' Delacroix); Graham Greene (Arlen Bitterbuck); Sam Rockwell (William 'Wild Bill' Wharton); Doug Hutchison (Percy Wetmore); Barry Pepper (Dean Stanton); Patricia Clarkson (Melinda Moores); Jeffrey DeMunn (Harry Terwilliger); Harry Dean Stanton (Toot-Toot); Dabbs Greer (Old Paul Edgecomb); Eve Brent (Elaine Connelly); William Sadler (Klaus Detterick); Gary Sinise (Burt Hammersmith); Mack C. Miles (Orderly Hector); Rai Tasco (Man in Nursing Home); Edrie Warner (Lady in Nursing Home); Paula Malcomson (Marjorie Detterick); Christopher Ives (Howie Detterick); Evanne Drucker (Kathe Detterick); Bailey Drucker (Cora Detterick); Brian Libby (Sheriff McGee); Brent Briscoe (Bill Dodge); Bill McKinney (Jack Van Hay); Rachel Singer (Cynthia Hammersmith); Scotty Leavenworth (Hammersmith's Son); Katelyn Leavenworth (Hammersmith's Daughter); Bill Gratton (Earl the Plumber); Dee Croxton (Woman at Del's Execution); Rebecca Klingler (Wife at Del's Execution); Gary Imhoff (Husband at Del's Execution); Van Epperson (Police Officer); David E. Browning (Reverend at Funeral).

CHRISTIAN SCIENCE MONITOR, 12/10/99, P. 15, David Sterritt

Hollywood is having a banner year, so the box-office fate of any particular new movie is hardly a make-or-break question. This week is an interesting one in terms of judging audiences tastes, however. Which would-be blockbuster will rule the roost: "The Green Mile," with its sentimental suspense story; "Cradle Will Rock," with its starry-eyed historical saga; or "The Cider House Rules," with its cautious mixture of button-pushing subjects and old-fashioned emotionalism?

Odds are that *The Green Mile* will be the breakaway success of the week, and conceivably of the whole holiday season. Until recently, its three-hour-plus length would have been considered a liability, but hits like "Titanic" and "Saving Private Ryan" have changed the rules.

"The Green Mile" borrows other tricks from those movies, too, including a prologue and epilogue that gift-wrap it as a string of memories in the mind of an aging survivor. Some viewers will squirm with impatience as the misty-eyed prison yarn inches toward its conclusion, but others will willingly succumb to its storytelling spell—or at least to the nearly constant presence of Tom Hanks, one of the most ingratiating stars in the Hollywood firmament.

He plays a death-row prison guard in a Deep South penitentiary during the Depression years. His job is more routine than it sounds, but this changes when an unusual prisoner enters his unit: John Coffey, an African-American man with an enormous body, a simple mind, and a horrifying crime on his record. John is a marginal character for much of the movie, which focuses largely on the death-row guards and two other prisoners. Unexpected events bring out unexpected qualities in John, though, including a gift for healing that he himself doesn't fully understand.

The best thing about "The Green Mile" is that it deals with two substantial issues—spiritual healing and capital punishment—that Hollywood usually finds too serious or controversial to tackle. Unfortunately, it fails to probe these themes with the thoughtfulness they deserve. The death penalty is treated as a plot device rather than a moral concern, and the scenes of healing are closer to "E.T—The Extra-Terrestrial" than to any effort at religious insight.

The result is an overlong drama that would reach a higher level if its makers thought more about stimulating our minds and less about opening our tear ducts. Frank Darabont directed the movie from his own screenplay, as he did with "The Shawshank Redemption" five years ago. Both films are based on works by famed author Stephen King, who has wittily remarked that Darabont has the narrowest specialty of any filmmaker around: prison pictures based on King stories. This recipe has advanced the director's career so far, but it's time for him to try a new bag of tricks.

"Cradle Will Rock" also takes place in the 1930s. but it paints a much larger canvas, visiting the New York theater scene during a tumultuous era when artistic and political adventures often overlapped. Written and directed by Tim Robbins, it scampers through various story lines about everything from the ambitions of a starving actress to the love-hate relationship between an American millionaire and a Mexican muralist. The climax pits boy-wonder Orson Welles against government officials who want to veto his production of an opera that celebrates the labor movement—or glorifies class warfare, depending on your point of view.

Some moviegoers may find "Cradle Will Rock" too crowded and preachy to serve as a meaningful history lesson. But it will delight anyone who thinks or cynical age could benefit from recalling the vigorous idealism and venturesome artistry of the years before World War II.

"The Cider House Rules" is based on John Irving's novel of the same title, which may be a warning signal for viewers who found earlier Irving adaptations ("The World According to Garp," "The Hotel New Hampshire") mannered and contrived. Irving has improved as a storyteller, though. he no longer strains so hard to prove how inventive he can be, and the new movie is the best one so far to carry his name.

The hero is an orphan who grows up under the guidance of a kindly physician, drifts toward a different kind of life in a community of African-American laborers, and undergoes emotional trials that eventually bring him to the orphanage where he started.

Superb performances by Tobey Maguire and Michael Caine bring a bracing sense of humanity to the story, which has the courage to include issues as controversial as abortion and racial discord among its themes.

Alone among recent releases, the film suffers from being too short—it leaves out elements of Irving's novel that are needed for context and balance—but its acting alone is worth the price of admission.

LOS ANGELES TIMES, 12/10/99, Calendar/p. 1, Kenneth Turan

The face of Hollywood today is the face of power. Director's power. The power of special effects. Together, they can create wonders, but if unchecked they can also lead to things that are not so wonderful, things that are done simply because the power to do them is there. Witness "The Green Mile."

That there's a good story in "The Green Mile" is not much of a surprise. Stephen King's serial novel mixed new age miracles with age-old "behind these walls" prison melodrama cleverly enough to sell 20 million copies and have its six parts last a total of 93 weeks on the Publishers Weekly bestseller list.

What is a surprise is how deeply, almost fatally buried that story is in three hours and eight minutes of ultra-leisurely storytelling by a filmmaker too fond of his own work to cut a frame, and too powerful to be amenable to changing his mind. Not even the excellent, elevating acting of Tom Hanks as the head guard on death row and some pleasing supernatural moments can make up for a film that moves with the suffocating deliberateness of a river of molasses.

"The Green Mile's" writer-director is Frank Darabont, whose last film was another adaptation of a King prison story, "The Shawshank Redemption." Its seven Oscar nominations (including best picture) notwithstanding, "Shawshank" revealed a filmmaker with a sure instinct, even a gift for the obvious. Similarly, though the dramatic beats in "The Green Mile" are highly polished, they also couldn't be more pronounced and predictable.

The heart of the problem (and one of the causes of the film's length) is the overly earnest attitude Darabont takes toward the material. "The Green Mile" sold as many copies as it did not because its themes are lofty and profound but because it's a page-turner. What we have here is basically pulp material (albeit of a high order), and pulp material doesn't gain in effectiveness by being treated as if it were written by Henry James.

"The Green Mile's" other unpleasant surprise is what it makes you endure in the way of on-screen horrors. Three executions via electric chair are shown, and while none of them is exactly pleasant, the death of Eduard Delacroix (Michael Jeter) is gruesome and stomach-turning beyond reason. How many lovingly constructed and very realistic shots of a man's head consumed by flames does any sane person need to experience?

Yes, this sequence is critical to the plot and comes directly from the book, but so is a spate of illness-related profanity by a female character that, presumably out of a desire not to offend, is alluded to but not reproduced. Just because special effects technology and a director-as-brutalizer attitude make it possible to fry the audience's sensibilities as well as the victim's body, is that sufficient reason to do it? Making the visuals as graphic as possible doesn't make the film richer and more meaningful; if anything, it's so horrific it throws you right out of the movie and makes it more difficult to get reinvolved with the narrative.

"The Green Mile" opens in a more bucolic spot, a Southern retirement home where longtime resident Paul Edgecomb is something of a mystery to both staff and fellow boarders. One day, a glimpse of a Fred Astaire and Ginger Rogers film on TV triggers a teary breakdown, and Paul tells his friend Elaine things he hasn't spoken about in 60 years.

Back we go to 1935, where a younger Edgecomb (Hanks) works in Louisiana's Cold Mountain Penitentiary as the guard in charge of the Green Mile, named for the walk from death row to the electric chair because the cement floor is painted a glowing lime green. That's the year Edgecomb was suffering from an excruciating urinary infection and the year that John Coffey (Michael Clark Duncan) took up residence on the Green Mile as the convicted killer of two little girls.

Coffey turns out to be a giant of a black man (7 feet tall in the book and wonderfully played by the 6-foot-5-inch, 300-plus-pound Duncan), someone whose staggering size is matched by the timidity of his man-child behavior. Coffey's considered somewhat simple-minded by the guards (David Morse is especially effective as Brutus "Brutal" Howell) but he turns out to have inexplicable powers (some involving swarms of exhaled insects left over from "The Mummy") that have consequences both terrible and wonderful.

There are other prisoners on the Green Mile, the most notable being the unfortunate Delacroix, who makes friends with a performing mouse named Mr. Jingles who's known for his ability to roll an empty spool of thread, and William "Wild Bill" Wharton. A smiling psychopath (convincingly played by Sam Rockwell), Wharton is so thoroughly evil that his very presence complicates things on the Mile.

Wild Bill's opposite number on the law and order side is Percy Wetmore (Doug Hutchison), an unapologetic sadist who is protected from the consequences of his misdeeds by being the favorite nephew of the state governor's wife. "He's mean, careless and stupid," Edgecomb says, "a bad combination in a place like this."

All these characters and lots more, including Warden Hal Moores (James Cromwell) and Edgecomb's wife, Jan (Bonnie Hunt), don't dare to have more than a single dimension. Ordinarily that's not a problem for this kind of a story, but then again ordinarily this kind of story doesn't put the excessive demands on our time this particular one does.

The only exception to all this is Paul Edgecomb, and Tom Hanks is the reason why. An actor who effortlessly adds fairness, decency and humanity to any role he plays, Hanks makes even a character in a melodrama like this seem real, complex and convincing. His work elevates "The Green Mile," giving it a level of interest and integrity it wouldn't otherwise have. It can't completely rescue this bloated film, but it's certainly the best reason to see it.

NEW YORK, 12/20-27/99, p. 161, Peter Rainer

The Green Mile, like *The Sixth Sense*, is a movie that takes its supernaturalism with a great deal of *largo* seriousness, and it may end up striking the same kind of emotional chord with audiences. Set mostly in a southern penitentiary in 1935 and starring Tom Hanks as a prison guard supervising death row, it's about innocence and forgiveness, and coming back from the dead, or the near-dead; the film's quasi-biblical vibes and slow-crawl pacing give it a ponderous grandiosity. Frank Darabont, who wrote and directed The *Shawshank Redemption,* is once again working on Stephen King source material set in prison. The film's three-plus hours length, not entirely justified by the subject matter, is almost a rebuke to the MTV generation. *Sit still for this,* it says. I'm sympathetic to Darabont's complaint: If we lose the ability to sit through the longueurs of a fairly good and well-acted movie like *The Green Mile,* then we probably won't be making it through the epic-size great stuff, either.

Much of *The Green Mile* resembles a long-form version of one of those "meaningful" *Twilight Zone* episodes that always came with a moral lesson attached. The lesson here is that grace sometimes appears in the guise of the grotesque. Hanks's Paul Edgecomb, whom we also see as a present-day old man in the film's framing device, is in charge of conducting the prison's electrocutions, and into his death row one day comes a behemoth of a black man, John Coffey (Michael Clarke Duncan), convicted on circumstantial evidence of murdering two young white sisters.

Coffey, who, despite his appearance, is as childlike as Lenny in *Of Mice and Men,* turns out to be a magical healer; he clears up Edgecomb's searing bladder infection and then moves on to bigger things. Coffey is a holy fool, and by emphasizing the man's shambling, menacing, big-buck bulkiness, Darabont comes uncomfortably close to racial stereotyping. The point here seems to be that one must look beyond the packaging, but the point is not always well made. In a movie in which everybody seems to be a symbol for something or other—usually pure goodness or utter depravity—Coffey may be carrying more than his quota.

Set alongside him is Percy (Doug Hutchison), a snot-nosed sadist of a guard whose uncle is governor; Eduard Delacroix (Michael Jeter), a sweet-souled Creole death-row prisoner whose closest friend is a cell-block mouse, Wild Bill (Sam Rockwell), a multiple-murderer yahoo—and, of course, Edgecomb, who fears divine punishment for setting up for execution "an angel of God." Edgecomb is depicted as a good and decent man who must carry out orders.

Though there is ample reason to do so, neither he nor anyone else attempts to overturn those orders; there's no suggestion that on some deeper level he may not even be aware of, Edgecomb is complicit in pushing through the execution. Edgecomb is like a simplistic version of Melville's Captain Vere, with Coffey as the Billy Budd he hastens to his end. Darabont works big but thinks small, or at least without great complexity. The *green mile* in the title refers to the stretch of green floor leading from the cells to the death chamber, and the film, puffed with significance, is a fable about how we all walk our own mile in our own time.

NEW YORK POST, 12/10/99, p. 47, Jonathan Foreman

You might expect "The Green Mile" to be little more than shmaltzy Oscar bait (as I did). After all, it's a film about the relationship between a wrongly convicted, retarded black man on Louisiana's death row—who just happens to have E.T.-like healing powers—and a decent, humane prison guard played by Tom Hanks.

But you'd be wrong. "The Green Mile" turns out to be a terrific, powerful movie—a deeply affecting fable that, thanks to superb performances and masterful direction, holds you fast for almost all of its three-plus hours.

Sure, it's underedited, but there aren't too many films that have the emotional wallop to make a hardened reviewer laugh one minute and bring tears to his eyes the next. "The Green Mile" is a reminder of just how good Hollywood storytelling can be.

Like writer-director Frank Darabont's "The Shawshank Redemption," "The Green Mile" is adapted from a Stephen King tale. (King seems to translate exceptionally well to the big screen. Witness "Stand by Me," "The Shining" and "Misery.")

Most of the action takes place at a Louisiana prison in 1935. The "Green Mile" is the local nickname for the death row in the E-wing at Cold Mountain State Penitentiary, and Paul Edgecombe (Hanks) is the guard who runs it.

Edgecombe has the task of keeping his little world quiet and comfortable down to a fine art. He treats doomed prisoners, like Graham Greene's Bitterbuck and Michael Jeter's remorseful Cajun Delacroix, with dignity—allowing the latter to keep a strangely daring and intelligent mouse in his cell.

And he takes the ghastly ritual of execution by electric chair (a process you get to see in all its inefficient cruelty) with appropriate seriousness.

But his life has recently been made harder by an excruciating bladder infection and the presence on his team of Percy Wetmore (Doug Hutchison), a sadist whose family connection with the governor makes him unfireable.

Then two new prisoners arrive: Wild Bill (Sam Rockwell), a vicious redneck sociopath, and the huge, gentle John Coffey (Michael Clarke Duncan), who has been convicted of the rape and murder of two 9-year old girls.

Hanks is as good as he's ever been here, and he's surrounded by first-rate actors at the top of their form, among them James Cromwell as Warden Moores and Barry Pepper (from "Saving Private Ryan") as a young, impetuous guard.

David Morse, a wonderful, underrated character actor, is particularly good as Edgecombe's best friend, Brutus "Brutal" Howell, and Harry Dean Stanton is funny as an inmate-trusty who helps the guards rehearse executions.

While it's rare to find an ensemble cast doing work this outstanding, the film depends on Duncan's performance as the Christ-like John Coffey to ensure that its supernatural and sentimental scenes don't become cheesy or cloying. And the "Armageddon" actor succeeds brilliantly.

All of these remarkable performances make it even more of a shame that writer-director Frank Darabont thought it necessary to retain the tale's modern-day bookends, footage that contributes little or nothing to the story (like in "Saving Private Ryan") but adds more joint-twisting minutes to the film's excessive length.

Still, "The Green Mile" may be the holiday season's most satisfying movie experience, and should be a shoo-in for a Best Picture nomination.

NEWSDAY, 12/10/99, Part II/p. B8, John Anderson

As everybody knows, the name Stephen King is synonymous with horror. Dementia. Rabid dogs. Arsonous children. But besides being a writer of no such limitations, his vast popularity has just as much to do with an unflinching belief in the existence/determination of good and evil—disembodied or otherwise. We come for the creepiness. We stay for the reassuring morality.

This balancing of fictional impulses may be an easy thing to understand (and sell) but it's a much harder thing to accomplish—something that's quite apparent in "The Green Mile," director Frank Darabont's first film since "The Shawshank Redemption"—which makes it his second King movie, his second prison film and, given the season, might have been called "Miracle on Death Row."

"The Green Mile" has everything necessary to wring tears from the eyes and dollars from the pockets—earnest sentiment, high ideals, unspeakable cruelty and Tom Hanks. It's also one of those movies that's about as long as a baseball game (which is OK, since movies will soon cost as much to see as a baseball game). Like that other Hanks blockbuster, "Saving Private Ryan," it's also based on the reminiscence of a seemingly nondescript senior citizen—teaching us, once again, never to underestimate the narrative power of senior citizens. Or to try and figure out the logic behind Hanks' career path. It's a movie full of lessons, like that January missive from MasterCard.

Shortly after we meet him, the older Paul (screen veteran Dabbs Greer) is stricken with emotion during a retirement-home screening of "Top Hat" and Fred Astaire—singing "Cheek to Cheek." As he pulls himself together, he confesses to a friend (Eve Brent) the story of his life—which includes, in addition to the very obscure "Cheek to Cheek" reference, the story of John Coffey (Michael Clarke Duncan), an enormous, hulking and apparently simpleminded black man whose arrival at the Cold Mountain Penitentiary changes Paul's life and that of every other guard on death row.

In bringing us into the penitentiary—and into the story—Darabont is at best elemental in his establishing of time, place and mood. Once inside—where "The Green Mile" can comport itself like a play—he creates real atmosphere with real people: The guards, including Paul, his pal Brutus (a very likable David Morse) and Percy Wetmore (Doug Hutchison), the vicious little sadist with political connections who provides the movie's considerable hate factor. And the prisoners—Eduard Delacroix (an equally likable Michael Jeter), Barry (Harry Dean Stanton) and "Wild Bill" Wharton (Sam Rockwell), another vicious little man (did Randy Newman co-write the script?) and the manifestation of pure evil. As a dramatic construct, the movie is as balanced as a checkbook.

The mouse—isn't there always a mouse?—is Mr. Jingles, who's adopted by Delacroix, trained to do tricks and whose untimely accident prompts John Coffey to demonstrate something that causes no small amount of discomfiture on the cell block. He's cured Paul of a painful urinary tract infection (along with "A League of Their Own," Hanks can now claim two of the most famous peeing scenes in movie history). So is he guilty? What we've been given, via flashback, is Coffey at the scene of his alleged crime—sitting on a riverbank, cradling the bloodied bodies of two small girls and moaning the words, "I tried to take it back, but it was too late." What Coffey meant, and what he means, becomes as increasingly clear as Paul's doubts about his guilt.

And as long as Darabont is following the narrative—which includes justifiable homicide, well-intentioned mayhem and crowd-pleasing justice—"The Green Mile" stays the course and provides all the sturdy entertainment of any well-calculated crime drama. Darabont just doesn't know when to quit. Or to accept that his audience might actually get it, long before the soliloquies and postscripts and epilogues and addenda manage to dilute whatever emotional pitch he's reached. My advice: Take that long-awaited bathroom break around Act 5, make like Hanks, and forget to come back.

NEWSWEEK, 12/13/99, p. 86, David Ansen

Looking back on his long life, the former death-row prison guard Paul Edgecomb (Tom Hanks) reckons he never saw the likes of John Coffey (Michael Clarke Duncan), the convicted killer who arrived in shackles at his Southern prison one day in 1935. A looming seven-foot black man condemned to death for the rape and murder of two 9-year-old white girls, Coffey turns out to be a regular sweetheart. Gentle, childlike, ignorant and afraid of the dark, he doesn't strike the observant Paul as a man capable of such atrocities.

If the guard (or the audience) has any doubts about Coffey's innocence, these doubts are pretty much erased one hour into "The Green Mile," the second adaptation of a Stephen King prison tale from writer-director Frank ("The Shawshank Redemption") Darabont. In the movie's first—and nearly last—surprising moment, Coffey reaches outside his prison bars and yanks Edgecomb up against his face. Placing his huge hands on the guard's groin, Coffey proceeds (with the help of growing lights, blowing fuses and soaring music) to magically cure the guard of a painful urinary-tract infection. Aha! So "The Green Mile" isn't just another wronged-man prison drama, and John Coffey isn't just your run-of-the-mill, old-fashioned Noble Savage. No, he's a saintly, New Age Noble Savage—which, in 1999, doesn't make the stereotype much less offensive.

Darabont's movie, trawling for Oscars, arrives amid a flurry of expectation and hope. What's up there on screen, however, is a lumbering, self-important three-hour melodrama that defies credibility at every turn. Who are these people? What planet are we on? Not only is Hanks's blissfully married character the nicest, most sensitive prison guard in the history of the Southern penal system, his three death-row colleagues (played by David Morse, Barry Pepper and Jeffrey DeMunn) are nearly as caring and genteel. Running a close third is the warden (James Cromwell), whose loving wife is dying of cancer (can you guess where that plot strand is heading?). In keeping with the movie's Old Hollywood view of reality, the villains are painted in strokes broad enough for any 2-year-old to hate them. Every scene in which the sadistic guard Percy (Doug Hutchison) appears stomping on an inmate's pet, gloating at executions, then peeing in his pants when scared—makes the same point: this man is BAD! Ditto for "Wild Bill" Wharton (Sam Rockwell), a snarling psychotic serial killer who pisses in more aggressive ways. (What's with this movie's urinary obsession?) "The Green Mile" seems to have been directed to the tick of a metronome set in the 1950s—everything's given equal weight (heavy); nothing is left for us to discover ourselves.

"Shawshank" had wonderful narrative surprises that pulled the rug out from under us. "Green Mile's" plotting—perhaps because King originally wrote it in serial form—barely makes sense. *Stop reading here to avoid major plot revelations.* Though Edgecomb is convinced of Coffey's innocence—and even knows who the real killer is—he makes no effort to stop the execution. We're supposed to believe it's hopeless, but it seems anything but. (It's interesting that the warden, who could help—and whose wife Coffey heals—disappears from the end of the movie.) King and Darabont want Coffey to make a sacrificial, Christ-like exit in the electric chair so we can all feel bad for him and good about ourselves. Like so many well-meaning, unconsciously racist Hollywood dramas of the past, the black man's death serves mainly to highlight his white defender's exquisite sensibilities. Of course the mysterious Coffey isn't a man at all, but a trumped-up symbol of the triumph of the human spirit. Which is helpful. The next time we run into a dumb but gentle seven-foot black saint with mystical powers, we'll be sure to be nice.

SIGHT AND SOUND, 3/00, p. 44, Rob White

In a US retirement home in the present, elderly Paul Edgecomb reminisces to his friend Elaine.

Flashbacks reveal events in 1935: Edgecomb is a death-row warder in a southern state prison. He takes custody of John Coffey, convicted of murdering two little girls. Another warder, Percy Wetmore, who treats the prisoners sadistically but is protected by powerful allies, asks to take part in the next execution. One day, Coffey calls over Edgecomb, who is afflicted by a urinary complaint, and heals him by touch. Afterwards Coffey breathes out a stream of tiny 'insects'. Later, Percy deliberately bungles an execution so the prisoner dies a horrible death.

Edgecomb and the other warders sneak Coffey out of the prison during which the drugged prisoner 'Wild Bill' is briefly roused and grasps Coffey as he's led past. They take Coffey to the prison governor's house where he heals the governor's terminally ill wife. Coffey holds the insects in and breathes them into Percy's mouth back at the prison. In a trance, Percy shoots Bill. Taking Edgecomb's hand, Coffey lets Edgecomb 'see' what he had found out when Bill touched him: Bill was the real killer of the murdered girls whom Coffey, when he was found, was trying to heal. Coffey is executed. In the present, Edgecomb tells Elaine Coffey's healing greatly extended his life span: he's now 108.

Near the beginning of *The Green Mile*—adapted by Frank Darabont, the director of *The Shawshank Redemption* from Stephen King's serialised novel—the ageing protagonist Paul Edgecomb is watching Fred Astaire sing 'Cheek to Cheek' in *Top Hat* (1935). The most joyful of Irving Berlin songs ("Heaven, I'm in heaven ..."), it makes him weep uncontrollably, forcing him to run out the retirement-home television room. Where does his sorrow come from? The rest of the film unravels the answer to this as Edgecomb recalls several weeks in 1935 when he worked as a death-row warder and met telepath and healer John Coffey, convicted of murdering two young girls. The bond between them is the heart of both book and film. Often King's God-fearing middle-aged protagonists are blandly stolid representatives of God-fearing middle-American decency. Here, unexpectedly, we see the Mom-and-apple-pie virtue which Tom Hanks so often personifies demystified: Edgecomb first benefits from then exploits his prisoner's power. He can continue with his professional duties towards Coffey in these circumstances only because he's capable of moral evasion, taking advantage of Coffey's powers without sufficiently repaying the debt he owes.

In fact, there are all sorts of hidden costs in the film's moral accounting. Coffey, played remarkably by Michael Clarke Duncan (whose few previous roles have mostly been bit parts as bouncers or bodyguards), is black and enormous. His body, covered with the scars from numerous beatings, is fetishised as a kind of primal physicality. He's illiterate and, until being imprisoned, itinerant. (In one location scene the economic conditions of the time are sketched in by a sign reading, "No jobs here: transients turn back." King's novel is clearly influenced by John Steinbeck's Depression era fiction.) Though Coffey is *The Green Mile*'s most sympathetic figure, he's concocted more than any other character out of a bundle of folkloric stereotypes whose origins in bigotry don't seem entirely acknowledged. A prisoner eats a Sambo chocolate bar. The leader of the search party (lynch mob) sent after the two missing girls spits in Coffey's face. His own lawyer compares "negroes" to violent mongrel dogs. The language of the prison—"boy", "boss" and so forth is also the language of racist contempt.

In another way, however, "boy" is right. Coffey's childlike quality is emphasised: he's afraid of the dark; when he's briefly released under supervision to attend the wife of the prison governor he takes intense pleasure in the sight of stars and the feel of wet leaves. Yet his acts of healing are depicted as almost sexual. To cure Edgecomb's urinary complaint he grasps Edgecomb's groin. To draw out the cancer in the governor's wife, and then pour it forth again into a sadistic warder, he must kiss them. The poignancy in this mock sexuality comes from Coffey's insufferable loneliness. "I want it to be over and done with," he says. "Tired of all the pain, like pieces of glass in my head." On being touched by a fellow prisoner, Coffey perceives all the prisoners murderousness. Coffey is an innocent forced to become aware of and be implicated in atrocious acts—like the child in *The Sixth Sense* (and other cursed telepaths in King's work and elsewhere). Both of these mainstream genre films belong to that strange branch of mass entertainment that is more than melodrama, and dwells on extremely traumatised protagonists who can expect little relief. What makes such films so interesting is that, for all their formulas, they never let go of their melancholy premises. *The Green Mile* is suffused with Coffey's deep and terrible grief at what he sees around him, and Edgecomb's guilty proximity to this grief. Watching Astaire reminds him that, in the end, he could do nothing or would do nothing for Coffey except arrange for him to watch *Top Hat* in the prison. Coffey watched in rapture, but for Edgecomb, so many years later, it's unbearable—just as a great deal else is unbearable. He's a very old, broken man hoping to die before he has to witness the deaths of more loved ones. How many blockbusters deal with that kind of grief?

TIME, 12/13/99, p. 97, Richard Corliss

For Frank Darabont, "doing time" means taking it. As the adapter and director of two Stephen King prison stories, Darabont is a man with a slow hand. He wants you to share the agony of ennui felt by jailbirds whose only job is marking time while scheming to escape or waiting to die—just like the rest of us. In *The Shawshank Redemption* he managed to invest this anxious leisure with tension and transcendence.

Odd how a style that looked spare in one movie can feel bloated in the next. That's the case with *The Green Mile*, reverently taken from King's serialized novel. It's 1935, and we're on a Southern prison's death row, where the only recreation is watching a mouse commandeer the corridor. Enter a new inmate, John Coffey (Michael Clarke Duncan), a giant black man with a gift of preternatural empathy; he can literally suck the pain out of people. Paul Edgecomb (Tom Hanks), the chief guard of E Block, is in awe of this white magic. He benefits from it, uses it to help a friend and, eventually, pays for it.

The piece has some eerily effective moments. The sponging of a condemned man's head makes electrocution seem a sacrament: baptism and extreme unction in a single dab. The healing scenes will evoke tears, some of them earned. And there's a lot of sharp acting, led by Hanks' pained restraint. The two villains are vigorously portrayed: a sadistic, craven guard (Doug Hutchison) and a strutting, rabid inmate (played with a daringly lunatic, dark-star quality by Sam Rockwell), whose crimes are even worse than we feared. At the core, though, one finds a slacky, sappy film. The human mystery that breathed so easily in *Shawshank* is often forced here. Grandstanding reaction shots of teary guards cue us to John Coffey's miraculous power as surely as the big man's initials hint at his majesty.

And there's no excuse for the movie to run, or meander, for more than three hours. Darabont must believe his film will move audiences, or he wouldn't have had the nerve to end it with the line "Oh, Lord, sometimes the green mile is so long." To more than a few viewers, this one will feel like a life sentence.

VILLAGE VOICE, 12/14/99, p. 188, Michael Atkinson

When the fiction foundry/movie mine/paradigm spigot that is Stephen King tries for an all-American magical-realism—his fave location for which is early-century prisons, his fave tone a rueful mushiness—what spills out is more like a cheddar-esque *Saturday Evening Post* yarn pasteurized, as it were, by a corporatized sense of self-importance. *The Green Mile*, written and directed by Frank Darabont like a testament to the humanity of its author, is in every aspect an attempt at restriking the Oscar-greased lightning of *The Shawshank Redemption*, plus some. The iron gravitas of Morgan Freeman is exchanged for sub-Cocoon digital doodads, but there's no lack of glowing saints and glowering sinners.

You'd think that with the movie flagging in at three methodical hours Darabont was under the impression he was adapting Pasternak, but Lean-like length is hardly the least honor Hollywood can bestow upon its primary vendors and brokers. Darabont's movie of course messes very little with King's scenario, in which a Depression-era Louisiana death row as cozy as Will Rogers's lap confronts one John Coffey (Michael Clarke Duncan), a seven-foot black refrigerator of a man with a kitten's gentleness, the tendency to weep at others' suffering, and the empathic ability to heal by touch. Cell-block chief Tom Hanks gets his bladder infection fixed up, warden James Cromwell's wife (Patricia Clarkson) is cured of a brain tumor (but not before it turns her into *The Exorcist*'s Regan O'Neill), and an intelligent mouse (a backwoods relation of Stuart Little?) is reconstituted after being crunched. The various inmates and guards on the Mile struggle to understand how such an angelic figure could've murdered two little girls.

Like his master, Darabont takes his folksy time, and it's refreshing for a while, but King has a third-grade gym wimp's ideas of plotting—one-dimensional cruelty and evil are answered by cosmic comeuppance—and *The Green Mile* is irritatingly repetitive and piled high with long-foreseen conclusions. (Distributor Warner Bros. warns us not to divulge the ending; which of the four or so endings they want kept secret is unclear.) Of the actors, only Duncan distinguishes himself, despite having to vomit fly swarms and to spit rays of Spielbergian light; Coffey's stunning first lines about being afraid of the dark are delivered in an embarrassed sob that stays in your ears deep into the movie. Hanks is himself, naturally, less an actor that anyone really finds interesting than yet another brand name from whose movies the public have learned to expect a substantial degree of professional Hollywood homogeneity. Seen this way, Darabont has hit one out of the park.

Also reviewed in:
CHICAGO TRIBUNE, 12/10/99, Friday/p. A, Michael Wilmington
NATION, 1/24/00, p. 35, Stuart Klawans
NEW YORK TIMES, 12/10/99, p. E17, Janet Maslin
NEW YORKER, 12/20/99, p. 103, David Denby
VARIETY, 11/29-12/5/99, p. 56, Todd McCarthy
WASHINGTON POST, 12/10/99, p. C1, Stephen Hunter
WASHINGTON POST, 12/10/99, Weekend/p. 44, Desson Howe

GUINEVERE

A Miramax Films release in association with Millenium Films of a Jonathan King and Bandeira Entertainment production. *Executive Producer:* Avi Lerner, Danny Dimbort, Trevor Short, Beau Flynn, Harvey Weinstein, Bob Weinstein, Stefan Simchowitz, John Thompson, and Boaz Davidson. *Producer:* Jonathan King and Brad Weston. *Director:* Audrey Wells. *Screenplay:* Audrey Wells. *Director of Photography:* Charles Minsky. *Editor:* Dody Dorn. *Music:* Christophe Beck. *Sound:* Glenn R. Gaines. *Casting:* Linda Lowy. *Production Designer:* Stephen McCabe. *Art Director:* Jason De Bart. *Set Decorator:* Danielle Berman. *Set Dresser:*

David K. Wolfson and Tijana Agic-Gaudio. *Costumes:* Genevieve Tyrrell. *Make-up:* Carol Strong. *Make-up (Gina Gershon):* Lori Jean Swanson. *Running time:* 104 minutes. *MPAA Rating:* R.

CAST: Stephen Rea (Connie Fitzpatrick); Sarah Polley (Harper Sloane); Jean Smart (Deborah Sloane); Gina Gershon (Billie); Paul Dolley (Walter); Francis Guinan (Alan Sloane); Jasmine Guy (Linda); Tracy Letts (Zack); Sandra Oh (Cindy); Carrie Preston (Patty); Emily Procter (Susan Sloane); Grace Una (April); Gedde Watanabe (Ed); Carlton Wilborn (Jay); Sharon McNight (Leslie); Oded Gross (Gary); Michelle Aurthor (Denise/Jazz Singer); Dorit Sauer (French Diva); Rose Mallett (Toilet Paper Woman); Kim Flowers (Pretty Woman); Scott Kaske (Transsexual); Trevor Edmond (Jeremy); Danny Kovaks (Cop); Brian Frank (Wedding Guest #1); Debra Engle (Wedding Guest #2); Kevin Brief (Dentist); Martin Yu (Modern Boyfriend); Paulina Sahagan (Mexican Seamstress); Kai Ephron (Positano's Regular); Alexandra Hilden (Angelic Girl).

LOS ANGELES TIMES, 9/24/99, Calendar/p. 4, Kenneth Turan

[*The following review by Kenneth Turan appeared in a slightly different form in*
NEWSDAY, 9/24/99, Part II/p. B7.]

Both true and contrived, genuine and slick, "Guinevere" details one of the world's oldest stories: the relationship, at once mentoring and romantic, between an older man and a much younger, beautiful woman. We have a right to yawn, but we don't, and Sarah Polley is the reason.

Praising this exceptional Canadian actress is not to minimize the good work of Audrey Wells, a screenwriting veteran with a decade's experience ("The Truth About Cats and Dogs," "George of the Jungle"), who makes a solid directing debut with a shrewd script that was a winner of the Waldo Salt Screenwriter Award at Sundance earlier this year.

But to see Polley take a scenario that's awfully familiar and convincingly convey that, as her young and naive character Harper Sloane truly believes, something this unique and wonderful has never happened to anyone before, is to witness acting talent of a very high order. Polley has made a strong impression in other films, "The Sweet Hereafter" and "Go" among them, but "Guinevere" will be the one that makes her a full-blown star.

We hear Harper's voice before we meet her, speaking in the confident been-there tones of a 25-year-old describing tasteful nude photographs she posed for in the distant past, i.e. when she was 21. The photographer? "He was the worst man I ever met, or maybe the best, I'm still not sure," she says. "If you're supposed to learn from your mistakes, then he's the best mistake I ever made."

Back we go five years, to Harper's gilded-cage existence as the youngest daughter of a San Francisco family of legal barracudas led by a take-no-prisoners mother (a splendid Jean Smart), who's both incisive and terrifying.

It's the wedding day of Harper's older sister, and Harper, though strikingly beautiful, sees herself as so awkward and gawky that she tries to hide in the pantry with only champagne for company. Not surprisingly, she attracts the attention of Cornelius Fitzpatrick (Stephen Rea), who, we can be sure, has had experience with young women like this before.

Though he's working today as the wedding photographer, Connie, as everyone calls him, proves to be exactly what his appearance advertises: the grand artiste with the looks and the loft to complete the package. Unshaven, with unruly hair and a white scarf knotted casually around his neck, he is Mr. Irish Bedroom Eyes, and when we find out that he drinks whiskey straight and listens to cool jazz far into the night, it merely completes the picture.

Though he's old enough to be her father, Connie and Harper become fast pals, in immediate complicity, and soon he's calling her his Guinevere, after King Arthur's queen, and she is visiting him in his hipster's loft, completely oblivious to the fact that, as everyone from Connie's ex-girlfriends to a seamstress who works down the hall knows, she's not the first to walk down that particular path.

Harper is supposed to follow in the family tradition and go to Harvard Law, but her infatuation with Connie, especially the way he informs her, based on nothing anyone else has noticed, that she has the makings of a great photographer, changes her plans.

Telling her mother she's living with a friend, Harper moves in with Connie, who, presenting himself as a one-man artists' colony, says she can stay only if she commits herself to study and the creative process.

Though she protests, saying, "You're mistaking me for someone with potential," Harper is obviously pleased that someone so, uh, mature, is paying attention to her, just as Connie is pleased that someone so young and beautiful is paying attention to him.

You don't have to have sat through all three versions of "A Star Is Born" to know every inch of this territory, but the wonderful thing about Polley's performance is that she keeps her character from letting on or even realizing she's living out a gigantic cliche.

An actress of enormous skill and poise (she started working at age 4 and had a major TV following in Canada), Polley can convey any emotion you can name, and a few you can't put your finger on. There is a quiet force to her work, plus an ability to instinctively go for the truth in every scene. To watch her face during the film's big seduction scene is to see a combination of confusion, hesitation and anticipation that couldn't be more real and compelling.

Rea, though an undeniably fine actor ("The Crying Game," "Interview With the Vampire"), feels hamstrung, as Polley is not, by his familiar part and by having to say lines like, "You take a picture when it hurts so bad you can't stand it." Smart, by contrast, makes the absolute most out of her small part, using her brief but indelible scenes to convey that, as writer-director Wells puts it, "she is the rightest person in the movie," albeit a terribly nasty one.

Wells is sensitive to the implications of the Harper-Connie relationship for both parties and to how much it can mean for anyone to have confidence in you, no matter (as "The Muse" also points out) who that person turns out to be. Despite its ever-present obviousness, "Guinevere" is involving enough to make us look forward to Wells' next work. And, it goes without saying, to Polley's as well.

NEW YORK POST, 9/24/99, p. 42, Lou Lumenick

A knowing take on the venerable theme of May-September romance, "Guinevere" showcases the luminous Sarah Polley as an insecure 20-year-old swept off her feet by a photographer 30 years her senior.

He's Connie, a magnificently shaggy Irish drunk—played by Stephen Rea of "The Crying Game"—whom Harper (Polley) encounters while he's photographing her snooty sister's San Francisco wedding.

He begins a sneaky, low-key flirtation that reaches a slow simmer when she goes to his loft to pick up the pictures—including a romantic portrait of herself that sets her swooning.

Harper, long ignored by her WASP family, is swept off her feet by his intensely focused attention. She chucks plans to attend Harvard Law and takes up Connie's invitation to move in—provided she devote herself to "the arts" under his tutelage, and share his bed, of course.

The heart and soul of "Guinevere" is watching Harper blossom from a girl so painfully shy she won't express an opinion to a confident, sexually aware young woman who becomes conscious of Connie's increasingly desperate manipulations to keep her—including preying on her upper-class guilt.

Harper is beautifully matched with Rea's Connie, whose considerable Gaelic charms barely mask a burned-out artist who's mentored a long line of young women he's ironically named "Guinevere"—after the queen who left King Arthur for a younger man.

Harper will inevitably follow her predecessors, but screenwriter Audrey Wells ("The Truth About Cats and Dogs"), here making her directing debut, homes in like a laser on Harper's relationship with Connie, which takes increasingly dire turns as he sinks into paranoia and alcoholism.

"No woman with any experience would stand in front of you with awe," Harper's unhappily married mother (Jean Smart of TV's "Designing Women" in a well-etched cameo) tells Connie, hitting the nail perhaps a little too squarely on the head.

The strong cast—Gina Gershon is especially delicious as a sassy ex-Guinevere who tries to wise up Harper to Connie's game—balances out an uneven script, which includes bursts of feminist preachiness and a way-over-the-top romantic coda set four years later.

Wells stages scenes with confidence and avoids exploiting Polley—and the material—by discreetly cutting away before serious lovemaking gets under way.

"Guinevere" should make Polley, memorable in "The Sweet Hereafter" and "Go," into a bona-fide star.

VILLAGE VOICE, 9/28/99, p. 126, Amy Taubin

A mainstream version of Jennifer Montgomery's controversial *Art for Teachers of Children, Guinevere* is notable as a showcase for Sarah Polley, a mercurial young actor with a wide, seemingly effortless range. Nothing could be further from the steely, working-class survivor that she played in *Go* than Harper Sloane, the shy, sheltered daughter of a wealthy, rather despicable San Francisco family.

Harper has just been accepted to Harvard Law School when she meets Connie Fitzpatrick (Stephen Rea), a nearly burnt-out photographer who's 30 years her senior. Connie sees a kindred outsider spirit in Harper, and within days of her first visit to his dilapidated studio, he's convinced her to put her plans on hold and move in. Although sex plays a part in their relationship, their attraction has more to do with their belief in each other's fantasies. Harper sees Connie as an uncompromising great artist and the teacher who can change her life; Connie makes Harper believe that she also has the potential to express a unique vision as well. By the time Harper discovers that she's only the latest in a long line of Connie's "Guineveres," she's too involved to cut herself free.

Writer-director Audrey Wells doesn't take a moral position against this classic May-December relationship, which is what's admirable about the film. Although Connie exploits the youth of his Guineveres, he suffers more than they do because he's the one left behind when his nurturing pays off. Rea is convincing as a romantic, alcoholic wreck, but he lacks the narcissistic blinders that would allow Connie to repeat the same relationship with a half dozen women.

As a director, Wells is too conventional for her own material, and much of the time the film plays like soap opera. Except for Polley and Rea, the performances are heavy-handed. Still, I was willing to cut *Guinevere* some slack until the excruciating final scene—a rip-off of *All That Jazz* and twice as maudlin.

Also reviewed in:
NEW YORK TIMES, 9/24/99, p. E24, Janet Maslin
VARIETY, 2/1-7/99, p. 54, Todd McCarthy
WASHINGTON POST, 10/1/99, p. C5, Rita Kempley
WASHINGTON POST, 10/1/99, Weekend/p. 47, Desson Howe

HANDS ON A HARD BODY

A Legacy Releasing release. *Producer:* Kevin Morris, Chapin John Wilson, and S.R. Bindler. *Director:* S.R. Bindler. *Editor:* S.R. Bindler. *Director of Photography:* Michael Nickles, Chapin John Wilson, and S.R. Bindler. *Music:* Neil Kassanoff. *Running time:* 97 minutes. *MPAA Rating:* PG.

WITH: Russell Welsh, Kerri Parker, Kelli Mangrum, Greg Cox, Norma Valverde, Janis Curtis, J.D. Drew, and Benny Perkins (contestants); Blake Long (Contest Host).

NEW YORK, 2/15/99, p. 56, Peter Rainer

Hands on a Hard Body is about one of those real-life homegrown gothic events just crying out to be chronicled. Every year in Longview, Texas—population 70,000—an auto dealership stages a contest in which entrants are required to stand around a fully loaded Nissan hard-body pickup with at least one hand on the truck at all times (minus five-minute breaks every hour; fifteen every six). The last person standing wins—and past winners have taken it up to 83 hours. S. R. Bindler, an NYU-film-school graduate, video-taped this contest in 1995 for less money than what the truck is worth—around $15,000. The results aren't all they might have been; we don't get very far into the character of any of the contestants, and the camera often hovers and whirls when you want it to just sit still and observe. But Bindler doesn't poke fun at these people or turn them into freaks. It's clear right away that most of them are going through this for the very good reason that they're unprosperous and need a truck to pay the bills.

Jammed around the hard-body, the original 24 men and women are like a squadron of bombardiers on a dangerous mission-they know they're not all going to make it. Roly-poly Ronald McCowan consumes kilos of Snickers. The devoutly Christian Nonna Valverde, wearing headsets, pumps herself up with spirituals. The fortyish Benny Perkins, a winner two years ago, is back again, and in pretaped interviews he talks about the event as if he's a recovering POW. "It's all about who can maintain sanity the longest," he says, and sure enough, round about the third day, people start getting loopy and giggly. Eating jumbo burgers and fries during the breaks is the clearest mark of insanity. "That'll take you down," says Benny, who knows and knows. A filmmaker such as Werner Herzog or Errol Morris could have turned this subject into a creepy-crawly sideshow, but I'm glad they didn't get wind of it. Weirdness this good deserves the plain treatment.

NEW YORK, POST, 2/5/99, p. 63, Rod Dreher

The racy title of S.R. Bindler's wonderful slice-of-life documentary—"Hands on a Hard Body"—refers to the contest at the hilarious heart of this compulsively entertaining, off-the-wall picture.

Each year, a Nissan dealership in Longview, Texas, has a popular competition in which 24 people place a hand on a brand-new pickup truck. The last person left standing with a hand on the vehicle—that's "vee-HICKel" to you, Yankee—drives away with it. Because this contest can last for three days or longer, folks get downright loopy as the hours march stolidly on.

Far from being a "get a load of this" take on a goofy Texas ritual, "Hands on a Hard Body" is a "Lifeboat"-style passion play about the limits of endurance and the quirks of character that manifest themselves under duress.

Deep into the contest, after the punishing hours have blasted away the easygoing bonhomie of the surviving members of the group tethered to the truck, you hear them talking with grim ambivalence of those who dropped out, as if they had slipped under the waves into the darkness of oblivion. The atmosphere surrounding the pickup is so tense and riveting you may laugh at yourself for wanting to cry when favorite contestants collapse in fatigue.

After two days of relentless standing (interrupted by a five-minute break every hour), minds begin melting down. Waves of delirious laughter circle the truck, exhilarating some and unnerving others. Several, including a scary toothless crone, begin suspecting others of cheating, and lash out spitefully. Others form peculiar but lovely bonds with their fellow contestants.

The considerable allure of "Hands on a Hard Body" lies in its subject, not its style. This documentary, which has been bouncing around film festivals and art houses for a couple of years now, was shot fairly crudely on video by NYU film-school grad (and Longview native) Bindler, and his small crew.

Unfortunately, they weren't always on the scene to record crucial moments, like the woozy surrender of a "Hard Body" stalwart whose source of strength tragically proves to be an Achilles' heel in the last, desperate hour.

Still, "Hands on a Hard Body" is such a rousing wallop of screwball profundity, and so unlike anything else in theaters right now, that complaining feels niggardly. (Fight ignorance, use that word!) It's a hoot and a holler, and you'd be crazy to miss it.

NEWSDAY, 2/5/99, Part II/p. B11, Jack Mathews

The body in S.R. Bindler's documentary, "Hands on a Hard Body," belongs to Jack Long Nissan in Longview, Texas. It's a brand new 1995 Nissan pickup truck. The hands in the title belong to the 24 people who want to win the truck so badly they're willing to stand next to it, touching it, until only one of them is left.

The best thing about "Hands on a Hard Body" is that somebody thought to make a movie about it. The Nissan dealership had been conducting the promotional contest for several years before Bindler, a Longview native, brought his home video camera to the occasion in 1995 and captured the answer to the age-old question: How far will people go to get something for nothing?

Of course, nothing is a relative term to those contestants who last into the second or third day, with no more than periodic 5 and 15-minute breaks, and experience the genuine pain, anguish, disorientation and—in some cases—spiritual challenge of the quest. I wouldn't attempt this for anything less than a Porsche.

Don't tell that to Keni Parker, a 30-something woman whose sole means of transportation is her bicycle. Or Russell Welsh, a farmer who'd had to sell his old truck to pay his bills. Or J.D. Drew, an oldtimer with a young heart who intends to take the truck home as a gift for his wife.

Some of the entrants are in it for a lark, and are gone in a blink. Some are in it to prove something to themselves. For others, it's "Wide World of Sports," a test of skill, endurance, and training that holds for the winner the thrill of victory and for the losers the agony of de-feet.

Bindler devoted 90 hours of home video to the event and its participants and has edited from them a 97-minute documentary that is amazing for what it reveals about character and desire. Asked what it felt like to be the last one standing in a previous contest, Benny Perkins, the current event's favorite, searches for the right words and compares it to that feeling "you have when you kill your first big animal."

Now, I don't know how that feels, and don't want to know. But I understand from the look on Benny's face and the excitement in his voice what it means to him. It's the same feeling, one assumes, that all first-time winners of marathon events have, whether they're competing for a pickup truck or a gold medal. What some people won't do...

VILLAGE VOICE, 2/9/99, p. 65, Dennis Lim

Twenty-three hopefuls gather outside a Nissan dealership in Longview, Texas, place their hands on a shiny new pickup, and try to keep them there as long as they can. The last person left standing drives home with the truck. (The runner-up staggers away with $250.) Scrappy, likable, and immensely absorbing, S.R. Bindler's chronicle of the "Hands on a Hard Body" contest (typically a four-to-five-day marathon) exploits the towering absurdity and unlikely intensity of its subject matter, without ever succumbing to yokel-Americana condescension.

The annual contest is, fundamentally, a surreally sadistic publicity stunt, a point certainly not lost on Bindler. But, as one of the participants stresses, it's also "a human drama thing." The 1995 competition filmed by Bindler featured an ex-marine, a rabidly devout Christian woman, a bubbly twentysomething, and a middle-aged farmer. The by-default star of the film, though, is ruminative former champion Benny, who eloquently describes the bittersweet thrill of seeing a fellow competitor go down ("I'd compare it to the first time you kill a really big animal") and remarks on the event's allegorical quality. "It's like a movie that I once saw. It's called *Highlander.*"

The contestants start to lose it by the second day—swollen limbs, hallucinatory episodes, uncontrollable laughter (as one of the religious woman's supporters notes, "The joy of the Lord started manifesting itself in her"). Bindler is an astute observer, as vigilant as his visibly minuscule budget allows. Offering close-ups of stricken, sleep-deprived faces, he watches as mind-numbing boredom accelerates into sanity-threatening torture and conveys a sense of the subtle mindfucking at work. Gripping and cathartic, the culminating face-off packs a punch most big-budget blowouts would be hard-pressed to match.

Also reviewed in:
CHICAGO TRIBUNE, 2/26/99, Friday/p. N, John Petrakis
NEW REPUBLIC, 3/8/99, p. 30, Stanley Kauffmann
NEW YORK TIMES, 2/5/99, p. E18, Anita Gates
VARIETY, 11/3-9/97, p. 101, Todd McCarthy

HAPPY, TEXAS

A Miramax Films release in association with Marked Entertainment of an Illsley/Stone production. *Executive Producer:* Jason Clark. *Producer:* Mark Illsley, Rick Montgomery, and Ed Stone. *Screenplay:* Ed Stone, Mark Illsley, and Phil Reeves. *Director of Photography:* Bruce Douglas Johnson. *Editor:* Norman Buckley. *Music:* Peter Harris. Music Editor: Brian Kirk and Ron Finn. *Choreographer:* Kelly Devine. *Sound:* Ed White and (music) Scott Cochran. *Sound Editor:* Michael Payne. *Casting:* Joe Garcia. *Production Designer:* Maurin Scarlata. *Art Director:* Tobey Bays. *Set Decorator:* Phoebe O'Connor. *Set Dresser:* Ed Servaites, David Buckband, Wayne Alton, Maxwell Britton, Ricky Zamudio and James L. Eddy. *Costumes:* Julia Schklair. *Make-up:* Pico and Karen Scherer. *Stunt Coordinator:* Bobby C. King. *Running time:* 96 minutes. *MPAA Rating:* PG-13. *Running time:* 96 minutes. *MPAA Rating:* PG-13.

CAST: Jeremy Northam (Harry Sawyer); Steve Zahn (Wayne Wayne Wayne Jr.); Ally Walker (Josephine 'Joe' McLintock); Illeana Douglas (Ms. Schaefer); William H. Macy (Sheriff Chappy Dent); M.C. Gainey (Bob Maslow); Ron Perlman (Nalhober); Paul Dooley (Judge); Mo Gaffney (Mrs. Bromley); Jillian Berard (Madison); Scarlett Pomers (Jency); Melissa Arnold, Cassie Silva, and Tiffany Takara (Other Happy Girls); Tim Bagley (David); Michael Hitchcock (Steven); Ed Stone (Alton); Rance Howard (Ely); Derek Montgomery (Bully Boy); Kiva Lawrence (Pageant Judge); Carly Fink ('Little Light Girl'); David Shackelford (Varnel); Kim Story (Guard).

LOS ANGELES TIMES, 10/1/99, Calendar/p. 2, Kevin Thomas

"Happy, Texas" is a hoot, a hilarious comedy that's smart and caring, yet sexy and ingenious enough that it just might stir up some of that elusive "Full Monty"-style box-office appeal. It marks a nifty directorial debut for Mark Illsley, a second-unit veteran, and it sparkles with deliciously spot-on, career-advancing performances from Jeremy Northam, Steve Zahn, Ally Walker and Illeana Douglas, and boasts a portrayal from William H. Macy that's such a comic gem it's sure to remain a high point in Macy's splendid filmography.

Illsley and co-writers Ed Stone and Phil Reeves cleverly slip a pair of convicts, the handsome and smooth Harry (Northam) and the wistful and clumsy Wayne (Zahn), a couple of petty criminals, away from a Texas chain gang. They land in the small town of Happy, Texas, where they find themselves mistaken for a pair of professional pageant producers hired to shape up a bunch of small girls so that they might qualify for the Little Miss Squeezed Pageant, a goal that has eluded the community for 25 years. It's an unexpected opportunity for the escapees to elude the authorities in pursuit, but there is a catch: The actual pageant guys are known to be gay and also to be lovers.

Harry cons Wayne into coaching the girls despite his total inexperience in show biz. Meanwhile, Harry cases the local bank in order to crack its safe, which involves him getting to know its attractive owner, Joe (Walker). She feels comfortable in confiding her romantic problems to Harry in her belief that he's gay, not realizing that the ultimate effect is to make him fall in love with her.

As Wayne starts to get the hang of working out a kiddie act, he in turn attracts their vivacious schoolteacher, Ms. Schaefer (Douglas). Despite the frustration of disguising their true sexual orientation, Harry and Wayne—though they are loath to admit it—are beginning to feel happier in Happy, Texas, than they have ever been in their heretofore wastrel existences.

Illsley plays the repressed sexual longing between Harry and Joe for all it's worth, then throws in a wholly unexpected complication involving the sweet-natured local sheriff, Chappy (Macy), which provide some great comic as well as surprisingly tender moments.

With each twist and turn of the plot, Illsley et al raise the ante when it comes to the final payoff; the more complications multiply, the more the audience wonders how you're going to unravel them in a satisfying manner. The filmmakers are inspired enough to avoid letdown and wise enough to resist an abrupt finish, but there's no denying "Happy, Texas" requires quite a bit of time to play everything out. You probably won't mind, however, because the picture's such fun, with fine contributions from M.C. Gainey, Ron Perlman and Mo Gaffney.

It's also sensitive and imaginative, a nice blend of satire and sweetness as Harry and Wayne are suddenly thrust into their new identities. As affectionate as it is zany, "Happy, Texas" looks to send both straights and gays home happy.

NEW YORK, 10/11/99, p. 102, Peter Rainer

Happy, Texas is one of those low-budget high-concept comedies in which the concept is none too high—a pair of escaped convicts (Jeremy Northam and Steve Zahn) from a west Texas chain gang end up impersonating a gay couple who stage Junior-miss beauty pageants—but I would be remiss if I didn't champion the performance of William H. Macy as a forlorn small-town sheriff smitten by one of the escapees. He's immensely touching, which is more than this balderdash deserves.

NEW YORK POST, 10/1/99, p. 63, Jonathan Foreman

"Happy, Texas" was the hit of the Sundance Film Festival—and for good reason. It's a funny and occasionally poignant movie that gives Steve Zahn ("Out of Sight") a starring role at last and includes a superb, moving performance by William H. Macy ("Fargo," "Boogie Nights") that should be a lock for a Best Supporting Actor Oscar nomination.

It also shows just how comfortable Hollywood has become with homosexuality.

Two small-time crooks, Harry Sawyer (Jeremy Northam) and Wayne Wayne Wayne Jr. (Steve Zahn), escape from a chain gang and steal an RV belonging to two gay pageant producers on their way to the small town of Happy, Texas.

With cops all over the highways, the two outlaws decide that their best bet for freedom is to lay low in Happy in the guise of the two producers—and therefore as a couple. They also decide that the local bank would be worth knocking off.

Their new identities require that one of the two criminals coach the town's pre-teen school girls for the Little Miss Squeezed Pageant. Wayne is the one who ends up assisting their teacher, Miss Schaefer (Illeana Douglas), in this task, while Harry sets out to befriend Josephine (Ally Walker), the bank's attractive owner, with an eye to finding out about its security systems.

Harry quickly becomes Josephine's confidant, and she asks him for advice about men, while Wayne struggles to teach the school girls how to sing and dance. But when the local sheriff, Chappy Dent (Macy), starts snooping around, he focuses on Harry, who finds himself having to go further and further into his assumed character.

Chappy, it turns out, has a secret agenda of his own.

It's all predictable stuff—the basic plot is in many ways a retread of "Some Like It Hot." And it's clear from the start that the two cons will fall for the single women played by Douglas and Walker—even though you never get a sense that Wayne and Miss Schaefer are attracted to each other until they're in each other's arms.

But the film's real weakness is the obvious difficulties the writers had fashioning an ending that satisfies without completely defying belief.

Northam, the English actor who excelled in "The Winslow Boy" and "An Ideal Husband" (he was also the bad guy in "The Net"), revealed in the disastrous remake of "Gloria" that he has real problems with American accents, and he hasn't solved them.

But he's a good-looking leading man and he has enjoyable chemistry with Ally Walker, the lovely star of TV's "Profiler."

The only joker in the pack is Douglas, who seems miscast as a ditsy high school teacher.

Refreshingly, first-time director and co-writer Mark Illsley ensures that the inhabitants of Happy look and sound like real Southerners. He refrains from depicting them as ridiculous hicks or cutesy eccentrics.

NEWSDAY, 10/1/99, Part II/p. B6, John Anderson

"Happy, Texas" was the movie voted most likely to have cost $8 trillion at this year's Sundance Festival (speculation about its Miramax deal went on for days), and Steve Zahn won a special jury prize for Comedic Performance (which he couldn't pick up personally, because no one gave him a ticket to the awards); what got lost in the hubbub was whether the movie could possibly be as funny as any of its very partial observers said it was.

Answer? Nothing could be that funny. Still, "Happy, Texas" definitely is amusing, with a few decided qualifications.

A kind of "We're No Angels" mixed with a Hope-Crosby road movie—a cross-dressing Dorothy Lamour impersonator wouldn't have been entirely inappropriate—"Happy, Texas" also carries a genetic strain of "Some Like It Hot": Two fugitive prison inmates are mistaken for a pair of gay "pageant coordinators" hired by the town of Happy in a last-ditch effort to get their little girls into the annual Little Miss Fresh-Squeezed competition. Thinking initially that they're being re-arrested, the two cons are more than happy to take the job, especially if it means they can continue their flight, and maybe rob the local bank before they do.

That this subterfuge requires them to behave like lovers is the comedic crutch—excuse me, crux—of the movie, meaning that the vast bulk of the humor in "Happy, Texas" is based on the hilarity inherent in either being gay, being mistaken for being gay, mistaking people for being gay, or just being a hick. It's not necessarily homophobic, but it's certainly sophomoric.

At the same time, the movie's got a pair of terrific performances. Zahn, as professional prisoner and short-fuse specialist Wayne Wayne Wayne Jr., has moments of inspired silliness, especially when his con man partner, Harry Sawyer (a miscast Jeremy Northam), leaves him to instruct the girls in the finer points of modern dance (think George Balanchine tumbling across the prairie). Harry, meanwhile, cases both the bank and its owner, the lonely-but-lovely Joe (for Josephine) McClintock (Ally Walker). Back at the ranch, Wayne Wayne Wayne develops his own chemistry with the girls' teacher, Ms. Schaefer (Illeana Douglas). And the local sheriff, Chappy Dent (William H. Macy), gets wild about Harry.

Macy is just hilarious and might easily have made the deeply closeted Chappy—who woos the nerve-racked Harry like a character out of "Our Town"—into a country two-stepping burlesque. Instead, he gives his character a deep reserve of fragile dignity and that makes all the difference. It makes Chappy a lot funnier than he might have been, too: It's not the sheriffs homosexuality that's the gag, really; it's his fractured chivalry that generates the laughs. And the pathos as well.

Director Mark Illsley is no Preston Sturges, although "Happy, Texas" blows in that direction—small-town foibles, awkwardly mannered comedy, the delicate scent of absurdity drifting across the plains.

It's too bad that the film has to go out with a bang, more or less, when a third escapee, played by the hulking M.C. Gainey, shows up to rob Joe's bank, which turns Harry honest, sparks the seemingly inevitable chase scene and brings things to a climax just as the girls are hitting the stage for their big Little Fresh-Squeezed number. So where, exactly, is "Happy, Texas"? Somewhere between Surprise and Predictable, a stone's throw from Interesting, but a good day's drive from Deep in the Heart of Anywhere.

SIGHT AND SOUND, 1/00, p. 51, Philip Kemp

On a Texas chain gang, convict Wayne Wayne Wayne Jr picks a fight with the brutal Bob Maslow, alarming a third felon on the chain, conman Harry Sawyer. When the van taking them to solitary crashes, Maslow takes off. Harry and Wayne hijack a rundown Winnebago and find themselves escorted to the small town of Happy, Texas, by the local sheriff Chappy Dent. The van actually belongs to two gay beauty-pageant producers, David and Steven, hired to stage a pre-teen pageant in Happy. Harry and Wayne adopt the gay pair's identities.

Harry hatches a plan to rob the town bank during the pageant. Leaving Wayne to coach five small girls for the event, he sets about gaining the confidence of the bank president, Josephine 'Joe' McLintock, to whom he becomes attracted. Meanwhile Chappy finds Harry arousing his latent homosexuality. Wayne discovers an aptitude for stagecraft and wins the admiration of schoolmistress Ms Schaefer. When the girls qualify for the semi-finals, she and Wayne have sex. On the day of the pageant, Harry and Wayne decide to abandon their bank heist but Maslow reappears and forces them to go through with it. Harry summons the Texas marshals. Chappy, devastated by Harry's rejection, is wounded while heroically foiling Maslow's attack on the bank. Maslow takes Joe hostage, but is captured after a chase. Back in jail for a short spell, Harry and Wayne are visited by Joe and Ms Schaefer, while Chappy finds happiness with a Texas marshal.

Two minutes into *Happy, Texas,* one convict clouts another over the head with a dead armadillo. This suggests we're in for some undemandingly broad humour in the Zucker or Farrelly Brothers style. But although it reverts to slapstick for its set-piece chase finale, for most of its length Mark Illsley's debut film offers an unexpectedly gentle, even sentimental comedy of sexual identities, a less raucous version of *The Adventures of Priscilla Queen of the Desert.*

Here, as in Stephan Elliott's film, most of the comedy derives from the clash of cultures, and from the effect on a backwoods world as its denizens open up, under the influence of the anomalous outsiders, to suppressed aspects of their own sexuality. However, the edge is taken off the humour by the film's overall air of benevolence. This is one Texas burgh where homophobia is utterly unknown. The people of Happy (The Town Without a Frown) regard their supposedly gay visitors with nothing more aggressive than bemused curiosity and go out of their way to be tactful. Even the macho Wayne, initially horrified at the subterfuge, soon starts getting in touch with his feminine side. ("First I gotta make little polka dotted flowers for the girls' hats," he protests when Harry summons him for a heist conference.)

If *Happy, Texas'* central plotline—of the two conmen coming to care about the small-town folk they were planning to dupe—is hardly unexpected, it's worked out with some warm and sensitive scripting, especially in the exchanges between Harry and Joe. Jeremy Northam turns in a neatly understated comic performance, well matched by Ally Walker. As the secondary couple Steve Zahn and Illeana Douglas get less support from the script and tend to ham it up accordingly. But acting honours are stolen, not for the first time, by the peerless William H. Macy as the lovelorn sheriff. His Texas shuffle number, in the gay bar where he takes Harry on a date, withstands comparison to Jack Lemmon's tango in *Some Like It Hot* (1959), and his tearful response to Harry's rejection is genuinely moving. Cutting through the general fluffiness, the scene injects a moment of real pain into a film that, though bright and likeable, is otherwise a touch too good natured for its own good.

TIME, 10/4/99, p. 94, Richard Corliss

At last January's Sundance Film festival, the big finds were *The Blair Witch Project* and *Happy, Texas.* The first film, which its makers sold to Artisan Entertainment for $1.1 million, went on to become the feel-scared (or -shafted) movie of the summer and to earn nearly $140 million at the domestic box office. By this yardstick, *Happy, Texas,* which Miramax Films picked up for about $6 million, should sweep the Oscars and outgross *Titanic.*

In movies, of course, the rules of mathematics apply less universally than the law of the fluke. *Blair Witch* was a cunning fluke; *Happy, Texas* is just the kind of smart, communal comedy *(The Opposite of Sex, Happiness, Election, Go)* to which the mass film audience has shown serial resistance. Yet here you will find an easy charm, a cleverly unforced sense of humor and a benignity toward all its genially oddball characters that Hollywood would do well to emulate. If moviegoers skip this one, they'll be missing a real treat.

Two cons—Harry the thief (Brit throb Jeremy Northam, doing a nice imitation of all four Baldwin brothers) and Wayne Wayne Wayne Jr., the career loser (appealingly whiny Steve Zahn)—have escaped from prison and landed in "the town without a frown." The camper they have stolen belonged to a couple of pageant producers, so Harry and Wayne must pretend to be gay men, with an encyclopedic knowledge of show tunes and sewing as they prepare five avid little girls for the 18th annual Little Miss Fresh Squeeze Preteen Talent Competition. They are also expected to be the most sensitive guys west of Dallas, tending to the emotional needs of a teacher (Illeana Douglas), a bank president (Ally Walker) and a sheriff (William H. Macy, great as always).

Doesn't this look like a cynical mix of every indie trope of the past few years? Guys on the run, heartland town, a goofy pageant, the career-gal blues. Oh, and some *real* gay people. All of which proves there's nothing new under the sun. And nothing so original as a writer who can make comic haute cuisine out of the ingredients for hash.

That would be Ed Stone. Collaborating with first-time director Mark Illsley on the script, he creates drama by placing decent folks in uncomfortable situations. It's as simple as having a man or a woman fall in love with someone wildly unsuitable, and as difficult as making all the parties pleasant and plausible—in the best sense, human.

The character defects that got Harry and Wayne into trouble are precisely those that appeal to the Happy, Texans. The town loves the danger they suggest, or perhaps just their novelty. In a place where everybody knows everybody, the unknown is sexy; it offers a last hope for change, adventure, escape. Jettisoning propriety means the locals have never felt so alive. If the fling ends in one's getting flung ... well, as the sheriff says, "That's what life is about, isn't it—finding out?"

What does it take to get people to see a lovely comedy that offers flawless ensemble performances and acres of good cheer? Try this blurb: Funnier than *The Blair Witch Project*.

VILLAGE VOICE, 10/5/99, p. 216, Dennis Lim

If *Happy, Texas*, the subject of a heated bidding war at Sundance this year, has any use at all, it's as an illustration of festival-induced delirium. Lazily directed by first-timer Mark Illsley (who also cowrote the clueless script), this mistaken-identity comedy about gay-acting straights sputters to a dead halt right out of the gate. Every wheezy gag is implicit in the one-joke premise.

On the lam, two bumbling convicts—slow-witted goofball Steve Zahn and his very bland foil Jeremy Northam—steal a motor home and, upon arriving in the small town of Happy, Texas, are enthusiastically greeted as the gay pageant consultants (a couple, no less) who've been hired to help stage the Little Miss Fresh-Squeezed Pageant. One labored scenario follows another. Profanity-prone Zahn is stuck teaching little girls JonBenet routines with the help of a sexually frustrated schoolteacher (Illeana Douglas). Roving-eyed Northam sets about wooing the pretty local banker (Ally Walker) with sensitive-gay-man behavior, while fending off the advances of the town's real homosexual, William Macy's sad-sack sheriff.

The film strikes a perverse balance between gay jokes and redneck jokes, and makes them all equally toothless. Thanks to the genial performers, the questionable material comes off, for the most part, merely tiresome (though Zahn's comic timing and self-deprecating capacity for buffoonery is more than the movie deserves). No more or less offensive than the overrated *In and Out, Happy, Texas* is, at best, too dumb to hate; at worst, it's *Birdcage* lining.

Also reviewed in:
CHICAGO TRIBUNE, 10/8/99, Friday/p. B, Michael Wilmington
NEW YORK TIMES, 10/1/99, p. E25, Stephen Holden
NEW YORKER, 10/11/99, p. 106, Anthony Lane
VARIETY, 2/1-7/99, p. 61, Emanuel Levy
WASHINGTON POST, 10/8/99, p. C5, Rita Kempley
WASHINGTON POST, 10/8/99, Weekend/p. 53, Desson Howe

HARD

An Jour de Fete Films release of an M.P.H. production. *Producer:* John Matkowsky, Noel Palomaria, and John Huckert. *Director:* John Huckert. *Screenplay:* John Huckert and John Matkowsky. *Director of Photography:* John Matkowsky. *Editor:* John Huckert. *Music:* Phil Settle and John Huckert. *Sound:* Steven A. Morrow. *Production Designer:* John M. Plume. *Make-up:* Wendy Wixon. *Special Make-up:* Michael Valenzuela and Eric Jerstad. *Running time:* 102 minutes. *MPAA Rating:* Not Rated.

CAST: Noel Palomaria (Detective Raymond Vates); Malcolm Moorman (Jack); Charles Lanyer (Detective Lucky Tom Ellis); Michael Waite (Andy); Arron Zeffron (Doug); Steve Andrews (Detective Hendrickson); K.D. Jones (Detective Jenkins); Bob Hollander (Capt. Foster); Ken Narasaki (Detective Chyun); Steve Gonzales (Detective Dominguez).

LOS ANGELES TIMES, 6/25/99, Calendar/p. 10, Kevin Thomas

John Huckert's "Hard," one of the best films from Outfest '98, is an ambitious and successful first effort, a taut, chilling police procedural that plays the plight of a closeted gay cop (Noel

Palomaria) against the rampaging of a savage serial killer (Malcolm Moorman).   "Hard" represents an imaginative, provocative use of genre that is rightly deeply disturbing in its implications.   "Hard" is hard to take in some of its imagery, but it's not irresponsible; it emphasizes the consequences of violence over the acts themselves.

Moorman's Jack is a gay man's nightmare. Rugged and handsome, he's physically a fantasy figure come to life, but he's also possessed of a psychopath's fearlessness. When he comes on to a man in a bar in his insinuating yet forceful way, he has little reason to expect much resistance. Jack is an insatiable seducer but is in the grip of such intense internalized homophobia that he feels compelled to kill his lovers; in this way he has much in common with Jeffrey Dahmer as an attractive yet lethally self-hating gay man. Hitchhikers and hustlers are especially vulnerable to Jack's deadly instincts.

Arriving in Los Angeles to continue his killing spree, Jack cannot resist observing from a bridge a police investigation of the corpse of one of his victims. His gaze rests upon Palomaria's Raymond, a rookie homicide detective. Later on at a gay bar, when Jack recognizes Raymond as one of the cops at the crime scene, he comes on to the policeman; at the same time he hits upon a particularly diabolical scheme.

Huckert and his co-writer John Matkowsky gradually intensify Raymond's predicament as a gay cop who leaves himself open to all manner of homophobia if he comes out of the closet but who eventually may face even worse consequences if he does not. That homophobia persists in America's police departments is well-documented, manifesting itself not only in the harassment of gay cops but often in indifference to gay murder victims. These concerns emerge implicitly within "Hard" and not in a preachy manner.

Palomaria and Moorman head a list of outstanding actors. Charles Lanyer lends the entire film dimension and maturity as Raymond's veteran partner, a seen-it-all cop who teaches the rookie the ropes and is secure and wise enough to take in stride Raymond's homosexuality when it inevitably surfaces.

Michael Waite, who has a Billy Bob Thornton quality, is wonderful as a naive bisexual security guard who gives Jack shelter. Mitchell Grobeson, the Los Angeles Police Department sergeant who filed the first lawsuit in the U.S. by a law enforcement officer to prohibit discrimination based upon sexual orientation, has an effective cameo.

With a whopping 40 locations and 56 speaking parts, culminating in North Hollywood's El Portal theater, "Hard" had challenging logistics for a picture that cost only $87,000. With co-writer Matkowsky's resourceful camera work and a suitably ominous score composed by Huckert and Phil Settle, "Hard" proves that imagination and craftsmanship can still count for more than money.

NEW YORK POST, 3/26/99, p. 71, Rod Dreher

The wholly dreadful gay serial-killer thriller "Hard" begins unpromisingly enough with repulsive dialogue in the opening scenes: vomitous prattle about ingesting semen, locker-room haw-haw about an epileptic hooker with a menacing case of jaw spasms and a character's suave gambit for another man's affections. It's downhill from there.

Director John Huckert really puts the "low" in low-budget, mangling genre conventions as badly as his villain mutilates corpses, and staging sinister encounters in a sex torture dungeon that come off as grisly and disgusting without being the least bit chilling.

When a butch drifter who calls himself Jack (Malcolm Moorman) arrives in L.A., bodies begin piling up. He seduces men, mostly hustlers, and strangles them off screen.

The film is so amateurishly scripted that you suspect the violence isn't being shown not because director Huckert is discreet but because he can't figure out how to stage a killing.

The case falls to Ramon Vates (Noel Palomaria), a deeply closeted homicide detective. Ramon, unawares, brings Jack home.

Psycho Jack tauntingly outs himself as the killer and puts Ramon in a compromising position: In order to catch the killer, Ramon will have to tell his homophobic police colleagues that he's gay.

In the hands of a smarter director, this material could have been dynamite. But huckster Huckert is interested only in selling lurid exploitation.

"Hard" makes the notorious "Cruising" look good; it's a complete stiff.

VILLAGE VOICE, 3/30/99, p. 126, Dennis Lim

An explicitly gay serial-killer flick, *Hard* might be expected to counteract, or at least undermine, the dubious take on sexuality endemic to its Hollywood counterparts, from *Cruising* to *Basic Instinct* to *The Silence of the Lambs*. But as much as John Huckert's first feature strives for a mix of slasher chills and anti-hate emoting, the film's forte is clearly exploitation. Indeed, on its own lurid terms, *Hard* counts as a competent and confident example of low-budget genre moviemaking.

Mutilated bodies of young hustlers are piling up around Los Angeles. The killer (whose identity is established immediately) is a bearded, leather-jacketed gay drifter (Malcolm Moorland) who calls himself Jack. Raymond (Noel Palomaria), the young LAPD detective assigned to the case, is recently divorced and deeply closeted (not to mention surrounded by an entire precinct of raving homophobes). From this schematic setup, *Hard* proceeds to home in on the erotically charged relationship between hunter and hunted. (The film sticks to formula even in the details, down to the inevitable final descent into the killer's dank torture-chamber of horrors.)

Mid-investigation, Raymond is picked up by Jack, only to experience a particularly rude morning-after shock. Having handcuffed Raymond to the bed, Jack taunts the cop, steals his badge, and before long has implicated him in the murders. The only way for Raymond to clear his name and catch the killer is to do the unthinkable: come out at work. The film's main theme is self-loathing—it's what fuels the murderer's God complex, and it's at the heart of the cop's personal and professional dilemmas. It's also well-worn psychological terrain—which Huckert and his cowriter John Matkowsky bulldoze their way right through, opting for leaden declamations even when the subtext is sufficiently loaded. There's a racial component here, too— Raymond is Filipino American (he never uses his real name, Ramon, at work)—but the filmmakers don't factor this into the equation in any interesting way.

Hard is a triumph of resourcefulness more than anything else—Huckert also edited the film and cowrote the score, Matkowsky shot it and did the production design. The movie wants to be more than a genre piece (hence cringe-inducing laments like "Where does all the hate come from?"), but there are serial-killer-movie references strewn all over, often without any real purpose. The look, tone, and pace are freely informed by *Seven* and *Silence of the Lambs*. Early on, Jack charms his way into a creepy *Henry: Portrait of a Serial Killer* domestic situation. His absurdly casual body-disposal method is reminiscent of *Man Bites Dog*. The filmmakers' indiscriminate cut-and-paste approach lets them down most glaringly in the final scene, a standard but-is-he-really-dead? coda—in this case, it's a cheap parting shot that makes absolutely no sense.

Also reviewed in;
NEW YORK TIMES, 3/26/99, p. E29, Stephen Holden
VARIETY, 6/29-7/12/98, p. 41, Dennis Harvey

HARMONISTS, THE

A Miramax Films release of a Bavaria Film International and Betafilm presentation. *Executive Producer:* Joseph Vilsmaier. *Producer:* Hanno Huth, Reinhard Kloos, and Danny Krausz. *Director:* Joseph Vilsmaier. *Screenplay (German with English subtitles):* Klaus Richter. *Based on an idea by:* Juergen Buescher. *Director of Photography:* Joseph Vilsmaier. *Editor:* Peter R. Adam. *Music:* Harald Kloser. *Choreographer:* Regina Weber. *Sound:* Heinz Ebner. *Casting:* Barbara Voegel. *Production Designer:* Rolf Zehetbauer. *Art Director:* Bernhard Henrich. *Costumes:* Ute Hifinger. *Running time:* 114 minutes. *MPAA Rating:* R.

CAST: Ben Becker (Robert Biberti); Heino Ferch (Roman Cycowski); Ulrich Noethen (Harry Frommermann); Heinrich Schafmeister (Erich A. Collin); Max Tidof (Ari Leschnikoff); Kai Wiesinger (Erwin Bootz); Meret Becker (Erna Eggstein); Katja Riemann (Mary Cycowski); Dana Vavrova (Ursula Bootz); Noemi Fischer (Chantal); Otto Sander (Bruno Levy); Michaela

Rosen (Ramona); Guenter Lamprecht (Eric Charell); Gerard Samaan (Roman's Father); Rolf Hoppe (Streicher); Susi Nicoletti (Mrs. Grünbaum).

LOS ANGELES TIMES, 3/12/99, Calendar/p. 13, Kenneth Turan

Given its melodious title, it's not a shock that music is central to "The Harmonists," but what will be pleasantly surprising for most audiences is how charming and infectious the sounds it features turn out to be.

Set in Germany in the years between 1927 and 1934, "The Harmonists" is based on the career of the Comedian Harmonists, little known in this country but considered one of the great vocal ensembles of modern times. It's the seamless, syncopated vocalizing of the original Harmonists (remastered from vintage discs) that's heard on the soundtrack, and their sound turns out to be the film's most engaging character.

Inspired by an American group called the Revellers, the Harmonists specialized in intricate, insouciant five-part harmonies with piano accompaniment. Their lyrics couldn't be more insubstantial ("Veronica, spring has sprung, the girls are singing tra-la-la" ran one), but the way their voices blended was completely intoxicating and made the group an enormous success throughout Europe.

The modern interest in the Harmonists was sparked by a massive, eight-hour 1988 documentary by Eberhard Fechner called "Six Lives." Completely fascinating but never released in this country, it told one of those stranger-than-fiction stories that dramatic filmmakers can never resist retelling.

Directed by Joseph Vilsmaier ("Stalingrad") from a script by Klaus Richter, "The Harmonists" is not going to win any awards for originality. Predictably conventional and mainstream, it cheerfully serves up numerous stock situations, from love at first sight to neighbors banging so hard on a musician's walls that pictures fall off their hooks.

Yet such is the power of the Harmonists' music that even well-scrubbed stereotypes like prostitutes as glamorous as movie stars come off as good-natured and easy to take. And the story of the group's rise and fall is always involving, even when told in a way calculated not to mar a highly polished surface.

"The Harmonists" opens in 1928, with the group's triumphant Berlin debut. Germany may be in despair but, as a theatrical impresario tells the men, "the darker the times, the brighter the theater lights," and so the Harmonists' world avoids glimpses of bread lines in favor of monocles, cigarette holders and evening clothes.

From that night, the film flashes back to a year earlier and a young man named Harry Frommermann (Ulrich Noethen). He's so poor he eats the birdseed intended for his parrot Paganini, but Frommermann is a dazzling arranger, and he dreams of a vocal group that can breathe life into his charts.

A want ad corrals Robert Biberti (Ben Becker), a bass whose extensive music world contacts, including the serious former opera singer (Heino Ferch) and the Bulgarian singing waiter—Lothario Ari Leschnikoff (Max Tidof), soon bring the group to capacity.

"What I'm planning is totally new, at least in Germany," Frommermann announces, telling the men that his arrangements are not only extremely difficult but must be made to look easy. Months of overcoat-wearing rehearsals in unheated rooms, plus a stint in a cooperative brothel, follow, and though the group often chafes at the needed discipline, even bad feelings aren't too troublesome in "The Harmonists."

While all this is going on, the shy Frommermann is doing his best to court winsome record store clerk Erna Eggstein (Meret Becker), who also catches the eye of the much more decisive Biberti. Though both men prefer to avoid it, a romantic battle is clearly unavoidable.

Despite their considerable success, what is also in the offing is a confrontation with the omnipotent Nazi regime. At first the shadow of the swastika doesn't daunt the singers; they believe that, as Erna's Jewish employer Mr. Grunbaum puts it, "We still live in Germany, there is law and order here and it will stay that way."

But half of the Harmonists' six members are Jewish, and they soon learn that the regime's strict racial laws may prevent them from performing. As with the rest of the film, this dilemma is dramatized in a most conventional way, but the reality behind it adds intrinsic interest to the situation.

Time and again, however, it's that catchy music and re-creations of the group's long-forgotten stage numbers that come to the rescue of "The Harmonists." Both then and now, just hearing those inimitable sounds simply makes you smile.

NEW YORK, 3/22/99, p. 100, Peter Rainer

In 1927 Berlin, the legendary a cappella ensemble the Comedian Harmonists began an international career that abruptly ended seven years later; three of the vocalists, including its founder, Harry Frommermann, were Jewish. In many ways, the movie *The Harmonists* that German director Joseph Vilsmaier has made about these men is strictly Hollywood: The mild-mannered Harry and another singer, the blustery, cigar-chomping Biberti, are in love with the same woman; the group's rising fame is charted as if they were the Supremes; a few of the Nazis, such as the notorious Julius Streicher, are shown to have a soft spot for schmaltz; and so on. But the story of the Comedian Harmonists, who brought to the waning days of Weimar a bubbly frivolity, is a rich one. Rich enough to keep you watching and wanting to know more. The destruction of the arts in Germany by the Nazis is usually framed in terms of high culture. Here's an instance of pop culture being blown apart.

NEW YORK POST, 3/12/99, p. 47, Rod Dreher

If the story told in "The Harmonists" weren't true, it undoubtedly would have been invented for the movies. Whenever a scene in this pleasant but conventional German import seems too contrived, it helps to remember this stuff really did happen.

The "stuff" in question is the rise and fall of the Comedian Harmonists, a wildly popular Berlin singing group that was the toast of Europe before the Nazis came to power and forced a breakup. Much of the group's repertoire was written by Jewish or black composers—verboten under the new laws—and half the band was Jewish.

Joseph Vilsmaier's film shows the quintet (and their piano player) struggling to find their sound. The moment they hit the right notes—in a bluesy improv while drowning their sorrows in a bar—is beguilingly cheerful. The film follows the boys as they go from ragtag rehearsing in friendly bordellos to the most prestigious stages on the Continent. You could call this movie "Der Commitments."

Aside from the sweet-sounding songs, which are digitally remastered versions of original Comedian Harmonists recordings, what makes "The Harmonists" work is its deeply felt performances, which show the band's friendships to be as complicated as their harmonies. The offstage drama centers on tensions between Frommerman, the troupe's muse, and Robert Biberti (Ben Becker), the blond, barrel-chested bass who manages their money. Mousy Frommerman has been trying to romance a shop clerk named Erna Eggstein (Meret Becker), but Biberti won't be content to wait on Harry to make his move.

And the Nazis have even less patience with the group, its adoring public notwithstanding. There are heartbreaking scenes of the boys being harassed by the authorities as the imposition of cultural laws brings all artistic expression under the vise grip of the state. "The Harmonists" turns tragic when the group decides to put its faith in their popularity with the German people.

The print ads tout "The Harmonists" as "a true story that proves the voice is mightier than the sword." But that's exactly wrong. If anything, the film proves how insanely hard it is for friendship and marriage, to say nothing of art, to survive totalitarianism. The Comedian Harmonists were a merry flight of Jazz Age butterflies broken on history's grim wheel. It's a sentimental, lovely film.

NEWSDAY, 3/12/99, Part II/p. B11, John Anderson

With one brand new musical telling their story on Broadway, another by Barry Manilow apparently in the wings and a minor resurgence of their music on the radio (National Public Radio, at any rate), the Comedian Harmonists are enjoying one of those coalescing twitches in the zeitgeist. Which means that not many viewers will approach the film unaware that the group suffered professional murder at the hands of the Nazis. Or that they provide a near-perfect parable about the mismatch of naivete and evil.

Inspired by the black American group the Revellers, the Comedian Harmonists brought champagne-happy vocal music (which included their uncanny impersonation of musical instruments) to a German idiom—a mixed marriage, but a successful one. As music, it was four-fifths charm, one part facile sophistication. "This looks hard," one prospective member says of the group's arrangements. "What's worse," says founder Harry Frommermann (Ulrich Noethen), "is that it's supposed to sound easy."

Because we know what happens, Joseph Vilsmaier's dramatic version of the tale—from enormous struggle to enormous success to disbanding by Nazi edict because half the members were Jewish—carries a bittersweet aura. Every little triumph is doom postponed; the musical triumphs take on the overtones of tragedy. Although it occasionally bogs down in the sentimental morass of its characters' love lives, "The Harmonists" is a solid story with a moral purpose, a big, emotional musical finish and an air of fantasy that seems appropriate for a musical group—for that matter, a world—that shut its eyes to the political realities breathing down its neck.

As a reflection of the evils of Nazism, "The Harmonists" is as dramatically relevant as any we have this year—and this isn't suggested just because Noethen looks like a more urbane version of Roberto Benigni. Unlike the so-called "degenerate art" of Max Beckmann or Otto Dix that the Nazis banned, there was little furthering of frontiers in the Harmonists' music, just simple pleasure wrapped in five-part vocals. It's the most difficult kind of art to defend, of course, but that it would even come under the Third Reich's microscope exemplifies the relentless, useless waste perpetrated by hate.

But perhaps art for sensuality's sake is the most subversive act. If so, the Harmonists' humanizing/ syncopating of German music may have been perceived as the most degenerate of art. While the Revellers sang in American English, the Harmonists injected buoyant frivolity into a language not exactly known for its effervescent qualities. The promoters of the master race clearly couldn't handle the insult.

There's not enough music in "The Harmonists"—although this might be a misconception, since what is there is so infectious. The performances are uniformly good—particularly Noethen, Ben Becker as the thick-necked Robert Biberti, and Max Tidof, as the crazed Bulgarian member Ari Leschnikoff, sweet voiced and sex mad. It's interesting to imagine what Richard Lester ("A Hard Day's Night") might have done with the Comedian Harmonists, or even Alan Parker ("The Commitments"). But Vilsmaier has done well by them, making a movie that's musical and potent. With echoes.

VILLAGE VOICE, 3/16/99, p. 123, J. Hoberman

The Harmonists, as Joseph Vilsmaier's Comedian Harmonists has been retitled for American release, is framed as a sort of retrospective concert—the VH-1 of pre-V-1 Germany. It's the pinnacle of Berlin's Jazz Age, and an audience of swells in monocles and evening clothes anticipates the premiere of a hot vocal group. As the elegantly attired ensemble—two tenors, a baritone, a bass, and an imitator of orchestral instruments, accompanied by their pianist—burst into their lilting close harmonies, the crowd is transfixed.

What was old is new again. Like Germany itself, the pop stars whom The Harmonists' publicists are pleased to compare to the Beatles are back together and never was a group so appropriately named. With their trained voices, clockwork precision, and perfect pitch, the Comedian Harmonists invented a distinct form of Euro-scat—a sort of doowop lieder as convoluted as a fugue and as intimate as a whisper. The group's precise versions of American show tunes ("Night and Day") or syncopated German chestnuts ("Veronika") are both funny and glorious. The sound is stirring, yet soothing—the music of some celestial, hi-de-ho glockenspiel.

As the German movie of 1998, The Harmonists confirmed Vilsmaier, maker of the 1994 World War II superproduction Stalingrad, as the leading purveyor of the German nostalgia film. In its local context, The Harmonists celebrates the restoration of a lost cultural wholeness. A unified nation looks back and is delighted to find a mixed German-German Jewish-Balkan ensemble that was, once upon a time, the toast of Europe—until the Nazis came to power. Vilsmaier, a former cinematographer, clearly enjoys putting the period on widescreen display, although the glossy bits of Weimar depravity are tame even by comparison to Hollywood's Cabaret.

Less than the divine decadence suggested by its print ads, *The Harmonists* has the happily crass and vapid quality of an early 1950s Doris Day musical. Anyone familiar with the group's oeuvre will enjoy watching their stage act, rife with innuendos and visual humor, as recreated by actors lip-synching digital remasters from the original 78s. But, performances aside, the movie is dull and perfunctory. Harry Frommerman (Ulrich Noethen) conceives of the Comedian Harmonists; bluff Robert Biberti (Ben Becker) propels the group to the top. A requisite success montage allows the pre-rock-'n'-roll Harmonists to enjoy their fame—acting big and banging babes—and screenwriter Klaus Richter concocts a stale romantic subplot in which Harry and Robert compete for the affections of pert Erna Eggstein (Meret Becker) while waiting for the Nazis to appear.

We know that the driven little Harry is a Jew not only because he visits his deceased parents in a prophetically old and overgrown cemetery, but because he is into "irony." Robert, however, doesn't realize that the group has any other Jewish members until October 1933, when he's summoned to Nazi central, innocently wondering who are "our friends are in high places." The Harmonists struggle briefly with the New Order—at one point giving a command performance for Julius Streicher, the most rabid anti-Semite in the Nazi hierarchy. The premise of this sequence is so grotesque that I can only assume it's based on some kind of actual incident—the inference is that even the worst Nazi was a closet Harmonist fan.

Harassed by brownshirts, the band is invited to New York. In reality, the tour was something of a flop. In the movie, the Harmonists frolic like the Beatles in Central Park and perform aboard an aircraft carrier in New York Harbor. (It is symptomatic of Vilsmaier's benign history that he imagines a racially integrated U.S. navy in 1934.) The three Jewish Harmonists are tempted to remain in New York, but Robert persuades them to stage their breakup on German soil.

As detailed by Eberhard Fechner's definitive three-hour documentary (shown here in 1991 and ripe for reissue), the Jewish Harmonists then left for Vienna, toured the Soviet Union, recorded with Josephine Baker in Paris, and relocated briefly to Australia, before settling in the U.S. Meanwhile, the group's Aryan faction dropped their Jewish wives, recruited three new singers, and, changing their name to Der Meister Sextette, performed a more martial—as well as racially pure—form of pop, until they were banned again for their "Marxist tootling." As all this would have required considerable exposition, *The Harmonists* ends with a grand auf Wiedersehen concert and tearful farewells. The Jewish Harmonists head straight for America with the somewhat self-pitying suggestion that, although expelled from their homeland, they were the lucky ones.

Although the group's records were long available in West Germany, *The Harmonists* coincides with a new American interest. The staged concert *Band in Berlin* has opened this month, beating a rival show with music by Barry Manilow to Broadway. In Germany, Harmonist mania harks back to the last moment when East and West shared a permissible common culture. Here, perhaps, it is the longing for an honest-to-God, surefire Holocaust musical. Can anyone doubt that even now someone somewhere is writing songs for an imagined Broadway version of *Life Is Beautiful?*

Also reviewed in:
CHICAGO TRIBUNE, 3/19/99, Friday/p. P, John Petrakis
NEW REPUBLIC, 3/29/99, p. 28, Stanley Kaufmann
NEW YORK TIMES, 3/12/99, p. E14, Lawrence Van Gelder
VARIETY, 3/9-15/98, p. 41, Derek Elley
WASHINGTON POST, 3/19/99, Weekend/p. 42, Desson Howe

HAUNTING, THE

A Dreamworks Pictures release of a Roth/Arnold production. *Executive Producer:* Jan De Bont. *Producer:* Susan Arnold, Donna Arkoff Roth, and Colin Wilson. *Director:* Jan De Bont. *Screenplay:* David Self. *Based on the novel "The Haunting of Hill House" by:* Shirley Jackson. *Director of Photography:* Karl Walter Lindenlaub. *Editor:* Michael Kahn. *Music:* Jerry Goldsmith. *Music Editor:* Ken Hall. *Sound:* David MacMillan and (music) Bruce Botnick and Robert Fernandez. *Sound Editor:* Frank Eulner and Ethan Van der Ryn. *Casting:* Randi Hiller.

Production Designer: Eugenio Zanetti. *Art Director:* Tomás Voth. *Set Designer:* Andrea Dopaso, Easton Michael Smith, William Hawkins, Aric Lasher, Lori Rowbotham, Gerald Sullivan and Luis Hoyos. *Set Decorator:* Cindy Carr. *Set Dresser:* Tyler Patton. *Special Effects:* John Frazier. *Visual Effects:* Phil Tippett and Craig Hayes. *Costumes:* Ellen Mirojnick. *Make-up:* Cindy Jane Williams. *Make-up (Liam Neeson):* Jean A. Black. *Make-up (Special):* Greg Nicotero, Howard Berger, and Wayne Toth. *Stunt Coordinator:* Tim Davison. *Running time:* 117 minutes. *MPAA Rating:* PG-13.

CAST: Liam Neeson (Dr. David Marrow); Catherine Zeta-Jones (Theo); Owen Wilson (Luke Sanderson); Lili Taylor (Eleanor 'Nell' Vance); Bruce Dern (Mr. Dudley); Marian Seldes (Mrs. Dudley); Alix Koromzay (Mary Lambetta); Todd Field (Todd Hackett); Virginia Madsen (Jane); Michael Cavanaugh (Dr. Malcolm Keogh); Tom Irwin (Lou); Charles Gunning (Hugh Crain); Saul Priever (Ritchie); M.C. Gainey (Large Man); Hadley Eure (Carolyn Crain); Kadina Halliday (Rene Crain).

CHRISTIAN SCIENCE MONITOR, 7/23/99, p. 15, David Sterritt

Everyone enjoys a lively visit to a haunted house, as long as it's safely contained in a novel or a movie.

This doesn't mean everyone will line up to see Jan De Bont's picture, "The Haunting," which can't quite decide whether it's an out-and-out thriller, a psychological drama, or a systematic demonstration of the latest computer-generated effects. But it should attract big crowds for a weekend or two on the strength of its attractive stars and deliciously spooky setting.

Some literature buffs may also journey to their local multiplexes, drawn by the perennial appeal of Shirley Jackson's original novel "The Haunting of Hill House," first published 40 years ago. Not that director De Bont has much interest in the "beautifully written, quiet, cumulative shudders" that critic Dorothy Parker praised in Jackson's book.

De Bont specializes in fun-ride movies like "Speed" and "Twister," designed less for quiet shudders than jolting shocks. The DreamWorks team headed by him has wrought huge changes in Jackson's tale, starting with the premise that probably led her to write it. Her sardonic novel is a story of four discontented people haunted by their mistrustful minds. On the screen, "The Haunting" is a story of four discontented people haunted by the audiovisual technologies of a wealthy Hollywood studio.

Liam Neeson plays Dr. Marrow, a psychologist who studies fear. Deciding that shadowy Hill House is the ideal place for an experiment, he lures three strangers there under false pretenses. They think he's researching sleep disorders, and that his discoveries might cure the insomnia that motivated them to answer his phony ad. What he really plans is to scare them silly and study their behaviors.

The movie's biggest mystery is how such a hotshot psychologist could forget that people have ... psychology. From the moment they walk into Hill House, his unwitting subjects start responding to their surroundings and each other in complicated ways that have little to do with clinical graphs. If the movie allowed this to continue, it might have been as unpredictable as Jackson's novel, which takes the complexities of human nature as its abiding interest. But that would deprive the digital-effects department of a chance to show its stuff, so De Bont begins focusing on the book's more externalized aspects, such as the brooding atmosphere of the house.

Even here the picture falls short of Jackson's teeming imagination, paying more attention to a ponderous historical subplot—about a sweatshop operator who exploited children—than to the architecture of the house, whose supernatural qualities are described in the novel with almost mathematical precision, or the personality quirks that cause each character to experience the horror in a subtly different way.

This notwithstanding, the best reason to see "The Haunting" is the sheer sumptuousness of its creepy-crawly set designs. The second-best reason is Lili Taylor, whose sincerity and conviction could make any script come at least partly alive. Owen Wilson also has amusing moments as Marrow's only male subject, and Marian Seldes is wonderful as the gloomy old housekeeper who keeps the gloomy old house.

It's worth a footnote to mention that the movie's producers include Susan Arnold, whose father (Jack Arnold) directed fantasy classics like "Them!" and "The Incredible Shrinking Man," and Donna Arkoff Roth, whose father (Samuel Z. Arkoff) ran American International Pictures, once a cornucopia of low-budget horror epics. How many chills Hollywood managed to create before computer graphics were ever dreamed of!

LOS ANGELES TIMES, 7/23/99, Calendar/p. 15, Kenneth Turan

"The Haunting" is such a feeble fright fest that even its characters seem irked at it. "You brought us here to scare us, is that it?" is the disbelieving reaction of the lovely Theo (Catherine Zeta-Jones), a sentiment that people who end up watching the film instead of participating in it will likely share.

A picture with an impressive pedigree, "The Haunting" is based on Shirley Jackson's admired novel, "The Haunting of Hill House" and was expertly filmed under the same name by director Robert Wise with stars Julie Harris and Claire Bloom back in 1963.

But the current big-bucks version, directed by Jan De Bont ("Speed," "Twister," the abysmal "Speed 2: Cruise Control"), demonstrates that scaring people is harder than it looks. In fact, this "Haunting" almost serves as a reverse image of a successful film, demonstrating by what it lacks exactly what is needed to do things right.

While the original film sensibly featured a scientific type studying paranormal phenomena, this time around Dr. David Marrow (Liam Neeson) is investigating the dynamics of fear. What he tells his subjects, however, is that he's studying people who have trouble sleeping. "You don't tell rats they're actually in a maze," the doctor says in his own defense, ignoring the question of how you'd go about informing rats even if you wanted to.

Aside from the glamorous Theo, grandly introduced as a bisexual artist with a complicated love life but soon reduced by David Self's tepid script to Just Another Pretty Face, two other subjects face the music with the doctor.

One is Luke (Owen Wilson), a likable cynic who exists mainly to look cute. More central is the character of Eleanor, familiarly known as Nell (Lili Taylor), an initially tentative young woman who's spent the last decade caring for her dying, demanding mother.

These folks all gather in Hill House, a grand pile built in the Berkshires over one hundred years ago by Hugh Crain, a childless textile magnate who, like the owner of San Jose's Winchester Mystery House, just kept adding and adding to what was a fairly sizable mansion to begin with.

Though it's meant to be "The Haunting's" pride, that house is the source of problems. First of all, it doesn't take a study of the credits (which reveal it to be England's Harlaxton Manor) to know that architecturally this place has as much chance of being in the Berkshires as Buckingham Palace. Fright often depends on verisimilitude, and that gets sacrificed right off the bat.

More to the point, though Hill House's caretakers (Bruce Dern and Marian Seldes) moan and groan about needing to be miles away by dark, the plain fact is that this mansion is way too lavish and pristine, too sumptuous in its appointments, to unnerve anyone except a less-is-more devotee of the Bauhaus School.

Top-drawer production designer Eugenio Zanetti ("What Dreams May Come" and the Oscar-winning "Restoration") outdid himself here, filling some of the largest, most elaborate sets ever created with fabulous statuary, breathtaking furniture, doors the size of redwoods and a dazzling mirrored ballroom with a revolving floor.

The house is truly, as one of the characters says, "Charles Foster Kane meets the Munsters," but though decorators will no doubt be studying the video for years to come (with the sound off, to be sure), all that luxury turns out to have a deadening, soporific effect.

The same situation occurs with "The Haunting's" elaborate and expensive computer-generated special effects. Shapes form in curtains, immovable objects take on life, doors turn into arms and huge heads morph out of ceilings, but instead of making the film scary, all this technological gimmickry simply weighs it down.

The problem with computer-generated images in a film like "The Haunting" is that it's all too easy for filmmakers to believe that what money can buy is a suitable replacement for what money can't. If we just get the effects right, the feeling seems to be, the fright will take care of itself.

In fact, as the black and white original "Haunting" demonstrated, what makes a film scary has more to do with sensibility, conviction and an understanding of the dark places of the human psyche than an ability to orchestrate expensive set pieces. "The Haunting" has the hardware, but it takes more than that to terrify, even now.

NEW YORK, 8/2/99, p. 56, Peter Rainer

When it comes to putting horror on the screen, less is almost invariably more. In *The Haunting*, adapted from Shirley Jackson's novel *The Haunting of Hill House,* more is almost always less. It hurls so many special effects at us that after a very short while the audience feels under assault—it's more war movie than horror movie. The point of all this tumult is presumably to give us a thrill ride, but a certain condescension is built into the approach: By doing all the work for us, the filmmakers don't allow us to use our own imaginations. They must think pummeling trumps the power of suggestion. They couldn't be more wrong.

Shrieking together is one of the communal pleasures of watching a horror movie with a big audience. At the press screening I attended, the communion was all about laughter—of the unintended variety. (The audience seemed resolved to have a good time, even if it wasn't the kind the filmmakers were aiming for.) The silliness starts early, when Nell (Lili Taylor), a mousy shut-in who had been caring for her invalid mother, arrives at the forbidding 130-year-old Hill House, in a remote area of the Berkshires, to take part in what is misleadingly billed as an insomnia research study. She's ushered onto the grounds by the caretaker, played by—who else?—Bruce Dern. The mansion is supposed to be frightful, but the production designer, Eugenio Zanetti, under the guidance of director Jan De Bont, has gone hog-wild for Moroccan, Indian, Gothic, Neo-Classic, Baroque, Romanesque, Disney World-esque, Xanadu-esque, *Addams Family*- esque. (The sets were constructed in the same space in Long Beach, California, that once housed Howard Hughes's *Spruce Goose,* which must be some kind of poetic justice.) It's robber-baron kitsch, and in a comedy it might have made giddy sense. But the effect here is to suffocate the horror by piling on the ornateness. When the huge Moroccan doors and circular mirrored rooms start to rumble and sway, you figure that, for what they cost, they had *better* do something.

The real research study being conducted in Hill House is not about insomnia but about "the dynamics of fear." Besides Nell, the annoyingly intense Dr. David Marrow (Liam Neeson) has convened Luke (Owen Wilson), a wisecracking cynic who early on suspects the study is a sham, and Theo (Catherine Zeta-Jones), a bisexual gadabout who seems to have a change of clothes for every scene—no, make that every shot—she's in. Theo comes on to just about everyone and everything; even the statues and the moldings don't appear to be off-limits. With all this concupiscence at her disposal, why would this insomniac ever worry about sleeping? Dr. Marrow doesn't seem to notice Theo's allurements, though. He's too busy being dubious about all the clangings and clonkings Nell claims to be experiencing. Instead of trying to help the poor stricken woman by bundling her out of Hill House, he perseveres, which makes him something of a sadist, although the film just views him as "driven." With Marrow, the scientific method is just a little out of control, that's all. Kind of like filmmakers who don't know when enough is enough.

Jan De Bont made his fame as the director of *Speed* and *Twister*, and he brings to the party a smash-and-grab style that's almost at the opposite extreme from what Robert Wise brought to his 1963 version of Jackson's novel. Wise's *Haunting* was infinitely scarier, and the scares were almost all suggestive. Julie Harris as Nell was the neurasthenic spinster whose every twitch seemed to trigger a shift in the shadows; Claire Bloom's Theo was the lesbian as sloe-eyed Village sophisticate. What happened to these people mattered to us, because they were, well, *people*—not, as in De Bont's version, merely distractions from the décor. (De Bont's talented cast is almost uniformly awful, right on a par with the script; having given the worst performance of his career, Liam Neeson must feel relieved he can't sink any lower). Robert Wise had worked with the low-budget horror maestro Val Lewton in the forties on such genre classics as *Curse of the Cat People,* and he brought to *The Haunting* same spare stylistics. Like just about all good scare pictures, it included the audience as full collaborator, recognizing that what the director puts on the screen can never be quite as scary as what we might imagine.

It's a touching approach in retrospect. Imagine! Using a feather instead of a sledgehammer! Even back in 1963, Wise was already out of touch with the show-it-all shock tactics coming into vogue. (The film was not a commercial hit.) Today, much more so than three decades ago, a film like Wise's *Haunting* might seem like an affront to moviegoers who expect constant instant gratification. The pleasures of suggestion, of delayed gratification, seem lost on audiences, older as well as younger, who have been pounded into submission by movies until they think the pounding *is* the movie. The current whirlybird style of high-powered muscularity has crossed over from the Hollywood action picture into the horror genre: You come out of a movie like *The Haunting* or *The Mummy* feeling like you just sat through *Armageddon*. With its cheesy-scary monumentality, *The Mummy* was a big hit. Despite the laughter at the screening, *The Haunting* may end up a hit, too. If sensation is all, who cares if the sensations make any sense, or if they stay with you for even a millisecond after you leave the theater?

NEW YORK POST, 7/23/99, p. 51, Rod Dreher

"The Haunting" is a scream, all right, but in exactly the wrong way. A preview audience this week hooted and giggled through much of the alleged horror picture, and no wonder: It's so clumsy, bloated and wretchedly overdone that you laugh for the same reason you'd snicker at a hippopotamus in the Kentucky Derby.

Director Jan De Bont has spared no expense in this remake of the genuinely scary 1963 thriller of the same name (which in turn was based on Shirley Jackson's ghostly novella "The Haunting of Hill House"). The Pharaonically gaudy sets, dripping with rococo frippery, suggest Siegfried & Roy's dream home in Transylvania. And the computer-generated-effects budget in this insanely overproduced monstrosity must have run to eight figures.

But you can't order imagination from Industrial Light & Magic at any cost, and that's the one thing this movie disastrously lacks. Like this summer's occult smash "The Blair Witch Project," the original "Haunting" understood that what you can't see is far more frightening than what you can. For De Bont, more is more; his frenzied piling on of thrill-ride effects only makes the film's creative bankruptcy ever more conspicuous.

The drama, if you can call it that, takes place at a gloomy old pile in the Berkshires, where parapsychology researcher Dr. David Marrow (Liam Neeson) has gathered an unsuspecting threesome to the premises under the guise of doing sleep experiments. In fact, he wants to observe their fearful reactions when he plants a false scare story within the group.

Trouble is, Hill House really is haunted, and violently so. Though jockish Luke (Owen Wilson) and sexpot Theo (Catherine Zeta-Jones) both experience things going bang in the night, the poltergeist activity centers on mousy Eleanor (Lili Taylor). The poor dear has stumbled into the crucible of conflict between the demonic ghost of Hugh Crain, the mad robber baron who built Hill House, and the spirits of those he abused. No fair giving details, but be warned that the whole nightmare ends up in a hysterical showdown in which Lili Taylor takes a courageous stand for family values in the face of an unsympathetic demon.

She's less Sigourney battling the alien than Kathie Lee giving a press conference about sweatshops. Taylor has been taken prisoner by David Self's rotten screenplay, one that has her character express her modest personal ambitions by saying, "Adventures are for soldiers, and for women [that] bullfighters fall in love with."

De Bont, who proved his mettle as an action director with "Speed" and "Twister," badly mishandles his duties here. What made the original "Haunting" so intriguing was not only its supernatural suggestiveness (as opposed to the new version's ham-handed literalness), but also the story's eerie psychological dimension. You weren't sure what was real and what was imagined by the freaked-out protagonist. That's out the window here; it's all an in-your-face fun-house romp.

DreamWorks executives have suggested that the movie's computer-generated whirligigs had to be added to make "The Haunting" relevant to modern audiences. But the astonishing critical and box-office success of "The Blair Witch Project" shames Hollywood by exposing the emptiness of that argument.

"Blair Witch" is a no-budget horror flick that's scaring sellout houses around the country without benefit of stars, special effects or elaborate sets.

It says something about the state of Hollywood moviemaking when a major director and his leading studio are spectacularly shown up by two Florida film students and a cast of three unknowns.

NEWSDAY, 7/23/99, Part II/p. B3, John Anderson

Any discussion of "The Haunting"—Jan ("Speed") De Bont's hard-to-call-it-a-remake of the classic 1963 psycho-thriller—seems to require at least passing genuflection toward the current "Blair Witch Project." One is a movie that spares no animatronic advantage to more or less bludgeon you into a fright state. The other is genuinely terrifying because of what you never really know.

A personal preference, perhaps, but there's little question that "Blair Witch" is the truer heir to Robert Wise's original "Haunting," one of the scariest movies ever made (my brother and I, circa 9 and 10, slept in the same bed after one of its rare TV airings) and a film in which almost nothing overt occurs.

Whether it was the supernatural or mere madness at the heart of Wise's film although there was certainly something going on in that house—the creepiness created was purely psychological. Julie Harris, who seemed to accomplish the neat trick of walking erect while in a fetal position, was a weirdly ethereal narrator and star, and may have been warming up to play the Belle of Amherst, albeit one who could commune with the dead.

While the scariest thing in De Bont's film may be its art director's budget, it is an entertaining movie, energetic, even if the attempts to create a psychological infrastructure are blown off at the end in an orgy of special effects. Lili Taylor, re-creating the Harris role of Eleanor, is likable, but certainly no raw nerve. She is, by comparison, wide open, a naif. She, too, has cared long-term for a demanding invalid mother, been deprived of a life and, after all her service, is being tossed out of her apartment by an unfeeling sister (Virginia Madsen) and a badly written will. But she's far too self-possessed to be a convincing doormat, or as needy (a la Harris) as one expects a supernatural conduit to be.

But then, the setup is no longer about assembling a group of psychically sensitive souls to act as magnets for the demonic forces of Hill House. It's about an experiment in the "dynamics of fear" being conducted by Dr. David Marrow (Liam Neeson), who advertises for insomniacs—people with a high degree of "suggestibility"—so he can then subject them to a high-stakes round of mind games. As he tells his more ethics-minded assistant, Mary (Alix Koromzay), "You don't tell the rats they're in a maze." (The plot hook should have been our assumption that Marrow is behind the strange things that overtake the house, but De Bont—as if unable to resist—gives us glimpses right from the start of things his characters never see, thereby dulling the movie's psychological edge.) The other kids at the sleepover from hell include Theo (Catherine Zeta-Jones), a globe-trotting adventuress and flamboyant bisexual (an aspect only hinted at by the original's Claire Bloom); Todd (Todd Field), who takes Mary to the hospital after a vicious harpsichord attack and never returns, and Luke Sanderson (Owen Wilson), the resident wiseacre whose relentless stream of quips points up another disparity, not just between a movie like "Blair Witch" and "The Haunting" but between the '90s fright flick and its ancestry: Rather than horror films with comedy relief, we get comedies accessorized with shock cuts and gore. The audience laughs at the jokes, and then laughs again nervously after the cook with the cleaver (Marian Seldes) appears innocently behind the door.

When does it quiver in fear? Not too often, although Hill House itself is an architectural nightmare. Imagine Christopher Wren, Goya and King Ludwig of Bavaria taking a wrong turn at East Baroque and heading straight into South Rococo: Grecian column mating with Byzantine turrets beside Romanesque steeples atop English baronial gravity, everything multiplied like a triple exposure into structural madness (the house actually exists, we're told, near Lincolnshire, England). Inside, there are rooms with water, rooms that spin, rooms adorned with the faces of tortured satyrs and vacant cherubs, all of which come alive as the house attempts to expel the foreign agents within it.

The house, its visitors are told, was built by Hugh Crain, a Concord, Mass., textile manufacturer who wanted to fill the house with the laughter of children. How he went about it is at the root of the house's spiritual unhealth, which affects Eleanor much more so than the others—and for reasons presented by screenwriter David Self that were met at one recent screening with as much derisive laughter as greeted the first shot of the house's Hugh Crain portrait—something akin to Mr. Hyde-meets-the-Wolfman. It's a strange mix of literal-mindedness and fantasy that infects "The Haunting," which is enjoyable enough, but despite itself.

NEWSWEEK, 8/2/99, p. 63, David Ansen

A ghost has to work overtime to haunt Hill House, the gargantuan mansion Eugenio Zanetti designed for Jon De Bont's lavish remake of "The Haunting."The imposing Romanesque pile in the 1963 version (directed by Robert Wise) was a modest cottage compared with this looming, cavernous Gothic-Italianate-Moorish-Baroque hodgepodge. If something went bump in the night here, you'd never hear it: things have to rumble, screech and crash like a 50-car collision to get the attention of the three freaked-out human lab rats lured to the house by Dr. David Marrow (Liam Neeson) for his study on the physiology of fear.

The terrified trio consists of Lili Taylor (in the mother-dominated Julie Harris role), Catherine Zeta-Jones (as a sexually ambiguous jet-setter) and the amusingly quirky Owen Wilson (as the group skeptic). Keeping admirably straight faces, they must undergo an elaborate trial-by-special effects in this expensive-looking horror movie, which turns the original's scare strategy on its head. Where Wise worked by suggestion, never showing the spirits haunting Hill House, De Bont and his visual-effects team adopt a more-is-more philosophy. Doors turn into giant hands, walls sway, ceilings attack, statuary comes alive and the angry ghost of the house's dead patriarch rages around the mansion like a cyclone in De Bont's "Twister." It's all very impressive—and counterproductive. The more the computer-generated images take over, the sillier "The Haunting" gets. By the end, the computers have chased all the scares away.

Where the no-budget "The Blair Witch Project" shows how you can make something out of next to nothing—a camera, a forest, a few actors—the best-that-money-can-buy technology of "The Haunting" shows how little you can make of too much.

SIGHT AND SOUND, 11/99, p. 44, Kim Newman

Eleanor 'Nell' Vance devoted her life to the care of her recently deceased mother. One day a phone call draws her attention to an ad for volunteers for a study of insomnia. The study's supervisor Dr David Marrow is actually investigating fear and is assembling a small group of maladjusted adults to spend a week in Hill House. The reputedly haunted mansion was built in the 1870s by textiles tycoon Hugh Crain for the children he never had because of his wife's suicide.

At Hill House Nell meets sophisticated artist Theo and slacker Luke Sanderson, the other subjects of the experiment. After an accident involving a harpsichord drives Marrow's assistants away and a message of welcome is written in blood on a portrait, Nell becomes convinced the house is trying to communicate with her. She learns the ghosts are Hugh Crain and the many children he took out of his mills and murdered, but the others don't believe her. The subjects learn the nature of the experiment. Nell almost has a breakdown thanks to her persecution by the ghosts. The four try to escape the house, but the gates are chained and Luke is beheaded by a chimney flue. Nell stands up to the ghost of Hugh Crain—whom she realises is her great-great-great-grandfather and forces him to leave earthbound limbo for hell. As she lies dying, her soul joins the departing spirits of the children whom she has freed from Crain's tyranny.

Though director Jan De Bont must take the blame for *The Haunting*'s over elaborate visuals, unsuspenseful pace and mistimed scare scenes, David Self's dreadful script is the chief culprit in this botched remake of Robert Wise's 1963 film of Shirley Jackson's 1959 novel *The Haunting of Hill House*. Every single change, update and 'improvement' is a gross mistake that undoes Jackson's careful tapestry of fear and melancholy. The substitution of a bogus sleep experiment for the original's psychic investigation skews *The Haunting* seriously from the start: Liam Neeson's Dr Marrow comes across as an unsympathetic semi-villain and the film has to scuttle down a false trail in suggesting that he's faking the ghostling himself to prod his subjects into fear. (A rational pay-off would be as unthinkable in this context as a real ghost in a vintage *Scooby-Doo* episode.)

Although it's not crudely spelled out, the suggestion in the book and (to a lesser extent) in the first film is that Hill House is not haunted until Nell arrives. The remake, however, reconfigures the plot as a truly absurd mystery melodrama, with a mid-nineteenth-century baddie (a lookalike for the *Planet of the Apes'* Dr Zaius) who seems to have been half wicked Dickensian industrialist and half paedophile serial killer. The set-up here, with its three types of ghost, is so complex the film spends a lot more time having the luckless Lili Taylor as Nell explain it than it does being scary or insightful.

Like a lot of recent genre pictures, *The Haunting* is desperate to show how aware it is of its predecessors, co-opting bits from classic literary ghost stories by M. R. James, Oliver Onions and Wilkie Collins. This would be more appreciated if it weren't for the way the admittedly impressive gothic art direction (tormented cherubs in friezes, a revolving room like a giant music box, a fallen statue in a fountain, bedboards like cathedral frontages, and so on) keeps coming alive in unthreatening CGI to loom at the cast. *Rushmore*'s co-writer Owen Wilson, who works in an irrelevant rant about the Teletubbies, is summarily decapitated, and perhaps escapes most easily: One suspects he was allowed to do his own dialogue, which is much sharper than everyone else's. Neeson and Zeta-Jones are just lost, concentrating on their looks at the expense of characterisation.

It's a shame that this should be independent mainstay Lili Taylor's first shot at carrying a major studio film (though she is criminally billed fourth). She is one of the few actresses working today who might have matched Julie Harris' reading of the typical Jackson heroine, timid and introspective but with a perverse streak of strength. Her introductory scene, which finds her at the mercy of her horrid sister and a truly appalling child, establishes Nell perfectly. Throughout Taylor struggles to make the lines work, but she is defeated by passages where she is repeatedly called upon to channel the plot explanations. The finale, which has her confronting the black cloud of Hugh Crain and departing beautifully to heaven surrounded by glowing children, is kitsch eschatology far beyond even the bathes of *Ghost* or the horror-comedy of *The Frighteners*. It plays distinctly less well than the afterlife of Kenny in *South Park Bigger Longer & Uncut*. In a season that also includes *The Sixth Sense* and *The Blair Witch Project* both of which have no CGI effects and know a shout of 'Boo!' is only scary if it comes after a period of relative quiet— this bristling, attention-grabbing carnival funhouse of a picture hasn't got a snowball's chance in hell.

VILLAGE VOICE, 8/3/99, p. 59, J. Hoberman

Inspired amateurism and shoestring ingenuity may not be to every taste, but anyone who thinks *The Blair Witch Project* has been oversold should take a gander at this summer's big Hollywood psychological-horror flick. *The Haunting,* DreamWorks's high-powered version of the Shirley Jackson ghost story that was first filmed back in 1963, means to be something more than a loud and gory slimefest. But its anemic chills are only further diminished by the megamillions projected on the screen.

The Haunting's setup is the same as in its earlier incarnations, albeit less resonant and more irrational. An enthusiastic if unscrupulous professor engaged in some dubious form of research gathers together three neurotics in an isolated, spooky old New England mansion. The scientist is openly ghost-hunting; the ensuing supernatural occurrences are precipitated by the presence of his most disturbed subject, the childlike, lonely, and sexually repressed Nell, a no-longer-young woman recently set free after a decade caring for her demanding invalid mother.

It's a premise straight from Psych 101, but the 1963 movie (directed by Val Lewton alum Robert Wise) was a flop. Indeed, reporting on the audience hostility she observed during its release, Pauline Kael cited *The Haunting* as an example of a perfectly understandable movie that sailed over the heads of the new TV-addled audience. Be that as it may, director Jan De Bont and scriptwriter David Self have made certain that the DreamWorks remake will provide nothing whatsoever to think about. Whereas the supporting neurotic, Theo, was a deviously clairvoyant lesbian in the Wise film, she's played here by dishy Catherine Zeta-Jones as a vacuous clotheshorse; where Julie Harris's unloved and unlovable Nell was filled with rage, Lili Taylor is a spunky, big-hearted eccentric. (If Owen Wilson's bland third subject is an improvement, it's mainly because the part was played by teen idiot Russ Tamblyn in 1963.)

The single character with any complexity is the professor (despite being played by Liam Neeson in action enigma mode). Rather than chasing poltergeists, he's studying the human panic reflex under cover of gathering data on insomnia. The premise is less ridiculous than it is weirdly self-reflexive: Having planted what he terms an "experimental 'haunting' fiction" in the minds of his suggestible subjects, he has set himself up as a surrogate filmmaker—attempting to produce "group fear and hysteria."

Would that it were so. De Bont's two previous features—*Speed* and *Twister*—were elaborately visceral neo-disaster flicks. But *The Haunting* (remaking a movie that Steven Spielberg has cited as a favorite) is more ambitious. For much of the film, the digital effects are relatively restrained. Just as Nell is the focal point of much mild spookiness (spirits calling, chains rattling), so most of the directorial energy seems displaced onto the hugeness of the set. The haunted house is played by the monumentally gingerbread Harlaxton Manor in Lincolnshire, England, and the movie doesn't lack for swooping shots of the grounds—De Bont is far better at posh camera maneuvers than scene construction.

Flagging the movie's high aspirations, the house seems to be a museum bigger than the Met. The interiors are staggering: Nell and Theo's adjoining bedrooms seem a full football field apart (thus preventing De Bont from reusing the memorable Wise image of the two terrified women huddled together in bed). In addition to the requisite glaring portraits and malevolent Chippendale, the place features lysergically patterned floors, a small army of wide-eyed lacquered cherubs, a hall of mirrors within a built-in merry-go-round, and a full-sized pastiche of Rodin's *Gates of Hell*.

Every cornice is a dagger and each chandelier an invitation to an impaling, but that's as far as the power of suggestion goes. Once she starts to hallucinate, Nell finds a literal skeleton in the closet—rather than the traumas buried in her psyche. Still, Taylor has her best scenes ranting at her costars from the incomprehensible depths of her soon-to-be-universalized bad trip. *The Haunting* could almost have succeeded as a study in derangement had a greater distinction been made between Nell's consciousness and that of the other characters. As it is, the perspective shifts wildly from moment to moment.

The climactic *Walpurgisnacht* is so absurd that one might well miss the way in which the downbeat closer has been spun for Spielbergian uplift. The mansion turns out to have been built by the 19th-century king of New England's satanic mills and haunted by the ghosts of his abused child laborers. Hard to know just how Nell's sacrifice will help but, at least, "it's about family," as she declaims, having seen the light.

Also reviewed in:
CHICAGO TRIBUNE, 7/23/99, Friday/p. A, Michael Wilmington
NEW YORK TIMES, 7/23/99, p. E13, Janet Maslin
NEW YORKER, 8/2/99, p. 88, Anthony Lane
VARIETY, 7/26-8/1/99, p. 34, Todd McCarthy
WASHINGTON POST, 7/23/99, p. C1, Stephen Hunter
WASHINGTON POST, 7/23/99, Weekend/p. 38, Desson Howe

HEAD ON

A Strand Releasing release of a Great Scott production in association with the Australian Film Finance Corporation and the assistance of Film Victoria. *Producer:* Jane Scott. *Director:* Ana Kokkinos. *Screenplay:* Andrew Bovell, Ana Kokkinos, and Mira Robertson. *Based on the book "Loaded" by:* Christos Tsiolkas. *Director of Photography:* Jaems Grant. *Editor:* Jill Bilcock. *Music:* Ollie Olsen. *Choreographer:* Zois Tsikas. *Sound:* Craig Carter, Livia Ruzic, and (music) Roger Savage. *Casting:* Dina Mann. *Production Designer:* Nikki Di Falco. *Art Director:* Paul Heath. *Costumes:* Anna Borghesi. *Make-up:* Christine Miller. *Stunt Coordinator:* Zev Eleftheriou. *Running time:* 104 minutes. *MPAA Rating:* Not Rated.

CAST: Alex Dimitriades (Ari); Paul Capsis (Johnny, 'Toula'); Julian Garner (Sean); Elena Mandalis (Betty); Tony Nikolakopoulos (Dimitri); Damien Fotiou (Joe); Eugenia Fragos (Sofia); Dora Kaskanis (Dina); Maria Mercedes (Tasia); Alex Papps (Peter); Vassili Zappa

(Vassili); Andrea Mandalis (Alex); Chris Kagiaros (Groom); Ourania Sideropoulos (Bride); Anthony Lyritzis (Boy in Car); Ana Gonzalez (Woman Sweeping); Maya Stange (Janet); Aimee Robertson (Nose Ring Girl); Nathan Farinella (Young Ari); Paul Farinella (Young Peter); Allan Q (Vietnamese Man); Aris Gounaris (Dealer); Fiv Antoniou (Card Player); Nicholas Polites (Costa); Wasim Sabra (Charlie); Robert Henry Price (Fishing Cap Man); John Rakkas (Barman); Katerina Kotsonis (Ariadne); Nicholas Pantazopoulos (George); Michael Psomiadis (Grey Beard); Nikos Psaltopoulos (Stav); Chrystal Kyprianou (Mary); Diana Stathis (Woman); Marnie Statkus (Punk Girl); Costas Kilias (Taxi Driver); Ayda Daher (Charlie's Mum); Neil Pigot (Senior Constable); Fonda Goniadis (Wog Cop); Gary McMahon (Thin Man); Okan Husnu (Rat); Blake Osborn (Good-Looking Guy); David Chisholm (Shaved Head).

LOS ANGELES TIMES, 9/3/99, Calendar/p. 6, Kevin Thomas

Ana Kokkinos' "Head On" plunges straight into the eye of the storm that is the life of Ari (Alex Dimitriades), a handsome, ultra-masculine gay 19-year-old Greek Australian youth who finds himself in rapidly escalating conflict with his claustrophobic ethnic community, with its strong machismo and allegiance to rigid family values. Anyone of any generation who has ever felt at odds with his or her environment can identify with the characters in "Head On."

"Head On" spotlights a new star in Dimitriades, who has already been summoned to Hollywood, and marks an impressive feature debut for Kokkinos, who first came to international attention five years ago with her powerful short film "Only the Brave," also a coming-of-age odyssey involving a Greek Australian lesbian.

Adapted from Christos Tsiolkas' novel "Loaded," the film unfolds in Melbourne in the course of 24 hours—a fitting adherence to the Aristotelian unities, intended or not—during which one incident after another is propelling Ari toward an inescapable confrontation with himself. He's a layabout in his immigrant parents' home, certain that there are no decent jobs available to him and determined not to take the menial work that's always accompanied by bigotry aimed at minorities; he's not made the connection that his life is stalled because he feels compelled to stay in the closet, open only with a drag-queen pal Johnny (Paul Capsis), who's as gutsy as he is reckless, and with his friend Betty (Elena Mandalis). Ari loves Betty but cannot connect with her sexually. Ari and Betty are increasingly turning to drugs for escape.

Photographed by Jaems Grant in rich, dark hues in images and movements that convey perfectly the chaos enveloping Ari, "Head On" captures the oppressiveness of his existence in his volatile relationship with his hard-working father, Dimitri (Tony Nikolakopoulos), an expansive bear of a man; and his loving, hyper mother, Sophia (Eugenia Fragos).

Naturally, Ari and his younger sister Alex (Andrea Mandalis) want to go out on their own, but their parents still believe the family should go out together. Whether in homes or clubs there's so much Greek music and dancing that its communal warmth and high spirits become suffocating—the hard-edged rock music that attracts Ari and his friends never sounded so welcome. In any event, Ari soon breaks away from his parents to go out on the town, which means a rush of drugs and back-alley sex that is invariably a struggle for dominance in which Ari rejects all possibilities of tenderness as weakness; sex for him is in fact a way of releasing his ever-present rage and frustration.

Through Ari's journey toward self-discovery, we discover the terrific pressure on young people to marry; the lingering, ferocious hatred of some Anglos toward Greek immigrants—and of Greek hatred of Asian newcomers.). Hypocrisy runs rampant in Ari's world, and Ari's perceptive Aunt Tasia (Maria Mercedes) utters the film's key line when she bluntly tells her nephew: "Find a girl, get married, and then it doesn't matter what you do." Later on, after receiving a savage beating from a homophobic cop of Greek origin (under the enraged gaze of an Anglo cop, both homophobic and xenophobic), Johnny tells Ari that "you've got to stand up against hypocrisy; it's the only way you'll make a difference."

When we take leave of Ari neither he nor we know whether he will ever be capable of giving and receiving love from another man or of attaining the courage of Johnny. But he's been faced with these choices and he can no longer escape self-knowledge, even if it should ultimately destroy him.

NEW YORK POST, 8/13/99, p. 62, Rod Dreher

Despite a title ripe for Beavis-style wisecracks, "Head On" is a surprisingly sophisticated gay coming-of-age drama. In terms of storytelling and production values, it's miles ahead of the recent crop of ploddingly earnest gay pictures, though its shallow protagonist quickly grows tiresome, and its frequent episodes of raunchy sex are gross and distasteful.

Ari (Alex Dimitriades) is a restless 19-year-old gay man living with his parents in a Greek immigrant community in Australia. He's deeply closeted, meeting men for furtive anonymous encounters in alleyways and bathrooms, while maintaining a pretense of heterosexuality for his friends and family.

"Head On"—the title describes director Ana Kokkinos' filmmaking style, obviously influenced by the "Trainspotting" lads—follows a day in the life of Ari as his anger, frustration and petulance lead him through a series of lurid sex-and-drugs adventures.

Ari's problems have to do with his family's high expectations. They fought and scrimped and saved to give him a good life in Australia, and here he is a jobless, party-boy layabout. Ari knows he'll never fit in with the traditional Greek subculture, yet he doesn't want to shed his Greek identity.

So he loses himself in massive amounts of drugs and equal quantities of sex ("Head On" seems like a kitchen-sink of teenage acting-out). It's a form of daddy-hating rebellion which every young male goes through, though it generally does not lead to repulsive encounters with obese grocery men behind garbage bins. The film isn't rated, but the Quad Cinema is not letting in anyone under 18, owing to the soft-core porn element in many scenes.

"Head On" seems to treat Ari as a tragic character, a man whose hatred of his own father completely controls his emotional life. Ari debauches himself by having sex with strangers in public places as a way of asserting his own freedom. But he's far too dull and bratty to rise to the level of tragedy. In the end, he blames Daddy for everything. Yawn.

Actor Alex Dimitriades shows great confidence and flair, but his irritating character wears out our sympathy long before the movie ends. Dimitriades is strikingly handsome, and flashes plenty of attitude, but the emotional stakes are too high in this story to build a sympathetic character on the basis of style and attitude alone.

SIGHT AND SOUND, 11/99, p. 46, Mark Sinker

Australia, the present. After attending a Greek wedding, young Greek-Australian Ari stays over at his brother Peter's flat, where he meets Sean. Home again, he finds his father Dimitri angry and mother Sofia worried. He leaves, scores some drugs, which he loses, gambles some money he borrows from his friend Johnny, buys more drugs and sells them to Joe. Joe's mother Tasia tells him his fortune: someone called 'S' wishes to care for him. He tells Tasia he intends to leave home. Back home, Ari's sister Alex tells him she's going to have sex with her boyfriend Charlie that night. After Dimitri and Ari dance an authentic Greek dance, the family sit down to a meal, which is curtailed by arguments.

At Tasia's, Joe and Dina announce their engagement. Ari does drugs with Dina and has partial sex with Betty. Sofia tries to dissuade Ari from leaving home. After dropping Alex off with Charlie, Ari goes to a club where he meets Sean. He leaves when Johnny arrives in drag; Sean follows him and says he loves him. Taking a taxi with Johnny, Ari checks up on Alex and Charlie, but Alex makes him go. The taxi runs a red light; Ari and Johnny taunt the police and end up in a cell. Johnny is beaten up by a sergeant. Released with Johnny, Ari goes to a club where he meets Sean. At Sean's, they have sex, until Ari starts a fight, is beaten and thrown out. He dances, Greek-style, on the docks.

"I don't take it up the arse," says Ari to Betty. "Course you do," says Betty. "You're Greek. We all take it up the arse." A pitiless study of the conflict between freedom and identity, Ana Kokkinos' debut feature is not so much about what it's like to be young, Greek and gay in Australia today as it is about what it's like to *detest* being young, Greek and gay in Australia today. Ari and his friends refer to their fellow Greeks as "dumbfuck wogs", not as some in-your-face insult appropriation, but more from misery and self-disgust. Of all those around him, Ari can best use his looks and grace to slip across frontiers and dodge the ties that bind, and in doing so arouses admiration and panicked hostility in his friends and relatives. In particular his father, a working-class Marxist, is reduced to bombastic lectures on work, responsibility and earning the right to freedom. But less strident requests that he compromise are even less convincing to Ari: at least his father's insults make him stronger, and respect the threat he poses.

"This isn't Europe any more: we're in Asia!" Ari yells from the car at passersby—and *Head On*'s visual style confirms this, at times resembling the lunge and blur of cinematographer Chris Doyle's work with Wong Kar-Wai, establishing around Ari a sense of drug-induced solipsism (although it's less the lacerated melancholia of Wong's films than a self-absorption born of a furious if inarticulate idealism). It's not that Ari doesn't believe in better things, rather that he refuses to believe that his father's value—or for that matter anyone else's—amount to much more than a half-baked collusion with self-hatred, a plea for the gentrification of the soul. Yet Ari well knows he often fails to live up even to his own truths. By forcing Sean to beat and reject him, he appears to be punishing himself for not standing by Johnny, while he recognises the wrongness of his earlier over-protective intrusion on his sister Alex's freedom ("You're worse than Dad," she tells him).

The history of the youth movie is the (often enjoyable) history of the recuperation of Jean Genet as the poet of outlaw love, from Brando's *Wild One* all the way up to the Shangri-Las "Leader of the Pack" ("He's good-bad, but not evil"). But *Head On* could not be less of a rites-of-passage/getting-of-wisdom movie—the poetry and pain of outsider love are not redeemed, no haven of loving acceptance is found, no possibility of reconciliation is glimpsed. For importantly (and impressively) Kokkinos has placed centre stage that element in Genet most commonly side-stepped as wholly unpalatable: his "original and disturbing notion that homosexuality is congenial to betrayal and, further, that betrayal gives homosexuality its moral value," as critic Leo Bersani put it in *Homos*.

Ari, as he himself insists, is no poet, no scholar. He barely knows why he does what he does, only that he must do whatever his emotions tell him. Perhaps to drive this home, Kokkinos' approach to narrative is intense and sometimes over-condensed. The movie is compact, its surface polished, unyielding and unforgiving, and viewers will surely find in it a reflection of their personal obsessions, possibly mistaking this for deep content. Certainly the centrality of Genet's influence that's proposed here is in no way a clarification of his perhaps irresponsible commitment to betrayal as a radical political act—indeed some will consider it more a critique than an endorsement. But equally, *Head On* is seductively clear about the lyricism, and lure of pure irresponsibility and about the cruel light this sheds in on all those who resist lyricism and lure and build such resistance into their politics.

VILLAGE VOICE, 8/17/99, p. 68, Jessica Winter

Speaking of eyes wide shut, the erotic encounters in *Head On* are soaked with the strip-club reds and blues that permeate the Kubrick film (and your average Showtime late movie), and just like Tom, our hero cruises at night but doesn't get laid. *Head On*'s Ari is gay and Greek in Australia, and though a well-meaning friend tells him, "Fuck politics. Let's dance," the surly heartthrob sports a chip on his well-muscled shoulder to rival the most dangerous Backstreet Boy, or even the young Donnie Wahlberg. The movie trails Ari for 24 restless hours as he spars with his old-world parents, jaws with his lethargic friends, and surfs the local bars and dance clubs, while spastic handheld cameras, smeary slo-mo interludes, and incessant jump-cutting try to foist a sense of urgency on the proceedings. Ari seems to be heading toward a happy ending, but the film's close is grim and ambivalent, a choice that would be commendable if the movie had not so stubbornly held the same dour tone for two hours already, and if Ari weren't as boring as he is bored.

Also reviewed in:
CHICAGO TRIBUNE, 10/22/99, Friday/p. M, Michael Wilmington
NEW YORK TIMES, 8/13/99, p. E24, Stephen Holden
VARIETY, 6/8-14/98, p. 69, David Stratton

HELL'S KITCHEN

A Cowboy Booking International release. *Producer:* Tony Cinciripini, Valerie Bienas, and Randy Gardner. *Director:* Tony Cinciripini. *Screenplay:* Tony Cinciripini. *Director of Photography:* Michael Spiller. *Editor:* Steve Silkensen. *Music:* Joseph Arthur. *Production Designer:* Natalie Bienas. *Running time:* 101 minutes. *MPAA Rating:* Not Rated.

CAST: Rosanna Arquette (Liz); William Forsythe (Lou); Angelina Jolie (Gloria); Mekhi Phifer (Johnny); Johnny Whitworth (Patty); Stepehn Payne (Boyle); Jade Yorker (Ricky).

NEW YORK POST, 12/3/99, p. 50, Jonathan Foreman

Everything about "Hell's Kitchen"—a slow-moving crime film that piles cliché upon cliché—seems third-hand and out of date. It's as if an alien receiving TV signals from 20 years ago tried to make an American gangster movie.

It begins with a gang attempting a burglary, during which one of them is killed. Johnny (Mekhi Phifer) is arrested and does time. On his release one of the prison officials sets him up with boxing trainer/manager Lou (William Forsythe).

Johnny's career races forward until he's asked to throw a fight by a crooked promoter. But he's more worried about Gloria (Angelina Jolie), the sister of the kid who was killed in the burglary. Johnny likes her but she blames him for her brother's death and wants him dead.

Meanwhile, her boyfriend Patty (Johnny Whitworth), another member of the gang, has started sleeping with Gloria's junkie mother (Rosanna Arquette).

Cinciripini's writing is simply atrocious. The dialogue's ludicrously fake-sounding and everyone speaks in a hopelessly bad Noo Yawk accent.

Phifer has such presence that the film almost comes to life when he's on screen.

Although the film is well-lit, Cinciripini's heavy-handed direction ensures that everyone shouts as if they're in a spoof of a John Cassavetes film.

It's a mystery how such an impressive cast could end up in such a lame project.

VILLAGE VOICE, 12/7/99, p. 149, Jessica Winter

Matching *A Map of the World* in bad justice and penny-dreadful melotrauma, *Hell's Kitchen* pokes its craven snout around the wreckage of a drug deal gone awry: Kids die, an innocent man (Mekhi Phifer) goes to prison, a grieving mom (Rosanna Arquette) seeks refuge in drugs. Angelina Jolie, as Arquette's daughter, nabs the tastiest bits, including teary confrontation ("You killed my brudda!") and not one but two chances to catch her boyfriend nailing her mother ("You fucked my mudda!"). You can't possibly hate a movie this thunderously stupid.

Also reviewed in:
NEW YORK TIMES, 12/3/99, Lawrence Van Gelder
VARIETY, 12/21/98-1/3/99, p. 79, Leonard Klady

HIDEOUS KINKY

A Stratosphere Entertainment release of a The Film Consortium and BBC Films presentation in association with the Arts Council of England of a Greenpoint film co-produced with L. Films and AMLF developed with the assistance of BBC Films/Greenpoint Films and with the support of The European Script Fund supported by the National Lottery through the Arts Council of England. *Executive Producer:* Mark Shivas and Simon Relph. *Producer:* Ann Scott. *Director:* Gillies MacKinnon. *Screenplay:* Billy MacKinnon. *Based on the novel by:* Esther Freud. *Director of Photography:* John de Borman. *Editor:* Pia Di Ciaula. *Music:* John Keane. *Sound:* Bruno Charier. *Sound Editor:* Zane Hayward. *Casting:* Susie Figgis. *Production Designer:* Louise

Marzaroli and Pierre Gompertz. *Art Director:* Jon Henson. *Costumes:* Kate Carin. *Make-up:* Mel Gibson. *Stunt Coordinator:* Stuart St. Paul. *Running time:* 99 minutes. *MPAA Rating:* R.

CAST: Kate Winslet (Julia); Saïd Taghmaoui (Bilal); Bella Riza (Bea); Carrie Mullan (Lucy); Pierre Clémenti (Jean-Louis Santoni); Abigail Cruttenden (Charlotte); Almed Boulane (Ben Saïd); Sira Stampe (Eva); Amidou (Sufi Sheikh); Michelle Fairley (Patricia); Kevin McKidd (Henning); Peter Youngblood Hills (Hippy); Mohcine Barmouni (Aziz); Annouar Zrika (Hicham); Mohamed Chekaoui (Hadaoui); Abderrahim Bergache (Doctor); Khaldi Cherif (Village Elder); Ahmed Madha (Poet); Frédérique Zepter (Translator); Salah-Dine Fenijirou (Blank Clerk); Roukia Bent H'Mad (Bilal's Wife); Hassan Bajja (Policeman); Abdellatif Jamal Saadi (Sufi Gate Man); Lisa Orgolini and David Baxt (Tourists); Abdelkader Lotfi (Ticket Clerk).

LOS ANGELES TIMES, 4/16/99, Calendar/p. 12, Kevin Thomas

How do you follow up the most successful film of all time? If you're "Titanic" star Kate Winslet, you return to making the distinctive, venturesome small films that established your career. Indeed, "Hideous Kinky" is the riskiest picture Winslet has made since "Heavenly Creatures," the surreal New Zealand feature about real-life teen killers, which first brought her international acclaim in 1994.

Winslet plays Julia, a 25-year-old woman who has fled to Marrakech, Morocco, from London, where her lover, a famous, trendy writer-poet, has moved on to more women (and more children). The time is 1972, and Julia, a creature of the '60s, craves new experiences, a fresh start and inner peace.

She is determined not to be daunted by her lack of funds, severely limited means of employment and decidedly erratic child support payments from her ex-lover. Julia is a lovely, intelligent woman, brave and open to life, but her financial situation is perilous in the utmost.

Then along comes Bilal (Said Taghmaoui), a wiry, exuberant acrobatic street performer who quickly wins the hearts of Julia and her girls, serious, wise-beyond-her-eight-years Bea (Bella Riza) and Lucy (Carrie Mullan), an adorable 6-year-old. Bilal moves in with Julia and her daughters in the Hotel Moulay, the epitome of picturesque poverty though in reality a tenement popular with local prostitutes. Bilal takes a brutal job in a rock quarry, but soon the lovers and the kids are off on a series of adventures.

"Hideous Kinky" was directed by Gillies MacKinnon, a Scotsman with an idiosyncratic filmography that includes "The Playboys," "A Simple Twist of Fate" (a reworking of "Silas Marner" with Steve Martin), "Small Faces," "Trojan Eddie" and "Regeneration," every one of them dealing with unconventional or marginalized lives. This film was adapted by MacKinnon's brother, Billy, from Esther Freud's acclaimed 1992 semi-autobiographical novel. (Freud is the daughter of painter Lucian and great-granddaughter of Sigmund.)

Lucy was Freud's alter ego, and she has explained that she and her older sister loved the word "hideous" and that it and "kinky" were favorites of a friend of her mother. "To us, the words meant anything beautiful, absurd or frightening," wrote Freud in her novel, and that pretty well describes this film and Julia's odyssey.

By and large the film establishes a tone of adventure recollected with humor and high spirits, but as it progresses it does not soft-pedal the fact that Julia gets herself and her daughters into one potentially, disastrous situation after another. The girls are pretty good-natured, all things considered, though Bea is not afraid to speak out and question her mother's judgment. You sympathize entirely with Bea when she says, "I want to go to school, I don't want another adventure." Yet there is some truth to Julia's belief that living on the edge in Morocco beats working 14 hours a day in London "with nothing to show for it" and the girls watching too much TV.

The role of Julia allows Winslet a wide range, for this woman is endearing and exasperating, heroic and foolish, often all at the same time but ever-admirable for the value she places on self-knowledge. Winslet's co-stars are equal to her in well-written roles.

With its authentic locales, "Hideous Kinky," photographed by John de Borman, is gorgeous and exotic. Romantic and blithe in spirit, "Hideous Kinky" arguably rambles too much for its own good. Just like its heroine.

NEW YORK, 4/26/99, p. 74, Peter Rainer

What must Kate Winslet think? As one half of the romantic team in the biggest-grossing movie of all time, she might reasonably, expect something like hysteria surrounding her next screen appearance.

Leonardo DiCaprio and his posse, after all, are trailed by the press from here to Timbuktu; his upcoming movie projects, his salary, his main squeezes, are examined with the kind of scrutiny, normally, reserved only for the chief executive of our land. Meanwhile, here's Winslet in a new movie, *Hideous Kinky*, playing an English mother with her two daughters in Morocco—and no tom-toms are sounded.

It's as if the success of *Titanic* was linked in the popular imagination entirely to DiCaprio, with Winslet the lucky stiff who just happened to be cast alongside him. The deafening near-silence in the press surrounding the post-Titanic Winslet—except, tellingly, for the snipes about her "weight problem"—is a slap in the face to an accomplished actress.

Standards of beauty tend to go in and out of phase, and what I fear may soon be upon us is another stultifying cycle of movie-star-looking movie stars: Call it the Gwyneth Syndrome. We've been down this road before. In the Grace Kelly fifties, the height of attractiveness was how well you looked in a tiara. The waxworks handsomeness and hyperprettiness of many of the Hollywood screen actors of the sixties—the Doris Day-Rock Hudson era—was a big reason why films from that period were so bland. I have nothing against movie-star beauty, but is it asking too much for a little something to be going on behind the stars' eyes? One of the most exciting developments in movies over the past few decades has been the opening-up of acting—of stardom—to the less-than-picture-perfect types. It enlarges the range of experience on the screen. (The great movies of the early seventies are unthinkable without the collection of unruly faces they introduced.) How depressing—how patrician—it would be to return to a celebration of glossy, whittled physical perfection.

In the current pop-celeb derby, Kate Winslet loses out to Gywneth Paltrow's tiara twinkle. This despite the fact that, aside from *Titanic,* where she managed to hold her own with the boat, Winslet's work in *Heavenly Creatures* and *Sense and Sensibility* and *Jude* and *Hamlet* show her off to be the better actress. Not to mention being the one with the authentic British accent. But authenticity may not be as valued these days as the sparkling counterfeit, and Winslet, unless James Cameron cooks up some kind of DiCaprio-ized prequel to *Titanic,* is probably slated for an unglitzy career in which she is merely excellent.

Her new film is a no-stars, non-Hollywood, medium-budget affair. It seems an odd follow-up to *Titanic*—but that may be the point. *Hideous Kinky* is the un-*Titanic.*

It's far from great, but it gives Winslet a chance to explore different sides of her talent. (Her next film, due at the end of the year, co-stars Harvey Keitel and is directed by Jane Campion; I hope this doesn't mean she'll be playing a mute.) In our megabucks movie climate, it takes courage for a hot commodity to refrain from inserting herself into the next empty blockbuster; but what may take more courage in the long run is trying to extend one's craft. You can, after all, be just as unadventurous in an empty small movie as in an empty big one.

In *Hideous Kinky,* set in 1972, Winslet is playing Julia, who has left London with her two small daughters (Carrie Mullan and Bella Riza) for the all-spice exotica of Marrakech. Surviving tenuously on checks from her British ex-lover, a playboy poet and the father of her girls, Julia camps out in a hotel peopled by prostitutes who filch her undies and then contemptuously swagger about in them in full view of her. For her daughters, Marrakech is an *Arabian Nights* adventure, but Julia seeks enlightenment from a Sufi in Algeria. To reach him, she drags her kids through escapades in a remote mountain village, and then a Moorish villa occupied by European émigrés who seem to have stepped out of a Paul Bowles story. (Their host is played by Pierre Clémenti, best remembered as the leather-jacketed john with steel-capped teeth in Buñuel's *Belle de Jour.*) She takes up with a Moroccan acrobat (Saïd Taghmaoui) who keeps appearing and reappearing throughout the odyssey as a combination stud muffin and guardian angel.

Winslet captures the ways in which Julia's allegiances are always in flux. She cares for her children, but she's part child herself; she resents how being a mother breaks her own self-absorbed gaze. Gillies MacKinnon, directing from a script by Billy MacKinnon based on a novel by Esther Freud, doesn't soft-pedal the irresponsibility behind Julia's wanderlust, and yet you can't entirely blame her. The people and the landscape and its colorations—which at times resemble Matisse's Moroccan paintings—pull us in, too. Julia's children, who are under no illusion that they are on the road to salvation, are more clearheaded than she is. One of the movie's continuing jokes is that Julia becomes more childlike as her daughters come to resemble miniature Englishwomen of breeding. A sensualist who has eroticized her own spiritual quest, Julia's the apotheosis of hippieness.

It augurs well for the long-term integrity of her career that Winslet in this movie doesn't try to ingratiate herself with the audience; a role like this needs to be approached honestly—with an appreciation for the ways in which wantonness can fog our good sense. Near the end of her quest, Julia says, "I want to know the truth," but she doesn't, really. She's just looking for a more aromatic species of lie.

NEW YORK POST, 4/16/99, p. 48, Jonathan Foreman

The lovely-looking but slow-moving and undramatic "Hideous Kinky" works wonderfully as a photographic love letter to a sanitized, superficial Morocco but not at all as a movie.

Set in the early '70s, it is based on Esther Freud's autobiographical novel about two little girls dragged around that country by their dippy-hippie mother.

But the MacKinnon brothers focus more on the mother than the children, and halfheartedly transform a story about the price of parental irresponsibility into a thinly sketched cross-cultural romance.

Julia (Kate Winslet) is a self-obsessed, amazingly unobservant single mom who leaves London with her two little girls in order to find and/or lose herself in Marrakesh.

A typical hippie traveler of the time, she wears the local clothes (they look great against her tan) but has acquired no real knowledge of the language or culture.

Her two little daughters, Bea and Lucy (played with assurance by Bella Riza and Carrie Mullan), are more perceptive and have more common sense than she does, and they are miserable.

Julia takes Bilal, a drifter-cum-acrobat (Said Taghmaoui from "La Haine")—whom she meets in the street—as a lover. He is a decent guy, he supports the whole menage with some manual labor, and he cannot help playing surrogate dad to Bea and Lucy.

But he's also on the run from the law, so the four of them travel all over the country, from one stunning landscape to another.

What makes "Hideous Kinky" such a frustrating experience is that it is virtually impossible to sympathize with a character as shallow and irresponsible as Julia, even though the filmmakers seem undecided as to whether or not she's kind of cool (as if they cannot get over their own hippie nostalgia).

And the film is structured like a series of snapshots: Julia getting her clothes stolen by prostitutes in one place, everyone getting sick in another, Julia visiting a Sufi monastery in a third.

It's all lushly photographed but as vague and half-baked as Julia's own spiritual search.

It doesn't help that strings of unbelievable dialogue inspire some terrible line-readings by Winslet. And the contrast with a standout performance by French-Moroccan actor Taghmaoui does her no favors.

She looks great though. The rich cinematography makes almost as much of her un-Hollywoodish beauty, her extraordinary eyes and skin, as it does of the stunning locations.

The weird title comes from a nonsense phrase made up by Bea and Lucy.

NEWSDAY, 4/16/99, Part II/p. B7, John Anderson

Although it's a trap, "Hideous Kinky," the title of Gillies MacKinnon's seductive new film, is provocative enough that you might want to consult Mr. Webster—who will happily agree that "hideous" can mean morally offensive and confirm, obliquely, that "kinky" implies self-indulgence. Given that the Esther Freud autobiographical novel on which the film is based is about an indigent English beauty dragging her bewildered kids around the spiritual slums of '70s North Africa, the fait certainly seems accompli.

But multiplicity of meanings—either of words, character or cultures in counterpoint—are the hinge on which "Hideous Kinky" swings. And swing it does.

Putting as much distance as possible between herself and her last known whereabouts (James Cameron's ship-swallowing North Atlantic), a radiantly grimy Kate Winslet plays the desert-bound Julia, well-bred, Sufi-besotted mother of Bea (Bella Rizza) and Lucy (Carrie Mullan). A well-intentioned but basically clueless westerner, Julia and the girls are stranded in Marrakech, a city that promises enlightenment and succor but delivers just about as well as Julia's "husband," a London poet whose support checks never fail not to arrive. In a pleasant holiday touch, he does manage to send them a Christmas package intended for his other children.

Bea is growing angry; she wants school and central heating ("I want to be normal"). Lucy, the younger, is sweetly adoring and bemused. Both seize hungrily on Bilal (Said Taghmaoui), a good-natured hustler-acrobat who becomes Julia's lover and the girls' putative father. His abilities as a provider are little better than Julia's, however, and as a bonus he's wanted by the police.

Rolling lustily through its dusty, inscrutable African landscape, "Hideous Kinky"—the girls' all-purpose exclamation for the unfathomable, or incredible is intensely atmospheric, occasionally hallucinatory and a movie with only skeletal plot. More problematically, it has no real heroes—something MacKinnon ("Small Faces") handles deftly. Julia's independent streak and occasionally ferocious maternity is admirable; her abandonment by the London poet makes her sympathetic, but her treatment of her daughters is borderline abuse. Bilal, for all his noble self-sacrifice, also has a wife he has abandoned. The girls are above reproach—as are the young actresses Bella Riza and Carrie Mullan—but in the philosophical scheme of things they are props.

Had "Hideous Kinky" been released at the time in which it's set, it might have been seen as a metaphor for Vietnam—westerners blundering into cultures they don't understand on the foolhardy presumption that their values are universal. From a 1999 vantage point, the blundering serves a similar symbolic point, but Julia also serves as a near-archetype of feminist backlash—much of whose sting has to do with men being the beneficiaries of women's emancipation. In other words, Julia may be a free spirit, but she still has the kids.

There's a wealth of subtle irony in "Hideous Kinky," much of it fueled by the soundtrack—provided by a smattering of late '60s-early '70s avant-pop groups like Love, the Incredible String Band and, best of all, the ersatz raga of Jefferson Airplane's "White Rabbit" (whose dirge-like qualities were culturally absolved at the time by its East Indian modalities). It's a perfect song for Julia "Alice in Wonderland" imagery, surface-skimming cultural appropriations and pseudo-exotica. Like the recycling of 19th-Century Orientalism, the fascinations of "Hideous Kinky"—like its political analogies—are cyclical and, for the moment at least, seem inescapable.

SIGHT AND SOUND, 2/99, p. 43, Philip Kemp

1972. Julia, a young Englishwoman, is living in Marrakesh with her daughters Bea (age 8) and Lucy (age 6). Julia hopes to study Sufism but, with money from the girls' father arriving only rarely, she scrapes a living making dolls for sale. The girls meet Bilal, an acrobat, and he and Julia become lovers. Bea persuades Julia to let her attend school.

When Bilal loses his regular quarrying job, all four set off for Bilal's home village. They are welcomed, but Bilal, uneasy at the presence of his neglected wife, insists they leave again, and goes to Agadir to find work. Back in Marrakesh Julia and the girls meet a Frenchman, Jean-Louis Santoni, and his English friend Charlotte, who invite them to stay in their grand villa. A cheque arrives from London; Julia proposes to hitch to the Sufi college in Algiers but Bea chooses to stay with Charlotte and go to school.

In Algiers the Sufi's leader makes Julia realise she isn't ready to leave her old life. She and Lucy return to Marrakesh to find Jean-Louis and Charlotte have departed, and Bea has run away. Julia tracks her to an orphanage run by a priggish nun and reclaims her daughter. Bilal returns, wearing a resplendent uniform for a tourist spectacular. Bea falls ill, and Julia realises she must return to London. Bilal sells his uniform to buy tickets for her and the girls, then flees to escape his employer's wrath. As Julia and the girls sit in the speeding train, they see Bilal racing alongside in a truck waving goodbye.

Gillies MacKinnon is one of those stimulating film-makers who hates to repeat himself. Each film is different from his previous ones, and especially from the last. As if in reaction against the shell-shocked stasis of *Regeneration,* all chilly blues and greys in a desolate winter landscape, *Hideous Kinky* finds him plunging with infectious relish into the vibrant sun-baked colours, sounds and turmoil of Morocco. What's more, both films include nightmares, but in *Regeneration* the camera seemed to hover over the hellish trenches in mesmerised horror, trapped and helpless. The nightmare that opens *Hideous Kinky,* reprised later, is a tumult of noise, panic and headlong flight, as a small girl rushes terrified down narrow alleys, harried by clutching hands and grinning faces.

Despite appearances, though, this nightmare isn't being dreamt by either Bea or Lucy, the young English girls plunged into this fascinating, bewildering country, but—as if on their behalf—by their mother Julia. Though she insists, both to the girls themselves and to her compatriot Charlotte, that Morocco is a wonderful place for her daughters, far preferable to a dreary cold flat in South London, her dreams betray her. Subconsciously she's haunted by the potential dangers to them. It's not surprising either that Julia seems to live her nightmare through her daughters' eyes, since in some ways she's more of a child than they are: more naive, less ready to confront reality. Much of the film's comedy derives from the contrast between her flower child fantasies and the children's laconic, down-to earth appraisals. To Julia, the longed-for visit to the Sufi will bestow 'annihilation of the ego', magically solving everything. The girls, having pretty healthy egos of their own, are less than convinced. "What the hell is a Sufi anyway?" mutters Lucy in voice-over, eventually concluding that: "They live in a mosque, they pray all day and they never go out."

The set-up, if not the surroundings, recalls Bill Forsyth's underrated melancholic comedy *Housekeeping.* There too a would-be free-spirited mother-figure tries to bring up two young girls according to her own wayward lights, only to collide head on with the innate conservatism of childhood, and there too the elder girl insists on embracing what she sees as "normality". Bea, at that stage in a child's development when she wants to stand out as little as possible from the crowd, yearns for the conventional. And, as if in one of those fairy stories where you get *exactly* what you wished for, she finds it in the form of the pious orphanage matron Patricia.

Indeed, in many ways *Hideous Kinky* can be read as a fairy tale, not least for its loose, episodic structure and its mood of enchanted unreality. From this angle, Patricia serves as the wicked stepmother or maybe as the Wicked Witch of the West, with Charlotte as the well-meaning but disorganised Witch of the South, and the charmingly unreliable Bilal, with his acrobatic tricks and dicey juggling (an engaging performance from Said Taghmaoui, who featured in *La Haine)* as a younger, handsomer Wizard of Oz. There's even a magic slipper to wish on, and the title comes from the secret, half understood phrase that the two children repeat like a mantra in moments of stress. But the film's superb final image evokes a far older story-telling tradition: Bilal, standing in the speeding truck, waving madly as he recedes into the distance, his scarlet turban unravelling like a banner across the sky, is pure *Arabian Nights.*

TIME, 4/19/99, p. 77, Richard Schickel

It's a catchy title—*Hideous Kinky*—but it doesn't mean anything. It's just a nonsense phrase that sets two little girls named Lucy and Bea (Carrie Mullan and Bella Riza) to giggling. Certainly it doesn't catch the patient, tender tones of this gently exotic movie or the spirit of the girls' mum, Julia (Kate Winslet). "Sweetly addled" comes closer to the mark. Or maybe "daftly dreamy."

Back in the '70s, when Morocco was to the counterculture what France was to the Lost Generation of the 1920s—a place to find your bliss on an agreeable currency-exchange rate—Julia has dragged her kids from chilly London to sunny Marrakech, where she vaguely hopes to achieve spiritual transcendence by linking up with the mystical Sufi sect.

Unfortunately, the support checks from the girls' faraway father arrive only erratically. Julia takes up with a sometime acrobat named Bilal (Said Taghmaoui), whose charm is matched by his fecklessness. They are all blown this way and that by minor mishaps, passing acts of grace, and the suspense of the movie derives from our wondering whether Julia will come to her senses before irretrievable disaster overtakes these innocent adventurers.

The film's strength, however, comes from another place: the unblinking objectivity with which it views their trials. The children are not sentimentalized (though we worry about the emptiness of their days as they drag along in the grownups' wake). Bilal is not idealized (his generosity is balanced—or maybe one should say unbalanced—by his impetuosity), and neither is Julia. Caring and good-natured though she is, we can't help being disturbed by the fact that all her motherly alarm bells seem to be disabled.

Looking chunky and suburban, yet glowing with hope, Winslet is the opposite of her Titanic character. There she grasped heedlessly at her destiny; here her reach is more tentative, her manner more reactive than active. There's bravery in that acting choice, and in the refusal of director Gillies MacKinnon, working from a script adapted by his brother Billy of a novel by Esther Freud, either to romanticize or trash the hippie past. They permit us to see it for what it was—another silly, doomed, very human attempt to evade responsibility's inescapable embrace.

VILLAGE VOICE, 4/20/99, p. 143, J. Hoberman

Gillies MacKinnon's robustly directed, fiercely pictorial, drastically sanitized, and ultimately bungled adaptation of Esther Freud's 1992 novel, *Hideous Kinky,* is not what it might have been. Still, thanks in part to Kate Winslet's adventurous performance, it's a more vivid and even affecting movie than it deserves to be.

The tale of a London flower child wandering through the teeming souks, hash dens, and crash pads of late-'60s North Africa with two small daughters in tow, Freud's novel was most striking for being told, semiautobiographically, from the perspective of the younger child and, hence, with a child's acceptance of adult antics. Gillies MacKinnon's movie, directed from his brother Billy's screenplay, is considerably less focused. The first scene is a vision of an English girl lost in the Marrakech medina's maze of narrow alleys. This anxiety dream may be appropriate (Esther Freud is the great-granddaughter of Sigmund himself, but, as attributed to the child's mother, Julia (Winslet), it has the effect of immediately confusing the movie's point of view.

Actually, it is Julia who is lost in the labyrinth. *Hideous Kinky* is purposefully elliptical in its narrative development and deliberately incoherent in its spatial geography. Waiting in vain for her feckless poet-husband to send her a check from London, free-spirited Julia moves from one dump to another, dreaming of Sufis, ineptly trying to hustle wealthier tourists, and taking up with the marketplace acrobat Bilal, a sweet-tempered vagabond played by Saïd Taghmaoui (the fastest talking of the three banlieuards in Mathieu Kassovitz's *Hate*).

Flushed with excitement and damp with sweat, Winslet throws herself into the role of Julia the way Julia hurls herself at Morocco. As her performance has a disarming absence of vanity, so the character reveals a complete lack of self-awareness. Here, even more than in the novel, where Julia can be quite resourceful, five-year-old Lucy (Carrie Mullan) and seven-year-old Bea (Bella Riza) are pointedly less childlike than their impulsive, unrealistic 25-year-old mother.

Perhaps attempting to protect Julia from further viewer disapproval, the filmmakers downplay her casual kef smoking and eliminate the kids' fondness for the local hashish fudge, majoun. Still, *Hideous Kinky* promotes an atmosphere of clamorous sensory overload. MacKinnon favors a moving camera and is fond of shock-cut disorientation. When the whores next door steal Julia's clothes, the ensuing courtyard squabble is staged like a high-velocity squash match. Such mad chaos is scarcely inappropriate to the milieu, although one suspects that, for those under the influence, such scenes would have unfolded in slow motion. Parachuting into Marrakech for the Christmas 1968 "love-in," British alternative journalist Richard Neville found an international freak show populated by all manner of "mystics, Maoists [and] stray Living Theatre members" and confessed that "all attempts to retrieve a few unstoned moments" from his sojourn would prove "fruitless."

Although the novel takes place around 1968, the filmmakers push the time frame forward a few years—perhaps to squeeze more early-'70s Richie Havens onto the soundtrack (but not, perversely, the Crosby, Stills and Nash choo-choo chestnut that likely drove the stake through the heart of romantic Marrakech and would seem perfect for the dippy closing moments). In any case, if the movie's most far-out musical touch is the brief shot of a banjo-playing hippie in the souk, the weirdest bit of period resonance is the appearance of Pierre Clementi—a French high-'60s icon long gone MIA—as a continental bon vivant who briefly looks after Julia.

It's being promoted as a love story, but *Hideous Kinky* (which takes its title from a pet phrase invented by Bea and Lucy) is basically the story of a heroically self-indulgent single mom. With its murky blend of perspectives, however, the movie doesn't sufficiently draw out the family relations—nor, pace Freud, does it illuminate Julia's psychology. When, at one point, she parks disapproving Bea with an expat couple and takes off with compliant Lucy, her giddy lack of responsibility is mirrored by the inarticulate ecstasy of the acid-ripped European hippie they encounter on the road. Just before Julia's nightmares come true, she tells Lucy that what she is seeking is "pure joy, blissful emptiness, no pain"—what Freud somewhat disapprovingly described as the oceanic feeling.

Hideous Kinky's perfunctory happy ending is unfortunate, and it only highlights the movie's deficiencies. Canned Heat and sun-dazed local color are not enough to conjure the cracked cosmology and cannabis-fueled exaltation that could send a woman like Julia heedless into the Sahara, searching for the "annihilation" of her ego.

Also reviewed in:
CHICAGO TRIBUNE, 4/23/99, Friday/p. B, Michael Wilmington
NEW REPUBLIC, 4/26 & 5/3/99, p. 74, Stanley Kauffmann
NEW YORK TIMES, 4/16/99, p. E13, Janet Maslin
VARIETY, 10/12-18/98, p. 39, Lisa Nesselson
WASHINGTON POST, 4/23/99, Weekend/p. 50, Desson Howe

HIGHWAY

A First Run/Icarus Films release of a Dune/Leapfrog production coproduced with ZDF/ARTE/BBC/YLE/TSI/NRK and France 3. *Executive Producer:* Chantal Bernheim. *Director:* Sergeï Dvortesvoy. *Screenplay (Kazakh with English subtitles):* Sergeï Dvortesvoy. *Director of Photography:* Alisher Khamidkhodjaev. *Editor:* Sergeï Dvortesvoy. *Sound:* Sergeï Dvortsevoy, Gulsara Mukataeva, and (music) Milos Zajdl. *Running time:* 57 minutes. *MPAA Rating:* Not Rated.

NEW YORK POST, 12/29/99, p. 42, Hannah Brown

In the desolate steppes of Kazakhstan, a young man lies on broken glass while his father, drops a 32-kilo weight on his chest, then passes the hat among spectators.

That's the opening scene of "Highway," a fascinating and original documentary that follows the members of a Kazakh circus family as they travel through remote areas.

The highway of the title connects Central Asia and Russia, and is located 2,000 kilometers from Moscow.

The family passes through towns so isolated that their circus, which consists solely of family members performing difficult and dangerous acts (toddlers walk on glass, a boy holds a weight with his teeth as his father pounds it with a sledge-hammer), is apparently quite a draw for the locals.

The performers travel in a rundown bus that needs to be cranked up in order to start and live a life that is almost completely untouched by modern culture and technology.

Russian director Sergey Dvortsevoy provides no background about the family or narration of any kind, which may be frustrating for some viewers. However, this allows the audience to be drawn unobtrusively into the rhythm of life on the road.

It's an approach that makes for a slow-paced film, but one that creates an atmosphere of rare intensity.

The tone is set by the stark and haunting Kazakhstan landscape, which is a central presence in the film and is a symbol for the family's isolation and hardship.

In one scene, the children are playing by the side of the road and find an eagle, which the family adopts. This magnificent bird, which is just a baby and can't fly yet, perches protectively over the youngest child of the family as the mother sings him to sleep.

Other moments are more commonplace. As the children squabble over the miles and miles of stark road and the mother loses her temper, the scene could be any family on a road trip.

This mixture of the everyday and the exotic is what makes "Highway," such an unusual experience.

It's showing with a similar short film by the same director, "Paradise," also set in Kazakhstan, which follows the life of a nomadic shepherd and his family.

Also reviewed in:
NEW YORK TIMES, 12/29/99, p. E7, Lawrence Van Gelder

HOLY SMOKE

A Miramax Films release of a Miramax Films production. *Executive Producer:* Bob Weinstein, Harvey Weinstein, and Julie Goldstein. *Producer:* Jan Chapman. *Director:* Jane Campion. *Screenplay:* Anna Campion and Jane Campion. *Director of Photography:* Dion Beebe. *Editor:* Veronka Jenet. *Music:* Angelo Badalamenti. *Music Editor:* Julie Pierce. *Choreographer:* Tobin Saunders. *Sound:* Roger Savage. *Casting:* Alison Barrett. *Production Designer:* Janet Patterson. *Art Director:* Tony Campbell. *Special Effects:* Studio Kite, Steve Rosewell, Warren Beaton, and Marcus Erazmus. *Visual Effects:* Andy Brown. *Costumes:* Janet Patterson. *Make-up:* Noreen Wilkie and Kylie Marr. *Stunt Coordinator:* Lawrence Woodward. *Running time:* 120 minutes. *MPAA Rating:* R.

CAST: Kate Winslet (Ruth Barron); Harvey Keitel (PJ Waters); Julie Hamilton (Miriam, Mum); Tim Robertson (Gilbert, Dad); Sophie Lee (Yvonne); Dan Wyllie (Robbie); Paul Goddard (Tim); George Mangos (Yani); Kerry Walker (Puss); Leslie Dayman (Bill-Bill); Samantha Murray (Prue); Austen Tayshus (Stan); Simon Anderson (Fabio); Pam Grier (Carol); Savrash and Saurabh Srinivasan (Dancing Boys); Dhritiman Chaterji (Chidaatma Baba); Genevieve Lemon (Rahi); Robert Joseph (Miriam's Taxi Driver); Valerie Thomas (Miriam's Double); Arif (Boy Who Runs with Taxi); John Samaha (Chatiwall, Shiva's Diner); Jane Edwards (Priya); Miranda Cleary (Priya's Daughter); Tamsin Carroll (Jodie); T'mara Buckmaster (Zoe); Ante Novakovic (Man with Trolley); Diana Kotatko and Patricia Lemon (Women with a Trolley); Ethan Coker (Toddy Barron); Ellie Burchell (Tiffany Barron); Eleanor Knox (Meryl); Mark Gray (Dope Peddler); Cameron McAuliffe and Tim Rogers (Seducers); Johannes Brinkman (Ruth's Boyfriend); Eric Schussler, Joan Bodgen, and Robert Lee (Cult Video Reporters).

CHRISTIAN SCIENCE MONITOR, 12/3/99, p. 15, David Sterritt

Jane Campion's new *Holy Smoke!* seems a largely squandered opportunity. Kate Winslet, of "Titanic" and "Sense and Sensibility" fame, plays a young Australian woman who's moved to India and joined the following of a mystical guru. Luring her home on false pretenses, her parents hire a self-styled deprogrammer (Harvey Keitel) to clear her mind of cultish delusions. Alone in a rural hut, the devotee and the skeptic try to wear each other down in a drawn-out war of conflicting belief systems.

Campion has earned international acclaim for movies like "The Piano" and "Portrait of a Lady." but here she reduces her fascinating subject to a two-character psychodrama that doesn't work particularly well on either spiritual or psychological levels. Winslet's superb acting and Keitel's feisty presence may win the film a fairly wide audience, though.

LOS ANGELES TIMES, 12/3/99, Calendar/p. 18, Kevin Thomas

"Holy Smoke," a high-risk, darkly comic triumph, is the most unabashedly outrageous movie Jane Campion has made since her debut, "Sweetie," a decade ago. Like that film's heroine "Holy Smoke's" Ruth is at intense odds with her crass working-class family. But whereas "Sweetie's" lead character was mentally unbalanced, seriously overweight and truly grating, Ruth (Kate Winslet) is beautiful, intelligent and quite endearing.

Ruth has fled the Sydney suburb Sans Souci, a tract of virtually identical red-brick bungalows, for the dense, picturesque squalor of Delhi, where she is captivated by a local guru. Her horrified friend Prue (Samantha Murray) rushes home to tell Ruth's family what's happened to her. Ruth's sweet but dim mother (Julie Hamilton) rushes off to India to retrieve her, telling her that her father (Tim Robertson) is at death's door.

A blissed-out Ruth responds that maybe she'll see him "in another life." An authentic panic attack on the part of her mother jolts Ruth into returning with her to Sydney, where, expense-be-damned, America's most successful cult deprogrammer, PJ Waters (Harvey Keitel), awaits Ruth to put her through his proven ritual of winning her respect only to break her down, culminating in a teary reunion with family. You know from the get-go that Ruth's deprogramming is not going to go according to plan.

Written with Campion's filmmaker sister Anna, "Holy Smoke" begins as a satire of the whole guru trip but moves swiftly to a bold struggle of a man and a woman to break through all the conventions that restrict a possible relationship between them. Before Ruth and PJ arrive at this main event she is subjected to a torrent of outrages by her well-meaning, male-dominated family.

There's no evidence to suggest that there is anything at all unscrupulous or exploitative about Ruth's particular guru; in fact he's given her a sense of being in harmony with herself and the universe. Nor is there anything zombie-like or deranged about her. She is perfectly capable of intelligent discussion of her spiritual enlightenment—which is taken by her profoundly unsophisticated relatives as but further proof of how thoroughly brainwashed she has become.

Arriving in black cowboy gear, complete with boots and jet-black dyed hair and mustache, PJ looks for the world like the archetypal aging country-and-western singing star. PJ is Ruth's dad and brothers and their macho pals' kind of guy—even her gay brother Tim (Paul Goddard) and his lover join in this male solidarity as they encircle Ruth as if she were a cow to be branded.

PJ boasts of the 189 successful deprogrammings as Ruth is in effect taken prisoner by her own kin to be transported to an isolated cabin in the outback where PJ is to do his stuff. In the meantime, Ruth's sultry sister-in-law (Sophie Lee) has been coming on to PJ while confessing to him that when her husband (Dan Wyllie) is making selfish, uninspired love to her she imagines she's with Brad Pitt and other screen idols.

PJ, however, has his work cut out for him with Ruth. Fueled by understandable outrage at such barbaric treatment, Ruth is smart and forthright, quite up to sparring with PJ on intellectual and spiritual levels. Ruth is also young, radiantly beautiful, statuesque in her glowing abundance; the cumulative impact of all these qualities upon PJ is understandably dizzying and, not surprisingly, ultimately and profoundly seductive. Ruth's war on PJ's machismo, much to his surprise, is liberating in its effect, and he has the curiosity to go wherever she wants to take him. But what of the emotional consequences of this love-hate power struggle? How do men and women escape power playing? How do they break down the walls of gender without destroying each other?

Campion is, of course, a feminist. But like her fellow director Catherine Breillat ("Romance"), her feminism reaches the level of an all-embracing humanism, and in "Holy Smoke" she and her sister Anna realize fully what women's lib can cost men.

With its smart, tart use of pop music past and present incorporated in Angelo Badalamenti's glorious score, their film traverses a tremendous range of emotional terrain, and they've got just the actors—including the ever-majestic Pam Grier as PJ's belatedly arriving assistant—to go the distance.

"Titanic" has not diverted Winslet from taking risks, and it's not easy to imagine a young actress who could so convincingly hold her own on all levels with a formidable, endlessly resourceful pro like Keitel. Thank goodness for filmmakers like Abel Ferrera ("Bad Lieutenant") and Campion, who can inspire Keitel—Campion first directed the actor in 1993's "The Piano"—to hold nothing back. As in "The Piano," Campion presents Keitel as a sex object without that view limiting or demeaning him; indeed, she celebrates his enduring masculine appeal even as he grows older and less physically appealing.

At once hilarious and serious, cruel and tender, and bristling with vitality, "Holy Smoke" is the right movie for the millennium, envisioning new possibilities in the way people view and relate to one another.

NEW YORK, 12/13/99, p. 72, Peter Rainer

In Jane Campion's *Holy Smoke!*, Kate Winslet may be playing an Australian girl who falls under a guru's spell while traveling in India, but she's the true spellbinder of the piece: Whether her Ruth is smoldering in a sari or cavorting on an emu ranch, Winslet keeps you watching. The film, otherwise something of a botch, is about what happens when Ruth, lured back to her family, squares with a cult deprogrammer (Harvey Keitel). The sexual politics between them is like *Feminism for Dummies*, and Keitel's held-in performance doesn't credibly account for his transformation from cock of the walk to whimperer. It probably all looked good on paper, but the playing out is something else again.

NEW YORK POST, 12/3/99, p. 50, Jonathan Foreman

Jane Campion's "The Piano" had its detractors but was undoubtedly well-made. "Holy Smoke," on the other hand, is just a dreadful mess.

With enough unintentional laughs to compete with "Eyes Wide Shut," it lurches ineptly from lame comedy to hokey melodrama, while smugly espousing a crude Aussie version of American hippie attitudes circa 1970.

It's also shot through with anti-male sexism and snobbish contempt for Australia's allegedly crass lower classes—an unappetizing stew that cannot be saved even by fine photography or the excellent acting of Kate Winslet. It doesn't help that Harvey Keitel turns in a singularly bad performance.

You meet Ruth (Winslet) as she tours India with a friend and falls under the spell of a guru. When the friend comes back to Sydney with the news that Ruth has been "brainwashed" and isn't coming home, Ruth's absurdly stupid and bigoted suburban parents decide to take action.

Her mother (Julie Hamilton) flies to India where, being a working-class buffoon, she's freaked out by the crowds and poverty. Her plan is to tell Ruth that her father is dying so that the girl will come home and there be "cured." Ruth, however, couldn't care less about her father. But when mom collapses, Ruth ends up escorting her home.

The whole family goes out to the desert, where Ruth is imprisoned in a cabin and subjected to the attentions of a professional cult-deprogrammer imported from America. The greasily macho P.J. (Keitel) sports cowboy boots and a dyed-black mustache and calls women "ladies."

Unlike Ruth's ignorant parents, P.J. is at least capable of discussing religious issues seriously (he's read the key Hindu texts), but the debates between him and Ruth soon fall flat. It isn't because of the (unbelievable) sexual tension between them but because the Campion sisters' joint script is just too careless and confused.

The screenplay takes on serious issues of gender and power, but then dispatches them in a startlingly complacent way, reaching a nadir in the scene in which P.J.—now a broken man—crawls into the desert wearing lipstick and a dress.

On the other hand, the film does confirm Kate Winslet's amazing screen presence (and attractiveness, despite an un-Hollywood-like full figure). Her performance in the face of such a screenplay is the film's only saving grace.

And the fine Pam Grier is wasted in a small role as P.J.'s assistant.

NEWSDAY, 12/3/99, Part II/p. B7, John Anderson.

As my colleague Jan Stuart noted last week (vis-a-vis "Flawless"), it's not a bad time for fans of the toe-to-toe dramatic duets and, when reduced to its essence, that's what Jane Campion's "Holy Smoke" is: a psychosexual shoot-out between a middle-aged American cult deprogramer (or "exiter") and a young, spirited Australian woman whose family has duped her into returning from India so they can wash the ashram right out of her hair.

But Campion ("The Piano") is a genuine filmmaker despite the poverty of her script (written with sister Anna), so we get something more than a two-character filmed stage play: a beautifully photographed, but also very broad and mean-spirited lampoon of a particularly lumpen Aussie middle class, against whose spiritual dead weight the questing Ruth Barron (Kate Winslet) seems a bird in flight. And in which the songs of Neil Diamond ("Holy Holy," "I Am... I Said") take on sardonic intent.

We also get an interpretation of the hipster American male (as embodied by Harvey Keitel) who, when posed against the combined forces of the Campion sisters and the radiant Winslet, seems like a Bryl Creamed fish in a barrel.

Winslet, as usual, is immediate and thrilling; Keitel, who has a tendency to play Keitel much of the time and isn't known for nuance, gives an uncharacteristically complex performance, probably his best since "The Piano," which means he should work with Jane Campion as often as possible. When his character P.J. sleeps with Ruth—violating every tenet of the deprogramer's trade and thus shifting the balance of power from his court to hers—we get a portrait of wounded vulnerability, plus lust, plus stupidity.

Despite the good performances and Campion's visual reach, her characters are too specific/eccentric to transcend their storyline and make us feel that there's something to be absorbed from the P.J.-Ruth imbroglio. Movies don't necessarily need morals or lessons or an epiphany, but it would be nice to get the point.

SIGHT AND SOUND, 4/00, p. 48, Stella Bruzzi

Delhi, India. Young Australian Ruth Barron joins a cult, leaving her friend Prue to return to Sydney alone. Prue tells Ruth's horrified family of her friend's conversion. To lure her back, Ruth's mother Miriam travels to Delhi and pretends Ruth's father Gilbert is dying. They fly home.

P.J. Waters, an American "cult exiter", is hired by Ruth's family. He begins his three-day deprogramming of Ruth in a shack in the outback. On the evening of day two, Ruth starts to break. P.J. shows the family a video about cults and brainwashing. Later, Ruth and P.J. have sex. On day three, Ruth joins her gay brother and mates at the local pub, where P.J. saves her from being gang raped. Carol—P.J.'s partner—arrives unexpectedly. Ruth and P.J., who is now besotted with Ruth, argue about religion among other things. She dresses him up in women's clothes. The family arrive. P.J. locks Ruth in the boot of his car so she won't reveal what's happened between them, but her sister in-law Yvonne lets her out. Ruth runs off, chased by a hallucinating P J., who offers to return to the cult with her. In the bed of the family truck, Ruth and P.J. embrace. One year later. Ruth is living in India, and P.J. and Carol have twins. P.J. and Ruth continue to correspond.

Holy Smoke is an exquisite and unexpected film. Frank Auerbach once remarked that fellow British painter Michael Andrews was a great artist because he only ever produced masterpieces; a similar tribute could almost be paid to Jane Campion, despite the odd blip, such as *The Portrait of a Lady,* a film weighed down by the expectations generated by *The Piano.* Paradoxically, despite the echoes in *Holy Smoke* of earlier work such as *Sweetie* and *Passionless Moment,* the latest film is mature and finely polished. Both in style and subject, Campion has abandoned the earnest precision of the crinoline genre and has resuscitated the light, witty touch she displayed in her films set largely in modern times. For all its stylistic richness, *The Piano* lacked spontaneity; *Holy Smoke*—the story of recent cult convert Ruth Barron's confrontation and eventual relationship with "cult exiter" P.J. Waters—is vibrant, alive, and comes more from the heart than the head.

Symptomatic of this shift towards imaginative exuberance is Campion's abandonment of Stuart Dryburgh's lush but convoluted camerawork (his swooping, vertiginous helicopter shot over the New Zealand cliffs in *The Piano* is now an oft-imitated cliché). Shot by Antipodean DP Dion Beebe *(Crush), Holy Smoke*'s style is more playful. Its *mise en scène* juxtaposes mundane detail with pyrotechnic flights of fancy (for instance, the garish, hypnotic Pierre et Gillesesque sequence marking Ruth's conversion, or P.J.'s hazy, love-fuelled-vision of Ruth as a six-armed goddess). In both *The Piano* and *The Portrait of a Lady* such extravagances jarred (remember the 'talking' lima beans in *Portrait?*); here they're tropes integral to the narrative and keys to understanding Ruth and P.J.

Holy Smoke is ostensibly a film about cults and cultism, in much the same way as *Sweetie* and *Angel at My Table* were about mental illness. But as with those films, what makes *Holy Smoke* so joyous (as if Campion herself is finding the means to express her liberation from the costume film's stays) is the fact that the subject matter never constricts the film. It's only one element in a much richer narrative centring on the ambiguities of characters and relationships, Campion's most consistent preoccupation.

On paper, the love affair between cult member Ruth and her deprogrammer P.J. sounds like a cliché. But in Campion's hands their liaison becomes emblematic of how power trickles back and forth between lovers. By degrees, P.J. and Ruth's roles are reversed as she becomes *his* guru. *Holy Smoke* doesn't judge their mutual dependence: Ruth's susceptibility is an imaginative need, a craving for a life freed from banality, hence the preponderance of subjective fantasy, sequences. At first P.J. is characterised by a lack of fantasy, but by the end he has discovered a comparable desire for imaginative liberation as he permits her to dress him in a provocative red dress, to daub his lips with matching lipstick and to transform his life. Existence is a chain; we learn from and mimic each other.

In this way, cultism may be the catalyst for the action in *Holy Smoke,* but it is essentially a film about the tenuousness of most people's sense of self—our decentredness, our malleability, our vulnerability in the face of our own desires and the manipulative skills of others. Everyone in the film, not just Ruth, is impressionable (there's her mother who returns to India with her at the end; there's her sister-in-law who, when she isn't imagining sex with film stars, falls for P.J. in much the same irrational way as Ruth did), and they all, in the chaos that pervades the whole film, are attracted to each other in a desperate attempt to flee from themselves.

Certainty and identity are learned, not innate. In delivering this idea, *Holy Smoke* is Campion's most superficial film, brimming with visual trickery, sudden changes of direction, unpredictable characters. It is ultimately about reconciling imagination with reality. Just as the film marries fantasy and realism, so the characters, having undergone their own tortured and extreme awakenings, become reconciled to compromise. Across continents Ruth and P.J. become virtual lovers, a state of being, the film suggests, we're all in. *Holy Smoke* can be read as a text of reconciliation: between realism and surrealism, earnestness and irreverence, oneself and the world. It is an immense, emotional, engrossing film that nevertheless wears its brilliance casually.

TIME, 1/31/00, p. 73, Richard Schickel

Harvey Keitel enters the movie wearing snakeskin cowboy boots and an arrogant attitude. Before it's over, he'll be wearing a red dress, lipstick and an air of considerable moral confusion.

Kate Winslet comes on as a dull yet impressionable girl seeking spiritual redemption in the ashram of a slightly suspect Indian maharishi. Before *Holy Smoke!* ends, she will be found wandering the Australian outback, naked as a jaybird and horny as a toad, seeking quite a different sort of redeeming experience.

How Keitel, playing P.J. Waters, an American who specializes in deprogramming youthful cult followers at the behest of their parents, and Winslet, as Australian Ruth Baron, who specializes mainly in self-absorption, find themselves alone in a shack, arguing for one another's souls, is the substance of Jane Campion's curiously exhilarating and often quite funny film.

Indeed, it represents something of a leap forward for Campion from the strained improbabilities of *The Piano,* the choked feminism of *Portrait of a Lady.* There's a looseness about *Holy Smoke!* that's not quite improvisatory but not entirely locked down either. This spirit freshens the film and gives it somewhat the quality of being surprised at its own journey.

That begins with Ruth's conventionally disorganized family. Their morality is determinedly conventional, but their hypocrisies are many. Mom (Julie Hamilton) is a caregiver, though given to hysteria. Dad (Tim Robertson) is a secret womanizer. One of their boys is gay, and they have a daughter-in-law obsessed with sex. You can see why Ruth, on a visit to India, is drawn to her maharishi's promises of peace and purity.

You can also see why the family is drawn to P.J. He's a no-nonsense, know-it-all kind of guy, a typical New York City type. His strategy with creatures like Ruth is simply to isolate them in a one-on-one situation and impose his formidable will on their confusions.

The thing is, though, that Ruth—as presented in the script written by Campion and her sister Anna, and as embodied by Winslet—is not as pliable as she appears. There's real need in her desire to escape the crushing banality of her family, and a real willingness to experiment with alternatives—especially P.J.

He's surely drawn to her, but it's equally certain she's the seducer here. And something more than that too. She's the true reprogrammer, getting the macho P.J. quite hilariously, yet quite sweetly, in touch with his feminine-side. Their sexual battle is fierce and believable. The befuddlement of her family is told with unpatronizing honesty. And, best of all, both combatants emerge, finally, as better people—more tolerant, more human. That goes for Campion too. Her film may contain a kind of feminist parable, but she's less tense about it than she has been, more open in the exploration of her characters and more wayward (and charming) in the way she permits them to develop.

VILLAGE VOICE, 12/7/99, p. 139, J. Hoberman

I don't know if anyone has ever named God as a divorce-case third party, but it's a possibility the tormented male protagonists of Jane Campion's rambunctious *Holy Smoke!* and Neil Jordan's more sober *The End of the Affair* could well appreciate. Blame it on the power of love or millennial consciousness: Both films humble their smug heroes with divine retribution for attempting to possess women consecrated to the supreme Alpha Male.

Holy Smoke!—which had its premiere at the New York Film Festival and opens Friday for a one-week qualifier—is the more affirmative, complex, and entertaining of the two movies. Campion's latest, directed from an original screenplay cowritten with her sister Anna, is lusty and tumultuous—as willful as its heroine. Filled with flashy sight gags, overwrought performances, and madly overlapping dialogue, *Holy Smoke!* alternates the crass hyperbole endemic to Australian film comedy with a scarcely less confrontational affair between the young acolyte of a Hindu cult and the middle-aged American "cult exiter" her parents hire to deprogram her.

Traveling through India and ripe for the picking, Ruth (Kate Winslet) finds God in the person of the guru Baba—her illuminating vision illustrated in appropriately garish pink and orange. After a distraught friend returns to Sydney to report this transfiguration ("some sort of freaky hypnotism happened"), Ruth's mother is dispatched to Delhi, where she proves humorously ill-equipped to deal with India's crowds, toilets, and undeniable thereness. Mother's fortuitous collapse precludes Ruth's participation in a group wedding to Baba, and under wildly false pretenses, daughter is transported back to the bosom of a grotesquely caricatured family.

A scene in which Ruth is literally corralled by her male relatives presages the appearance of legendary cult-buster PJ Waters (Harvey Keitel), who materializes out of the desert in the all-black outfit of a western gunfighter. Campion heralds this apparition with a majestic chorus of "'I Am,' I Said." (One of *Holy Smoke!'s* pleasures is its sense of being an operetta scored to the unselfconscious rhinestone excess of Neil Diamond; Ruth prefers to sing along with Alanis Morissette.) Antagonists in place, *Holy Smoke!* proceeds as a three-day psychic showdown between two utterly committed, fearless performers—with Winslet in particular placing her lush physicality in the service of her character's personal liberation struggle.

Engaging Ruth in a spurious dialogue, pompous PJ is initially an advocate of reason, but by the end of the second day, his flighty subject has intuited his Achilles' heel and begun to fight back on less rational terrain. When she appears to PJ naked and asking for love, he can't resist her (later lamely explaining, "I was trying to be comforting"). Mischievously deconstructing the May-September sexual relationship between an old Method actor and a brazen ingenue, most elaborately romanticized in *Last Tango in Paris,* the Campion sisters are themselves pretty programmatic.

Holy Smoke! justifies its exclamatory title as a sort of emotional slapstick in which characters react to stimulation as directly as they would to a kick in the pants. A scene of family celebration in some sort of outlandish outback honky-tonk with the now cured Ruth chugging beer and dancing with her sister-in-law sets up the jealous PJ for an epic arguing, teasing, taunting, crawling, confusing one-on-one, the battle for control interrupted, but only temporarily, by the timely arrival of PJ's irate girlfriend (Pam Grier).

As the prophet once said, when your heart's on fire, smoke gets in your eyes. By the time the cowboy deprogrammer has been himself sufficiently deprogrammed to trade his Hopalong Cassidy duds for a flaming red dress, he's hopelessly in love. In the movie's most pathetic, poignant moment, smitten PJ offers up a prayer to the very deity he set himself against. "We'll see Baba. He could help us."

Also reviewed in:
CHICAGO TRIBUNE, 2/11/00, Friday/p. A, Michael Wilmington
NATION, 1/31/00, p. 35, Stuart Klawans
NEW REPUBLIC, 2/7/00, p. 26, Stanley Kauffmann
NEW YORK TIMES, 12/3/99, p. E24, Janet Maslin

VARIETY, 9/13-19/99, p. 45, David Rooney
WASHINGTON POST, 2/11/00, p. C5, Stephen Hunter
WASHINGTON POST, 2/11/00, Weekend/p. 43, Michael O'Sullivan

HOME PAGE

A Copacetic Pictures/Home Box Office/ZDF-Arte release. *Producer:* Doug Block, Jane Weiner, and Esther Robinson. *Director:* Doug Block. *Screenplay:* Doug Block and Deborah Rosenberg. *Director of Photography:* Doug Block. *Editor:* Deborah Rosenberg. *Music:* Beo Morales. *Sound:* Otto Gain. *Running time:* 102 minutes. *MPAA Rating:* Not Rated.

WITH: Justin Hall, Lucy Block, Doug Block, Patrick Farley, Julie Petersen, Jim Petersen, Howard Rheingold, Judi Rose, John Seabrook, Marjorie Silver, Josh Silver, Carl Steadman and J. Carew Kraft.

NEW YORK POST, 11/19/99, p. 58, Jonathan Foreman

"Home Page" is a strange, disorganized, self-involved film about cyberexhibitionists and Internet gurus, circa 1996.

Documentarist Doug Block had a vague idea of making a film about the Internet. He heard from his son at Swarthmore College about Justin Hall, a student there who had achieved fame as one of those people who put their whole lives on the Web.

So Hall became the subject of the documentary and Block followed him to San Francisco, where Hall started working with Internet guru Howard Rheingold.

Block also interviewed other Internet exhibitionists and publishers, but most of the film that doesn't feature the glib but amiable Hall is actually about Block and his family—and how they deal with him making the film in the midst of a mild midlife crisis.

Unfortunately, all that makes for a less interesting subject than he realizes. And the discussions about the opportunities for "community" offered by the Web are now mainly interesting as history, because the film was shot three years ago, largely before live Internet video became common.

Still, if you don't mind the chaotic structure and the out-of-date talk about the Web's potential, "Home Page" does bring you into the lives of some fascinating people. And if you have ever considered posting the intimate details of your life on the 'Net, you should definitely see "Home Page" first.

NEWSDAY, 11/19/99, Part II/p. B10, John Anderson

It's a paradoxical sign of the times that "Home Page," begun by Doug Block as a cutting-edge documentary in 1996, now seems like a time capsule. Although its take on the World Wide Web has necessarily become a timepiece—because life online moves so quickly—it's also a testament to rumination, cogitation and reflection, if only because those qualities are so glaringly absent among the young and/or desperate to achieve some kind of temporal online celebrity.

It's also apt that the 40-something Block, an established, prize-winning documentary cameraman, director and producer ("Silverlake Life," "Jupiter's Wife," "To Heck With Hollywood") made this film at all. (He actually set out to make a film about his daughter, but got waylaid.) Block, unlike so many he interviews, has no cultural tie to the Internet, no investment of ego, no sense of indentity that can only survive online. His cultural compass is essentially divorced from the Web (although he does get seduced). His view isn't jaundiced, it's just blunt.

And so is his interview technique. Although Block never stoops to mocking even the most needy "Web celeb" who comes under his microscope, neither does he shrink from the uncomfortable question. "What's with the clothes?" he asks Justin Hall, his main object of attention, a wild-haired Swarthmore College Webster with a proclivity for clashing ties, Hawaiian shirts, Fijian skirts and revealing the most intimate details of his life (sex included) online. "Is it an extension of what you're doing on the Web? ... Or is it more Justin screaming for attention?" Later—and much more excruciatingly—he asks the husband of a Web designer, "How bizarre was it to read about your wife's adventures with her lover on the Web?" Block doesn't always get the answers he wants, but the silences and digressions are eloquent.

And unlike some Web-happy navel gazer, he bridges the obvious (to us) gap between mano-a-mano human relationships and the fabricated "intimacy" of people interacting on the Web. Howard Rheingold, the middle-aged Web guru who hires Justin for his "Electric Minds" virtual community, is asked by Block when Justin is going to learn there are costs to putting everything on the Web.

"When someone punches him in the nose," Rheingold replies, displaying a wisdom—and connection to real life—so often lacking among the younger denizens of "Home Page."

VILLAGE VOICE, 11/23/99, 142, Michael Atkinson

Doug Block's *Home Page* is almost about the real world, documenting the uneventful life of goofy-haired college narcissist/home page diarist Justin Hall, who can best be characterized as a couch-grown Pokémon of the Snore variety, with special Silly Clothes power. As Perplexichu and I watched this aimless but sweet first-person doc, in which fortysomething Web neophyte Block tries to understand cyberculture through Hall's minor celebrity, it became clear that Block is several years behind the curve, and that Hall's Web-evangelizing road tour was aimed at retirees in Des Moines. The interviews with the boys at suck.com are quietly pungent, but most of *Home Page* is Pokédull.

Also reviewed in:
NEW YORK TIMES, 11/19/99, p. E22, Stephen Holden
VARIETY, 2/8-14/99, p. 81, Dennis Harvey

HOUSE ON HAUNTED HILL

A Warner Bros. release of a Dark Castle Entertainment production. *Executive Producer:* Dan Cracchiolo and Steve Richards. *Producer:* Gilbert Adler, Robert Zemeckis, and Joel Silver. *Director:* William Malone. *Screenplay:* Dick Beebe. *Story:* Robb White. *Director of Photography:* Rick Bota. *Editor:* Anthony Adler. *Music:* Don Davis. *Music Editor:* Joe E. Rand. *Sound:* Vince Garcia and (music) Armin Steiner. *Sound Editor:* Dane A. Davis. *Casting:* Lora Kennedy. *Production Designer:* David F. Klassen. *Art Director:* Richard F. Mays. *Set Decorator:* Lauri Gaffin. *Set Dresser:* Marco Lopez, Douglas McKay, Efren Perez, and David Ladish. *Special Effects:* T. "Brooklyn" Bellissimo and Charlie Belardinelli. *Visual Effects:* Marc Kolbe. *Costumes:* Ha Nguyen. *Make-up:* Joyce B. Etheredge. *Make-up (Special Effects):* Robert Kurtzman, Gregory Nicotero, and Howard Berger. *Stunt Coordinator:* Gregory Brazzel. *Running time:* 96 minutes. *MPAA Rating:* R.

CAST: Geoffrey Rush (Stephen Price); Famke Janssen (Evelyn); Taye Diggs (Eddie); Peter Gallagher (Blackburn); Chris Kattan (Pritchett); Ali Larter (Sara); Bridgette Wilson (Melissa Marr); Max Perlich (Schecter); Jeffrey Combs (Dr. Vannacutt); Dick Beebe (Male Nurse); Slavitza Jovan (Twisted Nurse); Lisa Loeb (Channel 3 Reporter); James Marsters (Channel 3 Cameraman); Jeannette Lewis (Price's Secretary); Janet Tracy Keijser (Girl on Wires); Peter Graves (Himself).

NEW YORK POST, 10/30/99, p. 45, Lou Lumenick

A good cast can't save the slow-moving, yawn-inducing remake of "House on Haunted Hill," which provides far fewer scares than your typical ride on the A train.

Director William Malone had Geoffrey Rush made up to eerily resemble Vincent Price, the star of William Castle's hokily entertaining 1956 original, right down to the pencil thin mustache. They've even renamed the character Price, in case anyone misses the point.

But Rush, the Oscar-winning star of "Shine," seems slightly embarrassed as the bitchy, amusement-park magnate who invites four strangers to spend the night at a notorious former mental institution. Providing his guests with guns as party favors, he offers $1 million (up from $10,000 in the original) to anyone who survives.

It's a birthday celebration for his beautiful but greedy wife Evelyn (Famke Janssen), whom he may or may not be trying to kill. Or she may be trying to kill him.

Or the rising body count may be the work of one of the guests—including a former professional baseball player (Taye Diggs, who gets to keep his shirt on for once), a doctor (Peter Gallagher) and a descendant of the building's original owners (Chris Kattan).

Just before the house's special-effects ghosts—who bear an unfortunate resemblance to mold—show up, one of the characters remarks, "There's a lot of energy in here." The same can't be said of this joyless film.

SIGHT AND SOUND, 3/00, p. 45, Kim Newman

1931. At the Vannacutt Psychiatric institute for the Criminally Insane, an art deco fortress atop a Californian cliff, abused patients rebel against the sadistic and murderous Dr Vannacutt. He traps them inside and allows them to burn to death. Only five staff members escape.

The present. Evelyn, wife of amusement-park tycoon Stephen Price, convinces her husband to rent the institute, now the property of Watson Pritchett, for her birthday party. A mysterious force hacks into Stephen's computer and changes his guest list. On the night of the party, Price welcomes the guests: office-worker Sara (who stole her boss' invite), baseball player Eddie, aspirant celebrity Melissa and physician Blackburn. Price offers £1 million to anyone who survives a night in the house, which Pritchett explains is alive and malicious. Shutters trap the guests and Schecter, Price's special-effects man, is killed before he can do any of the planned stunts. Evelyn is conspiring with Blackburn, her lover, to have Price murdered by framing him for her own apparent death and so terrorising the guests that one of them (Sara) will shoot him. However, the Darkness, a supernatural force, has brought together descendants of the five 1931 escapees to die and fulfil the curse. All but Sara and Eddie are killed. They are saved by Pritchett's ghost, who has resisted joining the Darkness and opens a shutter so they can escape.

Producers Robert Zemeckis, Joel Silver and Gilbert Adler are veterans of the cable series *Tales from the Crypt* and the films *(Demon Knight, Bordello of Blood)* spun off from it. They turn their attention here to one of the first filmmakers to be influenced by the 50s horror comics which inspired the Crypt series: producer (and sometime director) William Castle. Remembered for gimmicks like Emergo (a skeleton puppet dangled over the audience) and Percepto (small seat-buzzers to tingle spines), Castle really came into his own as a horrormeister with *House on Haunted Hill* (1958). He amused himself with a rollercoaster pacing (wittily literalised in this remake, whose protagonist is a rollercoaster tycoon) piling shock on shock. But he also combined solid old-fashioned horror premises with cynical characterisation and casually lunatic plot devices to provoke constantly a reaction of befuddled astonishment.

Though it contains the bones of the old Robb White script, this new *Haunted Hill* adds a genuinely supernatural plot wound around the old business of the duplicitous wife contriving to knock off her husband but being one-upped by his even more ingenious counterplots. It's a bit like having two skeletons in one body. The film shifts rapidly from the explicable but far-fetched business to the plot-thread about the house's wispy blob of damned souls seeking further victims, so both strands suffer. However, the try-anything approach of writer-director William Malone (another *Crypt* alumnus) is actually very much in the spirit of Castle (whose daughter Terry joins the production team), and so this noisy, scrappy, effects-heavy rethink manages to respect the original's intentions far more than such recent remakes as the 1999 versions of *The Mummy* and *The Haunting*. There's no point in complaining that the blood pools, dismemberment and rampaging spooks cheapen the purity of a property that was always supposed to be disreputable, and Malone may even be essaying a further homage by yoking in some of the apparitions from Castle's *Thirteen Ghosts* (1963).

The 1958 film house (a Frank Lloyd Wright exterior) was built around one of Vincent Price's first elegant, verge-of-camp horror performances. The new development (a wonderful streamlined cliff-top shape) luckily secures Geoffrey Rush playing a character named after the old star. With his sad eyes and a pencil moustache, Rush is the image of Price.   Malone has him quoting Vincent Price's key line ("The house is alive!") from Roger Corman's *House of Usher* (1960), another major Price horror film, and even throws in a mad dream sequence with tossed-around severed heads from the Corman-Price *Tales of Terror* (1962).   The super Famke Janssen, like Carol Ohmart, stands up to her domineering co-star and has one wonderful moment when, improvising as her murder scheme falls apart, she flirtatiously suggests to her dim lover she has a crazy idea that might work if a fresh corpse can be procured—and then stabs him in the stomach with a scalpel as a demonstration.

The supporting stooges have no more chance of surviving than they did in the old film, though *Saturday Night Live* alumnus Chris Kattan delivers an extended homage to Elisha Cook Jr's speciality, squirming alcoholic cowardliness, and pleasingly saves the day in spectral form.   The mix of laughs, shocks and gruesomeness is much the same as in the two *Tales from the Crypt* movies, but Malone coaxes a slightly fresher flavour, taking on board the influence of David Fincher and even Lars von Trier.

The opening asylum revolt—a closeshot of a pencil being sharpened is enough to tip off the squeamish viewer to shut their eyes for a minute or so—is *guignol* nastiness of the first order. This strong meat recurs as the ghastliness begins in earnest, with Price trapped in a basement isolation chamber, bombarded with flash-cut images and monsters (one a top Dick Smith design made for but cut from *Ghost Story)* that, along with a loud soundtrack of groans and rumbles, make a good case for the hit-you-over-the-head style of horror movie in an era where the subtle creepy chill is in the ascendant.

Also reviewed in:
NEW YORK TIMES, 10/30, p. B18, Lawrence Van Gelder
VARIETY, 11/1-7/99, p. 87, Joe Leydon

HUNDRED AND ONE NIGHTS, A

A Cinema Village Features release.   *Producer:* Dominique Vignet.   *Director:* Agnès Varda. *Screenplay (French with English subtitles):* Agnès Varda.   *Director of Photography:* Eric Gauter. *Editor:* Hugues Darmois.   *Running time:* 101 minutes.   *MPAA Rating:* Not Rated.

CAST: Michel Piccoli (Simon Cinema); Marcello Mastroianni (Italian Friend); Henri Garcin (Firmin, the Butler); Julie Gayet (Camille); Mathieu Demy (Mica); Emmanuel Salinger (Vincent); Fanny Ardant, Jean-Paul Belmondo, Sandrine Bonnaire, Catherine Deneuve, Robert De Niro, Gérard Depardieu, Harrison Ford, Anouk Aimée, Gina Lollobrigida, and Jeanne Moreau (Themselves).

NEW YORK POST, 4/16/99, p. 56, Rod Dreher

Agnes Varda's 1995 tribute to cinema's first 100 years, "A Hundred and One Nights," is a shallow indulgence. She gathers a "That's Entertainment"-style collection of famous clips and presents them as part of an embarrassingly silly plot, a gasbag of Gallic whimsy that has to be seen to be disbelieved.

It's this: An eccentric centenarian (Michel Piccoli) named—get this—"Simon Cinema" hires Camille (Julie Gayet), a fetching young film student, to come by every day for movie chitchat. He's a senile cinephile who thinks he is and has been a number of great characters and personages from film history.

Camille is surprised one day to find Marcello Mastroianni visiting Monsieur Cinema. They're old friends, as it happens, and keeps happening: The movie tosses up cameos from superstars of French cinema (including Alain Delon, Jean-Paul Belmondo, Catherine Deneuve) and international moviemaking (Harrison Ford, Robert De Niro, Clint Eastwood).

It's fun to see all these luminaries glamming their way fleetingly across the screen, but it's not worth having to put up with this dull and sentimental dialogue.

Camille is involved in a subplot with her aspiring film auteur boyfriend, Mica (Mathieu Demy, son of the director and the late Jacques Demy).   A new generation of up-and-coming moviemakers jabber gaily about their love of movies, and decide at last to cast M. Cinema in their project. C'est un kitschy coup! Yuck.

VILLAGE VOICE, 4/20/99, p. 148, Elliott Stein

Made in 1994 and inspired by the centenary of the movies, Agnés Varda's *101 Nights* is a work of unbridled whimsy in which Michel Piccoli plays a near-hundred-year-old director who inhabits a château filled with movie memorabilia. Perturbed by his loss of memory, he employs a film student to stimulate him with chatter on Welles, Buñuel, and Renoir. Varda punctuates their meetings with clips from movie classics and visits from old colleagues (Delon, Mastroianni, Moreau, et al.), but the clips are by the numbers, and the illustrious callers can't do much with the inane script. A waste of talent, *101 Nights* could have used 50 rewrites.

Also reviewed in:
NEW YORK TIMES, 4/16/99, p. E20, Janet Maslin
VARIETY, 1/30-2/5/95, p. 51, Lisa Nesselson

HURRICANE, THE

A Universal Pictures and Beacon Pictures release of an Azoff Films/Rudy Langlais production. *Executive Producer:* Rudy Langlais, Thomas A. Bliss, Marc Abraham, Irving Azoff, Tom Rosenberg, and William Teitler.   *Producer:* Armyan Bernstein, John Ketcham, and Norman Jewison. *Director:* Norman Jewison. *Screenplay:* Armyan Bernstein and Dan Gordon. *Based upon the book "The Sixteenth Round" by:* Rubin "Hurricane" Carter. *Based upon the book "Lazarus and the Hurricane" by:* Sam Chaiton and Terry Swinton. *Director of Photography:* Roger Deakins. *Editor:* Stephen Rivkin. *Music:* Christopher Young. *Music Editor:* Thomas Milano. *Sound:* Bruce Carwardine and (music) Robert Fernandez. *Sound Editor:* Michael O'Farrell and Wayne Griffin. *Casting:* Avy Kaufman. *Production Designer:* Philip Rosenberg. *Art Director:* Dennis Davenport. *Set Decorator:* Gordon Sim. *Set Dresser:* David Evans. *Special Effects:* Kaz Kobielski. *Costumes:* Aggie Guerard Rodgers. *Make-up:* John Caglione, Jr and Irene Kent.   *Make-up (Denzel Washington):* Carl Fullerton.   *Stunt Coordinator:* John A. Stoneham, Jr. *Running time:* 120 minutes. *MPAA Rating:* R.

CAST: Denzel Washington (Rubin "Hurricane" Carter); Vicellous Reon Shannon (Lesra Martin); Deborah Kara Unger (Lisa Peters); Liev Schreiber (Sam Chaiton); John Hannah (Terry Swinton); Dan Hedaya (Vincent Della Pesca); Debbi Morgan (Mae Thelma); Clancy Brown (Lt. Jimmy Williams); David Paymer (Myron Beldock); Harris Yulin (Leon Friedman); Rod Steiger (Judge Sarokin); Badja Djola (Mobutu); Vincent Pastore (Alfred Bello); Al Waxman (Warden); David Lansbury (U.S. Court Prosecutor); Garland Whitt (John Artis); Chuck Cooper (Earl Martin); Brenda Thomas Denmark (Alma Martin); Marcia Bennett (Jean Wahl); Beatrice Winde (Louise Cockersham); Mitchell Taylor, Jr. (Young Rubin); Bill Raymond (Paterson Judge); Merwin Goldsmith (Judge Larner); John A. Mackay (Man at Falls); Donnique Privott (Boy at the Falls); Moynan King (Tina Barbieri); Gary Dewitt Marshall (Nite Spot Cabbie); John Christopher Jones (Reporter at Bar); Gwendolyn Mulamba (Nite Spot Woman); Richard Davidson (Paterson Detective); George Odom (Big Ed); Tonye Patano (Woman at Prison); Fulvio Cecere (Paterson Policeman); Phillip Jarrett (Soldier #1 in U.S.O. Club); Rodney M. Jackson (Soldier #2 in U.S.O. Club); Judi Embden (Woman in U.S.O. Club); Terry Claybon (Emile Griffith); Ben Bray (Joey Giordello); Michael Justus (Joey Cooper); Kenneth McGregor (Detective at Hospital); Frank Proctor (Pittsburgh Ring Announcer); Peter Wylie (Pittsburgh Referee);   David Gray (Pittsburgh TV Announcer);   Joe Matheson (Philadelphia Ring Announcer);   Bill Lake (Philadelphia TV Announcer);   Robin Ward (Reading, Pa. TV Announcer); Harry Davis (Reading, Pa. Referee); Pippa Pearthree (Patty Valentine); Jean Daigle (Detective); Robert Evans (Detective at Lafayette Bar); Scott Gibson (Reporter at

Banquet); Ann Holloway (Cashier); Jim Beardon (Lieutenant); Peter Graham (Prisoner with Camera); George Masswohl (Mechanic); Lawrence Sacco and David Frisch (New Jersey Policemen); Ralph Brown (Federal Court Assistant Prosecutor); Dyron Holmes (Reporter); Ryan Williams (Elstan Martin); Bruce Vavrina (St. Joseph's Doctor); Brenda Braxton (Dancer with John Artis); Christopher Riordan (Jury Foreman).

LOS ANGELES TIMES, 12/29/99, Calendar/p. 1, Kenneth Turan

Denzel Washington's career has not lacked for exceptional roles; he's been nominated for Oscars and even won one. But nothing really prepares us for what he does in "The Hurricane." With power, intensity, remarkable range and an ability to disturb that is both unnerving and electric, it is more than Washington's most impressive part, it sums up his career as well, encapsulating the reasons why he's one of the very best actors working in film today.

That this role would be good for Washington was no surprise to the man himself. He tried to buy the right to former middleweight contender Rubin "Hurricane" Carter's stranger-than-fiction life story nearly a decade ago, and he told eventual co-writer and co-producer Annyan Bernstein, "Just know that I want this, and I'm always going to want this." Once Washington got the part, he trained as a fighter for more than a year and lost enough pounds to physically transform himself into the lean and deadly boxer with a cobra's instinct for the kill.

Given this, it's regrettable, if perhaps inevitable, that the rest of this film is not up to the mark set by Washington's work. Co-written by Bernstein and Dan Gordon and directed by the veteran Norman Jewison, "The Hurricane" is fairly standard middle-of-the-road fare, simplistic, conventional, and, when the camera is not focused on Washington, lacking in things to hold our attention. Still, with a story so full of twists it's hard to believe it wasn't invented (and, as with "The Insider," some of it was), a certain amount of interest is built in.

If you're more a refugee from the counterculture than a boxing fan, Hurricane Carter will be familiar from the Bob Dylan song about him featuring classic protest lyrics like "This is the story of the Hurricane, the man the authorities came to blame." For Carter was falsely convicted of a bloody triple murder in Patterson, N.J., in 1967 and served nearly two decades in prison before a jaw-dropping series of events ended up winning him his freedom.

"The Hurricane," to its credit, is an ambitious film, as witness the complicated back-and-forth structure its screenwriters have come up with to hopscotch through several decades of the boxer's life.

In what looks like a stylistic nod to "Raging Bull," Carter is introduced via a black-and-white re-creation of his 1963 fight against Emile Griffith. With his trademark goatee and hostile stare, Carter was intimidation itself in the ring, someone who, as he later says, would "take all the hatred and skill I could muster and send a man to his destruction."

Next we see Carter behind bars, willing to put his life on the line to protect the manuscript of the autobiography he's written in prison. With that book, "The Sixteenth Round," published in 1973, Carter discovered writing as a weapon—"more powerful than a fist could ever be."

Years later, a copy of that book falls into the hands of Lesra Martin (Vicellous Reon Shannon), a Brooklyn-born teenager living in Toronto with three socially conscious Canadians (John Hannah, Deborah Kara Unger, Liev Schreiber) who have taken an interest in his welfare. (And if that sounds inexplicable that's just the way the movie presents it.)

Pompously prompted by one of the Canadians ("Sometimes we don't pick the books we read, they pick us"), Lesra begins to read "The Sixteenth Round," enabling us to see, via flashback and voice-over, the circumstances of Carter's life and why he ended up in prison.

Many of Carter's on-screen difficulties seem to stem from a "Les Miserables"-type vendetta against him by the fictional Det. Vincent Della Pesca that began when Carter was a boy of 11. (According to an article by Selwyn Raab, the New York Times reporter who covered the original case, several aspects of Carter's personal and legal history have been changed and simplified.) Della Pesca is played by Dan Hedaya, best known for his portraits of Richard Nixon, and his character is so blackhearted and devious he makes the former president at his worst look like Kris Kringle by comparison.

Never an easygoing individual, once Carter is imprisoned for murders he didn't commit as a result of Della Pesca's machinations, he focuses on not allowing himself to want or need anything. "Freedom came," he says, "in not having anything they could deprive me of."

So it's next door to miraculous (yet true) that this hardened convict both read and responded to a letter Martin sent him after finishing the book, and that the Canadians the young man lived with became seriously involved in the movement to free Carter, even if the film makes them more significant players than they were.

It's in dealing with these Canadians that "The Hurricane" is at its weakest. It's almost painful when the camera moves from the magnetic Carter to a trio of blander-than-bland individuals who hardly seem real. In fact, the problem is they're not.

According to "Hurricane," an excellent new authorized biography by James S. Hirsch about to be published by Houghton Mifflin, between eight and 10 Canadians were involved with Carter, not three, and both the group's dynamic and relationship to Carter (particularly that of Lisa Peters, played by Unger, who later married him) was much more psychologically complex than the film felt comfortable getting into. Still the awkward and stagy treatment of the Canadians does no one any favors, and edges the film's story into standard inspirational territory much more than it deserves.

Fortunately, "The Hurricane" has the honesty and skill of Washington's performance to combat its tendency toward tedium. The actor's work is especially impressive not only because Carter was a terrifying exemplar of barely controlled fury for much of his life—when he looked at you, you knew you'd been looked at—but also because the experiences of his life ended up changing him in not always foreseeable ways.

It's Washington's gift to be able to connect us with Carter even when he's at his angriest and most hostile and to make all the stages of his gradual evolution distinct and believable. He even takes what could be a cliched scene, Carter's personality splitting into three parts during a particularly harsh stretch of solitary confinement, and makes it an unforgettable moment. This is the last great performance of 1999, and arguably the best of the lot as well.

NEW YORK, 1/10/00, p. 45, Peter Rainer

In its early boxing scenes, *The Hurricane* shows us a fighter who takes a grim-faced pleasure in pulverizing his opponents. Denzel Washington's Rubin "Hurricane" Carter uses his body as a honed weapon, and his shaved head gives him a scary, projectile-like appearance. Carter's career as a leading middleweight contender was cut short when, in the fall of 1966, three white people were killed by two black gunmen in a Paterson, New Jersey, bar—leading to his arrest and that of John Artis, a young fan of his, both of whom happened to be riding in a car near the crime scene when the police stopped them. Convicted and sentenced, along with Artis, to three consecutive life terms, Carter spent nearly nineteen years in prison before winning his exoneration and release. The judge who overturned his second trial conviction, played in the movie by Rod Steiger, said that the findings were "based on racism rather than reason, and concealment rather than disclosure."

It's a tribute to Washington's performance that, in his many prison scenes, he never lets Carter go all gooey on us. He dropped 45 pounds for the role and worked himself into fighting trim; locked up, agitating for his freedom, his Carter is *still* a human projectile. Washington makes us understand how someone in prison might need to close himself off from all earthly wants in order to transcend the place that holds him. He also demonstrates the emotional toll on Carter; fortressed inside himself, the prisoner lets almost no light in. The actors uncompromising work stands in stark contrast to the rest of the film, which has a liberal-humanist slogginess. In an effort to turn Carter's story into a moral triumph of near-mythic proportions, the filmmakers, director Norman Jewison and screenwriters Armyan Bernstein and Dan Gordon, undercut Washington's fine, feral quality—his caged heat. To be truly memorable, the rest of the film needed to be as ferocious as its star.

The Hurricane simplifies Carter's odyssey. Instead of fully dramatizing how racism was rampant in the criminal-justice system that convicted him, it opts for a less sweeping indictment. What we get instead is a monomaniacal, partially fictionalized cop, Della Pesca (Dan Hedaya), who pursues Carter from the time of his boyhood right up to the final appeal and who is so openly malevolent that he makes Inspector Javert in *Les Misérables* seem like Officer Joe Bolton. What the movie doesn't probe is how, according to *Lazarus and the Hurricane*, the book on which the film is partially based, Carter, because of his growing aversion to passive resistance and his friendship with Malcolm X, had already been targeted for harassment by the New Jersey police and the FBI years before his arrest. The context of Carter's militancy is softened for mass consumption.

Della Pesca is balanced out by a trio of white, goody-goody social-activist Canadians (Liev Schreiber, Deborah Kara Unger, and John Hannah), who live commune-style in Toronto with Lesra (Vicellous Reon Shannon), the black, underprivileged Brooklyn boy they have "adopted." Years after Carter's initial conviction, Lesra picks up for a quarter a dog-eared copy of Carter's 1974 autobiography, *The Sixteenth Round,* and, his life changed, begins corresponding with Carter in prison, enlisting his guardians in a full-scale, and ultimately successful, campaign for the boxer's release. In real life, the three Canadians were nine, and according to Lewis Steel, one of Carter's defense attorneys, writing in the January 3 *Nation,* "none of the Canadians' investigative efforts played a role in the final outcome." Be that as it may, all this paints a pretty picture: Lesra, Carter's surrogate son, raises his idol Lazarus-style from the dead. The pillars of justice, photographed with stately splendor, vibrate with vindication.

The movie's dogged humorlessness, and its sixties-style cant, don't do justice to all the political crosscurrents in this story. Carter played out his cause from prison with remarkable media savvy; he became the darling of celebrities, including, of course, Bob Dylan, only to be set aside by many of them after his loss in his second trial. The movie alludes to this disenfranchisement in passing, but we never get a real sense of what a circus Carter's cause had become, or how it fit into the radical social activism of the time. You leave the film with the calm assurance that racial harmony has KO'd racial discord and that all is indeed right with the world.

NEW YORK POST, 12/29/99, p. 41, Lou Lumenick

Denzel Washington delivers a knockout performance that makes him the top contender for the Best Actor Oscar in "The Hurricane," an expertly crafted, deeply moving film.

He soars as boxer Rubin "Hurricane" Carter, a middleweight contender who was tried and convicted (along with a fan named John Artis) of a brutal triple homicide in a Paterson, N.J., bar in 1966.

Carter and his supporters—including Muhammad Ali and Bob Dylan, who wrote a famous song about the case—contended that Carter and Artis were innocent, framed by racist cops who bribed two witnesses to place them at the crime scene, and who altered and suppressed other evidence.

Carter, sentenced to three consecutive life sentences, spent nearly 20 years in jail—during which he published a best seller about his case, won a retrial and was convicted by a second, all-white jury.

He was finally freed, in 1985, in a highly unusual ruling by federal Judge H. Lee Sarokin, who found that Carter's civil rights had been grossly violated by the investigations and trials. (Artis had been paroled by this point.)

Washington, who lost 40 pounds for the well-staged boxing scenes, is magnificent as the fiercely defiant Carter, who copes with the brutal prison system by refusing to wear stripes and rarely leaving his cell.

He gets under your skin the way Burt Lancaster did in "Birdman of Alcatraz"—and it will be a tough performance for Kevin Spacey and the other Oscar hopefuls to beat.

After losing his retrial, Carter cuts himself off from the world, forcing his wife (Debbi Morgan) to divorce him. He only regains hope, years later, through a correspondence with Lesra Martin (Vicellous Reon Shannon), a black teenager from Brooklyn whose life was changed by reading Carter's book, "The Sixteenth Round."

The movie then goes on to suggest that Carter was freed largely through the superhuman efforts of white members of a Canadian commune with whom Lesra lived—an inspiring story that may be a bit of a factual stretch.

As my colleague Jack Newfield reported recently, the movie minimizes the contributions of the lawyers—and journalists—who labored for years to help Carter get his freedom.

The movie does depict Carter making a dramatic plea to Judge Sarokin (Rod Steiger). In reality, Carter wasn't even in the courtroom (though I consider this to be acceptable dramatic license).

"The Hurricane" is certainly high-velocity, thoughtful entertainment. Returning to the civil-rights themes of his most memorable films ("In the Heat of the Night," "A Soldier's Story"), veteran director Norman Jewison directs with a passion and precision that's been missing from his recent work.

The acting is first-rate, including young Shannon and Liev Schreiber, John Hannah and Deborah Kara Unger as the crusading Canadians (in real life, there were nine of them, including one who eventually married Carter).

The only one-note performance comes from Dan Hedaya ("Dick") as a Paterson detective who improbably dogs Carter from 1949 (when the boxer was busted as a juvenile offender) right up until his release 36 years later.

Make no mistake about it, thanks to Washington's layered acting, "The Hurricane" packs a real punch.

NEWSDAY, 12/29/99, Part II/p. B2, John Anderson

A personal note/admission: This reviewer grew up quite close to Paterson, N.J., land of William Carlos Williams, Allen Ginsberg, silk mills and the Lafayette Bar and Grill—where, on June 17, 1966, two gunmen murdered three people and kicked off the legal acrobatics that led to the 20-year imprisonment of middleweight contender Rubin (Hurricane) Carter and a young fan named John Artis.

There was never, to my recollection, any doubt among the locals (particularly the local police) that Carter was guilty. The "free-Carter" movement of the '70s, led by such celebrities as Muhammad Ali and Bob Dylan (rasping the folk-journalistic "Hurricane"), was seen as so much fashionable posturing. When Carter and Artis were re-convicted in December, 1976—after the New Jersey Supreme Court had ruled that the prosecution withheld evidence in the first trial—the air was out of the balloon. The two went back to prison for another dozen years.

The point is that at the center of "The Hurricane," the story of Carter as told by Norman Jewison, is nationalized, institutionalized racism. Carter didn't suffer just because a few cops in Paterson needed a fall guy and Carter was in the wrong place at the wrong time. Carter suffered because he was the right guy for a wrong age.

And while director Jewison can't help but push our righteous indignation buttons with "Hurricane," and gets a formidable performance out of Denzel Washington, the story never radiates much beyond the corruption of Carter's lifelong enemy, Paterson detective Vincent Della Pesca (a nicely vicious Dan Hedaya), who serves as the deserving, but all-too-obvious, whipping boy of the story, absolving the world of its sins.

"The Hurricane" is based on two books: Carter's own "The Sixteenth Round" (titled back when championship fights were actually 15 rounds), which inspired everyone from Dylan to young Lesra Martin, a Brooklyn teen living in Canada (Vicellous Reon Shannon); and "Lazarus and the Hurricane," by Terry Swinton and Sam Chaiton, two of the three social-activist Canadian lawyers who were Lesra's guardians and, at his behest, launched the legal campaign that eventually set Carter free.

Granted, there's only so much a filmmaker can do with a character serving a two-decade prison term (although Carter's introductory stint in solitary is one of the better things Washington's ever done). So Jewison—a Canadian, by the way—devotes much of the film to Lesra's story, his guardians (played by John Hannah, Liev Schreiber and Deborah Kara Unger), his bonding with Carter, and his impassioned efforts to set his hero free.

Because of this secondary story line, one never feels that Washington really gets to mount a sustained performance; he's an accessory to his own movie, seen in flashbacks and placed somewhere outside the emotional core of the film. He's beatified, in a way, made more or less flawless and immaculate, and less of a man than a billboard for the crimes that he's suffered—and for which Jewison never really hands up an indictment.

NEWSWEEK, 1/10/00, p. 60, David Ansen & Allison Samuels

Denzel Washington may make almost $10 million a movie, but he's not afraid to take a punch. When he took on the role of Rubin (Hurricane) Carter—the real-life middleweight contender imprisoned for 19 years for a murder he didn't commit—Washington trained as if he'd been given a shot at the title. He lost 44 pounds, and spent day after day taking punches: "I put my heart and soul into it. We were doing a lot of the full-body boxing, which I loved, but I began getting headaches and memory loss—that was a problem. It's a tough sport. I knew that already, because I know [Tyson] and Ali. But I can't give it up. It's addictive."

Washington gives a heavyweight performance in Norman Jewison's powerful movie "The Hurricane." Jewison, who also directed Washington in his breakthrough role in "A Soldier's Story," claims that by the end of filming he couldn't tell the actor from Carter himself: "He had his walk, the way he spoke, the way he carried his body. This role is probably his best work." Jewison is biased, but he may be right. Washington has been extraordinary before—as Stephen Biko in "Cry, Freedom," as Malcolm X in Spike Lee's epic and as the '40s sleuth in "Devil in a Blue Dress". But playing Carter stretches him in new ways. The hero of Jewison's movie— whom Bob Dylan commemorated in his anthem "Hurricane"—is a man who kept reinventing himself to survive. In trouble with the law since childhood, Carter was a soldier and then, because of his devastating punch, a celebrity with a wife, a daughter and a shot at the title. All that ended in 1966 when he and another innocent man were framed for killing three people in a Paterson, N.J., bar.

In "The Hurricane" Carter struggles to stay sane in prison, as rage and despair battle for the upper hand. Knowing that hope makes him vulnerable, he turns inward—refusing even to see his wife and daughter. Washington perfectly captures the steeliness of Carter's will. It's a moving, fiercely compacted performance that invites us to marvel at the resilience of the spirit. "The Hurricane" has a lot of ground to cover, and it jumps back and forward in time, not always gracefully. Carter's saga alternates with the story of Lesra Martin (the excellent Vicellous Reon Shannon), a black teenager who reads the boxer's jailhouse autobiography, then helps him overturn his conviction. Lesra has been adopted by three white Canadian idealists who will ultimately devote their lives to freeing Carter. Who on earth *are* these people? The truth is they're composite figures boiled down from the nine commune members who worked for Carter's release—though not quite in the Hardy Boy manner the movie presents.

The screenplay takes a more dubious liberty by inventing a racist and corrupt New Jersey detective (planned by Dan Hedaya) with a lifelong vendetta against our hero. This melodramatic device succeeds in getting the blood boiling—audiences like their villains unregenerate—but by putting the onus on one evil white man, it diminishes the systemic racism that kept Carter behind bars. Perhaps these are the compromises Hollywood filmmakers have to make to get a true story of a black hero made. It would be nice if "The Hurricane" trusted the audience to swallow a less simplistic view of reality. (Was Carter always a victim of injustice? At every step of his life?) Still, this rousing tale of hideously belated justice throws knockout blows. "Hurricane" may get sidetracked in its "O Canada" salute—Jewison was born in Toronto—but whenever Washington is on screen, it hums with intensity and conviction.

With due respect to Will Smith, Washington has been the pre-eminent black actor of the '90s, and he clearly feels some responsibility to present an upstanding image. He had no interest in playing slave roles like the leads in "Beloved" and "Amistad," and he has shied away from interracial love stories. Washington dropped out of the romance "Love Field" with Michelle Pfeiffer and, before making "The Pelican Brief" with Julia Roberts, lobbied to have what he believed were out-of-character love scenes cut from the script. "I know that a large part of my audience is black women," he says. "I also know there aren't many black love stories they can see on the big screen—and that's an issue."

While the star projects a straitlaced image, he's loose and funny in person. When the cameras aren't rolling, the 6-foot-1 actor favors baggy sweats, tennis shoes and baseball hats. He glides into the Four Seasons in Beverly Hills with his signature *I'm the man* strut, and the businessmen in ties look up in awe. Washington is a sports fanatic (he has Lakers floor seats across from Jack Nicholson's) and an emphatic lover of hip-hop (he can recite a DMX or Nas verse smoother than a 15-year-old in Brooklyn).

Washington grew up middle class in the city of Mt. Vernon, N.Y., and his parents divorced when he was 14. The actor himself has been married to the same woman, Pauletta Pearson, for 17 years. They have four kids, and Washington is determined to be there for them in ways his own father couldn't be. His father was a Pentecostal minister. He spent a lot of time at work and wasn't the type for hugs and kisses. "When my first child was born it was clear where my commitment was going to be," says Washington. "I make the recitals, the football game, whatever, because you can't tell your kid, 'Sorry I can't raise you now—I have a career.' My father didn't have the option—he didn't have the money I have." Whether or not it's his first priority, Washington's career has been dazzling. He expects that black actors of his children's generation will make even greater strides. "The term they use is being kept down by the glass ceiling. I tell people: the ceiling is glass, not lead. Which means we can break it down."

SIGHT AND SOUND, 4/00, p. 50, Richard Kelly

1973. Black middleweight boxer Rubin 'Hurricane' Carter is in prison. 1966. Three whites are killed in a New Jersey barroom, and two black men are seen fleeing in a white car with out-of-state plates. Carter and young black friend John Artis, driving a similar vehicle, are arrested by detective Vincent Della Pesca.

Years later. Lesra Martin, a black boy tutored by three Canadian educationalists, reads Carter's autobiography. As a boy, Carter was railroaded into juvenile detention by Della Pesca. He escaped, joined the army and became a promising fighter, but Della Pesca oversaw his recapture. Carter emerged from prison to become a middleweight contender and public figure. Della Pesca convinced two petty criminals to testify they saw Carter and Artis fleeing the New Jersey barroom. In 1967 an all white jury convicted the two men. Despite a prominent campaign supporting Carter and Artis, they lost a second trial in 1976. Lesra corresponds with Carter, visits him in prison, and introduces him to the Canadians. After a lost appeal that dispirits Carter, the Canadians offer support to his defense counsel. Della Pesca threatens them and their car is sabotaged, but they uncover papers which reveal that Della Pesca falsified evidence against Carter. In 1985 Carter gambles on appealing to a federal court. Judge Sarokin nullifies the convictions as unconstitutional.

Norman Jewison barely gets 10 minutes into this workmanlike liberal biopic before his soundtrack makes the first of several nods to Bob Dylans 'Hurricane', a magisterially detailed ballad about the iniquities that befell Rubin Carter. Jewison's film dutifully visualises what civil-rights students and Dylan fans already know of this notorious triple murder frame. But its narrative structure and final act are indebted to *Lazarus and the Hurricane,* a book by Canadians Sam Chaiton and Terry Swinton about their relationship with Lesra Martin and their role in the efforts to win Carter's freedom.

In the opening reels, the structure of *The Hurricane* seems restless and inventive: we wonder if the film will tell us something sharp and unsettling about race hate in the US. After all, Carter and Artis were wrongly convicted in the incendiary summer of 1967 and Carter was politically outspoken. Here, Carter is seen shaking his head over news footage of the Harlem riots, and an off-the-record barb about hunting down 'nigger hating cops' winds up in print, earning him a brick through his window. Meanwhile, in the film's present, young Lesra imbibes enough of Rubin's fierceness to accuse his Canadian teachers of salving their liberal guilt by undertaking his education.

But otherwise *The Hurricane* fights shy of evoking the climate of prejudice that condemned Carter and refuses to disquiet us by linking his plight to racist disgraces in the US today. As the synopsis above might attest, the drama is hung on a vendetta between a flawed but honourable man and a doggedly bad cop. Yes, it's Valjean and Javert, together again. Jewison frames Dan Hedaya's detective Della Pesca forever lurking at street corners and doorways, or stepping from the shadows to mutter some foul racist oath. *The Hurricane*'s producers have insisted the film mounts an indictment of institutional racism which encompasses judges and prosecutors too, but you might have trouble figuring this out from what you're shown.

Moreover, the film's account of prison exposes the points where mainstream cinema always fumbles stories as harsh and unhappy as Carter's. As *The Hurricane* serves out his first stretch, he tells us in voiceover that bitter experience convinced him to train himself as a man-machine, his body a weapon. But this tragic, dehumanised sentiment is somehow rendered movie-sexy by a montage in which star Denzel Washington executes inverted push-ups as though auditioning for the *Con Air* sequel. Later there's a crucial, adventurous sequence, after Carter has refused prison fatigues in protest at his conviction and lands in solitary confinement ("The Hole") for weeks on end. There, Jewison tries to convey Carter's personality in collapse and Washington effects a convincing tussle between Carter's warring selves: a child who wants to sob, a fighter who wants to lash out, and the wiser head who knows the worst is still to come.

Nevertheless, the standard movie ellipsis fails to give us much more than an inkling of how such deprivation might maim the spirit. An entire film could have been conjured out of that Hole. Thereafter, with the help of a very controlled performance from Washington, Jewison presents Carter as a stoic jailhouse intellectual, "Buddha in a ten foot cell," as Dylan had it. Then there's a lousy, inevitable scene where the Canadians pay Rubin a visit. Carter rebuffs them tersely for their inability to understand the claustral, inhumane hell that is imprisonment. Trouble is, Jewison hasn't really given us the images to fit Carter's description. He's even issued Carter with a prison-guard pal, and when Carter is finally freed, there's a ticker-tape celebration in the jailhouse.

Of course, Jim Sheridan's drama of wrongful imprisonment *In the Name of the Father* was equally studio-slick and cavalier with the facts, but it worked because its Gerry Conlon protagonist was seen to be dime-a-dozen: a bit of an eejit, always likely to get himself in the wrong place. Rubin Carter, though, is plainly extraordinary. "How can the life of such a man be in the palm of some fool's hands?" Dylan complained. But lesser men still fall into the same hands, and still find the law discriminates against class and colour. Very few can muster the resilience and dignity of Rubin Carter, and their stories are unlikely to be deemed sufficiently inspirational for Hollywood. While doing the rounds of US breakfast television for *The Hurricane*'s opening weekend, Rubin Carter himself was respectfully asked if he was surprised by anything in the film. "I never knew," he professed with a very engaging grin, "that I was so pretty."

TIME, 12/27/99, p. 176, Richard Schickel

Maybe Rubin Carter was a hurricane in the ring, but the movie version of his story—the middleweight contender who was framed on murder charges based on racism—downgrades him to a tropical storm. In Washington's finely shaded performance he's a low-pressure system, illuminated by distant flashes of lightning.

Despite what you might imagine, this is not a bad thing. For once he absorbed the outrage of false conviction, Carter turned fiercely inward. He wrote a good autobiography about his case, read spiritually uplifting books and learned to avoid everyone who might offer him false hope. He had to find the strength to endure entirely within himself.

The austerity of Carter's prison life does not offer many opportunities for electrifying moviemaking, but *The Hurricane* is nevertheless a thoughtful and even inspiring film. That's not just because of the way it celebrates Carter's self-discipline, but because the director, Norman Jewison, enforces the contrast between his stoicism and the efforts of the unlikely team of '60s activists that eventually came to his rescue.

There were nine of them in reality, just three of them in the movie (for the sake of narrative convenience), and their relentless determination to free a man they came to know only after they took up his cause is impressive. That's especially so since they are led by a teenage black youth, Lesra Martin (very well played by Vicellous Reon Shannon), who happens to pick up Carter's book, enters into correspondence with him and then drags his Canadian guardians into the long, complicated fight to redeem him. He's an irresistible kid, maybe the only sort of person who could break down Carter's wall of reserve. *The Hurricane* may be a little too leisurely in its development, but the unlikely triumph of Carter's saviors is an authentically moving one.

VILLAGE VOICE, 1/4/00, p. 108, Amy Taubin

Rising above his filmic circumstances, Denzel Washington delivers a mesmerizing, volatile performance as Rubin "Hurricane" Carter, the New Jersey boxer who spent 20 years in prison for a triple homicide he didn't commit. Washington is a more experienced actor than he was when he played Malcolm X—as impressive as he was in that film, he has even more depth and concentration here. But he's limited by a director and scriptwriter who prefer to paint Carter as a saint and a martyr than as a complicated human being, unfairly treated by a racist justice system.

A talented boxer and a defiant black nationalist who never hesitated to show his contempt for the white establishment, including the media, Carter is a great subject for a biopic. *The Hurricane,* however, asks him to share equal time with a trio of white Canadian social activists (played by Deborah Kara Unger, Liev Schreiber, and John Hannah) and an African American boy (Vicellous Reon Shannon) whom they're fostering and who brings *The Sixteenth Round*, the autobiography that Carter wrote in prison, to their attention. In the film, this quartet then devotes itself full-time to Carter's appeals, eventually uncovering the evidence that wins him his release.

As Lewis M. Steel, one of Carter's lawyers, writes in the January 3 issue of *The Nation*, the Canadians provided Carter with much needed psychological support but had almost nothing to do with the discovery of evidence or the legal processes. By concocting a fictional drama around their investigations, the film blurs the way an entire racist-tainted system of justice was rigged to reward and protect those who convicted Carter and to keep truth from being told. Similarly the film reduces institutionalized racism to the vindictiveness of one bad-apple cop (Dan Hedaya), who had it in for Carter from childhood. And most improbably, it provides a counterbalance for the bad cop in the form of a corrections officer who bends the rules to secure special privileges for Carter during his 20-year stay in the pen.

It's a Hollywood adage that the political must be personalized and another that in order to attract a "crossover" audience, a film that features a black hero must provide white heroes as well. *The Hurricane* plays by those rules and as a result is far too tepid to either do right by Rubin Carter or expose the racism that exists unchanged in the 35 years since he was railroaded into prison. Does anyone think Giuliani would play the same race card that Carter's prosecutors did if it wasn't still the key to political success?

Also reviewed in:
CHICAGO TRIBUNE, 1/7/00, Friday/p. A, Michael Wilmington
NEW REPUBLIC, 1/31/00, p. 30, Stanley Kauffmann
NEW YORK TIMES, 12/29/99, p. E1, Stephen Holden
NEW YORKER, 1/10/00, p. 91, David Denby
VARIETY, 12/20/99-1/2/00, p. 56, Emanuel Levy
WASHINGTON POST, 1/7/00, p. C1, Stephen Hunter
WASHINGTON POST, 1/7/00, Weekend/p. 37, Desson Howe

I STAND ALONE

A Strand Releasing release of a Les Cinémas de la Zone production with the participation of Love Streams Productions and Canal+. *Producer:* Gaspar Noé. *Director:* Gaspar Noé. *Screenplay (French with English subtitles):* Gaspar Noé. *Director of Photography:* Dominique Colin. *Editor:* Lucile Hadzihalilovic and Gaspar Noé. *Sound:* Olivier Le Vacon. *Sound Editor:* Valerie Deloof. *Running time:* 92 minutes. *MPAA Rating:* Not Rated.

CAST: Philippe Nahon (Jean Chevalier, the Butcher); Blandine Lenoir (Cynthia, his Daughter); Frankye Pain (His Mistress); Martine Audrain (Mother-in-Law); Zaven (Moralistic Man); Jean-François Rauger (Estate Agent); Guillaume Nicloux (Supermarket Manager); Olivier Doran (Voice of Presenter); Aïssa Djabri (Doctor Choukroun); Serge Faurie (Nursing Home Manager); Fréderic Pfohl (Male Hospice Nurse); Stéphanie Sec (Female Hospice Nurse); Arlete Balkis (Dying Woman); Gil Bertharion, Jr. (Truck Driver); Rado (Hotel Caretaker); Nicolas Jouhet (Café Owner); Ahmed Bounacir (Café Customer); Roland Gueridon (Old Friend); Hervé Gueridon (2nd Friend); Sophie Nicolle (Interim's Daughter); Paule Abecassis (Drug Addict); Marie-Madeleine Denecheau (Roland's Wife); Robert Roy (4th Friend); Joel Lecullée (1st Butcher); Denis Falgoux (2nd Butcher); Marc Faure (Abattoir Director); Gérard Ortega (Bar Owner); Stéphane Derderian (Bar Owner's Son); Alain Pierre (Bar Owner's Friend); Sylvie Raymond (Nurse); Monsieur Billot (3rd Butcher).

LOS ANGELES TIMES, 5/7/99, Calendar/p. 6, Kevin Thomas

Gaspar Noe's "I Stand Alone" has an exhilaration that comes from looking at life at its meanest so unflinchingly that you can actually be amused by the absurdity of the human predicament.

His story of a brutal and brutalized butcher is of a man managing to survive at society's lower rungs only to have his life unravel hopelessly in a moment of enraged misunderstanding. A rugged man with a furious gaze and doughy nose who looks much older than the 41 years of age he's supposed to be in the year the film is set, 1980, the butcher (Philippe Nahon) speaks to us continually in voice-over, revealing a fierce, reflective intellect that bespeaks of a self-awareness that heightens rather than relieves his profound despair. He knows a truth Noe is unafraid to tell: that many people live lives that are ultimately without meaning. This is the fate that the butcher, in a mounting rage and frustration, becomes determined to avoid but realizes he has yet to find a way to do so.

We learn that he was abandoned at age 2 by his mother, that his father, a communist, ended up in a German death camp. As a boy he managed to learn the butcher's trade, eventually setting up his own shop in a drab industrial section of Paris. When his lover abandons him and their baby daughter he raises the child, buying a flat for the two of them. Unprepared for the onset of menstruation, the daughter, a mute, heads for her father's shop, but he mistakes the blood on her skirt as evidence of rape. His ensuing moment of rage is enough to destroy his meager existence: He loses everything while serving time, even his daughter, who is sent to an institution.

(All of this is covered in a quick montage drawn from "Carne," the film to which "I Stand Alone" is a sequel; but the latter film can in fact stand alone.)

Once out of prison, the butcher takes a job at a bar and begins an affair with the ample proprietress (Frankye Pain), who becomes pregnant and with whom he moves to Lille with the false hope that she will stake him to a meat market. Instead he winds up in a cramped apartment with this loathsome woman and her elderly mother (Martine Audrain). In no time he's heading back to his old Paris neighborhood, foolishly expecting to find "real human beings" who will help him get started on a new life.

Yet the conflicted, highly emotional moment of truth to which Noe brings us is not at all predictable, and is full of ambiguity and contradictions. It is an amazing, explosive moment, preceded by a buildup so relentlessly grim and nasty, so brutalizing to the butcher, that "I Stand Alone" actually verges on comedy in the darkest way imaginable.

Nahon is a ferocious presence, a wounded beast of a man, who recalls the late Neville Brand. In both predicament and temperament this butcher has much in common with none other than that Stephen Sondheim protagonist, Sweeney Todd. (Noe regards a butcher "as the last on the chain based on a violent act, all for the survival of the strongest species.") His butcher also brings to mind Franz Biberkopf, the hero of R.W. Fassbinder's monumental "Berlin Alexanderplatz," a lower depths everyman, also fresh out of prison. He is also not unlike James Ellroy's cops, cursed with too much self-knowledge while caught up in a corrupt system.

Stylistically, "I Stand Alone" is a tour de force in black-and-white wide-screen, shot crisply in actual locales with sharp cutting punctuated by what sounds like gun shots. Noe has said his film is about survival rather than hate, and he certainly accomplished what he set out to do, creating "a real melodrama written in blood, semen and tears." You can't come with a better description of "I Stand Alone" than that.

NEW YORK POST, 3/17/99, p. 40, Jonathan Foreman

First shown at last year's New York Film Festival this pretentious and desperate-to-shock film was hailed by some of the more credulous critics as a brilliant Gallic "Taxi Driver" filtered through Dostoyevsky by way of Godard."

But for all its efforts to be degenerate, writer/director Gaspar Noe's "I Stand Alone" achieves only an adolescent (life is like, so meaningless) nihilism.

The film's unnamed antihero (Philippe Nahon) is a unemployed, middle-age horsemeat butcher, drunk on self-pity and impotent rage. A human toilet, overflowing with bitterness and bigotry, he rants endlessly about "f ---- ts in suits" when he's not alternatively fantasizing about murder and incest with his autistic daughter. Clearly, he is supposed to represent the dark side of French life—the stuff of which fascism is made.

Set in 1980, the film begins with a voice-over synopsis of the protagonist's life. We hear how his communist father was murdered in a Nazi death camp; how he impregnated a factory worker who abandoned him and their child before committing suicide; and how he himself went to prison (and lost both his shop and his daughter) for stabbing a man he erroneously believed had seduced the girl.

Now he is in Lille, France, living with (and supported by) his pregnant girlfriend and her aged mother, both of whom he hates.

When the girlfriend wrongfully accuses him of unfaithfulness, he savagely beats her, steals a gun and flees to Paris. There he takes a room in the same fleabag hotel where he conceived his daughter, and begins looking for a job in the meat business, his murderous misanthropy and bitterness redoubling with every setback.

There is something despicably compelling about this character's journey, but any social point (and there seems to be cheap existentialism behind all this) is undermined by the director's stylistic indulgences: Giant titles appear on screen saying things like "Morality" or "Death Opens No Doors," loud bangs accompany sudden close-ups, and large chunks of the film are taken up by the protagonist staring blankly into space while his voice-over narration explains the emptiness of all human relationships.

Noe's enthusiasm for ugliness doesn't help either. There's an ultra-realistic murder with blood 'n' brains on the floor and a long genital close-up from a porn movie. There is also a nauseating scene in which the heavily built protagonist tries to kill the baby in his pregnant girlfriend's womb.

The viewer is clearly supposed to think all this stuff is terribly daring; however, it's just the flailing of a technically adept "auteur," with a craving for attention but nothing to say.

NEWSDAY, 3/17/99, Part II/p. B13, John Anderson

Easily the most disturbing and talked-about entry in last year's New York Film Festival, Gaspar Noe's "I Stand Alone" has achieved a notoriety that hinges mostly on outrage and repulsion, locating it on the great "Les Demoiselles d'Avignon"-to-Karen Finley continuum of international art. Ultimately, it's a work that may require years to fully appreciate because its mere attitude is such an appallingly obvious byproduct of premillennial nihilism.

But ... is it a great movie? If the criteria are visual grace, an exhaltation of the human condition and dramatic fluidity, perhaps not; if the standards include a torquing of one's worldview and an unforgettable trip into a pestilential mind, there's no question "I Stand Alone" will stand.

Told from the point of view of an unnamed butcher (the mournful-looking Philippe Nahon), "I Stand Alone" is a great example of "in your face" cinema, in which the Butcher's ruminations exhibit every racist, sexist, paranoid and especially self-loathing aspect of the unexamined life. Noe lets him give his own backstory—unknown father, faithless mother, abusing teachers, grinding poverty—through the time when he, mistakingly thinking his daughter had been raped, stabs a man (the wrong man in any event) and goes to prison, loses his horsemeat shop, sees his daughter institutionalized and then loses touch with her. Released from prison, he hooks up with an obese matron (Frankye Pain), whom he impregnates, moves with to Lille and winds up brutally assaulting before fleeing back to Paris, with no money and a loaded gun.

A marriage of sorts between Dostoyevsky's "Notes From the Underground" and the work of Jean-Luc Godard, "I Stand Alone" is singularly brutal in its unveiling of the butcher's fevered mind. His deprived background might demand sympathy, but the enthusiasm of his hate makes us rule it out. So does the extent to which he follows his basest impulses down into a sewer of degradation. Noe's supertitles ("You have 30 seconds to leave the theater ... "), the gunshot accompaniment he give his closeups and the sense of no boundaries makes "I Stand Alone" a deeply unnerving experience. But of course, so does the nagging fear that the Butcher might not be so strange, or even so far away.

SIGHT AND SOUND, 4/99, p. 58, Tony Rayns

1980. Embittered and misanthropic, horse-meat butcher Jean Chevalier (long abandoned by his wife and fresh out of jail for maiming an immigrant he wrongly suspected of seducing his autistic daughter Cynthia) settles in Lille with his pregnant mistress and her mother. The mistress postpones funding the butcher's shop as she has promised him, and so Chevalier begins working as a nightwatchman in a hospital for geriatrics. When his mistress falsely accuses him of infidelity, Chevalier beats her up (hoping to abort the baby), steals her gun and hitchhikes back to Paris.

All but penniless, he rents a sleazy hotel room in the northern suburbs—it is the room where his daughter was conceived and tries to look for work. But the job centre has no jobs and old friends and acquaintances are broke and pessimistic. Two humiliating experiences (getting the brush-off at an interview for an abattoir job and being expelled from a bar after picking a fight) push him over the edge. He retrieves Cynthia from the institution where she has been in care and brings her back to the room. He imagines raping her or mercy-killing her before surrendering to a rapturous fantasy: their mutual love will transform them and empower them to make a stand against a hostile world.

Although its storyline picks up exactly where Gasper Noé left off in his 1991 featurette *Carne*, this is less a sequel than an elaborated remake. Many elements are identical, including the cast, the theme, the locations, the flashy 'Scope cinematography and the bad mantra voiceovers; even the most aggressive tic of style—the whip-pan or jump-zoom underlined by a loud gunshot on the soundtrack—made a brief guest appearance in the earlier film. In other words, Noé's fundamental project hasn't moved an inch in the last seven years. The director (who had a cosmopolitan, liberal, middle class upbringing and describes himself in the press notes as, "a straight kind of guy and a bit of a wimp") tries to get inside the head of a dangerously disturbed man from a specifically French underclass. The aim is to gob on what Noé sees as the social and cultural complacency of mainstream French cinema and television. And, of course, to 'shock' the viewer with a not very metaphorical barrage of visual and verbal provocations.

A brief prologue in which a loudmouth in a bar defines "morality" as a tool of the rich and "justice" as the gun he carries establishes the film's confrontational style and reductivist context. Like the average radio phone-in caller, the horse-meat butcher Chevalier is barely capable of joined-up thinking. His almost continuous voiceover delivers a stream of evasions, denials and contradictions. The revered thought that the father he never knew was a communist martyr, slaughtered by the Nazis, blurs into the dismissal of France as a country of cheese and collaborators. Diatribes against 'faggots' crash into denunciations of the hypocrisy of family values. (One of the few details not reprised from *Carne* is that film's casual revelation that Chevalier had a seemingly tender gay relationship with his cell-mate in prison.) Misogyny shades into misanthropy, from which the only escape is a dream of incestuous bliss with his autistic daughter. Meanwhile a visit to a porno cinema yields the perception that life is never more than brute physical functions. Noé extrapolates from this torrent of verbiage some neo-Darwinian slogans which he splashes across the screen as captions: "Living is a Selfish Act", "Surviving is a Genetic Law".

This blitzkrieg of bar-room philosophy rationalised by Chevalier's joblessness, poverty, and hunger, is less a cry from the heart in the Céline tradition than a rhetorical performance: as loud, repetitive, obnoxious and calculated to offend a notional bourgeois audience as a very extended punk three-chord thrash. As such, it's mildly diverting, especially when Noé reaches for the pre-punk spirit of William Castle by bringing up a caption offering the viewer 30 seconds to leave the theatre before the climactic scenes between Chevalier and his daughter kick in. Any viewer in tune with the cruel burnout of this gesture (what other kind is going to pay to see this film?) will probably find *Seul contre tous as* a whole engaging for two reasons. First, the performances are strong and fearless; Philippe Nahon embodies Chevalier with almost reckless credibility, and even those cast primarily for their grotesque appearance or manner are more believable than, say, anyone in the Jeunet/Caro films. Second, the deliberate mismatch between the grungy material and the amphetamine-charged editing syntax is just about surprising and/or irritating enough to sustain interest for 93 minutes.

Sadly, though, there's a typically punk hollowness at the core of Noé's rhetoric. Despite opening and closing with an outline map of France, the entire film rests upon an evasion: the only obvious reason for setting the story in 1980 is that it lets Noé off the hook of dealing with the appeal of Le Pen to mentalities such as Chevalier's and thus of confronting the social-racial-economic realities of France now in the way that such contemporaries as Kassovitz and Dumont have tried to do. But even as a black, socially disengaged existential fable, *Seul contre tous* betrays its own hard-man stance in its final scenes. The mercy-killing of Cynthia is shown in graphic, lingering detail (the first bullet leaves her choking on her own blood; the second splatters her brains on the floor), but then bracketed off as Chevalier's paranoid fantasy. The real ending which follows is supposed to be even more shocking in its 'unexpectedly' elegiac way: Chevalier cosies up to Cynthia on the bed, imagines thrusting his hand between her milky thighs, and drifts off into a reverie about their mutual love being all either of them needs.

Earlier, in two of the film's few actual jokes, Noé has mocked the very idea of high culture: the terminal station for geriatrics where Chevalier works as a nightwatchman is named Residence Debussy and the high-rise slum where he batters his loathsome mistress is called Pablo Picasso Tower. But the elegiac ending has, of all things, Pachelbel's 'Canon' swelling portentously on the soundtrack while the camera, in a probably unconscious echo of Mizoguchi's *Sansho Dayu* turns its attention to the street outside where Life Goes On. The old maxim is as true as ever: scratch a punk and you'll find an art-college wannabe inside.

VILLAGE VOICE, 3/23/99, p. 125, J. Hoberman

I Stand Alone, a movie that did much to hone the edge of the last New York Film Festival, is lacerating in its precision. This hair-trigger first-feature by 35-year-old Gaspar Noé is constructed to spring shut like a steel trap—if not a guillotine.

Part circus stunt, part social tract, the movie opens by aggressively restating the "wisdom" of 1968—morality is made by and for the rich, power comes from the barrel of a gun and then proceeds to prove the point. *I Stand Alone*, which is interspersed throughout with Godardian intertitles, calls itself "the tragedy of a jobless butcher struggling to survive in the bowels of his nation." A slide-show biography synopsizes Noé's 1992 short, *Carne*, in which a World War II orphan becomes a dealer in horse meat, then winds up in prison for stabbing some guy who he imagines has raped his autistic daughter; *I Stand Alone* picks up the story.

The nameless, now 50-year-old butcher is played by Philippe Nahon as a glowering, bilious block of rage—if this were a David Cronenberg film, his head would explode. A late-20th-century Underground Man, he's as philosophical as he is disgruntled. Perhaps 90 percent of the soundtrack is devoted to his endless misogynist, xenophobic, class-conscious complaints. (As this internal mutter rises in volume, the butcher suggests a crazed R. Crumb character trudging through a desolate urban landscape under the weight of an oppressive thought-balloon.) Almost the most remarkable thing about *I Stand Alone* is this furious, despairing diatribe, a nihilist stream of consciousness that flushes through the movie like raw sewage into the void.

The butcher has most recently worked as a bartender and, having impregnated his sour, obese employer, has relocated with her to her mother's apartment in Lille—a cramped space in a housing tract named, rather too obviously, Pablo Picasso Towers, that only serves to further incubate his seething alienation. As his inability to smile insures that he won't get a job behind a supermarket deli counter, the butcher works briefly as the night watchman at an old-age home. In what amounts to an existential revelation, he helps a young nurse tend to an old woman who dies like a child, crying, "Daddy ... don't leave me alone." The butcher then goes off to a porn flick (like many of the most confrontational European art films of the past few years, *I Stand Alone* as a hardcore insert), and when his mistress picks a fight, he punches her out—reducing the baby in her womb to "hamburger meat." The sequence is so brutal one barely wonders how exactly the butcher acquires the gun with which, having turned his back on domesticity, he then splits back to Paris.

I Stand Alone is strong stuff but it's not depressing—in part because Noé's filmmaking is so energetic in its calculations. The movie is a veritable sonata of social disgust in which the director underscores his explosive cuts and percussive camera moves with a noise that resounds in the brain like a cell door slamming. Shot largely in deliberately composed, widescreen close-ups, *I Stand Alone* is at once focused and abstract, unfolding in a bleak world of empty corridors and vacant, industrial streets—at once prison and abattoir. When the butcher hitchhikes back to Paris, a brief nocturne in which a trucker blasts his music against a windshield montage of onrushing highway provides the designated lyrical interlude.

Renting the flophouse room where his daughter was conceived 15 years before, the butcher looks for work but mainly finds humiliation. (Meanwhile, the gun he's carrying begins to burn a hole in his brain.) At one point, he's picked up by a half-mad junkie hooker. Naturally, she calls him "Daddy"; this is a world of fathers, real and imagined, for the filmmaker no less than his protagonist. (Among other things, *I Stand Alone* gives *Taxi Driver*—to which Noé pays homage—a stringent, sardonic Fassbinder makeover.) Inevitably, the butcher goes to the institution to retrieve his silent, dough-faced daughter and "show her the Eiffel Tower."

As noted here by Gavin Smith last June, Noé resurrects a gimmick from schlockmeister William Castle's 1961 *Homicidal* by giving the audience a 30-second warning to either leave the theater or avert their eyes. He's not altogether kidding. The climax is long and bloody, although the butcher's prolix torrent of insane thoughts are tempered by the cliché strains of Pachelbel's Canon. But if *I Stand Alone* tricks the viewer, it does so honestly—the entire movie is preparation for a choice between rival forms of what Marxist film theorists used to call *unpleasure*.

In interviews, the Argentinian-born Noé has expressed contempt for the gentility of current French cinema, locating his film in the tradition of Luis Buñuel's *Los Olvidados* or such 1970s provocations as *Salo, Straw Dogs*, and *Taxi Driver*. Five years in the making, *I Stand Alone* was fueled by "the desire to finish a film that no one in French film circles wanted to see." Be that as it may, *I Stand Alone* has been praised by French critics across the political spectrum—many citing the corrosive, first-person novels of fascist modernist Louis-Ferdinand Céline as literary precedent for *I Stand Alone'* s nonstop talk-radio rant.

Noé's antihero may call France a "shithole of cheese and Nazi lovers," but like Céline's *Journey to the End of the Night, I Stand Alone* can be seen as bizarrely patriotic. However beleaguered his national culture, the miserable, martyred, misanthropic butcher of Paris will not go quietly into oblivion. *I think therefore I am,* the movie's antihero bellows, knowing that his ferocious diatribe has the power to amaze *tout le monde*—the whole world will hear this French dog bark.

Also reviewed in:
CHICAGO TRIBUNE, 7/9/99, Friday/p. A, Michael Wilmington
NEW YORK TIMES, 3/17/99, p. E7, Stephen Holden
VARIETY, 6/15-21/98, p. 102, Lisa Nesselson

I WOKE UP EARLY THE DAY I DIED

A CQN Releasing release of a Muse Productions/Cinequanon Pictures International production. *Executive Producer:* Jordan Gertner and Bradford L. Schlei. *Producer:* Chris Hanley and Billy Zane. *Director:* Aris Iliopulos. *Screenplay:* Edward D. Wood, Jr. *Director of Photography:* Michael F. Barrow. *Editor:* Dody Dorn. *Music:* Larry Groupe. *Sound:* Bryan Franklin. *Production Designer:* Maia Javan. *Running time:* 90 minutes. *MPAA Rating:* Not Rated.

CAST: Billy Zane (Thief); Sandra Bernhard (Sandy Sands); Ron Perlman (Cemetery Caretaker); Tippi Hedren (Maylinda); Andrew McCarthy (Cop); Will Patton (Preacher); Carel Struycken (Undertaker); Max Perlich (Assistant Undertaker); John Ritter (Robert Forrest); Eartha Kitt (Cult Leader); Ann Magnuson (Loan Secretary); Maila Nurmi (Vampira); Abraham Benrubi (Bouncer); Karen Black (Honey Child); Conrad Brooks (Old Cop); Summer Phoenix (Girl at Beach); Christina Ricci (Teen-Age Hooker); Rick Schroder (Cop); Nicollette Sheridan (Ballroom Woman); Jonathan Taylor Thomas (Bystander); Steven Weber (Cop); Kathleen Wood (Lady).

NEW YORK POST, 9/10/99, p. 56, Rod Dreher

Contemporary audiences like Ed Wood movies because they're so awful. But what makes them campy is that Wood, the poor deluded cross-dresser, thought he was making art.

Who knows what director Aris Iliopulos thought he was up to when he took on "I Woke Up Early the Day I Died," a Wood screenplay that was never inflicted upon celluloid.

It's about a Thief (Billy Zane) who escapes from an insane asylum, commits a robbery, and loses the money while sleeping in a graveyard.

There's no dialogue; it plays like a silent film comedy, with Zane wordlessly chewing scenery as he trips over cameo performers like Sandra Bernhard, Christina Ricci, Eartha Kitt, Tippi Hedren and others.

Presumably Zane & Co. had a lot more fun filming this inexplicable low-budget indulgence than any sane person will have watching it.

VILLAGE VOICE, 9/14/99, p. 133, J. Hoberman

He's not quite Van Gogh, but Ed Wood Jr., declared the "world's worst filmmaker" barely two years after his ignominious death in a dive off the wrong side of Hollywood Boulevard, is turning out to be one of the great posthumous success stories. First came the bad-movie festivals, then the reissues, the biography, the *Plan 9 From Outer Space* musical, and the Tim Burton biopic—remade this summer, after a fashion, as Steve Martin's *Bowfinger*. Now, Wood's last "screenplay" has been exhumed from the vault and brought to the screen—with maximum faux-naïveté and much interpolated stock footage—by Italian director Aris Iliopulos.

The script, which has no dialogue, has something to do with a thief (coproducer Billy Zane) who stashes his ill-gotten gains in a coffin and loses the money to some graveyard habitué. Iliopulos has managed to cast a number of well-known suspects, including Sandra Bernhard (allowed to do a striptease), Tippi Hedren (permitted to punch out Zane's lights before he hurls her into the Pacific), Eartha Kitt, Christina Ricci, and authentic Wood star Maila "Vampira" Nurmi. Zane, in and out of drag, has the Wood look down (at least as it was invented by Johnny Depp) and can play physical comedy too—for what it's worth. *I Woke Up Early* isn't narrative-driven but neither is there much documentary subtext. At its best, it suggests the exuberant Bronx rooftop epics produced in 8mm 30-odd years ago by the Kuchar twins. Wood's bargain-basement aesthetic is impossible to parody. That this mime show works better than it should is, in a sense, the ultimate dis.

Also reviewed in:
NEW YORK TIMES, 9/10/99, p. E20, Anita Gates
VARIETY, 10/12-18/98, p. 44, Glenn Lovell

IDEAL HUSBAND, AN

A Miramax Films release of a Fragile Film production in association with Icon Productions/Pathé Pictures/The Arts Council of England. *Executive Producer:* Susan B. Landau, Ralph Kamp, and Andrea Calderwood. *Producer:* Barnaby Thompson, Uri Fruchtmann, and Bruce Davey. *Director:* Oliver Parker. *Screenplay:* Oliver Parker. *Based on the play by:* Oscar Wilde. *Screenplay Adaptation:* Oliver Parker. *Director of Photography:* David Johnson. *Editor:* Guy Bensley. *Music:* Charlie Mole. *Music Editor:* Mike Higham. *Choreographer:* Sue Nye. *Sound:* Peter Lindsay and (music) Steve Price. *Sound Editor:* Max Hoskins. *Casting:* Celestia Fox. *Production Designer:* Michael Howells. *Art Director:* Rod McLean. *Set Decorator:* Katie Lee. *Special Effects:* Paul Dimmer. *Costumes:* Caroline Harris. *Make-up:* Elizabeth Tagg. *Running time:* 97 minutes. *MPAA Rating:* PG-13.

CAST: Peter Vaughan (Phipps); Rupert Everett (Lord Goring); Minnie Driver (Mabel); Cate Blanchett (Gertrude); Ben Pullen (Tommy Trafford); Marsha Fitzalan (Countess); Julianne Moore (Mrs. Cheveley); Lindsay Duncan (Lady Markby); Neville Phillips (Mason); John Wood (Lord Caversham); Jeremy Northam (Sir Robert); Nickolas Grace (Vicounte de Nanjac); Simon Russell Beale (Sir Edward); Anna Patrick (Miss Danvers); Delia Lindsay (Lady Basildon); Denise Stephenson (Gwendolen); Charles Edwards (Jack); Nancy Carroll (Cecily); Andy Harrison (Algernon); Jill Balcon (Lady Bracknell); Janet Henfrey (Miss Prism); Toby Robertson (Canon Chasuble); Michael Culkin (Oscar Wilde); Oliver Parker (Bunbury); Douglas Bradley (Brackpool); Stephen May (Burlington); Jeroen Krabbé (Baron Arnheim); Susannah Wise (Young Mother); Peter Parker (First MP); Oliver Ford Davies (Sir Hugo Danforth); Neil Mendoza (Second MP); John Thompson (The Speaker).

LOS ANGELES TIMES, 6/18/99, Calendar/p. 10, Kevin Thomas

What is so swiftly striking about Oliver Parker's exhilarating and elegant film of Oscar Wilde's "An Ideal Husband" is how very contemporary it is in its consideration of morality—or lack of same—in both personal and public life. Wilde was always about lots more than witty repartee, and as sparkling as his play is as drawing-room comedy, it reveals his concern with the timeless values of unselfish love and forgiveness. Parker has shaped the play to make it more film-friendly and relevant, but he has done so with such subtlety you would have to be a Wilde authority even to notice.

Britain a century ago was the world's superpower that America is now, and its hero, Sir Robert Chiltern (Jeremy Northam), a member of Parliament heralded as "the last decent man in London." He is poised on the threshold of a brilliant career, with the prime minister's office the ultimate goal, surely. He has a vision of a responsible empire embodied in his slogan, "Commerce with a conscience, which sounds lots like a certain presidential candidate's advocacy of "compassionate conservatism." Yet there is a dark secret in his life, one that most people would find far more damaging than l'affaire Lewinsky, one that makes him vulnerable to the bewitching blackmailer, Mrs. Cheveley (Julianne Moore).

Mrs. Cheveley, whose unabashed glamour and insinuating manner set her apart from more proper women, has descended upon the dashing Sir Robert at his grand London residence (looking only slightly less posh than Buckingham Palace) during a glittery soiree presided over by Sir Robert's gracious and devoted wife, Gertrude (Cate Blanchett), a lovely young woman of noble character and intelligence. Mrs. Cheveley is nothing if not direct with Sir Robert: He is to stand up in Parliament and endorse a fraudulent scheme for a canal in Argentina in which she has heavily invested or she will make public a letter that will reveal just how he, born poor but clearly well-connected, made his fortune. (Moore is as memorable an adventuress as Paulette Goddard was in Alexander Korda's 1948 film version of the Wilde play.)

When a desperate Sir Robert turns for help to his friend Lord Goring (Rupert Everett), "An Ideal Husband" at once broadens and deepens its scope, heightens its humor and shifts its focus to Goring, who becomes the film's dominant presence, especially as played with such scene-stealing wit and style by Everett.

There is a great deal of Wilde in both men, for like Sir Robert, Wilde was a loving, though in his case flagrantly errant, husband, and like Lord Goring in that his mastery of the epigram belied a fundamental seriousness. The kind of epic-scale scandal that threatens to engulf Sir Robert as the millennium approaches of course in fact did destroy Wilde—while in fact "An Ideal Husband" was playing in London.

Mischievous, indolent and given to outrageous yet knowing pronouncements almost every time he opens his mouth, Lord Goring is just the man of the world to deal with the opportunistic Mrs. Cheveley, to whom he was once briefly engaged. She insists on taking a "We're birds of a feather" approach to a man she would still like to land, thus seriously underestimating Lord Goring's actually quite formidable strength of character, solid values and unflinching courage.

Yet as Lord Goring commences to act, he also inadvertently sets himself on a course of responsible conduct that will endanger his cherished bachelor status, making it harder to resist his own candidacy as an ideal husband—to Sir Robert's strong-willed yet enchanting sister Mabel (Minnie Driver) who chafes at the propriety of not making perfectly clear her love for him. What's more, Lord Goring's father, Lord Caversham (John Wood), is eager to see his son tie the knot. An amusing confusion on the part of Lord Goring's redoubtable butler (Peter Vaughan) allows fate to interact with character in the unraveling of an increasingly complicated plot.

Parker reveals the same deftness here in bringing Wilde to the screen as he did in Shakespeare's "Othello," with Laurence Fishburne a striking Moor of Venice. As before, purists may object to Parker's streamlining a stage classic in adapting it to film. The rest of us, meanwhile, can be delighted that his "Ideal Husband," like "Othello," is a real movie rather than a filmed play. We can also take pleasure in how he's turned his stars into a stunning ensemble who are at once able to bring out the humor as well as the seriousness in Wilde.

You have the feeling that the actors are enjoying themselves—a feeling that is felicitously contagious. It is a special joy to see Blanchett shine, freed once again from the self-important ponderousness of "Elizabeth," as admirable as she was in last year's Oscar-nominated hit. The film also consolidates the wide appeal and recognition Everett established with "My Best Friend's

Wedding," and in the wake of "The Winslow Boy" confirms the formidable talent and charisma of Northam.

Not surprisingly, "An Ideal Husband" is also the kind of glorious period piece the British do so well, with sumptuous settings and costumes that in this instance, however, never overwhelm story and character. Say what you will about the constrictions of corsets, trains and elaborate hairstyles in this era of the liberated, natural-looking woman, Caroline Harris' 1890s costumes remind us how deeply romantic and highly flattering they could be; you could say the same for the men's handsome, well-cut formal attire. Vital and buoyant, "An Ideal Husband" continues in an impressive manner the resurgence of interest in Wilde as the centennial of his death approaches.

NEW YORK, 6/28-7/5/99, p. 128, Peter Rainer

The characters in Oscar Wilde's *An Ideal Husband*, at least on the page, are so brittle with pith and rectitude they might as well be sporting hairline fractures. Onscreen, in the adaptation by Oliver Parker, they're fleshier, sexier. The, cast is almost *too* right: Rupert Everett, with his aristocratic hair and sly eye, plays the foppish bachelor Lord Goring; John Wood is Goring's infinitely critical, infinitely doting father Lord Caversham; Jeremy Northam, last seen as the crusading barrister in *The Winslow Boy,* is Sir Robert Chiltern, Parliament's rising star, who is being blackmailed by Mrs. Cheveley, played by Julianne Moore, in connection with a secret financial scandal of his from years before. Sir Robert's wife, Lady Gertrude, who believes her husband is ideal and can't bear the imputation of scandal, is played by Cate Blanchett. Minnie Driver is Mabel, Sir Robert's sister, with designs on Lord Goring. This isn't a cast, really—it's a stock company.

Our familiarity with the actors, and their comfort in this period setting, lend the piece an unexpected air of naturalism. Parker hasn't simply reproduced Wilde; he's bolstered certain characters, especially Mrs. Cheveley and Mabel, and also done some wholesale rewriting, notably in the end, when he concocts a bet between Mrs. Cheveley and Lord Goring that threatens to turn the proceedings into a cliff-hanger. Sacrilege aside, all this plays rather well, but I wish Parker had tried to preserve even more of the Wildean tone—that is to say, the sense of life as an exquisite, farcical artwork. Parker closes the gender gap a bit more than Wilde did—the sexual byplay seems more modern than late Victorian—and he also punches up the connection the play makes between moral stricture and political scandal. I realize this is meant to highlight the material's "universality," but it's disconcerting here to be tweaked, even ever so gently, into drawing contemporary parallels: One doesn't really want to be thinking of Bill Clinton while watching Oscar Wilde.

Still, the movie achieves the play's primary effect: what Wilde's biographer Richard Ellmann described as a "gradual expansion of tenderness." Lord Goring may be the archetypal Wildean dandy, but what that also means is that his dandyism masks surprising depths of feeling. His triumph is that, acting as unofficial emcee, he rescues everybody, even himself, from hypocrisy. This is a victory for upper-class manners, but it doesn't smack of snobbery. It just seems like the right way to behave. These characters inhabit a world in which all human interaction is a form of commerce, but they learn to move beyond that—into a world where love can't be auctioned off. The ideal husband turns out to be as much a figment as the ideal wife, and in that realization lies a happy salvation.

NEW YORK POST, 6/18/99, p. 49, Jonathan Foreman

"An Ideal Husband" shows how a play by a genius can transcend both clumsy direction and an adaptation for the screen that amputates some of its best scenes and dialogue.

And while you can imagine a better filmed version of Oscar Wilde's comedy (far from his best play, by the way), this one is still very enjoyable.

Set in 1895, the film stars Rupert Everett as the elegant Lord Goring and Jeremy Northam as his best friend, Sir Robert Chiltern. Goring is famously rich, single, cynical and idle. Chiltern is an ambitious, wealthy politician with an envied reputation for integrity and a successful marriage to Gertrude (Cate Blanchett).

Into their lives comes the twice-married Mrs. Cheveley (Julianne Moore), a sophisticated adventuress who was Gertrude's enemy at school, and who, it turns out, knows something about Sir Robert that could destroy his career and perfect marriage. In ruthless fashion, she blackmails him to use his Cabinet post to promote her investments in a canal-building scheme.

Because his wife puts so much stock in his virtue, the only person Sir Robert can confide in is Lord Goring. But Goring's efforts to dissuade Mrs. Cheveley only make things worse for the Chilterns, and they threaten his own friendship with Sir Robert. In the meantime, Goring is under tremendous pressure from his father (John Wood) to marry, and is disturbed by his attraction to Sir Robert's young, sassy sister Mabel (Minnie Driver).

Writer-director Parker seems to understand that Wilde's play is surprisingly moral in its own way: "An Ideal Husband" is a comedy in praise of white lies told for good and important ends.

The hero is Goring, who is cynical but fundamentally kind and loyal. The villain is Mrs. Cheveley, a predator who knows just how to use morally utopian Victorian standards to exploit and destroy decent people.

And while Julianne Moore cannot really pull off an English accent, she does makes an excellent Mrs. Chevely. Hers is the best-written character in the film, and Moore invests it with just the right combination of sex appeal (despite an unflattering hairstyle) and lethality.

Still, as good as Moore is, Cate Blanchett is simply extraordinary. She not only fills out and makes believable a thinly written role, but her peculiar beauty is more beguiling than ever, and her presence makes every scene she's in leap off the screen.

Rupert Everett, on the other hand, mumbles through his nose even more than he did in "A Midsummer Night's Dream." If he didn't have so many wonderful lines, it would be impossible not to notice just how narrow his range is.

As it is, his insincerity seems so bogus that you rarely forget that it is Rupert Everett up there, playing a witty guy in white tie.

The oddest thing about this adaptation, though, is the way it fluffs the period atmosphere. The costumes are right, but the manners are wrong—and the interiors and exteriors are strangely cramped. Which helps make this "Ideal Husband" rather less than ideal.

NEWSDAY, 6/18/99, Part II/p. B11, John Anderson

The assessment of a movie has to hinge at least somewhat on the intention of its makers. And since the intention of the people behind "An Ideal Husband" was to get out of Oscar Wilde's way, you have to say, "well done."

The liberality of Wilde's times were mostly in his head, as he came to discover. In ours— and to our credit—it's at least a bit more tangible, and no better evidenced than by the resurrection of the author. Call it a campaign if you like, one that began with Richard Ellman's epic '80s biography, was supported by Broadway's Tony-nominated "An Ideal Husband" in 1996 and the Off-Broadway hit "Gross Indecency" in 1997, continued by the '98 Stephen Fry vehicle "Wilde," and now culminates, more or less, with an all-star production of "An Ideal Husband," directed by Oliver Parker ("Othello," 1995).

All in all, Wilde seems less infamous than celebrated these days, less the victim of his "scandalous" history (he was a rather chaste sodomite, if one cares) than the martyr, revered for the epic humanity of his writing and his life. We should feel good about Wilde, a man who was more than the sum of his bon mots, just as Wilde makes us feel good about ourselves.

The Wilde world, after all, is beautiful and everyone far too witty to be real; people are as effortlessly charming as Wilde's humor. Nothing in his work, of course, is everyday—his scope seldom fell below a certain economic class, or degree of hyperbole. But at the same time, his were comedies of manners—manners constituting the machinery and oil of everyday life, something that, in itself, makes what happens to his characters a lot less frivolous than the atmosphere suggests.

Take Sir Robert Chiltern (Jeremy Northam), a polished politician with all the necessary assets, including a beautiful wife (Cate Blanchett) and the support of his party. He's the perfect candidate, the "ideal husband," but there's a chink in the armor (and if this begins to sound familiar, just wait). First, the American adventuress Mrs. Cheveley (Julianne Moore) threatens to disclose a career-destroying secret from Robert's past. Then, when cornered, he turns for help inexplicably—to Arthur Goring (Rupert Everett).

Goring, of course, is a womanizing reprobate whose lifestyle is scandalizing his father (John Wood) and making him renowned throughout London for an abundance of wit and corresponding scarcity of substance; to paraphrase Wilde himself, Arthur can resist anything but temptation. But when Robert asks Arthur to save him from Arthur's old flame, Mrs. Cheveley, Arthur rises to the occasion and a Wildean system of interconnecting devices and desires engages, to sinister and comic effect.

"An Ideal Husband" is blessed with a cast that can slide effortlessly into this kind of high-handed, high-toned farce, but none as blithely as Everett. He's already brought a Wildean irony to some unlikely projects ("My Best Friend's Wedding," for one), and when faced with the genuine article, manages to make this movie his own. For her part, Moore is deliciously venal, riper than usual and harboring a reservoir of bile that makes Mrs. Cheveley as dangerous as she is seductive.

Blanchett gives a rather wan performance, but she also has the least gratifying role—The Wife. Northam, however, is as versatile and charming an actor as is currently in circulation. (Who else could star in both "Mimic" and "The Winslow Boy"?) He's also one of those odd men who looks more callow than rakish in a mustache. But he needn't worry. Robert needs a mustache.

SIGHT AND SOUND, 5/99, p. 49, Peter Matthews

London, 1895. Sir Robert Chiltern MP is happily married to the high-minded Gertrude. One evening, the Chilterns hold a reception. Among the guests are Sir Robert's sister Mabel, his best friend Arthur Goring—and Mrs Laura Cheveley. Laura asks Robert for his public support of an Argentinian canal scheme in which she has invested heavily. Robert turns her down, but Laura reveals she has an incriminating letter he once wrote. She threatens to expose the fraud on which Robert built his wealth if he will not do her bidding. Robert agrees to back her scheme in the Commons.

Gertrude persuades Robert to write to Laura and withdraw his promise, whatever it is. Robert confides his woes to Arthur. Receiving Robert's note, Laura visits Gertrude and reveals to her Robert's secret. Disillusioned with her "ideal husband", Gertrude sends an urgent note to Arthur, requesting a private interview. Expecting Gertrude, Arthur instructs s butler Phipps to admit an unidentified lady and no one else. When Mrs Cheveley unexpectedly arrives, Phipps escorts her to Arthur's study, where she steals Gertrude's note. Now Robert appears, desperate for advice. Hearing a noise in the study, he finds Laura and storms out. Laura suggests a wager to Arthur: she will return Chiltern' s letter if he condemns the canal scheme in parliament; if he endorses it, Arthur must marry her.

Robert condemns the scheme, and Laura hands the letter over to Arthur but posts Gertrude's compromising note to Robert. Mabel claims the note was from her to protect Gertrude. Arthur proposes to Mabel and she accepts but Robert objects to the engagement, believing Arthur is conducting an affair with Mrs Cheveley. Gertrude comes clean and Robert is delighted to discover his perfect wife suffers from human frailty.

A few years ago, Oliver Parker directed a smooth, uninspired film version of *Othello*, notable for some radical pruning of the text and an attempt to 'open out' the play that consisted largely of velvety shots of torch-lit gondolas. Sadly, conspicuous consumption plus the odd camera flourish do not a memorable Shakespeare adaptation make. For all its prettiness, Parker's *Othello* ended up in a dull halfway house between theatre and cinema. His new translation of Oscar Wilde's *An Ideal Husband* shows a similar infirmity of purpose, but with the opposite result. Far from being insufficiently cinematic, it isn't stagy enough. While Shakespeare's muscularity arguably lends itself to full-blooded spectacle, the whole point of Wilde lies in his coruscating effeteness. The overbred dandies of his plays turn tinkling triviality into a badge of honour—they are always acting, even in their own drawing rooms. A smart Wilde production should pursue the air of stilted theatricality to the very limit.

Wilde's epigrammatic prolixity poses obvious hazards for film-makers. Just about the only adaptation to strike the requisite note of overripe preciousness was Anthony Asquith's splendidly stagnant *The Importance of Being Earnest* (1952). Parker seems to have assumed that Wilde at full throttle would antagonize rather than captivate the *hoi polloi*. So he has shorn *An Ideal Husband* of some of its more egregiously fey dialogue (one certainly misses the jabbering Lady

Markby), though what remains still makes for fairly *recherché* entertainment.   Probably as a favour to rising star Minnie Driver, the ingenue Mabel's part has been beefed up; and now Sir Robert delivering his firebrand oration at the House of Commons is actually seen.   It's understandable that Parker should want to ventilate Wilde's hothouse flowers a bit, yet the cinematic filigree he adds merely counterfeits movement.   There are a few too many shots of messengers scampering across London charged with fatal letters; and one or two montage sequences (of feet dancing or people dressing for dinner) reach new heights of visual redundancy Trying for pace and variety, the movie whips between picturesque locations, often in midspeech: characters are apt to begin a *pensée* in a parlour and complete it in a steam room.   Parker's shuttlecock technique only succeeds in throwing Wilde's cascading rhythms seriously out of whack and makes it hard to attend to the language as fully as one would like.   Fortunately, the play has the kind of sturdy Victorian backbone that stands firm whatever latterday tinkerers choose to do with it.

Now and then, Parker scores a scrupulously balanced composition (as in the ceremonial two-shots announcing the reunion of the estranged Chilterns), and it becomes clear that he's fishing about for an equivalent to Wilde's formalism.   But on the whole, his cinematic elaborations work to sentimentalise the tone.   Where Wilde's imponderable ironies keep you guessing as to whether his characters are quite the twittering, creatures they appear, the realism inseparable from 'opening out' implicitly obliges you to take them as human beings.

Still, the actors are superbly accoutred down to the last footman, projecting high elegance even when the direction doesn't. Wearing his new camp image like a queenly mantle, Rupert Everett performs an immaculate turn as the closet moralist Arthur Goring.   Cate Blanchett makes an exquisitely distressed Lady Chiltern, while Minnie Driver gurgles and pouts as if possessed by the phantom of Joan Greenwood.   However, the show belongs to the phenomenally gifted Julianne Moore, who goes from playing a suburban housewife *(Safe)* to a porn star *(Boogie Nights)* to the conniving *grande dame* here, and manages to be fresh and different every time.   Perhaps in the interest of softening the role, Mrs Cheveley has been robbed of the great *coup de théâtre* when she is exposed.   But even so, Moore gives the best display of female Machiavellianism since Bette Davis held court over *The Little Foxes* (1941).

VILLAGE VOICE, 6/22/99, p. 152, Amy Taubin

Adapted from Oscar Wilde's romantic comedy of manners about an ambitious politician with a scandalous secret hanging over his head and the morally upstanding wife who wrongly believes he is perfection itself, *An Ideal Husband* is set in end-of-the-19th-century London, but it might as well be end-of-the-20th-century D.C. Director Oliver Parker doesn't belabor the parallels, which in any case are not exact.   But the implication that politics has always been a dirty business is one of the pleasures of the film.

Parker, who also wrote the script, keeps most of Wilde's jokes, but he tightens the talk and adds a plot device of his own.   His film is hardly memorable, but it's amusing enough for two hours, and it never panders or cloys.   That's more than can be said for the ludicrously written *Notting Hill,* in which Julia Roberts and Hugh Grant seem to be engaged in a head-cocking, lip-biting, eyebrow-raising, teeth-baring contest of their own devising.   It's as if their faces had become muscle-bound from the strain of delivering star power in every close-up.

No such burden is placed on Rupert Everett and Cate Blanchett; they still have the luxury of being actors rather than megastars.   Everett plays Lord Arthur Goring, a 35-year-old bachelor who's feeling the pressure to end his party-boy existence and get about the business of marrying and breeding.   "Other people are quite dreadful.   To love oneself is the beginning of a life-long romance," said Wilde, using Lord Goring as a mouthpiece.   It's the mark of Everett's excellent performance that for two hours he causes you to all but forget about Wilde and believe instead that Lord Goring issues such witticisms on the fly.

Everett also lets you understand that beneath Lord Goring's dedicated superficiality is a serious person, capable of great loyalty to his friends, in this case Sir Robert Chiltern (Jeremy Northam) and his wife (Blanchett).   Sir Robert is being blackmailed by a scheming femme fatale (Julianne Moore), who has proof that he once leaked a government secret and reaped sufficient funds for his indiscretion to jump-start his brilliant political career.   If she goes public with this information, his career and his marriage are over. Lord Goring, who believes that no life is without some indiscretion and that those who would bring Sir Robert down are hypocrites with checkered pasts of their own, sets an elaborate scheme in motion to save his friend and in the process discovers that he values marriage more than he knew.

Of the three characters in this peculiar triangle, Sir Robert is the least developed (or perhaps Northam's performance is a bit too stolid). Blanchett, however, continues to amaze. She suggests a strength of character reminiscent of the young Ingrid Bergman, and her precise comic timing never distracts from the seriousness of her character's dilemma. A proto-feminist who tries to use her privilege for the common good, Lady Chiltern cannot make truly moral choices until she recognizes the contradictions in society and within human beings that make it impossible for anyone, including herself, to live up to her ideals. Some of the other actors fare less well. Julianne Moore as the heartless blackmailer and Minnie Driver as the willful young woman determined to marry Lord Goring simply work too hard.

Parker lacks any distinctive directorial style, although he does a credible job of opening the play up, as they say, for the screen. The first scene, with most of the major characters on horseback (women as well as men), crossing paths and exchanging small talk, sets the tone for everything that follows in this brisk and funny film.

Also reviewed in:
CHICAGO TRIBUNE, 6/25/99, Friday/p. A, Michael Wilmington
NEW REPUBLIC, 7/19 & 26/99, p. 30, Stanley Kauffmann
NEW YORK TIMES, 6/18/99, p. E18, Stephen Holden
NEW YORKER, 7/5/99, p. 89, Anthony Lane
VARIETY, 4/26-5/2/99, p. 43, Derek Elley
WASHINGTON POST, 6/25/99, p. C1, Stephen Hunter
WASHINGTON POST, 6/25/99, Weekend/p. 47, Desson Howe

IDLE HANDS

A Columbia Pictures release of a Licht/Mueller Film Corporation and a Team Todd production. *Executive Producer:* Jeffrey Sudzin. *Producer:* Andrew Licht, Jeffrey A. Mueller, Suzanne Todd, and Jennifer Todd. *Director:* Rodman Flender. *Screenplay:* Terri Hughes and Ron Milbauer. *Director of Photography:* Christopher Baffa. *Editor:* Stephen E. Rivkin. *Music:* Graeme Revell and John Houlihan. *Music Editor:* Ashley Revell. *Sound:* Joseph Geisinger. *Sound Editor:* Michael O'Farrell. *Casting:* John Papsidera. *Production Designer:* Greg Melton. *Art Director:* Roland G. Rosenkranz. *Set Designer:* Scott Herbertson. *Set Decorator:* Evette Frances Knight. *Special Effects:* Lou Carlucci. *Costumes:* Julia Caston. *Make-up:* Scott Eddo. *Make-up (Vivica A. Fox):* Rea Ann Silva. *Stunt Coordinator:* Charles Picerni, Jr. *Running time:* 92 minutes. *MPAA Rating:* R.

CAST: Devon Sawa (Anton); Seth Green (Mick); Elden Henson (Pnub); Jessica Alba (Molly); Christopher Hart (The Hand); Vivica A. Fox (Debi); Jack Noseworthy (Randy); Katie Wright (Tanya); Sean Whalen (McMacy); Nick Sadler (Ruck); Fred Willard (Dad); Connie Ray (Mom); Steve Van Wormer (Curtis); Kelly Monaco (Tiffany); Timothy Stack (Principal Tidwell); Joey Slotnick (Burger Jungle Manager); Tom DeLonge (Drive Thru Jockey); Sabrina Lu (News Reporter); Kyle Gass (Burger Jungle Guy); Mindy Sterling (Lady Bowler); Donna Scott (Nurse); Randy Oglesby (Sheriff Buchanan); Molly Maslin and Carl Gabriel Yorke (Chaperones); Dexter Holland (Band Lead Singer).

LOS ANGELES TIMES, 4/30/99, Calendar/p. 6, Gene Seymour

[The following review by Gene Seymour appeared in a slightly different form in
NEWSDAY, 4/30/99, Part II/p. B2.]

It may not be fair to castigate Rodman Flender's low-rent comic pastiche for using a gimmick that goes all the way back to 1946's "The Beast With Five Fingers," even though this movie doesn't do much more with it than attach it—literally—to the "slacker" mystique.

This time, it's a blithe, perpetually stoned teenage couch potato named Anton (Devon Sawa) who finds himself stuck with a right hand with a homicidal mind of its own. He's so out of it that it takes him several hours after getting out of bed to realize that he has slaughtered Mom and Dad.

Fellow basement-dwellers Mick (Seth Green) and Pnub (Elden Henson) find themselves the next victims of Anton's demonically possessed hand, only to decide in true slacker fashion that they'd rather hang out with Anton's remote control and refrigerator than Move Toward the Light. So they become real zombies as opposed to the aspiring zombies they were in life. Anton thinks cutting off and microwaving the offending appendage will save himself and humanity. But the marauding hand seeks victims on its own and no one, except a no-nonsense druidic princess (Vivica A. Fox, camping it up), has any answers to its mayhem. Meanwhile, there's a Halloween dance at the local high school that's about to be scarier than anyone expects ...

Count the number of horror classics you recognize from that brief synopsis. "Idle Hands" is both shameless and affectionate toward its precursors. But after several editions of "Scream" and other teen-horror franchises, even the act of goofing on the genre has passed the point of critical mass. It doesn't take long for the you-know-what's-going-to-happen-next archness of "Idle Hands" to congeal into a been-there-done-that pallor.

But what "Idle Hands" lacks in originality, it makes up for in energy and insolence. It takes guts for a movie to indulge as much as this one does in proto-hippie humor and you find yourself tickled, in spite of yourself, by the movie's nerve, if not its jokes. And after the anxiety of so many recent high school epics, it's almost a relief to come across one that slouches at a cool, hazy distance from class conflict.

It may not be the best live-action splatter cartoon money can buy. And those 1940s Tom and Jerry cartoons weren't as well made or ingenious as the Tex Avery shorts made by the same studio. Admit it. You laughed anyway, right?

NEW YORK POST, 4/30/99, p. 63, Jonathan Foreman

"Idle Hands" starts with a creepy murder sequence before it degenerates into a disastrous attempt to mix comedy and horror. With the exception of a handful of good jokes during the first half-hour, it's boring and lame, and after a while you begin to feel embarrassed for the cast.

Ultra-lazy stoner Anton (Devon Sawa) wakes up on Halloween, smokes some pot and discovers that his parents have been murdered by a killer terrorizing the California town of Bolan. Immediately he goes around to see his pals Mick (Seth Green) and Pnub (Elden Henson) to get some more weed. When the three boys come back to Anton's house, it dawns on all of them that Anton must be the killer. Actually, it's his hand, which is possessed by the devil.

The hand kills both of Anton's friends but they come back as greenish un-dead beings, like the victims in "An American Werewolf in London."

Anton now fears that he'll end up killing Molly (Jessica Alba), the underdressed girl next door, so he chops off the offending hand and microwaves it. But it promptly disappears on its own steam, just like the one in Oliver Stone's "The Hand" (1981), or Thing in "The Addams Family."

Meanwhile, druid priestess Debi Lecure (Vivica A. Fox) arrives in town with her sacred dagger, determined to battle the forces of darkness.

Sawa is adequate but uncharismatic in the lead role but Green's lackluster performance is a disappointment after his efforts in last year's "Can't Hardly Wait." Fox rushes through her lines hyperactively as if she were in a Leslie Nielsen spoof, and her over-the-top-performance wrecks every scene she's in.

SIGHT AND SOUND, 6/00, p. 45, Kim Newman

Bolan, California, a few days before Halloween. The parents of slacker teenager Anton are murdered by a mysterious force, but Anton doesn't notice. He continues to hang out with his dope-smoking friends Mick and Pnub, and fantasise about Molly, the cool girl who lives across the street. Meanwhile, Druid priest Debi is tracking an evil force which takes possession of the lazy and turns them into serial killers.

Anton finds his parents' corpses and calls Mick and Pnub over, only to have his hand—which is possessed—murder them. While Anton tries to get Molly to help, the hand makes advances to her that Anton follows through on. Mick and Pnub come back to life as zombies and suggest Anton consults with heavy-metal kid Randy on the subject of Satanic powers. Anton hacks off his possessed hand but it continues to make mischief. Debi hooks up with Randy, who leads her to Anton. They track the hand to the school dance, where more teenagers are killed but Anton saves Molly. Later, Mick and Pnub return from Heaven as angels.

This likeable, if minor, slacker horror comedy is a reworking of the intermittently popular crawling-hand theme, exemplified classically by *The Beast with Five Fingers* (1946), although the splatter-comic elements here also seem inspired by a subplot from *Evil Dead II* in which Bruce Campbell battled with his possessed, amputated hand, a plight closely resembling that of *Idle Hands'* luckless Anton.

It's an infallibly funny gambit, and Devon Sawa's writhing fingers create a real separate character. There's an undeveloped suggestion that the evil hand is acting out Anton's desires, as when it gropes Molly, thus landing the timid slacker the girlfriend he would otherwise never have got round to approaching. The film's nugget of irony—based on the proverb "Idle hands are the Devil's playground"—is unforced, but also rather thrown away.

Roger Corman-stable veteran Rodman Flender (director of *Leprechaun 2)* worked previously in television *(Tales from the Crypt, Dark Skies)*. He marshals sick slapstick very well, using a Dario Argento-inspired colour palette still unusual in American horror movies. The amiably blank Devon Sawa, credible as a clod who uses a backscratcher to scoop a remote control when it's out of reach, performs impressive contortions before the evil hand is hacked off his wrist, pulling off the hard trick of approaching Bruce Campbell's skill at battling an apparently rebel body part. Once chopped off and microwaved, the hand is 'played' by Christopher Hart, who handled Thing in the *Addams Family* films. Hart matches Sawa's moves and creates a distinctively different crawling hand from his earlier character: Thing was perky and inquisitive, this hand is sneaky and cruel. Among many horrid japes, the funniest and crassest moment comes during the obligatory teenage backseat make-out scene, as a girl realises her breasts are being fondled by three hands.

As is the fashion with teenage horror films at the turn of this century, *Idle Hands* is more of an ensemble piece than a solo venture. This diffuses its potential for real scariness but also means potential dead spots are filled by scene-stealing supporting players. While Jessica Alba is appealing, most of the work is done by double acts, such as Vivica A. Fox and Jack Noseworthy as, respectively, the Amazonian Druid priestess and the bewildered heavy-metal kid, and especially the vastly underrated Seth Green and Elden Henson as Mick and Pnub, who return from the dead because "Some voice said, 'Walk into the light,' but it was, like, really far, so we said, 'Fuck it'." Raised from the dead, the teens pull a few *Re-Animator* routines: Pnub has to carry around his severed head or jam it back onto his stumbling body with a fork, but the nicest joke is that these zombies would rather lie on the sofa watching MTV eating cheesy snacks than consume human flesh.

Also reviewed in:
CHICAGO TRIBUNE, 4/30/99, Friday/p. B, Monica Eng
NEW YORK TIMES, 4/30/99, p. E21, Lawrence Van Gelder
VARIETY, 4/26-5/2/99, p. 45, Robert Koehler
WASHINGTON POST, 4/30/99, Weekend/p. 64, Desson Howe

ILLUMINATA

An Artisan Entertainment release of an Overseas Filmgroup presentation in association with CDI Compagnia Distribuzione Internazionale, JVC Entertainment Sogepaq of a Greenstreet Films production. *Executive Producer:* Giovanni Di Clemente. *Producer:* John Penotti and John

Turturro. *Director:* John Turturro. *Screenplay:* Brandon Cole and John Turturro. *Based on His Play:* Brandon Cole. *Director of Photography:* Harris Savides. *Editor:* Michael Berenbaum. *Music:* William Bolcom and Arnold Black. *Sound:* Gary Alper. *Sound Editor:* Lynn Sable. *Casting:* Todd Thaler. *Production Designer:* Robin Standefer. *Art Director:* Stephen Alesch. *Set Decorator:* Donna Hamilton. *Set Dresser:* Paul Roer. *Costumes:* Donna Zakowska. *Running time:* 111 minutes. *MPAA Rating:* R.

CAST: John Turturro (Tuccio); Katherine Borowitz (Rachel); Christopher Walken (Bevalaqua); Susan Sarandon (Celimene); Beverly D'Angelo (Astergourd); Bill Irwin (Marco); Rufus Sewell (Dominique); Georgina Cates (Simone); Matthew Sussman (Piero); Ben Gazzara (Old Flavio); Leo Bassi (Beppo); Donal McCann (Pallenchio); Aida Turturro (Martha); Henri Behar (Pitou); Maurizio Benazzo (Passerby); Fernando Bolles (Boy #2); Jeff Braun (Duke); David Cale (Journalist); Kenny Cranna (Scruffy Man); George DiCenzo (Jailor); Tim Doyle (Aristorat #1); Alexander Goodwin (Crying Boy); Amo Gulinello (Pupo); Chris Papadopoulos (Boy #3); Mary Lou Rosato (Duchessa); Suzanne Shepherd (Marco's Mother); Rocco Sisto (Prince); Richard Spore (Stagehand); June Stein (Angry Woman); Henry Stram (Captain); Kohl Sudduth (Concubine #1); Arjun Bhasin (Concubine #2); Matthew Sussman (Piero); David Thornton (Orlandi); Amadeo Turturro (Boy #1); Jeremy Knaster (Military Policeman); Richard Termini (Gypsy Musician on Guitar); Joe Paparone (Grand Inquisitor); William Preston (Old Toothless Man).

LOS ANGELES TIMES, 8/6/99, Calendar/p. 2, Kevin Thomas

John Turturro's "Illuminata," a rhapsodic celebration of love and life in the theater, is about as close to an all-out art film in the grand traditional manner as an American movie ever gets, recalling such films as Max Ophuls' "La Ronde" and Ingmar Bergman's "Smiles of a Summer Night."

According to Turturro, who with Brandon Cole adapted Cole's play for the screen, he was influenced by Jean Renoir's "The Rules of the Game" and also took inspiration from Georges Feydeau's farces and Michael Powell and Emeric Pressburger's "Red Shoes." All this should tell you that you're in for something out of the ordinary, something that those unwilling to go along with this heady treat might well dismiss as "arty." Ironically, were "Illuminata" either an Italian or French film, it might be an easier sell.

Set in 1905 Manhattan, it has as its principal setting a charming, old-fashioned theater with a very high proscenium flanked by tiers of box seats that is owned by Astergourd (Beverly D'Angelo) and her husband Pallenchio (the late Donal McCann). Currently in residence is an acting company drawing upon much immigrant talent arriving in the city in that era and headed by the incandescent Rachel (Katherine Borowitz), a Pre-Raphaelite beauty and consummate actress. (It may be no accident that Rachel is the name of the sublime French actress heralded across Europe a generation before Sarah Bernhardt.)

The troupe is performing "Cavalleria Rusticana," until an illness fells one of the actors. Turturro's Tuccio, a talented but still struggling playwright and Rachel's lover, doesn't hesitate to step forward in front of the footlights and announce that the play he wrote for Rachel, "Illuminata," will be presented at the theater the very next night. After such a public announcement, Astergourd, who has been stalling Tuccio, has little choice but to comply.

When "Illuminata," a play about infidelity and forgiveness espousing the value of imperfect love as all that mere humans are capable of, goes on the next night, it sets off a chain of Feydeau-like complications. The all-powerful critic Bevalaqua (Christopher Walken), who comes across as a hilariously burlesqued Oscar Wilde, hates the play but is smitten with Marco (Bill Irwin), cast as a Harlequin-like figure.

Now if Marco could be persuaded to accept Bevalaqua's fevered invitation to come over for a visit at his exotic digs, and be prepared to give at least hope to the critic that he might succumb to the love that dare not speak its name, well maybe "Illuminata" could be resuscitated.

Meanwhile, Susan Sarandon's Mme. Celimene, an international stage legend of a certain age with the bravura manner of a Bernhardt, wants "Illuminata" as the vehicle that will allow her to return to the Paris stage in triumph—and with Tuccio in tow as her latest lover.

As the fate of the play unfolds, the company's self-absorbed leading man Dominique (Rufus Sewell) carries on with the ingenue Simone (Georgina Cates), while Astergourd and Pallenchio unknowingly swap partners, at least for a night, as Astergourd vamps the beefy, aging clown Beppo (Leo Bassi), whose plump lover Marta (Aida Turturro) sets her sights on Pallenchio.

Turturro and his formidable cast carry off all these tempestuous shenanigans with admirable aplomb. The themes of Tuccio's play surface in his relationship with Rachel, who without much reflection accepts the gossip buzzing about Sarah and Tuccio as truth. Jealousy and anger, as Rachel comes to realize, make her love for Tuccio something less than perfect.

Look, feel and tone are crucial to the success of such a potentially precious and flighty undertaking. Yet everything falls into place and seems exactly right: the brisk tempo, the crisp, witty performances, the slightly sooty touch—think of all those Czech comedies of the '60s—to cameraman Harris Savides' lovely images that capture so beautifully the evocative settings and costumes of Robin Standefer and Donna Zakowska, respectively.

They no doubt cost a fraction of those for Martin Scorsese's "The Age of Innocence" yet are far more consistently authentic.

Typical of the resourcefulness and subtlety of this film's approach is the use of the baroque-style Loew's Jersey, one of the greatest surviving movie palaces; it wasn't built until two decades after this film takes place, so the filmmakers use only glimpses of it to suggest opulence, whereas a more literal use of the theater would be thuddingly anachronistic. Completing the picture is William Bolcom's irresistibly romantic yet never overdone score.

The light, right touch prevails throughout, with Turturro inspiring glorious performances from his very large cast that includes Ben Gazzara as Rachel's father, a theater stalwart whose memory is beginning to fade.

The film's comic tours de force are Bevalaqua's vigorous attempt to seduce Marco, who is neither as young nor as handsome as he is in the critic's eyes—and almost certainly as gay as his pursuer, but heavily repressed; and Celimene's equally flamboyant attack on Tuccio.

NEW YORK POST, 8/6/99, p. 51, Hannah Brown

"Illuminata" is like a thick slice of ham—tasty, elegantly prepared and served—that aspires to be gourmet fare but in the end turns out to be only half-baked.

The story of a troupe of flamboyant actors in New York at the turn of the century, it's a pretentious but lively look at how the theater and life are connected.

Directed and co-written by John Turturro, who also stars, it features a wonderful ensemble cast.

Susan Sarandon revels in her role as a promiscuous diva who still plays 19-year-old virgins, and Christopher Walken is over the top but undeniably entertaining as a critic who looks like a combination of Oscar Wilde and Quentin Crisp, and sounds like Bela Lugosi in "Dracula."

Best known for his quirky roles in movies by the Coen brothers and Spike Lee, Turturro is more restrained than usual here as Tuccio, the company's resident playwright.

He's tolerated only because his wife, (played by Katherine Borowitz, his real-life spouse) is the lead actress and director of the troupe. (The film is a real Turturro family affair: his son and a cousin, Aida Turturro, also have roles.)

Tuccio longs to abandon the heavy-handed melodramas of the period and present a more naturalistic style of theater, but everyone doubts his talent—including his wife.

Set against a bawdy background of sex and low comedy backstage, the drama between Tuccio and his wife starts to mirror his latest play, and "Illuminata" comes to resemble "Shakespeare in Love." Unfortunately, though, it can't match that film's charm, grace and wit.

The biggest difference, of course, is that the play rehearsed and performed in "Shakespeare in Love" is "Romeo and Juliet," while the lines written by Tuccio do not suggest that his work will be an enduring masterpiece. Sample dialogue: "If you look for someone to love you imperfectly, look no further, for I am she."

While Turturro occasionally pokes fun at his character's vanity and single-mindedness, Tuccio is meant to be admirable, a slave to his art.

But Tuccio's struggle pales beside the terrific performances from a cast that includes Ben Gazzara, Beverly D'Angelo, and, in one of his last roles, Donal McCann, who died last month.

The costumes and sets are dazzling and create a vivid sense of the period.

With its combination of fun and high-mindedness, "Illuminata" will probably be enjoyed most by people who go to movies only when they can't get theater or opera tickets.

NEWSDAY, 8/6/99, Part II/p. B6, John Anderson

There's a sense of circus act in John Turturro's "Illuminata"—a comic bouquet to love, the stage and the latter's imperceptible distance from life. And not just because of its sprawling, big-top atmosphere. Or its acknowledgment of theater's very populist roots. Or even the presence of clown genius Bill Irwin.

It's because Turturro's doing a juggling act while walking a high wire, something that seizes your admiration even before you notice whether he's keeping the balls—or himself—in the air.

Set among a Little Italy acting troupe at the turn of the century, "Illuminata" meaning, essentially, an enlightened one—rambles about the theater of Astergourd (Beverly D'Angelo) and Pallenchio (the late Donal McCann), giving us snapshots of actors rehearsing, insulting each other, in distress and—in the case of Simone (Georgina Cates) and Dominique (Rufus Sewell)—in flagrante delicto.

Politics is raging: Piero (Matthew Sussman) has been given the disgruntled Dominique's part in "Cavalleria Rusticana." The critic/assassin and "macaroni queen" Umberto Bevalaqua (Christopher Walken) is in the house, as is aging prima donna Celimene (Susan Sarandon), who's never met scenery she couldn't chew. The stage is set for chaos, which occurs when Piero faints, the playwright Tuccio (Turturro) tells the audience the actor really died and the house demands that Tuccio's new play—to star the popular and luminescent Rachel (Katherine Borowitz)—be staged immediately.

Ruthlessness, art, sexual musical chairs and the "slender curtain between theater and life," as Celimene puts it, are the stuff of "Illuminata," which in its casting and its enthusiasm manages to capture the energy of the very acting troupe it portrays. Balanced with the farce—the antics of Beppo (the wonderful clown Leo Bassi, in his first film role), or the Brooklyn-accented stage mama Marta (Aida Turturro) or the pursuit of Marco (Irwin) by the lecherous Bevalaqua—we also get the contrapuntal autopsy of love embodied by Tuccio's play (think Chekhov as staged by the Wooster Group) and the troubled, inexplicable love of Rachel for Tuccio.

It's rather difficult, given the fulcrum of the story—the established star involved with a struggling playwright—to ignore the fact that while Turturro has had a flourishing film career, his wife, Borowitz, has made few films relative to her talents. Maybe that's why her director-husband deprives her no opportunity to look radiant. On the other hand, she doesn't have to try very hard.

But the Turturro-Borowitz, shall we say, situation does take the entire conceit a step further than where it would be otherwise. This is a film—based on a play by Brandon Cole and co-scripted by Cole and Turturro—whose thrust is all about life as theater. Among its more poignant moments are the actual death of Piero, the actor who never returned to the stage after being pronounced dead there by Tuccio. His collapse is inexplicable, unless you accept—as "Illuminata" does that the stage is life. Add to this the frozen tableaux of mourners Turturro arranges around the deathbed, suggesting, if nothing else, the idea of theater after death.

As good as his cast is—Borowitz, Cates and Sarandon are marvelous, sometimes marvelously hammy, and Walken is a ghoulish hoot—Turturro may not be his own best director. Although Tuccio is supposed to be the egoiste/artiste, Turturro maintains too austere a tone for the rest of the film. He's told by Rachel at one point that she's going to do Ibsen because they have to eat. "You and your eating!" he says. "What about my play?" What should be a laugh line arrives like an announcement that your train is leaving the station.

The play-within-the-play is somewhat tedious; ending with the cast-as-credits is a good idea, because it lightens what is a breathlessly delicate ending of the film proper. Still, "Illuminata"—the Tuccio play at the heart of "Illuminata"—is essential to the wholeness of the film. Its ending, that of a near-tragic love story, becomes a point of contention between Tuccio and the theater owner Pallenchio, and, at one point, an exasperated Rachel, too.

"She doesn't leave him. She doesn't hurt him. She just goes on loving him!" she says of her character. In this, Turturro's movie goes full circle: not life turned into theater, but theater breaching life.

VILLAGE VOICE, 8/10/99, p. 7, Ethan Alter

John Turturro points the camera at the stage in *Illuminata,* a loving ode to the theatrical world. The subject is, as one character describes it, "the slender curtain between theater and life." Set in turn-of-the-century New York, the film follows the farcical misadventures of a struggling repertory company, which contains all the requisite stock characters, including the luminous leading lady (Katherine Borowitz), the tortured playwright (Turturro), and the boisterous clown (Leo Bassi). Rounding out the cast is Christopher Walken, who hams it up gloriously as a foppish theater critic.

Turturro directs the film with great confidence; through an imaginative visual style and ornate production design, he believably re-creates the look and feel of an early-20th-century playhouse. But he is unable to present an equally convincing depiction of the world outside the theater. This makes it difficult for viewers to remain involved as it meanders to a bland conclusion. For all its ambitions, *Illuminata* sheds only murky light on what separates theater from life.

Also reviewed in:
CHICAGO TRIBUNE, 8/20/99, Friday/p. A, Michael Wilmington
NEW YORK TIMES, 8/6/99, p. E32, Janet Maslin
VARIETY, 5/25-31/98, p. 59, Emanuel Levy
WASHINGTON POST, 8/20/99, p. C5, Stephen Hunter

I'M LOSING YOU

A Strand Releasing and Killer Films release of a Lions Gate Films presentation. *Executive Producer:* David Cronenberg, Michael Paseornek, Jeff Sackman, John Dunning, and Andre Link. *Producer:* Pamela Koffler and Christine Vachon. *Director:* Bruce Wagner. *Screenplay (based on his novel):* Bruce Wagner. *Music:* Daniel Catán and Randall Poster. *Director of Photography:* Rob Sweeney. *Editor:* Janice Hampton. *Casting:* Billy Hopkins, Suzanne Smith and Kerry Barden. *Production Designer:* Richard Sherman. *Costumes:* Theadora Van Runkle. *Running time:* 102 minutes. *MPAA Rating:* Not Rated.

CAST: Andrew McCarthy (Bertie Krohn); Rosanna Arquette (Rachel Krohn); Frank Langella (Perry Needham Krohn); Salome Jens (Diantha Krohn); Buck Henry (Philip Dragom); Elizabeth Perkins (Aubrey); Gina Gershon (Lidia); Amanda Donohoe (Mona Deware); Laraine Newman (Casting Person).

LOS ANGELES TIMES, 7/16/99, Calendar/p. 16, Kevin Thomas

In bringing his highly acclaimed novel "I'm Losing You" to the screen, writer-director Bruce Wagner attempts something quite unusual: His film portrays a wealthy Los Angeles family capable of dignity in the face of a string of catastrophes that would test the spirit of Job. This is an elegant, stately film of considerable acrid wit but of even greater compassion and wisdom that glows with polished ensemble performances from a notable cast.

The Krohns are not the nouveau riche philistines of typical depictions of show biz families. They are smart, educated, sophisticated people capable of reflection who do not let the onslaught of tragedy erase their appreciation of the good fortune they have known.

"I'm Losing You," a phrase that refers to a fading call on a cell phone as well as impending death, opens with Perry Krohn (Frank Langella) getting very bad news on the eve of his 60th birthday: He has terminal lung cancer and no more than a year to live. Krohn, who looks and feels fine, cannot help but express the irony of learning such dire news at a time he's making $8 million a year as producer of a "Star Trek"-like TV series, an accomplishment he views with pride diluted with a certain degree of self-disdain.

Krohn lives in a hilltop estate of impeccably tasteful contemporary splendor with his elegant wife, Diantha (Salome Jens), a psychiatrist who dedicates herself to unlocking the secrets of her patients while keeping a few whoppers of her own. In addition to their son, Bertie (Andrew

McCarthy), an actor whose brief moment in the limelight has passed, Diantha and Perry have also raised as their daughter Perry's niece Rachel (Rosanna Arquette), an appraiser at a fancy auction house who was orphaned as an infant.

Bertie is not the usual Hollywood scion who can't get it together. While open to acting gigs when they come along, he is committed to supporting himself and his little daughter as best he can. Currently, he's selling life insurance policies of AIDS patients in order to obtain a cash advance for the dying. He's about to get a commission for his part in getting a dentist and his wife to buy such a policy—a scene of exceedingly subtle humor.

By coincidence, the policy belongs to a former costume designer (Buck Henry) on Perry's series; although gay, the designer appreciates the dark irony of having become infected with AIDS via a blood transfusion, for he is a hemophiliac. Divorced from a serious substance abuser (Gina Gershon), Bertie, in his new gig, meets and falls for Aubrey (Elizabeth Perkins), a chic socialite with a small son; Aubrey is on the verge of entering the terminal stages of AIDS, which she acquired under bizarre circumstances. Meanwhile, Rachel, reeling from the discovery of the true circumstances of her parents' death, finds herself unexpectedly drawn to the rituals of Judaism.

Wagner undercuts all the tragedy by maintaining a calm, understated tone with a flicker of recognition of life's absurdities. Most adults know that the advent of one impending loss scarcely makes one immune to another, so the chain of dire events that shower upon the Krohns do not really defy credibility. In any event, what concerns Wagner is how the respective Krohns rise to the occasion.

Arquette and McCarthy have had challenging roles before, but perhaps not quite so demanding as these, and they are every bit as impressive as the more seasoned Langella and Jens. Perkins manages the tricky business of making Aubrey appealing rather than pathetic or insufferably brave or noble. Amanda Donohoe is beguiling as a stunning, coolly mature British actress who takes a key role in Perry's series and his life. Everyone else in the large cast also hits just the night notes.

"I'm Losing You" has a sleekness that is epitomized in Theadora Van Runkle's typically distinctive costumes. The film is too adult and too perceptive, its people far too well-drawn and persuasive, to seem either as contrived or as depressing as a description of it almost surely sounds. A sharp observer with a dry satirical edge, Wagner dares to ask us to discover in his highly contemporary people something of the stature of the heroes of Greek tragedy.

NEW YORK POST, 7/16/99, p. 46, Jonathan Foreman

It's supposed to be art. After all, it's about miserable Hollywood folk confronted by disease and death, and the characters have a pronounced—if improbable—tendency to quote Emily Dickinson and drop literary references into their conversation.

But "I'm Losing You" is really just an ultra-gloomy episode of "Melrose Place," filled with self-conscious intellectual name-dropping and a lot of mannered, supposedly mordant dialogue. (It's even shot like TV, with an excess of close-ups.)

This self-important dreck may pass for highbrow in the Hollywood Hills, but it's as phony as can be. It's also slow, talky and almost comically morbid, as if Bruce Wagner, who adapted his novel of the same name, thinks that filling the plot with a lot of death (mostly from AIDS, but also by cancer and car crashes) is the hallmark of high-minded seriousness.

Perry (Frank Langella), a rich and powerful TV producer, is told he has 12 months to live. Then his niece and adopted daughter Rachel (Rosanna Arquette) finds out that her parents didn't really die in a car crash. The truth is that her mother was having an affair with Perry, and her father shot her before he killed himself.

On finding out the truth, Rachel decides to take up "Tahala," the ritual cleansing of corpses according to Jewish tradition. Naturally, one of the first bodies she encounters turns out to be a beloved relative.

Meanwhile, Perry's failed-actor son Bertie (Andrew McCarthy with a goatee) is making a living by selling the life insurance benefits of people dying of AIDS, but he refuses to accept a role on his dad's "Star Trek"-like show. He meets and falls for hard-bitten HIV-positive widow Aubrey (Elizabeth Perkins). In the throes of passion he begs her to infect him with the disease ... Tragedy does strike him, but from quite another quarter.

In between the deaths are various betrayals and overwrought confrontations. Here and there are some affecting moments, but most are undermined by Wagner's straining to be witty and sardonic (Perkins says to McCarthy, "So you're an actor... that's kind of like being HIV [positive]") and by his general desperation to establish intellectual bona fides.

At one point, he actually makes poor Rosanna Arquette say that she was a grad student at Oxford who "studied Coleridge and cabala before either were hip."

When "I'm Losing You" does work, despite all I the glibness and doomy pretentiousness, it's thanks to the efforts of a fine cast in the wrong place at the wrong time.

NEWSDAY, 7/16/99, Part II/p. B6, John Anderson

Listen to lines like "Bergman's been debunked" and "television Strindberg" in a movie as morose and mordant as "I'm Losing You," and you can't help but think that something peculiar's going on. And when characters refer to the soap-opera aspects of their lives—in a film filled with as much tragedy, emotional self-flagellation and contrived coincidence as this one—you're sure there's a satirical agenda at work, a sending up of the hand-wringing theatricality of so much of what passes for popular drama.

Then again, maybe not. "I'm Losing You"—written and directed by Bruce Wagner from his 1997 novel—was never going to be the feel-good film of '99. Perry Krohn (Frank Langella), producer of a "Star Trek"-style TV phenomenon, discovers on his 60th birthday that he has inoperable cancer. His son, Bertie (Andrew McCarthy), a wildly unsuccessful would-be actor, is involved in "selling short" life-insurance policies of the terminally ill. His sister, Rachel (Rosanna Arquette)—who's actually his cousin, is taking instruction in the Jewish ritual of washing the dead. Bertie's ex-wife (Gina Gershon) is a drug addict, and the woman he's in love with (Elizabeth Perkins) is HIV-positive.

While all this might sound like a rollicking good time, Wagner—altering his book to a considerable degree does get some terrific performances out of his actors, especially when he has them working one-on-one. Langella and Buck Henry, who plays Perry's AIDS-infected costume designer, have a morbidly funny discussion about death. Perkins is a real eye-opener, as the fatalistically funny Aubrey. And even McCarthy, who has seemed in need of bearings since outgrowing his Brat Pack days, is affecting as the rudderless Bertie, a lad at sea amid so many tragedies and people unhinged.

The film—whose double-entendre title refers both to incipient death and the cry of the fading cell-phone connection—walks naturally through the confines of upscale Hollywood and tangles gracefully with a lot of tough issues that, like child abuse, addiction, AIDS and cancer, have become dramatic clichés through overuse and clumsy handling. Wagner's script is too clever by half—the occasional lazy line might have given it some rhythm—but he has made a film that's rather courageous in what it tackles and how. On the other hand, just because your characters acknowledge that their lives are full of an outlandish amount of Sturm und Drang doesn't mean your movie isn't, too.

VILLAGE VOICE, 7/20/99, p. 135, Abby McGanney Nolan

Welcome back to L.A. The title of Bruce Wagner's directorial debut is a reference to hazy mobile-phone connections and, more heavy-handedly, to the unstable relationships of some sorry inhabitants of Hollywood. Wagner has adapted his sharp and wide-reaching 1996 novel by reconfiguring five characters into one family and foisting far too much of the book's plot detail upon them.

Perry (Frank Langella), the hugely successful TV producer of a show that eerily resembles *Star Trek* ("May you wander and wonder with the stars"), has just found out he's dying. Rachel (Rosanna Arquette), his adopted daughter, learns her parents weren't killed in a car crash after all and delves into her Jewish roots. Failed actor Bertie (Andrew McCarthy) dotes on his sickly sweet daughter and woos HIV-positive Aubrey (Elizabeth Perkins). Perry's wife, Diantha (Salome Jens), meanwhile has little to do, even as Perry initiates an affair with an English actress on his show (Amanda Donohoe).

From here we get death, more betrayal, and more death. These events are all supposed to be attributable to Hollywood's toxicity. More likely, Wagner thought he needed some drama to drive his movie along. But as Rachel describes some revelation she's unearthed, "It's like television Strindberg." The film then devolves into TV-movie land, complete with treacly music and tearful goodbyes.

That said, the cast is uniformly solid, with an impressive turn by Perkins (in a role that's overly but somehow refreshingly hard-bitten) and all-too-brief bits by Buck Henry and Laraine Newman. Wagner also has plenty of good one-liners (like Bertie's commentary on his acting career—"I'm too cable, not too mention boyish and endearing"). Where the novel was stuffed with references to then current Hollywood projects and stars (with a few making walk-on appearances), the film is full of quotations from movies and literature. Emily Dickinson's "First —chill—then stupor—then the letting go" is given at least three readings, and it ends up approximating the movie's effect.

Also reviewed in:
NEW YORK TIMES, 7/16/99, p. E13, Janet Maslin
VARIETY, 9/28-10/4/98, p. 40, Todd McCarthy

IN DREAMS

A DreamWorks Pictures release of a Stephen Woolley production. *Producer:* Stephen Woolley. *Director:* Neil Jordan. *Screenplay:* Bruce Robinson and Neil Jordan. *Based on the novel "Doll's Eyes" by:* Bari Wood. *Director of Photography:* Darius Khondji. *Editor:* Tony Lawson. *Music:* Elliot Goldenthal. *Music Editor:* Curtis Roush. *Sound:* James J. Sabat and (music) Joel Iwataki. *Sound Editor:* Douglas Murray. *Casting:* Janet Hirshenson and Jane Jenkins. *Production Designer:* Nigel Phelps. *Art Director:* Martin Laing. *Set Designer:* Mark Morgenstein. *Set Decorator:* Gretchen Rau. *Set Dresser:* Juliet Carter, Jeffrey DeBell, Jim Schneider, Ted Suchecki, Kathy Rosen, Todd Bakerian-Devane, and Robert Schleinig. *Special Effects:* Yves De Bono. *Costumes:* Jeffrey Kurland. *Make-up:* Lori Hicks. *Make-up (Annette Bening):* Carrie Angland. *Make-up (Special Effects):* Billy Messina and Bill Johnson. *Stunt Coordinator:* Jery Hewitt. *Running time:* 112 minutes. *MPAA Rating:* R.

CAST: Annette Bening (Claire Cooper); Katie Sagona (Rebecca Cooper); Aidan Quinn (Paul Cooper); Robert Downey, Jr. (Vivian Thompson); Paul Guilfoyle (Detective Jack Kay); Kathleen Langlois (Snow White); Jennifer Berry (Hunter); Amelia Claire Novotny (Prince); Kristin Sroka (Wicked Stepmother); Robert Walsh (Man at School Play); Denise Cormier (Woman at School Play); John Fiore (Policeman); Ken Cheeseman (Paramedic); Dennis Boutsikaris (Doctor Stevens); Devon Cole Borisoff (Vivian Thompson, as a Boy); Stephen Rea (Doctor Silverman); Prudence Wright Holmes (Mary); Lonnie Farmer (Nurse Rosco); Margo Martindale (Nurse Floyd); June Lewin (Kindly Nurse); Pamela Payton-Wright (Ethel); Krystal Benn (Ruby); Dorothy Dwyer (Foster Mother); Geoff Wigdor (Vivian Thompson, as a Teenager); Wally Dunn (Walter); Eric Roemele (Security Man, 1970's); Dossy Peabody (Vivian's Mother); John Michael Vaughn (Helicopter Pilot); Brian Goodman (Policeman in Squad Car); Michael Cavanaugh (Voice of Judge).

CHRISTIAN SCIENCE MONITOR, 1/15/99, p. 15, David Sterritt

Apples are a wholesome symbol of the New England countryside, but Neil Jordan's thriller "In Dreams" gives them a sinister twist.

The heroine, aptly named Claire, is an apparently normal woman plagued by clairvoyant nightmares that prominently feature the color red: an apple orchard, lipstick, a little girl named Ruby. Her life turns nightmarish when her young daughter is killed by an elusive madman. It gets worse when she realizes that the murderer is paying her mysterious visits by penetrating her sleeping and waking thoughts.

Jordan has directed movies as varied as "The Crying Game" and "Michael Collins," but his interest in horror recurs as often as one of Claire's bad dreams—from "The Company of Wolves" to "Interview With the Vampire"—and he isn't afraid of explicit violence, as "The Butcher Boy" reminded us. "In Dreams" delivers a hefty amount of gore, although most of it springs from the screen so abruptly that ifs over almost as soon ifs begun.

The picture is also strong on moods and maneuvers borrowed from better chillers, from "The Shining" and "Don't Look Now" to the notorious "Blue Velvet," which put Roy Orbison's pop song "In Dreams" to purposes even creepier than the ones Jordan dishes up here.

The movie's sanguinary suspense should keep horror fans happily howling; others may watch portions through their fingers. If so, they'll miss an enormously creative performance by Annette Bening as the tormented heroine, and solid work by Robert Downey Jr. as her evil nemesis.

The screenplay contains pointed references to psychiatric experts who think they know more than their patients. These raise more thought-provoking questions about the modern medical establishment than the self-congratulatory "Patch Adams," now in theaters, manages to do in its entire running time.

LOS ANGELES TIMES, 1/15/99, Calendar/p. 8, Jack Mathews

[The following review by Jack Mathews appeared in a slightly different form in **NEWSDAY, 1/15/99, Part II/p. B7.]**

The key to the demented mind of a serial killer, and to his connection with a neighborhood clairvoyant, is to be found in a child's bedroom in a town at the bottom of a lake formed by a flood 30 years ago. The water, it should be quickly noted, isn't the only substance piled high in Neil Jordan's ludicrous horror-thriller "In Dreams."

Adapted from an out-of-print pulp novel, "Doll's Eyes," with apparent additional inspiration from "Nightmare on Elm Street" and, perhaps, a few Dionne Warwick psychic infomercials, "In Dreams" tells of the psychological war between children's book illustrator Claire Cooper (Annette Bening) and the madman who haunts her premonitory dreams.

Claire doesn't even have to be asleep to dream of this killer's deeds, which involve—but are not limited to—the kidnappings and murders of small girls, whose bodies are invariably found in the sunken ghost town. He has somehow gained access to Claire's mind, does some of her thinking for her, even uses her teeth to bite through her husband's lip when the mood strikes him.

As the body count and bitten lips mount in the small New England community, so too do the clues of the killer's identity, at least in Claire's porous mind. There is a recurring children's nursery rhyme, an apple orchard, a boy's bedroom, chains, the flood. Naturally, husband Paul (Aidan Quinn), detective Jack (Paul Guilfoyle) and her psychiatrist (Stephen Rea) think Claire's insane, so it is up to her to turn her power against her mind's possessor.

Speaking of possession, we can only wonder what drew such high-powered talent as Jordan, Bening and her co-stars Quinn and Robert Downey Jr. (as guess who) to such wretched B-movie material. The script, by Oscar nominee Bruce Robinson ("The Killing Fields"), is direct-to-video stuff, a run-on of preposterous psychic horror cliches.

At the root of all evil in "In Dreams" is child abuse, begetting child abuse. Where there's a serial killer, you can be sure there was once a sadistic authoritarian parent, and an inciting event, all of which makes, in this case, for some graphically jolting flashbacks.

The underwater images, of both the flooded town and the circumstances of young Vivian Thompson's escape from it, have the haunting atmosphere typical of Jordan's past horror films, "Interview With the Vampire" and "The Company of Wolves." If this were a portrait of a demented mind, "In Dreams" might have been worthwhile. (Of course, Jordan just did that, with last year's brilliant "The Butcher Boy.")

In any event, the psychic connection overwhelms every other element of realism. "In Dreams" doesn't even work on its own level of fantasy. Claire's clairvoyance (come on, guys, you can do better than that!) isn't the major theme; it's Vivian's ability to enter her mind. And why does he do that? Because, Claire reasons, he wants to get caught. Please.

Bening works this role like a sore muscle, or a tooth that needs pulling. It's a courageous, anti-glamour effort, one of those sweat-and-drool "Snake Pit" performances that drives hair and makeup crazy, not to mention mental-health-care providers.

She's nothing if not a pro.

Others in the cast were less inspired. Quinn plays Claire's husband, a 747 pilot, like a guy losing at poker and looking for a reason to quit. The low level of energy that Rea brings to the psychiatrist makes you wonder if the character hasn't been sneaking the Thorazine.   And Downey, well, you want psycho, he'll give you psycho.

NEW YORK, 1/25/99, p. 47, Peter Rainer

What in the blazes happens to Neil Jordan when he makes movies in this country?   You can just about bet the farm on the likelihood that his British- and Irish-made films will be wonderful and his American films will be bad.   And yet he keeps trying to make a go of it in Hollywood.   He's followed *The Butcher Boy,* one of last year's finest, with *In Dreams,* a dollop of supernatural claptrap starring Annette Bening.   Completed many months ago, it's finally making its appearance in the January compost heap traditionally reserved for stinkos the studios didn't have the nerve to release earlier into a more competitive field.

Bening's Claire Cooper is a children's-book illustrator whose dreams are being commandeered by a killer (Robert Downey Jr.).   He does a Vulcan-mind-meld number on her in which she is made to see the murders he will soon commit.   Unable for a long time to persuade her jet-pilot husband (Aidan Quinn) or the local police detective (Paul Guilfoyle) or psychiatrist (Stephen Rea) to take her warnings seriously, she loses her daughter to the creepo and ends up in a padded cell, complete with bullyboy orderlies and stone-faced headshrinkers.   Even though we're in rural Massachusetts, you'd think this film was taking place in some medieval dungeon.   The only things missing are the toads and the tongs.   The American Psychiatric Association should sue.

By making it clear from the beginning that Claire is dreaming real murders, Jordan discounts any alternative, psychological explanation for her unraveling which under the circumstances would have been more interesting.   But he still seems vaguely drawn to that approach: Claire's messed-up marriage, for example, sometimes provokes her visions.   And although Bening is supposed to be playing an essentially sane seer, her performance is prime bughouse.   Everything she speaks sounds italicized—stentorian—and she does a lot of eyeball-rolling under her close-cropped hair. (She looks sheared.) When she finally has her showdown with the killer, you're afraid he's going to boost the fruitcake quotient, but no, Downey plays it cool.   He's a slow-motion nut in a flibbertigibbet pageant.

Jordan is the wrong director for a supernatural horror thriller in which we are supposed to draw a line between the "real" and the imagined.   At his best, he's beyond such distinctions; his genius is for conveying the visionary in the everyday.   It's a peculiarly Irish gift, which is why, when his movies really sing, you think not of other filmmakers but of, say, Yeats or Heaney.   Maybe the reason he can't be an artist in Hollywood is that he lacks the peculiarly American gift of turning dross into gold.   He requires rich material from the get-go.   The trash essence of *In Dreams* works upon his talent like battery acid.

NEW YORK POST, 1/15/99, p. 47, Rod Dreher

It was directed by Neil Jordan and stars Annette Bening as the heroine and Robert Downey Jr. as the villain.   Stephen Rea and Aidan Quinn have supporting roles.   How bad could the serial-killer suspenser "In Dreams" be?

Here's a clue about this film with such prestigious names attached: If "In Dreams" were any good, would DreamWorks SKG be releasing it in the bleak midwinter?   They've dumped it like a barrel of sludge into the post-Christmas moviegoing Marianas Trench, where it will sink without leaving so much as a ripple.   Deservedly, alas.

To its credit—and pay attention, because this is the only praiseworthy element in the whole preposterous shebang—"In Dreams" has a terrifically spooky opening sequence, showing divers exploring the underwater graveyard that used to be a village, before it was evacuated and flooded to make a reservoir.   Some dark secret lies buried underneath all that water, and Jordan instantly draws us to the edge of our seats, expecting a severed head or some such thing to come tumbling out of a murky cranny, a la "Jaws."

The submerged New England village happens to be the dumping ground for little girls abducted and slaughtered by a serial killer.   It so happens that area resident Claire Cooper (Bening) keeps having horrible nightmares about kidnapped children.   Her nocturnal misery is so great that it's threatening her marriage to her airline pilot husband (Quinn).

When their own daughter is stolen and later found dead in the lake, a grief-stricken Claire tries to kill herself. Waking from a coma weeks later in a hospital, she comes to believe that her dreams predict the future. Her husband and her shrink (Rea, in a Thorazine-glazed performance) believe Claire has lost her mind.

She hasn't; rather, the killer has found her mind. The mysterioso murderer (Downey, unseen until well into the picture) has established a psychic connection with Claire and invades her subconscious to make his thoughts her own.

What makes this premise so frightening is the loss of control over the most private aspects of one's identity. It's why supernatural horror shows like "The Exorcist" are more frightening than standard slasher films. You can always run away from a nut with a hatchet, but how do you escape a malicious being who can capture your soul?

"In Dreams" never makes this fear palpable. Bening wiggles and wails and gnaws poor Quinn's lips bloody, but we don't for a second feel her terror. It doesn't help that an "Amityville Horror"-type of scene involving a garbage disposal vomiting apple butter is apt to make audiences cringe, for all the wrong reasons.

Worse, this is the kind of mediocre material that depends on incredible coincidences and a stupid heroine. If a serial killer were on the loose and you believed he was particularly interested in your scalp, would you go running off into the woods at every opportunity? Would you disarm yourself when one shot would dispatch the killer and end the movie? Do you think characters in a horror movie by the likes of Neil Jordan ought to behave that way?

Eventually the greater horror of "In Dreams" is wondering how a script this cheesy took over the minds of people like this fine director (who graced us last year with a truly scary film, "The Butcher Boy") and his top-flight cast. There's a place for ludicrously plotted B-movie horror, but this lot are slumming (Jordan is no John Carpenter, and Bening is no Jamie Lee Curtis).

And if you think that Downey will save this mess when he at long last appears on the scene, all too briefly—keep dreaming, pal.

SIGHT AND SOUND, 5/99, p. 50, Richard Kelly

In 1965, the New England town of Northfield is evacuated, then flooded to create a reservoir. In the present, illustrator Claire Cooper lives near the reservoir with her husband Paul, a pilot. Their marriage is fraying, due to Paul's frequent absences and Claire's recurrent nightmare visions of an abducted child, which she thinks may be relevant to a local murder investigation. Claire's daughter Rebecca is snatched and her body is fished from the reservoir. Realising her visions were premonitory, Claire attempts suicide. She is treated by psychiatrist Dr Silverman, but the visions only get fiercer, and she slashes her wrists. She tells Silverman that the killer is "inside her head".

Paul agrees to have her committed. Claire foresees Paul's murder, but can't convince Silverman to prevent it. In her hospital room, Claire discovers a poem, familiar from her dreams, inscribed by ex-inmate Vivian Thompson. Claire breaks out by following Vivian's own escape route. Inspecting Thompson's file, Silverman learns that the child Vivian was left for dead by his mother during the Northfield flooding. Claire lures Vivian from hiding, and accompanies him to his home a derelict cider factory where he is holding another child, Ruby. Claire helps Ruby escape and flees herself, pursued by Vivian. The police arrive but fail to prevent Claire plunging to a watery death. Ruled insane, Vivian is recommitted, only to be haunted by bloody visions and Claire's voice.

Plainly, Neil Jordan is not an artist who's much arrested by naturalism. He has a flair for all things fantastic, hence his happy teaming with Patrick McCabe on *The Butcher Boy,* a film in which any sane man should take delight. So you have to wonder why Jordan continues to make movies for Hollywood studios. Whether the matter at hand be pretty-boy vampires or the birth-travails of the Irish Free State, the results always seem to bear the rabid tooth-marks of preview testing. His latest undertaking amounts to not much more than just another serial-killer thriller, and from Jordan that isn't nearly enough.

The pity is that there's some grand stuff here. Having formerly found a soulmate in the late Angela Carter, Jordan is comfortable with eerie invocations of fairy tales amid a rural bourgeois idyll. Claire Cooper's visions, if compounded of familiar dreads, come forth in great torrents and have a nerve-straining intensity: the boy Vivian chained and thrashing in his watery bedroom tomb; a fair child and her killer, holding hands in a musty orchard; an apple ominously crushed underfoot. (Kudos must be due to the excellent Tony Lawson, whose editing feels taut throughout.)

A real treat is the sequence where Claire's moppet daughter Rebecca is stolen away from her school production of *Snow White*. As realised by Jordan and designer Nigel Phelps, the play is an uncommonly glamorous affair, bound to induce envy in any parent who has squirmed away an evening in a draughty assembly hall. The setting is authentically deep, dark woodland, lit with lanterns, and the kids are wonderfully costumed, not least Rebecca as the sprite inside the mirror on the wall. Suddenly, enchantment is translated into terror: Rebecca vanishes, police and a distraught Claire tramp the woods, only to discover a bereft pair of angel wings snared on a briar. A fast track past Rebecca's bewildered classmates finishes on the hapless little Wicked Queen, who earlier made such a lisping *tour de force* of her jealous tirade to the mirror.

Throughout, Darius Khondji's camera moves with giddiness and guile, seeming to assume assorted personages—even at one point that of Claire's dog Dobie. Claire's premonition of her suicidal plunge into the reservoir packs a tremendous, vertiginous point-of-view punch. Later, grieving Claire confesses to a sense of disembodiment, of watching herself from a distance as the camera watches her from a distance. At other times, we feel the watchful, wraithlike presence of the killer in the camera-eye. The commingling of these intimations duly comes, as Claire sees herself making love to Paul and is joined in the shadows by Vivian. They share complicit whispers, even a kiss—until Claire bites into his lip. Of course, ever since *The Silence of the Lambs* broke the box office, Hollywood has fed us gifted, wistful killers, whose dearest desire is to murmur endearments in the ear of some fine-boned WASP woman. Jordan flirts with a few variations on this theme of unnatural union, and there's one inspired passage of doubling, as Claire uncannily retraces Vivian's steps out of her asylum incarceration. But finally Vivian wants only to fashion a surrogate family for himself, and when that comes to naught, he settles for just giving Claire a nasty nip.

Since her spirited early roles in *Valmont* and *The Grifters,* Annette Bening has looked marooned on-screen as a middle-class mommy. But as Claire becomes an increasingly unhinged and resourceful heroine, Bening serves a reminder of her spark. The supporting players are given only bones to suck. Duplicitous husband Aidan Quinn is marked as dead meat from the start. Stephen Rea plays the sceptical spare-part shrink with a flawless accent. (Clearly, and not unreasonably, Jordan can't stand to be without him.) As for Robert Downey Jr, with his rather sensual man-child mien and ragamuffin demeanour, it was probably inevitable that he would eventually get a go in the cinematic nut-house. But his delayed entrance to the proceedings is the point where the film descends unerringly into formula. One is forced to reflect that few horror films have been as good as Gary Sherman's *Death Line (1972)* in giving us a lovelorn bogeyman who's both loathsome and pitiable.

As *In Dreams* unravels, its lineage is laid bare (Freud and fairy-tale psychoanalyst Bruno Bettelheim, *Psycho* and *The Shining*), and the plausibles take a pasting. An unpleasant epilogue exposes yet again just how deeply the serial-killer thriller responds to the US obsession with capital punishment. Jordan clearly felt for Patrick McCabe's murderous butcher boy, but this time out his heart is harder—or maybe just not in it. The likely fate of this movie is to wind up in digital double-bills with *Jennifer 8* or maybe *Candyman*. That could be counted a success only if Jordan's present ambition as a film-maker is to become quite nasty. His fans know better, and expect that his next one, an adaptation of Graham Greene's *The End of the Affair*, will see him in finer fettle.

VILLAGE VOICE, 1/26/99, p. 64, Amy Taubin

Neil Jordan's *In Dreams* is a nuclear family nightmare—nakedly auteurist and not at all nice. It's part possession-genre flick, part Grimm fairy tale, part Irish ghost story. No wonder DreamWorks has dumped it in the dead of winter. It's as if Jordan had gone fishing with the kid in the sickly sweet DreamWorks logo and hooked something even scarier than a Great White.

Claire Cooper (Annette Bening) has a close relationship with her nine-year-old daughter. She has a husband (Aidan Quinn) who pilots 747s, which means that he's not always there when she needs him. The family lives in a rustic New England house at the edge of a forest near a big lake. Claire is a children's-book illustrator who suffers from terrifying dreams in which little girls are abducted and murdered. It may be that her drawings have caught the eye of a psychopathic child-murderer, or perhaps her drawings (and her dreams) are psychic projections from a killer who has taken possession of her unconscious. Whatever the explanation, when the killer strikes at Claire's own flesh and blood, she goes over the edge. The doctors think she has had a psychotic breakdown, but there's method in Claire's madness. Only by surrendering to the killer with whom she's in such intimate rapport can she destroy him and save the children. ("I must save the children," whispers Deborah Kerr in *The Innocents,* Jack Clayton's airtight adaptation of Henry James's *Turn of the Screw,* a film that I suspect was much on Jordan's mind.)

Adapted from Bari Woods's pulp novel *Doll's Eyes, In Dreams* could have been a streamlined horror film á la *Nightmare on Elm Street,* with a knife-wielding superhuman killer appearing on cue. There is a killer here (Robert Downey Jr.) and he brandishes a lethal-looking scythe, but he's framed in a narrative that's as fragmented and amorphous as a real nightmare when we try to take hold of it the next morning. That's an ambitious structure, and the screenplay isn't quite up to it. The film lacks a compelling character to act as an anchor. Claire is a bunch of bits and pieces with no center, her husband is no more than the sum of his absences, and the killer is too much a pastiche of damaged goods from other movies (he's a double whammy of Norman Bates and the cross-dressing, breathy-voiced nutcase from *Silence of the Lambs).*

But if *In Dreams* isn't as fully realized a film as *The Butcher Boy,* it has more than enough haunting moments, not to mention a complete catalogue of Jordan's obsessions: blood-streaked walls; transvestism; scary, punitive mothers; tender, angelic mothers; and frighteningly fragile children on the edge of becoming predators or prey. Jordan has a rich and complicated vision of childhood. Claire's daughter has one line in a class production of *Snow White,* a delirious extravaganza no school could afford. At one point, a hunter enters through the mist on a white horse. And yet the children have a sturdiness and spontaneity that can't be imagined away. When Claire frantically searches the troupe of diaphanous-winged fairies for her missing daughter, it's about as panic-inducing a moment as you'll ever experience in a movie theater.

In Darius Khondji, Jordan has a cinematographer who can bring his imaginings to light. The film opens with an extended silvery green underwater sequence that's technically brilliant and provides the film with its basic metaphor. There's a whole town under the water. It's the world of the unconscious and of memory and if you go too deep and stay too long, you drown.

Khondji shot *Seven,* and he's still carrying a bit of its baggage. (I could have done without the images of a decaying corpse in a dank, crumbling room.) Still, so much of Jordan's method involves absorbing pop culture archetypes and pushing them over the top. Who else but Jordan would have the heroine and her psycho-killer alter ego slow-dance to the '50s relic "Ebb Tide"? That takes guts.

Bening has some finely overwrought moments but she hasn't a strong enough personality to compensate for the absence of character in the script. Downey is exactly the opposite kind of talent. His presence is never less than electrifying, but given a stock serial killer to play, he tends to showboat shamelessly. Neither performance is a disaster in terms of the film as a whole, since what's remembered of dreams is a quality of light, a streak of movement, a string of words, and the sense of something lost underneath.

Also reviewed in:
CHICAGO TRIBUNE, 1/15/99, Friday/p. A, Michael Wilmington
NATION, 2/8/99, p. 35, Stuart Klawans
NEW YORK TIMES, 1/15/99, p. E14, Janet Maslin
VARIETY, 1/18-24/99, p. 43, Emanuel Levy
WASHINGTON POST, 1/15/99, Weekend/p. 32, Desson Howe

IN THE PRESENCE OF A CLOWN

An SVT Drama in collaboration with DR, NRK, YLE1, and ZDF. *Producer:* Pia Ehrnvall and Mans Reutersward. *Director:* Ingmar Bergman. *Screenplay (Swedish with English subtitles):*

Ingmar Bergman. *Director of Photography:* Tony Forsberg and Irene Wiklund. *Editor:* Sylvia Ingemarsson. *Music:* Franz Schubert. *Sound:* Magnus Berglid. *Production Designer:* Goran Wassberg. *Set Dresser:* Rasmus Rasmusson. *Special Effects:* Lars Söderberg. *Costumes:* Mette Möller. *Running time:* 118 minutes. *MPAA Rating:* Not Rated.

CAST: Börje Ahlstedt (Uncle Carl Akerblom); Marie Richardson (Pauline Thibault); Erland Josephson (Osvald Vogler); Pernilla August (Karin Bergman); Peter Stormare (Petrus Landahl); Anita Bjork (Anna Akerblom); Agneta Ekmanner (Klovnen Rigmor); Lena Endre (Märta Lundberg); Gunnel Fred (Emma Vogler); Gerthi Kulle (Sister Stella); Johan Lindell (Johan Egerman); Folke Asplund (Fredrik Blom); Anna Björk (Mia Falk); Inga Landgré (Alma Berglund); Alf Nilsson (Stefan Larsson); Harriet Nordlund (Karen Persson); Tord Peterson (Algot Frövik); Birgitta Pettersson (Hanna Apelblad); Ingmar Bergman (Mental Patient).

VILLAGE VOICE, 6/8/99, p. 64, Jessica Winter

In conjunction with the U.S. premiere of Ingmar Bergman's stage production of *The Image Makers*, the Brooklyn Academy of Music is screening three kindred films: Victor Sjöström's silent *The Phantom Carriage* (the inspiration for *The Image Makers)*, the Sjöström-influenced *Wild Strawberries*, and Bergman's latest film, *In the Presence of a Clown*. Shot for Swedish television, the movie arranges the 1920s meeting of two psychiatric patients, the inventor Carl Akerblom (also seen in *Fanny and Alexander)* and the professor Osvald Volger. They hope to collaborate on the first talking picture, a biopic of Franz Schubert. Bergman's films frequently make reference to each other, but *Clown* more than any of them reads as cumulative—and slipshod—pastiche, engaging themes of cathartic violence (as in *The Hour of the Wolf,* personified death *(The Seventh Seal)* female speechlessness-as-purity *(Persona),* the mystic powers of cinematography ("cinematography" was *Persona's* original title), man's insuperable loneliness (all of Bergman's films). The only new wrinkle, regrettably, is a tiresome anal fixation. For completists.

Also reviewed in:
NEW YORK TIMES, 6/4/99, p. E23, Stephen Holden
VARIETY, 5/25-31/98, p. 61, Emanuel Levy

IN SEARCH OF KUNDUN WITH MARTIN SCORSESE

An In Pictures and Hollywood Independent Film Distribution release of a Compagnie Panoptique production in association with Ray Productions and Canal+. *Producer:* T. Celal, Jean Labib, Dale Ann Steiber, and Michael Henry Wilson. *Director:* Michael Henry Wilson. *Screenplay:* Michael Henry Wilson. *Director of Photography:* Jean-Jacques Flori and Frederick Vassort. *Editor:* Rick Blue. *Music:* Ken Lauber. *Sound:* Patrice Mendez. *Running time:* 84 minutes. *MPAA Rating:* Not Rated.

WITH: Roger Deakins; Dante Ferretti; Tencho Gyalpo; Dalai Lama; Melissa Mathison; Lobsang Samten; Martin Scorsese; Tulku Jamyang Kunga Tenzin; Tenzin Thuthob Tsarong; Jigme Tsarong.

NEW YORK POST, 4/29/99, p. 48, Rod Dreher

God knows all decent people despise China's brutal occupation of Tibet and look forward to that captive nation's liberation, but sitting through Martin Scorsese's "Kundun," a beautifully photographed but snoozy Dalai Lama biopic, was not my idea of suffering for the cause.

Now comes an equally dull companion piece, a "making of" documentary called "In Search of Kundun With Martin Scorsese."

Director Michael H. Wilson should have gone in search of a narrator. His film is not without its moments, but its collage of interviews and snapshots from the set desperately needs organizing into a coherent narrative.

The best parts of the film show the great Scorsese directing Tibetan children. Who knew that the choreographer behind such grand ballets of violence as "Raging Bull" and "GoodFellas" could be so sweet and tender with little ones?

Equally affecting are interviews with the amateur Tibetan actors humbled and moved by the opportunity to portray leading figures in what they describe as their nation's worst-ever calamity.

But most of "In Search of..." meanders around the "Kundun" project, touching on but never satisfactorily exploring the challenges an American filmmaker and his Western crew face in telling a story about the avatar of an ancient, peaceful religion clashing with ferocious, atheistic modem ideology.

Judging from this documentary, Scorsese clearly loves and respects Tibetan culture, but neither he nor screenwriter Melissa Mathison offers any illuminating insight into their subject. Which probably explains why "Kundun" was a gorgeous dud.

VILLAGE VOICE, 5/4/99, p. 116, Amy Taubin

A cross between a Hollywood religious biopic and an interiorized meditation on faith, loss, and transcendence, Martin Scorsese's *Kundun (1997)* was unjustly dismissed as "Tibetan chic" by critics anxious to drag it down to their own level. But Scorsese's depiction of the boyhood and coming of age of the Dalai Lama was, among many other things, a passionate attempt to put on celluloid the culture that was all but decimated by the Chinese invasion.

"What I'm trying to do is to create an impression of a world that doesn't exist anymore," a gracious and accommodating Scorsese explains in *In Search of Kundun With Martin Scorsese*. "It may be the only way to preserve the heart of that culture. We have documentary footage of it, but what I'm trying to do is capture the emotion and the spirit." Its overblown title notwithstanding, Michael Henry Wilson's documentary is a lively and often illuminating behind-the-scenes look at a master filmmaker at work. Wilson, who collaborated on the film-history doc *A Personal Journey With Martin Scorsese Through American Movies,* was on location in Morocco for the entire production and had good access to the director and his team-production designer Dante Ferretti, screenwriter Melissa Mathison, cinematographer Roger Deakins. The documentary is most useful when it shows Scorsese on set—directing his cast of Tibetan nonprofessional actors, choreographing shots, peering with worried eyes over the top of his reading glasses, improvising solutions to endless problems, making jokes to keep a lid on his temper. ("There must be a photography shop open late in Casablanca. What time is it? 3:20 a.m.?")

Fluidly edited, *In Search of Kundun* segues between the Dalai Lama, videotaped at his residence in exile in Dharamsala, India, and Scorsese on location in Morocco directing reenactments of the events the Dalai Lama is describing. Wilson fills out the picture with old newsreels of Tibet and clips from the completed version of *Kundun.* There are extremely moving interviews with some of the Tibetans who acted and advised on the film. Its a cliché that on long location stints lonely people, for better or worse, bond as surrogate families. Here the Tibetans, many of them related by blood or marriage, come from the ends of the earth and reunite to keep their story alive.

Also reviewed in:
NEW YORK TIMES, 4/29/99, Stephen Holden
VARIETY, 8/31-9/6/98, p. 99, Derek Elley

IN TOO DEEP

A Dimension Films release of a Suntaur Entertainment Company production. *Executive Producer:* Don Carmody, Bob Weinstein, Harvey Weinstein, Jeremy Kramer, and Amy Slotnick. Producer: Paul Aaron and Michael Henry Brown. *Director:* Michael Rymer. *Screenplay:* Michael Henry Brown and Paul Aaron. *Director of Photography:* Ellery Ryan. *Editor:* Dany

Cooper. *Music:* Christopher Young. *Music Editor:* Charles Martin Inoye. *Sound:* Tom Mather. *Casting:* Aisha Coley. *Production Designer:* Dan Leigh. *Art Director:* Kenneth Watkins. *Set Decorator:* Ken Clark and Sean Kirby. *Set Dresser:* Andrew Yerex, Jim Duffy, and Kerry Spurrell. *Special Effects:* Michael Kavanagh. *Costumes:* Shawn Barton. *Make-up:* Mario Cacioppoo. *Make-up (Omar Epps):* Laini Thompson. *Stunt Coordinator:* Steve Lucescu. *Running time:* 104 minutes. *MPAA Rating:* R.

CAST: Lloyd Adams (Ray-Ray); Philip Akin (Minister); Anna Alvim (Esperanza Batista); Karina Arroyave (G.G.); Richard Blackburn (Officer #1); Richard Brooks (Wesley); Elio Campbell (J.Reid/Jeff Stand-in); Ron Canada (Dr. Bratton); Kevin Chapman (O'Hanlon); Ivonne Coll (Mrs. Batista); Chris Collins (Lookout); Shane Daly (Batista Cop #1); Brenda Thomas Denmark (Mrs. Coy); Guillermo Diaz (Miguel Batista); Jermaine Dupri (Melvin); Aujanue Ellis (Denise); Omar Epps (Jeff Cole/J. Reid); Dolores Etienne (Grandmother); Sticky Fingaz (Ozzie); Wendji Fulford (Mrs. Connelly); Brian Furlong (Batista Cop #2); Julie Gonzales (Nude Stand-in); Pam Grier (Det. Angela Wilson); Gano Grills (Frisco); Jackie Hargrave (Mrs. Johnson); Hill Harper (Breezy T.); Don Harvey (Murphy); Edward Heeley (Professor); Howard Hoover (Officer #2); Tatum Hunter (Connelly, 4 Years); Camille James (Doreen); Claire Johnson (Connelly, 2 Years); Hassan Iniko Johnson (Latique); David Patrick Kelly (Rick Scott); Robert Lasardo (Felipe Batista); Dustin Leonard (Marcus, 8 Years); Jordan Leonard (Marcus, 3 Years); Latoya Lesmond (Female Cadet); LL Cool J (Dwayne Gittens, God); Nia Long (Myra); Yvette Martin (Lisa); Michi Mi (Martha); Mya (Loretta); Toby Proctor (Red-Haired Cadet); Alex Restrepo (Dancer); Victor Rivers (Romeo Concepcion); Shyheim (Che); Stephen Graham Simpson (2nd Cop); David Spates (K. Dee); Lenore Thomas (Angie); Angel Torres (Ramon); Katherine Trowell (Judge); Stanley Tucci (Preston D'Ambrosio); Avery Kidd Waddell (Cashman); Veronica Webb (Pam); Jake Weber (Daniel Connelly).

LOS ANGELES TIMES, 8/25/99, Calendar/p. 2, Gene Seymour

[The following review by Gene Seymour appeared in a slightly different form in **NEWSDAY, 8/25/99, Part II/p. B3.]**

The one thing a thriller should never do is waste your time. The whole point of spending 90 minutes in the dark is to avoid the far more worthwhile tasks you're supposed to pursue. So that shadow play on the screen better get you sufficiently lost. Or else.

For the most part, "In Too Deep" fulfills this requirement with enough fire and grit to make you forget the by-the-numbers nature of its plot about an undercover cop (Omar Epps) who gets too caught up in pretending to be a down-and-dirty street criminal.

Epps' Jeff Cole is a Cincinnati policeman so fresh out of the academy that he barely has time to get the shrink-wrap off his badge. Though greener than fresh Astroturf, Cole convinces a senior investigator (Stanley Tucci) to toss him onto the streets as a faux small-time dealer.

Cole's trial run as a professional infiltrator is a near-botch. He is nonetheless given a bigger, more carnivorous fish to fry: drug kingpin Dwayne Gittens (LL Cool J), whose dominion over people's lives is so broad and deep that no one questions his assuming the nickname "God."

Taking the cue from his character's omnipotent moniker, LL Cool J plays Gittens like a Cheshire cat combination of ward leader, avuncular supervisor and strict daddy. Only in a few explosive scenes (one of them an especially gruesome torture sequence in God's rec room) does Cool J's character resemble the snarling drug lords of many "blaxploitation" thrillers.

As one could have guessed, Cole, posing as J. Reid, a snarky dealer from Akron, Ohio, finds himself doing what movie audiences often do in gangster movies: admiring, in spite of himself, the bad guy's magnetism and power.

Indeed, Gittens' cuddly-puppy manner informs the template of moral ambiguity contrived by producer-writers Michael Henry Brown ("Dead Presidents") and Paul Aaron as an ethical obstacle course for Cole, whose pose is so effective that he starts to scare himself, his dancer-girlfriend (Nia Long, steely and subtly effective in what could have been a standard-issue role) and his captain, who's ready to pull the plug at any moment.

If you think you've seen all this before, you have. And there isn't much in the bread-and-butter direction of Michael Rymer to make you think otherwise. Still, Aaron and Brown's script resounds throughout with astringent dialogue and stark authenticity. And Epps makes an impressive, more-than-stolid showing in his schizoid leading role. One thing, though: No movie should get off easy for not giving Pam Grier more to do than she does here as a tough veteran cop. Are we back to begging once again for more starring roles for this legendary lady?

NEW YORK POST, 8/25/99, P. 53, Jonathan Foreman

How far will an undercover cop go to be accepted by a vicious criminal gang? After months in their company, will he still be able to betray the men he has befriended? Will he get so into character that he loses touch with his own personality and values?

It's hard to go wrong with the drama and conflict inherent in undercover police work. That's why there have been so many movies on the subject—some of them excellent, like "Donnie Brasco."

Yet "In Too Deep" pales before even a second-rate example of the genre, like "Deep Cover" with Laurence Fishburne.

Sure, it touches the usual bases. And there are some tense scenes when the protagonist is almost "made" for a cop, but for the most part it's slow and predictable, and the characters are so poorly written that it's hard to react to them in any way.

Jeff Cole (Omar Epps) wants to get into undercover work straight out of the Cincinnati police academy and is convinced he's perfect for the task.

Police supervisor Preston D'Ambrosio (Stanley Tucci) thinks that the strain of the job requires something more than just being a tough kid from the projects but puts him to work anyway.

Eventually he is sent to infiltrate a gang led by a crime lord nicknamed "God" (LL Cool J), who we're told controls most of the city's crime—though we see little evidence of the gang's size or power.

God is intelligent and charismatic, but also ruthless and sadistic. (He organizes a Thanksgiving dinner for the folk in the projects, but he also inflicts Louima-style torture on a friend who looks the wrong way at his wife.)

Cole becomes obsessed with bringing down God, even as he becomes so immured in street culture that he alienates his beautiful dancer girlfriend. D'Ambrosio realizes that Cole is in too deep.

But when he tries to pull him out, Cole abuses him and goes behind his back to the district attorney and the Drug Enforcement Agency to ensure that he stays on the case. By the time Cole is in position to pull the plug on God, he's so messed up, you almost wonder if he'll be able to tell right from wrong.

To its credit, "In Too Deep" has more moral integrity than many better-executed movies that deal with the gangster milieu.

Screenwriters Michael Henry Brown and Paul Aaron don't glamorize the thug life while pretending to condemn it. (Just when you're warming to God, you see him break a man's arm in a car door while his own toddler watches from a car seat.)

Still, themes that should be powerful—like the contest between God and D'Ambrosio for Cole's soul—fall flat because the script tells us too little about either man.

It doesn't help that Australian director Michael Rymer ("Angel Baby") evokes such a small, limited performance from Epps. Despite their underwritten parts, the actors in secondary roles are all so charismatic that they almost make Epps disappear.

This is true not just of Tucci and Pam Grier who's terrific in little more than a cameo—but also LL Cool J. The rapper (who was the best thing in this summer's "Deep Blue Sea") injects his crime-lord character with real charm, thus making his brutality—and there's some disgusting violence in this movie—all the more shocking.

SIGHT AND SOUND, 8/00, p. 48, Danny Leigh

Chicago, the present. Detective Jeff Cole instructs a class of police cadets in the art of undercover work. Two years earlier, in Cincinnati, Cole approaches senior officer Preston D'Ambrosio and asks to join his undercover task force. Involved in the arrest of a Latino cocaine dealer, Cole is dispatched to infiltrate the latest operation of crime boss Dwayne Gittens, also known as God. Cole adopts a new identity as J. Reid and ingratiates himself with Gittens. After a gunfight with a pair of young criminals, Cole is pulled from his assignment by D'Ambrosio and sent to the country for a period of recuperation. There, he meets Myra, a dancer with whom he begins a relationship.

Summoned to Cincinnati by D'Ambrosio, Cole again assumes the identity of J. Reid, rapidly becoming Gittens' right-hand man. His dealings with both Myra and his senior officers suffer as a result of his adopted criminal pose. During an argument with Myra, Cole is arrested by the local police. A confrontation ensues, but D'Ambrosio allows his charge one last chance to seal Gittens' arrest. Cole accompanies Gittens to a cocaine deal, where the latter is finally captured. Cole testifies at Gittens' trial; the crime boss is sentenced to life imprisonment. Cole reunites with Myra. The pair leave for Chicago.

Right down to its title, the memory of Bill Duke's 1992 thriller *Deep Cover* hangs over *In Too Deep* like a trace of cheap cologne. Yet, despite having lifted that film's premise—black cop gets seduced by criminal life while undercover director Michael Rymer clearly has higher aspirations than the slick, glitzy tropes of Duke's film. It's something like the complexity of Mike Newell's *Donnie Brasco,* notably the insight into the moral confusion suffered by a cop while working undercover, that Rymer is after.

It's an ambition that seems some way beyond the slender resources of Rymer, his script or most of his cast. The comparison *In Too Deep* invites so explicitly could only ever be to its detriment for a film in which ambivalence and ambiguity are such central themes, it displays no appreciation of either (Newell's project had both in spades). While in *Donnie Brasco* FBI agent Joe Pistone's turmoil was exquisitely captured by Johnny Depp, here Omar Epps relies largely on changes to his hairstyle to portray the disorientation his character Jeff Cole experiences when going undercover (neatly trimmed dreadlocks as a cop; shaven head while playing the gangster).

Equally, despite briefly giving the character of crime boss Dwayne Gittens a speech in which he holds forth with some eloquence on the nature of poverty, the script loses the courage of such equivocal convictions at the very point where they might have rescued the film. Instead, we have to be shown an expedient litany of scenes in which Gittens tortures his acolytes and abuses various crackheads. Of course, these thumpingly obvious reminders that Gittens is a real *bad guy* make it much simpler for Rymer to dispense his easy, upbeat resolution: again look for the desperate poignancy of *Donnie Brasco*'s ending, with the broken, betrayed gangster played by Al Pacino preparing for his mob execution, and you'll be searching in vain.

But, while this lack of subtlety compromises *In Too Deep,* its aura of made-for-television prosaicness also fatally diminishes it (in true film-of-the-week fashion, the pre-credits declare: "This is based on a true story"). Certainly, Rymer and director of photography Ellery Ryan handles the look of the film competently enough and the script's narrative is free of glaring logical flaws. But Rymer seems unable to work up any degree of tension or, more to the point, believability. If someone as blatantly hokey as Jeff Cole can get past a feared underworld boss like Dwayne Gittens, it's a wonder there are any criminals left.

It should therefore come as no surprise that none of the cast is at all convincing. Ironically, with Epps' prissy cop playing a double role and LL Cool J's parodic bogeyman at its centre, *In Too Deep* ultimately brings to mind Robert Townsend's engaging film-industry satire *Hollywood Shuffle.* Watching Epps implausibly vowing to "keep it real, nigga," you can't help thinking of Townsend's cry after his casting as yet another African-American superfly streetsmart criminal: "Hey, there's always work at the post office."

VILLAGE VOICE, 8/31/99, p. 115, Gary Dauphin

The new cops-and-crack thriller *In Too Deep* is a heavily cut bag of passing gangsta highs, empty at the core but superficially diverting. Ripping off the now venerably old-school *New Jack City, Deep* recasts the familiar, undercover cop's dilemma of overassociation as a Method-acting misfire. Jeff (Omar Epps, doing his best big-screen work since *Juice*) is the Cincinnati narc with a knack for worming his way into drug dealers' confidence. Though hot on the trail of kingpin LL Cool J throughout, our hero does drift away from his superiors (including Stanley Tucci, playing his drug warrior like a worried, overmatched shrink), disobeying orders and carrying an increasingly violent undercover persona into his aboveground life. (Black-bohemian Nia Long offers the requisite romantic flipside to the mayfly-pretty crack-groupies Jeff starts squiring around.)

Director Michael Rymer keeps *Deep* moving at a respectable clip. Although the writing (from Michael Henry Brown and Paul Aaron) would be best described as semishallow, the film does have a canny appreciation for how ghetto realness is acted out, with cops and crooks following mental scripts that inevitably have serious holes in them. *In Too Deep* doesn't do much with this insight, but as rides to nowhere go, this one isn't half bad.

Also reviewed in:
NEW YORK TIMES, 8/25/99, p. E3, Janet Maslin
VARIETY, 8/30-9/5/99, p. 53, Joe Leydon
WASHINGTON POST, 8/25/99, p. C1, Stephen Hunter

INSIDER, THE

A Touchstone Pictures release of a Mann/Roth production. *Producer:* Michael Mann and Pieter Jan Brugge. *Director:* Michael Mann. *Screenplay:* Eric Roth and Michael Mann. *Based on the Vanity Fair article "The Man Who Knew Too Much" by:* Marie Brenner. *Director of Photography:* Dante Spinotti. *Editor:* William Goldenberg, Paul Rubell, and David Rosenbloom. *Music:* Lisa Gerrard and Pieter Bourke. *Music Editor:* Curt Sobel. *Sound:* Lee Orloff and (music) Robert Fernandez, John Kurlander, and Dan Wallin. *Sound Editor:* Gregg Baxter and Gregory King. *Casting:* Bonnie Timmerman. *Production Designer:* Brian Morris. *Art Director:* Marjorie McShirley. *Set Designer:* Lynn Christopher, Kelly Hannafin, and Darrell L. Wigh. *Set Decorator:* Nancy Haigh. *Set Dresser:* James Meehan. *Special Effects:* John Gray. *Costumes:* Anna Sheppard. *Make-up:* Bill Myer. *Make-up (Russell Crowe):* Greg Cannom. *Running time:* 155 minutes. *MPAA Rating:* R.

CAST: Al Pacino (Lowell Bergman); Russell Crowe (Jeffrey Wigand); Christopher Plummer (Mike Wallace); Diane Venora (Lione Wigand); Philip Baker Hall (Don Hewitt); Lindsay Crouse (Sharon Tiller); Debi Mazar (Debbie De Luca); Stephen Tobolowsky (Eric Kluster); Colm Feore (Richard Scruggs); Bruce McGill (Ron Motley); Gina Gershon (Helen Caperelli); Michael Gambon (Thomas Sandefur); Rip Torn (John Scanlon); Lynne Thigpen (Mrs. Williams); Hallie Kate Eisenberg (Barbara Wigand); Michael Paul Chan (Norman the Camerman); Linda Hart (Mrs. Wigand); Robert Harper (Mark Stern); Nestor Serrano (FBI Agent Robertson); Pete Hamill (NY Times Reporter); Wings Hauser (Tobacco Lawyer); Clifford Curtis (Sheikh Fadlallah); Renee Olstead (Deborah Wigand); Michael Moore (Himself); Gary Sandy (Sandefur's Lawyer); Willie C. Carpenter (John Harris); Paul Butler (Charlie Phillips); Jack Palladino (Himself); Megan Odabash (Sandra Sutherland); Rogert Bart (Seelbach Hotel Manager); Alan DeSatti (Hezbollah Interpreter); Sayed Badreya (Hezbollah Head Gunman); Chris Ufland (Doug Oliver, FDA); Doug McGrath (Private Investigator); Bill Sage (Intense Young Intern); Joseph Hindy (Baldo the Editor); Dennis Garber (FBI Agent #1); Tim Grimm (FBI Agent #2); Paul Perri (Geologist/FBI Man); Wanda De Jesus (Geologist/FBI Woman); Robert Brink (Policeman); V.J. Foster (Bill Felling); James Harper (FBI Agent #3), Lyal Pudell (Lowell's Son); Breckin Meyer (Sharon's Son); David Roberson (John Telafarro); Gregg E. Muravchick (Private Security Guard); William P. Bradford II (Subpoena Man); David Carr (Local Newscaster); Ann Reskin (Seelbach Hotel Desk Clerk); Claire Slemmer (Edie Magnus); Steve Salge (Dan Rather); Derrick Jones (Mississippi Reporter); Donald F. Burbrink II (B & W Male Security Officer); Vyto Ruginis (Junior Lawyer); George R. Parsons (B & W Uniformed Security Officer); Isodine Loury (Mississippi Court Stenographer); Charlene Bosarge (Mr. Scruggs' Assistant); Saemi Nakamura (Japanese Waitress); Ronal G. Yokley (Police

Detective); Bob Lazarus (Stage Manager); Robert Ragno, Jr. (Photographer - New Media); Alvin L. Welch (Judge); Nathan Lewis Hill (Production Assistant); Paula Bisbikos (Mike Wallace's Assistant); Christi Evans (CBS News Producer); Knox Grantham White (Soundman); Amy L. Caudill (Student).

CHRISTIAN SCIENCE MONITOR, 11/5/99, p. 15, David Sterrit

New movies as different as "The Straight Story" and "Boys Don't Cry" are based on real-life occurrences, but none is more revealing than "The Insider," starring Al Pacino as crusading "60 Minutes" journalist and Russell Crowe as a tobacco industry whistle-blower whose life is almost ruined by his decision to take a stand against corporate greed and deceit.

Informed moviegoers will already know about this story from news accounts, but its dramatization in Michael Mann's devastating film makes it as vivid and compelling as the most attention grabbing headline.

Pacino plays Lowell Bergman, a producer of "60 Minutes," the CBS news show. When the case of scientist Jeffrey Wigand comes across his desk, he takes an interest for more than one reason. Wigand is bursting with inside information, since as a former research chief at tobacco giant Brown & Williamson, he knows everything worth knowing about the company's activities. Just as important, Wigand seem ready to go public with evidence of tobacco industry's nastiest secret: that despite loud denials made under oath during a congressional investigation, leaders knew they were peddling a poisonous and addictive product.

If Bergman can get Wigand before camera and present their interview to the enormous audience of "60 Minutes," the producer can impact perceptions tobacco marketing and its consequences for public health.

But problems loom. For one, Wigand's anger at his former employer isn't necessarily strong enough to override his anxieties about the damage he might suffer—harassment, lawsuits, even criminal prosecution—if he breaks a contractual obligation to keep his mouth shut about company policies and practices.

For another, his family life isn't solid, and the added strain of a public controversy could shatter it for good. The corporation seems ready to fight, mobilizing a smear campaign that sets even Bergman reeling with its suddenness and ferocity.

On top of all this, Bergman himself unexpectedly battling his corporate bosses. Despite its commitment to hard news, CBS gets cold feet toning down its revelations and eliminating Wigand's testimony despite the harrowing experience he's endured for the sake of the program.

Is this decision based on sound journalistic reasoning, as claimed by Bergman's superiors and associates including Mike Wallace, also involved in the segment—or is it because a high-profile controversy could endanger the network's impending sale to a conglomerate with very deep pockets?

"The Insider" operates on two different but related levels. It's an engrossing human drama, posing a difficult moral question—how much private contentment should a person be expected to sacrifice in the service of a greater good? It explores the answer through a series of tightly written, pungently acted episodes as powerful as anything Hollywood has given us in ages. It's also a rare example of keenly relevant muckraking by a Hollywood studio that dares to point fingers and name names.

This doesn't mean the picture is a documentary-type study. It's a movie melodrama complete with appealing stars, neatly scripted dialogue, and crisply constructed scenes (some that are being contested by real-life figures in the story) designed to convey a traditional motion-picture punch.

As such, it's more effective at some points than at others, and its first half—focusing on the early stages of Wigand's torturous decision-making process—works somewhat better than its later portions, when big-business representatives (tobacco-industry executives, "60 Minutes" honchos, and CBS managers) slug it out.

This notwithstanding, "The Insider" is one of the most stirring movies of this increasingly strong year. Mann and collaborators deserve great credit for their achievement, as does the Walt Disney studio for releasing it as part of stimulating a 1999 slate that has already given us "The Straight Story" and "Summer of Sam," among other pictures. Congratulations to all.

LOS ANGELES TIMES, 11/5/99, Calendar/p. 1, Kenneth Turan

Unlikely material can inspire exceptional films: witness "The Insider." What could sound less promising than the legal fuss surrounding one man's indecision about telling what he knows about cigarettes, unless it's the internal wranglings of a television network's news division? But it is the triumph of this Michael Mann-directed film that those iffy scenarios result in a compelling drama, as notable for the importance of what it has to say as for the riveting skill with which it's said.

Mann's involvement, as co-screenwriter (with Eric Roth) as well as director, is the tip-off that something is afoot. As his credits ("Heat," "Thief," "The Last of the Mohicans," TV's "Miami Vice") indicate and this film underlines, Mann practically mainlines intensity, and he uses his instinct for dramatic storytelling to fill every bit of this two-hour, 38-minute film with passion and tension.

In fact the argument could be made that Mann's career has been preparation for telling the based-on-fact parallel stories of Jeffrey Wigand, arguably the most significant anti-smoking source to come from the heart of Big Tobacco and one of the keys to a recent $246-billion settlement against the industry, and Lowell Bergman, the "60 Minutes" producer who fought to get his story on the air. Not only is "The Insider" fiercely directed, not only does it have memorable starring performances from Al Pacino and the marvelous Russell Crowe, but it has a tale to tell that is both substantial and significant.

For as much as anything else, "The Insider" is a paradigmatic slice of 20th century America, a look at who we are and at what drives us as individuals and a society. It's a scathing attack on the power of serious money and the chilling effect corporate might can have on the ability to disseminate the truth.

At its core, however, "The Insider" is a story of, as someone says, "ordinary people under extraordinary pressure." It shows how difficult and torturous it can be to do the right thing on an individual level and, most important, what bravery actually means and how little the faces and personalities of heroes fit our often simplistic preconceptions.

To tell this story, screenwriters Roth (an Oscar winner for "Forrest Gump") and Mann, working from Marie Brenner's excellent Vanity Fair piece, have made considerable and unapologetic use of dramatic license. Hardly a documentary (and even they manipulate), "The Insider" uses real names but does not hesitate to embellish or fictionalize situations when it suits its purposes, which include greatly enhancing Bergman's role in events to build him into more of a conventional hero. But peripheral fabrications notwithstanding, the core story the film tells, the issues it raises, remain dead-on accurate.

"The Insider" starts in the most unlikely place, an unidentified Middle Eastern city where a man is being blindfolded for a meeting with a leader of the terrorist Hezbollah organization. The man is Bergman (Pacino), a producer for "60 Minutes," and when the sheik in question asks why he should agree to an interview with "the pro-Zionist American media," Bergman unhesitatingly replies, "Because it's the highest-rated, most respected television newsmagazine in America."

That opening establishes several crucial points, not the least of which is Bergman's loyalty to and belief in "60 Minutes" and its mainstay Mike Wallace (Christopher Plummer), whose producer and alter ego he's been for 14 years. It also shows Bergman as the pragmatic go-to guy, the producer-as-fixer adept at convincing even the most reluctant subjects to come forward and talk.

An operative both within and against the system—a role that in some ways echoes the actor's earlier work in "Serpico"—Bergman is one of Pacino's best, most alive characterizations. It allows him to be natural and powerful, to hold the screen and convince us of someone's sincerity without resorting to mannerisms or well-worn tricks.

Able to match him stride for stride is the virtuoso Australian actor Crowe. Known to art-house viewers for his award-winning roles in that country's "Proof" and "Romper Stomper," Crowe's ability to project internal complexity electrified a wider audience as the love of Kim Basinger's life in "L.A. Confidential." A powerhouse actor who joins an old-fashioned masculine presence with an unnerving ability to completely disappear inside a role, Crowe not only has made himself look like Wigand, he even duplicates the complex personality journalist Brenner described as "prickly, isolated and fragile ... There's a wary quality in his face, a mysterious darkness."

When Wigand is introduced on a sunny afternoon in 1993, he and Bergman are not even aware of each other's existence. It's not a good day for the pin-striped scientist, head of research and development for Brown & Williamson, one of the biggest tobacco companies. He's just been fired, in part, we eventually learn, for objecting to measures the company wants to take to make its products more addictive.

With a comfortable lifestyle, a Southern belle wife (Diane Venora) and two children, one of whom has expensive medical problems, Wigand is not eager to jeopardize his B&W settlement or the health insurance that comes with it. Prodded by company president Thomas Sandefur (Michael Gambon), he signs a pair of confidentiality agreements, but though he doesn't necessarily look it, Wigand is a person who does not respond well to being pushed around. There is an unexpected fury in him, a rigid core that cannot be quashed or ignored, a core that Bergman will come to both fear and admire.

At work on a different tobacco story, one having to do with fire safety and smoking in bed, Bergman receives an anonymous box of tobacco company documents that he needs "translated into English." A colleague gives him Wigand's name, but when Bergman calls the scientist at home for this simple task, the unexpected resistance Wigand puts up is a goad to the producer's savvy instincts.

Though he has no real idea who Wigand is and not even a clue about what the man knows, Bergman, like a bull facing a cape, can't resist charging. And the more Wigand demurs from talking, the more Bergman increases the pressure, especially after he learns who this difficult, elusive man is and what he knows about the cigarette industry's willingness to lie about its product's effects. "He's the ultimate insider," the producer says. "He's got something to say and I want it on '60 Minutes.'"

The extended cat and mouse interplay between journalist and source is one of "The Insider's" most involving dynamics. An elaborate ritual dance of courtship, a seduction pure and not so simple, it pits Bergman's insistence that he can be trusted ("When I talk to people in confidence, it stays that way") and Wigand's fears about his settlement and whether what he does will make any kind of a difference.

"I'm a commodity to you," he says. "Thirty million people will hear you," Bergman replies, unfazed, "and nothing will ever be the same again."

While this elaborate scenario is being played out, the tenor of Wigand's life changes in ways that ups the ante on his decision. He hears intruders in his backyard, he's followed, he finds threatening messages on his computer, he finds a bullet in his mailbox. He's supposed to be scared, but what he gets instead is angry. (The Times reported last week that Brown & Williamson, which has a history of attacking Wigand, claims the scientist manufactured his death threats. A federal law enforcement official said the evidence either way was not conclusive.)

Alternately closed-off and furious, needy and suspicious, with his marriage now in trouble, the tightly wound Wigand finds himself drawing closer to Bergman as he comes to terms with what seems like a compulsion to come clean. If he decides to talk, finally, it will be because he cannot imagine not doing so.

Compelling as this is, "The Insider" has two more dramas to play out. One is whether or not Wigand will testify in the Mississippi-led multi-state case against the tobacco industry (one of the areas where Bergman's influence has apparently been exaggerated) and the other is the crisis at CBS.

Led by an attorney (an appropriately slick Gina Gershon) worried about something called "tortious interference" and the remote possibility of a massive lawsuit, CBS corporate strong arms its news department in general and "60 Minutes" in particular not to air the Wigand segment. How much and when Wallace resisted this edict has become a major bone of contention between the journalist and the filmmakers, but of one thing there is no doubt: What happened at "60 Minutes" was a major debacle. (The New York Times calls it "one of the low points in the history of CBS News.")

Even if you know every detail of this much-reported situation, it can't overemphasize how effectively Mann and company have ratcheted up the tension to involve us in the immediacy of the Wigand/"60 Minutes" story, to emphasize the chaotic personal dynamics, the battle of wills, that lurked behind all the headlines.

Shot with exceptional crispness by Dante Spinotti (who also did "L.A. Confidential") and energetically edited by William Goldenberg, Paul Rubell and David Rosenbloom, "The Insider" also benefits from Mann's passionate attention to detail. The strong, atmospheric score is by former Dead Can Dance mainstay Lisa Gerrard and her new writing partner Pieter Bourke (with a notable contribution by Gustavo Santaolalla on the Argentine mandolin), and even relatively small roles, like Lindsay Crouse as Bergman's wife and Bruce McGill's firebrand Mississippi attorney, are smartly cast.

"To get the truth out has been such an effort," Wigand said in a recent newspaper interview. "It's still an effort." More than anything else could, "The Insider" not only explains why that effort was worth making but also how hard it was to make.

NEW YORK, 11/15/99, p. 68, Peter Rainer

The Insider begins with a man, *60 Minutes* producer Lowell Bergman (Al Pacino), being whisked blindfolded in a car to a secret powwow with an Islamic terrorist. Bergman is there to set the stage for a forthcoming interview with Mike Wallace (Christopher Plummer), and he's in his element: Boasting of the "integrity" of *60 Minutes,* he's a muckraking freewheeler par excellence. When Wallace finally comes on the scene, Bergman pampers and cajoles him as if he were a diva. The film appears to be saying: Forget the Hezbollah, this guy can handle *Mike Wallace.*

The real terrorist in the film is, of course, Big Tobacco; this prologue in Lebanon is like a featherweight preliminary bout before the main bone-crusher event. Early on, Bergman's stage-managing is intercut with unrelated scenes depicting the abrupt departure of Jeffrey Wigand (Russell Crowe) as chief of research at Brown & Williamson, the nation's third-largest tobacco company. (Wigand was fired as a probable consequence of his outspoken in-house concerns about the product's health risks.) Like gunslingers at high noon, these two men are fated to meet—except, of course, they end up slinging for the same side. Bergman at first is interested in Wigand's expertise in deciphering a load of clandestine tobacco-related documents, but he quickly sizes up the racked, somnolent scientist as the "ultimate insider" who can, with careful coaxing, deliver a whopping scoop for CBS and, incidentally, become the point man in the war against the tobacco industry. (He became the key witness in legal action taken by seven states seeking reimbursement of Medicaid expenses for smoking-related illnesses.)

With its big, gleaming righteousness and gangster-movie undertow, *The Insider* is like an elongated cross between *Silkwood* or *All the President's* Men and the sort of hyperbolic, noirish stylefests peculiar to its director, Michael Mann (*Thief, Heat,* TV's *Miami Vice*). As a filmmaker, he's a lot like Lowell Bergman here—driven and messianic, and hammy. The fact-based story he's telling, derived primarily from Marie Brenner's 1996 *Vanity Fair* piece "The Man Who Knew Too Much," is essentially in the standard ripped-from-the-headlines glamorama-Holly-wood-thriller mode, but he gives it a doomy largeness. We're on a holy crusade here, with a full house of tormented souls and ogres and ordinary people made extraordinary by a higher calling.

As substantial a subject as Big Tobacco is for *The Insider,* the lying and evasions of Brown & Williamson aren't its real meat. Neither is the humiliating backdown of *60 Minutes,* which initially nixed the full airing of a damning interview between Wallace and Wigand for fear of being massively sued by B&W—and also, perhaps, for fear of derailing an impending sale of CBS to Westinghouse. (The interview finally aired on February 4, 1996, after much of Wigand's testimony was already a matter of public record following a suit against the tobacco companies, and after the New York *Times* and *Wall Street Journal* had detailed the cave-in at CBS.) The film's real subject, instead, is how the stakes have become so high in modern corporate culture that the whistleblowers end up playing by the same rules as the ones being whistled at. They all kowtow to the same greenback god.

Except for a chosen few, of course. Bergman rages against his superiors at CBS to get the incriminating interview aired while Wigand, his life a scary funk of harassment and recrimination, is left twisting in the wind. These two are portrayed as temperamentally opposite yet united by a passion for payback. Bergman, his hair blow-dry-shaggy in a most uncorporate way, still trails fumes of his counterculture past as a writer for *Ramparts;* he's the last best hope of his generation, and when the creator and executive producer of *60 Minutes,* Don Hewitt (Philip Baker Hall), accuses him of being a "fanatic, an anarchist," the sanctification is complete. Bergman is enough of a political animal to respect compromise, but his vainglory is that, when the screws are put to him, he refuses to back down.

Mann and his co-screenwriter, Eric Roth, are so busy propping up Bergman as an authentic hero out of his time that about halfway through this 155-minute movie, they lose sight of Wigand's story, which, at least the way it's been done here, is more emotionally complex, if less flamboyant. Al Pacino gives a real showboat performance, with full-body shimmies and burning stares and foursquare speeches, and Mann makes everything even more florid by positioning the actor against wide-screen, Valhalla-size backdrops as the overwrought soundtrack swells. (In one dark-lit long shot, Bergman stands knee-high in the ocean as he converses with a distraught Wigand on his cell phone).

By contrast, Wigand is a stolid sufferer for much of the movie, but Russell Crowe gives him a seething core. With his hair lightened and thinned for the role, and a paunch added, Crowe is hardly recognizable from the bully-boy cop he played in *L.A. Confidential.* Wigand may have believed himself to be a man of science who could devise a "safe" cigarette, but he also wasn't above self-aggrandizement; as Marie Brenner wrote, "It is conceivable that B&W had sized Wigand up psychologically. He surely appeared to be highly ambitious, money-hungry, a potential captive to the firm." What gives *The Insider* its power, despite all the glossiness and excess, is that Wigand's dispossession and retribution come across as a key drama for our corporate-circus times. For Wigand, the price of reform is catastrophic. Testifying against B&W, he enters a night-world where his family is endangered and everything becomes commodified, including himself; he's a potential ratings-grabber for CBS until the network figures out it has more to lose than to gain from his appearance. Even iron-faced Mike Wallace—splendidly played by Plummer, with each syllable honed to a cutting edge—doesn't stand up for him. (Later, according to the film, Wallace sees the light.)

At one point, Bergman tells Wigand, "We're running out of heroes. Guys like you are in short supply," and the line has a hollow ring because it seems to come out of a movie about old-style heroism, and what we have with Wigand is something new. (Bergman's heroics, as depicted here, are something old.)

Wigand's rage at B&W is more about pride than about doing good; if the company, after terminating him, hadn't insulted him by pressing for a more severe confidentiality agreement, he probably would have clammed up forever. Wigand as a hero feels right to us, more contemporaneous, precisely because, for a long time, he *doesn't* act on principle. He acts on pique and fear and gall. And yet he seems stunned—hollowed out—by his betrayal at the hands of B&W, and then again by CBS. This ultimate insider becomes the ultimate outsider. We're accustomed to the bland facelessness of the Corporate Man, but this film gives that anonymity a darker twist: When the first, bowdlerized *60 Minutes* show is aired, Wigand sees himself being sound-bited on TV with his face blanked out and his voice patterns disguised. What should be his coming-out party is instead a sick joke, a further retreat into nowheresville.

It's a good thing Wigand isn't a conventional, come-to-the-rescue hero in *The Insider,* because, although Michael Mann tries for a victory dance, there's ultimately little cause for cheer. A few good men here got out with their honor intact, but Big Tobacco is still Big: In September, the Justice Department, after five years and millions of dollars spent, acknowledged that its criminal investigation of the tobacco industry was closed, opting instead for a civil lawsuit accusing the companies of racketeering and fraud. "It was a case," a Justice Department official was quoted in the *Times* as saying, "that the criminal division decided it was not likely to win." This is the real-world backdrop against which the righteous theatrics of *The Insider* play themselves out. It's a world in which there are many whistleblowers and yet the tune remains pretty much the same.

NEW YORK POST, 11/5/99, p. 52, Jonathan Foreman

"The Insider" is a beautifully shot, well-acted movie that manages to make a complicated, real-life story without much drama feel like a thriller. But it's also far too long, and overflows with a sense of its own importance.

It's about tobacco-industry whistleblower Jeffrey Wigand (Russell Crowe) and CBS producer Lowell Bergman (Al Pacino), who fought to broadcast an interview with Wigand on "60 Minutes" despite the opposition of network brass.

The script stays fairly close to the true story, distorting things mainly to make Bergman's and Pacino's—role more important. But the film works less as a parable about evil tobacco pushers or the subversion of press freedom by corporate ownership than as a double tale of betrayal—and counter-betrayal—in the ruthless modern workplace.

Wigand is a well-paid scientist at Brown & Williamson when he's fired for what the company calls "poor communications skills" and what he later says is his opposition to the use of carcinogens to boost the nicotine fix in cigarettes.

At this point, Wigand has no intention of spilling any beans about the company. He's become a schoolteacher, has a generous severance package (and a daughter with severe asthma) and has signed a confidentiality agreement.

But by pure chance, Wigand is suggested to Bergman as a consultant on a tobacco story. After he secretly meets with Bergman, the company forces Wigand to sign a much wider confidentiality agreement.

Furious, he agrees to tell Bergman about his work for Brown & Williamson. To get past the confidentiality agreements, Bergman persuades Wigand to testify in a lawsuit filed against the company by the Mississippi attorney general's office. That means defying a Kentucky restraining order and becoming an open enemy of his former employer.

Wigand then receives an e-mailed death threat and a bullet in his mailbox. The local FBI agents seem to be somehow corrupted by the company, so Bergman arranges 'round-the-clock bodyguards for the Wigand family. Mrs. Wigand (Diane Venora), a spoiled Southern housewife, can't take the pressure and leaves her husband, taking their daughters with her.

Just when things seem as if they cannot get any worse for Wigand, Bergman is told by the CBS suits that the network must not run the interview with him. Both anchor Mike Wallace (Christopher Plummer), with whom Bergman has worked for years, and producer Don Hewitt (Philip Baker Hall), agree with the corporate muckety-mucks.

Michael Mann ("Last of the Mohicans" "Manhunter" and "Heat") is a superb stylist. But there's something showoffy and desperate about the way he uses dramatic compositions and the film's terrific soundtrack to pump up the tension.

Russell Crowe ("L.A. Confidential") is magnificent as the stolid, volatile Wigand—an Oscar-winning performance. And Al Pacino is much less over-the-top than usual: The ranting, roaring persona he adopted in "Scent of a Woman" seems finally to have worn off.

British actor Michael Gambon pulls off an OK Southern accent as ruthless B&W CEO Thomas Sandefur, and character actor Bruce McGill has one terrific courtroom scene. But it's the great Plummer ("Sound of Music," "Star Trek V") who steals the movie with his brilliant, devastating impersonation of Mike Wallace.

"The Insider" is clearly supposed to be an "All the President's Men" for our time, but, unless you're a media insider yourself, there just isn't enough at stake here. It's not as if the fate of the republic depends on the public being told the news that cigarettes are dangerous, and that cigarette companies can be ruthless and dishonest.

NEWSDAY, 11/5/99, Part II/p. B3, John Anderson

It seems fairly safe to say that Hollywood's on-screen relationship with the media has been on a downhill trajectory ever since 1976's "All the President's Men." Certainly, the news business has become more cutthroat and callous. But having once exalted reporters (and filled up the J-schools), the film industry has rarely missed an opportunity since to portray any and all news gatherers as slavering, craven, scoop-hungry parasites who would cheerfully run over their mothers on the way to a zoning board meeting. And this is just in kids' movies.

So imagine the glee that must have accompanied the genuinely shameful disclosure at the heart of "The Insider": that the revered "60 Minutes" had rolled over and buried an interview in a Big Tobacco story, because the expert in question-ex-Brown & Williamson executive Jeffrey Wigand—had signed a nondisclosure agreement with his former employer. Hallelujah, you can hear them saying: The fourth estate has shot itself in the foot. Let's help bury the body.

Nothing is quite as simple as that, at least not in Michael Mann's "The Insider," which stars Al Pacino as producer Lowell Bergman, the wondrous Russell Crowe as Wigand and Christopher Plummer in a scathingly callow and physically uncanny portrayal of the show's pre-eminent raker of muck, Mike Wallace. A movie about integrity and a movie about risks, Mann's epic-length dramatization of this low point in American journalism is visually electric, expertly acted and, unfortunately, a bit narratively fuzzy.

It's a little difficult at times to assess just what's going on, at least at the outset. Did Bergman just stumble onto Wigand while looking for some expert testimony in an unrelated tobacco story? Are those boxes of tobacco documents Bergman has the same ones Wigand took with him when he left—in slo-mo—Brown & Williamson? Is Wigand playing cat and mouse with Bergman, or does he sincerely want to abide by his confidentiality agreement? Is someone after Wigand, or is his paranoia getting the better of him? Equally intriguing: Has Al Pacino taken up permanent residency in some ethereal zone of perpetual intensity and righteous dudgeon, or is he consciously trying to make Bergman into an unctuous weasel? If it's the latter, he does a good job. His character is a self-important, manipulative, name-dropping operator who keeps pictures of Che Guevara, Allen Ginsberg and Geronimo on his office wall to remind himself of the days he wrote for Ramparts and had some vestige of integrity. But Bergman is only the second-string hero of the tale. It's Wigand who's the real thing and Crowe who carries the movie with one of the best performances of the year in one of the least gratifying roles.

Wigand is an Everyman, one with a closet full of flaws. He has two daughters, one an asthmatic, and a wife (Diane Venora) who seems a few hands short of a bridge game. A scientist who already feels he's sold out by working for Big Tobacco, Wigand is unceremoniously sacked by B&W for his outspoken manner, but never entertains any ideas of revenge—until company CEO Thomas Sandefur (Michael Gambon) questions Wigand's honor by demanding he sign a second and more binding agreement.

With a belly full of indignation and the sins of the cigarette industry hanging on his conscience, Wigand is a genuinely tortured character whom Crowe elevates—by dint of a moral conscience and outrage absent everywhere else in the movie—to the status of mythic, tragic hero.

In other words, Wigand is that rare movie creature, a complex human being. And it's to Mann's credit that character—rather than the social and moral aspects of the story—is kept at the forefront of the film. Despite the title, it's not an "inside" movie, not about law, or news, or tobacco. It's about people—few of them lovable, but most of them seeming very true to life.

Most people going to see "The Insider" will probably know the story—that Wigand turned central witness in the lawsuits brought by Mississippi and the other 49 states that resulted in the landmark $246 billion settlement by the tobacco industry. And that "60 Minutes" yanked the Wigand portion of its tobacco story. So the irony comes on fast, early and nonstop. The film opens, for instance, with Bergman trying to convince some mysterious Arab sheik in some mysterious Mideast country to do a "60 Minutes" interview. "You know our reputation for integrity and objectivity," Bergman answers, when the sheik asks why he should. (Yes, even Shiite fundamentalists know Mike Wallace.) Later, after the show's executive producer Don Hewitt (Philip Baker Hall) and Wallace have acquiesced to the corporate lawyers, and Wigand's been smeared by the media assassins of Big Tobacco and Bergman has not quit in protest and the credibility of "60 Minutes" is in tatters, Wallace has a moment with Bergman (Plummer is really good) where he says that a man of his age and stature starts to worry, "How will I be regarded in the end?" What he's afraid of is being known as the man who allowed CBS to be destroyed from without. Not within.

Which is the biggest irony of all.

NEWSWEEK, 11/8/99, p. 98, David Ansen

Logically, Michael Mann's "The Insider" shouldn't be the edge-of-your-seat, gut-churning thriller that it is. A movie about Jeffrey Wigand, the guy who blew the whistle on the tobacco companies? Don't we know how that story turned out? A movie about how "60 Minutes" caved under corporate pressure and pulled its Wigand interview off the air? We read about it in the paper. Besides, everybody knows nicotine is addictive. This is news?

Yes, indeed, when it's told by a filmmaker as accomplished as Mann. What he and his co-writer Eric Roth have chiseled out of this public drama is a wrenching personal tale of two men engaged in mortal combat with the corporate dragons. One is Wigand (Russell Crowe), the R&D man who is fired from his job at Brown & Williamson and decides to expose the tobacco company's courtroom lies. The other is Lowell Bergman (Al Pacino), the "60 Minutes" producer and reporter who must seduce Wigand to go public with what he knows, and protect him against the smears, the byzantine lawsuits and the death threats that follow. Bergman, who works with Mike Wallace (Christopher Plummer), doesn't foresee that his crusade, like Wigand's, is going to put him in a head-on collision with CBS's business interests. "The Insider" is a parable any employee can take to heart: as flies to wanton boys are we to the CEOs. They crush us for their sport.

Mann could probably make a movie about needlepoint riveting. Employing a big canvas, a huge cast of superb character actors and his always exquisite eye for composition, he's made the kind of current-events epic that Hollywood has largely abandoned to TV—and shows us how movies can do it better. Crowe makes Wigand a fascinating, mulish hero. Under his pudgy, blond and bland exterior lurks a cranky, complex and proud man caught in an impossible dilemma. It's hard to believe this is the same actor we saw in "L.A. Confidential." Pacino is rock solid, and more restrained than usual. The movie takes some liberties with the facts, giving Bergman credit for things he didn't do. Whether it's unfair to Wallace (as the veteran journalist claims) we may never know for sure, but Plummer wittily captures the man's florid style and aura of self-importance. Philip Baker Hall plays the capitulating CBS heavyweight Don Hewitt, and Bruce McGill as lawyer Ron Motley has an extraordinarily satisfying courtroom moment when he puts the smug corporate litigators in their place. Powerfully and elegantly, "The Insider" reveals a chilling reality: how hard it is to tell a simple truth when big business doesn't want it told.

SIGHT AND SOUND, 3/00, p. 46, Mark Kermode

The US, the present. Lowell Bergman, producer of Mike Wallace's segments for the news programme *60 Minutes* on CBS, receives anonymously sent documents concerning tobacco research. He approaches Jeffrey Wigand, recently fired from research and development at tobacco giant Brown and Williamson (B&W), to interpret the findings and senses Wigand has a story to tell. B&W threatens to withdraw Wigand's medical benefits unless he signs a further confidentiality agreement. Despite this, Wigand tells *60 Minutes* on camera several incriminating facts: the company deliberately manipulated nicotine levels in cigarettes; an additive called comaurin was used after it had been shown to cause cancer in rats; cigarette companies knew they were in the business of 'nicotine delivery' even though the seven CEOs of the biggest tobacco companies (including B&W president Thomas Sandefur) swore before an April 1994 congressional hearing that they did not believe nicotine to be addictive.

After receiving death threats, Wigand accepts bodyguards into his home. As his marriage collapses, Wigand's reputation is smeared by a B&W-funded investigation. Wigand travels to Mississippi to give a deposition in the state's ongoing case against the tobacco industry, even though a Kentucky ruling forbids him to do so. As *60 Minutes* prepares to air its story, CBS lawyer Helen Caperelli warns of 'tortious interference', a legal precedent which may endanger CBS for encouraging Wigand to break his confidentiality agreement. When the story is aired without Wigand's interview, Bergman leaks information to the *New York Times* which accuses CBS of spiking the story to avoid damaging a merger deal with Westinghouse. After extracts from Wigand's deposition are made public and his smearing is widely debunked, Wigand's interview appears unexpurgated on *60 Minutes*.

"There is no question," wrote journalist Marie Brenner in her head-turning *Vanity Fair* article 'The Man Who Knew Too Much', "that [Jeffrey] Wigand's presence in the tobacco wars is an accident, without grand design." There is also little question that few film-makers could fashion an engrossing thriller around the complex web of deceit which surrounds the modern tobacco industry, and fewer still could do so without recourse to easily discernible heroic central figures, pitiable victims or the reduction of the story to simple plot points. That Michael Mann has resisted the temptation to dumb down this material for *The Insider* reaffirms his position as one of the most important and intelligent directors currently working in mainstream cinema. He has created a tense psychological suspenser as complex and uncompromising as it is engaging and enthralling. It is, in short, a masterpiece, a brilliant dissection of recent US politics and the media by a scalpel-sharp screen sensibility.

Flying in the face of accepted movie law which states real events must be drastically simplified for on-screen use, *The Insider*'s edgy screenplay (by Mann and Eric Roth) sticks surprisingly close to the rambling, nitty-gritty facts outlined in Brenner's original article. Proudly stretching towards the three-hour mark that few films genuinely merit, *The Insider* remains, brisk, brave and ballsy enough to allow events to speak for themselves. It's indeed a surprise to learn the one or two overtly 'dramatic' moments which appear to have been concocted for the benefit of the viewer (Bergman's midnight calls and subsequent anonymous hotel meeting with Wigand; Wigand's last-minute arrival at the Mississippi courthouse) are lifted directly from fact. Real names, rather than the customary legally protective pseudonyms, are used throughout, lending *The Insider* a cool air of credibility so often lacking in latterday's political potboilers. One is tempted to compare it to *All the President's Men* (1976), but that hardly does service to *The Insider*'s brash effrontery. After all, everyone knew that Nixon was corrupt and had resigned by the time Alan Pakula's movie hit the screens. He was, therefore, a sitting duck, while Mann's target (the tobacco corporations) is still powerful and on the move.

Eschewing any action set-pieces (other than the unconnected opening salvo showing producer Bergman negotiating with Middle-Eastern militiamen), Mann's direction expands on the paradoxically intimate use of widescreen showcased to such involving effect in *Heat*. He zeroes in on the facial and physical convolutions of characters locked in intense conversation, finding action in the minutiae of apparent inaction. Pacino's dark features drift in and out of shadow, exquisitely choreographed by Dante Spinotti's cinematography which treats the landscape of human features and inhuman cityscapes with the same sense of awe. Rising to the challenge of such close-quarter encounters, Pacino plays the *éminence grise* to the hilt, relishing a part for which he is perfect in terms of physique, charisma and reputation.

More startling, however, is the transformation of Russell Crowe, the formerly lithe star of such muscular vehicles as *Romper Stomper*. Here he seems to have shrunk in height and ballooned in girth, metamorphosing from the glamorous thug cop he played in *L.A. Confidential* into the humbling, harried picture of awkwardness trapped at the centre of this infernal feud. Whether it is his eyes, constantly avoiding the gaze of both camera and other characters; his fingers, fidgeting incessantly, or his speech patterns, broken into a form of Morse code, Crowe brings Wigand to the screen in all his unlikeable splendour, resisting any temptation to make him any more than a man manoeuvred into actions with accidentally heroic consequences.

The supporting performances are also uniformly handsome, from Christopher Plummer's ever-so-slightly slimy Mike Wallace and Michael Gambon's satanically smooth-tongued B&W president to Gina Gershon's spiky corporate lawyer and Diane Venora's increasingly exasperated (but never caricatured) wife. What a pleasure, too, to see the vastly underrated Wings Hauser getting the chance to flex his spectacular lantern jaw as the attorney from hell. Add to this Mann's usual sensual use of music and *The Insider* ought to walk off with a basket of Oscars in March. The fact that it won't says more about the state of the international film industry and the ticket-buying/cigarette-smoking public than it does about Michael Mann and his movie. Both are magnificent: they should be proud to be outsiders.

VILLAGE VOICE, 11/9/99, p. 135, J. Hoberman

[*The Insider* was reviewed jointly with *Rosetta*; see Hoberman's review of that film.]

Also reviewed in:
CHICAGO TRIBUNE, 11/5/99, Friday/p. A, Michael Wilmington
NATION, 12/6/99, p. 50, Stuart Klawans
NEW REPUBLIC, 12/6/99, p. 28, Stanley Kauffmann
NEW YORK TIMES, 11/5/99, p. E1, Janet Maslin
NEW YORKER, 11/8/99, p. 102, David Denby
VARIETY, 10/4-10/99, p. 84, Todd McCarthy
WASHINGTON POST, 11/5/99, p. C1, Rita Kempley
WASHINGTON POST, 11/5/99, Weekend/p. 47, Desson Howe

INSPECTOR GADGET

A Walt Disney Pictures release. *Executive Producer:* Jon Avnet, Barry Bernardi, Aron Meyerson, Jonathan Glickman, and Ralph Winter. *Producer:* Jordan Kerner, Roger Birnbaum, and Andy Heyward. *Director:* David Kellogg. *Screenplay:* Kerry Ehrin and Zak Penn. *Story:* Dana Olsen and Bruno Bianchi. *Based on characters created by:* Andy Heyward and Jean Chalopin. *Director of Photography:* Adam Greenberg. *Editor:* Thom Noble and Alan Cody. *Music:* John Debney. *Music Editor:* Bob Badami and Andrew Silver. *Choreographer:* Adam Shankman. *Sound:* Arthur Rochester, Andrew Rovinsm, and (music) Shawn Murphy. *Sound Editor:* Lon E. Bender. *Casting:* Amanda Mackey Johnson and Cathy Sandrich. *Production Designer:* Michael White and Leslie Dilley. *Art Director:* Geoff Hubbard. *Set Decorator:* Kate Sullivan. *Special Effects:* Peter M. Chesney. *Visual Effects:* Christopher Raimo. *Costumes:* Mary Vogt. *Make-up:* Christina Smith. *Special Animation:* Stan Winston. *Stunt Coordinator:* Brian Smrz and Gregg Smrz. *Running time:* 85 minutes. *MPAA Rating:* PG.

CAST: Matthew Broderick (Inspector Gadget/RoboGadget/John Brown); Rupert Everett (Sanford Scolex/Claw); Joely Fisher (Brenda Bradford/RoboBrenda); Michelle Trachtenberg (Penny); Andy Dick (Kramer); Cheri Oteri (Mayor Wilson); Michael G. Hagerty (Sikes); Dabney Coleman (Chief Quimby); D.J. Hughley (Gadgetmobile Voice); René Auberjonois (Artemus Bradford); Frances Bay (Thelma); Cliff Emmich (Bus Driver); Brian Tibbetts (Boy on Bike); W. Bob Gaynor (Robotic Foot Dancer); Richard Penn (Doctor); J.P. Manoux (Mayor's Assistant); Sam Brown (Officer McMurphy); Brad Blaisdell (Officer Johnson); Sonya Eddy (Hospital Secretary); Katsy Chappell and Katherine M. Darcy (Nurses in Hallway); Brian George (Guru); Alexander Witt (Businessman); E.J. Callahan (Hot Dog Vendor); Chad Parker (Assistant Car Thief); Frank Masi (Photographer); Mary Chris Wall (News Anchor); Linda Cevallos and Lora-Lyn Peterson (Showgirls); Amy Derrick (Zaftig Woman); William Smith (Little Man); Jim Thiel and Jeff Thiel (Bartenders); Matthew Murray (Autograph Kid); Mark Leahy (Father of Kid); Rick LaFond (News Reporter); Tadao Tomomatsu (Japanese Tourist); Adrienne Wehr (Waitress on Bridge); Richard Rauh (Man with Toupee); THE MINION RECOVERY GROUP: Richard Kiel (Jaws); Mr. T (Himself); Richard Lee-Sung (Odd Job); Robert N. Bell (Tattoo); Hank Barrera (Tonto); Keith Morrison (Igor); Bob Bell (Peter Lorre); John Kim (Number One Son); Jesse Yoshimura (Kato); Aaron Meyerson (Himself); Don Adams (Voice of Brain).

LOS ANGELES TIMES, 7/23/99, Calendar/p. 8, Gene Seymour

[The following review by Gene Seymour appeared in a slightly different form in NEWSDAY, 7/23/99, Part II/p. B10.]

Maybe it's a generational thing, but "Inspector Gadget," the animated adventure series that flourished in the '70s and '80s, never quite caught my fancy in the way that, say, its lesser-known contemporary, "Danger Mouse," did.

"DM" never took itself too seriously and liked to wink at the kids to show that it knew how corny it could get. "Gadget," whimsical as its concept was, never seemed to acquire the self-deprecating edge that could have made it more than a nice midafternoon baby-sitter.

Nevertheless, those responsible for bringing "Inspector Gadget" to big-screen, live-action, high-concept ... whatever, try to bring such self-aware hipness to the tale of a security guard (Matthew Broderick), who is blown to bits by the sinister Claw (Rupert Everett) and rebuilt as a sort of Rube Goldberg notion of RoboCop; "a walking hardware store," as Broderick's Inspector calls himself.

Broderick's mechanized man is welcomed to the police by the town mayor (Cheri Oteri), but is put on cat-recovery duty by the crusty police chief (Dabney Coleman), who thinks Gadget's nothing more than a circus act with a badge.

Why, you ask, would such a weapon be squandered? Thanks to cyber-scientist Brenda Bradford (Joely Fisher), Gadget has all these levers, propellers, flames, springs and fluids bursting from his limbs. He also gets his own self-propelled Gadgetmobile (the voice of comic D.L. Hughley). "Gotta wear a seat belt!" the car announces at one point. "This is a Disney movie!"

Indeed it is. And despite such slick asides to the audience that lead you to think it'll be another "George of the Jungle," "Gadget" instead ends up as another mindless, noisy thrill ride that gorges its audience on bright effects and leaves it queasy from overconsumption.

The doodads and knickknacks that spring unbidden from Gadget's body and car are charming for about five seconds at a time. But after a while, they induce the same languor that the animated series did. One thing the movie picks up from the series: Once again, it's left to Gadget's niece Penny (Michelle Trachtenberg from "Harriet the Spy") to save his bacon.

Gadget's showdown with his Claw-constructed evil twin (Broderick with big, white teeth) would seem a waste of energy if it weren't for the fact that Broderick strikes the proper balance of earnestness and goofiness. Though "Gadget's" a far different slice of pizza than "Election," both movies would seem to prove, in their distinct ways, that Broderick has found himself a cinematic niche as the prototypical wide-eyed, klutzy galoot.

NEW YORK POST, 7/23/99, p. 50, Jonathan Foreman

Based on the TV cartoon of the same name, "Inspector Gadget" is "Robocop" reworked as wacky children's comedy. It has going for it a lot of expensive-looking special effects, but little in the way of wit or excitement. Frenzied but stale, it's a short movie that feels a lot longer than 80 minutes.

Dumb but nice John Brown (Matthew Broderick) is a security guard who has always wanted to be a police officer. He finally gets the chance after being blown up by an exploding cigar. Brenda Bradford (Joely Fisher), the scientist whose lab Brown was protecting from evil crooks, replaces most of his body with an amazing amount of low-tech mechanical gadgetry, and he is hired by the Rivertown force as "Inspector Gadget."

Although he gets to spend lots of time with Brenda—whom he has long loved from afar the mechanically enhanced Brown finds it hard to adjust to a new life as a cross between the Six Million Dollar Man and a Swiss army knife.

All too often the wrong stuff pops out of his body when he utters the "go-go gadget" password. His streetwise talking car (D.L. Hughley) keeps making fun of him. And Chief Quimby (Dabney Coleman) just wants to get him out of the department.

If this weren't bad enough, one-handed supervillain Sanford Scolex (Rupert Everett) who was responsible for blowing up Brown is developing an evil version of the Gadget robot, using technology stolen from Bradford.

The evil robot—identifiable by his shiny fake teeth—is a lot more fun than the good one, and Everett, using a mid-Atlantic accent that almost comes off, makes a surprisingly lively Disney villain.

Broderick is blandly goofy, and the only interesting thing about Fisher is the way her bust seems to get bigger as the movie trundles along.

The most enjoyable thing about "Gadget" is the supporting cast. Cheri Oteri from "Saturday Night Live" perks things up from time to time as a cynical mayor. And Andy Dick from "NewsRadio " is a scientist employed by Scolex who keeps trying to persuade himself that his work might be used for good ends.

"Gadget" contains little real violence or content otherwise inappropriate for children, does include some outrageous product placement.

SIGHT AND SOUND, 1/00, p. 52, Jamie Graham

Artemus Bradford and his daughter Brenda are attempting to advance robotics by combining body tissue and machinery. One night, evil rival Sanford Scolex steals the Bradfords' invention. The laboratory's security guard John Brown gives chase, and in the ensuing car crash Artemus is killed and Brown critically injured.

Scolex loses a hand, leading to a hook replacement and a new moniker: Claw. Brenda saves Brown by fusing his broken body with technology to create Inspector Gadget, a robocop equipped with numerous crime-fighting contraptions. Gadget is also provided with the Gadgetmobile, a talking, self-driving car. While Gadget is assigned only menial tasks by the police, Claw hires

Brenda to work at Scolex Industries. Using Brenda's files, Claw makes RoboGadget, an evil identical twin of Gadget programmed to wreak havoc.

To save his credibility, Gadget breaks into Scolex Industries headquarters, only to be detected and destroyed. Meanwhile, Brenda discovers Claw used her to build RoboGadget and, along with John Brown's niece Penny, sets out to save the city. They discover Gadget and piece him back together. The two Gadgets face off and tussle for supremacy. Claw kidnaps Brenda but the triumphant Gadget flies to the rescue, snatching Brenda to safety. Claw is captured. Penny clears up the whole mess by telling the police about the evil robot lookalike and Inspector Gadget's name is cleared while he is heralded a hero.

Adapted from an 80s animated series in which a private investigator fights crime with the help of a trench coat and trilby laden with gimmicks, *Inspector Gadget* is a suitably cartoonish children's feature. Bulging with colourful production design, slapstick chases, throwaway jokes, inventions and special effects, all bumped together by breakneck edits and garish cinematography, it achieves a razzle-dazzle effect akin to riffling through a *Bash Street Kids* annual for 78 non-stop minutes.

That children will find plenty to amuse them is virtually a given; but, as the likes of *Toy Story* and *Antz* have demonstrated in recent years, it is no longer enough to cater for infants' tastes while parents go hungry, and director David Kellogg (who also made some films in alliance with *Playboy* magazine and the Vanilla Ice vehicle *Cool as Ice)* tries hard to sprinkle some sustenance for grown-ups amid the incandescent confectionery, largely by updating *Gadget* for the new millennium. Now a "sophisticated network of tissue, hardware and software", Gadget could have wandered in from a David Cronenberg movie were it not for his chipper smile and quest for justice. Technology is further scrutinised and its dangers highlighted by the creation of an arch nemesis in the form of RoboGadget, an evil *doppelgänger who* sets out to destroy the city and Gadget's reputation. The battle that ensues plays out like some bizarre kiddies' version of *RoboCop*, every bit as ballistic and baleful if not nearly so brutal.

Unfortunately the 'adult' humour is less successful, often lazily peddling tired postmodernist knowingness with its constant game of 'spot the film reference', not so much nodding to as head-butting the likes of *Batman, Top Gun, Mission Impossible, Godzilla, The Last of the Mohicans* and *The English Patient.* Frequent self reflexive quips further add to the smugly 'knowing' tone: Inspector Gadget, admirably played by Matthew Broderick, is referred to as "Columbo and Nintendo all rolled into one," while Gadget's car, the Gadgetmobile, reacts to the Inspector's amazement at its ability to talk by saying, "What do you expect? This is a Disney movie!"

More rewarding, though, is a running joke in which characters accidentally collide with the camera, a quasi-Brechtian device almost as old as cinema itself that's perhaps forced a little too far when Broderick looks straight at the audience and grimaces following a particularly bad gag.

VILLAGE VOICE, 8/3/99, p. 66, Nico Baumach

Inspector Gadget (Matthew Broderick) is hysterical, not to say hysterically funny. The hero of Disney's live-action version of the '80s cartoon series literally can't contain himself. Ostensibly designed as a gentle Robocop, he is made of gadgets that are mostly frivolous accessories, many of which produce some sort of liquid or goo and threaten to erupt without warning. And if this weren't embarrassing enough, he wears his heart on his hat.

In an intriguing reversal, the brains of this outfit are the women. Until they revert to their more traditional female roles, scientist Brenda (Joely Fisher) and precocious niece Penny (Michelle Trachtenberg) help focus and control the emasculated hero's wayward appendages. Meanwhile, Gadget's rival, Claw (Rupert Everett), a smarmy diva who also has a predilection for wacky machinery, is too silly to be more than a phantom menace. The values of the old fashioned everyman are affirmed as John Brown a/k/a Gadget, self-proclaimed "nice guy," learns to come to terms with his diminished stature in a technology-driven world. Aiding him in these efforts is the Gadgetmobile, with a voice that might as well have been supplied by Jar Jar Binks, but more jive-talking hep cat than Steppin Fetchit.

Known primarily for television commercials, director David Kellogg hasn't charted any new territory here. Shot mostly in close-up, with nearly every action accompanied by a sound effect, the film itself is slightly hysterical. It ignores narrative—or any other sort of—logic; much of its humor is derived from references to pop culture and numerous references to pop culture and numerous brand names. Kids today appreciate a good joke about merchandising tie-ins as much as they do scatological humor. *Inspector Gadget* suggests that the two might be closer than we'd thought.

Also reviewed in:
CHICAGO TRIBUNE, 7/23/99, Friday/p. A, Mark Caro
NEW YORK TIMES, 7/23/99, p. E20, Lawrence Van Gelder
NEW YORKER, 8/2/99, p. 89, Anthony Lane
VARIETY, 7/26-8/1/99, p. 35, Joe Leydon
WASHINGTON POST, 7/23/99, Weekend/p. 37, Desson Howe

INSTINCT

A Touchstone Pictures and Spyglass Entertainment release of a Barbara Boyle and Michael Taylor production. *Executive Producer:* Wolfgang Petersen and Gail Katz. *Producer:* Michael Taylor and Barbara Boyle. *Director:* Jon Turteltaub. *Screenplay:* Gerald DiPego. *Suggested by the novel "Ishmael" by:* Daniel Quinn. *Director of Photography:* Philippe Rousselot. *Editor:* Richard Francis-Bruce. *Music:* Danny Elfman. *Music Editor:* Bob Badami. *Sound:* Peter J. Devlin and (music) Shawn Murphy. *Sound Editor:* Kelly Cabral and Wylie Stateman. *Casting:* Renée Rousselot. *Production Designer:* Garreth Stover. *Art Director:* Chris Cornwell. *Set Designer:* Mark E. Garner and Stéphanie S. Girard. *Set Decorator:* Larry Dias. *Special Effects:* James L. Roberts. *Costumes:* Jill Ohanneson. *Make-up:* John Blake. *Special Character Effects:* Stan Winston. *Stunt Coordinator:* Jim Vickers. *Running time:* 124 minutes. *MPAA Rating:* R.

CAST: Anthony Hopkins (Ethan Powell); Cuba Gooding, Jr. (Theo Caulder); Donald Sutherland (Ben Hillard); Maura Tierney (Lyn Powell); George Dzundza (Dr. John Murray); John Ashton (Guard Dacks); John Aylward (Warden Keefer); Thomas Q. Morris (Pete); Doug Spinuzza (Nicko); Paul Bates (Bluto); Rex Linn (Guard Alan); Rod McLachlan (Guard Anderson); Kurt Smildsin and Jim Coleman (Guards); Tracey Ellis (Annie); Kim Ingram (Lester Rodman); Paul Collins (Tom Hanley); Marc Macaulay (Foley); Jim Grimshaw (Boaz); Gary Bristow (Federal Marshal); Rus Blackwell and Bruce Borgan (Government Aides); Louanne Stephens (Marjorie Powell); Ajgie Kirkland (Captain Kagona); Chike Kani Omo (David); Christopher John Harris (William); Ivonne Coll (Doctor Marquez); Pat McNamara (Doctor Josephson); Vivienne Sendaydiego (Catherine); Roger Floyd (Gilbert); Dave Deever (Man in Car); Tim Goodwin (Helmet Man); John Travis (Mike, Bartender).

CHRISTIAN SCIENCE MONITOR, 6/4/99, p. 15, David Sterritt

"Instinct" stitches together such a patchwork of tried-and-true story ideas that it might have been titled "The Silence of the Gorillas."

Looking like Hannibal Lecter with a beard, Anthony Hopkins plays another demented scientist: Ethan Powell, a primate researcher who's been arrested after killing some park rangers in Africa, where he spent years observing a gorilla colony. Now he's incarcerated in an American prison for the criminally insane, where he refuses to speak with the authorities.

Enter an ambitious young psychiatrist (Cuba Gooding Jr.), who believes he can break Powell's silence and learn the secrets lurking in his heart of darkness.

Hopkins and Gooding are gifted actors, and "Instinct" gives high-octane scenes to each of them. Still, its borrowings from other, better pictures are so constant that a cloud of *déjà vu* hangs distractingly over the whole project. Call it Hollywood's instinct for popular ingredients, or kleptomania by filmmakers who couldn't find ideas of their own. Either way, even Hopkins and Gooding don't have the charisma to overcome it.

LOS ANGELES TIMES, 6/4/99, Calendar/p. 2, John Anderson

[*The following review by John Anderson appeared in a slightly different form in*
NEWSDAY, 6/4/99, Part II/p. B3.]

Anthony Hopkins may no longer hold the title of World's Greatest English-speaking film actor (the un-Oscared Ian McKellen would seem the better candidate, given Hopkins' recent, careless choices), but he's still a weighty, penetrating presence. Cuba Gooding Jr., conversely, could dance across a carpet of potato chips without displacing any salt. So while their matchup may not be quite heaven-sent, it seems at least to be the stuff of weirdly intriguing dynamics.

But the real marriage within "Instinct," director Jon Turtletaub's primatology-meets-psychology howler, is among movies, not men. Hopkins' portrayal of the brilliant but deadly Ethan Powell—mute after his imprisonment for mass murder in the jungles of Rwanda—is an all-too-obvious echo of Hannibal Lechter; his look, for that matter, is straight out of "Mask of Zorro" (with a touch of Papa Hemingway).

Mostly, though, "Instinct" is a greatest-hits collection of plot devices and emotional cues from such films as "Gorillas in the Mist" and "One Flew Over the Cuckoo's Nest," making it something of a trained chimp, one that apes a lot of good movies while making itself look ridiculous. And as long as we're cataloging "Instinct's" debts, let's not forget "The Miracle Worker," "Cool Hand Luke" and "The Snake Pit."

The prison where Powell is being held is an underfunded hellhole for the criminally insane, directed by the bureaucratized Warden Keefer (John Aylward) and muscled by Dacks (John Ashton) and his gang of thuggish jail guards. George Dzundza, impersonating an unwashed bag of laundry, is Dr. John Murray, the wornout resident psychiatrist who's resigned himself to order over healing.

Enter Theo Caulder (Gooding), go-getter shrink with just enough idealism to temper his overwhelming ambition when he confronts the career-making case of Powell. Of course, not only is Powell too cagey for the feel-good mind-bending of Caulder and his mentor, Ben Hillard (Donald Sutherland, doing his now-patented Mephisthophelean shtick), but his "miraculous" work among mountain gorillas in Rwanda—and his own heart of darkness—have given him an insight into human behavior that has turned him silent. That is, of course, until he meets Caulder, who touches something in the blackened soul of Hopkins' brooding ape man.

That any of this needed to be remotely believable—the setup, the relationship or the bloodless revolution Powell inspires within the prison population—seems to have eluded Turtletaub, director of "Phenomenon," "3 Ninjas" and "While You Were Sleeping."

Skirting gracefully around the mixed-race romance blooming between Theo and Powell's estranged-but-devoted daughter Lyn (a very nice Maura Tierney), "Instinct" undermines its own tension with cheap laughs, mostly at the expense of the psychiatric prisoners. When Powell reminisces about his "terrifying and wonderful" encounters with the silver-back gorillas, what we get is neither terrifying nor particularly wonderful (although the special effects are pretty convincing). But Turtletaub has no idea when to stop and the emotional manipulation spins completely out of control.

Gooding is an attractive actor who brings a lot of energy even to this underwritten (or perhaps just underdeveloped) role. You might say that Hopkins could have phoned his performance in, but who would have answered? Maybe director Milos Forman ("Cuckoo's Nest"), whose pockets have been picked most greedily by "Instinct," but who is hardly its only victim.

NEW YORK, 6/14/99, p. 54, Peter Rainer

Anthony Hopkins gets down with the gorillas in *Instinct,* an unintentionally risible drama about a famous primatologist who hid out for four years in Rwandan jungles with the Silverbacks and their brood and then went a bit bonkers. Interned in a Florida prison for the criminally insane, Hopkins's Ethan Powell resembles a cross between Hannibal Lecter and Papa Hemingway. He's malevolently bushy. His psychiatrist, Theo Caulder, is played by Cuba Gooding Jr. In the end, Powell thanks his doctor for sharing the journey, but audiences who sit through this zoologically daft back-to-nature clinker may feel far less charitable.

732   FILM REVIEW ANNUAL

NEW YORK POST, 6/4/99, p. 49, Jonathan Foreman

"Instinct" is one of those schizoid cross-breed movies: You can imagine it being pitched as "Gorillas in the Mist" meets "Brubaker," or "Mighty Joe Young" crossed with "One Flew Over the Cuckoo's Nest." But despite a remarkably silly premise, this gumbo of formulae somehow ends up satisfying entertainment.

The ridiculous story combines the sadistic screws-vs.-convicts myth from classic prison movies with a romanticization of madness and a half-baked idealization of the natural world. You might not want to make policy based on these themes but they have an eternal, irrational appeal.

Ethan Powell (Anthony Hopkins), a famous, Hemingway-bearded primatologist, follows a band of mountain gorillas deep into the jungles of Rwanda and is eventually accepted by them. They even let him hold their cute babies.

But the group is butchered by Rwandan park rangers—presumably taking a break from slaughtering other Rwandans. Powell takes out two of the bastards with a club and is imprisoned for murder.

Powell's school gets him out of Africa. Pending a competency hearing he's locked up in the psych wing of an old-fashioned Florida jail, a silent long-haired wild man with amazing strength.

Ambitious shrink Dr. Caulder (an unconvincing Cuba Gooding Jr.) volunteers to figure out what happened to Powell in Africa. Of course, once Caulder breaks through Powell's silence, their sessions quickly become an opportunity for Powell to liberate his doctor.

Powell, you see, was transformed when he realized that civilization is a bad thing. All the cruel stuff in the prison—like the abuse of the mental-ward prisoners—is added proof of this.

His consciousness raised, Caulder starts to fight the evil prison regime in between swallowing more of Powell's sub-hippie blather about an Edenic pre-civilization only 10,000 years ago—a time before the "takers" took over with their craving for control, when men lived in harmony in nature.

Hopkins is the James Mason of the '90s—an actor who can make compelling the most idiotic material—even "Instinct." No one conveys cunning or inner ferocity so well.

George Dzundza is also excellent here as the compromised prison shrink. But no performance could distract you from a script built on philosophically moronic cliches: The only way out of society's hell is to live by instinct.

Murder isn't nearly so bad as soul-murder. We are all in prison until we give up "the illusion of control" over nature. You'll know you're free when you stand in the rain and don't mind getting wet.

SIGHT AND SOUND, 10/99, p. 47, Ken Hollings

Florida, the present. Psychiatric resident Theo Caulder is selected to evaluate the mental competence of anthropologist Ethan Powell to stand trial for murder. Powell has been extradited from Rwanda where he has already served a year in prison for killing and wounding members of a search party sent to find him. Having spent two years in the jungle living among the gorillas, Powell displays an affinity with animals and responds violently to other humans. He has been completely silent since his arrest.

Caulder's first attempts to get him to talk are frustrated by the brutal methods employed at the correctional facility where Powell is being held. He seeks help from Powell's daughter who describes how her father's obsession with gorillas left little room for his own family Eventually Powell speaks, offering Caulder insights into his life with the apes, whose company he found far superior to human society. He also reveals he attacked his rescuers only after they had opened fire on the gorillas, slaughtering several of them. Just before his trial, however, Powell assaults a guard who has been terrorising a fellow inmate and then withdraws into silence again. Using a pen unwittingly supplied by Caulder, Powell escapes and is last seen wandering alone through the jungle.

With a title sequence that contrasts lush scenes of gorillas ruminating peacefully in their green jungle habitat with dank images of human captivity as Powell is manacled for extradition to the US, *Instinct* has its arguments locked and loaded pretty much from the start. Human society, exemplified this time by the demands and strictures of the Florida penal system, is once more found wanting compared with the order and wonder of the natural world. (Director Jon Turteltaub and writer Gerald DiPego previously collaborated on the cod-mystical *Phenomenon.*)

With his customary subtle authority Anthony Hopkins plays Powell, a highly educated scientist who has returned from the wilderness having become a violent representative of what state appointed shrink Caulder describes as 'ungoverned man', a noble savage responsible for clubbing to death two fellow humans and wounding three more. Florida being one of the first states to reintroduce the death penalty for murder nearly 20 years ago, a lot more than Powell's liberty is at stake. A stooped, shuffling figure in drab prison fatigues and heavy restraints, his features partially obscured by a grizzled beard and straggling, unkempt locks, Powell bears an alarming resemblance to Charles Manson on his way to prison in 1971.

The similarities don't end there. Caulder's cautious probings of Powell's psyche quickly become philosophical exchanges in which Powell imparts to his unwilling pupil lessons that could have come straight from the Book of Charlie. The vast majority of humanity are "takers", exploiting and abusing the world around them. Freedom and control are nothing but illusions, a point which Powell demonstrates forcibly by threatening to break Caulder's neck with his bare hands. Following the doubts about screen violence which he expressed after his performance as serial killer Hannibal Lecter, Hopkins is back playing a kinder, gentler sociopath.

But what happens when we get in touch with our inner gorilla? More importantly, what happens when we don't? If the Harmony Bay correctional facility is a stark cypher for modern society, it is one manifestly devoid of women. In fact, there are only two female characters of any substance in the entire movie: Powell's daughter, whom he finally accepts; and a female gorilla who invites Powell to share in the nurturing of her baby and is promptly shot by park rangers for her trouble. *Instinct* depicts the gorillas existing happily within a benign patriarchy watched over by a powerful male leader, but you never see how this position is maintained or challenged within the group. A mother defending her child is about as ugly as it gets. Meanwhile, the Harmony Bay inmates are shown fighting over playing cards, inflicting indiscriminate injury upon themselves and each other. All in all, *Instinct* comes across as an updated version of *Bambi* (1942). Made at a time when gorillas were still chasing the Ritz Brothers around haunted houses, Disney's animated feature warned audiences that "Man has entered the forest" with a similar, if less extreme, blend of sentiment and brutality. Even the wordless choruses Danny Elfman uses so effectively on the soundtrack here carry awestruck echoes of Frank Churchill and Edward Plumb's *Bambi* score. From cartoon deer to animatronic gorillas, however beautifully designed, is only a small step.

Cuba Gooding Jr brings a brash, kinetic fun to his portrayal of Caulder, whether bluffing a patient into doubting her own paranoiac delusions, laughing too loudly at a colleague's jokes or addressing a barman by his first name. But the demands of the plot gradually erode his position, leaving him by the end a passive accomplice to Powell's escape. Like Hannibal Lecter before him, Powell has to disappear because there is nowhere left for him, or the story, to go. But whereas the highly cultured Lecter only needed the top from a psychiatrist's pen to attain his freedom, the more primitive Powell now requires the whole thing.

VILLAGE VOICE, 6/15/99, p. 150, Gary Dauphin

The new psychodrama *Instinct* tells the not very compelling tale of Dr. Ethan Powell (Anthony Hopkins), a primatologist who kills some African game wardens after disappearing into the bush with his furry study group. Convicted on the Dark Continent, Powell is saved by the feds and shipped back to the States, where he falls under the care of Dr. Theo Caulder (Cuba Gooding Jr.), a shrink who's imagining a bestselling case study long before he meets his patient. Caulder gets Powell to tell him about the murders, but he quickly loses control of their sessions, as Powell rants about the evils of "taking" *(Instinct's* shorthand for the rat race, civilization, whatever). As directed by Jon Turtletaub (the equally dippy *Phenomenon),* *Instinct* moves along at a competent clip, but it's mostly a tease, suggesting that Hopkins is a Lechter-ape when he's really more of a nature-loving Shaolin monk. The absurdities pile up, like Gooding's constant, earnest demand that Hopkins tell him about "the jungle." Not that show-me-the-money man should have any expertise in such matters, but it wouldn't have killed *Instinct* to acknowledge there's something curious about the white-haired Hopkins teaching the woolly-haired Gooding Jr. about humanity's African roots.

Also reviewed in:
CHICAGO TRIBUNE, 6/4/99, Friday/p. A, Michael Wilmington
NEW YORK TIMES, 6/4/99, p. E14, Lawrence Van Gelder
NEW YORKER, 6/14/99, p. 91, David Denby
VARIETY, 5/31-6/6/99, p. 27, Dennis Harvey
WASHINGTON POST, 6/4/99, p. C5, Rita Kempley
WASHINGTON POST, 6/4/99, Weekend/p. 54, Desson Howe

IRIS BLOND

A Miramax Films release of a Cecchi Gori Group Tiger Cinematografica production. *Executive Producer:* Bob Weinstein and Harvey Weinstein. *Producer:* Vittorio Checchi Gori and Rita Cecchi Gori. *Director:* Carlo Verdone. *Screenplay (French and Italian with English subtitles):* Francesca Marciano, Pasquale Plastino, and Carlo Verdone. *Director of Photography:* Danilo Desideri. *Editor:* Antonio Siciliano. *Music:* Lele Marchitelli. *Casting:* Gerda Diddens, Fons Feyaerts, and Shaila Rubin. *Art Director:* Maurizio Marchitelli. *Set Decorator:* Laura Casalini. *Costumes:* Tatiana Romanoff. *Make-up:* Stefano Fava. *Running time:* 100 minutes. *MPAA Rating:* R.

CAST: Carlo Verdone (Romeo Spera);   Claudia Gerini (Iris Blond);   Andréa Ferréol (Marguerite); Nuccia Fumo (Fortune Teller); Nello Mascia (Vincenzo Cecere); Mino Reitano (Himself); Didier De Neck (Julien); Alain Montoisy (Renè Discografico); Patrice De Mincke (Daniel); Liesbet Jannes (Jacqueline).

NEW YORK POST, 5/14/99, p. 48, Hannah Brown

The banal "Iris Blond," the story of a down-on-his-luck Italian musician who helps a waitress become a singer, should have been called "Iris Bland."

The movie stars its director, Carlo Verdone, as Romeo Spera, an Italian singer who was briefly a Euro-pop star in the '70s.

After an ill-fated liaison with Marguerite (Andrea Ferreol), an over-the-hill cabaret singer, Romeo meets Iris (Claudia Gerini), who fits the predictions of a fortuneteller he visits at the beginning of the film.

Iris is the kind of gorgeous, free-spirited young woman whom European movies often present as charming.

She shoplifts, moves casually from man to man and—most important—displays her sleek body in revealing clothes.

Soon, Romeo dumps Marguerite, Iris quits her job at a fast-food joint and they begin to collaborate on songs based on her maudlin poems.

Calling themselves Iris Blond and the Freezer, they create the kind of mindless, grating Europop that makes Madonna sound like Mozart.

"Iris Blond" was co-produced by Miramax, which recently scored big with "Life Is Beautiful," another film by an Italian actor/director, Roberto Benigni.

"Iris Blond" is evidence that not all Italian clowns are created equal.

NEWSDAY, 5/14/99, Part II/p. B10, Bob Heisler

Here's an interesting movie plot: Former pop singer-composer, nearing 50, finds his muse in a free-spirit chick singer and is reinvented as half of a hot, underground Euro-techno duo. But the big time whistles and she goes running, leaving our hero alone onstage as fans cry out for more—trapped in his new identity, all attitude, no amore.

What happens next, how the relationship is resolved, how their worlds collide. Who knows? Starring Billy Joel, say, and Angelina Jolie ...

This is not the plot of "Iris Blond." But give director-star Carlo Verdone credit for suggesting a far better movie than he delivers.

Instead, we are stuck with the story of Romeo Spera, the oddly passive odd man out in a Roman pop band love triangle, whose character moves from hapless victim to object of pity as he tries to make a fortune teller's mysterious predictions of true love come true.

Suddenly Romeo is transplanted from a cruise ship lounge to a Brussels supperclub, where his woman of destiny makes mincemeat of the Jacques Brel songbook for the teary, gray-haired couples, while he chafes under his black turtleneck. You'd question fate, too, locked into "Ne Me Quitte Pas" night after night.

And then there's Iris, the kind of diner waitress who sits down at your table, borrows your lighter and sets fire to your heart before you can say, "Check, please." A flirt, liar, thief and generally scattered liver of life, Iris, too, matches the fortune teller's description of Romeo's Juliet.

Yo, Romeo, can't you see it coming? Again?

In quick order, he is smitten by the prospect of being with her and she is transformed by the prospect of turning her poetry into music with him. Together they find a rhythm and a language that resonate with the young crowd at a rock club. She is Blond, Iris Blond. So cool she dyes her hair black. He is The Freezer. The Eurythmics they're not, but they'll do.

By the time, naturally, she is offered a gig in Paris, alone, Romeo can't see it coming. Finally, he's angry and throws her out. Finally, he visits her father's home to extract at least a financial settlement. Instead, he is honored at a gathering of Italian expatriates—for the pop hit he recorded several lives ago. He arrives as Billy Idol; they treat him like Jerry Vale.

Verdone, looking a bit like Monty Python's Terry Jones, has made several movies here. Perhaps Roberto Benigni raised the bar on the genre of sophisticated Italian comedy. Perhaps Verdone just picked the wrong situation to call comedy. Either way, there's more to think about than laugh at in "Iris Blond."

VILLAGE VOICE, 5/18/99, p. 126, Yael Schacher

Cross Phil Collins, Paul Shaffer, and a heavy Italian accent, and you get Romeo Spera, a balding, buzzed, bespectacled musician, playing keyboard to the pseudo-poetic lyrics of Iris Blond. Actually, Romeo (director Carlo Verdone) looks better in the bohemian-black turtlenecks he used to wear while backing up vampy chanteuse Marguerite. But having fallen for Iris, a Patti Smith wannabe who's more like a Spice Girl, he resolves to help her launch her career. Had Verdone stuck to straight slapstick rather than attempted a romantic musical, the film might have struck more of the right chords.

Also reviewed in:
NEW YORK TIMES, 5/14/99, Lawrence Van Gelder

IRON GIANT, THE

A Warner Bros. release. *Executive Director:* Pete Townsend. *Producer:* Allison Abbate and Des McAnuff. *Director:* Brad Bird. *Screenplay:* Tim McCanlies. *Story:* Brad Bird. *Based on the book "The Iron Man" by:* Ted Hughes. *Director of Photography:* Mark Dinicola. *Editor:* Darren T. Holmes. *Music:* Michael Kamen. *Music Editor:* Christopher Brooks. *Sound:* Randy Thom and (music) Steve McLaughlin. *Sound Editor:* Dennis Leonard. *Casting:* Marci Liroff. *Production Designer:* Mark Whiting. *Art Director:* Alan Bodner. *Animation:* Tony Fucile. *Running time:* 86 minutes. *MPAA Rating:* G.

VOICES: Jennifer Aniston (Annie Hughes); Eli Marienthal (Hogarth Hughes); Harry Connick, Jr. (Dean McCoppin); Vin Diesel (Iron Giant); Christopher McDonald (Kent Mansley); James

Gammon (Marv Loach/Floyd Turbeaux); Cloris Leachman (Mrs. Tensedge); John Mahoney (General Rogard); M. Emmet Walsh (Earl Stutz).

CHRISTIAN SCIENCE MONITOR, 8/6/99, p. 15, David Sterritt

Are movies targeted at youngsters becoming a tiny bit more responsible where gun violence is concerned?

Neither of the newest pictures for young audiences, "The Iron Giant" and "Mystery Men," can be called gentle, and "Mystery Men" has plenty of the grossout humor that's currently in fashion. Both movies have violent episodes, and their producers haven't resisted the temptation to flash guns aggressively across the screen.

But you won't find the continual gunplay that even respectable genres—westerns and thrillers—flaunt on a regular basis. And both pictures take a moment to question the value and morality of guns, indicating a new skepticism about their necessity in popular entertainment. Lots of progress is still needed, but even small steps in this area should be acknowledged and welcomed.

The Iron Giant, easily the summer's funniest and cleverest animated feature, takes its title from one of the main characters: an enormous robot that falls to Earth from outer space, landing in the forest near a Maine village. Stories of the event immediately start flying, thanks to a fisherman who saw it happen, but most of the locals dismiss his account as too crazy to believe. The only person who really knows what's going on is Hogarth Hughes, a nine-year-old boy who stumbles on the giant and becomes its only friend.

The challenge facing Hogarth is wacky enough to be written as a joke: How do you hide a 50-foot giant in a rural town where everyone knows everyone? But the boy has good reason to keep his discovery under wraps. The year is 1957, and rumors about the robot have reached the government's ears. A stranger who lives in the woods, looks peculiar, and behaves differently from everyone else? Communists must surely be involved!

So a special agent barges into the village, determined to sniff out Hogarth's secret and save Maine from subversive elements. It doesn't help that the giants idea of a good meal is whatever piece of metal he can get hold of, including the special agent's car. It also doesn't help that Hogarth's only ally is the local beatnik, almost as suspicious to the G-man as the robot himself.

"The Iron Giant" gains much of its sharp-edged humor from its satirical view of the 1950s, when cold-war prejudices ran amok and children like Hogarth were taught to cheerfully "duck and cover" if an atom bomb ever exploded outside their window.

But the movie is relevant to our own time, too, especially when the giant learns about the destructiveness of guns and tries his clumsy best to oppose their power. So while the movie's animation is more efficient than exciting, its screenplay (based on a Ted Hughes novel) has worthwhile things to tell the mostly young audience it's likely to attract. Grownups may also enjoy the sprightly vocal performances by Jennifer Aniston, Eli Marienthal, Harry Connick Jr., and many others.

Mystery Men is a more violent and vulgar movie, with several scenes punctuated by comic-book mayhem. But this rambunctious atmosphere makes it all the more striking when we discover that one of the main characters won't ever use a gun, even though his job is fighting crime. The heroes also get help from an eccentric scientist who invents weapons that can't kill. Forget the flame-thrower; how about a blame-thrower, instead?

The movie starts with an amusing premise. Captain Amazing, a superhero, spends half his time conquering criminals and the other half endorsing products. But when he's beaten every bad guy around, the public loses interest in his exploits. So he arranges to have an archvillain released from jail, only to fall immediately into the archvillain's clutches.

The only folks who can save him are the city's amateur superheroes, armed with nothing more exotic than shovels, bowling balls, and dinner-table cutlery.

Can this rag-tag bunch rescue Captain Amazing, or will his nemesis triumph? The movie will disappoint people expecting a genuine superhero epic or an over-the-top spoof. But those in the mood for an offbeat satire with a gifted cast (Ben Stiller, Janeane Garofalo, Paul Reubens) will have a surprisingly good time.

LOS ANGELES TIMES, 8/4/99, Calendar/p. 1, Kenneth Turan

Straight-arrow and subversive, made with simplicity as well as sophistication, "The Iron Giant" remembers the wonder of being a child and understands how to convey that in a media-savvy age. Both a step back and a step forward from the trends of modern animation, it feels like a classic even though it's just out of the box.

While charming Disney animated features from "Beauty and the Beast" through the current "Tarzan" have provided hours of wonderful entertainment, there is nevertheless a sameness about their peppy musical formats and the wised-up patter of their characters. "The Iron Giant" does things differently.

Directed by Brad Bird, "The Iron Giant" is loosely based on something Ted Hughes, Britain's poet laureate, wrote for his children after the death of their mother, Sylvia Plath. It's a simple, straightforward tale of a small boy and his oversized, otherworldly friend, and Bird has wisely chosen both traditional and modern ways of visualizing it.

In a decision that fits well with the film's 1957 setting, Bird has utilized old-fashioned, flat two-dimensional animation to tell most of his story. That makes sense for creating the Norman Rockwell-inspired town of Rockwell, Maine, and also makes for frames that look more like carefully drawn storybook illustrations than much of modern animation can manage.

When it comes to animating the 50-foot metal behemoth that gives the film its name, however, Bird and company went to computer-generated images to underline the creature's differentness and to give this giant metal object a kind of grace and personality it might not otherwise have.

The key dramatically to "Iron Giant's" success is a parallel ability to adroitly blend competing sensibilities. Written by Tim McCanlies from a screen story by Bird, the film has the same honest warmheartedness that marked the writer's previous "Dancer, Texas Pop. 81." But though it's got heart, "Iron Giant" is far from square, exhibiting a dryly humorous Rocky and Bullwinkle -influenced anti-establishment sense of humor fueled by one of its main characters, an espresso-drinking hipster named Dean McCoppin (perfectly voiced by Harry Connick Jr.) who wears shades and listens to cool jazz far into the night.

Dean's character is not the only time that "Iron Giant" makes good use of its 1957 setting. Various amusing segments remind us that this was an era characterized by science-fiction films about alien invaders as well as the intertwined fears of the Communist menace and the atomic bomb. Maybe people didn't lock their doors, but there was considerable fear in the air.

Nine-year-old Hogarth Hughes (Eli Marienthal), by contrast, is completely unafraid, a feisty and independent tyke who lives with his hard-working waitress mother Annie Hughes (Jennifer Aniston) and is always game for adventure.

When Hogarth hears a local fisherman talk of sighting an enormous metal monster, he's all ears. And when he hears suspicious noises outside his house one night, naturally Hogarth investigates. What he finds, to his complete shock, is a classic 1950s-type metal-eating robot, 50 feet tall, which the film's opening shots have shown arriving from outer space.

Because Hogarth, in an "Androcles and the Lion" maneuver, helps the giant out of some difficulty, and because the iron man is something of a big kid itself, the two become friends. And though his voice (courtesy of Vin Diesel) sounds like a garbage disposal attempting to speak, the giant even learns to appealingly express himself in English.

Some of "Iron Giant's" most appealing moments convey the pure glee Hogarth feels at having this completely delightful playmate. "My own giant robot," he says, genially puffed up with pride. "I am the luckiest kid in America."

But happy though he is, Hogarth is smart enough to know he has to hide the giant from the rest of Rockwell. "People just aren't ready for you," he says before choosing the junkyard run by hipster (and would-be sculptor) Dean as the most likely refuge.

A refuge proves especially necessary when officious government agent Kent Mansley (Christopher McDonald), a 1950s version of an X-Files investigator, starts snooping around town, trying to get on Hogarth's good side by calling him "chief," "scout," "sport," "skipper" and any other bogus appellation he can think of.

"The Iron Giant" takes special glee in poking fun at the pipe-smoking, trenchcoat-wearing Mansley, the epitome of wrongheaded, xenophobic authority whose thoughts about the giant boil down to, "we didn't build it, that's reason enough to blow it to kingdom come."

While it does turn out that the giant is not always a benign figure, the lessons this film wants to teach are of the gentle variety. It is against guns, against killing, against nuclear weapons (which make a scary cameo appearance) and for the existence of souls and personal self-determination: Both Hogarth and the giant learn that "you are what you choose to be."

In addition to calling the boy Hogarth after the British artist, the makers of "Iron Giant" pay specific tribute to other comic illustrators, from the makers of Superman to Will Eisner, creator of the cult-favorite Spirit. The film also echoes earlier efforts like "King Kong," "Frankenstein" and "E.T." but with a refreshing spirit of bemused, nonaggressive hipness that is completely, and delightfully, its own.

NEW YORK POST, 8/4/99, Part II/p. 44, Rod Dreher

In most respects, "The Iron Giant" is one of the better animated children's films in recent memory, which makes its strident political correctness all the more frustrating.

Leave it to Hollywood to transform "The Iron Man," a beloved 1968 English children's book, into a left-wing fable about McCarthyism and nuclear warfare. Ethel and Julius Rosenberg, this robot's for you.

It's a pity that politics, and of an especially pernicious kind, intrude into a discussion of this entertaining, heartwarming kids' movie. But director Brad Bird forces the issue by reinventing the story as a forthright allegory of America's anti-Communist "paranoia."

It starts in 1957, with a meteor speeding past the orbiting Sputnik and crashing into the ocean off Maine. The meteor is actually a 10-story robot, which hides in the woods outside the quaint village of Rockwell (as in Norman).

One night, while his single mom (voice of Jennifer Aniston) is working the late shift at the diner, little Hogarth Hughes (voice of Eli Marienthal) discovers the Iron Giant caught in the sparking wires of an electrical power station. The robot appears to be dying until Hogarth flips the off switch.

Hogarth and the Iron Giant become friends, meeting secretly in the woods because, as Hogarth says, "People always wig out and start shooting when they see something different."

The giant's persecutor emerges in the guise of Kent Mansley (voice of Christopher McDonald), a government agent looking to make his career by rooting out Commie infiltrators. He suspects the Russkies may have a secret weapon skulking around Rockwell and harasses Hogarth into ratting out his steely pal.

Things head to an atomic showdown with the U.S. Army, which is willing to destroy Rockwell in order to kill the "Red." "He's a gun that walks!" shrieks a government guy.

That he certainly is, but the Iron Giant seeks peaceful coexistence and will only use his sophisticated weaponry in self-defense. That's what Soviet apologists said about the U.S.S.R., too.

"The Iron Giant" cannily tips its hat to the way sci-fi films of the late 1950s sublimated the country's Cold War jitters. But what's so infuriating is how the film perpetuates the lie that the Soviet Union was no threat at all, and that the search for Soviet spies was about nothing more than persecuting misunderstood innocent outsiders.

None of this will likely matter to children, who'll see a beautifully told fable about a boy and his secret friend, and the noble sacrifice that friend makes for the boy's love. The writing is vivid and bright, the voicing accomplished, and the storytelling emotionally satisfying.

The animation, while nowhere near Disney's sophisticated standard, is exuberant and as appealing as the movie's history and politics are appalling.

NEWSDAY, 8/6/99, Part II/p. B2, Gene Seymour

Its unlikely rescuer is a winsome, bright-eyed, 50-foot- tall, battleship-gray mechanical man whose heroism extends beyond the feats he performs on, the big screen.

Indeed, the title character of "The Iron Giant" has done more than save an imaginary town and a generally soporific summer movie season. He has pulled the once-legendary reputation of Warner Bros. animation from the doldrums and allowed it to recover the hip, edgy irreverence of yesteryear while giving Disney a run for its money in projecting full-length dramatic power.

And all of this is carried out without one song to goose the emotions.

After seeing a movie as startlingly well-wrought as "The Iron Giant," your thoughts scatter in several directions, frantically searching not for superlatives so much as for reasons. How did director Brad Bird and company pull off such a sleekly designed, perfectly balanced combination of dry wit and sweet feeling? The question is especially vexing, given the many ways this material could have cloyed like caramel. Bird, a one-time Disney animator who has also worked on "The Simpsons" and "King of the Hill," took liberties with the source (a 1968 children's book by the late poet Ted Hughes) and set the fable in a town in Maine shortly after Sputnik's launch in 1957.

It's in the woods outside that town that 9-year-old Hogarth Hughes (voice by Eli Marienthal) first encounters the big gray guy who apparently fell to Earth from Somewhere Out There and acquired a bump on its head.

Hogarth, who lives with his single mom (voice by Jennifer Aniston), rightly believes himself to be the world's luckiest kid. He's also smart enough to know that most of the grown-ups in the vicinity aren't going to understand that this metal-munching amnesiac poses no threat to their lives, especially with foreign objects sending beeps from above the stratosphere.

So Hogarth stashes the robot (voiced by Vin Diesel) in what appears to be the perfect hideout: a junkyard where it will have plenty to eat. Even better, the place is owned by a beatnik artist (voice by Harry Connick Jr.), who reluctantly goes along with the plan, probably because, as he puts it, "We kooks have to stick together." By then, however, the robot has done enough damage to cars, tractors and power lines to attract the attention of eager-beaver federal investigator Kent Mansley (voice by Christopher McDonald), who, putting it mildly, lacks Fox Mulder's poetic grace. Hogarth manages to match Mansley's bullying with his gifted-student guile. But not for long.

Just from this plot description, you can imagine many places where the sap could start leaking in buckets. "The Iron Giant" simply refuses to go to those places, and by keeping the sentimental volume on "mute," the movie earns your emotional engagement. It passes along its antiviolence messages without beating you senseless. (Hogarth's toy gunplay unwittingly triggers the giant's frightening defense mechanisms.) And the movie's plea for tolerance is made more convincing by its broad, knowing satire of the Cold War paranoia.

Parents of a certain age will laugh with rueful recognition at the "duck-and-cover" civil-defense cartoon in Hogarth's class. They also will likely get a kick out of the parodies of period black-and-white sci-fi horror movies and hard-sell TV ads. The kids may not get all the jokes. But they'll love Hogarth's coffee jag and the tsunami effect caused by the giant's cannonball dive into a lake. Conceptually, the movie wears its elaborate design with seeming effortlessness. It fills the eye, but without gratuitous overload of detail.

In fact, the only gratuitous moment in all of "Iron Giant" is a dead-deer sequence which, even if it was a parodic nod to "Bambi," doesn't need to be in there. And the ending, without giving anything away, also hints at a mild compromise with the conventions of full-length animation.

But great movies are allowed to have little things wrong with them. And "The Iron Giant," as much as Disney's "Pinocchio" or, for that matter, Warner's "Duck Dodgers in the 24½ Century," deserves to be ranked with the greatest of animated cartoons.

NEWSWEEK, 8/9/99, p. 69, David Ansen

This beguiling animated feature is set in the paranoid 1950s. Even in the small Maine town where 9-year-old Hogarth Hughes lives, the shadow of the A-bomb hovers, and cold-war rumors about Russian espionage abound. Imagine, then, what fears are unleashed when Hogarth finds, and befriends, a 50-foot giant robot that feeds on metal. With the help of his beatnik artist friend Dean, Hogarth tries to hide his giant metallic playmate—especially from the suspicious eyes of a commie-obsessed federal agent. But it's only so long before the robot is forced to unleash its lethal powers to defend itself.

This is not exactly standard children's fare, but kids (and their parents) should be smitten by its wit and wisdom. Loosely based on poet Ted Hughes's book "The Iron Man," it has been turned by writer-director Brad Bird into a multilevel fable about violence, free will, the continuity of life and—more topically—gun control. At once simple and sophisticated, Bird's "Iron Giant" makes it clear that Disney isn't the only animation game in town.

SIGHT AND SOUND, 1/00, p. 54, Leslie Felperin

Rockwell, Maine, 1957. An enormous iron man crash-lands on Earth, reassembles itself and sets about consuming the metal it needs to live. Nine-year-old Hogarth Hughes, son of single mother Annie, happens on the giant one night in the woods and saves its life when it tries to eat a power station. Rockwell's strange goings-on bring government agent Kent Mansley to town. Hogarth persuades local beatnik Dean McCoppin to keep the giant at the junk yard Dean owns where it will have enough to eat. Hogarth teaches the giant English and teaches it not to use its destructive powers.

Eventually, the giant is discovered. Convinced it is a weapon, Mansley calls in the military. Seeing that conventional weapons are of no use, Mansley gets the army to launch a nuclear attack on the giant. Hogarth persuades the giant not to fight. It launches itself into the sky, detonating the bomb safely in outer space but seemingly destroying itself in the process. Some time later, Dean has made a statue in the giant's honour and is now part of a family with Annie and Hogarth, who still mourns the giant. But all over the world, pieces of the giant are slowly finding each other ...

Not only is *The Iron Giant* one of the more emotionally satisfying films of the year, but it also affords a cheering opportunity for all those who'd like someone other than Disney to have a cartoon hit. Given its illustrious record with shorts starring Bugs Bunny and crew, it's surprising it's taken Warner Bros this long to make a serious stab at original features.

It was a particularly smart move to hire *Simpsons* veteran Brad Bird to direct. In collaboration with screenwriter Tim McCanlies, Bird brings with him a very Simpsonian knack for mixing burnout with sentiment so that the morality never clots into indigestible preaching. This means the "you can be whatever you want" message Hogarth teaches the Iron Giant emerges as a subtle lesson in free will. Similarly, the *Simpsons* line in nimble parody emerges with a hilarious pastiche of a 50s safety film 'Duck and Cover' while unforced allusions to 50s atomic-horror films, vintage comics, *The X Files* and the Beat Generation oxygenate an already bubbly story. Even the clean, stylised animation, although distinctive, conjures up the gestural simplicity of Bird's training ground at its best.

In the film's knack for darkness and emphasis on line, there's a trace memory of Andrew Davidson's woodblock illustrations for Ted Hughes' original story on which this is loosely based. Purists might demur at *The Iron Giant*'s radical departure from its source, the significantly differently titled *The Iron Man*. Gone is the truly blood-frosting image it conjures of the space-bat-angel-dragon, as big as Australia and bent on licking life from the planet. Perhaps such stuff would be a little too scary for children if given visual form. The giant here is more like E.T. crossed with a Transformer than Hughes' mysterious emanation of the Earth, but this adaptation still incorporates delicious memories from the original—the giant munching thoughtfully through a junkyard of metal, the sense of his awesome scale and his gift for self-assembly (an ability many parents would wish on the presents opened on Christmas morning)—that sweeten the near tragic, genuinely moving climax. Given the film's enormous box-office success so far, expect the inevitable follow-up, although the film-makers probably won't use Hughes' own harrowing sequel *The Iron Woman*.

TIME, 8/16/99, p. 65, Richard Schickel

A lonesome little boy, hyper-active and hyper-imaginative. A big, scary monster who doesn't know his own strength—especially the strength of his sweet soul. An uncomprehending world that would rather exercise its many itchy trigger fingers than try to understand that which is strange to it.

Been there? Done that? Well, sure. But Brad Bird, who directed *The Iron Giant*, and Tim McCanlies, who wrote this handsomely animated feature, have given it a special urgency by the simple expedient of setting it in exactly the right time and place. That would be 1957 in a small town in Maine. It's a moment when cold war paranoia is at its height and isolated rural communities are the targets of choice for aliens in dozens of cheapo sci-fi epics.

Not that the movie is most significantly a satire of an essentially self-satirizing genre (though it is entirely hip in its cross-references). Rather, it uses the archetypes of its time to impart a certain moral and melodramatic force to its story. Its kid hero, Hogarth, is full of bounce and bravery; the car-gnawing, train-wrecking giant is enthusiastically educable in his genially klutzy way. But the largest fun lies in the other characters: jut-jawed Kent Mansley, the funny-dumb government agent who has bought into the whole duck-and-cover thing; Dean, the beatnik junk sculptor whose cool helps thwart Kent's heat; Hogarth's mother, an old-fashioned, benignly clueless sitcom mom. Together they create a smart live-and-let-live parable, full of glancing, acute observations on all kinds of big subjects-life, death, the military-industrial complex—that you can talk about with the kids for a long time to come.

VILLAGE VOICE, 8/10/99, p. 59, J. Hoberman

Set at the dawn of the space race, Brad Bird's *The Iron Giant* is steeped in a mythos of sputniks, spooks, and classroom shelter drills. It's a deft, economical, and uncloyingly sweet-natured movie that even invokes the ultimate Cold War nightmares nuclear missile arcing out of the sky over Main Street.

Bird, a Cal Arts and Disney alum who had an early involvement with *The Simpsons,* has freely adapted a children's book by British poet Ted Hughes; however, the feel is hardly literary. If anything, the movie hews too closely to the *E.T.* scenario. Hogarth, the nine-year-old son of a harried single mom (dubbed by Jennifer Aniston), finds, saves, and protects the humongous robot who drops from the sky-educating him as well with his collection of comic books.

The story's a tad simpy but the character animation and action interludes are so matter-of-fact in their brilliance that it scarcely matters. Set pieces range from a storm at sea and a pursuit sequence involving air force bombers to a mess precipitated in the local diner by Hogarth's pet squirrel and a kindred sequence with a giant robot hand scuttling through the boy's house. With an insatiable appetite for scrap metal and an uncanny ability to reassemble his scattered parts, the giant himself is a sturdy comic conception as well as a fully realized icon—ratchet jaw and headlight eyes are encased in a bullet-shaped cranium, an imposing torso pivoting on a Tinker Toy construction. (That only the giant appears to be computer-animated is among the many unobtrusive touches that make *The Iran Giant* so satisfyingly coherent.)

If Bird appears to have logged a few hours studying *Duck Dodgers in the 24½ Century* and the Superman cartoons of the early 1940s (not to mention King Kong and Ultra Man, among other Japanese robots), *The Iron Giant* is in no way derivative. Incredibly, it suggests a cartoon remake of *The Day the Earth Stood Still* that might have been made in 1957—a sensation promoted by the *Forbidden Planet* poster that Hogarth has in his bedroom, the cleverly incorporated period ad he watches on TV, and the invented "duck and cover" civil defense cartoon shown in school. The characters, angular rather than cuddly, are set against fully rendered backgrounds. At once stylized and detailed, jazzy and classic, the animation picks up where Warner and Disney left off when they cut back their theatrical cartoon units in the mid '50s.

The music doesn't flood the script with sentiment or canned nostalgia, and the movie is even restrained in its toilet jokes. Remarkably unassuming, genuinely playful, and superbly executed, *The Iron Giant* towers over the cartoon landscape.

Also reviewed in:
CHICAGO TRIBUNE, 8/6/99, Friday; p. A, Mark Caro
VARIETY, 7/26-8/1/99, p. 33, Lael Loewenstein
WASHINGTON POST, 8/6/99, p. C1, Stephen Hunter
WASHINGTON POST, 8/6/99, Weekend/p. 44, Nicole Arthur

JAKOB THE LIAR

A Columbia Pictures release of a Blue Wolf Productions film with Kasso Inc. *Executive Producer:* Robin Williams. *Producer:* Marsha Garces Williams and Steven Haft. *Director:* Peter Kassovitz. *Screenplay:* Peter Kassovitz and Didier Decoin. *Based on the book "Jakob der Lügner" by :* Jurek Becker. *Director of Photography:* Elemér Ragályi. *Editor:* Claire Simpson. *Music:* Edward Shearmur. *Music Editor:* Craig Pettigrew. *Sound:* Clive Winter and (music)

Stephen P. McLaughlin. *Sound Editor:* Patrick Dodd. *Casting:* Billy Hopkins, Suzanne Smith, Kerry Barden, Vanessa Pereira, Simone Ireland, Zsolt Csutak, Magda Szwarchart, and Risa Kes. *Production Designer:* Luciana Arrighi. *Art Director:* Branimir Babic and Tibor Lázár. *Set Decorator:* Ian Whittaker. *Set Dresser:* Agi Menyhert. *Special Effects:* Ferenc Ormos. *Costumes:* Wieslawa Starska. *Make-up:* Kati Jakóts. *Running time:* 114 minutes. *MPAA Rating:* PG-13.

CAST: Robin Williams (Jakob Heym); Alan Arkin (Frankfurter); Bob Balaban (Kowalsky); Hannah Taylor Gordon (Lina); Michael Jeter (Avron); Armin Mueller-Stahl (Professor Kirschbaum); Liev Schreiber (Mischa); Nina Siemaszko (Rosa Frankfurter); Mathieu Kassovitz (Herschel); Justus von Dohnányi (Preuss); Mark Margolis (Fajngold); Gregg Bello (Blumenthal); Éva Igó (Lina's Mother); István Balint (Lina's Father); Kathleen Gati (Hooker); János Gosztonyi (Samuel); Adám Rajhona (The Whistler); Antal Leisen (Peg-Leg); Peter Rudolf (Roman); Jan Becker (Young German); János Kulka (Nathan); Grazyna Barszczewska (Mrs. Frankfurter); Judit Sagi (Mrs. Avron); Ilona Psota (Grandmother); Agi Margitai (Miss Esther); Iván Darvas (Hardtloff); Lászlo Borbély (Doctor); Zoli Anders (Meyer); Miroslav Zbrojewicz (SS Officer 1); Jozef Mika (Soldier); György Szkladányi (SS Officer 2); Zofia Saretok (Neighbor); Michael Mehlmann (Escaping Man); Mirtill Micheller, Orsolya Pflum, and Beatrix Bisztricsan (3 Lady Singers).

LOS ANGELES TIMES, 9/24/99, Calendar/p. 9, Kenneth Turan

Robin Williams, enough already. Enough with the compassionate roles, the humanitarian roles, the caring and concerned roles. Enough with the good deeds, for pity's sake. Remember being funny? Maybe you could try that again. How hard could it be?

"Jakob the Liar," in which Williams plays a poor soul who brings, yes, hope to his fellow Jews imprisoned in a World War II ghetto, is the latest in what feels like an endless string of movies ("Patch Adams," "What Dreams May Come," "Good Will Hunting," to name a few) in which the actor's parts have ruinously overdosed on sentimentality and schmaltz at the expense of humor and even sanity.

Following "Schindler's List" and "Life Is Beautiful," "Jakob" stands in clearer relief than it otherwise might as everything a Holocaust film shouldn't be. A painful miscalculation, this is the kind of bogus production only completely sincere but misguided individuals can come up with.

Set "somewhere in Poland in the winter of 1944," "Jakob" wants to move us, to make us cry, and sets about doing it in absolutely the worst way possible. And don't forget the laughs, the gallows humor that we all know makes tragedy bearable. Laughter through tears ... how does that sound?

It sounds good to Jakob, who reminds us in his overly earnest voice-over that humor is how the Jews who did come out alive managed to survive the war; "everything else," he tidily points out, "the Germans had taken."

A former cafe owner who specialized in apricot pancakes, Jakob's troubles begin when he sees a page of a newspaper floating through the ghetto's windblown streets. Since all news is at a premium, Jakob tries to catch it, but in his eagerness doesn't realize he's wandered into a forbidden Germans-only zone.

While explaining himself to a military official, Jakob accidentally overhears an equally forbidden radio broadcast announcing Russian victories in nearby towns. He's elated at the news, but once he's back in the ghetto he's afraid to pass the information on because only collaborators come out of Nazi headquarters alive. Plus he now also has to worry about 10-year-old Lina (Hannah Taylor Gordon), an escapee from a death-camp train he's rescued from the streets.

But while talking to hotheaded young boxer Mischa (Liev Schreiber), Jakob's news leaks out. Still unwilling to reveal his sources, Jakob allows the talkative Mischa to assume that he, Jakob, owns a strictly forbidden radio and is regularly receiving broadcasts from the outside world.

Soon, everyone in the ghetto is in awe of Jakob and his putative radio. Emboldened by the good news, Mischa even asks his sweetheart Rosa (Nina Siemaszko) to marry him, much to the disgust of her overbearing father, Frankfurter (Alan Arkin). Even the ghetto's beloved Dr. Kirschbaum (Armin Mueller-Stahl) credits the news of Jakob's radio with cutting down on suicides. And so an unlikely hero is born.

While this scenario may sound (barely) passable, several factors work against it in practice. Though "Jakob" is based on a novel by ghetto survivor Jurek Becker (which was previously made into an East German film in the mid-'70s), and though director and co-writer Peter Kassovitz had to be hidden with a Catholic family during the war, nothing about the film, not even the carefully distressed costumes and art-directed ghetto streets, manages to sound an authentic note.

That's because the script (by Kassovitz & Didier Decoin) assumes that it's impossible for Jews to communicate without sounding like a gathering of Borscht Belt comedians. This is especially true when Jakob talks to best pal Kowalsky (Bob Balaban), but lines like "If you hang yourself, I'll kill you," "I'll burn that bridge when I get to it" and "Chosen people... why didn't he choose someone else?" are so prevalent that if a Henny Youngman type had shown up and said, "Take my wife... please," he would have fit right in.

Along with burdening everybody with bogus-sounding accents (too bad space couldn't be made for Eddie Murphy, whose Jewish intonation is at least as good as anyone here), "Jakob" is such a stranger to restraint that this plays like the kind of Holocaust film cynics feared "Schindler's List" would turn out to be but wasn't.

"Jakob" also fares poorly compared with Roberto Benigni's "Life Is Beautiful," which had its own kind of unlikely integrity and didn't overstuff audiences on trumped-up poignancy quite so shamelessly as this crew does.

"Jakob the Liar" is so forced that only the interest of a star of Williams' magnitude could have gotten it made, which is another reason why it would be nice if the actor was willing to focus his talents on something he's brilliant at. That used to be humor. Let's hope it still is.

NEW YORK, 10/4/99, p. 52, Peter Rainer

Having seen *Jakob the Liar* on the heels of *Patch Adams* and What *Dreams May Come,* I see clearly that Robin Williams is not satisfied with his Oscar: What he's really bucking for is the Nobel Peace Prize. So give it to him already, and maybe he'll stop trying to melt our hearts. In this latest film, he's playing a poor soul in a Polish Jewish ghetto run by the Germans, and he's as misty-eyed as all get-out. He suffers his way into sainthood. The film itself is soberer and less dishonest (except in its outrageous final scene) than *Life Is Beautiful,* but the end point is about the same: Living through the Holocaust is made to seem like a great way to build character.

NEW YORK POST, 9/24/99, p. 51, Jonathan Foreman

"Jakob the Liar" is yet another attempt to wring melancholy laughter—and big bucks out of the Holocaust.

Made two years ago, before Roberto Benigni's overrated "Life Is Beautiful," "Jakob" is meant to be an absurdist fable about an everyman whose good, unselfish side is brought out by nightmarish circumstances, and there are several moments (notably the final sequence) when you can detect the powerful and moving film it could have been.

But "Jakob the Liar" isn't powerful or moving, mainly because it's written with astonishing crudeness.

The film's French co-writer and director, Peter Kassovitz, is so tone deaf in his attempts at gallows humor that chunks of the film could be scenes from "Shoah: The Sitcom." And Robin Williams' standardized moist-eyed screen persona overwhelms the material.

Williams is Jakob Heym, the widowed owner of a long-closed cafe in an unnamed Polish ghetto in the winter of 1944. He is always saying things like "I know that we're the chosen people, I just wish the Almighty had chosen someone else!" and "I'll burn that bridge when I come to it."

During a brief arrest by the Germans—who speak English in accents out of "Hogan's Heroes"—he overhears a radio news bulletin announcing Soviet advances.

The same night, Jakob meets little Lina (Hannah Taylor Gordon), who has escaped from one of the trains going to the concentration camps. Although it might put him in some danger, Jakob decides to hide the girl in his house in the ghetto, and they begin a predictably cutesy relationship that distracts from the main story.

Jakob tells his friend Mischa (Liev Schrieber, excellent as always) about the Russian advance but doesn't say where he heard the news. Mischa then tells everyone that Jakob has a forbidden radio set—an offense punishable by death.

Jakob decides not to reveal the truth when he realizes what a powerful morale-boosting effect the mythical radio has on almost everyone in the ghetto.

Jakob's barber friend Kowalsky (Bob Balaban) decides to put off hanging himself And Mischa decides to marry his girlfriend because he now thinks there's a chance they could survive the war.

Only prideful actor Alan Arkin and two bearded religious guys think that the presence of a radio in the ghetto is a bad thing.

Jakob finds himself in the difficult position of having to make up news that he has heard on his radio. You only hear one of these stories at length, and it's obvious tripe about the arrival of American troops on the Russian front accompanied by jazz bands. For the men of the ghetto to believe Jakob's lies, they'd have to be moronic as well as desperate.

Portraying Polish Jews who are due to be murdered by the Nazis as a collection of amusingly gullible, argumentative fools is in questionable taste, at best. At worst, it's a particularly gross exploitation of the Holocaust for financial gain.

NEWSDAY, 9/24/99, Part II/p. B2, John Anderson

When Robin Williams more or less abdicated his status as America's most unhinged comic in order to become the hardest-working hankie salesman in Hollywood, it seemed like a professional left turn into solid, respectable hackdom. As it turns out, he was just completing an orbit.

In "Jakob the Liar"—Williams' latest and the latest in feel-good Holocaust movies—the actor comes full circle, back to situation comedy. Rather than an episode of "Mork and Mindy," the "situation" involves the Warsaw Ghetto, Nazis and the systematic extermination of the Jews. But as comedy—and it is supposed to be comedy—the structure is basically the same. Longer, but the same.

In director Peter Kassovitz' Warsaw, death is indiscriminate—except, of course, when it isn't. Jakob Heym, restaurateur without restaurant, meanders about the mile-square, walled ghetto with his cohorts—Mischa the boxer (Liev Schreiber), Kowalsky the barber (Bob Balaban), the learned Dr. Kirschbaum (Armin Mueller-Stahl)—doing the business of the storyline. Meanwhile, passerby Jews are beaten (not too severely), others are arrested (but not if they have speaking parts) and Yiddishisms are sprinkled across the script like poppy seeds.

The deliberate casualness of all this "reality" recalls a moment in Barry Sonnenfeld's otherwise undistinguished "For Love or Money" when a posse of Brooklyn Hasids chase a culprit through the background of a scene for no narrative reason whatsoever. That was funny, because it was absurd. Warsaw was absurd, but it's not funny at all.

Neither is Jakob. But could he be? While detained by the Nazis for a curfew violation, he overhears a German radio broadcast about Soviet incursions into Poland. Since he's afraid of being mistaken for an informer—any Jew released from Nazi headquarters is assumed to be an informer—he tells his friend Mischa that he actually owns a radio, even though owning a radio is punishable by death. The news of Jakob's radio circulates through the ghetto like cholera, and Jakob is thereafter expected to deliver daily updates, resulting in an expanding fabric of optimistic lies that reduce the suicide rate in the ghetto but spin wildly out of control.

Within the Borscht Belt-meets-"Schindler's List" sensibility of "Jakob the Liar," the nonexistent radio provides the device by which Williams gets to exercise his gifts as a mimic and to interrelate with a child—in this case Lina Kronstein (Hannah Taylor Gordon), a 10-year-old who has escaped a train to the camps and taken refuge in Jakob's house. In what is more or less the comic centerpiece of the movie, Jakob, in a thoroughly unconvincing series of antic gestures, acts out a radio broadcast behind a curtain. Lina buys it wholesale.

But then Lina is perhaps the great missed opportunity of the entire movie. Although no one—least of all director Kassovitz—seems to realize it, Lina is completely mad. Her state of denial about what's going on around her is so extreme that she acts like a normal movie child, perhaps one who has gotten lost at the mall and is waiting for Mom to pick her up.

She's fanciful, mischievous and has absolutely no connection to any reality. As such, she might easily have been the most frightening thing in a movie that otherwise takes unadulterated horror and turns it into ethnic humor.

"Jakob the Liar" is a movie that takes its credibility from history and proceeds to change history for emotional convenience. The ending, although "tragic" for the few, is resolved for the many, who are saved by a bit of whimsy that suggests that the camp-bound trains were intercepted by the Soviets late in the war. But since the Warsaw Ghetto was emptied of Jews in 1943, this seems to be taking dramatic license to an obscene extreme.

"Life Is Beautiful" assumed that audiences wanted to feel good about the Holocaust, which by all indications they did. For those who believe the Holocaust should be treated with silence, the question is whether a movie that imposes comedy on the Final Solution can be anything but a philosophical outrage. Kassovitz, born in Hungary, saw his parents taken to the camps (they survived), so his heart has to be in the right place. But consider some alternatives: Can Ezra Pound be considered a great poet? Or Leni Reifenstahl a great director? Sure.

And if a movie about the Holocaust was a comedic masterpiece, there might be an argument about its right to exist. With "Jakob the Liar," as it happens, no such dilemma exists.

SIGHT AND SOUND, 12/99, p. 48, Peter Matthews

Nazi-occupied Poland, 1944. Jewish café proprietor Jakob overhears a broadcast reporting the defeat of the Soviet army in a nearby town, which actually means the Allies are close to winning the war. He meets Lina, a ten-year-old girl who has just escaped from a train bound for the death camps, and hides her in his attic. Later, Jakob discloses the news about the Russians to his friend Mischa. Assuming Jakob has a radio, Mischa quickly spreads the word. Jakob asks Mr Frankfurter for his daughter Rosa's hand in marriage.

The optimistic rumours lead Jakob's friend Herschel to an act of defiance that ends in his death. Jakob unsuccessfully tries to tell community leader and doctor Kirschbaum he doesn't own a radio. A faction headed by Frankfurter demand to hear a broadcast on Jakob's radio, but a power cut intervenes. Jakob is elected leader of the resistance. The Gestapo demands Kirschbaum attend a highranking SS officer with a heart condition who informs the doctor the ghetto will be shipped to the camps in the morning. He can save himself if he reveals the name of the radio owner. Kirschbaum commits suicide instead. The Gestapo take hostages who will be killed if the culprit doesn't step forward. Jakob turns himself in; under torture, he confesses there is no radio. He is marched to a public square and ordered to say the radio is a myth, but he merely laughs and is shot dead. The ghetto residents are sent to the camps. During the journey, Lina spies the Russian troops advancing in the distance.

In prospect, *Jakob the Liar* sounds like one of those inspirational turkeys we jaded critics love to sharpen our knives over. Set during the Nazi occupation of Poland, the story tells how a simple Jewish man brings hope to his ghetto neighbours by fabricating radio bulletins about an impending Allied victory. The premise offers the kind of portentous irony that tempts Hollywood to make a sanctimonious meal of it. By way of further soggy discouragement, the star is Robin Williams, herein afforded an opportunity to resume his duties as Holy Fool of the Universe. I was expecting *Life Is Beautiful* meets *Good Morning, Warsaw*, but *mea culpa* the actual film doesn't invite a cynical response. While it never scales any great heights, *Jakob* remains a doggedly honest work.

Jurek Becker's best-selling 1969 novel *Jakob der Lügner* was previously adapted by East German film-maker Frank Beyer in 1974, and it's worth remarking how Jakob's Teutonic 'k' has survived into this version. That foolhardy decision alone will probably scotch the movie's chances at the multiplex, but it suitably betokens a production that feels solidly European in temper. A veteran of French television, director Peter Kassovitz lacks the technical bravura of his more celebrated son Mathieu of *La Haine* fame (who has a minor role here). After a few experimental camera twirls, the senior Kassovitz hunkers down to a meditative rhythm which allows the gravity of faces and settings plenty of leisure to sink in. It might be stretching a point to say the film possesses a Bressonian austerity. Yet in their less rigorous way, Kassovitz and screenwriting partner Didier Decoin follow an analogous policy of dedramatising situations that would ordinarily head straight for the jugular.

For instance, the young deportee whom Jakob squirrels away in his attic is plainly meant to evoke Anne Frank. However, the movie draws upon this card only to underplay it, keeping the character a muted presence in the background and granting us the freedom to discover the tremulous beauty of the child actor Hannah Taylor Gordon for ourselves. The same drive towards asceticism leads the film-makers to throw a wet blanket over the possibilities for comedy. ostensibly, *Jakob* is a robust folk fable which shows how the traditional mordancy of Yiddish humour serves as spiritual capital against hard times. In broad accordance with this idea, the plot device of the apocryphal radio involves much quasi-farcical scurrying around and hiding in closets as a wide array of types vainly attempt to discern its whereabouts. Yet it's difficult to laugh when Kassovitz's scrupulously aloof staging drains away the emotional colouring in nearly everything. He gets sizeable help from DP Elemér Ragáyi, whose minimalist palette varies muddy blues and browns with overcast greys. The monochrome gloom scarcely lifts even in the big cathartic sequence where, bruised and bloodied, Jakob defies his SS captors on the scaffold. At long last, a shaft of sunlight breaks through to punctuate the little man's moral triumph but it's an extremely watery beam that you have time to register only subliminally before it fades. Kassovitz doesn't supply epiphanies on cue, the audience is expected to use its own capacity for feeling.

The main exception to this rule is the final scene, which slaps on a pretty touch of magic realism to leave the viewer at least vaguely smiling. While the *deus ex machina* is duly tagged as ironic, it still comes across as a gimmicky concession to popcorn sensibilities. Otherwise, the movie is selfless and that includes Williams, who tones down his usual sad-sack clowning to give an impressively interiorised performance. *Jakob the Liar* has neither the cinematic panache nor the fascinating ambiguity of *Life Is Beautiful*. It's a decent, dignified, slightly mouldy picture whose virtues are largely negative ones. But movies of true integrity aren't so frequent that they can be easily passed up.

VILLAGE VOICE, 9/28/99, p. 128, Michael Atkinson

Hope. Hope divine, hope springs eternal, Star *Wars: A New Hope,* Hope Lange, the Hope Diamond, Bob Hope. You can't help it—hope's what buckjumps into your head while you're immersed in the feel-good gravy that is *Jakob the Liar*, Robin Williams's newest expression of his own saintliness. Bringing hope, chuckles, and joy to the Vietnam War and cancer-morbid children was just the warmup; bringing a smile and maybe a rueful tear to the Holocaust is the main event.

Yes, hope as looming and insurmountable as, well, a mountain of teeth. Holocaust heartwarmers have become big business, but it's not too late to be properly qualmish about the ongoing cultural project dedicated to making corpse-piled recent history safe and delicious for middle-class moviegoers. *Jakob the Liar,* from the sharp-tongued Jurek Becker novel, succeeds in being less Benigni-rific than stale, menschy schmaltz, and though Williams is The Clown That's Still Crying, he owes little to that Jerry Lewis ghost film and more to grandpa Jonathan Winters, improvising routines from kitchenware and doing Churchill impressions. As Jakob, a ghetto Jew during the Occupation who tells his neighbors about a radio broadcast overheard in the Gestapo's office (the Russians are coming!) and then must concoct a litany of stories afterward to keep their spirits up, Williams has at least the opportunity to be beleaguered by history. His compulsive laugh-getting emerges mostly with Lina (the dreary Hannah Taylor Gordon), a 10-year-old orphan whose secret shelter in Jakob's attic gives the latke maker concern when everybody, including the Gestapo, wants his hidden radio, which doesn't exist.

But Robin keeps on tikkun. *Jakob the Liar,* written and directed by Peter Kassovitz (father of Mathieu, who shows up, and a prolific manufacturer of French TV movies) and shot in the usual Holocaust catalogue tones of charcoal, olive, and taupe, avoids sick-making uplift until the coda, but avoids emotional wounds as well. Even the casting—sarcastic patriarch Alan Arkin, nervous barber Bob Balaban, bullying yenta Liev Schreiber—telegraphs a Borschty lightness ("That schmendrick Hitler!"), and the Nazis are *Indiana Jones* villains. Things get truly dire when Lina goes feverish, and wizened doctor Armin Mueller-Stahl tells Williams that the best medicine for her is more cock-and-bull stories.

The implication at this point seems to be that the world in general could heal its many wounds if only we let Robin Williams twist the truth. But *Jakob the Liar* also feels creepily like an unconscious metaphor for Williams's entire career: he will say or do anything at all to please us, even if martyrdom is his reward. We can only hope.

Also reviewed in:
CHICAGO TRIBUNE, 9/24/99, Friday/p. A, Mark Caro
NEW REPUBLIC, 10/25/99, p. 32, Stanley Kauffman
NEW YORK TIMES, 9/24/99, p. E12, Janet Maslin
VARIETY, 9/13-19/99, p. 51, Todd McCarthy
WASHINGTON POST, 9/24/99, p. C5, Stephen Hunter
WASHINGTON POST, 9/24/99, Weekend/p. 45, Desson Howe

JAWBREAKER

A TriStar Pictures release of a Kramer-Tornell production in association with Crossroads Films. *Producer:* Stacy Kramer and Lisa Tornell. *Director:* Darren Stein. *Screenplay:* Darren Stein. *Director of Photography:* Amy Vincent. *Editor:* Troy Takaki. *Casting:* Lisa Beach and Sarah Katzman. *Production Designer:* Jerry Fleming. *Costumes:* Vikki Brinkkord. *Make-up:* Carol Strong. *Stunt Coordinator:* Scott McElroy. *Running time:* 85 minutes. *MPAA Rating:* R.

CAST: Rose McGowan (Courtney Shayne); Rebecca Gayheart (Julie Freeman); Julie Benz (Marcie Fox); Judy Evans Greer (Fern Mayo); Chad Christ (Zach Tartak); Ethan Erickson (Dane Sanders); Charlotte Roldan (Liz Purr); Pam Grier (Detective Vera Cruz); Carol Kane (Miss Sherman); Tatyana Ali (Brenda); Kall Harrington (Super Star #1); Alexis Smart (Superstar #2); Lisa Robin Kelly (Cheerleader #2); Michael McClafferty (College Stud); Alexandra Adl (Cheerleader #1); Joni Allen (Make-up Monger #1); Vylette Fagerholm (Make-up Monger #2); Ann Zupa (Gothic Girl); Jan Linder (Customer); Brian Gattas (Drama Student #1); Claudine Claudio (Drama Student #2); Jessica Gaynes (Wannabe #1); Jane Connelly (Wannabe #2); Tommy McKay (Officer); Marita Black (Dreamgirl #1); Dan Gerrity (Dreamperson #2); Rebecca Street (Mom Freeman); Jeff Conaway (Marcia's Father); William Katt (Mr. Purr); P.J. Soles (Mrs. Purr); Sandy Martin (Nurse); Rachel Winfree (English Teacher); Sophia Abu Jamra (Biology Teacher); Donna Pieroni (Cooking Teacher); Rick Lindland (Auto Stud); Allison Robertson (The Donnas #1); Brett Anderson (The Donnas #2); Maya Ford (The Donnas #3); Torry Castellano (The Donnas #4); Billy Butler (High School Stud #2); Allison Thayer (Superstar #3).

LOS ANGELES TIMES, 2/19/99, Calendar/p. 14, Kevin Thomas

"Jawbreaker," Darren Stein's wickedly hilarious sendup of high school mores, takes its title from that hard candy about the size of a pingpong ball. Although not as serious or sophisticated, this zesty film rekindles fond memories of "Heathers" of some years back in its dark view of teenagers.

Courtney (Rose McGowan), the icy undisputed queen of Reagan High, comes up with what she insists on calling a "clever prank" even after it goes lethally awry. To celebrate the 17th birthday of one of her three veritable ladies-in-waiting, Courtney decides that she and the others will kidnap the girl, bind and gag her, and put her in the trunk of a car and release her for a surprise breakfast. Guess what? When the girls open the trunk, they discover that the birthday girl has asphyxiated because Courtney decided to gag her with a jawbreaker.

What fun Stein has in taking it from there. From the get-go, Rebecca Gayheart's Julie, who actually has a sense of decency lurking beneath her allegiance to the all-powerful Courtney, wants to go to the police, but she's overruled by this callous campus leader, seconded by Julie Benz's Marcie, an airhead who sucks up Courtney's every word. Very swiftly, however, there's a major complication: Wistful class nerd Fern (Judy Greer) inadvertently learns what happened.

No sooner has Julie declared to Courtney, "You can't hide a murder with a make-over" than Courtney has done just that, transforming Fern, re-christened Vylette, into a lovely swan in return for her silence.

Designer Vikki Brinkkord has come up with closets full of trashy chic finery so that the girls will cut a swath the second they step out of their boudoirs, and Carol Strong's makeup and hairstyles complete their picture to brazen perfection.

Something will, of course, give before the end, but when it does it is as inspired as the rest of the film. While Courtney is coaching Vylette to become a campus star so intently she fails to realize she may be creating a rival, Julie becomes increasingly alienated from Courtney, rediscovering her values and wrestling with her conscience. (A blackmailing Courtney points out that Julie, like it or not, has allowed herself to become an accomplice.) Meanwhile, Pam Grier—yes, the one and only—plays a canny police detective investigating the death of the girl in the trunk.

Courtney is one of the bitchiest dames on the screen since Joan Crawford's Crystal in George Cukor's "The Women." Her soulless prattle is consistently amusing, and the silly chatter between her and her followers becomes the heart of the film, which suggests—admittedly not for the first time, but wittily all the same—that to true believers popularity and the intoxicating power it confers is so all-important that nothing else matters, not even death.

Stein deftly keeps things crackling between his actresses, while Grier easily commands the screen every second she's on camera and Carol Kane contributes a delightful portrayal of the prim but firm principal of Reagan High (a composite of the local Dorsey and University high schools). This is actually Stein's second film, and it leaves us looking forward to Stein's debut film, the soon-to-be-released "Sparkler."

NEW YORK POST, 2/19/99, p. 54, Jonathan Foreman

Bad movies come in many forms. Some just don't work. Some are too corny or cheesy to digest. But a very few of them, like this one, make you want to shower in disinfectant.

Even within the overworked genre of dark comedy, the loathsome, ruthlessly unoriginal "Jawbreaker" scrapes the bottom of the barrel.

It's about someone getting killed by accident during some high jinks, and the trouble nasty people get into trying to cover it up.

The movie isn't funny or scary or cool. It's slimy and sleazy and, thanks to atrocious writing and crude directing, it wastes the looks and talent of two gorgeous young actresses, Rose McGowan and Rebecca Gayheart.

"Jawbreaker" begins as an inept rip-off of "Heathers," with the first of many slow-mo, floor-level shots of four high school beauties walking down a corridor in miniskirts and improbably high heels.

A confusing voice-over tells us at length which of the four is which, and what they think of each other.

Cut to the birthday kidnapping of Liz (Charlotte Roldan) by the other three. They gag her with a baseball-sized jawbreaker and throw her into the trunk of a car.

When they open the trunk, they find she has choked to death on the giant candy.

Courtney (McGowan), the ringleader, decides to take the corpse back to Liz' Beverly Hills house and make it look as if she had been raped and murdered.

They are in the house, arranging the body, when Fern (Judy Greer), the school dork, arrives with Liz's homework.

Courtney persuades Fern not to spill the beans in exchange for a makeover—new clothes, bleached hair and a new name.

Julie (Gayheart) decides she doesn't like any of this. She leaves the new fabulous foursome and takes up with a drama student named Zack (Chad Christ, who looks like Ethan Hawke, down to the fuzz on his chin).

Pam Grier, in a small part as the investigating police detective, gives the only believable performance.

McGowan, usually so magnetic, is terrible throughout, and Gayheart, despite the exposure given her perfect cheekbones, does her fledgling acting career no favors.

But the fault presumably lies not with the unfortunate cast but with the ugly vision and rotten lines provided by writer-director Darren Stein.

NEWSDAY, 2/19/99, Part II/p. B7, Gene Seymour

The most arresting visual image in "Jawbreaker" is the recurring slow-motion shot of four dangerously well-dressed vixens sauntering and swaggering down the middle of a high school corridor as if it were their private runway.

One feels guilty bringing up, say, the climactic showdown in "The Wild Bunch," as a comparison. But then again, a movie like "Jawbreaker" is practically begging from the start to be a guilty pleasure.

In fact, writer-director Darren Stein's darkly comic homage to "Heathers," "Carrie" and other chronicles of high school social mayhem seems so brazen in its bid for camp cultdom that you can almost see the stress lines. Still, while "Jawbreaker" doesn't quite rise to the level of its predecessors, those who hated high school for whatever reason may find some cathartic release in its nasty little soul. Eventually.

Stein's setting is Ronald Reagan High School, whose social pyramid is topped, like a fake cherry on a sundae, by the aforementioned dressed-to-kill quartet whose fearsome beauty and fashion sense is so dazzling that everything and everyone around them fades. As far as Courtney Shane (Rose McGowan), their snarling, domineering ringleader, is concerned, nothing else in life matters except their mere existence.

Then, one morning, three of the girls decide to give the fourth a 17th birthday she'll never forget by kidnaping her from her bed, gagging her with a jawbreaker, tying her with duct tape and tossing her in the trunk as a joke. The joke's on them when they open the trunk and find their friend has gagged on the gag.

Courtney, as usual, takes charge. No cops, she commands. She and the others improvise a cover-up which hits a snag when Fern Mayo (Judy Evans Greer), the school doormat, accidentally overhears their plans. Rather than add to the body count, Courtney offers Fern the makeover of her dreams in return for her silence. Now, Fern's in with the in-crowd while ex-clique member Julie (Rebecca Gayheart) is on the outs because of an afflicted conscience.

Stein gives "Jawbreaker" a garish veneer and a cluttered design that owes as much to low-rent horror movies as it does to exploitation epics of the 1970s. But for all the quirky, kinky moments and the occassional casting coup (Let's hear it for Pam Grier as—honest!—Detective Vera Cruz!), the movie often risks choking on its own sticky campiness.

Ultimately, it's McGowan who, unlike her character, prevents such suffocation and takes full advantage of the fact that she has all the best lines. Her Courtney belongs to the gallery of insightful, witty villains whose comeuppance, however well-deserved, is a bit of a shame. The only stretch in "Jawbreaker" that matters is McGowan's bravura turn.

VILLAGE VOICE, 2/23/99, p. 120, Dennis Lim

"Dork," as we know, is the indie flavor of the month; it's also, as done by cross, witless (and, almost invariably, young white male) writer-directors, a *very fucking bad thing*. Case in point *Jawbreaker*, in which three fabulously popular high school vixens kidnap a friend as a birthday prank, and stuff the titular candy down her throat. Not surprisingly, she dies, leaving the evil one (Rose McGowan), the brainless one (Julie Benz), and the remorseful one (Rebecca Gayheart) to deal with it in very different ways. They're soon found out by class nerd Fern (Judy Evans Greer); can a Faustian makeover be in the cards? There are blatant references to *Heathers* and *Carrie*, among other teen staples, because *Jawbreaker* is, you see, a "spoof" or "homage." Only it isn't—director Darren Stein's script is slack and tin-eared, too feeble to pass for satire, and inadequate even by lazy-pastiche standards. Only the soundtrack (the Donnas, Imperial Teen) and the irrepressible McGowan make it fractionally more bearable.

Also reviewed in:
CHICAGO TRIBUNE, 2/19/99, Friday/p. B, Mark Caro
NEW YORK TIMES, 2/19/99, p. E10, Janet Maslin
VARIETY, 2/8-14/99, p. 79, Emanuel Levy
WASHINGTON POST, 2/19/99, p. C1, Stephen Hunter
WASHINGTON POST, 2/19/99, Weekend/p. 37, Desson Howe

JEANNE AND THE PERFECT GUY

A Strand Releasing release of a Les Films du Requin production in association with Le Studio Canal Plus/France 2 Cinema/M6 Films/Orsans Productions. *Producer:* Cyriac Auriol and Pauline Duhault. *Director:* Olivier Ducastel and Jacques Marineau. *Screenplay (French with English subtitles):* Oliver Ducastel and Jacques Martineau. *Director of Photography:* Mathieu Poirot-Delpech. *Editor:* Sabine Mamou. *Music:* Philippe Miller and Jacques Martineau. *Choreographer:* Sylvie Giron. *Sound:* Jean-Jacques Ferran and Jean-Pierre Laforce. *Art Director:* Louis Soubrier. *Costumes:* Juliette Chanaud. *Running time:* 98 minutes. *MPAA Rating:* Not Rated.

CAST: Virginie Ledoyen (Jeanne); Mathieu Demy (Olivier); Jacques Bonnaffe (Francois); Valerie Bonneton (Sophie); Frederic Gorny (Jean-Bapitste); Denis Podalydes (Julien); Laurent Arcaro (The Messenger); Michel Raskine (The Plumber); Damien Dodane (Jacques); David Saracino (Remi); Nelly Borgeaud (Jeanne's Mother); René Morad (Jeanne's Father); Jean-Marc Rouleau (Friend Olivier); Sylvain Prunenec (Jerome); Emmanuele Goizc (The Bookseller); Marie Guittier (The Nurse); Judith Guittier (The BDE Lady); Christiane Millet (The Night Nurse); Cedric Brenner (The BDE Guy); Nicolas Seguy (Edouard); Johanna Menuteau (Nathalie); Axelle Laffont (Helene); Grégory Sauvion (Richard); Linh Bui My (Self Maid); Juliette Chanaud (Cinema Cashier); Philippe Mangeot (Act Up Militant); Elise Caron (Jeanne, Voice).

LOS ANGELES TIMES, 2/19/99, Calendar/p. 14, Kevin Thomas

Olivier Ducastel and Jacques Martineau's effortlessly charming musical "Jeanne and the Perfect Guy" is likely to remind you of the classic "Umbrellas of Cherbourg," and not just because its leading man, Mathieu Demy, is the son of "Umbrellas'" late director, Jacques Demy.

Ducastel and Martineau's songs, like those of "Umbrellas"' Michel Legrand, have a sweetness and buoyancy, and flow naturally out of everyday life. Similarly, its stars are not trained singers and dancers, which makes for a refreshing lack of slickness.

For all its celebration of romance and young love, however, "Jeanne and the Perfect Guy" is inevitably a much darker film. When Jeanne (Virginie Ledoyen), a receptionist at a chic Paris travel agency, locks eyes with Demy's Olivier aboard a Metro train, she knows in a flash she's at last found "the perfect guy." A liberated modern woman, Jeanne is upfront about the considerable "research" she's done in her quest for Mr. Right; "if the sex is no good, it can't be love," she remarks to Olivier.

Olivier, who may be a student, is more boyish than the debonair but ultra-bourgeois executive (Frederic Gorny) or the hunky messenger (Laurent Arcaro) who have been pursuing Jeanne at work, but her newest lover drives her wild.

After an ecstatic night of love, Olivier levels with Jeanne: a drug user some six years earlier, he has tested HIV-positive. She responds easily that it's not a problem for her because he used a condom. Their romance blossoms, but you sense that Olivier fears that time is running out for him. Ledoyen, one of the most promising of the new generation of French actresses, and Demy, who has the dark, expressive eyes of his mother, director Agnes Varda, are most appealing and poised.

"Jeanne and the Perfect Guy" is not the first film musical to play the exhilaration of the musical form against the specter of AIDS, but Ducastel and Martineau develop the contrast with stunning emotional impact, illuminating not only Jeanne and Olivier's relationship but also AIDS activism in all its impassioned commitment. The poignancy of their romance becomes underlined by the fact that they are both acquainted with Francois (Jacques Bonnaffe), a member of ACT UP, yet are unaware of the coincidence, which proves to be crucial.

The way in which Ducastel and Martineau bring their story to a conclusion is inspired in its tough-mindedness. American audiences may feel that the film seems dated in that its emphasis on the importance of AIDS awareness is scarcely news, at least in the U.S. (You may also be wondering, whether Olivier is in any special treatment program or, for that matter, why he's still smoking.) Yet, sad to say, "Jeanne and the Perfect Guy," while avoiding heavy-handed preachiness, will be relevant until there's a cure for AIDS.

NEW YORK, 4/26/99, p. 75, Peter Rainer

Jeanne and the Perfect Guy is a French musical about a frisky woman (Virginie Ledoyen) with a panting horde of boyfriends. Her truest love turns out to be an HIV-positive heartthrob (Mathieu Demy, son of Agnes Varda and Jacques Demy). The filmmakers try for a bittersweet lyricism à la Jacques Demy's *The Umbrellas of Cherbourg* but end up with something closer to his genial misfire *The Young Girls of Rochefort*. The movie's combination of froth and political activism doesn't gel, and the song-and-dance numbers never achieve liftoff, perhaps because nobody involved can sing or dance.

NEW YORK POST, 4/16/99, p. 66, Jonathan Foreman

Tone deaf, if occasionally charming, the new French musical "Jeanne and the Perfect Guy" has pretensions to saying something about AIDS. But it works mainly as a hymn to bralessness as practiced by fetching young French actresses.

It also proves that "The Umbrellas of Cherbourg" was a fluke.

The fact is, the French have the same cultural block when it comes to movie musicals that they do with rock'n'roll. They don't seem to understand the importance of catchy tunes and lyrics, or that a performer who can only dance like a giraffe in ski boots probably shouldn't dance at all.

And even in musical-land, people should only break into song when the moment is right.

Jeanne (Virginie Ledoyen) is an exceptionally pretty young woman who works as a receptionist. In the first and most enjoyable section of the film, we see her managing her active sex life with Parisian elan, juggling several lovers while keeping an eye out for Mr. Right.

One day she meets Olivier in the Metro and the two of them have such chemistry they actually do it on the train. (You cannot imagine an American musical being so generous with nudity and sex.)

But the morning after, the perfect guy confesses he's HIV positive. The revelation doesn't dampen Jeanne's ardor; in fact she begins to jettison her other lovers. But soon Olivier falls ill.

Meanwhile there's a farcical, subplot involving an ACT-UP activist who knows them both but doesn't know they're a couple.

The music is awful sickly-sweet stuff, though it tries to span a range of styles. The first number—performed by a squad of black and Arab immigrant janitors—is a cheery syncopated world-beat effort with grim lyrics about racial exploitation.

And "Jeanne" even fails on a technical level: the lip-synching is so off that the song-and-dance numbers look like sleepy imitations of scenes from a Bombay masala musical. Although the cameraman of a Bombay musical would know better than to cut the dancers off at the knees.

NEWSDAY, 4/16/99, Part II/p. B7, John Anderson

What is this? Characters, conducting their lives more or less normally, who suddenly burst into song? Who translate their emotional inner lives into lyrics? Who dance in the middle of a critical moment, and in the middle of the street?

Anyone with an MGM-inspired immunity never asked the question, but yes, it's the movie musical, the singing-dancing hallucination on which an entire subculture was founded and survives to this day. And in creating "Jeanne and the Perfect Guy," a confection with a heart of glass, there's no doubt directors/writers Olivier Ducastel and Jacques Martineau knew the deal: They work in absurdity the way Stanley Donen and Gene Kelly worked in suspended disbelief.

The form has been exploded before, very notably by the French—in 1996, Jacques Rivette's "Haut/Bas/Fragile" deglamorized the musical, put it in street clothes and gave it an edge that the pirouetting Jets and Sharks never thought about. But even in Rivette's film, the milieu more or less matched the message. In "Jeanne and the Perfect Guy," the candy-coated aspect of fantastical theater is in such direct opposition to the "facts" of the story that the result is at least satiric, at best tragic.

Jeanne (Virginie Ledoyen) is, well, Ducastel-Martineau's faux Doris Day. While working as a receptionist for Jet Tours and conducting a whirlwind social life, she's really looking for the perfect man. Unlike Doris—or Ann Miller or Debbie Reynolds (although we have our suspicions about Betty Garrett in "On the Town")—Jeanne isn't "saving herself" for marriage: Hers is a more-than-active sex life, a bouncing from bed to bed with little regard for permanent attachment or commitment or disease. And then she meets Olivier (Mathieu Demy), with whom she falls—as they might have said at MGM—head over heels. And then she discovers he's HIV-positive. And on the fast track down.

So much for fairy tales and happy endings, but the juxtaposition of social realism with the bonbon of Philippe Miller's music is intoxicating, as is the cast. Ledoyen, who was most recently seen in "A Soldier's Daughter Never Cries," is not so technical an actress that she can disguise her natural youth or attitude and, as a result, she's naturally joyous to watch—even if she doesn't sing her own songs, and her dance numbers are roughed out and purposely un-slick.

That her costar is Mathieu Demy, whose father, Jacques, directed the most romantic French musical of all time—the all-singing "Umbrellas of Cherbourg"—is coincidental, but only that. Where "Cherbourg" was sugar melting in the rain, "Jeanne and the Perfect Guy" is a slap in the face by Tinkerbell. Yeah, it hurts. And it's surprising.

VILLAGE VOICE, 4/20/99, p. 143, Justine Elias

Here's something you don't see very often: an ACT UP march in Paris in which the principals burst into song. But the scene's strange mix of emotions—joyous musical outbursts in the midst of a politically charged occasion—is typical of *Jeanne and the Perfect Guy,* a contemporary musical in the tradition of Jacques Demy's *Umbrellas of Cherbourg.* The new movie's heroine (a radiant Virginie Ledoyen) is a travel agency receptionist who leaps from one sexual entanglement to the next, hoping to find her ideal man. Trouble is, she has only a vague notion of what she's searching for, so virtually any man her age—from the denim-clad motorcycle messenger who brings her packages to the vain executives at her travel agency office to a handsome stranger on the Métro—is worth a try.

Though she's something of a wildcat in bed, Jeanne has a short attention span when it comes to relationships. The exception is Olivier, played by Mathieu Demy, the son of directors Jacques Demy and Agnés Varda. But Olivier has a secret: he's HIV positive. As usual, Jeanne's morning-after reaction is breezy denial: "That's okay," she chirps. "We used a condom." At this point, the film seems to divide in half: the less interesting story follows Jeanne's almost delusional faith in love as a great healer. The other thread involves François (Jacques Bonnaffee), a gay professor-activist who knows both Jeanne and Olivier, and has far more depth. As a musical, *Jeanne and the Perfect Guy* suffers from a treacly sameness in its songs (the only notable exception is a number performed by the African cleaning staff at Jeanne's office). As a love story, the movie is alternately charming and grim. In the end, the alternately charming and grim. In the end, the message is, the more people profess—and sing about—love, the less they feel it.

Also reviewed in:
NEW YORK TIMES, 4/16/99, p. E20, Stephen Holden
VARIETY, 2/23-3/1/98, p. 80, Derek Elley

JEW IN THE LOTUS, THE

A Blind Dog Films release of a Blind Dog Films production. *Producer:* Laurel Chiten. *Director:* Laurel Chiten. *Based on the book "The Jew in the Lotus:* A Poet's Rediscovery of Jewish Identity in Buddhist India":* Rodger Kamenetz. *Director of Photography:* Peter Wiehl. *Editor:* William Anderson. *Music:* Paul Chiten. *Sound:* Richard Bock. *Running time:* 60 minutes. *MPAA Rating:* Not Rated.

CAST: Rodger Kamenetz (Himself).

NEW YORK POST, 1/29/99, p. 61, Hannah Brown

What is the sound of one ego rapping? This riddle, which has not plagued masters of Eastern mysticism for centuries, has been solved: It would sound like Rodger Kamenetz, the writer and subject of the documentary, "The Jew in the Lotus."

The film, directed by Laurel Chiten, tells the story of Kamenetz's journey, along with a group of rabbis and scholars, to see the Dalai Lama in India.

The Dalai Lama, the Tibetan Buddhist leader, has lived there since fleeing Tibet in 1959, 10 years after the Chinese invaded. He invited these Jews to advise him on "the secret of spiritual survival in exile."

Kamenetz, who wrote a highly regarded book about this trip (also called "The Jew in the Lotus"), went along "as a scribe."

The heart of the film tells how this spiritually troubled writer felt the experience brought him closer to his own Jewish roots, and not to Eastern mysticism, as he assumed it would.

A worrier who says "nervous is my religion," Kamenetz admits he was an unlikely candidate to attain Nirvana.

Distraught since the death of his infant son—the most moving section in the film describes how he and his wife coped with this loss—Kamenetz is at a loss for words only when he talks about this tragedy.

The rest of the time, he and those whom he accompanied on the trip (including a childhood friend, a mystical Hasid and Jews from various parts of the religious spectrum) spout glib pseudo-profundities.

At times, the film seems to be crying out for the "Sleeper"-era Woody Allen to pop up with a line like, "Those achieving oneness can move on to twoness."

However, admirers of Kamenetz's book will undoubtedly adore every minute of "The Jew in the Lotus." Those who haven't yet achieved oneness would probably get more out of renting "Kundun"—or "Bananas."

Also reviewed in:
CHICAGO TRIBUNE, 1/29/99, Friday/p. G, John Petrakis
NEW YORK TIMES, 1/29/99, p. E20, Lawrence Van Gelder

JEWISH SOUL, AMERICAN BEAT

A First Run Pictures release.   Producer: Barbara Pfeffer.   *Director:* Barbara Pfeffer. *Screenplay:* Barbara Pfeffer. *Director of Photography:* Joe Friedman. *Editor:* Cindy Kaplan Rooney. *Running time:* 60 minutes. *MPAA Rating:* Not Rated.

WITH: John Zorn; Annette Insdorf; Moshe Waldoks; Ephraim Buchwald; Egon Mayer; Ann Roiphe; Arthur Hertzberg; Leonard Fein; Alexander Schindler; Yaffa Eliach; Rachel Cowan; Steve Reich; Cynthia Ozick; Tony Kushner; Elizabeth Swados.

NEW YORK POST, 5/27/99, p. 64, Jonathan Foreman

Barbara Pfeffer's 1997 documentary "Jewish Soul, American Beat" tries to illustrate the debate about whether American Jewry is doomed to evaporation through intermarriage and assimilation, or whether it will be refreshed and sustained by a new craving for Jewish roots.

It's a fascinating question. And the best parts of the film are those in which interviewees such as composer Steve Reich explain their dissatisfaction with Jewish upbringings that erred on the side of assimilation or replaced an intellectually rigorous religion with a secular Jewish identity centered on Israel or social activism.

Unfortunately, most of "Jewish Soul" is predictable, superficial stuff that bounces between long, home-movie-style scenes of people at Passover Seders and interviews with an odd selection of Jewish notables.

The only fresh, enlightening material here is in the section dealing with converts—among them an African-American woman who found Reform practice too shallow and became Orthodox.

VILLAGE VOICE, 6/1/99, p. 124, Gary Susman

This documentary's title dares to find something harmonious in the thorny issue of Jewish assimilation in America. Pfeffer bucks conventional wisdom to argue that, despite the moaning about secularism and intermarriage threatening Jewish survival, an encouraging reawakening is sending previously nonobservant Jews back to their religious roots. Pfeffer's evidence—Downtown artists like John Zorn who incorporate their renewed passion for Judaism into their work, Russian émigrés in Brighton Beach eagerly practicing rites forbidden to them for generations, the SRO Shabbat services at the Upper West Side's B'nai Jeshurun—would seem stronger if it were less anecdotal and extended beyond New York City. She also includes the opinions of doubters, including Arthur Hertzberg, who decries as inauthentic the "picking and choosing" approach to Judaism, and Cynthia Ozick, who finds the revival's focus on the "spiritual" a squishy New Age-ism foreign to the Jewish tradition of rigorous study. But while Pfeffer's brief survey raises more questions than it can answer, her optimism, like the apparent joy of her subjects, is refreshing.

Also reviewed in:
NEW YORK TIMES, 5/27/99, p. E5, Lawrence Van Gelder

JOE THE KING

A Trimark Pictures release of a 49th Parallel Productions/Forensic/291 Films/Lower East Side Films production. *Executive Producer:* Janet Grillo and John Leguizamo. *Producer:* Robin O'Hara, Scott Macaulay, Jennifer Dewis, and Lindsay Marx. *Director:* Frank Whaley. *Screenplay:* Frank Whaley. *Director of Photography:* Michael Mayers. *Editor:* Melody London and Miran Miosic. *Music:* Robert Whaley and Anthony Grimaldi. *Sound:* David Alvarez. *Sound Editor:* Tim Walston. *Casting:* Billy Hopkins, Suzanne Smith, and Kerry Barden. *Production Designer:* Daniel Ouellette. *Art Director:* Mylene Santos. *Costumes:* Richard Owings. *Special Effects Make-up:* Rob Benevides. *Stunt Coordinator:* Kristopher Medina. *Running time:* 100 minutes. *MPAA Rating:* R.

CAST: Noah Fleiss (Joe Henry); Val Kilmer (Bob Henry); Karen Young (Theresa Henry); Ethan Hawke (Len Coles); John Leguizamo (Jorge); Austin Pendleton (Winston); Max Ligosh (Mike Henry); James Costa (Ray); Harlee Ott (Dawn); Camryn Manheim (Mrs. Basil); Travis J. Feretic (Rory); Benjamin Styx (Little Ray); Alice Blythe (Alice); Linda Key (Mrs. Williams); Rob Bergenstock (Little Mike); Richard Bright (Roy); Amy Wright (Mary); Michael Taylor (Man in Jerry's Apt.); Lori Eastside (Woman in Jerry's Apt.); Robert Whaley (Jerry); Craig Levine (Dave); Kate Mara (Allyson); Rachel Miner (Patty); Lyn Nagel (Jenny); Sarah Vitale (Brandy); Laura Ligosh (Fooseball Girl); Raymond De Felitta (Mr. Brazer); Jack McNamara (Mr. Dawson); Christopher Wynkoop (Mr. Margolis); Reggie Montomery (Andy); Anthony Todisco (Kenny Orzo); Caitlin Clark (Pat); Raynor Scheine (Doctor); Mitchell Fleiss (Cop #1); Louis Zorich (Judge); Danny Wiseman (Ticket Taker); Guy Griffis (Old Man); Jenny Robertson (Waitress); P.J. Pesce (Detention Security); Tali Cherniawsky (Len's Assistant).

LOS ANGELES TIMES, 10/15/99, Calendar/p. 6, Jan Stuart

[*The following review by Jan Stuart appeared in a slightly different form in* NEWSDAY, 10/15/99, Part II/p. B6.]

High school yearbooks are filled with guys like Joe Henry, the teenager at the troubled heart of "Joe the King." He would be the one with a gray square reading "picture not available" where his graduation photo should be. The one with nothing listed under "Activities." The one who writes defiant adages under "Motto" like "It's better to rule in hell than to serve in heaven."

Ruling in hell would seem to be a legitimate aspiration for this 14-year-old delinquent (a fine Noah Fleiss), who—from the evidence at hand in Frank Whaley's earnest screenwriting and directing debut—has been groveling there since infancy. He is forever tardy at school, where he must slink under the shadow of his janitor father (Val Kilmer), an alcoholic who owes money to half the town. When not being abused by his teachers or taken to task by his parents, he is hit up for his dad's debts and chewed out by the manager of the town restaurant where he is illegally employed.

Joe's only consolation comes from his ex-con work mate (John Leguizamo) and his older brother Mike (Max Ligosh), who is of an age when he would rather be hanging out with his friends. Left to his own devices, Joe takes to stealing everything from a box of Yodels to precious jewelry. Under the circumstances, the only questions left to the viewer are when will the final shoe drop and how.

Whaley, a much undervalued actor, populates his semi-autobiographical story with a credible assortment of townies. He resists the tendency of first-timers to stuff his characters' mouths with poet's flights of fancy, as well as the temptation to fashion some heroic deus ex machina from Joe's guidance counselor (Ethan Hawke).

If anything, "Joe the King" is antisentimental to a fault. Whaley is so determined not to pander, he all but clobbers us with Joe's sufferings. From an over-baked prologue in which a 9-year-old Joe is spanked by a venomous teacher (played by Camryn Manheim like something out of Grimm's Fairy Tales), "Joe the King" trots out the tribulations with an overemphatic hand. By the time Joe reaches into the fridge to draw some succor from a carton of milk, you know the milk has to be putrid.

Much will be made of Kilmer's dissolute turn (look, he let his belly go!) but it's all surface: He never entirely gets down with the role. Karen Young is a revelation. As Joe's beleaguered mom, she telegraphs a spectrum of feelings in a single glance that easily transcends the monochromatic landscape surrounding her.

NEW YORK POST, 10/15/99, p. 58, Jonathan Foreman

"Joe the King" starts off badly, with Camryn Manheim going over the top as a vicious school teacher in an unbelievable school-room scene.

But it eventually grows into a poignant, graceful little film about a teenager growing up poor and lonely in a small town in upstate New York.

It's a bleak story. But actor turned writer/director Frank Whaley, who is supposed to have drawn upon his own youth, tells Joe's tale in an admirably unsentimental, low-key way.

As a result, unlike so many films that deal with unhappy poverty-stricken childhoods in dysfunctional families, this one is never so depressing that you just don't want to know what happens next.

Joe (played at first by Peter Tambakis, and then, for the bulk of the film, by Noah Fleiss) is the second son of Bob (Val Kilmer with a big beer gut), a some-time school janitor and full-time no-goodnik.

Bob is also a drunk and a deadbeat, and Joe cannot go to school or the restaurant where he washes dishes without an adult reminding him of his father's debts. And when Bob gets angry, he's capable of beating Joe's mother Theresa (Karen Young).

Skinny, badly dressed and always hungry, Joe is perpetually late for school. He's also foul-mouthed and a petty thief, though not a bad kid under it all.

In his inarticulate way, he loves both his parents and his older brother. When he steals, it's to help pay off his father's creditors and to replace his mother's record collection (destroyed by Bob in one of his drunken rages).

Eventually, though, Joe's thieving gets him into real trouble.

Fleiss does a fine job of making Joe a sympathetic character, so that you hope things will turn out well for him, even though you know they probably won't. Kilmer, Young and Ethan Hawke as a kindly teacher are all good.

Apart from the odd, hard-to-believe line, Whaley's script is strong and fat-free. His direction gets more assured as the film goes on, and there are some powerful, deftly drawn scenes.

One odd thing is that Whaley depicts the 1970s as the time before shampoo: all the characters sport lank, greasy hair, all the time.

VILLAGE VOICE, 10/19/99, p. 140, Amy Taub

A slight, poignant, sharply detailed coming-of-age film, *Joe the King* is set in a blue-collar community and revolves around a yearning, resourceful 14-year-old who never gets the attention he deserves from his parents. Joe (Noah Fleiss) works as a dishwasher in a greasy spoon so he can pay off the loan sharks threatening his alcoholic father (Val Kilmer) and replace the Johnny Ray records his mother (Karen Young) cherished (his father broke them during a violent argument). What's interesting about Joe is that despite bad parenting he's a friendly, outgoing kid.

The debut feature of the actor Frank Whaley, *Joe the King* starts on a rocky note. The acting is too broad, although the worst offender, Camryn Manheim, quickly disappears from the screen. Whaley seems to have figured out how to direct as he went along, and in the end, he draws a complicated performance from Young as a woman who is a little bit stupid and has been bashed around so much she can't even focus on her kids. Kilmer is appropriately bloated and boozy and menacing, but it sometimes seems as if he thinks he's doing everyone a favor by even showing up.

But the film belongs to Fleiss, and he makes Joe's inner life so transparent that it's heartbreaking to watch the boy dig himself into a hole. Whaley gives Fleiss the space he needs to turn a conventional film into one filled with small, specific revelations about growing up without much money or support or any promise of a better future.

Also reviewed in:
CHICAGO TRIBUNE, 10/22/99, Friday/p. D, Michael Wilmington
NEW YORK TIMES, 10/15/99, p. E18, Stephen Holden
VARIETY, 2/8-14/99, p. 79, Dennis Harvey
WASHINGTON POST, 10/29/99, Weekend/p. 43, Desson Howe

JULIEN DONKEY-BOY

An Independent Pictures/Fine Line Features release of an IP production in association with Forensic/391 Films. *Producer:* Cary Woods, Scott Macaulay, and Robin O'Hara. *Director:* Harmony Korine. *Screenplay:* Harmony Korine. *Director of Photography:* Anthony Dod Mantle. *Editor:* Valdís Oskarsdottir. *Music:* Tracy McKnight. *Sound:* Brian Miksis. *Casting:* Billy Hopkins, Suzanne Smith, Kerry Barden, and Lori Eastside. *Production Designer:* Carrie Fix. *Set Decorator:* Steve Beatrice. *Set Designer:* Jeremy Buhler. *Stunt Coordinator:* Manny Siverio and Jeff Ward. *Running time:* 94 minutes. *MPAA Rating:* Not Rated.

CAST: Ewen Bremner (Julien); Chloë Sevigny (Pearl); Werner Herzog (Father); Evan Neumann (Chris); Joyce Korine (Grandmother); Chrissy Kobylak (Chrissy); Alvin Law (Card Playing Neighbor); Brian Fink (Pond Boy); Miriam Martinez (Teenage Girl); Edgar Eriksson (Bearded Man); James Moix (Dancing Man); Victor Varnado (Rapper); Carmel Gayle (Clothing Store Cashier); Herman Reimmer (Man in Clothing Storre); Virginia Reath (Gynacologist); Mary O'Hara (Nun); Donna Smith (Dancing Woman); Gary Bergman (Piano Player); Tom Mullica (Magician); Archie MacGregor and Jeanmarie Evans (Amnesiac Patients); Ricky Ashley (Hasidic Boy); Courtney Deblis, Marybeth Grunstra, and Heidi Vanderhoof (Skaters); Hy Richards, Barry Wernick, and Clinton Wright (Doctors); Carmela Garcia (Nurse); Punky (Himself).

LOS ANGELES TIMES, 10/15/99, Calendar/p. 20, Kevin Thomas

Harmony Korine's "julien donkey-boy," a film of piercing beauty and pain, takes its title from a thin, intense schizophrenic of perhaps 20. In a prologue that reverberates throughout the film

Julien (Ewen Bremner) comes upon a little boy playing with some turtles by a pond and abruptly snuffs out his life, burying him in a shallow grave accompanied by prayers.

This sudden, shocking act of violence on the part of an otherwise gentle, though profoundly disturbed man, is never explained, but it's surely significant that Julien is much taken with the concept that Jesus died for our sins. Quite possibly Julien was so overwhelmed by the child's innocence that he saw the boy as a perfect candidate for religious sacrifice. Or perhaps he was under the impression that the child was treating—or would treat—the turtles cruelly. Indeed, the terrible act may have been motivated by some or all of the above reasons, and it echoes the opening of Georg Buchner's "Woyzeck," filmed by Werner Herzog, who plays Julien's father.

In a graceful montage Korine introduces Julien's family, each of its members alone, suggesting right from the start their essential isolation. The Queens row house's bleak tone is set by Julien's martinet of a father (Herzog, the erstwhile enfant terrible of the New German Cinema), an immigrant who may or may not be retired but who is suffused with a sense of defeat and longing for his dead wife. He seems to be in denial over Julien's mental state, regarding him, in anger and contempt, as merely stupid. Of his pregnant daughter Pearl (Chloe Sevigny), he denounces as "a dilettante and a slut" as she plays a harp. He reserves his greatest rage and abuse for his younger son Chris (Evan Neumann), a high school wrestler, in whom he sees his only ray of hope.

Living in her own world and only rarely speaking is the children's grandmother (Joyce Korine, the filmmaker's grandmother, whose home serves as the film's main set). Pearl is very loving of Julien, and sometimes, while talking with him from upstairs, allows him the delusional comfort of believing that he is talking to their mother from heaven—shades of J.D. Salinger's "Franny and Zooey." Already under severe pressure from their father, Chris is easily exasperated by the overly intense, easily rattled Julien. Julien, however, is sufficiently functional to work as a kindly and conscientious aide at a school for the blind, where he becomes captivated by Chrissy (Chrissy Kobylak), an 11-year-old whose severe visual impairment has not prevented her from becoming an accomplished ice skater.

Having mapped out his film, which progresses steadily to a shattering yet tender denouement, Korine, after easing his actors into character, allowed them to improvise in the belief that once they had arrived at that state they could do no wrong. As a visionary and inspiring director Korine makes this bold, risky approach work, with Bremner in particular giving a portrayal of wrenching conviction (for which he prepared by working four months as an assistant at New York's Wards Island for the Criminally Insane).

Korine's method fit right into the principles of filmmaking espoused by Danish filmmakers Lars von Trier and Thomas Vinterberg, and thus "julien donkey-boy" became the first American film of their Dogma '95 manifesto intended to reclaim the cinema from what they see as its current state of malaise.

As a result, Korine netted the cinematographer, Anthony Dod Mantle, and the editor, Valdis Oskarsdottir, from Vinterberg's "The Celebration," which probes a far wealthier but easily as dysfunctional a family as Julien's.

Korine, now 25, first came to their attention as the 18-year-old screenwriter of Larry Clark's "Kids" (1995), which he followed with "Gummo" (1997), his group portrait of kids adrift in an impoverished dead-end semirural community in Middle America, which marked his directorial debut.

"julien donkey-boy" was shot in digital video with multiple hand-held cameras, which at once gives it a quality of immediacy in its intimacy and restless camera movement but also a crucial distancing with its grainy, high-contrast imagery. Without its highly expressive jagged, stylized quality, the film, in its raw emotional intensity, might well have been unbearable. So steady is Korine's gaze, and of such a depth of compassion and understanding, that "julien donkey-boy" acquires a spiritual dimension that allows it ultimately to become an act of redemption.

NEW YORK POST, 10/11/99, p. 47, Jonathan Foreman

As sucker bait for the sort of credulous cinast who'll buy anything ugly and boring that looks like it's avant-garde, "julien donkey-boy" could hardly be improved.

Writer-director Harmony Korine tries to prove his rancid stew of cheap shocks, sleaze and phony artiness isn't just a bid for easy notoriety by including lots of scenes featuring people with severe handicaps, and masturbating nuns.

Julien (Ewen Bremner) is a drooling, incomprehensibly chattering 21-year-old who lives with his squalid family in a miserable house in Queens. His ballerina sister Pearl (Chloe Sevigny) is heavily pregnant with Julien's baby, his father (Werner Herzog) is crazy, and his relatively normal brother Chris (Evan Neumann) is a high-school wrestler.

When the father isn't knocking back cough syrup or listening to music while wearing a gas mask, he rants at Chris, telling him to be more manly and less of a loser. (Some of these scenes of calculated eccentricity, which have the feel of improvisation, are mildly funny.)

When Julien isn't having imaginary conversations with Hitler, he's hanging out with blind people at a bowling alley and jumping up and down at a Baptist church.

There are also some unconnected scenes involving a man with no arms who plays the drums with his feet. Towards the end of the movie, Pearl falls down on an ice rink and has a miscarriage. Julien takes the dead fetus home on the bus.

Shot on digital video according to the restrictive conventions of Dogma 95—the vow of cinematic chastity developed by Danish director Lars von Trier—the film has a moments of visual beauty thanks to cinematographer Anthony Dod Mantle.

But for the most part, "julien" looks and feel like a student film, though it's hard to imagine a student film as cynical as "julien donkey-boy," with its sideshow exploitation of the blind and crippled.

NEWSDAY, 10/8/99, Part II/p. B8, John Anderson

The briefly celebrated and now seemingly defunct "Dogme 95 " manifesto created by Lars von Trier, Thomas Vinterberg and several other Danish directors was intended—more or less tongue-in-cheekly—as a refutation of bourgeois slickness and conventionally "decadent" Hollywood moviemaking. So for a virtually anti-narrative nihilist like Harmony Korine to jump on the Dogme bandwagon is a little like the Pope embracing Catholicism.

But jump he has, if not far enough. "Julien Donkey-Boy"—which follows "Gummo," which Korine directed, and "Kids," which he wrote—adopts a number of the "dogma" constraints in its jittery, abstract route to visual unease: no opening director credit, no stationary cameras, no artificial lighting or music. The movie does, however, seem to begin with one "dogma" taboo, murder: the idiotic Julien (Ewen Bremner) strangling a child and burying him beneath the soft and unmistakably excremental earth of Queens, never to be heard from again.

Whether this happens—what's reality and fantasy, or whether Korine is suggesting there's a difference—are matters never quite defined in "Julien Donkey-Boy," which co-stars Chloe Sevigny as Julien's tutu-busting, ballet-dancing sister Pearl (whom Julien may have impregnated) and the great German director Werner Herzog as their martinet father. But then, clarity of narrative is never an issue in "Julien" (another reason its "dogma" pretensions are just that).

Korine, working in the relatively new realm of handheld digital video because of the "intimacy" (his word) it provides, gives us some moments of genuine emotion, mostly through Bremner and Sevigny, sometimes via the mere juxtaposition of imagery. But he's attempting to create a portrait of a schizophrenic mind (whether Julien is actually suffering a personality disorder or mere imbecility seems open to debate). And here his technique is inherently flawed. The definitive schizophrenia experiment, Lodge Kerrigan's "Clean, Shaven" (1995) was both terrifying and sympathetic, specifically because it looked within from without. Korine can create a disordered film, but re-creating a disordered mind is a bit more of a leap. And since he can't seem to resist the cheap laugh or gratuitously queasy visual, the film certainly seems to be more about him than Julien.

As an artist, Korine is primarily a provocateur—Jean-Luc Godard may be the easy reference, especially vis-a-vis "Julien"—but Korine's real role model is Madonna. At one point, Julien, our drooling protagonist, declares at the family dinner table that he wants to recite a poem; you can feel fists clenching the silverware. "Morning, chaos," he begins. "Evening, chaos; dinner, chaos; morning, chaos, evening, chaos; dinner, chaos ..." "Stop it," orders Father (Herzog is a consistently humorous aspect to the movie). "This is all artsy-fartsy stuff," he says, proceeding to tell the family what he does like—via a mangled recount of the final scenes of "Dirty Harry."

The confrontation is apparent, the opponents clear: the recycled cinema of his critics vs. the spontaneous filmic poetry of Harmony Korine.

Unsurprisingly, Korine, pugilist and referee, wins the round.

Does he win the war? Hardly. "Julien" may be that rarest of cultural oysters—the experimental film getting a theatrical release. For that, there should be gratitude. For "Julien" itself, however, very little indeed.

SIGHT AND SOUND, 10/00, p. 47, Xan Brooks

New Jersey, the present. Wandering in a local park, schizophrenic Julien attacks a small boy whom he finds playing with a turtle. Julien works as an attendant at a school for the blind, but the majority of his time is spent at the family home he shares with his father, his grandmother, pregnant sister Pearl and aspiring athlete brother Chris.

Julien's mother died giving birth to Chris, but Pearl preserves Julien's fantasy by masquerading as their mother and phoning him from a nearby room. In the meantime, Julien's father rules the roost: lecturing his offspring over the dinner table, devising fitness regimes for Chris and pouring scorn on Pearl, who is unmarried and will not name the father of her baby. Julien befriends Chrissy, a young blind girl who dreams of being an ice-skater. He travels with her and Pearl to the local skating rink. Picking her way across the ice, Pearl falls heavily and is rushed to hospital, where she loses the baby. Julien tells the nurse that the baby is his, and escapes from the hospital with the foetus. Back home, he clambers into bed and cradles the dead baby.

Julien Donkey-Boy is topped and tailed with tragedies. In its first moments, the title character is seen attacking a small boy and then brushing earth over what appears to be a shallow grave. In its dying minutes, Julien's sister Pearl suffers a miscarriage while carrying what turns out to be his child. Tragedy number one arrives abruptly and is never referred to again (was it a hallucination?). Tragedy two is signposted with a spectral subtlety throughout: little clues sprinkled amid the seeming chaos. In this way the second film from *Gummo* creator Harmony Korine follows its own scrambled sense of plot logic and runs to its own rhythm.

One could argue that, in this respect, Korine's film is in perfect symbiosis with its lead character. Ewen Bremner's Julien (a suburban Nosferatu with raisin-black eyes and detachable dentistry) is a schizophrenic, and *Julien Donkey-Boy* toils to provide an approximation of the schizophrenic's take on the world. Its narrative is scattered, a burst of freeform vignettes. Its editing switches between stuttering jump cuts and leisurely freeze frames. Its soundtrack is muddied and discordant (some of the dialogue sounds as if it's been recorded from a tannoy). Whatever its merits, *Julien Donkey-Boy* is never an easy film; Korine flouts its awkwardness like a badge of honour.

That said, this low-life burlesque is a constant fascination: a maddening, showoffy assault on the senses. Julien's garbled fixation on religious teaching ("cursed be he who sleeps with his sister") hints at the film's denouement, while certain scenes (the fevered Gospel meeting, the wrestling bout) flare up startlingly amid the murky drift that surrounds them. In acting terms, *Julien Donkey-Boy* swiftly becomes a two-horse race. With Chloë Sevigny as Pearl an oddly watery presence here, the real stand-off is between Bremner's central character and director Werner Herzog—compelling as Julien's pedantic, tyrannical father. Certainly, Herzog's earnest description of the climax of *Dirty Harry* ("I truly like that stuff") provides the film's bizarre comedic highlight.

Julien Donkey-Boy is not without precedent. In spirit, the film falls within a strain of kooky family dramas, its portrait of an oddball household harking back to the likes of *Arsenic and Old Lace* (1944) and television's *The Munsters*. In style, it reprises the stream-of-consciousness techniques that Korine honed in his 1997 debut *Gummo*. The fact, then, that *Julien Donkey-Boy* is the first US picture shot under the *Dogme 95* vow of chastity (and uses *Festen* cinematographer Anthony Dod Mantle) finally seems of little significance. Although shot on pixellated, handheld digital video, the film marks no grand departure from Korine's earlier work.

This, perhaps, is the film's final failing. *Gummo* provoked wildly differing responses. Was this a jumbled, non-narrative *tour de force* or a cheap freakshow in arthouse bunting? Was it the one truly revolutionary film of the past 25 years (as Bernardo Bertolucci claimed) or one of the worst pictures ever made (as *New York Times* critic Janet Maslin reckoned)? So *Gummo* exploded, and *Julien Donkey-Boy* repeats. Second time around, the shock of the new just isn't shocking any more.

VILLAGE VOICE, 10/12/99, p. 139, J. Hoberman

A handheld and grainy exercise in cine-stupefaction, Harmony Korine's *julien donkey-boy* was shot on digital video according to the strictly "naturalistic," well-hyped precepts of the Danish Dogma group. It also shares Dogma's unwritten but trademark fondness for cretinous overacting. The movie opens with its eponymous protagonist (Ewen Bremner) punching out the camera, dripping snot and drooling through his metal teeth.

Opening fluid-fest aside, fans of Korine's genuinely disgusting *Gummo* (hyped by Janet Maslin as the worst movie of 1997) may be disappointed. *julien donkey-boy* is more feeble and less unpleasant than Korine's debut—the big shocks in this cattle-tranquilizer are a masturbating nun, an armless drummer, a cigarette-swallowing geek, a potty-mouthed kid with *payess,* and the miscarriage suffered by Julien's sister (poor Chloe Sevigny) after her ludicrously telegraphed tumble on a skating rink. The oh-wow look sugarcoats the inane action. The movie's only really tasteless scene uses a black Baptist church service as a backdrop for Julien's antics.

Korine has suggested that his lowlife, Queens-set family drama is in some sense autobiographical. Be that as it may, filmmaker Werner Herzog plays Julien's punitive father, lugubriously lecturing a second son (Korine look-alike Evan Neumann) to be a "man" and a "winner." After a while, Herzog seems to be commenting on the movie itself: "If I were so stupid I would slap my own face." Well put but, even at that, *julien donkey-boy* is too spastic to connect —the movie just flails the air.

Also reviewed in:
CHICAGO TRIBUNE, 11/5/99, Friday/p. B, John Petrakis
NEW YORK TIMES, 9/29/99, p. E1, Janet Maslin
VARIETY, 9/13-19/99, p. 46, David Rooney
WASHINGTON POST, 10/22/99, Weekend/p. 46, Desson Howe

JUST A LITTLE HARMLESS SEX

A Phaedra Cinema release of an Isn't It Romantic and Miss Q production. *Producer:* Deborah Capogrosso and Rick Rosenthal. *Director:* Rick Rosenthal. *Screenplay:* Marti Noxon and Roger Mills. *Director of Photography:* Bruce Surtees. *Editor:* James Austin Stewart. *Music:* Tito Larriva and Jen Miller. *Music Editor:* Terry Delsing. *Sound:* John Boyd, Stewart Pearce, and (music) Reinhold Mack. *Sound Editor:* Xavier Sol. *Casting:* Rene Haynes, Cathy Henderson-Martin, and Dori Zuckerman. *Production Designer:* Amy Danger. *Art Director:* Joseph Dunn. *Set Decorator:* Dianne Kalemkaris. *Set Dresser:* Brendon Crigler. *Special Effects:* José Ignacio Alvarez. *Costumes:* Kelly Zitrick. *Make-up:* Lorena Lopez. *Stunt Coordinator:* Chuck Waters. *Running time:* 98 minutes. *MPAA Rating:* R.

CAST: Alison Eastwood (Laura); Robert Mailhouse (Alan); Rachel Hunter (Marilyn); Kimberly Williams (Allison); Lauren Hutton (Elaine); Tito Lariva (Chuey); Jonathan Silverman (Danny); Jessica Lundy (Terianne); Michael Ontkean (Jeff); William Ragsdale (Brent); Robin Blazak (Cyndi the Drive-By Hooker); Nuno Bettencourt (Vince the Pizza Guy); David La Mano (Bouncer); Pat Murphy (Racid Guy); Tom Pettit (Married Guy); Daniel O'Connor (Yoga Boy Matt); Tom Rhodes (Yoga Boy Jeremy); Jen Miller (Hostile Creek); Peter Atanasoff (Chuey and the Spatular Guitar); Lyn Bertles (Chuey and the Spatular Violin); Jennifer Condos (Chuey and the Spatular Bass); Nick Vincent (Chuey and the Spatular Drums); Johnny Hernandez (Chuey and the Spatular Percussion); Keith Coogan (Loudmouth Guy).

LOS ANGELES TIMES, 6/11/99, Calendar/p. 6, Kevin Thomas

Rick Rosenthal's sharp, funny yet serious romantic comedy "Just a Little Harmless Sex" shows that not all the possibilities have been mined in that familiar turf, yuppie emotional angst.

Inspired by an incident in his own life, Rosenthal had yet another inspiration: to have Marti Noxon, co-producer of TV's "Buffy the Vampire Slayer," write the women's scenes and Roger Mills, a former assistant director, write the men's scenes, then have them collaborate on the final sequences.

This approach gives the film a welcome edge, suggesting that when it comes to discussing sex, women, among themselves, can get just as raunchy as men. More important, we're made to feel that when members of either sex are getting down and dirty in their sex talk, it is but a prelude to what really concerns them, and that is being in love with someone who loves them in return.

None of this is exactly news, but the film has such verve, such zingy dialogue and such a good ensemble cast that it is a brisk, shrewd delight. Its makers know better than to allow themselves to be caught up in the self-absorption of their characters and therefore create ways in which their people can convincingly learn to look beyond themselves.

A young man, Alan (Robert Mailhouse), driving home after an evening at a strip club to celebrate a friend's birthday, encounters a beautiful young woman (Robin Blazak) with a stalled car. He stops to help, she comes on brazenly and, before you can say Hugh Grant, the cops arrive in force. Alan has no idea the woman is a hooker, and she, as it happens, hits on him at the very moment he's feeling a little uncertain about having the child his lovely wife Laura (Alison Eastwood) wants.

Stunned at the news, Laura gathers her pals Terrianne (Jessica Lundy) and Allison (Kimberly Williams) around her, and they decide to head to a favorite hangout. Wouldn't you know that they arrive not long after Alan and his best pals Danny (Jonathan Silverman) and Brent (William Ragsdale) have left, accompanying Alan home, where he intends to have it out with his wife. No sooner do the guys arrive at Alan and Laura's house than Laura's glamorous mother Elaine (Lauren Hutton) arrives.

A stunning woman of much sophistication, she has wisdom to dispense to her distraught son-in-law while having a little flirtatious fun with his pals, who are knocked out by this dazzling older woman of any young man's fantasies, Elaine is a wonderful role for Hutton—one of her best yet—and she has assured, sultry fun with it.

Elaine is the worldly adult who makes her daughter, son-in-law and their friends look mighty childish in their behavior, yet she also understands that their pain and confusion are very real. When Laura and Alan and their pals finally do confront one another, they start discovering the ways in which they need to grow up.

When Terrianne and Danny, the most brash members of the group, actually start talking to each other, they start dealing with the reasons why their marriage broke up. This is the film's strongest scene, in which an embarrassed Danny discusses a harmless idiosyncrasy wrongly interpreted by Terrianne, who in turn reveals her own hang-ups. To be sure, other revelations ensue before the evening is over. Each the film's key characters has his or her moment of truth, and the ensemble cast responds with skill and passion, especially Williams, when she confesses her true love.

Helping Hutton provide a mature perspective is actor-musician Tito Larriva (formerly of the Plugz and the Cruzados and now of Tito and the Tarantula, he also composed the music for the film). As Chuey the club's chef and proprietor, he observes of the men—and he could be speaking of the women as well—that they all have nice cars, nice homes and all the money they need, but that they are all messed up when it comes to love. These are members of the privileged "want-it-all" yuppie class who are moving toward their 30s and beyond and beginning to fear that they're not going to get everything they want.

Others contributing stellar moments are Rachel Hunter as an observant waitress, Michael Ontkean as seductive yoga instructor and Nuno Bettencourt as a pizza deliveryman with no lack of curiosity.

A TV and film veteran, Rosenthal knows how to make "Just a Little Harmless Sex" zip along breezily with style and assurance yet invite us to reflect as well as laugh. It's a fun diversion that also makes a rash of young actors look good.

NEW YORK POST, 6/11/99, p. 48, Jonathan Foreman

Every overworked battle-of-the-sexes cliche of the decade gets the microwave treatment in "Just a Little Harmless Sex"—an attempt at wry flipness filled with dialogue that ranges from sitcom material desperately in need of a laugh track to squirm-in-your-seat rottenness.

It's an ensemble piece peopled by characters who range from the merely annoying to the truly loathsome.

It opens with three guys in one of those fancy strip clubs that Hollywood types adore. On the way home, married Alan (Robert Mailhouse both wooden and insubstantial) stops to pick up a female motorist stranded in the rain.

Without a word she rewards him with some oral sex. But the police arrive and it turns out that she's a hooker. Alan is arrested, and the cops call his wife, Laura (Alison Eastwood), with the news.

The next thing you know, Laura's thrown Alan out and he's drowning his sorrows with buds Brent (William Ragsdale) and Danny (Jonathan Silverman) at a bar/club straight out of "Ally McBeal."

Meanwhile, Laura has her two best friends Danny's promiscuous ex-wife, Terrianne (Jessica Lundy), and shy Allison (Kimberly Williams)—over for a girls' bonding session replete with dancing and naughty sex talk.

Eventually, the men drive over to the house so that Alan can tell Laura he loves her. But by the time they get there, the women have gone to the club in the hope of picking up some guys "with big hands." The boys go back to the bar but just as they arrive, Laura is fooling around with her yoga instructor.

The scenes with the men are written by Roger Mills, the ones with the women by Marti Noxon. (They co-wrote the predictable last act.) The male characters at least sound like different people.

The only decent performances come from Williams (late of "Father of the Bride") and Lauren Hutton as a sexy mom-in-law (presumably not a stretch).

But given that everyone fluffs their line-readings you wonder if blame for the whole debacle shouldn't fall on veteran director Rick Rosenthal.

NEWSDAY, 6/11/99, Part II/p. B6, John Anderson

Think of the aircraft carrier. During war-time, it serves a very essential purpose. It gets people and devices where they need to be. And yet, although it's hard to ignore, it isn't really what the battle's all about. It needs airplanes. It needs closure.

Think of the set-up to "Just a Little Harmless Sex," a battle-of-the-sexes comedy, as a kind of narrative aircraft carrier, one around which a lot of attractive combatants buzz and strafe and, like Alan (Robert Mailhouse), occasionally crash land.

Leaving a birthday party at a strip club, Alan does the decent thing, stopping in the rain for a stranded woman motorist—a hooker who puts him in the classic Hugh Grant position just as the cops arrive to bust him (in multiple vehicles, in the rain) and, worst of all, call his wife.

A nightmare scenario, as well as a complete contrivance. Fortunately for everyone, this intro to marital hell is over quickly, leaving us with the question of whether Laura (Allison Eastwood) will ever forgive Alan, and with a fairly charming cast of characters to find the answer.

"Just a Little Harmless Sex" is a dialectical prize fight about gender-based anxiety and screenwriting. Written by Marti Noxon and Roger Mills—she wrote the women's lines, he wrote the men's—it sometimes feels like a game of chicken, a can-you-top-this of sexual frankness which Noxon wins, and not prettily. Alan and his buddies Danny and Brent (Jonathan Silverman and William Ragsdale) explore, boorishly, the male side of romantic haplessness while Allison and Terriane (Kimberly Williams and Jessica Lundy) help Laura examine what women really want—and what they do. The overall impresssion is that there are some things either sex would be just as happy to know nothing about.

The cast, however, is a winner. Williams ("Father of the Bride") steals most of her scenes, especially when her repressed Allison does, an impromptu striptease at the HiJinx, the club where most of the film takes place. Silverman (of TV's "The Single Guy") is slimily sympathetic as Danny, who's estranged from wife Terrianne.

VILLAGE VOICE, 6/22/99, p. 154, Jessica Winter

Just in time for Hugh Grant's second coming, a film arrives whose pivotal incident entails a hooker, a front-seat blowjob, and a police bust. Instead of consignment to emasculated docility in movie hell with Julia Roberts, however, transgressor Alan receives more-customary punishment: recent wife Laura just boots him out (though she does get one Anna Scott moment of her own—in a snit that shrieks of *Mommie Dearest*, Laura scissors Alan's head out of their wedding photos). Laura then tosses back some margaritas with the girls (orgasm-challenged Terrianne, exotic dancer-wannabe Allison) and hits the town. Groveling Alan follows with pals in tow (serial dater Brent, ex-girlfriend-hater Danny). This death march ends at the chillingly Roxbury-like HiJinx club, where zany antics play out like a bad episode of *Friends* set at Melrose Place. Mitigating factor for the leonine pizza boy pursuing Allison, the filmmakers have excavated Nuno Bettencourt, late of Extreme and as fetching as he was in his "More Than Words" heyday. His performance mainly consists of tossing his long black hair like he just don't care.

Also reviewed in:
NEW YORK TIMES, 6/11/99, p. E12, Lawrence Van Gelder
VARIETY, 6/14-20/99, p. 33, Lael Loewenstein

JUST THE TICKET

A United Artists Pictures release of a CineSon production. *Executive Producer:* Andie MacDowell and Yoram Pelman. *Producer:* Gary Lucchesi and Andy Garcia. *Director:* Richard Wenk. *Screenplay:* Richard Wenk. *Director of Photography:* Ellen Kuras. *Editor:* Christopher Cibelli. *Music:* Rick Marotta. *Music Editor:* Darrell Hall. *Sound:* Les Lazarowitz and (music) David Mitchell. *Sound Editor:* Lena Marcel. *Casting:* Amanda Mackey Johnson and Cathy Sandrich. *Production Designer:* Franckie Diago. *Art Director:* Henry Dunn. *Set Decorator:* Karin Wiesel. *Set Dresser:* Roman Greller, Eric Metzger, Joe Taglairino, and Jeff Rollins. *Costumes:* Susan Lyall. *Make-up:* Sharon Ilson. *Stunt Coordinator:* Jeff Ward. *Running time:* 115 minutes. *MPAA Rating:* R.

CAST: Andy Garcia (Gary Starke); Andie MacDowell (Linda Paliski); Sullivan Cooke ("Blinker"); Richard Bradford (Benny Moran); Alice Drummond (Lady with Cash); Fred Asparagus (Zeus); Louis Mustillo (Harry the Head); Anita Elliott (Refund Lady at the Met); Patrick Breen (San Diego Vinnie); Laura Harris (Cyclops); Don Novello (Tony); Ron Leibman (Barry the Book); Michael Willis (TV Customer); Jack Cafferty (Newscaster); Molly Wenk (Catholic Schoolgirl Fanny); Daniella Garcia-Lorido (Catholic Schoolgirl Lucy); Abe Vigoda (Arty); André Blake (Casino); Michael P. Morgan (Fat Max); Ronald Guttman (Gerrard, Culinary Director); Helen Carey (Food Critic); Bobo Lewis (Mrs. Dolmatch); Paunita Nichols (Rhonda); Irene Worth (Mrs. Haywood); Brian Schwary (College Kid in Jail); Chris Lemmon (Alex); Davenia McFadden (Social Security Checker); Lenny Venito (Stanley); Richard Wenk ("Good Call Johnny" D.J.); George Palermo (Undercover Cop); Anthony DeSando (Kenny Paliski); Elizabeth Ashley (Mrs. Paliski); Robert Castle (Uncle Donald); Sully Boyar (Uncle Tony); Donna Hanover (Realtor); Luis Aponte (Maury, Funeral Director); Joe Drago (Father V. Crespo); Joe Frazier (Himself); Alfredo Alvarez Calderon (Yankee Stadium Security Chief); Gene Greytak (The Pope); Bill Irwin (Ray Charles); Joanna P. Adler (Vickie); John Tormey (Taxi Cab Driver); Michael Higgins (Confessional Priest); Austin Lyall Sansone (Baby in Womb).

LOS ANGELES TIMES, 2/26/99, Calendar/p. 4, Kevin Thomas

No wonder Andy Garcia signed on as co-producer as well as star of the romantic comedy "Just the Ticket"; writer-director Richard Wenk came up with a juicy part for him as a Manhattan ticket scalper desperate to hold on to the love of his life. She's the radiant Andie MacDowell (who's co-executive producer) as Linda, a Macy's TV saleswoman and culinary student.

Both Garcia and MacDowell have charisma and sexual magnetism to spare and if "Just the Ticket" takes a while to pull its heartstrings taut, it finally kicks in for a strong finish. It's just the ticket for a date night.

As the film opens, Linda has in fact dumped Garcia's Gary. That's not about to stop him, but the truth is that his life is falling apart just as Linda's is taking off. She has a new boyfriend (Chris Lemmon), solid and stable, and has applied to Paris' legendary Cordon Bleu cooking school.

Meanwhile, Casino (Andre Blake), a smooth, well-heeled guy with a Caribbean accent, has moved in on Gary's territory just as he's come up with what he thinks will be the perfect idea for winning her back.

Now Casino is threatening his chance to make a big killing on scalping tickets for the pope's upcoming appearance at Yankee Stadium.

Garcia and MacDowell make Gary and Linda's attraction—and their attraction for each other—palpable, but it's all too understandable why Linda worries about what kind of future she will have with a man who doesn't even possess a Social Security card or any identification to prove that he even exists. Gary knows that Linda is the love of his life, the best thing that ever happened to him, but for all his desperation he cannot even begin to conceive of how to live a regular life. Garcia and MacDowell generate plenty of compassion for Gary and Linda's plight, which they make real and involving.

Not so involving, however, is the time spent in the dicey world of ticket scalpers, which is not all that fascinating and gets a sentimental Runyon-esque gloss. "Just the Ticket" needs to cut to the chase quicker—less time on Gary's grandstanding as fate seems to go against him and more time with Linda. Yet there's no denying Garcia, a most appealing and talented actor, is skilled at pulling out all the stops.

"Just the Ticket" works but its stars are better than it is as a whole.

The film's other solid pleasure is its formidable supporting cast in roles as smartly written by Wenk as they are well-played under his assured direction. Richard Bradford, as Gary's pal and partner, has a career high as an aging ex-fighter and onetime corner man for Joe Frazier; it's the film's Burgess Meredith "Rocky" part. Elizabeth Ashley is on hand as Linda's earthy and wise mother, and Irene Worth, no less, is an amusingly cheap grande dame.

Laura Harris is a heartbreaker as a wistful, pregnant young woman, one of Gary's associates, who's struggling to stay drug-free. Among many others who impress are Paunita Nichols and Bobo Lewis as Linda's neighbors, Ron Leibman as a bookie who tries to give Gary a dose of reality, Bill Irwin as an unctuous insurance man and Michael Higgins as a priest who hears out Gary in the confessional but can't resist asking, "By the way, can you get me a pair of tickets for the Knicks for Friday night?"

"Just the Ticket," which has a zesty score, is lots more Hollywood than John Cassavetes, whom director Wenk has said he wanted to emulate. Since his film is at heart traditional escapist entertainment that is doubtlessly just as well.

NEW YORK POST, 2/26/99, p. 48, Rod Dreher

Why can't Andy Garcia find a hit? In "Just the Ticket," he looks terrific, and his performance is energetic, charismatic and immensely appealing. Yet the picture is a thorough drag, a slapdash mess, another misfire movie choice for a talented actor whose career is by now running on fumes.

Garcia plays a New York City ticket scalper named Gary, a lovable rogue who has never held a straight job. Gary scams his way through harried Manhattan days, making deals on the street, dodging undercover cops and hanging out with his buddies.

The gregarious grifter is eagerly anticipating a windfall scalping tickets for the pope's upcoming visit, which should score him enough capital to get his life in order and leave his low-rent profession.

Problem No. 1: He has to avoid trouble from the cops and a sleazy competitor (Andre Blake) trying to upend his business, and keep his game going until the Holy Father shows up.

Problem No. 2: He's still stuck on the lovely Linda (Andie MacDowell), a former girlfriend he can't get out of his mind.

"Just the Ticket" jumps jitterishly from romantic comedy to caper picture, and wobbles on something in between. None of it is very interesting, but leaving the non-starter romance alone for the incipient madcappery around Gary's peculiar job situation would have made by far the better film. It's same song, umpty-second verse, for MacDowell, who, as ever, plays a bland beauty whose job it is to stand there waiting for Mr. Man to get his act together.

Garcia is so good he nearly salvages the picture in the last half hour, which spends more time on the friendship between Gary and his big-hearted elderly mentor, Benny (Richard Bradford). The bright, graceful denouement gets the emotional pitch perfect—a sweet, touching ending for a third-rate movie.

NEWSDAY, 2/26/99, Part II/p. B6, John Anderson

Since Muslims got pasted in "The Siege" and Jews had to pay "A Price Above Rubies," maybe it's just karma that Catholics now get sideswiped in "Just the Ticket."

It's hard to say what's weirder in this antic romance by Richard Wenk, aka the Andy Movie—Andy Garcia as ticket scalper extraordinaire Gary Starke and Andie MacDowell as his ex-girlfriend Linda Paliski, who has big plans that don't include Gary. Is it that Gary needs to make a big killing on the Pope? That one priest wants illicit Knicks tickets while another is drunk at a funeral? Or that they both apparently missed Vatican II because they're still speaking Latin?

Maybe these are just distractions calculated to take our mind off the idea that a ticket scalper—a certified urban parasite if there ever were one—is the hero of what is essentially a western set in Manhattan, about Gary and his band of merry men (which includes one pregnant junkie played by Laura Harris) and the Caribbean hustler Casino (Andre Blake) who's muscling Gary off his turf. Given the unlikely complexion of the rest of the movie, Casino's blackness probably needs addressing, but let's deal with one smear campaign at a time.

Linda, a talented chef who wants to go to the Cordon Bleu, has tossed Gary off, but just as tenaciously as he pursues tickets to the appearance by Pope John Paul II (played at one idiotic point by look-alike Gene Greytak), Gary stays hot on Linda's heels. His attempts at respectability are sincere, but since he has no proof of residence or even birth (apparently having been raised by wolves under the West Side Highway), Gary can't enter the world of the documented and legitimate. His is a tax-free existence defined by Madison Square Garden and the New York Coliseum.

In what is pure fantasy and a hugely sentimental, if misdirected, bouquet to New York (largely about the types of people Mayor Rudolph Giuliani has been chasing off the streets), illogic and inanity dance blithely down the street to the sounds of Harold Arlen, Dr. John and the Voices of Gospel, First African Methodist Episcopal Church, Los Angeles (this during the Pontiff's New York appearance ... oh, never mind).

Beautifully shot by the stealth cinematographer Ellen Kuras and produced by Garcia and Gary Lucchesi, it makes use of thoroughly unlikely locations and, if you can divorce yourself from the fact that bad taste knows no religious restrictions, it may be—brace yourself—just the ticket.

SIGHT AND SOUND, 6/99, p. 47, Geoffrey Macnab

New York ticket tout Gary Starke learns that the Pope is coming to give a mass at Yankee Stadium. Seeing this as an opportunity to secure his future and convince girlfriend Linda he is more than just a hustler, Gary tries to get hold of as many tickets as he can. But he has a rival, Casino, a tout with mob connections. Exasperated by Gary, Linda has started dating another man and now plans to study cookery in Paris.

Gary's old partner Benny lends him the money to buy more tickets and dies soon after. Gary gives the oration at his funeral, to which ex-heavyweight champ Joe Frazier turns up, giving substance to Benny's stories about his past exploits as a boxing coach. Disguised as a nun, Gary does brisk business selling tickets at Yankee Stadium. His cover is blown and he is arrested, but he sees the Pope from his cell. Once released, Gary brawls with Casino and is beaten up. Skulking in his one-room apartment, Gary is visited by a man who tells him he is the sole benefactor of Benny's life insurance and presents him with a cheque. With the cash, he is able to buy Linda the premises for a new restaurant. She abandons her trip to Paris.

Gary Starke, the ticket-tout hero of writer director Richard Wenk's *Just the Ticket* could be a character from a Damon Runyon short story. A street hustler, a scalper with an eye for the main chance, he wears the clothes (gaudy Hawaiian shirts and baggy trousers) and speaks the patter. His associates are lowlifes like him, but all with their own code of honour.

So far, so familiar: in its early scenes, *Just the Ticket* seems to be developing into a likable comedy-romance set against the backcloth of the touts' murky world. Wenk (director of *Vamp*) shot most of the film on location in New York. He captures the frenetic quality of big-city street life, complete with touts who seem to see themselves as urban cowboys. ("There are no rules ... it's the wild west here," one character observes.) In theory, combining the rough-edged, street-level drama with a love story should not have presented a problem. Chaplin did it in *City Lights* (1931) and countless other film makers have followed suit. Nevertheless, in *Just the Ticket* there is a dispiriting sense that two different, largely incompatible films have been yanked together.

Whenever Andy Garcia (who also produced this particular film) and Andie MacDowell are on screen together, the tone changes. The edgy, improvisatory quality is lost and the storytelling becomes blander and less credible. In his scenes with MacDowell, Garcia seems so witty and resourceful that it's hard to credit that this is the same character who lives in a shabby apartment and doesn't even have the wherewithal to get himself a social-security number. MacDowell's is a thankless role. While she is holed up in the kitchen (she dreams of becoming a chef), Garcia gets the chance to clown around. She is the straight man to his comedian. At times, for example when he offers to sell a television on her behalf in return for a date, her sole function seems to be to set up his one-liners.

The whimsy grates. Garcia's routines with his pet dog and his habit of bouncing a ball wherever he goes are more irritating than endearing. Easily the strongest scenes are those when he is out and about, hustling, passing on tickets or tips, or trying to steal a march on rival tout Casino. The street sharks, who all have names like Barry the Book or Harry the Head, are sharply and affectionately observed. Gary's relationship with oldtimer Benny (beautifully played by Richard Bradford) provides the few moments of grace and pathos. The rest of the crew dismiss Benny as a broken-down has been—wrongly, it transpires, when ex-heavyweight champ 'Smoking' Joe Frazier (playing himself) turns up at his funeral.

After Frazier's cameo, Gary's bizarre encounter with the Pope seems anti-climactic, as indeed does the rest of the film. *Just the Ticket* peters out in as contrived and mawkish a way as any tearjerker. By glossing over the harshness, seediness and violence of Gary's ticket-tout life on the streets, Wenk ends up hiding precisely what made the premise for the film so vivid and arresting in the first place.

VILLAGE VOICE, 3/9/99, p. 124, Jessica Winter

Familiar sparks are in bountiful supply throughout *Just the Ticket*, about Gary (Andy Garcia), a New York ticket scalper trying to woo back his former love, aspiring chef Linda (Andie MacDowell). In the first half-hour alone, Gary calls Linda "my amazing grace," hopes for "a light at the end of the tunnel," and pleads aloud for "something to hang my hat on"—Linda points out that in Gary's presence "I just melt," and comments upon his "puppy-dog eyes." Once Linda gazes into those canine orbs and intones, "You're special," one aches for Courtney Love to show up, send Linda back into the kitchen, dare Gary to fuck her, and then hit him up for Knicks tickets. After all, since *Just the Ticket* eventually equates winning a woman's heart with buying her off, the film should be more forthright about its own vulgarity.

Also reviewed in:
VARIETY, 3/1-7/99, p. 78, Oliver Jones

KING AND I, THE

A Warner Bros. release of a James G. Robinson presentation of a Morgan Creek production in association with Rankin/Bass Productions and Nest Entertainment. *Executive Producer:* Robert

Mandell. *Producer:* James G. Robinson, Arthur Rankin, and Peter Bakalian. *Director:* Richard Rich. *Screenplay:* Peter Bakalian, David Seidler, and Jacqueline Feather. *Adapted for animation by:* Arthur Rankin. *Based on the musical by:* Richard Rodgers and Oscar Hammerstein II. *Music Editor:* Douglas Lackey. *Animation:* Patrick Gleeson and Colm Duggan. *Character Design:* Bronwen Barry, Elena Kravets, and Michael Coppieters. *Editor:* James F. Koford, Paul Murphy, and Joseph Campana. *Music:* Richard Rogers and Oscar Hammerstein II. *Music Editor:* Douglas Lackey. *Choreographer:* Lee Martino and Lisa Clyde. *Casting:* Geoffrey Johnson and Vincent Liff. *Running time:* 100 minutes. *MPAA Rating:* G.

VOICES: Miranda Richardson (Anna Leonowens); Christiane Noll (Anna Leonowens, singing); Martin Vidnovic (King of Siam); Ian Richardson (Kralahome); Darrell Hammond (Master Little); Allen D. Hong (Prince Chululongkorn); David Burnham (Prince Chululongkorn, singing); Armi Arabe (Tuptim); Tracy Venner Warren (Tuptim, singing); Adam Wylie (Louis Leonowens); Sean Smith (Sir Edward Ramsey); J.A. Fujii (First Wife); Ken Baker (Captain Orton); Ed Trotta (Sir Edward's Captain); Anthony Mozdy (Burmese Emissary); Alexandra Lai (Princess Ying); Katherine Lai (Princess Naomi); Mark Hunt (Steward); B.K. Tochi (Soldier).

LOS ANGELES TIMES, 3/19/99, Calendar/p. 18, Gene Seymour

[*The following review by Gene Seymour appeared in a slightly different form in* **NEWSDAY, 3/19/99, Part II/p. B11.**]

The Disney juggernaut for feature animation must, for its competitors, seem like one of those stains on the rug that just won't come off, no matter how much industrial-strength chemistry is applied.

So why shouldn't Warner Bros. come up with the notion of using a Broadway musical as the basis for a full-length cartoons. Instead of paying for derivative music by hacks, they can use songs already written by masters like Richard Rodgers and Oscar Hammerstein II. And who knows, they might, in the process, introduce kids and parents to a classic theatrical work.

But sadly the music is the only thing worthwhile about this animated version of "The King and I," transformed by ex-Disney hand Richard Rich ("The Fox and the Hound") into a dismal pastiche of threadbare plot devices and not-so-comic interludes.

There may have been sound marketing reasons for pushing to the background the relationship between Anna (Miranda Richardson), the English governess, and Siam's mule-headed but ultimately good-hearted king (Martin Vidnovic). Making the Crown Prince (Allen Hong) into a buff kick-boxer and giving the king a hot-air balloon to stage a hoked-up rescue mission typify the nitwit pandering to young audiences.

There may even have been legitimate reasons for cluttering the landscape with funny animals and villains that come across as road-show rejects from Disney's "Aladdin." The addition of an evil sorcerer (Ian Richardson) with a magic gong (!) is bad enough. But the sin is compounded by saddling him with a sidekick named Master Little ("Saturday Night Live's" Darrell Hammond), who's more goofy than funny—and more racial stereotype than not.

All these extras are brash, noisy distractions for smaller children. But there's little reason to think that kids of all ages won't feel as if they've seen all this schlock before. Curiously, and not surprisingly, it's when the animators stick closely to the original (as in the march of the king's children and the climactic waltz between Anna and the king) that it looks fresh. If they didn't have the confidence to go all the way with the original, why'd they bother at all?

NEW YORK POST, 3/19/99, p. 47, Hannah Brown

Movie buffs who loved the classic 1956 musical "The King and I" should skip the animated version and preserve their fond memories.

This pretty but utterly charmless retread cannot match the excitement generated by the performances of Deborah Kerr and Yul Brynner in the earlier film of the Rodgers and Hammerstein show.

Instead, it offers a dumbing-down of the story line, presumably to appeal to children.

The well-loved songs are all still there (including "Shall We Dance?" and "Getting to Know You") and they're sung prettily enough.

Christiane Noll sings the part of Anna (Miranda Richardson provides her speaking voice) and Martin Vidnovic is the king.

But the moviemakers have taken this gentle period tale—the story of a British schoolteacher who brings Western culture to the king of Siam and finds herself drawn to this barefoot despot—and added so much action that the film resembles a video game.

This new version offers a jarring mixture of the politically correct and incorrect.

While there are preachy lessons against poaching and in favor of servants being educated, the film also features the most grating Asian stereotype since Mickey Rooney played the Japanese photographer in "Breakfast at Tiffany's": a nearly toothless character called Master Little (voiced by Darrell Hammond of "Saturday Night Live").

Many parents will assume that this film, which features many child characters, is suitable for the youngest viewers.

Unfortunately, perhaps to make the plot similar to that of "The Lion King," the moviemakers have made the king's disapproving associate (Ian Richardson) an evil schemer with supernatural powers.

In the opening scene, he scares Anna and her son by sending a huge, fire-breathing sea monster to menace their ship.

Later, he creates giant spiders that pursue two runaway lovers through the jungle.

The sight of these creatures made many children in a preview audience burst into tears. More than a few toddlers were carried out howling.

While the movie terrified younger viewers, older kids will probably be too jaded to enjoy it.

This is the first time the estate of Rodgers and Hammerstein has allowed one of their musicals to be adapted into an animated film.

Maybe it should be the last.

SIGHT AND SOUND, 7/99, p. 42, Leslie Felperin

The mid-nineteenth century. Widowed Englishwoman Anna arrives in Siam with her son Louis to take up her post as schoolteacher to the King of Siam's children. While the King's aide the Kralahome schemes to overthrow the King, Anna defies custom by taking the royal children out to see the city beyond the palace walls, which provokes a quarrel with the King. The Crown Prince falls in love with servant girl Tuptim, but the laws forbid his marrying a commoner. The Kralahome manipulates Anna into thinking the King is a tyrant so she'll help him to persuade the British to overthrow the King and crown him instead. However, despite their verbal sparring, Anna and the King develop an affection for one another and he learns to be less autocratic.

At an official banquet for the British ambassador, the King makes a good show of being 'civilised', but his cover is blown when he learns of the Crown Prince and Tuptim's romance and threatens to execute Tuptim. He relents but later the Prince and Tuptim run off to elope. They fall into a river after the Kralahome uses magic to sabotage the bridge they're crossing. The King saves them in his hot-air balloon, despite the Kralahome's attempts to kill him with fireworks aimed at the balloon. The Kralahome is caught and punished. The King rewards Anna with a house of her own.

Ever since Disney's *Snow White and the Seven Dwarfs* (1937), feature length animated films have tended to use the musical as their generic template. The connection between the two forms was cemented recently when Disney bought the New Amsterdam Theatre on New York's 42nd Street, sent in its 'imagineers' to restore it and now shows there a musical version of its successful cartoon *The Lion King*, thus rehabilitating and sanitising what was once a thoroughly seedy neighbourhood. It recently followed this success with a stage show of *Beauty and the Beast*.

It was inevitable that once the fairytale well started to run dry someone would get around to translating a classic Broadway show into cartoon form, rather than the other way around. Presumably Disney is disinclined to dip into this source since it would have to share the profits with other copyright holders. So here comes Richard Rich, one time Disney director and perpetrator of the shoddy and unlikable *Swan Princess* films, doing a service to an entire industry by providing a template for how not to adapt a classic musical into cartoon form: don't dilute the haunting sense of mortality the original contained by keeping a major character alive at the end just because you're afraid of upsetting the kiddies (the King doesn't die here; thank god they didn't take on *Carousel); don't* add pointless and deeply unfunny slapstick; and most importantly, don't trick out the film with irritating 'cute' animals just to ape Disney's successes.

True to Rich's earlier form, his version of *The King and I* is ugly and bereft of faintly memorable characters, some mean feat considering the original stage version is a gift, with a colourful setting and characters to match. For those fond of this version or the fine 1956 movie with Yul Brynner and Deborah Kerr, this animated rendition will be nothing short of sacrilegious, like seeing a majestic oak brutally pruned and trussed up with plastic swings and a tawdry playhouse. The animation itself is so poorly directed and disjointed one could almost guess which sections were executed by which international team of collaborators. The only interesting sequence depicts CGI stone statues coming to life, creeping stealthily up on the King like the topiary animals in the novel of *The Shining.* Look very closely and their faces almost resemble the wrathful features of Richard Rodgers and Oscar Hammerstein II, bent on revenge.

Also reviewed in:
CHICAGO TRIBUNE, 3/19/99, Friday/p. A, John Petrakis
NEW YORK TIMES, 3/19/99, p. E13, Anita Gates
VARIETY, 3/15-21/99, p. 39, Robert Koehler
WASHINGTON POST, 3/19/99, p. C5, Stephen Hunter
WASHINGTON POST, 3/19/99, Weekend/p. 44, Michael O'Sullivan

KING OF MASKS, THE

A Samuel Goldwyn Films release of a Shaw Brothers (H.K.) production. *Executive Producer:* Mona Fong and Hong Pou Chu. *Producer:* Wu Tianming. *Director:* Wu Tianming. *Screenplay (Mandarin with English subtitles):* Wei Minglung. *Director of Photography:* Mu Dayuan. *Music:* Zhao Jiping and Chen Wengui. *Art Director:* Wu Xujing. *Running time:* 101 minutes. *MPAA Rating:* Not Rated.

CAST: Zhu Xu (Bian Lian Wang); Zhou Ren-ying (Doggie); Zhang Riuyang (Tien Che); Zhao Zhigang (Liang Sao Lang).

LOS ANGELES TIMES, 5/21/99, Calendar/p. 4, Kevin Thomas

Director Wu Tianming, former head of the progressive Xian Film Studios and mentor to China's two greatest directors, Zhang Yimou and Chen Kaige, at last returns to the screen, after a long political exile, with "The King of Masks," an exquisitely wrought period piece set in the Sichuan province in the '30s, an era plagued by both natural disasters and increasing political instability. A film of much humor and sentiment, it celebrates the resilience of the human spirit.

The film opens as an elderly man in a boat emerges from the mists hovering over a river. He is Bian Lian Wang (Zhu Xu, a wonderfully witty and expressive veteran actor) known as the King of Masks. He's a lifelong street performer, adept at working up his audiences before treating them to his confounding act, which enables him to replace one fearsome mask with another with lightning speed.

Living on his boat and plying his trade as he travels up and down the river, the King is a hearty, tough old man, proudly self-sufficient and philosophical. But as his only son died at age 10 more than 20 years earlier, he has no one to whom to pass on his art, handed down from father to son for untold generations. He longs for an heir and also someone to look after him should the infirmities of age eventually overtake him.

Terrible floods have pushed peasant families to start selling off their infant daughters for a pittance, but the King holds out for a boy, as tradition dictates that the secret of the masks can be passed only to males. Just as he is leaving the shadowy, heart-rending market in infants and babies a child (Zhou Ren-ying, adorable and talented) with cropped hair, a radiant smile and a direct gaze stops him in his tracks. The King cannot resist the child he calls Doggie, who, as you might have guessed, turns out to be a girl.

The relationship works: Doggie gratefully not only cooks and cleans but under the King's training becomes a skilled contortionist to provide him with an opening act. And the King can't help but care for Doggie, even if she is only a girl. There is a timeless quality to the King and Doggie's simple way of life, but of course time never stands still, and the fabric of Sichuan society becomes dangerously frayed as the plight of China relentlessly worsens.

The ways in which gifted writer Wei Minglung reshaped a script submitted to Wu by Hong Kong's venerable Shaw Bros. Film Productions suggest Wu's identification with the film's central characters, having experienced a long exile as well, feeling like someone living on the margins of society. The King rightly sees himself as an artist, but he's nonetheless a poor and lowly street entertainer, and as a female, Doggie has virtually no status at all.

Photographed superbly by Mu Dayuan and scored in appropriately stirring fashion by Chen Wengui, "The King of Masks" is gorgeous to behold, with its enchanting authentic vintage settings and beautiful natural locales. There's tremendous affection for his people on the part of Wu, who respects their tenacity, good humor and kindness. One of the characters sums up the meaning of the film when he remarks: "The world is a cold place, but we can bring warmth to it."

NEW YORK POST, 4/28/99, p. 50, Hannah Brown

The last thing this world needs is another movie about a crusty loner bonding with an adorable orphan, but Chinese director Wu Tianming has managed to rework this tired plot into a graceful, moving film.

"The King of Masks" is set in the 1930s during the chaotic, pre-Communist era, when warlords ruled China.

Wang (Zhu Xu) plays the king of the title, an elderly master of the ancient art of making gorgeous masks. He can also change quickly from one mask to another by performing sleight-of-hand tricks.

Eking out a living by performing on the street, he wins the admiration of Master Liang (Zhao Zhigang), the star of the local opera, who offers him a place in his troupe—if Wang will teach him the secrets of the masks.

But Wang declines, explaining that tradition forbids him from teaching his art to anyone but a male heir. Since his son died many years ago, Wang is resigned to the fact that he will carry his professional know-how to the grave.

But this conversation stirs something in Wang, and as he passes a market where poor farmers desperately try to give away their unwanted daughters, he sees a man selling an 8-year-old boy (Zhou Ren-ying). He makes a deal with the man and takes the boy, whose arms are scarred from beatings, to be his apprentice.

When Wang discovers the boy is really a girl, he is angry that he has been duped. But he accepts the situation and teaches the girl to be an acrobat.

Though it does have its saccharine moments, "The King of Masks" succeeds because it sets the story of the love between Wang and the child against the background of a society that treats children—and especially girls—with shattering cruelty.

This is the first feature in eight years by Wu, who spent several years following the Tiananmen Square massacre in the United States.

NEWSDAY, 4/28/99, Part II/p. B11, John Anderson

Historically, "The King of Masks" marks the return to filmmaking of Wu Tianming, onetime head of China's celebrated Xian Film Studios, mentor to his country's most celebrated filmmakers—Chen Kaige, Zhang Yimou—and, until recently, a Tianamen Square-inspired U.S. exile.

Emotionally, Wu's is a potent, affecting film, one whose subject matter—lonely, good-hearted old man crossing paths with irresistible waif—avoids the tarpits of bathos via Wu's elegantly naturalistic approach to what is essentially a fable.

Politically? Therein lie many questions.

"The King of Masks" has already been honored all over the world, including in China, where its script apparently met no resistance from the censors and where it even won China's "Oscar," the Golden Rooster. At the same time, it posseses a social conscience so relevant and provocative that how it got made seems as remarkable as the film itself.

Old Wang (Zhu Xu), an aging magician, travels the province of Sichuan aboard the boat he calls home, making his living from the small crowds that watch his awe-inspiring act of "face-changing"—the rapid-fire switching of masks, akin to the costume changes of kabuki. He is observed one day by the "Living Bodhisattva," Master Liang (Zhao Zhigang), the nation's most celebrated female impersonator, whose performances of Buddhist dramas attract thousands.

Liang offers Wang a job, but the old man thinks Liang wants the secrets of his craft, which can be handed down only to a son. Liang is sincere in his admiration for the old man's skills—but knows that, as a homosexual, he wouldn't qualify even as an adopted heir of Wang's. They form a mutual admiration society, one rooted as much in their status as societal outsiders as it is in their art.

But the meeting makes Wang realize that without a male heir his art will be lost. So he ventures into alleys of Sichuan where the poor sell their children. There he finds Doggie (Zhou Ren-ying), a short-haired 8-year-old whom he believes to be a boy. Discovering soon enough that the oft-adopted child he's bought is a girl, his hopes are crushed and their once-warm relationship is ruined. Unable to simply cast her off, Wang orders her to call him "boss" instead of "grandpa," and to work hard for her keep.

The evolution of their relationship is handled with great care by Wu and he has two intoxicating actors in old Zhu and young Zhou; "spunky" doesn't begin to describe her, as Doggie defends the old man to bullying Chinese soldiers or climbs across rooftops in one of the movie's multiple climaxes. As exciting and emotionally satisfying as "King of Masks" is, however, Wu is acting not only as filmmaker but critic, one whose aim is not just at contemporary politics but at Chinese tradition itself.

Making a film set in the 30s, a time of transition between the remnants of Chinese feudalism and Mao's communism, absolves Wu of making specific political criticisms. But the second-class status of female children is as essential to "The King of Masks" as the iceberg was to "Titanic." The Chinese girls being adopted by Americans every day are abandoned on convent steps for two specific reasons: The tradition of male children being responsible for the care of their elderly parents (married women are responsible for their husband's parents) and the one-family, one-child policy imposed by current day Beijing. It's a two-headed monster that Wu seems to be is attacking.

We'd like to say we're wrong, of course, because we need more films from a director like Wu. On the other hand, and if we're right, you have to admire the subtlety of a director who can make such a crowd-pleasing picture with this kind of soul.

VILLAGE VOICE, 5/4/99, p. 116, Gary Susman

The King of Masks is a conventional melodrama whose dialogue has the stale ring of fortune-cookie aphorisms. Yet, as one character notes, you would have to have a heart of stone not to be moved by the plight of its protagonists.

The King (Zhu Xu) is a street performer in 1930s Sichuan who practices a rare, remarkable sleight-of-hand act that involves the quick changing of elaborate masks. Lacking a male heir to inherit his secrets, the old man is persuaded by a prosperous drag diva, to buy from a destitute farmer an eight-year-old named Doggie (Zhou Ren-ying). The King is shattered when he learns that Doggie is really a girl but keeps her on as a servant. Doggie reveres the old man, but her curiosity about the forbidden art sets off a horrifying chain of events that lands her on the streets and the King on death row. To save him (and prove her worth as both artist and grandchild), Doggie makes a desperate, operatic sacrifice.

Wu has spent much of the last decade away from both China and the camera, which may explain the creaky plotting. He does, however, have an eye for vivid color and folk art, and makes deft parallels to contemporary China, where materialism trumps art, and girls are still of little value. But the power of the film lies in the performance of Zhou Ren-ying, whom Wu disturbingly puts through some perilous stunts and whose character responds to all manner of abuse with heartbreaking emotional directness.

Also reviewed in:
CHICAGO TRIBUNE, 5/21/99, Friday/p. M, John Petrakis
NEW YORK TIMES, 4/28/99, p. E5, Janet Maslin
VARIETY, 3/4-10/96, p. 77, Derek Elley

KNOCKIN' ON HEAVEN'S DOOR

A Myriad Pictures release of a Mr. Brown Entertainment production. *Producer:* Thomas Zickler and Andre Hennicke. *Director:* Thomas Jahn. *Screenplay (German with English subtitles):* Thomas Jahn. *Director of Photography:* Gero Steffen. *Editor:* Alexander Berner. *Music:* Franz Plasa. *Sound:* Stefan Colli. *Production Designer:* Monika Bauert. *Set Decorator:* Wolfgang Küchler and Heike von Polheim. *Make-up:* Susanne Wörle. *Stunt Coordinator:* Ernst Reimann. *Running time:* 89 minutes. *MPAA Rating:* Not Rated.

CAST: Til Schweiger (Martin Brest); Jan Josef Liefers (Rudi Wurlitzer); Thierry Van Werveke (Henk); Moritz Bleibtreu (Abdul); Huub Stapel (Frankie); Leonard Lansink (Kommissar Schneider); Ralph Herforth (Assistant Keller); Cornelia Froboess (Martins Mutter); Rutger Hauer (Curtiz); Willi Thomczyk (Autoverkäufer); Christiane Paul (Verkäuferin in der Boutique); Hannes Jaenicke (Motorradpolizist); Vladimir Weigl (Harald Rohwitz); Jenny Elvers (Schwester Labor A); Corinna Harfouch (Schwester Labor B); Tobias Schenke (Junge); Hark Bohm (Polizeipsychologe); Jürgen Becker (Tankwart); Wolfgang Kamen (Dr. Graf); Bernd Hoffmann (Dr. Wortmann); Muriel Baumeister (Schwester in der Ambulanz); Helen Duval (Puffmutter); Christoph Ott (Polizist am Fahrstuhl); Henry Lupprian and Benny Lappmann (Hotel Boys); Georg Roth (Hotelmanager); Florian Fitz (Polizist im Hotel); Xenia Seeberg (Polizistin im Hotel); Dana Schweiger (Junge Frau am Bahnhof); Valentin Schweiger (Baby im Bahnhof); Mick Schweiger (Rodriguez Bruder, #1); Salvatore Pascale (Rodriguez Bruder, #2); Evangelos Pananos (Rodriguez Bruder, #3); Gustav Adolph (Carlos); Anton Rattinger and Ayman Vanelli (Polizist im Autor); Ludwig Boettger (Apotheker); Clelia Sarto (TV-Reporterin); Eva Mannschott and Nicolaus Brodyk (Bankangestellter); Lauren Stark (Kleines Mädchen); Sönke Wortmann (Regisseur); Ursula Schreiber (Frau mit Capri); Corinna Flock (Frau Puff, #1); Janine Kunze (Frau Puff, #2); Thomas Jahn (Taxifahrer); Szusanne von Griensven and Susanne Brandauer (Tänzerin); Bernd Eichinger (Typ mit Geld).

NEW YORK POST, 8/20/99, p. 61, Rod Dreher

Who is Til Schweiger, and why hasn't Hollywood discovered this guy?

Schweiger, who comes off as a youthful cross between George Clooney and Johnny Depp, is Germany's biggest male movie star. And he shows more than enough charisma and screen presence in "Knockin' on Heaven's Door" to make him an international star (but how's his English?).

Unfortunately, this buddy road movie is only a tad better than OK. Still, Schweiger and co-star Jan Josef Liefers, who looks like Stephen Rea with his jowls pinned back, work wonders with Thomas Jahn's hackneyed screenplay. The two are such great company here I kept wishing they would emigrate to a better movie.

They play a pair of mismatched adventurers who meet in the hospital when both are diagnosed with terminal illnesses. Timid, bookish Rudi (Liefers) initially can't stand Martin (Schweiger), a stocky, handsome nonconformist who insists on chain-smoking in the room they share.

After a bottle of tequila and a session of Martin's alluring "what the hell?" fatalism, the duo turns into the Thelma und Louise of the cancer ward. Stealing a baby-blue Mercedes convertible from a couple of low-rent gangsters (Moritz Bleibtreu and Thierry Van Werveke), Martin and Rudi set out on a quest to fulfill Rudi's dream of seeing the ocean before they die.

Initially cautious, Rudi falls under Martin's spell as the merry mayhem of their road trip takes in robbing gas stations and banks, confounding their pursuers and pitching a tent in the poshest suite of the Hotel Metropole. "Knockin' on Heaven's Door" is a pleasant ride for the most part, but its low-brow sentimentality and lack of originality blunt the good will the likable actors earn.

Writer-director Jahn baldly and lamely steals from American movies and TV shows. This kind of thing is dumb in American movies, but at least it has the courage of its lack of conviction. This Euro movie comedy is a lot like Euro rock'n'roll: an ersatz knockoff of a genre done much better by Yanks, but sweet-natured fun all the same.

VILLAGE VOICE, 8/24/99, p. 126, Jessica Winter

Surely many hoped that *Lock, Stock and Two Smoking Barrels* represented the last gasp of the Woo-via-Tarantino genre of ironic bloodbath capers, yet here comes the latest cinematic hoodlum (this one from Germany), ready to pistol-whip a bullet-riddled dead horse. Or at least, such would seem the sad case at the outset of *Knockin' on Heaven's Door*: we watch two reservoir slobs running errands for their don, just before their cash and Mercedes land in the hands of two terminal hospital patients who escape their sickbeds for one last road trip.

The story line is thus bipolar, but the requisite car chases and shoot-outs are so lazily staged that we know our closest attention is meant for the deepening friendship between the ailing road warriors.

This aspect of the film never wanders too far into maudlin terrain, mainly due to the performances of sad-eyed Jan Josef Liefers and Til Schweiger, who radiates Ewan McGregor's cagey intelligence and comic grace. Why anyone felt compelled to dress up a gimpy yet charming, sweet-souled buddy movie in a cheap black suit accessorized with skinny tie and a .45 is obvious from a commercial standpoint, but no less dully depressing.

Also reviewed in:
NEW YORK TIMES, 8/20/99, p. E21, Stephen Holden
VARIETY, 12/22/97-1/4/98, p. 61, Derek Elley

LAKE PLACID

A Fox 2000 Pictures release from Phoenix Pictures of a Rocking Chair production. *Executive Producer:* Peter Bogart. *Producer:* David E. Kelley and Michael Pressman. *Director:* Steve Miner. *Screenplay:* David E. Kelley. *Director of Photography:* Daryn Okada. *Editor:* Marshall Harvey and Paul Hirsch. *Music:* John Ottman. *Music Editor:* Amanda Goodpaster. *Sound:* Larry Sutton and (music) Tim Boyle. *Sound Editor:* Frank Eulner. *Casting:* Lisa Beach. *Production Designer:* John Willett. *Art Director:* William Heslup. *Set Decorator:* Tedd Kuchera. *Special Effects:* Dean Lockwood. *Creature Effects:* Stan Winston. *Costumes:* Jori Woodman. *Make-up:* Dana Michelle Hamel. *Stunt Coordinator:* Jacob Rupp. *Running time:* 88 minutes. *MPAA Rating:* R.

CAST: Bill Pullman (Jack Wells); Oliver Platt (Hector Cyr); Bridget Fonda (Kelly Scott); Brendan Gleeson (Sheriff Hank Keough); Betty White (Mrs. Delores Bickerman); David Lewis (Walt Lawson); Tim Dixon (Stephen Daniels); Natassia Malthe (Jaine); Mariska Hargitay (Myra Okubo); Meredith Salenger (Deputy Sharon Gare); Jed Rees (Deputy Burke); Richard Leacock (Deputy Stevens); Jake T. Roberts (Officer Coulson); Warren Takeuchi (Paramedic); Ty Olsson (State Trooper).

LOS ANGELES TIMES, 7/16/99, Calendar/p. 8, John Anderson

[*The following review by John Anderson appeared in a slightly different form in*
NEWSDAY, 7/16/99, Part II/p. B6.]

OK, campers, this is a standard inspection. Please have your checklists ready:

Aerial shot—introducing picturesque hills, forest and lake where nothing should go wrong but everything will?

Got it.

Murky underwater shots—implying threat from below but actually showing nothing? Check.

Soundtrack that suggests heartbeat?

Yup.

Federal official displaying insufficient respect for local law enforcement and thereby ensuring his own gruesome death?

You bet.

False alarms by the boatload? Check.

Rip-offs of "Jaws"? Check.

Incredibly lame jokes meant to relieve nervous tension? Check.

No nervous tension? Check.

Welcome to "Lake Placid," in which a remote body of water that is not the former Winter Olympics site is terrorized by an enormous crocodile. And in which a cast that includes Bridget Fonda, Bill Pullman, Brendan Gleeson and Oliver Platt finds itself up "Dawson's Creek" without a paddle.

Director Steve Miner—the man behind "Halloween: H20," Chapters 2 and 3 of "Friday the 13th," "Forever Young" and the pilots of several successful TV series—also directed the first year of "Creek." And he and producer-writer David E. Kelley ("Ally McBeal," "Chicago Hope") have contrived an alleged horror movie that has the sensibility of a teen TV series. The few moments of shock and mayhem are effective enough (and will have people clutching each other in the backs of theaters everywhere, which is the point) but only because they've ripped off Steven Spielberg.

The rest of the film has its actors reciting dialogue silly enough to equal the scenes themselves—the four mostly sizable stars, for instance, jammed into two wobbly canoes on a lake where the monster croc has been biting people in half. This is funny stuff, but only if you think the movie is laughing with you and not at you.

"Placid" certainly treats its characters as jokes. Kelly Scott (Fonda), a paleontologist at New York's Museum of Natural History, is dispatched to Maine to identify the tooth removed from the remaining half of the wildlife inspector. No Fed Ex in Maine, you ask? Sure, but Kelly has just broken up with her boss (Adam Arkin) and in order to get her out of his hair he's sending her off to Maine, where she gets to play the aggravating New Yorker, whining about the bugs, the weather, the rubes and the fact that there are no toilets in the woods.

More absurd—but in this movie, you don't necessarily notice—is Hector Cyr, a wealthy mythology professor and crocodile aficionado. "He thinks they're divine conduits," Kelly says, seriously. Hector, played by Platt with as much brio as possible, drops in by helicopter to join Sheriff Keough (Gleeson) and game warden Jack (Pullman) in their search for a reptile capable of snatching grizzly bears right off the shore of the lake (Grizzly bear attacks in Maine? Hey, crocodiles in Maine?)

Betty White gets to play an eccentric old weirdo and recite lines salty enough to have given the rest of the Golden Girls cardiac arrest (well, maybe not Bea Arthur). Like White, the crocodile is having a long-awaited day in the New England sun. After enormous snakes ("Anaconda"), various apes, mobs of frogs ("Frogs"), and whatever that mechanical spider is supposed to be in "Wild Wild West," the lowly crocodile is more than due.

NEW YORK POST, 7/16/99, p. 47, Jonathan Foreman

An off-beat, lighthearted creature feature that would be the perfect thing for a night at the drive-in—if there still were any—"Lake Placid" combines humor and thrills with remarkable deftness.

It's an affectionate spoof of the "Jaws" genre just a quarter-turn away from the real thing and couldn't be further from the Leslie Nielsen/Zucker brothers school of broad satire.

A scuba diver from the Maine department of Fish and Game gets chomped by something big and nasty during a routine check of Black Lake. What looks like a dinosaur tooth is found in what's left of his body. So paleontologist and city girl Kelly Scott (Bridget Fonda) is sent up to investigate by a boss and former lover only too happy to get her out of town.

Neither the irascible local sheriff Keough (Brendan Gleeson), nor the fish and game warden (Bill Pullman) investigating the diver's death wants to have her around. They become even less keen on her presence when the creature beneath the dark, still water of the lake starts biting the heads off incautious deputies.

Then wealthy, crazy mythology professor Hector Cyr (Oliver Platt) descends on their camp in his helicopter, determined to swim with what he believes is a gigantic crocodile.

The special effects and music are all perfectly serious, and might indeed make you think twice about going for a solo dip in a dark lake miles away from anywhere. But what makes "Lake Placid" such a pleasure is the crackling repartee between the four main characters.

Screenwriter David E. Kelley (the creator of TV's "Ally McBeal" and "The Practice") fills the script with an updated (i.e. obscenity-laced) version of the sardonic, snappy dialogue you associate with the better American comedies of the 1930s. (Though it's tempting to repeat one or two of his best lines, too much about "Lake Placid" has already been given away by the trailer.)

Platt, Fonda and the excellent Irish actor Brendan Gleeson gleefully make the most of Kelley's writing. Fonda in particular revels in a sassy role that suits her looks and talents and contains more than a touch of Carole Lombard. (Pullman by contrast doesn't really get enough to say). And Oliver Platt is an exuberant pleasure.

The result is a sunny, witty, well-proportioned pastiche that avoids excess in any way and manages to obey the rules of the genre without plumbing its clichés.

There are no crazed local mayors who put tourist lives at risk to protect the local economy, no bloodthirsty hunters out to exterminate a beast that's merely defending its habitat, no animal rights fanatics so misanthropic that they all but deserve to die.

Indeed there's nothing outsized about "Lake Placid" (except the big lizard itself), but the sum of its small pleasures make for a very entertaining summer night.

SIGHT AND SOUND, 4/00, p. 51, Jamie Graham

Black Lake (nicknamed by the locals "Lake Placid"), northern Maine, the present. A Department of Fish and Game diver is killed while trawling the depths of the lake. Sheriff Hank Keough sees him killed from a boat. In New York, palaeontologist Kelly Scott is sent on her first field assignment to the lake to investigate. She establishes that a tooth pulled from the diver's torso belonged to a crocodile, and joins Keough and game warden Jack Wells in their quest to capture the reptile.

They are joined by Hector Cyr, a mythology professor who has swum with every type of crocodile. The four of them come across Delores Bickerman, an old woman who sacrifices cows to the crocodile. Catching woman and crocodile mid-meal, Cyr dives into the lake to swim with the 30-foot beast. A helicopter is brought in to lift him to safety but is attacked by the crocodile, a diversion which allows Cyr to escape. A hovering helicopter then lowers a cow into the water as bait. The crocodile strikes, the helicopter crashes and the reptile gets trapped in the wreckage, allowing its hunters to drug it. A second giant crocodile appears, but is blown up immediately. The Florida Fish-and-Game team arrive to take care of the drugged crocodile, and the four battered hunters depart. But back at the lake, Delores is feeding a batch of baby crocodiles.

Just as the serene waters of Lake Placid belie the presence of the marauding crocodile lurking within its depths, Steve Miner's wonderfully trashy, frequently hilarious movie is not all it seems at first. Initially, Miner is delighted to nurture notions that *Lake Placid* is going to be just another po-faced *Jaws* rip-off. Opening with a helicopter shot that scuds high above the water's surface, the film quickly establishes an ominous tone as the camera swoops into the lake's murky depths. Even the most cine illiterate viewer couldn't fail to spot the parallels with Steven Spielberg's film: the creature's-eye viewpoint, the kicking diver high above, the rapidly diminishing distance between the two.

Rather than thrash around in stagnant waters, though, *Lake Placid* quickly veers into unexpected territory. The first hint comes with the death of a Fish-and Game Department diver, whose body is hauled from the churning lake, sans legs, by Brendan Gleeson's horrified sheriff. Coming as the bloody climax to the aforementioned mechanical predator-in-the-depths build-up, it's unclear whether we should laugh or gag, but there's a clue in the half-bod reference to *Alligator* (scripted by John Sayles), which was also healthily aware of its own preposterousness. (Miner already has a track record in self-aware horror cinema, having directed *Friday the 13th Part 2* with its strong echoes of Mario Bava's *Bay of Blood,* 1971, and *Halloween H20* with its *Scream*-style self-referentiality.)

In place of Sayles' typically wry tone, however, *Lake Placid*'s screenwriter David E. Kelley (creator of *Ally McBeal*) goes for broad humour, stuffing his characters' mouths full of scathing sarcasm.   Much of the comedy bleeds out of the head on collision of dropping New York palaeontologist Bridget Fonda amid a landscape and people for whom her only reference point is *Deliverance.*   Consequently, she spends much of the film's refreshingly brief duration dishing out condescending one-liners. (Although Oliver Platt's mythology professor is given the best line: "The sooner we catch this thing, Sheriff, the sooner you can get back to sleeping with your sister.") Indeed, the withering put-downs are the film's main attraction, coming with more force and snap than any of the colossal reptile's sudden attacks.

Of course, such low humour delivered with staggering frequency will not be to everyone's taste, but then neither will a movie about a 30-foot Asian crocodile hiding out in northern Maine. Genre buffs, on the other hand, will be delighted by this spirited 'B' movie which recaptures the winning horror-comedy formula Sayles made his own in the late 70s (he also penned *Piranha*). Admittedly, the third act is weakened by the crocodile's long-awaited revelation, proving to be just another jerky creation ill-rendered by CGI, but *Lake Placid* is nonetheless a triumph compared to such recent, lazy additions to the genre as *Anaconda, Deep Rising* and *Deep Blue Sea.*

Also reviewed in:
CHICAGO TRIBUNE, 7/16/99, Friday/p. H, Michael Wilmington
NEW YORK TIMES, 7/16/99, p. E13, Janet Maslin
VARIETY, 7/12-18/99, p. 38, Robert Koehler
WASHINGTON POST, 7/16/99, p. C5, Stephen Hunter
WASHINGTON POST, 7/16/99, Weekend/p. 45, Michael O'Sullivan

LAST CIGARETTE, THE

A New Yorker Films release of a Drifting Smoke Productions/Cologne Cartoon/BBC/Bayerischer Rundfunk/Arte/Learning Channel production. *Producer:* Gerd Hecker, Steve Hendel, and Kevin Rafferty. *Director:* Kevin Rafferty and Frank Keraudren. *Director of Photography:* Kevin Rafferty and Frank Keraudren. *Editor:* Frank Keraudren. *Sound:* Margaret Crimmins and Paul Hsu. *Running time:* 82 minutes. *MPAA Rating:* Not Rated.

NEW YORK POST, 6/9/99, p. 44, Rod Dreher

In 1982, filmmaker Kevin Rafferty put together "The Atomic Cafe," a hilarious and wildly subversive documentary satirizing the U.S. government's attempts to mold public opinion about the bomb.

The film was a brilliant pastiche of archival footage, which included 1950s clips aimed at schoolchildren, chirpily urging them to "duck and cover" if an atomic fireball should appear outside their schoolhouse window.

Between guffaws, you had to shake your head and ask, "What the hell were we thinking?"

"The Last Cigarette" does for smokes what "The Atomic Cafe" did for the bomb: offers an amusing collage of archival footage to send up our culture's schizoid relationship with a lethal weapon.

Rafferty, who made this film, too (with partner Frank Keraudren), has a gift for unearthing bizarre film artifacts and stylishly editing them to give his polemic comic punch.

The movie centers around congressional testimony given in 1994 by the heads of the nation's tobacco companies. Under the Torquemada-like torture of Rep. Henry Waxman (D-Calif), the ciggie chieftains squirmed and protested and screamed bloody murder, but wouldn't back away from their preposterous claims that nicotine is non-addictive and that cigarettes don't necessarily kill people.

A Philip Morris scientist tells members of Congress that the word "addictive" has no meaning because people speak of exercise and chocolate as "addictive." Even those resentful of the anti-smoking hysteria gripping the culture can't help but be alternately disgusted and amused by this Clinton-esque mendacity.

But it's been going on for a long time. As vintage TV commercials show, there was an outrageous campaign to associate the habit with beauty, health, hygiene and the good life.

Words like "clean," "smooth" and "fresh" keep cropping up, and there were even claims of wholesomeness, such as Philip Morris' insistence that smoking their brand made one "feel better."

And there's sex. Countless big-screen lovers have done a slow burn for each other over lit cigarettes, and the filmmakers have uncovered an underground industry in smoking fetish films, in which women puff suggestively for the prurient pleasures of the home-video fan.

Toward film's end, there is a bit suggesting that anti-smoking zealots sometimes go too far in their reactions. One flight attendant suing the tobacco companies over the smoke she breathed from passengers' cigarettes, says, "Breathing secondhand smoke is rape."

The funny and highly entertaining "Last Cigarette" could have given a fuller picture of the social anxiety sparked by the evil weed by paying more attention to anti-tobacco hysterics, who can be just as obnoxious as the smokers they attack.

"The Last Cigarette" makes you wonder about media lies that we take as gospel truth today and how they will look in 2050, when documentary filmmakers of the future turn current propaganda into acid social comedy.

VILLAGE VOICE, 6/15/99, p. 143, J. Hoberman

Advertising, as any American child can tell you, is largely based on imbuing a specific brand of a particular product, the more useless the better, with an array of magical associations. In this sense, *The Last Cigarette*—a meditation on the pleasures and perils of smoking tobacco—reflects its subject almost too well. Kevin Rafferty and Frank Keraudren's found-footage documentary is a movie made from other movies. As with cigarettes, the image is more important than the thing itself.

Actually, *The Last Cigarette* has something of a thesis. It's no secret that, in the wartime '40s at least, people learned to smoke by watching the movies. Smoking is presented as an integral part of America's national identity, as when the filmmakers juxtapose clips of action and intellectual icons John Wayne and Edward R. Murrow invoking "freedom" while ostentatiously sucking their coffin nails. The film begins with Christopher Columbus—or rather, Columbus as embodied by Fredric March in the 1949 movie—landing on Hispaniola to find the locals thoughtfully puffing on flaming cigars. How uncivilized, the explorer exclaims, cueing a quick cut to Humphrey Bogart in evening clothes, demonstrating why no less an authority than Cuban writer G. Cabrera Infante would anoint him "the greatest cigarette smoker in moviedom."

That greatness can only be burnished by the knowledge that Bogie died a miserable death of lung cancer—a martyr to cool. The idea that cigarettes provide the cheapest, most public way to live fast and die young (if not leave a good-looking corpse) underscores most of *The Last Cigarette*—although it's not something that the movie ever wants to visualize. The argument is held together largely by excerpts from the C-SPAN telecast of 1994 congressional hearings on "the single most dangerous consumer product ever sold." Husky-voiced, tough-talking tobacco company CEOs fence with posturing Democratic representatives—each side attacking the other as "fanatics."

The filmmakers intersperse this patriotic debate with an assortment of vintage cigarette ads and movie clips conjuring up a familiar variety of mythological beasts—the Philip Morris bellhop, the Marlboro cowboy, Joe Camel, cowboy Gary Cooper and Bogie's eventual widow Lauren Bacall manufacturing ciggies together in *Bright Leaf*. As the CEOs deny scientific evidence that smoking is harmful, so the old TV spots are filled with even more barefaced lies. And as the ads traffic in blatant showbiz, so the representatives grandstand wildly, at one point producing a camera-poised asthmatic seven-year-old to whom they attempt to compel the CEOs to apologize.

Rafferty's previous documentaries—*The Atomic Café, Blood in the Face,* and *Feed* (the last two made in collaboration with *Voice* writer James Ridgeway)—have all taken a bemused look at the American scene, positioning themselves as part exposé and part hokum. Here the two aspects are indistinguishable. *The Last Cigarette* offers as "evidence" found news footage of a chimp who likes to smoke and a dog that hates cigarettes—there are antismoking ads which show fetuses dragging on cancer sticks and the antismoking satire of Robocop busting a hapless nicotine-head. More provocatively, there is also the recent phenomenon of crypto-pornographic videos that showcase dolled-up sex-toys who langorously smoke and suggestively talk about it.

While these fetishistic smokesploitation films cross-reference the old TV ad in which a sultry chanteuse promises that "you get a lot to like in a Marlboro," the selection here is frequently capricious—where is the stone-age *Dream of a Nicotine Fiend* or Paul Henreid lighting two cigarettes and passing one to Bette Davis in *Now Voyager?* The structure is sometimes so loose as to seem almost random—or maybe free-associational. That the movie is steeped in '40s-ness is more likely a factor of the filmmakers' own fantasies. While there are times in this 82-minute doc when the filmmakers succeed in leeching out all interest, *The Last Cigarette* is at its best once dreamlike cigarette commercials are intercut with scientific charts and shocking experiments—a mouse poisoned before our eyes with a single drop of pure nicotine. More concerned with propaganda than smoking, these outrageously synthesized attraction-repulsion films are appropriately salted with comic overreaction shots and tied together by the moody, menacing themes from various Hitchcock movies.

Although the film's title promises some closure on the fin de siècle Edison mutoscope *Her First Cigarette, The Last Cigarette* rummages around the archives but doesn't really go anywhere. Didactic as it seems, the movie is a readymade campy goof for neo-Rat Pack *fumistes*. No less cynical than the commercials it plunders, *The Last Cigarette* should carry its own warning label: This media history light and heavily filtered.

Also reviewed in:
NEW YORK TIMES, 6/9/99, p. E1, Janet Maslin
VARIETY, 9/6-12/99, p. 62, Dennis Harvey

LAST DAYS, THE

An October Films release of a Steven Spielberg presentation in association with the Survivors of the Shoah Visual History Foundation. *Executive Producer:* Steven Spielberg. *Producer:* June Beallor and Ken Lipper. *Director:* Jim Moll. *Director of Photography:* Harris Done. *Editor:* James Moll. *Music:* Hans Zimmer. *Music Editor:* Adam Smalley. *Sound:* Claude Letessier and (music) Alan Meyerson. *Sound Editor:* John Reese. *Historians:* Michael Berenbaum and Randolph Braham. *Running time:* 88 minutes. *MPAA Rating:* Not Rated.

WITH: Irene Zisblatt; Renée Firestone; Alice Lok Cahana; Bill Basch; Tom Lantos; Randolph Braham; Hans Munch.

LOS ANGELES TIMES, 2/5/99, Calendar/p. 6, Kevin Thomas

At the beginning of the eloquent Holocaust documentary "The Last Days," a vigorous retired businessman named Bill Basch tells us how the Nazis might have managed to draw out World War II by as much as six months had they not been so intent on carrying out the Final Solution.

Basch knows of where he speaks; he is one of five Hungarian Holocaust survivors who for this film agreed to return to the concentration camps and hometowns they had not seen for more than half a century in order to give us a sense of the full impact of the horrors that must never be forgotten.

Indeed, the familiar atrocity images here are, in fact, stronger and more substantial than in most other, if not all other, Holocaust documentaries. But they are sustained by the humanity, intelligence and dignity of these five people who witnessed and survived the atrocities firsthand. All of them are longtime American citizens, and all are either in their late 60s or early- to mid-70s. They are all well-dressed people who live in nicely furnished homes. They do not look like victims, and, in fact, they are not. They are survivors who endured the unspeakable, who lost everything but who had the courage and determination to build new, rewarding lives in a new country.

Both Renee Firestone and Irene Zisblatt were born in storybook Czech towns that were annexed to Hungary. They speak of their idyllic childhoods shattered by the German invasion of Hungary on March 19, 1944. For two years, Prime Minister Miklos Kallay's government had resisted implementing the Final Solution, but after the Germans' arrival, Hungary's Jewish community was systematically eradicated with desperate, unprecedented brutality. In 1941 Hungary had a Jewish population of 825,000, but by the time the war was over, 620,000 of them were dead.

Having grown up integrated within the Gentile community, Zisblatt recounts her shock at the anti-Semitism that erupted once her town, a mineral springs resort, had been annexed to Hungary. Congressman Tom Lantos, who tells us how he owes his life to the efforts of Swedish diplomat Raoul Wallenberg, speaks of the naive patriotism of the Hungarian Jews. Lantos survived in his native Budapest in a Wallenberg safe house, but artist Alice Lok Cahana, another Budapest native, ended up in Bergen-Belsen. Firestone and Zisblatt were sent to Auschwitz, where Zisblatt was selected for medical experimentation, and Basch was sent to Buchenwald. All of them would lose their immediate relatives in the camps.

What these five and others have to say may be familiar to many by now, but the experiences they lived through are so terrible and told in such riveting detail it's as if you're hearing about the Holocaust for the first time.

And there are those personal touches that make their stories unforgettable. Firestone tells us of trying to save a bathing suit as a memento of far happier times, and Zisblatt talks of her determination to preserve the diamonds sewn into her clothes by the mother she would never see again. Cahana, intent upon learning of the fate of her beloved sister, has an astounding, chilling interview with the very doctor who apparently performed experiments upon her sibling. Dr. Hans Munch was acquitted at Nuremberg because he seemingly was able to prove that he performed harmless experiments on prisoners as a way of helping to extend and thereby save lives. Yet with Cahana he proves evasive, stating that it was "only normal" that after six months in captivity her sister should die.

"The Last Days" is the first theatrical feature produced by the Survivors of the Shoah Visual History Foundation, founded by Steven Spielberg in 1994, who served as the documentary's executive producer. It was directed with the utmost sensitivity by James Moll, and has a score by Hans Zimmer that is at once understated and elegiac. The words of the survivors are augmented by a trove of deftly interwoven archival material, much of it unfamiliar and all of it overwhelmingly powerful. What "The Last Days" ultimately evokes, beyond celebrating these five remarkable people, is the sense that evil is eternal within human nature. "Evil is always with us," Lantos says. "We must fight it every moment of our lives."

NEW YORK, 2/15/99, p. 57, Peter Rainer

In March 1944, when the Nazi War machine was almost spent, Germany invaded Hungary and, in less than four months, virtually annihilated one of Europe's largest Jewish populations. The Survivors of the Shoah Visual History Foundation, founded by Steven Spielberg, has been preserving on film since 1994 the testimony of thousands of Holocaust eyewitnesses. The documentary *The Last Days*, directed by James Moll, centers on five Hungarian survivors. Their recollections, interspersed with rare footage including wartime photos taken in Auschwitz, are memorializations of experience. Because these people, including California congressman Tom Lantos, have sustained their lives, the film's tone is ostensibly inspirational. But the abomination of their past stays with one, too. The film's straightforward accounting is perhaps the only respectable way to deal with the enormity. Metaphor would be a paltry substitute—which is why Roberto Benigni's *Life Is Beautiful,* for all its goodwill, offends. No subject is exempt from dramatization, but Benigni's transformation of the camps into a bloodless fairy-tale fable between father and son etherealizes the agonies that *The Last Days* so devastatingly describes.

NEW YORK POST, 2/5/99, p. 63, Jonathan Foreman

As powerful and disturbing as you would expect, "The Last Days" is the first feature-length documentary from Steven Spielberg's Shoah Visual History Foundation.

Unlike previous, wider-ranging Holocaust documentaries, it deals solely with the terrible fate of Hungary's Jewry in the waning days of World War II, and it depicts that fate by focusing on the experiences of just five people.

As a result, "The Last Days" is not only remarkably calm and, for the most part, unmanipulative for a project associated with Spielberg, it does a superb job of making the Holocaust vividly immediate.

By giving his subjects a pre-war context, by showing that the pajama-clad, shaved-head skeletal beings in the camps had normal lives before night fell in March 1944, director James Moll gives them back some of their humanity.

It was then that Hungary, a Nazi ally, became the last country to be invaded by the Germans, and that the deportations and high-speed destruction of its 850,000 strong, highly assimilated Jewish community began.

The film follows the five survivors—Tom Lantos, Alice Lok Cahana, Renee Firestone, Bill Basch and Irene Zisblatt—back to their former homes in Hungary and to various ghettos and camps. The filmmakers selected five unusually articulate people with radically different pre-war lives. Indeed, all that the five had in common at the beginning of 1944 was Jewish faith.

Background information is provided by newsreels, a historian-survivor and Dr. Hans Munch, a Nazi doctor in charge of medical experiments on human beings at Auschwitz. There's an extraordinary, chilling moment in the film when one of the five asks Munch what procedures were performed on her murdered sister.

There is remarkable power in the little details the five tell us of the last days before cattle trains. But perhaps the most amazing thing about "The Last Days" is the never-before-seen color footage from a liberated death camp that takes these familiar horrors out of history and makes them shockingly immediate and real.

That's why it is all the more irritating that, in the last third of the film, Moll drops his strict documentary integrity. Some scenes of the survivors turning up in their old hometowns and meeting Hungarians they once knew clearly were staged. The locals, who never once glance at the American camera crew, have obviously been prepped, if not rehearsed.

More disturbing are some gratuitous scenes of the survivors wandering about Auschwitz and other camps. The problem is not simply that they are obviously under pressure to say something ringing about man's inhumanity to man. What's galling are the unnecessary shots of them breaking down in tears.

What we have already seen and heard is distressing enough; there is something almost pornographic about taking Holocaust survivors back to a death camp so you can film them crying.

NEWSDAY, 2/5/99, Part II/p. B7, John Anderson

Let's pity the Holocaust deniers—not just for willful stupidity, but because with each new document, their black hearts leap with hope that this will be the one to exhaust the subject, make it trivial, expose the flaws in the collective memory of millions and finally establish the existence of a propaganda conspiracy that makes the TV-studio-staged moonwalk theory look like kid stuff.

Pity them especially for "The Last Days," director James Moll's nonfiction memory play about the last-ditch campaign against Hungary's Jews, which proves that there may, in fact, be no limit to what we can learn about Hitler's Final Solution: that as long as there are persons left to remember firsthand, we have one more fresh piece of the puzzle, itself the great mystery of our self-revelatory age.

Produced by Ken Lipper and June Beallor and executive produced by Steven Spielberg and his Shoah Foundation, "The Last Days" introduces us to five survivors, all of whom were living in Hungary in March, 1944, when Hitler knew the war was lost and launched a desperate campaign of extermination. A lot of what we see at first seems like "generic" documentary material. But after the reminiscences about the yellow stars and the friends who turned against them, the movie suddenly presents us with Hans Munch, a doctor at Auschwitz who is so matter of fact in his recounting of medical experiments that the film takes a sharp right turn into the Dante-esque.

Often, director Moll tries too hard to put poetic punctuation on his subjects' memories; they don't need the help. But a lot of what he's unearthed and installed in this film is remarkable—horrific, but remarkable, not the least of which is a short color sequence of emaciated camp survivors, who walk away from the camera like a troupe of sickly comic marionettes.

When Renee Firestone travels to her old family home, an old neighbor asks embarrassed questions. "I have only seen it in the movies," he says. "Unfortunately," Firestone says, "it was much worse than what they show in movies." Even "The Last Days" can't do "justice" to the Holocaust. But as tribute and testimony, it couldn't be better.

SIGHT AND SOUND, 11/99, p. 48, Mark Cousins

Five Hungarian-American Holocaust survivors describe their experiences during the last days of World War II, when 438,000 Hungarian Jews were deported to Auschwitz in less than six weeks. They recall the early rumours of anti-Semitic beatings, the arrival of the SS in Hungary on 19 March 1944, their forced removal from their homes, ghettoisation and the intervention of Swedish diplomat Raoul Wallenberg, who saved many lives.

Some were deported first to, Buchenwald or Dachau but most went straight to Auschwitz-Birkenau, where they were 'selected' and separated from family members, many of whom were immediately gassed. Irene Zisblatt, Renée Firestone, Alice Lok Cahana, Bill Basch and Tom Lantos describe their various experiences in Birkenau. Lok Cahana revisits it with her son. Zisblatt goes to the ghetto with her daughter. Lantos takes his grandchildren back to show them where he was involved in the underground. Basch returns to Dachau with his son. As we hear about their lives today Lantos is a US congressman, Lok Cahana a painter, Firestone an educator, Basch a businessman, Zisblatt a grandmother—all five reflect on how their experiences during the last days of the Holocaust have formed their view of the world.

If any subject can make film-makers rethink their technique from first principles, then surely the *Shoah*—Nazi Germany's attempted genocide of European Jews—will. The crime is so vast that mere texts, certainly conventional ones, seem inadequate as a means of reporting it. Writer George Steiner and others advocated literary silence and painters produced square fields of blackness. Claude Lanzmann extended the experience of watching his film *Shoah* to nine and a half hours, refusing ellipsis.

For its first hour at least, *The Last Days* attempts no such fundamental rethink. People in their late sixties and early seventies sit in their homes and recall a time of barbarism. Their tripod-shot, 35mm, widescreen interviews dissolve into slow-motion archive footage of the things they describe. Hans Zimmer's sombre music underscores. Director-editor James Moll, taking his cue from executive producer Steven Spielberg's Survivors of the Shoah Visual History Foundation, builds much of his film out of seated portraits of people in the present describing events in the past.

He does other, better things too, but it is the passivity of this basic approach, the aesthetically easy way in which the past dissolves into the present, which makes the film feel under-imagined. The fact that these people are relatively young, and that they—especially Irene Zisblatt speak with such freshness, means their accounts are accessible and of great educational value. Occasionally striking, unfamiliar details emerge: Zisblatt's town was taken by just two SS men on motorbikes, as most of its residents were sympathisers. Others were coaxed from the ghettos by being told they were going to work in vineyards.

If this history had not been so well documented elsewhere, if the film-makers had discovered substantial new archive film, documentation or eye-witness accounts, then their presentation in any form would have been fully justified. But since *The Last Days* doesn't break really new ground, the nature of its presentation becomes an issue. Moll's sensitive humanism is deeply compassionate and tasteful, but there is a danger that such survivor interviews become the only way the horrific past is accessed. The unforgettable moment in Lanzmann's *Shoah* when Jan Karski walks away from the camera, unable for a time to face the pain of recollection, has always seemed to me to be about the impossibility of filmically turning back the clock.

There are surely more inventive ways of exploring the themes raised in *The Last Days*. Imagine what a surrealist like David Lynch might make of the Shoah Foundation's extraordinary collection of half a million survivors talking. Imagine how well Maximilian Schell's techniques in his documentary film about Marlene Dietrich—where he interviewed her in sound only, then recreated her apartment in a studio—might work for this gigantic resource. What would the artist Douglas Gordon do with such material?

The Last Days grows in stature in other sequences, however. Each participant visits some of the places he or she has described and at such times the film becomes more layered. At several points the cinematic ease is broken by the appearance of Hans Munch, an off-hand Nazi doctor. Renée Firestone discovers her sister was experimented on in the "institute" where Munch was director. She meets him and shows him a list that confirms it. He says, "It's nothing. All is good." Afterwards she comments, "I tried to be civilised. He was very evasive. I became very angry." She then visits Crematorium V where her mother died. These moments are as moving as anything I have ever seen and they are charged with the unique qualities of documentary film. They stand head and shoulders above the editorial smoothness of much of what has gone before, which amounts to a philosophical underestimation of what happened in the last days of World War II.

VILLAGE VOICE, 2/9/99, p. 70, Gary Susman

Though it's full of the conventions of Holocaust documentaries—survivors who burst into tears in midstory, indelible footage of the walking dead—*The Last Days* is a bracingly unsentimental, moving retelling, focusing on Hungary, to which the Holocaust spread only in the last year of World War II. Director James Moll devotes the first half of the film to familiar-sounding testimony from five survivors; the second half shows them passing down history by returning to their hometowns and to the camps with their descendants. But instead of closure, says survivor Renee Firestone, there are only "new questions and new doubts." Firestone, whose sister Klara underwent medical experiments before she died in Auschwitz, confronts the evasive Dr. Hans Munch, whose successful defense against war crimes charges was that, as long as he kept performing "harmless" trials on such subjects as Klara, he kept them from the gas chamber. Unanswered and unanswerable questions abound, not just why the genocide happened but also how those spared were to live with the memories. Says survivor Alice Lok Cahana, "For us, liberation wasn't the last day."

Also reviewed in:
CHICAGO TRIBUNE, 2/12/99, Friday/p. I, Michael Wilmington
NATION, 3/1/99, p. 35, Stuart Klawans
NEW REPUBLIC, 3/8/99, p. 30, Stanley Kauffmann
NEW YORK TIMES, 2/5/99, p. E16, Stephen Holden
VARIETY, 10/19-25/98, p. 76, Dennis Harvey
WASHINGTON POST, 4/9/99, p. C1, Marc Fisher
WASHINGTON POST, 4/9/99, Weekend/p. 51, Desson Howe

LAST NIGHT

A Lions Gate Films release of a Rhombus Media production with the participation of Telefilm Canada in association with the Canadian Broadcasting Corporation and La Sept Arte. *Executive Producer:* Caroline Benjo and Carole Scotta. *Producer:* Niv Fichman and Daniel Iron. *Director:* Don McKellar. *Screenplay:* Don McKellar. *Director of Photography:* Douglas Koch. *Editor:* Reginald Harkema. *Music:* Alexina Louie and Alex Pauk. *Music Editor:* Colin Baxter, Hans Lucas, and Christopher Donaldson. *Sound:* John J. Thomson. *Sound Editor:* Steve Munro. *Casting:* Diane Kerbel. *Production Designer:* John Dondertman. *Art Director:* Kei Ng. *Set Decorator:* Patricia Cuccia. *Special Effects:* John LaForet. *Costumes:* Lea Carlson. *Make-up:* Sarah Fairbairn. *Stunt Coordinator:* Peter Szkoda. *Running time:* 98 minutes. *MPAA Rating:* Not Rated.

CAST: Don McKellar (Patrick Wheeler); Sandra Oh (Sandra); Callum Keith Rennie (Craig Zwiller); Sarah Polley (Jennifer Wheeler); David Cronenberg (Duncan); Robin Gammell (Mr.

Wheeler); Roberta Maxwell (Mrs. Wheeler); Tracy Wright (Donna); Michael McMurtry (Menzies); Charmion King (Grandmother); Trent McMullen (Alex); Arsinée Khanjian (Streetcar Mother); Geneviève Bujold (Mrs. Carlton); Jessica Booker (Rose); Karen Glave (Lily); Chandra Muszka (Streetcar Daughter); Brian Renfro (Angry Driver); François Girard, Daniel Iron, and Bruce McDonald (Wild Guys); Pierre Elrick (Cousin Ernie); Kirsten Johnson, Regan Moore, and Darren O'Donnell (Revellers); Bob Martin (TV Newscaster); Michael Barry (Marty); Nathalie Shats (Marty's Girlfriend); Tom McCamus (Radio DJ); Jackie Burroughs (Runner).

LOS ANGELES TIMES, 11/5/99, Calendar/p. 19, Jan Stuart

[The following review by Jan Stuart appeared in a slightly different form in **NEWSDAY, 11/5/99, Part II/p. B12.**]

The world is coming to an end at midnight. How would you spend your last night? With whom would you spend it? Would you behave? Would you break the rules? Would you be in a helping spirit, or every man for himself? What, at the end of the day, really matters?

These are the questions that wash over us as we take in "Last Night," a mordantly funny and shrewdly understated millennial fantasy from Don McKellar, a Canadian actor and writer ("The Red Violin") who is making his directing debut.

No reasons are offered for the apocalypse awaiting the characters whose lives overlap in "Last Night," but they have all made their peace with it. A 30-ish widower named Patrick (McKellar) puts in a token dinner appearance with his family but prefers to spend these last hours in solitude. Patrick's buddy Craig (Callum Keith Rennie) chooses to fulfill his every last sexual fantasy, using the Internet to round up willing participants. And Alex (Trent McMullen), a former schoolmate, elects to give his first, and last, concert hall recital during the final hour.

As Patrick returns home past roving gangs who are looking for cheap thrills, he meets a married woman named Sandra (Sandra Oh), who is trying without success to get back to her own home. Despite his own isolationist resolve, Patrick finds himself being drawn to the woman, who intends to commit suicide with her husband at the stroke of midnight.

For all the mayhem and violence spilling onto the streets, "Last Night" is a relatively polite speculation on human behavior in dire circumstances. Perhaps only in Canada would a gas company executive (touchingly played by David Cronenberg) methodically call each one of his customers to thank them for their business.

Not everyone is as well-mannered. Patrick's mother (the estimable Roberta Maxwell) tries to make him feel guilty about abandoning the family, while an elderly relative grumbles that some of the sympathy pouring out to children should be reserved for older folk such as herself, who have survived so much suffering.

Resolutely unsentimental to the not-so-bitter end, McKellar spikes his drama with memorably droll encounters. Chasing over to Craig's to see if he can borrow a car for Sandra, Patrick intrudes on one of his pal's trysts, a former French teacher of theirs (Geneviève Bujold), who gives the startled Patrick a pop language quiz. When Patrick presses his reluctant buddy for one of his cars, Craig relents grudgingly, saying, "I wanted to die a man with three cars."

The soundtrack is peppered with trashy bubble-gum hits as heard over the radio. Perhaps the most disturbing notion put forth by "Last Night" is the understanding that the potentates who rule the airwaves have so successfully robbed their listeners of choice, we may be forced to spend our final minutes on Earth listening to "Taking Care of Business."

NEW STATESMAN, 7/5/99, p. 45, Jonathan Romney

There's a priceless piece of teaser copy on the publicity for the new Canadian film *Last Night:* "Nothing to wear ... Love life a mess ... Can't get a cab. Nothing on TV ..." Then the pay-off. "It's not the end of the world ..." (place a sly, pregnant pause here). "There's still six hours left."

Don McKellar's film is the perfect antidote to those fire-and-fury apocalypse packages in which blazing portents of destruction streak across the skies only to be halted at the last moment by a few stout American hearts—*Armageddon, Independence Day* and the weirdly sanctimonious *Deep Impact,* in which the final computer-generated tableau of redemption could have been the airbrushed painting on a Jehovah's Witnesses pamphlet. McKellar treats Doomsday the smart way—he rules out salvation from the start, and chooses to treat the biggest topic imaginable in a scrupulously minor key. Be honest, what are you more likely to be doing on the very last night of the world: praying for Bruce Willis as he struggles against cosmic forces, or hoping the farewell roast is going to be cooked in time?

Last Night is set in Toronto between six and midnight on the last night of 1999. The world will end at the stroke of 12, quite simply, and in broad daylight. *Last Night* doesn't explain why the world is ending, or why there's no night—astronomers and science-fiction buffs can draw their own conclusions. Toronto is a wasteland, practically empty, although occasionally party crowds move through the barren streets, as do looters, lunatics and the odd frustrated motorist who may be rushing to hire the last dinner jacket in town. The mood isn't so much one of expectation and dread, more that of the fag-end of a party in the small hours, with the sky already light and everyone hanging on with weary patience till they can crawl off to bed or breakfast.

McKellar's small group of characters all have some business to conclude, mostly with a degree of everyday *sang froid*. Sandra (Sandra Oh), the film's most frazzled character, is trying to get across town to fulfil her suicide pact with her husband (David Cronenberg, guesting with his usual cordial mortician's calm), who's staying late at the gas company to make polite corporate thank-you-and-farewell calls to everyone in the phone book. Narcissistic hipster Craig (Callum Keith Rennie) is assiduously working through all his unrealised sexual fantasies, and by mid-evening has moved on to a liaison with his old French teacher (a languid, wryly melancholic Geneviève Bujold).

Life, meanwhile, goes on in what we can only assume unless McKellar is being very cruel—is typical Canadian fashion. On the radio, a DJ is playing the top tunes of the millennium, and it's only halfway through the film that we realise the selection is no one's but his own: he's just indulging himself with cringesome MOR pulp (some of it rather good, although it's unlikely that forgotten 1970s names like Burton Cummings or the DeFranco Family can count on the film reviving their careers). The best Canadian in-joke is the announcement that thousands have chosen to end their days at a giant guitar jam hosted by Randy Bachman, of the wretched rockers Bachman-Turner Overdrive.

Writer-director McKellar, whose face you'll know from Cronenberg and Atom Egoyan films, plays Patrick, the centre of an Altmanesque ensemble of characters. Patrick's main anxiety is to get through a family dinner in one piece (Mom in beaming denial, Grandma peevishly hacking through a generation's worth of family videos) and return home to brood in solitude over his lost love. Of course, it's nothing but interruptions from there on. This soured loner—McKellar is a master of testy sarcasm—does have a redemptive moment in store, but it's handled with sublime lightness in the film's final moments, to the tune of "Guantanamera" (the subject, earlier on, of one of those pop trivia discussions mandatory since *Reservoir Dogs*—and one of the better examples of the genre, too).

Among other things, *Last Night* is an extraordinary feat of atmospherics, with the cinematographer Douglas Koch effectively finding a whole new spin on the film technique of "day for night". Here we're convinced that broad daylight effectively is night-time. The light is cast by a glaucous sun, whose unnatural, creeping progress across the sky we infer as it moves from point to point across the bleakly hip interiors of Craig's apartment.

The script's bone-dry wit has a serious philosophical edge: everyone seems pretty certain about what will be the most important thing in life when the crunch comes, and yet everyone might well be wrong and have the appropriate revelation with seconds to spare. If anyone in this film does get redeemed, it's in a sweetly farcical way: the indefatigably priapic Craig is humanised by a timely attack of impotence.

Only in Canada can you get away with films like this (although *Last Night* was originally commissioned for a French millennium series). Even in the American independent sector, it would have been considered impossible—global oblivion is not what you'd call all an upbeat ending. And yet, with extraordinary bravado and *joie de vivre*, as well as a lovely Hitchcockian circling shot, McKellar brings history to a close with a burst of pure elation. When the film was screened for the first time in Cannes last year, you could have heard a pin drop in this closing moment—until someone's mobile went off. And when the time comes, that's probably exactly how it will all finish—with neither a bang nor a whimper but a Motorola.

NEW YORK POST, 11/5/99, p. 61, Jonathan Foreman

"Last Night" is a rare and welcome reminder of how original, provocative and moving a low-budget independent film can be.

Nicely timed for the millennium—and essential viewing for the 18 percent of Americans who believe that the apocalypse will happen in their lifetime—it's a film about the ways a selection of quirky Canadians choose to spend the last night of the planet.

How or why the world is ending is never explained (although darkness no longer falls), but when the movie opens there are six hours to go, and the timing of the end has been to known to everyone for two months.

The central character is Patrick (Don McKellar), a mildly obnoxious and self-involved architect. Although his parents—who throw a guilt-laden Christmas dinner on the last evening—want him to stay with them for the end, Patrick is determined to be alone and in his apartment.

But when he gets there he finds Sandra (Sandra Oh) on his doorstep. She's been trying to get home to her husband after her car was destroyed by part of the crowd of people filling their last night with pointless vandalism.

Sandra enlists Patrick's help and he takes her to the apartment of his friend Craig (Callum Keith Rennie) to borrow a car. Craig has spent his last weeks trying every kind of sex that's ever caught his fancy, and as Patrick arrives, Craig's high school French teacher (Genevieve Bujold, still beautiful) is just leaving.

There are moments when "Last Night" feels like a slow episode of the "Twilight Zone," and others when it feels more like a play than a film. Despite this staginess, it's unpredictable and ruefully romantic, and Sandra Oh is very good in a role that could not be more different from her Rita Wu in TV's " Arli$$."

Sarah Polley has a tiny, insubstantial role as Patrick's sister.

SIGHT AND SOUND, 7/99, p. 44, Richard Kelly

A Canadian city, 6 pm. The world is due to end at midnight. Patrick Wheeler attends a last 'Christmas' dinner with his family. His sister Jennifer and her boyfriend Alex are going to a party. Patrick's parents try in vain to dissuade Patrick from leaving to spend the final hours alone. Gas-company executive Duncan and his colleague Donna attempt to keep services running until the end. Sandra is trying to join her husband at home, but her car is wrecked by revellers, civil order having collapsed. Craig makes love to a succession of women, including his high-school French teacher Mrs Carlton.

Patrick meets Sandra on his doorstep, and takes her to Craig's where she borrows a car. Craig tells Patrick he is attempting to fit in every conceivable sexual activity, but Patrick declines Craig's proposition to have sex with him. Sandra is unable to drive through the throng of revellers in the city. Duncan is killed in his home by a stranger. As midnight approaches, Craig relieves Donna of her virginity. Sandra (Duncan's wife) returns and asks Patrick to replace Duncan in a suicide pact the couple had planned. They hold guns to each other's heads, but at the last moment, they kiss.

"Millenniums," disgraced MP Peter Mandelson once wrote with customary acuity, "only come once in a thousand years." Good job too, since they are widely supposed to provoke all manner of feverish atavism in the populace. But as we now face down the year 2000, our fevers seem to find expression only in senseless pop songs and disaster movies about meteors. Fair play then to actor-director Don McKellar few millennarian dramas have been so muted and mild-mannered as his directorial debut.

One would like to forswear cultural stereotypes, but as a vision of terminal chaos and decadence, *Last Night* is deeply bourgeois-Canadian. There's a lot of finicky emoting, not much in the way of liberating gut-laughter, and it all see to unfold in a series of tasteful Toronto apartments. David Cronenberg once described the experience of making his film *Shivers* (1974) in a Montreal apartment block: "We all wanted to rip that place apart and run naked, screaming, through the halls." Here, however, the cultivated sterility of early Atom Egoyan pervades the proceedings. One's heart sinks with the appearance of Egoyan regular Arsinée Khanjian in a typically haunted, waxen cameo.

McKellar's cleverest visual trick is that the entire drama is played out in broad daylight: darkness never falls, even at the bitter end. But his refusal to explain exactly why the end is nigh is a very contemporary cop-out. The dialogue has much sport at the expense of mobile phones, mainframes and internet pick-ups, so there's a nagging sense throughout that humankind has meekly consented to its own destruction, in a devil's pact with impersonal technologies. But some vague nostalgia for human spirit and solidarity can be discerned for example when Patrick lectures Sandra on the socialist significance of Pete Seeger's version of José Marti's 'Guantanamera'.

To his great credit, McKellar has picked some fine performers, and engineered a good number of grace notes. As the keen libertine Craig, Callum Keith Rennie has a wiry, raffish sexual presence, his bedroom chores accompanied always by Parliament's 'I've Been Watching You'. As one of Craig's last partners, the wonderful Geneviève Bujold brings a draft of wanton elegance to the affair. Tracy Wright does an endearing turn as virginal office stalwart Donna, hoping finally to escape her fruitless workplace. And David Cronenberg himself is well cast as the aspirant suicide Duncan, forced to confront the reaper before his self-appointed hour. The reasoning purr of Cronenberg's voice, and his blankly sinister face (into which all available shadows seem to fly) are ideal for the task.

McKellar's only mistake was to craft the niggling central role of Patrick, and then play it himself. His prickly, nebbish persona can't give the movie a spine. When Patrick and Craig are alone and Craig makes a modest proposal that they get horizontal, the audience anticipates Patrick's wary flinch well before it comes. If he had stuck his tongue down his fellow actor's throat, he'd have sent us careering off into a much livelier movie.

Instead, the final, calculated exchange of fates is a bit of a let-down. Duncan dies alone, and we're denied what would have been an intriguing last intimacy between him and Sandra. Patrick steps in to deputise, and at last we learn the excuse for his quavering reticence throughout the film: his saintly girlfriend Karen a kindergarten teacher, of course—was lately and cruelly snatched from him by death. Thus as all humanity faces extinction, Patrick wants to be loved for his very own personal tragedy. The sentiment feels strangely late-twentieth century in its towering conceit, but it's at least as old as 'September 1, 1939'. "Not universal love/But to be loved alone": this craving Auden ruefully skewered as the commonest of human failings, before proposing that "we must love one another or die."

VILLAGE VOICE, 11/9/99, p. 140, Amy Taubin

To the inventory of ecstatic film finales add Don McKellar's version of the end the world in *Last Night* . McKellar combines Pete Seeger's recording of "Guantanamera," a riff on *Vertigo*'s whirling 360-degree embrace, and radiant faces (his own and Sandra Oh's) The unlikely fusion results in a moment that rivals Giulietta Messina smiling into the camera in *Nights of Cabiria,* or the seaside sunset in Eric Rohmer's *The Green Ray.*

A comic stealth weapon in Ato Egoyan's *Exotica* and David Cronenberg's *eXistenZ,* McKellar has flown almost entirely under U.S. radar. In his native Canada, he's best known as the writer and star of the inspired sitcom *Twitch City,* in which he plays an agoraphobic couch potato whose sex appeal is as undeniable as it's mysterious. Although he's cowritten two features—*32 Short Films About Glenn Gould* and *The Red Violin*—*Last Night* is his feature directorial debut.

Playing on millennial anxieties, *Last Night* proposes a familiar existential question: what would you do if you—and everyone else on the planet—had only six hours to live? McKellar's characters have had two months to ask themselves what matters most to them and to plan their final moments accordingly. Patrick, who's played by the filmmaker and is the film's governing consciousness, is adamant about spending his last hours alone. This puts him in the usual conflict with his clingy, guilt-tripping mom, and, less predictably, with his best friend Craig (Callum Keith Rennie). Craig is working his way through a list of sex acts hitherto only fantasized, and wants Patrick to participate in a guy-and-guy experience. In other words, the end of the world, while removing pesky mate questions like what you have to do to pay next month's rent, still leaves you the everyday dilemma of balancing your own desires against the demands of family, friends, and society, not to mention your neurotic superego.

Like the character he plays, McKellar is a romantic with a taste for the absurd—the kind of romantic who might feel that it's a privilege to be present at the end of the world, especially since no one was around to witness the beginning. Patrick is testy, stubborn, and almost terminally ambivalent. Love does not come easily to him, but by a quirk of fate, he's thrown an opportunity to affirm Eros in the face of oblivion and he takes it. On his doorstep he finds Sandra (Sandra Oh), whose plan to get across town and home to her husband—with whom she plans to commit suicide—has been derailed by gangs of marauders. (The end of the world doesn't bring out the best in everybody.)

Bare-bones filmmaking, *Last Night* is nothing special to look at, but it has a witty, trenchant script, lots of complicated characters, and a few actors who turn human frailty into something nearly sublime. With his worried-aardvark face and his half-choked, half-drawling voice, McKellar matches defensiveness with vulnerability. Oh's impulsiveness and emotional intensity make her a great foil for him. David Cronenberg as the buttoned-up manager of the gas company and Genevieve Bujold as a high school French teacher who's spending her final hours looking up former students are silly, sweet, and valiant. Bujold is particularly hilarious when, departing Craig's apartment (their 15-year-old fantasies happily coincided), she encounters Patrick, and demands to know what he's been doing with himself. Patrick dutifully delivers his résumé in halting French and bids her "au revoir." Not au revoir, she answers, drawing her coat close to her breast, diva style. "Adieu." It's a Hollywood adage that audiences will flock to films that make death seem less than final. Existential to the core, *Last Night* takes the opposite tack. In the inevitable adieu is the meaning of life.

Also reviewed in:
CHICAGO TRIBUNE, 12/24/99, Friday/p. H, Mark Caro
NEW YORK TIMES, 11/5/99, p. E16, Stephen Holden
VARIETY, 6/1-7/98, p. 36, Leonard Klady
WASHINGTON POST, 12/3/99, p. C1, Stephen Hunter
WASHINGTON POST, 12/3/99, Weekend/p. 55, Desson Howe

LATE AUGUST, EARLY SEPTEMBER

A Zietgeist Films release of a Dacia Films and Cineaco co-production with the participation of Le Studio Canal+, the Centre National de la Cinématographie, and Soficas Sofinergie et Sofygram. *Executive Producer:* Françoise Guglielmi. *Producer:* Georges Benayoun and Philippe Carcassonne. *Director:* Olivier Assayas. *Screenplay (French with English subtitles):* Olivier Assayas. *Director of Photography:* Denis Lenoir. *Editor:* Luc Barnier. *Sound:* François Waledisch. *Sound Editor:* Stéphanie Granel and Marie-Christine Ruh. *Casting:* Antoinette Boulat. *Production Designer:* François Renaud. *Set Decorator:* Cécilia Blom. *Costumes:* Françoise Clavel. *Make-up:* Thi-Than Tu Nguyen. *Running time:* 105 minutes. *MPAA Rating:* Not Rated.

CAST: Mathieu Amalric (Gabriel Deshayes); Virginie Ledoyen (Anne Rosenwald); François Cluzet (Adrien Willner); Jeanne Balibar (Jenny); Alex Descas (Jérémie); Arsinée Khanjian (Lucie); Nathalie Richard (Maryelle Deshayes); Mia Hansen-Love (Véra); Eric Elmosnino (Thomas Deshayes); Olivier Cruveiller (Axel); Jean-Baptiste Malartre (Editor); André Marcon (Gérard Hattou); Elisabeth Mazev (Prospective Buyers); Olivier Py (Prospective Buyers); Jean-Baptiste Montagut (Joseph Costa); Olivier Torres (Marc Jobert); Joanna Preiss (Receptionist); Jean-François Gallotte (Documentary Producer); Fejria Deliba (Lucie's Friend); Bernard Nissille (Frédéric); Béatrice de Roaldès and Jean-Loup Taleghani (Couple at Dinner); Elisabeth Marre and Thierry Angelvi (Apartment Buyers); Damien Dodane (Axel's Friend); Alexandra Yonnet (Production Office Junior); Ozal Descas (Jérémie's Daughter); Julien Vieville (Véra's Little Friend); Marion Hanania (Véra's Friend); Catherine Mouchet and Elli Medeiros (Themselves).

LOS ANGELES TIMES, 8/20/99, Calendar/p. 14, Kenneth Turan

"Late August, Early September" is involving and intimate as only other people's lives deftly observed can be. An insightful film that takes us on a nuanced emotional journey with a group of friends trying to make sense of the romantic choices they've made, it has the sympathy and psychological acuity we've come to recognize as the hallmark of French cinema at its best.

"Late August" is the seventh feature for 44-year-old writer-director Olivier Assayas, but only the second (after the very different "Irma Vep") to find commercial distribution in this country. Its title refers not to a specific time on the calendar but to a time in life, when the easy indolence of youth is ending and it's necessary to get serious, to figure out where you are and what you want to do.

At the center of the film's circle of acquaintances is the oldest of the group, author Adrien Willner (the Dustin Hoffmanish Francois Cluzet). His four novels have given him something of a cult status, but at 40, Adrien feels at a crossroads, not sure if he's done the right things with his life, worrying about never having gotten through to a wider public.

Though he can be distracted and difficult, Adrien has the force of personality necessary to dominate his little circle, which is consequently shocked when he announces that an unnamed illness is going to put him in the hospital and possibly threaten his life.

Most affected is Gabriel, the film's co-protagonist and Adrien's disciple. As played by Mathieu Amalric (who has an urchin-like Dead End Kid look and previously starred in Arnaud Desplechin's "How I Got Into an Argument ... My Sex Life"), the uncertain and insecure Gabriel feels both close to and intimidated by his mentor.

Gabriel is introduced at an awkward moment; he's trying to sell the Parisian apartment belonging to him and his former girlfriend. She is Jenny (Jeanne Balibar), a lively woman with a crooked grin, who agreed to the split but is more regretful than Gabriel that it's occurred.

That's because Gabriel already has a new girlfriend, the beautiful Anne ("A Single Girl's" Virginie Ledoyen), a clothing designer who is both younger and more impulsive than the rest of Gabriel's friends, a situation that Assayas underlines by shooting most of her scenes with a hand-held camera.

Because character and emotions are his main concerns, Assayas and Denis Lenoir, his director of photography, employ a lot of close-ups that increase the film's sense of intimacy. But there is also room for the fluid cinematography that is the director's trademark, including some lightning moves that camera buffs are going to want to play back again and again once the film comes to video.

Assayas uses on-screen titles to break his story up into segments, like chapters in a novel, offering us glimpses of relationships in transit as his characters navigate through crises both real and imaginary. Over the course of a year, they worry about the boundaries of friendship and love, the pain of romance and possible death, struggling to make the best of their situations while balancing the needs and neuroses that inevitably get in the way.

In a film like this, it's the journey as much as the destination that affords pleasure, as people change and new characters—as well as new revelations about old characters—gradually get added to the mix. Almost imperceptibly, "Late August, Early September" accumulates an emotional impact that is both powerful and unexpected.

Beautifully made (including exquisite use of the haunting guitar work of Mali's legendary Ali Farka Toure), this confident, accomplished work gains by being part of the great tradition of Gallic cinema. As Arnaud Desplechin said a few years ago when he introduced "How I Got Into an Argument" at the New York Film Festival, "for a French guy, this sort of film is like a western for Americans."

NEW YORK, 7/19/99, p. 73, Peter Rainer

The 44-year-old French director Olivier Assayas, best known for *Irma Vep*, offers up his own variation on the vagaries of companionship and amour and mortality in *Late August, Early September*, a mellifluous contemporary roundelay about Parisian friends in their thirties. It has some of the same resonance as Claude Sautet's 1974 *Vincent, François, Paul and the Others,* but it's about a somewhat younger and scroungier crowd. The cast, including Virginie Ledoyen,

François Cluzet, and Mathieu Amalric, is as well coordinated as a fine chamber-music ensemble; their entrances and vanishings and re-entries play like recurring motifs.

NEW YORK POST, 7/7/99, p. 48, Rod Dreher

Three years ago, when asked at a New York Film Festival press conference why nobody was interested in French film anymore, writer-director Olivier Assayas shrugged. He said as long as he thought he was doing good work, and his friends agreed, that was all he cared about.

Not surprisingly, "Late August, Early September," Assayas' latest, is the kind of pretentious picture only a Ministry of Culture grant-giver could love.

It's a purposely unfocused slice-of-life movie about a group of dithering thirtysomething Parisians and the way they react to the imminent death of their older friend basically, by breaking up, changing apartments, chain smoking and having sex. Imagine the dreary "Singles" written and directed by a French intellectual, and you get the idea.

The writer is Adrien (Francois Cluzet), a cult novelist in his 40s, whose illness forces him to consider that he may die without ever having written a book that reached more than a few people. When he's not angsting boringly over the Meaning of It All, Adrien passes his time with blond gamine Vera (Mia Hansen-Love), his teen-age hottie girlfriend.

Meanwhile, his friend and admirer Gabriel (Mathieu Amalric), is preoccupied with ending his relationship with Jenny (Jeanne Balibar) and selling their apartment. Gabriel's new girlfriend, Anne (Virginie Ledoyen), is a tempestuous fashionista with a weakness for "Betty Blue"-style tantrums.

"Late August, Early September" follows this group over the course of a year. The look of the film, some of which is shot with a hand-held camera, is realistic, as is the dialogue. But Assayas isn't interested in plot; he just observes his characters going about their aimless lives: meeting over coffee, finding jobs, arguing, and the like.

MTV's diarylike "The Real World" is a model of narrative force and concision compared with this, and even Eric Rohmer's stultifying talkfests at least seem to be about something.

Assayas never accounts for the choices his characters make, either by having others confront them or forcing them to explain themselves. They are a self-absorbed bunch, whose banal lives have no weight or consequence. Despite sensitive, naturalistic performances from the cast, we don't know or care about them much more at film's end than we did at the beginning.

A lengthy interview with Assayas that came with the press notes clarified what he was attempting to do philosophically with the film, with reference to Proust, Hegel and the artist Joseph Beuys.

That's probably why "Late August, Early September" is less a living, breathing movie than a dry exercise in theory.

VILLAGE VOICE, 7/13/99, p. 57, J. Hoberman

The title of Olivier Assayas's *Late August, Early September* refers to a season of life, and that's scarcely the only Rohmerian aspect to the French cineaste's adventurous if disappointing follow-up to his art house firecracker *Irma Vep*. Assayas's portrait of a half-dozen still-youngish Parisians is deliberately structured, steeped in dailiness, and filled with constant conversation—it's very much a series of one-on-one scenes concerned with issues of love, work, and real estate.

Of course, the hyperkinetic Assayas style has almost nothing in common with Rohmer's understated understatement. Rather, Assayas has a showy facility for long, fluid takes and complicated ensemble acting. Shot vérité-style in Super-16, *Late August, Early September* exults in this. The elliptical opening sequences, mainly hectic handheld close-ups, introduce a surplus of characters and material. Much of the action thereafter is disconcertingly oblique and brusque-albeit softened and distanced by African musician Ali Farka Toure's elusive fretted-instrument score.

If the film's focus is not immediately apparent-lost in a clutter of purposefully banal interactions—it may be that Assayas is treating us to a somewhat older cohort than in his earlier films. Mainly in their thirties, most of his characters are already burdened by history—emotionally tied to their ex-lovers or jointly owned apartments, worried about their career choices, and haunted by a sense of failure. The focal point is the group's senior member, a serious novelist named Adrien (François Cluzet); the protagonist is his admirer Gabriel (Mathieu Amalric), a would-be writer caught between his relationship with the warmly nostalgic Jenny (Jeanne Balibar) and a gorgeous, but manic, younger woman (Virginie Ledoyan).

The boyish and slightly feral Amalric—who played a not dissimilar role several years ago in Arnaud Desplechin's *My Sex Life … Or How I Got Into an Argument*—is not always easy to read, but then all the characters lack definition. Or rather, they are defined only in relation to each other. Assayas is at his best with a close-up pan through the crowd at a smoky nightclub or choreographing the emotional complexity of a scene in which a gaggle of old friends reminisce. But too often, the movie sinks into an amorphous state of emotional torpor.

Late August, Early September unfolds over the course of a year. Gabriel ends one relationship and embarks on another, gets (and quits) his first "real" job, and loses a friend to death. The movie exits leaving a trail of vignettes that seem to have been designed to show that life goes on. It's a pretty slight payoff for such a diffuse plot. In the end it seems to be the filmmaker, not Gabriel, who is working something out.

Also reviewed in:
CHICAGO TRIBUNE, 9/17/99, Friday/p. F, John Petrakis
NEW YORK TIMES, 7/7/99, p. E5, Janet Maslin
VARIETY, 10/12-18/98, p. 44, Derek Elley

LEGEND OF 1900, THE

A Fine Line Features release of a Medusa Film and Sciarlo production. *Executive Producer:* Laura Fattori. *Producer:* Francesco Tornatore. *Director:* Giuseppe Tornatore. *Screenplay:* Giuseppe Tornatore. *Based on the stage monologue "Novecento" by:* Alessandro Baricco. *Director of Photography:* Lajos Koltai. *Editor:* Massimo Quaglia. *Music:* Ennio Morricone. *Choreographer:* Leontine Snel. *Sound:* Roberto Petrozzi and (music) Fabio Venturi and Damiano Antinori. *Sound Editor:* Michael Billingsley. *Casting:* Fabrizio Sergenti Castellani, Jeremy Zimmermann, and Valerie McCaffrey. *Production Designer:* Francesco Frigeri. *Set Decorator:* Bruno Cesari. *Costumes:* Maurizio Millenotti. *Make-up:* Luigi Rocchetti and Renato Francola. *Running time:* 110 minutes. *MPAA Rating:* R.

CAST: Tim Roth (1900/Danny Boodman T.D./Lemon Novecento); Pruitt Taylor Vince (Max Tooney); Bill Nunn (Danny Boodman); Clarence Williams III (Jelly Roll Morton); Peter Vaughan (Music Shop Owner); Melanie Thierry (Girl); Niall O'Brien (Plymouth Harbor Master); Easton Gage (Young 1900 I); Gabriele Lavia (Farmer); Cory Buck (Young 1900 II); Alberto Vasquez (Mexican Stoker); Cory Buck (Lemon, age 8); Norman Chancer (Disc Jockey); Sidney Cole (Black Guy); Luigi De Luca (Neapolitan Stoker); Agostino Di Giorgio (Banjo Player); Harry Ditson (Captain Smith); Femi Elufowoju, Jr. (Black Stoker); Nigel Fan (Chinese Stoker); Easton Gage (Lemon, age 4); Eamon Geoghegan (Sergeant); Piero Gimondo (Clarinetist); Kevin McNally (Senator Wilson); Luis Molteni (Commissioner); Roger Monk (Irish Stoker); Aida Noriko (Mattress Maker); Vernon Nurse (Fritz Hermann); Bernard Padden (Boatswain); Stefano Pagni (Bass/Tuba Player); Bryan Pringle (Ship's Recruiter); Michael Supnick (Trombonist); Ivan Truol Troncosco (Stowaway); Adriano Wajskol (Percussionist); Heathcote Williams (Doctor Klauserman); Wilson Du Bois (Radio Operator); Leonid Zashavski (Polish Stokero); Steven Luotto ('Blind' Helmsman).

CHRISTIAN SCIENCE MONITOR, 12/3/99, p. 15, David Sterritt

[*The Legend of 1900* was reviewed jointly with *Sweet and Lowdown*; see Sterritt's review of that film.]

LOS ANGELES TIMES, 10/29/99, Calendar/p. 2, Kevin Thomas

Giuseppe Tomatore's "The Legend of 1900" is a beautiful and venturesome companion piece to the director's beloved "Cinema Paradiso," for both are deeply moving affirmations of the power of the imagination.

Adapted by Tornatore, in an assured English-language debut, from Alessandro Baricco's theatrical monologue "1900," "Legend" is so unusual that its universal appeal is not nearly as immediate as in the earlier film, which drew upon everyone's childhood memories of discovering the movies. But as this exquisite fable unfolds, we're increasingly able to recognize ourselves in Tornatore's unlikely hero—and Tornatore is able to find in it unexpected meanings—perhaps even more than in "Cinema Paradiso."

Tantalizingly structured to intrigue us night from the start, it opens with a middle-aged man (Pruitt Taylor Vince), unshaven and clearly down on his luck, entering a used musical instrument shop in what proves to be post-World War II London. Vince's Max, a jazz musician, has come to sell his trumpet. The shopkeeper (Peter Vaughan) drives a hard bargain, and Max starts to leave but says he must play his cherished instrument one more time. When the shopkeeper hears him, he is inspired to play a jazz record. Shocked at what he hears, Max is moved to tell the shopkeeper an amazing story.

We cut to the year 1900, when a hearty laborer, Danny (Bill Nunn), who shovels coal aboard the ocean liner Virginian, a vessel with the grandeur of the Titanic, discovers an abandoned baby boy nestled in a fruit box. Wanting to spare the infant the orphanages of the day, Danny, with the support of his co-workers, informally adopts the boy, calling him 1900. For eight years, 1900, who officially does not exist, goes undetected by the captain as the Virginia travels between Southampton and New York and other routes. But then Danny is killed in a shipboard accident, and 1900 escapes deportation by the captain through a virtuoso display of piano playing.

The Virginian sails gracefully into the Roaring '20s, its Beaux Arts elegance undiminished, and in 1927, Max and 1900 (Tim Roth) meet when Max joins the ship's red-hot jazz band. By now, 1900, the band's star attraction, can play any kind of music dazzlingly well and cuts a dapper figure in white tie and tail. He even takes on Jelly Roll Morton (a spot-on Clarence Williams III), the epitome of proud, cocky splendor as the father of jazz, but he finds the notion of competition abhorrent and pointless. The witty and urbane 1900 has mingled with the likes of Sigmund Freud, Arturo Toscanini and Erich Maria Remarque, yet, as Max learns, much to his astonishment, his new friend has never set foot on land.

Tornatore discovers in 1900 a metaphor rich in meaning, indeed, a metaphor for no less than the human experience. At first, we—and Max—see 1900 as in a state of limbo, a man who has escaped into his art and resists stepping into the muck of everyday life. But 1900 sees the land as a rat race, a place of overwhelmingly infinite choices and perils. The longer 1900 stays aboard, the more intimidating the idea of standing on terra firma becomes.

Ultimately, Tornatore finds a larger meaning in 1900's predicament: Namely, that while most of us have not experienced so unusually proscribed an existence as 1900 has, it is also obviously impossible for us to experience all of life in all of its aspects. Therefore, we have to rely upon our imagination to understand others as well as ourselves. It is finally impossible also not to see 1900 as a symbol of the individual's essential solitariness.

As this beguiling, splendid-looking film progresses, moving deftly between past and present, we become charmed by the brilliant 1900 and also by the loyal Max, both men played with flawless persuasiveness by Roth and Vince, respectively. But the Virginian can't keep on sailing forever, can it? What happens to Max becomes a source of increasing concern and suspense, and "Legend," gratifyingly, is one film in which the payoff is actually more than equal to the buildup. (You are left wanting to see the original 170-minute version—even if the film was badly received at that length at the Locarno festival.)

Ennio Morricone's score soars, ranging from jazzy to operatic, and "The Legend of 1900" becomes a particularly apt picture for the millennium's close. When Max remarks that "nobody is really done for as long as you have a good story to tell and someone to listen," he's giving us the very reason why Giuseppe Tornatore is likely to be around for a long time.

NEW YORK POST, 10/29/99, p. 45, Lou Lumenick

Giuseppe Tornatore's exquisitely beautiful "The Legend of 1900" is the enigmatic story of a musical Flying Dutchman—a jazz pianist who chooses to live his entire life on a luxury liner.

His full name is Danny Boodman T.D. Lemon 1900—discovered by a stevedore (Bill Nunn) in a lemon crate aboard the Virginian on the first day of the new century.

When his foster father is killed in an accident, 1900, now 8, gets to stay on board by demonstrating his considerable prowess entertaining passengers as a keyboard prodigy. As he grows into adulthood, it's clear that 1900 (Tim Roth) could write his own ticket anywhere—but he refuses to leave the Virginian, the only home he's ever known.

Leisurely structured as a two-hour series of vignettes, "The Legend of 1900" has one standout sequence, the first meeting between 1900 and Max (Pruitt Taylor Vince of "Heavy"), the jazz trumpeter who serves as the film's narrator.

The ship is swaying wildly on the ocean, and 1900 bids Max, who is violently seasick, to remove the brakes from his piano and join him at the bench. Max reluctantly does, and 1900 performs as the piano gracefully lurches around the ship's grand ballroom, then finally through a plate-glass window.

It's a stunning moment, not matched even by the film's climactic shipboard piano duel between 1900 and jazz legend Jelly Roll Morton (played with verve by Clarence Williams III).

These scenes are intercut with scenes set in the late 1940s, when a down-and-out Max pawns his horn and discovers a copy of the only recording 1900 ever made. He also learns that the Virginian, which had been turned into a hospital ship during World War II, is slated to be dynamited.

Max sets out to find and rescue 1900, along the way telling the story behind the recording, and that of the beautiful young immigrant who inspired it (French model Melanie Thierry) and briefly tempted 1900 to leave his ocean-going home.

Roth, who usually plays thugs in movies like "Pulp Fiction," is effectively cast against type as the sweetly naive and passive 1900, who doesn't say much except in the movie's somewhat over-wrought final scene.

Working with great assurance in English for the first time, Tornatore (who directed the wonderful "Cinema Paradiso"), calls his movie "a universal fable built around a very modern metaphor for the human condition—representing nothing less than the precariousness of life itself."

That's an awful lot of metaphorical cargo for any movie to carry, and this one is often more interesting than involving.

But with considerable contributions from cinematographer Lajos Koltai, production designer Francesco Frigeri and costume designer Maurizio Millenotti, "The Legend of 1900" transports us back to the early part of the century in grand style.

NEWSDAY, 10/29/99 Part II/p. B11, Jan Stuart

There must be something in the Italian soil that nurtures fantasies of extraordinary isolation. Admirers of fabulist writer Italo Calvino will recall the story of the young baron who lived amid the branches of treetops, never to alight upon the ground. And now "Cinema Paradiso" director Giuseppe Tornatore has concocted an ocean-going variation on this eternal outcast theme with "The Legend of 1900," an angst-driven saga that will have you longing for terra firma well before it's over.

Derived from a dramatic monologue by Italian novelist Alessandro Baricco, "The Legend of 1900" traces the life of a man who is, literally and otherwise, at sea. Named for the year in which he was born and abandoned in the hull of an ocean liner, 1900 (Tim Roth) is raised into boyhood by the coal room worker who discovers him. He soon emerges from the shadows of the coal room to become the ship's celebrated pianist, and there he remains, shuttling between ports without ever disembarking to land.

Even with its exotic premise, 1900's saga is beset by clouds of deja vu blowing in from a barely vanquished memory called "Titanic." Once more, a lavish evocation of luxury liner days gone by (The chandeliers! The fashions! The love theme! The third class poseur slipping in with the swells!) is related through the time-tripping device of a witness' testimony. In this case, the observer is an admiring musician named Max (Pruitt Taylor Vince) who became 1900's closest ally.

Cast against type, Roth puts on a great show. One of the few contemporary actors with a real Bogart, wise-guy appeal, he effortlessly captures the characters ethereal, lost-soul side. But "The Legend of 1900" doesn't really hook us until midway with a droll piano competition scene at the expense of jazz great Jelly Roll Morton (Clarence Williams III), a real-life figure who drops in "Ragtime"-style and is exaggerated for effect as an arrogant, obnoxious Narcissus.

As an evocation of a lost world, "The Legend of 1900" impresses with Lajos Koltai's kinetic cinematography and Francesco Frigeri's dazzling wreck of a shipboard set. But the score's the thing. Composer Ennio Morricone, who gave "Cinema Paradiso" its heart-tugging pulse has once again whipped up a boldly elegiac theme that dares us not to be touched.

Morricone's orchestra works overtime for our tears and big sound track sales, but the film is curiously unmoving. Neither the protagonist's friendship with Max nor his late-blooming ardor for a passenger (Melanie Thierry) are sufficiently nuanced to lend much urgency to the denouement. As metaphor, 1900's land-loathing dilemma is both artificial and meaningless. It's a tabula rasa on which we can dump whatever baggage we happen to drag into the theater. Clocking in at a draggy, airless two hours, "The Legend of 1900" often feels like cinema purgatorio.

SIGHT AND SOUND, 1/00, p. 56, Mark Sinker

Plymouth, England, the 40s jazz trumpeter Max sells his horn to a musicshop owner who lets him play it one last time. The tune reminds the owner of a record he has come by. Max recognises the music, and tells the owner the tale of the greatest pianist whoever lived: 1900, whom Max met aboard the *USS Virginian*.

Named for his birth year, foundling 1900 was raised aboard the ocean liner and never left it. Miraculously able to play piano from a young age, 1900 became the ship's entertainer. In 1927 Max came to work on the ship, and during his time aboard Max saw 1900 beat 'Jelly Roll' Morton in a jazz duel, got him recorded and watched as he fell in love with an unnamed girl. 1900 smashed the one copy of the recording; Max hid the pieces in the ship's piano. Later 1900 considered leaving the ship, but turned back. Max left the ship in 1933. In the present, the now-derelict *Virginian* is due for dynamiting; the shop owner had bought the piano at the port. Max searches for his friend on the ship. Finally, 1900 appears and explains why he cannot leave. Distraught, Max leaves and the ship is blown up. The shop owner gives Max his trumpet back.

This first English-language movie by Giuseppe Tornatore, director of *Cinema Paradiso,* has been dubbed already by wags *Ship of Fool:* it centres on a solitary man ship-bound for almost 50 years, even though he's supposedly the greatest pianist who ever lived. Touting itself as a fable, this blodged, peculiar, overloud post-*Titanic* epic hints it has a compelling metaphor somewhere in it, but the more we try—striving to be agnostic about Tornatore's humour-free sentimentality and leaden ear for English speech patterns—the less we find.

Star Tim Roth coolly junks the unplayable notion of 1900 as a placeless genius and goes for a watchable performance as an unassuming murmur of a fellow—which unfortunately shows up the graceless mugging everyone else gets away with. As Jelly Roll Morton, who claimed to have invented jazz, Clarence Williams III at least brings real dignity to his cameo (which demands a genuine historical black figure be humiliated by a pasty white fiction). However, this implicit racial slur is dwarfed by the broader contempt the film seems to have for the music at the story's core.

Since it costs 1900 no effort to gain his musical gift, it never feels as if it matters to anyone whether it is preserved. Certainly the record we hear of 1900 playing is highly anachronistic—deeper and plusher than any hi-fi reproduction the real life Morton had access to. Pre-electric recording today has immense force through our sense of the dead all but physically caressing these objects. To amplify or boost such documents is to dilute their power as mementoes—so paradoxically this story about music could perhaps only have worked as a silent film. Instead, 1900's disc blares out at us in full Dolby surround-sound. Give or take dabs of post-production crackle and wobble, it's not different enough from the films live performances to convey any sense of loss. Besides, how is it that, of all the people who heard 1900 play, his 'legend' only haunts one listener, Max?

Only three moments of phantasmagoria puncture the platitudes. The first is when Max meets 1900 during a storm at sea and they careen together on an unmoored piano around the ballroom and down corridors, past shoes set out to be shined which shuffle and slither on the plunging deck. The second is the vista of New York 1900 sees when he's about to leave the ship, a matte which is no 20s sprawl but a sinister H.R. Giger Babylon, with seagulls like pterosaurs menacingly circling.

The third haunting vision is the engine room of 1900's infanthood, a firelit Tartarus. If 1900's piano-playing had been imagined so as to encompass this Dantean hell, 1900's first apprehended soundworld, only someone like black free-jazz titan Cecil Taylor could possibly have performed the soundtrack. And Taylor, a world-historical legend with a genuine claim to the greatest-ever title, is a pianist even Jelly Roll Morton might have taken defeat from, honour unsullied.

VILLAGE VOICE, 11/2/99, p. 140, Dennis Lim

It's a testament to Tim Roth's sheer grace and adaptability that *The Legend* of 1900—a fanciful tale of a baby born at sea who grows up to be a piano virtuoso—doesn't run aground as often as it should. Wading through pools of icky sentiment, Roth remains charismatic and improbably serene, fine-tuning his performance for maximum resonance and comedy. He's also confident enough to avoid signaling his superiority to the material. In fact, Roth's tacit respect for the prevailing hokeyness might be the most moving thing about the film.

Adapted by Giuseppe Tornatore (*Cinema Paradiso*) from a stage monologue and novel by Alessandro Barrico, *The Legend of 1900* is what is often euphemistically called an old-fashioned movie—meaning it's pretty, unwieldy, and glazed with enough fake emotion to earn it a Foreign Film Oscar (indeed, you keep forgetting the movie is in English). Though the premise is vaguely magic-realist, the mode is less mystic than misty. An infant is discovered atop a grand piano in the ballroom of a transatlantic liner and named for the year of his birth. Played as an adult by Roth, the prodigiously talented 1900 spends his life on the *Virginian* shuttling between New York and Southampton as house-band pianist and resident legend. His story unfolds in flashback, told by trumpeter ex-bandmate Max (Pruitt Taylor Vince), who's trying to postpone the demolition of the ship because he's convinced that his friend is still on board. Turns out that, like all musical geniuses in movies, 1900 suffers a life-threatening affliction—in his case, a paralyzing inability to set foot on land.

Tornatore's lazy structure leaves the movie disproportionately reliant on set pieces. The most outrageous ones work best: Max and 1900 sit at the piano as it slides across the room, crashes through a window, and rumbles down a corridor; an absurdly dramatic duel between 1900 and a disdainful Jelly Roll Morton (Clarence Williams III). Cinematographer Lajos Koltai lavishes the requisite attention on period finery (and on the looming Manhattan skyline), but Roth's heavy-lidded, mournful eyes provide the film with its most enduring image. It's not clear if 1900's condition is agoraphobia or a more generalized existential despair, but Roth somehow makes it poignant, even pulling off a climactic declamation that requires him to compare the big bad scary world with the "infinite keys" on "God's piano."

Also reviewed in:
CHICAGO TRIBUNE, 11/19/99, Friday/p. J, Michael Wilmington
NEW YORK TIMES, 10/29/99, p. E26, Stephen Holden
VARIETY, 8/23-29/99, p. 110, David Rooney
WASHINGTON POST, 11/19/99, p. C5, Rita Kempley
WASHINGTON POST, 11/19/99, Weekend/p. 51, Michael O'Sullivan

LEILA

A First Run Features release of a Mehrjui and Farazmand Film production. *Producer:* Dariush Mehrjui and Faramarz Farazmand. *Director:* Dariush Mehrjui. *Screenplay (Farsi with English subtitles):* Dariush Mehrjui. *Based on a story by:* Mahnaz Ansarian. *Director of Photography:* Mahmoud Kalari. *Editor:* Mustafa Kherqepush. *Music:* Keivan Jahanshahi. *Sound:* Asghar Shahverdi and Sasan Nakhaf. *Art Director:* Zhila Mehrjui, Fariar Javaherian, and Rita Qazal-Ayaq. *Running time:* 102 minutes. *MPAA Rating:* Not Rated.

CAST: Leila Hatami (Leila, the Wife); Ali Mosaffa (Reza, the Husband); Jamileh Sheikhi (Reza's Mother); Mohamad Reza Sharifinia (Leila's Uncle); Turan Mehrzad (Leila's Mother); Amir Pievar (Reza's Father); Shaqayeq Farahani (Second Wife).

LOS ANGELES TIMES, 8/13/99, Calendar/p. 8, Kevin Thomas

"Leila" is the latest in a long line of superb films that have placed Dariush Mehrjui in the front ranks of filmmakers not only in his native Iran but in international contemporary cinema. For more than 30 years, Mehrjui, a UCLA alumnus, has depicted the harshness of life in his native country with an unflinching yet detached power that frequently verges on the poetic. "Leila" deceptively fits comfortably within the universal genre of socially conscious drama but is as eloquent and devastating as anything he has ever done.

When we meet Leila (Leila Hatami) and Reza (Ali Mosaffa), they strike us as much like any affluent, attractive young couple, deeply in love, with a bright future ahead of them and already living in a spacious, smartly designed contemporary-style home in Tehran. Their views seem as modern and liberated as their decor; Reza steadfastly insists that it matters not in the least that his wife is unable to conceive, and they reject adoption as well as the more drastic measures available to them to attempt to have a child, although they might well have not so decisively dismissed artificial insemination if they had had an inkling of what lay ahead of them.

They don't reckon with the implacability of Reza's mother (Jamileh Sheikhi) in her determination that her son have children. She has the shamelessness of the truly ignorant as she begins to bear down on her daughter-in-law, tapping into her guilt over being unable to fulfill her childbearing duties as a traditional wife. It would be a mistake to write off the mother merely as a monster, as destructive as she is, for she is as much a victim of the tradition as those she unleashes it upon in such a crushing manner. With a psychological validity that is all the more terrifying for being so utterly persuasive, Leila, weighed down by her mother-in-law's incessant pressure, starts convincing herself that her love for her husband can and must be strong enough for her to withstand him taking into their home a second wife who can give him an heir.

The irony here is that just about everyone else in Reza's family is outraged at Leila's worsening plight and arguing that the couple should stand up to the overbearing matriarch. That neither can do so in any meaningful way reveals the full and overwhelming force that tradition—embedded in a rigid, even distorted reading of religious beliefs—continues to exert on Iranian society. Even so, Mehrjui is too wise to judge, trusting instead to the sheer power of illuminating the predicament of the young couple, so very well played by Hatami and Mosaffa.

NEW YORK, 5/17/99, p. 59, Peter Rainer

As the young middle-class wife in the Iranian film *Leila*, the actress Leila Hatami has an extraordinary look: Dressed in black, she has an ancient gravity, yet she wears her chador with a crisp chicness and her features are as fine-boned as any famished super-model's. Leila is a living, breathing contradiction: a modem woman blurred into the most traditional of guises. The film, which was co-written and directed by Dariush Mehrjui, is about how Leila, with her own complicity, is pulled apart by the opposing forces in her life. Discovering shortly after her marriage to Reza (Ali Mosaffa) that she's infertile, she falls prey to the calculations of her mother-in-law (Jamileh Sheikhi), who presses Leila to stand aside for a second wife who will bear a male heir. (Polygamy in Iran is sanctioned.) At first, Reza, who genuinely loves his wife and claims he doesn't want children, has only contempt for his mother's ministrations. But gradually, horrifyingly, he follows through with the plan. What gives the film its fascination is that Leila's participation in her mother-in-law's campaign represents more than simply a capitulation to Islamic orthodoxy. Leila, who adores her husband, believes she is being punished for her infertility and willingly conspires in her own destruction. Her demolition of her marriage draws on something deeply disturbing within her: a lust to be humiliated. She is not only aghast at what

Reza has wrought; she's mortified, and captivated, by her collaboration. (No one else in either family camp condones her complicity.) The film, in its resolution, invokes *A Doll's House,* which Mehrjui once adapted for the screen, and it also recalls, in a less layered and lyrical mode, Satyajit Ray's films about women and the strictures of class and tradition, particularly his *Home and the World.*   It's a quiet heartbreaker.

NEW YORK POST, 5/14/99, p. 48, Rod Dreher

"Leila," a psychologically sophisticated melodrama from Iranian director Dariush Mehrjui, traps its title protagonist between Islamic traditionalism and modern romantic sensibilities. The movie opens with the prosperous families of Leila (played by Leila Hatami) and her new husband Reza (Ali Mosaffa) celebrating their wedding feast. When Leila learns she is barren, Reza says he loves her and will stay with her anyway.

But his resolve melts under pressure from his mother (Jamileh Sheikhi), a harridan who insists that Reza must take a second wife to guarantee an heir. She harasses Leila mercilessly, manipulating the shy young bride into believing that if she really loved Reza, she would consent to a polygamous arrangement.

"Leila" proceeds inexorably to a tragic conclusion that casts a harsh light on the way inflexible social tradition can deform minds and defeat individual will—with women, ironically, their own worst oppressors.

The movie is marked by the stiff, gawky formalism characteristic of contemporary Iranian films, which makes for less than fluid storytelling. Yet those put off by the preoccupation with clunky neorealism and preoccupation with children in other Iranian movies will be pleasantly surprised by "Leila."

VILLAGE VOICE, 5/18/99, p. 126, Amy Taubin

I didn't make time to see a single film in the Dariush Mehrjui retrospective at the Walter Reade this past autumn. I knew that Mehrjui was regarded as one of Iran's finest filmmakers, that he was the only Iranian filmmaker whose primary subject was personal relationships among the upper-middle-class intelligentsia, and that he'd made a quartet of films about women. One of these, an adaptation of J.D. Salinger's *Franny and Zooey,* titled *Pari,* brought the author's wrath and the threat of a lawsuit down on the Film Society of Lincoln Center, the sponsor of the retrospective. But why would Salinger care that some obscure Iranian filmmaker had paid him homage with a meditation on his heroine, a late-'50s, New York-bred college student who is obsessed with the concept of "praying incessantly" and whose nervous breakdown is accelerated by her dinner date's remark that Flaubert "lacked testicularity"?

Now that I've seen *Leila,* Mehrjui's provocative and wise depiction of a promising marriage gone to hell (at the moment, it seems like the most brilliant depiction of a marriage gone to hell that I've ever seen), I'm furious at myself for having missed his retro. My resistance to Mehrjui had to do with my nitwit belief that a male filmmaker working in a culture where women are required to wear the chador would have nothing relevant to say about the particular contradictions in my American life, where women are supposedly equal under the law but misogyny rules too often in practice. What *Leila* makes evident is that, in terms of the innermost layers of the psyche and the feelings of love and loathing rooted therein, the differences between American and Iranian society are not as great as a self-interested American woman (me, me, me) would expect. As it turns out, Mehrjui is the perfect filmmaker to understand what a time bomb Salinger planted with that seemingly casual remark about Flaubert's lack, a time bomb that Franny and the readers who identified with her (myself included) were incapable of disassembling. We could only respond with an inchoate sense of having been deeply dissed, and we would not begin to understand why until the feminist movement exploded a decade later.

So, too, is the heroine of *Leila* deeply dissed. Her resulting anger—directed against both her husband and herself—has a kind of ascetic purity that makes it seem like devotion. Leila's problem is the female equivalent of what Franny's date inflicts on Flaubert. Blissfully married for one year, she learns that her hormonal levels are so low that it's unlikely she will be able to have a child.

Leila (Leila Hatami) and Reza (Ali Mosaffa) seem a perfectly matched couple. Attractive twentysomethings from prosperous families, they mix modernity (fooling around while watching *Doctor Zhivago* on video) with tradition (he goes to work; she stays home and prepares his dinner). They never question their love until they learn that they will probably never have children together. Then the seeds of doubt are sown. Reza tells Leila that he's married her for herself alone, that he doesn't care whether they have children or not. But she isn't convinced. Neither are we, for that matter.

How could Reza be immune to the values of the society in which he's been raised, where women who cannot bear children are considered cursed by God? That's how Leila views herself, and her self-hatred makes her push Reza away. Still, the situation might have been worked out if the couple had been left to their own devices. Instead, Leila's doubts about her worthiness as a wife are exacerbated by Reza's mother, the most villainous woman to appear on the screen since Snow White's stepmother. This manipulative, venomous woman is determined to make Leila acquiesce to Reza's taking a second wife so that her husband's family name does not die. Oddly enough, Reza's father considers her action reprehensible, though he stops short of forbidding her to interfere. Similarly, Reza claims that he doesn't want a second wife, but he never tells his mother to get lost. Instead of taking responsibility, he claims he'll do anything Leila wants him to do, and Leila, who's been persuaded by her mother-in-law that Reza will eventually leave her if she doesn't allow him to take a fertile second wife, encourages Reza to court other women.

It's a classic double bind—self-hating women who manipulate passive-aggressive men to their own disadvantage. The marriage goes from bad to worse as the couple become emotionally addicted to cycles of anxiety and relief. In a particularly agonizing stretch, Reza takes Leila with him in the car when he goes courting, dropping her off to window-shop or wander through the park alone while he drives on to his assignations. Each time he returns with the verdict that the woman was unsatisfactory, the two of them have a moment of release that passes for happiness. But then, the cycle starts again.

Mehrjui is an amazingly subtle, almost self-effacing filmmaker. His style is so fluid that you may be amazed to realize at the end of the film (an end that strikes some viewers as fraught with possibility and others as the final nail in the coffin) that about 10 years have passed. But he also understands the power of a close-up—the one image you might take away from the film is the pearl-encrusted hem of the second wife's bridal gown hitting the staircase as she ascends to the bedroom from which Leila has been exiled.

Or should I say the bedroom from which Leila has exiled herself? The confusion and conflation of action and reaction, especially within the symbiotic construction of marriage, is very much the issue of this film. That it's couched entirely in Leila's point of view doesn't make it one-sided. Mehrjui keeps us constantly at Leila's side without coloring the film with her subjectivity. Although we see nothing on the screen that occurs outside her presence, our access to her interiority is as limited as it is to that of the other characters. What went wrong here and who is to blame? You and your significant other could debate that for hours. Among its most unexpected virtues, *Leila* is a great date movie.

As far as imaginable from the monstrous mother of *Leila* is Larisa Loktev, a Russian immigrant and former computer programs analyst who now spends all her time caring for her husband, Leonid Loktev, also a former computer analyst, who was severely brain damaged when he was hit by a car while crossing a road between two yard sales in his Colorado neighborhood on April Fool's Day 1989. Their daughter, Julia Loktev, has made a documentary, *Moment of Impact*, about her parents' daily life that is as discomforting as it is brilliant.

Shot with a handheld home video camera, the film is an intimate, unsparing view of a dread situation. Since the accident, Leonid has been capable of almost no autonomous physical movement and only the most limited speech. How much he understands is another matter—there are clues that he might be thinking far more than he can express. Larisa takes care of him 24-7 because she can't stand how limited his life would be if he were in a nursing room and because her insurance company has denied home assistance. "I'm just a person placed in circumstances," says Larisa, when her daughter grills her about her choices. "In principle, a responsible, reliable person, and he has no one else."

If I were not so moved by the mother, I might be more disturbed than I was about the way the camera intrudes on her life and that of her husband. There's no way of knowing how Leonid feels about having his vulnerability exposed, but he seems, at moments, to resent his filmmaker daughter intensely. The daughter is not unaware of the problem, but she toughs it out. "The only time I don't feel invisible is when I go to aerobics," says the mother. Thanks to this film, the witnesses to her life may be counted in the thousands.

Also reviewed in:
NEW YORK TIMES, 5/14/99, p. E14, Stephen Holden
VARIETY, 2/23-3/1/98, p. 92, David Rooney

L'ENNUI

A Phaedra Cinema release of a Gemini Films/Ima Films production. *Producer:* Paulo Branco. *Director:* Cédric Kahn. *Screenplay (French with English subtitles:* Cédric Kahn and Laurence Ferreira Barbosa. *Based on the novel "La Noia" by:* Alberto Moravia. *Director of Photography:* Pascal Marti. *Editor:* Yann Dedet. *Sound:* Jean-Paul Mugel. *Sound Editor:* Pascal Villard. *Casting:* Antoinette Boulat, Antoine Carrard, Anne Marepiano, and Sarah Tepper. *Production Designer:* François Abelanet. *Set Decorator:* Sabine Delouvrier. *Costumes:* Françoise Clavel. *Make-up:* Corinne Maillard. *Running time:* 120 minutes. *MPAA Rating:* Not Rated.

CAST: Charles Berling (Martin); Sophie Guillemin (Cécilia); Arielle Dombasle (Sophie); Robert Kramer (Meyers); Alice Grey (Cécilia's Mother); Maurice Antoni (Cécilia's Mother).

LOS ANGELES TIMES, 10/15/99, Calendar/p. 12, Kevin Thomas

Cedric Kahn's relentless "L'Ennui" is such a rigorous exploration of sexual obsession that it proves to be a most demanding film. Virtually devoid of eroticism and sensuality, it depicts with the utmost realism a 17-year-old girl and a fortysomething philosophy professor engaging frequently in raw, intense sex that leaves the girl content and the man craving for much more in the way of fulfillment.

Life has turned sour for Charles Berling's Martin. He and his sophisticated wife Sophie (Arielle Dombasle) have split up some six months earlier. Teaching no longer gives him pleasure or meaning, and he can't get started on the book he means to write. He hasn't made love since his marriage broke up.

One aimless night he wanders into a tawdry bar where a doorman starts beating up an older man (Robert Kramer, the noted independent filmmaker) when he can't pay for his drinks. Martin comes to the man's rescue and in short order learns that he is a painter whose passion for his teenage model Cecilia (Sophie Guillemin) proves fatal mere hours after their meeting. Martin is immediately intrigued and swiftly replaces the painter in Cecilia's life.

With a lush body and a doll-like face, Cecilia, whose maddening simplicity is her strength, combines a robust sexual appetite with minimal personality. Although not stupid, she is resolutely unreflective and not curious. She says she loves Martin and may mean it, but she's too obdurate by nature for Martin to ever possess her. Her implacable ordinariness provides Martin with a challenge that only heightens her attraction for him, driving this totally self-absorbed and neurotic intellectual to the brink of madness.

That she is also involved with an actor more her age gets the instantly callous Martin really teetering on the brink. It's not that Cecilia is manipulative—in fact she accommodates herself well to so possessive a lover—but that Martin, in his despair and desperation craves from her the kind of rapture that is beyond the teenager's depth. Cecilia seems lacking in capacity as well as inclination.

Since the nature of the glum, complex Martin and the stolid, uncomplicated Cecilia's relationship, as well as the radical differences in their temperaments and intellects are clear from the start, "L'Ennui" becomes grueling to watch, even as it commands respect for its uncompromising, clear-eyed perspective.

Even so, Berling and Guillemin are remarkably selfless and authentic in their portrayals, and "L'Ennui", adapted from a vintage Alberto Moravia novel, rewards the patient with an ending that strikes just the right note.

(Note: In 1964, the same novel was reworked unsuccessfully as "The Empty Canvas," in which painter Horst Buchholz was obsessed with model Catherine Spaak; Bette Davis, no less, played Buchholz's mother.)

NEW YORK POST, 10/11/99, p. 50, Hannah Brown

There are lots of movies about Lolita-esque young women who drive older men crazy, but the twist in "L'Ennui" is that the temptress is an ordinary, chubby teen without much to say.

At first, Martin (Charles Berling), a lonely academic, disdains the lack of intellect he sees in Cecilia (Sophie Guillemin), a zaftig 17-year-old who visits him daily for quick sexual encounters. But he falls apart when Cecilia, who is not as naive or artless as she seems, starts seeing another man. He begins stalking her and begging her to marry him.

This film, with fine performances by Berling and Guillemin, is a haunting portrait of a man obsessed. But it's also talky, overlong and, ultimately, just as predictable and repetitive as the maddening relationship it depicts.

VILLAGE VOICE, 10/12/99, p. 146, Elliott Stein

Alberto Moravia was one of the first Italian authors of his day to write honestly about sex—it was therefore no surprise when, in 1952, his novels were declared immoral by the Vatican and placed on its "Index of Forbidden Books." Forbidden or not, over the years his works were snapped up by the movies—Bertolucci's *The Conformist*, De Sica's *Two Women*, Godard's *Contempt*. Cedric Kahn's *L'Ennui*, based on the writer's 1961 novel, *La Noia*, does contain at least a good half-dozen steamy bedroom scenes, but they're in the service of a fairly absorbing account of a philosophy professor's gradual descent into nightmarish obsession with a teenage girl. In this loose adaptation (with the action transferred from 1960s Italy to contemporary Paris), fortyish Martin (Charles Berling) meets the insatiable Cecilia (Sophie Guillemin) after she has apparently fucked to death her elderly painter lover (director Robert Kramer). The pretentious prof enters into a passionate affair with the inarticulate working-class model. He goes around the bend, stalking her every movement and submitting her to near Sadeian interrogation rituals. His nutty antics and the increasingly brutal love scenes become a tad tedious, but the film is endowed with some richly comic moments, including a grotesque Buñuelian passage during which Martin calls on Cecilia's clueless parents. While Berling is excellent as the tormented intellectual, somehow managing to evoke sympathy for the creepy dude, the plump, Rubenesque Guillemin steals the show. Her understated simplicity is her strength—this is one of the major movie debuts of recent years.

Also reviewed in:
CHICAGO TRIBUNE, 1/28/00, Friday/p. F, John Petrakis
NEW YORK TIMES, 10/8/99, p. E9, Stephen Holden
VARIETY, 9/14-20/98, p. 90, Brendan Kelly

LET IT COME DOWN: THE LIFE OF PAUL BOWLES

A Zeitgeist Films release of a Requisite Productions film. *Executive Producer:* Daniel Iron. *Producer:* Nick de Pencier and Jennifer Baichwal. *Director:* Jennifer Baichwal. *Director of Photography:* Nick de Pencier and Jim Allodi. *Editor:* David Wharnsby. *Music:* Paul Bowles. *Sound:* Denise Holloway. *Running time:* 73 minutes. *MPAA Rating:* Not Rated.

WITH: Paul Bowles; William S. Burroughs; Phillip Ramey; Jonathan Sheffer; Ned Rorem; Gustavo Romero; Marguerite McBey; Joe McPhillips; David Herbert; Mohammed Mrabet; Mohammed Choukri; Allen Ginsberg; Amina Bakalia; Tom McCamus (Reader).

NEW YORK POST, 4/28/99, p. 54, Jonathan Foreman

"Let It Come Down: The Life of Paul Bowles" is about the cult author (and composer) who lived as an expatriate in Morocco for 60 years and whose most famous novel, "The Sheltering Sky," was filmed by Bernardo Bertolucci, with Debra Winger and John Malkovich starring.

Among other flaws, "Let It Come Down" assumes not only familiarity with Bowles' literary output, but that the audience will share the worshipful stance of the filmmakers. But even Bowles fanatics may be disappointed by the film's shapelessness, its poor production values and its reluctance really to get under its subject's skin.

Because the interviews are limited to Bowles and some of his surviving friends, you don't get a sense of his place in the 20th century or of the texture of his life in Tangiers.

Instead, director Jennifer Baichwal strains to connect Bowles with the Beat Generation writers who in the 1950s visited or joined the homosexual expatriate community of which Bowles was the dean. And much of "Let It Come Down" is taken up by a meeting in 1996 of Bowles with Allen Ginsburg and William S. Burroughs in a Manhattan hotel.

But the most interesting thing about this film is the way it reveals how unhip—and charmingly old-fashioned—Paul Bowles really is. Not just his startlingly aristocratic accent, but his discretion about his own private life could not be less "Beat."

The best thing about "Let It Come Down" are Tom McCamus' readings from Bowles work. It's a shame and a mystery that so few of those readings are accompanied by shots of the spectacular Moroccan landscapes that Bowles says were the inspiration for his work.

VILLAGE VOICE, 5/4/99, p. 120, Elliott Stein

From the outset of Jennifer Baichwal's *Let It Come Down: The Life of Paul Bowles, it's* clear that the director has succeeded in cultivating enough of a personal relationship with the Morocco-based recluse to worm out unexpected revelations from the famously reticent writer. A talking-head movie, yes—but what heads. Ned Rorem, the highly photogenic doyen of American composers, provides a keen assessment of Bowles's other creative body of work—his music. Before he began the career for which he's best known, Bowles had turned out a number of elegant chamber works and music for stage productions by Orson Welles and Tennessee Williams. There are precious scenes in which Baichwal captures Bowles's final meeting with William Burroughs and Allen Ginsberg.

If hardly a "life"—it's too fragmentary—this is a deeply engaging film portrait, full of memorable nuggets. Bowles is blistering on the subject of Gertrude Stein and her "house of humiliation"; his verdict on Bertolucci's adaptation of *The Sheltering Sky* is a curt "idiotic." And the 88-year-old writer speaks with less restraint than in earlier interviews about his life with Jane Bowles, who died in 1973. Although the couple cared for each other deeply, both were primarily homosexual and pursued a number of same-sex relationships during the course of their stormy marriage. One of the director's major coups is her footage of the notorious Amina Bakalia ("Cherifa"), the Moroccan peasant woman who was Jane's lover for 20 years, considered by nearly everyone in their entourage to have practiced black magic on Jane and Paul and to have poisoned her.

Jane Bowles, for Truman Capote "that genius imp, that laughing, hilarious, tortured elf," unfortunately gets short shrift in the film. A marvelous writer and a profoundly original talent, she deserves a movie all her own.

Also reviewed in:
NEW YORK TIMES, 4/28/99, p E5, Stephen Holden
VARIETY, 12/20/99-1/2/00, p. 58, Brendan Kelly

LIBERTY HEIGHTS

A Warner Bros. release of a Baltimore/Spring Creek Pictures production. *Executive Producer:* Patrick McCormick. *Producer:* Barry Levinson and Paula Weinstein. *Director:* Barry Levinson.

Screenplay: Barry Levinson. *Director of Photography:* Chris Doyle. *Editor:* Stu Linder. *Music:* Andrea Morricone. *Music Editor:* Suzana Peric. *Choreographer:* Jerry Mitchell and Luis Perez. *Sound:* Steve Cantamessa and (music) Fabio Venturi. *Sound Editor:* Tim Holland. *Casting:* Ellen Chenoweth. *Production Designer:* Vincent Peranio. *Art Director:* Alan E. Muraoka. *Set Decorator:* William A. Cimino. *Set Dresser:* Liz Weber. *Special Effects:* Douglas Retzler and Michael Bird.. *Costumes:* Gloria Gresham. *Make-up:* Betty Beebe. *Make-up (Bebe Neuwirth):* Patricia Reagan; *Stunt Coordinator:* Conrad Palmisano. *Running time:* 134 minutes. *MPAA Rating:* R.

CAST: Andrien Brody (Van Kurtzman); Bebe Neuwirth (Ada Kurtzman); Joe Mantegna (Nate Kurtzman); Ben Foster (Ben Kurtzman); Rebekah Johnson (Sylvia); Justin Chambers (Trey); Carolyn Murphy (Dubbie); Orlando Jones (Little Melvin); David Krumholtz (Yussel); Richard Kline (Charlie); Vincent Guastaferro (Pete); James Pickens, Jr. (Sylvia's Father); Frania Rubinek (Rose); Anthony Anderson (Scribbles); Kierstan Warren (Annie); Evan Neuman (Sheldon); Kevin Sussman (Alan); Gerry Rosenthal (Murray); Charley Scalies (Louie); Shane West (Ted); Cloie Wyatt Taylor (Gail); Susan Duvall (Teacher 2); Carlton Smith (James Brown); Elizabeth Ann Bennett (Mary); Ellyn O'Connell (Anne Whittier); Doug Roberts (Assistant D.A.); Al Brown (Baliff); Kenny Raskin (Burlesque Comic); Peter Wilkes (Butler); Kimberlee Suerth (Buxom Nurse); Mary Lynn Ray (Woman in Court 1); Marty Lodge (Defense Attorney); Gideon Jacobs (Ben, Aged 8); Jan Austell (Judge); Timothy J. Scanlin, Jr. (Nick); Ralph Tabakin (Phil); Shelley Stokes (Box Office Attendant); Patsy Grady Abrams (Woman in Court 2); Jay Hillmer (Matt); Stan Brandorff (Morris); Katie Finnerman (Mrs. Johnson); Kate Kiley (Nurse); Jake Hoffman (Turk); Joseph Patrick Abel (Lenny); Sekiya Billman (Halloween Stripper); Brenda Russell (Singer); Barry Black (Cantor); Dennis N. Math (Rabbi); Judith Knight Young (Teacher 1, 1944); Stephen Williams (Wilbert Mosley); Ty Robbins (Sylvia's Mother); Emily Chamberlain (Ben's Teacher); Christain T. Dockins, Kenny Pitt, and Zahmu Sankofa (Three Flames); Paul Majors (Party Fight Guy).

LOS ANGELES TIMES, 11/17/99, Calendar/p. 1, Kenneth Turan

For writer-director Barry Levinson, "Liberty Heights" is one from the heart.

The fourth film to be set in his native Baltimore (following "Diner," "Tin Men" and "Avalon"), this is a mature, accomplished piece of work, both funny and deeply felt, personal cinema of the best kind. Older now, seeing more, understanding more but caring just as much, Levinson has made the memory film we always hoped he would.

Though its focus on Baltimore's Jewish community in the fall of 1954 couldn't be more specific, the issues and themes "Liberty Heights" raises, its focus on the dreams, diversions and disappointments of an increasingly multicultural America, have a universal taste of life about them.

Levinson has done this, ironically, by embracing specificity, by having characters (unlike those in "Avalon," who never mention their Jewishness) proudly screaming out car windows as they drive from their Liberty Heights neighborhood into a Gentile area, "Get ready, folks, Jews are coming."

For Baltimore in 1954 was still a place where you could divine people's religion and ethnicity by asking where they lived. But the Supreme Court had just desegregated the schools, barriers of all kinds were breaking down, and the reality of a more open America was beckoning everyone, even Nate and Ada Kurtzman (Joe Mantegna and Bebe Neuwirth) and their sons Van and Ben (Adrien Brody and Ben Foster).

"Liberty Heights" is at its funniest exposing the contours of the Kurtzmans' doomed all-Jewish world, complete with an irascible old-country grandmother (Frania Rubinek), who insists "if it's in the Bible, it's for a reason." And what specifically might that reason be? "A good reason."

Reading from a school essay describing his still younger years, Ben recounts (and we hilariously see) his concision at coming across Wonder bread at a small friend's house. "Everything was white, there's too much white stuff," he wails to his mother, who nods and says ominously of the visited family, "They're the other kind."

Though Ben, now in high school, has already learned that "99% of the world is not Jewish," there's a lot he and the college-going Van don't know about what it's like to be "the other kind." For both brothers, forbidden romance will aid in the getting of wisdom, and "Liberty Heights" expertly intertwines their stories with another cross-cultural difficulty, one their father has managing his unconventional business.

The world and, more important, the IRS, think the source of Nate Kurtzman's income is a collapsing burlesque house on Baltimore's famous Block. But it actually comes from the numbers business, a gambling enterprise so beyond the pale it's never even mentioned at home. Desperate to drum up more customers, Nate and his associates come up with a bonus system, but when a small-time black drug dealer named Little Melvin (Orlando Jones) hits his number big, Nate faces a crisis that taxes even his considerable toughness and ingenuity.

Ben, meanwhile, has become fascinated with Sylvia (Rebekah Johnson), the only black student in his homeroom. The daughter of a prominent surgeon, elegant and self-possessed, Sylvia is not only a world away from Little Melvin, she is a world away from Ben as well.

Still, despite opposition from both sets of parents—her father has a rule against white boyfriends and his mother simply says, "Just kill me now!"—Ben and Sylvia find themselves really liking each other and wanting to spend time together.

Theirs is the sweetest of friendships, even extending to a joint visit to a lovingly re-created James Brown concert, but like everything else about "Liberty Heights," it manages to be clear-eyed and unsentimental as well as warm. Both Ben and his friends have accumulated considerable prejudice, old wives' tales and just plain ignorance and misinformation about blacks (not to mention about sex, but that's another story), which this relationship gracefully and often amusingly disabuses him of.

Van's romantic entanglement is just as forbidden. At a Halloween party in a Gentile neighborhood, while his friend Yussel (David Krumholtz) is getting into a bravado-induced fight for refusing to admit he's Jewish, dark and poetic-looking Van gets intoxicated with Dubbie (model Carolyn Murphy), a kind of ultimate shiksa goddess who is involved with a wealthy fellow socialite named Trey (Justin Chambers) who drinks too much and drives too fast.

The experienced Brody ("King of the Hill," "Summer of Sam") brings a fine poetic grace to the part of Van, and it is a tribute to Levinson's sensitive direction (and Ellen Chenoweth's adroit casting) that he gets equally strong performances out of the film's numerous first-time feature actors, including Foster, Johnson, Murphy, Chambers and Jones. Not even born when this film takes place, they've managed to recapture its nuances with remarkable fidelity.

But it's Levinson who's given them such rich and often comic things to say, who understands how to structure great riffs that seem to come out of nowhere. So we have Ben and his pals, faced with a sign reading "No Jews, Dogs or Colored," wondering how Jews got the first position, or Yussel's tirade about anti-Semitism. "They all pray to a Jew," he fumes. "I guess it's OK to have a dead Jew hanging over your bed but not to have one come in the front door."

Levinson's storytelling style has always been on the discursive side, and "Liberty Heights," ebbing and flowing like a river of memory, shows that technique to its best advantage. There's almost a free-form quality to the narrative as stories weave in and out of one another, meandering a bit but never losing their novelistic grasp of feeling and atmosphere.

Aiding in the creation of that atmosphere is an eclectic soundtrack (from the Midnighters' "Annie Had a Baby" to Mandy Patinkin singing the Yiddish classic "Mein Shtetele Belz") that is a living presence in the film, as well as the fine work of the film's production talents. These include previous Levinson collaborators Stu Linder (editor) and Vincent Peranio (production designer) as well as the brilliant Hong Kong-based cinematographer Chris Doyle, a master of color and mood.

Though the film's advertising tag line ("You're Only Young Once, but You Remember Forever") sells it that way, "Liberty Heights" is hardly an exercise in simple nostalgia. Strains of darkness, pain and regret are visible through the comedy, and some of the societal/racial issues the film brings up have yet to be resolved. "A lot of images fade," Ben says at one point. "If I knew things would no longer be, I would have tried to remember better." Barry Levinson, thankfully, has remembered enough for us all.

NEW YORK, 11/29/99, p. 130, Peter Rainer

Barry Levinson's Baltimore movies clearly mean more to him than most of his more frankly commercial jobs, and his fourth entry in the semi-autobiographical Baltimore series, *Liberty Heights*, set in 1954, has all the earnestness and manicured social consciousness of a personal project. I like it less than his previous outings in this terrain, *Diner* and *Tin Men* (the two best by far, I think) and the uneven *Avalon*. In its approach to the past, if not in its dialogue, the film is reminiscent of some of Neil Simon's mood-memory plays, especially *Brighton Beach Memoirs*. It has the same sense of forced nostalgia and self-congratulation; Levinson takes great pride in bearing witness to the supposed naïveté of those coming-of-age years.

And yet there are lovely moments throughout: the warming, tentative relationship between Ben Kurtzman (Ben Foster) and the radiantly intense Sylvia (Rebekah Johnson),the first black student in his high school; a scene where they go to a James Brown concert and rave it up, the look of hangdog bliss on the face of Ben's older brother, Van (Adrien Brody), when he first gazes upon a Gentile goddess (Carolyn Murphy) at a Wasp bash he and his friends have slipped into—the performance of Joe Mantegna as the boys' burlesque-house-owner father, who ducks out of Rosh Hashanah services to check on the new Cadillacs in a local showroom. As a writer-director, Levinson has become a lot slicker since the rawness of his *Diner* days, but when he slows down and goes inside himself, as he does in snatches of *Liberty Heights*, he can still find ways to move us.

NEW YORK POST, 11/17/99, p. 57, Lou Lumenick

"Liberty Heights," Barry Levinson's latest love letter to the Baltimore of his youth, is a touching and frequently hilarious chronicle of a Jewish family's struggle with their self-consciousness as outsiders.

At 16, Ben Kurtzman (newcomer Ben Foster) has already learned that "99 percent of the world were the other kind," or, as his mother (Bebe Neuwirth) calls them, "the others." A sign at an exclusive country club reads "No Jews, Dogs or Coloreds Allowed," prompting Ben and his friends Sheldon (Evan Neuman) and Murray (Gerry Rosenthal) to debate just how the club decided that Jews were a bigger threat to decorum than dogs.

Ben is enough of a rebel to dress up as Adolf Hitler for Halloween, much to the horror of his parents, who promptly ground him in one of the movie's funniest scenes. "Put the Fuhrer on the phone," instructs Ben's long-suffering dad Nate, played to perfection by Joe Mantegna, as his Yiddishe grandmother (the scene-stealing Frania Rubinek) walls, "Couldn't you have gone as a pirate or a reindeer?"

Ben tests the limits by pursuing a friendship with the beautiful and self-assured Sylvia (Rebekah Johnson), one of the first black students at his school. While Ben's parents aren't thrilled ("Just kill me now," moans his mom), their relationship is much more of a problem for Sylvia's father (James Pickens Jr.), a wealthy doctor who's angered at finding a middle class Jew hiding in his daughter's closet when he arrives home unannounced one afternoon.

Levinson deftly intercuts Ben's story with those of the Kurtzman family's other males over a particularly eventful year.

Less naive than his younger brother, college student Van (Adrien Brody) is ruefully aware of the risks entailed when he courts Dubbie (Carolyn Murphy), a blond, horse-riding gentile.

When he and his friends Yussel (David Krumholtz) and Alan (Kevin Sussman) first venture out of the Jewish enclave of Liberty Heights for a party (as "Strangers in Paradise" fills the soundtrack), Yussel narrowly escapes a beating—and won't return without a new hair color (blond) and a gentile-sounding name (Yates).

Van forms an unsettling friendship with the perverse, hard-drinking Trey (Justin Chambers), who he doesn't realize is Dubbie's boyfriend. Through Trey, Van gets a bittersweet education in the ways of WASPS.

Nate, meanwhile, has plenty of problems of his own.

His numbers operation is failing to keep up with the price of the new Cadillacs Nate purchases every Yom Kippur, and he's forced to greatly exaggerate the take from the struggling burlesque house he uses as a front to bamboozle the IRS.

In desperation, Nate and his partners—portrayed with panache by Charley Scales, Richard Kline and Vincent Guastaferro—institute a numbers bonus scheme that backfires, putting them hugely in debt to Little Melvin, a small-time black drug dealer (the hilarious Orlando Jones).

As the three (sometimes contrived) storylines converge over the course of just over two hours, writer-director Levinson pulls you along with razor-sharp dialogue ("I've got a stripper who dresses like my cousin Marsha," Nate complains when a burlesque dancer insists on going on in her street clothes when her costumes don't arrive).

His storytelling is greatly abetted by an astonishing re-creation of place and time on a scale (including a James Brown concert) that in ways exceeds even "Avalon," the most recent film in the Baltimore series.

Besides a stunning collection of vintage cars, there are painstakingly detailed decors that delineate the characters' varying social statuses, from the Kurtzmans' wood-paneled basement to Trey's antique-filled home.

"Liberty Heights," which includes a couple of scenes set in the "Diner" diner, is the best film in the series since that 1982 sleeper, which it also recalls in its flawless (though much larger) ensemble cast. The new film, though more heavily plotted than its predecessors, is easily one of the year's best movies.

NEWSDAY, 11/17/99, Part II/p. B3, Jan Stuart

Toward the end of Barry Levinson's "Liberty Heights," three teenage Jewish boys invade the outdoor pool of a restricted country club and plop themselves down with the letters J.E.W. scrawled on their naked bellies for all to see. It's one of those uplifting, thumb-nosing moments that occur mostly in Hollywood movies, where characters are devised to realize all of the fantasies we haven't the temerity to act out in real life.

Forced and unlikely as the gesture plays, it speaks to film history with a poignancy that transcends the 1954 Baltimore in which the film is set. A crowd-pleasing, out-and-proud entertainment about growing up Jewish in America, "Liberty Heights" has the air of a filmmaker's gently defiant response to the marginalization of Jewish identity in Hollywood movies for the better part of the 20th Century.

Of course, assimilationist Jewish moviemakers were at the vanguard of that practice during the heyday of the studio system, and Levinson has done his own part to carry the torch. In "Diner" and "Tin Men," his first two period comedies, ethnicity was mostly encoded in the jokey-combative shtetl fraternizing of a bunch of guys hanging out at a greasy spoon. "Avalon" was his Jewish coming out, albeit with a tree-grows-in-Baltimore cuddliness that appealed to the nostalgia bug in us all.

From an early scene in which a young Jewish boy complains about the unrelenting whiteness of a meal at a WASP home, Levinson lets you know exactly what kind of neighborhood this Liberty Heights is. The middle-class family of Levinson's teenage hero Ben Kurtzman (Ben Foster) is contentedly tribal and affably unkempt. Ben's father, Nate (Joe Mantegna), subsidizes income from his fading burlesque theater with a numbers racket. His mother, Ada (Bebe Neuwirth), is a bit of a nag. And the otherwise bright Ben himself is clumsy enough not to appreciate just how boorish it would be to show up at a Halloween party dressed as Adolf Hitler.

Surrounded exclusively by clannish rites and influences for all of their lives, both Ben and his older brother Van (Adrien Brody) yearn for forbidden fruit.

Van pines for a blond WASP princess (Carolyn Murphy) who is a lot more troubled than her pristine veneer first conveys, while Ben is smitten with a black student (Rebekah Johnson) who has just enrolled thanks to the blessings of Brown vs. the Board of Education.

"Liberty Heights" examines the liberties that two young Jewish men are able to gingerly exercise in an America caught between the rigid old divisions and dissolving social borders. It shares with Levinson's other Baltimore films a relaxed disregard for plot, relying instead on a wealth of demonstrative, sharply defined male characters and a handful of promising female characters who are ultimately relegated to cliche status.

It also revels in an attention to what one of his "Diner" characters would call "nuance": the little grace notes of pop culture and period detail that speak ironic volumes about the characters and their milieu. Where an aluminum siding salesman in "Tin Man" obsesses over the inauthenticity of "Bonanza," Ben and company contemplate the de-ethnicizing of the Loman family in "Death of a Salesman." Ultimately, the Kurtzmans' Baltimore that we glimpse is a little too cozy and safe for this viewer's taste, given the social tensions percolating. Although people occasionally behave badly and even go to jail for it, there is a scrubbed sheen to the film epitomized by the vintage automobiles, which all look as if they've dropped in fresh off the assembly line. Cars have always been an important motif of Levinson's Baltimore movies, but here he practically fetishizes them. "Liberty Heights" often looks like an auto show disguised as a memory play.

NEWSWEEK, 11/29/99, p. 94, David Ansen

Not a minute too soon, the floundering Barry Levinson ("Sleepers" and "Sphere") has returned to Baltimore, the inspiration for his best, most personal movies—"Diner," "Tin Men" and "Avalon." "Liberty Heights," a languorous, funny and lovingly detailed memory film, is set in 1954 in a Jewish suburb at a time when signs at a country club still announce baldly: NO JEWS, DOGS, OR COLOREDS ALLOWED. That would soon change. Integration is just around the corner, and white teenagers like Ben Kurtzman (Ben Foster), who can't keep his eyes off the only black girl (Rebekah Johnson) in his classroom, are about to discover the glories of Ray Charles and James Brown.

Ben is not the only member of the Kurtzman family dealing with what his mother calls "the other kind." His older brother, Van (Adrian Brody), becomes obsessed with a rich, blond shiksa goddess (Carolyn Murphy). Their father, Nate (Joe Mantegna), who always drives this year's Cadillac, doesn't buy it with the money he makes at his dying vaudeville theater but by running numbers. When a small-time drug dealer named Little Melvin (Orlando Jones) wins 100 grand on a number—more than Nate has—Kurtzman has to play dirty to stay afloat, with unexpected consequences for his family.

Fifties coming-of-age tales have become a cliche unto themselves, but Levinson's reverie feels handcrafted. By focusing on such a specific milieu, he keeps the genre alive with his great ear for small talk, an elegant eye and a warm, forgiving heart. This is nostalgia bottled and aged with care.

SIGHT AND SOUND, 11/00, p. 56, Andrew O'Hehir

1954. Life in the Jewish neighbourhood of north-west Baltimore known as Liberty Heights is changing. Sixteen-year old Ben Kurtzman, his older brother Van and their friends are meeting gentiles, white and black. Their father Nate, who has seen his burlesque business dry up, runs an illegal numbers racket. Ben is interested in Sylvia, a black girl at school, while Van falls in love with a blonde he meets at a party. Sylvia's father forbids her to see Ben. Van befriends a rich WASP named Trey, not realising his girlfriend is Dubbie, the blonde from the party.

A drug dealer named Little Melvin wins Nate's lottery, but Nate can't pay him, Little Melvin kidnaps Ben, Sylvia, and two other teenagers from outside a James Brown concert. Nate then surrenders the business to him, but soon gets it back. After Trey is injured in a crash, Van and Dubbie sleep together. Ben bids Sylvia farewell and heads off to college; Nate is arrested and imprisoned.

Outside of New York and Los Angeles perhaps no US city has been as passionately chronicled on screen as Baltimore, which has Barry Levinson and John Waters as its competing Virgils. In its very red brick ordinariness and its marginal metropolitan status as a place where black and white, North and South come together, Baltimore appeals to its advocates as a miniature America in a way more illustrious cities do not.

Liberty Heights is the fourth and most ambitious film in Levinson's Proustian saga of Jewish life in post-war Baltimore (after *Diner, Tin Men* and *Avalon*). Here, he brings the resources commanded by a major Hollywood director to bear on the project, employing a big cast, lavish costumes and locations and a narrative structure that interweaves the stories of all three male members of the Kurtzman family as they confront what the family matriarch calls "the other kind". Levinson is clearly after something like the epic social vision found in Scorsese's and Coppola's larger films, and his climax, in which scenes of younger brother Ben and his black girlfriend Sylvia at a James Brown concert are delicately intercut with older brother Van and his sweetheart Dubbie at a WASP bonfire party, is impressive and moving.

Yet *Liberty Heights* is also a creaky, didactic mechanism that labours long and mightily before gathering some semblance of dramatic momentum. Levinson's characters almost all speak the same awkwardly self-conscious dialogue: the boys' father Nate tells one of his cronies, "The last time I looked, running a numbers racket was illegal." Later, his friend informs us what year it is, by way of explaining why Ben might think it acceptable to dress as Hitler for Halloween: "The war ended when he was seven years old. it's now nine years later." Levinson's men still conduct earnest running arguments about girls and popular culture, but now that Quentin Tarantino *et al* have perfected the form, it isn't as fresh as it once was. If *Liberty Heights* is a larger spectacle than Levinson's previous Baltimore films, the genial spontaneity that made *Diner* and *Tin Men* among the surprises of the 80s has mostly been lost. When several characters gather at Levinson's trademark Fells Point Diner to shoot the breeze, you can feel the director trying to rekindle a flame that has pretty well gone out.

Levinson has spoken of his desire to counter stereotypes with this film, to emphasise that in 50s Baltimore Jews could be racketeers as well as lawyers and blacks could be doctors as well as hoodlums. This is no doubt a noble point, but it's essentially essay material rather than drama. Sylvia, for example, is an implausibly perfect angel; her first conversation with Ben is about the meaning of the 23rd Psalm. Despite the efforts of Rebekah Johnson, the role is, in its own way, just as thin a racial stereotype as Orlando Jones' incompetent, jive-talking Little Melvin.

The weakness of the Ben-Sylvia relationship also suggests that Levinson isn't sure who his protagonist is. Ben is obviously the authorial stand-in but his story isn't as compelling as Van's or Nate's. Adrien Brody is suave and Mediterranean-handsome as Van, and Carolyn Murphy nearly makes the *shiksa*-goddess role of Dubbie believable. But you can't help thinking that Nate, who sets his family on the path to assimilation yet destroys himself in the process, should have been the centre of the film. Played by Joe Mantegna without an ounce of self-pity, Nate is a man of doomed pride and flawed principle, who celebrates Rosh Hashanah every year by going to the synagogue, then to the Cadillac dealer to see the coming year's new models. He is the great creation of *Liberty Heiqhts*, the living embodiment of the world Levinson has worked so long and lovingly to recapture.

TIME, 11/29/99, p. 78, Richard Schickel

It's the 1950's—the last time, we nostalgically think, when the American middle-class narrative was coherent, predictable: everyone in his place and a preordained place for everyone.

This was, of course, an illusion, maybe even a dangerous one. It is writer-director Barry Levinson's business in *Liberty Heights* to shatter that illusion, pick up the shards and rearrange them into a somewhat more realistic, though scarcely revolutionary, pattern. The result is a loose, lively, lovely film that enfolds everything in its embrace from the death of burlesque to the birth of rock 'n' roll, but is mostly concerned with the ways in which Jews, blacks and Wasps, most of them more puzzled than angry, take their first wary, halting steps out of ethnic isolation.

The setting is again the Baltimore, Md., of Levinson's youth, source of *Diner, Tin Men* and *Avalon*. This time his alter ego is a smart, sweet-souled teenager named Ben (Ben Foster), who, having lived all his life in a Jewish enclave, is astonished to discover that most of the world is not, after all, Jewish. That's particularly, true of Sylvia (the uncannily cool, wise and beautiful Rebekah Johnson), who is one of the token blacks in his newly integrated school. Their relationship is handled with great delicacy: this is a friendship that yearns to be, deserves to be, richer. But—and this maybe the most poignant thing about Liberty Heights—these kids are ahead of a time that is still waiting to happen, a time when people will be sympathetically supported when they try to speak gently, lovingly across the color line.

Sylvia's doctor father sternly forbids contact between them; it endangers his hard-won position. Ben's father Nate (Joe Mantegna) is distractedly against it too, though most of his attention is focused on his two troubled businesses—a failing burlesque house and a numbers racket threatened by an obstreperous black man named Little Melvin (Orlando Jones), who portends the violent, irrational '60s, just a historical nanosecond away.

Little Melvin will bring Nate—a decent guy despite his shabby work—to an uncomfortable end. Indeed, no one in this movie gets what he or she really wants or deserves. Even the romance between Ben's older brother Van (Adrien Brody) and his Wasp princess Dubbie (Carolyn Murphy) ends badly, when her ethereal perfection turns out to be only skin- (and coiffure-) deep.

But somehow that doesn't matter. Neither does the fact that Levinson packs his movie with more melodrama—including Little Melvin's kidnapping of Ben and Sylvia from an early rock concert—than you would think it could hold. What's important is the casual, even digressive, movement of the piece. It plays like a memoir, not a conventional three-act movie. There's room here for Ben to shock his family by dressing as Hitler for Halloween, for a faux-naive stripper to electrify Nate's theater, for the strange power of a new-model Cadillac to cloud the mind of a '50s male. In short, *Liberty Heights* seems to encompass all the humor, sadness and weirdness of ordinary life in an utterly winning, morally acute way.

VILLAGE VOICE, 11/30/99, p. 146, Michael Atkinson

You cannot, apparently, take the Baltimore out of the boy with a lock wrench, and so Barry Levinson returns again, with *Liberty Heights,* to the fading metropolis he wistfully remembers from his youth. It'd be easy to flay him for his inexorable trips to this particular well—so much else about his career is craven and naive—but the truth is, *Diner* hums its middle-class/middle-century/Middle America tune better than any film of its decade, and Levinson's Baltimore movies are by far his most watchable. He does get the details right, and *Liberty Heights,* which focuses on being Jewish and being a teenager in 1955 B-town, is rife with them; more time and attention is spent watching two kids listen to r&b records than on a gunpoint kidnapping. More so than *Tin Men* or *Avalon, Liberty Heights* is buoyant with quiet smiles and unpretentious fondness. Even racial politics, inherent in every scene, are treated as no more or less a sign of the times than the carpets, the kitchens, and the looming-cliff hairdos.

Also reviewed in:
CHICAGO TRIBUNE, 12/10/99, Friday/p. A, Mark Caro
NEW YORK TIMES, 11/17/99, p. E1, Stephen Holden
NEW YORKER, 11/29/99, p. 139, Anthony Lane
VARIETY, 11/15-21/99, p. 87, Todd McCarthy
WASHINGTON POST, 12/10/99, p. C5, Stephen Hunter
WASHINGTON POST, 12/10/99, Weekend/p. 44, Desson Howe

LIFE

A Universal Pictures and Imagine Entertainment release of a Brian Grazer production. *Executive Producer:* Karen Kehela and James D. Brubaker. *Producer:* Brian Grazer and Eddie Murphy. *Director:* Ted Demme. *Screenplay:* Robert Ramsey and Matthew Stone. *Director of Photography:* Geoffrey Simpson. *Editor:* Jeffrey Wolf. *Music:* Amanda Scheer-Demme and Wyclef Jean. *Music Editor:* Allan K. Rosen. *Sound:* Russell Williams II and (music) John J. Cevetello. *Sound Editor:* Michael Hilkene. *Casting:* Margery Simkin. *Production Designer:* Dan Bishop. *Art Director:* Jeff Knipp. *Set Decorator:* John Anderson. *Set Designer:* Maria Baker, Mary Finn, Joshua Lusby, and Lori Rowbotham. *Set Dresser:* Dale E. Anderson, Frank Anderson, Sam Anderson, Mark Boucher, Larry Haney, John Horning, Ronald A. Papazian, and David Elton. *Special Effects:* Dan Sudick. *Costumes:* Lucy Corrigan. *Make-up:* Judy Murdock and Joseph M. Regina. *Make-up (Eddie Murphy):* Toy R. Van Lierop. *Make-up (Martin Lawrence):* Kim Davis. *Stunt Coordinator:* Alan Oliney. *Running time:* 105 minutes. *MPAA Rating:* R.

CAST: Eddie Murphy (Rayford Gibson); Martin Lawrence (Claude Banks); Obba Babatundé (Willie Long); Nick Cassavetes (Sgt. Dillard); Anthony Anderson (Cookie); Barry Shabaka Henley (Pokerface); Brent Jennings (Hoppin' Bob); Bernie Mac (Jungle Leg); Miguel A. Nuñez, Jr. (Biscuit); Michael "Bear" Taliferro (Goldmouth); Guy Torry (Radio); Bokeem Woodbine (Can't Get Right); Ned Beatty (Dexter Wilkins); Lisa Nicole Carson (Sylvia);

O'Neal Compton (Superintendent Abernathy); Noah Emmerich (Stan Blocker); Rick James (Spanky); Clarence Williams, III (Winston Hancock); Heavy D (Jake); Bonz Malone (Leon); Ned Vaughn (Young Sheriff Pike); R. Lee Ermey (Older Sheriff Pike); Sanaa Lathan (Daisy); Allyson Call (Young Mae Rose); Poppy Montgomery (Older Mae Rose); James D. Brubaker (Judge); Walter Jordan (Slim); Brooks Almy (Billy's Mama); Hal Havins (Billy); Hildy Brooks (Nurse Doherty); Kenn Whitaker (Isaac); Ernie Banks (Bathroom Attendant); David Alexander (Doctor); Johnny Brown (Blind Reverend Clay); Armelia McQueen (Mrs. Clay); Nate Evans (Juke Bartender); Todd Everett (Deputy at Mansion); Don Harvey (Man with Lantern); Venus De Milo Thomas (Juke Joint Waitress); Zaid Farid and Keith Burke (Shady Cardplayers); Haskell Vaughn Anderson III (Junkie); Steven Barr and Pete Zahradnick (Firemen); Kenneth White (Deputy); Leonardo O. Turner (Superintendent Burke); Garcelle Beauvais (Yvette); Augie Blunt (Man in Prison); Keith Burke, Quantae Love, and Sean Lampkin (Trustees at Line); James Emory, Jr. (Goldmouth's Son); Bill Gratton (Fire Inspector); Reamy Hall (Mrs. Dillard); Corrie Harris and Ayanna Maharry (Sylvia's Girls); George Hartmann (Prison Guard); Zack Helvey (Captain Tom Burnette); Kimble Jemison and Jordan Mahome (Gang Bangers); William Taylor and Jay Arlen Jones (Bagmen); Oscar Jordan (Juke Joint Guitarist); Jordan Lund (Funeral Chaplain); Bridget Morrow (Cocktail Waitress); Ronald Lee Moss (Bouncer); Betty Murphy (Mrs. Abernathy); Walter Powell, Jr. (Waiter); Chris Prevost (Pilot); Joseph Rappa (Disgruntled Fan); Dawn Robinson (Club Crooner); Leon Sanders (Barkeep).

LOS ANGELES TIMES, 4/16/99, Calendar/p. 1, John Anderson

[The following review by John Anderson appeared in a slightly different form in **NEWSDAY, 4/16/99, Part II/p. B3.]**

Life is full of surprises. Eddie Murphy coming back to earth after "Holy Man," for instance. Or the oft-crazed Martin Lawrence revealing an unsuspected gift for understatement. Or a movie starring the two of them that's so gracefully bittersweet and balanced that you forget they were in "Boomerang."

It's not just a weird time of the year for movies, it's a weird year. The comedies have actually been funny ("Analyze This" and "10 Things I Hate About You," at least), so the planets are obviously out of alignment. Further confusing things is "Life," director Ted Demme's latest and the long-awaited reunion of Murphy and Lawrence, which confirms the suspicion that some things, at least, are going unnervingly right.

From graveside at a sparsely attended prison burial, "Life" flashes back 50-odd years to the incarceration of Ray Gibson (Murphy) and Claude Banks (Lawrence), two hapless small-timers framed for the murder of a black gambler by a white sheriff in Prohibition-era Mississippi. It's the prison-as-legalized-slave-plantation and the Depression-era version of being disappeared.

Prisons are a great source of primitive comedy—brutality, criminality, imminent sodomy—it's all hilarious. And the last thing you want to call a comedy is thoughtful; that would be the kiss of death. But while "Life" is certainly no treatise on race, crime or the bad sense it took to be black and in Mississippi circa 1932, it never forgets the plausibility of its story.

The focus of the camp itself manages to turn from hard labor to baseball games and barbecues; there's a terrific fantasy sequence in which Ray imagines the nightclub he's going to open in New York, and his bunkmates join in—the irritating Claude is cast as a waiter. But there's always an underlying sense of loss and an awareness that men like Claude and Ray could easily have been forgotten inside Mississippi's legalized plantation system.

Which gives all the jokes (some of them eagerly crude or enthusiastically homophobic) a connection to, yes, life. Demme finally lays it on the line with an obvious but undeniably poignant sequence in which the passage of Ray's and Claude's lives are marked by their prison mates vanishing one by one, intercut with a roll call of history—the history they've missed: Jackie Robinson, Martin Luther King Jr., Malcolm X, the moonwalk. Murphy and Lawrence are funny, of course, but "Life" is also ennobled by the sense that injustice was, is and, as far as we can tell, ever will be, with us.

"Life's" lessons? Never play poker in a town you don't know; never touch a blood-soaked body when the sheriff needs a fall guy; never try to escape from prison without a decent map and a boat (didn't they ever see "Papillon"?) and—this spring at least—don't judge a movie by its poster.

NEW YORK POST, 4/16/99, p. 48, Rod Dreher

How is "Life"? Not so hot. The dream-team comedy pairing Eddie Murphy and Martin Lawrence, last paired in 1992's disappointing "Boomerang," again proves a major letdown. Murphy and Lawrence are two of the most able comic actors on the planet, but this prison dramedy's muddled, episodic script seems to have gone on a hunger strike for humor, leaving the funnymen starving for material.

"Life" covers a lot of ground in its nearly two-hour running time. It opens in 1930s Harlem, with jabbery Ray (Murphy) negotiating a lifesaving deal for himself and virtual stranger Claude (Lawrence). To settle their accounts with a mob boss ("VH1's Behind the Music" fave Rick James), Ray negotiates a deal in which he and Claude agree to make a bootlegger's run to Mississippi.

The road trip establishes their "Odd Couple"-ish personalities. Ray's the rascally confidence man whose scheming and city-slicker cockiness does a number on solid, squarish Claude. Down in the Delta, the hapless Yankees get framed by a white Mississippi sheriff for murder, and draw a life sentence—this, a full half-hour into director Ted Demme's sluggishly paced picture.

Their small rural prison camp is a sort of informal "Hogan's Heroes" set-up, presided over by a harsh guard (Nick Cassavetes), and populated by a most likable crew of murderers and rapists. They learn the rhythms and realities of prison life. The personality clash between Claude and Ray (who is forever hatching getaway plans) does spark scattered laughs, with the best stuff coming from an energized Murphy, who has Pop Rocks in his mischievous motormouth. Lawrence fares less well, in part because he's got the straight-man role, but also because he never really connects with the rage at Claude's core over the injustice that has befallen him.

The key problem with "Life," though, is its frustrating thematic and tonal ambiguity. Screenwriters Robert Ramsey and Matthew Stone unsatisfactorily attempt to split the difference between flat-out comedy and humanistic drama. Halfway through, scripters Robert Ramsey and Matthew Stone go "Shawshank Redemption" on us, uneasily trying to expand the reach of the movie into poignant consideration of the life denied Ray and Claude. It lets what little head of comic steam Murphy and Lawrence have built up seep out around the margins.

Though "Life" begins and ends with the aftermath of a prison barracks inferno that appears to have taken the pair's lives, the only time this more-or-less watchable film really catches fire is during a throwaway scene near the end, in which crotchety centenarian Ray, profane and garrulous, warns a young inmate off snorting coke. It's the kind of laugh-out-loud moment you expect a movie starring Eddie Murphy and Martin Lawrence to come bursting with.

VILLAGE VOICE, 4/27/99, p. 136, Justine Elias

Don't be dissuaded by the crude, unfunny trailer, and don't mind that the screen writers' only previous effort was the rotten *Destiny Turns on the Radio*. *Life*, starring Eddie Murphy and Martin Lawrence, is an uneven but extremely funny throwback to '70s hits like *Uptown Saturday Night* and *Stir Crazy*. The story, covering 60 or so years, begins in Prohibition Harlem, where Ray (Murphy) is a con artist and Claude (Lawrence) is an earnest bank teller. They quickly run afoul of a bootlegger (an unrecognizable Rick James) and are forced into a dangerous moonshine run. During the overlong, choppy setup, they bungle the deal, lose the bootlegger's money, and find themselves on a Mississippi prison farm with no hope of parole.

At this point, it looks as though the story will be a slog through some dreary men-in-the-slammer gags, but trust director Ted Demme *(The Ref)* to balance the grim setting and episodic structure with free-form verbal comedy and showcase moments for the stars. Nothing flashy: the movie's best scenes feature the inmates simply razzing one another about women, baseball, and their respective criminal records. (At one point, Ray's dreamy chatter about a Harlem nightspot explodes into a full-scale musical fantasy, with each inmate imagining himself in tuxedoed splendor.)

Strangely, Life bears some resemblance to *Life Is Beautiful,* which put a sugary gloss on the Holocaust. But *Life* is a comic tall tale rather than a bogus fairy tale, and it never lets you forget that Claude and Ray have been robbed by bigotry and injustice. (When a seventyish Claude is briefly allowed outside the prison walls, he finds himself bewildered by the changed world and grieving for the life he has been denied.) Both leading men have had their troubles recently and it's gratifying to see both stars at their best, in a movie that transforms a clichéd buddy comedy into something worthwhile.

Also reviewed in:
CHICAGO TRIBUNE, 4/16/99, Friday/p. M, Michael Wilmington
NEW YORK TIMES, 4/16/99, p. E9, Janet Maslin
VARIETY, 4/12-18/99, p. 63, Todd McCarthy
WASHINGTON POST, 4/16/99, p. C1, Stephen Hunter
WASHINGTON POST, 4/16/99, Weekend/p. 43, Desson Howe

LIGHT IT UP

A Fox 2000 release of an Edmonds Entertainment production. *Executive Producer:* Kenneth Edmonds. *Producer:* Tracey E. Edmonds. *Director:* Craig Bolotin. *Screenplay:* Craig Bolotin. *Director of Photography:* Elliot Davis. *Editor:* Wendy Greene Bricmont. *Music:* Harry Gregson-Williams and Michael McQuarn. *Music Editor:* Richard Whitfield. *Sound:* Scott D. Smith and (music) Alan Meyerson. *Casting:* Robi Reed-Humes. *Production Designer:* Lawrence G. Paull. *Art Director:* Karen Fletcher Trujillo. *Set Designer:* Kurt Sharp. *Set Decorator:* Patricia Schneider. *Set Dresser:* Ron Grenko and Matthew Tufano. *Special Effects:* Don Parsons. *Costumes:* Salvador Perez. *Make-up:* Neal Martz. *Make-up (Vaness L. Williams):* Kate Best. *Stunt Coordinator:* Rick LeFevour, Jim Fierro, and Tom Lowell. *Running time:* 98 minutes. *MPAA Rating:* R.

CAST: Usher Raymond (Lester Dewitt); Forest Whitaker (Officer Dante Jackson); Rosario Dawson (Stephanie Williams); Robert Ri'chard (Zacharias "Ziggy" Malone); Judd Nelson (Ken Knowles); Fredro Starr (Rodney J. Templeton); Sara Gilbert (Lynn Sabatini); Clifton Collins, Jr. (Robert "Rivers" Tremont); Glynn Turman (Principal Armstrong); Vic Polizos (Capt. Monroe); Vanessa L. Williams (Audrey McDonald); Gaddiel Otero (Arturo Orosco); Frank Dominelli (Sgt. Tortino); Reggie Theus (Intel. Officer #1); Jennifer Say Gan (Intel. Officer #2); Kevin Morrow (Boy, Gangbanger); Kevin Robert Kelly (O'Connor, Security Guard); LaTaunya Bounds (Bridget); Erica Hubbard (Girl One, Bathroom); Melissa Gonzalez (Girl Two, Bathroom); Patrick Nugent (Police Officer Kelly); Sharif Atkins (Gunman); Stephen R. Key (Rookie Cop); Eric Avilis (Vernon); Shawn Isom (Straggler #1); Deborah J. Crable (WPIX Anchor); Amy Landecker (Reporter #2); Rengin Altay (NY Post Reporter #3); Sam Samuelson (NY Post Reporter #4); Rhomeyn Johnson (Spotter, S.W.A.T.); Llou Johnson (Radio DJ); Daren Flam (Cop, Shooting at Kids); Rick Johnson (Paul Miller/Sniper #1); Erick Garcia (Armondo); Olumiji Aina Olawumi (Student Council Secretary); Dan De Casual (Mr. Miller); Serena Altschul (Herself); Liza Cruzat (MTY Employee); Sabrina Dames Crutchfield (BET Reporter); Charles Brougham (Team Leader); Eddie Fernandez (Tactical Cop #2, Shooter); Donna Hanover (Fox News Anchor); Tara Hickey (Secretary); Darlene Komar (Principal Armstrong's Secretary); Velma Austin Massey (Lester's Mom); Robert Minor (Lester's Dad); Marvin Nelson (S.W.A.T. Team Member); Eriq F. Prince (Security Officer); Gary Anthony Ramsay (News Anchor #1); Dale Rivera (Security Guard, Bob); Sue Simmons (WNBC Anchor); Adam G. (Cop #2); LeShay N. Tomlinson (Student).

NEW YORK POST, 11/10/99, p. 61, Lou Lumenick

"Light It Up" would be a strong candidate for the year's most irresponsible movie—if it were remotely believable.

In writer-director Craig Bolotin's frenzied imagination, a group of students takes a police officer hostage at a Queens high school following the dismissal of a popular teacher. The teacher's crime: He took his civics class to a local eatery to escape a classroom at fictional Lincoln High, where snow is blowing in through broken windows. Oh, and he ends up foiling an armed robbery by a former student.

During a confrontation with the principal (Glynn Turman), one of the students struggles with the cop who's been assigned to the school (Forest Whitaker) and ends up wounding up him with the officer's gun. The students decide to take the cop hostage and, lionized by the media (yeah, right), they begin issuing demands: They want the windows fixed, more textbooks and—no kidding—a career day.

Though one character is briefly seen preparing Molotov cocktails that are never seen again, "Light it Up" contains so little violence it suggests a hasty post-Columbine re-editing job.

What's left is a preachy, inner city, aren't-we-all-victims version of "The Breakfast Club" (which its producers frankly cite as a model—they've even miscast that film's Judd Nelson as the fired teacher).

To be fair, the youthful ensemble cast of "Light it Up" is appealing, especially R&B star Usher Raymond as the group's leader, Robert Ri'chard as a graffiti artist and Sara Gilbert as a purple-haired student expecting a baby.

But the dialogue is ridiculous and condescending—one character actually describes himself as "a chalk-mark waiting to happen"—and midway through, the movie drops its posturing about the school system and turns into a diatribe against the NYPD (Raymond's character's father, it turns out, was shot by officers who mistook his asthma inhaler for a gun).

Though set in Queens, "Light It Up" was actually shot in Chicago. Perhaps that explains the eerie lack of parked cars near the school and the filmmakers' belief that a student from Crown Heights would commute to a school in Queens.

NEWSDAY, 11/10/99, Part II/p. B3, Gene Seymour

From the moment you see stressed-out, short-tempered NYPD patrolman Dante Jackson (Forest Whitaker) roughing up scruffy, gentle Ziggy Malone (Robert Ri'chard) for drawing pictures on a crowded high-school stairwell, you suspect that a long day is in store for the borough of Queens.

And before you can say "Blackboard Jungle," the following ensues: A popular teacher (Judd Nelson) is suspended for taking his class off school grounds because there was no available space in the underheated, overcrowded building for him to do his job. Several students, including the class president (Rosario Dawson), the star basketball player (Usher Raymond) and the friendly drug dealer (Clifton Collins Jr.) are all threatened with suspension for protesting this decision.

Then chaos. The basketball star, whose name is Lester, gets in the middle of a scuffle between Officer Jackson and Ziggy, who accidently shoots the cop in the leg with the latter's own sidearm. Somehow the gun ends up in Lester's hands.

Early dismissal. Everybody gets to leave, except Lester, Ziggy, Jackson, the class president and the dealer. They are soon joined by a gang member (Fredro Starr) who'd love to show Lester what he could do with that gun, and a pregnant punk-ette (Sara Gilbert), who was asleep in the library when all the commotion started.

Soon, this demographically perfect team of accidental guerillas is making demands over the World Wide Web for things they couldn't get through normal channels, like textbooks, new windows and respect. Lester, who has reasons for his bitterness toward the police, seems to be speaking to more than the wounded cop when he says, "You had your minds made up about us the minute you got here." It is as a plea for tolerance and compassion that "Light It Up" functions best.

When you see the dreary, impossible conditions at the school, you share the sense of helplessness and abandonment pervading many urban public schools. An inventory of such grievances would have been gripping enough without reprising "Dog Day Afternoon," right down to the street rabble's rousing cheers for the hostage-takers.

But a hostage drama, cliches intact, is what we get. And despite the firm resolve of Vanessa L. Williams' police negotiator to bring closure with no more spilled blood, you just wait for the inevitable payback that somebody in this crowd is going to get for daring to Break The Law. The presence of Raymond, Starr and Williams, recording stars all, gives "Light It Up" the feel of a familiar pop standard given a new synthetic polish and not much else.

VILLAGE VOICE, 11/23/99, p. 144, Gary Dauphin

Even as it hews close to the familiar rhythms of the misunderstood-teen flick, *Light It Up* is unexpectedly satisfying feel-good agitprop. The social sparks that set off this tale of student rebellion in a dilapidated Queens public high school are hot-button enough to have been, you know, ripped from the headlines (crumbling educational infrastructure, police brutality, teen pregnancy, thickheaded technocrats, the Web), but the film's conceit that there are kids out there who'd react to such ills with what amounts to armed insurrection is a breath of fresh air, even with its quaint whiff of old-school lefty political fantasy.

Written and directed by first-timer Craig Bolotin, *Light It Up* introduces the motley crew who'll rise to the film's unlikely challenge in music-vid style. There's Lester (played credibly by singer Usher Raymond), the basketball star struggling with the Diallo-style execution of his father; there's Stephanie (Rosario Dawson), the smart future doctor who just can't get over how few books there are in class; and there's Ziggy (Robert Ri'chard), a homeless graffiti artist who screams martyr the moment his softly beautiful face appears on screen. Lester has long played protective big brother to Ziggy, so when a hard-nosed cop (Forest Whitaker) assigned to sandlot duty accosts them, the expected accidental hell breaks loose, leading to what the cops outside call a hostage situation.

The "hostage takers" (rounded out by a couple of self-proclaimed white trash rejects and a thuggy hothead) soon decide that since their lives are basically over, they might as well hold on to the cop and ask for something big.   The meeting where they cobble together their demands—more books, fix the windows, rehire a beloved teacher—is *Light It Up*'s most poignant moment, as the kids come into a kind of political self-awareness. *Light It Up* ends exactly how you'd expect it to—not as harshly as it would in the real world, not as happily as it would in a perfect one either—but you're left with the unexpected conviction that it wasn't the kids on-screen who faltered.

Also reviewed in:
NEW YORK TIMES, 10/10/99, p. E5, Lawrence Van Gelder
VARIETY, 11/15-21/99, p. 89, Robert Koehler
WASHINGTON POST, 11/10/99, p. C1, Rita Kempley

LIMBO

A Screen Gems release of a Green/Renzi production. *Producer:* Maggie Renzi. *Director:* John Sayles. *Screenplay:* John Sayles. *Director of Photography:* Haskell Wexler. *Editor:* John Sayles. *Music:* Mason Daring. *Music Editor:* Patrick Mullins. *Sound:* Judy Karp and (music) Michael Golub. *Sound Editor:* Philip Stockton. *Casting:* Lizzie Martinez. *Production Designer:* Gemma Jackson. *Art Director:* Keith Neeley. *Set Designer:* Marco Rubeo. *Set Decorator:* Brian Kasch. *Costumes:* Shay Cunliffe. *Make-up:* Lori Hicks. *Running time:* 126 minutes. *MPAA Rating:* R.

CAST: Mary Elizabeth Mastrantonio (Donna De Angelo); David Strathairn (Joe Gastineau); Vanessa Martinez (Noelle De Angelo); Kris Kristofferson (Smilin' Jack Johansson); Casey Siemaszko (Bobby Gastineau); Kathryn Grody (Frankie); Rita Taggart (Lou); Leo Burmester (Harmon King); Michael Laskin (Albright); Herminio Ramos (Ricki); Dawn McInturff (Audrey); Tom Biss (Baines); Jimmy McDonell (Rabdy Mason); Marit Carlson-Van Dort (Stacy); Monica Brandner (Corky); Maria Gladzisewki (Denise); Dan Rinner (X-Man); Stephen James Lang (Vic); Ron Clarke (Cruise Director); Charlotte Carroll (Loan Officer); Joaqlin Estus (Teacher); Andy Spear and Dave Hunsaker (Bad Guys).

CHRISTIAN SCIENCE MONITOR, 6/4/99, p. 15, David Sterritt

American movies didn't make a big showing at this year's Cannes Film Festival, but of the few that did appear, some were commendably thought-provoking. One was "Limbo," by John Sayles, a leading light of the non-Hollywood "indie" movement.

Although he's directed a dozen pictures during his two-decade career, he has never seemed a natural-born filmmaker. There's often an awkward touch to his camera work and editing, and his stories rarely flow as gracefully as they might. What distinguishes his best pictures is their social commitment—see "The Brother From Another Planet" and "Men With Guns" for good examples—and the clear sense of language that reflects his experience as a writer.

"Limbo" wears these qualities lightly, but they're crucial to the picture's success. The setting is Alaska, and the heroine is a single mother (Mary Elizabeth Mastrantonio) working to raise her teenage daughter (Vanessa Martinez) while pursuing a new boyfriend (David Strathairn).

While these sound like ingredients of a standard domestic drama, Sayles makes an unusual choice by probing the inner lives of the characters rather than the larger-than-life emotionalism that a more commercially minded filmmaker might stress. When the story turns melodramatic—complete with life-threatening danger—it poses a slew of ethical and emotional problems. "Limbo" has stilted and unpersuasive moments, but its determination to explore bedrock human values places it among Sayles's most worthwhile movies.

LOS ANGELES TIMES, 6/4/99, Calendar/p. 6, Kenneth Turan

Writer-director John Sayles' "Return of the Secaucus Seven" helped launch the current American independent film movement in 1980, and now "Limbo," his 12th and latest feature, reminds us what true independence means.

Moving and empathetic but also unsettling and curiously structured, "Limbo," like much of Sayles' output, insists on satisfactions that branch out beyond the conventional. If much recent independent work has been as wearily formulaic as the studios at their worst, this film takes another path, ebbing and flowing in eccentric, unexpected ways.

The storytelling in "Limbo" is not merely multilayered, it comes in different forms, from the personal and melodramatic to the cultural and sociological. A filmmaker who casually puts more into his work than others do by huffing and puffing, Sayles has in this case skirted the edge of overreaching. While his diverse elements are engrossing on their own, they do not always mesh with each other as tightly as we would like.

"Limbo" follows the Sayles pattern of setting each new project in a different part of the U.S. and using film to explore the culture and the people of that particular region. Getting the nod this time is Alaska, with shooting done in the capital city of Juneau (renamed Port Henry for the film).

Even though it's not his primary focus, Sayles supplies an informative meditation on life in a state hovering between traditional industries like fishing and logging and the new boom in tourism, symbolized by cruise ships pointedly characterized as "floating nursing homes." In a world where movies rarely touch on issues, this kind of real-world concern is frankly bracing.

Working with superb cinematographer Haskell Wexler (who also shot "Matewan" and "The Secret of Roan Inish" for him), Sayles provides strong images of Alaska's natural beauty and the grittiness of both fishing and fish processing, images that securely ground the story in its setting.

It's always the people, however, and not the pictures that Sayles cares about most: Few directors are more instinctively caring, or provide for more moments of grace between characters. In this case the key people are a man and a woman who need to decide whether what they've gone through in life leaves them with the wherewithal to attempt a relationship one more time.

Donna De Angelo (Mary Elizabeth Mastrantonio in a welcome return to form) is a singer exasperated—both by her "so-called career" and her sullen teenage daughter Noelle ("Lone Star's" Vanessa Martinez). The film opens with Donna singing at a wedding and then publicly stomping out of yet another relationship that's proved less satisfying than she had hoped.

If Donna is a wanderer, someone who's worked in 36 states and Puerto Rico, homeboy Joe Gastineau (Sayles veteran David Strathairn) has only been as far as Seattle—and there just a couple of times. Reserved and distant, Joe has a tragedy in his past, something that has kept him away from fishing for 25 years and made him especially tentative where relationships are concerned.

Both Strathairn, who manages to be sensitive and intensely masculine, and the gifted Mastrantonio, who sings beautifully and has a presence that lights up like a fire, do a wonderful job conveying the kind of wary tenderness their parts require and their relationship turns out to be one of the most affecting Sayles has put on film.

But whenever you think you know where "Limbo" is going, it heads off in another direction like an ornery prospector determined to stake one last claim. Different parts of Joe's past, including a slippery half-brother (Casey Siemaszko) and a pilot he has unfinished business with (Kris Kristofferson) reappear in his life, and suddenly we are in a completely different movie whose concerns for physical survival and verbal storytelling are intriguing but unexpected.

The same goes for "Limbo's" resolution, a scenario that is consistent with the film's title and intentionally leaves a problematic taste. Determined to use melodrama as a vehicle to get to other places and explore other possibilities, Sayles simply assumes the audience will go along with him. His skill is such that we invariably do, but the journey, like that of his characters, is not always an easy one.

NEW STATESMAN, 1/24/00, p. 46, Jonathan Romney

The dictionary definition of "limbo" on the poster of John Sayles's film of that name is "a place of arrested possibilities; a condition of uneasiness or apprehension". This driest of poster tag lines is unlikely to enhance box-office receipts. Still, you can't fault it for accuracy. *Limbo* is very much about apprehension and suspension which is something more radically unsettling than the traditional suspense you might be expecting. *Limbo* drops us, along with its characters, in the middle of nowhere, then leaves us wondering whether there's any chance of a safe passage back. As a narrative strategy, this is as radical and as pitiless as you'll find in mainstream American cinema.

You might not expect narrative extremity from as dependable a figure as the American independent stalwart Sayles. He has long embodied a go-it-alone ethic, making enjoyable, accessible films that are nevertheless considered uncommercial because they are serious-minded, unglamorous and politically informed. But recent films have become stranger and increasingly complex: *Lone Star* was a time-jumping Tex-Mex mystery that confronted Oedipal trauma with racial politics, while even the comparatively simple *The Secret of Roan Inish*—ostensibly an Irish-set children's tale about magical seals—was really concerned with the relations between oral narrative and local history.

Limbo is Sayles's boldest stroke yet. Its first half is an ensemble drama set in a small community—the sort of narrative that Sayles has often excelled at, notably in his sprawling industry tale *City of Hope*. So we think we're in for two hours of getting to know the population of a troubled Alaskan fishing town. Alaska is about to become one huge theme park—local businessmen are planning to market evocative place names such as Whale's Causeway and Island of the Raven People, and to peddle adventure and the "illusion of risk". The characters roll by—two middle-aged lesbian entrepreneurs, the town's glamorous no-gooder (craggier-than-ever Kris Kristofferson) and Joe, an ex-fisherman with a painful past (Sayles regular David Strathairn). Then there are the newcomers—lounge singer Donna (Mary Elizabeth Mastrantonio), who's seen too much of life and the road, and her tormented teenage daughter Noelle (Vanessa Martinez), who's seen too much of her mother.

Things are heading for a glorious sprawl, and the film teasingly promises to explore every imaginable path. And then Sayles yanks away the carpet, suddenly limiting his narrative options with one audacious stroke. If you don't want to know how, skip the next paragraph. If you can stand to find out, he does it by dropping his three main characters in limbo, taking Joe, Donna and Noelle on an unexpected fishing trip and leaving them stranded on a remote island. This is both outrageous narrative string-pulling and something like real life, in which things are more likely to happen suddenly and inexplicably than by the reasonable types of chance permitted by Hollywood narrative. The three are forced to become a nuclear family under rather more urgent conditions than they'd planned. And when Noelle discovers a journal left on the island a century earlier, she takes control as a storyteller in a way that opens up psychological resonances considerably more disturbing than the stage-managed chills of *The Blair Witch Project*.

Simple as it is, *Limbo* is a film so richly complex that Sayles is almost obliged to pull in his net before it all spins out of control. His journalistic, investigative streak is always to the fore: when fish is served at a business lunch, we already know the fish's history. And few US directors get the same depth of characterisation from their actors. Donna could have been another stock *chanteuse* on the skids, but she's given a hard backbone of angry, compassionate anxiety by

Mastrantonio. Newcomer Martinez sends ripples of ambivalent disturbance flowing under the surface of Noelle's pasty, vulnerable ordinariness, flying in the face of the repertoire of teenage stereotypes currently dominating even the smarter US movies.

Strathairn continues to be America's most underrated actor—it's somehow appropriate to Joe's character that the lines around Strathairn's jaw are taking on a distinct shade of Gary Cooper. But Joe is less like a western hero than another brand of strong, silent hermit: Sayles set out with Joseph Conrad's characters in mind. There's a distinct echo of Conrad's island novel, *Victory*, in which, if A-level memories serve, a character professes: "He who forms attachments is lost." *Limbo* is about connections between people and the danger of those connections, and consequently it really does feel like a dangerous ride in uneasy company. It's appropriate that a film about fishing should expertly reel us in and then, like the salmon in the ominous credit sequence, leave us helplessly floundering.

NEW YORK POST, 6/4/99, p. 46, Rod Dreher

I'm trying to be a grown-up about this, but the way John Sayles ended "Limbo"—it's one of those "Lady or the Tiger"-type finales that leave you hanging in (ha!) limbo—has to be one of the most enervating, let's-burn-down-the-art house conclusions ever.

It's not so much that the ending leaves you with no hope of resolution—although let's not downplay the pull-your-hair-out annoyance of that. It's the way Sayles completely falls apart as a storyteller.

Writing is usually his strong suit, but in "Limbo," he slowly, slowly convinces us to invest emotions in his characters, then drops the bottom out with a lunatic plot turn that seems to have come from another movie entirely. It feels like a manipulative con job.

"Limbo" takes place in Port Henry, an Alaskan fishing village (Juneau, actually) where people seem fated to live dead-end, vaguely depressive lives.

Hippy-dippy Donna (Mary Elizabeth Mastrantonio) is a nightclub singer who drifts from man to man, much to the displeasure of her self-mutilating teen-age daughter Noelle (Vanessa Martinez).

Eventually this leggy piece of driftwood washes up on the unspectacular shore of quiet handyman Joe (David Strathairn), a former fisherman who left the sea after a tragic accident years earlier.

Sayles takes forever to bring these two together, but it's time well spent, because he gently and methodically uncovers the spiritual crisis riving the coastal community.

The town is undergoing an uneasy transition between its past as a traditional fishing and manufacturing base, and a future that looks to be based on tourism. Sayles' overarching theme—the anxiety resulting from an uncertain future—is made manifest in a number of well-written, brilliantly acted character studies.

Why he trashes his characters, his actors and our expectations in the film's second half is beyond telling. It starts when Joe's shifty brother Bobby (Casey Siemazsko) returns from California, and convinces Joe to join him on a cruise up the coast.

Joe invites his new girlfriend and her daughter along for the ride. Bad move: The trip turns into a wilderness survival experience, in which Joe, Donna and Nicole reveal themselves to be far more boring than we expected.

The bizarre leap "Limbo" makes wastes the exceedingly tender and detailed acting done by Strathairn, a Sayles vet, and Mastrantonio. Cinematographer Haskell Wexler does a fine job capturing the brooding skies and rough natural beauty of the Alaskan landscape.

Too bad the disappointing "Limbo" proves such a purgatory of dashed potential.

NEWSDAY, 6/4/99, Part II/p. B7, John Anderson

Since every other review of the new John Sayles film is going to begin with the words "the ending of 'Limbo' is ... " let's hop aboard the bound-for-Alaska bandwagon: The ending of "Limbo" is the least of its problems.

That ending—and we're not giving anything away—has been bothering people so much that it's dominated all early discussion of the film either here or in Cannes, where it was in the festival's competition last month. And the conclusion is a conversation piece, to be sure. But while there are many things to like about "Limbo"—not the least of which is Mary Elizabeth Mastrantonio's wonderfully mature and welcome performance—you have to wonder if that parting shot was intended purely as a distraction.

In many ways this, his 12th, is the quintessential Sayles movie, with all ingredients present and accounted for: Social commentary. Human drama.

Humankind's propensity for befouling its soul and/or its world. And a plot turn in which debt/duty/familial obligations get good people in hot water.

Those good people include Joe Gastineau (Sayles regular David Strathairn), a former athlete, former fisherman and all-around decent guy whose life has stalled out because of a fatal accident. Donna De Angelo (Mastrantonio), an itinerant bar singer making her way around the clubs of Alaska, and Donna's daughter, Noelle (Vanessa Martinez), a unhappy teenager with a gift for both fiction writing and self-mutilation.

In getting us to "Limbo's" ultimate destination—the coming together of these three unsettled people on a remote island after a violent crime—Sayles first sets up the entirety of contemporary Alaska, with its cynically avaricious developers, a couple of carpetbagging and pronouncedly lesbian lawyers, and the locals—some conniving, some not—who need to get out of the way of the souvenir stands and tour boats that are turning the unspoiled North into one more theme park. Industry is disappearing; the people who chose Alaska because it demanded so little are finding that Unattainable Success has tracked them north to harass them. Without offering much in the way of solutions, Sayles fires off a shot that's more angry than wise.

The problems arise where you least expect them. Sayles' scriptwriting talents are legendary; at least part of the money that's gone into creating the director's oeuvre—"Men With Guns," "Lone Star," "Matewan," "Brother From Another Planet," et al.—has come from the director's work as a screenwriter and script doctor. So it's surprising how much awkwardly expository dialogue permeates the early part of "Limbo's" script. Characters who've known each other for years sit around telling each other things they already know.

Villains laying out the economic realities of Alaska's tourist potential sound like they're teaching Exploitation 101. All this clunkily constructed history is unworthy of Sayles, who, all things considered, didn't seem to make much of an effort.

But Strathairn and Mastrantonio, in their several scenes alone together, are marvelous. They can make even the worst lines sing and endow their wounded characters with all the crazing and fractures life's left on them.

That such performances should come from two such seasoned performers is hardly as surprising as the rest of what happens in "Limbo." But it's what you'll remember, long after that ending is done playing with your head.

SIGHT AND SOUND, 2/00, p. 47, Philip Kemp

Port Henry, Alaska, the present. Joe Gastineau works as a handyman at a guest lodge run by Frankie and Lou. An ex-fisherman, Joe quit 25 years ago when his boat sank, drowning two of his friends. At a party he meets singer Donna De Angelo, and helps her move into a flat at the Golden Nugget saloon, her new place of work.

When Frankie and Lou persuade Joe to go out fishing, he rediscovers his joy in the job. He and Donna become lovers, arousing her teenage daughter Noelle's jealousy Joe's half-brother Bobby, who runs a charter business, asks Joe to help him crew a boat up the coast to meet clients. Joe invites Donna and Noelle along for the ride.

En route, Bobby confesses his clients are drug dealers. They show up and shoot Bobby; Joe, Donna and Noelle escape to a nearby island. They take refuge in a hut. Noelle finds a diary left by a previous owner and starts reading from it; as the narrative grows more doom-laden, Donna realises Noelle, now feverish, is making it up. Jack Johansson, a pilot from Port Henry, arrives in a small seaplane. He admits he's working for the drug dealers, but promises to fetch help. Soon, a larger plane approaches. The three await rescue or death.

John Sayles is one of the most politically tuned in of American independents. But the downside to his social awareness can be a tendency to didacticism, where the narrative moves predictably towards closure. Not this time, though. *Limbo* is Sayles' most unexpected film to date: not so much in its themes, which connect with his previous work, as in the shape of the story and the way it's resolved or rather, in the way it isn't resolved. *Limbo*, as Sayles defines it, is a condition of unknowable outcomes, and this is exactly the point he leads us to.

Locations are crucial to Sayles' work, and he has always explored cultural territory far from his own New Jersey roots. With *Limbo* he veers northwards to Alaska, which he presents as frontier territory. Not a frontier in the adventurous, uncharted sense of the Old West, but a last-resort frontier for washed up characters who have wearily arrived here with their disillusionments in tow. Most of them take a perverse pride in living in such a God-awful place. A running gag involves the regulars of the local saloon swapping ghoulish tales of drownings and fatal freezings.

For the first half of the film we're in familiar Sayles terrain. As in *City of Hope* or *Lone Star* he evokes a community with its feuds and social cross-currents, often via his signature shot: a long unbroken take meandering from group to group, picking up phrases and showing how all these people connect up. But midway Sayles works a switch on us, lifting his three main characters out of this busy environment and dropping them into isolated jeopardy to play out a tight psychological drama.

Each of the trio carries weighty emotional baggage. Ex-fisherman Joe Gastineau is haunted by an accident where he caused the death of two friends; torch singer Donna De Angelo is the survivor of a string of transient relationships; her teenage daughter Noelle has taken to self-mutilation in response to her insecure lifestyle. Trapped on an island, and with the Alaskan winter closing in, the three are forced into close interdependence, exacerbating the fears and tensions between them. It's still a community, but shrunk down, distilled and intensified, all its edges sharpened.

They're joined by a ghost: the diary of a young girl who once lived on the island with her parents. Noelle finds the diary, reads aloud from it and starts using it as a weapon, rewriting it as she goes to mirror her own situation and get back at her mother. This set-up recalls Sayles' 1994 film *The Secret of Roan Inish,* where a family also wind up on an offshore island haunted by past presences. But that was far lighter in tone; *Limbo* introduces a harsh, unsettling note that's new in his work. Though the three confront their demons, we're left with no assurance that they'll find redemption.

As ever, Sayles gives his actors plenty to chew on. David Strathairn hits the exact note of wary gentleness, and Mary Elizabeth Mastrantonio's taut, ravaged beauty has never been better used. Haskell Wexler makes the Alaskan wilderness look at once alluring and forbidding; a shot of icy mist drifting over wooded hills has a Japanese delicacy. Over two hours long, the pace occasionally drags. Certain characters and elements—such as Noelle's crush on Joe—feel underdeveloped, almost as if the film had been boiled down from the longish novel. But when, as here, a filmmaker strikes out on a daring new track, the odd minor imperfection goes with the territory.

TIME, 6/7/99, p. 76, Richard Schickel

John Sayles is a filmmaker at home everywhere in the world—mythical South American countries (*Men with Guns*), Texas border towns (*Lone Star*), West Virginia a long time ago (*Matewan*). But wherever he goes, he finds ordinary people who turn out to have extraordinarily complicated back stories—stories that often have kinks in them that even they are unaware of.

As a stylist he's always seemed sort of prematurely mature, more earnest than flashy. But that gravity is also the source of his ripening strength; at a time when characterization is in short supply at the movies, Sayles keeps finding troubled, intelligent life in venues that are at once exotic and quotidian.

For example, the Juneau, Alaska, of *Limbo*. It seems to have a limitless supply of his kind of people—aging slackers muddling inconclusively along. Chief among them are Joe Gastineau (Sayles regular David Strathairn) and Donna De Angelo (Mary Elizabeth Mastrantonio). He's a handyman, an omnicompetent fixer-upper, who has abandoned the life he loves, as a fishing-boat captain, because he feels responsible for the death of two men on a long-ago voyage. She's a wandering bar singer—a very good one—encumbered by a sulky, judgmental adolescent daughter (Vanessa Martinez) but blessed by good nature. Like Joe, Donna deserves more from life; unlike him, she has a mysterious ability to bounce back from disappointment. She's not chirpy or fierce. Rather she just glows expectantly.

Sayles feels the life of this pair persuasively—no patronizing, but no false hopes either. There's nothing flighty about their romance. They come together warily, but also with a certain subtle, last-chance resolve. That's largely owing to the playing. Strathairn is one of those rare actors who make you believe it when they mime thinking. But it is Mastrantonio who is the revelation.

She's an actress who can take us from the relaxed romantic clarity of her songs (she sings all the vocals herself) to the damp miseries of *Limbo*'s melodramatic (and harshly ambiguous) conclusion without our being aware of the downshifting. But then, for much of this decade, Mastrantonio has been a performer in search of a defining role. Or maybe not sufficiently in search of one—at least not with the teeth-gritted ferocity of her peers.

For she has chosen to live in London with her husband, director Pat O'Connor, raising their two sons. She had thought she could maintain her formerly bustling career, which included an Academy Award-nominated role in Martin Scorsese's *The Color of Money*. But "if you're not available in the U.S., you're just not seen," she says. And, besides, "I've never been a person to make sure I'm seen." She worked intermittently, of course, but became increasingly aware that "the phone hasn't rung and that you're not being offered things, and when you are, it's in soft focus."

On the other hand, she unaffectedly loves her family life. As she puts it, "You don't act better in a $20 million picture than you do in a $2 million one. The only thing that informs the acting is your life. My life has taken huge changes and shifts. And if I come back out of it and do a good performance, I have to think, really, that I wouldn't have done this performance 10 years ago."

Having known Mastrantonio, Sayles wrote Donna for her, infusing the character with what he calls her "resilience" and then creating a stern, surprising test for it. Civilization in Alaska is, after all, a thin membrane stretched across a vast wilderness, and the writer-director devises a way for Donna, Joe and her daughter to fall into the darkness. On a seemingly innocent cruise with his half brother, they are beset by murderous demons out of the brother's shady past and become castaways on a deserted island—their resources (and survivalist skills) scant, the knowledge that the criminals must seek them out certain. The mood shift is wrenching—this is almost a self-contained second movie. But it's a pretty good one also, resolving as it does the relationship between adults and child and also giving Mastrantonio the chance to let some cracks in her composure begin to show. The movie may be called *Limbo*, but it definitively rescues Mastrantonio from the land of the lost. If her next film, the small Scottish family drama *My Life So Far*, grants her similar opportunities, she may look forward to, if not $20 million pictures, then the sharp-focus roles she so richly deserves.

VILLAGE VOICE, 6/8/99, p. 59, Michael Atkinson

Nobody can make a John Sayles movie like John Sayles, and if you dig large side dishes of multicultural sermonizing and overproud anti-formula with your literate-indie veggie burger, you're likely to be a repeat customer. But Sayles's grip on visual storytelling has always been wobbly, his preachiness can be stultifying, and in strenuously bypassing some clichés, he often backs into others. Homily-free and unpretentious, *Limbo* bears its Saylesian dharma lightly, focusing for the first hour on a few worn-out, middle-aged nobodies with no axes, just burdens, and the small Alaskan fishing community around them. Then the script goes off-road in a way that could redefine "left field." Just like life, Sayles might say, but *Limbo* feels by turns spontaneously original and blandly calculated.

You can't help but side with Sayles on principle—the movie dispenses with "arc," defiantly lollygaggling around with Joe and Donna (David Strathairn and Mary Elizabeth Mastrantonio), a brooding ex-fisherman and bar singer, respectively, who start a tentative romance despite his haunted past (accidental fishing deaths) and her unhappy, self-mutilating teenage daughter Noelle (Vanessa Martinez). The rhythms of chitchat are beautifully realized, and Sayles carefully carves out a convincing reality in the town gin mill, a locus of tale-spinning seen in a montage of conversational fragments. It's a sweet strategy: we've spent so much downtime with the movie's people that when the plot proper kicks in—Joe's huckster brother (Casey Siemaszko) sets up a shady deal and gets Joe, Donna, and Noelle stranded on an isolated, sub-Arctic island—we're more aware of what's at stake for them than we're used to.

Limbo is assembled with such high intentions and respect it's a shame it never coalesces dramatically, or lets the characters do anything surprising. Like many Sayles movies, this one has a way of staying on the page. Still, in the current field, it might be the only studio film made for adults—Lucas-resistant codgers, this Bud's for you.

Also reviewed in:
CHICAGO TRIBUNE, 6/4/99, Friday/p. A, Michael Wilmington
NEW YORK TIMES, 6/4/99, p. E14, Stephen Holden
VARIETY, 5/31-6/6/99, p. 28, Todd McCarthy
WASHINGTON POST, 6/11/99, p. C1, Stephen Hunter

LIMEY, THE

An Artisan Entertainment release. *Producer:* John Hardy and Scott Kramer. *Director:* Steven Soderbergh. *Screenplay:* Lem Dobbs. *Director of Photography:* Ed Lachman. *Editor:* Sarah Flack. *Music:* Cliff Martinez and Amanda Scheer-Demme. *Sound:* Jim Webb and (music) Leanne Ungar. *Sound Editor:* Larry Blake. *Casting:* Debra Zane. *Production Designer:* Gary Frutkoff. *Set Decorator:* Kathryn Peters. *Special Effects:* Kevin Hannigan. *Costumes:* Louise Frogley. *Make-up:* Rick Sharp. *Stunt Coordinator:* John Robotham. *Running time:* 89 minutes. *MPAA Rating:* Not Rated.

CAST: Terence Stamp (Wilson); Lesley Ann Warren (Elaine); Luis Guzman (Ed); Barry Newman (Jim Avery); Joe Dallesandro (Uncle John); Nicky Katt (Stacy); Peter Fonda (Terry Valentine); Melissa George (Jennifer 'Jenny' Wilson); Amelia Heinle (Adhara); William Lucking (Warehouse Foreman); Matthew Kimbrough (Tom); John Robotham (Rick); Steve Heinze (Larry); Nancy Lenehan (Lady on Plane); Wayne Péré (Pool Hall Creep); Allan Graf (Gordon); Carl Ciarfalio, George Ruge, and Lincoln Simonds (Warehouse Thugs) Rainbow Borden (Warehouse Sweeper); Michaela Gallo (Young Jennifer); Carol White (Jennifer's Mother); José Perez and Alex Perez (Teen Gun Dealers); Brandon Keener (Excited Guy); Jim Jenkins and Mark Gerschwin (Party Guys); Johnny Sanchez (Valet); Brooke Marie Bridges (Child Actress); Randy Lowell (Director); Eva Rodriguez (Ed's Sister); James Earl Olmedo (Ed's Nephew); Jamie Lon Olmedo (Ed's Niece); Clement E. Blake (Pool Hall Bartender); Tom Pardoe (Party Bartender); George Clooney (Himself, on "Access Hollywood").

CHRISTIAN SCIENCE MONITOR, 10/8/99, p. 15, David Sterritt

Many filmmakers are in the opposite of a feel-good mood just now. Some of the most talked-about new pictures treat unsettling subjects with disturbing directness.

Exhibit A is "The Limey", directed by Steven Soderbergh, who gave American independent cinema a major boost when his "sex, lies, and videotape" became a runaway hit 11 years ago. His career has endured more downs than ups since then, but "The Limey" could improve his fortunes if US moviegoers take to it as enthusiastically as audiences at the Toronto filmfest did.

And this might well happen, thanks to Terence Stamp's searing portrayal of a British hit man who visits Los Angeles in search of the criminals he blames for his daughter's death. Revisiting the "film noir" style that Soderbergh explored so evocatively in "The Underneath," the movie blends jarring violence with sincere respect for the inarticulate love felt by the main character for his lost child. Stamp continues the impressive comeback he started with "The Adventures of Priscilla, Queen of the Desert," and Peter Fonda is amazing as a sleazy Hollywood producer.

LOS ANGELES TIMES, 10/8/99, Calendar/p. 6, Kevin Thomas

Steven Soderbergh follows up the critically lauded "Out of Sight" with "The Limey," a sleek, stylish contemporary L.A. noir, a solid genre film that offers the satisfactions of the familiar while deriving its resonance through its specific and telling references to the '60s.

Fittingly it stars two '60s icons, Terence Stamp and Peter Fonda, with Barry Newman, star of the 1971 cult film "Vanishing Point," and Andy Warhol regular Joe Dallesandro in key supporting roles. What's more, it has a lovely leading lady in the wonderful Lesley Ann Warren, who knows her way around genre as well. "The Limey" is just the ticket for those who remember the '60s; it has more depth than "Out of Sight" but probably won't have as wide an appeal.

Stamp has the title role as Wilson, who's just completed his third term (of nine years) for armed robbery. While still in prison, the long-widowed Wilson has received word that his daughter Jennifer, who was an infant when he was first convicted, has been killed in a fiery car crash on Mulholland Drive. Wilson has become convinced that it was no accident and heads for L.A. to get some answers.

Soderbergh and writer Lem Dobbs are thus able to inject complexity and ambiguity in the stoic Wilson right from the start. You feel that this steely, silver-haired, very tough man is seeking a redemption that could boomerang—that Wilson could find himself confronted with the truth that he is ultimately responsible for his daughter's fate, regardless of whether he accepts that responsibility.

Jennifer turns out to have been that L.A. archetype, the pretty aspiring actress. The man who sent word of her death to her father is Ed (Luis Guzman), a likable ex-con living in East L.A. who has straightened out his life and had been Jennifer's friend and drama coach. Ed learned of her death from another of Jennifer's friends, Elaine (Warren), an actress for whom stardom proved elusive but who is a resourceful survivor. Elaine felt Wilson should be notified, even if his daughter thought of him as a ghost.

Wilson's key target is Terry Valentine (Fonda), a successful rock 'n' roll promoter back in the '60s, who could well have been tempted to engage in some decidedly unsavory dealings to maintain the lavish lifestyle to which he has become accustomed. Although Valentine can get momentarily wistful over the '60s, he is essentially shallow, a glib man who dresses expensively and has held on with all his might to his looks. (Could Terry's surname be a reference to the late Elmer Valentine, co-owner of the Whisky and a Sunset Strip celeb of eras past?)

He's just the kind of seemingly rich and powerful guy who easily ensnares ambitious though naive women young enough to be his daughters. He lives in a spectacular cantilevered house in the Hollywood Hills with his current squeeze, the delectable Adhara (Amelia Heinle).

Danger, violence and plot convolutions quickly envelop Wilson and everyone with whom he comes in contact, taking us into the town's murkiest margins. We've been down these mean streets many times before, but in its writing and adroit casting, "The Limey" evokes the lost idealism and dreams of the '60s. Stamp's Wilson is rightly the fearless, implacable monomaniac, but Soderbergh gives him a past, courtesy of Ken Loach, from whose memorable 1967 "Poor Cow" the director and Dobbs borrow some key sequences. We see how the father's thievery impacts his little daughter, but we also glimpse the affable, smiling young Wilson strumming a guitar and singing, entertaining little Jennifer and her mother (Carol White).

Warren's Elaine is the true adult here, and her smarts and charm represent what might have been for Wilson, had he been somehow deflected from his course. Newman is Valentine's top aide, as ruthless as he is loyal, and Dallesandro plays a laid-back hired killer teamed with the nervy, jumpy, much younger Stacy (Nicky Katt), for whom the dream of L.A. success has gone sour.

Soderbergh unleashes a flourish of flash-forwards here and there that reveal Wilson's resolve of iron and become part of the elegant nonchalance that is the film's stylized quality. Ed Lachman's photography of locales high and low is lush, varied and supple, and all aspects of the film contribute toward making it a sophisticated entertainment of considerable subtlety.

NEW YORK, 10/18/99, p. 54, Peter Rainer

Few actors have aged onscreen as remarkably as Terence Stamp. He looks whittled and severe, with a swatch of bright white hair and a laser stare. In Steven Soderbergh's *The Limey*, written by Lem Dobbs, he's playing an English career criminal named Wilson who has recently been let out of prison after nine years and seems none the worse for it. Wilson's elegance is like a blade: It cuts through the crap. He travels to L.A. because his daughter from whom he's long been estranged, has been killed in an accident and Wilson, with his crook's radar, suspects foul play. Striding into enemy fire, he charges forward in his quest as implacably as Lee Marvin in *Point*

Blank. Wilson is almost otherworldly in his indestructibleness; he represents the invincibility of vengeance.

Soderbergh's last movie, *Out of Sight,* was marred by time-jump trickery, but mostly it was a sexy, stylish spree; he's at his best, as in that film and his undervalued *King of the Hill,* when he isn't attempting to wow us with a lot of experimentation. In *The Limey,* he's going for deep-dish pulp noir, but he also wants to make a tasty art-house canapé. The movie has lots of drive, and it keeps Stamp front and center almost continuously, even in flashbacks, which are lifted from his performance as a hood in Ken Loach's 1967 *Poor Cow.* But it also plays up Soderbergh's show-offy side, which tends to denature pulp: Though the film is shot all over California, from the barrios of L.A.'s Boyle Heights to Big Sur, it's remarkably low on atmosphere. It's too fancy for that.

Peter Fonda, who, all things considered, has aged pretty well, too, plays the record producer who faces off with Wilson. His pairing with Stamp is billed as dueling sixties icons, but I doubt many in the audience will get dewy-eyed about the casting coup. What these actors represent—the bygone fripperies of Mod London and ashrams and hippie communes and what all—doesn't really carry much meaning for this film. On the other hand, I think the team of Stamp and Fonda would be a natural for the next Austin Powers movie.

NEW YORK POST, 10/11/99, p. 50, Jonathan Foreman

"The Limey" has cult film written all over it. Wistfully moody, stylized and exquisitely self-conscious, it's filled with 1960s movie references and makes maximum use of the iconic status of two stars from that era: Terence Stamp and Peter Fonda.

It's clever, cool fun and it looks great. But it doesn't work nearly as well as "Out of Sight," Steven Soderbergh's terrific last movie, which also used lots of jump cuts and flashbacks.

It's a much smaller, slower, arty piece of work that veers between taking itself seriously as a revenge thriller and playing the story for laughs as a collection of jokey genre references.

Wilson (Stamp) is a tough, Cockney-speaking English career criminal who has been released from prison after the death of his daughter Jenny in L.A. He crosses the Atlantic to investigate what he believes was her murder.

First he enlists Ed (Luis Guzman), a Mexican-American cook who was a friend of his daughter, and then Elaine (Lesley Ann Warren), who was her acting teacher. With their help, he discovers that Jenny had been seeing Valentine (Peter Fonda), a wealthy record producer with a sideline in drugs. Despite receiving a severe beating in the course of his investigation, Wilson decides to exact revenge for his daughter's death.

The weakest thing about "The Limey" is a script by Lem Dobbs that reaches for laconic simplicity but comes off as underwritten, prone to the odd cliché and occasionally crude.

The great Stamp doesn't act much. And sometimes when he delivers his lines, he looks like he's repeating something someone just whispered in his ear. But, like Fonda, he just exudes presence.

NEWSDAY, 10/8/99, Part II/p. B9, Jan Stuart

Since the indelible premiere of "sex, lies, and videotape," Steven Soderbergh has groped and stumbled like a director in search of a genre. After several years knocking about independent land with "Kafka" and "King of the Hill," it took a big studio film to end the quest. Last year's "Out of Sight" was like a homecoming for the filmmaker, who spoke the rough-and-tumble language of crime suspense drama as if to the manner born.

"The Limey" offers further evidence that Soderbergh has a master's grip on the taut demands of pulp fiction. Returning him to the land of the indies with a narrative economy that recalls the best "B" thrillers of the '50s as it pushes the form into the next century, "The Limey" is a lean and mean treat for savvy action lovers.

Veteran British actor Terence Stamp does a ferocious star turn as Wilson, a career criminal who doesn't waste any time getting his hands dirty again after nine years in the slammer. Flying from his native England and into the jet-set heartland of California, Wilson prowls the coastline as he goes after the people responsible for the murder of his daughter.

The chief target of his search, which takes him from Los Angeles warehouses to tony house parties in Big Sur, is a record producer named Terry Valentine (Peter Fonda). After the tight-lipped requirements of "Ulee's Gold," it's a pleasure to see Fonda open up into the more unctuous skin of this show-biz glamor-puss, who is living high off the rock territory he chartered back in the '60s. Fonda's casting offers a sly and deliberate reference to the sensational impact of the actor's "Easy Rider" turn in 1969.

Far from wallowing, Soderbergh and writer Lem Dobbs send up empty nostalgia.

When someone waxes nostalgic about the glory days of the counterculture, Valentine dryly replies, "It was just '66 and early '67." "The Limey's" cunning self-referential methods extend to Valentine's antagonist. Cutting between past and present with a prismatic use of time that keeps the viewer teetering off balance, Soderbergh layers in black and white clips of the young Terence Stamp in Ken Loach's 1967 debut film "Poor Cow," in which Stamp played a thief also named Wilson.

The juxtaposition offers an unexpectedly poignant resonance to a resolutely tough-minded film. Wilson mows down his underworld opponents with a fierce, uncompromising determination, confounding everyone with his period English colloquialisms. Dobbs' dialogue is uncommonly stinging and witty, without ever sinking to the wiseacre, make-my-day-lethal action pabulum favored by action stars who shall remain nameless.

SIGHT AND SOUND, 1/00, p. 57, Philip Strick

Released after a nine-year prison term, Cockney criminal Wilson flies to Los Angeles in response to news that his daughter Jenny has been killed in a car accident. Interrogating her friend Ed, Wilson learns she was having an affair with rock promoter Terry Valentine. Attempting to locate Valentine, Wilson is beaten up by thugs apparently associated with him. He shoots them, mystifying Valentine and his security chief Avery.

Acting on information from Jenny's former voice coach Elaine, Wilson gatecrashes a party at Valentine's home, kills a bodyguard and wrecks Avery's car. Avery hires an underworld contact, Stacy, to kill Wilson. Avery, Valentine and Valentine's girlfriend Adhara then retreat to a hideout in Big Sur. Stacy's attack on Wilson and Elaine is thwarted by narcs who reveal Valentine's new location. Wilson finds the place protected by guards. In the ensuing gunfire, complicated by another attack from Stacy, Avery and his various employees kill each other off. Wilson confronts the wounded Valentine on the beach. Recognising that Valentine's relationship with Jenny closely mirrored his own, Wilson leaves and flies back to London.

It was around the middle of filming *The Underneath* that director Steven Soderbergh admits he lost interest in what he was making. There must have been a brisk mood change because *The Underneath* is undervalued and something of a treat to watch. But such crises of confidence are surely the secret behind the Soderbergh style, which habitually offers an assortment of disclaimers, distractions and second thoughts. Like most of his leading characters, Soderbergh appears to personify a combination of bravado and vulnerability, two extremes which constantly challenge each other. His protagonists are neither wholly innocent nor irremediably criminal; they are simply trapped by their own fallibility. Which is why the dominating image of Soderbergh's latest film, *The Limey,* is a wall.

With its montage of flashbacks and flashforwards, images as much from imagination as from memory, *The Limey* is almost a story that never happened, a fantasy briefly dreamed by airline passenger Wilson, perhaps on his way to Los Angeles, perhaps not. His quest, announced in the darkness punctuating the opening credits, is for knowledge. "Tell me," he says, "about Jenny." The demand is not just for information about his daughter's death but for an understanding of the girl he hasn't seen in nine years. There is now a wall of time and silence between them. Soderbergh fills the screen with it, a towering barricade with Wilson's bowed and labouring figure at its base, heading towards an uncertain turning for as long as it takes. The obstacle reappears as part of the litany of ciphers that flash throughout the film, giving way to less forbidding structures as Wilson achieves progress. Soderbergh has an appreciative eye for angular environments: both *Kafka* and *The Underneath* were precisely framed, and *The Limey* is set against a striking series of elegant confinements until, on the final seashore, the walls have all crumbled.

There is also a satisfying geometry about the relationships in the film, a collection of triangles derived from the matrix represented by Wilson/Valentine (Jenny's lover)/Jenny. As well as the underlying symmetry of two car crashes, there is a near-pedantic matching of Wilson as he arrives and as he departs. One suspects, as Soderbergh goes off at a brief tangent, that his attention has again proved capricious and that the fun of, say, intercutting two bloodied hands (Wilson's and Valentine's) transcends any awkward questions about where he blood came from. He cheerfully whips up a stir of allusions, for example, by filming Wilson through Jenny's former voice coach Elaine's security bars. With singular economy, their unyielding framework represents exclusion, restraint, a reminder of the intruder's criminal background, and, in a wild stretch, the barcodes that are Elaine's stock-in-trade (she moonlights as a checkout girl). Few images are simple when Soderbergh's visual vocabulary is at full volume.

And language itself is a continuing theme: where experiments in French, Italian and Japanese represented attempts for a man and wife to communicate in *Schizopolis,* words in *The Limey* are a passport to an era of the Who, the Hollies and other late-60s rock phenomena. "Freedom is a word I rarely use," says Wilson, quoting Donovan to his uncomprehending questioner (who replies: "The thing I don't understand is every word you're saying") while his use of rhyming slang requires frequent—if ponderous—translation. While Terence Stamp and Peter Fonda rest knowingly on their 60s laurels (the concluding extract from *Poor Cow,* 1967, reprises Donovan but is otherwise more distraction than asset), the film is subtly stolen by Amelia Heinle, joining such actresses as Andie MacDowell, Elisabeth Shue, Betsy Brantley and Jennifer Lopez as the latest in a line of Soderbergh's saving graces.

VILLAGE VOICE, 10/12/99, p. 139, J. Hoberman

A jaggedly impressionistic reverie, Steven Soderbergh's *The Limey* works best as a brutal yet delicate gloss on the Orpheus myth. A man journeys to the underworld looking for his lost love (in this case a child) only to lose her again—albeit through the filmmaker's backward glance, a rueful immersion in the old-movie hall of mirrors.

A British ex-con known simply as Wilson (Terence Stamp) arrives in Los Angeles to conduct his own investigation into the mystery of his daughter's accidental death. *The Limey,* which Soderbergh directed from Lem Dobbs's somewhat undernourished script, harks back to the stylized quest of the original neo-noir, *Point Blank,* among other British crime films of the late '60s and early '70s. As in *Point Blank,* an implacable, single-named protagonist—as fearless as he is irate—bulls his way through a suspiciously mental terrain, further abstracted by flashy montage, seeking vengeance on the fat cats who betrayed him.

Stranger in a strange land, Wilson is worldly enough to purchase his weapons from a couple of school kids and sufficiently naive to mistake the parking valets outside a posh Malibu party for hired muscle. Like the antihero of *Point Blank,* he is also a walking anachronism. *The Limey* cascades with Wilson's dated cockney rhyming slang. ("Do you even understand half the shit this guy is saying?" someone demands after a particularly flavorsome diatribe.) Perhaps existing only in his own mind, Wilson is constructed to defy the past. The 60-year-old Stamp is impressively trim; his character is impossibly tough, capable of absorbing a monstrous beating (then coming back for more), as well as tossing a 250-pound bodyguard off a cliff.

The Limey feasts on character performances, yet much of it feels like a solo. Wilson picks up sometime sidekicks in his daughter's acting teacher (Lesley Ann Warren) and fellow student (Luis Guzman, the punchy-looking restaurateur from *Boogie Nights),* before finding an appropriate nemesis in the person of her ex-lover, the powerful music promoter Valentine, played by Peter Fonda. Supposedly the man who packaged the counterculture, this smug and pedantic hustler lives in a house filled with austerely framed psychedelic posters and perched on the edge—a point where "you could see the sea out there if you could see it."

Thanks to Fonda, *The Limey* is well-stocked with *Easy Rider* references (although his narcissistic character might have been inspired by the account of hipster mogul Bert Schneider that appears in *Easy Riders, Raging Bulls).* In a particularly neat bit of casting, the job of Valentine's security expert is filled by Barry Newman, a minor and appropriately bitter Peter Fonda-type back in the day. Wilson's own past, meanwhile, is supplied by flashbacks lifted from Ken Loach's 1967 *Poor Cow,* in which the young Stamp played a good-hearted petty thief and even sang a Donovan song. The original color footage is here printed in monochromatically to enhance its past-ness; it supplies another level of fantasizing and regret in this densely edited time-twister.

Soderbergh's third recent genre film—following his overly schematic *Criss Cross* remake *The Underneath* (1995), and last year's romantic succès d'estime, *Out of Sight*—is moodier and less overweening than its precursors. Indeed, *The Limey* might be taken as a productive experiment in deploying a contemporary crime-flick vernacular predicated on movie references, industry riffs, sight gags, carefully selected vintage pop, and historically resonant casting. The recipe, which was more or less invented by Robert Altman in *The Long Goodbye,* is close to the Quentin Tarantino formula, but Soderbergh has a lighter hand.

For all its flourishes, *The Limey* is an economical movie—as well as a curiosity in which the independent filmmaker whose early success paved the way for Tarantino at Sundance and Cannes reinvents himself as the most skillful of Tarantino disciples. *The Limey*'s narrative is absurdly straightforward but the movie has a casual, tossed-off feel—less the logic of a nightmare than a daydream.

Also reviewed in:
CHICAGO TRIBUNE, 10/8/99, Friday/p. A, Michael Wilmington
NATION, 11/1/99, p. 35, Stuart Klawans
NEW YORK TIMES, 10/8/99, p. E15, Janet Maslin
NEW YORKER, 10/11/99, p. 106, Anthony Lane
VARIETY, 5/24-30/99, p. 71, Emanuel Levy
WASHINGTON POST, 10/8/99, p. C5, Stephen Hunter
WASHINGTON POST, 10/8/99. Weekend/p. 53, Desson Howe

LITTLE BIT OF SOUL, A

A Phaedra Cinema release of a Faust Film production. *Executive Producer:* Tristam Miall. *Producer:* Peter Duncan, Simon Martin, Martin McGrath, and Peter J. Voeten. *Director:* Peter Duncan. *Screenplay:* Peter Duncan. *Director of Photography:* Martin McGrath. *Editor:* Simon Martin. *Music:* Nigel Westlake. *Sound:* Chris Alderton. *Production Designer:* Tony Campbell. *Costumes:* Terry Ryan. *Running time:* 84 minutes. *MPAA Rating:* R.

CAST: Geoffrey Rush (Godfrey Usher); David Wenham (Richard Shorkinghorn); Frances O'Connor (Kate Haslett); Heather Mitchell (Grace Michael); John Gaden (Dr. Sommerville).

NEW YORK POST, 8/6/99, p. 50, Jonathan Foreman

The hapless, misfiring Australian comedy "A Little Bit of Soul" has grand ambitions but a distinctly collegiate feel.

It's about a pair of scientists who spend the weekend at the country house of a wealthy, powerful couple who turn out to be Satanists, and much of the shtick is lamely ripped off from "The Addams Family" and "The Rocky Horror Picture Show."

It's a shame because it wastes the comic talent of Geoffrey Rush (from "Shine," "Elizabeth" and "Shakespeare in Love"), the charms of Heather Mitchell, who was so appealing in "Love and Other Catastrophes," and the screen presence of David Wenham, who deserves to be better known in this country.

Dr. Richard Shorkinghorn needs money to continue his chicken-based research on the aging process. So does his ex-girlfriend and ex-research assistant, Kate (O'Connor). Neither expects to see the other or to have to compete for a grant when they turn up at the country retreat of Grace Michael (an overacting Heather Mitchell) of the Michael Foundation.

Nor are they prepared for the antics of Grace's husband Godfrey Usher (Rush), Australia's eccentric, innumerate Federal Treasurer, or the apparent suicide of another guest.

"Soul" isn't unwatchable—it's just jejune and shamelessly unoriginal, down to the use of a jaunty jazz soundtrack to indicate wackiness. It climaxes in a spoof courtroom scene apparently stolen outright from TV's "The Simpsons"—in which Rush's bad guy has to do the "You want the truth? You can't handle the truth!" bit from "A Few Good Men" before being hoisted on his own arrogance.

Sideshow bob and Lisa Simpson did it better for free.

VILLAGE VOICE, 8/10/99, p. 64, Katherine Wolff

A flustered romp of supposedly Faustian proportions, Peter Duncan's *A Little Bit of Soul* moves from one chaotic scene to the next, which is strangely appropriate considering that much of the ranting in it embraces disorder. Filled with rhythm-and-blues songs that signal random plot details, the film follows two scientists (Frances O'Connor and David Wenham) who find funding for their anti-aging virus through a couple (Geoffrey Rush and Heather Mitchell) who soon morph from oversexed weekend hosts to pragmatic Satanists. Thrown into the mix are such issues as sexual repression, abuse of governmental office, and burial rites. That none of these gives rise to moralizing is one of the small joys of this film; the cast-particularly Rush and Mitchell—seems to revel in the shameless detachment and morbid efficiency with which their characters operate. The camp quotient is obvious, but only becomes enjoyable when the movie takes on the aesthetic of a *Tales From the Darkside* episode, replete with an overactive fog machine and a bow-tied savior.

Also reviewed in:
NEW YORK TIMES, 8/6/99, p. E32, Anita Gates

LOCK, STOCK AND TWO SMOKING BARRELS

A Gramercy Pictures release of a PolyGram Filmed Entertainment, Summit Entertainment, The Steve Tisch Company and SKA Films presentation of a Matthew Vaughan production. *Executive Producer:* Steve Tisch, Peter Morton, Stephen Marks, Angad Paul, and Trudie Styler. *Producer:* Matthew Vaughn. *Director:* Guy Ritchie. *Screenplay:* Guy Ritchie. *Director of Photography:* Tim Maurice-Jones. *Editor:* Niven Howie. *Music:* David A. Hughes and John Murphy. *Sound:* Simon Hayes. *Sound Editor:* Danny Sheehan. *Casting:* Celestia Fox and Guy Ritchie. *Production Designer:* Ian Andrews and Eve Mavrakis. *Set Decorator:* Jacalyn Hyman. *Special Effects:* Ken Lailey. *Costumes:* Stephanie Collie. *Make-up:* Catherine Scoble. *Stunt Coordinator:* Glenn Marks. *Running time:* 106 minutes. *MPAA Rating:* R.

CAST: Jason Flemyng (Tom); Dexter Fletcher (Soap); Nick Moran (Eddie); Jason Statham (Bacon); Steven Mackintosh (Winston); Nicholas Rowe (J); Nick Marcq (Charles); Charles Forbes (Willie); Vinnie Jones (Big Chris); Lenny McLean (Barry the Baptist); Peter McNicholl (Little Chris); P. H. Moriarty (Hatchet Harry); Frank Harper (Dog); Steve Sweeney (Plank); Huggy Leaver (Paul); Ronnie Fox (Mickey); Tony McMahon (John); Stephen Marcus (Nick the Greek); Vas Blackwood (Rory Breaker); Sting (JD); Jake Abraham (Dean); Robert Brydon (Traffic Warden); Stephen Callender-Ferrier (Lenny); Steve Collins (Boxing Gym Bouncer); Elwin David (Nathan); Vera Day (Tanya); Jimmy Flint (Don); Alan Ford (Alan); Sydney Golder (Phil); Alex Hall (Slick); John Houchin (Doorman); Danny John-Jules (Barfly Jack); Bal Jusar (Gordon); Victor McGuire (Gary); Mark Mooney (Serg); Suzy Ratner (Gloria); David Reid (Samoan Jo); Graham Stevens (Policeman); James Tarbuck (John O'Driscoll); Andy Tiernan (Man in Pub); Richard Vanstone (Frazer); Matthew Vaughn (Yuppie in Car).

LOS ANGELES TIMES, 3/5/99, Calendar/p. 14, Kenneth Turan

"Lock, Stock and Two Smoking Barrels" is dark, dangerous and a great deal of wicked, amoral fun. A film that manages to be as clever, playful and mock violent as its title, "Lock, Stock" was a major hit in its native Britain and its cheeky tone, simultaneously calculated and off the cuff, is as hip as anyone could want.

The feature debut of 30-year-old writer-director Guy Ritchie (currently so esteemed in Hollywood that Sony backed his next picture, "Diamonds," without reading a finished script), "Lock, Stock" does several things well, starting with presenting a clever plot delirious enough to tempt viewers to diagram its farcical intricacies.

Focusing on a quartet of young Londoners who get in over their heads with the local underworld and have to contend with a contingent of knuckle-headed desperadoes, "Lock, Stock" enjoys nothing more than being unexpected. Complications bounce off each other like bumper cars in a fun house as the film intercuts the exploits of half a dozen distinct groupings of incorrigible and amusing East End rogues.

Ritchie concocted this story, and he manages to tell it with considerable cinematic energy, making good use of an eclectic soundtrack and tossing in a variety of enlivening visual tricks he mastered while making commercials and music videos.

Though head-banging is prevalent in this world and all its characters can be casually brutal when the mood strikes them, Ritchie often (but not always) shies away from showing excessive violence, giving us an unmistakable taste but leaving the most graphic portions safely off-screen.

Helping leaven the carnage is "Lock, Stock's" lively and often unexpected sense of humor. With lines like "That wad's like Liberia's deficit," "This is turning into a bad day in Bosnia" and "It's kosher as Christmas," the deadpan Britspeak dialogue is wised up and sarcastic. In this world, if you don't have an attitude, comic or otherwise, you simply don't survive.

Ritchie was particularly concerned in how he cast "Lock, Stock," wanting to ensure that his actors had what he calls criminal credibility, that they looked as tough as they talked. So the key role of Barry the Baptist (so named because he next to drowns people to make them talk) went to Lenny McLean, a Cockney former bare-knuckle boxing champion, and debt collector Big Chris was played by Vinnie Jones, an ex-soccer star known for being a disciplinary problem.

Both of these men work for Hatchet Harry (P.H. Moriarty, who played Razors in "The Long Good Friday"), one of the criminal pillars of the East End, someone equally at home selling sex toys or using them to beat people to death.

Harry also runs a very high stakes card game where players need 100,000 pounds to pull up a chair. Handsome Eddie (Nick Moran), a wizard with cards "since he could lift them," wants in, and he gets three pals to match his 25,000-pound stake. They would be the entrepreneurial Tom (Jason Flemyng), the muscular Bacon (Jason Statham) and Soap (Dexter Fletcher), so named because he's the only one of the quartet who cares about keeping his hands at least metaphorically clean.

"Lock, Stock" wouldn't be much of a movie if everything worked as these lads planned. After a number of dizzying twists, they end up having only a few days to come up with half a million pounds or else Barry will go after their fingers with one of Harry's hatchets while casting covetous eyes at the bar owned by Eddie's dad, JD (Sting).

Meanwhile, Barry has hired a pair of lunatic Liverpool natives (identifiable by their accents) to burglarize a stately home that has a pair of antique shotguns Harry's taken a fancy to, shotguns that amusingly figure in the plot again and again. Also part of the criminal stew are a quartet of upper-class toffs who grow marijuana for profit but are too stoned to close their security gate, the ruthless Dog (Frank Harper) and his band of reprobates, and drug kingpin Rory Breaker (Vas Blackwood), respectfully described as "a psychotic black dwarf with an afro."

Though Eddie apparently had a girlfriend in an earlier cut, "Lock, Stock" as it now stands is a completely masculine vision that's brash enough to orchestrate a complex criminal shootout to Mikis Theodorakis' classic dance music from "Zorba the Greek." Described by a participant as "a farce with action," this is one film that's not over until it's over, and maybe not even then.

NEW YORK, 3/15/99, p. 58, Peter Rainer

The current British cinema lurches between genial little nothing movies like *The Full Monty* and *Waking Ned Devine* and scabrous jags like *Trainspotting*, with time out for the odd costume epic. *Lock, Stock and Two Smoking Barrels* is in the scabrous mode, and I like it better than *Trainspotting*—it doesn't pretend its shenanigans are revolutionary. It's about four petty hoodlums—well played by Jason Flemyng, Nick Moran, Jason Statham, and Dexter Fletcher—

who, after a rigged poker game, find themselves owing £500,000 to underworld boss Hatchet Harry (P. H. Moriarty). Coming up with the debt, they throw in a double-cross of their own. Guy Ritchie, a first-time writer-director, sets his rumbles in London's East End, with four separate gangs going at it like a serial gunfight at the O.K. Corral. An MTV-generation Peckinpah, Ritchie stages the splatter with a hideous giddiness. He's one to watch.

NEW YORK POST, 3/5/99, p. 59, Jonathan Foreman

Fresh, fast and very funny, this rollicking movie joins a spate of hits denoting a welcome transformation in British cinema. (Think "Trainspotting," "Shallow Grave," "Sliding Doors" and "Hilary & Jackie.")

After years of costumed preciousness, elitist artiness and relentless grittiness, Brits are once again making movies that are good fun rather than good for you.

"Lock, Stock" is an exuberant, unpretentious crime caper that combines the old-fashioned charm of the Ealing comedies of the '50s and the remorseless energy of Scorsese's "GoodFellas." With its flashy camera work and groovy soundtrack, it is also superficially reminiscent of Quentin Tarantino's movies. But it has a charm and an underlying warmheartedness entirely absent from Tarantino's slick but cold work. The four main characters are not the one-dimensional, pop-culture-obsessed killers who inhabit the Tarantino universe. And while there is violence aplenty in "Lock, Stock," there is little or no gore, and most of the shootings and beatings take place out of sight.

The story follows four all-for-one best mates from London's working-class East End who make the mistake of staking their (mostly ill-gotten) savings on Eddie's (Nick Moran) card skills in a big game against local gangster Hatchet Harry. The game is fixed, and Eddie finds himself owing $800,000, to be paid in a week. If he doesn't pay up, a fearsome debt collector will break one of his fingers every 24 hours—unless Eddie's dad (played by Sting) hands over his popular bar to Hatchet Harry.

When the boys, who are all decent fellows, discover that a gang of vicious thieves is planning to rob some upper-class marijuana growers slumming in the neighborhood, they decide to rob the robbers and sell the weed to the equally ferocious leader of an all-black gang. The mayhem that follows is stylishly filmed and cleverly plotted.

First-time director Ritchie likes to show off his repertoire of camera tricks, but he also gets perfectly pitched performances from a cast that includes a number of real-life ex-criminals. Most memorable of the oddly formal villains that populate this neighborhood is enforcer Big Chris, played by Vinnie Jones, an English soccer star famous for an outrageous foul caught on national television.

Another pleasure of "Lock Stock" is the delight its characters take in language. Their speech is filled with vivid metaphors, unusual obscenity and lots of Cockney rhyming slang—a dialect that takes a little getting used to (even for most English people) but which is usually comprehensible.

This said, "Lock, Stock and Two Smoking Barrels" has been the victim of excessive media hype since its smash success in the U.K.—and an inevitable critical backlash. The carping is undeserved: This is an exciting, technically accomplished action-comedy with a wicked sense of humor and underlying decency that makes it utterly original.

NEWSDAY, 3/5/99, Part II/p. B11, John Anderson

For all the broken noses, trigger fingers, pot farmers and knee-breakers that parade through Guy Ritchie's Brit-wit gangster comedy "Lock Stock and Two Smoking Barrels" the moral of the story comes courtesy of that noted English pub crawler, Francis (Frankie) Bacon. To wit, knowledge is power.

For instance, had Eddie the cardsharp (Nick Moran) really had a clue, he would never have gotten into the big card game with London's capo-di-East-End Hatchet Harry (P.H. Moriarty), which was, of course, being rigged by the Luka Brasi-esque Barry the Baptist (the late Lenny McLean), thus putting Eddie and his three pals and financiers—Tom (Jason Flemyng), Bacon (Jason Statham) and Soap (Dexter Fletcher)—500,000 pounds in debt.

And if Dog (Frank Harper) had known that the money and marijuana he was ripping off Winston (Steven Mackintosh) and his dilettante clique of drug dealers really belonged to the lethal Rory Breaker (Vas Blackwood) he would never have ripped them off. Nor would Eddie and Co. have tried to sell the pot—which they subsequently stole from Dog—back to Rory, who's considerably out of sorts.

And had two second-story men known the value of two antique shotguns stolen during a Barry-orchestrated burlgary, they would never have sold them to Tom, who used them against Dog before losing them to Chris (Vinnie Jones), who gave them back to Harry. Nor would they have tried to get them back from Harry when they were working for Harry in the first place.

Alongside the "Reservoir Dogs" meets-"Trainspotting" allusions of "Lock, Stock and Two Smoking Barrels"—the pallor of which matches its characters'—is a fine analogy for multinational business techniques and the advantages of diversity, synergy and, naturally, hostile takeovers. Harry, for instance, doesn't just rely on gambling, he's into pornography and money lending. When Rory loses his pot and money, it all comes back to him in the end because he controls his territory. And even though Chris is a thug, he loves his son (Peter McNicholl), thus keeping matters in proper perspective.

In such an intimate circle of cutthroats, rip-off followed by payoff inevitably leads to tip-off. The tipoff on "Lock, Stock" is that director-writer Ritchie's debut feature is a tongue-in-cheek, genre-saturated romp whose most satisfying aspect is its mix of gangsterized civility and casual brutality. The end result is a array of things we've seen before, but not the way we've seen them.

NEWSWEEK, 3/22/99, p. 75, David Ansen

The British crime comedy *Lock, Stock & Two Smoking Barrels* starts off with such showy, hip, "Trainspotting"-indebted commotion—the camera whirling and stopping as if in the grip of Saint Vitus' dance—that it seems this movie will surely wear out both the viewer and its welcome very fast. But hang in there. Once you sort out the main characters—four cheeky East London schemers whose plan to make a killing in a poker game backfires disastrously—and once the plot kicks into action, it becomes clear that under the shameless MTV pyrotechnics lies a structure as intricately crafted as a Feydeau farce.

First-time writer-director Guy Ritchie has a giddy gift for storytelling. His quartet of con artists are out £500,000 to a dangerous porn king who threatens to remove their digits one by one. The lads' solution to their bleak predicament is to rip off their next-door neighbors—a gang of thugs who are themselves planning to rip off a cash-rich clutch of ganja-growing college kids. Everyone in this almost exclusively male milieu is up to no good, and as all their felonious plans go bloodily awry, the disasters pile up as fast as the corpses. But Ritchie, a clever man, knows just how much gore a comedy can tolerate, and how to calibrate the fine line between sadism and slapstick. Danny Boyle and Quentin Tarantino may have inspired the flashy, fashionably vicious style, but "Lock, Stock's" eager-to-please comic spirit goes back as far as the 1951 caper classic "The Lavender Hill Mob." That film whispered and this one shouts, but the twinkle in the eye isn't all that different.

SIGHT AND SOUND, 9/98, p. 46, Danny Leigh

London. Four friends—Bacon, Soap, Tom and Eddy—pool their savings for Eddy's card game with porn baron Harry. Eddy ends the game owing Harry £500,000. He must repay the debt or forfeit his father's bar. Eddy overhears his drug-dealing neighbour Dog planning to rob an upper-class rival, Winston. Unwittingly buying a pair of stolen antique shotguns mislaid by two burglars working for Harry, Eddy and friends hijack Dog's haul after his gang's raid on Winston. They leave the money at Eddy's. Later, Dog and his gang break into the empty flat, only to be discovered by Winston's paymaster Rory and his gang. The subsequent gun battle leaves all the participants dead. Harry's debt collector Big Chris arrives, finding his boss' £500,000 among the bodies. Harry is shot dead by one of his incompetent burglars. Big Chris disappears with the cash. Tom keeps the guns, but his friends insist he dispose of them. Big Chris informs Eddy of their value. Frantically, the group call Tom on his mobile phone. Hanging over a bridge, about to throw the guns into the Thames, he attempts to answer with the hand holding the rail, while the other clutches the shotguns ...

Despite featuring a card game as a central motif, *Lock Stock and Two Smoking Barrels* is unexpectedly eager to reveal its hand. The storyline moves indefatigably along and is amusingly open ended, but music-video and commercials director Guy Ritchie's cinematic territory is marked pre-credits.

Bacon, one of the film's quartet of essentially amiable, mid-twenties rogues, sprints from the police, the camera matching him step for breakneck step. Over adrenal-pumping rock music, the shot freezes, and an elucidatory voiceover begins. This is an exhilarating device, just as it was in *Trainspotting*, from which it is duplicated almost exactly. Tellingly, the one divergence from the *Trainspotting* template is musical: while Danny Boyle employed the edgy, sardonic Iggy Pop, Ritchie opts for famously boorish retrorockers Ocean Color Scene.

Although nothing that follows is as derivative (well, not much) this single moment encapsulates the whole. Superficially, both in dizzying style and studiedly laddish content, the exploits of the four young chancers and their supporting cast of London lowlife are quintessentially 90s. High on spectacle, low on identity, the audience is presumed to have a cinematic frame of reference largely confined to Quentin Tarantino. Yet the farcical tone is closer to a 60s caper movie, as are the anachronistic crime lords, while the expectation of laughs at the mere mention of "copious amounts of ganja" simply smacks of condescension.

Though the sundry plot twists are well executed and the voluminous dialogue yields some piquant one-liners, the minimal characterisation betrays a fundamental laziness. It's as if Ritchie thinks such things are unnecessary: that as long as the pace remains relentless, the characters can function as ciphers, random mouthpieces for his often excruciatingly self conscious 'Mockney' parlance. And while it would be facile to sneer at the director's background in commercials and music videos, he does himself no favours by routinely falling back on the gimmickry of those forms: stylised wildly at every turn, the film often appears less a movie and more the work of someone demonstrating a special feature of their new camcorder.

Lock, Stock is redeemed by several of its performances, particularly those of *The Long Good Friday* veteran P. H. Moriarty as an understated Harry and the appealingly whimsical football hardman Vinnie Jones as Big Chris. But the party trick of balancing broad comedy with 'authenticity' collapses, a failure epitomised by Eddy and friends beating up a traffic warden, which is neither gritty nor particularly funny.

TIME, 3/1/99, p. 68, Richard Corliss

The movie is about some guys who lose £500,000 in a card game and have to come up with the money in a week, or they'll start losing fingers and other precious protuberances. And in a case of life imitating art, the guy making the movie—Guy Ritchie, that is, three days before shooting his first feature, the British crime comedy *Lock, Stock and Two Smoking Barrels*—found that the financing had fallen through, and he needed to raise dough pronto. Forget all the bad guys in the script; worry about some of the ex-cons cast in the film. "We had real villains in the movie who were ready to break our legs if the money didn't come," says producer Matthew Vaughn. "I even spoke to some Mob people about financing it. They hemmed and hawed." Damn! Just the folks you'd think could make a quick executive decision.

LS&2SB, as we'll call it did get made and became a big Brit hit: $22 million so far, which puts it in the blockbuster class in the U.K. The movie may not go stratospheric here, if only because its East London accents are thicker than its hail of artillery. ("Americans will get used to the language," says Jason Flemyng, one of the film's flotilla of engaging young actors, "We had to get used to *Boyz N the Hood*.") But *LS&2SB* has all the early signs of success. Tom Cruise's early enthusiasm for the film helped it land a U.S. distributor. The picture got ballistic buzz this year at Sundance. A spin-off series is planned for British TV. And Ritchie, 30, is a bicontinental rising star. It's not just the deal he has with Sony for his next film. It's that he's been, well, squiring Madonna. The writer-director is typically a chatty bloke, but he goes all coy when asked about his famous friend. "She's a very ... well, we all know what she is!"

We know what she is, Guy, but what are you? The next Mr. Quentin Tarantino? Probably not: Ritchie's idea of film pizazz is to dip into his TV commercials bag of fast-mo, slo-mo and stop-mo, until you may cry out, "No mo'." The movie is frolicsome but pushy, the triumph of flash over style. But for narrative savvy and direction of actors, Ritchie is up there with Q.T.

He takes the basic Gang of Four plot (four streetwise young men fall into a lot of trouble) and expands it exponentially. His story has *four* gangs of four, and three other tough-guy twosomes, all trying to screw or do in their rivals. Since Tarantino revived the crime genre, it has devolved into a contagion, a virtual pulp affliction, of high body counts and low quality; it needed new blood, and not just from the effects department. That's where Ritchie comes to the rescue.

The plot is too good to spoil and too complex to spill. Just know that our gang (Flemyng, Jason Statham, Nick Moran and Dexter Fletcher), scrounging to find that half a million quid, overhears the goons next door plotting to steal money and drugs from four ganja growers nearby; our lads hope to cash that booty in with an Afro-Cockney gang. (Clear?) Then it all goes as wrong as a bad day in Bosnia. "Could everyone stop getting shot?" one of the goons pleads—and this is before a shoot-out that makes the St. Valentine's Day Massacre look like a heart-shaped box of Cadbury chocolates.

Yet the film so tightly holds on to its sense of humor, its love of East End patois, its fascination with lowlifes and the low deaths waiting for them, that the carnage is mostly punctuation. The movie is as buoyant as a floating corpse in a clown costume. Or, as one of the "good" guys says, "A little pain never hurt anybody."

Ritchie is not a film-school wonderboy. "He has no awareness of movie history, and in a way that's refreshing," notes executive producer Steve Tisch. "It sounds funny saying it but Guy is a guy's guy." If he had given in to other impulses, he could have been, as other wise guys say, a made man. "I left school at 15," Ritchie says, "and got distracted by the ways of the underworld." He was arrested for (but not charged with) robbery after a police search of his home yielded TVs, VCRs and stereos with no serial numbers. Ultimately Ritchie determined that the outlaw life was "not a sensible vocation for me. I felt the only profit I could take from that world was to make a film about it."

Before directing TV spots and music videos, he traveled through Africa ("I discovered that if it moves, you can eat it") and dug trenches at sewer sites in Greece ("That gave me an appreciation for money that's invaluable now"). Ritchie shot *LS&2SB*, with its dozens of speaking roles and locations, for just $1.6 million. "When it comes to film budgets, I'm lethal."

That's just the sort of killer instinct Hollywood loves: an unerring commercial sense at the price of a street vendor's Rolex. Time will tell if Ritchie is the real goods. But as *LS&2SB* proves, he can blast out 107 minutes of hard, dark fun.

VILLAGE VOICE, 3/9/99, p. 113, J. Hoberman

From the original *Scarface* to *Superfly* to *Reservoir Dogs*, the urban gangster film has thrived on a combination of violence, attitude, and masculine style. The mobster is a fashion plate with pow and the disjunction between brute and dandy can approach self-parody. Perhaps this is why, almost since the beginning, the genre has lived a shadow life as a source of hard-boiled comedy.

Three films opening Friday try to have it both ways—reveling in cool while going for yuks, staging elaborate pratfalls amid a mounting body count. The most self-consciously hip of the trio, *Lock, Stock and Two Smoking Barrels*, has been hyped as the hottest British crime film since the wildly overpraised *Trainspotting* upchucked onto the local multiplex scene three summers ago. This debut feature by 30-year-old music-video director Guy Ritchie pillages *Trainspotting* but it's a fizzier, less-overweening action cartoon—without the slightest pretense toward strung-out realism.

Positioning itself as "fun" with a playful panoply of freeze-frames, fast-motion bits, and droll voiceovers (albeit waiting too long for the laughs to roll in), *Lock, Stock* sets up shop at the intersection of several simultaneous criminal capers. The parallels are clever, Ritchie appears to have graphed the action as much as written it. Having gone wildly into debt in a crooked card game with the local porn king, a vaguely likable quartet of youngish East End hustlers attempt to recoup their losses by robbing a more professional criminal gang.

This second outfit, more villainous for being led by a hard-bitten fish-and-chips de Sade, are themselves planning to rip off a twittering gaggle of upper-class, postgrad dope dealers. Thus establishing a modicum of sympathy for its otherwise forgettable East End antiheroes, the caper doubles back on itself as an intricate three-gang gavotte, with several rugged individualists in subplot orbit—one of them, a fearsome enforcer (played by soccer star Vinnie Jones), collecting debts with his 10-year-old son in tow.

The lad is key to the movie's sensibility. Ritchie's principals are a colorful, highly verbal lot and masters of schoolyard one-upmanship: "A minute ago this was the safest job in the world—now it's turning into a bad day in Bosnia." Its humor largely based on chirp and cheek, this is a very British comedy. Nearly all the players have some sort of *Goon Show* accent and, as in *Reservoir Dogs*, virtually every one of them is male. Ritchie's precursor as a hyperkinetic, gag-driven director, however, is less mad Quentin Tarantino than mod Richard Lester (whose retro conveniently begins this weekend at AMMI). Given its boundless sarcasm, running-jumping-standing-still ambience and hyperbolic Guignol violence, *Lock, Stock* aspires to be something like the Beatles meet the Wild Bunch. Too bad it doesn't have even a rubber soul.

With everyone getting mixed up in one another's business, the laborious table-setting does eventually draw blood—in buckets. The final doom-show convergence is a cross-cut lock-and-load scored to the theme from *Zorba the Greek*. (Here, as elsewhere, the lively audio track insures that the movie sounds better than it looks.) "It's been emotional" is the punch line. The joke, of course, is that it hasn't.

Also reviewed in;
NEW REPUBLIC, 4/5/99, p. 29, Stanley Kauffmann
NEW YORK TIMES, 3/5/99, p. E22, Janet Maslin
NEW YORKER, 3/8/99, p. 95, Anthony Lane
VARIETY, 8/24-30/98, p. 28, Derek Elley
WASHINGTON POST, 3/12/99, p. C1, Stephen Hunter
WASHINGTON POST, 3/12/99, Weekend/p. 43, Desson Howe

LOLA AND BILLY THE KID

A Picture This Entertainment release of a Zero Film production in association with WDR/Arte, C & O Produktion, Boje-Buck Film. *Executive Producer:* James Schamus. *Producer:* Martin Hagemann. *Director:* Kutlug Ataman. *Screenplay (Turkish and German with English subtitles):* Kutlug Ataman. *Director of Photography:* Chris Squires. *Editor:* Ewa J. Lind. *Music:* Arpad Bondy. *Choreographer:* Hakan Tandogan. *Sound:* Axel Arft and (music) Marc Elsner. *Casting:* Annette Borgmann, Cornelia Partmann, Yuzler Sesler, and Elif Esin Cokünal. *Production Designer:* John Di Minico. *Art Director:* Mona Kino. *Set Decorator:* Otu Tetteh, Mathias Nitschke, Markus Leuwer, Joao Gonzaga-Silveira, Anslem Breig, and Alexander Liebenthron. *Costumes:* Ulla Gothe. *Make-up:* Axel Zornow. *Running time:* 94 minutes. *MPAA Rating:* Not Rated.

CAST: Baki Davrak (Murat); Gandi Mukli (Lola); Erdal Yildiz (Bili); Michael Gerber (Friedrich); Murat Yimaz (Iskender); Inge Keller (Ute); Hakan Tandogan (Fatma Souad); Cihangir Gümüsturkmen (Lale Lokum); Celal Perk (Sehrazat); Mesut Ozdemir (Kalipso); Ulrich Simontowitz (Man in Tiergarten); Hasan Ali Mete (Osman); Willi Herren (Rudy); Mario Irrek (Hendryk); Jan Andres (Walter); Hatice Tolgay (Neighbor); Nisa Yildirim (Fatma); Aykut Kayacik (Bili's Friend); Gundula Petrovska (Hella); Katharina Voss (Schoolteacher); Isabell Wernitz and Madeline Bommert (Girls in Schoolbus); Sabine Winterfeldt (Tilly); Azisa-A (Nightclub Singer); Ursula Staack (Flower Seller); Andreas Leupold (Man in Chinese Restaurant); Andreas Kruse (Businessman); Carla Hagemann (Little Girl); Mohammed Herzog (Islamic Priest); Erden Alkan (Taxi Driver); Axel Page (Dancing Man).

NEW YORK POST, 11/19/99, p. 59, Lou Lumenick

"Lola and Billy the Kid" is a decently acted, out-of-the rut coming-of-age story set in Germany's gay Turkish community.

Baki Davrak, who looks a bit like Leonardo DiCaprio, plays a teen named Murat, who feels stirrings for other men, something not very well tolerated by his fellow Turks—and especially not by his ultra-macho older brother Osman (Hasan Ali Mete), who tries to arrange his sexual initiation with a prostitute.

Things get complicated when Murat learns he has a third brother—a drag queen who goes by the name Lola (Gandi Mukli), and who was run out of the house years earlier by Osman.

Murat tracks down Lola, who lives with Billy the Kid (Erdal Yildiz), another ultra-macho type who's in denial about his own homosexuality and keeps pestering Lola to have a sex-change operation so they can live as husband and wife.

Director Kutlug Ataman deftly balances the violence Murat and Billy face from other Turks and neo-Nazi skinheads with a comic subplot about an aging architect who tries to get his mother to accept his much-younger male lover.

"Lola and Billy the Kid" flounders with a poorly staged, action-packed climax that seems to have wandered in from a different movie. But until then, it captures its milieu in fresh and interesting ways.

SIGHT AND SOUND, 4/00, p. 53, Paul Julian Smith

Berlin, the present. Murat, a closeted gay Turkish teenager, lives with his widowed mother and homophobic brother Osman. Meanwhile, Lola, a transvestite dancer in a nightclub, lives with her macho lover Bili, a rent boy. Lola and her friends are menaced by neo-Nazi youths. When Lola attempts to make contact with Murat's family, Murat discovers Lola is his brother, previously thrown on to the streets by Osman. In a subplot, wealthy, older German Friedrich becomes involved with another young rent boy Iskender, to the consternation of Friedrich's conservative mother.

Murat visits Lola's nightclub and arranges to meet her the next day. After a nocturnal birthday party in the park, Lola argues with Bili and, leaving alone, is threatened by thugs. Later she is found dead. Bili vows to take revenge on the neo-Nazis. Dressing Murat as a transvestite whore and luring the thugs to an abandoned building, he mutilates and kills two of them but is shot dead. Murat escapes and returns home. Still in drag, he confronts Osman, who had murdered Lola himself and whose homophobia is a front for his own homosexuality. When their mother hears this she slaps Osman in the face and leaves the family home with Murat.

Director Kutlug Ataman opens his second feature *Lola + Bilidikid* (his first was *The Serpent's Tale)* with silent nocturnal pacings through the cruising ground of Berlin's Tiergarten. But he quickly cuts to a Turkish transvestite nightclub, all music, light and saturated colour. This is typical of a film that treats serious issues such as racism and homophobia in an engaging and humorous way. Parallel plotlines are organised to maximum dramatic and ironic effect. Young Murat is victimised by his homophobic brother Osman, just as his older sibling the transvestite Lola is oppressed by his/her macho lover Bili (indeed, one prescient queen observes that, despite flagrant differences, Osman and Bili are two of a kind). Or again, Murat's kindly downtrodden Turkish mother is mirrored by Friedrich's steely aristocratic German parent; in spite of appearances, each woman seeks only the happiness of her gay child. While their eventual teaming up seems implausible, they reflect the optimism of the film, one that at no point minimises the difficulties of Turkish gays in contemporary Berlin.

Friedrich's mother attempts to buy off her son's lover with the priceless heirloom of a cameo. When he throws it from the car window in disgust, it is retrieved later by lucky queens. Ataman consistently uses visual motifs of this kind to tell his story. For example, Murat returns to Lola the red wig she had worn when she came out to her family, only to wear it himself after she is murdered. And Ataman, who is also the author of a video installation called *Women Who Wear Wigs,* is clearly up to speed on theories of gender and performance.

Perhaps the most important feature of this first Turkish film with explicit homoerotic content is its exploration of different national forms of homosexuality and masculinity. Brutish Bili favours the traditional Mediterranean model in which "a man is a man and a hole is a hole." But this does not hold for younger gays such as Lola and Murat who believe that two men can love one another without one becoming a woman. If some of the dialogue sounds suspiciously close to Almodóvar ("A woman's got to look after her dick"), Ataman, who is both scriptwriter and director, spices things up with less familiar phrases ("May Allah render his semen putrid"). In spite of its fascinating cultural distinctiveness, then, *Lola* follows other national cinemas (Cuba's *Strawberry and Chocolate* comes to mind) in allowing a first treatment of homosexuality to emerge only under the sign of ostentatious camp.

Casting seems to follow the *Beverly Hills 90210* convention (Baki Davarak is clearly a decade over-age for the 17-year-old hero), but performances are professional, locations atmospheric, and production values surprisingly high. Mainstream narrative and characterisation make the film all the more subversive, because challenging content is presented in an accessible form. The winner of prizes in both Berlin and Turin, *Lola* was screened in Turkey, only in the face of death threats to the director (now an exile in London) and thanks to the courageous efforts of co-producer Zeynep Ozbatur. In the final sequence Murat abandons his symbolic red wig as his mother removes her equally emblematic headscarf. A brave political and cinematic success, *Lola* suggests a similar alliance between gay men and women in the interests of Turkish democracy.

VILLAGE VOICE, 11/23/99, p. 142, Elliott Stein

The best new film from Germany is Turkish. Kutlug Ataman's *Lola and Bilidikid* takes place in the gay and transvestite subcultures of Berlin's immigrant Turks. Its protagonist, Murat (Baki Davrak), a German-born Turkish teenager, alienated from his repressive traditional family, is hesitantly experimenting with his sexuality in parks and bars. He's drawn to nightclub performer Lola (Gandi Mukli), who turns out to be his older brother, thrown out by the family years before. Lola is in a stressful ménage with ultramacho Bili (Erdal Yildiz), who, fed up with being "a fag living with a fag," is pressuring Lola to undergo a sex change so they can get married, return to Turkey, and "live like others."

Ataman skillfully interweaves Murat's voyage of self-discovery with a number of other story lines involving neo-Nazi punks, seamy gigolos, and German aristocrats who have fallen on hard times. The ending is a shocker, but leavened, as is most of the movie, by mordant humor. One droll subplot is a lopsided triangle concerning Bili's male whore best friend, the middle-aged German architect he hustles, and the john's mother, a dowager-from-hell, impeccably played by octogenarian stage diva Inge Keller. Although Ataman's heartfelt, handsome drama took top prize at this year's Istanbul Film Festival, the openly gay director was obliged to flee his homeland to escape the death threats that followed its release.

Also reviewed in:
NEW YORK TIMES, 11/19/99, p. E29, Anita Gates
VARIETY, 3/22-28/99, p. 42, Eddie Cockrell

LOSS OF SEXUAL INNOCENCE, THE

A Sony Pictures Classics release of a Summit Entertainmen presentation in association with Newmarket Capital Group of a Red Mullet production. *Executive Producer:* Patrick Wachsberger. *Producer:* Mike Figgis and Annie Stewart. *Director:* Mike Figgis. *Screenplay:* Mike Figgis. *Director of Photography:* Benoît Delhomme. *Editor:* Matthew Wood. *Music:* Mike Figgis. *Sound:* Pawel Wdowczak. *Sound Editor:* Nigel Heath. *Casting:* Jina Jay and Russell Gow. *Production Designer:* Jessica Worrall, Mark Long, Mark Long, and Giorgio Desideri. *Art Director:* Anita Bryan, Alberto Tosto, and Adel Chelbi. *Set Decorator:* Julie Harris. *Costumes:* Florence Nicaise. *Make-up:* Katya Thomas and Essia Baaziz. *Running time:* 101 minutes. *MPAA Rating:* R.

CAST: Julian Sands (Adult Nic); Saffron Burrows (Twins); Stefano Dionisi (Lucca); Kelly MacDonald (Susan Brown); Gina McKee (Susan's Mum); Jonathan Rhys-Meyers (Nic, aged 16); Bernard Hill (Susan's Father); Rossy De Palma (Blind Woman); John Cowey (Nic, aged 5); Nina McKay (Mixed-race Girl); Dickson Osa-Omorogbe (Wangi); Jock Gibson-Cowl (Old Colonial Man); Justin Chadwick (Flash Man); Femi Ogumbanjo (Adam); Hanne Klintoe (Eve); Johanna Torell (Nic's Wife); Geraint Ellis (Nic's Son); George Moktar (Nic, aged 12); Mark Long (1st Detective); Mike Figgis (2nd Detective); Joe Cunningham (Policeman); Wesley

Kipling (Nic's Brother); James Bradley, Nick Figgis, and David Medleycott (Band Members);
Mark Long (Man in Dream);   Clare Jones and Zoe Jones (Baby Twins);   Marina Ilina and
Fabrizia Farra (Novice Nuns);   Roderic Leigh (Boring Businessman);   Rachel Boss (Italian
Woman);   Bruno Bilotta (Italian Man);   Rodney Charles (Charlie);   Phil Swinburne (Games
Teacher);   Cite Chebbla (Blue Child);   Neziha Youssef (Blue Mother);   Rami Chebbi (Blue
Father).

LOS ANGELES TIMES, 5/28/99, Calendar/p. 8, Kevin Thomas

Nobody could ever accuse Mike Figgis, Oscar nominated for "Leaving Las Vegas," of not
taking chances, but he has never gone for broke so completely as with "The Loss of Sexual
Innocence," his most venturesome, most personal—and least accessible film to date. If you open
your mind and trust him completely, it's possible to experience the wrenching impact of this
ravishingly beautiful and highly distinctive film.

But be prepared to accept that there are moments and images that will remain puzzling; it's as
if Figgis is suggesting that if there are so many loose ends in life, why should you be able to
make all the connections in art? What Figgis wants is the audience to respond to his film with
emotion rather than reason, and wait until the film is over to start thinking about it. (And there
is plenty to think about.) At bottom, Figgis is paying us the compliment of inviting us to
participate in his film instead of just sitting there passively in the dark.

Elliptical, perhaps to a fault, "The Loss of Sexual Innocence" is short of exposition, except for
the very occasional subtitle telling us where we are and when—a couple of more of these would
help a lot and not detract from Figgis' rigorously nonlinear storytelling.

Jumping back and forth in time and place in the life of Nic (Julian Sands)—whom we eventually
learn is a filmmaker—we gradually realize that he is drifting in and out of his memories. He and
his wife (Johanna Torrel) and young son (Geraint Ellis) are driving to their handsome manor
house in the countryside of the north of England, where he awaits a call that will send him off
to London to fly to Italy. From there he will proceed to the Tunisian desert with a filmmaking
crew that is composed of two assistants (Saffron Barrows, Stefano Dionisi) and a driver. This
narrative thread, however, does not emerge clearly until the film's climactic sequence. And for
Figgis' purposes, it shouldn't.

When Nic's mind wanders, the memories that flood over him are of himself at ages 5, 12 and
16 when he is experiencing primal scenes in regard to sex. In this approach Figgis is suggesting
how such moments, which may be traumatic in varying degrees but are inevitably affecting, shape
our emotions and how we, in turn, express them sexually. In Nic's case, we discover that he is
sexually aggressive with his wife, an icy blond who responds to him sexually but not at all
emotionally. The lack of emotion between man and wife surely is key in propelling Nic to his
ultimate fate.

Figgis sees in Nic, who seems clearly the filmmaker's alter ego, and the arc of his sensual life
a meaning to be found in the parable of Adam and Eve and their fall from innocence in the
Garden of Eden. Figgis actually interpolates the biblical tale, played out by Femi Ogumbanjo as
Adam and Hanne Klintoe as Eve in a sylvan setting whose location is not revealed until the film's
finish.

By the time Figgis has evoked the fear and guilt that too often hover over sexual love, he
broadens his perspective even further: A loss of sexual innocence gives way to a loss of innocence
in general, and along with it the responsibilities and temptations of knowledge. Figgis is
suggesting, while avoiding a lethal literalness, that there's a direct connection between the world's
ills and the ways in which our sexuality is formed and directed.

The oblique, graceful way in which Figgis evokes such thoughts for us to contemplate is no
small accomplishment, to say the least. But for the committed, it's well worth accepting a certain
degree of perplexity. Most viewers are likely to be puzzled over the fact that Barrows is playing
twins, born in Italy to a 15-year-old unwed mother and given up for adoption, with one girl raised
in England. As adults they encounter each other briefly at an airport. What this means is
elusive, at least on a first viewing of the film.

Since this is a film of images rather than words, it requires a great deal of presence and
expressiveness on the part of the actors. Happily, Figgis has chosen well, with Sands effortlessly
carrying by far the most demanding role of a man of isolating self-absorption.

"The Loss of Sexual Innocence," for which Figgis composed a rich, seductive score, is never less than ravishing, with its kaleidoscopic hues, ranging from cool blues to burnished golds and scorching oranges; Benoit Delhomme ("The Scent of Green Papayas," "The Winslow Boy") is the film's consummate cinematographer. More than most films, "The Loss of Innocence," which had a gestation period of more than 15 years, gives the sense that it has emerged precisely the way its maker intended. Make of it what you will.

NEW YORK, 6/7/99, p. 87, Peter Rainer

Mike Figgis's new movie is called *The Loss of Sexual Innocence*, but there's not much sex on view and even less innocence. Figgis is a strange amalgam of *artiste* and pulpster, and, disconcertingly often in his career, the *artiste* wins out. When he makes a smart, vicious Hollywood crime melodrama like *Internal Affairs*, from somebody else's script, he's a surefooted ace; he even roused Richard Gere into a fire-breathing portrayal as a precinct Iago. Figgis came out of the multimedia-performance art circuit in England, and he's also a jazz musician; at his best, in *Internal Affairs* and parts of *Stormy Monday* and the overrated *Leaving Las Vegas*, he gets a rhythmic swing going in his imagery that's elegantly woozy. But his "personal" films, like *Liebestraum* and *One Night Stand*, which he mostly writes himself, are a tough sit. His new movie has something to do with a documentary filmmaker (Julian Sands) and the various traumatic stages in his life, shown in flashback, as a 5-, 12-, and 16-year-old—all of it crosscut with grainy, yellow-filtered sequences featuring Adam and Eve—a black man and a Nordic white woman—and their fall from grace. My press notes tell me—the film certainly didn't—that we're watching a drama about not only the loss of sexual innocence but "the humanity of our species." Yet what I experienced was a lot of fetid experimental-film folderol perfumed by Chopin nocturnes on the soundtrack. Adam and Eve look like they wandered over from Woodstock Nation. In their finest hour, they achieve oneness by stepping into the shimmering river of life and making pee-pee. The Serpent shows more restraint.

NEW YORK POST, 5/28/99, p. 59, Jonathan Foreman

There are some good scenes in "The Loss of Sexual Innocence." So it is a shame that Mike Figgis' autobiographical art film is almost comically pretentious—and that his meditations on the way sexual desire can lead to bad stuff like death are so jaw-droppingly trite.

To the extent that it has a story, this slow-moving film drops in on the life of an English filmmaker called Nic. We see him first as a 5-year-old in colonial Kenya, then as a teen-ager in the North of England and finally as a married but unfaithful father in his 40s.

The boy (John Cowey) witnesses the strange humiliation of an African girl by an old white man. The teen-age Nic (Jonathan Rhys-Meyers) is betrayed by his girlfriend during a drunken wake for her father. The adult Nic (Julian Sands) has a bad relationship with his wife and sleeps with a stunning Italian (Saffron Burrows) while on location in Tunisia—a liaison that predictably ends in tragic, brutal violence.

Intercut with these episodes are wordless scenes from the biblical tale of Adam and Eve. Adam, who is black, emerges fully formed out of a pond. Eve, who is a white redhead, follows soon after.

They are both naked, but only Eve is shown in full frontal until a later scene when they watch each other urinating into the pond. Once Adam and Eve have tasted the forbidden fruit, they are chased from the garden—which appears to back onto an abandoned Italian villa—by fascists with dogs.

There's also a well-handled scene in which two twins almost meet at an airport—but it has no connection to the rest of the story.

There isn't much dialogue, but some of it especially the middle-aged Nic's envirobabble—has the deadened, clumsy quality of stuff improvised by actors.

The movie has the lush look Figgis always brings to his work ("Leaving Las Vegas," "Internal Affairs"), but this time the visuals are just too slick. A scene with a Land Rover racing along a road beneath Tunisian mountains looks for all the world like a car commercial. And even the movie's best sequence, a wordless flirtation between two stunning Italians on a railway platform, could easily be a sophisticated pitch for upmarket aftershave.

"The Loss of Sexual Innocence" isn't a dead loss, but it's close.

NEWSDAY, 5/28/99, Part II/p. B6, Gene Seymour

It begins with the blond, blue-eyed face of a young boy who, we are told, lives in Africa in the early 1950s. Happy in his bucolic, if harsh-looking surroundings, the boy is playing one bright day before he finds himself in front of a house. He peeks through distorted glass and beholds a strange act of what can only be characterized as chaste kinkiness.

No further explanation ensues before we move ahead to what we presume to be the same boy (Jonathan Rhys-Meyers), age 16, living in an industrial British town and then abruptly to a clear lake from which emerge a naked black man (Femi Ogumbanjo) and a naked white woman (Hanne Klintoe), who appear to be Adam and Eve, suddenly realizing they exist.

We'll get back to them soon enough—though, if you know the story, you can guess what happens as soon as a snake appears.

At some point, we then meet what we, once again, assume is the grownup boy, whose name is Nic (Julian Sands), driving his wife and young son to a country house. We have to connect lots more dots on our own before we figure out that Nic is a filmmaker who broods a lot about his past, especially those parts where bad stuff happens because of sexual longings and frustrations.

I don't know if I have the exact order of events right, but you get the idea. And, hard as it may be to believe, it's part of what makes one want very much to declare "The Loss of Sexual Innocence" the artistic success that its narrative daring deserves.

Mike Figgis, whose "Leaving Las Vegas" remains one of the decade's movie touchstones, lays waste to the traditional three-act structure and lets the resulting fragments tell his story of a man's fall—or, if you want to get biblical about it, fall from grace.

Given Figgis' penchant for jazz-inspired motifs, it's irresistible to compare "Loss of Sexual Innocence's" loosely threaded, allusive strategy to one of Miles Davis' slippery, enigmatic mid-1960s recordings. And again, you wish the movie worked on that level as well as one of Wayne Shorter's solos.

The trouble is that while some of the digressions work—notably a hypnotic set piece in an Italian airport in which a woman (Saffron Burrows) working on Nic's film has a brief, stunning encounter with her long-lost twin—others seem to slip under your memory the way insects scurry beneath woodwork.

All these various flashbacks of Nic's youth and the intercutting of the Adam and Eve fable all coalesce around an African misadventure whose triangular romantic tension and split-second tragedy is reminiscent of Hemingway's "The Short, Happy Life of Francis Macomber." Figgis' own African story is compelling enough on its own to make you wonder if all that other stuff was necessary. He thinks it was. You may think otherwise.

SIGHT AND SOUND, 12/99, p. 49, Charlotte O'Sullivan

The film follows the experiences of the protagonist Nic at various times in his life. Intercut with this are Adam and Eve's creation, their discovery of sex and banishment from the Garden of Eden.

In 50s Kenya, five-year-old Nic spies a young girl exchanging education for sexual favours. Years later in Newcastle, Nic attends a funeral for his girlfriend Susan's father. At the party afterwards, he catches her kissing another man. Now an adult, Nic travels with his wife and child to a holiday cottage. On the way they argue. We see scenes from Nic's childhood involving a gruesome murder.

Nic's marriage breaks down and he leaves to direct a film in the Sahara. He stops in Rome to meet a beautiful Italian girl whose boyfriend Lucca will be the film's sound recordist. Unbeknown to this girl, she has a twin (they were separated at birth) travelling to Rome on the same plane as Nic. At Rome airport the twins see each other, but are distracted and 'miss' each other. On location, Nic and the Italian twin are attracted to each other; Lucca picks up on this and records the sound of their love-making one night. He plays it back as the group are travelling across the desert. In his jealous rage, Lucca drives over and kills a child. The boy's tribe demand one of the party stay behind while the others go off to get the police. The girl insists on staying. The tribespeople kill her.

Mike Figgis claims to have learned the hard way "that you do yourself no favours by holding onto things that do not belong within the big structure." If that's so, how does one explain his lush art movie *The Loss of Sexual Innocence,* a film entirely devoid of a big structure?

There are so many faces, so many "things" competing for our attention here, it's hard to feel much about any of them. Far from appearing surreal or jagged, many of the vignettes prove predictable. As soon as we see the protagonist Nic's teen-years girlfriend Susan talking drunkenly to a rakish fellow at her father's funeral party, we guess she's going to grind herself into betrayal. As soon as the female twins parted at birth begin their separate journeys to Rome airport, we know they will meet (if only briefly). Even Nic's and his wife's Dennis Potteresque dreams feel familiar. And we all know exactly where Adam and Eve are headed. The actors are faced with the impossible task of bringing tableaux to life; most seem too self-conscious to make this work. Saffron Burrows has too few lines to break the spell of her beauty. Femi Ogumbanjo (Adam) and Hanne Klintoe (Eve) seem too inexperienced. Trying to convey awe, they look witless.

You don't have to prefer Figgis' more polished efforts *(Leaving Las Vegas, One Night Stand)* to find all this grating. The Adam and Eve sequences are perhaps the most hackneyed, and when white horses appear, we're really lost. Benoît Delhomme, *The Scent of Green Papaya*'s DP, knows how to make earth come shudderingly to life, but the ideas behind the beautiful images aren't complex enough to hold our attention. What does Figgis add to the creation myth? And what lies beyond Eden makes no sense. The paparazzi (such easy targets) are as one with a brutal police force, but can an obsession with celebrity be so easily equated with fascism?

When in doubt, Figgis throws in humour, but it sits uneasily with the film's somewhat pompous tone. We don't know Nic well enough to know if the asides are meant to be his view of the world. More often than not, they seem to come straight from Figgis, with more than an edge of contempt. Thus the subheading "Her father which now art in heaven" appears before a scene in which teenage Nic tries to go all the way with Susan. Similarly, when Nic fondles his unnamed wife in their kitchen, the camera rests on a phallic cucumber. We may not care about these people but that doesn't mean we want to laugh at them. Meanwhile, we are prepared for a number of climaxes. The first, in which the twins meet, is ludicrous. The brassy music builds while a subplot involving a clumsy British businessman reminds us how ridiculous the rest of humanity is. In fact, it's the businessman you warm to.

But the film has a few more crescendoes, and the next one comes off the moment where Burrows, as the Italian twin, is murdered is astonishingly powerful. Suddenly the cloud of poise and misery hovering over her explodes and for once the sub heading—"Justice" comes into its own. Burrows' character stays with the tribespeople because she thinks that a female will defuse the situation. That she gets it so wrong seems a judgement neither on her nor on the tribespeople and is thus genuinely tragic, a question about sexual and racial identity that can't be answered. For this scene alone, *The Loss of Sexual Innocence* is worth our attention.

VILLAGE VOICE, 6/1/99, p. 126, Dennis Lim

Mike Figgis's *The Loss of Sexual Innocence* is a serious miscalculation—the film isn't short on ideas, it's just that those ideas are dumbfoundingly pretentious and trite. The movie opens in elusive, mildly seductive mode, but as soon as the director's designs become clear, it's one long free fall.

Composed entirely of fragments, *The Loss of Sexual Innocence* is, on one level, a psychological sketch of Nic, a filmmaker and quite likely Figgis's alter ego, whom we see at four different ages, and who's played as an adult by Julian Sands. Nic's story is intercut with scenes of a biblical idyll on the verge of being shattered—a black Adam and a white Eve rise from a lake, discover each other's privates, pee into the lake; a white horse, a snake, fruit, and sex are also involved. Think *The Blue Lagoon,* as brought to you by Benetton.

The mood is stone-faced and heavy-lidded, exacerbated by Kieslowski-esque plot turns, ridiculously frequent fades-to-black, and a sanity-threatening score (repetitive loops of numbingly familiar classical piano pieces—"Moonlight Sonata," Chopin nocturnes). The movie obsesses pointlessly over connections between sex and death (and between sex and bad stuff in general).

The lustrous, couture-ish photography by Benoit Delhomme (who's worked with Tran Anh Hung) actually has an adverse effect—it makes the movie seem even more like torturous Eurotrash.

Also reviewed in:
CHICAGO TRIBUNE, 6/18/99, Friday/p. D, Barbara Shulgasser
NEW YORK TIMES, 5/28/99, p. E10, Stephen Holden
VARIETY, 2/1-7/99, p. 59, Emanuel Levy
WASHINGTON POST, 6/25/99, Weekend/p. 48, Desson Howe

LOST AND FOUND

A Warner Bros. release of an Alcon Entertainment presentation of a Wayne Rice/Dinamo Entertainment production. *Producer:* Andrew A. Kosove, Broderick Johnson, Wayne Rice, and Morrie Eisenman. *Director:* Jeff Pollack. *Screenplay:* J.B. Cook, Marc Meeks, and David Spade. *Director of Photography:* Paul Elliott. *Editor:* Christopher Greenbury. *Music:* John Debney and Michael Dilbeck. *Sound:* Kim Ornitz and Glenn Berkovitz. *Casting:* Jackie Burch. *Production Designer:* Rusty Smith. *Art Director:* Alec Hammond. *Set Decorator:* Stephanie Ziemer. *Set Designer:* Mindi Toback. *Set Dresser:* Matthew Altman, Eric Fishman, Pete Flynn, Guy Owen, and Edward Tamayo. *Costumes:* Susan Bertram. *Make-up:* Ron Berkeley. *Special Effects:* Dean Miller and Joel Blanchard. *Stunt Coordinator:* Kim Koscki. *Running time:* 98 minutes. *MPAA Rating:* PG-13.

CAST: David Spade (Dylan); Ever Carradine (Ginger); Stephanie Chang (Restaurant Patron #2); Neal MacMillan (Restaurant Patron #1); Mitchell Whitfield (Mark); Lloyd Garroway (Waiter); Artie Lange (Wally); Coby (Jack); Sophie Marceau (Lila); Carole Cook (Sylvia); Estelle Harris (Mrs. Stubblefield); Marla Gibbs (Enid); Rose Marie (Clara); Natalie Barish (Mrs. Elderly Couple); Phil Leeds (Mr. Elderly Couple); Christian Clemenson (Ray); Dee Dee Rescher (Sally); Faye DeWitt (Blind Lady); David Hartman (Cello Student); Larry Raben (Peter); Brett Banducci, Mary Ingersal and Nicole Garcia (Mall Quartet Players); Patrick Bruel (Rene); Alessandra Toreson (Park Girl); Michelle Clunie (Gail); Abidah Viera (Vet); Shannon Dang (Girl at Pet Store); Carl Michael Linder (Brat); Karen Rosin (Brat's Mother); Nicolas Greenbury and Andrew Greenbury (Rollerblade Kids); Frankie Muniz (Movie on TV "Boy"); Alicia Leigh Willis (Movie on TV "Big Sister"); Lael Pollack (Movie on TV "Little Girl"); Jeff Haley (Guard at Hollywood Bowl); Jon Lovitz (Uncle Harry); Jason Stuart (Jewelry Store Clerk); Jim Meskimen (Good Samaritan); Frank Mercuri (Bartender); Candy Rich (Party Guest); Martin Sheen (Millstone); Maree Cheatham (Mrs. Millstone); David Garry (Joby the Valet); David Seewack (Valet at Millstone's); Wolf Muser (Ubermann); Della Miles (Singer #1); Erika Nann (Singer #2); Cynthia Bass (Singer #3); Fred Golt (Table Guest); Pina De Rosa (Maria, the Cook); Danny Woodburn (Mover); Harper Roisman (Mr. Norton); Pearl Shear (Mrs. Norton); Robert Del and Robert Schroer (Construction Workers); Daphnee Lynn Duplaix (Flight Attendant); J.B. Cook (Jan-a-tor); Marc Lynn (Homeless Guy); Ovis (Pet Store Employee); Frankie Pace (Sal); Hal Sparks (DJ); Don Perry (Guest at Millstone's); Jennifer Farrell (Window Washer Girl); Audrey Wasilewski (Pet Store Saleswoman).

LOS ANGELES TIMES, 4/23/99, Calendar/p. 12, Eric Harrison

Bodily secretions and abused pooches aside, the most startling quality of "There's Something About Mary" was the way it married the romantic comedy genre to the teen gross-out movie. All of that raunchy stuff that had audiences either squirming or rolling in the aisles might've shook up the folks who flock to Meg Ryan movies, but it has long been the bread and butter of a certain kind of flick that caters to, shall we say, less delicate tastes.

The Farrelly Brothers' accomplishment was getting both audiences together in the same theater, and satisfying them both. "Mary" made it seem easy. "Lost & Found," David Spade's new movie, shows how hard it truly is. Even for those who didn't find "Mary" as funny as the rest of the world seemed to, its mix of crudity and sweetness, explicitness and charm, offered the shock of the new. "Lost & Found" is nothing but a cynical, astonishingly inept attempt to copy "Mary's" formula.

Spade, playing essentially the same smug, smart-alecky character he plays on the NBC sitcom "Just Shoot Me," is enraptured by his pretty new neighbor (French actress Sophie Marceau). In what passes for logic in this movie, he tries to win her affections by kidnapping her dog. The plot's other particulars don't really matter. We've seen it all before, if not in other movies then in creaky TV sitcoms.

Spade co-wrote this movie, and he apparently had the good sense to realize that he can't carry an entire film. So "Lost & Found" is stuffed with extraneous bits featuring funnier (but often misused) TV comedians like Jon Lovitz, Estelle Harris, Rose Marie and Marla Gibbs. Probably Spade's biggest splash in the movies were in the two comedies he made with the late Chris Farley, "Tommy Boy" and "Black Sheep." This movie features a corpulent Farley-like character (Artie Lange) in a misguided attempt at duplicating that chemistry.

Of course, just about everything in this movie is an attempt at duplicating something else.

Like "Mary," this movie is about a short, not particularly attractive guy who is fixated on an unattainable, good-hearted and great-looking woman. Both movies also are set in seaside communities and have disgusting old lady homebodies as supporting characters. Both have annoying doggies that are just begging to be abused.

The most glaring similarities, though, are in the movie's attempt to shock.

Some of the low points: Spade makes his dimwitted flunky (Lange) poke around with his fingers' in mounds of dog feces for a missing ring. Then, just for fun, he tricks the idiot into smearing the stuff on his face.

Then, let's see? There's the scene where Spade tosses the dog into a clothes dryer. We hear the pooch yelp and whimper as it slams again and again against the sides.

And let's not forget the scene where Spade knocks out a little kid in a pet store.

These scenes go beyond distasteful, they're just cruel. All of these actions are true to the jerky, weaselly persona Spade has made his calling card, but they make him a difficult suitor to root for. The smug way he dispenses pain and humiliation isn't easy to laugh at.

All of this points to the two major differences between "Mary" and "Lost": Ben Stiller's character in "Mary" was likable (if pathetic), and "Mary" was sporadically funny.

NEW YORK POST, 4/23/99, p. 59, Jonathan Foreman

As well as being the second film in a year to capitalize on the sensual appeal of the cello, "Lost and Found" is yet another movie that exploits the comic possibilities of a restaurant kitchen.

(Perhaps running a restaurant—a fashionable hobby for yuppie/foodie actors—is about as close as Hollywood types can get to as an idea of the working world.)

The other interesting thing about "Lost & Found" is the presence of two famous French actors, Sophie Marceau and Patrick Bruel, both of whom display a remarkable facility for comedy in English—but whose charm and talents are largely wasted in a David Spade vehicle that goes nowhere.

To be fair, "Lost & Found" has some very funny moments. But it feels like an extended TV sitcom. Spade's core shtick (a weaselly wimp who makes wise-ass comments and gets away with it) may have worked as a counterpoint to the late Chris Farley's antics in "Tommy Boy," but it plays a lot better on the small screen.

Spade is Dylan, a snide, sarcastic restaurateur who has just broken up with his stripper girlfriend. Dylan's neighbor Lila (Marceau) is an underachieving cellist who has fled France and Rene (Bruel) the handsome, successful musician boyfriend who undermined her confidence.

Lila has a terrier named Jack who disappears for solo jaunts along the pier. Dylan kidnaps the dog so he can eventually "rescue" it and look like a hero. But his plan begins to go wrong when Rene turns up in L.A. and insists on helping in the search for Jack.

Rene caps his natural advantages in the competition for Lila's affections by promising to introduce her to the chairman of the Philharmonic.

(Weirdly, Rene and Lila talk to each other in accented English rather than French.)

In the meantime there's some business with a loan from the bank that Dylan needs to expand his restaurant, and a diamond anniversary ring that Dylan's partner entrusts to him for safekeeping.

Jack the dog has some very amusing scenes, as does Estelle Harris (Mrs. Costanza from "Seinfeld") and her klatsch of lascivious elderly poker players. But Marceau steals the show with her surprising comic timing.

Unfortunately, her beauty undermines the credibility of the plot. It's impossible to believe that the faintly repellent Dylan could win her over.

Not only is he physically unprepossessing (though you could easily see her with Steve Martin, Woody Allen or even Danny DeVito) his persona lacks grace, wit, integrity or any other redeeming, endearing feature.

The script tries to make up for this with a halfhearted Nike moment, but when Dylan tells Lila to go all out for her career there's cheese in the air, not romance.

NEWSDAY, 4/23/99, Part II/p. B11, Gene Seymour

On the small screen, David Spade is a huge talent. He deflates pretense with tiny darts dipped in smarm. His gift for stealth malice is never more welcome than when it shatters the decorum of a solemn board meeting—as it frequently does on "Just Shoot Me," the underachieving sitcom that would stagnate without Spade.

As with Don Rickles, whose brassy invective is a precursor to Spade's leaner model, the former thin white duke from "Saturday Night Live" owns the kind of persona you count on to mess up somebody else's context rather than inhabit one of its own.

Who on earth wants to see a bomb-thrower like Rickles or Spade cast as a romantic lead? It'd be a waste of valuable resources.

But the concept of "waste" doesn't seem to faze the people (Spade included) who went ahead and made "Lost & Found." Indeed, many of the movie's jokes are fixated on waste, dog vomit and feces especially. Such humor suggests that the film's producers were paying close attention to the—um—grosses of "There's Something About Mary" and other doofus comedies.

But that kind of shamelessness works best with a protagonist who's either slack-jawed stupid or wide-eyed hapless. Spade's image is far too slick to be either. Which is why he's cast here as Dylan Ramsey, sly, sharp-tongued restaurateur who's looking to expand his business while also keeping an eye cocked longingly at his sexy next-door neighbor Lila Dubois (Sophie Marceau), a French cellist whose dog keeps running away.

Dylan, plagued by a magazine rack of issues regarding intimacy, decides that the only way to connect with Lila is to kidnap her wandering pooch and offer her his services as a dog finder. Among the many complicating factors to this scheme are a dimwitted delivery boy (Artie Lang), who's decided to make Dylan his role model, and Lila's overbearing ex-fiance Rene (Patrick Bruel).

Then, there's the dog himself, whose dietary mishaps compel Dylan, at one point, to pour a bottle of Pepto Bismol down its doggy gullet. You're probably laughing at this idea. Trust me: As with just about every other gag in this movie, it sounds funnier than it plays.

"Lost & Found" suffers from a curious lack of conviction. Neither the movie nor its star can decide whether to seduce the audience with coy cuteness or fragment—bomb them with arch grossness.

In the cuteness department, it's a close call between Spade and the dog. Most of the time, the gross-out stuff misfires badly. (And in case you wondered, the obligatory Jon Lovitz cameo can be found among the flotsam.)

Marceau and Bruel get high marks for good sportsmanship. And Spade isn't entirely a washout as a screen lover. But the movie goes to such embarrassing extremes to appeal to the mall-rat demographic that you wish there were somebody on screen to let the air out of the misbegotten enterprise. Somebody very much like ...David Spade.

Maybe we'll see that dry guy with sharper weapons next time around.

Also reviewed in:
CHICAGO TRIBUNE, 4/23/99, Friday/p. A, Mark Caro

NEW YORK TIMES, 4/23/99, p. E18, Stephen Holden
VARIETY, 4/19-25/99, p. 47, Oliver Jones
WASHINGTON POST, 4/23/99, Weekend/p. 51, Nicole Arthur

LOVE ETC.

A Phaedra Cinema release of an Aliceleo/France 3 Cinéma/le Studio Canal+ production in association with Studio Images 3 and Cofimage 7 and participation of Canal Plus. *Producer:* Patrick Godeau. *Director:* Marion Vernoux. *Screenplay (French with English subtitles):* Dodine Herry and Marion Vernoux. *Based on his novel "Talking It Over":* Julian Barnes. *Director of Photography:* Eric Gautier. *Music:* Alexandre Desplat and Leonard Cohen. *Additional music from his opera "Turandot":* Giacomo Puccini. *Running time:* 105 minutes. *MPAA Rating:* Not Rated.

CAST: Charlotte Gainsbourg (Marie); Yvan Attal (Benoit); Charles Berling (Pierre); Susan Moncur (Susan); Thibault de Montalembert (Bernard).

NEW YORK POST, 7/2/99, p. 49, Hannah Brown

Burdened by a banal title and familiar love-triangle plot, "Love Etc." triumphs over its conventionality to paint a quiet, painfully intense portrait of love and loneliness.

Based on a novel by Julian Barnes, "Love Etc." tells the story of odd-couple friends: Pierre (Charles Berling), a confident, handsome literature teacher who's constantly meeting (and dumping) women, and Benoit (Yvan Attal), a shy foreign-currency expert at a bank.

We've seen duos like this in lots of movies, but here it's not played for laughs.

When Benoit decides to answer a personal ad, he's so insecure he sends Marie (Charlotte Gainsbourg) a photo of Pierre.

Marie, an art restorer, is just as solitary as Benoit. She's sleeping with her married downstairs neighbor and feels the chances of meeting a man she both respects and is attracted to are as small as hitting the lottery.

She doesn't mind Benoit's trick with the photo, since she's attracted by his sincerity and flattered by his love for her. The two are soon are married.

But at their wedding, Pierre decides that he's in love with Marie and has to win her away from Benoit.

The gangly Marie, who has never been pursued like this, at first rejects his advances, but he gradually wears her down.

Director/screenwriter Marion Vernoux creates an emotionally satisfying movie about dilemmas with which everyone can identify.

The characters do the kinds of things people really do when they're feeling desperate, like listening to a maudlin Leonard Cohen song over and over. Only an insubstantial epilogue mars the flow of the film.

But that's a minor flaw. The awkwardness and drama of finding and losing love has rarely been portrayed so gracefully on screen in recent years.

VILLAGE VOICE, 7/6/99, p. 70, Leslie Camhi

Few cinematic passions have proved more enduring than the love of a man for his best friend's wife. *Love Etc.* adds a touch of millennial fever and some stylistic flourishes. Adapted from Julian Barnes's bestseller, *Talking It Over,* Marion Vernoux's third feature retains a good measure of the novel's comic elegance, but its characters drown in excessive verbiage and familiar posturing. As Pierre, Charles Berling plays his perennial role—a lust-ridden, angst-filled, eternally adolescent intellectual. His best friend, Benoit (Yvan Attal), a pathologically shy banker blessed with domestic virtues, meets Marie (Charlotte Gainsbourg), a pretty art restorer, through the personals. When they wed, Pierre discovers his sensitive side and true feelings. Smartly shot in chic apartments, with a soulful Tom Waits score, *Love Etc.* is stuffed with talent, though I'm not sure what part belongs to the director. The admirable Gainsbourg refrains from overacting, but her leading men never quite transcend the emptiness and inanity of their characters' dilemma.

Also reviewed in:
CHICAGO TRIBUNE, 12/24/99, Friday/p. S, John Petrakis
NEW YORK TIMES, 7/2/99, p. E13, Lawrence Van Gelder

LOVE GOD

A Good Machine release of a Good Machine production. *Executive Producer:* James Schamus, Ted Hope, and Shimpei Okuda. *Producer:* Anthony Bregman. *Director:* Frank Grow. *Screenplay:* Frank Grow. *Director of Photography:* Terry Stacey. *Editor:* David Frankel. *Music:* Tracy McKnight. *Casting:* Peggy Adler. *Production Designer:* Clay Brown. *Art Director:* Kristin Loeffler. *Costumes:* Melissa Toth. *Make-up (Special Effects):* Keith Edmier. *Running time:* 95 minutes. *MPAA Rating:* Not Rated.

CAST: Will Keenan (Larue); Shannon Burkett (Helen); Kymberli Ghee (Kathleen/Kali); Kerri Kenney (Darla); Michael Laurence (Victor); Dale Soules (Connie); Yukio Yamamoto (Dr. Noguchi).

NEW YORK POST, 12/3/99, p. 50, Jonathan Foreman

Unwatchably bad, "Love God" is the ultimate proof that there's too much money available for indie films.

It looks like its downtown hipster cast had fun making the film but were too pleased with themselves to notice that it's a tedious, incoherent mess.

Larue (Will Keenan), a mental patient who suffers from "compulsive reading syndrome," lives in a halfway house, where he meets a guy with chronic bad hygiene who is attacked by a prehistoric parasitic worm.

Meanwhile, a self-mutilating, blue-skinned woman who thinks she's the goddess Kali is stalked by a monster that looks like the poop demon in "Dogma."

Most of the time you can't tell what's going on. The writing and direction are unbelievably amateurish, and the special effects are dreadful.

The filmmakers seem to have been aiming at a '60s psychedelic feeling, but it's doubtful that it would seem anything less than dumb and boring, even to a heavily medicated audience.

NEWSDAY 12/3/99, Part II/p. B6, John Anderson

Pulsing, throbbing, powered by sheer lunatic energy and heavy-metal thrust, "Love God" may be the perfect midnight movie, one that borrows from the Troma aesthetic and then takes it places no mutant has gone before.

Set in a 1996 New York, where mental-health cuts are prompting the premature release of some seriously troubled people, Frank Grow's '97 Sundance favorite is really an old-fashioned romance—except that the principals are some seriously troubled people.

The medication-averse Larue (Will Keenan), deposited in a seedy Manhattan SRO after his mandatory discharge, suffers from Compulsive Reading Syndrome—he's driven to read everything he sees and then tear it to pieces. Between roaming the streets in super-thick glasses (so he can't see) and making totemic sculptures out of chewed bubble gum, he gets involved with Helen (Shannon Burkett), a strange mute compulsive who works crime-scene cleanup and lives with her clean-freak mother (Dale Soules). Mom loses her grip when she thinks Larue has touched her daughter. But it's worse that his medium is gum.

Meanwhile, the clearly unhinged Dr. Noguchi (Yukio Yamamoto) is searching for his prehistoric tapeworm, which escaped into the sewer system and is preparing to wreak havoc among the down, out and weird. They include the blue-faced Kathleen (Kymberli Ghee), who imagines herself to be Kali, homicidal wife of the Hindu God Shiva, and the hilarious Victor (Michael Laurence), a Bible-reading punk rocker with a bad case of Tourette's syndrome.

Grow tosses it all into the mix—slime monsters, animation accents, ingenious editing and the "loooove god"-intoning Play-Doh face that vaguely resembles the classical mask of comedy—but it works. The energy level is consistently high, the humor is broad but good-natured and most of the time you can't believe what you're seeing.

Also reviewed in:
NEW YORK TIMES, 12/3/99, p. E22, Anita Gates
VARIETY, 2/10-16/97, p. 66, Godfrey Cheshire

LOVE LETTER, THE

A DreamWorks Pictures release of a Sanford/Pillsbury production. *Executive Producer:* Beau Flynn and Stefan Simchowitz. *Producer:* Sarah Pillsbury, Midge Sanford, and Kate Capshaw. *Director:* Peter Ho-sun Chan. *Screenplay:* Maria Maggenti. *Based on the novel by:* Cathleen Schine. *Director of Photography:* Tami Reiker. *Editor:* Jacqueline Cambas. *Music:* Luis Bacalov. *Music Editor:* Sharon Smith. *Sound:* John Patrick Pritchett and (music) Mark Kalm. *Sound Editor:* Victoria Rose Sampson and David Hankins. *Casting:* Mali Finn. *Production Designer:* Andrew Jackness. *Art Director:* Carl Sprague. *Set Decorator:* Tracey A. Doyle. *Set Dresser:* Steve Brennan. *Special Effects:* J.C. Brotherhood. *Costumes:* Tracy Tynan. *Make-up:* Melanie Hughes. *Running time:* 88 minutes. *MPAA Rating:* R.

CAST: Kate Capshaw (Helen); Blythe Danner (Lillian); Ellen DeGeneres (Janet); Geraldine McEwan (Miss Scattergoods); Julianne Nicholson (Jennifer); Tom Everett Scott (Johnny); Tom Selleck (George); Gloria Stuart (Eleanor); Bill Buell (Officer Dan); Alice Drummond (Postal Clerk); Erik Jensen (Ray); Margaret Ann Brady (Selma); Jessica Capshaw (Kelly); Walter Covell (Post Office Customer); Patrick Donnelly (Bookstore Customer); Lucas Hall, Christian Harmony, and Christopher Nee (Garbage Men); Marilyn Rockafellow (Vivian); Breanne Smith (Emily); Sasha Spielberg (Girl with Sparkler).

LOS ANGELES TIMES, 5/21/99, Calendar/p. 12, Kevin Thomas

"The Love Letter" is a romantic comedy of much charm and wisdom, set in a storybook New England village, that takes a bemused look at the capriciousness of fate in determining the course of our lives.

Kate Capshaw, Blythe Danner, Ellen DeGeneres, Geraldine McEwan, Julianne Nicholson, Tom Everett Scott, Tom Selleck and Gloria Stuart form a sterling ensemble cast that glows under the breezy yet tart direction of Peter Ho-sun Chan, a top Hong Kong director making his Hollywood debut.

Chan turns out to be an excellent choice for bringing Maria Maggenti's brisk script from Cathleen Schine's novel to the screen. He's established his flair for bringing both humor and seriousness to the often confused and conflicted passions of the heart in a series of sparkling successes, including "Comrades: Almost a Love Story" and "He's a Woman, She's a Man."

Capshaw's Helen is the film's key figure, an attractive divorcee with a child to support, a bookstore to operate and a stately, though run-down, home to maintain. Luckily, she has her good friend Janet (DeGeneres), who's as organized and efficient as Helen is not, to manage the store, where Scott's Johnny and Nicholson's Jennifer have summer jobs.

Sitting on a couch in the store to go through the day's mail, Helen comes across a letter, sans envelope, salutation or signature, wedged between the cushions. It is a scorching declaration of love that hits Helen like a truck, awakening in her a deep sense of longing that starts her daydreaming. She becomes convinced that Johnny, a tall, handsome, sweet-natured 20-year-old, has sent the letter to her, and a quick turn of the plot makes Johnny thinks she's intended it for him.

Learning about the letter, Janet quite logically points out that it could just as easily have been intended for her as for Helen, and Janet is hoping that it came from Selleck's George, the local fireman who's just going through a divorce. (Alas, he's been secretly in love with Helen for years; however, this doesn't automatically mean that he wrote the letter.) Meanwhile, Jennifer pines for Johnny. Threading through the story is McEwan's Miss Scattergoods, a chain-smoking aristocrat, astringent and independent. Just as Helen is being carried away by dreams of a man half her age, her free-spirited grandmother Eleanor (Stuart) arrives—with her period furniture no less—and her globe-trotting daughter, Lillian (Danner).

It's a bit startling to see Danner cast as Capshaw's mother, even though Danner has been "aged" for the role (Danner is only about 11 years older than Capshaw). No matter: Danner is such a skilled actress that we don't dwell on the fact that she's too young to play Capshaw's mother.

No one familiar with this large cast can be surprised at how effective everyone is in taking the crisply defined roles in often quite unexpected directions.

More than anyone else, Selleck stands out as a man who is in love but is diffident about showing it. This means Selleck must hold back his emotions when he's with Helen yet reveal to us the depth of his feelings for her, and Selleck makes George's predicament at once funny and poignant. In any event, Selleck's approach pays off handsomely.

Photographed by Tami Reiker, "The Love Letter" captures the beauty and mellowness of its locale (Rockport, Mass.) and boasts graceful yet understated costume and production design by, respectively, Tracy Tynan and Andrew Jackness. Luis Bacalov's score complements both the film's emotional complexity and its buoyant mood and tempo.

"The Love Letter" suggests how vulnerable we are to pure chance but also makes the point that there's something to be said for making declarations of love directly to the other person and not entrusting them to written missives.

NEW YORK, 5/31/99, p. 97, Peter Rainer

As Helen MacFarquhar in *The Love Letter*, Kate Capshaw has a marvelous look—voluptuously frazzled. A single mother whose 11-year-old daughter is in camp for the summer, Helen is a woman at odds with herself. Living in a ramshackle New England town called Loblolly-by-the-Sea, she runs her bookstore with a distracted efficiency.

We see her jog on the beach, and it's clear from her flailing, hectic gait that she's running away from something. Either that, or she's running—ravenously—into something new. If only she knew what it was?

Helen is punch-drunk from the sensual possibilities in the salt air; the wide vistas in Loblolly have a golden clearness, and the townspeople stand out against them in all their fleshy singularity. The setting is almost comically ripe for romance, and so it's a magical touch that Helen should find, in a bundle of mail at the store, a passionate, anonymous love letter. She, of course, believes it was written for her. Later, the letter is spied upon by others—including Johnny (Tom Everett Scott), the buff 20-year-old college student working for the summer in her store—and they join the erotic rondelay. Who the letter's author is becomes less important than the fantasies it inspires.

At its best, *The Love Letter*, based on the 1995 Cathleen Schine novel, is a lyrical little lark about the embarrassments of love. Peter Ho-sun Chan, a Hong Kong director making his American debut, has a deft touch. His camera slides among the Loblollers with a sly, insinuating speed; it's as if we were watching the trajectory of a hot rumor. The actors have a shaggy, Americana kind of familiarity, and yet, because they're always doing surprising things, they don't turn into friezes. Working from a script by Maria Maggenti, Chan understands the loony affliction of being love-struck.

The younger players in the lineup, such as Johnny, or his co-worker Jennifer (Julianne Nicholson), are jangly and impulsive. (Jennifer shears her tresses the day after Johnny apologetically rebuffs her advances.) The adults are equally scrambled—lust is the great leveler. When, inevitably, Helen and Johnny bed down, he's full of romantic ardor while she, stunned by where her senses have led her, is flummoxed. "I've never felt this way before," he says to Helen. "Of course not," she replies. "You're 20." (Capshaw can be wonderfully deadpan.) Johnny has his grown-up counterpart in Tom Selleck's gentle George, the town's soon-to-be-divorced fireman, who loved Helen when they were back in their twenties and warms at the prospect of another go-round.

The film's farcical structure keeps the rondelay spinning in mid-air. Even the cynics are swept up. As Janet, Helen's wisecracking assistant and best friend, Ellen DeGeneres keeps shooting darts into everybody's love balloons, but she's as desirous of rapture as anybody else. She roots out the love letter, imagining it was addressed to her, and can't abide Helen's spoilsport insistence that it wasn't. In the course of the movie, just about every romantic mood is at least glancingly struck. It's a very *democratic* love story.

The chalkboard in Helen's bookstore carries daily messages, and one of them is from Shakespeare: "This is heavy midsummer madness." Not quite. The filmmakers are wrong to underscore a tone they haven't fully achieved. At times, *The Love Letter* resembles nothing so much as a folksy, "knowing" TV series on the order of *Picket Fences*. Loblolly is a little *too* quaint; the people can seem that way, too. And some of the actors one wants most to see, such as Blythe Danner and Gloria Stuart, playing Helen's mother and grandmother, barely make an appearance. There's a glibness to some of the frolics, as in the scene where Johnny peels an orange for Helen and we see the luscious fruit pulled apart. This is right out of the food-equals-sex *Tom Jones* handbook, and it's too obvious and uncouth for Chan's delicate balancing act.

One of the pleasures of Cathleen Schine's novel is the way Helen's bookishness is itself a kind of romance; the novel is about how one can be seduced not only by the flesh but by language—by the taste and smell and feel of words. Schine made the literary sensibility—of all things—arousing. That's the book's wit. The movie adaptation is gaga in more conventional ways, but that doesn't mean it's a conventional movie. Unlike most so-called romantic comedies these days, it doesn't seem prepackaged, and that's because the filmmakers are tickled by the vagaries of amour. The love letter frees everybody to play out his or her erotic wishes, and everything goes blissfully, ruefully awry.

NEW YORK POST, 5/21/99, p. 53, Rod Dreher

The one thing that sticks with you about Kate Capshaw's—that is, Mrs. Steven Spielberg's—drowsy vanity project "The Love Letter" is its bizarre attempt to pass off Blythe Danner as Capshaw's mother. Hel-lo! There's only 10 years difference in their ages. Dame Spielberg, 45, is a lovely woman, but why didn't someone point out to her that she, too, is old enough to be Gwyneth Paltrow's mother—and looks it?

If "The Love Letter" were set in an Arkansas trailer park, this might make sense. But its setting is a picturesque New England coastal village called Loblolly-by-the-Sea (think Garrison Keillor meets Martha Stewart).

How picturesque, how quirky, how postcard-perfect is it? The beefy fireman George (Tom Selleck) loves opera. The town biddy, Miss Scattergoods (Geraldine McEwan), putters about on her bicycle making flinty observations.

Yes, if this eccentric burg were a farm, you'd call it Pepperidge.

It even has a "You've Got Mail"-ish bookstore that no paying customers ever seem to visit but even so makes enough money to afford a staff of three.

They all labor for owner Helen (Capshaw), a divorcee who runs on the beach to work off the frustration of never having a date.

"The Love Letter's" MacGuffin makes its entrance when Helen discovers an anonymous amorous epistle between the cushions of a sofa. She thinks it's a mash note from thick-headed but sexy Johnny (Tom Everett Scott), the hunky college student working in the bookshop during the summer.

When Johnny sneaks a secret peek at the letter, he assumes Helen wrote it to him. They smolder, they grope, but farce never once threatens to break out.

Meanwhile, George continues his fruitless crusade to interest Helen in age-appropriate dating. That internal letter causes more problems when, out of the blue, Helen's sexy mother (Danner) and dotty grandmother (Gloria Stuart) turn up abruptly for mysterious, letter-related reasons.

There's no lightness or magic in any of this, and I think the problem is mainly Capshaw. Her Helen is cold and charmless, all sculpted body and aloof hardness. We need to sense that underneath that forbiddingly firm shell there's a soft, gooey core just waiting to come gushing out. But the most that can be said for Helen is that she's in great shape for someone her age.

Believe it or not, Ellen DeGeneres is easily the best thing about this depressing picture. She plays Janet, the bookshop's business manager, and though she too complains that no man will look at her, Janet is the one female character who seems to have a sense of humor.

NEWSDAY, 5/21/99, Part II/p. B3, Gene Seymour

You have to admire a major studio production that protects its quirks to the very end. Without giving anything away, the denouement of "The Love Letter" keeps a respectful enough distance from what's expected of a Hollywood romantic comedy to get bonus critical points for effort.

Good thing, because just about everything else about this adaptation of Cathleen Schine's witty novel about May-September love in a New England town is slick, coy and sitcom-cozy. (So was the book, to some extent.) The movie is equivalent to an indolent, undemanding and, hence, relaxing beach read. If only there were something sharp and pungent—besides Ellen DeGeneres' wisecracks—to keep you from drifting off.

DeGeneres' character Janet works in a bookstore owned by Helen McFarquhar, played by Kate Capshaw with a dourness that's almost unsettling. Helen is a role model for 40-ish women all over the cute little Connecticut town of Loblolly-by-the-Sea. She's smart, tough and impervious to all manner of mindlessness.

Until she comes across, by accident, an unsigned love letter whose passion and eloquence make even Helen's well-schooled heart gooey and moist. Who could have left this thing in her midst? A good candidate, in more ways than one, is George Mathias (Tom Selleck), the warmhearted fire chief who was once in love with Helen when both were in high school.

She concludes, for some reason, that the letter could have only come from Johnny (Tom Everett Scott, from "That Thing You Do"), a college student working in her store for the summer. Somehow, Johnny comes across the same letter and gets the idea that Helen had written it for his eyes only. After much preliminary twitching and ducking, older woman and younger man fall into each other's arms.

The letter hasn't finished its mischief. Janet finds it in the store shortly after George leaves, leading her to believe that its for her. From him. Meanwhile, Jennifer (Julianne Nicholson in a neat, spiky turn), the other student working in the store, is fighting her own crush on Johnny with proto-feminist rhetorical force fields. Then, just as things start to calm down, here come Helen's grandmother (Gloria Stuart) and mother (Blythe Danner) with their own baggage, literally and figuratively.

The device of a floating, mysterious mash note is as appealing a hook as it was in Schine's book. But while Maria Maggenti's screenplay captures some of the book's off-kilter sweetness, there's little magic in Peter Ho-sun Chan's direction. We're constantly told of Helen's magnetism and dynamism, but we don't feel any of it. And while some of the love scenes with Scott and Capshaw give off heat, you still aren't sure what they see in each other, though Scott manages to bring lots of charm and a little mystique into what could have been an empty role.

SIGHT AND SOUND, 10/99, p. 51, Leslie Felperin

Helen is a divorced single mother who owns a bookshop in Loblolly-by-the-Sea, Massachusetts. One day while opening the mail, she finds an unsigned love letter, addressed only to 'Darling', which speaks of the impossibility of the writer ever being with its addressee. Assuming it was meant for her, Helen wonders who her admirer could be. Her college-boy employee Johnny finds the letter and thinks Helen wrote it and intentionally left it for him to find. He drops a hint to let Helen know he's read it, which makes her think he's the letter's author. Meanwhile, Helen's best friend, the shop's manager Janet, finds the letter and assumes local fireman George wrote it for her, even though he has been carrying a torch for years for Helen. Meanwhile, Helen has started a secret affair with Johnny but still goes out on a couple of dates with George. When Helen tells Janet the letter wasn't for her, they argue and fall out.

Meanwhile, young Jennifer has developed a crush on Johnny and cuts all her hair off when he rebuffs her advances. Helen's mother Lillian and grandmother Eleanor return from an extended holiday, and Lillian comes out as a lesbian to Helen, revealing she's been in love for years with local historian Constance Scattergoods. The town's policeman Dan finds the letter and, pretending he wrote it, proposes with it to his girlfriend. Helen breaks off with Johnny in favour of George. Constance and Lillian find the letter and sit musing on how it had been lost—Constance had written it to Lillian years ago.

A romantic comedy focusing, unusually this year, on characters past puberty, *The Love Letter* seems genetically engineered to serve as video popcorn fuel for girlie nights in, its theatrical release a mere formality (although it has done surprisingly well at the box office in the US). Although ineffably slight with its soapy focus on a mature single mother torn between two equally toothsome if bland suitors, this film more than adequately meets its target audience's demands for cheerfully lachrymose drama. A certain bittersweetness—like milk chocolate chased with cheap beer—bubbles out its thematic concern with the 'wrong' turns and missed opportunities of love. Because Helen never found a secret note in a postcard sent years ago, she didn't get it together with George; in the present, because she finds an anonymous letter she ends up embroiled in an affair with the ardent young Johnny.

It's the sort of too-neat parallelism that screenwriting courses encourage, though presumably the conceit originates in Cathleen Schine's source novel, which is probably also to blame for the sickly, homey prose of the titular love letter in which the author waxes lyrical about its correspondent "when I tie my shoe ... when I peel an orange."

Funnily enough, the inspiration to make the film apparently sprang from it's leading actress and producer Kate Capshaw reading a review of the book. Legend has it that she bought the rights to the book out of her own pocket, but the $30,000 wasn't even noticed missing from the family cookie jar by her husband, Steven Spielberg. Nonetheless, his DreamWorks studio has produced the film, and a happy-slappy family atmosphere cosies over the proceedings like a backseat tartan rug (one of the Spielberg *enfants* even has a walk-on part).

Director Peter Ho-Sun Chan (formerly based in Hong Kong and director of *Comrades, Almost a Love Story*) coaxes warm, low-key and likeable ensemble performances from his cast of television actors and lesser-known stars and creates the occasional soft-focus effect by shooting through age-warped windows. On the evidence of the easy competence he displays here, he shouldn't have much trouble securing future work in Hollywood.

VILLAGE VOICE, 6/1/99, p. 119, Justine Elias

Helen MacFarquhar, a bookstore owner in a sleepy New England town, is the sort of wry, slightly disappointed heroine that Joan Fontaine used to play. It's not that love has passed her by—it's more like love stopped in when she was out doing errands. At the start of *The Love Letter*, a charming romance starring Kate Capshaw, Helen sorts through her mail, sees nothing but bills, and promptly forgets what she's doing. Surrounded by travel guides and maps, she's barely conscious of the missed connections in her own life.

Then a letter, minus its envelope, catches her eye. The message is a simple, earnest declaration of love, unsigned and addressed only to "my dearest." To Helen, celibate since her divorce, the letter reads like a prank—until she dares herself to wonder who might have written it. Though there's a funny sequence in which Helen imagines that everyone she sees—from her business partner (Ellen DeGeneres) to a truckload of firefighters—is reciting lines from the mysterious letter, the likely author is either Johnny (Tom Everett Scott), her young summer employee, or George (Tom Selleck), a pal from high school who's just gotten divorced himself.

Peter Ho-sun Chan, who directed *Comrades: Almost a Love Story*, lets *The Love Letter* unfold like a lighthearted thriller, and Capshaw, who has never had a better role, gives a thoughtful, understated performance. Capshaw developed this adaptation of the Cathleen Schine novel as a vehicle for herself, but the story finds time for a few other romances, all sparked, or reignited, by the same letter. Unlike recent epistolary love stories like *You've Got Mail* or *Message in a Bottle*, *The Love Letter* approaches romance with a real sense of humor. (Johnny, a college student who can explain the libretto of *Tosca*, is also cloddish enough to leave Helen a note that says, "I love you more than my car.") And it is rare to see a love scene that focuses on the man's, rather than the woman's, ecstatic face. It hardly matters, in the end, who actually wrote the love letter. Everybody, including the audience, will get the message.

Also reviewed in:
CHICAGO TRIBUNE, 5/21/99, Friday/p. A, Mark Caro
NEW YORK TIMES, 5/21/99, p. E16, Stephen Holden
VARIETY, 5/24-30/99, p. 37, Joe Leydon
WASHINGTON POST, 5/21/99, Weekend/p. 16, Desson Howe

LOVE REINVENTED

A Jour de Fête Films release of a compilation of 12 short films: *Director "Close To":* David Ottenhouse. *Director "Cherish":* Stephen Jones. *Director "So What?":* François Dupeyron. *Director "One Moment":* Pierre Salvadori. *Director "All Is Not Black":* Philippe Faucon. *Director "Night Hustler":* Anne Fountaine. *Director "Pregnant or Lesbian?":* Françoise Decaux-Thomlet. *Director "Inside":* Marion Vernoux. *Director "Tears of AIDS":* Paul Vecchiali. *Director "Burn Rubber":* Merzak Allouache. *Director "The Seagull":* Nils Tavernier. *Director "An Ordinary Night":* Jean-Claude Guiguet. *Screenplay (French with English subtitles). Running time:* 72 minutes. *MPAA Rating:* Not Rated.

LOS ANGELES TIMES, 11/25/99, Calendar/p. 22, Kevin Thomas

"Love Reinvented," is composed of 10 vignettes underwritten by the French government to depict the gay experience in the age of AIDS. The omnibus takes its name from one of the segments, each written and directed by young filmmakers. Jour De Fete, its American distributor, has added David Ottenhouse's "Close To" at the beginning and Stephen Jones' "Cherish" at the end to create a 72-minute feature.

The American bookends are the strongest of the dozen episodes. In the swift, succinct "Close To," Alexis Arquette plays a gay man who comes on to a handsome blond guy (Steve Wood) in a Manhattan subway train, but passion, once subsided, gives way to volatile, conflicting emotions and actions. Jones' "Cherish" is a heart-tugger in which a young man (John Adam), preparing to go on his first night out since the death of his lover (Russell Paige) from AIDS, is flooded with tender and passionate memories.

All 12 vignettes are concerned strictly with the young and good-looking, but the French entries go for a typically Gallic fatalism and cool detachment. Only two of the French 10 deal with women coping with AIDS. A number of them touch on AIDS directly, with one couple having sex first and thinking about safety after the fact; another couple takes off for a weekend with one of the men realizing he forgot to bring condoms. One of the most erotic segments features a handsome bodybuilder (Jean-Michel Monzoc) with a penchant for nude sunbathing who recalls a lover lost to AIDS. One of the most effective finds a young man passing himself off as a male hustler simply because he's lonely for companionship. All these and other vignettes have been done with finesse and dispatch. "Love Reinvented" adds up to an effective feature.

NEW YORK POST, 10/1/99, p. 62, Lou Lumenick

"Love Reinvented" is an uneven collection of largely dated shorts with gay and lesbian themes, mostly commissioned for a French government-funded television special as part of an AIDS-prevention campaign.

The 10 shorts were shot in 1996, just as a breakthrough in drug therapies was beginning to dramatically reduce the death toll from this modern-day plague.

Several of the stories are quite good, with the best being Jean-Claude Guiguet's "An Ordinary Night," in which a man sings happily as he bicycles through Paris to see his dying lover. But other segments, including several revolving around condoms (one featuring French screen legend Gerard Depardieu's hunky son Guillaume), feel more like public-service announcements.

VILLAGE VOICE, 10/5/99, p. 216, Dennis Lim

Love Reinvented is a package of 12 shorts—10 French films loosely dealing with AIDS and sexuality commissioned by the prolific production company ARTE, bookended by David Ottenhouse's *Close To,* a flashy anonymous-sex fantasy, and *Cherish,* a personal study of grief by Australian director Stephen Jones. Many of the French shorts play like stylized safe-sex commercials—in Pierre Salvadori's *One Moment,* for instance, the handheld camera assumes the perspective of an HIV-positive man, consumed by lust and out of rubbers. Only one entry, Jean-Claude Guiguet's *An Ordinary Night,* has lasting impact. A young man, visibly exhilarated, rides his bike through Paris on his way to, it turns out, a quiet, erotic evening with his hospitalized lover. A deft orchestration of numerous small, offhand gestures, Guiguet's film achieves a tenderness and poignancy that makes virtually everything else in the program seem glib or preachy.

Also reviewed in:
NEW YORK TIMES, 10/1/99, p. E27, Anita Gates

LOVE STINKS

An Independent Artists release of a Baumgarten/Prophet Entertainment production. *Executive Producer:* Craig Baumgarten and Jeff Franklin. *Producer:* Adam J. Merims and Todd Hoffman. *Director:* Jeff Franklin. *Screenplay:* Jeff Franklin. *Director of Photography:* Uta Briesewitz. *Editor:* Richard Candib. *Music:* Bennett Salvay. *Sound:* Phillip Seretti. *Casting:* Ferne Cassel. *Production Designer:* Pamela A. Marcotte. *Set Decorator:* Greta Grigorian. *Costumes:* Ileane C. Meltzer. *Running time:* 90 minutes. *MPAA Rating:* R.

CAST: French Stewart (Seth Winnick); Bridgette Wilson (Chelsea Turner); Bill Bellamy (Larry Garnett); Tyra Banks (Holly Garnet); Steve Hytner (Marty Mark); Jason Bateman (Jesse Travis); Tiffani-Amber Thiessen (Rebecca Melini); Shanna Moakler (Tawny).

LOS ANGELES TIMES, 9/10/99, Calendar/p. 4, Gene Seymour

[The following review by Gene Seymour appeared in a slightly different form in
NEWSDAY, 9/10/99, Part II/p. B9.]

Look, I'm as tired as you are of lame wish-fulfillment fairy tales being passed off as romantic comedies. I could use a stiff chaser of pure, uncut ribaldry as an antidote to the sappy "Runaway Brides" and "Sleepless in Seattles." And, just maybe, a movie with a title like "Love Stinks" could be expected to provide that bracing shot.

It's a shot all right. Straight through the groin and out the other end. Low comedy doesn't get any lower than "Love Stinks." And if you're willing to pay for the privilege of laughing at cats tortured for no good reason and beautiful women dehumanized into grotesque demons, then dig in. Just don't expect the rest of us to join you.

Writer-director Jeff Franklin, the culprit behind this crime against American comedy, is a veteran of such "family hour" sitcoms as "Full House" and "Hangin' With Mr. Cooper." He's taken his penchant for dumb, obvious jokes and cheesy, equally obvious complications to the big screen in telling this story of a successful TV producer named Seth (French Stewart) who falls for a blond, beautiful interior decorator named Chelsea (Bridgette Wilson).

Seth's skittishness toward commitment crashes violently against Chelsea's near-pathological urge to get married. She is goaded in her single-minded run to the altar by her friend Holly (how is it possible for Tyra Banks to look as unappealing as she does in this movie?), whose husband Larry ("MTV Jams" host Bill Bellamy) is Seth's writing partner. "When all else fails," Holly tells Chelsea, "don't underestimate the power of tears."

Tears, threats, ultimatums, deception—nothing Chelsea tries can get Seth to commit. So she takes legal action and sues for palimony. Told by his attorney that there's little he can do to avoid paying big money in this process, Seth says, "I could kill her and get away with it. This is L.A.!"

As anyone who's watched "3rd Rock From the Sun" will tell you, Stewart is a funny guy. His Harry Solomon is one of the great geek archetypes of network TV. But he's wasted here—to say the least—as a romantic lead. That is, if you can call someone who breaks wind in bed to annoy his would-be fiancee a "romantic" anything. "You are so unfunny!" Chelsea screams at Seth in one of the few moments of insight the movie permits her.

Any redeeming qualities? Yeah. The part where Seth and Chelsea dance along with an Elvis Presley/Ann-Margret clip from "Viva Las Vegas"—Chelsea dressed like Elvis, Seth like Ann-Margret.

Interesting, even vaguely kinky. But there's no follow-through. If you're going for bad taste, the least you can do is have the courage of your low-flying convictions.

NEW YORK POST, 9/10/99, p. 57, Rod Dreher

Anyone who survived "Life Stinks," the death rattle of Mel Brooks' filmmaking career, will approach any movie with the word "stinks" in the title with extreme caution.

That's good advice for "Love Stinks," a lame TV sitcom with big-screen ambition that's almost touching in its hopelessness.

"Love Stinks" is an audience pleaser, at least to judge by the raucous laughter at the screening. And to be honest, there are a handful of very funny scenes that keep the pic from being a total waste of time.

By and large, though, the comic sensibility at work here is a racier version of the lowbrow, broadly accessible style that made writer-director Jeff Franklin rich as the creator of "Full House."

Franklin's TV background is all over the "Love Stinks" plot. Seth Winnick ("3rd Rock from the Sun's" French Stewart) is a successful sitcom producer who falls head over heels for the hooterrific Chelsea (Bridgette Wilson) at the wedding of their pals Larry (Bill Bellamy) and Holly (supermodel Tyra Banks).

Chelsea's perfect: tall, gorgeous, fun to be with, and equally crazy about Seth. But she moves aggressively to take over Seth's life and force him to propose.

When he won't, Chelsea bares her fangs, blowing her cutesy manipulative-minx act up into a gynecological Gotterdammerung, complete with a palimony suit, a restraining order, and dirty tricks involving guy hair-care products.

"Love Stinks" is a forthrightly misogynistic movie, but the anti-female attitude is fairly jovial, about on the same level as Comedy Central's "The Man Show."

Thematically, the movie most resembles "The War of the Roses," but Franklin lacks either the chutzpah or the chops to bring off a gender-war satire as caustic and clever as that one.

His "Love Stinks" script does have its moments (including a smart, nervy ending), but his idea of cutting-edge comedy writing runs to the kind of vulgar, unfunny shtick that puts the gag in "gag."

He also lacks a first-rate cast. For "Simpsons" fans who may have wondered how actor Troy McClure ("You might remember me from... ") would be in a real-life movie, Stewart's mannered, stand-uppy performance as Seth gives a pretty good idea.

As for Wilson's acting, let's just say her va-va-va-voomish turn as a scantily clad lollapalooza represents career peaks.

Also reviewed in:
CHICAGO TRIBUNE, 9/10/99, Friday/p. D, Barbara Shulgasser
NEW YORK TIMES, 9/10/99, p. E23, Anita Gates
VARIETY, 9/13-19/99, p. 42, Robert Koehler

LOVERS OF THE ARCTIC CIRCLE

A Fine Line Features release of a Sogetel production. *Executive Producer:* Txarli Llorente and Fernando de Garcillán. *Producer:* Fernando Bovaira and Enrique López Lavigne. *Director:* Julio Medem. *Director of Photography:* Gonzalo F. Berridi. *Screenplay (Spanish with English subtitles):* Julio Medem. *Editor:* Iván Aledo. *Music:* Alberto Iglesias. *Sound:* Ivan Marin. *Sound Editor:* Polo Aledo and Dulce Juanita. *Casting:* Sara Bilbatua. *Production Designer:* Satur Idarreta, Karmele Soler, Estibaliz Markiegi, and Itziar Arrieta. *Art Director:* Satur Marreta and Montse Sanz. *Set Decorator:* Jukka Uusitalo. *Costumes:* Estibaliz Markiegi. *Make-up:* Karmele Soler. *Running time:* 112 minutes. *MPAA Rating:* Not Rated.

CAST: Fele Martinez (Otto); Najwa Nimri (Ana); Nancho Novo (Alvaro, Otto's Father); Maru Valdivielso (Olga, Ana's Mother); Peru Medem (Otto as a Child); Sara Valiente (Ana as a Child); Victor Hugo Oliveira (Otto as a Teenager); Kristel Diaz (Ana as an Adolescent); Pep Munné (Javier, Otto's Teacher); Jaroslaw Bielski (Alvaro Midelman); Joost Siedhoff (Otto Midelman); Rosa Morales (Ana's Teacher); Beate Jensen (Otto's Mother); Petri Helmo (Aki); Outi Alanen (Messenger); Maria Isasi-Isasmendi (Shop Assistant); Angela Castilla (Boarding House Landlady).

LOS ANGELES TIMES, 4/23/99, Calendar/p. 23, Kenneth Turan

Passion. Fate. Eternal Love. Romantic Destiny. "Lovers of the Arctic Circle" is so emotionally emphatic, and so self-conscious, that it's hard to talk about it without resorting to capital letters. A poetic meditation on the price demanded by deep and true attachment, this new work by Spanish filmmaker Julio Medem is a litmus test that will separate the deep-dish die-hard romantics from the rest of the crowd.

A gifted writer-director, Medem has constructed an elaborate film that deals with one of life's biggest questions—is there someone out there just for me?—in a way that's delicate, accomplished and just on the right side of excessive. Complexly constructed, "Lovers" whirls you around like a carousel as it ponders the nature of soul mates and wonders if, in fact, it's inevitable that they'll spend the rest of their lives together.

While Medem's concerns have a lot in common with the ones animating fellow Spanish-language director Luis Mendoki in "Message in a Bottle," the moviemaking attitude couldn't be more different. Where "Message" is mainstream studio filmmaking all the way, "Lovers" is a stylish European art film that has fragmented its story into a thousand pieces, thrown them up in the air and fed it all back to us in a display of narrative legerdemain that makes intuitive sense even when we're not quite following it from point to point.

The film's protagonists are Otto (Fele Martinez) and Ana (Najwa Nimri), and if you noticed that both their names are palindromes, you'll probably also notice that the film features two Alvaros, another Otto, and all kinds of elaborate wordplay.

It's not only the words and character names that get repeated; visual motifs and images, like flying and near-collisions with streetcars, appear again and again as well. The film alternates telling the story from Otto's and Ana's points of view, but it should be clear by now that relating it strictly chronologically would be too boring for this adventurous a director.

Otto's voice-over is heard first. After a flash of him as an adult, we're taken back to Otto the 8-year-old child (Peru Medem, the director's son), trying to come to grips with the breakup of his parents' marriage and vowing his belief in the durability of eternal love.

Chasing an errant soccer ball, Otto ends up following fellow 8-year-old Ana (Sara Valiente) running for reasons of her own, trying to escape the knowledge that her father has just died. When she and Otto come face to face, he falls in love while she wonders if maybe her father's spirit has come to rest in this boy.

Being at several kinds of cross-purposes, psychological and otherwise, is one of the constants that defines Ana's and Otto's lives during the 17 years that "Lovers" covers. Another is that coincidence (the film, which treats chance as destiny, is rife with all manner of them) is a major player in everyone's lives.

Making things more complex is that Ana's mother, Olga (Maru Valdivielso), and Otto's father, Alvaro (Nancho Novo), fall in love—a development the children unintentionally influence. Which creates yet another layer of difficulties when the pair (now played by Victor Hugo Oliveira and Kristel Diaz) become mutually besotted teenagers.

"Lovers of the Arctic Circle" (a title that, not surprisingly, ends up having both literal and metaphorical meanings), does not hold anything back, drenching us in its own waves of emotion. Because of the fragmented way in which it's told, we are both ahead of and behind its characters, knowing and not knowing where things are headed. That's fate for you, after all.

NEW YORK POST, 4/9/99, p. 58, Hannah Brown

The ideal audience for "Lovers of the Arctic Circle" would be 18-year-olds in love for the first time.

Perhaps only this group—and college literature majors—could fully appreciate the mix of romance, symbolism, coincidence, foreshadowing and ponderous solemnity of Julio Medem's latest feature.

The highly praised Spanish writer/director has chosen an ambitious approach to a complicated love story.

"Lovers" uses several pairs of actors to tell the story of a passionately intense love affair between Otto and Ana, who meet at age 8, become lovers as teenagers, and play a global game of hide-and-seek when they are in their 20s.

Told alternately from the point of view of each of the two main characters, "Lovers" begins with a meeting of the adult Ana and Otto (Najwa Nimri and Fele Martinez), then backtracks to explore the history of their relationship.

The story unfolds as an elaborate series of coincidences involving accidental deaths, planes, car crashes, palindromes, a German soldier who bombed Guernica and, most significant of all, a fascination both the lovers have with the Arctic Circle.

The two meet in Spain, just after the death of Ana's father in a car crash, and Otto's father's announcement that he is moving out. Ana is convinced that the spirit of her father is returning to her through Otto.

When Otto and Ana are teenagers, their passion turns sexual.

But Otto is stricken with guilt after his mother dies suddenly, and he runs away.

He becomes a courier pilot on an airline that flies between Spain and Finland. Separately, both he and Ana are drawn to the Arctic Circle.

Alas, the many coincidences don't have the emotional resonance for audiences that they apparently had for the director.

The film begins to feel unpleasantly contrived instead of romantically inevitable.

It's a shame, because the story is imaginative, the direction lyrical and evocative, and the acting (particularly by the younger children) sensitive.

NEWSDAY, 4/9/99, Part II/p. B11, John Anderson

If the director is God—and plenty of actors, grips and caterers will tell you that one part of any filmmaking team believes this to be true—then the resident deity should be unseen and unobtrusive; the moving hand should not leave messy (albeit divine) fingerprints. And even if there is no free will, the viewer should be able to believe in one—or else, whatever happens is merely caprice.

In "Lovers of the Arctic Circle," a very ambitious but overly godly movie by Julio Medem ("Cows"), two lovers find themselves at the top of the world and remember their intertwined pasts: How little Otto (Peru Medem) and little Ana (Sara Valiente)—twin palindromes, in case the foreshadowing was not obvious enough—meet at school; Otto's father, Alvaro (Nancho Novo) will leave Otto's mother for Ana's (Maru Valdivielso); they become less than siblings but more than lovers, and their indivisible hunger and love for each other will progress throughout their lives.

Romantic and earnest but stylized to the point of parody, "Lovers" does ring true in its sense of eros-inspired self-absorption—that is, if we are to accept as fantasy so much of what seems to be just that. The older Otto and Ana (Fele Martinez, Najwa Nimri) must weather the guilt and anguish of their paired-up parents and the death of Otto's mother—which is greeted by such unhinged grief and irrational anger that it disturbs the psychology of the film. But then, so many things do. I couldn't help feeling, after one too many coincidences, a deep feeling of suspicion.

"Sliding Doors" anyone? That film's "what if" scenarios were derivative, too, but they worked better than those of "Lovers of the Arctic Circle." Actually, when Krzysztof Kieslowski was devising the Chinese boxes of "Double Life of Veronique" or the "Three Colors" trilogy, the enchantment came via the utter frankness with which he presented the fantastic elements of his characters' lives and connections, as well as the audacity that allowed him to do it. In "Lovers of the Arctic Circle," Medem exhibits audacity, but there seems little chance that any audience is going to achieve a suspension of disbelief. Most of the elements—from the Terence Davis-inspired flourishes to the coincidences that pepper the plot, are strictly Medem, wholly Medem and nothing but Medem. It's pranksterism in the guise of poetry and as such left at least one viewer cold.

SIGHT AND SOUND, 2/00, p. 48, Jonathan Romney

Madrid, the present. Schoolchildren Otto and Ana become fascinated with each other. After Otto's parents separate, his father Alvaro and Ana's mother Olga become lovers. Later, the adolescent Otto leaves his mother to move in with Ana, Olga and Muaro. Otto tells Ana he is named after a German pilot encountered by his Basque grandfather after the bombing of the town of Guernica. Although their parents see them as siblings, Otto and Ana become lovers and develop a mutual fascination for Lapland.

Years later, Olga is approached by a man named Alvaro Midelman who recruits her as a television newsreader, she also becomes his lover. After finding his mother dead, Otto becomes angry and self-destructive, and is nearly killed in a sledge accident. He leaves home and takes a job as a pilot flying mail to Finland. Ana takes up teaching and moves in with Javier, Otto's old schoolteacher. When Olga moves to Australia, Ana too feels the need to leave; Midelman tells her she can use his father's cabin in Rovaniemi, Finland, on the Arctic Circle. She writes to Otto, telling him that Alvaro Midelman's father was the German pilot after whom he was named.

Otto flies back to Finland, but bales out of his plane, landing close to the cabin. Hearing news of the plane's crash, Ana returns to Rovaniemi, and is happily reunited with Otto. In another ending, however, Ana is run over and killed just as Otto arrives in town.

Basque director Julio Medem may be cinema's last full-blown symbolist. Not only does he fill his films with recurring images, but he also encourages us to read philosophical significance into them. So *The Lovers of the Artic Circle* begins with the midnight sun skating across the Finnish horizon, while the hero's voiceover narration ponders the notion of a life ruled by circles.

The flip side of such questionable profundities is the possibility that everything is simply a formal game generated from abstractions (opposites, doubles, mirror images) and the occasional multilingual pun (finish/Finnish; the Spanish word *aqui*, and the Finnish name Aki). *Lovers of the Arctic Circle* ostensibly adopts a more realistic mode than Medem's last film *Tierra*, where the rural setting could well have been another planet. *Lovers* is a relatively small scale story of romance and destiny, but its geometrical construction and deployment of outrageous coincidence make it a genuinely alien confection. What looks at first sight like a grand *Zhivago*esque tale of fated love and separation keeps devolving into a compendium of polarities and circles. There are two characters named Otto, two named Alvaro, two lovers both acutely aware of having reversible names; the narrative too is built on repetition, doubling, circularity and presumably—although this really issues a challenge to analysis—the palindrome principle.

The story defies easy synopsis, partly because it requires reassembly from Otto's and Ana's alternating chapters, and partly because the lovers are played at different ages by three different sets of actors. To complicate things further, the actors (Fele Martinez and Najwa Nimri) who play the mature lovers appear in the flashback showing the German pilot ("Otto el piloto") meeting his future wife, a sequence which duplicates Otto and Ana's first meeting.

As if this jigsaw principle weren't alienating enough, Medem tests us further by spinning us what purports to be a narrative of grand destiny, while repeatedly exposing its twists as cavalier string-pulling. Without warning, Medem will send his characters' lives in an unforeseen direction by having a man walk in out of nowhere to seduce Olga—a man who happens to share the name of her lover Alvaro. The notion of plausibility is swallowed up in an intricate game, in which every element is there simply to reflect another, and in which every part has to be accounted for before the game can reach a satisfying conclusion.

But would this love story seem any more plausible stripped of Medem's manipulations? Or is he, rather, following the classic strategy of self reflexive fiction, using the ready-made label destiny to expose those petrified conventions we like to think of as the natural, organic shapes of narrative?

Lovers seems to be even more explicitly about narrative than Medem's other films, and so this means *Lovers of the Arctic Circle* invests slightly less in visual artifice. The images themselves, apart from an extravagant snow-bound sequence, are low key by his standards: classrooms, the generally prosaic Finnish landscape, cramped interiors suffused with a distancing and already polar blue chill. Medem here seems less interested in specific images than in the way they interlock. This is an intensely edited film, with emphasis on staggering leaps: a lurching car in a near-miss accident abruptly vaults the narrative several years into the future.

Medem's cinema often depends heavily on the performers' charisma, and his repertory casting has established his work as an autonomous zone in which films refer to each other. Here his customary leads Emma Suárez and Carmelo Gómez are gone, replaced by the slightly pallid duo of Martinez and Nimri (rather more arresting are the eerily blank-eyed pair who play their childhood selves).

The only familiar face is the saturnine Nancho Novo, here playing a rapidly ageing patriarch, as if to suggest that Medem's cinema is pulling up roots, moving on. Medem's Basque imagery already going underground in *Tierra* also continues to recede. The scene has shifted to Madrid (Otto and Ana have a beautifully choreographed non-encounter in the Plaza Mayor), while the only explicitly Basque factor is the reference to Guernica, which allows for a multiple flourish of taboo busting: not-quite siblings Ana and Otto neck on the sofa, as her mother on television reads a news item about German reparations for the bombing. The scene supplies more grist to the film's already complex incestuous thematics, and it's only appropriate, after all, that a film about quasi-incestuous passion should be this audaciously, self-devouringly involuted.

VILLAGE VOICE, 4/13/99, p. 150, Jessica Winter

Hard as it is to begrudge a film as meticulously constructed and deeply felt as Julio Medem's *Lovers of the Arctic Circle*, this avowedly whimsical, magic-realist take on destiny remains pinned to the ground by the obsessive exactitude of its own symbolism. It seems as though its every image has a twin in metaphor, and every tossed-off remark is meant as a secret maxim. Like the clandestine sweethearts of its title, this Spanish-language movie leads a double life, and soon enough begins to slip up and exhaust itself.

The film's stamina is tested by a daunting plot, told in alternating chapters titled "Otto" and "Ana." They meet at age eight, when Otto's parents are breaking up and Ana's father has just died; she convinces herself that her father's spirit has entered Otto's body. Remarkable timing of a different sort figures in when, as teenagers, Otto and Ana consummate their love about the same time that their parents decide to move in together. Tragedy soon spurs Otto's departure and disappearance; he becomes a pilot, flying between Spain and Finland, while troubles of her own impel Ana, incredibly, toward Finland as well. There she meets another Otto, an old man, and decides he is the German pilot for whom her Otto was named.

Ana feels that this final coincidence is a harbinger of (unspecified) destiny; she sits down outside her cottage and literally waits for fate to happen. Ana's chosen religion is one of ironic accidents, while Otto locates a guiding creed in the motions of orbits and cycles. But Otto's repeated declaration that "Life is a circle"—a belief underscored by his and Ana's palindromic names—would grate even if Elton John hadn't beaten him to that punch, while Ana's passive notion of destiny leaves her simply idle. Najwa Nimri's brittle, melancholy performance, however, beautifully evokes Ana's restless inertia; her huge eyes are deep pools stirred from beneath.

Desire is just about all Ana does, and though desire's literal objective may be death, there needn't have been so much of it here; the messier, better scenario would have let more folks stick around and try to resolve things themselves. Since writer-director Medem takes the melodramatic easy way out, he invites surely unwelcome comparison between his film and *Sliding Doors,* with

LOVERS OF THE ARCTIC CIRCLE   855

its rotating narrative and fixation on what-if coincidences. *Lovers of the Arctic Circle* exhibits
no more recognition than Ana does that chance can't be contrived; though the wonderful Nimri
braces her character for a revelation, the film's final events seem as predictable as the path of a
compass.

Also reviewed in:
CHICAGO TRIBUNE, 5/7/99, Friday/p. A, John Petrakis
NEW YORK TIMES, 4/7/99, p. E1, Janet Maslin

LUCIE AUBRAC

An October Films release of a Renn Productions/TF1Films production with the participation of
Rhône-Alpes Cinema and the Centre national de la cinématographie (CNC) with the participation
of Canal+. *Executive Producer:* Pierre Grunstein. *Producer:* Claude Berri. *Director:* Claude
Berri. *Screenplay (French with English subtitles):* Claude Berri. *Based on the novel "Ils
partiront dans l'ivresse":* Lucie Aubrac. *Director of Photography:* Vincenzo Marano. *Editor:*
Herve de Luze. *Music:* Philippe Sarde. *Sound:* Gerard Lamps. *Sound Editor:* Michel
Klochendler. *Casting:* Gerard Moulevrier. *Production Designer:* Olivier Radot. *Costumes:*
Sylvie Gautrelet. *Make-up:* Michel Deruelle and Jacques Clemente. *Running time:* 116 minutes.
MPAA Rating: R.

CAST: Carole Bouquet (Lucie); Daniel Auteuil (Raymond); Patrice Chereau (Max/Jean
Moulin); Jean-Roger Milo (Maurice); Eric Boucher (Serge); Heino Ferch (Barbie); Bernard
Verley (Charles-Henri); Jean Martin (Paul Lardanchet); Marie Pillet (Marie); Maxime Henry
(Booboo); Alain Maratrat (Lassagne); Franck de la Personne (Aubry); Pascal Greggory
(Hardy); Jean-Louis Richard (Mr. Henry); Hans Wyprachtiger (German Colonel); Andrzej
Seweryn (Lieutenant Schlondorff); Gregiore Oestermann (Pierrot the Forger); Olga Grumberg
(Judith); Jacques Marchand (Justice of the Peace); Remy Darcy (Colonel Schwartzfeld); Hubert
Saint Macary (Dr. Dugoujon); Jean-Claude Bourbault (Colonel Lacaze); Yves Neff (Bruno);
Jacques Bonnaffe (Pascal); Alain Sachs (Claude B.); Roland Amstutz (Attorney); Jean-Claude
Grumberg (Raymond's Father); Daniele Goldmann (Raymond's Mother).

LOS ANGELES TIMES, 9/24/99, Calendar/p. 12, Kevin Thomas

Claude Berri's "Lucie Aubrac" has it all: a tender romance, acute suspense, terrific acting, and
a camera style and score that are beautiful yet understated. Most important, it has an impeccable
sense of period and draws from a true story that casts light on one of France's darkest, most
painful eras.

This is a major work, possessing breadth, depth and passion, by a formidable writer-director
whose string of hit comedies has rightly become overshadowed by his more recent evocations of
the past drawn from literature, most notably Pagnol's "Manon of the Spring" and its sequel "Jean
de Florette" and Zola's "Germinal." "Lucie Aubrac" looks to be a best foreign film Oscar
contender—from a filmmaker who won an Oscar on his first try, for the short film "Le Poulet"
(The Chicken) in 1963.

To counter the strategy of the wily attorney for Klaus Barbie, the sadistic Gestapo chief of
Lyon, at last brought to trial for crimes against humanity in the 1980s, Resistance heroine Lucie
Aubrac decided to write her memoirs, published in France in 1984 and in the U.S. in 1993 as
"Outwitting the Gestapo." She was specifically concerned about the attorney calling into question
certain members of the Resistance's attitudes toward the arrest of leader Jean Moulin, who was
attempting to unite groups of differing political allegiances in the common cause of sabotaging
the Germans.

With the blessing of Aubrac and her husband, Raymond, Berri brought their story to the screen
accurately but with some freely acknowledged—and actually relatively minor—dramatic license
in regard to the activities of the Resistance for reasons of structure and pacing. This enabled the
film to play like a romantic thriller—the essence of the Aubracs' tale.

Aubrac was the Resistance code name for Raymond Samuel (Daniel Auteuil), a Jew, and Lucie Bernard (Carole Bouquet), a Gentile, who married nearly 60 years ago and decided to keep their wartime name. When the film opens, in March 1943, the couple and their infant son are living in a charming 19th century home on a fine old tree-shaded avenue in Lyon. Raymond takes on daring missions for the Resistance, while Lucie is a dedicated and inspired grade school teacher concerned that her pupils understand the importance of learning from the past and remembering for the future all they are living through in the present. On the surface Lyon seems not only a beautiful place but also one marked by civility, despite the Nazi occupation. But as anyone who has seen Marcel Ophuls' Oscar-winning"Hotel Terminus: Klaus Barbie—His Life and Times" (1988) knows, the city was a place of constant and lethal danger under the Butcher of Lyon's reign of terror.

Yet the Aubracs respond to the increasingly tense atmosphere with a passionate love for each other that flowers and strengthens in times of peril. When Raymond is arrested in an apartment that is ostensibly headquarters for a black market operation in sugar and noodles and the state attorney suspects rightly that it is a front for a Resistance meeting place, Lucie boldly pays a visit to the attorney. Threatening him with assassination in the name of the Resistance and its leader, Charles De Gaulle, she swiftly wins her husband's release.

The next time will be tougher, for Raymond is caught as he is about to join a high-level meeting with "Max"—the mysteriously betrayed and soon-to-be-martyred (at the hands of Barbie) Moulin (Patrice Chereau). (The June 21, 1943, meeting was in the office/home of a Dr. Dugoujon, who had as a patient Berri, who would turn 11 on July 1; the same Dr. Dugoujon allowed Berri to shoot inside that very abode.) Lucie becomes immediately determined to stop at nothing to save her husband's life and those of his imprisoned colleagues.

Berri brings to bear the authority and ease of 35 years of filmmaking to make Lucie's story, a wondrous interplay of luck and pluck, totally persuasive with his writing and direction. Bouquet and Auteuil make the Aubracs seem a couple of exceptional devotion, character, intelligence and courage. Berri shows just how barbarous Barbie and his minions could be, without lingering over their savagery, and Berri manages to make the Aubracs' story seem as authentic as it is entertaining; indeed, "Lucie Aubrac" plays like Fred Zinnemann's suspenseful and exciting 1973 classic "The Day of the Jackal," based on Frederick Forsyth's bestseller about a plot to assassinate De Gaulle.

The occupation, which brought out the best and the worst in the French, and the role of the Resistance have been tackled by French filmmakers of the caliber of Jean-Pierre Melville and Rene Clement, but have rarely been dealt with since Ophuls' scathing 1971 documentary "The Sorrow and the Pity" opened up old wounds. More than enough time has passed since then for "Lucie Aubrac" to make a fresh impact, both as a love story and as commentary on a treacherous time for good people.

NEW YORK, 9/27/99, p. 81, Peter Rainer

Claude Berri's *Lucie Aubrac*, set in 1943, is based on the true account of a woman in the French Resistance (Carole Bouquet) who engineered the liberation of her husband (Daniel Auteuil), also a Resistance fighter, from Montluc prison in Lyon during the German occupation. It's not a particularly artful piece of work, but the best parts—the way Lucie methodically, implacably sets up the Germans and the French Fascist—have the dash of first-rate melodrama.

NEW YORK POST, 9/17/99, p. 51, Jonathan Foreman

"Lucie Aubrac," the Resistance code name of a still living French heroine who risked her life to spring her husband from a Gestapo prison, is a restrained, oddly undramatic film by Claude Berri (the maker of "Jean de Florette").

Berri keeps to the facts in telling Aubrac's remarkable story, but he's unable to resist various cliches, especially those that exaggerate the impressiveness of French opposition to the Germans.

When Resistance fighter Raymond Aubrac (Daniel Auteuil) gets arrested by the French police for black marketeering, his wife, Lucie (Carole Bouquet), gets him released by visiting the French prosecutor at home and threatening him with assassination by Gaullist agents.

Raymond then changes his name and identity, and carries on with his important underground work in Lyons.

But a key meeting with Jean "Max" Moulin (Patrice Chereau), De Gaulle's Resistance chief, is raided by the Gestapo. Raymond is again arrested, along with Max and all but one of the Resistance members at the meeting.

All are interrogated by the infamous Klaus Barbie, and one of them cracks. As a result, Raymond is sentenced to death. Lucie pregnant with her second child—then hatches a new and daring escape plan.

Auteuil, a fine actor who's ugly yet handsome in that Gallic way, gives a typically subtle and accomplished performance as a quiet hero.

Bouquet, who's better known as a beauty than an actress, is steely and all but inscrutable in the title role: You see her passion in her deeds rather than in her face.

SIGHT AND SOUND, 2/98, p. 46, Chris Darke

Lyon, March, 1943. Resistance activist Raymond Samuel, known under the pseudonym "François Vallet", dynamites a train and is arrested. Raymond's wife, who goes under the pseudonym "Lucie Aubrac", manages to get her husband released by threatening the local prosecutor with Free French reprisals. In facilitating Raymond's release, Lucie is upholding a pact that, come what may, they will be together every May 14, their anniversary. Raymond is renamed "Claude Ermelin" and is temporarily put in charge of the Resistance's Northern Zone. In June, betrayed by an internal informer, Raymond and others are captured at a meeting by the Gestapo. One of their number escapes. The group is imprisoned and tortured by Police Chief Klaus Barbie, who is intent on discovering the identity of their leader, Max. Barbie knows that Raymond is "François Vallet", and has him sentenced to death.

Lucie plans a way to liberate her husband and determines to kill the escapee, Hardy, who is assumed to be the informer. Discovering that she is pregnant with Raymond's second child, she asks Barbie to release "Claude Ermelin" but he refuses. Via a Resistance contact in the Paymaster General's Office, Lucie is finally able to request a marriage *in extremis* to Raymond in order to spare her family the shame of her giving birth out of wedlock.

A meeting between the two is set up by the Nazi superiors and Lucie arranges with her Resistance cell to spring Raymond during his transport back to prison. The plan fails when a getaway car stalls. When the couple are married, though, the plan is successfully executed. Lucie and Raymond escape south where they learn that Raymond's parents have been arrested. The family is flown to Britain, where they are to join up with Charles de Gaulle's Free French.

Most contemporary French films about the Resistance are necessarily revisionist accounts. They attempt to reconcile present-day French attitudes to the past which, when it comes to the still thorny issue of the Occupation, oscillate awkwardly between national shame at collaboration and the celebration of Resistance heroism. Jacques Audiard's *A Self-Made Hero* had the virtue of inscribing the revisionist approach into the fabric of its own deeply sceptical fiction, with its hero airbrushing his personal history to blend in with the Resistance movement.

It's the precarious balance between the first person, anecdotal account of history and the Grand Narrative approach that always underlies the 'history film'. Claude Berri's *Lucie Aubrac* proves no exception. Based on Aubrac's true-life account of wartime exploits, *Ils partiront dans l'ivresse (Outwitting the Gestapo)*, Berri's film bills itself as "a true love story". The instant critical reflex is to dismiss it as yet another lavishly budgeted French costume drama, doing for the occupation what *Indochine* did for French end-of-Empire traumas. The standard argument against mainstream French film accounts of the Resistance is that they create a too easy *post hoc* identification with the freedom fighters, mythologising the national resistance to Nazi occupation rather than subjecting it to awkward enquiry.

In presenting itself as a true-life love story with a Resistance setting, *Lucie Aubrac* is more concerned with the emotional than the political lives of Lucie and Raymond. In itself, this is a potentially fascinating subject, suggesting a study of the incredible pressures that Resistance fighters had to endure in combining armed subterfuge with everyday anonymity. The basic dramatic dynamic is the constant threat of discovery or betrayal but, strangely enough, *Lucie Aubrac* does little to exploit this element.

Rather, dramatic tension arises more from the physical separation of the two characters—Lucie's constant scheming to get Raymond released while he languishes in prison under the threat of execution. Their separation and the promise of their being reunited works to up the emotional ante and delivers one of the film's strongest scenes. Lucie, claiming she was abandoned by Raymond after he impregnated her, demands to be married to him *in extremis* in order to avoid shaming her military (by implication, Vichy supporting) family. She confronts him in the office of a Nazi functionary where the couple must act as if they barely know one another and Berri skilfully uses the dynamics of denial and suppressed emotion generated across the film to construct a powerfully emotional scene. Auteuil is well cast as Raymond, and ably reprises his now stock-in-trade depiction of emotional repression previously refined in *Un coeur en hiver* and *La Séparation*.

In fashioning an emotional portrait of Resistance heroism, *Lucie Aubrac* fits alongside other accounts dramatising the role of women fighting against Nazi occupation—notably René Clément's *Le Jour et l'heure* (1962) and Jean-Pierre Melville's *L'Armée des ombres* (1969), both with Simone Signoret. Moreover, the film plays explicitly on discourses of the family, featuring both real families and familial social groups, up to the national level. Thus different plot strands concern Lucie, the mother of Raymond's son, expecting their next child, and Raymond's parents, who refuse to conceal their Jewish identity by changing their surname Samuel. These elements are bought together in a scene when, having been saved by the Resistance and in hiding with Lucie, Raymond learns that his parents have been arrested. The implication is clear: they will die for his freedom and as he weeps for them, Lucie cradles his head on her belly, his child kicking inside her.

There's a certain pleasure to be had in the role-reversal that Berri effects in this scene and others, with Auteuil as the terrified Resistance fighter and Carole Bouquet (who replaced Juliette Binoche after a month's shooting) as a ruthlessly resourceful matriarch. But it's a strange kind of war thriller that sacrifices much needed suspense in order to generate the oceanic feeling of the French as one big anti-Nazi family.

VILLAGE VOICE, 9/28/99, p. 126, Leslie Camhi

"What's history for?" a schoolgirl asks in *Lucie Aubrac*, Claude Berri's film about the eponymous French Resistance fighter, transforming her memoirs into a period piece, tidy and dour as a history lesson. Glamorous Carole Bouquet is woefully miscast as Lucie—wife, mother, teacher, and, with her husband Raymond (Daniel Auteuil), a key figure in Resistance circles. Berri's film focuses on an incident in 1943, when Raymond, at an undercover meeting in Lyon with their leader, Jean Moulin (Patrice Chéreau), is caught by the Gestapo. Aubrac's liberation from prison was orchestrated by his wife, with the help of their companions-in-arms.

This extraordinary story still sparks controversy in France, but in Berri's hands, it never comes alive. Auteuil provides some warmth, but Bouquet's performance is one-dimensional, and Chéreau, stiff in his hat and scarf, resembles an animated photograph. The physiognomies of certain Jewish characters come perilously close to caricature. And when Lucie tries to comfort Raymond, who learns that his Jewish parents have been deported, she strikes a note as jarring as Roberto Benigni's little boy, who screams "We won!" after leaving Auschwitz.

The passion that unites them remains a mystery, illuminated only briefly when Raymond's former cellmate meets with Lucie, and, to gain her trust, recounts intimate details her husband has told him of their life together. The scene is uncommonly moving, but it also signals what's missing from the rest of this movie, which remains a shadow play of historical icons, rather than a portrait of people in love.

Also reviewed in:
CHICAGO TRIBUNE, 10/29/99, Friday/p. C, Barbara Shulgasser
NEW REPUBLIC, 9/13 & 20/99, p. 36, Stanley Kauffmann
NEW YORK TIMES, 9/17/99, p. E29, Stephen Holden
VARIETY, 2/24-3/2/97, p. 80, Derek Elley

LUCINDA'S SPELL

A Zero Pictures release of a Golden Shadow Pictures production in association with Motion Picture Capital. *Executive Producer:* Joe Chavez. *Producer:* Michael Kastenbaum. *Director:* Jon Jacobs. *Screenplay:* Jon Jacobs. *Director of Photography:* Jaime Reynoso. *Editor:* Clayton Halsey. *Music:* Niki Jack. *Sound:* John Delpin. *Production Designer:* Andy Peach and Jana Pasek. *Art Director:* Jay Poggi and Ricky B. *Costumes:* Keith Sayer. *Running time:* 104 minutes. *MPAA Rating:* Not Rated.

CAST: Jon Jacobs (Jason, First Horn); Christina Fulton (Lucinda Bale); Shannah Baltz (Beatrice); Leon Herbert (Maddison); Angie Green (Chickory); Alex Koronzay (Natalie); J. C. Brandy (Betsy); John El (Geroge); Fatt Natt (Jules); Brother Randy (Jim); Ajax Davis (Severain); Judy Garwood (Ms. Worth); Bliss Davis (Gloria).

NEW YORK POST, 9/10/99, p. 56, Hannah Brown

"Lucinda's Spell," the story of a free-spirited New Orleans prostitute who dabbles in witchcraft, looks and sounds great.

Unfortunately, despite its MTV-video design and eclectic soundtrack, it gets bogged down in a mawkish, New Age sensibility.

Director/writer/star Jon Jacobs plays Jason, a descendant of Merlin who comes to New Orleans not knowing he has a child with Lucinda (Christina Fulton).

This frenetic indie features lots of raunchy talk and some artfully staged sex scenes, but exotic beauty Fulton gives an overly energetic performance that grates.

And she's not helped by the cliched script (sample: "In layman's terms, I believe love is magic").

"Lucinda's Spell" just isn't as sexy or outrageous as it wants to be.

VILLAGE VOICE , 9/14/99, p. 146, Jessica Winter

Kicking and screaming for inappropriate reactions of any kind is the wannabe-cult movie *Lucinda's Spell*, a pillowcore mishmash of catfights, covens, and frustrated mother love. Out to win a spell contest and win back custody of her son, the eponymous prostitute and sometime witch is played by Christina Fulton, who chicken-stomps her way through the role with Elizabeth Berkley-esque gusto. Lucinda's willing and able, but the movie bearing her name is a cold cocktease, fettered by a surfeit of story and a disgraceful dearth of sex. Reverse the plot-to-shtup ratio and you'd have yourself a boffo porno with some posh set design and fabulous costumes, and then you'd be getting somewhere.

Also reviewed in:
NEW YORK TIMES, 9/10/99, p. E10, Anita Gates
VARIETY, 6/22-28/98, p. 54, Leonard Klady

MAGNOLIA

A New Line Cinema release of a Joanne Sellar/Ghoulardi Film Company production. *Executive Producer:* Michael De Luca and Lynn Harris. *Producer:* Joanne Sellar. *Director:* Paul Thomas Anderson. *Screenplay:* Paul Thomas Anderson. *Director of Photography:* Robert Elswit. *Editor:* Dylan Tichenor. *Music:* Jon Brion. *Music Editor:* Paul Rabjohns. *Sound:* John Pritchett and (music) Dennis Sands. *Sound Editor:* Richard King. *Casting:* Cassandra Kulukundis. *Production Designer:* William Arnold and Mark Bridges. *Art Director:* David Nakabayashi. *Set Designer:* Conny Boettger-Marinos. *Set Decorator:* Chris Spellman. *Set Dresser:* Martin Milligan, Richard Anderson, Bryan Hurley Shupper, Matt Shepherd and Wes Long. *Claudia's Artwork:* Fiona Apple and Melora Walters. *Special Effects:* Lou Carlucci. *Costumes:* Mark

Bridges. *Make-up:* Tina K. Roesler. *Make-up (Tom Cruise):* Lois Burwell. *Make-up (Julianne Moore):* Elaine Offers. *Stunt Coordinator:* Webster Whinery. *Running time:* 180 minutes. *MPAA Rating:* R.

CAST: Jeremy Blackman (Stanley Spector); Tom Cruise (Frank T.J. Mackey); Melinda Dillon (Rose Gator); April Grace (Gwenovier); Luis Guzman (Luis); Philip Baker Hall (Jimmy Gator); Philip Seymour Hoffman (Phil Parma); Ricky Jay (Burt Ramsey); Orlando Jones (Worm); William H. Macy (Quiz Kid Donnie Smith); Alfred Molina (Solomon Solomon); Julianne Moore (Linda Partridge); Michael Murphy (Alan Kligman, Esq.); John C. Reilly (Officer Jim Kurring); Jason Robards (Earl Patridge); Melora Walters (Claudia Wilson Gator); Michael Bowen (Rick Spector); Henry Gibson (Thurston Howell); Felicity Huffman (Cynthia); Emmanuel L. Johnson (Dixon); Don McManus (Doctor Landon); Eileen Ryan (Mary); Danny Wells (Dick Jennings); Pat Healy (Sir Edmund William Godfrey); Genevieve Zweig (Mrs. Godfrey); Mark Flanagan (Joseph Green); Neil Flynn (Stanley Berry); Rod McLachlan (Daniel Hill); Allan Graf (Firefighter); Patton Oswalt (Delmer Darion); Ray Gonzales (Reno Security Guard); Brad Hunt (Craig Hansen); Jim Meskimen (Forensic Scientist); Chris O'Hara (Sydney Barringer); Clement Blake (Arthur Barringer); Frank Elmore (1958 Dectective); John Kraft Seitz (1958 Policeman); Cory Buck (Young Boy); Tim Sorenen (Infomercial Guy); Jim Ortlieb (Middle-aged Guy); Thomas Jane (Young Jimmy Gator); Holly Houston (Jimmy's Showgirl); Benjamin Niedens (Little Donnie Smith); Veronica Hart and Melissa Spell (Dentist Nurses); James Kiriyama-Lem (Doctor Lee); Jake Cross and Charlie Scott (Pedestrians); Juan Medrano (Nurse Juan); John Pritchett (Police Captain); Cleo King (Marcie); Michael Shamus Wiles (Captain Muffy); Jason Andrews (Doc); John S. Davies (Cameraman); Kevin Breznahan (Geoff, Seminar Guy); Miguel Perez (Avi Solomon); David Masuda (Man Coroner); Neil Pepe (Officer 1); Lionel Mark Smith (Detective); Annette Heide (Woman Coroner); Lynne Lerner (Librarian); Scott Burkett (WDKK Page 1); Bob Brewer (Richard's Dad); Julie Brewer (Richard's Mom); Nancy Marston (Julia's Mom); Maurey Marston (Julia's Dad); Jamala Gaither (WDKK p.a.); Amy Brown (WDKK Page 2); Meagan Fay (Doctor Diane); Patricia Forte (Mim); Patrick Warren (Todd Geronimo); Virginia Pereira (Pink Dot Girl); Craig Kvinsland (Brad the Bartendar); Patricia Scanlon (Cocktail Waitress); Natalie Marston (Julia); Bobby Brewer (Richard); Clark Gregg (WDKK Floor Director); Pat Healy (Young Pharmacy Kid); Art Frankel (Old Pharmacist); Matt Gerald (Officer 2); Guillermo Melgarejo (Pink Dot Guy); Paul F. Tompkins (Chad, Seduce & Destroy); Mary Lynn Rajskub (Janet, Frank's Assistant); Jim Beaver, Ezra Buzzington and Denise Woodfork (Smiling Peanut Patrons); Bob Downey, Sr. (WDKK Show Director); William Mapother (WDKK Director's Assistant); Larry Ballard (WDKK Medic); Brett Higgins and Brian Higgins (Mackey Disciple Twins); Michael Phillips (Mackey Disciple in Middle); Lillian Adams (Donnie's Old Neighbor); Steven Bush, Mike Massa, and Dale Gibson (Paramedics); Scott Alan Smith (ER Doctor).

CHRISTIAN SCIENCE MONITOR, 12/17/99, p. 15, David Sterritt

"Magnolia" is Paul Thomas Anderson's third movie, not his second, but in every other way it's a textbook example of the sophomore slump.

This energetic young writer-director made an impressive debut with the small-scale "Hard Eight" and then became a star with the large-scale "Boogie Nights," his Oscar-nominated portrait of the 1970s porno-film business. His new picture, "Magnolia," is just as sweeping and ambitious. Yet it seems more contrived and less absorbing than its predecessor, as if Anderson were straining so hard to cook up a great encore that he forgot to make his tricks and gimmicks add up to anything.

The cast of characters is varied, ranging from a woman-hating sex lecturer (Tom Cruise) and an insecure policeman (John C. Reilly) to a dying entertainment tycoon (Jason Robards) and his grief-stricken young wife (Julianne Moore), to name just a handful.

The intermittently clever screenplay unites most of them through their diverse connections with the world of quiz shows. Linked themes of aging, illness, and death prevent the multiple subplots from becoming a complete hodgepodge.

All this constitutes an impressive display of moviemaking logistics, but it provides little to think about, despite the screenplay's comic-philosophic musings about fate and coincidence.

It's not very original either—it often seems like a remake of Robert Altman's epic "Short Cuts," another channel-surfing picture that took place in L.A., hopping around a multitude of story lines. Anderson is still a solid talent, but he should remember to explore his ideas in depth as well breadth.

LOS ANGELES TIMES, 12/17/99, Calendar/p. 1, Kenneth Turan

"Magnolia" is drunk and disorderly on the pure joy of making movies. A frantic, flawed, fascinating film that is both impressive and a bit out of control, often at the same time, "Magnolia" may occasionally overshoot its mark, but it's the kind of jumble only a truly gifted filmmaker can make.

That would be writer-director Paul Thomas Anderson, whose last film, "Boogie Nights," was a nervy, assured and empathetic look at pornography in the 1970s, San Fernando Valley style. Also set in the Valley and also involving numerous interlocking stories, "Magnolia" is if anything more involved and ambitious than its predecessor.

Taking place during a single 24-hour period in today's Valley, "Magnolia" uses the interconnected tales of its nine protagonists (acted by Anderson veterans such as John C. Reilly, Julianne Moore, William H. Macy, Philip Baker Hall and Philip Seymour Hoffman and newcomers including Tom Cruise, who almost steals the picture) to form a frenzied slice of our life and times.

"Magnolia's" people are searching for happiness, having trouble making human connections, and, more specifically, trying to come to terms with what's come before. "We're through with the past," is how one character puts it, "but the past isn't through with us."

Another key element, perhaps the key element, in this scenario is the role played by coincidence and chance. In fact, "Magnolia" starts with a bravura prelude that shows three examples of truly boggling coincidences, alleged to be as true as they are strange, that took place in 1911, 1958 and the early 1980s. This crackling sequence, filled with jazzy visuals tossed off casually but with genuine cinematic flair, is the film's most irresistible. It overflows with Anderson's unstoppable zest for cinema (the 1911 sequence was even shot with a vintage hand-cranked Pathe camera) and its infinite storytelling possibilities.

When it comes to introducing the film's horde of characters, Anderson, cinematographer Robert Elswit and editor Dylan Tichenor employ a similarly dazzling rapid-fire approach. With Aimee Mann's haunting vocals washing over everything (Anderson says her music was a key source of inspiration), "Magnolia's" people are presented so rapid-fire it feels as though we're meeting them all at the same time.

"Magnolia" eventually slows down and allows its characters to intersect, both tangentially and deeply, but some things remain constant, especially the energy, confidence and panache that mark Anderson's directing style. Even when we have no clear idea where he's heading, we're more than happy to take the trip with him.

Which is a good thing because, inevitably, some of "Magnolia's" characters are more interesting than others. And the dark-night-of-the-soul nervous breakdowns/screaming fits all of them seem to be having simultaneously leads to a level of nonstop emotional intensity that borders on the exhausting.

If there is anything else that unites "Magnolia's" characters it's that almost all of them have some kind of connection to television. Earl Partridge (Jason Robards), for instance, is a wealthy television producer, but now he's dying of cancer and his much younger wife, Linda (Moore), and his nurse Phil Parma (Hoffman) are pursuing different roads in trying to make his last hours as he'd want them to be.

Game show host Jimmy Gator (Hall) has been on TV for a long time—12,000 hours over 30 years by one count—but now he's dying as well and wants to reconcile with his angry daughter Claudia (Melora Walters).

Heavily into meaningless sex and intense drug use, Claudia refuses, but one of "Magnolia's" more genial coincidences brings her into contact with LAPD Officer Jim Kurring (Reilly, excellent as always), a decent if awkward policeman, deeply religious and on the square, who likes his job because of the chances it gives him to right the world's wrongs.

Jimmy Gator is currently employed hosting a show called "What Do Kids Know?," in which a panel of adults competes with a group of youngsters. Smartest of the kids, in fact the smartest person on the whole show, is young Stanley Spector (Jeremy Blackman), who finds that being brilliant does strange things to his relationship with his dad.

"What Do Kids Know?," as it happens, has been on the air a long time, and Macy plays a former champion, perennially known as "Quiz Kid Donnie Smith," who has difficulty getting his adult life in order. One of "Magnolia's" most amusing scenes has Donnie trying to convince Solomon Solomon (Alfred Molina) and Avi Solomon (Miguel Perez) of Solomon Electronics that they shouldn't fire him for terminal ineptitude.

Easily the most dynamic person on the small screen (and, as played by Cruise, on the large as well) is the wonderfully named Frank T.J. Mackey, a television motivational speaker with a most peculiar calling. Handsome, cocky, with a magnetic line of gab, Mackey is the ultimate male chauvinist with a phone number that says it all: 1-877-TAME HER. Preaching and teaching a profanity-laced philosophy of penile supremacy he calls "Seduce and Destroy," Mackey gives Cruise the chance to cut loose by doing amusing riffs on his charismatic superstar image. It's great fun, expertly written and performed, and all the more enjoyable because the self-parody element is unexpected.

Exciting as "Magnolia" can be to watch, it wouldn't be fair to the writer-director and his considerable potential to call it completely successful. Some of the film's emotional payoffs are predictable and less than profound, some revelations are not that revealing, and we don't connect with all of "Magnolia's" characters as much as might be hoped. Still, it's an impressive piece of work with some fine acting that makes holding our interest for three-plus hours seem easy. Maybe, for someone as talented as Paul Thomas Anderson, it is.

NEW STATESMAN, 3/20/00, p. 45, Jonathan Romney

Over the past decade, the mainstream of American cinema has been increasingly mired in the same weary paths, and many people blame that on the rise of the scriptwriting gurus and their prescriptions for homogenised narrative. If you believe their manuals, storytelling should be a nice orderly matter—three-act structures, story arcs, character development and the rest, all making for tidy packages, easily comprehensible, perfectly coherent and safely confined within genre boundaries.

This does not, however, account for Hollywood's increasing inability to tell tight, well-managed tales. Quite the opposite: we are getting ungainly concoctions that have precious little to say and cannot say it in less than two hours—for example, the featherlight. *Meet Joe Black* and the death-row schmaltzer, *The Green Mile,* both clock in at over three hours.

Magnolia is a three-hour wonder that makes a virtue out of excess. Its sprawling effusiveness often hits the outer limits of coherence and plausibility. But the third feature from the wildly talented Paul Thomas Anderson—director of porn-world panorama, a *Boogie Nights,* and the lesser-known gambling miniature, *Hard Eight*—is so brimful of energies, so much the story of its own uncontainable enthusiasms, that you simply have to go along with it. Just take a deep breath every now and then.

Magnolia's story of lost souls in the San Fernando Valley is close to *Boogie Nights,* not just because several of its superb cast reappear, but also because its overlapping stories again aspire to limn the spirit of a city. Anderson is shaping up as LA's own movie-brat Balzac, although *Magnolia's* nearest equivalent is really Tony Marchant's recent BBC series, *Holding On,* a London tableau of everyday madness. *Magnolia* is also very close to Robert Altman's LA ensemble piece, *Short Cuts:* it, too, has a surprise catastrophe climax, but Anderson's *deus ex machina* is so utterly bizarre, so flamboyantly biblical, that I wouldn't dream of blowing the gaffe (even though some of the advertising material already has).

This bizarre apocalypse gives the clue to Anderson's notion of structure. He works by accumulation, piling detail on detail, moment on moment, small telling revelation on revelation, until finally something has to blow: the characters explode, the world boils over, the narrative house of cards caves in on itself. This catastrophe theory of narrative may be inherent to portrayals of a city perched on a fault line, and you can see its effects in the acting: watch how Julianne' Moore's nervy, disconsolate fussing at last erupts in her magnificent outburst in a pharmacy.

The story takes place over one day and one night, with the characters immobilised by a relentless downpour: the film is an incomparable monument to pathetic fallacy. The cast includes Tom Cruise, luxuriantly horrible as a strutting sex guru peddling seduction as a technique of militaristic attrition; a dying TV magnate (Jason Robards), his young wife (Jullianne Moore) and his patient carer (the always majestic Philip Seymour Hoffman); a former child-quiz champ (William H Macy) and a boy (Jeremy Blackman) undergoing the same ordeal on the same show, hosted by a weary showbiz pro (Philip Baker Hall); a nervous, well-meaning cop (John C Reilly); and a bitter, coke-frazzled young woman (Melora Walters) he falls for.

It is a lot to take in, but Anderson doesn't want us to take it all in easily. He zaps from strand to strand with blinding speed, in hyperanimated fugue-like montages, noisily through-scored on the soundtrack, in blurs of camera-work (he is a shameless abuser of the steadicam). But, at key points, he slows down to let us spend a little quiet time with his characters. At one point, everything stops and all the main players sing along contemplatively to Aimee Mann's song, "Wise Up"—a sudden audacious conflation of soap opera and musical.

Anderson has a special knack of reminding us that we don't know as much as we think we do, especially when we think we are just watching another movie. He repeatedly overturns our expectations: Cruise's character, in a critical dismantling of the star's own screen persona, flirts gruesomely with a female TV interviewer, but we gradually realise that she is doing the search-and-destroy job on him.

This is also a very self-reflexive film. Anderson rather indulges himself by kicking off with a jaunty but rather pedantic disquisition on outrageous real-life coincidences. Characters keep measuring life against film: Hoffman, realising he is living out a screen-style moment of high emotion, says: "They have those scenes in the movies because they're true." And when Anderson finally tests our credulity to the maximum, he cuts to a line of text in a picture on the wall: *"But it did happen!"*

You come out of *Magnolia* exhilarated and a little battered, feeling that you've had an authentic blast of the pulse of life—not life as it is usually packaged by the movies, but life in all its cacophony and incoherence, not to mention the excessive coherence that is coincidence. Anderson is not a sensible director: he can't stop himself from cramming it all in, but it's been a longtime since anyone in American cinema has shown such an unbounded appetite—not just for images but for the world. Let the script manuals explain that away if they can.

NEW YORK, 1/10/00, p. 46, Peter Rainer

I wish I could join in the chorus of praise for Paul Thomas Anderson's *Magnolia*, because I think he's extravagantly gifted. But this San Fernando Valley-based epic of alienation features often remarkable actors (Julianne Moore, William H. Macy, Jason Robards) in mostly unremarkable situations. The movie I saw seemed more like a concatenation of soap-opera stories with an epistemological overlay than like something deserving of the comparisons it's been receiving to prime Robert Altman or, heaven forfend, Eugene O'Neill.

NEW YORK POST, 12/17/99, p. 53, Lou Lumenick

Most great movies have three or four memorable scenes—at most, half a dozen. "Magnolia," hands-down the best movie of the year, has nearly 20 of them—stunningly performed by an incredible cast.

It's an audacious, hilarious, deeply affecting three-hour tapestry that follows a dozen walking-wounded characters during a single day in Los Angeles' San Fernando Valley.

Connected by blood and chance, they're united in two positively electrifying sequences—all singing along with an Amy Mann tune called "Wise Up" on the radio, and caught up in a biblical plague that literally rains down on them.

At the movie's center is Big Earl Partridge (a deeply moving Jason Robards), a dying television producer who wants to see the son who hasn't spoken to him in 10 years: Frank Mackey (an Oscar-worthy Tom Cruise), a preening self-help guru who coaches men to "seduce and destroy" women.

Also succumbing to cancer is Jimmy Gator (Philip Baker Hall), the host of Big Earl's long-running game show "What Do Kids Know?," which pits young contestants against adults.

Jimmy, wracked by dark secrets that belie his family-values image, wants to reconcile with his daughter Claudia (a spectacular Melora Walters), who's hooked on cocaine, loud music and anonymous sex.

Then there are the quiz kids (everything in this movie comes in twos): Stanley Spector (Jeremy Blackman), a genius who's being pressured by his selfish dad (Michael Bowen) to keep winning; and Donnie Smith (William H. Macy, even better than in "Fargo"), a contestant from the 1960s who's desperate for love and money.

The movie's twin moral centers are Phil Parma (the ubiquitous Philip Seymour Hoffman, in his best work of the year), a male nurse who tries desperately to broker a meeting between Earl and his son; and Jim Kurring (the highly affecting John C. Reilly), a bumbling but sweet LAPD officer who romances Claudia—and helps Donnie out of a tight spot.

Delivering big time on the promise he showed with "Boogie Nights," 29-year-old director Philip Thomas Anderson has written a banquet of great scenes for his huge cast.

The actors include Julianne Moore (in her fifth and best film role of the year) as Linda, Big Earl's promiscuous, guilt-wracked and drug-addicted spouse; Melinda Dillon (her best part since "Close Encounters of the Third Kind") as Jimmy's long-suffering wife; and Henry Gibson in a wry turn as an older gay man in competition with Donnie for the attention of a hunky bartender.

What makes this brilliantly edited (and visually arresting) film an instant classic is that Anderson keeps cutting back and forth between various scenes, building a kinetic energy that leaves you gasping with wonder.

"Magnolia" (the title refers to a briefly glimpsed street sign and a couple of barely seen photographs) demands a lot from its audience; a single viewing is barely adequate to absorb the details.

But Anderson has his hand so firmly on the pulse of millennial America that I wish could give it more than four stars.

NEWSDAY, 12/17/99, Part II/p. B8, John Anderson

At the risk of starting a bicoastal culture war, Paul Thomas Anderson's "Magnolia" is one of those films that raises serious questions about the culture of Los Angeles. It's not just that people there seem to be defined by their problems. It's that others find them interesting.

You, however, may not. Choreographing eight or nine "main" characters and several satellite victims into a seamless chimera of premillennial angst, languor and regret, Anderson takes the kind of thing he did in "Boogie Nights" to a technically more sophisticated place. And a running time close to that of "Titanic."

"Boogie Nights," however, had a solid subtext of family, lost and found, which is why it transcended its milieu of '70s porn and achieved something like grace. "Magnolia" may have its recurring themes—cancer, sex, child exploitation, death-bed remorse—but they never coalesce into anything greater than the parts.

In a lot of ways, "Magnolia" is a perfect movie to close out the '90s, because it extrapolates from all the vices of '90s mainstream cinema: vacuous visual agility, big-name actors in search of a point and a black hole where its soul should be.

Several of the actors—no, almost all of the actors—are first-rate. They include an edgy Tom Cruise, whose Frank Mackey—founder of the embittered men's group Seduce & Destroy—is the Tony Robbins of unwanted testosterone; John C. Reilly as Officer Jim, thick-headed sendup of the LAPD; Julianne Moore, former golddigger-cum-devoted wife of the dying Earl Partidge (Jason Robards), and Melora Walters, whose coke-snorting Claudia is the would-be lover of Jim and the daughter of Rose (Melinda Dillon) and Jimmy Gator (Philip Baker Hall), longtime host of the TV quiz show "What Do Kids Ynow?"—which years ago ruined the life of Donnie Smith (William H. Macy) and is now doing the same to young brainiac Stanley Spector (Jeremy Blackman).

Are there more? You bet, all playing out within close proximity of Magnolia Street. Or is it avenue?

Or do we care? We don't, really, because while Anderson gives us a lot, he never gives us any opportunity to invest in his characters, or a sense of purpose to his pageant of unhappiness. The film's opening salvo—three supposedly factual vignettes about weird coincidences and six degrees or less of separation—casts everything else in the film as a contrivance. If the three strange anecdotes are meant to persuade us that truth is stranger than fiction, what's the subsequent three-hour fiction supposed to mean? "Magnolia" is trite enough that we accept anything Anderson tells us. We just never believe it.

NEWSWEEK, 12/20/99, p. 42, David Ansen

Normal movies take time to rev up their engines. Paul Thomas Anderson's "Magnolia" achieves instant liftoff, with a dazzling prologue chronicling three bizarre tales of chance. Next comes an exhilarating passage that introduces nine characters in Los Angeles's San Fernando Valley, whose oddly interlinked stories we'll follow. Even before the movie proper has begun you know several things. That you are in the hands of an extravagantly talented filmmaker. That you are about to see a wildly ambitious, boldly unconventional film. And that a three-hour movie that starts on such a high note could turn out to be a masterpiece or a folly.

"Magnolia" is about fathers and children, about the horrible deeds of the past that return to haunt us, about trying to do the right thing and finally about forgiveness. Anderson ("Boogie Nights") doesn't have any cinematic small talk in him—he pitches us straight into the writhing hearts of his lost, haunted characters. Two of the fathers are dying of cancer. One is a TV, producer (a gaunt, brilliant Jason Robards) who's trying to locate his long-lost son. The other is the beloved host of a TV quiz show, (Philip Baker Hall) who has dark skeletons in his closet and a daughter (Melora Walters) strung out on coke. The current star of his quiz show (Jeremy Blackman) is a child genius whose father treats him like a performing seal. There's also a former quiz kid (William H. Macy) whose life has fallen to pieces; a heavily medicated trophy wife (Julianne Moore); a sad-sack guardian angel of a nurse (Philip Seymour Hoffman) who hovers over Robards's death bed, and a humbling, good-hearted cop (John C. Reilly) who is the tale's surprising moral center. And in the boldest performance of his career, Tom Cruise places Frank T.J. Mackey, the preening macho guru of "Seduce and Destroy," a self-help program for men who want to score with women.

"Magnolia's" flaws are sins of excess. It's all too much—too much emotion, too much intensity, too many climaxes. It's never boring, but it can be exhausting. Still, why complain in the face of so much bounty? At its best, "Magnolia" towers over most Hollywood films this year.

One has to be in awe of how much the 29-year-old writer-director knows about the human heart. Unlike other movie-savy young directors with flashy techniques, Anderson doesn't hide behind irony and cool—he's an old-fashioned humanist. He takes huge chances here, producing a startling apocalyptic finale that could be something out of a García Márquez novel—or the Book of Exodus.

SIGHT AND SOUND, 4/00, p. 56, Leslie Dick

Los Angeles and the San Fernando Valley, the present. The lives of several characters intersect over the course of a day. Television producer Earl Partridge, whose production company makes the game show *What Do Kids Know?* is dying of cancer. He asks his nurse Phil Parma to help him contact his estranged son Jack, now a guru on the art of seducing women who goes by the name Frank T.J. Mackey. Earl's wife Linda, who married him for money but only now realises how much she loves him, spends the day gathering prescriptions from various doctors. Jimmy Gator, presenter of *What Do Kids Know?* also has cancer and tries unsuccessfully to reconcile with his estranged daughter Claudia, a coke addict. Reported by the neighbours for playing music too loud, Claudia is later visited by police officer Jim Kurring who asks her for a date.

Jimmy presents what will be his last show; one of the contestants is Stanley, a child genius, whose father Rick bullies him. Donnie Smith, the show's star contestant in the 60s, is fired from his job that day and gets drunk in a bar where he declares love to barman Brad. The show falls apart due to Jimmy's failing health and Stanley's refusal to participate in the final round. At home, Jimmy indirectly confesses to his wife Rose he abused Claudia as a child; she leaves him.

Driving home after his awkward date with Claudia, Jim sees Donnie trying to break back into his employer's offices to return money he stole. Frank arrives at Earl's for a final confrontation before Earl dies. Stanley tells Rick he has to be nicer to him. Jimmy shoots himself just as a sudden bizarre rain of frogs descends over the area which also knocks Donnie off the building and causes the ambulance carrying Linda who has attempted a drug overdose—to crash.

In the morning, Earl has died but Linda is recovering. Jim helps Donnie return the money and then visits Claudia; they seem poised to begin a relationship.

Magnolia is a street that runs east-west through the San Fernando Valley, parallel to Burbank and Ventura boulevards. And *Magnolia* isn't a Hollywood movie; it's a Valley movie, like *Earth Girls Are Easy*. The Valley is an indeterminate space of multiple overlapping soap operas, a place without distinguishing features or final destinations. *Magnolia*, like the Valley in microcosm, somehow incorporates no less than 12 major characters and innumerable unlikely plots and subplots into a whirlwind structure that periodically, with exhilarating insouciance, insists on its own antirealism. (When they switch off the rain, as the weather report appears in neat text across the screen; when characters separated by space and emotional distance sing the same song together, accompanying the soundtrack; when one of the 10 plagues of Exodus erupts in these nondescript fleshpots, the thrill is something else.)

Magnolia ends up being about narrative, as it moves with an indescribable intensity between and within these various stories. The film begins (and ends) with a voiceover paean to coincidence, as if, without coincidence spatial, temporal—there would be no tales to tell, no relations between people whatsoever. Fundamentally, it is a film against patriarchy, in which (almost) every position is doubled, as if to underline the point. There are two dysfunctional families, each headed by a powerful old man who is dying, each with one estranged child (Frank, Claudia) who can only scream with inarticulate rage when faced with a dying father. Each old man has a wife, one popping prescription drugs and eventually attempting suicide, the other apparently permanently sozzled on large tumblers of vodka with ice. All the women without exception have substance abuse problems (Claudia is the cokehead to end all cokeheads), which make them extremely unappealing, an ironic byproduct of this film so deeply critical of patriarchal structures. Paradoxically, in charting the damage done by fathers to their children (and wives), *Magnolia* can't help reinscribing a whole set of tired old misogynist clichés.

Then, as if we have missed the point, *Magnolia* presents not one but two additional damaged kids, both child geniuses: Stanley is a young boy performing brilliantly on a television quiz show called *What Do Kids Know?*; Donnie is an adult ex-whiz kid, famous (in a pathetic, Valley way) from the same show in the 60s. The child Stanley is demonstrably at the mercy of his single father and the oblivious adults from the show, which is shown to be a theatre of cruelty, transforming his intelligence into mere fodder for the spectacle. The quiz show scenes are harrowing, as in the heartbreaking moment where Stanley simply refuses (on live television!) to take part in the final round. Later he tells his insane father, "Dad, you have to be nicer to me." If only it were that simple. (You can't help wondering where this poor kid's mother is—in rehab, maybe?) Meanwhile, both powerful old men are television people: Jimmy Gator is the 30-year veteran presenter of *What Do Kids Know?* Earl Partridge is the show's producer. In some sense, the station is understood to be the television industry's institutionalisation of fatherly abuse, as these evil old men carry over into their careers the ruthless exploitation that occurs within their families.

Within all this, there are a series of amazing performances, some extremely funny scenes, held together by Robert Elswit's radical cinematography and Paul Thomas Anderson's sheer nerve. Although *Magnolia* runs over three hours in length (his previous film *Boogie Nights* was nearly as long), nothing is superfluous to Anderson's project, and the film is worth seeing for Tom Cruise's performance alone. He plays Frank T.I. Mackey, inspirational guru for Seduce and Destroy, an organisation which instructs men how to exploit women sexually. Abandoned by his father at 14, left to nurse his cancer-stricken mother, Frank's tragedy lies in the way he is doomed to repeat his father's sins.

To continue the doubling, there are more Capraesque figures, who wander through this forest of neurosis and psychic damage like Bambis in the woods. First, there's the innocent cop Jim, who falls in love with the cokehead Claudia in a case of severe wishful thinking: the idea that these two might make a go of it is both the only hopeful note and the most implausible dimension of the film. And Stanley the child genius has his youthful counterpart in the boy the cop encounters, a sophisticated child who functions as the Greek chorus to the movie, appearing intermittently to save somebody's life, steal a gun or recite hip-hop rhymes the cop can't understand. At least the cop is only a klutz, not a sadistic shit like the other men Claudia knows.

And he really does want to know who she is, paralleling the brilliant woman reporter who cross-questions Frank into sulky silence.

The other innocent is Phil Parma, hospice nurse, who gently, tearfully places a dropper of liquid morphine in Earl's mouth, thereby saving him from the pain of remembering who he is or what he's done. Both these innocents abroad are benevolent, but their kindness is wildly at odds with the cruelty and pain all around them, and here Anderson seems to want to weave a thread of pure sentimentality into the film, which doesn't really wash. The old men talk, deathbed-style, about their crimes ("I cheated on her! I cheated on her!" they whine, as if that's the worst thing anyone could do to anyone), and then (as the film's bizarre catastrophe strikes) they die, miserably. With them out of the way, there is the tiniest vestige of a possibility of change.

This film moves between various sites—Earl's deathbed, the show, the electronics store, the gay bar, Frank's seminar, Claudia's apartment—mapping out not only a narrative connectedness, but an emotional geography. *Magnolia* has a rhizome structure: like the Valley, it is without centre, spreading in all directions, with proliferating nodes or intersections providing the sites of concentration. Rhizome like, it duplicates itself structurally, as each element is repeated, with variations. It's a gambler's strategy—double or nothing and *Magnolia*'s gamble pays off.

TIME, 12/27/99, p. 165, Richard Schickel

Paul Thomas Anderson is out to prove the obvious: that we live in a chance universe, that coincidence and mishap play a larger role in our destinies than we like to think. In *Magnolia* he intertwines four disparate (but equally glum) stories of people living in California's San Fernando Valley and show how they touch—or fail to touch—one another in the course of a single, very long day.

The result is a hard-striving, convoluted movie, which never quite becomes the smoothly reciprocating engine Anderson (who did *Boogie Nights)* would like it to be. Indeed, only one of his tales is fully persuasive. That's the one about the Partridge family, which is not to be confused with the nice folks from '70s TV. The patriarch, Earl (Robards), is dying of cancer, a metaphor for decay that Anderson likes too much. Earl's trophy wife (Moore), who married him for his money, has decided she actually loves the old guy and is in a guilty frenzy to prove it. He, meantime, is desperate to reconcile with his estranged son (Cruise), who, under an alias, runs viciously sexist seminars teaching men how to have their way with women. Earl has a nurse (Hoffman) who tries to get everyone what they want before it is too late.

Everything about the Partridges rings tense and true—Moore's brilliantly rendered hysteria, Cruise's near parodistic charisma when he's leading his group and, even more astonishing, the way his biographical falsities, his emotional denials crumble under probing from a gently persistent TV interviewer. Anderson knows and feels for these people in some true, instinctive way.

Everyone else in his movie is, by comparison, an easy construct—a TV host with a guilty secret; his damaged, drugged out daughter; game-show contestants, current and has-been, wrestling with the consequences of brief, cheesy fame; a humbling cop betrayed by his good nature. These characters are all well played, but we don't fully connect with them. Or, finally, with an endless movie that mostly mistakes inflation for importance.

VILLAGE VOICE, 12/21/99, p. 143, J. Hoberman

Topsy-Turvy [see Hoberman's review] is a film about a midcareer crisis that throws its maker's own career into a new light. (Is it possible that Leigh has always thought of himself as doing comic opera?) Paul Thomas Anderson's more perverse *Magnolia* is a potential crowd-pleaser that risks losing its audience before the credits are over.

A manic meditation on karmic craziness, *Magnolia*'s elaborately fast, cheap, and out of control setup restages a 1911 snuff film, plants a scuba diver in a treetop, and diagrams the way in which a failed suicide becomes accidental manslaughter as a prelude to plunging into the maelstrom of present-day Los Angeles. Anderson's third feature is a mosaic of dark cross-purposes in which just about each scene plays like The Big One and every well-honed speech is designed to rhyme with something else in the movie.

The cast, which includes Anderson regulars Philip Baker Hall, Philip Seymour Hoffman, William H. Macy, Julianne Moore, and John C. Reilly, lives large and loud. Anderson allows his actors long ranting scenes, but they repay his generosity. Flat on his back with a tube up his nose, Jason Robards is hypnotic in his rambling soliloquies while, as his trophy wife, Moore obliterates her plaster saint performance in *The End of the Affair* with a blast of focused hysteria. Meanwhile, interviewed in his Jockey shorts, Tom Cruise plays a sexual self-help guru as an outrageous parody of the pumped-up roles he played in *Cocktail* and *Top Gun*. (A later scene in which he emotes is mercifully short.)

Nearly as impressive as Anderson's rapport with his actors is his use of parallel action to juggle their performances. *Magnolia*'s geo-narrative structure engages Robert Altman's *Short Cuts*, but its time-bending montage is crazy enough to evoke *Intolerance*. Anticipating the *Who Wants to Be a Millionaire?* gestalt, Anderson uses the telecast of *What Do Kids Know?* ("America's longest-running quiz show") as the set piece for his movie's middle hour. The format, which hilariously pits kids against adults, recapitulates the generational anguish that characterizes the movie. (Two fathers are dying—both the show's host and its producer—and, as Jim Morrison once said, all the children are insane.)

What Do Kids Know?, which suffers its own spectacular on-air crack-ups, is crosscut with an existential TV interview, a pharmaceutical odyssey, a cop's attempt to make time with a strung-out cokie, a former contestant's barroom antics, and a male nurse trying to fulfill the Robards character's last request. ("You know the scene in which the dying man tries to get in touch with his long-lost son," he tells the office assistant who puts him on hold. "This is that scene.") As global-village as all this is, it's not even the most elaborate device Anderson uses to link his suffering characters—moving from a broken 360-degree pan through an Aimee Mann ballad to a full-scale Old Testament plague.

Magnolia is not a perfect film. The performers are a lot more believable than their characters. There's too much backstory, some overly intellectualized connections, and a facile racial subtext. Nevertheless, Anderson takes enormous risks. As *Boogie Nights* had the effrontery to engage Martin Scorsese, so *Magnolia* even more boldly rewrites Altman. As Anderson is not yet 30, I'd read this showbiz apocalypse as a sign of hope.

Also reviewed in:
CHICAGO TRIBUNE, 1/7/00, Friday/p. A, Michael Wilmington
NATION, 1/3/00, p. 36, Stuart Klawans
NATION, 2/7/00, p. 34, Stuart Klawans
NEW YORK TIMES, 12/17/99, p. E15, Janet Maslin
NEW YORKER, 12/20/99, p. 102, David Denby
VARIETY, 12/13-19/99, p. 105, Emanuel Levy
WASHINGTON POST, 1/7/00, p. C1, Rita Kempley
WASHINGTON POST, 1/7/00, Weekend/p. 36, Desson Howe

MAN OF THE CENTURY

A Fine Line Features release of a Sun-Telegram Pictures production. *Director:* Adam Abraham. *Screenplay:* Adam Abraham and Gibson Frazier. *Director of Photography:* Matthew Jensen. *Editor:* Frank Reynolds. *Music:* Michael Weiner. *Production Designer:* Zeljka Pavlinovic. *Costumes:* Claudia Hill. *Running time:* 77 minutes. *MPAA Rating:* R.

CAST: Gibson Frazier (Johnny Twennies); Cara Buono (Virginia Clemens); Susan Egan (Samantha Winter); Dwight Ewell (Richard Lancaster); Anthony Rapp (Timothy Burns); Frank Gorshin (Roman Navarro); Madame Du Froid (Margaret Twennies); Lester Lanin (Lester); Bobby Short (Chester); David Margulies (Mr. Meyerscholtz).

CHRISTIAN SCIENCE MONITOR, 10/29/99, p. 15, David Sterritt

This week's other exercise in self-reflexive cinema fancy term for movies about movies [The reference is to *Being John Malkovich*; see Sterritts' review.]—is *Man of the Century*, a time-warping comedy about a '20s sort of guy who happens to live in the '90s.

His name is Johnny Twennies, and he bangs out a New York newspaper column when he isn't squabbling with his wealthy mom, dodging crooks who want to rough him up, or romancing his girlfriend, a thoroughly '90s woman who runs a trendy art gallery. Johnny doesn't just dream about the '20s, he actually lives there, at least in his own mind. And the movie is completely on his side—depicting his adventures in black-and-white cinematography and filling the soundtrack with old-fashioned music.

"Man of the Century" is basically a one-joke movie as it plays two American eras off each other for laughs and occasional pathos. It's clever enough to combine strategies from pictures as different as "The Purple Rose of Cairo" and "The Brady Bunch Movie," though, and modest enough to deliver all its goods in a snappy 77 minutes. Comedy fans and nostalgia buffs will find enough pleasures here to justify the price of a '90s ticket.

LOS ANGELES TIMES, 10/29/99, Calendar/p. 21, Eric Harrison

The biggest sleeper of the year, this summer's "Blair Witch Project," may look as if it was cobbled together from raw footage found in the woods, but if it starts a trend toward faux amateurishness—as it already seems to be doing, naturally—don't expect Adam Abraham to join in.

Abraham's new movie, the charming "Man of the Century," could be called the anti-"Witch." Joyously retro in and design, this black-and-white movie aspires to a kind of innocence and old-fashioned polish that were out of style before Abraham was born.

"In the '30s and '40s there was a craft to making movies and a caring that is in stark contrast to what we see in movies today," said Abraham, sounding like a fogy even though he is only 28. When he started writing the movie in 1995 with his friend Gibson Frazier, another 28-year-old who also stars, "we were disappointed with what was coming out of both the major studios and the independents," Abraham said. "I asked why can't I make films that have that [old Hollywood] kind of quality and craft in it?"

"Century," which won this year's audience award at Slamdance, a satellite festival to the Sundance Film Festival in Utah, is about a modern-day newspaper reporter who dresses and acts as if he thinks he's a character from the 1930s newspaper tale "The Front Page." He speaks the snappy patter of early Howard Hawks movies as he saunters through Gotham enthusiastically pursuing stories about ribbon cuttings—until he gets embroiled in the story of the century, which just might get several people killed.

It sounds a bit like an extended "Saturday Night Live" skit, and it is similar to one. But Abraham achieves a persuasive 1930s movie look on a budget of less than $2 million, and he presents it without a shred of irony or condescension—audiences either get it or they don't. And while the movie has been enthusiastically received at festivals (with viewers mimicking the fun, old-timey dialogue for days after seeing it), it leaves others cold. It took Abraham more than a year to find a distributor for it, although he blames this partly on his ignorance about what to do with the film once he finished it in 1998. "We really didn't know what to do next," he said. "Somehow we'd forgotten that part."

Realizing that their movie plays better in theaters than on video, they resisted handing tapes to potential distributors. Unfortunately, head honchos usually would see it no other way. One after the other said no until New Line picked it up. Even studio execs who liked it passed because they didn't know what demographic it would appeal to, Abraham said.

"Sweet" isn't a term often applied to low-budget movies from first-time indie filmmakers. "Edgy" is more the norm. But "Century" is as far from edgy as it gets. It isn't hip. It isn't cynical. And it isn't about navel-gazing twentysomethings coming of age and falling in love. Rather, it has Frazier as Johnny Twennies doing the jitterbug with his gal pal (Susan Egan). It has people saying things like, "Stick with me, kid, and everything's gonna be jake." And it has the likes of crooner Bobby Short fronting a big band. What was Abraham thinking?

Abraham doesn't look like the kind of filmmaker you might expect to helm such a movie. With his long hair and dressed in black, he could be just another Hollywood hipster as he lunched at Musso & Frank's the other day, sitting across the table from Frazier. Although they both are from Philadelphia, the director met the UCLA graduate in Los Angeles while working on an earlier short film that Abraham made. Quite by chance, they found that their sensibilities were in sync.

With his jutting Dudley Do-Right chin and a way of speaking that would not be out of place in an old Katharine Hepburn movie, Frazier makes a jaunty impression as the irrepressible Johnny Twennies. He's so persuasive, in fact, that he says he's found that some casting agents have already typecast him: He's good, they say, but can do anything else? This, even though he has good stage credentials and has played a variety of roles with the Buffalo Nights Theatre Company he founded in 1991.

While it's questionable whether the duo's first movie will launch a young fogy movement of retro filmmakers, they said they made "Century" the way they did in reaction to most contemporary films, mainstream and independent, which they find mean-spirited and "anti-human."

Abraham gets worked up talking about this, as perhaps only the young and uncorrupted can. Most Hollywood pictures, he said, follow a simple formula: "You get talking heads—close-up after close-up after close-up of the movie stars, and then you get an explosion at the end." As for independent movies, he says "99.9%" of them are "low-brow sociology," primarily concerned with observing "lifelike" behavior in whatever milieu it happens to be set.

NEW YORK POST, 10/29/99, p. 44, Lou Lumenick

"Man of the Century" takes a premise that might sustain a clever five-minute short—a present-day Manhattan reporter acts like he's living in the 1920s—and stretches it out to 77 minutes.

Gibson Frazier, who co-wrote the screenplay with first-time director Adam Abraham, gives such a monotonous performance that he turns his character, Johnny Twennies, into Johnny One-Note. Mostly it consists of him wearing high collars, smiling like an idiot and dropping names like Theodore Dreiser, and trotting out corny bons mots like "Gee, you look swell!"

This never-explained affliction—or is it an affectation?—grows tiresome rather quickly. Not much diversion is provided by Johnny's slow-moving attempts to break up a drug ring and win back his estranged girlfriend (Susan Egan of Broadway's "Cabaret"), a downtown art dealer who can't understand Johnny's lack of interest in sex.

Cabaret legend Bobby Short and bandleader Lester Lanin perform a couple of numbers on screen, providing about the only entertainment in this black-and-white oddity.

NEWSDAY, 10/29/99, Part II/p. B12, John Anderson

To his fellow inhabitants of 1999 Manhattan, Johnny Twennies (Gibson Frazier) seems like a slim, well-mannered, overly dapper fellow who wears vintage clothing and knows about opera. They don't think much about it. They just assume he's gay.

But inside the head of Johnny, the retro-silly hero of "Man of the Century," exists a parallel universe of speakeasies, the Social Register, the bare-knuckle journalism of the Roaring '20s and a chivalric code as hidebound as the Sherman Antitrust Act. Lacking any other explanation—and, wisely, no other explanation is offered—he seems quite mad, actually. And, as one might expect, there's a certain wisdom to his madness.

A strictly giddy exercise in suspension of sense, "Man of the Century," seems to be setting us up for one of those lessons in how much better life was Way Back When. But that's where director Adam Abraham and his co-writer Frazier throw us a Lefty Grove curveball. Straddling its separate eras, "Man of the Century" offers a bit of the good and bad of each, enough for the viewer to question his or her own reflexive nostalgia. Johnny is a gentleman, at least to Samantha (Susan Egan), the downtown art dealer who's getting a tad impatient waiting for her sex-oblivious boyfriend to get busy. He's devoted to writing his column at the failing Sun-Telegram and stands up to two mob heavies who are trying to get him to write a fictitious obit about their gangland boss.

On the other hand, Johnny treats an old girlfriend like trash and moves through the blatant racial stereotypes of the movie's re-created Hollywood musical numbers—to say nothing of the casting of singer Bobby Short as a restroom attendant—as if nothing has ever changed. If that weren't enough, he smokes like a chimney and eats fried beef and onions. He'll never make it to the '90s.

Modern Manhattan—shot in glorious black and white by cinematographer Matthew Jensen—is a mix of crime, rubbish and chaos, but it's also inhabited by relatively liberated people, so the point is made. The cast—particularly Egan, the original Belle in Broadway's "Beauty and the Beast," and Dwight Ewell as her gallery assistant—are all attractive and bright. And although Johnny's alleged competition, the Journal-American, wasn't formed until 1937 and "Dancing in the Dark" wasn't written till the early '30s, "Man Of the Century" is a movie that has its finger on the pulse of the '20s.

VILLAGE VOICE, 11/2/99, p. 140, Dennis Lim

Another case study of pathological denial [The reference is to *The Legend of 1900*; see Lim's review of that film.] the protagonist of the black-and-white indie *Man of the Century* believes he was born in 1900 (or thereabouts). The joke is, he lives in 1999. Johnnie Twennies (played by the film's cowriter Gibson Frazier) is a newspaper man with a quaint way with words, a rat-tat-tat delivery, and what the movie seems to think of as 1920s values—though he's not so much gentlemanly as sexless and weird. Johnnie's seamless delusion is never explained, which is perhaps just as well, and the film uses it as an excuse for affectionate musical numbers and much pseudo-screwball anachronist comedy. Johnnie has a girlfriend who works in a Soho art gallery, Johnnie is assigned to work with a gay photographer, Johnnie baffles gangsters with his fearlessness and integrity. Good-natured but labored, the film clings to its lone gimmick with increasing desperation. By the mechanically farcical conclusion (all the characters are thrown together for a big-band blowout), the whimsy has long curdled.

Also reviewed in:
CHICAGO TRIBUNE, 11/5/99, Friday/p. D, John Petrakis
NEW YORK TIMES, 10/29/99, p. E13, Stephen Holden
VARIETY, 3/29-4/4/99, p. 71, Joe Leydon
WASHINGTON POST, 11/26/99, p. C1, Stephen Hunter

MAN ON THE MOON

A Universal Pictures and Mutual Film Company release of a Jersey Films/Cinehaus production in association with Shapiro/West Productions. *Executive Producer:* George Shapiro, Howard West, and Michael Hausman. *Producer:* Danny DeVito, Michael Shamberg and Stacey Sher. *Director:* Milos Forman. *Screenplay:* Scott Alexander and Larry Karaszewski. *Director of Photography:* Anastas Michos. *Editor:* Christopher Tellefsen and Lynzee Klingman. *Music:* R.E.M. and Anita Camarata. *Music Editor:* Shara Schwartz Johanson. *Choreographer:* Jaymi Marshall. *Sound:* Chris Newman and (music) Pat McCarthy. *Sound Editor:* Ron Bochar. *Casting:* Francine Maisler. *Production Designer:* Patrizia Von Brandenstein. *Art Director:* James Truesdale. *Set Decorator:* Maria Nay. *Set Dresser:* Mara Massey, Dale Anderson, Brooke Bacon, Brent Blom, and Brooke Sartorius. *Special Effects:* Larry Fioritto. *Costumes:* Jeffrey Kurland. *Make-up:* Bill Corso. *Make-up (Jim Carrey):* Sheryl Ptak. *Stunt Coordinator:* Buddy Joe Hooker. *Running time:* 118 minutes. *MPAA Rating:* R.

CAST: Jim Carrey (Andy Kaufman); Gerry Becker (Stanley Kaufman); Greyson Pendry (Little Michael Kaufman); Brittany Colonna (Baby Carol Kaufman); Leslie Lyles (Janice Kaufman); Bobby Boriello (Little Andy Kaufman); George Shapiro (Mr. Besserman); Danny DeVito (George Shapiro); Budd Friedman (Himself); Tom Dreesen (Wiseass Comic); Thomas Armbruster (Improv Piano Player); Pamela Abdy (Diane Barnett); Wendy Polland (Little

Wendy); Cash Oshman (Yogi); Matt Price and Christina Cabot (Meditation Students); Richard Belzer (Himself); Melanie Vesey (Carol Kaufman); Michael Kelly (Michael Kaufman); Miles Chapin (SNL Assistant); Isadore Rosenfeld (ABC Executive); Vincent Schiavelli (Maynard Smith); Molly Schaffer (Maynard Smith's Assistant); Howard West, Greg Travis, and Maureen Mueller (ABC Executives); Phil Perlman (Mama Rivoli's Angry Guy); Tony Clifton (Himself); Jessica Devlin (Mama Rivoli's Diner); Paul Giamatti (Bob Zmuda); Jeff Thomas (Andy's Stand-in); Randall Carver (Himself); Peter Bonerz (Ed Weinberger); Howard Keystone (Taxi Marching Man); Howdy Doody (Himself); Brent Briscoe (Heavyset Technician); Ray Bokhour and Patton Oswalt (Blue Collar Guys); Caroline Gibson (Sorority Girl); Conrad Roberts (College Promoter); Jeff Zabel (College Student); Marilyn Sokol (Madame); Angela Jones and Krystina Carson (Hookers); Gerry Robert Byrne (Taxi AD/Stage Manager); Mark Davenport (LA Times Reporter); Bert F. Balsam, Lonnie Hamilton, Ron Sanchez, and Billy Lucas (Taxi Security Guards); Patricia Scanlon (Ed Weinberger's Secretary); Max Alexander (Harrah's Booker); Ed Mitchell (Harrah's Conductor); Reiko Aylesworth (Mimi); Michael Villani (Merv Griffin); Courtney Love (Lynne Margulies); Maria Maglaris (Irate Merv Spectator); Heath Hyche (Merv's Guest Coordinator); Robert Holeman (Boxing Trainer); James Ross (Wrestling Commentator); Tamara Bossett (Foxy Jackson); Gene Lebell (Foxy Jackson Referee); Bob Zmuda (Jack Burns); Brian Peck (Friday's Announcer); Caroline Rhea (Friday's Melanie); Mary Lynn Rajskub (Friday's Mary); Phil Lenkowsky (Friday's Tech Director); Rob Steiner (Friday's Control Booth Tech); Claudia Jaffee (Friday's Floor Director); Mando Guerrero (Jerry Lawler Referee); Lance Russell (Ring Announcer); Ladi Von Jansky (Stadium Photographer); K.P. Palmer, Mark Majetti, and Deana Ann Aburto (Memphis Paramedics); Mews Small and David Elliott (TM Administrators); Fredd Wayne (Bland Doctor); Tracey Walter (National Enquirer Editor); David Koechner and Jeanine Jackson (National Enquirer Reporters); Johnny Legend (Wild-Haired Guru); Doris Eaton Travis (Eleanor Gould); Greg Sutton (Carnegie Hall Conductor); Sydney Lassick (Crystal Healer); Yoshi Jenkins (Jun Roxas); Lance Alarcon (Comedy Store Patron); D.J. Johnson (Comedy Store Waiter); Melissa Carrey (Comedy Store Waitress).

CINEASTE, Vol. XXV No. 2, p. 52, David Sterritt

Man on the Moon joined the list of 1999's most misunderstood movies within hours of its first press screenings, as assorted critics started complaining they'd been cheated of the Andy Kaufman biopic they'd apparently come to see. The film's lukewarm box-office reception probably had a similar cause, abetted by lingering memories of Kaufman's actual career, which still conjures up extremely mixed vibes in the popular imagination. Universal Pictures didn't help, promoting the movie with publicity stunts designed to merge Jim Carrey's star power with Kaufman's own persona—a peculiar decision, considering Kaufman's rocky relationship with the public, not to mention the fact that Carrey's younger devotees aren't likely to have much awareness of Kaufman beyond *Taxi* reruns on late-night television. Nor did Universal give *Man on the Moon* an effective launch on the film-festival circuit. This was an obvious option, given the *auteur* eminence of director Milos Forman and the precedent of his previous picture, *The People vs. Larry Flynt,* opening the New York filmfest in 1997. But the studio apparently feared that any trace of 'art-film' stigmata might scare away Carrey fans before they had a chance to line up on opening weekend.

The result was a lackluster showing on all fronts for a serious, ambitious movie that deserves more thoughtful attention. To confront the most glaring misperception first, *Man on the Moon* is no more a biopic than *Solaris* is a space opera. It doesn't fail to show the 'real' Andy Kaufman and reveal what 'made him tick.' It takes virtually no interest in those tasks, focusing instead on the substance of his trailblazing work—his radical challenge of entertainment norms as a performance artist *avant la lettre* who had the audacity to conduct his experiments in the populist arenas of comedy clubs and commercial TV.

Since the movie's value rests on its faithfulness to the spirit (if not always the specifics) of Kaufman's career, a bit of synopsis is in order here. Kaufman climbed the comedy-club ladder in the early Seventies, gaining his first national attention on *Saturday Night Live* in 1975. Acquiring a following and an agent, he joined the fledgling *Taxi* sitcom, where he turned the

Foreign Man character from his stand-up act into Latka Gravas, a mechanic who makes up in amiability what he lacks in language skills. This confirmed Kaufman as a mainstream success by industry standards but an Establishment sell-out by his own. He soon reasserted his orneriness by inventing "intergender wrestling" and becoming the self-declared bad guy of the sport, pushing the envelope of professional wrestling's already dubious show biz conventions. He also played the nightclub circuit in the guise of Tony Clifton, his uproariously obnoxious alter ego. As satirical as they clearly were, these deliberately abrasive moves caused great confusion among Kaufman's erstwhile admirers and nearly wrecked his career. He died in 1984 from large-cell carcinoma, an uncommon form of lung cancer. He was 35 and a nonsmoker.

Man on the Moon begins with a comic disclaimer vis-à-vis its fidelity to the facts: Speaking to the camera, Carrey/Kaufman/ Foreign Man complains of changes made in the story "for dramatic purposes," noting "all the baloney" these have brought into the picture. This won't persuade Kaufman loyalists to overlook the movie's most flagrant rearrangements of the record, but what matters in the film is less its journalistic accuracy than its commitment to the cultural resonances of his work. Here it excels by virtue of Forman's efficient stylistics, Carrey's surprisingly nuanced performance, and the ingenious *mise-en-abime* structure devised by screenwriters Scott Alexander and Larry Karaszewski, whose previous pictures include Tim Burton's admirable *Ed Wood* and Forman's own *Larry Flynt* epic.

Just as *Man on the Moon* has been underrated by critics mistaking it for a biopic, Kaufman's career was undervalued by audiences mistaking him for a comedian. He resisted this, but the label he preferred "song and dance man"—was even further off the mark, as he surely (and mischievously) knew. In actuality he was, as I've suggested above, a performance artist whose laboratory was the art-unfriendly world of mainstream entertainment, and whose obsessions were more far-reachingly subversive than that world could begin to comprehend, much less put up with.

His career had clear ties with comedy, of course, and one important aspect of his work was its bold refiguring of stand-up comedy conventions. The dominant style of middlebrow-to-highbrow comedy in the Fifties and Sixties, from Steve Allen and Mort Sahl to Jean Shepherd and Lenny Bruce, relied on making the audience into coconspirators with the comedian, sharing a nebulous sort of hipness that contrasted with the out-group squareness of everyone not in the room. Kaufman discombobulated this pattern with a vengeance, largely by keeping his audience in a state of continual uncertainty as to what in the world he might do next. Questions of the most basic kind—is he kidding? Is this part of the act? Is the show over yet?—moved from the margins to center stage, and stayed there for disconcertingly long stretches of time. Not surprisingly, this drove spectators crazy, and not surprisingly, Kaufman took that as a triumph. "This is the hippest audience in television," says Kaufman's agent in *Man on the Moon,* telling his client that even *Saturday Night Live* viewers want nothing more to do with him. Kaufman gets the message, but the movie has taught us that he's secretly thrilled at such events. He's made people feel, and what they feel is almost beside the point.

Kaufman's desire to rework the dynamics of comedy is one facet of his interest in what performance theorists call "breaking the frame," which has a long pedigree, from Dada and Surrealism to performance art per se. This tradition was very much alive in the Sixties, when Kaufman was crystallizing his ideas as a teenager, and it produced an explosion of innovative concepts in the Seventies, the very decade when Kaufman made his first public impact. Its practices are often associated with boundary-blurring uses of the performative body, which is precisely what Kaufman specialized in as he confounded speech and action with silence and stillness; merged performance spaces with the outside world; and refused to distinguish a 'real' self from an 'acting' self, to the point where his most hyperbolic fans reportedly saw his death as the last and best prank of an unstoppable artist who'd turned indeterminacy into the ultimate expressive form.

I won't claim that *Man on the Moon* is as radical or resolute as the work it celebrates, but Alexander and Karaszewski have been remarkably successful at weaving Kaufman's sensibility into their screenplay, using intermittent appearances by his loony Clifton character to muddle the lines between performative reality, biographical reality, socio-cultural reality, and various combinations thereof. Carrey provides brilliant support for their endeavor in at least three ways: his portrayal of Kaufman is uncannily accurate; his childish demeanor foregrounds Kaufman's subtextual messages about the persistence of infantile traits in adult thought and behavior; and his fitful efforts to broaden his own career (e.g., *The Truman Show*) lend poignancy to his depiction of a colleague who found a different kind of slippage between professional and personal goals. Lest his acting be dismissed as mere impersonation, I hasten to add that Carrey has crafted a genuinely creative portrait that interprets aspects of Kaufman's personality in unexpected ways. Compare his Tony Clifton with Kaufman's, for instance, and observe how Carrey adds a forward-thrusting neckline that combines with a fiercely jutting lower lip to suggest a grueling self-satisfaction that Kaufman himself didn't conjure up quite so ferociously.

I suspect much of the resistance to *Man on the Moon* has stemmed front its refusal to provide such conventional pleasures as a reassuring biopic format and production values as spiffy as the show-biz milieu that Kaufman inhabited. I further suspect Kaufman would have been pleased with it. It's often been noted that comedians are less interested in wooing their audiences than subduing them, and Kaufman carried this also to extremes, unmasking the sadomasochistic components of comic performance as few other American entertainers have done. He turned the well-timed tease (He's on the stage—why isn't he saying anything yet?) into the finely tuned torture (He's really insulting that guy—is it art of the act?) and savored the discomfort this brought on everyone concerned.

Man on the Moon seems methodically in league with his irascible agenda, from the sitcom-style flatness of Anastas Michos's cinematography to the over-the-top edginess of its wrestling sequences; even the ready-made nostalgia of the *Taxi* scenes are calculated to shrivel our romance-hungry souls with their views of a desperately aging Judd Hirsch and Christopher Lloyd cavorting on the tackiest set you ever saw. It's a spectacle only Tony Clifton could love, and here it is in a Jim Carrey picture that Universal itself couldn't figure out how to sell. Oh, yes, Kaufman would have cheered.

LOS ANGELES TIMES, 12/22/99, Calendar/p. 1, Kenneth Turan

Pleased with itself for taking on unusual subject matter, "Man on the Moon" takes pains to introduce us to the strange mind of Andy Kaufman as soon as possible, to thrust us into the Andy Zone without unnecessary delay.

"I am Andy and I would like to thank you for coming to my movie," Jim Carrey says in the clipped Foreign Man accent that was one of Kaufman's several personalities. "I wish it was better. It is stupid. Everything is mixed up for dramatic purposes."

To emphasize his point, Kaufman encourages the audience to leave the theater, even running the film's final credits to squeaky music played on a tiny portable phonograph. But people don't leave (although some will wish they had) and Kaufman, switching to what for him is a normal voice, explains that he only did the last bit to "get rid of folks who wouldn't understand me." Which, it turns out, may be just about everyone.

Certainly Kaufman, the eccentric 1970s comic who died at the age of 35, couldn't have asked for a better forum to have his strange ideas on comedy and performing presented to a wide audience. Director Milos Forman and writers Scott Alexander and Larry Karaszewski are dedicated to the notion that Kaufman was a brilliant visionary, a performance artist before that was a well-known term, years ahead of his peers in his postmortem notion that it was more than OK to have your audience hate you, it was a state close to Nirvana.

Neither could a better choice for the lead role than Carrey even be imagined. Besides sharing a birth date with Kaufman, Carrey is a major fan and seems to have an intuitive understanding of his bizarre subject. His performance is a brilliant, almost terrifying impersonation, and he's so committed to the role he seems to understand Andy better than Andy did himself.

Starting as a New York nightclub stand-up, so delighted in having an act that is "totally original, no one else is doing it" that he doesn't notice that more people are walking out than staying, Carrey's Kaufman is a provocateur, a show-biz anarchist whose mantra is "I'm not a comedian, I don't do jokes, I don't even know what's funny."

What Kaufman wants to do most of all is mess with people's minds, mock their hard-earned sense of reality. The real world was a tenuous concept for him at best (the institutionalized women in "Girl, Interrupted" seem saner than he does), so it's not surprising that everything was a put-on for Kaufman, that he got so far into his own head he couldn't get out if he'd wanted to.

Unfortunately for "Man on the Moon," Kaufman is definitely a person more interesting to hear about than to experience, an acquired taste few will be tempted to acquire. Caring only about amusing himself and fueled by contempt for his audience, Kaufman could be such an unpleasant provocateur that even those closest to him would ask, "Is it an act or are you just addicted to causing trouble?" Not even as consummate a director as Forman and writers who have made a career of heroic portraits of marginal figures ("Ed Wood," "The People vs. Larry Flynt") can make us care about someone who could not be bothered to return the favor.

Given how out-there Kaufman was, it's surprising that "Man on the Moon," its opening sequence notwithstanding, is structured like a standard "Somebody Up There Likes Me" biopic, with Danny DeVito playing the straightest role of his career as Kaufman's discoverer and agent, George Shapiro, who utters the classic words, "You're insane, but you might also be brilliant."

It was Shapiro who procured the role that made Kaufman's national reputation, the lunatic Latka Gravas on television's "Taxi." Kaufman, not surprisingly, hated the part and the show, and took his revenge on unsuspecting fans by using a tour of college campuses to read "The Great Gatsby" aloud in a pompous British accent.

Kaufman had a number of safety valves, including transcendental meditation, when the pressures of his borderline sane life got too much for him, and the most obnoxious was Tony Clifton. Given lots of attention here, Clifton was Kaufman's alter ego, a boorish Las Vegas lounge singer who projected higher levels of abrasive, anti-audience hostility than even Kaufman was willing to express himself.

The ultimate Kaufman situation, allowing him to combine varying levels of role playing, hostility and vanity, was his foray into professional wrestling in general and wrestling with women (he styled himself the World's Intergender Champion) in particular.

It was in the ring that Kaufman met Lynne Margulies (Courtney Love, beaming a lot), the girl who, despite initial reservations, inevitably ends up looking at him with adoring eyes. "Why do you pretend to be an expletive ?" she asks at one point, to which Kaufman guilelessly replies, "It's what I'm good at."

Given that Kaufman often seemed to be from another planet, "Man on the Moon," taken from an R.E.M. song about him, seems like a fitting title. If it ever turns out to be true, as some people persist in thinking, that the moon landing was faked somewhere here on Earth, Andy Kaufman would have been the perfect person to pull that off.

NEW STATESMAN, 5/8/00, p. 41, Jonathan Romney

To American audiences in the 1970s and 1980s, the comedian Andy Kaufman was a legendary figure whose confrontational routines turned show-business conventions upside down.

In Britain, where he was known mainly as the ingratiatingly kooky Latka in the TV sitcom *Taxi*, Milos Forman's biopic *Man on the Moon* won't mean quite so much. There's an uncomfortable sense of "you had to be there": we must take it on trust that Kaufman was a media revolutionary, a pop situationist and a performance artist who used prime-time TV as his medium.

Nevertheless, Kaufman's career remains startling, however accustomed we are today, to the wind-up strategies of a Chris Morris. Despite his success in *Taxi*, Kaufman professed to despise the sitcom itself and showbiz in general; yet he claimed to be a song-and-dance man at heart. He courted affection and loathing in equal measures, finally baiting his audience so thoroughly that he short-circuited his career almost entirely. On the one hand, he would play a childlike clown lip-syncing to the *Mighty Mouse* theme song; on the other, he spouted outrageous macho rhetoric challenging women to wrestling matches. He devised an alterego, a foul behemoth of a lounge singer called Tony Clifton, who became an autonomous golem and turned up to disrupt the taping of *Taxi*. Today's imaginary stars, such as Ali G, barely approach such extremism. People came to assume that Kaufman was having them on when he wasn't. The supreme irony of his life, which the film treats with some poignancy, is that neither the public nor his parents believed him when he announced that he had terminal cancer (he died in 1984).

To reproduce Kaufman's life as a canon of notorious stunts inevitably reduces terrorist strikes to greatest hits. Forman's film does just that, although it feigns not to, presenting itself as a parody of biopic conventions. It plays, sometimes excruciatingly, on the tradition of highlighting significant moments, such as the discovery of Kaufman by the agent George Shapiro. ("Heh, heh, you're insane—but you could also be brilliant!") But the fact that Shapiro is played by Danny

DeVito, Kaufman's co-star in *Taxi,* is not so much anti-illusionistic as plain cosy. There are too many friends and associates involved—in cameos, as consultants and coproducers—to make this anything other than a friendly tribute.

Jim Carrey is a wildly narcissistic performer who trades on his constant awareness of being watched; this alone makes him an appropriate candidate to play Kaufman, who was similarly never off air. As far as one can tell, Carrey genuinely transforms himself into Kaufman in both looks and mannerisms. Yet the closer Carrey gets, the more ambivalent the performance becomes: the more he vanishes into Kaufman, the more we see the feat of impersonation, obscuring Kaufman himself. One of Kaufman's best-known routines was as a nervous man of vague foreign origin, who turned out to be a dynamite Elvis impersonator. In the film, this act becomes dizzying: Carrey doing Kaufman doing the foreign man doing Elvis. But finally we just marvel at Carrey's plate-juggling ability to pull off three impersonations at once.

In effect, Carrey wears the Kaufman persona like "an expensive suit"—to quote *Being John Malkovich,* that incisive commentary on the lure of borrowed identity. In this respect, *Man on the Moon* is a film of its time: our current entertainment culture, starved for original turns, is morbidly obsessed with off-the-peg appropriations, living holograms of dead acts. The film is of a piece with the fad for pop revivals by proxy, tribute bands doing Abba or The Doors. It is close to, but not nearly as insightful as, Terry Johnson's recent stage and TV evocations of the Carry On Team. And it is perhaps closest to the British artist Gavin Turk's sculptures of himself as Sid Vicious and Che Guevara: Forman effectively presents an animated waxwork of Carrey in Kaufman's clothes.

The screenwriters Scott Alexander and Larry Karaszewski are veterans of such reanimation, having written Tim Burton's *Ed Wood* and Forman's *The People versus Larry Flynt.* The *raison d'être* of such biopics is ironic hindsight, as if nobody had understood at the time that these lives were exemplary American narratives. *Man on the Moon* successfully presents Kaufman as a tormented package of contradictions, a one-man deconstruction of showmanship and its discontents. Yet the film is neither very entertaining nor illuminating: you come out uncertain whether Kaufman was a genius or a disturbed time-waster. It invokes the inner child, but offers little insight into the adult: we learn that Kaufman was turned on by wrestling women and that he married a nice woman called Lynne (played like an afterthought by Courtney Love and, in real life, a creative consultant on the film). Nor does it reveal much about the *folie à deux* he shared with his accomplice Bob Zmuda (the co-executive producer).

This is the approved, authorised Kaufman story. He may have been most interesting when demolishing his own charm, but the stunt the film cherishes is a Carnegie Hall spectacular featuring the Rockettes, Santa Claus and milk and cookies for the whole audience. After celebrating his abrasive destroy-all-certainties ethic, the film concludes by revealing that Kaufman was a happy vaudevillean, after all. It's like a Sex Pistols biopic in which Johnny Rotten finally redeems himself as an entertaining guest on *Blankety Blank.*

NEW YORK, 1/3/00, p. 85, Peter Rainer

This must be the week for nowhere men in the movies. We have, besides *Ripley, Man on the Moon,* starting Jim Carrey as the late Andy Kaufman. Its pivotal moment comes when Andy tells his girlfriend, Lynne Margulies (Courtney Love), that she doesn't know the real him, and she responds, "There *isn't* a real you," and he says, "Oh, yeah, I forgot." Director Milos Forman and his screenwriters, Scott Alexander and Larry Karaszewski, have attempted to make a movie about a human nullity, and a fair amount of screen time is taken up with Kaufman's bizarre routines and shenanigans. He doesn't reveal himself onstage, and he doesn't offstage either; whether he's playing Latka Gravas on *Taxi* or the crumbum Vegas entertainer Tony Clifton, he never breaks character.

The usual Hollywood approach to celebrity bio is two-pronged: Freudian-ize and canonize. *Man on the Moon* goes heavy on the canonization—that's its major weakness—but it doesn't pretend to "explain" Kaufman. No childhood trauma, no Rosebud, awaits our discovery. The movie assumes that performers are authentic only when they're performing, and so the Andy that Milos Forman gives us is always on. He needs to be entertained by audiences—by their cheers and jeers—at least as much as they need to be entertained by him.

What the movie doesn't explore is how Kaufman might have been deeply pained by his multiple-man mind-set, and it also doesn't suggest the cruelty behind some of his so-called performance art. When he refuses to play Latka for a clamorous college audience and, instead, submits the few of them who remain to a cover-to-cover, English-accented reading of *The Great Gatsby*, the scene is played as if he were asserting his right to be an artist and not just a sitcom personality. But when he wasn't taking them out for milk and cookies, Kaufman regularly rebuffed his audiences, and he didn't do it because he was protecting the purity of his gifts. He did it because he probably couldn't help himself, and because flop sweat for him was just as sweet as the nectar of adulation. Heckling was music to his ears; that's why he made such a big deal out of wrestling women in his self-created "intergender" championship matches. Strutting and playing the villain inside the ring, he could provoke a direct-action response from audiences even more effectively than in the comedy clubs. *Man on the Moon* makes the same mistake that Bob Fosse's *Lenny* made: It gives the abrasiveness of its subject a saintly glow.

Perhaps part of that glow exists because many of the people who were important to Kaufman's life and career—including George Shapiro, his agent; Bob Zmuda, his friend and writer; and Lynne Margulies, his girlfriend—acted as advisers and, in some cases, co-producers on the film as well as being depicted in it. A lot of the action has a scrubbed, authorized feel. Thus, when Shapiro, played as a lump of human kindness by Danny DeVito, first connects with Kaufman, he tells him, "You're insane, but you might also be brilliant." In a nightclub, Paul Giamatti's Zmuda plays the stooge to Andy's Tony Clifton, getting razzed before an unsuspecting audience and having a drink thrown in his face, and afterward it's all fun and games between them. We don't see how Zmuda might have reacted to this kind of usage, or what resentments or competitiveness may have been behind it. Courtney Love's Lynne first encounters Andy when she loses to him in one of his wrestling matches, but soon after she turns into a drab, devotional caregiver. Their relationship is depicted as a love match, but there's virtually no sexual dimension to Kaufman in this film: he's almost as infantilized as Pee-wee Herman.

Jim Carrey plays Kaufman onstage with an uncanny exactitude, but what are we watching exactly? He's doing more than mere impersonation, and yet Kaufman never comes to full-blooded life for us, any more than Carrey's Truman, another hologram of a person, did. When I did a brief interview with Kaufman in L.A. in the early eighties, I thought I was talking to somebody out of *The Manchurian Candidate*. There was a propulsive, gaga rhythm to his patter. I was hoping *Man on the Moon* would prove an enlightenment, but by conceiving of Kaufman as a holy hollow man who lived only through his guises, the filmmakers have deprived Carrey of the opportunity to go behind the comic's fixed blank stare. If there's no there there, why should he, or we, bother? The movie is intended as a celebration of Andy Kaufman, but it's the kind of celebration that denatures its subject. It's not the "real" man we're missing. We're missing a man, any man, period.

NEW YORK POST, 12/22/99, p. 51, Lou Lumenick

When comedian Andy Kaufman died in 1984 of lung cancer at the age of 35, his reputation as a prankster was so notorious that many people thought the death was his ultimate hoax.

Kaufman is uncannily brought back to life by Jim Carrey in an extraordinary, Oscar-worthy impersonation in Milos Forman's "Man on the Moon," an audacious celebration of a mad genius who challenged audiences with material crafted to make them uncomfortable.

Best remembered for playing the sweet, English-fracturing immigrant Latka Gravas on the TV series "Taxi" (which he loathed), Kaufman virtually destroyed his career with a series of ever-more elaborate stunts.

He was barred from "Saturday Night Live" (then TV's edgiest show) after a poll revealed only 28 percent of viewers wanted him to remain on the program.

"Man on the Moon" (also the title of an R.E.M. song about Kaufman) is less a conventional biography than a performance film—one that stuns and delights.

Forman and screenwriters Scott Alexander and Larry Karaszewski ("Ed Wood," Forman's "The People vs. Larry Flynt") signal their intention to skip pat psychological observations by having Kaufman's Foreign Man character denounce the movie as inaccurate at the outset—and ordering the audience home as the closing credits roll.

A sensation on the first episode of "Saturday Night Live"—posing silently while lip-synching only the refrain of the "Mighty Mouse" TV theme—Kaufman joins "Taxi," represented in the film by a montage featuring original cast members (among them Judd Hirsch and Marilu Henner) surrealistically playing themselves of 20 years ago.

But Kaufman's career is on the skids well before "Taxi" ends its six-year run.

Aided by his demented writing partner Bob Zmuda (played by a terrific Paul Giamatti), Kaufman turns off audiences by creating an obnoxious, bloated lounge-singer alter ego named Tony Clifton who Kaufman famously insisted wasn't himself (a fiction respected in the movies credits).

Even more alienating is Kaufman's obsession with wrestling women, including a bout on Merv Griffin's TV show in which, the movie has it, Kaufman meets his girlfriend Lynne Margulies (a miscast Courtney Love in a brief role).

There is also his notorious (and staged) coffee-flinging incident with wrestler Jerry Lawler on "Late Night with David Letterman."

By this point, Kaufman's harried manager George Shapiro (Kaufman's old "Taxi" castmate Danny DeVito, who served as one of the movie's producers) begins to panic.

After Kaufman is diagnosed with cancer, he stages a spectacular comeback with a Carnegie Hall concert featuring Santa Claus, bogus Rockettes and a phony Mormon Tabernacle Choir. He then takes the audience out for milk and cookies.

It makes a great climax for the film, even if the concert actually happened several years earlier. (The film ignores Kaufman's disastrous movie career and his adolescence, during which he impregnated another girlfriend and they gave their child up for adoption.)

"You don't know the real me," Kaufman at one point complains to Margulies, who replies: "There isn't a real you."

"Man on the Moon," one of the year's most entertaining movies, has the courage to leave you wondering if she was right.

NEWSDAY, 12/22/99, Part II/p. B2, John Anderson

You wonder whether Andy Kaufman would have appreciated the irony. Described as everything from "the first true performance artist" to "the Zen guerrilla" to "the nihilistic elf," the late, confrontational comedian now finds himself the subject of a bio-pic as formulaic as "Man on the Moon." It sounds like a prank Kaufman would have played on himself.

Another in director Milos Forman's catalog of fractured-genius pictures ("Amadeus," "The People vs. Larry Flynt"), "Man on the Moon" stars Jim Carrey in a role many have been predicting will get him the Oscar nomination he was denied for "The Truman Show." It very likely will. Although the two comics ar antithetical—Carrey will clearly do anything for a laugh; Kaufman would do nothing—Carrey is otherworldy, abandoning all of his own trademark tics and flourishes and creating a fully realized character known as Andy Kaufman.

The problem—which belongs to Forman; his writers, Scott Alexander and Larry Karaszewski, and whatever lawyers might have been waiting in the wings—is that Carrey's Andy Kaufman is little more than an Andy Kaufman character. "Our story begins in Great Neck, Long Island" the film tells us, but the story might well have ended there, too, because there's nothing we don't already know. There's Andy doing Elvis; there's Andy on "Saturday Night Live," lip-synching "Mighty Mouse"; there's Andy putting a college audience to sleep by reading "The Great Gatsby"; there's Andy on Letterman, getting slapped out of his seat by wrestler Jerry Lawler, a hoax so convincing the wire services ran it as fact. There's Andy inviting his Carnegie Hall audience for milk and cookies. Hey, there's Andy with cancer, getting outpranked by a Filipino shaman's sleight of hand.

Since you could get most of this off an Andy Kaufman highlights reel, one wonders why Forman—who once upon a time, remember, directed "One Flew Over the Cuckoo's Nest"—wasted his time with a screenplay so superficial. Movies about artists—and like him or not, Kaufman was some kind of artist—should be about what makes that artist tick. "Man on the Moon" is sturdy, entertaining, funny and travels the rutted road of the standard show biz biography: Talent rises, falls, rises again, tries something new, is misunderstood and, in Kaufman's case, succumbs to a rare lung cancer at 35.

Paul Giamatti is terrific as Kaufman's collaborator, Bob Zmuda. Courtney Love, a lot tamer than she was in "Larry Flynt," is fine as Kaufman's love interest, Lynne Margulies. Forman makes some mischief, mostly with Tony Clifton, the Las Vegas lounge singer and Kaufman alter ego, whom the movie portrays not just as a separate entity from Kaufman but as his survivor. The truly Kaufmanesque moment, however, is when Forman assembles the current-day alumni of "Taxi"—the show Kaufman reputedly hated, but which made him famous—and you realize that Danny DeVito (who's busy playing Kaufman's manager, George Shapiro) is missing.

What's also missing, however, is some kind of revelation about Kaufman. "Man on the Moon" is basically the version of Andy Kaufman's life that Andy Kaufman would have told himself. And if the movie's clear about anything, it's that you couldn't trust Andy Kaufman.

NEWSWEEK, 12/20/99, p. 44, David Ansen

Jim Carrey may be a better Andy Kaufman than Andy Kaufman. In director Milos Forman's quirky, very entertaining "Man on the Moon," Carrey pulls off a neat trick—he gets deeply inside a man, who, by his own admission, had no inside to get into. What Carrey plays are the many characters Kaufman portrayed in lieu having a personality of his own. For most people, this meant the benignly-out-of-it Latka on "Taxi". Others" knew him as the belligerent guy who tossed women around in the wrestling ring. Most alarming of all was Kaufman's boorish alter ego Tony Clifton, a talentless Vegas lounge singer. Carrey resurrects them all and they seem, in his elastic hands, a little funnier than we'd remembered.

Carrey's totally committed performance captures both Kaufman's mania and his strange detachment. Kaufman was more interested in making people uncomfortable than in making them laugh. He took an often hostile delight in blurring the line between performance and reality. Was his coffee-throwing fight with wrestler Jerry Lawler on the "Letterman" show for real or a setup? Ambiguity was his weapon and his disguise. What's most striking about Forman's movie is that it makes no attempt to psychoanalyze or explain its subject. Screenwriters Scott Alexander and Larry Karaszewski ("Ed Wood"), specialists in oddball biopics, are content to take Kaufman at face value—as a man of many masks, none more authentic than the next.

Forman hasn't made a movie this light on its feet in years. But what's missing is much of the danger that was a crucial part of Kaufman's act. Because he's dead, and because it's the movie star Jim Carrey playing him, the audience has a safety net. We can laugh at the concert where he read the entire "The Great Gatsby" in a phony British accent: we're spared that live audience's pain. But Forman's decision to stick to the surface is probably, in the end, a wise one. Kaufman always wanted to keep us guessing, and this movie respects his wishes.

SIGHT AND SOUND, 4/00, p. 57, Leslie Felperin

The comedian Andy Kaufman introduces the story of his life. As a child, he fantasises about performing on television. By the mid 70s, he is working clubs in LA as a stand-up comedian. George Shapiro, an agent, signs Andy and gets him an appearance on the comedy show *Saturday Night Live*. This brings an offer of a regular role on a new sitcom called *Taxi*. Andy reluctantly takes the part on condition the producers guarantee a guest slot for his friend Tony Clifton, an obnoxious lounge singer who insults his audience. George learns Clifton is really Andy, working with a plant, Bob Zmuda, his partner who sometimes plays Clifton as well.

Taxi becomes a hit, but Andy yearns to push his comedy further. He gets the opportunity to make a special, but the material proves too bizarre for the network. He starts a new act wrestling women. Through this he meets his future wife Lynne, and eventually falls afoul of professional wrestler Jerry Lawler, although their antagonism is staged. Many of his fans turn against Andy, deciding he's either offensive or not funny any more. *Taxi* is cancelled. Andy discovers he has a rare form of lung cancer. He gives a triumphant performance at Carnagie Hall but dies soon after. His funeral is stage managed as he wanted it. Some time later, Tony Clifton performs at an LA club, sparking rumours Andy is still alive.

Clearly, if you're going to spend $52 million making a movie about a now-obscure comedian from the 70s, you have to believe his life is extraordinary in some way. (It's probably rule number one in the textbook for film school courses called *Advanced Screenwriting: Biopics*.) Indeed on paper, Andy Kaufman's life story sounds thrillingly unlikely. Here's an introverted situationist *manqué* who rose to fame and fortune by singing along to the theme tune from *Mighty Mouse*, pretending to be a inept refugee and physically assaulting people. As every good biopic protagonist should, he duly died tragically young, of lung cancer at the age of 36. (Allegedly he didn't even smoke, which is in itself pretty funny.)

The problem is that while Kaufman's life story has its required quota of bizarre yet true events, it's doomed to failure as mainstream entertainment because Kaufman wasn't terribly likeable as a person. More importantly, he was the master of a comedy style that, as his agent George in the film tells him, is "only funny to two people in the universe." He means Kaufman and his partner Bob Zmuda, although we should clearly include *Man on the Moon*'s director Milos Forman and star Jim Carrey among the fans of Kaufman's particular brand of wit and whimsy.

It's to their and the film's credit that it only half-heartedly tries to sweeten these acrid pills. Kaufman, uncannily and superbly impersonated by Carrey right down the flaring eyelids and gratingly fey Latka voice, remains in the movie a bit of an arrogant prick, whose psychology the film either audaciously refuses to flesh out or spinelessly can't because of the risk of litigation from surviving friends and relatives. (This makes Lynne Margulies, Kaufman's wife, no more than a functional straight man in a peasant blouse throughout.) In many ways, Kaufman is kin to the hero of Forman's last film, *The People vs. Larry Flynt*. Both Kaufman and porn-magnate-turned-first-amendment-champion Flynt are dodgy, deeply flawed characters whom Forman (a Czech refugee who has always revered his adopted country's ideal of self-realisation, no matter how obnoxious the result) delights in heroising. While Kaufman doesn't have the same historical importance as Flynt, he has supporters who champion to this day his 'subversive' performances, such as reading *The Great Gatsby* deadpan on stage for hours—stunts almost always more amusing when described than when observed.

Again you have to give the film credit for not wussing out and for letting Carrey's recreations of Kaufman's turns risk boring us. At a key point, Kaufman asks his transcendental-meditation guru what the secret of comedy is, to which comes the reply: "Silence." As often as not, this finds a correlative in the sound of no hands clapping and no one laughing at his act, but it's linked to the way Kaufman would push comic timing to the limits of tolerance. In one excellent scene, we see him arguing with the network executives producing his special about exactly how many seconds the show can mimic the vertical-hold fritzing on viewers' televisions before it will set off a nationwide bout of set banging.

Likewise, the movie tries to encapsulate Kaufman's subversiveness formally in little self-reflexive frills and trimmings. We see Kaufman in a montage working on the set of *Taxi*, with all its original cast members playing themselves (the years have been more unkind to some than to others), apart from Danny DeVito who is already playing George (he was the show's biggest discovery apart from Kaufman and Christopher Lloyd). Jerry Lawler and David Letterman reenact a famous fight on the latter's show between Kaufman and Lawler, edited in such a way to maximise the revelation in the next scene that this too was just another pre-planned stunt. *Man on the Moon* opens with Kaufman telling us he thinks the film is so bad he's decided to cut straight to the end. So the final credits roll before Kaufman comes back to explain that was just to frighten off the people who wouldn't understand it. Unfortunately, there's not as much to understand as Kaufman, Forman, Carrey *et al* think.

VILLAGE VOICE, 12/28/99, p. 121, J. Hoberman

The second coming of the late Andy Kaufman is an appropriately self-reflexive affair. As star Jim Carrey staged a fame mock-Kaufman disruption at the *Man on the Moon* junket, so the movie itself opens with a pastiche of Kaufman's 1978 television special, *Andy's Fun House* (currently showing at the Museum of Television and Radio), which serves to introduce his key tropes of childhood, TV, and failure.

Cutting from the child Andy, singing a kid's song for his sister, to grown-up Andy 20 years later, provoking an incredulous Improv audience with an equally sincere rendition of the same inane song, *Man on the Moon* poses the central Kaufman enigma. Was this guy the holy innocent of stand-up comedy? A real-life Chauncey Gardner mimicking everything he learned on television? A conscious practitioner of Zen slapstick? A mass-market performance artist? A postpolitcal yippie? (And if he was just doing his thing, what was that? Borderline autism? Split personality? Arrested development?)

"I'm not a comedian. I don't do jokes," Kaufman tells his prospective agent (played by *Taxi* costar Danny DeVito) in *Man on the Moon.* "I don't even know what's funny." Basically, Kaufman confounded expectations with a deadpan refusal to break character and a fearless willingness to bomb. Even at his late-'70s height, Kaufman was pretty much a cult taste. He placed himself beyond the pale as an outrageously sexist wrestler-villain, taunting the crowds while offering $500 to any woman who could pin him.

Movie as boxed CD set, *Man on the Moon* offers an anthology of Kaufman's greatest hits: the hilariously unfunny Foreign Man, uncanny Elvis, minimalist rendition of the Mighty Mouse song on *Saturday Night Live,* chaotic scuffle on the set of the live show *Fridays,* and Carnegie Hall milk-and-cookies concert. The acts hold up but, for Foreman, it's the same thing over and over. Repeatedly, as if by some contractual agreement, he cuts to the reaction of Kaufman's baffled parents: "That kid is totally meshugge."

Man on the Moon is as hyperreal in its way as *Ed Wood* (also written by Scott Alexander and Larry Karaszewski). The movie is stocked with celebrities, from David Letterman to the cast of *Taxi,* who are pleased to appear as themselves. Carrey nails his character's distinctively avid, wide-eyed stare-at once frozen-faced and shifty—even as he gives Kaufman an additionally wired and paranoid edge. The effect is not unlike one of Richard Estes's insanely detailed representations of storefronts on upper Broadway. It's an obvious performance, but wasn't that always the point? (indeed, Carrey's imitation of Kaufman's sometime alter ego—the supremely obnoxious lounge singer, Tony Clifton—might be even better than Kaufman's.)

Carrey seems to have conceived Kaufman as a sort of Truman Burbank turned inside out—a man who knowingly treated the world as his TV show. But, television aside, there's no social context. The movie is considerably less expansive than Foreman's last essay in American craziness, *The People vs. Larry Flynt.* The filmmakers don't even attempt to give Kaufman an inner life. (The big revelation Andy remains a '50s kid at heart. He still gets choked up at *Lassie.)* The dragged-out ending avoids bathos thanks only to Kaufman's particular genius. There's a sense of that genius in *Man on the Moon* but even more to be found in *Andy's Fun House.*

Also reviewed in:
CHICAGO TRIBUNE, 12/22/99, Tempo/p. 1, Michael Wilmington
NATION, 1/24/00, p. 36, Stuart Klawans
NEW YORK TIMES, 12/22/99, p. E1, Janet Maslin
VARIETY, 12/13-19/99, p. 109, Todd McCarthy
WASHINGTON POST, 12/24/99, p. C1, Stephen Hunter
WASHINGTON POST, 12/24/99, Weekend/p. 32, Desson Howe

MANSFIELD PARK

A Miramax Films and BBC Films release in association with The Arts Council of England of a Miramax, Hal Films production. *Executive Producer:* Trea Hoving, David Aukin, Colin Leventhal, David M. Thompson, Bob Weinstein, and Harvey Weinstein. *Producer:* Sarah Curtis. *Director:* Patricia Rozema. *Screenplay:* Patricia Rozema. *Based on the novel "Mansfield Park" and letters and journals by:* Jane Austen. *Director of Photography:* Michael Coulter. *Editor:* Martin Walsh. *Music:* Lesley Barber and Bob Last. *Choreographer:* Jane Gibson. *Sound:* Peter Glossop. *Sound Editor:* Glenn Freemantle. *Casting:* Gail Stevens. *Production Designer:* Christopher Hobbs. *Art Director:* Andrew Munro. *Set Decorator:* Patricia Edwards. *Special Effects:* Richard Van Den Berg. *Costumes:* Andrea Galer. *Make-up:* Veronica Brebner. *Running time:* 105 minutes. *MPAA Rating:* PG-13.

CAST: Hannah Taylor Gordon (Young Fanny); Talya Gordon (Young Susan); Lindsay Duncan (Mrs. Price); Bruce Byron (Carriage Driver); James Purefoy (Tom Bertram); Sheila Gish (Mrs.

Norris); Harold Pinter (Sir Thomas Bertram); Elizabeth Eaton (Young Maria); Elizabeth Earl (Young Julia); Philip Sarson (Young Edmund); Amelia Warner (Teenage Fanny); Frances O'Connor (Fanny Price); Jonny Lee Miller (Edmund Bertram); Lindsay Duncan (Lady Bertram); Victoria Hamilton (Maria Bertram); Hugh Bonneville (Mr. Rushworth); Justine Waddell (Julia Bertram); Embeth Davidtz (Mary Crawford); Alessandro Nivola (Henry Crawford); Charles Edwards (Yates); Sophia Myles (Susan); Hilton McRae (Mr. Price); Anna Popplewell (Betsey); Danny Worters (Boy with Bird Cart); Gordon Reid (Dr. Winthrop).

LOS ANGELES TIMES, 11/18/99, Calendar/p. 52, Kenneth Turan

With its self-effacing heroine and deeply moral concerns, "Mansfield Park" is Jane Austen's unlikeliest candidate for screen success, but that hasn't stopped writer-director Patricia Rozema from trying. She's turned what is perhaps the novelist's least appealing work into a vision of what Austen would have written if she were a fearless and committed 20th century feminist instead of an early 19th century spinster with the most subtle insights into human nature. If, in other words, she'd had the good fortune to be as self-consciously clever and politically correct as Rozema.

Though it takes some getting used to, Rozema's subversive "Mansfield Park," surely the first Austen adaptation to be rated PG-13 for "brief violent images, sexual content and drug use," does have its points. It's sensitively acted and Rozema's belief in her audacious vision is so strong it brings a fine intensity to the material.

But though it's never dull, this "Mansfield Park" has too much of its own agenda and too little of Austen's to completely succeed. What's implicit in the novel is made blatant and explicit here, what was merely hinted at with exquisite skill is now screamed from the rooftops. It's an interesting take, and it always holds our interest, but it's finally too ham-fisted to be a completely winning one.

Rozema has done all this by more or less ignoring heroine Fanny Price as written and turning that character into a version of Jane Austen herself, a controversial choice memorably skewered by columnist Ron Rosenbaum in a recent New York Observer piece. "They've taken a heroine whose identity was in the integrity of her resistance to being lovable," he wrote about a film he variously calls "Mansfield (Theme) Park" and "Mansfield Park Nice," "and made her into an audience-friendly, happenin' babe."

From the film's introduction of 10-year-old Fanny Price telling stories to her younger sister Susie, this is a character bent on creating imaginary worlds, a talent she is going to greatly need in her about-to-change circumstances. For impoverished Fanny is going to leave home to live with the wealthy Bertrams of Mansfield Park and be put under the care of the grave and grumpy Sir Thomas (Harold Pinter, of all people), his substance-abusing wife (Lindsay Doran) and Fanny's other aunt Mrs. Norris (Sheila Gish). She is fated to be the classic poor relation, looked down on by all and sundry and treated like a servant by Maria and Julia, the snooty Bertram sisters.

Fanny, however, has two secret weapons: her male cousin Edmund, an all-around swell fellow, and her restless urge to write. Letters on top of letters flow back home to Susie, and soon the fictional Fanny is using up piles of paper scribbling clever histories and satires that were in fact written by the real Jane Austen.

As Fanny/Jane grows up into the attractive Frances O'Connor (memorable in the Australian comedy "Love and Other Catastrophes"), Maria (Victoria Hamilton) and Julia (Justine Waddell) still look down on her. And her best audience remains the always faithful Edmund (Jonny Lee Miller, unrecognizable from "Trainspotting"), who as the younger son (older brother Tom who stands to inherit the family fortune is a complete wastrel) is thinking of a career in the clergy.

While the novel's Fanny, "as fearful of notice and praise as other women are of neglect," rarely had the nerve to say boo, this one is a regular firebrand, with a tongue "sharper than the guillotine" and way concerned with class differences, the position of women and the evils of slavery.

In fact, capitalizing on the fact that the Bertrams' money comes from slave-run plantations in the West Indies, Rozema makes a bigger deal out of the horrors of that institution than comfortably fits into the picture, including commissioning a song called "Dijongna" ("Slavery") by the great Malian singer Salif Keita and introducing an X-rated illustrated journal showing graphic scenes of rape and torture. Now there's a touch Austen surely would have used if only she'd thought of it herself.

Into this confusing atmosphere, half modern and half traditional, come the Crawfords, Mary (Embeth Davidtz) and Henry (Alessandro Nivola), a brother and sister pair of sophisticated city mice who dazzle the countrified Bertrams.

Henry flirts with anything in skirts, and Edmund (oh, the fool) is very much taken with Mary, a woman much given to cigars and low-cut gowns who is never too busy to cast an unmistakably lascivious eye on our attractive Fanny.

An area where "Mansfield Park" the movie has more success than the novel is in one of the book's pivotal situations, the suddenly serious infatuation flirtatious Henry develops for Fanny. Fanny resists ("No man died of love but on the stage, Mr. Crawford") but the quandary of how much and how sincerely a scamp can reform is given full treatment, as is the question, much closer to Rozema's heart, of the almost unbearable pressures brought on women to marry for fiscal advantage.

Though Rozema's radicalized vision is energetic and different, and she certainly can't be accused of timidity, her film's determination to be modern no matter what the consequences finally does it in. "Mansfield Park" is insistent to the very un-Austenish point of stridency about the horrors of insensitive men and the sad state of put-upon women; Rozema is so embarrassed at the tale's inevitable conventional happy ending she can barely film it. And for every unexpected grace note there is a thudding line like "This is 1808, for heaven's sake." For heaven's sake indeed.

NEW STATESMAN, 4/3/00, p. 46, Jonathan Romney

The poster blurb for *Mansfield Park* proclaims this to be "the newest and steamiest Jane Austen adaptation". And just how steamy, pray, ought an Austen adaptation to be? These days, we're used to them being passably torrid, ever since Mr Darcy's wet-shirted swim in the BBC's *Pride and Prejudice*—a version based partly on the proposition that its heroine, Elizabeth Bennet, should be, as the adapter Andrew Davies put it, "wonderful in bed".

Patricia Rozema's *Mansfield Park* similarly proposes a world in which almost everyone is hot to trot. It's also very much a revisionist rewrite: Rozema has described the story in flatly modern terms as being about "a dysfunctional family with an absentee slave-trader father". *Mansfield Park* is famously the novel which many Austenites dislike, for which special excuses have to be made, largely because of the intractably dry figure of Fanny Price. She is the timid poor relation brought to live with the rich Bertrams and treated as their inferior, but who, through self-denial and firmness of character, becomes the household's moral centre. Alternatively, she is simply a tight-arsed bore.

A film that manages to make a compelling heroine out of that Fanny would be a complex one indeed, but that's not the path taken by Rozema, the Canadian director whose films *I've Heard the Mermaids Singing* and *When Night is Falling* are rather arch fables of lesbian self-affirmation. Rozema remakes Fanny as a tough, sprightly minx, and weaves in extracts from Austen's own letters and journals in order to replace Fanny the desiccated wallflower with Fanny the dashing literary ironist.

Frances O'Connor is very good in the role: brisk, mischievous and even convincing when she is giving wry conspiratorial looks to camera. This Fanny is wont to storm boldly out of arguments and go riding in the rain. Dashing in black with a white collar, she looks in one scene like a cross between a bluestocking Byron and a sparky Angela Brazil prefect.

Here, Fanny's moral probity is restricted to being rather less of a sexpot than everyone else. The real hot numbers are the glamorous Crawford siblings, Henry and Mary, who, as played by Alessandro Nivola and Embeth Davitz, fairly crackle with libertine glamour. They don't just crackle: Henry eventually gets his bout of bare-bottom rampancy, and Mary turns suavely Sapphic as she helps Fanny out of her wet clothes. When the Bertrams and Crawfords rehearse their amateur dramatics, the heaving loucheness is like backstage at the Hellfire Club.

Rozema also underlines, rather heavy-handedly, the reading that Edward Said and other critics have made more or less standard: *Mansfield Park* as a story about slavery. From a wind-lashed cliff, Fanny sees a slave ship out at sea and hears distant voices raised in African song: the crassly Spielbergian touch is a beautifully arranged number specially written by a Malian pop star, Salif Keita. When the Bertrams' dissolute son Tom falls ill, the real cause appears to be trauma induced by horrors witnessed in Antigua. Sure enough, Fanny finds Tom's book of sketches, which depict Sir Thomas (a grimly monolithic Harold Pinter) looming over his slaves like Simon Legree: they look like storyboards for *Mandingo* or some such 1970s plantation melodrama. Just to make it clear where we are to stand on the matter, there's this juicy exchange: "The abolitionists are making inroads." "That's a *good* thing, isn't it?"

The film goes really off the rails when Fanny visits her impoverished family in Plymouth. The place isn't just shabby-genteel, but crawling with maggots. Lindsay Duncan plays both Fanny's rich, spoilt aunt and her poor, cadaverous mother—a literal-minded illustration of what different social conditions can do to people. It is even suggested between the lines that her father is a brutal child molester: this is not a film that is soft on patriarchs.

You want to cry out, as Mary archly does in this version: "This is 1806, for heaven's sake!" Rozema's film, all superior 1990s hindsight, feels like an A-level gloss designed to make the story "relevant" to audiences more socially and sexually enlightened than poor Austen could have been. All Rozema does is elide the book's difficulties by painting over them with unsubtle glamour.

I admit I'm hard to please when it comes to literary adaptations. I get edgy if I feel a film is selling short a complex book; but then, if it's too faithful, I'm likely to complain that it ought to engage more critically with the text. Still, I'm always open to persuasion. A recent modernisation of the 17th-century *La Princesse de Clèves* very plausibly had the heroine fall for a Portuguese rock star. Conversely, the Emma Thompson/Ang Lee *Sense and Sensibility* was an object lesson in bringing Austen alive through scrupulous fidelity. But there is something at once gauche and presumptuous in Rozema's undertaking to rescue both Fanny and Austen from the restrictive conventions of their day. A bit of swagger is very fine in its place, but *Mansfield Park* probably isn't the place. As Austen herself once said—and might have said again on seeing her shrinking Price girl become a proto-Spice Girl—"What is become of all the shyness in the world?"

NEW YORK POST, 11/18/99, p. 59, Jonathan Foreman

"Mansfield Park" is one of those rare movies that turns out to be a success despite the intentions of the people who made it.

It's extremely romantic, clever and funny—a cracker of a date movie, in fact mainly because the Jane Austen novel on which it's based is all these things and more. (Unlike so many of the late 20th-century literary novels that have been adapted as movies in recent years, this 1814 classic has a good, strong plot.)

But while writer-director Patricia Rozema often captures the spirit of Austen's humor, she arrogantly and foolishly tries to make the story more relevant by gluing crass new sub-plots and themes onto the original tale.

Jane Austen's novels have been popular for nearly 200 years, thanks to their combination of psychological subtlety, moral seriousness, and brilliant ironic wit: They are mostly incapable of improvement by someone with Rozema's sledgehammer sensibility.

Fortunately, her crude additions do comparatively little damage.

Fanny Price (Hannah Taylor Gordon as a child, Frances O'Connor as an adult) lives in poverty with her family in Portsmouth because her mother married a sailor for love. One of her two aunts, on the other hand, married a wealthy landowner, Sir Thomas Bertram (Harold Pinter). So when Fanny is 10 she's sent across the country to Mansfield Park to be brought up with Sir Thomas' family.

She's treated from the start as a poor relation, particularly by Sir Thomas' daughters Maria (Victoria Hamilton) and Julia (Justine Waddell), and by her mother's other sister, the snobbish Mrs. Morris (Sheila Gish).

But Fanny bonds immediately with Sir Thomas' gentle younger son Edmund (Jonny Lee Miller), with whom she shares a love of reading and riding.

However, when quietly passionate Fanny reaches marrying age, she finds herself the love object of handsome, wealthy rake Henry Crawford (Alessandro Nivola), who has come to stay at Mansfield Park together with his seductive, ruthless sister Mary (Embeth Davidtz).

In a world without divorce—one in which a woman's mistakes last a lifetime—Fanny has to make some terrible choices.

All the performances are first-rate. But Frances O'Connor, the pretty Australian actress so good in *Love and Other Catastrophes*, is superb as Fanny, capturing with real grace the character's intelligence and humor.

In the one alteration to the book that does work on screen, Rozema has made the heroine less passive by combining her personality with that of Jane Austen herself—as gleaned from her letters.

Still, the lesbian scene, the nude adultery scene and the modern-looking art by Sir Thomas' disturbed older son are pure overkill, as is the biggest new theme forced into the story: Rozema's notion that gentry life at this time somehow depended on slavery.

Right at the beginning, Fanny hears haunting music from a slave ship off Portsmouth. Historically, it's extremely unlikely that a ship full of singing slaves would be sitting off the coast in 1806, given that there was no slavery (or slave markets) in England and that the trade routes went from Africa to the West Indies and the U.S., bringing only money and goods back to Britain.

Other false notes include Mansfield Park itself, a Regency country house weirdly bereft of art, and women's costumes that belong to a later date.

More bothersome, though, than any anachronisms are those moments when the characters break the fourth wall and address the audience directly—as if this were a spin-off of a TV teen comedy.

NEWSDAY, 11/18/99, Part II/p. B3, John Anderson

"More respected than loved" has long been the line on Jane Austen's third and least user-friendly novel, "Mansfield Park," largely because the book defies the expectations of the Austen reader as well as the conventions of the 19th-Century "woman's novel." Its heroine, Fanny Price, is socially reticent, morally upright and has a seemingly perverse attitude about the marital merry-go-round at the center of the earlier Austen books ("Pride and Prejudice," "Sense and Sensibility"). Its portrait of the English gentry is Shakespearean in its social and emotional complexities. It is, in short, a radical book.

Apparently, however, not radical enough.

In Patricia Rozema's "Mansfield Park"—a movie most charitably described as underpopulated, underfurnished and intellectually undernourished—we get a Fanny Price (Frances O'Connor) with assertiveness training; a feminist Cinderella who speaks out against the injustices around her, including the slave trade—something Austen may have alluded to in the novel, but which is hardly its central issue. The decidedly dysfunctional Bertrams, who take their impoverished cousin Fanny into Mansfield Park as a child (played here by "Jakob the Liar's" insufferable Hannah Taylor Gordon) have become the morally unconscious beneficiaries of Antiguan slave labor. Lady Bertram (Lindsay Duncan) is an opium addict; her daughters, Julia and Maria (Justine Waddell and Victoria Hamilton), have become the homely wicked stepsisters. And slavery provides the easy metaphor for the plight of women—to whom Austen always ascribed social power and mental vigor, and whom Rozema makes mere victims.

Rozema may be inept—the camera movements, just for example, are incomprehensible when they aren't comic—but she knows enough to co-opt an unassailable historic grievance in an effort to give an anemic movie some gravity.

And she knows enough to pander to any existing audience she has. Known for her lesbian-inflected features ("I've Heard the Mermaids Singing," "When Night Is Falling"), Rozema includes a completely delusional, sexually precious boudoir scene between Fanny and the scheming Mary Crawford (the seductive Embeth Davidtz, who makes everyone else in the movie seem pre-adolescent). All the male characters, meanwhile, have become weaklings, idiots or predators—most egregiously, Sir Thomas Bertram (Harold Pinter, for no known reason), who in Austen was Fanny's loving protector and whom Rozema portrays as a debauched lecher.

Sir Thomas' embrace of Fanny upon his return from Antigua—a pivotal and emotional moment in the book, in which Fanny's ambiguous status and self-worth are both exalted—has her squinting here with sexual embarrassment. Her dissipated father (Hilton McRae), gets roughly the same treatment: At their reunion, his line, "Nice to have another girl around the house," provokes a look of worried indictment from Fanny's younger sister, Susan (Kate Winslet-lookalike Sophia Myles). What horrors have transpired in the Price home? We can only imagine. When Fanny's mother (Lindsay Duncan again) serves Fanny's suitor, Henry Crawford, dinner on their maggot ranch of a kitchen table, it looks like reheated religious sacrifice.

This movie was inevitable, we suppose; out of the six Austen novels, only "Northanger Abbey" now needs such loving treatment. And inevitable is how it feels. A production of Miramax and its British associate, HAL Films, (who should all be talking to their lawyers), "Mansfield Park" may be a genuinely bad movie, but it's a first in the history of English literature: The word "vulgarity" can now be associated with Jane Austen.

NEWSWEEK, 11/29/99, p. 96, David Ansen

The movies "Persuasion," "Sense and Sensibility" and "Emma" inevitably took a few cosmetic liberties with Jane Austen. The intent was not to rethink the novels, just to mold them into cinematic shapes. Patricia Rozema's "Mansfield Park" is another story. The Canadian writer-director ("I've Heard The Mermaids Singing") has performed major surgery on Austen's third novel. Both film and book follow Fanny Price (Frances O'Connor), an impoverished girl plucked from her Portsmouth family to be raised by her wealthy relatives, the Bertrams, at Mansfield Park. It's a Cinderella-like fable built atop the solid foundation of Austen's cool, astute social satire.

The movie's Fanny, however, is a far cry from the passive, repressed—and to many, unlikable—heroine on the page. Using Austen's own letters and notebooks as source material, Rozema makes Fanny a more forthright, morally decisive figure. Now a budding writer, she's a composite of Fanny and Austen herself. Dramatically this works: now she's more like the heroine of "Persuasion." We are duly appalled that this splendid girl is treated hardly better than a servant by the silly Bertram sisters, and bossed about by her aunt, the officious Mrs. Norris (Sheila Gish).

Her status at Mansfield Park begins to change with the arrival of the glamorous brother and sister, Henry and Mary Crawford (Alessandro Nivola and Embeth Davidtz). While the two Bertram girls fall into a swoon over the eligible and charming Henry, his eye is caught by Fanny—the one woman is wise enough to see through his narcissism and frivolity. Fanny's true love is for her cousin Edmund (Jonny Lee Miller), her soulmate since they were children together. But the sophisticated Mary Crawford has Edmund sized up for marriage, and Fanny is too afraid to reveal her feelings to him (a fear that doesn't entirely jibe with this proto-feminist Fanny).

Rozema's handling of the entangled amours and social gamesmanship at Mansfield Park is delightful. O'Connor radiates Austenian intelligence, and the casting of playwright Harold Pinter as the powerful patriarch, Sir Thomas Bertram, is a coup. Glowering and deep-voiced, Pinter turns Sir Thomas into a fascinatingly complex figure—at once a model of courtly civility and a sinister slave trader with sexual secrets in his past.

Slave trader? Sexual secrets? If this doesn't sound like Jane Austen, it's because it isn't. Far more distracting than Rozema's revamping of Fanny Price, or her un-Janeish sexual explicitness, the director has grafted a 20th-century political sensibility onto the material, imposing a slave-trade subplot and taking P.C. potshots at these early-19th-century figures. This sort of historical back-seat driving can leave a smug aftertaste. But not enough, fortunately, to seriously mar one's enjoyment of a tale well told. The open-minded moviegoer will have a hard time resisting Rozema's stylish and stirring movie. It's impure Austen, but potent movie-making.

SIGHT AND SOUND, 4/00, p. 58, Andy Richards

England, the early 19th century. Fanny Price leaves her home in Portsmouth to live with wealthy relatives on their vast country estate Mansfield Park. There, she is treated as a social inferior by her aunt and uncle, Sir Thomas and Lady Bertram, and her cousins Tom, Maria and Julia. Only Edmund, the Bertram's second son, treats her kindly.

Fanny grows into a spirited young woman. Sir Thomas departs on a business trip to his plantations in Antigua, accompanied by Tom. The Mansfield routine is disrupted by the arrival of charismatic siblings Henry and Mary Crawford. Henry flirts with Maria, despite her engagement to Mr Rushworth; Mary has designs on Edmund. Tom returns from Antigua, and proposes putting on a play. The rehearsals are a pretext for much unseemly flirtation by the Crawfords, but the performance is prevented by the return of Sir Thomas.

Maria marries Mr Rushmore. A debut ball is held in honour of Fanny, where Henry declares his love for her. Secretly in love with Edmund, she spurns him, enraging Sir Thomas who sends her back to Portsmouth. She is abruptly recalled to Mansfield Park when Tom falls ill. While nursing Tom, Fanny discovers some of his sketches of abuses against the Antiguan slaves. She also finds Henry in bed with Maria, who then runs off with him. Mary's callous behaviour repels Edmund. Soon after Tom recovers, Edmund confesses his love for Fanny which she reciprocates.

Given the recent spate of Jane Austen adaptations (notably, Ang Lee's *Sense and Sensibility*, Douglas McGrath's *Emma* and the BBC productions of *Persuasion* and *Pride and Prejudice)*, one could be forgiven for anticipating diminishing returns from what is widely viewed as the author's least satisfying and most intractably moralistic work. But that would be to reckon without the contribution of Canadian director Patricia Rozema who, disdaining a purist approach, offers some smart and suggestive variations on the usual Regency rituals.

Rozema's previous features (*I've Heard the Mermaids Singing* and *When Night Is Falling)* have all dealt with meek, repressed female protagonists who are initiated into new social and cultural worlds, before attaining self-sufficiency. In this respect, Austen's Fanny, who arrives at Mansfield Park a timid and socially unsure young woman only to become an indispensable member of the household, would seem to be another variant on Rozema's heroines.

Yet the Fanny of Rozema's film, as incarnated by a radiant Frances O'Connor, is resolutely all the things the Fanny of the novel is not: vivacious, artistic, even sexy—a self-confessed "wild beast". This Fanny is, in fact, something of a hybrid of Austen's heroine and the novelist herself (Fanny's stories and her updates to her sister Susan are based on Austen's own early writings and letters). In Fanny, Rozema creates a screen heroine we can root for (more in the mould of *Pride and Prejudice*'s Elizabeth Bennet), and a film that stands alongside the rest of her oeuvre as a paean to female artistic and romantic independence.

Rozema's emancipatory agenda is significantly different from the novel's more sober, stoic preoccupation with the upholding of true moral consciousness through abstinence and self-denial. Austen's Fanny, as the unimpeachable repository of older, High Tory values, must strike modern sensibilities as something of a prig. Rozema's heroine, on the other hand, is a modern woman oppressed by an antiquated patriarchal society. To throw this theme into sharper relief, Rozema has chosen to make the slavery issue (fleetingly alluded to in the novel) explicit. At one point, Fanny mortifies her family by raising the subject of abolition. The scene in which she discovers Tom's sketches of atrocities (gang rape included) committed against the slaves on his father's Antiguan plantations is shocking in its deliberate rupturing of the film's predominantly genteel *mise en scène*.

Rozema's point is that Mansfield Park, and the amorous escapades of its wealthy inhabitants, are founded on and sustained by this debased form of exploitation. This is certainly an intriguing opening-out of the novel, but in doing so the film appropriates the moral high ground in a way that further distances it from the delicacy and ambiguity of Austen's insights.

Rozema might shift the moral dynamics of the tale to suit our modern broad-stroke sensibilities, but she also has fun with the novel's romantic conventions. The initial entrance of the glamorous, seductive Crawfords is played as a comic cliché, a languorous camera tilt up their bodies intercut with hot flushes from the assembled onlookers. The central ball scene—filmed with candle-lit intimacy and rhapsodic camera swirls—and a couple of fanciful sapphic interludes between Fanny and Embeth Davidtz's serpentine, cigar-smoking Mary Crawford also confirm this as the most overtly erotic of Austen adaptations to date.

VILLAGE VOICE, 11/23/99, p. 142, Justine Elias

At her best, Fanny Price, the heroine of *Mansfield Park*—Jane Austen's third and most problematic novel—displays remarkable forbearance. She endures innumerable slights and simply waits for the man she loves to recognize her affection. At her worst, Fanny's an annoying little prig who lives like a servant in the home of her rich cousins. Patricia Rozema's adaptation—based on the novel as well as "the author's letters and early journals"—doesn't merely invest Fanny with a more appealing inner life. As played by Frances O'Connor, Fanny has become a veritable Jane Austen Action Figure With Kung Fu Grip, galloping around during thunderstorms, frolicking with her beloved cleric-to-be cousin Edmund (Jonny Lee Miller), and taking her scary uncle (Harold Pinter) to task for his involvement in the slave trade. Fanny's no longer a poor relation; she's the houseguest from hell. Still, she seems positively polite compared to the spoiled, sybaritic Crawford siblings who bedazzle the entire household. Mary Crawford (Embeth Davidtz) fixes her eye on Edmund, much to Fanny's chagrin, while her brother Henry (Alessandro Nivola) has the smug, sated look of the cat who's eaten the canary, the vicar, the vicar's daughter, and half the countryside. The Crawfords are so much fun, in fact, that you wonder why Fanny, hellion that she's supposed to be, doesn't throw her lot in with them. Anyone familiar with Austen's world, though, knows the danger lurking within characters universally described as "most agreeable." It's a term that could also apply to Rozema's movie, which, in trying so hard to entertain, ends up sabotaging itself.

Also reviewed in:
CHICAGO TRIBUNE, 11/24/99, Tempo/p. 1, Michael Wilmington
NEW YORK TIMES, 11/18/99, p. E1, Stephen Holden
NEW YORKER, 11/29/99, p. 140, Anthony Lane
VARIETY, 9/6-12/99, p. 66, Derek Elley
WASHINGTON POST, 11/24/99, p. C1, Stephen Hunter,
WASHINGTON POST, 11/26/99, Weekend/p. 45, Desson Howe

MAP OF THE WORLD, A

A First Look Pictures release of a Kennedy/Marshall Company production. *Executive Producer:* Willi Bar.   *Producer:* Kathleen Kennedy and Frank Marshall.   *Director:* Scott Elliott. *Screenplay:* Peter Hedges and Polly Platt. *Based on the novel by:* Jane Hamilton. *Director of Photography:* Seamus McGarvey. *Editor:* Craig McKay and Naomi Geraghty. *Music:* Pat Metheny. *Sound:* Claude Le Haye. *Casting:* Avy Kaufman. *Production Designer:* Richard Toyon. *Art Director:* Megan Less. *Set Decorator:* Megan Less. *Costume Designer:* Suzette Daigle. *Running time:* 125 minutes. *MPAA Rating:* Not Rated.

CAST: Sigourney Weaver (Alice Goodwin); Julianne Moore (Theresa Collins); David Strathairn (Howard Goodwin);   Ron Lea (Dan Collins);   Arliss Howard (Paul Reverdy);   Chloe Sevigny (Carole Mackessy);   Louise Fletcher (Nellie);   Dara Perlmutter (Emma);   Kayla Perlmutter (Claire);   Marc Donato (Robbie).

LOS ANGELES TIMES, 12/3/99, Calendar/p. 6, Kevin Thomas

The title of the powerful "A Map of the World" refers to a drawing a child makes to try to grasp where her dying mother might be going. Now as an adult, Sigourney Weaver's Alice Goodwin finds herself heading into uncharted territory as her life starts unraveling.

Adapted by Peter Hedges and Polly Platt from Jane Hamilton's novel, "A Map of the World" is a serious film that has provided Weaver with what is arguably the richest and most challenging role of her career, possibly even more complex than that of primatologist Dian Fossey in "Gorillas in the Mist." Under Scott Elliott's perceptive direction, Weaver responds with a luminous portrayal that misses no nuances or implications. The same can be said for her co-stars Julianne Moore and David Strathairn.

Weaver is a natural aristocrat with her commanding intelligence, physical stature and striking looks. No matter how contemporary she may be, no matter how ferocious a Wonder Woman taking on one alien after another, she is innately regal at the core—think Eleanor Roosevelt or Ethel Barrymore. (She could be a great Medea.)

Alice has moved from the city with her quiet, unassuming husband, Howard (Strathairn), to a Wisconsin farm with their small daughters, the stubborn, defiant Emma (Dara Perlmutter) and the younger, more docile Claire (Kayla Perlmutter). Alice is a good sport as a farm wife and mother but is an outspoken woman of astringent wit and irony, qualities that are pretty much lost on her unsophisticated neighbors, with the exception of Moore's demure Theresa Collins, who appreciates and perhaps envies Alice's wry, candid sense of humor.

Out of nowhere tragedy strikes, leaving Alice so consumed with guilt that she considers herself to be in the throes of a nervous breakdown—one that, as she remarks, nobody will let her have. Only weeks later, Alice, a nurse at the local grammar school, is arrested and hauled off to jail, accused of sexually abusing the troubled son (Marc Donato) of a local waitress (Chloe Sevigny) whom Alice has criticized as a bad mother. Public opinion instantly turns against Alice, this "outsider" who is overly blunt and direct by conservative community standards, a woman sensed as a threat because of a natural superiority she neither hides nor allows to lapse into condescension.

In its broadest outlines, "A Map of the World," a traditional-style narrative, follows a course that can be predicted, but along the way the filmmakers take full advantage of making each character as distinctive and individual as possible. In the Racine County Jail, Alice discovers that she is the only white woman other than her cellmate, an overweight young woman who murders her newborn twins so that her mother won't know their father was black. In short, Alice couldn't find a riper locale for the redemption she craves. In the meantime, Howard valiantly copes as best he can, his incarcerated wife too self-absorbed to comprehend fully at first his ordeal.

Alice's predicament allows us to see how a marriage can work between committed people of differing temperaments. On the surface, Alice and Howard don't seem the perfect match; she overwhelms him in personality and intellect, yet he is a man of calm, steady strength who complements her well. Even so, he and Theresa, who possesses a noble and forgiving nature without a trace of the insufferable, seem better suited to each other. Louise Fletcher, as Howard's well-meaning but dense mother, and Arliss Howard, as Alice's shrewd attorney, lend vital support.

In all ways, "A Map of the World" is an accomplished film that continually takes us beyond our first impressions of people and situations. It is a remarkably assured and graceful work for a first film; director Elliott is making his screen debut following a distinguished career in the New York theater. "A Map of the World" rewards us for trusting that it will aim higher than socially conscious drama and instead become Alice's odyssey of self-discovery. Alice requires nothing less than a heroic portrayal—and that is precisely what Weaver gives her.

NEW YORK POST, 12/3/99, p. 43, Jonathan Foreman

An adaptation of one of those best-selling women's novels by Jane Hamilton, "A Map of the World" turns out to be a surprisingly gripping and moving experience, thanks partly to fine acting—including a vivid starring performance by Sigourney Weaver—and skillful direction by first-time helmer Scott Elliott.

Alice Goodwin (Weaver) helps her husband with his farm in rural Wisconsin, works part time as an elementary school nurse and tries to bring up her two young daughters—despite being unsuited temperamentally to all of these activities.

Alice's abilities as a wife and mother are contrasted with those of her best friend Theresa (Julianne Moore). It seems to be Alice's fault that her older daughter is such a rude little brat (although children in Hollywood movies are almost always badly behaved).

Though mouthy, eccentric and prickly, Alice is basically a decent person. But when Theresa's daughter dies in an accident while in Alice's care, guilt hurls Alice into a deep depression that makes her seem even more selfish and difficult than usual.

Destiny isn't through with her, however. Soon after the accident, Alice is arrested for allegedly sexually abusing the children she's treated at the local school. The first accusation comes from a sluttish welfare mom (Chloe Sevigny) with whom Alice has fought, but there is no immediate explanation for the ones that follow.

Alice's husband, Howard (David Strathairn), cannot raise bail to get her out of the county jail without selling his beloved farm. Meanwhile, all their friends and neighbors—except Theresa, who's away—turn against them.

In the county lockup, Alice is the only white inmate apart from her cellmate, an overweight white racist who murdered her own half-black babies. She's also a target for the jailhouse bully (Aunjanue Ellis).

But in a perverse, guilt-stricken way she enjoys her imprisonment, and even fails to tell the whole truth to her ruthless lawyer (Arliss Howard).

Weaver always radiates an imperious, intelligent, sardonic quality, and there are times when you wonder if the character is supposed to be quite so superior to everyone else. (There are also moments, especially during the jail-house scenes, when you half expect her to deploy the physical toughness of the Ripley character from the "Alien" movies.)

The film's main flaws lie in the writing. None of the main characters is particularly likable. Strathairn in particular is such a pathetically useless mama's boy that you wonder how a woman like Alice could possibly have been drawn to him. And the ending leaves a little too much unresolved.

But all of the characters in this story of love, guilt and redemption feel like real people, facing real dilemmas, and you truly care about what happens to them.

NEWSDAY, 12/3/99, Part II/p. B6, John Anderson

It's easy to see why tart-tongued, transplanted urbanite Alice Goodwin (Sigourney Weaver) would be resented to the point of prosecution by the agricultural folk of Farm Failure, Wis. As the local school nurse, she's quick to chastise negligent parents. At home, she spoofs the one-eyed egg lady in front of her kids, but can't keep the place clean. She's the kind of city slicker who gags on franks and beans. She's ripe for a fall.

That it comes, and hard, is not a surprise in Scott Elliott's "A Map of the World," based on the Jane Hamilton novel and structured as a good, old-fashioned righteous-indignation movie about a small-minded town and the outsider framed for child abuse. It might have been a Movie of the Week. But between Elliott's apparent fidelity to the book and Weaver's bitingly ironic disposition of Alice, "A Map of the World" operates at a level far beyond nighttime soap and knee jerk sociology.

Despite solid support from both David Strathairn, as her husband, Howard, and Julianne Moore, as her close friend, Theresa, it's Weaver's movie, and if she got an Oscar nomination, it wouldn't be at all surprising (despite the complexities of her performance). Academy voters love to see glamorous Hollywood stars play desperate and disheveled, especially if they get to go to jail, too. But there's much more to Weaver's performance than that. The actress, who has played heroic ("Alien, etc." "Gorillas in the Mist") and bitchy ("Working Girl," "The Ice Storm"), and once in a while has been miscast ("Death and the Maiden"), has never had a chance to play a character so in sync with her strongest natural instinct, irony. Alice, the reluctant farm wife, is an outsider by nature. She lacks Theresa's Martha Stewart gene. She's overwhelmed by her children—particularly the borderline sociopath Emma (Dara Perlmutter)—and she certainly lacks any regard for realpolitik, which makes it easy for her to tongue-lash the likes of Carol Mackessy (Chloe Sevigny, our nation's foremost interpreter of the trailer-trash mystique), a waitress who consistently sends her son to school sick.

Alice can convincingly feign neither maternity nor civility. So she doesn't.

And she pays. A freak accident—the drowning of Theresa's younger daughter in Alice's pond—sets the stage for community-wide resentment, an accusation by Carol's son that escalates into a re-enactment of the McMartin and Kelly Michaels child-abuse fiascoes, and Alice's incarceration in the county jail. Where she more or less thrives. "I've never seen someone take to it so well," says her lawyer (the excellent Arliss Howard).

What Alice has wanted all along is escape from a world in which she doesn't fit. And within the nuances of her performance, Weaver provides enough interpretive space to let viewers decide on their own whether Alice is fighting for her freedom, or just looking for a small, quiet cell of her own.

VILLAGE VOICE, 12/7/99, p. 149, Jessica Winter

From a bizarrely overenunciated, hooked-on-phonics voice-over, through a diva fit at a child's funeral as if the church were Jennifer Lopez's makeup trailer, to a jailhouse paroxysm of split-selved masochism brutal enough to make David Fincher squirm, Sigourney Weaver in *A Map of the World* kamikaze-dives her mission-impossible part with action-hero zest, turning what could have been a made-for-Lifetime drama starring Meredith Baxter into a made-for-Lifetime drama starring Farrah Fawcett. Weaver's Alice, a school nurse, becomes distracted one day while watching her daughters and those of neighbor Theresa (a serene Julianne Moore, who escapes not just unscathed but weirdly ennobled by this catastrophe); Theresa's child drowns in the backyard pond. Then a trashy waitress (Chloe Sevigny) accuses Alice of sexually abusing her son, and Alice lands in jail; her spacey husband (David Strathairn) has to pony up their farm and move the kids into a rat-hole apartment to get bail money. Alice seems little more than annoyed by her tribulations; when her lawyer asks why she's taking her blows so unnervingly well, she replies, "Didn't you ever want to run away to a desert island?" The line doesn't make sense in context either, except that the whole movie is one big shrieking non sequitur. By the time Alice speaks of her family as "outcasts making a perfect circle," we see her martyrdom as self-empowerment at the expense of a broken spouse, several traumatized children, and a dead baby. Scott Elliott's palsied directorial debut, from a mine shaft-ridden script, is a sick joke, and Weaver's part in it screams of temporary insanity.

Matching *A Map of the World* in bad justice and penny-dreadful melotrauma, *Hell's Kitchen* pokes its craven snout around the wreckage of a drug deal gone awry: Kids die, an innocent man (Mekhi Phifer) goes to prison, a grieving mom (Rosanna Arquette) seeks refuge in drugs. Angelina Jolie, as Arquette's daughter, nabs the tastiest bits, including teary confrontation ("You killed my brudda!") and not one but two chances to catch her boyfriend nailing her mother ("You fucked my mudda!"). You can't possibly hate a movie this thunderously stupid.

Also reviewed in:
CHICAGO TRIBUNE, 2/4/00, Friday/p. A, Barbara Shulgasser
NEW REPUBLIC, 1/31/00, p. 30, Stanley Kauffmann
NEW YORK TIMES, 12/3/99, p. E24, Janet Maslin
NEW YORKER, 2/7/00, p. 96, David Denby
VARIETY, 9/20-26/99, p. 82, Emanuel Levy

MARCELLO MASTROIANNI: I REMEMBER

A First Look Pictures release of a Mikado and Istituto Luce production in collaboration with Cinecitta, RAI, and Tele+. *Executive Producer:* Mario Di Biase. *Director:* Anna Maria Tato. *Director of Photography:* Giuseppe Rotunno. *Editor:* Anna Maria Tato. *Music:* Armando Trovaioli. *Sound:* Marco Di Biase. *Running time:* 198 minutes. *MPAA Rating:* Not Rated.

WITH: Marcello Mastroianni.

LOS ANGELES TIMES, 10/1/99, Calendar/p. 10, Kevin Thomas

Anna Maria Tato's three-hour, 18-minute "Marcello Mastroianni: I Remember" is the kind of full-length career portrait that every great actor deserves but rarely receives.

When Mastroianni died at 72 in Paris on Dec. 19, 1996, he had been acting half a century and had become the leading European international star of his generation. On screen and off, Mastroianni was a man of infinite charm, a quality that suffused a remarkably wide range of roles. He was the definitive handsome leading man, possessed of a certain passiveness that made him wildly attractive to several generations of women. As skilled with comedy as he was with tragedy—and every permutation in between—he avoided playing saints and heroes. Consider some of his most famous roles; in "Divorce Italian-Style" he was a pompous cuckolded count with Brilliantined hair and a silly mustache; in "La Nuit de Varennes" he was the aged Casanova, gallant but decayed, heavily and unevenly rouged and powdered.

Mastroianni loathed the inevitable Latin lover tag that went along with the renown "La Dolce Vita" brought him 40 years ago when he played a world-weary Rome cafe society columnist, marking the beginning of his celebrated collaboration with Federico Fellini that ended only with their deaths. The desire to dispel this myth prompted him to agree to allow Tato, a distinguished documentarian and Mastroianni's companion of more than two decades, to make this film, which they had kept putting off for a decade.

The irony is that even though the documentary steers entirely clear of his romantic life it actually reinforces that "despised" image. It's easy to imagine that the humility, wisdom and passion with which he speaks of his craft, which he loved as much as life itself, would only heighten his appeal to women.

Mastroianni loved playing an impotent husband in the anti-machismo "Il Bel Antonio" and a gay man in the anti-Fascist "Special Day"; in both, he's just the sympathetic, sensitive kind of man whom women love to fantasize "saving" from themselves. And surely, most everyone drawn to this enthralling and deeply moving documentary most likely knows of his romances with Catherine Deneuve—their daughter is actress Chiara Mastroianni—and Faye Dunaway, among others. The point to make about Mastroianni being viewed as a Latin lover is how effectively he could play against the stereotype and how far away he could move away from it without ever truly escaping it. Thus Mastroianni emerged as a very modern male who possessed weaknesses as well as strengths, more human than heroic.

The film is superbly structured. On one level it unfolds as Mastroianni is on location in Portugal for Manoel De Olveira's elegiac "Voyage to the Beginning of the World," which would prove to be a most effective epitaph to a glorious screen career. On another, it allows Mastroianni to discuss his career in chronological order, but both these overall narrative lines allow for plenty of rich free association and for him to converse with us in many locales—Mastroianni loved to travel and loved architecture. He might be railing against the mindlessness of mainstream TV while acknowledging his affection for nature documentaries, which in turn triggers his thoughts of documentaries on World War II and in turn his own experiences in Mussolini's Italy. In some sections Mastroianni had grown noticeably gaunt and pale yet his enthusiasm dims not an iota.

Mastroianni had the good fortune to become a part of Luchino Visconti's acting company, and early in his career he appeared in productions of "Three Sisters," "A Streetcar Named Desire" and "Death of a Salesman"; Chekhov would remain a passion of Mastroianni, who would have great success with "Dark Eyes," Nikita Mikhalkov's enchanting film drawn from several Chekhov short stories. For Mastroianni, Chekhov, in his understatement, would always move him more than Shakespeare.

He had in addition to Fellini close collaborations with Vittorio De Sica (teamed unforgettably with Sophia Loren), Marion Monicelli, Ettore Scola and the ever-venturesome and darkly humorous Marco Ferreri.

Mastroianni insisted that Tato include entire sequences—hence, the lengthy running time—and not just the usual ultra-brief clips. He was right to do so, for you get the measure of his performances and the quality of the films themselves.

Monicelli's "The Organizer" is rightly near the beginning of the film and near the top of Mastroianni's favorites among his films. This 1963 masterpiece finds Mastroianni cast as a diffident yet determined university professor who attempts to help turn-of-the-century Turin factory workers form a union. Of course, we see once again the most famous moment in all of Mastroianni films, from "La Dolce Vita": embracing the goddess-like Anita Ekberg in Rome's Fountain of Trevi (which was turned off in honor of Mastroianni's death—and turned on again in a ceremony involving the city's mayor and his widow, from whom he had long been amicably separated).

Of the approximately 170 films in which Mastroianni appeared he reckoned that about 20 were "really rotten," undertaken to afford a flashy car, a chance to visit a foreign locale (e.g., two months in Budapest) or to pay off back taxes. Yet Mastroianni arguably made more outstanding films than any actor of his generation. Mastroianni was a lover of cities, with a special affection for Naples, where the film concludes.

"Life is an appearance on a balcony, and then the shutters close," says Mastroianni, quoting his Naples hotel's night porter. Lest this seem too sentimental, too apt, Mastroianni characteristically hastens to add that not only did the man expect a tip for such an aphorism but also had to be reminded, "That's what you said last night, too."

NEW YORK, 8/23/99, p. 52, Peter Rainer

Because of the plangent humility that came through in his performances, I often regarded Marcello Mastroianni as the perfect Chekhovian actor, although, with the exception of *Dark Eyes,* which drew on several of the author's stories, he never attempted Chekhov onscreen. How gratifying, then, it is to discover, in the wonderful documentary *Marcello Mastroianni: I Remember*, that he played Chekhov several times onstage in his career, notably in a production of *Uncle Vanya* directed by Visconti, and that the playwright was the actor's favorite. Mastroianni had an international reputation for playing the Latin lover—a designation he hated and which, given the wide range of his roles, was almost insultingly erroneous. This documentary, running almost three and a half hours and directed by Anna Maria Tató, his companion for two decades until his death in 1996, is a feast of clips and extended reminiscences by the actor recorded near the end of his life, while he was on location in Portugal. The most Chekhovian movie Mastroianni ever made turns out to be his own spiritual autobiography.

NEW YORK POST, 8/13/99, p. 62, Rod Dreher

Marcello Mastroianni, who died in 1996, was one of the all-time greats, but "Marcello Mastroianni: I Remember" is an exhausting, overindulgent film, at least for American audiences.

Clocking in at a skull-cracking three hours and 18 minutes, the film offers no more than the genial actor staring at the camera, relating anecdotes from his life—with clips from his films inserted amid the reminiscences.

At times, it feels like you're sitting rapt at the feet of a grand and generous paterfamilias of the movies; for most of its duration, though, the experience feels like Grampa Simpson meets "Cinema Paradiso."

Shot in Portugal during the last year of the actor's life, "I Remember" begins charmingly, with the 73-year-old star recalling the iconic place movie theaters held for youth of his generation. "It was a place for escape, but more than escape, the cinema let you dream," he says. Nice. Then he starts crabbing about TV the kids today love to watch so dang much.

Mastroianni rarely left Italy to act, and this rambling documentary depends on a familiarity with his work that most contemporary American audiences aren't likely to possess. Worse, director and editor Anna Maria Tato apparently has never met a Marcello observation, no matter how trivial, she didn't think worthy of committing to film. She was Mastroianni's companion for the last two decades of his life, and she was far too close to her subject to bring him into focus.

Actually, there are obviously many anecdotes she chose to ignore. This soft-pastel portrait bypasses anything remotely controversial about Mastroianni's vivid life—like that torrid romance he had with Catherine Deneuve.

Who wouldn't rather hear Mastroianni's thoughts on la dolce Deneuve than his chuckly musings on nature films and the anti-smoking attitudes of Americans? This film is a sentimental journey for diehard Marcello fans only.

VILLAGE VOICE, 8/17/99, p. 66, Leslie Camhi

Anyone who has interviewed actors knows that even the greatest can say little to illuminate their largely intuitive art.

Mastroianni, who died in 1996, was no exception. The son of a carpenter, he found his calling while still an adolescent, pestering De Sica for work as an extra on the back lots of Cinecittà, and for the next 60 years, he was never far from the camera. In this three-hour-and-20-minute documentary, made in the last year of his life by his longtime companion, Mastroianni looks back over his 170 films, a small history of Italian cinema; his discretion and straightforward approach to his craft, though laudable, make for a very long movie.

Postwar audiences at home first knew him as everybody's favorite proletarian, before a kiss with Anita Ekberg in Fellini's *La Dolce Vita* transformed him into an international icon of the Latin lover. The mantle stuck, though the actor claimed to loathe it. (A hilarious clip from a 1960s profile of Marcello at his swinging Roman villa, trying on fur coats while surrounded by bathing beauties, might suggest otherwise.)

Still, he did much to shed the title, playing failures, cuckolds, the poor, the impotent; in Maria Luisa Bemberg's *I Don't Want To Talk About It*, he even married a midget. His performance as a closeted homosexual, opposite Sophia Loren's frowsy housewife, in Ettore Scola's *A Special Day* remains indelible. He kept an artist's open mind to the great film experiments of his day, and he wasn't afraid to look ugly or ordinary.

But even Mastroianni cannot hold our attention for over three hours. And when interest flags, there's no dirt to appeal to baser instincts. (The closest the film comes to a personal confession is a silent pan around an unidentified Parisian apartment belonging to ex-wife Catherine Deneuve.) Priceless anecdotes about Fellini or his family are scattered amid sprawling reflections on television nature documentaries and smoking in America. It seems that director Anna Maria Tato was so enamored of her late great mate, she simply couldn't bear to say "cut."

Also reviewed in:
NEW REPUBLIC, 8/30/99, p, 28, Stanley Kauffmann
NEW YORK TIMES, 8/13/99, p. E20, Lawrence Van Gelder
VARIETY, 5/19-25/97, p. 55, David Rooney

MARY JANE'S NOT A VIRGIN ANYMORE

A Station Wagon Productions release. *Producer:* Sarah Jacobson. *Director:* Sarah Jacobson. *Screenplay:* Sarah Jacobson. *Director of Photography:* Sarah Jacobson and Adam Dodds. *Editor:* Sarah Jacobson. *Music:* Rama Kolesnikow. *Sound:* Lara Maciejewska, Tyler Hubby, Allyn Hardyck, and Lynn Struiksma. *Running time:* 98 minutes. *MPAA Rating:* Not Rated.

CAST: Lisa Gerstein (Mary Jane); Greg Cruikshank (Dave); Beth Ramona Allen (Erika); Chris Enright (Tom); Marny Snyder Spoons (Grace); Bwana Spoons (Ryan); Andrew David DeAngelo (Matt); Shane Kramer (Steve).

LOS ANGELES TIMES, 3/12/99, Calendar/p. 18, Kathleen Craughwell

The second feature from San Francisco-based writer-director Sarah Jacobson, "Mary Jane's Not a Virgin Anymore," is a study of slacker culture in a Midwestern city, but despite its tantalizing title, Jacobson doesn't give her characters much of interest to say or do.

The film's protagonist, Mary Jane (her friends just call her Jane), is a high school senior from the suburbs who commutes into the city to work part time in a revival-house theater. Although she's an honor student, Jane (Lisa Gerstein) is not too interested in traditional high school activities like the prom—she's far happier hanging out with her co-workers at the theater, a motley crew of ambition-impaired twentysomethings that serves as a surrogate family to the teen.

The opening scene is of Jane losing her virginity in a cemetery (somehow not as exotic as it sounds) with a good-looking but completely insensitive acquaintance. Disappointed with the experience, Jane resolves never to have sex again. But talking with her friends at the theater about their "first times" reinvigorates her interest; they all talk about sex in the way characters in Henry Jaglom's "Eating" discuss food though with much less passion. Jane gets sympathy from the theater's manager Dave (Greg Crulkshank), a kind, gay man who at the ripe age of 30 serves as the group's paternal figure.

More importantly, she gets advice from the forthright and big-sisterly Erika, a tattooed punk princess (musician Beth Allen, who gives the film's best and most spirited performance).

Jane is destined to have one more lover before she leaves for an unnamed college in Boston, yet another co-worker named Tom (Chris Enright). Tom, who also functions as the linchpin for the rest of the film, including two other plot points that wouldn't be fair to give away, is nice to look at but otherwise a dullard.

In fact, a lot of the characters and what happens to them is dull. In their down time at the theater, the young men spend as much time as possible getting as drunk as possible. The young women? Mostly they watch the guys get wasted. Wow.

The film also feels dated, which isn't surprising since Jacobson made it in 1996 (it played at Sundance in 1997 and has been on the indie and art-house circuit since). But even three years ago the slacker film genre had peaked, and this film doesn't come close in originality to, say, Kevin Smith's "Clerks" or Richard Linklater's "Slackers."

Jacobson did, however, manage to make a decent-looking film on a shoestring budget, and she does have a fan base that includes many punk rock musicians (hence the film's killer soundtrack, which includes cuts from Babes in Toyland and Mudhoney).

NEW YORK POST, 1/15/99, p. 46, V.A. Musetto

The heroine of "Mary Jane's Not a Virgin Anymore" is deflowered in a cemetery in the opening minutes of the film.

The frumpy, high-school honor student (Lisa Gerstein) spends the rest of the 98-minute, shoestring-budget indie playing with herself, having sex with a guy in the back seat of a car and talking about sex with her stoned friends at the funky moviehouse where she works.

"Mary Jane" is the debut feature by Sarah Jacobson, 27, who wrote, directed and edited. Too bad her hard work doesn't pay off. She regurgitates every indie-movie cliche you can think of, tries too hard to make her characters hip and gives them inane dialogue to recite. You end up feeling embarrassed for the young actors.

Jacobson's editing isn't so hot either. She needs a few pointers on how to insert closeups.

But she does manage to come up with an interesting fantasy sequence. And she deserves credit for taking on a controversial subject and for self-distributing the movie, getting it into theaters around the U.S., including Manhattan's Cinema Village, where it opens today.

Maybe she'll be able to put her energy to better use next time out.

Also reviewed in:
NEW YORK TIMES, 1/15/99, p. E20, Stephen Holden
VARIETY, 2/10-16/97, p. 68, Joe Leydon

MASCARA

A Phaedra Cinema release of an Amamorph Films production. *Producer:* Crocker Coulson. *Director:* Linda Kandel. *Screenplay:* Linda Kandel. *Director of Photography:* Francois Dagenais. *Editor:* Jane Pia Abramowitz. *Music:* Steven Medina Hufsteter. *Sound:* Jack Lindauer. *Production Designer:* Thomas Thurnauer. *Art Director:* Eduardo Sarabia. *Costumes:* Jennifer Levy and Lisa-Ann Cabasa. *Running time:* 94 minutes. *MPAA Rating:* R.

CAST: Ione Skye (Rebecca); Lumi Cavazos (Laura); Amanda de Cadenet (Jennifer); Steve Schub (Donnie); Steve Jones (Nick); Barry Del Sherman (Ken); Tara Subkoff (Daphne); Corey Page (Andrew); Karen Black (Aunt Eloise).

LOS ANGELES TIMES, 5/14/99, Calendar/p. 15, Kevin Thomas

Linda Kandel's "Mascara" is a feature-length soap opera zeroing in on three female friends unnerved by the prospect of turning 30. While working on a decidedly modest budget, Kandel reveals admirable commitment to her characters but is not sufficiently detached from them to provide her material with depth and perspective.

The sad truth is that all three women are vapid and offer little to engage our concern. They rely on one another but show no interest in anything beyond an all-consuming need to love and be loved in return. Kandel seems to identify with her heroines so intensely that she offers no comment on such awesome self-absorption. Such a state is of course all too credible but is quickly off-putting; Kandel might well have considered setting off her compassion with a satirical edge.

She sets her story in motion with the impending marriage of Laura (Lumi Cavazos) to an immature jerk (Steve Schub) who, later, manages to run up a $ 47,000 credit card bill a mere seven months after the wedding. Meanwhile, Jennifer (Amanda de Cadenet), who has a small daughter and is married to a hard-working, successful attorney (Barry Del Sherman), has turned into an alcoholic tramp because her life is so empty and her husband is so busy; she justifies her behavior as revenge upon him.

Ione Skye's Rebecca seems a happier spirit, although she feels compelled to flit from one job to the next. She seems happy enough in a relationship with a middle-aged photographer (Steve Jones, once lead guitarist of the Sex Pistols), but becomes dismayed by what she considers his daughter's unhealthy attachment to him; meanwhile, she becomes carried away by his good-looking son (Corey Page). Virtually the only true adult in the film is Rebecca's aunt, well-played by Karen Black in an all-too-brief appearance.

Kandel makes the trio's anguish palpable, but they indulge in so much self-pity you find yourself caring little as to what happens to them long before the picture is over. Kandel's actresses try hard, and Cavazos, who starred in "Like Water for Chocolate," manages to make Laura more intelligent and worthy of attention than she really is. But game as they are, there's not much Skye and De Cadenet can do with Rebecca and Jennifer. Since there's so little to care about in these people, there's little to care about in "Mascara."

NEW YORK POST, 5/21/99, p. 52, Rod Dreher

Everything "Mascara" writer-director Linda Kandel knows about life she learned from reading Cosmopolitan.

That's the only conclusion that makes sense after seeing this dreadful paean to female bonding, in which three excruciatingly vapid Los Angeles women rely on their friendship to carry them through various appalling crises. Imagine "Melrose Place" without the irony, the moral seriousness and the dramaturgical finesse.

Our heroines are horrified at the prospect of—oh, the humanity—aging. Sweet-faced Laura ("Like Water for Chocolate's" Lumi Cavazos) marries a jerk (Steve Schub) so she won't hit the big three-oh alone. Free-spirited Rebecca (Ione Skye) has second thoughts about her wrinkly live-in boyfriend (former Sex Pistol Steve Jones), and glammy sot Jennifer (Amanda de Cadenet) retreats into the bottle and cheap affairs to escape her unhappy marriage.

With the possible exception of Laura, none of these needy, self-centered ditzes are the least bit likable, though in the absence of anything else to engage one's attention, there's something to be said for Rebecca and Jennifer's compulsion to take off their tops at the slightest provocation.

But the dialogue sounds like it came gift-wrapped from Hickory Farms. Here's dipso dingbat Jennifer, in mid-canoodle with a Spanish boy:

"Where did we meet?"

"Outside my high school, remember?"

"Rico, I can't stay with you in this motel any longer!"

Oy. We hear a dancer described as liking to "boogie," and a swank beau—pointedly not meant to be a figure of fun—chatting up Jennifer with, "Are you a Pisces?" Later, when one of these floozies meets a shaggable hunk, she whips her shirt off and coos, "Do you want to make it?"

Yeah, baby! In a non-Austin Powers context, this is only slightly less dated and ridiculous a come-on line than, "Do you like pina coladas?" But what do you expect from a movie whose idea of a moment of truth comes when one character confesses to her friends that her husband was the only man with whom she'd ever had an orgasm? And they say feminism's dead.

Also reviewed in:
VARIETY, 5/17-23/99, p. 54, Joe Leydon

MATING HABITS OF THE EARTHBOUND HUMAN, THE

An Independent Artists release of an Earthbound Humans Productions production. *Producer:* Larry Estes. *Director:* Jeff Abugov. *Screenplay:* Jeff Abugov. *Director of Photography:* Michael K. Bucher. *Editor:* Stephen Myers. *Music:* Michel McCarty. *Production Designer:* Helen Harwell. *Art Director:* Craig Keller. *Costumes:* Kristin M. Burke. *Running time:* 90 minutes. *MPAA Rating:* R.

CAST: David Hyde Pierce (Narrator); Mackenzie Astin (Billy Waterston, The Male); Carmen Electra (Jenny Smith, The Female); Markus Redmond (The Male's Friend); Lucy Liu (The Female's Friend); Lisa Rotondi; Sharon Wyatt; Jack Kehler; Leo Rossi.

LOS ANGELES TIMES, 10/8/99, Calendar/p. 19, Kathleen Craughwell

"The Mating Habits of the Earthbound Human," a mockumentary that charts and analyzes the courtship behavior of two healthy, young Homo sapiens, begins with the disembodied voice of an intellectually advanced extraterrestrial (David Hyde Pierce) informing us that "of all the beings in the universe, none possess the mating ritual as complex as the earthbound human." How true.

Writer-director Jeff Abugov, whose background is in television sitcoms, got the idea for his feature film debut while watching one of those nature documentaries on the reproduction process of some obscure animal species and listening to the droning narrator describe, in clinical detail, the fine points of seduction and copulation. What might a completely objective observer think of the way humans approach reproduction (or in many cases, the avoidance of reproduction)?

It's a novel premise for what would otherwise be a standard boy-meets-girl romantic comedy and the film's greatest strength is the deadpan narration of Hyde Pierce (whose cadence as the know-it-all alien is similar to that of his fussy "Frasier" character Niles). Abugov's script too is quite funny and there are several laugh-out-loud scenes, particularly in the movie's first half, as well as some surprisingly deft insights into the quandaries of finding a mate, or for that matter, a date.

The light tone, however, shifts to being slightly off-putting as the relationship between the Male, a.k.a. Billy (Mackenzie Astin), and the Female, a.k.a. Jenny (Carmen Electra), progresses. After several months of dating (and sleeping together) Jenny begins to yearn for more stability while Billy is content with their level of commitment. It could be funny but perhaps because it's such familiar territory, in real life and in movies, you find yourself cringing instead of laughing.

And because Astin and Electra are playing archetypes—and Hyde Pierce is carrying the bulk of the comedy load—there is not too much call for heavy-duty acting. It's the situations that are funny, and as the situations become less funny, so does the movie.

"Mating" is at its best when skewering the sometimes absurd aspects of dating, like the well-intentioned but often ill-advised advice of friends who suddenly become relationship experts, provided they're discussing someone else's.

For example, when Billy's best friend and co-worker tells him that if he really likes Jenny he should not call her for at least a week, because if he does call right away she might think he likes her, our friendly narrator interrupts to tell us that there is in fact no problem with the transmitting signal; we are hearing the friend's courting advice correctly even though it doesn't make sense. It's a human thing.

Overall, it's a cute movie, and Astin and Electra are pleasant leads. But a special mention needs to be made of Kurt Bryant, the "stunt and sperm coordinator" (surely a first), and the brave actors who played the spermatozoa (Bobby Bums, Brett Jones, Cole McKay, Anthony Perkins Jr., Dana Reed, Patrick J. Statham, Michael-John Sama) for some of the film's funniest segments in which the alien explains the actual process of fertilizing a human ovum. It's an alien thing.

NEW YORK POST, 10/11/99, p. 51, Lou Lumenick

"The Mating Habits of the Earthbound Human" does not become Electra—Carmen Electra, that is.

This is a witless and vulgar romantic comedy wrapped inside a mock documentary about human behavior as it might be observed by a clueless extraterrestrial.

David Hyde Pierce dryly reads the pretentious narration for this trite vanity project, written and directed by TV producer Jeff Abugov, whose credits include "Grace Under Fire."

Accountant Billy (Mackenzie Astin) meets Jenny (Electra) at an L.A. club, makes a jerk of himself, apologizes, gets her phone number. He loses her phone number, tracks her down and they begin to date.

They begin having sex—but not, the narrator insists, for procreation. The film dramatizes this by showing actors dressed as sperm—a concept Woody Allen used more effectively decades ago in "Everything You Always Wanted to Know About Sex"—bouncing off a rubber barrier representing a condom.

This gag is repeated at least a dozen times (with a special variation for use of spermicide)—until Billy and Jenny have unprotected sex and she becomes pregnant.

The movie drones toward marriage and parenthood, all accompanied by endless narration.

The charm of lines like "ready for procreation, the male slips his tongue into the female's mother" wear out their welcome quickly.

The actors—especially the erstwhile Mrs. Dennis Rodman, who's kind of charming—deserve better than "The Mating Habits of the Earthbound Human."

Also reviewed in:
NEW YORK TIMES, 10/8/99, p. 29, Anita Gates
VARIETY, 9/27-10/3/99, p. 49, Brendan Kelly

MATRIX, THE

A Warner Bros. release in association with Village Roadshow Pictures-Groucho II Film Partnership of a Silver Pictures production. *Executive Producer:* Barrie M. Osborne, Andrew Mason, Andy Wachowski, Larry Wachowski, Erwin Stoff, and Bruce Berman. *Producer:* Joel Silver. *Director:* Andy Wachowski and Larry Wachowski. *Screenplay:* Andy Wachowski and Larry Wachowski. *Director of Photography:* Bill Pope. *Editor:* Zach Staenberg. *Music:* Don Davis. *Music Editor:* Lori Eschler Frystak and Zigmund Gron. *Choreographer:* Yuen Ping. *Sound:* David Lee and (music) Armin Steiner. *Sound Editor:* Dane A. Davis. *Casting:* Mali Finn and Shauna Wolifsohn. *Production Designer:* Owen Paterson. *Conceptual Designer:* Geofrey Darrow. *Art Director:* Hugh Bateup and Michelle McGahey. *Set Designer:* Sarah Light, Jacinta Leong, Godric Cole, Judith Harvey, Andrew Powell, and Deborah Riley. *Set Decorator:* Tim Ferrier, Lisa Brennan, and Marta McElroy. *Special Effects:* Robina Osborne. *Animatronic Designer:* Trevor Tighe. *Costumes:* Kym Barrett. *Make-up:* Nikki Gooley. *Special Effects Make-up:* Bob McCarron. *Stunt Coordinator:* Glenn Boswell. *Running time:* 115 minutes. *MPAA Rating:* R.

CAST: Keanu Reeves (Thomas Anderson, "Neo"); Laurence Fishburne (Morpheus); Carrie-Anne Moss (Trinity); Hugo Weaving (Agent Smith); Joe Pantoliano (Cypher); Gloria Foster (Oracle); Marcus Chong (Tank); Julian Arahanga (Apoc); Matt Doran (Mouse); Belinda McClory (Switch); Anthony Ray Parker (Dozer); Paul Goddard (Agent Brown); Robert Taylor (Agent Jones); David Aston (Rhineheart); Marc Gray (Choi); Ada Nicodemou (Dujour); Deni Gordon (Priestess); Rowan Witt (Spoon Boy); Bill Young (Lieutenant); David O'Connor (FedEx Man); Jeremy Ball (Businessman); Fiona Johnson (Woman in Red); Harry Lawrence (Old Man); Steve Dodd (Blind Man); Luke Quinton (Security Guard); Lawrence Woodward (Guard); Michael Butcher (Cop Who Captures Neo); Bernie Ledger (Big Cop); Robert Simper and Chris Scott (Cops); Nigel Harbach (Parking Cop); Martin Grellis (Helicopter Pilot).

LOS ANGELES TIMES, 3/31/99, Calendar/p. 1, Kenneth Turan

"Imagine you're feeling a little like Alice, tumbling down the rabbit hole," someone says in the dazzling and disorienting "The Matrix," and who has the strength to argue?

A wildly cinematic futuristic thriller that is determined to overpower the imagination, "The Matrix" combines traditional science-fiction premises with spanking new visual technology in a way that almost defies description. Like it or not, this is one movie that words don't come close to approximating.

Written and directed by the Wachowski brothers, Larry and Andy, "The Matrix" is the unlikely spiritual love child of dark futurist Philip K. Dick and the snap and dazzle of Hong Kong filmmaking, with digital technology serving as the helpful midwife.

Yet because this tale has been on the Wachowskis' minds for so long—it was written before their 1996 debut film, "Bound"—"The Matrix" never feels patched together. And its story, constructed though it is from familiar elements and pseudo-mystical musings, is nevertheless strong enough to support the film's rip-roaring visuals.

Thomas Anderson (Keanu Reeves), a software programmer in a world very much like our own who goes by his nighttime hacker moniker of Neo, has heard the Matrix whispered about his whole life, but no one knows what it is. All the beautiful Trinity (Carrie-Anne Moss of TV's "Dark Justice") can tell him is that "It's looking for you," which is certainly scary but not a great deal of help.

For that Neo has to turn to Trinity's partner, the legendary Morpheus (Laurence Fishburne), considered the most dangerous man alive by the authorities. What he says is more than frightening: What Neo thinks is the real world is no more than a computer-generated dreamscape, a virtual reality created by the artificial intelligence that really controls things to distract our human minds while our bodies are systematically plundered as an energy source to keep those nefarious machines up and running.

Sometimes those machines take human form as agents, robotic parodies of FBI men, like the chilling Agent Smith (Hugo Weaving of "Proof" and "The Adventures of Priscilla, Queen of the Desert"), who wear security earpieces, sunglasses and white shirts with ties and are terrifyingly close to indestructible.

These Matrix men have a special interest in Neo. There's a feeling in the air, one that Morpheus and his ragtag colleagues (including "Bound" veteran Joe Pantoliano) are tempted to share, that Neo might be the One, the foretold liberator who has the power to destroy the Matrix and free the human race. But only the Oracle (a fine cameo by Gloria Foster) knows for sure, and everything she says is, well, oracular.

Obviously, there's a great deal that's familiar about "The Matrix," starting with its sturdy themes of alternate realities, the deadly rivalry between men and machines, the resilient power of the human mind and the creeping dangers of conformity. And the film's fake-Zen dialogue, lines like "Don't think you are; know you are" and "There's a difference between knowing the path and walking the path," isn't going to win any ovations for originality.

On the other hand, the somber quality of the dialogue suits the apocalyptic quality of "The Matrix" story, and the gravity of the actors, especially the always magisterial Fishburne and the magnetically phlegmatic Reeves, makes the words more bemusing than bothersome.

Helping most of all are the riveting visuals shot by Bill Pope. The Wachowskis do have a taste for the bizarre (witness an electronic bug that turns into a body-piercing insect) but this tendency pays off in bravura moments like a mesmerizing vista of a body farm without end (inspired by the work of comic-book artist Geof Darrow) where humans are relentlessly harvested for energy like so many replaceable Eveready batteries.

Just as exciting are "The Matrix's" two kinds of action sequences. One strata involves John Woo-type expenditures of massive amounts of ammunition shot in super slow-motion and the other uses both Hong Kong-style stunt work and a technique the press notes refer to as "bullet-time photography" that involved shooting film at the computer-aided equivalent of 12,000 frames per second.

"The Matrix" cast members who were involved in the film's eye-catching kung fu fight sequences also apparently committed to four months of pre-production work with Hong Kong director and stunt coordinator Yuen Wo Ping, someone who specializes in the technique, known as wire fighting, that gives H.K. films like "Drunken Master," "Once Upon a Time in China" and "Fist of Legend" their distinctive high-flying look.

Not everything in "The Matrix" makes even minimal sense, but the Wachowski brothers, said to be major fans of comic books and graphic novels, are sure-handed enough to smoothly pull us over the rough spots. When a film is as successful as this one is at hooking into the kinetic joy of adrenalized movie making, quibbling with it feels beside the point.

NEW STATESMAN, 7/12/99, p. 38, Jonathan Romney

[*The Matrix* was reviewed jointly with *Star Wars: Episode One—The Phantom Menace*; see Romney's review of that film.]

NEW YORK POST, 3/31/99, p. 73, Rod Dreher

"The Matrix" is a bug-eyed blast, a slick sci-fi thriller with spectacular special effects and hellzapoppin' action sequences among the most memorable ever put to film.

A more technically dazzling synthesis of action choreography and cutting-edge computer graphics has not been seen since James Cameron's "T2." "The Matrix" will do enormous business among genre fans alone.

But that script—oy!

You expect screenplays for movies like this to be striplings on which to hang flashy action and visuals. "Matrix" suffers from the opposite problem. The Wachowski brothers, twentysomething writer-directors whose last feature was the Sappho-vs.-the-Mob drama "Bound," have jammed so many interesting but half-baked ideas into their overlong (two hours-plus) picture that none of them gets a satisfactory workout, and in fact they gum up the storytelling.

It's difficult to discuss "The Matrix" in detail without revealing too many of its mysteries. Its narrative pleasures come from the striptease revelations about the true nature of the Matrix of the title. It has to do with the nature of reality, but, like the press notes say, "No one can be told what The Matrix is. You have to see it for yourself."

But I can, in good faith, tell you this much: The hero is Neo, a mild-mannered hacker geek played by the android-like Keanu Reeves. He is inadvertently drawn into a dark underworld when a strange voice in a phone call warns him that he is being pursued by baddies. After a "Men in Black"-type squad captures him and performs an exotic interrogation, Neo falls in with a shadowy group of cyber-rebels and is spirited away to their hideout.

Their leader is Morpheus (Laurence Fishburne), who gives Neo the choice to learn the truth about the world he inhabits and be initiated into their cell or to remain blissfully ignorant. Of course Neo chooses truth, else there'd be no movie. He undergoes a brain-frying (his and ours) "rebirth" "tumbling down the rabbit hole," it's called—that's brilliantly phantasmagorical.

Neo then begins a Luke Skywalker-like apprenticeship under Morpheus, learning the rules of the game and how to use his cool new powers to fight the "MiB" tyranny ruling the planet.

The Wachowskis don't always follow the rules they establish for themselves (bullets, for example, hurt people—except when they don't). And the performances leave something to be desired. Overwrought direction turns chief Man in Black Hugo Weaving into a bus-and-truck Tommy Lee Jones.

It is, however, very easy to overlook this movie's faults when confronted by the razzle-dazzle visual effects the Wachowskis pioneer here.

The actors dodge bullets, leap over chasms, engage in terrifically choreographed (by Yuen Wo Ping) martial-arts sequences—all of which are presented with breakneck speed, visual seamlessness and breathless realism from unusual points of view. It's like animation come to three-dimensional life, and f/x addicts as well as sci-fi fans will not want to miss a split-second.

NEWSDAY, 3/31/99, Part II/p. B2, John Anderson

In what might have been a collaboration between William Gibson and Immanuel Kant, "The Matrix" presumes a future where everything we see is an illusion: The entirety of reality—a concept that grows more and more amorphous as the movie rolls on—has been preempted by an insidious power that has disguised the ravaged present with a veil of normality. In other words, it's like television.

What also seems to be happening is that the brothers Wachowski, Andy and Larry, are ankle deep in the homage-is-hip school of derivative filmmaking. As they proved in their debut "Bound," they have a sense of humor (it was, after all, a gangster-murder-lesbian-caper movie), but also a flair for creative kleptomania.

When not borrowing wholesale from "2000," "Terminator 2" or the memorable abduction sequences of "Fire in the Sky," they would like us to consider the universe of "The Matrix" according to the Christian concept of a temporal world that can be transcended only through faith.

Then they'd have us consider Laurence Fishburne's Morpheus as computer-hacking approximation of John the Baptist. Morph is waiting on "The One"—an individual who will break the chains of perception imposed by the Matrix (that veil of unreality) and liberate the world.

Take one more step—ooooh, it's a doozy—and consider Keanu Reeves (alias Neo, ultra-hacker and dealer in illicit software) as the putative Messiah. And you have the theological underpinning of one fairly pretentious sci-fi thriller.

"The Matrix" is really about filmmaking style rather than context, though—and here enters the question that's bound to haunt us: If state-of-the-art, computer-driven special effects allow moviemakers to produce just about anything, is there anything left to get excited about? Has Hollywood's almost routine resorting to blue screens and morphing driven any residual magic out of the movies?

As if trying to shove the answer in our collective face, the fraternal filmmakers have produced a film in which impenetrability equals profundity—unless of course they're just kidding.

The characters—who include the lethal good-girl Trinity (Carrie-Anne Moss), the treacherous Cypher (Joe Pantoliano), Morpheus, Neo and their unstoppable pursuers, the "Agents" (especially Hugo Weaving's comically businesslike Smith)—pass through so many different computer programs that there seems little chance of keeping track of what "reality" is actually supposed to be. The result is the kind of distancing Brecht never dreamt of—we've had our perception questioned so many times we're immune to any illusion of peril. Or, for that matter, any illusion at all. Ergo, it's a small step outside the movie entirely. Call the Wachowskis self-destructive geniuses, or complete idiots.

Fishburne is having fun behind his cheaters and grins. Pantoliano is a convincing weasel. Moss is an attractive distraction when she's not paying tribute to Demi Moore. Only Reeves seems to be taking it all seriously, and he's probably the only actor in existence who could. Consider, for instance, the action-convenience factor: When they need to, windows in an ultramodern office building actually open; characters, empowered by whatever program they happen to be in, can vault from building to building. And yet, they run up stairs when the action calls for a neck-and-neck chase scene.

Outside of the scenes of hysterical destruction and moderate suspense, the rhythms of "The Matrix" are positively languorous; where there isn't hard-core action, shots shift like water lapping against a disinterested shore. But perhaps that's part of the Wachowskis' post-post-post-modernist message: that despite every sensory escape hatch the future will have to offer, the thing we won't be able to escape is ennui. Guess what? The future is here.

NEWSWEEK, 4/5/99, p. 70, David Ansen

What if everything we thought was real—these streets, this city, the year 1999—was merely a computer-generated program in our heads, a cyberdream of reality? That, in short, is the premise of *The Matrix*, which appears to be set in the present—that is where its hero, Neo (Keanu Reeves), thinks he is—but is actually set in 2199, when artificial-intelligence machines rule the world, and humans are merely the crops they grow to supply energy.

In Larry and Andy Wachowski's flamboyantly energetic action movie, Neo gets clued into the real deal: humans are just slaves to the machine. He's chosen by the rebel hacker Morpheus (Laurence Fishburne) to lead the Resistance against man's mechanical masters.

"The Matrix" throws a lot at you—mythic quests, pop Pirandello, kung-fu fight scenes and an encyclopedia of quotations from "Alien" to "Blade Runner" to Cocteau's "Orpheus." The Wachowskis, who made the bouncy lesbian crime comedy "Bound," have a true passion for pulp, a boldly dynamic visual style, an affection for cheesy acting and a gift for explosive action. With an arsenal of cool f/x at their disposal, they've come up with a dizzyingly enjoyable junk movie that has just enough on its mind to keep the pleasure from being a guilty one.

SIGHT AND SOUND, 7/99, p. 46, Philip Strick

Menial office worker Thomas Anderson operates by night as computer hacker Neo. Warnings from unknown girl Trinity fail to prevent his detention by law-enforcement agent Smith, who demands Neo help capture notorious subversive Morpheus. Refusing to co-operate, Neo is released. Trinity takes him to meet Morpheus, leader of the struggle against the Matrix, an artificial intelligence that controls the world. Morpheus explains that the planet's long-derelict citizens are trapped in the illusion of 1999 (really the distant past) until converted into food and energy to power the Matrix itself.

Joining Morpheus' team, Neo endures an agonising awakening process. Although his body is on a life-support system, a mental projection of his digital self roams the Matrix's simulation of the everyday. He can also be programmed with phenomenal skills. Morpheus is convinced they have found in Neo the fabled leader, The One, who can rescue the planet. Betrayed by fellow crewmember Cypher, Morpheus is captured by Smith, desperate to prise from him the location of Zion, the last stronghold of humanity. Rushing to the rescue, Neo and Trinity battle enormous odds to save him. As Matrix forces close in, Smith traps Neo and shoots him down. But when Trinity declares her love to Neo's body his digital self is miraculously resurrected. He blows Smith apart and returns to his body just in time to thwart the Matrix invaders. Embracing Trinity and accepting his role as The One, he prepares to revitalise a dormant world.

The Wachowski Brothers wrote and sold the script for *The Matrix* before they made their first film, the mesmerising crime thriller *Bound*. They have since reported that between comic-book conception (a spin-off from their work at Marvel on the *Hellraiser* stories) and production go-ahead, "the script that nobody understands" underwent considerable fine-tuning, thanks to studio insistence on explanatory dialogue. Even so, for a breathlessly vertiginous first quarter *The Matrix* scorns offering any rationale behind its attention-grabbing assaults and chases, leaving only its peevish spokesperson to mutter legitimate protests on our behalf ("This is insane! Why is it happening to me? What did I do?") until reasonably concluding he must be half-asleep. At which point naturally, he falls into the grasp of Morpheus.

The Wachowskis are good at names, as they demonstrated with the title and main trio of *Bound*: Corky (buoyant), Violet (clinging) and Caesar (dictatorial). Conjuring up a flock of evocations—Cypher, Tank, Switch, Apoc, Mouse for *The Matrix*, they invest the film's gradually uncovered crusade with a rich blend of messianic implications blatantly signalled by warrior priestess Trinity. Her unifying presence links—and exchanges—the powers of Morpheus the dreammaster with those of the long-sought saviour Neo (note the anagram) who is at once the New Man (as in, by useful coincidence, Neo-Tokyo, subsumed by *Akira)* and the neophyte disciple.

More squarely, the film is an ironic rereading of *Logan's Run* (1976), with a nod to *Soylent Green* (1973) and more than a dash of *Zardoz* (1973). The Wachowskis unveil a seedy utopia where mankind is preserved, protected and endlessly recycled by its own mega-computer. The alternative to this artificial stasis is, as usual, well beyond the wit of mortal proles. Necessarily, *The Matrix* ends much where it started, its newborn visionary poised—like Logan or *2001*'s Starchild or *THX 1138*'s hero or even like Luke Skywalker (prime exponent of the "Why me?" syndrome)—on the brink of literally unimaginable new benefits. Away from the meddlesome tyranny of the machine, the superhero will be in charge. There's always One.

The prospect is less than reassuring and the Wachowskis don't hide their misgivings. Played by Keanu Reeves with a certain gloomy helplessness, Neo gives a good impression of being incapable of original thought (he is, after all, as programmed as any Matrix slave) and little sign of inspiring social reform. But two voices speak loudly and persuasively on behalf of the Matrix: the traitorous terrorist Cypher celebrates it for colourful comforts unmatched by the drab post-apocalyptic real world, and the fearsome man-in-black humanoid Agent Smith (not quite Winston Smith, but the Wachowskis, recognising an affinity, have mischievously appended a Room 101) spells out its evolutionary task by dismissing humans as "a plague—and we are the cure". The same dispassionate logic was prologue to *The Terminator* and more recently at the core of *Virus*.

But if the Wachowskis claim no originality of message, they are startling innovators of method. As with *Bound*, the film is a feast of unexpected fidgets and perspectives, punctuated by trademark overhead shots and teasing detail and detour, such as the squeal of washed windows as Neo is reprimanded by his boss, or the White Rabbit subtext culminating in a glimpse of *Night of the Lepus* (1972) on a television. Just as in *Bound*, telephones play a vital role, while the fetishistic use of shades and black leather tells yet another story, encompassing Smith's chipped lens and Neo's triumphal final outfit. Primarily, *The Matrix* is a wonderland of tricks and stunts, light years from Kansas, combining computerised slow-motion with the extravagant choreography of martial-arts movies to create a broadside of astonishing images. As Neo turns cartwheels, blazing away behind wildly exploding decor, it seems clear that the Wachowskis have discovered a gleeful utopia of their own.

TIME, 4/5/99, p. 68, Richard Schickel

All the time you thought it was the media. Or maybe the swollen federal bureaucracy. Or just possibly the irreducible idiocy of humankind. That is to say, like Neo (Keanu Reeves), the reluctant but deeply curious hero of *The Matrix*, you had a vague sense that something was not quite right about life as we live it, that something was preventing you from realizing all your potential.

Luckily, the Wachowski brothers, Larry and Andy, have finally figured it all out: the machines really have taken over the world. Yeah, sure, you had that idea a couple of sleepless nights ago and immediately dismissed it as farfetched. But that's why your life remains Dilbert-like and why the giddily self-confident Wachowskis are (potentially) the dauphins of the new Hollywood.

Clever lads that they are, they offer us a world in which most of the population consists of dronelike clones created and managed, without their knowing it, by superintelligent humanoid machines (men in black, of course). Even more cleverly, they posit, in Reeves' character, a modern Everyman—a computer hacker, naturally—who may be the Messiah whom the remnants of authentic humanity have long awaited. These resisters, called Zionists, live near the earth's core and are represented up top by the very brainy Morpheus (Laurence Fishburne) and a small band of rebel fighters, living by their wits and their martial-arts skills (nicely enhanced by special effects). A lot of what they do and endure consists of spins on the sci-fi past. There are references to everything from the *Alien* movies to *The Terminator* to *Soylent Green*, but that's what we have for a living mythology these days, and the Wachowskis are bold and knowing in their deployment of it. They're acknowledging a tradition, not ripping it off.

The same thing applies to their reflections on such matters as artificial intelligence, alternative realities and the space-time continuum. You feel they have at least read the better magazine articles on these topics—enough to provide a little more subtext than we expect to find in little more subtext than we expect to find in enterprises like *The Matrix*. Besides, there's real wit in their presentation of the Zionist oracle (who turns out to be a motherly black lady baking cookies in an old-fashioned kitchen), and real sexiness in Carrie-Anne Moss as super-buff Trinity, leading Neo to his destiny. Given a budget that encourages their kinesthetic skills, the filmmakers tend to go on a bit, but it's mostly a kind of quick, glancing hipness that's being indulged here. And that's a rare and welcome commodity in mass-market moviemaking these days.

TIME, 4/19/99, p. 75, Richard Corliss

Bunch of guys at a Manhattan 'plex watching *The Matrix*. Carrie-Anne Moss kicks some 'droid butt, makes a streetwide leap from one building top to the next, then crash lands through a small window. "The bitch is bad," one of the guys opines. "Go, girl!" Then Laurence Fishburne shows up as Morpheus—a morphing Orpheus, a black White Rabbit, an R.-and-B. Obi-Wan Kenobe, a big bad John the Baptist, a Gandalf who grooves; every wise guide from literature, religion, movies and comix. Though he's in a dark room in the dead of night, and as if he needed to be more cool, Fishburne is wearing these teeny black shades. Another guy at the 'plex says approvingly, "Those glasses are fabulous!"

To deliver a futurismo fashion statement and a can of whup-ass in the same movie—this is smart filmmaking. Larry and Andy Wachowski, the Chicago-bred brothers who wrote and directed *The Matrix*, are smart in a way moviegoers love and Hollywood moguls cherish: the picture, shot in Australia for $63 million, had the year's strongest opening weekend and pulled in a robust $50.7 million in its first nine days. The film's producer, Joel Silver, says the boys have a sequel in mind, and cannily adds, "The more success the movie has, the more willing they'll be to write it down." Suddenly Larry, 33, and Andy, 31, are giving Peter and Bobby Farrelly (*There's Something About Mary*) competition as the hottest brother act in town.

But the Wachowskis, whose first directorial effort was the seductive femme-noir drama *Bound*, have deeper fish to fry. "We're interested in mythology, theology and, to a certain extent, higher-level mathematics," says Larry. "All are ways human beings try to answer bigger questions, as well as The Big Question. If you're going to do epic stories, you should concern yourself with those issues. People might not understand all the allusions in the movie, but they understand the important ideas. We wanted to make people think, engage their minds a bit."

And blow their minds a lot. The film posits that life as we know it is a computer simulation: it is, Morpheus says, "the world that has been pulled over your eyes" by some creepezoid machines that look like spidery octopi. Who can free a mankind that doesn't know it's enslaved? Morpheus believes the cybermessiah is Neo (Keanu Reeves), a computer hacker. Early in the film Morpheus offers two pills to Neo. Take the blue one, you wake up and remember nothing. Take the red pill, "you stay in Wonderland. And I show you how deep the rabbit hole goes."

Naive viewers may think *The Matrix* is just a cool way to pass the time while sitting in the *Phantom Menace* waiting room. They should think again, breathe deep, get strapped in for a brain-popping trip. *The Matrix* is a careering cyberride without the headset, a virtual masterpiece. Every other movie out there is the blue pill. This one is the red.

An anthology of dystopic science fiction, *The Matrix* plunders *Blade Runner* and *The Terminator*: bad machines, grungy rebels and rain, rain everywhere, even indoors. It invokes the kung furiosity of prime Jackie Chan and the heroic bloodshed and long coats of John Woo movies; the Hollywood-Hong Konglomeration has never meshed so suavely as in this film's fight scenes and wire-work aerobatics. Never seen the mega-imaginative, ultraviolent Japanese cartoons known as anime (*Akira, Ghost in the Shell*)? Now you have—in whirling live action.

Those are just the movie references. The Wachowskis, both dropouts from good colleges (Larry from Bard, Andy from Emerson), want to weld classic lit, hallucinogenic imagery and a wild world of philosophical surmises to pop culture. The Bible meets Batman; Lewis Carroll collides with William Gibson; Greek and geek mythology bump and run. Hell, you may find string theory in *The Matrix*.

As the children of a businessman and a nurse, the boys created comic books, and the obsession continued into their 20s. "Jack Kirby comics interested us," says Andy. "We liked the idea of punching guys through brick walls and over-the-top action like that." But they connected as well with older, more revered sources. "The Bible seeks to answer a lot of relevant questions for man," says Larry. "In the film we refer to the story of Nebuchadnezzar; he has a dream he can't remember but keeps searching for an answer. Then there's the whole idea of a messiah. It's not just a Judeo-Christian myth; it also plays into the search for the reincarnation of the Buddha."

The search—the quest—informs Greek myths ("We have Orpheus and Morpheus in the film," says Larry) as well as Alice's Adventures in Wonderland: "It's a story about consciousness," says Larry, "a child's perception of an adult's world. *The Matrix* is about the birth and evolution of consciousness. It starts off crazy, then things start to make sense." It can also be read as a variant on Gibson's *Neuromancer,* the 1986 cyberpunk classic about a computer cowboy on the run. "It'd be near impossible to make a movie out of that," says Larry. "We knew the way to make it relevant was to turn what we view as the real world into a virtual reality."

And now, for extra credit: theoretical mathematics. The lads became fascinated, Larry says, "by the idea that math and theology are almost the same. They begin with a supposition you can derive a whole host of laws or rules from. And when you take all of them to the infinity point, you wind up at the same place: these unanswerable mysteries really become about personal perception. Neo's journey is affected by all these rules, all these people trying to tell him what the truth is. He doesn't accept anything until he gets to his own end point, his own rebirth."

Great, guys, but is Joe Popcorn supposed to carry a *Matrix* concordance in his head? "We wrote the story for ourselves and hoped others would pick up on it," says Larry. "Every studio we showed it to thought no one would understand it. We told them it would be complex and dense, but we were also going to shoot the best action scenes and coolest computer graphics ever. Even if audiences didn't get all of the references, we knew they'd at least have a good time with the visuals."

Kind of like *Star Wars*, eh, where the kids came for the laser show and stayed for the course in Joseph Campbell? Well, maybe not. "The Force is good, fun stuff," says Larry. "I grew up on those movies. But we were hoping to do something a little more sophisticated with *The Matrix.*"

Comparisons aside, the brothers have shown they can make a science-fiction epic that both probes and throbs. George Lucas' May tricks are a month away, but Andy and Larry have proved that right now they're the big Wachowski.

VILLAGE VOICE, 4/13/99, p. 150, Dennis Lim

Working off the transcendently paranoid, made-for-movies premise that reality might be the grandest illusion of all, *The Matrix* comes on like an all-or-nothing mindfuck, hot-wired into the intense existential panic that courses through millennial anxiety attacks like *The Truman Show* and dystopian sci-fi trips from Philip K. Dick to last year's inventively convoluted *Dark City*. But the second film by Andy and Larry Wachowski (the brothers' follow-up to *Bound,* their obnoxious lesbian-chic-for-straight-guys neo-noir) turns out to be a tunnel-visioned crowd pleaser, and the spook factor that initially juices the movie evaporates in the interests of quick-fix set pieces. With big guns. And kick boxing.

There's plenty of plot to spill, so in the broadest possible terms: the world is in deep shit, but oh look, a Savior is on hand. *The Matrix* wears this biblical allusion like a bumper sticker, with a dopey, self-congratulatory smirk. The metaphor gets even more insane when you consider that The One (as he's repeatedly referred to) is, um, Keanu Reeves. In yet another blankly effortful performance, Reeves plays a computer nerd nicknamed Neo, who's led to his dubious destiny by a couple of enigmatic, leather-clad figures: the vixenish Trinity (Carrie-Anne Moss, underacting an underwritten role) and the stoic Morpheus (a no-bullshit Laurence Fishburne). They toy with Keanu's pretty little head for a while, but when the revelations arrive, they're suitably momentous, so I won't give them away—suffice to say, it's not really 1999 after all.

The Matrix has all the makings of a cult—for starters, there's the too-much-information syndrome that fanboys revel in. Their central idea is vivid and enormously suggestive, but the Wachowskis' screenplay is composed mostly of mile-a-minute gobbledygook and mystic hogwash, and while the natural temptation is to deconstruct the mess, I suspect the film won't get any more coherent on subsequent viewings (finally, a movie tailor-made for Keanu's perpetual look of befuddlement). Virtual reality is relatively fresh and obviously fertile terrain for movies (it's the theme of David Cronenberg's upcoming *eXistenZ*, which is both more playful and more ingenious), and here, you wish it was more than simply a neat way of introducing really cool effects.

Ultimately, *The Matrix* settles for technically dazzling comic-book shtick. Some might count this as a good thing, but I'm not a fan of the Wachowskis' more-is-more aesthetic, which they unleashed in the inappropriately florid *Bound,* and which has since turned even more grotesque. The visual effects (especially a shooting technique called "bullet-time photography" that applies animation tricks to live action) are impressive, but the movie's overall style is wearing. The camera (or computer program, as the case may be) calls attention to itself more than to what's within the frame, all swooping overheads and nutty angles. The John Woo-on-speed shoot-outs and martial-arts tomfoolery, though tongue-in-cheek, are similarly histrionic (even if the virtual-reality context provides some sort of explanation for the gravity-defying acrobatics). The cumulative effect is perversely deflationary: long before it's over, the film has flushed the paranoia from its system.

Also reviewed in:
NATION, 4/26/99, p. 34, Stuart Klawans
NEW YORK TIMES, 3/31/99, p. E1, Janet Maslin
NEW YORKER, 5/3/99, p. 194, David Denby
VARIETY, 3/29-4/4/99, p. 67, Todd McCarthy
WASHINGTON POST, 3/31/99, p. C1, Stephen Hunter
WASHINGTON POST, 4/2/99, Weekend/p. 41, Michael O'Sullivan

MEN CRY BULLETS

A Phaedra Cinema release of an Idiot Films production. *Executive Producer:* Harry Ralston, Tamara Hernandez, and Jessica Rains. *Director:* Tamara Hernandez. *Screenplay:* Tamara Hernandez. *Director of Photography:* Michael Grady. *Editor:* Garth Grinde and Scott Balcerek.

Sound: Lionel J. Ball. *Production Designer:* Ivana Letica. *Running time:* 106 minutes. *MPAA Rating:* Not Rated.

CAST: Steven Nelson (Billy); Honey Lauren (Gloria); Jeri Lynn Ryan (Lydia); Harry Ralston (Freddy Fishnets); Michael Mangiamele (The Paper Boy); Sabrina Bertaccini (Collete); Trish Elliott (Gloria's Mom); Hugh Bogan (Gloria's Dad); Bob Sherer (Bootser).

NEW YORK POST, 10/22/99, p. 67, Jonathan Foreman

A lobotomized attempt to make a no-budget John Waters movie, "Men Cry Bullets" is a painful reminder of just how bad indie cinema can be—especially when it plays with gender roles. It's desperately unfunny and dreadfully acted, written and directed.

Ultra-meek drag queen Billy (Steven Nelson) has his act wrecked by loud-mouthed writer Gloria (Honey Lauren). She then violently seduces him and he becomes obsessed with her.

Gloria's Texan cousin Lydia (Jeri Ryan with a terrible accent) comes on the scene, and Gloria is driven to violence by Billy's apparent interest in her. In between all the heavy-handed outrageousness, Billy has frequent black-and-white flashbacks to domestic violence in his childhood.

Ryan plays Seven of Nine on TV's "Star Trek Voyager" but her big-eyed sex appeal is wasted here.

VILLAGE VOICE, 10/26/99, p. 168, Nico Baumbach

A rape/seduction scene in which the woman is the perpetrator and the man is the victim: shocking and subversive, or just indie high concept? The irony of Tamara Hernandez's scrappy first feature, *Men Cry Bullets,* is that it feels most conventional when trying to be provocative. Fortunately tongue isn't so firmly planted in cheek to prevent genuine pathos from seeping through in the depicted relationship between meek drag queen Billy (Steven Nelson) and his aggressor, bad-girl writer Gloria (Honey Lauren). A film about dependency, it never absolves itself of its own dependency on the tropes of gritty indie cleverness. Nonetheless, this amateurish no-budget effort has earnest charm, and a sensitivity to the tragic dimension of *amour fou* that saves it from lapsing into shtick.

The psychosexual drama plays out around the premise that the would-be honeymoon killers must avenge the death of a pig. Don't ask. More to the point, Billy, who makes a living impersonating his late mother, is ultimately driven to maintain this masochistic performance offstage, with ill-fated results. Meanwhile Gloria, when she can't force her lover to be a real man, must become one herself. While the film delights in the perversity of its role reversals, it has the courage to admit that such pleasure is not utopian. Billy's need for the abusive Gloria feels like a necessary though ultimately fatal attempt at resistance, as does Gloria's need to destroy what she loves. As melodrama exploring the relation between power and gender, *Men Cry Bullets* is no *Bitter Tears of Petra von Kant.* On the other hand, as the tale of losers struggling for relief from that apparent sham, the normal American family, it maintains a lighter touch but still "looks closer" than the infinitely more polished contrivance *American Beauty.*

Also reviewed in:
NEW YORK TIMES, 10/22/99, p. E26, Anita Gates
VARIETY, 3/30-4/5/98, p. 44, Joe Leydon

MESSAGE IN A BOTTLE

A Warner Bros. release in association with Bel-Air Entertainment of a Tig production in association with Di Novi Pictures. *Producer:* Denise Di Novi, Jim Wilson, and Kevin Costner. *Director:* Luis Mandoki. *Screenplay:* Gerald DiPego. *Based on the novel by:* Nicholas Sparks. *Director of Photography:* Caleb Deschanel. *Editor:* Steven Weisberg. *Music:* Gabriel Yared. *Music Editor:* Robert Randles. *Sound:* Lance Brown and (music) John Richards. *Sound Editor:*

Bruce Stambler. *Casting:* Amanda Mackey Johnson. *Production Designer:* Jeffrey Becroft. *Art Director:* Steve Saklad and Mark Zuelzke. *Set Designer:* Masako Masuda, Andrea Dopaso, Mike Cukers, and Nancy Deren. *Set Decorator:* Dorree Cooper and Elaine O'Donnell. *Special Effects:* David Kelsey. *Costumes:* Nick Scarano. *Make-up:* Kathrine James. *Stunt Coordinator:* Lance Gilbert and Norman Howell. *Running time:* 110 minutes. *MPAA Rating:* PG-13.

CAST: Kevin Costner (Garret Blake); Robin Wright Penn (Theresa Osborne); Paul Newman (Dodge Blake); John Savage (Johnny Land); Illeana Douglas (Lina Paul); Robbie Coltrane (Charlie Toschi); Jesse James (Jason Osborne); Bethel Leslie (Marta Land); Tom Aldredge (Hank Land); Viveka Davis (Alva); Raphael Sharge (Andy); Richard Hamilton (Chet); Rosemary Murphy (Helen at the B&B); Steven Eckholdt and Susan Eckholdt (David); Susan Brightbill (Catherine); Patricia Belcher (Annie); Steve Mellor (Man on Dock); Lance Gilbert (Man on Sinking Boat); Jenifer Lamb (Woman on Sinking Boat); Hayden Panettiere (Girl on Sinking Boat); Walt MacPherson (Pete the Cop); Justin DiPego (Typewriter Repairman); Meagan Riley-Grant (Mary); Karen Fowler (Mother in Car); Caleb Deschanel (Man at the B&B); Maurice Ochmann (Mall Boy); Anthony Genovese (Photographer); Elizabeth Guindi (Christine); Donald Watson (Diner Patron 1); Claphan Murray (Diner Patron 2); Gregg Trzaskowski (Johnny's Friend); Philip Traynor (Boy in Car); Daniel V. Trefts (Policeman on Boat); Christin Bergstron and Norman Fessler (Officers); Mark Thomason (Garret Photo Double); David W. Paris and Robert Kenney (Helicopter Pilots).

CHRISTIAN SCIENCE MONITOR, 2/12/99, p. 17, David Sterritt

Kevin Costner hasn't exactly been on a roll since "The Postman" became the most embarrassing flop of the late '90s, but you'd never know it from "Message in a Bottle," his new picture.

The screenplay establishes his character as the most warmhearted, sympathetic, and desirable man on the planet, making us long for the moment when he'll show up on screen. Then it delays his entrance, tantalizing us with a surprising number of Costnerless scenes. When he finally does arrive, his fans will be ready to swoon and even skeptics may feel a tingle or two at the payoff.

This is Hollywood at its most shamelessly manipulative, but hey, it's the sort of trick that's been selling tickets for as long as movie stars have existed. Does it still work its magic? Box-office returns will tell, but odds are that Costner's slump is a thing of the past. The story begins when a woman named Theresa, still smarting from a failed marriage, discovers a bottle washed ashore on a beach that's as lonely as she is. It contains a letter written by a forlorn lover to a woman who's vanished from his life. Theresa shares this with friends at the Chicago newspaper where she works. Another message surfaces, then a third, seemingly written by the same romantic hand.

Tracking down the author to the North Carolina shore, she finds a man whose experience of life and love has been as disappointing as her own. They fall for each other, but it's a hesitant relationship that won't be able to blossom as long as memories retain their grip.

Costner can play this sort of wistful hero in his sleep (and has, on occasion), so it's no surprise that his doe-eyed performance is one of the movie's most dependable assets. Robin Wright Penn also makes a fetching impression, and Paul Newman almost steals the show as the hero's crusty dad.

The producers surround this trio with oodles of scenery gorgeously filmed by Caleb Deschanel; and Luis Mandoki directs with every sentimental stop pulled completely out. Moviegoers looking for a good, long cry (at well over two tearful hours) need search no further.

LOS ANGELES TIMES, 2/12/99, Calendar/p. 1, Kenneth Turan

"The fault is not in our stars," Shakespeare wrote once upon a time. and though he wasn't referring to "Message in a Bottle," he could have been. Kevin Costner, Robin Wright Penn and Paul Newman do everything major attractions can do to make "Message in a Bottle" into a three-hankie extravaganza, but they're finally let down by a film that tampers both too much and not enough with what looked to be a sure thing.

"Message" is based on a novel by Nicholas Sparks. a.k.a. "the king of read-it-and-weep," which sold 600,000 copies and counting in hardback and spent months and months on major bestseller lists. Producer Denise Di Novi was such a fan that she convinced Warner Bros. to buy the book when it was still partially in outline form, and—or so the press notes claim—she was so convinced that Costner should play the lead that she dreamed about him in the part. Yet even with this kind of audience-proven pedigree, the makers of "Message," including director Luis Mandoki and screenwriter Gerald DiPego, couldn't leave well enough alone. In typical studio development fashion, they've fussed and worried over everything in the story, especially its last third, making what was quick and clean in the book labored and overly elaborate. The result is exposition overkill and a dragged-out finale that turns what should have been a Tear Duct Special into a deflating experience, making what worked in the book unacceptable on the screen.

It's not that "Message," with its picture-book exteriors swooningly photographed by Caleb Deschanel, was ever destined to be anything but a complete romantic fantasy for which reality checks need to be checked at the door. But because the acting is so right for this kind of production, the film threatens to get to us until faulty exposition abruptly pulls the rug out from beneath our feet.

Simultaneously energizing "Message" and holding it together is Wright Penn, whose performance should catapult her into more major leading roles. Wright Penn has not lacked for work since her debut in "The Princess Bride," but because her previous films ("State of Grace," "She's So Lovely," "Moll Flanders" among them) have come and gone under most moviegoers' radar, her classic beauty, formidable integrity and complete believability even in a flimsy role are fresh enough to make an impact.

Wright Penn plays Theresa Osborne, a single mother who works as a researcher for the Chicago Tribune. After dropping her son Jason (Jesse James) off with his remarried father, she takes a vacation on Cape Cod, where she finds, embedded in the sand on one of those dazzling, pristine beaches that movies like this specialize in, a bottle with—that's right—a message in it.

And not just any message. It's a letter from a man to a woman, a letter so filled with romantic longing and poetic passion that Theresa, not to mention all the people back at the Chicago Tribune she ends up sharing the message with, are simply flabbergasted that such a paragon of sensitivity might actually be walking on the Earth.

Soon enough, the wheels of the great newspaper start turning, and Theresa discovers that the writer's name is Garret (with one "t," though the book insists on two) Blake, that the woman he's written to is his beloved late wife Catherine, and that the man himself is alive and well on the Outer Banks of North Carolina. Though her editor (an amusing Robbie Coltrane) warns her, "You're thinking Heathcliff and this guy is probably Captain Ahab," Theresa feels compelled to go directly to the North Carolina shore and seek the bottler out, though she doesn't feel compelled (O foolish woman!) to tell him the truth about why she's there.

As boat builder and restorer Garret Blake, Costner is completely in his element and gives a surprisingly successful performance. The kind of complete earnestness that led the actor to invest himself in "The Postman" and caused him to tell Madonna, in a celebrated moment in the documentary "Truth or Dare," that her stage show was "neat," is exactly what's called for in the part of a sturdy straight-arrow with the most reassuring of masculine presences. Costner is an actor we don't want to be trying too hard, and here, as the wary, withdrawn Garret, he doesn't have to.

Theresa. that genteel bundle of energy, is, of course, just the type of woman to successfully draw Garret out, and director Mandoki, whose last film was the equally soggy "When a Man Loves a Woman," makes the most of their natural interaction, of interchanges like his "I used to be better with people; I used to be charming" and her "Sorry I missed that." Even simple moments like Garret telling Theresa, "I make a perfect steak; it's the best thing I do," benefit from their joint charisma.

The third wheel in this scenario, and someone who might have played Costner's role if he were younger, is Newman as Dodge, Garret's grumpy old coot of a father. Newman has reached the stage of his career where he has so much presence and skill to call upon that each new role feels like a gift we are not quite worthy of. His Dodge is a gem of a performance as Newman makes things look easy that other actors couldn't begin to accomplish.

The double-bind of "Message's" plot is that the very thing that attracted Theresa to Garret, the intensity and duration of his apparently endless love for his dead wife, is the quality that stands in the way of the two of them being happy, should she ever get around to telling him the truth about how they met. Wright Penn and Costner are so sincere in their attempts to work through this conundrum that the film's bollixed final sections are especially unfortunate. You almost wish "Message in a Bottle" had discarded this part of the story with the same alacrity used in jettisoning Garret's superfluous final "t." It just gets in the way.

NEW YORK, 2/22/99, p. 114, Peter Rainer

In the new Kevin Costner movie *Message in a Bottle*, said bottle washes up on shore and *Chicago Tribune* researcher Theresa (Robin Wright Penn) reads its contents, a rapturous love letter from a man to a woman he lost. You may not shed a tear with Theresa; you may find, as I did, that the letter is purest Hallmark. The whole movie is purest Hallmark, as is, I gather, the Nicholas Sparks best-seller upon which it's based. (I couldn't make it more than twenty pages into the book without wanting to drain a bottle of distinctly different vintage.) This is the sort of four-hankie extravaganza that usually gets palmed off as a "woman's movie"—meaning, I suppose, that one can appreciate its lachrymosity only if possessed of the right biogenetic equipment. I question this. In the Hollywood-studio hierarchy, for example, male executives are just as willing as women to cry all the way to the bank.

In the tearjerker genre, there's bull that wins you over and bull that just sits there. *Message in a Bottle* is inert from the first frame. Director Luis Mandoki is fortunate in his choice of cinematographers: Caleb Deschanel turns all those standard-issue shots of crimson sunsets and wheeling gulls into something more than picture postcards (though less than art). But one still has the feeling this film was designed to lull you into dumb-dumb land, the better to pick your pocket. Even in dense coastal fog, you can see it all coming a mile away. Theresa tracks down Garret (Costner), the lovelorn message-maker, in North Carolina, and damned if this boat-builder isn't an all-around dreamboat. Except he's still grieving over the loss of his wife two years before. He doesn't grieve very strenuously, though: Costner's acting has gone from minimal to marginal. In their scenes together, Paul Newman, playing Garret's crotchety, wisdom-dispensing fisherman father, steals what little there is to steal. Robin Wright Penn is a shimmer of banked fires. Her Theresa is so unconscionably understanding of Garret's grief that even the snifflers in the audience may guffaw. "I think it's so beautiful the way you love her," she says to him after he commemorates his wife for the umpteenth time. Yeah, sure.

NEW YORK POST, 2/12/99, p. 44, Jonathan Foreman

"Message in a Bottle" is a pretty, artificial romance drenched in designer schlock, the sort of shameless chick flick in which every outdoor scene takes place in front of a sunset, full moon or giant rainbow, and the female yuppie's love object is a handsome widowed guy who works with his hands. It devotes so much energy to postcard vistas, perfect interiors, matching pillow cases and beautiful clothes that you almost forget the by-the-numbers love story.

Still, it does give a starring role to one of the most beautiful women in movies, an actress whose mainstream sightings have been all too rare. And while hers is no Oscar-worthy performance, Robin Wright Penn's presence keeps your interest and the movie afloat.

The story begins with divorced single mom Theresa Osborne (Wright Penn) jogging on a spectacular beach and finding a bottle containing someone's moving, typewritten love letter to his dead wife. Here at last is a man who can express his emotions!

Back in Chicago, where she works as a researcher at a lavishly appointed newspaper, Theresa tracks down not only another letter-containing bottle by the same hand, but also the whereabouts of the man himself.

Down to North Carolina she goes, already in love with the letter writer. The man who sends his emotions out to sea turns out to be Garret Blake (Kevin Costner), a handsome repairer of boats who also knows his way around a kitchen, lives in a stunning house out of a Ralph Lauren catalog and can handle himself in one of those fist-fights that break out in rural diners soon after dawn.

Naturally, there's instant chemistry between these two lonely, pretty people (you know they're failing in love because they're soon throwing marshmallows at each other). But Garret is carrying a lot of baggage, thanks to his wife's death two years earlier, and the road to romance will not be smooth—especially as Theresa neglects to mention finding the letter in a bottle.

Still, once the two get together, the magical therapy of love enables both of them to get on with their unrealized career ambitions: her writing and his building (rather than repairing) a boat.

People have compared Harlequin-style fantasy-romance to pornography for the way it fosters unrealistic, unhealthy expectations. And the underlying message of "Message in a Bottle" is no exception: It says that you can only really love someone who is thousands of miles away or dead.

All the best acting in mediocre American movies comes from supporting actors, and this film is no exception. John Savage is as fine as ever, Robbie Coltrane is terrific as Theresa's canny boss and Newman steals every scene he's in until you wish that he, rather than Costner, could get the girl.

NEWSDAY, 2/12/99, Part II/p. B10, John Anderson

Wearing what seems to be the accumulated hurts of a thousand bad reviews, Kevin Costner moves through "Message in a Bottle" like an abused pet, which suits his performance as widowed hero/reluctant lover. But that shouldn't be perceived as anything even close to remorse; coming in the wake of "Waterworld" and "The Postman," the casting of producer-actor Costner as a letter-writing shipbuilder shows a stubborn resiliency, if not downright defiance.

But add to this the fact that "Message in a Bottle"—an unhappy marriage of "Sleepless in Seattle" and "Rebecca"—lasts two hours-plus, and Costner's reputation for, well, overdoing it seems planted on pretty firm ground.

On the other hand, for those who cry at AT&T commercials, "Message" may be the perfect Valentine's card: A paean to fated love, with a dash of death and a take on the world that's pure picture postcard (with just as much soul, despite being shot by the talented Caleb Deschanel). Our heroine, Theresa (Robin Wright Penn), a single mom with a job at the Chicago Tribune, finds a bottle on the beach while vacationing in Cape Cod. Inside is a note, written by a heartbroken lover, whose sentimental excesses would earn a walk on the plank at Hallmark ("You were my true north," he writes to who-knows-who). But Theresa buys it wholesale and reads the letter to her friends at the paper, prompting her editor (Robbie Coltrane) to run it in a column, which results in a reader response so great that Theresa is dispatched on the Search for Mr. Sensitive.

When the trail leads to the Outer Banks off North Carolina and Garret Blake (Costner), the mutual mooring of Theresa and her boatwright-in-mourning seems all but inevitable. As does his emotional recovery and the eventual cessation of hostilities with his late wife's family (led by a particularly crazed John Savage).

But at the same time, the nagging questions that have been lurking at the back of your mind start overflowing and obscuring your vision. Why is Theresa, a Tribune researcher, sent on this story? Why doesn't she ever call her editor? Why doesn't her editor call her? Why, in what seems a violation of all ethics, does she keep her professional status such a big secret? Well, we know why. Because it provides the segue to the big betrayal-of-trust scene when Garret finds out what she's really about. But the whole thing is so artificial as to preclude emotional engagement—unless of course, you ignore even the most elementary question: Why Garret would so carefully place his messages in bottles if he didn't expect them to be read?

For all this, "Message in a Bottle" does have Paul Newman, whose performance as Costner's father (now there's a Hollywood-mythic concept) acts like CPR on this otherwise comatose movie whenever he appears on screen. Wright Penn is no slouch, either: She's profoundly beautiful but manages to make a convincing physical argument that she's also a beleaguered single mother with a bad job despite her magnificent Chicago townhouse, her Dolce & Gabana wardrobe and the office her editor gives her after writing one front-page piece for the Tribune. Anyone familiar with "Dilbert" and the tyranny of corporate decor knows this is pure fantasy—although fantasy is suppposed to be fun, and "Message in a Bottle" is anything but.

SIGHT AND SOUND, 5/99, p. 53, Jamie Graham

On a shoreline, Theresa Osborne discovers a bottle in the sand and is moved by the contents: a heartfelt love letter addressed to someone named Catherine and signed "G". Theresa shows the letter to her colleagues at the *Chicago Tribune* where she works as a researcher Columnist Charlie Toschi prints it, and the public response is enormous. Two readers send in other letters, found under similar circumstances, which appear to be the work of the same author. *The Tribune* traces the epistles to Garret Blake, a sailboat builder living in Saint Clair, California. Theresa visits Garret to research a follow-up. A hesitant courtship unfolds between them, and it transpires that Catherine—Garret's childhood sweetheart and wife—died two years ago during childbirth. Determining that Garret is still in mourning, Theresa returns to Chicago. Weeks pass, during which Garret completes work on a boat crafted in memory of his wife. He visits Theresa in Chicago where they make love for the first time. But Garret discovers his love letters and Toschi's newspaper column in her bedside drawer and leaves, disgusted by her deceit. Theresa attends Garret's boat launch in Saint Clair, telling him to come for her when he's ready. Garret types another letter and sets sail to deliver it. In a storm, he chances upon a capsized family and loses his life while saving them. Theresa attends the funeral and talks to Garret's father, who shows her his son's final letter—a farewell note, telling his wife of his new love, Theresa.

Message in a Bottle's first 30 minutes will lead many viewers into a misconception. Having discovered a love letter on a deserted shore, divorcee Theresa Osborne pours over its poignant prose with feverish intensity. By the time she decides to track down its mysterious author Garret, she has clearly fallen blindly in love. At this point it seems as if *Message in a Bottle* is about to encroach on similar epistolary territory to Nora Ephron's *You've Got Mail* (itself an update of *The Shop Around the Corner)*. However, rather than explore how love can be unleashed by written sentiments rather than physical interaction, *Message in a Bottle* quickly reveals itself to be something altogether different: a purely cinematic movie that tries to represent love transcendent through imagery and lush music alone.

Director Luis Mandoki *(When a Man Loves a Woman)* seems quite uninterested in observing courtship through pingpong witticisms and aggressive dialogue, the staple diet of Ephron's and her imitators' romantic films. Instead, he's grasping for hidden meanings in the intangible. Each awkward pause says far more than the sentence that follows it, and few films outside the oeuvres of Antonioni and Malick rely so much on landscape to co-ordinate themes and portray psychology: Garret seems like a piece of the coastal town he lives in; Theresa is tentatively rooted in the urban world she's on the verge of escaping.

But while Mandoki's intention to rise above generic boundaries and represent love on a higher, almost spiritual level is commendable, the execution is less so. Gabriel Yared's orchestral score ebbs and flows like the ocean that plays such an integral role, but it rarely buoys the heart and never sweeps the emotions away. Likewise, the cinematography is strangely lifeless, the drab colours proving more dull than dreamlike. Potentially rhapsodic compositions of rustling treetops and windswept meadows fail to attain the sensual lyricism of, say, *Picnic at Hanging Rock* (1975) or Powell and Pressburger's *Gone to Earth* (1950), and what fragile beauty there is collapses under the weight of its symbolic baggage.

VILLAGE VOICE, 2/23/99, p. 109, Jessica Winter

Theresa (Robin Wright Penn) is a recently divorced *Chicago Tribune* staffer. Since she is wan and frizzy-haired with a cheerful yet slightly strained manner, we know that all she needs is a good man and those cheeks will flush with her second spring and she'll get that promotion. During a Cape Cod vacation, Theresa finds a bottle washed up on shore with a letter inside to "Catherine," whom we can presume is either the writer's long-lost love or his human-resources contact at Hallmark: "I feel I've been lost, no bearings, no compass... You were my true north." Theresa decides to track down the note's directionally challenged originator, and finds Garret Blake, a sailboat builder in North Carolina. Since he is played by Kevin Costner, we know that he's an oddball outsider, a strong, silent type who gets into bar fights. Catherine turns out to be Garret's dead wife, though her demise is the film's one real mystery. "Pregnancy just took the stuffing right out of her. I took care of her the best I could," Garret explains with the simplicity we're supposed to mistake for gravity; I was just left wondering if the Blakes were Christian Scientists, since I'm not prepared to accept the film's apparent conjecture that there aren't any doctors in redneck country (though Garret probably wouldn't be able to find them anyway). The screenplay hums along like clockwork: city girl and country boy meet cute, court awkward, fall in love, have a fight, and reconcile just in time for a big ending, a tacked-on tragedy that unfolds to the strains of Gabriel Yared's score. Since it retreads Yared's music for *The English Patient,* we're only reminded of another movie about maps and memory, an infinitely more accomplished proof of a bad idea: that cosmic doom, above all else, is damn sexy.

Also reviewed in:
CHICAGO TRIBUNE, 2/12/99, Friday/p. A, Michael Wilmington
NEW REPUBLIC, 3/15/99, p. 27, Stanley Kauffmann
NEW YORK TIMES, 2/12/99, p. E26, Janet Maslin
NEW YORKER, 2/22-3/1/99, p. 186, David Denby
VARIETY, 2/8-14/99, p. 74, Todd McCarthy
WASHINGTON POST, 2/12/99, p. C5, Rita Kempley
WASHINGTON POST, 2/12/99, Weekend/p. 46, Desson Howe

MESSENGER, THE: THE STORY OF JOAN OF ARC

A Columbia Pictures release of a Gaumont production. *Producer:* Patrice Ledoux. *Director:* Luc Besson. *Screenplay:* Andrew Birkin and Luc Besson. *Director of Photography:* Thierry Arbogast. *Editor:* Sylvie Landra. *Music:* Eric Serra. *Sound:* Vincent Tulli and (music) Didier Lozahic. *Casting:* Lucinda Syson, Nathalie Cheron, and Todd Thaler. *Production Designer:* Hugues Tissandier. *Art Director:* Alain Paroutaud. *Set Decorator:* Alain Pitrel and Robert Le Corre. *Set Dresser:* Guy Monbillard and Bruno Salord. *Costumes:* Catherine Leterrier. *Make-up:* Kuno Schlegelmilch. *Stunt Coordinator:* Philippe Guegan. *Running time:* 130 minutes. *MPAA Rating:* R.

CAST: Rab Affleck (Comrade); Stephane Algoud (Look Out); Edwin Apps (Bishop); David Bailie, David Barber, and Timothy Bateson (English Judges); Christian Barbier (Captain); David Begg (Nobleman, Rouen's Castle); Christian Bergner (Captain); Andrew Birkin (Talbot); Dominic Borrelli (English Judge); John Boswall (Old Priest); Matthew Bowyer (Bludgeoned French Soldier); Paul Brooke (Domremy's Priest); Bruce Byron (Joan's Father); Vincent Cassel (Gilles de Rais); Charles Cork (Vaucouleur's Priest); Patrice Cossoneau (Captain); Tony D'Amario (Compiegne's Mayor); Daniel Daujon (Church's Peer); Tonio Descanvelle (Xaintrailles); Philippe du Janerand (Dijon); Faye Dunaway (Yolande of Aragon); Sylviane Duparc (Mary of Anjou's Lady's Companion); Barbara Elbourn (Aunt); Christian Erickson (La Tremoille); Tara Flanagan (Woman, Rouen's Castle); Bruno Flender (Poitiers' Inquistor); Serge Fournier (Church's Peer, Coronation); David Gant (Duke of Bedford); Sydney Golder (Cell's Guard); Jessica Goldman (Duchess of Bedford's Lady's Companion); Framboise Gommendy (Joan's Mother); Robert Goodman (Blackbeard); Jean Pierre Gos (Laxart); Joanne Greenwood (Catherine); Pascal Greggory (Duke of Alençon); Bernard Grenet (Senlis' Bishop); Valerie Griffiths (Hag); Timothee Grimblat (Conscience, Child); Richard Guille (English Guard, Rouen's Castle); Thierry Guilmard (Assessor); Jerome Hankins (Nobleman, Rouen's Castle); Desmond Harrington (Aulon); Jacques Herlin (Orlean's Priest); Len Hibberd (Comrade); Dustin Hoffman (Conscience); Didier Hoarau (Assessor); Vera Jakob (Woman at the Cemetry); Michael Jenn (Duke of Burgundy); Toby Jones (English Judge); Milla Jovovich (Joan of Arc); Tcheky Karyo (Dunois); Gerard Krawczyk (Church's Peer, Coronation); Richard Leaf (Conscience, Young Man); Frank Lebreton (Assessor); Joseph Malerba (Beaurevoir's Guard); John Malkovich (Charles VII); Dominique Marcas (Poitiers' Inquisitor); Eric Mariotto (Young Monk); Rene Marquant (Rouen's Priest); Carl McCrystal (Glasdale); Gina McKee (Duchess of Bedford); Phil McKee (Redbeard); Simon Meacock (Teeth Soldier); John Merrick (Regnault De Chartres); Joseph O'Conor (Poitiers' Chief Inquisitor); Quentin Ogier (Louis); Kevin O'Neill (Scribe at Process); Melanie Page (Young Girl in Bath); Brian Pettifer (Executioner); Brian Pettifer (Torturer at Process); Philip Philmar (English Judge); Enee Piat (Monk at Coronation); Irving Pomepui (Louis XI, 5 Years Old); Brian Poyser (English Judge); Olivier Rabourdin (Richemont); Vincent Regan (Buck); Rene Remblier (Dijon's Assistant); Joseph Rezwin (Poitiers' Inquisitor); Ralph Riach (English Judge); Mark Richards (Corridor's Guard in Rouen); Richard Ridings (La Hire); Malcolm Rogers (Bishop); Tara Romer (Gamaches);

Julie-Anne Roth (Young Girl in Bath); Olga Sekulic (Mary of Anjou); Joseph Sheridan (Canon); Eric Tonetto (Captain); Vincent Tulli (Orleans' Physician); Jane Valentine (Joan, 8 Years Old); Jemima West (Girl); Tat Whalley (Raymond); Peter Whitfield (English Judge); Timothy West (Cauchon); Frederick Witta (Poitiers' Inquisitor).

CHRISTIAN SCIENCE MONITOR, 11/12/99, p. 15, David Sterritt

Religious subjects are coming to the screen more frequently these days, and not everyone is happy with the form they're taking. This week brings two contrasting examples that should generate some lively discussion.

"The Messenger: The Story of Joan of Arc," by French director Luc Besson, presents itself as a celebration of a martyr's faith but shows more interest in the violence and hatred that surrounded her life. "Dogma," by American filmmaker Kevin Smith, presents itself as a foul--mouthed satire but winds up making unexpectedly smart points about the value of religion as a living force.

The Messenger takes its cue from the long Hollywood tradition of biblical epics and "hagiopics," as some critics call them, dramatizing the lives of famous saints. Joan of Arc has received many treatments, and the results have often been undistinguished, even with major stars like Ingrid Bergman and gifted directors like Otto Preminger.

With the melodrama "La Femme Nikita" and the fantasy "The Fifth Element" in his list of credits, Besson is hardly the first director you'd think of for a thoughtful exploration of the courageous French teenager whose "voices" led her to assemble an army, defeat her country's English invaders, and perish at the stake rather than renounce the justness of her cause or the authenticity of her divine guidance.

True to form, Besson reveals his agenda in an early scene where Joan watches helplessly as her sister is murdered and raped (in that order) by an English soldier. The film doesn't maintain this level of nastiness for all of its 140 minutes, but spectacle is much higher on its priorities list than insight. It doesn't help that Milla Jovovich plays the heroine with a bravado more closely resembling movie-star charisma than saintly fortitude.

John Malkovich's fey Dauphin and Faye Dunaway's steely Yolande D'Aragon add touches of conviction, and Dustin Hoffman shows up for a few minutes as Joan's conscience. Still, only a handful of isolated scenes—when Joan is overwhelmed by the bloodshed her army has caused, for instance—suggest that the filmmakers have anything on their minds beyond exploiting the story's action-adventure elements. There's little on the nature of inspiration, the challenge of interpreting revealed wisdom, and the tension between worldly actions and spiritual ideals.

Dogma has been stirring up controversy ever since its May premiére at the Cannes filmfest. It arrives in theaters today from Lions Gate Films, which acquired the movie after Disney vetoed distribution by its Miramax subsidiary. Protesters have already raised an outcry against its irreverent story—about two fallen angels hoping to reenter Heaven by exploiting a loophole in Roman Catholic dogma—and its steady stream of sexual humor and four-letter language.

Moviegoers offended by raunchiness will be especially outraged by its presence in a picture that takes religion as its central theme. Some are hailing the film as a rare attempt to grapple with faith-related issues in a way that might attract a large, young audience, though, and filmmaker Smith has been outspoken about his longtime status as an active churchgoer. His claims of sincerity are bolstered by insightful moments in "Dogma" itself—as when a character criticizes negative creeds that make religion a burden rather than a blessing, or when another says religous "ideas" are more valuable than "beliefs," since ideas can blossom and mere beliefs constrict.

However the arguments over "Dogma" play out, more religiously oriented films are on their way. "The End of the Affair" adapted by Neil Jordan from Graham Greene's novel, begins as a sexually explicit love story and ends as an affirmation of divine intervention. "Holy Smoke," by Australian filmmaker Jane Campion, pits Harvey Keitel as a psychological "deprogrammer" against Kate Winslet as a cult member. "Genesis," by Cheick Oumar Sissoko, transports the biblical story of Jacob and Esau to West Africa. "Kadosh," by Amos Gitai, poignantly tells of two Israeli women trapped in unfulfilling marriages to men gripped by religious and political conservatism.

Together such releases point to a growing discourse about religion in the public square of popular cinema. Earthy characteristics may lead some observers to wonder if the good aspects of this trend outweigh its problematic side. But expression related to faith takes a huge variety of forms; there must be room for all of them in a genuinely free marketplace of relogous ideas.

LOS ANGELES TIMES, 11/12/99, Calendar/p. 1, Kenneth Turan

Who was responsible for Joan of Arc? Who put those wild and crazy ideas in the impressionable head of the future saint and savior of France? "The Messenger: The Story of Joan of Arc" has a few suggestions.

Perhaps it was that kindly 15th century country priest, the one who told a God-fearing little girl to listen to her voices. Or maybe it was yet another priest, responding to the girl's survival guilt after witnessing a brutal massacre with a reassuring "the Lord always has a good reason. Perhaps he needs you for a higher calling." Perhaps indeed.

The story of Joan—the illiterate teenage peasant girl who changed the course of history by inspiring France's liberation from the British and was eventually canonized by the same church that helped burn her at the stake—is as inherently dramatic a yarn as anyone could want, and between a 1916 Cecil B. DeMille silent and the recent Leelee Sobieski-starring TV miniseries, numerous attempts, including versions starring Ingrid Bergman, Jean Seberg and Maria Falconetti, have made it to the screen.

"The Messenger," starring Milla Jovovich and directed by Luc Besson from a script he co-wrote with Andrew Birkin, is one of the more curious Joan interpretations, wildly ambitious but only intermittently successful. Old-fashioned enough to open with a map of Europe slowly overflowing with blood, it blends great cinematic energy with an awkwardly mixed multinational cast and aggressively over-modernized dialogue. When you throw in Dustin Hoffman as, of all things, Joan's conscience, you know you are in for some heavy weather.

Demurely subtitled "The Story of Joan of Arc," "The Messenger" opens with our girl as a happy child of 8, a baby zealot who goes to confession three times a day and would be happy to spend her entire life inside a church.

Joan's personality gets understandably less sunny when she (and, regrettably, we as well) witnesses the extremely violent and graphic rape of her sister by British troops who have terrible teeth and swinish eating habits in the bargain.

A few years pass and the scene shifts to the royal court, where the uncertain Dauphin, France's uncrowned king (John Malkovich), has heard news of a young girl who wants to see him and claims to be a messenger from God. He's reluctant, but his mother, Yolande of Aragon (Faye Dunaway, costumed like an elaborate Continental queen bee), thinks he should because the little people are on Joan's side: "Suddenly," she thuddingly theorizes, "there's a spark of hope in their simple minds."

Joan in the flesh so convinces the Dauphin of her sincerity and belief that he allows her to go to Orleans to help his army lift the British siege of the city. And, at least in these early stages, Jovovich convinces us as well.

Best known for her role opposite Bruce Willis in Besson's previous "The Fifth Element," Jovovich's very physical Joan-as-Tank Girl take on the future saint is a persuasive one. An actress of great force more than skill, she brings energy, nerve (she did many of her own stunts, including a daunting backward fall from a ladder) and combativeness to the enterprise, adding an essential level of conviction to lines like "I don't think, I leave that to God" and "I am calm; it is God that is angry." When she powerfully screams, "Follow me, I will give you victory," she would be difficult for anyone to resist.

Besson, whose pre-"Fifth Element" films include "La Femme Nikita," "The Big Blue," "Subway" and "Le Dernier Combat," is a potent visual director who brings a fine sense of epic, wide-screen movie-making to the proceedings. The Thierry Arbogast-photographed battles around Orleans, with heaving, roiling masses of humanity engaged in truly savage combat at close quarters, are Besson (who donned a costume to get close to the action and shoot hand-held battle footage himself) at his brutal but beautiful best.

But after Joan wins enough victories to allow the Dauphin to be crowned Charles VII at Rheims, the battles largely cease and "The Messenger" gets as confused as Joan, who starts to notice all the carnage she's caused and wonders if this could really be the Lord's plan.

It's also at about this point that "The Messenger's" willfully pedestrian dialogue (co-writer Birkin also scripted Richard Gere's clunky "King David") becomes more noticeable. "To hell with your voices," someone says to Joan, "it's time to face facts," and Malkovich's Dauphin whines at his coronation like a pouty starlet, "That's meant to be a crown? Can't you get something more regal?" Mixing native and normative English speakers does not help this situation, and neither does Besson's congenital aversion to subtlety.

Things enter a whole other level of strangeness when Joan is captured by the British and has to contend not only with beatings and hostile clergymen of the most obtuse kind but also with Hoffman, cowled like a monk. Personifying Joan's doubts is an acceptable idea, but Jovovich is too broad an acting instrument and Hoffman is too much a time traveler from a different century to make it credible. Nothing less than a miracle saved France, "The Messenger" tells us, and nothing less than a miracle would be needed to rescue this film from itself.

NEW YORK, 11/22/99, p. 87, Peter Rainer

In *The Messenger: The Story of Joan of Arc*, we first glimpse the fabled warrior maiden as a young peasant sprite gamboling through multicolored fields. She also spends quality time in the confession booth badgering the local priest with her piety—he can't believe this little sprig has so much that she wants to be forgiven for. When the British invade Joan's village, she watches her older sister first murdered and *then* raped by a soldier in need of a shave and some heavy orthodonture. Is it any surprise Joan will grow up to defeat the English at Orléans? The only surprise here is her transformation from Pippi Longstocking look-alike to her adolescent incarnation as runway model for the latest in fifteenth-century armorwear. As personified by Milla Jovovich, Joan is lanky and statuesque, with stylishly sheared hair and accented cheekbones. Her perfect teeth are whiter-than-white. When it comes to dentistry, the French win this Hundred Years' War hands down.

Director Luc Besson, who never met a camera move he didn't like, is perhaps best known in this country for *La Femme Nikita,* and there's a lot of Nikita, who also looked like a supermodel, in this Joan. She's a righteous assassin prone to hissy-fit outbursts of remorse. (Apparently, it never dawned on her that people fighting a war actually get slaughtered.) The timing for Besson's take on Joan was inevitable: After George Bernard Shaw and Dreyer and Bresson (what a difference an "r" makes); after Jean Seberg and Maria Falconetti and Ingrid Bergman, the world is finally ready for Joan of Arc as the prototype of grrrl power (Joanie the Brit-slayer). Storming the British battlements at Orléans, she takes an arrow full in the chest and, retreating to safety, urges her warriors to press on. (This part of the spectacle could be called "Start the Revolution Without Me"). But then Joan plucks out the bloody thing and rejoins the fray. The battle scenes are in the *Braveheart* tradition: The score sounds like cannonballs trying to mate, while legions of armored and voluminously hairy bellowers clank to be free. In their verbal ripostes to the French, the British here are far from flowery. They respond to Joan's entreaties to yield to the Kingdom of Heaven with a hearty, "Go fuck yourself!" Historical accuracy can be so limiting, *nest-ce pas?*

Besson and his co-screenwriter Andrew Birkin are offering up Joan as mystic, maiden, martyr (choose any one or combination). The maiden part doesn't work because of Joan's high diva quotient; the martyr part is tempered by our desire, after listening to so much of Joan's holier-than-thou yowling, to see her taste the flames and be done with it. The mystic part has potential, but Joan's visions are about on the level of a Bjork music video, and Besson introduces a character known to Joan as the Conscience, who tests her faith, or something, but is impossible to take seriously because he's played by Dustin Hoffman in hooded robe and beard. Hoffman delivers his lines in a kind of dry, oracular patter; he could be Obi-Wan George Burns. I don't think Hoffman has ever been sillier, though he's not meant to be, exactly.

Contrast him with John Malkovich, playing Charles VII. With his dauphin's haircut and ceremonial duds, this king is a fruity fanatic, and Malkovich gives him a gaudiness that's the most entertaining thing in the movie. Watching the actor here, it occurred to me that the reason he was so perfectly cast in *Being John Malkovich,* where he spends some of his screen time inhabited by a woman, is that, as a performer, he projects in almost equal measure feyness and macho belligerence. With Malkovich, you may not always know what you're getting, but it all adds up. He's turned the omni-weirdness of his screen presence into a remarkably supple comic instrument capable of spanning centuries- Whether he's appearing in the deadpan futurism of *Being John*

Malkovich or the deadweight antics of *The Messenger*, Malkovich is oddly, absolutely *right*. He's just about the only reason to pace yourself through this movie, but maybe not reason enough. I suspect its audiences will be ahead of the British in sounding the retreat.

NEW YORK POST, 11/12/99, p. 58, Jonathan Foreman

"The Messenger: The Story of Joan of Arc" feels like "Braveheart" crossed with "The Sound of Music"—with some hints of "I Never Promised You a Rose Garden" thrown in for good measure.

In French writer-director Luc Besson's flashy version, performed in a very stilted English, we first meet Joan as a little peasant girl of the early 1400s who loves to go to confession and believes God is communicating to her directly.

After one of her visions, she goes home to find her village is being sacked by demonic English soldiers. After the attack, Joan is adopted by relatives—and the next thing you know, she's 17, played by the gorgeous Milla Jovovich, and famous enough to call on Prince Charles, the heir to the throne of France (John Malkovich).

Charles cannot be crowned king because the zone of English occupation includes the ancient capital at Rheims. Joan convinces the prince that she is God's messenger and that she will help liberate France to ensure he becomes king.

At first, the French generals are not inclined to listen to a teenage girl. But the troops are inspired to uncharacteristic aggression by her fearlessness, and Joan's battle plans take the English by surprise.

The king is crowned at Rheims, but instead of rewarding Joan with more troops for the liberation of the whole country, he decides to save money, enjoy his rule and betray his savior.

So when Joan mounts an underfunded attack on Burgundy—a state allied with England she's captured, ransomed by the English and put on trial in ecclesiastical court for heresy and witchcraft.

During her imprisonment, Joan is visited by a supernatural presence, played by Dustin Hoffman, who makes her question the source of her earlier visions. It's unclear if Hoffman is Satan or God. The production notes list him as "The Conscience."

The battle scenes are extremely gory and ridiculously one-sided—as in "Braveheart" the enemy is so easy to defeat you wonder how they could possibly have taken over the country in the first place.

While the mace-swinging slaughter is brilliantly photographed and often terrifying, the armies seem surprisingly small for such an expensive-looking production.

Besson has it both ways when it comes to Joan's visions. At first he shows them as real; later he implies that she may just be a charismatic nutcase. Certainly Jovovich plays her with the ranting speech and mannerisms of a schizophrenic.

But the movie's most damaging weakness is its inconsistent tone. Besson is unable to weave the comic scenes together with the serious gory ones, so both seem increasingly jarring and unbelievable.

Still, it's hard to imagine Americans or Brits making a historical movie as fervently patriotic as this—so much so that it's weirdly reminiscent of Nazi propaganda films.

Partly it's the scenes in which Joan of Arc (Jovovich) has boyishly cropped blonde hair and looks likes a golden Aryan youth in shining white armor.

Partly it's the depiction of the Anglo-Saxon enemy as foul-mouthed hairy savages with a taste for raping fresh corpses.

It's all rather disturbing.

NEWSDAY, 11/12/99, Part II/p. B7, Jan Stuart

Luc Besson's production of the life and death of Joan of Arc is truly a film for our times: bloated, excessive, noisy, techno-heavy, celebrity-conscious and ultra-violent. You could almost say that "The Messenger: The Story of Joan of Arc" has something for everyone, except those hoping for a restrained and contemplative look at one of the most enigmatic spiritual figures of the past millennium.

In casting model-singer Milla Jovovich in the lead, Besson obviously subscribes to the Jean Seberg school, which presumes that Charles VII's army would hardly take seriously the call to arms of a teenage girl who merely had personality to recommend. Jovovich isn't awful in the role: She does ardent and determined with the best of them, but her alluring beauty is always a distraction. No matter how bloodied and battered this Joan gets, she always gives the impression that she'd rather be storming the Pret-a-Porter runway with a silver nail file.

Besson plants the seed early on that Joan may not have been acting out of the most divine of motives when she convinced Charles (John Malkovich, in his campy peel-me-a-grape aristocrat mode) to let her lead the siege against the English at Orleans. While the child Joan claims to hear voices that exhort her toward a spiritual life (a medieval-age Jesus is always cropping up in science-fiction visions, souped up with choirs and portentous drums), it isn't until after she witnesses her sister brutally slaughtered and raped by an English soldier that she is moved to action.

Joan receives an audience with Charles, thanks to his Machiavellian mother-in-law Yolande (Faye Dunaway, looking like queen of the Coneheads), who knows a populist heroine when she sees one. Even after conquering the royal family, Joan still has to deflect all the same male chauvinist derision that Helen Mirren had to contend with on the police force in "Prime Suspect." But conviction, chutzpah and face by Lazlo win the day.

The middle third of "The Messenger" is devoted to graphic, elaborately costumed and staged battle sequences that the action-prone Besson ("La Femme Nikita," "The Professional") settles into with palpable pleasure. The blood and thunder audience may have little patience with the film's discursive final third, a pseudo-Shavian argument in which Dustin Hoffman (as the embodiment of Joan's voices) emerges from the wings to challenge Joan on the nature of her violent calling.

For all the high-flown rhetoric, "The Messenger" is one of those movies that would appeal most to the adolescent mobs for whom it should be least available.

It's a smorgasbord of beheadings, dismemberments, crushings, impalings, necrophilia and, for dessert, immolation. The Motion Picture Association of America, in its infinite tolerance for violence, has seen fit to award "The Messenger" an R. So go ahead, take the kids. Your Beavis and Buttheads will thank you.

SIGHT AND SOUND, 4/00, p. 50, Ginette Vincendeau

Domrémy, France, 1420. Eight-year-old Joan's village is pillaged by rampaging English soldiers. Joan witnesses the brutal rape and murder of her sister. Ten years later, this trauma as well as divine inspiration (materialised by voices and apparitions) propel the deeply religious Joan to seek out the Dauphin Charles, the disinherited heir to the throne. Her voices tell her to rid France of the English and put Charles—confined to a court in Chinon by the Duke of Burgundy in alliance with the English—back on the throne. Partly thanks to the manoeuvres of Charles' mother-in law Yolande of Aragon, Joan is assigned an army.

Her army defeats the English at Orléans and the Dauphin is crowned Charles VII at Reims cathedral in 1429. Joan wants to throw the English out of France but the king and his entourage withdraw their support. Joan's army is defeated at Paris and Compiègne. She is captured by the Burgundians who sell her to the English. In Rouen, she is tried by the Church for heresy. Under pressure she signs a confession but as she recants she is accused of witchcraft. She is burned at the stake in 1431.

Since the 1898 film L'Exécution de Jeanne d'Arc, which condensed in a few minutes her trial and burning, there have been innumerable films about Joan of Arc. Some are classics, such as Carl Dreyer's La Passion de Jeanne d'Arc (1927), Roberto Rossellini's Joan of Arc at the Stake (1954), Otto Preminger's Saint Joan (1957), Robert Bresson's The Trial of Joan of Arc (1962) and Jacques Rivette's Jeanne La Pucelle (1994). In addition there are numerous historical accounts, novels, plays, operas and paintings about Joan, who has always been an object of fascination and controversy. Politically she has been claimed by both the left and the right, including Le Pen's National Front. She has been an equally ambiguous figure for the Church, who accused her of heresy and then canonised her in 1920.

On the evidence of Joan of Arc, Luc Besson is not interested in these debates. His Joan is neither a political catalyst nor a mystic. As we might expect from his track record, her story becomes a spectacle but, despite the 1,500 extras and 200 horses, a surprisingly dull one. Besson's *Joan* is an uneasy mix of *cinéma du look* and 'new heritage' film. *La Reine Margot* and *Elizabeth* are two examples of such new heritage movies, ones which introduced sex, gore and grunge into the hitherto refined genre. The opening sequence here encapsulates this clash: young Joan dances ecstatically, *Sound of Music*-style, through the fields just before filthy soldiers rape and murder her sister.

The battle scenes have their gory quota of ravaged bodies and beheadings as well as the odd crude joke. But they lack the streamlined brilliance of Besson's action pieces in, say, *Nikita, Léon* or *The Fifth Element*. His showy trademarks appear here and there: striking compositions with Joan's face in extreme close up and her army in the background; the camera-as-arrow (recalling the camera-as-bullet in *Nikita*). The scene where Joan's virginity is verified is a classic in this respect, with its flashy changes of camera angle, exaggerated sound effects, asymmetrical compositions and polished lighting. Also, *Joan of Arc* is new heritage in its international cast. British actors play the English and the rest are an assemblage of the usual suspects: John Malkovich hams it up as the Dauphin; Pascal Gregory and Vincent Cassel, who appeared in *La Reine Margot* and *Elizabeth* respectively, play two of Joan's captains; Faye Dunaway's Yolande d'Aragon is a cover version of Virna Lisi in *La Reine Margot* (those scheming mothers-in-law!). None of the film's faults would matter if it had a strong Joan. Besson frames his star Milla Jovovich with stunning closeups and poses her inspirationally on horseback. But if Jovovich is pretty enough to withstand the haircut, she lacks charisma. And where, for example, Renée Falconetti in Dreyer's film and Sandrine Bonnaire in Rivette's radiated intensity during the trial, Jovovich just seems neurotic and shrill.

Erasing her mystical dimension, Besson has turned Joan into a 15th-century Nikita, the Babe of Orléans, a dangerous phallic virgin who nevertheless cries because "underneath she is vulnerable." Nikita's massive gun is swapped for a sword, both weapons imbued with heavy-handed significance. Replacing the religious dilemmas of Joan (the earlier films' focus) with psychology is not in itself uninteresting and could have been developed further. The jury is still out on Joan of Arc's exact historical significance, but as a heroine—virgin, tomboy, religious fanatic, tragic victim of male authority—she is a potent myth. Besson's film neither sheds new light on her nor succeeds in entertaining much in the telling of her extraordinary story.

VILLAGE VOICE, 11/16/99, p. 129, J. Hoberman

Another comic book of revelation [The reference is to *Dogma*; see Hoberman's review of that film.] Luc Besson's *The Messenger: The Story of Joan of Arc* stars Milla Jovovich as the Babe of Orleans. The battle scenes are stirring in a brainless way. Besson is something of a wiseacre and there are moments, including a major steal from *The Sound of Music*, that are almost as funny as *Dogma*. "She's nuts," someone says of Joan in the heat of combat. Still, the movie would have been nearly as improved by a Kevin Smith script polish as *Dogma* would have benefited from Besson's chintzy panache.

Besson's conception takes a bit from the no-frills four-hour *Jeanne la Pucelle* that Jacques Rivette directed with Sandrine Bonnaire in 1993. As in the Rivette film, Joan is baffled by the carnage she precipitates, while her inquisitors seem to regard her worst sin to be cross-dressing. (After *Boys Don't Cry*, it's impossible not to make the connection to Brandon Teena.) But, unlike Rivette, Besson seems to have no sense that Joan herself was giving a performance. The lanky, lush-lipped Jovovich appears to be in a state of permanent arousal—not the least when she models her form-fitting chain-mail ensemble.

Inexplicable as it is, the Joan of Arc story encourages contemplation of ourselves as a species. *The Messenger* is more apt to prompt meditation on the nature of show business. Although nominally French, the movie was made in English with a cast of high-powered Hollywood actors, including a petulantly queeny John Malkovich (who now seems permanently possessed by *Being J.M.*), an imperiously queeny Faye Dunaway, and, most bizarrely, Dustin Hoffman in a burnoose. In a conceit worthy of Kevin Smith, Hoffman plays Joan's "conscience," appearing to her in prison as a sort of Old Testament shrink who, after explaining that she saw visions because she wanted to see them, answers most of her questions with his own.

Also reviewed in:
CHICAGO TRIBUNE, 11/12/99, Friday/p. A, Michael Wilmington
NEW REPUBLIC, 11/29/99, p. 24, Stanley Kauffmann
NEW YORK TIMES, 11/12/99, p. E14, Janet Maslin
VARIETY, 11/1-7/99, p. 87, Todd McCarthy
WASHINGTON POST, 11/12/99, p. C5, Stephen Hunter
WASHINGTON POST, 11/12/99, Weekend/p. 47, Desson Howe

METROLAND

A Lions Gate Films release of a Pandora Cinema presentation of a Blue Horizon/MACT/Filmania production in association with the Arts Council of England with the participation of BBC Films, Canal+, the European co-production fund (UK), Eurimages, and Sogepaq. *Producer:* Andrew Bendel. *Director:* Philip Saville. *Screenplay:* Adrian Hodges. *Based on the novel by:* Julian Barnes. *Director of Photography:* Jean-François Robin. *Editor:* Greg Miller. *Music:* Mark Knopfler. *Sound:* Brian Simmons and (music) Chuck Ainlay. *Casting:* Deborah Brown. *Production Designer:* Don Taylor. *Art Director:* Mark Kebby. *Set Decorator:* John Bush. *Costumes:* Jenny Beavan. *Make-up:* RoseAnn Samuel. *Running time:* 87 minutes. *MPAA Rating:* R.

CAST: Christian Bale (Chris); Emily Watson (Marion); Lee Ross (Toni); Elsa Zylberstein (Annick); Rufus (Henri); Jonathan Aris (Dave); Ifan Meredith (Mickey); Amanda Ryan (Joanna); John Wood (Retired Commuter); Brian Potheroe (Woody); Bill Thomas (Commuter); Daisy Fairban (Amy); Bethan Fairban (Amy); Claire Wilkie (Girl at School Dance); Boris Terrel (Jacques); Lucy Speed (Punk Girl).

LOS ANGELES TIMES, 4/9/99, Calendar/p. 12, Kevin Thomas

"Metroland," a satisfying story of love and marriage told with humor and insight, finds Christian Bale's Chris and Emily Watson's Marion married eight years, living comfortably in a leafy London suburb with a baby daughter. The year is 1977 when up pops Chris' boyhood friend Toni (Lee Ross), after a long absence, to challenge Chris' assertions of happiness.

Toni is an unpublished poet who bums around the world, taking the odd teaching job and supported by a rich American girlfriend. "I do what I want," he says.

From the moment Toni moves in for a visit of an indeterminate length he's accusing his old friend—a former '60s rebel like himself—of selling out and settling for Metroland, that suburban sprawl at the end of the London Underground Metropolitan Line. Toni spouts so many anti-Establishment cliches that he unwittingly verges on caricature. Yet Chris cannot help but recall his Paris idyll in the tumultuous '60s, triggering a long flashback that is so archetypal as to be ever so slightly satirical.

We see Chris as an aspiring photographer in Paris, apparently subsidized by his parents. Chris lives in a charming garret, presumably on the Left Bank, and meets a lush, lovely young Frenchwoman, Annick ("Mina Tannenbaum's" talented Elsa Zylberstein), who good-naturedly relieves him of his virginity and teaches him to value French directness over evasive English tact. Chris is radiantly happy, feeling completely unfettered and hip, while he and Annick go out a lot and take in "the new Bresson" and "the new Truffaut."

When Chris encounters Marion, playing cricket with two young Englishmen in a Paris park, he has not sold a single photograph. As he prattles on about the freedom and joy of the bohemian existence, swearing he'll never return to stultifying England and settle down to married life, Marion stops him cold, saying, "Oh, I think you will. You're not original enough not to." Marion, who has an astringent wit, knows exactly what she wants, and what she wants is Chris. She knows herself and knows Chris lots better than he or Annick do.

By the time director Philip Saville and writer Adrian Hodges, who adapted Julian Barnes' 1980 novel, "Metroland," returns us to 1977 their film bristles with uncertainties and possibilities. Has

Chris, who works in an advertising agency, in fact sold out? And will Toni, so eager for Chris to break out of his sedate life, prove the catalyst that strengthens or destroys Chris and Marion's marriage? Once "Metroland" has established this premise it proceeds to its resolution revealingly and persuasively.

At first you wonder why Watson, the formidable young actress who received Oscar nominations for her performances in "Breaking the Waves" and "Hilary and Jackie," would accept what seems such a secondary role. One ought to know better; slowly but surely Marion emerges as a strong woman, smarter and more perceptive than her sweet-natured but essentially ordinary and conventional husband. You can see why Marion appealed to Watson; she is as cool and controlled as her two previous heroines were tempestuous.

Yet such is the force of Watson's presence, here deliberately understated, that even when she is off-screen, sometimes for substantial lengths of time, her Marion is rightly the film's dominant figure. Ross is amusing as the essentially phony Toni, and Bale brings Chris fully alive, defining his character through more than a decade of changes. "Metroland," which has an evocative score by Mark Knopfler, formerly of Dire Straits, is a handsome film that offers a gratifyingly adult take on the virtues and travails of growing up.

NEW YORK POST, 4/9/99, p. 58, Rod Dreher

The word "Metroland," the title of Philip Saville's modest but acutely poignant melodrama, is Londonspeak for "suburbia," the draggy, gray neighborhood where husband and father Chris (Christian Bale) finds himself measuring out his routinized days in teaspoons.

The year is 1977, and Chris, in his early 30s, has settled down comfortably with a wife (Emily Watson), an infant and a respectable job. A surprise visit from his old drinking buddy Toni (Lee Ross) plunges Chris into crisis. Scruffy bon vivant Toni is still living the high life, traveling the world, a girl in every port, partying hard and to all appearances gleefully sucking the marrow out of life with the gusto of a fat kid with a Slurpee.

Toni's visit sends Chris on an extended reverie back to his idealistic student days, when he left boring old Britain behind and established himself as a bohemian student in Paris. Art! Romance! A sexy French girlfriend! Chris' naked romps in an attic flat with Annick (Elsa Zylberstein) are the stuff the dreams of every 18-year-old fan of Hemingway's "A Moveable Feast" are made of.

Yet it's there he meets fellow English student Marion (Watson) and begins to fall in love with her. Chris comes to understand, in spite of himself, that familiarity can breed a more sublime and lasting kind of love. Revisiting those memories helps Chris understand the intrinsic value of the unglamorous choices he made, and to see Toni's extended adolescence in a different light.

As an old bourgeois pensioner tells Chris on the train, "Metroland is a state of mind." He means that the quotidian life of work, wife, kids and mortgage is only bland and unsatisfying if, against all experience, you buy into a youthful romantic's worldview.

It's not an especially sexy lesson to build a film around, but it has the incontrovertible advantage of being true. And, in Adrian Hodges' knowing, wryly amusing screenplay adaptation from Julian Barnes' novel, persuasive.

The actors beautifully portray these oh-so-recognizable characters. It's great to see Watson, so memorably hysterical in "Breaking the Waves" and "Hilary & Jackie," playing a normal person. And Bale deftly handles the transitions between Chris' extravagant Paris years and the tentativeness and uncertainty with which he tiptoes toward early middle age.

NEWSDAY, 4/9/99, Part II/p. B7, John Anderson

The Metroland of Philip Saville's new-old film is, not surprisingly, a terminus—a benign "Dead End," a sane "Grey Gardens." It's a place where people and/or dreams have come to rest—in this case, the area where the London Underground grinds to a halt amid a robust suburban sprawl.

In other words, it's a metaphor with the subtlety of a hand grenade. In "Metroland," onetime Parisian esthete and now-dedicated bourgeois Chris (Christian Bale) is shaken out of his state of domestic torpor by Toni (Lee Ross), an old mate who shows up and tries to recycle Chris into the swinging scene they once shared. Toni's problem, obviously, is arrested adolescence. Chris' dilemma is little more involved—a youth too ripe not to revisit, as well as a mind too callow not to succumb.

There are a number of curious circumstances surrounding the release of Saville's "Metroland," a movie so uninflected it just had to be made for television. One is the appearance of Emily Watson as Marion, Chris' saintly wife (half spouse, half deity). Watson, of course, was most recently seen here in "Hilary and Jackie," for which she received a Best Actress Oscar nomination; her fellow Oscar nominee, Rachel Griffiths, can be seen recently in another by-the-numbers English import, "Among Giants." This illustrates, for one thing, that no matter how well one does on the British screen, one must continue to work.

The other dividend is getting to see the estimable Watson playing a fairly routine character—as opposed to the disturbed visionary of "Breaking the Waves," the disturbed cellist of "Hilary" or the taciturn IRA martyr of Jim Sheridan's "The Boxer."

Conversely, and for those opposed to change, we have the very palatable Bale playing a character almost identical to the one he portrayed in Todd Haynes' "Velvet Goldmine"—a veteran swinger looking back on his errant but very enjoyable youth in the '60s from the vantage point of the '70s. In Chris' case, this includes a chapter in Paris with a very sexy libertine named Annick (Elsa Zylberstein) and some arty escapades as a fledgling photographer.

Adapted from the Julian Barnes novel, "Metroland" has a highly likable cast, but it carries the burden of being a '90s movie based on an '80s book in which a '70s hero is reminiscing about the '60s. Add to this the television technique of insipid musical cues and obvious camera work and the rather pedestrian problems of Chris are hardly enough to breathe passion, or even oxygen, into this tepid soap opera.

SIGHT AND SOUND, 8/98, p. 51, Demetrios Matheou

Eastwood, a leafy suburb on the further reaches of the Metropolitan line, 1977 Chris Lloyd, an advertising executive, his wife Marion and their baby are visited by Toni, Chris' oldest friend. Toni travels the world and has never settled down, enjoying a polygamous relationship with his American girlfriend. His arrival starts to make Chris doubt the choices he has made.

A series of intercut flashbacks fills in the events until this time. In 1963, Chris and Toni were schoolboys: bemoaning life in 'Metroland', looking upon the people around them with contempt and dreaming of travel. In 1968, Chris lived in Paris. He aspired to be an art photographer but worked part-time in a bar, where he met a confident young Parisian, Annick, who became his lover. But Chris met Marion, and their increasingly close, if platonic, friendship drove Annick away.

Back in 1977, Toni arranges for a young woman, Joanna, to seduce Chris at a party; though tempted, Chris changes his mind when he realises that Toni set her up to ask him. The next day he fights with Toni, whom he suspects of having slept with Marion. She tells Chris she rejected Toni's propositions, but does admit to having had a fling with someone else in the past. A few days later Toni announces that he is returning to the US and asks Chris to join him. Chris declines, stating that he is not sure he is content with life in Metroland.

Love, etc., the recent French adaptation of Julian Barnes' novel *Talking It Over*, may seem like a poor man's *Jules et Jim* with a trio of unappealing central characters and little new to say about relationships, but it's far preferable to *Metroland*, a weak adaptation of Barnes' book of the same name. This is Barnes' first and one of his least interesting novels (why not *Staring at the Sun*, or *Porcupine*?). And key changes in the adaptation have conspired to obscure its redeeming wit and irony. The result is that a slight, though charming tale about a man's acceptance of his bourgeois inclinations is transformed into another male menopausal dirge, akin to such poor 70s television sitcoms as *The Cuckoo Waltz* and *Man about the House*.

Barnes' book is told in the first person, in three evenly balanced sections through which its protagonist Chris recalls how he abandoned his pretensions to be anything other than his suburban self. The gentle rebukes from Chris' friend Toni, who continues to play out a semi convincing lifestyle as a poetry-writing traveller and political activist, create a mild dialectic on the nature of convention and aspiration, between one man stagnating in his roots, the other rootless.

The key decisions made by director Philip Saville (best known for television's *Boys from the Blackstuff* and scriptwriter Adrian Hodges are all damaging: the film builds Toni's role into something more conniving, loses the first-person voice over, and concentrates on the 70s part of the story. *Boogie Nights*, *The Ice Storm* and the forthcoming *Velvet Goldmine* all successfully mine the 70s in order to illustrate wider cultural issues. But more is needed (Mike Leigh, perhaps) to extract anything fresh from the torpor and embarrassment of British suburban life—leafy residential streets, identikit detached houses, matching gardens—in that period.

Saville actually displays a fondness for his drab 70s suburb, and when he moves away from it to Toni's "bohemian" party for instance he seems as much out of his depth as his protagonist. The placing of a copy of the Sex Pistols' *Never Mind the Bollocks* on a cabinet to ram home a trendy authenticity seems a hollow gesture. There is a similar lack of conviction in presentation and tone when the film shifts to 60s Paris. A panoply of sub-Cartier-Bresson canal shots and rooftops, Gauloises cigarettes, and croissants and coffee push home the francophilia, accompanied by a gratingly cheesy soundtrack by Mark Knopfler. We assume that Chris' artistic pretensions are being mocked, but the film—indulging as it does in visual clichés and bereft of the ironic distance a voice-over might have provided—fudges the point.

While at least knowing in the book, here Chris is an easily manipulated buffoon with little access to his emotions. His wife Marion is a smug example of bland rosy Englishness (who tellingly manages to usurp Chris' first girlfriend Annick, the only character in the film to display charm or passion), while Toni is a sad old hippie, jealous of rather than disappointed by his friend and lacking the genuine convictions he has in the novel. As such, the film presents a central trio as unengaging as that of *Love, etc.*

Now and again there is a glimpse of the tougher moments in the book: when the "retired commuter" whom Chris meets on the train (a poignant cameo by John Wood) riles at the "bourgeois dormitory" which is Metroland, "25 miles from Baker Street and a pension at the end of the line"; or when Marion asks Chris what he has to panic about and he replies "nothing, that's what worries me." But while Barnes gives you something to think about and laugh at on the way to his essentially conservative conclusion, the film alternately whines and whimpers its way to a soporific end.

TIME, 4/19/99, p. 76, Richard Schickel

He has it all "creative" job, sensible wife, pretty child, starter home in *Metroland*, the generic name for London's middle-class suburbia. Chris (Christian Bale) also has something he doesn't need: his best friend from the swinging '60s, a wandering poet named Toni (Lee Ross), who lurches back into his life in the late '70s to taunt and tempt him. The taunts are about the road not taken—abandoned career in photography, abandoned girlfriend (sweet, sexy Elsa Zylberstein) from his years in Paris. The temptation is to return to youthful irresponsibility.

Uh-oh—another wistful study of quiet desperation among the symbol manipulators, another examination of how the anarchic spirit of the '60s got sold out. But this adaptation of Julian Barnes' first novel, by director Philip Saville and screenwriter Adrian Hodges, has some good things going for it. They understand that it isn't politics, Pop Art or drugs that would come permanently to haunt the memories of that brief, lost time for people like Chris. It's the sex, stupid. And the freedom that era offered to pursue it across all sorts of formerly formidable barriers.

There's honesty and energy in the film's flashbacking pursuit of that thought. But Chris' lasting luck is his wife Marion. Emily Watson plays her as a kind of dream nanny—knowing, ironic, tolerant of his erotic nostalgia and not as prim as she looks. She, and *Metroland*, finally make a good, subtle case for the bearable weightiness of middle-class being, for the higher morality of muddling through.

VILLAGE VOICE, 4/13/99, p. 145, Justine Elias

It's official: Emily Watson is eminently capable of playing ordinary, well-adjusted characters, too. *Metroland*—shot after *Breaking the Waves* but before her cello-mad performance in *Hilary and Jackie*—is an unflashy tale of memory and desire in suburban London. The memories and desires belong to the story's hero, Chris (Christian Bale), who craves rebellion and escape but ends up nine-to-fiving it back in his boring old hometown.

Metroland, based on the novel by Julian Barnes, moves back and forth through time from 1963, when Chris is a wisecracking schoolboy, to 1968, which finds him in Paris, living *la vie bohème* as a struggling photographer, to the late 1970s, when he's returned home to marriage, fatherhood, and a boring but secure job in advertising. The catalyst for Chris's soul-searching, at each stage in his life, is the appearance of Toni (Lee Ross), a drifter and malcontent who goads him into taking risks and tossing aside bourgeois comforts. Bale conveys the torments of all three stages of British lad-hood, but Ross has a more difficult job—Toni is supposed to be a charismatic rebel, but he's mainly irritating and cruel. As is typical of stories of young men's crises, the women have it all figured out and must wait for their men to catch up. Watson, as Chris's wife, here has an endearingly tart sense of humor that masks a soulful sadness.

To convey the quotidian life, director Philip Saville seems to have chosen the grayest, dullest settings in all of England; even the bed linens appear worn out and dirty. The whole movie has an uncomfortable intimacy, and the close-ups are lit as unforgivingly as and the close-ups are lit as unforgivingly as an old Polaroid. (Ross's face, in particular, seems to be shot in terrifying Pore-O-Rama.) The message seems to be: you can go home again, but Jesus, dim the lights.

Also reviewed in:
CHICAGO TRIBUNE, 4/16/99, Friday/p. 5, Mark Caro
NEW REPUBLIC, 4/12/99, p. 28, Stanley Kauffmann
NEW YORK TIMES, 4/9/99, p. E22, Janet Maslin
VARIETY, 9/22-28/97, p. 48, David Rooney
WASHINGTON POST, 4/30/99, Weekend/p. 63, Michael O'Sullivan

MICKEY BLUE EYES

A Castle Rock Entertainment release of a Simian Films production. *Producer:* Elizabeth Hurley and Charles Mulvehill. *Director:* Kelly Makin. *Screenplay:* Mark Lawrence, Adam Scheinman, and Robert Kuhn. *Director of Photography:* Donald E. Thorin. *Editor:* David Freeman. *Music:* Basil Poledouris. *Music Editor:* Dominic Gibbs. *Sound:* Danny Michael and (music) Geoff Foster. *Sound Editor:* Martin Evans. *Casting:* Laura Rosenthal. *Production Designer:* Gregory P. Keen. *Art Director:* Tom Warren. *Set Decorator:* Susan Kaufman. *Special Effects:* Albert Griswold. *Costumes:* Ellen Mirojnick. *Make-up:* Lynn Campbell. *Stunt Coordinator:* Peter Bucossi. *Running time:* 102 minutes. *MPAA Rating:* PG-13.

CAST: Hugh Grant (Michael Felgate); James Caan (Frank Vitale); Jeanne Tripplehorn (Gina Vitale); Burt Young (Vito Graziosi); James Fox (Philip Cromwell); Joe Viterelli (Vinnie); Gerry Becker (Agent Connell); Maddie Corman (Carol); Tony Darrow (Angelo); Paul Lazar (Ritchie Vitale); Vincent Pastore (Al); Frank Pellegrino (Sante); Scott Thompson (Agent Lewis); John Ventimiglia (Johnny Graziosi); Margaret Devine (Helen); Beatrice Winde (Mrs. Horton); Mark Margolis (Gene Morganson); Helen Lloyd Breed (Emily Basset); Carmine Parisi (Luigi); Sybil Lines (Caroline Cronwell); Alexis Brentani, Rose Caiola, and Felicia Scarangello (Bridesmaids); Joseph R. Gannascoli (Gina's Doorman); Rocco Musacchia (Carmine); John DiBenedetto (Harold Green); Bruno Gioiello (Technician); Rich Topol (FBI Chief, Truck); Frank Senger (Delivery Driver); Lori Tan Chinn (Chinese Waitress); Marsha Dietlein (Woman); Steve Mellor (FBI Chief, Leader); John DiResta (Traffic Cop); Ephraim Benton (Boy Student); Ed Wheeler (Reporter); Aida Turturro (Waitress); Tony Sirico (Risolli Man 1); Lorri Bagley (Antoinette); Brian Davies (Priest); Melissa Marsala (Carla); Joe Rigano (Mr. Risolli); Michael Kennedy (Jeffrey); Leonard Sessa and Andy Redmond (FBI Chiefs); Chris Mcginn (Tourist Woman); David McConeghey (Tourist Man); Stephen Dym (Cromwell Employee); Shelagh Ratner and Tom King (Art Patrons); Sara Cotton and Kevin Kean Murphy (Auction Bidders).

CHRISTIAN SCIENCE MONITOR, 8/20/99, p. 15, David Sterritt

Hugh Grant once told an interviewer that his acting range is "sinisterly narrow." While that's refreshingly candid, it must be added that he's an extraordinarily likable performer as long as he's within that narrow range.

The trick for filmmakers is to find new ways of exploiting his charm—giving center stage to his reliable bag of tricks, while surrounding him with new sets of characters, situations, and plot twists.

The gimmick behind "Mickey Blue Eyes" is one of the wilder stabs at pulling this off. Grant plays his usual sort of character: mild-mannered art auctioneer Michael, who leads a usual sort of life, plying his trade and wooing the woman of his dreams (Jeanne Tripplehorn). Trouble starts when she inexplicably turns down what ought to be his irresistible marriage proposal.

This induces Michael to meet her relatives, who turn out to be a family in the darker sense of that word: a "Godfather" clan, with racketeers, loan sharks, and hit men. No respectable person would marry such a mob, but respectability may grow shaky when the heart asserts itself. Discovering that his girlfriend hates the family's nefarious activities, Michael vows that they'll never get involved with the Mafioso branch of the family—a promise more easily made than kept, as they discover when their wedding draws near.

As Grant waltzes through this farce, his handsome face sports its lopsided smile at every opportunity; his hair flops gracefully as he trots down a Manhattan sidewalk; and his British accent provides for some hilarious spoofs of Hollywood gangster-speak. The rest of the cast is just as entertaining, from Tripplehorn's smart fiancée—her exotic looks make a beguiling contrast with Grant's dimply demeanor—to James Caan's effortless performance as the gun-toting father of the bride.

Moviegoers tired of ethnic humor will find plenty to complain about in "Mickey Blue Eyes," which builds its story on the gulf between Grant's smooth Englishness and the Italian-American stereotypes—Burt Young's snarling patriarch, Joe Viterelli's pudgy henchman, and so on—that share the screen with him. The movie clearly takes its major cues from the "Godfather" trilogy: Even the advertising tag ("A romantic comedy you can't refuse") is a "Godfather" knockoff, and Caan's portrayal evokes fond memories of the saga's first episode.

This doesn't mean "Mickey Blue Eyes" will ever become a classic, with its uneven humor, sometimes heavy-handed visual style, and occasional echoes of "The Freshman," which twitted the Mafioso genre more imaginatively. It has some highly amusing moments, though, and Grant fans will be gratified by his presence in almost every scene. It's not the worst movie prospect in this slow pre-Labor Day season.

LOS ANGELES TIMES, 8/20/99, Calendar/p. 1, Kenneth Turan

If he'd been on the Titanic, fewer lives would have been lost. If he'd accompanied Robert Scott to the South Pole, the explorer would have lived to be 100. That's how good Hugh Grant is at rescuing doomed ventures. And while "Mickey Blue Eyes" was never going to be a certifiable disaster, Grant goes a long way toward saving it from itself.

Starring Grant, James Caan and Jeanne Tripplehorn, "Mickey Blue Eyes" follows "Analyze This" and "Mafia!" films that insist that there is something terribly funny about Italian Americans who terminate lives for a living.

Certainly Michael Felgate (Grant), a Brit turned Manhattan fine arts auctioneer, would never guess that the Mafia would be good for a laugh, or even figure in his life. He's madly in love with the vivacious Gina Vitale (Tripplehorn), so much so that he's determined to marry her after only three months of dating even though she's never introduced him to her family.

But Michael's farcical proposal scene, at a non-romantic Chinese restaurant with the obdurate owner hanging on every word, ends badly, with Gina bursting into tears and fleeing the room, insisting that she loves him but that marriage is impossible.

Trying to find her, Michael ends up at the La Trattoria, the Italian restaurant run by Gina's father, Frank (Caan). Inside he meets a lot of sullen guys named Carmine, Vinnie and Uncle Vito. "Are you all family?" he asks brightly, an unknowingly charged question that gets answered with a gruff "mostly."

As we know instinctively and Michael finds out once he locates Gina, Uncle Vito is Vito "The Butcher " Graziosi (Burt Young), head of a prominent crime family, and this is the mob the young man's thinking of marrying into. Except Gina won't let him.

"Everything they touch ends up spoiled and corrupted," Gina says, fearful that Michael will get caught in a web of favors given and received and become complicit in organized crime before he knows what's happening. Michael's confidence that this won't happen gets Gina to agree to the marriage, but we know he can't be right or there wouldn't be any movie.

It turns out, for instance, that Vito has a hot-headed, unstable son named Johnny (John Ventimiglia) who took up painting as part of his therapy, and Vito wonders if Michael can help with the sale of striking efforts like Johnny's portrait of Christ with a machine gun. Michael agrees and all of a sudden his once-surly truckers treat him with respect, there's a fire of suspicious origin at archrival Sotheby's and the genteel art auctioneer realizes he's in trouble.

This is a clever conceit (the script is by Adam Scheinman and Robert Kuhn) and director Kelly Makin, best known for his work with the Canadian comedy troupe the Kids in the Hall, manage to start things off agreeably with sly moments and smart lines.

"Mickey Blue Eyes"' biggest asset is, of course, Mr. Grant. Nobody does dazed and confused like he does, and this script, which was rewritten specifically with him in mind, gives the actor numerous opportunities to be humorously humbling and befuddled. Especially diverting is the scene in which Frank, in an attempt to pass Michael off as mobster Mickey Blue Eyes (don't ask), tries to teach the man how to say, "Fuggedaboudit."

But though it begins with promise, "Mickey Blue Eyes," like many an unlucky gangland figure, comes to a bad end. Though they are classic comedy characters, Michael, Frank, Gina and company end up getting involved in very real violence, and the mixture makes for an awkward fit. Add in preposterously convoluted plot twists, and not even Grant in full rescue mode plus an Italian American soundtrack with Frank Sinatra, Dean Martin and Louis Prima are enough to make us smile all the way through to the end.

NEW YORK, 8/30/99, p. 166, Peter Rainer

Hugh Grant was the co-star of *Notting Hill,* but rightly or wrongly, its commercial success was attributed almost solely to Julia Roberts. If his new film, *Mickey Blue Eyes,* turns out to be boffo, there will be no one else to credit; his co-stars, after all, are Jeanne Tripplehorn and James Caan, names unlikely to cause a box-office stampede. Given what passes for funny these days, *Mickey Blue Eyes* probably will be a hit, which means we're in for a lot more of Hugh Grant's effetely charming tic shtick.

Grant's ascension as a leading man may have something to do with the plenitude of slobs onscreen these days. Between the youth-pic gross-out gang and the Sean Penn-Nicolas Cage misfit generation, there aren't many romantic leads in the movies anymore who seem to know the difference between a salad fork and a dinner fork—or whether to use a fork at all. Grant is popular, I think, because his mannerisms are all about *manners.* Trying to keep up the proper front in a world inhabited by the unruly, he's forever flustered.

Although he's careful not to play the snob, there's an element of snobbery, or at least connoisseurship, in the American audience's embrace of Grant. For one thing, he has that Oxbridge diction that sets him apart from Hollywood's other leading men. You can actually make out what he's saying. We have a weakness for royalty, for good breeding, and Grant, stammering and self-effacing, allows us to keep our self-respect by making fun of the very thing that draws us to him. He's like a fussier David Niven, or, at his most clownish, a spiffier Stan Laurel. He's fun to watch in limited doses, but his act is so one-note that his performances blend into one another. From *Four Weddings and a Funeral* to *Nine Months* to *Notting Hill* to *Mickey Blue Eyes,* he's working the same narrow track. I'm not suggesting Grant suddenly hit us with his *Hamlet,* but there was a time a while back, in movies like *The Lair of the White Worm* and *Impromptu,* when he had a bit more dash in his stride. It's too early in his career for him to be neutering himself into an upper-crust bumbler.

Mickey Blue Eyes plays up the chasm between the goons of the world and Grant's agitated articulateness. He plays Michael Felgate, who works for a New York auction house. To his surprise, his girlfriend, Gina (Tripplehorn), to whom he has just proposed, turns out to be a Mafia princess, plunging him into a world of slugged syllables and good-natured chops to the solar plexus. In the past, Gina's family, including her father, Frank (Caan), and "uncle" Vito (Burt Young), have pulled her paramours into a life of crime against her wishes. (She's a very unprincessy princess—she teaches underprivileged schoolkids.) Inevitably, Michael's attempts to lure her to the altar bring on the mob; figuring he's practically one of the family anyway, the goombahs start using his art auctions to launder money. Lies, murder, double crosses ensue, all purportedly comical. At one point, Frank, trying to pass off his prospective son-in-law as mobster Mickey Blue Eyes from Kansas City, counsels Michael in the proper way to pronounce *fuhgeddaboudit.* Haven't we already been through this voice lesson in *Donnie Brasco?* It's time to fuhgeddabout *fuhgeddaboudit.*

There are some funny moments early on, before it dawns on Michael exactly what sort of family he's joining. It might have worked out better for the film if he never quite figured it out—Michael is much funnier clueless than criminal. The best scene in the movie, however, has nothing to do with the mob at all: Michael botches his proposal to Gina in a Chinese restaurant and brings on the wrath of the owner, played by Lori Tan Chinn with such crack comic timing that the film never recovers from her exit. We're left with a lot of recycled jokes about whacking and wheezing.

If reports in the press are to be trusted, the Mafia is on the wane in this country. So why is it that movies and TV shows about the Mafia are on the rise? Just in the past year, we've seen, in rapidly descending order of quality, *The Sopranos, Analyze This,* and now *Mickey Blue Eyes.* In Hollywood these days, family entertainment is where you find it.

NEW YORK POST, 8/20/99, p. 52, Rod Dreher

How many times can Hollywood reheat the same old pot of spaghetti before it loses all flavor? "Mickey Blue Eyes" proves the Italian mob comedy still has some tang, provided you toss a pasty Englishman in the mix.

That would be Hugh Grant, and this obvious but still light and charming picture would be unthinkable without him. Once again, he does that stammering, beguiling Hugh Grant thing, this time as a respectable British gentleman trying to accommodate himself to his New York Italian future in-laws. "Welcome to the family" takes on a new and alarming meaning here.

Grant plays Michael Felgate, a Manhattan fine-arts auctioneer who's madly in love with Gina Vitale (Jeanne Tripplehorn). In a hilarious scene involving a misplaced fortune cookie, Michael proposes to his beloved in a Chinatown restaurant, only to be shocked when she flees in tears.

Gina says she can't marry Michael—because she can't inflict her family upon him. "They corrupt everything they touch!" she protests. A trip to the family business, a Little Italy pasta joint called the La Trattoria, explains Gina's anxiety.

In addition to Gina's dad Frankie (James Caan), Michael meets her "Uncle" Vito Graziosi (Burt Young), and sundry surly goombahs—most notably Vito's hot-tempered son Johnny (John Ventimiglia), who fancies himself an artist.

Before you can say "ba-da-bing," poor bumbling Michael has been strong-armed into auctioning Johnny's hideous paintings—an avenging machine-gun Jesus, for example—as part of a money-laundering scheme. The FBI shows up, there's an accidental shooting, and Michael ends up having to pretend that he's a Kansas City gangster called "Little Big Mickey Blue Eyes" to save himself from a rival gang.

Everything you need to know about the movie comes in a very funny scene in which Frankie gives the newly christened Mickey Blue Eyes emergency elocution lessons. "Fuggedaboutit," Frankie says. "Foogeedabutteet," a distressed Michael responds, rather unconvincingly.

Grant's amusing fish-out-of-water flopping recalls Matthew Broderick's boyish monkeyshines in "The Freshman," though the plotting is most reminiscent of the recent hit "Analyze This." "Mickey Blue Eyes" is not as jokey as that one, and the screenplay, by Adam Scheinman and Robert Kuhn, can't sustain its comic energy much past the halfway point, losing Grant's blithe spirit in the contrived plotting, which leads like clockwork to the inevitable wedding finale.

Still, there are wonderful performances in this movie. Grant is always a pleasure to watch, and Caan looks like he's having the time of his life, bouncing on the balls of his feet from scene to scene.

Young is priceless as the serpentine Uncle Vito, "Analyze This" vet Joe Viterelli turns up with that magnificent meatball mug of his, and as the snooty auction-house owner, the hysterical James Fox out- Brit-twits Grant, if such a thing can be imagined. Only Jeanne Tripplehorn is a dud as Gina, but hers is a minor role.

Ultimately, "Mickey Blue Eyes" is an enjoyable minor-league lark. But another "Notting Hill"? Fuhgeddaboutit. Foogeedabuttet. Whatever.

NEWSDAY, 8/20/99, Part II/p. B7, John Anderson.

All comedies are contrived, at least to a certain degree. Could Chaplin's Tramp even have gotten to the Yukon much less eaten his shoes when he got there? Would anyone really believe Jack Lemmon as a woman? How about a mouse that talks? A wistful pig? A mad scientist named Fronkenshteen? All comedies are contrived, some just take it too far—"Mickey Blue Eyes," to name one, which features Hugh Grant on full charm alert and some inspired incidental laughter via director Kelly Makin ("Brain Candy: Kids in the Hall"), but isn't funny enough to be this ridiculous. Produced by Simian Films—the Grant-Elizabeth Hurley company responsible for "Extreme Measures"—the film suffers from a script whose reliance on ethnic jokes is feeble and whose sense of direction is worse.

It takes, for instance, a solid half hour to get to the point: that Michael Felgate (Grant), urbane English manager of a tony Manhattan auction house, is getting married to the mob. Michael is stunned—he's often stunned—when Gina (Jeanne Tripplehorn), girl of his dreams and inner-city schoolteacher, flees the Chinese restaurant when he asks her to marry him. Was it the mishandled proposal-via-fortune cookie? The outrageously stereotyped restaurant owner? The moo shu pork? No. But only after we've seen every Italo-mob cliche in existence and a lineup of mugs that suggests an alumni meeting of the Scorsese Academy of Dramatic Arts does she come clean, tell him about the family business, and admit she just didn't want to get him involved.

At which point you want to say: We know, we know. And so does he. And he doesn't care. And neither do we. But at least get on with it.

So they do. Michael, who's had trouble with deliveries to the auction house, suddenly has Teamsters showing up early. Sotheby's mysteriously catches fire.

And in return for these unsolicited favors, Uncle Vito (Burt Young) merely asks that Michael auction off some paintings by his son Johnny (John Ventimiglia)—garish pastel allegories featuring machine-gun-wielding Christs and surrealist rubouts. It's a way of laundering the family's money. Michael suddenly is in, he's in deep, and "We Are Family" is playing on the jukebox.

Grant certainly has a winning way about him, at least in small doses, and he shuffles his way through the story, always valiantly attempting to maintain his dignity—it's shtick, but it's all his. He can certainly deliver an understated laugh line. At one point, when his father-in-law-to-be Frank Vitale (James Caan) has introduced him as out-of-town mobster Mickey Blue Eyes, Grant even affects a rather amusing mock-mob accent that mixes Oxford with Seaford. The weird thing about Grant is that he plays Michael so consistently, nonplussed Michael behaves the same regardless of whom he's with, be it his clipped British boss (James Fox) or the woman he wants to marry. The shtick never stops and it precludes any sense of emotional reality in a movie that desperately needs some.

Director Makin, knowing he has to embellish if he's going to get any laughs at all, makes good use of his subordinate characters—a daffy FBI agent played by former Kid in the Hall Scott Thompson, or Gina's brother Ritchie (Paul Lazar), who is inexplicable and inexplicably goofy. The entire project could, and does, exist solely on personality, at least for a while. But the story shoots itself.

An accidental murder. The overcooked mob cliches. Would Vito really want his niece Gina dead, even for the accidental killing of his son Johnny? Not in this man's mob-movie world. There are some things that shouldn't be tampered with.

Or, for that matter, committed to film.

SIGHT AND SOUND, 9/99, p. 50, Philip Kemp

Englishman Michael Felgate works in New York as auctioneer for art dealers Cromwell's. He's in love with high-school teacher Gina Vitale, but when he asks her to marry him she reacts badly.

She reveals that her father Frank Vitale is a member of the Graziosi crime family, headed by Vito Graziosi. She's certain that Michael will become corrupted by her father and his associates. Michael meets Frank, Vito, Vito's son Johnny and other mobsters, but assures Gina he'll remain uncorrupted. They become engaged.

Unbidden, Vito leans on some truck drivers who have been messing up Cromwell's deliveries. In return, he expects Michael to auction one of Johnny's terrible paintings as a money-laundering scam. Michael reluctantly does so. Vito has Sotheby's burnt down and wants another of Johnny's paintings auctioned. Through a mix up, it sells way over its reserve price. Suspecting Michael of deception, Johnny beats him up in front of Gina. Gina accidentally shoots Johnny dead.

Michael tells Frank he shot Johnny and gets him to help him dispose of the body. Meeting some other mobsters while doing so, Frank introduces Michael as "Mickey Blue Eyes", an out-of-town hitman. Vito sees through Frank's evasions and insists he shoots Michael at the wedding. Frank and Michael appeal to the FBI, who set up a fake shooting to incriminate Vito. This misfires, and Gina is shot instead. Vito is arrested. In the ambulance Gina, who had arranged her own fake shooting, revives and forgives Michael for his deceptions.

A few years back, hard on the heels of *Four Weddings and a Funeral*, Hugh Grant starred in another Mike Newell film, an adaptation of Beryl Bainbridge's novel An *Awfully Big Adventure*. An uneven but atmospheric movie, it featured Grant's most unexpected performance to date—as a supercilious, manipulative theatre director, utterly uningratiating and far removed from the loveable ditherer of *Four Weddings*. Hugh Grant made a far more interesting villain than hero. Advance accounts of *Mickey Blue Eyes,* in which he portrays a Mafioso—or at least someone pretending to be a Mafioso—raised hopes that he might once again be playing nasty.

No such luck. Grant does indeed briefly impersonate the supposedly lethal Mickey Blue Eyes; but the whole point of the joke—and a pretty thin one it is—is that he's quite useless at it, unable even to produce a passable American accent. That apart, it's back to good old loveable ineptitude. We even get a gag about floppy hair.

Grant's performance, though, fits snugly into a film which mostly relies on well worn stereotypes. All the old comic clichés about New York mobsters being folksy, murderous and pasta-loving are trotted out—and were better done anyway in Andrew Bergman's *The Freshman* from which *Mickey Blue Eyes* lifts chunks of plot. Just to be culturally even-handed, we're also treated to a painfully overdone display of English silly-assery from James Fox. Most of the rest of the cast get submerged in the backwash, with James Caan and Jeanne Tripplehorn both looking lost though there's a neat cameo from Scott Thompson (Hank's gay sidekick in *The Larry Sanders Show*) as a puppyishly eager FBI agent. And, as the resident godfather, the veteran Burt Young craftily steals a scene or two.

The best of the film comes early on. Grant's establishing scene in the auction room is capably handled, and there's a funny, well-timed episode in a Chinese restaurant. Thereafter the plot becomes tiresomely over-contrived, with a particularly inane subplot involving a deaf old lady (who of course drops her hearing aid at a crucial moment). Assured comic direction might have overcome some of the weak scripting, but Kelly Makin, previously known for *Kids in the Hall Brain Candy*, turns in a lacklustre job, with the final big set piece—the protracted shoot out at the wedding—especially ill-handled.

The ragged pacing may partly be down to last-minute excisions: judging from the press material some bedroom action between Grant and Tripplehorn has gone missing, which might at least have given us a raunchier, less anodyne movie. If this had been a far darker comedy in which Grant's character, like Al Pacino's in *The Godfather Part II*, finds within himself a capacity for viciousness and violence, that could have been a Hugh Grant performance worth watching.

TIME, 8/30/99, p. 66, Richard Schickel

If there were still a British Empire, one could imagine Hugh Grant bestriding one of its far-flung ramparts, trying to bring order to unruliness. Mostly that would be a matter of self-deprecating humor, romantic chivalry, honorable business dealings, and, of course, irresistibly floppy hair.

Colonialism being at something of a discount nowadays, Grant is obliged to ply his undeniable charms in cross-cultural comedies like *Mickey Blue Eyes*. In it, he plays a Manhattan art auctioneer named Michael Felgate, in love with a schoolteacher Jeanne Tripplehorn) who reciprocates his affections but refuses his engagement ring.

She has her reasons. They have names like Vito, Vinnie, Angelo and Ritchie, to say nothing of her father, Frank James Caan), who runs a family restaurant in Little Italy. That's "family" in the full post-Puzo sense of the word. But Vito (Burt Young), who is the godfather here, sees opportunity in this chance—a chance to off-load some of his talentless son's paintings and do a little money laundering via Michael's auctions. Before you know it, Michael has acquired his eponymous Mob nickname, is burying stiffs in Brooklyn and, finally, wearing a wire for a comically clueless FBI, whose forces include a hearing-challenged agent.

Director Kelly Makin has a gift for casually tossed-off farce. And along with Michael's bemused unflappability, his weird British conviction that somehow he will muddle through to a happy ending, that good-natured spirit carries one over some of the logical lacunae of the script by Adam Scheinman and Robert Kuhn. But not quite past the presence of Caan. It was only 27 years ago that his crazy volatility ignited *The Godfather*. Now he's almost beamish as a wary fixer. He's still funny, but his new characterization, like the success of *The Sopranos* and *Analyze This*, reminds us how quickly we have converted palpable menace to pure ethnic comedy. Is this progress? Not really. But in the context of *Mickey Blue Eyes* it's easy to fuhgeddaboutit.

VILLAGE VOICE, 8/31/99, p. 128, Jessica Winter

Let's give Hugh Grant some credit where credit is due: he's not waving his shtick around quite so much anymore. In his dumb, affable new comedy *Mickey Blue Eyes,* there's nary a swipe through the hair, the stammering quotient dips as low as his blood pressure in *Notting Hill,* and the only notable quirk left intact is the compulsive blinking that must leave him thinking his world is lit with a strobe. Grant plays an art auctioneer who proposes wedlock to Jeanne Tripplehorn, but finds himself married to the mob: Tripplehorn's father (James Caan) is a Mafia operative, and Grant is soon inadvertently laundering money through the auction house and getting involved in the accidental murder of a don's son. The last half-hour bogs down badly, with a cynical fake-out ending and a final scene that borders on nonsensical, but until then *Mickey Blue Eyes* plays a friendly, forgettable song, squarely thumping keys of broad physical comedy. Caan, sly and droll, underplays every half-baked line; he and a crackerjack team of bit players—notably James Fox as Grant's bemused, indulgent boss and Scott Thompson as an uptight, glassy-eyed FBI man—hover weightlessly above the material, while a partly reformed Grant knots his brow trying to keep his masochism in check.

Also reviewed in:
CHICAGO TRIBUNE, 8/20/99, Friday/p. A, Michael Wilmington
NEW REPUBLIC, 9/27/99, p. 30, Stanley Kauffmann
NEW YORK TIMES, 8/20/99, p. E10, Stephen Holden
VARIETY, 8/16-22/99, p. 28, Lael Loewenstein
WASHINGTON POST, 8/20/99, p. C1, Rita Kempley
WASHINGTON POST, 8/20/99, Weekend/p. 43, Desson Howe

MILKY WAY, THE

A Kino International release of a Sanabil production with assistance of The Fund For The Promotion of Israeli Quality Films. *Executive Producer:* Muhammad Bakriah. *Director:* Ali Nassar. *Screenplay (Arabic with English subtitles):* Ali Nassar and Ghalib Sha'ath. *Director of Photography:* Amnon Salomon. *Editor:* Era Lapid and Tova Asher. *Music:* Nachum Heiman. *Running time:* 104 minutes. *MPAA Rating:* Not Rated.

CAST: Muhammad Bakri (Mahmmud); Suheil Haddad (Mabruq); Mihaela Mitraki (Jamilah); Makram Khoury (Mukhtar); Yussef Abu Warda (Military Governor); Mahmmud Abu Jazi (Ahmad, Teacher).

NEW YORK POST, 1/20/99, p. 44, Hannah Brown

"The Milky Way," a Palestinian film produced with the assistance of the Israeli government, proves that Arab filmmakers have now achieved equality with their Israeli brethren in at least one way: They have the freedom to make earnest, confusingly plotted, allegorical films.

Director and co-screenwriter Ali Nassar, an Israeli Arab, focuses on the tensions in an Arab village in Galilee. The year is 1964, when Israel still imposed a military government on this region.

The Israeli military casts an oppressive shadow over the village, ruled by a corrupt official, the Muktar (Makram Khoury), a post that combines the functions of mayor and village elder. For all his petty tyranny, the Muktar is under the thumb of the local Israeli military governor (Yussef Abu Warda). For instance, he is too concerned about staying in the governor's good graces to be of much help to villagers seeking permits to work in Israeli cities.

(One of the main threads of the convoluted plot concerns the governor's discovery of forged work permits and the Muktar's failure to help a teacher who is wrongly accused in this incident.)

Another strand follows the story of Mahmmud (Muhammad Bakri), an ironworker who vies with the Muktar's no-good son for the hand of the woman he loves. The good news is that Bakri, who starred in the 1984 Israeli hit "Beyond the Walls" and appeared in Costa-Gavras' "Hanna K.," is the sexiest actor to come out of the Middle East since Omar Sharif.

Here, though, his chiseled good looks (he has been called the Palestinian Clint Eastwood) are obscured by a thick mustache and bad lighting. Still, he gets a chance to display his acting talent and make the most of his raspy, seductive voice.

His adopted brother, Mabruq (Suheil Haddad), is the village idiot, a naive clown who was orphaned in 1948 and has never recovered. He spends his days wandering the village and dreaming of marrying Jamilah (Mihaela Mitraki), another orphan who lost her mother in a massacre.

The various subplots do come together when the Muktar's son is killed in a fight with Mahmmud. However, this scene, and so many others in the film, is confusing. And although there is a brief explanation of the military rule in Galilee at the beginning, the plot is likely to baffle anyone not extremely familiar with Israeli-Palestinian history.

That's a shame, because Nassar is an accomplished director with a great deal to say and, for the most part, he and co-screenwriter Ghalib Sha'ath give a refreshingly balanced point of view. If only he had paid more attention to developing one or two characters and telling a more straightforward story. When the climax of the film comes, it would have so much more power to move audiences if they had understood everything that led up to it.

NEWSDAY, 1/20/99, Part II/p. B9, John Anderson

An Israeli-financed film with a Palestinian point of view, "The Milky Way" turns out to to be as dramatically engaging as it is politically ambitious—something that may not require surprise, but generates it nonetheless.

Set in a Galilean village in 1964, the last year of Israeli military rule, "The Milky Way" is a survivor's tale. As the prelude tells us, the 1948 war left many of the village's people killed or in flight, "leaving behind their relatives." It's these relatives we're about to meet, and by defining them strictly in terms of the dead, their story automatically becomes secondary, subsidiary—as they are, especially in the eyes of their oppressors. "Let them kill themselves," says the Israeli commandant, just as long as national security isn't involved.

But like Shohei Imamura's current "Dr. Akagi," which is set in Japan during the closing days of World War II, the military foe in "Milky Way" is almost a benign evil. The real well-waking, goat-shaking crises erupt out of the intramural tensions of a village caught between ancient tradition and modern politics, religious chastity and western carnality, maybe even a latent Marxist impulse rubbing up against the fealty the people instinctively show their presumed betters—a tradition they seem ready to throw over, were the Israeli presence not threatening their cultural identity.

The hero of the piece is Mahmmoud (Muhammad Bakri), local blacksmith and modern man, whose leadership qualities and sundry virtues arise from within unlike the Mukhtar, a village leader craven enough to be held in general contempt but who commands obedience nonetheless. Like the nightly news, or the Dallas Cowboys.

Between Mahmmoud and the Mukhtar swirls a panoply of dysfunction. And while the acting is a bit broad for American tastes, the characters are indelible: Mabruq, the village idiot whose flashbacks recall a small boy crying on a road littered with slaughtered relatives; the similarly afflicted Jamilah, whom Mabruq loves; Suad, Mahmmoud's betrothed, and Mohammad, the Mukhtar's corrupted son, who wants Suad and will do anything to get her.

There are elements of daytime-nighttime TV drama in "The Milky Way"—the title refers not just to the stars, but to the village's pathway to the markets—but the film has a firm sense of how history reverberates and maims and occasionally engulfs the present. "He ran around as if he were at home," Mabruq tells the children, while making up a story about an arrested Arab. Like the movie that surrounds it, Mabruq's fairy tale contains all the truth of fiction.

VILLAGE VOICE, 1/26/99, p. 104, Leslie Camhi

Little is heard about Israel's one million Arab citizens—those Palestinians (and their descendants) who stayed after the 1948 war and Israel's independence when others were killed or fled into exile. In the continuing tug-of-war over the West Bank and Gaza, they're a source of political speculation and uncertainty.

The Milky Way, a first feature by Israeli Arab director Ali Nassar, explores this largely uncharted territory. Set in the Galilee in 1964, this vivid portrait of an Arab village uncovers the lingering scars of war in private life and society. At its center is Mabruq (Suheil Haddad), a childlike man, still crazed and wounded by the 1948 massacre of his family. Most of the villagers take pity on Mabruq; he lives off odd jobs and charity. His closest friend is Mahmmud, a local ironworker played by Muhammad Bakri (who's been dubbed "the Palestinian Clint Eastwood") as a rangy, taciturn figure with a dash of tenderness and a strong code of honor.

The social costs of military occupation include corruption within the community, curfews, seizures, arrests, and border closings. Yet against this backdrop of fear, Nassar lovingly recreates a texture of Israeli life that barely exists today: donkeys and herds of sheep crowd the narrow clay lanes of villages; tribal justice decides disputes over goats and gardens. In the midst of all this ancient beauty, flashbacks to the violence of 1948 appear decontextualized and largely unexplained. Funded by an Israeli government ministry in the brief interlude after Oslo and before Netanyahu, and made with an Arab cast and Jewish crew, this film, simple and moving as a child's drawing, seems like a first step in the telling of the Israeli Arab story; let's hope there will be more.

Also reviewed in:
NEW YORK TIMES, 1/20/99, p. E5, Lawrence Van Gelder
VARIETY, 9/22-28/97, p. 60, Dennis Harvey

MINUS MAN, THE

A The Shooting Gallery and Fida Attieh Productions release in association with Donald Carter. *Executive Producer:* Larry Meistrich, Steve Carlis, Joseph J. DiMartino, and Keith Abell. *Producer:* David Bushell and Fida Attieh. *Director:* Hampton Fancher. *Screenplay:* Hampton Fancher. *Based on the novel by:* Lew McCreary. *Director of Photography:* Bobby Bukowski. *Editor:* Todd Ramsay. *Music:* Marco Beltrami. *Music Editor:* Jim Flatto. *Sound:* Tom Brandau and (music) John Kurlander. *Sound Editor:* Stuart Stanley. *Casting:* Mary Vernieu and Anne McCarthy. *Production Designer:* Andrew Laws. *Art Director:* Austin Gorg. *Set Decorator:* Laser Rosenberg. *Set Dresser:* Jeff Damal and Leon Hoiles. *Costumes:* Kimberly Adams-Galligan. *Make-up:* Ann Pala. *Running time:* 112 minutes. *MPAA Rating:* R.

CAST: Owen Wilson (Vann); Sheryl Crow (Casper); Dwight Yoakam (Blair); Dennis Haysbert (Graves); Alex Warren (State Trooper); Mercedes Ruehl (Jane); Chloe Black (Karen, Age 18); Brian Cox (Doug); Eric Mabius (Gene); Larry Miller (Paul); Lois Gerace (Lois); Erik Holland (Coach); Daniel Rey (Arthur); Janeane Garofalo (Ferrin); Axel Ovregaard (Joe La Moine); Brent Briscoe (Chief of Police); John Vargas (Priest); Lew McCreary (Man in Diner); Shannon Kies (Wendy); Madeleine Ignon (Karen, Age 5); Marla Diaz (Anchorwoman); David Warshofsky (Pate); Mark Derwin (Creech); Matt Gerald (Arresting Officer); Little Jake (General).

CHRISTIAN SCIENCE MONITOR, 10/1/99, p. 15, David Sterritt

[*The Minus Man* was reviewed jointly with *Stigmata*; see Sterritt's review of that film.]

LOS ANGELES TIMES, 9/10/99, Calendar/p. 14, Kevin Thomas

At the beginning of Hampton Fancher's eerie, quietly compelling "The Minus Man" a young man washes his pickup truck and takes off from a rural area, and after driving a spell, pulls up to a roadside tavern, looking for food, not drink. He amiably gives a lift to an inebriated young woman (Sheryl Crow).

At a rest stop the man returns to his truck to discover the woman shooting up. Undismayed, he offers her a drink from a shiny flask. Soon he's propping up her dead corpse in the restroom, making it look like she's a victim of overdose. We figure at first that the guy just doesn't want to get involved in an OD he really had nothing to do with—until it sinks in that whatever killed her was in that flask.

Vann, the young man (Owen Wilson), turns up in a small city somewhere along the West Coast and rents a room in the comfortable old home of a troubled middle-aged couple, Doug (Brian Cox) and Jane (Mercedes Ruehl), whose lives have been blighted by the fate of their only daughter, who has either disappeared or has died—we're never certain which. The reserved, wary Jane wants to avoid making Vann feel a part of the family, but the lonely Doug can't resist befriending such a likable young man. Doug is soon lining Vann up with a job sorting mail at the post office, where he works. And when Vann learns that the one bright spot in Doug's life is a gifted local athlete, for whom he has high hopes, you can be sure Vann arranges to pass him his fatal flask.

Affable serial killers are not exactly unknown on the screen, but in adapting Lew McCreary's 1990 novel, Fancher, a veteran writer whose credits include "Blade Runner," in his directorial debut, makes "The Minus Man" a fresh and mesmerizing experience. The film goes for a minimalist approach and is all the stronger for it. Whatever forces formed Vann, heredity or environment or a combination of the two, would most likely be depressingly prosaic--brain damage, brutal parenting, etc; what's of interest is that Vann is as compulsive as Peter Lorre's child-killer in Fritz Lang's "M" and is so haunted by being caught he imagines that a pair of tough, smart cops (Dennis Haysbert and Dwight Yoakam) are always catching up with him.

What is of even greater interest is the impact Vann, an All-American guy seemingly at his most benign, has on everyone around him. Relentlessly nice, he is in fact a blank, which enables people to make of him what they will. His accommodating nature and cheerful demeanor brightens Doug and Jane's lives, but will lifting their spirits only serve to let them down with a dangerous thud? And at the post office, Vann gives a pretty co-worker (Janeane Garofalo) no encouragement whatsoever, which has the effect of making her all the more attracted to him.

Ultimately, Vann's impact on these people and others reflects their loneliness, and in some instances, outright desperation. Can it be that Vann embodies such longing himself in its most extreme form, welling up from some dark, destructive region of his being?

In any event, "The Minus Man," which has a simple, seductively flowing style, gives its cast plenty to work with, especially Cox, who makes Doug an appealing, idiosyncratic man with a gnawing neediness that gives way at times to self-inflicted pain. It's only three years since Wilson came to attention with Wes Anderson's "Bottle Rocket," which he co-wrote, yet he carries off this most enigmatic of protagonists with nary a misstep.

"The Minus Man," flawlessly photographed by Bobby Bukowski, fresh off "Arlington Road," has its moments of humor—it would not be nearly as persuasive if it didn't--but it is above all such an unsettling experience you find yourself still taking it all in well after the lights have gone up.

NEW YORK POST, 9/10/99, p. 56, Jonathan Foreman

"The Minus Man" is about someone so bland and lacking in personality that people attribute qualities to him that he doesn't really have.

He also happens to be a serial killer who is truly a nice guy when he's not poisoning people—so appealing that you're supposed to like him, too, and then be troubled by it.

The filmmakers clearly thought there was something profound in such a character, that it says something important about America or humanity or serial killers. But whatever that something is, it's not apparent on the screen.

What you have instead is a slow, self-consciously low-key, very dull film that strains for eeriness with long silences and affectless performances. "The Minus Man" is merely an exercise in slick emptiness.

Vann Siegert (Owen Wilson), a blond, affable drifter with a twangy voice, turns up in a roadside bar, buys junkie Sheryl Crow a drink, gives her a lift and finishes her off with a shot of poisoned Amaretto.

Then Vann turns up in one of those superficially perfect West Coast towns and rents a room from a slightly creepy middle-aged couple whose daughter is either missing or dead (you never find out which).

Jane (Mercedes Ruehl) is wary of the new tenant, but Doug (Brian Cox) takes to him and gets him a job in the local post office, where Vann soon gets promoted to a delivery route.

He also wins the amorous interest of co-worker Ferrin (Janeane Garofalo) and murders the town's high school football hero.

In between, Vann has weird dreams in which he's visited by a pair of FBI detectives (Dwight Yoakam and Dennis Haysbert) who have his m.o. all figured out.

What interest the film has is from an impressive cast. Cox gives a strong performance and Wilson does a fine job of incarnating Vann.

But the best things about "The Minus Man" are the always terrific Mercedes Ruehl and Janeane Garofalo, who achieves a career breakthrough. For once, she drops her usual sarcastic persona and is completely believable (and surprisingly attractive) as the vulnerable, endearing Ferrin.

NEWSDAY, 9/10/99, Part II/p. B9, Gene Seymour

The most frightening monsters are the ones who seem quite plausible and, worse, reasonable. This truth seems so self-evident that one would think it's grafted within the brains of moviemakers both within and outside the Hollywood sausage factory.

Yet these same moviemakers really think they're scaring you to death with over-the-top psycho killers and Grand Guignol nightmare figures when all they're doing is increasing your comfort level.

After all, the Freddy Krugers, Max Cadys and Norman Bateses, however distinctive they are as personalities, are nonetheless such familiar archetypes that you never feel you're in danger of meeting the real thing. The guess here is that you wouldn't know what to do with a mass murderer who gives off absolutely, positively no creepy vibes whatsoever.

So please welcome to our stage, ladies and gentlemen, Vann Siegert (Owen Wilson), a blond, blue-eyed drifter with just the right mixture of shyness and charm to make you trust him to give you a lift to the next gas station. Whatever you do, don't accept his offer to drink out of his flask. It's spiked with poison that'll put you out quickly, but gently.

Vann picks his victims randomly, but carefully. It's OK, maybe, to send a junkie (Sheryl Crow in a fiery cameo) home for good. There may even be some rough logic to killing a high school football hero who wants to join the FBI someday.

In the Pacific coastal town where he chooses to hang out for a while, however, Vann's not inclined to do any harm to his post office co-worker (Janeane Garofalo), who's sweet on him. Nor is he interested in offering his toxic substances to the couple who give him room and board in their home—though they're a fairly toxic compound in their own right.

Doug (Brian Cox) seems on the surface like a warm-and-fuzzy Regular Guy with unexpected flashes of poetry and passion. But he also has a habit of literally beating himself up over some private torment he can't name. His wife Jane (Mercedes Ruehl) is likewise a welter of mood swings, leaving many things unsaid about her marriage and the daughter who won't come home.

Within these shadows, Vann seems the brightest, healthiest presence in town, even if he's on the prowl for whomever he believes is worthy of being dispatched. Whatever second thoughts he may have about such acts come to him in the form of imaginary interrogations by a pair of rough, tough detectives (Dwight Yoakam, Dennis Haysbert). It's a dream to Vann, but it all seems plausible.

As, for that matter, does this impressive directorial debut by veteran screenwriter Hampton Fancher ("Blade Runner," "The Mighty Quinn"). "The Minus Man" stands out from other, similar efforts in psychological suspense in the almost organic way it achieves its eerie effects. The blank spaces in the characters' lives provide the source of the film's terror rather than the kind of over-the-top nerve goosing that even the best filmmakers can't resist in movies like this.

Fancher isn't entirely immune from the hiccups in visual flow that typify writers' maiden directorial efforts. Nonetheless, he has a good eye for off-kilter composition and—not surprising—a firm hand in narrative pacing. He's also lucky to have a cast like this. Garofalo has rarely been as magnetic as she is here while Cox and Ruehl are, in their different ways, scarier to watch than Wilson's Vann, who is as canny a creation as any charming movie monster you've ever seen. Or can imagine.

VILLAGE VOICE, 9/14/99, p. 144, Dennis Lim

The ad campaign for *The Minus Man* is what you might call an exercise in ironic suggestibility, all sneering warnings ("Don't Bring a Dumb Date") and promises ("Running Time: All Night [In Your Head]"). It's a smug tactic—marketing a movie as a conversation piece (the tag line, in fact, is "Conversation Usually Follows")—but in this case, the cocky pose is also misleading, at glaring odds with the meditative, almost trance-like, tone of this willfully low-key serial-killer flick. Directed by *Blade Runner* screenwriter Hampton Fancher (and based on a 1990 novel by Lew McCreary), *The Minus Man* is less interesting for what it has to say about evil—namely, that it's banal/unknowable/random/everywhere—than for the microsurgical procedures it performs on genre conventions and expectations.

The murderer here is a smiling cipher, a drifter named Vann (Owen Wilson), bland, blond, agonizingly polite. (There's a hint of danger, though—is it the crooked smile? the squinty eyes? the resemblance to Sean Penn?) Vann's m.o. is unremarkable—he drives around in a pickup with a tiny flask of poisoned Amaretto. (We see only one act of physical violence, and, perhaps too obviously, it's triggered by a moment of physical intimacy.) After a summary disposal early on of a strung-out Sheryl Crow, he moves in with an unhappy suburban couple—tense, troubled Jane (Mercedes Ruehl) and good-guy-with-dark-side Doug (Brian Cox) -whose woes apparently have much to do with their absent daughter. Vann finds a job at the local post office as well as a somewhat puzzled admirer in his coworker Farrin (a well-used Janeane Garofalo, in a keen performance composed of more than the snide wisecracks typically required of her).

Vann kills—that's all we know, and all we need to know. Motivation and backstory are beside the point, though there is the vague suggestion that Vann's victims are, as he sees it, begging to be put out of their misery. Shifty and paced like a reverie, the film lodges itself inside its protagonist's head without attempting to make sense of what it discovers—case in point: Vann's imagined conversations with two detectives (Dwight Yoakam and Dennis Haysbert) and fantasies about his eventual capture. In an oddly effective use of voice-over, Fancher floods the soundtrack with abrupt bursts of Vann's drawling monotone. But the point of the stream of consciousness isn't necessarily to illuminate-the opacity of the delivery is more seductive, and arguably more significant, than the faux—profundity of the content. The same might be said of the film as a whole.

Also reviewed in:
CHICAGO TRIBUNE, 9/24/99, Friday/p. D, Michael Wilmington
NEW YORK TIMES, 9/10/99, p. E20, Stephen Holden

VARIETY, 2/1-7/99, p. 59, Glenn Lovell
WASHINGTON POST, 9/24/99, p. C5, Rita Kempley

MISS JULIE

A United Artists release of a Moonstone Entertainment presentation of a Red Mullet production. *Executive Producer:* Annie Stewart, Willi Baer, and Etchie Stroh. *Producer:* Mike Figgis and Harriet Cruickshank. *Director:* Mike Figgis. *Screenplay:* Helen Cooper. *Based on the play by:* August Strindberg. *Director of Photography:* Beniôt Delhomme. *Editor:* Matthew Wood. *Music:* Mike Figgis and Louise Hammar. *Choreographer:* Scarlett Mackmin. *Sound:* Pawel Wdowczak and (music) Mark Tucker. *Sound Editor:* Nigel Heath. *Casting:* Jina Jay. *Production Designer:* Michael Howells. *Art Director:* Philip Robinson. *Set Decorator:* Totty Lowther. *Special Effects:* Alan Senior. *Costumes:* Sandy Powell. *Make-up:* Peter King. *Running time:* 100 minutes. *MPAA Rating:* R.

CAST: Saffron Burrows (Miss Julie); Peter Mullan (Jean); Maria Doyle Kennedy (Christine); Olivia Coles, Santi Rieser, and Oliver Swan Jackson (Children); Sinead Jones, Griselda Sanderson, and Christian Weaver (Musicians).

CHRISTIAN SCIENCE MONITOR, 12/10/99, p. 15, David Sterritt

"Miss Julie" comes from Mike Figgis, whose filmmaking has ranged from mainstream movies like "Leaving Las Vegas" to experimental fare like "The Loss of Sexual Innocence," his most recent picture.

This season he's turned to August Strindberg's great melodrama—also memorably filmed by Alf Sjöberg almost 50 years ago—about the psychologically complex love affair of an aristocratic young woman and an ambitious servant in 19th-century Sweden. Stressing fundamental human emotions over historical details and eye-catching effects, Figgis creates a visually claustrophobic yet steadily absorbing atmosphere in which the barely controlled feelings of his characters take on an almost palpable reality.

He deserves hearty praise, as do stars Saffron Burrows and Peter Mullan, for bringing Strindberg's study to convincing life 100 years after it was written.

LOS ANGELES TIMES, 12/10/99, Calendar/p. 4, Kevin Thomas

In Mike Figgis' edgy, rigorous filming of Strindberg's "Miss Julie," its heroine couldn't strike a less sympathetic introductory note. Saffron Burrows' Julie is tall, regal—and hateful. It's midsummer's eve 1894, and Julie, with nothing better to do, has ventured into the huge ground-floor kitchen of what must surely be a palatial ancestral estate. (As it happens, her father, a count, is away.)

There's a sense of pagan carnal celebration in the air, but she's feeling left out. In the kitchen she encounters her father's footman Jean (Peter Mullan), a virile, bearded, compact man of perhaps 40. Also present is the count's cook, a pretty, dark-haired, sensible young woman named Christine (Maria Doyle Kennedy), who considers herself engaged to Jean and is now dozing off in a rocker out of sheer exhaustion.

Overflowing with condescension, Julie commences baiting Jean, who proves to be more resilient, more self-respecting than she perhaps anticipated. He is not impudent in response but neither is he humble, which to her makes him all the more attractive.

Swiftly, Julie's behavior turns seductive, and this erotic charge gradually turns the encounter into simultaneously a battle of the sexes and class warfare. From the start Jean warns her that she's embarked on a dangerous course, but she has no conception of just how dangerous.

But then Julie has no conception of what the hard life of a servant must be like or that an oppressive existence from which there is no realistic hope of escape could breed such contempt for the unfeeling, exploitative upper classes. Jean is too intelligent, too innately ambitious to be content with his lot, and his close observation of his masters has made him sufficiently well-spoken and polished to pass for a gentleman.

But a lifetime's resentments have had their withering effect, leaving him mean-spirited, vengeful and small-minded. Julie, in turn, has been raised to be a freer spirit than most young women of her class—but her outspoken, uninhibited manner has just caused her fiance to jilt her. Neither of these two fit comfortably within the rigid societal structure of their time, but we begin to wonder, once their mutual attraction catches fire, whether either has the courage or resources to flee, either together or separately.

Strindberg is scarcely the playwright to ask us to like his tormented—and tormenting—men and women, but we do come to understand and feel compassion for Jean and even for Julie, so insulated as to be clueless.

The plight of an aristocrat entangled with her father's manservant doesn't strike an exactly contemporary note, yet surely the contemporary corporate world in which so many men and women spend most of, their lives can be as autocratic and treacherous as the society in which Julie and Jean exist.

Strindberg, the eternal modernist, was among the earliest writers to grasp the neurotic, destructive elements within relationships, and the seesawing, power-tripping between Julie and Jean could scarcely be more timeless. Figgis, in turn, elicits the unsparing, no-holds-barred emotions from Burrows and Mullan that he did from Nicolas Cage and Elisabeth Shue in "Leaving Las Vegas."

It's been said the test of a director is whether he can communicate on purely a visual level. The seriously flawed sound recording for "Miss Julie" inadvertently puts Figgis to that test. The sound is so muddy and unbalanced, fluctuating between whispery and bombastic, that at least a third, perhaps even more, of screenwriter Helen Cooper's vital, idiomatic rendering of Strindberg's dialogue is virtually unintelligible, with Figgis' own score, aptly spiky and intense, so loud that it threatens to overpower everything else.

Yet, even in those moments when you despair of comprehending any dialogue at all, Figgis remains a compelling storyteller, holding you with the intensity of his vision and his mastery of nuance.

But a Figgis film, not to mention a Strindberg play, deserves to be heard as well as seen.

NEW YORK POST, 12/10/99, p. 55, Lou Lumenick

August Strindberg's "Miss Julie" is one of the least-filmed great plays, and with good reason. With the action—mostly a lengthy discussion of sex and class—confined largely to a single set, this intense psychosexual drama doesn't easily lend itself to the camera.

No one has even attempted to film the play since Swedish director Alf Sjoberg's classic 1950 version, which opened up the action and added characters.

Now, director Mike Figgis has taken the opposite tack. He and his screenwriter, Helen Cooper, flaunt the staginess of their minimalist, bare-bones adaptation, shot largely with a hand-held camera.

With the exception of a brief trip outdoors into a highly stylized garden set, the story takes place entirely in the kitchen of a Swedish count's estate. It's 1894 and the household is celebrating a summer holiday, a rare occasion for socializing between aristocrats and their servants.

Miss Julie (Saffron Burrows), the count's daughter, takes the opportunity to flirt openly with the footman Jean (Peter Mullan), much to the disapproval of his fiance, Christine (Maria Doyle Kennedy).

When Miss Julie orders Jean to dance with him, it sparks gossip among the staff. Miss Julie manipulates Jean, who admits admiring her since childhood, into seducing her (a scene pointlessly shot in split screen) as the housemaids sing about the "bitch in heat" who's slumming beneath her class.

Jean, who despises the landed gentry, wants to manipulate Miss Julie to steal her father's money, so he can escape the estate with her and Christine and open a hotel in Lake Como.

Miss Julie, a man-hating feminist who's reluctant to give up the privileges of her class, has very different fantasies, and the clash between these two very strong-willed individuals ends with tragic results.

Unfortunately, neither of the leads really offers more than a one-dimensional portrait. Mullan's Jean seethes with arrogance, but the charm that's supposed to attract Miss Julie is in very short supply.

Burrows ("The Deep Blue Sea"), who towers over Mullan by at least a head in height, isn't really up to the intricate text. And her "Miss Julie" seems about as vulnerable as a Mack truck.

NEWSDAY, 12/10/99, Part II/p. B9, John Anderson

In an interview about a year ago, director Mike Figgis discussed his plans to make a film version of August Strindberg's 1889 "Miss Julie," a one-act in one room. "But it's an interesting room," he told Newsday. "Seriously. The challenge is 'don't open it,' for crissakes, because the whole play is based on claustrophobia. It's a submarine movie. It's the 'Das Boot' of the thinking man."

Now that Figgis' "Miss Julie" has arrived—starring Saffron Burrows and Peter Mullan, not Juliette Binoche and Nicolas Cage, as he'd originally intended (and which now seems like a disaster averted)—it's clear that Figgis has opened up the play, at least in terms of its sexuality (his split-screen clinch of Burrows and Mullan is astounding, for many reasons). He also imposes the visual aspects of an ending that was only implied on the page. But Strindberg's kitchen a la Figgis—where we see the seduction/ruination of the title character by the house servant Jean—is a suffocating crucible of pain for the playwright's anxieties about class and marriage, an enormous, yet inescapable space.

Strindberg's mother was a servant, his father was a ruined aristocrat and their son put his lifelong concerns about heredity and sex into the play; the early lines about Miss Julle's angst about her dog having mated with a stray foreshadow with venom the oncoming tragedy of Miss Julie, whose familiarity with the servants earns only their contempt and whose flirtation with the self-educated, contemptuous Jean leads to her "fall." Some of the conceits in "Miss Julie" sound passe, perhaps, but they don't come across that way via Figgis, who makes us feel that the chasm of class is as unbreachable as ever.

For audiences in 1890s Sweden, "Miss Julie" would certainly have been an NC-17 production (it was 25 years before anyone staged it there), but Figgis' more explicit version is R, which says something—if only that a classic of the 19th Century can still provoke, especially if the societal constraints are removed and its author's implicit intentions allowed some light. If there's a reservation to be had with Figgis' film, it's in the casting—not because Mullan and Burrows don't give riveting performances, but because of their stature. Literally. Mullan is so much shorter than the statuesque Burrows (whose extraordinary face Figgis clearly worships) that it disturbs the dynamic. Sure, a thirst for conquest is always among Jean's motivations in "Miss Julie." But even if Strindberg was a visionary, inferiority complexes had to wait for Freud and the rest of the psychoanalysts.

SIGHT AND SOUND, 10/00, p. 51, Peter Matthews

The north of Sweden, midsummers night, 1894. In the kitchen of a country estate, the cook Christine upbraids her fiancé Jean, the footman, for dancing with the Count's daughter Miss Julie. Julie commands Jean to dance with her again. On his return, he and Christine fondle each other. Julie interrupts them and orders Jean to put on clothes befitting a gentleman. When Christine falls asleep, Julie asks Jean to drink beer with her. Then she insists he kiss her shoe. In the garden, Julie flirts with Jean, but slaps him when he kisses her. Back in the kitchen, Jean describes his impoverished childhood and confesses his desire to rise. When revellers erupt into the kitchen, Jean hides Julie in his room and there seduces her. Afterwards, he confesses his dream of owning a hotel and proposes that they run away.

Jean suggests Julie rob her father to finance the scheme. Drunk, Julie leaves to search the Count's desk. Christine appears and surmises what has occurred. She demands that Jean accompany her to church, and tells him to shave. Julie returns with the stolen money and a suitcase. When she tries to take a pet bird along on the journey, Jean kills it. After a confrontation with the pair, Christine goes to church alone. Julie asks Jean to give her the razor. The Count rings from upstairs, and Jean hastens to attend him. Julie slashes her wrists.

Though August Strindberg's 1888 play *Miss Julie* is one of the great war horses of western theatre, few film-makers have been drawn to the material, and it's easy to see why. Strindberg himself worried that audiences used to the pomp and circumstance of 19th century stagecraft would not accept a brooding chamber piece where just three characters (Miss Julie, the well-heeled daughter of a Count, and servants Jean and Christine) are confined to a single set. Striving for a heightened realism, the Swedish dramatist arranged the action in an unbroken flow and (shocking at the time) instructed the players to turn their backs on the spectators now and then.

In this regard, *Miss Julie* anticipated the sustained voyeuristic illusion that is cinema; still, screen adapters have largely steered clear of a work that puts so many obstacles in the way of conventional opening out. Once an unassailable classic, Alf Sjöberg's 1951 version seems to have fallen off the map of late, despite the stunning virtuosity of its flashbacks, through which the tortured heroine's past was made to occupy the same physical space as her present.

The one indulgence director Mike Figgis permits himself in his bargain basement version (the film was shot chronologically over a relatively short period of time) is a brief split screen sequence showing the erotic grappling of Julie and her footman lover Jean from fractionally varied angles. Other than this redundant bit of punctuation (which anticipates his extended split-screen experiment *Timecode)*, Figgis has burned off the slightly disreputable swank that characterised such earlier pictures as *Internal Affairs*. Far from opening out the theatrical frame, he closes it down, not only keeping to Strindberg's kitchen set, but pinioning the actors with a mock-*vérité*-style that emphasises every blemish and fleck of lip spittle. The movie was shot on Super 16mm using two handheld cameras, which judder and lurch as though whipped up by the stormy passions; the editing could have been done on a butcher's block, so prodigal are the mismatched eyelines and jarring reverses in screen direction. While Figgis isn't quite as root and branch in his asceticism, it would appear that *Dogme 95* has spawned another fellow traveller. By sacrificing the frills of mainstream filmmaking, he presumably hopes to free the play's primal anger. In this, he follows Strindberg, whose jagged psychodramas were an assault on the stuffy conventions of bourgeois theatre.

High-born Julie is possessed by a fantasy of wallowing in the mud, while the rising young Jean entertains few illusions about his motives in seducing the Count's daughter. Their liaison carries a kinky sadomasochistic charge, and that's perhaps what caught Figgis' interest—it's hard to miss the parallels with the destructive symbiosis of the couple in *Leaving Las Vegas*. Screenwriter Helen Cooper faithfully preserves the play's vituperative atmosphere, and indeed amplifies it by a coarsening of the language (when Jean narrates a childhood recollection, his monologue builds into a scatological aria). Since it was only censorship that inhibited Strindberg from spelling out the earthier implications of his naturalism, this is one case where vulgarisation makes sense. Indeed, the film shows thought and care in practically every detail; so it's a real cause for regret that it never catches fire. Saffron Burrows gives a technically accomplished performance as Miss Julie, but is perhaps working too hard to arouse much pity and fear. Or perhaps the wobblyscope technique is at fundamental odds with Strindberg's tightly deterministic structure, and ends up cooling things down when it should heat them up. Simplicity, you're left thinking, may be the toughest goal to achieve in movies.

VILLAGE VOICE, 12/21/99, p. 148, Amy Taubin

Smack in the middle of *Miss Julie*, Mike Figgis's frenetic and grossly self-aggrandizing adaption of Strindberg's worse-for-wear two-hander about the battle between the sexes and the classes, the neurotic lady of the house (the beautiful but appallingly inept Saffron Burrows) is deflowered by her father's ambitious footman (Peter Mullan, who at least is not as embarrassing as his costar). Figgis splits the screen in two for no discernible reason, since both perspectives on the pounding and grunting are equally gratuitous. I thought this might be his riff on Warhol's *Chelsea Girls*—until I read that Figgis's digital project for the new millennium, *Time Code 2000*, quarters the screen. The only imaginable thing more atrocious than one or two versions of Figgis's *Miss Julie* is four.

Also reviewed in:
CHICAGO TRIBUNE, 3/3/00, Friday/p. O, Michael Wilmington
NEW REPUBLIC, 1/3/00, p. 26, Stanley Kauffmann
NEW YORK TIMES, 12/10/99, p. E10, Stephen Holden
VARIETY, 9/20-26/99, p. 82, Emanuel Levy

MR. DEATH: THE RISE AND FALL OF FRED A. LEUCHTER JR.

A Lions Gate Films release of an Independent Film Channel presentation in association with Channel 4 of a Fourth Floor/Scout production. *Executive Producer:* Jonathan Sehring, Caroline Kaplan, and John Sloss. *Producer:* Michael Williams, David Collins, and Dorothy Aufiero. *Director:* Errol Morris. *Director of Photography:* Peter Donohue. *Editor:* Karen Schmeer. *Music:* Caleb Sampson. *Sound:* Steve Bores. *Production Designer:* Ted Bafaloukos. *Running time:* 91 minutes. *MPAA Rating:* PG-13.

INTERVIEWS WITH: Fred A. Leuchter, Jr.; Robert Jan Van Pelt; David Irving; James Roth; Shelly Shapiro; Suzanne Tabasky; Ernst Zündel.

CHRISTIAN SCIENCE MONITOR, 12/31/99, p. 16, David Sterritt

This has been a strong year for documentaries, or "nonfiction films," to use a term considered more friendly at the box office.

But varied as they were, most fell into a few categories that have dominated this genre for decades. "American Hollow," about a poor rural family, and "American Movie," about an aspiring horror-film director, are *cinéma-vérité* pictures that seek to capture spontaneous views of life as it happens.

"42 Up," continuing a decades-long film series about a diverse group of British citizens, uses interviews and time-jumping editing to explore its subject. "Buena Vista Social Club" hops between travelogue-style footage and concert performances.

All have their merits, but I'd argue that the year's best nonfiction movie fits into none of these stylistic pigeonholes. "Mr. Death: The Rise and Fall of Fred A. Leuchter Jr." has a distinctive personality for two reasons. One is that its topic—the career of a self-made entrepreneur whose success is based on the darkest sides of human existence—has few precedents to which critics might compare it. The other is that it's directed by Errol Morris. a hugely important American filmmaker whose work has revolutionized nonfiction cinema.

Morris has won awards and honors, but since he isn't a household name, it's worth recalling his contributions. He became, a director in the late 1970s, when nonfiction film had already passed through several stages of evolution.

From the '30s through the '50s, most documentaries were either "educational" or "poetic" in style—explaining a topic with the help of an all-knowing narrator or evoking a subject through impressionistic images and music.

This changed in the '60s, when a general tendency to question authority led to *cinéma-vérité* or "direct cinema," claiming to represent reality in an undiluted form, with no omniscient arbitrator to coach its into viewing it through a particular set of ideas or preconceptions.

This was a dubious assertion, since all films manipulate their viewers. Still, many people accepted the notion that *cinéma-vérité* presents the unvarnished truth of life.

Morris questioned this view with a vengeance. Rejecting the *cinéma-vérité* conventions that audiences had learned to associate with realism—shaky camera work, jumpy editing, grainy film—he moved in a radically different direction.

Rather than catch the "characters" of his films in spur-of-the-moment situations, he interviewed them in well-prepared settings. And breaking the ultimate taboo of the *cinéma-vérité* era, he didn't hesitate to re-create material—complete with unrealistic effects like slow motion and expressive sound.

The result was a series of groundbreaking films. "Gates of Heaven," completed in 1978, explores the world of pet cemeteries so vividly that critic Roger Ebert has called it one of the finest movies ever made. "Vernon, Florida" captures a rural town with a realism that borders on surrealism.

Morris's greatest work, "The Thin Blue Line," reopened a criminal case so incisively that the movie's central figure—a man on death row for murder—was cleared and freed after its release. Subsequent films include "A Brief History of Time," about physicist Stephen Hawking, and "Fast, Cheap & Out of Control," a mind-bending essay interlocking the careers of a lion tamer, a robot designer, a topiary gardener, and the leading authority on a type of African rodent.

"Mr. Death" continues the unique Morris tradition. It focuses on Fred A. Leuchter, a Massachusetts man who went into business as designer of equipment for capital punishment, seeing himself as a humane individual who could reduce suffering by ensuring the speedy demise of condemned prisoners.

In the late '80s, he was hired as an expert witness in the Canadian trial of a German publisher charged with spreading false information about the Nazi era.

Leuchter rose to this challenge by making the incredible argument that Jews and other Holocaust victims could not possibly have perished in gas chambers.

From here Leuchter became a full-fledged member of the "Holocaust denial" movement, writing and lecturing against the reality of the 20th century's most horrific crimes.

"Mr. Death" treats Leuchter with more dignity than Leuchter allows Holocaust victims. While another filmmaker might have used *cinéma-vérité* spontaneity to catch him in unguarded moments, Morris lets Leuchter present himself to the camera in a straightforward manner.

This makes "Mr. Death" a riveting movie. What makes it an important one is the concern that lies below it surface: the fascination with death that subtly pervades our supposedly civilized society. We live in a world that still harbors a multitude of problems and a multitude of solutions (such as capital punishment) that some consider just as bad.

By connecting two forms of state-sanctioned killing—the Holocaust and capital punishment—Morris does not argue that they are equivalent or even similar to each other, but he does call attention to a contemporary affinity with death that most of us don't like to think about too deeply. While his film isn't the cheeriest way to usher in the new year, moviegoers aren't likely to find a more stimulating and thought-provoking picture.

LOS ANGELES TIMES, 12/29/99, Calendar/p. 4, Kevin Thomas

The less you know about the subject of Errol Morris' latest documentary, "Mr. Death: The Rise and Fall of Fred A. Leuchter, Jr.," the more startling the impact.

As a chronicler of bizarre Americana without peer, Morris seems to have found the ideal subject in Leuchter, who tells us how his concern for humane execution led to a career in improving electric chairs and gas chambers in America's state prisons. Leuchter, who reveals no interest in the debate over the death penalty, is a voluble, middle-aged man with big glasses, a pronounced New England accent and an anonymous, nerdy demeanor. He seems to fit right in with the operators of pet cemeteries and assorted oddballs who have intrigued Morris over the past 20 years.

As we watch this film with the fascination combined with a sense of creepiness that is Morris' calling card, we are completely unprepared by the tack the film suddenly takes. When Ernst Zundel, a Canadian neo-Nazi, was on trial in 1988 for publishing two books, "Did Six Million Really Die?" and "The Hitler We Loved and Why," he was advised to send a gas chamber expert to Auschwitz on a fact-finding mission. He came across Leuchter, and off he went to Poland, combining research—with his honeymoon. Zundel sent a film crew—their footage is included in "Mr. Death"—along with Leuchter to show him taking measurements and illegally chipping away at the remnants and ruins of Auschwitz and its Birkenau annex.

Smuggling the fragments out with bags of dirty laundry, Leuchter returned home to Malden, Mass, where he submitted them to a laboratory chemist, James Roth, without telling him where the fragments came from or what the purpose of the testing would be. Roth discovered significant levels of cyanide in specimens from the concentration camp's delousing building but little or no traces in bricks from the crematoria. In a flash, Leuchter became the darling of the Holocaust denial movement.

Leuchter became an extreme example of the human capacity to believe what you want to believe. Roth bluntly states that he was essentially asked to perform the wrong tests and details why they do not support Leuchter's contention. For example, Auschwitz's delousing building remains intact, while its crematoria were dynamited by the Germans as the defeat of the Third Reich became imminent, with the ruins Leuchter tested exposed to the elements for more than four decades before he arrived to chip away at them.

A history major at Boston University, Leuchter, his scientific and engineering skills self-proclaimed, never bothered to study the Auschwitz archives. The more the neo-Nazis embraced Leuchter, the more publicity he received, and the more resoundingly discredited he became, his career and marriage destroyed. (Faced with business reverses, Leuchter actually took out this classified ad: "EXECUTION DEVICE. Control module for lethal injection machine. Being sold for nonpayment. $ 10,000.")

Eventually, Morris tracked down Leuchter in California. Leuchter insists he's a reluctant revisionist and not anti-Semitic but clings steadfastly to his belief in the validity of the study he made of Auschwitz. With his elegantly elliptical style and mordant tone, Morris trusts us to appreciate for ourselves the way in which irony compounds irony within Leuchter and his fate, and how his capacity for denial in regard to the quality of his own "scientific" endeavors connects to the larger question of the denial that the Holocaust ever happened.

Zundel describes Leuchter as "a mouse of a man" who is "totally sincere, a total innocent," and you come away from "Mr. Death" suspecting that Zundel is probably right in his appraisal. Morris once told reporter Mark Singer that what interests him is that "anybody can think he's a hero," which cuts to what Singer calls an important Morris principle: "We never truly know what we presume we know." Thus, "Mr. Death," which is shot through with one dark absurdity after another, emerges as a cautionary tale if ever there was one.

NEW YORK, 1/10/00, p. 46, Peter Rainer

It's impossible to describe Fred A. Leuchter Jr., the subject of Errol Morris's new nonfiction film *Mr. Death*, without invoking the word *geeky*. He looks like Toad, the character Charlie Martin Smith played in *American Graffiti*, brought into middle age. Leuchter, who had a thriving Massachusetts-based business designing more "humane" electric chairs and lethal-injection systems, unwittingly initiated his own downfall when he prepared a report for the defense of a neo-Nazi on trial in Toronto alleging that, upon inspection, Auschwitz and Birkenau were not the sites of any gas executions. (The judge refused to allow the report into evidence.) Leuchter represents the banality of banality, and one may perhaps be forgiven for feeling that Morris made him up altogether: This death-obsessed dweeb, who drinks 40 cups of coffee and smokes six packs of cigarettes a day, is such a perfect Errol Morris person that it's as if Leuchter's entire life were a clarion call for the filmmaker's attentions. But perhaps Leuchter is too perfect for Morris. Having found him, the director doesn't quite know what to do with him; the camera brings Leuchter up close, and the effect is a bit like staring at a big-screen bug in *The Hellstrom Chronicle*. Morris is trusting that the man's blank affableness will eerily resonate, but the only revelation I got is just further confirmation that creeps do indeed walk among us. Clearly Morris wants us to see a bit of ourselves in Leuchter and, in so doing, admit that the Holocaust was perpetuated not by monsters but by duped, deluded ordinary types. But Morris's idea of ordinary isn't necessarily yours or mine. Leuchter is too singular to be anybody's Everyman—even Morris's.

NEW YORK POST, 12/29/99, p. 42, Lou Lumenick

"Mr. Death: The Rise and Fall of Fred A. Leuchter Jr.," a new documentary from the brilliant Errol Morris, tells the chilling story of a self-taught American execution expert who lent his reputation to an unspeakable lie: that the Holocaust didn't happen.

Leuchter explains at length how he got into the death business. As an engineer, he was called in to overhaul an electric chair, which he redesigned to make executions more humane. He was hired by other states and, though they have absolutely nothing in common, eventually branched out into gas chambers and gallows.

He built a thriving business, Leuchter admits, largely because not many people wanted the work and because he quoted good prices.

Leuchter, a mild-mannered son of a prison employee who boasts that he drinks 60 cups of coffee a day, unself-consciously discusses the pros and cons of various methods of execution.

Leuchter's growing reputation did not escape the attention of lawyers for Ernst Zundel, a Canadian neo-Nazi who was being tried under an statute that makes it a crime to tell lies that promote hate crimes.

Leuchter was put on a plane to Poland with a bizarre mission: to prove that no one was gassed to death at the Auschwitz death camp.

Leuchter, whose limited professional training in no way prepared him for this job, set about methodically drawing meticulous renderings of the remaining Auschwitz buildings.

Without permission, he chipped away hundreds of brick samples from the national monument, which he sent to a Canadian laboratory for analysis. (All of this was documented by a film crew hired by Zundel's lawyer; Morris effectively combines some of this footage with expertly staged re-creations.)

Zundel's lawyers unsuccessfully tried to enter into evidence Leuchter's report, which claimed the buildings lacked the sort of ventilation systems required by gas chambers, and that a chemical analysis of the chips showed no residue of the Zyklon-B gas used to exterminate millions of Jews and others.

The chemist who did the tests—he had no idea where the chips came from—angrily debunks the findings. An Auschwitz historian points out that there is ample documentation of the gas chambers (and their ventilation systems) contained in camp records, which Leuchter didn't bother to look at.

Zundel was convicted, and Leuchter's findings, published as a book, made Leuchter a celebrity on the neo-Nazi circuit. It also made him a pariah, even to the capital punishment establishment. Contracts were canceled, his professional credentials were questioned, and he was ruined financially.

Leuchter's ex-wife (who disgustedly describes how the Auschwitz trip served as her honeymoon) explains that he was seduced into continuing to tell lies that made him the center of attention. Leuchter professes bewilderment at what happened to him.

"Mr. Death," Morris' most gripping film since "The Thin Blue Line," is the year's scariest movie.

TIME, 12/27/99, p. 188, Richard Corliss

To do good you don't need a graduate degree, just a smart idea. To do harm you don't need bad intentions, just a plodding arrogance. Those truisms are at the heart of the latest documentary enthraller from artful Errol Morris (*The Thin Blue Line, A Short History of Time*). Fred Leuchter won renown for devising more "humane" electric chairs, gallows and gas chambers. Now considered an expert in all aspects of state torture, Leuchter was hired by Ernst Zundel, a prominent denier of the Holocaust to use his expertise to determine if the Nazi concentration camps had in fact been death camps. Leuchter went to Auschwitz with his bride (it was their honeymoon!) and discovered no trace of cyanide. His methods were faulty, his conclusions inane. He was discredited and, suddenly, unemployed.

Morris, an elegant and scrupulous filmmaker, is fair both to Leuchter and his aggrieved accusers. The movie makes clear that Mr. Death's sin was not race hatred but hubris; he simply could not, does not doubt his qualifications to do a job beyond his expertise. Morris takes this quietly agitated fellow (he consumes about 40 cups of coffee and 100 cigarettes a day) at face value, letting Leuchter explain how tinkering with science led to his rise and fall. It's the fascinating film equivalent of a humane execution.

VILLAGE VOICE, 1/4/00, p. 101, J. Hoberman

No matter who *Time* sees fit to anoint Man of the Century, it's difficult not to view World War II—and specifically, the Holocaust—as the 20th century's defining event. Indeed, it is the problem that Auschwitz poses to one's faith that creates the context for millennial movies as otherwise disparate as Errol Morris's new documentary and Agnieszka Holland's theological thriller.

Mr. Death, Morris's troubling portrait of the execution-technician and Holocaust-denier Fred Leuchter, began as part of Morris's *Fast, Cheap, and Out of Control* and begins with a tacky thunderstorm out of a grade-Z '50s horror flick. Is Leuchter a mad scientist—or a Frankenstein monster? Son of a man who worked for the Massachusetts penal system, Leuchter went into the family business. Having invented an electrocution "helmet," he went on to design lethal-injection machines, gallows, and gas chambers.

Morris, who more or less invented the ironic documentary, seems to struggle here for an appropriate tone even as he allows Leuchter more than enough rope to hang himself. Leuchter proudly describes his product—death—and frames himself as a humanitarian. His graphic descriptions of electrocution are gruesome enough to wipe the smirk off anyone's face. Without meaning to, this specialist vividly makes the case against capital punishment—foreshadowing the way in which Morris's own treatment of the material is at once snide and reserved, bluntly straightforward and surprisingly oblique.

A self-designated engineer, Leuchter adopts a rational and persuasive tone that soon comes to seem unhinged. Monumentally self-absorbed, his huge ego inflated by 40 cups of coffee a day, the guy is a natural nerd, but Morris piles on the slo-mo to make him look totally crazed. There's a sense that the filmmaker is laughing, although it's not exactly funny when Leuchter reports that he married a waitress he met at Dunkin Donuts and that their honeymoon was spent in Auschwitz. He made the trip after the neo-Nazi white-supremacist Holocaust-denier Ernest Zündel, on trial in Canada for publishing "false history," recruited him as an expert witness on gas chambers.

Searching for proof that there were no mass gassings at Auschwitz, Leuchter illegally scraped the walls of the abandoned gas chambers for traces of cyanide. The expedition was videotaped: Ridiculous-looking Leuchter grins inanely while scrambling around the most death-haunted site in European history. ("It was kind of spooky," he tells Morris in voice-over.) The footage is additionally distressing for it not being clear that this moron is actually Leuchter. (The movie credits cite a "re-enactment cast" and Polish crew.) It does, however, provide a setup for Morris to demolish his subject's methodology.

A Dutch expert who spent 10 years on the archaeology of Auschwitz makes clear Leuchter's total ignorance of both historical and archival evidence. Even more devastating, Morris interviews Leuchter's own chemist, who explains that the samples Leuchter obtained were untestable: Cyanide does not permeate brick but remains, if at all, on the surface, and whatever traces that might have remained after 40-odd years would have been destroyed in the pulverized stone. Leuchter nonetheless used his "research" as the basis for a pseudoscientific report debunking the existence of gas chambers at Auschwitz and other extermination camps.

"We have a hard job executing one man. Why didn't they just shoot them?" Leuchter asks. Genocide is irrational and Leuchter's apparently nonideological willingness to discount the Holocaust because it doesn't "make sense" is one reason the neo-Nazis adore him. His British publisher approvingly calls Leuchter a "simpleton," which is one way of characterizing his willful self-deception. At the end of the movie, Morris is heard (for the first time) asking if Leuchter thinks he could have made a mistake. Mr. Denial doesn't even hear the question. "I did everything possible to substantiate the existence of the gas chambers," he claims—stupidly satisfied in his failure to convince himself.

Also reviewed in:
CHICAGO TRIBUNE, 2/4/00, Friday/p. C, Michael Wilmington
NATION, 1/24/00, p. 36, Stuart Klawans
NEW YORK TIMES, 12/29/99, p. E1, Stephen Holden
VARIETY, 10/18-24/99, p. 40, Todd McCarthy

MOD SQUAD, THE

A Metro-Goldwyn-Mayer Pictures release. *Executive Producer:* Aaron Spelling and David Ladd. *Producer:* Ben Myron, Alan Richie, and Tony Ludwig. *Director:* Scott Silver. *Screenplay:* Stephen Kay, Scott Silver, and Kate Lanier. *Based upon characters created by:* Buddy Ruskin. *Director of Photography:* Ellen Kuras. *Editor:* Dorian Harris. *Music:* BC Smith and Randy Gerston. *Music Editor:* Ellen Segal. *Sound:* Ken Teaney, Marshall Garlington, and (music) Tim Boyle. *Sound Editor:* Andrew DeCristofaro. *Casting:* Christine Sheaks. *Production Designer:* Patrick Sherman. *Art Director:* Andrew Max Cahn. *Set Designer:* Cat Smith. *Set Decorator:* Patricia Elias. *Set Dresser:* Matt Gilbert. *Costumes:* Arianne Phillips. *Make-up:* Jill Cady. *Make-up (Claire Danes):* Kathy Jeung. *Make-up (Special Effects):* Lance Anderson. *Stunt Coordinator:* Shane Dixon. *Running time:* 94 minutes. *MPAA Rating:* R.

CAST: Claire Danes (Julie); Giovanni Ribisi (Pete); Omar Epps (Linc); Dennis Farina (Greer); Josh Brolin (Billy); Steve Harris (Briggs); Richard Jenkins (Mothershed); Larry Brandenburg (Eckford); Lionel Mark Smith (Lanier); Sam McMurray (Tricky); Michael O'Neill (Greene); Stephen T. Kay (Bald Dude); Bodhi Pine Elfman (Gilbert, Skinny Freak); Holmes Osborne (Mr. Cochrane); Dey Young (Mrs. Cochrane); Toby Huss (Red); Michael Lerner (Howard); Monet Mazur (Howard's Girlfriend, Sally); Mariah O'Brien (Tiffany); Steve Chambers, Thomas J. Huff, and Gary McLarty (Howard's Muscle); Jason Maves (Kirk); Casey Verst (Kevin); Ricky Lesser (Kris); Caarmen Llywellyn (Alley Prostitute); Pilar Biggers (Pickup Girl); Khristian Lupo (Tiffany's Boyfriend); Joey Day (Billy's Other Girlfriend); Dean Marisco (Bartender); Skip Evans (Pilot); Eddie Griffin (Sonny).

LOS ANGELES TIMES, 3/26/99, Calendar/p. 1, Kevin Thomas

Don't go to "The Mod Squad" expecting a replication of the TV series that ran from 1968 to 1973, for director Scott Silver and his co-writers have delivered something better than nostalgia. Using the series premise, which takes three young people in trouble with the law and gives them the chance to straighten themselves out by becoming undercover cops, Silver creates a portrait of three engaging individuals trying to get their lives together.

Julie (Claire Danes), arrested for assault; Pete (Giovanni Ribisi), for robbery; and Linc (Omar Epps), for arson, are loners who have been taken under the wing of tough but avuncular Capt. Adam Greer (Dennis Farina) of the LAPD. Defending his decision to give them a second chance, Greer points out to precinct skeptics that "they can get in a thousand places we can't."

Specifically, he wants the trio to investigate reported drug dealing and prostitution at a popular downtown L.A. club. This routine assignment, however, triggers a flurry of plot developments that leaves them in danger from corrupt policemen as well as criminals. The three, who have begun to respond to the concerned discipline and direction of Greer, are suddenly stranded. Their only hope of survival is to pull together, and in fact the entire point of the plot is to build to Linc's observation: "We can't trust anybody; it's just us."

Danes, Ribisi and Epps are all on the threshold of major careers, and there's no way they would have accepted this film if it didn't offer them substantial roles. Julie, who has beaten a drug habit, and Linc have developed the kind of focus and sense of responsibility that suggests a career in law enforcement is theirs if they want it. Pete, a screwed-up Beverly Hills rich kid, who's smart, sweet and likable, is also such a loose cannon you have to wonder how Greer can trust him with any kind of assignment. Should he make a mistake it could cost not only his life but Julie's and Linc's as well.

In Julie, Pete and Linc, who are as well-played as their characters are well-written, we recognize the sense of betrayal and disillusionment they experience, along with their feelings of isolation and vulnerability, as universal, transcending the workings of a thriller plot with a premise that is gimmicky at best. (Did these three, you have to wonder, go through any kind of police academy training before being turned loose on the streets?)

In any event, Silver directs his stars with an assured sense of neo-noir style and pace, set off by some welcome humor, much of it provided by Michael Lerner's eccentric, exuberant rock promoter. Josh Brolin makes as vivid an impression as Danes' smooth, handsome former boyfriend who unexpectedly reenters her life. Farina's strong presence lends credibility to the very notion of his special squad.

Cinematographer Ellen Kuras and production designer Patrick Sherman give the film a cool, deliberately impersonal urban atmosphere, creating the feeling that the film could be unfolding anywhere. And if Silver plays real people against a formula plot, then composer BC Smith plays a remarkably rich score, incorporating a wide range of songs, against an admirably lean movie. "The Mod Squad" is a great-looking picture that zips along with grace, light on its feet but possessed of just enough gravity to allow us to take its people rather than its old TV series premise seriously.

NEW YORK POST, 3/26/99, p. 61, Rod Dreher

Very late in "The Mod Squad," a 94-minute movie that feels as long as a root canal done with a pencil eraser, an obese drug lord (Michael Lerner) asks black Mod Squadder Linc (Omar Epps) to waltz with him to "My Favorite Things." The scene is surrealistically awful, but only slightly less insane than anything else in this catastrophically crummy movie.

It's long past time for Hollywood to quit trying to mine old TV programs for material. Note to studio heads: Quit whining about how mean old Miramax keeps winning all the Oscars, and start making movies as good as theirs. Harvey Weinstein wouldn't have touched this "Mod Squad" project with a pooper-scooper.

Who has any nostalgia for the cop show that ran on ABC-TV from 1968 to '73? Certainly not the teenagers and young adults who are this picture's natural audience. Most of them weren't alive when "The Mod Squad" was on; and—unlike, say, "The Brady Bunch"—the program didn't air in syndication on after-school television.

Besides, the TV cop show's cachet was very much a thing of its moment. The basic idea—cool juvenile delinquents who plea-bargain into the clear by agreeing to work with The Man fighting crime undercover—seemed a lot edgier amid the fevered rebellion of the counterculture.

Thirty years later, that kind of cool has long since been co-opted. A successful fin-de-siecle "Mod Squad" might have imagined a crime-fighting trio from the ghetto and the barrio.

But fine-boned blondie Claire Danes as Julie? What are these people smoking? Dennis Farina (playing their police handler) introduces her in voice-over, saying, "This little girl was as hard as they come." Yeah, maybe clawing her way to the front at a Miu-Miu trunk sale—but it's obvious that sassy Dee from that '70s show "What's Happening" could mop the floor with missy.

Epps doesn't embarrass himself as Linc, probably because the three credited writers (whose names we won't repeat here, as an act of charity) couldn't figure out how to screw up his character. He's the brotha of the trio, but has about as much street cred as Al Roker.

And then there's Giovanni Ribisi, normally a fine actor. Someone forgot to tell him he was no longer playing the retarded guy in "The Other Sister."

The chemistry is nonexistent, the plot hardly more in evidence. As far as I could tell, the three young people are caught in some kind of drug scheme run by evil cops within the force. One scene leads to another for no compelling reason other than the laws of physics—you can't stop time.

It ends up in a preposterous shoot-out at a desolate air hangar, which Danes and Ribisi mock as being a TV cliche—as if acknowledging the hackneyed plotting allowed them some distance from it.

"The Mod Squad" is not offensive, just moronic and dull.

NEWSDAY, 3/26/99, Part II/p. B7, John Anderson

One black. One white. One blonde. So went the teaser for "The Mod Squad" when it was the hippest show on network TV (remember network TV?). It was so excrutiatingly cool that you didn't even care that, yeah, the blonde was obviously white, too, so the whole thing didn't make too much sense. But a lot of things fall apart if you pay too much attention.

So don't pay too much attention to "The Mod Squad" movie, which will evaporate under too much scrutiny. Just appreciate its strangely adolescent purity: the way it plunges into the rolling action in a sweaty stab at immediate gratification; the way it eschews any sense of history among its characters; the way only the most immediate problem (broken romance, broken taillight, broken nail) can get those characters' attention. It may be a facetious re-creation of a TV show that was facetious to begin with. But if "The Mod Squad" were a teenager, it would be in its room listening to Third Eye Blind and piercing its own body parts.

Despite their apparent lapse in judgment, Claire Danes, Giovanni Ribisi and Omar Epps—who play attitudinal delinquents-turned-cops Julie, Pete and Line are the real thing, particularly Ribisi, who's not just a good actor but has a sallow, sleepless look that's endearingly antiglamor. Danes, currently affecting the ubiquitous faux-Gwyneth Paltrow-Cate Blanchett-lank-blonde silhouette, is magnetic, as is Epps, even if he lacks the period militancy of the original Linc Hayes (Clarence Williams III.

None of the characters—who were spared jail in order to work undercover for their soon-to-be-late mentor Greer (Dennis Farina)—is particularly swift. Nor is there much of a pursuable plot—although, amid the music-video posturing and moorless attitude, it really matters very little. It's a style movie and director Scott Silver ("johns") certainly appreciates the retro-cheesy flourishes of an old Quinn-Martin production.

Owing to their youth and hipness, streetwise Julie, rich-boy Pete and homeboy Linc are sent into the nightclubs and side streets of Los Angeles to ferret out drug dealers. What they find is a scheme involving Julie's old boyfriend (Josh Brolin), a drug kingpin (Michael Lerner, camping it up) and a couple of dubious cops (Sam McMurray, Richard Jenkins) whose skeptical view of the Mod Squad may be well-founded, if based on corruption.

Could someone really have championed the idea of making these three head cases into police officers? "Dirty cops, the drug thing," moans Pete. "These things really happen?" For all their alleged grit and hipness, the Mod Squad is a consistently disillusioned bunch. Sex, adults, authority, drivers in Los Angeles—the entire adult world contains the potential for betrayal. And they take it hard.

Only their movie-image view of police work allows them to be such cowboys—an idea Silver might have explored further, although the fact that it's here at all is a miracle.

They don't carry guns, they're "not real cops" as we so often hear and they seem to have a code of honor that precludes their turning in other kids. But they're basically informants. In the '60s, the hip-cop thing was a bit more audacious and counter-counter-cultural than it is today, but it still seems like a dicey premise for a youth-culture movie. Good thing, then, that Silver has laid on the "Homicide"-inspired stutter shots and staggered close-ups and kaleidoscopic quick cuts. It'll give his audiences something to believe in.

VILLAGE VOICE, 4/6/99, p. 121, Justine Elias

You'd pretty much have to be, in the edited-for-television language of the youthquake, out of your ever-loving mind to enjoy this feeble movie version of the Aaron Spelling series, which aired from 1968 to 1973. Along with the obligatory car chases and wacka-wacka-wacka guitar solos, there's a listless plot involving dirty cops, briefcases full of cocaine, and skeevy informants getting thrown against chain-link fences. After an early scene in which the squad's mentor (Dennis Farina) touts his baby-faced charges' ability to infiltrate "a thousand places" ordinary cops cannot, the trio's cover is immediately blown. But then again, even if they hadn't been unmasked, this Mod Squad wouldn't have uncovered anything useful. Ordered to infiltrate a drug-infested nightclub, Julie (Claire Danes, alternately brittle and weepy), a recovering alcoholic, ducks into a restroom to fuck an old acquaintance (Josh Brolin); Pete (a hyperactive Giovanni Ribisi) gets wasted and humps a girl on the dance floor; and Linc (Omar Epps, brooding like he's doing *Richard II*) makes a great show of lurking at the bar and looking as though he's spying on the club's management.

There are enough utterances of the words "freak," "right on," and "man" to suggest that those involved in the production get a kick out of the manners and mores of TV-hippie culture; even the film's cinematography (faded Kodachrome-style blues and grays) and production design (thrift-shop chic) reek of Nixon-era anomie. But if the makers of the new *Mod Squad* had really studied their source material, they would have noticed how weak it was to begin with, and ended this mess after 60, rather than 94, minutes of pain.

Also reviewed in:
CHICAGO TRIBUNE, 3/26/99, Friday/p. A, Mark Caro
NEW YORK TIMES, 3/26/99, p. E20, Lawrence Van Gelder
VARIETY, 3/29-4/4/99, p. 68, Todd McCarthy
WASHINGTON POST, 3/26/99, p. C1, Stephen Hunter
WASHINGTON POST, 3/26/99, Weekend/p. 65, Desson Howe

MOLLY

A Metro-Goldwyn-Mayer release of a Cockamamie/Absolute Entertainment production. *Executive Producer:* Amy Heckerling. *Producer:* William J. MacDonald. *Director:* John Duigan. *Screenplay:* Dick Christie. *Director of Photography:* Gabriel Beristain. *Editor:* Humphrey Dixon. *Music:* Trevor Jones. *Music Editor:* Jim Harrison. *Choreographer:* Joann Fregalette Jansen. *Sound:* Mark Ulano and (music) John Richards. *Sound Editor:* David Giammarco. *Casting:* Amanda Mackey Johnson and Cathy Sandrich. *Production Designer:* Sharon Seymour. *Art Director:* Bruce Allen Miller. *Set Designer:* Robert Harbour. *Set Decorator:* Maggie Martin. *Set Dresser:* Merdyce McClaran. *Special Effects:* J.D. Streett. *Costumes:* Carol Oditz. *Make-up:* Rebecca Alling. *Make-up (Elisabeth Shue):* Desne Holland. *Stunt Coordinator:* Charlie Croughwell. *Running time:* 103 minutes. *MPAA Rating:* PG-13.

CAST: Elisabeth Shue (Molly McKay); Aaron Eckhart (Buck McKay); Jill Hennessy (Susan Brookes); Thomas Jane (Sam); D.W. Moffett (Mark Cottrell); Elizabeth Mitchell (Beverly Trehare); Robert Harper (Doctor Simmons); Elaine Hendrix (Jennifer Thomas); Michael Paul Chan (Domingo); Lucy Liu (Brenda); Jon Pennell (Gary McKay); Sarah Wynter (Julie McKay); Lauren Richter (Molly McKay, 7 Years Old); Tanner Prairie (Buck McKay, 8 Years Old); Nicholas Pryor (Doctor Prentice); Mark Phelan (Highway Patrolman); Jay Acovone (Jack); Julie Ariola (Joyce Lacy); Patricia Belcher (Margaret Duffy); Robert Neches (Randall Prescott); James Krag (Courtney Pratt); Michael Yama and Rachen Assapimonwait (Asian Clients); Musetta Vander (Maxine); Ana Christina (Fiona); Brian George (Director); Roger Davis (Sheriff); Erl (Sex Therapist); Vinny Argiro (Manager); Liz Lang, Kiki Susan Hall, and Heather Bell (Nurses); Michelle Rock (Receptionist); Julio Oscar Mechoso (Fan); Athena Massey (Lauris); Lisa Mollick (Juliet); Terence Heuston (Romeo); Charles Hoyes (1st Base Umpire); Mark Christopher Lawrence (Angels' Manager); Irene Olga Lopez (Carmen); Jennifer O'Dell (Actress); Elisha Choice (Clerk); Kristina Malota (Small Girl); Joe Everett Michaels (Security Guard); Dick Christie (Maitre D'); Alexa Jago (Haughty Woman).

LOS ANGELES TIMES, 10/22/99, Calendar/p. 10, Kevin Thomas

"Molly" seems like a TV movie masquerading as a big-screen feature; its saving grace is that it offers Elisabeth Shue a splendid part in the title role. At 28, Molly, who is autistic but highly functional, has lived in an institution since the death of her parents 15 years before. She has been well cared for and formed a bond with one of the staffers, Sam (Thomas Jane).

Molly suffers from a severe learning disorder, but a cutoff in government spending is thrusting her into the outside world. She is to live, at least temporarily, with her older brother Buck (Aaron Eckhart), who's about to lose his job at a hotshot ad agency.

Only 17 himself when he lost his parents, Buck has had little contact with Molly over the years between Christmas visits. Now he's thrust with the responsibility of a woman with a laundry list of special needs. Buck is a nice guy who tries hard but is relieved when Molly qualifies for an outstanding facility where Sam conveniently now works. What's more, Molly proves to be an excellent candidate for experimental brain surgery that may well render her fully functional in society.

Under the direction of Australia's John Duigan, always a skilled director of actors, Shue is radiant as Molly, at last blossoming, able finally to tap into her full potential as a woman, her erratic, fearful behavior gradually fading away and growing calmer and more assured with each passing day.

Writer Dick Christie deftly manages some worthy consciousness-raising in telling Molly's story. He shows that Buck never realized the level of awareness Molly possessed even when trapped in her autistic state, with its vulnerability to fear and need for rigid order and routine. As Sam points out to Buck, Molly was a person, one he has always cared for deeply even before the seemingly miraculous surgery.

As Molly emerges from her autistic state, she discovers how "normal" people learn to dissemble their true emotions to the extent that they can unknowingly cut themselves off from themselves and, beyond that, from all that is beautiful and sustaining. Christie's attempts at comic relief, however, are hit and miss—some of them amusing, others overly contrived.

"Molly" is a bit too obvious as a message movie for current big-screen tastes, and may well find its most responsive audience when it hits the tube. But it is moving and has been well-crafted with much care, and it allows Shue, Eckhart, Jane and Jill Hennessy as Molly's doctor to make solid impressions.

NEW YORK POST, 10/22/99, p. 57, Lou Lumenick

"Molly" is a moist, heavy-handed vehicle for Elisabeth Shue, who's been looking for a suitable follow-up ever since she hit the jackpot with her Oscar-nominated turn as a hooker in "Leaving Las Vegas."

Good golly, it certainly isn't "Molly," wherein she portrays an autistic young woman who undergoes an experimental operation that allows her—at least temporarily—to function normally.

Even worse, Shue's Molly McKay is required to impersonate a 10-year-old's idea of Scarlett O'Hara and perform an excruciating dance version of "We're Off to See the Wizard."

She also announces that "I have all these emotions I really don't understand"—and boasts that "my vocabulary's grown exponentially."

Yikes.

There are also dreadfully whimsical scenes in which Molly tries to stop a lobster from being boiled at a restaurant—and interrupts the final scene in "Romeo and Juliet" to stop the hero from killing himself.

"Molly" very gingerly explores the relationship between Molly and her brother, who—for reasons that are never satisfactorily explained—is forced to take her in when the nursing home where she's lived for years closes.

Buck (Aaron Eckhart of "In the Company of Men"), a California advertising executive who's been embarrassed by his sister for years, is thrilled when Molly starts to become, in his words, "normal"—and furious when she starts to revert to her former self.

Whenever things threaten to get interesting as when Molly starts thinking about having sex with her brother—the movie shies away. It's so choppily edited that although one scene reveals her parents died in their 40s, it never gets to telling you how they met their demise.

Australian director John Duigan ("Lawn Dogs") can't do much with this shallow and blatantly manipulative variation on "Awakenings" in which every plot development is telegraphed.

Shue comes perilously close to offensive caricature as the afflicted Molly—and her "normal" Molly isn't a whole lot more interesting.

The only performer who survives "Molly" with his dignity intact is Thomas Jane, who's affecting as Sam, a retarded young man who falls for Molly. He demonstrates an understated grace and sensitivity that are otherwise sorely lacking.

NEWSDAY, 10/22/99, Part II/p. B5, Gene Seymour

Not since her Oscar-nominated performance in 1995's "Leaving Las Vegas" has Elisabeth Shue been given the opportunity to do the things she does in "Molly." As a mentally challenged woman made lucid by science, Shue takes the kind of role that even good actors are prone to overplay and brings the kind of guileless sensuality and wounded vulnerability that made her "Vegas" hooker so resonant.

By no means is her Molly as great a performance. But at least it keeps Shue in the running as a major actress in ways that post-"Vegas" cipher roles in "The Saint" and "Deconstructing Harry" didn't. Maybe she'll now get better roles in better movies.

And that means better movies than "Molly," whose core plot suspiciously resembles that of "Charly," the 1968 adaptation of Daniel Keyes' short story, "Flowers for Algernon" about a mentally handicapped man transformed by brain surgery into a genius.

The same thing happens to Molly, except for the "genius" part. Autistic since birth, she's released into the custody of her brother Buck (Aaron Eckhart), a self-absorbed advertising man whose laid-back Angelino lifestyle is upended by having to take care of her. "There's a real person in there," Sam (Thomas Jane), a learning-disabled friend of Molly's, assures Buck. "She's trying to get out." Toward that end, Buck agrees to let a surgeon (Jill Hennessy) perform an operation that will allow Molly's faculties to grow. Within weeks, Molly's mind is surging toward adulthood at an alarming rate, consuming science articles, history books and Jackie Collins novels by the metric ton. Intellectual matters are easier to grasp than emotional ones such as love, jealousy and, worse, the growing fear that this change won't last. (This is also from "Charly," which has either been dissed or forgotten by time.) "Molly" has many funny moments; sometimes intentionally so, more often not.

(Did I hear Sam right when he tells Buck, "I sense things"? If so, did Jane wonder at that moment why he was there?) It's left to Shue to keep the package from being a total waste and, by the inevitable ending, she does some of those amazing things with her eyes that one remembers so well from "Leaving Las Vegas." Watching her face at that moment, your own may start feeling warm. And not from the flu.

Also reviewed in:
NEW YORK TIMES, 10/22/99, p. E17, Stephen Holden
VARIETY, 10/18-24/99, p. 45, Lael Loewenstein

MOMENT OF INNOCENCE, A

A New Yorker Films release of a Pakhshiran/MK2 Productions coproduction. *Executive Producer:* Mohamed Azin. *Producer:* Abolfazi Alagheband. *Director:* Mohsen Makhmalbaf. *Screenplay (Farsi with English subtitles):* Mohsen Makhmalbaf. *Director of Photography:* Mahmoud Kalari. *Editor:* Mohsen Makhmalbaf. *Music:* Nadjid Entezamic. *Sound:* Zezam Kiai. *Art Director:* Reza Alagheband. *Running time:* 78 minutes. *MPAA Rating:* Not Rated.

WITH: Mirhadi Tayebe (Policeman); Ali Bakhshi (Young Director); Ammar Tafti (Young Policeman);   Marjam Mohamadamini (Young Woman);   Mohsen Makhmalbaf (Director); Moharan Zinai Zadeb.

NEW YORK POST, 11/10/99, p. 61, Jonathan Foreman

[*A Moment of Innocence* was reviewed jointly with *The Silence*; see Foreman's review of that film.]

VILLAGE VOICE, 11/16/99, p. 136, Leslie Camhi

Cinephiles may reproach Mohsen Makhmalbaf for changing styles from film to film. But for a man who started out as a political revolutionary, was jailed and tortured by the shah, became a cultural leader of the Iranian revolution, and then its most prominent dissident, formal consistency must seem a minor consideration.

Like Makhmalbaf's other great films, *Moment of Innocence* (1996) maintains uneasy alliance with reality. The director takes as his point of departure the incident that landed him in prison, when, at 17, he stabbed and wounded a policeman. Twenty years later, Makhmalbaf decides to restage the attack with his former target—he and the ex-policeman will each choose and direct young men to play their teenage selves. The result is a meditation-brilliant, humorous, a moving-on history and memory. Perhaps what so disturbed Iranian censors (who shelved the film for years) is the suggestion that the past is up for grabs—a bomb waiting to explode. We long to reconstruct according to our interpretation and have it universally upheld.

The Silence (1998) returns to the remote, quasi-surrealist terrain of the director's magnificent *Gabbeh* (1996) to infinitely lesser effect. Filmed in Tajikistan, it's the story of a blind boy whose mother worries every morning about their coming eviction. Yet he is remarkably carefree, easily distracted on his way to work by strains of music and women's voices. Makhmalbaf's distinctive visual poetry informs this story about the rich gifts to be extracted from a simple life. But his symbolism is often heavy-handed, and as a figure for the artist, the boy's perpetually closed eyes suggest a disturbing, mystical self-enclosure. Let's hope the director moves beyond that.

Also reviewed in:
CHICAGO TRIBUNE, 2/18/00, Friday/p. N, John Petrakis
NATION, 11/29/99, p. 51, Stuart Klawans
NEW YORK TIMES, 10/10/99, p. E5, Stephen Holden
VARIETY, 9/16-22/96, p. 73, Derek Elley

MUMFORD

A Touchstone Pictures release of a Kasdan Pictures production. *Producer:* Charles Okun and Lawrence Kasdan. *Director:* Lawrence Kasdan. *Screenplay:* Lawrence Kasdan. *Director of Photography:* Ericson Core. *Editor:* Carol Littleton and William Steinkamp. *Music:* James Newton Howard. *Music Editor:* Jim Weidman. *Sound:* John Pritchett and (music) Bill Schnee. *Sound Editor:* Robert Grieve. *Casting:* Jennifer Shull. *Production Designer:* Jon Hutman. *Art Director:* Wray Steven Graham. *Set Designer:* Dawn Swiderski. *Set Decorator:* Beth Rubino. *Set Dresser:* Nicholas A. Meeks. *Special Effects:* Ron Bolanowski. *Costumes:* Colleen Atwood. *Make-up:* Leonard Engelman. *Stunt Coordinator:* Charles P. Croughwell. *Running time:* 115 minutes. *MPAA Rating:* R.

CAST: Loren Dean (Mumford); Hope Davis (Sofie Crisp); Jason Lee (Skip Skipperton); Alfre Woodard (Lily); Mary McDonnell (Althea Brockett); Pruitt Taylor Vince (Henry Follett); Zooey Deschanel (Nessa Watkins); Martin Short (Lionel Dillard); David Paymer (Dr. Ernest Delbanco); Jane Adams (Dr. Phyllis Sheeler); Dana Ivey (Mrs. Crisp); Kevin Tighe (Mr. Crisp); Ted Danson (Jeremy Brockett); Jason Ritter (Martin Brockett); Elisabeth Moss (Katie Brockett); Kirk Fox (Gregory); Scott N. Stevens (Ben Crisp); Robert Stack (Himself); Eddie Allen (Gilroy); Rick Dial (Correctional Officer); Joy Carlin (Judge Otto); Helene Cardona (Candy); Priscilla Barnes (Landlady); Kelly Monaco (Landlady's Daughter); Steven Sennett (Young Pharmacist); Amanda Carlin (Mumford's Sister); Randall King (Revenue Officer McLure); Arell Blanton (Brother Timothy); Eddie McClintock (Unsolved Mumford); Molly Schaffer (Attractive Date); Simon Helberg (College Roommate); Lucie Laurier (Pretty Coed); Sam Sako (Edmond Warris); Penny Safranek (Mrs. Warris); David Doty (Samuel Gorbeck); Pamela Paulshock (Sutter's Young Wife); Kathryn Howell (Co-Worker IRS); Sulo Williams (Gas Station Co-Worker); Simone Kerrick (Lionel's Teacher); Barbara E. Tuss (Elizabeth); Ronald B. Morefield (Factory Co-worker); Dick Mallon (Dino); Gea Carr (Jennifer); Chase Allen (Tough #1); Bryan Close (Tough #2); Jim Hiser (Tough #3); Tim Hayes (Prosecutor); Roger Oyama (Revenue Officer); Naomi Sample (Janitor); Joe Peer (Garbage Co-worker); Ron Kaell (Pest Control Co-worker); T.J. Blair (Irate Taxpayer); Holt McCallany (Newcomer); Charles Okun (Charlie).

LOS ANGELES TIMES, 9/24/99, Calendar/p. 1, Kenneth Turan

"Mumford," the latest film from writer-director Lawrence Kasdan, is a slight yet amusing doodle that depends for its success on audience tolerance for the whimsical antics of the small town's worth of genial eccentrics it conjures up.

Which is kind of poetic justice, because the film's protagonist, young Dr. Mumford (Loren Dean), has to be tolerant in his line of work. He's the newest and most successful psychologist in a mythical small town, also called Mumford, where everybody knows everybody else's business.

Maybe it's because he's so young (Dean, last seen in "Enemy of the State," looks barely old enough to drive), but Dr. Mumford's approach to therapy is a bit unconventional. He occasionally visits patients in their homes, throws them out of his office if he thinks things aren't going well, and even gossips about their problems to other townsfolk.

But while no one can argue with Dr. Mumford's success or with his ability to empathize with "wanting to leave a problem behind," there is something undeniably odd in his manner, something reserved, even unknowable. Patients naturally reveal themselves to him, and all he offers in return is a cipher-like noncommittal smile.

Though he's written his share of blockbusters, from "Raiders of the Lost Ark" through "The Bodyguard," much of what Kasdan directs as well as writes has been small-scale and reflective, on the order of "The Big Chill" and "Grand Canyon." His current fable-like effort, which feels like something out of the 1940s, gradually introduces nearly a dozen of the doctor's patients and friends. These include:

* Althea Brockett (Mary McDonnell), wife of rapacious investment banker Jeremy Brockett (Ted Danson), who buys so much merchandise by mail that her house looks like an overstocked storeroom;

* Lily (Alfre Woodard), a friend, not a patient, who runs the town's coffee shop and tells anyone who's interested that she's had it with men;

* Henry Follett ("Heavy's" Pruitt Taylor Vince), the town's overweight pharmacist, who has a strong fantasy life that seems to come right out of James M. Cain's "The Postman Always Rings Twice";

* Lionel Dillard (the always amusing Martin Short), the town's slick and aggressive criminal lawyer;

* Nessa Watkins (Zooey Deschanel, daughter of the fine cinematographer Caleb Deschanel), a teenager who's prone to acting out in very teenage ways;

* Skip Skipperton ("Chasing Amy's" Jason Lee), the skateboarding young billionaire who founded Panda Modem, "the Monarch of Modems," a company that employs just about everybody in Mumford;

* Sophie Crisp (Hope Davis), a sickly but acerbic young woman who has returned to her hometown suffering from chronic fatigue syndrome and general heart-weariness.

Though Mumford the town couldn't be more bucolic (it was shot in several Northern California locales), "Mumford" the movie does have several problems to overcome. Not all of its people are as interesting as the film thinks they are, and this includes an uninvolving performance in the title role. Fortunately, thanks to the idiosyncratic strength of actors Lee and Davis, key characters Skip and Sophie are a pleasure to be around.

Also, the picture's lackadaisical pacing, which pays dividends in its final section, strains our tolerance early on. "Mumford" takes a good long while getting anywhere interesting, counting more on its shaggy dog charm than it perhaps ought to.

But even if it takes awhile to happen, everything comes together nicely by "Mumford's" final credits. Writer-director Kasdan has a nice way with his oddball crew, and though the resolution may be too tidy for some tastes, those who enjoy the old-fashioned Hollywood pleasure of seeing divergent threads neatly pulled together will be more than satisfied.

NEW YORK, 10/4/99, p. 51, Peter Rainer

The new psychologist in quiet, residential Mumford is also named Mumford. As played by Loren Dean, Dr. Mumford is a clean-cut cipher: After only four months on the job, he's the talk of the town, but nobody knows much about him. He's a good listener—that's the key to his rapid rise—and yet he's also a straight shooter. When, for example, a smart-ass local lawyer (Martin Short) takes to the couch and starts singing his own praises, Mumford can't take it and throws him out. Written and directed by Lawrence Kasdan, *Mumford* is about the ways we help, and hide from, one another, and it's a bit too genial, too beneficent. You would think that a movie centering on the deep-rooted troubles of people would be more troubling, but Kasdan assiduously works the middle ground, where he's most content.

What we see is a can-do version of therapy stripped of psychoanalytic jargon or psychotropic drugs (which Mumford, not being an M.D., can't prescribe anyway). It's all about good listening, straight talk, direct action, but Kasdan is also realistic about the benefits. The changes worked by Mumford on his patients are noticeable but not monumental. He might not be doing much more for them than what a chummy bartender or a minister might do. His psychologist's credentials certify his expertise, yet when those credentials are cast in doubt, it hardly seems to matter in the end. People want to talk about their problems, and Mumford hears them out. That makes him something of a guru to the town's many malcontents, who are never listened to.

Most of the movies we've been seeing lately about the underside of white-picket-fence Americana—such as *The Truman Show, Pleasantville*, and *American Beauty*—exaggerate the hypocrisy and the horror. (The exaggeration can be as much of a crock as the sunniness it replaces.) *Mumford* emphasizes the mildness; the underside isn't very different from the topside. For Kasdan, psyches don't run deep, and the goodness people project isn't a false front—as it so often is in those other films—but a true rendering. What's more, people, and their problems, don't really change from era to era. The town of Mumford seems to be caught, along with its inhabitants, in a kind of time warp: It's vaguely fifties, but shards of practically every other decade in the century also show through.

Mumford seems the most old-fashioned when it attempts to be topical. Sofie Crisp (Hope Davis), who has come home to live with her uncomprehending family because she believes she has chronic-fatigue syndrome, gets taken out for walks by Mumford, and their genial strolls are like excursions in Mayberry. Another patient, Althea Brockett (Mary McDonnell), who is married to a high-octane investment banker (Ted Danson) probably more in need of therapy than she is, has a compulsive shopping habit fed by the mail-order mill. She's about as disturbing as a sitcom matron. A chubby pharmacist named Henry Follett (Pruitt Taylor Vince) recounts his sex fantasies to Mumford, which are enacted on the screen as naughty, imaginary film-noir playlets. Skip Skipperton (Jason Lee), who gets around on his skateboard, is virtually friendless because, as the billionaire founder of a computer-modem company based in Mumford, he employs a good part of the townspeople, and they're not comfortable hanging out with the boss. Skip hires Mumford to be his pal, but you get the feeling they'd be pals anyway; they play catch and amble into the hills overlooking the neighborhood. Skip's top-secret project, which he confides to Mumford, is the building of a "gender-specific sex surrogate"—a sex doll that responds like the real thing. The way the film presents this novelty, we might as well be looking at a super-duper student-science-fair project. This movie has a way of cleaning up *everything*.

Kasdan may think he's offering up a jargon-free movie about the ways of therapy, but actually he's operating in a zone of psychobabble. With Mumford acting as their sounding board, his patients come to realize their own innately decent selves; he instinctively knows what they want, and he's nonjudgmental. The purity of their hearts transforms his own. And he's not only a healer but a matchmaker—many of his people end up pairing off. There's a sweetness to some of the stories: Hope Davis, especially, has such a marvelously expressive face that it's painful to see her zonked by whatever is zonking her, and when she warms to Mumford the flesh tones come back into her features and the film briefly becomes magical.

But Mumford himself never transforms before our eyes into something spectacular. Dean plays him like a blank with a mystery in his past. When we find out the mystery, he's *still* a blank. The film is about how we all have it in our power to start over—to leave our lives for another, better one. It's a peculiarly American notion, I suppose, and in this context, it's not very convincing. Although we're meant to regard his life changeover as the exercise of a free man in a free society, Mumford is actually pretty creepy. He comes across more like a con man than like a lost soul who has found redemption; the humbled person he finally becomes seems just another guise. In a darker movie this might be effective, but Kasdan isn't working that side of the street. For him, Mumford is a homespun original whose duplicity serves a higher truth.

What you feel watching *Mumford* is that its director has been bamboozled right along with the good doctor's patients. It's a classic case of transference: Kasdan has fallen in love with his therapist.

NEW YORK POST, 9/24/99, p. 42, Jonathan Foreman

"Mumford" is just delightful, the kind of movie that leaves you with a big silly grin on your face.

Sure, it's as sappy and predictable and implausible as any 1940s comedy. And it's based on one of those vaguely sappy, New-Agey Hollywood premises: A person who listens and really cares is as good a healer as any trained psychotherapist.

But it doesn't matter. "Mumford" is a crowd-pleasing ensemble piece, whose story goes exactly where you want it to. And it's perfectly executed by a fine cast under Lawrence Kasdan's deft direction.

Dr. Mumford (Loren Dean, who uncannily resembles a young Charles Grodin) has recently set up shop as a shrink in a small town, also named Mumford. He's actually a fraud without any training in psychology. Still, his clients like him because he's attentive, unusually frank and completely without professional arrogance.

He's a placid fellow, leading a pleasant enough life. He has more clients than the town's other two shrinks put together. One of the clients, Skip Skipperton (Jason Lee) is a skateboarding, twentysomething computer billionaire, on whom the local economy depends.

He's so lonely he's making a female android in his lab, although he does have an eye for Dr. Mumford's friend and neighbor Lily (Alfre Woodard).

Among Mumford's other clients are an overweight pharmacist (Pruitt Taylor Vince) whose sexual fantasies have wrecked his marriage, and a promiscuous, anorexic high school girl addicted to fashion magazines (Zooey Deschanel).

There's also Althea (Mary McDonnell), whose unhappy marriage to a ruthless big businessman (Ted Danson) has triggered an overwhelming compulsion to order expensive things by mail.

Feeling guilty because he's been indiscreet, telling Skip about his other clients, Mumford reveals to him that he's not really a shrink. Things don't get complicated until Mumford takes on the case of Sofie (Hope Davis), a young woman with one of those fatigue-causing illnesses.

As part of her therapy, he takes her for walks and listens to her like no one has listened to her before. It works, but as she starts to feel better Mumford realizes that he is falling in love with her.

At the same time, Lionel Dillard (Martin Short) a client Mumford turned away because he was so obnoxious, has begun to investigate his background.

Writer-director Lawrence Kasdan, began his career with "Body Heat" and "The Big Chill." Some of his later work like "Grand Canyon" and "French Kiss" has been too preachy or saccharine or both. But here he ensures that scenes that could have been cliché come off as charming and sweet.

Part of Kasdan's recipe for success is in allowing the cast to make the most of small, sharply written roles, without letting any of them overwhelm the film's balance.

There's a price to be paid in that some of the performers have too little time on screen, particularly David Paymer, newcomer Deschanel, and Woodard, the beautiful and talented actress who should have won an Oscar for her work in "Passion Fish."

But Hope Davis deserves much of credit for making "Mumford" work. She's one of those screen presences who looks like a normal person, yet grips your attention as completely as any of the industry's glamour queens.

NEWSDAY, 9/24/99, Part II/p. B3, John Anderson

I laughed my ... well, let's just say I laughed quite a bit at "Mumford," so it would be thoroughly dishonest to blame it for being what it is: a Terrarium Movie-aka, an examination of (human) nature, set in a tiny universe where any intrusion of real nature would cause the entire system to decompose.

But Lawrence Kasdan's genre films, including "Silverado," the underappreciated romantic comedy "French Kiss," or even "The Big Chill" (its own genre, granted), have usually managed to be both Terrarium Movies and charming—which "Mumford" is, largely because of a first-rate assortment of supporting characters who serve as various symbols of the modern condition.

They include a devious egomaniac (Martin Short) who happens to be a lawyer. A sexually obsessing pharmacist (Pruitt Taylor Vince). A shop-at-home-aholic (Mary McDonnell) compensating for her nouveau riche husband (Ted Danson). The local restauranteur/normal person (Alfre Woodard). And my favorite, the computer geek/billionaire (Jason Lee), who spends his many off hours skateboarding around the very village in which he's the major source of employment. "He gets hit by a truck," someone observes, "and the whole town shuts down."

"Mumford" has a rich cast that includes Jane Adams and David Paymer, as two rival therapists who begin to question the credentials of their colleague Dr. Mumford (Loren Dean), who has come to the town that shares his name and become the hottest ticket in psychotherapy. How? By listening, essentially, although not to everyone equally. He "fires" the obnoxious Lionel (Short), for instance, because he simply can't stand him. He tells Skip Skipperton (Lee) things about his other patients' sessions. And he pays particularly close attention to Sofie Crisp (Hope Davis), who seems to be suffering from chronic fatigue syndrome but may just be worn out by her raving witch of a mother.

That all is not quite what it seems with Dr. Mumford isn't a big secret to anyone—not anyone in the audience, at any rate. Although it's apt casting in its way, Dean is something of a blank page, whose Dr. Mumford affects the disinterested wisdom of the beard-stroking Freudian although he has no beard and no particular philosophy, either. Dean is more than balanced out by the delightful Davis, though, who continues to prove herself one of our best actresses, a gifted comedienne and potentially a major star, if Hollywood could ever see that someone with unconventional good looks might still be beautiful (to say nothing of talented).

Davis aside, the problematic point of "Mumford" seems to be that if they were only offered a sympathetic ear, most people could realize what's wrong with themselves and make themselves happy. As Hemingway once wrote about blissful illusions, wouldn't it be pretty to think so. "Mumford" thinks so. It's pretty, too.

VILLAGE VOICE, 10/5/99, p. 201, J. Hoberman

Mumford opens promisingly in black and white, with a burst of jazzy music and a faux-noir voice-over. A hunky young drifter arrives in a "two-bit town," rents a room from a hot and bothered landlady, and ... cut. It's the fantasy of a balding, overweight, sweat-soaked pharmacist free-associating on his psychotherapist's couch. Thus inoculated, we can now proceed to the main fantasy.

Written and directed by the generally soulless veteran genre-mechanic Lawrence Kasdan, *Mumford* is less a midnight fireworks display than a pallid ray of sunshine. Young "Doc" Mumford (Loren Dean) is the most popular shrink in the picture-postcard town of Mumford (don't ask, I won't tell), in the Pacific Northwest. Given that Mumford is a place where everyone knows your name, Doc's methods are a bit unorthodox—perhaps even post-Lacanian. He terminates sessions early and summarily rejects a sleazy lawyer (well-oiled Martin Short) as a patient. He makes house calls and tells tales out of school particularly once he's hired to befriend the local cybermogul Skip (boyish Jason Lee).

Dean has a bluff, pushed-in face and a mildly hard-nosed style. The joke of his analytic personality almost works. *Mumford* is not quite *Northern Exposure,* but it's basically a sitcom way of knowledge. The near-total absence of narrative tension suggests that Doc Mumford might be engaged in some sort of scam. But then isn't psychoanalysis itself a kind of confidence game? In any case, Mumford has already established himself as the town's guardian angel and most accomplished matchmaker—even before he develops a positive chemistry with a young divorcee, Sophie (Hope Davis), suffering a mysterious form of yuppie flu.

Spontaneously applauded by the press in Toronto, *Mumford* is good for a few chuckles and not nearly as egregious or cloying as it might have been. Like last year's *Pleasantville*, it's a pro-Hollywood allegory. A charismatically self-confident fake who is everything to everyone, Doc is the idealized embodiment of popular entertainment. He can cure one patient of her addiction to trashy magazines, while treating another through an infusion of other trashy magazines. (Given his underlying "don't dream, be it" ideology, it would be interesting to see how the good doctor would have counseled Teena Brandon.)

Entertainment gives and entertainment takes away. Appropriately, Mumford's secret identity is exposed by a real television show, *Unsolved Mysteries*. The movie's most magical shot has the shrink walking out into the small-town night and sensing the tele-glow of simultaneous awareness all around him. There's no unconscious in this town, just a wonderful collective illusion. This movie might have been made to illustrate the Frankfurt School koan that mass culture is psychoanalysis in reverse.

Also reviewed in:
CHICAGO TRIBUNE, 9/24/99, Friday/p. A, Michael Wilmington
NEW REPUBLIC, 10/25/99, p. 32, Stanley Kauffmann
NEW YORK TIMES, 9/24/99, p. E9, Stephen Holden
NEW YORKER, 10/4/99, p. 117, David Denby
VARIETY, 9/20-26/99, p. 82, Todd McCarthy
WASHINGTON POST, 9/24/99, p. C5, Stephen Hunter
WASHINGTON POST, 9/24/99, Weekend/p. 46, Desson Howe

MUMMY, THE

A Universal Pictures release of an Alphaville production. *Executive Producer:* Kevin Jarre. *Producer:* James Jacks and Sean Daniel. *Director:* Stephen Sommers. *Screenplay:* Stephen Sommers. *Story:* Stephen Sommers, Lloyd Fonvielle, Kevin Jarre. *Director of Photography:* Adrian Biddle. *Editor:* Bob Duscay and Kelly Matsumoto. *Music:* Jerry Goldsmith. *Music Editor:* Ken Hall. *Sound:* Chris Munro and (music) Bruce Botnick. *Sound Editor:* Leslie Shatz. *Casting:* John Hubbard and Ros Hubbard. *Production Designer:* Allan Cameron. *Art Director:* Tony Reading, Giles Masters, Clifford Robinson, Peter Russell, and Ahmed Abounouom. *Set Decorator:* Peter Howitt. *Special Effects:* Chris Corbould. *Mummy Designer:* Mark Moore, Alex Laurant, Derek Thompson, Benton Jew, Brian O'Connell, Miles Teves, and Carlos Huante. *Costumes:* John Bloomfield. *Make-up:* Aileen Seaton. *Make-up (Brendan Fraser):* Ben Nye Jr. *Stunt Coordinator:* Simon Crane. *Running time:* 134 minutes. *MPAA Rating:* PG-13.

CAST: Brendan Fraser (Rick O'Connell); Rachel Weisz (Evelyn); John Hannah (Jonathan); Kevin J. O'Connor (Beni); Arnold Vosloo (Imhotep); Jonathan Hyde (Egyptologist); Oded Fehr (Ardeth Bay); Omid Djalili (Warden); Erick Avari (Curator); Aharon Ipale (Pharaoh Seti); Patricia Velasquez (Anck-Su-Namun); Carl Chase (Hook); Stephen Dunham (Henderson); Corey Johnson (Daniels); Tuc Watkins (Burns); Bernard Fox (Winston Havelock); Mohammed Afifi (Hangman); Abderrahim El Aadili (Camel Trader).

LOS ANGELES TIMES, 5/7/99, Calendar/p. 1, Kenneth Turan

Oh, to be a young teenage boy with the prospect of "The Mummy" before him.

A silly and cartoonish remake of the 1932 horror classic starring Boris Karloff, this very modern "Mummy" has all the elements dear to the hearts of the juvenile male audience, from an apocalyptic story line and frequent special effects to a smidgen of near-nudity, a smart-aleck attitude and a squirm factor too strong to be ignored.

Energetically written and directed by Stephen Sommers, "The Mummy" is harmless enough and poses no great threat to the moral fiber of America, but it would be nice if it had more to get excited about than the ability to create a massive spooky face out of a mountain of sand.

Sommers and screen story collaborators Lloyd Fonvielle & Kevin Jarre have gone for inspiration to the Indiana Jones films and their predecessors, the classic Saturday matinee serials of decades past. As a result, "The Mummy" is crammed with such familiar genre elements as secret brotherhoods and savage hordes on horseback, ancient booby-traps and characters who exclaim, with as much of a straight face as they can manage, "Beware of the curse" and "What have we done?"

But because this is 1999, the ampage has been upped. While Karloff's original mummy was a danger only to those unfortunate enough to be in his immediate vicinity, this new mummy, once unleashed, would neither eat nor drink nor sleep (that's a quote) until he'd sated his compulsion to decimate the entire planet.

Not for this '90s mummy (South African actor Arnold Vosloo) a pitiful covering of unwinding linen. In fact, as envisioned by Industrial Light & Magic, he isn't even covered by skin but just stumbles around as an ambulatory pile of decaying flesh.

Speaking of decay, the least pleasant aspect of "The Mummy's" modernization is the film's determination to be as yucky as possible. Unlikely to please the squeamish are hungry scarabs, plagues of vermin unleashed on the unwary and several moments that are calculated to have the audience collectively twist and groan in their seats.

The biggest puzzle surrounding "The Mummy," however, is whether it knows how inane its dialogue and situations are. Sometimes, the words seem to be making an attempt to be tongue-in-cheek, while at others the language is just plain inept.

The film's gossipy prologue, set along the Nile in precisely 1290 BC, is as crazily over the top as an Egyptian version of "Hard Copy." Here we meet Imhotep, lord of the dead; Seti, Pharaoh of all Pharaohs; and the great one's mistress, the seductive Anck-Su-Namun (Patricia Velasquez, in an abbreviated costume Cher would envy). "No other man," we are informed in no uncertain terms, "was allowed to touch her"; even accidentally brushing against her in a post office line would presumably be seriously frowned upon.

It turns out that Anck and Imhotep have a thing going on that Seti, despite being Pharaoh of all Pharaohs, doesn't know about. He surprises them together and loses his life for his pains. Anck's reaction is equally deadly: "My body," she tells Seti's suitably thunderstruck guards, "is no longer his temple."

Anck is executed for her passion, but a worse fate is in store for Imhotep. It's a curse so awful, so horrible, that even an eternity locked in a room with Yasser Arafat and Benjamin Netanyahu would be a picnic by comparison. The long and the short of it is that though Imhotep yearns to reincarnate Anck, he must spend forever in Hamunaptra, the City of the Dead, being chewed alive by flesh-eating scarabs and turning into, yes, the Mummy.

Flash-forward to Egypt in the 1920s and the jaunty character of Rick O'Connell (Brendan Fraser). A former officer in the French Foreign Legion who we've glimpsed fighting on the outskirts of Hamunaptra, he is about to be executed in a Cairo prison when a plucky librarian named Evelyn (Rachel Weisz of "Land Girls" and "Swept From the Sea") and her raffish brother Jonathan ("Sliding Doors" John Hannah) save his life.

Evelyn, a budding Egyptologist, wants to go to Hamunaptra to further her research, and only Rick knows how to get there. Also looking for the city are a bunch of loutish, treasure-hunting Americans (is there any other kind?) who are led by Rick's nemesis, the weaselly Beni (Kevin J. O'Connor). Hoping to head everyone off before they unwittingly wake the sleeping monster are the descendants of Seti's plucky guardians, who've been keeping watch over the burial site for 3,000 years without taking so much as an afternoon off.

Given that Evelyn considers Rick "filthy, rude and a complete scoundrel," it's inevitable that they fall in love, especially with her wandering around the sands in a clingy black number thoughtfully provided by helpful desert nomads. Both Weisz and the always agreeable Fraser, who seems to have used this role as a warmup for his upcoming "Dudley Do-Right," are capable and attractive performers, but the film drags its uninspiring action out too long for anyone's good—even for anyone who's not 14.

"Maybe this place is cursed," someone finally says, and maybe that's the simplest explanation after all.

NEW YORK POST, 5/7/99, p. 45, Jonathan Foreman

"The Mummy" is a delightfully old-fashioned adventure yarn that pays no heed to political correctness or modern fashion. If you've missed movies with battles in the desert, biplanes, proud Berber tribesmen, human sacrifice, villainous foreign officials and a handsome hero in jodhpurs and riding boots who is sure to get the girl, then "The Mummy" is for you.

Unlike the Indiana Jones movies it resembles, "The Mummy" feels no need to mix swashbuckling action with New Age mysticism or gross sadism. Instead it remains faithful not just to the original 1932 Bon's Karloff movie but to great pulp novels about lost cities and ancient curses by authors like H. Rider Haggard and Edgar Rice Burroughs.

To his credit, writer-director Stephen Sommers avoids the temptation to make too much fun of the genre. He keeps the camp quotient at about 25 percent, so that the laughs—and there are plenty of them—don't undermine the thrills.

The movie opens with a prologue set in a colorful and impressive—if slightly fake-looking—ancient Egyptian city. A voice-over narrator relates the story of the powerful sorcerer Imhotep, who was caught in an affair with Pharaoh's beautiful mistress, murdered his master, and was then punished with an agonizing, endless living death in a cursed tomb in the cursed city of Hamunaptra.

Three thousand years later, who should come upon this lost city with its fabled wealth but American soldier of fortune Rick O'Connell (Brendan Fraser). He arrives with a battalion of Legionnaires (from Libya, although it was an Italian colony in 1923) that is immediately annihilated by desert tribesmen led by the descendants of the Egyptian high priests.

O'Connell makes it back to Cairo and is about to be hanged for an unspecified crime, when antiquities expert Evelyn (Rachel Weisz) and her roguish brother Jonathan (John Hannah) rescue him so that he can lead them to the lost city.

Once they set out down the Nile, they find themselves in competition with a more ruthless Anglo-American expedition. But when the two expeditions jointly find Hamunaptra, they unleash the undead Imhotep with his awesome powers of destruction. Soon Imhotep turns up in Cairo, assimilating the internal organs of those who've awakened him, commanding an army of zombies, and inflicting the 10 biblical plagues on the city.

If the good guys don't stop him, not only will Imhotep take over the world, but along the way he'll sacrifice Evelyn, so as to bring his ancient mistress back to life. And the only way to stop Imhotep is to defy his magic and his swarms of man-eating beetles, and invoke the spells in an ancient book of incantations hidden at Hamunaptra.

As a traditional roughneck hero, Fraser does early Harrison Ford with verve and assurance. Rachel Weisz, a doll-like English beauty, handles her mostly comic role well and looks great in a veil. But the show is all but stolen by South African actor Arnold Vosloo as the handsome, terrifying Imhotep, who is willing to do anything to restore his lost love.

Sensitive filmgoers accustomed to more pious depictions may be shocked by the traditional if mild and fairly even-handed stereotyping. The men are masculine, the woman is feminine. Americans are mercenary but tough, Brits are eccentric but brave. Berbers are romantic and mysterious, and most other foreigners are corrupt and cowardly but viciously dangerous when in the grip of superstition.

"The Mummy" isn't art. It's cheerful, slightly cheesy entertainment that uses the latest special-effects techniques to breathe life into a venerable film tradition. The best of these is the sandstorm-with-a-face whipped up by Imhotep, but the Harryhausen-esque animated skeletons that hack at Brendan Fraser are remarkably lifelike.

NEWSDAY, 5/7/99, Part II/p. 3, John Anderson

Let's face it: you've seen one attack by decaying corpses, you've seen them all. Oh, the ooze. Oh, the slime. Oh, the frozen grimace of death itself.

But the good news is that "The Mummy"—just the thing for Mother's Day weekend—doesn't remake the old Boris Karloff shocker (or, for that matter, anything out of the Peter Cushing-

Christopher Lee-Lon Chaney Jr. catalog). It remakes a lot of other movies, but never that "Mummy"—no lurching, no bandages, no muffled death threats.

Instead, we get the very watchable Brendan Fraser, the eminently watchable Rachel Weisz and a lot of watchable sidekicks—with the exception of several gross Arab stereotypes for which the filmmakers should be ashamed of themselves—rollicking and rolling their way through crypts, curses, flesh-eating insects and some rather intemperate corpses-come-to-life.

There's seldom been a movie so infatuated with its own special effects, and "The Mummy's" special effects say something about special effects. From the opening sequences—in which the dialogue is subtitled, as if someone knew what ancient Egyptian sounded like—there's a veneer of unreality, imposed by Industrial Light and Magic and the literally hundreds of people listed among the technical credits. The vast cities of Thebes and Hamunaptra, the City of the Dead—where, in introductory flashback, the high priest Imhotep (Arnold Vosloo) is buried alive for his illicit romance with the Pharaoh's mistress, Anck Su Naman (Patricia Velasquez)—look like something out of "Prince of Egypt" rather than a film featuring real (quasi) people. The cartoon quality, of course, excuses the rampant violence, which has the excuse of being, yes, a cartoon.

The people are a little more reality-based. Evelyn (Weisz) is an ancient Egyptian scholar, whom we meet atop a ladder, balancing between book shelves, which she then topples like dominoes—one by one, all around the room, each and every shelf, you can't believe they're showing us the whole thing, which was old when Buster Keaton was a lad—thereby receiving a reprimand from the curator (Erick Avari). He reminds her that she only has the job because of her late parents philanthropy. And he reminds us that the reason "The Mummy" is set in the 20s is because filmmakers can therefore have free rein with such out-of-date devices as ditzy-but-decorative women, smelly, sneaky avaricious Arabs and less-than-progressive but beautiful men.

Namely, Rick O'Connell (Fraser), adventurer, treasure hunter and Indiana Jones clone who's the only living westerner who knows the whereabouts of Hamunaptra. Rick has his pistols and a granite jawline; Evelyn has a vast knowledge of ancient Egypt and a sappy brother named Jonathan (John Hannah). Together, they will unearth whatever there is to unearth.

Luckily, they run across a group of Americans who seem to be on a spiritual retreat from Goldman Sachs and who give the Rick-Evelyn team a run for its money. I say luckily, because someone has to supply the blood and body parts Imhotep is going to need to fully restore himself while unleashing the 10 plagues of Egypt (and thereby incorporating the Old Testament into a movie already fattened with weird references). Add the gross-out sight gags and relentless power of Imhotep and what we've got is one messy and occasionally tedious movie.

But when it's rolling, it's rolling. Director-writer Stephen Sommers knows what to purloin and where, from "Night of the Living Dead" to "Dune" to "Raiders of the Lost Ark" to some John Woo moments during Rick's battles with the Egyptian Ninja warriors led by Ardeth Bay (Oded Fehr), whose name sounds like something out of "Flash Gordon," an old movie serial amply represented by all the cliff-hangers hung throughout "The Mummy."

What you get, essentially, is something like this: Imhotep gives a display of his awesome power. Rick says "We're in trouble." Imhotep immediately gives an even bigger display of his awesome power. Rick says, "We're in big trouble." And so it goes, for most of the film. Not exactly big trouble, admittedly, but on the other hand, you've been warned.

SIGHT AND SOUND, 7/99, p. 48, Kim Newman

Egypt, 1290 BC. The high priest Imhotep conspires with royal mistress Anck-su-Namun to murder Pharaoh Seti. Anck-su-Namun kills herself to escape Pharaoh's guards, trusting Imhotep to raise her from the dead with sorcery. But Imhotep is buried alive in Hamunaptra, the City of the Dead.

In 1923, American Rick O'Connell discovers the now-lost Hamunaptra but he is driven off by tribesmen. Three years later, English wastrel Jonathan brings his librarian sister Evelyn an artefact from Hamunaptra he filched from O'Connell who is imprisoned in Egypt awaiting execution. Evelyn persuades the warden to free O'Connell in exchange for a share of Hamunaptra's treasures. O'Connell's treacherous former comrade Beni guides a rival expedition to the lost city. Both sets of adventurers are attacked by warriors under the command of Ardeth Bay.

At Hamunaptra, Beni's associates open a casket thus invoking a curse, while Evelyn reads aloud from a book which revives the beetle-eaten, mummified Imhotep. Using supernatural powers, Imhotep pursues the adventurers to Cairo, overcoming his skeletal state by killing and absorbing assorted adventurers. Imhotep makes Beni his servant and captures Evelyn, intending to sacrifice her to revive Anck-su-Namun. O'Connell and Jonathan join forces with Bay, whose people have been guarding against Imhotep's return for millennia. At Hamunaptra, Jonathan reads from a book of counter-spells and the sacrifice is interrupted. Imhotep is destroyed and Beni trapped inside the sinking city. O'Connell and Evelyn pledge their love.

Made shortly after Universal Pictures had transformed *Dracula* (1931) and *Frankenstein* (1931) into franchises, Karl Freund's *The Mummy* (1933) combined *Frankenstein*'s star (Boris Karloff) with a rewrite of *Dracula*'s plot, all dressed up with cursed Egyptologists and reincarnated lost loves informed by newspaper legends of 'the curse of Tutankhamun.' In *The Mummy* Karloff is briefly glimpsed as the bandaged relic Imhotep but he spends most of his time as a parchment-faced sorcerer named Ardeth Bey. *The Mummy's Hand* (1940), and three lookalike sequels, stirred footage from the original into the brew, but split the Karloff roles between the bandaged, stumbling killer Kharis (Tom Tyler, later Lon Chaney Jr) and a succession of befezed evil high priests. When Universal licensed remake rights to Hammer, Terence Fisher's *The Mummy* (1959) mixed together elements from all five Universal films. Hammer made unrelated but imitative follow-ups, and *The Mummy*'s homages consist of such unofficial remakes as *La momia azteca* (1957), the porno film *Mummy Dearest* (1990) and *The Mummy Lives* (1993).

Universal has been developing a new *Mummy* for over a decade, with Clive Barker and John Sayles among others attempting scripts. This action-picture retread juggles all the elements, while copping bits of business from almost all previous bandagers. A prologue tongue-cutting is cribbed exactly from previous bandagers. A prologue tongue-cutting is cribbed exactly from Fisher and a sequence with a short-sighted victim menaced by a blurry monster comes from the most despised of all mummy movies, Hammer's negligible *The Mummy's Shroud* (1966).

Director Stephen Sommers *(Deep Rising)* doesn't skimp on ingredients, but overeggs the pudding. The high concept was to do *The Mummy* as a *Raiders of the Lost Ark*-style period adventure. So we have a grinning Brendan Fraser and a fetchingly distressed Rachel Weisz facing a non-stop series of perils: marauding tribesmen, creepy crawlies, living sandstorms, rivers of blood, brainwashed Cairo hordes, a cadre of zombie warriors who take us briefly into Ray Harryhausen territory, and a self-burying city lifted from Howard Hawks' *Land of the Pharaohs* (1955). A side effect of this business is that the plot darts all over North Africa rather casually (making Hamunaptra one of the more accessible lost cities), deploying vast disasters—the plagues of Egypt are tossed in with an amazing disregard for logic, history, and the discrete myth bodies of Egypt and the Israelites—that threaten the end of the world.

With all this going on, there's sadly little time for the atmosphere, mystery and romance that make the Freund movie such an enduring gem. Karloff's Imhotep is a tragic but frightening figure yearning for his lost love; but Arnold Vosloo's smirking sorcerer here is first seen in an ancient version of a *Double Indemnity*-style triangle, and spends his post-resurrection time striding about and ripping body parts off his victims while indulging in CGI mouth-opening and plague-unleashing stunts. Even Anck-su-Namun is a nasty piece of work, coming back to life for a one-on-one slugfest with Evelyn in the amazingly crowded finish.

The Mummy is a mostly entertaining series of theme-park rides, but sorely misses out on magic, with its cardboard villains, fundamentally unlikable heroes, and endless irritating comic bits. It also offers offensive Egyptian stereotypes—the locals are all smelly, venal, lecherous, cowardly, boil-ridden, murderous or ugly here—which were unacceptable in the dignified 1933 movie. At least it manages to be an equal-opportunitities offender by characterising all Brits as stuffy, pompous and humbling and all Yanks as violent, avaricious and philistine.

VILLAGE VOICE, 5/18/99, p. 121, J. Hoberman

"If the plastic arts were put under psychoanalysis, the practice of embalming the dead might turn out to be a fundamental factor in their creation." So André Bazin provocatively began his famous essay "The Ontology of the Photographic Image." It was Bazin's thesis that the artistic impulse was rooted in a "mummy complex"—his playful name for the primitive desire to preserve life through its representation.

Applied to *After Life,* [see Hoberman's review] Bazin's theory imbues Koreeda's vision with an additional poignance. But it won't do much to explicate *The Mummy*—an elaborately high-spirited, low-comic, action-horror vaudeville written and directed by Stephen Sommers. Crudely remaking the 1932 Universal original (and shamelessly pillaging the pharaoh's hoard that is *Raiders of the Lost Ark),* Sommers's *Mummy* substitutes slapdash, if expensive, digital effects (including a dazzlingly orange-hued desert) for the earlier film's clammy atmosphere, and goofy attitudinizing for the dark erotic frisson between Boris Karloff's resurrected corpse and the half-possessed Zita Johann, whom he believes to be the reincarnation of his ancient inamorata.

Doggedly literal-minded, *The Mummy* tunnels into its subject. The action takes place largely in tombs infested by flesh-eating beetles while, not too tightly wrapped, the eponymous monster appears mainly as a manic moldering corpse. Alternately clownish and bemused, Brendan Fraser rehearses his Dudley Do-Right campiness in the requisite role of the brash treasure hunter (it's a footnote to the part he played as muse to James Whale in *Gods and Monsters).* As the season's second ample and tousle-haired Brit gal of the Sahara, Rachel Weisz shares Fraser's sense of humor—she's introduced toppling the bookcases of an entire library. All characters are imagined as types, although the presence of several crude American cowboys can scarcely compensate for the sort of egregious Arab bashing that seems far harder to eradicate in Hollywood than the dread Mr. Mummy.

Like the newly dead of *After Life,* the Mummy is stuck with a single memory—albeit not a happy one. If the monster were placed under psychoanalysis (as he was by film theorist Bruce Kawin), he might be diagnosed as a symptom come to life—an ambulatory "repetition compulsion," forever doomed to reenact the frustrated sacrilege and consummate the passion that got him mummified in the first place. Drop the romantic aspect and that analysis would equally well describe the mindless force behind Sommers's larky remake.

Also reviewed in:
CHICAGO TRIBUNE, 5/7/99, Friday/p. A, Michael Wilmington
NEW YORK TIMES, 5/7/99, p. E13, Stephen Holden
NEW YORKER, 5/10/99, p. 104, Anthony Lane
VARIETY, 5/3-9/99, p. 83, Todd McCarthy
WASHINGTON POST, 5/7/99, Weekend/p. 49, Desson Howe

MUPPETS FROM SPACE

A Columbia Pictures release of a Jim Henson Pictures presentation. *Executive Producer:* Kristine Belson and Stephanie Allain. *Producer:* Brian Henson and Martin G. Baker. *Director:* Tim Hill. *Screenplay:* Jerry Juhl, Joseph Mazzarino, and Ken Kaufman. *Director of Photography:* Alan Caso. *Editor:* Michael A. Stevenson and Richard Pearson. *Music:* Jamshied Sharifi. *Music Editor:* Kim Naves. *Choreographer:* Toni Basil. *Sound:* Carl S. Rudisill and (music) Nick Wollage. *Sound Editor:* Sandy Gendler. *Casting:* Mike Fenton and Allison Cowitt. *Production Designer:* Stephen Marsh. *Art Director:* Alan J. Cassie and William Glenn Davis. *Set Designer:* Christopher Scott Baker, Helen Williams, and Alan Hook. *Set Decorator:* Marthe Pineau. *Set Dresser:* Gregory H. Messer. *Special Effects:* Michael Alan Schorr. *Visual Effects:* Thomas G. Smith. *Muppet Effects:* Tom Newby. *Costumes:* Polly Smith. *Make-up:* Cecelia M. Verardi. *Running time:* 82 minutes. *MPAA Rating:* G.

MUPPET PERFORMERS: Jeffrey Tambor (K. Edgar Singer); F. Murray Abraham (Noah); Rob Schneider (TV Producer); Josh Charles (Agent Barker); Ray Liotta (Gate Guard); David Arquette (Dr. Tucker); Andie MacDowell (Shelley Snipes); Kathy Griffin (Female Armed Guard); Pat Hingle (General Luft); Hollywood Hogan (Man in Black); Veronica Alicino (TV Stage Manager); David Lenthall (Mikey the Cameraman); Richard Fullerton and Mark Joy (Gate Guards); Carl Espy (TV Associate Producer); Deron Barnett (Child); Christine Mullins (Little

Girl); Elaine Nalee (Mashed Potato Lady); Dave Goelz (Gonzo/Bunsen Honeydew/Waldorf/The Birdman); Steve Whitmire (Kermit the Frog/Rizzo the Rat/Beaker/Cosmic Fish #1); Bill Barretta (Pepe the Prawn/Bobo as Rentro/Bubba the Rat/Johnny Fiama/Cosmic Fish #2); Jerry Nelson (Robin/Statler/Ubergonzo); Brian Henson (Dr. Phil Van Neuter/Sal Minella); Kevin Clash (Clifford); Frank Oz (Miss Piggy/Fozzie Bear/Animal/Sam Eagle).

LOS ANGELES TIMES, 7/14/99, Calendar/p. 6, Robin Rauzi

Lest anyone be worried that the folks at the Jim Henson Co. were getting lazy, content to remake classic tales with puppets, along comes "Muppets From Space." Smart and winning, this sixth Muppet feature film comes closest to recapturing the pure joy of the 1979 original, "The Muppet Movie." Kids will like it; parents who grew up with the Muppets may like it even more.

Gonzo—that strange hook-nosed creature referred to as a "whatever" in earlier films—is at the center of this adventure. When he begins to receive messages from outer space though his breakfast cereal, he determines that he is, in fact, an alien. He tries to contact his distant relations, but is quickly intercepted by K. Edgar Singer (Jeffrey Tambor), who heads a secret government agency. It's up to Kermit, Miss Piggy, Fozzie Bear, Rizzo the Rat and Animal to rescue him.

In only 82 minutes, "Muppets From Space" manages more plot than the last four Muppet films combined—largely because it has dropped the song-and-dance numbers. Instead, the movie is set to an infectious funk beat by the Commodores, James Brown, the O'Jays, and Earth Wind and Fire. It's a surprising fit and somehow adds to the Muppets' timeless-yet-modern quality.

Also, unlike "The Muppet Christmas Carol" and "Muppet Treasure Island," in which the Muppets were characters within characters (e.g. Kermit as Bob Cratchit), here they are back to being themselves. They make their way in the world, working odd jobs, living together in a large boarding house. All the favorites are there as well, if only for a minute: The Swedish Chef cooks in the kitchen and Dr. Bunsen Honeydew and Beaker cook up experiments in the basement. (Sadly missing, for some reason, is Gonzo's longtime chicken girlfriend, Camilla.)

The scene-stealer is a new addition to the Muppet clan, a smart-mouthed Spanish shrimp named Pepe, who hollers, "I am not a shrimp! I am a king prawn!" Actor Bill Barretta, who performs Pepe and Bobo the Bear, gives both characters a distinct edge that complements the more familiar Muppets.

As K. Edgar Singer, Tambor plays well with the Muppets, especially Bobo, his giant brown-nosing underling. Andie MacDowell, too, is an appropriate rival for Miss Piggy—attractive and assertive.

None of the other human cameos quite measures up—David Arquette, Kathy Griffin, Ray Liotta, Hollywood (formerly Hulk) Hogan, Pat Hingle. Some are better in their bit parts than others, but it's a far cry from "The Muppet Movie"—made at the height of the popularity of "The Muppet Show"—in which brief appearances by Bob Hope, Richard Pryor, Cloris Leachman and Orson Welles made each scene a potential surprise.

In addition, Steve Martin, Mel Brooks and Dom DeLuise added humor that was goofy for the kids, but nuanced for the grown-ups. The jokes, likewise, aren't quite as adult. But director Tim Hill—making his feature debut—is subtly funny with his visual references to "Close Encounter of the Third Kind," "E.T.: the Extra-Terrestrial" and "The X-Files," all clearly put in for mom and dad.

Twenty years after "The Muppet Movie" and 30 after the beginning of "Sesame Street," there is still life in these creations of felt, foam rubber and fake fur. With care, they will easily entertain and educate a third or fourth generation of children. The magic is back.

NEW YORK POST, 7/14/99, p. 44, Rod Dreher

Anybody who grew up with the Muppet menagerie in the '70s will always have a soft spot for the fuzzy buggers. But on evidence of the likable but draggy and awfully thin "Muppets from Space," Kermit & Co. are showing their age.

Miss Piggy is about five years away from Norma Desmondhood, and Kermit is ready for his pipe and cardigan, Mr. DeMille.

Actually, Gonzo the Great, a heretofore uncelebrated member of the Muppet tribe, gets top billing in this sixth feature-film Muppets outing. The movie starts with a stern Noah (F. Murray Abraham) turning Gonzo away from the Ark because there's only one of him.

It's just a dream, but it reveals Gonzo in the throes of an existential crisis, feeling all alone of his blue crook-nosed species in the universe.

When he begins to receive cryptic messages in his alphabet cereal and elsewhere, Gonzo convinces himself he's a wayward space alien whose intergalactic brethren and sistren are trying to establish contact.

The Muppet family—Kermit, Miss Piggy, Fozzie Bear and others, all of whom share a wonderful tumbledown house—tries to put up with Gonzo's larkiness.

But when Miss Piggy puts Gonzo on a TV show called "UFO Mania," touting him as an alien scoop, the whole world takes notice.

Especially K. Edgar Singer (Jeffrey Tambor), a bumbling but evil space program bureaucrat who is trying to capture a bona fide space creature. He has his goons kidnap Gonzo, and take him to a lab to have his brains removed and analyzed.

Gonzo's roommate, Rizzo the Rat, is also captured, and placed in a cage with other adorable vermin, where a maniacal scientist (David Arquette) performs cruel lab experiments on them.

The plot turns on whether the Muppets will rescue Rizzo and Gonzo, and get Gonzo to the seashore in time to rendezvous with the aliens.

"Muppets from Space" may have a "Babe 2" problem. Though it begins with the cheerful wackiness characteristic of all things Muppetational much of the life and color drains away once Gonzo and Rizzo become captives inside a gray, sterile lab.

Will very small kids—used to antic Muppet clowning—be unduly distressed by the prospect of Gonzo having his brains sucked out? Maybe not, but once into the high-security lab, the movie has to work hard to maintain the lively, colorful sense of celebration you expect from the Muppets.

Fans of Muppet films will miss the original musical numbers, which have been replaced here with a funk standards soundtrack. "Muppets in Space" introduces a new character, Pepe the King Prawn, who shows promise.

There are several star cameos from the likes of Andie MacDowell, Rob Schneider and Ray Liotta, and Muppet vets Dave Goelz, Steve Whitmire, Frank Oz and others do their customary great work providing Muppet voices.

Parents will appreciate having something wholesome and worthwhile, on balance, to take their children to this summer. At the same time, it's a little startling and a little sad to see old friends have such little relevance to contemporary pop culture—especially when the kind of sweet, zany humor they provide to kids, and kids-at-heart, is so desperately needed.

SIGHT AND SOUND, 1/00, p. 58, Leslie Felperin

Unidentifiable creature Gonzo awakes from a dream in which Noah is refusing him access to the ark because there is only one of him. During breakfast at the boarding house Gonzo shares with his other muppet friends, he finds a message warning him to "watch the skies" spelled out in cereal letters. A bolt of lightning induces a vision in Gonzo of two cosmic fish who explain that he's an alien from another planet and that his relatives will be returning soon to retrieve him.

Miss Piggy, newly made an anchorwoman, interviews Gonzo on television about his alien status. Government agent K. Edgar Singer sees the interview and Gonzo and Rizzo are brought by Singer's minions to their headquarters for tests. Fortunately, Kermit and Piggy come to his rescue. Rizzo also escapes and helps free other laboratory rats. Gonzo and his friends travel to Area 51 to meet the mothership from Gonzo's planet. When it arrives, the reunion is joyous. Gonzo contemplates returning home with the other aliens, but ultimately decides to stay behind with his Muppet friends.

The sixth feature-length film in the Muppet franchise, *Muppets from Space* may seem misleadingly titled for fans of the original television show who remember *Pigs in Space,* one of the series' more delicious running spoof skits. Note that central preposition change, because this latest film struggles to get off the ground in every sense. Like its hero Gonzo, abandoned on Earth by his alien brethren, this sweet-natured but unchallenging film seems left behind by the greater sophistication of current children's films and, indeed, by the increasing sophistication of child viewers themselves, who expect flashy effects almost as a birthright.

Now that kids have *The Phantom Menace* and its digitally-created ilk to keep them entertained, cloth-foam-and feather puppets are likely to elicit little more than a yawn except from the very young. Gagwise, only a couple of moments in the middle section match the old muppet gold standard: Rizzo the rat and vermin pals escape their laboratory cage, *Shawshank Redemption* style, through a hole in the wall covered by a Mice Girls poster; the operation to remove Gonzo's brain is stalled while the baddies check to see if his HMO will cover the co-pay. Otherwise, *Muppets from Space* overlabours its parody-cum-homage to *Close Encounters of the Third Kind* (a pretty old target).

With presiding genius Jim Henson now gone, some of the life in the franchise seems to have vanished. Where the series and movies used to pull in pretty big names (Michael Caine, Orson Welles), the human actors here are a sad, B-list lot (Ray Liotta, Andie MacDowell). At least we can be thankful, albeit puzzled, that the film makers have plumped for a soundtrack of welcome if slightly predictable 70s funk classics instead of the usual ersatz showtunes favoured by children's films.

VILLAGE VOICE, 7/20/99, p. 142, Ethan Alter

Ever since Jim Henson's death, his successors have wrestled with a dilemma even more serious than finding a vocal replacement for Kermit: keeping the Muppets relevant to today's audience. After all, compared to a certain computer-generated floppy-eared alien, a talking piece of multicolored cloth seems quaint. But the Henson Company's first solution—plugging the characters into classics like *A Christmas Carol*—resulted in movies that resembled a bad game of Mad Libs. For their latest feature, the filmmakers have concocted an original story, which revolves around Gonzo's discovery that he is—surprise!—not of this Earth. Unfortunately, Gonzo is not the only alien in the movie; all of the characters have been replaced by humorless pod creatures. You know something's wrong when Kermit's first words are "Way to get down with your bad selves." It's painful how hard the filmmakers try to make the Muppets "cool," overlooking the fact that character, not attitude, has always been the source of their appeal. Stripped of their humanlike personae, Kermit and the gang are reduced to something they never were in Papa Henson's day: puppets.

Also reviewed in:
CHICAGO TRIBUNE, 7/14/99, Tempo/p. 1, Michael Wilmington
NEW YORK TIMES, 7/14/99, p. E5, Lawrence Van Gelder
VARIETY, 7/19-25/99, p. 26, Joe Leydon

MUSE, THE

A USA Films release of an October Films presentation. *Executive Producer:* Barry Berg. *Producer:* Herb Nanas. *Director:* Albert Brooks. *Screenplay:* Albert Brooks and Monica Johnson. *Director of Photography:* Thomas Ackerman. *Editor:* Peter Teschner. *Music:* Elton John and Bonnie Greenberg. *Music Editor:* Michael T. Ryan. *Sound:* Kim H. Oritz and (music) Simon Rhodes. *Sound Editor:* Michael J. Benavente. *Casting:* Victoria Burrows. *Production Designer:* Dina Lipton. *Art Director:* Marc Dabe. *Set Designer:* Christopher S. Nushawg. *Set Decorator:* Anne D. McCulley. *Set Dresser:* David Newell. *Costumes:* Betsy Cox. *Make-up:* Nina Kraft. *Make-up (Sharon Stone):* Tricia Sawyer. *Make-up (Andie MacDowell):* Beth Katz. *Make-up (Jeff Bridges):* Edouard Henriquez. *Running time:* 97 minutes. *MPAA Rating:* PG-13.

CAST: Albert Brooks (Steven Phillips); Sharon Stone (Sarah Liddle/Christine); Andie MacDowell (Laura Phillips); Jeff Bridges (Jack Warrick); Mark Feuerstein (Josh Martin); Steven Wright (Stan Spielberg); Bradley Whitford (Hal); Mario Opinato (European Man); Dakin Matthews (Doctor Jacobson); Concetta Tomei (Nurse Rennert); Cybil Shepherd (Herself);

Monica Mikala (Julie Phillips); Jamie Alexis (Mary Phillips); Marnie Shelton (Jennifer); Catherine MacNeal (Anne); Lorenzo Lamas (Himself); Jennifer Tilly (Herself); Skip O'Brien (Universal Studio Guard);   Aude Charles, Ange Billman, and Gannon Daniels (Spielberg Secretaries); Jennie Ventriss (Older Secretary); Bobby Ender (Boy at Sarah's House); Stacy Travis (Phyllis); Michele Crosby Jones (Tiffany Saleswoman); Paul C. Jensen (Four Seasons Porter); Steve Valentine (Four Seasons Assistant Manager); Greg Grunberg (Four Seasons Hotel Security); Rob Reiner (Himself); Alexandra Kaplan (Rob Reiner's Daughter); Steven Anthony Lawrence (Rob Reiner's Son); Wolfgang Puck (Himself); James Cameron (Himself); Jill Tobin (Female Attendant); Martin Scorese (Himself); Walter Wiliamson (Bruno); A.J. Orta (Boy in Cookie Store).

LOS ANGELES TIMES, 8/27/99, Calendar/p. 1, Kenneth Turan

Who hasn't wondered where today's ideas for movies could possibly have come from. Or why some writers seem to flourish while others, equally talented, get bogged down in the slough of despond. Albert Brooks lets you in on a need-to-know show business secret: It's all due to "The Muse."

In Greek mythology, the Muses were nine daughters of Zeus, each responsible for inspiring a different facet of creativity. But what if one of these remarkable women were alive today and found her way to Hollywood? Whom would she be able to help, how would she manage it, and what kind of chaos would it cause to have a Muse on your payroll?

This is the charming conceit of "The Muse," starring, directed by and co-written (with longtime collaborator Monica Johnson) by Brooks, just the person to turn out the sharpest inside Hollywood comedy in quite awhile.

A poet of exasperated comic desperation who grew up in the business (his father was a celebrated performer known as Parkyakarkus), Brooks did stand-up before he went wider with his singular brand of humor and hard-wired it into films like "Mother," "Defending Your Life," "Real Life," "Lost in America" and "Modern Romance."

Because Brooks' comedy is inextricably linked to his on-screen persona of someone frantically trying to cope with existence without benefit of the proper instruction manual, his co-stars are especially important. And when he cast Sharon Stone as Sarah the show-biz Muse, he made a wonderful choice.

Though her career has been built on very different kinds of roles, one of Stone's earliest parts was in another inside Hollywood comedy, the underappreciated "Irreconcilable Differences," and her sure-handed, gleeful work in "The Muse" plays well against Brooks' anxiety and underlines her own real gift for confident verbal humor.

When we first meet Brooks' character, screenwriter Steven Phillips, he's sharing the pride of a Hollywood humanitarian award with his wife, Laura (a warm Andie MacDowell, also well cast), and the thought that he might need the help of a Muse, or anyone else for that matter, is far from his thoughts.

But come the following week, at a lunch with heartless studio executive Josh Martin (a clever Mark Feuerstein) to discuss his new script, the ax falls. "Let me put it in a form that isn't too insulting," Josh says, overflowing with bogus concern. "It's no good."

The script is so no good, it transpires, that it's beyond notes, beyond even keeping Steven on his current studio retainer. "The problem with the script is you," the exec insists, presumably still trying not to be too insulting. "You've lost your edge."

Flailing around for any source of support or advice, Steven goes to see old friend and lately very successful screenwriter Jack Warrick (Jeff Bridges in a rare small role). When he drives up to his pal's Bel-Air house, he sees Jack solicitously putting Sarah into a taxi and though he thinks there's a sexual connection, Jack proceeds to set him straight.

Remember that Greek myth about the Muses?, he asks. "What if I told you they still exist." With Sarah's help, he says, sounding like a convert to creative Viagra, "you'll write better than you've ever written in your whole life." "I want in. This is what I need," Steven insists, setting the stage for a movie that proves, once again, that it pays to be careful what you wish for.

For Sarah turns out to be very much of an L.A. Muse: a bossy, super-demanding prima donna who has to be courted with gifts from Tiffany and set up in rooms—and, mind you, not just any rooms on any floor—in the posh Four Seasons Hotel. Plus, Sarah doesn't seem to really do anything. She just ... inspires.

Naturally, all this makes even Steven's understanding wife, Laura, more than a little suspicious, but Sarah smooths that over. In fact, she's soon making changes in Laura's life as well, and, like the Muse Who Came to Dinner, moving into the Phillips' Pacific Palisades home without any immediate plans for departure.

Brooks and co-writer Johnson have a great ear for the cultural rites and foibles of Hollywood, and "The Muse" is enlivened at numerous points by deft pokes at studio mores, like the humiliations Steven has to endure, including the lack of a coveted drive-on pass, when he wangles an appointment to meet with Steven Spielberg on the Universal lot.

Helping the satiric edge is the film's adroit use of real-life cameos. Studio exec Josh, for instance, takes time out from telling Oscar-nominated Steven he can't write to assure handsome Lorenzo Lamas that his script is brilliant. And both James Cameron and Martin Scorsese make brief, pleasantly self-deprecating appearances as directors who have been helped by Sarah, though when Rob Reiner shows up and thanks her for "American President," it's hard not to wonder who is kidding whom.

Underneath all its humor, "The Muse" manages to casually deal with some fascinating issues, such as the nature of creativity and inspiration and the important role belief has in making things happen. After all, as someone says, "This is Hollywood. People here believe anything."

NEW YORK, 9/6/99, p. 53, Peter Rainer

At his best there is no funnier or sharper comic in America than Albert Brooks, but in his new movie *The Muse*, which he also directed, and co-wrote with Monica Johnson, he's nowhere near top form. He's playing a Hollywood screenwriter, Steven Phillips, who has lost his "edge," and Brooks may be all too invested in the role. Steven has a lumpy, haggard look, and Brooks seems haggard playing him; the portrayal and the person are all of a piece. In his other movies Brooks has often lolled in the doldrums, but there was also something spiky and bearish about him. The classic Brooks persona—best represented by the intrusive TV documentarian in *Real Life* and the rampaging adman in his Winnebago in *Lost in America,* both of which he directed—is part con artist, part crybaby, part heckler, all narcissist. He isn't likable, really, but you put up with him because you never know what zigzag inklings will issue from his brainpan. After awhile, putting up with him becomes part of the fun. His maddening, self-absorbed malaise is more jocose than everybody else's good manners.

The Muse is supposed to show how a washed-up screenwriter recovers his inspiration by hooking up with what appears to be a real-life daughter of Zeus. Sarah (Sharon Stone) is the secret muse of a chosen few in Hollywood; Steven's moviemaker best friend, Jack (Jeff Bridges), whose fortunes have skyrocketed, first turns him on to her services, and subsequently Rob Reiner, James Cameron, and Martin Scorsese, playing themselves, put in appearances as grateful clients. (Scorsese, in a scattershot, rat-a-tat cameo, divulges his latest Sarah-inspired bright idea: a remake of *Raging Bull* featuring "a really thin guy.") Sarah doesn't do any real creative work herself, she's more like a pop-psych therapist, coaxing brainstorms from Steven that revive his confidence and set him on the road to manna.

Beyond being told that Steven isn't good at "action," it's never made clear to us what kind of screenwriter he is or even if, despite his one Oscar nomination, he was ever truly good. And there's a logic to this, since *The Muse,* despite its premise, isn't really about regaining inspiration; it's about being bankable—staying in the game. It's a Hollywood comedy that plays by Hollywood rules: Brooks doesn't question the win-win values of the schlock factory even though, implicitly, his entire career until now has pretty much been a slam at those values.

Brooks is a child of show business—his father, Harry Einstein, worked with Eddie Cantor and was Parkyakarkus on the radio. By the time he'd recorded comedy albums in the mid-seventies like *A Star Is Bought* and made his short films for *Saturday Night Live's* debut season, Brooks had already been a regular on the big TV variety and talk shows hosted by Dean Martin, Ed Sullivan, Merv Griffin, Johnny Carson. Smart and almost deliriously hangdog, Brooks was a screwball prodigy; he appealed to the *Hollywood Palace* crowd, but he also appealed to audiences who wanted to storm the palace.

The Muse might have been redeemed if Brooks had gotten inside his own love-hate romance with the crassness of Hollywood—if he'd made a comedy about the passion for trash that goes hand in hand with the passion for success. This is what Steve Martin achieved in *Bowfinger,* in which a bargain-bin movie producer goes from schlockmeister to auteur and connives his way to glory. What ultimately made *Bowfinger,* for all its satirical jabs, such a sweet experience was the notion that junk dealers crave transcendence, too. In *The Muse,* we observe Steven Phillips tooling around in his Mercedes or admiring his friend's Bel-Air estate, and there's no irony in what we see—no "edge," to co-opt the film's terms. Steve doesn't really get turned on by the business, or even, beyond their commercial potential, by his own ideas. He's a rather blah presence, and so is his wife, Laura, who also gets helped by the muse and is played by Andie MacDowell as if she hadn't quite shaken off a hypnotherapy session.

Sharon Stone is at the opposite extreme from MacDowell: She's motormouthed and strenuously flitty, like a madcap comedian who hasn't figured out why she's being funny. Not that she has a whole lot to work with. Sarah, in exchange for her services, demands from Steven a limo and a suite at the Four Seasons; she calls him at all hours and has him shop for her and do her dry cleaning, and when that isn't enough, she moves into his house. She's like a movie diva ravenous for perks. It's a one-joke role: the muse who came to dinner. What Sarah doesn't comprehend is that her sessions with Steven are basically a lost cause, since, win or lose, he doesn't really have it in him to be happy anyway. Maybe he's meant to, but with Brooks's blotto-ness here, who can tell?

What's happened to Brooks in this movie—and to a lesser extent in his last two films, *Mother* and *Defending Your Life*—can't all be explained away by lackluster material or personal doldrums. It must be that he sees this funk as a higher truth. In the movies he appears in directed by others, such as, most recently, *Out of Sight* and *Critical Care,* he seems unfettered in a way he doesn't with his recent "personal" projects—which bring out in him the sogginess of good intentions. *Mother* got high marks from critics for being more than just a Brooksian mother-son satire, when some of us would have been pleased to have had just that instead of the touchy-feely psychodrama it turned into. *The Muse* wants us to know that we don't need a muse, that we have it in us to be successful if only we trust ourselves. If this movie is a product of that philosophy, we're all in trouble.

NEW YORK POST, 8/27/99, p. 48, Rod Dreher

Who doesn't root for an Albert Brooks movie? His smart, urbane, casually genteel style of comedy is so out of sync with today's fashionably vulgar comic filmmaking as to be positively countercultural. Go, Albert Brooks!

Alas, for those of us starved for evidence that tastefulness and humor are still on speaking terms at the movie house, "The Muse" is a major letdown. It's good for some sterling one-liners and a generous handful of sparkling scenes, but after a strong, peppery start, the movie collapses into bland mush for want of anything interesting to say.

Middle-aged Brooks must be feeling acutely his alienation from the Hollywood mainstream, in which Adam Sandler rakes in kabillions for his pee-pee jokes and a movie featuring sex with a pastry proves a hit with young audiences.

In "The Muse," his usual incarnation of his amusingly neurotic self is called Steven Phillips, and he's a veteran screenwriter in desperate need of a hit. Steven has reached the point in his career where he's receiving awards for his good works, as distinct from his good work. Leaving a ceremony at which her dad was feted, Steven's little girl asks, "Daddy, what's a humanitarian?"

"Somebody who hasn't won the Oscar," he answers. Steven suffers through a humiliating meeting with a callow young Paramount executive (Mark Feuerstein), who tells Steven he's lost his edge and terminates the studio's deal with him.

Desperate, sad-sack Steven visits his hot, Oscar-winning screenwriter friend Jack (Jeff Bridges, of whom we see too little here), seeking the secret of his success. Jack's muse really is a Muse, and she lives in the guest house nearby. The Muse is played by Sharon Stone, who spins the minor goddess as a delicious caricature of a petulant film diva.

The flighty Muse agrees to help Steven write a hit, as she's helped so many of Tinseltown's players (there is a string of very funny cameos by the likes of Rob Reiner, Martin Scorsese and

James Cameron, all kvelling over the Muse's powers)—but only if he'll cater to her every whim. This proves costly, given her exotic tastes (baubles from Tiffany's, a suite at the Four Seasons, and so forth). Eventually, she demands to move in with Steven's family, much to the suspicious chagrin of his wife, Laura (Andie MacDowell).

But the Muse then turns her helpful affections (she's like the Martha Stewart of career redecorating) to Laura, whom she encourages to start her own business—leaving needy and jealous Steven fuming over whether he'll ever be rid of this capricious creature.

"The Muse" is a satire of Hollywood's congenital obnoxiousness and epidemic insecurity. Brooks skewers a movie biz that desperately chases after "edgy," whatever that is, and which fosters creative types so insecure they're willing to believe in anyone, even a New Age mystic who promises to guarantee them a hit.

That's not exactly news, but for the first half of "The Muse," Brooks mines jeweled jibes and insiderly laughs on the shopworn premises. I don't know why Brooks' own muse seems to have hit the road at the halfway point here, but as soon as Sharon Stone moves in with the family, the delicate "Muse" deflates like a souffle.

The beautiful Andie MacDowell's usual dullness sucks the life out of every scene, even with Stone showing real comic flair (who knew?!), doing her energetic best to pump life into this wheezer.

The real problem, though, is that Brooks and co-screenwriter Monica Johnson run out of inspiration long before the finish, leaving "The Muse," which begins so briskly and promisingly, to stumble aimlessly and flat-footedly toward a surprise finale.

That'll teach Brooks to skimp on the tributes from Tiffany's.

NEWSDAY, 8/27/99, Part II/p. B3, John Anderson

In the Medea-suckled Hollywood of Albert Brooks' "The Muse," the words "no edge" have the finality of a death sentence. The ace of spades at the fortune-teller's tent. The suspended click of Madame Defarge's knitting needles. The big thumb down (and not from Roger Ebert). The words mean—well, they mean nothing, actually. And neither does "The Muse."

In his last movie, "Mother," Brooks' long-suffering persona took the form of a middle-aged novelist trying to understand his relationship with Mom—which meant, basically, getting her to love him unconditionally while still seeing things his way. In his new film, Brooks plays a successful screen writer named Steven Phillips, rejected by Hollywood at what should be the pinnacle of his career because he's allegedly lost his "edge." The word is out: His new script stinks. His career is in the toilet. His life has become a Kafkaesque nightmare perpetrated by people who can't spell Kafka-esque.

And so, having spent the first half hour of the movie establishing that the film industry is run by phonies, cretins and parasites, Brooks gives us a hero who spends the rest of the film desperately trying to get Hollywood to love him.

This is one of Brooks' Big Jokes—that a guy as intelligent as Steven would define his own worth by the standards of an industry run on rumor, fear and cowardice (his portrayal, not ours). Or that he'd be so umbilically attached to the place he would resort to the help of a muse named Sarah (Sharon Stone), one of the nine daughters of Zeus, for a little creative inspiration.

Brooks, who has also directed himself in "Lost in America," "Modern Romance" and "Real Life" (all co-written with Monica Johnson, is great at supplying those Big Jokes, which include "Player"-like cameos by Hollywood second-raters and a "break through" script idea that's totally ludicrous and unfilmable. But Brooks neglects the little jokes, the ones that are actually supposed to keep us with the film and entertained.

His character is too-long-suffering, whining in a frequency that only dogs should be able to hear. Stone, however, is spectacular, luminescent even, and fulfills her Carole Lombard potential as the free-loading Sarah, a muse who expects baubles from Tiffany's, a room at the Four Seasons and Steven on call 24 hours a day. This puts something of a strain on the relationship between Steven and wife Laura (a perfectly capable Andie MacDowell), whom Sarah muses into a successful cookie tycoon and supplier to Los Angeles' best restaurants (Wolfgang Puck and Spago must have done Brooks' catering to get this kind of product placement). Steven, meanwhile, struggles to finish the script upon which his entire future rests.

James Cameron, Martin Scorsese and Rob Reiner all traipse through the picture, paying tribute to Sarah and taking her advice religiously (no "Titanic" sequel, Cameron keeps repeating). You wonder if Cameron knew about the scene at the beginning of the film, when Steven accepts his humanitarian award ("It's what they give people who never win the Oscar") and declares "I'm the king of the room!" That they all stare at him blankly suggests the disposability of even the heaviest hitters.

Hollywood's propensity for instant amnesia and the queasy foundation upon which the whole film industry rests. Big ideas, well-thought-out, but not, in "The Muse" at least, particularly funny.

SIGHT AND SOUND, 1/00, p. 58, Mike Higgins

Hollywood screenwriter Steven Phillips is fired by his studio employers because his latest script "lacks edge". Jack, a successful screenwriter friend of Steven's, puts him in touch with Jack's Muse: Sarah, a divine descendent of the god Zeus. She agrees to help Steven as long as he indulges her every whim at his expense, such as a suite at the luxurious Four Seasons Hotel. Steven's wife Laura is initially wary. A trip to an aquarium with Sarah proves inspirational for Steven, but a succession of other writers and filmmakers occupy her time.

Sarah moves in with the Phillips family, and Steven grows envious when she inspires Laura to begin a cookie business. A second trip to the aquarium at Sarah's suggestion enables Steven to complete his screenplay. One day, a visiting psychiatrist and nurse inform Laura and Steven that Sarah is really an escapee from a mental hospital suffering from multiple personality disorder. Sarah disappears. Steven's former studio offers to make his latest screenplay. He meets the new studio executive who commissioned it: Sarah.

For anyone not familiar with the work of the unfairly neglected director Albert Brooks, this hit-and-miss satire on the vulnerability of screenwriters reiterates some of his characteristic themes and techniques. As in *Defending Your Life,* myth supplies the comedy's ironic premise, while the same jaundiced view of the Hollywood machine ventured in *Modern Romance* is reprised here. Struggling screenwriter Steven's fractious relationship with the maternal figure of Sarah the Muse has obvious echoes of Brooks' film *Mother.* Unfortunately, these disparate elements cohere only occasionally in *The Muse,* its flagging *jeu d'esprit* propped up only by a clutch of amusing insider skits.

The sharpest of these involves the director-and-star's familiar persona, the Woody Allenesque harassed *mensch* brimming with rueful one-liners, doing futile battle with his agent and a young, bullish studio executive. However, Steven cuts a much less engaging dash away from the studio lot. Fellow-screenwriter Jack is held up as an object of envy by dint of his huge house and rolling gardens, but given Steven's own conspicuously comfortable lifestyle and happy family, his kvetching rings more than a little hollow. A good deal of the film's comedy falls victim to the same short-sightedness. While a running gag involving Sarah's inspirational collaborations with good sports Martin Scorsese, James Cameron and Rob Reiner, each playing himself, allows them to indulge in some self-deprecating amusement, a redundant sequence featuring 'celebrity' restaurateur Wolfgang Puck illustrates that the star cameo is a device best used sparingly.

Acute though some of these sketches are (Scorsese in particular caricatures himself brilliantly), they're essentially comic asides. Even though Brooks and his co-writer Monica Johnson are capable of satirical insightfullness, neither the screenplay, the casting nor the direction of *The Muse* does their talent justice, The insipid Andie MacDowell's Laura, for example, is disappointing enough, but her venture into cookie-making is nothing more than an extension of the character's twee housewifery. The narrative leans too heavily on the single joke that Sarah appears to inspire everyone but Steven. What's more, *The Muse* itself is barely a cut above the sort of screenplay Sarah eventually rouses Steven to write (a potential Jim Carrey vehicle). Only occasionally does a pertinent, if not quite subversive, observation about the Hollywood creative process puncture the surface.

As played by Sharon Stone, the capricious, demanding and selfish Sarah is less an inspiration to great art in the classical or Romantic sense than an embodiment of the big studios' corrupted values to which screenwriters must pander. (It's one of the film's better jokes that no one doubts she's the real thing.) Stone's grating performance, however, blunts the point. The final revelation that all have been taken in by a mentally disturbed sanatorium escapee plays like the creaking macguffin it patently is. All in all, *The Muse* is a not-dishonourable addition to that genre of Hollywood satire of which *The Player* is the best example, but Brooks can only yet dream of Altman's complexity and assurance.

VILLAGE VOICE, 8/31/99, p. 115, J. Hoberman

The Muse is light summer fare about a middle-aged Hollywood screenwriter so desperate to brainstorm a light summer fare he hires a Greek goddess to help him. The premise feels practically weightless, but because the writer is played by the doggedly earthbound Albert Brooks (who also cowrote and directed), *The Muse* is as consistently funny as it is smartly tooled.

A harried Beverly Hills paterfamilias with a wife (Andie MacDowell) and two little girls, Brooks is introduced at a dinner ceremony where an unimpressed Cybill Shepherd—the golden shiksa he lusted after so long ago in *Taxi Driver*—presents him with Hollywood's lowest form of recognition, a humanitarian award. "I'm the king of the room," he quips to total silence. Nor is it much solace that the award itself, as his daughter observes driving home in the car, "looks like a penis."

That joke may be *The Muse*'s single concession to the youth market, but it serves to direct the movie toward the psychosexual. *The Muse* is a tale of midlife crisis rendered additionally fanciful and self-reflexive for being steeped in Hollywood, as well as generational, paranoia. Brooks is summoned for a story conference in which his typically sarcastic one-liners are jotted down by the same glib young junior executive who has just rejected his latest script (and terminates his contract) for lack of "edge."

The writer's immaculately staged humiliation continues after he requests a meeting with his "old friend" Steven Spielberg. As related by Brooks in his recent Playboy interview, Spielberg refused to allow his onetime buddy to film the scene at Amblin; thus, Brooks was free to invent an imaginary "Spielberg Building" as the site for his character's suitably Kafka-esque confrontation with the omnipotent (and unrepresentable) personification of show business law. But perhaps Spielberg is not the only deity on Mount Olympus. Who, in this premillennial year, doesn't believe in magic, witchcraft, angels? Certainly not screenwriters looking to enchant the American public.

Brooks discovers the equivalent of a secret Hollywood cult when his Oscar-winning, aggressively youthful colleague (Jeff Bridges) reveals that the source of his recent success has been his professional relationship with a real-life muse, which is to say, an actual daughter of Zeus. "I must look pretty pathetic that you have to be soothing me with this fairy tale," Brooks snaps even as he grovels for Bridges to set up a meeting. The muse, as all New York City pedestrians know, is Sharon Stone, and, her sense of fun something of an untapped resource since *Basic Instinct*, the actress spoons down the role like vanilla ice cream.

Stone is a New Age vision of flowing scarves and sparkly outfits, delicate fan-fluttering, and mad, irrevocable impulse. This flighty creature would have doubtless struck mythologist-poet Robert Graves as a vulgar travesty of his Triple Goddess, but having carved out a niche somewhere between a shrink and an agent, she wafts through the movie as pure eau de celeb. Deigning to take on Brooks as a client, she immediately begins demanding her sacrifices. "How long will this muse-ing process take?" he can't help but grumble when she requests a $1700-per-day suite at the Four Seasons and a 24-hour limo—albeit knocking down the price somewhat by taking the chauffeur job himself.

The Muse inspires only indirectly, obliging Brooks to read her whims as oracular. When she insists on going to the Long Beach aquarium, the initially annoyed writer is driven to an epiphany: This could be the location for a possible Jim Carrey movie! (Graciously indulgent, the muse takes credit for Carrey's own breakthrough—"I'm very proud of *The Truman Show*"—before snapping her fingers to erase the admission from Brooks's mind.) As if to confirm her powers, Rob Reiner shows up to thank her profusely for *The American President* and, by way of appreciation, spontaneously hand over his gold watch.

Brooks is instantly jealous and, once the muse sets up residence in his house, becomes all the more so. Stone transfers her attentions to MacDowell, who is encouraged to embark upon a sensational new career even as her resentful husband keeps tripping over the likes of James

Cameron and Martin Scorsese making emergency muse consultations on his dime. The comic nightmare reaches a climax of sorts at a Spago success party thrown for MacDowell—where, however thwarted, insulted, or ignored, Brooks is never at a loss for a line.

Although providing Brooks ample opportunity to exercise his trademark combination of single-mindedly self-absorbed neediness, aggrieved obsession, and tormented, sarcastic self-consciousness, *The Muse* lacks *Mother*'s surefire psychological hook. Closer to *Defending Your Life*, Brooks's earlier parody of the supernaturalist film blanc, *The Muse*'s deceptive slightness masks a darker purpose. The Brooks character is stuck searching for his script's missing third act when the movie unexpectedly provides one. In a plot device more characteristic of Alfred Hitchcock than *American Pie*, *The Muse* uncorks a revelation that radically shifts its conceptual grounds.

Not the least impressive thing about Brooks's light comedy (as well as Stone's comic performance) is that the industry satire deepens on a second viewing. This Hollywood may be no less deluded than the one presented in Steve Martin's *Bowfinger*, but fear and trembling is a far greater part of the equation. Knowing the muse's secret only hones *The Muse*'s edge.

Also reviewed in:
CHICAGO TRIBUNE, 8/27/99, Friday/p. A, Michael Wilmington
NATION, 9/20/99, p. 66, Stuart Klawans
NEW YORK TIMES, 8/27/99, p. E1, Janet Maslin
NEW YORKER, 9/13/99, p. 107, David Denby
VARIETY, 8/16-22/99, p. 28, Todd McCarthy
WASHINGTON POST, 8/27/99, p. C5, Rita Kempley
WASHINGTON POST, 8/27/99, Weekend/p. 37, Desson Howe

MUSIC OF THE HEART

A Miramax Films release of a Craven/Maddalena Films production. *Executive Producers:* Harvey Weinstein, Bob Weinstein, and Amy Slotnick. *Producer:* Marianne Maddalena, Walter Scheuer, Allan Miller, and Susan Kaplan. *Director:* Wes Craven. *Screenplay:* Pamela Gray. *Based on the documentary "Small Wonders" and the life of:* Roberta Guaspari. *Director of Photography:* Peter Deming. *Editor:* Patrick Lussier. *Music:* Mason Daring and Sharon Boyle. *Music Editor:* Bill Abbott. *Sound:* Michael Barosky and (music) John Richards, Tim Boyle, and Dennis Sands. *Sound Editor:* Todd Too. *Casting:* Avy Kaufman. *Production Designer:* Bruce Miller. *Art Director:* Beth Kuhn. *Set Decorator:* George DeTitta, Jr. *Set Dresser:* Kevin Brink, Steve Kriegler, Gary Brink, and Michael Cavotta. *Special Effects:* Al Griswold. *Costumes:* Susan Lyall. *Make-up:* Matiki Anoff. *Make-up (Meryl Streep):* J. Roy Helland. *Stunt Coordinator:* Peter Bucossi. *Running time:* 110 minutes. *MPAA Rating:* PG.

CAST: Meryl Streep (Roberta Guaspari);   Cloris Leachman (Assunta Guaspari);   Henry Dinhoffer (Lexi at 5);   Michael Angarano (Nick at 7);   Robert Ari (Supervisor);   Aidan Quinn (Brian Sinclair);   Teddy Coluca (Taxi Driver);   Angela Bassett (Janet Williams);   Josh Pais (Dennis Rausch);   Barbara Gonzalez (Janet's Secretary);   Jade Yorker (DeSean at 11);   Victoria Gomez (Lucy at 10);   Justin Pierre Edmund (Bongo Kid);   Justin Spaulding (Naeem Adisa at 9);   Zoe Sternbach-Taubman (Guadalupe at 9);   Christopher Lopez (Adam);   Ruben Jared Seraballs (James);   Lucy Nonas-Barnes (Becky Lamb);   Rosalyn Coleman (Mrs. Adisa);   Kevin Miller (Hall Boy);   Hazel J. Medina (Alice Crowley);   Gloria Estefan (Isabel Vasquez);   Iraida Polanco (Landlady);   Asha Sapp (Tanisha);   Betsy Aidem (Mrs. Lamb);   Julie Janney (Flight Attendant);   Cole Hawkins (Lawrence at 5);   Arthur French (Ernie the Electrician);   Edmund Wilkinson (Sheetrock Man);   French Napier (Painter);   Socorro Santiago (Lucy's Mother);   Dominic Walters (Justin Brady);   Jean Luke Figueroa (Ramon Olivas);   Sam Fox Royston (Leonard Hood);   Jane Leeves (Dorothea von Haeften);   Eva Loomis (Vanessa Klein);   Melay Araya (Rachel);   Charlie Hofheimer (Nick at 17);   Kieran Culkin (Lexi at 15);   Asease Korankyi (Shandra Wilson);   Myra Lucretia Taylor (Beverly Wilson);   Olga Merediz (Roman's Mother);   Christian Berreondo

(Ramon's Brother); Leilani Irvin (Myesha); Sophia Guaspari (Rosario); Adam Lefevre (Mr.
Klein); Rafael John Alan Hines (Simon); Jordan Ware (Kenny); Amanda Muchnick (Stephanie);
Ian Quinlan (Carlos); Naeem Jones (Toussaint); Jay O. Sanders (Dan Paxton); Mateo Gomez
(Ramon's Father); Rosalyn Benniman (Woman at Opus Meeting); Leon Addison Brown (Mr.
Adams); Arnold Steinhardt (Himself); Scott Cumberbatch (Lawrence at 15); Majid R. Khaliq
(Naeem at 19); Molly Gia Foresta (Guadalupe at 19); Cristina Gomez (Lucy at 20); Omari
Toomer (DeSean at 21); Tarik Lowe (Teamate #1); Justin Daly (Teamate #2); Isaac Stern
(Himself); Isaiah Sheffer (Carnegie Hall Concert Director); Mark O'Connor (Himself); Michael
Tree (Himself); Charles Veal, Jr. (Himself); Karen Briggs (Herself); Itzhak Perlman (Himself);
Sandra Park (Herself); Diane Monroe (Herself); Joshua Bell (Himself); Jonathan Feldman
(Himself); Dyllon Rogers (Horse Hair Boy); April Davis (First Grade Girl); Anibal Crooklyn
Cuevas (Frog Hair Boy).

LOS ANGELES TIMES, 10/29/99, Calendar/p. 16, John Anderson

[The following review by John Anderson appeared in a slightly different form in
NEWSDAY, 10/29/99, Part II/p. B7.]

Based on the Oscar-nominated documentary "Small Wonders," "Music of the Heart" (formerly
titled "50 Violins") stars Meryl Streep as Roberta Guaspari, the East Harlem violin teacher who
has introduced thousands of underprivileged students to the joys of music.

It includes cameos by violinists Isaac Stern, Itzhak Perlman and Arnold Steinhardt of the
Guarneri Quartet. It marks a fording of genre by horror director Wes Craven. Gloria Estefan
sings the title song. And if it seems as if we're stalling, we are.

A movie with its heart in all the right places—music education in the schools, after all, certainly
deserves such a big wet kiss—"Music of the Heart" is not what anyone would call up-tempo.
Opening with Roberta being dumped by her husband (the Navy officer for whom she presumably
sacrificed her musical career), the film traces her grief-driven move to East Harlem, where she
finagles herself a violin program, fights entrenched attitudes and dubious parents and is vindicated
by a school concert at which the pupils shine and their families are rapturous.

It's quite moving, actually. Then you realize that the movie still has more than an hour to go.
Few moments in Craven's "Nightmare on Elm Street" were as scary as this.

Streep, arguably, has never given a bad performance and she's quite convincing here. Although
hardly as prickly as the real Guaspari of "Small Wonders," Streep's Roberta is no saint. She's
short-tempered and impolitic and she has a spontaneous affair with an old friend (Aidan Quinn),
the one who sends her to East Harlem in the first place.

She's a bit blinkered about the adjustment problems of her sons, both to Harlem and to the
divorce. And she's short with her students, to the point of being chastised by principal Janet
Williams (Angela Bassett), the one who has to cancel Roberta's program 10 years later when the
Board of Education slashes all those "luxury" courses such as music and art.

This sets the stage for the tear-jerking and rather belabored route to a fund-raising concert at
Carnegie Hall, featuring Roberta, her kids and an all-star lineup that even includes bluegrass
genius Mark O'Connor.

By this point, however, luster has long left the film, because of the cheesy quality of both the
script (written, presumably too quickly, by "A Walk on the Moon's" Pamela Gray) and the
production itself (there's an embarrassing series of alternating shots at the end, between
performers on the Carnegie stage and Streep, who may have been in another state entirely when
she was filmed). Basically, "Music of the Heart" has a lot of heart and a lot of music. It just
doesn't sing.

NEW YORK, 11/8/99, p. 64, Peter Rainer

In *Music of the Heart*, directed by Wes Craven, Meryl Streep plays real-life Roberta Guaspari,
a Navy wife who, dumped by her husband, moves to East Harlem and talks her way into a job
teaching violin to school children. (Guaspari's story also was the basis for an Oscar-nominated
documentary, *Small Wonders.*) The film's climax arrives when Roberta's classes, a fixture in the
inner-city schoolscape, are cut. In order to raise money, and a ruckus, she launches a successful

charity fund-raiser at no less than Carnegie Hall, with her students concertizing en masse with the likes of Itzhak Perlman and Isaac Stern (both playing themselves, with Stern presiding over his scenes like Yoda). The tone of inspirational uplift is familiar from movies like *Stand and Deliver* and *Mr. Holland's Opus*—which is to say, it's familiarly awful. Streep plays her role like a rowdy den mother. Everybody involved must think they're striking a blow for the compulsory funding of music education in our schools, but the implicit, and misguided, message here seems to be that superhuman efforts can always save the day. What about all those hardworking, marginalized music teachers who *aren't* chummy with Isaac Stern?

NEW YORK POST, 10/29/99, p. 44, Lou Lumenick

Watching Meryl Streep act can be an exhausting experience—and never more so than during "Music of the Heart," in which she relentlessly tugs at your heartstrings as an imperious violin teacher in an East Harlem elementary school.

Streep never lets you forget that she's acting up a storm in this overwrought tearjerker, directed without a shred of subtlety by horror-meister Wes Craven as part of a deal that includes his delivering "Scream 3" for Christmas.

"Music of the Heart" is based on a documentary about Roberta Guaspari, a real-life teacher who saved her music program from Board of Ed cuts with a benefit concert at Carnegie Hall.

It's been inflated into "Ms. Streep's Opus"—a smug feminist celebration that thrusts Streep front and center in nearly every scene.

She's at least a decade too old to play the Roberta of the first part of the film, a woman whose husband has dumped her for another woman and left her to raise two young sons. Brian (Aidan Quinn), an old friend, suggests she put her musical background to work as a teacher.

Roberta doesn't have any real teaching experience, but she does have 50 kid-size violins and a lot of gumption, so the principal (an improbably glamorous Angela Bassett) hires her as a substitute. Roberta hectors her uninterested students into shape and wins over their sometimes skeptical parents.

The kids and parents are condescendingly treated as cliches, and the top of the film is given over to Roberta's uninteresting love life. (Brian, like all the men here, is a stereotype who bolts when she demands commitment.)

Among the friends helping Roberta mount the benefit are Gloria Estefan (in a cameo as a fellow teacher) and Jane Leeves as violinist Arnold Steinhardt's wife.

Steinhardt, Isaac Stern and Itzhak Perlman appear as themselves in the film's hugely self-congratulatory final sequence, with Streep impressively mimicking violin playing.

It may well get her another Oscar nomination.

SIGHT AND SOUND, 2/00, p. 49, Kay Dickinson

New York, the present. Roberta Guaspari, a navy wife and talented violinist, is abandoned by her husband. Left to fend for herself and her two sons, she is encouraged by her friend Brian (who later becomes her lover) to teach music at an East Harlem high school as a substitute. Eventually she convinces the sceptical principal to give her a permanent job. After initial classroom chaos, Roberta becomes a successful teacher. She buys a house in Harlem, but ends her relationship with Brian because she senses his lack of commitment.

Ten years later, the still-single Roberta is running three violin programmes at various schools on which photo journalist Dorothea is writing an article. Roberta's two sons take out a lonely-hearts advertisement in her name. Dan, who works at a journalism school, replies to it but Roberta remains wary. When her courses suddenly lose their funding, Roberta organises a "Fiddlefest" charity concert, encouraged by Dorothea. Dan and Dorothea help to publicise her plight in various newspapers. When the venue for the Fiddlefest is flooded, Dorothea uses contacts including her husband, the famous violinist Arnold Steinhardt to rebook the concert at Carnegie Hall with guest appearances from several prestigious violinists. The concert is a resounding success and Roberta's project is rescued.

One might wonder why horror director Wes Craven has taken time off from his usual fare to visit that schmaltziest of subgenres, the teacher film, with *Music of the Heart*. Yet after a quarter of a century of making slash'em-ups, one can hardly begrudge him a holiday, even if geared to gain him the respect of the over-25s or maybe even some kind of Oscar nomination. After all, the probable inspiration for *Music of the Heart*, the documentary *Small Wonders* (1996) about the real-life violin teacher Roberta Guaspari, was nominated for Best Documentary. No doubt the box-office success of *Dangerous Minds*, which has virtually the same plot, was also a factor. Something as beloved but staid as the teacher film perhaps works best when abiding by audience expectations. Having bought our tickets, we anticipate a protagonist's battle and an inevitable triumph over an assembly of doubting Thomases. Obedient to these rules, Meryl Streep's naive Roberta enters a rough Harlem school and gradually charms staff and students alike with her plucky post-divorce resolve and her dedication to music education.

However, the standard plotline of a teacher bearing the torch of liberal enlightenment to an educationally bereft group comes off rather dubiously here. Early on, an irate mother withdraws her son from class, indignant at Roberta's blinkered devotion to "the music of dead white men". Roberta wins her over in the end, but there's too much emphasis on endless Bach concerti and not enough on Harlem's own rich musical heritage. Although rap and Hispanic pop pound out intermittently from the soundtrack, they merely act as entry signs into the ghetto during various establishing shots.

Nothing about *Music of the Heart* really merits a two-hour-plus running time or the focus on a single character. Traditionally well worn plot footholds such as student crises (here drive by shootings and domestic violence) are barely put to use. The unwillingness to linger over points of dramatic climax, to wallow in trauma, tragedy and eventual survival leaves us with no one to warm to and no indication of Roberta's specialness as a teacher.

Both Streep and Craven fail to muster the unabashed humanism vital to an enjoyable teacher film. Usually adept at handling ensemble casts, Craven is manifestly less capable when dealing with a solo lead. The plight of the struggling individual is not his forte nor, despite her best efforts, is it Streep's who seems eerily detached from her role. Endowed with less feminist spirit than Bette Davis in *The Corn Is Green* (1945), less tearerking than Robin Williams' character in *Dead Poets Society* and less rootable for than Sidney Poitier in *To Sir, with Love* (1967), Streep leaves us questioning the allure of this supposed pedagogical enchantress who may beguile her pupils, but is unlikely to bewitch anyone living outside the film's narrative.

If the charm of a nativity play (or school concert) multiplies the more one has invested in its child performers, then *Music of the Heart*'s youngsters fail to inspire audience pride. Pamela Gray's rather stingy script hands out only one or two lines per pupil, making rounded characterisation nearly impossible. In fact the coy amateurishness of Isaac Stern, who plays himself towards the film's end, is distinctly more endearing. Apart from Stern's contribution, the ratio of heart-strings to violin strings being plucked is decidedly lop-sided.

VILLAGE VOICE, 11/9/99, p. 148, Jessica Winter

Would that the mind's powers of self-persuasion were stronger, and it were possible to convince oneself that Wes Craven's *Music of the Heart*, or Sam Raimi's recent *For Love of the Game*, is a stealthy joke on complacent audiences hungry for stand-up-and-cheer, Jeanne-Wolf-blurb-goes-here tearjerkers—a gag so unwinking and reckless it would do Andy Kaufman proud. There's promise in smart scary-movie mavens trying their hand at a horror genre of a different, deadlier sort, especially since Craven has already proven his talents as metaphysician: Hankering for escape from his own genre ghetto, he made *Scream,* a slasher flick about slasher flicks. So why not meta-mush this time, starting with that doozy title?

Alas, *Music of the Heart* is inspirational fare of the *Stand and Deliver/Mr. Holland's Opus* variety, glossing the true story of Roberta Guaspari, a navy wife and homemaker who one day found herself dumped for another woman and left to fend for herself and her two young boys. She began teaching violin in an East Harlem elementary school and proved excellent at it, and when city budget cuts lopped her funding, she did what any sensible gal would do—she threw a benefit concert in Carnegie Hall featuring Isaac Stern, Itzhak Perlman, and her students. Solid raw material, but the execution is overcooked: The kids are cutesy, and Meryl Streep as Roberta is hyperaddled and indecisive about which outer-borough accent to affect. Only Angela Bassett (as the no-bullshit principal) really acquits herself, worse off are requisite love interest Aidan Quinn and teacher-in-arms Gloria Estefan. And once we've seen the boom mike wave to us from above for the third time, the possibility that Craven didn't actually bother to direct his actors grows more distinct. The climactic concert should be a shamelessly rousing no-brainer, but Craven subverts the action with endless wowee-zowee reaction shots from the adoring audience; he might as well be filming the Emmys. He might as well be filming anything, really—Craven is asleep at the wheel, having crashed hard from a sugar high.

Also reviewed in:
CHICAGO TRIBUNE, 10/29/99, Friday/p. A, Michael Wilmington
NEW YORK TIMES, 10/29/99, p. E13, Janet Maslin
VARIETY, 9/13-19/99, p. 50, David Stratton
WASHINGTON POST, 10/29/99, p. C1, Stephen Hunter
WASHINGTON POST, 10/29/99, Weekend/p. 41, Desson Howe

MY BEST FIEND: KLAUS KINSKI

A New Yorker Films release of a Werner Herzog Filmproduktion/Cafe Production/Zephir Film co-production for the BBC, in collaboration with WDR, Arte, BR, YLE, with the participation of the Independent Film Channel. *Executive Producer:* Andre Singer and Christine Ruppert. *Producer:* Lucki Stipetic. *Director:* Werner Herzog. *Director of Photography:* Peter Zeitlinger. *Editor:* Joe Bini. *Sound:* Eric Spitzer. *Running time:* 95 minutes. *MPAA Rating:* Not Rated.

WITH: Werner Herzog (Narrator), Claudia Cardinale, Eva Mattes, Beat Presser, Guillermo Rios, Andrés Vicente, Justo González, Benino Moreno Plácido.

LOS ANGELES TIMES, 3/10/00, Calendar/p. 8, Kevin Thomas

Director Werner Herzog and actor Klaus Kinski were made for each other, and their five films together, beginning with their 1972 masterpiece "Aguirre, Wrath of God," reveal Herzog's obsession with exploring the outermost limits of human experience and Kinski's mesmerizing gift in portraying men driven to risk madness in attaining all but impossible goals.

Kinski's Aguirre is a 16th century Spanish conquistador who becomes a cruel, savage monster in his unrelenting search for El Dorado in the wilds of the Peruvian Jungle. Similarly, in the title role of "Fitzcarraldo" (1982) Kinski is an opera-loving Irishman, a failed railroad builder and a struggling ice manufacturer who realizes he must belatedly join the Peruvian rubber boom if he is to realize his absurd dream of building an opera house in Iquitos, which he intends his idol, Enrico Caruso, to inaugurate. To do this, Fitzcarraldo ends up trying to haul a steamship over a mountain in order to harvest rubber.

Herzog and Kinski went on to do a stylish 1978 remake of "Nosferatu," an homage to F.W. Murnau's silent original, with Kinski a perfectly cast Count Dracula. They followed it up with a bleakly brilliant film of Georg Buchner's "Woyzeck," in which Kinski's desperate, haunted army private is a virtual slave to his captain and is made to be a guinea pig in a crazy starvation diet experiment staged by a 19th century Dr. Mengele.

Their partnership ended in 1988 with "Cobra Verde," with Kinski cast as an exploited Brazilian peasant turned bandit, who is sent off to revive the slave trade in West Africa only to end up leading a rebellion against the mad King of Dahomey. "Cobra Verde," widely regarded as a disappointment, was scheduled for a local release only to be withdrawn, never to resurface.

Now Herzog has made a heartfelt homage to Kinski that's alternately funny, tender and downright scary—"My Best Fiend," in which he recounts his tempestuous relationship with the actor. Kinski was every bit as driven as the director but had considerably less self-control, to put it mildly, although Herzog owns up to his own moments of madness, recorded memorably in Les Blank's "Burden of Dreams," his documentary on the making of "Fitzcarraldo."

A world-class egomaniac given to volcanic eruptions of rage on the slightest provocation, Kinski could also be a caring and thoughtful man, as both Eva Mattes and Claudia Cardinale, his leading ladies of "Woyzeck" and "Fitzcarraldo," respectively, attest. Kinski was small and wiry and fair-haired; he had a striking, mobile face with a strong jawline and large, expressive eyes and sensual lips. In rare moments of repose he could seem handsome, but his most characteristic look was that of a tormented gnome. Off-screen he could be charming and likable despite a blazing intensity that could leave one feeling drained and exhausted.

Herzog, who revisits key locales in both his friendship and professional relationship with Kinski, even returning to the Peruvian jungle, can never say he didn't know what he was getting into when he sent Kinski a script of "Aguirre." That's because he actually met the actor when he was only 13, and he and his mother and two brothers were all living, in the mid-1950s, in one room of a bohemian Munich boardinghouse (now restored to Architectural Digest splendor) where Kinski, establishing himself both in films and the theater, was living in a tiny servant's room off the kitchen. Indeed, Herzog's first recollection of Kinski was when he holed himself up in the bathroom in a 48-hour fit of rage during which he wrecked everything he could. (We get to see Kinski in awesomely sustained high dudgeon over a meal not to his liking during the shooting of "Fitzcarraldo.")

Somehow director and actor had enough understanding and respect for each other for long enough periods of time to make their five films, glimpsed in an array of fine clips, although Herzog says that both Kinski and their working relationship were burning out by the end of "Cobra Verde." Herzog sticks only to what he knew of Kinski from first-hand experience and does not speculate as to the source of the actor's stormy emotions.

You couldn't get Kinski, born in 1926 of Polish descent, to open up about his formative years. In any event, he left you with the sense that, whatever he might volunteer, beyond leaving an impression of youthful hardship and poverty, might not be reliable anyway. "My Best Fiend," in fact, leaves you feeling that it is nothing less than a miracle that Herzog was actually able to work with Kinski at all. Herzog nevertheless has said that the notion that Kinski might actually have been insane "can only be justified from a petty and mediocre standpoint." Herzog says simply that Kinski, "the most fascinating actor I know," had "burned out" when he was found dead at 65 in his Northern California home in 1991.

NEW YORK POST, 11/3/99, p. 51, Lou Lumenick

"My Best Fiend—Klaus Kinski" is German director Werner Herzog's fascinating, fond and often bitchy documentary recalling the late star of his most celebrated movies, among them "Aguirre: The Wrath of God" and "Fitzcarraldo."

It's partly a rebuttal to "Kinski Uncut," the actor's posthumously published memoir, in which Kinski described Herzog as "a miserable, hateful, malevolent, avaricious, money-hungry, nasty, sadistic, treacherous, cowardly creep."

Herzog, who appears as the movie's on-screen narrator, reads the description aloud—and insists he helped Kinski, with whom he had a love-hate relationship, come up with those adjectives to help sell the book.

Kinski, he says, was "impulsive, unpredictable, half-mad—a peculiar mixture of physical cowardice and bravery."

The director takes relish in telling horror stories about the famously intense actor, whom he first met when they shared an apartment. Herzog was 13 at the time, and during a tour of his old digs he horrifies the present tenants with a story of how Kinski locked himself in a bathroom for 48 hours and demolished its contents in a murderous rage.

Herzog (whose comments in German are translated by an English voice-over) next met Kinski when he cast the notoriously difficult and egotistical actor as a mad 16th-century conquistador in "Aguirre." When Kinski threatened to walk away from the grueling location in the Bolivian jungles, the director says he threatened to shoot him on the spot.

Kinski stayed put, and the obsessive Herzog returned the favor. He says he declined an offer by the film's Indian extras—who were terrorized by Kinski's screaming fits—to kill the actor.

Most interesting are the recollections of Herzog and co-star Claudia Cardinale of the famously ill-starred production of "Fitzcarraldo, " which was begun with Jason Robards (seen briefly in an outtake with Mick Jagger) in the lead. When Robards took ill while shooting in Bolivia, Herzog contemplated taking the role himself—then begged Kinski, whom he had vowed never to work with again, to take the role.

In terrific production footage, Kinski is seen literally risking his life in one shipboard sequence—and berating the production manager, at length, over the quality of the food he was served.

"My Best Fiend—Klaus Kinski" ends with Herzog admitting, "We complemented one another. I need him as much as he needed him." And their films together prove it.

NEWSDAY, 11/3/99, Part II/p. B9, John Anderson

Any American film buff who came of age in the '90s (and lived in a bubble) might be forgiven for associating the name Werner Herzog solely with documentary moviemaking. Since 1988's "Herdsmen of the Sun," his U.S. releases have been strictly nonfiction, including the Kuwati-oil-fire meditation "Lessons of Darkness" and the true-life POW thriller, "Little Dieter Needs to Fly." It would be just as tidy to conclude that the 1991 death of Klaus Kinski—manic actor and star of five Herzog films, including the Amazon epics "Aguirre, the Wrath of God" and "Fitzcarraldo"—somehow dampened Herzog's passion for feature filmmaking. Tidy, yes, but untrue. "There were films before Kinski, and films after Kinski," Herzog has said, omitting the fact that he's also staged operas, published books and has several fiction films in the works, the first of which should appear early in the new year.

There might, however, be something in the suspicion that the Kinski-Herzog collaboration forged a hellish kind of bond between the actor and the director, whose latest documentary, "My Best Fiend," is a scathingly naked depiction of Kinski—as well as an admission of the creative link between two seminal figures in the New German Cinema.

The film opens with Herzog revisiting the Munich apartment where the 13-year-old and his mother lived—as did a number of the postwar impoverished, including a lunatic named Klaus Kinski, whom Herzog recalls either tearing the apartment up or locking himself in the bathroom for a 48-hour rave. If there's any doubt about the comedy Herzog wants to generate in this film, one need only look at the apartment's current, middle-class owners: The husband smiles politely throughout Herzog's tales of horror; the wife looks as if she wants to have the place repainted.

It is a very funny movie, as well as a harrowing one. Between Herzog's various reminiscences, delivered in the South American jungle setting of his and Kinski's greatest battles, we get Kinski on stage during his early '70s solo "Jesus" tour, where he read poetry from the stage and baited the audience members to the point of violence; during "Aguirre," Herzog's first major film, and on the set of "Fitzcarraldo," having a screaming, uncontrollable fit about God knows what.

There's never any doubt about his intensity off screen, but its manifestation on film is set up ingeniously by the master structuralist Herzog, with outtakes of an aborted version of "Fitzcarraldo" that was cast with Jason Robards and Mick Jagger. Able actors, for sure, but when Kinski's face suddenly appears as the obsessed title character, the wild-haired, white-suited hysteric who wants to build an opera house in the middle of a jungle—and drags a boat over a mountain to do it—we are left in awe of the kinship of compulsive-obsessive that still exists between an actor with no self-control and a director who really did drag that boat over that mountain.

VILLAGE VOICE, 11/9/99, p. 135, J. Hoberman

It will be a remarkable year for cine-histrionics if anything tops Klaus Kinski's posthumous turn in Werner Herzog's *My Best Fiend*—a first-person doc assembled largely from footage taken in the course of the five features they made, being madmen together. Herzog introduces his alter ego on stage, in the lunatic midst of his ranting "Jesus tour," and reveals that, back in the '50s, Kinski briefly occupied the same Munich pension where 13-year-old Herzog lived with his mother and brothers. As anyone who has suffered through *julien donkey-boy* knows, Herzog is no mean performer—his account of the day Kinski trashed the house, locked himself in the toilet, and raved for 48 hours is not the last of *My Best Fiend*'s fantastic tales.

The first and greatest Herzog-Kinski collaboration, *Aguirre, Wrath of God*—shot under extreme conditions in the Amazon rain forest—provided momentum for the less-hallucinated features that followed, including its near-remake *Fitzcarraldo* (where the stars tantrums so rattled the Indian extras that, according to Herzog, they offered to kill Kinski for him). Coaxing a last vehicle from the late actor's outtakes, Herzog—who is only now beginning his first fiction film since working with Kinski on *Cobra Verde* in 1987—offers some evidence of Kinski's "great human warmth," somewhat more of his "rage of unimaginable proportions," and a good demonstration of Kinski's uncanny capacity to corkscrew his way into the frame. There is also a priceless scene of the frighteningly tanned and blond actor in diva mode, graciously swanning through the Telluride Film Festival to greet its insider-director, "Oh, so you're Tom Luddy."

Also reviewed in:
CHICAGO TRIBUNE, 2/11/00, Friday/p. E, John Petrakis
NEW YORK TIMES, 11/5/99, p. E5, Janet Maslin
VARIETY, 5/24-30/99, p. 69, Todd McCarthy

MY BROTHER, MY SISTER, SOLD FOR A FISTFUL OF LIRE

A Jungle Films release. *Director:* Basile Sallustio. *Screenplay (English and Italian subtitles):* Basile Sallustio. *Director of Photography:* Marcello Montarsi, Olivier Pulinckx, and Giuseppi Schifani. *Editor:* Evelyne Bertiau and Anne-Laure Guegan. *Running time:* 90 minutes. *MPAA Rating:* Not Rated.

NEWSDAY, 7/21/99, Part II/p. B9, John Anderson

The intractable Pia Dilisa, the heroine of her nephew's documentary "My Brother, My Sister, Sold for a Fistful of Lire," is like an Alp on wheels. In her hunt for her brother and sister—who were sold away from the family in the early '50s, amid Italy's crushing post-war poverty—she is obstinance on the march, whether it's pursuing a slender thread of information about the post-war adoption market or bringing a dissembling, 96-year-old prelate to the point of hysterical exasperation.

Her story is certainly compelling: The only child left at home when her needy, widowed father gave up his other children to Italy's church-run child-trade network, the 56-year-old woman spent much of her life with no idea what became of her siblings—who became part of a Vatican-connected traffic in Italo-American adoptions that continued until 1965.

But under the direction of Basile Sallustio, all we really get of Dilisa is an almost comic stolidity as she moves stiffly through a narrative whose various episodes that have all the spontaneity of a traffic light—and whose narration (delivered by the director) is portentious to the point of parody. New York, where Dilisa's pursuit eventually brings her, is a "concrete city made of steel, fury and noise ..." A breakthrough with Catholic Charities means that "the long chain of silence is broken at last ... probably a weak link in the fine machinery of lies and secrets." How, Sallustio asks, "can Pia change the course of destiny singlehandedly?" The answer is she can't *change* anything. She certainly can't retrieve the life she might have had with her family. But you do cheer her on in her quest for a reunion, or at least some answers to the fate of her kin.

The one really remarkable scene in the film comes when Dilisa confronts the aging priest who was responsible for coordinating Pope Pius XII's child-welfare program and who reacts to her persistent queries about his role in child traffic with what seems to be guilty outrage. Here, Sallustio just sits back and observes, which is the thing to do. Elsewhere, though, the film meanders wildly—a trip to Ellis Island, where nothing is learned, is a typical waste of footage. And since the viewer also gets the distinct feeling that Sallustio is the engine behind everything—the search as well as the film—there's a sense of contrivance within "My Brother, My Sister" that the director simply can't conceal.

VILLAGE VOICE, 7/27/99, p. 64, Amy Taubin

A more oblique view of the devastation of war, [The reference is to *Cabaret Balkan*; see Taubin's review.] Basile Sallustio's *My Brother, My Sister, Sold for a Fistful of Lire* is a documentary about a middle-aged Italian woman's attempt to find the siblings whom her father gave up for adoption nearly 50 years earlier. During the decade that followed World War II, thousands of Italian children were sent to America for adoption, some because they were orphaned, some because their parents were too poor to feed them. Pia Dilisa, who still lives on the farm where she was born in southern Italy, was troubled since girlhood by the loss of her younger brother and two sisters and also by the persistent rumor that her father had, in fact, sold them to the church.

Accompanied by the filmmaker, a nephew by marriage, she embarks on an investigation that takes her from the local church to the Vatican, and finally to New York and Chicago. Dilisa only wants to find out what became of her sibs, but her questioning inevitably leads to questions about the church's role and specifically about who profited from these adoptions. The treatment she receives from almost all officials of the church, ranging from shamefaced stonewalling to blatant attacks on her motives and integrity, is the meat of the film. The lure is Dilisa herself, a sturdy, forthright, intelligent woman who's more than a match for all these men with their self-importance and their secrecy. Like all investigations, *My Brother, My Sister* has an element of suspense, but I have to say, I never doubted that God was on Dilisa's side.

Also reviewed in:
NEW YORK TIMES, 7/21/99, p. E5, Stephen Holden

MY FAVORITE MARTIAN

A Walt Disney Pictures release of a Jerry Leider/Robert Shapiro production. *Executive Producer:* Barry Bernardi. *Producer:* Robert Shapiro, Jerry Leider, and Marc Toberoff. *Director:* Donald Petrie. *Screenplay:* Deanna Oliver and Sherri Stoner. *Based on the TV series by:* John L. Greene. *Director of Photography:* Thomas Ackerman. *Editor:* Malcolm Campbell. *Music:* John Debney. *Music Editor:* Andrew Silver. *Sound:* Robert J. Anderson, Jr. and (music) Dennis Sands. *Sound Editor:* Michael Hilkene. *Casting:* Janet Hirshenson and Jane Jenkins. *Production Designer:* Sandy Veneziano. *Art Director:* Christopher Burian-Mohr. *Set Designer:* Nancy Mickleberry. *Set Decorator:* Michael J. Taylor. *Set Dresser:* Sara Gardner Gail. *Special Effects:* Rich Ratliff. *Visual Effects:* Phil Tippett and John T. Van Vliet. *Animatronic Martian Effects:* Alec Gillis and Tom Woodruff, Jr. *Costumes:* Hope Hanafin and Nancy McArdle. *Make-up:* Kenny Myers. *Stunt Coordinator:* Ernie Orsatti and Noon Orsatti. *Running time:* 88 minutes. *MPAA Rating:* PG.

CAST: Jeff Daniels (Tim O'Hara); Christopher Lloyd ("Uncle Martin"); Elizabeth Hurley (Brace Channing); Daryl Hannah (Lizzie); Christine Ebersole (Mrs. Lorlei Brown); Wallace Shawn (Dr. Elliott Coleye); Michael Lerner (Ben Channing, Newspaper Editor); Jeremy Hotz (Billy); T.K. Carter (Lenny); Shelley Malil (Felix); Ray Walston (Armitan, "Neenerd"); Zoot (Himself); Dawn Maxey (Salesgirl); Steven Anthony Lawrence (Nurplex Kid); Michael Chieffio (Earl Metz); Troy Evans (Captain Dalton); Arthur Senzy (Commander Murdoch); Charles Chun (Radar Controller); Michael Dempsey (Van Gundy); David St. James (Prescott); Dee Ann Helsel (Dressing Room Woman); Joe Garrett (Hardware Store Employee); Lorin McRaley (Cool Dude); Ken Thorley (KTSC Floor Manager); Tom Hallick (Howard Greenly); Barry Pearl (News Director); Buck Kartalian (Senior Citizen Muscle Man); Steve Bond (The SETI Group Driver); Sylvester Terkay (Huge Guard); Michael Bailey Smith (Big Guard); Jean-Luc Martin (Guard at Gate); Christian Keiber (Guard at Clearing); Richard Kleber (Mr. Butz); Debra Christofferson (Mrs. Butz); Howard H. Ross (Newspaper Man); Frank Cavestani (Tanning Contest Emcee).

LOS ANGELES TIMES, 2/12/99, Calendar/p. 15, Kevin Thomas

"My Favorite Martian" lands on the big screen with a thud, but if Disney is lucky, this may not matter much to children, who could be captivated by the clever special effects, or to diehard fans of the popular TV series of the same name that ran on CBS from 1963 to 1966.

Nonetheless, the film is loud and labored— its sense of adventure kicking in so late that it scarcely matters.

When a Martian (Christopher Lloyd) lands by the ocean near Santa Barbara, feckless local TV reporter Tim O'Hara (Jeff Daniels), a nice-guys-finish-last prototype, naturally figures that here's his chance to save his career in a really big way. But the Martian, who has the ability to assume human form, among many other magical gifts, wants to keep his presence secret, insisting on passing himself off as Tim's Uncle Martin.

This keys no end of wrangling and a plethora of incidents of little interest, eventually making Uncle Martin the target of an obsessed scientist (Wallace Shawn).   Meanwhile, Tim is so bewitched by the beautiful but clueless daughter (Elizabeth Hurley) of his erstwhile fire-breathing boss (Michael Lerner) that he overlooks lovely station camerawoman Daryl Hannah.

The film is so busy, contrived and clunky that at times its strained writers (Sherri Stoner and Deanna Oliver) and heavy-handed director (Donald Petrie) seem to defy you to pay attention to it. (Penelope Spheeris' "The Beverly Hillbillies," which brings an affectionate, sophisticated sensibility to bear upon cornball material, remains the standard by which all films from old TV series are measured.)

The cast of reliables is game, serving to remind us that they have all been seen to better advantage in numerous other pictures. The only truly inspired touch in the entire film is the way in which the TV series' martian, Ray Walston, has been integrated into the plot. What's more, Walston displays a crisp wit and blithe sense of whimsy otherwise lacking in this loser.

NEW YORK POST, 2/12/99, p. 53, Rod Dreher

Disney, originally set to release "My Favorite Martian" last summer, finally pulls the agonizingly dreadful movie off its shelf and unloads it into theaters nationwide this weekend. Note to real-life "A Civil Action" lawyer Jan Schlichtmann: Rush right down to your local cineplex, buddy, because toxic dumping this outrageous has got to be actionable.

"My Favorite Martian" is the kind of leering, obnoxious picture that seizes you by the neck and gnaws at your skull like a giant, snot-nosed, Ritalin-deprived child who won't let up until he chews through to the soft, creamy center and sucks it clean. It does have a certain rare purity: You don't often see movies so pristinely crapulous, so 100 percent laugh-free, so utterly and completely unenjoyable.

The picture is based on a lousy 1960s TV show about a space alien who secretly keeps house with a tolerant schmo, posing as his uncle. The schmo is Tim O'Hara (Jeff Daniels), and the alien, who goes by the name Uncle Martin, is impersonated by Christopher Lloyd. They "meet cute" when TV producer Tim and Brace (Elizabeth Hurley), the turbo-bitchy on-air reporter on whom he has a massive crush, investigate what may have been a UFO crash.

The Martian stows away in Tim's trunk and is discovered the next day wreaking havoc in Tim's living room. Martin initially is a hostile nut case, but gradually Tim is won over by his wacky charm.

At least it works on somebody.

Must be the antennae. It's certainly not his silvery spacesuit, which has a voice (provided by Wayne Knight) of its own, and dances around spastically, making irritating wisecracks and framing product placements shameless even by Hollywood's low standards. Daryl Hannah plays the supposedly homely camerawoman who carries a torch for dorky Tim, and despite her ridiculous pigtails, she fails to convince that she's a Betty to Hurley's Veronica.

Blame "Casper" scribes Sherri Stoner and Deanna Oliver for the hopeless screenplay, which embarrassingly cribs its denouement from "E.T." For heaven's sake, if you can't figure out how to extricate yourself from your own asinine plotting, don't steal from the best-known kiddie alien film ever.

In any case, an evil scientist played by Wallace Shawn conspires with a secretive government heavy (Ray Walston, TV's original Uncle Martin) to capture the Martian and perform gruesome experiments on him—none more gruesome, alas, than the agonizing endurance test the movie performs on the audience.

Despite some mild sexual innuendo, "My Favorite Martian" appears to be meant for children. Not the Rev. Jerry Falwell's children, mind you. The movie's about a male couple who share a house, with the one who poses as an uncle telling his handsome blond "nephew" after an intense embrace that he's "never had feelings for a human before." What's up with that?

NEWSDAY, 2/12/99, Part II/p. B3, John Anderson

That's five years and $17 trillion well spent!"
The budget on "My Favorite Martian"? No, but certainly the best line in the movie: A NASA engineer's verdict on a Pathfinder-style probe, which runs out of juice only microns away from crossing one more sand dune and discovering the Martian equivalent of Las Vegas.

It's not just the film's best joke, it's virtually the only joke in this remake of the less-than-lamented '60s sitcom, in which a marooned man from Mars (Ray Walston) moved in with an addled reporter (Bill Bixby), both of whom tried with enormous success to keep his identity a secret. It lasted two years and then faded into Nick-at-Nite-less obscurity— that is, until fate rescued it via Hollywood's ongoing hunger for regurgitated TV comedies.

Yes, there are a few giggles, most of the "Uranus" variety best appreciated by the under-7 set. Unfortunately, that particular target audience wasn't taken into consideration when the rest of the movie was put together. There's too much, well, stupid violence, sexual innuendo, scary monsters and one sequence involving a shrunken car and a trip through a toilet bowl ... which of course will be tickling the single-digit set. Who will have to be accompanied by their parents. Who may see things differently.

Basically, what someone should have asked is this: Would "My Favorite Martian" have been a good idea for a movie without the television connection?

And the answer, of course, is no. A mischief-making creature from another planet moving in with a naive and besieged earthling? Gee, what a concept. If you wanted, you could argue that "I Love Lucy" used the same idea in 1951. These days, any similar proposal— lacking the TV pedigree— would be used by a studio's script readers to carefully wrap fish. But then, had there been any actual thinking here, they wouldn't have had to reach back to 1963 for a motive to make a movie.

Christopher Lloyd, lacking any of Walston's wryness, tries very hard with very little as the Martian-cum-Uncle Martin, who sports twin antennae on his head ("Most of our young these days are born cable-ready") and drives TV news producer Tim O'Hara (Jeff Daniels) to distraction.

Daniels, looking like he rues the day he ever heard the words "Dumb and Dumber," drives a New Frontier-inspired Plymouth Valiant (it's got to be a '64), has a thing for the aptly named on-air personality Brace Channing (Elizabeth Hurley) and thinks he has the story of the century. He's dissuaded from exposing Uncle Martin, whose presence on Earth has already been detected by an evil scientist (Wallace Shawn) and a mysterious government agent, played as is the habit of this particular genre— by the original series' star, Ray Walston.

There's a Milky Way's worth of talent lying stagnant in "My Favorite Martian," from the underused Hurley to Shawn, who must use his salary from these throwaway movies to go off and write plays like "The Designated Mourner." Actually, "My Favorite Martian" would have been a good movie for little kids had its makers eschewed the crude. As is, the movie is simply and desperately frantic— either in its efforts to find a joke or to just get through to the end credits, either of which is a noble pursuit indeed.

SIGHT AND SOUND, 6/99, p. 48, Kim Newman

Television-news producer Tim O'Hara, fired for embarrassing newsreader Brace Channing, notices a crash-landing spaceship which shrinks to toy size. Tim takes the ship home, and its pilot— a Martian who can assume human form by chewing special gum, and is bonded to his sentient spacesuit—Zoot hides in his car. Disguised as Tim, the Martian picks up on Tim's attraction to co-worker Lizzie and kisses her.

The Martian then adopts the identity of Tim's Uncle Martin, and enlists Tim's help in repairing his spaceship. Hoping to win his job back with a big scoop, Tim videotapes the Martian in alien form, but, growing fond of him, decides against exposing him. Brace— contacted by Dr Coleye, a scientist with the Search for Extra-Terrestrial Intelligence programme—steals the tapes and plans to broadcast them. Attempting to get them back, Martin and Tim are captured by Coleye. Martin seems to die under dissection. Lizzie chews some of the alien's gum and briefly becomes a giant monster, enabling Tim to resuscitate Martin. Coleye's boss Armitan turns out to be a Martian stranded on earth since 1964 and hitches a ride back with Martin. Coleye is transformed into an alien and captured for study. Tim and Lizzie begin to have a relationship, whereupon Martin returns and announces that he is moving in with Tim.

Thirty-five years on, the 1963-65 television sitcom *My Favorite Martian*, which starred Bill Bixby and Ray Walston as Tim and Martin, stands out among similarly plotted couple-with-a-secret domestic fantasy shows *(Bewitched, I Dream of Jeannie, My Mother the Car)* for its thinly disguised gay subtext. Each week, the harried Tim, desperate to blend in, would try to conceal the truth about his flamboyant, epicene, antennae sprouting 'uncle' from his regulation suburban neighbours. This late 90s Disney remake is clearly designed to haul in parents who remember the old show and their pre-teen kids. (However, parents of children young enough to get anything out of this frenetic mess are more likely to remember a brief 1973 cartoon reprise, which effectively outed Martin by casting camp icon Jonathan Harris from *Lost in Space* in the role.)

Because it needs to dilute any lavender flavour, there is a great deal of heterosexual faffing about: Jeff Daniels is torn between Daryl Hannah and a nasty-but-dim Elizabeth Hurley while Christopher Lloyd gets to make time with Christine Ebersole's glamorous widow. Admittedly, it's not quite as obnoxious in its romantic attitudes as *The Mask* in which the glamorous but shallow girl rather than the sensitive but mousy one turns out to be right for the hero—but the non-stop up-and-down relationships of characters do add to the generally overwrought feel of the film.

As usual, the score samples the original theme tune, and the surviving star (Walston, who played the Martian in the series) gets a cameo appearance which establishes the film as a combination of sequel to and remake of the old television show, though there's a sense that everyone wants to get it over with quickly. (Walston doesn't even sprout his trademark antennae.) There's also an attempt, as with DC Comics' revamp of the 50s Martian Manhunter character, to square the show's silly premise with what is now generally known about Mars. In an opening snippet that is wittier than the rest of the film a terrestrial probe conks out after "exploring nine new rocks", while just over the rim lies a vast Martian civilisation.

Apart from a few references (not even jokes) that evoke *Men in Black, E.T* and *The X Files, My Favorite Martian* largely comprises special effects slapstick set-pieces that manage to be resolutely unfunny and faintly ugly: a shrinking car escaping through the sewers and enlarging itself in a toilet bowl, for instance, or Martin 'drunk' on ice cream producing a messy telekinetic food hurricane.

Amid such energetic charmlessness, Jeff Daniels is prodded into one of his rare misjudged performances as the harassed human, while Christopher Lloyd cuts loose in search of laughs that aren't in the script. The CGI living spacesuit Zoot ranks as one of the most irritating miracles of special effects ever to make it into a film, and its non-stop incoherent patter is weighed down with earth references that render its alien origin meaningless. ("Are you one of the Spice Girls?" it asks a hulking guard.)

A decade ago, the legacy of fantasy sitcoms was evoked by such films as *Splash* and *Earth Girls Are Easy*, which at least tried to adapt to the different social milieu of their time. Now, the old stuff is served straight, filtered through those 80s movies. That mad-scientist subplot, which didn't work in *Splash* but has unaccountably become its most imitated aspect, is trotted out again here—with more hideous effects and loud noises than the mind can stand ladled in. Only the total collapse of Hollywood can save us from a reprise of *My Mother the Car*.

Also reviewed in:
CHICAGO TRIBUNE, 2/12/99, Friday/p. A, Michael Wilmington
NEW YORK TIMES, 2/12/99, p. E20, Lawrence Van Gelder
VARIETY, 2/15-21/99, p. 58, Joe Leydon
WASHINGTON POST, 2/12/99, Weekend/p. 47, Desson Howe

MY LIFE SO FAR

A Miramax Films release in association with the Scottish Arts Council Lottery Fund of an Enigma production in association with Hudson Film. *Executive Producer:* Bob Weinstein, Harvey Weinstein, and Paul Webster. *Producer:* David Puttnam and Steve Norris. *Director:* Hugh Hudson. *Screenplay:* Simon Donald. *Based on the book "Son of Adam" by:* Denis Forman. *Director of Photography:* Bernard Lutic. *Editor:* Scott Thomas. *Music:* Howard Blake. *Sound:* Ken Weston, Rudi Buckle, and (music) Mike Ross. *Casting:* Patsy Pollock. *Production Designer:* Andy Harris. *Art Director:* John Frankish and Alain Chennaux. *Set Decorator:* Gillie Delap. *Costumes:* Emma Porteous. *Make-up:* Caroline Noble. *Stunt Coordinator:* Paul Weston, Pat Bailey, Del Baker, John McQuillian. *Running time:* 93 minutes. *MPAA Rating:* PG-13.

CAST: Colin Firth (Edward); Rosemary Harris (Gamma); Irene Jacob (Heloise); Mary Elizabeth Mastrantonio (Moira); Malcolm McDowell (Uncle Morris); Robert Norman (Fraser); Tcheky Karyo (Gabriel Chenoux); Kelly MacDonald (Elspeth); Roddy McDonald (Rollo); Daniel Baird (Finlay); Jennifer Fergie (Brenda); Kirsten Smith (Meg); Sean Scanlan (Andrew Burns); John Bett (Uncle Crawford); Anne Lacey (Aunt Eunice); Olivia Preston (Debs Haig); Sarah Turner (Ruth Haig); Moray Hunter (Jim Skelly); Jimmy Logan (Tom Skelly); Brendan Gleeson (Jim Menzies); Eileen McCallum (Mrs. Henderson); Carmen Pieraccini (Sissie); Elaine Ellis (Aggie); Julie Wilson Nimmo (Sarah); Elspeth McNaughton (Marnie); Freddie Jones (Reverend Finlayson); Stewart Forrest (Donald Burns); Caroline Spencer (Cassie Burns); Ralph Riach (Sir David Drummond); Andrea Hart (Lillian); Terry Neason (Hector); Jenni Keenan-Green (Caroline); Jenny Foulds (Frances); Clive Russell (Tramp); Paul Young (Doctor Gebbie); Pamela Kelly (Euphemia Gebbie); Eric Barlow (Miner); Gordon McCorkell (Young Miner); Neil McMenemy (Miner's Son); Lorenzo Boni (Baby Fraser); Robyn Cochrane (Baby Brenda); Ross Anderson (Young Rollo); Joanne Turner (Young Debs Haig); Nicole O'Neill (Young Elspeth); Victoria Campbell (Young Meg); George Knight (Old Gardener).

CHRISTIAN SCIENCE MONITOR, 7/23/99, p. 15, David Sterritt

Family dramas and comedies and have always drawn crowds to the movies. Their continuing appeal is illustrated by the important roles they play in recent offerings as different as the excellent "Election" and the offbeat "Limbo." More stories emphasizing the eccentricities in family ties are now arriving on multiplex screens.

My Life So Far plugs into one of the most commonplace family-film formats: the "Life With Father" scenario, based on memories of long-ago experiences with a dad who's not quite ... perfect.

The way his son Fraser remembers him, Edward Pettigrew is one part genius and one part screwball. Edward divides his time between flamboyant schemes—experimenting with airplanes, building Europe's only moss factory—and self-centered whims that drive his household crazy.

Other strong personalities inhabit the bucolic 1920s Pettigrew estate, including Edward's long-suffering wife and a sympathetic maid who helps young Fraser through the trials of growing up. Their lives take a tumultuous turn when visitors show up. Among them are Uncle Morris, a no-nonsense businessman who plans big changes when he inherits the family fortune, and his fiancée, Heloise, whose continental charms work too much magic on innocent Fraser and his not-so-in-nocent father.

"My Life So Far" orchestrates these ingredients into an inspired tale. The story isn't helped by too-familiar plot twists (young Fraser gets curious about sex) and characters who'd be more interesting to know if today's entertainment weren't so crowded with them (yet another gay best friend).

The cast is excellent, though, from young Robert Norman as Fraser to Colin Firth as his dad, Mary Elizabeth Mastrantonio as his mom, Malcolm McDowell as the ominous uncle, and Irene Jacob as the fiancée. The picture was directed by Hugh Hudson, who hasn't scored a hit since the overrated "Chariots of Fire" in 1981. "My Life So Far" isn't likely to be a box-of-office giant, but it's leagues above Hudson flops like "Revolution" and "Greystoke: The Legend of Tarzan, Lord of the Apes." It should appeal to audiences tired of the summer's flashier fare.

LOS ANGELES TIMES, 7/23/99, Calendar/p. 18, Kevin Thomas

Hugh Hudson's "My Life So Far" lulls you into thinking you're watching yet another of those charming British memoirs of a childhood spent in a large, aristocratic household between the wars. This sumptuous film is all that, but there's a twist: It's the father who comes of age rather than the son. It's also a film that proceeds from one vignette to another; only when it reaches its climax do you realize that it's been quietly adding up all the while.

Directed with verve and subtlety by Hudson, whose affinity for British period pieces has also informed both the Oscar-laden "Chariots of Fire" and "Greystoke," "My Life So Far" has been skillfully adapted by Simon Donald from "Son of Adam," the childhood memoir of renowned television executive Sir Denis Forman. (The film is dedicated to the late co-star of "Chariots of Fire," Ian Charleson.)

The father in question is Edward Pettigrew (Colin Firth), a largely feckless inventor with twin passions, the Bible and Beethoven. He and his wife, Moira (Mary Elizabeth Mastrantonio), a woman whose forbearance equals her beauty, and their children live in a vast faux castle in the Scottish Highlands, nestled between a lake and the mountains. The estate is that of Moira's family, and it is run with a kindly, if magisterial, hand by Edward's widowed mother-in-law (Rosemary Harris).

Edward is quixotic, to say the least. He's great with kids—and the estate seems overrun with relatives and visitors—but he can swiftly turn severe. His experiments are many and largely impractical, but his key interest is in running the only moss factory in Europe. Edward had been among the first to appreciate the medicinal properties of the plant, which was put to good use during World War II.

He's processing the moss to make soap, a cologne and an unguent. Moira's older brother Morris (Malcolm McDowell), who made his fortune in Liverpool before moving to London, periodically turns up to throw his weight around. He does little to mask his contempt for Edward and complains loudly that the estate needs to be generating a profitable income, but his mother, whose word is law, points out that the estate is a home, not a business.

Since the time is circa 1933, in the depths of the Great Depression, you have to wonder if the matriarch is just a tad out of touch. (You also have to wonder whether primogeniture is still in force and if so, what will be its effect on the family's fortunes.) The larger point is that Edward and Morris are men with both strengths and failings. But their chronic personality clash takes on a new dimension when Morris arrives with his fiancee, Heloise (Irene Jacob), a beautiful cellist, who at 24 is less than half Morris' age. Firth is a stocky man of sensual features and, like early movie star Richard Dix, whom he resembles, is skilled at playing forthright yet priggish men who unexpectedly find themselves overcome with passion. In short, Edward makes a pass at the indignant Heloise, an act that has unforeseen consequences.

Despite all the escalating tensions, Edward and Moira's bright, inquisitive 10-year-old son Fraser (Robert Norman) is a happy child, basking in such a glorious environment and in the affection of so many doting relatives and servants. Fraser is old enough to express his desire to live always at the estate at just the moment we in the audience—if not all the adults on the screen—are experiencing the feeling that in a rapidly darkening world of economic depression and slowly gathering war clouds, this privileged way of life surely cannot go on undisturbed for much longer. At the very least the peacekeeping matriarch cannot be expected to live forever.

Hudson's actors form a perfectly modulated ensemble in which the principals glow, revealing the complexities and contradictions of their characters. (Stick with the picture and you will discover why Mastrantonio accepted so seemingly secondary a role.) As so many British pictures do, the handsome "My Life So Far" recaptures a vanished way of life, but it's not all nostalgia.

NEW YORK POST, 7/23/99, p. 58, Rod Dreher

What a pity that "My Life So Far" goes nowhere, and takes its own sweet time doing so. Shot in a glorious house on a misty loch, the film is lovely to look at, but there's not much to it.

There hasn't been such a collusion of class, handsomeness and chipper eccentricity in the service of a futile cause since William F. Buckley ran for mayor of New York City. Set in 1934, "My Life So Far" follows a year in the life of one Fraser Pettigrew (Robert Norman), a curious 10-year-old growing up on his family's splendid manor in the Scottish Highlands. Fraser's father,

Edward (Colin Firth), is a kooky entrepreneur who's hero-worshiped by his little boy, who finds his dad's extravagant Rube Goldberg schemes fascinating, as only a little boy can.

Fraser's mother (Mary Elizabeth Mastrantonio) and stout-hearted grandma (Rosemary Harris) keep things in order, though his grumpy businessman Uncle Morris (Malcolm McDowell) scowls and harrumphs at Edward's stewardship of the estate.

Nasty old Morris hopes to inherit the house when grandmother dies and brings home an exotic, much-younger French fiancee to impress the family. Heloise (Irene Jacob) impresses everyone, but stirs Edward a bit too much. His unruly attraction to the French filly serves as the catalyst for a family crisis.

Meanwhile, precocious Fraser's been up in the attic learning about the birds and the bees from his dead grandfather's musty library.

Possessing intriguing new knowledge without understanding causes Fraser to make faux pas like suggesting his mum and auntie become prostitutes for extra money, and to ask if fellatio is like a trombone.

Obviously, director Hugh Hudson and producer David Puttnam, who last worked together on "Chariots of Fire," are trying to make a coming-of-age tale with a storybook feel. But for all the beautiful Scottish locations and marvelous acting talent on display, Simon Donald's screenplay is little more than a compendium of cliches.

There's a bosomy wet nurse waiting to be splashed in the tub by naked Fraser. There's a creepy troll hiding in the forest. There's an infallible father proved to be something less than perfect in front of his adoring son. There's a French aviator who swoops down out of the sky for no apparent reason other than it's time for something zany to happen.

Each of these elements has dramatic potential, but none blend particularly well, and there's no special insight brought to bear on Fraser's experiences. A wan whiff of whimsy burbles up from time to time, but for the most part, the chef who assembled all these delectable ingredients in the kettle forgot to turn on the heat.

NEWSDAY, 7/23/99, Part II/p. B10, Gene Seymour

The words "arrested development" were invented to describe Edward Pettigrew (Colin Firth), who lives in a castle in the Scottish highlands in the 1930s. His stiff-backed moral puritanism is offset by a bumptious obsession with tinkering, inventing and the many uses of sphagnum moss, which he sells and markets for use all over the world. Teddy Roosevelt would have shouted "Bully!" if he knew such a Scotsman existed.

His wife Moira (Mary Elizabeth Mastrantonio) bears Edward's bombastic absorption in his scientific activity crackpot theories with stoic grace while their children are alternately amused and annoyed. Moira's mother MacIntosh (Rosemary Harris), who owns the castle, barely tolerates the din and clatter. Not surprisingly, their 10-year-old son, Fraser (Robert Norman), is the only one who understands or identifies with Edward's tearing about.

Then Moira's brother Morris (Malcolm McDowell), a suave, worldly businessman who takes a dim view of Edward's moss-bound activities, arrives from Paris with his young French-born fiancée, Heloise (Irene Jacob), whose sultry presence sets off hormonal alarms in both Edward and Fraser. The latter can only watch as his impulsive dad makes a move on Heloise, whose firm but gentle rebuff resonates for some time.

From this description of "My Life So Far," adapted from the memoirs of British TV executive Sir Dennis Forman, there doesn't seem to be much that you haven't in some way seen before from a thousand and one coming-of-age stories in several countries. Yet director Hugh Hudson, making his best film since the 1981 Oscar-winning "Chariots of Fire," gets a lot of resonance and charm out of the material by simply keeping a warm, steady eye on both the actors and their setting.

Since the story is told from Fraser's (and we assume Forman's) point of view, the grown-up actors have to enact their roles from the corners of a boy's perception. All of them respond to the challenge with keenly honed professionalism. Firth may well have the most difficult part of all since it's hard to be an overgrown adolescent without getting on the audience's nerves. By the time the movie's over, Edward's character assumes a well-earned maturity that makes all the glandular antics that preceded it more poignant in retrospect.

It's nice to see McDowell playing an avuncular part with his edgier persona concealed until needed. Meanwhile, as with most stories about a boy's coming-of-age, the women—Mastrantonio, Jacob and even Harris—are depicted in broad, enigmatic strokes. They fill in the shadows using their individual acting resources and, for the most part, that's sufficient. You do wish, at times, there was more of Moira than barely contained hurt. Or, for that matter, more of Fraser's sisters who have romantic confusions of their own to reconcile. Never mind. It's Fraser's story, and newcomer Norman makes an agreeable enough guide to the action.

SIGHT AND SOUND, 6/00, p. 48, Edward Lawrenson

Argyll, Scotland, 1920. Twelve year old Fraser Pettigrew lives with his parents (Moira and Edward) and two siblings on Kiloran estate, owned by Moira's mother Gamma Macintosh. Moira's brother Morris who disapproves of Edward introduces the family to his 24 year-old French bride Heloise. Edward is attracted to Heloise and forces himself on her in one of the estate's outhouses.

Fraser devours Gamma's dead husband's library of sexually explicit literature, stored in the attic. Morris and Heloise return from their travels. At a curling contest on a frozen lake, the ice under Gamma's feet gives way; she dies from pneumonia weeks later. Edward inherits the estate and boasts to Morris that he slept with Heloise. They fight, confirming Moira's suspicion that Edward has been unfaithful. Morris and Heloise leave. Moira reluctantly forgives Edward. With the family reconciled, Fraser is sent away to boarding school.

It's not long into *My Life So Far* that alarm bells will start sounding for anyone even vaguely familiar with the sad old bag of clichés filmmakers have tended to delve into when making movies about Scotland. The moment comes when dashing French pilot Gabriel lands his aeroplane in the grounds of Kiloran estate, takes in the gorgeous Argyll landscape and comments, "I seem to have landed in Shangri La." Portraying Kiloran very much as a timeless idyll, *My Life So Far* proves the ghost of Brigadoon just won't go to rest, no matter how hard cultural theorists might try to exorcise it.

Apart from airing a pretty dusty line in comedy Scots (the drunken minister; the abstemious housekeeper who keeps the cooking sherry under lock and key), director Hugh Hudson ends up with a film embarrassingly patrician in outlook by falling back on this cheerily bucolic vision of Scotland. The servants (played by such fine Scots actors as Jimmy Logan) are gossipy, good-hearted folk, earthy types (Andrew knows a lot about geology) if not vaguely pantheistic (the old servant Tom namechecks Greek mythology in a pep talk with Fraser). It's clear the Macintosh family have the best interests of these people at heart: raising money for unemployed miners, treating the downstairs staff with friendly respect, setting great store in their stewardship of the land, Gamma the Macintosh matriarch and her extended family exude benevolent authority and kindly concern. Like BBC's unspeakably naff series *The Monarch of the Glen*, *My Life So Far* plays like a subtle endorsement of the (largely inept) private ownership of vast tracts of rural land in Scotland. When Gamma orders Edward to stop using explosives for one of his harebrained land-development schemes, she explains that the noise bothers the sheep. This might cause a rather wry reflection on the role her ancestors had in the Highland clearances (where tenant farmers were turned off their land to make way for woolly livestock), but any irony here is surely unintended.

Not that *My Life So Far* is visually unimpressive (Bernard Lutic's camerawork is outstanding), but the picture postcard aesthetics gloss over a darker, more interesting film. Fraser's father Edward—childish, jealous, dogmatic—is clearly a flawed, if not unsuitable parent. But as portrayed by Colin Firth, he's no more than a loveable eccentric, the kind of playful patriarch who used to turn up in those cute and cloying movies produced by the Children's Film Foundation. In a film devoid of dramatic incident, his unwelcome advances towards his sister-in-law Heloise spark off a major crisis, but the question of whether he raped or not is skirted over, cited obliquely in terms of a family disgrace, much as it would be in a Victorian melodrama. There are some delicate and lively touches—Fraser's unknowingly crude language during the hushed civility of a dinner party; Malcolm McDowell's caddish portrayal of Morris—but for the most part *My Life So Far* is a hard slog, like trudging shin deep through heather on a pointless albeit very pretty Highland excursion.

VILLAGE VOICE, 7/27/99, p. 70, Jessica Winter

The life in question is that of 10-year-old Fraser, an inquisitive boy who lives in the Scottish highlands with his saintly mother (Mary Elizabeth Mastrantonio) and inventor father (Colin Firth), who, as Fraser begins to realize, is equal parts lout and loon. The facade is broken by the arrival of Heloise (Irene Jacob), a beautiful French apparition. We watch through Fraser's eyes Dad's attempts to seduce Heloise, and his intransigent pride following her rejection makes it seem as if his adulterous advances have succeeded. *My Life So Far* draws an unforced parallel between the childish narcissism shared by father and son, but it confuses the youngster's innocence with the grown man's fatuity. The film falls in love with its characters' various cases of willed blindness, celebrating their naiveté. As Fraser tells us at the end, his "parents remained happily married for the rest of their lives."

Also reviewed in:
CHICAGO TRIBUNE, 8/6/99, Friday/p. J, Barbara Shulgasser
NEW YORK TIMES, 7/23/99, p. E22, Stephen Holden
VARIETY, 5/31-6/6/99, p. 29, Todd McCarthy
WASHINGTON POST, 8/6/99, p. C5, Rita Kempley

MY NAME IS JOE

An Artisan Entertainment release of a Parallax Pictures and Road Movies Vierte production with the support of the Scottish Arts Council National Lottery Fund, the Glasgow Film Fund and Filmstifung Nordhein-Westfalen. *Executive Producer:* Ulrich Felsberg. *Producer:* Rebecca O'Brien. *Director:* Ken Loach. *Screenplay (Glasgow English with English subtitles):* Paul Laverty. *Director of Photography:* Barry Ackroyd. *Editor:* Jonathan Morris. *Music:* George Fenton. *Sound:* Ray Beckett and (music) Geoff Young. *Casting:* Gillian Berrie and Steven Mochrie. *Production Designer:* Martin Johnson. *Art Director:* Fergus Clegg. *Costumes:* Rhone Russell. *Make-up:* Anastasia Shirley. *Running time:* 105 minutes. *MPAA Rating:* Not Rated.

CAST: Peter Mullan (Joe Kavanagh); Louise Goodall (Sarah Downie); David McKay (Liam); Anne-Marie Kennedy (Sabine); David Hayman (McGowan); Gary Lewis (Shanks); Lorraine McIntosh (Maggie); Scott Hannah (Scott); David Peacock (Hooligan); Gordon McMurray (Scrag); James McHendry (Perfume); Paul Clark (Zulu); Stephen McCole (Mojo); Simon Macallum (Robbo); Paul Gillan (Davy); Stephen Docherty (Doc); Paul Doonan (Tattie); Cary Carbin (Sepp Maier); Martin McCardie (Alf); James McNeish (Shuggy); Kevin Kelly (Jake); Brian Timoney (Scooter); David Hough (Referee); Sandy West (DSS Investigator); John Comerford (DSS Supervisor); Carol Pyper Rafferty (Rhona); Elaine M. Ellis (2nd Receptionist); Stewart Ennis (Doctor Boyle); Andy Townsley (Husband); Ann Marie Lafferty (Wife); Bill Murdoch (Postman); Kate Black (Kiosk Attendant); Rab Affleck (Lorry Driver).

LOS ANGELES TIMES, 2/5/99, Calendar/p. 2, Kenneth Turan

"My Name Is Joe" is a romance that pulsates with the disturbances both large and small of the hard-knock life. A tough, fearless piece of work that cares desperately about its people—and respects them too much to provide an easy way out—"Joe" is yet another terribly moving and eloquent film from the old master of British cinema, Ken Loach.

A director who's been close to canonized by his peers for efforts like "Cathy Come Home," "Kes," "Raining Stones" and "Land and Freedom" created over a 30-year career, Loach is without equal when it comes to combining acute social commentary with a warm sympathy for the humanity of his characters. His gaze doesn't flinch as he focuses on life on the fly, and though we frequently find ourselves laughing, it's never at anyone's expense.

In all his decades of work, Loach may never have had as handsome and charismatic a leading man as Peter Mullan, a ringer for a young Paul Newman, who plays the Joe Kavanagh of the title. With a compelling naturalness that makes his character someone we take to at once, Mullan not only won the best actor award at Cannes but also delighted the audience by accepting it in a kilt.

"Joe" is set in one of Glasgow's poorest neighborhoods, a place where humor is critical because life is not easy. One of the things Loach and screenwriter Paul Laverty insist on is a thoroughgoing authenticity in matters of speech: "There's so much humor and richness in the rhythms of the way people talk; their whole history is in their language," the director explained at Cannes.

What that means for American audiences is that distributor Artisan Entertainment has taken the unusual but necessary step of subtitling the dialogue to make it easier to understand. The language and the slang would make "Joe" a challenge to decipher without this kind of help, and the subtitles don't distract any more than they would in a foreign language film.

Anyone familiar with AA meetings can guess that "My name is Joe" is the first part of a sentence that ends with "and I'm an alcoholic." "Joe" starts with Kavanagh detailing his drinking history in a Glasgow meeting, proud of his year of sobriety and hoping to continue to make more of his life.

Though, like almost everyone else he knows, Joe is on public assistance, he's not idle. He spends much of his time coaching a ragtag soccer squad, the city's worst, a group he is as involved with as if they were his flesh and blood. He especially cares about his nephew Liam (David McKay) and Liam's wife, Sabine (Anne-Marie Kennedy), young parents who are shakily coming back from a drug-addicted past.

It's because of Liam and Sabine that Joe meets Sarah Downie (Louise Goodall), a public health worker so intent on getting to their house for an appointment that her car nearly crashes into his van.

Emotionally self-sufficient and gainfully employed, Sarah is not looking for a relationship. Neither, for that matter, is Joe, who'd like to be on firmer psychological footing before getting seriously involved with anyone.

But it is one of the pleasures of "Joe" that we feel how impossible it is for these two to resist each other. Joe is attracted to Sarah's straight-forwardness, to the way she "doesn't mess about," and Sarah is attracted, as we are as well, to Joe's breathtaking honesty, profane sense of humor and visible appetite for life.

Yet we, as well as Sarah, also see the difficulties in this relationship. Joe's vital energy has a history of turning into a terrifying temper, and though Sarah has the gift of seeing the best in him, both these people have an understandable wariness about committing to a relationship with someone so different from themselves.

Laverty's script is not afraid to make use of melodrama and contrivance, from doors that lock people out when they least expect it to the ominous presence of a local crime boss named McGowan (David Hayman) and his strong-arm hooligans.

It's a grounding in reality that makes these conventions acceptable, plus the irresistible vigor of Mullan's performance. Added to that is Loach's impeccable empathy as a director, and his unspoken insistence that society's inequalities are the underlying cause of its citizen's troubles. Combining all these divergent strains is what Loach does best, and "My Name Is Joe" is one of his most appealing works.

NEW YORK, 2/1/99, p. 48, Peter Rainer

The title character in Ken Loach's *My Name Is Joe* is a recovering alcoholic who lives on the dole when he isn't sneaking odd jobs or coaching a soccer team of wayward boys from the poorest section of Glasgow. Taut and compactly built, Joe (Peter Mullan) is like an ex-fighter who has sworn off fisticuffs but is always tensed for action. He approaches the world with an exhilarated wariness; the years of booze and bad living are never more than an inch away from his mood.

The film is just fine as long as Loach stays with Joe's personal reclamation project, The tentative relationship that develops between this ardent man and a health counselor (Louise Goodall) drawn to his decency is immensely touching; we can sense that for both of them something very new and yet inexplicably sad is being played out. But Loach doesn't trust the simple back-and-forth expressiveness of these two. Although he's renowned for his social realism, in his own obtrusively unobtrusive way he can be just as meddlesome as the melodramatists. He balls up Joe's story into a running-from-the-local-mob thing, and it's not where we want to be. Plenty of directors can do this stuff better than Loach—when it's worth doing at all. What he can do surpassingly well is provide an actor with the oxygen to create a thriving, humane portrayal. (It's a gift he shares with his countryman Mike Leigh.) Peter Mullan gives the kind of performance that keeps expanding before our eyes: He prepares us for everything—Joe's princeliness and lyricism and bullish loyalty. It's a near-great piece of work, and one of the least condescending working-class characterizations I've ever seen.

NEW YORK POST, 1/22/99, p. 47, Jonathan Foreman

Director Ken Loach has a deserved reputation for putting out well-made but gloomy movies about working-class life—gritty social realism interspersed with Marxist lectures that do well only in France. Which makes his new film, "My Name Is Joe," even more of a pleasant surprise—there's no overtly political content, and much of it is taken up by a delightful, heartwarming, grown-up love story.

To be sure, "My Name is Joe" is not for the filmgoer who wants a few lighthearted laughs on a Saturday night. But it's a moving, powerful film that—thanks to the winning combination of some first-rate direction, terrific performances and an intelligent script laced with understated humor—is completely involving. Its characters stay with you long after the credits have come rolled.

The film is set in Glasgow, a once-prosperous Scottish city now notorious for its heroin addicts, its brutal gangs and its total economic dependence on the state. Joe (Peter Mullan) is a 37-year-old unemployed former alcoholic who coaches a soccer team for delinquents. He's worried about one of the players, Liam (David McKay), a former addict who is trying to pull his own life together for the sake of his little son and his slatternly junkie wife. Because of his wife, Liam owes the local gangsters money he cannot pay back.

Picking up Liam for a soccer game, Joe meets nurse Sarah (Louise Goodall), a social worker. Although—or perhaps because—they come from different worlds (she's lower-middle as opposed to working class) there's an immediate attraction that gradually blossoms into romance. Not only has Joe turned his life around; his whole world is expanding. But then Liam's worsening predicament forces Joe to go back into the criminal underworld and risk everything he has achieved.

The relationship between Joe and Sarah is wonderfully real. And as a result of this and the fine performances by Mullan and Goodall, the love scenes between these two middle-aged people have an erotic charge that's all too rare in Hollywood productions. (Mullan won a deserved best actor award at last year's Cannes Film Festival for this role.)

Unfortunately, the creaky crime plot elements of the movie tend to slow it down. Loach and screenwriter Paul Laverty employ a traditional movie cliche: the hero who is on the straight and narrow but must, for the best of reasons, commit one last crime. But the way they resolve the situation, and the movie, is disappointing and half-hearted.

Still, "My Name is Joe" is a heartwarming film. Its intended message is: look at the terrible situations people are forced into by unemployment. But this portrait of slums where everyone lives off the state—except for the hookers and drug dealers—says more about the psychological devastation wrought by the welfare culture than about poverty, In a mindset strange to most American sensibilities, the notion of moving to where the jobs are rather than complacently settling down to a life on the dole simply never occurs to these characters.

NEWSDAY, 1/2/99, Part II/p. B6, Jack Mathews

You know you're in for some uncompromised filmmaking when the characters' English dialogue is accompanied by English subtitles. And when you see the name of director Ken Loach attached, you know you're in for some uncompromised human emotion, as well.

Both are true of "My Name Is Joe," Loach's latest journey into the tortured souls of the British working class. It's the story of Joe Kavanagh (Peter Mullan), an unemployed recovering alcoholic whose blossoming, strengthening and rehabilitative romance with a health worker is threatened by old habits and old debts.

Played by Mullan with the same level of intensity and brilliance that Chrissy Rock brought to the title role of an alcoholic welfare mother in Loach's "Ladybird, Ladybird," Joe is an exposed nerve flailing in the streets and alleys and soccer fields of the underclass neighborhood of Ruchill, in Glasgow. He's a heavily traveled roughneck, hanging onto his new sobriety by his fingertips, working odd jobs and filling his time in between managing a local soccer team made up of delinquents blessed with more enthusiasm than talent.

When Joe meets Sarah (Louise Goodall), his life takes on an additional spark of hope. We can read in his eyes, and in his almost stumbling schoolboy eagerness, his realization that his sobriety may do more than rescue him from the abyss, but make it possible to scale the heights, to have a fulfilling, lasting relationship. Life could be good, life could be beautiful.

Then, again...

Joe's rose-colored crystal ball is soon clouded by ominous threats to one of his soccer players, Liam (David McKay), a recovering junkie in debt to the drug-dealing neighborhood thug McGowan (David Hayman). Accepting the risks to his relationship with Sarah, and their future together, Joe goes to the aid of Liam by agreeing to do work for McGowan.

The English subtitles are helpful. I saw "My Name is Joe" at Cannes without them, and it was a struggle. Not so much in the scenes with Joe and Sarah, where body language and facial expressions clarify any confusion. But in Joe's collegial scenes with the soccer team, and his emotional outbursts with Liam and his junkie girlfriend Sabine (Anne-Marie Kennedy), the Scottish accents have a ricocheting effect that renders dialogue almost incomprehensible.

With or without the subtitles, there's no mistaking the brilliance of Mullan's performance. The veteran Scottish stage and television actor fills Joe with a combination of energy, tension, charm, confusion, hope and dread; he's portraying, with painful verisimilitude, a man balanced on a razor's edge.

Goodall provides a strong, complementary figure in Sarah, though her character is not as well defined as Joe. As charming as he can be with her, it seems a bit of a stretch that someone with as much experience with emotional wrecks would go so willingly into a relationship with one.

Nonetheless, Mullan and Goodall have tremendous chemistry, an essential fact that will have audiences empathetically agonizing over their characters' eventual choices.

SIGHT AND SOUND, 11/98, p. 58, Judith Williamson

Glasgow. Joe, a dried-out alcoholic, testifies to an AA meeting that he "can no longer drink with safety". Later, driving a vanload of youths to a football match, he stops off to collect team member Liam. He has a caustic exchange with Sarah, a health visitor checking on Liam's and his partner Sabine's baby. When Joe and Sarah meet again he offers to wallpaper her flat. A social-security spy catches him working, but Sarah writes to the DSS office to get him off the hook, and they become close. When she asks why he stopped drinking he tells her he once attacked a girlfriend when drunk and has not touched alcohol since.

They spend the night together and their relationship develops. Joe is trying to help Liam, an ex-junkie, stay clean. Sabine, a client of Sarah's, is still hooked, and works as a prostitute. The young couple are in thrall to dealer and gangleader McGowan, to whom they owe money. To settle their debt, Joe agrees to do three drug runs. Sarah discovers she is pregnant, but is morally outraged when she finds out about the drug runs. Joe tries to explain but she throws the story of his earlier violence in his face. He begs McGowan to let him off the last run, but this ends in a fight; he goes home and hits the bottle. Liam comes round but, finding his mentor blind drunk and McGowan's men at the door, hangs himself. At Liam's funeral, Joe stands with Sabine and the child, while Sarah stands apart. As the film ends, they walk nearer to one another through the graveyard.

Like much of Ken Loach's work, *My Name Is Joe* is fundamentally about the kinds of desperation created by poverty. It starts off as a quite upbeat story with that element of 'universality' that characterises the mainstream: Joe's conquered alcoholism and his blossoming romance with Sarah invite us to focus on a Man and his Feelings and Battles. But Joe is not an abstract Man, he is a working-class man living on the dole—as we are swiftly reminded when the light-hearted scene where Joe and his mate decorate Sarah's flat, singing 'Hi Ho Silver Lining', is interrupted by a Department of Social Security spy. The class differences between Joe and Sarah, a health visitor, have been merely cultural up to this point, a source of banter; now, crucially, we see that they are also material, and the rest of the film shows, almost like a Marxist textbook, how these two dimensions are inseparable. More subtly, the tension between them creates the mess that results in tragedy at the story's climax as Joe, financially bound into an underworld Sarah doesn't understand, tries to adopt her moral values in order not to lose her.

Tellingly, their romance is charted through Joe's acquisition of a range of middle-class markers. When Sarah first comes to his flat she is surprised to find a tape of Beethoven's 'Violin Concerto in D Major'. This is the night she first sleeps with him, after hearing how he stopped drinking after beating up a previous girlfriend. The classical music counterbalances this otherwise off-putting information: how would the scene have worked without a Beethoven sensitivity-indicator on the soundtrack? What if he was a recovered working-class alcoholic who listened to heavy metal? Joe's emotional and cultural reclamation is highlighted further in a sequence where their shared domesticity takes the form of his slicing *celery*. He even continues holding the redemptive bowl of celery during a love-making scene, as if to guarantee their new found happiness.

Yet this doesn't last, because celery or no celery, there are debts to be paid. The pivot of the plot is a precise sum of money, the £1,500 Liam and Sabine owe their dealer McGowan, who threatens to break Liam's legs and even attack Sarah (something she never finds out) if they don't deliver. A sum which a middle-class person might spend on doing up their kitchen becomes the bind which ties these working-class characters to a gangland of extreme ruthlessness. There is a powerful echo here of Loach's *Raining Stones,* another story where relatively small sums of money entangle the central characters in violence and degradation. Joe tries first to settle the debt by drug running, and then to extricate himself from the situation when Sarah freaks out. In fact, it is not his involvement but his attempt to back off which causes the final, brutal fight, returning him to the bottle, and leading to the unexpectedly sad ending. The moral is contained in Joe's keynote speech (in Loach films there is always a keynote speech) to Sarah in which he tells her he doesn't live in a "tidy wee world" like hers, and asks her what she would have done. The simplest message is, don't listen to middle-class do-gooders, especially when they are as irritating as Sarah (not that the film intends her to be so irritating as I personally find her).

The clarity of this message is at once the film's strength and its weakness. Besides Loach, who is making films that really address the harsh choices faced by millions of people on the dole? Stripping may be a feel-good solution to debt in movie terms, but *My Name Is Joe* presents us with precisely the scenario that *The Full Monty* rollickingly avoids. It also, through the character of Sarah, shows the limitations of what even the most well-meaning of social and healthcare professionals can achieve. But this is at the price of a deeper investigation of some of the more general themes the film itself raises: for instance, the issue of dependency—on both people and drugs which is invoked when Sarah tells Joe he should stop protecting Liam.

Unfortunately, she picks a moment when Liam might get his legs broken, so the more subtle question of how much or little to support others—the issue of 'codependency'—becomes quickly pushed aside. Sarah herself sleeps with Joe right after she learns his worst secret, whispering, "It's okay, it's okay", as if she were able to make things all right, which she patently isn't. There are interpersonal questions here which *Leaving Las Vegas,* for example, made into a whole film. But as Brecht acknowledged in the 30s: "Solely because of the increasing disorder/In our cities of class struggle/Some of us have now decided/To speak no more of cities by the sea, snow on roofs, women/The smell of ripe apples in cellars, the sense of the flesh, all/That makes a man round and human ..."

Loach has battled with this Brechtian dilemma for decades, and has never given up the attempt to speak both of the class struggle *and* of what makes people round and human. *My Name Is Joe* gets closer than many of his earlier films to a sense of beauty and possibility—without which there can be no sense of what, besides money, society's 'losers' are deprived of. The film has a sharper aesthetic than the grimly ugly *Raining Stones,* and its camera finds order and pattern even in tenement railings or a diagonal shot of a grey street. The opening sequence of restless visual movement suggests an energy propelling the central characters, balanced by the final slow shot in the graveyard where we scrutinise the movements of the mourners to see whether Sarah and Joe will come together again. There is a touching visual and social joke when Joe's gangly football team play in borrowed strips of various world teams culminating in their successful stealing of a full set of Brazilian outfits. A film's lesson may be contained in its plot, but its gift to its audience is its imagery. Here, for once, Loach has not only taught us something (which we might have known already) but given us something which, for all the film's shortcomings, I was glad home.

VILLAGE VOICE, 1/26/99, p. 64, Amy Taubin

Nothing could be further from Jordan's lyrical hyperrealism and his sense of how the unconscious floods daily life than Ken Loach's character-driven social dramas. [The reference is to *In Dreams*; see Taubin's review of that film.]

Returning from the romantic epic sweep of his Spanish Civil War film, *Land and Freedom*, and his semi-disastrous attempt to depict Latin American political struggle, *Carla's Song*, Loach zeros in on an ordinary Joe named Joe, a recovering alcoholic from Glasgow with few economic options and too many old connections to a heroin-drenched underworld.

As played by the vibrant Peter Mullan, who's as cocky and tender as the young-ish Paul Newman, Joe is a character who commands your attention and your heart. He wants nothing so much as to live a clean, productive life, but, like everyone he knows, he's on the dole, with no prospects of extricating himself from a poverty-based economy. (It seems as if the only legitimate jobs in Glasgow are providing social services for the poor.) He falls in love with a family counselor who's wary of committing to him because of his violent past. He feels responsible for a hapless kid on his soccer team who's in debt to the local mob boss. If Joe tries to save him, he risks losing himself, not to mention his girlfriend, in the process.

Mullan has an amazing energy and range. He lets you understand that Joe's optimism is an act of will, his only defense against his terrible anger. Without being mushy, the film raises difficult questions about forgiving oneself, forgiving others, and the irreparable damage a word or an action can do to a relationship.

The last uncompromising leftist filmmaker, Loach shows how the economic and political system leaves basically good guys like Joe, trying to live one day at a time without hurting themselves or anyone else, little room for anything except bad choices. This is Loach's best film since *Riff-Raff* and, like *Riff-Raff*, it's being released in the U.S. with subtitles. Loach's commitment to the Glasgow dialect makes it difficult, even for most British audiences, to understand the dialogue. It's regional filmmaking at its radical best.

Also reviewed in:
CHICAGO TRIBUNE, 2/26/99, Friday/p. A, Michael Wilmington
NEW YORK TIMES, 1/22/99, p. E14, Janet Maslin
NEW YORKER, 2/1/99, p. 85, Anthony Lane
VARIETY, 5/18-24/98, p. 72, Derek Elley
WASHINGTON POST, 3/5/99, p. C7, Rita Kempley
WASHINGTON POST, 3/5/99, Weekend/p. 42, Desson Howe

MY SON THE FANATIC

A Miramax Films release of a BBC Films presentation in association with Canal+, Image International amd The Arts Council of Great Britain of a Zephyr Films production. *Executive Producer:* George Faber. *Producer:* Chris Curling. *Director:* Udayan Prasad. *Screenplay based on his story:* Hanif Kureishi. *Director of Photography:* Alan Almond. *Editor:* David Gamble. *Music:* Stephen Warbeck and Charlie Gillett. *Sound:* Albert Bailey and (music) Steve Parr. *Sound Editor:* Nick Adams. *Casting:* Simone Ireland and Vanessa Pereira. *Production Designer:* Grenville Horner. *Art Director:* Colin Blaymires and Sara Kane. *Costumes:* Mary-Jane Reyner. *Make-up:* Penny Smith. *Stunt Coordinator:* Clive Curtis. *Runnning time:* 86 minutes. *MPAA Rating:* R.

CAST: Om Puri (Parvez); Rachel Griffiths (Bettina); Stellan Skarsgard (Schitz); Akbar Kurtha (Farid); Gopi Desai (Minoo); Harish Patel (Fizzy); Bhasker Patel (Maulvi); Sarah Jane Potts (Madelaine Fingerhut); Judi Jones (Mrs. Fingerhut); Geoffrey Bateman (Chief Inspector

Fingerhut); Bernard Wrigley (Drunk Man); Moya Brady (Druggy Prostitute); Badi Uzzaman (Man in Mosque); Andy Devine (Comedian); Shiv Grewal (Waiter); Omar Salimi (Rashid); Dev Sagoo (Taxi Controller); Rowena King (Margot); Olwen May and Alison Burrows (Prostitutes); Parvez Qadir and Shakher Bassi (Acolytes); Balraj Singh Somal and Rez Kempton (Drivers).

CINEASTE, Vol. XXIV, No. 4, 1999, p. 42, Leonard Quart

Hanif Kureishi is the son of a British mother and Pakistani father, a novelist, essayist, playwright, and one of those rare screenwriters whose strikingly written scenarios define and dominate the films on which they collaborate. Kureishi's new work, *My Son the Fanatic* follows in a much less flashy manner, the pattern of his films like *My Beautiful Launderette, Sammy and Rosie Get Laid*, and the four-part BBC serial, *The Buddha of Suburia*, that he adapted with Roger Michell front his own novel. *My Son the Fanatic* explores the nature of love, the relationships between fathers and sons, and what it means to live as a member of an ethnic minority seeking a new life and identity in a country where much, of the population doesn't accept you. Like Kureishi's other films, it also seamlessly mixes the satiric, the political, the romantic, and the sexual in a richly-layered fashion.

The film takes place in Bradford—a Northern English industrial city (woolens and synthetic fibers) with a large Asian population that has seen better days. There is a brief, pointed look at a comedian telling racist jokes to the approval of his working-class audience in a Bradford night club. The film's prime focus, however, is not on the city's social structure or problems, but on the emotional life of an intelligent, middle-aged taxi driver, Parvez (Om Puri), who spends long, exhausting nights ferrying hookers and their customers. Parvez has lived in England for twenty-five years, has a dutiful, traditional wife, Minoo (Gopi Desai), and a son, Farid (Akbar Kurtha), whom he adores and maintains great hopes for. It's a limited, routinized existence, but Parvez has, on the surface, made his peace with it.

Two events send Parvez's life spinning out of control, and lead to profound personal changes. First of all, Farid stuns and breaks Parvez's heart by abruptly dropping his English fiancé—the local chief inspector's daughter—and selling his possessions. He has rejected acculturation, embraced his roots, and become a Muslim fundamentalist. What is more significant, Parvez is engaged by a decadent, contemptuous German businessman, Schitz (Stellan Skarsgard), to introduce him to the local prostitutes and be driven around town. Parvez develops a friendship with Schitz's favorite prostitute—hardened but empathetic Bettina (Rachel Griffiths) that turns into a poignant romantic and sexual relationship.

The film's strength lies in the complexity and attractiveness of Parvez's character. Kureishi has a genius for creating vibrant, multidimensional father figures like the exploitative, materialistic, and generous Nasser (Saeed Jaffrey) in *My Beautiful Launderette* and the charming, murderous ex-Pakistani cabinet minister, Rafi (Shashi Kapoor), in *Sammy and Rosie*. The fathers in his films, played by actors with great emotional range and feeling for nuance, usually have more energy, and personality than their sons. It's no different in this film. Parvez, whose point of view is the film's, is a bulbous-nosed, pockmarked, economically struggling and culturally divided figure who has not tapped into the depths of his psychic imagination and courage. He knows he's treated as an outsider in England, but in an avidly comic fashion, pushes Farid to marry into the white chief inspector's family. He's decent and gentle, but is also emotionally blind to his son's turmoil (he thinks his son's problem is drug addiction or homosexuality) and wife's discontent. Although Parvez has removed himself from a traditional Muslim way of life—rejecting religion, undisturbed by intermarriage, and finding solace in whiskey and American jazz and r&b records—by never taking his wife anywhere, he quietly binds her to the house and to a life of submerged anger and recrimination.

Parvez's personal transformation is subtly rendered as he becomes more deeply involved with white British Bettina. He talks intimately to her about the troubles with his son, they take walks in the country together, and he calls her a "magnificent special woman." Ultimately, they go beyond yearning looks when she kisses and touches him—something she has dreamt of doing—and they go to bed, the scene fading out into a flaming red screen. It all feels genuinely tender and believable—the hungry sexuality and longing much more real than the mechanical, impersonal sexual athleticism of mainstream American cinema. Despite their differences in age and background, the relationship flowers, and both are transformed. Parvez becomes a more knowing, wiser, tougher man—finally, getting angry at the odious and patronizing Schitz (who through the film derisively calls him "little man") and throwing him out of his cab. Bettina's warmth and wish for something better from life emerges from beneath her calloused persona without her becoming a clichéd prostitute with a heart of gold.

Parvez, however, is conflicted about Bettina being a prostitute, and maintains a residual loyalty to his wife. He also has to deal with his fellow immigrants' rejection, and his son's uncontrolled rage about his relationship with Bettina. The film's most glaring weakness lies in the character of Farid, whose abrupt turn to religion doesn't derive from seemingly anything inside himself, but from the needs of Kureishi's social vision. Farid is much more a representative of a position than a character with a life of his own. He rejects capitalism, materialism, acculturation, and is opposed to (in one of Kureishi's more felicitous phrases) "the empty accountancy of things," but that's all we know about this stiff zealot and ideologue.

In his pursuit of purity and rejection of 'degenerate' Western culture, Farid invites a Muslim teacher and his followers to his father's house. The *maulvi* takes over—banishing Minoo, who serves them, to the kitchen, toting up an enormous phone bill, and spending his days watching cartoons. The *maulvi*, who wants to get a green card and emigrate to England, is not quite a grotesque but is seen as absurd—the object of the film's ridicule. Kureishi's work has always abhorred the puritanical and affirmed the spontaneous and sexual. He has written that "all authority should be viewed with suspicion and constantly questioned" and that "the desire for more freedom, more pleasure, more self-expression" is basic to life. Consequently, there is little that is positive in this portrait of fervent fundamentalists who beat up prostitutes and try to burn down the city's red-light district.

The film's prime interest, however, is not in exploring the fundamentalist ethos or the dilemma of multicultural identity, but in the love story between Parvez and Bettina. At the film's conclusion, Farid leaves without even a look back at Parvez, and Minoo, who is much stronger than Parvez ever realized, takes a stand and leaves for India, unwilling to accept his inability to have more than obligatory feelings for her. Though confused and feeling bereft, Parvez has Bettina and the relationship provides more emotional satisfaction and depth than anything Minoo could ever give. The film ultimately affirms Kureishi's belief that "friendship can be found in the funniest places" and that "there is more than one way of being a good man."

Kureishi's films have always found rogues appealing, and embraced contradiction and disorder. Parvez, of course is a good man, but he has ironically discovered the possibility of a more fulfilling existence during a time when his traditional notions of loyalty and morality have been subverted by chaos, loss, and his own betrayal of his wife. For Kureishi, emotional risk and the pain that accompanies it are not much better than living a moribund life. Parvez has rejected "life sitting behind the wheel without having a human touch" for something much less predictable.

My Son the Fanatic is a much less politically ambitious and dazzling work than films like *My Beautiful Laundrette* and *Sammy and Rosie*—a work that brilliantly preens and postures. Still, this small film, directed in a solid, unobtrusive manner by Udayan Prasad, is blessed with Kureishi's literate and animated dialog and a memorable central character that make *My Son the Fanatic* an emotionally moving work.

LOS ANGELES TIMES, 6/25/99, Calendar/p. 2, Kenneth Turan

"My Son the Fanatic" opens with what should be a high point in the life of Parvez (Om Puri), born in Pakistan, but for the last 25 years a cabdriver in the northern English city of Bradford.

Parvez and his wife are having tea with their presumptive future in-laws, the Fingerhuts, celebrating the engagement of their son Farid (Akbar Kurtha) to the daughter of one of the town's top officials. "This boy of ours, I can assure you he's all-around type going whole hog," Parvez says in his charmingly mangled immigrant's English, so delighted he doesn't notice the cross-cultural discomfort everyone else in the room is feeling.

Best known for "My Beautiful Laundrette," writer Hanif Kureishi calls his latest work "a romantic film with ideological edges," and what makes it exceptional is how much subtlety and compassion Kureishi and director Udayan Prasad bring to both halves of that equation.

Effortlessly well-written, with nuanced characters that easily come to life on the screen, "My Son the Fanatic" does justice to the unlikely love story it uncovers as well as the troubling underlying reality of adapting to a new country and a new culture. Intelligent, poignant and witty, it involves us in real issues without stinting on their complexity and without forgetting to be caring toward people caught in the undertow of forces they cannot begin to control.

Even without this impending marriage, Parvez initially feels content. He still loves his wife, Minoo (Gopi Desai), though over the years their relationship has grown distant and pro forma. He doesn't even envy the success his best friend, Fizzy (Harish Patel), has had in the restaurant business. Then, like an emotional pincers attack, three factors combine to bring his life to a crisis.

Most devastating is the change in Parvez's only child. Once a boy who loved clothes and considered modeling, Farid is now intent on getting rid of all his worldly possessions, including his music and even his cherished guitar. "You always said there were more important things than 'Stairway to Heaven,'" he tells his baffled father, "and you were so right."

Parvez initially suspects drugs, but the truth is even more devastating. In a reverse twist on the usual scenario of traditional parents and modern children, it is the searching son who embraces the Muslim fundamentalism the father rejected. "Our cultures cannot be mixed," Farid insists, and flays modern Britain for being "a society soaked in sex."

As if to underline that point, Parvez becomes the regular driver for a visiting German ("Breaking the Waves'" and "Good Will Hunting's" Stellan Skarsgard), an amoral businessman, more obtuse than anything dangerous, who seems to live only for pleasures of the flesh and says things like "Don't you love the sound of silk on skin?"

That last remark is inspired by Bettina (Australian Rachel Griffiths, Oscar-nominated for "Hilary and Jackie"), a local prostitute who uses Parvez's taxi for late-night service. Almost without knowing it, this pair of societal outsiders begin to depend on each other for the honesty and quiet decency they can obtain nowhere else. With all his moorings gone, desperate for tenderness, Parvez finds himself emotionally drawn to Bettina even as he realizes how impossible their situation would be.

Celebrated Indian actor Puri, a veteran of dozens of films from "Gandhi" to the works of Satyajit Ray, gives a moving, captivating performance as the capsized Parvez, struggling to believe that the truths he's always held are still valid. Griffiths is also outstanding as a woman who knows what reality is but also knows what she wants and needs.

Director Prasad (a British TV regular whose feature debut was "Brothers in Trouble"), always sensitive and empathetic, is impressive in the way he honors the script's determination to give all aspects of this complex situation their due.

For though "My Son the Fanatic" is at times bemused at Farid's zealotry, it leaves no doubt that the racism and lack of respect he decries in British society is both real and pervasive. And while Parvez is equally convinced that the rigidity of fundamentalism and its insistence on purity and conformity is not a solution to anything, he has difficulty formulating an alternative that has any meaning for his son.

While "My Son the Fanatic" is too subtle and thoughtful to offer simple solutions—Parvez's declaration that "there are many ways of being a good man" may be as close as it gets to a summing up—Kureishi and Prasad have given this story a nuanced, bittersweet ending that has more staying power than a more conventional finale would. For if the answers to these pervasive problems were simpler, if the tangled emotions these peoples' lives call for them were easier to sort out, "My Son the Fanatic" wouldn't behalf the memorable film it turns out to be.

NEW YORK, 7/12/99, p. 50, Peter Rainer

Parvez (Om Puri), the middle-aged Pakistani cabdriver in the marvelous *My Son the Fanatic*, moved to the industrial north of England 25 years ago with his wife, Minoo (Gopi Desai), and, against the evidence of his eyes, still sees his adopted country as a fabled and pleasant place. He's a naïf who has internalized the rewards of Empire far more than have the native English. When his only child, Farid (Akbar Kurtha), who still lives at home, drops his white fiancée, forsakes his possessions, and becomes an Islamic fundamentalist, Parvez is stung by this renunciation of his own dream; at first he thinks the boy must be on drugs.

Hanif Kureishi, who wrote the screenplay based on his *New Yorker* short story, doesn't frame this conflict as a generational grudge match. It's more like an upside-down father-son love story in which the usual sides are reversed: The father is much more liberal than the son. Kureishi, with the director Udayan Prasad, understands the allures of orthodoxy, the way it can focus rage. And yet when Farid brings a Muslim priest and his followers to live in their home, and Minoo is quietly shut off from the dining room to eat alone, the consequences of that orthodoxy seem unutterably sad. Parvez is dumbstruck by his son's fanaticism and begins to confide in Bettina (Rachel Griffiths), a prostitute he's been ferrying around on assignations. The relationship that develops between them is so acutely observed that what might seem odd instead seems inevitable—Bettina shares Parvez's despairing, triumphal sense of what their lives could be like. Bewildered by what their country has become, they are the true inheritors of England's dashed glories.

NEW YORK POST, 6/25/99, p. 57, Rod Dreher

While Dad skulks in the basement drinking whisky and listening to jazz, Junior sits upstairs studying Scripture and wondering what the hell's happened to the morals of parents these days.

That's the delicious irony on which screenwriter Hanif Kureishl's "My Son the Fanatic" is based. It's a bittersweet comedy about a hardworking Pakistani immigrant cabdriver driven crazy by his only son's conversion to militant Islam.

Kureishi ("My Beautiful Laundrette," "The Buddha of Suburbia") made his reputation as an acute and witty chronicler of culture clashes in multicultural Britain. In his latest work, he sympathetically and amusingly observes the tribulations of beleaguered Everyman Parvez (Om Puri), who is painfully trying to keep his family together.

Parvez thinks he's hit the assimilationist jackpot when son Farid (Akbar Kurtha) gets engaged to the constable's daughter.

But then Farid abruptly breaks up with the girl and joins a rigid Islamic sect of sons of immigrants who consider their parents backsliding lackeys of the Brits.

When easygoing Parvez confronts Farid about his intemperance, the son spits, "It is you who has swallowed the white and Jewish propaganda!" This ain't "Family Ties."

With his wife, Minoo (Gopi Desai), an embittered shrew, Parvez has only one pleasure: the people he meets while driving his taxi. He is encouraged by Mr. Schitz (Stellan Skarsgard), a hedonistic German businessman who may not be quite the friend he pretends to be. And Parvez falls for a hooker named Bettina (Rachel Griffiths), who does him the treasured kindness of listening tenderly to his problems.

Things boil over when a Muslim cleric moves to town and starts a violent campaign against "decadent" Western values (while secretly trying to take advantage of the liberal, prosperous society that has welcomed him).

The film's perfect balance between comedy and tragedy never wavers, and Puri's brilliant performance in this subtle, gratifyingly complex role makes this Pakistani cabbie's blues strike a universal chord.

NEWSDAY, 6/25/99, Part II/p. B7, Gene Seymour

It must be drugs, thinks Parvez (Om Puri), a Pakistani taxi driver living in a north England industrial town. What else could explain the erratic behavior of his cherished only son, Farid (Akbar Kurtha)? Parvez has worked long and hard to make a decent life for his wife, Minoo (Gopi Desai), and son, even to the degree of picking up extra dollars to fix up some of his passengers with local prostitutes.

So now, here's Farid all set to marry the daughter of the local police chief and suddenly he breaks off the engagement and is meeting strange people on street corners and selling off all his belongings. Drugs, Parvez thinks. He couldn't be more wrong.

Farid has decided to cast his life and soul with a fundamentalist Islamic sect. He rejects his father's blithe Western values as sources of corruption. Worse, Farid has invited the leader of his sect to move into Parvez' home. The bewildered Parvez can only find solace playing jazz LPs in his basement and talking out his troubles with Bettina (Rachel Griffiths), a prostitute who is enchanted by Parvez' stubborn sense of decency, even in the most sordid situations.

In "My Son the Fanatic," Hanif Kureishi, whose screenplays for "My Beautiful Laundrette" and "Sammy and Rosie _____ " have engaged volatile issues of race, class and sex with devil-may-care wit, expanded his own short story—which focused tightly on the father-son clash—into a complex portrait of Parvez, who is victimized by the same demons of corruption and racism that push his son to extremes, but fights back with stoicism and tolerance.

"There are many ways to be a good man," he tells Farid, who only becomes more intransigent as his sect engages in physical assaults on the prostitutes—including Bettina, with whom, almost in spite of himself, Parvez has fallen in love.

Puri's performance as Parvez brings a warm center of gravity to the movie. His shoulders sag with melancholy and confusion, but never defeat. Though Griffiths' hooker-with-a-heart-of-gold may come across as the only hackneyed convention in an otherwise clever variation on gener-ation-clash motifs, her low-boiling eroticism and sloe-eyed intelligence make it easy to understand how a devoted family man like Parvez can tumble from fidelity.

Director Udayan Prasad is a veteran of British TV, and the movie often slips into the visually cramped pace of made-for-TV melodrama. And though her relative absence probably couldn't be avoided, Desai's droll Minoo seems abandoned by her family and her creator. Her isolation is worthy of another movie. Meanwhile, this one will do fine thanks to Puri's crusty, touching resilience and Kureishi's brilliant dialogue.

SIGHT AND SOUND, 5/98, p. 53, Rachel Malik

Residents of a northern English town, Parvez and his wife Minoo, both originally from Pakistan, are looking forward to their son Farid's marriage to Madelaine, who is white. Parvez works as a cab driver. Many of his regulars are prostitutes, one of whom, Bettina, he has a soft spot for, while his relationship with Minoo is increasingly distant.

Parvez gets a job chauffeuring a visiting German businessman, Schitz. Hoping to do Bettina a favour, he mentions her to Schitz, who hires her. Parvez is shocked when Farid breaks off his engagement on the grounds that a mixed marriage will not work. Wanting only to become a proper Muslim, Farid invites a *maulvi* (or holy man) over from Pakistan to instruct him. The *maulvi* and his acolytes take over the house. Meanwhile, Parvez and Bettina fall in love. Rumours about his father reach Farid. He and his companions campaign against the local prostitutes, culminating in the torching of Bettina's house. Parvez, en route for the airport with Schitz, intervenes to help and finds himself exposed. At home, Parvez discovers that both Minoo and Farid are leaving. Minoo is going to Pakistan, perhaps for good; Farid no longer wants to know his father. He and Bettina face an uncertain future together.

Offering an explanation to his father Parvez of why he broke off his engagement to a white girl, Farid explains that "you can't mix keema and strawberries". It's a fittingly domestic metaphor for *My Son the Fanatic,* Udayan Prasad's follow-up to *Brothers in Trouble,* in which cooking and western-Asian relations were also central. Written by Hanif Kureishi and based on his own short story, the film follows the transformation of Farid from would-be accountant to fervent fundamentalist through the eyes of Parvez.

Parvez, however, is not a simple 'assimilated Asian', there merely to counterpoint his increasingly zealous Islamic son. Indeed, he views Farid's broken engagement as filial disobedience, a challenge to his position as master of his own home. But when a *maulvi* (an Islamic holy man) and his acolytes arrive at Farid's invitation, the social space of the house and Parvez's place within it are transformed. Parvez's wife Minoo must eat separately from the men while Parvez's jazz records are drowned out by Koranic incantations. Meanwhile, as driver and fixer for the seedy visiting businessman Schitz, Parvez is forced into servility. Both Schitz and the *maulvi* are tourists and exploiters: the *maulvi*'s studied authenticity masks his bid for permanent UK residency, while Schitz's smoothness barely conceals violence.

Clearly, Kureishi and Prasad want to parallel the subordinated positions of Parvez and Bettina, the young white hooker he falls in love with. Moreover, for an the apparent unlikeliness of their relationship, this is in essence a very conventional love story, not unlike *The Crying Game* with its own seemingly mismatched protagonists. To play off this 'true love' against the tawdry world of Schitz, the sex party Parvez helps Schitz organise is shot like a cross between a pop video and a soft-porn film, and is contrasted with the privatising red blur that climaxes Bettina and Parvez's first sexual encounter.

However, what is particularly successful about *My Son the Fanatic* is its representation of fundamentalism as solidly modern. Radical Islamic politics are essentially bound up with youth, which functions, here as so often, as a signifier for the modern. The house overflows with fanatical young men. Parvez's final sight of his son, glimpsed from behind as he strides down a side street with his fellow acolytes, is a parody of 'laddism'—another contemporary form of gender separatism. The film thus avoids the common binary opposition which sets enlightened secularism against pre-modern fanaticism. And to further undermine this flawed binary, the film teems with seemingly inappropriate keema-and-strawberries juxtapositions. The *maulvi* giggles at kids' cartoons. Bettina the hooker snorts cocaine in suspenders with Schitz, but drinks tea in a tracksuit with Parvez. Juxtaposition of this kind is a signature of Kureishi's writing and is here, as elsewhere, the site of comedy. But it has a more general function in texts which explore cultural hybridity, such as *Bhaji on the Beach*. For Farid, such juxtapositions are undesirable. For Parvez and Bettina they are simply the complex conditions of living.

But romance also neutralises these complexities and the film is less able to explore the contemporary appeal of fundamentalism that it proposes. Parvez himself is ill-equipped to comprehend the attraction. But his and Farid's dissatisfactions are reactions to the same crisis. Love and religion are two forms of quest or escape. Both Parvez and Farid are trying to escape "the empty accountancy of things": the son through religion, Parvez through his love for Bettina. For all the deliberate specificity of the film's context—this is a post *Satanic Verses* world where stand-up comics make jokes about *fatwas*—love and religion are finally timeless absolutes. The romantic narrative, though it ends ambiguously, despecifies the contemporary. Prostitution may be a figure for capitalism but it is also the world's oldest profession. Love can be seen finally to parenthesise the complexities of contemporary culture, which are refigured as so much roughness in the way of it running its true course.

VILLAGE VOICE, 6/29/99, p. 148, Amy Taubin

Issues of race, racism, and integration loom large in *My Son the Fanatic*, an absorbing, wonderfully acted, and subtly written film about a middle-aged Pakistani man named Parvez (Om Puri) who has lived in the north of England for 25 years, works as a cabdriver, and is trying to integrate himself and his family into English life. In a twist on generational relationships, Parvez's teenage son joins a Muslim fundamentalist sect whose principal occupation is attacking the prostitutes who are frequent customers of his father's taxi.

The film is a complicated study of a' man brought up with traditional values who can't help feeling guilty about his involvement in the sex industry (Parvez lines up dates for visitors he picks up at the airport), but who also wants to embrace the swinging lifestyle that he identifies with Western culture. Puri, one of India's most skilled actors, has a big, homely face that's made to convey mixed emotions, never more so than when this married man is forced to acknowledge that he's in love with one of the prostitutes (Rachel Griffiths). Caught between his past and his future, Parvez takes refuge in his basement to listen to the '40s jazz that fueled his boyhood dreams of the New World. He's a compelling character, but director Udayan Prasad is not altogether comfortable with the point-of-view structure he's set in motion. Sometimes it's not just Parvez who moves in fits and starts, but the film itself as well.

Also reviewed in:
CHICAGO TRIBUNE, 7/2/99, Friday/p. A, Mark Caro
NEW REPUBLIC, 8/9/99, p. 30, Stanley Kauffmann
NEW YORK TIMES, 6/25/99, p. E14, Janet Maslin
VARIETY, 5/12-18/97, p. 76, Derek Elley
WASHINGTON POST, 7/2/99, p. C5, Jane Horwitz
WASHINGTON POST, 7/2/99, Weekend/p. 40, Desson Howe

MYSTERY, ALASKA

A Hollywood Pictures release of a Baldwin/Cohen-Rocking Chair production. *Executive Producer:* Dan Kolsrud. *Producer:* David E. Kelley and Howard Baldwin. *Director:* Jay Roach. *Screenplay:* David E. Kelley and Sean O'Byrne. *Director of Photography:* Peter Deming. *Editor:* Jon Poll. *Music:* Carter Burwell. *Music Editor:* Adam M. Smalley. *Sound:* Larry Sutton and (music) Michael Farrow. *Sound Editor:* George Anderson. *Casting:* Linda Lowy and John Brace. *Production Designer:* Rusty Smith. *Art Director:* Andrew Neskoromny. *Set Decorator:* Elizabeth Wilcox. *Set Dresser:* Gordon Brunner. *Special Effects:* Gary Paller. *Costumes:* Deena Appel. *Make-up:* Victoria Down. *Stunt Coordinator:* Guy Bews. *Running time:* 118 minutes. *MPAA Rating:* R.

CAST: Russell Crowe (John Biebe); Hank Azaria (Charles Danner); Mary McCormack (Donna Biebe); Burt Reynolds (Judge Walter Burns); Colm Meaney (Mayor Scott Pitcher); Lolita Davidovich (Mary Jane Pitcher); Maury Chaykin (Bailey Pruitt); Ron Eldard ("Skank" Marden); Ryan Northcott (Stevie Weeks); Michael Buie (Connor Banks); Kevin Durand ("Tree" Lane); Scott Grimes ("Birdie" Burns); Jason Gray-Stanford (Bobby Michan); Brent Stait (Kevin Holt); Leroy Peltier (Ben Winetka); Adam Beach (Galin Winetka); Cameron Bancroft ("Tinker" Connolly); Michael McKean (Mr. Walsh); Rachel Wilson (Marla Burns); Beth Littleford (Janice Pettiboe); Megyn Price (Sarah Heinz); Judith Ivey (Joanne Burns); Stephen Hair (Jack Danby); Joshua Silberg (Michael Biebe); Regan Sean O'Byrne MacElwain (Joey Biebe); Terry David Mulligan (Dr. Henry Savage); Rod Jarvis (Referee); Lindsay Jarvis (Linesman); Mike Myers (Donnie Shulzhoffer); Jim Fox (Himself); Doug McLeod (Himself); Phil Esposito (Himself); Betty Linde (Mirabelle Houle); Randall Arney (TV Director); Little Richard (Himself); Gary Murdoch (Bodyguard); Genevieve Fraser (Student Charlotte); Taylor Smith (Student Tommy); Matt Clarke (Joe); Scott Olynek (Bob); Zane Snow (Jeff); Joe Turvey (Walt); Brenda Shuttleworth (Deputy Betty Fisher); Michael Auger (Gordon Herrod); Shaun Johnston (D.A. Dollof); Karen Gartner (Jury Foreman); Bruce Nozick (NHL Lawyer); Gerry Becker (Players' Union Lawyer); L. Scott Caldwell (Judge McGibbons); Steve Levy (Himself); Barry Melrose (Himself).

LOS ANGELES TIMES, 10/1/99, Calendar/p. 6, Kenneth Turan

"Mystery, Alaska" is a film that believes, in the words of hockey player and ladies' man Skank Marden, that "skating and fornicating are the most fun you can have in the winter." While that may or may not be accurate in life, on screen it's half true at best.

For while the hockey scenes in this "Rocky on Ice" fable are enjoyable, attempts to expand the film's horizons to include both juvenile sexual humor and quasi-serious examinations of troubled relationships come off as stiff as a frozen flounder. Dozing off during the exposition and waking up for the on-ice action is definitely the way to go.

Co-written (with Princeton hockey teammate Sean O'Byrne) and co-produced by David E. Kelley, the creator of "Ally McBeal" and "The Practice," "Mystery" is set in that mythical "Northern Exposure"-ish Alaska hamlet, population 633.

While it's unclear what most people do for a living in Mystery, hockey is the place's No. 1 obsession, a passion that focuses on a local phenomenon called the Saturday game.

Once a week during the winter, the best players in town—so chosen by a committee of Mystery's leading citizens—get together and play against one another on a frozen pond for love of the game and the edification of the local citizenry. The team's hardiest veteran is Sheriff John Biebe (Russell Crowe), a scrappy playmaker who's been in the Saturday game for a record 13 years.

The film opens at a point when Mystery's game is about to get some national exposure. Charles Danner (Hank Azaria), a local boy who left Mystery (mostly because he was one of the town's worst skaters) for a writing career in Manhattan, has gotten a story on the weekly ritual into Sports Illustrated.

More than that, the owners of the New York Rangers were intrigued enough by the piece to consider a good-for-publicity exhibition game in Mystery, pitting the NHL powerhouse against the local legends. "It'll be good for the economy," one resident says, while another responds, "What economy?"

When "Mystery" sticks to ice-related doings, like the possibility that the sheriff might be bumped from the squad, it rarely loses its footing. The team's players, even if they are familiar types like sex machine Skank (Ron Eldard), hot young prospect Stevie Weeks (Ryan Northcott) and Tree Lane (Kevin Durand), the big guy who doesn't know his own strength, are amusing en masse, and David vs. Goliath sports events have an undeniable heartwarming appeal.

Though a comic cameo by Mike Myers as a hockey legend turned TV commentator is highly effective, it is Australian Crowe, a previous non-skater, who gives the film's standout performance. Almost unrecognizable from his breakthrough in "L.A. Confidential," Crowe is one of those blessed leading men who can convincingly disappear inside a variety of roles.

It's unfortunate that "Mystery, Alaska" can't stick to hockey, because the other things on its mind are best forgotten. Examining local marriages, like that of Mayor Scott Pitcher (Colm Meaney) and his straying Mary Jane (Lolita Davidovich) or the sheriff and wife Donna (Mary McCormack), who was Charles Danner's girlfriend in 12th grade, couldn't be a duller exercise. In fact, it's notable that director Jay Roach (best known for his two "Austin Powers" films) can get the actors to play this pro forma material without flinching.

"Mystery, Alaska's" other interest is even more tiresome. Echoing Kelley's naughty boy tendencies in "Lake Placid," which had Betty White cursing like a stevedore, this film takes the most childish delight in comic profanity and inappropriate remarks coming out of youthful mouths. It sounds like a minor tendency, but it's so overly cute it makes you want to gag.

Coming after the even more ill-starred "Lake Placid," "Mystery, Alaska" increases the impression that writer-producer Kelley can't be bothered to give big-screen projects his full attention. If he released material this halfhearted on television, there would be a lot fewer Emmys for him to call his own.

NEW YORK POST, 10/1/99, p. 54, Lou Lumenick

"Mystery, Alaska," which tries to cross "Slap Shot" with "Northern Exposure," doesn't quite achieve its goal, but this overgrown little movie does offer solid laughs, engaging performances and a captivating setting.

That would be the remote little village of the title, where the residents have two main interests.

"I play hockey and fornicate," explains one character, "because they're the two most fun things to do in cold weather."

When they aren't hopping into one others' beds, the good folk of Mystery are obsessing about their Saturday hockey game on an ice pond, a decades-long tradition.

But the purity of that experience is challenged when a former-resident-turned-sportswriter (a wonderfully smarmy Hank Azaria) returns with a stunning offer. He wants the Mystery men, whose skills he's hyped in a magazine article, to play the New York Rangers in Alaska as a televised stunt.

The town judge and resident hockey expert (Burt Reynolds in foxy-grandpa mode) warns the pond players they haven't a prayer against professionals and he refuses, at least at first, to coach the team.

But civic pride wins out, and the mayor (Colm Meaney) pressures the sheriff (Russell Crowe) to take on the job—though he just cut the 34-year-old sheriff from the squad after 13 seasons to make room for a high-school phenom (Ryan Northcott).

To make things worse, the sportswriter is flirting with his ex-sweetheart, the sheriff s wife (Mary McCormack). Crowe also has to arrest the team's star player, a grocery clerk (Michael Buie), for shooting a representative of a Wal-Mart-style chain (Michael McKean) in the foot.

And the mayor's wife (Lolita Davidovich) is fooling around with yet another player (Ron Eldard).

You practically need a scorecard to keep track of the players in this amiable ensemble piece, which springs from the fevered brains of TV uber-producer David E. Kelley ("The Practice," "Ally McBeal" and this summer's unfortunate big-screen misfire "Lake Placid") and Sean O'Byrne, a writer on Kelley's fondly remembered "Picket Fences."

Indeed, "Mystery, Alaska" throws in so many quirky subplots, it often feels like a very long (127 minutes) TV episode, with lots of obscenity and sexual activity added.

But it has a terrific cast (including Judith Ivey as Reynolds' wife, and priceless cameos by Mike Myers as a sportscaster and Little Richard as himself).

Crowe ("L.A. Confidential") is wonderful as the hang-dog lawman who watches helplessly as the town slides into giddy self-delusion. Maury Chaykin is funny and touching as the town lawyer, who goes to New York to plead Mystery's case in court when the Ranger players balk at the Alaska junket.

Director Jay Roach (who helmed the two Austin Powers movies) gets maximum laughs of out the material, though his staging of the climactic game is sometimes a mite confusing. (No, the Rangers don't play themselves, and it's far from "Hoosiers" on skates).

"Mystery, Alaska" is not a great movie, but it's consistently entertaining and almost worth seeing just for the beautifully photographed setting, a town the filmmakers created from scratch at the base of a mountain in Alberta, Canada.

NEWSDAY, 10/1/99, Part II/p. B6, Gene Seymour

Could "Mystery, Alaska's" pedigree possibly be any weirder? The creator of TV's "Ally McBeal," "The Practice" and "Picket Fences" helped write and produce it, while the guy who directed it has both "Austin Powers" movies on his resume. With David E. Kelley and Jay Roach respectively on board, it's a safe guess this hockey movie spares little in the way of cuddly quirkiness, over-the-top speechmaking and raunchy suggestiveness.

All present and accounted for. And the movie's heart is as slick as a patch of ice on blacktop. You can almost smell the corn and cheese through the snowy landscape.

Empty as the calories are, however, you compulsively gobble the gratuitous poignance and "Rocky"-esque melodrama. "Mystery, Alaska" is fun to watch, even if you're not a hockey fan, thanks to an appealing cast and some exciting game scenes ... if, that is, you don't mind waiting for them.

Kelley, who wrote the script with fellow hockey amateur Sean O'Byrne, borrows not a little from his "Picket Fences" formula to build another small town—the title character, if you will—with a wise sheriff (Russell Crowe), a corpulent litigator (Maury Chaykin) and a crusty judge (Burt Reynolds), along with a scattering of good moms, bored wives, lusty hunks and a few "colorful" types scattered about.

All of whom are passionately engaged in the town's ongoing ritual of Saturday morning hockey games, in which the young male population pairs off in two teams that play at a competitive level close to major league. Word of Mystery, Alaska's hockey obsession is no longer a mystery, thanks to a Sports Illustrated cover story by one of the local exiles, a journalist (Hank Azaria) who, for reasons never clearly explained, has a mutually mistrustful relationship with his hometown.

Soon the town's mayor (Colm Meaney) gets word that the New York Rangers have been tagged to play an exhibition game with Mystery's all-stars; one of whom, a notorious ladies man named Skank (Ron Eldard) is carrying on an affair with the mayor's wife (Lolita Davidovich).

Both the aforementioned judge and sheriff worry that the town will become a global joke if it loses. The game somehow manages to survive a gauntlet of complications, from the shooting of a supermarket corporation heavy (Michael McKean) by the town's best goal scorer to frictions between husbands and wives, fathers and sons, boyfriend and girlfriends. And it's sometimes just too much to bear, all these cozy-quirky contrivances that are ready made for home video.

Still, the bright, snappy performers carry out their bright, snappy parts to great effect. The role of avuncular scold seems an odd fit for Reynolds, but he handles it gracefully. Crowe, as the town conscience and aging team captain, is a solid presence, while Davidovich, Mary McCormack (as Crowe's wife) and the other women are so good, they make you forget how relatively inconsequential women are in the all-but-inevitable outcome.

VILLAGE VOICE, 10/5/99, p. 212, Jessica Winter

Where the hockey's good, the compass points north, and the ladies stay warm all night. Mystery, Alaska, is a tiny burg, little more than a post office and a plow stranded in the middle of freezing white *nada-y-pues-nada,* where the locals block the encroaching tentacles of conglomeration with muskets and moxie (early on, a surveying suit from a Wal-Mart-type plunderbund visits the hardware store and takes a bullet in the foot for his trouble). The townies are intrigued, however, when another big-city hotshot, prodigal son Hank Azaria, engineers a publicity stunt that brings the New York Rangers to Mystery for a game of pros-versus-provincials hockey, on a real pond no less; the gimmick occasions plenty of self-affirmation and sexual healing as the ad hoc teammates hone their stick action.

This boreal *Rocky* (oh, wait, that was *Rocky IV*) could at least deliver a suspenseful David-and-Goliath rumble for its climax, but director Jay Roach (who helmed both Austin Powers movies) has filmed possibly the first hockey match bereft of a single semiaerial shot—instead of the spontaneous give-and-take choreography of a good game, all Roach offers is the actions of individual players in rapid succession; your brain can't keep up with what your eye is seeing. In lieu of exciting outdoor sports, the slack, saccharine script (cowritten by bland TV juggernaut David E. Kelley) bears down hard on the troubled state of indoor sports in Mystery: Colm Meaney's mayor catches his puck-slut spouse (Lolita Davidovich) offside with a strapping left wing; the stoic, bearlike sheriff played by Russell Crowe suffers a marriage that can't get the brakes off its skates; and miscellaneous utility players log skates; and miscellaneous utility players log time in the sexual penalty box. But sleep well: however cold it might seem, we're still in Disney territory, where everyone rides his or her Zamboni into the great good night.

Also reviewed in:
NEW YORK TIMES, 10/1/99, p. E27, Stephen Holden
VARIETY, 9/27-10/3/99, p. 36, Robert Koehler
WASHINGTON POST, 10/1/99, p. C5, Stephen Hunter
WASHINGTON POST, 10/1/99, Weekend/p. 45, Desson Howe

MYSTERY MEN

A Universal Pictures and Lawrence Gordon release of a Golar/Lloyd Levin/Dark Horse production. *Executive Producer:* Robert Engelman. *Producer:* Lawrence Gordon, Mike Richardson, and Lloyd Levin. *Director:* Kinka Usher. *Screenplay:* Neil Cuthbert. *Based on the Dark Horse Comic Book Series:* Bob Burden. *Director of Photography:* Stephen H. Burum. *Editor:* Conrad Buff. *Music:* Stephen Warbeck. *Music Editor:* Alex Gibson. *Choreographer:* Anita Mann. *Sound:* Douglas B. Arnold and (music) Dennis Sands. *Sound Editor:* Fred Judkins. *Casting:* Mindy Marin. *Production Designer:* Kirk M. Petruccelli. *Art Director:* Barry Chusid. *Set Designer:* James Bayliss, Nathan Crowley, Mary Finn, Chad Frey, Liz Lapp, Richard Mays, Marco Rubeo, Domenic Silvestri, Paul Sonski, and Sally Thornton. *Set Decorator:* Victor Zolfo. *Set Dresser:* John Maxwell, Gregory Griffith, Wayne Haas, Paul Mugavero, and Rick Staves. *Special Effects:* Terry Frazee. *Visual Effects:* Lori J. Nelson. *Costumes:* Marilyn Vance. *Make-up:* Scott Edo. *Stunt Coordinator:* Mickey Gilbert. *Running time:* 100 minutes. *MPAA Rating:* PG-13.

CAST: Hank Azaria (Blue Raja); Janeane Garofalo (Bowler); William H. Macy (Shoveler); Kel Mitchell (Invisible Boy); Paul Reubens (Spleen); Ben Stiller (Furious); Wes Studi (Sphinx); Greg Kinnear (Captain Amazing/Lance); Eddie Izzard (Tony P); Prakazrel Michel (Tony C); Lena Olin (Dr. Annabel Leek); Geoffrey Rush (Casanova Frankenstein); Ernie Lee Banks (Ted); Gerry Becker (Banyon); Ned Bellamy (Funk); Corbin Bleu (Butch); Philip Bolden (Roland); Jake Cross (Thugs); Claire Forlani (Monica); Ricky Jay (Vic Weems); Louise Lasser (Violet); Emmy Laybourne (Reporter); Jenifer Lewis (Lucille); Mason Lucero (Young Kid); Monet Mazur (Becky Beaner); Joel McCrary (Funk); Chris Mugglebee (Reporter); Olivia Lauren Todd (Tracy); Frederick Usher (Thug); Kinka Usher (Moe); Gayle Vance (Sally); Tom Waits (Dr. Heller); James Dukes (Big Tobacco); Michael Bay, Riki Rachtman, and Noah Blake (Frat Boys); Michael Chieffo, Gil Christner, and Carl Strano (Suits); Artie Lange (Big Red); Margaret Wheeler (Old Lady); Billy Beck and Robert Lieb (Old Men); Sarah Kane and Florence Stone Fevergeon (Old Party Goers); Ed Denette (Old Veteran); Kiyoko Yamaguchi, Kiko Kiko, and Nori T. Gehr (Back-up Singers); Mark Mothersbaugh (Band Leader); Nancye Ferguson

(Singer); Stacey Travis and Joann Richter (Powerwomen); Larkin Campbell (Supervacman); Oliver Clark (Reverse Psychologist); Jack Plotnick (Mr. Pups); Dane Cook (Waffler); Robert Musselman (Ballerinaman); Vince Melocchi (Mailman); Doug Jones (Pencilhead); Vincent Bowman (Son of Pencilhead); Vylette Fagerholm (Little Miss Vengeance); Dana Gould (Squeegeeman); Branden Williams (Maintainer); Aaron Priest (Artiste); Robret B. Martin, Jr. (Big Billy Hill Billy); Gabrielle Conferti (PMS Avenger); Jeff Z. Danziger (Radio Man); Wilbert Sampson and Kenneth W. Watts (Pigs); Elliot Durant, III (Martial Artist); Anthony Sebastian Marinelli (Gorilla);   Drinda E. Shaneyfelt (Evil Devil Woman);   Felix Castro (Globalman); Michael Craig (Gardener); Ronald Lasky (Bullfighter); David Still (Stilt Man); Jonathan Khan (Fisherman); Jerry Farmer (Thirstyman).

CHRISTIAN SCIENCE MONITOR, 8/6/99, p. 15, David Sterritt

[*Mystery Men* was reviewed jointly with *The Iron Giant*; see Sterritt's review of that film.]

LOS ANGELES TIMES, 8/6/99, Calendar/p. 1, Kenneth Turan

It's their names that gives them away:

Mr. Furious, "a ticking time bomb of fury" who has trouble getting a date.

The Blue Raja, "the master of cutlery," who lives at home with his erratic mother.

The Shoveler, implement at the ready, decked out in his son's Little League chest protector and in-line skating kneepads.

These are real superheroes? Fighters against the blight of crime and corruption like the celebrated Captain Amazing? It's got to be some kind of joke, right? Well, yes and no.

For while Furious (Ben Stiller), Raja (Hank Azaria) and the Shoveler (William H. Macy) are serious about their quest to be crusaders against evil in Champion City, "Mystery Men" is a tongue-in-cheek hipster celebration of the humor inherent in their determination.

Inspired by a Dark Horse comic created by Bob Burden, this high-style parody of the superhero ethos (written by Nell Cuthbert and directed by commercial whiz Kinka Usher in his feature debut) has all the qualities so often missing in film: It's clever, amusing, clever, visually inventive, clever, well-cast... did anyone say it was clever?

For watching "Mystery Men" is a bit like sitting next to a brilliant person at a dinner party who just won't shut up. Because this film is so self-conscious and, like Mr. Furious and friends, has a tendency to try too hard, it's an effort you end up admiring more than completely loving. Influenced by its betters, films such as "Brazil," "Buckaroo Banzai" and even "Blade Runner," it's destined to join them all in cult film heaven.

Our trio of heroes make their entrance during an attempted robbery of a retirement home by the heartless Red Eyes gang. With the Blue Raja erratically hurling forks and spoons (knives wouldn't be sporting), the Shoveler unloading on the wrong targets and Mr. Furious not as mad as he'd like to be, these wannabes do as much damage to themselves as to the badguys.

Fortunately, the justly famous Captain Amazing (Greg Kinnear), Champion City's resident superhero, puts in an appearance and sets things right. It's back to the coffee shop for this lot, where Mr. Furious has his eye on a new waitress (Claire Forlani) and all three engage in the kind of "what's holding us back" post-mortems that is their forte.

Unknown to the group, Captain Amazing has his problems, too. We catch up to the local hero in his limo, where he's berating his agent (Ricky Jay) about losing the lucrative Pepsi endorsement. That's right, this superhero shills for products like Mighty Whitey toothpaste and has as many logos on his chest as a stock car champion.

The problem is that the Captain is so good at what he does that he's already eliminated the kind of worthy opponents that keep sponsors happy. His solution is a novel one: He connives to have his greatest rival, Casanova Frankenstein (Geoffrey Rush), released from an asylum and put on the streets again.

Casanova, obviously, is not without his wiles, and soon enough our three "jive superheroes," as a scoffer calls them, realize that if anyone is going to save Champion City from a wave of Casanova crime, it has to be them.

Considerably daunted, their first thought is to increase their number. Against their better judgment, they add Invisible Boy (Kel Mitchell), who's only invisible when no one's looking, and the pestilent Spleen (Paul Reubens), who has turned flatulence into a nearly fatal art form.

Joining up as well are the Bowler (Janeane Garofalo), who carries around the skull of her genuine superhero father, Carmine, in a crystal bowling ball, and the mysterious Sphinx (Wes Studi), whose strength lies in such baffling aphorisms as "He who questions training only trains himself in asking questions." And don't forget the eccentric Dr. Heller (Tom Waits), a genius at designing nonlethal weapons. Next stop, Cha-teau Casanova.

All this takes place in an extravagant visual world, part Batman's Gotham but with a loopiness of its own devising, contributed to by production designer Kirk M. Petruccelli, costumer Marilyn Vance and a small handful of visual effects houses.

With expert and well-matched comic actors such as Stiller, Macy and Garofalo on the team, "Mystery Men" has no trouble creating a consistent flow of amusement. Typically, however, the film undercuts three of its most potent performers (Rush, Azaria and Reubens) by giving them all either accents or vocal mannerisms that are more grating than entertaining. Knowing when to stop is as much an asset for a film as knowing where to go, and "Mystery Men," having skillfully mastered one, would benefit by showing more of the other.

NEW YORK POST, 8/6/99, p. 42, Rod Dreher

What's good about "Mystery Men": the prospect of spending two comedy-filled hours in the company of an inspired comic cast, including Ben Stiller, Janeane Garofalo, the great William H. Macy and—ta-daaa—Paul "Pee-wee Herman" Reubens, returning to the big screen after too long in exile.

Don't be taken in. What's bad about it is everything else. And not even the bizarrely amusing spectacle of Pee-wee Herman farting like a mule can save this inane stinker, this year's "The Avengers." It could only be less entertaining if it were in Latvian, without subtitles.

"Mystery Men" is a "humorous" action fantasy about a trio of would-be superheroes mired in the pits of perpetual loserdom. The three are the Blue Raja (Hank Azaria), an effete mama's boy who throws silverware, affects a limey accent and dresses like Carnak the Magnificent; the Shoveler (Macy), a dutiful working-class father whose specialty is conking villains on the head with his spade; and Mr. Furious (Stiller), a leather-clad neurotic who tries to subdue baddies through displays of his rotten temper.

The Mystery Men labor in the towering shadow of Captain Amazing (Greg Kinnear), Champion City's leading superhero, a celebrity in his own right. Having put away all the city's super-villains, Amazing secretly worries that he'll lose his product endorsements for lack of anything to do. He quietly conspires to have the Lecter-like Casanova Frankenstein (Oscar winner Geoffrey Rush, for Pete's sake) released from prison.

His scheme backfires, though, when C.F. has Amazing kidnapped, and bound and gagged, leaving Champion City open to C.F.'s ghoulish pleasures—and creating an opportunity for the hapless Mystery Men. They attempt to transcend their fourth-rate status by recruiting new members—the bitchy Bowler (Janeane Garofalo), the pimple-faced flatus-spewer Spleen (Reubens) and the rather nontransparent Invisible Boy (Kel Mitchell)—to take on the fiendish C.F.

It must have sounded like a good idea in the pitch meeting: Gather some of the funniest and most talented actors around, and have them send up superhero comic-book conventions. But in the event, it's awful. A handful of snickery moments aside, "Mystery Men" is a feature-length skit that wastes the time and talents of everyone involved.

NEWSDAY, 8/6/99, Part II/p. B6, Gene Seymour

"Mystery Men" manages to exalt both the terminally weird and the frighteningly mundane with such flamboyant good spirits that you overlook its occasional dead zones and dull patches. Try as it might to prop up its static plot, the movie is more comic revue than action comedy. Viewed within these parameters, "Mystery Men" is as satisfying as a heaping helping of Abbott-and-Costello shorts. And much smarter than the average doofus blockbuster.

Adapted from "Flaming Carrot" comic-book creator Bob Burden's series, "Mystery Men" deals with a gang of losers who walk the streets of Champion City under the delusion that they are superheroes. There's the Blue Raja (Hank Azaria), a silverware-slinging faux British fop who is really a mother-dominated wimp.

There's the Shoveler (William H. Macy), whose long-suffering African-American wife wishes he would put away that silly shovel and spend more time with the kids.

There's the pockmark-faced Spleen (Paul Reubens, the artist formerly known as Pee Wee Herman), who is to passing wind what Keith Richards is to rhythm guitar. Last and least, there's Mister Furious (Ben Stiller), whose "super power" is Getting Really, Really Mad.

No one takes these misfits seriously—especially since they routinely get the crap beaten out of them by gangs like the Disco Boys. Indeed, the city's reigning super guy, Captain Amazing (Greg Kinnear), barely notices them. He's too busy noticing the slow erosion of his commercial endorsements.

To remedy that situation, Cap's secret identity (whom everyone knows anyway) engineers the parole of his arch nemesis, the creepy Casanova Frankenstein (Geoffrey Rush), who proceeds to pick up where he left off by capturing his benefactor and holding him hostage.

Suddenly, the Mystery Guys find themselves the city's last best hope. Sensing correctly that they need help, they recruit Invisible Boy (Nickelodeon network star Kel Williams), who can only turn invisible when no one else is looking. A poolside party held at the Shoveler's house to audition costumed help yields the smart-alecky Bowler (Janeane Garofalo), whose bowling ball contains the skull of her martyred hero-dad. With the maddingly oracular Sphinx (Wes Studi) giving them spiritual advice, and chicken farmer-mad scientist Tom Waits arming them with "nonlethal" hardware, these high-strung wannabes are ready to meet their destiny.

Director Kinka Usher brings to this crowded story the same antic verve he used in his Taco Bell talking-chihuahua commercials. Even the least self-aware nerd will recognize the shrewdness with which the movie inquires into the very nature of comic-book obsession.

Best of all, the apparent enjoyment of everyone involved is so infectious that you laugh the occasional languors away. If the unspeakable happens and a sequel is made, one presumes that a tighter, leaner script will be in order since, by then, everyone will know what these guys can—and can't—do.

SIGHT AND SOUND, 2/00, p. 50, Jonathan Romney

Champion City, USA. Irascible Roy and his friends Eddie and Jeffrey are aspiring superheroes, fighting crime under the guises of the Furious, The Shoveller and the fork-throwing Blue Raja. But their efforts are eclipsed by the sponsorship-conscious Captain Amazing.

Worried about his declining profile, Captain Amazing engineers the release from prison of mad criminal Casanova Frankenstein, only to be captured by him. The trio recruit equally inept sidekicks the flatulent Spleen, the all-too visible invisible Boy—and finally become a team with the addition of The Bowler, who carries her father's skull in a bowling ball. They also find a mentor, the enigma-spouting Sphinx. In a rescue attempt, Captain Amazing is accidentally killed by the team; but they eventually defeat Frankenstein with the aid of eccentric weapons expert Doctor Heller. Despite looking from the artwork and the casting to be a more appealing proposition than the usual run of comicbook spin-offs, *Mystery Men* proves a grotesquely wasted opportunity. No expense has been spared to provide a cast that evokes off-beat modishness, but what went wrong can pretty much be guessed from the CV of Kinka Usher, a commercials director making his feature debut here after doing the business for Miller Lite, Nissan and Nike.

Mystery Men crassly parodies superhero comics without acknowledging that the smartest comic strips have been tilting at their own absurd conventions at least since the renaissance of Marvel in the 60s (the Blue Raja's relationship with his mother looks like a poor shadow of Spiderman's early domestic tensions with his aged Aunt May). Like most recent superhero films, *Mystery Men* takes Tim Burton's *Batman* as a starting point, particularly in its dystopian urban setting Champion City. But the clumsy, often condescending parody is sanctioned by a comic book company, Dark Horse Comics, one which ought to have known better given that it is already responsible for such overblown effects laden movies as *The Mask* and *Barb Wire*.

Mystery Men, which spun off from the austerely bizarre *Flaming Carrot* comics, has a one-joke premise: its costumed heroes barely have basic competence, let alone superpowers, and believe that the only qualifications needed are the right rhetoric and a snappy costume.

In fact, the film finally endorses that view: the team only come into their own once they replace their makeshift look with diligently hand-sewn costumes in glittery fabrics (costume upgrades seem to have become a feature of the genre when Joel Schumacher inherited the Batman franchise, although there are no rubber nipples here).

A desperately hit-and-miss affair, *Mystery Men* depends largely on the personalities of its top-heavy cast. There are a few star turns: William H. Macy's home-loving regular Joe, Paul Reubens as a grotesque zit-faced *pétomane*, and Hank Azaria as an American momma's boy apeing the tones of a 30s English fop. And Wes Studi is largely responsible for buoying up the film's final third, intoning portentous one liners: "You must be like the wolf pack, not like the six pack."

But there's a frightening waste of talent too, making you wonder just how much of whose screen time was cut: Tom Waits, Eddie Izzard (who should have known to avoid henchman roles after *The Avengers*), as well as a briefly glimpsed Lena Olin. The greatest shame is that Janeane Garofalo, memorably abrasive on *The Larry Sanders Show*, still hasn't found a big-screen venture that knows what to do with her.

A lazy script works on the one-note premise that superheroes are just deluded schmucks with too much nervous energy. But the writers finally play it safe by calling on unearthly powers to wrap things up. Usher, seduced by what looks like a gargantuan design budget, directs like someone who either doesn't love comics at all or loves the wrong sort too much. *Mystery Men* is a horrible mess with little to recommend it, except for nice touches in DP Stephen H. Burum's and designer Kirk Petruccelli's colour palette. Unfortunately, few strident reds and purples don't make a movie.

TIME, 8/9/99, p. 66, Richard Corliss

Are we not all dreamy or daft enough to think of ourselves as superheroes in the comic book of our lives? Are we not tickled to think that the world is somehow dependent on our skills and charisma? And do we not come to understand, in the bleak clarity of reality, that some heroes—especially the one staring at us in the bathroom mirror—will never be truly super?

It was the inspiration of comic-book artiste Bob Burden to answer these ornate rhetorical questions. He created, in his *Mystery Men* stories, "a bizarre hodgepodge crew of second string, blue collar, milltown heroes." Now Burden's words are made flesh in a movie version that, for all its fights and stuff blowing up, dares to deflect action-adventure expectations to pursue off-kilter character comedy.

Each of our heroes has a tiny, not very useful skill. Mr. Furious (Ben Stiller) works himself into a fine rage. The Blue Raja (Hank Azaria) flings silverware. And the Shoveler (William H. Macy)—as he says, "I shovel well. I shovel *very* well." While glitzy Captain Amazing (Greg Kinnear) routinely saves Champion City with his bravado and big ego, the Mystery Men must scrounge to find the perils they believe they were born to overcome.

Neil Cuthbert's clever screenplay is a parable of class. The three main Mystery Men may not be much, but when they audition other heroes in preparation for battle against evil genius Casanova Frankenstein (Geoffrey Rush), they discover there are nicely delineated levels of mediocrity.

The Waffler, with his magic Truth Syrup, White Flight and the Black Menace ("We work together")—all are unworthy of joining even this pickup team. But there is talent out there. The Bowler (Janeane Garofalo) has a magic ball with her father's head inside; Dad nags her from beyond the grave. Spleen (Paul Reubens) unleashes fart darts, silent but deadly. The Sphinx (Wes Studi) has a profoundly inane aphorism for every tight spot. Invisible Boy (Kel Mitchell) may one day live up to his name. In unity these losers find strength and cool. The unholy three become the Seven Glamourai.

What's cool about *Mystery Men* is that it is what it's about. Expected to underachieve in a season of teen-boy farces, it triumphs by being its smart, shambling self, though it takes a while to get there. In the opening scene, director Kinka Usher tries to get a Tim Burton flavor of dark comic hipness and blows it; he is flailing even as Mr. Furious does at first. Usher feels his way to the right tempo and tone, and when he finds it he doesn't let go.

He gets seamless ensemble work from the year's most agreeable, most cannily chosen cast. These, after all, are not-quite stars playing not-quite supermen. They grow in the roles as they grow comfortable in them. By the end they have cobbled together an A-minus comedy about B-plus people. Every other action picture is about the impossibly outsize Them; this one is about the just barely heroic Us. It's about making the best of your small talents—about looking in the mirror and, despite all evidence to the contrary, smiling back.

VILLAGE VOICE, 8/10/99, p. 64, Gary Dauphin

The loser superheroes of the unexpectedly smart comic book send-up *Mystery Men* are a pretty pathetic lot. There's Mr. Furious (professional neurotic Ben Stiller) who gets really, really mad, the Shoveler (a painfully nice William H. Macy) who does semi-nifty things with a shovel, and the self-described fop Blue Raja (Hank Azaria) who throws forks with not-so-pinpoint accuracy. Bumbling in the shadow of a real superhero, the corporate-logo-adorned Captain Amazing (a perfectly smug Greg Kinnear), the trio hope for just one legit feat of derring-do, when what they really need (or at least needed 15 years ago) is a long, all-body soak in a powerful astringent.

The team gets its chance for redemption when Captain Amazing, stung by low super-fight ratings and the loss of his Pepsi endorsement, has his biggest arch-nemesis Casanova Frankenstein (an appropriately loony Geoffrey Rush) paroled. Frankenstein of course has other plans—not only kidnapping Amazing but setting about the de rigueur destruction of the world. Furious, Shoveler, and Raja stumble into action, holding a super-friend tryout pool party that nets only the ball-throwing Bowler (Janeane Garofalo), a fart-aiming Spleen (Paul "Pee Wee" Reubens), and the Invisible Boy (Kel Mitchell), a black kid who can apparently disappear, but only when no one is looking.

Skillfully adapted from Bob Burden's indie comic series, *Mystery Men* is less interested in high-flying bang-ups than in the side-business of slaying personal dragons, like Furious's daily humiliations at the hands of his boss or the Shoveler's African American wife, who wants to know just when he's going to give this superhero foolishness up. As with the best tales of loser supermen, *Mystery Men* is wryly sentimental stuff, but it's also pretty sharp, imagining a low-brow universe where the primal secret origin isn't a radioactive spider's bite but the ever-transformative purchase of that first comic book.

Also reviewed in:
CHICAGO TRIBUNE, 8/6/99, Friday/p. D, Mark Caro
NATION, 9/6 & 13/99, p. 35, Stuart Klawans
NEW YORK TIMES, 8/6/99, p. E14, Janet Maslin
VARIETY, 8/2-8/99, p. 32, Godfrey Cheshire
WASHINGTON POST, 8/6/99, p. C5, Rita Kempley
WASHINGTON POST, 8/6/99, Weekend/p. 43, Michael O'Sullivan

NEVER BEEN KISSED

A Fox 2000 Pictures release of a Flower Films/Bushwood Pictures production. *Executive Producer:* Drew Barrymore. *Producer:* Sandy Isaac and Nancy Juvonen. *Director:* Raja Gosnell. *Screenplay:* Abby Kohn and Marc Silverstein. *Director of Photography:* Alex Nepomniaschy. *Editor:* Debra Chiate and Marcelo Sansevieri. *Music:* David Newman, Mary Ramos-Oden, and Michele Kuznetsky. *Music Editor:* Tom Vilano. *Choreographer:* Marguerite Derricks. *Sound:* Keith A. Wester and (music) John Kurlander. *Sound Editor:* Michael D. Wilhoit. *Casting:* Justine Baddeley and Kim Davis. *Production Designer:* Steven Jordan. *Art Director:* William Hiney. *Set Designer:* Susan E. Lomino. *Set Decorator:* Suzette Sheets. *Set Dresser:* Addam Olszewski, Peter J. Bates, Rick "Gramps" Manalia, Glenn S. Matayoshi, and Lisa Ozanne. *Special Effects:* John Hartigan. *Costumes:* Mona Way. *Make-up:* Kimberly Greene. *Stunt Coordinator:* Joni Avery. *Running time:* 97 minutes. *MPAA Rating:* PG-13.

CAST: Drew Barrymore (Josie Geller);   David Arquette (Rob Geller);   Michael Vartan (Sam Coulson);   SUN-TIMES: Molly Shannon (Anita);   John C. Reilly (Gus);   Garry Marshall (Rigfort);   Sean Whelan (Merkin);   Cress Williams (George);   Octavia L. Spencer (Cynthia); Sarah DeVincentis (Rhoda);   Allen Covert (Roger in Op/Ed);   Rock Reiser (Dutton);   David Doty (Hairplug Bruns);   Derrick Morgan (Armcast Henson);   Kathleen Marshall (Sun Times Worker); Jenny Bicks (Miss Haskell);   SOUTH GLEN SOUTH: Leelee Sobieski (Aldys);   Jeremy Jordan (Guy Perkins);   Jessica Alba (Kirsten);   Marley Shelton (Kristen);   Jordan Ladd (Gibby);   Katie Lansdale (Tracy);   Branden Williams (Tommy);   James Edward Franco (Jason);   Gregory Sporleder (Coach Romano);   Martha Hackett (Mrs. Knox);   Jennifer Parsons (P.E. Teacher); Andrew Wilson (School Guard);   Giuseppe Andrews (Denominator);   Alex Solowitz (Brett); Niesha Trout (Sera);   Chad Christian Haywood (Matz);   Cory Hardrict (Packer);   Chad Todhunter (Stoner #1);   Daniel Louis Rivas (Stoner #2);   Mark Edwards (School Guard #2);   Denny Kirkwood (Billy Prince);   Marissa Jaret Winokur (Sheila);   Carmen Llywellyn (Rob's Girlfriend); Sara Downing (Billy's Prom Date);   Mike G. Moyer (Monty Malik);   Steven Wilde (Bouncer); Maya McLaughlin (Lara);   David Douglas (Rasta);   Russell Bobbitt (Carny);   Tara Skye (Tyke); Mark Allen (D.J.);   Conor O'Neil (Gibby's Prom Date);   Joe Ochman (Prom Judge #1);   Don Snell (Prom Judge #2);   Jason Weissbrod (Big Bad Wolf);   Tinsley Grimes (Little Red Riding Hood);   Joshua Fitzgerald (Tarzan);   Amanda Wilmshurst (Fruit Headdress Woman).

LOS ANGELES TIMES, 4/9/99, Calendar/p. 2, Kenneth Turan

It's taken some years, but Drew Barrymore's career has finally come full circle. After she became America's moppet sweetheart in 1982's "E.T.," the actress' work and image took a series of hairpin turns, but now, with "Never Been Kissed," she's as warm and appealing as she ever was. Maybe even more.

An easygoing and amusing romantic confection, "Never Been Kissed" solidifies the work Barrymore did in last year's "The Wedding Singer" and "Ever After." At this point in time, there may be no American actress with the same combination of spunkiness and adorability, someone we so desperately want to see live happily ever after.

Frankly, it's difficult to imagine "Never Been Kissed" and its story of a dowdy 25-year-old going back to high school as an undercover journalist succeeding without Barrymore's core likability. With an improbable plot line that has the emotional texture of an episode of "Happy Days," "Never Been Kissed" presents its star with speeches that would have flummoxed gee-whiz 1940s girl-next-door June Allyson. Yet Barrymore not only makes us buy this piffle, we even end up liking it.

Director Raja Gosnell edited the first two "Home Alone" movies (and directed the third), but there is none of John Hughes' trademark maliciousness here. Taking advantage of the good-natured high spirits of the Abby Kohn & Marc Silverstein script, Gosnell's sense of fun makes all his characters engaging. Especially Josie Geller (Barrymore).

Josie's a copy editor at the Chicago Sun-Times who's great at correcting grammatical mistakes, but she yearns for something more, both personally and professionally.

Despite having Anita ("Saturday Night Live's" Molly Shannon), the paper's Ms. Promiscuity, as her best friend, the borderline hefty Josie lives with her pet turtles and hasn't been out on a real date in years. Frustrated with desk work, she's eager to be a hard news reporter, though her rumpled editor Gus (John C. Reilly) tells her she isn't the investigative type.

Then, as it often does in the movies, fate intervenes. Gus' tyrannical boss Rigfort (Garry Marshall) decides he wants a story called "My Semester in High School" and picks Josie almost at random to get it done. She's ecstatic, at least until her underachieving brother Rob (David Arquette at his most likable) reminds her of how awful her high school years really were.

We're not just told how grim the old days were, we're shown them as well. Barrymore, an actress clearly without excess vanity, added weight and makeup to portray the pitiful 17-year-old "Josie Grossie" in all her nightmarish agony. The re-creation is so convincing that the film is seduced into going back to Grossie more than it should: These painful, humiliating moments are no more fun for us than they were for her.

Barrymore's splendid gameness stands the film in better stead when her character registers as a senior at South Glen South High. It turns out that high school, with its trio of too-hip girls who set the fashion standard, has not changed, and neither, at least at first, has Josie. She's still just as much of a klutz as ever, still prone to spilling food on her clothes and making a total fool out of herself. More than that, Josie turns out to be not the world's greatest reporter, something that, in a "Truman Show" type riff, the entire newsroom gets to witness via a miniature video camera-pin attached to her clothes.

There are, however, compensations this time around. Like a handsome guy named Guy (Jeremy Jordan) who looks just like the lout Josie had a crush on in high school. And there's the dreamy English teacher (Michael Vartan) who befriends Josie and strikes a chord with the undercover reporter when he tells her class, apropos Shakespeare's "As You Like It," "in disguise we feel freer, we do things we wouldn't do in ordinary life."

Josie also gets befriended by Aldys (LeeLee Sobieski), the class brain and the ringleader of a group of math types called "The Denominators" who are her first pals. Aldys could be a throwaway part, but as performed by this excellent young actress ("A Soldier's Daughter Never Cries," the TV miniseries "Joan of Arc" and Stanley Kubrick's forthcoming "Eyes Wide Shut"), it isn't. While "Never Been Kissed" belongs heart and soul to Barrymore, Sobieski's natural poise and assurance reminds us that her own prime time is not so very far away.

NEW YORK POST, 4/9/99, p. 59, Jonathan Foreman

Drew Barrymore is so good in "Never Been Kissed" that you can overlook the execrable writing—and the fact that you've already seen all the best jokes in the movie's trailer. The child-star turned Hollywood sexpot doesn't just carry this movie, she all but transforms it from formula trash into something almost as charming and funny and perceptive as she is.

Effortlessly convincing as a smart, klutzy, Marilyn Monroe-ishly vulnerable but prematurely spinsterish romantic, Barrymore displays here a comic talent equal to Goldie Hawn's or Meg Ryan's at their best. If only she'd had the screenwriters from last week's much more literate "10 Things I Hate About You."

Josie Geller (Barrymore), a mousy, weepy, virginal copy editor in yet another absurdly unrealistic newspaper office, gets an assignment to go undercover in a Chicago high school. Josie's own high-school years were filled with humiliation and "Carrie"-esque cruelty. (In the wince-inducing flashbacks, Barrymore is brilliant as a braces-wearing, greasy-haired, acne-afflicted Ur-nerd with a hideously obvious crush on the school hunk.)

But when she returns to school eight years after her first graduation, coolness and popularity continue to elude her. She ends up joining the geek clique by default. (LeeLee Sobieski is particularly good as the queen of the nerdy smart kids.)

The newspaper isn't interested in calculus competitions, and Josie is ordered to befriend the beautiful people (a trio of vicious, overdressed nymphets straight out of "Heathers") or else. Fortunately, Josie's slacker brother Rob (David Arquette) decides to register at the same school so he can play baseball. And (in one of the movie's more unconvincing sequences) he persuades the people who count that Josie really is cool despite her goofiness and bad fashion sense.

Now that Josie has made "the transition" from nerddom, the most glamorous boy in school becomes interested in her. But a handsome teacher (Michael Vartan) is entranced by her understanding of Shakespeare, and Josie begins to fall for him too.

As in all of this year's teen movies, everything comes to a predictable but still enjoyable head at the senior prom.

"Never Been Kissed" is one of those movies with multiple writing credits—always a warning sign. Interesting themes, like the way your high-school social status effects the rest of your life, are raised and then buried under teen-movie cliche. While one of the three screenwriters has come up with some very funny lines, the others are responsible for dreadful, embarrassing dialogue. Indeed, some of the clunky expository speeches in the first third would be walk-out bad if it weren't for Barrymore's timing and charm.

NEWSDAY, 4/9/99, Part II/p. B7, John Anderson

Here's one for the copy desk: In "Never Been Kissed," Drew Barrymore plays a Chicago Sun-Times copy editor with an office. And an assistant. And she has all day to edit two stories.

Is there any question this is a comedy?

No, but whether anyone will actually laugh is another story. In a movie that preys wholesale on the pain and/or sadism of most audience members' high school memories, Barrymore's Josie Geller, pedantic wordsmith and social train wreck, is picked by her tyrannical-yet-endearingly-wacky editor (Garry Marshall, who else?) to infiltrate a local high school and get the goods on what's going down. She looks young enough—and that's where the qualifications desist.

Josie, known in her high school days as Josie Grossy, is basically assigned to be hip. And Josie, possessing all the physical grace and social skills of a yak, anticipates her return to academe the way most people would look forward to full-body orthodontics.

This is funny—maybe, if you're one of the people who made Josie's life miserable. And therein lies the problem. Who's the movie for? The flashback-Josie is so grotesque, and the present-tense-Josie so unbelievable (professionally or psychologically) that "Never Been Kissed" is essentially an exercise in humiliation.

The point seems to be deflating the myth of high school—that the so-called cool people, by which so many people define themselves for life, are really just billboards for the world to come: walking hype and advertising. But in its undernourished attempt at humor, it more often exploits the very presumptions it's supposed to be exploding.

Josie gravitates naturally to the so-called nerd class—including calculus club president Aldys (LeeLee Sobieski)—but struggles to be accepted by the troika of supermodel wannabees (Jessica Alba, Marley Shelton and Jordan Ladd) while getting giggly over Guy Perkins (Jeremy Jordan), the kind of guy who treated her like garbage when she was 17.

Meanwhile, her fated romance blooms with teacher Sam Coulson (Michael Vartan), who's a little closer to her age although no one knows it. And all of this would be fine—if "Never Been Kissed" was funny; comedies don't, after all, have to make sense. Billy Crystal, for instance, probably should have joined the Witness Protection Program at the beginning of "Analyze This," but no one cares because it's hilarious. "Never Been Kissed," on the other hand, is so remarkably lifeless it begs for an autopsy.

Drew Barrymore is unquestionably cute, which is why she gets away with making mindless movies like "The Wedding Singer" and "Never Been Kissed"—wherein the tactic seems to be keeping the audience off balance with so many questions of logic that there's no time to think about how bad the jokes are. Josie's a fairly successful woman, after all, so why would she show up for the first day of school wearing a moth-eaten feather boa and white lipstick? Why would she fall prey to the same social faux pas that ruined her original high school years? Why would she care what anybody thought? But then, why would she be there in the first place?

"Never Been Kissed" tries very hard to be smart. Occasionally it succeeds: David Arquette, as Josie's jock brother, is a far more cutting example of adolescent salesmanship—when he returns to school, his lumpen behavior knocks everybody dead. On the other hand, Molly Shannon, as Josie's man-crazy girlfriend Anita, is playing a character that was probably available in the commissary vending machines of the old MGM. Ultimately, you wish that the oft-debased Josie would turn into Carrie and incinerate her classmates past, present and future. Maybe she will, in the sequel.

SIGHT AND SOUND, 9/99, p. 51, John Wrathall

Josie Geller, a straitlaced 25-year-old copy editor on the *Chicago Sun-Times,* gets her big break as a reporter when she is commissioned to write an undercover exposé on life in high school. Posing as a teenager, she enrols at South Glen South, where her attraction to class heart-throb Guy reawakens memories of humiliation during her real schooldays, when her dream prom date pelted her with eggs. Since that trauma she has never had a boyfriend or been 'properly' kissed.

Befriended by brainy girl Aldys, Josie joins the school maths club and flirts with English teacher Sam Coulson. But her editor Gus demands she get in with the cool crowd. To help her out, Josie's brother Rob, a former high-school baseball star turned slacker, enrols at the school too and spreads juicy rumours—which convince everyone Josie is cool. Guy asks her to the prom. However, the attraction between Josie and Sam is showing; Gus demands she concentrate on writing an exposé of teacher/pupil relationships.

At the prom, Josie is voted queen, but she blows her cover to save Aldys from having dog food tipped over her. As a result, Sam realises he has been set up, and Josie's story is scooped by a rival paper. Her planned exposé scrapped, Josie instead writes a soul-baring article in which she apologises to Sam and announces she will wait for him to come and kiss her at the school baseball game that night. The article is a huge success. At the game, Josie is cheered by the crowd, and when Sam eventually shows up they kiss. Rob, having rediscovered his passion for baseball, gets a job coaching the school team.

With its mature protagonist returning to high school to relive character-forming experiences, *Never Been Kissed* has obvious credentials as a teen-nostalgia movie. The flashbacks to Josie's actual high-school days feature caricatured 80s fashions and provide the excuse for 'period' songs on the soundtrack, a vein of 80s nostalgia which Drew Barrymore previously exploited in her biggest hit to date, *The Wedding Singer*.

Less predictably, *Never Been Kissed* also functions as a teen-movie-nostalgia movie. Director Raja Gosnell is an alunmus of the John Hughes school of film-making, having made his name as editor of the first two instalments and director of the third in the massively successful Hughes-produced *Home Alone* franchise. Though there's an early gag involving the metal detector at the school entrance, the student body is conspicuously free of the gun-toting homeboys of the 90s high-school movie. Instead, it's populated by the same archetypes (brainy nerds, bitchy glamour queens, good-hearted free spirit with wacky dress sense) as any John Hughes high school circa 1984. Wearing a white shirt and shades without trousers, Josie's brother Rob (the cool, crazy one, in Hughes terms) even comes to the (present-day) fancy-dress prom as Tom Cruise in *Risky Business* (not a Hughes film, but a Bratpack milestone).

Cannily, Rob is played by David Arquette, best known for *Scream*, the 90s dark mirror to the 80s high-school movie. Covering all bases, the film also pays lip-service to the current post-*Clueless* teenmovie craze: high-school versions of the classics (see *10 Things I Hate About You; Cruel Intentions;* the forthcoming *O*). Although *Never Been Kissed* isn't by any means a direct reworking of *As You Like It* (the play which Sam teaches in his English class), the love story between Sam and the 'disguised' Josie chimes in with the disguise theme of Shakespeare's comedy.

Tailor-made for Drew Barrymore by her own company Flower Films, *Never Been Kissed* displays a commendable willingness on the star's part to appear mousy and dumpy, so that Josie's eventual ugly-duckling-to-swan transformation carries some conviction. There's a neat visual gag early on when the camera, closing in on a crowd of commuters, picks out the expected glamorous blonde, only to swerve aside at the last minute and settle on the real, plump brunette Barrymore. (The positive appeal of Barrymore's chubbiness is pointed up by a catty joke at the expense of the trio of diet-crazed school beauties who finally decide to be nice to Josie due to a rumour she is the heir to the Ex-Lax fortune.)

The script efficiently contrives a spiral of dilemmas and challenges to bring about Josie's ultimate blossoming. The only drawback of such an expertly manufactured package, however, is the way it glosses over any riskier business thrown up along the way. Josie's parallel love affairs, with Guy and Sam, are both in some sense transgressive: in one case, 25-year-old woman with teenage boy; in the other, male teacher with pupil (whom he believes to be underage).

A less determinedly feelgood film might have made more of this imbroglio. As it is, at least it throws up one choice one-liner, from Rob to Josie at the teen party where both are on the verge of copping off with underage partners: "See you around the cell block, Mrs Robinson."

VILLAGE VOICE, 4/13/99, p. 154, Justine Elias

Despite her tabloid status as a former child star, recovering alcoholic, and whiplash bride and divorcée, Drew Barrymore, as an actress, erases her public image every time she's onscreen. In *Never Been Kissed,* as fledgling newspaper reporter Josie Geller, she again gets the chance to play her ideal role—a wised-up young woman with a little girl's wistful face. The setup for Josie's transformation from mousy, pedantic copy editor to a revised version of her geeky high-school self is both familiar *(Fast Times at Ridgemont High,* the book, anyone?) and ridiculous (her Chicago daily happily bankrolls her months-long undercover project, plus an electronic surveillance team to keep an eye on her), but with Barrymore at center stage, the contrivance hardly matters. Determined to rewrite her humiliating high-school years, Josie tries to infiltrate the popular crowd, but only the school nerds (led by LeeLee Sobieski) will accept her. Josie's other champion is a distractingly handsome English teacher (Michael Vartan), who is delighted by her mature understanding of Shakespeare's *As You Like It*. Josie, like Rosalind, has found her true love while in disguise.

So far, so good. But the movie becomes strictly formulaic when Josie, at the urging of her scandal-mongering editor, must dump her brainy pals in favor of the hard-partying in-crowd. By this time, her brother (David Arquette), a one-time high-school baseball star gone to seed, has joined her undercover, and embarks on a ludicrous gossip campaign to pump up Josie's reputation. Though director Raja Gosnell seems to want to rush to the movie's prom-night climax, *Never Been Kissed* is a lively tribute to the awkwardness and power of adolescent girlhood.

Also reviewed in:
NEW YORK TIMES, 4/9/99, p. E13, Stephen Holden
NEW YORKER, 5/31/99, p. 94, David Denby
VARIETY, 3/29-4/4/99, p. 67, Lael Loewenstein
WASHINGTON POST, 4/9/99, p. C4, Rita Kempley
WASHINGTON POST, 4/9/99, Weekend/p. 49, Michael O'Sullivan

NEW ROSE HOTEL

An Avalanche Releasing release of an Edward R. Pressman production. *Executive Producer:* Jay Cannold, Greg Woertz, and Alessandro Camon. *Producer:* Edward R. Pressman. *Director:* Abel Ferrara. *Screenplay:* Abel Ferrara and Christ Zois. *Based on the short story by:* William Gibson. *Director of Photography:* Ken Kelsch. *Editor:* Anthony Redman and Jim Moll. *Music:* Schoolly D. *Production Designer:* Frank De Curtis. *Costumes:* David C. Robinson. *Running time:* 93 minutes. *MPAA Rating:* R.

CAST: Willem Dafoe (X); Christopher Walken (Fox); Asia Argento (Sandi); Yoshitaka Amano (Hiroshi); Annabel Sciorra (Madame Rosa); John Lurie (Distinguished Man); Ryuichi Sakamoto (Hiroshi's Executive).

LOS ANGELES TIMES, 10/8/99, Calendar/p. 20, Kevin Thomas

Over the years, ceaselessly venturesome independent filmmaker Abel Ferrera has been drawn to dangerous, ultra-volatile heroes, often criminals living violent lives who nonetheless crave spiritual redemption, as epitomized by Harvey Keitel's tormented cop in "Bad Lieutenant." It takes actors like Keitel and Christopher Walken to play these roles—mature, forceful men with intellect to match their intensity.

Willem Dafoe is also such an actor, and he has now teamed with Walken to star in, as well as produce, Ferrara's "New Rose Hotel," which Ferrara adapted with Christ Zois from a short story by cyberpunk writer William Gibson.

Elliptical and stylized to the max, "New Rose Hotel" becomes primarily a chamber drama—the chambers being luxe hotel rooms in various cities around the world. It's as emotion-charged as any Ferrara film ever, yet whatever violence ensues happens offscreen. Plot counts for little—but allows for a bold experiment in structure and repetition. "New Rose Hotel" is a bravura mood piece, a fatalistic fable about a central character with the delusions of grandeur of an Orson Welles hero.

The film takes us "five minutes into the future," a time when Walken's Fox, who has spent his whole life making shady deals, is in Tokyo. There he and his longtime junior partner and pal, X (Dafoe), are planning to deliver from one corporation to another a brilliant geneticist, Hiroshi (Yoshitaka Amano, the renowned fantasy artist). Elaborate surveillance on the part of Fox has shown that Hiroshi has grown restless and frustrated in the workplace—and bored with his German-born dominatrix wife. He has found a corporate chief in Tokyo to pay him and X a whopping $100 million to deliver the geneticist.

Fox believes he has also found in Sandi (Asia Argento), a European working as a bar girl in Tokyo, just the woman sultry and shrewd enough to seduce Hiroshi away from job and wife for a fee of $1 million.

There may be a hitch, however: X has grown tired of Fox's endless wheeling and dealing and is also drawn to Sandi, with whom he falls in love as he instructs her on the finer points of seduction.

Naturally, all does not go as planned, but what interests Ferrara is to draw from Dafoe and Walken portraits of middle-aged angst in a bleak near-future in which government and the corporate universe are virtually one—and totally corrupt. Dafoe's X is a sensualist longing for love and substance; Walken's Fox wants only to continue with his grandiose schemes of corporate/industrial espionage, for they are his only defense against old age and loneliness.

What Sandi really wants becomes the big question mark here. We're asked to simply accept the plot, never mind the details, and concentrate on the three principals, who in fact are most persuasive. Their murky, risky world may strike us as pure fantasy, but Fox, X and Sandi seem very real, with Argento sexy and poised enough to be so formidable a seductress. (X and Sandi may scorch the screen, but Ferrara wisely leaves Sandi's snagging of Hiroshi entirely to our imaginations.)

Cinematographer Ken Kelsch, a longtime Ferrara collaborator, and composer Schoolly D. have been crucial in helping the director create and sustain the dark, glittery and transient world of Fox, X and Sandi. "New Rose Hotel" is no place for literalists, but Ferrara fans should be pleased with this tale.

NEW YORK POST, 10/1/99, p. 63, Jonathan Foreman

"New Rose Hotel" represents the sadly failed union of two cult sensibilities. It's a low-budget adaptation by director Abel Ferrara (who made "Bad Lieutenant" and the brilliant "King of New York") of a short story by William Gibson, the father of the cyberpunk genre of science-fiction.

It's moody and atmospheric. But with the exception of a few cool moments that remind you of Ferrara at his best, it's dull and written with little attention paid to basic storytelling.

And with the exception of a mini-orgy in Japan, almost all the action takes place off screen. In its place you get the main characters having long, rambling conversations in full hipster-philosophical mode.

The story is set in a high-tech near-future in which corporations hire industrial espionage specialists to arrange kidnappings and defections of top executives and researchers.

Fox (Christopher Walken) is one such specialist. With his pal X (Willem Dafoe) he hatches a plan to secure the defection of top scientist Hiroshi from a German company to a Japanese one.

The key to the plan is Sandi (Asia Argento), a hooker who should be just Hiroshi's type once X has psychologically prepared her to fall in love with him.

The first problem is that X falls in love with Sandi. The second is that both X and Fox are out of their depth.

Once things have gone horribly wrong—and you hear about it rather than see it—X has to take refuge in the New Rose Hotel. And the last third of the film is made up of his flashbacks, repeating scenes from the first hour.

Walken is as magnetically watchable as ever, but even he becomes tiresome as he spouts a mixture of wisdom and existential claptrap. Dafoe, on the other hand, just looks pained throughout the film. Argento is appealing, but she looks more like an Italian starlet with a tatooed belly than a hooker.

But what really spoils "New Rose Hotel" is its failed storytelling. Ferrara and his co-writer, for example, have their characters explicitly say that they are looking for redemption as if afraid to let the film's themes come out by themselves.

VILLAGE VOICE, 10/5/99, p. 206, Amy Taubin

William Gibson's short story "New Rose Hotel" has been a Holy Grail for directors in love with the ominous, seamy atmosphere of futuristic noir. Kathryn Bigelow had it on her agenda for a decade, but financing of *Blade Runner* proportions proved elusive. Two years ago, Abel Ferrara took over the project, cowrote a down-and-dirty adaptation that could be made for next to nothing, and cast Willem Dafoe and Christopher Walken in the leading roles. With two such icons of decadence in place and a director whose entire oeuvre seemed to lead him to the precincts of the New Rose Hotel ("a coffin rack ... in a concrete lot off the main road to the airport"), the film seemed foolproof.

Instead, what's on the screen is so dreadful that it inspires the ontological question "What are films and why is this not one of them?" Not that *New Rose Hotel* doesn't have its moments, but most of them are inspired by utter desperation. There will always be a special place in my heart for Walken's aborted soft-shoe routine or the image of Dafoe, lying on his pallet in the New Rose, sorting through the discards from his lost love's handbag. On such occasions, you can see how *New Rose Hotel* might have achieved a level of cinematic meltdown to rival Jack Smith's *Flaming Creatures*. But instead, commercial considerations appear to have pushed the film, such as it is, into softcore porn with much baring of breasts (though no dick), several threesomes, and, as I counted, one fivesome involving an utterly passive Dafoe and four Japanese beauties, filmed, mercifully, in long shot.

The narrative is archetypical noir. Walken plays Fox, a broken-down middleman in the world of high-tech industrial espionage, who enlists the help of X (Dafoe), his loyal disciple, in a risky scheme to get Hiroshi, the star research scientist of a German company, to defect to its Japanese rival. The lure is Sandi (Asia Argento), a gorgeous hooker who needs to convince Hiroshi that she's in love with him so that he'll give up his job, his wife, and everything else to please her. Fox's instruction to X: "You have to teach her to fall in love without falling in love yourself." The nature of the libido is such that, on receiving an order, it will do the opposite. Which is how X winds up alone at the New Rose, running images of Sandi in his paranoid imagination and wondering exactly when her betrayal began.

Left high and dry by their director, who seems to have been unable to provide them with a context for their characters' actions, the actors try in various ways to cope. Walken, who gave one of the greatest performances in film history in Ferrara's *King of New York,* feints and parries with gutter wisecracks and deranged stares. Dafoe stoically distances himself behind an expression of universal pity. Argento has the easiest job since she only has to look inviting, which she does. What the film lacks, however, is any sense of heat, even of the imploded dark-star variety.

Also reviewed in:
NEW YORK TIMES, 10/1/99, p. E70, Janet Maslin
VARIETY, 9/14-20/98, p. 37, David Stratton

NIGHTS OF CABIRIA

A Rialto Pictures release of a Dino De Laurentiis production. *Producer:* Dino De Laurentiis. *Director:* Federico Fellini. *Screenplay/Story:* Federico Fellini, Ennio Flaiano, and Tullio Pinelli. *Dialogue:* Pier Paolo Pasolini. *Director of Photography:* Aldo Tonti. *Editor:* Leo Catozzo. *Music:* Nino Rota and Franco Ferrara. *Sound:* Roy Mangano and Oscar Di Santo. *Art Director:* Piero Gheradi. *Costumes:* Pierro Gherardi. *Make-up:* Eligio Trani. *Running time:* 110 minutes. *MPAA Rating:* Not Rated.

CAST: Giulietta Masina (Maria Ceccarelli, "Cabiria"); François Périer (Oscar D'Onofrio); Franca Marzi (Wanda); Dorian Gray (Jessy); Aldo Silvani (Magician); Ennio Girolami (Amleto, the Pimp); Mario Pasante ("Uncle", the Cripple); Christian Tassou (Man); Amedeo Nazzari (Alberto Lazzari, the Movie Star); Franco Fabrizi (Giorgio); Polidor (Brother Giovanni); Maria Luisa Rolando (Marisa); Pina Gualandri (Matilda, Cabiria's Enemy); Loretta Capitoli (Rosy); Leo Catozzo (Man with Sack); Sandro Moretti (Pimp); Giovanna Gattinoni (Aunt).

LOS ANGELES TIMES, 7/1/98, Calendar/p. 3, Kenneth Turan

Wistful and willful, delighted and heartbroken, there has never been a face quite like Giulietta Masina's. To see her in the beautifully restored 1957 "Nights of Cabiria" is to witness the indomitability of life itself, to experience one of film's most memorable characterizations, a performance that remains as fresh and irresistible as it was 40-plus years ago.

"Cabiria" was a sensation when it was first released, winning the best actress award for Masina at Cannes and earning the best foreign film Oscar for its director (and Masina's husband) Federico Fellini.

The duo had also collaborated on 1956's Oscar winner, "La Strada." Partially because that film stars Anthony Quinn, it's better known in this country than "Cabiria," which has also been hampered by poor print quality and indifferent subtitles.

Now, in a clean new print that has been retranslated and restores a missing sequence for the first time in decades, "Cabiria" is once again among the living. To see it at the Royal in West Los Angeles is to understand why some critics, including Pauline Kael, consider this classic of Italian cinema to be Fellini's best work, and to know how it is that Masina, with only a small handful of films to her credit, has become a legend among actresses.

Episodic by nature, "Nights of Cabiria" is a warm yet pitiless work that explores the life of a Roman prostitute (Masina) who's taken the name Cabiria. Made in a neo-realistic, almost documentary style, the film examines a considerable swath of Roman society through this woman's wide eyes.

An elfin but dynamic presence, with a bantam swagger and toughness that alternate with a touching naivete and a willingness to be hopeful no matter what, Cabiria is knowingly reminiscent of Chaplin's Little Tramp. The film is in fact filled with bits of physical business, like her getting caught in the curtains of a fancy nightclub entrance, that are conscious slapstick echoes of silent comedy.

Cabiria lives in a tiny one-room house she's managed to buy from her earnings. With her uniform of tight skirt, ratty fake fur top, trusty portable umbrella and ankle socks, she is such a vital presence that it's impossible not to feel that everything we see is actually happening to her.

No sooner do we catch sight of Cabiria, walking with her boyfriend near the Tiber on the blighted high-rise outskirts of Rome, than he pushes her in the river in order to steal her purse. Bad judgment in men, a willingness to be fatally attracted to deadbeats, is Cabiria's eternal weakness, one she knows well. "I'm such a moron," she hisses to herself, soaking wet and furious at her own gullibility.

Because Rome is Rome, Cabiria has spiritual experiences as well as secular ones. She accompanies some of the other prostitutes and a disabled former pimp on an unsatisfactory pilgrimage to a local shrine. Also, in a moving sequence that was cut from the film for reasons that have never been clear, Cabiria meets "the man with the sack," a self-effacing individual dedicated to helping Rome's destitute poor.

One of the film's best-known episodes, and a delightful one, has Cabiria getting picked up by Alberto Lazzari, a major Italian movie star (played, in roguish self-parody, by Amedeo Nazzari). Cabiria's delight in her good fortune, her astonishment at the star's amusingly palatial villa, even the way she walks into a glass door, are delightful to behold.

The next man in Cabiria's life, and her hope of happiness, is an accountant named Oscar (French actor Francois Perier), whom she meets after a local vaudeville show in which, under hypnosis, she's revealed the hopes and dreams she still cherishes. What happens between these two is the climax of Cabiria's story, and the source of one of the most indelible of all of Fellini's closing sequences.

The director was especially fortunate in his collaborators. Writer Pier Paolo Pasolini, later a celebrated filmmaker, brought an authenticity to the language of Rome's streetwalkers that the newly translated subtitles restore. And composer Nino Rota did one of the best of his numerous Fellini scores, in turn inspiring Broadway to turn this story into the musical "Sweet Charity."

Finally, however, any discussion of "Cabiria" must come back to Masina. An actress who conveys emotions with a crystalline intensity, who can bring audiences to tears and laughter almost simultaneously, Masina makes Cabiria so indelible that Fellini said in later interviews that "I myself have worried about her fate ever since." Though we share his concern, we also know that in a sense we don't have to. Through this unforgettable performance, Cabiria will endure as long as anyone cares to watch transcendence projected on a screen.

NEW YORK, 7/20/98, p. 46, David Denby

In one of the most famous sequences in the history of the cinema, Federico Fellini ends his 1957 masterpiece *Nights of Cabiria* with a benumbed Giulietta Masina walking along a street as a bunch of carefree teenagers serenade her. The boys and girls swirl around the lonely, grief-stricken woman, passing in and out of the frame, singing, riding a motorcycle around her, until, finally, Masina smiles, even grazing the camera with a glance, as if to signal to us her permission to enjoy the moment. One can analyze this movie, which has just been rereleased in a restored, uncut version, in terms of its technique and its cinematic language—patterns of light and dark, figures in the foreground and background intricately moving together, and so on. But emotion is a language, too—the language that the cinema forgot and when watching *Nights of Cabiria*, one is amazed by how close Fellini keeps us to the moment-by-moment feelings of Masina's aging, unhappy little prostitute. That final sequence pulls together the seemingly random meanings of everything that has come before; it completes Masina's character and releases us into tears. *Nights of Cabiria* remains the most perfectly beautiful and touching of Fellini's movies.

At the end of the war, Fellini began his career in film by writing screenplays for Roberto Rossellini, who was creating, with other directors, a new, raw-streets style that came to be known as neorealism. *Nights of Cabiria,* which marks the end of Fellini's first period as a director, can be seen as a final stopping place for that style. The heavily symbolic *La Dolce Vita* came next, and then the many Fellini extravaganzas in which the fate of no single human being seemed to matter very much. *Cabiria* shares the neorealist emphasis on poverty and unhappiness—the sense of social betrayal, the rapacity of street life—but the movie at its most expressive is moving away from realism and toward fable and even religious myth.

Masina's Cabiria is no longer young; she's been around, and she talks tough, insisting on her independence, refusing the services of a pimp. She has something—her own house. But it's the most comfortless of refuges, an isolated cement box surrounded by empty lots and a few blank modern buildings. In the neighborhood where she works, pimps and clients drive up, the other girls strut and shout, and sometimes lewd parties break out on the street. It's a Fellini movie, and there's always a lot of life going on. But the prostitutes and their clients are struggling to cheer themselves up, struggling to keep at bay the loneliness and impersonality of the huge, tawdry city. For all her tough talk, Cabiria is entirely vulnerable; she believes what people tell her. She unwittingly poses a test of their honesty and loyalty.

At the beginning of the movie, a man Cabiria loves throws her in a river and grabs her purse. She is pulled out by a bunch of kids and turned upside down until the water drains out. As soon as she can, she's up and fighting, enraged and hurt but ready for more. Battling for every bit of respect she can get, she responds to everything, little slights and moments of temporary advantage. Masina's performance draws on the circus, and on the Chaplin Tramp figure, but it has a delicacy that goes even beyond Chaplin. Cabiria can't conceal anything; her feelings show up on her face, a clown's mug with saucer eyes and big round lips. At a pretentious nightclub, she starts dancing like a music-hall performer, kicking and grinning—Cabiria is not stupid, but she's guileless. She lives deep in fantasy and emotion while hardly seeing what's in front of her.

Even after her gruesome experience in the river, Cabiria is looking for love, or at least a little companionship. It was a principle of neorealism that incident mattered more than plot—that reality not be squeezed into a preset pattern. *Nights of Cabiria* seems at first rather wandering and random. But Fellini quietly creates a structure that echoes and resonates. If you think of the movie as both a Christian fable and a sorrowing defense of illusion, everything in it makes sense. The movie becomes a panorama of betrayal—by art, by the church, by men. Only a silent man with a sack, walking about the outskirts of Rome and handing gifts to the broken-down old whores living in caves—a secular saint—redeems this wasteland.

Nights of Cabiria, we think, should be a tragedy. But Fellini renounces tragedy; he insists that life without illusion is not possible. He offers a Christian optimism that draws nothing from doctrine or clergy and everything from love. It would be nice to say that *Nights of Cabiria* could redeem the cinema, too, but some things are not possible. Yet this 41-year-old movie provides an extraordinary contrast to the summer-season monstrosities as they blaze their way into oblivion.

NEW YORK POST, 7/1/98, p. 38, Thelma Adams

"Masterpiece" is an overworked term these days. "Classic" can be any old black-and-white on AMC. The devaluation of the superlative (what new fashion isn't "amazing," "fabulous," "exquisite," "a revelation"?) challenges a contemporary critic facing the restoration of Federico Fellini's "Nights of Cabiria" (1957).

"Cabiria" follows the life and near-death of a low-rent hooker working Rome's archaeological district. The black-and-white picaresque stars Fellini's wife, Giulietta Masina, in her greatest role.

The two were coming off a high: The triumph of "La Strada" (1954) gave Fellini his first Oscar and cemented his international reputation. With "Cabiria," Fellini became a name that could ride before the title.

As the plucky prostitute, Masina's touching, spirited performance cinched the best actress award at Cannes in 1957 and secured Fellini's second Oscar for foreign-language film. The movie inspired the Gwen Verdon Broadway musical "Sweet Charity" and its Hollywood film version, starring Shirley MacLaine.

Cabiria lives in a squalid little house on the outskirts of Rome. She has money in the bank. This financial security affords her a smidgen of self-respect; she wants romance, followed by a husband and kids.

But this is still the era of neorealism. Cabiria, the outcast, gets dirt, despair and, in a final moment that pushes the film to brilliance, a golden glimpse of grace.

What separates her from the stock golden-hearted hooker is her unapologetic stance, her desperate need to love and be loved and Pier Paolo Pasolini's gritty dialogue.

Fellini, without being sexually explicit, allows no illusions about Cabiria's work. In the shorthand of a dark moment, a truck follows Cabiria up a rain-slicked road. A faceless voice calls, "Hey, Shorty." Cabiria climbs into the cab. The door shuts.

Cut to Cabiria walking through a desolate field, trying to find her way home after being dumped by the trucker like a used condom. In her ratty fur stole, cigarette skirt and sandals with bobby socks, a black umbrella clutched in her hand, Cabiria is not an idealized figure, a bombshell.

At Cannes, French critics called Masina "Charlot." It was a compliment, a comparison of Masina's greatest screen performance with Charles Chaplin's. The lady was a Little Tramp—and Fellini acknowledged that "City Lights" had influenced him.

"Nights of Cabiria" appears deceptively loose, moving in long arcs that bounce off each other into the night. It opens with a "suitor" stealing Cabiria's purse and tossing her into the Tiber River. Later, she hangs out with the girls on the corner, joins a religious pilgrimage, spends time with a famous Italian movie star and reveals her secret desires to a sideshow hypnotist—and a packed auditorium of spectators.

The restored 35mm "Cabiria" includes a sequence unseen since Cannes '57. Italian censors banned the "man with the sack" scene. Cabiria tours Rome with a man who feeds the homeless and sees her future in the filthy face of a once-wealthy prostitute living in a cave.

The Samaritan's lack of religious ties may have offended the Catholic Church, but the segment is key: He is the only man to whom Cabiria confides her full Christian name.

"Cabiria," is a masterpiece because it improves with age. Masina's hooker is a contemporary heroine, trying to balance love and grace with economic necessity. She snatches our hearts as easily as her lover stole her purse, but she doesn't push us into a river of sorrow. She opens the audience to a rare celebration of life.

Her final gift is a joy in the present moment where young people sing, our feet find their own rhythm and the night brings us the comfort of our own beds.

NEWSWEEK, 7/27/98, p. 58, David Ansen

Federico Fellini's *Nights of Cabiria* may have been first released in 1957, but it seems fresher than just about every movie around. Reissued in a sparkling new print that includes seven minutes never seen before, and with more accurate subtitles, this is a sterling opportunity to see

Giulietta Masina (Fellini's wife) give the performance of a lifetime. Her Cabiria is a streetwalker from the outskirts of Rome, a waifish, wide-eyed spark plug with a childlike belief, in the face of all evidence, in the redemption of romance. Attired in bobby sox and a ratty fur, she cuts a figure of Chaplinesque poignancy as she bounces from betrayal to misadventure to the brink of tragedy, never losing her innate, wonderfully irrational optimism. Fellini said he had Chaplin's "City Lights" in mind when he concocted the comic sequence in which she finds herself picked up by a famous Italian movie star—only to spend the night locked in his bathroom while he reconciles with his glamorous girlfriend. The most heartbreaking work in Fellini's career, it was made before "La Dolce Vita" turned him into an international celebrity. It's not as flashy and fantastical as his later movies—whose star was always Fellini himself—but it may be the most emotionally direct. Its final, transcendent images of Masina's face will stay with you forever.

SIGHT AND SOUND, 10/99, p. 53, Geoffrey Macnab

Cabiria, a prostitute living on the outskirts of Rome, is thrown into the river by her lover Giorgio who runs off with her money. She nearly drowns, but is fished out by some local boys. Later, she witnesses a row between movie star Alberto Lazzari and his girlfriend. Lazzari whisks Cabiria off to a nightclub, then on to his apartment. When his girlfriend returns, Alberto hides Cabiria, eventually helping her slink out after the girlfriend falls asleep. Dumped in the wasteland on the edge of town, Cabiria meets a man giving out food to homeless people, among whom is the once-renowned prostitute La Bomba. Cabiria goes to church, but she is disillusioned by the shabby, market-like atmosphere. She visits a vaudeville club, where she is called up on stage by the hypnotist. Under hypnosis, she reveals her dreams of romantic love. The audience ridicules her. Outside the club, she meets Oscar, an accountant, who claims to have been moved by her honesty. She agrees to a date with him. They begin courting.

Eventually, Oscar offers to marry her. Radiantly happy, Cabiria sells up her house, withdraws her life savings and prepares to set up home with him. He leads her through the woods to a cliff top. She realises he intends to kill her. He spares her life but takes her savings. Distraught, she stumbles back to the road. Serenaded by a procession of young dancers and singers, she wipes away her tears and smiles. In spite of everything, her optimism has returned.

In an interview he gave to Charlotte Chandler, Fellini cited Chaplin's *City Lights* as a key influence on *Nights of Cabiria*. Instead of the little man in the bowler hat, he offers us a prostitute (played by his wife, Giulietta Masina) ekeing out an existence in scrubland on the edge of Rome. Screaming abuse at boyfriends, haranguing other women on the street, Cabiria is an infinitely more fiery character than Chaplin's tramp. "She's got nine lives, like a cat," someone observes after she is saved from drowning. She needs to be resilient, if only because she is constantly betrayed by menfolk.

At times, *Nights of Cabiria* seems like a picaresque folk tale. Nino Rota's playful music, Masina's live-wire, clownlike performance and the cruel humour which runs throughout the film suggest Fellini was no longer constrained by the tenets of neorealism. There are moments here—for instance the grotesque sequence in which the cripple is led into church in search of a miracle, attempts to walk unaided and promptly falls flat on his face—which wouldn't look out of place in a Buñuel film. The flights of fancy, such as Cabiria's evening with the handsome, world-weary movie star, anticipate equally magical and improbable happenings in the director's later work. Nevertheless, we're left in little doubt about the practical difficulties which beset Cabiria. She is a home owner, "with water, electricity, everything," but she knows that if she slips up, she may end living rough like La Bomba, the bedraggled ex-prostitute who now sleeps in a hole in the ground.

Their encounter comes when Cabiria accompanies a mysterious stranger who distributes food and blankets to the homeless. "The man with the sack" sequence, as it is known, has been missing from most prints since the film showed in Cannes in 1957. There are different theories why. Biographer John Baxter suggests the church took exception to the fact that the benefactor was a layman, not a priest. But producer Dino De Laurentiis claimed the scene was cut simply to shorten the film. Whatever the reasons, the restored sequence seems pivotal. It's here that Cabiria is given an intimation of what may happen to her. The benefactor is also the only truly trustworthy man she meets in the entire film.

Masina plays Cabiria as an eternal optimist, almost cartoonishly picking herself up every time she's knocked down. She is nothing if not mercurial. One moment, she'll be happily dancing a mambo in the street; the next, having a catfight with a fellow prostitute who has taunted her about her latest no-good boyfriend. (It is striking how closely Masina resembles the equally close-cropped, equally volatile Shirley MacLaine, who played a character based on Cabiria in *Sweet Charity*, 1968.)

In outline, *Nights of Cabiria* sounds bleak and depressing, Unlike the young narrator of *I Vitelloni* (1953), who was finally able to escape his provincial home town, Cabiria has no way out. She's a Sisyphean figure, destined always to land back where she started. Given his acknowledged debt to Chaplin, Fellini might have been expected to play up the pathos in her plight. Cabiria's story is indeed heartrending, but neither director nor actress allow her time for self-pity. She may be robbed, betrayed and almost killed, but despair is never more than a passing emotion with her. Fellini ends the film ambiguously. Cabiria has lost her home. We don't know whether she'll suffer the same fate as La Bomba or pick herself up yet again. "I myself have worried about her fate ever since," the director confessed to Charlotte Chandler. Audiences are liable to leave the film's feeling equally concerned.

VILLAGE VOICE, 7/7/98, p. 117, J. Hoberman

Acclaimed as something like a masterpiece when it opened here in 1957, Federico Fellini's Oscar-winning *Nights of Cabiria* has been so obscured—both by the director's subsequent movies and the partial eclipse of his once titanic reputation—that Rialto's impeccably restored re-release feels surprisingly, fresh.

A new print of *8 1/2* is also scheduled for revival this summer, but the time scarcely seems ripe for a full-scale Fellini rehabilitation. After all, his favorite tropes (deserted piazzas, sprightly, circus music, near-empty nightclubs with bored sophisticates watching hot voodoo) remain the stuff of Madonna videos, fashion shoots, and bank commercials. Still, given the allegorical back-beat in recent films as disparate as *Buffalo 66, Henry Fool,* and *He Got Game, Cabiria's* stylized, performance-driven exercise in mystical humanism would wow them at Sundance—especially now that the film's hooker outfits, not to mention the mambo, are back in fashion.

I first encountered Fellini's schematic fable of an indomitable little streetwalker, played by his wife Giulietta Masina, in battered 16mm at a college film society screening and found its Disneyfied vision of the lower depths a bit old-fashioned—at least as compared to the aggressively contemporary *Fellini Satyricon.* Seen again in a pristine black-and-white print, *Cabiria* seems suggestively pre-"Fellini," less the premise for a Broadway musical than the missing link between Charlie Chaplin's richly emotional *City Lights*—Fellin's acknowledged model—and Jim Jarmusch's stringently controlled *Stranger Than Paradise.*

Coming off her world-famous performance as the sad clown in Fellini's international breakthrough, *La Strada,* Masina elaborated on the friendly little hooker briefly introduced in her husband's first solo feature, *The White Sheik.* The attempt to map her milieu would prove Fellini's last attempt at neo-neorealism. The filmmaker made much of researching the lives of Roman streetwalkers and even hired notorious young poet Pier Paolo Pasolini to slang up the dialogue. Cabiria, however, is less a character than a mythological construct—the innocent whore. What's amazing is how Masina, sexless yet adorable in her cartoon outfit (striped dress, ratty fur, bobby socks), makes this abstraction breathe.

A tiny, hot-tempered pixie with huge eyes and a sardonic smirk, her Cabiria is never required to turn a trick. Or rather, her trick has something to do with investing everything she does with childlike spontaneity—squabbling with the other hookers, telling off a passel of nuns, cutting loose on the dance floor, cavorting alone to the hurdy-gurdy Nino Rota soundtrack that apparently plays in her head.

Pilgrim's Progress in the guise of a one-woman variety show, *Cabiria* opens in long shot—our heroine frolicking with some guy on the outskirts of Rome until he grabs her pocketbook and pushes her into the river. The scene is played for uneasy comedy, but Cabiria's strident denial that she was robbed suggests suffering to come. The most famous sequence is transposed from Chaplin's adventure with the drunken millionaire in *City Lights*. Cabiria is picked up by a morose movie star (Amedeo Nazzari) who has just had a public breakup with his luscious girlfriend, and is brought back to his palatial mansion—a Xanadu of exotic pets and delicacies. Masina's eyes couldn't possibly be any wider. She plays the scene with enough pratfalls and double takes, to stock an episode of *I Love Lucy,* but the mode turns inexorably wistful when the star's girlfriend returns and the luckless Cabiria is stashed in the bathroom, watching the couple's reconciliation through the keyhole.

The crucial moment is the star's refusal to respect Cabiria's refusal to take money—the episode is one more instance of her humanity denied. In a subsequent instance of disillusionment, she accompanies her cronies to a religous festival seeking a miracle cure for a pimp's crippled uncle. Cabiria's naive truth is such that she becomes upset when no one is transformed. But, despite the happily half-cracked priest who encourages Cabiria to seek God's grace, Fellini salvation is not to be found in the Church—in a scene cut from the movie after its sensational Cannes debut, reportedly for its anti-clerical implications, Cabiria encounters a selfless individual who devotes himself to bringing food and blankets to those who live in ditches just outside the city.

A final inversion of Catholic ritual has Cabiria into a neighborhood vaudeville house, where, seeking some sort of communion, she is coerced up onstage to serve as a hypnotist's foil. Her trance takes her back to an idealized state of maidenhood. She imagines meeting her fiancé Oscar in a beautiful garden and dances with him to "The Merry Widow Waltz," a flowered garland on her head. More than just a public humiliation, this painfully funny performance—in which Cabiria reveals the depths of her conventional, romantic yearnings—sets in motion the events which will bring about her downfall and beatification.

Showman that he was, Fellini more than once saved a movie with a boffo closer. *8 1/2*'s self-reflexive circus-ring finale has been stolen so often that the maestro might have made a small fortune leasing the rights to Woody Allen alone. The utter desolation with which *La Strada* ends nearly redeems the preceding hundred minutes of strained and sentimental whimsy. *Nights of Cabiria* has a Mack truck denouement that one sees coming miles away—since the picture's first scene, in fact—and a brief postscript which, again quoting from Chaplin, is nearly transcendent.

Whether our heroine ultimately achieves divine grace in this world or (more "realistically") imagines it among the angels in the next one—and even if *Cabiria*'s haunting final minutes are understood materially, as the equivalent of Masina's curtain call for her brilliant, career performance—Fellini has orchestrated a passage that defies synopsis. Seeing is believing. Words cannot describe the emotions that flicker across Masina's face—so simple and mysterious. Watching it is like hearing the sound of a heart break.

Also reviewed in:
NATION, 9/21/98, p. 42, Stuart Klawans
NEW REPUBLIC, 8/10/98, p. 24, Stanley Kauffmann
NEW YORK TIMES, 10/29/57, p. 34, Bosley Crowther

NÔ

A New Yorker Films release of an In Extremis Images production with the participation of Telefilm Canada and Sodec. *Producer:* Bruno Jobin. *Director:* Robert Lepage. *Screenplay (French and English with English subtitles):* Robert Lepage and André Morency. *Director of Photography:* Pierre Mignot. *Editor:* Aube Foglia. *Music:* Michael F. Côté and Bernard Falaise. *Music Editor:* Robert Langlois. *Sound:* Véronique Gabillaud and (music) Robert Langlois. *Casting:* Paul Cauffopé. *Production Designer:* Monique Dion. *Set Designer:* Claude Jacques and Jean Le Bourdais. *Costumes:* Marie-Chantale Vaillancourt. *Make-up:* Marie-Angèle Breitner-Protat. *Running time:* 83 minutes. *MPAA Rating:* Not Rated.

CAST: Anne-Marie Cadieux (Sophie); Marie Brassard (Hanako); Alexis Martin (Michel); Marie Gignac (Patricia); Richard Frechette (Walter); Éric Bernier (François Xavier); Patrice Godin (René); Jules Philip (Cop 1); Jean Charest (Claude); Tony Conté (Cop 2); Normand Bissonnette (Harold Buchanan); Ghislaine Vincent (Madame Petypon); Jean Leloup (Delivery Man); Walter T. Cassidy (Nô Actor); Ron Korb, Darren Hitoshi Miyasaki, Gary Kiyoshi

Nagata (Nô Musicians); Jim Asano and Milton Tanaka (Nô Assistants); Hitomi Ashahata (Nô Saleswoman); Yosh Tagushi (Doctor); Michel Lee (Étienne); Robert Bellefeuille (Feydeau Priest); Lynda Lepage-Beaulieu (Freydeau Lady); Noriko Hisatomi (Expo Osaka Hostess); Katia Bassanoff (Ghost); Julie Shimotakahara (Waitress); Nathalie d'Anjou (Concierge); Denis Gaudreault and Denys Lefebvre (Apartment Visitors); Abdul Aziz Rasuli (Aziz); Yoshihisa Shimazu (Karaoke Announcer); France Larochelle and Annie Larochelle (Air Hostesses from Québec); Robert Norman (SQ cop).

NEW YORK POST, 4/23/99, p. 59, Jonathan Foreman

There are moments when "No" is so comically pretentious, you think it has to be a spoof along the lines of "This Is Spinal Tap." But there's no such luck with this French-Canadian film, based on part of director Robert Lepage's seven-hour theatrical opus "The Seven Hours of the River Ota." And "No" is exactly what you might expect from someone who specializes in improvised, collectively written works subsidized by the Canadian government.

The action of the film is split between the October 1970 World's Fair in Osaka, Japan, and the separatist crisis in Quebec the same month. The Canadian scenes are in black and white, and the Japanese ones in color.

The title refers both to "Noh," the highly stylized traditional Japanese theater form that makes use of masks, and the "No" vote cast in the referendum on Quebec independence in 1980, and the film labors to link the two.

The idea is to say something deep and insightful about the way we all live in masks, and to contrast the "colonized" nature of Quebecois cultural identity with Japanese authenticity.

Sophie (Anne-Marie Cadieux) is a lead actress in a farce by the French playwright Feydeau that is being performed as part of the Canadian contribution to the Osaka Expo.

On the last night of the production she discovers she is pregnant (she is not sure by whom) and decides to stay over in Osaka for an extra week to have an abortion, the procedure being illegal in Canada.

Meanwhile, back in Montreal, her boyfriend, Michel (Alexis Martin), a radical aspiring playwright, is part of an amateurish urban-guerilla cell. He and his fuzzy-headed friends are making bombs when Canadian Prime Minister Trudeau invokes martial law to deal with Quebecois terrorism.

(The Canadian government crackdown is made to look far more sinister, and the radical separatist movement much less nasty than they really were).

The revolutionaries' plan goes haywire while Sophie spends a bizarre drunken evening with a sleazy Canadian diplomat and his snobbish, French-educated wife.

Director Lepage uses so many closeups that the whole thing feels and looks like TV. It's a technique that emphasizes the unevenness of the film's lead performances.

There are some deliberately amusing scenes when the filmmakers drop their own high-minded masks and play around with farce and low comedy (like the scene where the flight attendants make fun of the size of Japanese condoms). But for the most part, "No" just doesn't work.

NEWSDAY, 4/23/99, Part II/p. B11, John Anderson

Perverse and bipolar, Robert Lepage's "No" is clearly unafraid of pulling any metaphoric muscles. The title refers to the Japanese theater form, as well as Canada's resounding rejection of the Quebec separatist vote of 1980, and since the movie takes place almost entirely in 1970, and the No actors are seen for, oh, about five minutes, you may suspect—and you may be right—that there's a lot more going on.

Primarily—or, rather, cosmetically—"No" is a farce within a farce, or parallel farces bound by a political banner. A Canadian acting troupe, including the pregnant Sophie (Anne-Marie Cadieux), is performing a work by the French farceur Feydeau, in French, for a French director, as part of Canada's representation at the 1970 Osaka World's Fair. The implication is, you want separation, you got it. Back in Canada, however, Pierre Trudeau has invoked the War Measures Act in response to some high-level kidnapings. And in response to Trudeau, Sophie's boyfriend Michel (Alexis Martin) and his fellow Keystone terrorists are planning to blow things up.

Which swings us back around to Japan, because the Osaka World's Fair is commemorating the end of the Second World War and, by implication, the Hiroshima bombing, which left Sophie's friend and translator, Hanako (Marie Brassard), blind. There's an epiphany in "No," and we see it through—or, rather, in—the eyes of Hanako, the one character who knows what's really important, which isn't bombs or politics. Of course, a blind woman as the sole character with vision is about as subtle a message as a mushroom cloud. But it is a lovely moment, nonetheless.

Getting there involves some frenzied farce of Lepage's own creation, including Sophie's coitus-diplomatus with dullard Canadian cultural attache Walter (Richard Frechette), which may be revenge against Michel, or the attache's wife, Patricia (Marie Gignac). The sparring shrews played by Cadieux and Gignac in the tatami room of a Japanese restaurant are delicious and wicked—as is Patricia's invasion of Sophie's boudoir, which morphs into a staged curtain call in which all the players take a bow and a bemused Sophie walks up the aisle and toward the exits.

You will not be compelled to follow her, even if "No" does amble a bit through the brambly structural thickets that surround what is, at heart, a sweetly simple movie, just one that happens to be ensnared by devices and conceits. Lepage, one of Canada's more distinguished/contentious theater figures, likes to flay the Canadian cinema a bit.

SIGHT AND SOUND, 4/99, p. 50, Richard Falcon

1970. At the French-Canadian pavilion for the Osaka World's Fair, Sophie Maltais is performing in a Feydeau farce. She learns she's two months' pregnant and rings her political-playwright boyfriend Michel to say she's staying in Japan to have an abortion. But when she discovers he is receiving a visitor even though it is 4:00 am Quebec time, she doesn't tell him. Imagining Michel is having an affair, Sophie rebuffs her besotted co-star François-Xavier but accepts a dinner invitation from Canadian cultural attaché Walter and his wife Patricia. Sophie gets drunk and sleeps with Walter, but Patricia catches them *in flagrante delicto*.

Michel's visitors in Quebec are members of a radical separatist theatre troupe hiding from the police. They plan to plant a bomb to protest against the introduction of repressive anti-terrorist measures. The plans go disastrously wrong when Michel sets the bomb on Osaka time. The group just make it to safety before it detonates. Sophie learns about the imposition of martial law at home, abandons her plan to abort the baby and returns to the devastated apartment where she is arrested and immediately miscarries.

1980. Sophie and Michel watch the results of the referendum on Quebec's independence. After the 'No'-to-independence lobby wins, Michel starts to persuade Sophie to have a child with him.

Robert Lepage's first feature *Le Confessionnal* informed us that, "Quebec carries its past on its shoulders like a baby. *Nô*, the theatrical maestro's third feature (after *The Polygraph),* extends his preoccupation with Quebecois cultural identity by setting itself at perhaps its most difficult historical juncture. In 1970, then Canadian Prime Minister Pierre Trudeau responded to separatist terrorists' kidnapping and murder of a government minister by instituting martial law, stationing armed forces on the streets of the province. Given the seriousness of Lepage's first two features, what surprises here is the sly and absurd humour he deploys to tell the story against this backdrop.

As he did with *Le Confessionnal*, Lepage interlinks two complementary narratives in *Nô*, although far less intricately in the Japanese sequences, he also introduces an overt theatricality, a contrast with the earlier films' self-conscious meditations on cinema and reality. Derived from the final section of his seven-hour play *The Seven Branches of the River Ota, Nô* contrasts the controlled elegance of a Noh play—with the measured tread of its performers, the impassively elegant masks and costumes—with the garish, frenetic Feydeau farce Sophie is performing in, chosen to represent French-Canadian culture to the world. In the dinner scene with the genially lecherous Canadian cultural attaché Walter and his loquacious, vinegary wife Patricia, a preoccupied Sophie responds to Patricia's needling with a drunken outburst about the awfulness of the play that turns into a rant about the liberation of Quebec. Patricia provokes this outburst by favourably commenting on the play's Victorian costumes, a clear code for saying it stinks.

Lepage foregrounds the kitsch 70s fashions worn by Sophie and makes us aware of Walter's outrageous sideburns and his suit, both of which could pass muster in the Feydeau farce. These deliberately colourful and stagy Japanese sequences build to a not entirely successful *coup de cinéma* after Patricia discovers Walter has slept with Sophie, the film space morphs into the stage of the French farce and the characters take a bow before a rapturous audience. This is audacious and fun stuff, but does little more than overemphasise one central idea: that official attempts to sell French-Canadian culture abroad at this time were farcical.

The real farce, though, occurs in the film's black and white Montreal scenes with Sophie's boyfriend Michel and his would be separatist terrorist theatrical friends. While Michel bickers with his comrades about the syntax in their communique, in another room two policemen on a stakeout argue about whether there are three or four terrorists in the room on the basis of their takeaway order. The absurdity of these sequences makes for entertaining and appealing comedy, with Lepage and his performers maintaining the same dominant tone of indulgent mockery informing the Japanese scenes.

Although the visual coding here is blunter than in Lepage's screen debut *(Le Confessionnal* employed different film stocks to distinguish sequences set in Quebec in 1952 and 1989; here we alternate between colour and black and white), the transitions between the two narratives are still visually flamboyant. This is particularly the case in the shock cut from actor François-Xavier, sitting in a photo booth and lashing out at the glass in front of the lens, to Michel's bomb shattering the window of his apartment.

Colour enters the Quebec scenes with Sophie's return to Michel's wrecked apartment where she loses the baby, the camera tilting to show the blood running down her legs. Is Lepage suggesting that the abortive conclusion to this farcical quest for cultural identity and self-determination is the endangering of the future? Or is he saying the opposite? It's deliberately vague, but points to tragedy behind the farce just as Alfred Hitchcock in *Le Confessionnal* finally declares film's narrative to be not suspense but tragedy.

Behind the impressive facade of the Noh play also lies the reality of a Japanese culture in which Sophie's blind Japanese translator Hanako is ostracised for being an *ibakusha*—a person disabled by the Hiroshima bomb. At this point, Lepage inserts a shot of an atomic mushroom, drawing vague comparisons with the Quebec bomb. This must have been clearer in Lepage's original theatre version, inspired by a visit to Japan in 1994, just before the fiftieth anniversary of the Hiroshima bomb. Here, the weight of the image and its connotations exceed *Nô*'s design and prompt a fleeting, unfavourable comparison with the most famous movie about a Francophone actress' brush with Japanese history, Alain Resnais' *Hiroshima mon amour* (1959)

Nô's coda is an affirmative one. The title also stands for the result of the 1980 referendum on Quebecois independence. It resolves the two narratives by uniting the couple for the first time on the screen together, but leaves us ultimately perplexed about the film's wider perspective on the issues it has alluded to. *Nô* is witty, always intriguing and amusing, and maintains the director's reputation as an inventive cinematic stylist. But set against the visual and creative richness of *Le Confessionnal, Nô* can't help looking both insubstantial and claustrophobic.

VILLAGE VOICE, 4/27/99, p. 131, J. Hoberman

A frisky Canadian fiction set in an alternate reality—namely late 1970, when, responding to Quebec separatists, Prime Minister Pierre Trudeau effectively placed the nation under martial law—Robert Lepage's third feature, Nô, opens in off-putting schematic mode before running cheerfully amok.

Lepage, Quebec's best-known experimental theater director, asserts his mastery of time and space by cutting back and forth between a theatrical performance in full-color Osaka, Japan, and a countercultural dump in black-and-white Montreal while offering a barrage of possible perspectives (backstage, onstage, from the audience, and through various cameras, including surveillance). But then, without sacrificing its cerebral premise, Nô—which is adapted from a part of Lepage's epic theater piece *The Seven Streams of the River Ota,* a 50th anniversary memorial of Hiroshima—settles into a highly satisfying low comedy.

Free-spirited Sophie (Anne-Marie Cadieux), a Montreal actress playing in a mediocre French Canadian production of a hokey Feydeau bedroom farce at the Osaka World's Fair, discovers that she's pregnant and telephones Montreal to inform her lover just as, unbeknownst to her, his would-be terrorist friends stumble in, seeking shelter from the police. The ensuing misunderstandings and increasingly comic parallel action—which involves amorous diplomats, ideological rants, jealous wives, and ticking bombs—unfold in two time zones, even as Sophie's own behavior oscillates wildly between the passive and the volatile.

Lepage doesn't stint on walking metaphors (his longtime associate Marie Brassard plays a translator blinded as a child by the bomb that fell on Hiroshima). Still, more than contrasting vision with insight, or East with West, Lepage is rehearsing the familiar '60s merger of the personal and the political—as brought home in the coda to this deft and unexpectedly economical farce.

Also reviewed in:
NATION, 5/17/99, p. 43, Stuart Klawans
NEW YORK TIMES, 4/23/99, p. E23, Stephen Holden
VARIETY, 8/31-9/6/98, p. 97, Brendan Kelly

NOBODY

A Phaedra Cinema release. *Producer:* Toshifumi Ogura, Tsugio Hattori, and Seiichi Kyoda. *Director:* Shundo Okawa. *Screenplay (Japanese with English subtitles):* Shundo Okawa. *Director of Photography:* Hiroshi Ogata. *Editor:* Yoshio Kitazawa. *Music:* Kiyoshi Kazizawa. *Running time:* 100 minutes. *MPAA Rating:* Not Rated.

CAST: Masaya Katoh (Taki); Jimpachi Nezu (Detective Karaki); Riki Takeuchi (Nanbu); Hideo Nakano (Konishi); Hiromi Nakajima (Rika); Yumi Nishiyama (Reiko).

NEW YORK POST, 8/20/99, p. 61, Rod Dreher

"Nobody" is a slick, but overstylized and mostly uninspired Japanese film noir about a trio of Tokyo advertising executives ensnared by a revenge fantasy.

Taki (Masaya Katoh), Nanbu (Riki Takeuchi) and Konishi (Hideo Nakano) are out late drinking in a yuppie bar when one of them makes a smart-alecky comment about the three men knocking back a few at the next table.

Our heroes clear out before a fight starts, but when pudgy, fearful Konishi returns for his umbrella, the mysterious threesome clean his clock but good.

Taki and Konishi want to forget about it, but hot-headed Nanbu goads the mild-mannered salarymen toward revenge. As luck would have it, the three run into one of the original brutes in an alleyway, and beat him senseless.

The next day, one of the three receives a mysterious phone call: "Your victim has died. We know who you are. And you're not going to get away with it."

Until this point, "Nobody" is an impressively cool take on male rage. The characters are only roughly sketched in the screenplay, but the actors effectively embody three credible and contradictory male responses to violence (Taki's reasoned calm, Nanbu's seething rage, Konishi's fearful passivity).

As the protagonists descend into paranoia, writer-director Shundo Okawa loses his sure touch with the plot, substituting hoary theatrics for character development.

The film's early promise steadily devolves into a bombastically cliché action movie, filled with ho-hum car chases, gun battles and increasingly absurd plotting.

And Okawa's heavy-handed approach to creating atmosphere—drench everything in blue light and trot out minor-key jazz Muzak seems dated and amateurish. "Nobody" is for hard-core genre fans only.

VILLAGE VOICE, 8/24/99, p. 122, Dennis Lim

A riff on, among other things, wounded masculinity and white-collar facelessness, the Japanese revenge thriller *Nobody* opens with three ad executives getting into an altercation at a bar with a disconcertingly similar (though more bloodthirsty) trio at the next table. The film plays out as a predictable spiral of retaliatory ugliness, working up a paranoid sweat that eventually evaporates into stylish, if entirely unoriginal, ultraviolence. Timid, chubby Konishi is beaten to a pulp—twice; hair-trigger Nanbu vows to track down his colleague's attacker; nominal hero Taki is left to take stock of the bloody fallout (and cope with the advances of a mysterious woman who wanders into his life one rainy night). Throughout, the identity of the bad guys remains a mystery—are they crooked cops? yakuza? sociopaths? the undead?—and their anonymity is the essence of the mindfuck. Shundo Okawa's direction is both slick and ham-fisted, overreliant on generic score and camera trickery for suspense and on rigorous color schemes—overbearing metallic blues (night), bleached-out blandness (day)—for mood. The film's most agreeable quality is its playful streak, evident in a slyly mocking brand-name fetish (the initial argument starts when Nanbu calls one of the antagonists' Rolex "tacky") and the supernaturally unkillable villain of the finale. Too interminable to be suspenseful, it provides a kind of surreal thrill all the same.

Also reviewed in:
NEW YORK TIMES, 8/20/99, p. E21, Lawrence Van Gelder

NOTTING HILL

A Universal Pictures release of a PolyGram Filmed Entertainment presentation in association with Working Title Films of a Duncan Kenworthy production from Notting Hill Pictures. *Executive Producer:* Tim Bevan, Richard Curtis, and Eric Fellner. *Producer:* Duncan Kenworthy. *Director:* Roger Michell. *Screenplay:* Richard Curtis. *Director of Photography:* Michael Coulter. *Editor:* Nick Moore. *Music:* Trevor Jones. *Music Editor:* Peter Clarke. *Choreographer:* Geraldine Stephenson. *Sound:* David Stephenson. *Casting:* Mary Selway. *Production Designer:* Stuart Craig. *Art Director:* Andrew Ackland-Snow and David Allday. *Set Decorator:* Stephanie McMillan. *Costumes:* Shuna Harwood. *Make-up:* Jenny Shircore. *Make-up (Julia Roberts):* Richard Dean. *Running time:* 105 minutes. *MPAA Rating:* PG-13.

CAST: Hugh Grant (William Thacker); Richard McCabe (Tony); Rhys Ifans (Spike); James Dreyfus (Martin); Julia Roberts (Anna Scott); Dylan Moran (Rufus the Thief); Roger Frost (Annoying Customer); Julian Rhind-Tutt ("Time Out" Journalist); Lorelei King (Anna's Publicist); John Shrapnel (PR Chief); Clarke Peters ("Helix" Lead Actor); Arturo Venegas (Foreign Actor); Yolanda Vasquez (Interpreter); Mischa Barton (10-year-old Actress); Tim McInneny (Max); Gina McKee (Bella); Emma Chambers (Honey); Hugh Bonneville (Bernie); Henry Goodman (Ritz Concierge); Dorain Lough, Sanjeev Bhaskar, Paul Chahidi, and Matthew Whittle (Loud Men in Restaurant); Melissa Wilson (Tessa); Emma Bernard (Keziah); Emily Mortimer (Perfect Girl); Tony Armatrading (Security); September Buckley (Third Assistant Director); Philip Manikum (Harry the Sound Man); Sam West (Anna's Co-Star); Dennis Matsuki (Japanese Business Man); Patrick Barlow (Savoy Concierge); Ann Beach (William's Mother).

LOS ANGELES TIMES, 5/28/99, Calendar/p. 1, Kenneth Turan

"What am I doing with you?" Julia Roberts' Anna Scott—a.k.a. "Hollywood's biggest star by far"—says to Hugh Grant's William Thacker, the shambling and seemingly ordinary bookstore owner she is in the process of being smitten with. But if Anna doesn't know, everyone watching "Notting Hill" surely will.

For if all romance is a process of recognition, of noticing someone else who notices us, movie romance ups the ante. No matter who they're pretending to be on screen, even if they're royalty and regular people (like Audrey Hepburn and Gregory Peck in "Roman Holiday" or even Carrie Fisher and Harrison Ford in "Star Wars"), it's the first law of cinema that stars recognize each other and find a way to be together, no matter what the circumstances.

A collateral descendant of "Four Weddings and a Funeral," the film that made Grant an international star, "Notting Hill" is a smartly cast and consistently amusing romantic comedy.

As with its predecessor, the key to this film's considerable charm is the script by Richard Curtis, his first solo credit (he collaborated on "Bean") since "Four Weddings."

The idea (and Curtis says it came from his fantasizing about turning up at dinner with friends with someone like Madonna or Princess Diana) is that megastar Anna wanders by chance into William's travel bookstore in the happening Notting Hill section of London. He shyly recommends a book ("I think the man who wrote it has actually been to Turkey"); she ignores him and buys another, and in that brief moment the scent of mutual attraction, faint but unmistakable, passes between them.

Naturally, there are problems, a whole caboose of them, ranging from his deranged Welsh roommate Spike (a zany Rhys Ifans) to a gap in their fame and status so considerable that neither one can believe at first what is happening to them.

Given how familiar and predictable this scenario is, it's much to Curtis' credit that he regularly surprises us with either a situation or a line of dialogue, that creates contagious laughter. Like when William spills orange juice on Anna in a classic cute-meet situation and promises to have her quickly "back on the street again, but not in the prostitute sense."

Taking advantage of Anna's star-of-stars status, some of "Notting Hill's" funniest situations deal with the movie business, like Anna discussing the ins and outs of her contract's nudity clause or William helping her run her lines in a script that smoothly skewers "Armageddon" and its ilk.

Best of all is an extended sequence in which William, mistaken for "Britain's preeminent equestrian journalist" on assignment from Hare and Hounds, participates in a press junket for Anna's latest film and finds out firsthand (as if he didn't already know) just how inane those Q&A sessions can be.

Speaking of Hollywood, one obstacle "Notting Hill" has had to clear that "Four Weddings" wasn't burdened with is its status as a mixed marriage of character-intensive contemporary British comedy with mainstream studio moviemaking.

The Hollywood influence is visible in the film's intrusive "get in the mood or else" Trevor Jones music and its use of sandwich board songs like "How Can You Mend a Broken Heart" and "Ain't No Sunshine When She's Gone." And it shows up in the way "Notting Hill" occasionally gives in to more sentiment than the moment really demands.

But under the able direction of Roger Michell (whose version of "Persuasion" is close to the best of the recent Jane Austen adaptations), "Notting Hill" has the enviable ability to right itself before it gets too far gone, to follow a borderline saccharine moment with just the right biting line or tart scenario.

It also helps to have the right actors delivering those lines, and Grant especially has a delightful time with Curtis' arch dialogue. Convincing as a bumbling sophisticate, a hangdog Cary Grant, this Grant has such an expert way with words that it's no surprise that Anna is taken with him despite herself

While Grant wins us over immediately, Roberts has a tougher time. This is partly because, despite the actress' insistence that a picture about heroic nuns ministering to lepers in equatorial Africa couldn't be further from her life than this one, "Notting Hill" does seem within at least shouting distance of a self-portrait.

Finally, though, it is the connection—acknowledged or not—that Roberts makes with this material that make her portrait surprisingly effective. To see her in moments of diva pique, to hear her forlorn tone of voice when she talks about how "every time your heart gets broken newspapers splash it around like it's entertainment," is to see the genuine vulnerability without which her character would not be believable or sympathetic.

The inevitable compromises made with Hollywood make "Notting Hill" creak around the edges in a way "Four Weddings" did not, but the film's romantic core is impervious to problems. Roberts and Grant are the most glowing of stars here, the people who keep us alive in the darkness, and we want so much for their characters to be happy in their turn.

NEW YORK, 6/7/99, p. 86, Peter Rainer

Anna Scott (Julia Roberts) in *Notting Hill* is the world's most famous movie star, but something is missing from her life. The fame game has left a void in her celluloid soul, and the gent she elects to fill it is a stammering travel-bookstore owner, William Thacker (Hugh Grant), who appears to love her for herself and not her celebrity. In other words, what we have here is another self-congratulatory play-it-both-ways Hollywood romance: William is saluted for having the proper values while, at the same time, we're encouraged to lap up the luxuries of stardom.

In London to promote her latest movie, a sci-fi epic called *Helix,* Anna first meets William at his Notting Hill store when he interrupts a sales pitch to deter a shoplifter; later, he accidentally bumps into her on the street and drenches her in orange juice, which brings her into his nearby apartment for a freshen-up and a surprise kiss. (She smooches him as she exits; he smiles wanly.) The plotting throughout the movie, courtesy of screenwriter Richard Curtis, remains at this clunky level, although the clunkiness may be intentional—as a way to point up the love affair's wacky improbability.

But there's a difference between improbable and untenable. These two, despite what we're meant to believe, are not exactly lovers for the ages. The best they do for each other is demonstrate a kind of pronounced affection, and so it's tough to get worked up about their voided souls. William, recently divorced, shares his flat with a Welsh layabout named Spike (a scene-stealing Rhys Ifans), who trots about in his day-old undies and wears T-shirts with messages like FANCY A FART? He's certainly got more inner life than his roomie, with his aggregation of tics and blinks and winks, and, for a while, one holds out the faint hope that Spike will be the guy to land Anna. (The wanker certainly wants to.) But this, after all, is a romantic comedy with "heart," which means we have to go through the standard two-step about finding true love by finding your own true self.

In Anna's case, her true self turns out to be connected to all the "real people" things we simple folk take for granted. During a dinner-party game hosted by William's friends, in which the winner is the one who tells the most self-pitying tale, Anna triumphs. Her tale trumps even a woman permanently wheelchair-bound (Gina McKee) who laments that she can't have kids. How does Anna do it? In measured tones, she tells the assemblage that she's been dieting for a decade, that she's had cosmetic surgery, that she'll eventually lose her looks and be referred to as someone who used to be famous. After this recitation, the director Roger Michell holds the camera on her face for that extra beat that says *feel her pain.* Of course, earlier in the evening, Anna one-upped a guest by citing her standard acting fee—$15 million—but apparently money doesn't mean much to her. Her sobby litany is meant to tenderize her glamour, but it comes across like royalty slumming with the help.

The movie-star-playing-a-movie-star-who-wants-to-be-a-real-person conceit also has an odd, chilling effect on Julia Roberts, whose appeal, overwhelmingly, is based on her seeming just like the rest of us—only more gorgeous and winning. By playing a diva unhappy with the trappings of stardom, she cancels out her attractiveness; we don't want to see her bemoaning her success, we want her to be as delighted as we imagine we would be in her place. I mean, this is a *fantasy,* folks.

The movie makes it easy for Anna to be disengaged from her good fortune: She's had a history of crumbum boyfriends (including one played, in a cameo, by Alec Baldwin); she's hounded by paparazzi; she gets no particular pleasure from her craft. We see a clip from *Helix* that makes her look like just another high-priced Hollywood automaton. But what if we saw her in something where she really showed off her joy in acting—or whatever it is that makes Anna the world's biggest movie star? Suppose William was attracted not just by her simple self but also by her abilities, her allure? Since he's apparently all but ignorant of her movies, or anybody else's, it's easy for William to seem untainted by her fame. But isn't it a cheat to set up the movie in this way—as if there were something inherently impure in the notion that we might be turned on by things like talent, power, and moolah?

The kicker, of course, is that William gets to have it all anyway. He gets the girl and he also gets to politely disdain the razzmatazz she represents. Even though most of their excursions together are all about her priorities and not his—he reads over her scripts with her and shows up at her press junkets and movie locations—he still pulls the heartstrings. In his own befuddled way, William's a real smoothie: Waking up in bed with him, Anna complains about the way she looks and he answers, "You look lovelier than ever," and the way he says it, it's not just a line. William acts so "real" around Anna that he's completely unreal. You want to tell him to take his lovely sincerity and stuff it.

NEW YORK POST, 5/28/99, p. 51, Rod Dreher

"Notting Hill" s a blatant but worthy attempt by the creative team behind "Four Weddings and a Funeral" to recapture the giddy magic of that film, one of the best romantic comedies of the decade. Lightning doesn't strike twice, alas, but with the can't-lose casting of Julia Roberts and Hugh Grant as romantic leads, "Notting Hill" comes close enough to strike plenty of sparks and generate a satisfying tingle.

Roberts plays herself, basically. Her Anna Scott is a glamorous, aloof American film star shooting on location in London. And though he plays a charmingly bumbling bookstore-owner named William Thacker, Grant is essentially reprising the "Four Weddings" role that rocketed him to international fame. No complaints here: He wears that rumpled role well.

One fine day, Anna happens by the shambling little bookshop William runs in London's Notting Hill neighborhood. He knows who she is but, perhaps out of shyness, treats her like a normal person. She's amused, and begins a flirtation with him. Anna invites William to see her at her hotel, whereupon he gets caught up in the ridiculous phenomenon known as the movie junket (he pretends to be a reporter for Horse & Hound magazine).

Impressed by his kindness and the gentle everydayness of his life, Anna accepts William's invitation to come to a homey dinner in honor of his sister. How would your friends and family react if you brought Julia Roberts (or Hugh Grant) home to dinner? It's a wonderful scene, with William's grab-bag of eccentric, very funny pals impressing Anna with their love for each other and a very British game of group one-downsmanship.

When tabloids unearth some embarrassing photos, Anna hides out with William and his laughably grotty roommate Spike (newcomer Rhys Ifans), a skinny Welshman who looks like a Cro-Magnon in a diorama at the Museum of Natural History. But Anna's inability to trust anyone sends her into celebrity bitch mode, and gentlemanly William's heart is ever being stomped flat.

Roberts is the big star here, but it's really Grant's movie. His character is smart, generous, handsome and self-deprecating, a complete pleasure. But the screenplay shortchanges Roberts. We never really see why a guy like him should fall for a goddess like her. She's stunning, of course, but we never see what's beyond the glorious facade—aside from a confused, brittle, lonely and deeply needy young woman. Anna's a real person, but as Anna is written, she's little more than a collection of character traits.

Still, when a repentant Anna stands in front of the man she's treated so badly and says with that trembly voice: "Don't forget, I'm just a girl standing in front of a boy, asking him to love her," your heart melts like a Snickers bar under a sun lamp. Though the comedy is sharper and more appealing than the romance, and the resolution is rickety, to say the least, the frothy, feel-good "Notting Hill" is about as enchanting as movies get these days.

NEWSDAY, 5/28/99, Part II/p. B3, John Anderson

She's a tabloid-frequenting Hollywood superstar whose face—sculpted nose, flayed-anchovy mouth—adorns every bus stop in town. He's a decidedly less prominent Brit with a self-deprecating air, a winning smile and the emotional range of a crumpet.

So: Is "Notting Hill," the alleged romantic comedy starring Julia Roberts and Hugh Grant, mere docu-drama? More or less. It may mark a new low in the dissolving of that fabled fourth wall between news and fiction, being as it is a celebration of celebrity (one starring the celebrities it's celebrating). And when it isn't shoplifting plot devices from Grant's hit "Four Weddings and a Funeral," it seems to be insisting that its suffering-star theme is the stuff of dubious fact instead of the welcome fairy tale it might have been.

"Notting Hill" is also of the opinion that William Thacker—Grant's romantically impaired bookshop owner—is the only sensible, right-thinking person in all of Notting Hill, the funky-chic Vanity Fair where he and his eccentric circle (including a sister beamed up from "Funeral") live a life they can't possibly afford in an area antiseptically free of the ethnic melange of present-day London.

Divorced and rooming with Rhys Ifans' disgusting Welshman, Spike (take note of distancing ethnicity), William is nobly fatalistic about his nonexistent love life, which is abruptly upturned when Anna Scott (Roberts) makes a Garbo-esque visit to his shop.

As the star revealed—what did she expect?—Roberts exudes a sour rudeness that William stoically ignores as he helps her avoid paparazzi and is rewarded with a passionate kiss. At this juncture, the picture has already leapt into the Fantasy Kingdom, but that would be all right if there were an underlying romantic sparkle to the story, rather than the faux-realism it's trying to jam down our throats.

Director Roger Michell, obviously, is caught on the horns of a box-office dilemma: Exercise the satisfying, character-defining inflections he brought to the Jane Austen adaptation "Persuasion"? Or make a Hollywood star vehicle in which no nuance of Roberts' Anna need agree with another, as long as the ultimate outcome is happily vapid? What he does is give us two endings: The one that makes sense and leaves William crushed but wiser. And the kind that satisfies exit polls and the wisdom of committees.

"Notting Hill" gets almost every emotional echo wrong (especially the music: "Ain't No Sunshine When She's Gone" when Anna goes away? Please. The timing is enough to make you cringe). So it's no surprise that it can't even skewer its enemies properly.

During one of their evasions, as they try desperately to sidestep celebrity and embrace true love, William has to impersonate a journalist at a junket for Anna's latest blockbuster (Title: "Helix." Sequel: "Double Helix."). Stumbling through a series of embarrassingly inept interviews with the movie's actors, he makes it more than clear he hasn't seen the movie and consistently asks the most inappropriate questions.

It would, of course, have been far more biting (to say nothing of realistic) if William, clever lad that he is, had sailed through the junket asking the most innocuous, obvious questions and been rewarded with an offer of a big PR job or a post on a London tabloid. But that would have demeaned everyone involved in the process of starmaking and star-stroking, and thereby undermined the underlying message of "Notting Hill," which is all about celebrity as martyrdom and the sins of the seduced.

NEWSWEEK, 5/24/99, p. 71, Jeff Giles

So you can't get into "Star Wars"—or you've read the reviews and no longer want to. Half of Hollywood is hoping to catch you on the rebound, but "Notting Hill" is the first place you should turn. Roger Michell's adorable, if uneven, romantic comedy is essentially a fairy tale, as Julia Roberts's best movies tend to be. Our princess is an American movie star named Anna Scott (Roberts). Our commoner is William Thacker (Hugh Grant), who owns a foundering travel bookstore in London. Anna and William meet. They fall in love. They surmount—well, not very big obstacles, come to think of it. Still, "Notting Hill"—written and produced by the folks who gave us "Four Weddings and a Funeral"—has a mountain of British charm.

When Anna first walks into the bookshop, William nimbly chats her up even as he admonishes a shoplifter who's put a book down his pants. What follows is, for the first hour anyway, a hilarious, deadpan variation on the theme of worlds colliding. William introduces elegant Anna to his roommate, Spike (Rhys Ifans), a disgusting Welshman who obliviously spoons down a cup of mayonnaise ("There's something wrong with this yogurt"). Later William sneaks into a press junket for Anna's new sci-fi movie by pretending to be a journalist from, of all places, Horse and Hound magazine. William is entranced by Anna's world—and mortified by his own. Soon we discover—and this is where the movie stalls out—that Anna's really the one with the problems.

Grant gives a great, unaffected performance—he piles on the charm and goes easy on the stuttering and eyelid fluttering. Roberts has some sparkling moments, but becomes increasingly less lovable as we get to know her character better. When old porn pictures of Anna turn up in the tabloids, she gets hounded by the paparazzi, turns nasty and rants at William about the price of fame. Frankly, Roberts is so convincingly uppity that you wouldn't wish her on anybody. This being a fairy tale, however, the movie lurches toward a happy ending you're only half rooting for. Grant and a sublime supporting cast still manage to carry the day. "Can't we just laugh about this?," William implores, as the photographers swarm. It takes Anna forever to get a sense of humor. Us? We're laughing all along.

SIGHT AND SOUND, 6/99, p 49, Charlotte O'Sullivan

Divorcee William Thacker runs an ailing travel bookshop in Notting Hill, a London neighbourhood. One day a film star, Anna Scott, buys a book from him. Shortly afterwards, they messily collide in the street. William invites Anna back to his house to clean up, where impulsively she kisses him. Some days later, William discovers that Anna has phoned. The couple arrange a date—it's William's sister Honey's birthday, so they all meet at William's friends Bella and Max's house. Afterwards, Anna invites William up to her hotel room but they find Anna's boyfriend there on a surprise visit. William beats a swift retreat.

Salacious shots of Anna appear in the newspapers, and she seeks refuge at William's house where they have sex. The following morning, the press are at the door. Furious, Anna accuses William of setting her up, although it was his flatmate Spike who accidentally tipped off the press. Seasons pass. Filming a Henry James adaptation in London, Anna invites William to meet her on the set. She seems pleased to see him, but William overhears her dismissing him to a fellow actor, so he sidles away.

A contrite Anna appears at the bookshop, but William rejects her. Realising his mistake, he chases after her. He arrives at her press conference and declares his love. Some time later, Anna is pregnant with William's child.

Notting Hill is a sly film. Although in many ways it exploits the *Four Weddings and a Funeral* formula screenwriter Richard Curtis created, it's actually quite a different beast. In *Four Weddings*, 'vulgar' America is in thrall to cultured, wealthy Britain. But aside from such embarrassing worship, the US barely figures in it (Andie MacDowell's character could have been any nationality). In *Notting Hill* there's no competition: big, bold, glamorous America is on top; Britain has banana slipped from importance to impotence. In *Four Weddings,* Hugh Grant's character knew one of the "sixth richest men in Britain"; here all his friends are financial failures. America is shown to have a clear identity, while Britain is all at sea. Anna is a somebody; William (mistaken first for a journalist, then a room-service cleaner) could be anybody. Such an antagonism can be enjoyable, and the sections of the film that deal with Anna/America's narcissistic prowess are remarkably acute. Grant, meanwhile, makes the most of his role, the perfectly pained martyr to comic calamity. It's the emphasis on William and Britain's high-brow "crapness" that fails to convince because *Notting Hill*—a British film, after all—is obsessed with money and success. When Anna gives William a Chagall painting, his friends ask, "Is it the original?'—in other words, is it valuable? Learning it is, they give the relationship the go-ahead. In the film's scheme of things, Henry James is also good because a slice of his classy prose gets Anna an Oscar.

Of course James—that great chronicler of doomed Anglo-American relations would have been horrified by this film's disingenuous attitude to economics (we never find out where William gets the money to afford such a posh address). Nor would James have understood the presentation of the British as 'innocents'. Each time we're asked to watch William the Non-Conqueror, all we can think is how well his tribe has colonised Notting Hill. That's why the US has to appear so dominant and knowing, the *uber*-colonial power. Who else could make Willy *seem* like an underdog? In *Four Weddings,* we enjoyed cheering on the British rich. Now we have to be tricked into it.

But does *Notting Hill* really want its cynical project to succeed? We're asked to see William/Britain and Anna/America as polar opposites and yet, on some strange, murky level, we're led to suspect they're the same. When Anna's sexual indiscretions come back to haunt her via the tabloids, it's hard not to remember Grant's own true life brush with scandal. When she compounds her error by sleeping with him, she says, "Newspapers last forever—I'll regret this forever." This is uncannily significant dialogue. Who would understand this sentiment more than Grant?

The film is also intent on reminding us of the duplicity of actors, not least Anna, who, as her reference to *Gilda* makes clear, comes from a long line of snaky females. In fact the whole tribe are bad—as we see with Anna on the Henry James set, they're notoriously 'indiscreet'. But Grant's public image and charm are inextricably tied to his unreliability. In the homage to his personality that was Four Weddings, his character's bitchy indiscretion was intriguingly turned into a virtue. In this film, when asked why his wife left him, he winces and says, "She saw through me." We're meant to see this as marvellous self-deprecation, but it's one of the few lines that rings true. Anna is the official actor in this relationship, but William—an instinctive actor—appears equally untrustworthy.

Viewed in this light, intentional or not, it makes perfect sense that William's proposal is offered (and accepted) in front of hundreds of journalists. For both Anna and William, the media provide a stage and audience. If we're to draw any conclusions from this slight but canny film, it's that the Anglo-American contest is a fake: after centuries of conflict, these two countries are culturally one and the same and really do deserve each other.

TIME, 5/31/99, p. 87, Richard Schickel

The problem with romantic comedy has never been getting the lovers together. The trick is to keep two people, obviously meant for each other, apart until they—and we—are crazed with frustration.   But in the modern world, all the traditional barriers—most notably class distinctions—are breached all the time. There is apparently nothing to keep the boy from getting the girl for more than about two reels of a movie.

Nothing, that is, but the most obviously addling issue of all, the one that obsessively preoccupies everyone, namely celebrity. Why no one up to now has thought to use fame as true love's great obstacle is a nice question. But here, at last, is *Notting Hill,* and it makes something utterly charming—and very smart—out of the efforts of the world's most famous and desirable movie star, Anna Scott (Julia Roberts), and William Thacker (Hugh Grant), the world's most anonymous bookseller, to get together.

Their meeting isn't particularly cute—she just wanders into his shop on London's Portobello Road one day—and their attraction is distinctly muted. William's charm is of a musing, terribly English sort. He knows his place, which is deliberately narrow, unthreatening. She, in turn, has the wariness of the constantly stalked. She doesn't have a place. She is a bird of passage, always about to leave one movie location for the next. The film's comedy and crises arise out of their attempts to find a refuge where she can settle down and he can open up.

It is a process that screenwriter Richard Curtis *(Four Weddings and a Funeral)* and director Roger Michell *(Persuasion)* allow to develop confidently, digressively. William, for example, finds himself obligated to pretend he's a journalist for a fox-hunting magazine interviewing all those connected with Anna's latest release, a horseless sci-fi epic, at a press junket. On another occasion, he's mistaken for the room-service waiter and patronized by her movie-star boyfriend (a funny, uncredited Alec Baldwin, trying hard for noblesse oblige and delightfully missing the note).

But William's place is not entirely peaceful either. He has a hilariously loutish roommate (Rhys Ifans) who keeps muddling the relationship with Anna, a shop assistant who mistakes her for Demi Moore, a sister who becomes giddily unhinged by close proximity to the famous. Above all, he can't protect Anna from the media frenzy attending discovery of some dirty pictures she posed for prior to her fame.

The movie turns persuasively on that point, but it is finally its casual knowingness on everything from Anna's salary to the contractual prohibitions against excessive bodily exposure in her love scenes that gives the picture honest weight. That and the lead performances. There's winning tentativeness in the way Grant makes his way back to life from depression, an irresistible glow to Roberts when she forgets what she has become and is simply a girl who has found her unlikely Mr. Right. They are edgy charmers, and you have to wonder if the happy ending that concludes the picture will be permitted to last. But you can't help—hoping gratefully—for the best.

VILLAGE VOICE, 6/1/99, p. 126, Dennis Lim

The tagline for *Notting Hill* reads, "Can the most famous film star in the world fall for the man on the street?" A more honest version would be "Can the moviegoing public fall for the same old crap again?" Yes, on both counts, apparently. *Notting Hill* cynically merges Hollywood gloss and smarminess with an overwrought but highly exportable English taste for quirk. It is not, the filmmakers stress, a sequel to *Four Weddings and a Funeral* (which writer Richard Curtis was also responsible for), but it fits the latter-day Hollywood definition of the term—same movie, only worse.

Julia Roberts plays Anna Scott—"Hollywood's biggest star by far," we're informed in a tacky opening montage of flashbulb explosions and magazine covers. Hugh Grant is William, the man on the street (though the street happens to be situated in a snooty-boho West London enclave), a divorcé who owns a not very profitable travel bookshop (signifying *smart, sensitive, vulnerable*). One day Anna walks into William's store. He's flustered, she buys a book and leaves; shortly after, on the street, he spills a drink on her. From this serendipitous double whammy begins an exasperating, desperately predictable, start-stop romance—scored in literal-minded fashion to r&b-lite love songs and packed with cloyingly cute setups. William crashes a junket and pretends to be a journalist; Anna hangs out with commoners and discovers the pleasures of slumming; William declares his love—at a press conference.

All the bumps in this relationship arise from Anna being a self-absorbed bitch who's prone to actress-y hissy fits. Which brings us to the prespun, media-ready question at the heart of *Notting Hill*: is Julia Roberts playing herself? A moot point, really, since there are few moments where Anna Scott resembles an actual person. Curtis spikes his screenplay with smirky gestures that pass for porno self-deprecation. Within minutes of meeting William's pals, Anna reveals to all that she's been on a diet for 10 years, that she's had plastic surgery twice, and that she is, in fact, a terrible actress. When Anna and William are besieged by paparazzi, she shrieks at him that the scandal will be in her "clip file" forever—not unlike Divine Brown, she neglects to add.

As in *Four Weddings*, the Grant character is surrounded by a gaggle of less attractive friends whose primary concern in life, it seems, is his emotional well-being. Curtis has switched some defining traits around: for instance, the kooky chick isn't Grant's flatmate but his sister, there's still a kooky flatmate, but he's a Welsh slob. The mawkish resolution is, even by Nora Ephron standards, risible, hinging on a single objectionable line ("I'm just a girl, standing in front of a guy, asking him to love her"). Roberts is called upon to deflect plot glitches and bad dialogue with her klieg-light beam. Grant, as usual, relies on exaggerated social clumsiness—a curious, passive-aggressive variation on charm that's growing uglier by the minute.

Also reviewed in:
NEW REPUBLIC, 6/21/99, p. 30, Stanley Kauffmann
NEW YORKER, 6/7/99, p. 96, Anthony Lane
NEW YORK TIMES, 5/28/99, p. E7, Janet Maslin
VARIETY, 5/3-9/99, p. 83, Derek Elley
WASHINGTON POST, 5/28/99, p. C1, Stephen Hunter
WASHINGTON POST, 5/28/99, Weekend/p. 49, Desson Howe

OCTOBER SKY

A Universal Pictures release of a Charles Gordon production. *Executive Producer:* Marc Sternberg and Peter Cramer. *Producer:* Charles Gordon and Larry Franco. *Director:* Joe Johnston. *Screenplay:* Lewis Colick. *Based on the book "Rocket Boys" by:* Homer H. Hickman, Jr. *Director of Photography:* Fred Murphy. *Editor:* Robert Dalva. *Music:* Mark Isham. *Music Editor:* Tom Carlson and Joe E. Rand. *Sound:* Mary Ellis and (music) Stephen Krause. *Sound Editor:* Howell Gibbens. *Casting:* Nancy Foy. *Production Designer:* Barry Robison. *Art Director:* Tony Fanning. *Set Designer:* William G. Davis and Alan Hook. *Set Director:* Chris Spellman. *Set Dresser:* Eric J. Luling. *Special Effects:* Joey DiGaetano. *Costumes:* Betsy Cox. *Make-up:* Lynn Barber. *Special Effects Make-up:* Bill Johnson. *Stunt Coordinator:* Cliff Cudney. *Running time:* 100 minutes. *MPAA Rating:* PG.

CAST: Jake Gyllenhaal (Homer Hickam); Chris Cooper (John Hickman); Laura Dern (Miss Riley); Chris Owen (Quentin); William Lee Scott (Roy Lee); Chad Lindberg (O'Dell); Natalie Canerday (Elsie Hickam); Scott Miles (Jim Hickam); Randy Tripling (Leon Bolden); Chris Ellis (Principal Turner); Elya Baskin (Ike Bykovsky); Courtney Fendley (Dorothy Platt); David Dwyer (Jake Mosby); Terry Loughlin (Mr. Dantzler); Kaili Hollister (Valentine Carmina); David Copeland (Coach Gainer); Don Henderson Baker (Jensen); Tom Kagy (Lenny); Donald

Thorne (Trooper One); Justin Whitsett (Kid); Larry Rue, Neva Howell, and Terry Nienhuis (Neighbors); Brady Coleman (Anderson); Rick Forrester (Roper); Terrence Gibney (Basil Thorpe); Doug Swander (Corvette Guy); Keeli Hale Kimbro (Corvette Girl); Mark Jeffrey Miller (Vernon); Blaque Fowler (Reverend); Don Tilly (Rescue Worker); Rockford Davis (Chemistry Teacher); John Bennes (Doctor); Jonathan Fawbush (Barney); Larry Black (Fred Smith); Frank Schuler (Moonshiner); Tommy Smeltzer (Man at Mine); Charles Lawlor and Tom Turbiville (Miners); Ida Ginn (Quentin's Mom); Richard Lumpkin (Judge at Welch); Mark Whitman Johnson and Don Taylor (Union Officials); Don G. Campbell (Mr. Morris); Elizabeth Byler (Ivy League Girl); Bradford Ryan Lund (Ivy League Boy); Frank Hoyt Taylor (Judge at Indy); David Hager (Head Judge); Ray Elder (Tom Webster); Andy Stahl (Jack Palmer); Joey DiGaetano (Wernher von Braun); Thomas Taylor (Miner in Elevator); David Ducey (Man in Crowd); Jenny Patterson (Nurse); O. Winston Link (Locomotive Engineer).

CHRISTIAN SCIENCE MONITOR, 2/19/99, p 15, David Sterritt

In many ways, "October Sky" is exactly the sort of Hollywood picture we need to see more often: cleanly written, capably filmed, and focused on a young person who's determined to turn his life in constructive, creative directions.

But movies are complicated beasts, and to leave the review at that would be to overlook shortcomings that weaken the films value. When all the evidence is considered, the verdict on "October Sky" has to be more a mixed recommendation than an unqualified rave.

The time is the 1950s, and the hero is Homer Hickam, a teenage boy growing up in the aptly named West Virginia town of Coalwood, where the chosen destiny of nearly all males is to finish as much of high school as seems convenient and then head straight to the local mine for a lifetime of picking, shoveling, and inhaling mineral dust.

That was good enough for Homer's father, who rose to the rank of superintendent and expects his son to follow a similar path. But a couple of factors are snarling this neat scenario. One is the changing nature of Coalwood's mining industry, hit with labor unrest and signs that the mine's yield is diminishing.

The other is Homer's growing awareness that a mining life isn't for him, even if Coalwood's veins keep flourishing forever. Emulating his father's career doesn't seem like a sure-fire route to contentment, and more important, he has a passion of his own: rocketry, a growing and glamorous science that makes his head whirl with fantastic possibilities.

He's so eager to become a rocket scientist that he can't wait for the usual training, or four years of college, or even his parents' permission. Helped by like-minded friends and slightly bewildered grownups, he starts practicing his would-be profession in his backyard with results that range from almost comical to literally explosive.

Right down to its title, "October Sky" takes inspiration from the nights in 1957 when the Soviet satellite Sputnik first streaked through the heavens, during the boyhood of the real Homer Hickam, whose memoirs gave the movie its basic plot. Many viewers may feel a nostalgic shiver at the very mention of that history-changing time, when the complacency of the immediate postwar years gave way to both anxiety and excitement as the Space Age moved from science-fiction stories to newspaper headlines. The filmmakers ably capture this mixture of emotions as it affected ordinary people, who wondered what impact these events might have on their own quiet lives.

The movie is capably acted, too, most notably by Jake Gyllenhaal and Chris Cooper as Homer and his dad. Also noteworthy are Natalie Canerday as Homer's mom, William Lee Scott and Chad Lindberg as his closest friends, Chris Owen as a high-school science geek, and Laura Dern as a teacher who believes in Homer when others think his head has vanished entirely into the clouds.

One problem with "October Sky" is a weakness for clunky storytelling. The director, Joe Johnston, treats even the most heavy-handed patches of the screenplay as if they were subtle points that we might fail to notice if he didn't noisily hammer them home.

More serious is the movie's poorly thought-out conception of individuality, which is one of its main themes. Celebrating individualism is wonderful when it affirms the right of a young man like Homer to realize his dreams on his own terms. But it's not so appealing when it leads to cynical views of group activity and community action, as in the portrayal of Coalwood's mining union, which is viewed in insultingly simplistic and negative terms. Some may also question the movie's hero-worshiping treatment of Homer's role model, Werner von Braun, who's depicted as an all-American icon with no acknowledgment of his earlier career in Nazi Germany.

These oversimplified aspects of "October Sky" don't scuttle its worthwhile qualities, and many parents will cheer it clean and friendly approach. Here's hoping other filmmakers will follow it spirit, if not all of its methods.

LOS ANGELES TIMES, 2/19/99, Calendar/p. 10, Kenneth Turan

"October Sky" is one of the most unfashionable movies of the new year, and one of the more appealing. Made with a gee-whiz earnestness and simplicity that's so out of style it's rather refreshing, this reality-based tale of a West Virginia teenager's hopes and dreams is not only a stranger to cynicism, it also manages to be unapologetically sentimental without the excessive emotional pandering that's become so much the rule with films of this type.

The story "October Sky" tells is the one Homer H. Hickam Jr. related in his well-reviewed 1998 memoir, "Rocket Boys," a finalist for the National Book Critics Circle Award. It tells of a young man growing up in the 1950s with a passion for exploring outer space in a town, Coalwood, W. Va., that sent every healthy male in exactly the opposite direction, down deep below the surface into labyrinthine pits to mine for coal.

Having spent much of his career as an Oscar-winning creator of visual effects—a helpful background for the director of "Honey, I Shrunk the Kids" and "Jumanji"—Joe Johnston may seem an unlikely choice for this kind of film. But Johnston also directed the similarly innocent "The Rocketeer," and working with screenwriter Lewis Colick, he has turned out a film so gosh darn old-fashioned it might have emerged from a time capsule.

With Chris Cooper and Laura Dern as its best-known acting names, "October Sky" banks on the impact little-known faces can have and, with the help of casting director Nancy Foy, that faith has paid off. Jake Gyllenhaal is appropriately Huck Finn-ish as Homer, and William Lee Scott, Chris Owen and Chad Lindberg play his three pals and fellow rocket boys (cut down from the book's grand total of six) with the requisite spunk and enthusiasm.

So soft at times it uses the classic '50s rock on its soundtrack for edge, "October Sky" is especially well served by Cooper, whose feature roles include a key part in John Sayles' "Lone Star." An intense, focused actor, Cooper plays Homer's father, John, the mine superintendent in tiny Coalwood, and his portrait of a caring but rigid and unbending figure gives the film a kind of backbone it wouldn't otherwise possess.

Lovingly re-created in Tennessee (with a nod to the visual look of celebrated West Virginia photographer O. Winston Link, who has a tiny cameo as a train engineer), Coalwood was a town that wouldn't exist without the inky-black fuel that gave it its name.

The news that the Russians have put a Sputnik into orbit around the Earth is unnerving enough to shake up people in 1957, even here. Young Homer joins his fellow townspeople watching the October skies for the satellite's appearance, and the sight of it has a lasting effect. "I'm thinking of building a rocket," he tells his parents (Cooper and Natalie Canerday) and his brother Jim (Scott Miles) at breakfast the next morning, shocking them as much as if he'd announced he was about to move to the Soviet Union.

Homer, however, is hard to discourage; as the local football coach tells him when he tries out for the team in the film's opening sequence, "You sure got guts, but you got to know when to quit." Working first with best pals Roy Lee (Scott) and O'Dell (Lindberg), he sets out to build rockets with whatever homemade parts and assistance he can muster, even writing to NASA scientist Wernher von Braun when he feels especially put upon.

It's a mark of Homer's determination to succeed that he risks committing social suicide by enlisting the aid of glasses-wearing classmate Quentin (Owen), the school's nerdy science and math whiz. An even bigger help is science teacher Miss Riley (a small, restrained but remarkably effective performance by Dern), who encourages him to work hard enough to enter the local science fair. "You can't," she says, "just dream your way out of Coalwood."

There are barriers to the rocket boys' quest, but because "October Sky" is based on reality, some of them turn out to be unexpected. Homer's most durable obstacle is, however, not surprising: a hard-headed, no-nonsense dad who refuses point-blank to understand what his son's passion is all about.

A father who can't connect across the generations couldn't be more of a stock figure, as are many others in Colick's screenplay. But "October Sky's" evident sincerity, its air of decency as it explores the power of a dream, help make these people more substantial than might be expected.

"October Sky" has another anachronistic characteristic—and that is its vision of an America we'd like to believe in, an America where hard work and determination can make something happen, an America we see in the home movie glimpses of the real Homer and his friends that end the film. It's a country we want to feel existed once upon a time, a country we'd like to live in even now.

NEW YORK, 3/1/99, p. 93, Peter Rainer

October Sky, about a coal miner's son who becomes a rocket scientist, is an inspirational drama without a whit of inspiration. The visuals, the dialogue, the sentiments all seem lifted right out of the *Boy Scout Handbook*. The film is supposed to be based on a true story, but who can believe a minute of it? That's the problem with mediocrity—it makes even verity seem fraudulent. Homer Hickam (Jake Gyllenhaal, in a respectable performance)—whose father (Chris Cooper, ditto) is the no-nonsense mine supervisor in the company town of Coalwood, West Virginia—doesn't want to spend his life underground inhaling black dust. Inspired by the recent Sputnik launch, he reads up on rockets and, enlisting three high-school mates, starts boosting his own. Crude cherry-bomb contraptions soon give way to smarter stuff, and eventually Homer and the boys win top prize in the National Science Fair and college scholarships. We're supposed to applaud Homer for rising above his roots, but the effect is condescending. It's as if the filmmakers were saying, *If these hillbillies could do it, why not you?*

NEW YORK POST, 2/19/99, p. 55, Jonathan Foreman

If it weren't an amazing but true story, "October Sky" would be unforgivably corny.

And even knowing that the basic plot is true doesn't make up for the hopeless hokiness of many of its scenes.

Yet, if you can endure the drippiness and the stately pace, "October Sky" ends up a sweet, uplifting, even inspiring movie.

Based on "Rocket Boys," the memoir of NASA scientist Homer Hickam Jr., the film is set in 1957 in the mining town of Coalwood, W. Va.

It's an unforgiving place, where a boy ends up working in the mines, as his father did—unless a football scholarship takes him to college.

Homer (Jake Gyllenhaal) is the younger son of mine superintendent John Hickam (Chris Cooper) and, unlike his older brother, he's too small to play football.

When Russia launches Sputnik, the first man-made satellite, Homer is one of the townspeople who watch in awe and fear as it crosses the night sky.

He decides that he will help his country catch up in the space race by building a rocket with his two best pals. But he's not much of a scholar, especially when it comes to math.

So building a rocket—which rapidly becomes an obsession necessitates befriending school nerd Quentin (Chris Owen).

With the backing of Miss Riley (Laura Dern), a determined teacher, and the assistance of some of the guys in the mine's machine shop, the four youths become "the Rocket Boys."

Homer even starts writing to the brilliant German rocket scientist/war criminal, Dr. Werner von Braun.

But John Hickam, an obstinate but courageous and decent man, thinks that making rockets is a silly distraction, and he does everything he can to hinder the project—even though there's a slim chance that it might lead to a science prize and even a college scholarship for his younger son.

Dad believes Homer should be preparing to follow him down the mine. Later, Homer is forced to drop out of high school, abandon his hopes of winning any science prizes and start working in the pit.

But all is not lost, and it's giving nothing away to say that Homer and the Rocket Boys will end up winning not only that state prize but maybe even a prize at the National Science Fair in Indianapolis, thus catapulting them out of Coalwood.

And along the way, the Rocket Boys will capture the imaginations and the hearts of everyone in the town, except Homer's father ...

"October Sky" is the kind of movie in which characters say things such as, "Things will never be the same again." Yet, all the characters—save the father—are underwritten.

You never know why Homer should be fascinated by Sputnik or by rockets. And the motivation of the other boys is even more of a blank.

By-the-numbers direction by Joe Johnston does the script no favors. But the four young actors who play the Rocket Boys are solid and believable—especially Gyllenhaal.

Dern once again invests a relatively small role with wonderful energy, and Cooper, the subtle, powerful actor who was so terrific in "Lone Star," gives a superb performance.

The two of them raise the whole tone of the movie so that you almost don't mind the way that every sappy moment is milked within an inch of its life.

Still, as relentlessly cornpone, lazily written, and predictable as it is, "October Sky" works. You cannot help but root for these West Virginia kids in their struggle to get out of the mines, and when they do, it leaves a catch in your throat.

NEWSDAY, 2/19/99, Part II/p. B3, John Anderson

To paraphrase Hermann Goering, when I hear the words "based on a true story" I reach for my revolver. However, just because people are plotting against you doesn't mean you're not paranoid. And just because a story is heartwarming and sentimental to the point of disbelief doesn't mean it isn't true.

"October Sky," based on Homer Hickam's "Rocket Boys" (a 1999 National Book Critics Circle nominee in autobiography and a much better title) takes a few liberties with his magical, account of growing up in a '50s coal camp in West Virginia. There are four "rocket boys" here rather than the original six, for instance. And there's no way the town of Coalwood was possessed of this much serendipity and sentiment (both of which are laid on with a trowel by director Joe Johnston, who, by the way, directed "The Rocketeer"). But basically, it's Hickam's story: How the 1957 launch of the Soviet Sputnik satellite shook up the scientific community in general, and a bunch of boys in Coalwood specifically.

It's hard to imagine "October Sky" ever being made if it hadn't been true, because it's almost too good to be true. The story has the feel-good component every other screenwriter seems to be striving for in '90s movieland. It contains an omnipotent metaphor in the juxtaposition of coal mine to outer space. And it has a classic case of father vs. son, pragmatist vs. fabulist, the gravity of fate vs. the airborne dynamic of dreams.

The Coalwood we meet is a place where sons are expected to follow their fathers down into the mines and where only football scholarships offer a ticket out of the red (debt) and black (lung). Homer's father, John (Chris Cooper), the mine superintendent, expects his younger son will take his place someday—the other son, a football star, is ipso facto exempt. Homer is no athlete, but he and his fellow rocket boys—Roy Lee (William Lee Scott), Odell (Chad Lindberg) and Quentin (Chris Owen)—dare to look up, persevere through dozens of failed attempts to launch their relatively simple rockets, learn the chemistry, do the math and grope their way to a larger, wider world. What "October Sky" is, is "Breaking Away"—except that instead of bicycles, its heroes are riding potassium nitrate, sulphur and zinc dust on a vicarious trip to the moon.

Gyllenhaal makes his way through most of the film with a goofy grin; it's Cooper, one of our more interesting actors, who gives the movie weight. He also gives it authenticity-by-association, by way of his work in John Sayles' films, including the coal movie "Matewan." Of course, John Hickam's virulent anti-union bias would never fly with Sayles. And it's a little distracting here. It may be John's job to be anti-union, but since that labor is represented in "October Sky" only by a drunk, a mob and a would-be sniper's bullet, the prejudices seem a little overheated. And, since we're talking about coal mines here, misplaced.

Otherwise, "October Sky" is an inspiring and involving story, part coming-of-age, part student-teacher (a la Laura Dern as the dedicated mentor Miss Riley), part coming-of-age, Cold War-at-home and even entertainment-as-education: A lot of the fun stems from the boys' inept attempts at rocket-launching, their search for solutions and their initiative at research and financing—tearing up old railroad tracks, for example, so they can sell the rails for scrap. But then, it's a scrappy movie, finally, for all its starry-eyed skywatchers and plucky heroism.

SIGHT AND SOUND, 1/00, p. 59, Kevin Maher

On the night of 5 October 1957, the residents of the mining town Coalwood, West Virginia, watch Sputnik pass through the night sky. The next morning, teenage Homer Hickam decides to build his own rocket. After his first attempt fails, he constructs a more powerful rocket assisted by his schoolfriends Quentin, Sherman and Roy Lee. It flies into the mines where Homer's father John works. Banned from mine property, the boys continue their testing at a slack-dump just outside town.

Arrested for setting fire to the forest, the boys give up their experiments. When John is injured in an accident, Homer starts working down the mine. In his spare time he studies trigonometry and realises that his rocket wasn't to blame for the fire. He quits work, goes back to school, and enters his rocket in a nationwide competition which he wins. Closing titles reveal Homer is now a NASA engineer.

Rarely has a movie in recent years been as blatantly flag-waving as *October Sky*. With its small-town setting, where the houses are ringed with white picket fences and where Homer and his friends dream of rocket ships while sipping soda pop in diners, *October Sky* brings to mind Norman Rockwell's rosy vision of folksy Americana. There are also echoes of *The Man Who Shot Liberty Valance* (1962). Rocket enthusiast Homer recalls James Stewart's Ransom Stoddard, being a harbinger of modernity (his science obsession) and a symbol of the town's and by extension America's—Manifest Destiny. His father John, on the other hand, is like John Wayne's Doniphon, a man of action who rushes into collapsing mine shafts without thinking. As with *Liberty, October Sky*'s sympathies lean towards the powerful man of action John: Homer says admiringly to him, "Dr Von Braun is a great scientist, but he isn't my hero—I only hope I can be just as good a man as you are!"

But unlike Ford's film, which radically explored the tensions opened up by the two differing models of masculinity represented by Wayne (with whom we are encouraged to identify) and Stewart, *October Sky* tries to have it both ways by celebrating both John and Homer as idealised versions of American masculinity. Here the movie retreads the soggy ground staked out by *Field of Dreams*, with sentimental tears and group hugs as the answer to conflicting ideological standpoints.

Like one of Homer's rockets, *October Sky* has a predictably linear trajectory. When Homer announces, "I'm going to build a rocket like Sputnik," it's only a matter of time before his picture appears in the final credits as Homer Hickam, NASA Engineer. Along the way, whenever the momentum starts to flag, we're treated to countless musical montages. Even a few spirited turns from an otherwise adequate cast can't transcend the film's mood of earnest naivety. When a girl approaches Homer at the school dance and tells him, "It sure was exciting watching your rockets go up," you can be sure that the scene is not being played for *double entendres*.

VILLAGE VOICE, 2/23/99, p. 114, Gary Dauphin

In the age of cyberspace, there's something remarkably quaint and corn-fed about the image of a boy craning his neck to follow the smoke trail of a model rocket. The kids in *Rocket Boys*, the recent memoir of a Sputnik-era coming of age, do an awful lot of craning and in *October Sky*'s unabashedly nostalgic translation, their pastime is more than just a fond childhood memory. Looking up and projecting your desires into the sky say some basic things about what it means to be human in ways that have little to do with X-Files paranoia, rubber ears, and Trek conventions.

Homer Hickam Jr. grew up to be a NASA scientist (and bestselling author), but in 1958 he was just another white-trash kid in a Kentucky coal-mining town. Initially the picture of averageness, Homer is destined for the mine, Jake Gyllenhaal effectively playing him as a mild kid with perpetually hunched shoulders and a slow-dawning but wide smile. Homer's life is changed when the Russians launch Sputnik in October 1958, his previously underutilized imagination not only fired up but directed into the creation of increasingly powerful projectiles.

Since *Sky* is aiming for a certain tear-jerking movie uplift, Homer faces the expected struggles: his borderline abuser father fulminates about "this rocket business"; the school principal warns that there's no escaping the mines' gravitational pull; his best friends think he's gone plain crazy, what with all the girls around town. Homer presses on anyway and, after a kindly teacher (Laura

Dern, syrupy and saintly as can be) tells him about fabled science fairs where small-town boys can win college scholarships, he risks his school-yard reputation by befriending the school outcast-science whiz in exchange for insights into combustible solid fuels and exhaust nozzles. Homer's enthusiasm infects two more friends and the resulting quartet become the "Rocket Boys," a nickname that starts out as a slur but is soon the stuff of local legend.

As directed by Joe Johnston, *October Sky* is a professionally crafted family film that reserves all its challenging moments for its characters, letting the audience bask comfortably in the approach of a predetermined warm and fuzzy ending. Still you can't help but be moved when the inevitable "where are they now" coda rolls: Homer may be the only one who made it to Cape Canaveral, but *October Sky*'s real clincher is the more modest fact that the three other rocket boys also escaped the mines.

Also reviewed in:
CHICAGO TRIBUNE, 2/19/99, Tempo/p. 4, Michael Wilmington
NEW YORK TIMES, 2/19/99, p. E14, Janet Maslin
NEW YORKER, 2/22-3/1/99, p. 184, David Denby
VARIETY, 2/8-14/99, p. 75, Joe Leydon
WASHINGTON POST, 2/19/99, p. C1, Stephen Hunter
WASHINGTON POST, 2/19/99, Weekend/p. 38, Desson Howe

OFFICE SPACE

A Twentieth Century Fox release. *Executive Producer:* Guy Riedel. *Producer:* Michael Rotenberg and Daniel Rappaport. *Director:* Mike Judge. *Screenplay:* Mike Judge. *Based upon the "Milton" animated shorts by:* Mike Judge. *Director of Photography:* Tim Suhrstedt. *Editor:* David Rennie. *Music:* John Frizzell. *Music Editor:* Abby Treloggen. *Sound:* Stacy F. Brownrigg and (music) Rick Winquest. *Sound Editor:* Robert Shoup. *Casting:* Nancy Klopper. *Production Designer:* Edward McAvoy. *Art Director:* Adele Plauche. *Set Decorator:* Carla Curry. *Set Dresser:* Roy G. Huth, Marc Dabrusin, Steve Sawhill, Michael Bayer, April L. Crump, and Colleen Saro. *Special Effects:* Paul Lombardi. *Costumes:* Melinda Eshelman. *Make-up:* Felicity Bowring. *Stunt Coordinator:* Rob King. *Running time:* 97 minutes. *MPAA Rating:* R.

CAST: Ron Livingston (Peter); Jennifer Aniston (Joanna); David Herman (Michael Bolton); Ajay Naidu (Samir); Diedrich Bader (Lawrence); Stephen Root (Milton); Gary Cole (Bill Lumbergh); Richard Riehle (Tom Smykowski); Alexandra Wentworth (Anne); Joe Bays (Dom Portwood); John C. McGinley (Bob Slydell); Paul Willson (Bob Porter); Kinna McInroe (Nina); Todd Duffey (Chotchkie's Waiter); Greg Pitts (Drew); Michael McShane (Dr. Swanson); Linda Wakeman (Laura Smykowski); Jennifer Jane Emerson (Female Temp); Josh Bond (Initech Security Guard); Kyle Scott Jackson (Rob Newhouse); Orlando Jones (Steve); Barbara George-Reiss (Lumbergh's Secretary); Tom Schuster (Construction Foreman); Ruperto Reyes, Jr. (Mexican Waiter); Jackie Belvin (Swanson's Patient #1); Gabriel Folse (Swanson's Patient #2); Jesse De Luna (Cop at Fire); William King (Chotchkie's Manager); Justin Possenti (Spectator); Jack Betts (Judge).

LOS ANGELES TIMES, 2/19/99, Calendar/p. 6, Kevin Thomas

With the sharp and funny "Office Space," Mike Judge, the creator of "Beavis and Butt-head," makes his zesty live-action feature directorial debut with a picture that works both as a white-collar romantic comedy and as a crisp satire of today's corporate realities. Bristling with shrewd observation, inspired humor and all-around smarts, "Office Space" is a winner about a guy who's beginning to feel like a loser.

Ron Livingston's Peter Gibbons is an amusingly average young man who is becoming bored to death working as a computer programmer in a vast generic office of an engineering company situated in an industrial park that looks exactly like a zillion others. He lives in a perfectly decent but seemingly immense apartment structure that also resembles countless others. He is as much "one of the crowd" as was James Murray in King Vidor's silent classic "The Crowd" more than 70 years ago.

Peter is increasingly dissatisfied with his job but remains essentially timid in the face of his awful boss, played to scene-stealing perfection by Gary Cole as one of those dapper tyrants who rule with a casual, presumptuous drawn-out drawl. Then his soon-to-be-former girlfriend insists he see a hypnotist who casts a spell over Peter.

The spell is cast with such intensity that the effort proves fatal to the hypnotist. But it leaves Peter so relaxed and uninhibited that he starts turning up to work only when he feels like it. His termination surely would be immediate were it not for the arrival of the two deliciously unctuous Bobs (John C. McGinley and Paul Willson), efficiency experts to whom he is so breathtakingly candid that they see in him material for promotion; after all, how many employees would be honest enough to say that they're bored because the boss doesn't challenge them enough?

At this point a more conventional film would show Peter coping with a higher rung up the corporate ladder, but Judge, through the presence of the Bobs, veers his film in an all-too-topical direction instead, toward downsizing, that harsh reality of the modern workplace. Once Peter discovers that his two best friends at work, Michael (David Herman) and Samir (Ajay Naidu), are in danger of losing their jobs, "Office Space" takes flight as a zany adventure, including a romance for Peter with Jennifer Aniston's pert, level-headed Joanna, a waitress at a nearby theme restaurant where everyone has to wear buttons to show their "flair."

What makes "Office Space" such an amusing treat is that it is chock-full of deftly defined characters. Starting with its stars, virtually every actor on whom the camera lingers even briefly gets to shine: Diedrich Bader as Peter's laid-back next-door neighbor, a contented construction worker; Stephen Root as the apprehensive, dithering and vaguely threatening most-put-upon worker in the entire office; and Todd Duffey's obnoxious waiter are but three standouts in a cast that includes Richard Riehle, Joe Bays, Orlando Jones and William King, who also contribute equally fine work.

Judge constantly finds humor in everyday exasperation: Michael coping with the coincidence that his last name happens to be Bolton; Joanna having to put up with King's relentless boss, who insists that 15 buttons with silly sayings on them don't show enough "flair" when Duffey sports a whopping 37; everyone in Peter's office wrangling with a computer printer constantly breaking down.

Working with astute production designer Edward McAvoy, Judge subtly evokes the creeping, relentless homogenization of modern life and the piling on of trivial soul-withering regulations that reflect a steady, mindless insistence on workers to conform, eroding them of their sense of individuality and freedom—even while insisting that they "express themselves."

The more you peer beneath the surface humor of "Office Space" the scarier and more serious its vision of contemporary existence becomes.

NEW YORK, 3/1/99, p. 92, Peter Rainer

Office Space opens with a massive traffic jam in which the drivers, encased in their cars, give play to their secret selves. The straight-arrow looking Peter (Ron Livingston) comes apart; meek Michael (David Herman) blasts rap music but is careful to lock his doors when a black peddler wedges into an adjoining lane. It turns out these guys are computer programmers en route to their jobs at the monolithic Initech Corporation. This daily commuter snarl may be their only occasion to blow off steam. Slotted into look-alike cubicles at work, they peep over the partitions like rodents, sniffing the air for danger. Locking eyes with their boss Bill (Gary Cole) invites trouble: He'll ask you to work the weekend.

This is the first live-action feature from writer-director Mike Judge, creator of *Beavis and Butt-head* and co-creator of the TV series *King of the Hill*. He gives the film an uncluttered, almost abstract look that allows us to home in on the visual jokes, the way we might in a Jacques Tati film. That Initech office complex is so sterile it's unnerving; it's the prototype for every soul-deadening job we've ever had. Gazing into it is like staring at the floor plans for your prison block.

Judge is sharp about the jangles and subterfuges of office politics. He knows how to decode the doublespeak. When a team of efficiency experts shows up at the office to interview the staff, you don't need to be told that layoffs are pending. The drones at Initech are preternaturally sensitive to upper-management bull; they always know when the next punch is coming, and the best they can do is take it full on the chin. Judge gets the corporate details just right: the flat lighting that isolates the wage slaves as if they were lab specimens; the soft tread on acrylic carpet of slit-eyed company honchos; the chirpy secretary whose endlessly repeated telephone greeting has turned her into a human tape loop. *Office Space* is a white-collar comedy for the generation of lowered expectations. The toilers at Initech are the children and grandchildren of the Organization Men of the fifties. Spending their lives staring into a computer screen, they have to fight off becoming computers themselves. For most, it's a battle long since lost.

The standout rebel is Peter, who starts out in such dire straits that he finally seeks relief front an "occupational hypnotherapist." "Is there some way you can zonk me out?" he asks during his session, and then, just after Peter goes into a trance, the therapist suddenly keels over dead. Locked into his hypno-bliss, Peter is a changed dude. Showing up late to work, or not at all, he's so cavalier in his unconcern that, instead of being fired, he's recommended for an upper-level position. It's a rich joke: The less he cares, the more he's valued. But Peter is no sellout. He devises a scheme with Michael and another co-worker, Samir (Ajay Naidu), to bilk Initech, and he also enlists a newfound waitress girlfriend, Joanna (Jennifer Aniston), who has her own job woes. (She works at a place called Chotchkie's, where her boss, played by Judge, has criticized her for not pinning enough "flair"—personally chosen buttons and pins and what-not—to her uniform.)

Judge has a good eye for casting—a cartoonist's eye. The people in *Office Space* are live-action versions of his animated nerds and creeps and blubberers. One of them, Milton (Stephen Root), is actually based on a character from judge's animation work. He's portrayed in the movie as a whimpering poor soul with matted hair who keeps getting marginalized until he finally ends up in an unlighted cubicle in the basement. Laid off, he refuses to leave—he's Melville's Bartleby the Scrivener for the Dilbert generation. Boss Bob is so unctuous and android-like, so boneless, that he might have been fashioned from poured plastic. And then there's Michael, chinless and mop-haired, who looks like a geekier Bill Gates, and whose last name, Bolton, compounds his agonies. (On first acquaintance, people are always asking him if he is related to the singer, whom Michael detests.) Judge isn't being especially cruel in accentuating the peculiarities of these people. It's just how he sees things. He's an equal-opportunity caricaturist who enjoys tickling himself.

Office Space is so enjoyable that you wish it were even better. It's targeted for the bright-young-adult audience, and that's fine but also limiting. Until now, there hasn't been a comedy about the attitudes of white-collar kids mired in corporate purgatory; the subject is so good that you want to see it blown up big-time. Judge is a bit like Joanna the waitress—she could benefit from a bit more flair, too. Once the scheme to bilk Initech is set in motion, the off-kilter humor flattens into a take-this-job-and-shove-it thing, and the ending seems pooped-out. Judge may not be fully aware of how wildly talented he is, which, in a Hollywood culture swarming with relentless blowhards, makes him something of an anomaly. He has it in him to make classic comedies. The nut-brain *Office Space* is a good warm-up act to the main event.

NEW YORK POST, 2/19/99, p. 44, Jonathan Foreman.

Very funny though uneven, Mike Judge's first live-action feature, "Office Space," takes irreverent satire beyond the domestic realm of his "Beavis & Butt-head" and "King of the Hill" cartoons.

No film has better captured cubicle hell and the weirdly Dickensian world of today's white-collar factories.

It's all here: the horrible fake informality, the flatulent management-speak, the drudgery, the hidden little hierarchies, the ruthless downsizing and the fantasies of revenge.

And it's not just the high-tech office world that meets Judge's satirical blade, it's also the service sector: The main character's love interest works in a ghastly theme restaurant in the same bland business park.

Peter (Ron Livingston) hates his programming job and his bosses at Initech—especially the unctuous Lumbergh (Gary Cole). But like his two buddies at the company, Michael Bolton (David Herman) and Samir (Ajay Naidu) there's nothing he can do about it.

All three are only a few steps up from the office ultra-victim Milton (Stephen Root), whose workspace is continually shrinking.

One day, the "occupational hypnotherapist" Peter has been seeing at his girlfriend's request dies mid-session, with Peter still in a hypnotized "I don't care" mode.

As a result, Peter starts blowing off weekend work and coming in late—very late. This change in behavior happens to coincide with the arrival of consultants at Initech, whose real purpose is deciding who to "downsize."

Bolton and Samir are toast. But Peter's new attitude—he tells the consultants (played by John C. McGinley and Paul Willson) that he likes to kill time in the mornings—has the perverse effect of getting him promoted.

Anyone this confident is clearly "a straight-shooting, upper-management type."

Despite the promotion, Peter masterminds a plan to rip off Initech, using a computer virus and the help of his two fired buds.

It works—but too well. Peter's new waitress girlfriend Joanna (Jennifer Aniston) doesn't approve of his stealing. And all three of them may well face jail—unless Milton is driven crazy first.

The genius of this film is in its abundance of sharp-edged gemlike details: the way the unctuous Lumbergh always begins one of his dreaded little talks with a "So ... what's happening?" or the way we first meet the wimpy Michael singing along to gangsta rap in his car and then see that his cube is decorated with posters of Navy Seals ...

Judge makes good use of a fine cast. Ron Livingston makes a convincing everyman and clearly enjoys lines like, "I did absolutely nothing, and it was everything I thought it would be."

Gary Cole is particularly good as his malevolent boss. And Aniston, who showed she can be more than Rachel from "Friends" in Ed Burns' "She's the One" holds her own in a limited part.

The main flaw of "Office Space" is the sudden plot shift from Peter's career turnaround to the ill-fated embezzlement plan. The first half definitely contains most of the really great jokes.

But this movie will strike home with anybody who has ever worked in a contemporary cube-farm—and strike fear into the little hearts of evil bosses everywhere.

NEWSDAY, 2/19/99, Part II/p. B7, Gene Seymour

The target audience for "Office Space" would seem to comprise wage slaves convinced that the people they work for are meaner and stupider than they are.

Are we talking big numbers here or what?

Of course, the not-so-subtle irony within Mike Judge's first live-action feature is that even among the wage slaves themselves, there can be found many ways to be dim-witted or cruel. Only one person in the whole movie—a waitress named Joanna (Jennifer Aniston)—is neither. And she's such a secondary element of this enterprise that she doesn't even get a last name.

But did I already mention this was a Mike Judge movie? Thought so. If you know "Beavis and Butt-head" and "King of the Hill," you're aware that Judge's satire is the kind that takes few prisoners, leaves nothing out of ridicule's path. The only mystery was whether Judge could handle flesh-and-blood characters with the same pitiless mirth as he moves Hank Hill's animated neighbors through their drab lives.

He can ... and does by taking the grainy surfaces and languid pace of the generic slacker movie to fashion a rambling reminder to America of just what it is that slackers work so hard to avoid.

Judge's white-collar Candide is Peter Gibbons (Ron Livingston), a computer programer who spends eight hours a day cocooned in a cubicle at something called INITECH. Anyone who's ever been told by three different supervisors to do the same meaningless task can relate to Peter's sense that pieces of his soul are being shaved off with the passing of each mind-numbing hour.

Also trapped in this corporate purgatory are Peter's fellow cyber-drones Michael Bolton (David Herman), who just hates his famous namesake, and Samir ("Lateline's" Ajay Naidu) who shares his pain. There's also a strange little man named Milton ("NewsRadio's" Stephen Root) who isn't even on the payroll and yet keeps getting his desk moved closer to the storage room. All are bonded by a common, futile hatred for supervisor Bill Lumbergh (Gary Cole), the kind of weasel-in-suspenders that leans over your desk and prefaces his newest mind-game by cooing, "Whaaaat's happening?"

One day, two "consultants" are called into INITECH to check the place out, prompting well-founded panic over the prospect of layoffs. Peter, oddly, isn't sweating it. In fact, thanks to a post-hypnotic suggestion, he starts acting like ... a slacker, not coming in until noon or 1 p.m. Or not at all, if he feels like it.

Instead of putting Peter among the pink-slip crowd, the consultants take this attitude as a sign that Peter's got a mind of his own. "Upper management written all over him," one says. "Uuuuuuhhhh ...," Lumbergh says.

Once Peter's back on the fast track, Judge really has nowhere to go with this story, but plenty of movie left. So he suddenly has Peter and his buds planning a high-tech rip-off inspired, says Michael, by the "very underrated ... 'Superman III.'" The aforementioned Joanna, who's now dating Peter, thinks this is a bad idea.

The anecdotal drift of "Office Space's" narrative is closer to a sitcom or a comic strip (guess which one most comes to mind) than a movie and the approach frequently threatens to weaken the whole process. Fortunately, Judge takes your mind off the sags in the plot with lots of shrewdly observed details about life in the shopping-center-industrial-park-subdivision universe that hardly ever makes it on the big screen. (Even though it's where all the multiplexes are.)

VILLAGE VOICE, 2/23/99, p. 120, Justine Elias

It's nine o'clock on a weekday morning—do you know where you are? If you've ever stumbled into work more than a few minutes late, bleary-eyed and defeated, desperate to avoid the boss, here's a fine excuse to sneak out of the office for an early afternoon movie. But don't expect your special chair or favorite stapler to be there when you get back.

Office Space, the first live-action feature by Mike Judge, creator of *Beavis and Butt-head* and cocreator of *King of the Hill*, is a surprisingly good-natured comedy about the suppressed rage and paranoia of unappreciated employees. Every irritating character found in corporate culture is well represented here, from the ever-perky receptionist who blathers on about having "a bad case of the Mondays," to a senior VP, played by the fabulously unctuous Gary Cole, who greets his employees with a sneering "So ... what's happening?" before reprimanding them, for the eighth time, for using the wrong cover sheet on a report. There's even a demonic printer that seems to require a blood sacrifice before it will work properly.

Judge's earliest animated shorts, which ran on Comedy Central, followed a middle-aged office peon who suffers endless indignities at the hands of a tyrannical corporate vice president. Ordered to move his desk farther and farther away from a window, he eventually ends up seething in a basement storage room. Though the muttering, eccentric Milton reappears in *Office Space*, he exists as a counterpoint, an example of what can happen in the minds of workers who cling too tightly to their lousy jobs. The movie follows three guys in their twenties, all programmers at a high-tech company in a bland, nameless city, who are still rebellious enough to see a way out of their dead-end jobs before they crack up or get laid off. That their screw-the-company scheme is inspired by the plot of *Superman III* should be ample evidence of just how naive they are about white-collar crime. The ringleader is Peter, a likable bum whose dream isn't really wealth or revenge, but the chance to lounge around watching reruns of *Kung Fu* with a friendly waitress (Jennifer Aniston).

Peter's not a terribly dynamic hero, particularly after a fateful visit to a hypnotherapist who treats stress, but it helps that the actor who plays him, Ron Livingston of *Swingers*, has the most insanely expressive eyebrows since Vincent Price. Peter's office mates include Samir (Ajay Naidu), a dapper, scrupulous immigrant from the Near East, and the unfortunately named Michael Bolton (David Herman), a squirrely-looking outsider who decorates his cubicle with toy soldiers and posters of Navy Seals, and seems to live his life with a gangsta rap soundtrack running through his head. Unlike most stories of paranoia and revenge in the workplace, *Office Space* manages to find room for a happy ending that doesn't involve ripping anyone off, including the audience.

Also reviewed in:
CHICAGO TRIBUNE, 2/19/99, Friday/p. A, Michael Wilmington
NEW YORK TIMES, 2/19/99, p. E14, Stephen Holden
VARIETY, 2/15-21/99, p. 58, Joe Leydon
WASHINGTON POST, 2/19/99, p. C1, Rita Kempley
WASHINGTON POST, 2/19/99, Weekend/p. 37, Desson Howe

OLYMPIC GLORY

An International Olympic Committee, Megasystems and Pacific Title/Mirage release. *Executive Producer:* Kathleen Kennedy. *Producer:* Frank Marshall and Scott Swofford. *Director:* Kieth Merrill. *Screenplay:* Thomas Keneally. *Director of Photography:* T.C. Christensen, George Griner, James Neihouse, Reed Smoot, Jack Tankard, and Rodney Taylor. *Editor:* Christopher Rouse and Mark Fitzgerald. *Music:* Sam Cardon. *Special Effects:* Ivan Gulas. *Visual Effects:* Kelly Granite. *Running time:* 42 minutes. *MPAA Rating:* Not Rated.

WITH: Stacy Keach (Narrator); Midori Ito; Picabo Street; Philip Boit; Hermann Maier; Tara Lupinski; Michelle Kwan; Masahiko Harada; Bjorn Daehle.

NEW YORK POST, 1/22/99, p. 55, Jonathan Foreman

The breathtaking large-format film "Olympic Glory" was shot at the 1997 Winter games in Nagano, Japan, and is essential viewing for Olympic buffs and winter sports fans.

Seeing the world's best athletes do amazing things on the eight-story-high IMAX screen doesn't merely dwarf the experience of watching them on TV—it may be superior to actually being at the Games in person. Most effective and dramatic are the scenes shot by the large-format camera, placed on the front of a luge as it screams down the icy chute.

And although "Olympic Glory" also gives you samples of figure skating, hockey, snowboarding, Nordic Skiing and speed skating—including cool wipe-out shots—40 minutes of this kind of spectacular action just isn't enough.

But for all its stunning visual power, "Olympic Glory" could have been far better, given the amazing photogenic possibilities of its subject and an all-star team of producers Kathleen Kennedy ("ET" and "Jurassic Park") and Frank Marshall (the Indiana Jones trilogy), director Kieth Merrill and writer Thomas Kenneally (who wrote the novel on which "Schindler's List" was based).

Purely in terms of photography, "Olympic Glory" doesn't reach the dramatic heights achieved by great skiing/snowboarding filmmakers like Warren Miller. And although billed as an action-adventure film, it is really a documentary, but unfortunately not the kind of documentary that gets beneath the surface of its subject or one that lets the visual glory of the games speak for itself.

Instead, "Olympic Glory" feels like more like a long advertisement for the Games, thanks to over-the-top music and Kenneally's bland, relentlessly corny narration—read by Stacy Keach with what sounds like a bad cold. This is filled with the usual treacly hypocritical Olympic hokum about everybody who takes part being a champion and oodles of cheesy nonsense about unquenchable flames.

Fortunately, there are large swathes of the film unblemished by voice over. But you cannot help wondering if 40 minutes of pure photography and action—or a genuine documentary that took a less shiny, happy, sappy look at Olympic competition—would not have been better than an a mix of incredible spectacle and saccharine-soaked corn.

There's something particularly odd about the amount of ultra-expensive IMAX film "Olympic Glory" expends on sumo rituals, Japanese athletes winning the gold, Rising Sun flags and adorable Japanese children cheering on the fatherland's victorious athletes.

But just as you begin to wonder if you're watching something put out by the Japanese ministry of propaganda, the film switches to the American women's hockey team as it triumphs over the Canadians. And as the American athletes stand for their medals, it's hard not to be moved. There's something about this giant screen that amplifies the emotional power of film to an extraordinary degree. It's just as well that IMAX technology wasn't available to the totalitarian regimes of our century.

NEWSDAY, 1/22/99, Part II/p. B6, Bob Heisler

WARNING: After seeing "Olympic Glory," and you should, you'll want to go home and punch your puny, inadequate television.

Now this is how to watch sports. Imagine the thrill of victory, the agony of defeat on an eight-story-tall screen with a script written—a bit overwritten—by Thomas Keneally, who wrote "Schindler's List." It's like ABC's "Wide World of Sports" died and went to technology heaven.

Easily the most cinematic of the recent IMAX films, the "official large-format film of the Winter Olympics" (that's the 1998 Games in Nagano, Japan) fills its brief, 40-minute run with large-scale spectacle and large-heart emotion, finding heroes to match its heroic size.

Some wise choices have been made to temper the part-thrill-ride, part-state-fair exhibit nature of pervious IMAX films. Yes, there are a couple of disorienting luge runs, and a couple of the sports are deconstructed with the help of a distracting computer-generated character, but for the most part, "Olympic Glory" offers a set of interesting, human-sized storylines against a ton of pomp and circumstance.

Figure skating and ice hockey are seen from angles—at once closer and with a deeper visual perspective—you've never seen before. Dominic Hasek leads the Czech Republic to a gold medal, but the focus of the hockey segment and the movie's emotional high point is the victory of the U.S. woman's team.

Three stories stay with you: Japanese ski jumper Masahiko Harada, who personally lost his team's gold medal in 1994 and who faced the same possibility again in front of the hometown crowd; cross-country skier Philip Boit from snowless Kenya, who had never seen snow until he started training and who finished last in his single race but still can call himself an Olympian, and fellow skier Bjorn Daehlie from Norway, who became the most decorated and successful Winter Olympian at the Games, but who waited at the finish line to congratulate Boit.

The visual images and the speed of both the athletes and the narrative are completely involving and, at times, overcome the cynical observation that "Olympic Glory" is well timed to counter the International Olympic Committee bribery scandal unfolding in Salt Lake City, site of the next Winter Games.

It's hard to suggest a special trip to the West Side to see a 40-minute movie, but find an excuse.

Also reviewed in:
NEW YORK TIMES, 1/22/99, p. E14, Lawrence Van Gelder

ON THE ROPES

A WinStar Cinema release of a Highway Films production. *Executive Producer:* Jennifer Fox and Jonathan Cohen. *Producer:* Nanette Burstein and Brett Morgen. *Director:* Nanette Burstein and Brett Morgen. *Director of Photography:* Brett Morgen. *Editor:* Nancy Baker and Nanette Burstein. *Music:* Theodore Shapiro and Web Davis. *Sound:* Juan Carlos Martinez. *Running time:* 94 minutes. *MPAA Rating:* Not Rated.

WITH: Harry Keitt; Tyrene Manson; George Walton; Noel Santiago; Mickey Marcello; Randy Little; Ebony Pile; Equana Pile; Martin Goldman; James Pullings, Jr.; Eddie Mustafa Muhammed; Aida Santiago; Judge Finnegan.

LOS ANGELES TIMES, 9/24/99, Calendar/p. 19, Kevin Thomas

"On the Ropes" is another in a stream of documentaries that explore the potential of the form so effectively that they become as involving and suspenseful as the best fictional films. Nanette Burstein and Brett Morgen are the very models of contemporary documentarians: They win the trust of their subjects to the extent that they are the proverbial flies on the wall, eavesdropping on life. Eschewing on-camera interviews, they concentrate on building trust to gain the most comprehensive opportunities possible to observe their people in as many revealing circumstances as they can.

They then assemble their footage in a straightforward, unpretentious manner that makes us feel that we are witnessing the unfolding of their subjects' lives with the kind of detachment and fullness that allows us to decide for ourselves how we feel about these people and their fates—precisely the kind of distancing the most gifted filmmakers have always created.

Actual people and their lives have to become for us as real on the screen as characters brought to life by writers, directors and actors. And in telling the stories of four individuals whose lives intersect at Brooklyn's New Bed-Stuy Boxing Center, Burstein and Morgen—who is also the film's sensitive cinematographer—allow their four main characters to captivate us like stars.

Harry Keitt is the center's trainer, a wise yet challenging father figure to young people in need of self-respect and direction, inspiration and hope to make something of their lives against often overwhelming odds. The filmmakers focus on Keitt and three of these young people. Keitt sees in Noel Santiago both intelligence and boxing talent, but while Noel can work up considerable dedication in the ring, he is a chronic truant, one of the children of a single mother and a former drug addict. Keitt is hoping that a desire to win in the ring will ignite in Noel the urge to become confident and constructive in his life.

Motivation is no problem for Tyrene Manson, a pretty, bright young woman aiming for a career in boxing while trying to act as a mother to her two young cousins, whose father is a drug addict with AIDS. Tyrene has moved into a small rented house with all three, determined to do the best she can for the children but caught up in a drug bust triggered by the father's sale of cocaine to an undercover cop.

Tyrene finds herself in a courtroom the very day she is preparing for her Golden Gloves bout that evening. Tyrene's predicament just begs for the filmmakers to load on the sympathy, but by quietly recording events as they unfold they achieve a more dramatic impact.

Under Keitt's coaching, muscular, affable George Walton wins a number of championship matches and is now eager to turn professional, attracting the attention of manager Mickey Marcello, who wants him to go to Las Vegas to train under Eddie Mustafa Muhammed, former world light-heavyweight champion. This development brings us to the heart of Keitt's own troubled personal history, which he has struggled successfully to overcome. Determined to help young people avoid the mistakes he made, he nonetheless would like to hitch his wagon to a star—but not at the youths' expense.

He is willing to step aside as George's trainer, as painful a disappointment as it is for him, for the good of the highly promising fighter. The question is, will Walton be able to realize that Keitt has his priorities straight or come to see him simply as wanting a piece of the young fighter's action, like everyone else? Walton is clearly intelligent and reflective but his inexperience in the ways of the world of professional boxing has the potential to turn him cynical all too soon.

In recording life as it unfolds in the course of a year, "On the Ropes" not only defies prediction as to its outcome but is in some ways downright confounding. By the time it is over the only certainty seems to be Keitt himself, he'll never give up on himself or the young people who come to him for guidance and caring as much as to attain skill in boxing.

"On the Ropes" also leaves us realizing how pervasive drugs and the crime, disease and heartbreak that go with them remains in America's inner cities, how vulnerable the impoverished minorities are to injustice, and how boxing, for all the criticism it draws as a sport, stubbornly remains a promising way out for so many young people.

NEW YORK, 8/30/99, p. 167, Peter Rainer

On the Ropes, a documentary by Nanette Burstein and Brett Morgen, follows for about a year the careers, in and out of the ring, of three young boxers and their trainer, Harry Keitt, at the Bed-Stuy Boxing Center in Brooklyn. George Walton, who has already won the Golden Gloves, is poised to make it in the pros; Noel Santiago, a welterweight, has been held back in the ninth grade three times and seems held back in the ring as well—his confidence is wanting; Tyrene Manson, who is up for the Golden Gloves finals at Madison Square Garden, is implicated in a drug bust, although she is almost certainly innocent of any wrongdoing.

What makes this film so extraordinary is that it takes the clichés we've grown accustomed to about boxing and the inner city and fleshes them out—makes them shudderingly real. Burstein and Morgen have a hair-trigger instinct for capturing offhand moments of grief and wariness. When Harry, who has brought up all these boxers in the ring and is part father figure and part preacher to them, first meets a big-talking manager interested in handling George, we can see right away in his eyes the presentiment of his fighter's betrayal. Harry was a promising puncher himself before drugs did him in; after spending time in Sing Sing and Attica, he made it back to Bed-Stuy. He is a boxing priest in search of redemption, and George, a possible champion, is his ticket to heaven—and now he's being lured away. It's a familiar story made fresh by the filmmakers' resounding empathy.

Tyrene's situation culminates in her court trial, which, for sheer lacerating power, beats anything I've seen onscreen all year. It's one thing to read about the injustice of the criminal-justice system—the way it can bludgeon the already beaten-down. But hearing Tyrene's harrowing defense of herself, of her life, in an atmosphere of such stark indifference, is almost unbearable: It's like watching a life flame out before your eyes.

NEW YORK POST, 8/18/99, p. 47, Rod Dreher

"On the Ropes" is a kind of "Hoop Dreams" of the boxing ring, a documentary sketch of three working-class amateur Brooklyn boxers struggling against obstacles most people can scarcely imagine.

What the film lacks in freshness—sports as a metaphor for life's trials has been done many times—it makes up for in its sympathetic and compelling portrayal of its subjects.

You come away from Nanette Burstein and Brett Morgen's slice-of-life movie both cheered by the tenacity of the human spirit and sobered by the hard cold fact that when the odds are stacked so powerfully against you, good intentions aren't ever enough.

The stage is the ring at the scruffy New Bed-Stuy Boxing Center, where trainer Harry Keitt serves as a guru to neighborhood kids trying to make something of their lives. "We don't have a lot of equipment, we don't have a lot of glamour," Harry observes. But they do have a history of producing champions, like Riddick Bowe and Mark Breland.

What Harry, a veteran of the city streets and jails who is trying to redeem his misspent youth, does offer his boxers is hope and a firm hand of guidance.

Noel Santiago is a rangy welterweight Golden Gloves aspirant whose biggest opponent is his own lack of discipline and self-confidence. Fatherless and directionless and raised by a single mom who used to be strung out on drugs, flighty Noel's only realistic chance of getting his life in order is through Harry. But will Noel have the courage to take it?

The tautly muscled George Walton has already won the Golden Gloves and is on the verge of turning pro. Harry has been his trusted mentor, but now smooth-talking career management types are courting George. "Everybody ain't your friend," Harry warns him. Then again, is Harry the man to take George's career to the next level?

The most involving story is that of Tyrene Manson, a female boxer with a guileless stare and a fiercely competitive style in the ring. She's the de facto matriarch of an extended family, raising her dead druggie sister's children under the same roof as their AIDS-suffering crackhead father.

Boxing keeps Tyrene powerfully focused, but her inability to find the clarity and strength to kick out the shiftless bum affects her career in the most tragic way.

Harry, of course, is the real unsung hero of "On the Ropes," and his courageous life inspires the Bed-Stuy youth to keep trying. Says Harry, "Quitting's not even in my vocabulary. The day I quit is the day I die."

NEWSDAY, 8/18/99, Part II/p. B7, John Anderson

Columnizing in 1962 on the ring death of Benny Paret, the late Red Smith defended boxing as one of the purest of art forms. "Yet," he added, "there is no quarrel here with those who sincerely regard it as a vicious business that has no place in a civilized society." The hitch, of course, is defining a civilized society. In "On the Ropes," a compelling if not entirely satisfying look at three Brooklynites with boxing dreams, the world outside the ring consists of crackheads, domestic violence, a lackadaisical court system and a failing school system. Cruising the streets of Bedford-Stuyvesant and peering into the lives of their would-be champs—the promising George Walton, the passionate Tyrene Manson and the uninspired Noel Santiago—directors Nanette Burstein and Brett Morgen make a convincing argument for the sanctifying power of physical violence. Certainly, the mere bodily punishment endured by the fighters—along with the improbable prizes at the end of their sweat-stained rainbow—makes the sport of boxing seem like an oasis of sanity, especially if compared to the civilized world.

The sports documentary by which all others are measured—at least in terms of psychological insight, since Leni Riefenstahl never cared about anything but bodies—is "Hoop Dreams." But its directors had the luxury (not that they would call it that) of spending three years with the two basketball players at the heart of their non-Oscar-nominated film. Burstein and Morgen had only one. You wish they had more. They get close to their subjects, but never get past the point where those subjects aren't aware of the camera, and acting for it.

This is particularly noticeable with Harry Keitt, the committed trainer at the New Bed-Stuy Boxing Center whose most promising fighter, Walton, wins the 1996 Golden Gloves and draws the attention of manager Mickey Marcello (one-time member of the Long Island rock band the Good Rats and who is credited as "music supervisor" on the film). What the movie doesn't do is tell us that Marcello never handled a boxer before; what it does do is essentially portray him as a predator.

To his credit, Marcello takes Walton out of Brooklyn, puts him in a Las Vegas training camp and hires former lightweight champ Eddie Mustafa Muhammed as a trainer. Keitt, who saw Walton as his own ticket out of Brooklyn, watches everything slipping away. But while Walton seems destined for great things, the business of boxing—or just the lack of short-term reward—sucks the passion out of his career. He's left in a pugilistic limbo.

Santiago is pegged from the beginning as a non-starter, a boxer lacking heart. Tyrene Manson, on the other hand—living with the crack-addled uncle and multiple cousins she's adopted—is all heart. And soul. Running, training, sparring, praying, she makes her way to the Golden Gloves finals at Madison Square Garden and then gets sucker punched by a drug bust instigated by her uncle for which she may face a 12-to-25-year sentence for selling cocaine.

If this were a movie of the week, you'd know how it comes out. But this is a documentary and as such has neither a predictable course nor a real ending—the lives don't end, just the credits— and there are a lot of unanswered questions, specifically about Walton's future and even Manson's culpability. At the same time, the film does make a convincing argument for the existence of boxing itself. Recalling the backroom brawls and bareknuckled epics of another era, Red Smith wrote, "They are wrong, those who think boxing can be legislated out of existence." Especially when, as "On the Ropes" so eloquently observes, it's the lesser of two evils.

VILLAGE VOICE, 8/24/99, p. 122, Gary Dauphin

Hailing from a completely different point on the global and generic maps, [The reference is to *Perfect Blue*; see Dauphin's review.] Nanette Burstein and Brett Morgen's earnest, forthright doc *On the Ropes* is also an industry cautionary tale, focusing on the trials of a group of amateur boxers and trainers from the Bed-Stuy gym that produced Riddick Bowe.

Ropes begins with the solid presence of Harry Keitt, who has trained fighters out of a storefront gym for 16 years. Harry's charges give him reasons for hope and despair in equal measure: George, a smiling potential champion, flirts with a big-name manager's promises of fame and fortune. The teenaged Noel finally decides to try his best only to find he can't quite overcome his limitations as a boxer. Most heartbreaking is Tyrene, who trains with heroic drive despite having what seems to be a bogus drug charge hanging over her head. Except for the intrusion of a limply de rigueur hip-hop soundtrack, Burstein and Morgen take all this in from an unobtrusive middle distance, letting the subjects themselves slowly complicate the profusion of athletic and ghetto-real clichés that fly scattershot in the early going. Harry shouts familiar platitudes about hard work and dedication but throughout exudes the distracted nervousness of a man trying hard not to remember past disappointments. He provides *On the Ropes* with its main visual motif and enduring emotional note anyway: win or lose, Harry still gets up early every day to lift the gym's metal gates, hopeful that a champion will be walking in soon.

Also reviewed in:
CHICAGO TRIBUNE, 12/17/99, Friday/p. I, John Petrakis
NEW YORK TIMES, 8/18/99, p. E3, Stephen Holden
VARIETY, 2/1-7/99, p. 61, Glenn Lovell

ONEGIN

A Samuel Goldwyn Films, Seven Arts International, Starz Pictures release in association with Samuel Goldwyn Films of a Canwest Entertainment presentation of a Baby Productions film. *Executive Producer:* Ralph Fiennes. *Producer:* Ileen Maisel and Simon Bosanquet. *Director:* Martha Fiennes. *Screenplay:* Michael Ignatieff and Petre Ettedgui. *Based on the verse novel by:* Alexander Pushkin. *Director of Photography:* Remi Adefarasin. *Editor:* Jim Clark. *Music:* Magnus Fiennes. *Choreographer:* Eleanor Fazan. *Sound:* Ivan Sharrock and (music) Pete Lewis. *Sound Editor:* Eddie Joseph. *Casting:* Mary Selway. *Production Designer:* Jim Clay. *Art Director:* Chris Seagers. *Set Decorator:* Maggie Gray. *Costumes:* Chloe Obolensky and John Bright. *Make-up:* Peter Owen. *Stunt Coordinator:* Terry Forrestal. *Running time:* 106 minutes. *MPAA Rating:* Not Rated.

CAST: Ralph Fiennes (Evgeny Onegin); Liv Tyler (Tatyana Larin); Martin Donovan (Prince Nikitin); Toby Stephens (Vladimir Lensky); Lena Headey (Olga Larin); Jason Watkins (Guillot); Alun Armstrong (Zaretsky); Harriet Walter (Madame Larina); Irene Worth (Princess Alina); Francesca Annis (Katiusha); Gwenllian Davies (Anisia); Simon McBurney (Triquet); Geoff McGivern (Andrey Petrovich); Margery Withers (Nanya); Tim McMullan (Dandy 1); Tim Potter (Dandy 2); Richard Bremmer (Diplomat); Elizabeth Berrington (Mme. Volkonsky).

LOS ANGELES TIMES, 12/17/99, Calendar/p. 18, Kevin Thomas

"Onegin" is an elegantly wrought, deeply felt film based on Alexander Pushkin's 1831 novel in verse, which in turn inspired Tchaikovsky's 1879 opera. The very model of a literary adaptation to the screen, it stars a perfectly cast Ralph Fiennes and marks a remarkably assured feature directorial debut for Fiennes' sister, Martha, and also a splendid opportunity for their brother Magnus, who composed the film's spare yet evocative score. As a period piece the film is breathtaking in its beauty and authenticity, its production design a work of symbolically decayed grandeur.

Like the novel, the film plays an effortless simplicity of style against a rich complexity of character in flawless fashion. Fiennes' Onegin is a St. Petersburg aristocrat, a jaded, bored playboy swiftly running through his inheritance. He receives a magnificent reprieve when he inherits from his uncle a vast country estate, complete with a Greek Revival palace and serfs beyond count. He arrives in a quizzical state of mind, delighted to escape the numbing formality and routine of St. Petersburg society yet too cynical not to be his usual candid and direct self with the landed gentry, who are intimidated by his sophistication.

He immediately scandalizes his neighbors with his declaration that he intends to lease his land to his serfs, a notion that strikes a sympathetic note with the lovely Tatyana Larin (Liv Tyler), who is more intelligent and imaginative than most others in her rural world. More significant is the mutual attraction between Tatyana and the dashing newcomer, to whom she impetuously sends a letter declaring her love.

Onegin, though attracted, does not return the ardor and tells her so in a manner that she herself acknowledges as honorable. In the meantime, Onegin's relentless candor has had dire and unintended consequences, sending him into a six-year exile. When he next encounters Tatyana she has become the regal wife of his cousin, a prince (Martin Donovan) whose home would seem to be The Hermitage, no less. Now it is his turn to become love-struck.

"Onegin" is more than a romantic tragedy; it is the tragedy of a man who does not know himself—and his heart in particular—as well as he thinks he does. There is within Fiennes' personality and manner a clenched quality that sometimes works against him, as in "Oscar and Lucinda," but here is just right for a polished man who opens his heart too late. Under his sister's direction, Fiennes is at his most poised and least mannered; the result is one of the most effective, best modulated portrayals to date.

Tyler is very much Fiennes' equal as Tatyana, who matures before our eyes yet, try as she may, cannot stop loving Onegin. Lena Headey is Tatyana's equally attractive but far less complicated sister Olga, and Toby Stephens is memorable as Olga's handsome, sweet-natured suitor who befriends Onegin only to be disastrously confounded by Onegin's insistence on speaking his mind at all costs. Among the gifted supporting players is that wondrously formidable grande dame, Irene Worth as a princess who gives Tatyana and her mother (Harriet Walter) some bluntly realistic advice.

"Onegin" is a pleasure in all ways, including Jim Clay's resourceful yet consistently stunning production design and Remi Adefarasin's lush yet rightly somber camera work. In bringing to life the long-vanished world of the Russian nobility, "Onegin" strikes a timeless note of eternal love and loss.

SIGHT AND SOUND, 12/99, p. 51, Julian Graffy

The early nineteenth century. Bored St Petersburg dandy Evgeny Onegin inherits his uncle's estate and decamps to the countryside. There he meets a neighbouring landowner, the young poet Vladimir Lensky, and through him the Larin family: widowed mother and daughters Tatyana and Olga.

Naive Lensky is engaged to flighty Olga but Tatyana, who is deep, is drawn to Onegin and writes him a declaration of love. At Tatyana's name-day party Onegin rejects her and flirts with Olga, which infuriates Lensky. They quarrel and Lensky challenges him to a duel. Lensky misses and Onegin shoots his opponent dead. A horrified Tatyana comes to visit him but he has left. Tatyana's mother introduces her into society and she marries a prince. Six years later, Onegin returns from his wanderings and is captivated by Tatyana's beauty and distinction. He now writes her a passionate letter. Though she still loves him she remains true to her husband.

Onegin opens with a sequence of startling beauty of a horse-drawn carriage crossing a vast expanse of snow. It is perhaps the major distinction of first-feature director Martha Fiennes' film to have made the settings of this story—the melancholy birch groves; the country estates with their contrasting interiors (the Larins' house bright and lived in, Onegin's romantically bereft); the splendour of imperial St Petersburg; a scene of people skating on a frozen river—so consistently enthralling, a triumph of cinematography, lighting and production design. Fiennes wears her background in commercials and music videos lightly—*Onegin* in is much more visually restrained than *Mumu*, the version of the Turgenev story directed last year by the Russian commercials director Yuri Grymov.

This film is also uniformly well acted, with Liv Tyler compelling as the brooding Tatyana, her still demeanour somehow suggestive of the dark passions swirling beneath the surface. Lena Headey is equally persuasive as the shallow, impetuous Olga, so physically like her sister and so emotionally different. There is a hilarious turn from Simon McBurney as the girls' oleaginous French tutor, and a memorable vignette from Irene Worth as the society *grande dame* Princess Alina. Executive producer Ralph Fiennes in the title role and Toby Stephens as Lensky also give thoughtful performances but both, alas, are about ten years too old for the parts they play. This renders Onegin precociously racked and seedy at the start, though it makes Fiennes persuasive in the (over-elaborated) concluding episodes. Lensky, however, is 18 in Pushkin's original and having him played by a noticeably older actor makes all his poetic petulance and hypersensitivity risible and exasperating without the saving grace of extreme youth. It also draws attention to the conventionality and predictability of the plot.

Martha Fiennes has spoken of her desire to keep as close as possible to the original story of *Eugene Onegin*, but as she (and every Russian schoolchild) knows, to concentrate on the plot is to risk banality, removing precisely what makes this verse novel unique: the extraordinarily vivacious authorial commentary and the famous ironic and subversive digressions through which Pushkin paints a compendious picture of a society and an age.

This itself begs the question—who is this new *Onegin* for? The film got its world premiere in Moscow in June as a central part of the lavish celebration of the bicentenary of Pushkin's birth. It provoked great and respectful interest, partly because the Russian film commissioned to mark the anniversary, Aleksandr Proshkin's *Russian Riot* an epic version of Pushkin's story 'The Captain's Daughter', was not completed in time, and partly because the Russians, whose cinematic history is littered with Pushkin adaptations, have never filmed *Eugene Onegin* (though there is a film version of Tchaikovsky's opera known as *Ievgeny Onegin* starring Galina Vishnevskaya, made in 1958).

So maybe the film's ideal audience is in Russia. But for Russians an *Onegin* without the familiar lines of poetry is not *Onegin* and the various minor inaccuracies, such as a waltz danced to an orchestration of a famous Russo-Japanese War song, are inescapable and unsettling. In fact there *was* an earlier attempt to film Pushkin's *Onegin*, for the centenary of his death, in 1937 (the occasion of huge Soviet celebrations). The Formalist critic (and husband of Mayakovsky's lover) Osip Brik spent two years working on a script, even attempting to preserve the authorial voice by inventing a system of what he called "resounding sur-titles"—lines of the poem in Pushkin's handwriting would appear briefly on screen while being simultaneously spoken by a narrator but the project was eventually aborted.

Of course none of these problems would be apparent to most western viewers, who would not see rows of Russian graves on Manchurian hillsides as they listened to the (charmingly orchestrated) waltz. No, the danger with western audiences may be that they will wonder what all the Russian fuss is about, finding the story of love spurned and love lost melodramatic and predictable, and the wit only occasionally approaching the level sustained in recent film adaptations of Jane Austen.

Onegin then, is a film for which the adaptation of the literary source presented fundamental difficulties, ones the Fiennes and their collaborators were well aware of and which had defeated their illustrious predecessors. In a sense the whole enterprise is a misguided act of literary piety. And yet its achievements are far from negligible. It is respectful and sincere; it is never less than visually splendid; and at its best it takes the romantic plot of *Eugene Onegin* into the realms of tragic grandeur.

VILLAGE VOICE, 12/28/99, p. 130, Dennis Lim

As Evgeny Onegin, the luckless hero of Pushkin's cruelly ironic tale of romantic reversal, Ralph Fiennes—his thin lips locked into a rueful half-smile—at least looks the part. But *Onegin*, directed by his sister Martha (their brother Magnus composed the overweening score), is never more than costumed frippery. Upon inheriting a country estate from his uncle, jaded aristo-dandy Onegin leaves behind St. Petersburg debauchery for a taste of rural life. He flirts with an impressionable, bookish girl, Tatyana (an expressionless Liv Tyler), and spurns her declarations of love, only to fall for her years later after she has married his cousin.

Pushkin's verse novel is notoriously difficult to translate, let alone film. Unable to capture either its wit, psychological acuity, or formal rigor, the movie essentially reduces the schematic, seesaw narrative to doomy clichés. Martha Fiennes, an established music video director, gives the material a theatrical flash, which only highlights the abundance of lampoon-ready Russian-lit signifiers: a horse-carriage rumbling across snowy tundra, a fatal duel on a misty morning (try not to think of Woody Allen's *Love and Death)*, an ice-skating interlude. It's been said, as a testament to its writer's craft, that Pushkin's story is one in which "nothing happens, twice." With the Fiennes family's version, you can unfortunately take that observation at face value.

Also reviewed in:
CHICAGO TRIBUNE, 3/31/00, Friday/p. F, Michael Wilmington
NEW YORK TIMES, 12/22/99, p. E6, Stephen Holden
VARIETY, 9/27-10/3/99, p. 34, Derek Elley

OPEN YOUR EYES

An Artisan Entertainment release of a José Luis Cuerda production for Sogete/Les Films Alain Sarde/Lucky Red. *Executive Producer:* Fernando Bovaira and José Luis Cuerda. *Producer:* José Luis Cuerda. *Director:* Alejandro Amenábar. *Screenplay (Spanish with English subtitles):*

Alejandro Amenábar and Mateo Gil. *Director of Photography:* Hans Burmann. *Editor:* Maria Elena Sainz de Rozas. *Music:* Alejandro Amenábar and Mariano Marin. *Sound:* Berg Goldstein & Stein and (music) José Vinader and Eduardo Ruiz Joya. *Sound Editor:* Nacho Royo and Pelayo Gutierrez. *Art Director:* Wolfgang Burmann. *Set Decorator:* Carola Angulo. *Special Effects:* Reyes Abades. *Costumes:* Concha Solera. *Make-up:* Paca Almenara and Silvie Imbert. *Make-up (Special Effects):* Colin Arthur and Dream Factory. *Running time:* 110 minutes. *MPAA Rating:* R.

CAST: Eduardo Noriega (César); Penélope Cruz (Sofia); Chete Lera (Antonio); Fele Martinez (Pelayo); Najwa Nimri (Nuria); Gérard Barray (Duvernois); Jorge de Juan (Department Head); Miguel Palenzuela (Commissar); Pedro Miguel Martinez (Chief Doctor); Ion Gabella (Paranoic Recluse); Joserra Cadiñanos (Guard); Tristan Ulloa (Waiter); Pepe Navarro (TV Presenter); Jaro, Walter Prieto, and Carola Angulo (Doctors); Fanny Solorzano (Secretary); Luis Garcia and Javier Martin (Jury Guards); José Luis Manrique (Policeman); Richard Cruz (Driver); Raul Otegui (Service Boy).

LOS ANGELES TIMES, 4/16/99, Calendar/p. 6, Kenneth Turan

"Open Your Eyes" can be heard two ways, as a physical command or a metaphysical warning to be aware, to pay attention to what's happening around you. When the characters in this nervy and unnerving psychological thriller don't do both, they end up in serious trouble.

A major hit in its native Spain, "Open Your Eyes" is part of a current spate of films, including "The Matrix" and David Cronenberg's forthcoming "eXistenZ," that deal with the always provocative notion of how we tell appearance from reality, madness from sanity, the physical world from a dream.

Although it eventually involves loopy science-fiction elements, "Open Your Eyes," co-written (with Mateo Gil) by director Alejandro Amenabar, has sensibly chosen to focus on its realistic elements. What results is a complex, disturbing, occasionally terrifying story that wreaks determined havoc with our own fragile sense of what's real and what is not. From its opening scene, when protagonist Cesar (Eduardo Noriega) has an experience that turns into a dream without our knowing it, "Open Your Eyes" is a puzzle picture, a tricky artistic head trip that is always daring us to figure out exactly what is going on at any given moment. All we often know for sure is that what we're watching is both disorienting and disquieting, a feeling that's intensified by music co-written by Amenabar and Mariano Marin.

Cesar is young, extremely handsome and very rich. When we initially meet him, he's a spoiled urban playboy, teased by lonely best friend Pelayo (Fele Martinez) about never sleeping with the same woman twice.

At his 25th birthday party, however, Cesar meets the stunning Sofia (Penelope Cruz, the best thing in Stephen Frears' "The Hi-Lo Country") and thinks he might be falling in love. Never the most considerate of men, Cesar isn't concerned that Sofia came as Pelayo's date or that her presence infuriates Nuria (Najwa Nimri), a previous conquest who is partial to intense jealousy.

As this story begins to play out, however, the first of the movie's several other layers reveals itself. Meeting Sofia is not happening now but in the past; in fact, that encounter is being related to a concerned psychiatrist named Antonio (Chete Lera) who's visiting Cesar in prison, where he's accused of committing a murder he doesn't remember. Even more confusing, Cesar is wearing a mask that completely covers his face and that he adamantly refuses to remove.

It turns out that at some point Cesar did have an accident, which he survived—but at the price of a face distorted to look like a modern-day Quasimodo. That experience made Cesar extremely bitter, and his mood isn't helped by the difficulties this causes with Sofia, who is not particularly interested in a beauty and the beast relationship.

That much is fairly clear, but everything that comes after—as Cesar and the psychiatrist sort through the detritus of his confused mind and try to pin down reality—is anything but. Did Cesar and Sofia get back together? Was Cesar's face repairable after all? Why is he wearing a mask? What is the meaning of the cryonics infomercials Cesar can't quite remember? Who was murdered and why? All you can say for sure is that nothing is what it seems.

While it's inevitable that the ending of "Open Your Eyes" would be a letdown after this kind of driving, insistent buildup, it's by no means unacceptable, and the film as a whole was good enough to interest Tom Cruise's production company, which has purchased the remake rights.

Adept at creating unease, director Amenabar, whose first film, "Tesis," won seven Goya awards (the Spanish Oscar), has put together a metaphysical thriller that recalls the French classics "Diabolique" and "Yeux Sans Visage." For full appreciation, you have to take the advice one character gives another: "Don't think about it," he says, "or you'll go crazy."

NEW YORK POST, 4/16/99, p. 65, Rod Dreher

Open Your Eyes (Abre los Ojos) "is yet another sci-fi variation on the "what is reality?" theme so popular these days.   While this comparatively modest Spanish import shares the same preoccupation with the difference between image and reality as "The Truman Show" and "The Matrix," writer-director Alejandro Amenabar's no-tech thriller seeks to mess with your mind the old-fashioned way: by jiggering the narrative. The results are decidedly mixed.

Rich, gorgeous and obscenely vain, Madrid yuppie Cesar (Eduardo Noriega) fops his way Hugh Grantishly through life, picking up and discarding women with casual charm and Eurotrash ease. His comparatively homely best friend Pelayo (Fele Martinez) slinks around, complaining about how he doesn't stand a chance with women with Don Juan around. Cesar promptly steals the poor shlump's date, the lovely Sofia (Penelope Cruz). Trouble turns up in the person of Cesar's spurned ex-lover Nuria (Najwa Nimri), the kind of tightly wound sexual nutcase role that will be played by Jennifer Jason Leigh in the American remake. Feeling invulnerable, Cesar hops in the car with Nuria on the promise of a quickie, and she drives the car off a cliff in a mad suicide-murder bid. Cesar survives, but his movie-star good looks have been savaged beyond repair.

Now what? Amenabar's script is best when it explores Cesar's turbulent emotions when the one thing that gave him a sense of worth, his looks, are ripped away. His entire world is upended, his illusions smashed, and though we're tempted to say "Serves you right, jerk," Noriega just you watch, he's the next Antonio Banderas) reveals surprising pathos in his shallow character's plight.

Despite fine performances, "Open Your Eyes" derails itself with a confusing, ultimately maddening, exercise in shuttlecocking the audience back and forth between dreams and reality. Cesar finds himself in the criminal ward of a psychiatric hospital, having committed murder. A sympathetic psychiatrist (Chete Lera) patiently tries to help the patient, who wears a plastic mask, sort out his hallucinations from his legitimate memories. Cesar recalls having received a "miraculous" cure from surgeons that completely restored his looks. But did it really happen? And who is that mysterious man shilling for cryogenic technology on TV?

Amenabar and co-scripter Mateo Gil have constructed a needlessly labyrinthine plot to convey the movie's basic philosophical point: that there's a difference between what we see and the way things really are. But the intriguing point gets lost when the film starts playing annoying head games with the audience. Is this real? Can we trust what we're seeing? More to the point: when does this higgledy-piggledy mess end"

NEWSDAY, 4/16/99, Part II/p. B 13, Gene Seymour

"Open Your Eyes" is a sultry dance of the veils, with each gauzy layer peeled off to reveal yet another until at the end you're left with … maybe nothing, maybe more veils.

It's closer in spirit to the reality-bending exercises of Philip K. Dick and Jorge Luis Borges than to the Alfred Hitchcock who made "Vertigo" and "Marnie." Probably it could have used more Hitchcock and less from the other guys to make it easier to absorb. But even with its conceits peeking from the edges, "Open Your Eyes" rarely tempts you to close yours.

It begins like a contemporary Spanish love song in a minor key. Cesar (Eduardo Noriega), a handsome, spoiled brat, thinks he's ditched his latest quickie conquest only to find that the woman (Najwa Nimri) just won't leave him alone. He finds himself drawn to an actress (Penelope Cruz) whose graces are such that he's tempted to renounce his wicked ways. Too late. The other woman, who has stalked him to the actress' lair, offers him a ride home and instead drives them off a cliff.

Cesar survives, but his once-crystalline features are mutilated and his psyche in ruins. He is certain that the actress is the love of his life and just as certain that she rejects him because of his disfigurement. He wants to die. From here, it's hard to say what happens without giving away too much. Suffice to say, there's a peculiar subplot involving cryogenics, plastic surgery and a murder investigation in which Cesar is the prime suspect.

It would appear that director Alejandro Amenabar, who wrote the script with Mateo Gil, has built this labyrinth to make his audience aware of the potential for subterfuge behind every human transaction.

This may not be stop-the-presses information for most, but the movies that bother to engage such issues are rare. Even more rare are the movies that mess with your own head with as much concentrated enthusiasm as this one. More than "The Truman Show" (which was the better movie), this may leave you feeling around the open air for trapdoors and hidden tunnels.

SIGHT AND SOUND, 3/00, p. 50, Paul Julian Smith

A prison cell in an unnamed city, the present. César, a 25-year-old in a prosthetic mask, tells his story to psychiatrist Antonio. Flashbacks reveal the following events. Good-looking César is attractive to women. At his birthday party he flirts with Sofía, the girlfriend of his best friend Pelayo. The next morning, he accepts a lift from his obsessive ex-lover Nuria. She crashes the car, committing suicide, and César is horribly disfigured, beyond the help of cosmetic surgery. Sofía prefers Pelayo again.

Drunk, César falls asleep in the street. On awakening everything has changed—Sofía now claims to love him and the surgeons restore his lost looks. But while making love to Sofía one night, she apparently changes into Nuria. Horrified, César murders her, yet finds everyone else believes Nuria was indeed Sofía.

While he is confined to the prison, fragments of his past return to him as if in a dream. César realises he visited a company called Life Extension. Returning to their headquarters, under strict supervision by prison officers, he discovers they specialise in cryogenics with a twist: 'artificial perception' or the provision of a fantasy based on the past to clients who are reborn in the future. Convinced his life since the drunken night in the street is simply a nightmarish vision created by Life Extension, César leaps from the roof of the company's high-rise headquarters, resolving to open his eyes once more to real life outside the cryogenic fantasy.

Alejandro Amenábar is the archetypal Spanish movie brat. Born in Santiago, Chile, in 1972 and taken to Spain as a child after the fall of Allende, Amenábar attended the film school at Madrid's Complutense University, where he famously failed the narrative component of the course. His revenge at the age of just 24 was *Tesis/Thesis*, a sleek, taut thriller on the theme of snuff movies in which the serial killer, a professor of media studies, was given the same name as Amenábar's own luckless tutor. Shown in the UK only at the London Film Festival, *Tesis* was a sensation in Spain, where it had almost a million domestic admissions and won a clutch of Goyas, the Spanish Oscars.

Both *Tesis* and its successor *Abre los ojos* are shot in Madrid, but set in an abstract modern metropolis emptied of all local reference, their cinematic predecessors are not Spanish but American films. Like his US heroes, Amenábar knows no world but cinema. This is clear not only from the explicit references to, say, *Vertigo* scattered throughout *Abre los ojos*, but also from the way film-making is woven into a plot in which reality and illusion become indistinguishable. At the very start, in the credit sequence, a film crew is shooting in Madrid's Gran Vía as main character César cruises by in his sports car; half way into the film, the plot segues into fantasy, an invisible transition described by one character with the cinematic term 'splice'.

The most successful moments, however, are not those which cite Hitchcock (such as the camera circling the embracing César and Sofía, shadowing Scotty and Madeleine), but those that reveal Amenábar's own distinctively chilly style: the traffic-choked Gran Vía is suddenly emptied of life, or a crowded discotheque inexplicably falls silent. One of the few directors young enough to give a convincing account of youthful hedonism, Amenábar can also turn that same facile pleasure inside out, revealing the hollowness of the cult of looks so prized in both clubs and cinema. The big budget Amenábar won after the success of *Tesis* is all on the screen here, in the sexy interiors (César's sterile loft, all glass brick and gunmetal blue) and the spectacular exteriors (the Picasso Tower skyscraper on whose roof the climax is played out).

There are some apposite ironies in the casting also. Handsome Eduardo Noriega (César) and plain Fele Martinez (best friend Pelayo) were previously teamed in *Tesis,* and once César is disfigured, their positions are reversed (Pelayo wins back Sofía, whom César had taken from him). The theme of identity as performance is fully explored, with characters constantly changing roles and repeating each other's dialogue: the fact that the Spanish words for face and mask are so similar (*cara* and *carete*) helps here. Since *Abre los ojos* was wrapped, Martinez has been teamed by Julio Medem with Najwa Nimri (Amenábar's scarlet woman Nuria) in *The Lovers of the North Pole* while Penélope Cruz (sweet Sofía) has won fame abroad as the sacrificial nun in Almodóvar's *All About My Mother.*

Amenábar's next project is an English language feature with Nicole Kidman and remake rights for *Abre los ojos* are said to have been sold to Tom Cruise. It's not surprising *Abre los ojos'* flashy visuals have brought Amenábar to the attention of Hollywood; he shares the US thriller genre's lack of concern for narrative logic. *Abre los ojos,* chilling in parts, especially when the truly disturbing Nimri is in the driving seat, runs out of steam before the final plot twists, and there's too much expository dialogue dutifully describing psychiatry and cryogenics. Nonetheless, Amenábar's virtuoso style and connection to the youth audience, both of which are resented by the Spanish film establishment, make him a plausible model outside Spain for a European cinema that bridges the gap between arthouse and mainstream.

VILLAGE VOICE, 4/20/99, p. 148, Gary Dauphin

There's nothing more maddening than being dropped into a movie, getting to know its characters, walking with them through twists and turns only to be told that—surprise, stupid!—it was all a dream/lie/virtual-reality simulation. From "Who Shot J.R.?" to the ongoing crop of was-it-real-or-Playstation? movies, the whole "I lied" thing has become an overused gambit, making for punch-line-based flicks that are only watchable once. *Open Your Eyes* wants to offer a less bird-flipping spin on such tricky filmmaking, and in most ways it does, taking the audience on a trip through the messed-up head of Madrid pretty boy César (Eduardo Noriega). *Eyes* opens in one of César's nightmares, but before he can get too freaked out, he awakes next to his latest conquest, Nuria (Najwa Nimri), a combination of sex appeal and psychosis. Despite her stalker vibes, Cesar toys with her and uses her as a stepping stone to the actual woman of his dreams (Penelope Cruz). Nuria takes revenge by going Elephant Man on César's fine features, after which *Eyes* starts messing with everyone's head in earnest, as Cesar slips in and out of dreams about his troubles all being, well, dreams. (*Eyes* doesn't settle for that particular trick ending, it settles for another.) Writer-director Alejandro Amenabar handles these changes agilely enough, and despite its flashy premise, *Eyes* provides some affecting moments, as when it lingers over a disfigured Cesar losing himself in the anonymity of a dance floor. Amenábar may drop the ball with a surprise happy ending, but the real shock is that when César finally opens his eyes, you feel he's earned it.

Also reviewed in:
CHICAGO TRIBUNE, 4/30/99, Friday/p. B, Monica Eng
NEW YORK TIMES, 4/16/99, p. E20, Lawrence Van Gelder
VARIETY, 1/12-18/98, p. 64, Jonathan Holland

OTHER SISTER, THE

A Touchstone Pictures release of a Mandeville Films production. *Executive Producer:* David Hoberman.   *Producer:* Mario Iscovich and Alexandra Rose.   *Director:* Garry Marshall. *Screenplay:* Garry Marshall and Bob Brunner. *Story:* Alexandra Rose, Blair Richwood, Garry Marshall, and Bob Brunner. *Director of Photography:* Dante Spinotti. *Editor:* Bruce Green. *Music:* Kathy Nelson and Rachel Portman. *Music Editor:* Bill Abbott. *Sound:* Thomas Causey and (music) John Richards. *Sound Editor:* Todd Toon. *Casting:* Gretchen Rennell Court. *Production Designer:* Stephen J. Lineweaver. *Art Director:* Clayton R. Hartley. *Set Designer:*

George Lee and Domenic Silvestri. *Set Decorator:* Jay Hart. *Set Dresser:* Troy Peters and Bryan Hill. *Special Effects:* Gary Zink. *Costumes:* Gary Jones. *Make-up:* Bob Mills. *Make-up (Diane Keaton):* Kelsey Fry. *Make-up (Hector Elizondo):* Coree Lear. *Stunt Coordinator:* Jimmy Romano. *Running time:* 131 minutes. *MPAA Rating:* PG-13.

CAST: Juliette Lewis (Carla); Diane Keaton (Elizabeth); Tom Skerritt (Radley); Giovanni Ribisi (Danny); Poppy Montgomery (Caroline); Sarah Paulson (Heather); Linda Thorson (Drew); Joe Flanigan (Jeff); Juliet Mills (Winnie); Tracy Reiner (Michelle); Hope Alexander-Willis (Marge); Harvey Miller (Dr. Johnson); Hector Elizondo (Ernie); TECH SCHOOL: Almayvonne (Rachel); Marvin Braverman (Uncle Sam Teacher); Laura D'Arista (Statue of Liberty Teacher); Linda Hawkins (Student Marilyn); James Emery (Computer Teacher); Steve Lipinsky (Tough Guy Phil); Giuseppe Andrews (Tough Guy Trevor); Jake Wall (School Registration Man); Zaid Farid (Tech Principal); Debra Wiseman (Tech School Student Student Alice); Sunny Hawks (Broken Toe Student); THE WEDDINGS; Dennis Creaghan (Caroline's Minister); Jim Meskimen (Carla's Minister); Julie Paris (Wedding Coordinator); Pierson Blaetz (Assistant Coordinator Mark); Steve Restivo (Bakery Boss Vitello); Shannon Wilcox (Danny's Mom Ruthie); Phil Redrow (Ruthie's Boyfriend Tex); Adrienne Smith (Bridesmaid Ginger); Gretchen Bingham (Bridesmaid #1); Mariah Dobson (Bridesmaid #3); Tom Hines (Best Man); Gregg Goulet (Cousin Teddy); David Sterns (Usher #1); Benjamin Linder (Usher #2); Ryan Hart (Usher #3); Connie Engel (Cousin Anne); Barbara Marshall (Guest Cynthia); Frank Campenella (Guest William); Norma Jean Jahn (Guest Grace); COUNTRY CLUB: Allan Kent (Country Club Bartender); Joe Ross (Maitre 'D); Catherine McGoohan (Country Club Lady #1); Julia Hunter (Country Club Lady #2); Stephanie Kissner (Country Club Member Stephanie); Joy Rosenthal (Country Club Member Joy); OTHER PLAYERS: Patrick Richwood (Real Estate Agent); Jeanette Lee (Pool Player-Black Widow); Cassie Rowell (Truck Girl Jenny); Anthony Russell (Train Passenger); Bob Brunner (Train Conductor); Richard Stahl (Train Ticket Seller); Steven Daniel (Band Master); Gerald Miller, III (Drum Major); Bud Markowitz (Roselake Juggler); Jodi Johnson (Roselake School Teacher); Shiri Appleby (Free Sample Girl); Steve Moloney (College Maintenance Man #1); David Ketchum (College Maintenance Man #2); Monette Magrath (Store Clerk); Jason Cottle (Dog Trainer); Jenn Byrne (Stewardess #1); Ali Gage (Stewardess #2); Robert Malina (Bus Driver); Bill Ferrell (Bus Station Bartender); Charles Guardino (Limo Driver); Natalie Ramsey (Body Shot Girl); Scott Egan (Body Shot Guy); Kendra Krull (Young Carla); Brooke Garrett (Young Caroline); Brighton McCloskey (Young Heather); Jennifer Leigh Warren (Dr. Johnson's Secretary); Colin Mac Donald (Mean Young Boy).

CHRISTIAN SCIENCE MONITOR, 2/26/99, p. 15, David Sterritt

[*The Other Sister* was reviewed jointly with *20 Dates*; see Sterritt's review of that film.]

LOS ANGELES TIMES, 2/26/99, Calendar/p. 4, Kenneth Turan

There are, as has often been reported, two kinds of people in the world: those who look forward eagerly to a shamelessly heart-tugging, feel-good romance between two "mentally challenged" young people, and those who, quite frankly, would rather turn the page.

"The Other Sister," directed by that determined sentimentalist Garry Marshall, is not a film likely to bridge the gap between these two categories. While it's hard to fault the film's intentions or get too upset about how it executes them, it's even more difficult to think completely positive thoughts about a film that treats its two main characters like charming ceramic figurines, so winsome you want to chuck them under the chin, rather than as actual human beings.

Written by Marshall & Bob Brunner, "The Other Sister" is one of a line of films that considers those with special needs to be wiser, more honest, more genuine, in fact all-around better human beings than those who do not fall into that category. While it wouldn't be accurate to call Carla Tate and Danny McMahon caricatures, the way they're portrayed runs the risk of condescending both to them and to us.

Carla (Juliette Lewis) is a daughter of privilege whose parents, proud country-club members in the mythical Bay Area suburb of Sutter Hills, have the resources to send her to a posh special school. When the film opens, she's graduating and heading home, much to the delight of her softhearted father, Radley (Tom Skerritt).

Carla turns out to be a very single-minded young woman, determined to live her own life and explore all her options. Her zest for living and her capabilities are so clear, only a criminally obtuse, overbearing and intrusive mother wouldn't get the message soon enough. Which is just the kind of parent the script helpfully provides.

Elizabeth Tate (Diane Keaton) turns out to be wound as tight as the cables on the Golden Gate Bridge. She loves her daughter, but this kind of broad-strokes movie couldn't exist if she was even the slightest bit sympathetic to or understanding of her concerns.

What the script hypothesizes instead is a mother so dense everyone in the audience can feel superior to her, a mother so oblivious to who her daughter is that she insists, in one particularly egregious scene, that Carla go one on one with a tennis machine and learn the game all well-bred young ladies know.

Still, with the support of sisters Heather (Sarah Paulson) and Caroline (Poppy Montgomery) and Caroline's fiance, Jeff (Joe Flanigan), Carla persists in trying to be her own person. She wants to go to college, she wants her own apartment, and, completing the triptych, she wants a boyfriend.

That would be Danny ("Saving Private Ryan's" Giovanni Ribisi), a fellow student at Bay Area Polytech.

Danny has his own apartment, with kindly Vietnam vet Ernie (Marshall favorite Hector Elizondo) serving as manager; he is passionate about marching band music; and, most impressive to Carla, he even has a job making cookies for a local baker.

Young people who are "mentally challenged" are especially difficult to portray on screen; in recent years only Leonardo DiCaprio's exceptional work in "What's Eating Gilbert Grape" was good enough to make you forget that a well-known face was in fact playing a part.

While Lewis and Ribisi eventually win you over, both their performances are more studied and less flexible than DiCaprio's. As talented professionals, they have a good grasp on the appropriate mannerisms and verbal cadences, but we are aware more than we'd like to be that they're both acting, so to speak, to beat the band.

More of a problem than the performances is the film's almost complete lack of spontaneity. There are warm moments, but there's almost not one that isn't oversimplified or completely schematic, from talks about sex ("I wonder who thought up sex in the first place"/"I think it was Madonna") to a dreary subplot about Elizabeth's difficulty accepting daughter Heather as a lesbian. By coddling viewers and micromanaging our responses, "The Other Sister" shows almost as little respect for the audience as Elizabeth does for her feisty, underappreciated daughter.

NEW YORK POST, 2/26/99, p. 40, Rod Dreher

Is there a soul alive who wouldn't be made extremely squeamish by the prospect of a Garry Marshall comedy starring Juliette Lewis as a mildly retarded woman in search of independence and sexuality?

The premise is dicey, to be sure, and mainstream slickster Marshall, who brought his trademark breeziness to film treatments of prostitution ("Pretty Woman") and sadomasochism ("East of Eden"), gives the story a customarily heavy dusting of powdered sugar. But, God knows how, it's OK. Really.

Given its ghastly premise, the picture is better than it has a right to be, thanks to the against-all-odds credibility of Lewis and Giovanni Ribisi as the mentally challenged lovebirds. Despite chronic cutesiness, dialogue that just begs for mockery (Lewis, irately: "Daniel! Why did you tell evwybody our love see-cwet?!"), and scenes of questionable taste, the entire cast is more than likable, and the ending softens all but the flintiest hearts.

"The Other Sister" opens with Carla Tate (Lewis) coming home to her wealthy family after finishing at a boarding school for the mentally disabled. She's 24, and believes she's ready to be out on her own. Rich bitch mother Elizabeth (Diane Keaton) won't hear of it, but puffball Dad (Tom Skerritt) backs Carla's wishes.

At school, she meets Daniel (Ribisi), also retarded but able to function at a Benny-on-"L.A. Law" level. They fall in love, and in their screwball innocence, make a deliberate plan to chuck virginity. There they are, going over "The New Joy of Sex," picking out positions that look interesting and commenting on them like a couple of 6-year-olds with a Sears Wish Book. We're meant to find this charming, but it made me want to crawl under my seat.

"The Other Sister" provokes conflicted responses because while it calls into question our assumptions about retarded people, it does so in a manipulative way that steamrolls over practical and moral questions that complicate its sentimental message.

It has to be said that all this would be easier to deal with if Carla didn't sound so much like Lisa Loopner, which makes you spend half the film stifling guilty snickering and feeling like you'd really rather be watching a Farrelly Brothers movie.

Still, Lewis and Ribisi do grow on you, and by the storybook conclusion I was cheering them on, against all critical instinct. The movie is hard to recommend, but if the premise seems interesting, "The Other Sister" is worth a look.

NEWSDAY, 2/26/99, Part II/p. B6, John Anderson

There's an argument to be made that Garry Marshall, whose new movie, "The Other Sister," concerns the romantic plight of the mentally handicapped, is merely tripping down Memory Lane. His early successes on television, after all, included "Laverne and Shirley" and "Happy Days," so he's knows something about the intellectually challenged.

That may not be funny, but neither is the use of mentally handicapped characters for purposes of pathos—or the equally condescending notion that they serve as emblems of innate goodness and naive wisdom, or provide some pre-Fall reflection of the world at large. It's always comedy in which they're used, of course—a totally serious movie on the subject would be box office death. Inevitably, the differences between the "normal" and the not become the engine of the humor, no matter how sensitive a director's treatment, or even his intentions.

At the same time—despite haphazard editing, runaway sentiment and a sense there was no director present for a lot of the movie—"The Other Sister" is unavoidably affecting. Thanks solely to the performances of Juliette Lewis and Giovanni Ribisi.

Lewis, for whom many have an understandable allergy—for sucking De Niro's finger ("Cape Fear"), disemboweling rednecks ("Natural Born Killers") or polluting the future ("Strange Days")—is hard to resist as Carla Tate, a young woman whose upscale family can't quite come to terms with her disability, or anything else. Among the many things that are so wonderful about her characterization is that it's not just believable, it's consistent—she doesn't "get better" as so many challenged people seem to in this type of film. Nor does her performance rely on tics, spasms or some other physical crutch. She plays Carla as human first, with the disability just part of the total makeup.

At least as good if not better is the dark-eyed Giovanni Ribisi, late of "Saving Private Ryan" and a young actor who seems intent on taking on difficult roles and difficult movies and turning them into tours de force. As Danny, Carla's counterpart at a local technical college (and her eventual love interest), he's heartbreakingly emotional, nakedly candid to the point that you almost do want to embrace him as a metaphor.

Elsewhere, frankly, the movie is a mess. Marshall never knows when to stop ladling out the treacle, and following the exposition is like running an obstacle course. Facts about the Tate family dribble out in narrative-hobbling increments, making the flashbacks ungraceful, if not impossible to follow. Carla's mother, Elizabeth (Diane Keaton in perhaps the most awkward performance of her career), is established as a shrew, one who wants the young Carla sent off to school, while husband Radley (Tom Skerritt) wants her home. Only later do we learn Dad was drinking heavily (and that he's a doctor). That Carla's sister Heather (Sarah Paulson) is gay and Mom won't except her lover. That, as a child being abused by neighbor children, Carla pushed one down a flight of stairs.

This is virtually storytelling in reverse; if Marshall is experimenting with postmodernist narrative techniques, someone should tell him to stop. He does, however, get standout performances out of both Ribisi and the surprising Lewis, performances good enough, perhaps, to cure an allergy.

SIGHT AND SOUND, 12/99, p. 52, John Wrathall

San Francisco, the present. After spending her childhood in a residential special school, 'mentally challenged' Carla returns home to her upper-class family. Against the wishes of her over-protective mother Elizabeth, Carla enrols at a local vocational school where she meets the equally 'challenged' Danny. Romance blossoms and Carla persuades her family to set her up in her own flat. When Danny fails his exams, his father cuts off his allowance; he will have to go and live with his mother in Florida. Carla asks Elizabeth if Danny can move into her flat, but Elizabeth refuses.

After much prevarication, Carla finally has sex with Danny. But when the family takes Danny along to a Christmas dance at the local country club, he announces this to everyone. Carla freaks out and tells Danny she never wants to see him again. While Carla's family prepare for her sister's wedding, Danny catches the train to Florida. But half way there he gets off and hitches back to San Francisco where he disrupts the wedding by proposing to Carla. This time everyone is charmed, but Elizabeth refuses to agree to Carla and Danny's marriage. Carla goes ahead and arranges it on her own. On the day, Elizabeth refuses to come to the church with the rest of the family. Carla and Danny are married. Then Elizabeth turns up after all. The family is reunited.

About ten years ago, the success of *Pretty Woman* and *Beaches* made Garry Marshall one of the most prominent directors in Hollywood. Until the success of *Runaway Bride* his star seemed to be waning with the failure of *Exit to Eden* and *Dear God* which both went straight to video in the UK. *The Other Sister*, made before *Runaway Bride*, fared little better. Marshall first made his name in television, producing such hit shows as *Happy Days* and *Laverne and Shirley*. *The Other Sister*, which he co-wrote with his *Happy Days* associate Bob Brunner, marks a return to old-fashioned small-screen values. Beyond the quality of the cast, and the long drawn-out running time, there's little to distinguish this from an 80s made-for-television 'movie of the week' exploring mental-health problems in sensitive, soft-focus style. This is the sort of film in which a mother can say of her own daughter: 'She has significant social adjustment problems.'

With an over-protected, ugly-duckling daughter emerging from the shadow of her overbearing mother, *The Other Sister* echoes the Bette Davis classic *Now, Voyager* (1942). But Marshall, ever the feel-good merchant (he even made prostitution look fun), shies away from any psychodrama inherent in the situation. As a love story, it's equally coy: a montage of the young lovers Carla and Danny getting to know each other is accompanied on the soundtrack by Jewel singing, "Please be careful of me, I'm sensitive." Although the 'mentally challenged' Danny is prone to embarrassing public outbursts and is driven above all by his desire to have sex with Carla, there's a cosiness about him summed up by his two great passions in life: *The Graduate* (1967) and marching bands—tastes which seem to say more about the sensibilities of the 60-year-old writers than they do about those of their 20-year-old creations.

That this film is watchable at all, especially at 130 minutes, is down to the efforts of the cast. Previously a specialist in child-woman antics, Juliette Lewis is refreshingly restrained as Carla, limiting her tics to a strangely tongueless way of talking and a tendency to open her eyes very wide. Though the performance isn't going to win her an Oscar, it's hard to think of another actress of her generation who could have carried it off. The up-and-coming Giovanni Ribisi, meanwhile, spices up the wonderfully vacant persona he perfected as Phoebe's brother in *Friends* with some low-key rocking and blinking, and an endearingly goofy grin.

VILLAGE VOICE, 3/2/99, p. 150, Dennis Lim

Being a Garry Marshall movie, *The Other Sister* reflexively translates mental retardation as maniacal cuteness. Juliette Lewis, Young Hollywood's patron saint of emotionally unstable behavior, plays a well-to-do young woman with a learning disability, who, after 10 years in a "special" boarding school, returns home to a control-freakish mom (Diane Keaton), docile, ex-alcoholic dad (Tom Skerritt), and two barely distinguishable sisters (though, in a feeble stab at a halfway modern subplot, one is, it turns out, a lesbian).

The Other Sister breezily charts Carla's journey to independence, though, headstrong from the outset, she never seems like she has very far to go. She enrolls in college, meets a cookie-baking marching-band enthusiast (Giovanni Ribisi), falls in love, moves into her own apartment, and loses her virginity. Exhaustingly upbeat, *The Other Sister* exists in some embalmed universe where tough situations are glibly acknowledged, then deflected with smirky laughs.

Plunging headfirst into mush at every opportunity, Marshall brings out the worst in his actors. Lewis is as full-throttle as ever—it's a method that has seldom served her well, and this slack-jawed, wide-eyed naïf comes off, disturbingly, as a cuddly version of her usual drawling, hair-trigger kook (given the circumstances, you can't help wishing she would revert to type here, grab hold of a sharp object, and shed some blood). A fine actor increasingly forced to play below his IQ, Ribisi is no better. Their courtship is the film's centerpiece, as well as its most patronizing element—the pair thumb through *The New Joy of Sex,* marking page numbers, and we're supposed to giggle at the adorable awkwardness of it all.

"Stop laughing at me!" Carla shrieks after a climactic country-club meltdown (which is, of course, the movie's idea of ultimate mortification). It's a dismayingly hollow plea, not least because every other scene in the film has no qualms about encouraging precisely that reaction.

Also reviewed in:
CHICAGO TRIBUNE, 2/26/99, Friday/p. A, Mark Caro
NATION, 3/29/99, p. 34, Stuart Klawans
NEW REPUBLIC, 3/29/99, p. 28, Stanley Kauffmann
NEW YORK TIMES, 2/26/99, p. E16, Stephen Holden
VARIETY, 2/22-28/99, p. 54, Lael Loewenstein
WASHINGTON POST, 2/26/99, p. C5, Rita Kempley
WASHINGTON POST, 2/26/99, Weekend/p. 39, Desson Howe

OUT OF SEASON

An I.M.J. Productions and Jour de Fête Films release of a Picture This Entertainment production. *Producer:* Jeanette L. Buck. *Director:* Jeanette L. Buck. *Screenplay:* Kim McNabb. *Director of Photography:* Ed Talavera. *Editor:* Sharon Teo. *Music:* Miki Navazio, Janine DeLorenzo, and Kenni Feinberg. *Sound Editor:* Missy Cohen. *Casting:* Elizabeth Boykewich. *Running time:* 85 minutes. *MPAA Rating:* Not Rated.

CAST: Carol Monda (Micki); Joy Kelly (Roberta); Dennis Fecteau (Charlie); Nancy Daly (Shelley); Rusty Clauss (Jane); Al Faris (Store Clerk).

NEW YORK POST, 6/11/99, p. 48, Rod Dreher

If, as the Talking Heads once sang, heaven is a place where nothing ever happens, then the lesbian lovers in "Out Of Season" are dwelling in paradise on the Jersey shore. "Anybody ever die of boredom around here?" one character asks of the sleepy townspeople. Yeah, sister, this movie does.

Jeannette L. Buck's debut feature brings surly, troubled Micki Silva (Carol Monda) to Cape May to take care of her ailing Uncle Charlie (Dennis Fecteau).

Her leather jacket, chain-smoking and ever-present scowl telegraph T-R-O-U-B-L-E. Uncle Charlie helpfully provides the movie's thesis sentence when he asks his niece, "Micki, what are you running from?"

Answer: Responsibility. Micki has spent her wayward life looking for love, but running away from any relationship that would tie her down. Then she goes into Zoe's Diner for a cup of coffee, and upends the prissy waitress (Nancy Daly) by asking her if she knows how good it tastes to kiss a woman after she's finished a cigarette. This talk pricks up the ears of cook Roberta (Joy Kelly), who happens to be both an out lesbian and Uncle Charlie's best friend.

Micki starts chasing standoffish Roberta, inviting her to play along when her grabby girlfriends come to visit. There's a funny scene detailing the classification of lesbian phyla (Grunge Girls, Pinstripe Lesbians, etc.), but the dramatic arc flatlines because scriptwriter Kim McNabb can't figure out how to make the tension between Micki and Roberta palpable.

The dialogue tells us very little about the women, and we don't see why Roberta should be interested, or not interested, in persistent Micki. McNabb evades the hard work of writing emotionally plausible and revealing dialogue by having her would-be lovers emerge from a movie with cold-fish Roberta inexplicably in rapid thaw. Her warming to Micki seems as stilted and perfunctory as her initial resistance.

Half the battle would have been won if Monda and Kelly, both good actresses, had the least bit of chemistry or even lightness. The inevitable love scene has a dreary, forced-trot quality that's pleasurable only because it signals we can soon shut the barn door on this swaybacked old mare of a movie.

VILLAGE VOICE, 6/15/99, p. 148, Jessica Winter

Micki is a drifter, a rebel. She pulls at her cigarettes like they were straws in an obstinate Slurpee, turns heads at the local diner when she orders breakfast at three in the afternoon, and never sheds her black leather jacket—she even sports it around the Jersey seashore house where she's come to care for her dying uncle, Charlie. Despite Micki's badass facade, she's mostly content to sit around and stare at diner employee Roberta, an old pal of Charlie's who plays on Micki's team but has benched herself indefinitely. There are many dramatic possibilities in an interracial lesbian romance set in a provincial town, but *Out of Season* focuses on the women's fears of commitment, which would be fine—even refreshing—if they seemed to, well, like each other or something. The listless, lustless duo ends up confirming the pervasive straight assumption that any two gay folks with mutual friends were made for each other.

Also reviewed in:
NEW YORK TIMES, 6/11/99, p. E12, Lawrence Van Gelder
VARIETY, 4/13-19/98, p. 30, Mark Woods

OUT-OF-TOWNERS, THE

A Paramount Pictures release of a Robert Evans production in association with Cherry Alley Productions and the Cort/Madden Company. *Executive Producer:* Christine Forsyth-Peters and Philip E. Thomas. *Producer:* Robert Cort, David Madden, Robert Evans, and Teri Schwartz. *Director:* Sam Weisman. *Screenplay:* Marc Lawrence. *Based upon the screenplay by:* Neil Simon. *Director of Photography:* John Bailey. *Editor:* Kent Beyda. *Music:* Marc Shaiman. *Music Editor:* Dan DiPrima. *Choreographer:* Adam Shankman. *Sound:* David M. Kelson and (music) Dennis Sands. *Sound Editor:* Robert L. Sephton. *Casting:* Illene Starger. *Production Designer:* Ken Adam. *Art Director:* William F. O'Brien and Charles Beal. *Set Designer:* Darrell Wight and Jack G. Taylor, Jr. *Set Decorator:* Kathryn Peters, Marvin March, and George DeTitta. *Special Effects:* Alan E. Lorimer and Bill Traynor. *Costumes:* Ann Roth. *Make-up:* Kenneth Myers, John Elliot, and Margot Boccia. *Stunt Coordinator:* Chris Howell. *Running time:* 91 minutes. *MPAA Rating:* PG-13.

CAST: Steve Martin (Henry Clark); Goldie Hawn (Nancy Clark); John Cleese (Mr. Mersault); Mark McKinney (Greg); Oliver Hudson (Alan Clark); Valerie Perri (Stewardess); Steve Mittleman and Randall Arney (Passengers); Carlease Burke (Airline Representative); William Duell (Lost Baggage Clerk); J.P. Bumstead (Boston Cab Driver); Peggy Mannix (Sweeper Woman); Anne Haney (Woman in Bathroom); Charlie Dell (Janitor on Train); Jordan Baker (Rental Car Clerk); Tom Riis Farrell (Andrew Lloyd Webber); Dani Klein (Michelle); Daniel T. Parker and Karen Elizabeth White (Desk Clerks); Alyson Palmer and Elizabeth Ziff (Shoplifters); Diane Cheng (Korean Grocer); Christopher Durang (Paranoid Man); Mo Gaffney (Paranoid Woman); Mary Testa (Dominatrix); Monica Birt (Supermodel); John Elsen (Deli Guy); Babo Harrison (Well Dressed Woman); Josh Mostel (Doctor Faber); Gregory Jbara (Edward); Amy Ziff (Edward's Friend); Cynthia Nixon (Shena); French Napier (Sexaholic); Joseph Maher (Mr. Wellstone); Constance McCashin (Mrs. Wellstone); Steve Bean (Greg's Friend); James Arone (Room Service Waiter); Philip Earl Johnson (Hotel Security Man); Ernie

Sabella (Getaway Driver); Jack Willis (Robber); John Pizzarelli (Band Leader); Rudolph Giuliani (New York Mayor); Scotty Bloch (Florence Needleman); Chris McKinney and Joe Grifasi (Arresting Cops); Jerome Preston Bates (Prisoner 1); Jack McGee (Sergeant Jordan); Jacinto Taras Riddick (Prisoner 2); L.B. Fisher (Howard the Bellman); Janna Lapidus (Central Park Woman); T. Scott Cunningham (Paul); Mandy Sigfried (Receptionist); Jenn Thompson (Lisa Tobin); John Gould Rubin (Bill); Christopher Duva (Barry the Bellman); Arthur French (Cab Driver); Jessica Cauffiel (Susan Clark).

LOS ANGELES TIMES, 4/2/99, Calendar/p. 12, Kevin Thomas

"The Out-of-Towners" teams Steve Martin and Goldie Hawn as an attractive baby-boomer couple from Ohio who fly off to Manhattan for the husband's interview at a top ad agency only to be plunged into a nightmare of foul-ups. If the film's title and premise sound familiar that's because back in 1970 Neil Simon, director Arthur Hiller, Jack Lemmon and the late Sandy Dennis made a movie of the same name, at once funny and rueful, about just how many things can go wrong for newcomers in the Big Apple.

The new version, however, is much more a free reworking than a remake, a glossy two-star vehicle, rewritten by Marc Lawrence as a glamorous romantic comedy-adventure fantasy tailored for Martin's and Hawn's personalities and comedic gifts. They are a terrific team and look great, but their film is a throwback to old Hollywood hokum in which shiny production values have been applied to much that smacks of the contrived and the synthetic.

Whereas the original film was very much rooted in everyday reality, artfully exaggerated only slightly for humor and poignancy, this new version is ultra-sleek escapist fare that depends heavily upon your being able to be carried away by its stars. Martin and Hawn do have as much charm as they have a gift for comedy, but ultimately the film is not as consistently effective as they are.

Both films start out similarly with the missed connections and lost luggage we've all experienced. But once Martin and Hawn, who are swiftly mugged and left nearly penniless, have arrived in Manhattan, they've also landed in fantasy land, with a string of wildly improbable incidents—some hilarious, others merely strained—that test their spirits, their marriage and their capacity for renewal and perseverance.

The truest moments have to do with two people, married 27 years, learning to depend upon and trust each other as never before. The set piece of the film finds Hawn coming on to a personable but eventually irate Hollywood agent (Mark McKinney) so that she can snag his expensive hotel suite so that she and Martin can call room service for dinner, freshen up and maybe even get a little rest before the guy comes back from a play. Hawn is sly and sexy, and this substantial sequence, beautifully sustained under Sam Weisman's smooth direction, is comedy that grows out of character rather than slapstick, and is all the more effective for it.

Hawn's wife is lots more daring and resilient than Martin's husband ever realized, but suffering from empty nest syndrome, Hawn needs to start putting Martin first again, just as he needs to be lots more assertive. You couldn't ask more of both stars, who deliver in high style, and they get splendid support from McKinney and from John Cleese, as the most unctuous hotel manager since Franklin Pangborn. You may want to take a chance on this new "Out-of-Towners" because of its stars, but keep in mind that while its characters take chances, the picture itself plays it awfully safe.

NEW YORK POST, 4/2/99, p. 39, Rod Dreher

"Thank God for John Cleese," one peeved moviegoer said on the way out of the dispirited remake of Neil Simon's "The Out-of-Towners." Lord, yes. It is always meet and right to thank Our Heavenly Father for John Cleese—never more so than after digesting the woebegone blandness of this comedy, a bucket of cottage cheese in which he is one prickly pepper.

As the Basil Fawlty-ish manager of a posh Manhattan hotel, Cleese condescends magnificently to the Ohio rubes played by Steve Martin and Goldie Hawn. It's not that Cleese has much to work with in Marc Lawrence's slack update of Simon's 1970 screenplay; it's just that you're grateful to his superbly pitched superciliousness for keeping you awake.

Whatever the faults of the original Jack Lemmon-Sandy Dennis version, it wasn't boring. Lemmon's jitteriness, on the cusp of full-blown mania, made sure of that. He plays a small-town Ohio business executive headed with his patient wife (Dennis) to New York City for a job interview that could vault him into the Big Leagues. The trip turns into a comically hellish misadventure, as lost luggage, a transit strike, a stickup and all manner of urban mayhem descend upon the poor couple in the course of one long, long night.

The Simon-scripted version turned on one scrappy Buckeye's refusal to be defeated by the worst that grubby 1970 New York could throw at him. So how do you tell this story in 1999, when Manhattan has become safer, lovelier and altogether more pleasant than the places most out-of-town visitors come from? Scripter Lawrence reimagines it as an empty-nest marriage crisis brought to the fore by Manhattan misfortune.

The film opens with Henry and Nancy Clark (Martin and Hawn) sending their college-age son (Hawn's real-life son Oliver Hudson) on a school trip to Europe. Distraught over the sudden silence of their suburban house, Nancy tags along with Henry on his scheduled business trip to New York. What she doesn't know is he's lost his job, and doesn't so much want this interview as desperately needs it.

Unlike Lemmon's protagonist, Martin's Henry doesn't idolize Manhattan, so he has no bright-lights-big-city illusions to be robbed of. Instead, he has the far more mundane problem learning that his marriage isn't as wonderful as thought. I smell Very Special Episode.

A miscast (too smart, too ironic) Martin and an agreeably golden-retrieverish Hawn cavort from crisis to crisis—crashing their rental car in Chinatown, being mugged by a crook pretending be Andrew Lloyd Webber, suffering the humiliation of an invalid credit card, and so on—without much enthusiasm.

And why should they? Every potentially funny setup—wandering into a sex-addicts anonymous meeting, for example—peters out with Lawrence's sitcommy dialogue, pre-chewed for the convenience of audiences who think Martin's "Father of the Bride" films are laff riots. Simon's simple, snappy, lowbrow little chase movie is ruined by turning it into yet another gasbag vehicle for middlebrow Boomer angst.

Incidentally, director Sam Weisman gets the geography of the city all wrong. The couple walk from Times Square to the East Village in no time flat, and walk out the door of their Park Avenue hotel (the Plaza Athenee, at East 64th) past the Metropolitan Museum, headed uptown for a Financial District appointment. But out-of-towners won't know the difference.

NEWSDAY, 4/2/99, Part II/p. B3, John Anderson

Timing is usually Hollywood's strong suit. Multiple Shakespeare movies are in the works. Queen Elizabeth is hip. Last year we had duplicate asteroid movies and a few years before that, multiple Christopher Columbi.

So why "The Out-of-Towners"? Why, indeed. Originally released in 1970 with Jack Lemmon and Sandy Dennis, it's the ultimate lost-in-New York "comedy" about two rubes who hit Gotham and experience virtually every nightmare scenario afforded by the modern urban experience. Lost luggage, canceled reservations, hotel exile, muggings, lack of food, lack of sleep, jail, Central Park as Skull Island. Everything, in other words, that New York is not supposed to be about now.

Amadou Diallo aside, crime is down; the economy is up; Disney is vaporizing every last trace of unsavory "color" it comes across, and there hasn't even been a major garbage strike in 10 years. OK, it rains now and then. But is the idea of two Ohioans—especially nice ones like Steve Martin and Goldie Hawn—having a bad time in Manhattan really supposed to be funny? You more or less have to ignore the basic premise of the movie to enjoy it, and that's asking a lot.

Too much, in fact, despite the charm of its two leads: Martin as advertising man Henry Clark—who hasn't told his wife he's lost his job—and Hawn as Nancy Clark, who tags along with Henry not knowing how important his Monday morning job interview is. With the kids moved out, she just wants a little more juice in the marriage. When their plane is redirected to Boston, she gets it.

Much of what happens is pretty improbable, given ATMs, credit card services, and the fact that the world is just a lot smaller than it was in 1970. (The Clarks think a mugger is Andrew Lloyd

Webber? Don't they have PBS fund drives in Ohio?) The movie gets a lift from the always-droll John Cleese as the hotel manager who unceremoniously evicts them when their credit card is rejected which would likely never happen at this class of hotel. But then, the story line by Neil Simon—is not just inherently flawed, it's rabidly anti-New York, and the cameo by Rudolph Giuliani proves nothing except how desperately he wants to raise his national profile.

The original "Out of Towners" was excrutiatingly unfunnny, so you'd probably have to call the new one a success. Still, much of the humor is simply tepid, from the reheated slapstick (Hawn upsetting a flight attendant's tray; Martin running up the conveyor belt on a luggage carousel) to the tame sex jokes (Nancy vamps a traveling Hollywood agent so she can get in his room and order food). Some of the situations are so torturously contrived you can't believe anyone thought this would work, but part of the film's appeal may be the opportunity to watch Martin and Hawn, two of Hollywood's smarter entertainers, running around like buffoons. They have nothing to lose, and it makes us feel closer to them.

SIGHT AND SOUND, 12/99, p. 53, Kim Newman

Henry Clark, an Ohio advertising executive, hasn't told his wife Nancy he's been laid off. He's pinning all his career hopes on an interview with a New York agency. Nancy, depressed because her son has left for college and her daughter has dropped out of medical school to become an actress, decides to join Henry on his trip. Their plane is diverted to Boston, where they miss their connecting train to New York and are forced to rent a clapped-out car. Arriving in Manhattan, they are mugged. Next, they're humiliated at a luxury hotel managed by the supercilious Mr Mersault because their daughter has maxed out their only remaining credit card. In the hotel bar, Nancy tries to vamp hotel guest Greg to gain access to his room so she and Henry can freshen up. But Greg returns early with amorous intentions and the couple flee out of the window, incidentally observing Mersault dressed up in a lady guest's gown and jewels.

The Clarks sleep rough in Central Park and Henry is arrested for relieving himself in public. Nancy blackmails Mersault into paying for Henry's bail so he can make his job interview. But Henry is given a hallucinogen by a fellow prisoner and turns up at the ad agency just as his high crashes into manic depression. He ends up pitching an idea for a New York tourism campaign and gets the job. Some time later the Clarks attend the opening of a play starring their daughter.

Neil Simon's original 1969 screenplay of *The Out of Towners*, as directed by Arthur Hiller, was (along with *The Prisoner of Second Avenue*, 1974) a work in which the playwright had his surrogate self suffer through the horrors of an especially vicious mid-life crisis. Jack Lemmon and his spouse, the earnestly awkward Sandy Dennis, were actually younger than the stars of this remake. Nonetheless, at that point in history (the era also of *Coogan's Bluff* and *Midnight Cowboy*) their straight-laced Midwesterners in the big city seemed stranded on the wrong side of a generation gap and a cultural divide. The Hiller version of *The Out of Towners* is more excruciating than funny, evoking Kafka and Sisyphus as well as Wile E. Coyote. It climaxes horribly with Lemmon cracking a tooth before the crucial job interview and has the couple fleeing in defeat from Manhattan only to have their plane hijacked to Cuba, by implication preferable to the Big Apple.

For this version, screenwriter Marc Lawrence takes the broad outline of Simon's script and softens it into the comedy of errors the original, which wasn't much appreciated on its release, might have liked to be. By starting the Clarks' run of bad luck in Ohio, as their marriage is crippled by Henry's covert unemployment (a theme lifted from *The Prisoner of Second Avenue)* and Nancy's bad case of empty-nest syndrome, the film diminishes Simon's vision of Manhattan as an infernal maelstrom. Delaying the city jitters by getting bogged down in the frustrated road trip, this initial misstep is extended further by the lengthy side trip to Boston, recalling Steve Martin's turn in *Planes, Trains & Automobiles* right down to the conflicts with blankly malevolent travel clerks. In another case of a stale marriage healed through crazy comedy, the horrors of the trip force the stuffy couple to cut loose—to become, in effect, Steve Martin and Goldie Hawn—and rediscover each other in adversity. While Lemmon and Dennis were crushed, Martin and Hawn finally triumph, picking up the necessary survival skills (seduction, blackmail, mendacity, borderline insanity) not only to get by in New York but to conquer it.

In its in-flight movie way, the film has a few genuinely funny incidental characters and situations, like the mugger who poses as Andrew Lloyd Webber and the hotel desk clerk who reacts to Nancy's plea of "couldn't you just trust us?" with a perfect doubletake. Since Martin (pre-*Bowfinger*) and Hawn fall into that sad category of 'not as funny as they used to be', the film has to haul in John Cleese as a rude hotel manager who's a lot more amusing before his exposure as a silly-walking transvestite. *The Out-of-Towners* has the look and feel of too many mock-sophisticated city comedies. There are sparkly lights even in the run-down sections of the city and a sop to Mayor Rudy Giuliani (who has a cameo) and his campaign to clean up the streets of New York, thus making them safe for Henry and Nancy Clark but invalidating the premise of Neil Simon's story.

Also reviewed in:
CHICAGO TRIBUNE, 4/2/99, Friday/p. A, Michael Wilmington
NEW YORK TIMES, 4/2/99, p. E8, Lawrence Van Gelder
VARIETY, 4/5-11/99, p. 30, Joe Leydon
WASHINGTON POST, 4/2/99, p. C5, Stephen Hunter
WASHINGTON POST, 4/2/99, Weekend/p. 42, Michael O'Sullivan

OUTSIDE PROVIDENCE

A Miramax Films release of an Eagle Beach production. *Executive Producer:* Bob Weinstein and Harvey Weinstein. *Producer:* Michael Corrente, Peter Farrelly, Bobby Farrelly, and Randy Finch. *Director:* Michael Corrente. *Screenplay:* Peter Farrelly, Michael Corrente, and Bobby Farrelly. *Based upon the novel by:* Peter Farrelly. *Director of Photography:* Richard Crudo. *Editor:* Kate Sanford. *Music:* Sheldon Mirowitz. *Music Editor:* David Carbonara. *Choreographer:* Gerrianne Genga. *Sound:* Peter Schneider. *Sound Editor:* Jeff Stern. *Casting:* Sheila Jaffe and Georgianne Walken. *Production Designer:* Chad Detwiller. *Art Director:* Tom Walden. *Set Decorator:* Karen Weber. *Set Dresser:* Arthur Wood, Greg Morell, Shawn Gamache, and Kenji Messenger. *Costumes:* Annie Dunn. *Make-up:* Joe Rossi. *Make-up (Alec Baldwin):* Carl Fullerton. *Stunt Coordinator:* Brian Smyj. *Running time:* 95 minutes. *MPAA Rating:* R.

CAST: Shawn Hatosy (Tim Dunphy); Tommy Bone (Jackie Dunphy); Samantha Lavigne ("Clops"); Jonathan Brandis (Mousy); Adam Lavorgna (Tommy the Wire); Jesse Leach (Decenz); Jon Abrahams (Drugs Delaney); Alec Baldwin (Old Man Dunphy); Richard Jenkins (Barney); Mike Cerrone (Caveech); George Wendt (Joey); Robert Turano (Fran); Kristen Shorten (Bunny Cote); Tim Crowe (Mr. Funderburk); Gabriel Mann (Jack Wheeler); George Martin (Dean Mort); Jack Ferver (Irving Waltham); Chris Jewett (Brackett); Alex Toma (Billy Fu); Sean Gildea (Math Teacher); Bernie Sheredy (History Teacher); Amy Smart (Jane Weston); Jimmy Landi (Ticket Taker); Amy Van Nostrand (Mrs. Weston); Mark O'Connell (Jizz Flashback Older Boy #1); Seth Meier (Jizz Flashback Older Boy #2); Nicholas Cardi (Cornwall Student #1); Vincent Mesolella (Cornwall Student #2); Joshua Moore (Cornwall Student #3); Scott Rabideau (Cornwall Student #4); David Vaillancourt (Cornwall Student #5); Libby Landgon (Mrs. Dunphy); Johnny O'Hern (Young Tim Dunphy); Kyle Pepi and Ryan Pepi (Young Jackie Dunphy); Gus Albero (Stoner); T.J. Paolino (Maggie); Eric Brown (English Teacher); Robert W. Jordan (Shorty); Harry Cooper (Man at Bar #1); Steve Cerrone (Man at Bar #2); Johnny Cicco (Jensen); Kevin Gilmore (Kelleher); Max Ricci (Student in Dining Hall); Kate Lohman (Secretary); Nigel Gore (Dean John S. Rogers, Jr.).

LOS ANGELES TIMES, 9/1/99, Calendar/p. 1, Kevin Thomas

"Outside Providence" is a coming-of-age story of exceptional warmth and humor that represents a felicitous teaming of writer-director Michael Corrente and the brothers Farrelly, Peter and

Bobby. Corrente's gift for evoking the lives of blue-collar men that made his debut film, "Federal Hill," so appealing blends perfectly with the antic sensibility of the Farrellys.

Peter Farrelly's 1988 novel, the basis for the film's script, on which the Farrellys and Corrente collaborated, represents a broader scope for all concerned. "Outside Providence" reveals further development as a filmmaker for Corrente while it allows the Farrellys to explore on the screen more serious concerns while offsetting them with moments of hilarity typical of their comedy classic "There's Something About Mary." What's more, it provides young Shawn Hatosy a star-making role and for Alec Baldwin the kind of performance that will be remembered come awards season.

Hatosy's Tim Dunphy is a likable 17-year-old who lives in seedy Pawtucket, R.I., with his widowed father (Baldwin) and younger brother Jackie (Tommy Bone). The year is 1974, and Tim and his pals are preoccupied with getting high, allowing for lots of Cheech and Chong-style pothead humor. Tim is brighter, more responsible than the others, but he is not fully aware that he is. He is a wonderful older brother to Jackie, who uses a wheelchair after a fall from a rooftop. He's loving yet won't let Jackie feel sorry for himself, believing that he won't "fit in" if he succumbs to self-pity. The boys' father spends virtually every evening playing poker with his buddies in his old frame house, from which the paint is peeling seriously. The father is a tough parent, and he's especially hard on his older son for reasons not readily apparent.

One night Tim, although he does not have a license, is driving his father's car, which is packed with his pals, all of them high as a kite, when he crashes into a parked police car. What looks to be the kind of catastrophe that can potentially ruin a life turns out to be Tim's salvation. One of his father's poker regulars, Caveech (Mike Cerrone), a used-car salesman rumored to be "connected," proves to be just that. Instead of reform school or worse, Tim, through Caveech's efforts, winds up at Cornwall Academy, a posh, venerable New England prep school. It's so strict, however, that it is virtually a reform school, albeit one for the upper classes.

In short, Tim becomes the classic fish out of water, and the Farrellys and Corrente make the most of his predicament. Tim becomes drawn to pretty, well-bred Jane (Amy Smart), good-humored and unpretentious but also a disciplined student intent on being accepted at Brown. Most important, Tim discovers that he is more intelligent than he ever realized, that he has the capacity to learn and earn good grades and to feel fulfilled in doing so. Tim is beginning to change, and this gives him some perspective on his troubled relationship with his father and the confidence to confront him when the time comes. He even begins to think of college for himself, which would be a family first.

Corrente and the Farrellys manage Tim's emergence with admirable deftness, moving between Cornwall and visits home, between the serious and the comic, in a manner that gives Tim's story a richness of variety expressed in a graceful, buoyant shifting in mood and tone. They demand a lot from young Hatosy, and he delivers with ease and naturalness.

He has a sweet-natured, unforced masculinity and clear intelligence that give him an easy yet commanding presence. His Tim is a sturdy foil to his father's blunt, working-class machismo, a shield against painful loss that also hides a capacity for insight and reflection. Old Man Dunphy is one of Baldwin's best parts ever, and his present beefiness only adds to the authenticity of his portrayal. In addition to Bone and Smart, there are terrific supporting performances all around, especially from Tim Crowe as a headmaster who could teach Mrs. Tingle a few tricks in gleeful killjoy nastiness; Jack Ferver as Tim's skinny, hyper roommate; and George Wendt as one of Dunphy's poker players, a guy who packs a walloping surprise.

By the time it's over, "Outside Providence" has belied the negative spiritual implication of its geographical title. If ever a teen hero discovered redemption, it's Tim Dunphy.

NEW YORK POST, 9/11/99, p. 51, Jonathan Foreman

Another movie set in the '70s with an enjoyably nostalgic soundtrack, "Outside Providence" is a sometimes poignant coming-of-age story punctuated with moments of the ribald, absurdist humor that the Farrelly brothers brought to their comic masterpiece, "There's Something About Mary."

The Farrellys wrote the screenplay for "Outside Providence" with director Michael Corrente ("Federal Hill"). The movie that issues from their combined sensibilities is sweet-natured and entertaining, but it's also disjointed and, in the end, disappointing.

It's as if too many people had come up with some great ideas and there just wasn't room to develop them. You meet all these terrific, promising comic characters in the first half, and then you barely see them again in the second. You also get the sense that the filmmakers got stuck in their own '70s nostalgia trip, because "Outside Providence" turns into a '70s movie two-thirds of the way through, with a corny love montage, a mawkish reconciliation between son and gruff dad, and an unbelievable climactic scene in the office of a Brown University dean. Timothy "Dunph" Dunphy (Shawn Hatosy) lives in a ramshackle working-class section of Pawtucket, R.I., with his tough dad (Alec Baldwin), his wheelchair-bound kid brother and a three-legged dog.

Dunph and his going-nowhere pals spend their nights getting wasted and watching less-uptight people dance in discos. When a car driven by Dunph crashes into a parked cop car, dad uses a "connected" friend to keep the boy out of jail—and to get him into a tony Connecticut prep school.

Dunph is unprepared for the school in every way. But, this being the early '70s, a shared enthusiasm for good weed is all it takes to smooth over class differences between the kid from Pawtucket and his rich schoolmates.

But Dunphy's stoner proclivities do not help his relationship with one particularly nasty teacher, Mr. Funderburk (Timothy Crowe), or his precarious academic status.

Then Dunph meets Jane Weston (Amy Smart), a blond beauty in the long-tressed '70s style who turns out to be smart, down-to-earth and remarkably unprejudiced even when it comes to hanging out with his friends in Pawtucket.

There are good performances all around. But Alec Baldwin is a particular pleasure as a tender-hearted grouch, and George Wendt has a small but enjoyable role with some great lines.

NEWSDAY, 9/1/99, Part II/p. B3, Gene Seymour

Just because someone looks like a romantic leading man doesn't necessarily mean he should be one. To support this premise, Exhibit A—as in Alec Baldwin—is submitted to the court.

Baldwin's dashing good looks have dared producers to make him into some kind of slick-hunk franchise. That this effort hasn't borne fruit after more than a decade of films has confounded the great minds of moviemaking. (And if those last four words don't equal an oxymoron, I'll eat my paycheck.)

Perhaps it's because Baldwin, who is far more intelligent than anybody who's tried to put his persona in a box, finds greater satisfaction playing heels, dolts and sociopaths than he ever could as another Action Jackson superhero.

One senses that all Baldwin ever wanted—or needed—is the kind of role where both his insatiable yen for edgy comedy and his hair-trigger sensitivity toward human pain could be adequately sated. He seems to have found it at last as the rheumy, loutish working-class patriarch in "Outside Providence," a scruffy coming-of-age story set in early-1970s Pawtucket, R.I.

Baldwin's character is simply known as the "Old Man" to Tim Dunphy (Shawn Hatosy), a teenager getting through his so-called life on Pawtucket's gloomy streets with his widower dad, his handicapped kid brother and a three-legged dog with an eyepatch. Tim appears to be on a one-way ticket to the kind of dead-end future shared by his beer-swilling dad and dope-smoking friends. Then, after one screw-up too many, he's told by the Old Man that he's spending his senior year at Cornwall Academy, an exclusive prep school in neighboring Connecticut.

Why prep school?, Tim asks his dad. Replies the Old Man: "It's to prepare you to not get your neck broke by me."

Once at Cornwall, Tim finds himself in trouble with one of the deans (Timothy Crowe) even before he has a chance to do anything wrong. It doesn't take long for him to fall in with the school misfits, dopers and ne'er-do-wells. But just as he's resigned himself to stumbling his way toward further failure, he falls for the classiest girl in the school, Jane Weston (Amy Smart). Things, in a way, start looking up. But never too far up.

This is a '70s movie in content and style. Which means that it has a loose, improvisational texture that lacks—or seems to lack—a solid plot structure. While you're watching "Outside Providence," you're almost certain there's something wrong with it. But you're enjoying the ride too much to look for it.

Knowing that this story comes from Peter and Bobby Farrelly will make those professing refined tastes believe that something has got to be wrong. But those who recognize the sweetness and charm lingering beneath the outrageous gross-out surfaces of the Farrellys' "Dumb & Dumber," "Kingpin" and "There's Something About Mary" won't be surprised by "Outside Providence's" humane wit—or, for that matter, its moments of dark and bawdy humor. The screenplay, adapted by the Farrellys and director Michael Corrente ("Federal Hill") from Peter's novel, maintains the thick, yeasty feel of a work of fiction.

NEWSWEEK, 9/6/99, p. 67, David Ansen

If you've seen the ads for "Outside Providence," you've been deceived. This is not, as Miramax would like you to believe, "There's Something About Mary" meets "Dumb & Dumber." Yes, it was written by the Farrelly brothers (along with Michael Corrente, the director) and based on Peter Farrelly's novel—and, yes, it's often very funny. But gross-out farce is neither its style nor its objective. A memory piece set in 1974, it's the coming-of-age story of a working-class teenager, Tim Dunphy (Shawn Hatosy), from Pawtucket, R.I. Tim's got a gruff but loving widowed dad (Alec Baldwin) who calls him Dildo, a kid brother in a wheelchair, a three-legged dog, a small circle of stoner friends and a view of the world that doesn't stretch farther than the end of his bong. All that begins to change when, to get him off the hook with the law, he's sent for his senior year to the preppy Cornwall Academy for Boys. Cornwall is just the sort of uptight, disciplinarian institution a blue-collar kid like Tim—who doesn't know how to tie his tie—was born to disrupt.

It's also just the sort of place where he'll fall in love with a thoroughbred beauty (Amy Smart) and discover there's more to life than listening to the Allman Brothers. All coming-of-age stories tell essentially the same story. If they rise above cliché and "Outside Providence" does, several contrived moments aside it's because they play telling variations on an old theme. Whether it's Tim giving his girl a double roach clip for a Christmas present, or the convincing way Baldwin and Hatosy navigate their ambivalent feelings toward each other, the movie gets a lot of the details right.

Director Corrente ("Federal Hill"), who grew up in Providence, has a nice feel for the '70s, and a simple but sensitive style. He turns this cast of largely fresh faces into an impressive ensemble. (But why do the wigs have to be so obvious?) Baldwin once again shows that he's a far more interesting character actor than Hollywood leading man. Of course, no project Bobby and Peter Farrelly worked on would be complete without masturbation, vomiting and a couple of crashing wheelchair gags—but Corrente puts them in a human, not cartoon, context. This is a sweet, funny little movie, and with luck it can survive the marketing con job. "Outside Providence" is winning enough on its own terms.

TIME, 9/13/99, p. 74, Richard Schickel

Bad attitude, bad wardrobe, bad study habits. Tim Dunphy (Shawn Hatosy) arrives at snooty Cornwall Academy with all that baggage spilling out of the trash bag he carries in lieu of the suitcase he can't afford.

In his working-class back-story there are drugs, drink and a feckless but funny bunch of buddies. Also a paraplegic brother, a three-legged dog and a widowed father (Alec Baldwin) for whom tough love is a family tradition, not a catch phrase. It is he who has sentenced his son to a last-chance senior year in prep school, which strikes him as a better, if more expensive, alternative to reform school.

Outside Providence—the title refers to Tim's native habitat, Pawtucket, R.I., as well as to the silence of God when it comes to doofus teenagers—works in mysterious ways its wonders to perform. For the coming-of-age cliché's don't stop once Tim settles in at Cornwall. There are a sadistic housemaster, a hidebound headmaster, a geeky roommate and a duplicitous pal to contend with, and the prettiest girl on campus (Amy Smart) to woo, ruin and redeem. One finds oneself asking how such familiar stuff breeds contentment instead of contempt.

Part of the answer, paradoxically, may lie in the way the film shamelessly, even joyously, keeps piling on that familiar material. At some point the sheer mass of it simply overwhelms dubiety. The fact that everything that happens in the movie comes as a surprise to its participants helps too. They apparently have not seen all the movies or read all the books about adolescent angst. So their responses are fresh. And felt.

That's particularly true of Hatosy. He's not so much a goofball as a radical innocent trying to pick up the clues to the preppie lifestyle but at the same time remaining fiercely loyal to his family and friends back home. It's a touching quality, and the actor engagingly lives it. Ditto Baldwin as his roughneck father, who has a depressive's shrewdness about other people's weaknesses as well as a depressive's inability to do anything about his own life, which consists mainly of railing at his children and playing poker with his boozy cronies.

These are both wonderful performances, with Baldwin's—coming on top of his superb movie-star parody in *Notting Hill*—opening up rich new territories for him to explore. But *Outside Providence* is full of glorious actor's moments, and may finally owe its success to them. One begins to think, if all these people believe so wholeheartedly in this enterprise, maybe I ought to as well.

Certainly it leads one to re-examine the premise of Peter and Bobby Farrelly. Up to now they have been our gross-out geniuses (*Dumb & Dumber, There's Something About Mary*), and Miramax wouldn't mind if you thought *Outside Providence* was more of the same. But adapting a novel by Peter and working with director Michael Corrente, the siblings, who also produced this film, maintain their best quality, which is a kind of unblinking frankness about our basic humanity, while slopping the bathroom jokes. You won't miss them at all.

VILLAGE VOICE, 9/7/99, p. 113, Amy Taubin

Cross *Rushmore* with Cheech and Chong and you might get *Outside Providence,* an unassuming fish-out-of-water, coming-of-age movie for stoners. Based on a novel by Peter Farrelly (of the Farrelly brothers) about growing up working-class in Rhode Island in the mid '70s, it's directed with great affection for the characters and milieu by fellow Rhode Islander Michael Corrente.

High-school senior Tim Dunphy (Shawn Hatosy) lives with his morose, bellicose father (Alec Baldwin), spunky, wheelchair-bound kid brother (Tommy Bone), and a three-legged dog in a weather-beaten house in Pawtucket. He spends most of his time getting wasted with his friends. An unfortunate accident leads to Tim being sent away to Cornwall Academy, a strict boarding school where, much to his surprise, he falls in with some hardcore potheads almost as congenial as the ones he grew up with. The only difference is that these boys are rich and college-bound. And when Jane (Amy Smart), the foxiest girl on campus (most of the time she seems like the only girl on campus), takes a shine to him, prep school no longer seems like jail. Jane likes to get wrecked every now and then, as long as it doesn't interfere with her studies.

Nothing much happens in *Outside Providence*, which is one of its charms, the other being its affirmative attitude toward marijuana. I think the message is that it's okay to party (or at least it was in the '70s) as long as you're not driving, but if you're so stoned all the time that your friends call you "Drugs," you probably won't live a long life.

Tim eventually proves himself by standing up for the woman he loves. I guess she knew from the moment she saw him misfire a Frisbee that he was the kind of guy who would watch her back. There's no other discernible reason for her to be enamored of him—especially not after he takes her home to meet his family and his friends, one of whom gets drunk and barfs all over Tim. That's the only vomit scene in *Outside Providence* which is quite restrained about body fluids. There is, however, one pretty funny sight gag involving masturbation and another in which someone does something truly disgusting with spaghetti.

Hatosy, who's almost never off the screen, has a refreshingly unaerobicized bod and a broad, mobile face distinguished by teeth that look like he borrowed them from one of Maurice Sendak's *Wild Things*. Scruffy without being threatening, he's the embodiment of Corrente's vision. Originally a theater director, Corrente has a no-frills cinematic style that relies on performance for energy and excitement. The disadvantage is that the actors, particularly the adults, work too hard. That's especially true of Baldwin, who's so determined to do a good job playing a character at some remove from his leading-man image that you can see his acting wheels grinding away. Watching Baldwin slumped in his lounge chair with a half-gallon of ice cream as he tries to get up his courage to say something more heartfelt to his son than "Bye, Dildo" just makes you realize what a great character actor someone like Dustin Hoffman is.

Corrente does have a knack for getting out of a scene at exactly the right moment, which is always a couple of beats earlier than you might expect. Those beats add up. An unassuming 95 minutes in length, *Outside Providence* doesn't wear out the small welcome it's won.

Also reviewed in:
CHICAGO TRIBUNE, 9/1/99, Tempo/p. 1, Mark Caro
NEW YORK TIMES, 9/1/99, p. E1, Janet Maslin
VARIETY, 8/30-9/5/99, p. 52, Dennis Harvey
WASHINGTON POST, 9/3/99, Weekend/p. 43, Desson Howe

OXYGEN

A Unapix Films release of a Curb Entertainment International Corporation presentation in association with Paddy Wagon Productions and Abandon Pictures. *Executive Producer:* Karen J. Lauder and Marcus Ticotin. *Producer:* Carol Curb Nemoy and Mike Curb. *Director:* Richard Shepard. *Screenplay:* Richard Shepard. *Director of Photography:* Sarah Cawley. *Editor:* Adam Lichtenstein. *Music:* Rolfe Kent. *Sound:* Dave Paterson. *Casting:* Laura Rosenthal and Ali Farrell. *Production Designer:* Rowena Rowling. *Art Director:* Betsy McDonald. *Costumes:* Barbara Presar. *Running time:* 92 minutes. *MPAA Rating:* R.

CAST: Maura Tierney (Madeline); Adrien Brody (Harry); Terry Kinney (Tim Kirkman); James Naughton (Clarke Hannon); Laila Robins (Frances Hannon); Paul Calderon (Jessie); Dylan Baker (Jackson).

LOS ANGELES TIMES, 11/5/99, Calendar/p. 14, Kevin Thomas

"Oxygen" could use a little fresh air. At its core it offers a raw, compelling confrontation between a troubled cop (Maura Tierney) and a clever psychopath (Adrien Brody), who is trying to force her to admit that she recognizes her dark side in him while she is trying to get him to tell her where he has buried a woman alive.

Tierney's Madeline and Brody's Harry are convincing and involving, and while the film is never less than tense—sometimes acutely so—much that surrounds this key situation smacks of the contrived, highlighted by an elaborate chase sequence through crowded Manhattan streets.

Writer-director Richard Shepard, whose whimsically offbeat "Linguini Incident" teamed Rosanna Arquette and David Bowie, has created challenging roles for his stars, but the rest of the film is a standard police procedural in which most of the supporting players are rather too obviously acting. Indeed, you're always aware of them hitting their marks, and too much of the movie plays like clenched, emphatically acted TV series melodrama.

But Tierney has the seen-it-all look and feel of a real policewoman, even if some of her moves are dubious. She and Brody, who makes Harry truly a man you love to hate, get the sparks flying in earnest, and this may be enough to make the movie worth the effort for some viewers. Harry is a gangly, smirky type whose hero is Houdini, and he's grabbed the wife (Laila Robins) of a rich man (James Naughton) in hope of shaking him down for a cool million. Things go drastically wrong for Harry, but he's still the only person who knows where he's buried his kidnap victim. Robins and Naughton are both effective.

Madeline has followed in the footsteps of her father, a cop legendary for perfectionism, which has left her so screwed up that she takes refuge in the bottle and in the arms of a sleazy-looking sadist (Olek Krups) with a penchant for stubbing out his lighted cigarettes on her arm. This tips off the alert Harry that Madeline may not be quite the totally in-charge professional she strives to project.

Certainly, "Oxygen" is fast-paced and professional, but the symbiotic relationship between cop and criminal has been explored in a more convincing context in the past, most notably Richard Tuggle's 1984 "Tightrope" with Clint Eastwood as a New Orleans policeman forced to admit that he has much in common with the sexual psychopath he is pursuing.

NEW YORK POST, 11/12/99, p. 58, Lou Lumenick

"Oxygen" is a middling psychological thriller containing a terrific performance by Adrien Brody as a psychopathic killer who taunts a troubled female NYPD detective.

The riveting Brody plays a changing but devious young man who will give his name only as Harry (after Harry Houdini). He abducts the wife (Laila Robins) of a wealthy art dealer (James Naughton) and buries her alive in a wooded area in upstate New York.

When Harry demands $1 million ransom, the husband goes to the cops. Led by the deeply troubled Detective Madeline Foster (Maura Tierney), they stake out the money drop at Houdini's tomb in Queens—and she nabs him following a high-speed chase into Manhattan.

But Harry won't tell the cops where he's stashed the wife, whose air supply is running out. During repeated questioning, he spots cigarette burns on Madeline's arm and senses a fellowship with the deeply guilty detective, who cheats on her husband (and supervisor) Capt. Tim Kirkman (Terry Kinney) in a sadomasochistic relationship.

Brody, who was so good as the young Bronx man suspected of being the serial killer in "Summer of Sam," is even better as the devious Harry. Tierney is OK in the less showy role of Madeline, who in the film's opening scene is seen chasing a suspect on an elevated subway train in a sequence that owes much to "The French Connection" but lacks that classic's flair.

Writer-director Richard Shepard keeps things moving at a fair clip, but he fails to develop Madeline's character or get us to believe the plot's more incredible contrivances. Would an NYPD captain really be allowed to supervise his own wife? Would a detective really be allowed to run a major kidnapping case, with minimal backup?

And would Madeline really be left alone to question a dangerous criminal like Harry, especially by authorities well aware of her psychological vulnerabilities?

"Oxygen" is not so breathlessly exciting that you won't be wondering.

VILLAGE VOICE, 11/16/99, p. 136, Amy Taubin

Oxygen is not strictly a serial-killer movie but a no-frills psychological thriller about a nasty sociopath who kidnaps a woman and buries her alive, knowing that there's enough air in her coffin for her to survive for 24 hours. His ostensible motive is ransom, but, in fact, he's turned on by the prospect of her dying a slow, horrible death. Directed by Richard Shepherd, *Oxygen* is so low-key as to seem like real life, which makes it disturbing in the extreme. It benefits from an excellent cast: Terry Kinney, James Naughton, and particularly Maura Tierney as a detective whose deep masochism makes her a doppelganger for the kidnapper. As the kidnapper, Adrien Brody is in another league entirely. Brody has gone deep inside himself, searching out empathy, pity, compassion, and guilt, and turning them off at the source, The killer is like a dark star—emitting light or heat even when he explodes in violence. If *Oxygen* gets more than a very limited release, Brody risks being typecast for life.

Also reviewed in:
NEW YORK TIMES, 11/12/99, p. E14, Lawrence Van Gelder
VARIETY, 5/10-16/99, p. 63, Ken Eisner

PAULINA

A Turbulent Arts release of a CineMamas production in association with the Banff Centre for the Arts. *Executive Producer:* S. Diamond. *Producer:* Jennifer Maytorena Taylor and Vicky Funari. *Director:* Vicky Funari. *Screenplay (Spanish with English subtitles):* Vicky Funard, Pauline Cruz Suarez, and Jennifer Maytorena Taylor. *Director of Photography:* Marie Christine Camus. *Editor:* Vicky Funari. *Music:* Pauline Oliveros. *Running time:* 88 minutes. *MPAA Rating:* Not Rated.

CAST: Paulina Cruz Suarez (Herself); Mathyselene Heredia Castillo (Paulina, Young Adult); Mariam Manzano Duran (Paulina, Age 8); Erika Isabel de la Ramirez (Paulina, Age 13);

Emigdia Hernandez Suarez (Franca); Rual Amado (Facundo); Rene Pereyra (Mauro); Maira Serbulo (Placida); Alicia Ortega (Luz Maria); Lolo Navarro (Woman on Bus); WITH: Carlos Arturo Corona; Mario Islas Alvarez; Jesus Barrios; Griselda Velazco Rojas; Reina de Luna de Marin; Josefina Hernandez Jeffroy.

NEW YORK POST, 4/2/99, p. 47, Jonathan Foreman

"Paulina," an earnest documentary about a Mexican woman's horrific childhood and escape to independence as a maid in Mexico City, is all but derailed by its amateurishness and film-school pretentiousness.

Fortunately, Paulina herself is so engaging a storyteller that the film holds your interest, despite all the unnecessary, self-conscious re-enactments inserted by director Vicky Funari to hammer home their point about misogynist oppression and poverty in rural Mexico.

Apparently, Paulina Cruz Suarez was traded as a kind of captive mistress to a local landowner by her own father at the age of 13.

After several brutal years as the landowner's youngest concubine, Paulina ran off to Mexico City where she worked as a maid for a series of wealthy families—including the family of the film's director.

She was able to achieve a life of genuine dignity and had a daughter of her own who has successfully become a member of the middle class.

The documentary follows Paulina back to the village of her childhood and re-creates an earlier visit, when she responded to a sexual assault on a bus by biting the offender's hand.

In a typical example of where this documentary goes wrong, Funari shows how one woman on the bus saw her as a hooker, a little girl pictured her as a female superhero and an American tourist pictured her as an Aztec deity.

Still, Paulina is clearly an extraordinary woman. And the combination of her narrative and the interviews with her relatives provides an extraordinary glimpse into a bizarrely cruel rural society.

NEWSDAY, 4/2/99, Part II/p. B11, Gene Seymour

A poem in Rita Dove's new collection yields the following observation: "Women invented misery/but we don't understand it./We hold it close and tell it everything, cradle the ache/until it seeps in and he's/gone just like the wind when the air stands still."

Though this stanza wasn't written with the subject of "Paulina" in mind, you can't help hearing its echoes as you follow one woman's attempt to come to terms with the traumatic theft of her childhood. And the near-loss of her self-respect.

For her first film, writer-director Vicky Funari found an irresistible subject in the life story of her one-time domestic, Paulina Cruz Suarez, a middle-aged woman who escaped to Mexico City from a horrific upbringing in a poor village. A freak accident caused the 8-year-old Paulina to injure her genitals, which gave her parents the notion to, in effect, sell her off to a rich local in exchange for property rights.

Paulina's own story is interspersed with re-enactments of this nightmarish process and all the bad stuff that happened afterward: her isolation from others in town, including her family; repeated physical and sexual abuse by her polygamous, thuggish "owner," and finally her escape, as a teenager, from the town.

The reconstructed sequences are plainly staged, but presented in a near-surreal fashion that gives Paulina's story the texture of cutting-edge Latin-American fiction. Such a tone gives the film flavor, but it also comes perilously close to taking the edge off the terrors being depicted.

Which is why the most intriguing sequences show the real Paulina returning to the town to find that not only has the quality of life remained impoverished and perilous, but that many of those still living, including her parents, are in anguished denial over the damages inflicted on her.

What is even more fascinating is Paulina's discovery that the wealthy property owner responsible for so many agonizing childhood memories is given such a small, sorry-looking grave.

This is one of the ironies that Funari's film sometimes applies with a trowel. But it also effectively amplifies the triumphs of Paulina's own life self-sufficiency, pride in her work as a housekeeper and an intelligent daughter with a mind of her own. Given machismo's dreary persistence, manifested in callow form by the daughter's would-be fiance, she'll need every bit of that independence.

VILLAGE VOICE, 4/6/99, p. 130, Yael Schacher

Forty years after escaping the sexual abuse of the local landowner and the disdain of her community, Paulina Cruz Suarez, a middle-aged Mexican maid, returns to her impoverished village, along with director Vicky Funari, to "make a film of her life." The result is an exploration of identity that combines documentary footage with impressionistic reenactments of Paulina's childhood trauma. Her past is almost too horrible to be true and made more difficult to watch by Funari's heavy-handed treatment. In one segment, snapshots of Paulina are accompanied by a voice-over asking, "How do I define myself?" The film has moments of psychological complexity—Funari astutely presents the desires for revenge and reconciliation that complicate Paulina's relationships with her parents and her lovers. Perhaps the film's most powerful message is that the sexual inequalities of Paulina's youth persist. As an interview with Paulina's daughter's machismo-ridden boyfriend suggests, the wounds of an earlier generation have not yet healed.

Also reviewed in:
CHICAGO TRIBUNE, 10/22/99, Friday/p. G, Michael Wilmington
NEW YORK TIMES, 4/2/99, p. E16, Anita Gates
VARIETY, 4/20-26/98, p. 48, Howard Feinstein

PAYBACK

A Paramount Pictures release of an Icon production. *Executive Producer:* Stephen McEveety. *Producer:* Bruce Davey. *Director:* Brian Helgeland. *Screenplay:* Brian Helgeland and Terry Hayes. *Based on the novel "The Hunter" by:* Richard Stark. *Director of Photography:* Ericson Core. *Editor:* Kevin Stitt. *Music:* Chris Boardman. *Music Editor:* Jim Harrison and Michael T. Ryan. *Sound:* Geoffrey Lucius Patterson and (music) Frank Wolf, Tom Vicari, and John Richards. *Sound Editor:* Michael Chandler, Ben Wilkins, Miguel Rivera, Keith Bilderbeck, and John K. Adams. *Casting:* Marion Dougherty. *Production Designer:* Richard Hoover. *Art Director:* Troy Sizemore. *Set Designer:* Adam Scher and Gina B. Cranham. *Set Decorator:* Sandy Struth and Daniel B. Clancy. *Special Effects:* Bob Stoker. *Costumes:* Ha Nguyen. *Make-up:* Beauty Bucket, Julie Hewett, Medusah, Mindy Hall, and Jennifer Bell. *Stunt Coordinator:* Mic Rodgers. *Running time:* 110 minutes. *MPAA Rating:* R.

CAST: Mel Gibson (Porter); Gregg Henry (Val Resnick); Maria Bello (Rosie); David Paymer (Stegman); Bill Duke (Detective Hicks); Deborah Kara Unger (Lynn Porter); John Glover (Phil); William Devane (Mr. Carter); Lucy Alexis Liu (Pearl); Jack Conley (Detective Leary); Kris Kristofferson (Bronson); Mark Alfa (Johnny's Friend 2); Kwame Amoaku (Radioman); Justin Ashforth (Michael, the Bartender); Len Bajenski (Fairfax Bodyguard 1); Kate Buddeke (Counter Girl); Price Carson (Bronson's Heavy 1); Roddy Chiong (Chow's Thug 2); Art Cohan (Bronson's Heavy 2); Andrew Cooper (Whipping Boy); James Deuter (Tailor); Doc Duhame (Fatboy); David Dunard (Doctor); Nathan Effron (Johnny's Friend); Tom Equin (Razor Clean 1); Brian Heinberg (Bartender 2); Alex Henteloff (Varrick's Manager); Jeff Imada (Chow's Bodyguard); Michael Ingram (Chow's Thug 1); Robert Kim (Chow's Courier); Robert Kurcz (Oakwood Arms Manager); Turk Muller (Black Suit); Chet Nichols (Oakwood Arms Tough 1); George O'Mara (Driver); Yasen Peyankov (Panhandler); Ed Pfeifer (Ed Johnson); Katrina Phillips (Teller); Freddy Rodriguez (Punk Messenger); Michael Skewes (Fairfax Bodyguard 2); Alex Skuby (Oakwood Arms Tough 2); Trevor St. John (Johnny Bronson); Lee Stepp (Bar Patron); Daniel Patrick Sullivan (Razor Clean 2); Tedd Taskey (Waiter); Manu Tupou (Pawnbroker); Marc Vann (Gray); James Coburn (Justin Fairfax).

CHRISTIAN SCIENCE MONITOR, 2/5/99, p. 15, David Sterritt

"If you don't understand it, get rid of it," says an ignorant thug in "Payback," the new Mel Gibson movie.

The villain is telling a henchman to eliminate a possible enemy, but his words reveal the formula for this kind of filmmaking.

Every plot twist is hammered home with the subtlety of a sledgehammer, and anything that might deepen or enrich the picture—anything that might require a smidgen of thought or attention from the audience, in other words—is rubbed out by a burst of violence and nastiness.

This is hardly new territory for Hollywood, or for Gibson, whose box-office clout is largely based on the "Lethal Weapon" series.

But he's also made movies like "Hamlet" and "The Man Without a Face," which showed signs of wanting to raise the level of American moviemaking. What's his goal this time around: to sink the very ship he tried to launch? A film as vicious as "Payback" raises serious questions about the priorities such an influential star ought to be cultivating.

Gibson plays a criminal named Porter who's been filled with rage against his ex-wife and former partner ever since they robbed him of $70,000 and left him for dead. Determined to get the money back and not a penny more, since his "principles" wouldn't allow that, he relentlessly tracks them down, casually killing anyone standing in his way. Murder is commonplace in this kind of movie, of course, but "Payback" adds hefty doses of torture and sadomasochism to the bargain. It's hard to remember a mainstream picture that has aimed so much gleeful mayhem at women.

The movie wouldn't be worth any attention if so many high-profile talents weren't involved in it. Brian Helgeland, the director and cowriter, helped script "L.A. Confidential" two years ago. The interesting cast ranges from James Coburn and David Paymer to Kris Kristofferson and Deborah Kara Unger plus Gibson, who certainly can't claim he did this because he needed the money.

Perhaps the excesses of "Payback" reflect a momentary miscalculation by film-industry professionals who will recognize their mistake and hurry back to a more responsible course. If it turns out to signal a new trend for more pictures where even the advertising prods us to, "root for the bad guy," Hollywood will have a lot to answer for.

LOS ANGELES TIMES, 2/4/99, Calendar/p. 1, Kenneth Turan

"Parker steals. Parker kills. It's a living." Or so claimed the paperback blurb copy for the series of drop-dead hard-boiled novels about a nerveless professional criminal that Donald Westlake wrote in the 1960s and '70s under the Richard Stark pseudonym.

With an amoral antihero who said, in a calmer moment, "I'm going to chew up his heart and spit it into the gutter," the Parker novels struck a nerve with filmmakers; even Jean-Luc Godard apparently made a version with Anna Karina as the Parker character. The most famous Parker adaptation, taken from "The Hunter," the first novel in the series, was the 1967 John Boorman-directed "Point Blank," starring Lee Marvin in a bravura performance as the relentless Walker, a man preternaturally determined to revenge himself on his betrayers and to recover a sum of money that was owed him.

Writer-director Brian Helgeland is also, apparently, a Parker fan, for his first film after his career-making co-writing job on "L.A. Confidential" is "Payback," taken from the same novel that "Point Blank" was based on and starring Mel Gibson as an amoral antihero named Porter who, yes, is bound and determined to get what's owed him no matter what.

To his credit, Helgeland was not intimidated by "Point Blank," a film many critics consider one of the high points of the decade. As "L.A. Confidential" proved, he understands the genre inside out, and in its opening segments, "Payback" has the makings of that rarest of ventures, an adaptation that is true to the spirit of the original as well as its own time and place.

But as "Payback" wends its way toward its conclusion, its promise dissipates and its pleasures wane. It's undone not so much by the shadow of Lee Marvin falling heavily on it (which it does) as by the twin obstacles of big star image and, more to the point, excessive violence. To be entertained by "Payback," you have to be willing to endure the agonizing beatings and torture it inflicts on its characters, and that is not a price worth paying.

"Payback" does manage to start auspiciously, with Porter, "a real Cro-Magnon-looking bastard," roaming the streets of the film's gray, washed-out world. He's looking first for Lynn (Deborah Kara Unger), the wife who was disloyal, and then for Val (Gregg Henry), the partner who betrayed him, left him for dead and used his money to gain entry into the "outfit," the kind of crime organization that was called the "syndicate" once upon a time.

Though most of his career has been spent in conventional heroic roles, Gibson did play a revenge-minded individual in his Australian debut, "Mad Max." And in the early going, he does a convincing job as the lethal, implacable Porter—someone without a moral qualm in his body, an irresistible force you can't even imagine withstanding.

Helgeland's gift for nasty and sarcastic humor helps here as well, and, once we are in on the joke, it can be amusing to see the nominal hard guys Parker meets up with think they are tough enough to take him on. Parker can be momentarily outsmarted, but he can't be out-toughed, and his determination to wreak untold havoc just to get what's owed him never ceases to amaze his adversaries.

In the course of his quest, Porter runs into a crooked taxi operator (David Paymer); a crooked cop who wants in on his take (Bill Duke); a mistress of pain (Lucy Liu); and Rosie (Maria Bello of "ER" and "Permanent Midnight"), a call girl who, hey, just might have been the love of his life.

As Parker did in "The Hunter" and Walker did in "Point Blank," Porter also finds that the higher he gets in the outfit, the more it starts to resemble any major corporation, peopled by executives like Carter (William Devane) and Bronson (Kris Kristofferson), who are not used to his less than subtle methods.

But as Porter works his brutal way up the corporate ladder, the balance in "Payback" shifts and the film becomes less about humor and more about gut-clutching violence. It's interesting to compare this with "Point Blank," a movie that felt violent but used unconventional scenes, like Walker terrifying someone with a hair-raising car ride, to get across the same points that "Payback" can't manage without beating almost everyone on screen, plus the audience, to an unpleasant pulp. Times certainly have changed, and not at all for the best.

Also changed, apparently, is how Helgeland envisioned the movie. As has been reported in the media, reworking of the film was done by Terry Hayes, an Australian writer who shared screen credit with Helgeland and has worked with Gibson before.

What's likely, though unconfirmed, is that the star, despite the film's "Get ready to root for the bad guy" tag line, was uncertain about playing so much of an unapologetic savage and had both Porter's inhuman personality and how his story ends softened. Too bad he didn't think to soften some of the excessive violence while he was at it.

NEW YORK, 2/22/99, p. 114, Peter Rainer

As Porter, the thug-on-a-mission in the startlingly funny *Payback*, Mel Gibson is as mad as he's been since he was Max. His bootblacked hair is color-coordinated with his black jackets and blacker mood. He's a human projectile blasting into crime's inner sanctums. Shot and left for dead after a heist by his double-crossing partner, Val (Gregg Henry), he thinks of only two things: revenge and getting back his share—$70,000. The insanity of setting himself up as the walking dead for such a paltry sum never penetrates Porter's brainpan. It's a matter of honor that he retrieve the money; it's also a matter of honor that he not ask for a penny more.

Brian Helgeland, the gifted screenwriter who wrote the undervalued Gibson-Julia Roberts thriller *Conspiracy Theory* and cowrote, with Curtis Hanson, *L.A. Confidential*, makes his directorial debut with *Payback*. His source material is the same book—*The Hunter*, written by Donald Westlake under the pseudonym Richard Stark—that John Boorman used in 1967 for *Point Blank*. Boorman's film was a flagrant pulp hallucination, with big-limbed Lee Marvin manfully striding through crime-world corridors; with his blockhead and broad, flared nostrils, he was like a cartoon brought to furious life, the Terminator with a heartbeat.

Gibson takes a different tack. He's more like an avenging angel made flesh. When we first see Porter, he's stretched out in a squalid room as a drunken quack takes bullet slugs out of his back. He survives, but he should be dead. The key to Porter's fearlessness is that in a sense, he already sees himself as history. Rosie (Maria Bello), the hooker from his past whom Porter strives to protect, knows as much. "All those stories about you being dead are true," she says to him. "You're just too thickheaded to admit it."

Porter has his perversities: We're never entirely sure if this avenger isn't on his rampage in order to get the crap beat out of him. Most of the characters in *Payback* have a disconcerting ability to morph back and forth between sadist and masochist. When Val invites a dominatrix hooker (Lucy Liu) into his scuzzball boudoir, she greets him with a gratefully accepted smash to the solar plexus; he returns the compliment, and then Porter enters the fray. The thin red line between gangland retribution and S&M is erased in *Payback:* At times, we might be watching a Three Stooges movie for the whips-and-chains set. (David Paymer, who turns in a terrific cameo as a small-time hood, actually looks like the Stooges' Larry.) The atmosphere is almost comically lurid, and the mob honchos who successively face off against Porter—played by William Devane, an unbilled James Coburn, and Kris Kristofferson—have boom-box voices.

Payback has had a troubled production history. Near the end of filming, Helgeland reportedly walked off the set rather than tenderize, at Gibson's behest, Porter's character at the fade-out; Terry Hayes, who scripted several of the *Mad Max* movies, was brought in and shares screenwriting credit with the director. Gibson may have backed off from making Porter unrelentingly unredeeming, but what we get is still pretty truculent. And vicious. Despite evidence of tampering—the henchman played by John Glover, for example, has a wisp of screen time—Helgeland has come up with a crazy-quilt horror show that's often funniest when it's at its most ghastly. Even allowing for Gibson's star power, it may be difficult for squeamish audiences to absorb Helgeland's barrage. They may take offense because he's crafted a killing comedy. Quentin Tarantino makes killing comedies, too, but he clues us that his carnage is too, too hip; his movies are about how swell we look when we're drawing blood. Helgeland is just as movie-mad as Tarantino—the unnamed Gotham in this film, with its sinister Deco power buildings, owes a lot to *Batman,* and the dialogue is a *film noir* compendium—but he isn't a smart aleck about it. He bumps together the suspense thriller and the screwball farce with moody-blues melodrama and even Hong Kong-style free-for-all because he wants to hear what kind of clang they make. Porter may be relentlessly onetrack-minded, but Helgeland goes every which way, and that's what's exciting about *Payback*. He realizes instinctively, as did Boorman in 1967, that you can't make a thriller in the same old ways. If it doesn't get all over the place, it doesn't belong in your face.

NEW YORK POST, 2/5/99, p. 54, Jonathan Foreman

"Payback" is the film equivalent of Frankenstein's reanimated monster: It has all the freshness you'd expect of something assembled from the body parts of other movies. Except for a few good S&M jokes, everything in "Payback" has been lifted whole from a better film.

Its corporate mobsters, a hero who eliminates enemies by casually flicking his cigarette onto spilled gasoline and grisly comic-book violence played for laughs (you may have seen earrings ripped out before, but what about a nose ring?) add up to a cheesy mess.

Mel Gibson plays Porter, one of those middle-aged, small-time robbers with superhuman fighting abilities and GQ looks. Ripped off and left for dead by colleague Val (the excellent Gregg Henry), who's in cahoots with his own junkie wife, Porter returns to town to get his money back. He ends up battling a syndicate of WASP mobsters led by Kris Kristofferson, William Devane and James Coburn.

The believability threshold for any thriller isn't high, but "Payback" has trouble even with that. While Mel Gibson's character looks and dresses like the zillionaire in "Ransom," he lives like the cabby in "Conspiracy Theory," in a scuzzy little apartment, and goes only for hooker types. This is convenient, as the only women in the movie are hookers.

There have been rumors that Gibson took over from Brian Helgeland as director of "Payback," and the movie's tone does vary wildly, as if two incompatible sensibilities were at work. But whoever directed it was operating from an awful script credited to Helgeland (who co-wrote "L.A. Confidential," but who also scripted "The Postman" and "Conspiracy Theory") and Terry Hayes.

But the rotten screenplay doesn't excuse the movie's crude overreliance on music, sound effects (souped up so that each punch lands like a watermelon on asphalt) and pointless stylistic gestures.

Not only is "Payback" set, like "Seven," in a crumbling, art deco city with no name (and tinted blue rather than yellow, to make everything look sorta sad and noirish), but all the cars are from the '80s and the telephones have dials rather than buttons.

It doesn't help that Gibson—miscast in a role tailor-made for someone like Bruce Willis or George Clooney—treats his lines as if they had Philip Marlowe punch and James Bond wit. In the voiceover, he makes his voice all deep and gravelly, and the narration is so portentous, it come right out of "The Naked Gun."

Gibson's performance seems worse than it is thanks to the presence and skill of fine supporting actors such as Devane, Kristofferson, Coburn, David Paymer and Bill Duke. They make the most of the material, as does Lucy Liu (of "Ally McBeal"), in her film debut as a fierce dominatrix/whore/gangster.

NEWSDAY, 2/5/99, Part II/p. B3, Jack Mathews

At first blush, Brian Helgeland's "Payback" looks every bit a match for John Boorman's classic 1967 film, "Point Blank." Both are adapted from Donald E. Westlake's "The Hunter" (written under the pseudonym Richard Stark), and both star lovable actor-rogues as principled revenge killers. "Point Blank" had Lee Marvin, "Payback" has Mel Gibson.

But we aren't too far into "Payback" when we begin to sense the corrupting influence of the marketing and star-dominated New Hollywood, where the guiding principles are "Nothing succeeds like excess" and "Silence is leaden."

"Point Blank" was violent, but its fistfights and shoot-outs, done in highly stylized black and white, were kid stuff compared to the new film's noisy, blood-splattered array of killings, explosions and torture beatings, and its use of sadomasochistic sex as a running gag. "Payback" is "Point Blunderbuss."

Westlake's novel and the two adaptations tell the story of a thief who will stop at nothing to recover his share of an ill-gotten fortune taken from him by his wife and her lover, who'd double-crossed him and left him for dead. He doesn't want more than he has coming to him, nor will he settle for anything less.

Marvin played this character with the expressions and flexibility of the Sphinx, giving one of the great near-silent performances. Gibson, while more restrained than usual, is too much of a motormouth wise guy to let opportunities slide. His Porter is not only a stand-up guy, but a stand-up comic, as well.

"Do you have a light?" Porter asks a man lying at his feet.

"No," says the man, leaking from two bullet holes Porter had already put in him.

"Then what good are you?" Porter says, shooting him in the head.

Helgeland, an Oscar-winning screenwriter ("L.A. Confidential") making his feature film directing debut, seems to have intended what would be, at least partly, tongue-in-cheek film noir. Though the film is set in '70s Chicago, some of the dialogue is '30s Warner Bros. A gun is called a "roscoe" (better than gat, I suppose), and at one point, Porter tells two thugs to keep their hands up or "I'll drill you."

The narration, read by Gibson while apparently attempting to swallow the microphone, has an overripe Raymond Chandler flavor to it, and the bad guys standing between Porter and his $75,000 are cardboard caricatures. Since they exist to be mowed down by Porter, they're more like ducks in a shooting gallery.

With the exception of Kris Kristofferson, who overplays the cynical top mob boss, the actors cast in the traditional villain roles are mugging so badly it's a surprise they don't wink at the camera. Playing the black hats are Gregg Henry, as Porter's errant associate and wife stealer; David Paymer, as the head of a taxi ring of drug dealers; William Devane, as a local ganglord, and James Coburn, as a man more into the perks of crime than the deeds.

If you remember "Point Blank," you'll recall that Marvin was ably supported by costar Angie Dickinson, as a feisty old girlfriend enlisted to help him on his quest. That role has been down-sized to a passive love interest here and is filled by Mario Bello ("ER's" Dr. Del Amico). In a badly conceived comic subplot, Lucy Liu ("Ally McBeal's" Ling Woo) plays a dominatrix for whom no amount of violence is too much of a good thing.

As if all that weren't enough, Helgeland adds a pair of corrupt cops (Bill Duke, Jack Conley) and a gang of Chinese thugs. If each of the people killed in the move had chipped in a hundred bucks, they might have paid Porter his $75,000 and saved themselves—and us—a lot of grief.

SIGHT AND SOUND, 4/99, p. 53, Nick Roddick

Criminals Porter and Resnick rob some Chinese gangsters; Porter's wife Lynn drives the getaway car. But Lynn and Resnick betray and shoot Porter, leaving him for dead. They take off with the $140,000 proceeds. However, Porter survives and decides to get back his share of the money and take revenge on Resnick. His first stop is Lynn, whom he tries to cure of her heroin addiction. But she overdoses on a hidden stash. Porter tracks down the heroin's supplier, Stegman. While confronting Stegman, he attracts the attention of two corrupt cops, Hicks and Leary, who decide to keep tabs on Porter and take the money if he finds it. Porter links up with ex-girlfriend Rosie, a callgirl who works for the same syndicate—"the Outfit"—which Resnick used the money to buy into.

Rosie tells Porter where to find Resnick, which he does, demanding his share of the money Resnick enlists the help of Outfit boss Carter and alerts the Chinese gangs to Porter's whereabouts through his dominatrix Pearl. Porter is rescued from the Chinese by Hicks and Leary. He eliminates Resnick and Carter, and kidnaps the son of Outfit boss Bronson. Pursued by the Chinese and watched by Hicks and Leary, Porter closes in on his $70,000 against steadily increasing odds.

"Unattractive rehash of *Point Blank* with much more gratuitous violence." So reads the tenth edition of *Halliwell's Film Guide* entry on *The Outfit*, John Flynn's 1973 movie adapted from the novel *The Hunter*, which had also inspired John Boorman's 1967 film. Frankly, *Payback* deserves the same one-line dismissal, even given the talents involved and the handful of gracenotes that make it sporadically watchable. Like its two predecessors, it abandons the novel's title for one which stresses the story's elemental side but without aspiring to any of the metaphyscial trappings that elevate Boorman's movie.

Accompanied by a voiceover that rivals Nick Nolte's in *The Thin Red Line* for world-weariness, Mel Gibson strides through the bleached-out colours of the all purpose US city (actually Chicago), meting out his own brand of justice in a series of locations—seedy pool halls, ornate gangster hotels—which belong more to *film noir* than to reality. If the same could be said of Gibson's character and the handling of the action by director Brian Helgeland, *Payback* would be a much better film. Both star and director seem to be more interested in playing off perceptions of Gibson's on-screen persona than in actually telling the story, which lurches along from one violent set piece to the next. "No More Mr Nice Guy" is the promotional tag for the film, and Gibson rams the point home in the early scenes, stealing money from a beggar, cigarettes from a waitress and the wherewithal to begin his vendetta from an anonymous passer-by whose pocket he picks.

But that is only the beginning, as Gibson's Porter whacks, slices and drills holes in anyone coming between him and his money, while the Outfit and its thugs reciprocate with a series of even more unpleasant acts (one involves a large hammer and two of Gibson's toes). But while Helgeland helped to write the book as far as post-modernist *film noir* is concerned (he co-scripted *LA Confidential* with Curtis Hanson), he keeps falling off the log when it comes to balancing violent action with ironic lightness of touch. Even Sergio Leone (scarcely the most understated of directors) did a less heavy-handed job with Henry Fonda's fall from grace in *Once Upon a Time in the West* (1968).

All that's left is: a series of occasionally witty one-liners; over-the-top performances by Brian De Palma regular Gregg Henry as a sexually hung-up psychopath and *Ally McBeal*'s Lucy Alexis Liu as his leather-clad dominatrix; a string of character actors either underused (Bill Duke, Deborah Kara Unger) or simply uncredited (James Coburn as an entertainingly epicene mob boss who winces when a cohort spills some of Porter's blood on his suit); some Chinese gangsters midway between the racism of Cimino's *Year of the Dragon* and the knockabout of Laurel & Hardy; and the running gag of Porter trying to make the Outfit understand that he is only after his share of the loot: $70,000, not the whole $140,000 that Resnick paid them. Imagine Gibson's resigned rolling of the eyes—one of the actor's trademark tics—as yet another hood says

"$140,000", add in a lot of heavy-handed gore and you pretty much have *Payback*. Everyone—including Gibson—deserves better.

Also reviewed in:
CHICAGO TRIBUNE, 2/5//99, Friday/p. A, Michael Wilmington
NATION, 3/1/99, p. 35, Stuart Klawans
NEW YORK TIMES, 2/5/99, p. E14, Stephen Holden
VARIETY, 2/8-14/99, p. 74, Emanuel Levy
WASHINGTON POST, 2/5/99, p. C1, Stephen Hunter
WASHINGTON POST, 2/5/99, Weekend/p. 39, Michael O'Sullivan

PERFECT BLUE

A Manga Entertainment release of a Rex Entertainment Co. Ltd. production in association with Kotobuki Seihan Printing Co. Ltd./Asahi Broadcasting Corp./Fangs Co. Ltd. *Executive Producer:* Koshiro Kanda and Yuichi Tsurmi. *Producer:* Hitomi Nakagaki, Yoshihisa Ishihara, Yutaka Toga, Masao Maruyama, and Hiroaki Inoue. *Director:* Satoshi Kon. *Screenplay:* Sadayuki Murai. *Based on the novel by:* Yoshikazu Takeuchi. *Based on the character design by:* Hisashi Eguchi. *Director of Photography:* Hisao Shirai. *Editor:* Harutoshi Ogata. *Music:* Masahiro Ikumi and Tetsu Saito. *Choreographer:* Izumi. *Sound:* Masafumi Mima. *Character Design:* Hideki Hamazu and Satoshi Kon. *Animation:* Hideki Hamazu. *Running time:* 80 minutes. *MPAA Rating:* Not Rated.

VOICES: (*Japanese Version*) Junko Iwao (Mima); Rika Matsumoto (Rumi); Tsuji Shinpachi (Takodoro); Masaaki Okura (Uchida); Yosuke Akimoto (Tejima); Akira Shioya (Shibuya); Hideyuki Hori (Sakuragi); Emi Shinohara (Eri); Masashi Ehara (Murano); Kiyonobu Harita (Director); Toru Hurusawa (Yada); Shiho Niyama (Rei); Emiko Furukawa (Yukiko); Shocker Ono (M.C.); Makato Kitano (Special Appearance); Kaori Minami (Special Appearance); (*English Language Version*) Ruby Marlow; Wendee Lee; Gil Starberry; Lia Sargent; Steve Bulen; James Lyon; Frank Buck; David Lucas; Jimmy Theodore; Elliott Reynolds; Sparky Thornton; Bambi Darro; Melissa Williamson; Dylan Tully; Kermit Beachwood; Sam Stong; Carol Stanzione; Ty Webb; Billy Regan; Darl Mackenzie; George C. Cole; Syd Fontana; Sven Nosgard; Robert Marx; Devon Michaels; Robert Wicks; Mattie Rondo.

NEW YORK POST, 8/20/99, p. 60, Jonathan Foreman

"Perfect Blue," a feature-length adult cartoon from Japan, is primarily interesting as anthropology, thanks to its combination of brutal, graphically depicted violence and a creepy, vaguely pedophile sexuality.

It's a common combination in Japanese adult comics, by which standards this psychological thriller's faintly repulsive fixation with miniskirted teenage girls, rape and grisly murder are actually relatively mild.

Mima Kirigoe is the miniskirted lead singer of Cham, a moderately successful sugar 'n' spice all-girl pop group. She has enormous eyes, long legs and we keep seeing her little white underpants every time she sits down on her bed.

Under pressure from her sleazy manager, Mima gives up pop idoldom for small parts on the small screen, much to the dismay of her devoted fans.

As Mima's career on TV slowly progresses, one of those disappointed fans starts sending anonymous threatening letters, and then a letter bomb.

At the same time Mima discovers a home page on the Web (purporting to be run by her) that contains information that could only be known by someone spying on her. She also starts seeing a doppleganger who berates her for leaving the world of music.

Nevertheless, Mima is persuaded by her manager to pose nude for a magazine and then to take part in a graphic gang rape scene. Soon after, the porn photographer and then the director of her TV program are brutally murdered. And Mima finds bloody clothes in her closet...

Did she herself stab her own director in the eyes with a screwdriver? Or was it the weirdo with a gray face she kept seeing hanging around the set? Did the murder really happen or is she going crazy and confusing the life of her TV character with her real life?

It's too easy to play the game of "was that whole episode real or was it a fantasy/a nightmare/a scene from her show?" in an animated film, and after a while the device becomes irritating and the plot incoherent. And the ending, when it comes, is unbelievable, even by the standards of the genre.

The animation is neither beautiful nor as imaginative as the cyberpunk landscapes of "Akira," although the maker of that film, Katsuhiro Otomo, is listed as a special adviser to the production.

NEWSDAY, 8/20/99, Part II/p. B7, Gene Seymour

One of the tastier ironies of this all-but-spent movie summer is that the full-length animated features have been more sophisticated than most, if not all, of their live-action counterparts. Though not as polished a product as "Tarzan" or "The Iron Giant," "Perfect Blue" may well be the most sophisticated in execution.

This very adult Japanese anime may sometimes seem a tad too sophisticated for its own good. Still, those expecting to see a longer, naughtier version of a "Sailor Moon" or "Pokmon" episode with banalities intact will be surprised by both the intensity and complexity of its storytelling.

Indeed, it's hard to imagine too many Hollywood movies, live-action or not, dealing with the stiff dues of contemporary pop celebrity as vigorously as this tale of Mima Kirigoe, lead vocalist for a girl group who decides to leave bubble-gum rock behind and take her chances as a third-tier actress on a TV soap opera.

The pressures of establishing herself in a new field are bad enough for Mima.

What only makes things worse is that she's being stalked by a sallow-faced, dead-eyed fan who calls himself "Mimamaniac" and deplores the new turn her career has taken. What especially ticks him off is the way Mima is so intent on making a name for herself in the grown-up world that she's willing to sacrifice her wholesome image for strip scenes and nude photo layouts for slick magazines.

Soon, things start to get really weird. A Web site run by the Mimamaniac transmits false quotes attributed to her, but also frighteningly true facts about her private life. Then a couple of people involved with her new career are found stabbed to death. The lines between the emotionally tortured, physically endangered character Mima plays on TV and her real life begin to bleed together in disorienting ways. And then, there are these disturbing visits in the night by Mima's erstwhile frilly pink persona who apparently wants the real Mima hacked to pieces.

No, this is definitely not Saturday-morning fare. Nor, for that matter, is it merely a live-action story done with pictures. Director Satoshi Kon makes full use of the anime style to goose the suspense and to exploit the layers-within-layers motifs of Sadayuki Murai's screenplay. Soon, Mima's own doubts about the reality around her become our doubts as well. The hallucinatory shifts in tone and locale coalesce into a kind of running commentary on the nature of Japanese animation.

The movie keeps messing with your head so much that you forget, until its climax, that the solution to the mystery was revealed at or near the very start. Which will bother no one except the narrative purists in the audience.

"Perfect Blue" may not be perfectly made. But it's a surprise package where surprises leap out at you with jolting regularity.

SIGHT AND SOUND, 8/99, p. 50, Jonathan Romney

Mima, one third of the girl vocal group Cham, shocks her fans by leaving to pursue an acting career. But her role in television soap *Double Bind* proves disappointing, and she begins to miss her popstar past. On a fan's website, she is shocked to read what is supposedly her own diary. Mima is plagued by hallucinations of her former pop self, and is stalked by obsessive fan Uchida, aka "Mimaniac", who sees the new Mima as an impostor. As a soap actress, Mima acquires a raunchy new image that further alienates her old fans.

Meanwhile, people involved with her new career are murdered. Increasingly cracking up and haunted by her former self, Mima begins to fear she is herself responsible for the killings. Uchida is killed, but as the series ends and Mima is acclaimed as an actress, she has a further showdown with her vengeful former self—which proves all along to have been her confidante Rumi, her manager Tadokoro's business associate. Visiting the deluded Rumi in hospital, Mima can at last accept her own identity.

Perfect Blue could almost be the Kylie Minogue story in reverse. Its heroine Mima abandons pop for a career in a television soap, not only alienating the male fans of her squeaky-clean, white-knickered past, but causing her former self to return as a vengeful succubus. The film's most telling images of fan fantasy revolve around Mimaniac, a dead-eyed ghoul cupping his hand to make it seem as if Mima is dancing in his palm.

In narrative terms, Satoshi Kon's *anime* doesn't wholly make sense. The phantom Mima seems to be at once the ex-singer's own psychic projection and someone else. But *Perfect Blue* has much to say about fame as an addiction for star and audience—a mutual dependency heightened these days by the internet. To know herself, Mima has to read her own diary as compiled by a psychotic fan. In essence, *Perfect Blue* is a traditional *doppelganger* nightmare. Mima's artificial pop self one of three near-identical fluffy Lolitas that comprise Cham—revolts by taking on a life of its own, and all Mima can do is guiltily suffer its taunts, while trying to exorcise it in her new soap role. It's no accident that Mima's television character is dressed as a soft-porn version of the Cham look in her rape scene.

Satoshi and screenwriter Sadayuki Murai develop a complex structure for Mima's psychosis, interleaving layers of the real with Mima's dreams and the appropriately named show *Double Bind* in one scene from the series, it seems that Mima's character Yoko is suffering from multiple-personality disorder, and is convinced that she's really Mima a baffling moment soon revealed as only a provisional representation of Mima's predicament. Elsewhere, the carpet is pulled from under our feet several times in quick succession. A traumatic scene proves to be a dream as Mima wakes, but that reality is collapsed in turn as Mima wakes yet again in a replay of the same scene—a brilliant use of the hallucinatory repetitiveness of commercial animation.

The reality-dream divide is memorably worked out in the images. Satoshi—a manga artist who worked on *Roujin Z*—goes for a flat, flimsy look, often reducing background figures to faceless cut-outs, but dropping in jolts of visual complexity, quoting pop and manga images as manufactured product. At one point an excessively baroque flash of manga art—a generic big-eyed space girl—invades the screen, looking much more three-dimensional than the film's real world. The execution becomes a complex metaphor for Mima's reality, in which the everyday becomes a colour-drained place of exile from the pop universe. This dilemma is resolved in a bizarre conclusion, as Mima simply exchanges one kind of stardom for another: a career in soaps hardly seems the best way to get a purchase on reality. Even so, *Perfect Blue* is a delirious, culturally astute invention, and you can't help thinking it would make instructive viewing for former Spice Girl Geri Halliwell.

VILLAGE VOICE, 8/24/99, p. 122, Gary Dauphin

Hyped since its Japanese release in 1997 as a movie Hitchcock could have made, Satoshi Kon's *Perfect Blue* is a deliriously impressive, albeit sometimes overblown, animation. Telling the freaky tale of a cute-as-a-button, B-list pop singer named Mima, *Blue* immediately breaks out of character, with Mima interrupting a concert to announce she's decided to pursue a career as a serious actress. Her choice has a downbeat ring that sets the tone for the film: her agents bicker, the invasive fans behind an encyclopedic Mima Web site howl, and our hopeful heroine retreats to a tiny, teddy bear-strewn apartment to prepare for her big break—one line in a sleazy television drama.

Mima's on a slow train to nowhere until the show's producers decide her goodie-two-shoes pop-idol profile would make her the perfect (i.e., unlikely) candidate to play the series' resident rape victim and revenge-murder suspect. Ratings skyrocket, but soon the various men who engineered her makeover start turning up dead. Besides the corpses, Mima's rise is complicated by her own fear that she's sold herself out. She starts getting creepy visits from what may or may not be herself—Old Mima done up in the abandoned schoolgirl-idol drag, giggling maniacally that New Nima is dirty and tarnished and nasty.

Blue puts some predictably sketchy gender politics in play, and its climax is luridly hysterical, overloaded with dream sequences and Mima's "Am I crazy?" freak-outs. Still, the film is tawdrily insightful in the way it uses the hot lights of the entertainment industry to illuminate anime's peculiar duality as the mirror of both wholesome and not-so-wholesome fantasy, and this with nary a tentacled demon-dick in sight.

Also reviewed in:
CHICAGO TRIBUNE, 9/17/99, Friday/p. G, John Petrakis
NEW YORK TIMES, 8/20/99, p. E20, Anita Gates
VARIETY, 11/1-7/99, p. 88, Dennis Harvey

PHOTOGRAPHER

A Seventh Art Releasing release of an Apple Film production in co-production with Broadcast AV and TVP S.A. Channel 1/the Committee of Cinematography/APF/Canal Plus Poland/MDR/ARTE in cooperation with Canal Plus France. *Producer:* Darius Jablonski. *Director:* Darius Jablonski. *Screenplay (Polish, German, and Yiddish subtitles):* Andrzej Bodek, Arnold Mostowicz, and Darius Jablonski. *Director of Photography:* Tomasz Michalowski. *Editor:* Milenia Fiedler. *Music:* Michal Lorenc. *Sound:* Piotor Domaradzki and Jena Hasler. *Running time:* 80 minutes. *MPAA Rating:* Not Rated.

NARRATOR: Arnold Mostowicz.

LOS ANGELES TIMES, 6/25/99, Calendar/p. 12, Kevin Thomas

In 1987, around 400 color slides from the early 1940s turned up in mint condition in a Vienna antique shop. They had been taken by Walter Genewein, the Austrian chief accountant for the Nazis of the Lodz Ghetto, and their subjects were the inhabitants of the ghetto itself. The irony is staggering: A man who participated in the Nazis' "Final Solution"—indeed, he got the German government to pay the ghetto workers 20% of their salaries and remit the rest to his office—inadvertently became one of its chief chroniclers.

"Photographer" is a uniquely devastating film even among Holocaust documentaries. Polish filmmaker Dariusz Jablonski frames his film by having Arnold Mostowicz, who had been a doctor in the Lodz Ghetto and is an Auschwitz survivor, viewing them along with us. As he looks at them, he tells us his terrible story. Jablonski further cuts very precisely between the settings of Genewein's photos and those locales today, often virtually unchanged, giving the film movement, tempo and also relief from endless images of gaunt faces ridden with despair and occasionally contempt at being photographed.

"Our only way is work!" was the slogan of Chaim Rumkowski, the head of the ghetto's Council of Jewish Elders, who were entrusted to set up a model economy. The ghetto, enclosed by barbed wire on April 30, 1940, imprisoned 156,000 Jews, with the population later increased by 20,000 Jews from Germany, Bohemia and Austria, and by 18,000 from towns around Lodz. In increasingly overcrowded and filthy conditions, the Jewish workers manufactured a wide array of items for Germany's home-front market and for the armed forces.

It was a tremendously profitable and efficient operation, for Rumkowski saw that responding to the Germanic zeal for efficiency was the only hope of saving his people; indeed, Genewein's purpose in taking the pictures was to make a record of the ghetto's success. It apparently never occurred to him that others might view his images quite differently, as a chronicle of horrendous human suffering and systematic dehumanization. As the war dragged on, conditions grew worse, and the sick, the very young and the elderly were deported to extermination camps.

By August 1944, when the ghetto had to be evacuated in the face of the heavy Allied bombing of Lodz, its population had dwindled to about 70,000, who were then sent to Auschwitz.

Mostowicz is among the 15,000 of that number who survived; he surmises that had the assassination attempt on Hitler earlier in the year been successful, Rumkowski would have been able to save some tens of thousands of Jewish lives.

As Mostowicz recounts one horror after another, Jablonski counterpoints his excruciatingly painful memories with extracts from Genewein's testy correspondence with Agfa, the German film company, in which he complained about the quality of their printing and occasional use of out-of-date stock. (The photos he took were among the first color slides ever produced.) Genewein, who confiscated his camera from a Lodz Jew, seems the ultimate monster of detachment. Those who believe that what comes around, goes around, should take notice: Genewein died a respected citizen of Vienna in 1974 at the age of 73.

NEW YORK POST, 4/14/99, p. 46, Rod Dreher

In 1987, nearly 400 color slides were found in a secondhand book shop in Vienna. They had belonged to Walter Genewein, a pensioner who died more than a decade earlier, a respectable Austrian citizen whose real legacy is preserved in these images.

Genewein had been a civil servant appointed by the Nazis as an accountant charged with overseeing the finances of the Lodz ghetto, the most notorious of the Jewish work camps in occupied Poland. Genewein used his photography hobby to impress his superiors with proof of "subhumans in the process of being civilized by the German culture of work and organization."

The result was a remarkable, if deceptive, visual record of daily life in the Lodz ghetto, which has in turn been brought hauntingly to life in Polish filmmaker Dariusz Jablonski's harrowing documentary, "Photographer."

Jablonski dramatically juxtaposes Genewein's placid color images with testimony from Arnold Mostowicz, one of the last living Lodz ghetto survivors.

Even more disturbing are quotes from letters, ledgers and other documents evidencing the grotesque moral indifference Genewein and his fellow bureaucrats brought to their work. Genewein, for instance, wrote a letter to film supplier Agfa complaining about the poor quality of the slide hues. That the slides depicted people he was driving to their deaths never troubled him.

VILLAGE VOICE, 4/20/99, p. 143, J. Hoberman

Photographer, by Krysztof Kieslowski's onetime assistant director Dariusz Jablonski, is a taut and expressionistic evocation of the giant slave-labor sewing factory that was the wartime Jewish ghetto of Lodz.

The first ghetto established in occupied Poland (and the last liquidated), Lodz was administered by the Nazis through their appointed "Jewish elder," a failed textile magnate named Chaim Rumkowski, who, placed in a terrifying and untenable moral position, bought time for many Jews by feeding Nazi deportation quotas with those too sick, too old, or too young to work including, inevitably, the parents and children of his captive subjects. Before he was gassed at Auschwitz, Rumkowski ran the Lodz ghetto as a personal kingdom, complete with social welfare programs, security police, and a bureau of statistics that chronicled every aspect of Jewish communal life.

The 1982 Swedish documentary *The Story of Chaim Rumkowski and the Jews of Lodz*—one of the simplest, least sentimental, and most devastating accounts of the Holocaust—is almost entirely based on the photographs Rumkowski commissioned. *Photographer* draws on a trove of 400 color slides made by SS accountant and photo-hobbyist Walter Genewein (discovered 40-odd years later in a Vienna secondhand bookstore) and, less austere than the Swedish film, involves two witnesses. Genewein's slides—which he described as images of "subhumans in the process of being civilized by the German culture of work and organization"—are juxtaposed with the recollections of Arnold Mostowicz, a now elderly Lodz ghetto survivor who had worked, under Rumkowski, as a young doctor.

Jablonski repeatedly dissolves the underpopulated streets of present-day Lodz into the wartime ghetto—an eerie juxtaposition of a ghostly, slow-motion, black-and-white present and the frozen Agfachrome past (displays of store mannequins in SS uniforms, piles of confiscated clothing, transports leaving for the east). The oddly posed photos of Jewish work-details are the most compelling—grim, hopeful, curious faces with haunted eyes and hunger-sharpened features. Interrogating these images, Jablonski often brings his camera so close that resolution breaks down.   These traces can't speak, but Genewein's smug self-portraits are underscored by Mostowicz's mournful recollections of his own coldness and cowardice in the struggle to survive.

The images are further accompanied by a collage of bureaucratic reports—including Genewein's letters to the Agfa company and memos to Adolf Eichmann, as well as Rumkowski's official missives (read in the original Yiddish). *Photographer* may strike some as overly baroque. But its initially distracting clutter of staged photos, stark statistics, and angst-producing drone-music coalesces into an unsettling miasma and then a vortex into Europe's heart of darkness.

Also reviewed in:
CHICAGO TRIBUNE, 4/5/99, Friday/p. Q, Michael Wilmington
NATION, 5/3/99, p. 35, Stuart Klawans
NEW YORK TIMES, 4/14/99, p. E1, Lawrence Van Gelder
VARIETY, 3/8-14/99, p. 60, Lael Lowenstein

PIZZICATA

A Milestone Film release of a Horres Film & TV/Classic/Suddeutscher Rundfunk/Les Films du Paradoxe co-production. *Producer:* Edoardo Winspeare, Dieter Horres, and Fratelli Guercia Sammarco. *Director:* Edoardo Winspeare. *Screenplay (Italian with English subtitles):* Edoardo Winspeare. *Director of Photography:* Paolo Carnera. *Editor:* Carlotta Cristiani. *Sound:* Giuseppe Napoli. *Sound Editor:* Jérôme Harley. *Set Designer:* Sonia Peng. *Production Designer:* Edoardo Winspeare. *Costumes:* Silvia Nebiolo. *Running time:* 93 minutes. *MPAA Rating:* Not Rated.

CAST: Cosimo Cinieri (Carmine Pantaleo); Fabio Frascaro (Tony Marciano); Chiara Torelli (Cosima Pantaleo); Anna Dimitri (Immacolata Pantaleo); Ines d'Anbrosio (Nzina Pantaleo); Paolo Massafra (Pasquale); Lamberto Probo (Donato Pantaleo).

LOS ANGELES TIMES, 4/30/99, Calendar/p. 14, Kevin Thomas

Edoardo Winspeare's "Pizzicata" is a lovely, low-key film that takes us into the timeless world of the Salentino peninsula, a beautiful though impoverished region in the heel of Italy.

Winspeare sets his story in the summer of 1943, when an American fighter plane is shot down. The sole survivor by chance happens to be an Italian American, whose parachute lands him in a tree, where he is discovered unconscious and wounded, though not too seriously, by the Pantaleos, a peasant family who grows olive trees.

Unhesitatingly, Carmine (Cosimo Cinieri, the film's sole professional actor), a middle-aged widower with three daughters and a son off fighting in Greece, offers the soldier shelter. As soon as Tony Marciano (Fabio Frascaro) regains consciousness he starts becoming a part of the family. Not only does he speak Italian but also was born not too far away; hard times forced his family to emigrate to America 15 years earlier.

Since he closely resembles the son of Carmine's cousin, who lives in Lecce, the capital city of the region, it is easy for Tony to pass himself off as that relative, explaining that he is on leave, having been wounded in Africa and here to help Carmine work his land.

Life goes on smoothly, and Winspeare, a native of the region descended from English Catholics who in 1700 fled persecution in their homeland, celebrates the Pantaleos' ancient rustic way of life, one that's close to God and nature. This idyll is endangered as attraction starts developing between the handsome Tony and the pretty Cosima (Chiara Torelli), who is pursued by the good-looking and rich Pasquale (Paolo Massafra).

The unraveling of the lovers' fate, which evolves with a refreshing lack of melodrama, unfolds through the region's folk dance, the pizzica, which takes three forms: the pizzica de core, an elegant and sensual courting dance; the danza della schenna, a duel-like sword or knife dance performed by men; and the frenzied pizzica tarantata, a therapeutic dance of exorcism performed by women who find themselves in the grip of grief or sexual repression.

The way in which Winspeare incorporates the various forms of the pizzica seems not in the least contrived or artificial. As a result "Pizzicata" emerges as a most effective work of folklore, easy and graceful. This film may have been a labor of love—three years in the making—on the part of Winspeare, in his feature debut, and his colleagues, but there is nothing labored about "Pizzicata," a film that casts a spell as potent as its seductive music and dancing.

NEW YORK POST, 2/3/99, p. 45, Jonathan Foreman

"Pizzicata" is word made up from the names of two dances: the Pizzica (dance of love) and the Tarantella (dance of death) and both music and dance figure strongly in this film, set in the Salentino region of Southern Italy during World War II—a place where all the men have glowering good looks and all the women go barefoot, even in the fields.

"Pizzicata" is a pretty, sensual film that reminds you how even the smallest gestures—especially during a whirling hands-off folk dance—can be powerfully erotic in a society that rigidly forbids physical contact between unmarried men and women.

Unfortunately, because of a predictable plot, occasionally crude writing and uneven acting, "Pizzicata" is mainly enjoyable on the level of a travelog or ethnography.

Tony (Fabio Frascaro) an American pilot of Italian parentage who has parachuted from a crashing bomber, is found by the three daughters of a widowed farmer. The family takes him in and hides him from the fascist police.

He and the middle daughter, Cosima (Chiara Torelli) fall in love but Pasquale (Paola Massafra), the obnoxious son of the local rich man—and the only young man in the whole village who has not gone off to the war—wants to marry her.

If this were a Hollywood movie you would be sure that all would end up just fine. But it is made clear from the start that the film will end with the "tarantella"—a strange, disturbing dance of female grief that looks a lot like possession and is believed by the local peasants to be an affliction caused by a tarantula bite between the legs.

VILLAGE VOICE, 2/9/99, p. 65, J. Hoberman

The more conventional [the reference is to *Dry Cleaning*; see Hoberman's review] sexy stranger in *Pizzicata* is an American bomber pilot who bails out over southern Italy (and into the arms of the local peasantry) during the summer of 1943. World war notwithstanding, the provinces here are far more appealing than in *Dry Cleaning*. The landscape where the American finds himself is a timeless paradise of zephyr breezes and twittering birds.

The pilot is discovered by a peasant paterfamilias and, naturally, this grizzled pillar of gruff dignity (who, were *Pizzicata* a Euro-pudding dubfest, would have doubtless been played by Maximilian Schell) has fathered two ripe, barefoot babes with perfect posture and teeth to match. Considering this excellent luck, it seems no particular miracle that the American—representative of a realm even more fabulous than the dives where the Queens of the Night strut their stuff—would turn out to be Italian-born, scarcely wounded, and, once he regains consciousness, eagerly on the make. The family passes him off as a visiting relative, which, given his relative absence of personality, presents little problem.

Studied, sun-soaked, and somewhat elliptical, *Pizzicata* is a movie that aspires to the elemental. Winspeare, directing his first feature after a number of documentaries, favors a visual style based on fixed camera positions and deliberate lateral pans across rows of symmetrically arranged performers. As befits this schematic mise-en-scène (and insofar as power is transferred from the family to the community), civilization is much more powerful here than in *Dry Cleaning*, not to mention more obviously exotic.

Sublimation—if not discontent—is manifest in a series of funerals, festivals, and local rituals ranging from courtship to exorcism. The dancing here is better too, not to mention the hysterical female dervish writhing.

The American disrupts the social order with his desire for the peasant's daughter who has been promised to the son of the town's richest citizen. But, although *Pizzicata* shares the same doomed trajectory as *Dry Cleaning*, the means by which society exacts its toll lacks an equivalent tension.

If the situation is Freudian, the characters are prepsychological. This is the sort of movie where the women naturally sing in the fields and there is no shortage of carefully framed picturesque customs. (The glorified ethnography has the flavor of Tony Gatlif's gypsy movies without their nutty intensity.)

In the end, *Pizzicata* is less a drama than a sound-and-light show performed for tourists in the main square of a picture-postcard town. Although Cosimo Cinieri, who plays the old peasant, is the movie's lone professional actor, the rest of the cast might just as well have been handpicked by Giorgio Armani.

Also reviewed in:
CHICAGO TRIBUNE, 3/3/00, Friday/p. O, John Petrakis
NEW YORK TIMES, 2/3/99, p. E5, Janet Maslin
VARIETY, 9/16-22/96, p. 72, Derek Elley

PLAYING BY HEART

A Miramax Films and Intermedia Films release in association with Morpheus of a Hyperion production. *Executive Producer:* Paul Feldsher, Bob Weinstein, Harvey Weinstein, Guy East, and Nigel Sinclair. *Producer:* Meg Liberman, Willard Carroll, and Tom Wilhite. *Director:* Willard Carroll. *Screenplay:* Willard Carroll. *Director of Photograhy:* Vilmos Zsigmond. *Editor:* Pietro Scalia. *Music:* John Barry. *Music Editor:* Clifford Kohlweck and Adam Kay. *Sound:* Arthur Rochester and (music) Dennis Sands. *Sound Editor:* Kelly Cabral and Wylie Stateman. *Casting:* Irene Cagen. *Production Designer:* Melissa Stewart. *Art Director:* Charlie Daboub. *Set Designer:* Patte Strong and Mark Poll. *Set Decorator:* Cindy Carr. *Set Dresser:* Dwain Wilson, Carl Denoover, Scott Jones, Paul Dominick Mugavero. *Costumes:* April Ferry. *Make-up:* Christina Smith. *Make-up (Body):* Jane English. *Stunt Coordinator:* Dan Bradley. *Running time:* 100 minutes. *MPAA Rating:* R.

CAST: Gillian Anderson (Meredith); Ellen Burstyn (Mildred); Sean Connery (Paul); Anthony Edwards (Roger); Angelina Jolie (Joan); Jay Mohr (Mark); Ryan Phillippe (Keenan); Dennis Quaid (Hugh); Gena Rowlands (Hannah); Jon Stewart (Trent); Madeleine Stowe (Gracie); Patricia Clarkson (Allison); April Grace (Valery); Alec Mapa (Lana); Jeremy Sisto (Malcolm); Matt Malloy (Desk Clerk); Christian Mills (Philip); Kellie Waymire (Jane); Tim Halligan (Director, Cook Show); Michael Emerson (Bosco); Nastassja Kinski (Melanie); John Patrick White (Pete); David Clennon (Martin); Amanda Peet (Amber); David Ferguson (Drag Queen); Joel McCrary (Bartender, Drag Bar); Worthie Meacham (2nd Drag Queen Performer); Michael Buchman Silver (Max); Hal Landon, Jr. (Actor "Commissioner"); Marc Allen Lewis (Actor "Harpagon"); Ron Boussom (Actor "Jacques"); Daniel Chodos (Actor "Anselme"); Mark Lewis (Waiter); Jim Abele (Doctor); Chris Conner (Harry); Marcus Printup (Trumpet Player); Larry Antonio (Bass Player); Tom Chuchvara (Drummer); Robert English (Saxophonist); Ryo Okumuto (Pianist).

LOS ANGELES TIMES, 12/30/98, Calendar/p. 8, Kevin Thomas

Willard Carroll's "Playing by Heart" is a fine example of the traditional-style, multicharacter love story featuring an all-star ensemble cast, beautifully headed in this case by Gena Rowlands and Sean Connery. In structure and in its Los Angeles locale it brings to mind such films as Alan Rudolph's "Welcome to L. A." and Robert Altman's "Short Cuts"—though it could be set just as easily in New York or Chicago.

That's because its terrain is emotional, not geographical, and Carroll probes it deeply and engagingly. He serves his cast—and thereby his audience—impressively in directing his actors in notably well-written roles. If "Playing by Heart" is the kind of film that used to be known as a "woman's picture," it certainly provides more emotional nourishment than most other mainstream movies generate these days.

"Playing by Heart," in for a one-week Oscar-qualifying run at the Royal and reopening in national release on Jan. 22, is quite an accomplishment for a filmmaker known primarily for "The Runestone," a handsome but routine and pretentious 1992 horror picture.

Rowlands and Connery are so absolutely night for each other it's a wonder no one ever teamed them before. She is beautiful, he is handsome and the chemistry is palpable. Their Hannah and Paul make a stunning couple as they approach their 40th wedding anniversary. The impending milestone is darkened, however, by an unexpected turn of events and intensified by a flash of jealousy experienced by Hannah as she is inadvertently reminded of her husband's attraction to another woman 25 years earlier.

It is gratifying to watch two mature adults, clearly deeply in love with each other, working their way through crisis with refreshing honesty and directness—and not without humor, either. Rowlands and Connery, who play a TV chef of Julia Child-like status and her producer-husband, are a pure joy to behold, and they provide a ballast and resonance that enriches the entire film.

Carroll cuts between them and several other stories. Angelina Jolie's Joan is a brash but likable aspiring actress who, in the midst of splitting up with her boyfriend by phone in a nightclub, finds herself attracted to a bystander, Ryan Phillippe's Keenan, who inexplicably resists her considerable charms even though he is clearly drawn to her.

Gillian Anderson's Meredith, in turn, is a success as a stage director but has been so unlucky in love she reflexively tries to send Jon Stewart's charming and intelligent architect packing before she even gets a chance to become acquainted with him.

Meanwhile, Madeleine Stowe's Gracie is caught up in a hot affair with Anthony Edwards' Roger, who is eager to take their relationship to a more serious level despite the fact that both are married to others.

Ellen Burstyn's Mildred is trying to comfort her son Mark (Jay Mohr), who is trying to get his mother to accept that he is in the final stages of AIDS-related diseases.

Finally, there's Dennis Quaid's Hugh, who seems to have a penchant for getting drunk in bars and restaurants, making heavy-duty passes at Patricia Clarkson's Alice, Nastassja Kinski's Melanie and even an upfront, compassionate drag queen, played with humor and wisdom by Alec Mapa, who is one of the film's strongest presences.

Carroll's key inspiration is in how he brings his film to a conclusion, one that is not merely surprising but also deeply satisfying, giving "Playing by Heart" unexpected breadth and depth. Throughout the film Carroll has the strong assistance of Vilmos Zsigmond's expressive camerawork and John Barry's mood-enhancing score, but it's the film's bravura concluding sequence that takes the full measure of Zsigmond's and Barry's contributions. "Playing by Heart" takes aim and hits the bull's-eye.

NEW YORK, 2/1/99, p. 48, Peter Rainer

Playing by Heart is one of those tedious multicharacter split-story jobs in which all the seemingly unconnected plot strands are tied up at the end. It's about looking for love in all the wrong/right places, and it features a large and impressive cast doing, for the most part, small and unimpressive things. The writer-director, Willard Carroll, seems to have broken open the story lines for a season's worth of soap operas and then scrambled them. The banalities bubble up at an alarming rate. Among the actors—including Sean Connery, Dennis Quaid, Gena Rowlands, Ellen Burstyn, and Madeleine Stowe—the flippiest is Angelina Jolie, whose smoochy, beestung kisser is amusingly florid. So's her performance.

NEW YORK POST, 1/22/99, p. 46, Rod Dreher

"Playing by Heart" is an unfortunately generic title that doesn't begin to suggest the quirky pleasures in this minor, but observant and brilliantly acted comedy-drama.

The original title, "Dancing About Architecture," would have been better; it comes from a line spoken by Angelina Jolie in the movie's opening scene. "Talking about love," she says, "is like dancing about architecture." By which she means that the essence of love is to be found in the experience of loving, not in holding it up to analysis.

And that's what the neurotic Los Angeles couples in this gently provocative movie just can't stop doing. The action and there's not much of it in this cool talkfest—centers around six variations-on-a-theme stories of male-female love.

You may go bug-eyed when Sean Connery and Gena Rowlands (now *that's* casting!) turn up as a couple suffering a crisis in the twilight of their long and happy marriage. They are so good together I wouldn't have complained had the movie spent its entire two hours on their characters, Paul and Hannah. Paul is dying of a brain tumor, and Hannah, no doubt displacing her anxiety over his imminent demise, keeps lighting into him about an affair he may or may not have had many years earlier.

Even better, and even more surprising, are sexpot Jolie and Ryan Philippe, of all people, as lovelorn L.A. club kids. Motormouth Joan (Jolie) is crazy for Keenan (Philippe), an icy blue-blonde Adonis who remains aloof from her charms for a mysterious reason. Jolie, who has never been better, carries on like the kind of knockout who is used to getting exactly what she wants; Philippe's blasé reaction humbles her, and ultimately leads to a startling, heartbreaking revelation.

Elsewhere in the city, Gillian Anderson is Meredith, a theatrical producer who has locked herself in an impregnable tower to keep her oft-broken heart safe. Jon Stewart plays the charming and patient suitor who sees Meredith's true worth, and tries to hold out against her bitchy slings and arrows.

Madeleine Stowe plays a married woman having a clandestine affair with Anthony Edwards, who would like to proceed beyond the slam-bam-thank-you-ma'am stage. She resists, preferring not to fudge her physical pleasure with romantic complications.

An exceptionally moving Dennis Quaid plays a miserable loner who makes sport of sidling up to women in bars and spinning elaborate, emotionally manipulative tales while getting soused. And finally, Ellen Burstyn plays an emotionally restrained mother who jets to the bedside of her AIDS-ravaged son (Jay Mohr), whose imminent demise encourages the two to share intimacies they've avoided all their lives.

Five story lines and 11 characters in two hours' time—that's a lot to keep airborne at once, so it's not all that surprising that writer-director Willard Carroll drops the ball on the AIDS segment, which seems too abbreviated, forced and out of place here.

But that feels like quibbling, considering how strong most of this material is. The structure of Carroll's screenplay is admirably complex, disclosing surprise connections and tying things up nicely by the end. The dialogue sounds real, and the confused, struggling characters, fumbling and staggering their way along a conversational gauntlet, all too real. Carroll's point is that love may not consist in talking, but that's the only way to break down the barriers of fear, mistrust and deception that keep love at bay.

"Playing by Heart" will not be not to everyone's taste. Some will no doubt find it too vignettey and low-key to hold their interest (there's a reason Chet Baker's moody, downbeat jazz compositions figure prominently in the soundtrack). Patience: despite the lack of dramatic crescendos, the characters do grow on you, and the calm, constant rhythm of the film mesmerizes. Carroll's terrific cast, and his cool, steady, insinuating style make "Playing by Heart" more mature and rewarding than the throwaway title would suggest.

NEWSDAY, 1/22/99, Part II/p. B7, Jack Mathews

The multiple characters in Willard Carroll's cleverly constructed, superbly cast "Playing by Heart" seem as fragile as crystal bubbles in an L.A. earthquake. Each of these Angelinos, who range in age from 25 to about 65, is at a crisis point over love—the pursuit of it, the fear of it, the desire to protect it—and each is about to learn something very profound about it.

Given the number of central characters involved—11—Carroll has set a mighty task for himself, and he doesn't completely succeed. Even at a roomy two-hour running time, some of the individual stories move too fast and cover too much emotional ground to have much plausibility.

In fact, two sets of couples who pair up during the film get off to such unpleasant beginnings, you have to take it on faith that the attractions between the fated lovers are strong enough to overcome them.

But Carroll, a TV writer and executive with little work in features behind him, has crafted such a winsome, gracefully paced series of stories (whose relationships to each other aren't revealed until the film's final scenes) that you don't devote much energy to deconstructing them. And his cast, for the most part, gets you through the weakest elements in his script.

The showcase couple is Paul and Hannah (a perfectly matched Sean Connery and Gena Rowlands), an affluent, deeply respectful couple facing their 40th anniversary with the tragic news of Paul's inoperable brain tumor. It's the first major crisis in their marriage since another woman nearly came between them 25 years earlier, and it compels them, once again, to reassess their life together.

Elsewhere, in fragments that build on each other, we meet: Joan (Angelina Jolie), a flamboyantly romantic Gen Xer prowling L.A.'s club life for Mr. Right, and Keenan (Ryan Phillippe), whose sulking, aloof manner makes him seem like the last person she'd suspect; Meredith (Gillian Anderson), a stage director whose past romantic tragedies have left her colder than a fish at the Fulton Market, and Trent (Jon Stewart), the handsome, catch-of-the-day architect who persists in pursuing her; and Gracie (Madeleine Stowe), a married woman carrying on a "sex and no regrets" affair with a married man (Anthony Edwards) who can't get enough of her.

Love of another sort is explored in the relationship between Mildred (Ellen Burstyn) and her gay son Mark (Jay Mohr), who is dying of AIDS. Her last days with him in the hospital are reality sessions, with each revealing to the other who they really are.

Finally, there is Hugh (Dennis Quaid), who roams from one bar to another finding sympathetic strangers who will listen to his spectacularly tragic lies.

The link between all these stories is so well concealed, the movie might have ended without the dots being connected, and still been OK. But the last scenes do create the sense of a satisfying punchline. Suddenly, your mind adds up the clues given throughout, and the puzzle is sensibly complete.

Still, the greatest strengths of "Playing by Heart" are the performances. Connery and Rowlands, whose careers haven't crossed before, play off each other as if they'd done it a dozen times and grown old together. Their banter playful at times, pointed at others—has a lived-in comfort level. Paul and Hannah have been through a lot in 40 years, and while the scars show, nothing is more apparent than the depth of their love.

Overall, "Playing by Heart" may be thought of as the flip side of Todd Solondz' dark, ironically titled "Happiness." Both films deal with the complications of love, family and relationships, but in Carroll's film, happiness actually seems attainable.

SIGHT AND SOUND, 9/99, p. 52, Mike Higgins

Los Angeles. The personal relationships of an apparently disparate group of characters are depicted over eight days. Joan is a skittish clubber who falls for the brooding Keenan. Hugh props up bars spinning fictional hard-luck yarns to whoever will listen. Retired television producer Paul and his wife Hannah, a television chef, are coping with the recent diagnosis of his brain tumour. Trent is a single, attractive architect who by chance meets and invites out Meredith, a workaholic theatre director. Unhappily married Gracie is having an affair with Roger, also married. Meanwhile, Mildred is at the bedside of her gay son Mark, who is dying of Aids.

Keenan reveals that he is HIV+ to Joan who, to his relief, is undaunted. Gracie, it transpires, is married to Hugh, whose tale-telling turns out to be part of an improvisation class. Paul admits to Hannah to falling in love with an assistant 25 years ago. Meredith succumbs to the persistent Trent before being called away to the funeral of her ex-husband Mark. Paul and Hannah renew their wedding vows watched by their three daughters—Gracie, Meredith and Joan—and the daughters' partners with whom they are all, more or less, reconciled. Roger is the officiating minister.

Following on the heels of David Kane's *This Year's Love*, Neil LaBute's *Your Friends & Neighbors*, Tony Gerber's *Side Streets* and even Todd Solondz's *Happiness*, *Playing by Heart* is yet another film in which a daisy-chain narrative links by coincidence and fate the lives of sundry characters. But any resemblance between director of *The Runestone* Willard Carroll's soft-centred comedy-drama and those other films is only skin deep.

To begin with, Carroll is too discrete with character and storyline to let the various narratives overlap with anything other than the most fleeting of connections. Before we know they're related, for instance, each of the sisters drops the epithet "anger ball" into conversation. It's nothing more than a frivolous clue to the film's ending, but that phrase itself speaks volumes about the simplistic way in which Carroll approaches *Playing by Heart*'s basic theme: emotional crisis. Everyone from youngest child Joan to her father Paul—is defined by little else but the single problem confronting them. So the most important thing we learn about Paul is that in the early 70s he had a crush on a fellow member of staff, a confession which enrages his wife Hannah. Besides this problem Paul's other major concerns—his brain tumour, even his children feel trivial.

Hand-in hand with this reductiveness is the film's refusal to distinguish between the numerous quandaries of its characters. Mark's dying moments with his mother are clearly of a more intense order than Hugh and Gracie's marital difficulties, so why lard both with the same teary-eyed schmaltz? The same naivety is apparent in the unwavering integrity ascribed to each character. In the same way certain couples decide who gets which side of the bed, the adolescent Joan and Keenan breezily agree on the etiquette of a relationship in the shadow of Aids. This uniformity isn't only skewed psychologically, it scuppers any diversity in terms of tone or pace. One has to worry when the most challenging screen presence belongs to Joan's mangy, one-eyed cat.

This being a Los Angeles-set ensemble drama, Robert Altman's *Short Cuts* looms large, but *Playing by Heart* suffers by comparison. Carroll clearly wants to make the case for the universal significance of his parochial cast of emotional casualties. At strategic points, the sun and moon rush across the cityscape in a time-lapsed round. Even the screenplay's lumbering final twist—the revelation that what we've been watching are the soap operatics of an extended family—is meant to stand as a reassuring metaphor for the all-encompassing nature of emotional turmoil. Set against Altman's panoramic web of stories, though, Carroll's milieu is resolutely middle class and the crises encountered all too predictable.

TIME, 1/25/99, p. 74, Richard Schickel

Willard Carroll is a cockeyed optimist. The writer-director of *Playing by Heart* thinks our dysfunctions are curable. Or at the very least transcendable. With a little help from the great cinematographer Vilmos Zsigmond, he bathes this radically unfashionable idea in a glow so romantic that even Los Angeles, where most of his multicharacter, multigenerational saga takes place, is transformed. The world capital of road rage is returned, in his vision to something like the balmy prettiness of its prelapsarian prewar era.

This is no accident. It is something like a moral imperative for Carroll. He wants us to understand that a prescription compounded of kindness, patience, civility and a touch of irony can work wonders on anger and despair—even when their cause is mortality itself. For at the heart of *Heart* are two stories in which couples are obliged to confront death. In one of them, a mother (Ellen Burstyn) and a son who is dying of AIDS (Jay Mohr) try to bring their troubled relationship to a peaceful conclusion in the few days remaining to them. In the other, a long-married couple (Sean Connery and Gena Rowlands) are coping successfully with her incurable illness—until she finds evidence of a past betrayal that threatens to destroy the trust on which they have based their happy, privileged life.

These four are intended as exemplary figures. As we watch them struggling toward acceptance of harsh fates, we are encouraged to believe that everyone else in the film, whose bedevilments are merely romantic, can work things out as well. A colorful, often comic crew includes a woman (Gillian Anderson) so mistrustful of men that she keeps a mastiff to ward them off, a guy (Dennis Quaid) mysteriously given to alternately angry and self-pitying (but always noisy) rants in restaurants; a married woman (Madeleine Stowe) coldly addicted to a sexually stirring but loveless affair; a lonely young actress (Angelina Jolie) hiding neediness under a brassy surface. Most of them find someone willing to help still the insanities that Carroll regards as only temporary.

Each comes to some understanding of his or her miseries and to a degree of hope for better times ahead.

Is there something a little too comfortable—and comforting—in the way this movie works out? Possibly so. On the other hand, its emotional range is extraordinarily generous, the conflicts it permits its unimprovable cast to explore are well beyond the call of their usual duties. And Carroll orchestrates the several variations on his redemptive theme expertly, ultimately resolving them all in a way that is both surprising and satisfying. With the bitter taste of movies like Todd Soldonz's *Happiness*—this film's dark double—still on our tongues, still all the rage, one has to wonder whether the audience for serious movies is still capable of suspending disbelief in the common decency and common sense of middle-class Americans, whether it is willing to try a little tenderness—if only as a relief from chic transgressiveness.

VILLAGE VOICE, 2/2/99, p. 57, Justine Elias

There's exciting telecommunications news out of Los Angeles—you no longer have to wait for your phone calls to go through. Just drop a coin, hit a few numbers, and start yapping. In *Playing by Heart,* one of the city's magic pay phones works so well for Joan (Angelina Jolie), a radiantly egotistical actress, that she tries her hand at a magic monologue: an arch, irritating verbal assault that eventually captures the love of a morose young man (Ryan Phillipe) who can't get a word in edgewise. Elsewhere, a series of similarly dumbstruck strangers fall prey to a barroom bullshitter (Dennis Quaid), who waylays them with patently false tales of domestic tragedies; a set of adulterous lovers (Madeleine Stowe and Anthony Edwards) engage in a talky affair; a mother and her dying son (Ellen Burstyn and Jay Mohr) are reunited; and a long-married couple (Gena Rowlands and Sean Connery) bicker, apparently for the first time, about infidelity and mortality.

Nearly everybody in this well-acted drama of disconnection seems to live in a shelter magazine, but only a nervous romance between Gillian Anderson and Jon Stewart manages to be more fascinating than the pricey furniture. The movie's previous title, *Dancing About Architecture,* was derived from writer-director Willard Carroll's misapprehension of the old musician's put-down of music criticism. Joan misquotes the line as "Talking about love is like dancing about architecture" and attributes it to "a trumpeter friend," so it should come as no surprise that when that trumpeter appears in the film, these supposedly bosom pals don't bother to acknowledge each other. (She's a wedding guest; his band is working the party.) In this movie, music, like language, is mere decoration: you notice it only when it gets on your nerves.

Also reviewed in:
CHICAGO TRIBUNE, 1/22/99, Friday/p. D, Mark Caro
NEW YORK TIMES, 1/22/99, p. E12, Stephen Holden
NEW YORKER, 2/1/99, p. 84, Anthony Lane
VARIETY, 1/4-10/99, p. 98, Lael Loewenstein
WASHINGTON POST, 1/22/99, p. E5, Rita Kempley
WASHINGTON POST, 1/22/99, Weekend/p. 38, Desson Howe

PLUNKETT & MACLEANE

A U.S.A. Films/Gramercy Pictures release in association with The Arts Council of England of a Working Title production. *Executive Producer:* Gary Oldman, Douglas Urbanski, Douglas Urbanski, Selwyn Roberts, and Matthew Stillman. *Producer:* Tim Bevan, Eric Fellner, and Rupert Harvey. *Director:* Jake Scott. *Screenplay:* Robert Wade, Neal Purvis, and Charles McKeown. *Based on his original screenplay by:* Selwyn Roberts. *Director of Photography:* John Mathieson. *Editor:* Oral Norrie Ottey. *Music:* Craig Armstrong. *Music Editor:* Tom Sayers. *Choreographer:* Blanca Li. *Sound:* Mark Holding and (music) Geoff Foster. *Sound Editor:* Glenn Freemantle. *Casting:* Jina Jay. *Production Designer:* Norris Spencer. *Art Director:* Petr Kunc and Jindrich Koci. *Set Decorator:* Jenny Dyer. *Special Effects:* Jaroslav Stolba. *Costumes:* Janty Yates. *Make-up:* Graham Johnston. *Stunt Coordinator:* Pavel Voukoun. *Running time:* 102 minutes. *MPAA Rating:* R.

CAST: Jonny Lee Miller (James Macleane); Iain Robertson (Highwayman Rob); Robert Carlyle (Will Plunkett); Ken Stott (Chance); Tommy Flanagan (Eddie); Stephen Walters (Dennis); James Thornton (Catchpole); Terence Rigby (Harrison); Christian Camargo (Lord Pelham);

Karel Polisenky (Newgate Priest); Neve McIntosh (Liz); Matt Lucas (Sir Oswald); David
Williams (Viscount Bilston); David Foxe (Lord Ketch); Jake Gavin (Newgate Gent); Alexander
Armstrong (Winterburn); Ben Miller (Dixon); Jan Kuzelka (Peruquier); Vladimir Javorsky
(Headbutted Tailor); Milena Sajdkova (Horse Dealer); Alan Cumming (Lord Rochester);
Michael Gambon (Lord Chief Justice Gibson); Liv Tyler (Lady Rebecca Gibson); Karel Dobry
(Lewd Young Man); Daniel De La Falaise (MP); Tom Ward (Backbench Heckler); Nicholas
Farrell (P.M.'s Secretary); Gordon Lovitt (Ranelagh MC); Claire Rushbrook (Lady Estelle);
Tim McMullan (Bridegroom); Jeff Nuttal (Lord Morris); Dana Jurzova (Duchess of Stoke);
Martin Serene (Josh); Dean Cook (Older Highwayman Kid); Jacob Yentob (Younger
Highwayman Kid); Annabel Brooks (Widow with Garter); Tony Maudsley (Older Cleryman);
Alex Palmer (Younger Clergyman); Victoria Harrison (Maria); Emma Faulkner (Young Girl
Prostitute); Noel Fielding (Brother Gent); Jack Walters (Duel Referee); Pavel Greg (Surgeon);
Susan Porrett (Lady Newbold); Nichola McAuliffe (Lady Crombie); Anna Keaveney (Lady
Marchant); Jacques Mathou (French Count); Michael Culkin (Judge Berestade); Murray
Lachlan Young (Gallows Poet); Dave Atkins (Landlord); Karel Augusta (Hangman); Drahomir
Miraz (Hangman's Assistant).

LOS ANGELES TIMES, 10/1/99, Calendar/p. 6, Jan Stuart

[The following review by Jan Stuart appeared in a slightly different form in
NEWSDAY, 10/1/99, Part II/p. B7.]

It is entirely possible that a movie more unpleasant than "Plunkett & Macleane" will open in
the roughly three months prior to the year 2000, but you wouldn't want to put money on it.

Working Title Films, the generally sane British production company behind "My Beautiful
Laundrette," "Four Weddings and a Funeral" and "Dead Man Walking," has obviously banked
a lot of sterling on this dark, noisy and nasty tale of debauchery in 18th century England.

"Trainspotting" cohorts Robert Carlyle and Jonny Lee Miller reunite to play a pair of formerly
respectable citizens turned coach robbers.

Will Plunkett (Carlyle) is a wily, lower-class rascal, a onetime apothecary who teams up with
the well-bred James Macleane (the inspiration for "The Threepenny Opera's" Macheath, played
by Miller) to plunder from the wealthy. Their daytime seductions and nocturnal robberies pit
them in the middle of a power struggle between the Lord Chief Justice Gibson (Michael Gambon)
and the fiendishly corrupt Chance (Ken Stott), a cad in Puritan's clothing who is hell-bent on
bringing the pair down.

The two rogues are cheered on and abetted by hedonist extraordinaire Lord Rochester (Alan
Cumming) and Gibson's comely niece, Lady Rebecca (a ravishing and dull Liv Tyler), a vixen
at heart who falls for Macleane's charms.

Everyone else in the film is so creepy and unpalatable that Plunkett and Macleane become
heroes by default. Writers Robert Wade, Neal Purvis and Charles McKeown have created a
British Tourist Authority's nightmare of olde London, teeming with squalid prisons, unctuous
gaming parlors and surly residents.

Stereotypes take a holiday: The upper-crust preen insufferably, homosexuals wear heavy
makeup, and the French ambassador quaffs cognac with a gun to his temple while grousing about
how foreigners mutilate his language. First-time director Jake Scott tarts up these tired
conventions with pointedly anachronistic rock music and editing that is so quick on the draw you
spend the first 10 minutes wondering who is doing what to whom, where they are doing it and
whether you should care.

Everything is stunningly photographed by John Mathieson, but to paraphrase Gertrude Stein,
a cockroach is a cockroach is a cockroach.

NEW YORK POST, 10/1/99, p. 62, Jonathan Foreman

"Plunkett and Macleane" should have been good, swashbuckling fun—a buddy action comedy
set in the era of three-cornered hats, pirate boots and overflowing bodices that happens to star
Robert Carlyle from "Trainspotting" and "The Full Monty."

Unfortunately, it's a noisy, amateurish mess that doesn't work on any level—an extended, cliché-ridden MTV video set to anachronistic bad music.

It's 1740. Capt. James Macleane (Jonny Lee Miller) is a British officer and gentleman reduced to poverty. Will Plunkett (Carlyle) is a ruined apothecary turned highwayman. They get to know each other a little in jail before bribing their way out using a combination of Plunkett's swallowed loot and Macleane's upper-class manners.

Plunkett then recruits Macleane into a life of crime. The idea is that Macleane will frequent high society (while Plunkett pretends to be his manservant) researching who really has money and jewelry worth stealing. Then Plunkett (who is a crack shot) will plan and lead the actual robberies.

It works, thanks to Macleane's friendship with the bisexual fop Lord Rochester (Alan Cumming). Soon the papers are full of stories about "The Gentleman Highwayman." But when the duo rob a coach carrying the Lord Chief Justice (Michael Gambon) and his beautiful niece Rebecca (Liv Tyler), Macleane falls in love with the girl—and the authorities get serious about catching and hanging the pair.

The film is shot almost entirely in underlit close-ups, as though first-time director Jake Scott seems to think that it's uncool to show anyone's whole face.

But while Scott's flashy incompetence is irritating, the screenwriters also have a lot to answer for. The plot could hardly be more formulaic, and the dialogue more jarringly modern and crude. Worse, it fails to establish Plunkett or Macleane as likable characters in a real friendship.

SIGHT AND SOUND, 4/99, p. 54, Philip Strick

London, 1748. Bankrupt James Macleane encounters Will Plunkett, who proposes a partnership: financed by Plunkett, Macleane will mingle with high society and identify its wealthiest and most vulnerable members, whom they will rob. The scheme ideally suits both men: Macleane is an ardent party-goer and womaniser with a passion for gambling, while Plunkett is amassing funds for a passage to America. Befriended by the dissolute Lord Rochester, Macleane is soon among the idle rich, selecting Lord Gibson as the first target. Gibson's niece Lady Rebecca is with him when the two masked horsemen stop his coach, and is impressed by their courtesy. Overnight they become known as "the Gentlemen Highwaymen".

Gibson's deputy Chance makes it his personal vendetta to track down the robbers. Although upset when Macleane squanders most of their booty, Plunkett still loyally rescues his partner when he's wounded in an ambush. Eager to claim Gibson's job as well as his niece, Chance sets up a trap with the unwilling assistance of Rebecca, who by now has guessed the miscreants' identity. Plunkett and Macleane intercept Gibson's coach but evade Chance's horsemen; Chance shoots Gibson himself. Challenging Rebecca for her supposed betrayal, Macleane is captured and sentenced to hang for Gibson's murder. As Macleane is hauled aloft on the gallows, Plunkett rescues him with Rebecca and Rochester's help, galloping off pursued by Chance and his men. Plunkett turns back to confront Chance and shoots him before heading for freedom with Rebecca and Macleane.

Like the movie versions of Butch and Sundance, *Plunkett & Macleane*'s two bandits and a girl make their final exit in a blaze of glory, severed from the tedious weight of historical accuracy. One might generously suppose that their story's concluding scenes are in *Incident at Owl Creek* (1961) territory, a representation of the condemned captive's fevered imaginings. This would excuse the implausible nature of the rescue operation and its aftermath. Viewed less generously, its peculiar climactic twists serve mainly to confirm the structure of *Plunkett & Macleane* as an opportunistic patchwork designed more to please or titillate than persuade. Quite why the film's protagonists elect to blunder through storm-drain tunnels, or why Plunkett puts himself at such risk from Chance, or where the exuberant Lord Rochester is galloping off to at the end, are evidently of minor concern—like the fact that the original Macleane died unrescued at Tyburn prison in 1750. Genetically modified for today's tastes, the Gentlemen Highwaymen have been packaged as iconic superheroes, flawed (of course) but immortal and irresistible in an anti-authoritarian kind of way.

Fortunately, despite a certain amount of posturing for the sake of felony, they are played for grime as much as glamour. In fact their objectives appear tolerably rational against the lurid background. Relishing exaggeration and absurdity, the film offers four distinct contexts: a resplendently untouched countryside, a terrain exploitable not for its Englishness or its reminders of the hills of various Gainsboroughs but for its seclusion as a shooting range. At the opposite extreme, all artifice and old lace, is London society, powdered and plastered beyond reason, ripe with potential plunder. Meanwhile, the braying club-crowd, weaving haughtily from one party to the next, is parodied on the London streets (actually filmed in Prague) where Pythonesque assemblies of gap-toothed extras celebrate a riotous programme of hangings and other indignities.

Underlying these deliberately dubious reconstructions is another vision entirely—that of the seasoned film fan. Described by its producer as a *Butch Cassidy and the Sundance Kid* for the 90s, *Plunkett & Macleane* is an anthology of echoes, not just of Westerns, but of cinema as a whole. Opening with a mist-shrouded graveyard to suit any Corman classic and a macabre bloodletting to match Terence Fisher (*The Curse of Frankenstein*, 1957) at his most clinical, the film proceeds to steal gleefully from numerous precedents: *Tom Jones, The Draughtsman's Contract, The Company of Wolves* and so on. When it gets around to paying due tribute to Scott *père*, the only surprise is that the duellists favour pistols instead of swords. And if some of the allusions may be unintentional—a masked nod to *Batman* say, or a hint of *A Clockwork Orange* in the brothel sequence—there's little doubt that the stagecoach riddled with bullets is a lift from *The Gauntlet* with Robert Carlyle trying on the Eastwood role for size and finding it a capable fit.

Well primed by a string of music videos, Jake Scott achieves a flashy if noncommittal feature debut. His soundtrack, sure enough, is militantly anachronistic, a terrorzone of back-beats and electronics. But he has a connoisseur's eye for costume and decor, and his widescreen vistas, when he remembers to use them (economical close-ups dominate the film), are elegantly enjoyable. Probably his best shot is of a ballroom's patterned floor, although he studies Liv Tyler with a similar symmetry, his experience in commercials evidently continuing to inspire a preference for form over content. While he can be accused of having subverted the account of an intriguing partnership into little better than a noisy romp, an opportunity for Ken Stott to pop an eyeball or two and for Alan Cumming to dress up as Boy George, he does so with enough energy and style to suggest that, like the other film-makers in his family (father Ridley and uncle Tony), he has excellent prospects.

VILLAGE VOICE, 10/5/99, p. 206, Gary Dauphin

Director Jake Scott's aesthetically unmoored period action flick, *Plunkett and Macleane,* is so desperate to be a hipster swashbuckler that—like its eponymous heroes—it'll shamelessly steal from and sleep with anyone. Although concerned with the true-crime adventures of one of Britain's endless string of Gentlemen Highwaymen (the "... and give to the poor" requirement is dropped from the Robin Hood credo here), this film could have easily been set anywhere and anywhen guns blaze, electronics thumps, guttersnipes put on Dickensian airs, and gilded aristocratic fops joke about "swinging both ways" while their pox-carrying ladies cruise for rough trade. (It doesn't count for much in the end, but there's some kind of dubious accomplishment in making 1743 London seem like the mayor's vision of Saturday night at a Gatien-owned club.)

The tag team of Plunkett and Macleane itself is as much an odd hybrid as everything else onscreen. Plunkett (Robert Carlyle, a walking physical anachronism in other films, but perfect here) is a career robber who has a flash of criminal inspiration when he happens upon Macleane (Jonny Lee Miller), a beggar and drunk who, as he so eloquently puts it, "knows da rich." Plunkett convinces the pretty and well-mannered Macleane to case the houses of the upper classes, the two riding in on horseback afterward to rob various powdered dukes stumbling home after a night of gambling and cockfighting. It's just a gig to our Plunkett, but Macleane, who clearly suffers from some serious title envy, is soon impressing robbery victims with his polite erudition—this when he's not on the circuit with the queenly Earl of Rochester (Alan Cumming, of course) making eyes at a cabinet minister's niece (Liv Tyler, essentially playing a well-girdled bosom).

That Macleane's romantic fantasies will lead to disaster is, of course, clear to both the audience and Plunkett, setting up the expected team-busting conflicts, declarations of love, brushes with the law, last-minute escapes, etc., all of the film's climactic bits delivered Hollywood action-movie style. The film's fundamental instability could be mistaken as an aesthetic choice, except that its excess isn't period or down-and-dirty ribald but plain desperate. Carlyle gives a credible performance, but most of the other acting boils down to a procession of accents, and the script is as full of holes as some of the highwaymen's bullet-riddled victims—why not throw a drum-and-bass track over everything?

Also reviewed in:
NEW YORK TIMES, 10/1/99, p. E8, Stephen Holden
VARIETY, 4/5-11/99, p. 32, Derek Elley

POKEMON: THE FIRST MOVIE

A Warner Bros. Family Entertainment release of a Kids! WB presentation of a Pikachu Project '98-Shogakokan production in association with 4Kids Entertainment. *Executive Producer:* Alfred R. Kahn, Masakazu Kubo, and Takashi Kawaguchi. *Producer:* Norman J. Grossfeld, Choji Yoshikawa, Tomoyuki Igarashi, and Takemoto Mori. *Director:* Kunihiko Yuyama and (English adaptation) Michael Haigney. *Screenplay:* Takeshi Shudo. *Based on characters created by:* Satoshi Tajiri. *English adaptation:* Norman J. Grossfeld, Michael Haigney, and John Touhey. *Director of Photography:* Hisao Shirai. *Editor:* Toshio Henmi, Jay Film, and Yutaka Ito. *Music:* Ralph Schuckett and John Loeffler. *Music Editor:* Julian Schwartz and Susan Shufro. *Sound:* Gary Chester, Nobuhira Mima, and (music) Martin Kloiber. *Sound Editor:* Richard Q. King. *Art Director:* Katsuyoshi Kanemura. *Animation:* Akihiro Tamagawa and Sayuri Ichishi. *Animation (Special Effects):* Noriyuki Ota. *Running time:* 90 minutes. *MPAA Rating:* G.

VOICES: Veronica Taylor (Ash Ketchum); Philip Bartlett (Mewtwo); Rachael Lillis (Misty Williams/Jessie of Team Rocket/Togepei/Others); Eric Stuart (Brock Harrison/James Morgan of Team Rocket/Others); Addie Blaustein (Meowth of Team Rocket); Ikue Otani (Pikachú).

LOS ANGELES TIMES, 11/10/99, Calendar/p. 1, Robin Rauzi

Children. Their attentions wander. But not fast enough to prevent "Pokemon: The First Movie."

The Pokemon franchise, Japan's most popular export since the Toyota Camry, started as a Nintendo Game Boy. Its success begat a TV cartoon, which begat trading cards. And now, like "Rugrats," "Mighty Morphin Power Rangers" and "Teenage Mutant Ninja Turtles" before it, Pokemon is a feature film.

For kids already indoctrinated into the cult of Pokemon, the movie may add something to the ever-growing mythology surrounding the characters. For most others, it will be an appealing diversion, though by no means an exhilarating one. For those completely on the outside (read: adults), the Pokemon world is baffling, even somewhat troubling.

The Pokemon universe is complicated; there are 151 Pokemon characters, for instance, about 20 of which make appearances in the film. The human protagonist, Ash Ketchum (voiced by Veronica Taylor), and his buddies Misty and Brock are trainers. They capture these "pocket monsters," the Pokemon, teach them, and pit them against those of rival trainers. The Pokemon is a willing gladiator. The trainer is a general—he issues the commands he hopes will win the battle. The prize: possession of the Pokemon.

"Pokemon: The First Movie," sub-subtitled "Mewtwo Strikes Back," is about a powerful Pokemon gone bad. Mewtwo, a cat-like biologically engineered Pokemon clone, has more supernatural strength than any regular Pokemon. (One of the handful of adult laughs comes from Mewtwo's decidedly feline character. Pathetic humans, he tells his creators, I will not serve you. I am superior to all of you.)

Superiority complex aside, Mewtwo is racked with existential angst. "Why am I here?" he says after destroying the lab where he was created. "What is my purpose?" Well ... fear leads to anger. Anger leads to hate. And hate leads to suffering, right? Mewtwo sets out to wipe the trainers and their lackey Pokemon off the face of the planet.

Great Japanese animation "Pokemon" is not. ("Princess Mononoke" is still in theaters, if that's what you're after.) "Pokemon" isn't even good animation, unless the standard of measure is the crude LCD graphics of a Game Boy. The characters are flat—apparently deliberately so, to resemble the TV drawings. But unlike the TV program, the film at least contains movement that is somewhat fluid, and director Kunihiko Yuyama creates surprising angles and unexpected extreme close-ups.

The film has, however, been "Americanized." Producer Norman J. Grossfeld, voice director Michael Haigney and John Touhey essentially wrote an American script that lays like a template over the 75-minute Japanese movie. It's impossible to tell whether Yuyama's vision of the film remains intact. The most obvious change is a jarringly bad pop soundtrack that even second-graders can tell doesn't suit the film.

But it seems the Americans have made other, more subtle changes. Writer Stephanie Strom made a good case in Sunday's New York Times that the "Pokemon" TV show is steeped in Japanese values: responsibility, empathy, respect for elders, cooperation, obedience and humility. One wonders what happened to the film, then. There are no elders present or even mentioned. Only the Pokemon are obedient. There's very little teamwork between Ash and buddies. To the contrary, Ash hollers at the wicked Mewtwo, "I won't let you do that!" That's pure, undiluted American individualism.

But like most children's entertainment, the "Pokemon" themes seem disturbingly unexamined. Aspirations for world domination aside, Mewtwo objects to the enslavement of Pokemon to their trainers. Viewed in that context, Ash's declaration that he cares for his Pokemon seems eerily antebellum. The whole competition between trainers starts to look like cockfighting, or worse.

But elementary schoolers, for whom the world is still fairly two-dimensional, probably won't be bothered by such thoughts. It's the parents who might be, as they take their kid back to the theater for the fourth time to get that last "exclusive" Pokemon trading card. They will look at their child's overstuffed binder of cards, the well-worn Game Boy, and wonder if they've been had. And then the title may start to seem like a threat: "Pokemon: The First Movie."

NEW YORK POST, 11/10/99, p. 59, Hannah Brown

Out of the Gameboy and onto the big screen comes "Pokemon: The First Movie," a full-length version of the Japanese TV cartoon.

Poke-maniacs, the crazed young fans who have spent billions of dollars on trading cards and other merchandise based on the video game and TV show, won't be disappointed.

This is strictly a kids' movie, but parents may be relieved to sit back and enjoy the fact that for two full hours, they won't have to hear the kids asking them to buy any more Pokemon trading cards.

For the uninitiated, "Pokemon" is the condensed form of "Pocket Monsters."

These Pokemon—the word can be used in the singular or plural—can roll themselves up into little balls, but turn into giant warriors, some of which look like fish, dinosaurs, eagles, etc. when they fight. They are trained by humans who, by a combination of skill, compassion and instinct, teach the creatures how to battle.

Ash, the hero, is a boy who longs to be the greatest Pokemon trainer ever, and whose favorite monster is the cute yellow Pikachu.

In the movie, which plays like a long episode of the TV series, some unthinking scientists clone Mew, a rare, cat-like Pokemon. The clone, Mewtwo (which bears an uncanny resemblance to Dr. Evil's hairless cat Mr. Bigglesworth in "Austin Powers"), is miffed at being a mere experiment and vows revenge on humanity. Luring all Pokemon masters to an island, he pits his army of savage clones against the Pokemon.

The movie is laced with sarcastic humor meant to send the under-10 set into stitches. Mewtwo sounds like a James Bond-movie villain and gets lots of lines like, "Mew—so finally we meet."

The film was already released in Japan, where it was a big hit, but it has been retooled for American audiences. Its pop score features artists like Christina Aguilera and Emma Bunton (a.k.a. Baby Spice). Visually, it's a strange mixture. Some of the backgrounds and colors are strikingly beautiful, especially the scenes of storms on the ocean. But in other sections, they vary from crude to downright headache-inducing. The people are especially unimaginative and the final battle scene is static and repetitively staged.

The film is preceded by a comic short, "Pikachu: The Movie," which will delight very young children and provide clueless adults with some inside snippets on the habits of the Pokemon.

NEWSDAY, 11/10/99, Part II/p. B7, Gene Seymour

When a kid-cult phenomenon goes from the tube to the big screen, there's usually an accompanying impulse to introduce—some would say, it, indoctrinate"—grown-ups and other outsiders to the particulars of said phenomenon. "Pokemon: The First Movie," however, assumes from the get-go that if you're in the theater in the first place, you know enough about the little critters and their handlers to bypass any explication.

So if you're inclined to use the occasion of "The First Movie's" release to figure out the rhyme or reason behind this global, multi-tiered and highly lucrative Pokemon thing, you shouldn't expect much. Indeed, one gets the sense from watching the movie that even its creators are asking themselves why and how Pokemon got so big, so fast.

But let's not get ahead of ourselves, shall we? Let's give a little of our valuable space to those who have spent the last year-and-a-half in underground ice caverns. Pokemon is short for "pocket monsters" and they first entered public consciousness from Japan via a portable Nintendo game three years ago.

Since then, it's become an animated TV series that's so popular, it sometimes swallows up the whole WB network's Saturday morning schedule.

Both the game and the show involve these cute, inventively designed creatures with "special powers" that are captured and deployed in a kind of martial-arts-with-critter-proxies by trainers such as plucky Ash Ketchum and his pals Misty and Brock. Ash's prized possession is Pikachu, a lovable little yellow whatchamacallit that, when necessary, can fry a whole room with tons of voltage. The little guy gets his own short subject, "Pikachu's Vacation," to help us understand what these creatures do when they're not in their trainer's pockets waiting for action.

This review has neither the space nor the inclination to mention the approximately 150 other Pokemon. If you need help, open a window and call out for a collector. It won't take long for one to show up.

The movie's story involves the creation of a man-made Pokemon: a super-powered model named Mewtwo, who's not only a state-of-the-art pocket creature but a gifted trainer in his own night. He's a scary guy, but he's asking the right question: "Why am I here?" He doesn't know whether he's been created to be mankind's "slave" or its master.

It turns out he's been cloned by scientists who should know better from the hairs of a rare Pokemon named Mew, who, like the others, is cute but packs a wallop if aroused. Mewtwo, in turn, decides to clone every Pokemon into a meaner version of the original. Flawed copies, huh? Sounds like a message to all those card collectors out there to be wary of counterfeit Pokemon cards.

The ensuing battle of clones vs. originals eventually yields a "positive" message to its young audience. Somehow, such sentiments seem at odds with the acquisitive nature of the phenomenon. Which, make no mistake, is reinforced throughout this movie. As with every other kid-cult movie, "Pokemon: The First Movie" will only make its already hooked target audience want to "catch some more." And, as noted, the movie won't be able to explain why.

SIGHT AND SOUND, 6/00, p. 50, Ken Hollings

Japan, the present. Cloned from the remains of Mew, an ancient forebear, Mewtwo is the most powerful of the species of creatures know as the Pokémon. Refusing to obey his human creators, he destroys their island laboratory and vows to use his psychic abilities to conquer the world. Shortly afterwards Ash, a young Pokémon trainer, receives an invitation to a Pokémon championship on New Island, where selected trainers can challenge the World's Greatest Pokémon Master.

On arrival, Ash discovers the competition is a trap set by Mewtwo, who separates the Pokémon from their human trainers, then uses their DNA to create clones with which to rule the planet. Unable to withstand Mewtwo's powers, the Pokémon are soon fighting with their clones. Ash attempts to intervene, assisted by Mew, who has been restored to life. Accidentally killed while trying to stop Mew and Mewtwo from destroying each other, Ash is revived by the tears of the mourning Pokémon. Moved by such devotion, Mewtwo leaves New Island, taking his clones with him, to seek his true purpose in life.

To the adult mind, which in this case probably constitutes anyone above the age of 12, a mass-media marketing phenomenon such as Nintendo's *Pokémon* appears as a dark conspiracy to foster confusion and dread among grown ups. Suddenly children are speaking in strange tongues and worshipping graven images. Unfortunately, the first feature-length animated film to star the Pocket Monsters makes very few concessions to the uninitiated. Plot strands and background stories from both the games and the television series are shuffled on and off the big screen without explanation. This leaves the conflict between Mewtwo and Ash centre stage as the sole narrative focus. Brooding, articulate and vengeful where the other Pokémon remain bright blobs of wordless energy, Mewtwo alone justifies the film's enhanced production values and grandiose score. Like a troubled elder brother, Mewtwo represents an older order of experience. it is perhaps no accident scenes depicting his creation and early life contain strong echoes of such anime classics as *Ghost in the Shell*, *Akira* and *Evangelion*, all of which are geared to teen and adult audiences.

At the same time there's something very affecting about the ferocious loyalty Ash and Pikachu, his Pokémon companion, display for each other. The movie may have been designed to shift Pokémon product but it also comes down hard on the side of friendship, mutual respect and resourcefulness. Similarly, the sight of an arena filled with Pokémon mindlessly bludgeoning their cloned doubles to a standstill offers a strong message about the futility of violence for its own sake—especially after *Pikachu's Vacation*, the short film packaged with *Pokémon*, has revealed that Pokémon do not usually battle without their trainers.

At its best, this is pure gothic eye candy. Mewtwo's refuge resembles an evil amusement park, complete with rotating windmills, steeply angled slides and glittering towers, while his underground laboratory boasts an equally imposing array of mechanical arms, conveyor belts and chemical vats. The arena itself, setting for the film's final conflict, has a shadowy three-dimensional grandeur that only serves to highlight the sparkling web of tears cast over it by the grieving Pokémon. Not surprisingly, with Ash restored to life, the story ends with the happy promise of further adventures to come. Whether parents and teachers alike will find the Pocket Monsters as menacing the next time around still remains to be seen.

TIME, 11/22/99, p. 82, Richard Corliss

A movie critic is no more likely to ask for mercy than he is to dish it out. And his first rule is: never plead ignorance. But this time a confession and a request are in order.

Know this, Pokémoniacs: your world is alien and barren to me. I have never so much as held a Game Boy—though in my role as uncle, I have held boys who were playing the game. I don't know the Pokémon toys, cards or comic books. I once watched 10 minutes of the Pokémon TV show, and that particular episode must have been the antidote to the one that provoked seizures in 700 Japanese kids; it put me near to sleep. So as I describe my exasperation with *Pokémon: The First Movie*, be gentle in your derision. Sometimes the young have to indulge their elders.

I was ready to return the favor as I watched *Pikachu's Vacation*, a harmless, mildly inventive short cartoon that precedes the feature. The plot, eventually, is about the communal effort to pull a dragon's head out of a drainpipe. But the fun comes before, as the whole gang cavorts—heads rolling, bodies warping—in a cheery Dadaist vaudeville that echoes Bob Campell's 1938 Looney Tunes triumph, *Porky in Wackyland*.

Then comes the feature, and charm is replaced by the dull treatment of a way-too-familiar scenario. As in the James Bond film *The Man with the Golden Gun*, an evil genius lords it over a mountainous island patrolled by a supermonster. The monster here is Mewtwo, a kitty clone or copycat of cuddly Mew. And as in *Toy Story*, the old-fashioned toys (like Mew) have to teach the mechanized ones (like Two) a bit about human values.

Now it someone would instruct the filmmakers about cartoon values. This picture has none. It lacks visual wit and expressiveness of movement. It has no pace, or even much of a pulse. As a Rastafarian moviegoer might say, "It's pokey, mon."

Last confession: I'm as eager to pretend understanding of a hot fad as any journalist. And I do like things kids like; this summer I read all three Harry Potter books, aloud and enthralled, to my wife. So I'm no grinch. Honest. I'm just a guy who loves good cartoons and, when he sees a bad one, gets a little ... *bit... UPSET.*

VILLAGE VOICE, 11/23/99, p. 142, Michael Atkinson

Stand aside, for I am the master of Perplexichu, the 152nd Pokémon species of the Head-Slapping variety, with the special power of Gape! In combat, my Pokémon can muster the Alarmed Gaze, before which poorly trained moviemakers crumble! My Pokémon can even transform into Irkadon, a highly evolved Pokémon of the Cranky Critic variety! Hmm!

Upon confronting *Pokémon the First Movie,* as Pokémon Master declare, yes! Under my command, there will be a thousand more Pokémovies! Without my own Pokémon to battle other Pokémon just as some have illegally set fighting cocks on each other for fun and profit, I might've thought, five minutes into the lysergic introductory short *Pikachu's Vacation,* that I'd died and gone to very-bad-acid hell. In fact, entire hunks of the feature (about a cloned, psychic feline Pokémon endeavoring to take over the world by cloning more Pokémon, the bastard!) made me wish I was Dopechu, air Pokémon of the Peyote variety. Amid the low-grade *Akira* brimstone, noxious cuteness, and stone-knives animation, the Pokémon universe reveals itself here to the newcomer as possibly the most deranged, pointlessly complex, automatic-writing-like, cultural manifestation outside the cosmologies of the more creative psychotics. It makes the *Star Wars* mythos play like Pong.

Reeling in Poké-sorrow as the movie climaxed with the evil clone Pikachu pounding the peacefully protesting original Pikachu, Perplexichu didn't buy the antiviolence message any more than I did, since Pokémon live to serve masters like me! and fight! Grown-ups will be stunned into a brain-blockaded silence, but kids everywhere, for whom this is a motivational training film for increased binging on trading cards and video games, will bask as if in an opium fog.

Also reviewed in:
NEW YORK TIMES, 11/10/99, p. E1, Anita Gates
VARIETY, 11/15-21/99, p. 88, Robert Koehler
WASHINGTON POST, 11/10/99, p. C1, Mark Jenkins
WASHINGTON POST, 11/12/99, Weekend/p. 49, Michael O'Sullivan

PORT DJEMA

A Shadow Distribution release of a Paradis Films/Orly Films/La General d'Images/Classic Srl/Theo Angelopoulos Productions films. *Executive Producer:* Bernard Lorain. *Producer:* Marc Soustras. *Director:* Eric Heumann. *Screenplay (French with English subtitles):* Eric Heumann, Jacques Lebas, and Lam Le. *Director of Photography:* Yorgos Arvanitis. *Editor:* Isabelle Dedieu. *Music:* Sanjay Mishra. *Sound:* François Waledisch. *Casting:* Frédérique Moidon. *Production Designer:* Danka Semenowicz and Yves Bernard. *Costumes:* Valerie Delafosse. *Running time:* 93 minutes. *MPAA Rating:* Not Rated.

CAST: Jean Yves Dubois (Dr. Pierre Feldman); Nathalie Boutefeu (Alice); Christopher Odent (Jérôme Delbos); Edouard Montoute (Ousman); Frédéric Pierrot (Dr. Antoine Barasse); Claire Wauthion (Sister Marie-Françoise).

NEW YORK POST, 1/1/99, p. 33, Hannah Brown

"Port Djema," a moody look at the perils of colonialism, is visually stunning but emotionally unsatisfying.

The emptiness at the core of this ambitious and earnest movie, which is set in a fictional East African country, is primarily the fault of its sketchy script. The characters simply aren't fully realized.

But it's still an accomplished debut by director Eric Heumann (the producer of "Indochine"), who won the best director prize at the Berlin Film Festival.

"Port Djema," which was filmed in the haunting deserts and ports of Eritrea, tells the story of Pierre (Jean-Yves Dubois), a man in unfamiliar territory.

He's a Parisian surgeon who comes to Port Djema to investigate the death of his friend and former colleague, Antoine (Frederic Pierrot).

Antoine was drawn into the bitter civil war that is tearing the country apart, and worked for the Muslim rebels in the north. Pierre retraces his friend's steps to try to find a child befriended by Antoine.

France's policy in Port Djema is ambiguous, according to the vaguely sinister consular official (Christophe Odent) who follows Pierre.

It's clear that there is danger and a great deal of suffering in this impoverished region. But Pierre simply withdraws when confronted by Port Djema's troubled citizens. He helps a soldier who has been shot, but ignores a woman and her sick baby in rebel territory.

While this may be psychologically accurate (how many people would risk their lives for strangers?), it's a letdown dramatically. The viewer keeps waiting for Pierre to experience an epiphany that will inspire him to help the victims of the war.

But it doesn't happen. Even when he meets a sultry Swiss photographer, Alice (Nathalie Boutefeu), they merely speak in loaded, very French parables about life and death, smoke a few cigarettes and go their separate ways.

While Heumann's refusal to give pat answers is admirable, the many unanswered questions raised by this literate script become frustrating.

Bertrand Tavernier's much more direct "Coup de Torchon" (1981) gave a clearer portrait of French colonialism.

But "Port Djema" shows enough promise to suggest that Heumann's next film will be worth seeing.

Also reviewed in:
CHICAGO TRIBUNE, 3/19/99, Friday/p. P, Michael Wilmington
NEW YORK TIMES, 1/1/99, p. E12, Anita Gates
VARIETY, 2/24-3/2/97, p. 82, David Stratton

PORT OF LAST RESORT, THE

A release of The National Center for Jewish Film of a Pinball Films production in association with Estrafilm. *Producer:* Joan Grossman and Paul Rosdy. *Director:* Joan Grossman and Paul Rosdy. *Screenplay:* Joan Grossman and Paul Rosdy. *Director of Photography:* Wolfgang Lehner. *Editor:* Joan Grossman and Paul Rosdy. *Music:* John Zorn. *Sound:* Vincent Tese. *Running time:* 79 minutes. *MPAA Rating:* Not Rated.

VOICES: Barbara Sukowa; Otto Tausig; Jaromir Borek; Erika Deutinger; Fritz von Friedl; Brigitta Furgler; INTERVIEWS WITH: Fred Fields; Ernest Heppner; Illo Heppner; Sigmar Simon.

NEW YORK POST, 12/9/99, p. 58, Hannah Brown

"The Port of Last Resort," a documentary that is a fascinating look at the intense clash of cultures that occurred when 20,000 Jews fled Hitler's Europe for Shanghai in the late '30s and early '40s.

Co-directors Joan Grossman and Paul Rosdy resist the temptation to be anything but straightforward as they combine home movies, excerpts from letters, refugees' reminiscences, newsreels, music and other archival material to explore a little-known chapter in Jewish history.

Their restraint pays off. "Port" is a moving look at survival in alien and harsh surroundings, one that will touch a chord not only in those who follow Holocaust history, but in anyone who has ever been homesick.

Jews ended up in China, the film explains, not out of any interest in Chinese culture but because few other countries were willing to take them then.

Recalls former refugee Fred Fields: "There is one place on earth where you can go without any paper, no permit, no affidavit, no visa. You just get there—that's Shanghai."

Arriving by ship, with just eight German marks apiece, the Jews lived on charity at first, then managed to build a thriving Jewish community, complete with newspapers, theater and cafes.

While some dreamed of Europe, America or Israel, others found themselves attracted to the Far East. "God forgive me, [Shanghai] was the most exciting and unique city in the world. She was poison, and the old-time Shanghai-landers were addicts who could never free themselves from being in love with her," wrote one man.

But after the Japanese tightened their hold on Shanghai in 1942, the Jews were forced to live in a ghetto and suffered from severe malnutrition and disease.

In spite of their mixed feelings about the years they spent in their Far Eastern refuge, several admitted that they wouldn't want to have missed the experience of living there, and this compelling film makes clear.

It's playing with John Burgan's "Memory of Berlin," a documentary about an Englishman's search for his birth parents in Berlin.

VILLAGE VOICE, 6/15/99, p. 150, Ryan Deussing

Joan Grossman and Paul Rosdy's *Port of Last Resort* tells the little-known story of nearly 20,000 Central European Jews who—in the face of growing persecution from the Nazis—fled to Shanghai in the years leading up to World War II. A collage of stunning archival footage, letters, newspaper clippings, and interviews with former refugees, the film succeeds in conveying the peculiar combination of relief and despair that developed as these stateless exiles eluded European concentration camps only to be deposited in a seething, foreign metropolis largely controlled by Hitler's allies. Though they sought only a temporary safe haven, most of these Jews remained in Shanghai for nearly a decade, moving from so-called Little Vienna, which sprung up as immigrants flocked to the free port, to Hongkew, the wretched ghetto overseen by the Japanese.

The material that forms the backbone of the film ranges from color footage of Vienna in 1938, in which storefronts are smeared with anti-Semitic graffiti, to a document printed by the German consulate in Shanghai warning residents that Jewish immigrants would bring with them "crime, sin, and intrigue." A particularly moving newsreel outtake shows starving Chinese—who also suffered during Shanghai's Japanese occupation—sweeping the street for individual grains of rice.

"It wasn't like China welcomed the Jews," explains Rosdy. "Shanghai (pre-Pearl Harbor) was under Japanese control, and the Japanese thought the presence of the Jews could help their relations with America. They believed America was under Jewish control—they even thought Roosevelt was a Jew." One former refugee explains that throughout the war, rumors were afoot that Hitler had sent a special envoy to Shanghai charged with bribing the Japanese to murder Jewish refugees.

Though many refugees did die in Shanghai, especially in the ghetto, the film is ultimately a survival story, documenting the refugees' passage from persecution to freedom. The extraordinary circumstances of their exile in Shanghai are depicted in personal terms, through letters as well as through interviews with survivors, who ultimately abandoned Shanghai as the Communists took control. The recollection of one refugee depicts the city as a dangerous pleasure: "She was the most exciting and unique city in the world. She was poison, and the old-time Shanghailanders were addicts who never could free themselves from being in love with her."

VILLAGE VOICE, 12/14/99, p. 180, Leslie Camhi

In the 1930s, Shanghai was the world's only free port—no papers or payment required for entry. So at the start of World War II, nearly 20,000 Jewish refugees from Nazi-occupied Europe set out for the city, then under siege by Japanese forces. They bartered Impressionist paintings for a place on ship, or crowded aboard the Trans-Siberian railroad. Once there, they re-created a lost world of Viennese coffeehouses, German newspapers, and kosher restaurants. *The Port of Last Resort,* a richly detailed documentary by directors Joan Grossman and Paul Rosdy combines newsreel footage with home movies, photographs, letters, and reminiscences by four former refugees, to recall this twilight of European Jewish culture, existing in the shadow of the Orient's great den of iniquity.

John Burgan's *Memory of Berlin* (also screening at Anthology) follows a more private journey that this English director took back to the German city he had visited as a child, with his adoptive family, at the height of Cold War tensions. Even then he had sensed that Berlin's divisions mirrored his own half-understood personal history. When the wall came down he returned there, and set about searching long-distance for his birth parents in London and Australia. His strangely affecting film is a poetic meditation on a city that remains deeply split in time and psychology, and on an adoptee's sense of being haunted by an alternative history. Yet it walks a thin line between emotional reticence and avant-garde affectlessness, and sometimes the latter wins.

Also reviewed in:
NEW YORK TIMES, 12/9/99, p. E5, Anita Gates
VARIETY, 12/6-12/99, p. 87, Ken Eisner

PORTRAITS CHINOIS

A Phaedra Cinema release. *Producer:* Georges Benayoun. *Director:* Martine Dugowson. *Screenplay (French with English subtitles):* Martine Dugowson and Peter Chase. *Director of Photography:* Vincenzo Marano. *Editor:* Noelle Boisson. *Music:* Peter Chase. *Sound:* Jean-Pierre Ruh. *Production Designer:* Pierre Guffroy. *Running time:* 105 minutes. *MPAA Rating:* Not Rated.

CAST: Helena Bonham Carter (Ada); Romane Bohringer (Lise); Marie Trintigant (Nina); Yvan Attal (Yves); Jean-Philippe Ecoffey (Paul); Elsa Zylberstein (Emma); Sergio Castellitto (Guido); Miki Manojlovic (Alphonse); Jean-Claude Brialy (Rene Sandre); Sophie Minon (Agnes); Emmannuelle Escourrou (Stephanie); Pierre Ballot (Monsieur Verdoux).

LOS ANGELES TIMES, 5/19/00, Calendar/p. 9, Kevin Thomas

With her second feature, "Portraits Chinois," Martine Dugowson takes a wry look at a group of Parisian thirtysomethings steeped in self-absorption, sporting slightly shaggy looks and searching for love wherever they can find it and with little regard to the consequences. While this film hasn't the scope or the depth of Dugowson's standout debut feature, "Mina Tannenbaum," a story of the ups and downs of a lifelong friendship between two women, it is sharply observant in an amused way and maintains the light, brisk touch crucial for a film more comedy than drama.

At the center of a clutch of entangled lives is Helena Bonham Carter's Ada, an Englishwoman who for 10 years has been a top designer at a Paris fashion establishment run firmly by its proprietor, Rene Sandre (Jean-Claude Braily). She and her lover of a decade, Paul (Jean-Philippe Ecoffey), have taken a vast apartment in an old building that is perhaps a bit beyond their means. Since things haven't been going all that great between them, Ada instantly decides she must have been out of her mind to have made this move with Paul but decides to make the best of it.

In the meantime Sandre announces he is taking on a young designer, Lise (Romane Bohringer), and adds that he is concerned that Ada has become a bit too sure of herself. As if this weren't enough for Ada to deal with, Lise has had a crush on Paul for years, ever since as a young teenager she waited on Ada and Paul's group at her father's cafe. Now Lise is coming on strong to Paul, and her timing may be just right, for Paul not only is feeling edgy about Ada but also is struggling with his writing partner, Guido (Sergio Castellito), to come up with a script long overdue for their producer Alphonse (Miki Manojlovic) and director Yves (Yvan Attal).

Yves is married to the lovely Nina (Marie Trintigant), who is adored by Guido. Mixing in this tricky group is Emma (Elsa Zylberstein), a would-be actress and cabaret artist whose only talent seems to be for compulsive shopping. (Bohringer and Zylberstein were "Mina Tannenbaum's" stars.)

"Portraits Chinois" has an effortless flow, a lively sense of spontaneity, a first-rate cast, and it makes an entertaining case for the importance of looking beyond yourself and growing up. The result is a minor but stylish work that pleases because it doesn't promise more than it can deliver.

NEW YORK POST, 11/5/99, p. 61, Lou Lumenick

[*Portraits Chinois* was reviewed jointly with *Some Fish Can Fly*; see Lumenick's review of that film.]

VILLAGE VOICE, 11/16/99, p. 140, Justine Elias

In Martine Dugowson's debut film, *Mina Tannenbaum*, there's a superbly apt description of the tumultuous relationship between two longtime female friends. "With time," one of them realizes, "she preferred the memory of her friend to her presence." That bittersweet sentiment is again explored in Dugowson's *Portraits Chinois*. The setting is Paris, where a group of smart, stylish friends—all involved in film production, fashion design, or both—fall in and out of love with each other. Ada (Helena Bonham Carter), an English designer, lives with her screenwriter boyfriend, Paul (Jean-Philippe Ecoffey). At their housewarming party, various insecurities emerge: A seemingly meek coworker named Lise (Romane Bohringer) covets both Ada's job and her man, and Paul's writing partner, the hopelessly gauche Guido (Sergio Castellito), is distracted by his pathetic love life. If the situation sounds like a dozen other American independent films about postcollegiate clusterfucking in the big city, it's not. *Portraits Chinois* lets its intertwined stories emerge with considerable warmth. As in *Mina Tannenbaum*, people always seem to be sounding out arguments in their heads—and the director allows the audience to hear their secret thoughts, whispered in voice-over. The performances are uniformly strong, and Bonham Carter has no trouble fitting into this particularly Parisian ensemble. Speaking French, she seems freer to explore the vulnerability beneath her sometimes brittle screen persona. In *Portraits Chinois*, she, like the story, has room to breathe.

Also reviewed in:
NEW YORK TIMES, 11/5/99, p. E20, Lawrence Van Gelder

PRINCESS MONONOKE

A Miramax Films release of a Tokuma Shoten Nippon Television Network, Dentsu, and Studio Ghibli presentation of a Studio Ghibli production. *Executive Producer:* Yasuyoshi Tokuma, Bob Weinstein, Harvey Weinstein and Scott Martin. *Producer:* Toshio Suzuki. *Director:* Hayao Miyazaki. *Screenplay and story:* Hayao Miyazaki. *Screenplay (English Adaptation):* Neil Gaiman. *Editor:* Takeshi Seyama. *Music:* Joe Hisaishi. *Animation:* Masahi Ando, Kitaro Kosaka, and Yoshifumi Kondo. *Sound:* Shuji Inoue, (music) Masayoshi Okawa and Makoto Morimoto. *Sound Editor:* Steve Schwartz and Charlotte Stobbs. *Voice Direction:* Jack Fletcher. *Running time:* 135 minutes. *MPAA Rating:* PG-13.

VOICES: Billy Crudup (Ashitaka); Billy Bob Thornton (Jigo); Minnie Driver (Lady Eboshi); John Di Maggio (Gonza); Claire Danes (San); John De Mita (Kohroku); Jada Pinkett-Smith (Toki); Gillian Anderson (Moro); Ketih David (Okkoto); ADDITIONAL VOICES: Corey Burton; Tara Charandoff; Keith David; John De Mita; Julia De Mita; Debi Derryberry; John DiMaggio; Alex Fernandez; Jack Fletcher; Patrick Fraley; John Hostetter; John Rafter Lee; Jessica Lynn; Sherry Lynn; Matt Miller; Marnie Mosiman; Tress MacNeille; Matt McKenzie; Michael McShane; Adam Paul; David Rasner; Dwight Schultz; Pamela Segall; K.T. Vogt.

NEW YORK, 11/8/99, p. 64, Peter Rainer

I only have room here to say that there are ravishments to be found in the legendary Japanese animator Hayao Miyazaki's *Princess Mononoke*, set in a mythic fourteenth century where forest creatures and demons and humans war against a wash of exquisite watercolor vistas. Utilizing traditional hand-drawn cels and some computer-generated imagery, Miyazaki brings out the animism in this emerald vision and gives it a spaciousness rarely found even in live-action epics.

NEW YORK POST, 10/29/99, p. 45, Jonathan Foreman

With the exception of "Titanic," Hayao Miyazakai's epic "Princess Mononoke" is Japan's highest grossing film ever, and for good reason.

It's the "Star Wars" of animated features, a haunting, beautiful film that holds your attention despite its length and its complex plot, which is rooted in Japanese folk tales and animist mythology.

"Mononoke" is a cartoon in the tradition of anime rather than Walt Disney, in that it's aimed at adults as much as children (it includes some graphic limb-lopping violence but no songs). But it eschews the cyberpunk influence and panty-flashing of other well-known anime films like "Perfect Blue" and "Akira."

The action takes place in medieval Japan, as the world, once dominated by animal and tree spirits, increasingly comes under the control of human beings.

Ashitaka (Billy Crudup) is a prince of the dying Emishi clan, who inhabit a remote mountain village in northern Japan. When a demon in the form of a giant wild boar attacks the village, Ashitaka kills it. But in doing so he is touched by the creature, and therefore inherits its curse.

The village's wise-woman tells that him that eventually he will die from the curse and that he must leave forever. Ashitaka travels far to the West on his red elk in search of a powerful Forest Spirit who might be able to lift his curse.

On his way he comes upon Iron Town, a community of the rejected, ruled by the imperious but benevolent Lady Eboshi (Minnie Driver). Iron Town has a giant smelting works, operated by former brothel girls recruited by Lady Eboshi. It sells iron to both the emperor and predatory samurai, and it has a powerful thirst for charcoal.

That thirst for fuel requires the stripping the forest of its trees. This has provoked an escalating conflict with the forest gods, including the giant white wolf Moro (Gillian Anderson), her two pups, and her adopted human child Mononoke, also known as San (Claire Danes). (Moro and the other characters seem like intelligent but threatening beasts rather than the cuddly, anthropomorphic Disney creatures.

Mononoke hates the Lady Eboshi and tries to kill her. Ashitaka stops the assassination but also stops the townspeople from killing Mononoke. He sympathizes with both sides, but the animals and their protectors are just as unreasonable as the human beings, and a catastrophic war is inevitable.

The animation is only inferior to Disney in the way that faces are drawn (the characters have those odd "Speed Racer" eyes).

But Miyazakai's strange and lovely creatures, brilliant details (like sunlight flashing off sword blades), and vast battle scenes reminiscent of Kurosawa's films, make this a visually stunning film.

NEWSDAY, 10/29/99, Part II/p. B6, John Anderson

One of the biggest money-makers in the history of Japanese cinema, "Princess Mononoke" is that almost-unheard-of item, the animated movie for adults. It's not just the violence-severed heads, severed, limbs, roiling rivers of blood—that should probably keep the Pokémon crowd at home. It's more the sentiments of the movie—and its elegiac qualities, its lack of belief in an imminent Apocalypse—that make it more suited for audiences with a developed sense of environmental justice.

Based on Asian folklore and being sold as the crowning achievement of anime, or cutting-edge Japanese animation, "Mononoke" is set in a far off mystical time where demons and spirits are as common as squirrels. The ruined, dying Emishi clan is under attack by a churning, pulsing, gore-spewing monster and the young warrior Ashitaka (voice of Billy Crudup) rises to the occasion and kills the beast, at the center of whose throbbing, anemone-like outer surface is a wounded boar, whose body has been slowly ravaged internally by a mysterious iron ball.

Ashitaka, too, has been wounded, on the arm—a wound that he's told will eventually spread throughout his body, drive him mad and kill him.

So Ashitaka, searching for redemption from the elusive Spirit of the Forest/Nightwalker, becomes the proverbial wanderer of legend. And the various factions he encounters on his way—the smelters and forgers of Iron Town, for instance, ruled by the despotic Lady Eboshi

(Minnie Driver)—provides a political metaphor for everything from suburban sprawl to the burning of the rainforest.

Romance, as it must, arrives via Princess Mononoke herself (Claire Danes), a warrior girl reared by the wolf goddess Moro (Gillian Anderson) and set on killing Eboshi, who is intent on killing the Forest Spirit and thus making the land safe for iron foundries, subdivisions and, in all likelihood, theme parks.

Feverish and obvious, yes, but there's also a majesty to "Princess Mononoke," whether in the Monet-evoking landscapes or the sequences of misty mountain serenity that separate one blood-splattered battle scene from another. The film does, however, contain a lot of those techniques that American audiences—those raised on anything from "Speed Racer" to "Hello Kitty"—would recognize as distinctly Japanese: static backgrounds, an economy of movement, a reliance on repeated movements and a kind of pulsing rhythm within those movements. Also, an overly hasty, quasi-hysterical delivery of dialogue.

The effect, for anyone more comfortable with the glass-like surfaces of Disney animation, can come across as relatively cheesy. But "Princess Mononoke" is a movie seemingly unbound by financial restraints; its aesthetic is intentional, calculated and at a curious variance with the luxe cartoon that Americans consider state-of-the-art.

The really curious thing, though, is how westernized director Hayao Miyazaki's characters look. The big eyes and sculpted noses, part of what's become a Japanese animation tradition, seem to be a striving for a beautiful blankness, an anonymity of physical characteristic—except for the hair, in fact, Princess Mononoke and Ashitaki could be twins.

Usually, the vocal performances in an animated film are too unremarkable for mention, but not so in "Mononoke." As the title character, Danes is borderline whiny; the princess doesn't say "whatever," but she might. As Moro, Anderson lowers her register and heightens the tension. And Driver, who can be a tad irritating in the flesh, is terrifically haughty as Lady Eboshi. After her equally impressive turn as Jane in Disney's "Tarzan," she may have found her new, or true, calling.

NEWSWEEK, 11/1/99, p. 87, David Ansen

"Princess Mononoke," the most successful anime film in Japanese history, breaks most of the animation rules Walt Disney lived by. Hayao Miyazaki's wonderous 14th-century tale about the never-ending battle between man and nature isn't the usual bouncy and compact 75 minutes but a leisurely (though action-packed) 2 ¼ hours. No animals trot out their borscht-belt routines. No one bursts into song. The handsome prince and the beautiful princess don't get married. Most remarkable of all, good and evil are not conveniently packaged in separate, clearly marked containers, but spread about equally in almost every character—man, woman, beast or god. This, you see, is the thinking kid's cartoon.

Infused with a mystical animist spirit, this lyrical and often savage epic tells of a young prince who has fallen under a curse for killing a demon boar. Hoping to free himself from the lethal curse, he journeys to the forest—ruled by the magical Forest Spirit—where trees and animals are being destroyed by humans. The prince finds himself in the middle of a war between man and nature, the latter represented by gods in the form of wolves and boars. But this is no simple Nature Good/Man Bad ecological fairy tale. Everyone has his reasons, and no one has a lock on virtue. This English-language version—using the voices of Billy Crudup, Claire Danes, Billy Bob Thornton and Minnie Driver—has a few lapses into banality, but the beauty and scale of Miyazaki's vision shines through. You'll see why, in animation circles, Miyazaki himself is considered one of the gods.

VILLAGE VOICE, 11/2/99, p. 133, J. Hoberman

The highest-grossing movie (save *Titanic*) in Japanese history, Hayao Miyazaki's *Princess Mononoke* is a complex, superbly rendered, and wildly eccentric anime—even by Miyazaki's own standards. This epic folk pageant, set in an exquisitely detailed 15th-century world of lava-lamp deities and teeming marketplaces, posits an apocalyptic pantheism in which endangered species turn demonic. The theme recalls Miyazaki's ecological sci-fi *Nausicaä* (1984), albeit with greater graphic violence. The characters include a possessed boar who writhes like an animated plate of spaghetti, a princess who runs with the wolves, a tribe of red-eyed apes, and a forest full of toadstool sprites—not to mention an iron foundry staffed by lepers and ex-prostitutes. The mystical Shinto premise is an agreeable jumble—not understanding adds to the pleasure. Indeed, U.S. distributor Miramax scarcely familiarizes the material even with the dubbed-in voices of Minnie Driver, Billy Bob Thornton, and (being Princess Mononoke) Claire Danes.

Also reviewed in:
CHICAGO TRIBUNE, 10/29/99, Friday/p. A, Mark Caro
NEW YORK TIMES, 9/27/99, p. E1, Janet Maslin
VARIETY, 2/2-8/98, p. 28, Leonard Klady
WASHINGTON POST, 11/5/99, p. C5, Stephen Hunter
WASHINGTON POST, 11/5/99, Weekend/p. 49, Desson Howe

PRIVATE CONFESSIONS

A Castle Hill/First Run Features release of Sveriges Television Drama production in collaboration with NRK/DR/YLE-2/RUV-TV and the Nordic-TV Coproduction fund, with support by the Swedish Film Institute. *Executive Producer:* Kaj Larsen. *Producer:* Ingrid Dahlberg. *Director:* Liv Ullmann. *Screenplay (Swedish with English subtitles):* Ingmar Bergman. *Director of Photography:* Sven Nykvist. *Editor:* Michal Leszczylowski. *Music:* Jan B. Larsson. *Sound:* Bengt Wallman, Gunnar Landstrom, and (music) Owe Svensson. *Production Designer:* Mette Möller. *Costumes:* Inger Pehrsson. *Make-up:* Cecilia Drott-Norlén. *Running time:* 125 minutes. *MPAA Rating:* Not Rated.

CAST: Pernilla August (Anna); Samuel Fröler (Henrik); Max von Sydow (Jacob); Kristina Adolphson (Maria); Thomas Hanzon (Tomas Egerman); Gunnel Fred (Marta Gärdsjö); Hans Alfredsson (Bishop Agrell).

LOS ANGELES TIMES, 1/7/00, Calendar/p. 6, Kevin Thomas

Legendary director Ingmar Bergman and actress-turned-director Liv Ullmann have had some remarkable collaborations in the past—"Persona," "Cries and Whispers," "An Autumn Sonata," etc. Now Ullmann has directed "Private Confessions" from Bergman's script drawn from events in the lives of his own parents, whose unhappy marriage he also dissected in his script for "The Best Intentions" (1989), directed by Bille August.

The result, filmed in 1996, is as oppressive, alas, as it is impressive: The performances are luminous—with Pernilla August and Samuel Froler repeating their roles from "Best Intentions"—and its perceptions are profound. But it is so weighty and protracted you suspect that Ullmann has been overly respectful of the words and thoughts of her illustrious mentor. Ultimately, the film is worth the considerable effort it demands, but you can't help thinking that a less measured, far terser approach might have given the film considerably more vitality and impact.

Superbly structured, the film is composed of five extended conversations, confessional scenes dealing with a pivotal moment in the life of an unfaithful wife who at 45 at last can participate in the ancient Christian ritual of communion she could not at 18. "Private Confessions" charts a longing for spiritual redemption in the wake of an adulterous affair, but it also suggests that in matters of love women are capable of more strength and honesty than men.

The film opens in 1925, when August's Anna, after some hesitance, confesses to her beloved Uncle Jacob (Max Von Sydow), a man of the cloth, that she has been unfaithful to Henrik (Froler), a zealous theologian whose superior is none other than her uncle. She tells him that she has plunged into a passionate affair with a young theology student, Tomas Egerman (Thomas

Hanzon). Jacob is wise, compassionate and nonjudgmental but advises that the only valid course for his niece to take is to tell her husband the truth.

At the moment of confession, Anna feels only an overwhelming relief, especially since her husband initially makes a real effort to be understanding, but soon she is swept over by guilt, just as he is by anger. Yet in a quintessentially Bergman-esque remark, Anna urges, "Let's at least be miserable together." She has already forthrightly declared that she responded to rather than resisted Tomas because she "hoped to enjoy the experience of love just once in my life." But 10 years later, when she is summoned by a now-dying Uncle Jacob to tell him how her life has been, we can see how high a price she has paid and how she has yet to forgive herself. You are left to wonder whether Anna would have been unfaithful had she known the long-term effect of her actions.

August and Von Sydow possess the stature and range their characters demand, and no small degree of Froler and Hanzon's effectiveness lies in their striking similarity in their bland good looks. Both are persuasive as men not up to dealing with the predicament that entangles them.

Photographed with the usual luster by longtime Bergman collaborator Sven Nyqvist, "Private Confessions" looks rather than feels like a Bergman film. Too much of it lacks that essential spark that enlivens even Bergman's gloomiest films.

NEW YORK POST, 1/7/99, p. 48, Jonathan Foreman

"Private Confessions" is a technically superb but joyless exercise in Bergmanesque filmmaking by the great Swedish director's acolytes and protegees.

Written by (the officially retired) Ingmar Bergman, and directed by his ex-mistress, the Norwegian actress Liv Ullmann, it retells—in five non-chronological episodes—the unremittingly gloomy story of Bergman's mother's unhappy marriage, her love affair with a divinity student, and her return to the marriage on the dubious advice of a priest.

It's a wordy, literal screenplay (writing explicitly about his own family seems to bring out the worst in Bergman). And Ullmann treats both it and her fine cast of actors with claustrophobic reverence, following one static, stagey scene with another, presumably in the mistaken belief that the master's dialogue will somehow infuse the whole with life and energy.

It is a shame, because the performances are uniformly excellent, as one would expect from superb actors such as Max von Sydow and Pernilla August (wife of the director Bille August). And the photography by the great cinematographer Sven Nykvist is as beautiful as ever.

Unfortunately, except for one episode set in a hunting-lodge-turned-love-nest, Nykvist's efforts are mostly confined to the cold, gloomy, depression-inducing interiors that seem to have been the preferred dwellings of upper-middle-class Swedes in the '20s and '30s.

You cannot help but wonder if it was not such surroundings that smothered whatever lightness and humor existed in their culture. But whatever the reason, the characters in "Private Confessions" are as remote and unsympathetic as space aliens. They have nothing but their angst, and caring about their problems is next to impossible.

There is one brilliant tension-filled episode centering on the taking of Communion in the house of a dying priest. But otherwise the film seems aimed exclusively at those filmgoers whose masochistic devotion to the Bergman mystique predisposes them to tolerate large doses of Nordic misery.

It's clearly meant to say something profound about the way people lie to themselves, and about the way that life forces them to compromise their ideals. But the results are vague and unsatisfying.

In the end, "Private Confessions" is more a technical exercise than a movie: a puritanical, earnest experiment in stripping the pleasure out of film, making it an art form to be endured rather than enjoyed.

TIME, 1/25/99, p. 75, Richard Corliss

In most people's lives, high drama is not an asteroid heading for Earth or a battle on Omaha Beach. It is the agony and suspense in an intimate conversation. Do you love me? Have you betrayed me? Will you leave me? The answers to those questions make the heart soar or sink; they leave lasting marks on the soul, like a trophy or a gravestone. Years later, we look back and think: from that moment everything was different. Yet movies rarely touch on this form of domestic convulsion. They offer escapism—not just from daily drudgery but from our most exalted apprehensions.

Ingmar Bergman has been listening to, and making, these confessions for half a century—in films, such as *The Seventh Seal, Through a Glass Darkly* and *Persona*, that define the age of anxiety. And though Bergman retired from film directing in 1983, he has continued to write for the screen, wrestling with his Lutheran God, facing up to his household demons, making them the stuff of astringent artistry.

Private Confessions (known in Europe as *Private Conversations,* after Martin Luther's term for his version of the sacrament of penance) is the last of a trilogy of films about his parents. All three—the others are the 1982 *Fanny and Alexander* and the 1992 *Best Intentions*—were made as Swedish TV serials, then condensed for theatrical release. This film, directed by Bergman's lustrous actress Liv Ullmann, is the finest of the three. It distills four lives into a series of chats, revelatory confessions, between a woman and the men in her life.

First conversation, July 1925: Anna (Pernilla August) tells her uncle, Pastor Jacob (Max von Sydow), of her affair with Tomas (Thomas Hanzon), a divinity student; Jacob advises her to reveal the affair to her husband Henrik (Samuel Froler), also a clergyman. Second conversation, a few weeks later: Anna tells Henrik. Third, a few months before: Anna and Tomas have their tryst. Fourth, 10 years later: Anna talks with Jacob about her marriage and the affair. Final conversation, May 1907: the 18-year-old Anna makes a confession to Jacob.

Two people talking—drama and life in its essence. The camera, manned by Bergman's master cinematographer, Sven Nykvist, holds on the actors' faces as they pour or spit out their lines. The film could lie there, inert and artless as an episode of an afternoon soap opera. It doesn't; it brings old rancors and flames alive. These troubled folks might be your parents, or you.

Bergman is back in the haunted house he built for himself. He sets his favorite obsessions—God and sex—at war in all these desperate creatures. The men try balancing their clerical duties with their clumsy passions. Henrik's first reaction on hearing of Anna's infidelity is to console her, as a minister would a sinner; Tomas kneels before Anna as a communicant receiving the Eucharist, or a child before its mother. Love is a sacrament of which neither man is worthy. Henrik and Tomas are really complementary halves of one weak man: the Bergman man. Henrik tastes the truth as if it were a bitter plum, and the corners of his mouth tighten in rage and impotence.

Anna, whose conflicted intelligence exercises itself in passion (when that was the only outlet allowed a middle-class woman), is more than a match for her husband or her lover. Her passion is as potent as Tomas' guilt or Henrik's rage. She can plan an adulterous weekend as if it were a state dinner and tell Henrik that "the thought of your seed in my body was unbearable." She can dish out the awful truth or a blessed lie, and her men don't know the difference. Her only proper adversary is a disapproving God.

And her only pipeline to the Almighty is Jacob, who watches her judiciously, lovingly, over the 28 years of this story. Von Sydow, a Bergman stalwart since he played the knight in *The Seventh Seal,* has graduated to a severe serenity. His face carries all Bergman's hopes and fears for Anna.

Great filmmakers create, or attract, great actors. Bergman's performers, especially his actresses—Ullmann, Eva Dahlbeck, Bibi and Harriet Andersson—have transformed his dour testaments into radiance. August (who will play the young Darth Vader's mother in the new *Star Wars* film) is an excellent heir to that magnificent tradition. Emotions don't play on her face; they live there in all their complexity and contradiction. They flush into a mischievous grin or produce tears as natural as a summer shower. Her face is a book. Read it for two hours and know the triumph and pain of a strong woman's love.

At the end of the film, the man who may have been her heart's truest desire caresses Anna's face with his large hand. An older Anna looks back on that moment with a smile that understands and accepts everything. For out of these private conversations, Bergman says, something beyond anguish or exaltation may emerge. Something like wisdom.

VILLAGE VOICE, 1/12/99, p. 61, Amy Taubin

The mother/whore dichotomy is hard to shake. In Christian cultures, the story of Jesus and his two Marys is mainlined into the unconscious from birth. One variant on this triangle is what Freud dubbed "the family romance," wherein the young boy fantasizes that his mother is a whore (or more politely, an adulteress) and that the identity of his real father is therefore up for grabs. This fantasy confers several benefits. It diminishes the authority of the father, who in the child's imagination becomes a mere cuckold, and it allows the child to libidinize his mother, to obsess over her imagined sexual transgressions and the punishments they deserve. (Freud wrote about this syndrome only from the male point of view, but there's obviously a female version as well.)

Among the filmmakers inspired by the family romance are Hitchcock (*Psycho* is the most blatant, but hardly the only, example) and Ingmar Bergman, whose scripts have become more specifically autobiographical since he allowed others to direct them. In 1992, Bille August directed *The Best Intentions* from a script that Bergman wrote about his parents. *Private Confessions,* written by Bergman and directed by Liv Ullmann, is something of a sequel to that film, with Pernilla August and Samuel Froler again playing the roles of Bergman's parents, the long-suffering Anna and the obnoxious Henrik.

The directorial credit notwithstanding, this is very much a Bergman film. The light has that Bergmanesque blue cast that's at once cold and soft, as if the film were shot through the mist rising from a glacier (and, indeed, the cinematographer is Bergman favorite Sven Nykvist). The drama is narrowly focused on marriage and religion, to the exclusion of everything else in the world. The atmosphere is heavy with guilt and suffering. Ullmann scrutinizes her actors' tears in interminable close-ups, much as, years ago, Bergman scrutinized her own.

The film is structured as a series of five conversations between Anna and all the important people in her adult life—with the significant exception of her children. (Such is Bergman's repression vis-à-vis the family romance that little Ingmar and his sibling, while frequently mentioned, never appear onscreen.) These conversations are focused exclusively on an affair that Anna had when she was in her midthirties with a man much younger than herself. For Anna, the affair, though too laden with guilt to afford any pleasure except of the most masochistic variety, is the defining event of her life.

What's strange is that everyone else is as obsessed with it as she is. Poor Anna, the doubts that have colored her religious practice from adolescence have had the effect of throwing her into the arms of zealots. Her husband is a church official, her lover is a divinity student, her closest female friend is a missionary, her uncle (Max von Sydow) is a minister who's still worrying about Anna's sex life on his deathbed. The Republican right could take lessons from this crew, although unlike Bill and Monica's adolescent hanky-panky, Anna's affair is depicted as more a matter of disrobing than groping.

I doubt that Bergman's script would have made much of a film even if he had directed it himself, but it might have been less confused. According to an interview in a Swedish paper, Ullmann believes the script is "a religious drama" and that Bergman would have had difficulty making it himself because of his lifelong struggle with faith and doubt. But the problem is that the script has nothing to say about religion that we haven't heard a thousand times over. On the other hand, Bergman does have a secular insight into the deployment of power within a marriage, and the ways that Christianity both exacerbates and masks sadomasochistic sexuality. The marriage depicted in *Private Confessions* is a dreadful relationship that brings out the worst in both husband and wife. I can't imagine any viewer not wanting Anna to do a Nora and just leave, but that doesn't seem to be the film's position, if indeed the film has a position. Perhaps Ullmann hoped that by nailing nothing down (someone please tell me what all those tiny smiles at the end are about), she'd provoke discussion. It didn't work for me. I just wanted to put every morose minute out of my mind as soon as possible.

Also reviewed in:
NEW REPUBLIC, 2/1/99, p. 24, Stanley Kauffmann
NEW YORK TIMES, 1/6/99, p. E1, Janet Maslin
VARIETY, 5/26-6/1/97, p. 67, David Stratton
WASHINGTON POST, 8/13/99, Weekend/p. 45, Desson Howe

PUNITIVE DAMAGE

A First Run/Icarus Films release of a New Zealand Film Commission presentation of an Occasional Productions production in association with New Zealand on Air, U of Auckland. *Executive Producer:* Gaylene Preston. *Producer:* Annie Goldson and Gaylene Preston. *Director:* Annie Goldson. *Director of Photography:* Leon Narbey. *Editor:* John Gilbert. *Music:* Stephen Taberner. *Sound:* Ken Saville and Brian Shennan. *Sound Editor:* Mike Hedges and John Boswell. *Production Designer:* Saskia Kouwenberg. *Running time:* 77 minutes. *MPAA Rating:* Not Rated.

CAST: Helen Todd (Kamal's Mother); Constancio Pinto (Resistance Leader); Alan Nairn (Journalist).

NEW YORK POST, 10/29/99, p. 44, Lou Lumenick

"Punitive Damage" is a thought-provoking and timely documentary about East Timor, the tiny former Portuguese colony whose controversial, 23-year occupation by Indonesia was ended this month.

New Zealand filmmaker Annie Goldson looks at the situation there through the eyes of Helen Todd, a countrywoman whose 20-year-old son Kamal, a political activist, was shot to death along with 271 unarmed East Timorese—by government troops in 1991. Todd, sent a corpse she believes probably wasn't her son's body, sued an Indonesian general in a Boston federal court and was awarded $22 million.

Drawing on court transcripts, surreptitiously shot news footage and extensive interviews, "Punitive Damage" paints a damning picture of political repression under Indonesian President Suharto, who resigned last year after the documentary was completed.

NEWSDAY, 10/29/99, Part II/p. B12, John Anderson

To adopt the vernacular of the diplomatic corps, the recent "unpleasantries" in the breakaway nation of East Timor were hardly the first. Neither, for that matter, was the 1991 massacre by the Suharto regime—armed with U.S. weaponry and U.S. political support and protection—of 200 students during anti-government protests. Most of the victims disappeared. Many were allegedly tortured before they died.

One of the few whose death was accounted for was Kamal Bamadhaj, a 21-year-old from New Zealand, who had long been active in the East Timorese cause and who, according to "Punitive Damage"—Annie Goldson's documentary chronicle of a mother's search for justice—was probably marked for death. Although Kamal's body was buried after his shooting, it was subsequently recovered and sent to Helen Todd—who couldn't identify her son, but certainly had enough anger for an international court battle.

"Punitive Damage" gives a blow-by-blow account of Kamal's upbringing and political sympathies, the casual brutality of the U. S. backed Suharto regime and the nightmare of life in East Timor. It also offers interviews with East Timorese insurgents, U.S. and Australian journalists and lawyers from the late William Kunstler's Center for Constitutional Rights in New York, who helped Todd sue the general responsible for the massacre—who was on "sabbatical" at Harvard University—under an old piracy law intended for enemies of humanity.

Eventually, Todd was awarded a total of $22 million—while, not surprisingly, the general fled to Indonesia, calling the verdict "a joke." Todd's symbolic victory—made more satisfying because of her evident dignity and strength—gives "Punitive Damage" enough emotional power to counterbalance some of Goldson's tactical errors. One is the effective but confusing device of shooting Todd and lawyer Beth Stephens in black and white, against a black backdrop, while having them go through what is apparently—we're never told for sure—their courtroom testimony. Another is the use of footage showing demonstrations and Indonesian military violence without identifying where and when the actions took place. There are also a dramatic recreation or two that seem totally unnecessary.

Certainly, none of this changes the fact that the story behind "Punitive Damage" remains moving and important. You just wish the director hadn't taken for granted our uninterest in fact.

Also reviewed in:
NATION, 11/15/99, p. 31, Stuart Klawans
NEW YORK TIMES, 10/29/99, p. E16, Anita Gates
VARIETY, 6/28-7/11/99, p. 71, David Stratton

PUSHER

A First Run Features release of a Balboa Enterprise production.. *Executive Producer:* Peter Aalbaek Jensen and Teddy Gerberg. *Producer:* Henrik Danstrup. *Director:* Nicolas Winding Refn. *Screenplay (Danish with English subtitles):* Nicolas Winding Refn and Jens Dahl. *Director of Photography:* Morten Soborg. *Editor:* Anne Osterud. *Music:* Peter Peter and Povl Kristian Mortensen. *Sound:* Peter Schultz. *Production Designer:* Kim Lovetand Julebaek. *Running time:* 105 minutes. *MPAA Rating:* Not Rated.

CAST: Kim Bodnia (Frank); Zlatko Buric (Milo); Laura Drasbaek (Vic); Slavko Labovic (Radovan); Mads Mikkelsen (Tony); Peter Andersson (Hasse); Vanja Bajicic (Branko); Lisbeth Rasmussen (Rita).

NEW YORK POST, 5/7/99, p. 53, Jonathan Foreman

"Pusher" is a realistically depressing low-budget movie about Copenhagen drug dealers collecting and incurring debts. It makes the Danish criminal life look miserable, bleak and pretty dull during the stretches when people aren't threatening or beating each other.

Nasty and seedy, it's another film clearly inspired by Tarantino's work (especially the obligatory torture scene), and by Abel Ferrara's "Bad Lieutenant," but its predictable, derivative plot is unleavened by sympathetic characters or amusing dialogue.

Instead, "Pusher"'s cast of thugs, hookers and junkies is authentically inarticulate and pathetic. This combined with the director's pseudo-documentary style (is there some law in Denmark that demands the use of a hand-held camera and minimal lighting?) gives "Pusher" a grinding quality that makes you wish that the protagonist would hurry up and get killed by the big shots to whom he owes all the money.

Frank (Bodnia) is a tough small-time thirtysomething drug dealer, in hock to bigger Yugoslav dealer Milo (Buric), who's sort of his friend. When not pushing or doing cocaine, Frank tools around Copenhagen with his sidekick Tony (Mads Mikkelsen) playing the car stereo at top volume, while both of them swear a lot and talk crudely about women. Frank has extreme intimacy problems with his waifish junkie hooker, girlfriend Vic (Laura Drasbaek).

Things really start to go wrong for Frank when a deal with a Swedish stranger is interrupted by the cops and he is forced to dump Milo's very expensive heroin in the lake.

Unfortunately, Milo isn't interested in his excuses: he just wants his money back and quickly. Frank beats Tony to a pulp with a baseball bat for talking to the cops, and then runs around town for a week desperately trying to raise the money before Milo and his goon Radovan catch up with him.

It's a shame that the dialogue is so weak, the plot so familiar, the pace so meandering, and the lighting so poor, because "Pusher"'s cast is uniformly excellent. Kim Bodnia, who vaguely resembles Bob Hoskins, does a particularly fine job. He somehow manages to make you care about Frank, even though the character has no redeeming qualities.

VILLAGE VOICE, 5/11/99, p. 72, Dennis Lim

As botched-drug-deal tales go, *Pusher* digs surprisingly deep—its surface clichés give way to an existential despair that finally swallows the movie whole. Tracking a precipitously horrible week in the life of a small-time Copenhagen smack dealer, this first feature by Danish director

Nicolas Winding Refn is a model of a downward spiral. And it doesn't pause for pop-cult free associations, art-directed trippiness, or smirking wisecracks on the way. When a shotgun goes off in someone's face, it's decidedly not a punch line.

Frank (Kim Bodnia), an impassive tough-guy type, orchestrates an elaborate deal that unfortunately involves inflating his already sizable debt to Croatian kingpin Milo (Zlatko Buric). Within days, the transaction has of course fallen apart spectacularly—the cops show, Frank ends up with neither cash nor stash, and Milo, up till now creepily hospitable in a manner that suggests Christopher Walken for the American remake, decides it's time to collect.

Pusher's antihero is an emotional wreck beneath his stoic exterior; though obviously happy to turn on the smut-talk bravado for his hair-trigger skinhead buddy, Frank is incapable of any kind of physical contact with his long-suffering hooker girlfriend. Refn, who was 25 when he made the film, gives *Pusher* a self-consciously edgy look—it's shot with available light and handheld jitters—but he doesn't OD on style. The editing is especially sharp—dynamic and disorienting without resorting to shock cuts.

Abrasive from start to finish, *Pusher* has something of the headlong inevitability of Matthieu Kassovitz's *Hate*, but it is, in some ways, a more thoughtfully configured movie. It begins in free-form, faux-vérité mode, but as Frank's predicament becomes more dire, the narrative tightens like a noose, culminating in a sequence of events that's perversely exhilarating in its precision, lucidity, and understatement. Frank's options fall away, one by one, until his condition has been distilled to one of pure desperation.

Also reviewed in:
CHICAGO TRIBUNE, 7/9/99, Friday/p. M, Michael Wilmington
NEW YORK TIMES, 5/7/99, p. E23, Anita Gates
VARIETY, 3/31-4/6/97, p. 89, Gunnar Rehlin

PUSHING TIN

A Fox 2000 Pictures and Regency Enterprises release of a Linson Films production. *Executive Producer:* Alan Greenspan and Michael Flynn. *Producer:* Art Linson. *Director:* Mike Newell. *Screenplay:* Glen Charles and Les Charles. *Based upon the article "Something's Got to Give"* by: Darcy Frey. *Director of Photography:* Gale Tattersall. *Editor:* Jon Gregory. *Music:* Anne Dudley. *Music Editor:* Michael Connell. *Sound:* D. Bruce Carwardine and (music) Roger Dudley and Steve Price. *Sound Editor:* Sue Baker. *Casting:* Ross Clydesdale. *Production Designer:* Bruno Rubeo. *Art Director:* John Dondertman. *Set Designer:* Elis Lam and Gordon White. *Set Decorator:* Clive Thomasson and Steve Shewchuk. *Set Dresser:* Greg Pelchat. *Special Effects:* Michael Kavanagh. *Costumes:* Marie-Sylvie Deveau. *Make-up:* Christine Hart. *Make-up (John Cusack and Billy Bob Thornton):* Lynne Eagan. *Make-up (Angelina Jolie):* Janeen Schreyer. *Stunt Coordinator:* Rick Forsayeth. *Running time:* 115 minutes. *MPAA Rating:* R.

CAST: John Cusack (Nick Falzone); Billy Bob Thornton (Russell Bell); Cate Blanchett (Connie Falzone); Angelina Jolie (Mary Bell); Jake Weber (Barry Plotkin); Kurt Fuller (Ed Clabes); Vicki Lewis (Tina Leary); Matt Ross (Ron Hewitt); Jerry Grayson (Leo Morton); Michael Willis (Pat Feeney); Philip Akin (Paul); Mike O'Malley (Pete); Neil Crone (Tom); Matt Gordon (Ken); Joe Pingue (Mark); Shaun Majumder (New Controller); Dwight McFee (Veteran Controller); Rob Smith (Bob); Catherine Lloyd Burns (Tanya Hewitt); Star Jasper (Julie Clabes); Molly Price (Crystal Plotkin); Sarah Knowlton (Beverly); Kiersten Warren (Karen); Andrew Dan (Diner Cook); Tennyson Loeh (Diner Waitress); Michael Hyatt (Trudy); Jillian Cameron (Falzone Girl); Michael Cameron (Falzone Boy); Carolyn Scott (Mrs. Connor); Cody Jones (Timmy); Jimmy Ruderman (Scared Student); Paul Brogren (Supermarket Clerk); Gene DiNovi (Enzo Sorrento); Emile Belcourt (Tenor); Robyn Stevan (Sara); Amanda Delaney (Bodybuilder); Ferne Downey (Serrento Customer); Joe Matheson (Announcer); Gina Clayton (Dynajet Flight Attendant); Matthew Bennett (Dynajet Steward); Jim Millington (Dynajet Captain); Ramona Milano (TV Reporter); Ray Paisley (K-9 Cop); Rita Tuckett (Lady Sparta);

Bob Bidaman (Near Miss Pilot);   Dick Callahan (TRACON Guard);   Brian King (Honeymoon Man);   Julia Paton (Honeymoon Woman);   Jenny Parsons (Flight Attendant);   John Lefebvre (Pilot);   John Robinson (Co-Pilot);   Todd Faithfull (Tina's Boyfriend).

LOS ANGELES TIMES, 4/23/99, Calendar/p. 1, Kenneth Turan

With the manic world of air traffic controllers as a backdrop, it's both fitting and unnerving that "Pushing Tin" has the feel of a near-miss. It's an intriguing film, one of the year's most interesting, but involving as much of it is, it leaves an unsatisfied taste when it's over.

Directed by Mike Newell and written by Glen Charles and Les Charles (based on a New York Times Magazine cover story by Darcy Frey), "Pushing Tin" is at its best in its opening sections. These unveil the fascinating and frightening subculture of controllers, men and women who pride themselves on having more lives in their hands on a single shift than a surgeon will in an entire career.

The work controllers do guiding planes to a safe landing is especially intense in the New York City area, where Tracon (Terminal Radar Approach Control) is responsible for three major and 47 lesser airports. That adds up to 7,000 aircraft a day in 150 square miles of air space—more planes closer together than anywhere on Earth. So no one argues when a controller says: "The universe tends toward chaos and we're the last line of defense."

In truth, pretty much no one argues with controllers no matter what they say. "Driven" is a kind word for these high-energy, extremely focused individuals who, whether getting airplanes to line up on approach with Rockettes-like precision or ordering complex take-out at the nearest diner, know exactly what they want and when they want it.

King of the hill at Tracon is Nick Falzone (John Cusack), familiarly known as "the Zone." Whether speaking fast and crisp to a gaggle of pilots or sweet-talking his wife, Connie (Cate Blanchett, who makes an unnervingly perfect transition from Elizabeth the queen to Long Island housewife), Falzone has the affect of someone who knows he can't afford to be wrong.

As long as "Pushing Tin" (the concept of moving planes briskly through the skies is called "pumping tin" in the original story) stays within that intense, hermetic world, it is hard to fault—though the candor of its look inside a control room can't help but increase fear of flying nationwide. But because this is a movie and not journalism, dramatic situations needed to be created and grafted onto the setting, and that's where the film starts to wander off-course.

What "Pushing Tin" comes up with is the specter of a new gun in town arriving out of the west, a lean, mean controlling machine named Russell Bell (Billy Bob Thornton at his most magnetic).

Risk-addicted, seemingly nerveless, Russell shows up with his own chair, a feather on his head (he's part Choctaw, it turns out) and a reputation of being crazy enough to let a 747 fly over his head so he can experience the turbulence.

Bell's presence, not to mention that of his stunning young wife, Mary (a very effective Angelina Jolie), causes all kinds of ripples in the tight controller society. Falzone, not surprisingly, feels especially threatened by his reckless rival. "There's an aluminum shower in that guy's future," he says, darkly, competitive to the core.

Unfortunately, the macho rivalry between Falzone and Bell, which begins over their work and extends to their wives, is not any more diverting than most macho rivalries—and that's not much. The engaging ambience of the control room, the film's strongest point, gets lost in the morass of rivals facing off like sumo wrestlers intent on muscling each other off the floor.

While the usual problem with films that are not entirely successful is that some elements are smarter than others, that's not the case here. Rather "Pushing Tin" is hampered by a cultural clash between two different but conflicting kinds of smart.

The film's script, as befits something written by the two brothers who wrote and produced "Taxi" and co-created "Cheers," is sharp, wacky and decidedly offbeat. But good as it is, its humor, and its plotting, belong more to the world of the superficial than Mike Newell's direction.

Newell did make the irrepressible "Four Weddings and a Funeral," but mostly his gift is for the kind of intelligent, nuanced filmmaking and compelling acting that characterized films like "Dance With a Stranger" and "The Good Father" as well as parts of "Pushing Tin." But the script for "Tin," especially its flaky, sitcom resolution, is too insubstantial to support this more serious thrust of Newell's direction. A near-miss can have its moments, but it's a near-miss just the same.

NEW YORK, 5/3/99, p. 114, Peter Rainer

A *M*A*S*H*-style comedy about air-traffic controllers, *Pushing Tin* is not exactly the high-concept brainstorm of the year. I mean, whose bright idea was it—given all the people in the audience already afraid of flying—to produce a film in which our friendly skies are shown to be at the mercy of a gaggle of hypercaffeinated yahoos? Hollywood is supposed to be ruled by the marketeers these days, but clearly, if a movie like *Pushing Tin* can make it through the maze, the watchdogs aren't all that vigilant. Normally this kind of laxity would be cause for celebration in a standardized world, but, as it turns out, *Pushing Tin* barely rates faint praise.

On second thought, maybe the marketeers had a lot to do with this film after all. In every respect except its subject matter, *Pushing Tin* bears the telltale traces of a movie that's been run through the audience-survey grinder. The filmmakers throw in just about everything: not just *M*A*S*H* but heavy dollops of *Top Gun* along with a smattering of frat-boy humor and Zen and sit-com. The screenwriters, Glen Charles and Les Charles, are TV-sitcom pros; over the years, they've written and produced for, among many others, *The Mary Tyler Moore Show, The Bob Newhart Show,* and *Cheers*—and *M*A*S*H*. Good shows all, and a lot smarter than *Pushing Tin.* Television comedy used to be the place where you plugged away until you got to strut your stuff in the movies. Now the reverse is often true.

The cast is a spiffy assortment of talent, mostly wasted. John Cusack, in his motor-mouth mode, plays the gutsiest controller at Long Island's Terminal Radar Approach Control center. Billy Bob Thornton, a new arrival to the center, is his super-cooled-out rival. He's the kind of guy who, for kicks, stands under a revving 747 and gets blown out by the wake of its turbulence. Cate Blanchett shows up as Cusack's wife, and her Long Island accent, if not her dialogue, is impeccable. Thornton's wife is played by Angelina Jolie, and her tarty, vodka-guzzling turn perks the film's flagging joke-o-meter. Jolie is a bombshell with great comic timing—an irresistible combo.

In the right hands, the pressure-cooker lives of air-traffic cowboys would probably make for a bang-up black comedy or white-knuckler, but director Mike Newell is too straitlaced for the job. He turns a terrific, new-to-movies subject into a gagfest because he doesn't want to upset viewers with anything resembling reality. They'll probably be upset anyway, especially if they're frequent flyers. At least *Pushing Tin* won't be showing up as an in-flight movie—although a friend of mine swears he once saw *The Buddy Holly Story* on TWA.

NEW YORK POST, 4/23/99, p. 58, Rod Dreher

"Pushing Tin," a comedy about air-traffic controllers and the women who love them, bumps along without ever really getting off the ground. Thanks mostly to the exceedingly enjoyable cast, the film does have some buoyant moments that show us what flights of fancy a sharper script would have provided.

The film's odd title is slang for what air-traffic controllers do: guide giant metal birds whose bellies are packed with people safely through crowded skies. As we learn in the movie's buzzy, chaotic opening scenes in the Long Island facility tracking planes headed in and out of JFK, Newark and LaGuardia, managing that kind of responsibility is enough to drive a man crazy.

Not Nick Falzone (John Cusack), the cocky ace who's the undisputed king of the control room. His gum-smacking confidence is shaken one day when a taciturn new controller named Russell Bell (Billy Bob Thornton) arrives on the scene. Bell has a reputation for being a cowboy on the scopes, but he's cool and stoic no matter how intense the pressure. Which sends alpha-male Nick into a testosto-tizzy of competitive aggression.

Nick's happily married to Connie (an unrecognizable Cate Blanchett), but covets Russell's va-va-va-voom young wife, Mary (Angelina Jolie). Dark, seductive and unstable—everything his housewife isn't—Mary proves an irresistible challenge for Nick. He finds Mary sobbing in the supermarket and invites her to dinner. Cusack and Jolie, the luscious sexpot for whom chapped lips are a major medical emergency, have an intoxicating scene in which they bond over chianti and weltschmerz.

Billy Bob finds out, of course, but his nutcase refusal to show anger only rattles the guilt-ridden Nick further. "Pushing Tin" takes a long, steady nose dive as it tries to figure out what to do with all the macho posturing.

The film's strength is as a quirky character piece, but it has serious problems trying to resolve the increasingly ludicrous conflicts and dilemmas. Writers Glen and Les Charles fritter away the credibility and affection we've developed for these characters by putting them in idiotic situations out of desperation to bring this big, two-hour baby in for a landing before it runs out of gas.

NEWSDAY, 4/23/99, Part II/p. B7, John Anderson

Fashioning glitzy new wrappers for previously owned goods is a Hollywood tradition. The sports movie, for instance, has been reworked so many times they've run out of sports (rumor has it Scotland is working on a curling epic). The western? The figurative horses are so tired they've circled the wagons and are going nowhere.

What passes for innovation is combining two weary genres and then getting by on personality—which is the route of "Pushing Tin," a dramatic comedy about stressed-out air-traffic controllers that has the Mysterious Stranger element of the western and the late-inning resolution of a million sports movies. Thankfully, it has enough of that personality to avoid a massive midscreen collision.

At Long Island's Terminal Radar Approach Control building—nerve center of the metropolitan airways—we meet the boys (Vicki Lewis plays the token female controller, but she's a bodybuilding enthusiast, so it almost doesn't count). To no surprise, we're introduced to their frat-house work space with the kind of rapid-fire, jargon-rich technobabble that's guaranteed to be totally incomprehensible while impressing us with just how capable these oddballs are. Choreographing the aerial ballet taking place over the New York skyline—it really makes you want to hop on a plane—well, ma'am, it's dirty work, but these cowpokes can do it in their sleep.

Almost, anyway. And the most savant of these idiots is Nick Falzone, aka The Zone (John Cusack), the most adept at what they call "pushing tin"—getting the unwieldy air traffic concentrated around Kennedy, Newark and LaGuardia Airports onto the ground in one piece (that would be each plane in an individual piece, of course, not a single, smoldering heap). Nick is married to the loving and lovely Connie (a virtually unrecognizable and fabulous Cate Blanchett), and he suffers from big-fish, small-pond syndrome: He's the best in his building and deals with it with as much hipster bravado as possible—until the arrival of one Russell Bell (Billy Bob Thornton), who does everything Nick does so much better that The Zone starts to come apart like an airborne 747 missing its rivets.

Plenty about "Pushing Tin" is quite enjoyable, particularly the acting. Blanchett, Oscar-nominated for "Elizabeth" this year, gives the kind of performance that never gets prizes but is so contrary to everything we think we know about her that it's a constant wonder to watch her work. Similarly, Thornton ("Sling Blade," "A Simple Plan"), gaunt but glamorous, leaves behind the geeks-and-freaks roles to achieve a kind of Jedi-master grace as Russell, a wounded sort whose reputation for edgy behavior has preceded him to New York.

The movie relies heavily on "M*A*S*H"-style gallows humor—the controllers have betting pools, for instance, on how far burned-out-but-returning ex-colleagues will get before running back out the door. Of course, in a movie that lives and dies by the credibility of its story, that credibility is stretched to fit the jokes when certifiable nervous wrecks are even allowed back in the building.

But the whole air-traffic thing is background for the story of Nick—and, with him, "Pushing Tin" suffers from what we might diagnose as "My Best Friend's Wedding" syndrome. Like Julia Roberts' nuptial-saboteur, Cusack is the star of the film, but only because the credits says so. His character is not admirable, or even likable. He's glib and he's shallow. He can summon up no humility in the face of Russell's superior traffic-controlling, and he sleeps with Russell's inexplicably vulnerable wife, Mary (Angelina Jolie), not because his own wife makes him unhappy—on the contrary, she's a casserole-making goddess—or because he feels anything particularly romantic for her.

He does it for one of two reasons: Because she's fabulous-looking (which makes him banal) or to get back at Russell (which makes him a creep). The movie never bothers to explain its most important plot turn—about which Russell finds out, and Connie finds out—so you have to draw your own conclusions.

Not that you needed any more reason to like Russell more than Nick, but: When Russell squeezes converging planes into unforgiving airspace, he does it because he cares whether passengers make their connecting flights. How can you not love him?

Besides the fact we don't care about Nick (although Cusack is good), "Pushing Tin" has an ending so sappy you may reach for the air-sickness bag. Then realize you're in the wrong kind of seat. Then you'll realize, having watched these maniacs, that you're glad you are. And ultimately glad you came. Because, among other things, you certainly won't be seeing "Pushing Tin" on a plane flight any time soon.

NEWSWEEK, 4/26/99, p. 69, David Ansen

Air-traffic controllers call what they do "Pushing Tin." It's a maximum-stress job that calls for split-second reflexes, nerves of steel and high levels of testosterone. Mike Newell's comedy, written by "Taxi" and "Cheers" veterans Glen and Les Charles, takes us inside the Long Island radar tower where the safety of 7,000 daily flights into and out of JFK, La Guardia and Newark rests in the hands of cocky pros like Nick Falzone (John Cusack). Nick, who prides himself on being the best in the business, mans his radar screen like a guy playing the ultimate videogame, with life-or-death stakes.

The gamesmanship doesn't end with office hours. The macho competition extends into the men's private lives, as we discover when Nick's status is threatened by the arrival of the laconic, motorcycle-riding Russell Bell (Billy Bob Thornton), whose Zen-like cool instantly rubs Nick the wrong way. Nor does it help that Russell is accompanied by a luscious, adoring wife (Angelina Jolie). Though Nick is happily married to Connie (Cate Blanchett), his obsession with one-upping Russell fuels his libidinous interest in the other man's wife.

"Pushing Tin" unfolds with a loose, "M*A*S*H"-like sense of community. You're not sure where it's headed, but with an ensemble this good the aimlessness seems invigorating. It's when the plot kicks in that Newell's movie gets less interesting. The focus narrows to the pissing match between two overgrown male egos, and the film then turns into a contrived romantic comedy. Will the estranged Cusack and Blanchett get back together? Why should we care? Their relationship was never what the movie was about.

It's frustrating to see such a promising premise, and such a delightful cast, wasted. "Elizabeth" fans will find the chameleon-like Blanchett almost unrecognizable as a Long Island housewife; Thornton is a mesmerizing underplayer; Cusack a charming, quicksilver comedian, and Jolie almost steals the show as the tattooed, vodka-swilling, poignant Mary Bell. They're all revved up; if only they had somewhere interesting to go.

SIGHT AND SOUND, 11/99, p. 49, Andrew O'Hehir

Nick Falzone is the top controller at NYC-New Jersey air-traffic control centre TRACON. When new controller Russell Bell arrives, Nick feels his supremacy is challenged. At a barbecue, Nick and his wife Connie meet Russell's wife Mary. Nick wins $100 from Russell in a basketball contest and the rivalry grows.

Later Nick meets a distraught Mary: Russell has gone off on a trip and her favourite plant has died. Nick takes her to dinner and they sleep together. Mary confesses this to Russell; Russell tells Nick he forgives him, and hints that he is interested in Connie, making Nick paranoid. At the funeral of Connie's father, Nick admits his infidelity. Later a bomb threat is phoned in to TRACON; Nick and Russell remain to land the incoming planes, but Nick is depicted as a coward in the television coverage while Russell is lionised. Connie leaves Nick. He nearly causes two mid-air collisions. Russell and Mary leave for Colorado. Nick follows them. Nick and Russell end their conflict by standing together on a runway as a 747 flies over them. Nick goes back to work at TRACON and convinces Connie to give their marriage another try.

The unjaundiced outsider's eye that British director Mike Newell brought to lower-middle-class Italian-American culture in *Donnie Brasco* is again in evidence in *Pushing Tin* a social comedy rich in appealing characterisations, dense dialogue and delightful visuals. The film's plot might be overcooked and too crowded with improbable incidents to be coherent, but this at least reflects the film-makers' ambition to make a comedy aimed at an adult audience. Whatever its flaws, any movie that can offer Billy Bob Thornton and Cate Blanchett performing a duet of 'Muskrat Love' while Angelina Jolie wraps herself around Thornton, python-like, has an irresistibly eccentric spirit.

Pushing Tin tries to pack three different movies into its ungainly 124 minutes, but Newell can't quite get the difficult combination to pay off. Based on an article about the hyper-competitive world of air-traffic controllers, the rapid-fire script by brothers Glen and Les Charles (creators of *Cheers)* is a misbegotten child of one of Hollywood's newfangled 'synergies'. So we begin with the jargon-thick world of TRACON, essentially a roomful of men playing video games with thousands of lives at stake. Newell vividly depicts Nick and Russell's workplace as an arena of psychological warfare where surface camaraderie barely masks fear and hostility. In one sequence we seem to leap inside Nick's radar screen to see the blips as moving objects in 3-D, as Nick and his colleagues must do.

Newell and the Charleses seem more interested in the suburban comedy of manners that grows out of this setting. Manhattan is often seen in movies but few film-makers (beyond native son Hal Hartley) venture into the New Jersey and Long Island hinterlands where much of New York's middle classes live. Saturated with that distinctively Northeastern watery haze, this is a landscape so drab that when we first see Nick drive home from work he mistakenly parks in the driveway of the house next door. But Newell is not out to ridicule the private lives of the controllers, more to demonstrate their almost surreal isolation. Like Blanchett's eerily convincing Jersey-girl accent, the *arriviste* leisurewear at the backyard barbecue—a thicket of silk and velvet shirts—is deadly accurate, just a millimetre short of parody.

A control freak in an Adidas sweatsuit, constantly self-ironising, Nick Falzone is the perfect role for the twitchy, intellectual style of John Cusack. When Mary Bell, played by Jolie as a luscious New Age sphinx, asks him acidly, "Are, there people who find you charming?" he rakishly replies: "Well, they pretend because I try so hard." As enjoyable as Thornton is at issuing low-rent gnostic wisdom, Russell is really only Nick's foil. The conflict between them has its amusing moments—when Nick drives like a maniac, seeking to rattle Russell, the latter simply falls asleep. But after the romantic quadrangle gives way to a predictable fable of *mano a mano* combat, *Pushing Tin* reaches its least interesting narrative level. No movie that's this unsure about what it wants to be can be considered a success. But from the terrific ensemble cast to the meticulous cinematography and subtle score, *Pushing Tin* is one of the most consistently enjoyable US films of the year. Hollywood could use more failures like this one.

VILLAGE VOICE, 4/27/99, p. 131, Michael Atkinson

Nick Falzone (John Cusack), a/k/a the Zone, is a zany air-traffic-controller scalawag who mans his console dressed in a what-do-I-care-I'm-that-good Rangers jersey and who gets a reckless surge every time he fills his airspace with enough planes to give an ordinary ATC an aneurysm. He's the cock of the walk, the number one hun—until laconic Zen daredevil Russell (Billy Bob Thornton) comes to town on a Harley, a mystery man with nerves of steel. These two rugged individualists face off over a pair of radar screens (the suspense! the Pong-like blips! the technical gibberish!), determined to see who has the biggest cubes by juggling more planes than the next guy and, by the way, putting as many anonymous airline passengers in mortal jeopardy as possible.

Think the swinging-dick mentality of *Top Gun,* but in an ergonomic desk chair. Written by the cocreators of *Cheers, Pushing Tin* pivots on our dubious fascination with professional erection duels, which are a sad substitute for dramatic conflict. Director Mike Newell could've been Michael Caton-Jones or Michael Apted for all the distinction he brought to this studio sheepwash; Cusack, Thornton, and Angelina Jolie as Thornton's grumpy young bride coast like skiers. If *Pushing Tin* will be remembered for anything, it'll be for Cate Blanchett as Cusack's sweet but savvy Nassau County wife, Connie. Forget that Blanchett nails a working-class L.I. accent better than any imported actress ever has—she shows up the natives, too, including several Long Island-bred costars. She's also the only 3-D human being in sight. Hell, anybody could lord it up as a monarch; *here's* the true measure of an actress, defending her career against mediocre scripting and direction and coming out on top.

Also reviewed in:
CHICAGO TRIBUNE, 4/23/99, Friday/p. A, Michael Wilmington
NEW REPUBLIC, 5/17/99, p. 34, Stanley Kauffmann
NEW YORK TIMES, 4/23/99, p. E25, Janet Maslin
VARIETY, 4/19-25/99, p. 46, Todd McCarthy
WASHINGTON POST, 4/23/99, Weekend/p. 49, Desson Howe

RAGE, THE: CARRIE 2

A United Artists release of a Red Bank Films production. *Executive Producer:* Patrick Palmer. *Producer:* Paul Monash. *Director:* Katt Shea. *Screenplay:* Rafael Moreu and Howard A. Rodman. *Based on characters created by:* Stephen King. *Director of Photography:* Donald M. Morgan. *Editor:* Richard Nord. *Music:* Danny B. Harvey. *Music Editor:* Danny Garde. *Sound:* Steven Smith. *Sound Editor:* Barney Cabral. *Casting:* Gretchen Rennell Court. *Production Designer:* Peter Jamison. *Art Director:* Geoffrey S. Grimsman. *Set Designer:* Beverli Eagan. *Set Decorator:* Linda Spheeris. *Set Dresser:* Adam Cameron, Carl Hector, and Mike Marcelli. *Special Effects:* Roy H. Arbogast. *Costumes:* Theoni V. Aldredge. *Make-up:* John R. Bayless. *Stunt Coordinator:* Charlie Croughwell. *Running time:* 97 minutes. *MPAA Rating:* R.

CAST: Emily Bergl (Rachel Lang); Jason London (Jesse Ryan); Dylan Bruno (Mark); J. Smith-Cameron (Barbara Lang); Amy Irving (Sue Snell); Zachery Ty Bryan (Eric); John Doe (Boyd); Gordon Clapp (Mr. Stark); Rachel Blanchard (Monica); Charlotte Ayanna (Tracy); Justin Urich (Brad); Mena Suvari (Lisa); Elijah Craig (Chuck); Eddie Kaye Thomas (Arnie); Clint Jordan (Sheriff Kelton); Steven Ford (Coach Walsh); Kate Skinner (Emilyn); Rus Blackwell (Sheriff); Harold Surratt (School Principal); David Lenthall (English Teacher); Kayla Campbell (Little Rachel); Robert D. Raiford (Senior D.A.); Katt Shea (Deputy D.A.); Deborah Meschan (Party Girl); Robert Treveiler (Smiling Patient); Gina Stewart (Female Vet); Claire Hurst (Night Nurse); Albert E. Hayes (Head-Banging Patient); Colin Fickes (Tuba Player); Rhoda Griffis (Saleswoman); Eric Hill (Jesse's Spotter); Jennifer Nicole Parillo (Fleeing Party Girl); Jessica Cowart (Smoking Girl); Tiffany LeShai McMinn (Gardening Girl); Steven Culbertson (The Ref).

LOS ANGELES TIMES, 3/12/99, Calendar/p. 6, Kevin Thomas

What makes "The Rage: Carrie 2" much more than just a sequel to the 1976 Stephen King-Brian De Palma horror classic is the astute direction of Katt Shea, a master of genre, from Rafael Moreu's intelligent script.

It's all a matter of emphasis and tone, and what rightly interests Shea and Moreu more than the supernatural elements is how key members of a small-town high school football team have formed a competition to see who can seduce the most girls, rating each victim according to a point system, and then dropping them immediately. (It may be that the filmmakers took their inspiration from an actual incident that occurred in Lakewood several years ago.) Many of the girls comply, believing that it will be their entry into the school's golden social circle, only to be brutally dismissed as losers.

One girl, Lisa (Mena Suvari), takes her cruel rejection so hard she jumps to her death from the high school roof. As it happens, she is the only friend of Rachel Lang (Emily Bergl), who's the school pariah because she's openly smart and doesn't conform. Worse still for her, Rachel has a mother (J. Smith-Cameron) in a mental institution and poor blue-collar foster parents.

Just as she begins to go after her friend's seducer, the cloddish Eric (Zachery Ty Bryan), she begins connecting with Jesse Ryan (Jason London), one of the most popular boys in school, a football star whose intelligence matches hers.

Even though he is as much an insider as she is an outsider, he is capable of thinking for himself. As smart as she is, Rachel does not comprehend the treacherous situation in which she is entering: Her flowering relationship with Jason, which forces his set to accept her, poses a twofold threat. On the one hand, she has incurred the jealous wrath of his longtime girlfriend, a bosomy cheerleader (Charlotte Ayanna); on the other, she does not realize that she is on the verge of discovering the seduction ring in her effort to make sure that Eric takes responsibility for Lisa's suicide. She is also vulnerable to the distracting illusion of social acceptance.

Meanwhile, Amy Irving's Sue Snell, the only survivor of the original "Carrie's" carnage, has become the high school's counselor, and she understandably becomes alarmed when she begins to detect that Rachel is developing telekinetic powers she doesn't know she possesses. Sue knows full well that history could repeat itself if Rachel doesn't get professional help to learn how to control it. Rachel, of course, is getting into precisely the kind of predicament that has the potential to provoke her wrath, which, in turn, could telekinetically unleash a catastrophe.

You have the feeling that Shea accepts the telekinetic gimmick as an obligatory plot device and she cleverly plays against it, concentrating on the mindless cruelty of a bunch of jocks who would cause girls such pain simply as an affirmation of their masculinity and popularity. In doing so, she makes the point that real horror lies in human behavior more than in the forces of the supernatural.

Rachel, moreover, is not the helpless creature that Sissy Spacek's pre-prom Carrie was, and Shea is more interested in exposing the excesses of machismo—and the young women who go along with it—than in inciting us to root for a telekinetic revenge. Yet when the moment of truth arrives, Shea handles it with the panache that you would expect from a Roger Corman alum.

Indeed, Shea's ability to play various elements in Moreu's adroit script against one another gives "The Rage" a welcome complexity and tension. Bergl emerges as yet another lovely and talented young actress of exceptional presence and range who can command the screen with ease; remember, it was Shea who consolidated Drew Barrymore's move from child actress to blossoming movie star with her wickedly funny "Poison Ivy." Bergl is well-matched by London, and a fine supporting cast is anchored by Dylan Bruno, whose brawny good looks nicely set off the self-aware evil of his character.

Instead of the bravura Grand Guignol and bristling wit of "Carrie," an outrageous baroque triumph, "The Rage" dares to take a different tack, taking its young people seriously in a more realistic context. If ever there was a director ready to graduate from genre films, it surely is Shea.

NEW YORK POST, 3/12/99, p. 47, Jonathan Foreman

As much remake as sequel, "The Rage: Carrie 2" sticks tightly to the format of the original "Carrie," including scenes of doors slamming shut and a nasty shock at the end.

This precludes any surprises or real scariness. But "The Rage" is surprisingly effective when it's being a high school movie (imagine "She's All That" with decapitations) rather than a horror show. And it contains a remarkable debut performance by Emily Bergl that sustains your interest to the bloody, fiery end.

It's set in the same town where, 20 years ago, a high school graduation class was slaughtered by much-abused but telekinetic Carrie White—only everyone thinks that that holocaust was some kind of accident. (Everyone except for school counselor Sue Snell (Amy Irving), who was there.)

The new Carrie figure is Rachel (Emily Bergl) and she's much tougher and more together than Sissy Spacek's innocent teenagers But she's still an outsider—after all, she has curly black hair, pale skin, a tattoo and strange good looks—and she lives in a trailer with horrible foster parents because her real mother has been in an asylum since Rachel was a little girl.

Rachel is not really aware that she has the power to move objects with her mind. (She remembers that her mother was convinced that she was possessed by the devil when they took her away.) We see evidence of that power before she does. When she sees that her best friend, Lisa (Mena Suvari), has committed suicide, all the school locker doors fly open. Lisa, it turns out, was the victim of a nasty group of football players who make a competitive game of bedding girls for points and then dropping them.

But Jesse (Jason London), one of the guys on the team, is smart and nice, and he notices Rachel in English class. They become friends after he helps rescue her dog. Then they become more than friends.

But the bad guys, who know that Rachel knows why Lisa jumped off a roof, and the bad popular girls who are jealous of Rachel's relationship with Jesse plot to split them up and simultaneously humiliate her. This involves an absurdly elaborate plan that depends on Rachel suddenly becoming a credulous innocent, desperate to be popular. But it culminates at a post-game party in a vast house with a swimming pool and lots of plate glass ...

The film takes far too long to reach its climax of abuse and telekinetic revenge. But when it does, it's suitably vicious. In fact, the finale also contains one of the most gruesome scenes of mutilation ever to appear in a mainstream film: You see something happen to one of Rachel's enemies that makes the roughest parts of "Saving Private Ryan" look tame and tidy by comparison.

The assured Ms. Bergl is supported by an able and attractive young cast (check out those nubile cheerleaders!), which makes it all the more unfortunate that Amy Irving gives such a terrible performance as the counselor who wants to help Rachel before she starts throwing stuff around.

Several flashbacks using footage from the original serve to remind you how brilliantly creepy the Brian DePalma film was. They also make Katt Shea's attempts at directorial flash—the loud knife sounds every time Rachel uses her powers, the meaningless shifts into black and white—look silly and trashy.

NEWSDAY, 3/12/99, PartII/p. B6, Gene Seymour

They didn't leave Carrie White alone 23 years ago and they're not leaving "Carrie" the movie alone now. Doesn't anybody learn? Don't these impulsive brats know that bad things happen when you go too far without thinking?

Guess not. They went ahead anyway and made a sequel to one of the best "nerd-vengeance" movies ever. Even placed against the present surge of teen-angst movies, Brian DePalma's 1976 adaptation of Stephen King's novel stands firm and tall. Part of the reason is the pure catharsis it offers to the young outcasts in the audience. The mandate of its unforgettably apocalyptic climax was clear as a class bell: Forget trying to fit in or find common ground with the popular kids. Crush them like the insects they are!

More seriously, the other thing that made "Carrie" a classic was the way it shamelessly deployed the base elements of teen exploitation fantasies and then turned up the intensity to a fever pitch while capturing some painfully shrewd observations on the cruelty of the high school caste system.

Which, in case you didn't know, never changes. Poor, shy girls like Rachel Lang (Emily Bergl) are still treated like doormats by what passes for the aristocracy at Bates High. That means, jocks like sociopathic Mark (Dylan Bruno), stupid Eric (Zachary Ty Bryan) and sensitive Jesse (Jason London), whose chief sport besides football is scoring points with as many girls as possible. One of those girls, who happens to be Rachel's only friend, is so distraught when Eric dumps her that she takes a header off the school roof.

Rachel, whose mother is in an asylum, withdraws deeper into her shell with only Jesse and a guidance counselor (Amy Irving, gamely reprising her role in the original) willing to reach out, trying to break through. Jesse finds something soulful in Rachel and she begins to feel less defensive, less lonely. The counselor notices that Rachel can move things around without using her hands. This ominously reminds the counselor of a girl she once knew in high school. Another lonely outcast who was pushed so far that she blew the previous Bates High to smithereens with her mind. A girl named Carrie ...

Like Mark, the head creep, "The Rage" knows it's "lower than scum" and once in a while has the humor to wallow in its contrivances. (Hey, kids! There's even a winning touchdown in a big game!) But that doesn't keep the film from looking and sounding like a cheaply stylized cover of a rock-and-roll standard. It's probably good for a campy night out, but that's about all it's good for, despite an avid performance by Bergl in her film debut and some well-timed jolts scattered here and there.

SIGHT AND SOUND, 12/99, p. 54, Kim Newman

Bates High School, Ca., the present. Rachel Lang, raised by foster parents because her mother Barbara is institutionalised, is shocked when her best friend Lisa commits suicide. Lisa had been deflowered and dumped by Eric, a star football player, as part of a contest organised by team mate Mark: members of the Bates High Bulldogs compete to see who can seduce the most girls.

Guidance counsellor Sue Snell, sole survivor of the prom night 20 years ago when Carrie White burned down the school, notices Rachel has abilities similar to Carrie's. She visits Barbara in the asylum, and learns Rachel is Carrie's long-lost sister.

Rachel brings Eric's crime to the attention of the authorities, exciting the enmity of Mark and the team. She also starts a relationship with sensitive football-player Jesse Ryan, which sets Jesse's ex-girlfriend Tracy and her friend Monica against her. An apparently conciliatory Monica and Mark incite Rachel to a big party but she is humiliated there when Mark screens a video of Rachel and Jesse having sex. Lashing out with telekinesis, Rachel murders Eric, Monica, Mark, Tracy and most of other guests. She also accidentally kills Sue, who has sprung Barbara from the asylum. Barbara rejects Rachel whom she believes is possessed by the Devil. Rachel resists Jesse's attempt to stay with her, telekinetically throwing him to safety while she burns to death. A year later, Jesse is still haunted by dreams of Rachel.

Given that a film-going generation has come and gone since Brian De Palma's 1976 film of Stephen King's 1974 breakthrough novel *Carrie*, it's surprising that the rights-owners have opted to go the tardy sequel route rather than mount a 90s take on the same basic story as a straight remake (like the 1978 *Invasion of the Body Snatchers*). *The Rage Carrie 2*, however, goes the whole sequel hog. Amy Irving, sole survivor of the original production, reprises her role, her 'where did my career go?' bewilderment appropriate to her high-school princess cum psychological cripple. Tiny snippets of Sissy Spacek are glimpsed in flashbacks, and while it's a touch shoddy that Irving's Sue should remember Carrie's subjective fantasies, at least continuity is respected in a visit to the still ruined site of the old school. In the book, telekinesis is passed down from mother to daughter, but this jiggles the premise to introduce a hitherto unknown sister of the definitively killed-off Carrie.

There are noteworthy changes in the characterisation. Rachel is a tougher outcast than Carrie, tattooed and sharp. This plays well during the long build-up that tries to feel like a teen movie distantly influenced by *Kids*. But it undercuts the finale in which Rachel has total control over her telekinetic powers (she can even rewind videotapes) and is thus a malignantly vengeful fury in contrast to the lost, desperate Carrie. Rafael Moreu's script just scrambles the elements, taking all the plot points and characters from De Palma and King and trotting them out again in light disguise: the caring gym teacher becomes the caring counsellor, the callous bitch becomes a callous stud, the strict mother becomes neglectful foster folks, the nice girl who tries to help becomes a nice guy, the prom becomes a post-game party (with a considerable loss of iconic teenpic status) and Sue's last-minute nightmare of Carrie's hand reaching up from her grave is ineptly reprised as Jesse's vision of a fragmenting ghostly Rachel.

For a project that could hardly be anything but a waste of space, the film is fitfully engaging for at least two-thirds of its running time. Aside from one minor exercise in post-*Scream* jokiness, the standard teen stuff is enlivened by good performances from the kids (the adults, mostly are dreadful). Katt Shea, who took over direction at the last minute from Robert Mandel, strives to recreate some of the class and sex issues of *Poison Ivy*, his most successful film. But *The Rage* falls apart when it ought to go into overdrive during the climactic holocaust. The more contrived gruesomeness (a spear impales one jock to the door and also skewers Sue on the other side, for example) tends to get laughs. That producer Paul Monash, who handled the original, has a franchise in mind is confirmed by the veiled suggestion that Ralph White, father of Carrie and Rachel, might have other unknown daughters out there.

VILLAGE VOICE, 3/23/99, p. 130, Amy Taubin

Emily Bergl is a young actor of uncommon talent, great integrity, and no particular beauty. I doubt that any male director would have cast her as the central character in a horror film update aimed at a teen audience. She's neither a toughened-up but fashionably proportioned object of desire (à la Neve Campbell in *Scream)* nor a barely formed, barely human wraith whose very fragility is a mask for the monster within (à la Sissy Spacek in the original *Carrie*).

The brilliance of the original *Carrie* lies in the explicit connection it makes between Carrie's telekinetic power and menstruation, the body function that, come adolescence, irrevocably separates the girls from the boys. The fear and hatred, i.e. the horror, that Carrie inspires is primal. It's the horror of the feminine body, the body that bleeds, the body of the all-powerful mother, the body that must be kept under wraps lest it overwhelm the patriarchal social order. "Plug it up, plug it up," scream Carrie's female classmates, as they pelt her with tampons.

If women can be complicit in their own oppression, they also can be exhilarated when one of their kind rises up and takes revenge. Like *Carrie*, *The Rage* is a revenger's tragedy, but its grisly denouement is its least interesting aspect. Director Katt Shea, who got her start working for Roger Corman and surfaced into the mainstream (or a prominent tributary thereof with *Poison Ivy*, is perhaps a shade too willing to cater to the teenage exploitation crowd. "That was really disgusting," said one teenage girl to her friend as they exited the preview screening. (It didn't sound like a recommendation.) She was, I presume, referring to the orgy of shattered glass and sheared bodies that climaxes the film. Heads roll—literally, they do.

Undistinguished as filmmaking and too over-the-top to be at all scary, this finale could blind audiences to the many virtues of *The Rage*, which include Shea's dead-on articulation of how class operates in the formation of high school hierarchies, how misogyny is an essential element of jock culture, and how women lose their lives when they allow men to determine their value. What makes the film startling, however, is Bergl's performance as a young woman whose traumatic childhood taught her to trust no one other than herself. Like Claire Danes, Bergl has a strikingly real presence. She seems less like an actress and more like a person you might actually know. Which might get you wondering about why you've never seen anyone quite like her onscreen before.

Rachel Lang (Bergl) has been raised by foster parents since her schizophrenic mother was committed to a mental institution. Rachel knows there's a one-in-eight chance that she's inherited her mother's schizophrenia, and indeed, when objects in her vicinity start crashing about seemingly of their own accord, she fears that she's becoming delusional. What Rachel doesn't know is that her father was also Carrie White's father (the infamous Carrie who 22 years earlier caused the local high school to burn to the ground) and that the gene for telekinesis is transmitted by fathers.

The loss of her mother has made Rachel extremely wary of relationships. Her only close ties are to her dog, a shambling, arthritic bloodhound, and to a girl in her class (Mena Suvari) who shares her taste for dime-store goth clothing but who otherwise is her opposite—and maybe her ideal. Rachel is small and sturdy with a head that seems slightly too large for her body; her friend is as ethereal as a Pre-Raphaelite muse. When she's seduced and summarily dumped by one of the school's reigning jocks, she commits suicide. Her death makes Rachel more guarded, but not invulnerable to the attention shown to her by Jesse (Jason London), a star athlete who's begun to have doubts about his membership in the high school elite.

Fathers, father surrogates, and boys who unquestioningly emulate their dads are the collective villain of *The Rage*. Shea tears through the macho facade of jock culture to show the squirmy castration anxiety underneath. "Bend over and pull down your pants," yells the coach at a player who has been slacking off. "I thought I'd find a tampon string hanging from your ass." It's a neatly feminist twist on the shower scene in *Carrie*, and there are about half a dozen other twists that are just as sharp. Shea gets into trouble, however, when she uses bits of the original *Carrie* as flashbacks (the two films don't seem to take place in the same world, let alone the same small town). The film nearly goes down the tubes in the scenes where Amy Irving recapitulates her role as Sue Snell, one of the only survivors of Carrie White's senior-prom shenanigans. I never could stand Sue Snell, and given the fate assigned her here, I suspect Shea felt likewise.

Inside *The Rage: Carrie 2*, a smart, realist drama is taking form. If Shea could free herself from the genre trap, she might make some great films in the future. Still, you take what you can get, and I wouldn't be surprised if this one winds up on my 10-best list for '99.

Also reviewed in:
CHICAGO TRIBUNE, 3/12/99, Friday/p. N, John Petrakis
NATION, 4/5 & 12/99, p. 64, Stuart Klawans
NEW YORK TIMES, 3/12/99, p. E29, Anita Gates
VARIETY, 3/15-21/99, p. 40, Dennis Harvey

RANDOM HEARTS

A Columbia Pictures release of a Rastar/Mirage Enterprises production. *Executive Producer:* Ronald L. Schwary and Warren Adler. *Producer:* Sydney Pollack and Marykay Powell. *Director:* Sydney Pollack. *Screenplay:* Kurt Luedtke and Darryl Ponicsan. *Based on the novel by:* Warren Adler. *Director of Photography:* Philippe Rousselot. *Editor:* William Steinkamp. *Music:* Dave Grusin. *Music Editor:* Ted Whitfield and Stuart Grusin. *Choreographer:* Luis Perez.. *Sound:* Danny Michael. *Sound Editor:* Scott A. Hecker. *Casting:* David Rubin. *Production Designer:* Barbara Ling. *Art Director:* Chris Shriver. *Set Decorator:* Susan Bode. *Special Effects:* Jonathan C. Brotherhood. *Costumes:* Bernie Pollack. *Costumes (Kristin Scott Thomas):* Ann Roth. *Make-up:* Naomi Donne. *Make-up (Harrison Ford):* Michael Laudati. *Stunt Coordinator:* Mickey Giacomazzi. *Running time:* 131 minutes. *MPAA Rating:* R.

CAST: Harrison Ford (Dutch Van Den Broeck); Kristin Scott Thomas (Kay Chandler); Charles S. Dutton (Alcee); Bonnie Hunt (Wendy Judd); Dennis Haysbert (Detective George Beaufort); Sydney Pollack (Carl Broman); Richard Jenkins (Truman Trainor); Paul Guilfoyle (Dick Montoya); Susanna Thompson (Peyton Van Den Broeck); Peter Coyote (Cullen Chandler); Dylan Baker (Richard Judd); Lynne Thigpen (Phyllis Bonaparte); Susan Floyd (Molly Roll); Bill Cobbs (Marvin); Kate Mara (Jessica Chandler); Ariana Thomas (Shyla Mumford); Nelson Landrieu (Silvio Coya); Brooke Smith (Sarah); Christina Chang (Laurie); Michelle Hurd (Susan); Reiko Aylesworth (Mary Claire Clark); Ray Anthony Thomas (Officer Clayton Williams); Edie Falco (Janice); S. Epatha Merkerson (Nea); Jack Gilpin (David Dotson); Mark Zeisler (Steven Driker); John Carter (Peyton's Father); Davenia McFadden (Cassie); Barbara Gulan (Maureen); Molly Price (Alice Beaufort); Brian Schwary (Tad Baker); Priscilla Shanks (Susan's Customer); Lynette Du Pre (Nurse Nancy); Ken Kay (Peter Suchet); Susan Hatfield (Claire Suchet); Jenna Stern (Sally Gabriel); Tom McCarthy (Dick Shulte); Jan Austell (Joe Parella); Aasif Mandvi (Electronics Store Salesman); Todd Malta (Supermarket Stockboy); Jordan Lage (Assistant Prosecutor); Judith Knight Young (Clara); Fenton Lawless (Officer Lawrence); Deirdre Lovejoy (Officer Isabel); Terry Serpico (Evidence Technician); Liam Craig (Waiter at DC Restaurant); C.S. Lee (Luncheonette Counterman); Ellen Foley (Young Woman at Fundraiser); Judy Jamison, Steven Mark Friedman, Becky Veduccio (TV Reporters at Hospital); Susan Allenback (Airline Spokesperson); Don Scott, Dina Napoli, and Tracey Neale (News Anchors); Will Thomas (Field Reporter); Andy Fowle (Orderly).

LOS ANGELES TIMES, 10/8/99, Calendar/p. 1, Kenneth Turan

A fearlessly traditional romantic melodrama done up in grand Hollywood style, "Random Hearts" is not lacking in good things, from Sydney Pollack's polished direction to emotional and involving performances by stars Harrison Ford and Kristin Scott Thomas.

Yet as satisfying as this film is at moments, it's hard to shake the feeling that it's throwing good money after bad. The fault is not in the acting, directing or script (by Kurt Luedtke, who won an Oscar for Pollack's "Out of Africa") but rather that the film's underlying concept is so irredeemably screwy and far-fetched that no amount of fine work can hope to make it convincing.

That notion comes from a 1984 Warren Adler novel about an unlikely romance that has not surprisingly defeated several earlier attempts to film it. This is the story not just of two people who, to quote the ad copy, would never have met in a perfect world, but of two people we're not convinced should ever have been brought together even on a movie screen.

Using artful cross-cutting, "Random Hearts" (the title echoes the equally improbable classic weepy "Random Harvest") unhurriedly introduces Dutch Van Den Broeck and Kay Chandler, protagonists who start out in completely different Washington, D.C., worlds.

Dutch (Ford) is an 11-year veteran of the D.C. police force, a drinks-beer-from-the-bottle kind of guy who's now a sergeant in Internal Affairs, working with partner Alcee (Charles S. Dutton) to root out crooked cops. Apparently happily married, Dutch thinks nothing of it when his wife, a Saks fashion employee, says a business trip is taking her away on short notice.

Kay (Scott Thomas) is also unconcerned about her husband's flying out of town. A congresswoman from New Hampshire who's looking at a tough reelection campaign against a well-financed loose cannon, Kay is a Yankee aristocrat with high principles she hopes to pass on to her 15-year-old daughter.

What Dutch and Kay don't know is that their spouses, far from traveling anywhere on business, are seated next to each other on a flight to Miami, headed for the latest chapter in an elaborately hidden extramarital affair. The only detail the cheaters haven't counted on is a plane crash that will kill both of them and reveal their infidelity.

Make that "gradually reveal," because "Random Hearts" is so stately, so intent on taking its own good time, that Dutch and Kay don't even meet until about 45 minutes into the picture. Pleasant though a little regal gentility can be, it's hard not to wish that the film had more of the insistent energy that, ironically, Pollack provides as an actor in his role as Kay's sassy and realistic media consultant Carl Broman.

When the pair do meet, at Dutch's instigation, their interaction is hardly promising. While Kay's primarily worried about the mental health of her daughter, Dutch, ever the persistent policeman, is getting practically demented in his mania to find out all the details of an affair that is now literally as cold as the tomb.

Also, Kay has her campaign to worry about, while Dutch, who starts out as an officer who believes passionately in the difference between right and wrong, gets so bent out of shape about his wife's deception that it starts to affect his professional judgment. (The lumbering subplot about Dutch and Alcee's investigation of a rogue detective played by Dennis Haysbert is the script's weakest aspect.)

Perhaps inspired by the necessity of conveying a romantic notion so far-fetched it's hard to even write it down, both Ford and Scott Thomas create characters more believable than it would have seemed possible.

Though much of his career has been spent with either action roles or light comedies, Ford is strong and convincing in this romantic drama. Both his intensely masculine, weathered look and his tendency not to over-emote work for him here, though the almost demented way he reacts to his wife's duplicity can be more than we want to deal with at times.

As for Scott Thomas, her work as always leaves you grasping for superlatives. Helped by much better chemistry with her co-star than she had with Robert Redford in "The Horse Whisperer," the actress makes the confusion and despair inherent in her situation both real and alive. When she says, "Who is this woman who is wearing my clothes, using my body?," her dismay comes from the heart.

But as difficult as it is for Kay and Dutch to trust what's happening to them, it's even harder for us to believe it. Perhaps the good work Pollack and the actors have done toward making the characters realistic is counterproductive, for as this romance tentatively develops, the temptation to scream "no, no, no" at the contrived on-screen doings increases. Fatally neither here nor there, this is the story of a couple we can't happily envision either together or apart, and that is not a happy state of affairs.

NEW YORK, 10/18/99, p. 54, Peter Rainer

Sometimes a big Hollywood production goes so wrong that the spectacle of its collapse is far more compelling than the screen story we're watching. *Random Hearts*, a thick shroud of a movie starring Harrison Ford and Kristin Scott Thomas and directed by Sydney Pollack, has all the right big-ticket Hollywood credentials, and yet, almost from the get-go, it's a dud. In a way, this is reassuring: It's nice to know that the movie studios, with all their techno skills and demographic surveys and bottom lines, are still capable of screwing up so blatantly. Besides, it's a film this misbegotten can come off the assembly line, maybe there's a chance something really good can slip by too.

Harrison Ford plays an internal-affairs cop in Washington, D.C., who goes by the name of Dutch. Kristin Scott Thomas is Kay Chandler, a Republican congresswoman from New Hampshire. When a plane bound for Miami crashes into Chesapeake Bay. Dutch's wife and Kay's husband—longtime lovers on their way to a tryst—are among the dead. For Dutch and Kay, who never crossed paths before, the discovery of the adultery is like a double whammy. With his good cop's instincts, Dutch pieces together the puzzle, obsessively, while Kay, with an election coming up, doesn't want to deal with the emotional fallout. Naturally, they end up attracted to each other. (Their initial meeting is like a depresso version of meeting cute.) The chemistry is standard yin and yang: Dutch is gruff and grievous; Kay is decorous and in denial. He's a beer drinker; she sips vodka on the rocks. The only thing they seem to have in common is that neither was in a marriage that was ecstatic.

There's a strong premise buried beneath the bathos: A man whose job is to ferret out the truth is deceived by a wife he can't even mourn properly because he's too caught up in his own rage. If only Pollack and screenwriter Kurt Luedtke, adapting Warren Adler's 1984 novel, had jettisoned the cumbersome lovers-in-shock plot contrivance and focused instead on how Dutch is pulled apart and patched together. But then again, would we want to see such a film if Harrison Ford remained the center of it? As an actor, he's heavy weather; he soldiers through this movie without the slightest fillip of grace or nuance. Ford used to have a rowdy, antic spark, back in his *Star Wars-Indiana Jones* period, but his idea of playing heroes these days, particularly lumpen heroes like Dutch, is to ratchet up the self-righteousness. He plays every emotion squarely and thuddingly, as if he were a heavyweight hitting the bag.

Scott Thomas doesn't match up with him at all: she's become so hperrefined that practically any co-star she appears with now seems brutish by comparison. (Watching her opposite Ralph Fiennes in *The English Patient* was like seeing double; they deliquesced in unison.) Kay Chandler is supposed to be a politician of some repute, and yet she acts more like a library supervisor. The filmmakers work up the usual guff about the chicanenry of the political process and the intrusiveness of the media—Pollack himself turns in a free-wheeling cameo as Kay's media consultant—but all this appears to be taking place on another planet from the one Kay is inhabiting. Scott Thomas doesn't have the tight comportment to play a Republican congresswoman; she's patrician without the steel or the savy. No wonder so many actors these day's want to run for office. On the evidence of *Random Hearts*, it's pretty easy work.

NEW YORK POST, 10/11/99, p. 44, Lou Lumenick

"Random Hearts" is the cinematic equivalent of enduring a cross-country airplane flight trapped in a seat next to a manic depressive. It's sporadically riveting but more often tedious.

Harrison Ford, never glummer, plays Dutch Van Den Broeck, a Washington, D.C., internal-affairs sergeant whose life is shattered when his wife is killed in a plane crash.

Suspicious about the circumstances, he discovers she was on her way to a romantic weekend in Miami with a lover Dutch didn't know about.

Digging further, he discovers the lover (fleetingly played by Peter Coyote) was the husband of New Hampshire Rep. Kay Chandler (Kristin Scott Thomas)—to whom he grows increasingly close.

No, this is no "Two Funerals and a Wedding." This glum romantic thriller is more like "Airport '99: Dazed and Confused."

Dutch is so hurt and angry at his cheating spouse that he starts beating up on suspects (i.e., dirty cops) at work—and obsessing about getting the sordid details of his late wife's secret life. Were she and her lover planning a life together? Why did the wife (Susan Thompson) insist on making love with Dutch just before she left for her fatal rendezvous?

To that end, Dutch badgers Kay, who'd really rather not know her late husband's secrets and who wants to protect her 15-year-old daughter and her uphill re-election campaign (she's supposed to be a liberal Republican) from scandal.

But Dutch won't take no for an answer, and goads the traumatized, stiff-upper-lip Kay into an excursion to Miami, where their straying spouses were headed for their rendezvous.

One night of warm tropical breezes and Kay, who has good reason to have Dutch arrested for stalking her, is in a clinch with him in a parked car in the congressional reserved-parking section of Ronald Reagan airport.

It makes no dramatic sense. Ford's Dutch relentlessly gloomy, glowering and sporting an improbable gold earring—may be the least-appealing character he's ever played. But at least he's convincing as a cop. We don't buy Thomas as a congresswoman for a second and wouldn't even if the British actress weren't struggling with an American accent.

She's forced to play a scriptwriter's fantasy of a naif who's shocked, shocked, to learn her opponent would slime her with her late husband's misdeeds.

The script, credited to Darryl Ponicsan and Kurt Luedtke (the movie, based on a novel by Warren Adler, was in development for 15 years) contains more than its share of howlers.

"I'm not going to make small talk so there won't be any junk between us," Dutch tells Kay before a romantic clinch at his cabin in the mountains.

After a promising start and an amusing sequence in which the dogged Dutch grills his wife's former colleagues at Saks Fifth Avenue, legendary director Sydney Pollack (who also walks through a role as Kay's spin doctor) allows the proceedings to bog down in exposition and a prolonged subplot about one of Dutch's investigations. Charles Dutton has a thankless role as Dutch's partner.

Despite so many scenes of arrivals and departures at various airports that you'll feel entitled to frequent-flyer miles, "Random Hearts" goes nowhere—for 131 grueling minutes. Fasten your seat belts.

NEWSDAY, 10/8/99, Part II/p. B3, John Anderson

When a commuter plane goes down outside Washington, D.C., strapped in beside each other are Peyton Van Den Broeck (Susanna Thompson) and Cullen Chandler (Peter Coyote), who've registered as Mr. and Mrs. and aren't anything of the kind. If they weren't already dead, they'd probably die of embarrassment.

But there's plenty of embarrassment to go around, however, in Sydney Pollack's "Random Hearts." Exhibit A? Internal Affairs investigator "Dutch" Van Den Broeck (Harrison Ford), a veteran D.C. cop so unsullied that when a colleague (Edie Falco) suggests a little unconstitutional jail time for an uncooperative murder witness, he reacts like Rudolph Giuliani being pelted with elephant dung.

Exhibit B? Congresswoman Kay Chandler (Kristin Scott Thomas), who can't believe that a self-financed right-wing candidate really stands a chance against her re-election bid in New Hampshire. "The question is whether someone totally unsuited for public office can buy his way into the Congress," she says. With a straight face. Hello, baby? Give me Reality Central.

Having established his characters as inhabitants of the World of the Blissfully Naive, director Pollack (working off a script by Kurt Luedtke, of the equally quaint "Absence of Malice") proceeds to construct a two-hours-plus movie based on the pained idea that Dutch, a cop whose investigations are based on betrayals of trust, would spend all his time and energy re-creating, reimagining and reconstructing the infidelities of his wife, while also imagining that Kay would want to help him do it.

Given that Pollack casts himself as a kind of Roger Ailes-ish spinmaster attached to Kay's campaign, the movie is not unaware of the realities of the modern electoral process. But it's happy to ignore those realities, if the payoff is a love story between the two survivors of co-mutual adulterers.

Is this straining the bounds of believability? Is that an English accent we hear leaking through the line readings of Kristin Scott Thomas? The love story, frankly, becomes one of the more feasible aspects of a movie whose basic foundation is near-mythic in its disregard of dramatic logic.

Another essential difficulty regarding "Random Hearts"—the plot of which includes Dutch's almost purely tangential pursuit of a corrupt D.C. cop (Dennis Haysbert) and an almost totally wasted Charles S. Dutton—is the sense that everything we're seeing is preliminary to some larger story we're not seeing.

Can the seedy cheating of a congresswoman's husband and the wife of an under-appreciated cop really be the crux of a movie constructed—so slickly, so glossily—as a state-of-the-art contemporary thriller? Yes, it can. (Well, at any rate, it is.) And whether anyone ultimately will care has a lot more to do with Harrison Ford's lingering star quality than it does with plot, dialogue, logic or emotional potency. In fact, it's the only thing that matters.

NEWSWEEK, 10/11/99, p. 85, David Ansen

A lot of very talented people—director Sydney Pollack, writer Kurt Luedtke, stars Harrison Ford and Kristin Scott Thomas—have inexplicably entangled themselves in the lugubrious "Random Hearts," an adult love story that's trying for stiff-upper-lip poignancy. Ford is a Washington, D.C., police sergeant and Scott Thomas a New Hampshire congresswoman up for re-election whose spouses die in a plane crash. Ford discovers that the departed spouses were secret lovers, and becomes obsessed with uncovering the details of their adulterous affair, boorishly dragging Scott Thomas into his search for the awful truth. The film assumes that we will find his quest interesting. It isn't. Even less gripping is a jerry-built subplot about Ford's pursuit of a crooked cop. It takes forever for this portentous drama to get to the inevitable moment when the chilly congresswoman melts in the dogged cop's arms, and when it does, the heat generated by these two attractive stars barely rises above room temperature. This is Hollywood's idea of adult?

SIGHT AND SOUND, 12/99, p. 55, Liese Spencer

When a plane bound for Miami crashes leaving no survivors, internal-affairs police officer Dutch Van Den Broeck suspects his wife Peyton may have been on board. Although she is not named among the passengers, Dutch knows Peyton took a flight that day to Miami. After some enquiries, Dutch discovers that her "business trip" was fabricated and that she was travelling with another man. Leaving Washington and an investigation into a corrupt cop, Dutch travels to New Hampshire where he confronts Kay Chandler, whose husband Cullen accompanied Peyton on he plane. A congresswoman running for reelection, Kay is reluctant to talk, even when Dutch tells her he is going to visit the hotel the dead couple had booked in Miami.

In Miami, Kay surprises Dutch at the hotel bar and they piece together the couple's affair. Flying home they sit separately, but kiss in the airport car park. Kay decides not to run for re-election but Dutch persuades her against quitting. Dutch goes to his log cabin in the country where Kay joins him for a romantic weekend. Dutch wants them to find the apartment their dead partners used for their affair but Kay resists. They return to their normal lives. When Dutch eventually finds the apartment, he finds Kay already there. They argue. Dutch leaves and is shot by the cop he was investigating. At the hospital Dutch and Kay are reconciled.

When the Zeebrugge ferry went down pathologists identifying the drowned found one body with 12 wallets: a pickpocket. Another victim was discovered to have been leading a double life, with one family in England and another in Holland. Laid bare by untimely death, such subterfuge lends a pathetically personal note to mass disaster, tempers the deifying grief of tragedy with human fallibility. So the idea of following such a story in *Random Hearts* is an intriguing one. Sydney Pollack's romantic thriller explores what it's like to deal not only with the death of a loved one and the shock of a deceit that can never be explained, argued over or excused, but also how two survivors might seek solace with each other. Sadly, it's neither romantic nor thrilling.

One problem is the ponderous performances given by the two stars. Typecast as the tough but honest cop, Harrison Ford barely opens his mouth, let alone his heart, so his portrayal of a cuckold has little impact. Instead of a man emotionally disembowelled by doubt, what we see is a sullen detective obsessed with uncovering the banal details of betrayal. Starched, sensible and struggling with an American accent, Kristin Scott Thomas offers little more than cool stoicism. If just one of them had let down their guard and cried, it might have ended the emotional impasse.

All these gloomy ponderings on the nature of love and trust should, of course, be offset by the unlikely affair that blossoms between them. Unfortunately, these two don't even seem to like each other, let alone fall in love. When they return from their mournful sojourn in Miami and fall on each other in the car park, there's a desperate inelegance about their embrace which strikes true. But with no spark the scene plays as slapstick.

Complexly structured and put together with Pollack's usual polish, the film is not without its pleasures. The first hour, in which he intercuts between the four main characters, the inexorable tragedy and its gradual discovery, is stylish and gripping. News bulletins about the crash murmur in the background before Dutch and Kay begin to pay them any attention. As Dutch goes about his doomed enquiries, the objects of his investigation sit side by side, seatbelts fastened and hair floating upwards like seaweed. But despite flashes of bitter brilliance, the film flags desperately in its talk-sodden second half. Certainly, a neat ending in which these two very different characters waltzed off into the sunset would have been wrong. But what we have instead is downright bathetic. It's Christmas. The lovers have been apart for months. Thomas comes out of the airport arrivals gate and Ford is waiting for her. They exchange pleasantries and she walks away. All that's left for the audience to do is to identify the corpse of a good idea.

TIME, 10/11/99, p. 83, Richard Schickel

After many years of study and practice, Harrison Ford has just about mastered the art of talking without moving his lips. Kristin Scott Thomas is newer at the game of masking her emotions, but chilly elegance has achieved near total mastery over the sexiness she exuded in *The English Patient*.

And that's pretty much all the news from *Random Hearts*, a grim and draggy romance in which even the clothes and sets are dismal. Ford is a Washington detective named Dutch Van Den Broeck; Scott Thomas is a Congresswoman named Kay Chandler. Both their spouses are killed in a plane crash, and he suspects—his obsessive nature and the habits of his profession driving him on that they were lovers. She perhaps agrees, but prefers denial and resumption of her re-election campaign.

This is very sensible of her, especially in light of Dutch's maniacal pursuit of the dreary details of the adulterous back story. This investigation of the painfully obvious is glum and endless and appears to have been designed by writer Kurt Luedtke (working from a Warren Adler novel) to show Dutch in the worst possible light. Apparently, though, Kay has a taste for sullen plodders. No other explanation is offered for her decision to enter into a brief, nervous affair with Dutch.

What director Sydney Pollack, one of the movies' great romantics *(Tootsie, Out of Africa)*, saw in this lugubrious tale is even harder to imagine. There's no heat, wit or glamour in his telling of it. The movie is like bad gossip: a scandalous premise that comes to no interesting—or even amusingly ironic point.

VILLAGE VOICE, 10/12/99, p. 146, Michael Atkinson

Mildly more acidic than your average middle-aged tragi-romance, Sydney Pollack's randomly titled *Random Hearts* almost shoots itself in the Bruno Magli. As a D.C. cop who in one bad day finds out that his wife died in a plane crash and was cheating on him (her lover, Peter Coyote, was also on the plane, which makes it a good day, too), Harrison Ford spends most of the film wearing the frown of the betrayed. Even as the tinkly piano music and misty gazes from costar Kristin Scott Thomas (Coyote's wife) tell us romance is afoot, Ford is hunting down secret love-nest keys and seething as if terrorists have besieged the White House again. The film has all the Hollywood-romance trappings—naked affluence, glamorous/rugged professions (she's a Republican congresswoman, he's a detective), misunderstanding friends offering misguided advice, a log cabin idyll. The only drama is in how long it'll take Ford to forget the dead tramp and start humming along with the politician, who's ingenuous enough to gasp, "My God, you people!" when her own manager suggests a post-trauma public appearance for her teenage daughter.

Look past the run-amok Stoli placements if you can, at least to the surprising presence of an earring in Ford's leathery left lobe, and the chilly ID—the body scene, done via grim video monitors. Color-coded in Hillary tones, Scott Thomas is a cool glass of creme de menthe beside Ford, who's more like a moldy pillow with gastritis. But everyone in the film is a walking cliché (Bonnie Hunt as the mushy friend, etc.) even the manipulative opportunities afforded by dead spouses are neglected.

Also reviewed in:
CHICAGO TRIBUNE, 10/8/99, Friday/p. A, Michael Wilmington
NEW YORK TIMES, 10/8/99, p. E1, Janet Maslin
VARIETY, 10/4-10/99, p. 84, Todd McCarthy
WASHINGTON POST, 10/8/99, p. C1, Rita Kempley
WASHINGTON POST, 10/8/99, Weekend/p. 54, Desson Howe

RAVENOUS

A Fox 2000 Pictures release of an Adam Fields/Heyday Films production. *Executive Producer:* Tim Van Rellim. *Producer:* Adam Fields and David Heyman. *Director:* Antonia Bird.

Screenplay: Ted Griffin. *Director of Photography:* Anthony Richmond. *Editor:* Neil Farrell. *Music:* Michael Nyman and Damon Albarn. *Music Editor:* Bunny Andrews and Terry Delsing. *Sound:* Mark Holding and (music) Austin Ince and Tom Girling. *Sound Editor:* Roger Mitchell. *Casting:* Billy Hopkins, Suzanne Smith, and Kerry Barden. *Production Designer:* Bryce Perrin. *Art Director:* Karel Vacek. *Set Decorator:* Jirí Zucek and Marco Niro. *Special Effects:* Terry Glass. *Costumes:* Sheena Napier. *Make-up:* Fae Hammond. *Stunt Coordinator:* Paul Weston. *Running time:* 110 minutes. *MPAA Rating:* R.

CAST: Guy Pearce (Captain John Boyd); Robert Carlyle (Ives/Colqhoun); Jeremy Davies (Toffler); Jeffrey Jones (Colonel Hart); John Spencer (General Slauson); Stephen Spinella (Major Knox); Neal McDonough (Reich); Sheila Tousey (Martha); Bill Brochtrup (Lindus); Joseph Running Fox (George); David Arquette (Cleaves); Fernando Becerril, Gabriel Berthier, and Pedro Altamirano (Mexican Commanders); Joseph Boyle (US Blonde Soldier); Damian Delgado and Fernando Manzano (Mexican Sentries); Alfredo Escobar and Gerardo Martinez (Soldiers); David Heyman (Janus); Tim Van Rellim (Mr. MacCready); Miezi Sungu (Jones); Abel Woolrich (Borracho).

LOS ANGELES TIMES, 3/19/99, Calendar/p. 16, Kevin Thomas

Macabre doesn't begin to describe the sly, grisly Grand Guignol horror of "Ravenous," which has all the ingredients for a cult film success but most definitely is not for everyone. It's stylish, sophisticated, venturesome—to say the least—and it's not the project you would have thought Guy Pearce and Robert Carlyle would choose to consolidate the acclaim and recognition that "L.A. Confidential" and "The Full Monty," respectively, brought them.

But then you have to remember that before he played an ambitious, straight-arrow L.A. cop, Pearce first came to attention as one of the dragsters in "The Adventures of Priscilla, Queen of the Desert" and that Carlyle made his name as the psychopathic Begbie in "Trainspotting." "Ravenous" offers further assurance that the handsome Pearce and the wiry Carlyle are not about to let themselves be typecast.

We first meet Pearce's Capt. Boyd at an elaborate meal celebrating a victorious battle in the Mexican-American War of 1847. Boyd had been overcome by cowardice, played dead and wound up under a pile of corpses to emerge as the unexpected hero of the charge. "Something ... something happened to me," he mutters, unable to eat a hearty dinner, seeing in his steak the faces of the dead. His uncomfortably ambivalent status and demeanor gets him transferred to a California fort in the western Sierra Nevada, in the command of the witty Col. Hart (Jeffrey Jones), who presides over a group of eccentrics straight out of a James Whale movie. Hart is doing a pretty good job of living with the paradox of having wanted to escape from everything only to want to escape the remote post.

The haunted-seeming Boyd has barely met the others, who include David Arquette's loopy cook Cleaves, Jeremy Davies' deeply religious Toffler, Stephen Spinella's boozy medico Knox and Neal McDonough's macho Reich, when Carlyle's Ives staggers to the fort, explaining that he is a member of a snowbound Donner-like party that was in fact forced to resort to cannibalism. He wants Col. Hart to lead an expedition to a cave, where he says two people in the party were still alive when he left them.

Director Antonia Bird and writer Ted Griffin, crediting Native American belief, envision—vividly, to put it mildly—a certain dire consequence of cannibalism, as that turns their film into an outrageous supernatural gore feast that they sustain with gruesome, gleeful ingenuity that will be kicky for some, a turnoff to others. They probably would like you to see the film as an allegory of All-American expansionist greed and pillage, the doctrine of Manifest Destiny carried to the extreme. That's more than a tad pretentious for what is at heart a high-class midnight movie that does leave us with the timeless notion that, since good and evil both lie within us, we may be forced to make a drastic choice between the two.

Starting with Pearce and Boyd, the cast plays with appropriate gusto, and "Ravenous" was shot superbly by Anthony B. Richmond in the Czech Republic and Slovakia, of all places, as well as the more familiar Durango, Mexico. Music is almost always crucial in a movie but never more so than here, and Michael Nyman and Damon Albarn's score, alternately blithe and ominous, actually seems to help drive and shape the narrative as well as set tone and mood.

NEW YORK, 3/29/99, p. 70, Peter Rainer

A black comedy about cannibalism. *Ravenous* is a bit like *The Thing* plunked down in the Donner Pass. Starring Guy Pearce and Robert Carlyle. it opens with a closeup of bloody steaks at a victory feast and eventually moves on to bloody corpses. Set in 1847 in a remote military outpost (is there any other kind?) in California's snowy Sierra Nevada mountains, it's a not-so-Grand Guignol grossout that posits the moral dilemma: Would you rather eat or be eaten? Make no mistake: In the movie business, where they devour their young, these questions are more than academic. The press book for *Ravenous* includes the recipes for numerous human taste treats and then, off to the side, in small letters, cautions: "All recipes are fictitious. Twentieth Century Fox does not condone cannibalism." That's reassuring. Don't go to this movie on a full stomach. Better yet, don't go.

NEW YORK POST, 3/19/99, p. 46, Jonathan Foreman

To mix horror and comedy and have it work—as in "An American Werewolf in London" or "Scream" you need a well-written script and a director with a sure hand.

"Ravenous" has neither. The result is a waste of a fine cast.

The movie starts off shakily, with hokey-jokey titles and a quotation from Nietzsche that misspells the philosopher's name. Things go mostly downhill from there.

"Ravenous" is one of those once-bitten movies with the werewolf/vampire theme replaced by cannibalism. It relies on the notion that if cannibalism is taboo, there must be something wonderful about human flesh: Either people meat is addictively delicious or it gives you super powers—or, as here, both. The only original aspect of the story is its setting, a remote Army base in the 1840s.

In 1847, during a battle in the Mexican-American War, cowardly Captain Boyd (Guy Pearce) pretends to be dead. After his unit is wiped out, he awakens in a pile of corpses with his commander's blood dripping into his mouth. In a moment of uncharacteristic courage, he crawls out and captures a Mexican outpost. The Army gives him a medal and sends him out to the California Sierras.

Fort Spencer turns out to be the home of some unlikely soldiers, including a religious maniac (Jeremy Davies) and a stoner who spends all his time smoking marijuana with Indians (David Arquette). The motley squad is led by the bookish, cynical Hart (Jeffrey Jones).

One snowy night, a stranger collapses inside the gates. Colqhoun (Robert Carlyle, of "The Full Monty" and "Trainspotting") says he was one of six winter-bound pioneers who took refuge in a cave and turned to cannibalism when the food ran out.

Hart leads a team to rescue the remaining survivors—despite learning of the Indian myth that a man who eats another steals his spirit, but then develops a craving for human flesh. Colqhoun accompanies the expedition, but it soon becomes horribly clear that he hasn't told them the whole truth.

What follows is gory stuff, although some scenes are suddenly, jarringly played for laughs, as if director Antonia Bird couldn't figure out a tone for her movie. She's also clueless when it comes to action sequences, and tries to overcome their unconvincing feel by including too many shots of blood gushing out of mouths.

Cheesy music doesn't help; neither does bad lighting and substandard photography. But what really dooms "Ravenous" is an amateurish script that often makes no internal sense (the story rides on the assumption that if there's no deli within walking distance, people face the choice of cannibalism or starvation). It also includes some undergrad drivel implying that cannibalism is a product of American capitalism's drive westward.

Yet "Ravenous" has kitschily enjoyable sections—if only because Carlyle makes such a terrific villain and Jeffrey Jones is so watchable.

But poor Guy Pearce—who resembles Brad Pitt under his beard and lank hair—seems to have been stunned by the awful writing into a blank, expressionless performance.

NEWSDAY, 3/19/99, Part II/p. B11, John Anderson

Cast in flickering firelight, unconquerable grime and the raging torrents of its own vital fluids, "Ravenous" doesn't deliver a message as much as demand one: Something must be going on here, you tell yourself, as each fresh evisceration suggests a movie in need of windshield wipers.

Cannibalism? Ahh. Perhaps the filmmakers are attempting to reflect the sadistic dictates of social Darwinism. Vampirism? Well, that would be AIDS, drug abuse ... you know, the usual. Old West-meets-Gold Rush setting? The soul-shriveling price of Manifest Destiny, a nation (sniffle) cursed by its own ambition.

As a full-color Rorschach test, "Ravenous"—which stars Robert Carlyle ("The Full Monty") as the incarnation of evil and Guy Pearce ("L.A. Confidential") as the soul on the brink of damnation—works pretty well. At least it keeps you wondering. But if its purpose is provocation and not simply midnight-movie cult status—which it likely won't achieve, because it's not quite silly enough—why does this atmospheric and deliriously bad motion picture try so hard to be so funny? Why does it feel like a movie in contention with itself.?

As the story goes, director Antonia Bird—who has worked with Carlyle in a number of films, including the controversial "Priest" in 1994—took over from the Macedonian director Milcho Manchevski ("Before the Rain") when it became apparent that his vision and that of the producers were less than sympathetic. Knowing that, or not, you can feel the disjunction: Bird's efforts to make this a very black comedy are largely out of sync with the basic thrust of the film. Carlyle, when he delivers the various mood-lightening one-liners, is shot alone, suggesting an ex post facto tweaking of mood. As much of that mood is imposed by the music (and, as scored by Michael Nyman with Damon Albarn of the British band Blur, it isn't bad), the hurdy-gurdy serenade suggests levity where, visually, none seems to have been intended.

The acting is certainly fine, considering that the cast is trying to pull off the Grand Guignol version of "F Troop." Pearce's Captain Boyd, the hero-coward of the Mexican-American War, lost his nerve in battle, survived by being stacked like cordwood among the bloody dead and then was captured his captors. As reward-punishment, he is sent to California's Fort Spencer, which is run by reluctant scholar-soldier Colonel Hart (Jeffrey Jones) and staffed by a cross-section of social misfits: Knox (Stephen Spinella), a drunk; Toffler (Jeremy Davies), a religious fanatic; Reich (Neal McDonough), the resident uber-soldier, and Cleaves the cook (David Arquette), who spends his days sampling local hallucinogens.

Losers and lunacy already are the motifs of the ghastly Fort Spencer when Colqhoun (Carlyle), barely alive, is discovered at the fort and delivers a variation on the Donner Party story: He and his fellow pioneers, caught in a snowstorm, survived in the mountains by eating each other. The party's lone female is still alive, but imperiled by a very hungry character named Colonel Ives. Hart decides it's their duty to save the woman, and off they go.

There are some twists in the tale and since they provide some amusement we won't give them away. Suffice it to say the overriding moral of the story—eat, or be eaten—has some topicality as the Dow reaches 10,000; Ives eats flesh because he's addicted to the curative and invigorating power contained within it. (Old Indian legends are credited with this bit of malarkey, but it sounds like Bram Stoker to us.) But anything remotely serious about "Ravenous" is deflated by its unavoidably comic overtones (made unavoidable by the gallons of meat juice that come cascading through it) and a reluctance to take that comedy far enough. The frontier West was probably even wider than the metaphors in this movie, but, as per "Ravenous," equally uninteresting.

SIGHT AND SOUND, 9/99, p. 53, Philip Kemp

1847. Following a dishonourable incident in the Mexican-American War, Captain John Boyd is transferred to Fort Spencer, an isolated outpost in the Sierra Nevada mountains commanded by the disillusioned Colonel Hart. Also at Fort Spencer are the drunken Major Knox, the ultra-religious Toffler, keen soldier Reich, peyote-addicted Cleaves, and two Native Americans, George and his sister Martha.

While Cleaves and Martha are off fetching supplies, a stranger stumbles half-dead into the fort. He identifies himself as Colqhoun, survivor of a group of settlers snowbound in a mountain cave. Prompted by the group's leader the settlers had begun eating each other. Colqhoun joined in, but escaped to avoid being eaten. Leaving Knox at the fort, the others go with Colqhoun to the cave, where they realise he had eaten all his companions. Colqhoun stabs Hart and kills Toffler, George and Reich; Boyd jumps off a cliff and breaks his leg. While it heals, he survives by eating the corpse of Reich.

Boyd limps back to the fort, but his story is disbelieved. General Slauson, the area commander, appoints a new CO: Colonel Ives, alias Colqhoun. Alone with Boyd, Ives recounts how, as a former invalid, he regained strength and health through cannibalism, and urges Boyd to adopt the same practice. Boyd attacks him, and is chained up. While Martha is dispatched to fetch Slauson, Knox and Cleaves are killed by Hart, whom Ives had turned into a cannibal. Repentant, Hart frees Boyd, who slits his throat. After a savage battle Boyd lures Ives into a huge bear trap, where they die together.

Ravenous was a troubled production: the original director, Milcho Manchevski, was fired, and Robert Carlyle persuaded (or, according to reports, practically blackmailed) Antonia Bird, with whom he'd worked on three previous films, to take over. Such events usually herald a turkey, but in this case the end result, though uneven and at times incoherent, has enough ideas going for it (maybe even a few too many) to sustain momentum, helped immeasurably by the headlong frenzy of Bird's direction.

Kicking off with a quotation from Nietzsche, and tossing in references to Benjamin Franklin and Native American myth as it goes, *Ravenous* makes free with its conceptual reference points. At its heart is the idea of cannibalism as a proselytising movement, eager to attract new blood in more ways than one: gaining strength not only from the victims who are dismembered and eaten, but also from new converts to the creed. The religious parallel is underlined by the Native American George who recounts the legend of the Weendigo, a creature who absorbs the power and very spirit of each person it eats, adding casually, "Like man eats Jesus Christ each Sunday."

There's also a hint at a political subtext, with Ives/Colqhoun musing ironically on the westwards-expanding doctrine of Manifest Destiny, and referring to America as, "a country seeking to be whole, consuming all it can." (In his case it's an even more self-serving doctrine than usual, since he foresees a steady stream of westbound pioneers heading his way to serve as sustenance.) Ted Griffin's script dangles these references as if to lure us into thinking we're watching something serious. But essentially *Ravenous* is an ingenious period-costume reworking of that reliable old staple the closed-community horror movie, of which *Alien* (1979) and John Carpenter's *The Thing* (1982) are other variants, though its eat-or-be-eaten theme suggests a sideglance at subversive one-offs like Bob Balaban's *Parents* (1988) or Brian Yuzna's *Society* (1989)—both of which worked through their ideas more cleverly.

Whether due to script problems or last-minute reshoots, *Ravenous* comes apart towards the end. An abrupt, unmotivated change of heart by the recent cannibal-convert Colonel Hart is used to slice through a plot crux, after which the showdown between Boyd and Ives degenerates into standard hayforks-in the-barn mayhem where something far more towering and apocalyptic was needed. Whatever his subsequent misgivings, Carlyle plays Ives with a fine edge of callous relish, though Guy Pearce, terrific as the straight-arrow cop in *L.A. Confidential,* here can't do much with a role that mostly asks him to react. No doubt conscious of the script's weaknesses, Antonia Bird's typically dynamic camera goes into compensatory overdrive, wheeling and careening and zip-panning in mounting hysteria at every menacing moment. By itself this would be fine, but the hyperactivity is compounded by the contributions of Michael Nyman and Damon Albarn, collaborating on what must be the loudest and most bombastic score since Maurice Jarre pulled out all the stops for *Ryan's Daughter.*

VILLAGE VOICE, 3/23/99, p. 125, J. Hoberman

There's also a marked '70s quality to the even gorier black comedy *Ravenous.* [The reference is to *I Stand Alone*; see Hoberman's review.]

Surprisingly, this Hollywood-financed, antimilitarist, gross-out Western by British director Antonia Bird is the first theatrical feature to draw on one of the grisliest episodes in American history—namely the 1847 California-bound Donner Party who, trapped by an early winter in the Sierra Nevadas, resorted to cannibalism.

That *Ravenous* will oscillate in tone between the spooky and the jocular is immediately signaled when a Nietzschean epigram is capped by the anonymous injunction "EAT ME." In a movie filled with anachronistic wise-guy performances, Guy Pearce's Captain John Boyd—a soldier who managed to survive a Mexican War battle by cravenly playing possum in a mass grave—is unusually sober. As his reward, he's sent to a remote fort high in the Sierra Nevadas—there to be the straight man to a crew of rowdy, sloppy misfits. Things grow even more lysergic when a mysterious stranger (Robert Carlyle) stumbles out of the wilderness one night, recounting the tale of a stranded wagon train whose starving members were compelled to butcher one another for food.

The fort dispatches a rescue mission and Bird gets her best scenes, midmovie, with Boyd and a handful of other soldiers heading heedless into horror, their guide ever freakier as they approach his haunt of fear. A succession of dripping corpses, not to mention Carlyle's hooting, Manson-esque character, suggest the missing link between the Old West and *The Texas Chainsaw Massacre*—although Ted Griffin's screenplay, which derives an additional spin by appropriating an Indian vampire myth, is ultimately too crude to sustain the mood. As Bird, too, overplays her hand, the movie dissolves into a bloody mess.

For all its high-flown suggestions that cannibalism might be a metaphor for Manifest Destiny, gold-hungry Americans, or an innate will to consume, *Ravenous* loses resonance as it proceeds. To stay to find out how this campfire story ends is to sit still for a debate on morality that the butcher of *I Stand Alone* would find laughable, amid one-liners that would make even him wince. "It's lonely being a cannibal," a character complains. "It's tough making friends."

Also reviewed in:
CHICAGO TRIBUNE, 3/19/99, Friday/p. D, Michael Wilmington
NEW YORK TIMES, 3/19/99, p E27, Janet Maslin
VARIETY, 2/1-7/99, p. 58, Todd McCarthy
WASHINGTON POST, 3/19/99, p. C1, Stephen Hunter
WASHINGTON POST, 3/19/99, Weekend/p. 44, Michael O'Sullivan

RED DWARF, THE

A Samuel Goldwyn Films release of an A.A. Les Films Belge/Mainstream/Classic production in association with Parma Film and with participation of Cana. *Director:* Yvan Le Moine. *Screenplay (French with English subtitles):* Yvan Le Moine. *Based on the short story by:* Michel Tournier. *Director of Photography:* Danny Elsen. *Editor:* Ursula Leziak. *Music:* Alexei Shelegin and Daniel Brandt. *Production Designer:* Philippe Graff. *Costumes:* Pierre-Yves Gayraud. *Running time:* 102 minutes. *MPAA Rating:* Not Rated.

CAST: Jean-Yves Thual (Lucien Lhotte); Dyna Gauzy (Isis Colombe); Michel Peyrelon (Circus Director); Arno Chevrier (Bob); Anita Ekberg (Contess Paola Bendoni); Carlo Colombaioni (Old Clown).

NEW YORK POST, 6/18/99, p. 57, Jonathan Foreman

"The Red Dwarf" seems to be a latter-day attempt by Belgian director Jean-Yves Le Moine to remake 1932's "Freaks" as a Fellini movie.

Shot in black and white and set in what looks like the early 1960s, it's a cloying and creepy story about a middle-age dwarf whose dronelike existence is transformed by a brief affair with a former opera star—whom he murders—before he runs off to join the circus, where he has fallen in love with a pre-teen trapeze artist.

Lucien the dwarf (Jean-Yves Thual) works in a dusty, starchy old-fashioned office, where his job seems to be forging sexually explicit letters for clients to use in divorce proceedings. The firm's most important client, aging opera star Countess Bendoni (Anita Ekberg) finds his work titillating and summons him to her luxurious villa.

After he exposes himself to her, they begin an affair. Lucien falls in love, but then discovers that she's getting back together with her gigolo husband, Bob (Amo Chevrier, who gives the film's best performance).

Enraged, Lucien sneaks into the villa, gets smashed on whiskey, dons a wig and makeup and strangles the countess. He also frames Bob, who goes on the run.

As so often in movieland, getting away with murder has a tonic effect on Lucien. He starts dressing better, going out more and developing a serious attitude problem at work. When his creepy boss calls him on the carpet, he defecates on his desk and leaves.

He then turns up at the circus, where Isis (Dyna Gauzy), the owner's daughter, is thrilled to see him, and he's offered a job as a clown.

The film has some moving and dryly funny moments, but for the most part, it doesn't work except as an exercise in stylish photography and production design.

NEWSDAY, 6/18/99, Part II/p. B11, John Anderson

Boasting grainy-gothic cinematography, a taste for the grotesque and an epic Anita Ekberg, "The Red Dwarf" is a trip to profundity washed up on the shoals of circus metaphors.

Your physique is your destiny? No kidding. The film, which stars the very effecting dwarf actor Jean-Yves Thual, posists its person as the allegorical repository of man's inhumanity to man—which is rather like suggesting Moby Dick as a symbol of a white whale filling in for God. Given director Yvan Le Moine's flamboyance and flair for the startling scene—and there are several—you can't help waiting for all the obvious gestures to add up to something novel. What we get instead are obvious object lessons: People who are different are treated cruelly. And be careful what you wish for, because you may get it (apologies to Oscar Wilde).

Lucien (Thual) works for a stiflingly proper law firm and serves the unique purpose of writing erotic correspondence to he used as false evidence in divorce cases. That he's so good at it is evidence of his unvented sexuality; that he's scorned despite his talents is proof that dwarves can't win. Summoned to the home of the Countess Paola Bendoni (la dolce Ekberg), who wants to divorce her gigolo husband, Bob (Arno Chevrier), Lucien makes a play for the bountiful countess. (There's a great shot in which Lucien, his naked reflection warped by the multiple mirrors in Paola's bathroom, looks like Michaelangelo's David). Their's is a furious sexual obsession to which Paola cools quickly. Lucien, rejected yet again, does not take it lying down. So to speak.

In the parallel universes that constitute Lucien's life we find Isis (Dyna Gauzy), a little circus girl whose lithe body, acrobatic talents and innocence are such an obvious counterbalance to Paolo's hefty voracity that you can barely believe your eyes.

Lucien, torn between Isis and the circus and the outside world—and more or less liberated by a combination of betrayal and murder—is a character who genuinely develops during the course of the story. And the film reportedly got a huge ovation when it premiered at the 1998 Cannes Film Festival (whose audiences regularly—and rather patronizingly—applaud movies about the mentally or physically challenged). But if Le Moine was trying to make anything other than the most obvious points about personal destiny and the ills of society, he's come up a little short.

VILLAGE VOICE, 6/22/99, p. 149, Jessica Winter

The leering bastard child of La Dolce Vita and Freaks, The Red Dwarf is a Belgian melodrama that never transcends its air of sentimentalized sideshow curiosity. Lucien (Jean-Yves Thual) is a dwarf and law-office drone who one day makes a house call to his firm's premier client, a faded opera diva played by Anita Ekberg; the actress has, alas, finally grown into her gargantuan breasts, while her girlish chirp has coarsened into a nicotined grunt worthy of Patty and Selma Bouvier. His loins girded by one glimpse of Ekberg's Countess Paola lounging walrus-like poolside—and his confidence boosted by the appearance of a freakier freak in his tightly circumscribed world—Lucien plunges into the fountain at her estate for a bath no doubt meant to evoke Ekberg's false baptismal in La Dolce Vita and then seduces the countess, who responds with fabulously ludicrous sweet talk like "Come and eat my tiramisu."

The murky black-and-white cinematography and cheerily vulgar angles—for the singular image of Lucien and Paola fucking, the camera advances from under the bed and ends up peering over them, as if tracking the movements of some zealous R.A.—lend the film some seedy midnight-movie charm, but this tone collides with the cloying parallel story involving Lucien's friendship with a little girl, Isis, a trapeze artist in the local carnival. Once Paola dumps him and Lucien locates his inner murderous rage (against the Big People, in case you were wondering), our hero flees into the anonymity of circus life, yet still can't find footing as One of Us. Only Isis really understands him, as we're informed with a brief color interlude in which the red-rubber-nosed Lucien gazes at his muse with a soppy smile, dredging noxious memories of Patch Adams. At this point, all the film has left to say is, I'm okay, you're okay.

Also reviewed in:
NEW YORK TIMES, 6/18/99, p. E10, Stephen Holden
VARIETY, 5/25-31/98, p. 62, David Rooney

RED VIOLIN, THE

A Lions Gate Film release of a Rhombus Media/Mikado co-production. *Producer:* Niv Fichman. *Director:* François Girard. *Screenplay:* Don McKellar and François Girard. *Director of Photography:* Alain Dostie. *Editor:* Gaëtan Huot. *Music:* John Corigliano. *Sound:* Marcel Pothier. *Production Designer:* François Séguin. *Art Director (Italy):* Emita Frigato; *(Vienna):* Susanne Quendler; *(Oxford):* Martyn John; *(Shanghai):* Sun Weido. *Set Decorator: (Vienna)* Maria Blümel; *(Oxford)* Judy Farr; *(Montreal)* Pierre Perrault. *Violin Construction:* Peter Beare. *Costumes:* Renée April. *Make-up: (Italy)* Rosario Prestopino; *(Vienna)* Adolph Uhrmacher; *(Oxford)* Pat Hay; *(Shanghai)* Gui Shaolin; *(Montreal)* Micheline Trépanier. *Running time:* 130 minutes. *MPAA Rating:* Not Rated.

CAST: Carlo Cecchi (Nicolo Bussotti); Irene Grazioli (Anna Bussotti); Anita Laurenzi (Cesca); Tommaso Puntelli (Apprentice); Aldo Brugnini (Assistant); Samuele Amighetti (Boy); Jean-Luc Bideau (Georges Poussin); Christoph Koncz (Kaspar Weiss); Clothide Mollet (Antoinette Poussin); Rainer Egger (Brother Christophe); Wolfgang Böck (Brother Michael); Florentin Groll (Anton von Spielmann); Johannes Silberschneider (Father Richter); Arthur Denberg (Prince Mansfield); Paul Koeker (Brother Gustav); Josef Mairginter (Brother Franz); Johann Gotsch (Funeral Monk); Geza Hosszu-Legocky, David Alberman, and Andrzej Matuszewski (Gypsy Violinists); Jason Flemyng (Frederick Pope); Greta Scacchi (Victoria Byrd); Eva Marie Bryer (Sara); Dimtri Andreas (Gypsy Father); David Gant (Conductor); Stuart Ong (Manservant); Sylvia Chang (Xiang Pei); Liu Zifeng (Chou Yuan); Tao Hong (Comrade Chan Gong); Cao Kunqi (Deputy); Han Xiofel (Young Ming); Tan Zengwei (Guard); Zhou Zhiqing (Senior Policeman); Wang Xiaoshuai (Junior Policeman); Quao Zhi (Elderly Woman); Tang Ren (Young Xiang Pei); Lidou (Pawnbroker); Zhang Kai (Rally Speaker); Samuel L. Jackson (Charles Morritz); Colm Feore (Auctioneer); Monique Mercure (Madame Leroux); Don McKellar (Evan Williams); Ireneusz Bogajewicz (Mr. Ruselsky); Julian Richings (Nicolas Olsberg); Russell Yeun (Older Ming); Sandra Oh (Madame Ming); Paula De Vasconcelos (Suzanne); Rémy Girard (Customs Agent); Marie-Josée Gauthier (Hotel Concierge); Dany Laferrière (Cabby); Dorothée Berryman (Secretary); David La Haye (Handler); Grégory Hlady (Coat Attendant); Herman Meckler (Registar); Sheena MacDonald (Ruselsky's Companion); Jody Shapiro (Autograph Seeker); James Bradford (Stagehand).

LOS ANGELES TIMES, 6/11/99, Calendar/p. 8, Eric Harrison

Grand in ambition, complex in design, Francois Girard's "The Red Violin" dares to deal with large and enduring themes, namely the inviolable power of love and art and the abilities of both to transcend even death.

This is Girard's first movie since the critically acclaimed "Thirty-Two Short Films About Glenn Gould" (1993), and even though this is a completely different kind of film, "The Red Violin" is equally steeped in music and equally unconcerned with traditional linear narrative.

The story spans three centuries and five continents as it tracks the "life" of a violin from its creation in 17th century Italy to its fate at an auction in modern-day Montreal. Samuel L.

Jackson plays a pivotal role as an expert who authenticates the instrument for the auction house and falls under its thrall.

He and Greta Scacchi, as a British novelist who crosses paths with the violin in 1893, are the members of the movie's ensemble cast best known to American audiences. But though Jackson's intense and morally ambiguous music expert dominates the movie's concluding scenes, the sanguine instrument of the title must be described as the main character.

It is the one physical entity that ties together the various pieces of this sprawling story. And while Girard and co-writer Don McKellar deftly and economically fill the various episodes with full-bodied characters, we care as much or more for the violin that seems to possess both a personality and a soul of its own.

After its maker dies the violin comes to be owned by, in succession, an Austrian monastery, an orphaned 6-year-old child prodigy, a band of nomadic Gypsies and a lascivious rock star-like British violinist before making its way to Shanghai. There, after decades languishing in a pawn shop, it is bought and given to a young girl who eventually will be caught up in the Chinese Cultural Revolution. Decades later, Chinese authorities send the violin to Montreal with other instruments to be auctioned. Jackson immediately recognizes it as the fabled red violin of Italian master Nicolo Bussotti (Carlo Cecchi).

Movies such as this that are largely composed of discrete episodes invite viewers to judge them based on the strength of individual stories.

But while it's possible to view this movie like a short-story collection, putting check marks beside the selections one likes best, to do so would deny the pleasure of experiencing this beautifully crafted, intricately designed story the way it was intended, as an organic whole.

"The Red Violin" would be moving even if it had no dialogue or visuals. Music is at the heart of this movie and, just this once, to call the score conspicuous is not a slur. Girard uses composer John Corigliano's music not only as an expressive tool and as the instrument's melancholy "voice" but also as a unifying force. (The music is performed by the London Philharmonia Orchestra, with solo violin by Joshua Bell.) Corigliano participated in shaping the movie from the earliest stages, and it shows. Though "The Red Violin" is intensely cinematic, it nevertheless is symphonic both in scale and concept.

We realize fairly early that when Bussotti's pregnant wife has her fortune read with Tarot cards, the seer is foretelling the future of the not-yet-completed violin. The instrument, Bussotti's masterpiece, is to be a gift to his unborn child. The dialogue and visuals of these early scenes comprise the filmic equivalent of a symphony's theme. The cards become a leitmotif The movie returns to them to introduce each new section, or movement.

The movie also is unified by recurring scenes of the present-day auction house at which the violin is about to be sold. Each time we return we see the scene from a different vantage point, through the eyes of a different participant.

This is the extraordinary achievement of this film's complex structure: Just as all of the various stories are elaborations of the fortune read at the movie's beginning, they all also comment on the present-day scene, explaining to us how the characters in the room are connected to the violin. The stories are Janus-faced, looking forward and backward simultaneously.

Like a classical symphony, the movie recapitulates its theme at the end. Jackson's violin expert, autocratic, supremely confidant and every bit the perfectionist, is a bookend to the uncompromising violin maker. For Bussotti the instrument is the pinnacle of his art, the masterpiece through which he'll achieve immortality, as well as the embodiment of his love for his wife and child.

For Jackson it is a sacred object, the Holy Grail that he has spent years searching for. During one scene, he listens while a great violinist plays. Jackson sits rapt, transported by the beauty of the sound as the violinist, who will become a rival for ownership of the instrument, proves himself unworthy by failing to recognize that he is holding perfection in his hands.

Only Jackson knows for certain, and while he covets the violin just like everyone else does, only he recognizes its true value and only he wants to do with it something roughly equivalent to what its maker had in mind.

Girard showed a similar love and keen understanding of music in "Glenn Gould," which also was co-written with McKellar. That quasi-documentary was composed of 32 segments, the exact number of pieces in Bach's "Goldberg Variations," which loomed large in Gould's career as a pianist. But unlike the cold and elliptical "Gould," which was as cerebral and eccentric as its renowned subject, "Red Violin" glows with passion.

NEW YORK POST, 6/11/99, p. 49, Jonathan Foreman

A film directed by a French Canadian that tells the history—in five languages—of a cursed musical instrument across three continents and four centuries, "The Red Violin" turns out to be entertaining old-fashioned hokum rather than an exercise in artiness. Indeed, it's hard to think of a recent movie with a sensibility as shamelessly romantic. It's a date movie for people who like subtitles and classical music.

Nicolo Bussotti (Carlo Cecci), a brilliant 16th-century Italian violin-maker, crafts a masterpiece as his wife dies in childbirth. Just before her death, she gets a tarot reading that foretells a long, tumultuous life. When the violin-maker mixes her blood into the varnish, the instrument somehow takes on the woman's soul—and the destiny predicted by the fortune teller.

The violin turns up at the end of the 18th century at an Austrian monastery, in the hands of an orphan prodigy who is taken to Vienna by a French music master to perform before Joseph II. On the boy's sudden death, the monks bury the violin with his corpse. Stolen by grave robbers, it ends up in the hands of gypsies, whose descendants take it to England.

There it is discovered in 1893 by Byronic landowner-virtuoso Lord Frederick Pope (Jason Flemyng from "Lock, Stock & Two Smoking Barrels"). When he plays his impromptu compositions, women are quite undone—including his novelist lover Victoria (Greta Scacchi), who makes love to him mid-performance. But Pope is destroyed thanks to the influence of the red violin, and it is taken to China by his opium-dealing manservant.

There it passes into the hands of a wealthy Shanghai family, and a generation later almost falls victim to the fanatic anti-Western hysteria of the Cultural Revolution (whose cruelties are massively underplayed—perhaps to ease permission to film in China).

Finally, the violin comes up for sale at an auction house in Montreal, having been authenticated by Charles Morritz (Jackson) using the latest high-tech gadgetry. He, too, has fallen in love with the instrument, but he cannot hope to match the offers coming in from all over the world.

A cynic might justly complain that it's all ridiculous, overwrought, artificial stuff—much of the melodramatic dialogue would seem comical if it were in English—but its good, lushly photographed fun all the same. It helps that Samuel L. Jackson is magnetic as always. And fans of the lovely Greta Scacchi will doubtless enjoy her nude scene with Flemyng.

NEWSDAY, 6/11/99, Part II/p. B3, Gene Seymour

What does it say about the goofy state of art and life these days that the year's most moving love story on film so far has a sculpted piece of wood as its protagonist?

Maybe it's best not to think too hard on this matter. Especially since the central conceit of "The Red Violin" wanders perilously close to the kind of contrived sappiness that has waylaid several so-called "romantic comedies" ground out by the Hollywood sausage factory.

But if there was ever a case where artsy calculation, as practiced by director-co-scripter Francois Girard, is a redemptive force, "The Red Violin" serves it up with aromatic panache. Even at its most implausible or overwrought, the movie is as seductive as the instrument that serves as its resilient, plucky (no pun intended) focus.

The violin is conceived in 17th-Century Italy in the wake of the death, during childbirth, of its maker's wife. Love and death stalk the instrument through the ages. A century later, it turns up in an Austrian monastery where its bright red color makes it a perennial reward to the best orphans who play there. The very best, a frail, frightened little boy (Christoph Koncz), is taken to Vienna by a renowned, if impoverished teacher (Jean-Luc Bideau) for further study and becomes so physically attached to the instrument that even a brief separation is harmful to his health.

Somehow, the violin turns up next in 19th-Century England where a saturnine young virtuoso (Jason Flemyng of "Lock, Stock and Two Smoking Barrels") and his novelist-lover (Greta Scacchi) find both musical and erotic inspiration from its sound. More turbulence, more pain and then the violin finds itself crossing two oceans before ending up in a Shanghai pawnshop where it is sold to the mother of a little girl.

Suddenly it's 1965 and the little girl is now a grown-up Communist Party functionary (Sylvia Chang), who worries that the violin will become sacrificed to the Cultural Revolution. She takes it to the home of a music teacher who agrees to shelter it along with other discredited western instruments.

The instruments are recovered decades later by the Chinese government and sent to a Montreal auction house to be assessed. By now, the legend of the red violin has become such that a renowned appraiser (Samuel L. Jackson) finds himself almost trembling when he finds it. The resulting auction, which provides one of several recurring tropes in the film's narrative, leaves you on the edge of your seat wondering where the battered little thing will next find a home.

You read right. This movie will actually have you sitting in the dark, fretting over the destiny of this inanimate object. Absurd, even for the enchanted melodrama stirred up for this tale. But it works.

Girard and co-writer Don McKellar, who also plays Jackson's assistant, last collaborated on "Thirty-Two Short Films About Glenn Gould." The ingenious storytelling that characterized that 1993 film is retained in "Red Violin," though there's nothing in the new film that approaches the simple eloquence of the chambermaid sequence in "Gould." There are more mood swings to deal with here, contained nicely by both the auction and the flashback to a Tarot-card prophecy that was supposed to apply to the doomed violin-maker's wife but instead predicts the violin's future. (There's actually a reason for this and rather than disclose it here, I'll just provide this clue: DNA.)

SIGHT AND SOUND, 3/99, p. 50, Nick Kimberley

When his wife becomes pregnant, the seventeenth-century violin-maker Bussotti vows to craft the perfect instrument for the child. The housekeeper Cesca foretells a long journey entailing happiness and disaster. When mother and child die, Bussotti uses his wife's blood to varnish his violin.

The instrument becomes the property of an Austrian monastery, where a century later the orphan prodigy Kaspar plays it. The impresario Poussin fosters Kaspar's talent but while auditioning for Prince Mansfeld the boy collapses and dies. He is buried with the violin, but gypsies steal it. Another century later, the English virtuoso Frederick Pope hears gypsies playing, buys their red violin and, fired by his passion for Victoria Byrd, writes his greatest music for it. When she finds Pope with another woman, she shoots his violin.

Laid low by love and opium, Pope commits suicide. His Chinese manservant takes the battered violin to Shanghai and pawns it. Decades later, it is bought for Xiang Pei. During Mao's Cultural Revolution owning such an instrument is dangerous, and she entrusts it to a music teacher with a huge collection of western instruments. Years later the teacher dies. The authorities, realising his instruments are valuable, put them up for auction in Montreal. Valuer Charles Morritz suspects the red violin must be the Bussotti instrument and compares it to Pope's nineteenth century replica. Morritz reluctantly reveals his discoveries. The red violin takes pride of place at auction. Bidding is fierce but nobody realises Morritz may have substituted Pope's copy, planning to give the original to his child. Cesca's prophecies have come true, but only for the violin.

If music is a universal language, why does it speak in so many mutually incomprehensible dialects? The narrative of the time- and globe-spanning film *The Red Violin* has more than a little of the fable about it. But it's not simply a fable about music's universalising, healing power, although that comes into it. What is more apparent is the misery the red violin carries in its wake, shattering lives and breaking hearts while it alone remains intact, identifiable despite the odd scar left by centuries of use and abuse. Of course the misery is not the instrument's doing. It begins because its maker not content with merely human beauty, strives for something inhumanly perfect. Bussotti's hubris generates the misery, not the violin itself.

And as the movie ends, can we take it that the violin has at last come to rest? Of course not. Unless I misread them, the closing moments contain the merest hint of the possibility that Morritz does not make off with the immensely valuable red violin, but makes do with the legitimately acquired replica. Perhaps he has glimpsed the original's destructive power. Even if, as the more likely outcome, he has made the switch and stolen the instrument, the theft must be discovered, his cupidity exposed, and the woe that accompanies Bussotti's creation prolonged. It's built into the film's episodic structure that each story leads to another, so it's appropriate that the apparent ending should only open up further possibilities: uncertainty is so much more rewarding than closure.

This daisy-chain structure makes character subordinate to event. Although each character is clearly enough described, we care more about what happens to them than who they are. Indeed, so diligent is the movie's pursuit of authenticity even location matters more than personality, which isn't necessarily a criticism. As the story moves through countries, periods and languages, the characters become mere bit players, sidelined by the forward movement of the narrative they find themselves in.

Although music may not be the film's subject, it matters a lot to the director François Girard, whose best-known film is *Thirty Two Short Films about Glenn Gould*. Girard apparently planned to use music from each of the eras the movie occupies: something baroque, followed by some Mozart for the early scenes for example, perhaps some Paganini for the episode with the virtuoso Pope. (This is the movie's least convincing segment, resembling as it does a French and Saunders satire on BBC costume drama.) In the event, John Corigliano persuaded Girard to allow him to write a score that binds the strands together with its chameleon-like mimicry of different styles and recurring motifs.

In fact, the movie might be described as a cinematic symphony in variation form, complete with its own little musical jokes. In one nicely unemphatic *jeu d'esprit* Joshua Bell, the virtuoso violinist whose playing the actors mime to, appears as a lowly member of the orchestra that accompanies Pope. And yet, despite its open-endedness and deft handling, it's hard to escape the feeling that the movie has itself fallen prey to the allure of the red violin. It seems to want to efface division and difference so as to enfold us in music's warm and, yes, healing embrace. That's no sin, but it does provide a sugary coating for what is otherwise a pleasingly sour little yarn.

VILLAGE VOICE, 6/15/99, p. 148, Dennis Lim

An omnibus film constructed around a single fetish object, *The Red Violin* spans three continents, four centuries, and five languages. On the surface, the movie has high-artsy aspirations—it means to be opulent, expansive, romantic, cultivated. But it sustains its purplish, epic sweep by thrusting broadly etched characters into extravagantly hokey situations, and registers mainly as a flamboyant joke—one that's most engaging when it's neither too knowing nor too clueless, when it's ambiguous about how seriously it's taking its absurdity.

The violin of the title is a model of late-17th-century Italian craftsmanship, a flawless instrument capable of the most exquisite sounds—it is, as Samuel L. Jackson's awestruck present-day musicologist says while affecting a moony Gwyneth Paltrow-esque expression, "the ultimate ... thing." The fate of the remarkably durable instrument, which conveniently changes hands at regular intervals, is revealed in disparate vignettes.

From Italy, where its creator's wife dies in childbirth, the violin is transported to Austria, where, a century later, it is inherited by a child prodigy—a frail orphan for whom a brief separation from his beloved violin proves unbearably traumatic. The subsequent, insanely florid English sequence features strutting virtuoso Jason Flemyng, his vampy novelist lover Greta Scacchi, and the violin as instrument of seduction, sex tool, and object of jealousy. Much more muted but no less ridiculous is the Shanghai episode, in which a closet violinist (Sylvia Chang) heroically saves the instrument from a Cultural Revolution burning.

Director François Girard and his cowriter, the actor Don McKellar (who has a small, typically nebbishy role here and whose own film, *Last Night*, opens later this year), previously collaborated on *Thirty-Two Short Films About Glenn Gould*, a biopic diffused into a surprisingly lucid mosaic. In formal terms *The Red Violin* is merely fussy, its musty chain-reaction anthology ensnared within a structure that's at once elaborate and obvious. Chronological bookends double as framing devices—the narrative flashes back repeatedly to a tarot card reading (in which it soon becomes clear that the foretold fortunes are not those of the Italian violin maker's doomed wife but of the instrument) and forward to an auction in present-day Montreal. The tarot portents pompously set up each segment, which in turn ends with the cursory introduction of a newly relevant party among the bidders clamoring to purchase the violin. Two parallel mysteries are teased out—one concerning the fate of the instrument (i.e., the outcome of the auction), the other concerning the secret of its perfect acoustics and radiant hue; you see both coming miles off. Still, *The Red Violin* is about as watchable as a massively flawed, woolly-headed two-hour-plus movie gets—this has much to do with John Corigliano's lively score, some unintentionally funny performances, and the fact that the vignettes are all shrewdly terminated just as dullness is setting in.

Also reviewed in:
CHICAGO TRIBUNE, 6/18/99, Friday/p. A, Mark Caro
NEW YORK TIMES, 6/11/99, p. E12, Stephen Holden
NEW YORKER, 6/14/99, p. 90, David Denby
VARIETY, 9/7-13/98, p. 74, David Stratton
WASHINGTON POST, 4/21/99, p. C1, Stephen Hunter

REGRET TO INFORM

An Artistic License Films release of a Sun Fountain production. *Executive Producer:* Janet Cole. *Producer:* Janet Cole and Barbara Sonneborn. *Director:* Barbara Sonneborn. *Screenplay:* Barbara Sonneborn. *Director of Photography:* Emiko Omori, Nancy Schiesari, and Daniel Reeves. *Editor:* Lucy Massie Phenix. *Music:* Todd Boekelheide. *Sound:* Julie Konop and Elizabeth Thompson. *Sound Editor:* Jennifer Ware. *Running time:* 72 minutes. *MPAA Rating:* Not Rated.

WITH: Barbara Sonneborn; April Burns; Lula Bia; Norma Banks; Phan Ngoc Dung; Diane C. Van Renselaar; Grace Castillo; Nguyen My Hien; Xuan Ngoc Evans; Charlotte Begay; Tran Nghia; Troung Thi Huoc; Phan Thi Thuan; Troung Thi Le; Le Thi Ngot; Nguyen Thi Hong.

CINEASTE, Vol. XXIV, No. 4, 1999, p. 37, Paul Arthur

In the context of our current culture, narratives based on first-person revisiting of a site of intense trauma have achieved the status of a necessary, and necessarily praiseworthy, public ritual—emerging as standard fodder in television talk shows, literary memoirs, and even pop music. If our media-ready version of politics has been consecrated at the altar of the Personal, so too, it seems, has our version of history. Moreover, the ostensible motives for this fascination with subjective journeys into a troubled past have less to do with mapping potential intersections of individual and social histories, as in traditional oral chronicles, than the quest for psychic healing, the survivor as linchpin in an ideology of self-therapy. It is in these terms that we may best understand a pair of documentaries devoted to the debacle in Vietnam, a national trauma that continues to fester with unresolved contradictions and human consequences.

Now that the war has been exhaustively refought, often with greater military success, in the arena of commercial movies, it is perhaps not surprising that documentaries have moved in once again in a sort of 'mopping-up operation,' recolonizing the contested terrain under the aegis of cathartic testimony. In the mass cultural marketplace, the narrow focus on individual experience provides an obvious advantage insofar as it sanctions the avoidance of thorny social or geopolitical issues. Freida Lee Mock and Terry Sanders's *Return With Honor* and Barbara Sonneborn's *Regret to Inform* (both 1998) are destined to be linked, compared, and likely confused due to the similar lilt of their titles, superficially identical structures, and book-ended thematic concerns. Both are shaped by the deft interweaving of participant interviews with amazing archival footage (much of it drawn from sources inside Vietnam). Both explore previously under-publicized subcultures, POWs and war widows; both utilize strong musical tracks for added emotional leverage. And of course both have been greeted with tired critical homilies—about 'courage' and the 'unbreakable human spirit.' However, make no mistake: these are vastly different, in important ways nearly antithetical, projects. Although both deploy familiar strands of nonfiction rhetoric, *Honor* chooses to nestle in a confident, self-validating envelope of fraternal crisis and camaraderie, while *Regret* bracingly opens its discourse to an unpolished agglomeration of voices, moods, and experiential perspectives.

Mock and Sanders, who collaborated on the Oscar-winning portrait *Maya Lin: A Strong Clear Vision* (1996), fashion their account of American pilots shot down in battle and incarcerated in the infamous Hanoi Hilton in an admirably clear, if finally suspect, linear trajectory. Following a descriptive set of opening titles, a curiously poetic prelude conjures the thrill of jet-propelled flight. Over gorgeous shots of planes performing vertiginous maneuvers, pilots speak of "flying along on top of the clouds" and learning to "play [the aircraft] like a violin." Implicitly, this brief section serves to explain why these men became Air Force and Navy pilots, and, aside from a subsequent sketch on the rigors of basic training, it is virtually the only background information we get; nothing is said of the subjects' social locations, their attitudes toward war, or their reckoning with the human consequences of indiscriminate bombing. Several pilots express frustration with the restrictive policies of LBJ and civilian bureaucrats—"We had both hands tied behind our back"—and later on there is some mild contempt directed at antiwar protestors. But for the most part the film sticks to a strict chronology of capture, incarceration, interrogation and torture, intragroup bonding, and eventual release.

Framed largely in dramatically-lit medium close-ups against a stark black field, approximately ten former POWs assume the principal burden of narration, augmented by more than a dozen others, including Senator John McCain and three African Americans, who make sporadic appearances. Descriptions of successive stages of their ordeal are intercut and, with accompanying voice-overs, played against generic newsreel footage and thirty-year-old images of the central figures—during their capture, in press conferences, and in publicity shots of prison activities—taken by their captors. Thus there are frequent uncanny juxtapositions of the same subjects in comfortable middle age and youthful extremis (indicating a possible criterion for the selection or emphasis of interview subjects). Inserted into the basic matrix of past and present-tense imagery are supporting materials such as a set of striking drawings depicting techniques of torture made by a Navy pilot, and embarrassingly restaged slow-motion 'atmospheric' shots of dungeon corridors and swinging lamps reminiscent of a grade-Z slasher movie. The film's unusually slick production values, the desire for airtight continuity amid the constant building of emotional tension, at times threatens to overshadow its core of engaging, hyperarticulate narrators. The stories they have to tell are indeed remarkable and they do so in a manner studded with wry humor, exacting detail, and poignant moments of despair.

They discuss ingenious methods of communicating with fellow inmates as well as with the outside world: information encoded in patterns of coughing, sniffing, spitting; tapping between cells that resembled a "din of runaway woodpeckers"; Jeremiah Denton blinking Morse code for the word "torture" during a recorded news conference. A level of interpersonal sensitivity and intimacy borne of arduous confinement is alluded to by one speaker who says he knew when a prisoner he had never seen face-to-face "was happy or when he was depressed" simply by the cadence of his tapping. POWs invented mental and physical exercises to maintain their sanity, writing poems or drafting architectural designs. Following the death of Ho Chi Minh, conditions in the prison steadily improved and, no longer in complete isolation, they began to "educate each other" in foreign languages, physics, even a course in golfing taught with a bamboo latrine stick.

The grist of such memories offers a non-fiction counterpart to Hollywood's heroic WWII POW sagas, and what they indicate about the survivalist spirit of the men who lived them is hardly less exhilarating in this context. Of course 'context' here is paramount, a question not of "their story told in their own words" (as *Honor* assures us in an opening title) but the filmic organization of images and sounds, of what is left unsaid as well as what has been chosen for inclusion. For starters, the Air Force is distinct from other branches of the military: whiter, better educated, and more middle-class than the average grunt in the field—and the men of *Honor* were almost surely volunteer career officers. Given the codes of conduct by which they were trained, they were bonded up to the eyeballs well before their tours of duty began and after their release probably resumed aviation-related jobs. The high degree of solidarity and unvocality inscribed in their stories is in part a function of extraordinary circumstances but it is also informed by their backgrounds and training. If accurate, this profile suggests that they were not disposed to later rethink either their attitudes towards their captors or the objectives for which they fought and suffered. What cannot be inferred is how they have managed since their release, the trials of readjustment, the well-documented reflexes of survivor guilt and unfocused anger.

As with other issues that creep in around the edges of this hermetically edifying work, Mock and Sanders maintain a tactful silence, as if posing certain questions of the participants or complicating the drama with incongruous subtexts were equivalent to subverting the moral authority of POWs. No film can or should be expected to provide the scope or level of analytical complexity routinely found in historiographic narratives. Nonetheless, the adoption of such a narrow aperture turns even ancillary references into ominous signs of complicity. For instance, *Return With Honor* begins with the endorsement of Tom Hanks, recently anointed as an icon of benign militarism. At the end, among a rather short list of funding sources is an acknowledgment of the Boeing-McDonnnell Foundation. Between the cultural cachet of Spielbergian mythic redemption and the financial assistance of aircraft manufacturers lies a myriad of unspoken allegiances, none of them very salutary.

Regret to Inform is a looser, homespun enterprise in which Sonneborn, a San Francisco multimedia artist, documents her trip to the exact place where her husband Jeff died in combat in 1968. On a train headed South from Hanoi she says that "for years I tried to put the war behind me" and her visit is explicitly couched as a quest for personal understanding and resolution of ambivalent emotions. The premise is quite similar to that of another recent documentary, Jerry Blumenthal, Peter Gilbert, and Gordon Quinn's *Vietnam—Long Time Coming* (1998), a diaristic record of a corporate-sponsored 1200-mile bicycle tour from Hanoi to Ho Chi Minh City made by a team of disabled and able-bodied American and Vietnamese vets. In each film, the structure of physical travel through a once-hostile landscape stimulates as it embodies internal struggles associated with psychic legacies of guilt, rage, and sorrow. Unlike the measured progress of the bike ride, the journey in Sonneborn's film, which begins and ends with poetic close-ups of a wooden oar creaking in a timeworn oarlock, keeps turning back on itself, figuratively retracing its steps and veering off on unexpected detours.

Acknowledging her place in a larger community of widows, and believing that "by hearing their stories I could understand my own more deeply," the filmmaker interviewed a diverse group of five American and twenty-four Vietnamese women, among them a fiery, former Vietcong district leader ("I feel anger when I'm talking to you now") and a Navaho widow still confounded by her husband's misguided patriotism in the service of a racist war. Before departing, Sonneborn enlisted the help of a local friend, Xuan Ngoc Evans, as guide and translator. Before long this woman and her excruciating story of wartime slaughter, deprivation, prostitution, and marriage to an American soldier achieves a prominence nearly equal to that of Sonneborn herself.

Unlike other war documentaries that strive to pay homage to the 'other side,' the doubly split focus on American and Vietnamese experiences, in-country and state-side, is integral and truly collaborative. Intercut once again with unfamiliar Vietnamese newsreels as well as government-issue bombing footage, the interview material is additionally punctuated with letters from long-dead husbands, travelog scenes, recounted dreams, abstract asides, and a concluding poem by Archibald MacLeish ("Our deaths are not ours; they are yours; they will mean what you make them."). The speakers here are less unified and less sure of themselves than the POWs in *Honor* and are thankfully given space to express conflicting judgments.

By the same token, Sonneborn is careful to devise moments of relative emptiness inviting viewers to filter in their own meditations and memories. The unforced pace is further attenuated by a musical track combining traditional Vietnamese songs with composer Ken Schneider's piano and string elaborations on Asian melodies (in stark contrast to Charles Bernstein's tensely spooky score for *Honor).*

Rivers and trains are venerable cinematic tropes for the movement of History—Pare Lorentz's *The River* (1937) and Claude Lanzmann's *Shoah* (1985) are two prominent examples—and Sonneborn invokes both in her scattered progress toward the field in Que Sanh where her husband died. Significantly, the terminus of the journey is anticlimactic ("After years of imagining it, it's so ... ordinary.", a recognition that the process itself, the series of expansive acts that led to the conversion of private pain into public spectacle, is more crucial to the goal of memorialization and therapeutic understanding than any physical destination or didactic conclusion. Although never addressed directly, what the filmmaker has made of her life in the intervening years is traced across the body of her film as justification for the estheticizing of personal trauma. That is, the creative impulses and techniques by which she has sustained a career in the wake of tragedy are inseparable from the themes, structure, and conditions of production which alternate *Regret to Inform*. Once again it is possible to reread something of the film's meaning through the evidence of its closing credits: a virtually all-female production staff; a patchwork quilt of local funding organizations and private donors; acknowledgment of an extensive supporting cadre of Bay Area activists and artists (including a well-known avant-garde filmmaker).

The temptation to employ essentialist gender distinctions to address the effect of Sonneborn's work versus that of Mock and Sanders is as fruitless as it is insulting. The openness of inquiry and generosity of spirit that infuses the film is less the result of onscreen subjects or any obvious feminist ideology than it is a function of documentary modalities. *Return With Honor* exhibits both the virtues and contradictions of institutional demands, of officially-sanctioned history delivered in and for a specific climate of mass-cultural assumptions about 'survivors' and the recuperation of wartime trauma.

Regret to Inform is a personal documentary not only in its angle of vision but also in its method of construction. If in the final analysis it is less provocative or radically reflexive than certain films for which the unhealed gap between present and past events, between verbal commentary and visual absence, is produced as central to the discourse of historical memory—as it is in work by Harun Farocki, Patricio Guzman, and Marcel Ophuls, among others—it retains a similar aspiration. And in our current state of trauma-overkill, that is no small blessing.

NEW YORK POST, 6/25/99, p. 56, Rod Dreher

The Oscar-nominated Vietnam-war documentary "Regret to Inform" is a worthy bookend to "Return With Honor," the recent documentary account of American POWs who survived the horrors of the Hanoi Hilton with their dignity intact.

The most exhilarating moments of "Return With Honor" come when the returning airmen greet their long-suffering wives on the tarmac. This new film is about soldiers' wives who never knew that joy: Their husbands were killed in the fighting.

On the day she turned 24, filmmaker Barbara Sonneborn received news that her husband, Jeff, had been killed at Khe Sanh. Twenty years later, and happily remarried, Sonneborn summoned the courage to make a pilgrimage to Vietnam to find the ridge where Jeff died and attempt to make some peace with the awful past.

The result was this film, in which she interviews war widows on both the American and Vietnamese sides, asking them to tell their stories. Sonneborn isn't interested in blame-mongering; she's concerned with meditating critically on war itself and its soul-crushing consequences for the women whose true loves were soldier boys.

Including the widows of enemy soldiers was a brave gambit, but it pays off in heart-rending testimony about the universal scourge of war. The rheumy eyes of a toothless Vietnamese peasant woman, her hands a mass of calluses, fill with tears remembering the husband and son she buried.

Xuan Ngoc Evans, a friend of the director's who also serves as her translator, tells of having to become a prostitute in Saigon brothels to support her family.

On the American side, the widows grieve for the pain their dead husbands endured, but also for the pain the exigencies of battle must have forced them to inflict on others. Concludes Sonneborn, "What haunts me is not only that Jeff died here, but that he had to be a part of this at all."

There is no happy ending to this mournful, profoundly humane anti-war film, and little closure. We're left to think on the terrible beauty of the lamentation sung by a peasant to the memory of her husband: "Even the love of country is not deeper than the love we have together."

NEWSDAY, 6/25/99, Part II/p. B7, John Anderson

In Feb. 29, 1968, eight weeks after Barbara Sonneborn's husband, Jeff, left to fight in Vietnam, he was killed trying to rescue his radio operator. When his personal effects were returned to his widow—on her 24th birthday—his dog tags and wedding ring were encrusted with blood.

These are just some of the things we learn from "Regret to Inform," Sonneborn's virtually 30-years-in-the-making documentary, an Oscar nominee and the winner of the best director and best cinematography prizes for nonfiction films at Sundance this year. The end result of a letter

Sonneborn began writing to her late husband some 20 years after his death, the film is ripe with the sense of "what if," and a corresponding pang of national remorse.

But all that past is also prologue: What 'Regret' is about is the current state and perspectives of the women whose lives were derailed by the carnage in Southeast Asia, and few documentaries of recent years have done what they've set out to—or captured the kind of naked emotion simmering beneath their premise as well as Sonneborn's frequently heartbreaking film.

While she may not be smashing any barriers in the field of personal documentaries, she certainly is giving voice to the unheard and, often, uncared for. And in light of the coincidental opening last week of the Vietnam POW documentary "Return With Honor (a movie that seems, in retrospect, more and more calculated as the days drift by), Sonneborn is a one-woman diplomatic corps. Among her interviewees are North Vietnamese and Viet Cong widows. (When she began filming in 1992—after machete-ing her way through jungles of red tape—it was impolitic for South Vietnamese widows to talk to her.) While the idea that grief and loss know no borders may be less than revelatory, Sonneborn makes it shine like a new wound.

Easily the most moving of her cast of widows is Xuan Ngoc Evans, who was Sonneborn's translator and grew up in a poverty-ravaged South Vietnamese village in the '50s—a village destroyed in 1968. Three years later her husband was dead, and she'd seen her cousin blown up by an American soldier. "When people decide to go to war," she says, "they don't ask people like me, "What's going to happen?'" No, they never have. Nor in all the cautionary blather about our involvement in "another Vietnam" does there seem to be much concern evident for people such as Evans. Such considerations require a Barbara Sonneborn, a modicum of understanding and an all-too-well-informed take on 30 years of international breast-beating.

TIME, 7/19/99, p. 72, Lance Morrow

[*Regret to Inform* was reviewed jointly with *Return With Honor*; see Morrow's review of that film.]

VILLAGE VOICE, 6/29/99, p. 150, Dennis Lim

More than 20 years after her husband was killed in combat, Barbara Sonneborn decided to visit the site of his death in Vietnam. The resulting documentary, more than closure-providing therapy for its maker, locates Sonneborn's pilgrimage within a studiously broad context, encompassing archival footage (well chosen if sometimes clumsily deployed) and interviews with other war widows. Balance and perspective are key—the subjects comprise a diverse group of American and Vietnamese women. (Representing both camps is the translator who accompanies Sonneborn, Xuan Ngoc Evans, who has lived in the U.S. since 1972 and whose horrific recollections are rendered in curious Oprahspeak.) The lush Vietnamese landscapes that had such an anesthetizing effect in the insipid *Three Seasons* here serve as a poignant counterpoint to the harrowing testimonials. *Regret To Inform* may claim an unusual point of view, but the anguish it uncovers is familiar from numerous previous accounts of the war. That it's the same tragic story however you come at it may in fact be the most enlightening aspect of this film.

Also reviewed in:
CHICAGO TRIBUNE, 10/29/99, Friday/p. H, Michael Wilmington
NEW YORK TIMES, 6/25/99, p. E7, Stephen Holden
VARIETY, 3/8-14/99, p. 59, Glenn Lovell
WASHINGTON POST, 11/4/99, p. C1, Myra MacPherson

RELAX ... IT'S JUST SEX

A Jour de Fête Films release of an Atlas Entertainment production. *Executive Producer:* Eli Kabillio and Cevin D. Soling. *Producer:* Steven J. Wolfe, Megan O'Neill, and Harold Warren. *Director:* P.J. Castellaneta. *Screenplay:* P.J. Castellaneta. *Director of Photography:* Lon Magdich. *Editor:* Tom Seid. *Music:* Lori Eschler Frystak and Ricky Frystak. *Sound:* Adam

Joseph. *Casting:* Shevonne Durkin. *Production Designer:* Timm Bergen. *Costumes:* Sharon Lynch. *Running time:* 106 minutes. *MPAA Rating:* Not Rated.

CAST: Jennifer Tilly (Tara Ricotto); Mitchell Anderson (Vincey Sauris); Cynda Williams (Sarina Classer); Lori Petty (Robin Moon); Serena Scott Thomas (Megan Pillsbury); Eddie Garcia (Javi Rogero); Timothy Paul Perez (Gus Rogero); Chris Cleveland (Diego Tellez); T.C. Carson (Buzz Wagner); Billy Wirth (Jered Bartoziak); Gibbs Toldsdorf (Dwight Bergman); Susan Tyrell (Alice Pillsbury); Seymour Cassell (Emile Pillsbury); Paul Winfield (Auntie Miriam).

NEW YORK POST, 3/5/99, p. 59, Jonathan Foreman

A truly awful movie, "Relax ... It's Just Sex" has the look and feel of a high-school play. Its script, acting and direction are all so atrocious that you cannot help wondering if the only reason this film is getting released is a patronizing reverence for its gay subject matter—and its relatively explicit sexual content.

A soapy ensemble piece with two token straight characters, it's the kind of shallow consciousness-raising exercise in which the filmmakers think all they have to do is touch the requisite bases in order to say something. One gay man discovers he's HIV-positive, another gets gay-bashed, and a black lesbian loses her white girlfriend to a man ... The only stereotype this travesty explodes (rather than promotes) is the notion that gay artists tend to be wittier than straight folk.

It starts promisingly with a scene from a mock educational movie explaining the terms "fag hag," "gym queen" and "lipstick lesbian." But it immediately moves to scenes of Vincey (Mitchell Anderson, dreadful throughout) having and discussing casual sex.

Vincey is a whiny playwright (understandably) unable to find Mr. Right. Tara wants a baby, but her boyfriend, Gus (Timothy Paul Perez), isn't ready. Gus' brother Javi (Eddie Garcia) has just discovered he's HIV-positive, and he announces it at Tara's dinner party, which is attended by the whole ensemble. Everything is predictable and dull, except for a bizarre scene in which Vincey catches and rapes a thug who joined in his gay-bashing.

This is the sort of film in which references to Vanessa Redgrave's performance in "Julia" pass for cleverness, and in which plot holes are filled in by the characters talking to a video camera. Given the shallowness of the film's characters, you can almost forgive the execrable line readings by a cast of actors who've been at least competent in other movies.

Given that there have been so many good gay-themed plays and films in the last few years, the existence of this crude, cloying and unsophisticated piece is a mystery. But it is one of those movies of such total badness that it's almost worth watching for freak value.

NEWSDAY, 3/5/99, Part II/p. B11, John Anderson

And as soon as our guard is down, we're tossed into bed with two bucknaked bodies. Let the games begin!

"Relax ... It's Just Sex" never quite recovers from the sophisticated mischief of that intro, because it never floats quite that high again. An ensemble piece about a group of friends wending their way through the brambles and thickets of two-party love—there's not a combination/variation Castellaneta hasn't included—"Relax" is a rather formulaic morality piece suffering from a big chill.

The cast of characters is certainly diverse: A love-starved gay writer (Mitchell Anderson of "Party of Five"); a hetero couple striving for pregnancy (Jennifer Tilly, Timothy Paul Perez); a lesbian couple (Serena Scott Thomas, Cynda Williams) that breaks up for a straight man and a truck driver (Billy Wirth, Lori Petty, respectively). An HIV-positive man and his artist boyfriend, who doesn't believe in AIDS (Eddie Garcia, T.C. Carson). And, in the movie's most theologically adventurous twist, a pair of gay male lovers (Chris Cleveland, Gibbs Toldsdorf) who also happen to be born-again Christians.

The rather pedestrian course of their love lives—their friendships are more interesting, ultimately—take a horrible turn when Vincey (Anderson) and Javi (Garcia) are attacked by a gang of gay bashers. They're saved by their friends—but not before Vincey enacts a bit of revenge that throws the whole crowd into a soul-searching tizzy. It's a well-handled moment, gripping without being exploitative, and puts a new angry angle on what has been up till then a rather soapish scenario.

"Relax ... It's Just Sex" was part of the Sundance Film Festival in 1998 and boasts a solid cast, a smattering of hammy acting and several surprising cameos, among them Paul Winfield, Seymour Cassel and Susan Tyrell. The pathology of bias usually demands that contact equals "infection" (octoroons, anyone?). As a result, "Relax... It's Just Sex," will be categorized as a gay film, even as it strives to be all-embracing. As they say at the mall (where this film won't be playing anytime soon), whatever. What the movie is about in the end is that sex comes in all flavors, as does prejudice and stupidity. But then, tell us something we don't know.

VILLAGE VOICE, 3/9/99, p. 122, Dennis Lim

On paper, *Relax ... It's Just Sex,* a queerish L.A. ensemble comedy, is one of those "dating in the '90s" movies that has little, if anything, to say, and thinks it can get by on witty small talk. There's even a character whose dialogue consists almost entirely of movie references. But writer-director P.J. Castellaneta gives his moderately engaging material the right affectionate touch, and the film succeeds on the sheer force of its good nature.

Relax opens promisingly with a mock-educational segment introducing viewers to "lipstick lesbians" and "gym queens," followed by an amusingly involved to-swallow-or-not bedroom dilemma faced by the luckless central character Vince (a charismatic Mitchell Anderson). The movie quickly becomes a lightweight *La Ronde,* tracking the romantic exploits of a demographically balanced group of friends, with Jennifer Tilly as the gossipy fag-hag mother hen. There's one jarring scene midway in which Vince is gay-bashed. Horny, drunk, enraged, not only does he fight back, he rapes his attacker. It's an absurd, shocking reaction, which Castellaneta glibly parlays into a plot device and ultimately glosses over. But the image and the complicated response it evokes stay with you—if only the film had the nerve to follow through.

Also reviewed in:
CHICAGO TRIBUNE, 7/23/99, Friday/p. 1, Monica Eng
NEW YORK TIMES, 3/5/99, p. E31, Antia Gates
VARIETY, 2/23-3/1/98, p. 87, Emanuel Levy

RETURN WITH HONOR

An Ocean Releasing release of a Sanders & Mock/American Film Foundation production. *Producer:* Freida Lee Mock and Terry Sanders. *Director:* Freida Lee Mock and Terry Sanders. *Screenplay:* Freida Lee Mock, Terry Sanders, and Christine Z. Wiser. *Director of Photography:* Eddie Marritz and Terry Sanders. *Editor:* Greg Byers. *Music:* Charles Bernstein. *Sound:* Jim Gilchrist. *Running time:* 102 minutes. *MPAA Rating:* Not Rated.

CINEASTE, Vol. XXIV, No. 4, 1999, p. 37, Paul Arthur

[*Return With Honor* was reviewed jointly with *Regret to Inform*, see Arthur's review of that film.]

LOS ANGELES TIMES, 6/18/99, Calendar/p. 13, Kevin Thomas

The prospect of reliving the Vietnam War through the memories of American POWs sounds both grueling and profoundly depressing, but prizewinning documentarians Freida Lee Mock and Terry Sanders, with their stirring yet understated "Return With Honor," offer the rare opportunity to feel some pride in our involvement in the drawn-out Southeast Asian conflict.

Doves and hawks alike can be deeply moved by the accounts of a group of American pilots shot down over North Vietnam and imprisoned for as long as six to eight years. They were subjected to torture, primarily by being bound by ropes that kept them in agonizing positions for long periods of time, along with isolation, beatings and brutal interrogations. But these men, now middle-aged, in response became determined to survive and not to betray their country.

They endured periods of suicidal despair, unspeakable loneliness and deprivation. They developed their minds as well as their bodies to the best of their abilities and devised myriad ways of strengthening their spirit for survival over the long haul. Whenever their captors finally succeeded in breaking them down they learned to give them misleading information, and whenever they were filmed or photographed or allowed to write home they used the opportunity to send coded messages with their eyes, their words and their gestures. You are simply too affected by the calm, matter-of-fact, even at times humorous, manner with which they recount their ordeal and how they endured it to be depressed.

Not surprisingly, such captured leaders as naval commanders Jeremiah (Jerry) Denton and James Stockdale were singled out by the North Vietnamese for the harshest treatment. (One of the most severely injured of the POW survivors was John McCain, the U.S. senator from Arizona, who as a lieutenant commander in the Navy was shot down in October 1967 and was not expected to live, yet refused an offer of an early release.)

One of the most impressive, among uniformly impressive individuals, is Navy Lt. John (Mike) McGrath, who also received exceptionally harsh treatment but who refuses to judge anyone who broke under pressure, saying that everyone has a breaking point. McGraw also dedicated himself to committing to memory everything he witnessed in prison so that he could draw it if he got out; the drawings he made in the month after his release punctuate this film dramatically. Latino and African American POWs also were singled out in an attempt to undermine their loyalty to their country.

McGrath's drawings are among the many remarkable archival materials that Mock and Sanders, who won an Oscar for their "Maya Lin: A Strong, Clear Vision," were able to draw upon in creating their exceptionally evocative documentary. Virtually every one of their witnesses is also seen in North Vietnamese newsreel footage, which invariably portrays the captives in humiliating circumstances, and the filmmakers repeatedly return to present-day views of such notorious prisons as the Hoa Lo—better known as the "Hanoi Hilton"—to convey just how primitive conditions were for the POWs.

As the war wore on with increasing unpopularity on the home front, the North Vietnamese made sure the POWs were subjected to American TV news reports of antiwar protests. But as one captive remarks, a North Vietnamese prison was no place for a U.S. serviceman to start considering the validity of—America's involvement in Vietnam. These were men who had agreed to live up to the U.S. military code of conduct and there is no question that their determination to do so against all odds was crucial to their ultimate survival.

Even so, the wife of Col. Tom Madison says she kept it quiet that her husband was a POW so that their young son wouldn't be singled out for any ridicule. However, by 1969, Stockdale's wife, Sybil, and a group of other wives of POWs at last defied government policy on keeping secret the plight of their husbands. Their actions, coupled with the death of Ho Chi Minh, improved conditions for the men, ending torture and isolation. Still, Lt. j.g. Everett Alvarez, the first U.S. pilot shot down and captured in the Vietnam War (Aug. 4, 1964) and the longest held in captivity (8½ years), says that survival depended on erecting so many emotional shields that when liberation came, he at first could not allow himself to feel anything.

"Return With Honor" takes its title from the goal to which all these POWs strived with such resolve. Air Force Capt. Douglas (Pete) Peterson, held captive 6½ years, was able literally to achieve that goal: In 1997, he became the first U.S. ambassador to the People's Republic of Vietnam.

NEW YORK POST, 6/11/99, p. 49, Rod Dreher

The exceedingly fine historical documentary "Return With Honor" takes its title from the creed American prisoners of war adopted while being held in Viet Cong prisons.

As Ed Mechenbier, one of the Air Force POWs interviewed here, explains, he and his fellow captives vowed that no matter what tortures they were to suffer, they would not only survive to return home but would survive without doing anything they would be ashamed of later.

Watching these men tell the story of how they succeeded is to confront the extreme of human cruelty and to see it redeemed by courage, endurance and quiet heroism so visceral and potent that it leaves you tearful and speechless. Says one ex-POW: "It was a matter of dignity. All we had left was our name and our honor."

In 1973, 462 American airmen shot down over North Vietnam were released by Hanoi under terms of the Paris peace accords ending the war there. Those Air Force pilots who appear in this film—including U.S. Sen. John McCain and erstwhile vice presidential candidate Jim Stockdale—testify how they were considered princes of the air before descending to earth in fireballs.

On the ground behind the lines, they became less than nothing. Never-before-seen footage from North Vietnamese archives shows dazed and broken fliers being led off by Viet Cong soldiers and screaming mobs surrounding them immediately after capture.

Images of a horribly injured and obviously terrified young McCain—familiar to us as a well-groomed Washington politician—telling his wife he loves her, are especially affecting. The men testify about the unspeakable tortures to which the North Vietnamese subjected them. Beatings, dislocated limbs, starvation, dehydration and worse were the norm. One man talks about lying on his cell floor for a solid year, his body a mass of boils and abrasions, until he gathered the strength to pull himself up and pop his elbow back into its socket.

A most effective torment was screening films of anti-war protests back home in hope of demoralizing the prisoners. Wives of the POWs reveal that they would often keep their grieving to themselves, for fear of opening their children up to the abuse of anti-war activists.

How did the men survive? Prayer and faith in God and country had a lot to do with it, as well as having wills of iron. They also devised an ingenious "tap-code" system of communication within the camps to pass information on, and to reinforce a sense of solidarity. Simple rituals, like saying Our Father and the Pledge of Allegiance every Sunday, meant the world.

All this might sound corny and sentimental, but only the nastiest cynic could think so after watching this film. Like "Saving Private Ryan," "Return With Honor" reinvests worn-out pieties with tremendous freshness and power.

Veteran documentarians Freida Lee Mock and Terry Sanders, Oscar winners for "Maya Lin: A Strong Clear Vision," know what they're doing here, allowing archival footage and the men's own simple words to tell this extraordinary story, without emotional embellishment.

"Return With Honor" mentions that at least one of the prisoners died under torture and others committed suicide, but it concludes with the survivors being joyfully repatriated and reunited with their families.

In the crowd welcoming them to Clark Air Base in the Philippines is someone holding a banner reading "Welcome home, beautiful men." Yes, absolutely.

NEWSDAY, 6/11/99, Part II/p. B6, John Anderson

The most striking of the many striking things in Freida Lee Mock and Terry Sanders' documentary "Return with Honor" is the absence of bitterness among the former POWs they've interviewed—men who were imprisoned for up to 8½ years in places like the notorious Hanoi Hilton, who were tortured, isolated and undernourished and who look back on the experience with a remarkable charity.

The second most striking thing is the film's nearly complete lack of perspective on the Vietnam War. As one of the ex-POWs points out, news of antiwar protests in the late '60s and early '70s was dismaying to men who were languishing in Hanoi prisons—hardly the place, as he says, to start re-evaluating one's commitment to the war. At the same time, if there's anything you want from people such as Sen. John McCain or onetime Ross Perot running mate James Stockdale—two of the former pilots who contribute so much to this film—it's their take on the justness of the war.

The third stunner is the timing of Sanders and Mock (the latter won an Oscar for her 1994 documentary, "Maya Lin"). Now that the political relationship between the United States and Vietnam is close to normal—and the emotional one between our countries seems somewhere close to forgiving—why make a film that portrays a virtually faceless and demonized Vietnam as a nation of torturers and villains without providing some context about the war, the country, its history of colonialization/ oppression or the machinations of U.S. politicians and military-industrial complex in keeping us in the war? Would it tarnish the tribute being given the reminiscing airmen? It's highly doubtful.

Lastly, there's the juxtaposition of present-day Air Force cadets—and their hazing, and their singing with the courageous, selfless stories about the men and the war, all of which is fine, one supposes, even if it makes the film seem like part of a Defense Department recruitment drive.

For all the filmmakers' folly, though, you can't deny the power and grace of the men whose stories form the spine of the film. Although their tales often involve brutality and loss, they also involve the survival techniques and ingenuity used during the years of captivity—the codes, for instance, used to communicate within the prisons (one pilot remembers exchanging messages for years with fellow inmates he'd never even seen).

Elsewhere, sadness permeates the memories. There is the knowledge that they were being used as part of the Vietnamese propaganda effort. There's a subtle if persistent shame glimpsed in the men who succumbed to torture, even though no one—not even the men themselves on a certain level—can hold them accountable for anything but courage. And there's a lingering resentment, however understated, that they hold against men such as Robert McNamara, who as one pilot puts it "thought he knew better than anyone in the world about targeting" even while the men flying the planes were being popped out of the sky.

That Mock and Sanders interview everyone separately—pilots and wives—gives the film a sense of prison chill, but it would have been gratifying to hear some of them interact. The documentary also contains a lot of remarkable archival footage, most effectively the 30-odd-year-old clips of the men being captured, marched through Hanoi or photographed for Life magazine. And, for that matter, the shots of them boarding the plane for their return to the United States—the "return with honor" they swore to achieve, because, sensibly enough, they felt that return with no honor would be as unsatisfactory as honor with no return.

VILLAGE VOICE, 6/15/99, p. 143, Michael Atkinson

Now that Spielberg and Benigni have succeeded in dulcifying the Holocaust, here come the Oscar-winning doc-makers of *Maya Lin: A Strong Clear Vision* to restart the John Wayne-ing of Vietnam. No American film since *The Green Berets* has portrayed the 'Nam battle dynamic with such confident jingoism as *Return With Honor,* the first major theatrical documentary about the war since *Dear America: Letters Home From Vietnam.* From that film's well-earned desperation to a stoic, all-American heroism—we've come a long way, baby. A talking-heads trip through the memories of the war's most prominent fighter-pilot POWs as they recount their experiences of capture and internment at the Hanoi Hilton, Freida Lee Mock and Terry Sanders's dull-eyed hymn sidesteps the bothersome issues of the war's futility and tragedy early on (with a single pilot saying he understood the war to be a "NATO-type" intervention), and then settles in for tales of torture and tough-guy survival amid the hordes of bloodthirsty communists.

The virtually all-white vets (including ex-VP candidate Admiral Jim Stockdale) all comport themselves modestly, unlike the filmmakers, who illustrate the often harrowing torture stories with drunken camera pans through jungles and old buildings. Since it's the only situation in that war free of ambiguities, the dynamics of withstanding torture are focused upon, and the boys would make the Duke proud. (More affecting is the pilot who ruefully remembers how his intercell tapping-code conversations with another pilot he'd never met were the most intimate he's ever had.) In this context, even being broken under shoulder-dislocating torture and spilling info to the Reds isn't shameful; these lads take what's being dished out and hold their Yankee heads high. Maybe the filmmakers went in wanting to make a POWs' *Shoah,* but obviously entranced by the eloquent resilience of their subjects, they came out with a flag-waver fit for a mall recruitment office.

Also reviewed in:
CHICAGO TRIBUNE, 11/5/99, Friday/p. D, Michael Wilmington
NEW YORK TIMES, 6/11/99, p. E12, Stephen Holden
VARIETY, 10/26-11/1/98, p. 52, Dennis Harvey

RIDE WITH THE DEVIL

A USA Films release of a Universal Pictures presentation of a Good Machine production. *Executive Producer:* David Linde. *Producer:* Ted Hope, Robert F. Colesberry, and James Schamus. *Director:* Ang Lee. *Screenplay:* James Schamus. *Based on the novel "Woe to Live On" by:* Daniel Woodrell. *Director of Photography:* Frederick Elmes. *Editor:* Tim Squyres. *Music:* Mychael Danna and Alex Steyemark. *Music Editor:* Pat Mullins. *Sound:* Drew Kunin and (music) Geoff Foster. *Sound Editor:* Philip Stockton. *Casting:* Avy Kaufman. *Production Designer:* Mark Friedberg. *Art Director:* Steve Arnold. *Set Designer:* Thomas Minton. *Set Decorator:* Stephanie Carroll. *Set Dresser:* Mike Shapiro and John Bromell. *Special Effects:* Allen Hall. *Costumes:* Marit Allen. *Make-up:* Rick Pour. *Make-up (Special Effects):* Jeff Goodwin. *Stunt Coordinator:* Douglas Coleman. *Running time:* 138 minutes. *MPAA Rating:* R.

CAST: Skeet Ulrich (Jack Bull Chiles); Tobey Maguire (Jacob Friedel Roedel, "Dutchman"); Jewel (Sue Lee Shelley); Jeffrey Wright (Daniel Holt); Simon Baker (George Clyde); Jonathan Rhys Meyers (Pitt Mackeson); James Caviezel (Black John); Thomas Guiry (Riley Crawford); Tom Wilkinson (Orton Brown); Jonathan Brandis (Cave Wyatt); Matthew Faber (Turner Rawls); Stephen Mailer (Babe Hudspeth); John Ales (Quantrill); Zach Grenier (Mr. Evans); Margo Martindale (Wilma Brown); Mark Ruffalo (Alf Bowden); Celia Weston (Mrs. Clark); Jeremy W. Auman and Scott C. Sener (Guards); Glenn Q. Pierce (Minister); Kathleen Warfel (Mrs. Chiles); David Darlow (Asa Chiles); Michael W. Nash (Horton Lee Sr.); John Judd (Otto Roedel); Don Shanks (George); Jay Thorson (Ted); Dean Vivian (Storekeeper); Cheryl Weaver (Storekeeper's Wife); Amber Griffith (Clark Girl); Ric Averill and Buck Baker (Commissioners to Jesus); Donna Thomason (Mrs. Evans); Cassie Mae Sears (Mary Evans); Martin E. Liebschner, Jr. (Encampment Singer); Marvin Frank Schroeder, Steven Price, and David L. Asher (Encampment Musicians); James Urbaniak and David Rees Snell (Poker Players); Dave Wilson (Quantrill's Lieutenant); Larry Greer (Federal Captain); Kevin Fewell (Federal Lieutenant); John Durbin (Skaggs); Michael Owen (Federal Recruits Captain); Jim Shelley and Addison Myers (Southern Gentlemen); Michael Linsley Rapport (Drunk Raider); Joseph Moynihan (Mr. Riggs); Jennie Nauman (Mrs. Riggs); Christine Brandt (Pleading Woman); Bill Grivna (Dulinski); Nora Denney (Elderly Woman); Harry Gibbs (Old Man); Clayton Vest (Young Boy); Roger Denesha, Jacob Kozlowski, and David Lee Burnos, Jr. (Lawrence Raiders); Jennifer Ackland (Grace Shelley Chiles); T. Max Graham (Reverend Wright).

LOS ANGELES TIMES, 11/24/99, Calendar/p. 6, Kenneth Turan

It's been decades since the phrase "Bleeding Kansas" and the dark figure of pro-Confederate raider William C. Quantrill, mentor to outlaws Frank and Jesse James and Cole Younger, were familiar on-screen presences. But once upon a time TV westerns and even B-pictures like "Dark Command," "Kansas Raiders" and "Quantrill's Raiders" often focused on this bloody sideshow of the Civil War, with friends fighting friends in vicious guerrilla warfare along the Kansas-Missouri border.

"Ride With the Devil," a serious film with a lot on its mind, is probably the most intelligent treatment of this period we've had, so far removed from the previous pulp versions of the era that it doesn't even try to work the James brothers into the story.

But while intelligence and restraint are good things, "Ride With the Devil" sounds more interesting than it plays. A long, finally baffling movie about young people attempting to find themselves amid the meaningless carnage of war, it's oddly distant and uninvolving for such a blazing subject, managing to feel bloodless despite re-creating a notably bloody period of American history.

Taiwanese director Ang Lee, in a pattern reminiscent of John Sayles' explorations of Americana, seems determined to use film to investigate wildly different aspects of the past. Following his great success with his contemporary "The Wedding Banquet" and "Eat Drink Man

Woman," he took on 18th century England in "Sense and Sensibility" and 1970s suburbia in "The Ice Storm" before turning to 19th century America this time around.

Unfortunately, as "The Ice Storm" demonstrated, Lee can be an almost anti-dramatic director whose dispassionate approach to passionate material leaves you wondering if there's a more exciting movie lurking around somewhere that never made it to the screen.

Not helping this situation is an unwieldy decision made by Ang and screenwriter and longtime collaborator James Schamus (who adapted the script from a 1987 novel by Daniel Woodrell called "Woe to Live On") to have the characters speak with an archaic and stilted formality. This may or may not be true to the period—there's no one alive to tell us, after all—but, authentic or not, that troublesome language creates an additional barrier between the characters and the audience.

While the excessive modernity of the words "The Messenger" gives Joan of Arc and her gang presents problems of its own, going to the other extreme and having an entire film filled with lines like "It surely does seem so, it surely does" and "It's not much to gaze upon but I reckon we could assay some hospitality" is just as off-putting and even more distancing.

Handling most of the dialogue are two childhood friends now all grown up: Jack Bull Chiles (Skeet Ulrich), a Missourian from a long Southern line, and Jake Roedel (Tobey Maguire), who feels Southern but is in fact the son of staunchly pro-Union German immigrants. "You'll always be a German to them, no matter who you're friends with," his wise old father tells him, but does Jake listen? No, he does not.

Though "Ride" opens just before the start of the Civil War, that conflict begins soon enough and Jack Bull and Jake are found riding with the Bushwackers, a group of irregulars who chose to do their fighting close to home. With their elaborate long hair and dandified clothes, the Bushwackers look like a '60s rock band—think the Allman Brothers with repeater rifles—but they kill as readily, if not more so, as their elders.

As his father predicted, Jake, known as Dutchie to his comrades because of his German origins, is not treated as one of the gang, and young psychopath Pitt Mackeson ("Velvet Goldmine's" haughty Jonathan Rhys Meyers) seems especially determined to mistrust him whenever possible.

Dutchie's outsider status slowly brings him closer to Daniel Holt (Jeffrey Wright), a freed slave who is fighting for the South alongside his former master and best friend George Clyde (Simon Baker). Further complications ensue when these men winter together near the home of Sue Lee Shelley (singer Jewel, in her film debut), a comely young war widow whose father is also a Southern sympathizer.

"Ride With the Devil" does not stint on battles, including a full-scale re-creation of Quantrill's infamous raid on the barely defended Union center of Lawrence, Kan., and Schamus' script has some effective if familiar moments, like Dutchie reading to his fellow Bushwackers stolen letters intended for opposing soldiers who will never get those comforting words from home.

Though the film's overall pace is so phlegmatic that nonprofessional Jewel's lack of experience barely registers, some actors do excellent work. Tony Award winner Wright, memorable in the title role of the otherwise forgettable "Basquiat," has been given less painfully archaic dialogue than his comrades-in-arms and benefits accordingly. And the once-boyish Maguire shows an increased maturity that suits him well.

But too much of "Ride With the Devil" is taken up with not very fascinating young people clumsily attempting to discover meaning in life, a scenario not any more compelling with a 19th century setting than a 20th. Unable to find a focus that holds our interest, what we have on screen is well described by a bit of its own pseudo-folksy dialogue: "It ain't right, it ain't wrong, it just is."

NEWSDAY, 11/24/99, Part II/p. B9, John Anderson

It's always been convenient to credit the freshness of Ang Lee's films, particularly those disparate period pieces "Sense and Sensibility" and "The Ice Storm," to his Taiwanese roots—as if it were unusual to find a filmmaker inclined to seek new ways of seeing every time he got behind a camera.

Lee's thirst for finding new aspects to established genres has never been more evident than in "Ride With the Devil," a Civil War epic set in "Bloody Kansas," where men shed blood until there's no more blood or no more reason. It's a film that makes us look at an overworked period of our history in a new way—the violence is much more realistic, the aftermath of violence is much more realistic, and a lot of the historical explanations for violence are reduced to alibis.

But there's a ... well, not a coldness exactly, but an emotional glitch within "Ride With the Devil," and that's primarily the fault of the script by Lee's longtime producer-screenwriter, James Schamus. Perhaps Schamus is hewing too closely to the tone of Daniel Woodrell's novel; perhaps he's just striving too hard to coin an elegance of language equal to Ang Lee's eye. Whichever, "Ride With the Devil" is burdened by dialogue so antiquely rococo (when it isn't being expository) that it keeps the story from achieving momentum and distracts from the development of character. The words—they may be historically accurate, but who cares?—make a particularly awkward exit from the mouth of the young actor Tobey Maguire, whose native smarm was perfect for the bemused teenager of "The Ice Storm," but it serves only to maintain a perpetual distance between him and the rest of "Ride With the Devil." Maguire is Jake Roedel, son of a German immigrant and a most unprepossessing guerrilla, who joins the fight against Yankee incursions. With him is Jack Bull Chiles (Skeet Ulrich) and together they join a unit led by Black John (James Caviezel of "The Thin Red Line"), which includes George Clyde (Simon Baker) and his ex-slave, Daniel Holt (Jeffrey Wright).

Holt—a black man fighting with antiabolitionists—is easily the most complex and intriguing character in the film (the evolving Jake is second), and Wright gives the best performance. But the film is largely stolen away by Jonathan Rhys Meyers, whose fervent Bushwacker-cum-homicidal maniac Pitt Mackeson is the personification of scoundrel/patriot, using political extremism as an excuse to let blood.

Rhys Meyers struts through the film like a rock star, while the real rock star—Jewel, playing war widow Sue Lee—is merely adequate and self-conscious.

Which is the problem with many of those aspects of "Ride With the Devil" that never really work. The film does have one of the great intentional non sequiturs, however: "Have you ever bedded a woman before?" Sue Lee asks Jake.

"Girl, I've killed 15 men," says Jake, which should clear up any questions about the movie's antiwar sentiments.

SIGHT AND SOUND, 12/99, p. 56, Peter Matthews

Missouri, the early 1860s. When the American Civil War breaks out, a small community near the Kansas border is torn apart by conflicting loyalties. Young Jake Roedel sides with the Southern Confederacy, while his father Otto supports the Union. Asa Chiles, father of Iake's best friend Iack Bull Chiles, is killed by Unionists. Swearing revenge, Jake and Jack Bull enlist in the Bushwhackers, Confederate guerrilla fighters. The local chapter is headed by Black John, and Jake's comrades-in-arms include Pitt Mackeson, George Clyde and Clyde's faithful former slave Daniel Holt. The Bushwhackers capture some Federal soldiers whom Black John proposes to free in exchange for two of his captured men. Jake suggests their prisoner Alf Bowden, his former neighbour, be sent to deliver their offer. Once freed, Alf kills Jake's father and is killed himself.

Winter comes and Jake, Jack, Clyde and Holt are offered protection by Mr Evans, a rich landowner. They are supplied with food by young war-widow Sue Lee Shelley. Jack and Sue Lee fall in love. While they consummate their relationship, Evans is killed by Union soldiers. In the ensuing dogfight, Jack is severely wounded and later dies. Jake and Holt deposit Sue Lee on the farm of Orton and Wilma Brown, then rejoin the Bushwhackers. Bushwacker captain Quantrill incites the men to attack the residents of nearby Lawrence, Kansas. Jake spares an elderly couple from the massacre, antagonising Pitt. In a decisive battle, Clyde is killed and Pitt shoots Jake in the leg. Back at the Brown farm, Jake and Holt discover Sue Lee has given birth to Jack Bull's child. The Browns insist Jake marries her. Jake and Sue Lee resolve to start afresh in California. Hearing that Pitt is still on the rampage, Holt agrees to accompany them on the first stage of their journey But when Pitt catches up with them, he unexpectedly makes peace. Jake and Sue Lee bid farewell to Holt, who heads off for Texas to find his lost mother.

Unless one is charitable enough to include a piece of mega-shlock like *Titanic* in the reckoning, Hollywood has pretty much given up on historical spectacle these days. Since the studios are happy to stake imperial sums on the latest sci-fi or action-adventure franchise, the reasons can't be strictly budgetary. The thinking probably is that teenagers at the shopping mall lack the rudimentary knowledge required to empathise with people from the past. When *Gone with the*

Wind was released back in 1939, most filmgoers could be trusted to have the rough co-ordinates of the antebellum and Reconstruction eras stored in their brains, but that may no longer be the case. (To be fair, in 1939 some viewers in their eighties may even have lived through the war.) In any event, projects with too culturally specific a flavour are far less apt to be green-lighted now that global saturation has become the industry rule.

In this dual context of popular ignorance and corporate greed, Universal Studios is to be congratulated for having the altruism, the courage or maybe just the plumb foolhardiness to underwrite director Ang Lee's Civil War drama *Ride with the Devil*. While the movie intermittently revs up for some showy combat scenes, its real *métier* is a texture of fine-grained observation that brings history to life on the molecular level. Lee's famed attention to detail isn't necessarily the most lucrative quality in box-office terms, however, and there are bound to be many viewers who find his meditative rhythms a tax on their patience.

I wouldn't entirely disagree, but I think the movie is to be honoured more for its risk-taking longueurs than for the conspicuous ruckus of its action sequences. The Taiwanese-born Lee is almost invariably described as a consummate miniaturist and it's understandable that he should wish to knock that Orientalist assumption on its head. In *Ride with the Devil* he exhibits a gift for raw brutality which couldn't have been guessed at from such sunnier entertainments as *The Wedding Banquet* (1993) and *Sense and Sensibility* (1995) or even from the psychological violence of his sombre masterpiece *The Ice Storm* (1997). The current film can boast one hideous amputation plus an assortment of gaping war wounds, and it culminates in a civic massacre that seems a deliberate nod to the opening bloodbath of Sam Peckinpah's *The Wild Bunch* (1969). Maybe Lee needed to beat his chest a little for the benefit of those studio powerbrokers who would forever typecast him as a purveyor of dainty chinoiserie. But he also knows this virile posturing is basically kids' stuff—just like the heroic swagger of the young guns whose story he tells.

It's no great mystery what attracted Lee and screenwriter-producer James Schamus to the source material, Daniel Woodrell's acclaimed 1987 novel *Woe to Live On*. Set along the border of Kansas and Missouri in the 1860s, the book rehearses an eerily familiar scenario of neighbour squaring off against neighbour in a mortal struggle over value and belief. There's more than a suggestion of such other historic trouble spots as Northern Ireland, Kosovo and Vietnam in Woodrell's depiction of an internecine strife whose cruelty intensifies as longstanding private vendettas get hopelessly tangled with ideology. It's the same order of domestic dysfunction Lee and Schamus have treated in all their films, only this time written larger and in letters of blood.

Much has already been made of the fact that the movie adopts the perspective of the American South—identifying not with its racism, certainly, but with the core of aggrieved humanity lying behind that culture. Actually, most Civil War pictures are from the Confederate point gracious and vanquished Dixieland offers better opportunities for pictorial elegy than the victorious North. If Lee feels a twinge of closet sympathy for the Southerners, it's doubtless because they embody a vital connection to tradition which the secular and forward looking Yankees have lost.

Lee's earlier, family-based dramas were scrupulously poised between celebrating and chastising our modernity for its loosening of the ties that bind. *The Ice Storm* appeared to tip the scale towards conservatism, but even there the suburban wife-swappers were made human and comprehensible in their fumbling attempts at self emancipation. *Ride with the Devil* simply extends this principled ambiguity to a broader canvas.

In one sense, the movie is about throwing off the bad old customs and acquiring the virtues of liberal democracy. Desperate to prove his mettle, second-generation foreigner Jake Roedel (Tobey Maguire) joins in the slaughter of Union troops by the marauding Confederate guerrillas, the Bushwhackers, until enlightenment dawns in the guise of former slave Daniel Holt (Jeffrey Wright), whom he learns to accept on an equal footing with himself. Holt, meanwhile (who has sided against his own interests out of misguided loyalty to his quondam master), discovers the sweet taste of freedom. A third object lesson is supplied in the person of Sue Lee Shelley (Jewel), feisty frontierswoman and standard-bearer of the proto-feminist cause. However, the rise of egalitarian values also means the defeat of a whole way of life founded on their denial. That's the lacerating irony at the heart of both book and film. The flower of liberty is gained through an act of conquest, thus setting in train primordial resentments that continue to fester today (the 'woe to live on' of Woodrell's punning title).

D.W. Griffith similarly recognised that the steamrollering of the Confederacy was the necessary condition for the birth of a nation. But in his blighted 1915 epic of that name he had the demoralised South rear up again proudly through the fairytale expedient of the Ku Klux Klan. Not surprisingly, Lee and Schamus give their own pack of roving vigilantes a wider berth. The Bushwhackers aren't begrudged a glamorous aura as they gallop over the countryside, buckshot blazing and unkempt tresses flowing in the breeze. Yet at the same time they are regarded as atavistic specimens whom the film makers would sternly admonish to grow up and get a haircut. Jake does in fact have that tonsorial operation performed on him in an emblematic scene, thereby acknowledging his conversion to civilised norms. In still another symbolically charged moment his shot-off pinkie finger becomes an impromptu nipple for a baby to suck on.

There is sure to be some clever queer critic who argues that our hero's eventual repudiation of the masculine bond and pacification by marriage express a rearguard political agenda. But that's just a fancy way of saying this is a classical Western, plumping itself at the crossroads between phallic lawlessness and feminised order almost by definition. *Ride with the Devil* wants the precise sensibility of Lee's best work (the logistics of mounting a super-production having thickened his brushstrokes somewhat). Still, there remain countless ineffable grace notes—the primeval greenness of woods in the midst of carnage or a fidelity to the autumnal crispness of a particular day—that amply confirm this director as the most mysterious talent at large in American cinema.

TIME, 12/6/99, p. 101, Richard Corliss

The fighting men of the Civil War, whether Blue or Gray, are recalled with sympathy, poignancy. They left their homes to fight in someone else's backyard for freedom or tradition. The truth, though, may be closer to the blind, bloody chaos depicted in Ang Lee's severe, handsomely rendered *Ride with the Devil*. In Border states like Missouri, a young man was at war not only with his brother but with his own best instincts as well.

Two Missouri bushwhackers, Jake Roedel (watchful Tobey Maguire) and Jack Bull Chiles (Skeet Ulrich, parading what may be star quality or merely attitude), start out with a few ideals —war's first casualty. They also serially entertain the young widow Sue Lee (Jewel, the singer). They are idiot savants at making war without flair or even instinct but with an awful proficiency. At making love they are just idiots. They haven't had the example of the movies or even mush literature to teach them courtship. They hide their feelings as clumsily as they express them. "So, do you want to marry me?" asks Sue. Jake replies, "No, not too bad." And for a moment we see the sweet awkwardness Lee induced in *Sense and Sensibility.*

You are welcome to debate the violence and the presentation of a Southern black (Jeffrey Wright, impeccably conflicted) fighting for the flag of slavery. But for all the period dressings, this could be a deadpan study of why kids in Sarajevo, Belfast or South Central pick up guns and start spraying the street. And for all the carnage, Lee's tone is contemplative. He pines for those quiet moments when a wounded man can sit holding a baby, the newborn sucking on the man's nubbin of a blasted-off finger.

VILLAGE VOICE, 11/30/99, p. 133, J. Hoberman

Where Burton and Walker rewrite Uncle Walt to unexpected effect, Ang Lee and James Schamus essay Papa John Ford to very little. *Ride With the Devil* is an ambitious Civil War pageant, pitting anti-slavery Kansas Jayhawkers against Southern-sympathizing Missouri Bushwhackers to dispiriting effect.

Made from a Bushwhacker point of view, the movie is not unintelligent but it is insipid. As if to emphasize that this fratricidal bloodbath was mainly fought by kids, Lee relies on a youthful cast of hotties—Tobey Maguire, Skeet Ulrich, Jonathan Rhys Meyers—and attempts to render their wounds naturalistically bone-splintering. Given the flat performances and Schamus's overexplanatory script, *Ride With the Devil* has the feel of undergraduate costume drama; reflexively ducking away from the camera, pop poetess Jewel is hardly the least expressive performer.

As the wise and taciturn slave Holt, Jeffrey Wright has the dignified Woody Strode role. In a similar Fordian mode, Maguire plays at Jimmy Stewart—his voice cracks and quavers although his coy sidelong glances and trademark stare of slackjawed wonderment are something other than acting. The cast members often seem nonplussed—as well they might, given the movie's perfunctory montage and indifferent camera placement. "It ain't right and it ain't wrong," young sage Maguire ultimately declares. "It just is." *Ride With the Devil's* set piece restages William Quantrill's raid on the abolitionist town of Lawrence, Kansas (a massacre which has figured in Hollywood movies largely as an early life experience for future outlaw Jesse James). The sequence is murderous but unconvincing—in a fabulously petulant beau geste, Maguire ends the carnage by courageously ordering breakfast in a restaurant on Main Street.

Recipient of a windy, bizarrely Olympian air kiss from David Thomson in the current issue of *Film Comment,* Lee shows little more here than the guts to tackle bloody action. He'll never be mistaken for John Woo but he does at least reward Jewel's fanboys—they need only be patient and accept that her undraped form will be attached to a nursing baby.

Also reviewed in:
CHICAGO TRIBUNE, 12/17/99, Friday/p. C, Michael Wilmington
NEW REPUBLIC, 12/20/99, p. 30, Stanley Kauffmann
NEW YORK TIMES, 11/24/99, p. E1, Stephen Holden
VARIETY, 9/13-19/99, p. 42, Todd McCarthy
WASHINGTON POST, 12/17/99, p. C1, Stephen Hunter
WASHINGTON POST, 12/17/99, Weekend/p. 45, Desson Howe

ROCK THE BOAT

A Tell the Truth Pictures release. *Producer:* Robert Hudson. *Director:* Bobby Houston. *Director of Photography:* Bobby Houston. *Editor:* Michael Lorenzo. *Music:* Kevin Hayes. *Sound:* Bobby Houston. *Running time:* 84 minutes. *MPAA Rating:* Not Rated.

WITH: Robert Hudson; John Plander; Mike Schmidt; Ted Taylor; Dennis Boecker; Bill Kijovsky; Steve Kovacek; Mike Burelle; Richard Bartol; Keith Ericson; Bobby Houston.

LOS ANGELES TIMES, 3/5/99, Calendar/p. 22, Bob Heisler

[The following review by Bob Heisler appeared in a slightly different form in
NEWSDAY, 3/5/99, Part II/p. B11.]

It's hard to make much more of "Rock the Boat" than this:

In 1997, 12 sailors of varying skill, united only by the fact that they were HIV-positive, sailed in the TransPac boat race from Los Angeles to Hawaii. Their boat leaked, creaked, ripped and bent, but held together long enough to cross the finish line—19th in a field of 37. Filmmaker Bobby Houston recorded the effort for this documentary.

Where you go from here depends not on your view of HIV-positive men but on your view of symbols and symbolism. If self-selected symbols make you queasy, be advised. Yes, the crew is defying death, but that's how it is every day in their AIDS-cocktail way of life. These folks aren't heroes or fund-raisers or consciousness-raisers. A couple are sportsmen, but most are just trying to answer the question: I'm already a survivor, so what am I doing with today because tomorrow may be different?

This is an adventure documentary only in the sense that there's a mission—like climbing a mountain or completing a marathon—that most of us wouldn't choose from a list of personal options. There is no sense of competition—although the efforts by the captain to push his boat and crew turn into the most dramatic action.

Houston's oddly polite film is essentially a one-camera show, with occasional jump-cuts to the folks back home reading the latest e-mail. Shooting at night in the blackness of the Pacific limits the dramatic tension and puts a tight focus on the crew. Focus is frequently lost completely in the pitch and yaw of the boat. Only hints are offered of developing relationships among crew members.

Each gets a moment to talk about when and where he learned he was HIV-positive. Like those war movie platoons, each man's story is different. One was married, another took ill within weeks of a drunken episode. And also like a war movie, the body count is high. Each crew member, including Houston, describes the friends, partners and lovers lost to AIDS—their names are painted on the hull of the rented yacht, briefly called the Survivor.

NEW YORK POST, 3/5/99, p. 58, Rod Dreher

"Rock the Boat" is a documentary about a crew of HIV-positive men who sail a racing yacht to Hawaii. It's got the kind of self-congratulatory sentimentality that can set your teeth on edge. You'd think from the hugs-all-around treatment writer-director Bobby Houston gives the subject that these dudes were Shackleton & Co. slugging across the frozen Antarctic.

Thing is, once the journey gets under way, you have to admit what these guys accomplish is pretty remarkable. They fight high winds, rough seas and their own fear for 10 punishing days, and even outrun a Pacific hurricane.

And the fact that some of these men have been at death's door in their fight against AIDS—and that all of them might have been expected to sit still and wait to expire instead of embracing the dangerous challenge of the Trans-Pacific race—makes their courageous feat worthy of admiration and attention.

The most interesting parts of the film, which crew member Houston did a terrific job of shooting on video, involve conflicts among the mates amid the grueling shipboard tasks. The captain is a ruthless competitor who loses patience with the less experienced members of the crew, particularly when the rickety boat and the perilous night seas unnerve them.

In the end, the men pull together to complete their task triumphantly. There's more to this journey than the boat ride.

VILLAGE VOICE, 3/9/99, p. 124, Elliott Stein

Rock the Boat may be a doc, but it's also a stirring adventure story—the account of an all-HIV-positive crew's odyssey in the TransPac yacht race, an epic sprint from California to Hawaii. The idea was the brainchild of Robert Hudson, who founded a support group for AIDS patients and brought on board filmmaker Bobby Houston. After an overchatty start, the movie takes off when the Survivor sets out from Long Beach in the 1997 TransPac, its hull inscribed with the names of friends lost to AIDS—and it becomes apparent that this is not another treacly saga of male bonding under pressure. These amateur gobs' nerves soon get frazzled and personality conflicts develop on the overcrowded vessel—we're treated to endearingly bitchy outbursts and cabin-feverish flare-ups. By the time they reach Hawaii, though, they've become a band of brothers. No, they don't come in first—they finish 19th. Yes, they are some kind of heroes. The kind who've earned the right to say, after they've circumvented a hurricane, "We've outrun worse things in our lives."

Also reviewed in:
NEW YORK TIMES, 3/5/99, p. E8, Stephen Holden

ROMANCE

A Trimark Pictures and Jean-François Lepetit release of a Flach Film/CB Films/Arte France Cinéma coproduction with the participation of Centre National de la Cinématographie, Canal+ and the support of Procirep. *Executive Producer:* Catherine Jacques. *Producer:* Jean François Lepetit. *Director:* Catherine Breillat. *Screenplay (French with English subtitles):* Catherine Breillat. *Director of Photography:* Yorgos Arvanitis. *Editor:* Agnès Guillemot. *Music:* D.J. Valentin and Raphaël Tidas. *Sound:* Paul Lainé. *Sound Editor:* Emmanuel Augeard. *Casting:* Michaël Weill, Estelle Bertrand, Nicolas Lublin, Guylène Péan, Jacques Grant, and Catherine Hofer. *Art Director:* Frédérique Belvaux. *Set Decorator:* Valérie Leblanc Weber. *Costumes:*

Anne Dunsford Varenne. *Make-up:* Clairee Monatte. *Running time:* 93 minutes. *MPAA Rating:* Not Rated.

CAST: Caroline Ducey (Marie); Sagamore Stévenin (Paul); François Berléand (Robert Weil); Rocco Siffredi (Paolo); Reza Habouhossein (Man on Stairs); Ashley Wanninger (Ashley); Emma Colberti (Charlotte); Fabien de Jomaron (Claude); Carla (Model); Pierre Maufront (Photographer); Antoine Amador (Hairdresser); Roman Rouzier (Echographist); Olivier Buchette (Senior Doctor); Emmanuelle N'Guyen (Midwife); Nadia Latoui (Nurse); Sylvie Drieu (Attendant); Mélissa (Marie's Stand-in); Christian Poutrasson (Man Alone).

LOS ANGELES TIMES, 10/1/99, Calendar/p. 8, Kenneth Turan

Should anyone need help understanding the difference between graphic sexual content and eroticism, or, for that matter, between tedious pseudo-philosophizing and real thought, "Romance" has arrived to clear the air. As pretentious as it is hard-core specific, this fiercely anti-erotic film makes even the chilly "Eyes Wide Shut" play like "The Big Easy." Who could have imagined that sex on screen could be so unbearably dull?

French writer-director Catherine Breillat (whose seventh film this is) is playing a dubious double game. On the one hand, we're supposed to believe that what makes "Romance" worth enduring are its windy metaphysical speculations on the nature of love and/or sex, but these thoughts are so pompous and banal that without the lure of hard-core material the audience for this film would be severely limited.

Yet those deluded enough to go to "Romance" for its unapologetic scenes of masturbation, oral sex, intercourse and intricate bondage are going to be even more angry and disappointed by the torpid, uninvolving quality they exude. Distant sex, no matter how explicit, and bogus posturing turn out to be a deadly cinematic combination.

A painfully simple-minded film that grabs every chance it gets to depict men as thuggish rapists or narcissistic fools, "Romance" lets us in on the tortured, unhappy life of a young elementary schoolteacher named Marie (Caroline Ducey).

Marie lives with self-involved fashion model Paul (Sagamore Stevenin), someone who'd much rather read Charles Bukowski by himself in a Japanese restaurant than have anything to do with her. In fact, Paul and Marie have not had sex for three or four months (the film can't make up its mind which), a situation that the faithful Marie is understandably unhappy about.

"You despise me because I'm a woman. I disgust you," she screams at the indifferent Paul while letting on, in similarly lighthearted fashion, that she feels like "a heavy invisible cage has descended on me."

In truth, Paul and Marie are such insufferable pills that they are likely made for each other, but sexual frustration is not something "Romance" takes lightly. So fed-up Marie, faithful no more, sets out to have as many sexual adventures as the film's running time allows.

First stop is handsome Paolo (Rocco Siffredi, apparently a well-known Italian porn star), picked up in a local bar. According to the press notes (the film is far too cerebral to stoop to making things clear on screen), Paolo satisfies her sexually but is incapable of love. A live-and-learn type, Marie moves on.

She doesn't have to move very far. It turns out that Robert (Francois Berleand), the principal of the school where Marie teaches, is an accomplished seducer with 10,000 women (but who's counting?) on his list of satisfied partners. What's Robert's secret? He takes the time to talk to women and listen to them. Really.

A fussy dominator, Robert ties Marie up with such a wide variety of exotic knots it's a shame an expurgated version of their sessions together couldn't be made available to Boy Scouts needing help with their merit badges. Even with the knots, this relationship, supposedly the most tender in the film, will not do anything but bore anyone not already bondage-inclined.

All this soporific sexual activity is punctuated by the kind of pointless but supremely self-important dialogue that French films have a weakness for. Comments like "He wants to conquer because he's a man" are frequent, but, though the competition is stiff, the one line you're most likely to remember is the question "Why do men who disgust us understand us better than men who appeal to us?"

Extremely hard to take as seriously as writer-director Breillat insists it deserves to be, "Romance's" sexual explicitness may be undeniable but its empty pomposity makes it play like a caricature of an art film. When Marie's boyfriend feebly suggests that "there's more to life than sex," it's a shame the entire film didn't take him at his word.

NEW STATESMAN, 10/11/99, p. 46, Jonathan Romney

There's a much overused phrase in the French press—*"celle par qui le scandale arrive"*, roughly meaning "she who guarantees good copy". The director and novelist Catherine Breillat has filled that role for 30 years. All her films address female sexuality fairly directly, and her new film *Romance* most directly of all. But while it confronts some cold sexual realities, it is as distant from realism as its literary near-relations *The Story of the Eye* or, in film, Oshima's *Ai No Corrida*.

Marie (Caroline Ducey) is a young teacher whose boyfriend Paul (Sagamore Stévenin) refuses to sleep with her. Feeling "dishonoured", she finds herself a priapic substitute, played by the Italian porn star Rocco Siffredi, then gets together with the headteacher Robert (François Berléand), a middle-aged Don Juan who introduces her both to bondage and to his prolix theory of seduction.

A film that could only possibly be French, *Romance* is genuinely in the tradition of de Sade, combining the two registers of hard sex and hard philosophy. The physicality is startlingly explicit: Ducey appears to perform real fellatio and appears to have penetrative sex with Siffredi; she definitely undergoes a gynaecological fingering by a rubber-gloved procession of medical students. There is also what must be the only come-shot seen in an uncut 18-certificate film—all the more alarming because Breillat abruptly cuts to an ooze of lubricant on Marie's belly during an ultrasound scan. But the most confrontational sight is an extreme close-up of childbirth. Breillat's transgressive project is to restore to the language of pornography its great unsaid—real anatomy, a woman's insides, and not just the fetishised outsides of those insides.

Just as disturbing is the way the film's verbal register combines with the action. In the tradition of de Sade's windbag libertines, Robert discourses as he fastidiously ties Marie up, announcing that "physical love is the trivial clashing with the divine", even explaining the Latin etymology of the word "seduce". Argument A, if you're trying to convince people that *Romance* is not a titillating film, must be this sequence, which trembles between nervous expectation and pedagogic earnestness—sexual apprenticeship as arcane book-learning.

Marie, too, largely in voice-over, holds forth about her feelings and desires. For British viewers the language, straight out of Georges Bataille, will cause more nervous titters than the sex. "I want to be a hole, a pit," Marie announces. "It's metaphysical. I disappear in proportion to the cock taking me." This will certainly seem mystifying in the current British climate, where the talk about sex (if not necessarily the practice) is flavoured with have-a-go hedonism. To a culture of born-again jolly shaggers, where Denise Van Outen represents the last word in female sensuality, Marie's philosophically informed drive to purification through abjection will seem downright foreign, not to say Catholic.

Romance may superficially resemble the classic *Emmanuelle* scenario: virginal young thing gets screwed every which way in a crash-course of carnal enlightenment. But the whole point is that *Romance* is directed and written by a woman, and one for whom female sexuality is the central issue. If Breillat shows us more of Ducey's body than anyone else's, it is because the film speaks, as it were, from within Marie's skin. Men get short shrift: Marie judges them largely by their bodies and their willingness to use them. Thin cocks, she says, are "ignoble", and she feels Paul's feminised delicacy as an affront: any man, the film suggests, who would rather spend the evening alone in a Japanese restaurant deserves what he gets.

The sex itself is used to confound expectations and categories. Rocco Siffredi is there not just because he can guarantee a hard-on: his very presence in the credits is a challenge, a statement of cross-genre intent. It's perhaps a superficial shock that the sex is filmed so coldly and analytically (Marie's first session with Paolo is a seven-minute single take). But by having her cast perform as if for real, Breillat makes us reassess the distance between the things people actually do and feel during sex, and those things and feelings as they are conventionally performed on screen: the oohs, aahs and thrusts of hardcore, as against the more complex, contradictory signals given out here.

The physicality has implications that viewers of "legit" cinema don't normally have to worry about. In the bondage scenes, Ducey suggests an awkward, trembling agitation that we can't easily distinguish from the real discomfort she may be feeling. We're never quite able to separate her considerable acting skills from her willingness to expose herself, to push herself to limits that may really be physically and emotionally painful. The film thus makes us question not just the power relations between Marie and her partners but also the potentially fraught contract between the actress and the female director who speaks through her.

The extremity of the spectacle is tempered by a cool, distancing execution: the photography is by Yorgos Arvanitis, who works with Theo Angelopoulos, and you can't get much chillier or loftier than that. Everything becomes diagrammatic—Marie's white dress, Robert's red shirt, the white flat that Marie and Paul seem to have rented from Antonioni. Despite the aesthetic alienation, *Romance* is a genuine turn on in parts, as female and male viewers have testified. But it can't easily be boiled down to a simple proposition or a simple effect, and that's what makes *Romance* a radical anomaly—a film that uses pornography not to produce pleasure but to start arguments.

NEW YORK POST, 9/17/99, p. 50, Jonathan Foreman

"Romance" is a bleak, indulgently highbrow but provocative exploration of the dark side of female sexuality by writer-director Catherine Breillat.

It may also be the most explicit non-pornographic film ever made. (Certainly it's the first mainstream movie to show an unquestionably real act of oral sex since Marco Bellochio's "Devil in the Flesh.")

Despite many flaws—including a glacial pace, inconsistencies of tone and reams of pretentious philosophizing by the heroine—"Romance" is unquestionably an important film.

It is powerful, disturbing and unashamedly politically incorrect. It brings to a complex subject a sophistication and intelligence that is incredibly rare—and which was completely absent from "Eyes Wide Shut."

Perhaps because it takes sexual desire so seriously, "Romance" is also about as unsexy as a film about sex could possibly be. Its funny moments only contribute to its lack of erotic heat (real porn on the other hand is almost always humorless).

Breillat's chief concern is with the sometimes shameful stuff people think about when they're having sex. It's why the film's nudity is for the most part not gratuitous: It helps make Breillat's point that sex is really something that takes place in the head.

Marie (Caroline Ducey), a scrawny but elegantly dressed schoolteacher is deeply in love with her model boyfriend Paul (Sagamore Stevenin). He, however, refuses to have sex with her.

It's not that he can't do it; it's just that he won't. He refuses even to embrace or caress her. And he insists on spending lots of time with his male friends at the bar.

Marie then has a series of sexual encounters, first with a handsome guy named Paolo (Rocco Siffredi, an actual Italian porn star), whom she meets in a bar. He is impressively fit, virile and extraordinarily well-endowed, but Marie doesn't seem to get much pleasure out of their interaction.

She spends most of their encounter philosophizing gloomily while he waits for permission to get started—and the camera lingers on his erect organ.

Next, she goes home with her employer, the middle-aged Robert (Francois Berleand), who claims to have made love to 10,000 women, including a Grace Kelly-like movie star. As he keeps saying, he's not handsome or rich, but he knows how to talk to women. He's also an enthusiast for bondage and S&M.

He's just about perfect for Marie, who, as she says at great length, is searching for degradation and self-obliteration. The masochistic Marie does seem to find some kind of satisfaction in her relationship with Robert.

All the same, she continues on her dangerous path. And the film implies that she only really gets close to fulfillment when she gets pregnant and gives birth—a development you see in all its gory glory.

The bondage scenes are funny, presumably deliberately so. The first time Robert ties her up, it takes forever, using a rope system so complicated that it could be a knot-tying class in Outward Bound.

The actors, with the exception of Siffredi, are an unprepossessing bunch, but they seem like real French people. His presence is perhaps the only really gratuitous element in the film.

Although you never know if any of Marie's adventures are real or fantasy, you cannot help thinking that Breillat cast the porn star just to shock an audience used to movies in which ordinary guys get Barbie doll girls rather than vice versa.

NEWSWEEK, 9/13/99, p. 66, David Ansen

Outside of porn movies, no film has ever explored sex more explicitly than Catherine Breillat's "Romance." This alone will make it a subject of controversy—one erect penis on a U.S. screen is more incendiary than a thousand guns, and "Romance" has more than one. What makes it even more groundbreaking is that the point of view is distinctly female. French director Breillat puts us inside the head of Marie (Caroline Ducey), a schoolteacher who is in love with a model named Paul (Sagamore Stévenin). But the narcissistic Paul, who shares her bed, refuses to have sex with her, and his erotic indifference sets her off on a sexual quest that is every bit the opposite of Tom Cruise's never-satisfied journey in "Eyes Wide Shut." This one provoked even the shock-proof French.

Paolo, Marie's first fling, is Paul's opposite—pure carnal desire. (He is played by a legendary Italian porn star, Rocco Siffredi.) Her second encounter, with the principal of her school, is as much mental as physical. Robert (François Berléand) isn't good-looking, isn't young, yet he boasts of thousands of conquests. His power is verbal, and he introduces Marie to the world of S&M. The bondage scenes are presented with remarkable matter-of-factness. Breillat is not making judgments, or aiming only to titillate. When Marie cries from the pain, her lover pulls back, and there develops between them a tenderness that is nowhere else to be seen in this tale. "Romance" is indeed an ironic title: Marie's exploration reaches its nadir in a brutal encounter on a stairway that leaves her shattered.

Throughout, Breillat counterpoints her shocking images with Marie's thoughts, which we hear in voice-over. Some viewers may have as much trouble with the words as the sights, not because they are "dim," but because they are so highfalutin. Breillat is on to something important here—for sex is at least as much in the mind as in the flesh—but the French, with their love of abstract discourse, don't talk about sex the way we do. The philosophically, fat-free American audience may find Marie's ruminations ("Physical love is triviality clashing with the divine") a bit too high-caloric for its taste.

Nonetheless, "Romance" can't be easily shrugged off. Breillat and her brave actors take us places we haven't been. For the audience, as well as Marie, it's a journey that has few signposts. We don't get to "know" these characters in the traditional dramatic way: motives and feelings are left enigmatic. In the realm of the senses, logic does not apply, and one's sense of identity can morph like a sci-fi special effect. For those who believe that movies are a proper place to explore the riddle of sex, no holds barred, this movie is *de rigueur*. For the rest, be warned.

SIGHT AND SOUND, 11/99, p. 51, Ginette Vincendeau

France, the present. Marie, a schoolteacher, loves her partner Paul, but is frustrated by his refusal to make love to her. She picks up a young Italian named Paolo in a bar, and later they have sex. Robert, the head of her school, tells her there is a problem with her work. He takes her home to discuss it but they begin a series of ritualised S&M sexual encounters. She has rough sex which shades into rape with a stranger. Finally Paul makes love to her and she becomes pregnant. She undergoes a gynaecological examination and has vivid sexual fantasies. As she is about to give birth, Paul gets drunk. She opens the gas on the cooker and leaves for the hospital with Robert. She gives birth, with Robert present. Her flat is destroyed in an explosion which presumably kills Paul. Marie fantasises about Paul's funeral, while she holds her baby, also called Paul.

Much has been made in the press of the fact that *Romance* is one of the most explicit heterosexual art films to date, prompting both accusations of indecency and laudatory comparisons with Oshima's *Ai No Corrida* (1976). Central to *Romance*'s scabrous image is the presence of Italian porn star Rocco Siffredi as the Italian stud Paolo who 'fucks' Marie in a graphic take. Both male (erect and soft) and female genitals are on display here, along with head-on shots of Marie's gynaecological examination and her baby's birth. As Marie's voiceover explains: "I just want to be a hole; the more gaping, the more obscene, the truer it is; it's metaphysical, it's my purity."

Yet as Marie's mixture of obscenities and existential considerations indicates, *Romance* addresses its audience not as a sex film but as an intellectual artefact about sex. Culturally it belongs to a French tradition that goes back to de Sade and encompasses the writings of Apollinaire, Bataille, Klossowski and Pauline Réage (author of *Histoire d'O*), in which eroticism is a cerebral matter. As a film-maker Breillat radically undermines her movie's potential for titillation and voyeurism in a number of ways, often by using prosaic details. A discussion of used condoms and tampons comically precedes sex with Paolo, for example.

Breillat's aestheticisation of sex is indebted to the stillness of Japanese cinema. Her *mise en scène* is bluntly realistic in some ways, but distanced from naturalism. *Romance*'s social anchorage is minimal: Paul is a model, Marie a teacher, but their social identity is as pared down as their white flat. Breillat's signature use of near-to-real time allows such scenes as Robert and Marie's bondage games to be presented in such hyper-realist detail they become almost abstract. Similarly the gynaecological examination is shocking not in a traditional moral sense, but because of the deadpan approach. "*Romance* would not be classified porn," Breillat has said, "not through self-censorship, but by finding another way of showing."

Inevitably, since Breillat is a woman, *Romance* prompts the question of whether this 'other way of showing' is connected to and whether *Romance* can be regarded as a feminine or feminist exploration of female desire. Like many French female film-makers, Breillat denies the concept of 'women's cinema', seeking to be identified with a general view of authorship. And yet from her earliest films (such as *36 Fillette*) she has focused single-mindedly on female sexuality. Both her recent *Parfait amour!* and *Romance* contain savage explorations of female desire and identity and critiques of French machismo and misogyny. Marie says at one point of Paul, "He dances because he wants to seduce, he wants to seduce because he wants to conquer, he wants to conquer because he is a man."

In other ways too Breillat foregrounds a female point of view and works in the tradition of the woman's film. For instance, Marie's voiceover dominates the soundtrack. The men are weak or merely instrumental—each of them fulfils a simple function (partner, father, mentor, and so on), after which he is discarded. By contrast, Breillat's women are complex. Contrary to stereotypical representations, they are not victims, mad or mysterious objects of desire. In *Romance* it is Paul who is a mystery.

Thus in many ways Breillat satisfies one of the key feminist demands in relation to women's cinema: that it should challenge patriarchal representations and give expression to the complexity of female desire. Her direct tackling of sexuality, unburdened by conventional morality and political correctness, is original and emotionally powerful. *Romance* is both fascinating and disturbing. Why, then, is it disappointing? One reason is that some of its erotic tropes are rather too close to old-fashioned, oppressive male fantasies: Robert's self-important Don Juan figure; the notion that genital penetration is less intimate than kissing; and, most problematic of all, Marie's longing to "meet Jack the Ripper." Is the price Breillat pays for auteur recognition that of endorsing male-pleasing fantasies of what 'masochistic' women supposedly want? As in the recent films of other French women directors (such as Tonie Marshall and Jeanne Labrune), Marie's sexual autonomy is gained at the expense of any other sense of worth. All this only seems to produce a profoundly pessimistic, even nihilistic, world view. There is a lot of sex in *Romance*, but not a lot of pleasure.

TIME, 10/4/99, p. 94, Richard Corliss

The French, it seems, are trying to revive their old reputation as a culture that is smart and naughty about sex. The modern version of French postcards is French cinema—not of the frothy old ooh-la-la sort but so serious that watching a woman caress a man's genitals is like taking an anatomy final at the Sorbonne. Four recent French films of high pedigree have featured sex that goes well beyond soft core. One, Cathérine Breillat's *Romance*, has just opened here. Now we'll see if France and America speak the same dirty language.

It would be pleasing to report that someone has finally made a knowing, attentive and, why not, explicit movie about what people do in bed. But *Romance* cannot live up, or down, to its fevered billing. It's a slow, morose little film about Marie (Caroline Ducey), who teaches school by day and at night gets primal lessons in sex, rough or tender. Bored with her beau, who declines intercourse, she has a tryst with hunky Paolo (Italian porn star Rocco Siffredi). But her real soul mate is the headmaster of her school (François Berleand), who binds and gags her while spouting aphorisms like "Physical love is triviality clashing with the divine." This is Marie's kind of relationship; it means "tying me up without tying me down."

Romance might work if it had an electrifying central performance or some volcanic camera passion. It has neither. Ducey shows nerve and a lot of flesh but zero screen sorcery. As for the naughty bits, there is plenty of flesh but no joy. It's mostly an ordeal—for actress and audience. If the French want to illuminate the world in matters of sex, they'll have to try harder.

VILLAGE VOICE, 9/21/99, p. 160, Amy Taubin

Romance, Catherine Breillat's succès scandale, is both dour and wickedly funny. Disconcerting combos are the mark of this film, whose heroine has the slight body of preadolescent, except for her bush—the thickest and darkest to hit the screens "legitimate" movie theaters since Marusch Detmar's in Godard's *First Name: Carmen*. Outside of pornography, cinematic sightings of female pubic hair are rare. The exceptions—Julianne Moore in *Short Cuts*, Deborah Kara Unger in *Crash*—are shocking and memorable. Of course, if you count flashers like Sharon Stone in *Basic Instinct* minor characters like the hooker in *Eyes Wide Shut*, or corpses, then the numbers climb.

But while Breillat's graphic depiction of sex has brought her notoriety and—for the first time in her close-to-25-year filmmaking career—a European box office success, *Romance* does not aim to please. Audience expecting titillation will be as disappointed a they were with *Eyes Wide Shut*, a film with which *Romance* has much in common. Had Breillat and Kubrick opted for straightforward titles—something along the lines of *Sexual Fantasies of a Wounded Narcissist*—they might have avoided a certain amount of confusion. But using mixed signals to provoke thought is part of their games.

In *Romance*, a woman named Marie (Caroline Ducey) is involved in a humiliating self-destructive affair with a man named Paul (Sagamore Stevenin). For a brief time they were passionately in love, but now he refuses to fuck her. And since withholding turns Paul on, and Marie doesn't know how to take no for an answer, the suffocating relations drags on.

The basic situation in *Romance* is almost identical to that in *Perfect Love!*, Breillat's last film. But *Perfect Love!* was a melodrama, and the power struggle between the lovers end in murder. In *Romance*, Breillat uses fantasy so that Marie can plumb the depths of her masochistic desires and come out the other side. For Breillat, following the temptation masochism is a kind of rebellion because it involves breaking the taboo against self-destruction. This bedroom philosophy doesn't exactly endear her to most feminists. And obviously the danger is that one could, psychologically speaking, drown in one's obsessions or, like the heroine of *Perfect Love!*, actually wind up dead. Marie, however, puts herself through a kind of exorcism and emerges triumphant. In the classical sense *Romance* is a comedy because it resolves in favor of its protagonist.

In order to get back at Paul and regain her power, Marie embarks on a series of sexual adventures. Whether these are real or imagined is not a distinction that Breillat bothers to make. Like her first film, *Une Vraie Jeune Fille* (which, after a 23-year ban, has finally been rereleased in France), *Romance* is part of the surrealist tradition of film a dreamscape. And if you accept the film as part fantasy, it will keep you from asking a lot of literal-minded questions like "How could she afford those clothes on a grade-school teacher's salary?" or "Couldn't she have spared the cat?"

While Paul hangs out in sushi bars reading Charles Bukowski or lounges in bed in their white-on-white apartment watching muscle men on TV, Marie has sex with (1) a gorgeous, thick-headed, as it were, stud (played by European porn star Rocco Siffredi); (2) the pudgy, middle-aged headmaster of her school (François Berleand), who turns out to be an expert in bondage and an accomplished Lothario, having fucked 10,000 women, including the ice queen herself, "Grace

Delly"; (3) a guy who offers her 20 bucks to suck her pussy and nearly becomes her Jack the Ripper.

A dark and unsparing study of female masochism and a brittle sex comedy of manners, *Romance* is unsettled in tone, to say the least. Much of the humor comes from the fact that, like anyone in the throes of sexual obsession, Marie can't see the absurdity in her situation. Thus, when she's in bed with a guy who's giving her the fuck her boyfriend has been denying her for months, she can't restrain herself from whispering in his ear such Lacanian sweet nothings as "I disappear in proportion to the cock that takes me."

Breillat settles perhaps too easily for a generic fashion-magazine look, or rather a send-up of the same. Her visual style is the least interesting aspect of her filmmaking. Her direction is extraordinary for the ideas she puts in play and the courage she inspires in her actors to risk baring their souls as well as their bodies. The two extended s/m scenes between Ducey and Berleand are remarkable. Berleand has a moment when he's searching for a missing piece of hardware that's as ridiculous and sublime as anything in Buñuel.

Marie finally transcends her obsession by getting pregnant, which, of course, may be just as much of a fantasy as everything else in the film. Without spoiling the shock ending, it's safe to say that in the annals of money shots, the climax of *Romance* qualifies as a first.

Also reviewed in:
NATION, 10/4/9, p. 34, Stuart Klawans
NEW REPUBLIC, 10/4/99, p. 34, Stanley Kauffmann
NEW YORK TIMES, 9/17/99, p. E14, Janet Maslin
VARIETY, 2/15-21/99, p. 60, David Rooney
WASHINGTON POST, 12/3/99, p. C5, Rita Kempley
WASHINGTON POST, 12/3/99, Weekend/p. 55, Desson Howe

ROOK, THE

A Phaedra Cinema release of an Ecco Films production. *Producer:* Eran Palatnik and Alan J. Abrams. *Director:* Eran Palatnik. *Screenplay:* Richard Lee Purvis. *Director of Photography:* Zack Winestine. *Editor:* Ahmad Shirazi. *Music:* Robert Een. *Sound:* Jan McLaughlin. *Production Designer:* Sebastian Schroeder. *Running time:* 84 minutes. *MPAA Rating:* R.

CAST: Martin Donovan (John Abbott); John A. MacKay (Bob Brice); Michael Finesilver (Donald Heller); Sean Clark (Fritz Fox); Harrison Baker (David P. Dawson); Diane Grotke (Dr. Abby Trent).

NEW YORK POST, 3/19/99, p. 46, Rod Dreher

There's a reason 1993's "The Rook" has spent most of this decade peregrinating from film festival to film festival, but only now has found a commercial venue in New York City—aside from the Terry Gilliam-esque production design, it's pretty awful.

Writer-director Eran Palatnik begins with an interesting and unconventional idea, but it peters away into perverse incoherence. "The Rook" stars indie stalwart Martin Donovan as John Abbott, a detective sent to a 19th-century New England town to solve a vexing murder case. You quickly see that this is not a typical period piece.

Though Abbott's dressed like a parson in a Hawthorne story, he uses peculiar high-tech devices to assist his investigation. "The Rook" is a futuristic philosophical mystery as it might have been imagined by a medieval sci-fi writer. Production designer Sebastian Schroeder deserves much praise for his moody sets and the clever collection of peculiar antiquities and anachronistic gewgaws he's dreamed up.

They're wasted on a turgid plot that creeps and crawls farther out on an increasingly fragile limb. Abbott, a religious man, finds his faith under trial as he burrows deeper into the case. We keep hearing about a "revolution" in the vicinity, against the government Abbott works for, and he worries about his family back home. And there's a secret code Abbott sweats over cracking. None of this is ever explained, and it amounts to nothing. Palatnik intends the plot to remain an open-ended mystery; even he claims not to know what "The Rook" means. "Solutions are boring," Palatnik says in the press kit. After sitting through "The Rook," this sounds suspiciously like a screenwriter's excuse for not knowing how to finish the story.

VILLAGE VOICE, 3/23/99, p. 134, Gary Susman

The real star of *The Rook* is production designer Sebastian Schroeder, who, with an obviously minuscule budget, has done some of the most inventive art direction since *Brazil*. Like that film, which crossed an Orwellian future with prewar nostalgia, *The Rook* suggests an eerie mix of eras, with steam-powered computers, crank-operated telephones, gloomy fluorescent lights, and horse-drawn carriages. Viewers should feel as disoriented as the film's protagonist, trying to solve a murder mystery that takes him into the revolutionary underground of an unnamed country.

But as they say on Broadway, no one ever left a musical humming the set design, and Schroeder's work can't hide the amateurish storytelling of Palatnik and screenwriter Richard Purvis or their threadbare philosophical conceits. Sleuth John Abbott (a dazed Martin Donovan) finds his Manichaean religious faith an archaic liability in a place where everyone may be a double agent, and his insistence on discovering a single, unambiguous truth leads to his destruction. The movie is a muddle that plays like a mistranslated Raul Ruiz film.

Also reviewed in:
NEW YORK TIMES, 3/19/99, p. E26, Anita Gates
VARIETY, 12/12-18/94, p. 82, Ken Eisner

ROSETTA

A USA Films release of a Les Films du Fleuve/RTBF/ARP Selection co-production. *Producer:* Luc Dardenne, Jean-Pierre Dardenne, Michèle Pétin, and Laurent Pétin. *Director:* Luc Dardenne and Jean-Pierre Dardenne. *Screenplay (French with English subtitles):* Luc Dardenne and Jean-Pierre Dardenne. *Director of Photography:* Alain Marcoen. *Editor:* Marie-Hélène Dozo. *Music:* Jean-Pierre Cocco. *Sound:* Jean-Pierre Duret and (music) Thomas Gauder. *Sound Editor:* Benoît de Clerck, Luc Plantier, Aurélie Muller, and Julie Brenta. *Art Director:* Igor Gabriel. *Costumes:* Monic Parelle. *Make-up:* Tina Kopecka. *Running time:* 95 minutes. *MPAA Rating:* Not Rated.

CAST: Emilie Dequenne (Rosetta); Fabrizio Rongione (Riquet); Anne Yernaux (Rosetta's Mother); Olivier Gourmet (Boss); Bernard Marbaix (Camping Area Guard); Frédéric Bodson (Personnel Chef); Florian Delain (Boss's Son); Christiane Dorval and Mirelle Bailly (Secondhand Shop Sales People); Thomas Gollas (Mother's Boyfriend); Léon Michaux and Victor Marit (Policemen); Colette Regilbeau (Madame Riga); Claire Tefnin (Cloakroom Girl); Sophia Leboutte (Woman Who is Made Reduntant); Gaetano Ventura (Shop Boss); Christian Neys and Valentin Traversi (Télé Secours Men); Jean-François Noville (ONEM Employee).

CHRISTIAN SCIENCE MONITOR, 11/5/99, p. 15, David Sterritt

Arriving on American screens is *Rosetta*, the Belgian drama that recently won the Cannes filmfest's highest prize. Played by teenager Emilie Dequenne, who shared the festival's best-actress award, the title character is a girl facing poverty and unemployment. Convinced that a regular job would save her alcoholic mother and herself from their problems, she makes a series of desperate efforts to set her life on a normal path.

"Rosetta" has less urgency than "La Promesse," the brilliant 1996 feature by directors Luc and Jean-Pierre Dardenne, but it carries a strong emotional charge along with its valuable reminder of the suffering that youngsters may undergo when a heedless society overlooks their needs.

LOS ANGELES TIMES, Calendar/p. 12, Kenneth Turan

"Rosetta" grabs you by the throat and won't let go. It's a killer of a film about a desperate young woman, someone we're both terrified by and for, yet it's so finely empathetic and insightful it also tears at your heart. A triumph of humanistic cinema, it won two awards at Cannes, the Palme d'Or for writer-directors Luc and Jean-Pierre Dardenne and a share of the best actress prize for its 18-year-old star, Emilie Dequenne, and both couldn't be more deserved.

"Rosetta" is the latest film by the Dardenne brothers, who, after spending decades making some 60 documentaries in their native Belgium, astonished the film world with their multiple award-winning 1996 film, "La Promesse," which details how the 15-year-old son of a ruthless father comes to discover the existence and importance of morality.

Aside from being savagely unsentimental, both films share a passionate concern for what it means to be poor and disadvantaged. And both explore the great and gripping drama inherent in reconnecting people to their core humanity, as well as the difficulty of reintegrating society's outcasts into a society that has completely rejected them.

Without prologue or preamble, "Rosetta" thrusts us immediately into its protagonist's furious world.   Red-faced, breathing heavily, a look of mixed anguish and aggression on her face, Rosetta hurls herself down a factory hallway, angry at the world in general and at her supervisor in particular. He's just fired her from a short-term provisional job, and she is so completely enraged it takes several policemen to remove her from the premises.

Precisely because it's tempting to ask, "Why care so much about a simple job?," "Rosetta" spends the rest of its intense 95 minutes in effect answering that question. With devastating emotional impact it explores how much it can mean to those outside the circle to simply have a job, how strong a basic human desire it is to be productive, to take one's place as an ordinary working person.

To help us more completely understand Rosetta's situation, what she is capable of in pursuit of her unlikely but all-important dream, Alain Marcoen's hand-held cinematography (Benoit Dervaux was the operator) shadows her like a second skin. Implacable, pitiless, the camera is so close to Rosetta, often literally in her face, that we feel for her and share in her life because the insistent visuals simply leave us no choice.

What we see up close is a sullen, closed-off young person, abrupt to everyone and counting on nothing from life but trouble and despair. Her fury, determination and need are almost unbearable, and it's painful to imagine (the film doesn't tell us) what life has done to this young woman to make her this way. What we see finally is a kind of small, determined animal, a ferret perhaps, always wary and watchful. Peering around corners to see if it's safe to emerge, lashing out at anything and anyone who comes too close, Rosetta takes refuge in increasingly desperate daily rituals like hiding her boots in a storm drain when she goes to the city and fishing for food with makeshift equipment.

Rosetta lives in a run-down trailer park outside the Belgian city of Seraing with her terminally alcoholic, sleep-around mother (Anne Yernaux), who in rare moments of sobriety repairs clothes that Rosetta sells. More than anything, the daughter lives in terror of descending into complete oblivion like her wastrel mother, and, in her graphic words, "falling into the rut."

Rosetta's coldness and distance are always daunting. Yet it is the gift of Dequenne's magical acting and the Dardennes' masterful and sure-handed writing and directing that her feral intensity and determination (underlined by the complete absence of music), coupled with the almost biblical spareness of her wants, make her a person we care terribly about.

It's at a waffle stand that Rosetta makes her first tentative contacts with humanity. Riquet (Fabrizio Rongione), a shy, decent boy who works behind the counter, is fascinated by her difficult nature, and she also makes a positive impression on the stand's owner (Olivier Gourmet, the father in "La Promesse"). But even with those faint hopes, don't imagine that life is going to turn into a movie fantasy for Rosetta; the Dardennes have too much skill, and too much integrity, for anything even close to that.

As difficult as Rosetta is, there are moments with her that are indelible. Going to sleep one night, she repeats a devastating mantra to herself. "Your name is Rosetta. My name is Rosetta. You found a job. I found a job. You've got a friend. I've got a friend." Simple dreams but so devastatingly difficult to attain.

NEW YORK, 11/15/99, p. 69, Peter Rainer

Emilie Dequenne, who plays the lead in the Belgian movie *Rosetta*, has a remarkable face for the camera: fine-cut yet feral. The character she plays lives in a trailer park with her alcoholic mother and wants only to get a job, however menial. In a way, the 17-year-old Rosetta is a model citizen, and yet her obsession with work—which is really an obsession with normality—has emptied her out. She's a furious cipher, and the closer the camera gets to her, the more unreachable she seems. The film, directed by the Dardenne brothers, Luc and Jean-Pierre, won last year's Palme D'Or at Cannes, and it extends the documentary-style techniques of their previous collaboration, *La Promesse*. It not as good as that film, maybe because so much in-your-face unreachableness tends to wear one down, but it contains some startling passages.

NEW YORK POST, 11/5/99, p. 60, Jonathan Foreman

A moving but austere work of social realism, "Rosetta" won the Palme d'Or prize at the Cannes Film Festival this year. This Belgian-French co-production is bleak, demanding stuff, and its hand-held documentary-style photography is harder on the stomach than "The Blair Witch Project."

But newcomer Emilie Duquenne gives an extraordinary performance as the title character, a Belgian teenage girl whose character has been deformed by poverty and unemployment.

Rosetta is 17 and lives in a trailer park at the edge of a drab, rainy Belgian city. She has lanky hair, bad skin and an alcoholic mother (Anne Yernaux) who prostitutes herself to the guy who runs the trailer park (Bernard Marbaix).

You first meet Rosetta as she's being fired from a job. She refuses to leave the factory and has to be dragged out, kicking and biting, by police officers. Afterwards, when she's not looking for work, Rosetta fishes in the swampy pond behind the trailer park using traps made from old bottles. Every so often she doubles over in pain from a presumably stress-related stomach ailment.

Finally, Rosetta gets a job at a bakery. Then a young man (Fabrizio Rongione) who works at one of the baker's waffle stands befriends her, despite her distrustful unfriendliness. But Rosetta is let go when her employer's son says he wants her job.

Her single-minded dedication to finding work and through it, some stability and dignity in her life—then prompts Rosetta to commit an appalling act of betrayal.

Writer-directors Luc and Jean-Pierre Dardenne are leftist documentarians who also made the critically acclaimed feature "La Promesse." Although their "Rosetta" could be seen as a Marxist tract, it goes beyond agitprop.

It implies that even the most menial work fulfills a deep emotional need, and it shows in a powerful, personal way that widespread youth unemployment—the price that countries like Belgium and France pay for their semi-socialist economies—extorts a terrible psychic cost.

NEWSDAY, 11/5/99, Part II/p. B7, John Anderson.

Opening with a bang and ending in a whimper, "Rosetta"—the winner of the top prize at this year's Cannes Film Festival—seems likely to become the most misunderstood movie of the year. As relentlessly mobile and wild as its besieged heroine, the film is certainly an extended metaphor. The question, it seems, is for what? Played by 17-year-old Emilie Dequenne—who shared best actress honors at Cannes—Rosetta lives in a Belgian trailer park with her hopelessly alcoholic mother (Anne Yernaux), for whom she acts as a combination temperance cheerleader and camp commandant, fending off the men who ply the older woman with beer, while trying to attain a "normal" life—one in which she has a job, maybe a future and where every day isn't a Sisyphean struggle. How she's forced to go about it is brutish, appalling and cruel.

Belgium's Dardenne brothers, Luc and Jean-Pierre, explored the economic fringe of contemporary Europe in their devastating debut feature "La Promesse," but "Rosetta" is the superior film. Each element is essential to the next; their hand-held camera, relentless and agile, shadows Rosetta through her daily rigors—getting unjustly fired from one job because her trial period has ended, from another because the boss' son needs a job, storming from one failed job interview to the next—and making the oppressive nature of Rosetta's existence as palpable as the menstrual cramps that consistently double her over and which are clearly a symptom of her unhappy state of mind.

"Rosetta" is, essentially, a survivalist: She hides valuables in the woods like a dog burying a bone; she fishes with a homemade bottle trap, sells clothes her mother mends to thrift shops (getting ripped off in the process) and basically has reduced herself to the status of a hungry animal. That she's forced to behave this way is certainly a swipe at the political system. Unable to keep a job long enough, she's ineligible for unemployment. There are inadequate social services for her mother. But anyone who interprets "Rosetta" as merely a knee-jerk leftist diatribe is willfully missing the much bigger picture.

"Rosetta" is a feminist film, not in any faux-fashionable way, but almost like a manifesto against nature itself The cramps that beset her are the essential symbol here: The male power structure is her immediate problem, but the film winds up railing against biology. When she's laid off at the waffle stand and then rats out the one friend she's made, Riquet (Fabrizio Rongione), she can do it because he's a man, and men—from her absent, unmentioned father to her mother's parasitic beaus—have been the cause of all her misery.

One could accuse the Dardenne brothers of being patriarchal and patronizing, perhaps, but Rosetta is a singular character, unlike any other, hobbled by her own sex and oppressed by the other, but not quite able to make the next logical step: Divest herself entirely of moral conscience and bite life in the throat.

"Rosetta" in the end is not just kinetic and emotionally naked. It's primal.

SIGHT AND SOUND, 3/00, p. 51, Lizzie Francke

Liége, Belgium, the present. Rosetta, a proud young woman, has just been made redundant. She returns home to the caravan site where she lives to find her alcoholic mother has been turning tricks in exchange for drink.

Determined to find new work, Rosetta asks about vacancies at a local waffle stand run by a young man named Riquet. Later, Riquet turns up at the caravan park to tell her a job is going at the head office. They develop a tentative friendship. She visits him at his bedsit and discovers he's cheating his boss. Her job at the waffle bakery is short lived and she finds herself back on the streets. Riquet offers her a job moonlighting at his stand, but she turns him down as she wants 'proper' employment. She ends up blowing the whistle on Riquet's scam.

The waffle boss gives her Riquet's concession. Rosetta sells waffles, while Riquet loiters near by. After work one night, she finds her mother passed out. Rosetta rings the waffle boss to tell him she won't be coming to work any more. She seals up the windows of the caravan and tries to gas herself, but the gas runs out. Rosetta buys another gas canister from the caravan-park owner. On her way back to the caravan, she is confronted by Riquet.

"Your name is Rosetta. My name is Rosetta. You've found a job. I've found a job. You have a friend. I have a friend. You have a normal life. I have a normal life. You won't fall into the rut. I won't fall into the rut." So runs the desperate mantra of the Dardenne brothers' extraordinary film, its heroine portrayed heartbreakingly by Emilie Dequenne, her feral roughness masking an inner grace. This dialogue of self and soul marks Rosetta out as a latterday Everywoman seeking survival in post-industrial Belgium. Stripped of her white factory uniform after being made redundant, Rosetta dresses in a jumbled livery of red jacket, thick yellow tights and gumboots. These practical togs make her into a vivid, harlequin figure in the sparse and sombre winter landscape, underscoring her near-medieval existence foraging for sustenance and striving for the armoury of a 'normal life' in a Western Europe gone wild.

Fierce and proud, her tactics are basic, even clumsy. She poaches fish with makeshift equipment, and bargains desperately in second-hand clothes shops. She will do anything, including betray a potential friend—anything but lower herself to begging. So she despises her slumped alcoholic mother, prostituting herself for the price of a beer. The rut Rosetta so fears gapes wide open; the trapper could be trapped herself, perhaps in the thick black river which borders the caravan park. At one point Rosetta and her estranged mum become embroiled in a fight on its borders, and Rosetta ends up in the dank waters, weighed down with a despairing motherlode.

This startlingly palpable expression of Rosetta's physical and emotional hardship is emblematic of the Dardennes' poetic style, one which repeatedly discovers resonance in the commonplace.

In scrutinised minutiae the one time documentarians find transcendental signs, in a way reminiscent of the work of Bresson (particularly *Mouchette*). Rosetta's struggle is literally embodied in her recurring stomach cramps (presumably period pains) and her wrestling bouts with Riquet, the friend whose job she takes. In the final scene, as she drags the gas bottle back to the caravan so she can finish off her and her mother's lives, the burden of mortality is harrowingly intimated. Such a sense of gravity is emphasised further by the films restless, handheld camera style, bearing down on the heroine as it follows her, perched almost on her shoulders. Indeed, in the opening factory scene we hardly glimpse Rosetta's face as she ricochets around, angry at her impending fate. The Dardennes thrust us into the defiant rhythm of her long march, evoking the films of Alan Clarke who so often focused on his characters' seemingly endless walking, the tread and dread of a relentless existence.

The starkness is compounded by the film's almost complete lack of music, apart from a scene where Riquet demonstrates his enthusiastic but amateurish drumming (it's the only thing he feels he does "nearly well"). Here, perhaps the film's one upbeat moment, Riquet tries to reach out and offer some warmth to the isolated young woman. It's an emotional connection which offers a mite of hope in the ending when Riquet, albeit unwittingly, interrupts her suicide attempt. But ultimately there is little respite in *Rosetta*, and that's what makes it a film of such eviscerating emotional intensity.

TIMES, 11/22/99, p. 104, Richard Corliss

What would you do for a job—a menial, drudging job in a bakery or selling clothes that never were in fashion? If you are Rosetta (Emilie Dequenne), a teenager in today's depressed Belgium, the answer is anything. Luc and Jean-Pierre Dardenne's *Rosetta*, which earned this year's Cannes Film Festival Palme d'Or and a Best Actress prize for Dequenne, is the close-up portrait of a girl for whom need has become obsession.

The way medieval saints believed in Jesus, with a fervor bordering on lust, Rosetta believes in employment. Work is her religion: when she gets it, she does it harder (and glummer) than anyone else. When she has no job, she focuses on getting one so maniacally that she is in danger of destroying herself and the one fellow who befriends her. In the trailer park where she lives with her slutty, alcoholic mother, she methodically does the chores. For Rosetta, living is one job she can't lose. Unless she fires—kills—herself. And when she does decide to commit suicide, she is still a model employee: before turning on the gas. She calls her boss to say she won't be coming in anymore.

In another country, or in lesser hands, a teenager's addiction to work could be a subject for comedy; the Dardenne brothers turn it into tragedy and transcendence. But this dour, powerful film might be just an anecdote without Dequenne, 18. She invests Rosetta with the weird ferocity of an alien creature: a wild angel or a madwoman. This novice actress's task—finding the shading of realism in what could be a cartoon of misery—is made all the more harrowing by the film's intense, handheld scrutiny of her face in almost every shot. The purity of Dequenne's performance inspires awe. To a grubby life she brings dignity, clarity, passion, glory.

VILLAGE VOICE, 11/9/99, p. 135, J. Hoberman

Lights, camera, agitation: Two current portraits of left-wing heroism and victimhood—the scrappy Belgian import *Rosetta* and Hollywood's high-powered *The Insider*—are exposés that make their points by churning up maximum tumult.

Rosetta's stylized rough-and-tumble vérité is established from the onset, as its teenage protagonist slams through a factory, fighting ineffectually and violently to keep the job from which, for reasons never specified, she's just been fired. The handheld camera is kept disorientingly close to Rosetta (Emilie Dequenne) and will remain so for nearly every minute of this pummeling, jagged, and extremely well-edited film. This is the second feature by the brothers Luc and Jean-Pierre Dardenne, after their terrific illegal-immigrant drama *La Promesse;* I like that 1997 release, it puts 20 years of social-documentary experience in the service of a powerfully single-minded metaphor.

Living in a trailer park with an alcoholic mother who mends old clothes for her to peddle, *Rosetta* is a furiously sullen bundle of energy. She's not quite pretty but too fresh-faced to be dowdy, often expressionless but also impulsive ("You only drink and fuck," she screams at her mother as the prelude to one of several scuffles). Most significantly, Rosetta lives in a state of existential dread. The woodland swamp that borders the trailer camp exemplifies the "rut" into which she fears she might fall. In her quest to forestall this fate by finding work, she is befriended by a young guy who operates a waffle stand. He treats her to a dinner of beer and fried bread, plays a tape of him practicing the drums, and tries to teach her to dance—at which point Rosetta doubles over in the stress-related stomach pain that plagues her throughout this fiercely compelling movie.

Devoid of music, elliptical in its narrative. Rosetta has not been universally admired. That it stormed out of nowhere to win the Palme d'Or at Cannes, while David Lynch's heartwarming *Straight Story* was overlooked, seems to have struck some Americans as a conspiracy orchestrated by the Evil Empire from beyond the grave. Others directed their animus against the Dardennes' unglamorous heroine. Unlike the protagonists of *The City*, a more sentimental excursion through lower-class misery, *Rosetta* is neither likable nor ennobled by struggle. She is, rather, some form of brute life force. Cunning as an animal, she scrambles, hides, and hoards. The movie makes a spectacle of her repeated dodging and ducking across the highway into the woods. Laid off by a baker (Olivier Gourmet, the father in *La Promesse*), she goes into a rage—clinging to a heavy sack of flour as though it were her life raft. Most appallingly, she betrays the only character who has shown her sympathy.

Rosetta was shot in the same drab neighborhoods as *La Promesse,* but one could easily imagine the movie transposed to the U.S.—although I wonder if a career-conscious American indie would care to present so needy and (relatively) unattractive a protagonist, or plot a trajectory of such sustained anxiety. Is *Rosetta* an abstract construct? The Dardennes have signaled their modernist ambitions by comparing her to the hero of Kafka's *Castle*. But their movie's ugly-duckling heroine, her repeated routines and spiritual anguish, as well as the harsh clarity of the ending, suggest a Marxist remake of Bresson's *Mouchette.*

Rosetta strives for a material state of grace. Her will to survive is identical to her overwhelming desire to find a "real" job in this world. During the brief period when she operates a waffle stand—the camera, as usual, fixed on her every moment—she becomes almost human, It's a small miracle; work is a pleasure.

More posh, but scarcely less hectic, Michael Mann's *The Insider* begins by juxtaposing a dicey *60 Minutes* interview in revolutionary Iran with a child's asthma attack in suburban Louisville and thereafter races from one high-stakes crisis to the next.

Based on the true story of Jeffrey Wigand, the research scientist who blew the whistle on Brown & Williamson Tobacco and laid the groundwork for the lawsuits that have done so much for our current budget surplus, *The Insider* is a tale of brave truth-tellers and corporate mendacity. Confusing self-importance with importance, the never laconic Mann inflates his potentially nifty thriller with superfluous scenes extra-padded by wasted motion. Mann rarely misses a chance to savor the brooding dusk from a skyscraper window, while in an ongoing search for the audiovisual equivalent of purple prose, underscores the high drama with a bizarre mélange of Gregorian chants and word-music yodeling.

At 155 minutes, *The Insider* may be pumped-up, but it's rarely boring. Mann keeps the pot aboil by stoking the viewers sense of a ruthless corporate culture that will stop at nothing to protect itself. Not only is Wigand subject to gross intimidation, but after he brings his story to *60 Minutes* producer Lowell Bergman, CBS lawyers begin pressuring *60 Minutes* to cut back on Wigand's on-air interview with Mike Wallace—presumably so as not to jeopardize the network's possible sale to Westinghouse.

The Insider is also entertaining thanks to Mann's showboat cast. Russell Crowe plays the volatile, heroic Wigand with Al Pacino as the equally volatile and no less heroic Bergman —identified as a onetime student of Herbert Marcuse. Their wives (Diane Venora and Lindsay Crouse) have somewhat less to do, but in any case, the movie is stolen by Christopher Plummer's hilarious Mike Wallace impersonation. The real Wallace's well-documented unhappiness may have less to do with the suggestion that he sold out Wigand and Bergman than the glib ease with which he's shown doing it. When the vindicated Bergman gets to tell Wallace off ("What got broken here doesn't grow back together again"), Plummer plays the CBS star as baffled—but only momentarily. His Wallace is the most naturalistic character in the film.

The news business is the object of some satire, although given *The Insider*'s own throat-clearing self-aggrandizement, the darts can rebound. "Excuse me gentlemen, Mr. Rather is complaining about his chair again," a CBS producer remarks— something that has surely never happened on one of Mann's sets. When Wallace tells Bergman that he doesn't intend to end his days "wandering in the wilderness of NPR," he couldn't possibly be speaking for the director.

Also reviewed in:
CHICAGO TRIBUNE, 1/7/00, Friday/p. A, Michael Wilmington
NATION, 11/22/99, p. 32, Stuart Klawans
NEW REPUBLIC, 11/29/99, p. 24, Stanley Kauffmann
NEW YORK TIMES, 10/2/99, p. B13, Stephen Holden
NEW YORKER, 11/8/99, p. 105, David Denby
VARIETY, 5/31-6/6/99 p. 27, Derek Elley

ROSIE

A New Yorker Films release of a Prime Time/The Flemish Film Fund/VRI production. *Producer:* Antonino Lombardo. *Director:* Patrice Toye. *Screenplay (Flemish with English subtitles):* Patrice Toye. *Director of Photography:* Richard von Oosterhout. *Editor:* Ludo Troch. *Music:* John Parish. *Sound:* Dirk Rombey. *Art Director:* Johan van Essche. *Running time:* 97 minutes. *MPAA Rating:* Not Rated.

CAST: Aranka Coppens (Rosie); Sara de Roo (Irene); Frank Vercruyssen (Michel); Dirk Roofthooft (Bernard); Joost Wijnant (Jimi).

CHRISTIAN SCIENCE MONITOR, 7/23/99, p. 15, David Sterritt

Another film that focuses young people and parents [The reference is to *My Life So Far*; see Sterritt's review of that film.] is *Rosie*, which hails from the Flemish-speaking part of Belgium. Filmmaker Patrice Toye wrote and directed it with quiet sensitivity.

The title character is a 13-year-old girl whose mother, Irene, was only 14 when she was born. Irene works hard to raise her daughter right, but feels so embarrassed by her youthful indiscretions that she presents Rosie to the world as her sister, even refusing to let the child call her Mom at home. It's hard to grow up with such a conflicted mother-daughter relationship, and Rosie develops emotional problems that increase when Irene meets a new boyfriend. This situation leads to a final revelation about the family that threatens to push Rosie over the edge.

"Rosie" is not a happy tale, but sensitive acting and perceptive filmmaking make it touching rather than harrowing to watch. Best of all is Aranka Coppens's portrayal of the young protagonist, carrying off a complex performance that might challenge an actress twice her age.

LOS ANGELES TIMES, 8/20/99, Calendar/p. 8, Kevin Thomas

In a way that almost sneaks up on you, Patrice Toye's "Rosie" packs a wallop that's even stronger because its story seems so familiar, its downward trajectory so inevitable. However, Toye, described in publicity material as the first woman to direct a feature film in Flemish, engages us in the fate of a troubled Antwerp teenager with the freshness of her vision and her ability to make her cast seem to be living rather than acting their roles.

When we meet Aranka Coppens' 13-year-old Rosie, she is undergoing her intake interview in some sort of juvenile detention center. A girl trying to befriend newcomer Rosie remarks: "Everybody here is either crazy or has killed someone." What brought Rosie to this place soon begins to unfold in flashbacks. In the meantime, Rosie, a pretty, self-possessed brunette who's clearly intelligent and assertive, has taken a defiant stance toward her interrogator, convinced that there's no point in telling the truth because nobody would believe her, which signals Toye's uncovering of that truth, bit by bit.

Rosie lives in a small apartment with her mother, Irene (Sara de Roo), in a vast, austere Antwerp housing complex. The attractive Irene, a nurse, struggles to make ends meet; her daughter tends to daydream. Rosie seems not to have any close friends and is caught up in a world of paperback romance novels, steamy yet fairy tale-like in their promise of rescue by the proverbial knight in shining armor. As puberty approaches for her, Rosie is in large part living in her imagination.

So far there's nothing so unusual about Rosie or her daydreaming, but two factors quickly emerge that are potentially ominous. First of all, Irene insists that Rosie refer to her as her sister rather than her mother to disguise the fact that Irene gave birth to Rosie when she was only 14. It also helps Irene in her own search for a Mr. Right to be regarded as a childless woman. Just as Rosie is captivated by a blond youth, Jimi (Joost Wijnant), who becomes her boyfriend only in her imagination, Irene allows her dead-broke brother Michel (Frank Vercruyssen), a scruffy layabout with a weakness for playing the ponies, to move in. Michel seems amiable enough but quickly starts behaving like a strict father to Rosie, who understandably resents him, believing he has no right to play the paternal disciplinarian.

As fate would have it, as life in Irene's cramped apartment grows more tense, Irene meets a man she really likes. A widowed chemist of perhaps 40, Bernard (Dirk Roofthooft) is by far the most mature and perceptive individual within this small group of people. He and Irene start falling in love—though, under the circumstances, why they don't carry on their affair in the privacy of his place rather than hers remains a puzzle—and Bernard makes a real effort to win Rosie's approval. Life would seem to offer brighter prospects for both mother and daughter than ever before, but that's not reckoning with Michel, threatened by the arrival of Bernard and determined not to be so easily dislodged from his sister's home and life.

Of course, a lot is going on beneath an increasingly volatile surface, but, at 13, Rosie is the first to be affected by the gathering storm and the last to comprehend its root causes. That Irene comes so close to making everything work for her and for her daughter, that makes the playing out of their predicament all the more wrenching.

"Rosie" derives much of its tension, its sense of potential tragedy, from Toye's making it possible to identify with the mother as well as the daughter. Irene is a lovely, intelligent woman, striving mightily to overcome a dark past to provide a better, happier life for her daughter. Her biggest mistake is to think she can help her destructive brother without endangering her and her daughter's chances for happiness. Almost everyone who has survived adolescence can identify with Rosie, whose discovery of the capacity of adults for dishonesty and deception takes on a far more extreme and shattering form than it does for most of us.

The look and feel of "Rosie," with its overpowering sense of emotional authenticity, suggests that Toye works intuitively. She lets us discover her story's truths and meanings as it unfolds. Most importantly, Toye, in only her first movie, reveals herself to be a filmmaker with a vision that makes you feel you have missed nothing intended. In short, "Rosie" is a notably fully realized film beyond its telling dialogue and its faultless performances, especially that of young Aranka Coppens, who has the primary responsibility in carrying the film.

There's never a sense of Toye imposing a style or shape upon the film; rather, every aspect of "Rosie" has emerged from its people and their interactions. What Toye has done so effectively is to drain most every scene of all but its essential people, which heightens their aura of isolation and loneliness—never, for example, do we see anyone except the principals in that apartment complex. Such an approach allows Toye to build assuredly to her biggest truth, the abiding need for individuals to be loved, to feel part of a family, a need so deep that if it is not answered in reality it surely shall in fantasy—regardless of the consequences.

NEW YORK POST, 7/23/99, p. 58, Rod Dreher

"Rosie" is a poignant, well-acted but tiring addition to the slate of gritty social-realist films that have come out of Belgium in recent years. This unsentimental tale of a neglected teen-ager living in a gloomy housing project in an industrial neighborhood is unpleasant to watch.

The sun never comes out for working-class teens in soggy Flanders, which is the point, I guess, but it makes for depressing viewing.

Still, the strengths of writer-director Patrice Toye's storytelling, as well as a terrific performance by young Aranka Coppens in the title role, make "Rosie" an emotionally involving experience and a disconcertingly relevant one. Toye's portrait of the despair and emerging criminal psychosis of a teen-age girl whose single mother is too involved in her own life to show her child the love and attention she craves unavoidably brings to mind the destructive anomie of the Littleton generation.

The year is 1980. Rosie lives with her mother Irene (Sara de Roo) in a small public-housing unit in a crummy suburb. Irene gave birth to Rosie when she herself was a young teenagers and has never warmed to the role of mother. She fears men will run away if they discover she has a 13-year-old daughter, so she insists that Rosie call her "sister."

Desperate for affection and some release from the anguished monotony of her life, Rosie reads romance novels and dreams of the dashing lives led by handsome knights and the czarinas they ravish. She finds a strangely chaste boyfriend, Jimi (Joost Wijnant), a here-comes-trouble rapscallion who initiates Rosie into a life of petty delinquency.

Meanwhile, Irene's lay-about brother Michel (Frank Vercruyssen) has moved into the flat while he's out of work. His malevolent presence looms as a threat to Rosie—there's the constant fear that he will prey sexually on her loneliness, and a whiff of incest lingers in the stale air—and to Irene's budding romance with the decent Bernard (Dirk Roofthooft). Well-meaning but slutty and self-absorbed, Irene's emotional neglect of Rosie pushes the desperately needy girl to the psychological margins.

I hate to say it about an admirable film, but watching "Rosie" is something of an endurance test. Director Toye errs in assuming that grime + white-trash sociopathy = authenticity. Maybe so, but who wants to spend 97 minutes having their nose rubbed in such ugliness?

NEWSDAY, 7/23/99, Part II/p. B12, John Anderson

Aranka Coppens, the self-possessed young actress who plays the merely possessed "Rosie," is so antimovie she can't help being totally magnetic. Fox-faced, snake-lipped, she gives the kind of oddly creepy, creepily needy performance that forgives—or at least distracts—from the quavering uncertainties of her character's story.

This Flemish film—its nationality makes it rare enough—is a psychological tragedy whose direction is clear, but whose ultimate destination is never quite certain until its final shattering moment. There are hints, naturally, but director Patrice Toye doesn't even really let us know at first what is a flashback and what is not.

Is the story rooted at the correctional facility where Rosie meets matricidal teenagers and ineffectual sociologists? Or at the apartment where she lives with her mother, Irene (Sara de Roo)—the mother who passes herself off as Rosie's sister? It's a lack of orientation that mirrors this life of Rosie, who can't even acknowledge that her mother is her mother, much less sort out the rest of her adolescent angst.

Her situation is aggravated by the arrival of her shiftless Uncle Michel (Frank Vercruyssen), whom Irene has an inordinate need to protect and defend and whom Rosie instinctively defies. The reasons become clear enough, soon enough, although other aspects of Rosie's existence are about as puzzling as they could possibly be.

Although her film is slow-moving and purposefully gray, Toye creates an obsessively personal portrait with "Rosie"—it's in her room, in her face, clinging to her the way Rosie wants to cling to Mummy. It also captures fairly effectively that amorphous state where girl meets woman, the former when Rosie roller-skates around the neighborhood, the latter when she's with her boyfriend, Jimi (Joost Wijnant), a blond heartthrob whose fascination with the girl seems more than a little odd.

Killing time in the kind of faceless suburb that breeds indolence and rebellion, Rosie escalates their small-time matters to car theft and baby-snatching, her neediness and apparent anger taking self-destructive paths with which the audience thoroughly sympathizes, because it's spent such an intimate amount of time with such a deeply troubled girl.

"Rosie," which is Toye's debut film, broke box-office records for a Belgian film in Belgium. It has a fresh feel, but a sage sense of how to marry youth to desperation. Toye claims to have watched Terrence Malick's "Badlands," about young love and serial murder, which makes a certain amount of sense. Rosie may not be quite that desperate, but you wouldn't want to try and convince her of it.

VILLAGE VOICE, 7/27/99, p. 64, Michael Atkinson

Decent films about adolescent girls are hardly a dime a dozen. Watching the new Belgian film *Rosie* veer alarmingly close to truthfulness and insight, you can't help but wish writer-director Patrice Toye had trusted in her young heroine more and in snake-pit melodramatics less. Toye has the tools: a moody working-class realism, a knack for adolescent observation, and the open-faced Aranka Coppens as the titular 13-year-old. Alert yet wary, Rosie lives in an Antwerp project with her mother (Sara de Roo), who tries to keep her parenthood a secret while dating, and hangs out with Jimi (Joost Wijnant), a sweet blond boy who might not be altogether real. Rosie herself feels genuine, but rather than flesh her out, Toye excavates white-trash clichés like incest, murder, and madness. Rosie has many breath-holding scenes—the poor girl delicately skating away after getting hit by a car, and later carrying off a stolen infant without any idea how to care for it—but by the end, the thrust is Belgian Gothic.

Also reviewed in:
CHICAGO TRIBUNE, 2/25/00, Friday/p. F, John Petrakis
NEW REPUBLIC, 8/9/99, p. 30, Stanley Kauffmann
NEW YORK TIMES, 7/23/99, p. E22, Janet Maslin
VARIETY, 9/28-10/4/98, p. 44, Glenn Lovell

RUN LOLA RUN

A Sony Pictures Classics release in association with Bavaria Films International of an X-Filme Creative Pool production. *Executive Producer:* Maria Köpf. *Producer:* Stefan Arndt. *Director:* Tom Tykwer. *Screenplay (German with English subtitles):* Tom Tykwer. *Director of Photography:* Frank Griebe. *Editor:* Mathilde Bonnefoy. *Music:* Tom Tykwer, Johnny Klimek, and Reinhold Hell. *Sound:* Dirk Jacob. *Sound Editor:* Markus Münz. *Casting:* An Dorthe Braker. *Art Director:* Alexander Manasse. *Set Decorator:* Attila Saygel and Irene Otterpohl. *Special Effects:* Gerd Voll and Roland Tropp. *Costumes:* Monika Jacobs. *Make-up:* Margit Neufink. *Stunt Coordinator:* Ruff Connection. *Running time:* 81 minutes. *MPAA Rating:* R.

CAST: Franka Potente (Lola); Moritz Bleibtreu (Manni); Herbert Knaup (Father); Nina Petri (Jutta Hansen); Armin Rohde (Herr Schuster); Joachim Król (Nozbert von Au); Ludger Pistor (Herr Meier); Suzanne von Borsody (Frau Jäger); Sebastian Schipper (Mike); Julia Lindig (Doris); Lars Rudolph (Herr Kruse); Andreas Petri (Cleaner); Klaus Müller (Croupier); Utz Krause (Casino Manager); Beate Finckh (Casino Cashier); Volkhart Buff (Ambulance Driver); Heino Ferch (Ronnie); Ute Lubosch (Mother); Dora Raddy (Old Woman); Monica Bleibtreu (Blind Woman); Peter Pauli (Supermarket Security Guard); Marc Bischoff (Policeman); Hans Paetsch (Narrator).

FILM QUARTERLY, Spring 2000, p. 33, Tom Whalen

Tom Tykwer's *Run Lola Run* (*Lola rennt*, 1998) blasts open doors for viewers in the late 90s the way Godard's *Breathless* (1959) did for viewers in the late 50s. In few other ways would I compare these two films. Godard's exercise is tinted cool, hip, his characters posturing cartoons; whereas Tykwer's is hot, kinetic, and his (at times animated) characters bristling realities. Though a profoundly philosophical and German film, *Run Lola Run* leaps lightly over the typical Teutonic metaphysical mountains. Tykwer's work doesn't have the Romantic receptive gaze of a Wenders or entertain the grapple with the gods of a Herzog, but instead possesses a lucid spirit willing to see life and art as a game. Nor, though as excited by the techniques of cinema as the film of a first-time director *(Run Lola Run* is Tykwer's eighth movie), is it the loose, dehumanized display of, say, *Pulp Fiction* (1994) or *Trainspotting* (1996). *Run Lola Run* is fast, but never loose. It's as tightly wound and playful as a Tinguely machine and constructed with care.

What are the constituent components of this energized mechanism? This essay proposes that the film's unifying principle is the Game: its unifying theme. Time and determinism; its dominant formal principle, the Dialectic: and its (subsidiary,) narrative systems those of the love story and fair tale. By examining each of these areas and related motifs, I hope to illuminate at least some of the rules of Tom Tykwer's game.[1]

I. THE GAME

As long as I can play the game,
I can play it, and everything is all right.
-Ludwig Wittgenstein

Of the films two epigraphs (the first by T. S. Eliot and the second by S. Herberger). the one that concerns me at the moment is the second: *"Nach dem Spiel ist vor dem Spiel."* "After the game is before the game." Or: When one game ends, another is about to begin. Hardly a pause, and even the pause is preparation for the next game. What dominates, whether before or after the game, is the game itself. So whatever else this epigraph might mean (and who might S. Herberger be? A German soccer coach, *natürlich),* it reminds us that while watching *Run Lola Run* we should never forget that we are in a sense watching a game. Or in several senses.

Games, like films, are usually time-bound, and Lola (Franka Potente) is a most time-bound character: she has 20 minutes to come up with 100,000 Deutschmarks in order to save the life of her boyfriend Manni (Moritz Bleibtreu). Games can also be played again; if you lose one game, you can always try again. So if film is like a game, then why not give Lola a second chance to win, or a third? "The space-time continuum is unhinged, so what?" Tykwer said in an interview, "We're at the movies!" *("Das Raum-Zeit-Kontinuum wird aus den Angeln gehoben, na und? Wir sind doch im Kino!* (Tykwer, 137).

Run Lola Run's film antecedent might well be the short *Same Player Shoots Again* (1967) by Wim Wenders. "For me," Wenders has said of this abstract "thriller" which basically repeats a single two-minute shot five times, "it had a lot to do with pinball machines. ... Visually, it's as if you had five balls. In fact, that was the idea, to edit it this way" (Dawson, 18). A man carrying a machine gun and wearing a long coat is shown from the torso down wounded and, like Lola, running. The two shots that precede the five repeated shots also contain elements one finds in *Run Lola Run.* In a room we see a television with a shot of hands shuffling cards in a Western. In the second shot we see an empty phone booth with the receiver dangling above the ground after a man has run out. The first shot recalls the television in Lola's mother's room at the beginning of each of the three "rounds" (Tykwer's term, *Runde,* also has a boxing connotation in German), though what is playing on the television is an animated Lola running outside the door, and as the camera moves into the television, the frame becomes all animation. The second shot of the Wenders film, it seems to me, is directly referenced by Tykwer whenever we see Manni in or leaving the phone booth. (Intertextuality can't be against the rules in this game.) Also, what Robert Kolker and Peter Beicken say about the Wenders' film is true of *Run Lola Run:* "While the gangster film clues do not add up to a full gangster story, they evoke a milieu, recall expectations, sometimes in a most circuitous way" (22). Though *Run Lola Run* is more narratively complete, it is equally abstract.

Two further thoughts: 1) Games exist, as much as possible, in a zone of safety. Like Wile E. Coyote, a game character can't (or shouldn't) be harmed. No one dies in *Run Lola Run.* 2) The player should be able to affect the outcome of the game. Lola is determined, beyond all logic (so determined that she rises above the logically possible), to win the game. But can a player affect the outcome even of a game of chance such as roulette? Yes, in this case especially roulette.

What is important while viewing *Run Lola Run* is to acknowledge the director's central conceit of life/art/film as a game. In the opening sequence, after the epigraphs, Tykwer again emphasizes the point. A clock's pendulum swings ominously back and forth across the screen. The camera tilts upwards, rises, and we plunge into a gaping black hole of Chronos's mouth. Swallowed by time, we are presented with a handful of characters, zoom-selected, like playing cards, from a crowd of figures. Then a man in a guard's uniform (Armin Rohde) holding a soccer ball tells us: "Ball is round, game lasts 90 minutes. That much is clear. Everything else is theory." *("Ball is rund, Spiel dauert 90 Minuten. Soviel is schon ma klar Alles andere is Theorie"* [Tykwer, 7].)

And then he says, " *Und ab!*" ("Go!"), kicking the ball high into the air and the camera soars up with it, while below the figures coalesce into the words LOLA RENNT.

II. TIME

Time is the substance I am made of.
-Jorge Luis Borges

Then the camera plunges back down toward the lone figure of the guard standing just inside the "O" of LOLA and then into the "O" tunnel of the animated credit sequence. How to escape this "O," the closed circle of time, is Lola's metaphysical problem. Tykwer's assessment that *Run Lola Run* is "an action film that carries a philosophical idea, woven in very playfully, however, not placed in the center" (130) masks the foregrounding of time in the narrative and its use as a frequent visual motif. Clocks, for example, are everywhere: from the film's first sound (the ticking of a clock), to the clock that swallows our gaze in the opening, to the three clocks in the animated credit sequence, to the "O" in LOLA, to the cross-cutting from Lola as she runs to meet Manni, to the clock Manni watches as he waits to see if Lola will arrive before the 20 minutes are up. We can't ignore Lola's temporal prison. So conscious is the film of time that several of its images serve as visual metaphors of clocks: an overhead shot of Lola running across a square (Round One) makes a circular fountain look like a clock; another overhead (Round Two), of Manni lying on the pavement after an ambulance has run over him, positions him as if his limbs were the hands of a clock.

Perhaps it's for the best that, while she stands in her room talking to Manni on the phone, Lola doesn't notice the tortoise walking past her left foot and thus misses this comic reference to Zeno's second paradox, which, as quoted "more or less in Zeno's words" in *A Newcomers Guide to the Afterlife,* reads:

Achilles must first reach the place from which the tortoise started. By that time the tortoise will have got on a little way. Achilles must then traverse that, and still the tortoise will be ahead. Achilles is always coming nearer, but he never makes up to it. (99)

Had she been aware that the tortoise gets a head start on her, she might have never have even attempted to reach Manni.

The animated running Lola of the credit sequence punches and shatters clocks one and two, but is swallowed up by clock three. But Lola's shattering of the clocks does foreshadow her developing powers as she becomes more and more aware of her situation -- that she is literally repeating, with variations, her 20-minute rounds. To this extent, *Run Lola Run* is a coming-of-age story, albeit a fast-track one, wherein Lola moves from dependence on her parents to independence, front ignorance (powerlessness) to knowledge (power) of her player status in the ganie universe. "We shall not cease from exploration," reads the film's first epigraph, from T.S. Eliot's "Little Gidding," "And the end of all our exploring/Will be to arrive where we started/And know the place for the first time." The circling back and back again to her problem's beginning allows Lola to "know the place," to understand her situation.

Two examples of how Lola learns from round to round should suffice: 1) Lola, in the animated sequence we move into on her mother's television, runs (Round One) past a dog and a punk kid hanging out on the landing; in Round Two the dog growls and the kid trips her, sending Lola sprawling down the stairs; in Round Three, Lola leaps over the growling dog and astonished kid, then growls back at the dog who whimpers in fright. 2) In Round One Lola runs parallel with then past an ambulance when it skids to a stop in front of a sheet of glass being carried across the street; running alongside the ambulance in Round Two, Lola asks the driver if he can take her, and, distracted, the driver crashes the ambulance through the glass (and shortly after this, he will run over Manni); by Round Three, a wiser Lola, when the ambulance skids to a stop in front of the glass, takes the opportunity to hop into the back, where she will take the hand of a heart attack victim and bring him back to life. (Pointing out that Lola seems to learn things from one round to the next, Tykwer said: "Logically speaking it's impossible, of course—but to secretly play down such elements is the beauty of film" [137]).

If Lola could stop time (and she can, but doesn't know it yet), she would. In her father's bank office (Round One), frustrated with his unwillingness to help her and learning that her "Papa" (Herbert Knaup) is having an affair with a woman (Nina Petri) who also works in the bank, Lola screams, shattering the clock on the wall and stopping for a moment, at least figuratively, her tormentor. Earlier she has screamed at Manni on the phone in order to shut him up, and the bottles on her TV break. But it is the third scream, in the casino at the roulette wheel, shot in a tight close-up (a visual shout), that is truly efficacious and fantastic. This time, besides shattering the drinking glasses on the sideboards and in the guests' hands, her scream is the manifestation of her immanent will which causes the ball rolling around in the wheel to rest finally on 20, the number, of course, of Lola's game—the temporal condition placed on her saving Manni's life and her bet.

The roulette wheel is another image of Lola's temporal circling. Lola herself, long before we enter the casino, seems to be in the middle of a wheel when she turns round and round as the faces of people she considers asking for the DM 100,000 appear before her, among them her father, who shakes his head "No," and an animated figure (later we'll recognize him as the live-action croupier [Klaus Müller] in the casino), who says, *"Rien ne va plus"* ("No more bets"). In one frame, Lola runs past a wall with a roulette wheel's spoke-like pattern, suggesting Lola is less player at this moment than she is the ball put into play (or is she the wheel's axis?). But the movement of a roulette ball isn't altogether circular. The ball moves clockwise to the wheel's counterclockwise motion, and the friction this creates causes it eventually to fall into the wheel's bowl. Thus, with a little opposition, a dialectical nudge, the circle becomes a spiral, and the spiral, as Vladimir Nabokov knew, "is a spiritualized circle. In the spiral form, the circle, uncoiled, unwound, has ceased to be vicious; it has been set free" (275).

III. THE DIALECTIC

I thought this up when I was a schoolboy,
and I also discovered that Hegel's triadic series
(so popular in old Russia) expressed
merely the essential spirality of all things
in their relation to time.
-Vladimir Nabokov

This dialectical shift from circle to spiral is visually represented in the sign for a nightclub, Die Spirale, that spirals (like an imploding clock) behind Manni on the corner where he phones Lola. The image is also see in the animated tunnel/spiral in the credit sequence, and in several camera movements: around Manni and Lola when they are surrounded by the police; in the 180o turn/reverse turn around Manni and the bum (Joachim Król) who has Manni's money bag; around Lola's mother (Ute Lubosch) before we enter the animate image on television of Lola running down the (spiral staircase. We even see a spiral pattern on Manni and Lola's pillows in the "transitional" between-life-and death scenes of our two characters in bed. These spirals remind us that Lola's journey is not essentially circular. Time for Lola (and for us) is not circular, but (dialectically) spiral.

On the narrative level, the tripartite structure functions as the film's fulcrum. In Round One (thesis) Lola dies; in Round Two (antithesis) Manni dies; in Round Three (synthesis) both live. In Round One Manni holds up a Bolle supermarket; in Round Two Lola holds up her father's bank; in Round Three both get lucky: Lola wins DM 100,000 at the casino and Manni recovers the DM 100,000 the bum picked up when Manni accidentally left his bag on the subway.

Other significant (and seemingly insignificant events deviate from round to round.

Lola and Papa

I: Lola's father agrees to marry his mistress, rejects Lola's plea for help, and shoves her out of the bank; II: Lola's father learns from his mistress he is not the progenitor of her pregnancy, and Lola steals the guard's gun and forces Papa at gun point to tell the bank teller (Lars Rudolph) to give her the money; III: Lola arrives at the bank too late; Papa has already left with Herr Meier (Ludger Pistor).

Lola and Herr Meier

I: Lola runs past a car leaving a driveway; distracted by Lola, the driver does not see the oncoming car containing Ronnie (Heino Ferch), the drug dealer for whom Manni made the drop and pick-up, and his two musclemen, and Ronnie's car slams into the driver's; II: Lola jumps onto and across the hood of the car leaving the driveway, distracted, the driver (we still don't know he's Herr Meier) slams into Ronnie's oncoming car; III: Lola lands on the hood of Herr Meier's car recognizes him, and he her; Herr Meier asks. *"Lola, alles in Ordinung?"* ("Lola, is everything O.K.?"), and Lola says "No," while Ronnie's car passes unharmed (for the moment —later in Round Three the two cars will be in an accident).

Lola and the bad-tempered woman
with the baby carriage

1: Lola almost runs into a bad-tempered woman (Julia Lindig) with a baby carriage, who shouts after Lola "Watch where you're going, you slut!" *("Pass doch auf, du Schlampe!");* II: Lola almost runs into bad-tempered woman with a baby carriage who shouts after Lola: "Hey! Watch out, you stupid cow!" *("Mensch! Augen auf, du blöde Kuh!")* and adds, *"Kackschlampe!"* ("Fucking bitch!"). III: Lola misses her entirely, and the bad-tempered woman just hisses after her but says nothing.

Lola and the bum

I: Lola brushes past the bum carrying Manni's drug money bag; II: Lola bumps straight into him, but again has no idea he holds the (or one) solution to he dilemma. III: Lola doesn't encounter the bum at all, because he has bought a bicycle from ...

Lola and the bicycler

I: Running parallel with a bicycler (Sebastian Schipper), Lola is offered the bike for DM 50, declines, and runs up the steps of a bridge; II: again, Lola is asked if she needs a bicycle and is offered it for DM 50, and the bicycler adds that it's "like new," but Lola says, "It's stolen!" (perhaps a true insight or she's recalling what made her miss her appointment with Manni in the first place, and thus the event that sets the dominoes of this tale tumbling: the theft of her Moped), and the bicycler pedals past her. (Lola's Moped and its thief will also be involved in the [third] accident between Herr Meier's and Ronnie's cars.); III: running onto the street to avoid the group of nuns she has in the previous rounds run through, she bumps into the bicycler, apologizes, runs on, and the biker turns off to an Imbiss kiosk where he sells the bum the bicycle, which causes Lola not to encounter him in this round, but allows Manni later to see him and chase him down.
    Like a pinball, the characters (objects) in *Run Lola Run* carom crazily from cushion to knob to flipper to (ding! ding!) post, and from round to round no character follows the exact same pattern. Each contact effects changes in all that follow (like the "run" of the stacked dominoes falling that we see on Lola's TV when she is talking to Manni on the phone in the narrative's opening), but the points of (present or absent) contact (chronologically: Lola's mother on the phone, the animated Lola and punk kid with dog, Lola and the bad-tempered woman with the baby carriage, Lola and Herr Meier, Lola and the nuns, Lola and the bicycler, Lola and the bum, Lola and the bank guard, Lola and Papa, Lola and the old woman in front of the bank she asks for the time, Lola and the ambulance, Lola and Manni) never change.
    That cause and effect (the smallest cause producing a great consequence) is definitely on Tykwer's mind is clear if we consider some of the film's rapid-fire flash forwards. "UND DANN" ("AND THEN") these sequences begin, and what follows is a series of still frames accompanied by the shutter click and whir of a still camera that reveals a minor character's

future. The three futures of the bad-tempered woman are, from round to round: 1) She becomes a social welfare case, loses her child, steals another in a park while the father is taking a piss in the bushes, and is last seen being chased by the father and two other people; 2) she buys a Lotto ticket and wins, purchases a new car, is last seen in a lounge chair beside her baby in a crib as she and her husband share a toast in the front yard of her new home; 3) she encounters a Jehovah's Witness on the street, prays in a church, her husband takes communion, and she is last seen with another woman on the street offering copies of Jehovah's Witness publications *Erwachet! (Awake)* and *Wachturm (Watchtower)*.

As chaos theory attests, the slightest variation can produce enormous changes for the characters. After Lola runs past the bicycler in Round One, his first future finds him chased and beaten up by hard rockers; then, his face still bruised and bloodied, he buys a meal in a cafeteria, is befriended by the cashier, and the two of them are last seen in their wedding clothes as they leave their wedding. In Round Two, now a bum with a beard, he begs in front of a supermarket, begs in the subway, blathers to a woman on a bench in the forest, and is last seen as a junkie passed out in a WC. In Round Three, when Lola leaves him, instead of a flash forward, the image shifts to video (this occurs whenever Lola or Manni are not in a scene), and we follow him to the Imbiss where he meets the bum with Manni's money who will buy his bicycle, which means Lola will not encounter him in Round Three, but Manni will. "Twirl follows twirl," Nabokov says, "and every synthesis is the thesis of the next series" (275). (Although I am using the term "dialectic," as does Nabokov, in a rather loose sense, a more rigorous Hegelian approach could be applied to *Run Lola Run:* the antithesis [Round Two] *does* negate the thesis [Round One], and the synthesis [Round Three] incorporates both, allowing Lola to land with a new, hard-won knowledge of her basic ontological ground, not "Being" as such but at least "Becoming," which, as Hegel said, "is the first adequate vehicle of truth" [122].)

The dialectic also generates much of the film's visual multiplicity. Tykwer's use of the split screen exemplifies *Run Lola Run's* dialectical strategy. In frame left, Manni outside the Bolle awaits Lola; in frame right, Lola runs desperately toward Manni, their faces almost touching in cinematic but not narrative space; then from bottom frame arises, up to Manni and Lola's necks, the top arc of the supermarket's clock as the second hand ticks to 12. In another split screen, we see frame left Manni foregrounded and Lola backgrounded, and frame right Lola foregrounded and Manni backgrounded—an example, one might say, of a simultaneous shot/reverse shot. The simultaneous dialectical move is also shown when Lola's image is wiped to the right while the Bolle's automatic door opens to the left.

The possibilities generated by *Run Lola Run's* dialectical drive, its oppositional play, links with the film's theme of "the possibilities of life." As Tykwer told his interviewer:

> A film about the possibilities of life, it was clear, needed to be a film about the possibilities of cinema as well. That's why there are different formats in *Run Lola Run;* there is color and black and white, slow motion and speededup motion, all elementary building blocks that have been used for ages in film history. George Méliès was already able to work with these effects, especially with double exposure and tricks ... Animation suggests: anything can happen in any given moment, and that gives the film additional power (131).

Black and white is used for Lola and Manni's memory sequences, when Lola remembers the theft of her Moped and Manni recalls how he lost the drug money. The animated moments are in the credit sequence, Lola running out of the apartment (first seen on her mother's television), and the single shot of the croupier saying *"Rien ne va plus"*. Video, as stated before, only occurs in those sequences which neither Lola nor Manni witness directly, but which fill in the narrative, for example the bum picking up the bag on the subway, Papa and his mistress in his bank office together before Lola arrives, and when the bicycler meets the bum at the kiosk.

"Run Lola Run is a movie about the possibilities of the world, of life, and of cinema," Tykwer told his crew (117). Tykwer's Indie sensibility shapes the film's formal qualities (the aesthetic rules of the game), as well as informing the film's themes: of time, determinism, and possibility. The dialectical play helps keep it all alive. And what is the life possibility driving the film's basic narrative? Well, love, of course, as in any typical Hegelian movie romance.

IV. LOVE STORY

> I shall have to say, for example, that there is
> on the one hand a multiplicity
> of successive states of consciousness,
> and on the other a unity which binds them together.
> -Henri Bergson

Lola loves Manni. That much is clear. Lola minus Manni makes no sense. Lola plus Manni is what matters. "I'm a part of you, dear," are the lyrics we hear when Lola is shot at the end of Round One; "My lonely nights are through, dear, since you said you were mine." Aren't the sentiments expressed here in part what brings Lola out of death, allowing her to begin her game again? Tykwer's "Union of the Heart" song in the film contains these lyrics: "Love is the only strain/ That lets me live through my pain." Not perhaps the most elegant rhyme, but the message is unmistakable. These two young people belong together, and Lola is ready to stretch and twist and transform the boundaries of logic to reunite with Manni.

And it is Lola, we must remember, who is the driving force here; Lola runs, whereas Manni is more often than not stationary. Lola is the player who must counteract the deterministic forces set against her winning the game. Still, these two are a pair, emotionally and visually. Thus the split frames that put them side by side and the liminal, between-life-and-death scenes that find them in bed together. There are even subtle, complex, near match-cuts of the two of them: In an overhead shot, Lola in frame left runs diagonally up left across a square in a grid pattern with a fountain (circle/clock/wheel) frame right. Cut to: a low angle shot of Manni frame left in the phone booth with its grid pattern and frame right the large spiral of the club Die Spirale. Thus, shots A/B: Lola/Manni to the left, circle/spiral to the right (circle to spiral in one stroke!). This from Round One. In Round Two, Tykwer changes the angle, but not the connection. In the overhead shot, Lola runs across the square, but the fountain is out of the frame and the square's grid is at a diagonal—Lola runs parallel with the gridline, not against it. Cut to: Manni in the phone booth shot at a low angle with the phone booth's grid in the same diagonal as the square's grid, and the spiral is out of the frame.[2]

Another dialectical conjoining of Lola and Manni occurs when Lola helps Manni rob the Bolle by knocking down the security guard. His gun slides (like a hockey puck) to Manni's feet, and Manni shuffles it back to Lola. In the transitional universe we slip into after each lover "dies," Manni and Lola are lying side by side. We see them only from their shoulders up lying on their pillows with their spiral patterns. After Lola's "death," she lies on Manni's arm; after Manni's "death," he lies on Lola's arm.

Lola's passion (it's never overtly a sexual passion, but one of love) and the film's manifest themselves, as I've already suggested, in the narrative and the multiplicity of cinematic techniques (animation, video, black and white, jump cuts, slow motion, rapid and sometimes collisive montage, Lola running in one direction dissolving into Lola running in another direction), but one could say the key emblem for this mercurial, exhilarating film's passion is the color red. Lola's phone is red and so is the bag with money. A red ambulance runs over Manni. A red light is foregrounded, a red car passes by. Red arrows on a wall point Lola in the direction she's running. The Bolle sign is red. Fades to red occur when Lola and Manni, respectively, die and enter a liminal zone shot with a red filter. And, of course, Lola's hair is red. A bright, dyed red, the film's visual lifeblood threading its way through this 24-frames-per-second labyrinth. "I wish I were a heartbeat/That never comes to rest," sings the voice of Franka Potente (Lola) during Lola's third and, at last, successful run.

At the end of the second round, when Lola appears before Manni can rob the supermarket, Manni looks lovingly at her, crosses the street, and gets run over by the ambulance. These two lovers only have eyes for each other. One would think that this would have been enough to keep at bay the critics who saw in the film's stylistic display and speed an anti-humanistic element. Janet Maslin, in her *New York Times* review (March 26, 1999), after praising the film as "playfully profound," continued her "praise" by calling *Run Lola Run* "post-human"—hardly an accurate term for the human moments evident in the desires and dilemmas of the characters (all the characters) and the director's aesthetic (humanistic) vision. Which is not to say that *Run Lola Run* is a realistic, in-depth, psychological character study; fairy tales never are.

V. FAIRY TALE

> Play only becomes possible, thinkable
> and understandable when an influx of mind
> breaks down the absolute determinism
> of the cosmos.
> -Johan Huizinga

For what is *Run Lola Run* if not a fairy tale, albeit of the self-conscious, philosophical variety. The film itself is clearly aware of its fairy tale status. Its tripartite structure is the same structural (and magical) three that underlies so many traditional fairy tales. In her "Wish" song, Lola sings "I wish I were a princess/With armies at her hand/I wish I were a ruler/Who'd make them understand." Lola is our princess and Manni our prince, though the genders, as is appropriate for the late 1990s (in the sense that the princess must save the prince), are reversed. True, these two are not your usual figures of royalty, but then neither at first were *Aschenbrödel* and *Schneewittchen* (Cinderella and Snow White). Lola's father isn't a stand-up papa (and possibly, according to what he tells her in Round One, he isn't even her real father), and her mother's an astrologically fixated drunk. But the bank guard Schuster recognizes on some level Lola's "royalty": in Round One he calls her the "house princess" (*"Holla, holla, Lolalola, die Hausprinzessin"*) and in Round Two he lectures her on the virtues of queens. It is their third encounter that reveals the film's deeper fairy tale status.

Lola, having just missed her father, stands in front of the entrance of the bank, shouting *"Scheisse, Scheisse!"* ("Shit, shit!") when Schuster, his fairy tale role as doorkeeper now altered, steps outside for a smoke break. "So you made it at last, darling," he says (*"Da bist du ja endlich, Schatz"*), which Lola finds not at all amusing. Schuster himself seems surprised by what he says. Something isn't right here. Lola's gaze rivets him. Does he recognize that this is the third time Lola has come to the bank, that somehow his world has been split three-ways? Do he and Lola realize that it's she who's controlling the game? How has he become a part of Lola's game of repetition with variations? Or is it possible that he recalls, if only faintly, his role in the film's prologue as the kicker of the soccer ball, the one who puts the (non-diegetic) ball into play? And if so, what are the ontological consequences of his recognition? Lola runs on, but Schuster stands still, and we hear the loud pounding of his heart.

Does Lola possess the power to affect the heart rate of the characters in her game? Certainly from run to run she has gained in knowledge and power. No need in this final round to ask the old woman for the time (she's not even in this round); instead, Lola enters the casino and twice wills the ball (the second time with the help of her scream) to land on 20. Then she climbs into the back of the ambulance and there on the stretcher is Schuster having his heart massaged, but to no effect. "What do you want here?" the attendant asks, and Lola says, "I belong to him" (*"Ich gehör zu ihm"*). Then she holds his hand and brings his heart beat back to normal.

No question now that we're headed for a fairy tale happy ending. Lola has the money to save Manni, and Manni, as it turns out, has found his missing money (with the help of the fairy tale-like blind woman outside the phone booth whose "gaze" he follows and sees the bum passing by on a bicycle) and returned it to Ronnie. As they hold hands, Manni asks Lola what's in the bag. Lola smiles. The End. But we should note the film's final dialectical move: ENDE enters front frame right and the credits roll from top down.

Life, *Run Lola Run* implies, is like a game of roulette; the player is not the spinner; nonetheless, the player can affect the outcome. Or as Tykwer puts it: "The world is a stack of domino stones, and we are one of them ... On the other hand, the most important statement is the end: Not everything is predetermined" (117).

Finally, fairy tales begin *"Es war einmal,"* "Once upon a time," and this omniscient point of view is echoed in *Run Lola Run*'s opening. What is the world of the film's prologue? Not exactly a diegetic one; more the open ground before the actual story begins, when a voice speaks to us, not the author, but a storyteller outside the limitations of time. Characters mill around and from them the camera selects those who will be in the game. And as it does, a voice says:

Man, probably the most enigmatic species on our planet. A mystery of open questions. Who are we? Where do we come from? Where are we going'? How do we know what we believe we know? Why do we believe anything? Innumerable questions searching for an answer, an answer that will generate a new question, and the next answer the next question, and on, and so on. But in the end, isn't it always same question, and always the same answer?

Hans Paetsch, the actor who delivers this voiceover "was God" for Tykwer as a child, "because he always knew everything. *Run Lola Run* is a game in which we claim the power, so to speak, to change bits and piece and to influence fate as well. Something that usually only gods can do. Hans Paetsch, with his soft, warm voice, brings irony into the construct and in this way expresses that *Run Lola Run* is a fairy tale as well (130). German viewers of all ages recognize in Paetsch's voice the omniscient narrator of fairy tale With this reflexive gesture ("influx of mind"), Tykwer begins his film's philosophical project of disrupting determinism, and for the next 81 minutes, like Lola, we, too, if we work at it, can become the player rather than the played.

Notes

I wish to thank Susan Bernofsky for her comments on this essay and Annette Wiesner for her suggestions, insights, and close readings, which made my work not only better but possible.

1. Throughout this essay I rely on the original German of the film, at times complemented by the shooting script. Credit for the translations, with minor emendations by me, is due to Annette Wiesner.
2. Annette Wiesner connected these four shots for me.

Works Cited

Dawson, Jan. *Wim Wenders*. Tr. Carla Wartenberg. New York: Zoetrope, 1976.
Heigel, G.W.F. *Hegel: The Essential Writings*. Ed. Frederick G. Weiss. New York: Harper & Row, 1974.
Kolker, Robert Phillip and Peter Beicken. *The Films of Wim Wenders: Cinema as Vision and Desire*. Cambridge, MA: Cambridge University University Press. 1993.
Nabokov, Vladimir. *Speak, Memory: An Autobiography Revisted*. New York: Putman. 1966.
Quinn, Daniel and Tom Whalen. *A Newcomer's Guide to the Afterlife: On the Other Side Known Commonly as "The Little Book."* New York: Bantam. 1997.
Tywkwer, Tom. *Lola rennt*. Ed. Michael Töteberg, Hamburg: Rowohlt. 1998.

LOS ANGELES TIMES, 6/18/99, Calendar/p. 2, Kenneth Turan

"Run Lola Run" is the message, but flame-haired Lola hardly needs the encouragement. Tireless, unstoppable, fueled by the energy of desperation, Lola flies through the streets of Berlin, dodging cars, parting columns of nuns, always moving, moving, moving.

Not only does Lola run, she takes this hyperkinctic pop culture firecracker of a film with her. Writer-director Tom Tykwer's restless, inventive work, the most energetic from Germany in recent years, is about the playful inventiveness inherent in the medium itself. Cinema is a contest without rules, a place where anything can happen, and if you don't believe it, just keep watching.

Tykwer not only wrote and directed, he also (with Johnny Klimek and Reinhold Hell) did the hypnotic, insistent techno-pop music that drives everything before it. As essential in its own way as Anton Karas' celebrated zither work was to "The Third Man," "Lola's" music is perfectly suited to the film's aims and just about addictive in its throbbing, insinuating rhythms.

Before all that running begins, Tykwer provides a brief prologue and a statement of cinematic philosophy couched in a homily about soccer: "The ball is round, the game lasts 90 minutes, all the rest is pure theory." Someone shouts, "Here we go," the ball is kicked, and everything begins.

It starts with a phone call, from desperate small-time operator Manni (Moritz Bleibtreu) to his girlfriend Lola (Franka Potente). "Help me, Lola," he screams from a public phone booth. "I don't know what to do.

Usually Lola picks Manni up after his quasi-legal transactions, but unavoidable circumtances made her late this time. Manni panicked, took the subway and ended up leaving a plastic bag filled with 100,000 marks on the train where an addled homeless man soon walked off with it.

In 20 minutes, Manni's unforgiving boss Ronnie, who has abbreviated lives for less, will show up and have to be told that the money is gone. So unless Lola can show up in 20 with the cash, Manni will be history. "Love can do anything," Lola determinedly proclaims, and sets out on a dead run across the city to round up the money and save her hysterical beau.

Lola's first thought is to reach her banker father, but this is always a movie where the journey is more important than the destination. Dressed for speed in pale green pants and a light blue top, Lola has a confident, all-out stride (actress Potente, surprisingly, is said not to be a runner off-screen) and it is exhilarating to watch her on the move.

Lola's journey puts her in contact with physical obstacles like cars and people whose path she happens to cross. And just because it's a jazzy thing to do, whenever Lola runs into anyone, filmmaker Tykwer edits in a quick and amusing flash-forward to that person's future life, added at no extra charge.

While "Run Lola Run" is in part a "High Noon" with a raffish punk attitude, given that Lola's 20-minute journey is shot in real time, it's to be expected that when that time is up this film still has any number of surprises to reveal.

Among the games that "Lola" plays is a kind of reshuffling of the deck of chance, showing how even the slightest change in small things can have a broad impact on what really matters. If that sounds murky, the film itself couldn't be clearer in its effects.

Fortunately for a picture that lives entirely on the surface, filmmaker Tykwer proves to be as tireless in terms of invention as his heroine is pounding the streets of Berlin. Working with cinematographer Frank Griebe and editor Mathilde Bonnefoy, he mixes up angles and cuts with aplomb, even turning Lola into an animated character when it suits him.

Lola and Manni can finally be understood as no more than pieces in a game. So it's impressive how great an air of urgency and involvement this film creates around them, and how thoroughly entertaining it is into the bargain.

Cleverness is "Run Lola Run's" greatest asset and extends even to the film's closing credits, which crawl onto the screen from the bottom to the top. While that's happening, the huge word "ENDE" edges slowly on the screen and off. Like the rest of this always lively film, we hate to see it go.

NEW YORK, 6/21/99, p. 60, Peter Rainer

Franka Potente, the star of *Run Lola Run*, has the lean-machine look of a champion sprinter. Pumping her arms and legs as she races around the city, the orange-punk-haired Lola is like a new-style industrial-age automaton: She's a sexy speedster. The 34-year-old German director Tom Tykwer has made a movie that really zips along; it offers some of the same pleasures as the silent slapstick comedies, particularly the Keaton films, with their sense of how sheer velocity carries its own wit. Tykwer, whose third film this is, belongs to a new generation of moviemakers who see the cinema as a species of techno romp—as the playing field on which to try out all sorts of conjunctions with video games and animation and computer graphics (all of which Tykwer utilizes in this film). He's interested in seeing how close he can come to making a movie with real people in real locations and yet have it all look like a great big cyber frolic.

His compositional eye and his pacing have a pared-down, lickety-split excitement; we always seem to be looking at precisely what we need to see and not a millimeter more. I am not, as a rule, a big fan of this movie-as-big-screen-computer-game trend; too often the filmmakers would rather dispense altogether with mere mortals, and the scenarios, as in, most recently, *The Matrix,* are thuddingly hocus-pocus-y. But Tykwer, along with his spiffy graphic sense, has an affinity for people. He knows what's really important here: the classic romance of a woman racing to rescue her man. It's what keeps everything winging along and on track. Tykwer has given the oldest story in the book a new cover.

The film recaps the same plot in three alternate ways. Lola's boyfriend, Manni (Moritz Bleibtreu), a low-level courier for a crime boss, accidentally loses his cash delivery of 100,000 marks and needs to make up the loss in twenty minutes or he's kaput. Lola, whose moped has just been stolen, darts into action, whooshing like an Olympian past a phalanx of nuns, an aggravated mother with a baby carriage, a pesky bicyclist; she snarls traffic, almost gets herself run over, and, each time we see this story played out, ends up in her father's bank office imploring him for the cash—which only leads to more sprinting and screeching. The story lines all end differently, but they link up with one another; when one twenty-minute spree closes out, it restarts—the rapid-fire turnover suggests the addictive rhythms of a video-game junkie.

Tykwer is a playful maniac. Although he opens the film with a quote from T. S. Elliot's "Little Gidding," he's not really hunting big game here. (I am nevertheless fully, if reluctantly, prepared for all the gassy critical exegeses about space-time and all that jazz this film will provoke.) What Tykwer is really after is the rush you get when you connect a primal, direct-action story to a love of speed. He knows how deliriously exciting it can be just to watch someone running; he's captivated by the moods and energies you can create by accelerating a maneuver, a gesture—or slowing it down. Interspersed with Lola's zigzag swiftness are moments when the action shifts into trancelike tableaux. In one horrifyingly comic scene, Lola's glass-shattering shriek transfixes an entire roomful of gamblers in a casino. She's like a human stun gun. But in the same scene, we're also—literally—placed behind the spinning white ball in a roulette wheel. Tykwer just can't keep away from speed, and he gets in real close.

He gets way up too: When Lola slants across a city square, he shoots from a dizzyingly elevated angle that brings out the Mondrian-like geometry in the terrain. This, we are made to feel, is how patterned the world looks if you get high enough. And yet even here, microscopic as she is, Lola remains central. Her smallness only emphasizes her pumping zeal, her ardor. Up close or miles away, she's still a heroine in love.

NEW YORK POST, 3/26/99, p. 62, Thelma Adams

What's a girl to do? Her boyfriend's lost a bag of mob cash, and if she doesn't come up with 100,000 marks in 20 minutes, she literally buries the relationship.

The answer? "Run Lola Run," German writer-director Tom Twyker's breathless post-MTV comedy that gives Lola (Franka Potente) three chances to trump fate and save her man.

Structured in three vignettes, the film is hard-wired to Potente's wiry energy. She's a punk Pippi Longstocking, her flame-dyed hair streaking behind her like Nike's wings.

We're energized just watching Lola course through Berlin at breakneck speeds, tumbling into her banker father's adulterous soap opera, sprinting past a flock of nuns, clipping the homeless bum who just happens to have the bag of cash Manni (Moritz Bleibtreu) accidentally left on the subway.

As Lola runs she changes the fate of those around her in minidramas presented like acid flash-forwards, quick-cut commercials.

What begins as fast and furious fun in the first 25 minutes catches its breath in the second lap. By the third, "Run Lola Run" runs out of track. It begins to feel like an omnibus film with three competing shorts in search of a false happy ending. But, before the novelty wears off, Potente muscles her way into our consciousness, a spunky, spiky romantic presence for whom we're willing to go the extra mile.

NEW YORK POST, 6/18/99, p. 56, Jonathan Foreman

Fast, smart and fun, "Run Lola Run" is Germany's remarkably cool answer to "Go" and "Lock, Stock & Two Smoking Barrels." It's not quite as funny as the Anglo-Saxon youth flicks—and it overdoes the MTV-influenced running, jumping, slow-mo, freeze-frame camera work—but it's charged with the same infectious, high-spirited energy.

In the fashion of "Sliding Doors" and "Twice in a Lifetime," this comedy-thriller explores notions of destiny and contingency by showing three variations on a story, which begins the same way but ends differently because of a single (tiny) changed circumstance.

In all three episodes, Lola (Franka Potente) is a spoiled, punky, rich kid with a junior-drug-dealer boyfriend named Manni (Moritz Blelbtreu).

One day he calls her, hysterical, from a phone booth. Because she didn't pick him up by moped, he had to take the subway back from a major deal. When some inspectors came into the car he jumped out, forgetting a bag of cash, which was promptly stolen by a bum.

Now, if he can't produce $60,000 in 20 minutes, his vicious boss will kill him.

Lola tells Manni not to panic. Manni says he'll rob a store at gunpoint in 20 minutes unless Lola can somehow come up with a solution. She runs out of the family apartment and races through the streets of Berlin to her banker father's office, hoping he'll give her the cash.

Along the way she collides with or avoids a series of people, and as she does, you see a rapid montage of slides of the rest of their lives. Finally she hooks up with Manni and, at least in the first version of the story, the result is tragic.

There are times when "Run Lola Run" seems like a long and expensive video for a (derivative) techno song: The electronic drums pulse and boom away as we see Lola running from the front, from behind, from the sidewalk and from above.

Bits of the story are told in animation, on a split screen and with footage shot on videotape. Some of the technical and story gimmicks become a little tiresome, especially Lola's glass-shattering scream.

But the superb editing and Franka Potente's oddly seductive screen charisma ensure that Lola keeps your attention for the whole breathless ride.

NEWSDAY, 6/18/99, Part II/p. B6, Gene Seymour

Cult phenomenon in Germany, "Run Lola Run" deserves to ring as many cash registers on these shores as any big-concept Hollywood thrill ride. It is a vibrant kinetic-energy device powered by toontown aesthetics, high-tech rock, metaphysics and the churning legs of Franka Potente, whose magnetic presence alone keeps you riveted to the screen.

As the tangerine-haired title character, Potente spends most of her time dashing frantically through the prenoon pall of a premillennial Berlin, a city unaware that she's trying to prevent her dim-bulb boyfriend, Manni (Moritz Bleibtreu), from self-destructively shattering the calm.

It seems that Manni, courier for a vicious drug dealer, has left a bag filled with 100,000 deutsche marks on a subway train at 11:30 in the morning. Within minutes, he's on the phone with Lola, blaming her for "being late" and thus discombobulating his fluffy brain. Manni swears that if he doesn't have the money back by noon, he will rob a nearby grocery store. Lola tells him not to do anything (else) stupid until she gets there.

Aaaaaand she's off in blue tank top and chartreuse jeans, she dashes through and around by-standers whose destinies are chronicled in amusing flash-shots before rejoining Lola on her quest. Her first stop is the office of her bank-executive father (Herbert Knaup), who's in the throes of his own life-changing situation. He turns her down. She presses on, hooks up with Manni. It all ends badly.

Or does it? The story goes into rewind to the point when Lola gets off the phone with Manni. She's off again, bumping into the same people (who are given different destinies this time around). The whole thing runs through a different, no less perilous course, ending badly yet again.

And then ... we're back in Lola's apartment, and she begins running the same gauntlet again. Guess we're going to keep on doing this until somebody gets it right.

All this plays a lot hipper and smarter than it sounds. Writer-director Tom Tykwer, gleefully borrowing from the books of Godard, Kieslowski and Tex Avery, flosses and glosses this time-shifting wonderland with philosophical inquiries on the ways in which everything, no matter how small, is affected by everything, no matter how inconsequential.

You don't really have much time to think too much about this stuff until after you've been through the maelstrom. And it's more likely that "Run Lola Run," like other great chase movies, isn't really "about" anything except its own mad-real dynamism. Still, isn't it nice, for once, to have a thrill ride in the dark that gives you something to pleasantly argue about when it's over?

SIGHT AND SOUND, 11/99, p. 52, Richard Falcon

Berlin, 11.40 am. Young tearaway Lola receives a phone call from her petty-criminal boyfriend Manni. He has botched a diamond-smuggling job for homicidal gangster Ronnie, and left DM

100,000 on a subway train where it was picked up by a tramp. If Lola doesn't get to him by 12 pm with a replacement sum, Ronnie will kill him. Lola runs to Manni and three contrasting narrative timelines follow.

In the first Lola sprints to the bank where her father is a director, only to interrupt her father's colleague and mistress Jutta Hansen's revelation that she is pregnant. The father turns on Lola, declares that she is not his daughter and throws her out. Lola runs to the phone box just in time to see Manni conducting an armed robbery at a nearby store. When she helps him, she is shot dead by the police.

In the second timeline Lola is tripped by a thug in the hallway. She arrives at the bank after Jutta has told her father that the baby isn't his. Lola robs the bank at gunpoint and escapes. As she arrives in time to prevent Manni from robbing the store, he is run over by a truck.

In the last timeline Lola runs to the bank but this time fails to cause a road accident which in the previous scenarios had prevented her father's colleague Meier from reaching the bank. She misses her father and he and Meier are involved in a road accident caused by Manni chasing the tramp. Lola gambles at a casino and wins the DM 100,000. Meanwhile, Manni has recovered the money and given it to Ronnie. Lola and Manni are reunited.

Tom Tykwer's supercharged, exhilaratingly hyperactive movie had audiences in Germany and the US cheering at the screen. Emphasising emotional insecurity and cinematic style as did his earlier work, *Run Lola Run* sets new standards for the cinema of hysteria. It opens with a stylish sequence picking faces out of a crowd which later coalesce to form the title, and which—ironically—looks like a television commercial for insurance or financial services (heroine Lola runs each time to a bank). The voiceover suggests a copywriter's search for the meaning of life ("Who are we? Why do we believe?") but also offers us the answer courtesy of a comically gnomic quotation by Sepp Herberger, the legendary football coach who took, Germany to victory in the 1954 World Cup: "The ball is round, the game lasts 90 minutes ... everything else is theory."

Chaos theory in particular seems to be Tykwer's concern here, for the course of each of Lola's attempts to save her boyfriend Manni is determined by incidental micro-events—whether she is tripped on the stairs, if she causes a man to crash his car, and so on. But there is little of the romantic-comedy irony of *Groundhog Day*'s repetitions or *Sliding Doors'* mirrored stories in the crisis that turns into three dramas for Lola. Nor is there an unwavering commitment to the existential crime-plot take on fate and chance that runs from Kubrick's *The Killing* (1956) to Tarantino. So many things have gone wrong by the time Lola receives her phone—call the theft of her moped, a taxi driver taking her to the wrong address in the east—that chaos seems the norm rather than a flaw in a masterplan. The only response is screaming, which Lola duly does, shattering glass like the dwarf Oskar Matzerath in *The Tin Drum* (1979), the benchmark German 'breakthrough film'.

With each repetition of Lola's itinerary we become more familiar with the elements of her environment, as with the levels of a computer game (the film uses a variety of mixed media—animation, video, 35mm stock as well as time lapse effects and all manner of editing trickery). When Lola dies, she begins her quest afresh. And when she succeeds at the end, we feel, irrationally, that she has earned this for her exertions over the three mutually exclusive stories, none of which is more real than any other. This meticulous representation of chaos is clearest in the asides in which the lifelines of incidental characters flash by in seconds. The extreme alternatives here include car crashes, child kidnapping, unforeseen meetings leading to marriage or sadomasochistic relationships, lottery wins and more. On one level this is slapstick (Tykwer cannot resist showing us the ambulance crashing through the plate glass it narrowly avoided, the first time around). But it is also the logic of interactive DVD and of gamesplaying where each decision has potentially disastrous but never mundane results.

With a Hollywood remake likely, *Lola* may, of course, be transformed into a Lara Croft-style digital heroine. What will be lost then, though, is extremely old-fashioned and precisely what makes *Run Lola Run* great: for all its Teutonic version of *cinéma du look* stylisation, pop-video aesthetics and pumping techno which keeps us breathless, we empathise with Lola, whose lover's pillow talk with Manni about love and death links the three narrative strands. That Tykwer maintains our flow of empathy while demonstrating and exploiting the potential of interactive cinema *manqué* is, in itself, an awesome achievement.

VILLAGE VOICE, 6/22/99, p. 149, J. Hoberman

Jean-Luc Godard has long been consigned to the margins of commercial cinema, but the "new wave" cinema epitomized by his 1959 *Breathless* lives on and on, sometimes in forms that are barely recognizable. Based as much on attitude as methodology, new wave movies were blatantly cinephilic and radically self-conscious—drawing attention to themselves as films not only through historicizing allusions to other movies, but through disjointed narratives, deconstructed genre references, sudden mood shifts, bizarre sight gags, and performances based on "movie acting."

Almost every film-producing nation had its '60s or '70s new wave equivalent; the Hollywood version stood Godard on his head with the seamless, reconstructed package that was *Star Wars*. Current neo-new wave filmmakers would include Wong Kar-Wai, the Olivier Assayas of *Irma Vep*, and, of course, the still-burgeoning Anglo-American tribe of Tarantinians. This week brings another variation on the formula in German filmmaker Tom Tykwer's bid for name-brand status, *Run Lola Run*.

An enjoyably glib and refreshingly terse exercise in big beat and constant motion, *Run Lola Run* hit the ground sprinting at the last Venice Film Festival. (Such was the reception that the movie's first North American showing—days later, in Toronto—occurred amid a buzzy crescendo of cell-phone static and ended with word that Sony Classics had clinched the U.S. distribution deal midscreening.) Unfolding in near real time, this third feature by the 33-year-old writer-director hotshot is a sort of power-pop variation on the mystical time-bending Euro-art movies made by the late Krzysztof Kieslowski. In this tale of three alternate futures, the eponymous Berlin punk goddess (Franka Potente) has a mere 20 minutes to raise 100,000 deutsche marks (approximately $60,000) and save the life of her gangster-wannabe boyfriend—a cute *dummkopf* named Manni (Moritz Bleibtreu) who, gofer in some sort of dope deal, managed to leave a bag full of banknotes behind him on the U-Bahn.

The doomed outlaw couple is a new wave standby, but *Run Lola Run* is far too businesslike to indulge anyone's romantic fantasy. (There is not a single musical interlude to tweak the viewer's nostalgia.) Nor is there the least hint of a class angle. That the film's heroine is a banker's daughter turns out to be mere plot contrivance. Ultimately less useful than the gift of her petulant supersonic, glass-shattering scream, Lola's provenance has scarcely more weight than the various robberies, shootings, and fatal accidents that occur in the several parallel universes.

Run Lola Run aspires to pure sensation. Whether the denouement of Tykwer's mock interactive, beat-the-clock chase is predicated on chaos theory or blind chance, Franka Potente personifies the movie's compact running time. Indeed, with her eye-catching vermilion hair, blue tank top, sherbet green dungarees, and expression of grim determination, she is a sort of all-purpose cinematic muse. Watching this virtual cartoon character dash through a nondescript residential district in summery Berlin, you can imagine her form enlivening anything from Muybridge's pre-cinematic locomotion studies to *Mad Max* to Metal Gear Solid.

Switching back and forth between 35mm and video, color and black-and-white, live action and animation, *Run Lola Run* suggests an 80-minute chunk of MTV. Still, unencumbered by the narrative weight of kindred neo-new wave style parades like *Trainspotting*, *Lock, Stock and Two Smoking Barrels*, and *Go*, *Run Lola Run* maintains its forward momentum through all manner of split screens, replays, and rapid-fire digressions.

Run Lola Run manages to be both philosophical and brainless. As its title suggests the name of the original new wave film, so this go-go abstraction feels as, inexorable as the millennium. Subtitles may keep the movie from being a hit, but given its punchy editing, pulse-pounding score, and calisthenically enriched protagonist, Lola could have a long nontheatrical afterlife in health clubs across the world as a hipster exercise video.

Also reviewed in:
CHICAGO TRIBUNE, 7/2/99, Friday/p. A, Michael Wilmington
NATION, 7/12/99, p. 34, Stuart Klawans
NEW YORK TIMES, 6/18/99, p. E10, Janet Maslin
VARIETY, 9/14-20/98, p. 36, David Rooney
WASHINGTON POST, 7/2/99, p. C1, Stephen Hunter
WASHINGTON POST, 7/2/99, Weekend/p. 39, Desson Howe

RUNAWAY BRIDE

A Paramount Pictures and Touchstone Pictures release in association with Lakeshore Entertainment of an Interscope Communications production. *Executive Producer:* Ted Tannebaum, David Madden, and Gary Lucchesi. *Producer:* Ted Field, Tom Rosenbrg, Scott Kroopf, and Robert Cort. *Director:* Garry Marshall. *Screenplay:* Josann McGibbon and Sara Parriott. *Director of Photography:* Stuart Dryburgh. *Editor:* Bruce Green. *Music:* James Newton Howard and Kathy Nelson. *Music Editor:* Jim Weidman. *Sound:* Keith A. Wester and (music) Shawn Murphy. *Sound Editor:* Robert L. Sephton. *Production Designer:* Mark Friedberg. *Art Director:* Wray Steven Graham. *Set Designer:* Thomas Minton and Charles McCarry. *Set Decorator:* Stephanie Carroll. *Costumes:* Albert Wolsky. *Make-up:* Randy Houston Mercer. *Stunt Coordinator:* Gary Combs. *Running time:* 110 minutes. *MPAA Rating:* PG.

CAST: Julia Roberts (Maggie Carpenter); Richard Gere (Howard Eisenhower "Ike" Graham); Joan Cusack (Peggy Flemming); Hector Elizondo (Fisher); Rita Wilson (Ellie); Paul Dooley (Walter Carpenter); Christopher Meloni (Bob Kelly, Coach); Donal Logue (Brian Norris, Priest); Reg Rogers (George Swilling, Bug Guy); Yul Vasquez (Gill Chavez, Dead Head); Jane Morris (Mrs. Pressman); Lisa Roberts Gillan (Elaine from Manhattan); Kathleen Marshall (Cousin Cindy); Jean Scherlier (Grandma); Tom Hines (Cory Flemming); Tom Mason (Final Wedding Pastor); Garrett Wright (Dennis, "Jailbait" Student); Sela Ward (Pretty Bar Woman); Marvin Braveman (Marvin, T-Shirt Vendor); Yvonne Pollack (T-Shirt Vendor); Joy Rosenthal (Limo Woman); John Goldman (Construction Man); Sandra Taylor (Shelby, Model); Thong Nguyen (GQ Fashion Shoot Photographer); Karen Stirgwolt (Frances, Office Worker); Lee McKenna (Mrs. Whittenmeyer); Patrick Richwood (TV Host); Marty Nadler (Traveling Salesman); Allan Kent (Lou Trout); Kevin Murray (Pete); James Richardson (Mr. Paxton); Duncan Lam (Dragged Little Boy); Julie Paris (Murphy, Reporter); Dina Napoli (Dina, Reporter); Jacqui Allen (Jacqui, Reporter); Jack Hoffman (Jack, Reporter); Cheryl Frazel (Cheryl, Reporter); Tiffany Paulsen (Tiffany, Reporter); Gregg Goulet (Church Organist); Shannon Wilcox (Luau Lady); Diana Kent (Hula Girl); Diane Frazen (Diane, Wedding Guest); Karla Pattur (Karla, Church Teacher); Linda Larkin (Gill's Girlfriend); Laurie Metcalf (Betty Trout); Larry Miller (Kevin, Bartender); Kathleen Robertson (GQ Photo Shoot Model).

CHRISTIAN SCIENCE MONITOR, 7/30/99, p. 15, David Sterritt

Hollywood loves novelty. But what it loves even better is a known quantity that's certain to prosper at the box office, especially in the summer season, when originality takes second place to air-conditioned entertainment value. This is why multiplexes keep filling with juiced-up adventure yarns like "Deep Blue Sea" and old-fashioned romantic fables like "Runaway Bride," which positively revel in the tried-and-true formulas they recycle.

Runaway Bride recycles a savvy creative team as well, uniting Julia Roberts and Richard Gere with director Garry Marshall for the first time since "Pretty Woman" became a walloping success nine years ago. Times have changed, though, and their new story has a more conservative slant. Instead of a jaded wheeler-dealer and a fun-loving prostitute, Gere and Roberts now play a jaded journalist and a fun-loving shopkeeper who take almost two hours of screen time to discover that—you guessed it they're made for each other.

Gere plays Ike Graham, a newspaper writer who needs a subject for his next column. He finds it when he hears about Maggie Carpenter, a hardware-store clerk who's become a small-time celebrity by ditching no fewer than three bridegrooms just as their weddings were about to start. Ike tells her story to his readers, meeting his deadline but losing his job when his editor (and former wife) doesn't like the column's tone.

Driving to her Maryland town, Ike tracks Maggie down to apologize—and meet her latest fiancé, a macho mountaineer who's convinced their nuptials will come off exactly as planned. Ike isn't so sure. Nor are many of Maggie's neighbors, who pass the time gossiping about her past engagements.

The screenplay for "Runaway Bride," written by Josann McGibbon and Sara Parriott, has enough love-struck speeches and cute one-liners to seem intermittently fresh and clever. Most of the writing is fairly flat, though, and moviegoers won't detect the hints of real-world class and gender tension that made "Pretty Woman" marginally interesting.

But the dramatic shortcomings of "Runaway Bride" count for little against the pretested chemistry of Roberts and Gere, backed by the supporting antics of Joan Cusack and Hector Elizondo, and the comfy atmosphere of the picture's small-town setting. "Runaway Bride" will almost certainly be a runaway hit.

Deep Blue Sea takes place in an oceanbound research facility, so it's appropriate to describe the picture with an equation: 3 great big sharks + 1 biological experiment = 3 eating machines considerably smarter than the humans they're chasing.

The heyday of movies like this was back in the 1950s, when meddling nuclear-power experts produced the giant ants of "Them!" and the of spider of "Tarantula." Considered in this context, "Deep Blue Sea" may also spring from anxieties induced by science, reflecting present-day paranoia over genetic engineering and the overweening ambitions of biotechnical corporations.

Be that as it may, the picture reflects an overweening ambition on the part of Warner Bros. to cash in on the unkillable popularity of "Jaws," still a source of Hollywood inspiration almost 25 years after its release. "Deep Blue Sea" is less inventive and amusing than Steven Spielberg's minor classic, which also plugged into the spirit of its age, casting politicians rather than scientists as its villains. The new movie packs enough surprises to keep spectators jumping in their seats, though.

Action specialist Renny Harlin directed the movie, which features gifted character actors Samuel L. Jackson and Michael Rapaport, one promising character actor LL Cool J, and a lot of high-tech effects (fireballs and everything!). It's just the thing for moviegoers wanting violent adventure, split-second editing, and enough water-drenched cinematography to make "Titanic" look parched.

LOS ANGELES TIMES, 7/30/99, Calendar/p. 1, Kenneth Turan

You've got to kiss a lot of frogs, contemporary T-shirts insist, to come up with a prince, and anyone eager to see Julia Roberts kissing Richard Gere in "Runaway Bride" will also leave with a bad taste in their mouths.

Ever since "Pretty Woman" topped out as the highest-grossing film of 1990, Hollywood has been desperate to re-team co-stars Roberts and Gere with that film's genial director, Garry Marshall.

It took the combined efforts of two studios, three executive producers, four producers, three co-producers and who knows how many agents, managers, attorneys and personal assistants to make "Runaway Bride" happen, and in their fiscally sound eagerness to get it done everyone ignored how flawed and unpleasant the film's conception is. It's not that sight of the two stars in love isn't all it's supposed to be, it's that all the frog-kissing that audiences will have to do to get there takes a lot of the fun out of the proceedings.

For one thing, "Runaway Bride's" Josann McGibbon & Sara Parriott script is so muddled and contrived, raising issues only to ignore them or throw them away, you wonder why so many people embraced it.

More to the point, pleasant though it is seeing Roberts and Gere interact, the truth is neither one of them is convincingly cast, a situation Marshall's lethargic, uninspired direction doesn't improve on.

"Runaway Bride" starts off on the wrong foot by having Gere play rumpled Jimmy Breslin-type New York newspaper columnist Ike Graham. Gere is about as believable at this as Breslin would be playing an American gigolo, and the film further confuses things by trying to convince us, via numerous visual plugs that couldn't have come cheap, that this Manhattan icon, recognized on every street corner in the big town, writes not for the Times, the News, the Post or even the Village Voice but USA Today.

Desperate for a column idea, Graham does what movie newspaper men have done since time immemorial—he goes to his favorite bar and listens to a story from a talkative drunk. The man tells him about a devious woman from his hometown who has abandoned so many grooms literally at the altar that it's causing a traffic jam at the church.

A misogynist at heart, Graham writes the story with full name and particulars but without checking a single fact.   Not surprisingly he gets lots wrong and when Maggie Carpenter (Roberts), the woman in question, writes to complain, Graham is fired by his current boss and former wife (Rita Wilson).

Seething with rage and thirsting for revenge, Graham decides to visit the cheerful hamlet of Hale, Md., where Carpenter helps run the family hardware store.   There he proceeds to make her life a living hell by shadowing her every move and interviewing anyone who ever crossed her path, all in the name of some vague magazine article that is to simultaneously clear his name and besmirch hers.

While Gere's misogyny is not convincing (though having women periodically whack him with a newspaper is the film's best running gag), he is, unfortunately, all too believable in behavior that plays like a deranged stalker, not a dedicated journalist.   More of a mean-spirited jerk than non-Gere fans will find forgivable, Graham and his smirking, smug condescension give the entire first half of the movie a sour, misanthropic cast it can never fully shake.

Roberts, as she was in the more successful "Notting Hill," is in full movie-star mode, lithe, smiling and game for all kinds of physical humor, including pratfalls and the making of comically ridiculous faces.   This is all great fun, but Maggie is such a terrific person it doesn't really fit with the film's need to paint her, at least in part, as someone who has thoughtlessly ruined any number of lives.

Periodically, like a sleeper awakened from a deep repose, "Runaway Bride" tosses in an unconvincing scene purporting to show Maggie doing something dastardly like (horrors!) mildly flirting with the husband of her best friend Peggy (Joan Cusack, delightful as always). But, like the scenes dealing with Maggie's father's alcoholism and the pain caused by her family's verbal potshots, these come out of nowhere and play that way.

It's a tribute to the often misplaced quality called star power that when, in a notably arbitrary turn of events, Ike and Maggie start to took fondly at each other, we hope it works for the best instead of viewing their potential connection as a national disaster.   In a movie filled with improbable sequences, this at least is one we're happy to see, but erasing the memory of what's come before is not so easily done.

NEW YORK, 8/9/99, p. 48, Peter Rainer

Runaway Bride bears about the same relationship to a full-bodied Hollywood romantic comedy as a stick-on tattoo does to the real thing.   Its sole reason for being is the reteaming, nine years after *Pretty Woman,* of Richard Gere and Julia Roberts.   Since *Pretty Woman* was one of the most commercially successful comedies ever made in this country, it's a safe bet that the two stars, angling for a reunion, waded through unsuitable scripts for a decade before once again taking the plunge. *Runaway Bride,* with its trumped-up mechanics, isn't much of a high dive.   In Hollywood's Golden Age of romantic comedy, even stars like Cary Grant and Katharine Hepburn needed a strong story and sharp dialogue in order to shine.   But celebrity is its own reason for being now.   We're not supposed to worry if these star vehicles have any gas in their tanks.

I bring up the Golden Age because *Runaway Bride,* starting with its title, halfheartedly hearkens back to an era of romantic comedies about madcap dames and saphead grooms and big-city newspapermen and small-town crotchets and the New York skyline at dusk.   Gere plays Ike Graham, a *USA Today* columnist and part-time misogynist who, hard up for inspiration, jots down the complainings of a barfly in his favorite watering hole and turns it into his next byline.   It seems there's a woman named Maggie Carpenter (Roberts) living in rural Maryland who has left a succession of grooms at the altar; with her latest wedding a week away, she's poised to do it again.   Apparently, she dumps men for kicks.   Graham runs the column without checking it out, gets his facts wrong—he writes, for example, that Maggie is on her seventh try when it's only her fourth—and is duly fired.   By his ex-wife, no less, now his editor (Rita Wilson).   Seeking vindication, Ike—who represents the scourge of New York manners and New York journalism—descends on Maggie's little burg and gleefully insinuates himself into her life and the lives of her friends and family.   He taunts Maggie about her upcoming nuptials to the local high-school football coach (Christopher Meloni) and how she'll surely run away again.   He mocks her, whistling the theme song from *The Andy Griffith Show.*   Because he did Maggie wrong, you might expect her circle to shun Ike. But except for receiving a surprise, unwanted punk dye job at the hands of Maggie's hairstylist best friend (the always terrific Joan Cusack), Ike all but becomes the town's honorary buddy—not because these folks are starstruck hayseeds but because they're decent and forgiving people who understand that Ike is really decent, too.

Isn't it a bit late in the day to offer up the boonies as an antidote to wicked city ways? Ike may liken Maggie's hometown, with its comfy neighborliness and its barbershop quartet, to Andy Griffith's Mayberry, but the filmmakers—director Garry Marshall and screenwriters Josann McGibbon and Sara Parriott—truly view it as an oasis of good values. Marshall was the creator of such TV series as *Happy Days* and *Laverne & Shirley;* it's likely this sort of sitcom idealization has its own reality for him. But for us? The truth is, the boonies aren't really the boonies anymore; those awful city ways are everywhere. *Runaway Bride* isn't just out of step; it's out of touch.

When it first came out, *Pretty Woman,* also directed by Marshall, seemed to be out of touch, too. Except it turns out everybody still wanted to buy into that old happy-hooker-Mr. Moneybags fantasy—at least as played by Julia Roberts and Richard Gere. Roberts was peerlessly charming in that film, and Gere, with his Armani threads and his silver-fox preening, was a deluxe dreamboat. Roberts is charming again in *Runaway Bride*; I liked her a lot better here than in *Notting Hill,* where, playing a movie star—as opposed to just *being* a movie star—she looked tense and miserable. In a scene in *Runaway Bride* with Cusack, she does a wonderful impression of a duck-billed platypus, and she's so spirited that, as in *My Best Friend's Wedding,* you don't really care that this character is a wedding-wrecker. Julia Roberts creates her own aura of sympathy; she could probably play Linda Tripp in a movie and audiences would still cheer her on. She's a movie star who, at her most incandescent, doesn't appear to be aware of it; that's the essence of her down-to-earth glamour.

Gere, on the other hand, is *always* aware of his star vibes, and, although that may have worked for *Pretty Woman,* where he was basically playing a fantasy stud, it messes up the chemistry in *Runaway Bride.* Gere can't quite give himself over to Roberts because he's too infatuated with himself; he's getting high inhaling his own aura. Maggie and Ike are supposed to discover happiness with each other by being true to themselves. But who are they? The filmmakers undermine the sheer uncomplicated glossiness of these stars by trying to build emotional levels into their characters. Maggie tells Ike near the end that "you know the real me," but the real her seems just about as beguilingly vacuous as the unreal one. And the film's explanation for why she runs away all the time seems bogus, tidied up. We're supposed to think she knows all those grooms were wrong for her even though she can't articulate why, but since Maggie also seems to have had her flirtations with practically every other guy in town—from her best friend's husband to the desk clerk at Ike's hotel—mightn't there be something else going on here besides holding out for true love?

Ike finally awakens to the fact that his marriage collapsed because he never listened to his wife; so in the best pop-psych tradition, he learns to listen to Maggie. His inarticulateness masks hidden depths. He has a hankering for the literary life over journalism—he's partial to Yeats. He's also a devotee of Miles Davis, and whenever "It Never Entered My Mind" comes on the soundtrack, you feel wrenched. Introducing that deep, moody funk into this failed fluff is a miscalculation: It reminds us of a world of real feeling.

NEW YORK POST, 7/30/99, p. 49, Rod Dreher

"Runaway Bride" is a runaway bore, but there are worse ways to waste two hours on a hot summer day than hanging out with Julia Roberts and Richard Gere.

It's glossy, wan, entirely predictable and makes not the slightest bit of sense. But in its favor, the movie stands out this dreadful summer for its sweet, old-fashioned (not to say hokey) sensibility. And those two are very easy on the eyes.

Gere plays Ike Graham, a curmudgeonly columnist for USA Today. At a bar, he listens to a sad-sack tale about a woman down in Maryland who makes a habit of leaving grooms standing at the altar.

But Ike gets the story wrong. "Journalism fact No. 1: You cook your facts, you get fired," his editor says. He clears out his desk before she explains Journalism Fact No. 2: "Then the Sunday

Daily News hires you to write from Boston." So Ike goes off to Maggie's hometown to do a magazine hatchet job on her.

The movie is directed by shlocky Garry Marshall, who never met a sentimental cliche he didn't embrace, clutch tightly to his breast and run with into the end zone. The town, unsurprisingly, is cloyingly fake, even boasting public performances by a barbershop quartet. Recognizing the evil scribe when he steps into her shop, Maggie's wacky beautician pal (the always winning Joan Cusack) dyes his frosty locks all the colors of the rainbow.

Ha ha. It's that kind of movie.

Maggie is set to make her fourth trip down the aisle, this time with amiable jock Coach Bob (Christopher Meloni). But only big-city Ike can really grasp what Maggie needs—the freedom to be herself within a commitment. And only Maggie can humanize the cynical divorced loner Ike.

The script, by Josann McGibbon and Sara Parriott, forces us to take these changes on faith. What does he really see in her? Why does she warm so quickly and so intimately to him? Because the plot demands it, that's why.

The reunion of the "Pretty Woman" duo guarantees an automatic audience. But the spectacular chemistry that launched Roberts' career nine years ago is hard to find here. Chronically stiff Gere is more animated than usual, and Roberts is her usual sparkling self. But after almost a decade, we've gotten used to her face.

"Pretty Woman's" success was all about the pleasure of watching a star being born. When that star signs on for material this ersatz and undemanding, it's all about a paycheck.

NEWSDAY, 7/30/99, Part II/p. B3, John Anderson

In the original "Frankenstein," the monster—the product of corrupted intelligence and misguided values—is last seen adrift on an iceberg. Doomed. Cold. Forsaken. And incapable, finally, of perpetrating any more damage on the world that created him.

While we certainly wouldn't want anyone to construe anything literal out of this, the idea of creatures floating away on lonely icebergs just sort of popped into our head during "Runaway Bride," the latest by arch-cynic/sentimentalist Garry Marshall, whose continuing career as a film director is a testament to H.L. Mencken's timeless observation about the profits to be made in underestimating the intelligence of the American people.

You have to give him one thing: He rips himself off as much as anyone else in reuniting Julia Roberts and Richard Gere and re-creating the "magic" of his 1990 hit "Pretty Woman," the world's most successful prostitution comedy.

But he's refined a few techniques since then. How better to sacrifice substance for sappiness. How best to mine the Freudian fantasies of adolescent female audiences. (Consider the opening scene alone: Julia Roberts. In a wedding dress. On horseback. Pleeeeaase.) And, apparently, how to divest oneself of any sense of guilt in condescending so thoroughly to the lowest common denominator. By the way, if you see the film? That's not a lump in your throat. It's lunch.

In keeping with current trends, the movie's indulgence in product placement is shameless—totally in keeping with Marshall's ethos, but shameless—including a torrent of plugs for the newspaper where Manhattanite columnist Ike Graham (Gere) works. A national publication—whose presence in New York is invisible unless you happen to be staying at a chain hotel and it arrives free with breakfast—it's read everywhere by everyone in "Runaway Bride." That is, until Ike pulls a Mike Barnicle and writes a story about the altar-fleeing Maggie Carpenter (Roberts) that's so full of holes even his editor/ex-wife Ellie (Rita Wilson) has no choice but to can him.

Ike's only similarity to any actual newspaper person is his column photo, which makes him look 20 years younger than he is. But he wangles a freelance magazine gig to write the "real" story about her—think of it as a 5,000-word correction—travels to her hometown somewhere in Maryland horse country, is welcomed by everyone close to the woman he's allegedly defamed and sets about falling in love.

Up to a point, Marshall is more or less ripping off "It Happened One Night" with Gere in the Clark Gable role of the reporter on the skids and Roberts doing the Claudette Colbert bit as a woman fleeing unpleasant marital prospects. In "Runaway Bride," however, Maggie has left three grooms-to-be at the altar and is currently engaged to victim No. 4, local football coach Bob

(Christopher Meloni of "Oz"). One of the real handicaps of the movie is Marshall's attitude toward Maggie's wedding record, which seems, if not psychotic, at least deeply hostile.

The reasons we eventually get for her actions—that she doesn't know herself, so how can she commit to someone else?—doesn't quite explain the caterer, the church, the family in the lurch or the choice of potential mates, one of whom turned to the priesthood after Maggie left him high and dry.

The story is preposterous, but so is the town of Hale, where Maggie works as a handywoman (that a joke?). A barbershop quartet sings seemingly round the clock, Prada-dressed triplets in three-seater strollers go tripping down the street, Ike gets to sit in on bottleneck guitar with an impromptu Main Street blues band, everyone has time for softball and lemonade, the decor hasn't changed since the Harding administration and the local beauty shop is called Curl Up and Dye (as it was in another Roberts movie, "Steel Magnolias"). Oh yes, and a local guy named Flemming has a morning radio show called "Wake Up With Flem."

It's not the bad or recycled jokes that make this a truly bad movie. Nor is it the Roberts performance, which consists of her serious look, her happy look and her occasional explosive laugh. Or the fact that Gere is sleepwalking and no one thinks to wake him up. It's Marshall's crystal-clear assumption that's he's put something over on us. And he probably has.

NEWSWEEK, 8/9/99, p. 68, David Ansen

The problem with "Runaway Bride" isn't the radiant Julia Roberts, whose star wattage has rarely burned so brightly. The problem isn't Richard Gere, who is loose, self-effacing and unusually charming. No one, certainly, can deny chemistry: almost 10 years after "Pretty Woman," it's still volatile and plain to see. So why does "Runaway Bride" feel *so off?* Why does it produce such halfhearted laughter?

This is the sort of Hollywood tale in which everything seems to have been decided by committee. Roberts is Maggie, a superskittish small-town girl who has abandoned three prospective grooms at the altar. Gere is Ike, a cynical, divorced, rather misogynistic New York reporter who comes to town to write about her on the eve of her fourth wedding, to a local gym teacher (Christopher Meloni). He wants vindication: his first piece on this runaway bride, riddled with untruths, cost him his job at USA Today. Maggie, who runs a hardware store (and of course, designs trendy industrial lamps on the side!), wants retribution herself for his slanderous column. One guess who turns out to be groom No. 4.

Director Garry Marshall's romantic comedy has the earmarks of a project that has been fussed over by too many hands for too many years. (Beware any movie that lists 11 producers.) It's not just that the movie is formulaic; it's disingenuous. While it serves up platitudes about self-knowledge, it doesn't have a clue who these two damaged, and damaging, characters really are. It relies on Roberts's smile to erase all misgivings. But all the stardust in the world can't disguise the fact that this is more package than picture.

SIGHT AND SOUND, 11/99, p. 53, Stephanie Zacharek

Ike Graham, a handsome, single NYC newspaper columnist, notorious for his anti-woman screeds, writes a vicious column about Maggie Carpenter, a young Maryland woman he has heard about but never met. Maggie has left three men at the altar, high-tailing it off the premises in full wedding garb. Enraged by the column, Maggie writes a letter to the paper pointing out its inaccuracies, and Ike loses his job. He travels to Maggie's small town to discover the true story and clear his name.

There he discovers Maggie is engaged to be married once again. He falls in love with her and slowly wins her over—and on the eve of her fourth attempt at marriage, she dumps the fiancé, deciding Ike is the one she wants to wed. Since the church is already booked, she simply switches grooms. The whole town wonders if she'll really go through with it this time, and she doesn't: she gets cold feet and escapes on a Federal Express truck. Ike goes back to New York to rebuild his life, and Maggie spends their time apart finding out who she really is. Showing up at Ike's apartment, bearing her old, worn-out running shoes, Maggie reassures him that she's ready to marry him and they do.

In its mad scramble to give us romantic-comedy heroines who are intelligent, self-assured and witty, why is Hollywood setting us up with women who are simply nasty? With *Runaway Bride* Garry Marshall may think he's giving us a modern day Barbara Stanwyck in Julia Roberts' Maggie Carpenter, a young woman who can't seem to break her habit of leaving men at the altar. Her jitteriness, at the expense of the poor fellows' feelings, is clearly supposed to be a crafty little turning of the tables. Men have got away with such behaviour for centuries: why shouldn't women have their chance?

Maybe it is time we had more movies proving women can be just as deceitful and thoughtless as men are said to be. But until we have the equivalent of Stanwyck to play their heroines—or hell freezes over, whichever comes first—not even the naturally charming Roberts can quite pull it off. Marshall desperately wants us to fall in love with Maggie despite the fact she has the sensitivity of a monkey wrench. She works in a hardware store, a good excuse for her to dress in aw-shucks overalls and flannel shirts, her chestnut mane usually tucked up into a messy tousle that's more baseball than bedroom. She's a dream girl written to the specifications of every regular guy in every regular town around the world. Little wonder everyone she jilts (in addition to all the men in her small town she hasn't yet dated) remains in love with her for ever and ever.

Of course Marshall and screenwriters Sara Parriott and Josann McGibbon provide a good excuse for Maggie's shabby behaviour: she doesn't really know who she is. In the late 90s, a man who uses that excuse gets thrown out of the house; in Maggie's case, it just means she gets to keep every engagement ring she's ever received. As written, she's not even remotely complex as a character, and it's little wonder Roberts has no idea how to play her. She tries valiantly to cruise on her charisma (as she did in the similarly ill-conceived *Notting Hill*. But when she blinks her liquid-brown eyes—supposedly signalling Maggie's inner turmoil—it becomes all too clear how her previous conquests became blinkered and that we are her next victims.

Runaway Bride is loaded with shapeless characters: since it takes place in a small town, we're treated to lots of loveable loonies (including Joan Cusack as the less-beautiful best friend and the misused Laurie Metcalf as the loopy local baker). It's unfortunate that one of the blobbiest of these characters is the male lead, Ike Graham. There's no motivation for Ike to fall for Maggie: one minute she's caused him to lose his job; the next he's transfixed by that dazzling smile and proposing undying love. That's especially frustrating given that Richard Gere—who used to be a stiff, inscrutable actor—has grown softer and warmer as he's got older. Here he's supposed to play an acerbic newspaperman who's met his match, but his slow, gentle smile only makes you wonder why he doesn't hold out for better. Clumsy sexual politics and bad chemistry aside, *Runaway Bride* doesn't even have much of a story and by the last third what's there feels laboured. By the time Roberts has dumped her fourth conquest we're ready to clobber her with her own bouquet. Perhaps we should be more tolerant. She is, after all, such a tragic little thing, unable to find her way in a world full of overpowering men—and she's got that drawerful of diamonds to prove it.

TIME, 8/9/99, p. 66, Richard Schickel

Maggie (Julia Roberts) runs a small-town hardware store. But she's more famous for leaving her bridegrooms at the altar. Ike (Richard Gere) is a newspaper columnist who writes a piece exaggerating her escapist exploits in terms sexist enough to get him fired. Are these people meant for each other or what?

Sure. Especially since they are the best-looking people on display in *Runaway Bride*, a movie that takes its good-natured time explaining Maggie's curious behavior and balancing it against Ike's less obvious failures (he has an intimacy problem, naturally). That time is for the most part cheerfully spent, however, as he arrives in town hoping to witness her bolt from the altar for a fourth time.

She does. But you can guess who the (temporary) victim is this time, can't you? And maybe you can guess—this question is a little harder—why the bride keeps running away. She renounces her needs in order to fit her current man's ideal. The script by Josann McGibbon and Sara Parriott makes these jilted guys plausibly awful, so we agree with Maggie's decisions to dump them.

Why she waits until the last minute is another matter, but that's the conceit director Garry Marshall obliges us to accept and it's no more strained than the premise Roberts and Gere worked

1192   FILM REVIEW ANNUAL

so successfully for him in *Pretty Woman*. They're all good at diversionary sleight-of-hand. Roberts' tentativeness is charming; she knows what she's doing, fights it, then succumbs with sad but perky resignation. Gere puts a nice flaky edge on his incisiveness. The supporting cast, led by Joan Cusack, surrounds them with funny common sense that doesn't fully assert itself until the happy end of this deft, if disposable, movie.

VILLAGE VOICE, 8/10/99, p. 68, Amy Taubin

If the psychological explanation of love at first sight is a kind of unconscious déjà vu, that's certainly the experience of *Runaway Bride* for viewers who've waited nine years for Julia Roberts and Richard Gere to again gaze into each others' eyes and know that this only happens once in a lifetime. In the near-decade that has elapsed since *Pretty Woman*, nothing about the two stars seems to have changed except the order of their billing.

Roberts plays Maggie Carpenter, the most beautiful small-town hardware store proprietor that ever lived. Maggie's fear of commitment takes unusual form; she gets engaged to inappropriate men and then leaves them, literally, at the altar. Gere plays Ike Graham, a boozy (though not unduly bloated), cynical, divorced columnist for *USA Today,* a gig that, inexplicably, makes him recognizable to every person in America and also pays well enough for him to afford a small but well-appointed terraced apartment on Central Park West. Ike writes a column about Maggie so filled with inaccuracies that he's fired on the spot by his editor, who's also his ex-wife. The only way for him to reestablish his reputation is to write a kind of New Journalism profile of the runaway bride. But there's no story unless she runs again.

Roberts and Gere inhabit this forced premise as comfortably as a pair of old shoes—a really attractive pair of old shoes. It's a relief that Roberts, who was so frozen-faced and leaden in *Notting Hill,* is back to coltish form. Gere is not very interesting except when he's looking quizzically seductive, and maybe not even then. Under Garry Marshall's direction, the film drags along for two-thirds and then briefly stirs to life in a wedding scene that has the bridesmaids charging down the aisle. At that point the mostly middle-aged, mostly female preview audience started laughing and didn't stop until the end. That's more goodwill than I could muster for such a lame vehicle. *Runaway Bride* isn't as offensive as most studio romantic comedies—just pointless and dull.

Also reviewed in:
CHICAGO TRIBUNE, 7/30/99, Friday/p. A, Michael Wilmington
NEW REPUBLIC, 8/30/99, p. 28, Stanley Kauffmann
NEW YORK TIMES, 7/30/99, p. E25, Janet Maslin
NEW YORKER, 8/9/99, p. 82, David Denby
VARIETY, 7/26-8/1/99, p. 33, Todd McCarthy
WASHINGTON POST, 7/30/99, p. C1, Rita Kempley
WASHINGTON POST, 7/30/99, Weekend/p. 45, Desson Howe

SAME OLD SONG

An Artistic License Films release of an Arena Films/Camera One/France 2 Cinema/Vega Films/ Greenpoint production with the participation of Canal+, Cofimage 9, Sofineurope, Alia Film, Television Suisse Romande and the European Coproduction Fund production. *Producer:* Bruno Pesery. *Director:* Alain Resnais. *Screenplay (French with English subtitles):* Agnès Jaoui and Jean-Pierre Bacri. *Director of Photography:* Renato Berta. *Editor:* Hervé de Luze. *Music:* Bruno Fontaine. *Sound:* Pierre Lenoir and (music) Didier Lizé. *Production Designer:* Jacques Saulnier. *Running time:* 120 minutes. *MPAA Rating:* Not Rated.

CAST: Pierre Arditi (Claude); Sabine Azéma (Odile Lalande); Jean-Pierre Bacri (Nicolas); André Dussollier (Simon); Agnés Jaoui (Camille Lalande); Lambert Wilson (Marc Duveyrier); Jane Birkin (Jane); Jean-Paul Roussillon (Father); Nelly Borgeaud (Doctor 3); Götz Burger (Von Cholitiz); Jean-Pierre Daroussin (Young Man with Cheque); Charlotte Kady (Restaurant Customer); Jacques Mauclair (Doctor 1);   Pierre Meyrand (Café Owner);   Claire Nadeau (Female Guest); Dominique Rozan (Elderly Man); Jean-Chrétien Sibertin Blanc (Young Fired Man);   Bonnafet Tarbouriech (Doctor 2);   Françoise Bertin (Little Lady on Tour);   Robert Bouvier (Guest); Frédérique Cantrel (Female Guest); Jerôme Chappatte (Guest); Romaine de Nando (Nurse);   Nathalie Jeannet (Female Guest);   Geoffroy Thiebaut (Marc's Colleague); Wilfred Benaiche (Restaurant Waiter); Déphine Quentin (Young Woman Kissing).

LOS ANGELES TIMES, 10/15/99, Calendar/p. 14, Kevin Thomas

"Same Old Song," a romantic comedy in which several generations of popular French songs pop out of the mouths of its characters, is not the picture you would have expected from Alain Resnais, whose elliptical "Last Year at Marienbad" and intimate epic "Hiroshima Mon Amour" remain New Wave landmarks.

But in the four decades since those challenging works Resnais has gown lighter in tone and ever-more effortless in style, just as Luis Buñuel did before him in his own way. Still, who would have thought that the cerebral Resnais would have ever made a film so close in spirit to his New Wave confrere Jacques Demy's "The Umbrellas of Cherbourg"? In any event, "Same Old Song," intended as a homage to the late Dennis Potter, whose "Pennies From Heaven" this film most resembles, is a sure-fire charmer, even if the songs Resnais quotes in snatches, are by and large unfamiliar to non-French audiences.

Resnais and his writers, Agnes Jaoui and Jean-Pierre Bacri, who are also among the film's six stars, let us know we're in for something different right at the start. A Nazi commander in the Occupation receives word from Hitler to destroy Paris but after Der Fuhrer is finished the voice of Josephine Baker singing her signature "Two Loves Have I" starts coming out of his mouth. (Don't be surprised if this is the only song you recognize, even if the singers represented range from Maurice Chevalier to Sylvie Vartan and Johnny Halliday.)

In a graceful cut to the present typical of the film's easy, flowing style, we're introduced next to Camille Lalande (Jaoui), a history major and Paris tour guide who is pointing out the window of the office of that Nazi who in fact did not follow Hitler's orders.

Camille's older sister Odile (Sabine Azema) is in the process of nudging her reluctant husband, Claude (Pierre Arditi), into letting Camille's hotshot realtor boyfriend Marc (Lambert Wilson) sell them a posh penthouse. In the meantime, Nicolas (Bacri), Odile's old flame, has looked her up, having come to Paris to hunt for a job and relocate there with his family after a two-decade absence. Simon (Andre Dussollier), who works for Marc, is in Camille's tour group and strikes up an acquaintance with her once they discover they share a passion for history.

While introducing us to these six individuals and thereby setting in motion a complex set of interactions among them, Resnais maintains a largely jaunty tone. But once things get going the film gradually takes on a more melancholy tone. Camille and Nicolas prove to be severely depressed; Marc is an unscrupulous businessman who sneers at the older Simon, a dreamy writer of historical radio drama. Odile becomes increasingly unlikable, a bossy, brittle, frivolous silly woman who's about to drive away the pleasant but increasingly fed-up Claude.

Only Simon seems to be happy and content, easily shrugging off Marc's contempt for him. But he too may be developing vulnerability when he starts falling in love with Camille but keeps his feelings secret as he is so much older than she.

The way in which Bacri and Jaoui have incorporated bits and pieces of 35 songs is amusing and witty in effect while always remaining an integral part of their text. The idea is not to stop the show but to tap the emotional pull of standards to enrich the audience's identification with the six characters' ever-changing hearts. Resnais retains masterful control of this deft integration of dialogue and song.

He directs his cast to beautifully nuanced portrayals and maneuvers an ever-shifting tone flawlessly with a lyricism that becomes the film's signal accomplishment. If Resnais sends us home happy, he does so with the subtlest reminders of life's fleetingness.

NEW YORK POST, 10/15/99, p. 58, Lou Lumenick

"Same Old Song," from legendary French director Alain Resnais ("Hiroshima, Mon Amour," "Last Year at Marienbad"), is a lightweight boulevard farce about a ditzy amateur historian (Agnes Jaoui) and her suitors.

The suitors include a real-estate agent (Lambert Wilson), who swindles the heroine's sister (Sabine Azema), and his distracted assistant (Andre Doussollier), who fancies himself a radio writer.

The film is styled as a tribute to British TV writer Dennis Potter ("Pennies from Heaven," "The Singing Detective"), who had actors lip-synch to old recordings to reveal their characters' inner feelings.

But while Potter used songs well known to his audience and usually had his actors sing them all the way through, Resnais uses only brief snippets from melodramatic French ditties ranging from operetta to rock—to replace lines of dialogue.

For American audiences, the familiarity and context isn't there. It's a gimmick that slows down a complex, clever story that could use faster pacing.

Still, the performances are often hilarious, and it's hard not to smile at a movie that opens with a flashback of Nazi Gen. Dietrich von Cholitz breaking into a Josephine Baker song when Hitler orders him to destroy Paris.

NEWSDAY, 10/15/99, Part II/p. B6, Gene Seymour

"Same Old Song," Alain Resnais' award-winning homage to the late British playwright Dennis Potter, is infused with a striking autumnal glow. You feel like ordering cognac to enhance the mood. Some caviar, perhaps. On second thought, skip the caviar. It would only be redundant, given the pungent subtlety of what amounts to a laid-back musical about high-strung people.

Much like caviar, Resnais' oeuvre, including such well-known mind games as "Hiroshima Mon Amour" (1959) and "Providence" (1977), is regarded as an acquired taste that some believe is too demanding to acquire. "Same Old Song," however, might surprise these skeptics with its relatively easygoing style.

Its "message," assuming you're looking for one, is likewise fairly accessible when compared with the knotty philosophical conundrums associated with Resnais' movies. Actually, there are a couple of messages to be found here: We don't know ourselves as well as we should. Happiness is a chimera that's still worth chasing, even when it's most elusive. Realtors' promises should be carefully inspected for dry rot. Still not profound enough? You were expecting maybe structuralist politics? Never mind. What's the story here? There are these two sisters living in Paris who have little in common except annoyingly driven personalities. Odile (Sabine Azema) is confident about the solidity of her marriage and the "rightness" of her judgments. Odile (Agnes Jaoui) is so utterly absorbed in medieval French history that she doesn't notice that Simon (Andre Dussollier), a real estate agent who writes radio plays on the side, is in love with her.

Simon's slimy boss Marc (Lambert Wilson) is about to sell Odile what she's certain is her dream flat. She is also certain that Marc is just the right match for Camille, who warily, but willingly starts a relationship with him.

Meanwhile, Odile's old friend Nicolas (Jean-Pierre Bacri) hangs around the edges of this roundelay, advising Simon on what to do, confounding Odile's otherwise enigmatic husband Claude (Pierre Arditi).

Resnais heightens the absurdity of this wacky interplay by borrowing Potter's device of having his characters lip-synch pop songs at various points in the plot, either to express their emotions or offer commentary (ironic or otherwise) on the events. One may leave "Same Old Song" wishing it were more buoyant or less unresolved. The glow and the pungency make up for a lot.

SIGHT AND SOUND, 12/98, p. 54, Philip Kemp

Camille Lalande, working as a Paris tourist guide while completing her thesis, bumps into Nicolas, her sister Odile's old flame. Odile invites Nicolas to dinner, to the dismay of her husband Claude. Married to an Englishwoman, Nicolas is looking for a Paris apartment so he can bring over his family. He tries to get Odile to give his brother a job, but she's unimpressed by the young man. Seeking a luxury flat, Odile consults a smart young estate agent, Marc Duveyrier. The same agency fobs Nicolas off with Marc's employee Simon who, obsessed with Camille, follows her tours when he should be working. Marc makes an appointment to meet Odile at an apartment. She's delayed, but Camille shows up and she and Marc are instantly attracted to each other, Camille confides her happiness to Simon.

Delighted with the apartment and its superb view and ignoring Claude's misgivings, Odile and Claude move in. Simon confides his misery over Camille's affair to Nicolas who admits he still feels attracted to Odile and fears his marriage is in trouble. Camille, presenting her thesis, suffers a nervous crisis and pours out her troubles to Simon over lunch. Marc catches them together and publicly humiliates Simon. At Odile's housewarming party Simon reveals that an apartment block is to be built right in front of the flat. Odile and Camille denounce Marc for concealing this. Simon consoles Camille, while Odile tells Claude how much she needs him.

Alain Resnais' ongoing love affair with British drama last gave us *Smoking/No Smoking*, an adaptation of Alan Ayckbourn's linked pair of alterative-scenario plays, *Intimate Exchanges*. Now we have *On connaît la chanson*, billed in its production notes as "inspired by the work of Dennis Potter". But where the earlier film stuck closely to its original, capturing the Ayckbournian melancholy comedy of stifled passions, missed opportunities and misread motives—even down to setting it in a studio-bound Gallic rendition of Yorkshire—the present film bears scant relation to any of Potter's works in plot or mood. The sole link is the device, much favoured by Potter in his later plays, of having characters express their feelings by lip-synching to popular songs within an otherwise realistic narrative framework.

Even this device is put to very different use by Resnais. In a play like *Pennies from Heaven*, Potter used the bland optimism of 30s ballads (typified by the title song) to point up the contrast between his characters' aspirations and their tawdry, circumscribed existence, implying they'd be far less discontented if they'd never been fed these saccharine dreams. There's no hint of any such social comment in Resnais' film. Instead, in so far as the lipsynch trick serves any dramatic purpose at all, it's played largely for comic incongruity. The very start of the film plunges us into what looks like a scene from René Clément's *Is Paris Burning?* (1966). A Nazi general, bawled out by Hitler, opens his mouth and out come the honeyed tones of Josephine Baker singing 'J'ai deux amours'.

Not surprising, then, that *On connaît la chanson* reveals not a trace of the gnawing obsessions that fuelled Potter's work: the entrapment of the past, the link between sex and disease, the all-pervasive, disabling sense of guilt. Instead, what we get is a light, beguiling romantic comedy where the lovelorn may suffer a little, but not too much; where everyone lives in a civilised Parisian milieu; and where all the characters discuss their love lives articulately and at length. The kind of movie, in short, that French film-makers do so well—and that some of them (Eric Rohmer, for one) have done rather better. Which wouldn't matter, except that this is the director who once challenged us with the mental and emotional labyrinths of *L'Année dernière à Marienbad* (1961), *Je t'aime je t'aime* (1968) and *Providence* (1977). *Providence*, oddly enough, with its ailing writer protagonist obsessively rewriting the past, manipulating people and events from his own life into a malign fantasy of political and sexual abuse, is a far more Potterian work than the present film. Or maybe it isn't so odd, given Potter's admiration for the film's scriptwriter, David Mercer.

The lip-synching, in fact, is all that lifts this film out of a rut and recalls the audaciously experimental Resnais of old. And it's not really enough, or not at any rate for non-French audiences. The trouble is that, despite the title, most Anglophone viewers *won't* know the song. Barring a few exceptions (Piaf, Trenet, Aznavour) post-war French popular music doesn't travel, and few people will be familiar with the oeuvre of, say, Sylvie Vartan. And without that shock of recognition and incongruity—and lacking the intertextual irony that Potter intended—the device largely goes for nothing, leaving us with a comedy that's amiable enough but nothing exceptional.

VILLAGE VOICE, 10/19/99, p. 144, Jessica Winter

Best known for solemn, austere dreamscapes like *Hiroshima Mon Amour* and *Last Year at Marienbad*, Alain Resnais's latest project pays homage to Dennis Potter, who invented the postmodern musical with *The Singing Detective* and *Pennies From Heaven*. By a Brechtian twist, instead of belting out songs, Potter's characters lip-synch to '30s standards. Herbert Ross's marvelous 1981 film adaptation of *Pennies From Heaven* is suffused with a Depression-era mix of Hollywood razzle-dazzle and everyday despair; we're aware of both our distance from the glamorous dream promised by the genre and our foolish need to believe in it.

In Same Old Song, Resnais puts Potter's conceit to work in contemporary Paris. Depressive Camille thinks she loves unctuous Marc, whose diffident employee Simon adores Camille; her sister, anxious Odile, frets while her husband, bemused Claude, pursues extramarital sports. Resnais explicates these travails with snippets from famous French songs both old and recent—the tunes steal in and out of the dialogue as asides, wittily evoking the plight of the forlorn lover who unwisely switches on the radio to discover that her tangled emotions are clichés long ago set to music. What the movie lacks, though, is a sense of whimsy. The lockstep camerawork and sedate performances don't exert enough pull to lift *Same Old Song* above affectionate scholarly exercise and into the realm of reverie.

Also reviewed in:
CHICAGO TRIBUNE, 1/7/00, Friday/p. O, John Petrakis
NEW YORK TIMES, 10/15/99, p. E22, Stephen Holden
VARIETY, 11/17-23/97, p. 64, Lisa Nesselson
WASHINGTON POST, 12/10/99, Weekend/p. 45, Desson Howe

SARAGOSSA MANUSCRIPT, THE

A Kamera Film Unit production. *Director:* Wojciech Has. *Screenplay (Polish with English subtitles):* Tadeusz Kwiatkowski. *Based on the novel by:* Jan Potocki. *Director of Photography:* Mieczyslaw Jahoda. *Music:* Krzysztof Penderecki. *Production Designer:* Jerzy Skarzynski and Tadseuz Myszorek. *Running time:* 180 minutes. *MPAA Rating:* Not Rated.

CAST: Iga Cembrzynska (Princess Emina); Zbigniew Cybulski (Capt. Alphonse van Worden); Aleksander Fogiel (Spanish Nobleman); Joanna Jedryka (Princess Zibelda); Barbara Kraftowna (Camilla); Kazierz Opalinski (Hermit); Franciszek Pieczka (Pachco).

LOS ANGELES TIMES, 6/17/99, Calendar/p. 18, Kevin Thomas

For roughly the first half of its 180 minutes, "The Saragossa Manuscript" is a masterpiece of the macabre, but the second is spoiled by mounting tedium. However, any judgment of this lavish, 1965 Polish production, must ultimately be tentative, because even with good subtitles one cannot hope to keep track of one of the most convoluted plots in the history of the movies. It is being presented by Francis Ford Coppola and Martin Scorsese, who with the Grateful Dead's late Jerry Garcia rescued and restored it for preservation at the Pacific Film Archive.

Indeed, that complexity is the whole point of Jan Potocki's witty 18th century classic, brought to the screen by director Wojciech Has with breathtaking splendor. Having entertained his ailing wife with the tales of "A Thousand and One Nights," Potocki decided to write for her a Polish "Arabian Nights," in which he pushed the device of a story within a story within a story almost to infinity.

Hero Alphonse van Worden, a young captain in the Wallonian Guards of the king of Spain toward the end of the Napoleonic era, encounters on his way to Madrid two Moorish princesses while staying overnight in a deserted inn in the rugged mountains of the Sierra Morena. They tell him that as the descendant of a powerful Moorish family, he has been entrusted with several missions, but he must first be tested to prove his honor.

What follows is a series of fantastic adventures that eventually lead Worden to an encounter with a magician and a mathematician, who struggle for control of his soul. Each tells myriad stories, with characters who in turn relate their tales—all of which takes us further away from the hero and creates an added challenge for those of us who do not speak Polish.

Even so, it's easy to praise the superb acting of the huge cast, headed by a dashing, aristocratic Zbigniew Cybulski, who is barely recognizable as the same man who won international fame as the bespectacled hero of "Ashes and Diamonds." Elaborate costumes and sets and stunning photography (which captures the antique quality of Goya prints) are flawless. The deft juxtaposition of striking images of beauty and terror is the equal of anything by Ingmar Bergman, a director with whom Has has much in common, both in style and themes.

VILLAGE VOICE, 5/25/99, p. 125, J. Hoberman

The Saragossa Manuscript, directed by Wojciech Has from Jan Potocki's episodic early-19th-century novel, is part *Alice in Wonderland,* part *Arabian Nights.* This three-hour Polish super-production-shot with actual people in sumptuous wide-screen black-and-white—is a convoluted succession of stories-within-stories-within-stories,with Zbigniew Cybulski (Warsaw's answer to James Dean) playing a Spanish officer lost in the Sierra Morena and mixing it up with all manner of hermits, ghosts, gypsies, cabalists, and bandits, not to mention smiling babes with bodice-bursting cleavage.

Has's comic, macabre extravaganza, in which everything turns out to be an elaborate stage-managed sham, first blew minds at the 1966 San Francisco Film Festival, attracting a New York hippie following six years later with a brief, post-El Topo midnight run at the old Elgin theater. Somewhere along the line, Jerry Garcia signed on as the movie's biggest booster. It was evidently the print he underwrote that was shown at the 1997 New York Film Festival.

Also reviewed in:
NEW YORK TIMES, 5/21/99, p. E19, Stephen Holden

SCHOOL OF FLESH, THE

A Stratosphere Entertainment release in association with Flach Piramide International of a Fabienne Vonier presentation of an Orsans Productions/V.M.P./La Sept Cinema co-production. *Executive Producer:* Fabienne Tsai. *Producer:* Vonier. *Director:* Benoit Jacquot. *Screenplay (French with English subtitles):* Jacque Fieschi. *Based on the novel "Nikutai no Gakko" by:* Yukio Mishima. *Director of Photography:* Caroline Champetier. *Editor:* Luc Barnier. *Sound:* Jean-Claude Laureux and Brigette Taillandier. *Casting:* Frederique Moidon. *Production Designer:* Katia Wyszkop. *Running time:* 105 minutes. *MPAA Rating:* Not Rated.

CAST: Isabelle Huppert (Dominique); Vincent Martinez (Quentin); Vincent Lindon (Chris); Marthe Keller (Laurence Thorpe); Francois Berleand (Soukaz); Daniele Dubroux (Daniele); Bernard Le Coq (David Cordier); Jean-Claude Dauphin (Louis-Guy); Roxanne Mesquida (Marine Thorpe); Michelle Goddet (Quentin's Mother); Jan-Michell (Marcus).

LOS ANGELES TIMES, 2/26/99, Calendar/p. 14, Kevin Thomas

France's Isabelle Huppert has one of the most direct, penetrating gazes of anyone on the screen, and the secret of its strength is that Huppert frequently turns it inward. This is especially true in Benoit Jacquot's superb "The School of Flesh," adapted by Jacques Fieschi from the Yukio Mishima novel, that affords Huppert one of the finest roles of her career.

Huppert is perfectly cast as Dominique, a beautiful, chic, self-possessed Paris business executive for a Japanese fashion designer. She leads an elegant, financially secure existence but is honest and courageous enough to have ended her marriage to a childhood friend when she became bored with him. Dominique flourishes among the haute bourgeoisie without apology but is not about to be dictated by conventional mores.

So when she locks gazes with a handsome, half-Arab youth, Quentin (Vincent Martinez), in a pickup bar with both a gay and straight clientele she doesn't hesitate in being prepared to pay for sex. When it comes to picking a hotel, Quentin coolly says, "You choose. The rest is up to me."

Dominique, a woman you would describe as being at the full flowering of her beauty rather than as 40ish, attracts Quentin as much as he attracts her, and, not surprisingly, he tries to refuse payment. But Dominique has gotten what she wants and is prepared to take out her checkbook to hold on to it. This is new for Dominique, who clearly has decided her life needs a thrill, but refreshingly she is not naive. She may have plunged into a passionate affair with a young and impoverished man, but her eyes are wide open.

Dominique's sense of responsibility and her self-respect allow Huppert to make this woman admirable in her strength and lack of self-pity; no victim, Dominique understands that the affair may cost her more than money.

Quentin's life is as hectic as Dominique's is ordered. Although he likes to box, he has no real moneymaking skills outside sex. He is a good son to his single mother, who works the counter of an airport cafeteria, and helps support her and his younger brother. Like lots of young hustlers, he hasn't entirely come to terms with the reality of being a prostitute yet likes the quick money and rush of power over others it brings him. Still, at one point, he asks, "Aren't I entitled to a normal life, too?" In comparison to Dominique he is a romantic, and "The School of Flesh" understands the difference between passion and love, even if the distinction becomes blurred for these two characters.

A woman who can risk her heart without losing her head, Dominique is a take-charge woman who learns all she can about her new lover as she goes about discreetly clearing up his debts and moving him into her ultra-contemporary apartment. She has an urge to control, yet the only way she can hope to hold on to Quentin is to grant him as much freedom as he wants—even as he craves emotional security. The truth is, however, that Dominique and Quentin, whose passion for each other is authentic, have little in common outside the boudoir and the questions become how long will their relationship endure and how will it end. The way in which "The School of Flesh" resolves Dominique and Quentin's relationship is uncommonly mature and satisfying.

Dominique is more than willing to listen to those more knowledgeable about the demimonde than she, notably Vincent Lindon's Chris, a transvestite who encourages her involvement with Quentin, and Francois Berleand's Soukaz, a distinguished-looking middle-aged attorney. These are gay men who've fallen for Quentin too, and in their differing ways let Dominique know what she is getting into. An especially vibrant presence is Marthe Keller as Madame Thorpe, one of Dominique's key clients, a rich woman of more style than substance. Bernard Le Coq as a virile, middle-aged businessman attracted to Dominique and Roxane Mesquida as Madame Thorpe's pretty daughter (who brings to mind a young Romy Schneider) round out a flawless cast, along with Daniele Dubrouz as Dominique's hard-drinking older friend for whom romance is a thing of the past.

"The School of Flesh," a title too literal and sensational for the film itself, is a handsome work of authoritative yet understated style, responsive to mood, subtleties and nuance in exploring its especially well-drawn and intelligent lovers. In his film debut, Martinez is as sensitive and expressive as he is sexy, a leading man as romantic as his older brother Olivier Martinez, well-known for "The Horseman on the Roof" and "The Chambermaid."

But "The School of Flesh" rightly belongs to Huppert, whose illuminating portrayal of Dominique is right up there with her best work, including the title roles in "The Lacemaker" and "Madame Bovary."

NEW YORK POST, 2/26/99, p. 48, Rod Dreher

Isabelle Huppert receives an unsentimental education in director Benoit Jacquot's "The School of Flesh," easily the best new French film to show here in ages. Based on a Yukio Mishima novel, the picture is a chic, intelligent, romantic melodrama with an appreciation for the nuances and contours of adult sexuality miles beyond standard American fare.

The title is misleading, because far from being a soft-core indulgence, "The School of Flesh" is a sophisticated exploration of the conflict between lasting love and ephemeral passion, and the politics implicit in erotic desire.

Though the film is shot through with sexual tension, Jacquot wisely restrains his depictions of lovemaking, which highlights his true theme: What to do with what's left when the moment of fleshly ardor has passed.

Dominique (Huppert) is a Parisian divorcee, rich, smart and successful, who takes a walk on the wild side one night by visiting a louche bar. She and a young hustler named Quentin (Vincent Martinez) immediately lock eyes. Though he has been a kept boy for older gay men, Quentin is actually a hetero opportunist. He's soon living with sugar mama Dominique. A rich male former lover of Quentin's warns Dominique: "Watch the silver."

The differences in the lovers' ages, genders and social classes make for acute clashes, none of which are forced or overdone in Jacques Fieschi's subtle and ambiguous screenplay. Both desperate, impetuous Quentin and icy but vulnerable Dominique are in thrall to frustrated narcissism, confusing the demands of the body with needs of the soul, and a tragic notion of freedom.

What's most darkly captivating about the story is how money, more than anything else, defines the rules of attraction between these insouciant amoralists—but how certain social and psychological realities remain immutable despite the power of cash. Dominique's wealth and social position give her the freedom to buy Quentin's attentions—a provocative reversal from the standard older man/younger woman trope American filmmakers have exhausted—but her largesse can't purchase his loyalty or genuine affections. A casually shocking revelation from Madame Thorpe (Marthe Keller), a society friend, discloses the high cost and futility of compromising one's heart for the pleasures of the flesh.

The supporting cast is nonpareil, particularly Vincent Lindon as Chris, a devious cross-dresser who schemes to manipulate Dominique's affair with the rough-trade lothario. But the film belongs to the astonishing Huppert, who convey fathoms of character and infinite shades of emotion with her eyes alone. Hers is a masterfully complex and dazzlingly assured performance—one of the best we're likely to see from any actress this year—in a movie that reminds you how terrific French filmmaking can be.

NEWSDAY, 2/26/99, Part II/p. B13, John Anderson

Although the odds of it happening are about the same as getting health reform through Congress, it would be fascinating to see a "Hillary Clinton Story" starring France's Isabelle Huppert. Strength, intelligence, a certain amount of mystery. The right haircut. And enough sex appeal to get major studio financing.

Well, that may be going too far, since Huppert is over the 18-year-old hill, but it's a delirious idea. Less delirious, perhaps, but more than intoxicating is Benoit Jacquot's "The School of Flesh," which pairs the intriguing actress with a director thoroughly intrigued by women.

Jacquot, faithfully adhering to the novel by Yukio Mishima (a book never translated into English) and transporting it to present-day Paris, pursues themes that are close to his heart and intellect, themes explored also in his recent "Seventh Heaven" and "A Single Girl." Gender politics, the cult of the physical, the price of sex, the myth of contentment. It's one of Jacquot's gifts that the director seems to be discovering things at the moment he reveals them to us.

Like Mishima's book, however, it's an inversion of roles Jacquot explores here, along with the subtleties of Huppert's acting. Her character, Dominique, a publishing executive on the town with a girlfriend, makes eye contact with Quentin (Victor Martinez), the bartender at a gay club. Advised by the bar's helpful resident transvestite Chris (Vincent Lindon, most recently of "Seventh Heaven") that Quentin swings both ways and is often paid, Dominique backs off. But her fate has been sealed.

There's never any doubt that it's an ill-fated, terminal love affair, fueled strictly by sexual heat and Dominique's perverse willingness to sublimate her natural assertiveness, if not her self-respect. She pays Quentin's debts, tries to get him a job, suffers his thoughtlessness ("When I'm old you'll be dead") and weathers the endorsements of his former friends ("Count the silver").

And while Huppert's Dominique seems destined to end up like Emil Jannings in "The Blue Angel," crushed and bankrupted by bad love, Jacquot/Mishima has no intention of following such hackneyed paths (the viewer's assumptions, thwarted, are thus refreshed). But this shouldn't be surprising: The director has made a film that is virtually fetishistic in its devotion to Huppert, who occupies the frame like Joan Crawford possessed (if that's not redundant). Quentin is, and will be, an afterthought, a castoff. He serves as a conduit into a territory of Dominque's soul which, once surveyed and exploited, is sealed off like a Pharoah's tomb. "The School of Flesh," although obsessed by passion, is ultimately ruthless, even cold in its enforcement of the personal, which is where Huppert has had us all along.

VILLAGE VOICE, 3/2/99, p. 139, J. Hoberman

Looking at looking: A middle-aged filmmaker whose career dates to the tide-pool stage of the French New Wave, Benoit Jacquot has made his belated local reputation as the director of gorgeous young women searching for self-actualization through the labyrinth of contemporary Paris.

Released here over a period of 20 months, Jacquot's real-time tour de force *A Single Girl;* his suave, creepy, superbly fragmented *The Disenchanted;* and last summer's posh, fluid, *Seventh Heaven* were offbeat projects that staked their maker's claim to a mode of filmmaking that infused an out-front gamine fixation with a mixture of formal intelligence and psychological bravado. *The School of Flesh,* Jacquot's first film to have an Uptown opening, is more blatantly upscale—an elegant account of mad love and cool vengeance, adapted as a vehicle for Isabelle Huppert by one of the busiest French screenwriters, Jacques Fieschi, from a relatively obscure novel by Yukio Mishima.

The movie has been poorly received in France, perhaps because it so aggressively locates itself in the mainstream of current French cine-sophistication. Slumming at a Paris gay bar, Huppert's Dominique—a divorced clothing designer of a certain age—spots a young, perhaps Arab, hustler (newcomer Vincent Martinez) with smoldering eyes and a boxer's pushed-in face. Her long, level gaze is met by his insolent stare.

Although the kid, whose name is Quentin, may have been the central figure in Mishima's novel, the movie is shot from Dominique's perspective—or, rather, from Jacquot's own fascination with her point of view.

Self-possessed and a little dreamy, Dominique likes to watch, and so too does Jacquot's camera—although the sex that defines her relationship with Quentin takes place largely offscreen. *The School of Flesh* is at least partially a spectacle of public passion—the movie's hottest scene has the couple kissing on the street. Meanwhile, Dominique plays with Quentin as though he were a doll—keeping him, dressing him, and even getting him a modeling gig. Social class seems more a flash point than age in this affair. Dominique searches through Quentin's things, surreptitiously visits the cafeteria where his mother works. Her love is a form of curiosity, but despite her desire to know, she scarcely sees what is in front of her. Indeed, for all Dominique's jealousy, there doesn't seem to be much erotic chemistry.

Predicated as it is on Huppert's pensive, provocative blankness, the action moves a bit slowly, although, as is often the case with Jacquot, events make more sense after the movie is over. *The School of Flesh* is reactive and cerebral, but the trip that Dominique and Quentin take to Morocco has a vivid, comic-strip economy that subsequently expands in the mind. Such brevity is the soul of Jacquot's wit. The director is a master of oblique conversations and half-conscious gestures. His is a cinema of sudden swoops, evasive interruptions, eliminated transitions, and emotionally charged silences. The key exchanges are almost all set across the landscape of a restaurant table.

If *The School of Flesh* is a good deal more conventional in its scenario than *Seventh Heaven,* Jacquot nevertheless creates a perverse subtext by cross-referencing the latter film's cast. Vincent Lindon, who played *Seventh Heaven*'s confused husband opposite his own real-life wife, is here extravagantly nullified as the bar owner who may or may not have been Quentin's former lover; as another one of Dominique's potential rivals, François Berléand, the *Seventh Heaven* hypnotist who cured Lindon's wife, is no less enigmatic here in the role of Quentin's former trick. Such subterranean connections are welcome; framed with flamenco stomps and cries, the *School of Flesh* narrative tends toward an abstract, quasi-ritual quality.

Despite its inevitability, this trajectory is not without its twists (although, at barely 100 minutes and even with its ellipses, *The School of Flesh* feels overlong). Still, if there's less street energy here than in previous Jacquot films, the stasis is redeemed by the glimpses Huppert permits the director into the depths of her turbulent psyche. The movie's climactic scene and its moving coda are as emotionally complicated as anything he and she have ever done.

Also reviewed in:
CHICAGO TRIBUNE, 3/26/99, Friday/p. B, Michael Wilmington
NEW YORK TIMES, 2/26/99, p. E16, Stephen Holden
VARIETY, 6/1-7/98, p. 36, Leonard Klady

SECRET DEFENSE

An Artificial Eye release of a Pierre Grise Productions/La Sept Cinema/T & C Film/Alai Films co-production with participation of Canal Plus. *Producer:* Martine Marignac and Maurice Tinchant. *Director:* Jacque Rivette. *Screenplay (French with English subtitles):* Pascal Bonitzer, Emmanuelle Cuau, and Rivette. *Director of Photography:* William Lubtchansky. *Editor:* Nicole Lubtchansky. *Music:* Jordi Savall. *Sound:* Bernard Le Roux and Eric Vaucher. *Art Director:* Manu de Chauvigny. *Costumes:* Anne Autran. *Make-up:* Joelyne Lemery. *Running time:* 170 minutes. *MPAA Rating:* Not Rated.

CAST: Sandrine   Bonnaire   (Sylvie);   Jerzy   Radziwilowicz   (Walser);   Laure   Marsac (Veronique/Ludivine); Grégoire Colin (Paul); Françoise Fabian (Genevieve); Christine Vouilloz (Myriam);   Mark   Saporta   (Jules);   Sara   Louis   (Carole);   Hermine   Karagheuz   (The   Nurse); Bernadette Giraud (Marthe);   Patrick Le Bouar (Robert);   Micheline Herzog (Sabine).

NEW YORK POST, 11/19/99, p. 58, Jonathan Foreman

"Secret Defense" is a kind of Ironman Triathlon for cinephiles, a pretentious French film so torturously long and slow that just to getting to the end is a triumph of endurance.

Once you've put up with an agonizing hour or so of watching the main character drink vodka or look out of a train window (this activity takes up a good quarter of the movie) plus a lot of downbeat, static conversation between affectless characters, you can actually become engaged in the story—albeit in a strange, masochistic way.

It's sort of a thriller, although director Jacques Rivette deliberately makes it as flat and unthrilling as possible, ensuring that the characters respond to extreme situations with a minimum of emotion. Everything moves at a snail's pace: the camera, the actors, the story.

Sylvie (Sandrine Bonnaire) is a cancer researcher. One day her brother Paul (Gregoire Colin) turns up at her office and tells her that their father's death five years before was not an accident. He was murdered by Walser, his partner at missile-maker Pax Industries. Paul wants to kill Walser, but Sylvie makes him hand over his gun.

Paul then disappears for a few days, and then turns up in a hospital. He has more evidence of Walser's guilt. Sylvie goes to Walser's country house intending to kill him, but she shoots his secretary/mistress Veronique (Laure Marsac) by mistake.

Walser, feeling guilty about having assassinated Sylvie's father, gets rid of the body for her. When Veronique's sister Ludivine (also Laure Marsac) turns up, Walser hides her sister's death and (of course) sleeps with her.

Now both Walser and Sylvie are, as Walser says, guilty yet innocent. And when Sylvie returns to Paris she learns from her mother (Francoise Fabian) that Walser may have had a good reason to kill her father.

But there is one more death to come.

No music accompanies the action, such as it is, and the film is visually uninteresting. Rivette is intent on a kind of ascetic filmmaking that is in fact extraordinarily self-indulgent, and that is so static it's really a waste of the medium.

SIGHT AND SOUND, 10/98, p. 53, Keith Reader

Thirty-year-old research scientist Sylvie Rousseau catches her younger brother Paul trying to steal a gun from her laboratory. Paul says that he needs the gun to avenge the death of their father, killed on a train five years before, supposedly by accident. Véronique, the secretary and mistress of Walser (now the head of Sylvie and Paul's father's company), visits Sylvie in her flat. She tells Sylvie that Paul has been threatening Walser. Paul later tells Sylvie he believes Walser is their father's killer.

She takes the gun and goes to Walser's Burgundy estate, where she accidentally shoots and kills Véronique. Walser disposes of the body and offers Sylvie shelter. Paul turns up and Sylvie explains that she acted to protect him. A telephone conversation makes it plain that Walser and Sylvie's sculptress mother Geneviève were once lovers. Ludivine, Véronique's almost identical sister, comes inquiring about her, but is sidetracked and seduced by Walser. He admits to Sylvie that he killed her father, but claims he had a good reason. Geneviève eventually explains that the father caused the suicide of Sylvie's 15-year-old sister Elizabeth many years before by 'selling' her to a business acquaintance in exchange for a lucrative contract. Ludivine, Paul and Sylvie confront one another at the estate, and a slip of Sylvie's tongue reveals to Ludivine that Sylvie killed her sister. The distraught Ludivine shoots Sylvie dead with the same gun that killed Véronique.

Jacques Rivette's career stamps him above all as the modern cinema's supreme master of length. The original version of *Out 1* (1971), in which Françoise Fabian also appears, ran for more than 12 hours, and recently the longer version of *La Belle Noiseuse* is a remarkable attempt at putting the time of artistic creation on screen. By contrast, *Secret Défense*'s almost three hours seem merely long. The production notes describe it as a 'tense thriller", but the long barren shots following Sylvie nervously making her way through the streets of Paris or the Burgundy countryside are about as tense as the elastic in Robbie Coltrane's oldest pair of underpants.

The differences of epoch and texture between the film's two locations yield some striking visual effects. Sylvie's hyper-modern Parisian world—all computers, answer phones and curiously coloured fluids under intent observation in the laboratory—is set against the rural serenity of the manor house. This calm is periodically undercut by troubling baroque details, such as the painting Sylvie anxiously scrutinises (an allusion to Resnais—*L'Année dernière à Marienbad* of 1961 or even *La Vie est un roman* of 1983). Yet these contrasting settings are only backdrops for a fairly old fashioned family romance whose only sting is the revelation that Sylvie's father was motivated by corporate greed rather than the incestuous urges we might have suspected.

Hitchcock trainspotters, however, will have a field day spotting the plot parallels and allusions, obviously to *Strangers on a Train* (1951), but also to *Vertigo* (1958, two women, one killed, played by the same actress), *Psycho* (1960, the anxiously seeking sister) and *Notorious* (the nuclear-secret 'macguffin' reprised in a brief sequence that gives the film its title). The trouble is that 'macguffins' are precisely what these are: cumbersome winks in the spectator's direction which fail to strike any real intertextual spark.

The performances are as good as such lifeless direction allows them to be. Grégoire Colin is suitably manic as the avenging brother whose fevered pursuit infects his sister. Sandrine Bonnaire, playing a career woman for the first time (unless you count *Jeanne la Pucelle*, also for Rivette) is as impressive as ever if more restrained than usual, while Jerzy Radziwilowicz, best known for his work with Wajda, exudes an odious self-possession as Walser. His initial refusal to divulge his first name to Ludivine (her name suggesting a plaything of the gods) hints at an emotional frigidity, buttressed by his matter-of-fact attitude and seemingly total absence of grief after Véronique's death.

Amid this gallery of basketcases and obsessives, Françoise Fabian's dignified Geneviève is a rare exception, along with Sylvie's ex-lover Jules. Youthful looking, his repeated turning up to invite her to their old haunts is the kind of irritant familiar from a host of Rohmer films, but here—wandering in from the wrong movie, so to speak—it comes as a breath of fresh air. Rivette's first feature, *Paris nous appartient* (1960), stretched the normally laconic thriller format to the then unwonted length of 140 minutes. The best part of 40 years (and an additional half hour) later, *Secret Defense* seems to do little that the earlier film didn't do, leaving this critic at least with a feeling of *déjà vu*.

VILLAGE VOICE, 11/23/99, p. 135, J. Hoberman

At once the most classical and the most experimental of nouvelle vague directors, Jacques Rivette makes no more compromises at 70 than when he was a kid navigating the murky currents of Left Bank paranoia in *Paris Belongs to Us*. It's in the nature of Rivette films to fly beneath the radar: *Secret Défense*, like its two immediate precursors, is having its local premiere at the appropriately forbidding Anthology Film Archives.

Just shy of three hours (and thus one of the director's medium-length features), *Secret Défense* is an elegant, ascetic, and rigorous meta-thriller that updates the Greek tragedy of Electra and infuses its tale of filial revenge with the detached fatalism the young Rivette so admired in the later movies of Fritz Lang. Research scientist Sylvie (Sandrine Bonnaire) has her routine rudely disrupted when her unstable younger brother, Paul (Grégoire Colin), confronts her with evidence that their father's accidental death, five years before, may have been a murder committed by his partner, Walser.

Bonnaire's Sylvie is serious, almost severe, while Colin plays Paul with a permanent glower. The performers are wearing masks, just as they would have for Euripides, and just as is the dourly mysterious Walser (Polish actor Jerzy Radziwilowicz). The action is slow to develop until, more convinced of Paul's craziness than Walser's guilt, rational Sylvie decides to protect her brother by shooting Walser first. The heart of the movie is then a 20-minute set piece in which, having resolved to commit murder, the driven Sylvie travels by train to Walser's château. There, she pulls a gun on him but the wrong person winds up dead—with Walser himself a seemingly willing accomplice after the fact. *Secret Défense* has so far moved relentlessly in one direction. Now, although no less deliberate in its pacing, the narrative takes a surprising turn. (It's a Hitchcockian maneuver and there's an additional echo of *Psycho* when the innocent victim's sister comes looking for her.)

Secret Défense—which can be translated as "Top Secret"—is a mystery made of long takes and empty spaces in which duration and distance exert their own irrational fascination. Hermetic and somewhat opaque, this perfectly symmetrical tragedy is not for every taste. For those willing to enter the Rivette zone, however, it's a chess puzzle devised by a grand master.

Also reviewed in:
CHICAGO TRIBUNE, 10/1/99, Friday/p. N, Michael Wilmington
NEW YORK TIMES, 11/19/99, p. E20, Stephen Holden
VARIETY, 3/23-29/98, p. 88, Lisa Nesselson

SHE'S ALL THAT

A Miramax Films release of a Tapestry Films and FilmColony production. *Executive Producer:* Bob Weinstein and Harvey Weinstein. *Producer:* Peter Abrams, Robert L. Levy, and Richard N. Gladstein. *Director:* Robert Iscove. *Screenplay:* R. Lee Fleming, Jr. *Director of Photography:* Francis Kenny. *Editor:* Casey O. Rohrs. *Music:* Stewart Copeland. *Music Editor:* Michael D. Dittrick. *Choreographer:* Adam Shankman. *Sound:* Mark Weingarten and (music) Jeff Seitz. *Sound Editor:* Paul Clay. *Production Designer:* Charles Breen. *Art Director:* Gary Diamond. *Set Decorator:* Jeffrey Kushon. *Set Dresser:* Steve Whiteside. *Costumes:* Denise Wingate. *Make-up:* Felicity Bowring. *Stunt Coordinator:* Gil Combs. *Running time:* 86 minutes. *MPAA Rating:* PG-13.

CAST: Freddie Prinze, Jr. (Zack Siler); Rachel Leigh Cook (Laney Boggs); Matthew Lillard (Brock Hudson); Paul Walker (Dean Sampson); Jodi Lyn O'Keefe (Taylor Vaughan); Kevin Pollak (Wayne Boggs); Anna Paquin (Mackenzie Siler); Kieran Culkin (Simon Boggs); Elden Henson (Jesse Jackson); Usher Raymond (Campus D.J.); Kimberly "Lil'Kim" Jones (Alex); Gabrielle Union (Katie); Dulé Hill (Preston Harrison); Tamara Mello (Chandler); Clea DuVall (Misty); Tim Matheson (Harlan Siler); Debbi Morgan (Ms. Rousseau); Alexis Arquette (Mitch); Dave Buzzotta (Jeffrey Munge Rylander); Chris Owen (Derek Funkhouser Rutley); Charlie Dell (Elderly Man); Michael Milhoan (Principal Stickley); Carlos Jacott (Prom Photographer); Ashlee Levitch (Melissa); Vanessa Lee Chester (Girl #2); Patricia Charbonneau (Lois Siler); Katherine Towne (Savannah); Wendy Fowler (Harmony); Flex Alexander (Kadeem); Bob Baglia (Beatnik); Debbie Lee Carrington (Felicity); Clay Rivers (Gustave); Sara Rivas (Vampire Girl); Amon Bourne, Takbir Bashir, and Anthony Rivera (Rappers); Jarrett Lennon (Naylon); Milo Ventimiglia (Soccer Player); Kenté Scott (Sophomore Boy).

LOS ANGELES TIMES, 1/29/99, Calendar/p. 6, Kevin Thomas

[*The following review by Kevin Thomas appeared in a slightly different form in*
NEWSDAY, 1/29/99, Part II/p. B7.]

The makers of "She's All That" have taken one of the movies' oldest stories and told it with wit and perception. The result is a teen comedy that actually puts a priority on intelligence and values and spans generations in its appeal, emerging as a special delight for anyone for whom high school was something less than nirvana.

Rachael Leigh Cook's Laney Boggs is her Southern California high school's most despised nerd. She looks frumpy, is always overladen with books and is unafraid to speak her piece. By contrast, Freddie Prinze Jr.'s Zack Siler is the freely acknowledged king of the campus. He's handsome, rich, a jock and class president. His deliciously shallow girlfriend Taylor (Jodi Lyn O'Keefe), a lush beauty, is naturally queen of the campus but over spring break has had a fling with the comically self-involved Brock Hudson (Matthew Lillard), who's become a TV series personality. (He asks Taylor to stop nibbling on his bare chest for fear that her perfume might somehow rub off on him just when he's less than two hours away from "the Spelling interview.")

Stunned by Taylor's infidelity, Zack is vulnerable to a bet proposed by the treacherous Dean (Paul Walker) that he pick out a real loser and within the six weeks to the senior prom turn her into a glamour girl. In time-honored screen fantasy, all Laney has to do is to take off her unflattering glasses to reveal a beauty ill-hidden by ugly specs in the first place. It takes Zack's spunky younger sister (Anna Paquin) about five minutes to do a make-over on Laney that has her looking as radiant as Jennifer Love Hewitt.

Writer R. Lee Fleming Jr. and director Robert Iscove know how to play against the conventions of a totally predictable plot that they honor with alternating amused affection and critical disdain.

The point they make about Laney is that it doesn't matter that she's so clearly a beauty when she's unable to acknowledge it herself. A serious art student who has lost her mother to cancer, she's busy running her home for her father (Kevin Pollak) and younger brother (Kieran Culkin) while holding down a part-time job at a pizza parlor. She has little time for appearances and even less for Zack until she realizes that there's more to him than just a stereotypical high school hero. He's resisting choosing a college because his overbearing father (Tim Matheson) has his life all mapped out for him.

Zack and Laney have a potential for tremendous positive impact upon each other in building each other's self-confidence and assertiveness; they are also attracted to each other, but there's that bet, naturally unknown to Laney, hovering over them ....

"She's All That" suggests that high school never changes, with its extreme pressures to conform and its premium on appearances and popularity. It's honest enough to show that once Laney, the perennial outsider, is invited inside that the campus social arbiters and party animals swiftly confirm her suspicions that they were beneath her in the first place. (Zack sagely counters that to open yourself to what's good in life also entails the risk of having to deal with what's bad about it.) Yet the film even goes deeper to reveal that the child-like cruelty that persists in what are, after all, young adults reflects a persistent insecurity even within the most popular students. In short, "She's All That" offers unexpected depth.

It also offers a substantial number of supporting roles to notable actors as well as to its stars, who are exceptionally impressive. Cook's sense of how long to hold a pause is especially astute in so young an actress; Prinze confirms his promise as an up-and-coming star; and Lillard is once again hilarious. "She's All That" benefits from actors of the caliber of Paquin, Pollak and Debbi Morgan (as Laney's challenging art teacher) and Alexis Arquette (as a pretentious performance artist) in smaller roles.

"She's All That" is an admirable example of how to get the most out of a genre film.

NEW YORK POST, 1/29/99, p. 60, Jonathan Foreman

As high school movies go, "She's All That" doesn't hold a candle to last year's "Can't Hardly Wait," let alone the classics of the genre. It tries to be an update of "Fast Times at Ridgemont High" crossed with "Pygmalion," but while it has some funny and even original moments, it's too predictable to be "all that."

It begins on a note of unusual authenticity for this sort of formula flick, with a bunch of mostly white Southern California kids, who almost look young enough to be in high school, talking in fashionable black street argot.

Major jock, honor student and sure-fire prom king Zack (Freddie Prinze Jr.) gets dumped by his superficial girlfriend, cheerleader Taylor (Jodi Lyn O'Keefe), in favor of one of the stars of

MTV's "The Real World." Zack's response is to make a bet with his best friend, Dean (Paul Walker), that he can make any girl into a prom queen.

Dean picks Laney Boggs (Rachael Leigh Cook) because she's an obvious dork who spends all her spare time daubing paintings about Bosnia. Following the John Hughes "Pretty in Pink" formula, Laney is also the daughter of the local poolman, and therefore poorer than the cool kids.

To Zack's surprise, Laney resists even his overtures of friendship. But he is persistent, and increasingly intrigued. He even joins her at a wonderfully ridiculous performance-art session. Inevitably, her suspicions soften to the extent than when Zack invites Laney to a party at a rich friend's vast house, she allows Zack's sister, Mack, to give her a glamorous makeover.

Meanwhile, someone proposes Laney for the prom queen competition and, thanks to support from every outsider in school, the underdog candidate has a chance to beat Taylor.

"She's All That" would have worked better if it weren't so obvious that Laney is really a babe under her dork's glasses—and if she had even a bit of the shyness that inhibits high school nerds in real life. (It takes more than a makeover to make a self-conscious girl into a prom queen.)

Director Robert Iscove ensures that his capable cast has consistent comic timing. But his and their efforts are undermined by a formulaic script that piles unconvincing psychological dilemmas and self-discovery (Can Laney make her art more personal? Will Zack be able to choose from among the Ivy League schools?) on top of the froth.

SIGHT AND SOUND, 7/99, p. 52, Geoffrey Macnab

An LA high school. Zack, the most popular student in his class and strongly tipped as prom king, has just split up from his girlfriend Taylor who dumped him for minor television star Brock. In jest, he bets his friend Dean he could make any girl he wanted prom queen. Dean can pick the girl. Into their sight walks Laney Boggs, a diffident, short-sighted misfit specialising in art. Zack is from a wealthy background, Laney's family is poor. Her widowed father is a pool repairman. At first Laney resists Zack's charms, but she's partly won over when he performs an inventive routine with a hackysack at the conceptual arts club she frequents.

Laney stands as prom queen against Taylor who has now split up with Brock. On the eve of the prom, Dean tells Laney about the terms of the bet. Furious, Laney breaks off with Zack who goes to the prom with his sister. Laney goes with Dean. Zack is elected prom king but Laney is narrowly defeated by Taylor. She leaves with Dean, who is planning to drug and seduce her. Zack goes after them. Laney escapes from Dean and returns home to find Zack; they embrace.

The gawky, plain Jane from the wrong side of the tracks who only needs to loosen her hair and take off her spectacles to become beautiful is one of the oldest stock types. From Ruby Keeler in musicals of the 30s to Molly Ringwald in *Pretty in Pink,* countless films have featured their own variations on the Cinderella myth. Robert Iscove's teen comedy *She's All That* follows in their wake, blithely invoking all the familiar high-school clichés. There's the handsome football hero, the bitch queen and the ugly duckling who soon turns into a beautiful princess. It's not as startling a transformation as the filmmakers suggest. Laney may be short-sighted and intellectual (the two go together in films), but she is never really as gauche as all that, just in need of a new dress and a better haircut.

Occasionally the film seems caught in a time bubble. When the kids are playing volleyball or performing their own set dance at the prom, it's as if we've slipped back into the world of Frankie Avalon. Where *The Faculty* (also made by Miramax) portrayed high school as a battlefield, with teenagers pitched against teachers, the mood Iscove strikes here is altogether more benevolent. There may be divisions between the jocks and the 'dweebs', but none of their lives is tarnished by drugs, guns or racism. Laney's dad, a likable loser, is a struggling pool repairman, but even he gets by happily enough. From time to time it's hinted Zack is at odds with his own father, but that doesn't seem to stop him getting top grades or being the star of the high-school soccer team.

A more daring film-maker might have laid bare the shallowness of a society in which popularity is programmed by athleticism and good looks. But Iscove doesn't seem interested in *Heathers*-style satire. Predictably, the most repellent characters are the most colourful. While Laney and Zack are almost terminally bland, Taylor (played with brassy élan by Jodi Lyn O'Keefe) is altogether more charismatic. Whether hurling abuse at her fellow students, dancing Salome-like in her bikini, or pouring a drink down Laney's cleavage, she gets all the best moments. Her only rival is Matthew Lillard as Brock, a belching, big-headed actor, so vain he even interrupts his lovemaking to watch reruns of his own show.

Iscove (whose background is in directing tele-movies) conjures up the occasional inventive moment, for instance Zack's "living art" performance with the hackysack, or the prom-night dance. Rachael Leigh Cook's appealing, if anodyne, performance rekindles memories of Olivia Newton-John at her most demure. What the film lacks, though, is any sense of teen spirit or rebelliousness. Adolescence was never supposed to be this wholesome.

VILLAGE VOICE, 2/9/99, p. 70, Justine Elias

In this inoffensive variation on John Hughes's frenetic Cinderella stories, April (post-spring break and post-college acceptance season) is the perfect time to upend the established social order. When the most popular girl in school (a vamping, foot-stamping Jodi Lyn O'Keefe) dumps her brainy, sensitive jock boyfriend (Freddie Prinze Jr.) for an obnoxious MTV star (Matthew Lillard, in a dead-on Puck impersonation), the stage is set for a cruel, Pygmalion-style bet. The spurned jock vows to transform the "scary, inaccessible" class dork into the next prom queen in six weeks.

Of course, the game would be a lot tougher if the victim (Rachael Leigh Cook) wasn't a Winona Ryder look-alike, complete with quavering voice and killer bod. It's never quite believable, either, that the heroine's sudden social ascent is a great thrill for every other unpopular student. She's a poor, motherless waif with only one friend (male), so it's a mystery, rather than a triumph, when this loner knocks them dead at the prom wearing a Dior-style prom dress and Audrey Hepburn do. Amid all the cameos (Anna Paquin, Usher Raymond, Lil' Kim), only Prinze, who has the ethereal, gentlemanly quality of a young Anthony Perkins, gets enough screen time to really make an impression.

Also reviewed in:
CHICAGO TRIBUNE, 1/29/99, Friday/p. A, John Petrakis
NATION, 2/22/99, p. 34, Stuart Klawans
NEW YORK TIMES, 1/29/99, p. E18, Stephen Holden
NEW YORKER, 5/31/99, p. 94, David Denby
VARIETY, 2/1-7/99, p. 55, Godfrey Cheshire
WASHINGTON POST, 1/29/99, Weekend/p. 41, Desson Howe

SHILOH 2: SHILOH SEASON

A Legacy Releasing release of a Dale Rosenbloom/Carl Borack production in association with Utopia Pictures. *Executive Producer:* Seth Willenson. *Producer:* Carl Borack and Dale Rosenbloom. *Director:* Sandy Tung. *Screenplay:* Dale Rosenbloom. *Based on the novel by:* Phyllis Reynolds Naylor. *Director of Photography:* Troy Smith. *Editor:* Tom Seid. *Music:* Joel Goldsmith. *Casting:* Laura Schiff. *Production Designer:* Joseph B. Tintfass. *Costumes:* Rikke Rosbaeck. *Running time:* 96 minutes. *MPAA Rating:* PG.

WITH: Michael Moriarty (Ray Preston); Scott Wilson (Judd Travers); Zachary Browne (Marty Preston); Ann Dowd (Louise Preston); Caitlin Wachs (Dara Lynn Preston); Joe Pichler (David Howard); Rachel David (Beckey Preston); Marissa Leigh (Samanatha); Bonnie Bartlett (Mrs. Wallace); Rod Steiger (Doc Wallace).

LOS ANGELES TIMES, 7/2/99, Calendar/p. 18, Robin Rauzi

There's a blond-haired boy in a movie this summer who struggles with the nature of evil, who wants to work for the greater good, but isn't always sure how.

His name is not Anakin Skywalker.

The protagonist of "Shiloh 2: Shiloh Season," 12-year-old Marty Preston (Zachary Browne), tackles some of the tough questions kids face as they approach adulthood, and he does it without a blaster or a spaceship. His sidekick: an adorable beagle named Shiloh.

Many a beagle no doubt was adopted on the heels of 1997's "Shiloh," in which Marty rescued the abused hunting dog from big meanie Judd Travers (Scott Wilson). The sequel, based on the second book of a trilogy by Newberry Award-winning writer Phyllis Reynolds Naylor, offers more of the same family fare. The filmmakers can proudly hold up their work before any congressional committee investigating movies marketed to kids. The only gun in sight is a hunting rifle, and it's owned by the unheroic Judd.

In this earnest but dull installment, the beer-swilling, tobacco-spitting Judd wants his dog back. His threats against the Preston family don't get him far, but they fill out the first half of the film. The second half has Marty contemplating whether a man as downright hateful as Judd—someone who drinks while driving, who (in the first movie) hit Shiloh in the head with a rifle butt—can change his ways.

Parents should be pleased with the messages provided by Dale Rosenbloom's script, which while occasionally creaky at least isn't too preachy. That's not to say adults will be entertained. Unlike the best of Disney's animated movies, which operate on separate levels for parent and child, "Shiloh 2" is strictly for the kids. Elementary schoolers might be transfixed; grown-ups, meanwhile, will be counting the unnecessary scenes that pad the movie out to its 96-minute running time.

Director Sandy Tung, who previously directed the Schoolbreak Special "The Day the Senior Class Got Married," draws a nice performance from Browne, who is smart and eager to please without being grating. Tung clearly kept the home video market in mind while directing "Shiloh 2"; the shots are composed for TV, save a few amateurish point-of-view shots that should have been excised completely.

Reprising the role of the father, Michael Moriarty delivers a performance that is too even; what worked for him as District Attorney Ben Stone on "Law & Order" seems just unemotional here. But the strangest bit of casting is Rod Steiger, whose role in the sequel is about two minutes longer than what constitutes a cameo. Wilson provides the sole interesting performance as the proud but emotionally damaged Judd.

NEW YORK POST, 7/2/99, p. 49, Rod Dreher

"Shiloh 2: Shiloh Season" is a rather less successful follow-up to the 1997 children's film about a boy and the beagle he saved from its cruel owner.

In the first movie, "Shiloh," the lad's compassion for a dog mistreated by its crusty old owner led him through a series of ethical dilemmas, wonderfully written and directed scenes in which the child's moral sense is developed through reason.

The story, adapted (like the sequel) from the novels of Phyllis Reynolds Naylor, was that rare children's film that seamlessly blends storytelling with ethical instruction. No wonder it became such a huge video hit.

"Shiloh 2" reunites most of the old cast, though with a new actor, Zachary Browne, replacing Blake Heron as the young Marty Preston. It is thematically darker than its predecessor and, unfortunately, overthought, measuring its synthetic moralizing out by the teaspoon.

Though "Shiloh" producer Dale Rosenbloom wrote both screenplays, this one feels canned and obviously assembled, whereas the first one flowed naturally and seamlessly.

The mean old coot from the first movie, Judd Travers (Scott Wilson), has gotten worse. He's developed a serious drinking problem and has come to the conclusion that Marty, who paid him fair and square for Shiloh, rooked him.

Judd has become a reckless poacher on Preston family land, as well as a threat to the community by driving his pickup while under the influence.

Marty's dad, Ray (Michael Moriarty), attempts to warn Judd about his trespassing, but he is sternly rebuked by the slobbering geezer, who makes threats against Shiloh and the Prestons. The story proceeds through a series of crises in which Judd's problems put various members of the Preston family in danger, and at last force a resolution to his suffering.

Whereas the first "Shiloh" was about Marty learning about the lengths to which one can responsibly go to protect a cute helpless animal, "Shiloh 2" is about Marty figuring out how to have compassion for an unlovable human creature.

Scott Wilson gives a remarkable performance here, making hateful Judd, who was beaten as a child, vividly human—and justifiably hard to take. His excellent work reveals the shortcomings of the other major players, though.

Poor zombified Moriarty is an alarming shadow of the character he played two years ago. Zach Browne, the new Marty, seems ill at ease in this rural setting, and too precious by half.

To be fair, though, Browne has to struggle against the script's oversweetening of his character. The kid's heart seems too easily turned to feeling sorry for Judd, and too readily persevering in charity. Most kids would hate and fear him, at least initially. We don't sense that the moral struggle here is in Marty's heart, but in Judd's.

The directing this time is by Sandy Tung, who doesn't have Rosenbloom's fluid style. A scene in which Judd's dogs attack Marty's sister in her yard seems obviously a put-up job, with the bad dogs running away at what appears to be their trainer's unheard call. Frequent use of saccharine, greeting-card shots of the adorable dog, which were avoided in the first movie, cheapen the sequel.

Still, "Shiloh 2" will likely enjoy a healthy run on video. It will be appreciated by kids, but probably more by parents, who have so very little in the way of uncynical, quality filmmaking to show their children these days.

NEWSDAY, 7/2/99, Part II/p. B12, Gene Seymour

When we last left Shiloh, the hunting beagle who once was the prized possession of embittered, abusive ne'er-do-well Judd Travers, he was happily ensconsed with his new pet boy Marty Preston and his loving family in the Mountainside community of Friendly, W. Va.

Meanwhile, Judd (Scott Wilson), who you would have thought had learned compassion and grace from losing Shiloh to his neighbors, has instead become a drunker, looser cannon than before; growling and snapping at the Prestons as if he were one of his own chained hunting dogs.

If the point of the first "Shiloh" movie was saving a canine life, then the sequel—which, like its predecessor, is adapated from a young-adult novel written by Phyllis Reynolds Naylor—is about the value of human life, even one as mean and misbegotten as Judd's.

Marty, played here by Zachary Browne (who's at least a mild improvement over his predecessor Blake Heron), is baffled and frightened by Judd's behavior. He not only worries that he'll lose Shiloh, but his life. (Nobody but the audience thinks to ask, "Where the heck's the sheriff?") Gradually, Marty begins to see Judd as having the same wounds on the inside that Shiloh used to have on the outside and, instead of retreating or fighting, he tries kindness, much to the bemused dismay of his postman dad (Michael Moriarty).

Any kids' movie that promotes compassion as determinedly as "Shiloh 2" merits some attention, egpecially these days. Sustaining attention, however, is one of the movie's key problems. What narrative drive there is gets bogged down by clumsy didacticism and balsa-wood dialogue. Rod Steiger, playing the town's doctor-grocer (honest!), is OK, but you wish there were more of Bonnie Bartlett as his feisty, acerbic wife, who doesn't get any serious screen time until Judd's excesses finally get the better of him.

Indeed, the movie only comes to life whenever Wilson is on the screen. His gift is being able to make Judd as frightened as he is frightening and never once does Wilson diminish Judd's presence to cliche or bathos. Why doesn't this guy get more and bigger roles?

Also reviewed in:
CHICAGO TRIBUNE, 6/25/99, Friday/p. B, Monica Eng
NEW YORK TIMES, 7/2/99, p. E13, Anita Gates
VARIETY, 4/26-5/2/99, p. 48, Joe Leydon

SHOW ME LOVE

A Strand Releasing release of a Memfis production in co-operation with Zentropa Productions/Film i Väst/SVT Drama Göteborg and with the support from the Swedish Film Institute/Charlotta Denward and the Danish Film Institute/Mikael Olsen. *Producer:* Lars Jonsson. *Director:* Lukas Moodysson. *Screenplay (Swedish with English subtitles):* Lukas Moodysson. *Director of Photography:* Ulf Brantas. *Editor:* Michael Leszczylowski and Bernhard Winkler. *Casting:* Anna Malini Ahlberg and Imor Hermann. *Art Director:* Lina Strand and Heidi Saikkonen. *Costumes:* Maria Swenson. *Make-up:* Maria Swenson. *Running time:* 89 minutes. *MPAA Rating:* Not Rated.

CAST: Alexandra Dahlstrom (Elin); Rebecca Liljeberg (Agnes); Erica Carlson (Jessica); Mathias Rust (Johan Hult); Stefan Horberg (Markus); Josefin Nyberg (Viktoria); Ralph Carlsson (Olof, Agne's Father); Maria Hedborg (Karin, Agne's Mother); Axel Widegren (Oskar, Agne's Brother); Jill Ung (Brigitta, Elin's Mother); Lisa Skagerstam (Camilla); Bo Lyckman (Man in Car); Daniel Teider (Johan's Little Brother); Nils Björkman (Bengsston); Per Larsen and Kenneth Larsson (Teachers); Karl Strandlin (Ice Hockey Coach); Peter Teider (Markus's Friend); Linda Malmqvist (Sobbing Girl).

LOS ANGELES TIMES, 10/22/99, Calendar/p. 14, Kenneth Turan

Numerous as tubes of Clearasil are films about teenagers in love, but unusual as an unblemished face are those that get it right. A completely charming reality-based romantic fantasy, both sweet-natured and sympathetic, "Show Me Love" is a leader of the pack.

An enormous hit in its native Sweden (where it was that country's official Oscar entry last year), "Show Me Love" casually resists oversimplification. A film of considerable warmth and intimacy, it knows that by bringing a level of truth to the pain and confusion of adolescent relationships, by being honest about the pressures to conform and the difficulty of staying yourself, it enhances its moments of pleasure as well.

First-time writer-director Lukas Moodysson, himself only 30, creates an irresistible sense of complicity with this story of a mad high school crush. Who can't empathize with those manic feelings, wondering if the other person even knows you exist, agonizing over whether to call or stoically wait by the phone. But for 16-year-old Agnes (Rebecca Liljeberg), an additional wrinkle makes all this riskier and even more intense: the object of her affections, the person whose name she can't stop writing over and over again, is another girl.

That would be Elin (Alexandra Dahlstrom), a petite blond who dreams of being Miss Sweden and who is dark-haired Agnes' opposite number in almost every way. If Agnes is restrained, thoughtful and almost friendless after two years in a new school, Elin is wildly popular and given to volcanic displays of emotion and temper, mostly directed toward her older sister Jessica (Erica Carlson).

Yet both girls share a sense of dissatisfaction with their life in the small town of Amal. (The film's Swedish title expressed that frustration in extremely graphic terms.) While Agnes is troubled by being different in a place that breathes conformity, Elin, world-weary as only a teenager can be, finds outlets for her boredom in getting high (anything, even Alka-Seltzer, has party potential) and making out with what her sister malignly characterizes as "70,000 guys." Desperate for up-to-the-minute distractions like raves, Elin complains that "when something's in, it takes so long to get here, its already out."

Agnes' crush notwithstanding, these two would likely never have gotten to know each other if Elin's fanatical desire to party hadn't led her to be practically the only guest at a birthday event Agnes' well-meaning but clueless mother throws for her resistant daughter.

Egged on by a bet with Jessica, as well as the school rumors that Agnes may be a lesbian, Elin engages in some foolishness with the birthday girl that only leads to Agnes' greater misery, including increased torment from the heartless gang at school.

But though she doesn't want it to be happening, that interaction with Agnes weighs on Elin's mind. In part it's guilt for having caused an innocent person pain, but new thoughts and confusions, ones Elin doesn't dare confide in anyone but that are plainly seen on her face, start to take root in her consciousness.

It's a mark of "Show Me Love's" resistance to oversimplification that characters who could be simply stock figures are fleshed out and given increased reality. Johan Hult (Mathias Rust), for instance, the doltish guy who is as attracted to Elin as Agnes is, is clearly no deep thinker, but the sincerity of his affection is never in doubt.

Similarly, Agnes' father (Ralph Carlsson) is a welcome departure from the usual teen movie dads. For one thing, he is thoughtful, empathetic and at the opposite pole from the clueless father Eugene Levy played in "American Pie," to cite a recent example. But, in an even more accurate twist, he is so far removed from his daughter's reality that his ability to help her is clearly limited.

"Show Me Love" also finds time to take some deft pokes at current European societal problems, highlighting the hollowness of adult lives spent watching strangers win at the televised lottery and teenagers who are obsessed with who has the slimmest, most streamlined mobile phone.

Made with welcome maturity and frankness, "Show Me Love" manages to exercise restraint while being true to the over-amped, out-of-control emotions of teenage love. The films's grainy, neo-documentary look is appropriate, and its use of incidental music, like a bit of Foreigner's "I Want to Know What Love Is" over a passionate kiss, is always appropriate.

Best of all, even though its central romance is between two girls, "Show Me Love" couldn't be further from a specialty film geared only toward a niche audience. In its understanding and empathy, this film makes room for all of us, creating a world we will cherish no matter who we are or whom we love.

NEW YORK POST, 10/18/99, p. 59, Lou Lumenick

"Show Me Love," Sweden's nominee for this year's foreign-language-film Oscar, is a sensitive portrait of a Swedish teenager discovering her lesbian longings.

Elin (Alexandra Dahlstrom), a blonde who harbors vague ambitions of being a model, is bored with life in a small city so remote that, she complains, even hip things tend to be out by the time they arrive there.

One evening, Elin and her sister Jessica (Erica Carlson) turn up by accident at the wrong birthday party. It's a very sparsely attended affair for Agnes (Rebecca Liljeberg), a bookish and not very popular brunette reputed to be a lesbian.

Elin, who's been drinking heavily, decides to take up Jessica's dare to kiss Agnes—who, unbeknownst to her, has long had a crush on her classmate.

Agnes, who's never been kissed before, is at first horrified (she tries to cut her wrists with a plastic razor)—and then thrilled at the possibilities.

But Elin, who seeks out Agnes to apologize and ends up with a long, soulful kiss in the back seat of a car, is frightened by the feelings all this arouses in her.

"Show Me Love" is mostly about Elin's efforts to escape her attraction, which include giving up her virginity to a hunky but clueless hockey player (Mathias Rust).

She can't escape her nature, of course, and the movie has a particularly sweet and funny ending that isn't at all exploitative.

A first-time film by poet Lukas Moodysson, "Show Me Love" reportedly gave "Titanic" a run for its money at the Scandinavian box office. Its portrait of adolescence seems so authentic that it puts most Hollywood products to shame.

NEWSDAY, 10/15/99, Part II/p. B13, John Anderson

The scenario is certainly familiar enough. One teenager is the blondest, bustiest, most bored adolescent in her sleepwalking little town. The other is a quiet, friendless loner with a strain of quiet charm and a crush a mile wide. Their trajectories are bound to intersect. The only question is when.

But while the basics of "Show Me Love" are endemic to the entire youth-movie genre, the hook to this Swedish romance are the particular lovers in question: Elin (Alexandra Dahlstrom), who is the most excitable underage party girl in the village of Amal, and Agnes (Rebecca Liljeberg), who has virtually no friends, no life and a heartbreaking yen for Elin.

But while the same-sex angle may be novel, what's really unique is how director Lukas Moodysson treats it. It helps that his two principals, Dahlstrom and Liljeberg, are adorable, but within the rough-hewn world of funky Amal, it's what Moodysson doesn't say that makes his film so genuine. Natural. And, to a great degree, provocative.

Elin, after all, is in many ways the "normal" teenager. She and her less attractive older sister, Jessica (Erica Carlson), are the product of a single-parent household. Both smoke, drink and have a bit too much sexual experience for girls of 16 and 14. But, then, they're also heterosexual (at least Elin thinks she is). Agnes, on the other hand, despite being heckled by her classmates and labeled a lesbian (if they only knew), is self-assured, dignified and serious to the point of bookishness. It's not Agnes but Elin who changes over the course of the film, Elin who discovers her true sexuality to the betterment of herself. If we can look a bit past the closing credits, it's Agnes who'd be the good influence on Elin. And as Moodysson knows, there are plenty of people who'd happily disagree with that assessment.

"Show Me Love" has a grainy, naturalistic look and an uncorrupted sense of adolescence that's so real it's painful. Agnes' father (Ralph Carlsson) is a warmly sympathetic character, but when he tries to console a despondent Agnes with some vague promise of future happiness, Agnes' reaction is classic. "I'd rather be happy now," she says, "than in 25 years." Likewise, Elin's fear of peer pressure and her snubbing of Agnes symbolize all the little wounds and bruises that come with growing up—in every sense of the word. Whether you've decided you have or you haven't—grown up, that is "Show Me Love" might have something to show you.

NEWSWEEK, 11/18/99, p. 78, David Ansen

The roller-coaster emotionalism that is teenage life is captured so naturally in the Swedish movie "Show Me Love" that you might mistake it for a documentary. This small but rousing movie struck such a deep chord in its native country that it gave "Titanic" a run for its money. Unlike most Hollywood teen movies, which are designed to flatter their audience, "Show Me Love" acknowledges how mean and nasty teenage girls can be—especially in a small town like Amal, where there is little to do except get falling-down drunk or spit at cars.

Writer-director Lukas Moodysson focuses on two girls at the opposite end of the high-school social spectrum. Blond, bored Elin (Alexandra Dahlström) is the beauty every boy wants to date. Brunette, bookish Agnes (Rebecca Liljeberg) is the school untouchable, rumored to be a lesbian. She sits in class stealing glances at Elin, confessing her love for her on her home computer. On a dare from her friends, Elin kisses Agnes at a party for money. Shattered as Agnes is when she discovers the truth, Elin's sense of herself is more deeply threatened. She begins to sense her attraction to Agnes wasn't just play-acting. In a town where homosexuality is considered a disease, Agnes and Elin's predicament is fraught with peril. But the film doesn't need false melodramatics to achieve its power. With honesty, charm and an uncanny sympathy for all its characters, it takes us deep inside the awkward and exhilarating experience of first love. It's no mystery why the Swedes took this movie to their hearts.

SIGHT AND SOUND, 3/00, p. 52, Liese Spencer

Amal, Sweden, the present. Unhappy and unpopular, Agnes doesn't want a party for her sixteenth birthday, but Karin, her mother, insists. At first no one comes, but when a wheelchair-bound girl from school arrives, Agnes insults her and sends her away. Later, trendy Elin and her sister Jessica arrive. Agnes has a crush on Elin but the girls are only there to humiliate her. Jessica dares Elin to kiss Agnes. They run out laughing, leaving Agnes crying. Agnes tries to slash her wrists with a disposable razor.

Elin and Jessica leave for another party where they tell their friends what happened. Elin gets drunk and goes back to Agnes' house to apologise. The girls go for a walk and try to hitch a lift out of town. They share a passionate kiss. The next day, Jessica is curious to know with whom Elin is in love. Scared of her friend's reaction, Elin doesn't phone Agnes but begins going out with Johan instead. At school the following day, Agnes is bullied about being a lesbian. When Elin ignores her, Agnes slaps her. Elin loses her virginity to Johan but is bored by their dates. After looking through Agnes' computer files, Karin discovers her crush on Elin.

At school, Elin hustles Agnes into a toilet to tell her she loves her. A crowd gather around the cubicle, banging on the door. Elin and Agnes come out together hand in hand.

Teenagers Elin and Jessica live in a cramped flat on a quiet housing estate in a small town where nothing ever happens. Exhausted by ennui, Elin suggests going to a rave, but Jessica has read in her style magazine that raves are "out". How typical, wails Elin, that raves should have come and gone from fashion without ever reaching Amal. Across town, 16-year-old vegetarian Agnes is sitting out an unwelcome birthday party with her parents, a roast-beef buffet and a wheelchair-bound outcast from school whom she doesn't even like very much.

Set in a suburban hinterland of empty parks and deserted sports stadiums, Swedish director Lukas Moodysson's first feature is strong on seething inertia. Lonely lesbian Agnes spends much of the movie lying on her bed. The 'Miss Sweden' of her class, Elin kills time fighting with her sister or playing television bingo with her silent boyfriend. As the romance between the girls develops, the inaction reaches fever pitch: Agnes waits for a phone call; Elin abandons a party to hang off a motorway bridge spitting on passing traffic.

In *Show Me Love*'s most exhilarating scene, Elin and Agnes try to hitchhike out of town. When a car stops, the girls get in and kiss in excitement. For a moment it's just them, the engine and the swelling sounds of Foreigner's 'I Want to Know What Love Is' before the driver orders them out. It's a sublime anti-climax in a series of disappointing deflations—Elin trying to get high on her mother's heartburn pills; kids aimlessly hanging around an outdoor cafe—but however banal their lives, Moodysson's characters are never boring to watch, thanks to the director's keen eye and ear for the epic bathos of adolescence.

Shot on reverse film stock, Moodysson's grainy, documentary-style drama gets inside the heads of its young protagonists to produce a believable teen-eye view of growing up. Slouching around in baseball caps and bad make-up, his cast of largely non-professional actors display all the awkward exuberance of real youth. Unlike the well-groomed stars of such Hollywood entertainments as *Cruel Intentions* or *10 Things I Hate about You,* these young people are not allowed to play at being adults, but are trapped in a real teen purgatory, waiting for childhood to end and life to begin. Instead of earnest narration or precocious coming-of-age speeches, Moodysson uses intimate close-ups to illuminate his characters' emotional uncertainty. With her high forehead and grave gaze, the beautiful Rebecca Liljeberg gives a wonderfully expressive performance in the largely reactive role of Agnes. Equally arresting is Alexandra Dahlström's fidgety, frustrated Elin, a bottle-blonde sulk of thwarted rebellion.

Structured around the classic house party, Moodysson's story may be an old one—the taboo romance between lovers from different ends of the school spectrum—but his sharp script refreshes old themes. In one tender scene Agnes' father tries to comfort her by describing his triumphant return to a school reunion. "Yes, but Dad," his unhappy daughter replies, "I don't want to wait 25 years. I'd rather be happy now." In another Freudian aside, a group of shuffling boys compare mobile phone sizes: "Mine's longer and thinner, but yours is thicker." Originally released under the more telling title of *Fucking Amal*, Lukas Moodysson's low-budget debut rivalled *Titanic* at the Swedish box office. Shot through with a wry burnout and compassion, his winning drama deserves to do just as well over here.

VILLAGE VOICE, 10/19/99, p. 144, Jessica Winter

Easily the best teen movie of the year, *Show Me Love* conjures with wry, empathetic precision the careening mood swings and casual emotional sadism of growing up disgusted and hormonal in the middle of nowhere. Fourteen-year-old Elin (Alexandra Dahlstrom) harbors a grudge for her Swedish hometown summed up in the film's glorious original title, *Fucking Amal*—the mercurial mini-Bardot unleashes a barbaric yawp whenever small-town tedium gets the best of her. Elin's cri de coeur is inadvertently answered by a loner classmate, Agnes (Rebecca Liljeberg), who's nursing a painful crush on Elin. The girls' first encounter—a fleeting kiss in Agnes's bedroom—results from bored, cruel impulse on Elin's part, but the newly curious drama queen returns to apologize, and the girls spend a confessional night wandering around town that culminates in a backseat make-out session (scored, in a priceless touch, to Foreigner's "I Want to Know What Love Is").

Confused by her new affections, Elin soon makes use of sweet, slow-witted Johan to dispense with her virginity and avoid Agnes. The lumbering, hapless boy is one of several sharply etched secondary characters, including Agnes's attentive father and Elin's complacent sister, and *Show Me Love* brims with mordant vignettes illustrating the cowing claustrophobia of Amal. First-time writer-director Lukas Moodysson draws subtle, unmannered performances from his young actors, and loves to study their faces in close-up. Indeed, Moodysson's tight, zoom-happy lens betrays a slightly Dogmatic ostentation, but this is a trivial flaw. Flushed with raw teenage emotion but never rose-tinted sentiment, *Show Me Love* leaves us with an uncertain glimpse of our heroines together, one both matter-of-fact and dreamily hopeful.

Also reviewed in:
NEW YORK TIMES, 10/15/99, p. E29, Anita Gates
VARIETY, 10/26-11/1/98, p. 47, Gunnar Rehlin

SIEGFRIED AND ROY: THE MAGIC BOX

An Imax Ltd. release. *Producer:* Michael V. Lewis. *Director:* Brett Leonard. *Director of Photography:* Sean MacLeod Phillips. *Editor:* Jonathan P. Shaw. *Music:* Alan Silvestri. *Production Designer:* Michael Hartog. *Running time:* 50 minutes. *MPAA Rating:* Not Rated.

CAST: Siegfried Fischbacher (Himself); Roy Uwe (Himself); Anthony Hopkins (Narrator); John Summers (Teen-Age Siegfried); Andrew Dunlap (Teen-Age Roy); Dillon McEwin (Young Siegfried); Cameron Alexander (Young Roy).

NEW YORK POST, 10/1/99, p. 62, Lou Lumenick

"Siegfried & Roy: The Magic Box" in IMAX is a match made in movie heaven, because 3-D is the perfect format to tell the story of this stellar, over-the-top duo.

This entertaining new feature intercuts footage from their spectacular, long-running magic-and-animals show at the Mirage Hotel in Las Vegas, with scenes re-creating their struggles as children and young adults (narrated by Siegfried, Roy and Anthony Hopkins).

Siegfried (the blond one, now 60) and Roy (the one with the codpiece and 55) both grew up in Germany, where their families were shattered by World War II. They launched their careers—and a lifelong partnership that the film neither ignores nor flaunts—after meeting on a cruise ship while performing.

This stylized biography, which makes extensive and often clever use of computer-generated virtual-reality settings, is a real crowd-pleaser. Forty years after ads for the first 3-D feature "Bwana Devil" famously threatened "a lion in your lap!" IMAX makes good on that promise—and then some.

VILLAGE VOICE, 10/5/99, p. 216, Dennis Lim

Not quite the high-camp experience it should have been (not even with the absurdly somber narration of Sir Anthony Hopkins), the Imax "biopic" *Siegfried & Roy: The Magic Box* does provide a few 3-D thrills early on—when Siegfried Fischbacher, the one with blond hair and a frozen smile, and Roy Uwe Ludwig Horn, the one with dark hair, a codpiece, and a frozen smile, flap their sequined cloaks in your face, while you squint through the dry ice and a white tiger rubs noses with you. Director Brett Leonard intercuts a (presumably typical) S&R Vegas extravaganza—a giddy display of pristine vulgarity—with hokey "reenactments" from the boys' childhood, using suitably stony-faced actors and deranged imagery (Siegfried perched atop a snow-peaked Alp, Roy curled up with a cheetah at the Bremen Zoo). Once the filmmakers run out of sanctioned narrative, the movie devolves into a confusing final sequence in which S&R frolic with their wildcats at home and speak in incoherent ecobabble (nature is the real magic, apparently). Smut hounds should note that no rumors of any sort are addressed in this family entertainment, though Roy does lock lips with a lion at one point.

Also reviewed in:
CHICAGO TRIBUNE, 10/15/99, Friday/p. H, John Petrakis
NEW YORK TIMES, 10/1/99, p. E24, Lawrence Van Gelder
VARIETY, 10/25-31/99, p. 38, Godfrey Cheshire

SILENCE, THE

A New Yorker Films release of an MK2 Productions/Makhmalbaf co-production. *Executive Producer:* Mohamad Ahmadi. *Director:* Mohsen Makhmalbaf. *Screenplay (Farsi with English subtitles):* Mohsen Makhmalbaf. *Editor:* Mohsen Makhmalbaf. *Director of Photography:* Ebrahim Ghafori. *Sound:* Behroz Shahamat. *Running time:* 77 minutes. *MPAA Rating:* Not Rated.

CAST: Tahmineh Normativa (Khorshid); Nadereh Abdelahyeva (Nadereh); Golbibi Ziadolahyeva (Mother); Araz M. Mohamadli (Wandering Musician).

NEW YORK POST, 11/10/99, p. 61, Jonathan Foreman

Some wonderful films have come out of Iran in the past few years, but "A Moment of Innocence," by highly regarded director Mohsen Makhmalbaf, is too smug and too self-indulgent to count as one of them.

"The Silence," on the other hand, which the same filmmaker shot in Tajikistan and which opens today with "Innocence" at Lincoln Center's Walter Reade Theater, is a gorgeous film that makes the most of a simple story and a fascinating, color-drenched setting.

Khorshid (Tamineh Normativa) is a blind 10-year-old who lives with his mother (Golbibi Ziadolahyeva). He supports the family by working for a musical-instrument maker.

Every day, a young female coworker (Nadereh Abdelahyeva) picks him up at the bus stop and leads him to the workshop. But all too often Khorshid hears a conversation or a song and follows the source of the sound off the bus and into the streets.

The instrument maker threatens to fire Khorshid just as the landlord threatens to evict his family. In response, Khorshid retreats into his own imaginary world, inspired by the sounds around him.

As a picture of life in Tajikistan—a former Soviet republic whose people seem to be an extraordinary racial mix with a taste for brightly colored clothing—"The Silence" is fascinating.

The rest of its appeal lies less in the slight story, the abundant symbolism inspired by Persian poetry or the acting (mostly very weak) than in Makhmalbaf's photography. One stunning, beautifully composed image follows another.

The director's painterly eye is present to a smaller degree in "A Moment of Innocence," a film set in a snow-covered Tehran.

The movie's implicit message—that different people can experience the same incident in a different way—was sufficiently subversive to get the movie banned in Iran. But it is such an artificial exercise in playfulness about art and reality—he uses non-actors in a film-within-a film format—that poor acting and the lack of action take a tedious toll.

In 1975 Makhmalbaf was an Islamic revolutionary who stabbed a policeman while trying to steal his gun, and he was imprisoned until the Khomeini revolution.

This film depicts in faux-documentary style his efforts to re-create that incident with the help of the policeman (Mirhadi Tayeb).

There are some touching and some funny moments, but it's the kind of film that makes you wish for a fast-forward button attached to your theater seat.

VILLAGE VOICE, 11/16/99, p. 136, Leslie Camhi

[*The Silence* was reviewed jointly with *A Moment of Innocence*; see Camhi's review of that film.]

Also reviewed in:
CHICAGO TRIBUNE, 2/18/00, Friday/p. N, Michael Wilmington
NEW YORK TIMES, 10/10/99, p. E5, Stephen Holden
VARIETY, 9/28-10/4/98, p. 48, David Stratton

SIMON SEZ

An Independent Artists release of a Signature Films production. *Executive Producer:* Rudy Cohen, Dan Frisch, and Kevin Jones. *Producer:* Moshe Daimant and Ringo Lam. *Director:* Kevin Elders. *Screenplay:* Andrew Miller and Andrew Lowery. *Based on a story by:* Moshe Diamant and Rudy Cohen. *Director of Photography:* Avraham Karpick. *Editor:* Alain Jakubowicz. *Music:* Brian Tyler. *Sound:* Barry Reed. *Production Designer:* Damien Lanfranchi. *Special Effects:* Maurice Zisswiler. *Costumes:* Jaleh Falker. *Stunt Coordinator:* Xiong Xin Xin. *Running time:* 90 minutes. *MPAA Rating:* PG-13.

CAST: Dennis Rodman (Simon); Dane Cook (Nick); Natalia Cigliuti (Claire); Filip Nikolitch (Michael); John Pinette (Macro); Jerome Pradon (Ashton); Ricky Harris (Micro); Henri Courseaux (Bernard); Xin Xin (Bodyguard); Emma Sjoberg (Dancer).

LOS ANGELES TIMES, 9/25/99, Calendar/p. 10, Kevin Thomas

With "Simon Sez," a lackluster international action adventure, that well-known performance artist and occasional basketball player Dennis Rodman has his first starring screen role as an ace Interpol agent based on the French Riviera. Rodman, who made an amusing impression in Tsui Hark's "Double Team" two years ago, keeps his cool even though this picture's not so hot.

Elegantly tailored and good-humored, Rodman moves with his athlete's grace and has a laid-back star presence. Movies and Rodman would seem to be made for each other, but the pictures will have to start getting better than this one.

A klutzy, dense private eye, Nick (Dane Cook), who flunked out of a training program to qualify for the CIA, was with the agency long enough to recognize on a Riviera beach Rodman's hard-to-forget Simon, who is ex-CIA, or so it would seem. Somehow Nick managed to get hired by an American weapons manufacturer (Clayton Day) to rescue his kidnapped daughter Claire (Natalia Cigliuti).

It seems the father, Bernard (Henri Courseaux), of Claire's handsome new boyfriend Michael (Filip Nikolitch), is attempting to get his hands on a disc containing details about her father's latest secret ultra-deadly weapon. Bernard in turn plans to sell the disc to crazed arms dealer Ashton (Jerome Pradon). In an instant Nick has caught up Simon in this increasingly dangerous turn of events.

Written by Andrew Miller and Andrew Lowery from a story concocted by the film's co-producer Moshe Diamant and one of its executive producers, Rudy Cohen, "Simon Sez" is not exactly a triumph of originality but supplies plenty of opportunities for martial arts exploits, chases and the like. Director Kevin Elders handles such action sequences with aplomb—just as he does his star—but no one could expect him or anyone else to do much with the script's feeble yet frequent attempts at comic relief, not only with the swiftly tiresome Nick but also with a pair of silly robot monks (Ricky Harris and John Pinette), who are Simon's sidekicks. Cook, Harris and Pinette are game but are torpedoed by terrible material.

Screen time would have been more profitably spent on building up the relationship with Simon's sexy ex-lover (Emma Sjoberg), a martial arts virtuoso known as the Dancer, who has been hired by Bernard but is seduced by Simon into switching allegiances. Simon and the Dancer are a tempestuous duo: They'd as soon as kick-box each other as make love—and in this film these activities are by no means mutually exclusive. Well-photographed by Avraham Karpick, "Simon Sez" has Rodman and the Riviera, but they're not enough.

NEW YORK POST, 9/25/99, p. 28, Lou Lumenick

Dennis Rodman isn't half bad as a blond, multiply pierced Interpol agent in "Simon Sez,"' his second attempt to bring his brand of histrionics to the big screen.

But the movie, set on the mouth-watering French Rivera, is no "To Catch a Thief."

Rodman's Simon is enlisted by a bumbling PI to help track down a supposedly missing heiress. Her disappearance is connected to a plot by an evil arms dealer to (yawn) take over the world.

Rodman does very well in the expertly staged fight scenes, and he can deliver the odd quip (though the ones provided him tend to the lame). He even has a romantic clinch or two with Swedish supermodel Emma Sjoberg, who plays a kickboxing champion.

But the Worm can only roll his eyes at the low comic antics of his co-stars, including Dane Cook as the PI, who has trouble unhoistering his pistol; John Pinette as a 400-pound monk who moonlights as an Interpol computer expert; and Jerome Pradon as the tiresomely simpering chief villain.

Directed with no particular flair by Kevin Elders (who wrote the "Iron Eagle" trilogy) from a confused and witless script by actors Andrew Miller and Andrew Lowery, "Simon Sez" is rated PG- 13.

That means Simon can slaughter half the population of France without spilling a drop of blood.

Also reviewed in:
CHICAGO TRIBUNE, 9/28/99, Tempo/p. 2, John Petrakis
NEW YORK TIMES, 9/25/99, p. B12, Lawrence Van Gelder
VARIETY, 9/27-10/3/99, p. 50, Joe Leydon

SIMPLY IRRESISTIBLE

A Twentieth Century Fox release of a Regency Enterprises presentation of a Polar production. *Executive Producer:* Arnon Milchan and Elisabeth Robinson. *Producer:* John Fiedler, Jon Amiel, and Joseph M. Caracciolo, Jr. *Director:* Mark Tarlov. *Screenplay:* Judith Roberts. *Director of Photography:* Robert Stevens. *Editor:* Paul Karasick. *Music:* Gil Goldstein and Christopher Brooks. *Choreographer:* Jerry Mitchell. *Sound:* Billy Sarokin and (music) Ed Rak. *Sound Editor:* John Nutt. *Casting:* Billy Hopkins, Suzanne Smith, and Kerry Barden. *Production Designer:* John Kasarda and William Barclay. *Art Director:* Beth Kuhn and Caty Maxey. *Set Decorator:* Justin Scoppa. *Special Effects:* Connie Brink, Sr. *Costumes:* Katherine Jane Bryant. *Make-up:* Caryn Brostoff. *Running time:* 100 minutes. *MPAA Rating:* PG-13.

CAST: Sarah Michelle Gellar (Amanda Shelton); Sean Patrick Flanery (Tom Bartlett); Patricia Clarkson (Lois McNally, Tom's P.A.); Dylan Baker (Jonathan Bendel); Christopher Durang (Gene O'Reilly); Larry Gilliard, Jr. (Nolan Traynor); Olek Krupa (Valderon); Amanda Peet (Chris, Tom's Girlfriend); Betty Buckley (Aunt Stella); Andrew Seear (Frank Rogers); Meg Gibson (Hannah Wallberg); Alex Draper (François); Drew Nieporent (Gil Shapiro); Anthony Ruivivar (Ramos); Andrew McLaren (The Poet); Steven Skybell (Herr Mueller, Chief Financier); Phyllis Somerville (Ruth); Bill Raymond (Howard); Yusef Bulos (Bill); Joseph Mosso (Abe); Harley Kaplan (Brian in Shoes Department); Molly Tarlow (Molly); Gabriel Macht (Charlie); Hal Robinson (Southern Cross Customer); Margaret Sophie Stein (Frau Mueller); Lily Semel (Lauren); Audrey Matson (Lauren's Mother); Debbon Ayer (Bendel's Sales Person); Marisa Zabbak (Reporter); Eric Rota (Sous Chef at Market); Kara Wethington (Singer); Leslie Lyles (T.J. Russo).

LOS ANGELES TIMES, 2/5/99, Calendar/p. 10, John Anderson

[*The following review by John Anderson appeared in a slightly different form in* NEWSDAY, 2/5/99, Part II/p. B7.]

When enchanted restaurant chef Amanda Shelton (Sarah Michelle Gellar, TV's "Buffy the Vampire Slayer") cries into her saucepan, the result is a dish that sends her diners into paroxysms of joyous tears. They can't help it: They're so happy, they're blubbering into the fig compote.

It's a scene that verges on charming. Probably the movie's most charming. So the fact that it's a shameless rip-off of "Like Water for Chocolate" should give you some idea of the heights of creativity being scaled in "Simply Irresistible," one of those movies that dares you to make fun of its title while not even suggesting the rock song it's named after.

Perfunctory direction, a dull-eyed color scheme, contrived narrative, flaccid acting—the movie virtually screams "contractual obligation."

That it was directed by Mark Tarlov—described as a one-time lawyer and "speech writer for Warren Berger" (instead of Burger)—and written by former Warner Bros. lawyer Judith Roberts shouldn't necessarily mean an inedible concoction. But "Simply Irresistible" features in Sean Patrick Flanery's Tom Bartlett a character only a lawyer could love: A smarmy, self-absorbed operator in a $200 tousled haircut and a white silk tie, who can compartmentalize like Bill Clinton and is in charge of creating Jonathan's at Henri Bendel, a deluxe restaurant named for the store founder's demanding grandson (Dylan Baker).

Not only do we get product placement worthy of "You've Got Mail," we get a semblance of its plot line, too. Amanda shares ownership of a fading but homey Manhattan boite that was owned by her late mother, but Amanda can't cook any better than her aunt Stella (Betty Buckley). However ... aided by a magic crab procured at the 14th Street Farmer's Market (where they treat Miss Buffy as if she were Werewolfgang Puck) and a magical cabdriver (Christopher Durang, who promptly disappears from the movie till the final shot), she gets uptown restaurant-conceptualizer Tom in her place and the romance is off and running.

Not that you care. Gellar is a remarkably unremarkable screen presence. Flanery is a David Cassidy look-alike. His soon-to-be ex-girlfriend is played by Julia Roberts manquee Amanda Peet. The plot is borrowed from eight movies—some of them teen sports movies—and the incidental music sounds like it was borrowed from a Lifetime drama about housewives-turned-prostitutes. Whatever's going on, you not only wish you were somewhere else, you think you're already there.

The supporting trio of Baker, Buckley and Patricia Clarkson brings a great deal of class to the production, but Tarlov tries to wring dividends out of emotional situations without having made any investment. The two leads are unappealing, the story is dragged on for days and the rather random magical element renders any human factor irrelevant. There's a completely inane plot point about Tom being obsessed by paper airplanes, which is nothing more than a setup for the final scene of Tom sailing Amanda a long-distance love note. If she were smart, she'd mark it "addressee unknown."

NEW YORK POST, 2/5/99, p. 61, Jonathan Foreman

"Simply Irresistible" is an early contender for one of 1999's 10 worst films, the sort of stupid, boring mess that you walk out of wondering if the direction was worse than the script or vice versa.

Sarah Michelle Gellar stars and her flat performance here is almost enough to alienate fans of her "Buffy the Vampire Slayer" TV show.

But it's probably not her fault. Her character is completely incoherent and nowhere near as endearing as it's supposed to be. The script has her turn from a shy girl to a forward, almost slutty one, and then back again without reason.

Her character, Amanda, works with her aunt at the restaurant her mother owns. While she is out shopping for ingredients at the Union Square greenmarket, a fairy-godfather type appears, tells her his name is Gene O'Reilly (Christopher Durang) and sells her some magic crabs.

He also ensures that she bumps into handsome but superficial Tom (Sean Patrick Flanery), who is setting up a restaurant in the (endlessly plugged) Henri Bendel department store.

When she brings the crabs back to the restaurant, one particular magic crab causes a perfect crab dish to appear just when she needs it—when Tom turns up for lunch there with his girlfriend (again thanks to O'Reilly).

From that moment on Amanda turns from an incompetent to a brilliant cook. And not only is she brilliant, her food has magical, mainly aphrodisiac qualities. It is clearly only a matter of time before it gets her both Tom and an opportunity to shine at his restaurant.

Gellar, whose hair has turned red-brown for the role and who wears blue eyeshadow, is desperately unsexy. Flanery's jerky Tom looks prettier but gets no further bringing his lame lines to life.

Fortunately, as often happens, an able supporting cast (with the exception of playwright Christopher Durang, who is agonizingly bad in his few minutes on screen) keeps the picture watchable.

Patricia Clarkson, Dylan Baker and Larry Gilliard Jr.—doing a male Whoopi Goldberg as Amanda's wise black friend make the most of this flick's few funny lines.

The feeble, forced whimsy of the magic-crab/enchanted-food story almost saves "Simply Irresistible" from its soupy saccharine attempt at romance. But the two never gel. The writer doesn't understand that real fairy tales have a primitive logic whose rules must be followed: Cinderella doesn't get supernatural help until it's shown that she deserves it. You can't just posit that someone is adorable and deserving and hope that the audience is dumb enough to buy it.

The filmmakers don't make food (or cooking) look sensual at all. This isn't food as sex (like in "Like Water for Chocolate") it's food as posh real estate. The film strains to connect the pleasures of eating with the pleasures of expensive shopping in a store like Bendel's.

These folks don't get the difference between labels and taste, or love and sex: When people eat Amanda's aphrodisiac dessert, the result is behavior that lurches between the priggishly prim and the joylessly smutty.

Maybe it's all an L.A. thing. After all the filmmakers think that the corner of Hudson and Jane streets is in TriBeCa and that TriBeCa is some kind of down and dirty working-class nabe. But that would be forgivable if the script were not so witless, and the direction so lazy. Joke after joke lands with a heavy, squishy thud. After a while you begin to feel embarrassed for the actors, and finally for yourself.

SIGHT AND SOUND, 11/99, p. 54, Kevin Maher

At a Manhattan market Amanda Shelton is given a free basket of crabs. Afterwards she meets businessman Tom Bartlett who is presently overseeing the opening of a new restaurant at Bendel's department store. Amanda goes back to the ailing Southern Cross restaurant in SoHo where she works as a chef. Tom and his girlfriend arrive there later for a meal. One of Amanda's crabs has supernatural powers and confers magical cooking skills upon her. Deeply affected by the meal, Tom's girlfriend breaks several plates and storms out. Impressed with the food, Tom offers to buy Amanda some new plates.

News of Amanda's cooking spreads, and business booms at the Southern Cross. Late at night, after eating one of her desserts, Tom and Amanda kiss and then float up to the ceiling. Scared, Tom accuses Amanda of witchcraft and leaves. Tom's boss tastes Amanda's cooking and hires her for Bendel's opening night. Her cooking on the night is a huge success, but Tom still refuses to talk to her. He sees her leaving the restaurant and calls her back. They reconcile their differences and rejoin the party.

A debut effort from writer Judith Roberts and director Mark Tarlov (producer of *Pecker)*, *Simply Irresistible* is a befuddled attempt at producing a star vehicle for Sarah Michelle Gellar (television's *Buffy the Vampire Slayer)*. Here a plot with obvious *Pretty Woman* overtones has incorporated moments from recent food-obsessed films such as *Big Night* and *Tampopo* to create a flat romantic comedy that's shockingly free of narrative momentum.

Everything in *Simply Irresistible* is telegraphed and writ large. Gellar's Amanda is an average chef who needs to move on to greater things, while Tom is a successful businessman who predictably just happens to have a new restaurant on his hands. That's the blunt set-up, and the rest of the film procrastinates until Amanda finally hooks Tom and his restaurant. During this time, rather than Amanda's gradually improving cooking skills, *Simply Irresistible* makes a fatal error by introducing the concept of the skill-bestowing magic crab.

A lazy contrivance, the crab punctures the film full of plot holes: because Amanda's improved cooking skills are exclusively derived from this magic crab, technically she's still an average cook throughout the film, and the Cinderella-style resolution—where she lays on the wildly successful spread for the Bendel's opening do—rings false. Amanda apparently doesn't know that the crab is responsible for her new-found culinary confidence, but then she refuses to kill it, commenting obliquely, "I just don't think he's your normal crab!" There are no rules for the crab's magic either—after eating, Tom's girlfriend explodes with uncontrollable rage and Tom and Amanda float up to the ceiling, while most customers simply groan in ecstasy.

These moments recall the gustatory orgasms of Alfonso Arau's *Like Water for Chocolate*, but *Simply Irresistible* suffers badly in comparison, the ethnicity and magical realism of the former replaced by the latter's Waspish ascendancy and crass fantasy. *Simply Irresistible* adheres rigidly to classic dialogue-led conventions, apart from one formal flourish—Amanda's musical flashback to her romantic moments with Tom—which is embarrassingly weak. The lack of ambient sound in the Southern Cross restaurant scenes is particularly jarring, especially since we often cut to them from a noisy Manhattan exterior, giving the film the artificial air that surrounds such studio-shot sitcoms as *Friends*.

Notable performers are wasted in the midst of all this. Patricia Clarkson and Dylan Baker, who gave such eviscerating turns in, respectively, *High Art* and *Happiness,* are barely stretched in supporting roles. And though this is Gellar's star vehicle, she must struggle through such banal lines as "My whole life was ordinary, and then we met and these amazing things started to happen!" The fact that she has to play a character who's little more than a crab's talentless stooge, who looks pretty in a Todd Oldham gown and can't wait to be swept off her feet by a millionaire playboy makes you wonder what attracted her to the role in the first place and only adds to the misjudged tone of *Simply Irresistible.*

VILLAGE VOICE, 2/16/99, p. 150, Justine Elias

Though it comes late in the current cycle of youth-oriented romantic comedies, this occasionally inspired combination of *Like Water for Chocolate* and classic movie musicals scores points for oddball charm. Any story that manages to find a place for delectable meals, a magical crab, and Christopher Durang (as a sort of culinary angel) is, at the very least, striving for something stranger than most modern fairy tales. The heroine, played by Sarah Michelle Gellar of TV's *Buffy the Vampire Slayer,* is Amanda, owner and chef of a failing family restaurant in Tribeca. Her late mother was a genius in the kitchen, but Amanda's recipes are missing a key ingredient: a sensual enjoyment of life. She discovers her gift in time to whet the appetite of a straitlaced playboy (Sean Patrick Flanery, who looks scarily like David Cassidy). Their culinary romance begins as an obnoxiously cute tale of opposites, but once Amanda's cooking begins to cast an almost erotic spell over the proceedings, *Simply Irresistible* becomes as enjoyable as a long-denied dessert.

Also reviewed in:
CHICAGO TRIBUNE, 2/9/99, Tempo/p. 2, John Petrakis
NEW YORK TIMES, 2/5/99, p. E22, Lawrence Van Gelder
VARIETY, 2/8-14/99, p. 75, Joe Leydon
WASHINGTON POST, 2/5/99, p. C5, Stephen Hunter
WASHINGTON POST, 2/5/99, Weekend/p. 40, Desson Howe

SITCOM

A Leisure Time Features release of a Fidélité Productions/Le Studio Canal+ production with the participation of Canal+. *Producer:* Olivier Delbosc and Marc Missonnier. *Director:* François Ozon. *Screenplay (French with English subtitles):* François Ozon. *Director of Photography:* Yorick Le Saux. *Editor:* Dominique Petrot. *Music:* Eric Neveux and Irène Toporkoff. *Sound:* François Guillaume. *Sound Editor:* Benoît Hillebrant. *Art Director:* Angélique Puron. *Costumes:* Hervé Poeydemenge. *Make-up:* Agnès Morlhigem. *Running time:* 80 minutes. *MPAA Rating:* Not Rated.

CAST: Evelyne Dandry (Hélène, the Mother); François Marthouret (Jean, the Father); Marina de Van (Sophie, the Daughter); Adrien de Van (Nicholas, the Son); Stéphane Rideau (David); Lucia Sanchez (Maria); Jules-Emmanuel Eyoum Deido (Abdu); Jean Duchet (Phychotherapist); Sébastien Charles (Guy with Courgettes, Group Session); Vincent Vizioz (Guy with Red Hair, Group Session); Kiwani Cojo (Pierced Guy, Group Session); Gilles Frilay (Guy with Moustache, Group Session); Antoine Fischer (Gregory, Neighbor's Little Boy).

NEW YORK POST, 4/9/99, p. 59, Thelma Adams

"Sitcom" boldly answers that burning question: Which wine goes with rat? Red or white?

We learn more than we ever wanted to know about the other, other white meat in the farcical sex shocker from the director of last year's New Directors/New Films "Mommie Dearest" thriller, "See the Sea."

When French director Francois Ozon exploits the sitcom format for a gleefully artificial story about a bourgeois clan in psychosexual disarray, John Waters meets Franz Kafka.

One day, Dad (Francois Marthouret) brings home a pet rat. The white rodent alters the household, releasing pent-up perversions from bestiality to incest.

While the patriarch retreats behind his newspaper, vermin-fearing Mom (Evelyne Dandry) worries, suicidal sister (Marina de Van) goes dominatrix and baby brother (Adrian de Van) announces: "I've got something important to tell you. I'm homosexual."

What's a love-starved mother to do? How about trying to redirect her son with a little maternal sexual-healing?

Amid standard sitcom tropes—the phone-interrupting dramatic moments, the sofa dialogues, the dinner table confabs—Ozon playfully views the nuclear family through the rusty bars of a rat's cage.

Campier and less disturbing than "See the Sea," "Sitcom" is a fetishist feel-good movie, a French double-cheek kiss to "Married With Children."

It is, as Ozon says, "the film of a perverse child."

NEW YORK POST, 6/18/99, p. 56, Jonathan Foreman

Imagine a John Waters comedy drained of Waters' wit, timing and clever dialogue and you've still got something better than "Sitcom—a slow French farce that strains desperately to be daring before collapsing in horror-comic silliness.

Along the way there's a supposedly hilarious teen suicide attempt and a family massacre. "Sitcom" also has lots of incest, and scenes in which people cook and masturbate with a rodent (though not at the same time).

But for all its forced perversity, "Sitcom" carries as much satirical punch as one of the weaker episodes of TV's "Married With Children." Writer-director Francois Ozon thinks he's making fun of sitcoms and/or "family values," but he could not have seen a sitcom since "Leave It to Beaver."

Living in a big house we find Jean, a middle-aged French businessman (Francois Marthouret), and his Stepfordesque wife, Helene (Evelyne Dandry).

They have a nerdy teen-age son, Nicholas (Adrien de Van), and a daughter, Sophie (Marina de Van), who cannot keep her hands off her hunky boyfriend (Stephane Rideau).

One day, the father brings home a white lab rat with red eyes, much to Helene's horror. And very quickly the rat upsets the family's equilibrium by somehow causing everyone's repressed (and predictable) sexual desires to burst into the open.

Nicholas announces that he's gay. And after using the rat as a sex toy, Sophie (for no apparent reason) jumps out of a window. A paraplegic as a result of the fall, she also becomes a sadomasochist.

Nicholas becomes popular, starts to dress well and fills his tiny room with roulette-playing boyfriends.

But "Sitcom" is essentially about the clueless way Helene deals with all these changes: She tries to cure Nicholas by sleeping with him.

She isn't just dense when it comes to the homosexuality of her son and maybe her husband, she's a paragon of naivete so extreme that the character crosses the line into misogynist caricature.

SIGHT AND SOUND, 1/99, p. 56, Jonathan Romney

A man arrives home on his birthday and shoots his family dead. Months earlier, his wife Hélène welcomes Maria, a new Spanish maid, and introduces her to the household: her children Nicolas and Sophie and Sophie's boyfriend David. Her husband Jean arrives home with a pet rat. Maria, invited to dinner, arrives with her Cameroonian husband Abdu, while Nicolas gets to know the rat. At dinner Nicolas announces that he is gay. Abdu is bitten by the rat, then seduces Nicolas. Sophie defenestrates herself and is left paraplegic. Later Nicolas has left school and organises orgies at home. After spending time with the rat, the newly sensual Hélène attempts to 'cure' her son by seducing him. Sophie flirts with her father, who rejects her advances.

Months later the household has become increasingly anarchic. Sophie is a harsh dominatrix to David, who is consoled by Maria. When Hélène suggests family therapy, her children agree, but Jean declines. He comes home one day and shoots them all but it turns out to be a dream, interrupted by a phone call from Hélène, asking him to dispose of the troublesome rat. Jean microwaves and eats the animal. Arriving home, Hélène, Sophie and Nicolas are attacked by a giant rat, which they overcome and kill. With Sophie now walking again, the happy family attend Jean's funeral.

François Ozon made a considerable splash recently in French cinema with a number of inventively perverse shorts, such as *Regarde la mer*, a two-bander with a young mother and a predatory female hitchhiker which gives a twist to the territorial unrest of Polanski's *Knife in the Water (1962)*. Ozon's first feature, however, proves a serious disappointment, partly because he seems so anxious to display a light touch, with paradoxically cumbersome results. *Sitcom* may look less familiar in the context of French cinema than it does elsewhere. There are heavy traces of Buñuel, Joe Orton, Almodóvar and (the model Ozon has explicitly evoked) John Waters. The film belongs in the by now altogether cosy French cinematic tradition of *épater les bourgeois,* although Ozon is perhaps the first to 'out' the tradition, taking it into queer territory.

As an attempt at a Waters-style assault on middle-class mores, *Sitcom* fits the template all too comfortably. Ozon begins with a painfully nice, well-heeled family (placid Dad, amiably fussy Mum, studious son and sexpot daughter), then turns their relationships upside down, one after the other. In fact the film's most perverse aspect may be this seriality: although sexual anarchy accumulates, there's no sense of a linear thread linking the various stages of chaos. Hélène's sexual repression is cured by her own incestuous attempts to 'cure' her son, but soon after she's her old self, yearning for normality.

Rather than telling a 'straight' story (in whatever sense), Ozon shuffles his elements like Happy Families cards into different permutations each time. The strategy of the sitcom is at play here too: after each episode's explosion into chaos, there's a return to base, to a tentative status quo. But the film's narrative elasticity—the loop back to the start, the 'only a dream' fake climax the leap into sci-fi horror, not to mention the distancing stage curtains at the start—finally makes for an anything-goes feel and an apparent lack of satiric rigour.

Ozon's recipe for family discord is to introduce a sexy intruder, a strategy familiar from Orton's play *Entertaining Mr Sloane* and Pasolini's film *Theorem* (1968). But to make matters more complex there are three intruders, each an exaggerated version of Otherness as it might appear to the French bourgeoisie: an African man and a Spanish woman, both of them sexually up for anything, and the laboratory rat which, with its blank gaze seen in extreme close-up and subjective shots through the bars, seems to be the narrative genius experimenting on the humans. Ozon's most acute stroke is never to identify the rat explicitly as the instigator of desire. When Jean eats it, he seems to become it. But this is also left to our imagination, close-ups of fur and a bloodied jumper letting us infer the worst.

Sitcom is more unnerving in its little tweaks rather than its raunchier nudges. Assorted hardcore characters arrive for Nicolas' orgy, but the most disconcerting guest is a dapper little man with a bag who announces himself politely as 'the doctor'. The film's most mysterious and genuinely

Buñuelian touch is its opening and closing phone calls from Hélène's friend Françoise, who seems to have caught some unnameable illness.

It's hard to know quite what Ozon is offering beyond the standard lampooning of repression. It's hardly that taboo-busting to reveal that under the squeaky clean appearance everyone's up for a romp with the domestics and a fistful of courgettes. The aspect of the film that remains hardest to pin down is the role of Jean. As a distant paterfamilias who hides behind a repertoire of banal proverbs, he's clearly the patriarchal instrument of oppression and therefore ripe for massacre. Yet he's also the one who, when Nicolas outs himself, delivers a reasoned, altogether Foucauldian lesson on homosexuality in classical Greece. This refusal to yield entirely to unequivocal caricature finally allows the film to breathe. *Sitcom* might not work that well as comedy but, with its displacements, it should provide debate for film-and-psychoanalysis classes for years to come.

Whatever *Sitcom*'s shortcomings, it's definitely the work of a confident stylist who's not afraid to acknowledge his borrowings. Ozon follows late Buñuel's use of an exaggeratedly bland shooting style. He also, like Almodóvar, has an appealing way of placing his decor on equal terms with his characters, for example the colonial fantasy of Nicolas' desert-island wallpaper and the candy-striped wall that fills the screen when David walks out of view. He's served well by an extraordinary cast, especially Evelyne Dandry, a sort of radiant, hot-to-trot June Whitfield, and the slyly rattish children, played by Marina and Adrien de Van. They are real-life siblings, which adds an extra *frisson* to their bath scene. It's encouraging to imagine that *Sitcom* isn't all talk, and that Ozon was happy to encourage taboo-breaking on set.

VILLAGE VOICE, 6/22/99, p. 152, Amy Taubin

Even at his best, as in the elegant psychological-horror film *See the Sea*, François Ozon lacks the subtlety of Zonca. *Sitcom*, a macabre domestic comedy that's getting a release after a year on the festival circuit, is something of a French surburban reworking of Freud's *Totem and Taboo*. The totem animal is a large white laboratory rat that the father brings home and whose presence liberates the id of every person with whom it comes in contact—except the one with whom it's most closely identified. Because the conceit is not convincing, the pileup of perversities—from incest to sadomasochism to cannibalism—seems like an exercise in *épater le bourgeois*. Ozon has a flamboyant sense of style, which he uses to mean-spirited ends.

Also reviewed in:
NEW YORK TIMES, 4/9/99, p. E24, Janet Maslin
VARIETY, 5/25-31/98, p. 62, Lisa Nesselson

SIX-STRING SAMURAI

A Palm Pictures release of an Overseas Filmgroup presentation of an HSX Film production. *Producer:* Michael Burns and Leanna Creel. *Director:* Lance Mungia. *Screenplay:* Lance Mungia and Jeffrey Falcon. *Director of Photography:* Kristian Berner. *Editor:* James Frisa. *Music:* Brian Tyler. *Production Designer:* Jeffrey Falcon. *Running time:* 81 minutes. *MPAA Rating:* PG-13.

CAST: Jeffrey Falcon (Buddy); Justin McGuire (The Kid); Stephane Gauger (Death); John Sakisian (Russian General); Gabrille Pimenter (Little Man); Zuma Jay (Clint); Monti Ellison (Head Pin Pal).

LOS ANGELES TIMES, 9/18/98, Calendar/p. 10, Kevin Thomas

Forget Sputnik. According to the tedious "Six-String Samurai" the big news of 1957 is not that the USSR beat the U.S. into space by launching a satellite but that Russia bombed us to smithereens and took over the country except for that desert oasis stronghold "Lost" Vegas. Forget, too, that Elvis died in 1977 but instead lived on another two decades, reigning in Vegas as the king of rock'n' roll.

It would seem, too, that Buddy Holly didn't die in that plane crash either, and he—or a Buddy (Jeffrey Falcon, also cowriter, action director and production designer) clearly patterned after him—appears in a desert landscape, trudging off to Vegas to claim Elvis' at-last-empty throne. Soon tagging after him is the Kid (Justin McGuire).

That's the idea behind Lance Mungia's disappointing first feature—basically the latest retread of "The Road Warrior" with a rock twist, a touch of "El Topo" and a smidgen of "The Seventh Seal" thrown in for good measure.

To the accompaniment of the energetic but eventually monotonous Red Elvises, seen briefly performing in the ghost town of Rhyolite, Mungia takes us down a way, way overly familiar road in which our dynamic duo is in constant menace from countless grungy types, some of whom have ramshackle vehicles. Helpfully, Buddy is a swordsman of such skill he'd put Zorro to shame, but Mungia's constant attempts at humor result only in a chuckle here and there.

There's a curiously lifeless quality to this substandard post-apocalyptic odyssey that's underlined by the post-synchronization of much of the film's dialogue, and "Six-String Samurai" really doesn't kick in until its concluding sequence, which is way too late to make much difference. "Six-String Samurai's" best hope is to land midnight movie slots, when audiences are up for free-wheeling zaniness, never mind if it's done well or been done before.

NEW YORK POST, 1/22/99, p. 54, Jonathan Foreman

"Six-String Samurai" is a witless, lead-footed attempt to apply the Quentin Tarantino spirit to the post-apocalyptic "Mad Max" genre. Its student makers have sufficient technical skill to put together a remarkably glossy film on a minimal budget, but their aesthetic sensibilities match those of 12-year-old boys, and they lack storytelling ability.

As a result, this film mostly feels like a home movie made by some precocious but dorky comic-book-obsessed high school freshmen—who must have had great fun putting in really cool scenes copied from favorite westerns, Chinese martial-arts flicks and "The Wizard of Oz."

Their fun, alas, doesn't rub off on the audience. I can only describe watching it as an experience so tedious, it's almost painful.

"Six-String Samurai" is set in a low-budget, post-nuclear America: Back in 1957, the Russians took over America except for the city of Lost Vegas, where Elvis was crowned King.

But, 40 years later, Elvis is dead. And a sword-swinging, guitar-playing, ultra-laconic superhero named Buddy (Jeffrey Falcon) is making his way to Vegas to claim the crown.

But there are other claimants, including Death himself, who wears a stovepipe hat and resembles the guitarist Slash of the band Guns N' Roses. Buddy, with his blue suit, thick glasses and weirdly high voice, must battle Death, Russians and a bowling team as he crosses the wastelands with an 8-year-old orphan (Justin McGuire) in tow.

The acting ranges from the merely bad to the unbearable, ensuring that you don't care for a second about the fate of Buddy or his tiresome child sidekick. What no one seems to have told screenwriter-director Lance Mungia and his co-writer, Falcon, is that all the knowing movie references in the world cannot make up for this or for abysmal writing and nonexistent pacing.

"Six-String Samurai" is only 90 minutes long, but it feels like it lasts for days.

Falcon is an impressive martial-arts expert, but the violence looks fake—and not in a deliberate or stylized way. The floppy bayonets on the Russian soldiers' rifles are obviously made of cardboard. If the film had a tenth of the witty, bizarre sensibility of the low-budget films put out by the folks at Troma (remember "The Toxic Avenger"?), this wouldn't matter.

"Six-String Samurai" tries desperately hard to be cool. But it's just a plodding, unfunny compendium of narrative and visual cliches that never gel. The only bright spots are some impressive photography and the accompanying music by the Red Elvises, a Russian rockabilly band.

NEWSDAY, 1/22/99, Part II/p. B11, Kevin Thomas

Forget Sputnik. According to the tedious "Six-String Samurai," the big news of 1957 is not that the USSR beat the U.S. into space by launching a satellite, but that Russia bombed us to smithereens and took over the country except for that desert oasis stronghold "Lost" Vegas.

Forget, too, that Elvis died in 1977 but instead lived on another two decades, reigning in Vegas as the king of rock and roll.

It would seem, too, that Buddy Holly didn't die in that plane crash, either, and he—or a Buddy (Jeffrey Falcon, also co-writer, action director and production designer) clearly patterned after him—appears in a desert landscape, trudging off to Vegas to claim Elvis' at-last-empty throne. Soon tagging after him is the Kid (Justin McGuire).

That's the idea behind Lance Mungia's disappointing first feature—basically the latest retread of "The Road Warrior" with a rock twist, a touch of "El Topo" and a smidgen of "The Seventh Seal" thrown in for good measure.

To the accompaniment of the energetic but eventually monotonous Red Elvises, seen briefly performing in the ghost town of Rhyolite, Mungia takes us down a way, way overly familiar road in which our dynamic duo is in constant menace from countless grungy types, some of whom have ramshackle vehicles. Helpfully, Buddy is a swordsman of such skill he'd put Zorro to shame, but Mungia's constant attempts at humor result only in a chuckle here and there.

There's a curiously lifeless quality to this substandard post-apocalyptic odyssey that's underlined by the post-synchronization of much of the film's dialogue, and "Six-String Samurai" really doesn't kick in until its concluding sequence, which is way too late to make much difference. "Six-String Samurai's" best hope is to land midnight movie slots, when audiences are up for free-wheeling zaniness, never mind if it's done well or been done before.

VILLAGE VOICE, 1/26/99, p. 106, Laurie Stone

Everything from *Pulp Fiction* to *The Wizard of Oz* to *Road Warrior* to *The Good, the Bad, and the Ugly* has been mulched into this postapocalyptic road movie by Lance Mungia, who made this first feature fresh out of college. Cowriter Jeffrey Falcon, who also designed the costumes, stars as samurai Buddy, his battered, black-framed glasses and dweeb suit inspired by Buddy Holly. Buddy's on his way to Lost Vegas, an Oz with an opening for a new Elvis, but it's a long, strange trip, imperiled by mutants and bogeymen whom he must battle. Falcon is an agile martial artist and deadpan clown, and his wild-child sidekick, The Kid (played by seven-year-old Justin McGuire), is equally appealing. There's one charming sequence, with vaudeville grace and tragicomedy worthy of Beckett, but the rest of the film, even with startling visual effects and some impish humor, is repetitious and derivative, playing like an endless commercial for bullet-hole chic.

Also reviewed in:
NEW YORK TIMES, 1/22/99, p. E20, Lawrence Van Gelder
VARIETY, 3/16-22/98, p. 68, Leonard Klady

SIX WAYS TO SUNDAY

A Stratosphere Entertainment release of a Prosperity Electric production. *Executive Producer:* Charles Johnson. *Producer:* Adam Bernstein, David Collins, and Michael Naughton. *Director:* Adam Bernstein. *Screenplay:* Marc Gerald and Adam Bernstein. *Based on the novel "Portrait of a Young Man Drowning by:* Charles Perry. *Director of Photography:* John Inwood. *Editor:* Doug Abel. *Music:* Theodore Shapiro. *Sound:* Antonio L. Arroyo. *Casting:* Billy Hopkins, Suzanne Smith, and Kerry Barden. *Production Designer:* Theresa Mastropierro. *Set Designer:* Christine Manca. *Costumes:* Edi Giguere. *Running time:* 97 minutes. *MPAA Rating:* R.

CAST: Norman Reedus (Harry Odum); Deborah Harry (Kate Odum); Elina Lowensöhn (Iris); Adrien Brody (Arnie Finkelstein); Isaac Hayes (Bill Bennet); Jerry Adler (Louis Varga); Peter Appel (Abie "The Bug" Pinkwise); Clark Gregg; Anna Thomson (Annibelle); Paul Lazar; Holter Graham (Madden).

LOS ANGELES TIMES, 3/12/99, Calendar/p. 4, Kevin Thomas

In Adam Bernstein's darkly comic "Six Ways to Sunday," "White Heat" meets "Psycho" with '90s candor as a crazed woman's extreme possessiveness propels her 18-year-old son into a life of crime.   In adapting Charles Perry's 1962 novel "Portrait of a Young Man Drowning," Bernstein reveals a sure sense of control of outrageous material, allowing his film to be simultaneously and alternately serious and comic without either element undermining the other. The result is a deft entertainment for those who like their movies low-budget, noirish and risky.

From the first shot, you sense that the past will hang heavily over the film's key figures. That shot is of an austere old brick row house in Youngstown, Ohio, in the heart of America's Rust Belt. The house is the drab, dingy home to a middle-aged single mother, Kate Odum (Deborah Harry), a still-beautiful woman who never fixes her hair and lives in her bathrobe. Yet she is nevertheless the seductive parent to her virginal son Harry (Norman Reedus), at the same time warning him that "all girls are sluts." Meanwhile, Harry, who works as a fry cook, in a city whose steel mills once offered a good livelihood to blue-collar workers, one day tags along with his childhood pal Arnie (Adrien Brody), who's collecting a delinquent debt from a strip joint owner for a local gangster, the avuncular but steely Louis Varga (Jerry Adler). The impact of a bar full of topless dancers sparks a frustrated, violent response in Harry, in whom Varga immediately sees a comer.

Harry becomes part of a tightly knit underworld that rewards him with warm camaraderie but in return expects him to turn hit man on demand. Harry thrives as a daring criminal, while his Oedipal relationship with his mother persists, rendering him impotent.

Bernstein unravels the plot twists and turns without losing his balance between the bloody and the bizarre, the droll and the poignant. "Six Ways to Sunday" is a fable speculating on the relationship between sex and violence, and it is kept afloat by a raft of risk-taking performances, especially on the part of Reedus and Harry. Brody, Peter Appel as the ruthless Varga's deadly yet sentimental second-in-command, Holter Graham as Harry's sleek imaginary alter ego Madden and Isaac Hayes as a crooked cop all help anchor "Six Ways" to reality. But nothing is more real or more crucial to making the film remain convincing through mind-boggling developments than the faded grandeur of Youngstown itself—abetted by some New York and New Jersey locales—a place of derelict factories and magnificent but grimy Beaux-Arts buildings at its core, all of them captured on film as effectively as the people themselves by John Inwood's camera, which is as expressive as Theresa Mastropierro's knowing production design.

NEW YORK POST, 3/5/99, p. 58, Jonathan Foreman

"Six Ways to Sunday" is the kind of cynical, creepy production that makes you feel vaguely nauseated afterwards, as if you've gulped down milk turned sour.

We meet Harry (Norman Reedus), a vacant, timid 18-year-old, being given a bath by his blowzy mother (Deborah Harry): Shortly after the bathroom scene, Harry accompanies his friend Arnie (Adrien Brody)—an errand boy for the local Jewish mob who talks and dresses like a gangsta—on a little mission.

While Harry watches Arnie slap around a guy who's late with his protection money, some strange inner demon takes over. Harry begins pounding the guy into the ground. The beating is so effective that Harry is immediately hired as an enforcer, and then assassin, by mobster Abie Pinkwise (Peter Appel). After a successful cold-blooded murder, Harry is introduced to Godfather Louis Varga (Jerry Adler) and welcomed as a member of the organization.

His brutality makes him Louis' favorite, even though he attempts to rape Iris (Elina Lowensohn), the crippled East European girl who works for the Godfather. They order him to make it up to her by asking her out. And he does, encouraged by Madden (Holter Graham)—a sharp-suited alter ego who appears to him at moments of stress.

There are a few good lines on the way. But it's hard to care whether the mostly passive main character lives or dies. Harry does have moments of humanity, but they are undermined by director Adam Bernstein's assumption that the way he kills ex-friend Arnie with an electric jackhammer is funny and cool.

Like so many movies of this type, "Six Ways" contains some excellent supporting performances by fine actors who deserve better material. Appel is terrific as Abie, and Isaac Hayes is thoroughly convincing as a corrupt cop. Debbie Harry too does a good job, although she looks terrible, and her performance as the overprotective mom who desires her son is at the heart of what makes this movie so unattractive.

NEWSDAY, 3/5/99, Part II/p. B7, Gene Seymour

"Portrait of a Young Man Drowning," a 1962 novel by the late African-American writer Charles Perry, is a harrowing exemplar of the straight-from-the-psychosis crime melodramas associated with Jim Thompson and David Goodis. Such a pedigree should have made it an easier mark for adaptation by French filmmakers than our own especially since the book's climax still seems too joltingly risque, even for the great American cutting edge.

But never underestimate the ability of today's ultra-hip ironists to turn grim Freudian determinism into deadpan dark comedy. Adam Bernstein's "Six Ways to Sunday" does more than deliver Perry's book from its 1930s setting and plant it in present-day Youngstown, Ohio, the Rust Belt's broken buckle. It sandblasts the source material's bleakness and replaces it with a dry whimsy that would be almost charming if you weren't feeling queasy in spots.

At the center of this touching, sordid slice of Americana is Harold Odum (Norman Reedus), a dim 18-year-old who is sheltered beyond reason by his slatternly mom, Kate (Deborah Harry). She gives him sponge baths and advice on the evils of the outside world's temptations, e.g. young girls.

When Harold's best buddy Arnie (Adrien Brody), a self-styled urban "gangsta" and errand boy for the local Jewish mob, takes him along on a shakedown, Harold pounds a deadbeat strip-club owner to a bloody pulp. This so impresses Arnie's bosses, Abie "The Bug" Pinkwise (Peter Appel) and Louis Varga (Jerry Adler), that Harold immediately becomes the mob's ace maniac—sorry, mechanic.

Harold's new and exciting life would be way cool if it weren't for the occasional run-ins with a corrupt, bullying cop (Isaac Hayes) and a troubling romance with Varga's physically-challenged ward, Iris (the beguiling Elina Lowensohn); troubling because Harold's subconscious, which takes the form of a swaggering sadist named Madden (Holter Graham), goads him toward Iris while Mom uses every devious means at her disposal to pull him closer to home.

Needless to say, a deft touch is required to maneuver through this muck and mire with any degree of style. Perhaps to the surprise of the few who saw Bernstein's only other film (the negligible "Saturday Night Live" offshoot, "It's Pat"), the director maintains a no-sweat balance between over-the-top melodrama and gimlet-dry humor. The performances help a lot. Reedus makes himself into a perfect cipher while everyone else in the cast, especially Brody, Appel and Harry (who revels in the irony and sleaze), get emotional in more obvious but no less appealing ways.

VILLAGE VOICE, 3/9/99, p. 113, J. Hoberman

If not quite the synthesis of *Lock, Stock* and *Analyze This*, [See Hoberman's review of these films.] *Six Ways to Sunday* is nevertheless a post-MTV Freudian gangster comedy. Produced and directed by music-vid vet Adam Bernstein, this well-heeled indie starts with a blowsy Deborah Harry giving her 18-year-old son Harold (Prada model Norman Reedus) a sponge bath and proceeds to work out his Oedipal scenario in explicit detail.

Set in Dean Martin's hometown of Youngstown, Ohio, *Six Ways* engages in another form of displacement by treating this rundown rust-belt city as the realm of unreconstructed 1930s-style Jewish gangsters. Those Yiddish songbirds, the Barry Sisters, are warbling on the soundtrack and, as aspiring enforcer Harold soon discovers, the Jews allow no liquor in their office. "We like coffee here," the big boss (Jerry Adler) explains. Harold soon becomes the goy in the shvitz, beating up deadbeats while absorbing the local wisdom. "Having money and not flashing it is strictly for gentiles."

As the dialogue suggests, *Six Ways to Sunday* is not a particularly subtle film. In fact, it's crassly cut and often clumsily staged. Bernstein has a near-fatal fondness for gross close-ups and broad performances. Although the flavorsome, oddball cast includes Elina Lowensohn (as Harold's deceptively timorous love interest), Adrien Brody (as his overly "yo" buddy), and Isaac

Hayes (as a cop nemesis), the movie mainly feasts on the spectacle of beefy tough guys pulling faces and rolling their eyes.

Still, in true gangster fashion, Bernstein does imbue the project with an aggressively stylish look and gives it a nitwit savoir faire—a flashback to the '70s with Harry singing "More, More, More." *Six Ways* is also true to its psychosexual underpinnings. Harold takes orders from his surrogate father and his real mother until ... The least one can say for the final crack-up is that (unlike *Analyze This)* it's less shtick than what used to be called sick.

Also reviewed in:
NATION, 3/29/99, p. 35, Stuart Klawans
NEW YORK TIMES, 3/5/99, p. E12, Lawrence Van Gelder
VARIETY, 9/29-10/5/97, p. 63, Lisa Nesselson

SIXTH HAPPINESS, THE

A Regent Entertainment release of a Kennedy Maylor production. *Executive Producer:* Frances-Ann Solomon and Ben Gibson. *Producer:* Tatiana Kennedy. *Director:* Waris Hussein. *Screenplay (based on his novel "Trying to Grow"):* Firdaus Kanga. *Director of Photography:* James Welland. *Music:* Dominique Le Genore. *Choreographer:* Patrick Cesar and Lynne Page. *Editor:* Laurence Mery-Clark. *Sound:* John Marchbank. *Sound Editor:* Stewart Henderson and Philip Alton. *Casting:* Emma Style. *Production Designer:* Lynne Whiteread. *Art Director:* Tom Bowyer. *Set Decorator:* Joanna Tague. *Costumes:* Amal Allans. *Make-up:* Jacquetta Levon. *Running time:* 97 minutes. *MPAA Rating:* Not Rated.

CAST: Firdaus Kanga (Brit Kotwal); Souad Faress (Sera Kotwal); Khodus Wadia (Sam Kotwal); Ahsen Bhatti (Cyrus); Nina Wadia (Dolly Kotwal); Mahabanoo Mody-Kotwal (Jeroo); Nisha K. Nayar (Tina); Indira Varma (Amy); Roger Hammond (Father Ferre); Sabira Merchant (Madame Manekshaw); Dina Chinoy (Musical Daughter); Vijay Damania (Bank Clerk); Meral Durlabhji (Boy at Party); Dolly Dotiwalla (Plump Wife); Goolistan Gandhi (Defarge); Aloo Hirjee (Old Woman at Funeral); Dilnaz Irani (Daughter in Air-raid Shelter); Meher Jehangir (Vera Dinshaw); Noshirwan Jehangir (Doctor); Mitho Jesia (Woman in Air-raid Shelter); Firdausi Jussawalla (Plump Husband); Arun Kannan (Rohit); Pratima Kazmi (Wagh Baba's Assistant/Brothel Madam); Dharam Khan (Taxi Driver); Vijoo Khote (Wagh Baba); Nimmi Kumar (Bank Assistant); Dara Madon (Old Parsee Man); Zeenia Mirza (Young Tina); Brenda Rodrigues (Bank Secretary); Meera Syal (Breathing Generator); Jaimishi Shivjiani (Young Dolly); Zubin Tatna (Dinsu Dinshaw); Pervin Wadia (Cheerful Mother).

LOS ANGELES TIMES, 11/5/99, Calendar/p. 10, Kevin Thomas

Waris Hussein's "Sixth Happiness" has been described as "My Left Foot" meets "My Beautiful Laundrette" meets "The Tin Drum," and that's a pretty fair approximation of this most unusual yet beguiling coming-of-age/coming-out movie.   It's based on Firdaus Kanga's semiauto-biographical 1990 novel "Trying to Grow," and it stars Kanga himself.

It is hard to imagine how anyone else could play Kanga. Now 38 and living in London, he was born in Bombay into a middle-class Parsee family, the Parsees having been driven out of Persia by Muslims some 1,000 years ago. Kanga suffers from a rare brittle-bone disease, which means that so much as a hiccup can cause a rib to break. It also means that he is only 4 feet tall and confined to a wheelchair because his spindly legs cannot carry his small body. But Kanga, who has remarkable dark eyes, is a compelling presence and brings to mind Truman Capote in his forceful personality and an acute sensibility that ranges from the eloquent to the catty.

After a screening of "Sixth Happiness," Hussein remarked that making this movie was like being on the edge of a precipice the whole time. That's understandable because the film simply could not have sustained any serious missteps in taste, judgment and credibility.

From the start, the veteran Hussein and Kanga introduce a darkly humorous sense of absurdity that gives the film a sustaining dry, vigorous wit. The baby boy's condition is apparent at birth, with his mother, Sera (Souad Faress), taking the news briskly in stride while her husband, Sam (Khodus Wadia), is devastated. When the baby's older sister Dolly (Nina Wadia) suggests, in a child's joking innocence, that they call him Brit as in "brittle," Sera goes for it immediately, having already adopted a defiant stance in regard to her son. Besides, it reminds her of Britain, and she is the most ardent of Anglophiles.

Kanga plays Brit from the age of 8 through 18, and he gets away with it under Hussein's exceptionally sensitive direction. (You have the feeling that he's changed little physically in the last two decades.) Luckily for Hussein, Kanga has a vivid personality and is clearly a natural actor.

The amount of insensitivity and even outright cruelty directed at Brit in his childhood is breathtaking. Sam, a handsome banker, cannot hide his shame and inability to accept his son's condition, and when medical science can do nothing for the boy, Sam starts taking him to dubious holy men and faith healers. All this might crush a lesser spirit, but Brit has flourished under his mother's and sister's devotion.

Sera is fiercely protective of Brit, yet takes him out into the world. Finally, a very grand but also shrewd and caring Lady Bountiful (Sabira Merchant) in the Parsee community sees to it that Brit gets a proper education and builds his self-confidence and self-esteem. Indeed, Brit can carry on like a spoiled maharajah, but as he matures he becomes less self-absorbed and more and more interested in the world around him—which includes a handsome new tenant, Cyrus (Ahsen Bhatti), a violin prodigy turned law student, to whom Sera rents a room.

Hussein, whose most recent film was the zesty period comedy "The Summer House," has accrued decades of experience in directing both for TV and the big screen—and that experience has served him well. He maintains a high level of awareness that allows him to make persuasive a wide range of circumstances, and that darkly comic sense of absurdity allows Brit and the audience to deal with some very harsh, out-of-the-blue developments in the course of his youth. Brit ultimately discovers salvation in writing.

Spanning 1962 to about 1980, "Sixth Happiness" is also a deft evocation of its period and an affectionate portrait of Parsee family and community life. Much that happens to Brit is calamitous, but he meets life's losses and setbacks with such a brave, determined spirit that "Sixth Happiness" exudes a quality of lightness that allows it to play far more as comedy than tragedy, rich in its survivor's sense of humor.

NEW YORK POST, 10/22/99, p. 67, Lou Lumenick

"Sixth Happiness," the best movie ever made about a gay Indian dwarf, features the novelty of screenwriter Firdaus Kanga playing the lead character in an adaptation of his own autobiographical novel, which covers ages 8 to 37.

After speaking directly to the camera as an adult, he takes us back to 1972 Bombay. Where he's seen in sailor suits and tights, being wheeled around in a stroller because he suffers from a condition that renders his bones so brittle, a cough can cause a fracture. Nicknamed Brit, he will never walk on his spindly legs nor grow taller than 4 feet.

Veteran TV director Waris Hussein gets excellent performances all around, including Souad Faress as Brit's dotty but devoted mom, Khodus Wadia as his long-suffering father and Nina Wadia as a nurturing sister.

"Sixth Happiness" is definitely one of a kind. But it takes a huge leap of faith to get past the idea of an 8-year-old with 5 o'clock shadow.

NEWSDAY, 10/22/99, Part II/p. B8, Jan Stuart

One of the more extraordinary double coups of this or any movie year comes from Firdaus Kanga, the diminutive Bombay-born star and writer of "The Sixth Happiness." In Brit Kotwal, a young man with a rare bone disease that prevents him from growing, he creates a memorably feisty character who gains in wit and heart what he lacks in stature.

What makes the feat even more triumphant is that Kanga is playing out his own story, more or less. Based on his autobiographical novel "Trying to Grow," this entertaining saga traces Brit's development from boyhood, when his bones are so fragile that an attack of hiccups breaks a rib, to young adulthood, when he comes of age with members of both sexes.

A compelling figure with Louise Nevelson eyelashes and a delicate British accent, Kanga plays Brit from age 10 on, narrating his surprise-laden tale with an abundance of grace and irony.

"The Sixth Happiness" takes its flavorful and eccentrically funny tone from the protagonist's quirky family of Persian-descended Parsees. The Kotwals' Bombay household is dominated by Brit's vivacious mother, Sera (the wonderful Souad Faress), whose Anglophilia is so engulfing that Brit is inspired to sing a stiff-upper-lip round of "The White Cliffs of Dover" as the family huddles in a storm cellar waiting for a Pakistani invasion.

Surrounding Brit are his tart and loving sister, Dolly (Nina Wadia), his dour, regretful father, Sam (Khodus Wadia), his salty, deaf cousin to whom he is promised in marriage at an early age, and a retinue of quacks and overeducated witches who try to cure Brit's malady.

Stepping into this delightfully cacophonous domestic carnival like something out of Tennessee Williams is a handsome drifter named Cyrus (Ahsen Bhatti), who unexpectedly awakens Brit's sexuality.

Under Waris Hussein's solid, unpretentious direction, "The Sixth Happiness" gushes forward with enough events to pad a mini-series. A buoyant spirit keeps it from devolving into pathos: Kanga gives us permission (and reason) to laugh at the human comedy prompted by his condition. Too itinerant to pass as great art, it's a delightful roller-coaster ride nonetheless, one that leaves you at the end wanting to stay on for one more spin around.

SIGHT AND SOUND, 10/98, p. 54, Charlotte O'Sullivan

Bombay, 1962. British born with osteoporosis, also known as 'brittlebone' disease. His anglophile Parsee mother Sera is unperturbed, but his father Sam is appalled. As he grows up, Brit comes to rely on his mischievous elder sister Dolly for support. Another ally is snobbish but feisty Madame Manekshaw, who secures his admission to a Catholic school.

Devastated by her husband's death, Madame Manekshaw commits suicide. Dolly falls in love with a New York doctor, causing Sam to commit suicide as well. Brit's deaf and dumb cousin Tina falls in love, only to disappear. Sera takes in a lodger, Cyrus, and Brit and he begin a relationship. Cyrus then discovers a new partner, Amy. Brit is initially hostile but he and Amy end up sleeping together. Tina's mother Jeroo goes mad with grief. Sera's mother dies in an accident. Brit is ready to start a new life.

The book *Trying to Grow*, published in 1999, offers a semi-autobiographical account of growing up with brittle bone disease. It's an irony presumably not lost on Firdaus Kanga, the book's 37 year old author, that in the film of the book he is physically qualified to play his 8-to-18-year-old self. Kanga makes a plausible protagonist, but not just because of his small sized parts. The visual dissonance between old head and young body chimes with his father Sam's victim-in-a-horror-movie response to his son's condition. Like Udo Kier's bloated baby in Lars von Trier's *The Kingdom II*, Brit is "unnatural" and uncanny. But the film also captures something else. As in Dennis Potter's *Blue Remembered Hills*, the unchanging shape of our hero hints at an unspoken truth of autobiography: "little" Brit is both a wide-eyed child *and* an experienced, time-travelling adult, an unmistakable mix of character and author.

The resulting performance is extraordinary. Brit's face is like a volcano, permanently on the point of erupting. His eyes register everything. When he sees Mrs. Manekshaw's dead body, suddenly as tiny and frail as his, his pupils dilate with shock. And the elegant whines that worm their way out of his throat, along with his urgent exhalations of breath, are constantly surprising. One or two cloying epiphanies aside, there's nothing soft focus about this portrait—Brit's charm comes out of his self-obsessed gloom, not in spite of it. Given an award by his headmaster for being "the bravest little boy", Brit moans: "He might have asked me first."

It's also nice to see pushy mothers getting a fair deal, Usually the victims of sitcomish caricature, here—in the forms of Sera and Jeroo—they bulge with three-dimensional life. Khodus Wadia's Sam is equally masterly. More surprising is an adroit turn from Indira Varma: monumentally vapid in *Kama Sutra,* in this she embodies just the right mixture of smugness and silly, young warmth. (However, the fact that we get to watch her and Brit having sex, when we see nothing of his coitus with Cyrus, seems a cowardly and/or cynical move on the film-makers' part.)

The film's title is a reference to the Ingrid Bergman movie *The Inn of the Sixth Happiness* (1958). But as far as the visuals are concerned, it's Bollywood's influence which proves the most intense.

Introducing Brit to her new lover, deaf and dumb Tina suddenly bursts into colour-soaked song as her hunk wiggles his shoulders in the background. Brit stands in this sequence for cooped-up real life; Tina has clearly fallen head over heels into fiction. But her excitement is genuinely heady and seductive. Until this point, the cousins have always bickered in sign language, but now Tina has access to a powerful 'voice'. It's a sublime moment—words versus song, conformity versus individuality, but it exposes a huge weakness of the film: when we see this, we realise what we've been missing.

For in between the film's deliciously quiet moments and its mania, *Sixth Happiness* proves stylistically all too flat. The most obvious problem is director Waris Hussein's reliance on Brit's studio bound observations (Hussein has extensive television credits, including *The Glittering Prizes* and *Edward and Mrs Simpson)*. These narrative intrusions not only break up the movie's rhythm, they set an entirely different mood. The points themselves are entertaining, but they belong in a worthy Channel 4 documentary (Kanga has appeared in a number of Channel 4 programmes, which doesn't help).

It is as if Hussein is drawn to, yet fearful of, allowing his film to take on a magical life of its own. *Sixth Happiness* is full of painful joy (not least in its last scene, with Brit ecstatically gyrating to his parents' favourite tango). Hussein should have trusted to such material and lost his (talking) head.

VILLAGE VOICE, 11/2/99, p. 140, Jessica Winter

As the doting, dotty mother tells her son in *Sixth Happiness* (based on Firdaus Kanga's autobiographical novel), the five essential sources of bliss are health, longevity, wealth, virtue, and peace; the sixth is a self-determined X-factor. But the boy—who goes by Brit, a name doubly ironic for reasons we'll get to—faces daunting battles before he can make it through the average day alive, much less contented. Born with "glass-bone" syndrome, Brit (played from childhood to the present day by Kanga himself) doesn't grow past four feet, has to move about in a wheelchair, and cracks a rib as easily as most folks crack their knuckles. Just as painful are his father's shame and the cruelty of his mother's friends. Kanga's maladies grant him the objective distance of an alien scribe amidst his Anglophilic Parsee milieu (Mum can often be glimpsed dusting her pictures of the Queen), and the expression of his emerging homosexuality both enhances his outsider status and allows him to defy his body's limitations. But both as post-facto narrator and homily-coughing child ("My bones break; I don't"), Kanga pats himself on the back with one hand while outstretching the other for congratulation.

Also reviewed in:
NEW YORK TIMES, 10/22/99, p. E24, Lawrence Van Gelder
VARIETY, 12/8-14/97, p. 113, Dennis Harvey

SIXTH SENSE, THE

A Hollywood Pictures and Spyglass Entertainment release of a Kennedy/Marshall/Barry Mendel production. *Executive Producer:* Sam Mercer. *Producer:* Frank Marshall, Kathleen Kennedy, and Barry Mendel. *Director:* M. Night Shyamalan. *Screenplay:* M. Night Shyamalan. *Director of Photography:* Tak Fujimoto. *Editor:* Andrew Mondshein. *Music:* James Newton Howard. *Music Editor:* Thomas S. Drescher. *Sound:* Allan Byer and (music) Shawn Murphy. *Sound Editor:* Michael Kirchberger. *Casting:* Avy Kaufman. *Production Designer:* Larry Fulton. *Art Director:* Philip Messina. *Set Decorator:* Douglas Mowat. *Set Dresser:* Sharon Potts, Frank Grasso, Susannah McCarthy, Charles J. Scott, Thomas Watkins, William F. Hennessy, Jr., Morgan Miller, and Patrick J. Trowbridge. *Special Effects:* Garry Elmendorf. *Costumes:* Joanna Johnston. *Make-up:* Michal Bigger. *Make-up (Bruce Willis):* Gerald Quist. *Stunt Coordinator:* Jeff Habberstad. *Running time:* 107 minutes. *MPAA Rating:* PG-13.

CAST: Bruce Willis (Malcolm Crowe); Haley Joel Osment (Cole Sear); Toni Collette (Lynn Sear); Olivia Williams (Anna Crowe); Trevor Morgan (Tammy Tammisimo); Donnie Wahlberg (Vincent Gray); Peter Tambakis (Darren); Jeffrey Zubernis (Bobby); Bruce Norris (Stanley Cunningham); Glenn Fitzgerald (Sean); Greg Wood (Mr. Collins); Mischa Barton (Kyra Collins); Angelica Torn (Mrs. Collins); Lisa Summerour (Bridesmaid); Firdous Bamji (Young Man Buying Ring); Samia Shoaib (Young Woman Buying Ring); Hayden Saunier (Darren's Mom); Janis Dardaris (Kitchen Woman); Neill Hartley (Visitor #2); Sarah Ripard (Visitor #3); Heidi Fischer (Visitor #4); Kadee Strickland (Visitor #5); Michael J. Lyons (Visitor #6); Samantha Fitzpatrick (Kyra's Sister); Holly Rudkin (Society Lady #1); Kate Kearney-Patch (Society Lady #2); Marilyn Shanok (Woman at Accident); M. Night Shyamalan (Dr. Hill); Wes Heywood (Commercial Narrator); Nico Woulard (Hanged Child); Carol Nielson (Hanged Female); Keith Woulard (Hanged Male); Jodi Dawson (Burnt Teacher); Tony Donnelly (Gunshot Boy); Ronnie Lea (Secretary); Carlos X. López (Spanish Ghost on Tape); Gino Inverso (Young Vincent); Ellen Sheppard (Mrs. Sloan); Tom McLaughlin (Anna's Father); Candy Aston Dennis (Anna's Mother); Patrick F. McDade (Shaken Driver); Jose L. Rodriguez (Husband).

CHRISTIAN SCIENCE MONITOR, 8/6/99, p. 15, David Sterritt

The Sixth Sense another new suspense movie [The reference is to *The Thomas Crown Affair*; see Sterritt's review.] is more ambitious and less successful, Bruce Willis plays a child psychologist whose latest patient, an eight-year-old boy, is haunted by ghostly visions that doctors' theories can't explain away. It's hard to say more without revealing the surprises, but the movie's best and worst features all stem from a highly unusual plot structure that builds to a genuinely startling conclusion.

Some moviegoers may feel the ending justifies the means used to achieve it, while others may reject the picture's leisurely pace and literal-minded depiction of supernatural events. It's unquestionably a mixed bag of a movie, but at least it has higher-than-average aspirations to fall short of.

LOS ANGELES TIMES, 8/6/99, Calendar/p. 10, John Anderson

The following review by John Anderson appeared in a slightly different form in
NEWSDAY, 8/6/99, Part II/p. B6.]

It would be rash—foolhardy, even—to imply that summer '99 has seen anything like a renaissance of the horror genre. "Lake Placid" and "Deep Blue Sea" were beached whales. "The Haunting" had all the psychological terror of a jury notice (far less, actually). "American Pie" probably offered some chills, if you were a pastry. Otherwise, it hasn't been a vintage season.

On the other hand, "The Blair Witch Project" continues to frighten and befuddle in new and unusual fashion (it's not a documentary). "Eyes Wide Shut," in its own way, is an experiment in disequilibrium. And now "The Sixth Sense," which has crept up onto summer '99 like a clammy chill, has arrived, proving if nothing else that there are avenues of terror still open to a filmmaker with nerve.

"Sixth Sense" is certainly a nervy film, one that director M. Night Shyamalan ("Wide Awake") has made so disarmingly eerie it's virtually guaranteed to rattle the most jaded of cages. Set in Philadelphia—hometown of its director and, coincidentally, near-home to New Jersey native Bruce Willis—the film concerns Malcolm Crowe (Willis), honored child psychologist and husband to Anna (Olivia Williams of "Rushmore"), who's confronted in his home one night by a patient who slipped through the cracks: Vincent Gray (a convincingly unhinged Donnie Wahlberg), blaming Crowe for the "possible mood disorder" that's still plaguing him, puts one bullet in the doctor and another through his own brain.

A few months later, a recovered but clearly chastened Crowe is sitting on a bench, watching the comings and goings of Cole Sear (Haley Joel Osment), a kid with oversized glasses and the posture of a beaten puppy. Cole, we learn, also has a "possible mood disorder." And Malcolm intends to do for Cole what he couldn't do for Gray.

But the creepiness has already set in. Mixing weird rhythms and gothic-Catholic iconography—static shots of church friezes, petrified statuary and the Latin muttered by Cole when he seeks sanctuary among the pews. "Sixth Sense" is off-kilter from the start, rich in a kind of matter-of-fact horror. Because what Malcolm doesn't know, what he can't possibly suspect until Cole eventually bares his soul, are the depths and echoes of the boy's possible "disorder."

These days, trailers are less often ads for movies than their abridged versions, so while we haven't actually seen any for "Sixth Sense," we're hoping they tell you nothing. There's little to say about the story that won't ruin some twist or turn, other than to say that the various lapses in logic will either be explained away or essentially won't matter, because the film goes so deftly about what it does.

So do the actors, for the most part. Toni Collette, who plays Cole's single and slightly brassy mother, is a virtual revelation (she was this good in "Velvet Goldmine," too). Williams, consigned to the small role of distanced wife, is also fine. Willis, as he's been in some of his better movies, is essentially a supporting player here. It's Osment, whose Cole is such an intelligent, tortured child, who easily gives the best kid performance of the year. In fact, if he were to get an Oscar nomination, it would be both historic and just.

Shyamalan's script is a clever construct, but also contains a great deal of sensitivity to the plight of the "different" child. When he drew pictures of a man with a screwdriver through his neck, Cole tells Malcolm, they called his mother into school. So he started drawing rainbows. "They don't have meetings about rainbows," Cole says.

If there's a complaint to be had with the film, it's that the ending goes on far too long, belaboring the points that have been made so alarmingly and well. It is as if someone wanted to reinforce the idea that this is a Bruce Willis Film, which it's not. He can, however, be proud he was in it.

NEW YORK POST, 8/6/99, p. 43, Rod Dreher

"The Blair Witch Project" has its justly ballyhooed thrills, but who would have thought a ghost story starring Bruce Willis, of all people, would be even more shriek-worthy and unnerving?

Believe it: "The Sixth Sense" may be far more subdued than the summer's other spectral sensation, but the chills imparted by its eerie depiction of a terrified child haunted by the undead are much harder to shake.

"The Sixth Sense," written and directed by a precocious young Philadelphian named M. Night Shyamalan, is the summer's biggest surprise, particularly for viewers who had gotten used to seeing Willis in moribund mainstream fare. In the film, Willis is Dr. Malcolm Crowe, a child psychologist shot in his home by a deranged and suicidal intruder (Mark Wahlberg) who once was his patient.

Willis is OK in this movie, but it's not his picture anyway. The film belongs entirely to an 11-year-old kid named Haley Joel Osment. This TV veteran (as an infant, he played Murphy Brown's baby) delivers what may be the greatest performance ever by a child actor, one that should be remembered as one of the most Oscar-worthy turns this year.

Osment is Cole Sear, a profoundly troubled little boy whom Dr. Crowe takes on as a patient a year after the attack. Cole has a terrible secret, which it takes him a long time to confess to Dr. Crowe. Because we've seen the trailer, we know it: He sees ghosts. Everywhere. All the time. And they scare him to death.

What do they want? Why are they leaving wounds on the boy's body? How can they be dispelled? Shyamalan reveals the spirits to us sparingly, scheduling their abrupt appearance for maximum terror. (I haven't heard screaming like that in a theater in ages; I haven't screamed like that in a theater in ages.)

For all the squealing, he paces the drama slowly, wrapping it in a frigid air of brooding contemplation. It will be too slow for some, but I found it perfect for allowing the depth of Cole's alienation and terror to seep in. The screenplay stands above the horror genre in being a minutely detailed and entirely convincing portrait of a suffering child's character, which has been misshapen by the paranormal.

It is impossible to take your eyes off Osment, who vividly conveys the hopelessness of a sensitive, intelligent child who bears burdens beyond all telling. Depressed, isolated, shunned as a freak by his classmates, Cole is misunderstood by his stressed-out mother (Toni Collette) and trapped in a nightmare no one could possibly believe.

Though you rarely see the ghosts, Osment performs with such sustained and concentrated intensity you feel his terror as your own. It's as virtuoso a major film debut as any since Edward Norton freaked audiences out and launched his brilliant career in "Primal Fear."

Cole reminds Dr. Crowe of the tormented patient who shot him before turning the gun on himself, and the shrink chooses to work with Cole in hope of seeking redemption—and perhaps a new lease on his failing marriage to his depressed wife (Olivia Williams).

But the spectacular twist ending clues us in that Cole might have done some choosing of his own. It's the only shock in "The Sixth Sense" greeted not with a shriek, but with a gasp at how masterfully plotted this superb film is.

SIGHT AND SOUND, 11/99, p. 54, Philip Strick

Philadelphia. Psychologist Malcolm Crowe is celebrating his latest award with his wife Anna when former patient Vincent Gray breaks in. Blaming Malcolm's therapy for his dementia, Vincent shoots him, then kills himself.

Months later Malcolm takes on the case of nine-year-old Cole Sear, a disturbed schoolboy living with his mother Lynn. While gaining the boy's confidence, Malcolm begins to have misgivings about his marriage, suspecting Anna of having an affair.

Malcolm enlists Cole's co-operation by telling him about Vincent, and at last Cole reveals his secret: he is visited by dead people only he can see, who plead for his help. Baffled by this delusion, Malcolm despairs of helping the boy, but Cole begs him not to abandon his case. Listening to the tape of his sessions with Vincent, Malcolm suspects a supernatural element and begins to reconsider Cole's claims.

One of Cole's 'visitors' Kyra leads Cole to a videotape that proves to the guests at her funeral that she was murdered. Cole is cheered by his schoolmates, previously his tormentors, for his performance in the school play. Able now to discuss his 'gift' with his mother, who accepts he has special powers, he and Malcolm agree there is no further need for therapy. Returning home, Malcolm recognises that his loving relationship with Anna will always survive Vincent's fatal bullet.

Constantly on the brink of explanation, *The Sixth Sense* in fact derives most of its fascination from explaining next to nothing. A mass of disquieting details, it takes a number of detours towards a final reversal that throws everything open to question. What was masquerading as one case history gradually becomes several, most prominently that of the psychologist but also those of the mother, the wife, the suicidal psychotic and an ever-widening circle of the troubled and dispossessed.

Inadvertent guide to these lost souls, whether they're alive or in some other limbo, is the bewildered schoolboy Cole. He eventually comes to terms with his power, graduating from crime buster to marriage counsellor while retaining the skills of a seaside-booth medium ("Grandma says 'Hi!'"). But what kind of future awaits him in the employment of his now-validated gift is left to the imagination.

Director/writer M. Night Shyamalan has been film-making since the age of ten, although primed for a top-grade medical career. Future retrospectives will doubtless reveal to British audiences his 45 short films, his acclaimed 1992 debut feature *Praying With Anger,* and his second film *Wide Awake* (1997). But for now, *The Sixth Sense* (and its huge US box-office success) looks to have materialised almost out of nowhere.

At least we can guess from the available clues that Shyamalan's main concerns are isolation (he took the role of his own 'ghost' in *Praying With Anger)* and the strains and tensions of family ties: *Wide Awake* is about the relationship between a Catholic schoolboy and his grandfather. And generous doses of autobiography can be detected in *The Sixth Sense,* both in the character of the cool-headed specialist who finds his career on the wrong path and in that of the child haunted by innumerable dramas in need of an audience.

These traits aside, the film's main appeal is the assurance with which it is made. Studiously versed in art-house classics as much as in Spielberg or Craven, Shyamalan's film is an attention-grabbing fusion of minimalism and overstatement. His horror story is shot as Tarkovsky might have shot it, with briefly glimpsed figures on the fringes and with constant ambiguities of action and attitude. Setting the mood, the opening scene in the wine cellar, the camera hiding furtively behind the racks, would persuade us that an unseen intruder is about to pounce, but he doesn't, and what we've gained instead is a sketch of a highly strung wife along with a timely reminder of the ritualistic status of wine. And *then* he pounces, in the bathroom where, moments earlier, the psychologist who is about to learn of failure has suggested they consign his latest award.

It fits together so smoothly that one feels that Shyamalan could leave almost anything on the screen for us to assimilate. Since, for instance, he knows Philadelphia, his home town, well, his glimpses of a landmark sculpture plainly add up to something more than the passage of time. But such references are part of the film's attraction as well as its weakness. Keeping us guessing before the full misery of Cole's predicament becomes apparent, there are curiously misleading hints of his paranormal powers, at their strongest in his mother's presence.

Leaving Cole in the kitchen for a moment, his mother returns to find every drawer and door open. Examining family photographs, she finds the same flash of light in each one. Such images have a vivid but unresolved potency, distracting us from more awkward matters. Where does the psychologist go between the Vincent episode and the Cole assignment? If Cole's visitors don't know they're dead, why do they want his help? The enigmas remain, but since another of Shyamalan's accomplishments has been to coax exquisite performances from his cast (including Haley Joel Osment and an intensely introverted Bruce Willis) we are happy to share their bewilderment rather than dismissing it.

VILLAGE VOICE, 8/10/99, p. 70, Michael Atkinson

Despite being an inflated, polished-to-an-anonymous-shine Disney deal, M. Night Shyamalan's *The Sixth Sense* has its nervous thumb on something, a sharp regard for miserable preadolescent disconnectedness, and for how everyday life can ripple with fear. Too bad it ends up being a play date in the *Ghost* neighborhood. Writer-director Shyamalan's previous efforts, *Praying With Anger* and *Wide Awake*, were forgettable misfires, but there were signs of melancholy life. *The Sixth Sense* is Shyamalan's big spec-script shot in the dark, and in the summer scheme of things his movie falls somewhere between *The Haunting*'s digital slavering and *Blair Witch*'s spine-juicing nighttime. With few F/X to speak of (the characters' icy breath is CGI'D, which must be cheaper than refrigerating the set á la *The Exorcist*), Shyamalan shows restraint and some screenwriting wisdom detailing the life of a Philadelphia nine-year-old (Haley Joel Osment)who appears to be emotionally disturbed, but is in fact terrorized by the presence of dead spirits day and night. We see only a few genuinely chilling ghosts; mostly, the film feels huddled in apprehension.

Bruce Willis, as the boy's psychologist, is simply the impassive venture capital that got Shyamalan's movie made (has a star ever been so competent, and yet so dull?)—its real resource is Osment. His pitifully scrunched brow, choked silences, and curdled voice, suggesting tortures so dreadful parents will tie themselves in knots, are the movie's best special effect. Shyamalan achieves his coldest moments when looking at something, mostly Osment, dead on, but too often the film gets lost in overlit opulence and the soundtrack going boo. But complain all you want about Willis's posturing and the rabbit-in-the-hat ending (predicated as it is on a vast plothole), the film is still a rarity, a studio horror movie focused on a child's traumatic stress.

Also reviewed in:
CHICAGO TRIBUNE, 8/6/99, Friday/p. A, Mark Caro
NEW YORK TIMES, 8/6/99, p. E14, Stephen Holden
NEW YORKER, 8/16 & 23/99, p. 200, David Denby
VARIETY, 8/2-8/99, p. 33, Todd McCarthy
WASHINGTON POST, 8/6/99, p. C1, Stephen Hunter
WASHINGTON POST, 8/6/99, Weekend/p. 41, Desson Howe

SLC PUNK!

A Sony Pictures Classics release of a Beyond Films presentation of a Blue Tulip production. *Executive Producer:* Jan De Bont, Michael Peyser, and Andrea Kreuzhage. *Producer:* Sam Maydew and Peter Ward. *Director:* James Merendino. *Screenplay:* James Merindino. *Director of Photography:* Greg Littlewood. *Editor:* Esther P. Russell. *Music:* Melanie Miller. *Sound:* Doug Cameron. *Sound Editor:* Elmo Weber and Walter Spencer. *Casting:* Risa Bramon-Garcia and Randi Hiller. *Production Designer:* Charlotte Malmlof. *Costumes:* Fiora. *Make-up:* Tania Goddard. *Stunt Coordinator:* Fenton Quinn. *Running time:* 97 minutes. *MPAA Rating:* Not Rated.

CAST: Matthew Lillard (Stevo); Michael Goorjian (Bob); Annabeth Gish (Trish); Jennifer Lien (Sandy); Christopher McDonald (Father); Devon Sawa (Sean); Jason Segel (Mike); Summer Phoenix (Brandy); James Duval (John "The Mod"); Til Schweiger (Mark); Adam Pascal (Eddie); Chiara Barzini (Jennifer); Kevin Breznahan (Chris); Christina Karras (Jamie); Russ Peacock (Jones); Christopher Ogden (Young Stevo); Francis Capra (Young Bob); McNally Sagel (Mom); Scott Brady (Bouncer); Vaughn McBride (Liquor Store Man); Janice Knickrehm (Liquor Store Woman); Marcia Dangerfield (Liquor Store Lady); Tom Jacobson (Liquor Store Fellow); Stephanie Shumway (Jules); Eric Robertson (Doctor); Micaela Nelligan (Nurse); Mary Bishop (Sean's Mother); Dominic Gortat (Poser); Evan O'Meara (GBH Singer); Elizabeth Westwood (Hot Babe); Glade Quinn and Brad Jessey (Cowboys); Don Walsh (Bob's Dad); Adam Lawson (Russ); Brandon Klock (Tom); Kassandra Metos (Little Girl); Brad Slocum (Teller); Joyce Cohen (Clothing Store Woman); Tracey Pfau (Fast Food Clerk).

LOS ANGELES TIMES, 4/16/99, Calendar/p. 16, Kevin Thomas

Matthew Lillard, who first came to attention as the frenetic Stuart in "Scream," has a potentially star-making role in James Merendino's sit-up-and-take-notice "SLC Punk." It's a sharp, funny and ultimately wise and subtle coming-of-age movie set in Salt Lake City in the '80s that, while not strictly autobiographical, draws upon some aspects of the filmmakers's own experiences.

Lillard has said that he's drawn to extreme characters, and this film's self-proclaimed anarchist Stevo is certainly that, but lots more. Stevo is a role demanding range and depth, and by the time this fast and furious film is over, Lillard recalls the youthful Peter Fonda, not only in his lanky presence but in his anti-Establishment stance. Stevo, however, requires of Lillard a zany, corrosive wit and combustible personality rarely if ever asked of Fonda.

What distinguishes "SLC Punk," which has a rip-roaring soundtrack featuring '80s bands, from most rebellious-youth movies is its up-front smarts. Stevo, who dyes his hair blue as part of his punk look, may hate Reagan, hate the grayness of Salt Lake City, repeatedly viewed from condescending helicopter shots, and embrace the Ramones, the Specials and the Dead Kennedys, but he exhaustingly poses all the big questions about life's meaning and lack of same. Stevo is a brilliant guy, a philosopher whether he admits it or not, just as he's a good student in spite of himself. Helping him embrace an exuberant nihilism is his sweetly crazed pal Bob (Michael Goorjian), who has a Mohawk haircut and is paranoid about taking drugs, medicinally or otherwise, but his stance does not exclude booze and cigarettes. As Stevo and Bob carom through their lives, brawling, spouting protests, raising hell in general, they hold that the worst thing anyone could be is a poseur. (One of their passing acquaintances, by the way, is played by German star Til Schweiger, of "Maybe ... Maybe Not.")

But what is Stevo to make of Bob when his friend starts saying that maybe Salt Lake isn't so bad once he has fallen in love with head shop proprietor (Annabeth Gish). And what of Stevo himself, when he senses from the start that he'll fall for a girl (Summer Phoenix), from a family as rich as his own, an attractive young woman who coolly points out that punk is a fashion and revolution comes from within. At this point we wonder: Could it possibly be that Stevo's ex-hippie father turned slick corporate attorney (a slyly bemused Christopher McDonald), with whom he has a humorously sparring relationship, knows him better than he knows himself?

Rambunctious, explosive, scabrous and relentlessly in your face, "SLC Punk" ringingly tells it like it is, but from an ever-widening perspective that illuminates Stevo's loud and calamitous progress toward a self-knowledge and self-awareness that he's too intelligent not to accept with a wry humor. "SLC Punk," which is actually gently satirizing all the outrageousness it seems merely to be reveling in, is in fact quite a grown-up movie.

NEW YORK POST, 4/16/99, p. 57, Jonathan Foreman

Despite some funny set pieces, "SLC Punk!" just doesn't work. It's virtually plotless, Matthew Lillard gives an amazingly shallow and unconvincing performance as the film's main character, and it's filled with wannabe-wacky directoral tricks—like having the main character turn and address the camera.

Lillard plays the thinly sketched Stevo, who has been a punk since high school. Now it's 1985, he's just graduated from college and is hanging around a graffiti-covered apartment with his friend Bob (Michael Goorjian), hoping to waste some time in good "anarchist" fashion.

So when they're not partying in a tiny downtown scene that includes various hippies and mods, they get into unrealistically brutal battles with rednecks. But as the voice-over narration tells us, a series of incidents sour him on the "anarchist" lifestyle and push him toward the dream of his hippie-turned-yuppie parents that he go to Harvard Law School.

The endearing, sweet-natured punk is a movie cliche, so of course, neither Stevo nor Bob are nearly as vicious as they look. "Heroin Bob" is actually terrified of drugs, and Stevo has an increasingly hard time suppressing a variety of bourgeois instincts. And these contradictions are at the heart of the anecdotes that pass for the film's structure.

Writer-director James Merendino clearly thinks there's something extraordinary about someone playing punk in Mormon-dominated Salt Lake, but it doesn't look like that big a deal. Nor does Salt Lake City seem half as awful as Stevo thinks.

There's a lot of talk in "SLC Punk!" about the difference between "real" genuinely rebellious punks and "posers" who are merely making a fashion statement, but it's impossible to see what that difference is.

Stevo rants a lot about how hardcore he and Bob are, and why there's no reason for them to kowtow to the British punk movement. But unlike the original punks of the '70s, Stevo is an upper-middle-class kid, his rebellion is a shallow, virtually cost-free one, and it's obvious from the git-go that he'll end up part of "the system."

Watching Stevo make that journey would have been a far more interesting ride if Merendino and Lillard had been able to make him a person rather than a mannequin on which to hang some punkish threads.

NEWSDAY, 4/16/99, Part II/p. B11, Gene Seymour

The genie unleashed back in the 1970s by the Sex Pistols (and, arguably, a decade before by the Velvet Underground) convinced millions of restless kids that "going punk" was the path to truth. Slam dancing, head-butting, what's-it-to-you hostility promised insulation from mediocrity, hypocrisy and, above all, conformity.

"SLC Punk!" may not be the first, but it won't be the last movie that shows the punk mystique, like others before it, as a means of Hanging Out until you figure out who you are. At least that's the impression one gets from writer-director James Merendino's feature in which punk's reach is shown to be so powerful that not even Salt Lake City was immune.

Once you get over that shock, "SLC Punk!" settles into a dry, wry groove as it tours the cutting-edge of Utah's capital, circa 1985, with Matthew Lillard from "Scream" as your hyperbolic guide. As Steve, blue-haired son of a rich, Harvard-trained lawyer (Chris McDonald), Lillard delivers a running spiel on the aimless drift from party to fistfight to party to fistfight. Which is pretty much the uncompromising life he leads with his best friend (Michael Goorjian), who's called "Heroin Bob" because he hates needles and, unlike most of his acquaintances, spurns drugs.

Borrowing from "trainspotting's" antic tone and static narrative, "SLC Punk!" strings together anecdotes about life as a Salt Lake 1980s bohemian, which (surprise!) isn't much different from life in other towns in other decades. Each tale, no matter how whimsical, has the feel of a cautionary fable, whether it's about the acid dealer (Devon Sawa) who ends up fried and blasted by his own medicine or the hair-trigger paranoia of another dealer (Til Schweiger). There's even a set piece about the nutty things that can happen to you and your weird friends when you cross state lines to buy beer.

Together, these reminiscences have the texture of a wistful afternoon spent in a bar, swapping lies about surviving sex, drugs and rock and roll. Whether you can hang with the experience depends on how much of Lillard's goofball skittishness you can take. There are times when you wish "Steve-o" would find another table to bother. But even those parts of the movie most weighed down by slack and drift are relieved by Goorjian's fascinating performance as Bob, who, beneath his anxiety and bluster, seems as bewildered by his current state as any super-straight Mormon.

"SLC Punk!" may not generate any frisson of recognition among those who spent their punk years in New York, London or Los Angeles. But Merendino's film comes frustratingly close to being a definitive statement—not about punk, but about the ongoing, quixotic effort of postwar kids to make their nowhere places feel like somewhere.

SIGHT AND SOUND, 5/00, p. 61, Charlotte O'Sullivan

The early 80s. Stevo is a young punk living in Salt Lake City, Utah. Stevo's divorced middle-class parents want him to go to Harvard to study law. He'd rather fight and party but it dawns on him that his "hardcore" friends are going soft. And he himself seems to be changing. Further confused when his father informs him he's got into Harvard (his father filled out the forms), Stevo's world finally comes apart when he sees his girlfriend Sandy getting off with another man. The girlfriend of Stevo's best friend Bob promises to set Stevo up with a pal of hers, Brandy. Stevo and Bob go to see Bob's father. It's his father's birthday, but the old man is so paranoid he doesn't recognise Bob and gets out his gun.

That evening they all go to Brandy's party. Stevo is immediately smitten by Brandy but Bob can't settle down, telling everyone he's got a headache. A girl gives him a mound of tablets; he becomes violent, so Stevo takes him home. In the morning Bob is dead. Stevo is ready to marry Brandy and go to Harvard.

A sweet film about punks seems almost a contradiction in terms. You expect messy, amateurish and obnoxious and *SLC Punk!* certainly manages to be these as well—but sweet? Surely they can't be for real, these American anarchists. Director/writer James Merendino's point, of course, is that no one's for real. Like the boys in Peter Yates' delightful *Breaking Away* (1979), Stevo's gang are just looking for a niche, and just as the underprivileged hero in that film adopted an Italian identity, overprivileged Stevo has embraced funny-coloured hair. It comes as no surprise when right near the end we learn Stevo and Bob are also Dungeon and Dragon playing nerds.

One of the film's many problems, however, is that Matthew Lillard is not a naturally sympathetic actor. Like Dennis Hopper and Jim Carrey, he's one of those faster-and-faker-than-life performers who always brings something new to the term OTT. Lillard is especially limited because he has only two expressions: the I-know-you-like-me smile, and the shit-you-don't-like-me-pout. His constant presence (he supplies not only the voiceover narration but talks endlessly to camera) soon becomes irritating and only a few scenes manage to trick him into doing something new, such as a scene where his father gradually seduces him into going to Harvard. Most of the time, though, you don't know where you are with Lillard/Stevo. So when his friend Bob dies (fatally traumatised, it would seem, by his lack of parental love and Spandau Ballet's 'She Loved Like Diamonds'), Lillard dives into a puddle of emotion, wailing, "Now I don't have any friends!" You wonder if Merendino is taking a sly poke at Stevo's narcissism. Or maybe he's just hoping we'll break down in floods of tears ourselves.

The voiceover compounds the confusion. It's unclear, for instance, whether we're meant to accept the fast forward in the narrator's perspective. Three-quarters of the way through the film, Stevo makes it clear he's no longer the boy he was. It's just the sort of self-deprecating voice of authority familiar from *The Wonder Years*. Again, if this is an ironic comment on how we seek to shape our lives then it's an interesting move. However, one suspects Merendino wants us to take it at face value. As a viewer, you can put up with a lack of structure—this is, after all, an anarchist's tale but the last minute attempts at order are harder to forgive.

SLC Punk! sticks far too closely to the rites-of-passage formula. And most of the bizarre encounters (whether with misfit friends or prejudiced locals) take us places we've been before. But ironically the place feels new. Salt Lake City's mud flats, the post-apocalyptic forests and miles upon miles of white sky manage to appear both unfriendly and banal. We're used to seeing America's wide open spaces through appreciative eyes (as the "promised land" the Mormons supposedly mistook Utah for). It's nice to view it for once as a bored teenager might, as necessarily inadequate, as a waste of space.   And then there's that sweetness, that acknowledgement that boys do cry which actually leaves more room for the female characters to shine. (Annabeth Gish does a nice turn as stem hippie goddess Trish, while Summer Phoenix is a revelation as the unaffected Brandy.) This, plus the spot-on music (Blondie, that cherry coloured bridge between punk and mainstream, plays at Brandy's party) make one look forward to whatever shambolic project Merendino gets around to next.

VILLAGE VOICE, 4/20/99, p. 152, Amy Taubin

The rewind to the '80s is already upon us with skateboarders sporting Dead Kennedys T-shirts and Mary Harron's adaptation of *American Psycho* wrapping production in Canada. One of the first punk revival films out of the gate, James Merendino's *SLC Punk!* strikes a brighter chord than the immortal Sid and Nancy, and although fresh and endearing are hardly words you associate with punk, the film doesn't feel like a cop-out until the very end.

Matthew Lillard stars as Stevo, a Reagan-era, Salt Lake City punk whose ex-hippie liberal parents tolerate his blue mohawk, trusting that eventually he'll follow their footsteps all the way to Harvard Law School.   The film is couched as a memory piece and Merendino's most innovative directorial strategy is to collapse present and past by having Lillard shout Stevo's reflections about his youthful rebellion directly at the camera, while the scene he's describing in the past tense takes place behind him. I know it sounds like a Brechtian affectation, but it works. Unlike most narrations, which leach energy out of the action, this one amps the film up.

There are a couple of excellent set pieces, including a poignantly evoked acid trip. For a film about a youth culture defined by its music, *SLC Punk!* skimps a bit on the score, but the selections by the Ramones, the Specials, and the Dead Kennedys are choice.

Also reviewed in:
NEW YORK TIMES, 4/16/99, p. E27, Janet Maslin
NEW YORKER, 4/19/99, p. 108, Anthony Lane
VARIETY, 2/8-14/99, p. 81, Dennis Harvey

SLEEPY HOLLOW

A Paramount Pictures and Mandalay Pictures release of a Scott Rudin/American Zoetrope production. *Executive Producer:* Larry Franco and Francis Ford Coppola. *Producer:* Scott Rudin and Adam Schroeder. *Director:* Tim Burton. *Screenplay:* Andrew Kevin Walker. *Story:* Kevin Yagher and Andrew Kevin Walker. *Based on the story "The Legend of Sleepy Hollow" by:* Washington Irivng. *Director of Photography:* Emmanuel Lubezki. *Editor:* Chris Lebenzon. *Music:* Craig Anderson. *Music Editor:* Ellen Segal. *Sound:* Tony Dawe, Gary Alper, and (music) Shawn Murphy. *Sound Editor:* Skip Lievsay. *Casting:* Illene Starger and Susie Figgis. *Production Designer:* Rick Heinrichs. *Art Director:* Les Tomkins. *Set Decorator:* Peter Young and Debra Schutt. *Costumes:* Colleen Atwood. *Make-up:* Elizabeth Tag. *Stunt Coordinator:* Nick Gillard. *Running time:* 110 minutes. *MPAA Rating:* R.

CAST: Jonny Depp (Ichabod Crane); Christina Ricci (Katrina Van Tassel); Miranda Richardson (Lady Van Tassel); Michael Gambon (Baltus Van Tassel); Casper Van Dien (Brom Van Brunt); Jeffrey Jones (Reverend Steenwyck); Richard Griffiths (Magistrate Philipse); Ian McDiarmid (Doctor Lancaster); Michael Gough (Notary Hardenbrook); Christopher Walken (Hessian Horseman); Marc Pickering (Young Masbath); Lisa Marie (Lady Crane); Steven Waddington (Killian); Claire Skinner (Beth Killian); Christopher Lee (Burgomaster); Alun Armstrong (High Constable); Miranda Richardson (Crone); Mark Spalding (Jonathan Masbath); Jessica Oyelowo (Sarah); Tony Maudsley (Van Ripper); Peter Guinness (Lord Crane); Nicholas Hewetson (Glenn); Orlando Seale (Theodore); Sean Stephens (Thomas Killian); Gabrielle Lloyd (Doctor

Lancaster's Wife);   Robert Sella (Dirk Van Garrett);   Michael Feast (Spotty Man);   Jamie Foreman (Thuggish Constable);   Philip Martin Brown (Constable 1);   Sam Fior (Young Ichabod Crane);   Tessa Allen-Ridge (Young Lady Van Tassel);   Cassandra Farndale (Young Crane);   Lily Phillips (Girl 2);   Bianca Nicholas (Little Girl);   Paul Brightwell (Rifleman);   Martin Landau (First Victim).

LOS ANGELES TIMES, 11/19/99, Calendar/p. 1, Kenneth Turan

"Heads Will Roll" is more than a clever tag line for Tim Burton's "Sleepy Hollow." It's a bemused truth-in-advertising warning from a director who's told interviewers, "I've always wanted to make a movie where one of the characters didn't have a head." With more than a dozen decapitations to its credit, "Sleepy Hollow" surely made its creator happy, but how pleased others will be depends on their tolerance for the ghoulish and the grotesque.

An exquisitely mounted effort created to the exact specifications of an adroit director whose sensibility is truly bizarre, "Sleepy Hollow" is kind of an ultimate Tim Burton movie. More creepy and flesh-crawling than overwhelmingly gory, it nevertheless takes pride in characters who get splattered with blood as often as take-out fries get doused with catsup.

Coexisting with all this is Burton's wacky tongue-in-cheek sense of humor that ensures that eyes will roll as well as heads. And the film's look is so exceptional that it's easy to imagine Burton as a medieval monk, spending endless happy hours illuminating a manuscript with a fiendishly detailed panorama depicting the tortures of the damned.

"Sleepy Hollow," as every schoolchild used to know, is taken from "The Legend of Sleepy Hollow," the 1820 Washington Irving short story animated by Disney once upon a time. Ichabod Crane is still the leading character, but given the involvement of both Burton and screenwriter Andrew Kevin Walker ("Seven," "Fight Club"), the point has been changed and the ambience considerably darkened.

Schoolteacher no longer, the film's Crane is now a crusading 1799 crime-stopper, a hotshot Manhattan constable who believes in rational methods of detection, much to the disgust of his supervisor (played by British Hammer Films veteran and Burton idol Christopher Lee). "I stand up for sense and justice," Crane proclaims. "To solve crimes we must use our brains," not to mention the cases full of chemicals and strange optical equipment he's invented himself.

As connected to Burton as De Niro once was to Scorsese, Depp has often done his best work ("Edward Scissorhands," "Ed Wood") for this director, and "Sleepy Hollow" follows that form. Despite being a prissy, self-satisfied know-it-all as well as a bit of a prig, Depp's Ichabod is always engaging and his increased discomfort level as the film progresses is consistently amusing.

Crane's superiors don't agree with his advanced ideas, however, and they assign him to a dead-end case (so to speak) in the isolated farming community of Sleepy Hollow in the wilds of upstate New York. Three people have had their heads lopped off (including "Ed Wood" co-star Martin Landau in an unbilled cameo) and Crane has to figure out who the culprit is.

Up in Sleepy Hollow Crane bunks with the Van Tassels, the town's wealthiest family, including husband Baltus (Michael Gambon); his wife, Lady Van Tassel (Miranda Richardson); and their daughter Katrina (Christina Ricci, unexpectedly blond and surprisingly neutral in the film's twisted equivalent of a Sandra Dee role).

Horrified at the carnage, the townspeople know exactly who the culprit is: a carnage-loving long-dead Hessian mercenary nicknamed the Headless Horseman (played in flashback by a vampirish Christopher Walken, in reality afraid of horses) who filed his teeth down to little points just for kicks and was finally killed during the Revolutionary War and buried in the Western Woods near town, "a haunted place where brave men will not venture."

Ever the rationalist, Depp (oh ye of little faith) refuses to believe that a spirit is doing all this damage. "We have murders in New York without benefit of ghouls and goblins," he huffily insists, but soon enough he finds that, then as now, people from New York don't know quite as much as they think.

Ravishingly photographed in rich muted color by Emmanuel Lubezki ("A Little Princess," "Like Water for Chocolate"), "Sleepy Hollow" is often carried by its brooding, autumnal atmosphere, enhanced by composer Danny Elfman, production designer Rick Heinrichs and costume designer Colleen Atwood. Sleepy Hollow looks so gorgeous (albeit a bit sinister) that hordes of New

Yorkers would be looking to purchase second homes there if it hadn't been built from scratch on a 20-acre estate north of London.

Though "Sleepy Hollow's" scares start out on the genteel side, the film gets creepier and creepier as it goes on and Burton, doing what he does best, relentlessly cranks up the volume on the weirdness. Whatever work of literature he may turn to next, don't expect it to be by Jane Austen.

NEW YORK, 11/29/99, p. 131, Peter Rainer

Tim Burton's *Sleepy Hollow*, starring Johnny Depp as a hyperrational, Sherlock Holmesian Ichabod Crane, is a lot closer to Gahan Wilson than to Washington Irving. Burton goes in for a heavy dose of the cold creeps; the film seems to have been made to show off as many close-ups of severed heads as possible. (The screenplay is by severed-head specialist Andrew Kevin Walker of *Seven)* The production design is a triumph of gnarled vistas and foggy woods and slime. The galloping eruptions of the headless horseman, played by Christopher Walken, are startlingly ghoulish, and the cast, which also includes Christina Ricci as a dour dumpling with eyes for Ichabod, is chosen with a horror maven's eye for terror. It's a peculiarly adolescent conception of terror, though; Burton, for all his skill, never ranges beyond the thrills of the obvious, he doesn't enlarge the meaning of the horror he shows us, the way a Brian De Palma might. As a filmmaker, he's in a perpetual state of Halloween: a sicko treat-or-treat specialist.

NEW YORK POST, 11/19/99, p. 50, Jonathan Foreman

"Sleepy Hollow" is a visual tour de force: It's every bit as dreamy and atmospheric as you would expect from a movie by Tim Burton—the near-genius behind "Batman" and "Edward Scissorhands."

But as a horror movie, even one inspired by the kitschy Hammer horror films of the 1950s, it's disappointing.

While it features brilliantly photographed chases and fights amid wonderful sets, the film is never frightening, and rarely all that creepy, at least by Burton's standards. And it goes on just long enough for the stunning effect of the director's virtuosity to wear off, so that you begin to wish the story were more involving, the main characters more sympathetic and the lead performance by Johnny Depp less jokey and over the top.

It's almost as if Burton was so involved with the look and feel of his film that he allowed his exceptionally talented star to get out of control—or at least out of step with the rest of the cast.

It's 1799, and Ichabod Crane (Johnny Depp) is a New York police constable (in the original short story by Washington Irving, he's a teacher). He's also an amateur scientist who believes that detective work and reasoning would be more effective than the brutal investigative measures preferred by his superiors.

Tired of his badgering, they send him upstate to solve three strange murders near the isolated village of Sleepy Hollow.

All three victims were beheaded, and the villagers insist that a headless horseman—the ghost of a Hessian mercenary killed during the Revolution—was responsible for the crimes.

Crane doesn't believe in ghosts, and he's sure that one or more of the village leaders—perhaps even his wealthy host, Baltus Van Tassel (Michael Gambon)—is somehow behind the slayings.

It's a suspicion that doesn't bode well for his budding relationship with Van Tassel's bewitching daughter Katrina (Christina Ricci), whose other suitor (Casper Van Dien) conveniently becomes another victim of the horseman.

But while Crane finds out that he's wrong about the horseman's supernatural nature, he's also right about human involvement in the ongoing murders.

Depp's Crane is prissy and cowardly. The characterization is funny at first but makes it hard to care about his fate or his chances with Ricci, and there's something just a little too hokey about Depp's performance. It feels campier than the rest of the film, and that imbalance of tone makes it harder to suspend one's disbelief.

Ricci, miscast as an ingenue, doesn't have enough to do or say and is uncharacteristically bland (and blond). Miranda Richardson as Lady Van Tassel unwisely attempts an American accent

—even though all the other actors, including Depp sound more like Englishmen—and is a much less substantial presence than usual.

But the rest of the cast is all excellent, in particular Gambon and Jeffrey Jones (the principal in "Ferris Bueller's Day Off").

The film was shot in England, and the landscapes lack the real grandeur of the Hudson Valley. But the fog-shrouded village, the corpse-like scarecrows, the riders repeatedly silhouetted against a gloomy sky, the blood-spurting "Tree of Death" and the saber-swinging horseman himself—all of them shot in hues of blue and gray—are masterpieces of the grotesque Burtonic aesthetic.

NEWSDAY, 11/19/99, Part II/p. 29, Jan Stuart

The year is 1799, when the ride to Westchester County from New York City took two days and you didn't need to be a chief executive to qualify for a mortgage there. No one is getting much sleep in Sleepy Hollow, where the Headless Horseman is lopping off heads faster than you can say Salome, and even the dead are disturbed from their rest in the hunt for this mad executioner.

Enter Ichabod Crane, a very earnest constable with a very silly bag of investigative tools.

As evidenced by the magical "Edward Scissorhands," Johnny Depp and director Tim Burton make dark and fabulous music together. The pair ride high again with "Sleepy Hollow," a sumptuously enjoyable campfire story of a movie that manages to be both giddy and gruesome in large, equal dollops.

Burton has obviously spared no expense on his vision of Washington Irving's haunted village. The sky is in a spectacular state of perpetual overcast, the trees are as gnarly as a witch's face, and the earth is suffocating under a luxurious carpet of dead leaves. When Ichabod (Depp) approaches Sleepy Hollow in his horse-drawn carriage, the Hudson River seems to shimmer with the sorrows of recent days.

Dispatched from New York City to track down a headless serial killer (played, when he has his head on straight, by Christopher Walken) who decapitates his victims, then makes off with the heads. Crane is hosted by esteemed Sleepy Hollow residents Balthus and Lady Van Tassel (Michael Gambon and Miranda Richardson). Shrugging off the locals' superstitious tales of a headless horseman ("Seeing is believing," says a half-blind villager in ominous tones), Crane stalks the killer with science.

Depp is drolly charming doing his dour and hapless thing, more Buster Keaton's Sherlock Jr. than Basil Rathbone's Sherlock Holmes as he manipulates absurd powders and complicated spectacles that detect what is obvious to the naked eye.

"Sleepy Hollow" is at its best when it casts its shadows over Depp's lily-livered savior and enables Burton's special effects team full reign to whip up bug- eyed witches and blood-spilling tree trunks. There is some stab made at romance, although pouty Christina Ricci (as the Van Tassels' daughter, Katrina) seems somewhat ill-at-ease doing the fair blond maiden bit. Depp finds a more able partner in Marc Pickering, a 13-year-old with a naturally spooked visage who plays Crane's intrepid young aide-de-camp.

Pickering's wide, tremulous eyes reflect the film's lurid appeal to youthful terrors. Be forewarned: "Sleepy Hollow" is ultraviolent, blood-dripping horror that, despite the director's protestations over the film's R rating, is most assuredly not for young children. For older kids, the fun never clots.

NEWSWEEK, 11/22/99, p. 91, Jeff Giles

Tim Burton's "Sleepy Hollow" has got to be the most gorgeous, sumptuous, painterly movie ever made about multiple decapitations. The director can make anything look beautiful—the picking of flowers, the exhuming of coffins, even the steady stream of heads that come rolling toward you through the leaves.

Ichabod Crane (Johnny Depp) is no longer a geeky schoolteacher, as in Washington Irving's famous story, but a geeky detective. Early in the movie, Crane annoys his superiors in New York City so thoroughly that they dispatch him to the countryside, where three noggins were recently lopped off "clean as dandelion heads." Once in Sleepy Hollow, Crane first hears the legend of the Headless Horseman (Christopher Walken), which is re-enacted in a ravishing, wintry flashback. It's said that a Hessian soldier was decapitated during the Revolution and now prowls the earth returning the favor. Crane champions reason and science above all else, and dismisses the Horseman legend as superstition. Then he sees the demon in action. Soon Crane is chasing the Hessian, as well as a young beauty named Katrina Van Tassel (Christina Ricci). The thought of catching either makes him tremble.

Depp's performance here is highly mannered and takes getting used to, but ultimately he makes Crane funny and human. How many movie heroes respond to danger by shoving the nearest woman or child in front of them? Ricci, by contrast, is so-so. Her courtship of Crane is touching, nonetheless, and their faces are luminous together in close-ups—they look like two passing planets. Andrew Kevin Walker ("Seven") is credited with the wry, sparkling screenplay here. But there's no mistaking the brittle humor of the playwright Tom Stoppard, who reportedly ghost-wrote a draft. Toward the end of the movie, Crane and an orphan named Young Masbath (a very fine Marc Pickering) battle the Horseman atop a windmill that calls Burton's "Batman" movies to mind. Afterward Young Masbath asks, "Is he dead?" "That's the trouble," says Crane. "He was dead to begin with."

What slows "Sleepy Hollow" down is the dull, byzantine search for the mortal who is somehow controlling the Horseman. Do we really need a conspiracy-type plot to explain the Horseman's killings? He has no head, and he's pissed about it—surely that's enough. (One of Burton's rare false steps visually is some lame Freudian imagery meant to evoke castration and the fear of sex. The Headless Horseman travels between upstate New York and hell by plunging in and out of a hole in a tree that looks like—well, like one of Georgia O'Keeffe's flowers, to put it mildly.) It's not until the end that "Sleepy Hollow" really begins to hurtle along, that it's as much a visceral experience as an esthetic one. Ultimately, it may not be as quirky and unforgettable as some of Burton's earlier movies—it lacks the sort of magical dust that settled over "Beetlejuice" and "Edward Scissorhands". Still, at its best it's a marvel: bold, exciting and full of visions.

SIGHT AND SOUND, 2/00, p. 54, Andrew O'Hehir

New York, 1799. Ichabod Crane, a young constable, is sent to the upstate village of Sleepy Hollow to investigate a series of mysterious beheadings. Leading citizens, led by landowner Baltus Van Tassel, tell Crane the killings are the work of the Headless Horseman, a Hessian mercenary beheaded during the Revolution who has come back from the grave. Crane does not believe this until he sees the town magistrate killed by the Horseman. Shocked, he collapses, and is nursed back to health by Van Tassel's daughter Katrina with whom he falls in love.

Guided by a mysterious witch, he and Katrina discover that the Horseman emerges from the roots of a tree that seems to be a portal to hell. Crane suspects Van Tassel is behind the killings, then, after Van Tassel is killed, suspects Katrina of witchcraft and decides to leave Sleepy Hollow. Learning from a book she has given him that Katrina's spells are meant to protect him, Crane turns back just in time to save her from her stepmother Lady Van Tassel, the evil witch behind the Horseman. His missing head restored, the Horseman takes lady Van Tassel to hell. Crane, Katrina and an orphaned village boy Masbath leave for New York City.

No longer a prodigy at age 41, Tim Burton has now become a problem; I still find myself watching his movies with bemused tolerance, thinking surely he'll be a great director when he grows up. Although it's loaded with pseudo-ghoulish detail and imbued with a distinctive atmosphere—both of which, as usual, seem drawn from a 70s teenager's comic-book and album-cover collection—Sleepy Hollow suffers from terminal vagueness and clutter. Its plot is a complicated skein of unrelated fairy tale elements and coincidences, punctuated occasionally by balletic beheadings, its characterisation almost entirely haphazard.

There have been several previous film and television versions of Washington Irving's short story "The Legend of Sleepy Hollow" (familiar to generations of American schoolchildren), and if nothing else Burton definitively captures its mood of wilderness paranoia. His opening scene, in which Martin Landau becomes the Headless Horseman's quarry as he drives a deserted stretch of road, is a classic of gothic terror. As the heads severed by the Horseman twist through the air, we always glimpse in them a moment of horrified comprehension death (or something that may be worse) has come for them on the lonely edge of this dangerous continent.

Even Burton's vaunted visual sensibility gets him into trouble at least as often as it rescues him. His early vision of Ichabod Crane's Manhattan as a grey, fetid city crawling with crime and fever—where the authorities abuse miscreants and throw them into horrible dungeons with scarcely a gesture in the direction of justice—is so fascinating one feels disappointed when the film abandons it. There's a wonderful moment after Crane arrives in drab, severe, and dead silent Sleepy Hollow, throws open the doors to the inn and enters a crowded party pulsing with colour and gaiety. We understand at a single stroke that terror has driven the town's social life indoors. Burton never returns to this theme either.

Johnny Depp's Ichabod Crane is a man of many parts, never conclusively adding up to a whole. Depp's willingness to push his characters in unsympathetic directions is always engaging, and he plays Crane as a Clouseau-like incompetent, his face a mask of involuntary tics and twitches. His scientific aspirations are portrayed as foolish and grotesque, his bizarre toolkit seems borrowed from Jeremy Irons' mad surgeon in *Dead Ringers,* his goggles make him look like a demon from the *Hellraiser* series. Yet, as we learn in a series of tedious flashbacks, Crane is also another of Burton's damaged naifs, a survivor who finds inner reserves of strength and wins Katrina's love, despite the fact that he is entirely wrong about her, the Horseman and everything else.

Of course Depp and Christina Ricci (resplendent in a lovely blonde wig) make a charismatic pair, smashingly done up in period costumes by Colleen Atwood, and audiences are likely to swallow almost any narrative strategy that sees them united by the film's end. Andrew Kevin Walker's screenplay, which bears little relationship to Irving's story, doesn't offer Katrina much to do beyond gazing at the bumbling Crane with what is meant to be a knowing, tolerant affection. Still, she's better off than Miranda Richardson as Lady Van Tassel, who scarcely appears in the film before being revealed as the wicked stepmother behind it all—and delivering a lengthy Dr Evil-style disquisition on her motives and methods. Similarly, such irreproachable actors as Michael Gambon and Jeffrey Jones make little impression against the scattershot story and Rick Heinrichs' alluring production design. Christopher Walken cuts a fine, fearsome figure in his cameo as the medieval looking Hessian mercenary, his teeth sharpened to vampiric points.

As ever, Burton quotes from his favourite films—there's an elaborate restaging of the burning windmill climax in the 1931 *Frankenstein.* Maybe there's something perversely honourable about this; Burton certainly isn't serving plot or character at such moments, just referring to a cherished memory for no particular reason, like a patient free-associating on a therapist's couch. Ever since *Pee-Wee's Big Adventure* in 1985, Burton has been all potential and no delivery (with qualified exceptions for *Ed Wood* and the first *Batman* film). Even with an almost mythic story at its foundation, *Sleepy Hollow* doesn't seem like the work of an eccentric visionary, as Burton has long been labelled. It's more like the good natured mess produced by a shallow sentimentalist, an undisciplined imitator with a keen sense of style.

TIME, 11/22/99, p. 102, Richard Corliss

For nearly 200 years the tale has kept children awake and atremble—or lulled them to sleep with Washington Irving's drolly orotund style. *The Legend of Sleepy Hollow* is still a bedtime staple in tonier households, and with its Headless Horseman hurling a grimacing pumpkin at the head of Ichabod Crane, the story helped create the American giddying-up of Halloween as a funny fright night. But like so many old fables, *Sleepy Hollow* is chiefly remembered in its Disney version. That 1958 cartoon short, a genial mix of comedy and anxiety, took its tone from the voice of its narrator: Bing Crosby. A lulling, a chuckle, then a little scare. Buh-buh-buh-*boo*!

Tim Burton will not let you go so easy into that dark night. The director wants to turn this fairy tale into a full-blooded ghost story—and a total Tim Burton experience. So for this end-of-the-century parable (it's set in 1799), he imports the bats from Batman, the jack-o'-lantern from *Nightmare Before Christmas* and, as Ichabod Crane, Johnny Depp from *Edward Scissorhands* and *Ed Wood.* Instead of the bright Halloween hues of the Disney version, Burton gives his film a swankly, dankly desaturated color scheme. And just to make sure he doesn't go soft, he hires Andrew Kevin Walker, author of the sleazorific *Se7en* and *8mm,* to write the screenplay. No one will fall asleep in this *Sleepy Hollow.* It revs up the gore.

Is there a Headless Horseman? Then he'd better cut off some heads—heads that, when detached by the whoosh of the Horseman's blade, go spinning, rolling, bobbing as if each were a top, a bowling ball, a Halloween apple on its way from Hollow to hell. (The terminally cool Tussaud effects are by Kevin Yagher, who also worked on the script.) Irving's Horseman, a long-dead Hessian mercenary, was most likely, a story to scare away intruders and, when Ichabod sees him, a human prankster toning with the gullible schoolteacher. Here, though, the creature must be realer than a nightmare—a galloping plague to purge Sleepy Hollow. He is embodied, occasionally, by Christopher Walken, who could terrify small children just by singing *I'm a Little Teapot*. In full Horseman drag, with his spiky teeth and Stygian melancholy, Walken is an R rating waiting to happen.

Crane's name was his frame: a gangly galoot and, when he fell for buxom Katrina Van Tassel, an easy prey for the burly lads of Sleepy Hollow. In Burton's revision and Depp's incarnation, Crane is a Manhattan constable sent upriver to solve a murder; predating Poe's Auguste Dupin by several decades, he is America's first detective. He is also a troubled soul, carrying literal scars from childhood and memories that roil his sleep. So handsome, so haunted, he proves irresistible to this Katrina (Christina Ricci). Yet Depp humbles and stumbles, just like the old Ichabod; he is the hero and the comic relief in one tightly wound package. Doesn't always work, but we've been admiring this actor's bravado and forgiving his excesses for ages. Why stop now? Besides, he ultimately makes Ichabod a truly, obsessive romantic hero: Byron by Ahab.

The story is still set just north of New York City (and visually quotes the Hudson River School of painters), but it was filmed in a studio near London and cast mostly with British actors. At first the accents are jarring; viewers will stop to wonder just when Americans finally learned to speak American. But the presence of Michael Gambon, Miranda Richardson and especially Christopher Lee will tip you to Burton's intent. He is making not an American folktale but a British horror movie—a tribute to the Hammer studio of the late '50s and later, to its *Dracula* and *Frankenstein* remakes, to the decorum punctuated by gore, the stake driven into the capacious bosom.

Funny thing is, those movies weren't very good. This one is: Burton's richest, prettiest, weirdest since *Batman Returns*. The simple story bends to his to twists, freeing him for an exercise in high style. *Sleepy Hollow* may be late for Halloween, but this trick is a real treat.

VILLAGE VOICE, 11/30/99, p. 133, J. Hoberman

Tim Burton has yet to tackle an "adult" theme but there isn't a bankable Hollywood director with a flintier sense of aesthetic integrity. More insolently pop than David Lynch and less eager for approval than Steven Spielberg, Burton has repeatedly twisted studio resources to his own dank and gibbering expressionistic purposes.

Burton's *Sleepy Hollow* is by no means as radical an anti-entertainment as his ill-starred *Mars Attacks!* but this splendid, shuddering contraption has a dazzling purity of vision. It's a Halloween spookarama in which the falling leaves hit their marks, the shutters rattle on cue, and the goblin entrances are lit by lightning. Although populated by flesh-and-blood actors, Burton's fun house is as ruthlessly stylized as the Disney animation that, half a century ago, breathed a comic chill (not to mention Bing Crosby's narration) into Washington Irving's ghostly yarn.

The most literary of Burton films, *Sleepy Hollow* opens in a dark and smoky 1799 New York City and, humorously fin de siècle, drifts rhapsodically to a foggy fairy-tale village in the sumptuously autumnal Hudson River valley. Elevated from Irving's gawky schoolteacher, Ichabod Crane is not only played by the beautiful Johnny Depp but transformed into a self-consciously modern and amusingly timorous police officer, sent upstate to meet a comic gaggle of well-upholstered British actors (notably Michael Gambon and Miranda Richardson), all bewigged and befuddled to grotesque effect.

Officially, Ichabod has come to solve a series of mysterious decapitations. Screenwriter Andrew Kevin Walker, who wrote *Seven* and *8MM*, has reworked Irving's classic American fake-lore as (what else?) the story of a serial killer. The Horseman, a hoax in Irving's tale as well as in the scary old Disney cartoon, is literal enough here—a monstrous Hessian mercenary forever searching for his lost head (Christopher Walken with filed teeth). Burton scarcely strays from the screenwriter's well-trodden path but, like all of his films, *Sleepy Hollow* is not so much a narrative as it is a place. The mood isn't grim but Grimm. Burton directs the grisly action as though it were a jolly puppet show, another *Nightmare Before Christmas*.

Prissy and pedantic, Ichabod is an inventor of elaborate detection devices. He's an artist manqué who, supremely rational, doesn't flinch from the occasional ghoulish operation. (There's a bit too much Dudley Do-Right to Depp's delivery but-as in *Edward Scissorhands, if not Ed Wood*—he's at the service of his director's spectacular mise-en-scène.) A typically traumatized Burton hero, Ichabod has mysteriously-puncturedpalms and revisits his childhood throughout the movie with regular trips to dreamland. There, his witchy mother (played—significantly? — Burton's significant other, Lisa Marie) presents him with the proto-cinematic optical toy, known as a thaumatrope, which serves as his talisman.

Ichabod shows the illusion-producingthaumatrope to Katrina Van Tassel (Christina Ricci), the most innocent of the movie's several witches, explaining to her that "truth is not always appearances." You may not believe your eyes either, each time the Headless Horseman emerges from between the roots of a bleeding, twisted tree—less sleepy hollow than a vaginal passage to hell. Rampant castration anxiety notwithstanding, *Sleepy Hollow* is essentially comic—although perhaps a bit gory for small children, most especially in the savage punishment visited upon the village midwife and her little boy. (Like young Ichabod, he was partial to optical amusements.)

Although Walker's script is both overcomplicatedand underwritten, *Sleepy Hollow* gallops along at a goodly clip, offering a number of breathless (or should we say, headlong) thrill rides. The main attraction in this magic kingdom is Burton's gorgeous production design. The images are as rich as compost; every clammy detail is subordinate to the whole. Still, Burton and Walker have done yeoman service in creating an indigenous gothic, mixing fear of the primeval woods with the guilt arising from colonial rebellion.

The Horseman serves as an all-purpose return of the patriarchal repressed—a mutilated, yet potent, remnant of the American Revolution. (It's as though the statue of George III that New Yorkers pulled down at the Battery came back as a living thing.) But the movie itself is an act of historical hubris and symbolic regicide. Disneyland is revised as rampantly Freudian—and historically resonant—Grand Guignol.

Also reviewed in:
CHICAGO TRIBUNE, 11/19/99, Friday/p. A, Mark Caro
NEW YORK TIMES, 11/19/99, p. E1, Janet Maslin
NEW YORKER, 11/22/99, p. 205, David Denby
VARIETY, 11/15-21/99, p. 87, Todd McCarthy
WASHINGTON POST, 11/19/99, p C1, Rita Kempley
WASHINGTON POST, 11/19/99, Weekend/p. 51, Desson Howe

SNOW FALLING ON CEDARS

A Universal Pictures release of a Harry J. Ufland/Ron Bass-Kennedy/Marshall production. *Executive Producer:* Carol Baum and Lloyd A. Silverman. *Producer:* Harry J. Ufland, Ron Bass, Kathleen Kennedy, and Frank Marshall. *Director:* Scott Hicks. *Screenplay:* Ron Bass and Scott Hicks. *Based on the novel by:* David Guterson. *Director of Photography:* Robert Richardson. *Editor:* Hank Corwin. *Music:* James Newton Howard. *Music Editor:* Jim Weidman. *Sound:* Eric Batut. *Sound Editor:* Hank Corwin. *Casting:* David Rubin. *Production Designer:* Jeannine Oppewall. *Art Director:* Bill Arnold. *Set Decorator:* Jim Erickson. *Set Dresser:* Scott Calderwood, Audra Neal, Laura Edmondsen, Andrew Hussey, Herb Noseworthy, Rick Pattison, Larry Gonzales, and Steve Lemare. *Special Effects:* Bill Orr. *Costumes:* Renee Erlich Kalfus. *Make-up:* Rosalina Da Silva and Norma Hill-Patton. *Stunt Coordinator:* Raleigh Wilson. *Running time:* 130 minutes. *MPAA Rating:* PG-13.

CAST: Ethan Hawke (Ishmael Chambers); Youki Kudoh (Hatsue Miyamoto); Reeve Carney (Young Ishmael Chambers); Anne Suzuki (Young Hatsue Imada); Rick Yune (Kazuo Miyamoto); Max von Sydow (Nels Gudmundsson); James Rebhorn (Alvin Hooks); James Cromwell (Judge Fielding); Richard Jenkins (Sheriff Art Moran); Arija Bareikis (Susan Marie Heine); Eric Thal (Carl Heine, Jr.); Celia Weston (Etta Heine); Daniel Von Bargen (Carl Heine, Sr.); Akira Takayama (Hisao Imada); Ako (Fujiko Imada); Cary-Hiroyuki Tagawa (Zenhichi Miyamoto); Zak Orth (Deputy Abel Martinson); Max Wright (Horace Whaley); Sam

Shepard (Arthur Chambers); Caroline Kava (Helen Chambers); Jan Rubes (Ole Jurgensen); Sheila Moore (Liesel Jurgensen); Zeljko Ivanek (Dr. Whitman); Seiji Inouye (Young Kazuo Miyamoto); Saemi Nakamura (Sumiko Imada); Mika Fujii (Yukiko Imada); Dwight McFee (Bus Driver); Bill Harper (Levant); Xi Reng Jiang (Nagaishi); Myles Ferguson (German Soldier); Noah Heney (Ship's Doctor); John Destrey (Bailiff); A. Arthur Takemoto (Buddhist Priest); Ken Takemoto (Monk); Larry Musser (Gas Station Attendant); Jamie Kang (Singing Girl); Lili Marshall (Strawberry Girl); Lisa Mena (Strawberry Woman); Jethro Heysen-Hicks (Parade Boy with Stick); Tom Heaton, Frank C. Turner and Marilyn Norry (Jurors); Peter Crook, Ron Snyder, and Mark Ainsworth Farrell (Fishermen); Jay Brazeau, Tom Scholte, and Tim Burd (Reporters); Gareth Williams and Anthony Harrison (FBI Agents); Adam Pospisil and Johnny Brynelsen (Heine Children).

LOS ANGELES TIMES, 12/22/99, Calendar/p. 8, Kenneth Turan

The fog is thicker, thicker than you can imagine. The sound of the sea is the only one heard. Out of nowhere, a pair of one-man fishing boats come face to face. Wary, disbelieving, the owners stare at each other—it's not a friendly stare. What happens between them isn't shown, but the next morning one is found dead and soon after the other is arrested for his murder.

This is how it begins for "Snow Falling on Cedars," the film version of David Guterson's thoughtful, evocative thriller that tracks the racial and social fissures in the fictional Pacific Northwest island community of San Piedro as they're gradually uncovered by that 1950 murder trial.

Because Guterson's book, a genuine word-of-mouth success, was so compelling, top creative talent attached themselves to this project, starting with director Scott Hicks (in his first time behind the camera since "Shine" and its seven Oscar nominations), screenwriter Ron Bass and Oscar-winning cinematographer Robert Richardson.

But while there are things to like about this film, the poetic realism of Richardson's cinematography and Jeannine Oppewall's production design high among them, "Snow Falling on Cedars" has to fight to hold our attention and it doesn't always succeed. That's because it's a film without a hero, at least a hero that can function in an acceptable cinematic manner.

On one level, of course, "Snow Falling" has an obvious hero in brooding Ishmael Chambers (Ethan Hawke), who runs the town's one-man newspaper, the San Piedro Review, as a legacy from his late father, Arthur (played in flashbacks by Sam Shepard).

Ishmael's pained expression rarely varies, and there are two reasons for it: the arm he lost in the South Pacific and the love he lost, also because of the war. As a high school student he became involved with Hatsue Miyamoto (Youki Kudoh), a member of the island's tight-knit Japanese community. It was a taboo relationship even before the war, and after Pearl Harbor, when Hatsue and her family were incarcerated in California's Manzanar camp, it became impossible. Hatsue ended up marrying Kazuo Miyamoto (Rick Yune), the man on trial for murdering Carl Heine.

A decorated war hero, Kazuo had a complicated relationship with the dead man and his family involving the local custom that made it unheard of for Japanese to own the local strawberry-growing land they often worked on. As Kazuo's wily legal practitioner Nels Gudmundsson (a scene-stealing Max von Sydow giving the film's best performance) conducts his defense, it gradually becomes clear how much the unspoken "those people" kind of prejudice against the Japanese existed even before the war.

Because it flashes between the present, the war and the prewar years, "Snow Falling" is not always at that trial, but even when Ishmael's not hanging around the courtroom looking morose he spends too much of the movie just sitting and thinking. In the book, we have the benefit of constantly hearing Ishmael's thoughts, but given the lack of more than a hint of his interior monologues, this quickly becomes unexciting. Hawke is a fine actor, but he is not alive when he's not doing anything, he doesn't own the screen the way Brad Pitt, for instance, does, and if you're going to have a character who doesn't talk much but has his face writ large, that is what you need.

Watching "Snow Falling" also emphasizes how much bravura performances by Geoffrey Rush, Armin Mueller-Stahl and others brought an essential energy to "Shine." Not only did they hold our interest, they diverted us from Hicks' tendency, apparent in both films, to be too on the nose and turn minor characters into unfortunate cliches.

Also, although the novel's success may have made this inevitable, "Snow Falling" seems too calculated and conscious of its own pedigree. It's a reserved film, and given its reserved subject matter, it has a tendency to fall into ponderousness at times.

Yet there are other times, like the extensive and sensitive treatment of Manzanar exile Hatsue and her family are forced into, when the film's poetic realism is a strength. (Keep an eye out for a brief, haunting home-movie clip of a girl ice skating alone; it's from the celebrated Topaz footage, the only home movie aside from the Zapruder footage to be inducted in the National Family Registry, shot by Dave Tatsumo at the Topaz camp in Utah.)

At its most effective, a great melancholy hangs over the events of "Snow Falling on Cedars," a somber, regretful film about the weight of the past, about great sadnesses that can only be healed over time and then only in part. The old-fashioned power of Guterson's story finally triumphs, but it's a much harder-fought victory than we might have hoped for.

NEW YORK POST, 12/22/99, p. 53, Lou Lumenick

"Snow Falling on Cedars," a lumbering adaptation of David Guterson's best seller directed by Scott Hicks ("Shine"), is the year's most beautiful movie—and surely one of the dullest.

Ethan Hawke, who wears the same pained expression throughout (except during some flashbacks in which he ridiculously impersonates a teenager), woodenly plays Ishmael Chambers, who edits a weekly newspaper on a fictional island in the Pacific Northwest in 1950.

He's covering the murder trial of Kazuo (the pretty but vapid Rick Yune), a local Japanese-American fisherman and childhood friend who's married to the love of Ishmael's life, Hatsue (the pretty but vapid Youki Kudoh).

Ishmael comes up with evidence pointing to Kazuo's innocence, but holds back. He's struggling with the lingering hurt from Hatsue's rejection when they were teenagers—she a prisoner in an internment camp for Japanese Americans, and he as a GI who loses an arm in World War II combat.

All of this is very ... slowly ... revealed in a laborious series of flashbacks (and flashbacks within flashbacks) intercut with Kazuo's trial.

The racist prosecutor (James Rebhorn), playing to lingering postwar anti-Japanese basis, spars with Kazuo's highly moral but ailing lawyer (Max von Sydow) under the watchful eye of the tough but fair judge (James Cromwell).

This powerhouse supporting cast—Sam Shepard turns up in flashbacks as Ishamel's crusading liberal newspaperman father—seems to be wading through molasses for most of the film, which feels like it was shot in slow motion.

Any time things threaten to get interesting, Hicks cuts to another flashback—or back to the mundane mystery surrounding the death of the man Kazuo is accused of killing, whose father cheated Kazuo's father out of some land during the war.

Also seriously adding to the 130-minute running time are endless scenic shots of the island, breathtakingly photographed by Robert Richardson.

Painfully earnest and self-important (the screenplay is credited to Hicks and Ron Bass), "Snow Falling on Cedars" seems longer that a double feature of "Magnolia" and "The Green Mile."

For a great movie about a one-armed World War II vet confronting anti-Japanese bias in a small town, you'd be far better off renting Spencer Tracy's "Bad Day at Black Rock," a taut thriller running a mere 80 minutes.

NEWSWEEK, 12/20/99, p. 44, David Ansen

Somewhere inside this misty, moody movie, buried under snow banks of gratuitous style, there's a potboiler screaming to get out. David Guterson's best-selling novel has a strong melodramatic story that shouldn't be hard to tell. There's a murder trial in the Pacific Northwest: a Japanese fisherman (Rick Yune) is accused of killing his white friend. There's a forbidden interracial love story, (Ethan Hawke and Youki Kudoh) made even more dangerous when war erupts. There's the searing injustice of Japanese-American internment camps. But the way director Scott ("Shine") Hicks and cowriter Ron Bass tell it, none of it gets the heart racing.

If ever there was an example of a director's getting in the way of a story, this is it. Hicks splinters his story into little shards as he jumps artily backward and forward in time. The movie is beautiful: the darkly poetic images are suitable for framing. But the actors, posed like models, rarely get to interact. Only Max von Sydow cracks the surface with a rousing courtroom speech. The movie is all shots and no scenes, which is nice for a picture book but deadly for drama.

SIGHT AND SOUND, 6/00, p. 54, Geoffrey Macnab

San Piedro Island, not long after the end of World War II. Local fisherman Carl Heine Jr has died at sea in suspicious circumstances. Kazuo Miyamoto, an American-born man of Japanese descent, is standing trial for his murder. Watching the case from the gallery is reporter Ishmael Chambers. As the trial progresses, the depth of the anti-Japanese feeling in this close-knit community becomes apparent. Years before, Kazuo's family had been offered the chance to buy seven acres of land from the Heines. With the onset of World War II, Kazuo's family were interned. When they came back, Carl's mother reneged on the deal. At the time of his death, Carl was contemplating whether or not to allow Kazuo back onto the land.

Ishmael, who was the childhood sweetheart of Kazuo's wife Hatsue, is still bitter about the loss of an arm in the war and Hatsue's abandonment of him. Nevertheless, he sees the flaws in the case against Kazuo and discovers that a freighter, passing by Carl's boat on the night of his death, may have caused him to fall from the mast. In court, Kazuo's lawyer Nels Gudmundsson makes an eloquent plea on his behalf, begging the jury not to allow themselves to be swayed by old anti-Japanese prejudices. With the jury in recess, Ishmael's new evidence is shown to the judge. The next day, the charges against Kazuo are dismissed.

It doesn't come as a surprise to learn that director Scott Hicks (Shine) is an accomplished stills photographer. His screen version of David Guterson's 1995 novel Snow Falling on Cedars is beautifully crafted, full of lovingly composed images of mountains, woods, water and mist. The intention here seems to have been to emulate Guterson's prose with equally subtle and self-conscious camerawork and editing. As we're dealt slow-motion sequences and exposed to director of photography Robert Richardson's artful focus-pulling, it seems at times as if we're watching some sort of experimental film poem. The problem is that all this magical imagery goes hand in hand with some very uncertain storytelling. Strip away the varnish and what is left is a conventional, rather clunky courtroom drama.

In uncovering the anti-Japanese prejudice which gripped wartime America, Hicks isn't exactly breaking new ground. We've been this way before, both in John Sturges' magnificent latter-day western Bad Day at Black Rock (1954), and in Alan Parker's more solemn Come See the Paradise. The defence lawyer (a scene-stealing turn from Max von Sydow) tells us that the jury are "marking a report card for the human race", but this kind of blandishment has been trotted out in so many other courtroom dramas that it no longer has much resonance. Besides, despite von Sydow's persuasive efforts, Kazuo is acquitted not because any jury's decision but because of new evidence.

Nor is there anything striking in the way Hicks excoriates what seems a peaceable little community, revealing the prejudices which lurk beneath the happy facade. When Horace, the weasel-like coroner, allows racism to contaminate his evidence, or the prosecutor invites the jury to look at the defendant's inscrutable face and to read guilt in it, they're behaving little differently from Robert Ryan and his small-town lynch mob in Sturges' film.

In probably the film's most heavy-handed scene, we see Japanese families rounded up as ominous drumbeats are heard on the soundtrack. They're wearing tags, just like concentration-camp inmates. We hear anonymous voices hurling abuse down the telephone at Chambers, the local newspaper editor who refuses to be caught up in the anti-Japanese hysteria which grips the town in the wake of Pearl Harbor. Hicks, however, is so busy filming seagulls and driftwood that his attempts at exposing the inhabitants as bigots lack bite.

Ishmael is an enigma. It's through his eyes that we see most of the flashbacks, but he is given precious little dialogue. He's bitter after losing his arm in the war and being deserted by Hatsue. On one level, the film is as much about his struggles to come to terms with his predicament as it is about Kazuo's trial but he is so sketchily drawn that we're given little sense of his internal conflict. What Hicks offers instead are endless lyrical flashbacks and montage sequences.

They're all exquisitely filmed but ultimately only serve to draw attention to the weakness elsewhere in plot and characterisation.

TIME, 12/27/99, p. 181, Richard Schickel

Snow Falling on Cedars is essentially a liberal soap opera. Its simple, anti-prejudice message is hidden (in David Guterson's novel) behind dense thickets of rich, writerly prose and a narrative that moves large numbers of characters back and forth in time as it proceeds, in its leisurely way, to solve the murder mystery that serves as its none-too-robust pacemaker. Readers in the millions took the book seriously because Guterson was so serious about is though it did not hurt that his setting—an island in Puget Sound, before, during and immediately after World War II—was fresh and exotic.

Director Scott Hicks' version is faithful to the story's main beats. There's Ishmael, the physically and emotionally wounded hero (Hawke); Hatsue (Kudoh), the forbidden and then lost love of his childhood; her husband Kazuo (Yune), charged with killing an Anglo neighbor after a land dispute; and all kinds of characters who behave well and badly as his trial unveils the community's hatreds and suspicions.

Screen time is different from novel time, and it takes a lot of it for Ishmael to rediscover his "good heart" and bring forth the hidden truth that will free the accused. While he dawdles and moons, the wind starts to whistle through the story's riggings and we begin to suspect that there was always less in it than met an eye distracted by Guterson's fancy writing.

VILLAGE VOICE, 12/28/99, p. 130, Dennis Lim

Scott Hicks's loud, bustling direction ensures there's no shortage of activity in his adaptation of *Snow Falling on Cedars*, but the inertia at the core of the movie is unmistakable. Set on a misty Pacific Northwest fishing village in the 1950s, David Guterson's novel is a leisurely courtroom whodunit with a self-congratulatory anti-prejudice message, fleshed out with painstaking topographic detail. The flashback-heavy narrative is framed by the trial of Kazuo Miyamoto (Rick Yune), a Japanese American war veteran charged with the murder of a fellow fisherman, with the deck stacked for neat moral dilemmas resolved via cathartic journeys to—in Guterson's words—"the chambers of the human heart." Ethan Hawke plays Ishmael, um, Chambers, the local newspaperman who's privy to information that may acquit Kazuo—but the accused man is married to Hatsue (Youki Kudoh), Ishmael's teen sweetheart who dumped him when he was serving in the South Pacific.

Faithful to Guterson's mechanical setup, the film (from a screenplay by Hicks and hack supreme Ron Bass) is distinguished by its vulgar notion of impressionism—the tastefully florid hyperreality of Hicks's *Shine* has here exploded into a grotesque strain of middlebrow experimentalism. With random cross-cuts, baffling montage, overlapping dialogue, and a swelling choral soundtrack, Hicks undermines the elegant slate-blue solemnity of Robert Richardson's cinematography (though as a longtime Oliver Stone collaborator, Richardson must by now be used to the Cuisinart treatment). Trying to act in this movie is like trying to stand upright in a blizzard. Hawke and Kudoh come off as purely decorative, and in any case, everyone is upstaged by Max von Sydow. As the wheezing, doddering defense attorney, the old pro gives his lines—not least an overwritten, throat-clearing closing arguments near-miraculous gravity. It's a heartening display of force of personality cutting through bullshit: He turns a digression about his own mortality into the most moving thing in the film by far, and seems amazingly unperturbed that the novel's unfortunate final line—the one about aortic compartments—has been assigned to him as dialogue.

Also reviewed in:
CHICAGO TRIBUNE, 1/7/00, Friday/p. A, Michael Wilmington
NATION, 1/24/00, p. 35, Stuart Klawans
NEW YORK TIMES, 12/22/99, p. E6, Stephen Holden
VARIETY, 9/13-19/99, p. 51, Todd McCarthy
WASHINGTON POST, 1/7/00, p. C1, Stephen Hunter
WASHINGTON POST, 1/7/00, Weekend/p. 37, Desson Howe

SOME FISH CAN FLY

An Artistic License release. *Producer:* Joseph A. Zock and Miriam Foley. *Director:* Robert Kane Pappas. *Screeenplay:* Robert Kane Pappas. *Director of Photography:* Jim Denny. *Editor:* Brian Cole. *Music:* Edward B. Kessel and Mark R. Hoffman. *Production Designer:* Rich Awad. *Running time:* 95 minutes. *MPAA Rating:* Not Rated.

CAST: Nancy St. Alban (Nora); Kevin Causey (Kevin); Rich Nagel (Z); Clarke Bittner (Lyle); Nina Howie (Madeline); John Rowe (Chris); Bridget Barkan (Siobhan).

NEW YORK POST, 11/5/99, p. 61, Lou Lumeneck

"What is this sappy stuff?" complains an actor in the movie-within-the-movie in "Some Fish Can Fly," a woeful attempt to transplant "Annie Hall" to Ireland.

"It's supposed to be funny," explains Kevin (Kevin Causey), a New Yorker who's making a movie about his on-again/off-again romance with Nora (Nancy St. Alban), an Irish nanny who has a stronger commitment to her hometown in Cork than to Kevin.

As written and directed by Robert Kane Pappas, "Some Fish Can Fly" isn't particularly funny, romantic or well-acted. It drags on endlessly as Kevin's struggle to make his movie is interrupted by flashbacks from 10 years earlier, when he pursued Nora to Ireland on Christmas Eve.

The Woody Allen influence is also present in the French "Portraits Chinois" ("Shadow Play"), which borrows its next-to-last scene from "Annie Hall"—except that writer-director Martine Dugowson makes it all come out happy in her film-within-the-film.

Something most have gotten lost in the translation.

Swearing profusely in French, Allen's erstwhile leading lady Helena Bonham Carter ("Mighty Aphrodite") has a succession of bad hair days and smokes endless Galoises as Ada, a sour fashion designer who's losing both her job and her screenwriter boyfriend Paul (Jean-Phillipe Escoffey) to Lise (Romane Bohringer), who's 10 years younger. They're part of an upscale, self-centered, bed-hopping circle that includes a studly film director, an impotent screenwriter, and a would-be singer who's addicted to shopping.

At one point, the filmmakers have just premiered a movie called "Born in Miami," and they watch in horror as a TV movie critic sums it up as "totally vapid ... pretentious ... I know what's funny and it didn't make me laugh." Unfortunately, the critic could be talking about "Portraits Chinois."

VILLAGE VOICE, 11/9/99, p. 148, Jessica Winter

[*Some Fish Can Fly* was reviewed jointly with *Music of the Heart*; see Winter's review of that film.]

Also reviewed in:
NEW YORK TIMES, 11/5/99, p. E32, Lawrence Van Gelder

SOURCE, THE

A Winstar Cinema release of a Calliope Films, Inc. production. *Executive Producer:* Hiro Yamagata. *Producer:* Chuck Workman. *Director:* Chuck Workman. *Screenplay:* Chuck Workman. *Director of Photography (Black & white):* Tom Hurwitz and Don Lenzer. *Director of Photography (color):* Andrew Dintenfass, Jose Luis Magnone, and Nancy Schreiber. *Editor:* Chuck Workman. *Music:* Philip Glass, David Amram, Dizzy Gillespie, Thelonious Monk, The Doors, Bob Dylan, Stan Getz, Gerry Mulligan, Ornette Coleman, The Rolling Stones, Sonic Youth, Natalie Merchant. *Running time:* 89 minutes. *MPAA Rating:* Not Rated.

WITH: Johnny Depp; Dennis Hopper; John Turturro; INTERVIEWS WITH: Allen Ginsberg; William Burroughs; Timothy Leary; Lawrence Ferlinghetti; Michael McClure; Ken Kesey; Gregory Corso; Ed Sanders; Amiri Baraka; Jerry Garcia; Tom Hayden; Gary Snyder; Robert Creeley; Philip Glass; David Amram; Jack Kerouac; Bob Dylan; Shirley Clark; Diane DiPrima; Robert Motherwell; Norman Mailer; Terry Southern; Neal Cassady. *Running time:* 89 minutes. *MPAA Rating:* Not Rated.

CINEASTE, Vol. XXIV, No. 4, 1999, p. 41, David Sterritt

"First thought best thought" was a career-defining motto for Jack Kerouac, whose novel *On the Road* put the Beat Generation onto the literary map and introduced the notion of "spontaneous bop prosody" to young culture-vultures who felt more at home with the creative fringes of the postwar era—bebop, abstract expressionism, the theater of the absurd—than with the company-man conformity pitched by the mainstream media. Inspired by jazz improvisation and action painting, Kerouac's extemporaneous writing aimed to capture the quicksilver flux of moment-by-moment thought in all its unpredictable vitality. Similar goals animated the long-line impressionism of Allen Ginsberg's bardic poetry and the cut-up deliriums of William S. Burroughs's gloriously anarchic novels.

Chuck Workman's new documentary, *The Source,* joins a growing number of nonfiction films about the Beat sensibility, ranging from celebratory lovefests like *Fried Shoes, Cooked Diamonds* (Costanzo Allione, 1978) to biopics like *The Life and Times of Allen Ginsberg* (Jerry Aronson, 1993) and *What Happened to Kerouac?* (Lewis MacAdams and Richard Lerner, 1985), plus sundry visits with quasi-Beats like *Paul Bowles: The Complete Outsider* (Catherine Warnow and Regina Weinreich, 1993) and *Lenny Bruce: Swear to Tell the Truth* (Robert B. Weide, 1998).

A curious fact about nearly all Beat-based documentaries, including *The Source,* is that they engage with their subject far more effectively in content than in style. With dutiful enthusiasm, they fill the screen with colorful Beat iconography (footage from home movies, excerpts from Beat-conscious commercial films, looking-back-at-it-all interviews) while showing remarkably little interest in the "first thought best thought" adventurousness that provided the Beat enterprise with many of its most exciting and original qualities. The fundamental problem lies less with the filmmaking skills of Workman and his predecessors than with the format they've chosen for their explorations: the well-made traditional documentary, currently exemplified by PBS and its educationally oriented ilk.

In some limited respects, this sort of movie shares built-in proclivities with the Beat esthetics predilection for montage and collage, a fondness for found materials, an openness to unexpected juxtapositions, a willingness to zip spiritedly around in time and space. Still and all, there's a deep-down contradiction in the impulse to make authentic Beat materials conform with the televisually correct formulas of standard nonfiction film. (Parts of *The Source* eerily recall Kerouac's occasional TV spots with ultrasquares like Steve Allen and William F. Buckley, Jr., which made sense by the standards of the period—audiences craved novelty, talk shows needed variety, and Kerouac was too drunk to care—but seem as squirmingly incongruous today as they did when they were aired.) If the mercurial currents of spontaneous bop prosody have an analogue in documentary moviemaking, one would do better to seek it in the spur-of-the-moment flow of *cinema-vérité* (or better yet, the unmoored avant-gardism of Robert Frank's uncategorizable *Me and My Brother)* than in the predictable patterns deployed by Workman and like-minded directors, who show more interest in conveying information than in wholeheartedly sharing its spirit. (Workman did much the same in *Superstar,* his 1990 Andy Warhol documentary.)

Another problem shared by *The Source* and some previous documentaries is a tendency to imply strong connections between the so-called Beat revolution and a broad swath of sociopolitical events that the Beats themselves were involved with loosely, indirectly, or not at all. Eagerness to link the Beats with such developments is understandable, given the films' clear investment in the relevance and influence of Beat activities, and it's true that Ginsberg brought aspects of the Beat project into highly politicized territory as the Sixties and Seventies took their course. But unwary viewers of *The Source* might get the misleading impression that the Beats were a feisty band of political agitators, when in fact their commitment went in a very different direction, calling for the revolutionizing of consciousness on a profoundly personal basis, and embracing the social consequences of this quest as valuable byproducts rather than ultimate goals. Their mutiny against convention was radical, far-reaching, and thoroughly in tune with more earthbound rebellions (student protests, human-rights movements, and the like) that began gathering steam in the same postwar years. It was rooted far more deeply in spiritual yearnings than in social or political agendas, however, and *The Source* would etch a more accurate picture if it gave proper weight to the hostile and even paranoid views of political activism held by Kerouac and Burroughs, among others.

These important caveats aside, *The Source* has substantial riches to offer in its generous selection of Beat words, images, personalities, and artifacts. Workman spent three years assembling it, drawing from scores of archival sources, and while the results aren't comprehensive enough to justify its publicity claim of being "a portrait of the counterculture of the past fifty years," it should prove eye-opening for young viewers who know the Beat movement only by hearsay, and will certainly bestir the memories of Fifties and Sixties types who didn't lose too many brain cells during the hippie era that succeeded it. Indeed, bridging this generation gap appears to be part of the picture's project, since it brings in a trio of present-day luminaries to recite from works by Beat authors they vaguely resemble—Johnny Depp doing Kerouac (smoldering sexiness), John Turturro doing Ginsberg (wired-up ethnicity), Dennis Hopper doing Burroughs (what planet did you say we're on?).

Along for the ride are various fellow-travelers of the Beat movement, who provide some of the film's most revealing moments. Bob Dylan gazes at Kerouac's tombstone (probably in 1975) and tells Ginsberg that he wants to be buried in an unmarked grave, not unaware that a movie crew is memorializing his modest words. Amiri Baraka proclaims he's a materialist to his bones, injecting the film's only significant note of skepticism toward the transcendental ideal that most Beat commentators have shown surprisingly little inclination to interrogate, much less challenge. Ken Kesey recalls the good old days when you looked at a range of woodsy knolls and imagined what mind-blowing thrills waited on the other side, only to make the trip and discover that "there was just more knolls."

The substance of *The Source* is sometimes as problematic as its style. It shows no interest in the differences between the literary styles of the core Beat authors (beyond the recitations of its Hollywood visitors) and provides no assessment of their artistic merit vis-à-vis other writers and cultural figures of their day. It contains little historical material that hasn't been presented or approximated in prior Beat documentaries—followers of the genre won't find much new or surprising here—and its credibility isn't strengthened by occasional carelessness in this area, as when a soundtrack comment on Kerouac's drinking accompanies an easily recognizable photograph (taken by Ginsberg in 1964) showing him in a drug daze, not an alcoholic stupor. I also question Workman's judgment in what might be called personnel matters. Philip Glass is an artist great and true, but what makes him an authority on the sociology of the Eisenhower era? More important, should a creep like Timothy Leary be lumped in with obsessively ethical Beats like Ginsberg and Kerouac, as if his self-serving propaganda were just another kind of self-expressive poetry?

Coupled with its reductive structure, such problems keep *The Source* from approaching what Kerouac would have called the "kick in the eye" of Zenlike cinematic satori. Yet serious films on the radical aspects of Fifties culture remain rare enough for even flawed efforts to be well worth a visit by people interested in the diverse manifestations of Beat-hipster thinking. And here's hoping someone releases an album of the movie's music, which sketches an exhilarating lineage from Charlie Parker and Thelonious Monk through Dylan and the Doors to Sonic Youth and others still going strong, effortlessly invoking the protean vitality of Beat-related jazz and rock over a full half century.

More broadly, casual observers who thought the Beat movement began and ended with Kerouac/Ginsberg/Burroughs will be mightily enlightened by brief encounters with role models like Neal Cassady, accomplices like David Amram, disciples like Jerry Garcia, and full-blooded participants like Gregory Corso, Lawrence Ferlinghetti, and Michael McClure. They and their confreres made the Beat scene as eclectic as it was eccentric, and while *The Source* remains too linear and limited to get beyond the enticing surface of their social-spiritual adventure, it provides a reasonably stimulating account of a phenomenon from which our own soul-deadened time could learn a great deal if only it cared and dared to.

LOS ANGELES TIMES, 10/15/99, Calendar/p. 10, John Anderson

[The following review by John Anderson appeared in a slightly different form in **NEWSDAY, 8/25/99, Part II/p. B7.]**

Jack Kerouac never seemed to enjoy any of the liberating benefits of the social revolution he helped foment. Fatally stung by critics like Truman Capote ("It's typing not writing"), who scorned the stream-of-consciousness excesses of his "On the Road," Kerouac followed early successes by soldiering through a number of undistinguished works, finally succumbing to alcohol-aggravated illness in 1969.

William S. Burroughs, meanwhile, shot dope, shot his wife and blew a few holes through national self-satisfaction with such novels as "Naked Lunch," "Junky" and "Queer." Allen Ginsberg? Before his death two years ago, he'd become nothing less than a third link in an American poetic tradition that includes Walt Whitman and William Carlos Williams.

Kerouac, Burroughs and Ginsberg (New England mill-town kid, Midwestern heir and Jersey Jew) had lives as unlikely as their friendships. But from the time of their meeting at Columbia University in the '50s until their respective deaths, they changed the world with words. And they are the source of Chuck Workman's "The Source," an ambitious and largely successful documentary testimony-tribute to the founders of the so-called Beat movement.

Workman's thesis is that the relatively subdued Beat-poetic upheaval of the '50s helped create the massive unrest of the '60s, and that its echoes are heard today. It's tough to argue with him, even before he makes his case. But make it he does—even if his entire film is about myth making, and his subjects' lives were about shattering myths (poetry, politics and/or sex). It may be incumbent upon "The Source" to take its various subjects—who include Lawrence Ferlinghetti, Michael McClure, Amiri Baraka, Ed Sanders and Gregory Corso—seriously. But one can only imagine Ginsberg smiling beatifically over the profundity of it all.

Workman is the beneficiary of what he admits was an enormous amount of cooperation in getting rights to various clips and songs; much of the time he uses only snippets of material but the cumulative effect is rich. And pointed: Television coverage of the Beats—from '50s news material to a William F. Buckley interview with Kerouac to the likes of Deborah Norville smugly reporting on emerging interest in the movement and its poetry—points up not only the disposable quality of TV news, but its inherent shallowness and unfailing ability to miss the point.

If "The Source" falters, it's in the dramatized readings by its star attractions—Johnny Depp (as Kerouac), John Turturro (as Ginsberg, reading "Howl" on the grounds of the Rockland County mental hospital where the poet was briefly treated) and Dennis Hopper as Burroughs. Only the latter works at all—it is typecasting, after all, and typecasting often works. But all three feel like interruptions to an otherwise graceful and poignant tribute to perhaps the three bravest cultural figures of the past 50 years, particularly Ginsberg, whose value as a writer, cultural witness and social gadfly can't be emphasized enough, even by Workman.

NEW YORK, 9/6/99, p. 54, Peter Rainer

The Source, a documentary about the Beats, brings together an astonishing assortment of clips from the past 50 years of counterculturedom and then Mixmasters them into a hailstorm of fragments interspersed with dramatized performances by Johnny Depp, John Turturro, and Dennis Hopper (who was born to read Burroughs). Director Chuck Workman, who assembles those great-moments-in-movies montages for the Oscars, applies the same technique here: Everything is so lickety-split that very little sinks in. What's the point of a movie about the Beats if it doesn't get you high?

NEW YORK POST, 8/25/99, p. 53, Rod Dreher

The title of Chuck Workman's documentary "The Source" refers to the director's hypothesis that the root of most latter-day American pop culture can be directly traced to the 1950s literary movement known as Beat, whose leading apostles and evangelists were the poet Allen Ginsberg and the novelists Jack Kerouac and William S. Burroughs.

The film is skillfully put together, mixing interviews with the three leading Beats (all now dead) with minor figures in the movement, and tracing the advance of Beat morality and the Beat aesthetic from the cafes of San Francisco and Greenwich Village, through the counterculture, and finally, as the baby boomers aged, to the establishment culture itself.

And in a clever stroke, Workman cast three top actors to do readings in the guise of the Beat gods themselves—Johnny Depp as Kerouac, John Turturro as Ginsberg, and most strikingly, Dennis Hopper as Burroughs.

The staged readings, more than any of the testimonials on display, give the viewer an understanding of what the big fuss was all about in the first place. However, as a work of historical documentation, "The Source" suffers from Workman's wholly celebratory take on the movement. Some distance from the subject matter would have been helpful simply for the sake of critical analysis.

Why were the Beats different from what came before them? What were their limits as writers? No one turns up here to put their work in any literary/historical perspective other than golden.

Worse, for a film that posits the Beats as the avatars of postwar American popular culture, "The Source" is strikingly unwilling to question Beat values.

The closest the film comes to offering a dissent from Workman's hagiographical stance is a snippet in which it is alleged that Beats treated women cruelly. That may be, but the larger point—that the Dionysian rebellion fomented by the Beats had tremendously harmful consequences for American society is not once admitted, even to be attacked.

From the vantage point of 1999, surveying the wreckage of lives and families and institutions caused by the wholesale triumph of Beat morality, with its emphasis on sex-and-drugs hedonism, only the most hardcore counterculture could fail to note at least the ambiguity in the Beat legacy.

If "The Source" is largely a work of propaganda, it's an entertaining one. Archival photographs and footage of the early Beat years are fascinating to watch, as are moments like the matter-meeting-antimatter time Kerouac was a guest on Steve Allen's show (offering in a single unintentionally amusing TV shot the outer extremes of 1950s white American culture).

Workman has the wit to include vintage parodies of the Beats, such as Alfred Hitchcock appearing in a goatee and beret, and Granny Clampett denouncing the movement on an episode of "The Beverly Hillbillies." Yet the biographical information provided here is (perhaps unwittingly) unsettling, and offers clues as to the chaos and destruction inherent in Beatness.

Poor Kerouac died early, probably of alcoholism (he's shown bloated and drunk on a "Firing Line" episode). Ginsberg, who penned paeans to his sphincter, flops around at 1960s "be-ins" in flowing robes, chanting gibberish. William S. Burroughs looks mad, bad and dangerous to know. The embittered Gregory Corso, a major Beat figure, appears to have escaped from the drunk tank or the mental ward.

That we esteem degraded men like this as our heroes and the source of our postmodern civilization offers a lesson to the living, though I'm sure it's not the one Workman wants us to glean from his film.

"The Source" is amusing and informative, and it's worth seeing if you have an interest in the period or the writers. But it's far too adoring of its subjects, for whom more blame than credit is due.

VILLAGE VOICE, 8/31/99, p. 120, Amy Taubin

At best a primer, at worst a hagiography, Chuck Workman's *The Source* is a documentary about the Beat Generation that rehashes the basic history and relies on horse's-mouth analysis. Almost all the usual suspects are present and accounted for in new on-camera interviews and/or archival footage. There are the Times Square/Columbia/Downtown Beats: Allen Ginsberg, William Burroughs, Jack Kerouac, Gregory Corso, Herbert Hunke, Amiri Baraka, Ed Sanders, and David Amram (the composer in residence). And there are the West Coast/North Beach Beats: Lawrence Ferlinghetti, Michael McClure, Gary Snyder, Philip Whalen, and Ken Kesey. And there are others, many others, all exuding charisma and camaraderie. (Peter Orlovsky, Ginsberg's longtime companion, is a notable absence.)

Workman has also put together much home-movie footage of the elusive Neal Cassady (immortalized as Dean Moriarty in *On the Road*). Since most of it is of the back of his head (he was filmed as he was driving by someone sitting behind him), it doesn't do much to explain the powerful hold he had over Kerouac and Ginsberg's imaginations.

The Source opens in 1996 with Ginsberg leafing through a book of photographs of the Beats. In the background, we hear Philip Glass's tender solo piano, which later segues into a Bach cello sonata. There's a whiff of college-dorm transcendence in the air. Soon we see Burroughs through the window of his Kansas farmhouse and we hear his voice-like the sound of cicadas on a tape slowed to half-time. Someone could make a great film simply by analyzing the sound and meaning of Ginsberg's and Burrough's voices—arguably the most influential of the second half of the century.

But nostalgia, rather than cultural or aesthetic criticism, is Workman's game. A flurry of movie and TV clips that send up Beat culture, a couple of Beat generation events on contemporary college campuses with many close-ups of worshipful young faces, and then we're back in New York in 1944 where Ginsberg, Kerouac, and Burroughs meet and change history. The thesis, such as it is, illustrated by chronologically ordered archival footage, follows a familiar trajectory. The Beat generation rebelled against the conformity and creeping consumerism of American post-World War II society. Poets and novelists, they were part of an art movement that also included abstract expressionist painting, bebop jazz, and underground film. Disconcerted when they were made the butt of the mainstream media, they dispersed to various corners of the world, but returned to become spokespersons of the '60s counterculture. Their celebration of the individual as outsider, bonded in rebellion with other outsiders, inspires successive generations of rock-and-rollers; their voices echo in the poetry slams of the '90s.

Given that modesty was never a Beat virtue, it's not surprising that a film relying on insider testimony would have a self-congratulatory ring. But if *The Source* isn't informed with current reevaluations of the Beats, it does attempt to include a small acknowledgment of a feminist critique. There's a clip of filmmaker Shirley Clarke saying, "They got away with murder because what they were proselytizing was the male artist hero." It's followed by a clip of Ginsberg countering, "I don't think we were practicing machismo. Burroughs and I were queer, very sensitive and literary," and a clip of Burroughs tossing out the sardonic rejoinder "Some of my best friends are women." Since Clarke appears for 20 seconds quite early in the film and her argument never resurfaces, she is effectively silenced by everything that follows. I left *The Source* feeling as put down as I used to feel in the '60s. It didn't help that I knew why.

Also reviewed in:
CHICAGO TRIBUNE, 11/12/99, Friday/p. O, Michael Wilmington
NEW YORK TIMES, 8/25/99, p. E1, Janet Maslin
VARIETY, 2/22-28/99, p. 64, Dennis Harvey

SOUTH PARK: BIGGER, LONGER & UNCUT

A Paramount Pictures and Warner Bros. release in association with Comedy central of a Scott Rudin and Trey Parker/Matt Stone production. *Executive Producer:* Scott Rudin and Adam Schroeder. *Producer:* Trey Parker and Matt Stone. *Producer (animation):* Frank C. Agnone III. *Director:* Trey Parker. *Screenplay:* Trey Parker, Matt Stone, and Pam Brady. *Editor:* John Venzon. *Music:* Trey Parker. *Music Editor:* Dam DiPrima. *Sound:* Chris Welch, Deb Adair, Barbara Harris and (music) Tim Boyle and Dennis Sands. *Sound Editor:* Bruce Howell. *Art Director:* J.C. Wegman. *Running time:* 88 minutes. *MPAA Rating:* R.

VOICES: Trey Parker (Stan Marsh/Eric Cartman/Mr. Garrison/Mr. Hat/Officer Barbrady); Matt Stone (Kyle Broflovski/Kenny McCormick/Pop/Jesus/Jimbo); Mary Kay Bergman (Mrs. Cartman/SheilaBroflovski/SharonManson/Mrs.McCormick/WendyTestaberg/PrincipalVictoria; Isaac Hayes (Chef); Jesse Howell (Ike); Anthony Cross-Thomas (Ike); Francesca Clifford (Ike); Bruce Howell (Man in Theatre); Deb Adair (Woman in Theatre); Jennifer Howell (Bebe); George Clooney (Doctor Gouache); Brent Spiner (Conan O'Brien); Minnie Driver (Brooke Shields); Dave Foley (Baldwin Brothers); Eric Idle (Doctor Vosknocker); Nick Rhodes

(Canadian Fighter Pilot);   Toddy E. Walters (Winona Ryder);   Stewart Copeland (American Soldier 1);   Stanley G. Sawicki (American Soldier 2);   Mike Judge (Kenny's Goodbye).

CHRISTIAN SCIENCE MONITOR, 7/2/99, p. 15, David Sterritt

[*South Park: Bigger, Longer & Uncut* was reviewed jointly with *Wild Wild West*; see Sterritt's review of that film.]

LOS ANGELES TIMES, 6/30/99, Calendar/p. 4, John Anderson

[*The following review by John Anderson appeared in a slightly different form in* **NEWSDAY, 6/30/99, Part II/p. B9.**]

You'll hate yourself in the morning. Still, "South Park: Bigger, Longer & Uncut," in which the little kids with the big eyes and foul mouths save the world from intolerance and Saddam Hussein, is so gleefully vulgar, so eagerly offensive, it's tough not to get down on all fours and beg for more.

As the title suggests, the half-hour animated sitcom, which has been playing on cable for almost two years, has been cut loose from its only marginal restraints on Comedy Central and allowed to fulfill the promise of its nasty, untidy vision—which includes a gratuitous streak of misogyny and more than a trace of hackneyed homophobia. Like a Colorforms set as designed by Lenny Bruce, or "Children of the Damned" as directed by Howard Stern, "South Park" the movie is a lot more clever than it is subtle.

But it is smart. And neither its timing nor its attitude could be better, given the cultural hand-wringing post-Littleton or the self-serving sanctimony of partisans on either side of the movie morality debate.

The fun starts when South Park's resident angst-ridden midgets—Kyle, Stan, Cartman and Kenny, who not only dies but goes to hell—attend the R-rated "Asses of Fire" starring Canada's Terrence and Phillip (who are so deliriously vulgar they make Cartman seem like Noel Coward). When the boys emerge even more uncontrollably foul-mouthed than before, their mothers, led by the Queens-accented Sheila Broflovksi, declare a cultural war on Canada. This leads to the imprisonment of Terrence and Phillip, armed conflict, the threat of global annihilation and the preeminence of Satan himself who turns out to be basically a nice guy on the losing end of an exploitative sexual relationship with Saddam.

Forming their own "La Resistance" and bolstered by a blatant parody of "Les Miserables" and the anthemic faux polka "What Would Brian Boitano Do?," the boys have to save the world from sanctimony and itself.

A lot of the laughs in the movie spring from the virtual torrent of vulgarity teeming off the screen, but it probably says something that language can still shock us, even if it has to be in mass quantities. The irony is that "South Park's" target audience, the one that's too young for its R-rating, will probably get into the film, but won't get the whole picture—part of which is a total mockery of the ratings system itself It's hardly Paramount's fault, but had this been an independent movie, history suggests it would have been slapped with an NC-17.

That the Terrence and Phillip movie is R-rated is a laugh, but the fact that it's within another R-rated movie is even more pointed. The idea that even Satan is less evil than Saddam Hussein is a shot at the politics of demonization; that Cartman gets a V-chip implanted in his head and then continually zaps himself with his own expletives is hilarious. And that a war should break out because Sheila Broflovksi thinks her kids—or any kids—could remain innocent in this culture may be the biggest joke of all.

Director Trey Parker and his producing-writing partner Matt Stone share most of the voice-over chores (Mary Kay Bergman voices most of the women). Brent Spiner is credited as Conan O'Brien, Minnie Driver as Brooke Shields, and Saddam is credited as himself; who knew his voice was so high? Must be the effect of the Kuwaiti oil fires. Elsewhere in "South Park" the Baldwin brothers are blown up, Bill Gates is shot and, as Kenny discovers, there are nude women in heaven. Somebody will have to tell him, because he's clearly too young for his own movie.

NEW YORK POST, 6/30/99, p. 50, Rod Dreher

If you were building a movie guaranteed to make family-film advocate Michael Medved spontaneously combust, you couldn't do better—or worse, actually—than "South Park: Bigger, Longer & Uncut."

Think of the most offensive mainstream movie you've ever seen. This is worse. It's obscene, disgusting, blasphemous, scatological, nauseating—and, at times, very, very funny.

Any movie that makes cruel fun of Canada, Bill Gates and the Baldwin brothers can't be all bad. The quite clever satirical moments in this crudely animated filth fest, though, are not remotely worth being dragged through the cinematic sewer.

Think it's like the TV show? Just you wait. That's like comparing a third-grader passing gas to the same kid voiding his bowels and smearing the stuff all over creation.

The movie opens in the "quiet little redneck podunk white-trash mountain town" of South Park with the gang—Kyle, Cartman, Stan and mush-mouthed Kenny—going to see "Asses of Fire," an R-rated Canadian import.

They emerge aping the extremely foul mouths of the film's stars, Terrence and Philip.

The town goes berserk, with Kyle's overbearing Jewish mom founding a hysterical organization called Mothers Against Canada. Terrence and Philip are arrested on Conan O'Brien's show and held as war criminals, charged with corrupting America's youth.

With Canada and the United States at war, it's up to the "South Park" kids to rescue Terrence and Philip before they're executed, and teach the adults about tolerance.

Meanwhile, Kenny dies (for real) and goes to hell, where he witnesses gay lovers Saddam Hussein and Satan cat-fighting while preparing to take over the world.

"South Park" creators Trey Parker and Matt Stone may be vile, but they're awfully smart. They lace parodic musical numbers throughout the film, including a hilarious fantasy sequence called "What Would Brian Boitano Do?"

And their assault on pop-culture pieties can be as acidly funny as it is indiscriminate and offensive.

But they go sickeningly over the line, and the film leaves you feeling slimed and sorry for having bothered.

Did we really need to hear the raunchy pillow talk as Saddam and Satan have rough anal sex? Who laughs at a kid, even one as repugnant as Cartman, witnessing his mother being defecated on in an Internet porn video?

And what's the point of having a French kid calling God "the biggest bitch of them all"?

NEWSWEEK, 7/5/99, p. 58, David Ansen

To find out how obscenitites save the world from Satan and Saddam Hussein; to understand why the United States has declared war on Canada; to hear the best (and only) song written in praise of Brian Boitano, and to witness the violent demise of Bill Gates, there is only one place to turn: "South Park: Bigger, Longer & Uncut." Every bit as tasteless, irreverent, silly and smart as the Comedy Central cartoon that catapulted creators Trey Parker and Matt Stone into the Hollywood catbird seat, "South Park" has a gag-to-laugh ratio even higher than the new "Austin Powers."

And it's filled with roof-raising musical numbers. That maybe the biggest difference from the half-hour show. Otherwise, all the familiar, strangely fatherless little devils are on hand: lovelorn Stan, still pining and puking for Wendy; obtuse Cartman, making anti-Semitic cracks at the neurotic Kyle, and the parka-shrouded, incomprehensible Kenny, who dies this time when a surgeon replaces his heart with a baked potato. How did he end up in surgery in the first place? He went up in flames in a failed attempt to light a fart.

Oh, yes, flatulence is central to "South Park's" adolescent appeal, but also to the movie's plot—and its sly politics. The trouble begins when the kids sneak into an obscenity-filled Canadian movie, "Asses of Fire," starring the infamous Terrence and Phil. Soon they are mimicking the stars' every dirty word, and just as soon Kyle's outraged mom is leading a campaign to protect the children of the nation. ("Blame Canada" is one of Parker and Marc Shaiman's rousing musical anthems.) A kind of crack-pot Madeleine Albright, she soon has Clinton's ear. When the Canadians, protesting the arrest and imminent execution of Terrence and Phil, bomb the entire Baldwin family to oblivion, the hellhounds of war are un-leashed. Better dead bodies than dirty words, the voices of morality decree, as Parker and Stone gleefully hurl satirical poop at the MPAA, and all who have tried to muzzle "South Park's" wicked tongue. This raunchy assault on authority, coming in the midst of the nation's increasingly surreal debate on the pernicious influence of the media, couldn't be more timely. It cuts through the pious finger pointing like, well, we shouldn't really say.

SIGHT AND SOUND, 9/99, p. 55, Leslie Felperin

South Park, Colorado. The present. Third-graders Stan, Cartman, Kyle and Kenny manage to see the 'R-rated film *Asses of Fire*, starring their favourite scatological comedians, Terrance and Phillip, who are both Canadian. The next day at school, the boys scandalise their teacher Mr Garrison by quoting filthy lines of dialogue from the film. Their mothers are notified and Kyle's mother Sheila starts a campaign to blame Canada for the corrupting influence of Terrance and Phillip, who are arrested and sentenced to death. War is declared between the US and Canada after the Canadians bomb the Baldwin brothers.

Meanwhile, Kenny is killed by accident and arrives in hell where Satan is having relationship trouble with his new lover, the recently deceased Saddam Hussein. Terrance and Phillip's death will be Satan's cue to take over the world; Kenny's ghost tries to warn the others. Cartman is fitted with a 'V-chip' that electrocutes him every time he swears. Stan forms a resistance movement, partly to foil Terrance and Phillip's execution and partly to win back his classmate Wendy's affection from a rival. At a huge USO show, the resistance foils the execution but war breaks out. Many are killed. Kyle stands up to his mother who nevertheless shoots Terrance and Phillip. Satan and Saddam are about to take over the world, but Kenny persuades Satan to kill the callous Saddam. A grateful Satan grants Kenny's wish to return everything to normal; Kenny bids his friends goodbye and ascends to heaven.

It's all too tempting for UK film goers to sneer at the excesses of US-based censorship and self-censorship in the film and television industry (and all too dangerous to be complacent when the track record of the BBFC and the broadcasters here is so patchy). But no community is more aware of the absurdities of the current climate and their own responsibilities than those who work in the American industry. The rancid atmosphere of genuine anxiety and hysteria hanging in air after the Colorado shootings in April is ripe for Swiftean satire.

So *South Park Bigger Longer & Uncut* couldn't have come out at a better time. Skewering the military, politicians, the media, xenophobic Americans and weirdly-accented Canadians, meddlesome Jewish mothers ("horrific depictions of violence [in film] is OK as long as no one says naughty words," says Kyle's mother Sheila), smug school counsellors and misogynist schoolteachers ("never trust anything that bleeds for five days and doesn't die," sums up Mr Garrison's advice on the subject of women), the acting Baldwin and Arquette families, Canadians Bryan Adams and Alanis Morissette, dim starlets Brooke Shields and Winona Ryder, gay relationships, suburban coprophiliacs, black machismo, people with car alarms, Disney movies (Satan's ballad "Up There" is a spot-on parody of many a lyrical montage of Disney protagonist suffering) and many more, the film seems hell-bent on making good on celluloid the television series' precredits warning that the following material is 'offensive' and 'should not be seen by anybody'.

Co-producers and *South Parks* creators Trey Parker and Matt Stone have revealed in interviews that the title's 'uncut' may be a bit of a misnomer: early versions of the script certainly offended the delicate sensibilities of the MPAA (the US version of the BBFC). Some of the compromises agreed seemed even more vicious to them, so if their account is true this may be the first case of censorship improving a script. Whatever the cause, *Bigger Longer & Uncut* is far tauter, more a laser-guided contraption than the often scattershot episodes of the series. The only element that doesn't work here is the character of Christophe, an atheist French kid whose contribution seems negligible. Fans of the show will bemoan more space couldn't be spared for favourite recurring characters such as Chef (but he does get to initiate a wonderful running gag about clitorises).

Even if *South Park Bigger Longer & Uncut* is unlikely to shame pro censorship critics into silence, at least the success of the film at the US box office and that of its soundtrack album in the record shops will be seen by history as a victory of sorts; the revenge of drama-club nerds, we might call it. Clearly Parker and Stone spent far more time than is healthy rehearsing productions of *Guys and Dolls* and *On the Town* in high school, because to all intents and purposes this film is a musical, and a damn good one at that. Kenny in heaven knows it's certainly an improvement on *Cannibal! The Musical,* Parker and Stone's first slapdash film. And they can also now be officially forgiven for their second film, *Orgazmo.*

TIME, 7/5/99, p. 75, Richard Corliss

Some people should probably skip *South Park: Bigger, Longer & Uncut,* the new feature based on the Comedy Central cartoon series. A short list would include celebrities teased in the movie: the Baldwin brothers (they are killed en masse by the Royal Canadian Air Force); Conan O'Brien (he commits suicide by jumping from the GE Building); Winona Ryder (she performs an unusual exercise with Ping-Pong balls); Bill Gates (he is shot dead because Windows 98 isn't fast enough); Saddam Hussein (he has a gay affair with Satan and toys shamelessly with the Horned One's affections); Barbra Streisand (for all the old reasons); Liza Minnelli (don't ask); and God (who is vilified by one of the movie's guest kid heroes). Also anyone who lacks a bottomless tolerance for inspired comic rudeness.

For the *South Park* film is that happy surprise, an idea that is enriched as it expands from 20 minutes of TV time to 80 movie minutes. It confounds those who suspected that the explosive blips of the *South Park* fad were ready to flatline and that a feature film—likely to bore the faithful and annoy everyone else—was the surest way to do a Conan off the window ledge of the show's fading notoriety.

The kids are still here: Stan, Kyle, Kenny and Cartman, the quartet of cutout third-graders in the "quiet little red-neck podunk whitetrash Mountain town" of South Park, Colo. A bit more is at stake this time: the fate of the world. The lads see a movie starring their favorite Canadian grossout comics, Terrence and Phillip, and parrot the naughty language. The South Park moms blame Canada, and in a trice we're war-ready. Meanwhile, Kenny (the dead one) goes to hell, where Satan and Saddam lurk. It takes a children's crusade—La Resistance—to get to the final rainbow.

All that and a gigantic talking clitoris should be enough for a short feature. But director Trey Parker (who wrote the film with Matt Stone and Pam Brady) figured he'd turn *South Park* into a wall-to-wall musical: 14 tunes, each evoking a familiar Broadway style. Cartman's perky *Kyle's Mom's a Bitch* echoes *Chitty Chitty Bang Bang,* with choruses in fake Chinese, Dutch and French. Saddam could be an Arabic fiddler on the roof as he struts his seedy charm in *I Can Change.* Satan has a hilariously solemn ballad in the Disney-cartoon mode; like the *Little Mermaid,* he wants to be *Up There.* There's a dexterous quartet of musical themes, A la *Les Miz.* And though a song whose refrain is, more or less, "Shut your fucking face, Uncle Flicka" would seem to have little room for musical wit, ace arranger Marc Shaiman turns it into an *Oklahoma* hoedown, with kids chirping like obscene Chipmunks.

Did we say obscene? Be warned: the raunch is nonstop and often noxious. Kids who take their parents (or Liza or the Baldwins) should be prepared for some gasps and a scolding. As Cartman says of the Terrence and Phillip epic, "This movie has warped my fragile little mind." To viewers with sturdier cerebellums, here's another warning: you may laugh yourself sick—as sick as this ruthlessly funny movie is.

VILLAGE VOICE, 7/6/99, p. 70, Gary Dauphin

The foul-mouthed adventures of four crudely rendered grade schoolers from South Park, Colorado—Stan, Kenny, Kyle, and Eric Cartman (all voiced by creators Trey Parker and Matt Stone)—proceed apace in *Bigger, Longer & Uncut.* The boys' trouble begins this time when they sneak into an obscenity-laced "Canadian film." They soon start sprouting bons mots like "ass licker" and "uncle fucka," leading Kyle's easily outraged Jewish mom to launch an anti-Canadian protest movement. Kenny is, of course, quickly killed (he goes to hell to find Satan being buggered by Saddam Hussein), and war breaks out between the U.S. and Canada, an international crisis that has to be defused by Stan, et al.

Park is a purposely offensive and scatologically excessive TV show to begin with, but the potty mouth on this R-rated cartoon is pretty mind-boggling. The extravagance also extends into matters of form, *Bigger* being a musical with about 12 interminable production numbers.

(Parker's first film was a thoroughly daft live-action musical about cannibals.) The ultimate truth, though, is that certain, probably arrested, personalities (like mine) just find this kind of shit pretty funny and any attempt to talk your way around that is, as Cartman would say, blowing bubbles out your ass.

Also reviewed in:
CHICAGO TRIBUNE, 6/30/99, Tempo/p. 1, Mark Caro
NATION, 9/6 & 13/99, p. 36, Stuart Klawans
NEW YORK TIMES, 6/30/99, p. E1, Stephen Holden
VARIETY, 6/28-7/11/99, p. 73, Dennis Harvey
WASHINGTON POST, 6/30/99, p. C1, Rita Kempley

SPANISH FLY

An Avalanche Releasing release of a Star Line/Portman Entertainment/Banfilm production. *Producer:* Juan Alexander. *Director:* Daphna Kastner. *Screenplay:* Daphna Kastner. *Director of Photography:* Arnaldo Catinari. *Editor:* Caroline Biggerstaff. *Music:* Mario de Benito. *Casting:* Joseph Middleton and Sara Bilbatua. *Production Designer:* Alain Bainee. *Costumes:* Maria De Cossio. *Running time:* 94 minutes. *MPAA Rating:* R.

CAST: Daphna Kastner (Zoe); Toni Canto (Antonio); Martin Donovan (Carl); Antonio Castro (Julio); Danny Huston (John); Marianne Sagebrecht (Rosa).

LOS ANGELES TIMES, 12/1/99, Calendar/p. 5, Kathleen Craughwell

"Spanish Fly" is a smart, funny and realistic romantic comedy from fledgling but talented writer-director Daphna Kastner.

The film opens with the lead character Zoe (Kastner), an American journalist researching a book on machismo, interviewing a sullen taxi driver in a Madrid bar. Because of Zoe's poor Spanish language skills the interview is a struggle, at best, until Zoe's interpreter Antonio (Toni Canto) finally arrives.

The attraction between Zoe and Antonio is obvious but things derail rapidly when Antonio discards the research questionnaire that Zoe has prepared and begins conducting his own interview with the taxi driver. He insists that "no Spanish man will talk to a foreign woman about sex with questions like these" and within a few minutes the interview is over and Antonio is fired.

Zoe is attractive and articulate but she's also insecure and more than a tad uptight, especially compared with the carefree Europeans she encounters in sultry Madrid. (She even looks out of place in her prim cardigans and chunky healed loafers.)

Weary from reams of astoundingly unenlightened interviews, Zoe retreats to her cozy sublet apartment and, from phone conversations she has with her mother who lives in New York, we glean that Zoe has recently been dumped by a supposedly "safe and sensitive" boyfriend. We soon realize Zoe's interest in machos and consequently, her inquiries about what men want from women and vice versa, is more personal than professional.

She struggles between her rational desire for an intellectual and emotional equal, like Carl (Martin Donovan), a former university professor with whom she begins a sexual but loveless relationship, and her primal attraction toward men like Julio (Antonio Castro), a swaggering flamenco guitarist with little to offer but his much boasted about sexual skills.

Thankfully (for Zoe and for the audience) Zoe runs into Antonio again, and, more out of desperation than anything else, she rehires him to assist with her research. Antonio is cocky and a bit of a Lothario but he's also intelligent, funny and very good looking and despite their differences, or perhaps because of them, the two complement each other nicely.

About midway through the film the plot takes a sudden turn when Zoe gets the news from her New York literary agent that no author working on an advance wants to hear: The publishers have decided to scrap the whole project.

Zoe and Antonio then head south to a romantic beach town to the very hotel where Zoe was conceived. It is here that Zoe confronts her past and the mystery of her parentage. It seems obvious that the two are falling in love but Zoe is so consumed by her own pain she consistently sabotages the budding romance. Unfortunately this subplot involving Zoe's parentage is less interesting (and definitely less fun) than the rest of the action and high jinks in Madrid.

Danny Huston, son of John and brother of Anjelica, is hilarious in his small role as John, Zoe's ex-boyfriend who shows up in Madrid while "re-tracing Hemingway's steps" with his Robert Bly-type men's group. John is a former wimp who now embraces fishing, chanting and drumming and who contends that "men have forgotten how to be providers" because women have held them back.

Overall the film is an intelligent and entertaining probe into modern relationships and a nice showcase for Kastner, Canto and Huston.

NEW YORK POST, 12/3/99, p. 48, Jonathan Foreman

As critic, one dreads independent films in which the writer/director casts him-or herself in the lead because such filmmakers often become blinded by self-indulgence.

But "Spanish Fly" is a frequently funny and sexy exception to that rule.

Unfortunately, this romantic comedy sags grievously during its last third, but the first 45 minutes of the film are so enjoyable you can almost forgive the final slow descent into mushy writing and hackneyed plotting.

Zoe is a cute, slightly Jappy, sexually dissatisfied New Yorker, who has moved to Madrid to research a book on machismo. She's attracted to handsome, aggressive Spanish men, like Julio the guitarist (Antonio Castro) and Antonio, her womanizing interpreter, but the uptight politically correct convictions she's picked up in her gender-studies classes won't allow her to give these guys a try.

Instead she falls into relationship with one of her former college professors (Martin Donovan), who has moved to Madrid to open a bookstore. Carl is close to the sort of man she thinks she should be with—he sounds sensitive and he talks about philosophy during sex—but he fails to float her boat.

Zoe is increasingly drawn to Antonio, especially when they take a trip to the South of Spain. They stay at a hotel (run by Marianne Sagebrecht from "Bagdad Cafe"), which just happens to be the place Zoe's mother was impregnated by the Spanish father Zoe never knew. And it's at this point, as Zoe deals with her parental issues, that the film becomes soppy and artificial.

It's a shame, because writer/director/star Daphna Kastner skillfully captures the intoxicating energy of modern Spain. She also has a clever, perceptive take on the confusion experienced by so many American women when their homegrown ideas about relationships clash with more freewheeling European sexual mores.

Also reviewed in:
NEW YORK TIMES, 12/1/99, p. E3, Stephen Holden
VARIETY, 8/10-16/98, p. 44, Leonard Klady

SPARKLER

A Strand Releasing release of a Sunshine Filmworks/Conspiracy Entertainment production. *Executive Producer:* J. Herbert Niles III, John J. McDonnell III, Walter L. Threadgill, and Pamela S. Calloway. *Producer:* Jennifer Amerine and Kimberly Jacobs. *Director:* Darren Stein. *Screenplay:* Catherine Eads and Darren Stein. *Director of Photography:* Rodney Taylor. *Editor:* Ryan Gold. *Music:* Dave Russo. *Sound:* David Waelder. *Sound Editor:* Dave Weathers. *Casting:* Joseph Middleton. *Production Designer:* Chris DiLeo. *Art Director:* Sandra Lea Grass. *Costumes:* Dalhia Schuette. *Make-up:* Myke Michaels. *Running time:* 96 minutes. *MPAA Rating:* R.

CAST: Park Overall (Melba May); Veronica Cartwright (Dottie Delgato); Don Harvey (Flint); Jamie Kennedy (Trent); Steven Petrarca (Joel); Freddie Prinze, Jr. (Brad); Sandy Martin (Ed); Grace Zabriskie (Sherri); Sheila Tousey (Hurricane); Gloria Le Roy (Maxine); Glenn Shadix (Announcer); Jack Wallace (Jesse); Frances Bay (Raspy); Octavia Spencer (Wanda); Googy Gress (Big Stew); Chris Ellis (Buddy #1); Robert Peters (Buddy #2); Wendy Worthington (Bar-Goer #1); William Hendry (Bar-Goer #2); Rhonda Dotson (Fawner); Catherine Rideout (Waitress); Judy Armstrong (Old Lady); Promise LeMarco (Card Dealer); Faith Johnson (Balloon Woman); Allison Jacobs (Charlene); Rachel Winfree (Beauty Client); Timi Prulhiere (Showgirl); Jackie Debatin (Showgirl #2); Mario Gardner (Captain Uhura); C.C. Carr (Sexy Face).

LOS ANGELES TIMES, 4/2/99, Calendar/p. 8, Kevin Thomas

In the title role of "Sparkler," a lively little movie with lots of heart and humor, Park Overall is Melba May, a late thirtysomething Victorville trailer park housewife who is an innocent without being stupid, who is kind and observant and ready to make the most of life. But when she catches her low-down trucker husband, Flint (Don Harvey, a comic rascal), in their bed with another woman, she moves in with her beautician mother (Grace Zabriskie), shopping and psychic network zealot. Then, a couple of plot developments later, she winds up in Las Vegas with three young guys, Jamie Kennedy's Trent, Steven Petrarca's Joel and Freddie Prinze Jr.'s Brad, who initially are none too eager to have her company but they admit she does have a lot of sparkle.

The guys are trying to win $3,000 at the gambling tables so that they can pay back rent on their L.A. apartment. (Brad passes himself off as an agent, although he's still in the mail room; his pals are unemployed.) After 15 years of marriage, Melba May is out to have herself some fun and intends to look up her high school friend Dottie Delgato (Veronica Cartwright), who went off to Vegas to become a showgirl but all these years later turns up as a stripper in a raucous joint run by Ed (Sandy Martin), a rough, tough lesbian who has become Dottie's possessive protector. Dottie couldn't be more eager to have a night on the town with Melba's three new young friends and zeros in on Brad in particular.

Director Darrell Stein, whose delightful second film, "Jawbreaker," opened a few weeks ago, and his co-writer Catherine Eads make imagination and humor count for more than budget. The result is a sweet little comedy that embraces the full range of sexual orientation affectionately and glows with lively performances. (There are cameos from those redoubtables Gloria LeRoy and Frances Bay.) Overall and Cartwright are especially winning, and Cartwright makes Dottie appealing in the vulnerability and longing that lurks beneath her hard, painted and bewigged surface. "Sparkler" lives up to its name.

NEW YORK POST, 3/19/99, p. 46, Rod Dreher

Does anybody really need another movie about how charmingly eccentric the inhabitants of trailer parks, roadside diners, strip clubs and the city of Las Vegas are? No, but thanks to TV star Park Overall in the title role, "Sparkler" is a lot more engaging than you might expect.

Overall, the "Empty Nest" siren, who looks like a cross between Joan Cusack and Beverly D'Angelo, plays Melba May, a 39-year-old desert princess whose castle is lovingly described as "the nicest trailer in the park." But when she discovers her greaseball trucker husband Flint (Don Harvey) having sex with her best friend, Melba May runs home to her hairdresser mama (Grace Zabriskie). She dolls herself up one night in gaudy, glittery clothes and hits a local singles bar.

There she meets three L.A. snots (Jamie Kennedy, Steven Petrarca, and Freddie Prinze Jr.) making a pit stop in this broken-down town on their way to Vegas, where they hope to win enough money to make next month's rent. The guys look down on Melba. "In her world, she's glamorous," says one; another characterizes her situation as, "Small life, big dreams, going nowhere."

Ugly, but true. Desperate Melba sees the trio as her ticket to the big time, but they ditch her pronto. She eventually makes it to the sleazy Oz, and searches out her high-school friend Dottie (Veronica Cartwright), a former showgirl about whom naive Melba enthuses, "She even wrote me that she was dating Siegfried and Roy!"

The truth proves comically otherwise, giving wide-eyed Overall and Cartwright some uproarious scenes in the most woebegone locales. Of course the unsinkable Melba May crosses paths with the L.A. boys again, whose callow disregard for Melba masks their own fear of failure. They're hungry strivers too, but they think they're superior to Melba because they have better taste.

Despite some incongruous raunchiness in the relatively thin screenplay (by director Stein and Catherine Eads), Melba's robust spirit and true-blue heart carry the day. "Sparkler" could have used more polish—in particular, the male threesome are a tad wan and underdeveloped—but it's best as a showcase for the punchy Cartwright and the irresistible Overall, who glimmers like a diamond in the rough.

NEWSDAY, 3/19/99, Part II/p. B7, Gene Seymour

"Sparkler" is an indulgence. It's comfort-food stuffed with all kinds of things that are wrong with it—and may, indeed, be bad for you. (OK, not exactly bad, but certainly not good.)

Yet if there was ever a movie made for midafternoon binging, this road comedy by Darren Stein ("Jawbreaker") is it. The movie is a lot like its heroine, Melba May (Park Overall). It's warm, flaky, kitschy and disoriented. But once in a while, it's lucky enough to trip over an insight or two.

Melba, who lives in the roadside town of Victorville, Calif., with her pond-scum trucker husband, Flint (Don Harvey), trips over her first insight when she overhears Flint and her best friend making whoopie in their trailer. She moves in with her high-strung hairdresser-mom (Grace Zabriskie), who encourages her to celebrate her freedom by spending a night on the town in a glow-in-the-dark prom dress.

By chance, she encounters three desperate, 20-something guys from L.A. who are driving to Las Vegas to win enough money to pay all their creditors. Trent (Jamie Kennedy) identifies with Melba's sweet, unaffected manner while Brad (Freddie Prinze Jr.), a smug Mike Ovitz-wannabe working in a talent agency's mailroom, gives her his card to shake her off. Joel (Steven Petrarca) likewise wishes she'd go away and leave him to a private torment barely concealed by his petulant cool.

Vegas doesn't sound like a bad idea to Melba. Besides hooking up with her new buds, she can check up on an old one from high school. But Melba gets a heavy jolt of reality when she tracks down ex-baton ace Dottie Delgato (Veronica Cartwright) in a low-life strip joint run by a butch lesbian named Ed (Sandy Martin). Meanwhile, Flint finds out Melba has won a million-dollar sweepstakes prize and suddenly feels the need to reconcile.

Stein's meandering tale, which he co-wrote with Catherine Eads, has a few of the virtues and all the flaws of '70s American cinema, including a nagging ambiguity toward his subject. (He's half in love with the tackiness he denigrates.) Nevertheless, much of the affection he bestows upon his characters in this calling-card feature was sorely needed in "Jawbreaker." He gives Overall, who's dropped off the radar somewhat since "Empty Nest" vanished, a lovely showcase while Cartwright, one of Hollywood's neglected treasures, shows characteristic fire and uncharacteristic vivacity.

VILLAGE VOICE, 3/23/99, p. 130, Justine Elias

A Vegas road trip goes awry in the genial but clichéd *Sparkler,* in which three broke L.A. housemates seek a jackpot that will cover several months of unpaid rent. One (Freddie Prinze Jr.) is a would-be talent agent, cocksure and snide, even though he's stuck working in the mail room; the others (Steven Petrarca and Jamie Kennedy) are unemployed and feeling hopeless. When they meet a local woman (Park Overall) who loves kitschy home decorations and magazine sweepstakes, and a trashy stripper (Veronica Cartwright), their luck begins to change. They—and the movie—gradually loosen up and lose their smugness. Though the movie was *Jawbreaker* director Darren Stein's industry calling card, it should serve as a reminder that its two likable leading women deserve to be seen in more remarkable films than this.

Also reviewed in:
NEW YORK TIMES, 3/19/99, p. E9, Stephen Holden
VARIETY, 10/27-11/2/97, p. 44, Brendan Kelly

SPEAKING IN STRINGS

A Seventh Art Releasing release of a CounterPoint Films presentation. *Producer:* Lilibet Foster and Paola di Florio. *Director:* Paola di Florio. *Director of Photography:* Peter Rader. *Editor:* Ellen Goldwater. *Music:* Karen Childs. *Running time:* 73 minutes. *MPAA Rating:* Not Rated.

WITH: Nadja Salerno-Sonnenberg.

LOS ANGELES TIMES, 10/29/99, Calendar/p. 4, Kenneth Turan

"Speaking in Strings" is an extraordinarily intimate, deeply affecting and revelatory documentary on how pain and passion can come together in a creative artist. Its portrait of controversial virtuoso violinist Nadja Salerno-Sonnenberg is as vivid and unstoppable as the woman herself. You don't need to know who she is or even much care about classical music to be gripped, even flabbergasted by what's on the screen.

That's because the genuine drama of Salerno-Sonnenberg's life reaches the level of grand opera and the woman herself is exceptionally intense. "She doesn't know how to phone it in," says a friend, a description that barely does justice to someone whose emotions are all out on the surface, a diva who admits that "feeling more than anyone I know" can be both phenomenal and, frankly, "a damn curse."

Director Paola di Florio has an extensive background producing and directing documentaries for television, but what served her best here was a childhood friendship with the violinist. Without that kind of personal connection and the trust it engendered, it's doubtful that the kind of intimacy that is the film's hallmark would have happened.

More than being intense, Salerno-Sonnenberg is compelled to be completely honest, to forthrightly confront the demons and crises that have accompanied her to a position as one of the world's premier violinists. "It's amazing what you endure," she says, "when you must."

These crises include a 1984 kitchen accident in which Salerno-Sonnenberg cut off the tip of her left little finger ("I thought my life was over as I had known it") as well as a more recent suicide attempt that was nearly successful. "I don't want to talk about this," Salerno-Sonnenberg says at first about that, literally doubled over in psychological pain, but finally, movingly, she does.

The core of everything for Salerno-Sonnenberg is her playing. "Classical music is like a drug, it's like food for your soul," she says of this all-consuming way of life. Strong-willed and iconoclastic, she's able to make powerful connections through her music even during moments of terrible personal crisis. "In fact when I put a fiddle under my chin I'm able to convey how I feel a lot better than speaking"—hence the film's title.

The other constant in Salerno-Sonnenberg's life is her stance as a battler. Moving to this country from Italy when she was 8, her thick accent (and her old country lunches) made her an outcast at school, "but I had that fighting attitude."

Salerno-Sonnenberg's father, now dead, abandoned both her and her mother when his daughter was 3 months old, and her refusal to meet with him when she got older typifies her loyal, unbending frame of mind. "What if we became friends? How would my mother feel?" she asks. "I didn't want to hurt my mother's feelings."

The turning point in Salerno-Sonnenberg's career came in 1981 when, as a student at Juilliard and against her teacher's advice, she entered the prestigious Walter W. Naumberg International Violin Competition, practiced 12 and 13 hours a day and ended up winning the prize.

From the beginning, Salerno-Sonnenberg's approach to her art divided people, a schism "Speaking in Strings" fully acknowledges. "I feel possessed sometimes when I play," she says, and the film's many clips of her at the violin show her face transported by emotion. But critics have charged that she puts too much personality into her work, battling the composer and overpowering the music in the process.

In addition to talking to her mother, her friends, fellow musicians and writers like Martin Bernheimer, formerly The Times' classical music critic, "Speaking in Strings" shows Salerno-Sonnenberg in any number of situations, from dinner parties to recording sessions to tending to her aging cat.

Volatile, high-strung but with a fine wise-cracking sense of humor, Salerno-Sonnenberg, unable to be anything but herself, is the opposite of today's run of stage-managed public personalities. Your heart can't help but go out to her because, in this exceptional film, hers goes out to you.

NEW YORK POST, 9/17/99, p. 50, Rod Dreher

Nadja Salerno-Sonnenberg is a tough, chain-smoking Italian chick from Jersey who plays the violin like an angel—or, to be more honest, a demon.

She has become one of the world's pre-eminent concert violinists, and, owing to her fierce, passionate performing style, one of the most controversial.

"Speaking in Strings" is a no-budget profile of Salerno-Sonnenberg, a fascinating figure who is a tortured artist straight out of central casting. But it gives us so little information about her personal life that we can only guess what really bedevils her. The movie isn't bad, only scattered and incomplete.

VILLAGE VOICE, 9/21/99, p. 166, Robert Hilferty

Violinist Nadja Salerno-Sonnenberg is no shrinking violet. When she's on the stage, you can't ignore her, and not only because of her slash-and-burn virtuosity. She can't keep still, her face distorted in agony and ecstasy as she plumbs the nether regions of this or that concerto. Her restless physicality is both distracting and magnetic—a combination that has won her friends and enemies. Offstage, she hunts alligators and sharks in cowboy boots with a cigarette dangling from her lips. In spite of her exotic double-decker name, she's as American as apple pie. No question about it: she's the Mike Tyson of the Stradivarius.

This 39-year-old tomboy has redefined the "femininity" of violin playing—she's not afraid to make her instrument sound harsh when she feels the music calls for it—and now, fittingly, she's the subject of a documentary with feminist undercurrents. *Speaking in Strings* is directed by Paola di Florio, and most members of the production team are women too. One of Salerno-Sonnenberg's female cronies says, "The classical music business is run by a certain clique of men," but the film goes on to show that many women are involved—at least in Nadja's circle—including record producers, recording engineers, publicists, and conductors.

The movie, a clumsy labor of love with unforgivable lapses—key footage is missing, and it fails to show why Salerno-Sonnenberg's controversial interpretations are so original and valid—sometimes rises to become a compelling portrait of a neurotic personality.

Sure, she's tough as nails, but she's a total mess. Although she claims that music "saved" her life, what we actually see is how it ruined her, an overriding obsession wedded to a merciless schedule. Things went berserk: she accidentally cut off the tip of her pinkie (while cooking; it was sewn back). She later tried to commit suicide—triggered (literally) by a failed romance.

Or so the film obliquely suggests. For a movie fashioned in the let-it-all-hang-out confessional mode, it's odd that it pussyfoots around a rather obvious point. Salerno-Sonnenberg, who has a fuck-off attitude, doesn't have to be the Ellen DeGeneres of classical music, but she could at least fess up. This is no mystery: just *cherchez la femme.*

Also reviewed in:
CHICAGO TRIBUNE, 10/8/99, Friday/p. N, Michael Wilmington
NEW YORK TIMES, 9/17/99, p. E23, Stephen Holden
VARIETY, 2/8-14/99, p. 81, Dennis Harvey

SPLENDOR

A Samuel Goldwyn Company release of a Summit Entertainment and Newmarket Capital Group presentation of a Desperate Pictures/Dragon Pictures production. *Executive Producer:* Heidi Lester, William Tyrer, and Chris Ball. *Producer:* Damian Jones, Graham Broadbent, and Gregg Araki. *Director:* Gregg Araki. *Screenplay:* Gregg Araki. *Director of Photography:* Jim Fealy.

Editor: Gregg Araki. *Music:* Daniel Licht. *Production Designer:* Patti Podesta. *Set Decorator:* Jennifer Gentile. *Costumes:* Susanna Puisto. *Running time:* 93 minutes. *MPAA Rating:* R.

CAST: Kathleen Robertson (Veronica); Jonathon Schaech (Abel); Matt Keeslar (Zed); Kelly Macdonald (Mike); Eric Mabius (Ernest); Dan Gatto (Mutt); Linda Kim (Alison).

LOS ANGELES TIMES, 10/1/99, Calendar/p. 16, Kevin Thomas

"Splendor" marks a new direction for filmmaker Gregg Araki, who had pretty much explored all he could about Gen X sex, drugs and despair in such provocative movies as "Nowhere," "The Doom Generation," "Totally F***ed Up" and "The Living End."

Araki hasn't lost his edge; he's matured and, in doing so, has discovered a brighter side of life. So at least for now he's moved away from such concerns as AIDS, heavy drugs and death and turned to romantic comedy. Not to worry, Araki, who never in fact lost his belief in love (or his sense of humor), brings to "Splendor" the bold, richly hued color, the sharp wit and the unconventional sensibility that characterized his most recent films. If anything, "Splendor" marks a return to his earliest no-budget works in which he viewed his contemporaries with an amused compassion as they struggled to sort out their lives and their emotions—which is pretty much what Kathleen Robertson's Veronica is doing here.

Veronica, who from time to time addresses the camera in telling us her story, informs us that she's from some suburban hell where the choices seem to be either an exciting life as a mall beautician or marriage to a guy with "Beer to Eternity" tattooed on his bicep. Being drop-dead gorgeous, Veronica heads for L.A., eventually admitting to us that she's an aspiring actress.

No sooner does she hit her first club, where a costume party is in progress, than she connects with a guy wearing a Prince Valiant get-up—he's Johnathon Schaech's Abel. Then her gaze falls upon the hunky blond drummer in the club band—Matt Keeslar's Zed. Abel is tall, dark and handsome and Zed is tall, blond and handsome; Veronica is equally attracted to both. Since she's such a beauty herself, she begins to wonder if she can get away with having her cake and eating it too.

Once they're past macho displays of righteous indignation, Abel and Zed decide that sharing Veronica would work too. Pretty soon Veronica finds herself in a state of bliss beyond her wildest dreams. Then she's up for a role in a TV movie and meets the director, Ernest (Eric Mabius). As a career beckons and Ernest begins his own pursuit of her, Veronica realizes that in comparison to this new man in her life Abel and Zed are pretty immature. Ernest has a lush home with a pool, is kind, considerate and clearly enamored. A couple of plot twists later, however, Veronica finds herself more miserable than she has ever felt in her life. Can it be possible that at least occasionally those who have it all have to pay for it one way or another?

"Splendor" is a "Design for Living" for the millennium that zooms with a giddy joy only to reveal that its beautiful people have been hit with genuine emotion, causing them pain that's totally unexpected. In the midst of his people's escalating angst, however, Araki never forgets that he's making a romantic comedy, which he gives a fresh spin while respecting its traditions.

"Splendor" reunites Araki with cinematographer Jim Fealy, who shot "The Doom Generation" and "Nowhere's" production designer Patti Podesta. Araki directed Schaech in "The Doom Generation" and Robertson in "Nowhere"—all of which has contributed to giving "Splendor" a sense of connection with his most recent movies. His three stars are entirely winning, as are Mabius, and Kelly Macdonald as Veronica's advice-giving best pal. The pleasing "Splendor" is surely more likely to appeal to a wider—audience than any of Araki's previous films.

NEW YORK POST, 9/17/99, p. 50, Jonathan Foreman

"Splendor" is an embarrassing misfire, a comedy by indie icon Gregg Araki that is neither funny nor clever. It feels like a long, slow TV pilot about L.A. twentysomethings, only it lacks the polish and wit of your average sitcom.

Veronica (Kathleen Robertson) plays an aspiring actress who must choose between an immature guy whom she loves (Matt Keeslar as a punk drummer) and a mature rich one whom she doesn't (Johnathon Schaech as a rock critic).

But just as she's tiring of both of them, she discovers she's six months pregnant—and then a rich young director named Ernest (Eric Mablus) puts the moves on her, taking her to his fabulous place in Maui. Veronica doesn't love this guy exactly, but he'd certainly make a better father than her two boyfriends put together ...

Robertson was fun to watch as Clare on TV's "Beverly Hills 90210," so her flat, characterless performance here is a real disappointment.

VILLAGE VOICE, 9/21/99, p. 170, Dennis Lim

Masquerading as a bubbleheaded update of *Design for Living, Splendor* is Gregg Araki's version of a family-values movie. The values in question are kinky, but only on the surface. And for the first time in an Araki film, there's nothing but surface—the vacuity is genuine. At best, *Splendor* offers a kinder, gentler, seemingly heartfelt affirmation of polymorphous sexuality. At worst, it soft-pedals its heady perversity into a moral of sorts—threesomes are good; they can work. (And while we're at it, sex is really good, and so are babies.)

The ménage à trois here revolves around struggling L.A. actress Veronica (Kathleen Robertson), who relates the events of her strenuously wacky life in a cutesy to-camera confessional that suggests Meg Ryan doing Ally McBeal. The fun starts one night when she meets brooding, sensitive rock critic Abel (Johnathon Schaech) and punk-drummer sexgod Zed (an agreeably Neanderthal Matt Keeslar) and decides not to choose. At first the guys are jealous, but a truth-or-dare session engenders a (tame) same-sex kiss. All three sleep together (offscreen; the guys, it seems, don't so much as lay a hand on each other), and before long are cohabitating in relative bliss.

For far too long, the film leans on the notion of unconventional domesticity for humor—not unlike *Three's Company,* which it namechecks. Araki has always exploited the tropes of bad TV, turning them inside out and rubbing them up against each other, with pleasing—if not necessarily profound—results. *Splendor,* however, might as well be bad TV. The broad acting (Kelly Macdonald, as Veronica's kooky-Brit lesbian best friend, deserves special mention for her skin-crawling performance) and leaden script cancel each other out. The overall tone is also problematic—satirical, mocking, and large, but without direction or context (it's a mark of how self-satisfied and literal-minded the film is when the end credits roll and New Order's "Bizarre Love Triangle" kicks in). At once in-your-face and out-of-it, *Splendor* is what happens when a director whose natural mode is subversion runs out of things to subvert.

Also reviewed in:
CHICAGO TRIBUNE, 9/24/99, Friday/p. K, John Petrakis
NEW YORK TIMES, 9/17/99, p. E20, Stephen Holden
VARIETY, 2/15-21/99, p. 62, Emanuel Levy

STAR WARS: EPISODE I—THE PHANTOM MENACE

A Twentieth Century Fox release of a Lucasfilm Ltd. production. *Executive Producer:* George Lucas. *Producer:* Rick McCallum. *Director:* George Lucas. *Screenplay:* George Lucas. *Director of Photography:* David Tattersall. *Editor:* Paul Martin Smith. *Music:* John Williams. *Music Editor:* Ken Wannberg. *Sound:* John Midgley and (music) Shawn Murphy. *Sound Editor:* Ben Burtt and Tom Bellfort. *Casting:* Robin Gurland. *Production Designer:* Gavin Bocquet. *Visual Effects:* John Knoll, Dennis Muren, and Scott Squires. *Art Director:* Peter Russell. *Set Decorator:* Peter Walpole. *Special Effects:* Geoff Heron. *Visual Effects:* John Knoll, Dennis Muren, and Scott Squires. *Costumes:* Trisha Igggar. *Make-up:* Paul Engelen. *Stunt Coordinator:* Nick Gillard. *Running time:* 132 minutes. *MPAA Rating:* PG-13.

CAST: Liam Neeson (Qui-Gon Jinn); Ewan McGregor (Obi-Wan Kenobi); Natalie Portman (Queen Amidala/Padmé); Jake Lloyd (Anakin Skywalker); Pernilla August (Shmi Skywalker); Frank Oz (Yoda); Ian McDiarmid (Senator Palpatine); Oliver Ford Davies (Sio Bibble); Hugh

Quarshie (Captain Panaka); Ahmed Best (Jar Jar Binks); Anthony Daniels (C₃PO); Kenny Baker (R₂-D₂); Terence Stamp (Chancelor Valorum); Brian Blessed (Boss Nass); Andrew Secombe (Watto); Ray Park (Darth Maul); Lewis MacLeod (Sebulba); Warwick Davis (Wald); Steven Speirs (Captain Tarpals); Silas Carson (Nute Gunray); Jerome Blake (Rune Haako); Alan Roscoe (Daultay Dofine); Ralph Brown (Ric Olié); Celia Imrie (Fighter Pilot Bravo 5); Benedict Taylor (Fighter Pilot Bravo 2); Clarence Smith (Fighter Pilot Bravo 3); Samuel L. Jackson (Jedi Night Mace Windu); Dominic West (Palace Guard); Cristina Da Silva (Rabé); Friday Wilson (Eirtaé); Candice Orwell (Yané); Sofia Coppola (Saché); Keira Knightley (Sabé); Bronagh Gallagher (Republic Cruiser Captain); Silas Carson (Republic Cruiser Pilot); John Fensom (TC-14); Greg Proops (Fode); Scott Capurro (Beed); Jabba (Himself); Margaret Towner (Jira); Dhruv Chanchani (Kitster); Oliver Walpole (Seek); Jenna Green (Amee); Megan Udall (Melee); Hassani Shapi (Eeth Koth); Gin (Adi Gallia); Khan Bonfils (Saesee Tiin); Alan Ruscoe (Pio Koon); Michelle Taylor (Yarael Poof); Silas Carson (Ki-Adi Mundi); Michaela Cottrell (Even Piell); Jerome Blake (Oppo Rancisis); Dipika O'Neill Joti (Depa Billaba); Phil Eason (Yaddle); Jerome Blake (Mas Amedda); Mark Coulier (Aks Moe); Silas Carson (Lott Dod);

VOICES: Lindsay Duncan (TC-14); Peter Serafinowicz (Darth Maul); James Taylor (Rune Haako); Chris Sanders (Daultay Dofine); Toby Longworth (Lott Dodd); Marc Silk (Aks Moe); Tyger (Tey How).

LOS ANGELES TIMES, 5/18/99, Calendar/p. 1, Kenneth Turan

Over the 20-plus years since its release, George Lucas' "Star Wars" has influenced so many lives that the writer-director's friend Francis Ford Coppola suggested, more or less seriously, that he turn its philosophy into an organized religion.

Whatever its virtues, and it certainly has them, "Star Wars: Episode I The Phantom Menace" is not going to change anyone's life or method of worship. It's only a movie, and, like the unmasked Wizard at the end of Oz's Yellow Brick Road, a much less impressive one than all the accompanying genuflection would have you believe.

That excessive hype has to be a factor in the perhaps inevitable disappointment we feel. Unlike its illustrious predecessor, this film was not able to sneak into America's consciousness on tiny intergalactic feet. Instead, it had its arrival trumpeted, it's been truthfully said, on the cover of just about every magazine except the New England Journal of Medicine.

But even without the pre-release hoopla, "The Phantom Menace" would be a considerable letdown, as Lucas and company either misjudged or did not care to re-create key aspects of what made "Star Wars" a phenomenon. While the new film is certainly serviceable, it's noticeably lacking in warmth and humor, and though its visual strengths are real and considerable, from a dramatic point of view it's ponderous and plodding.

Seeing "Phantom Menace" not only makes us miss "Star Wars," it also puts that film's success into sharper perspective. The original may have been on the primitive side technically by today's standards, but it was light on its feet, it had an esprit and it wasn't self-consciously aware, as this one invariably is, of being the successor to the most popular series of films ever made.

"Phantom Menace" also unintentionally underlines how much of "Star Wars"' success was due to the sassy elan of stars Harrison Ford and Carrie Fisher. No one in this film steps up and takes their place, no one delivers anything like the irresistible pleasure evident in Ford's self-mocking reading of lines like "Do you think a princess and me ... ?"

Part of the reason for this lack of wit is that "Phantom Menace" is intentionally skewed quite young. One of its key protagonists, as anyone who cares knows by now, is 9-year-old Anakin Skywalker, the future Darth Vader, and many of the film's characters and situations are set up to please tender minds. "We're doing it for the wide-eyed 13-year-old," one of the film's key technicians told Premier magazine, not necessarily a pleasant thought for the rest of us.

Premier also quotes creator Lucas saying that he's "never enjoyed writing that much, to me it's like doing a term paper." While that attitude didn't cripple "Star Wars"—and, in fact, Lucas brought in Lawrence Kasdan to work on the "Empire Strikes Back" and "Return of the Jedi" scripts—its effects, in combination with the grim persona of star Liam Neeson, weigh heavily on the current film.

As Qui-Gon Jinn, the senior of the pair of Jedi Knights who are called upon to deal with a ticklish interplanetary situation, Neeson is saddled with a seemingly interminable series of dull, expository lines. "There is something else behind this," "There is something about this boy," "Be wary, I sense a disturbance in the force." Each line is unobjectionable by itself, but the cumulative effect of them, especially filtered through Neeson's somber, funereal reading, is deadening.

Ironically, in Ewan McGregor, who plays Obi-Wan Kenobi in his youthful apprentice years, "The Phantom Menace" does have an actor with the zest and twinkle this film desperately needs. But though he will figure prominently in the next two episodes, McGregor's presence is no more than nominal here, his lively light hidden under a basket and the film unhesitatingly given over to Neeson's glum philosophizing.

Like "Star Wars," "The Phantom Menace" begins with moving type on the screen setting the interplanetary scene, letting us know that "turmoil has engulfed the galactic empire." The greedy ogres of the Trade Federation are blockading the peaceful, we're-just-plain-folks-down-here planet of Naboo, ruled by youthful but feisty Queen Amidala (Natalie Portman in a weird Brillo-pad hairdo).

While the windy Congress of Republics debates the issue, those previously mentioned Jedi Knights, "guardians of peace and justice in the galaxy," arrive in the neighborhood, precipitating an out-and-out attack on Naboo by an army of battle droids controlled by the Federation. The Jedi spirit the queen off the planet so she can personally plead her case before the congress, but before that can happen there's an emergency stop on the sandy planet of Tatooine (where Luke Skywalker will grow up) for rest and repairs.

On Tatooine, the Jedi and the queen come across young Anakin (Jake Lloyd), a strong-minded boy slave who, the knights discover, has an uncommonly potent amount of the Force within him. How to free Anakin from his nasty master Watto, save the threatened queen and her planet and avoid the two Dark Lords of the Sith, the nasty Darth Maul (effectively played by martial-arts-adept Ray Park) as well as the nastier and more shadowy Darth Sidious, is what the rest of "Phantom Menace" reveals.

It's on Tatooine that the film's most involving sequence, an eye-catching and invigorating introduction to a form of motorized chariot competition (think "Ben-Hur" with jet engines) called "podracing," takes place. Young Anakin turns out to be better at this than any non-alien has a right to be, and watching him race is easily this film's biggest thrill.

It's in this kind of visual creation of other worlds that "Phantom Menace" lives up to expectations and reveals its very real strengths. Not only in expected areas like spaceships and hardware but in the lovely imaginings of very diverse urban settings—the fabulous cityscapes of Coruscant, the elegant Nabooan capital of Theed (filmed in part at the Caserta Royal Palace near Naples) and Naboo's hidden underwater dwellings—this film evokes the sense of wonder that is lacking on its dramatic side. This is not the first epic to have considerably more feeling for alien worlds than human interaction.

"The Phantom Menace" also showcases the initial appearance of the all-wise Yoda, the helpful droids R2-D2 and C-3PO, as well as a youthful Jabba the Hutt. But unfortunately for a film that has three times more computer-generated shots than any previous effort, its biggest miscalculation is a computer-generated sidekick.

That would be Jar Jar Binks, one of a race of Naboo underwater residents known as the Gungan. Looking like a large and ungainly sea horse, Jar Jar, who inexplicably speaks in a kind of Caribbean patois, is a major miscue, a comic-relief character who's frankly not funny. The Gungan as a whole prove very difficult to understand, and when you can make out what they're saying ("You're in big do-do this time") you wish you hadn't.

Despite its many shortcomings, "The Phantom Menace" is certainly adequate, and given the story's strong core idea and the residual power lurking in the Force, it's not necessary to dismiss it out of hand. It's just that the tale it tells isn't all that interesting; in fact, if Lucas wasn't partial to the idea of trilogies, "Phantom" could have been condensed down to a brief prologue tacked on the beginning of the next installment.

To put the best possible face on things, maybe the Force's creator, like a canny strikeout artist, was willing to waste his first pitch before dazzling us with his best stuff next time around.

NEW STATESMAN, 7/12/99, p. 38, Jonathan Romney

In the current issue of *Sight and Sound*, the credits alone for *Star Wars Episode 1: The Phantom Menace* take up over one and a quarter pages, of which some six columns are devoted to the various technicians who worked on the film's digital effects. That's roughly three times as many as the magazine listed for *Jurassic Park* in 1992. What exactly does this prove? That the new *Star Wars* is the most artificial film ever made? That's plain the moment you look at it. That the digital realm of computer-generated imagery (CGI) is fast supplanting bricks-and-mortar reality on screen? That's a condition we've lived with for several years now. Watch any Hollywood blockbuster and you realise that we're already attuned to the textures of a numerical, immaterial cloud-cuckoo-land, in which images, even at their most solid, often have the most fluid, vaporous presence.

In the trade press, what's most often at stake in discussions of the digital explosion is the industrial implication. As ever more spectacular effects can be created by boffins sitting at workstations, will the old trades disappear—will stunt artists, set designers, even stars become redundant overnight? But a more immediate question, as far as viewers are concerned, is the aesthetic one. We know that any spectacle imaginable can be created digitally and look more or less real. But that's very different from looking effective or possessing a real imaginative tangibility. The new *Star Wars* is a good example of this. Some of its images are too familiar to have much effect—its breakneck pod-race sequence is the *Ben Hur* chariot routine remade as state-of-the-art arcade-game whizz-bang. And some of its aliens might as well have been made the old-fashioned way. Its already much-loathed clown, Jar Jar Binks, is created through motion capture, whereby the gestures of a real actor dictate those of a chimera, yet Jar Jar still has the feel of a floppy latex Muppet. There are, however, true wonders in *The Phantom Menace*—some grisly deep-sea behemoths, a glowing underwater city that resembles a hyper-kitsch furniture store specialising in 1970s light-fittings, and the capital of the planet Naboo, an architectural marvel of cod-Byzantine Victoriana.

But we don't get to dwell on any of this for very long. George Lucas wants to throw in as many sights as possible, ushering us on our way, like a brisk theme-park guide. It's as if he's afraid that too much contemplation will reveal the magical castle as the conjuring of thin light that it is. But we should be given the leisure to enjoy it as just that. In fact the most interesting CGI films are the ones that exploit the plasticity and unreality of the images—recently Hollywood has provided few experiences of such crafted aesthetic density as the animation *A Bug's Life*. Some films make CGI's properties a subject in themselves. Last year's ragged but fascinating science fiction film *Dark City* was set in an imaginary world where every night a gang of aliens erases everyone's memory and changes the shape of everything. Like industrious stagehands, the aliens stretch rooms, move buildings, even change the inhabitants' clothes. *Dark City*'s implicit theme is the new possibility—and the new irresponsibility it entails—of creating images of pure, malleable immateriality, with neither depth nor history. Its slender SF premise unfolds into an ethical argument about the way studio productions manipulate both the image and the viewer.

That debate is posed with greater acuity in the Wachowski brothers' current hit *The Matrix*. The matrix itself is a hallucination created by the robots that really rule the earth. In reality, humans are cheerfully dreaming the world as they unknowingly slop about in viscous fluid. The brilliance of *The Matrix* lies not so much in its razzle-dazzle FX as in its inversion of fakery and reality. The narrative doesn't really take place in a computer-generated world but is almost entirely set in a single location, the anti-matrix rebels' hovercraft: the film is really a chamber piece in which characters occasionally, lapse into dream. All its martial arts sequences are given a strange piquancy by our knowledge that Keanu Reeves's character Neo is just imagining that he's fighting, while he reclines in a dentist's chair. Yet in reality, in order to shoot these scenes, he and Laurence Fishburne had to undergo extensive martial arts training.

In a roundabout way, solid physical effort finds its way back into the most immaterial film—as if the Wachowskis want to assure us that film can still provide hard, measurable value for money. The most acute joke about illusion in *The Matrix* comes when a heavy enjoys a large juicy steak in a restaurant. The restaurant's not real, and neither is the steak—both are hallucinations within the matrix. Yet the glistening red stab we see in closeup patently isn't the work of hundreds of effects artists, but a fresh cut straight from the butcher. Such moments turn illusion against itself to make us question not just the CGI revolution, but the nature of cinematic deception.

Both *The Matrix* and *Dark City*, are old-fashioned parables of political resistance: they remind us that seductive images can be used to repress us and that, while we should enjoy those images to the full, we may as well understand how they're made. That's why *The Phantom Menace* seems so dull and distant. It's too concerned with denying its own construction, with appearing seamless, which is why its castles seem built of air. But *The Matrix* and *Dark City*) want us to know precisely what sort of air they use. The most daring moment in *The Matrix* comes when Neo sees what the world is made of: a corridor decomposes and turns into glowing green strings of digits, as if seen on a VDU. All at once you realise that these, rather than the opening weekend figures, are the numbers that the new Hollywood is really built on.

NEW YORK, 5/24/99, p. 67, Peter Rainer

George Lucas has been quoted as saying that "actors are still the best way to portray people," but, in watching his *Star Wars: Episode I—The Phantom Menace*, you get the feeling he wishes it wasn't so—that he could dispense with actors altogether. Ninety-five percent of this film was altered on computer; only about 200 shots were not created digitally. It's a computer-generated-imagery blowout, and the actors in it are upstaged to a fare-thee-well. Being human has never seemed more humdrum. And maybe this was Lucas's intention: By making his CGI creatures—his 'droids and globs and thingamajigs—so much more captivating than his people, he's striking a blow for the primacy of special effects over human effects. At this point in his career, he may not know, or care about, the difference.

Lucas's vaunted fascination with the mythic elements of storytelling—his Joseph Campbell side—is an extension of this syndrome. It's his way of turning the commonplaces of life into something larger: into something superhuman or, more exactly, inhuman. In Lucas's hands, myth becomes a species of special effects, too. It has also, by this time, played itself out.

The mythological structure in the original *Star Wars* trilogy was keyed to the fall and redemption of Darth Vader. *The Phantom Menace,* the first of a projected prequel trilogy, introduces the 9-year-old Anakin Skywalker (Jake Lloyd), who will grow up to be Vader. We're supposed to want to hang in for the next two installments of the prequel (ETA 2002 and 2005), which will dramatize Anakin's passage to the Dark Side. But will anybody except die-hard *Star Warriors* really care? Based on what we see here, it doesn't seem like such an ineffable mystery that this kid will end up a wheezing, intergalactic power-mongering control freak. A slave boy who already fashions himself a Jedi knight, Anakin is a precocious brat—the kind of kid who, in our own galaxy, might commandeer a playground and run everybody else off the jungle gym. If the psychological richness of the *Star Wars* movies is grounded in Darth Vader's movement in and out of the light, then it may be high time to create a new myth—i.e., a new franchise.

The other characters in *Phantom Menace* don't fare much better. Liam Neeson plays Qui-Gon Jinn, the Jedi Master who first spots Anakin's techno-wizardry and suspects him of being the Chosen One. Qui-Gon is always sensing a disturbance in The Force. You desperately wish this guy would lighten up; he solemnizes everything, even what appear to be his jokes. If this movie is indeed intended for bright 13-year-old boys—which Lucas, when he's not invoking Joseph Campbell, seems to imply—then why isn't Qui-Gon funkier? Any kid will tell you that you learn more from the cutups than from the drones. That's why Yoda, who shows up here as well, is the true sage of the series. Emanating from his green elfin grin, all that Zen mumbo jumbo about The Force has the bounce of a good limerick.

Lucas doesn't seem to understand the essence of his stars, various appeals; he turns them all into icons, which is not my idea of a fun time. Ewan McGregor is the young Obi-Wan Kenobi, apprentice to Qui-Gon, and he does a passable rendition of Alec Guinness's pinched, ruminative speech rhythms. But he doesn't have much to do in this installment except stride about with his light saber. He too is overly intense; he's got Qui-Gon-itis. Natalie Portman, as Queen Amidala of the endangered planet Naboo, is queenly, that's for sure—she always seems to be issuing curt pronouncements, and she's required to behave as spunk-free as possible. Other actors you might expect to be more present in the movie—like Samuel L. Jackson, playing a Jedi council member—are given glorified walk-ons. What a wingding it might have been to have Jackson strut his stuff as a Jedi badass.

The strongest impression in the cast comes from chief Dark Side bad guy Darth Maul (Ray Park), who has a furious saber duel with Qui-Gon that's choreographed like an intergalactic Tae-Bo workout. It's a sinister piece of calisthenics. (For a good laugh, you might reference *Time*'s April 26 cover story on the movie, featuring a conversation between Bill Moyers and Lucas on "the true theology" of *Star Wars;* both guys invoke heavy dudes like Dante and Milton to explain Maul's scare appeal, while, in another part of the magazine, Iain McCaig, who conceptualized him, cites Bozo the Clown as a chief inspiration.)

As impressive as many of the CGI effects are in *Phantom Menace,* few of them stay with you; they have the disposability of cartoons but without the carefree flippancy that often comes from the best animation. Even when Lucas hits on a resonant image, such as the underwater city of Naboo, which glows like an aggregation of Art Nouveau chandeliers, he doesn't stay with it for long; he's on to the next effect. Not surprisingly, the film's best set piece is also its most sustained: a pod race featuring Anakin whizzing his jerry-built speedster up and around the canyons of Tatooine in homage to the chariot race from *Ben-Hur.*

Now that computer-generated effects have become so technically sophisticated, there's a tendency to overhype their *aesthetic* value. Lucas creates in *Phantom Menace* the kind of elaborate epic-movie landscapes that live-action moviemakers for the most part can no longer afford. But ponderous is still ponderous, whether it's for real or computer-generated. What hasn't yet been solved by Lucas is how to make all this cyber stuff resonate emotionally. Creating a so-called modern legend, droning on about The Force and all the rest of it, is no substitute for the full engagement of our senses. And isn't that what a film like *Phantom Menace* should provide? The second *Star Wars* film, *The Empire Strikes Back,* directed by Irvin Kershner, was the sole exception to this: Its lush, doomful compositions and its primal conflict between Luke and Darth Vader had a real pop majesty. In our movies, we don't just want the beauty of technological effects; we want the beauty of emotion that can come out of those effects. Certainly *The Phantom Menace* is a pop cultural event, but it's not a movie event that really matters for me. It's the work of a visionary all right—a visionary capitalist. It doesn't take much to start a religion these days.

NEW YORK POST, 5/18/99, p. 56, Thelma Adams

"I have a bad feeling about this," Ewan McGregor's Obi-Wan Kenobi announces at the start of "Star Wars: Episode I—The Phantom Menace."

With its snoozy first hour and clunky plot, the pre-quel begs the question: If it had been the first, would there have been any more "Star Wars" movies?

Probably not, but I'm no devotee. For me, "Star Wars" is "Star Trek" without the challenging adult content. The '70s sci-fi adventure was a boy's fantasy movie junkyard, with spare parts rifled from "Flash Gordon," WWII aerial combat footage and "Triumph of the Will."

What's missing from George Lucas' heralded return to the screen is ... sex. Gone is Harrison Ford's easy banter, the screwball machismo that sparked with Carrie Fisher's thorny feminist princess.

In "Menace," Lucas squanders sexy McGregor, the "Emma" star who has dropped trousers in more films than some porn stars. Maybe he'll get more action in the pre-quel sequel.

As for Liam Neeson's Jedi master Qui-Gon Jinn, he's wound tighter than his hair extensions. The aging rebel has more chemistry with nine-year-old Anakin Skywalker (Jake Lloyd), the future Darth Vader, than with Natalie Portman's peacenik queen.

Among the non-humans, alien sidekick Jar Jar Binks is as annoying as Barney, but he'll appeal to "Star Wars" primary audience: kids. Pumpkin-headed villain Darth Maul makes less of an impression than a "Hellraiser" extra.

And yet, the pre-quel's overblown pleasures nearly counter the shortcomings. The adrenalized pod race recalls Lucas "American Graffiti" in outer space; an underwater sequence highlighted by the line "there's always a bigger fish" wonderfully weds live action and computer artistry. The intergalactic senate set where the evil corporate Federation out-maneuvers the bureaucratic Republic is eye candy.

"Menace"s' greatest weakness is that outcast-turned-big-fishLucas has lost touch with the times. The original trilogy offered mainstream audiences alienated from the bible an updated creation myth.   He offered New-Age theology cribbed from Joseph Campbell and Carlos Casteneda through a Saturday-matinee delivery vehicle.

The resulting Yodaism created an accessible battlefield for good and evil in an era when morality had become relative. Twenty years and countless millions later, Lucas's evil business versus zen humanism message seems a tad hypocritical.

NEW YORK POST, 5/18/99, p. 57, Jonathan Foreman

In an era when audiences all but expect filmmakers to work miracles of illusion, "The Phantom Menace" is an amazing technical achievement. So it is all the more unfortunate that gazing in wonder at the products of George Lucas' imagination and technical skill is the greatest pleasure provided by this fourth, least story-driven movie in the "Star Wars" series.

The first bad sign is in the opening crawl, which explains the political situation. In the first movie, it was simple stuff about rebels fighting an evil empire. In the fourth, the problem is a dull-sounding dispute about tax and trade between the planet Naboo and something called the Trade Federation.

It has led to a blockade of the planet by the Federation's ships, and two Jedi Knights, Qui-Gon Jinn (Liam Neeson) and Obi-Wan Kenobi (Ewan McGregor) have been sent by the Chancellor of the Republic to sort out the situation.

But as they arrive on the Federation leaders' ship, the traders are embarking on an invasion of Naboo. The two knights find their way to the planet's surface as the forces of young Queen Amidala (Natalie Portman) are overwhelmed by legions of war droids. They rescue her from her alien captors and flee on a ship to the semi-outlaw desert planet Tatooine. There they encounter slave boy Anakin Skywalker (Jake Lloyd) and his mother, played by Danish actress Pernilla August.

It soon becomes clear that The Force is unusually strong with the boy and Qui-Gon resolves to get him off the planet and train him as a knight. Meanwhile, evil in the tiger-faced form of Darth Maul and his shadowy master are looking for the Queen.

There's a stirring race between what look like jet-propelled go carts, and an exciting climactic sword fight. But you know exactly how both will end, because there isn't a surprise to be found anywhere in the movie.

That is not just because it's a prequel and you know that Anakin will have to get out of slavery on Tatooine so that he can eventually become Darth Vader, or that you know that Obi-Wan Kenobi must survive all three of the new movies. It's that everything is signalled and formulaic.

Besides Neeson, who invests his Samurai character with just the right note of rueful wisdom, the brighter spots are: Watto the blue-faced, unshaven, winged alien trader; Ian McDiarmid as the sinister Senator Palpatine; and Portman, who is fine when she gets to talk in her own accent and to go without Kabuki-style makeup intended to be reminiscent of Elizabeth I. McGregor seems preoccupied by the effort to reproduce Alec Guinness' accent.

To add insult to injury, Lucas' directorial attention is clearly not focused on the cast, most of whom seem slightly adrift. It is spent instead on the effects.

And the weird, New-Agey anti-democratic politics have become more pronounced. For all the talk of republics and senates, more than ever the good guys in the "Star Wars" universe are queens, princesses, viceroys and knights: all folks who have inherited power or position.

NEWSWEEK, 5/17/99, p. 58, David Ansen

Twenty-two years ago "Star Wars" came out of nowhere, and changed the world. "Star Wars: Episode I, The Phantom Menace" comes out amid a cacophony of media hype, carrying on its shoulders the wildest hopes of several generations of worshipful moviegoers. It's been 16 years since "Return of the Jedi," the last installment of George Lucas's trilogy. In a country with a notoriously short attention span, it's nothing less than miraculous that the passage of time made no dent in our appetite for this intergalactic adventure. It's not hype to say that "Phantom Menace" is the most eagerly awaited movie ever made. (Pilgrims started camping out in front of theaters a month before its May 19 opening.) You'll be hard pressed to find anyone who doubts for a moment that it will recoup its $115 million budget.

I will beat around the bush no longer. The movie is a disappointment. A big one. Will you take my word for it? Of course not. This massively marketed movie is virtually critic-proof. Everyone feels he must find out for himself.

The oddest thing about "Episode I" which takes us back to the childhood of Anakin Skywalker, who as we know will later become Darth Vader, father of Luke Skywalker—is that it's a tale that didn't need to be told. Or that should have been told in 20 minutes, so that we could get on to the good stuff. What we want to know is how Anakin Skywalker, Jedi knight, turned to the Dark Side. You won't find that out in "The Phantom Menace." Lucas presents us with a cute, towheaded 9-year-old (Jake Lloyd), a slave on the outlaw planet Tatooine (everyone's favorite sci-fi town), who is discovered by the Jedi warriors Qui-Gon Jinn (Liam Neeson) and his apprentice Obi-Wan Kenobi (Ewan McGregor). The two Jedi are trying, and failing, to prevent a war between the powerful Trade Federation and the peaceful planet of Naboo, and they have stopped off on Tatooine to find a hyperdrive generator for their battle-damaged spacecraft. The war seems to be about commerce, but Qui-Gon Jinn intuits a darker purpose behind it (just what that is also awaits in "Episode II"). Traveling with our Jedi heroes is Naboo's young Queen Amidala (Natalie Portman), who apparently is destined to marry Anakin (also in the next movie).

This boy, the Jedi instantly see, is special. It's even heavily hinted that he's been immaculately conceived. Knowing what we know about his future, we want to see hints in this sweet child of his future monstrosity. Astonishingly, Lucas plants no seeds of evil. Instead, we are just told (by our old friend Yoda, in his pre-hermit days) that he senses a danger in him. What a rudimentary failure of storytelling. What was Lucas thinking when he turned Anakin into a banal youngster who, upon hearing he's going to leave home to train as a Jedi, proclaims, "Can I go, Mom? Yipee!" There is nothing strange, special or particularly interesting about the future Darth Vader here, and the casting of the conventionally adorable Lloyd, who looks like he should he hawking cereal on TV commercials, is no help. Neither is his good old-fashioned bad acting.

There's no shortage of action in "Phantom Menace"—lightsaber fights, attacking armies, exploding spacecraft—but there's a curious lack of urgency. Our emotions are rarely engaged. It's been 22 years since Lucas directed a movie, and he's gotten rusty. His rhythm is off. Many of the scenes feel shapeless and flat—they're not ended, but abandoned. He doesn't seem to care about building a character. Ewan McGregor, one of the most vital and versatile young actors around, is completely wasted: Obi-Wan is given nothing interesting to do or say. Liam Neeson brings a grave, slightly weary dignity to Qui-Gon, but he's a rather somber character to carry what is meant to be a slam-bang adventure fantasy. There is no equivalent here to the irreverent, wise-cracking Han Solo, and his light touch is missed. For comic relief, we get the computer-generated Jar Jar Binks, a goofy, floppy-eared, vest-wearing toy serpent with a clumsy two-legged lope and an incomprehensible Caribbean accent. (He's a kind of extraterrestrial Stepin Fetchit.) Funny not he is, as Yoda would say. A more successful debut is made by the devilish Darth Maul, a horned, painted Sith lord who works for shrouded Evil Genius Darth Sidious. There's fresh menace in his mien.

The genuine magic in "Episode I" is all in its design. Conceptual artist Doug Chiang and production designer Gavin Bocquet give us breathtaking vistas, fabulous imaginary cities that range from the Florentine splendor of Queen Amidala's domain to the teeming metropolis of Coruscan. The vaultlike Galactic Senate, whose box seats float through the air, is a triumph of baroque futurism. The sunset-drenched, open-air Jedi council chambers (shades of "Blade Runner") glow like a remembered childhood picture book. (The art nouveau, glass-bubble undersea city, however, looks like a floating Lamps Plus showroom to me). The massive, tree-crunching tanks of the droid armies have a brutal beauty; there's visual wit in the insectlike robot soldiers who do the Trade Federation's dirty work. Indeed, there's often so much to take in you wish Lucas would hold his shots longer, and let us feast on the details.

This is the impressive fruit of what Lucas calls his "digital backlot." "Phantom Menace" uses more computer-generated shots than any movie in history (95 percent of the frames employ some digital work). The technical significance can't be denied—Lucas is blurring the line between live action and animation. When it works—in the spectacular pod-racing sequence on Tatooine, in which Anakin and his repulsive rival Sebulba fly like the wind through jagged desert canyons—the movie re-creates the buoyant adrenaline rush the original "Star Wars" so light-heartedly and consistently generated.

Lucas even uses digital techniques to tinker with the performances—seamlessly merging, for example, an actor's frown in take three upon his face in take six. This may be the first step toward a cinematic future in which virtual actors replace flesh-and-blood ones—and unfortunately it sometimes seems as if he's drained the flesh and blood from his own cast. The usually vibrant Portman is decked out in wonderful Kabuki-like makeup and dressed in beautifully bejeweled costumes, but most of the time she looks lost in space, stranded without a character to play. All the state-of-the-art technology in the world is no help to an actor saddled with Lucas's tinny dialogue. The original had its share of cheesy, B-movie performances: it was part of its retro "Buck Rogers" charm. But in these more extravagant settings, the lapses seem puzzling.

The arc of Anakin's story—a boy leaving home to become a Jedi and a hero, saving the day in battle—recapitulates Luke's story in "Star Wars." You can understand why Lucas would want to carbon-copy his golden oldies—why tamper with the most successful formula in movie history? But you can't go home again. Lucas's sensibility, which was never particularly sophisticated to begin with, hasn't evolved in two decades. "The Phantom Menace" is more of the same, without the innocence and without the juice. And in the year of "The Matrix," which offers a new style of special effects and a dystopian fantasy that hits closer to home, Lucas's childlike vision is beginning to look merely childish.

The interesting question is whether any of this will matter. Is the hunger for "Star Wars" so insatiable that the audience won't notice that this epochal event is actually a little ... dull? If "The Phantom Menace" surpasses "Titanic" as the most successful movie of all time, it may stand as the ultimate example of cultural auto-intoxication.

SIGHT AND SOUND, 7/99, p. 54, Andrew O'Hehir

The Galactic Republic is in jeopardy. Two Jedi knights, Qui-Gon Jinn and his apprentice Obi-Wan Kenobi, are sent to the distant planet of Naboo to negotiate a dispute between the planet's leaders and the nefarious heads of the Trade Federation. Qui-Gon and Obi-Wan are ambushed and barely survive; the Federation's blockade is a cover for an invasion of Naboo, sponsored by a shadowy Sith master, or dark Jedi. Landing on the planet, Qui-Gon and Obi-Wan befriend Jar Jar Binks, a member of the Gunga species. The invasion is successful, but Qui-Gon and Obi-Wan help Naboo's Queen Amidala escape. While escaping, the droid R_2-D_2 saves their ship from destruction, but needing repairs they stop on the trade planet of Tatooine. Meanwhile the Sith lord sends his apprentice Darth Maul after Amidaca.

On Tatooine, Qui-Gon meets a slave boy named Anakin Skywalker whom he identifies immediately as a born Jedi. Qui-Gon wins the boy's freedom—and spare parts for the ship—by betting against Anakin's master on a pod race which Anakin wins over his archrival. As the group leaves Tatooine, Darth Maul appears and duels with Qui-Gon. On the Republic's central planet, Amidala learns the Galactic Senate will not help Naboo. The Jedi Council is disturbed to hear a new Sith is at large, but refuses to let Qui-Gon train Anakin as a Jedi Knight, despite Qui-Gon's contention that Anakin is "the chosen one who will bring balance to the Force." Yoda believes Anakin is potentially vulnerable to the Dark Side.

Amidala decides to go back to Naboo to mount an insurrection against the Federation. Qui-Gon, Obi-Wan, Jar Jar and Anakin go with her. On Naboo, she convinces the Gunga to mount an assault, drawing droid forces away from the city, while her band sneak into the palace to capture the Federations viceroy. Just as the Gunga are losing the battle, Anakin pilots a ship that destroys the Federation's command vessel. Darth Maul kills Qui-Gon in a light-sabre duel, but is then killed by Obi-Wan, who takes Anakin as his apprentice after Naboo is liberated.

Any film that begins with a seven-word title and then includes the words 'taxation' and 'debate', in its first five seconds is either a deadly historical epic about the American Revolution or is taking its audience for granted. I'm tempted to suggest *Star Wars Episode I The Phantom Menace* fits both of these criteria, but George Lucas' allegories are so muddled it's impossible to make sense of them. Start with a distinctive New World lust for ancient traditions of aristocracy and order, toss in a misguided effort at multiculturalism and season with the Aryan myth of racial purity, an you've got a murky, talky prequel that emphasises all the series' weakest elements rather than its strongest ones.

In the last year or two, film-makers have finally reached the point of diminishing returns with computer-generated effects. It's now possible for films to spend vast sums on effects and still look laughably cheap (see, for instance, *The Mummy*). *The Phantom Menace* doesn't have that problem precisely, but almost nothing in it is based on photographing actual human beings in their environments. Every shot is such a complex technical achievement, so full of droids, aliens, spacecraft or gargantuan structures, that the movie itself takes on the hazy, ugly look of software. Even if this is deliberate, it doesn't work—the excessively electric-blue skies and green fields of the planet Naboo may be meant to remind us that we are not on earth, but what they really make us aware of is that what we're seeing isn't real.

Lucas has never been much of a visual stylist (at least, not since the days of *THX 1138, 1970*), but the characteristic cleanliness and contrast of his compositions—the brilliant, antiseptic white of the stormtroopers' uniforms, the lustrous blue-black of Darth Vader's helmet—have been abandoned here in favour of meaningless clutter. Certainly some of this film's grand set pieces are impressive. The great battle between the benevolent, amphibious Gunga and the Federation's droids, lightly echoing the Agincourt scene from Olivier's *Henry V* (1944), is marvellous to behold in a *Jurassic Park* way. The vast, ovoid interior of the Galactic Senate, with its regimented rows of desks curving away into infinity, is a splendid visual joke about the inefficacy of politics on a grand scale. But Lucas' imagery often seems rooted in nothing particular. Naboo's capital looks like the Babylon of D. W Griffith's *Intolerance* (1916) just because it *can* not because it should. Compared with the visual wit and imagination of such 90s science-fiction epics as *The Matrix* and *Starship Troopers*, *The Phantom Menace*'s aesthetic seems leaden and outdated.

In a laboured quest to recapture some of the first trilogy's (sorry, the *second* trilogy's) humour, Lucas and his enormous team of collaborators have created many cartoonish new species. The Gunga character Jar Jar Binks, with his rubbery platypus face, joke-Caribbean accent and jive walk right out of a 70s blaxploitation movie (with bell-bottom trousers to match) may amuse small children, but many adults will find *The Phantom Menace*'s quasi-racial typing patronising at best. When you consider that the Trade Federation leaders speak hackneyed Fu Manchu accents and the elephant-insect character who owns the slave Anakin Skywalker resembles a traditional caricature of the hook-nosed Jewish trader, the whole picture becomes much more disturbing. Of course I don't believe Lucas has any consciously racist agenda; what's involved here are multiple failures of common sense, good taste and imagination. You have to wonder whether he has spent so long in an alternative universe—both the one inside his own head and the one in Marin County—that he can't tell the difference between a sensitive depiction of cultural difference and offensive stereotypes.

But the biggest problem with *The Phantom Menace* is it that lacks narrative coherence. Lucas' intrusive use of diagonal and horizontal optical wipes only reinforces the sense that this movie is all stitches and no fabric. Logically, this wants to be the story of Obi-Wan Kenobi's early relationship with Anakin Skywalker (soon to become Darth Vader), but the two scarcely exchange a word until the movie's final scenes. Qui-Gon Jinn is arguably the central character, with Liam Neeson supplying the requisite combination of Zen gnosticism and kung-fu athleticism. But we learn nothing about his life, and his relationship with Obi-Wan adds up to little more than a lot of graceful tandem swordplay. As Obi-Wan Ewan McGregor is one of several outstanding actors given virtually nothing to do. Another is Pernilla August as Anakin's mother. We're told she and Anakin are passionately attached (and it's hinted that his love for his mother will be his downfall), but their scenes together are bland and generic and she surrenders him to Qui-Gon without a murmur.

Indeed, the film's extended sojourn on Tatooine mostly serves to set up Anakin's pod race, which may thrill younger viewers who haven't grown tired of Lucas' careening point-of-view shots, but doesn't really advance the story. Similar galactic-bazaar locations have been presented with equal vigour in earlier films, and we don't learn anything about Anakin's childhood we couldn't grasp quickly in a brief flashback. Beyond our general sympathy for David over Goliath, it's also not clear why we should care much about Naboo. As its Queen Amidala, Natalie Portman looks smashing in a series of Japanese-influenced getups and hairdos (did she escape with her hairdresser?) but neither she nor anyone else has anything like an adult emotional life. I understand the series' prepubescent asexuality is part of its appeal, but it might be nice to feel some sense of evolution or possibility. Lucas' narrative's mystical long arc the conflict between the Jedi and the Sith, the Force and the Dark Side—isn't foregrounded until Qui-Gon brings Anakin before the Jedi Council. The whole Jedi concept—a eugenic warrior caste guided by pure spirit and shaped by elite training—is so troubling it calls the entire political dimension of Lucas' universe into question. His desire to combine a faith in democracy with idealised systems of royalty, nobility and knighthood is almost comically American. But the *Star Wars* notion of democracy is no better than a fuzzy abstraction, a cover story for the mystical Manichaeanism of the Jedi, who by all appearances are a masculine cult of chastity and purity straight out of Wagner's *Parsifal*. Like the great Teutonic composer, Lucas has tapped into a tremendously powerful Jungian current of pantheistic myth. However one interprets it, this is where the heart and soul of the *Star Wars* saga lies, and the tiny tastes of it we get in *The Phantom Menace* make the rest of the movie seem like didactic dithering at the edges of some incomprehensible Asimovian empire.

Things certainly pick up in the final half-hour or so, with the spectacular Gunga battle sequence and a three-way light-sabre duel that ranks among the series' best combat scenes. Anakin's half-accidental destruction of the Federation ship self-consciously echoes his son's later/earlier destruction of the Death Star, but this is a mistake—*The Phantom Menace* can only suffer by comparison with the feckless energy and enthusiasm of the original *Star Wars*. The whole saga has never felt more like a 12-year-old's efforts to emulate Tolkien; this instalment feels less like an opening chapter than a stammering, parenthetical preface.

TIME, 5/17/99, p. 80, Richard Corliss

To get in, you needed a ticket, more precious than a passport out of Kosovo, and a fluorescent handstamp with the 20th Century Fox logo. Security guards, as imposing as the Fruit of Islam, eyed you through four separate checkpoints. Inside the theater, an official requested that audience members turn in anyone who might be camcording the event. George Lucas' *Star Wars* films may celebrate the spirit of communal rebellion, but the first critics' screening of *Episode 1: The Phantom Menace* in New York City last week had a sulfurous scent of the Empire about it.

Precautions may be indulged for the most avidly awaited, assiduously hyped film since *Gone With the Wind*. But they may also boomerang, by setting up expectations that few films could satisfy. That too was evident at the screening. Robust cheers greeted the first words of the sacred text ("A long time ago ...") and the blast of John Williams' brass as the title *Star Wars* appeared. Later there was mild applause at Yoda's arrival. By then the impulse to ecstasy had been diluted into rote nostalgia. For whatever reason, the audience was quieter at the end than at the beginning.

All right. We know that critics aren't human. And those rabid fans who sneaked into screenings last week, then peppered the Internet with their indifference, are not Kevin and Katelyn Moviegoer. But the early murmur of unrest dented *The Phantom Menace*'s doctrine of infallibility. Recall that last year's highly hyped, sure-hit fantasy adventure—*Godzilla*—was outgrossed at the North American box office by such modestly budgeted frippery as *There's Something About Mary, The Waterboy* and *Rush Hour*.

Somewhere beyond the critics' dispassion and the cultists' disappointment lies the likely response of the multiplex masses when the film opens May 19. As one woman said upon leaving the screening, "What do you want for $9?" What you get in *The Phantom Menace* is a panoramic entertainment with several terrific set pieces of action, stalwart acting from the Brits (and some very raw work by the kids), a precise, luscious visual design, a multilevel climactic battle and a funeral pyre that echo *Return of the Jedi*, and a triumphal coda from the first *Star Wars* film (1977). All that, and a lot of talk.

The plot is familiar to anyone with access to a computer or magazine. Jedi Master Qui-Gon Jinn (Liam Neeson) and his apprentice Obi-Wan Kenobi (Ewan McGregor), hoping to settle a dispute between the flabby Republic and an insurgent Trade Federation, find Queen Amidala (Natalie Portman) on the planet Naboo. Diverted to Tatooine, they meet the boy Anakin Skywalker (Jake Lloyd), who has a mysterious force—perhaps the Force. They amass for a fierce face-off against battle droids and the malefic Darth Maul (Ray Park).

The plot is more complicated than this—and much chattier. Even the opening is talky. "Turmoil has engulfed the Galactic Republic," the now familiar trapezoidal text-crawl tells us. "The taxation of trade routes to outlying star systems is in dispute." Immediately one is perplexed. A summary made sense in the earlier films; they were episodes IV, V and VI in the grand fable, and as continuations of an initially untold saga, they required some elucidation. But what's the need for back-story text in a tale that is just beginning? Can it be that Lucas was unable to dramatize these events, so he put them in the crawl? That would explain the gobs of dry exposition, devoted to blustering, filibustering debates on taxation and elections. It's all very edifying. Like ... school.

This is the work of Lucas the compulsive chronicler of his own imaginary galaxy. But there are other Lucases. One is the grownup kid who loves wise heroes and fast cars. That Lucas created a terse, looming Jedi knight in the person of Qui-Gon, and orchestrated a spectacular, turbo-thrust drag race through sculpted desert rock that consumes 12 minutes and most of the audience's adrenaline supply.

There is also the Lucas who wants to dazzle filmgoers with his luxurious bestiary. The Gungan klutz Jar Jar Binks, who talks (sometimes unintelligibly) like a Muppet Peter Lorre and walks as if he had Slinkys for legs, is more annoying than endearing. But the junk dealer Watto is a little masterpiece of design: cinnamon stubble on his corrugated face, chipped rocks for teeth, the raspy voice of Brando's Godfather speaking Turkish, hummingbird wings that give him the aspect of a potbellied helicopter. He, Jar Jar and the other computer-generated critters are seamlessly integrated into live action—a superb technological achievement for Lucas' team.

One suspects that Lucas was more interested in the aliens than the humans, and in the art direction than the direction of actors. The vistas of the imperial city Coruscant and the Gungan sea kingdom have a suave rapture; but some of the dialogue scenes are way too starchy, as if the actors had been left to their own resources while George minded the computerized menagerie. (The line readings of Portman and Lloyd are often flat, or flat-out wrong.) Neeson gives Qui-Gon a flinty dignity; Pernilla August, her weathered face streaked with love and foreboding, brings heft to the small role of Anakin's mother; and Ian McDiarmid is all oily ingratiation as Senator Palpatine. Ah, Palpatine: his name could be a hill of Rome, or a palpitating volcano—one that we know will explode in later episodes as he devolves into the dark Emperor.

We know so much in this first chapter—and not because of the prerelease hype. We know that plucky Anakin will grow up to be Darth Vader, so the crepe of Fate hangs over his ascendancy. We are meant to root for the boy when he finds himself in a plane cockpit during the climactic battle (he could be a kid sneaking a drive in his dad's Lamborghini yet we know that the budding hero will later be a supervillain, as if Aladdin were to grow up to be Jafar.

We know too—anyway, some of us do—that the original *Star Wars* was at times a stilted enterprise, and that as secret alliances and bloodlines were revealed, the series matured, grew into emotional resonance. For now, *The Phantom Menace* is a phantom movie, the merest hint of a terrific saga that the final-two episodes of the new trilogy may reveal. At least, that's what we, and Hollywood, want to believe. Hype, after all, is just moviespeak for hope.

VILLAGE VOICE, 5/25/99, p. 125, J. Hoberman

There's a rough justice in the way the 24-hour news cycle devours its own. Bill Clinton was the first American president to enjoy a preinaugural "honeymoon"—the day he took office his poll numbers were already falling. If spouse Hillary's Senate campaign has faded from overexposure even before it could be declared, the same is true for George Lucas's *Star Wars* prequel.

Star Wars: Episode I—The Phantom Menace may be the first movie to peak before its opening. Last year's *Godzilla* was dead on arrival, but *The Phantom Menace*—which (finally!) has its premiere today has enjoyed a six-month run in the media. Hence, the movie requires scarcely more than six minutes to wear thin. There is nothing in this noisy, overdesigned bore to equal the excitement generated by the mere idea of the trailer. Indeed, days before *The Phantom Menace*'s high-security press junket, fans who penetrated a top-secret distributor's screening were venting their disappointment over the Net. By junket time, the backlash was evident. Several local and national periodicals broke the cardinal rule of studio PR and jumped the opening by 10 days to pan the most anticipated movie in living memory.

This, of course, scarcely matters. However anticlimactic, *The Phantom Menace* is not only critic-proof but audience-resistant as well. The movie has already made its money back 10 times over through Pepsi's just launched merchandising blitz alone, and thanks to Lucas's pressure on theatrical exhibitors to guarantee lengthy exclusive runs (and the decision by rival distributors to cede him the rest of the spring), it would take the consumer equivalent of the Russian Revolution to keep *The Phantom Menace* from ruling the box office for weeks.

What else is new? In essence, *The Phantom Menace* remakes *Star Wars* with more elaborate effects, greater childishness, and weaker characters. The evil Darth Vader is here an innocent nine-year-old towhead named Anakin Skywalker (Jake Lloyd), while the absence of a Han Solo antihero further diminishes the humanity quotient. From the moment a pair of Jedi knights (Liam Neeson and Ewan McGregor) do battle with a treacherous gaggle of Trade Federation fish faces, the movie is steeped in déjà vu. If *Star Wars* was, as *Time* magazine once raved, a "subliminal history of movies," *The Phantom Menace* is a dreary recap of that synopsis. Thus cute li'l R2-D2 saves another spaceship, Jabba the Hutt presides over a drag race through a digital Monument Valley, and Lucas rewards the faithful with the revelation that the future Darth Vader, who we already know fathered Luke Skywalker, was also a precocious mechanical genius who invented the dithering C-3PO.

Yoda puts in a cameo, but the film's designated alien is Jar Jar Binks, a rabbit-eared ambulatory lizard whose pidgin English degenerates from pseudo-Caribbean patois to Teletubby gurgle. (Although Jar Jar can be construed as grotesquely Third World and the fish faces talk like Fu Manchu, the most blatant ethnic stereotype is the hook-nosed merchant insect who owns young Anakin.) Jar Jar and his fellow Gungans suck the oxygen out of every scene; their human costars seem understandably asphyxiated. In addition to dogged Neeson (whose presence gives Oskar Schindler a retroactive Jedi glow) and the embarrassed, smirky McGregor, the unhappy-looking cast includes the seemingly dubbed Natalie Portman as the elected queen of Naboo, a walking piece of Japanaiserie; a ridiculously earnest Samuel L. Jackson as an über-Jedi; and Terence Stamp as the galactical pol Lucas has designated the Clinton character. The big tease is the close-up of Portman gazing fondly down at Jake Lloyd. All true Star Woids know that this little kid will father her children, doubtless offscreen—if not between episodes.

Climaxing instead with four simultaneous battles, *The Phantom Menace* is a war movie that's all the creepier for making the combat virtually cost-free. The two human Jedis decimate, dismember, and destroy several dozen digital droid armies—but these pesky critters feel no pain. Similarly, little Ani learns the magic of strategic bombing (or is it a video game?), blasting away at largely unseen as well as nonhuman targets. The extended carnage has none of the horror that characterized the digitally produced human-insect struggle of *Starship Troopers*. The most exciting action is also the most conventional—the Jedis' leaping light-saber fight with a horned, orange-eyed, camouflage-faced bogeyman could have been choreographed for Errol Flynn.

The Phantom Menace may strike even some kids as excessively cartoon-like, but then, as a director, Lucas remains the greatest exponent of the theme park aesthetic. As each character in *The Phantom Menace* has been designed with a molded plastic collectible in mind, almost every sequence suggests either Mr. Toad's Wild Ride or a Fantasyland it would be a pleasure not to visit. The production design is astonishingly crass. If Naboo City is a gussied-up Victorian vision of ancient Rome, the Gungan underwater civilization seems modeled on a Bowery lighting-fixture emporium. Most hideous is the galactic capital—a nauseatingly dense combination of Manhattan and L.A. in which every interior is furnished like a Reno carpet joint and every window reveals a sky in whirlybird gridlock.

Nor is the script much better. Most of the dialogue sounds like silent movie intertitles ("The death toll is catastrophic—we must bow to their wishes"). The rest, mainly intoned by Neeson, seems to have been found in a fortune cookie. "Our meeting was not a coincidence—nothing happens by accident," he explains to his little protégé.

Representative of the Force, Neeson is the resident sage: "Fear leads to anger, anger leads to hate, hate leads to suffering"—which presumably promotes fear.

Religion may be a presence, but Lucas's magic kingdom is strikingly sterile. His creatures dwell in a perpetual present, devoid of sexual activity (Anakin, it is strongly hinted, was the product of an immaculate conception), historical consciousness, or even the most debased form of cultural expression (like advertising). Any of these would constitute a dangerous distraction.

The *Phantom Menace* is simply a billboard for itself. Anyone who sees it will be experiencing it for the second time. The hype was not about the movie, the hype *was* the movie.

Also reviewed in:
CHICAGO TRIBUNE, 6/3/99, Tempo/p. 6, John Petrakis
NATION, 6/7/99, p. 34, Stuart Klawans
NEW REPUBLIC, 6/14/99, p. 30, Stanley Kauffmann
NEW YORK TIMES, 5/19/99, p. E1, Janet Maslin
NEW YORKER, 5/24/99, p. 80, Anthony Lane
VARIETY, 5/17-23/99, p. 53, Todd McCarthy
WASHINGTON POST, 5/13/99, p. C1, Rita Kempley
WASHINGTON POST, 5/21/99, Weekend/p. 16, Desson Howe

STICKY FINGERS OF TIME, THE

A Strand Releasing release of a Crystal Pictures production. *Executive Producer:* Jean-Christophe Castelli, Louis Robles, Ruth Robles, and Steve Menkin. *Producer:* Isen Robbins and Susan Stover. *Director:* Hilary Brougher. *Screenplay:* Hilary Brougher. *Director of Photography:* Ethan Mass. *Editor:* Hilary Brougher and Sabine Hoffman. *Music:* Mike Navazio and Tracy McKnight. *Production Designer:* Teresa Mastropierro. *Costumes:* Wendy Chuck. *Running time:* 81 minutes. *MPAA Rating:* Not Rated.

CAST: Terumi Matthews (Tucker); Nicole Zaray (Drew); Belinda Becker (Ofelia); James Urbaniak (Isaac); Leo Marks (Dex); Samantha Buck (Gorge); Thomas Pasley (J.L.); Julie Anderson (Dental Assistant of Death).

LOS ANGELES TIMES, 10/7/99, Calendar/p. 16, Kevin Thomas

Writer-director Hilary Brougher certainly deserves an "A" for ambition for her no-budget yet elegant supernatural thriller "The Sticky Fingers of Time." Successful crime fiction writer Tucker Harding (Terumi Matthews) steps outside her East Village flat one day in 1947 and is whooshed 40 years into the future, where she's thrust into a sinister adventure. Brougher is adept at defining past and present but mars her solid directing skill with a needlessly complicated premise and an overly arch tone that, intentionally or otherwise, suggests a certain smug self-satisfaction that's a real turnoff. Much more effective is the subtle way in which Brougher suggests a lesbian subtext.

NEW YORK POST, 3/26/99, p. 62, Jonathan Foreman

"The Sticky Fingers of Time," a travel story with lesbian-romantic overtones, would make a fine "Twilight Zone" episode if someone stripped it of the East Village/indie self-indulgence that slows it to a snail's pace—and then purged it of its execrable lines delivered with absurd, often unintentionally comic portentousness.

Writer-director Brougher has come up with a genuinely clever plot about a 1950s sci-fi writer (Terumi Matthews) who finds herself in 1997 in the company of "time freaks" slipping back and forth in "non-linear" time. (It's all something to do with the H-bomb, though Brougher confuses atomic fusion with fission) They include her boyfriend, Isaac (James Urbaniak), another depressed but cute writer (Nicole Zaray) and some evil folk from the future led by a sexy black scientist (Belinder Becker) who wants to kill her.

If you can get through the longeurs of the self-consciously mysterious first half, "The Sticky Fingers of Time" begins to gather pace—and to make more sense. But key early encounters between the main characters are flat and unbelievable, and one scene after another collapses under the weight of laconic dialogue. Stretches of celluloid are wasted on empty, useless shots of people lighting cigarettes, walking around, etc.

VILLAGE VOICE, 3/30/99, p. 130, Amy Taubin

In another sphere of reality entirely [the reference is to *EDtv*] is Hilary Brougher's *The Sticky Fingers of Time*, East Village time-warp mystery for female sci-fi addicts who've never before had a film they fully could call their own. (The *Alien* series isn't exclusively for girls.) Brougher's protagonists are a '50s sci-fi writer and her slightly younger, slightly more scattered, '90s counterpart, who keep bouncing into each other's lives thanks to some mix-up in the DNA coding of their souls. The hydrogen bomb experiments of the '50s may or may not be a causal factor.

Brougher's conceit is that time has five fingers. In addition to past, present, and future, there is also "that which could have been and that which yet could be." These two realms, which literary theorists term the subjunctive, are where desire and the imagination function. And they're where these two women are drawn together by a maternal, erotic bond that triumphs over ordinary time and space.

The film is psychologically resonant despite the intermittently clunky performances. Given her tiny budget, Brougher achieves minor miracles in her recreation of New York circa 1953. The set and costume designs point up how time transforms fashion into fetish and back again; Ethan Mass's cinematography adds a subtle dreamlike edge. *The Sticky Fingers of Time* is one of the only Amerindies in recent years to match intellectual with formal ambitions. That it's fun to watch as well makes Brougher a filmmaker to be reckoned with.

Also reviewed in:
CHICAGO TRIBUNE, 10/15/99, Friday/p. J, Michael Wilmington
NEW YORK TIMES, 3/26/99, p. E28, Anita Gates
VARIETY, 10/13-19/97, p. 96, David Stratton

STIFF UPPER LIPS

A Cowboy Booking International release of a Cavalier Features/Impact Pictures production. *Executive Producer:* Nigel Savage. *Producer:* Jeremy Bolt and Gary Sinyor. *Director:* Gary Sinyor. *Screenplay:* Paul Simpkin, Gary Sinyor, Stephen Deitch, and Richard Sparks. *Director of Photography:* Simon Archer. *Editor:* Peter Hollywood. *Music:* David A. Hughes and John Murphy. *Sound:* Danny Hambrook. *Casting:* Emma Style and Louis Elman. *Production Designer:* Mike Grant. *Art Director:* Marcus Wookey, Francesco Chianese, and Aradhana Seth. *Costumes:* Stephanie Collie and Dolly Ahluwalia. *Make-up:* Jenny Sharpe. *Stunt Coordinator:* Roderick P. Woodruff. *Running time:* 85 minutes. *MPAA Rating:* Not Rated.

CAST: Peter Ustinov (Horace); Prunella Scales (Aunt Agnes Ivory); Georgina Cates (Emily Ivory); Samuel West (Edward Ivory); Sean Pertwee (George); Brian Glover (Eric); Frank Finlay (Hudson Junior); Robert Portal (Cedric Trilling); Richard Braine (Mr. Tweeb); David Ashton (Dr. Henry); Mac McDonald (American Husband); Kate Harper (American Wife); David Artus and Kevin Furlong (Hurdlers); Nicholas Selby and John Boswall (Dons); Jon Croft (Station Master); Charles Simon (Hudson Senior); Anna Livia Ryan (Rosie); Geoffrey Palmer (Voice of Eric's Butler); Rajendra Varman (Sitar Player); Miss Swati (Tea Server); Tigmanshu Dhulia (Stall Holder); Baron Baretto (Indian Boy); Sindhu Tolani (Indian Girl); Shri Vallabh Vyas (Defense Lawyer); John Winter (Prosecution Lawyer).

LOS ANGELES TIMES, 8/27/99, Calendar/p. 12, Gene Seymour

[The following review by Gene Seymour appeared in a slightly different form in **NEWSDAY, 8/27/99, Part II/p. B6.]**

Those austere, handsomely mounted Edwardian-era films with their green lawns, golden skies and repressed emotions—yes, I'm a little sick of them, too. Why has it taken so long for a movie like "Stiff Upper Lips" to get made? Was Mel Brooks that busy? Isn't there a corset that would fit Leslie Nielsen? And don't tell me that Emma Thompson had better things to do! She's enough of a satirist herself to know a fat, juicy target when she sees one, even if those costume dramas did make her an icon.

Oh, well. Overdue or not, the movie we got is about as good as one could expect from the genre—parody genre—which, despite its seemingly wild and scattershot trappings, has become almost as formulaic as the movies it parodies.

Director Gary Sinyor, who proved his mettle for socially observant visual humor in "Leon the Pig Farmer" (1992), top-loads "Stiff Upper Lips" with sight gags and class resentment. The movie isn't as elegant as "Howards End" nor as raucous as "The Naked Gun," and the line it walks between the two extremes is a wobbly one. Nevertheless, it's hard to dislike a movie whose heroine declares, "I want my sexual awakening and I want it now!" That would be Emily (Georgina Cates from "Illuminata"), a tightly corseted upper-class beauty, whose Aunt Agnes (Prunella Scales from "Fawlty Towers") is eager to marry her off to a properly schooled, well-heeled man of the same social background.

The best Agnes can do for the moment is Cedric Trilling (Robert Portal), a bookish and truculent sort who's friendly with Emily's nitwit brother Edward (Samuel West). Emily, naturally, hates Cedric, while the latter has "feelings" for Edward.

While these twits play croquet and say withering things to each other, the grimy lower classes butt heads and inhale grog at a tavern called Scum of the Earth. From their numbers emerges a lusty young rabbit skinner named George (Sean Pertwee), who is hired by Agnes as a servant to carry the family lawn as the brood tours Italy and India. Though Emily can barely imagine herself in the arms of a man several stations below her, her repression breaks down as it always does in these stories—with sweeping, neoclassical music, meaningless chases through the woods and letters exchanged from as far away as the next room.

To Sinyor's credit, you don't have to be familiar with the movies of James Ivory, Ismail Merchant and David Lean to laugh at this stuff. As with most of those directors' movies, however, "Stiff Upper Lips" panders to the erudition of its target audience even as it keeps its low-ball hum or humming at a mild frenzy. There's only so much a movie can do within those constrictions. But the cast's poker-faced daffiness makes up for a lot. It's especially nice to see veterans Peter Ustinov and Frank Finlay in the house; the former as eccentric great-uncle Horace who's got the hots for Agnes, the latter as the family butler who looks as sick of golden skies and green lawns as we are.

NEW YORK POST, 8/27/99, p. 56, Jonathan Foreman

"Stiff Upper Lips," a pathetic attempt to give British costume dramas the "Airplane" treatment, cries out for even a tiny bit of the wit the Zucker brothers and Leslie Nielsen brought to their spoofs.

Despite a talented cast, it plays like a satire of the Merchant-Ivory movies by someone who has never actually seen one—or by someone who was so transfixed by all their 19th-century elegance that he missed the plot.

Smug, crass and almost completely unfunny, "Stiff Upper Lips" also takes aim at "Chariots of Fire," "Upstairs Downstairs," "Brideshead Revisited" and their ilk—but every underpowered shot misses by a mile.

Upper-class twit Edward (Samuel West) takes Cedric (Robert Portal), his fellow Cambridge undergrad, home to "Ivory's End" (har har) to meet his sister Emily (Georgina Cates). Their Aunt Agnes (Prunella Scales) is desperate to marry Emily off, but Cedric is a prig who keeps quoting Homer and is more interested in Edward than his sister.

In any case, Emily has her eye on George (Sean Pertwee), a handsome, virile working-class fellow (and son of a rabbit-skinner) who saved her from drowning. Hoping that a holiday might bring Cedric and Emily together, Aunt Agnes takes them all off to Italy and India, accompanied by George, who has been blackmailed into becoming their servant.

The clueless illiterates who made "Stiff Upper Lips" don't seem to realize that the Merchant-Ivory movies and the E.M. Forster novels they adapt skewer the Edwardian class system and its accompanying sexual repression far more effectively than this crude effort ever could.

To make effective satire, you have to get what you are satirizing. But filmmakers Simpkin and Sinyor are so off the mark they think it's a clever, subversive jape to have the upper-class twits in their movie turn out to be gay.

While Merchant-Ivory films can be irritating and precious, the last thing they can be accused of doing is closeting the homosexuality in Forster's work. There's barely a Merchant-Ivory movie that doesn't have an all-male nude bathing scene.

It's ironic that Tony Blair's Cool Britannia should produce a crude, chip-on-the-shoulder dud like this when uncool Great Britain was the source of brilliant satire for three decades. Where have you gone, Monty Python?

SIGHT AND SOUND, 7/98, p. 54, Geoffrey Macnab

England, 1908. Edward arrives with his Oxbridge chum Cedric Trilling at the family home, the palatial Ivory Hall. The plan is to match Cedric with Edward's younger sister Emily. When Emily almost drowns, she is rescued by George, the son of a local farm worker. Although she won't at first admit it, she falls in love with him.

Emily's domineering aunt Agnes hires George as a servant to accompany the family on a grand tour, which takes them first to Italy and then to India. Further attempts are made to pair off Emily with Cedric, but after she is seduced and made pregnant by George, this plan is abandoned. George is put on trial for arson, and sentenced to 13 years in prison. The family returns to England.

Emily plans to marry Cedric rather than have a child out of wedlock. George, however, escapes prison and makes it to the church in time to stop the wedding. Emily admits that she loves him. Cedric and Edward admit that they love each other. Everybody lives happily ever after.

As Mel Brooks' long and lamentable list of misfires suggests, spoofs are much harder to pull off than they might appear. In taking heritage drama as his target in *Stiff Upper Lips,* writer/director Gary Sinyor *(Leon the Pig Farmer)* seems to be offering himself plenty of leeway. In the first five minutes alone, he aims pot shots at *Chariots of Fire* (the race around the college quad) and *Brideshead Revisited* (his two protagonists, Cedric and Edward, come across as even more effete counterparts to Sebastian and Charles in Evelyn Waugh's novel). As the film proceeds, he swipes in every conceivable direction, mocking E. M. Forster one moment and Merchant Ivory, *Upstairs, Downstairs* or Henry James the next. Brian Glover's sycophantic peasant might have stumbled out of a *Monty Python* sketch. His son George (engagingly played by Sean Pertwee) functions here much as did Mellors the gamekeeper in D. H. Lawrence's *Lady Chatterley's Lover.* Sinyor even lampoons *Death in Venice.* But the scattergun approach is only fitfully effective. As the gags repeat themselves ad nauseam and the ennui sets in, *Stiff Upper Lips* begins to resemble nothing so much as a very bad episode of Channel 4's spoof series *The Comic Strip Presents.*

There is nothing wrong with the trappings. The film is handsomely shot and boasts the same fetishistic eye for irrelevant detail as the costume dramas it purports to mock. Part of the problem is that Sinyor never seems at all sure of his tone. He oscillates wildly between bawdy, prurient humour (Hudson the butler pissing in the soup; Prunella Scales swooning at the sight of a phallic looking stump) and rarefied punning (Cedric spends much of the time talking in Latin).

The knockabout approach encourages rum, over-the-top performances, especially from the old-timers: Scales offers a fair impersonation of Edith Evans while Peter Ustinov hams it up shamelessly as a dyspeptic, lecherous old relic of the Raj. ("India has driven many people absolutely mad including myself," he says at one point.)

The sheer inanity of the humour quickly becomes wearing, but there are one or two choice moments along the way. Arch snobs Cedric and Edward seem unable to distinguish between a 'commoners' gait" and a 'communist goat', while *ingénue* Emily is only able to tie on her girdle tightly enough with the assistance of a runaway horse.

At least Gary Sinyor is upholding a tradition. After the failure of *Carry On Columbus,* the feeble, knockabout British comedy rooted in class tension and sexual innuendo looked like an endangered genre. With *Stiff Upper Lips,* Sinyor proves beyond all doubt that British film-makers, still have a knack for telling bad jokes at their own expense.

VILLAGE VOICE, 8/31/99 p. 128, Jessica Winters

For true masochists, there's the *Airplane!*-style comedy of mannerisms *Stiff Upper Lips*, which parodies the Merchant-Ivory adaptations of E. M. Forster books, gathering the story lines of *Howards End, A Room With a View*, and *A Passage to India* into one upper-crust English family's slapsticky trip around the world circa 1908. Trouble is, a satire can't work if your subject understands the joke better than you do—the movie has a hearty laugh about the novelist's precious characters and homoerotic subtexts, but Forster himself had a better one.

Also reviewed in:
NEW YORK TIMES, 8/27/99, p. E22, Stephen Holden
VARIETY, 11/24-30/97, p. 65, Derek Elley

STIGMATA

A Metro-Goldwyn-Mayer Pictures release of an FGM Entertainment production. *Producer:* Frank Mancuso, Jr. *Director:* Rupert Wainwright. *Screenplay:* Tom Lazarus and Rick Ramage. *Story:* Tom Lazarus. *Director of Photography:* Jeffrey L. Kimball. *Editor:* Michael R. Miller and Michael J. Duthie. *Music:* Billy Corgan and Elia Cmiral. *Music Editor:* Ken Karman, Mike Flicker, and Stephen Lotwis. *Sound:* David Kirschner and (music) Billy Corgan, Bjorn Thorsrud, and John Whynot. *Sound Editor:* Mark Mangini. *Casting:* Wendy Kurtzman. *Production Designer:* Waldemar Kalinowski. *Art Director:* Anthony Stabley. *Set Designer:* Clint Durst. *Set Decorator:* Florence Fellman. *Special Effects:* Al DiSarro. *Costumes:* Louise Frogley. *Make-up Effects:* Ve Neill. *Make-up:* Perri Sorel. *Make-up (Gabriel Byrne):* Michelle Bühler. *Make-up (Patricia Arquette):* Debbie Zoller. *Stunt Coordinator:* David Barrett. *Running time:* 102 minutes. *MPAA Rating:* R.

CAST: Patricia Arquette (Frankie Paige); Gabriel Byrne (Father Andrew Kiernan); Jonathan Pryce (Cardinal Daniel Houseman); Nia Long (Donna Chadway); Enrico Colantoni (Father Dario); Dick Latessa (Father Gianni Delmonico); Thomas Kopache (Father Durning); Ann Cusack (Doctor Reston); Portia de Rossi (Jennifer Kelliho); Patrick Muldoon (Steven); Rade Sherbedgia (Marion Petrocelli); Shaun Toub (Doctor); Tom Hodges (Nurse); Lydia Hazan (Attending Nurse); Duke Mooseekian (Doctor Eckworth); Valarie Trapp (Woman with a Baby); Kessia Kordelle (Cheryl); Frankie Thorn (Donna's Customer); Mariah Nunn (Sister Angela); Tom Fahn (MTA Man); Marilyn Pitzer (Homeless Woman); Jack Donner (Father Paulo Alameida); Richard Conti (Valet Priest); Mary Linda Phillips (Sister Agnes); Liz Cruz and Faith Christopher (Waitresses); Joe Ruffo and Federico Scutti (Guards); William Howell and Kristopher Davis (Aerialists); Devin Unruh (Flower Boy); Vera Yell (Jennifer's Costumer); Mary Marshall (Nun); Daniel Escalzo and Michael P. Dearth (Italian Businessmen); Mark Adair Rios (Deacon).

CHRISTIAN SCIENCE MONITOR, 10/1/99, p. 15, David Sterritt

"The Blair Witch Project" was only the appetizer.

That surprise hit of the warm-weather season—a striking-enough phenomenon to make the cover of Time magazine—captured the imaginations of young moviegoers so strongly that a gaggle of imitators may soon be aping its mix of low-tech cinema and high-intensity emotion.

But this is turning out to be a Year of the Thriller in other respects, too, as Bruce Willis's brooding drama "The Sixth Sense" zooms beyond the box-office take of last summer's superhit, "There's Something About Mary," a raunchy comedy at the other end of the spectrum.

A varied mix of suspense pictures is providing chills at multiplexes and art theaters alike. What the most memorable of them have in common is a refusal to explain the uncertainties of life through cut-and-dried whodunits. Instead they weave ambiguous tales in which Hitchcockian terror overlaps with the dreamlike and the uncanny.

The religion-themed *Stigmata* has gotten the most attention and sparked the most debate. Patricia Arquette stars as an ordinary young woman whose life has careened into chaos since she started manifesting signs of supernatural possession. She finds her experiences as incomprehensible as they are terrifying, but her case draws the notice of a Roman Catholic priest (Gabriel Byrne) who's also a scientist with a knack for orderly analysis of bizarre occurrences.

He begins to suspect that a mysterious messenger is using her as the vehicle for a theological revelation connected with the recent discovery of an ancient text from Jesus' time—which the Catholic establishment wants to keep hidden at any cost, since it would call into question traditional dogmas that have kept that establishment in power for centuries.

"Stigmata" spends most of its energy on horror effects, many of them shamelessly cloned from bygone hits like "The Exorcist" and "The Omen," which blazed this gory trail a quarter-century ago.

Beneath its sensationalistic surface, the movie has a worthwhile message—that spiritual growth is a matter of personal understanding, not institutional creeds—and its willingness to stake out such a position lifts it a notch above the crowd of more conventional thrillers. In the end, though, its makers are clearly more interested in violent jolts than religious ideas.

Violence is present but understated in *The Minus Man*, which brings welcome restraint to a story that still manages to be more engrossing and unsettling than its more boisterous competitors. Owen Wilson brings a patented brand of boy-next-door pleasantness to the protagonist, a wandering young man whose utterly bland exterior masks a horrible compulsion to murder strangers at random with an exotic poison he carries with him.

The movie gets its eerie power from lifelike performances by Janeane Garofalo and Mercedes Ruehl, among others, and from Hampton Fancher's inventively creepy screenplay, which throws just enough curves to keep the story fresh and surprising. Fancher's directing style is also impressive, depicting scenes that might have been grisly and gruesome with a quiet control that most of today's scaremongers would do well to study.

Too subtle to be called a horror picture and too mysterious for the "psychological thriller" label, "The Minus Man" may lose at the box office because it doesn't fit into standard marketing categories. Moviegoers who enjoy hovering on the edge of their seat should seek it out before ifs swept off the screen by the next wave of more aggressive entertainments.

Stir of Echoes is less original than "The Minus Man," but has found an audience by virtue of energetic promotion and—more important—the popular appeal of Kevin Bacon. He plays an every, day working man who gets zapped with supernatural visions after his wife's sister (Illeana Douglas) hypnotizes him as a party stunt.

These visitations grow increasingly intense, threatening to derail his sanity until he realizes they're linked with an awful crime that once happened in his house and still cries out for justice.

This would be a better movie if Bacon didn't appear insecure about the part he plays, growling and gesticulating his way through the story as if we wouldn't otherwise notice the character's working-class background and ordinary-guy personality. It's hard to say what came over this usually persuasive actor.

"Stir of Echoes" is a run-of-the-mill supernatural yarn. It may end up with the largest profits of the fall horror crop, but it's the least ambitious of the lot.

LOS ANGELES TIMES, 10/10/99, Calendar/p. 8, Kenneth Turan

If there is a lesson to be learned from "Stigmata," this is it: Never send your daughter a rosary stolen from the corpse of a recently deceased saintly priest who for mysterious reasons had hidden himself away in a tiny village in the hinterlands of Brazil. Don't even think about it.

Pittsburgh hairdresser Frankie Paige (Patricia Arquette) is that unfortunate daughter, a live-for-the-moment, "I love being me" graduate of Claudia's University of Cosmetology who is partial to tight clothes, big shoes, sparkles on her nails and drinking shots at trendy dance clubs.

But one day, soon after receiving that religious item as a gift from her vacationing mom, something stronger than her usual tequila hits Frankie. Hallucinations plague her, powerful invisible force fields toss her around, and her body exhibits the unmistakable signs of the stigmata, freely bleeding wounds that replicate the injuries inflicted on a crucified Christ.

Stigmata are a very real phenomenon (reference books say that some 300 cases have been attested) and screenwriters Tom Lazarus and Rick Ramage and director Rupert Wainwright have used them as a shrewd point of departure for what is essentially a late-'90s MTV version of "The Exorcist," a half-serious, half-silly piece of business that keeps us involved despite (or maybe because of) being more than a little overdone.

Wainwright, a veteran of high-powered commercial and music video shoots and a member of the You Can't Have Too Many Candles school of filmmaking, has a tendency to treat directing as a merciless assault on all the senses. Working with cinematographer Jeffrey L. Kimball, also a commercial vet, his undeniable stylishness and flair cross over into overkill, but it does get our attention. Similarly, "Stigmata's" story, despite its surreal plotting, has a kernel of genuine interest that is sporadically involving.

It's that core that has attracted a better-than-average cast for a supernatural thriller, including Arquette and Gabriel Byrne, who plays Father Andrew Kiernan, a scientist and a Jesuit whose job as a Vatican-based member of the Catholic Church's Sacred Congregation for the Causes of Saints is to show up at the sites of miracles and throw cold water on the susceptibility of those who believe.

We meet Kiernan in the film's prologue, arriving at that Brazilian village where the sainted Father Paulo Alameida has just died and where, presumably in the holy man's memory, his church's statue of the Virgin Mary can be seen crying tears of certifiably human blood. While Kiernan believes this might just be a genuine miracle, back in the Vatican his superior, the oily Cardinal Daniel Houseman (the estimable Jonathan Pryce), is definitely not interested.

Meanwhile, on the mean streets of Pittsburgh, a terrified Frankie is pulverized by continual stigmatic attacks, which, in addition to everything else, are hell on her haircutting business. Just in case we might be dozing off, these are briskly edited (by Michael R. Miller and Michael J. Duthie) to intense music, and intercut with lightning-bolt flashes of nails pounded into wrists, crowns of thorns thrust onto heads ... you get the idea.

When Father Kiernan finally gets sent to Pittsburgh to investigate Frankie's troubles (are you surprised?), the seizures go into high gear, and director Wainwright throws his technique into overdrive.

Any visual twist you can think of, including monster close-ups of eyes, lips and raindrops, and the use a color-muting process called "skip bleaching" that gives "Stigmata" a look similar to "Seven's," is called into service, not to mention putting Arquette into full eye-rolling Linda Blair levitating possession mode. There's even some speaking (apparently closely supervised by a UCLA professor of Northwest Semitic Languages) in an ancient Galilee dialect not heard (gasp) since Christ walked the Holy Land's hot and dusty roads.

While all of this technique has a distancing effect, making us care less rather than more about Frankie's predicament, it's at least not boring, and it works well with the great variety of religious art focusing on the Crucifixion that "Stigmata" puts on the screen.

Similarly, while much of the film's plot has no interest in making sense, once the complete explanation of everything that's been happening has been presented (by a very effective Rade Sherbedgia), it's a bit cleverer than anticipated. "Stigmata" is too out of control too often to be much more than a shameless guilty pleasure, but its baroque religious overlay makes us close to believers by the end.

NEW YORK POST, 9/10/99, p. 43, Rod Dreher

What a bloody disappointment "Stigmata" is!

The promising run of paranormal horror movies that began with "Blair Witch" and continued through "The Sixth Sense" and today's "Stir of Echoes" stalls out with this dull, irritating exploitation flick.

Not even a fine, subtle performance by Gabriel Byrne can redeem this movie's lost soul.

More seriously, for a movie based on a Catholic mystical phenomenon—the film even appropriates the legacy of the beatified stigmatic Padre Pio in its plotting and promotion—"Stigmata" is jaw-droppingly anti-Catholic.

These filmmakers have some nerve, implicating the beloved Italian friar in such a low, dishonest and despicable assault on the Catholic faith.

"Stigmata" is about Frankie Paige (a wooden Patricia Arquette), a Pittsburgh hairdresser who begins experiencing bizarre physical assaults by an unseen force. The gory attacks attract the attention of the Vatican, which dispatches Jesuit Father Andrew Kiernan (Byrne) to investigate.

Frankie appears to be receiving the stigmata, an extremely rare condition in which a person, for no apparent reason, suffers the wounds of the crucified Christ. But Frankie is a bratty, foul-mouthed atheist, whereas genuine stigmatics are devout believers. Father Kiernan initially dismisses the case.

But after witnessing the worsening assaults himself, the priest's heart goes out to poor Frankie, who begins channeling an apparently malevolent spirit. He stays on to protect her from whatever is causing the affliction, as well as solve the mystery.

Hint: It involves a dead Brazilian heretical priest, an ancient document, and a shadowy, power-mad cardinal (Jonathan Pryce).

"Stigmata" director Rupert Wainwright cut his teeth on commercials and music videos, and it shows in his garishly overdone set pieces, jackhammer editing and suffocating atmospherics (it's always raining, and the candle budget on this shoot must've been huge).

Worse, the story makes increasingly little sense as it unspools. (Dare I say "Stigmata" has holes in the plot?) Is Frankie's stigmata real, or is it a demonic counterfeit? The spirit manifesting itself through Frankie is obviously a demon; it tortures the woman mercilessly and compels her to attempt seduction of the priest, whose celibacy it blasphemously mocks.

But—and I can't give too many details without revealing major plot points—"Stigmata" concludes that the institutional Catholic Church is the truly evil force at work here. The film wants it both ways: to trade off the trappings and substance of Catholic mystical theology, while painting the church as a massive metaphysical fraud scheme.

Ah, Hollywood, ever faithful to its nasty little dogmas.

NEWSDAY, 9/10/99, Part II/p. B11, John Anderson

In a church outside Sao Paolo, beside the casket of a beloved Brazilian priest, a statue of the Virgin Mary cries tears of blood.

In Pittsburgh, a young woman with pinned-up hair and a tattooed navel receives a priest's stolen rosary in the mail and begins to manifest the wounds of Christ.

Jetting between the New World and the Old, a priestly investigator is having some doubts. The Vatican is getting nervous.

And why not? With "Stigmata," Hollywood goes back to its favorite source of substantiated gothic horror (and perhaps its favorite institutional villain), the Catholic Church, whose vestigial sense of the medieval is a great source of screen credibility for even the most outlandish of horror stories. Make the heroine pregnant, have her bite an apple: Suddenly, the movie isn't just trying to scare your pants off—it's trying to save your soul.

"Stigmata" is a gorgeous movie to look at—the way the film has been processed, colors are super-saturated, while inky shadows permeate every scene. The effect is both deep and fragile. Less adventurously, the film employs the same opening gambit as every similar thriller from "The Omen" to "The Mummy": The archaeological-theological intro that implies a scholarly foundation for what's basically a scary movie.

Instead of ancient Egypt, "Stigmata" offers modern Brazil and the soon-to-be-deceased Father Alameida (Jack Donner), leafing through a translated version of the Gospel of Thomas which, we learn, purports to include the verbatim dialogue of Jesus Himself. The priest is almost immediately dead. A Vatican investigator, Father Andrew Kiernan (Gabriel Byme) comes to the conclusion that the bleeding statue is real, but is told by Cardinal Houseman (Jonathan Pryce, who, a la Richelieu, wears a Mephistophelian goatee) to drop the matter immediately. Instead, Houseman sends Kiernan to Pittsburgh to investigate the case of a young hairdresser named Frankie Paige (Patricia Arquette), who is bleeding from her wrists, and, during a subway ride captured on video, seems to have undergone a scourging much like that of Jesus.

Kiernan is unconvinced—stigmata, the manifestation of Christ's wounds en route to his death on Calvary, are only supposed to appear in true believers, as they have from St. Francis of Assisi to the mystic Padre Pio. And Frankie, of course, has an active sex life, lives her nights in the clubs and doesn't even believe in God—which, according to the movie's interpretation of Catholic doctrine, means God doesn't believe in her, either.

"Stigmata" is more than a run-of-the-mill horror film: What Frankie goes through when she receives her wounds is unnervingly violent and bloody. The ideas are unusual, perhaps even enlightening in their own weird way. Director Rupert Wainwright (of the virtually unreleased but intriguing "The Sadness of Sex") creates a lot of tension and springs the brutal action with a ruthless disregard for our lunch.

But at the same time, the casual assumption of the movie is institutional corruption in the church and its reflexive suppression of what might be the most important document in Christian theologic history (the reputed Gospel of Thomas, as explained in a postscript, has been rejected by the church, but the simplification of the case makes an easy target even easier).

Wainwright also succumbs to the needs of the standard Hollywood thriller, which means romantic entanglement, mindless action, no ambiguity regarding good and evil and plenty of ambiguity regarding just what in God's name is going on: Is Frankie channeling Father Alameida? Or, as her "Exorcist"-style possession implies, is the cause of her misery simply ... Satan? A little bit of both, it seems, in a movie that's a little bit art, a little bit hooey.

SIGHT AND SOUND, 2/00, p. 55, Stephanie Zacharek

Pittsburgh, the present. Frankie Paige is a hairdresser who doesn't believe in God. After receiving a rosary in a package of Brazilian souvenirs, she begins spurting blood from wounds that have opened of their own accord which directly correspond with Christ's crucifixion wounds. Father Andrew Kiernan, who investigates religious phenomena, is sent from the Vatican to look at Frankie's symptoms. He dismisses them because she's an unbeliever, but he finds himself drawn in by her case.

Frankie's attacks worsen. Possessed by the spirit of a priest who died in the process of translating a newly discovered gospel, she begins writing texts in a language not used since Jesus' time. Kiernan fears Frankie's affliction will kill her, and the two begin to fall in love. When a power hungry and corrupt cardinal realises Frankie may have some knowledge of the newly discovered gospel which the Church is trying to keep secret, he pulls Kiernan off the case. The cardinal and his henchmen abduct Frankie and try to kill her. Kiernan rescues her in the nick of time.

The supernatural pseudo-mystical thriller *Stigmata* is something of a mess, a roughly chopped slaw of spiritual hokum and scaremongering ripped off directly from *The Exorcist* (1973). Director Rupert Wainwright's previous credits include music videos and commercials. This CV is written all over *Stigmata* with its convulsive cutting and ubiquitous, meaningless close-ups. Huge chunks of the plot make no sense (particularly a demonic possession subthread) and Patricia Arquette, generally a marvellous and graceful actress, gets lost in the movie's manic shuffle.

But for lapsed Catholics especially, *Stigmata* holds its share of perverse delights. Vehement in its distrust of the Catholic Church, it features demons and beasties and treacherous priesties, as well as lots of hyper-Catholic visuals like statues that cry tears of blood and fluttering flocks of doves that radiate out of thin air. Gabriel Byrne, playing a special task-force priest, looks more soulful and sexier in cassock and clerical collar than he does in normal street clothes. He's like the Vatican James Bond, only his job is a hundred times harder: he's a babe magnet and he can't do a thing about it.

Arquette is too good an actress to throw away the whole movie. Her smile is pure delight, with the gentle surprise of those funny eye teeth, and she and Byrne have some charming flirtatious scenes together. Otherwise, though, her Frankie has little to do but bleed profusely. And when the stigmata hits, it descends like a bad Warrant video, all furious cross-cutting and abrasive noise. We see spikes going through wrists; thorns pressing into tender flesh; and blood spurting, dripping, coagulating and doing just about everything blood can do—all set to jarring industrial clanking music. The effects move so quickly that you don't have much time to dwell on their grisliness, but they're still queasy-making and unpleasant, and only underscore *Stigmata*'s shortcomings. *Stigmata* is lethargic and self-consciously edgy at the same time. Instead of being elegiac and creepy, it scrabbles for a false kind of downtown grittiness.

And when Wainwright tries to strike a more spiritual note, *Stigmata* just gets plain goofy: after her episodes, Frankie becomes bathed in ethereal light as Enya-like noodlings waft by on the soundtrack. Draped in a snowy bedsheet and holding a dove in her hand, she does a remarkable impersonation of St Francis of Assisi. Many mysteries in *Stigmata* remain unsolved: why is it constantly raining inside Frankie's apartment? Why does the spirit of a supposedly benevolent priest speak through her in a voice deeper than Barry White's? And can stigmata really be caught from contact with a rosary? If so, wouldn't a little ringworm medicine or an aspirin take care of it?

Stigmata is interesting only because it isn't really very nice. It refuses to genuflect before one of the world's great religions. It doesn't seem to care whom or even if it offends, which makes if naughty, florid fun for ex-Catholics of all stripes. But that doesn't make it any good. At least Byrne is allowed to bring some glamour to it, a little ecumenical *savoir faire*. If only they'd given him an Aston Martin DB5.

VILLAGE VOICE, 9/21/99, p. 166, Michael Atkinson

For sheer liturgical ookiness, the millennially challenged Catholic bloodletter *Stigmata* practically breaks a hip trying to outgoose the competition. Billowing curtains, angsty priests, wacky contact lenses (red and yellow this time), girls talking in pro-wrestler voices—whatever happened to Linda Blair, anyway? Here, Pittsburgh hairdresser Patricia Arquette gets a rosary from her mom in the mail, except it's the rosary of a dead priest whose passing makes a local statue cry blood and who died busily translating an old scroll the Vatican wants to rebury. That means trouble, and Arquette starts enduring her own stations of the cross (in no particular order), getting crucified in her bathtub and invisibly whipped on the subway. Meanwhile, Gabriel Byrne is the fed-up Vatican investigator told to forget about that bleeding statue (Cardinal Jonathan Pryce almost says, "I'm taking you off the case!") and redirected toward this Pittsburgh phenomenon, which includes scribbling in ancient Aramaic and mysterious doves that appear out of nowhere and sound like helicopters.

Despite exposition delivered so redundantly and witlessly (a Vatican scholar telling another what a gospel is, etc.) you think you're in a Kaplan class, *Stigmata* manages to be incoherent, no more so than when Arquette, seemingly possessed by Sid Vicious for a time, tries to ball Byrne and then kicks the shit out of him. Director Rupert Wainwright shot this baby in the middle of the David Fincher monsoon season and edited it like he was acing the 40-shots-per-minute sprint. Similarly hysterical, the all-too-Dolby soundtrack sounds like the dialogue, an old sound effects record, and Billy Corgan's mood-swinging score are fighting it out with aluminum bats. (Heart patients, beware.) *Stigmata* raises more questions than it intends, that's for sure: do hairdressers in Pittsburgh really make enough to afford what looks like a venture capitalist's apartment? What does St. Francis of Assisi have to do with it all? What is it with Hollywood and Catholicism?

Also reviewed in:
CHICAGO TRIBUNE, 9/10/99, Tempo/p. 5, Barbara Shulgasser
NEW YORK TIMES, 9/10/99, p. E18, Stephen Holden
VARIETY, 9/13-19/99, p. 41, Dennis Harvey
WASHINGTON POST, 9/10/99, p. C1, Stephen Hunter
WASHINGTON POST, 9/10/99, Weekend/p. 45, Desson Howe

STILL CRAZY

A Columbia Pictures release with the participation of The Greenlight Fund of a Marmot Tandy production. *Executive Producer:* Dick Clement and Ian La Frenais. *Producer:* Amanda Marmot. *Director:* Brian Gibson. *Screenplay:* Dick Clement and Ian La Frenais. *Director of Photography:* Ashley Rowe. *Editor:* Peter Boyle and Niven Howie. *Music:* Clive Langer, Tarquin Gotch, and Steve Dagger. *Music Editor:* Dina Eaton. *Sound:* Colin Nicolson and (music) Mark Bishop. *Sound Editor:* Bob Risk. *Casting:* Gail Stevens. *Production Designer:* Max Gottlieb. *Art Director:* Sarah-Jane Cornish. *Set Director:* Rebecca Alleway. *Special Effects:* Stuart Brisdon. *Costumes:* Caroline Harris. *Make-up:* Morag Ross. *Stunt Coordinator:* Nicholal Powell. *Running time:* 96 minutes. *MPAA Rating:* R.

CAST: Stephen Rea (Tony Costello); Billy Connolly (Hughie); Jimmy Nail (Les Wickes); Timothy Spall (David "Beano" Baggot); Bill Nighy (Ray Simms); Juliet Aubrey (Karen

Knowles); Helena Bergstrom (Astrid Simms); Bruce Robinson (Brian Lovell); Hans Matheson (Luke Shand); Rachael Stirling (Clare Knowles); Phil Daniels (Neil Gaydon); Frances Barber (Lady in Black); Phil Davis (Limo Driver); Zoe Ball (Zoe); Andy Nichol (Gary); Frances Magee (Hockney); Justin Gratton (Not Morrissey); Delroy Atkinson (Jason); Julian Simms (Steve Greenblatt); Virginia Clay (Young Karen); Luke Garrett (Young Hughie); Sean McKenzie (Young Beano); Rupert Penry-Jones (Young Ray); Matthew Finney (Young Brian); Alex Palmer (Young Les); Gavin Kennedy (Young Tony); Lee Williams (Young Keith); Peter Baynham (Kevin); Margaret Blakemore and Candida Gubbins (Waitresses); Alphonsia Emmanuel (Camille); Mikayla Jones (Natasha); Jason Green (Adam); Christopher Wild (Apprentice); Dean Lennox Kelly (Pizza Boy); MacKenzie Crook (Dutch Kid); Donna Air (Dutch Hitch-hiker); Ralph Van Dijk (Club 4 Owner); Sabina Michael (Dutch Receptionist); Steve Ubels (Dutch Local); Danny Webb (Clive); Anita Carey (Tax Woman); David Henry (Tax Inspector); Daisy Donovan (Female Reporter); Bruce Byron (Snotty Reporter); Jeffrey Harmer (Dutch Policeman); Sheila Reid (Mrs. Baggot); Leelo Ross (Dutch Lady); Brian Capron (Senior Executive); Luke D'Silva (Spanish Bar Man).

LOS ANGELES TIMES, 12/11/98, Calendar/p. 16, Kevin Thomas

"Still Crazy," an irresistibly uproarious and heart-tugging tale of a British rock band attempting a comeback 20 years after breaking up, offers the warmth, humor and wisdom of "The Full Monty." It also recalls the endearing 1991 film about an Irish rock band, "The Commitments," which in fact was written by Dick Clement and Ian La Frenais, who serve as "Still Crazy's" writers and executive producers.

Instead of the pretentiousness and incoherence of "Velvet Goldmine," "Still Crazy" offers a screen full of engaging, sharply defined people, abundant broad comedy set off by incisive wit and keen, knowing observation. Brian Gibson, who did such a superb job with HBO's "The Josephine Baker Story" and the Tina Turner bio, "What's Love Got to Do With It," is the perfect choice as its director.

Gibson is an impassioned storyteller who knows how to integrate musical numbers deftly into the plot and how to get socko performances from a wide array of actors. He knows how to go for broke in the big emotional scenes and when to pull back for those crucially quiet, subtle moments. In contrast to Gibson's two earlier pictures, "Still Crazy" is a comedy, and what makes this film work so well is that he and his colleagues never forget that it is—despite wrenching revelations along the band's rocky comeback trail.

Stephen Rea's Tony Costello has the condom concession in Spain's Balearic Islands, and has dropped by a posh restaurant on a service call when he is recognized as the keyboardist of the seminal '70s band Strange Fruit. He has been discovered by a young man whose father presented the Fruit at a legendary open-air rock festival in 1977, a gig that proved to be the tempestuous group's catastrophic final performance.

The young man offers a chance for a comeback—if Tony can round up the band members for a Holland tour as a warmup for a splashy return at the same festival. (The idea for the film was inspired by a reunion tour of the Animals.)

To be sure, Tony has his work cut out for him in simply locating his bandmates, let alone in persuading them to reunite. Tony first tracks down the Fruits' personal assistant Karen (Juliet Aubrey), considerably younger than the band members and still very attractive. As it turns out, her temporary job is about over, and she's willing to sign on as the band's manager.

The other former Fruits are Jimmy Nail's Les Wickes, a singer-guitarist who felt he should have become the lead singer when its original lead burned out and OD'd. Les, the only Fruit still on his first marriage, has built up a good business as a roofer in a town in Northern England. Ray Simms (Bill Nighy), who became the lead singer, has tried to sustain a semblance of a musical career, although he's not quite the happening guy his ferociously, hilariously humorless and possessive second wife, Astrid (Helena Bergstrom), insists that he is.

Boisterous drummer Beano Baggot (Timothy Spall) has become a portly nursery worker evading the tax collector, and the Fruits' songwriter-guitarist Brian Lovell is believed to be dead. Hughie (Billy Connolly), a cynical veteran who serves as the film's narrator, is willing to return to satisfy his "terrible urge to chronicle human folly." The younger generation is represented by Bruce

Robinson as a guitar wizard recruited to fill in the gap left by Brian, and Rachel Stirling as Karen's teenage daughter.

The big question is not merely whether the Fruits still have what it takes—or whether the group really ever did—but also whether they can put aside considerable losses and grievances and pull together for what is all too clearly a last and decidedly dicey chance to make a mark in the ever-changing world of rock'n' roll. The Fruits are barraged with the unkind reality that they are no longer young and must find a way to connect with audiences too youthful even to have heard of them.

The film offers ensemble performances of breadth and depth, overflowing with both spontaneity and nuance. Nighy has perhaps the most challenging role, as a still-handsome but ravaged-looking man, his Ray never regarded as talented as the band's original singer. He's now decidedly fragile and often loopy yet tries to tell himself he's still a champ who "takes no prisoners."

One of the miracles of the movie, and crucial to its success, is the music itself, with some of the songs deliberately pretentious and dated, others possessing a timeless power to connect. Mick Jones of Foreigner and Chris Difford of Squeeze wrote the music and lyrics, respectively, with Jeff Lynne contributing additional songs. Gary Kemp of Spandau Ballet coached the cast as well as serving as the film's musical director.

Another film "Still Crazy" recalls is Rob Reiner's awesomely spot-on mock-rockumentary "This Is Spinal Tap." But whereas that 1984 film skewered the pretensions and excesses of its Brit rockers, this film takes an affectionate rather than satirical view of human foibles.

The look and feel of "Still Crazy," as well as its music, seems exactly right, and it offers such hearty yet wry fun that you hope it will connect with the young audiences that Strange Fruit itself is trying to reach.

NEW YORK POST, 1/22/99, p. 55, Rod Dreher

You don't have to be over 40 to enjoy "Still Crazy," but ... well, actually you do.

This flaccid but pleasantly tolerable British comedy about the regrouping of a fictional '70s rock band is meant to rouse aging baby boomers who fear they're uncool and too old to rock'n' roll—and fear impotence.

It's a ripe subject for satire, and "Still Crazy" could have been a rollicking, uproarious send-up of boomer vanity and rock cliches. But after a promising beginning, director Brian Gibson gives in to a therapeutic approach that flatters its haggard audience with an unabashedly sentimental pep rally—the cinematic equivalent of St. Joseph's Baby Viagra.

If you find charming and inspirational the idea that a twentysomething groupie is obsessed with giving the full Monica to a blubbery old hairball of a drummer, "Still Crazy" will be heartening.

The group is called Strange Fruit, a pompous, stadium-rock "hair band" in the mold of Aerosmith and Led Zeppelin. The Fruit broke up acrimoniously at a 1977 English rock festival. As the Fruit's roadie, Hughie (Billy Connolly), observes in voiceover, "I think God got sick of all that '70s excess. That's why he invented the Sex Pistols."

As the action begins, Fruit keyboardist Tony Costello (the ever-droopy Stephen Rea) handles the condom-machine concession in the Spanish resort town of Ibiza, where he has a chance encounter with the son of the festival's promoter.

The kid is planning an anniversary fest reunion, and asks Tony to re-form the group for the gig.

Tony hooks up with Karen (Juliet Aubrey), the band's former personal assistant, and sets out with her to find the surviving Fruits. Les (Jimmy Nail), a bass player-turned-roofer, joins hesitantly, while Beano (Timothy Spall), the doofus drummer, leaps in feet first, desperate to make enough money to pay off the tax man.

The best performance in a well-acted movie is Bill Nighy's turn as Ray—the Robert Plant-like, preserved-in-amber lead singer. Ray lives far beyond his means in a giant mansion with his haughty young Scandi-babian wife, Astrid (Helena Bergstrom), releasing solo albums nobody wants to buy and struggling to stay off the sauce.

Nighy is terrific as a once-Byronic figure who's as dessicated as beef jerky and utterly terrified of aging.

They undertakes a tour of clubs in Holland, trying to work the kinks out, but their old animosities and chronic insecurities threaten to put the kibosh on what they hope will be a triumphant return.

The cast may be endearing, but the wheezy material is mighty soft in the belly. While not without amusing moments, the screenplay by Ian La Frenais and Dick Clement takes the sweet old geezers through the expected motions and obvious gags, but there's not much wit or cleverness here.

It recalls the way Hollywood filed the fangs off the stage version of "Steel Magnolias" to confect a squishy tribute to sisterhood. And if the music were any good, that'd be one thing, but does anybody really long for the resurrection of that Emerson, Lake and Palmer brand of sludge?

In their big comeback number here, Strange Fruit bleats rock-goddishly (with lyric-writing assistance from Foreigner's Mick Jones) about "the flame [that] still burns/it's there in my soul."

Hey, Pops, that's just gas.

NEWSDAY, 1/22/99, Part II/p. B6, Jack Mathews

I would be eager to declare British director Brian Gibson's nostalgia rock comedy "Still Crazy" the first good movie of 1999, except that its U.S. distributor, Sony Pictures, slipped it into a theater in Los Angeles for a week in late December to qualify it for the 1998 Academy Awards.

Whether that gambit is successful, we'll know next month. It has already netted the film two Golden Globe nominations from the Hollywood Foreign Press Association, including one for best musical or comedy. The other was for best original song, "The Flame Still Burns," which might, in fact, go all the way to the Oscar show.

The song should probably have been the title of the movie. Its earnest lyrics, written by Chris Difford of the British pop band Squeeze, captures the lingering heat—not quite from a flame, more from a pilot light—of a modestly popular fictional 1970s rock group named Strange Fruit, which attempts a reunion after 20 years apart.

"Still Crazy" plays like an agreeable knockoff of both Rob Reiner's "This Is Spinal Tap," about a metal band trying to hang together, and Alan Parker's "The Commitments," about a young Irish group trying to get started.

The script for "Still Crazy" was written by "Commitments" writers Dick Clement and Ian La Frenais and it has the same crisp wit and savvy band member byplay. At the same time, the fatigue and desperation evident in a group struggling beyond its time in "Spinal Tap" is here, as well.

But if it's derivative, it's derived from the best bits. Gibson, who worked on numerous musical film projects for the BBC before directing the Tina Turner biography "What's Love Got to Do With It?," has assembled a superb ensemble cast, and directed them with a passion that serves, beneath all the hilarity, as a kind of sweet homage to the music and musicians of the '70s.

Strange Fruit has spread far and wide since the 1977 Wisbech Festival, which ended with a calamitous direct-hit lightning strike on the outdoor stage, where the group was performing at the time. Two decades later, organizers are planning a Wisbech II, and Strange Fruit is on their list of recalls.

But where is everyone? The original lead singer is dead. Ray (Bill Nighy), who took his place and is still struggling with a solo career, looks dead. Brian (Bruce Robinson), the lead guitarist, was last seen on his way to a mental institution. Drummer Beano (Timothy Spall) is a gardener. Keyboardist Tony (Stephen Rea) runs a condom machine concession at a beach resort. And bass guitarist Les (Jimmy Nail) is a roofer.

Getting the group back together is the task of Tony, who's recognized by one of the Wisbech organizers while making his condom rounds, and Karen (Juliet Aubrey), the group's one-time personal assistant and now single mom, who's lured away from her hotel PR job to become Strange Fruit's manager. When most of the members are on board, and set for a pre-Wisbech bus tour of Europe, they're joined by their old roadie Hughie (the always delightful Billy Connolly).

"Still Crazy" is in the new instant tradition of "The Full Monty." It's an uplifting tale of underdogs regaining dignity through music, and you become involved knowing—demanding!— that Strange Fruit makes it to Wisbech II in the final act.

But if there are no major surprises, there are plenty of small, pleasurable ones. Each of the characters is nicely fleshed out, and there are old antagonisms, old crushes and new issues to work out. And there's the music, which is a lot easier on the ears than the Spinal Tap screeching, and, in the case of "The Flame Still Burns," downright moving.

SIGHT AND SOUND, 11/98, p. 62, Andy Medhurst

At a 1977 rock festival, the successful group Strange Fruit give their last, disastrous performance.

Twenty-one years later, keyboardist Tony is asked to reassemble the group for a reunion show. He tracks down their manager Karen, bassist Les, drummer Beano and vocalist Ray. Despite a history of resentments and personality clashes, they decide to reform, pending the return of guitarist Brian. Karen discovers that Brian's royalties have been paid into a cancer foundation. Assuming Brian is dead, the group recruit a new guitarist, Luke, and, in order to prove their viability to a sceptical record company, embark on a tour of Holland accompanied by their old roadie Hughie.

This begins badly, and longstanding rivalries within the group resurface, but by the end of the tour they have gelled once again and are offered a record deal. In the studio, they see a television interview recorded on the early part of the tour, in which drunken group members heavily criticise each other. This prompts them to split up, seemingly for good.

Karen discovers Brian is still alive, having renounced his wealth and fame, but she persuades him to reconsider and this leads the group to play the festival reunion after all. A hostile press conference spooks Brian into not playing, and the set threatens to be a flop, but he eventually walks on stage and the crowd acclaims a triumphant performance.

The Full Monty for *Mojo* readers, *Still Crazy* targets a precise demographic: thirtysomething men with over-extensive record collections. Since that sad faction includes me, I enjoyed the film hugely, but on reflection certain flaws are all-too glaring. The role of Karen is a clumsy attempt to attract an otherwise excluded female audience, but this can't disguise the utter implausibility of a 70s rock group (something like Free) having a female manager.

Likewise, the eagerness with which the young guitarist Luke climbs aboard the rickety bus of old fogeys that comprise the band Strange Fruit defies credibility, since he has both the musicianship and the looks (Ewan McGregor meets early Manic Street Preachers) to succeed on his own terms. Finally, the way the young festival crowd reacts ecstatically at the final performance is the concluding proof that *Still Crazy* is sheer fantasy, a wet dream of popstardom for men weighed down by mortgages and CD box sets.

Just as in *The Full Monty*, the last scene ends on a frozen moment of peaking triumph, thereby evading the crucial question of what happens next, and it might be argued that *Still Crazy* apes the Sheffield stripathon throughout, offering a bittersweet comedy of male bonding and success over adversity. Such a claim would mangle history, however, since behind *Still Crazy* are screenwriters Dick Clement and Ian La Frenais, whose classic television series *The Likely Lads, Porridge* and *Auf Wiedersehen, Pet* provided the templates for all subsequent British comedies centred on male groups. In that sense, *The Full Monty* was hugely in their debt, so *Still Crazy* sees Clement and La Frenais returning home to reclaim their turf.

The vicissitudes of a band—all that bickering, jockeying, farting and fusing—are an ideal subject for a comic exploration of straight male egos; add the extra anxieties wrought by encroaching middle age and you have extremely rich material. *Still Crazy* doesn't quite cut as deep as it could, frequently sidestepping emotional complexity for another broad gag involving the lumpen drummer. Admittedly, these always work, and Timothy Spall is irresistible as dim, flatulent Beano, but it's hard to suppress thoughts of a better, tougher film sacrificed for *Still Crazy* surface delights.

Delights, nonetheless, are there in abundance, or at least they are for those of us who felt that reading Nick Hornby's *High Fidelity* was like looking in a mirror. The pop-culture in-jokes are unerringly and lovingly accurate (Brian, for example, is Fleetwood Mac's reclusive Peter Green, with a touch of Sid Barrett from Pink Floyd), the dialogue is agreeably sharp and salty, and several of the actors are outstanding.

Best of all, perhaps surprisingly given the bigger names surrounding him, is Bill Nighy. He turns Ray into a delectable caricature of rock-star pretensions, with a voice derived from the *Spitting Image* Rolling Stone puppets and an ability to self-dramatise even when underwater. It's a star turn that comprehensively steals the film.

VILLAGE VOICE, 1/26/99, p. 106, Dennis Lim

Theoretically an exercise in '70s nostalgia at its ugliest, *Still Crazy* is in fact a deft, small-scale Brit comedy, effortlessly knocked off from an age-old formula. A feel-good, character-driven lark, this goofy, unglamorous distant relative of *Velvet Goldmine* is brisk and entertaining enough to excuse its complete lack of originality. As unassumingly likable as *The Full Monty* (which it shamelessly echoes), and devoid of *Waking Ned Devine*'s sickly coyness, *Still Crazy* revolves around the cash-in reunion of "seminal" but little-remembered rockers Strange Fruit, who disbanded at "the 1977 Wisbech Rock Festival."

Twenty years on, keyboardist Tony (Stephen Rea), now a condom salesman in the Balearic Islands, is ready for a comeback. The Fruits' virtuoso wild-child guitarist has long since gone missing, but with the help of the band's loyal assistant (Juliet Aubrey), Tony tracks down the other guys: the bassist (Jimmy Nail), now a family man with a roofing business; the tubby, perennially groupie-less drummer (Timothy Spall); and Ray (Bill Nighy), pretty-boy singer turned train wreck.

Written by English TV veterans Dick Clement and Ian La Frenais (best known here for adapting *The Commitments*), *Still Crazy* is perfectly successful on its own low-key terms. True, some of the humor is broad and easy, most of the sentimental cues are hopelessly clumsy, and there's a surfeit of bloated prog-glitter on the soundtrack (original songs by, among others, Squeeze's Chris Difford and Foreigner's Mick Jones). But it's difficult to resist the good-natured casualness with which it's all thrown together, or the gifted actors, many of them maneuvering imaginatively within one-note roles. Nighy's Ray is especially memorable. His mental faculties visibly depleted, Ray is a ravaged, sequined picture of ridiculousness. In a comic tour de force, Nighy conveys Ray's absurd vanity and quiet despair, making his condition both heartbreaking and hilarious.

Also reviewed in:
CHICAGO TRIBUNE, 1/22/99, Friday/p. H, Mark Caro
NEW YORK TIMES, 1/22/99, p. E14, Janet Maslin
VARIETY, 11/9-15/98, p. 30, Derek Elley
WASHINGTON POST, 1/29/99, p. C1, Rita Kempley
WASHINGTON POST, 1/29/99, Weekend/p. 41, Eric Brace

STIR OF ECHOES

An Artisan Entertainment release of a Hofflund/Polone production. *Executive Producer:* Michele Weisler. *Producer:* Gavin Polone and Judy Hofflund. *Director:* David Koepp. *Screenplay:* David Koepp. *Based on the novel "A Stir of Echoes" by:* Richard Matheson. *Director of Photography:* Fred Murphy. *Editor:* Jill Savitt. *Music:* James Newton Howard. *Music Editor:* Jim Weidman. *Sound:* Tim Chau, Martin Maryska, and (music) Shawn Murphy. *Sound Editor:* Todd Toon and Carmen Baker. *Casting:* Mary Colqhoun. *Production Designer:* Nelson Coates. *Art Director:* David Krummel. *Set Designer:* Terry Baughman, Hugo Santiago, and Gary Speckman. *Set Decorator:* Susie Goulder. *Costumes:* Leesa Evans. *Make-up:* Linda Melazzo. *Make-up (Special Effects):* Tony Gardner and Jim Beinke. *Stunt Coordinator:* Rick Le Fevour. *Running time:* 99 minutes. *MPAA Rating:* R.

CAST: Kevin Bacon (Tom Witzky); Kathryn Erbe (Maggie Witzky); Illeana Douglas (Lisa); Liza Weil (Debbie Kozac, the Babysitter); Kevin Dunn (Frank McCarthy); Conor O'Farrell (Harry Damon); Jennifer Morrison (Samantha); Zachary David Cope (Jake Witzky); Luisa

Strus (Sheila); Stephen Eugene Walker (Bobby); Mary Kay Cook (Vanessa); Larry Neumann, Jr. (Lenny); Richard Cotovsky (Neighborhood Man); Steve Rifkin (Kurt); Chalon Williams (Adam); George Ivey (Security Guard); Lisa Lewis (Debbie's Mother); Mike Bacarella and Christian Stolte (Train Station Cops); Eddie Bo Smith, Jr. (Neil the Cop); Hyowon K. Yoo (Korean Woman); Jim Andelin (Elderly Man); Karen Vaccaro (Upset Woman); Antonio Polk (Homey); Rosario Varela (Latin Woman); Duane Sharp (Polish Priest).

CHRISTIAN SCIENCE MONITOR, 10/1/99, p. 15, David Sterritt

[*Stir of Echoes* was reviewed jointly with *Stigmata*; see Sterritt's review of that film.]

LOS ANGELES TIMES, 9/10/99, Calendar/p. 6, John Anderson

[*The following review by John Anderson appeared in a slightly different form in* NEWSDAY, 9/10/99, Part II/p. B3.]

Timing may be everything, but it's also a funny thing. How else to explain why "Stir of Echoes," in which a little boy sees dead people, should open at a time when the biggest movie in the country is about a little boy who sees dead people?

But the reason "Stir of Echoes" works as well as it does has nothing to do with any similarities to "The Sixth Sense"—or to "The Shining," Poe's "The Black Cat" or even the infamous Glen Ridge, N.J., rape case that seems to figure in the story (and which seems unlikely, since Richard Matheson wrote his book more than 35 years ago). Neither is it about the hokum-rich screenplay of director David Koepp. Or all the hallucinatory editing intended to keep us off balance and susceptible to spooks.

What gives the movie its teeth is the very earthy Witzky family, who behave so much like real people you might think they are. Maggie (Kathryn Erbe of "Oz") is pregnant. Tom (Kevin Bacon) wishes she wasn't.

Little Jake (Zachary David Cope) seems to talk to people who aren't there. Generally, though, the Witzkys occupy their blue-collar Chicago neighborhood like every other beer-drinking, high school football-supporting, classic-rock-loving family on the block. Until, of course, the supernatural moves in with them.

Life is normal until Tom and Maggie go to a neighborhood beer blast and Maggie's sister Liza (Illeana Douglas)—a yet-to-be-licensed hypnotherapist—puts Tom under a spell. Everybody thinks it's the world's greatest party trick, but Liza's post-hypnotic suggestion that Tom continue to keep his mind "open" makes Tom a receiver for otherworldly transmissions, which turn his life upside-down, inside out and leads him to a murder in his own backyard.

Which he digs up, literally, along with the cellar in his house and the floorboards in his kitchen, looking for whatever it is the otherworld is compelling him to seek. Maggie, meanwhile, has discovered that both her son and her husband are part of a subculture with a gift (see: "The Shining"). The neighbors, including the skirt-chasing Frank (Kevin Dunn), are discovering that Tom is on to something they'd rather he didn't pursue. And Tom just keeps digging until he gets the good sense to rent a Jackhammer.

Which is funny. But while all that digging may make a good trailer and allow Bacon to heroically obsessively compulse, the best parts of his performance are when he's just being Tom —working-class family man, maybe not the brightest light in the box but a genuinely decent, reasonably courageous husband/father. He and Erbe give Tom and Maggie enough mutual affection/benign irritation that they really seem like a couple in a long-term relationship. More important, they react to the strange and unnerving things that happen to them the way you expect people might—unlike so many characters in so many movies, who turn into aliens the minute life becomes less than rational.

Koepp, who as a screenwriter was responsible for such blockbusters as "Jurassic Park," "Mission: Impossible" and "The Lost World," is fond of arranging torrents of images to suggest the tumult of Tom's mind and also indulges in a lot of false alarms (quick cuts to nowhere) to keep his audience primed and lumpy.

The more impressive aspect of "Stir of Echoes," however—especially considering the contrived way he resolves the film and the rather mawkish way he ends it—are the performances Koepp gets out of his actors and the substantial character study they all leave behind. It may sound illogical, but the more reality in a ghost story, the more convincing the ghosts.

NEW YORK POST, 9/10/99, p. 43, Rod Dreher

In "Stir of Echoes," a little boy sees and talks to a dead person, an angry spirit who torments the living in a furious attempt to get them to pay attention. Gee, haven't we been there before?

Okay, so it's not "The Sixth Sense"—which is one of the year's best films—but "Sixth Sense" fans may well appreciate this satisfyingly eerie genre effort from writer-director David Koepp, whose underrated "The Trigger Effect" was one of 1996's tensest thrillers.

Based on Richard Matheson's 1958 supernatural suspense novel, "Stir of Echoes" is studded with potent fright scenes and built on a rock-solid performance by the ever-dependable Kevin Bacon, who plays an Everyman with whom it's eerily easy to identify.

He's Tom Witzky, a Chicago phone company lineman who lives with his wife, Maggie (Kathryn Erbe), and son Jake (Zachary David Cope) in a close-knit blue-collar neighborhood. Tom's doing all right, though he's a bit down over the ordinariness of his working-stiff existence.

Everything changes when Maggie's flaky New Age sister (Ileana Douglas) hypnotizes skeptical Tom at a party. She secretly plants a suggestion in his subconscious: that he keep his mind open. Suddenly Tom's mind acts like a receiver, capturing premonitions of danger and flashbacks of a shockingly violent crime.

He even espies the pale ghost of a teenage girl (Jenny Morrison), who appears to be trying to contact him. Is this the unseen "Samantha" to whom Jake's always talking? And what does she want? Tom becomes hysterically obsessed with finding out.

"Stir of Echoes" excels as a study of creeping madness. Like Richard Dreyfuss in "Close Encounters of the Third Kind," Tom becomes so single-minded in his desperate quest for answers that he begins destroying his marriage, his career and his house.

Pity that the film telegraphs the answer to us long before Tom gets wise to it and that Koepp, whose direction is so artfully restrained through most of the film, re-creates the savage crime that led to the otherworldly activity.

What gives "Stir of Echoes" such resonance is the way Koepp anchors the paranormal happenings within a particular world—and the lives of believable characters. This flawed but worthwhile suspenser gets beneath your skin because Koepp understands, as did the makers of "Blair Witch" and "The Sixth Sense," that the more familiar horror is, the more effective it will be on the audience.

The haunted Witzky family, driven mad by a poltergeist with a secret, seems not like movie people, but the folks next door. "Stir of Echoes" cuts too close for comfort—which is to say, Koepp gets it right.

SIGHT AND SOUND, 6/00, p. 55, Demetrios Matheou

The present. Tom Witzky, his wife Maggie and young son Jake have recently moved to Chicago. At a party, the sceptical Tom agrees to let Maggie's sister hypnotise him. While under, he sees indistinct but frightening images which continue after the session.

He foresees the suicide of his friend Frank's son and the attempted kidnapping of his own son by a babysitter, which he prevents. Tom becomes withdrawn and psychotic, moping about the house trying to understand what the visions mean. He realises both he and Jake are able to see the ghost of a girl named Samantha, who disappeared some months before. Maggie encounters a Chicago cop who reveals that, like himself, Tom and Jake are "receivers", able to perceive the supernatural. Tom starts obsessively digging up the house. He finds Samantha's body and immediately has a vision of her murder by Frank's two sons. Frank arrives intending to kill Tom but, in a moment of guilt, shoots his remaining son and another accomplice instead. The Witzkys move away.

From the opening scene, in which five-year-old Jake speaks straight to camera, the similarities between *Stir of Echoes* and *The Sixth Sense* are strikingly apparent. Like Haley Joel Osment in last year's hit, both Jake and his dad have a gift for supernatural perception which alienates them from others (here Tom's marriage is on the line as he cracks up), but which sends chills through the audience. In both films, the creepy but less than malign ghosts seek a kind of redemption.

However, there are enough differences to allow *Stir of Echoes* to stand on its own merits. For a start, writer/director David Koepp's source material is the novel by eminent horror writer Richard Matheson, which adds the patina of a conventional whodunnit thriller to the supernatural core of the story. Koepp relocates the action from California to Chicago, but the working-class milieu remains, adding a further, social dimension: Maggie is concerned not only that her man is losing his mind, but that he can ill afford to lose his job; Samantha's murder will destroy the district's strong sense of community.

Tom's discontent at the outset of the film, feeling he has underachieved by being no more than a telephone lineman, provides the fuel for the whole movie. Very early on, he states that, "I never wanted to be famous. I just never expected to be so ordinary." His extraordinary gift is a painful panacea. There are other satisfying themes. The fateful instruction from his acerbic sister in-law when Tom is under hypnosis, to be more "open-minded", inadvertently opens the door for all kinds of unwelcome signals and intrusions. Beyond the pun, what's interesting is the difference in reaction of father and son towards what they see. Tom is disturbed, Jake unperturbed: demonstrating how a child's innocence and indeed open-mindedness are lost to life experience.

Although Samantha's ghost provides the film's heart-stopping moments, the supernatural plotting of the film is under-developed, not least in the exposition involving the psychic cop. Ultimately, it is Bacon's blue collar conflict that resonates: his obsessive digging, reminiscent of Richard Dreyfuss' fun with mashed potato in *Close Encounters of the Third Kind* (Koepp scripted the *Jurassic Park* movies) evokes the notion, call it cinematic pipedream, that for ordinary people it takes something extraordinary to provide a sense of self worth.

VILLAGE VOICE, 9/14/99, p. 146, Michael Atkinson

When they work, not merely as genre pieces but dream-stealing windows on our civilized weaknesses and vanities, horror movies can achieve a kind of primal profundity, a psychosocial commentary you feel between your toes. Sadly, that zany film-students-in-the-woods movie aside, supernatural narratives almost always deteriorate into literalism and exposition—ghost stories, for instance, may be the most infantilizing form of irrational experience, but they nearly always climax by providing succor for the unhappy dead. Once the paranormal is made normal, where's the beef?

Stir of Echoes, like *The Sixth Sense*, makes the most of its psychological tortures before it cops a therapeutic plea. Adapted by David Koepp (whose *The Trigger Effect* began in its own hothouse of domestic uneasiness) from a Richard Matheson novel, *Stir* is ultimately structured like a whodunit but fraught with anxiety. Though not as palpably damaged as *The Sixth Sense*'s grade-schooler, Kevin Bacon's half-educated Chicago lineman suffers mightily after being hypnotized (by New Agey sister-in-law Illeanna Douglas) at a party and thereafter experiences a series of disorienting visions. Koepp sticks to the rules (there's apparently no getting by without that old open-then-closed bathroom mirror trick), but revels in dislocation when he has the chance: the ghost in question (Jenny Morrison) has genuinely jolting appearances, a very real kidnapping by a babysitter is jacked up into a confrontational frenzy, and a scary dream in which neighbor Kevin Dunn appears in Bacon's living room babbling about murder is even scarier once Bacon wakes up and it begins to happen all over again.

Throughout, Koepp has made an interesting but irrelevant parallel between the otherworld and movies—Bacon's hypno trances are actually set in a vast, idealized movie theater, and the old crime he eventually uncovers is witnessed at first as unedited images. But it's the mad siege of home and family, a classic Matheson drill, that Koepp focuses steadily on, down to the chilly ending: Bacon's spirit-conversant preschool son (Zachary David Cope) sits tiny and implacable before a rising soundtrack storm of needy whispers.

Also reviewed in:
CHICAGO TRIBUNE, 9/10/99, Friday/p. M, Michael Wilmington
NEW YORK TIMES, 9/10/99, p. E18, Janet Maslin

VARIETY, 8/23-29/99, p. 107, Joe Leydon
WASHINGTON POST, 9/10/99, p. C5, Rita Kempley
WASHINGTON POST, 9/10/99, Weekend/p. 43, Desson Howe

STORY OF US, THE

A Universal Pictures release of a Castle Rock Entertainment presentation. *Executive Producer:* Jeffrey Stott and Frank Capra, III. *Producer:* Rob Reiner, Jessie Nelson, and Alan Zweiber. *Director:* Rob Reiner. *Screenplay:* Alan Zweibel and Jessie Nelson. *Director of Photography:* Michael Chapman. *Editor:* Robert Leighton and Alan Edward Bell. *Music:* Eric Clapton and Marc Shaiman. *Music Editor:* Scott Stambler. *Sound:* Robert Eber and (music) Tim Boyle. *Sound Editor:* Robert Grieve. *Casting:* Jane Jenkins and Leigh French. *Production Designer:* Lilly Kilvert. *Art Director:* Chris Burian-Mohr, Jess Gonchor, and Francesco Chianese. *Set Designer:* John Perry Goldsmith and Anthony D. Parrillo. *Set Decorator:* Gretchen Rau. *Set Dresser:* Loren P. Lyons. *Special Effects:* Paul Lombardi. *Costumes:* Shay Cunliffe. *Make-up:* Michael Germain. *Make-up (Bruce Willis):* Gerald Quist. *Make-up (Michelle Pfeiffer):* Ronnie Specter. *Make-up (Rita Wilson):* Gina Lamendola. *Stunt Coordinator:* Dick Ziker. *Running time:* 90 minutes. *MPAA Rating:* R.

CAST: Michelle Pfeiffer (Katie Jordan); Bruce Willis (Ben Jordan); Rita Wilson (Rachel); Julie Hagerty (Liza); Paul Reiser (Dave); Tim Matheson (Marty); Colleen Rennison (Erin, Aged 10); Jake Sandvig (Josh, Aged 12); Red Buttons (Arnie); Jayne Meadows (Dot); Tom Poston (Harry); Betty White (Lillian); Casey Boersma (Josh, Aged 2½); Rob Reiner (Stan); Dylan Boersma (Josh, Aged 3); Ken Lerner (Doctor Rifkin); Victor Raider-Wexler (Doctor Hopkins); Albert Hague (Doctor Siegler); Daniel Henson (Josh, Aged 7); Tara Blanchard (Erin, Aged 5); Adam Zweibel (Camper); Alan Zweibel (Uncle Shelby); Bill Kirchenbauer (Andy Kirby); Lucy Webb (Joanie Kirby); Jessie Nelson (Realtor); Tommy Tang (Cooking Teacher); Yaping (Store Clerk); James J. Ritz (Maitre d'); Ryan Townsend and Michael Chapman (Waiters); Jordan Lund (Clergyman); Robert Alan Beuth (Obstetrician); Marci Rosenberg (Sonia); Art Evans (George); Reneé Ridgeley (Sara); Matthew Moreno (Tax Driver).

LOS ANGELES TIMES, 10/15/99, Calendar/p. 2, Kenneth Turan

When the smiling, photogenic Jordans sit down to dinner, parents Katie and Ben like to engage 12-year-old Josh and 10-year-old Erin in a game called "high/low" in which each family member has to sound off on his or her best and worst experiences of the day.

Similarly, "The Story of Us," the dramatic comedy about a make-or-break summer in Katie and Ben's relationship, shows us the highs and lows in a marriage that has lasted 15 years but is now floundering. With their kids safely out of the way in camp, the Jordans embark on a trial separation, trying to figure out how what was once so good got so bad.

"The Story of Us," which stars Bruce Willis and Michelle Pfeiffer as the troubled Jordans, wants to be an honest look at the problems that can beset a modern marriage, and be funny at the same time, but it doesn't have the skills or the temperament to pull all that off. Written by Alan Zweibel ("It's Gary Shandling's Show" and the disastrous "North") and Jessie Nelson (the teary double bill of "Corinna, Corinna" and "Stepmom") and directed by Rob Reiner, "The Story of Us" has some affecting moments, but its manufactured crises and too-glib jokes give it a facile, fraudulent air.

A wannabe sensitive film that's scared of cutting too deeply, "The Story of Us" doesn't want to be real enough to jeopardize its homogenized humor. While it's already hard to accept carefully photographed major stars like Willis and Pfeiffer as regular folks with everyday problems, it's even harder when both their fun and their fury seem slickly scripted. Not only don't we feel the Jordans' pain, it's not clear that we even want to.

A prototypic Westside couple down to their monster sports utility vehicle, Craftsman-style house and fondness for Thai food and the Oceana Hotel, husband and wife face the camera separately, directly giving audiences their own sides of the story as the film displays their personal highs and lows.

Ben and Katie met when they both had starter jobs and a great deal more hair. He was a writer on a TV show dreaming of going out on his own; she was an office temp eager to create crossword puzzles. He got her attention by throwing handfuls of paper clips in her direction. Truly, love is grand.

That dichotomy of chaos versus order became the road map of this relationship and marriage. Katie was the obsessive one who kept the calendar and made the trains run on time, while Ben, though he furiously denied it, was the family's third child, a spontaneous big kid who was partial to Hawaiian shirts and wacky improvisations.

By the time Katie and Ben are thinking about divorce and hiding their problems from their kids (Colleen Rennison and Jake Sandvig), they've gotten so tired of each other's proclivities that they can't even be bothered to laugh at their partner's jokes.

Though these kinds of difficulties are real enough, the things Katie and Ben say to each other face to face and to us in extensive voice-over are too practiced to be effective. Lines such as "Fighting becomes the condition not the exception," "Some hurts you never completely get over" and "The loudest silences are filled with everything that's been said" all seem to come right out of some "Can This Marriage Be Saved?" relationship video.

Making the situation worse is the smug and obnoxious pals both Katie and Ben have. His, played by comic actors Paul Reiser and Reiner himself, try to decide if phone sex counts as cheating, while hers, especially Rita Wilson's Rachel, are so glib and breezy they couldn't sound more artificial. It's when it wanders outside the family circle that "The Story's" preoccupation with wisecracks is at its worst.

Pfeiffer and Willis acquit themselves as well as the script and direction allow, though Willis' romantic comedy timing does seem to have gotten rusty since his "Moonlighting" days. Their movie-stars-yelling-at-each-other relationship doesn't feel much more real than the happily married act they put on for their kids. It may fool some of the people, but it won't fool them all of the time.

NEW YORK, 10/25/99, p. 81, Peter Rainer

In Rob Reiner's *The Story of Us*, scripted by Alan Zweibel and Jessie Nelson, Bruce Willis and Michelle Pfeiffer play a married couple, with two preteen kids, who agree to a trial separation on the heels of their fifteenth wedding anniversary. Most of the movie is taken up with flashbacks and flash-forwards about what went right, what went wrong; there's lots of talking directly into the camera, lots of smiling through tears and cuddling and gnashing.

Willis plays a writer who wants his wife to be the sprite she was when he married her; Pfeiffer, a crossword-puzzle designer, wants everything neatly in place. He accuses her of lacking spontaneity, and the same charge could be leveled against this exhaustingly schematic hunk of sitcom blubberiness. The relationship between Willis and Pfeiffer is so tricked-up and fractured that we often have trouble figuring out where we are not to mention what the "issues" are. By showing us only the high and low points of the alliance, the filmmakers seem to be concocting a greatest-hits album of marital-movie clichés, dragging down their stars in the process. The mating dance between men and women is, of course, presented as a great and ineffable mystery, with everybody in the movie offering up his or her cosmic 2 cents. For a film that proudly proclaims "there are no answers," it's awfully smug about knowing all the questions.

NEW YORK POST, 10/15/99, p. 52, Jonathan Foreman

"The Story of Us," a dramatic comedy about a couple on the brink of divorce after 15 years of marriage, doesn't live up to the promise of its trailers.

It has funny and poignant moments, fine performances by both Michelle Pfeiffer and Bruce Willis, and a message worth delivering. But it's so crammed with flashbacks that it loses momentum.

Its best quality—being honest about the difficulties of making a relationship work over time—is compromised by a tendency to pull the really devastating punches, and by some weak sitcom-esque scenes involving secondary characters.

When we meet comedy writer Ben (Willis) and crossword puzzle writer Katie (Pfeiffer) they are about to send their two kids off to summer camp—and to embark on a trial separation.

It's not clear which of them has initiated the separation, but family life has sapped the romance from their lives and the two of them can hardly spend five minutes together without getting into a fight.

They've been to counseling before. But neither Ben nor Katie has been able to deal with the fact that the qualities that drew them to each other years ago aren't enough to make life together seem tolerable.

He never wears a watch and she is a compulsively well-organized scheduler, forced by his spontaneity/immaturity to become the "designated driver" of the marriage.

"The Story of Us" refuses to take sides—and that's unusual for a movie about marital discord.

Pfeiffer works hard and gives a strong performance, though her otherworldly (and rather gaunt) beauty is so extraordinary that it tends to undermine the movie's believability. In the real world, someone like her couldn't walk down the street without causing cars to crash, but in the film no one seems to think her looks are anything special.

As for Willis, this is the best performance he has ever given. Sure, there are a couple of moments when he seems to be about to break into one of his trademark smirks. But he achieves genuine dramatic power in a couple of heartbreaking scenes.

Rita Wilson does a spot-on Carrie Fisher imitation as Katie's best friend. Paul Reiser, however, is wasted as Ben's cynical agent, who believes that online sex doesn't count as cheating.

Director Rob Reiner uses some of the same stylistic devices that worked more effectively in "When Harry Met Sally." In addition to copious flashbacks and voice-overs, he has his characters address the camera directly. He also has fun denoting the passage of time by changing their hairdos and clothes.

In some ways the film seems like a sequel to "Harry," though it doesn't hold together nearly as well. That's partly because the script, by Alan Zweibel and Jessie Nelson, doesn't find the right balance of bitter and sweet, and is itself a mix of the fresh and the very stale.

It may also be that the unromantic lesson that "The Story of Us" propounds—that while marriage is better than the alternative, it's also really hard work—just isn't the kind of thing people expect from a big-budget studio film.

NEWSDAY, 10/15/99, Part II/p. B7, John Anderson

The glibly anesthetized style of director Rob Reiner couldn't have been put to more irritating purpose than in "The Story of Us," the anatomy of a bad marriage, whose characters are relentlessly, tediously bitter, but whose cynicism is easily matched by our own: Given the vaguely comedic nature of the film, we know the payoff is going to be a happy ending. The effect is something like nausea.

Essentially, "The Story of Us" is a divorce movie made for 7-year-olds. Maybe. One of its more preposterous suggestions is that the children of the warring Katie and Ben Jordan (Michelle Pfeiffer and Bruce Willis), longtime marrieds and habitual screamers, wouldn't be the first to know that their parents' marriage was on the rocks. Regardless, Ben and Katie wait until the kids (Jake Sandvig, Colleen Rennison) go off to summer camp to go their separate ways. Almost immediately—and considering the crassly deafening battles we've seen, this is a bit hard to swallow—they can't stop calling each other. A coy courtship develops. They have dinner. And then Gettysburg breaks out all over again.

The entire movie bobs and sways with sea-sickening regularity—nasty battles, flashbacks to better times, talking-head interviews with Ben and Katie (Reiner, mercifully, abandons this quickly), a couple of extended gags that limp along gamely and several fantasy segments that don't work at all. (At one point, crusty vets Jayne Meadows, Tom Poston, Red Buttons and Betty White, playing the couple's parents, join the two in bed).

Reiner, however, is oblivious to the fundamental flaw in his movie: Nothing could be funny enough to counterbalance the venom exchanged by Ben and Katie (Willis and Pfeiffer, ironically, may be too effective for the movie to work). Then, too, only in a Rob Reiner movie could such a damaged union be mended so blithely. The lingering sense is of having been grossly insulted.

As if it didn't have enough trouble, "The Story of Us" is burdened by an uncharacteristically trite Eric Clapton song, "(I) Get Lost," which recurs with such inappropriate regularity that it becomes far more humorous than anything else in the film. The opening lyrics, bidding for the heights of banality, are "I'm sorry." At least someone's being honest.

SIGHT AND SOUND, 6/00, p. 55, Geoffrey Macnab

Los Angeles, the present. Ben and Katie Jordan have been married for 15 years. He's a writer, carefree and spontaneous. She works as a crossword compiler. They maintain the façade of a happy relationship for the sake of their two kids,—Josh, aged 12, and Erin, aged 10—but the cracks are beginning to show.

During the summer, while the kids are sent away to camp, Ben and Katie agree to a trial separation. Ben moves out of the family's suburban house. During their time apart, they reflect on their marriage, what they loved about each other and what went wrong between them. When they visit the kids in camp, they sleep in separate beds. Ben and Katie have dinner together and it looks as if they've recaptured their old spark. They go upstairs to the bedroom, but before they can sleep with one another they begin squabbling again.

They agree to a divorce and plan to meet the kids on the bus back from summer camp, take them out to dinner and tell about the split. But while waiting for the bus to arrive, Katie decides she can't go through with the divorce. She realises she still loves Ben. The family is reunited, seemingly now at last happy.

With *The Story of Us*, Rob Reiner attempts the near impossible: to make an upbeat romantic comedy about a marital breakdown. The film begins misleadingly. Early on, when Ben addresses the camera directly as if talking to his therapist, he seems to be discussing a relationship which is already over. Just to emphasise how bleak the prospects are for the once-loving couple, Reiner plays a lugubrious Eric Clapton ballad again and again on the soundtrack. "I wonder if there's anything more horrible than a man and wife who hate each other," Strindberg once wrote. The problem with *The Story of Us* is that Bruce Willis and Michelle Pfeiffer don't feel any animosity for one another. "Fighting became the language of the relationship," we're told, but we wait in vain for the pot-smashing, drunken spats and vicious insults which usually come with *Scenes from a Marriage*-style dramas. Instead, Reiner throws in some cutesy dinner table scenes, in which mom and pop play at domestic harmony for the sake of the kids, and one or two sequences in which they sit around discussing their love lives with their slick, superficial friends. In their bright little corner of affluent, suburban LA, nobody suffers much. Pfeiffer is grumpy Willis leaves her to do most of the organising and housework. ("I'm sick and tired of being the designated driver in this marriage," she complains.) Willis, for his part, is exasperated at how straitlaced she has become. This, it seems, is grounds enough for separation.

In some ill-judged flashbacks, we see the couple in their courtship days. To signal how carefree and happy they were way back then, both sport peculiar hairstyles. (Willis looks like a band member from Reiner's earlier comedy *This is Spinal Tap* while Pfeiffer is all unflattering curls.) In one redundant interlude, we see them go to Venice to try to reignite their romance. Reiner can't resist picture-postcard shots of them dancing at dawn by the lagoon or playing footsie on a gondola. The point seems to be that relationships don't break down in blazing rows. It's the little things—irritating habits, domestic oversights—which cause them to come unstuck. Couples grow apart almost without noticing it. This may be so, but it doesn't make for an exciting movie. Reiner therefore throws in some slapstick (tugs of war with the kids, lovemaking on the kitchen table) and wheels on several eccentric marriage-guidance counsellors for comic relief. The star casting doesn't help. It is hard to accept Willis and Pfeiffer as an ordinary couple, struggling with everyday problems.

Nothing is at stake. Pfeiffer starts seeing another man but the relationship is never serious. Willis moves into his own apartment, where he broods and learns to do his own shopping. The question isn't whether they'll get back together but when. Shorn of tension, the movie meanders along in its own enervating way to its pre ordained conclusion. Prettily shot, well-enough acted, it ends up seeming utterly inconsequential.

VILLAGE VOICE, 10/26/99, p. 164, Justine Elias

Ben and Katie Jordan are wealthy, attractive Californians with dream jobs (novelist and crossword-puzzle designer), a perfectly appointed house, a massive SUV, and two adolescent children who are neither gun-toting psychopaths nor drooling morons. Nobody's hitting, cursing, or fooling around, and they just took a nice, relaxing vacation in Italy.

Yet in *The Story of Us,* this is cause for serious complaint: As soon as Ben (Bruce Willis) and Katie (Michelle Pfeiffer) pack their kids off to summer camp, they set about getting a divorce. Why? Ben is carefree, Katie is rigid, and they have trouble listening to each other. In this maudlin, irritating marital drama directed with no particular sensitivity by Rob Reiner, the Jordans have nothing better to do than rehash their 15 years of marriage and numerous attempts at couples therapy—which are all laid out, movie-trailer style, as sketchy, disjointed flashbacks or deadly dull exchanges of pause-filled answering-machine messages.

It is possible, of course, that there is more going on here than meets the eye. Perhaps Ben and Katie are being driven insane, as the audience surely will be, by the film's mellow-mindfuck soundtrack, which reaches a fiendish climax with a reprise of "Classical Gas." Perhaps they are nauseated by their friends, played by Rob Reiner (obnoxious), Rita Wilson (loud), and Paul Reiser (unctuous), who are not real people but synthetic shtick-delivery systems. Or maybe *The Story of Us,* like Willis's most recent film, *The Sixth Sense,* is a quiet horror movie about seeing dead people-confused, restless spirits who really ought to move the hell on.

Also reviewed in:
CHICAGO TRIBUNE, 10/15/99, Friday/p. A, Michael Wilmington
NEW YORK TIMES, 10/15/99, p. E14, Janet Maslin
NEW YORKER, 11/1/99, p. 123, Anthony Lane
VARIETY, 10/11-17/99, p. 43, Emanuel Levy
WASHINGTON POST, 10/15/99, p. C5, Stephen Hunter
WASHINGTON POST, 10/15/99, Weekend/p. 43, Desson Howe

STRAIGHT STORY, THE

A Walt Disney Pictures release. *Executive Producer:* Pierre Edelman and Michael Polaire. *Producer:* Mary Sweeney and Neal Edelstein. *Director:* David Lynch. *Screenplay:* John Roach and Mary Sweeney. *Director of Photography:* Freddie Francis. *Director of Photography (Aerial):* David Nowell and David Butler. *Editor:* Mary Sweeney. *Music:* Angelo Badalamenti. *Music Editor:* Walter Spencer. *Sound:* Susumu Tokunow and (music) John Neff. *Sound Editor:* Ron Eng. *Casting:* Jane Alderman and Lynn Blumenthal. *Production Designer:* Jack Fisk. *Set Decorator:* Barbara Haberecht. *Special Effects:* Gary D'Amico. *Costumes:* Patricia Norris. *Make-up (Sissy Spacek):* Bob Harper. *Make-up (Special Effects):* Crist Ballas. *Stunt Coordinator:* Rick LeFevour and Jim Fierro. *Running time:* 110 minutes. *MPAA Rating:* G.

CAST: Richard Farnsworth (Alvin Straight); Sissy Spacek (Rose Straight); Harry Dean Stanton (Lyle Straight); Everett McGill (Tom, the John Deere Dealer); John Farley (Thorvald Olsen); Kevin Farley (Harald Olsen); Jane Galloway Heitz (Dorothy); Joseph A. Carpenter (Bud); Donald Wiegert (Sig); Tracey Maloney (Nurse); Dan Flannery (Doctor Gibbons); Jennifer Edwards-Hughes (Brenda); Ed Grennan (Pete); Jack Walsh (Apple); Gil Pearson (Bus Driver); Barbara June Patterson (Woman on Bus); Anastasia Webb (Crystal); Max Guidry (Steve); Bill McCallum (Rat); Barbara Robertson (Deer Woman); James Cada (Danny Riordan); Sally Wingert (Darla Riordan); Barbara Kingsley (Janet Johnson); Jim Haun (Johnny Johnson); Wiley Harker (Verlyn Heller); Randy Wiedenhoff and Jerry E. Anderson (Firemen); John Lordan (Priest); Russ Reed (Mt. Zion Bartender); Ralph Feldhacker (Farmer on Tractor).

CHRISTIAN SCIENCE MONITOR, 10/15/99, p. 15, David Sterritt

Starting today, the biggest surprise of this year's Cannes film festival will be stirring up talk in theaters. David Lynch, known for ultraviolent movies like "Blue Velvet" and surreal TV fare like "Twin Peaks," has found still another way to give audiences a jolt of astonishment: He's made a G-rated picture for the Walt Disney Company, spinning a tale so kind and gentle that it makes his previous career seem like a brilliantly filmed nightmare from which he's finally awakened.

In short, "The Straight Story" is a major turnaround from a filmmaker who has earned international acclaim as a chronicler of dark, disturbing dreams. But has this hugely original artist really changed course as abruptly as it appears? Or has he simply found a new vocabulary to express his longtime taste for extremes—directing a picture that's radically sweet, daringly goodhearted, humane, and compassionate to the point of extravagance?

Based on real events, "The Straight Story" centers on an ornery old man named Alvin Straight, played by Richard Farnsworth in a performance that should loom very large when Oscar time rolls around. Alvin lives with his daughter in rural Iowa, where their uneventful routine is interrupted by news that his brother, Lyle, has become ill.

The brothers haven't spoken since a quarrel 10 years earlier, and Alvin feels a flood of regret when he hears of Lyle's misfortune. His first impulse is to pay Lyle an overdue visit.

While Alvin is no longer able to drive a car, he wants to make the trip on his own. The solution: Hitching a supply wagon to the tractor of his rider-style lawnmower, he sets off for his brother's Wisconsin home at a speed so slow that the 300-mile-plus journey will take several weeks of solitary travel—if the aging engine manages to get him there at all.

The speed of Alvin's lawnmower sets the tone for the movie. In some ways, this is the flip side of Lynch's last picture, "Lost Highway," which was as fast and hallucinatory as "The Straight Story" is slow and lucid. Don't think the movie lacks humor or drama, though. Alvin's gradual voyage brings him into temporary contact with all sorts of people, most of them amazed at the audacity of his journey yet eager to help him reach the finish line. Few films have been more eloquent about the kindness of strangers and the redeeming power we tap into when we recognize our shared humanity.

Lynch has often said he turned to the shadowy side of moviemaking—starting with "Eraserhead," his boldly inventive debut film—because of the shock he experienced as a young man when he moved to an East Coast city and learned that life seems to have an evil side he'd never dreamed of during his Midwestern upbringing. Seen in this light, "The Straight Story" isn't so much a new departure for Lynch as a long-awaited return to the peaceful, easygoing territory that has always lain beneath the surface of his gloomier visions.

It's also important to note that "The Straight Story" has a dark side of its own, contradicting some critics who claim it views the world through a sappy, rose-colored lens. Alvin is an adorable figure in many ways, but he's also a deeply stubborn man whose self-willed insistence on doing things, his way—why doesn't he simply take a bus or train?—could sabotage the whole purpose of his journey if Lyle doesn't survive until he arrives. Lynch has long regarded human ego as a stumbling block to intuition and creativity, so this aspect of the film bears thinking about.

The movie's view of family values is also remarkably complex. We hear a lot about the importance of family life, but we never see an intact family on the screen, and the dialogue paints a subtly disturbing picture of the gap between rhetoric and reality in this all-important area.

Although it's largely a one-character show, "The Straight Story" benefits from strong performances by Sissy Spacek and Harry Dean Stanton, artful cinematography by the great Freddie Francis ("Glory," the 1991 version of "Cape Fear"), and sometimes overdone music by Angelo Badalamenti, whose "Twin Peaks" theme was almost a national anthem a few years ago.

FILM QUARTERLY, Fall 2000, p. 26, Tim Kreider and Rob Content

The Straight Story begins a lot like a David Lynch film, specifically like *Blue Velvet*: first we see a dreamy montage of slow-motion scenes from a small-town, middle-American Eden (cinematographer Freddie Francis filling in for Norman Rockwell and composer Angelo Badalamenti for Aaron Copland), and then the camera drifts down to a neatly mown suburban yard. A fat woman with goggles and a tanning reflector is sunning herself on a lawn chair, blindly groping for Hostess Sno-balls on a nearby plate—a characteristically Lynchian figure, the Felliniesque grotesque next door. Nothing happens for a Lynchianly long time. The woman runs out of Sno-balls and gets up to go in for more. Because we know we are watching a David Lynch film, there is a certain expectant air—that ominous, low-register thrum of imminent catastrophe. Then we hear a cry and thud from inside—recalling the stroke that felled Jeffrey Beaumont's father and began *Blue Velvet*'s dark adventure. And then, this being a David Lynch film, we await our inevitable descent into the black and crawly underbelly of this overbright world.

Which, as everyone by now knows, never happens. The most famous thing about *The Straight Story* is that it is rated G. (Who could have imagined, after seeing *Blue Velvet* in 1986, that we would ever see the credit "Walt Disney Pictures Presents a Film by David Lynch"?) It's been described by critics as sweet, simple, and sentimental; authentic, buccolic, and unironic. Its hero, Alvin Straight, is a genuinely good man, honest and direct, dispensing advice and helping folks when he can—a guy we can admire. And, even more incredibly, almost every character he encounters on his odyssey is also honest and friendly and helpful and just basically decent. There is none of the ugly sex and violence, the lurid, nightmarish surrealism, that lie at the heart of other David Lynch films. It appears, however amazingly, to be a film devoid of darkness or duplicity, without so much as a single cuss word.

Anthony Lane of *The New Yorker* dismissed The *Straight Story* as a "comic coda to *Lost Highway*." Although the film is clearly not comic at its heart, it does, like its predecessor, use one story to mask another, more sinister, one. *Lost Highway*'s protagonist Fred represses all memory of having murdered his wife in a jealous rage; he only glimpses himself howling over her dismembered corpse on grainy videotape, and, in the film's second half, re-imagines his story as a pulpy film noir with himself as the unwitting dupe of his wife (reincarnated as a femme fatale)—instead of as the villain he truly is. (As he tells two detectives in the film's first half, "I like to remember things my own way.") Similarly, Alvin Straight never brings himself to tell the straight story of his own past; he tells, instead, incomplete and disguised versions of it to the strangers he meets, hears echoes of it in the stories they tell him, and sees distorted reenactments of it in one scene after another.

The real story of *The Straight Story* turns out not to be very straightforward at all, but involuted and hidden—buried, as in *Lost Highway*, within the ostensible narrative like a repressed memory. This movie is about how a mean drunk named Alvin Straight lost his daughter's children to the state because he let one of them get burned in a fire. This is the only way the film makes sense as a unified whole, as anything other than the meandering picaresque most reviewers thought it was. Alvin Straight is riding his mower with its wagon all those hundreds of miles along highway shoulders not on an errand of forgiveness, but as an ordeal of atonement.

There is darkness here beneath the bright autumn colors, and evil concealed in Alvin's heart. There is the history of a family destroyed by alcoholism and abuse. There is fire and death.

Is this all really unexpected? *The Straight Story* is a David Lynch film, after all.

That a story is seldom truly "straight" is one of the defining insights of literary modernism; writers like James Joyce and Henry James took the unreliability of first-person narrators to new heights of self-consciousness and, sometimes, new depths of self-deception. And yet this mistrust of the ostensible "story," by now instinctive in reading literature, seems not to have penetrated criticism of the superficially more transparent medium of film. The title of David Lynch's latest is not just an obvious pun but a warning and a test; it warns us not to be deceived by appearances in this case, by an ingenuous claim of forthrightness, a frank demeanor, or an honest face.

The story that Alvin tells of his own past, piece by piece, to the various people he meets is full of conspicuous gaps and contradictions. Take his story about his hard drinking: that he'd developed "a mournful taste for alcohol" during the war in France and became a mean drunk, but was helped to give up drinking by a preacher after he got home. Or his story about his daughter Rose: that she had four children, but that the state, misinterpreting her speech (or neurological) impediment as evidence that she was an unfit mother, took them away when one of them was burned in a fire. Or Alvin's account of his falling-out with his brother Lyle: the one time he's directly asked what was at issue, he vaguely waves the question off ("anger ... vanity ..."). Or even his answering "I did" when Lyle, at the film's end, asks if he drove his mower "just to see" him. None of these stories is quite straight. In fact, none of them stands up to much scrutiny at all.

If Alvin gave up drinking shortly after his return from World War II, why did drink figure in the fight that estranged him from Lyle ten years ago? Why doesn't Rose at least get to visit her children, or talk to them? And why do we learn so little about Alvin's breach with his brother? The fact that the details of what is ostensibly the central conflict in the film are left so conspicuously blank suggests that we ought to ask what else the conflict might involve. What *is* the real reason Alvin's making this trip?

Alvin first tells a small part of his story to the pregnant runaway who shares his campfire. It's the story of what happened to Rose's children: "Someone else was supposed to be watchin' them, and there was a fire, and her second boy got burned real bad." Note the vague references—"someone else"—and passive constructions—"there was a fire" and "got burned." As he speaks, we see a series of dissolves from one allusive image of abandonment and emptiness to another: the bare yellow wall of Alvin and Rose's house with a fly-swatter hanging from a nail; a child's ball rolling slowly down the sidewalk; Rose's wistful face reflected in the window glass; cigarette smoke curling in the air. Alvin shares this piece of his past to impress upon the girl how much her own family must miss her: "There's not a day goes by that she doesn't pine for those kids." But Alvin's story is only tangentially relevant to the girl's predicament. He's leaving something out.

Kenneth Turan of the *L. A. Times* calls Alvin "the Ann Landers of the Open Road," who "seems to know just how to solve the problems of the people, young and old, he meets by the side of the road." But the advice he gives the runaway has more to do with his own regrets and wishes than with her dilemma. Here's Richard Corliss's account, from *Time,* of the parable he offers her:

> The old man tells her that he used to give each of his kids a stick and say, "You break that." Of course they could. Then he'd tell them to tie some sticks in a bundle and try to break that. And they couldn't. "Then I'd say, 'That bundle—that's a family.'" The next morning, the old man wakes up to find the girl gone, with the hint that she'll be returning home. On the ground is a bundle of sticks with a bow tied around it.

Well, this is nice. But it should be pointed out that Alvin's quaint metaphor for strength through unity, the bundle of sticks tied together, is not his own invention. The "fasces," a bound bundle of rods containing an ax with the blade protruding forward, was an object borne ceremonially before Roman magistrates as an emblem of imperial power. The term "fascism" is derived from this emblem, a symbol of invincible strength through monolithic solidarity and submission to a single will—typically that of a tyrannical patriarch who ends up getting people killed. Even if you tie a pretty bow around that, it's still ugly.

But, more explicitly, this scene is also an allusion to *Ran*, Akira Kurosawa's adaptation of Shakespeare's tragedy of a senescent patriarch and warrior. Hidetora, the Great Lord of the Ichimonji clan, uses exactly the same demonstration to instruct his three sons in the value of filial unity: he gives them each an arrow to break, which they do easily, and then challenges them to try to break a bundle of three arrows. Except that Hidetora's youngest son angrily smashes the bundle across his knee and calls his father on his blatant hypocrisy. "You've spilled an ocean of blood," he cries. "You showed no mercy, no pity. We, too, are children of this age, weaned on strife and blood. We are your sons, yet you count on our fidelity—in our eyes, that makes you a fool, a senile old fool." Alvin Straight, unlike Hidetora, goes unchallenged when he mouths platitudes about loyalty and peace that are utterly at odds with his own history of violence and betrayal.

Alvin's performance as patriarch of his own clan doesn't seem to have matched his rhetoric about the unbreakability of the family bond. His own family *has* been sundered. He hasn't spoken to his brother for ten years. His daughter Rose's children have been taken from her. The rest of his children, like Hidetora's, don't seem to have taken the lesson of the stick-breaking game straight to heart; there's no evidence of any contact between Alvin and any of Rose's six surviving siblings. (We overhear Rose on the phone discussing Alvin and Lyle's feud with someone, possibly a family member, but Alvin himself stays off the line.) Where has all his family gone? Dispersed across the country, like so many American families—or driven apart, like the Ichimonji brothers, by the divisive example of their father's cruelty?

It does not seem like too broad a generalization to say that families in David Lynch films are not happy families. They are more likely to be incestuous and violent, twisted or torn apart by repressed memories and unspeakable secrets: Fred in *Lost Highway* murders his wife; Marietta Pace in *Wild at Heart* is complicit in her husband's death and tries to seduce her daughter's boyfriend; Leland Palmer molests and kills his daughter Laura in *Twin Peaks*; in *Blue Velvet* Frank Booth obviously (and Jeffrey Beaumont, less obviously) has basic Oedipal issues to work through. And let it suffice to say of *Eraserhead* that Henry Spencer's dinner with his girlfriend Mary's family, the Xes, is among the least pleasant of all the strained and unpleasant family dinner scenes ever filmed (possibly excepting the one in *Fire Walk with Me)*, and that the nuclear family unit formed by Henry and Mary and their infant is also less than traditionally strong and nurturing. Given all that, we would be willing marks if we weren't skeptical about any family-values platitudes uttered by one of Lynch's characters, or suspicious of a Lynchian family that *didn't* conceal an internecine crime at its heart.

David Lynch tells the ugly truth in *The Straight Story* not in words but in images, powerfully suggestive visual metaphors. In the film's only scene of genuine action or suspense, Alvin Straight almost loses control of his makeshift mower/wagon coming downhill into a small town where the local fire department is conducting a training exercise on a burning abandoned house. As the old man desperately brakes and grapples with the wheel, hurtling faster and faster down-hill, out of control, the camera cuts back and forth in a blur between his frantic face and the blazing house nearby. The high scream of the mower's overstrained engine and the engulfing roar of the fire become one terrifying noise. Anthony Lane shrugs this scene off as one of Lynch's "bursts of calculated strangeness" those irrepressibly wacky trademark idiosyncrasies popping up again in a film where they're only distracting. But this burning house is not just a surreal non sequitur; it's one of the central images in the film. This scene functions as a flashback to the earlier fire, the one in which Alvin's grandchildren were burned. Alvin's face, bathed in sweat and flickering orange with firelight, and his eyes, bulging and rolling in his head like a frightened animal's, express a terror that transcends his immediate situation. When intercut with those quick, jarring shots of the blazing house, the real object of that terror is unmistakable. Alvin is the unnamed "someone" who was supposed to be watching Rose's kids. He let his grandson get burned. He caused his daughter's children to be taken away by the state. After he manages to stop his tractor, he sits panting and shaking in terror, staring at nothing, the burning house clearly framed in the background. He is trembling not just in reaction to his near-accident, but in an abreaction to that original trauma—another time when Alvin Straight lost control and events took on their own scary, unstoppable momentum.

This underlying, untold story makes sense of his whole journey, uniting episodes that have no other narrative connection and nothing else in common: the burning house, a woman hitting a deer on a highway, war stories told in a bar. These seemingly random meetings and tangential tales—Lynch's "bursts of calculated strangeness"—are all integral, each one another clue to the straight story. The situations Alvin encounters are reiterations of his own crimes and failures, confrontations with his own denial.

The driver hitting the deer is no self-indulgent directorial digression but a crucial episode. Again, as in the scene of the burning house, the camera focuses on Alvin's reaction, zooming in on his face in an almost subliminally rapid, staccato succession of increasingly close shots as he witnesses the offscreen accident that we only hear. Again, his horror is not just reaction but abreaction; he's hearing an echo of his own accident. Alvin pulls out his canes and hobbles up to a car that has slaughtered a deer in the road, and finds the driver hysterical, weeping and shrieking. She's tried everything, she explains—honking the horn, rolling down the window and banging her hand on the door, even playing Public Enemy real loud. That's thirteen deer she's hit in the last seven weeks. "And I *love* deer!" she blurts out before getting disgustedly back into her car and peeling out.

This is a strange episode, its absurdist comedy seeming false and hollow in contrast to the bleakness of the surrounding landscape and the ceaseless sound of the wind ruffling through the dry grass. This driver isn't telling a straight story, either. Although she rails against the perverse luck that keeps throwing sacrificial victims at her, her killing streak is her own fault. Sure, deer do have a regrettable way of jumping in front of cars on country back roads—but, *thirteen* in *seven weeks?* During the *daytime?* That's more than bad luck. The fact is, she was driving way too fast; her car veered around Alvin's rig just as he was riding by a NO PASSING ZONE sign. The reason she keeps hitting deer is that she's a reckless driver. "Where do they *come* from?" she demands, looking helplessly out at the few sparse, bare trees in the landscape. But these deaths aren't being visited upon her by any cruel, arbitrary fate. She is Alvin's counterpart in her continuing inability to take responsibility for the terrible (and not unpredictable) consequences of a heedless urgency. After she screeches out of sight, there is a long, mournful shot of Alvin standing there in the road, thoughtfully nudging the deer's limp head with the toe of his boot.

In the very next shot we see him that evening cooking venison over his fire, glancing uneasily over his shoulder at an inexplicable herd of statues of deer who seem to be watching him. This is not just a cheap sight gag; these stolidly haunting presences represent the accusing memory of his human victims. Although there are about a dozen statues in the field, the shot when Alvin looks back at them is framed so that we see four of them "staring" at him; Rose, we'll remember, had four children. In the next scene, the deer's antlers have been mounted like a hood ornament on the front of his rig, where they remain visible for the rest of the film. They're particularly prominent in the frame after he's almost lost control near the burning house.

Animal trophies figure prominently in Lynch's work as symbols of casual human violence. Scarcely an interior in *Twin Peaks* is without a stuffed carcass; the whole town is densely populated by the hunted and mounted. The series' preoccupation with the fierce passions that possess parents and claim their children as victims leaves little doubt as to the meaning of so much taxidermy: it symbolizes human hungers, both carnivorous and carnal. Alvin Straight, from what we can see, is exclusively carnivorous, subsisting solely on processed meat products. And as for carnality, he did father fourteen children—about as many deer as that woman's killed in the last few weeks. Most likely, it was another of Alvin's appetites—his "taste for liquor"—that got his grandson burned. The antlers are a token of his past sins and a symbol of his new penitence. (It's not incidental, either, that the lawnmower he needs to make his journey is a John *Deere*, its logo the silhouette of a rampant buck.) Alvin's trophy alludes to that same central disaster—an innocent creature harmed by the carelessness of someone who claimed to love it, who couldn't understand why this sort of thing kept happening to him.

Yes, kept happening—because, as we learn later, that fire wasn't the first time Alvin was at fault in a tragedy. Sitting in a bar with another old veteran, Alvin reveals that as a sniper in the war he accidentally shot and killed one of his own men, a Polish kid from Milwaukee named Kotz. Artists have often used pastoral settings to disguise commentaries on the corruption and betrayals of civil life (sometimes, most famously in Virgil's *Eclogues*, on the troubled fates of aged soldiers). In a pre-millennial year that saw more than its share of triumphalist rhetoric about the "painful but necessary job well done," David Lynch shows us memories of the Second World War which refuse to paper over the disillusionments of the postwar period. For Alvin, "homed" to rural Laurens, Iowa, what followed was a lifetime of secret remorse that expressed itself in drunkenness and cruelty, eventually estranging him from his family. The original trauma, an honest but fatal mistake, brought on the hard drinking that led to later, less forgivable, lapses of judgment.

Even the war stories these two old vets swap refer back to the unspoken story of the film—the fire. The tale the other vet tells is about all his buddies being killed, burned alive, by an incendiary bomb. We actually hear the explosion as he remembers, faint with the distance of decades—another echo of Alvin's own catastrophe. It is significant that the story Alvin does bring himself to share in response is a confession of long-repressed guilt, especially that he describes the man he killed as "a little fella." Groping to find a way to begin, he awkwardly repeats the phrase, emphasizing it—"He was a *little* fella,"—as though it explains what he's really trying to convey. (We shouldn't forget Alvin's horrified memory of the German adolescents—"moon-faced boys"—it was his job to kill.) Though harrowing enough, even this story is an evasion, another disguised allusion to his own grandchild, "a little fella" whose side Alvin was supposed to be on, someone else he was supposed to be watching out for, another one of his own whom he hurt without meaning to.

In this same scene, Alvin admits that he came back from the war an alcoholic. "I was *mean,*" he says. But, he says, a minister helped him "put some distance between [him]self and the bottle," as though he had gone on the wagon a long time ago. Later, however, talking to a priest in a cemetery, he acknowledges that liquor was a catalyst in his falling out with Lyle. The apparent inconsistency between these two stories makes us wonder what really occasioned Alvin's reform. The clearest glimpse we ever get of the man Alvin Straight has been all his life—quick-tempered, impulsive, and violent—is after he's been brought back from his first, failed attempt to leave town. He deliberately fetches his shotgun, takes it out in back of his house, aims, and executes his old, broken-down mower—which explodes into flames.

Images of fire recur throughout Lynch's films: a desert cabin implodes in a fiery cloud in *Lost Highway;* in *Blue Velvet* the monstrous image of Jeffrey smacking Dorothy Vallens dissolves in a sheet of fire; billowing flames fill the credits and gigantic flaring match heads punctuate the scenes of *Wild at Heart.* Also in *Wild at Heart,* Lula is never quite told the straight story about the fire that killed her father, the memory of which still makes her shudder: It was deliberately set by her mother's lover, Santos. It's already been intimated that there was more to the fire in *The Straight Story* than Alvin lets on. We see fire again and again in the film, not only in the conflagrations of the house and mower but in domesticated forms— in the campfires he builds every night, in the bonfire at the bikers' camp, and, of course, in the glowing ends of his cherished cigars. Isn't it implied that Alvin may have *set* the fire, passing out with a lighted Swisher Sweet, that burned his daughter's child?

The straight story of Alvin's life would seem to have gone more like this: World War II turned the strengths of his rural upbringing—his patience as a hunter, his skill as a marksman, his commitment to protecting his brothers-in-arms-into the makings of a tragedy and a source of shame. The psychological damage to him was permanent, only fermented and made more potent by his alcoholism and denial. Traumatized far beyond his own awareness of the damage, Alvin Straight lived out the next 40 years—his entire adult lifetime—as an abusive drunk who impregnated his wife fourteen times, injured one of his grandchildren through his negligence and caused four of them to be taken into the custody of the state, alienated his brother, and ended up living in near-isolation with his damaged, now childless daughter in a small, lonely, too-quiet house. This reconstruction, if even close to correct, makes new, more somber sense of Alvin's signature line (singled out by some critics as mawkish screenwriting): "The worst part of bein' old is remembering when you was young."

Seeing Alvin's journey as one of atonement rather than of forgiveness is the only way to make sense of its strange, self-imposed restrictions. Alvin won't accept an offered ride when his mower breaks down, and politely but obstinately refuses not once but three times to enter his benefactors' house even just to use their phone. (Like another old cowboy who almost killed one of his own, John Wayne's Ethan Edwards at the end of *The Searchers,* Alvin only stands in the doorway, denying himself the comforts of domestic civilization.) At night, camped out in their back yard, he watches wistfully as the lights go out in their windows. His trip is not just the necessary means of getting to his brother's house; it's an ordeal ritual, its rigors and privations rigidly maintained as a form of self-flagellation.

Alvin has undertaken this journey not just because his brother has had a stroke and may not live much longer, but because he knows he's not going to live much longer himself. He tells his daughter the doctor said he was "gonna live to be a hundred," but this is far from the straight story. What the doctor told him was that his hips were going, he was in the early stages of emphysema, his circulation was failing, and his diet was bad. "If you don't make some changes quickly," he concluded, "there'll be some serious consequences." But it's pretty clear that Alvin Straight isn't going to be making any changes; he's petrified just looking at the medical equipment in the clinic, and insists that he's not going to pay for an operation, or have X-rays taken, or even use a walker. And for the rest of the film he keeps right on smoking his Swisher Sweets and eating raw wieners and Braunschweiger. He's a stubborn man, as he admits, stubborn even in self-destruction. Our glimpse of Alvin's unclothed body in the clinic—wrinkled, swollen, and sagging, speckled with prominent moles—is, finally, the thing itself, unveiled, that David Lynch has portrayed before in so many nightmarish versions, from the "baby" in *Eraserhead* to the piteously malformed Elephant Man to the spectacularly obese and postulant Baron Harkonnen in *Dune:* all the horror and glory of imprisonment in flesh—the inevitability of age, disease, and dissolution.

Significantly, Alvin makes his pilgrimage in the autumn. He and his daughter listen to the far-off roar of a grain elevator the night he announces his intention to make the trip. "It's ... harvest time," she says. The agricultural machines we see in those sweeping aerial views are threshers and harvesters. Harvest is when the world begins to die around us, and it is also when we reap what we have sown. Alvin knows this trip will be his last long haul; his quest is not for his brother's redemption but for his own. On the last night of his journey, before finally rejoining Lyle, he sets his camp in a cemetery.

Pilgrimages are not fashioned as gifts to our earthly siblings; they are abasements of the soul before the almighty. (Maybe Alvin's chosen to make this offering to Lyle because, as he tells the bickering twins who repair his mower, "Your brother knows better than anyone else *who* you are and *what* you are.") And, although often prompted by premonitions of mortality and fired by sincere repentance, pilgrimages are not guaranteed success. *The Straight Story* begins and ends with an elegiac image of the starry sky—the same image that attends John Merrick's last sleep in *The Elephant Man*. But the stars are not an unambiguous image of serenity, of making peace with the past and coming to rest, as Alvin hopes to do. There's no divine grace or forgiveness in evidence for him, not even the vision of maternal tenderness granted the suffocating Merrick. Alvin's endlessly expanding starscape could just as easily signify vast emptiness and indifference, or the absurdity of human striving in the face of unsurpassable sublimity, or the profound gulf between human yearnings and any answering assurance. The point here is not to supply an answer to the open-ended question posed by this image, but to explicitly acknowledge that it remains open-ended.

When has there ever been an unambiguously happy ending in a Lynch film, anyway? When John Merrick is urged to stand up and acknowledge the applause of London society at the theater, how different is that from his being prodded with a stick and ordered to stand and exhibit himself for gawkers at the freak show? The image of his mother in the stars, "the face of an angel" assuring him that "nothing dies," is a beatific deathbed dream. Is normalcy really restored, and corruption fully exposed, in the idyllic denouement of *Blue Velvet,* when we see Jeffrey's father returned to good health and the two young lovers' families lunching together? And are we really supposed to accept at face value the intervention of Glinda, the Good Witch of the North, and the last-minute reconciliation of Sailor and Lula at the end of *Wild at Heart?* Lyle is obviously moved beyond words by Alvin's effort, but *The Straight Story* deliberately leaves uncertain whether he forgives his brother. Alvin's journey itself, and whatever hard-earned glimpses of earthly grace it may have given him—a replenishing thunderstorm over an Iowa cornfield, children waving from the back of a pickup truck, late afternoon sunlight flickering through autumn leaves—will have to have been enough.

Questions of forgiveness—whether it is possible and what it really means—are also raised by Alvin's relationship with Rose. At first the two seem naive and sweet—an eccentric, aging father-and-daughter couple living together and looking after each other. But in the light of the buried backstory, the history of betrayal and hurt between them, we might see instead a stunted and bereaved Cordelia alongside a middle-American Lear. Rose is spending her middle age caring for a father who lost her children to the state. Their life together does seem tender and innocent, but it's also lonely and terribly sad. Rose, her speech interrupted by abrupt glottal stops, seems just as withholding and unable to speak about the truth as Alvin. She occupies herself building bird houses, protective shelters for helpless creatures, and painting them with the same brightly colored trim we see on her own house. How are we to judge this household? Does it display heartwarming familial loyalty and forgiveness—an example of the sort of solidarity Alvin preaches—or pathetic codependency and denial? Lynch isn't saying.

In his essay on *Lost Highway,* "David Lynch Keeps His Head," collected in *A Supposedly Fun Thing I'll Never Do Again,* David Foster Wallace argues that Lynch has alienated both critics and audiences because he confounds the conventional, reassuring dichotomy between good and evil that most American films foist on us. Lynch's protagonists, he insists, are never just good or evil but always, discomfitingly, both. Just look back at them: the naive mechanic Pete in *Lost Highway,* menaced by his mistress's gangster boyfriend, is actually a jealous husband who's killed his wife; the angelic Laura Palmer in *Fire Walk with Me* is also a coke whore; the youthful rebels Lula and Sailor in *Wild at Heart* are in danger of becoming the corrupt elders they're trying to flee; the college-boy detective Jeffrey Beaumont in *Blue Velvet* is secretly as perverted and sadistic as the "sick" Frank Booth. When Doctor Treves in *The Elephant Man,* who both helps and exploits poor deformed John Merrick, finally asks himself, "Am I a good man? Or a bad man?" there is, in answer, only a fade to black.

Alvin Straight, like Treves, is in the end one of Lynch's more self-aware protagonists—having come through the flames of his own anger and guilt, he knows what he is capable of. But in his heart he is no different from the rest of them. Yes, as we can see from everything he does and says, Alvin is at last what we like to think of as a "good" man, offering kindness and wisdom to the people he meets. But we also know, from what he has done before and cannot quite bring himself to say, that he's a son of a bitch. His "goodness" is not exactly a delusion, like Fred's, or naivete, like Jeffrey's, or hypocrisy, like Treves's; it's harder, more complicated, maybe more authentic—the kindness of a man who knows he is capable of great meanness, the wisdom that comes only from remorse over past recklessness, the knowledge that light is inseparable from shadow.

The Straight Story is genuinely poignant and moving, in a way that, say, *Lost Highway* certainly isn't. But to call the film "sentimental," or discontinuous with Lynch's previous work, is simply to misunderstand it. Far from abandoning grotesques and eerie atmospherics for a fantasy of some middle America where folks are just as honest and decent as they seem, David Lynch's portrait of crooked Alvin Straight, and of the many crooked miles he's traveled, reveals the deep psychological complexity—that "vanity and vexation of spirit"—in any human life, and the difficulty, if not the impossibility, of attaining any sure atonement in it.

LOS ANGELES TIMES, 10/15/99, Calendar/p. 18, Kenneth Turan

The equivalent of David Lynch doing "Little House on the Prairie," "The Straight Story" is a suspect enterprise for the creator of "Twin Peaks" and "Lost Highway." Can the Wizard of Weird successfully direct a heartwarming G-rated Disney film based on the true story of a cantankerous codger who wants to ride his lawn mower into another state? Finally, he can't, but Richard Farnsworth makes it a very near thing.

Now 79, in pictures since 1937 (though mostly as a rider and stunt man until the 1970s), Farnsworth was nominated for an Oscar for "Comes a Horseman" and won awards for "The Grey Fox," but this part is the role of a lifetime. Acclaimed at Cannes, it likely would have won Farnsworth the best actor prize if a sane jury (instead of the psychotic one masterminded by director David Cronenberg) had been in place.

Playing 73-year-old Alvin Straight (hence the too-cute title), Farnsworth is exactly right as a stubborn old-timer who's not about to let anyone tell him what to do. His dignified yet irascible performance is characterized by complete and effortless integrity, something the film otherwise has in uncertain supply.

For though the Montana-born Lynch (working from a fake-folksy script by John Roach and Mary Sweeney) takes a stab at being one with the film's four-square Midwesterners, "The Straight Story" is too mannered and weird around the edges to be convincing. Add in a tendency to turn Straight into the Ann Landers of the Open Road, and the film needs every inch of Farnsworth's considerable presence to keep our respect.

When Alvin Straight is first seen, he's more concerned with getting up from having fallen on the kitchen floor than getting on the open road. A feisty enemy of tests, X-rays, operations and all things medical, he visits the doctor only under protest and doesn't enjoy being reminded about his bad hips, failing eyesight and circulation problems. Determined to be independent, Alvin would rather use two canes than submit to a walker.

Living with his adult daughter Rose (Sissy Spacek), a maker of birdhouses who's considered "a little slow" by fellow residents of Laurens, Iowa, Alvin's idea of a big time is hanging out with his quartet of codger pals or getting on his ancient John Deere mower and attacking the lawn.

Then Rose gets the news that Alvin's brother Lyle, who lives 370 miles away in Mt. Zion, Wis., has had a stroke. Though the two brothers have not spoken in 10 years, Alvin feels he simply has to visit. There's no one to drive him, and no direct bus service, but Alvin is not the type to be deterred. "I'm not dead yet," he reminds Rose and, in a plan that dumbfounds his cronies, he decides to make the trip on his lawn mower pulling a trailer for sleeping and supplies behind him.

That proves a trickier proposition than Alvin anticipated, but soon enough he is on the road. Lynch made a point of filming "The Straight Story" along the same route that the real-life Straight took back in 1994, and veteran cinematographer Freddie Francis (who previously worked with the director on "The Elephant Man" and "Dune") makes the Lawnmower Man's quirky progress through pleasant rural vistas one of the film's most successful aspects.

(It's worth noting that "The Straight Story" is kind of a family project for the Lynch filmmaking clan. Co-screenwriter Sweeney is Lynch's business and personal partner; actress Spacek is married to production designer Jack Fisk, a friend of Lynch's since college; and composer Angelo Badalamenti has scored numerous Lynch projects.

Less appealing, unless you have a taste for bogus homilies and contrived folk wisdom, is the way Straight, when he's not saying down-home things like "I wasn't worth a stick of stove wood," seems to know just how to solve the problems of the people young and old he meets by the side of the road. He tells a young runaway how difficult it is to break even thin sticks when they're tied in a bundle, solemnly adding "that bundle of sticks, that's family." And he benignly lectures a pair of feuding twins about the importance of sibling friendship. There's not much in this life a few words from Alvin can't set straight, so to speak.

As noted, Farnsworth is so invested in this role that we buy into him no matter what kind of nonsense he's saying. The rest of "The Straight Story," however, suffers from an inability to decide what kind of an attitude it's going to take toward its material.

While Farnsworth would be right at home in a genuinely earnest and honestly sentimental effort like Joe Johnson's "October Sky," the rest of what's on the screen would not. For despite its gee-whiz dialogue, the film can't live without classic Lynch oddities like sinister grain silos, an overweight sunbather carefully eating pink Sno Balls, and a woman who seems primed to set a local record for number of deer hit by a single driver. There's nothing wrong with touches like these—Lynch used them brilliantly in "Blue Velvet"—but they clash with, rather than enhance, the kind of feeling Farnsworth is working so hard to convey.

NEW YORK, 10/25/99, p. 80, Peter Rainer

There are two ways of regarding *The Straight Story:* As a movie, or as a *David Lynch* movie.

As the former, it's a sweet and ruminative odyssey about a crotchety, crippled oldster, Alvin Straight (Richard Farnsworth), who leaves his devoted daughter (Sissy Spacek) and travels clear across Iowa on his riding mower to visit his ill estranged brother (Harry Dean Stanton, in a brief appearance). If, however, one chooses to evaluate this film as the latest work from the director of *Blue Velvet* and *Twin Peaks,* it's surely one of the most perverse movies ever made. No pustules, no raging cretins are to be found. No boogying dwarves. The cornfields and sunset-tinged landscapes don't disguise a lurking rot; the people don't morph into the Other. In the context of Lynch's oeuvre, this seems far more bizarre than his usual fare.

Is the comfy, G-rated Disneyishness of it all simply Lynch's capitulation to commercialism and Hollywood's newfound wholesomeness after a flagging career as freak-out artist? I don't think so. For one thing, the film seems honestly made; it doesn't have the coerciveness of schmaltz, in which every emotion is handed to you gift-wrapped. The *Straight Story* has a winning modesty—it could be the best Hallmark Hall of Fame movie that Hallmark never made. The performances of Farnsworth and Spacek are strong; the bits of local color add up to a pretty palette. Still, Lynch isn't drawing here on the most livid and voracious aspects of his talent, and while that may not be such a bad thing given the brain-numbing terribleness of much of his recent film work, the results are still somewhat thin. Lynch doesn't really live in this calendar-art universe of homilies and home truths; perhaps he wishes he did. He's just a tourist—a visitor paying his respects.

NEW YORK POST, 10/15/99, p. 52, Lou Lumenick

Yup, the credits confirm that "Walt Disney Pictures Presents a Film by David Lynch" and "The Straight Story," Lynch's first G-rated feature, turns out to be one of the year's best films.

Veteran character actor Richard Farnsworth gives a hugely touching, Oscar-worthy performance as Alvin Straight, a real-life Iowa man who rode 350 miles to Wisconsin to visit his estranged brother, who had suffered a stroke—and Straight did it on a 1966 John Deere riding mower.

Alvin, who's 74 but looks a decade older, doesn't have eyesight good enough to drive a car. Though he suffers from diabetes and emphysema and needs two canes to walk, he stubbornly refuses glasses, drugs or operations. And he certainly doesn't feel like riding on a bus.

So, much to the alarm of his daughter Rose (Sissy Spacek) and the amazement of his neighbors, the frail old man builds a crude wooden trailer to sleep in, hitches it to the mower and sets off with an ample supply of wieners and smokes.

The heart of "The Straight Story" is the Midwest countryside—cornfields and sunsets lyrically photographed by legendary cinematographer Freddie Francis, who filmed "Dr. Zhivago"—and the people Alvin meets during the six weeks he dodges tractor-trailer trucks while crawling along at 5 mph.

Among the people he encounters are a pregnant teen runaway (Anastasia Webb), whom he convinces to return to her family; a hysterical motorist (Barbara Robertson) who keeps driving her car into deer; and a pack of bicyclists whom Alvin tells, "The worst part about being old is remembering when you were young."

When the mower is damaged in a near-fatal plunge down a hill near the Mississippi River, a compassionate farmer (James Cada) offers to drive Straight to his destination.

But Alvin is determined to do things his own way, even if it means risking what little is left of his life—and fighting with twin mechanics (John and Kevin Farley) who try to gouge him for the repairs in the movie's funniest sequence.

Setting aside the twisted noir sensibility, violence and inscrutability of recent films such as "Lost Highway" for this deliberately paced road movie, Lynch treats the material (written by John Roach and Mary Sweeney, the film's editor and Lynch's girlfriend) in a very straightforward manner.

He focuses on the magnificently wrecked Farnsworth, who delivers two long, touching monologues—one about how his speech-impaired daughter had her children taken away following a fire, and a second in which he recalls accidentally killing another GI in World War II.

In his first starring role since "The Grey Fox" 15 years ago, the 79-year-old Farnsworth (an Oscar nominee for "Comes a Horseman") vividly sketches an old man nearing death—the real Alvin died in 1996, two years after his journey—with many regrets from decades of hard drinking, including a fight with his brother Lyle (a nice cameo by Harry Dean Stanton) that's kept them from speaking for 10 years.

Spacek is excellent in her small but key role as Alvin's daughter, who worries about her dad's frailty but knows better than to resist his determination.

Lyrical, sweet and brimming with optimism about the human condition, "The Straight Story" is a wonderful surprise from the director of "Blue Velvet" and "Dune."

NEWSDAY, 10/15/99, Part II/p. B7, Gene Seymour

The camera drifts lazily through a town rendered all but immobile by the afternoon sun. The camera pulls up at a small, nondescript house. A plain, plump woman is sunbathing in its yard. She walks into the house. The camera doesn't follow her in, but sort of hovers outside. No sound for a while and then a sudden thump. Either a huge sack of wet laundry dropped or someone fell down. Hard. A little while later, the woman comes out as if nothing at all has happened.

All this takes place at or near the beginning of "The Straight Story" and, from what's described here, you'd probably have little trouble pegging it for a David Lynch movie. But for all the wry insinuation and ominous tone of that sequence, this particular David Lynch movie is a far different blend of coffee than what you're used to getting from the director of "Eraserhead" (1978), "Blue Velvet" (1986) and "Wild at Heart" (1990).

"The Straight Story" is a David Lynch movie the whole family can enjoy. And if you think that sentence reads like the set-up for a lame punch line, consider that Lynch, even at his most exotically surreal, never relinquishes a yearning for simple, homespun goodness of the kind exemplified here by Alvin Straight (Richard Farnsworth), a 73-year-old Iowa man who can't see or move around well, but is determined to make amends with his estranged brother Lyle (Harry Dean Stanton), who's recovering from a stroke somewhere in Wisconsin.

Trouble is, Alvin's poor eyesight keeps him from a driver's license, and he hasn't enough money or inclination to take a bus. About the only thing he can do without help is tend his narrow lawn with a riding mower. So, despite the skepticism of his speech-impaired, but "steel-trap smart" daughter Rose (Sissy Spacek in a lovely performance), Alvin hooks up a trailer stocked with groceries and bedding to a 1966 John Deere mower and sets off on a 320-mile odyssey to find Lyle.

Weird enough for Lynch? Eccentric enough, to say the least. But the fact that this story, written by John Roach and co-producer Mary Sweeney, is taken from real-life events (Straight, who died in 1996, actually took this trip two years before) only adds to its enchantment and wonder.

Odd as Straight's quixotic endeavor may be, it is treated by Lynch with gentle, yet elemental rigor. His determination to sustain a dry-eyed, irony-free tone throughout the movie gives it a wholeness that hasn't been found in a Lynch movie for many years. While the artist in Lynch is careful that his use of shadow and light never clogs into excessive sentiment, the craftsman in Lynch maintains a leisurely narrative flow.

Some in your family will find the pace a mite too leisurely at times. But the spare, evocative music by Lynch mainstay Angelo Badalamenti keeps snapping at your antennae. And the iconic presence of Farnsworth, who came out of retirement to do this role, is riveting. At one point, Alvin fibs to his daughter about his doctor's assessment of his long-term health, saying, "I'll live to be 100." The real Straight didn't make it that far. I wouldn't bet my retirement fund against Farnsworth's chances.

SIGHT AND SOUND, 12/99, p. 57, Kevin Jackson

Laurens, Iowa, 1994. Alvin Straight, a stubborn 73-year-old widower who lives with his adult daughter Rose, suffers a bad fall and is sent to the local clinic. The doctor warns him he is in dangerously poor health and needs to take better care of himself, but Alvin shows little sign of mending his ways. Rose takes a phone call and learns Alvin's estranged older brother Lyle has had a stroke. Despite Rose's warnings and the incredulity of his fellow townspeople, Alvin is determined to travel to Lyle's home in Mt. Zion, Wisconsin, and try to patch up their ancient quarrel—by an idiosyncratic means of transport: a motordriven lawnmower.

On his slow and often interrupted chug to Wisconsin, Alvin meets and befriends a variety of people, including coach tourists heading for a grotto; a pregnant teenage runaway; a woman whose daily commute to work usually involves crashing into and killing deer; volunteer firefighters; a generous family who allow him to live in their garden while his lawnmower is being repaired by identical-twin mechanics who constantly bicker with each other; a World War II veteran with whom Alvin shares anguished memories of combat; and a hospitable priest. At long last, Alvin reaches the ramshackle wooden house where Lyle lives. The two old men sit together on the porch, largely wordless though seemingly deeply moved by their long-deferred reunion.

All the usual elements are present and correct at the start: the mock-innocent lilt of an Angelo Badalamenti score; a threateningly bland vista of one-storey clapboard houses and trimmed gardens; the mildly grotesque figure of a plump, recumbent woman sunning herself with a reflector while gobbling unappetising foodstuffs; a chillingly slow, predatory camera move in towards the house on the left; a sudden thumping noise from deep within. Any minute now, you expect David Lynch to bring on the severed genitals, the dwarves who talk Atlantean, the psychopath who injects himself in the pineal gland while crooning hits from Broadway shows of the 20s. Something like that, anyway.

Well, forget it. Behind the eerily normal and wholesome facade of Laurens, Iowa, are eerily normal and wholesome folks living ordinary lives. If you sit through *The Straight Story* waiting for Lynch to cut the cornpone and turn weird and ugly, then you will pass 111 minutes in vain, for the film is pretty much as good as its punning title promises. Its narrative has digressions, but not a single kink.

To be sure, there are a few sequences showing Lynch in a more familiar vein, such as Alvin's encounter with a woman who has inadvertently become a serial 'bambicide' ("Every week I plough into at least one deer—and I love deer!"), or his dispute with the identical-twin mechanics who spend more time sniping at each other than tinkering with engines. And the film sometimes sounds as well as looks like a typical Lynch product: when Alvin and another old-timer sit at a quiet bar recalling the guilty horror of their war service, the air gradually becomes filled with the crash and wail of heavy artillery. On the whole, though, this is a film made by David Lynch the sometime Eagle Scout from Missoula, Montana, not David Lynch the inspired sicko behind *Blue Velvet* and *Eraserhead.*

Grant this disconcerting limitation, and there's a lot to admire about the film, from Freddie Francis' cinematography (it's hard to do much new with sweeping fields of Iowan corn, but Francis manages it: some of the aerial shots render these growths as burnished tweed) to the impeccable and moving tact of the final reunion between the two brothers. Harry Dean Stanton's appearance as Lyle is as haunting as it is brief, though the film's richest performance belongs to Sissy Spacek as Alvin's "simple" daughter Rose who, with her speech impediment and habit of building bird-houses, initially seems like a refugee from the Lynch carnival but gains in gravity with every scene. *The Straight Story* also has the best crane-shot joke in years: the camera catches Alvin's puttering progress from behind, rises into the sky with epic majesty, then gracefully sweeps down again to reveal Alvin, about four feet further down the highway.

But to enumerate redeeming features is to confess a need for redemption. Lynch's film risks being nothing more than sweet-natured, and its habit of treating ornery old Alvin like a kindly wizard who sets people's lives to rights with a twinkle and a yarn can be more than a trifle sickly. In its least beguiling moment, Alvin tells a sad runaway a little homily about binding sticks together into a bunch so they won't break. "That's family," he sums up; at which point, ill-natured viewers will snarl that the Romans used to call such wooden bundles *fasces* and look where that homely symbol ended up.

TIME, 10/25/99, p. 120, Richard Corliss

On an Iowa roadside, the old man chats with a pregnant runaway. For the girl, family is a prison, to be broken out of. The old man tells her that he used to give each of his kids a stick and say, "You break that." Of course they could. Then he'd tell them to tie some sticks in a bundle and try to break that. And they couldn't. "Then I'd say, 'That bundle—that's family.'" The next morning, the old man wakes up to find the girl gone, with the hint that she'll be returning home. On the ground is a bundle of sticks with a bow tied around it.

Alvin Straight (Richard Farnsworth), hero of David Lynch's *The Straight Story*, brings out the best in people—by talking or listening to them or just by the example of his tortoise-like quest. He is driving his John Deere lawnmower 350 miles to see his estranged brother. Alvin turns out to be your basic Lynch hero: a Kyle Maclachlan type, as average as apple pie, who follows his obsessions to heaven or hell. The supporting cast is normal too—and thus vastly weird, because Lynch presents them, as he did the sickos of *Blue Velvet*, without comment or condescension.

This true tale might seem to have all the narrative momentum of a lawnmower pulling the Cheops pyramid up an Alp. It does move, thanks to the script by John Roach and Mary Sweeney. It keeps finding new ways to make rural decency dramatic. But the soul of the film is in Farnsworth's eyes—great watery repositories of wisdom and regret. "The worst part of bein' old," he says, "is rememberin' when you was young." Alvin's tragic memories give perspective to the triumph of his trek, even as Farnsworth's weathered brilliance makes this movie a G as in gem.

VILLAGE VOICE, 10/19/99, p. 133, J. Hoberman

A 73-year-old man who needs two canes to walk, and whose dimmed vision precludes driving a car, stubbornly pilots his 1966 John Deere lawn mower 240 miles (at 5 mph) across Iowa to visit an estranged brother in Wisconsin. Prince of weirdness David Lynch always was a closet cultural conservative, and his new movie, *The Straight Story,* is Disney material with a vengeance.

Dramatizing the true story of Alvin Straight, Lynch revels in a premise so shamelessly feel-good and absurdly family-friendly it might embarrass Steven Spielberg or Kevin Costner. The title is, of course, a pun. Lynch begins with a parody of *Blue Velvet*'s small-town geekery. But, unlike that masterpiece of ecstatic creepiness, *The Straight Story* is not about what goes on behind closed doors. Everything is on the surface: "What's the number for 911!?" someone wants to know, quoting Homer Simpson without credit.

The Straight Story is as American in its wanderlust as *Boys Don't Cry* is in its paean to reinvention and *Blair Witch* is in its fear of the woods. Despite a few peculiar details (a biddy-filled tour bus, a scene underscored by the piercing squeal of a hacksaw cutting metal pipe, the repeated insistence that Wisconsin is a "real party state"), the movie is unpretentiously straightforward. Wrinkled within his wrinkles, Richard Farnsworth is enormously sympathetic in the title role—it's heart-stopping to watch the flicker of adrenaline-fueled panic crease his face as the lawn mower's brakes fail on a downhill grade. Sissy Spacek gives a pitch-perfect performance as his peculiarly disabled daughter.

Lynch treats this geriatric road movie as a biblical parable—a tale from the Book of Dutch. As summer turns to fall, Alvin encounters a pregnant runaway, a hysterical woman who claims to have run over 14 deer, a teenage bicycle tour, and a pair of squabbling twins.   These opportunities for him to dispense his homely wisdom are overemphasized, replete with reverential reaction shots, even when they're meant to be funny. Lynch tips his hand when Alvin goes for a beer with another geezer and, with a '40s ballad playing prominently in the background, they swap references to their World War II traumas. Even so, thanks to the evident decrepitude of the actors, the scene has an old-western pathos.

Sunny as *The Straight Story* appears, Lynch is still defamiliarizing the normal. Perhaps the clearest indication that Straight lives in a paradise is the absence of authority figures. No cop appears to question his vehicle, and even though he spends an evening in a church graveyard, roasting wieners with a friendly priest, the concept of God is never mentioned.

Also reviewed in:
CHICAGO TRIBUNE, 10/15/99, Friday/p. A, Michael Wilmington
NEW REPUBLIC, 11/15/99, p. 28, Stanley Kauffmann
NEW YORK TIMES, 10/15/99, p. E1, Janet Maslin
NEW YORKER, 11/1/99, p. 123, Anthony Lane
VARIETY, 5/24-30/99, p. 73, Emanuel Levy
WASHINGTON POST, 10/22/99, p. C1, Rita Kempley
WASHINGTON POST, 10/22/99, Weekend/p. 45, Desson Howe

STUART LITTLE

A Columbia Pictures release of a Douglas Wick and Franklin/Waterman production. *Executive Producer:* Jeff Franklin, Steve Waterman, and Jason Clark. *Producer:* Douglas Wick. *Director:* Rob Minkoff. *Screenplay:* M. Night Shyamalan and Greg Brooker. *Based on the book by:* E.B. White. *Director of Photography:* Guillermo Navarro. *Editor:* Tom Finan. *Music:* Alan Silvestri and Elliot Lurie. *Music Editor:* Kenneth Karman. *Choreographer:* Melinda Buckley. *Sound:* Mark Ulano and (music) Dennis Sands. *Sound Editor:* Lawrence H. Mann. *Casting:* Debra Zane. *Production Designer:* Bill Brzeski. *Art Director:* Philip Toolin. *Set Designer:* Aric Lasher, A. Todd Holland, and Stella Vaccaro. *Set Decorator:* Clay A. Griffith. *Visual Effects:* John Dykstra. *Animation:* Henry F. Anderson III. *Special Effects:* Eric Allard.   *Costumes:* Joseph Porro. *Make-up:* Bonita De Haven. *Stunt Coordinator (Animals):* Boon Narr. *Running time:* 92 minutes. *MPAA Rating:* PG.

CAST: Geena Davis (Mrs. Little); Hugh Laurie (Mr. Little); Jonathan Lipnicki (George Little); Jeffrey Jones (Uncle Crenshaw); Connie Ray (Aunt Tina); Allyce Beasley (Aunt Beatrice); Brian Doyle-Murray (Cousin Edgar); Estelle Getty (Grandma Estelle); Harold Gould (Grandpa Spencer); Patrick O'Brien (Uncle Stretch); Julia Sweeney (Mrs. Keeper); Dabney Coleman (Doctor Beechwood); Miles Marsico (Anton); Jon Polito (Officer Sherman); Jim Doughan (Officer Allen); Joe Bays (Race Starter); Taylor Negron (Salesman); Kimmy Robertson (Race Spectator); Tannis Benedict (Hot Dog Vendor); Chuck Blechen and Westleigh Michael Styer (Skippers); Larry Goodhue (Boat Registrar);

VOICES: Michael J. Fox (Stuart Little); Nathan Lane (Snowbell); Chazz Palminteri (Smokey); Steve Zahn (Monty); Jim Doughan (Lucky); David Alan Grier (Red); Bruno Kirby (Mr. Stout); Jennifer Tilly (Mrs. Stout); Stan Freberg (Race Announcer).

CHRISTIAN SCIENCE MONITOR, 12/17/99, p. 15, David Sterritt

[*Stuart Little* was reviewed jointly with *Anna and the King*; see Sterritt's review of that film.]

LOS ANGELES TIMES, 12/17/99, Calendar/p. 16, Kenneth Turan

Those who remember "Stuart Little" from the gentle, half-century-old children's book written by E.B. White may have trouble recognizing a creature with "the pleasant, shy manner of a mouse" in his new movie incarnation.

Voiced by Michael J. Fox with dialogue written by M. Night Shyamalan ("The Sixth Sense") and Greg Brooker, Stuart has been reborn as a kind of show-biz mouse, a hipster whose ready line of patter would allow him to fit right in as a regular on "Letterman."

That's not all that's different between the children's classic and its movie version. Gone completely is Stuart's best friend and the moving force behind half the book, Margalo the bird. In her place is so much movie jeopardy, including car chases and animal attacks, that it makes you search for Jerry Bruckheimer's name among the producing credits. (It's not there.)

Paradoxically, however, the main problem with "Stuart Little" is not that it's too exciting but that it's too dull. Except for admiring the computer technology that allows a mouse to walk and talk on screen, reasons to see this film are few. It won't harm the tiny viewers who will be its main audience, but there's nothing very involving about this Rob Minkoff-directed effort either.

Perhaps deciding that White's original premise of a mouse actually born into a human family was too strange for a live-action film, this "Stuart Little" has Mr. and Mrs. Little (Hugh Laurie and Geena Davis) going to a Manhattan orphanage to adopt a brother for their son George ("Jerry Maguire's" Jonathan Lipnicki).

The Littles' attention is immediately caught by Stuart: He is, after all, a 3-inch white mouse who dresses nattily and reads "Little Women" in his spare time. While the orphanage's Mrs. Keeper (an amusing Julia Sweeney) cautions "adopting children outside a species, it rarely works," the Littles are determined to go ahead.

Even though the Littles live in a world where Stuart can speak to humans and animals can talk to each other, that doesn't mean that a relative this tiny is what young George had in mind. "Are you all nuts?" he yells at one point, justifiably irked. "He's not my brother, he's a mouse."

Even less pleased is Snowbell, the family cat. Voiced by Nathan Lane, Snowbell is so much a comedian that it would surprise no one to have him say, "Take my fur ball, please." In between cracks like "Read my furry pink lips" and "I can't believe this, I'm arguing with lunch," Snowbell complains to Smokey (Chazz Palminteri), the king of the alley cats, about having a mouse for a master, and a nefarious plan is hatched to put Stuart in his place.

What fun there is in "Stuart Little" is in enjoying how small and cute the little guy is in his computer-generated rendition. The closer the movie Stuart sticks to what's in the book—for instance, helping out during a toy sailboat race in Central Park—the more satisfying his adventures are.

Less engaging are Stuart's worries about his past ("I feel an empty space inside me" is how he puts it), a situation that somehow ends up in a high-powered chase through Central Park, with cats making wisecracks like "The mouse is sleeping with the fishes" and generally acting like feline versions of the Bowery Boys.

As far as can be determined, the main lesson "Stuart Little" is trying to teach is how good it is to be part of a family. "That's something families do," the Littles say, "they take care of each other." The other, unintentional lesson taught here is that it's easier to make a mouse talk than to come up with something interesting for him to say.

NEW YORK POST, 12/17/99, p. 60, Lou Lumenick

Family movies don't come much more entertaining than "Stuart Little," which has such astounding computer-generated effects you'll suspend disbelief and root for the hero, a 3-inch talking mouse.

Very loosely adapted from E.B. White's classic 1945 children's book, this disarming movie by M. Night Shyamalan (writer-director of "The Sixth Sense") and Greg Booker takes place in a idealized, studio-set version of modern-day New York City, where the streets are spotless and traffic runs uptown on Fifth Avenue.

When the sweetly eccentric Mr. and Mrs. Little (Geena Davis and British actor Hugh Laurie) visit a municipal orphanage to find a brother for their son, they end up adopting Stuart (winningly voiced by Michael J. Fox), despite warnings that they should "adopt within their own species."

Stuart's arrival at the Littles' Fifth Avenue townhouse is less than welcomed by their young son George (Jonathan Lipnicki of "Jerry Maguire"), who was expecting a human brother.

And the prospect of becoming a mouse's pet throws their Persian cat Snowbell (hilariously voiced by Nathan Lane) into a positive tizzy.

"I can't believe this," he says. "I'm talking to lunch."

Stuart finally wins George's heart by taking over his disabled sailboat during an excitingly staged race in Central Park's model-boat basin.

But Snowbell is another matter. When the cat overhears that Stuart "feels an empty space inside" wondering about his birth parents, he conspires with a gang of alley cats (providing an opportunity for terrific voice work by Chazz Palminteri and Steve Zahn, among others.

They hatch an elaborate plot to kidnap Stuart by bringing in a pair of mice (voiced by Bruno Kirby and Jennifer Tilly) to pose as his parents, who were killed in an accident.

The Littles tearfullly send Stuart off on his way in his little red sports car, kicking off a series of adventures that include an exciting chase, and an opportunity for Snowbell to reconsider whether he really does accept Stuart as a member of the family.

The human actors—they also include Brian Doyle-Murray, Jeffrey Jones and Estelle Getty, as members of the extended Little family—are very good, but the real stars are the cats (played by real-life cats) and mice.

With real heart (Fox is particularly touching) and laughs (Lane, never funnier, outdoes his work for the same director, Ron Minkoff, in "The Lion King"), "Stuart Little" lets you forget the special effects and enjoy the show.

NEWSDAY, 12/17/99, Part II/p. B3, Gene Seymour

A whole shelf of plastic toys falls on a hardwood floor. Nothing breaks. But goodness, what a racket! Nothing exactly like this happens in "Stuart Little," but it's the best available analogy for the experience of watching it.

Which, for those who grew up loving the classic children's novel by E.B. White, will come as both a mild disappointment and no surprise whatsoever.

Then again, I'm not sure that a generation bred on Barney and now steeped in Pokmon would be able to relate to the wistful, somewhat disconcerting melancholy of White's original story. (He fashioned a richer concoction, later on, with "Charlotte's Web.") I'm all but certain that those who make and distribute movies in this country are incapable of relating to it. And why would they? Tie-in merchandise doesn't know from wistful melancholy.

So instead of White's dark-edged, whimsical fable about a walking, talking, well-dressed mouse whose existence is accepted, even taken for granted, by most of the New Yorkers around him, you get a shiny, cacophonous story with talking animals about Being Different in a perilous world. Nothing wrong with that.

"Babe" did the same thing. Only better. Much better.

This "Stuart Little," directed by Rob Minkoff, carries a flashy veneer of sitcom razzmatazz that was doubtlessly designed to connect with children and adults accustomed to the knockabout pace of after-dinner TV reruns. The jokes come so fast that you don't have time to consider their corn-and-cheese content. Come to think of it, eating corn-and-cheese crisps is an even better analogy for the experience of watching "Stuart Little," especially the noisy, messy, disposable part.

One thing about the movie that's not messy is Stuart himself. Designed by a visual effects team led by "Star Wars" veteran John Dykstra, the little guy is one of the most plausible-looking special effects you can ever imagine living in a Manhattan townhouse. (The grin is a little creepy, but we all have our quirks.) Throw in Michael J. Fox's voice at its most ingratiating and polished, and there's your one good reason for sitting through the whole thing.

In the beginning, it seems as if only the Littles (Geena Davis, Hugh Laurie) are beguiled enough by Stuart to bring him home as the adopted son who isn't exactly what their other son, George

(Jonathan Lipnicki from "Jerry Maguire"), had in mind when he asked for a "little brother." Snowbell (voiced by the indefatigable Nathan Lane), the family cat, is peeved that his prospective lunch is getting his own double bed and, through his mooching friend Monty (voiced by Steve Zahn), seeks redress from the sinister alley cat Smokey (voiced by Chazz Palminteri).

What else is there to know? Minkoff, who co-directed "The Lion King," orchestrates the chaotic story line with the same brash energy of that animated feature's Timon-and-Pumbaa sequences. The cool little roadster some of you remember from the book makes an appearance, but gets a far sterner road test than E.B. White ever imagined. And those dirty cats say some very naughty things as they chase Stuart through Central Park.

SIGHT AND SOUND, 8/00, p. 55, Leslie Felperin

New York City, the recent past. Mr and Mrs Little visit an orphanage to find a little brother for their natural son George. Charmed by one modest orphan, a talking mouse named Stuart, they adopt him. At first, George, disappointed with his new brother's diminutive stature, is stand-offish, but he eventually bonds with Stuart who later helms the boys' toy boat in the lake in Central Park. Snowbell, the family's Persian cat, is indignant at having a mouse for an owner and plots with his feline cronies to have Stuart removed.

The neighbourhood's top cat Red hires two mice, Mr and Mrs Stout, to claim they are Stuart's mouse parents. Thinking he has finally found his real family, Stuart bids a tearful goodbye to the Littles and leaves with the Stouts for Brooklyn, unaware of the mice's plan to hand him over to Red. Mr and Mrs Little learn that Stuart's biological parents died in a car crash and start searching for him. Meanwhile, the Stouts have a change of heart and tell Stuart the truth so he can escape. He makes it back to the house only to be pursued into Central Park by Snowbell and the cats. Realising his fellow cats plan to eat Stuart, Snowbell repents and helps him escape. The Little family is reunited at last.

Like the 1997 children's film *The Borrowers* with its hotchpotch *mise en scène, Stuart Little* is set in an imaginary period where people have 40s hairstyles, 50s lifestyles and late-90s appliances. Forming a stylised vision of New York where—most fantastically of all—a moderately affluent middle-class family can afford a house on Central Park West, these retro trappings are like a thread leading the film back to its source, E. B. White's 1945 picaresque novella about the mouse son of a kindly family of New Yorkers. With delightful indirection, White's first sentence skirts gingerly around the nature of Stuart's genesis, "When Mrs Frederick C. Little's second son arrived, everybody noticed that he was not much bigger than a mouse." But even so, the book implies throughout that Stuart is the Littles' natural son. Presumably working on the assumption that contemporary audiences won't accept—and might even be repelled by—the notion of a woman whelping a rodent, screenwriters M. Night Shyamalan (writer-director of *The Sixth Sense*) and Greg Brooker make it plain from the outset that Stuart is adopted by, and not born into the little family.

This takes the film in a whole new direction from White's novella. Gone are all the story elements that innocently present bestiality or at least vaguely perverse inter-species relationships as everyday events. (The book's Stuart falls in love with a bird and later dates a two inch-high teenager.) Bringing to mind Michel Foucault's analysis of the "repressive hypothesis" which explains how modernity mistakenly caricatures 19-century thought as devoid of carnal content when it was in fact obsessed with pathologising sexual behaviour, White's *Stuart Little* belies our stereotypical conception of 20th-century children's fiction as anodyne and innocent. Paradoxically, the film version is a much more wholesome affair, didactically exploring the emotional fragility of adopted children, sibling rivalry and blended family life. Where White's Stuart is a kind of young, 20s romantic, this Stuart is pre pubescent, modestly trousered and sexless. Where White's book swerves and dips with strange adventures for its hero and a startlingly oblique ending, *Stuart Little* the film runs on straight, conventional narrative rails, looping back to dramatic stasis as predictably as the toy railroad in the Littles' basement.

As such, it's perfectly entertaining fare, sprightly, funny and never too cloying. Director Rob Minkoff, who co-directed *The Lion King,* in collaboration with visual-effects supervisor John Dykstra *(2001: A Space Odyssey),* coaxes charmingly nuanced movements and facial expressions from the computer generated animals who carry the plot more than the slightly dazed-looking live actors. Michael J. Fox is impeccably cast for Stuart's voice, high pitched and happy natured. He's upstaged only by Nathan Lane's Snowbell, the family cat who, like Lucifer, gets all the best lines. Refusing to help Stuart escape from a washing machine, he saunters off, tail aloft, explaining that he's "got to stare at traffic, yawn, lick myself. And believe me, that can take hours if you do it right." Maybe there's a streak of perversity in *Stuart Little* after all.

VILLAGE VOICE, 12/21/99, p. 152, Michael Atkinson

E.B. White's tearful prepubescent semi-classic gets the Happy Hollywood treatment, but with disappointing results—Stuart himself is a winsome CGI with Michael J. Fox's sour-skim-milk voice, and White's ruminative fairy tale is reduced to a cycle of departures and homecomings childishly dolled up for the Catdog crowd with butt and fart jokes. Don't wait for the rueful poetry that snuck into *The Iron Giant* or *Toy Story 2* to surface here; the movie reneges on virtually every emotional punch the book delivered. Whereas White's Stuart was, strangely enough, born into the human Little family and convinced he was no different from them, just smaller, the movie's Stuart is an amiable adoptee. Instead of the aching search for Margalo the vanished bird-girlfriend, the movie (cowritten by M. Night Shyamalan) swabs Stuart in the adoption blues, presenting him with a conniving set of fake mouse birth-parents hired by evil cats. Geena Davis and Hugh Laurie (the unlikeliest movie marriage since Marlene Dietrich and Herbert Marshall in *Blonde Venus*) are the enthusiastic adopters as well as the parents of the obnoxious, bespectacled cherub Jonathan Lipnicki, who, along with the family's bitter Persian cat (voiced in full-on Billy Crystal yenta-ish by Nathan Lane) dismiss Stuart and then redeem themselves by loving him. Getting the nondigital felines to act is a dilemma never adequately solved (although Steve Zahn's boggle-brained alley cat has his moments), and the story is little more than overdetermined trials and triumphs. Kids won't care, but they won't fall for it either; unsurprisingly, it doesn't stand a chance of providing them with the memories the book provided their parents.

Also reviewed in:
CHICAGO TRIBUNE, 12/17/99, Friday/p. K, Mark Caro
NEW YORK TIMES, 12/17/99, p. E15, Stephen Holden
VARIETY, 12/13-19/99, p. 110, Lael Loewenstein
WASHINGTON POST, 12/17/99, p. C1, Rita Kempley
WASHINGTON POST, 12/17/99, Weekend/p. 43, Desson Howe

SUBURBANS, THE

A TriStar Pictures release of an Ignite Entertainment production in association with Motion Picture Corporation of America. *Executive Producer:* Marc Butan, Tim Foster, and George Linardo. *Producer:* Michael Burns, Brad Krevoy, J.J. Abrams, and Leanna Creel. *Director:* Donal Lardner Ward. *Screenplay:* Donal Lardner Ward and Tony Guma. *Director of Photography:* Michael Barrett. *Editor:* Kathryn Himoff. *Music:* Robbie Kondor. *Sound:* James Mase. *Casting:* Sheila Jaffe and Georgianne Walken. *Production Designer:* Susan Bolles. *Set Decorator:* Catherine Pierson. *Set Dresser:* Debra Sugerman, Ralph Roman, and Analisa Quilty. *Costumes:* Pamela Withers. *Make-up:* Charlotte Ostergren. *Stunt Coordinator:* Tom Harper. *Running time:* 90 minutes. *MPAA Rating:* Not Rated.

CAST: Amy Brenneman (Grace); Donal Lardner Ward (Danny); Tony Guma (Rory); Craig Bierko (Mitch); Will Ferrell (Gil); Jennifer Love Hewitt (Cate); Bridgette Wilson (Lara); Brian Chlebowski (Kenny); Perrey Reeves (Amanda); Willie Garson (Craig/Sponsor); Lisa Gerstein (Leslie Gonzalez); Antonio Fargas (Magee); Robert Loggia (Jules); Jerry Stiller (Speedo Silverberg); Ben Stiller (Jay Rose); Ben Kronen (Priest); Cleo Adell (Square Q Girl); Kurt Loder (MTV Personality); Emily Kuroda (Mrs. Lee Lee); David LaChapelle (Thorlakur); Karl

A. D'Amico (MC); Matt Cedano (Tito); Mary Jane Lardner (Amelia); J.J. Abrams (Rock Journalist); Mary Porster (Mrs. Farley); Nikki Dion (Punk Rock Waitress).

LOS ANGELES TIMES, 10/29/99, Calendar/p. 12, Gene Seymour

[The following review by Gene Seymour appeared in a slightly different form in **NEWSDAY, 10/29/99, Part II/p. B11.]**

Call it, if you want, "That Thing You Do: The Sequel." Except that, unlike that underrated Tom Hanks project from 1996 about one-hit wonders from the 1960s, "The Suburbans" gets its title from the name of an imaginary "fab four" from Long Island that streaked across the pop universe on the cusp of the Reagan administration and flamed out after one hit single.

Now it's the cusp of the millennium and the Suburbans have become, if anything, even more suburban. Drummer Rory (Tony Guma) is a struggling insurance salesman who's living with a high-strung ex-model (Bridgette Wilson) who's got two high-strung kids from a previous "marriage from hell." Lead guitarist Mitch (Craig Bierko) is a shopping-center podiatrist who can't let go of his rocker dreams. Bassist Gil (Will Ferrell), newly married, is more solicitous about his stock portfolio and expensive toys than he is about his musical chops.

And then there's Danny (Donal Lardner Ward), the leader, who seems to have the most idyllic life of all. He's a professional lifeguard who's been living in non-wedded bliss to a beautiful photographer (Amy Brenneman). But there's trouble in paradise. She's ready for children. He seems to feel some loose ends in his past that haven't been tied.

And that's when Cate (Jennifer Love Hewitt), a twentysomething record producer, steps into Danny's life after an impromptu performance by his very rusty band. She thinks the world has been waiting for a Suburbans reunion and coerces both the group and her bosses (Jerry Stiller and Ben Stiller) to produce a new album, a video and a forthcoming pay-per-view reunion.

Who cares if the group crashed and burned after one hit? Or that hardly anyone remembers anything about them except the sordid (never really specified) circumstances of their breakup? "The more pathetic you were then," Cate assures Danny, "the more sympathetic you are now."

Anyone who is addicted to VH1's autopsies of rock careers can relate to that line and its presence gives just a small tremor of the bounce in the script, which is co-written by Guma and director Ward. The latter, whose "My Life's in Turnaround" was also driven by a savvy "inside" view of show-biz, also has a puppyish charm as an actor. He does bewilderment especially well.

Even with its charm and promise, "The Suburbans" goes into a tailspin after its impressive setup. Its dramatic tactics become so tangled and diffuse that, by the end, you get the feeling that everything gets tied up too hastily. Also, as with a lot of directors who are fine writers, Ward's sense of visual composition is off-kilter by several degrees.

NEW YORK POST, 10/29/99, p. 45, Jonathan Foreman

"The Suburbans" is a good-natured but mostly unfunny rock'n'roll satire about a one-hit-wonder band getting back together nearly 20 years after their big success.

With a screenplay that unhappily combines the sensibilities of Woody Allen and "Dawson's Creek," it wastes the talents of a cast that includes genuinely funny actors such as Will Ferrell, and Ben and Jerry Stiller.

The film starts with a flashback to 1981, with the Suburbans, a Long Island group, appearing on "American Bandstand."

Then you meet the members as they are in 1999. Mitch (Craig Bierko) is a podiatrist who still dreams of a music career. Rory (Tony Guma) is an overweight insurance salesman dating a pregnant ex-model with two kids.

Danny (Donal Lardner Ward) is a lifeguard who runs a failing soul club and who is frightened to commit to his photographer girlfriend Grace (Amy Brenneman). And Gil (Will Ferrell) is a wealthy businessman about to tie the knot.

At Gil's wedding, the band performs their one hit, and Danny meets young record-company scout Cate (Jennifer Love Hewitt). She's been a fan of the Suburbans since childhood and believes it would be a great idea for the band to get back together.

The disaster-strewn process leads Danny and Rory to re-evaluate their lives and relationships.

There are a couple of very funny, possibly improvised scenes with Jerry Stiller and Ben Stiller as father-and-son owners of the record company. There's also an amusing moment when the band members aren't allowed into their own launch party because the doorman cannot find their names on the list.

But for the most part, the chuckles are both predictable and thin. Brenneman and Hewitt give the most believable performances, and Hewitt looks great in a number of revealing outfits.

Also reviewed in:
CHICAGO TRIBUNE, 10/29/99, Friday/p. I, Gary Dretzka
NEW YORK TIMES, 10/29/99, p. E16, Janet Maslin
VARIETY, 2/8-14/99, p. 80, Dennis Harvey

SUGAR TOWN

A USA Films/October Films release of a Film Four presentation of a Jack N' Zack production. *Producer:* Dan Hassid. *Director:* Allison Anders and Kurt Voss. *Screenplay:* Allison Anders and Kurt Voss. *Director of Photography:* Kristian Bernier. *Editor:* Chris Figler. *Music:* Larry Klein. *Sound:* Aletha Rodgers and Paul Marshall. *Sound Editor:* Galen Walker and Mark Innocenti. *Production Designer:* Alyssa Coppelman. *Set Dresser:* Delphine Lafont. *Costumes:* Anita Cabada. *Make-up:* Suzan Kaminga. *Running time:* 93 minutes. *MPAA Rating:* R.

CAST: Jade Gordon (Gwen); John Taylor (Clive); Michael Des Barres (Nick); Martin Kemp (Jonesy); Larry Klein (Burt); John Doe (Carl); Lucinda Jenney (Kate); Marion Moseley (In Utero Baby); Veronica Nommenson (Violet); Elena Nommenson (Rose); Amelia Nommenson (Daisy); Ally Sheedy (Liz); Nicholas Walker (Masseuse); Rosanna Arquette (Eva); Jeff McDonald (Kevin); Catherine Munro (Groupie #1); Kristina Hayes (Groupie #2); Alyse Pozzo (Groupie #3); Richmond Arquette (Rick); Lumi Cavazos (Rocio); Michael Rodgers (Journalist); Paige Dylan (Nerve's Mom); Vincent Berry (Nerve); Polly Platt (Maggie); Chris Mulkey (Aaron); Simon Bonney (Band Member #1); Kelly Jones (Band Member #2); Beverly D'Angelo (Jane); Antonia Bogdanovich (Maya); Kai Lennox (Alex); Kadu Lennox (Monte); Bijou Phillips (Autograph Girl); Ursula Brooks (Tracy); Lacey Rodine (Groupie #4); Philip Tan (Karate Instructor).

LOS ANGELES TIMES, 9/17/99, Calendar/p. 18, Kevin Thomas

"Sugar Town," a light, wry take on the slippery slopes of the local contemporary music scene, reunites Allison Anders and Kurt Voss, who with cinematographer Dean Lent made "Border Radio," a gritty 1988 gem that exuded an engaging aura of authenticity in depicting the dicey existence of a group of rock musicians living on the margins. Not nearly so persuasive or probing, "Sugar Town" is diverting and sometimes humorous but sticks to the superficial as it introduces us to a large number of interconnected characters. "Sugar Town" offers a number of accomplished performances but is finally not distinctive enough to make much of an impression.

The intricate plot's linchpin characters are deftly drawn by Rosanna Arquette and Ally Sheedy. Arquette is Eva, a fading B-picture starlet married to John Taylor's Clive, described as a "rock god of the '80s" who hasn't had a hit in years. Sheedy's Liz is Eva's close friend, a production designer eager for romance. Clive at last has a prospect when hotshot record producer Burt (Larry Klein, who also composed the film's serviceable score) plans to team Clive with Nick (Michael Des Barres) and Jonesy (Martin Kemp), two more survivors from the '80s in equally desperate need of a comeback.

Eva tries fixing Liz up with Burt, but she has unwittingly also passed on to her as a housekeeper Gwen (Jade Gordon), a rock star wannabe whose ambition and total lack of scruples leave "All About Eve's" Eve Harrington at the starting gate.

Meanwhile, another rock musician, Carl (John Doe), signs up to go on the road with Lumi Cavazos' sexy singer Rocio, leaving his eight-months'-pregnant wife, Kate (Lucinda Jenney), at home with their three small children—and his brother Rick (Richmond Arquette), who's fresh out of rehab. Other key figures are Beverly D'Angelo's rich, hard-as-nails Jane, who will back the comeback album provided the dashing, silver-haired Nick will come across sexually, and Chris Mulkey's Aaron, a health-food store clerk whom Liz rejects when she learns he's an actor eager to use her contacts; ironically, he's not nearly as bad a person as Gwen, whose deliberately disastrous advice Liz takes unquestioningly.

Everyone is now in place to set in motion a lot of developments, many of them foolish, some improbable, others truly nasty and some providential. "Sugar Town" works best when viewed as a comment on people who don't have a whole lot going for them anymore, those who may have had just enough of what it takes to have a moment in the spotlight and then are left to cope with the rest of their lives with not much in the way of resources, financial or otherwise. By the end of the film, however, you feel that at least Eva and Nick have matured.

Anders and Voss cannot be accused of making things easy for themselves. They've created a gallery of individuals (most of whom are deftly drawn by the ensemble cast) who are either none too bright, unlikable or both. Carl and Kate are by far the most appealing individuals in the film, but both seem inordinately vulnerable to serious lapses in judgment. The bottom line, though, is that if you are going to create characters who are not all that special, then you face the challenge of making them interesting anyway. Since it's tough to become very involved with the people of "Sugar Town," the film is likely to be as forgotten as its has-been rock stars.

NEW YORK POST, 9/17/99, p. 42, Jonathan Foreman

"Sugar Town" is a real pleasure, a sweet, funny, ensemble comedy about hitting middle age in the entertainment industry, with particular emphasis on the music business.

Written and shot in the space of three months, it starts off uneasily, with some scenes that look and feel like rehearsals rather than the finished product.

But it finds its pace. And by the time it ends (with odd abruptness), you've developed such affection for the characters you really don't want it to finish. If only it could become the pilot for another great HBO series.

It's utterly authentic, and those who follow music-industry gossip will spot lots of references to real people. But you certainly don't need any insider information to enjoy this film, with its light-handed but dead-on satire, and its enjoyably unwholesome—but for the most part decent—characters.

Gwen (Jade Gordon) is the exception, a gorgeous monster who pursues her goal of becoming a rock goddess with sociopathic ruthlessness. She's paying a junkie to write songs that will make her the next Alanis, while cleaning house for lonely, sexually frustrated, New Agey production designer Liz (Ally Sheedy).

Liz's best friend is Eva (Rosanna Arquette), a former scream queen who at 35 only gets offered acting roles as Christina Ricci's mother.

Eva is married to famous rocker Clive (John Taylor from Duran Duran). He and his bandmates, Nick (Michael Des Barres from Power Station) and Jonesy (Martin Kemp from Spandau Ballet), are desperately trying to relaunch their careers.

Eva sets lonely Liz up on a date with Clive's record producer, Burt (Larry Klein), but Gwen does her best to sabotage it and to hook up with Burt herself.

Eva and Clive's household is thrown into chaos when a berobed woman turns up on their doorstep with Nerve (Vincent Berry), a sullen teenage boy she claims is Clive's son.

Meanwhile, Burt finds an investor to pay for Clive's band's album in the form of Jane (Beverly D'Angelo). But Jane's conditions include an interlude with Nick, whose insecurity about aging precludes him "having sex with adult women."

All the actors look like they're having a great time with Voss and Anders' dialogue. Ally Sheedy, strong and convincing in an unattractive role, looks like a grown-up, ultra-skinny version of the character she played in "Breakfast Club."

And as is so often the case, the real-life aging rock stars in "Sugar Town" all show themselves to be remarkably able actors.

Director and co-writer Allison Anders' last movie, "Grace of My Heart," was also about the music industry. This film is even more on the mark, and much more successful as sheer entertainment.

NEWSWEEK, 9/27/99, p. 69, David Ansen

It isn't easy growing old in the land of youth and beauty. It's even hardier if you're a rock-and-roller who hasn't had a hit in decades, or a sexy leading lady now being offered parts as Christina Ricci's mother. "Sugar Town," an agreeably scruffy L.A. satire co-written and directed by Allison Anders and Kurt Voss, is filled with sharp, funny snapshots of the hustlers, has-beens, recovering junkies and Topanga Canyon earth mothers on the fringes of the Hollywood music biz.

The movie may lack visual dazzle—it was shot fast and cheap—but it knows its way around town. There's the 50-something Billy Idol type (Michael Des Barres) who has a phobia about sleeping with women his own age, and Beverly D'Angelo as the foul-mouthed heiress he needs to satisfy to secure backing for his new record. There's the neurotic New Age production designer (Ally Sheedy) whose dating life is a disaster, and the ruthless wannabe rock star (Jade Gordon) who'll rip off anyone to get ahead. There's the fading rocker (John Taylor, of Duran Duran fame) facing a paternity suit, the wild child named Nirvana who may be his son, the sober guitarist (John Doe) trying to remain faithful to his wife on the road and a half dozen other deftly sketched show-biz desperadoes who make this slight but tangy sleeper such an unpretentious delight.

TIME, 9/13/99, p. 74, Richard Schickel

Sugar Town opens with a wanna-be rock star (Jade Gordon) making a list about how to achieve that status. Attending the Grammys with an old, paparazzi-attractive guy is high on it. Tony Bennett will do. Also Tony Curtis.

Don't bet against her. This kid will steal anything—a boyfriend, clothes, jewels—to get to the top. And don't bet against *Sugar Town* either. It's the kind of movie Robert Altman might make if he ODed on Elavil—a multicharacter comedy about the Los Angeles rock scene. Make that the trashed rock scene. For it's mostly about people who once had it, then lost it, but would like to find it again.

Central to *Sugar Town*, which was written and directed with casual aplomb by Allison Anders and Kurt Voss, are the efforts of a new band, composed of old rockers trying to re-establish themselves. In the end, that comes down to getting one of them, played by Michael Des Barres, who is exclusively interested in teenyboppers, to sexually service a potential backer, the hilariously voracious Beverly D'Angelo. The look on his face when he discovers the joys of mature sex could serve as the emblem of this sweet-tempered movie, which eventually touches—wryly, knowingly, forgivingly—on at least a dozen lives.

Mostly, they all—including the likes of Rosanna Arquette, Ally Sheedy and a lot of people who, like the characters then play, deserve to be better known—get what they want. Or at least manage to make the right compromises. Like the lives it recounts, *Sugar Town* comes to no resounding conclusion. But that indeterminacy is part of its seductiveness, part of its truth.

VILLAGE VOICE, 9/21/99, p. 160, Amy Taubin

Romance, [see Taubin's review of that film] is a hard act to follow, and it's probably not helpful to Allison Anders and Kurt Voss that their female-oriented comedy *Sugar Town* opens on the same day. Like *Border Radio* (1989), their UCLA Film School collaboration, *Sugar Town* is set in the Los Angeles rock scene. Sorry to say, the follow-up is neither as lively nor as tough as the original, and compared to the hardcore punk of *Border Radio*, the score for *Sugar Town* sounds like Muzak.

Actually, the subject of the film is not so much sex or music as it is being over-the-hill at 40 in L.A. The narrative, which is shaped as an Altman-esque round-robin, concerns some once-famous rock stars trying to make a comeback, the women they're involved with, the women friends of the women they're involved with, and the women who try to cut the throats of the women the rock stars are involved with or the throats of the friends of etc., etc.

Given Anders's reputation as a feminist filmmaker, it's disturbing that she's so much gentler with her male than her female characters. The men in *Sugar Town* are kind of hapless, but they try. At worst, they seem like they don't know what hit them. At best, they're John Doe, who leaves the first lucrative gig he's had in years because the Latina star is putting the moves on him and he refuses to be unfaithful to his wife.

The women of *Sugar Town* fall into three categories: airheads played by Rosanna Arquette and Ally Sheedy; dragon ladies played by Jade Gordon (a low-rent version of Nicole Kidman in *To Die For*), Lumi Cavazos, and Beverly D'Angelo; and mothers, or rather one very pregnant mother (played by Lucinda Jenney). The film's message to women is that motherhood is sacred and if you haven't experienced it you are to be pitied. I had a moment of doubting my extreme negative reaction to the sexual politics of this film. Then I read the following note by Anders in the press kit: "We made fun of everything that was once precious to me with the exception of childbirth and children." Everyone to her own perversity, but I'll take Breillat's anytime.

Also reviewed in:
CHICAGO TRIBUNE, 10/1/99, Friday/p. H, Michael Wilmington
NEW YORK TIMES, 9/17/99, p. E23, Janet Maslin
VARIETY, 2/8-14/99, p. 78, Todd McCarthy
WASHINGTON POST, 10/15/99, Weekend/p. 45, Desson Howe

SUITS

A Tenafly Film Company release of a Taurus Entertainment Company presentation of an Eric Weber/Chris Giordano production. *Executive Producer:* Eric Weber and Chris Giordano. *Director:* Eric Weber. *Screenplay:* Eric Weber. *Director of Photography:* Peter Nelson. *Editor:* Nancy Novack. *Music:* Pat Irwin, Lisa Gotthell, and Naomi Putterman. *Sound:* Rick Dior. *Casting:* Lina Todd. *Production Designer:* Pam Shamshiri. *Art Director:* Pam Shamshiri. *Costumes:* Ivan Ingermann. *Running time:* 88 minutes. *MPAA Rating:* R.

CAST: Robert Klein (Tom Cranston); Tony Hendra (George Parkyn); Larry Pine (Peter Haverford); Paul Lazar (Mitchell Mitnick); Randy Pearlstein (Ken Tuttle); Frank Minucci (Robert Naylor Sr.); Edoardo Ballerini (Johnny Akida); Ingrid Rogers (Anita Tanner); James Villemaire (Doug Humphrey); Mark Lake (Harson Covington); Joelle Carter (Heidi Wilson).

NEW YORK POST, 9/24/99, p. 50, Hannah Brown

Inside "Suits," a self-indulgent satire of the advertising industry, is a terrific comedy sketch yearning to break free.

The film, written and directed by veteran adman Eric Weber (he's also the author of the best-selling "How to Pick Up Girls"), takes on one of the world's easiest targets—the alienated staff of a Madison Avenue agency—and gives it a new spin by detailing the conflicts between the "Suits" (the executives) and the "Creatives" (the copywriters, designers and directors who actually create the ads).

The problem is that we're supposed to feel sorry for the poor, oppressed "Creatives," forced to use their genius to churn out slogans to sell deodorant, and loathe the evil "Suits."

The truth is, though, that the film's hero Ken Tuttle (Randy Pearlstein), who's supposedly just one year out of college, doesn't seem to have such a bad deal. He's already a top copywriter at the agency, has his own office and wears jeans to work.

Not only that, but the "Suit" who runs his agency, Tom Cranston (Robert Klein), is actually a smart guy who recognizes Ken's talent, as well as that of Ken's mentor, George Parkyn (Tony Hendra).

But when Cranston is out of town, the fatuous "Suit" Peter Haverford (Larry Pine) and his team of toadies take over, get Parkyn fired, ignore Ken's brilliant ideas and botch the important ad campaign they're working on for a new sanitary napkin.

Alas, potentially hysterical scenes, like the one in which so many guys from the agency listen in on a focus group of teenage girls talking about tampons that they actually break through the one-way mirror, are sabotaged by clumsy pacing and broad acting.

Also reviewed in:
NEW YORK TIMES, 9/24/99, p. E14, Lawrence Van Gelder
VARIETY, 1/25-31/99, p. 75, Lael Loewenstein

SUMMER OF SAM

A Touchstone Pictures release of a 40 Acres and a Mule Filmworks production. *Executive Producer:* Michael Imperioli and Jeri Carroll-Colicchio. *Producer:* Spike Lee and Jon Kilik. *Director:* Spike Lee. *Screenplay:* Victor Colicchio, Michael Imperioli, and Spike Lee. *Director of Photography:* Ellen Kuras. *Editor:* Barry Alexander Brown. *Music:* Terence Blanchard. *Music Editor:* Maisie Weissman and Lori Slomka. *Choreographer:* Otis Sallid. *Sound:* Rolf Pardula and (music) Geoff Foster. *Sound Editor:* Kevin Lee. *Casting:* Aisha Coley. *Production Designer:* Thérèse DePrez. *Art Director:* Nicholas Lundy. *Set Decorator:* Diane Lederman. *Set Dresser:* Harvey Goldberg, Douglas Fetch, Henry Kaplan, Joanna Hartell, and Dana Neuwirth. *Special Effects:* Steve Kirschoff. *Costumes:* Ruth E. Carter. *Make-up:* Anita Gibson. *Make-up (Mira Sorvino):* Margot Boccia. *Stunt Coordinator:* Jeff Ward. *Running time:* 145 minutes. *MPAA Rating:* R.

CAST: John Leguizamo (Vinny); Adrien Brody (Ritchie); Mira Sorvino (Dionna); Jennifer Esposito (Ruby); Anthony LaPaglia (Detective Lou Petrocelli); Bebe Neuwirth (Gloria); Patti LuPone (Helen); Ben Gazzara (Luigi); John Savage (Simon); Michael Badalucco (David Berkowitz, Son of Sam); Michael Rispoli (Joey T); Miker Starr (Eddie); Roger Guenveur Smith (Detective Curt Atwater); Saverio Guerra (Woodstock); Brian Tarantino (Bobby Del Fiore); Arthur Nascarella (Mario); Ken Garito (Brian); Al Palagonia (Anthony); Joe Lisi (Tony Olives); James Reno (Crony); Jimmy Breslin (Himself); Spike Lee (John Jeffries); Lucia Grillo (Chiara); Nelson Vasquez (Officer Cruz); Darielle Gilad (Debbie Cadabra); Michael Harper (Raygun); Jessica Galbreath (Fire); Evan Cohen (Bite); George Tabb (Spider); Michael Imperioli (Midnight); Victor Colicchio (Chickie); Peter Maloney (Detective Timothy Dowd); Christopher Wynkoop (Sam Carr); John Turturro (Voice of Harvey the Black Dog); Ernie Anastos and Jim Jensen (Anchormen); Melba Tolliver (Anchorwoman); Phil Rizzuto (Yankee Broadcaster); Reggie Jackson (Himself); Danielle Burgio and Lisa France (Girls in Parked Car); Peter Epstein (Chuckie); Jill Stokesberry (Rose); Joseph Lyle Taylor (Ron); Kim Director (Dee); Bill Raymond (Father Cadilli); Mildrid Clinton and Emelise Aleandri (Italian Women at Murder Site); Michael Sorvino (Bowler at Diner); Phil Campanella (2nd Bowler at Diner); William H. Burns and Ernest Mingione (Officers); Frank Fortunato (Doorman); Dan Zappin (Simon's Male Friend); Murielle Cohen and Christina Kolbe (Simon's Female Friends); Charlotte Colavin (Neighbor); Clayton Barber (Punk); Joie Lee (Bed Stuy Woman Interviewed); Rome Neal and Mark Breland (Bed Stuy Men Interviewed); Susan Batson (Bed Stuy Woman Interviewed); Evander Holyfield (Man in Riot); Toneda Laiwan (Dot, Atwater's Girlfriend); Janet Paparazzo and Jodi Michelle Pynn (Young Women Shot by Son of Sam); Jennifer S. Badger (Woman Victim); Jeff DeRocker (Man in Car); Nick Oddo (Husband); Damian Achilles (Wounded Man); Joanne Lamstein (Woman in Car); Gabriel Barre (Johnny Nasso); Norman Douglass (Stunt Driver); Tara McNamee (Woman Victim); *L.E.S. Stitches Band:* John Michael (Singer); Damian Branica (Bassist); Lorne Behrman (Guitarists); Curtis Gove (Guitarists); James Baggs (Drummer); Rozie Bacchi (Brian's Girlfriend); Grace DeSena (Joe T's Girlfriend); Zoe Bournelis (Anthony's Girlfriend); Ashleigh Closs (Princess); Frank Cadillac (Patty aka Man with Weird Eyes); Daniel J. Courtenay (Guitar Store Owner); Michael Prozzo (Rocco); Kathryn Hudd (Rocco's Girlfriend); Antonio Torres (Man Pulled from Car); Pamela Wehner (Lady at Block Party); Dionna Colicchio, Victoria Galasso, and Danielle Tutelian (Girls at Block Party); Mario Machaluso (Italian Chef); Andrew Lasky (Officer Cruz's Partner); Richard Paul (Detective with Decoy Dummy); Ray Carlson (Crime Scene Cop); Alexander J. Vega (Bouncer); Steven Croft (Limo driver); Mary Jo Todaro and Jacqueline Margolis (Ladies in Window); Iris Alten (Lady in Car Window); Valerie Mazzonelli (Lady with Dog); Hal Sherman (Arresting Detective); Nicholas Brown (Young Detective Petrocelli).

LOS ANGELES TIMES, 7/2/99, Calendar/p. 1, Kenneth Turan

"Summer of Sam" is shorthand for New York City in the unbearably hot summer of 1977, when a serial killer known as Son of Sam terrorized the city and inspired state-of-the-art tabloid headlines such as "Killer to Cops: I'll Do It Again."

That summer, director/co-writer Spike Lee informed the media, has always held special meaning for him: It was when he decided to become a director and bought his first Super-8 camera. But despite both that personal connection and Lee's considerable filmmaking skills (this is, after all, his 13th feature), "Summer of Sam" is a glum and unpleasant experience, caught between what it wants to do and how it has chosen to do it.

Parents of Son of Sam's victims as well as the still-incarcerated murderer himself (real name David Berkowitz, who pleaded guilty in 1978 to six killings) have complained about having those long-ago horrors exploited on film, but "Summer of Sam" is not really about the killings per se. Rather, the Victor Colicchio, Michael Imperioli and Spike Lee script tries to use that crisis in the city to show the effect the chaotic 1970s, with its strong counterculture and pervasive sexuality, had on the mores of conventional society.

To tell this larger story, "Summer of Sam" concentrates on a staunchly Italian American neighborhood in the Bronx where some of the killings took place and more particularly on two couples united by the close friendship between the men in each. Lee's choices seem natural, but they don't turn out to be very satisfying.

The center of the neighborhood, and of the film, is the husband-and-wife combination of Vinny (an energetic and convincing John Leguizamo) and Dionna (Mira Sorvino). Their dancing skill gives them the sheen of royalty in the flashy local disco, but the reality is that their marriage is in trouble even though Dionna doesn't know it yet.

For Vinny, employed as a hairdresser, is an incorrigible womanizer who sleeps with anyone who's willing and available. But when he realizes that one of his back-seat assignations has narrowly avoided making him one of Son of Sam's victims, Vinny takes it as a sign from God to straighten up. If he can.

While Vinny is very much of the neighborhood, his best friend Ritchie ("The Thin Red Line's" Adrien Brody) still lives there but is desperate to get away. A would-be punk who favors exaggerated hairdos and the occasional fake British accent, Ritchie puts on unusual (to say the least) one-man stage performances in Manhattan and bonds with Ruby (Jennifer Esposito), the neighborhood bad girl and fellow outcast.

All these crises get heightened and intensified because of the pressures and paranoia caused by the Son of Sam murders, which so terrifies the neighborhood that the discos stand empty and women rush to dye their hair blond when the rumor circulates that the killer is partial to brunets.

"Summer of Sam's" greatest success is in its ability (helped by Ellen Kuras' brooding cinematography) to re-create a gritty New York street feel. The film evokes the tensions and in-your-face bravado of a neighborhood where everyone has an attitude and acknowledging, let alone respecting, other people's feelings are ideas so alien they might as well come from Mars.

But though Lee and company can make the neighborhood convincing, they can't make it interesting. Uniformly white (the director plays one of the film's few persons of color, a superficial TV news reporter from Manhattan) and filled with never-gonna-grow-up lost boys who don't hesitate to call one of their number Bobby the Fairy, this is one dense, thick-headed neck of the woods.

Equally uninteresting are "Summer of Sam's" central couples. Outcasts Ritchie and Ruby, constructs created to make a point, never make the leap to real people. Even less appealing are Vinny and Dionna, whose shaky marriage is subjected to an unfortunate chance exposure to the sexual license of Plato's Retreat. As husband and wife curse and scream at each other, it's too exhausting to care whether this tedious, dysfunctional relationship survives or not.

Also shocking and disturbing is the considerable physical violence—both endemic to the neighborhood and created by Son of Sam—that overshadows everything. The problem is not that the film's beatings and killings are rough and raw, it's that it's hard to see what purpose they serve.

For as all "Summer of Sam's" key relationships disintegrate into betrayal, intolerance, stupidity and both physical and verbal beatings, it becomes increasingly difficult to tolerate the chaos, let alone figure out what to make of it. Lee is a powerful filmmaker who certainly knows how to have an impact on an audience, but those who survive his ministrations are likely to wonder if in this case the battle was worth the bruises.

NEW YORK POST, 7/2/99, p. 40, Rod Dreher

Spike Lee's "Summer of Sam" is an interesting failure, an ambitious misfire from the director who, absent Martin Scorsese, one would have thought perfect to tell this New York story.

It's a sprawling, fevered, kitchen-sink movie that's less than the sum of its often bracing parts.

Some moments rank with the best work of Lee's career, and he gets a galvanizing, career-making performance from John Leguizamo.

But the movie is a ragged mess that only rarely connects with its audience or with a point. As ever with Lee (who co-wrote the screenplay with Victor Colicchio and Michael Imperioli), the visuals are far more sophisticated than the storytelling.

"Summer of Sam" is not about pudgy sicko David Berkowitz, though the brief scenes with the guy, played by Michael Badalucco, are terrifying. Rather, it concerns the way his killing spree affected a working-class Italian-American neighborhood in The Bronx during the scorching summer of '77. Leguizamo plays studly hairdresser Vinny, a guido Warren Beatty by day, a leisure-suited John Travolta on the disco floor by night.

He's got a bad conscience about cheating on his wife Dionna (Mira Sorvino), whose cousin he's shagging in a car one night when Son of Sam passes by. This brush with death scares Vinny straight, or at least into making an honest attempt. Had the screenplay stayed with Vinny's story, deepened his character and tightened its focus on Sam as the dark side of the era's hedonism, Lee might have had a great film.

But the film drags in too many characters with too little to do. Vinny's pal Ritchie (a superb Adrien Brody) is a Bronx boy whose imagination is captured by the nascent punk scene in downtown Manhattan. He dances in a sleazy gay cabaret for extra cash, and plays CBGB's with his girlfriend, slut-'n-the-hood Ruby (Jennifer Esposito).

Meanwhile, the neighborhood lunkheads put their fat heads to work trying to find the killer—who they suspect could be their freaky friend Ritchie.

Their pick-up vigilante mob has competition from the real Mob, as a Mafia chief played by Ben Gazzara (who is far better than his cliched role turns out to be) takes control of the area's streets during the blackout.

None of this amounts to much. You find yourself bored, wondering where the various narratives are going, and finally not caring what happens to these lowlife dullards.

Is Ritchie really gay?

Will Vinny zip his polyester double-knit trousers and save his marriage?

Can you stick with this thing for two hours-plus? "Summer of Sam's" real pleasures are in its textures: the grimy atmosphere of the city heat—stroking its way through summer, woozy from promiscuous sex, drugs, sweat, riots, murder and the Yanks.

There's an intense, jagged montage set to The Who's "Baba O'Riley" that distills the spirit of fear, paranoia and chaos Lee fails to bring to the rest of the film.

The movie's most indelible moment comes during an orgy at Plato's Retreat: Dionna's bored, sad face juxtaposed with Vinny's tortured but exalted visage tells us everything we need to know about this crashing-and-burning couple—and a lot about that moment in history, too.

The raunchy dialogue is wearing on the ears after a while, and though the movie does not center on Berkowitz, his abrupt appearances outside the cars of his victims are shockingly violent.

Another scene, in which Lee uses computer technology to give the dog Berkowitz believed was telling him to kill a voice and mouth movements like the Taco Bell chihuahua, is just awful.

NEWSDAY, 7/2/99, Part II/p. B3, John Anderson

The Summer of '77 was an absurdity, a Wagnerian steambath, a circus tent filling up with gas. Elvis self-immolated on a burning love of barbiturates and fried bananas. The pin-striped soap opera called the Yankees was lurching toward its first World Series victory since '62. The weather was infernal. And a loser named David Berkowitz was blowing the heads off young people on the lovers' lanes of a bankrupt—and, for one night, blacked-out city.

Employing Jimmy Breslin bookends, ironic disco, stylized horror and (soap) operatic overtones, Spike Lee certainly captures the inherent absurdity in "Summer of Sam." In his very deliberate way, and with the aid of the gifted cinematographer Ellen Kuras, he has created one of the more visually spirited movies of his career—even if, on occasion, he proves himself more than willing to suspend narrative clarity for the shot he wants to make. But to what end? A voyeuristic film about a voyeuristic killer that savages everyone and every character it touches.

For all the outcry from the victims' families about Berkowitz being "glorified" by Lee—and the alleged tears shed by the imprisoned killer over the pain the movie is going to cause—the Berkowitz character (Michael Badalucco) is a side show. We see him writhing in his squalid Yonkers apartment, tortured by both the heat and the incessant barking of neighbor Sam Carr's black dog (which will talk to Berkowitz before the movie is over) and adding a pathetic note to the murder scenes when his pudgy form scuttles off to the shadows. He's a misshapen ornament, a grotesquerie whose presence calls into question the very essence of the universe, but whose own essence is opaque.

Which would be fine, of course, if you cared about the people he's stalking, or their religious neuroses, or their sexual peculiarities—all of which make up a lot more of "Summer" than Sam. We get nothing about the victims, and everything about a raft of characters who function as walking stereotypes, be they ethnic (Italian), religious (Catholic) or class (blue-collar).

First among equals is Vinny (John Leguizamo), the philandering newlywed who can't ask his wife, Dionna (Mira Sorvino), for creative sex because his Catholic upbringing tells him it's a sin. So, he finds it everywhere else in the neighborhood, from Dionna's Italian cousin—with whom he narrowly escapes a Berkowitz bullet—to Gloria (Bebe Neuwirth), who owns the beauty shop where Vinny cuts heads. Whether he's praying for sexual redemption before a statue of the Virgin Mary—or, toward the end of the film, screaming with Dionna beneath a haloed crucifix—Vinny is the supplicant of love.

Everyone else in the movie—from Adrien Brody's punk-hustler Ritchie, to Jennifer Esposito's slut-rocker Ruby, to Ben Gazzara's mobster-patriarch Luigi, to the trio of mugs who close the streets and beat intruders during the riotous blackout—represents some aspect of the roiling cultural soup of '77. So you have to ask yourself: Vinny? Leguizamo can certainly carry a movie, even if he has to do it as an Italian (maybe they all look alike to Lee?), but his job is to portray the residual ugliness and ignorance of a guy who can't reconcile his religion with his gonads. It's interesting that William Donohue, the Catholic League and their punching bags at Disney are all doing backflips over the theology comedy "Dogma" and no one has uttered a word about the Catholic-baiting and ethnic bias of "Summer of Sam" (co-scripted by actors Victor Colicchio and Michael Imperioli). Maybe they will.

From Yankee Stadium to Plato's Retreat, Studio 54 to CBGB's, Lee's portrait of New York is as unwieldy as his style. There's a terrific sequence scored with The Who's "Baba O'Riley," a virtual collage of characters and atmospherics that has the kind of energy you crave more of in "Summer of Sam." Conversely, with each scene featuring Dionna and Vinny, the music disintegrates into a mawkish, cloying syrup that would be funny if you thought it were intentional.

Lee himself makes an appearance, as the John Johnson manque John Jeffries, making on-the-street reports from a city that seems very different from the one in the Bronx, where Vinny, Dionna, Ritchie and Ruby hang their Yankees caps. That's obviously one of Lee's elusive points. But by the end, you're not really sure what "Summer of Sam" was about, if not just biliousness and pain.

SIGHT AND SOUND, 2/00, p. 57, Geoffrey Macnab

New York City, the summer of 1977. Bronx married couple Vinny and Dionna dance at a nightclub; Vinny sneaks off to have sex with Dionna's cousin just near where serial killer 'Son of Sam' is about to kill another couple. On his way home with Dionna, Vinny sees the victims and thinks Sam may be stalking him. Ritchie, Vinny's best friend, has embraced punk rock; the local Italian-American guys think he's a freak. Ritchie's stepfather tells him to move into the garage. He strikes up a relationship with Ruby, one of Vinny's former girlfriends. Vinny claims to love Dionna, but continues to cheat on her.

The police ask local gangster Luigi for help in catching Sam. The city is sweltering and a lynch mob mentality is developing. Learning he's a dancer in a gay porn club as well as a punk, the local guys decide Ritchie must be Sam.   They try to get Vinny to help them catch him. Meanwhile, Vinny's marriage is breaking up. Dionna moves out of the apartment.   Full of self-pity and high on drugs, Vinny betrays Ritchie to the neighbourhood thugs who beat him up. Ritchie's stepfather rescues him, telling the thugs that the real Sam, David Berkowitz, has already been caught by the police.

Summer of Sam, set in New York during the heatwave of 1977 when serial killer David Berkowitz was terrorising the city, has been largely misrepresented by the press.   A *New York Times* article in June quoted relatives of Berkowitz's victims railing against its director Spike Lee. "He feels that murder is entertainment," said one.   Berkowitz himself, now serving six consecutive life sentences, expressed his disappointment that the film was raking up "what is best forgotten."

Berkowitz, however, is only a minor player in the movie he helped inspire: *Summer of Sam* could just as well have been called *Summer of Reggie* (while Berkowitz was on his killing spree, baseball player Reggie Jackson helped the Yankees win the World Series) or *Scenes from an Italian-American Marriage*.   Lee's real interest is in the relationships between members of a close-knit neighbourhood in the Bronx.   With tensions aggravated by the sweaty weather and the fear of a serial killer in their midst, it's a community which is close to boiling point—similar to the Bedford-Stuyvesant neighbourhood in *Do the Right Thing*.   Lee captures brilliantly the creeping sense of paranoia that affected the city and the strange, macabre thrill of having its own serial killer. (To avoid Sam, who reportedly favours brunettes, women begin dying their hair blond or wearing wigs.) With such craziness in the air, it doesn't even seem incongruous when the killer begins to think a black labrador is talking to him, enjoining him to "kill, kill, kill."

The film begins and ends with veteran journalist Jimmy Breslin speaking directly to camera about "the summer of Sam".   His presence at once evokes the metropolis we know from Weegee photographs and gritty cop dramas, and creates a strange kind of nostalgia.   In *Summer of Sam* as in Martin Scorsese's *Bringing Out the Dead* (set in the early 90s), we're seeing a New York which no longer exists.   Mayor Giuliani may have cleaned up crime (homicides are now at their lowest since 1961, Breslin tells us) but he has also taken the heart out of the city.   But *Summer of Sam* also fits loosely into the serial killer genre, a line which stretches from *M* (1931) to *Se7en*. Several plot points even rekindle memories of Hitchcock's *The Lodger* (1926): as the lynch-mob mentality gets out of control, an innocent man is targeted simply because he doesn't fit in.

Lee, who adapted an original screenplay by Victor Colicchio and Michael Imperioli, isn't above playing up the Italian-American stereotypes.   Family loyalty and religious guilt figure as prominently here as they do in Scorsese's movies.   Well over two hours long, *Summer of Sam* isn't taut, either.   It is an ensemble piece full of flamboyant minor characters (Tony Olives, Joey T), all of them played beautifully but none developed in any great depth.   Ben Gazzara's patriarchal mobster has one big scene in a restaurant, but is barely glimpsed after that; Bebe Neuwirth (Vinny's boss) and Patti Lupone (Ritchie's mother) seem similarly underused.

Lee's focus is more on Vinny's crumbling marriage to Dionna and his friendship with Ritchie. Mumbling, cursing, intensely physical, John Leguizamo's Vinny comes across like a diminutive version of Brando's Stanley Kowalski.   Adrien Brody is equally striking as the punk who wanders round New York "sounding like a British fag," and looking as if he has just escaped from Carnaby Street.   Berkowitz then is only there to provide the historical context for what turns out to be one of Lee's very best films—a sprawling, brilliantly acted character study which touches on love, friendship and betrayal, while also managing to recreate the last days of disco without a note of self-parody.

TIME, 7/5/99, p. 75, Richard Corliss

Summer in New York City, 1977. A record heat wave, a Yankee pennant drive, a blackout and a looting spree.

For the tabloids and news shows, and for six unlucky people who died at the business end of his .44, that scalding season belonged to the Son of Sam.

Someone could make a good movie about a tortured fellow who kills lovers in parked cars on the advice of a talking dog. But in Summer of Sam, a kind of Bronx *Boogie Nights*, Spike Lee has made a very bad movie with David Berkowitz deep in the background. It's mainly about whether a Bronx hairdresser would rat on his best friend if he didn't get deflated by his wife. How do you say "Huh?" in Italian?

In a Spike Lee môvie you can barely see the characters behind all the editorial placards. Da boys in this hood hang out under a big sign reading DEAD END. Vinny the hairdresser (John Leguizamo) cheats on his wife (Mira Sorvino), then takes her to Plato's Retreat for a disastrous evening of group sex. His best friend, Ritchie (valiant Adrien Brody), is a newborn punk who moonlights as a dancer-stud in a gay porno house. The local lowlifes think Ritchie is weird; he's not *neighborhood*. So he must be the Son of Sam.

Movies have had way too much fun with Italian-American stereotyping, but Lee plays it dead serious, unendurably shrill—and for an endless 2 hrs. 20 min. Still, we can't pin all the blame for ethnic defamation on Lee; his screenwriters are Victor Colicchio and Michael Imperioli. To them, we cry, like a stern Italian grandma, *"Vergogna!"* That's how you say "Shame on you" in Italian.

VILLAGE VOICE, 7/6/99, p. 65, J. Hoberman

Quick thinking as he is, Spike Lee rarely shoots a boring scene or makes an entirely coherent movie. The details are worked out; the structure is unbalanced. Lee has more-better ideas and weaker follow-through than any director in Hollywood.

As feverishly disjunctive as they were, the early films, and even *Malcolm X,* promised a new sort of political rhetoric—a showboat didacticism founded less on social content than social conflict. But since *Crooklyn,* Lee's movies have felt like brainstormed knockoffs. Whether low-budget miniatures or sweeping urban landscapes, they're broad-stroke canvases in which the paint runs and the figures are barely drafted. They're never less than must-see but very much less than fully achieved.

Summer of Sam, which is being rushed out for the Fourth of July weekend, is even more sprawling than *Clockers* or *He Got Game*—a tabloid epic that takes the terror reign of serial-killer David "Son of Sam" Berkowitz as a prism to refract the riotous disco-punk Sodom that was 1977 New York. From the moment that Jimmy Breslin, the then *Daily News* columnist to whom Berkowitz addressed his infamous missives, takes the screen to proclaim his ambivalent love for his hometown and swat the viewer with clichés, the movie rushes off in three separate—and frustratingly valid—directions.

Reworked by Lee from a screenplay by Victor Colicchio and Michael Imperioli, *Summer of Sam* is at once a psycho-killer procedural in the tradition invented by Fritz Lang's *M*; a panoramic and perversely nostalgic evocation of New York's sleazy '70s; and an analysis of mass hysteria —specifically, the projection of evil onto otherness. The last aspect is the most developed. A philandering Bronx hairdresser named Vinny (John Leguizamo), out cheating on his disco-queen wife Dionna (Mira Sorvino), barely escapes being Sam's seventh victim.

From that moment on, the Son of Sam case is tied into the vagaries of Vinny's libido and the prejudices of his insular Italian American neighborhood, particularly as both are provoked by the return of Vinny's friend Ritchie (Adrien Brody). An aspiring punk rocker, and sometime porn actor, Ritchie rehabilitates the local bad girl (Jennifer Esposito) while picking up spare change by dancing naked—and hustling patrons—at a downtown dive called Male World. That the narrative ultimately coalesces into a modified *Mean Streets*—tightly wrapped Vinny as ambivalent neighborhood insider and Ritchie as his outcast buddy—is only one Scorsese echo.

Summer of Sam lacks Scorsese's precise sense of place but there's no doubt that this is his town. The 1977 anthem "New York, New York" is the movie's final number and just about everyone lives in a Travis Bickle nightmare. The letters left by Son of Sam (Michael Badalucco) echo Travis's diary and are themselves transformed into Ritchie's punk anthems. Meanwhile, *Taxi Driver*'s overheated mélange of splattered brains, sexual disgust, and Forty Deuce expressionism are marshaled to represent the period. *Summer of Sam*'s look is beyond lurid; at once bleached-out and oversaturated, the color has the quality of an 8mm porn loop.

A borderline cacophony—with Terence Blanchard's score suavely percolating under everything from Abba and the Who to high-decibel domestic squabbles and Yankee play-by-play—*Summer of Sam* goes into overdrive when the killer shoots the demon dog that's been driving him crazy to trigger a mad montage of murder, dope, prayer, and Male World prancing, mostly in mega close-up and set to "Baba O'Riley." Add to this the summer's traumatic power outage and the director's own jarringly affectless cameo as TV newsreporter John Jeffries. (To compound the joke, Lee goes for a "darker perspective," doing an on-the-street interview with a giggling bystander played by his sister Joie.)

Although Lee ignores the fact that 1977 was also the summer of *Star Wars,* the result is a laundromat effect in which subplots and characters are mashed against the washing-machine glass and then recede into the swirl. Occasionally, the centrifugal motion slows down in a sodden tangle of exposition, as when Vinny and Dionna hop in one frenzied night from CBGB to Studio 54 to the orgy at Plato's Retreat. By the time Vinny is driven to pretend to believe that his friend is the terror of the city, the old neighborhood isn't the only thing out of control.

Twenty minutes too long (or two hours too short), *Summer of Sam* is a film in which many things seem to happen twice and others not at all. It's an immersion in pungent urban detritus—not unlike combing Coney Island beach on a Monday morning. The elements are there but the movie isn't.

Also reviewed in:
CHICAGO TRIBUNE, 7/2/99, Friday/p. A, Michael Wilmington
NATION, 7/26 & 8/2/99, p. 34, Stuart Klawans
NEW YORK TIMES, 7/2/99, p. E1, Janet Maslin
NEW YORKER, 7/12/99, p. 87, David Denby
VARIETY, 5/24-30/99, p. 36, Todd McCarthy
WASHINGTON POST, 7/2/99, p. C1, Rita Kempley
WASHINGTON POST, 7/2/99, Weekend/p. 40, Michael O'Sullivan

SUPERSTAR

A Paramount Pictures release in association with SNL Studios of a Lorne Michaels production. *Executive Producer:* Robert K. Weiss and Susan Cavan. *Director:* Bruce McCulloch. *Screenplay:* Steven Wayne Koren. *Based on a character created by:* Molly Shannon. *Director of Photography:* Walt Lloyd. *Editor:* Malcolm Campbell. *Music:* Michael Gore and Elliot Lurie. *Sound:* Dan Munro. *Sound Editor:* Randle Akerson and David R. Cohn. *Casting:* Phyliss Huffman. *Production Designer:* Gregory Keen. *Art Director:* Peter Grundy. *Set Decorator:* Doug McCullough. *Costumes:* Eydi Caines-Floyd. *Running time:* 88 minutes. *MPAA Rating:* PG-13.

CAST: Molly Shannon (Mary Katherine Gallagher); Will Ferrell (Sky Corrigan/Jesus); Elaine Hendrix (Evian); Harland Williams (Slater); Mark McKinney (Father Ritley); Glynis Johns (Grandma); Emmy Laybourne (Helen); Natalie Radford (Autumn); Karen Dwyer (Summer).

LOS ANGELES TIMES, 10/8/99, Calendar/p. 8, John Anderson

[The following review by John Anderson appeared in a slightly different form in
NEWSDAY, 10/8/99, Part II/p. B14.]

The funniest moment on the recent "Saturday Night Live" anniversary show belonged to comedian Chris Rock. Wow, he said, 25 years. Four of 'em funny. He then made the nervy if not particularly novel observation that "SNL" alumni had been responsible for some of the worst movies ever made.

Chalk up another. "Superstar," in which "SNL" regular Molly Shannon brings her love-hungry Catholic schoolgirl Mary Katherine Gallagher to the big screen, pining for one big kiss, will have you pining for another Butabi Brothers movie. As "SNL" and "Superstar" producer Lorne Michaels certainly knows, and certainly doesn't care, making a feature-length film out of the kind of TV sketch that overstays its welcome at five minutes requires a lot of filler. If "Superstar" were meatloaf—and that would be an improvement—the recipe would be 4 pounds bread crumbs to 3 ounces sirloin. Make that chuck.

It's tough to get too indignant about the Mary Katherine character, in her too-short plaid skirt, unflattering glasses and impossible dreams, because she lacks the aggressive imbecility of, let's say, the late Chris Farley, or Adam Sandler in some of his more profitable moments. But she's equally dishonest, since her purpose is to provoke both derision and pity for a character too pathetic to live, but who ultimately triumphs because ... well, because it's her movie.

Directed by former Kid in the Hall Bruce McCulloch, "Superstar" has a few funny moments—the off-handed comments of Mary Katherine's crush, high school hero Sky Corrigan ("SNL's" Will Ferrell), are often hilarious, though largely inaudible. A sequence in which Mary Katherine and her special-ed classmate Helen (Emmy Laybourne) fantasize a supermodel documentary is also a lot smarter than the rest of the movie, which chronicles Mary Katherine's pursuit of that Hollywood-style kiss, her audition for the talent show and her excruciating abuse at the hands of the vapid but beautiful Evian (Elaine Hendrix) and her cohorts Summer and Autum (Karyn Dwyer, Natalie Radford).

Glynis Johns is Gallagher's grandmother, proving, once again, that the only time an actress older than 60 gets into one of these movies is so she can say the f-word and drive the audience into a frenzy. Do popcorn counters sell hemlock? They should think about it.

Also reviewed in:
CHICAGO TRIBUNE, 10/8/99, Friday/p. I, Mark Caro
NEW YORK TIMES, 10/8/99, p. E30, Anita Gates
VARIETY, 10/11-17/99, p. 46, Dennis Harvey
WASHINGTON POST, 10/8/99, p. C5, Stephen Hunter
WASHINGTON POST, 10/8/99, Weekend/p. 55, Michael O'Sullivan

SWEET AND LOWDOWN

A Sony Pictures Classics release of a Sweetland Films presentation of a Jean Doumanian production. *Executive Producer:* J.E. Beaucaire. *Producer:* Jean Doumanian. *Director:* Woody Allen. *Screenplay:* Woody Allen. *Director of Photography:* Zhao Fei. *Editor:* Alisa Lepselter. *Music:* Dick Hyman. *Sound:* Les Lazarowitz and (music) Roy B. Yokelson. *Sound Editor:* Robert Hein. *Casting:* Juliet Taylor and Laura Rosenthal. *Production Designer:* Santo Loquasto. *Art Director:* Tom Warren. *Set Decorator:* Jessica Lanier. *Special Effects:* John Ottesen and Ron Ottesen. *Costumes:* Laura Cunningham Bauer. *Make-up:* Rosemarie Zurlo and Eva Polywka. *Stunt Coordinator:* Peter Bucossi. *Running time:* 95 minutes. *MPAA Rating:* PG-13.

CAST: Anthony LaPaglia (Al Torrio); Brian Markinson (Bill Shields); Gretchen Mol (Ellie); Samantha Morton (Hattie); Sean Penn (Emmet Ray); Uma Thurman (Blanche); James Urbaniak (Harry); John Waters (Mr. Haynes); Tony Darrow (Ben); Brad Garrett (Joe Bedloe); Vincent Guastaferro (Sid Bishop); Denis O'Hare (Jake); Molly Price (Ann); Kalli Vernoff (Gracie); Woody Allen (Himself); Ben Duncan (Himself); Daniel Okrent (A.J. Pickman); Dan Moran (Boss); Chris Bauer (Ace, Pool Player); Constance Shulman (Hazel, Hooker #1); Kellie Overbey (Iris, Hooker #2); Darryl Alan Reed (Don); Mark Damon Johnson (Omer); Ron Cephas Jones (Alvin); Steve Bargonetti and Benjamin Franklin Brown (Musician Friends); Vince Giordano (Ball Player #1); Emme Kemp, Clark Gayton, and Marcus McLaurine (Jam Session Musicians); Carolyn Saxon (Phyliss); Drummond Erskine and Joe Ambrose (Hobos); Joe Rigano (Stagehand); Dennis Stein (Dick Ruth, Club Owner); Nat Hentoff (Himself); Katie Hamill (Mary); Carole Bayeux (Rita, Opium Party Hostess); William Addy (Master of Ceremonies); Dick Monday (Chester Weems); Mary Stout (Felicity Thomson, Amateur Singer); Dick Mingalone (Birdman); Mr. Spoons (Spoon Player); Carol Woods (Helen Minton); Josh Mowery (Movie Director); Fred Goehner (William Weston); Eddy Davis (Bass Player #2); Ralph Pope (Panhandler); Douglas McGrath (Himself); Ray Garvey (Club Manager); Sally Placksin (Sally Jillian); Lola Pashalinski (Blanche's Friend); Simon Wettenhall, Orange Kellin,

and Brooks Giles, III (Jam Session Musicians);   Alfred Sauchelli, Jr. (Ned, Pool Player);
Michael Bolus (Lynch, Bar Room Friend);   Mick O'Rourke and John P. McLaughlin (Holdup
Men);   Chuck Lewkowicz (Police Officer);   Rick Mowat (Flat Tire Man);   Ted Wilkins (Gas
Station Propietor);   Michael Sprague (Django Reinhardt).

CHRISTIAN SCIENCE MONITOR, 12/3/99, p. 15, David Sterritt

Music lovers often think of their favorite art as a universal language with a unique capacity for
bringing people together.

Some of today's filmmakers appear to see the matter differently, though. A surprising number
of recent movies show musicmaking as all activity steeped in rivalry, competition, and eccentricity.

The latest example is *Sweet and Lowdown*, the first movie to combine Woody Allen's
filmmaking skills with his longtime love of classic jazz. The main character is Emmet Ray, a
guitarist of the '30s whose fingers make mischief as well as music. The movie chronicles his up-
and-down career and his love affairs with an aggressive society woman and a pretty laundress.
Also present are jazz connoisseurs like critic Nat Hentoff and Allen himself, commenting on the
fictional Emmet as if he were real.

The film needs this trick, since Allen's flimsy screenplay rarely makes Emmet into more than
a collection of jazz-musician clichés—forever drinking, womanizing, and carousing—despite,
Sean Penn's marvelous acting in the leading role. This weakness extends to the movies main
subplot, centering on the dread Emmet feels at the thought of meeting Django Reinhardt, the
superb (and real) guitarist, whose uncanny talent hangs over him like an intimidating shadow.
Allen treats the Ray-Reinhardt rivalry as a plot gimmick rather than a psychological reality. It's
one more letdown in a disappointing movie.

(The soundtrack CD is available from Sony Classical, incidentally. Its two tracks of authentic
classic jazz played by Bunny Berrigan & His Orchestra and Sidney Bechet with Noble Sissle's
Swingsters, stand out brightly alongside the 13 newly recorded tracks by the Dick Hyman Group
featuring Howard Alden.)

The Legend of 1900, all English-language epic by Italian director Giuseppe Tornatore, is
another current film to depict music in terms of competition and peculiarity. Tim Roth plays a
piano wizard who's born on a steamship in the first year of the 20th century and vows that no
temptation will ever lure him ashore.

Directed in the overcooked style that Tornatore first displayed in his popular "Cinema Paradiso," the film musters enough appealing images and music to be reasonably entertaining. But
its makers couldn't resist pitting the hero against Jelly Roll Morton, a real-life jazz genius (played
here by Clarence Williams III) who initiates a battle to will the applause of the ship's other
passengers. The episode turns musicianship into a vulgar contest, contradicting the movie's own
message about the inherent satisfactions of artistic achievement.

As a footnote, it's worth noting some recent reportage on the real-life circumstances that inspired "Music of the Heart," the Meryl Streep movie about a schoolteacher who creates a
successful music program in a New York City school. Observers familiar with the school assert
that it has a history of strong arts education, and that an accurate film would have shown the
teacher's partnership with administrators and parents instead of portraying her as a lone warrior
fighting apathy and ingnorance.

Again, a vision of music as battleground seems to have held sway over commercially minded
filmmakers.

LOS ANGELES TIMES, 12/10/99, Calendar/p. 2, Kenneth Turan

In "Sweet and Lowdown," Woody Allen has found a droll and amusing way to combine his two
favorite subjects: jazz music and himself, not necessarily in that order.

While he often protests that he's thinking nothing of the kind, it's inevitable that films like
"Husbands and Wives" and "Deconstructing Harry" come to be viewed within the context of
Allen's own life, and their protagonists end up doing double duty as variant versions of himself.

With "Sweet and Lowdown," Allen adds some new mock documentary changes to this scenario,
for the film's subject, though invented, is treated as if he were real. Facing the camera in classic

talking-head mode, genuine authorities like Allen, jazz critic Nat Hentoff and writer-director Douglas McGrath set the scene by describing the made-up antics of 1930s virtuoso Emmet Ray, the second-greatest jazz guitarist of his day.

Sean Penn, the latest and best Allen surrogate (John Cusack, Kenneth Branagh and others have had the job), plays Ray as a man described as "vain, egotistical, with genuine crudeness," a gifted creative artist who is less than zero as a human being. So part of the pleasure of watching "Sweet and Lowdown" is the gradual realization that Allen is having fun riffing on the less flattering public perceptions of his own Soon-Yi-era persona.

The other pleasure of "Sweet and Lowdown" is Penn's performance. Though many of his films have been grim and grimmer, his spaced-out Jeff Spicoli in "Fast Times at Ridgemont High" remains memorable, and he brings an essential energy and a nice deadpan comic sensibility to his portrait of the great and greatly flawed guitarist.

Preening, cocky and ridiculous, with a wavy pompadour overshadowing a thin mustache, Emmet Ray is a hapless dolt, a man whose idea of a compliment is "very good everybody, particularly me." Penn, who learned the fingering for Ray's complex solos (Howard Alden does the actual playing), has had no trouble finding the character here, even coming up with a funny kind of peacock walk, part prissy, part robotic, for the gifted gentleman.

Yes, Ray is a kleptomaniac (he once stole an alarm clock from Hoagy Carmichael) whose thuddingly dull hobbies include trainspotting and shooting rats at city dumps with a cannon-like .45. Yes, he's a vacant soul who, when asked what goes through his mind when he's playing, replies, "that I'm underpaid." But he does play ravishingly. That makes up for everything, doesn't it? Or does it?

Ray himself certainly thinks it does. "I can't have my life cluttered," he says at one point. "I'm an artist. A truly great artist. I need to be free." The film, however, as it takes us through the musician's various inane misadventures, leaves it an intriguingly open question.

Most of "Sweet and Lowdown's" time is taken up with Ray's various romances, particularly one with a laundress named Hattie he encounters on his day off, only to be chagrined to find that she's mute. "This is my one day off," he characteristically whines. "I want a talking girl."

But as played by the wonderfully expressive British actress Samantha Morton, Hattie is able to say more with looks than most people can with words. Pulling great long faces when things go wrong, as they often do, Morton's Hattie is a very sweet virtuoso performance that can stand comparison to the classic playful ingenues of the silent screen.

Aside from his various romances (Uma Thurman is particularly engaging as a would-be writer fascinated by extreme characters), Ray's most consistent relationship, and the film's most engaging running gag, involves the real-life jazz guitarist Django Reinhardt.

Born into a troop of Gypsies and raised in France, Reinhardt was perhaps Europe's first jazz star and the acknowledged (even by Ray) top guitarist of his day. "Mostly I'm untouchable," Ray is wont to say of his talent, "except there's a Gypsy in France." Ray saw Reinhardt live only once, with disastrous results, and his obsession with his rival plays out in very funny ways.

Though "Sweet and Lowdown" feels like minor Woody Allen, the filmmaker's passion for jazz gives the film a kind of lilting confidence that serves it well. It's a loving and comic tribute to a musical era Allen knows well, and when characters say pointed things like, "No genius is worth too much heartache," and "such is the ego of genius, I must get used to it," wondering who the joke is really on is an added bonus.

NEW YORK, 12/13/99, p. 69, Peter Rainer

Perhaps the best thing to be said for Woody Allen's new film *Sweet and Lowdown* is that its star, Sean Penn, isn't doing an impression of the maestro. This is news: In most of Allen's movies, not only the lead actors but also, in many cases, the lead actresses, are mimicking Woody. In his last film, *Celebrity*, Kenneth Branagh's mannerisms and speech patterns were so dead-on that he dropped the bottom out of a movie that didn't have much bottom to begin with. You couldn't figure out if Branagh's body jerks and cranky, wheedling nasality were intended affectionately; they seemed cruelly satiric at times, and yet the director, who wields a martinet's control over his movies, must have endorsed the actor's riffs. Maybe Allen, world-class narcissist that he is, decided it was better to be dissed than dismissed; any attention is better than none. When he made his previous film, *Deconstructing Harry,* he didn't need a surrogate;

playing a writer who philanders his way through his nasty squall of an existence, he dissed himself, or at least his public image of himself, and many people interpreted the results as scathing self-analysis. But the film wasn't all that scabrous, really; essentially it was an apologia for a man who can't function in life, only in art. And as every artist knows, art is more important than life, right?

But it helps if at least there's some real artistry going on, and most of Allen's forays into purported self-criticism are less interesting as artworks than as analytic sessions writ large. In *Sweet and Lowdown,* he's once again presenting for our approval and opprobrium a cad-genius—in this case, Sean Penn's Emmet Ray, a legendary (fictional) jazz guitarist of the thirties who quickly faded into oblivion. Jamming onstage, Emmet has a blissfully intense look, as if he were living out whole lifetimes with each chordal progression. Offstage, Emmet keeps himself emotionally detached; he derives his greatest solace from shooting rats in a city dump with a .45. In Chicago, when we first see him, he's not above doing a bit of pimping, and he doesn't have a particularly chummy rapport with the other jazz players. Women for him are a way to fill out the hours and strut his stuff.

The amorality of the artist is a rich and resonant subject, but what we see of Emmet's life is too narrowly focused. Except for a brief passage where he talks bitterly about his upbringing, we don't get any real sense of what formed him, or what he's reining in. We're meant to take Emmet as a given, a specimen. *Homo jerkus.* Allen constructs the film as a biopic, with talking heads such as Nat Hentoff and Douglas McGrath, and himself, blathering on about Emmet like the witnesses in *Reds.* What great mysteries of personality are being investigated here? Emmet, as a film subject, can't support the scrutiny. In a way, despite Penn's sharp-edged and unsentimental performance and Allen's unblinking directorial gaze, this guitarist is just as diaphanous as Zelig was. He's a cipher who's always just upstaged: Outclassed by the greatness of his idol Django Reinhardt, he's perpetually second-best; when he arrives with big plans in Hollywood accompanied by Hattie (Samantha Morton), the mute laundress who reveres him, it is *she* who ends up landing big-time movie work (by accident).

Allen invokes his own idols: *Deconstructing Harry* was configured along the lines of *Wild Strawberries,* and *Sweet and Lowdown* is modeled on *La Strada,* with Emmet as a variation on Anthony Quinn's Zampano, the strongman who realizes too late the sweet frailty of his waifish adorer. Samantha Morton can be thought of in the same terms as Giulietta Masina's Gelsomina. Her performance seems inseparable from her personality; both are in a state of grace. Allen had a real chance here to get inside the psychology of a man threatened by such grace, who needs to destroy it, or flee from it, in order to live with himself. If the director had gone all the way with the material, surely Morton, with her almost preternatural sensitivities, could have made us feel Hattie's every pang of persecution, equal to Lillian Gish's cowering before Donald Crisp in D. W. Griffith's *Broken Blossoms* (the model for *La Strada).* And Penn could certainly have made us feel the full self-loathing behind Emmet's bantam strut. Allen opted instead for something far less passionate: a high gloss on a pet theme.

NEW YORK POST, 12/3/99, p. 51, Lou Lumenick

"Sweet and Lowdown" is Woody Allen in a minor if pleasant key—a playful riff on "La Strada" starring Sean Penn as a 1930s jazz musician who neglects a woman he much later realizes was the love of his life.

Framed documentary-style by recollections of jazz experts (including Allen and Nat Hentoff), this gently comic fable recounts the career of the fictitious Emmet Ray, a brilliant guitarist of the 1930s and 1940s.

When first seen, Emmet is supplementing his income by pimping for a couple of prostitutes—though he prefers the term "manager" and insists on handing out business cards to prospective clients.

A world-class drinker and carouser who's constantly in danger of being fired—if he shows up for his performances at all—Emmet is a combustible bundle of energy, egotism and raging insecurity.

In one riotous sequence, a drunken Emmet insists on performing while perched on an elaborately painted wooden moon—which lurches into the audience's view with disastrous results.

But mostly, Allen skips the belly laughs for chuckles and bittersweet romance. Romance enters Emmet's life in the form of mute Hattie (Samantha Morton), a sweet if none-too-bright laundress he meets on a double date.

Hattie travels with Emmet across the country, enduring his insults, infidelities and financial excesses until he abruptly dumps her for another woman. Emmet marries the woman, a socialite (Uma Thurman, in a virtual spoof of her performance in "Henry and June") who's fascinated by his self-loathing—at least until she meets a killer (Anthony LaPaglia) who excites her sociological curiosity even more.

Resembling both Robert De Niro and 1940s comic Eddie Bracken at times, Penn has a field day as the creepily charming Emmet, whose behavior—his favorite activities are shooting at junkyard rats and watching trains—often borders on the pathological (Allen here spoofing the idea of the self-destructive artist).

Morton, a little-known outside her native Britain, is positively incandescent as the long-suffering Hattie—suggesting infinite longing and pain without so much as a word of dialogue.

No one else—including cult director John Waters, fleetingly seen as one of Emmet's exasperated managers—makes much of an impact in this surprisingly choppy movie (Allen's first in many years without his longtime editor Susan E. Morse), stunningly photographed by Chinese master Zhao Fei.

But the movie has ample delights, including a great oldies score and a sequence in which three "witnesses" disagree about an incident involving Emmet in a gas-station holdup—which is shown in three hilariously different versions.

Every Allen movie is examined for its possibly autobiographical elements, and this latest will be no exception.

Besides resembling Giulietta Masina's waif in "La Strada," Morton's Hattie is heavily reminiscent of parts played by Allen's erstwhile leading lady and lover, Mia Farrow. (The character and the film's period show-biz milieu—including Emmet's brief trip to Hollywood—eerily evoke "The Purple Rose of Cairo.")

Emmet lives to regret what he does to Hattie, and, inspired by that emotion, he goes on to create his finest work.

"Sweet and Lowdown" isn't Allen's finest work by a long shot, but an undeniable part of its fascination is trying to figure out what—if anything, even unconsciously—he's trying to say about how he treated Farrow.

NEWSDAY, 12/3/99, Part II/p. B3, John Anderson

Despite "Celebrity," "Deconstructing Harry" and "Mighty Aphrodite," there are those for whom Woody Allen can do no wrong. And we wish them well. Others have found it infinitely more amusing—well, diverting, at any rate—to scout the more recent of the director's 30-plus films for their Mia Farrow potshots, general misogyny, bilious worldview, aka inventories of dirty laundry. He's made it a very easy thing to do.

And having done so, he has also set us up. "Sweet and Lowdown," which charts the irregular ramblings/peccadilloes of one Emmet Ray (Sean Penn)—a fictional but historically genuine '30s jazz guitarist, liar, braggart, pimp and kleptomaniac—would be a funny, touching movie under any circumstances. Viewed as a roman à clef, however, it's philosophically as profound as anything Allen's done since "Crimes and Misdemeanors" and represents a capacity for self-examination and introspection that a lot of Allen watchers probably thought was long ago exhausted.

Like Allen's best films, "Sweet and Lowdown" is about humans in a perverse universe, equipped with little but the perverse penchant for emotional suicide. But it also attempts a kind of unified field theory about morality and art. Emmet, played to sordid perfection by Penn, is a moral bankrupt but an extraordinarily gifted musician. (That Penn obviously can't play at all adds a surreal touch to an already farcical film.)

Emmet steals useless things for no reason, drinks like a fish and when drunk likes to go to the city dump and shoot rats. He treats women—most significantly, the mute and muse-like Hattie (Samantha Morton)—a little better than he treats the rats. And he can't keep a job because his sense of responsibility is virtually nonexistent.

When Emmet (the guy who never stops talking) teams up with Hattie (the girl who can't), "Sweet and Lowdown" is as sweet as Emmet is lowdown. Morton, the British actress who was so emotionally naked in "Under the Skin," is an adorable, mesmerizing presence and gives the best nonspeaking performance since—who? Lillian Gish? That Emmet would abandon her for the shallow wiles of a leggy writer named Blanche (Uma Thurman) shows Emmet's lack of taste and soul and his inevitable appointment with tragedy—something belied by his music, but always there, like a particularly insistent bass line.

Emmet may be stupid, but he has the good sense to be haunted—by the real-life Django Reinhardt, the legendary Gypsy jazz guitarist from France, who had the full use of only two fingers on his fretting hand (the others were injured in a childhood fire). Emmet carries Reinhardt around the way all saxophonists carry Charlie Parker, or Christian Slater carries Jack Nicholson. Allen's chief nonnarrative device is to tell Emmet's story partially through talking-head interviews set in the present—some with real people (himself, Ben Duncan, Nat Hentoff), some with fabricated experts (such as A.J. Pickman, played by Daniel Okrent). Through them Allen weaves a fabric of myths, half-truths and "actual" events, including how Emmet once fainted while in Reinhardt's presence.

Can Emmet ever be as good as Django? "Sweet and Lowdown" posits that he can't, not until his heart is broken, or he learns the meaning of love. As a dramatic premise, it's what you call thin ice—a glance at history will show no shortage of brilliant artists who've been useless human beings, to say nothing of beautiful people who couldn't play a lick. But as the subtext to an Allen movie, it certainly shows a transition for the director, and unless it's one of the great con jobs of all time, an apologia. "Sweet and Lowdown" is a movie that serves as Exhibit A in its own case that generosity of heart is the first step toward great art—not a premise that's true, necessarily, but is infinitely reassuring.

NEWSWEEK, 12/6/99, p. 84, David Ansen

After the excruciating spectacle of Kenneth Branagh aping Woody Allen in "Celebrity" the Woodman had nowhere to go but up. Which is where he lands with his relaxed, amusing new comedy, "Sweet and Lowdown." It helps considerably that he has Sean Penn as his leading man. Penn is a hoot as jazz guitarist Emmett Ray, a mythical musical legend of the '30s. Both genius and louse, Ray is a dangerous combination of insecurity and bantam-cock bravado. "Very good, everybody," he compliments his band after a performance. "Particularly me."

Employing faux-documentary "Witnesses" such as jazz expert Nat Hentoff, the film recounts the tall tales of Ray's exploits and eccentricities—his stint as a pimp, his kleptomania, his obsession with shooting rats in city dumps. The closest Ray gets to love is with the mute, adoring laundry girl Hattie (the brilliant young English actress Samantha Morton). What a narcissist's fantasy: a woman who can never talk back! But Ray dumps her, and moves on to the aristocratic and unfaithful Blanche (Uma Thurman).

"I need to be free. I'm an artist": this is our antihero's credo, but of course it's been the *cri de coeur* of so many Allen protagonists. Is the artist above morality? Allen's been chewing guiltily on this one for decades (even more so post-Mia). Here he treats his theme mockingly, making sport of this selfish genius. Lovely to look at, the anecdotal "Sweet and Lowdown" doesn't add up to any big deal. But it's a likable, lively little ditty—one theme, some clever variation—that never wears out its welcome.

SIGHT AND SOUND, 7/00, p. 55, Jonathan Romney

Various jazz experts, including Woody Allen, tell the story of the great but obscure 30s guitarist Emmet Ray, a player second only to Django Reinhardt, but an obnoxious and dishonest womaniser. Cruising for girls on the New Jersey boardwalk, Emmet meets Hattie, a mute laundress, and they become lovers. She accompanies him on a cross-country trip to Hollywood, where he plays in a short film; Hattie is spotted by a director and enjoys a brief screen career. Emmet's recording career takes off but his manager warns him about his spending.

Later, after Emmet has left Hattie, he meets and marries Blanche, a wealthy would-be bohemian writer. When Emmet is sacked from a club, Blanche goes to intercede with its gangster owner and ends up running away with his henchman Al Torrio. Different versions are told of Emmet's pursuit of them. Emmet returns to New Jersey to see Hattie, but she tells him she is married with children. The experts say that at the end of his career, before he vanished, Emmet's playing became truly great.

Following the shapeless agitation of *Celebrity,* Woody Allen's cogent return to form in *Sweet and Lowdown* proves that he is fascinated less by celebrity and the noisy now, than by obscurity and the sublime mysteries of the forgotten. *Sweet and Lowdown* is one of Allen's occasional musings, *à la* E.L. Doctorow, on the apocryphal corners of modern American history *(Zelig, The Purple Rose of Cairo)* and another of his studies *(Bullets over Broadway, Stardust Memories)* of the contradictions between artistic brilliance and moral inadequacy. Apocryphal jazz guitarist Emmet Ray, Allen comments at the start, is "sort of pathetic in a way" but he's indisputably fascinating. He's a vain egotist who walks over people, just like the anti-hero novelist of *Deconstructing Harry*—except Emmet is worse, in that he has considerable charm and knows how to exploit it. As one character remarks, "No genius is worth too much heartache"—effectively the moral proposition under discussion in *Harry.*

Sweet and Lowdown is as simple and affecting as the title suggests—a series of anecdotes framed with commentary by jazz experts. But through this structure, Allen examines the difficulty of truly fathoming artists of the past, either through their work or through the stories told about them. The hard evidence about Emmet is in his recordings, while the catalogue of anecdotes about him is open to variation. We get several alternatives for Emmet's pursuit of his wife: Emmet gets hi-jacked by robbers, stages a melodramatic confrontation, or has a chance meeting with the nemesis he holds in awe, Django himself.

All stories are equally valid in this patchwork of fragments, and the Emmet Ray legend becomes all the more concrete the less the gaps are filled in. At one point, the story jumps from a time when Emmet and his mute mistress Hattie are inseparable to Emmet single again. We have to imagine his split with Hattie, an elision that makes their final meeting all the more resonant with the unspoken pain he has done her.

The film, in other words, uses muteness as metaphor, dramatising it in the figure of Hattie, Emmet's child-like, trusting and—everyone keeps assuming—mentally disadvantaged lover. Her intelligence comes into its own in their ambivalent reunion, when she tells Emmet that she is now married with children—all of this conveyed without a word from her. If we take her story at face value, it's sad enough that Emmet has lost his great love; but the outcome is that much richer if we imagine Hattie has invented it. Then it becomes not just a tactful way to reject the lover she knows can only hurt her, but also a gift—Hattie is offering him the heartbreak that makes the virtuoso a truly sublime player.

There's a terrible risk of cliché in this figure of the infinitely supportive mute muse—Hattie could so easily have been a return to Chaplin's eroticised waifs. What brings her alive is Samantha Morton's performance, silent but in its own way entirely musical—a subtle repertoire of reactions, gleeful surges and bursts of erotic fire, and much of it from under a horrible knitted hat. Morton and Penn (playing Emmet) duet astutely, her silences forming a complementary punctuation to his rakish bluster. Penn himself is on top form, portraying the musician not as a standard lovable rascal, but as a thoroughgoing creep, redeemed by his appetite and by the kinetic passion he puts into his music. Even more impressive than the fingering Penn learned for the guitar-playing scenes is the expression on Emmet's face as he plays, the look of a man captivated by his own congress with the sublime.

As you'd imagine from Allen, America's most famous enthusiast for a pre-bebop Eden, *Sweet and Lowdown* is told with real love for the period, and the film's look is typically flawless; Allen's regular designer Santo Loquasto is teamed here with DoP Zhao Fei (who has worked with both Zhang Yimou and Chen Kaige) to create a gently frosted image of the world seen as though through a haze of distant memory. Jazz fans, however, may be aggrieved by Allen's perpetual blind spot: his inability to handle black characters. Black musicians do appear, but only as background figures—Emmet jams with them at a party, then steals a lighter. This might be Allen's incidental comment on white musicians' appropriation of the spark of black jazz, but that, I suspect, would be stretching a point.

TIME, 12/6/99, p. 100, Richard Corliss

The past few Woody Allen films have flirted, in a provocatively meanspirited way, with the public aspects of his personality. *Deconstructing Harry* focused on Woody the selfish lover, *Celebrity* on Woody the capricious star. The new one has reverbs of Woody's Monday-night gigs in a classical jazz ensemble. *Sweet and Lowdown* is about one sour fellow, but it's another character who gives this minor movie a surprising lilt and afterglow.

Emmet Ray (Sean Penn) is the premier American jazz guitarist. His fingers sculpt gorgeous sounds from the six strings; *I'm Forever Blowing Bubbles* was never so poignant or supple as in his hands. But Emmet is also a pimp, petty thief, paranoid ... if there's a bad word that starts with *p*, he's likely to be it. Driven by ego, dogged by insecurity, he rationalizes his outrages as the spillage of an overflowing talent.

Penn does bold justice to this lowdown giant. But Samantha Morton, as Emmet's "mute orphan half-wit" of a girlfriend, is the sweet revelation. Rarely has a performer mined such complex and potent emotion from such simple materials: a smile, a shrug, an attentive winsomeness. She hardly nods or shakes her head in response to a question, yet always conveys the meaning and feeling. In an age of actors' tics and rantings, such austere clarity is worth cherishing. The interpretive magic that Emmet Ray achieves with six strings, Morton conjures with none.

VILLAGE VOICE, 12/7/99, p. 144, Amy Taubin

Woody Allen's *Sweet and Lowdown* looks like peaches and cream with a dime-store glass of pale gold brandy on the side. It's the prettiest movie of the year, maybe of Allen's career. Zhao Fei's cinematography and Santo Loquasto's production design evoke an early swing era that's both glowing and faded. The film also has a great jazz score (old recordings and some new arrangements), a bunch of funny lines, a fabulous running gag (not the one about Django Reinhardt, which is okay, but the completely outrageous one involving shooting rats in the dump), and a spectacular performance by Sean Penn that's like watching someone doing back flips on a high wire with only a worn-out safety net below him.

The net is the film itself, basically a series of anecdotes knotted together in the shape of a biopic about a little-known '30s jazz guitarist who is, in fact, a fiction. The there-is-no-there-there effect is quite deliberate. It's what you could call a formal tendency that runs through Allen's entire career, but which he puts aside in his best films, such as *Crimes and Misdemeanors* or *Hannah and her Sisters*. Related to this aesthetic is the notion of an art object whose formal perfection is recognized only by a handful of connoisseurs. The problem for Allen is that, as a form, the feature film, like the novel, is too unwieldy for perfection.

Sweet and Lowdown, therefore, is an attempt to make the film equivalent of an album of music, where the scenes are like separate tracks. You can have soaring moments and occasions of grace without worrying too much about how to hold the thing together. Allen's pretext for this narrative sleight of hand-or maybe just slighting of narrative—is the character of Emmet Ray, who was considered by critics and musicians in the know—including Ray himself—as second only to Django Reinhardt. Scenes from Ray's life are introduced by critics and musicians, each of whom have heard one or two stories about him. Allen self-consciously structures *Sweet and Lowdown* as an anti-*Reds* : Experts testify to the camera about the life and work of an imaginary person who defines the world as himself and his music. He's the apolitical artist par excellence.

The film is also a wish-fulfillment fantasy about the kind of artist Allen could be if he were not a celebrity. Ray is unknown except for his records, the greatest of which were made just before he vanished from sight. In these last recordings, Ray broke through the defensive, narcissistic shell that made him a less expressive musician than Reinhardt. Ray is awed and burdened by Reinhardt, just as Allen is by certain European directors in whose shadows he labors. Ray's anxiety about Reinhardt is so great that he faints when he meets him. It's Allen's riff on the famous story about Freud fainting when he encountered Jung after their break.

This is great material, but Allen is so careless in developing it that the film is more interesting to think about after than it is to watch. On the other hand, Penn's performance, which, in its grotesquerie, is a hair's breadth away from caricature, has to be seen to be believed. That it never slips over the line has to do with his meticulous linking of body and psyche in all their parallels and contradictions. Simultaneously scuttling and strutting, as if he were part crab and part cock of the walk, Penn reveals the insecurities and delusions-of-grandeur of a pathological narcissist who has no idea what figure he cuts in the world. His body seems to shrink in on itself as if he were an accordion when he's agitated, the movement of his eyebrows turns the deep lines in his forehead to pleats. The overactive brow, the preening smile, the exaggerated moustache all suggest that, at an impressionable age, Ray watched too many Chaplin movies. And yet when he plays music, he's some sort of hopped-up, blissed-out deity. (In preparation for the part, Penn learned the fingering for some 30 pieces, and Allen lets the camera linger on his hands as if daring us to perceive the discrepancy between what we see and hear.) Penn's hostility feeds his sense of comedy. In a move so perfectly timed it would do Allen Iverson proud, he flips a fresh-killed rat behind his back and into the lap of a date he loathes.

Sweet and Lowdown combines the talking-jag rhythms of '30s comedies with the physical humor of the silent era. The Chaplinesque Ray's main squeeze is a mute laundress; the talented British actress Samantha Morton plays her like a cross between Harpo Marx and Mary Pickford. Though Morton never cloys, Allen's misogyny vis-a-vis this character is so blatant that it almost defies mention. (She's beautiful, she's adoring, she can't talk back.) Uma Thurman fares worse as a femme fatale whose vanity matches Emmet's own, and the huge supporting cast is indistinguishable from the furniture. *Sweet and Lowdown* is too slight to accommodate more than one ego—a larger-than-life model of the filmmaker's own.

Also reviewed in:
NATION, 12/20/99, p. 35, Stuart Klawans
NEW REPUBLIC, 12/20/99, p. 30, Stanley Kauffmann
NEW YORK TIMES, 12/3/99, p. E10, Janet Maslin
NEW YORKER, 12/6/99, p. 170, David Denby
VARIETY, 9/13-19/99, p. 40, David Stratton
WASHINGTON POST, 12/24/99, p. C2, Rita Kempley
WASHINGTON POST, 12/24/99, Weekend/p. 31, Desson Howe

TALENTED MR. RIPLEY, THE

A Paramount Pictures and Miramax Films release of a Mirage Enterprises/Timnick Films production. *Executive Producer:* Sydney Pollack. *Producer:* William Horberg and Tom Sternberg. *Director:* Anthony Minghella. *Screenplay:* Anthony Minghella. *Based on the novel by:* Patricia Highsmith. *Director of Photography:* John Seale. *Editor:* Walter Murch. *Music:* Gabriel Yared. *Music Editor:* Robert Randles. *Sound:* Ivan Sharrock, Danny Michael, and (music) John Richards. *Sound Editor:* Pat Jackson. *Casting:* David Rubin. *Production Designer:* Roy Walker. *Art Director:* John Fenner. *Set Decorator:* Bruno Cesari and Carol Nast. *Special Effects:* Richard Conway. *Costumes:* Ann Roth, Gary Jones, and Carlo Poggioli. *Make-up:* Fabrizio Sforza and Tina Earnshaw. *Make-up (Special Effects):* Fabrizio Sforza. *Stunt Coordinator:* Franco Salamon. *Running time:* 135 minutes. *MPAA Rating:* R.

CAST: Matt Damon (Tom Ripley); Gwyneth Paltrow (Marge Sherwood); Jude Law (Dickie Greenleaf); Cate Blanchett (Meredith Logue); Philip Seymour Hoffman (Freddie Miles); Jack Davenport (Peter Smith-Kingsley); James Rebhorn (Herbert Greenleaf); Sergio Rubini (Inspector Roverini); Philip Baker Hall (Alvin MacCarron); Celia Weston (Aunt Joan); Rosario Fiorello (Fausto); Stefania Rocca (Silvana); Ivano Marescotti (Colonnello Verrecchia); Ama Longhi (Signora Buffi); Alessandro Fabrizi (Sergeant Baggio); Lisa Eichhorn (Emily Greenleaf); Gretchen Egolf (Fran); Jack Willis (Greenleaf Chauffeur); Frederick Alexander Bosche (Fran's Boyfriend); Dario Bergeslo (Police Officer); Larry Kaplan (Uncle Ted); Claire Hardwick (Gucci Assistant); Nino Prester (American Express Clerk); Lorenzo Mancuso (Bus Driver); Onofrio Mancuso (Priest); Massimo Reale (Immigration Officer); Emanuelle Carucci Viterbi (American Express Clerk); Caterina de Regibus (Dahlia); Silvana Bosi (Ermelinda); Gianfranco Barra (Aldo, Desk Manager); Renato Scarpa (Tailor); Deirdre Lovejoy and Brian Tarantina (Fighting Neighbors); NAPOLI JAZZ SEPTET: Guy Barker (Trumpet); Bernardo Sassetti (Piano);

Perico Sambeat (Alto Sax); Gene Calderazzo (Drums); Joseph Lepore (Double Bass); Rosario Giuliuni (Tenor Sax); Eddy Palermo (Electric Guitar). SAN REMO JAZZ SEXTET: Byron Wallen (Cornet); Pete King (Alto Sax); Clark Tracey (Drums); Jean Toussaint (Tenor Sax); Geoff Gascogne (Bass); Carlo Negroni (Piano); Beppe Fiorello (Silvana's Fiancé); Marco Quaglia (Silvana's Brother); Alessandra Vanzi (Silvana's Mother); Marco Rossi (Photographer); Roberto Valentini (Eugene Onegin Players: Onegin); Francesco Bovino (Lensky); Stefano Canettieri (Zaretsky); Marco Foti (Guillot); Ludovica Tinghi (Fausto's Fiancée); Nicola Pannelli (Dinelli's Café Waiter); Paolo Calabresi (Customs Officer); Pietro Ragusa (Record Store Owner); Simone Empler (Boy Singer); Gianluca Secci, Manuel Ruffini, and Pierpaolo Lovino (Policemen); Roberto Di Palma (San Remo Hotel Desk Clerk).

CINEASTE, Vol. XXV, No. 3, 2000, p. 41, Michael Bronski

The commercial success of Anthony Minghella's *The Talented Mr. Ripley* is a curious, if predictable, marvel. Who would have thought, in the late 1990s, that a film featuring a sympathetic gay psychopathic killer, structured around a fairly complicated 'thriller' plot, and peppered with what is essentially an antilove interest with Hollywood's *belle de jour* Gwyneth Paltrow would be a hit? Released on Christmas day 1999, Minghella's film proved that you can neither under nor overestimate the taste of American audiences. Indeed, *The Talented Mr. Ripley* works, for both art and commercial audiences, because Minghella understands perfectly, and can cater to, the nuances and expectations of American middle-brow taste. In a year in which most studio releases evidenced little thoughtfulness and less artistry, *The Talented Mr. Ripley* was taken seriously by many critics who praised it as "highly intelligent" and "art." Even the culturally staid *New York Times Magazine* heralded it, in a cover story, as a major artistic and sociological event. But Minghella, through his clever screenplay with its insinuation of 'large themes' and his stunning, if recycled, visual flair, has created not so much art as the illusion of art in which, as Talullah Bankhead once quipped, "There is less here than meets the eye."

The Talented Mr. Ripley is based on Patricia Highsmith's 1955 psychological thriller of the same name. Highsmith's novel had an earlier screen life in René Clement's 1960 thriller *Purple Noon,* a film that, upon its original release on the art-house circuit, was viewed more as a sexy French thriller than a serious art film. Most general American audiences have never seen *Purple Noon,* nor have they read Patricia Highsmith, although they probably have heard of both. And this appearance of 'cultural insiderness' is one of the keys to the success and reputation of Minghella's film. It is a common phenomenon in marketing 'art' to middlebrow audiences. This (for lack of a more precise term) *'Masterpiece Theater* syndrome' is at the heart of *The Talented Mr. Ripley*'s commercial popularity.

Central to the marketing of *The Talented Mr. Ripley* is Patricia Highsmith's novel. Although she published more than thirty books—twenty-one novels, seven collections of stories, and assorted nonfiction—before her death in 1995, Highsmith, despite praise by Graham Greene, Truman Capote, and a legion of serious critics, remained, as she began, a cult figure. Highsmith's cult status was authentic, but continually threatened by the possibility of mainstream fame: between 1975 and 1995 there were no less than five attempted Highsmith revivals, each with the re-release of back titles and a flood of attendant reviews and laudatory articles. Mirroring the ironic, cantankerous tone of her work, Highsmith's reputation rests on being not simply a cult figure, but a completely well-known cult figure.

This paradoxical literary status is, to a large degree, one of the reasons behind the popularity of *The Talented Mr. Ripley,* for it confers on the film the artistic legitimacy of semiobscurity along with the potential of mass viewership, an eccentric mixture of intellectual snob appeal and mainstream popularity. This, of course, was one of the main ingredients that made Anthony Minghella's 1996 *The English Patient* such a success. Michael Ondaatje's densely literary novel was one of those culture flukes—like Umberto Eco's *The Name of the Rose* or Toni Morrison's *Beloved*—critically praised but probably read by only a fraction of the millions who bought copies. With its literary veneer, classy David Lean-esque photography and serious' actors such as Ralph Fiennes, Kirsten Scott Thomas, Willem Dafoe, and Juliette Binoche, *The English Patient* resonated with both the high and low end of the *Masterpiece Theater* crowd. But at heart *The English Patient* is far closer to Mervyn LeRoy's sentimental, but highly praised 1942 weepy

Random Harvest with Ronald Colman as a British soldier with amnesia. It looked like art and had a literary seriousness about it that made middlebrow audiences feel smart.

This, in many regards, is the formula that made *The Talented Mr. Ripley* click at the box office. Minghella has a shrewd and successful ability to shape and market his films as high-tone cultural artifacts. In *The Talented Mr. Ripley*, as in *The English Patient*, he has packaged respected actors Matt Damon, Jude Law, Gwyneth Paltrow, and Cate Blanchett, has written a witty, literate, intelligent script from Highsmith's novel, and has photographed it in the elegant, Technicolor, high-kitsch style of late 1950s-early 1960s Hollywood. As a commercial package, it looks and feels great but falls short of anything resembling art, of provoking us the way that great art can and does.

Minghella effectively *'Masterpiece Theaterized' The Talented Mr. Ripley* by making subtle, but substantiative changes in adapting Highsmith's novel. In the original, Tom Ripley is a near homeless petty thief and chronic liar with sociopathic tendencies. Through a coincidence, he meets Herbert Greenleaf, a wealthy man who believes that Ripley is friends with his son Dickie. The younger Greenleaf is bumming around Italy with his casual girlfriend Marge Sherwood. At the father's behest, and on his money, Ripley travels to Italy to persuade Dickie to return. Once there, Ripley becomes accustomed to Dickie's ne'er-do-well life and begins both to fall in love with, and want to be him. He murders Dickie and assumes his identity. This leads to another murder, which Ripley convincingly blames on the dead Dickie. Ripley then forges Dickie's will and fakes the already murdered man's suicide. At the novel's end, Ripley inherits a comfortable income. Highsmith's Ripley is not a charming grifter who gets away with a crime, but a psychopathic, deeply disturbed homosexual whose need to bolster his fragile ego disallows him the nicety of a conscience. But Highsmith's genius is in making him the hero, with whom we completely identify.

Minghella has made his Ripley far more palatable. As played by the engaging Matt Damon, Ripley is softened, now more a confused gay man who is at a social disadvantage in a world in which his social betters are often mean to him. More guilty of looking for love in all the wrong places—and being rejected—than of being an amoral killer, this Ripley is far more palatable to middle-class audiences. Minghella has made smaller changes in his hero's rehabilitation: he is now a down-on-his-luck musician not a scam artist; he is less a misogynist and seems truly to like Marge; his killing of Dickie is not premeditated but brought on in anger by the latter's cruelly rejecting and insulting him. And to make Ripley even more sympathetic, Minghella has coarsened Dickie Greenleaf, making him less a shallow, spoiled rich kid and more a callous womanizer responsible for the death of his Italian mistress, as well as a murderous hothead. But the most radical change here is that Ripley now is capable of love—and by the end of the film, he has a boyfriend. This is completely at odds with Highsmith's conceptualization of Ripley, who would not have been a crowd pleaser. There's a big difference between a confused gay con man and a charming, unfeeling sociopath. Movie audiences may have rejected a Ripley—and a Matt Damon—who lacked certain conventional elements of sympathy. In his introduction to the published screenplay, Minghella is quite clear that, despite the novel's "uninflected brilliance ... its disavowal of moral consequences, Ripley's solipsism, [and] the author's acerbic judgement of everybody other than Ripley ... do not sit easily within the context of film." We're talking box office here.

Ironically, this is not the first time that Highsmith's morally sophisticated, frightening vision was muffled and distorted by Hollywood's need for box office. Screen writers Raymond Chandler and Czenzi Ormonde adapted her first novel, *Strangers on a Train*, for Alfred Hitchcock, whose 1951 film revitalized his flagging career. Hitchcock's film, an effective thriller, departed from Highsmith's story in one significant detail: in the film Guy (Farley Granger), the innocent dupe of the psychopathic Bruno (Robert Walker), attempts to warn the latter's father of his son's murderous intentions; in the book Guy, feeling trapped by Bruno's threats, actually murders the old man. In Hitchcock's dark vision, Guy is 'guilty' because he wishes his wife were dead; in Highsmith's even darker nightmare, 'innocent' Guy easily becomes a killer. In Highsmith's world such activity is, if not natural, to be expected. This is why, in her topsy-turvy moral universe, the amoral Tom Ripley is less an antihero than a hero.

The two most profound changes that Minghella wrought upon Highsmith's original—which brings his *Ripley* squarely into the realm of bourgeois morality—is that he has made Tom Ripley capable of love, and he has determined that Ripley must be punished for his crimes. At the end of the film, Ripley falls in love with Peter Smith-Kingsley (Jack Davenport), a minor character in Highsmith's novel. In his introduction Minghella writes, "the novel is about a man who commits murders and is not caught. And so the film is about a man who commits murders and is not caught. But it departs in one crucial sense by concluding that eluding public accountability is not the same as eluding justice. The film has a moral imperative: You can get away with murder, but you don't really get away with anything." At the end of the film, Ripley, in order to conceal the first two murders, kills Peter. Thus, by killing the person who means the most to him—echoes of Oscar Wilde's *Ballad of Reading Gaol* here and the idea that "each man kills the thing he loves"—Ripley is, in fact, punished enough to meet traditional standards of both Hollywood and conventional morality. This reflexive, traditional moralizing is a perversion of Highsmith's universe. In her novel, Ripley—the ultimate outsider—is not punished for rejecting what Highsmith sees as the truly immoral: the unthinking social and moral standards of normalcy. As she once remarked in an interview, "Ripley isn't so bad. He only kills when he has to."

It is not only in the script that Minghella makes Highsmith's story more palatable to mass audiences. A great deal of the charm of *The Talented Mr. Ripley* resides in its lush, if calculated, visual beauty. Minghella and his cinematographer John Seale have re-created a Hollywood fantasy of late 1950s Italy. In bright travelogue colors and panoramas, they take us through the countryside outside of Mongibello, the Riviera, the cafés of Naples, and Roman nightlife. This *mise-en-scène* is often beautifully rendered and purposefully evocative of high-end, classic, sophisticated Hollywood films set in chic, stylish European settings. Many of these were sentimental romances such as *Roman Holiday, Funny Face, Summertime, Three Coins in the Fountain*, and *Rome Adventure*. There was also a distinct genre of elegant thrillers such as Hitchcock's *To Catch a Thief* and *The Man Who Knew Too Much*, and Stanley Donan's *Charade*. All of these films promoted a new and distinctive use of European and continental locales in postwar Hollywood film. The vastness of Cinemascope and the luxurious Technicolor presented U.S. audiences with an elaborate fantasy of post-war Europe that banished the harsh black-and-white images of the war—either from *Life* magazine, Hollywood films like Billy Wilder's *A Foreign Affair*, or, most starkly, the work of the Italian neo-realists like Rossellini's *Open City* —replacing them with an imagined world of glamor, chic, and (mostly) innocent worldliness.

These films, for the most part and to varying degrees, reflected an American desire to rediscover and reimagine Europe as a cultured, elegant alternative to the United States. They also articulated a specific fantasy that placed 'innocent' Americans in a continental setting to let them discover the innate wholesomeness of their Americanism: few, if any, of these characters stay in Europe or view it as a replacement for their homeland. For films of the time, European locations provided an original and often quietly provocative critique of American life and mores. They were, to a large degree, updated and more optimistic versions of the classic Henry James novels in which the 'innocent' American going to Europe is corrupted. For James, this embrace of the old world often meant disaster—Isabel Archer, in *The Portrait of a Lady* is trapped in a hideous marriage; Daisy Miller dies; and Milly Theale in *Wings of a Dove* also dies. In the films of the late Fifties and early Sixties influenced by James, Americans go to Europe, discover eroticism, and become fuller Americans. Europe here is a hothouse that allows them to bloom sexually.

We are reminded of these films continually while watching *The Talented Mr. Ripley*, and with reason, since Minghella consciously draws upon them. The resonance is not only visual. Highsmith, a keenly literary writer, drops two hints in her novel that she is, in part, playing with Jamesian material—references to *The Ambassadors* in which the bourgeois American, Lambert Strether, is sent to Paris to retrieve the son of a woman to whom he is engaged. As usual with Highsmith's work, the detail is wantonly perverse, for the sociopathic Tom Ripley is hardly the innocent American of James's imagination. Yet, rather than play or engage with this idea, Minghella speedily retreats from it. This is reflected in the film's visuals, as Minghella shies away from the more radical possibilities of using European locales as the aforementioned films used them. These films—particularly *Three Coins in a Fountain, Rome Adventure*, and *Summertime*—presented mainstream American audiences with a critique, albeit a gentle one, of American morality. The characters questioned their personal and social values when faced with the new (sophisticated and sexualized) European surroundings, and audiences were invited to do the same, as they also savored the lush Technicolor beauty of the old world. Minghella, however, uses these same images simply to create an atmosphere of nostalgia. The travelogue-like backgrounds and location shooting that functioned as a commentary on U.S. social mores in the Fifties films, function simply as travelogue footage here.

In the end *The Talented Mr. Ripley* remains a very safe film. The enormous moral challenges that Highsmith offered in the novel are wiped away, and Minghella's reliance on traditional Hollywood-generated visual images functions only as a way to placate, not stimulate, audiences. It is true that a film conveying the highly ironic and disturbing moral complexity of Highsmith's novel would not have enormous box-office potential, a choice reflected in all of Minghella's artistic decisions. While entertaining and, at times, suspenseful, this *Mr. Ripley* shows more talent in merchandising acceptable middlebrow culture than in creating provocative art.

LOS ANGELES TIMES, 12/24/99, Calendar/p. 2, Kenneth Turan

"The Talented Mr. Ripley" is a wonderfully accomplished work that's unconvincing at its core. A lack of nerve, or perhaps a difference in temperament between filmmaker and author, has resulted in a beautifully mounted and directed film that, despite the presence of Matt Damon and Gwyneth Paltrow, is unexpectedly lacking in emotional impact.

Presented with one of the most unnerving, breathtakingly amoral characters in modern literature, writer-director Anthony Minghella worried that the audience would resist committing themselves to such a chilling protagonist. So he monkeyed with the delicate balance of forces and personalities that make the novel memorable, a move that ended up backfiring and making Tom Ripley less interesting rather than more.

Ripley and his chilling adventures are the subject of five novels by the late Patricia Highsmith, whose first book, "Strangers on a Train," was turned into the memorable Alfred Hitchcock film. Other filmmakers have been attracted to the Highsmith series; Alain Delon starred in an earlier version of "The Talented Mr. Ripley" (Rene Clement's "Purple Noon") and Wim Wenders did a version of "Ripley's Game," the Dennis Hopper-starring "The American Friend."

Writer-director Minghella, in his first film since the Oscar-winning "The English Patient," would seem to be an excellent choice for this project, and in many ways he is. Working with such top-of-the-line collaborators as cinematographer John Seale, editor Walter Murch, composer Gabriel Yared, production designer Roy Walker and costume designers Ann Roth and Gary Jones, Minghella has a fine grasp of both the film's gorgeous Italian atmosphere and its complex narrative line.

If only there was a compelling protagonist, all would be well. But there isn't.

"Ripley" begins in Manhattan in 1958 with Tom (Damon) borrowing a Princeton blazer to accompany a singer at a tony reception. Eyeing the jacket, shipping magnate Herbert Greenleaf (James Rebhorn) asks if Tom knew his son Dickie Greenleaf at the school.

Not only did Ripley not know young Greenleaf, he didn't go to Princeton and is presently employed as a men's room attendant. Naturally, he admits to none of this and when Greenleaf senior offers him $1,000 to go to Italy and convince his wastrel son, whose "only talent is for spending his allowance," to come home, Tom is eager to agree.

Wanting to blend in with Dickie, a jazz fanatic, Tom undertakes an intense study of the music before he leaves New York. In fact, Tom's entire experience can be looked at as the story of a young man finding his vocation, of someone with a talent for deception and impersonation, a gifted improviser with the truth, finding a life path that suits him.

Tom accidentally-on-purpose runs into Dickie (Jude Law) and his girlfriend Marge Sherwood (Paltrow) on the beach at Mongibello (most of the shooting was done on Ischia in the Bay of Naples). Despite having the whitest skin on the continent, Tom manages to ingratiate himself with Dickie, and he soon agrees to be a double agent, to string Mr. Greenleaf senior along even though his son is unlikely ever to return to the U.S.

The more Tom hangs out with Dickie, the more he experiences his sybaritic lifestyle, the more he finds it suits him. "I've gotten to like everything about the way you live," Tom tells Dickie at one point, carefully studying him like a book he wishes he'd written himself.

In the Highsmith novel, Tom is a shark among guppies, an ice-cold cleaver cutting easily through the soft putty of American expatriate lives. As played by Damon, very much out of character, Tom is all gawky earnestness, determined to get what he wants in a nerdy sort of way.

Insecure, vulnerable but disturbing, this Tom lacks the jaw-dropping fascination of Highsmith's character but has nothing of real interest to in its place.

Another critical change from the book is to make Tom more explicitly gay and his physical attraction to Dickie that much more specific. This was just under the surface in the novel and, frankly, it made for in dramatic tension that way. Plus, making Tom gay mandated further changes to an already contorted plot dramatic tension that way.

Damon does the best he can here, but this role is off-putting without playing to his strengths. Paltrow's as the long-suffering "I make a fabulous martini" Marge is also undernourished, but, on the other hand, Law, a top young British actor, brings the right kind of savoir-faire to Dickie Greenleaf, and Blanchett, last seen as "Elizabeth," is excellent as uncertain expatriate Meredith Logue. Best of all is the unstoppable Philip Seymour Hoffman. His role as the thuggish, arrogant, red-convertible-driving Freddie Miles, one of Dickie's best friends, is pitch perfect.

It's yet another of the memorable framing details that make us wish that the central portrait of "The Talented Mr. Ripley" was worth all this care.

NEW YORK, 1/3/00, p. 84, Peter Rainer

In the movies, pathology and murder are often framed in deep shadow, as if horror only bloomed in dark places, but true epicureans of depravity know that cold creeps are coldest in the bright sun shine. *The Talented Mr. Ripley*—based on the same 1955 Patricia Highsmith novel, the first in her "Ripley" series, that served as the basis for René Clément's *Purple Noon,* starring Alain Delon—is awash in the sensual yellows and caramels of Naples and Venice and San Remo and Rome. It's a gorgeously unsettling film. You can hide in the shadows, but luminescence exposes who you are, and the only escape is into another identity.

Tom Ripley (Matt Damon) is a kind of learning-on-the-job psychopath whose chief talent is slipping into the guises of others. In New York, he casually convinces Herbert Greenleaf (James Rebhorn), a wealthy shipbuilder, that the man's expatriate son, Dickie (Jude Law), was a Princeton classmate, which results in an offer from the father to travel to Italy and bring back the free-spending scion. But once ensconced in seaside Naples with Dickie and his expensive-looking blonde girlfriend, Marge (Gwyneth Paltrow), Tom is in no hurry to wrap things up, and so, by revealing his mission, he becomes, in effect, a double agent. He makes himself over as Dickie, first by co-opting Dickie's *dolce vita* lifestyle and then by co-opting the man himself by murdering him.

Tom's capacity for impersonation at first seems like the survival tactic of a rube among the well-heeled, but it turns out to be his essence. Writer-director Anthony Minghella keeps Tom in virtually every scene; his switching of identities from Dickie to Tom and back again, and his narrow escapes, are breathtaking. By keeping everything centered on Tom, Minghella makes us complicit in the young man's pathology. He's the outsider on the inside; the deeper his infiltration, the more blood he spills and the more unreachable he becomes.

Though Tom is shown at various points to be racked with remorse, he's not really someone you can project yourself onto (unless he's meant to be Everyman as No Man). If Minghella intends to demonstrate how, given the right circumstances, any of us could slide into murder with a fairly clean conscience, then he underestimates the way Matt Damon in this film comes across as a vacuum (albeit a seductively robust and personable vacuum). The setting and even some of the themes of the film are distinctly Jamesian, but Tom is like an existential version of the Jackal from *The Day of the Jackal;* this cipher mutates into whatever puts him out of harm's way.

It's this free-floating dread under a hot summer sun, and not the film's cautionary-tale aspects, that takes hold. The actors seem to have been chosen for their ability to reflect the light. Jude Law and Gwyneth Paltrow in particular, look like they were dipped in gold; the emollients of wealth have oiled them to a fine finish. The other performers, including Cate Blanchett as a textile heiress and the always marvelous Philip Seymour Hoffman as Freddie, Dickie's sneering uppercrust Princeton mate, bring some earth tones into all the blondeness. They seem to operate in a less hazy, more grounded world. It is Freddie who, with his instincts for the deceptions of the lowborn, roots out Tom in the film's most cloak-and-dagger-ish scene. The sequence probably belongs in a more conventional movie, and yet I'm not sorry it's here. We've been asked to identify so closely with the far-gone Tom that the intrusion of Freddie, with his sharp, rational suspicions, is a balm. He's someone we can get behind.

Too much should not be made of the cool amorality and character-doubling on display here. Although the film captures better than *Purple Noon* did the distinctive Highsmith tone of steady-state anxiety, it's essentially a glossy plaything of a thriller—which is what the Alain Delon film was, too. Minghella brings out the homosexual subtext and erotic ambiguities in the material, and he heightens the class resentments, but make no mistake: The big draw here is the luxuriousness of corruption, and Minghella, for all his pretensions, is enough of a showman to know it.

NEW YORK POST, 12/24/99, p. 31, Jonathan Foreman

The first hour of "The Talented Mr. Ripley"—one of the most glamorous films since director Anthony Minghella's own "The English Patient"—is terrific.

It's as seductive and stylish as its main characters—wealthy, pretty, young American expatriates, playing around in Italy's most beautiful locales in the late 1950s.

Unfortunately, this film of mistaken identity, murder, class envy and (bi)sexual tension doesn't live up to its own promise.

Even though Minghella has changed Patricia Highsmith's startlingly amoral novel to make it more of a tragedy (and to make its homosexual subtext explicit), and despite a starmaking performance by Jude Law, you find yourself becoming less and less emotionally involved in the story.

It's 1958, and Tom Ripley (Matt Damon) is playing piano at a tony Park Avenue party while wearing a borrowed Princeton jacket.

The host, a shipbuilding magnate named Greenleaf (James Rebhorn), assumes that Tom was at school with his son Dickie (Law), who has run off to sail in Italy with his girlfriend Marge (Gwyneth Paltrow).

Tom is, in fact, a bathroom attendant, whose main talent besides playing classical piano is, in his own words, "forging signatures, telling lies and doing impressions of people."

Greenleaf offers Tom $1,000—enough to live in Europe for six months—if he will go off to the Adriatic and persuade Dickie to come home. Tom accepts. But you get a glimpse of troubles to come when he tells a fellow passenger on the ship over—an heiress played by Cate Blanchett—that his name is Dickie Greenleaf.

When Tom arrives in Italy, he's so taken by Dickie Greenleaf and his wonderful life that he soon confesses to being an agent of his father.

Both Dickie and Marge are great-looking, confident people, but Tom is clearly stunned by Dickie's good taste, his ease in the world and his skill at anything he tries. Dickie, who has some of the careless arrogance of Tom Buchanan in "The Great Gatsby," likes having an acolyte around, so he kind of adopts Tom, lending him clothes encouraging him to accompany him and Marge everywhere.

It turns out to be a double seduction, and Tom's desire for Dickie is connected with a desire to *be* him. That desire takes over when fickle Dickie gets tired of Tom, and is then murdered by him in a sudden, shocking moment of violence.

Tom instantly decides to take over Dickie's life and to live in Italy on Dickie's allowance. It will mean avoiding Marge and other people who know the real Dickie Greenleaf, but Tom is brilliant at leading a double life.

Unfortunately, as time goes on, the requirements of that life cost him the only person who has ever loved him for himself.

The more you get into the story, the more you wonder if there hasn't been a mistake in the casting—if it shouldn't have been Law playing Tom Ripley and Damon playing Dickie Greenleaf. It's not that Damon is bad as Ripley, but you just don't sense the charm or smoothness Tom would have to have in order to insinuate himself into this charmed circle of wealthy American expats.

And while Law brilliantly carries off the role of golden boy Dickie—there are moments when he could almost be a young Redford—you could easily believe him as the kind of seductive chameleon a Ripley should be.

Philip Seymour Hoffman, on the other hand, is perfect as the upper-class bully whose own meanness gives him the ability to see through Ripley's act and into the uncertainties that motivate him.

But what Minghella does brilliantly is capture the feel of a magical time and place. There's one scene, in particular, in a jazz club, with young Italians rapturously singing their love of American culture, that is just thrilling.

NEWSDAY, 12/24/99, Part II/p. B2, Gene Seymour

Tom Ripley, the title character of Patricia Highsmith's 1955 novel, "The Talented Mr. Ripley," is one of the great American creations in literature, worthy of the Mark Twain who wrote such sour mash stories as "The Man That Corrupted Hadleyburg." Yet Americans have never quite taken to Highsmith's six Ripley novels in the same way that Europe and the rest of the world have embraced them.

It's not hard to understand why. Ripley is a distressing projection of what Americans both value and fear about themselves. He's a clever, industrious young man on the make, especially gifted at that all-American sport of reinventing the self in order to get ahead in life. Toward such ends, Ripley will do just about anything—even kill people when they get in his way.

Hollywood habitually flinches from the matter-of-fact treatment of amorality that drives Highsmith's books—even though Alfred Hitchcock made one of his finest movies in 1951 from Highsmith's "Strangers on a Train." No problem for the French, who put "The Talented Mr. Ripley" on screen in 1960 under the title "Purple Noon," with Alain Delon as Tom.

Cast as Ripley in writer-director Anthony Minghella's newer, longer and more sumptuous adaptation of the novel, Matt Damon cuts a far less dashing figure than Delon. Yet one suspects that for this end-of-the-'50s version, Minghella preferred a shy, bespectacled Tom as a more convincing and, certainly, more acceptable cipher. Damon's Tom is less a cunning sociopath than a criminal savant; a Tom Sawyer whose conscience is on life support when the movie begins.

And it begins with a billionaire shipbuilder named Greenleaf (James Rebhorn), who mistakes Tom for a Princeton classmate of his son Dickie (Jude Law), who's burning holes in his trust fund, gallivanting all over Europe with a prim blond novelist named Marge (Gwyneth Paltrow). The elder Greenleaf is willing to pay Tom's expenses if the latter will go to Italy and convince Dickie to come home.

Tom, leading a life of quiet desperation in the bowels of Manhattan, agrees.

Dickie, of course, has no idea who Tom is, but nonetheless draws him into his glittering, wayward life of leisure on the Italian south shore. Boating by day, clubbing at night, bathing the sunlit afternoons in Frascati and laughter ...

Tom, without seeming to realize it at first, wants Dickie's life as his own.

But the charismatic Greenleaf is also a moody chap with some heavy baggage of his own to answer for. Worse, Tom begins to feel more and more on the outside looking in on this idyllic party, especially after Dickie's boorish friend Freddie Miles (Philip Seymour Hoffman) arrives on the scene. One day, while he and Tom are alone on a rowboat, Dickie begins taunting Tom as a prelude to cutting him off entirely. In a violent fit, Tom slashes Dickie's head with an oar and can't stop pounding.

From that moment, "Ripley" shakes loose of its gilded revenue and becomes an intriguing, unsettling cat-and-mouse game in which Tom assumes Dickie's identity, sending everyone around him, especially Marge and Freddie, into confusion and suspicion. Complicating matters is the presence of another young American aristocrat, Meredith Logue (Cate Blanchett), whom Tom met off the boat from America and told her he was Dickie.

An Oscar winner for 1996's "The English Patient," Minghella here proves himself even more accomplished at the kind of grand, yet exacting narrative process that made icons out of David Lean and William Wyler. By tightening his focus on the ins and outs of Tom's dangerous deception, Minghella makes you feel almost as complicit as Ripley. Whenever Tom finds himself backed into a comer, you find yourself scrambling with him for a way out. Which is a tribute to Damon's timing and story sense as well as Minghella's respect for Highsmith's blithe mischief.

Still, you come to regret the way both men conspire to clutter Ripley's character with motivational tics as if they wanted to cut the cyanide aroma of Tom's cold-bloodedness. As noted, mass tastes in this country may not be ready for Highsmith's Ripley. But ultimately, you feel that what began as a potential genre groundbreaker has ended as a glossier psycho-killer potboiler.

Because of which, you feel guilty for giving in to the golden glow of both the setting and the cast. Hoffman's bluff seediness is almost a relief, because it sets off the blinding light cast by Law's princely Dickie and Paltrow's daisy-fresh Marge. Blanchett, though playing someone not in the book, may well be the most interesting person in the movie besides Tom, given that her desires are almost as desperate, if more constrained, than his.

NEWSWEEK, 12/20/99, p. 43, David Ansen

The indolent, sensual glamour of Italy in the late 1950s—a playground for young, rich American WASP expatriates—beautifully captured in "The Talented Mr. Ripley," writer-director Anthony Minghella's first film since "The English Patient." It is there that Tom Ripley (Matt Damon) first lays eyes on Dickie Greenleaf (Jude Law), a charming, jazz-loving playboy with a beautiful girlfriend (Gwyneth Paltrow), thoughtless self-confidence and money to burn. Dickie's father in New York has paid Ripley—whom he's mistaken as a friend of his son's from Princeton—to go to Italy to persuade the golden boy to come home. But the impoverished, covetous Ripley, a gifted mimic and quick study, falls in love with Dickie's lifestyle—and with Dickie himself. Minghella puts us inside Ripley's bedazzled head, inviting us to share his energy and giddy excitement even as we recognize his warped, sycophantic need to be someone he's not.

The depth of Ripley's sickness is revealed midway through the film, when he kills Dickie and assumes his identity. In that moment his life becomes a desperate, criminal improvisation. But it is here—when the thriller plot kicks in—that the movie constricts into something more clinical and conventional than its wonderfully seductive first half promised.

Damon's Ripley is considerably different from the charming sociopath in Patricia Highsmith's novel or the smooth Lothario played by Alain Delon in the 1960 French thriller "Purple Noon." Both his homosexuality and his conscience have been outed, turning him into a tortured, self-hating young man. What was a cool, premeditated murder in the book becomes a spontaneous crime of passion—making Ripley's subsequent evil harder to buy. In taking a more moral approach to Highsmith's famously amoral story, Minghella ends up diminishing Ripley. He's been turned into a case study, a gripping one, to be sure, but the giddy thrill is gone.

SIGHT AND SOUND, 3/00, p. 53, Charlotte O'Sullivan

New York, 1958. As a result of a misunderstanding, Tom Ripley is hired by wealthy American magnate Mr Greenleaf to rescue his son Dickie from a dissolute life in Italy. On the way, Tom meets heiress Meredith Logue and tells her he's Dickie Greenleaf. In Italy, Tom befriends Dickie, who's involved both with Marge, an American writer, and local girl Silvana. Tom and Dickie take trips together and Tom's semi-sexual attraction to Dickie grows. Silvana, pregnant by Dickie, drowns herself. Suddenly bored with Tom, Dickie begins to exclude him. During a motorboat ride, Tom and Dickie argue; he kills Dickie and hides the corpse.

Tom tells Marge Dickie decided to move to Rome. There, Tom assumes Dickie's identity. Problems arise when Dickie's old friend Freddie Miles pays a call. Tom kills Freddie. The police become suspicious, but Tom is saved when a new policeman is assigned to the case. Marge and Dickie's father arrive in town, the latter bringing with him a private detective. Tom bumps into Meredith in Rome. He juggles his two identities but when Marge finds Dickie's rings she's convinced of Tom's guilt. The private detective uncovers Silvana's suicide. Dickie's father, disappointed by his son's bad character, gives up the search. Tom has by now fallen in love with Peter, a friend of Marge's, and they go on a voyage back to the US, only for Tom to discover Meredith aboard. Tom kills Peter.

The Talented Mr. Ripley, an adaptation of Patricia Highsmith's 1955 thriller, is a film about the look that cannot speak its name. At one point, the eponymous Ripley sits on a rocking train, gazing at the object of his sexual and economic desire, Dickie Greenleaf. Suddenly, he (and we) realise Dickie knows he's being watched. Director Anthony Minghella keeps the camera fixed on the two men for just that little bit too long, a brilliant move which allows Tom's ambivalent adoration to float queasily before us, while Dickie decides how to react. He finally settles on contempt and (peeping) Tom's body seems to contract with shame. Like that otherworldly moment in *Persona* where wannabe 'double' Liv Ullmann steps on to a shard of glass, Tom's expulsion into the land of the single makes us wince.

There are many such episodes in this film. A tense, troubling thriller, marred only by problems of pacing (the middle section drags) and some implausible characterisation (Meredith's obsession with Ripley never convinces), it's full of vivid, miserable life. Philip Seymour Hoffman, for example, burns a hole in the memory as the viciously astute Freddie.

But is this film 'dangerous', as has been suggested by the US press? Minghella has obviously adapted freely from the novel, and has been credited with taking more risks, not less. Something has happened, for instance, to the novel's take on class. In the book, the social gap between Tom and Dickie is not as wide as in the film, where Tom is a one-time janitor. Highsmith's Tom is also the more culturally worldly of the two—it's Dickie who's the conventional one. In Minghella's version, the roles are reversed: Tom plays nerdish pauper to Dickie's Machiavellian *la dolce vita* prince. Minghella presumably intended to make Tom more sympathetic. He has, but in doing so he's also made him less interesting and drained him of his mercurial power. Instead of identifying with Tom, we feel sorry for him. By the same token, instead of feeling sorry for Dickie, we're intrigued. He, along with girlfriend Marge (no longer a stodgy Ohio bumpkin but a cut-glass golden girl), now represents a new, enticing moral order.

Dickie and Marge break rules, Dickie with his casual, catastrophic affairs, his "half-killing" of a boy at school, Marge with her gay friend Peter (in the book, all are horrified by ''queers'). The couple are also bright as buttons. Where Highsmith's Dickie is pitifully limited when it comes to *aperçu* (Tom waits in vain for "something profound and original from Dickie"), Minghella's charismatic cad manages to impress constantly (he likens his privileged friends to cream, because they're "rich and thick"). Similarly, while Highsmith pokes fun at Dickie's mediocre paintings, Minghella allows the young man's musical ability to charm not only Tom but a crowded room of Italians (the camera, swirling round the room, infects us with the appreciative mood). As for Marge, in the book she remains duped to the end. Here, she's the only one to realise Tom's a murderer. Thus, as in *The English Patient,* Minghella gets to portray certain aristocrats not only as supremely glamorous but also ahead of their time. Their remoteness, even cruelty, just makes them more attractive. Like Almásy and Katharine, Dickie and Marge are extraordinary, objects of sexual and economic desire perfectly formed to suit middlebrow tastes.

Minghella's other "radical" break with Highsmith's text involves sexuality, introducing a full blown homosexual affair into the story, which Minghella has predicted will "alienate Middle America". But Ripley does not "get away" with his sexual/moral deviation. A prisoner of his own device, he ends up a psychologically doomed man. In an afterword to *The Price of Salt* aka *Carol,* the 'lesbian novel' Highsmith wrote she talks about the typical fate of homosexuals in fiction: "punished for their deviation, they've slashed their wrists or collapsed alone into a depression equal to hell." Minghella's Tom conforms utterly to this description. By combining sex with an unhappy ending and a contrite beginning ("If I could just go back ..." intones Tom) Minghella more than satisfies mainstream requirements.

The Talented Mr. Ripley is worth more than a peep. It's only in comparison with Highsmith's book that its conservatism becomes clear. Minghella cautions that envy won't get us anywhere, even as he makes us giddy with covetous lust for the aristocratic élite. Highsmith teaches that envy gets you everywhere, even as she reminds us how unenviable the rich truly are. What a shame this lesson is available to the reader's eyes only.

VILLAGE VOICE, 12/28/99, p. 126, Amy Taubin

If you want to set yourself up for disappointment, you've only to look forward to a movie based on a book you love. But even taken on their own terms, there's little to recommend either Anthony Minghella's conspicuously picturesque depiction of beautiful rich Americans acting ugly in Europe in *The Talented Mr. Ripley* or Alan Parker's bland evocation of growing up grindingly poor in Ireland in *Angela's Ashes.*

Based on Patricia Highsmith's great, dark novel of the same name, Minghella's Ripley stars a miscast Matt Damon as Tom Ripley, an ambitious hanger-on who cons his way into an Ivy League smart-set and murders to secure a lifestyle he envies. Ripley, who is the antihero of five Highsmith novels, is a fascinating study in psychopathology. Shrinks would have a field day with his diagnoses: severe narcissistic character disorder; borderline paranoid schizophrenic; repressed, self-hating homosexual. What's most disturbing about Ripley is how normal he seems to himself.

Though written in the third person, the novels are confined to Ripley's perspective. Highsmith burrows into Ripley's mind and, from that vantage point, reports on how the world appears to him. Highsmith's relationship to her character mirrors the kind of boundary problems Ripley has with those to whom he becomes attached. And it rubs off on the reader. To put it crudely, Highsmith suggests that the ability to lose oneself in writing or reading a novel has something in common with Ripley's "talent"—with his perverse ability to picture himself leading someone else's life—and that such identifications can lead to murder.

Ripley's chameleon-like personality is what makes him so difficult to portray on the screen. There have been two prior adaptations of the Ripley novels. Rene Clement's *Purple Noon* starred Alain Delon, who lacked, through no fault of his own, the distinctly American qualities of the character. Clement also grafted a moral ending onto the narrative that was totally antithetical to Highsmith's purposes. Dennis Hopper was a much more successful Ripley in Wim Wenders's *The American Friend*. Easily Wenders's best film and, along with *Chinatown*, the most powerful '70s neonoir, it combines the second and third books in the series (*Ripley Under Ground* and *Ripley's Game*). Rather than focusing on Ripley's expatriate alienation, Wenders shows the devastating effect of American entrepreneurship on the European middle class. Ripley cons a terminally ill family man (Bruno Ganz) into becoming a hired gun so that he can leave his wife and child some money when he dies. The double-faced nature of guilt is Highsmith's great subject. It would seem that Ripley lacks guilt but in fact the reverse is the case. His guilt is so heavy that it compels him to take leave of his own skin lest he end up killing himself. Wenders mirrors Ripley's guilt with German postwar guilt.

Minghella, a would-be art film director who never takes his eye off the box office, doesn't allow himself to become embroiled in such complexity. He turns *The Talented Mr. Ripley* into a splashy tourist trap of a movie. The effect is rather like reading *The National Enquirer* in a café overlooking the Adriatic. Minghella seems to be aware of the Hitchcockian aspects of Highsmith, but rather than going for the claustrophobia of *Strangers on a Train* (the most successful Highsmith adaptation), he employs the panoramic mise-en-scène of *North by Northwest*. Transposing the setting of the film from Highsmith's early '50s to the more affluent late '50s, Minghella references Hollywood's initial infatuation with widescreen cinematography but gives it a decided '90s gloss. Were it not for the occasional reference to the value of a dollar ($1000 buys six months of footloose living in Europe), you might forget this is a period movie.

A poor orphan with expensive tastes, Ripley is sent to Italy by a wealthy shipbuilder who wants him to convince his son, Dickie (Jude Law), to come home. Ripley, whose gay desire is more exposed in the film than in the novel, becomes obsessed with Dickie in the way that a narcissist inevitably does when he finds someone more self-involved than himself. Ripley envies Dickie, he wants to be Dickie; Dickie, however, finds Ripley's attentions tiresome and weird. When Ripley realizes that Dickie is about to cast him out, he kills him and spends a frantic six months shifting between Dickie's identity and his own in an effort to cover his tracks.

In the novel, the murder is both premeditated and completely psychotic. Minghella, in a transparent attempt to make Ripley more sympathetic, transforms it into Ripley's response to Dickie's attack on him. Dickie contemptuously tells Ripley that everyone hates him for being a pathetic social climber and a closet case to boot. Ripley hits him, probably harder than he might have intended. Dickie hits back, and the fight escalates into a bloody kill-or-be-killed confrontation.

Damon, who does an uncanny imitation of Chet Baker's androgynous rendition of "My Funny Valentine" (thanks, I suspect, to the kind of vocoder mike that made Laurie Anderson the queen of performance art), shows signs of wanting to dirty up his American golden boy image (his strained, toothy grin just makes him look like Alfred E. Neuman), but Minghella keeps him on a short leash, and he's in over his head anyway. Law queens his way through the supposedly straight role, and Gwyneth Paltrow is more tiresome than usual indulging her specialty of scrunch-faced, tearless crying. On the other hand, Philip Seymour Hoffman is exactly on the mark as a supercilious preppie, as is Cate Blanchett as a floundering heiress. It's a sign of how watered-down the movie is that only the supporting actors have any bite.

Also reviewed in:
CHICAGO TRIBUNE, 12/24/99, Friday/p. A, Michael Wilmington

NATION, 1/24/00, p. 35, Stuart Klawans
NEW REPUBLIC, 1/17/00, p. 24, Stanley Kauffmann
NEW YORK TIMES, 12/24/99, p. E1, Janet Maslin
NEW YORKER, 12/27/99 & 1/3/00, p. 128, Anthony Lane
VARIETY, 12/13-19/99, p. 105, Todd McCarthy
WASHINGTON POST, 12/25/99, p. C1, Stephen Hunter
WASHINGTON POST, 12/24/99, Weekend/p. 31, Desson Howe

TANGO

A Sony Pictures Classics release of an Alma Ata International Pictures/Argentina Sono Film production in association with Astrolabio Productions, Adela Pictures, Beco Films and Hollywood Partners, with participation of Saura Films and Pandora Cinema. *Executive Producer:* Carlos Rizzuti. *Producer:* Luis A. Scalella, Carlos L. Mentasi, and Juan C. Codazzi. *Director:* Carlos Saura. *Screenplay (Spanish with English subtitles):* Carlos Saura. *Director of Photography:* Vittorio Storaro. *Editor:* Julia Juaniz. *Music:* Lalo Schifrin. *Choreographer:* Juan Carlos Copes, Carlos Rivarola, and Ana Maria Steckelman. *Sound:* Jorge Stavropulos and (music) Osvaldo Acedo. *Sound Editor:* Jorge Stavropulos. *Casting:* Maria Inés Teyssie. *Set Designer:* Emilio Basaldúa. *Set Decorator:* Mariana Sourroille. *Special Effects:* Tom Cundom and Jorge Avalos. *Costumes:* Beatriz Di Benedetto. *Make-up:* Mirta Blanco. *Running time:* 100 minutes. *MPAA Rating:* PG-13.

CAST: Miguel Ángel Solà (Mario Suárez); Cecilia Narova (Laura Fuentes); Mia Maestro (Elena Flores); Juan Carlos Copes (Carlos Nebbia); Carlos Rivarola (Ernesto Landi); Sandra Ballesteros (María Elman); Oscar Cardozo Ocampo (Daniel Stein); Martín Seefeld (Andrés Castro); Antonio Soares, Jr. (Bodyguard 1); Ricardo Diaz Mourelle (Waldo Norman); Ariel Casas (Antonio); Carlos Thiel (Doctor Ramírez); Johana Copes (Dance Teacher); Nora Zinsky (Woman Investor 1); Mabel Pessen (Woman Investor 2); Fernando Llosa (Man Investor 1); Julio Marticorena (Man Investor 2); Enrique Pinti (Sergio Lieman); Julio Bocca (Himself); Juan Luis Gallardo (Angelo Larroca); Viviana Vigil and Héctor Pilatti (Singers); Roxana Fontan (Young Female Singer); Cutuli (Master of Ceremonies); Néstor Marconi and Adolfo Gómez (Bandoneón Players); Juanjo Domínguez (Guitar Player); Norberto Ramos (Pianist); Dante Montero (Bodyguard 2); Ángela Ciccone (Palmira Fuentes); Fernando Monetti (Homero Fuentes); Ángel Coria (Assistant Choreographer); Sofía Codrovich (Ana Segovia); Mariano Moisello (Roy Ramos); Elvira Onetto (School Teacher); Vito Melino (Larroca's Father).

NEW YORK POST, 2/12/99, p. 52, Rod Dreher

Spanish filmmaker Carlos Saura is a terrific maker of dance movies, and as long as "Tango" sticks with dancing, it's lush and thrilling. But he frames "Tango's" engrossing dance performances with a story afflicted by two left feet. It doesn't ruin the picture by a long shot, but "Tango" would have been almost perfect had Saura followed the same pure-documentary path as he did with his 1995 masterpiece "Flamenco."

Despite its dramatic limitations, "Tango," which was nominated earlier this week for the foreign-language Oscar, is a ravishing homage to the legendary Argentine dance and the Buenos Aires culture from which it springs. The tango is celebrated as the ultimate expression of the volatile, romantic Argentine soul—the quintessence of artfully sublimated passion.

Mario (Miguel Angel Sola) is a theatrical director trying to put together a sophisticated stage revue that will achieve his politically dicey artistic vision, while pleasing the production's conservative financial backers. He falls into a dangerous love affair with Elena (heartstoppingly gorgeous Mia Maestro, who makes American beauties look like washerwomen), a lithe young company dancer, who also happens to be the girlfriend of the Mafioso helping bankroll his show.

This is quite beside the point of "Tango," which is all about the beauty of the dance, gorgeously lighted and lensed by Vittorio Storaro. The sinuous footwork of the dancers, their tight precision, allegro rhythms, emotional expressiveness, and the white-hot eroticism inherent in the tango itself—all this makes for an exhilarating film, even if you aren't a dancer yourself.

Saura uses the interiors of 1930s-style formal restaurants, ballrooms and clubs for many of his scenes, and Storaro's warm, buttery lighting makes Buenos Aires look like a lover's paradise. Without its clunky narrative, "Tango" would have danced all night.

NEWSDAY, 2/12/99, Part II/p. B7, Gene Seymour

Spanish director Carlos Saura has made it his business over the last couple of decades to reinvent the movie musical by sensually probing the song-and-dance traditions that catch his interest. As with "Blood Wedding" (1981), "Carmen" (1983) and "Flamenco" (1995), "Tango" breaks down the musical-making process into its elemental forms of rehearsal, staging and presentation to both explore and revel in the myriad possibilities within this Argentinean dance of passion.

Once again, Saura and cinematographer Vittorio Storaro, his collaborator on "Flamenco," have mounted a sumptuous buffet for the eyes, with dance routines given lavish colors and imaginative staging. They exploit every visual trick at their disposal (mirrors, and shadows projected on a backdrop, among others) to heighten the tension-release dynamics of the tango. The camera drinks up the simmering allure while remaining a relatively stationary witness to tangos performed in pairs, in groups, between men and women, women and women and men and men in various costumes and settings.

As with Storaro's camerawork, the choreography by Juan Carlos Copes and Carlos Rivarola engages in mischief that contributes to the filmmakers collective view of the tango as a game played not just between dance partners, but between reality and imagination. It's a provocative strategy that gets slightly trumped by its story, which echoes such movies-within-movies as "8½," "Day for Night" and "All That Jazz."

The story is about a brooding tango artist named Mario (Miguel Angel Sola), physically hobbled by an accident, emotionally hobbled by his separation from his dancer-wife (Elena Flores). As a means to recovery, Mario has thrown himself into directing and writing a movie, also called "Tango," which will encompass both the history of Argentina (including the murders and tortures that terrorized the nation during military rule) and the evolution of the dance itself.

Investors are nervous over the prospect of a movie that makes its audiences think too much. Mario is adamant about doing things his way—except in the case of the biggest investor, a shady restaurateur straight out of a Borges street yarn who wants Mario to cast his girlfriend Laura (Cecilia Narova) in the ensemble. (Think they'll fall in love in spite of the dire consequences? Take a guess.)

This thin, conventional plot tries to tango with the audience's expectations, leading to a final twist that leaves you both breathless and cheated. And yet the dancing and the music by Lalo Schifrin has captivated you so much by then that you don't care what flimsy excuse is concocted for their existence.

SIGHT AND SOUND, 8/99, p. 52, Geoffrey Macnab

Buenos Aires. Mario Suárez, a middle-aged theatre director, is left holed up in his apartment, licking his wounds when his girlfriend (and principal dancer) Laura leaves him. Seeking distraction, he throws himself into his next project, a musical about the tango. One evening, while meeting with his backers, he is introduced to a beautiful young woman Elena, the girlfriend of his chief investor Angelo, a shady businessman with gangster connections. Angelo asks Mario to audition Elena. He does so and is immediately captivated by her. Eventually, he takes her out of the chorus and gives her a leading role. An affair develops between them, but the possessive Angelo has her followed all the time.

The investors are unhappy with some of Mario's dance sequences. They don't like a routine which criticises the violent military repression and torture of the past. Angelo has been given a small part, which he takes very seriously. The lines between fact and fiction begin to blur: during a scene in the musical showing immigrants newly arrived in Argentina, two men fight over Elena. She is stabbed. Only slowly do we realise that her death is not for real.

In his autobiography *A Lifetime in Movies*, Michael Powell writes about the idea of the composed film, in which music is the master, but is combined with emotion and acting to make a complete whole. Carlos Saura's *Tango* is just such a film. It relies far more heavily on colour, movement and music than on dialogue or characterisation. Like Powell's *The Red Shoes* (1948) or Saura's own, earlier dance movies (for instance, *Blood Wedding* or *Carmen*), it blurs the lines between rehearsal, real life and performance. And it is just about possible to trace a line between Powell's films and *Tango*. Late in his career, Powell worked as a consultant at Francis Ford Coppola's Zoetrope where cinematographer Vittorio Storaro (who has shot four of Saura's films) was one of the key technicians. Storaro's lighting of some of the interiors in *Tango*, complete with iridescent colours and dramatic shadows, rekindles memories of equally stylised sequences he lensed for Coppola's *One from the Heart*.

Tango is nothing if not self-conscious. Yet another womanising, middle-aged director, exorcising his own personal demons through his work, *Tango*'s lead character Mario Suárez seems to have been borrowed directly from Fellini's *8½* (1963). Miguel Ángel Solá, who plays him, has the same crumpled charm as Mastroianni in Fellini's film. There have been countless other films about filmmaking and also many about tango (just recently, Sally Potter's *The Tango Lesson*, for example). Of all dances featured in the movies, it is easily the most common. Combining arrogance and sensitivity with raw sexuality, the dance originated in the slums of Buenos Aires in the late nineteenth century, but spread across Europe and the US like rampant syphilis. Saura (a Spanish film-maker) seems determined here to take the dance back to its South American roots.

A spellbinding but perplexing piece of film-making, *Tango*'s storyline could be written on the back of cigarette paper—a director puts on a musical' just about sums it up. There are some misjudged moments: given the lack of social and historical context, the dance sequence showing brutal military repression seems out of place. Nevertheless, Saura manages to hint at the foibles and neuroses of his characters. As in all the best backstage/backscreen musicals, he shows up the tension between the artists and the investors backing them. Somehow he also convinces us that Suárez (the name is suspiciously close to his own) really is going through some sort of midlife crisis. His voiceover is melancholy and poetic; he is, for all his grace and humour, intensely voyeuristic. When we see Elena, his beautiful new discovery, dancing with his ex-girlfriend Laura, we're in no doubt about his mixed feelings of lust, anger and jealousy.

Saura draws a subtle contrast between the febrile atmosphere at rehearsal, where every new routine seems as much a battle as a dance, and the documentary-style sequences showing the way tango is integrated into everyday Argentinian life. We see an old maestro (Juan Carlos Copes) dancing it with incredible grace and delicacy. At school dance class, a precocious young girl holds herself back rather than be paired with anybody else other than the oafish, big-footed boy she loves. Nevertheless, for all its technical polish and virtuosity, *Tango* has the roughness and spontaneity of a work-in-progress. There's a sense that the filmmakers, like the dancers, are working on the hoof. That's what makes their efforts so exhilarating to watch—even when they do trip up.

VILLAGE VOICE, 2/16/99, p. 148, Jessica Winter

Though the parallels between them are shaky, *Tango* unavoidably calls to mind Sally Potter's paean to this genre of choreographed foreplay, the charming, narcissistic curiosity *The Tango Lesson*. In Potter's film, dance is an embodiment—albeit an awkward one—of clashing artistic wills, power relations between the sexes, and idealized love and the disillusionment that follows it. She divides her story into "lessons," some about dance, and others about the messy reality for which dance can be explication, sublimation, or escape. Carlos Saura's movie, filmed just outside Buenos Aires, attempts a similar employment of tango as all-purpose metaphor, and even boasts another charming narcissist at its center. Mario Suarez (Miguel Angel Sola) is filming a tango musical (one that appears to be modeled after *West Side Story*), but autobiography keeps seeping into his frame, mostly in the form of the wife who left him and the dewy-eyed gangster's moll with whom he's now entangled. Ever-prudent Mario, true to form, has cast them as his two female leads. The auteur eventually abruptly decides to inject some historical allegory into his film, with overt allusions to the suffering of Argentines under years of military dictatorship. His newfound political impulses bring on a softer, more reflective Mario; he's no longer merely a cad, but a wistful Zen cad.

While *The Tango Lesson* drew a permeable boundary between life and dance, Saura's film sets up a two-way mirror. He'll give his audience a by-the-numbers scene of seduction or betrayal in one moment, then in the next recast it as a tango number, providing a welcome distraction from the hackneyed script. Lighting the performers in silhouette against a back screen may seem a hokey device, but Saura's austere approach maintains the hard-edged purity of a dance that is at once rigidly precise and impulsively erotic. These scenes are thrilling, but ultimately redundant; one wishes that Saura had followed his protagonist's lead and made the far more efficient, eloquent film that lurks in *Tango,* one in which dance does all the talking.

Also reviewed in:
CHICAGO TRIBUNE, 3/26/99, Friday/p. F, Michael Wilmington
NEW YORK TIMES, 2/12/99, p. E29, Janet Maslin
VARIETY, 6/1-7/98, p. 35, Jonathan Holland
WASHINGTON POST, 3/19/99, p. C5, Rita Kempley

TARZAN

A Walt Disney Pictures release. *Producer:* Bonnie Arnold. *Director:* Kevin Lima and Chris Buck. *Screenplay:* Tab Murphy, Bob Tzudiker, and Noni White. *Based on the story "Tarzan of the Apes" by:* Edgar Rice Burroughs. *Additional Screenplay Material:* David Reynolds and Jeffrey Stepakoff. *Editor:* Gregory Perler. *Music:* Phil Collins and Mark Mancina. *Music Editor:* Earl Ghaffari. *Animator:* Glen Keane, Ken Stuart Duncan, Russ Edmonds, John Ripa, Michael Surrey, Randy Haycock, Bruce W. Smith, Sergio Pablos, Dominique Monfery, Jay Jackson, Bruce W. Smith, T. Daniel Hofstedt, and Chris Wahl. *Casting:* Ruth Lambert and Mary Hidalgo. *Sound:* Scott Martin Gershin and (music) Frank Wolf. *Sound Editor:* Per Hallberg. *Running time:* 88 minutes. *MPAA Rating:* G.

VOICES: Brian Blessed (Clayton); Glenn Close (Kala); Minnie Driver (Jane); Tony Goldwyn (Tarzan); Nigel Hawthorne (Professor Porter); Lance Henriksen (Kerchak); Wayne Knight (Tantor); Alex D. Linz (Young Tarzan); Rosie O'Donnell (Terk); Taylor Dempsey (Young Tantor).

CHRISTIAN SCIENCE MONITOR, 6/18/99, p. 15, David Sterritt

Good news. Hollywood is recovering from its "Star Wars" bombardment, and even if the new "Austin Powers" picture can't exactly be called a step in the right direction, more varied fare is starting to arrive.

Leading the way is Disney's animated *Tarzan,* retelling the story of an orphaned child who grows up with gorillas in Africa, becomes a handsome vine-swinger with animal pals, but decides humanity might have its own attractions when a group of scientists—including Jane, an Englishwoman who happens to be just his type—barge into his neck of the jungle.

Some recent animations with a traditional approach, including Disney's own "Hercules" and "The Hunchback of Notre Dame," have wobbled at the box office, suggesting that high-tech feats like "Antz" and "A Bug's Life" are the wave of the genre's future. "Tarzan" is entertaining enough to turn this trend around. The action is lively, the art work is enticing, and the voices-only cast brings the characters to vivid life.

What keeps the picture from swinging to the top of the family-film tree is the absence of any thrilling, over-the-top sequence to make audiences tingle with excitement, like the "Under the Sea" number in "The Little Mermaid" or "Be Our Guest" in "Beauty and the Beast" or many moments in older Disney classics. One scene heads in this direction, as jungle-dwellers poke through the British camp, but doesn't build on its possibilities.

This aside, "Tarzan" is a smart and stylish entertainment that reconfirms the value of old-fashioned movie cartooning.

The General's Daughter comes from the opposite end of the Hollywood spectrum, telling a dark tale of military life.

John Travolta plays an army cop probing the bizarre murder of a female officer whose father, a high-ranking commander, is about to enter politics. His main ally is a rape investigator (Madeleine Stowe) who can be as tough as the men she interrogates. Their discoveries range from a cache of scandalous videotapes to a long-buried secret that complicates their quest for justice.

The movie is marred by clunky dialogue, a scenario with more twists than it can handle, and a weakness for pop psychologizing that makes the average Woody Allen picture seem positively Freudian by comparison. On the plus side, Travolta and Stowe are in good form, backed by a strong supporting cast.

The picture also provides a timely reminder of how hard it is to use the R rating as a catch-all label for socially questionable material. Of course, its psychosexual horrors deserve that designation, but how about its well-aimed attacks on male chauvinism? "The General's Daughter" isn't great cinema, but it provokes a thought or two, and that's more than Austin Powers has to offer.

LOS ANGELES TIMES, 6/16/99, Calendar/p. 1, Kenneth Turan

How deep and forbidding is the jungle? How piercing is an ape-man's cry? How eager is Hollywood to cash in on something that's been previously successful? That's how many times "Tarzan of the Apes," Edgar Rice Burroughs' 1912 tale of a man raised by gorillas, has been transferred to film.

Well, maybe not quite that many times, but historians report that "Tarzan" has been turned into nearly 50 features since Elmo Lincoln created the role in 1918, and that's not counting multi-part serials, TV series and Jimmy Durante's comic riff as Schnarzan in a 1934 film called "Hollywood Party."

Yet the current Disney version is the first time Burroughs' character has been done as animation, and, in the will-wonders-never-cease department, this umpteenth "Tarzan" (directed by Kevin Lima and Chris Buck) turns out to rank with the best of the group.

Combining adroit vocal casting (based on ability not box office) with an entertaining script, an unexpectedly energetic (and non-Disney musical) soundtrack and some splendid technical breakthroughs, the animated "Tarzan" underscores why this story has captivated so many people for so long.

When we think of Tarzan, moving easily through the trees is close to his defining characteristic, and that's where the Disney film sets a new standard. Helped by a recent computer software program called Deep Canvas, which adds noticeable levels of depth and dimension to backgrounds, this Tarzan can swing through the jungle in a much more exhilarating and breathtaking way than reality-based film can hope to match.

The ape-man's supervising animator, Glen Keane, who also did the honors for the Beast in "Beauty and the Beast," says his son's skateboarding was one of the inspirations for Tarzan's magical fluidity. Keane has also been careful to use animation's resources to give Tarzan the kind of physically convincing musculature that makes sense for someone who's lived almost his entire life among jungle animals.

Before Tarzan can dazzle with his vine-swinging, he has to get to Africa in the first place, and the story opens with an intense and convincing fire on a ship that leaves an infant boy and his parents stranded in a jungle treehouse.

The jeopardy in this film is consistently real, and Tarzan's parents are soon terminated by a fierce leopard named Sabor. That's the same animal who recently deprived silver-back gorilla parents Kala (Glenn Close, who dubbed Andie MacDowell's voice in the Tarzan film "Greystoke: The Legend of Tarzan, Lord of the Apes") and Kerchak (Lance Henriksen, whose live-action roles would horrify this film's intended audience) of their infant son.

After a terrifying encounter with Sabor (another example of the film's inventive visual style), Kala finds the boy and tells Kerchak she wants to raise him. "It's not our kind," Kerchak responds unenthusiastically, but though wives always win these kinds of face-offs in Disney films, Kerchak has the last word. The boy can stay, but he won't consider him his son.

With its theme of acceptance and belonging, of a son wanting to prove himself to a father figure thus set (does anyone think it's a coincidence that the film is opening just before Father's Day?), "Tarzan" can't be accused of not fitting snugly into the tradition of well-meaning Disney animation.

But while many of the studio's recent cartoon features have seemed disappointingly pro forma, "Tarzan" is an example of the formula operating on a higher level than usual, with individual elements better conceived and executed across the board.

For one thing, the film's comic sidekicks like gorilla galpal Terk (Rosie O'Donnell) and worrywart elephant Tantor (Wayne King) are actually funny. Also, though the script felt the touch of numerous hands (the studio publicity material mentions "Gorillas in the Mist's" Tab Murphy getting first crack, Bob Tzudiker & Noni White upping the family values quotient, and Dave Reynolds, who gets an "additional screenplay material" credit along with Jeffrey Stepakoff, punching up the dialogue), the result feels surprisingly of a piece.

Also effective was the decision to avoid the by-now overly familiar Broadway musical formula of having characters periodically break into song. Instead, singer-songwriter Phil Collins was retained, and he provides five original compositions that, along with Mark Mancina's score, give "Tarzan" a narrative overlay that adds coherence and energy to the proceedings.

The adult Tarzan (Tony Goldwyn), gifted with the squarest jaw since Fearless Fosdick, gets the surprise of his life when his jungle is invaded by creatures he thinks he's never seen: fellow human beings. Specifically it's pompous guide Clayton (Brian Blessed), a professor eager to learn more about gorillas (Nigel Hawthorne) and the professor's daughter (Minnie Driver), a charming young woman whose name just happens to be Jane.

Naturally, Jane gets into trouble (with some irascible baboons) and Tarzan has to step in, leading to Jane's shocked "I'm in a tree with a man who talks to monkeys." A "me Tarzan, you Jane" sequence is all but mandatory, and how pleasantly it's presented is one of this film's many surprises.

Though they apparently never worked face to face, Goldwyn and Driver are not only excellent on their own; the push-pull of their relationship is equally satisfying. "Tarzan's" story unfolds with dangers as well as warm humor; a jungle jam session called "Trashin' the Camp" is especially hard to resist. We may have seen it all before, but when it's done up like this, experiencing it all over again is a pleasure.

NEW YORK, 6/28-7/5/99, p. 129, Peter Rainer

In the new Disney animated feature *Tarzan* which has some first-rate animation and some second-rate storytelling the ape man glimpses his first human and wails to his ape mom, "Why didn't you tell me there were creatures who looked like me?" Actually, aside from his Rasta locks, the creature Tarzan most looks like is Fabio. He's been given that hyper-physiqued appearance that animators now so often equate with superheroism—even Moses in *The Prince of Egypt* had it. He's also been given a lustier yell; none of that Johnny Weissmuller jungle yodel for this guy. When he finally hooks up with Jane, he gets so worked up that he surfs the treetops. It's a high-flying form of autoeroticism, and it points up just how sublimated Tarzan is. He might not have been so deprived if the animators had seen fit to introduce a few Africans into the jungle, but there's nary a one: Perhaps Disney thought the best way to get around the ooga-booga stereotype was to eliminate blacks altogether. It's the neutron-bomb version of political correctness.

NEW YORK POST, 6/18/99, p. 48, Rod Dreher

Disney's "Tarzan," is not only the summer's most thrilling mainstream movie so far, it's also the best animated feature the studio has put out since "The Lion King."

Though 47 previous live-action features would appear to have exhausted Edgar Rice Burroughs' jungle-man legend—in the era of "The Matrix" and "The Phantom Menace," who wants to see some loinclothed actor swinging on a rope disguised as a vine?—animation makes the Tarzan character and his world surprisingly fresh and compelling.

For one thing, the medium frees Tarzan to perform acrobatic feats and swinging stunts far beyond the capacity of a real actor. Disney's Tarzan (voiced by Tony Goldwyn) swoops through the jungle canopy like a gravity-defying superhero, and surfs barefoot along limbs and tree trunks like a world-class skate punk.

The breakneck jungle chases in "Tarzan" rival the pod-race scene in "The Phantom Menace" for thrill-ride intensity—courtesy of a new animation technique called "Deep Canvas" that gives the richly hued background stunningly beautiful depth.

And animation opens up an entirely new emotional world, giving the gorillas who raise Tarzan voice and character, and enabling us to see how he relates to them. The movie begins with a stunning opening montage, a marvel of efficient visual storytelling that depicts the infant boy's jungle-dwelling English parents' deadly encounter with a leopard (the attack is suggested, not shown on screen), and the child being rescued by a kindhearted gorilla mom named Kala (voice of Glenn Close).

Kala's husband, Kerchak (voice of Lance Henriksen), the protector of the gorilla tribe, refuses to accept the bare-chested stepchild but allows him to stay. Scenes of mother-child bonding are amazingly poignant, even heart-rending, as are later moments showing the child Tarzan's rejection by his stepfather.

As a young adult, Tarzan has his first encounter with people: Professor Porter (voice of Nigel Hawthorne), daughter Jane (voice of Minnie Driver), and their Great White Hunter-ish guide, Clayton (voice of Brian Blessed). Tarzan finds himself attracted to the human world (complete with a raging case of jungle fever for Jane), and suffers an identity crisis. Is his proper place with the people who look like him, or the people—gorillas, that is who loved and nurtured him?

"Tarzan" is a welcome change from recent Disney animated fare in that the comic relief is actually witty and mercifully underplayed. Tarzan's jokey buddies are a tough little gorilla named Terk (voice of Rosie O'Donnell) and a dwarfish pachyderm called Tantor (voice of Wayne Knight). There's a hilarious moment when Tantor first sees the humans' camp and says, in a send-up of "Heart of Darkness," "The horror! The horror!" The animals also create a delightful, "Stomp"-like symphony while cheerfully wrecking the camp.

In another welcome departure from the Disney formula, "Tarzan" doesn't attempt to be a musical. Its five Phil Collins songs are kept in the background, the way the songs in "Toy Story" were. They all sound the same, but don't Phil Collins songs always?

"Tarzan" doesn't have the visual sweep and emotional majesty of "The Lion King," but it dazzles the eye and steals the heart more winningly than anything else out there. Watch out, Austin Powers: Tarzan may be square, but this jungle cat can swing like nobody's business.

NEWSDAY, 6/18/99, Part II/p. B3, John Anderson

Edgar Rice Burroughs was an American, but his apeman was British nobility—a foundling/jungle survivor who represented a hopeful, imperial response to post-Darwinian anxiety: Yes, he was a beast. But a very decent sort of beast.

Burroughs himself left to conjecture whether Tarzan's character was a credit to his English peerage or his simple humanity, so you really can't expect Disney—a company built on the Bambi-fication of nature—to get down and dirty with Mr. T.'s primal urges (much less explain the loincloth). Looking a lot like Daniel Day-Lewis, with a hint of Basil Rathbone during his funkier moments, Tarzan is less ape than he is half man, half deity (very Byronic). He also has great teeth—a ringing endorsement for raw cuisine—and an instinct for protecting white people when they're endangered by the ... well, yes, the animals who happened to raise him from infancy.

Anthropological questions and loyalty issues aside, "Tarzan" is a rollicking, funny, good-natured and very exciting adaptation, which, despite (or because) of the story having been adulterated, makes perfect sense as a Disney film. All of the studio's real masterpieces—from "Dumbo" through "Beauty and the Beast"—have been underdog stories, pleas for tolerance and enlightenment and vehicles for tepid if unassailable decency. And even if "Tarzan" is less dog than monkey, it fits the Disney formula to a T.

Tarzan (voice of Tony Goldwyn) is the classic outsider—not a naturally dominant species, but one who has trouble cutting it in Gorillaville. Discovered as a baby by a band of apes after his parents are killed by Sabor the leopard (Burroughs' adult Tarzan was living with his parents' skeletons; here the corpses are fresh), he's adopted by the grieving Kala (voice of Glenn Close), whose baby, too, was lost to Sabor. "He'll never replace the one we lost," says her mate, Kerchak (Lance Henriksen), whose unacceptance of Tarzan is the dramatic fulcrum of the story—a story, by the way, that has shifted from being about man among the lower species to one in which the lower species are infinitely more human than the humans.

Most human, and most entertaining, are Terk and Tantor, the former a feisty little gorilla played by Rosie O'Donnell, the latter an officious elephant with an aversion to bacteria (Wayne Knight). They, too, fit the formula for most of the more recent Animated Disney Event Movies—the comical sidekick characters without whom the movie would stall out on nobility and earnestness. But Terk and Tantor are particularly funny. You'll wish they were in the movie more.

Directed by Kevin Lima ("A Goofy Movie") and longtime animator Chris Buck, "Tarzan's" pacing is a bit off—not drastically, just noticeably—once we're introduced to the tourists who serve as serpents in the garden. Minnie Driver, in probably her best performance, supplies the voice of Jane, who, with her father, professor Porter (Nigel Hawthorne), and their guide, the bloodthirsty gorilla poacher Clayton (Brian Blessed), are looking for the great apes and find Tarzan along the way. Clayton and Tarzan clash; Tarzan and Jane don't exactly clinch, but the potential is there. The professor sputters. But the other characters sort of drop out, and the movie becomes more conventional—black-hatted evil vs. vine-swinging good—before everybody reassembles for the climactic and reassuring finale and battle scene.

The animation itself, as usual, is splendid. The characters are endearingly malleable creations, sometimes silly, sometimes nearly classical in stature; the jungles, conversely, which might have been rendered by JMW Turner or Caspar David Friedrich, are romanticized to the point of Impressionism. It's an interesting synthesis of styles, which more or less mirrors the conflicting metaphysics behind Burroughs' Tarzan, who, after innumerable movies, 20 novels and 20 million sales of same remains a philosophical enigma.

Disney's "Tarzan" is a lower-case romance, an adventure and a comedy that works for everybody. It's also a departure from the more recent Disney musicals in that the characters don't sing as many songs as Phil Collins. Or maybe it just seemed that way. I thought Collins was singing one song through the entire movie, but the credits account for three, plus a duet with Close and another about "Trashin' the Camp" that's mostly gorilla noises and vocals by O'Donnell. The Collins music is a very heroic kind of pop music, one that's evidently supposed to evoke darkest Africa and the indomitability of the human/ape spirit. It may, in fact, inspire you to strap on a pack and take a 10-mile hike—but not until the movie's over.

SIGHT AND SOUND, 11/99, p. 58, Leslie Felperin

The nineteenth-century. A man and woman are shipwrecked with their infant son off the coast of east Africa. They build a tree house and move in, but Sabor the leopard kills the adults. Kala, a gorilla who has lost her own child to Sabor, finds the infant human, names him Tarzan and adopts him, despite the misgivings of her mate Kerchak, the head of their gorilla tribe. Although Kerchak never fully accepts him, Tarzan grows up among the gorillas and is befriended by Terk, a sarcastic female gorilla, and Tantor, an elephant.

Tarzan reaches manhood. One day, a new sound is heard in the jungle: gunfire. Professor Porter, a zoologist, has arrived in the jungle with his daughter Jane to study the gorillas. They are guided by Clayton, an adventurer who is secretly planning to capture gorillas and ship them back to England. When Jane, separated from the others, is cornered by Sabor, Tarzan saves her. Kala explains to Tarzan his origins by showing him the treehouse. Eager to learn more about his race, Tarzan spends time at the humans' encampment where he learns English and the history of mankind. They persuade Tarzan to take them to the gorillas, Clayton's men attack and capture many of the gorillas, much to Jane and Porter's disgust. With Tantor's help, Tarzan sets the gorillas free and in doing so finally wins the mortally wounded Kerchak's respect. Jane and Porter prepare to return to England, but at the last moment, Jane turns back and decides to stay with Tarzan, now the head of his tribe.

One of the most frequently filmed stories in the cinema, Edgar Rice Burroughs' *Tarzan of the Apes* is adapted to suit the times and has become a useful yardstick of our changing attitudes towards nature, savagery and Africa. The first adaptation in 1918, with Elmo Lincoln in the loincloth, tended to emphasise the freakish nature of the apeman and was inflected by the still-very-hot debate about Darwinism and man's contested relation to apes. Later versions, starring Johnny Weissmuller through to Christopher Lambert and Casper Van Dien, have posited a Tarzan more noble than savage, a good man in Africa who upholds up the white man's burden by his unique sensitivity to the environment. Frequently, imperialism is naturalised through Tarzan; he is 'rightly' the king of the apes, a sovereignty that inevitably places him above even the African natives.

Tellingly, there are no Africans in Disney's latest version of the story, *Tarzan*, perhaps because issues of imperialism would be considered a distraction to this Discovery-channel, eco-friendly take on the classic story. Instead, the gorillas themselves, here literally given a voice for the first time, represent that which is native and threatened by European encrouchers. Meanwhile, with his dreadlocks and deep tan, despite his white parents this version's Tarzan is 'blacker' than any previous incarnation.

Regardless of any subtextual meanings, supervising animator Glen Keane's Tarzan is admittedly a triumph of caricature: feral, powerful, more animalistic than any other version as he walks on his knuckles like an ape. In the film's heirarchy of design, he is the missing link between the highly realistic rendering accorded to the apes and the much-more cartoonish, exagerrated humans (even the film's self-mocking Jane looks like something out of a late-UPA cartoon). Disney's clever twist on the story is to make the hero's confusion about identity, family and community the film's emotional meat, although there's little doubt that in the end he will find his true place among the animals that nurtured him, but with a mate thrown in as a bonus. And just in case there's any doubt, Tarzan uses technology in a strangely paradoxical way to counterpoint the human and natural worlds: to show Tarzan's point of view of the jungle as he swings and 'surfs' like an extreme-sport *aficionado* through the trees, the animators have used a new, state-of-the-art computer technique called 'Deep Canvas' to create a vertiginous, speeding effect. The best the humans can offer him, when Jane and her father introduce Tarzan to the history of his species, is a magic lantern slide show, perhaps a deliberate nod towards the most primitive form of animation.

TIME, 6/14/99, p. 220, Richard Corliss

Bill Clinton is a canny player of political poker. In criticizing movies for their grossness, as he has in the wake of Littleton and other teen tragedies, Clinton is playing his Dan Quayle card. It's not the wrong card, but it is a low one. You can ask for movies to be gentler, a tiny bit more attentive to the power of the repeated image over the young. But after criticizing what's there, think about what's missing. Can we please have a little grandeur and depth in movies? Not of armies on parade or edifying soap operas, but of stories that touch our essential humanity, told with care and flair. Is it possible for a film to resonate in a billion heads at once, holding adults as intensely as fairy tales once mesmerized kids? Can we have a film that is smart, pure and funny and, just by the way, a little profound?

We have one now. *Tarzan*, the new Disney animated feature, is the best news to hit cartooning, and perhaps Hollywood, in ages. It is the full-service, romance-and-adventure, laugh-and-cry movie that Disney and its new competitors have been trying to make, without quite succeeding, since *The Lion King* five summers ago. This is brisk, epic storytelling. Like a shaman in a village circle, the film spins the old saga, made familiar in the Edgar Rice Burroughs books and nearly 50 films, but with a fresh and affecting power. Now it is a safari into the interior of Tarzan's conflicted soul, where he searches not so much for his mate Jane as for his place in a society of men and apes. Though it would be nuts to predict *Lion King*-size revenues (that film and its ancillary markets made Disney $1 billion in profit), it is also hard to believe the mass audience will find *Tarzan* resistible. In its pace, wit and poignancy, this is the movie *The Phantom Menace* should have been.

Disney could use a hit; lately, the company has mostly been taking them. Profits are down, partly because of the slump in popularity of the post-*Lion King* animated features (and hence of the ancillary videos and merchandise). The company's stock is down too, losing 25% of its value in the past bull-market year. Costs have zoomed: a billion here for the Animal Kingdom theme park, $700 million there for a couple of cruise ships—eventually it adds up. And for months CEO Michael Eisner has been on the defensive in a suit brought by Jeffrey Katzenberg, who ran the film studio until he was pushed out in 1994, for a share of the company's profits. That could cost $500 million. After a palmy decade, Walt's successors are finding it's a jungle out there.

Tarzan to the rescue! If not fiscally, then artistically. From the first images, the picture chest-thumps its narrative expertise. A shipwreck brings the baby Tarzan's parents to the jungles of East Africa; they die violently in a leopard attack; a baby gorilla is killed by the same leopard, Sabor; the grieving gorilla mother Kala (voiced by Glenn Close) discovers the humans' corpses and their living child; she saves the child from Sabor and decides to rear the human as her own; Kala's mate Kerchak (Lance Henriksen) gruffly, suspiciously accedes to her wish. All this—basically, the start of *Robinson Crusoe* and the Moses story—is told in a few minutes, with the deftest narrative brushstrokes.

Directors Kevin Lima and Chris Buck, writers Tab Murphy, Bob Tzudiker and Noni White and the myriad artists at their command have taken the Tarzan iconography—vine swinging Jane, Cheetah, the jungle yodel—then freshened or deepened it. This apeman (animated by Glen Keane and voiced by Tony Goldwyn) is no longer a swinger; he rides the twisting highways of tree boughs like the coolest surfer. (Alert, all Disney park ride designers: have the Tarzan Twist ready by next spring.)

Jane is still the proper young Englishwoman abroad, but she and Tarzan are naïfs in each other's worlds, with resources of strength and feelings still to discover. And with Minnie Driver adroitly mining each nuance of social primness, Jane is the first Disney cartoon heroine to provide her own comic relief.

What can be done with Cheetah? Replace that nattering chimp with gorillas who are all too human. This is a film about parenting, about the pain and triumph of racial or social assimilation. Kala is a loving adoptive mother, her concern for the boy complicated by the loss of her own child and the knowledge that his difference, when he finally does understand it, may force him from her. To Kerchak Tarzan is a threat: a wiser form of machismo. And to the brash young Terk (Rosie O'Donnell), Tarzan is just another playmate—weird, but who isn't?

The Tarzan yell might seem the most superficial accessory, but the filmmakers see it as a key to the drama. They never let us forget that the lad is isolated, unaware of his origin and his destiny—and aware that he is unaware. He places his palm against Kala's paw (hands are a major motif in the film) and knows that his mother is different; or, rather, she is the norm, and he the outsider. Africa is his metaphor: the lost continent is his identity. Always he asks, Who or what am I? Where do I belong?

The boy Tarzan is determined to "be the best ape ever." Frustrated that he can't growl exactly like his ape friends, he is advised by Kala to "just come up with your own sound." He does, and he likes it. The Tarzan yell is a shout of young maturity, of his interspecies uniqueness. But later, when he falls in love with Jane yet feels obliged to stay with his ape family to protect them, the yell carries a wrenching pathos. It is the primal scream of someone who doesn't know if he's man or monkey.

We don't mean to frighten the kids; *Tarzan* is not *Oedipus Rex*. It's a Disney coming-of-age comedy-drama in *Lion King* territory, with five radio-friendly tunes written and sung by Phil Collins. It has a standard villain: a grating white hunter (whose musculature nicely mimics Kerchak's, thus suggesting their similarity as imperfect male role models for the boy). It has a reeeeally cute baby baboon. It enfolds our hero in a dream jungle, painted in the lushest of sherbetty forest colors and shot in a new, virtual 3-D format called Deep Canvas that vivifies the scenes. Its set pieces (Tarzan swipes a tail hair from Tantor the elephant, fights Sabor to the death, studies human history and teaches Jane how to sail through the jungle) are models of economy, energy, subtlety, heart.

Tarzan is a movie to restore a proud tradition of popular art. And it gives the Disney company something to yell about. From the treetops, in triumph.

VILLAGE VOICE, 6/22/99, p. 152, Richard Gehr

It's a jungle out in Hollywood, so it's no surprise that Disney sticks to the straight and narrow path once again with its latest visually rich yet numbingly formulaic animated feature. The familiar ingredients—absent parents, unthreatening yet princely hero, perky but ditzy heroine, swarthy villain, cute sidekicks, hugs, lessons, and a CD's worth of forgettable pop tunes—have served Disney since 1989's *The Little Mermaid*. But please, on behalf of parents everywhere, I beseech ye sons and daughters of Walt: give it a rest, OK?

Here the noble alpha lad is of course Tarzan (Tony Goldwyn), who struggles to assert himself ("I'll be the best ape ever!") amid the friendly tribe of gorillas that adopts him when a leopard massacres his parents. Tarzan evolves into an adolescent, ape mother Kala (Glenn Close) sings the de rigueur ballad (by Phil Collins), and conflict arrives in the form of a small expedition consisting of spunky Jane (Minnie Driver), her goofy-scientist father (Nigel Hawthorne), and their tall, dark, and evil guide (Brian Blessed). Will Tarzan—given the opportunity to wear pants and be with the girl of his dreams—abandon the apes? Not on your opposable thumbs.

The new Deep Canvas technique that adds another dimension of background detail to the animation process is *Tarzan*'s real star. The African jungle is rendered as a verdant fantasia of cliffs, mile-high waterfalls, and impossible flora. The ultimate action figure, Tarzan swings convincingly through the jungle's upper terraces when he's not sliding and looping down tree limbs like a skateboarder or passenger on some possibly forthcoming Disney World thrill ride. But the film comes most fully to life—as when Jane flees a tribe of irked baboons, or when a herd of elephants threatens to trample the apes—only when the animation process enhances special effects that Spielberg or Lucas might have conceived. Otherwise, it's a typical Disney knuckle dragger.

Also reviewed in:
CHICAGO TRIBUNE, 6/18/99, Friday/p A, Michael Wilmington
NEW YORK TIMES, 6/18/99, p. E10, Janet Maslin
NEW YORKER, 7/5/99, p. 91, David Denby
VARIETY, 6/7-13/99, p. 29, Todd McCarthy
WASHINGTON POST, 6/18/99, p. C1, Stephen Hunter
WASHINGTON POST, 6/18/99, Weekend/p. 47, Desson Howe

TAXMAN, THE

A Phaedra Cinema release of a Counterclock Pictures production in association with Open City Films. *Executive Producer:* Pascal Borno. *Producer:* Avi Nesher and Kathy Jordan. *Director:* Avi Nesher. *Screenplay:* Roger Berger and Avi Nesher. *Director of Photography:* Jim Denault. *Editor:* Alexander Hall. *Music:* Roger Neill. *Sound:* Robert Ghiraldini. *Production Designer:* Michael Krantz. *Costumes:* Carolyn Grifel. *Running time:* 104 minutes. *MPAA Rating:* R.

CAST: Joe Pantoliano (Al Benjamin); Wade Dominguez (Joseph Romero); Elizabeth Berkley (Nadia Rubakov); Michael Chiklis (Andre Rubakov); Robert Townsend (Peyton Cody).

LOS ANGELES TIMES, 10/1/99, Calendar/p. 12, Jan Stuart

[The following review by Jan Stuart appeared in a slightly different form in
NEWSDAY, 9/17/99, Part II/p. B11.]

Where would crime thrillers be without the amateur sleuth who pokes his or her nose into places where professional investigators are too stupid to tread?

Muscling into a field already dense with rabbis, Girl Scouts and little old ladies from St. Mary Mead is Al Benjamin (Joe Pantoliano), the eponymous Brighton Beach tax investigator of "The Taxman," who is looking for glory amid the number-crunching tedium of his daily routine. When six gas merchants are rubbed out in a bloody back-office slaughter, Al anoints himself crusading gumshoe over the sneering objections of his boss and the police captain on the case. The more abrasive their objections, the more certain we are that Al will get his man.

Al is abetted by Joseph Romero (Wade Dominguez), a hapless police trainee whose ineptness at basic cop duties is counterbalanced by enterprise, detective savvy and a proficiency in Russian. The latter talent helps the two worm their way into the complex network of Russian emigre mobsters behind the crime.

"The Taxman" is co-written by Israeli director Avi Nesher and Robert Berger, a tax investigator whose experiences provided grist for this.   For all of the greasy-knish authenticity lent by Nesher's Brighton Beach locales and Berger's insider knowledge, the high-concept premise (crude misfit tax investigator joins forces with poetic misfit cop) has the hit-machine aura of something whipped together by L.A. studio execs over avocado sandwiches and banana smoothies.

As TV pilot wannabes go, "The Taxman" finds an incalculable asset in the garrulous and frequently alienating persona of its antihero.   Given a rudely funny, bull-in-a-china-shop moxie by Pantoliano, Al is the consummate brash New Yorker, crashing into strangers' quarrels and sidewalk deliveries with a sense of entitlement that is jaw-dropping to behold.   Diminutive of frame and speaking with a pinched Brooklynese that suggests Ratso Rizzo's bureaucrat relation, Al is a mouse who roars far louder than he seems capable of at first glance.   Pantoliano is so quirkily charismatic that Robert Townsend, playing a federal prosecutor Al shanghais into taking on his case, all but fades into the woodwork.

Not to be discounted is the eager-beaver charm of Dominguez ("Dangerous Minds"), a graceful actor whose leading-man promise was cut short when he died of respiratory failure last year.

NEW YORK POST, 9/17/99, p. 50, Rod Dreher

What an odd, unexpectedly interesting little movie is "The Taxman."

The title character is Al Benjamin (Joe Pantoliano), a runty state tax inspector desperate for a taste of crime-fighting glory, which he gets while looking into a Brooklyn gas station's books and, eventually, a deadly Russian-mafia scam.

Though the cliched plot hamstrings the drama, Pantoliano is an unexpected pleasure as the scrappy terrier Al.   The detective story may be routine, but Al—and Pantoliano's perform-ance—are anything but.

VILLAGE VOICE, 9/21/99, p. 155, Katherine Wolff

The Taxman cometh—the government's most abused and underappreciated civil servant is reinvented as an unlikely hero in Avi Nesher's rambling crime drama.   Al Benjamin (Joe Pantoliano) is a New York State tax investigator who stumbles onto a large cartel trying to defraud the good state of New York.   Muddling his way through the case, Benjamin teams up with equally inept patrol cop Joseph Romero (Wade Dominguez) to expose the connection between the evil corporation and Brighton Beach's Russian mob.   Pantoliano and Dominguez run through a particularly strained form of buddy-cop dynamic, with the former as a loose-cannon, paper-pushing schmuck, and the latter, his quiet, misunderstood, and supposedly intelligent counterpart (he dons a pair of wire-rimmed frames for the scenes requiring thought-out commentary).   Throw in Elizabeth Berkley as a mob insider's daughter turned love interest, whose Russian accent isn't nearly as disastrous as one might imagine, but whose attempt to muster looks of concern for Daddy is more painful than a gut full of bullets, and you have a wintertime crime caper that truly leaves you cold.

Also reviewed in:
NEW YORK TIMES, 9/17/99, p. E23, Lawrence Van Gelder
VARIETY, 6/8-14/98, p. 74, Deborah Young

TEA WITH MUSSOLINI

A G^2 Films (an MGM Company) release of a Medusa Film/Cattleya/Cineritmo/Film and General Productions production.   *Executive Producer:* Marco Chimenz.   *Producer:* Riccardo Tozzi, Giovannella Zannoni and Clive Parsons.   *Director:* Franco Zeffirelli.   *Screenplay (based on "The Autobiography of Franco Zeffirelli"):* John Mortimer and Franco Zeffirelli.   *Director of Photography:* David Watkin.   *Editor:* Tariq Anwar.   *Music:* Alessio Vlad and Stefano Arnaldi.   *Sound:* Brian Simmons and (music) Steve Parr.   *Sound Editor:* Mike Wood.   *Casting:* Emma Style and Mirta Guarnaschelli.   *Art Director:* Carlo Centolavigna and Gioia Fiorella Mariani.

Special Effects: Giovanni Corridori. *Costumes:* Jenny Beavan, Anna Anni, and Alberto Spiazzi. *Costumes (Cher):* Ermanno Daelli. *Make-up:* Franco Corridoni. *Running time:* 117 minutes. *MPAA Rating:* PG.

CAST: Cher (Elsa); Judi Dench (Arabella); Joan Plowright (Mary Wallace); Maggie Smith (Lady Hester); Lily Tomlin (Georgie); Charlie Lucas (Luca, as a child); Baird Wallace (Luca); Massimo Ghini (Paolo); Paolo Seganti (Vittorio); Michael Williams (British Consul); Mino Bellei (Cesare); Paul Chequer (Wilfred); Paula Jacobs (Molly); Tessa Pritchard (Connie); Claudio Spadaro (Mussolini); Bettine Milne (Edith); Hazel Parsons (Hazel); Helen Stirling (Ursula); Kathleen Doyle (Norma); Giselle Mathews (Elderly Lady); Gianna Giachetti (Signora Badaloni); Chris Larkin (Major Gibson); Giovanni Nannini (Sacristan); Pino Colizzi (Dino Grandi); Jack Basehart (Count Bernardini); Giacomo Gonnella and Clemente Abete (Carabinieri); Roberto Farnese (Maurizio); Chris Tattanelli (Carmelo); Claudia Piccoli (Anna); Allan Caister Pearce (American Dealer); Herman Weiskopf (German Officer); Benedetta Magini (Giulia Meyer); Beppe Landini (Menotti); Giuseppe Rossi Borghesano (Butler); Marcellina Ruocco (Adriana); Ferdinando Ferrini (Professor Cassuto); Massimo Salvianti (Leading Facist).

LOS ANGELES TIMES, 5/14/99, Calendar/p. 4, Kevin Thomas

[The following review by Kevin Thomas appeared in a slightly different form in
NEWSDAY, 5/14/99, Part II/p. B7.]

Franco Zeffirelli's lively, fanciful "Tea With Mussolini" draws upon the Italian director's memories of growing up in Florence in the increasingly fascist Italy of the 1930s. Felicitously combining events real and imagined with his co-writer, English novelist and playwright—and longtime Tuscan resident—John Mortimer, Zeffirelli has created an amusing yet touching high adventure and an unusual coming-of-age tale.

Perhaps best of all, he and Mortimer have fashioned no less than five fine roles for five splendid actresses: Cher, Judi Dench, Joan Plowright, Maggie Smith and Lily Tomlin.

Whereas Dench, Plowright and Smith are stalwarts of the international cinema, Cher and Tomlin possess such distinctive personalities and talents that screen roles worthy of them don't come along all that often. But when they do, as is the case here, they know how to run with them.

Cher's Elsa is a brassy Ziegfeld Follies alumna with a penchant for marrying elderly sugar daddies. She's taken Europe by storm, like the Unsinkable Molly Brown before her, and has developed a taste for collecting modern art—and attracting handsome Italian men; her beautiful oval face would have transported Modigliani. Elsa is good-natured, generous and flamboyant and wears with panache the boldest of the '30s styles (designed for the film by Ermanno Daelli).

Florence is a magnet for her, and she's struck up a warm friendship with Tomlin's hearty archeologist, Georgie, who when it comes to dancing partners, doesn't hesitate in picking out a pretty girl instead of a man.

No wonder these two breezy, outspoken, unconventional American women have bonded, for they are regarded with undisguised disapproval by Lady Hester Random (Smith), widow of a former British ambassador to Italy, and the haughty leader of a small colony of British ladies, most of a certain age, who have long lived in Florence. Most prominent in Lady Hester's group are Dench's Arabella and Plowright's Mary.

Arabella is an artist who takes her fashion cues from the Pre-Raphaelites, but whose knowledge of Florentine art treasures and concern for their preservation is deep and impassioned. Having lost both her father and her fiance in the Great War, the sensible, staunch Mary lives modestly and is employed as a secretary/English translator to a no-account count (Jack Basehart), a playboy with an insanely jealous wife. He owns a small but elegant clothing fabric store, and he has fathered a son out of wedlock with a talented fashion designer—"better than Schiaparelli," declares Elsa—who has died.

Reluctantly at first, Mary takes in the small son, Luca (Charlie Lucas)—Zeffirelli's alter ego—unable to leave him consigned to an orphanage. The count hopes Luca turns out to be "a perfect English gentleman."

For a time, Luca's life is a colorful idyll with the five women focusing their loving attention on the boy and firing his imagination in ways that will shape his destiny. But Mussolini and his thuggish brown shirts step up their terrorist ways, targeting foreigners in particular.

Unfortunately, the British and American women alike are reluctant to take a hint; the staggeringly obtuse Lady Hester even arranges to have tea with Mussolini, coming away assured that she and her friends have nothing to fear. (This incident was inspired by an actual meeting the expatriate English intellectual Violet Trefusis had with the dictator.)

Time passes, Elsa comes and goes, returning eventually to her magnificent art-filled villa, and by the time Luca (now played by Baird Wallace, in a smooth, effective transition) has reached 17 it's 1942, World War II is underway—and the five women are stubbornly still there, eventually sequestered by the military in the 14th century town of San Gimignano. They have now entered a period of adventure and danger, a time in which their spirit and character will be severely tested.

At the beginning of the picture no two women could seem more unalike than Elsa and Hester—they mutually loathe each other. Yet in time we discover how much they are alike in their naivete and in their capacity to rise to the occasion. Cher and Smith play their big moment of truth scene with the aplomb of Bette Davis and Mary Astor in "The Great Lie."

There are some scary, somber moments in this lushest of period pieces, yet Zeffirelli wisely sustains a gallant, predominantly blithe spirit throughout. "Tea With Mussolini" leaves you feeling that, if in reality not everything that Zeffirelli recalls had quite so much dash, whimsy and gallantry, it's the way it should have been.

NEW YORK, 5/31/99, p. 98, Peter Rainer

Tea With Mussolini is directed by Franco Zeffirelli and based on his memoirs of growing up as a young kid in Florence just before and during World War II. Most of it is taken up with the circle of proper Englishwomen—played here by, among others, Joan Plowright, Maggie Smith, and Judi Dench—who care for the boy while otherwise acting haughty or dotty. The film may have its roots in reminiscence, but it doesn't feel like it comes from the heart: Zeffirelli's, as usual, is swathed in tinsel. Still, the villas on display are gorgeous, and watching those dowager martinets intimidate the Fascisti is fine sport. Lily Tomlin puts in an appearance as a lesbian archaeologist. With her long-drawn features, she's looking more and more like Virginia Woolf these days. Cher, playing a former Ziegfeld girl turned Peggy Guggenheim-ish art vulture, is sloe-eyed and sinuous; as an actress, she always manages to be both camp artifact and the genuine article.

NEW YORK POST, 5/14/99, p. 49, Thelma Adams

"Foolish women, fickle fascists" would be a better title for "Tea With Mussolini," Franco Zeffirelli's slice of autobiographical nostalgia.

Set in Italy before and during WWII, "Tea" cozies up to a circle of English-speakers living in Florence. The women are known as the "Scorpioni" for their stinging wit—a trait absent from Zeffirelli's script, co-authored with British novelist John Mortimer.

The dotty dowagers adopt their late dressmaker's illegitimate son (presumably the young Zeffirelli), molding the boy into the perfect English gentlemen while expecting Benito Mussolini himself to protect the enclave as tensions build between Italy and England.

The arresting cast, which runs the gamut from Judi Dench to Cher, charms and annoys in equal measure as the women stubbornly hold on to the past, refusing to let reality seep in. Aristocrat Maggie Smith, convinced she has Mussolini's ear, is as hard and crisp as an old tea biscuit, until the inevitable crumble.

Bohemian Dench dithers in burnished colors, trailing scarves and clutching a puppy, ever on the verge of bursting into an interpretive dance. Joan Plowright bustles around Florence like Sleeping Beauty's blue fairy made flesh.

Lily Tomlin's butch archaeologist makes Indiana Jones look femme. Cher, as the obligatory American Jewish free spirit, is forever full-throated with New World vitality. She sings "Smoke Gets in Your Eyes" as if about to deliver "Gypsies, Tramps and Thieves" to an arena of aging boomers.

On the plus side, the ensemble wears great linen. What really turns the tea tepid is not the muffed Merchant-Ivory touches, but the tragic realization that "Mussolini" is the product of a once-great talent. Zeffirelli's "Romeo and Juliet" remains the most ravishing screen Shakespeare; his "Taming of the Shrew" still stings; his "Hamlet" has soul.

I'd take cappuccino with a Zeffirelli video over "Tea With Mussolini" any day.

SIGHT AND SOUND, 4/99, p. 60, Andy Medhurst

Florence, Italy, 1934. Mary Wallace, one of a group of elderly expatriate Englishwomen nicknamed the Scorpioni, finds herself looking after Luca, the illegitimate son of her employer, after the boy's mother has died. Rather than abandon him to an orphanage, Mary decides to raise Luca, assisted by the other Scorpioni, including their self-appointed leader Lady Hester and the artistic but disorganised Arabella. Hester is dismayed by a visit from Elsa, a rich American-Jewish socialite, whom Hester regards as intolerably vulgar. However, Elsa sets up a trust fund for Luca before leaving Italy.

As the fascist regime tightens its hold, public-order disturbances prompt Lady Hester to contact Mussolini himself. He invites her to Rome for tea and reassurances, a gesture Hester attributes to her status as a diplomat's widow, but which is really a publicity stunt. Luca's father sends him away to school in Austria. When he returns years later, Italy is at war with Britain and the Scorpioni have been interned. Elsa secretly pays for the Scorpioni to be moved to more comfortable quarters. Covertly, she helps Italian Jews out of the country and enlists Luca in her mission, though his willingness to help dwindles when he sees Elsa becoming involved with a local lawyer, Vittorio. After Pearl Harbor, Elsa is also interned and Luca discovers that Vittorio is scheming to steal her wealth and send her to her death. Luca and the local partisans help Elsa escape. Allied troops liberate the town and the Scorpioni are freed.

Submerged under an avalanche of divas, costumed and attached to within an inch of its life, swathed in sentimental music and explanatory intertitles which make it feel like the third-best film of 1954, and boasting a moment where Maggie Smith stops a Nazi soldier from shooting Judi Dench by shouting, "Stop this nonsense at once", it's safe to say that *Tea with Mussolini* is not uncamp. Not so much a date movie or a chick flick as a film for the perfect evening out with your ageing gay uncle, it serenely glides along as if the last 30 years of cinema history had never happened.

All of which lends it a certain reprehensible charm. Franco Zeffirelli is 76-years-old after all and to expect him to modify the well-plumped plushness of his early middlebrow hits would be churlish. This is an old man's film or, to be precise, an old queer's film, awash in a rapt savouring of stellar femininity and endearingly predictable in its casting of inept but decorative young men. The plot takes elements from Zeffirelli's own childhood but embroiders them into a wider fabric by introducing fictional characters. The figure of Elsa, for example, is an invention, but who can blame Zeffirelli for wanting Cher in his young life, particularly a Cher dressed to the hilt in a succession of beyond-drag gowns?

The difference between Cher and the theatrical British cast's acting registers is deftly turned into a plot device, placing the clash of outlooks between their characters at the narrative's core. Smith does her party piece of pinched imperious haughtiness, Dench floats about twitchily like Sandy Dennis playing Isadora Duncan and Plowright embodies no-nonsense maternal dependability. Cher has little trouble slipping into the role of glamour personified, prompting an awestruck Italian to ask, "Are all American women as exciting as you?" "Alas," she replies, timing the pause to perfection, "no." Her later switch to doughty freedom fighter makes some demands on our incredulity, but she does pull off a to-die-for last scene, gorgeously stoical and irresistibly Garboesque as the partisans' boat rows her to safety.

Buried beneath the film's satin surface are some gestural attempts at addressing questions of sexual politics. The presence of lesbian archaeologist Georgie (played by Lily Tomlin as if she were auditioning for the role of Indiana Jones) signifies this, as does the curious subplot which sees Lady Hester's nephew Wilfred dressed as a woman to escape detection. When the strain of this becomes too much, he strips off, shouts (not with masses of conviction), "I'm a man," and runs away to join the partisans, instantly sprouting stubble in the process. The trouble is that he looks immensely more convincing in the first kind of drag than the second, implying perhaps that while anti-fascist guerrilla subversion may be a fine and noble cause, it's never as important in a Zeffirelli film as the swish of an epigram or the cut of a frock.

VILLAGE VOICE, 5/25/99, p. 130, Justine Elias

In this languid portrait of the halcyon days between the great wars, an era that seems to have spawned many irritating cinematic nostalgists, Franco Zeffirelli constructs a semiautobiographical story based on his charmed youth in Florence. There may be a gripping story buried somewhere in *Tea With Mussolini,* but it doesn't belong to the lightweight central character, little Luca Innocenti, who was born out of wedlock and raised by a gaggle of artistically inclined British expatriates. The group—dubbed the "Scorpioni" because of their supposedly biting wit—are played, predictably, by Joan Plowright (kindly), Judi Dench (intense), and Maggie Smith (fussy). Also on the scene are a couple of Americans: a brash archaeologist (Lily Tomlin, sunburned) and a braying, big-spending art collector (Cher, quite fixed in her facial expression). Amid swirls of nauseating music, the grandes dames step forward for their bravura moments (tears! songs! defiant curses!), which occur at painfully regular intervals. In the background, though, is a more fascinating story: that of the Smith characters mousy grandson. When the women are jailed as enemy aliens, the young man is forced by his grandmother to disguise himself as a girl so that they can be interned together. Ashamed, he finally strips off his dress and escapes to join the resistance. Luca's transformation from waif to budding artist may be the thrust of the film, but it's the psyche of the conflicted grandson that you wonder about.

Also reviewed in:
CHICAGO TRIBUNE, 5/14/99, Friday/p. A, Barbara Shulgasser
NEW REPUBLIC, 6/7/99, p. 30, Stanley Kauffmann
NEW YORK TIMES, 5/14/99, p. E14, Stephen Holden
VARIETY, 3/29-4/4/99, p. 68, Derek Elley
WASHINGTON POST, 5/14/99, p. C5, Rita Kempley

TEACHING MRS. TINGLE

A Dimension Films release of a Konrad Pictures/Interscope Communications production. *Executive Producer:* Bob Weinstein, Harvey Weinstein, Cary Granat, Ted Field, Scott Kroopf, and Erica Huggins. *Producer:* Cathy Konrad. *Director:* Kevin Williamson. *Screenplay:* Kevin Williamson. *Director of Photography:* Jerzy Zielinski. *Editor:* Debra Neil-Fisher. *Music:* John Frizzell. *Music Editor:* Abby Treloggen. *Sound:* Jim Stuebe and (music) Bill Schnee. *Sound Editor:* Todd Toon and Albert Gasser. *Casting:* Lisa Beach. *Production Designer:* Naomi Shohan. *Art Director:* David Lazan. *Set Designer:* Lauren Cory and Scott P. Murphy. *Set Decorator:* Daniel L. May. *Set Dresser:* Josh Elliott, Sara Jane Bos, Jimmy Gmuer, and Sean Langdon. *Special Effects:* Frank Ceglia. *Costumes:* Susie De Santo. *Make-up:* Carol Schwartz. *Make-up (Vivica A. Fox):* Re Ann Silva. *Stunt Coordinator:* Steve Davison. *Running time:* 93 minutes. *MPAA Rating:* PG-13.

CAST: Helen Mirren (Mrs. Tingle); Katie Holmes (Leigh Ann Watson); Jeffrey Tambor (Coach Wenchell); Barry Watson (Luke Churner); Marisa Coughlan (Jo Lynn Jordan); Liz Stauber (Trudie Tucker); Michael McKean (Principal Potter); Molly Ringwald (Miss Banks); Vivica A. Fox (Miss Gold); John Patrick White (Brian Berry); Robert Gant (Professor); Lesley Ann Warren (Leigh's Mother).
VOICE CHARACTERS: Stephen Apostolina; Moosie Drier; Iake Eissinmann; David Cowgill; Edie Mirman; Frank Welker; Jackie Gonneau; Mitch Carter; Philece Sampler; Richard Horvitz; Matthew Labyorteaux; Christina MacGregor; Claudette Wells.

LOS ANGELES TIMES, 8/20/99, Calendar/p. 12, Kevin Thomas

There seems to be a teacher in everyone's memory who punished rather than instructed, who belittled rather than inspired. More often than not such teachers tend to single out the most vulnerable kids and make life miserable for them. Even if you escaped being targeted yourself you never quite forget such a teacher; every now and then you wonder if your victimized classmates suffered any permanent damage.

In his knockout directorial debut writer Kevin Williamson taps into such universal memories with his shrewd and energetic dark comedy "Teaching Mrs. Tingle." Few of us, happily, had to endure anyone quite as monstrous as small-town Grandsboro High history teacher Mrs. Tingle, played to the delicious hilt by Helen Mirren, who tempers a Medea-like ferocity with just the right amount of humor to make her malevolence amusing.

However, for bright and pretty Leigh Ann (Katie Holmes) Mrs. Tingle is no laughing matter. She needs that A in history to land the college scholarship that will allow her to escape Grandsboro for a better life, one filled with opportunities and possibilities that eluded her supportive, loving single mother (a radiant, unbilled Lesley Ann Warren).

For her term paper Leigh Ann has chronicled a year in the life of a young woman who has become one of the victims of the nefarious Salem witch hunts. Her presentation is poised and engaging, and her scholarship is impressive. That makes no dent whatsoever on Mrs. Tingle, who skewers Leigh Ann for what she holds to be the misuse of the word "irony."

Clearly, Leigh Ann is going to have to shine extra brightly on the final exam if she is to land that all-important A. In the high school gym she's offered a copy of that exam by the well-meaning but lazy Luke (Barry Watson). She turns it down but is unknowingly carrying it with her just as Mrs. Tingle walks in. Also present is Jo Lynn (Marisa Coughlan), Leigh Ann's best friend and Luke's would-be girlfriend.

With all three sure to be expelled, Jo Lynn and Luke decide that they must go to Mrs. Tingle's spacious Victorian residence, along with Leigh Ann, and at the very least persuade her of Leigh Ann's innocence.

A swiftly orchestrated series of mishaps lands the predictably unyielding Mrs. Tingle a hostage in her own home. Being tied down in her own bed doesn't stop her from attempting to play the kids against one another, and tension builds as to how this drastic turn of events will play out. However, her captors learn just enough about Mrs. Tingle to allow us to draw our own conclusions as to why she has become so intent on wrecking the life of so promising a student as Leigh Ann.

Writer of "Scream" and "I Know What You Did Last Summer" (and creator of TV's "Dawson Creek" in which Holmes stars), Williamson has a true gift in creating believable, likable young people and throwing them in scary situations set off with humor. He's not afraid to present teenagers as intelligent achievers, and in regard to Jo Lynn and Luke, he shows them to be smarter and more resourceful than adults seem to realize.

"Teaching Mrs. Tingle" reveals Williamson not only to be as accomplished a director as he is a writer , but also his willingness to move beyond horror to psychological suspense. From as distinguished an actress as Mirren we expect the wit and panache she brings to the pitiless Mrs. Tingle; the pleasant surprise is that her young co-stars—particularly Holmes and Coughlan—hold their own in her company. Grandsboro High teachers and staffers are smartly played by Jeffrey Tambor, Michael McKean, Molly Ringwald and Vivica A. Fox. "Teaching Mrs. Tingle" looks great, with a fine, old Pasadena residence serving as Mrs. Tingle's house, and it's lots of fun—even if your high school years still haunt you.

NEW YORK POST, 8/20/99, p. 61, Jonathan Foreman

In the wretched tradition of "Jawbreaker," "Teaching Mrs. Tingle" is an ugly, failed attempt to pull off a "Heathers"-style, teen-oriented black comedy.

It's exploitative in a strangely joyless, sour way and so uneven in tone that it makes mediocre teen comedies like "Varsity Blues" and "She's All That" look like superior pieces of filmmaking.

The singular badness of "Mrs. Tingle" is all the more remarkable given that it is written and directed by Kevin Williamson. It's hard to believe that this amateurish script, reeking of contempt for its teenage audience, could have been penned by the Hollywood wunderkind who wrote the terrific "Scream" and created television's smart-alecky "Dawson's Creek."

It opens with a typically sickly scene between Leigh Ann (Katie Holmes) and her weepy waitress mother (Lesley Ann Warren), which establishes in plodding-by-the-numbers fashion that Leigh is a sweet, hardworking girl devoted to Mom who must get the valedictorian's scholarship or she won't be able to go to college and become a writer.

Leigh Ann's hopes for a future are threatened when history teacher Mrs. Tingle (Helen Mirren) is unimpressed by her homework, a painstaking re-creation of a diary penned by one of the victims of the Salem witch trials.

But those hopes evaporate altogether when Mrs. T. catches Leigh, her best friend Jo Lynn (Marisa Coughlan) and slacker-hunk Luke (Barry Watson) with questions from the semester's final exam that Luke has stolen.

In an effort to get sweet Leigh Ann out of trouble, all three teens turn up at Mrs. Tingle's house. And when their efforts at peaceful persuasion run out, they turn to violence.

The tone veers hopelessly from grand guignol horror to dark comedy to farce. Jokey scenes curdle into something meaner and creepier. Notoriously, the original title—"Killing Mrs. Tingle"—was changed by the studio after the Columbine High School massacre.

But when you see Luke fire a crossbow bolt at Tingle (whose only crime at that point is being a tough grader), it's hard not to be repelled by the way Williamson paints deadly violence against a teacher as something cool and funny.

But then the whole film panders to a presumably idiotic teenage audience. The giveaway is the characterization of Mrs. Tingle. You're supposed to think the authoritarian teacher is a monster who deserves to be brutalized by three kids in her own home.

After all, instead of making nice to her students to bolster their self-esteem, she criticizes them harshly and insists that they use words correctly.

Oh, and she's such an old-fashioned prune that she lives in a Victorian house without a TV.

Williamson's direction isn't as lazy as his writing, but the dialogue feels rushed and the action slow. He somehow leeches the life out of his cast—with the exception of the great Helen Mirren, who's so good she throws the movie out of balance.

For a while you find yourself rooting for her cunning, nuanced villain—and that makes the film's ramshackle, ridiculous ending all the more of a disappointment.

Katie Holmes, a good actress as well as a beauty, was far more impressive in 1997's "Disturbing Behavior," but Williamson seems to have underwritten her role in the assumption that audiences familiar with her persona on "Dawson's Creek" won't need any further characterization.

NEWSDAY, 8/20/99, Part II/p. B7, John Anderson

Helen Mirren is such a potent actress, both emotionally and technically, that she can steal any scene without saying a word.

Unfortunately for all of us, "Teaching Mrs. Tingle" is not a silent picture.

If it were, Miramax presumably wouldn't have needed first-time director Kevin Williamson, who wrote the Wes Craven films "Scream," "Scream 2," the equally popular "I Know What You Did Last Summer" and helped create TV's "Dawson's Creek." The Williamson trademark, the common thread among all his very successful projects, in case you're wondering, is parody: The "Scream" films mock, quite cleverly, the conventions of the horror genre; "Dawson's Creek" more or less lampoons itself.

But faced with making a more "original" teen movie (the idea of another one being made this summer requires quotation marks), what does Williamson deliver? For one thing, a film that feeds off the popular notion that life's obstacles are always someone else's fault.

Leigh Ann Watson (Katie Holmes of "Dawson Creek") is the fatherless daughter of an overworked waitress (Lesley Ann Warren), a pure, good, diligent girl, but only the second smartest student in school—at least according to the official record. For some reason—and considering how much wheel-spinning goes on in "Tingle," a little explanation wouldn't have hurt—Leigh Ann has to be class valedictorian to get the scholarship she so desperately needs (and, we hasten to add, richly deserves). She won't make it, though, because the vicious Mrs. Tingle has it in for her.

Why? We never really know. In fact, all the while Leigh Ann and her pals are wounding, binding and gagging Tingle—and are in turn being psychologically manipulated by her—we're not told much. The mentality of the teenagers is intriguing, though. When Leigh Ann and Co.— hot-to-trot actress-to-be Jo Lynn Jordan (Marisa Coughlan) and hunky slacker Luke Churner (Barry Watson)—try to reason with Tingle over her accusation of cheating, things go awry: Tingle is accidentally knocked unconscious and the kids don't know what to do. "Maybe we should just finish her," Luke suggests. Huh? Williamson must be confused: This is a horrible movie, not a horror movie.

It might have actually been an interesting generation-vs.-generation picture.

Mirren has one peachy speech late in the movie that articulates Tingle's utter contempt for the values of her students, and it suggests that some provocative ideas are perhaps simmering just below the surface. But they never get anywhere, because Tingle isn't much more than a cartoon. She's purely malicious, rather than convincingly self-righteous, so she simply doesn't work.

Without a real moral conflict or, at least, some reason why Tingle is a teacher to begin with, why should our blood start pounding? When Jo Lynn presents as her history project a breathy Marilyn Monroe impersonation, during which the "actress" claims to have advised JFK on the Cuban Missile Crisis, you can understand why the teacher is ticked. But when Tingle also sneers at Leigh Ann's entry—an imagined year-long diary of an accused Salem witch, bound in hand-laced leather and written on artificially aged paper—she becomes incredible. The movie has no place to go. Tingle is evil, the kids are not and it's clear that Williamson is interested only in pandering to the lowest common denominator of teenage resentment. That is, when he's not busy making awkward transitions or laying yet another mawkish alternative rock song over all those meandering scenes of a pensive Leigh Ann.

If the target market for this movie is as smart as the kids that are in it, audiences will be laughing at, not with, "Teaching Mrs. Tingle." Helen Mirren fans, on the other hand, will be less amused, not because she's in this film, per se, but because such a splendid, sexy actress is given so little to do in a country that makes so many useless movies.

TIME, 8/30/99, p. 66, Richard Corliss

She churns down the school corridors to music that sounds like the theme for *The Wizard of Oz*'s Wicked Witch of the West; students scatter rather than get caught in the laser beam of her cool rage. In history class she makes one think of Harry Potter's Professor Snape, so regal is her malevolence, so acute her gift for the demeaning remark that cuts through the skin of her best students and into their fragile egos. Her intellect has veered into artful cruelty. Her ambition has been curdled by this life sentence in a town she was dying to leave, and by having to teach idiots who may get a ticket out. A figure of fear, and possibly pity, Eve Tingle is a nightmare pedagogue—the teacher from Hell High.

A shame she's not in a better movie. *Teaching Mrs. Tingle,* a revenge comedy from Kevin Williamson, sets up a battle between twisted Mrs. T (Helen Mirren, the British classical actress who is in way under her head here) and sweet, studious Leigh Ann (Katie Holmes). When Tingle threatens to frame her for stealing an exam, Leigh Ann counts on two pals to bail her out: her best friend (Marisa Coughlan, quite funny as a carefully histrionic tyro actress) and the Depp-ish, droolworthy class rebel (Barry Watson). Before you can say *oops,* they have Tingle trussed to her bedposts and, the kids think, in their power. There are maybe six good lines, and many more dramatic chances wasted. Williamson, the writer of *Scream* and TVs *Dawson's Creek,* now directing his first movie, needs a crash course in choreographing screen tension.

The film was once called *Killing Mrs. Tingle*, until events at Columbine High made the notion of teacher homicide just a bit less amusing. But like last year's *Apt Pupil*, this really is a story about education—about the wary exchange in an old dark house between a nasty adult, seemingly trapped but still full of guile, and the bright teen who underestimates Satan's knack for temptation. No teen is likely to see the film and take a crossbow to his hated teacher's house. Indeed, nobody is likely to get much out of this slack parable. It is too empty to applaud, too insignificant to deplore.

VILLAGE VOICE, 8/31/99, p. 120, Dennis Lim

Yet another black comedy that misunderstands and misrepresents the genre—all them Very Bad Jaw breakers—Kevin Williamson's first (pre-*Scream*) script, also his first attempt at directing, is a take-that-you-bitch fantasy told from the point of view of an insecure, overachieving teen. Or, more precisely, a thirtysomething Hollywood hack trapped in the body of an insecure, overachieving teen. Williamson's *Dawson's Creek* star, Katie Holmes, plays Leigh Ann, a valedictorian-in-waiting who needs only an A on her history final to win a full college scholarship. The alternative, it's repeatedly emphasized, is a fate worse than death—small-town purgatory and an existence destined to parallel that of her down-and-out waitress mother (a bizarrely maudlin Lesley Ann Warren). The only obstacle to Leigh Ann's escape: her evil history teacher, Mrs. Tingle (Helen Mirren).

When Leigh Ann is caught with a crib sheet—actually procured by her ditzy best friend, Jo Lynn (Marisa Coughlan), and their mutual lust object, Luke (Barry Watson)—the trio traipse off to the Tingle mansion to negotiate with the harridan (for some reason, they bring a crossbow with them). A scuffle leaves Mrs. Tingle unconscious, and the teens' idea of damage control involves tying the witch to her four-poster bed and posing her for naughty, blackmail-worthy pictures. Williamson hallmarks are present in their crudest form: contrived moral dilemmas, a bland yet distracting tie-in soundtrack, dialogue that vacillates between self-satisfied one-liners and bouts of logorrhea. One running joke concerns Leigh Ann's feeble, post-Alanis grasp of the concept of irony (the nitpicky Mrs. Tingle takes pleasure in correcting her, time and again). *Teaching Mrs. Tingle* is too lazy to function as more than a morality tale (Leigh Ann's third-act conscience attack is excruciating to watch), and yet so self-conscious that it can't help reverting to amoral poses. This schizoid stance, Mrs. Tingle would probably agree, is the only real irony here.

Also reviewed in:
CHICAGO TRIBUNE, 8/20/99, Friday/p. A, Mark Caro
NEW YORK TIMES, 8/20/99, p. E20, Janet Maslin
VARIETY, 8/23-29/99, p. 107, Dennis Harvey
WASHINGTON POST, 8/20/99, p. C1, Rita Kempley
WASHINGTON POST, 8/20/99, Weekend/p. 45, Desson Howe

10 THINGS I HATE ABOUT YOU

A Touchstone Pictures release of a Mad Chance/Jaret Entertainment production. *Executive Producer:* Jeffrey Chenov and Seth Jaret. *Producer:* Andrew Lazar. *Director:* Gil Junger. *Screenplay:* Karen McCullah Lutz and Kirsten Smith. *Director of Photography:* Mark Irwin. *Editor:* O. Nicholas Brown. *Music:* Richard Gibbs. *Music Editor:* Shannon Erbe and Nick South. *Choreographer:* Marguerite Derricks. *Sound:* James Bayard Carey and (music) Robert Fernandez. *Sound Editor:* David Kern, Nils Jensen, and Nancy MacLeod. *Casting:* Marcia Ross, Donna Morong, and Gail Goldberg. *Production Designer:* Carol Winstead Wood. *Art Director:* Gilbert Wong. *Set Decorator:* Charles M. Graffeo. *Set Dresser:* Brady J. Condit. *Special Effects:* William Casey Pritchett. *Costumes:* Kimberly A. Tillman. *Make-up:* Mel Berns. *Stunt Coordinator:* Ben Scott. *Running time:* 94 minutes. *MPAA Rating:* PG-13.

CAST: Heath Ledger (Patrick Verona); Julia Stiles (Katarina Stratford); Joseph-Gordon Levitt (Cameron James); Larisa Oleynik (Bianca Stratford); David Krumholtz (Michael Eckman); Andrew Keegan (Joey Donner); Susan May Pratt (Mandella); Gabrielle Union (Chastity); Larry Miller (Walter Stratford); Daryl "Chill" Mitchell (Mr. Morgan); Allison Janney (Ms. Perky); David Leisure (Mr. Chapin); Greg Jackson (Scurvy); Kyle Cease (Bogey Lowenstein); Terence Heuston (Derek); Cameron Fraser (Trevor); Eric Reidman (Audio Visual Guy); Quinn Maixner (Beautiful Jock); Demegio Kimbrough and Todd Butler (Coffee Kids); Dennis Mosley (Cohort); Bianca Kajlich (Coffee Girl); Nick Vukelic (Drugged Out Loser); Benjamin Laurance (Wimpy Loser); Aidan Kennedy (Laughing Loser); Jelani Quinn (Crying Loser); Jesse Dyer (Screaming

Loser); Aaron Therol (Detention Student); Carlos Lacamara (Bartender); Heather Taylor (Drunken Girl); Joshua Thorpe (Jock); J.R. Johnson (MBA Guy at Party); Wendy Gottlieb (Heather); Brian Hood (Clem); Travis Miller (Cowboy); Ari Karczag (Kissing Guy); Laura Kenny (Judith); Alice Evans (Perky Girl); Jesper Inglis (Buckeroo Bartender); Nick Brown (Biker); Monique Powell and Brian Mashburn (Save Ferris Singers); Kay Hanley and Michael Eisenstein (Letter to Cleo Singers).

LOS ANGELES TIMES, 3/31/99, Calendar/p. 1, Kevin Thomas

Given the current popularity of Shakespeare on the screen and the dominance of young moviegoers at the box office, you'd expect that at least one of his plays would wind up as a high school comedy. But writer Karen McCullah Lutz's refreshingly free adaptation of "The Taming of the Shrew" and Gil Junger's on-the-money direction result in the witty, bristling "10 Things I Hate About You." As satirical as it is romantic, this is one teen film that is wise enough to span generations in its appeal.

Julia Stiles stars as Katarina Stratford, a Seattle high school senior of such surpassing superiority she has outgrown any interest in mere popularity. She says exactly what she thinks and cares not what others, teachers and fellow students alike, think of her in return. She can't wait to get to Sarah Lawrence, confident that her father, Walter (Larry Miller, that master in making frustration and outrage hilarious), will in the end let her go farther away from home than he would like.

Walter, a single parent and a doctor obsessed with teen pregnancies, has decreed that neither Kat nor her younger sister Bianca (Larisa Oleynik) will date until they've graduated from high school.

Maddeningly for Bianca, Kat couldn't care less, since she's decided nobody's good enough for her in the first place. But there's a new kid in school, the self-effacing but determined Cameron (Joseph Gordon-Levitt) who is so transfixed by the lovely Bianca he's just got to find a way to take her out. When the miserable Bianca persuades her father to agree that she can date whenever Kat decides to date, the complicated plot of "10 Things" is set in motion. The best that poor Cameron's shrewd operator pal Michael (David Krumholtz) can come up with is to get an affluent rival for Bianca's affections—a narcissistic novice model, Joey (Andrew Keegan)—to pay someone to take Katarina out.

There's only one possibility, Patrick Verona (Heath Ledger). He's a freewheeling loner, tall and handsome, smart and imaginative. He is sufficiently cool and self-confident to allow Katarina to discover for herself his worthiness. But even if Patrick could be persuaded to go along with the plan, and even if it just might work, Cameron still has to compete with Joey for Bianca. The filmmakers have built an anything-can-happen situation that's lots of fun to watch play itself out.

To be sure, along the way we get a better understanding of why Kat behaves the way she does. The great thing about Katarina, in the way she's conceived and expertly played by Stiles, is that she's not about to apologize for her sarcastic directness. She is capable of giving credit on those rare occasions she believes it is due, and she has, underneath her hard veneer, a capacity to be made as vulnerable by love as anyone else.

Lutz's dialogue is consistently sharp and snappy, and the large cast forms a sparkling ensemble under Junger's adept direction. Among adults, Allison Janney stands out as a high school counselor who divides her attention, without missing a beat, between her students and the porn novel she's writing on school time. Likewise, literature teacher Daryl (Chill) Mitchell manages to stay a step ahead of Katarina and not let her get away with anything.

"10 Things I Hate About You" is slick and brisk, but why do the filmmakers try to pass off Tacoma as Seattle when its key setting is Tacoma's landmark Stadium High School, a vast, magnificent turn-of-the-century brick castle originally intended as a resort hotel, overlooking the Cascade Mountains on a cliff high above Commencement Bay? It is so unique and perfect and dramatic a period setting for a film inspired by a Shakespearean comedy that Tacoma deserves to be identified in the film itself, not just in the end credits.

NEW YORK POST, 3/31/99, p. 72, Jonathan Foreman

Just as "Clueless" was a reworking of Jane Austen's "Emma," "10 Things I Hate About You" is a high-school update of "Taming of the Shrew." It's a romp that strip-mines a dozen teen romantic comedies, shamelessly recycling whole scenes from genre classics like "Ferris Bueller's Day Off" and "Animal House."

But still, "10 Things" is a funny movie, cute and genuinely romantic, featuring the megawatt screen presence and sex appeal of Julia Stiles as the shrew. Stiles is the gorgeous young actress who was the only good thing in NBC's awful "The '60s" miniseries.

Shakespeare's sisterly opposites are still called Kat (Stiles) and Bianca (Larisa Oleynik), but the setting is a Seattle high school called Padua, not the Italian city. Their overprotective gynecologist dad (Larry Miller) refuses to let popular Bianca go out on a date unless Kat is dating, too—something that is not likely to happen given Kat's sharp tongue and bad attitude.

New kid Cameron (Joseph Gordon-Levitt) is smitten by Bianca ("I burn, I pine, I perish," he exclaims, in one of the script's fluid shifts from teen-speak to Shakespeare). He knows that Bianca doesn't date, so he and best friend Michael (David Krumholtz) persuade obnoxious rich kid Joey (the terrific Andrew Keegan), who also likes Bianca, to pay school tough Patrick Verona (Heath Ledger) to take out Kat, as an experiment in "extreme dating."

Although they make Kat a handful, the filmmakers were clearly wary about making her a real shrew. Instead she's a bad-tempered smart babe who has given up social life (except for concerts by angry-chick rock bands) and adopted the persona of a strident campus feminist. She complains bitterly to streetwise English teacher Mr. Malcolm (Daryl "Chill" Mitchell) about having to study "patriarchal" authors like Hemingway.

As a result, "10 Things" increasingly becomes a generic story of mutual seduction rather than Shakespeare's problematic tale of womanly submission.

Generic—and derivative. As in "She's All That" and "Carrie 2," there's a party scene here where the girl discovers that the nice boy who's lured her out of her protective shell was doing it for a bet. There's also one of those slapstick, chasing-each-other-and-throwing-stuff scenes which have become Hollywood longhand for "look, these two are falling in love!"

Veteran TV director Gil Junger keeps things moving swiftly and gets good comic timing from his cast. He makes the most of the screenplay's small gems—like Allison Janney's dippy, pornography-writing school counselor. The whole movie is effectively accompanied by girl-band covers of old songs like Cheap Trick's "I Want You to Want Me."

But Stiles is the main attraction here. When a smile finally spreads across her face, it's like a slow-motion nuclear explosion.

NEWSDAY, 3/31/99, Part II/p. B7, John Anderson

High school as hellhole is a theme that's more or less on fire this season, and the Shakespeare-classics bandwagon is officially the Vehicle Most Likely to Be Hijacked. So you'd have to be totally clueless not to see that the two were fated for each other.

However: Having approached "10 Things I Hate About You" with every expectation of writing—at best—"10 Things I Hate About This Movie" (or, at worst, "10 Reasons Why a Lobotomy Is a Better Bargain"), we have actually seen the film and must reassess:

1. Since "10 Things" is based on "The Taming of the Shrew," there's some chance—slim, but some—that it will provoke some adolescent Bardolatry.

2. Although the "Clueless" comparisons come easy ("Clueless" was based on a classic, too, Jane Austen's "Emma"), they merely point up what's best about "10 Things." Both are good-natured fantasies, both are set in schools wealthy to the point of parody, and neither has a mean bone in its body.

3. Unlike "She's All That," in which the independent-minded heroine is tamed by a prom dress and Freddie Prinze Jr., or "Cruel Intentions"—which debases virtually every female character for the sake of tacky titillation—our caustic heroine, Kat (Julia Stiles), maintains her feisty-mindedness throughout (even Shakespeare's Kate eventually folded under pressure).

4. Bianca (Larisa Oleynik) may be the Stratford sister most likely to go to the prom, but her slo-mo goddess walk is director Gil Junger's sleight-of-hand: She's only about half as interesting as

Kat, who's capable of dismissing her male classmates as "unwashed miscreants" or demanding the addition of Simone de Beauvoir to her English Lit. reading list.

5. Larry Miller, who plays the sisters' father, a sex-fretful obstetrician who figures if he doesn't let Bianca date until Kat does ("Hello, Kat. Make anyone cry today?"), he'll be able to sleep at night ("the deep slumber of a father whose daughters aren't out getting impregnated").

6. David Krumholtz, whose Michael helps Cameron (Joseph Gordon-Levitt) devise a scheme by which Patrick (Heath Ledger), the scariest male in school, will date the scariest female, Kat, thus opening the way for Cameron to date Bianca. Nothing quite works out that easily. And Krumholtz makes the most of it.

7. Daryl (Chill) Mitchell (of TV's "Veronica's Closet"), who plays Mr. Morgan the English teacher and is even funnier than Krumholtz.

8. The script by Karen McCullah Lutz and Kirsten Smith, who actually may have met.

9. The fact that "10 Things" can survive the ickiness of Kat and Patrick riding a pedal-boat or pelting each other at a paint-ball range, and still maintain an edge.

10. That edge itself, which is mostly Stiles. Her characterization—in a genre that usually worships at the feet of shallowness, conformity and male adoration—is at least refreshing, at best inspiring. It also suggests that perhaps high school and adolescence are only stages, not permanent afflictions. In a major motion picture, this smacks of revolution.

SIGHT AND SOUND, 7/99, p. 55, Peter Matthews

Padua, a Seattle suburb. New high-school student Cameron is smitten with fellow student Bianca, but her father Walter will only let her date once her shrewish sister Kat starts dating. Cameron resolves to find a boyfriend for Kat and settles on sullen Patrick Verona. Joey Donner agrees to bankroll the romance because he wants Bianca for himself. Kat repels Patrick's advances but Bianca relays information about Kat's taste for him.

Eventually Kat agrees to go with Patrick to a party so Cameron can take Bianca. At the party, Bianca ignores Cameron and goes after Joey. A drunken Kat is rescued by Patrick. Touched, she asks him to kiss her. When he declines, she's mortified. Disillusioned with Joey, Bianca asks Cameron to drive her home and kisses him. Patrick guiltily pockets $300 to escort Kat to the prom. Kat reveals to Bianca that she lost her virginity to Joey, who then ditched her. At the dance, Joey argues with Cameron and Kat overhears Joey talking about the cash paid to Patrick. She leaves hurt and angry. But later in English class, Kat recites a sonnet telling Patrick she can't help loving him. Both sisters end up with their true loves.

In a scene from experienced TV director Gil Junger's *10 Things I Hate about You,* an English teacher informs a class that Shakespeare is, "a dead white guy who knows his shit," before assigning his pupils the task of translating a Shakespearean sonnet into contemporary vernacular, resulting in the heartfelt bit of doggerel which gives the movie its title. Real-life mall rats are duly cautioned that what looks to be a standard teen flick is actually a Boring Old Classic in drag. Even worse, this bubblegum *The Taming of the Shrew* is meant to be good for you, though the screenwriters are smart enough to keep their stabs at youthful edification subliminal. Now and then, a flowery phrase from the original ("I burn, I pine, I perish") surfaces inscrutably amid such homelier locutions as, "remove head from sphincter, then drive." It's doubtful whether this 'reading is cool' subtext will trigger the intended response since in every other respect the movie has the artistic integrity of a Pop Tart. But if Shakespeare can be brought to the postliterate masses only by such clandestine means, *The Taming of the Shrew* is a logical choice. One of the weakest of the comedies, it gives stage and screen adapters plenty of elbow room to exploit the knockabout potential of the running war between termagant Kate and her bullying pacifier Petruchio. Junger strains to pump up the cartoon aggression with a paintball fight and an archery lesson where a teacher predictably gets it in the butt, yet somehow the requisite hard edge never develops.

10 Things clearly wouldn't have been made without the lucrative example of *Clueless*, itself based on Jane Austen's *Emma*. But that film showed more flair in mapping the social niceties of Regency England on to Beverly Hills. The revisionists here are hamstrung by a premise that doesn't ring true even in Shakespeare: the despotic paternal law which prohibits Bianca from dating until her elder sister does. Their solution is to concoct a soggy backstory about their father never being the same since his wife deserted him. This expedient prompts a round of conciliatory hugs at fade-out, as does Kat's climactic shocker that her misanthropy is due to a callous defloration. But the toughest nut to crack remains the antediluvian stance towards the heroine, compelled to eat crow in the play's notorious last scene. No prizes for guessing that Shakespeare's *Ur*-bitch becomes here a feisty advocate of girl power. Yet a measure of the Bard's conservatism seeps through insofar as this feminist loose cannon is ultimately restored to the value system represented by her high-school prom. Given the core constituency for the movie, its makers plainly recognise on which side their bread is buttered.

VILLAGE VOICE, 4/13/99, p. 154, Justine Elias

Less accomplished, but more obviously derived from a Shakespearean source, is *10 Things I Hate About You*, a modern twist on *The Taming of the Shrew*. [The reference is to *Never Been Kissed*; see Elias's review of that film.] In yet another wildly privileged high school, where students drive fancy cars and chat about their Prada accessories, Katarina (Julia Stiles) is a proud, brash exception. She stalks around campus in fatigues and combat boots, shunning boys and the popular crowd, and turning every English-class discussion into a platform for her spirited feminist views. Her overprotective father has decreed that his popular younger daughter, Bianca, cannot date until Kat does. Naturally, this sets the stage for another one of those obvious, cruel bets that seem to occur only in movies about high school: Bianca's suitor begs the school tough guy to consider Kat an adventure in "extreme dating." Anyone who hates '80s pop will find this movie awfully tiresome, but Stiles and her underage Petruchio (Australian actor Heath Ledger, as hunky as his name) are charismatic and bold enough to carry any romantic comedy. And that, plus one really funny joke about the Bard himself, is plenty.

Also reviewed in:
NEW YORK TIMES, 3/31/99, p. E11, Stephen Holden
NEW YORKER, 5/31/99, p. 94, David Denby
VARIETY, 4/5-11/99, p. 30, Dennis Harvey

TESTAMENTO

A Portuguese National Television/ADR Productions/Cobra Films/Cineluz Cinematographic Productions/Cape Verdean Cinema Institute production. *Executive Producer:* José Luis Vasconcelos. *Director:* Francisco Manso. *Screenplay (Portuguese with English subtitles):* Mário Prata. *Based on the novel "Mr. Napumoceno's Last Will and Testament" by:* Germano Almeida. *Director of Photography:* Edgar Moura. *Editor:* Luís Sobral. *Music:* Tito Paris and Toy Vietra. *Sound:* Ansoos Alberto Lopes. *Casting:* Franciso Manso, Joao Cayette, and Joao Milagre. *Production Designer:* Augusto Mayer. *Costumes:* Rosario Moreira. *Running time:* 110 minutes. *MPAA Rating:* Not Rated.

CAST: Nelson Xavier (Napumoceno); Maria Ceiça (Graça); Chico Diaz (Carlos); Karla Leal (Adélia); Zezé Motta (Eduardo); Cesaria Evora (Arminda); Via Negromonte (Mari Chica).

NEW YORK POST, 4/30/99, p. 62, Rod Dreher

Like "Three Seasons," this week's other trip to a visually bountiful locale, "Testamento"'s strongest suit is its rich, sensual setting—the island nation of Cape Verde. Director Francisco Manso's debut is a mildly picaresque tale of a flashy entrepreneur whose last will and testament occasions lengthy flashbacks that tell the story of his long and colorful life.

The film opens with the death of venerable businessman Napumoceno da Silva Araujo. His greedy nephew, Carlos (Chico Diaz), hopes to inherit the import-export firm he's been managing for his ailing uncle. But when the will is read, the old man has left everything to Graca (Maria Ceica), his impoverished, illegitimate daughter from a long-ago affair.

Graca comes to know her father by listening to a series of cassettes he left for her that detail his rise to fame and fortune. These episodes reveal Napumoceno to be both a bantam Babbitt and a charming romantic rogue whose great successes in public life were matched by conspicuous private failures.

The tone is lighthearted and gently comic, aiming for an airy, "Il Postino" feel. But Mario Prata's screenplay (adapted from a novel by the Cape Verdean writer Germano Almeida) is dismayingly slight and uninvolving. The gracefully fading beauty of the town of Mindelo, built as a Portuguese colonial city on the island off the West African coast, is far more captivating, particularly during a torrential rainstorm that made umbrella-selling young Napumoceno his initial fortune.

Fans of the Cape Verdean style of fado, a kind of blues music originating in Portugal, will enjoy the lilting guitar music that Tito Paris and Toy Vieira have composed for "Testamento," and will relish a nightclub performance here by the incomparable fado diva Cesaria Evora.

One caveat: The movie's subtitles are often very difficult to read.

VILLAGE VOICE, 5/4/99, p. 120, Elliott Stein

Not too far from Morocco as the crow flies are the Cape Verde islands where *Testamento,* a picturesque Portuguese-Brazilian-French-Belgian coproduction, was filmed. The story, told in flashback, kicks off with the death of a wealthy merchant who leaves his entire estate to an illegitimate daughter. Having only thought of him as "that pervert who followed me around," she gets to know him after his death by listening to his taped memoirs and becomes obsessed with uncovering the details of her late papa's amorous adventures. Although it may sound like great fun, this slow-moving tale lacks punch. It marks the feature debut of Portuguese director Francisco Manso, whose background is in documentary-his eye-filling location shooting is *Testamento*'s strong suit. The flick could easily be promoted as a travelogue celebrating Cape Verde's natural beauty.

Also reviewed in:
CHICAGO TRIBUNE, 10/20/00, Friday/p. G, John Petrakis
NEW YORK TIMES, 4/30/99, p. E23, Stephen Holden
VARIETY, 7/20-26/98, p. 47, Daniel M. Kimmel

THAT'S THE WAY I LIKE IT

A Miramax Films release of a Tiger Tiger Films production in association with Chinarunn Pictures. *Producer:* Glen Goei, Jeffrey Chiang, and Tan Chih Chong. *Director:* Glen Goei. *Screenplay:* Glen Goei. *Director of Photography:* Brian Breheny. *Editor:* Jane Moran. *Music:* Guy Gross. *Choreographer:* Zaki Ahmad. *Production Designer:* Laurence Eastwood. *Art Director:* Andy Heng. *Set Decorator:* Mimi Hockman. *Costumes:* Ashley Aeria. *Running time:* 115 minutes. *MPAA Rating:* PG-13.

CAST: Adrian Pang (Ah Hock); Pam Oei (Mui); Medaline Tan (Mei); Anna Belle Francis (Julie); Pierre Png (Richard); Steven Lim (Boon); Dominic Pace (Guardian Angel); Caleb Goh (Leslie/Ah Beng); Kumar (Mr. Larry).

LOS ANGELES TIMES, 10/15/99, Calendar/p. 8, Kevin Thomas

[*The following review by Kevin Thomas appeared in a slightly different form in* NEWSDAY, 10/15/99, Part II/p. B13.]

Imagine "Saturday Night Fever" set down in Singapore, blend in a bit of "Strictly Ballroom" and include a nod to Bruce Lee, and you've got Glen Goei's delightful "That's the Way I Like It," a tale that's sweet-natured, funny and surprisingly touching. It has plenty of star power in Adrian Pang, who is as affable and assured as Jackie Chan, and it marks a terrific film debut for Singapore-born, London-based Goei, an award-winning theater actor-director.

It's 1977, and Pang's Ah Hock is a nice guy whose dream of owning a motorbike is part of his yearning for a better life. He's twentysomething, stuck in a supermarket clerk job and still living at home with parents who constantly make it clear how much more they care for his younger brother Ah Beng (Caleb Goh), a medical student. Hock hangs out with pals he's known all his life, and their group includes the pretty and personable Mui (Pam Oei). They bowl a lot and idolize Bruce Lee, who's already been dead four years.

Indeed, they're off to see a revival of Lee's "Fists of Fury" not realizing that it has ended its run and been replaced by something called "Forever Fever"—a faux version of "Saturday Night Fever"—which sounds like a movie set in a hospital to Hock. After seeing the film, Hock suddenly discovers disco, which transforms his life.

If he and Mui take lessons they can compete in a disco dancing competition, which promises more than enough in prize money to afford that motorbike. Pretty soon Hock is dreaming that "Forever Fever's" John Travolta stand-in (Dominic Pace) is coming down from the screen to offer tips to disco stardom.

Wouldn't you know that Hock, who now likes to be called Tony—as in Manero—and Mui are loaded with natural dancing talent? But no path to stardom, be it in a disco club or the silver screen, is ever smooth, and Hock incites the jealousy of the current disco king (Pierre Png) whose gorgeous girlfriend and dancer partner Julie (Anna Belle Francis) understandably catches Hock's eye. A totally unexpected subplot involving Ah Beng, well-played by Goh, brings to the film an added dimension.

Goei, however, has already stood on its head the conventional wisdom about the pervasiveness of American pop culture, which is that it amounts to a form of imperialism. Drawing from his own generation's experience of coming of age in the '70s, he instead sees our pop culture, as represented by the disco craze of the time, as an inspiring source of liberation—that in fact disco filled the gap left by Lee's sudden death and the relatively recent end of British colonial rule in Singapore.

Disco for Hock and his friends represents an escape from conservative parents and low-level jobs and also a way of forging a new identity without losing a traditional Asian sense of responsibility to family. You can see in this film, as in numerous Eastern European films, how potent a symbol of freedom American music and movies can be to the youth of other countries. This is scarcely a new observation, but this consistently amusing and entertaining film from Singapore gives it a fresh perspective and a delightful new spin.

NEW YORK POST, 11/15/99, p. 58, Jonathan Foreman

"That's the Way I Like It" is the first Singaporean movie to be distributed abroad, and it is far more interesting for the glimpse it gives into a fascinating English-speaking, multiracial Asian culture than for the cliché-ridden story it tries to tell.

Set in 1977, it's a sweet-natured homage to disco and the influence of the movie "Saturday Night Fever"—the basic plot of which it borrows.

Unfortunately, it's also amateurishly written and directed, and so predictable that it hurts.

VILLAGE VOICE, 10/26/99, p. 164, Justine Elias

Imagine *Muriel's Wedding* without Abba, and you've got a good idea of the trouble with *That's the Way I Like It,* an affectionate, subdued gloss on *Saturday Night Fever* set in late-1970s Singapore, when a certain disco-flavored movie (here called *Forever Fever,* apparently because the producers could not obtain the rights to the Travolta film) was sweeping the nation. *Forever Fever's* star (Dominic Pace, more Tony Danza than Tony Manero) emerges as a hip-shaking guardian angel to the hero, Hock (Adrian Pang), a twentyish grocery-store employee. (As in the original, the hero's stuck living at home with a family that doesn't "get" his newly feathered hairstyle.) Hock is so thrilled by the faux-Travolta's moves that he secretly enrolls in dance classes. As his Hustle improves he attracts the attention of Julie (the va-voomy Anna Belle Francis, a Singaporean pop star), a sophisticated nightclub fox with a jealous boyfriend.

The situation becomes disco-infernal during a big dance competition, where Hock hopes to win the $5000 first prize. Writer-director Glen Goei, a London stage actor, ably guides his likable cast through this by-the-numbers story, but he is hobbled by the film's lifeless soundtrack, which consists mainly of tinny cover versions of the Bee Gees' throbbing *Fever* songs. He also makes the mistake of introducing, as a minor counterpoint to Hock's comic bid for self-expression, the life-and-death ordeal of Hock's troubled transvestite brother, Richard (Pierre Png), a medical student who's being crushed by his parents' ambitions and prejudices. When Richard comes home, dressed in Holly Golightly splendor, to plead for his father's understanding, his anguish is far more affecting than any dance contest could ever be.

Also reviewed in:
CHICAGO TRIBUNE, 10/25/99, Tempo/p. 2, John Petrakis
NEW YORK TIMES, 10/15/99, p. E14, Lawrence Van Gelder
VARIETY, 8/3-9/98, p. 36, Derek Elley

THIRD MAN, THE

A Rialto Films release of a David O. Selznick release of a David O. Selznick/Sir Alexander Korda/London Films production. *Producer:* Alexander Korda, Carol Reed, and David O. Selznick. *Director:* Carol Reed. *Screenplay:* Graham Greene. *Story:* Graham Greene, Alexander Korda, and Orson Welles. *Director of Photography:* Robert Krasker. *Editor:* Oswald Hafenrichter. *Music:* Anton Karas and Henry Love. *Sound:* John Cox. *Sound Editor:* Jack Drake. *Art Director:* Vincent Korda. *Set Designer:* Joseph Bato, John Hawkesworth, and Vincent Korda. *Set Decorator:* Dario Simoni. *Costumes:* Ivy Baker. *Running time:* 104 minutes. *MPAA Rating:* Not Rated.

CAST: Joseph Cotten (Holly Martins); Alida Valli (Anna); Orson Welles (Harry Lime); Trevor Howard (Major Calloway); Bernard Lee (Sergeant Paine); Paul Hoerbiger (Porter); Annie Rosar (Porter's Wife); Ernst Deutsch ('Baron' Kurtz); Siegfried Breuer (Popescu); Erich Ponto (Dr. Winkel); Wilfred Hyde-White (Crabbin); Hedwig Bleibtreu (Old Lady); Herbert Halbik (Hansel); Paul Hardtmuth (Hall Porter at Sacher's); Nelly Arno (Kurtz' Mother); Leo Bieber (Barman, Casanova); Alexis Chesnakov (Brodsky); Geoffrey Keen (British Policeman); Frederick Schreicker (Hansel's Father); Paul Smith (Military Policeman); Jenny Werner (Winkel's Maid).

LOS ANGELES TIMES, 6/10/99, Calendar/p. 10, Kenneth Turan

Who speaks up for "The Third Man" and its director, Carol Reed? A major success in its day—it won the Palme d'Or at Cannes 50 years ago—it tends to be faintly recalled by film fans as something they saw and enjoyed once upon a time. Rarely has a film been so in need of a major reissue, and rarer still is the amount of moviegoing pleasure in store for those who revisit this classic in its weeklong run at the Nuart in West Los Angeles, which starts Friday.

Rialto, a company that specializes in landmark revivals (previous efforts include Jean-Luc Godard's "Contempt," Federico Fellini's "Nights of Cabiria" and Michael Powell's "Peeping Tom"), has provided an exceptional new print that showcases Robert Krasker's Oscar-winning black-and-white cinematography.

Glorying in a nocturnal atmosphere of deep and dangerous shadows, a dark world in every sense of the word, this new print underlines how right American Cinematographer magazine was in recently naming "The Third Man" one of the 10 best shot films of cinema's first half century.

The Nuart's print also brings "The Third Man" back to its original form. That means that 11 minutes of excised footage, mostly trims from existing scenes, have been restored. And instead of star Joseph Cotten reading the opening voice-over, it's director Reed, with a voice much better suited to the bemused cynicism of Graham Greene's script, who gets to archly comment, while the camera reveals an unidentified corpse floating face down in the water, that in terms of corruption "amateurs can't stay the course" in postwar Vienna.

The new print even features a few more minutes of the film's most characteristic element, the indelible zither playing of Anton Karas. The story goes that director Reed stumbled upon Karas playing in a small cafe outside Vienna and decided to use him on the spot. Wherever he was found, Karas' music became a worldwide sensation, leading to a U.S. ad campaign that promised, no kidding, "He'll have you in a dither with his zither!"

Just as much of a character as anyone played by an actor is Vienna in these lean and nasty days when the city was divided into sectors run by each of the great powers. "The Third Man" makes excellent use of specific real-life locations, all specified by Greene, like the Great Wheel of an amusement park, the lonely Central Cemetery and the slightly seedy nightclub.

Even more evocative are the city's magnificent buildings, often glimpsed half-crumbling or standing destitute next to enormous piles of rubble. The atmosphere Reed and company created is as thick as the local coffee, an ideal setting for a world without heroes where everyone is either a fool, a cynic, a criminal or, quite possibly, a combination of all three.

Into this cesspool of casual amorality comes Holly Martins (Cotten), a bumbling, self-righteous American (Greene didn't think there were any other kind) who has naive notions of justice and righteousness plus a great deal of misplaced confidence in his ability to get to the bottom of things. "The Third Man" is the story of his unsentimental education, of the hard road he travels in the getting of wisdom.

A self-proclaimed writer of "cheap novelettes" with names like "The Lone Rider of Santa Fe" and "Death at Double X Ranch," Martins has come to Vienna at the behest of his oldest friend and possible future employer, Harry Lime.

Unfortunately, everyone tells him, he has come just a bit too late. Lime has been killed, the victim of a random traffic accident, mourned only by his girlfriend, Anna Schmidt (Alida Valli), and a pair of epicene Viennese named Baron Kurtz (Ernst Deutsch) and Dr. Winkel (Erich Ponto).

Also at Harry's funeral is Major Calloway (a crisp Trevor Howard), a British military policeman who tells Martins that his erstwhile boon companion was a trafficker in adulterated penicillin, "the worst racketeer who ever made a dirty living in this city."

Filled with alcohol-inspired righteous indignation and never considering that he might be getting into something considerably out of his depth, Martins is determined to prove the major wrong and find out what really killed Harry, starting with trying to discover who the mysterious third man seen at the site of the accident might be. "Death's at the bottom of everything, leave death to the professionals," the major says but Martins is in no mood to listen.

Working closely with director of photography Krasker and showing a fondness for disconcerting camera angles, director Reed does exceptionally well conveying the topsy-turvy nature of this world of smiling insincerity where a man typically speculates on Lime's afterlife state by saying, "He's either in heaven pointing down or in hell pointing up."

Reed and Greene also combine to create vivid characters who are very much of their time and place, like the smirking Baron incongruously walking through a Viennese cafe holding a copy of Martins' "Oklahoma Kid" or the small boy (Herbert Halbik) living in Lime's apartment building who starts to resemble a sinister, malignant dwarf.

"The Third Man" provides superior roles for all its lead actors as well, especially for Orson Welles in a part that influential French critic Andre Bazin called a milestone in his career. Not that the American actor wasn't fussy: Reed later recalled that Welles initially rebelled against filming in underground Vienna by saying, "Carol, I can't work in a sewer. I come from California!"

Because it is conceded that Welles wrote parts of his own dialogue, including the celebrated speech comparing the relative merits of peaceful Switzerland and Italy under the bloody Borgias, film historians have sometimes argued how much of the credit for this exceptional film belongs to him.

But anyone familiar with the best of Reed's work, tightly drawn, literate, popular items like "Odd Man Out," "Fallen Idol" and "Outcast of the Islands," can see how smoothly "The Third Man" fits into that equation.

Given this film's success at Cannes so many years ago, it's interesting to speculate what this year's artier-than-thou David Cronenberg-led jury would have made of "The Third Man." In all likelihood, they would have scoffed at this great work as too accessible to mainstream audiences. Truly, film has come a long way in 50 years, and much of it in the wrong direction.

NEWSDAY, 5/7/99, Part II/p. B11, John Anderson

Psychotic angles, fear-wracked faces and the persistent zither of Anton Karas are the signature elements of "The Third Man," a film in which everything is posed almost perversely against the grain: The landscape is a ruin, the hero is a rube—posed, counter-Hitchcock, as lone accuser rather than lone accused—and the villain is the most charismatic character in the picture.

The result of all this alchemy was a mythic movie. Directed by Carol Reed from Graham Greene's adaptation of his novel, "The Third Man" returns to theaters today with the original narration spoken by Reed himself (Joseph Cotten's voice was dubbed for the original U.S. release) and 11 more minutes of previously excised footage. These are merely bonuses: The film was and is an electrifying, provocative thriller whose worldview is as jaded as its atmosphere is thick. Add Karas' macabre playing of the "Third Man Theme"—probably the most associative music in all of cinema—and the opening credits are enough to raise goosebumps.

Because his stylistic fingerprints are all over it, "The Third Man"—a typically Greene-ish parable about crime and stupidity in postwar Vienna—is more casually identified with Orson Welles than with either Reed or Cotten, the ostensible star of the film (as bumbling American Holly Martins). So it's always surprising how little Welles appears, while still dominating the picture. He doesn't even show up until well over half the movie is over—in that fabulous half-lit doorway, a shot Welles conceded was "pure Carol"—to the infamous "cuckoo clock" speech (which Welles did contribute to the script) and the climactic chase through the sewers of Vienna—which for a 'California boy' like Welles was pure misery.

Add to his actual screen presence the personal melodrama Welles brought on set: Trying to get his own "Othello" made, he made Alexander Korda—who shared producing credit if not quite the headaches with David O. Selznick—chase him all over Europe. And Welles wasn't even the first choice—the producers originally wanted Noel Coward as the insidious Harry Lime, a what-if of casting that would have altered the entire film.

As it is, "The Third Man's" return couldn't be more timely; the Kosovo parallels are as obvious as Holly Martins. A naive cowboy novelist from America, Martins arrives in partitioned Vienna looking for his boyfriend chum Harry—who, even in Martins memory, is something of an opportunist/sociopath—finding instead the blackest of black marketeers. As a hero, Martins is hard to like; he's clearly out of his element, oblivious to both the wartime suffering and post-war decadence of Europe and under the initial impression that Harry is dead, Martins treats the very patient Major Calloway (Trevor Howard) with self-righteous contempt. He demands, while having no right to demand. He always thinks he knows the right thing to do—the right way to treat Harry's heartbroken girlfriend Anna (Alida Valli), for instance when it's clear he never even really knew Harry.

Holly is a well-meaning fool who gets people killed and lives in a kind of moralistic dreamworld. It's amazing, amid the high-tension of Reed's direction and the virtuoso-in-brief performance of Orson Welles, what a picture Holly offers of an American in Europe: Well-meaning but profoundly ignorant, he's a writer who creates fantasy history that romanticizes the gun, then suffers the cruelest disappointment when his illusions—mostly about himself—are left crushed like Vienna's architecture. As a portrait of cultures in contrast, "The Third Man" is brutally frank, easily the most inglorious American portrait of its era. One wonders, considering the virtual cabal that was the Greene-Reed-Welles collaboration, just how timeless they imagined their portrait might become.

VILLAGE VOICE, 5/11/99, p. 65, J. Hoberman

However hoked-up and self-regarding, *The Third Man*, rereleased this week in a fully restored version on the occasion of its 50th anniversary, remains an indelible experience. Carol Reed's arty thriller, written by Graham Greene, is set in the broken heart of Europe—an uncanny Vienna populated by a multinational assortment of rogues and fools.   The movie is a fun-house *Casablanca*, its jaundiced geopolitical romance appropriate to the bleary dawn of the Cold War.

Although predicated on mass murder and framed by two funerals (both for the same character), *The Third Man* is very much a jape—a sardonic waltz set to the mocking gaiety of its infectious zither theme.   Too comic to be noir, the movie is nevertheless extravagantly expressionistic in its extreme angles, zigzag lighting schemes, and fondness for gargoyle faces in mega close-up. The compositions are insistently off-kilter—as Manny Farber wrote in his New *Republic* review, the "tilted camera that leaves you feeling you have [been watching] from a fetal position."

Rapturously received in its day, *The Third Man* won the Palme d'Or at the 1949 Cannes Film Festival, opening here the following February with "awesome hooplah," according to *The New York Times*.   *Time* hailed Reed as a new Hitchcock and, no less than the movie itself, Anton Karas's catchy theme became an international hit. ("He'll have you in a dither with his zither," the American trailer promised.) *The Third Man* caught a mood, but then it was conceived as a topical movie.

The possibility of a new war in Europe seemed real enough.   After the February 1948 coup that brought the Communists to power in Czechoslovakia, British producer Alexander Korda dispatched Greene to Vienna to write a scenario for Reed on the city's four-power occupation. Although it was the similarly "internationalized" Berlin that made news that summer when Stalin blockaded the city, divided Vienna provides an appropriately duplicitous backdrop for the befuddlement of American hack writer Holly Martins (Joseph Cotten), invited to town at the behest of his shady old friend, Harry Lime.

Reporting from Vienna in 1948, John Gunther thought the city—where "every other building [was] destroyed"—resembled "an empty broken stage set." And so it proves for Martins, who arrives to discover that his school chum has been run over by a truck and killed not 10 minutes earlier.   Ruined capital of a lost empire, experiment in urban modernism, city of Sigmund Freud and the young Adolf Hitler, Vienna is here a labyrinth of deserted cobblestone alleys, empty squares, and rubble-strewn lots. (in its semidocumentary quality, *The Third Man* belongs with Vittorio De Sica's 1948 *Bicycle Thief* and Jean Cocteau's 1950 *Orpheus* as a snapshot of Europe after the rain.) Yet however desolate its landscape, Vienna was filled with smugglers, secret agents, and East European refugees, many to be arrested and repatriated by the Soviet military police.

Much of *The Third Man* bobs along on such free-floating intrigue.   Everyone has their eye on Martins, particularly the supercilious British major (Trevor Howard) who has been investigating Harry Lime and to whom the ineffectually antiauthoritarian American takes an immediate dislike. Martins is continually told to go home while the absurd, sinister atmosphere of operetta cloak-and-dagger is amplified by extended passages of untranslated German, as well as Martins's unrequited yearning for the sad, vulnerable Anna (Italian star Alida Valli, originally billed as simply Valli), an actress who was Harry's lover.

The naive and confused author of Western novels, Martins is, of course, an unsympathetic caricature of America itself. (The idea of the innocent Yank floundering out of his depth in postwar Europe was revisited by Lars Von Trier's *Zentropa.)* Martins not only develops a conspiracy theory of Lime's demise but begins to believe himself living inside one of his own sagebrush sagas.   A figure of ridicule, he is blamed for a murder, followed in the street, hijacked by a cab driver, and repeatedly rebuffed by Anna (who can never remember his name).   Such are the burdens of world leadership.

No less than its location, *The Third Man* is divided terrain.   Although essentially British, the movie was just last year appropriated by the American Film Institute as Hollywood's 57th greatest effort.   A NATO production made before NATO existed, *The Third Man* is also (like *Casablanca)* a film of multiple authors.   If the package was assembled by Alexander Korda, his American partner David Selznick was largely responsible for the casting.

The movie's internal politics were also complicated.   French historian Marc Ferro has demonstrated how Carol Reed reworked Graham Greene's script to create a political allegory—pro-British, anti-Soviet, and critical of the U.S.A.   Reed added the sequences emphasizing the deadly result of Lime's black-marketeering, reconfigured the dynamics of the crucial café ambush, and changed the famous final shot—thus irritating Greene by depriving the movie of its conventional happy ending.   Reed also made Holly Martins a weaker character and

Anna a stronger one—improving her politics by making her a refugee from Red Czechoslovakia rather than the daughter of a Hungarian Nazi.

Capping its precursors *Odd Man Out* and *The Fallen Idol*, *The Third Man* is certainly Reed's most impressive movie and yet, as Ferro points out in *Cinema and History*, it was stolen out from under him. Two-thirds of the way through, the character who has been the subject of virtually every conversation and the object of almost all desires suddenly—finally!—appears. The cat finds its master. Conjured out of the night by the drunkenly shouting Martins and illuminated by a sudden (impossible) shaft of light, it's Harry Lime smirking in a building doorway.

Or perhaps we should say Orson Welles. Appearing without makeup, Welles makes one of the most dramatic star entrances in the history of movies. From that moment, *The Third Man* belongs to him. Disrupting Reed's schema by transforming the villain into an ambiguously charismatic figure, Welles rewrote his dialogue and largely directed his performance, most effectively in the scene where Lime meets Martins at the foot of the Ferris wheel in the empty Prater amusement park. Reed had already adopted a Welles-inflected expressionism for *Odd Man Out*. But it was due to Welles's elaboration of what might have been just a cameo that Reed extended *The Third Man*'s underground sequences and added an additional chase (including the shot, credit taken by Welles, where Lime's fingers flutter through the sewer grate).

Harry Lime turned out to be Welles's most celebrated movie performance after Charles Foster Kane. Indeed, the ruthless Lime is an alternative Kane—similarly worshiped and betrayed by Joseph Cotten. André Bazin would suggest that this role made Welles into a myth. Certainly, *The Third Man* provided Welles with his last radio persona—in the early '50s he starred in a BBC series based on the movie—and his most romantic embodiment. Not for nothing is *The Third Man* theme echoed by the player piano in *Touch of Evil*.

Holly Martins may not have been a viable metaphor for America. But, in his mixture of overripe charm and *Übermensch* rhetoric, heedless cynicism and doomed megalomania, Welles's Harry Lime was both the dark spirit of a haunted metropolis and the shadow of the actor's future self.

Also reviewed in:
CHICAGO TRIBUNE, 7/30/99, Friday/p. C, Michael Wilmington
NEW YORK TIMES, 2/3/50, p. 29, Bosley Crowther

THIRD MIRACLE, THE

A Sony Pictures Classics release of a Franchise Pictures presentation of an American Zoetrope and Haft Entertainment production. *Executive Producer:* Francis Ford Coppola, Ashok Amritraj, and Andrew Stevens. *Producer:* Fred Fuchs and Steven Haft, and Elie Samaha. *Director:* Agnieszka Holland. *Screenplay:* John Romano and Richard Vetere. *Based on the novel by:* Richard Vetere. *Director of Photography:* Jerzy Zielinski. *Editor:* David J. Siegel. *Music:* Jan A.P. Kaezmarek. *Sound:* Peter Shewchuk. *Casting:* Todd Thaler. *Production Designer:* Robert De Vico. *Art Director:* Andrew M. Stearn. *Costumes:* Denise Cronenberg. *Special Effects:* Michael Kavanagh. *Running time:* 119 minutes. *MPAA Rating:* R.

CAST: Ed Harris (Frank Shore); Anne Heche (Roxanna); Armin Mueller-Stahl (Archbishop Werner); Charles Haid (Bishop Cahill); Michael Rispoli (John Leone); James Gallanders (Brother Gregory); Jean-Louis Roux (Cardinal Sarrazin); Ken James (Father Paul Panak); Caterina Scorsone (Maria Witkowski); Barbara Sukowa (Helen O'Regan); WITH: Rob Jarvis; Ned Vukovic; Jake Smith; Monique Mojiea; Aron Tager; Norma Dell'Agnese; Steve Ferguson; Mark Huisman; Rodger Barton.

LOS ANGELES TIMES, 12/29/99, Calendar/p. 6, Kevin Thomas

Pay close attention to the fast-moving opening sequence of "The Third Miracle," Agnieszka Holland's complex, challenging and impressive film from the Richard Vetere novel. A title card announces that we're in Bystrica, a quaint town in Slovakia, 1944. Suddenly there's a strong rumble, marking not the onslaught of an earthquake but of an Allied bombing attack on German factories there.

A little Gypsy girl awakens with her large family, grabs a small statue of the Madonna and child, and instead of fleeing the center of town with everyone else, heads for Bystrica's central cathedral. There on its steps, she drops to her knees in prayer and notices another likeness of the Madonna and child adorning the building. Only two people notice her: the church's priest, who has urged her to flee, and a wounded German soldier lying in the back of a truck.

As the little girl prays, the scene suddenly goes silent, leaving us to wonder what has happened to the bombs. As "The Third Miracle" evolves into a spiritual odyssey and a detective mystery, you will want to remember as many details of this prologue as you can.

Director Holland cuts to Chicago, 1979, and cinematographer Jerzy Zielinski's fluid camera picks up a gaunt, ascetic-looking man (Ed Harris) with an intent, blue-eyed gaze among a large number of the city's street people. When a young priest (Michael Rispoli) seeks him out, we learn that Harris' Frank Shore is a priest who for the past two months has dropped out of the church.

Father Shore is a postulator for the Roman Catholic Church, charged with the most rigorous possible investigations of accounts of miracles and claims of sainthood. A series of flashbacks as terse and abrupt as the film's opening sequence reveals Father Shore to be haunted by the devastating impact of his latest investigation, for which he, in refuting claims of miracles, blames himself for "destroying the faith of an entire community."

But now there's a new reported miracle occurring in an impoverished, multicultural, inner-city neighborhood, and the forceful, tough-minded and politically astute Bishop Cahill (Charles Haid) wants Frank back on the job immediately.

It seems that five years earlier, an Austrian-born parish worker, Helen O'Regan (Barbara Sukowa), placed her hands on a very ill girl suffering from terminal lupus, curing her instantly. Flashbacks show Helen to be a selfless woman with a radiant smile who dedicated herself to the needy children of the neighborhood. Helen has since died, and the statue of the Madonna has started to bleed—only in November and only when it rains.

Parishioners claim that the tears that flow from the Madonna's eyes are the blood of Helen and that they possess the power to heal. Bishop Cahill has a burgeoning Lourdes on his hands and wants Frank to start investigating right now.

In his present state, Frank would rather prove than disprove Helen's miraculous gifts. This sets him against church hierarchy, which, from a political and an ecclesiastical view, would prefer miracles to be debunked. The more he applies scientific tests, the more convinced he is that Helen is a candidate for sainthood. His pursuit is not without irony: That 11-year-old girl saved by Helen is now a drug-addicted prostitute, and Helen's own daughter Roxanna (Anne Heche) remains bitter over her mother. Helen abandoned Roxanna when Roxanna was only 16—and fatherless by then as well—to move into the church's convent to work with the children. But who is Helen anyway? What is her full story?

These are the biggest questions facing Frank as he endorses Helen's candidacy for sainthood amid a convocation of august church authorities dominated by the Vatican's arrogant, rigid representative, Archbishop Werner (Armin Mueller-Stahl), whose strict adherence to dogma puts him immediately at odds with Frank. Meanwhile, the bluntly nonreligious, sharp and stunningly attractive Roxanna represents an unexpected temptation for Frank.

From her script collaborations with Poland's veteran master director Andrzej Wajda, Holland has moved on to an adventurous, international career. She first won acclaim for "Angry Harvest," in which Mueller-Stahl played a solitary Polish farmer who shelters a Jewish refugee during World War II, and was widely praised for most of her subsequent films, especially "Europa, Europa," the true story of a Jewish youth who survived World War II as a German soldier. Holland has become a vigorous, boldly authoritative director who demands the utmost concentration of audiences; let your attention wander for a second and you may lose the narrative thread of this most convoluted and elliptical film.

"The Third Miracle" seems a masterwork—provided you're caught up in it from a beginning calculated to throw you off balance. That Holland has been able to evoke the miraculous owes much to Harris, for he has the impassioned intelligence to sustain Frank's driving, obsessive quest, and Heche and Mueller-Stahl are in their differing ways expert foils; all three are smart and exceptionally articulate.   "The Third Miracle" has the gritty, intimate feel of an Eastern European film—and packs the power of a genuine revelation.

NEW YORK POST, 12/29/99, p. 42, Lou Lumenick

Ed Harris gives another terrific performance as a priest suffering from a crisis of faith in "The Third Miracle," a flawed drama offering a rare look at the Catholic Church's canonization process.

Harris plays Father Frank Shore, a "postulator," or clerical detective, whose job is to investigate miracles attributed to candidates for sainthood.

As the movie opens, Frank is living on the streets of Chicago as a lay person, his spirit in disarray after he exposed one candidate as a suicide—an episode that left him with the nickname "The Miracle Killer."

Frank's superiors track him down and hand him a new job. In a poor parish, a deceased immigrant woman is being credited with a bleeding statue of the Virgin Mary as well as the miraculous cure of a girl suffering from a brain tumor.

Father Frank very reluctantly tracks down the girl who has grown up into a prostitute (Barbara Sukowa), as well as the dead woman's agnostic daughter (Anne Heche), with whom he is drawn into a none-too-convincing romance.

The skeptical cleric comes to believe in the miracles, but needs proof of a third one. He learns that during World War II, the woman lived in an Austrian village where the Allied bombing abruptly stopped—after she prayed to a statue of the Virgin Mary.

The movie climaxes with a trial that pits Father Frank against a cardinal (a hammy Armin Mueller-Stahl) who serves as a devil's advocate against the canonization—and it's here where the movie self-destructs with a mind-boggling coincidence.

Agnieszka Holland ("A Little Princess"), who previously directed Harris in "To Kill a Priest" (in which he played a Polish secret police officer) lays out the story at a rather leisurely pace. It's not terribly clear when it's taking place; Heche's fake-fur-trimmed coats suggest the 1970's.

"The Third Miracle" is worth seeing mainly for Harris and its unusual subject matter.

NEWSDAY, 1/21/00, Part II/p. B3, Gene Seymour

After years of being regarded as the best supporting actor never to get an Academy Award for best supporting actor, Ed Harris gets a chance to show what he can do in a leading role. And he makes the most of it in a movie that isn't quite as good as he is.

As the Rev. Frank Shore, spiritual "gumshoe" for the Chicago Archdiocese, Harris brings contained intensity and catlike grace to the first two-thirds of "The Third Miracle," director Agnieszka Holland's adaptation of Queens-based author Richard Vetere's novel about establishing the truth behind sacred miracles.

After an opening flashback to a Polish town in World War II (which displays some of Holland's most effective filmmaking), the story begins in the late 1970s, when "Father Frank" can be found haunting homeless shelters and soup kitchens with the indigo melancholy of a wayward, wounded idealist; in short, the classic cynical American detective.

Shore's slow-motion slide began a few years before, when, as a postulator for the Catholic Church, he broke the hearts of a small Illinois town: His investigation into the life of a parish priest offered as a candidate for sainthood uncovered less-than-saintly facts.

But Chicago's politically shrewd Bishop Cahill (Charles Haid) tells Shore to shake the self-pity from his joints and get back in the game. It seems there's this woman named Helen O'Regan (Barbara Sukowa), who died not long ago. Members of her parish church claim several incidents connected to the woman—a church courtyard statue shedding blood, a sick child brought back from near death—could only be explained by the woman's intimate connection with God.

So is she worthy of sainthood? Shore has to find three miracles to answer that question. Part of him hopes she is, while the other part is braced for disappointment. He's not at all encouraged when he meets Roxanna (Anne Heche), Helen's faux-punk daughter, who tells Shore she was abandoned by her mother at age 16 and still can't forgive her for it.

Her rage isn't the only thing that smolders. She finds herself physically attracted to this shy, hunky Father Frank guy, who has one foot in the priesthood and the other dangling in the void. She looks at him the way a cat stares through a glass window of a bird sanctuary. Although nothing happens besides some steamy groping, the sexual chemistry between Heche and Harris is the most potent of any movie you'll see this season.

Both their monkey business and the process of investigating Helen's suitability for sainthood fascinates for as long as the story can stay with them. (The cool, taut dialogue by veteran writer John Romano helps a lot.) But as soon as Harris gets his faith recharged and the case becomes officially debated among the Catholic hierarchy, the movie becomes a welter of strident speeches and inflated righteousness. Matters aren't helped by Armin Mueller-Stahl's portrayal of a skeptical archbishop in the hoary tradition of snooty German baddies.

After Helen's "trial" is orchestrated to a fevered pitch, Holland suddenly chooses to leave things to the audience's imagination. It's a worthy gamble, but I think she loses. Too bad. It wouldn't have taken much of a miracle to bring "The Third Miracle" up to the level of its leading man.

VILLAGE VOICE, 1/4/00, p. 101, J. Hoberman

Scarcely less haunted by the Holocaust, [The reference is to *Mr. Death*; see Hoberman's review.] Agnieszka Holland's *The Third Miracle* is a drama predicated on faith in God rather than history. After a brief prologue in wartime Slovakia, the action jumps ahead 35 years to Chicago, where the call has gone out for Father Frank, a tormented soul currently residing on skid row. It seems that the Holy Virgin at St. Stanislaus Church is shedding tears of blood, which the parish takes as evidence that a recently deceased immigrant woman named Helen is a saint.

Played with extraordinary sympathy by Ed Harris, Father Frank is the reverse exorcist whom the diocese uses to debunk such local cults. "They call you the miracle killer," somebody cracks. Father Frank, who became a priest when God spared his cop father (but just for three months), plumbs the lower depths of Slavic Chicago. He asks questions, drinks too much, gets a yen for Helen's bitter, nonbelieving daughter (Anne Heche); *The Third Miracle* is a sort of Catholic noir. The first half has a nifty B-movie feel—it's a canny little movie with a big, big theme. (This is the precise opposite of *The Improbable Mr. Ripley,* a pumped-up parade float about very, very little.)

God moves in mysterious ways and so does *The Third Miracle*—at least until a German archbishop played by Armin Mueller-Stahl enters the narrative as the Vatican's forbidding devil's advocate. (Oh for the days when Barbara Sukowa, who plays Helen in flashback, destroyed Mueller-Stahl in Fassbinder's remake of *The Blue Angel.)* This supercilious snob gets us rooting for Helen's beatification even after the screenwriter resorts to the sort of dramatically convenient supernaturalism that would embarrass the *World Wide News.*

Unlike Dreyer's *Ordet,* Holland's movie requires no leap of faith. Nor does it directly address its central conundrum—why did God bother with one small miracle amid the horrific carnage of World War II? If you believe that the question is absurd, the third miracle will have less to do with Father Frank's faith than your own.

Also reviewed in:
NEW YORK TIMES, 12/29/99, p. E9, Stephen Holden
VARIETY, 9/20-26/99, p. 86, Derek Elley

THIRTEENTH FLOOR, THE

A Columbia Pictures release of a Centopolis Entertainment production. *Executive Producer:* Michael Ballhaus and Helga Ballhaus. *Producer:* Roland Emmerich, Ute Emmerich, and Marco Weber. *Director:* Josef Rusnak. *Screenplay:* Joseph Rusnak and Ravel Centeno-Rodriguez. *Based on the book "Simulacron 3" by:* Daniel Galouye. *Director of Photography:* Wedigo von Schultzendorff. *Editor:* Henry Richardson. *Music:* Harald Kloser. *Music Editor:* Andy

Dorfman. *Choreographer:* Kim Clever and David Frutos. *Sound:* Jose Antonio Garcia, Bobby Anderson, and (music) Friedrich Wilhem Roedding and Richard Oesterreicher. *Casting:* April Webster. *Production Designer:* Kirk M. Petruccelli. *Art Director:* Barry Chusid. *Set Designer:* Evelyne Barbier and Leslie Thomas. *Set Decorator:* Victor J. Zolfo. *Special Effects:* John S. Baker. *Costumes:* Joseph Porro. *Make-up:* Thomas Nellen. *Stunt Coordinator:* R.A. Rondell. *Running time:* 120 minutes. *MPAA Rating:* R.

CAST: Craig Bierko (Douglas Hall); Armin Mueller-Stahl (Hannon Fuller); Gretchen Mol (Jane Fuller); Vincent D'Onofrio (Whitney/Ashton); Dennis Haysbert (Det. Larry McBain); Steven Schub (Zev Bernstein); Jeremy Roberts (Tom Jones); Rif Hutton (Joe); Leon Rippy (Jane's Lawyer); Janet MacLachlan (Ellen); Brad Henke (Cop #1); Burt Bulos (Bellhop); Venessia Valentino (Concierge); Howrd S. Miller (Chauffeur); Tia Texada (Natasha's Roomate); Shiri Appleby (Bridget Manilla); Robert Clendenin (Bank Manager); Rachel Winfree (Woman Bank Customer); Meghan Ivey (Chanteuse); Alison Lohman (Honey Bear Girl); Hadda Brooks (Lounge Piano Player); Ron Boussom (Maitre'D); Ernie Lively (30s Cop); Toni Sawyer (Grierson's Wife); Brooks Almy (Bridget's Mom); Darryl Henriques (Cab Driver); Suzanne Harrer (Tired Dancer); Lee Weaver (30s Limo Driver); Geoffrey Rivas (Security Guard); Travis Tedford (Newspaper Boy); Jeff Blumenkrantz (Choreographer); Andrew Alden (Doorman); Johnny Crawford (Singer).

LOS ANGELES TIMES, 5/28/99, Calendar/p. 14, Kevin Thomas

If looks were everything, "The Thirteenth Floor," a sleek time-travel mystery that offers a rich and accurate re-creation of 1937 L.A., would have it made. But for all the soaring visual splendor of its past, present and future, it's hobbled by a murky plot that proves to be not all that original once it starts unraveling.

What's more, its stars, Craig Bierko and Gretchen Mol, do not possess strong enough personalities to overcome their colorless roles and keep us engaged in their fates as the film relentlessly switches between past and present.

Bierko's Douglas Hall is second-in-command at a $2-billion computer software enterprise headquartered in a downtown L.A. skyscraper. His boss, Hannon Fuller (Armin Mueller-Stahl), the firm's owner and a father figure to Hall, has been found murdered in an alley off Skid Row. Hall swiftly becomes the prime suspect of smart LAPD detective Larry McBain (Dennis Haysbert), while Hall becomes convinced that Fuller's shocking fate is connected to an ambitious and risky virtual-reality program he is developing. What to do but jack into the system, with the help of company employee Whitney (Vincent D'Onofrio), and see what gives?

Suddenly Hall is thrust into the virtual-reality world of 1937. There he becomes John Ferguson, a bank teller curious about the proprietor (Mueller-Stahl) of a high-end Pasadena bookstore with an eye for pretty girls, who are readily supplied to him by an insinuating bartender (D'Onofrio) at a lavish Deco nightclub the bookseller frequents.

The gist of myriad plot complications is to speculate that a simulated universe may be able to spawn a simulated universe itself—i.e., the film's present therefore may be no more real than its past; and to posit that certain individuals (Fuller and Hall) might somehow possess souls, even though they may not be actual human beings. Such speculations are hardly new, but they're treated here with awe-struck reverence. Mol is the movie's mystery lady, identifying herself as the daughter of Fuller that nobody knew he had.

Certainly, director Josef Rusnak, in adapting Daniel Galouye's "Simulacron 3" with co-writer Ravel Centeno-Rodriguez, is aiming for quality and seriousness—too much seriousness, it turns out, because the film could use a dose of relieving humor. Mueller-Stahl, D'Onofrio and Haysbert fare better than Bierko and Mol because they are actors of wit and presence and have more sharply defined roles.

But far and away the strongest element of the film is its imaginative production design by Kirk M. Petruccelli, augmented by wondrous special effects and Wedigo von Schultzendorff's gleaming camera work. "The Thirteenth Floor" is hardly the first—or the last—movie to look better than it really is.

NEW YORK POST, 5/28/99, p. 59, Jonathan Foreman

"The Thirteenth Floor" is an ultra-stylish science-fiction thriller that combines elements of film noir, "The Truman Show" and cyberpunk without relying on costly special effects. Unfortunately, this mix—and the film's philosophical aspirations—are let down by some mediocre acting, pedestrian dialogue and slow pacing, so that at times you almost find yourself missing the cartoon violence of "The Matrix."

There are also some logical problems, but to state them would give away the plot (based on the novel "Simulacron-3").

The film starts off in a hotel room in 1930s California, with Mr. Fuller (Armin Mueller-Stahl of "Shine") leaving a tip for a sleeping girl, donning his tails and then entrusting a letter to the barman who pimps for him. He then goes home to bed, and wakes up in a gleaming high-tech lab in present-day L.A.

Fuller is a computer visionary who, with his younger colleagues Hall (Craig Bierko) and Whitney (Vincent D'Onofrio) has created an experimental technology that maintains a simulation in cyberspace: a lifelike 1937 L.A. peopled with autonomous characters.

You can "download" your own consciousness into the body of one of these characters and live their life for an hour or two. During secretive travels back in time Fuller has discovered "an awful truth" that he must tell Hall. But before he can, he is murdered in an alley.

The next day, police Detective McBain (Dennis Haysbert of "Love Field") asks Hall where he was at the time of the slaying. He can't remember, but there's a bloody shirt in his sink. Then a beautiful blonde with a 1930s hairstyle (a weak Gretchen Mol) turns up claiming to be Fuller's daughter and urges him to shut the simulation down.

Understandably confused, Fuller decides to go for the first time into the simulation himself once there, he is stunned by the open vistas of the pre-war city, and by the vividness of the simulation. As he says to Whitney, the characters there "are as real as you or me."

They have ongoing lives, feel pain, and have no idea that they are just programs. It gets Hall to wondering ... Meanwhile someone is killing everybody around him.

Haysbert and Mueller-Stahl are convincing enough. But Bierko and Mol, admittedly burdened by uninspired lines and a perfunctory romance, are so lacking in charisma that it's hard to care about their characters.

Visually though, this film delivers. Dust-filled, slanting light out of "Blade Runner" half-illuminates vast, somber interiors. And while director Rusnak lovingly re-creates 1930s L.A., he makes something sinister and strangely empty out of its modern incarnation.

It's no coincidence that the city's gleaming black glass towers resemble the high-tech gadgetry in the simulation lab.

NEWSDAY, 5/28/99, Part II/p. B7, Gene Seymour

The success of both "The Truman Show" and "The Matrix" have helped kick open the door to all kinds of story ideas involving alternate realities and parallel universes. It's a narrative milieu that's just waiting for the cinematic equivalents of Lewis Carroll, Jorge Luis Borges or Philip K. Dick to mine for wit and sublimity.

Wait. What are we thinking? Wit? Sublimity? In a Hollywood science-fiction movie? Only in another universe, bucky! For the time being, movies such as "The Thirteenth Floor" will have to do.

At least for most of its early going, you think it'll do just fine. It opens on a dark night in Los Angeles in 1937. A man (Armin Mueller-Stahl) in evening clothes is riding in a limousine to a dance club. He hands a note to a bartender, asking it be delivered to someone who doesn't exist yet. He goes to a surprisingly modest home, gets in bed and then—*whomp!*—he wakes up in modern dress in a sterile room occupied by banks of computers. A few minutes later, he's slashed to death in an alley.

It turns out the dead guy is Hannon Fuller, one of a handful of corporate wizards working on a virtual-reality experiment that allows them to inhabit the brains of people living 62 years in the past. Fuller's partner, Douglas Hall (Craig Bierko), is chief suspect in the murder and there's all kinds of evidence linking him to the crime along with a crystal-clear motive. (He inherits the company.)

Hall, however, can't imagine himself killing Fuller any more than he can figure out why Fuller's daughter Jane (Gretchen Mol) shows up, literally from nowhere, to contest the will. Grouchy detective McBain (Dennis Haysbert) thinks the whole thing stinks. Meanwhile, Hall, with help from his chief geek, Whitney (Vincent D'Onofrio), decides to jack into their time-traveling program himself to see whether the answer lies in 1937.

Hall finds an answer all right. But it's far more frightening than the one he was looking for. He goes back to the present-day reality, wondering if even that's reality ... Once this premise is established, the movie doesn't know what to do with it except turn it into a standard-issue crime melodrama and not a very satisfying or logical one, either. ("I have so much to explain," Mol's Jane says at the very end. You're welcome to try, kiddo.)

With actors such as Haysbert, Mueller-Stahl and the always fascinating D'Onofrio around, you'd think anyone would have the means to drive this baby into all kinds of termite-terrace hijinks. But director Josef Rusnak plays things so straight and tight-jawed that you wish producer Roland Emmerich had stepped in to bring some of the light-hearted, antic spin, he brought, to "Independence Day" and even "Godzilla."

VILLAGE VOICE, 6/8/99, p. 68, Michael Atkinson

It'll make you cyberlaugh, it'll make you cybercry, just like cyberlife. Based on a 30-year-old SF novel, this Roland Emmerich-produced soft machine has not been usurped by *The Matrix* and *eXistenZ* so much as by the "Menagerie" episode of *Star Trek*. Even the F/X are dingy with vault dust. Here, a massive mainframe "experiment" jacks you into a fully functional repro of 1937 Los Angeles; when creator Armin Mueller-Stahl is murdered in the present, employee Craig Bierko plunges in to investigate. There are ideas—what do you do when, while plugged in, you end up preferring your evil mate's sweet-natured cyberidentity to the real thing?—but also a lot of technocrap and alligator-brain dialogue that only George Lucas could envy. (It doesn't help that Bierko comes off as a screen-saver merge of George Clooney and Nicolas Cage, with a cyberbeard that never grows out.) Has only David Cronenberg noticed that movies about alternate realities are kind of like novels about reading? One thing is certain: your boredom will be real.

Also reviewed in:
NEW YORK TIMES, 5/28/99, p. E23, Lawrence Van Gelder
VARIETY, 5/24-30/99, p. 37, Robert Koehler
WASHINGTON POST, 5/28/99, p. C5, Rita Kempley
WASHINGTON POST, 5/28/99, Weekend/p. 49, Desson Howe

13TH WARRIOR, THE

A Touchstone Pictures release of Crichton/McTiernan production. *Executive Producer:* Andrew G. Vajna and Ethan Dubrow. *Producer:* Ned Dowd, John McTiernan, and Michael Crichton. *Director:* John McTiernan. *Screenplay:* William Wisher and Warren Lewis. *Based on the novel "Eaters of the Dead" by:* Michael Crichton. *Director of Photography:* Peter Menzies, Jr. *Editor:* John Wright. *Music:* Jerry Goldsmith. *Music Editor:* Ken Hall. *Sound:* Robert Eber and (music) Bruce Botnick. *Sound Editor:* Alan Robert Murray. *Casting:* Pat McCorkle. *Production Designer:* Wolf Kroeger. *Art Director:* Helen V. Jarvis, Richard St. John Harrison, and William Heslup. *Set Decorator:* Rose Marie McSherry. *Set Dresser:* Joanne Quirk, Patrick Kearns, and Scott Calderwood. *Costumes:* Kate Harrington. *Make-up:* Jeff Dawn. *Stunt Coordinator:* Brent Woolsey. *Running time:* 103 minutes. *MPAA Rating:* R.

CAST: Antonio Banderas (Ahmed Ibn Fahdlan); Diane Venora (Queen Weilew); Dennis Storhoi (Herger, Joyous); Vladimir Kulich (Buliwyf); Omar Sharif (Melchisidek); Anders T. Andersen (Wigliff, King's Son); Richard Bremmer (Skeld, Superstitious); Tony Curran (Weath, Musician); Mischa Hausserman (Rethel, Archer); Neil Maffin (Roneth); Asbjorn Riis (Halga, Wise); Clive Russell (Helfdane, Fat); Daniel Southern (Edgtho, Silent); Oliver Sveinall (Haltaf,

Boy); Sven Wollter (King Hrothgar); Albie Woodington (Hyglak, Quarrelsome); John DeSantis (Ragner, Dour); Eric Avari (Caravan Leader); Maria Bonnevie (Olga); Richard Ooms (One-eyed Old Man); Dylan Gray Woodley (Screaming Boy); Bjorn Ove Pedersen (Wulfgar, The Boy-messenger); Scott Elam (Herald); Ghoncheh Tazmini (Shaharazhad, Arabian Beauty); Joe Bulatti (Shaharazhad's Husband); Mina Erian Mina (Caliph); Mona Storhoi (Sacrificial Woman); Turid Balke (Oracle, Old Woman); Suzanne Bertish (Hulda); Susan Willis (Wendol Mother); Yolande Bavan (Wendol Mother Companion); Claire Lapinski (Freyda); Tarik Batal (Arab Page); Brett Reyez (Caravan Lieutenant); Sven-Ole Thorsen (Would-be King); Alaina Lander (Sleeping Girl); Jeremy Van Der Driesen and Al Hachlaf (Arab Generals); Gunnar Skjavestad (Norseman on Ship); Malcolm Jolly (Wulfgar Retainer); Owen Walstrom (Wendol Guard).

LOS ANGELES TIMES, 8/27/99, Calendar/p. 4, Gene Seymour

[*The following review by Gene Seymour appeared in a slightly different form in* **NEWSDAY, 8/27/99, Part II/p. B6.**]

Movies like "The 13th Warrior" aren't meant for prime-time consumption. You should shove them into your system on a Saturday afternoon, the way you gobble a hot dog at a ballpark. Thinking too much about the contents will ruin what little pleasure there is in the experience.

While there's much in this movie that may make you nauseous (and this isn't just a reference to the severed limbs and sliced guts), it speaks enough to the bloodthirsty 11-year-old in most male adults to explain, if not justify, its existence. Two words, of course, are sufficient explanation: Michael Crichton. When you're perceived to have a "magic touch" the way Hollywood perceives the author-creator of "Jurassic Park," "Disclosure" and "ER," you can get anything you want on screen—even if it's a long-forgotten novel like "Eaters of the Dead," Crichton's 1976 tale of 10th century Norse warriors liberating a kingdom from fear.

Crichton is listed as one of the producers of this dour, fast-paced adaptation of his novel, given the presumably less-confusing title "The 13th Warrior," which refers to Ahmed Ibn Fahdlan (Antonio Banderas), an urbane Muslim poet-diplomat banished from his homeland for messing around with the Wrong Woman. Ibn, as he's called for short, is wandering the "northern lands" before he finds himself exchanging pleasantries with a gang of brawling Nordic slobs with names like Herger the Joyous (Dennis Storhoi), Helfdane the Large (Clive Russell), Skeld the Superstitious (Richard Bremmer) and so forth. The leader of this band is Buliwyf (Vladimir Kulich). That's all. Just Buliwyf. Being king means never having your unsightly characteristics advertised.

Anyway, Ibn reluctantly agrees to accompany these sword-wielding toughs on a mission to battle a mysterious tribe of saw-toothed savages who have been brutalizing a tiny kingdom across the sea. Once there, they find an elderly monarch (Sven Wollter) too sick to fight and a treacherous prince (Anders T. Andersen) whose agenda is never clearly defined. Neither is the wonderful Diane Venora, criminally underutilized here as the queen and forced to say stupid things like "I know a wise woman who can help." Which is at best misleading. No woman in this boy's blood-and-guts romance is allowed to be wise. Or anything else.

John McTiernan directs this cliche-ridden script by William Wisher and Warren Lewis with cold-blooded efficiency. The cast does the best it can under the circumstances. But really it's Banderas who makes this thing bearable. If he doesn't have the same bounce and vitality he displayed in "The Mask of Zorro," neither does he submit to the gloom and ponderousness of his surroundings. His light stays on all the time, even in a relatively lost cause like this one.

NEW STATESMAN, 9/6/99, p. 45, Ziauddin Sardar

Hollywood has portrayed Muslims and the Muslim world largely in terms of two firmly fixed stereotypes. There is the bloodthirsty terrorist hell-bent on destroying civilisation as we know it of such epics as *True Lies* and *The Siege*. Then there is this exotic land, somewhere east of the west, where life is seedy and cheap but sensual pleasures are aplenty. From Valentino's *The Sheik* (1921) onwards, Muslim societies have been depicted as arenas of sexual licence and perversion where women (and boys) are easy and unspeakable things happen. Here, women are always scantily clad and imprisoned in a harem by nasty despots, as in *Arabian Nights* (1942) or *Harem* (1985). The men are nasty, smelly and brutal, as we find them in *The Sheltering Sky* (1990) or, more recently, in *The Mummy*.

To these standard representations, we can now add a third: the well-educated, cultured Muslim of history. *The 13th Warrior*, the true story of the tenth-century Muslim explorer Ahmed Ibn Fahdlan, provides the character with his second outing. The first was the noble Moor, played by Morgan Freeman, in Kevin Costner's *Robin Hood*. The new representation can arguably be described as a sympathetic portrayal. Actually, it is a carefully constructed amalgam of historical verisimilitude and knowledgeable ignorance that leaves intact the overall representation of Muslims as the darker side of Europe.

The first thing to note is that these figures are firmly rooted in history—there is no danger of educated, accomplished Muslims existing today. If culture and scientific sophistication have actually touched the Muslims, then it was resolutely in the past. Contemporary Islam continues to be the land of lowlife, terror and sexual perversion.

But the sympathetic Muslims of yesteryear are framed within standard archetypes of Islamic culture. The Moor of *Robin Hood* is given a certain dignity and permitted to demonstrate a learning and philosophy beyond the experience of the Crusaders. But, right at the beginning of the film, it is made clear that he emerges from a brutal culture. *Robin Hood* opens with stock imagery of Muslim brutality: hands are being chopped off in a dungeon replete with engines of terror. The good Moor who saves Robin Hood from this fate is an anomaly.

Similarly, *The 13th Warrior* begins with standard icons of Islamic sexuality. Even before the titles have finished, we have witnessed the exotic Arabia of western imagination, complete with semi-clad veiled women, a Scheherazade, an ugly and conniving vizier and a despotic caliph. The Scheherazade in question is the cause of Ibn Fahdlan's banishment from Baghdad and his journey to the land of the Vikings.

En route to the court of the king of the Bulgars and accompanied by his wise manservant Melchisidek (a tongue-in-cheek Omar Sharif), Ibn Fahdlan meets a band of Norse warriors. He considers the rogues to be crude but colourful and views with undisguised cynicism their description of mysterious creatures plaguing their homeland. The creatures appear like a group of bears, emerge through the foggy shroud of night and consume every living thing in their path. An old sooth sayer appropriately warns that the band will fail to defeat the creatures unless they are accompanied by a 13th, foreign warrior. Ibn Fahdlan is reluctantly recruited, and we proceed to a string of spectacularly staged battles.

As played by Antonio Banderas, Ibn Fahdlan emerges as a noble and sophisticated urbanite finding his way among the "wild men" of Europe. He learns their language simply by listening and observing. He knows how to adopt and transform their technology. Eventually he comes to admire and appreciate the Vikings.

But Ibn Fahdlan of *The 13th Warrior* is totally devoid of his own historical content. He has been filtered through two layers. His account of his journeys is written with clinical precision as a formal report to the court of Caliph al-Muqtadir (d 908). He saw the Vikings not as crude warriors but as a precious people with a highly developed philosophy of life and a sophisticated understanding of both the sea and military technology. But the film presents the Vikings as stereotypical products of Anglo-Saxon propaganda. Indeed it is Ibn Fahdlan's detailed and accurate account that has, after a millennium, finally overturned the Anglo-Saxon misrepresentations of the Vikings.

The second layer comes in the form of Michael Crichton's novel *Eaters of the Dead*, on which the film is based. The novel turns Ibn Fahdlan's narrative, exciting and kaleidoscopic as it is, into a complete fable. So real events become dim and distant exploits, not far removed from Dungeons and Dragons. One has difficulty in believing even in the existence of Ibn Fahdlan, let alone the fact that an early tenth-century Arab could have travelled to Scandinavia and lived with and studied the Norsemen for three years.

The giveaway that this is a distinctly cardboard portrayal comes with the prayer. The daily prayer is the most common ritual of Muslim life. There is no mystery about it; anyone can see how Muslims pray by walking into a mosque. But never in the history of film has a Muslim character offered his prayers properly or uttered a meaningful sentence of invocation. This is a persistent piece of significant and deliberate ignorance that has been used to portray the irrationality of the Muslim mind, from the 1966 epic *Khartoum* to the recent *Executive Decision*. So its presence in allegedly sympathetic representations is more than just curious. In *Robin Hood* Morgan Freeman mouths nonsense and kneels, bends and knocks his head on the ground in straightforward parody. Just before the final battle, Banderas takes off his armour and throws himself on the ground as though he is jumping into a swimming pool. Still, I suppose we ought to be thankful for small mercies—and the sympathetic looting of our classics.

NEW YORK POST, 8/27/99, p. 49, Jonathan Foreman

Although the release of "The 13th Warrior" was held back for nearly a year, this adaptation of Michael Crichton's early novel "Eaters of the Dead" turns out to be a deeply pleasurable, old-fashioned blood-'n'-guts adventure film.

The dialogue is spare, the plot simple, and the images strong—often startlingly so. As movies about Norsemen go, it's not as witty as "The Vikings" with Kirk Douglas, but it holds your attention through sheer cinematic power.

It's a primal tale of men, armed with little more than courage and loyalty, facing down terrifying things that come out of the night.

Although the original novel is a take on the Beowulf saga, with clever things to say about the meeting of two utterly different cultures, John McTiernan's film is more of a war movie, almost an early-medieval "Platoon," with the Beowulf link more lightly traced.

With its themes of stoicism and self-sacrifice, and its basic story of a band of warriors defending a civilized settlement against a savage foe, it brings to mind various westerns, foreign legion movies and "Gunga Din." Most of all, it draws on Kurosawa's "Seven Samurai."

Ibn Fahdlan (Antonio Banderas), an ambassador from the medieval court of Baghdad, is sent to the farthest reaches of the known world (together with Omar Sharif in a cameo role).

At a river in Russia he comes upon a band of fierce Viking raiders, fighters so hardened that even the Tartar bandits fear them.

The Norsemen are in the midst of a drunken funeral, when a messenger comes summoning them back to the fjords: A Viking community is on the verge of being wiped out by a terrifying, legendary evil, the "eaters of the dead."

Fahdlan is dragooned into being the 13th member of the warrior team who makes the journey north, led by Buliwyf (Vladimir Kulich). They find a settlement bereft of adult males, terrorized by savage monsters who come out of the mist.

Despite opposition from the local king's son, the 13 organize the defense of the settlement against an enemy whom Fahdlan realizes may actually be human rather than supernatural.

Sure, it's a little too long. Jerry Goldsmith's score is sometimes overbearing, and the bad guys would have been even scarrier if the Vikings themselves were shown to be as ferocious as they were in reality.

But for the most part, "The 13th Warrior" is an epic that works. The battle scenes are particularly effective: swirls of bloody, fire-lit chaos that evoke the brutality of real combat, without sadistically shoving it down your throat.

It helps that everything feels so authentic: the weapons are heavy, the heroes and their horses are physically huge, and the storm at sea looks wet, cold and scary.

Banderas again shows that he is a legitimate movie star, blessed with an almost magical glamour. And his less well-known co-stars do a fine job, particularly Norwegian actor Dennis Storhoi.

But the true star of "The 13th Warrior" is "Die-Hard" director John McTiernan, who has fashioned a very pure movie experience. He uses the narrative power of film to evoke a universe in which human settlements are fragile but human solidarity is not.

SIGHT AND SOUND, 9/99, p. 57, Kim Newman

922 AD. Ahmed Ibn Fahdlan, an Arab poet, is sent abroad by the caliph as an ambassador. In Tartary, he meets some Vikings under the command of chieftain Buliwyf and, through a translator, communicates with Herger the joyous, Buliwyf's lieutenant. A messenger from the North tells of a settlement ruled by King Hrothgar under attack by monstrous creatures. A

seeress divines that 13 warriors must come to Hrothgar's aid but the thirteenth must not be a Norseman so Ibn Fahdlan is drafted.

At Hrothgar's settlement, the Vikings discover the attackers are man-eaters. Herger duels with the champion of Wigliff, Hrothgar's treacherous son, and Ibn Fahdlan gains the respect of his fellow warriors after a skirmish with the enemy. During an attack on Hrothgar's stronghold, Ibn Fahdlan realises the enemy, a tribe called the Wendol, are men wearing bearskins. The surviving warriors track the Wendol to their cave lair. Buliwyf kills the Wendol mother. The Wendol launch a revenge attack, during which Buliwyf duels with and kills the Wendol chieftan before himself dying. The Wendol retreat. Ibn Fahdlan returns home to write of his experiences.

Post-production of *The 13th Warrior* has been so attenuated the film has been beaten into cinemas by its director John McTiernan's subsequent feature *The Thomas Crown Affair*. In many ways; it's not hard to understand how this happened since *Warrior* bears the battle scars of having been through the preview process, losing a few subplots and character explanations along the way.

Michael Crichton's 1976 novel *Eaters of the Dead* which 'explains' the story of *Beowulf* suggesting that Grendel and his mother were survivors of a tribe of Neolithic cavemen, is one of his more eccentric efforts. Meanwhile, this adaptation violates several rules of the big summer event movie: the apparent hero is in effect an observer who leaves all the heavy lifting to the Vikings; the climax seems insufficiently climactic (their leader killed, the fearsome Wendol just up sticks and leave); and there is no romantic interest beyond a little wound-tending.

It might also be that the daring stroke of making the spokesman for civilised Islamic normality (which has a precedent in Sidney Poitier's turn in *The Long Ships,* 1963) is just too much of a stretch for US audiences. To get round this, we are assured that the literate, fastidiously clean, reluctantly violent Ibn Fahdlan worships one God while the pagan Vikings have a parcel of under-explained beliefs almost as alien as the primitive, Venus-venerating, cannibal Wendol.

Banderas, having swashbuckled in *The Mask of Zorro,* comes across at first as a rather camp figure with heavy eye-liner, but soon he shows the sneering Vikings the right stuff by demonstrating superior Arab horsemanship and whittling a heavy sword down into an effective scimitar. After that, he has little else to do, though the film seems to imply that Ibn Fahdlan (a real historical figure) will become the author of *Beowulf.* Despite its ineffectual lead, *The 13th Warrior* doesn't play effectively as an ensemble hero movie like *The Magnificent Seven* (1960) or *The Dirty Dozen* (1967). Buliwyf is always at two removes, even when taking command and improving himself by learning to write, and Vladimir Kulich's quiet reading of the role is never given enough screen weight to suggest the foundation of a legend which will last for a thousand years. The most charismatic, canny character is Herger, whose plot function is to mediate between the narrator and the chieftain. Of the other ten warriors, half barely get a line out before they are beheaded and the rest are allowed a character trait apiece, as signalled by their names (Skeld the Superstitious, Ragnar the Dour, Rethel the Archer, and so on).

The genre it comes closest to is the horror movie, with the lurking Wendol chief glaring from the shadows like the monster from McTiernan's *Predator.* The Wendol are inevitably less fearsome up close than when glimpsed, though their slinky matriarch is a memorable creation and the art direction in their skull-festooned lair has a real Norse Chainsaw Massacre feel. With a spirited score, misty forest locations, plenty of sword-hacking and a few lifts from Kurosawa in the pitched battles, the film might not hold its own with Richard Fleischer's *The Vikings* but its pleasing, good-humoured ludicrousness should pass muster with bloodthirsty schoolboys.

VILLAGE VOICE, 9/17/99, p. 118, Gary Dauphin

Long-delayed and rumored to be a laughable mess, the John McTiernan directed Viking adventure *The 13th Warrior* is actually a well-marbled, albeit derivative, slab of action-movie man meat. Essentially a time-displaced subspecies of those familiar military gambols where an untested civvy is thrown in with the violent, musty men, *Warrior* was adapted from *Eaters of the Dead,* Michael Crichton's "realistic" retelling of *Beowulf.* It opens in appropriately crypto-historical fashion with actual historical figure Ahmed Ibn Fahdlan (a game Antonio Banderas), a 10th-century Arab poet banished to an ambassadorship in the wilds of Norse Europe. His exile is a baffled tour of curious local ways until the locals' longhaired leader Buliwyf (a stony-eyed Vladimir Kulich) receives an appeal from another kinglet for aid against a mysterious threat.

Buliwyf and 11 of his warriors immediately suit up, dragging Ahmed along after the resident witch-woman decrees the 13th warrior cannot be a Norseman.

Given the rotely atrocious treatment meted out to Arabs in Hollywood action flicks, Ahmed's adventures do have a minorly refreshing cast to them. (That said, there is something typically unfortunate about the lack of an Arab actor for the lead, or the way it seems you have to reach back 1000 years in order to avoid most contemporary stereotypes.) Inverting the traditional big-screen take on noble savagery, the literate and darkly handsome Ahmed is the civilized eye observing the pale-faced Norse, who come off as the brutish, illiterate, swine-eating trailer trash of Europe. When he arrives at their hard-luck destination, a threatened Norse village, Ahmed's stunned that human beings still live in such primitive conditions, but once his group crosses swords with the enemy (a persistently neolithic band of cannibals), he realizes the one thing trailer trash do know loads about is killing. Ahmed's almost foppish facility with a one-handed scimitar (the broadsword-wielding Norse keep calling his weapon a girl's knife) soon makes him one of the guys, and his exile becomes a kind of medieval student exchange, Ahmed learning about cold-weather heroism and war craft while teaching Buliwyf smart-people stuff like readin' and writin' and monotheism.

Warrior's story line is a frayed bundle—there are unfulfilled intimations of supernatural hijinks and royal intrigue—but the loose ends are overshadowed by the expertly choreographed fight sequences, overwritten by the always moving spectacle of the legitimately heroic and well-met death. (Moving to me at least, or anyone with a thing for Tolkien or Arthurian legend or Klingons.) Ultimately the movie's biggest asset and problem is its basic anachronism—the visit to this epic, macho oasis is stirring even as it underscores just how thoroughly exhausted most action-adventure tropes have become. As one of the Norsemen tells Ahmed, "This is the old way; you will not see this again," and although *The 13th Warrior* doesn't quite know if it's trying to reinvigorate or eulogize its own genre, the curious thing is that he's right.

Also reviewed in:
CHICAGO TRIBUNE, 8/27/99, Friday/p. A, Michael Wilmington
NEW YORK TIMES, 8/27/99, p. E27, Stephen Holden
VARIETY, 8/30-9/5/99, p. 49, Todd McCarthy
WASHINGTON POST, 8/27/99, p. C1, Stephen Hunter

THIS IS MY FATHER

A Sony Pictures Classics release of a Filmline International and Hummingbird Communications production. *Executive Producer:* Elie Samaha and Kieran Corrigan. *Producer:* Nicolas Clermont and Philip King. *Director:* Paul Quinn. *Screenplay:* Paul Quinn. *Director of Photography:* Declan Quinn. *Editor:* Glenn Berman. *Music:* Donal Lunny. *Sound Editor:* Michel Bordeleau. *Casting:* John Hubbard, Ros Hubbard, Nadia Rona, and Rosina Bucci. *Production Designer:* Frank Conway. *Art Director:* Claude Pare. *Special Effects:* Kevin Byrne. *Costumes:* Consolata Boyle. *Stunt Coordinator:* Bronco McLoughlin. *Running time:* 120 minutes. *MPAA Rating:* R.

CAST: PRESENT DAY: James Caan (Kieran Johnson); Jacob Tierney (Jack, Kieran Johnson's Nephew); Colm Meaney (Seamus, Owner of the Bed-and-Breakfast); Moira Deady (Mrs. Kearney, Seamus' Mother); Susan Almgren (Betty); Pauline Hutton (Maria); Fiona Glascott (Nuala); Françoise Graton (Old Fiona); Joel Gordon (Brian Winters); Alexandra Spunt and Victoria Sanchez (Female Students); Terrence Scammell (Chicago Radio DJ); Pat Leavy (Farmer Woman); Aidan Conron (Bartender); Peadar Lamb and Sean Madden (Men in Pub);

1939: Aidan Quinn (Kieran O'Day); Moya Farrelly (Fiona Flynn); Maria McDermottroe (Mrs. Maney); Donal Donnelly (John Maney); Gina Moxley (Widow Flynn); Eamonn Morrissey (Father Mooney); Stephen Rea (Father Quinn); John Cusack (Eddie Sharp, the Pilot); Brendan Gleeson (Officer Jim); Pat Short (Officer Ben); John Kavanagh (Liam Finneran); Sheila Flitton (Mrs. Madigan); Nevin Finegan (Petie Madigan); Oran Finegan (Davey Madigan); Karen

Ardiff (Young Mrs. Kearney); Michael Byrne (Michael Finnegan); Marian Quinn (Concepta); Michael West (Nosey Nolan); Michael Devaney (Young Suitor); Karl Hayden and Gavin O'Connor (Town Lads); Kieran Hanrahan (Band Leader); Frank O'Dwyer (Dance Chaperone); Andrew Bennett (Mr. Kearney); Devan Murray (Christy); Brendan Conroy (Undertaker); Gary Merrigan (Child Finnegan).

LOS ANGELES TIMES, 5/7/99, Calendar/p. 11, Kevin Thomas

Paul Quinn's "This Is My Father" is a beautiful, heart-wrenching film in which a Chicago high school history teacher (James Caan), in the grip of middle-age malaise, unexpectedly finds himself heading to Ireland in search of his birth father's identity. His quest in turn triggers a flashback in which a passionate romance collides tragically with the dictates of religion and class.

In a most affecting first feature, Quinn has created a film of considerable complexity and impact in a unique collaboration with his actor brother Aidan and cinematographer brother Declan; collectively, the Quinns represent a formidable array of talent. Caan's performance ranks among his finest, and a young Irish actress named Moya Farrelly is beguiling in her film debut.

A lonely widower, Caan's Kieran finds himself increasingly disconnected from his students. He is further depressed over his mother, Fiona (Francoise Graton), being felled by a stroke, left bedridden and mute, in the care of his hard-pressed divorced sister, Betty (Susan Almgren), who has a troubled teenage son, Jack (Jacob Tierney). When Kieran and Betty come across a photo of their mother as a young girl locked arm in arm with a farmer, along with a book of poems inscribed "Kieran," he decides that as soon as he can get away he should make a trip to his mother's native land, taking along Jack, who could also use a change of scenery.

And what gorgeous scenery awaits Kieran and Jack, who put up at a bed-and-breakfast in Fiona's hometown. Their elderly landlady (Moira Deady), who has a comically smarmy and greedy son (Colm Meaney), has plenty to tell Jack—as long as he's willing to cross her palm with silver. Still, what the woman, a consummate storyteller, has to say has the ring of truth.

Moving back to 1939, when the young, headstrong Fiona (Farrelly) has been sent home from school after "a bit of a run-in" with the nuns. Her mother (Maria McDermottroe) is an elegant snob, a widow assuaging her grief and loneliness with drink. When 17-year-old Fiona initiates a flirtation with the shy adopted son (Aidan Quinn, in a portrayal of much depth and intelligence) of tenant farmers who is easily twice her age (but most likely a virgin like herself), she sets in motion a great love and even greater disaster in a village presided over by a hellfire-and-damnation priest (Eammonn Morrissey) who doesn't hesitate to lecture individuals on the state of their morals from his pulpit. (Even worse is his sex-obsessed colleague, played by Stephen Rea).

Paul Quinn is more interested in expressing compassion for one and all than in passing judgment. Yet he conveys that, for all its warmth and charm, Fiona's village is no less oppressive, steeped in narrow-mindedness and ignorance. (An extraneous cameo by John Cusack jars but does not derail the film.) Gradually, the humor and lighthearted tone of the flashbacks turn darker and darker. Nonetheless, as the film comes full circle, Caan's Kieran finds meaning in his quest, as his nephew Jack, on a less intense level, has matured and regained focus upon meeting a local girl (Pauline Hutton), as lovely as his grandmother was in her youth.

"This Is My Father" is a rewarding film of healing and a most personal, impassioned work on the part of Paul, Aidan and Declan Quinn.

NEW YORK POST, 5/7/99, p. 53, Rod Dreher

On the surface, there's nothing surprising about "This Is My Father," a downcast tribute by the filmmaking Quinn brothers (actor Aidan, director Paul and cinematographer Declan) to their Irish heritage.

The story is a Romeo-and-Juliet fable played as a somewhat hackneyed homage to the misery our Old World ancestors endured. And, this being set in 1930s Ireland, that means loads of drink, discrimination, superstition and, saints preserve us, rock-hard piety from the Catholic Church.

But the film is redeemed by Aidan Quinn's restrained, achingly beautiful performance—he has never been better—and his brother Declan's hypnotic, extraordinarily poetic photography. By the time "This Is My Father" reaches its tearful conclusion, the tragedy is no less crushing for being inevitable.

The movie opens with an American schoolteacher named Kieran (James Caan) who, tired of drifting through the lassitude of late middle age, travels with his teen-age nephew back to his aged mother's County Galway village in search of the father he never knew.

Caan appears for only a short time in the film, which is almost entirely told as a series of flashbacks. Quinn plays Caan's long-lost father (also named Kieran), and Moya Farrelly is the spirited young woman who would become his mother.

Quinn's Kieran is a strong-backed country boy, shy and stout-hearted but none too bright, who lives with the kindly tenant farmer couple (Donal Donnelly and Maria McDermottroe) who took him in as an orphan. He falls for flashy Fiona (Farrelly), daughter of uppity Widow Flynn (Gina Moxley), who won't hear of her Fiona taking up with a "poorhouse bastard" like Kieran.

The two carry out their illicit courtship secretly, and we know it cannot come to any good. What's most moving, though, is the accumulation of images and small details, which paint a powerfully evocative portrait of a society smothering under the weight of tradition and the gravity of their lives.

It's hard to see what the framing device with Caan adds to the film, and the subplot involving the rebellious teen-ager is a positive distraction. There's a weird scene in which John Cusack, playing an American aerial photographer, descends from the sky in an airplane, and visits with Kieran and Fiona on the beach. America equals freedom and lightness, get it? It's exactly what you'd expect from the sons of immigrants, as the Quinn brothers are. Theirs is a most moving piece of work.

NEWSDAY, 5/7/99, Part II/p. B6, John Anderson

Actor Aidan Quinn and his brothers—Declan, the renowned cinematographer, and Paul, the now writer/director—grew up splitting their time between Ireland and America. So it makes sense that their collaboration, "This Is My Father," would be a movie that has not only dual nationality, but two plotlines and two morals.

And while it probably betrays this particular reviewer's presumptions about Gaelic-American sentiment and the way it's usually portrayed on screen, what's surprising about the Quinn brothers' film is how refreshingly bittersweet, frank and ultimately unvarnished it is. Paul Quinn's direction is tender; Declan's photography thrives (especially in the twilight) and Aidan certainly gives the best performance of his career. It's a movie that resists the easy lure of nostalgia, leaving us with the idea that all times are tough, they're just tough in different ways.

Opening in a depressingly accurate urban America, "This Is My Father" finds Kieran Johnson (James Caan), a high school teacher whose powerful attempts to reach his ice-cold students are completely inconsequential. In the house he shares with a dysfunctional sister, her alienated son, Jack (Jacob Tierney), and his mother, who's completely incapacitated by stroke, he discovers a picture of a man who may be the father he never knew. His mother can't answer his questions. So he takes Jack and they head back to Ireland.

The story may ultimately be Kieran's—or Jack's, for that matter—and Caan is terrific as a man seesawing between wanting to know and not wanting to know. But most of the film is flashback, a romantic tragedy told to Kieran and Jack by their bed-and-breakfast owner, Seamus (Colm Meany) and his Tarot-reading mother (Moira Deady), who apparently doesn't know her son is gay. Seamus' situation is amusing, but it also serves to foreshadow the story Mrs. Kearney tells—over several days, to keep her guests from leaving about prejudice, ignorance, intolerance and the meanness that affects people who can't forgive the world their own disappointments and grief.

It's the story of Kieran O'Day (Aidan Quinn), a "poorhouse bastard" who's been raised by a farming couple and has the bad luck to fall in love with a local girl named Fiona (Moya Farrelly, in a memorable screen debut). Fiona's widowed, alcoholic mother (Gina Moxley) disapproves of the match and, when she learns that intimacy has broken out between Fiona and Kieran, takes her grievance to the police. And the church.

It's a rich, ironic portrait the Quinns paint of 1930s rural Ireland, sparing the viewer the kind of "Quiet Man"-style embellishments that turn one kelly green and charging headlong into the country's conflicted religiosity. Stephen Rea's contribution may be little more than a cameo, but his deliciously sanctimonious Father Quinn—who seems to have walked to the pulpit directly out of James Joyce—is the personification of hypocrisy and the suffocating morality that leads to the movie's ultimate heartbreak.

In the end, what the Quinn brothers have convinced us of is that while Kieran Johnson and his students may have it tough, life has always been a struggle. There were times, for instance, when intolerance wasn't such an evil. And the plumbing was a lot worse, too.

VILLAGE VOICE, 5/11/99, p. 65, Michael Atkinson

Cursed with a title that screams choked-up, 12-step '90s self-obsession, *This Is My Father*'s main claim to attention is its all-in-the-family credits: Aidan Quinn stars, brother Paul Quinn wrote and directed, brother Declan Quinn served as cinematographer, and all three coproduced. If that seems like a selling point to you, it's your kind of movie. A generational saga born of equal parts career-building indie guile and heartfelt tribal bonding, the movie reveals Taviani-like ambition, but the results are lackluster and tame. Full of deep, soft shadows, pasty complexions, stormy skies, peat wagons, and Catholic ordeal, the film seesaws between the present, in which lonely teacher James Caan goes to Ireland (with his snotty nephew Jacob Tierney) to discover who his father was, and 1939, when village nitwit Aidan Quinn and restless rich girl Moya Farrelly fall in love, to widespread consternation.

Aidan Quinn as James Caan's father? The casting isn't as ruinous as you'd expect (Caan is surprisingly gentle, even when he's asked to do what actors should never do: talk to gravestones), but the script resorts to cliché and cheap shots too often to be seriously. It's the kind of movie in which every time somebody spills a drink in the present, they uncover a clue to the past while mopping up. Cameos by Stephen Rea as an irate and perverted priest and Brendan Gleeson as a local cop are merely favors to their *Michael Collins* costars; then as now, Quinn's brogue is decidedly shaky. (An endearing bit by John Cusack as a hyperactive *LIFE* magazine photog landing his plane on the Galway beach is beautifully beside the story's point.) Still, atmospherically shot (Declan photographed *Leaving Las Vegas*) and sober about its inevitable Irish stereotypes, the movie has sincerity to burn, and if you have paternal issues of your own, you may bawl.

Also reviewed in:
CHICAGO TRIBUNE, 6/4/99, Friday/p. A, Mark Caro
NEW YORK TIMES, 5/7/99, p. E13, Janet Maslin
VARIETY, 9/7-13/98, p. 73, Leonard Klady
WASHINGTON POST, 6/11/99, Weekend/p. 41, Michael O'Sullivan

THOMAS CROWN AFFAIR, THE

A Metro-Goldwyn-Mayer release of an Irish Dream Time production. *Executive Producer:* Michael Tadross. *Producer:* Pierce Brosnan and Beau St. Clair. *Director:* John McTiernan. *Screenplay:* Leslie Dixon and Kurt Wimmer. *Story:* Alan R. Trustman. *Director of Photography:* Tom Priestley. *Editor:* John Wright. *Music:* Bill Conti. *Music Editor:* Chris McGeary. *Choreographer:* John Carrafa. *Sound:* Tom Nelson and (music) Dan Wallin. *Sound Editor:* George Watters II. *Casting:* Pat McCorkle. *Production Designer:* Bruno Rubeo. *Art Director:* Dennis Bradford. *Set Decorator:* Leslie Rollins. *Set Dresser:* Joseph DeLuca, Wayne Brackett, Damian J. Costa, Dennis Freeborn, Eric Lewin, and Richard Nelson. *Special Effects:* Conrad F. Brink. *Costumes:* Kate Harrington. *Make-up:* Steven Lawrence. *Make-up (Pierce Brosnan):* Bron Roylance. *Make-up (Rene Russo):* Shane Paish. *Stunt Coordinator:* Frank Ferrara. *Running time:* 114 minutes. *MPAA Rating:* R.

CAST: Pierce Brosnan (Thomas Crown); Rene Russo (Catherine Banning); Denis Leary (Detective Michael McCann); Ben Gazzara (Andrew Wallace); Frankie Faison (Detective Paretti); Fritz Weaver (John Reynolds); Charles Keating (Golchan); Mark Margolis

(Knutzhorn); Faye Dunaway (Psychiatrist); Michael Lombard (Proctor Bobby McKinley); James Saito (Paul Cheng); Esther Cañadas (Anna Knutzhorn); Mischa Hausserman (Crown's Driver); Daniel Oreskes (Petru); Dominic Chianese, Jr. (Dimetri); Ritchie Coster (Janos); Gregg Bello (Iggy); John P. McCann (Senior Detective); Gino Lucci (Freight Truck Driver); George Christy (Senior Museum Guard); Mike Danner (Forklift Operator); James J. Archer (J.J. the Security Guard); John Elsen (New York City Cop); Robert Spillane (Crown Security Officer); Daniel Jamal Gibson (Sam); Cynthia Darlow (Crown's Secretary); Tom Tammi (Businessman); Mark Zeisler and Mark Zimmerman (Bulldogs); Dan Southern and James Yaegashi (Crown Executives); Ira Wheeler (Old Man); David Adkins (Son); John A. MacKay (Company Lawyer); Melissa Maxwell (Teacher); Colleen Hamm (Schoolgirl); Timothy Wheeler (Museum Security Tech); Jeffrey Dreisbach (Junior Proctor); R.J. Remo and Caleb Archer (Smoking Kids); Dennis Creaghan (Lenox); Jeremy Nagel (Crown's Caddie); John C. Havens (Museum Operating Tech); Annie Rose Murray (Woman Spectator); Bill Tatum (Gentleman Yachtsman); Teddy Coluca and Michael Charles (Detectives in Restaurant); Orlando Carafa (Cipriani Waiter); Ben Epps (Male Associate); Kim D. Cannon and Douglas Kahelemauna Nam (Cleaning Men); Richard Russell Ramos (Art Inspector); John Seidman (Lab Technician); Robert Ian MacKenzie (Jeweler); Yusef Bulos (2nd Jeweler); Ray Virta (Detective, Museum); Thomas Michael Sullivan (Museum Special Police); J. Paul Boehmer (Museum Detective); Tony Cucci (Watching Cop); Paul Geoffrey (Another Cop); R.F. Rodgers (Uniform Cop); Thomas Richard Bloom (Crown Impostor); Kim Craven (Ticket Agent); Marion McCorry (Stewardess); Sean Haberle (Ramp Manager); Mikel Sarah Lambert (Wealthy Woman).

CHRISTIAN SCIENCE MONITOR, 8/6/99, p. 15, David Sterritt

James Bond has been absent from the screen this summer, but other movies have capitalized on his popularity. First the boisterous "Austin Powers: The Spy Who Shagged Me" spoofed his manly persona even more mischievously than the first Powers picture did. Then the gimmicky western "Wild Wild West" arrived, based on a vintage TV series that brought Bond's charismatic style to frontier territory.

Neither of those movies can exactly be called a homage, and if Bond really existed he'd be mad about the irreverent treatment his image has been receiving. He'd smile again, though, when he saw "The Thomas Crown Affair", adapted from a 1968 thriller of the same title. Fresh from starring in two actual Bond pictures, Pierce Brosnan gives the title character as much glamour and allure as Agent 007 himself has ever projected. True, he quickly turns out to be the villain, but that's just a detail. He's the one we're supposed to root for, even if we're also rooting for the gorgeous sleuth hot on his trail.

Treading much the same turf as Sean Connery in "Entrapment"' a few months ago, Brosnan plays a charming gentleman who just happens to be an incorrigible art thief. His latest acquisition is an insanely valuable Monet painting, which he's heisted from New York's inimitable Metropolitan Museum of Art cleverly imitated on a Hollywood sound stage, incidentally, since the real museum wouldn't cooperate with a movie that builds entire scenes around bad antitheft systems. It looks as if he's successfully pulled off the job, but then that gorgeous sleuth shows up, figuring out his secrets even as she falls in love with him.

The new "Thomas Crown" is a flighty affair, but it's colorfully acted and tautly directed by John McTiernan, who makes it look almost as handsome as the paintings that decorate the backgrounds. The season isn't likely to bring a better Bondian entertainment.

LOS ANGELES TIMES, 8/6/99, Calendar/p. 1, Kenneth Turan

"The Thomas Crown Affair" plays by the rules. A moderately diverting entertainment as sleek and aerodynamically sound as the glider its characters tool around in, it takes no extraordinary chances and delivers no major surprises. With one exception.

For though Pierce Brosnan, whose production company initiated the idea of remaking the 1968 Steve McQueen-Faye Dunaway caper film with an eye toward his eventual starring role, it's Rene Russo, his opposite number, who makes the most of this chance.

A former model, Russo has been in film for 10 years, holding down highly visible roles opposite some of Hollywood's biggest male stars: Clint Eastwood in "In the Line of Fire," John

Travolta in "Get Shorty," Kevin Costner in "Tin Cup," Dustin Hoffman in "Outbreak" and Mel Gibson in two episodes of "Lethal Weapon."

Yet it's a mark of how little space is left for women in male-dominated studio films that despite all that screen time, Russo's decade of sidekick-cupcake roles has never before given her the opportunity to create the kind of believable, engaging genre character she comes up with here.

Russo plays Catherine Banning, a smart, been-there insurance investigator for a major Swiss firm retained to look into the theft of a $100-million Monet from an unnamed New York museum that is a dead-ringer for the Metropolitan but, a prominent on-screen disclaimer insists, is a completely fictitious place.

"This is an elegant crime done by an elegant person," Banning announces to the disgust of salt-of-the-earth New York police detective Michael McCann (Denis Leary), whose role consists exclusively of being exasperated whenever Banning says or does anything he wouldn't have himself.

Banning's candidate is in fact the man we have seen commit the super-elaborate heist in the film's meticulous opening sequence, smoothly directed by John McTiernan of "Die Hard" and "The Hunt for Red October." That would be Thomas Crown (Brosnan), a completely suave individual in hand-tailored suits who wagers $100,000 on a golf shot with the kind of aplomb James Bond uses to order the perfect martini.

But, despite all his wealth, Crown is no hero to his psychiatrist (Dunaway redux, in an uncertain cameo). She knows that he has issues with trust, that he may be successful but that he's also a self-involved loner who has never met a woman he considers worthy of his regard. Which is why he is so tickled when he meets Banning, who tells him her suspicions straight away and boasts of always getting her man. Will she get him?, he wonders. "Oh, I hope so," Banning all but purrs.

The opportunity for playful cat-and-mouse sparring is the reason "Thomas Crown" was worth the trouble of remaking. In fact, in an unusual maneuver, two writers with different skills were hired to do the script, with Kurt Wimmer writing the crisp heist sequences and Leslie Dixon doing the dicier but acceptable romantic dialogue.

Once Banning and the gentleman thief set their sights on each other, part of "Thomas Crown" turns into a tepid "Lives of the Rich and Famous" travelogue, as the pair go glamorously hang-gliding and jet off to his charming island hideaway in Martinique.

More diverting is the psychological duel between these two game players, both powerfully allergic to being played for fools and uncertain if they can be both true to their unbending personal codes of behavior and still trust another person enough to let them into their lives.

In this battle there's no doubt that Russo, with a different hairdo that accentuates the angles of her face, invests her character with the most involving weapons. Her Catherine Banning, handsomely costumed by Kate Harrington, has a feisty self-confidence that's capable of morphing into fury and flummoxing all the men in the immediate vicinity. It's a star turn—complete with a sassy dance in a much-publicized Halston dress and even more publicized nude scene—that's especially welcome because it comes from an actress who has not obviously been a star.

One of the things that keeps "The Thomas Crown Affair" from taking full advantage of that performance is that Brosnan plays Crown like a human ice cube: cold, brittle and slippery. This character makes Brosnan's James Bond performances cuddly by comparison, and even McQueen, who was not the warmest actor going, registered as more of a recognizable human being.

Ignoring these limitations whenever he can, which is not always, McTiernan does a professional job of direction and delivers a civilized production that entertains well enough. And if this film's ending is less willing to be ambiguous than the original, that's just one more sign of the unadventurous movie times we live in. As if we really needed one.

NEW YORK, 8/16/99, p. 55, Peter Rainer

At a time when nerdy twentysomethings are cashing in their Website stock options for millions, it seems almost touchingly sentimental to make a movie about a gentleman-thief billionaire. *The Thomas Crown Affair*—an updated remake of the 1968 Steve McQueen-Faye Dunaway film, starring Pierce Brosnan and Rene Russo—is about the élan that extreme wealth can confer; it's also an implicit rebuke to the technogeeks who seem poised to become the new aristocracy. The faintly antique appeal of *The Thomas Crown Affair* works to its advantage; although contemporary, it tries to recapture the sort of show-offy rich-and-beautiful fantasies that flourished in the Depression thirties and again in the movies of the sixties but now have fallen out of favor. It's a fairly entertaining nostalgia trip for the decadently shallow in all of us.

Brosnan's Thomas Crown resides in a Manhattan townhouse that looks like an extension of the Frick Collection. He sails catamarans and has a hide-away with a fully stocked wardrobe in Martinique. He's as sleek and beveled as one of his own expensive art *objets*. When Steve McQueen played this role, he projected the cool insolence that was his trademark. His Crown was a Boston Brahmin, but an up-from-the-streets glint sparked his blue eyes; there was in his character a slight disconnect between form and function. With Brosnan, there's no disconnect at all, which makes him a more unified fantasy figure but also a less startling one. Skillful as he is, Brosnan exemplifies the pitfalls of "perfect" casting. His Thomas Crown, like his James Bond, is so full of finesse that he never seems truly imperiled; the hurts rained down upon him are no more damaging than they might be to an android.

Perhaps this is part of the fantasy, too—that extreme wealth can insulate you from the grubbiness of life and turn you into a connoisseur of pleasure without the complications that pleasure can bring. The film is punctuated by Crown's sessions with his psychiatrist—played, with a knowing smirk, by Faye Dunaway—but the conceit doesn't click; we can't imagine this man ever believing he'd need her services. Crown seems to be entirely without a psyche, so what is there to dredge out of him? He's all surface calculation, all gambit. When this tycoon meets his match in Rene Russo's insurance investigator Catherine Banning, the cat-and-mouse romance comes across as a species of self-love.

Catherine is brought into the proceedings after a daring museum heist of a priceless Monet. (The original film involved a bank heist—a more mundane enterprise.) To the hard-bitten detective assigned to the case (Denis Leary), she volunteers the insight that the theft is an elegant crime committed by an elegant man. Right from the start, she suspects Crown, and tells him so, point-blank. Crown operates on the principle that anything in life is obtainable; Catherine, even though she is on to him—or, more precisely, *because* she is on to him—becomes his prize catch. He's charmed by her connivances and brass, and he has the same effect on her.

It's part of the film's macho whimsy that Crown falls in love with Catherine without ever really being played for a sucker. He anticipates her moves, including her romantic moves. "I hate being a foregone conclusion," she tells him, but clearly she also likes it—she likes being taken seriously enough to be outmaneuvered. Having fashioned a woman with the wiles and the glamour to play in the high-stakes men's league, director John McTiernan and screenwriters Leslie Dixon and Kurt Wimmer never quite follow through. Catherine's expertise and cunning, unlike Crown's, can be tempered by love.

And so it ever was in these reactionary reveries. "Womanliness" will out. At least Crown isn't paired with a glamour-puss half his age—the standard approach these days. (In *Entrapment*, basically a knockoff of *The Thomas Crown Affair*, Catherine Zeta-Jones was matched with Sean Connery, and the age disparity was so pronounced the filmmakers took the unusual step of actually noticing it.) The fact that Crown doesn't dally with chickies is one more touch of class: he appreciates a good vintage in all things. And Rene Russo makes his preference credible. She's often cast opposite superstars without quite getting her own chance to shine. Even when she's doing comedy, as in *Tin Cup*, her square-cut high-fashion features can seem forbiddingly glossy. Here, however, her glamour is part of her equipment; and when it frazzles and falls away, she seems like a real person for perhaps the first time onscreen.

I mentioned before that the retro-ness of *The Thomas Crown Affair* has its antiquated appeal. But it's still a stopgap entertainment. We can bask, guiltily, greedily, in the luxe lifestyles on display, but the more interesting issue posed by the film is, what will the rich-and-famous fantasies of the new generation look like? The kids cashing in now may inspire movie romances equally frivolous, but my guess is they won't make such a fetish of swank stylishness.

NEW YORK POST, 8/6/99, p. 42, Rod Dreher

There's a word to describe Rene Russo in "The Thomas Crown Affair," and that word is hummmina! She's an absolute knockout in this stylish, adult pleasure, a slick caper jazzed to the hilt with sex, romance and swanky locales both on and off Manhattan island.

This superior John McTiernan remake of the 1968 Steve McQueen-Faye Dunaway promises nothing more than a high-gloss good time—and for the most part, it delivers.

Pierce Brosnan plays the title character, a suave, debonair sort who runs an extremely successful acquisitions company. Crown is a loner who has trouble trusting women, or so he confides to his shrink (Faye Dunaway, in McTiernan's nod to the original). For fun he goes to the Metropolitan Museum of Art to visit a $100 million Monet—which he steals in an elaborately planned operation.

Russo plays Catherine Banning, an insurance investigator who jets in from Europe to assist a police detective (Denis Leary) in tracking down the thief. She's a smartie and intuits that Crown is the likely culprit. The two play a cat-and-mouse game with each other, which leads to a steamy a deux and deepening romantic involvement.

Catherine intrigues Crown because he knows he has finally met his match. She, sly and worldly and deliciously sophisticated, returns the favor. They circle each other like wary lions, their terrifically tense erotic standoff taking them from the glam restaurants of Manhattan to an exotic love nest on a Caribbean mountaintop.

She's on to him, and he knows it, and that makes her desirable. But can Crown trust Catherine to give up her duty to the law and her employer and join him on the lam? And can Catherine stake her entire career on the promises of a cagey thief who has a suspicious relationship with a beautiful young blonde (model Esther Canadas)?

The film is emotionally lopsided, however, and that's no minor weakness. Russo is doing all the acting, all the emoting, and is the only one who seems to have anything at risk. Brosnan looks smashingly good, but he's also pretty wooden, a champagne-and-caviar Keanu for Upper East Side ladies.

So what? "The Thomas Crown Affair" has so much else going for it, like McTiernan's expert direction, particularly in a fabulous closing sequence at the Met, cleverly set to a Nina Simone torch song, and an electrifyingly sexy tango Russo and Brosnan perform at a charity ball. Russo is 45, but she's a jaw-dropper here, and in every other scene.

Watching the bombshell move from triumph to triumph in "The Thomas Crown Affair," you're reminded of how rare it is that women of her age are cast as romantic leads.

This summer, a no-budget fright flick has forced Hollywood to rethink its approach to horror movies. You have to hope that Russo's smart, scorching work here—really, she could devour the current herd of busty, young and interchangeable actresses on toast—will force the industry to reconsider its foolish disregard of middle-age actresses.

NEWSDAY, 8/6/99, Part II/p. B3, John Anderson

It's fun to watch two sexy people defy every scruple to make whoopee.

It's fun watching major institutions and inviolable authority besmeared and besmirched.

It's fun watching ruthless Wall Street bigwigs humiliate each other—like watching mafiosi gun down other mafiosi. Most of all, it's fun to watch money.

And there's plenty of it in "The Thomas Crown Affair," an inconsequential remake of an inconsequential movie (Norman Jewison's, starring Steve McQueen and Faye Dunaway circa 1968) but a money movie nonetheless. It's an indulgence, a froth, a cheap bauble caught in a particularly flattering light and age (the '90s, when every day-trader thinks he should be living like the opulent Thomas Crown). And although any reference to the eroticized chess game that defined the original film will be found only in this summer's edition of "Austin Powers," there's enough style and sex delivered via Pierce Brosnan and Rene Russo that the rampant illogic of the story shouldn't be much of an obstacle to total immersion.

John McTiernan, maker of the better "Die Hard" movies—and who directed a young Brosnan in the dread "Nomads" (1986)—knows how to move fluidly through difficult spaces, how to digress with style and even how to tell a story.

Thomas Crown (Brosnan), when not demolishing rival businessmen with ingeniously self-inflating deals, or racing (and scuttling) his $100,000 catamaran, or making enormous golf bets he can't win, wiles away his free time at the Metropolitan Museum of Art. There, he spends hours (well, minutes anyway) studying a certain Van Gogh. Which is all part of the plot: When his hired gang of (yes!) "Eastern European" stooges sneak into the Met—via an antique, dare we say Trojan, horse—they get caught mid-robbery. And Crown smoothly makes off with a Monet.

Why? Because it's his hobby. Money may be enough for us, but not for him. Like the thuggish henchmen, however, theft is just a red herring—what Hitchcock would call the movie's McGuffin. What "Thomas Crown" is really about is the romance that erupts between the seemingly unflappable Crown and Catherine Banning (Russo), a brilliant (naturally), beautiful (naturally) insurance investigator (not so naturally: The Met uses private investigators?) who, for lack of a better word, flaps him.

Russo is the soul of the movie, not just because she looks great, or because, in defiance of every Hollywood tradition, the 40-plus actress is playing opposite a man her own age. It's because the crisis is all hers. Brosnan wears suits better than anyone in the world, and his Crown is delightfully infallible in the execution of his various schemes. He also has unbounded gall: When the Monet disappears, he offers the Met a Pissarro from his own collection to fill its space on the gallery wall. (The Met, by the way, whose policy is to discuss security NOT AT ALL, had nothing to do with this movie, which is understandable, since it makes the museum look ridiculous. But McTiernan and Co. do an admirable job of replicating its interiors.) Catherine, who is not above using her wiles to get what she wants, doesn't know what she wants. The painting? Or Thomas? Victory? Or love? Vindication over the smug New York detectives, who include Michael McCann (Denis Leary), and who disapprove of her methods? Or an all-expense-paid life in the Caribbean? Things, as they say, are tough all over. But at least the moral issues of the film aren't completely written off.

There's a generous amount of heat generated by Brosnan and Russo; the dance that leads to their upstairs-downstairs sex scene is particularly smoky, mostly thanks to Russo, who moves through the movie as warmly tousled as Brosnan is wrinkle-free. There may be more holes in the plot than in Albert Hall and more than enough upscale product placements to fill two movies (including a plug by a certain jewelry company linking itself to an AIDS benefit, which seems particularly shameless). But if the point of "Thomas Crown" is vicarious affluence and vicarious sex, it more than fulfills its promise. And probably its potential.

NEWSWEEK, 8/9/99, p. 69, David Ansen

The heist that set the original 1968 "The Thomas Crown Affair" in motion was a $3 million robbery of a Boston bank masterminded by Brahmin millionaire Steve McQueen. How quaint that amount now seems. The new Thomas Crown (Pierce Brosnan) is a self-made billionaire who oversees the elaborate theft of a Monet worth $100 million from New York's Metropolitan Museum of Art. A man who has never let anyone get close to him, a man so decadent he can afford to wreck a catamaran just for the thrill of it, Crown finally meets his match in the savvy, chic insurance investigator Catherine Banning (Rene Russo), who instantly suspects him. He knows she knows he's the culprit, and she knows he intends to seduce her. What neither of these cutthroat charmers expects is to fall in love.

The tale was, and is, a gold-plated fantasy of conspicuous consumption, and the only way to play it is to revel shamelessly in the erotica of luxury. Which is precisely what director John McTiernan does in his slick, gaudily suave guilty pleasure of a movie, which is filled to the brim with private planes, Caribbean retreats, overdone hairdos and marathon couplings on marble stairways that would leave ordinary mortals black and blue. The emphasis has been changed from larceny to love, and the overt sexuality turned up a notch. Russo has to shed a lot more clothing than Faye Dunaway did; given some of the odd outfits she's got to wear, this was probably a relief. But it's nice to see a Hollywood movie that appreciates a mature female body for a change. And nice to see that "The Thomas Crown Affair" has survived its glossy, glam makeover so well.

SIGHT AND SOUND, 9/99, p. 58, Kim Newman

New York. Billionaire Thomas Crown orchestrates an assault on a museum, with a team of Romanian criminals botching an attempt on an entire roomful of impressionists as a feint so he can personally snatch a painting by Monet worth $100 million. Detective Michael McCann is teamed with insurance investigator Catherine Banning, who soon pegs Crown as the thief. Crown loans a Pisarro from his own collection to replace the stolen painting. Catherine lets Crown know she's on to him, but still joins him for a date, Catherine copies Crown's keys and later invades his home to steal back the Monet, only to find a forgery.

Crown and Catherine become lovers and take a trip to his tropical-island retreat, but neither is able to get over a suspicion that the other is interested only in deception: Crown to get away with his crime, Catherine to catch him for her reward money. Back in New York, Catherine and McCann concentrate on tracking the forger, having realised the copy must have been made from the original. Crown is preparing to liquidate his holdings and run, and asks Catherine to come with him. Suspecting him of secretly seeing a girl named Anna, Catherine refuses, and Crown offers to prove himself by putting the Monet back. McCann reveals Anna is not Crown's mistress but his forger, and Catherine unhappily goes along with a police scheme to trap Crown at the museum. Crown's Pisarro is actually the Monet, with a watercolour fake over it, and his return to the museum is designed to set off the sprinkler system and reveal the truth. The couple are reunited in the first-class cabin of a plane to Europe.

Until the 60s, Hollywood remakes were always excused as upgrades: a given property hadn't yet been done as a talkie, in Technicolor, in 3-D or with uncensored sex and violence. However, the original of *The Thomas Crown Affair* was made (by Norman Jewison, with Steve McQueen and Faye Dunaway) in 1968 and would seem, like the recently remade *Point Blank,* more suitable for a rerelease than a remake. Since the original screenplay by Alan R. Trustman was always a trifle, Jewison's movie is remembered mainly for cinematographer Haskell Wexler's co-opting of French *deuxième vague* flash into mainstream cinema. It also caught something of the moment with its blankly beautiful but neurotic leads, its modish deployment of split screen, soft focus and a dozen other bits of trickery long thought old hat even in hairspray commercials, and the catchily meaningless easy listening of Noel Harrison's one big hit, "The Windmills of Your Mind".

John McTiernan's version replaces the style of the original, which invested every scene with bogus sophistication through cinematic techniques, with simply photographed but heavily price-tagged things. In a tiny but symptomatic snippet a party of schoolchildren stand at the soon to-be-stolen Monet, bored by their teacher's drone about its importance in art history. Suddenly they're excited when she tells them how much it's worth.

The whole film is a lot like that. McTiernan stands admiringly before a series of luxury items. The museum's collection of old masters, Rene Russo's amazing wardrobe (many shots start at her smart shoes and work their way up to her fetchingly distressed hairstyle), Crown's Martinique lair and his Manhattan house, jewels by BVLGARI, archetypal supermodel Esther Cañadas, (so sexlessly beautiful that she gets laughs), hobby objects like a yacht ("a $100,000 yacht," we're told) and a glider, and a queue-free first-class airport check-in where the girl at the desk is sympathetic to an obviously breaking heart. All this high life gets so thick, the script has to tell us both Crown and Catherine come from poor families to prevent us from hating them.

In lieu of depth, we have Brosnan whose best work to date has been in self-mocking mode in *Mars Attachs!*—pouring out his shallow heart to his psychiatrist, played by original star Dunaway. Meanwhile Russo manages a kind of haggard loveliness all too rare in a screen era when only teenagers are allowed to be glamorous. It's hard, noting that the handsome, wealthy, unmarried Crown (Brosnan, born 1951, is playing a 42-year-old) loves shopping for clothes and lives with a Chinese boy assistant, not to suspect that the real reason Catherine shouldn't get together with him is that he's a barely-closeted gay (he even offers to cook).

The plot performs an elaborate shuffle around its crime, with Crown pulling off the heist only to put his booty back immediately, allowing McCann indulgently to let him get away with it since no real people have been hurt. (Denis Leary has a funny speech about the real criminals he has put away that week.) This conveniently overlooks the fact that Crown's scheme depends on sacrificing a bunch of Romanian pawns (mostly ugly baldie foreigners, so who cares?) who are left rotting in jail—ratted out by their own boss, who picks them out of a line-up—while Crown and Catherine jet off to a luxurious exile. In 1968, it was an exhilarating surprise that a film like *The Thomas Crown Affair* could end with a good-looking, non-violent criminal getting away with the loot; in 1999, such finishes are so accepted that it would be refreshing to see one of those ironic last-minute contrivances that undid the perfect plans in *The Killing* (1956) or *The Lavender Hill Mob* (1951), and close with the well-groomed cracksman going up the river for a long stretch.

VILLAGE VOICE, 8/10/99, p. 70, Michael Atkinson

There is, relatively, precious little at stake in *The Thomas Crown Affair*, a sealskin-slick, cat-and-mouse romance-caper trifle with a hard-on for wealth that feels downright Trumpian. The groovy 1968 Steve McQueen-Faye Dunaway original is notable only for its tedium, and if John McTiernan's new run-through provokes fewer occasions to examine the theater ceiling, credit Rene Russo, who at a saucy, frequently nude 45 (she often looks it, and looks mahvelous) becomes something like a Mary Baker Eddy for aging movie divas. She's a high-living, know-everything insurance dick simultaneously investigating and being seduced by the suave playboy-thief (Pierce Brosnan, who's wooden, but nice wood, like teak), and whenever the cutesy story or the litany of billionaire toys and pads threaten to knock you out, Russo smiles, disrobes, and laughs like a mule. As Chubsy Ubsy of *Our Gang* used to say, What ho! Bring on the dancing girls!

Also reviewed in:
CHICAGO TRIBUNE, 8/6/99, Friday/p. A, Michael Wilmington
NEW YORK TIMES, 8/6/99, p. E1, Janet Maslin
NEW YORKER, 8/9/99, p. 80, David Denby
VARIETY, 7/26-8/1/99, p. 34, Todd McCarthy
WASHINGTON POST, 8/6/99, p. C1, Stephen Hunter
WASHINGTON POST, 8/6/99, Weekend/p. 41, Desson Howe

THOSE WHO LOVE ME CAN TAKE THE TRAIN

A Kino International release of a Téléma/Le Studio Canal+/France 2 Cinéma/France 3 Cinéma/Azor Films production. *Executive Producer:* Jacques Hinstin. *Producer:* Charles Gassot. *Director:* Patrice Chéreau. *Screenplay (French with English subtitles):* Danièle Thompson, Patrice Chéreau, and Pierre Trividic. *Based on an idea by:* Danièle Thompson. *Director of Photography:* Éric Gautier. *Editor:* François Gédigier. *Music:* Eric Neveux, Charles Henri de Pierrefeu, Valérie Albert, Amélie de Chassey, and Anne-Marie Durox. *Sound:* Guillaume Sciama and Jean-Pierre LaForce. *Sound Editor:* Nadine Muse. *Casting:* Margot Capelier and Pascale Béraud. *Art Director:* Richard Peduzzi and Sylvain Chauvelot. *Set Decorator:* Dominique Castan, Raph Salis, Victor Leitão, Eric Chemel, Joël Lavrut, Gilles Viaud, Emmanuel Lavrut, Gilles Tissot, Vincent Grand d'Esnon, and Sylvie Espinasse. *Costumes:* Caroline de Vivaise. *Make-up:* Kuno Schlegelmilch, Evelyne Byot, Franck Berteau, Magali Ceyrat, Mario Messere, Florence Vayssieres, and Turid Follvick. *Running time:* 122 minutes. *MPAA Rating:* Not Rated.

CAST: Pascal Greggory (François); Valéria Bruni-Tedeschi (Claire); Charles Berling (Jean-Marie); Jean-Louis Trintignant (Lucien/Jean-Baptiste Emmerich); Bruno Todeschini (Louis); Sylvain Jacques (Bruno); Vincent Perez (Viviane); Roschdy Zem (Thierry); Dominique Blanc (Catherine); Delphine Schiltz (Elodie); Nathan Cogan (Sami); Marie Daëms (Lucie); Chantal Neuwirth (Genevieve); Thierry de Peretti (Dominique); Olivier Gourmet (Bernard); Geneviève Brunet (Marie-Rose); Didier Brice (Cédric); Guillaume Canet (Hitchhiker).

LOS ANGELES TIMES, 8/27/99, Calendar/p. 6, Kevin Thomas

When screenwriter Daniele Thompson was visiting the dying François Reichenbach, the documentary filmmaker suddenly announced, "By the way, I want to be buried in Limoges." When Thompson, trying for a light touch, joked, "No, not Limoges, it's a long way, who wants to go to Limoges?," Reichenbach's reply in turn provided the inspiration and the title of Patrice

Chereau's quixotic and beguiling "Those Who Love Me Can Take the Train," which he wrote with Thompson and Pierre Trividic.

In the film, Reichenbach's wonderful line is spoken on the soundtrack by a celebrated dying painter and teacher, Jean-Baptiste Emmerich (Jean-Louis Trintignant), a 70ish gay man as charismatic as he is manipulative. Although he officially succumbs to heart failure he reportedly also had grown bored with life, tired of painting and of playing games with his friends. But he can't resist making his large, complex and diverse retinue jump through one final hoop by requiring them to travel from Paris to Limoges, where his twin brother, Lucien (also Trintignant), years before reluctantly assumed the responsibility of running the family shoe-manufacturing business and stayed on in the gloomy grandeur of an ancestral estate.

Jean-Baptiste would seem to have always had his way with any man he wanted while turning women into devoted acolytes. It's a motley crew, to say the least, that has gathered at a Paris train station to head for Limoges, a journey of several hours.

Two sets of key figures emerge. There's Jean-Baptiste's nephew Jean-Marie (Charles Berling), long estranged from his widowed father, Lucien, and in a disintegrating marriage with Claire (Valeria Bruni-Tedeschi). Meanwhile, François (Pascal Greggory) is a trim, sensitive man of perhaps 50 who may have been the lover who cared the most for Jean-Baptiste. He is himself in a faltering relationship with Louis (Bruno Todeschini), a dark, intense man who looks to be in his late 30s and who at last encounters a moody young man, Bruno (Sylvain Jacques), who first caught his eye three years earlier. What he doesn't know is that Bruno is along for the ride because he seemingly was a lover of both the dead artist—and François. In an instant there's a shifting emotional triangle between the three men that is as volatile as Jean-Marie and Claire's marriage.

"Those Who Love Me" is a marvel of solid construction, with brisk movement and shrewd, witty observation of human strengths and weaknesses, its skittish moods buoyed by an inspired selection of mainly pop songs, including even James Brown's version of "My Way." Aboard the train there are plenty of fireworks, but the funeral, the actual lowering of Jean-Baptiste's body into the ground, with some 20 people taking turns in covering his coffin with shovelfuls of dirt, has a sobering effect on the mourners.

More displays of angst occur at the wake at the Emmerich chateau, but a lighter tone gradually emerges. At last Jean-Baptiste's friends, lovers and relatives are free of his compelling thrall; conceivably, he wanted them to gather one last time to experience a feeling of collective liberation from him.

In this final section two more key figures emerge; Lucien, who is not without his own charm but who has in effect lost his wife, son and in a sense his life to his more dazzling brother; and Viviane, one of Jean-Baptiste's legion of lovers, who was once Frederic but is now a pre-op transsexual, played with warmth and gallantry by Vincent Perez, one of the French cinema's top romantic stars. There's a moment of flirtation between Lucien and Viviane that is funny and touching; they may be the two wisest people in the film.

Chereau's splendid ensemble cast includes Marie Daems as the ebullient Lucie, whose claim to fame is that she had an affair, most likely at her instigation, with Jean-Baptiste in Madrid in 1952. She proclaims, in a burst of proud, deluded self-importance, that for the artist "I was woman!"

Chereau has admitted that while drawing upon Reichenbach's remark and his penchant for complicated, partitioned-off friendships, that for the character of Jean-Baptiste, barely glimpsed but whose presence is always felt, he drew inspiration from his own father. Yet he has also said that he sees himself "everywhere" in his film. In the end, "Those Who Love Me Can Take the Train" is in the grand French tradition of depicting the eternal human comedy with a compassion balanced by a wry, unsentimental detachment.

NEW YORK POST, 8/4/99, p. 45, Jonathan Foreman

Imagine a very French knockoff of "The Big Chill"—replete with a ridiculous and intrusive rock score—and you've got something very like this sprawling, aggravating but intelligent film by the talented director of "Queen Margot."

It begins with a confused opening sequence as a group of arty Parisians boards a train for Limoges and the funeral of a minor artist named Jean-Baptiste. It's all but impossible to tell who is who and how they are related to each other or the dead artist.

But if you can put up with the Gallic self-indulgence of it all for nearly an hour, you get the reward of an intriguing second act and a gripping third act. By the end you're completely hooked and desperate to know how—or if—it's all going to be resolved.

By the time all of the late man's lovers, students and relatives leave the funeral for the Jean-Baptiste's brother's mansion, the film has turned into a kind of serious soap opera, but one that displays an emotional sophistication all too rare in American film.

This is especially true in its intelligent, mature depiction of homosexual relationships. While many of the main characters are gay, it's not a "gay movie"—it's a movie about different kinds of conjugal and filial love.

You encounter a surfeit of characters. There's bitter bald guy François (Pascal Greggory), who plays a tape of an interview with the deceased. He's just split up with his boyfriend, Bruno (Sylvan Jacques), who's also on the train.

They're still in love, but the boyfriend is transfixed by young Louis (Bruno Todeschini), who looks like a glam-rock star and who seems to have been everybody's lover except his. There's also married couple Jean-Marie (Charles Berling) and Valeria (Valeria Bruni-Tedeschi), who've split up because one of them is a junkie. They also keep yelling at each other.

All the mourners (and there are many more) argue constantly and viciously about who was closer to the great man, and whether he was worthy of so much love and attention. Most of them are difficult, grating people, and they're all lit so as to give them an unhealthy blue pallor. The fact that you care about them more and more as the film trundles along feels like a kind of miracle.

It certainly isn't because of the camera work. Some of the photography on the train—shot in hand-held cinemascope—is bravura stuff. But for the most part, the way the camera rushes in one direction and suddenly reverses is dizzying and disorienting.

What makes "Those Who Love Me Can Take the Train" so beguiling by the end are the universally superb performances by Chereau's cast. Trintignant is wonderful as always (as Jean-Baptiste and his brother Lucien). But Vincent Perez (as the transsexual Viviane) and Valeria Bruni-Tedeschi are just extraordinary.

NEWSDAY, 8/4/99, Part II/p. B9, John Anderson

"Everybody picks a family. The family Jean-Baptiste picked is us." "Us"—the collection of interwoven sex drives, love lives and psychic disturbances that populate "Those Who Love Me Can Take the Train"—are the funeral-bound mourners of artist Jean-Baptiste (the epic Jean-Louis Trintignant). In a final gesture of perversity, he has demanded that he be buried in Limoges, not Paris. Which means his friends and acolytes have to travel. Together. For miles. Considering the emotional tyranny Jean-Baptiste liked to exercise, he knew what he was doing.

And so does Patrice Chereau, the 54-year-old director ("Queen Margot") whose latest film rolls out in near-symphonic style around its motley collection of characters, their homo-hetero entanglements and their various stages of grief.

Chaos grips the cars they ride—handheld camera work on a moving train is an apt reflection of emotional upheaval—but when Chereau suddenly cuts to the studio of Jean-Baptiste, regal in its silence and rightness, you get the point in spades: that only the artist could give meaning to these lives, which are unraveling like a ball of black crepe bouncing along the tracks.

Chereau, far less cool within his work than a lot of younger French filmmakers, is prone to the dramatic gesture, as well as the big shot. The transition to Jean-Baptiste's studio is subtle compared with the message that life is a train trip or that the artist personifies meaning. But when we reach the cemetery, its epic perspectives (think the burning of Atlanta in "Gone With the Wind") are risky, obvious, but irresistible. As is the sudden appearance of Trintignant—playing Jean-Baptiste's twin, Lucien—or Lucien's quite natural interaction with the transsexual Viviane (Vincent Perez) or the final, sweeping aerial shots that put everything in focus, remanding the oh-so-theatrical breakdown of Jean-Baptiste's clique to the dustbin of history. It's an ominous finale. And an intelligently, seductively structured film.

SIGHT AND SOUND, 9/00, p. 55, Chris Darke

At a Paris railway station, the friends and family of Jean-Baptiste Emmerich, a recently deceased painter, gather to travel to Limoges for his funeral. Among them are François, who listens to taped conversations with the painter recorded at the end of his life, Jean-Marie and Claire, a couple in the throes of divorce, Lucie, a former lover of Emmerich, and Louis, a close friend of François, who's fallen in love with Bruno, a young man who's HIV+. As they head towards Limoges, the mourners watch aghast as the car carrying Jean-Baptiste's coffin is driven recklessly alongside the train by their friend Thierry. During a short break on the journey Claire, an ex-drug addict who's discovered she's pregnant, argues violently with Jean-Marie.

At the Limoges cemetery Jean-Marie meets his father, Lucien, who is Jean-Baptiste's twin brother. Thierry arrives and sneaks off with Jean-Marie to take drugs together. At the graveside, Jean-Marie launches into a vicious tirade against families and declares he will never become a father. Claire is disgusted. The wake takes place at Lucien's family home where the atmosphere soon degenerates into arguments over who was closest to Jean-Baptiste. Claire discovers that a young woman at the wake, Viviane, is in fact Jean-Baptiste's son, Frédéric, who's had a sex change. Later that night, Thierry and Jean-Marie have an argument that ends in violence. The following morning, the mourners leave: François on his own, Claire and Jean-Marie reunited and Louis and Bruno having decided to forge ahead in a relationship.

While being firmly rooted in the present day, Patrice Chéreau's *Those Who Love Me Can Take the Train* shares the intimate focus and ensemble dynamics of the director's 1994 ballet of bloodletting *La Reine Margo*. Following an ill-matched group of mourners, travelling from Paris to Limoges for the funeral of a painter, Jean-Baptiste Emmerich, Chéreau breaks his film down into three distinct parts: the journey, the funeral and the wake, which is presided over by Jean-Baptiste's brother Lucien (played by Jean-Louis Trintignant). But where *Margot* set in the poisonous, back-stabbing atmosphere of Charles IX's court, was about blue blood gone bad, *Those Who Love Me* is more prosaic, concentrating on the sundered relationships around the Emmerich family and the competing claims of friends and kin over the memory of the dead painter. This may suggest Chéreau is mining a similar family plot to the ones recently excavated by André Téchiné in *Alice et Martin* and Olivier Assayas in *Late August, Early September,* where domestic drama is played out around the death of a loved one. But Chéreau's excursion into this familiar territory has extraordinary vigour about it, so much so that the first third of the film threatens to overwhelm what follows by being almost excessively vivid.

The journey to Limoges is a triumph both of exposition and choreography. Aided by co-screenwriters Danièle Thompson and Pierre Trividic, Chéreau manages to distinguish the individuals within the crowd of mourners that pile onto the train. But he does so through cinematic means that push at the borders of incoherence. Director of photography Éric Gautier's use of handheld 'Scope cinematography gives the feeling of both buffeting movement and swooping detail. The sense of intense physicality, of bodies in antagonistic proximity, conveyed in the extended sequences on the train brings to mind *La Reine Margot*. But Chéreau really ups the formal ante through his use of sound. Jean-Baptiste's voiceover, reminiscences recorded by his friend François, overlap with the loaded dialogue of the cortége and an insistent, almost pointedly illustrative use of music. At one point, a group of the train-bound mourners watch as Thierry, who's transporting Jean-Baptiste's coffin by road, guns his car to keep up with the speeding train. The welling guitar introduction to Jeff Buckley's "Last Goodbye" works with the camera as it closes on Thierry's vehicle and drives home a sense of headlong recklessness that counterpoints the song's mellow lyrics. These gusts of music carry like fumes from the smoker's carriage and thicken the film's emotional textures; at any moment it feels like the whole journey might spiral off into hysterical anarchy.

In the subsequent funeral and wake sequences the cast get a chance to steal the film back from their director's hyperactive choreography. And it's some cast: Charles Berling is Jean-Marie, the overwrought, feckless and tempestuous son of Lucien Emmerich; Valéria Bruni-Tedeschi as Claire, his ex-addict wife who's carrying his child, exudes desperation and resolve in equal measure (Bruni-Tedeschi, with her Anna Magnani-like mournful sensuality, was born to play Joan of Arc); Vincent Perez is affecting in drag as Jean-Baptiste's sex-change son; and Trintignant presides over family breakdown with sorrowful, seedy stoicism. Chéreau was recently in

London, shooting the film version of Hanif Kureishi's *Intimacy*. It's worth waiting to see if he's able to bring the operatic-kinetic tendencies visible in *Those Who Love Me Can Take the Train* and *La Reine Margot* to his adaptation of Kureishi's aptly named novel.

VILLAGE VOICE, 8/10/99, p. 68, Amy Taubin

Patrice Chéreau's *Those Who Love Me Can Take the Train* is a rarity—a near perfect match of feeling and form wedded by an intellect that's both caustic and compassionate. Chéreau, one of the great theater and opera directors of our time, relishes the aspects of film that distinguish it from the stage—the close-up, the moving camera, and the cut. He deploys them not only to heighten what's happening in the narrative, but for the excitement they generate in the abstract. *Those Who Love Me* has a superabundance of plot, characters, and relationships, but even when you lose track of who's done what to whom, you can feel the film the way you feel a piece of music. It's a roller-coaster ride for cinephiles with a taste for grand opera.

About a dozen lovers, friends, and students of a famous artist travel from Paris to his hometown of Limoges for his funeral. Limoges, a bastion of bourgeois complacency, boasts the largest cemetery in Europe; the 185,000 dead exceed the live population of the town by 40,000. What better setting for a film that's about how mortality conditions desire? But *Those Who Love Me* is not a Kane-like portrait of a dead man; it focuses on the mourners, thrown into crisis by the loss of a father figure who seems to have held them in thrall by making them compete for his affection.

The desire released by the death of this mythic figure is mostly male and homoerotic. Chéreau has made a gay, contemporary *Rules of the Game* (although you wouldn't know that from the poster, which shows what seems to be two women in a hot embrace, but in fact portrays a woman and a transvestite having a heart-to-heart talk). The film's governing conscience is François (Pascal Greggory), who may have loved the dead man more than did anyone else but who also has a steady boyfriend, Louis (Bruno Todeschini), and a secret lover, Bruno (Sylvain Jacques), an exquisite, fragile boy who hangs out in railroad stations picking up tricks. Louis and Bruno are seized by an attack of love at first sight in the lavatory of the train on the way to the funeral. Louis confesses to François that he's in love with another, and François retaliates by telling him that Bruno was his lover for a year and that Bruno is HIV-positive.

The scene is extraordinary for its mix of hilarity and anguish, and because the three men are so beautiful it almost hurts to look at them. There's another scene much later in the film involving the transvestite (Vincent Perez), the dead man's shoe-magnate brother (Jean-Louis Trintignant), and a pair of red spike-heel pumps that's just as rich in cross purposes and inchoate emotions. Chéreau loves his actors (although perhaps the women less than the men) and they all deliver for him, but none more so than Greggory and Trintignant.

Those Who Love Me is shot in handheld Cinemascope (a trip in itself) by the agile Eric Gautier. The camera movement would be excessively romantic if it wasn't so wittily undercut (dissected, to be more exact) by François Gedigier's editing. On a second or third viewing, bits of camera movement emerge and echo in the way motifs do in classical music, tying the parts into a whole. And speaking of music, there's too much of it and some of the choices are too obvious, although it's hard to quibble about a score that includes Mahler and "Save the Last Dance for Me."

American viewers, who've come to expect a film to spoon-feed them plot, characters, and motivations, tend to react with hostility to a film that can't be totally apprehended in a single viewing. They'd rather blame the film than doubt their own intellectual capacity. But I guarantee that if you find yourself confused, so does everyone else in the audience. I loved this film from the first time I saw it but it took me a second viewing to sort out the characters and relationships, and a third to begin to appreciate the intricacies of the form.

For a fetishist, this is the film of the year.

Also reviewed in:
CHICAGO TRIBUNE, 3/10/00, Friday/p. D, John Petrakis
NEW YORK TIMES, 8/5/99, p. E1, Janet Maslin
VARIETY, 5/18-24/98, p. 74, Lisa Nesselson

THREE KINGS

A Warner Bros. release in association with Village Roadshow Pictures/Village-A.M. Film Partnership of a Coast Ridge Films/Atlas Entertainment production. *Executive Producer:* Gregory Goodman, Kelley Smith-Wait, and Bruce Berman. *Producer:* Charles Roven, Paul Junger Witt, and Edward L. McDonnell. *Director:* David O. Russell. *Screenplay:* David O. Russell. *Story:* John Ridley. *Director of Photography:* Newton Thomas Sigel. *Editor:* Robert K. Lampert. *Music:* Carter Burwell and Ralph Sall. *Music Editor:* Bunny Andrews and Adam Smalley. *Sound:* Lance Brown and (music) Michael Farrow. *Sound Editor:* Bruce Fortune and John Leveque. *Casting:* Mary Vernieu and Anne McCarthy. *Production Designer:* Catherine Hardwicke. *Art Director:* Derek R. Hill. *Set Decorator:* Gene Serdena. *Special Effects:* Marty Bresin. *Costumes:* Kym Barrett. *Make-up:* Allan Apone. *Make-up (Special Effects):* Tony Gardner and Jim Beinke. *Stunt Coordinator:* Dan Bradley. *Running time:* 105 minutes. *MPAA Rating:* R.

CAST: George Clooney (Major Archie Gates); Mark Wahlberg (Sergeant Troy Barlow); Ice Cube (Staff Sergeant Chief Elgin); Nora Dunn (Adriana Cruz); Jamie Kennedy (Walter Wogaman); Mykelti Williamson (Colonel Horn); Cliff Curtis (Amir Abdulah); Said Taghmaoui (Captain Said); Spike Jonze (Private Conrad Vig); Holt McCallany (Captain Van Meter); Judy Greer (Cathy Daitch); Christopher Lohr (Teebaux); Jon Sklaroff (Paco); Liz Stauber (Debbie Barlow, Troy's Wife); Marsha Horan (Amir's Wife); Alla Shawkat (Amir's Daughter); Jabir Algarawi and Ghanem Algarawi (Hairdressing Twins); Bonnie Afsary (Western Dressed Village Woman); Jacqueline Abi-Ad (Traditional Village Woman); Fadil Al-Badri (Deserter Leader); Al No-Omani (Kaied); Sayed Badreya (Iraqi Tank Major); Magdi Rashwan (Iraqi Troop Carrier Major); Alex Dodd (Iraqi First Kill Soldier); Larry Jones (Berm Soldier/Truck Driver); Patrick O'Neal Jones, Shawn Pilot, and Brett Bassett (Berm Soldiers); Jim Gaffigan (Cut's Troy's Cuff Soldier); Al Whiting and Brian Patterson (Camp Soldiers/Truck Drivers); Gary Parker (Civil Affairs Company Clerk); Haldar Alatowa (Saudi Translator); Salah Salea (Iraqi Soldier with Map); Doug Jones (Dead Iraqi Soldier); Farinaz Farrokh (Iraqi Civilian Mother with Baby); Omar Alhegian (Bunker 1 Lying Iraqi); Hassan Allawati (Bunker 1 Friendly Iraqi); Sara Aziz (Pleading Civilian Woman); A. Halim Mostafa (Iraqi Civilian Man); Al Mustafa (Bunker 2 Store Room Captain); Anthony Batarse (Iraqi Interrogation Sergeant); Mohamad Al-Jalahma and Mohammed Sharafi (Bunker 2 Iraqi Rifle Loaders); Hillel Michael Shamam (Bunker 2 Store Room Guard); Joey Naber (Iraqi Radio Operator); Basin Ridha (Black Robe Leader); Peter MacDissi (Oasis Bunker Iraqi Republican Guard Lieutenant); Tony Shawkat and Joseph Abi-Ad (Oasis Bunker Iraqi Republican Guard Sergeants); Fahd Al-Ujaimy and Derick Qaqish (Oasis Bunker Troy's Interrogation Guards); Hassan Bach-Agha and Fadi Sitto (Oasis Bunker Troy's Republican Guards); Ali Alkindi, Abdullah Al-Dawalem, and Rick Mendoza (Deserters); Jassim Al-Khazraji (Oasis Bunker Republican Roof Guard); Jay Giannone and Sam Hassan (Oasis Bunker Republican Guards/Snipers); Brian Bosworth (Action Star); Donte Delila and Dylan Brown (Iraqi Children).

CHRISTIAN SCIENCE MONITOR, 10/1/99, p. 15, David Sterritt

One of the ads for "Three Kings" quotes a film critic calling it "the savviest, wittiest war movie in years." This raises the interesting question of whether wittiness is one of the qualities a war movie ought to have.

There's a great deal of dark humor in classics like "M*A*S*H" and "Dr. Strangelove," of course, but those are antiwar movies with pointed messages to deliver.

For a few welcome moments scattered here and there in the story, "Three Kings" makes sharp comments of its own, shining a bitter light on the cruelty and absurdity of war in general and the Persian Gulf War in particular.

But most of its running time is taken up with a noisy celebration of guns and gore, via a steady stream of shootings, explosions, chases, and the nastiest torture scene this side of a Mel Gibson movie.

While boisterous laughs aren't missing from the package, "wit" is hardly its most conspicuous trait, even if it was directed by David O. Russell, whose previous pictures—"Spanking the Monkey" and "Flirting With Disaster"—are justly respected comedies.

The overall shallowness of "Three Kings" is especially regrettable since so much genuine talent has gone into the picture.

George Clooney, Mark Wahlberg, and Ice Cube give ferocious performances as the main characters, American soldiers who segue from the Gulf War to a clandestine search for gold bullion hidden in Saddam Hussein's secret stash, eventually getting involved in the plight of terror-stricken refugees.

The filmmaking is even more impressive, as director Russell makes the screen swirl with hard-hitting images and boldly imaginative editing, then relaxes the pace at just the right moments to hammer home the screenplay's intermittent outrage over the horror and hatred that warfare inevitably brings.

If that outrage were more consistently felt and more coherently expressed, "Three Kings" would be an important movie on moral as well as technical grounds.

Its ideas and insights are ultimately drowned out by its sound and fury, though, making it a snazzily filmed entertainment rather than a meaningful experience. It may make money, but it won't make much difference in the way we think or feel.

LOS ANGELES TIMES, 10/1/99, Calendar/p. 1, Kenneth Turan

You could argue it's a pity the three-hunks-looking-heroic poster art for "Three Kings" looks so conventional, because this Iraqi war scam gone awry adventure extravaganza is anything but. You could say that, but you'd be wrong. Or would you?

Actually, the truth is that like the best efforts coming out of the big studios these days—and this is definitely one of them—the ambitious "Three Kings" is Hollywood with a twist, demonstrating how far a film can stray from business as usual and still deliver old-fashioned satisfactions. Unexpected in its wicked humor, its empathy for the defeated and its political concerns, this is writer-director David O. Russell's nervy attempt to reinvent the war movie and a further step in the evolution of an audacious and entertaining filmmaker.

Just as Russell's first film, the modest, Oedipal-themed "Spanking the Monkey," gave no hint of what he'd accomplish with the effervescent, hugely comic "Flirting With Disaster," so "Disaster" doesn't really prepare us for the scope of "Kings." Traditional in its conclusions, but anything but along the way, this film gives its protagonists and its audience considerably more than anyone anticipated.

"Three Kings" begins as the U.S. war against Saddam Hussein's Iraq is ending in March 1991. Its opening line of dialogue—a question by Army Sgt. Troy Barlow (Mark Wahlberg), plaintively wondering, with an Iraqi soldier in his sights, "Are we shooting people or what?"—perfectly encapsulates the bizarre uncertainty of a military action that plays at first like an extended fraternity party with automatic weapons thrown into the mix.

It's Barlow, assisted by worshipful hillbilly high school dropout Pvt. Conrad Vig (Spike Jonze), who discovers a key document hidden in the posterior of a captured soldier and thereafter known, via the film's scabrous sense of humor, as "the Iraqi ass map." On it are the directions to some of Saddam's secret bunkers, where all manner of spoils from the ill-starred invasion of Kuwait are likely hidden.

Also finding out about the map are God-fearing Staff Sgt. Chief Elgin (Ice Cube) and world-weary Special Forces Maj. Archie Gates (George Clooney), who thinks the document is the key to locating millions in gold bullion Saddam removed from Kuwait. "Bullion? You mean like those little cubes you make soup from?" Vig wonders. No, private, not like those.

Teaming up to raid the bunkers and get rich quick, these cynical, self-involved and opportunistic individuals initially come off as the usual amoral heroes for the modern age. As they head off in a Hum-Vee with Homer Simpson plastered on the front grill and explosive-filled footballs in the rear, they, and we, can be forgiven for thinking that this is going to be a tough guy joy ride, a quintessentially macho adventure yarn.

But writer-director Russell (who spent 18 months researching and writing the script, with story credited to John Ridley), has no intention of letting us off that easy. Yes, we're meant to enjoy the excitement, but not to the exclusion of knowing the cost, not to mention a whole lot of other things Russell has on his mind.

For the first thing that happens to the guys is a collision with the Iraqi civilian population and the gradual realization that internecine warfare is going on between those who naively heeded the U.S. call to rise up against Saddam and brutal government forces who are taking advantage of America's abrupt avoidance of all things Iraqi.

This chaotic war within a war, an irrational free-for-all where tankers filled with milk are treated as lethal weapons, is vividly captured by the high-energy, frenetic visual style used by Russell and cinematographer Newton Thomas Sigel. Brief, oddball sequences take us inside the human body to show exactly the kind of damage a bullet inflicts, and Sigel even utilizes three different film stocks to convey a variety of emotional states, including a grainy, disorienting use of Ektachrome, a film usually found in tourist's cameras.

Making the transition from "Flirting With Disaster" is Russell's trademark sense of humor, his feeling for the absurdly comic in the most potentially horrifying situations. Who else would put a glimpse of the Rodney King beating on Iraqi TV, or be able to fashion an unlikely running joke about whether it's Lexus or Infiniti that offers a convertible model.

Also intact is Russell's gift for eccentric characters, like Pvt. Vig, an excellent first acting job for video director Jonze, whose debut feature, "Being John Malkovich," opens later this month. Minor players like Walter (Jamie Kennedy), a soldier who wears night vision goggles during the day, and TV newswoman Adriana Cruz (Christiane Amanpour look-alike Nora Dunn) are treated with as much care as audience surrogates Barlow and Elgin. Especially effective is Clooney who perfectly conveys the combination of capability, authority and a touch of larceny the film insists on.

Russell is also someone who enjoys being provocative, a trait that comes out in the disquieting character of Iraqi Capt. Said (Said Taghmaoui), a sympathetic villain whose employment of torture as a means of political education is daring and effective.

Though the film's title nominally derives from the biblical three kings who followed the star to Bethlehem, it echoes, intentionally or not, the names of other pertinent films. There's "The Man Who Would Be King," also about Westerners who thought to get rich off of native peoples, and John Ford's "Three Godfathers," about tough guys who have a change of heart in the desert. Off-and-on cynical and sentimental, Russell's darkly comic tale shows how much can be done with familiar material when you're burning to do things differently and have the gifts to pull that off.

NEW YORK, 10/11/99, p. 102, Peter Rainer

Set during the Persian Gulf War, *Three Kings* begins in March 1991, just as the official cease-fire is announced. The soldiers at an American base camp in Iraq ring in the good news by boozing and whooping it up, but the spectacle has its ludicrous side: These ground troops, after all, have been cooling their heels for weeks while the war has been fought mostly from the air, high-tech-style. They're celebrating a triumph they didn't really contribute to as combatants, and, as soon becomes clear, the triumph is equivocal at best.

Writer-director David O. Russell piles on the ironies and sick jokes: We are reminded that many of the Iraqis fighting the Americans were trained earlier by the CIA to fight Iran; the battles being fought rack up predominantly civilian and not military casualties; beleaguered, defenseless Kuwait is chockablock with cell phones and Rolls-Royces, which the Iraqis regard as spoils of war. Iraqi rebels looking to George Bush for aid in ousting Saddam instead find themselves twisting in the wind.

Russell works on our nerve endings, seemingly intent on outdoing *The Road Warrior*. With his cinematographer, Newton Thomas Sigel, he's devised a bleached-out look for the film, especially in its early sections, that has a corrosive effect on our eyeballs; no beauty is allowed to filter into the flat Iraqi desert terrain, or into anywhere else, either. Russell throws in shock cuts and heads exploded by gunfire and close-ups of a wounded soldier's infected innards; he wants us to know that war—even an apparently absurdist war such as this one—is hell.

The action is carried forward by the film's four main protagonists—Special Forces captain Archie Gates (George Clooney), a square-jawed cynic who's set to retire into civilianhood in a few weeks; Sergeant Troy Barlow (Mark Wahlberg), with a wife and newborn baby back in

Detroit; Staff Sergeant Chief Elgin (Ice Cube), an airport baggage handler when not on active duty who believes Jesus protects him in the field; and Private Conrad Vig (Spike Jonze), a southern hick who didn't have a day job back home and looks up to Barlow. When a map to the hiding place of millions in gold bullion stolen from the Kuwaitis by Saddam is literally fished out of a prisoner's ass, these four, led by Gates, go awol to make the score, leaving camp at dusk and planning to be back by lunch. Predictably, things foul up, and they quickly become what Gates, especially, never intended: rescuers of Iraqi villagers set upon by their own troops.

Whacked-out and hyperkinetic as Russell tries to be, he still opts in the end for the most timeworn cynic-with-a-heart-of-gold clichés. Gates, for example, makes a big show early on of sticking up for No. 1, but his transformation into putty-tat is pretty pro forma. We're meant to recognize how the wigginess of the war maneuvers all four men into being the unlikeliest of heroes.

But since Russell never really allows us to develop a closeness to these men, it's difficult to get worked up about their exploits, even though they're onscreen practically nonstop and we see them get shot and tortured. After a while, except for Clooney, who's entertainingly hale, they blend into the blasted, and landscapes teeming with insurgents and predators. Russell is caught in a conceptual bind that he never really figures his way out of. How to make an anti-heroic war movie with real heroes. His solution, in effect, is to have it both ways: He avoids standard-issue movie-star iconography but, storywise, makes a beeline for bleeding-heart humanitarianism. And so the film, charged-up and smart as it often is, comes across as something of a con. Russell isn't just dramatizing the facts and the disgraces of the Gulf War but also using the war as a way to jazz up his own hokum. (In a stylistically very different way, this is what Terrence Malick did to World War II in *The Thin Red Line,* which aestheticized combat into a graduate-level course in metaphysics.) Hokum works best when it's presented unjazzed, like Rick in *Casablanca* coming down with a last-minute case of good-guy-itis.

One reason you can tell that Russell isn't functioning as an enraged, politically committed artist is that the violence in the movie doesn't deepen our responses to the people who are suffering it; the film begins with a head-exploding splat, and the splats that follow are mostly more of the same except bigger and louder. Are the adrenaline-rush stylistics and the hip attitudinizing in this film—its mix of snicker and slobber—a "cool" new-style response to war? Movies about World War II and Vietnam have been straightforward or hallucinatory, political or apolitical, but rarely have they seemed as flip or as flashy as this one. Even *M*A*S*H,* which was set in Korea, kept its high jinks rooted in gallantry; Elliott Gould and Donald Sutherland could roust the military brass because they were great surgeons and they saved lives. Unlike Vietnam or Korea or World War II, the Gulf War is the first full-scale American conflict that the majority of today's moviegoing audience actually lived through; and it was, for them, a remote-control war, a video game war. Not coincidentally, perhaps, there's something remote-controlled and rock-video-ish about *Three Kings,* and that may be enough to turn it into a hit.

The Gulf War was billed in this country as the exorcism of Vietnam—a point duly noted in *Three Kings*—but the Vietnam War didn't carry much meaning to the generation born after it. The Gulf War probably doesn't carry much jingoistic meaning for that generation either, especially since Saddam is still in power. (That fact gives the soldiers' exploits in *Three Kings* an existential kick.) Maybe the war would have meant more to people if they actually saw its human toll. But the real suffering that transpired in the Persian Gulf was mostly kept away from American audiences, at least on television. On CNN, the buildings and enemy installations that were hit seemed devoid of actual inhabitants; the wipeouts of civilians were played down. There's a great war movie to be made about the ways in which war itself has become an abstraction in the modern media consciousness, and judging from the best moments in *Three Kings,* I think Russell understood that. But ultimately, instead of drawing us in, his swagger and the dazzle of his pyrotechnics keep us at a remove from the savagery. They become abstractions, too.

NEW YORK POST, 10/1/99, p. 54, Rod Dreher

"Three Kings" is an extraordinary experience: an original and brilliant combination of comedy, action and sophisticated political comment.

Combining style with substance, it's the best American movie of the year thus far, and if there's any justice in these things it will win an Oscar nomination for writer-director David O. Russell.

On one level it's a boisterous, conventional tale of soldiers pulling off a scam but developing a conscience in the aftermath of the Gulf War. But it also has plenty of smart, humane points to make in its mostly light-handed way: from the way American pop culture has conquered the globe to the fact that even good wars carry a terrible human cost.

Sometimes Russell takes his anti-war message to the very edge of an unfair anti-Americanism. But it's one of those pictures you can enjoy even if you disagree with its flashes of political correctness, its cynicism about America's motives for throwing Saddam out of occupied Kuwait and its implicit call for a morally based foreign policy.

Just after the Gulf War ceasefire, GIs Barlow (Mark Wahlberg), Chief (Ice Cube) and Vig (Spike Jonze)—all reservists who haven't seen any action—find a map hidden on an Iraqi POW that gives directions to a bunker where Saddam has hidden some of the gold he stole from Kuwait.

Gates (George Clooney), a cynical special-forces major who's sick of shepherding around an aggressive TV reporter, hears about the map and teams up with the three guys to borrow a Humvee and steal the gold.

They find the town with the bunkers easily enough and are relieved that the Iraqi soldiers there don't care about them lifting the loot. The Iraqis are too busy suppressing the rebellion against Saddam called for by President Bush.

It's not America's war anymore, and these guys' priority is getting the gold. But at a certain point the brutality of the Iraqi troops against the civilian population becomes too hard for the AWOL Americans to stomach, and they end up trying to help the anti-Saddam resistance.

But it's what happens along the way that makes "Three Kings" such fun and so provocative. There's plenty of absurd comedy, but there are also some nasty and very effective shocks.

Russell uses all sorts of visual tricks (including different film stocks) to convey not just the surreality of the situation in which his heroes find themselves, but also their mental states. The experiment works.

It's just as well, because the three main characters—the film gives them a more or less equal amount of screen time—are sketchily drawn, perhaps deliberately so.

Still, Clooney, Ice Cube and Wahlberg all come up with punchy performances. Ice Cube is particularly impressive—his gangsta-rap persona is completely absent. Mykelti Williamson, Nora Dunn and Spike Jonze are strong in supporting roles.

Russell's previous films "Spanking the Monkey" and "Flirting with Disaster" were clever and funny but gave no hint that he could pull off a movie as strong and, in its own strange way, as serious and important as this one.

NEWSDAY, 10/1/99, Part II/p. B3, Gene Seymour

Don't let the combat fatigues, land mines and armored tanks fool you. In style and content, "Three Kings" is less a war movie than a classic western. Indeed, it may well be the best western Hollywood has released since "Unforgiven." And if it isn't, it's certainly the funniest, most entertaining western one can remember seeing in a very long time.

How else, after all, to characterize the movie's four renegade soldiers (that title is a little confusing at first) except as scruffy, low-down outlaws? Played by George Clooney, Mark Wahlberg, Ice Cube and Spike Jonze, these motley warriors ride a moral and physical wasteland as perilous and forbidding as any traversed by John Wayne or Joel McCrea.

Writer-director David O. Russell—an unlikely helmsman for this project, given that his previous two movies, "Spanking the Monkey" (1994) and "Flirting With Disaster" (1996), were acid-drenched domestic comedies—brings as much stark resonance to the war-ravaged Iraqi setting of "Three Kings" as grizzled old hands used to bring to visions of 1880s Tombstone.

Really, it's a post-Persian Gulf War movie, given that it takes place in March, 1991, just after Saddam Hussein's surrender to Allied forces. Reservists like sergeants Troy Barlow (Wahlberg), Chief Elgin (Ice Cube) and PFC Conrad Vig (Jonze) are exultant in victory, though it's possible they're just happy they lived through the two-month "liberation of Kuwait." Meanwhile, you can count soon-to-retire Special Forces Capt. Archie Gates (Clooney) among those who wonder just what this war was about.

Somewhere in the mopping-up operation, the two sergeants come across a map concealed in the gluteus maximus of an Iraqi POW. Gates figures out that the map leads to a bunker containing billions in gold bullion stolen from Kuwait by Hussein's army. Gates convinces Troy, Chief and Conrad to help him make a lightning strike at the bunker and steal the gold for themselves.

The heist succeeds. But just before they can ride off with their booty, this not-so-fabulous four finds dozens of imperiled Iraqi civilians, opposed to Hussein but lacking the support promised by the Bush administration. Disregarding their safety and the terms of the ceasefire, Gates and company find themselves at war once again to save the endangered men, women and children.

The movie straddles at least a couple of very thin lines and it doesn't always manage to strike a balance between satiric farce and static adventure, cynical tone and high ideals. Yet Russell's script, adapted from a story by neo-noir novelist John Ridley, succeeds for the most part in mixing cool-hand heroism with flash-point skepticism toward the vagaries of "new world order" policy-making.

Clooney's confidence as a leading man becomes more impressive with each movie. (Is he Steve McQueen or Cary Grant? No matter. He's got plenty of time to navigate his own road between the two.) Jonze's dim-bulb good ol'boy is a sweet, touching portrayal.

As good as they are in their roles, none of the four guys is as interesting as Nora Dunn's volatile, stressed-out network reporter who knows she's being taken, literally, for a ride by the Army. She looks as if she's wandered, by accident, from one of Russell's other dark comedies. It'd be nice if this sexy sourpuss could get a movie of her own someday.

NEWSWEEK, 10/4/99, p. 64, David Ansen

"Three Kings" keeps you off balance from its first moment. We are thrust into the middle of a vast, barren desert, the colors bleached out, the horizon stretched and distorted by a wide-angle lens. It's 1991, and the gulf war has just ended. An Iraqi soldier stands at a far distance atop a mound, his hands raised as the armed American soldiers try to estimate the threat he poses. "Are we shooting?" one of them asks, meaning, *Are we shooting people?* but the viewer might think he was talking to the director, inquiring whether the camera was rolling. Then a bullet, shockingly, blows the Iraqi away, and we have our first clue that this caper comedy about a quartet of renegade Yanks stealing gold bullion from Saddam, isn't going to be merely a jolly, macho update of "Kelly's Heroes." David O. Russell's remarkable movie can be blisteringly funny, but it's playing for keeps.

Russell, who's made two nervy independent movies, "Spanking the Monkey" and the neo-screwball "Flirting with Disaster," is making his first big-canvas, big-studio movie, but there's no sense of compromise. Blackly funny, unafraid to shift emotional gears from farce to horror, peppered with spectacular action, and bitingly critical of the way the U.S. abandoned the anti-Saddam resistance movement when the war was over, "Three Kings" works both as a rousing action adventure moxie and as a subversion of the genre.

According to George Clooney, who plans the Special Forces mastermind of the heist, Russell's mantra on the set was "Every bullet counts." "He said it a billion times," Clooney says. Russell wanted to make sure there was not one gratuitous gunshot.

"Every time you see a bullet come out of a gun," Clooney explains, "you see what it does to your insides, to your body, to your family. This is extremely responsible violence. I'm proud of that."

When Clooney says *insides,* he means just that. One of the most striking shots in recent memory is a close-up of a man's innards that shows in graphic detail exactly what happens when a bullet penetrates the body. "When I first saw it," says costar Mark Wahlberg, whose character absorbs lead in the course of the story, "I got grossed out. I don't even want to pick up a gun again. I see violence on TV, and I don't look at it the I did before." When Russell is asked how he got such gruesomely realistic effects—were they models' computer-generated images?—he reveals his secret: it's an actual corpse you're seeing "We filmed a bullet going through a cadaver," he says. "The studio was concerned. They said, 'If the preview audiences don't like it, take it out.' But the premier audiences found it fascinating."

They won't be alone. "Three Kings" is an adventure film with a singular, surreal personality. It takes us on a wild ride through the tangled allegiances and troubling politics of a war most of us experienced as a videogame on CNN. But instead of that Olympian aerial vantage point, Russell plunks us down on the ground, among the charred corpses and partying American soldiers who just won a war without seeing any combat. Having saved Kuwait—and its oil—the cynical ex-Green Beret Archie Gates (Clooney) thinks it's time to cash in. He gets possession of a map that shows the location of the gold Saddam has looted from Kuwait's sheiks and sets off to find it with his small, motely crew—Chief (Ice Cube), a deeply religious airport baggage handler from Detroit; Troy (Wahlberg), the patriot who wants to get back to his wife and daughter, and the hilariously geeky redneck Conrad Vig (Spike Jonze). First they have to make sure that scarily aggressive reporter Adriana Cruz (Nora Dunn) is thrown off their scent (fat chance).

Gates and his men find the gold easily enough, which is when things start to get complicated. The defeated Iraqi soldiers guarding Saddam's loot are surprisingly willing to let them abscond with the bullion, because their first priority is to subdue the Shiite Muslim rebellion against the regime. These rebels had been encouraged by President Bush to rise up against Saddam, but now that the war was over our forces were under orders not to help them. Archie Gates and his pals can get rich—if they are willing to abandon the rebels to their certain death.

"Three Kings" is in the great Hollywood tradition of stories about hard-bitten American cynics who, when push comes to shove, find their moral backbone (hello, "Casablanca"). But there's nothing formulaic about the way Russell tells his story. In movie terms, the gulf war is terra nova, and the director, revealing a visual imagination he hadn't shown before, conjures strikingly original visions—burning oil fields, exploding cows, bunkers filled with VCRs and mobile phones and stolen computers, soldiers washed away in a sea of milk. There are times when its absurdist style brings to mind Richard Lester's 1968 antiwar satire "How I Won the War;" at other times it's casual irreverence suggests "M.A.S.H." Using a film stock that bleaches out colors, Russell's breathlessly paced comedy often achieves an almost hallucinatory intensity. It was a war of weird juxtapositions and ironic alliances (the Iraqi soldier who tortures his American captive learned his craft from the U.S. military, when we were backing Iraq in its war with Iran). So it's somehow appropriate that the stars are an utterly eclectic mix—a TV star, a rapper, an ex-underwear-model-rapper, and a video and film director (Jonze)—all of whom mesh seamlessly. Clooney is a good team player here. But he still exudes an effortless, old Hollywood authority—a masculinity so comfortable with itself it doesn't need to be insisted upon.

  Russell found the heist story in Warner Bros.'s vault of unproduced screenplays. The gulf war setting reminded him of the months he had spent in Nicaragua after college "in this environment where everyone had guns and there was political chaos. "The violence and discord struck him as both horrific and hilarious. He then took 18 months to write his own script, researching the war and its aftermath, hiring experts to consult with him. If George Bush has any problems with this movie, Russell is unfazed. "I'm presenting fact," he declares. "George Bush has said himself that he has regrets about the way the war was ended." One of the consultants, Sgt. Maj. Jim Parker, who died of cancer during the filming of the movie, was the model for Clooney's character. "He was so excited about the gulf war," says Clooney. "He was like, 'Yeah, were going to go stop a bad guy—and he's *definitely* a bad guy'." But Parker emerged disillusioned. "At the end of it, they would go on midnight raids and kill some of [Saddam's] Republican Guard, because they would have to stand there during the day and let the Guard murder the Shiite Muslims."

These are the tales the public, busy tying its yellow ribbons and watching new's reports that were rigorously, controlled by the Pentagon, rarely got to hear. That they should arrive in the form of a Hollywood adventure comedy is surprising. That this dark comedy manages to be both disturbingly powerful and powerfully funny is the most welcome surprise of all.

SIGHT AND SOUND, 3/00, p. 54, John Wrathall

Iraq, March 1991. The Gulf War has just ended. US soldiers Troy Barlow and Conrad Vig find a map of the bunkers behind Iraqi lines where Saddam Hussein has hidden gold bullion looted from Kuwait. After getting wind of the story, Major Archie Gates convinces them, along with their staff sergeant Chief Elgin, to help him steal the gold. The four soldiers locate the bullion in a bunker concealed beneath a village well. Saddam's soldiers make no attempt to stop them because they are busy suppressing local rebels. Reluctant to abandon them to their fate, the Americans decide to take the villagers with them, even though it's against official US policy.

As they are leaving the village, they are gassed by Iraqi Republican Guards. Troy is captured and tortured. Gates, Conrad and Chief are rescued by rebels. In return for a share of the gold and an escort to the Iranian border, the rebels help to rescue Troy, but Conrad is shot dead by a sniper. Fulfilling their part of the bargain, Gates, Troy and Chief escort the rebels to the Iranian border, only to be arrested by Gates' superior Colonel Horn for acting against US policy. As a result, Iraqi border guards are able to recapture the rebels. But Gates convinces Horn to secure the rebels' safe passage into Iran; in return, Gates, Troy and Chief agree to give back the gold.

A big-budget war movie starring George Clooney might seem like a huge departure for the writer-director of two intimate, subversively comic dissections of family life, *Spanking the Monkey* and *Flirting with Disaster*. But from the opening minute of *Three Kings*, it's clear that David O. Russell's idiosyncratic vision has survived the transition unscathed. Spotting an armed Iraqi in the desert just after the Gulf War ceasefire, and unsure exactly what their orders are, Sergeant Troy Barlow asks his comrades: "Are we shooting?" But instead of giving him a clipped affirmative or negative, they misunderstand him, launching into a cross-purposes riff on possible meanings of the phrase. As the atrocities pile up, Russell's dialogue never loses this screwball edge—not even in the torture scene, where the Iraqi interrogator Captain Said batters Troy into admitting how screwed-up US society must be to have forced Michael Jackson to have plastic surgery in order to look white.

The film's visual touches are correspondingly bizarre, not least the full-colour close-ups inside a body to demonstrate the damage bullets do to internal organs. But the film's surrealism, whether showing desert bunkers piled with looted consumer goods or towers of flame reflected in lakes of spilled oil seems less a flip stylistic decision on Russell's part than a direct and honest response to the extraordinary conditions of the war itself.

Russell never lets his quirky asides get in the way of a streamlined and classically structured Hollywood action-movie plot. The story itself, for instance, isn't all that far removed from the Clint Eastwood vehicle *Kelly's Heroes* (1970). The satirical tone, meanwhile, owes more to a very different Hollywood war movie of that era, Robert Altman's *MASH* (1969). Russell may share Altman's irreverence and cynicism but, unlike Altman, he never lets go of his humanity. Everyone in this war has their reasons, even the torturer Said, who is given a moving speech (powerfully delivered by the French-Moroccan actor Said Taghmaoui) about the slaughter of his child by American bombs.

Beyond the hip comedy and slick, action-driven narrative, Russell also offers a serious indictment of the conduct of the war, not least the way George Bush encouraged the Iraqi population to rise up against Saddam Hussein, and then refused to go to their support. In venturing into Iraq, Gates and his team are motivated purely by greed; that they end up doing any good is entirely by accident—and only by going directly against official US policy.

What lingers in the mind far longer than the smart dialogue, the slightly cartoon characterisations or the neat feel-good ending is a vivid sense of the sickening nature of modern warfare: poison gas, land mines, cluster bombs, chemical pollution, torture chambers and the indiscriminate slaughter of civilians, among other things. But these horrors, to Russell's credit, are conveyed with a minimum of sanctimonious outrage. Among the rebels rescued by Gates is a little girl. Both her arms are in plaster, but Russell never directs our attention to this detail, nor stops to explain it. How her arms were broken is left to our imagination.

TIME, 10/4/99, p. 92, Richard Schickel

The soldiers burst through the underground bunker's door, safeties off, trigger fingers tense. If the purloined gold—some $23 million worth—is anywhere, it's likely to be here—heavily, nervously guarded.

They are somewhat nonplussed by what greets them. Someone is watching the Rodney King drama unfold on cable TV, while someone else listens to an Eddie Murphy hit and another works out on a NordicTrack. One of the defenders makes a placatory gesture, offering the intruders a Cuisinart. Down the hall, a captive is being tortured by electric shock, his tormentor chatting amiably with him in American slang between jolts.

The invaders have, as David O. Russell, who wrote and directed *Three Kings*, says, "fallen down the rabbit hole" into one of modernism's most disturbing places, where calculated brutality and mindless consumerism exist side by uneasy side, a place where a life may not be judged a fair trade for a Rolex. They are also, as Russell later recalls, part of a sequence "we were not going to finish before lunch." A producer worried about the budget suggested he "broom out" some of the details and move on. But the film's star, George Clooney, stood fast. It was scenes like this that had induced him to cut his price in order to make the picture. Besides, Russell was certain that back in Burbank he had Warner Bros.' support. One of its senior executives had told him that if he couldn't occasionally green-light a movie like this one, he didn't want his job.

There are not, however, too many current movies like *Three Kings*—except, perhaps, in crude outline. On that level, it sounds like dozens of other interchangeable action-adventure scripts. In the aftermath of a war—in this case 1991's Desert Storm—three American soldiers discover a treasure map (you don't want to know where the enemy soldier hid it) that holds the secret of where the Iraqis have stashed the gold they stole from Kuwait. Our heroes set out to find it. In the course of their journey they encounter members of the Iraqi resistance who have been abandoned by President Bush's policy. Eventually the squad—besides Clooney it includes Mark Wahlberg, Ice Cube and rookie Spike Jonze as their sidekick—must choose between greed and helping their new friends escape Saddam's clutches. That choice is pretty much a no-brainer. The End.

Except story is not the end of this movie. It's a beginning, a pretext, for what is, finally, a brilliant exercise in popular but palpable surrealism. The film has the bleached look of a carelessly shot videotape, with, occasionally, what Russell calls "very intense hits of color"—a Bart Simpson doll is one of them—burning through its low-contrast surface. This is how combat appears to us in the new technological age—no terrible beauty, just absurdity's flat, deadly record keeping.

That visual manner grounds the film in harsh reality, reminding us that as funny as this movie often is, deadly issues are at stake in it. Two G.I.s carry on an intensely muttered argument over whether it is Lexus or Infiniti that carries a convertible in its product line, a discussion that is finally settled when they come upon a cache of such high-performance cars—including a stretch limo—in the middle of the Iraqi nowhere. Before that happens, though, we see Iraqi troops casually murder a mother in front of her husband and young daughter. We also hear a U.S. soldier being taught the difference between gold bullion and the cubes you make soup from. A pair of Iraqis avow that the U.S. is the Great Satan, but that does not prevent them from dreaming of becoming hairstylists there. Of course, they first have to dodge the footballs the Americans have wired with high explosives capable of knocking a helicopter out of the sky. But for all that when a scoop-needy television reporter (Nora Dunn) insists that her stories, unlike those of a younger, cuter rival, are "substance-based" not "style-based," she could be describing this movie.

"Multilayered" is Russell's modest term for it; "genially bizarre" is the phrase that springs to a bedazzled critic's mind. Also, curiously enough, engagingly retro. For the 41-year-old director is a child of the '70s, who sees movies like *MASH* and *Shampoo* as models for the juxtaposition of serious issues and tossed-off comedy in contexts that keep the audience from settling into either mode.

Russell says he was also influenced by novelist Robert Stone, who was writer-in-residence when he was attending Amherst (class of '81)—so much so that he spent time in postrevolution Nicaragua seeking out the realities behind Stone's *A Flag for Sunrise*. He found them. "You'd be playing baseball or listening to an old Michael Jackson record and hear a gunshot. You wouldn't know if it was the contras arriving or just some guy who'd run a red light."

Obviously that experience influenced *Three Kings*. But Russell honed his transgressive chops with a couple of smart, sly independent comedies: *Spanking the Monkey* (about, of all things, incest) and *Flirting with Disaster* (about a man trying to find his long-lost birth parents). They were both chamber satires, on nowhere near the symphonic scale of *Three Kings*, which required a year and a half for Russell to research and write—sometimes nervously.

"I didn't want to spend 18 months writing this and then be sent away," he says. That didn't happen. Instead, as they used to do in the days of the movies Russell admires, a major studio risked major money (around $50 million) on what remains a film of determinedly independent sensibility.

We keep meeting the enemy on our various peacekeeping missions and discovering that he is very like us—wearing our sneakers and T shirts, lusting after our music, our gadgets, our more deadly hardware. As Russell notes, the son of Slobodan Milosevic even has an American-style amusement park up and running in what's left of the former Yugoslavia. This is not exactly what people mean when they talk about the American Century. But that's the way it has worked out. And David Russell has written its epitaph in blazing, user-friendly fire.

VILLAGE VOICE, 10/12/99, p. 139, J. Hoberman

At the very least, David O. Russell's bold and messy *Three Kings* deserves credit for rethinking the war movie in the weird we-are-the-world terms established by Operation Desert Storm. The action begins in March 1991, just as the Gulf War is declared over. "Are we shooting?" one private asks before nervously splattering the desert with befuddled "raghead" brains—much to his comrade's delight.

The morning after the American victory bacchanal, Russell's three noncommissioned "kings" (Ice Cube, Mark Wahlberg, and Spike Jonze) discover a treasure map stuffed up a captured Iraqi anus and, led by an opportunistic and dissolute career-soldier (George Clooney), hatch a very quick plan to zip behind enemy lines and make themselves rich. Their jocular attitude is rendered iconic in the close-up juxtaposing an American flag with a Bart Simpson doll.

As intimated by his nouveau screwball comedy *Flirting With Disaster*, Russell has a knack for choreographing mad confusion. Exciting adventures are here set amid sickening violence, the chaos heightened by eccentric camera placement. The movie is flamboyantly bleached-out and cruddy, shot as wildly spontaneous combat-vérité. There are almost no establishing shots, but when a cow gets blown up, you can bet its head will bang down on the hood of the kings' jeep.

There hasn't been so bloodthirsty a service comedy since *The Dirty Dozen*, although *Three Kings*'s supercharged, bongo-driven cynicism mixes absurd slapstick with intermittent nods to the helpless huddled Third World masses. Russell not only visualizes bombed Iraqi children and bullet-traumatized internal organs but has the guts to point out that the war was fought for oil and that the U.S. had armed Saddam against Iran. Then the movie (which is cluttered with too many dumb peckerwoods and inexpressive performers) starts searching for its own heart. The action stops short so Clooney can explain what's happening—"Bush told the people to rise up against Saddam. They thought they'd have our support. They don't. Now they're getting slaughtered."

Increasingly muddled, cumulatively monotonous, would-be heartwarming, *Three Kings* becomes its own entertainment allegory—searching, Hollywood style, for the point at which blatant self-interest can turn humanitarian, while still remaining profitable. The movie has a unique trajectory. It keeps trying to go conventional and ultimately does.

Also reviewed in:
NATION, 10/25/99, p. 42, Stuart Klawans
NEW REPUBLIC, 11/1/99, p. 28, Stanley Kauffmann
NEW YORK TIMES, 10/1/99, p. E10, Janet Maslin
NEW YORKER, 10/4/99, p. 115, David Denby
VARIETY, 9/27-10/3/99, p. 34, Todd McCarthy
WASHINGTON POST, 10/1/99, p. C1, Stephen Hunter
WASHINGTON POST, 10/1/99, Weekend/p. 46, Desson Howe

THREE SEASONS

An October Films release of an Open City Films production in association with The Goatsingers and Giai Phong Film Studios. *Executive Producer:* Harvey Keitel. Producer: Jason Kliot, Joana Vicente, and Tony Bui. *Director:* Tony Bui. *Screenplay (Vietnamese and English with English subtitles):* Tony Bui. *Story:* Tony Bui and Timothy Linh Bui. *Director of Photography:* Lisa Rinzler. *Editor:* Keith Reamer. *Music:* Richard Horowitz. *Sound:* Curtis Choy, Brian Miksis, and (music) James Nichols and Richard Horowitz. *Sound Editor:* Steve Hamilton, Dave Paterson, and Mary Ellen Porto. *Casting:* Quan Lelan. *Production Designer:* Wing Lee. *Art Director:* Pham Hong Phong and Michele De Albert. *Set Decorator:* Thai Van Hoang. *Special Effects:* Russell Berg and David Watkins. *Costumes:* Ghia Ci Fam. *Make-up:* Nguyen Kieu Thu. *Running time:* 110 minutes. *MPAA Rating:* PG-13.

CAST: Don Duong (Hai); Nguyen Ngoc Hiep (Kien An); Tran Manh Cuong (Teacher Dao); Zoë Bui (Lan); Nguyen Huu Duoc (Woody); Thach Thi Kim Trang (Little Girl); Harvy Keitel (James Hager); Minh Ngoc (Truck Driver); Hoang Phat Trieu (Huy); Diem Kieu (Singing Lotus Woman); Kieu Hanh (Giang); Le Hong Son (Binh); Nguyen Ba Quang (Don); Tran Huu Su (Ngon); Luong Duc Hung (Minh); Hoang Trieu and Tran Long (Men Who Chase Lan); Bui Tuong Trac (Man Who Buys Lotus Flowers); Huynh Kim Hong (Woman on Balcony); Michael Salamon (Man Who Steals Case); Nguyen Van Son (Shoeshine Boy); A Lu and Hong Phu Quang (Street Guardians); Tran Quang Hieu ("Fagan"); Duong Tan Dung (Cyclo Race Promoter); Ho Van Hoang (Khoi); Ho Kieng (Restaurant Owner); Ngo Quang Hai (Man in Taxi); Van Es Antonie (Body Builder for Mr. Keitel); Hong Khac Dao (Parlor Manager); Pham Van Tai (Parlor Friend); Othello Khanh (Phuong's Drunk Boyfriend); Lola Guimond (Phuong, Amerasian Daughter); Nguyen Thanh Son (Cyclo Race Official); Nguyen Thi Ngoc (Teacher Dao's Servant); Nguyen Thi Lien (Grandmother).

LOS ANGELES TIMES, 4/30/99, Calendar/p. 12, Kevin Thomas

Tony Bui's "Three Seasons" is the gentlest, most exquisitely beautiful of films, set in a place that has experienced one of the bitterest struggles in modern times. That place is Ho Chi Minh City and its environs, and Bui, a 26-year-old filmmaker in his feature debut, has returned to the land of his birth to tell three loosely linked short stories. They all reach their own moments of truth only to give way to a larger truth: that Ho Chi Minh City, and by extension, Vietnam, is in a time of wrenching change, with the charming old French colonial city of Saigon being erased by a modem metropolis of skyscrapers, luxury hotels and miles of neon.

Bui, who left Vietnam for America with his family at age 2, discovers the soul of the city and its people and celebrates their resilience, leaving us with the feeling that the Vietnamese will have to make important choices for themselves if they are to hold on to traditional humanist values in the face of the inevitable technological and industrial transformation of their country generated by foreign interests. You cannot watch "Three Seasons," the first fiction feature produced in Vietnam by an American company, without recalling "From Hollywood to Hanoi," the first documentary made by an American company in Vietnam, in which actress-filmmaker Tiana also returned to the land of her birth, expressing similar concerns.

A skilled director of actors, Bui introduces us first to Kien An (Nguyen Ngoc Hiep), a pretty, deceptively demure young woman who has been hired to pick lotus flowers in a large pond dominated by an ancient temple and then sell the flowers in city streets. Kien An joins a large group of women involved in this timeless task but inadvertently breaks rank when, following a song the women sing every day, she dares to sing her own song, one taught to her as a child by her mother. She is overheard by poet-teacher Dao (Manh Cuong), who recognizes it from his own childhood and who has not left the temple in years and has, in fact, never been seen by any of the women. He is a shadowy figure in a wheelchair, but Kien An retains her poise and dares to reach out to this solitary man living with a terrible secret.

In the city, Kien An will in time sell lotus flowers to both Hai (Don Duong) and James Hager (Harvey Keitel). (She will also find herself competing with proliferating sellers of plastic lotus flowers.) Hai is a cyclo driver, a cheerful man who's constantly reading and who becomes infatuated with a beautiful young prostitute, Lan (Zoe Bui, no relation to the director), to the extent of waiting for her to finish her work late at night at the city's luxury hotels.

On principle, Lan refuses to stay overnight with her johns but also has hardened her heart, determined to escape poverty by landing a husband among her upscale clientele. In the meantime, Hai's love for Lan increases along with his resolve in expressing it in the most effective way possible.

In the meantime, Hai notices the American, Hager, sitting in a folding chair, smoking day after day, in front of a small hotel across from his cyclo stand. Hai also keeps an eye on Woody (Nguyen Huu Duoc), a small boy who peddles watches, flashlights and trinkets from a wooden case he carries everywhere. Woody approaches Hager, an anguished Vietnam veteran searching for the grown daughter he has never met. Hager offers the boy his first taste of beer in the nearby Apocalypse Now Cafe, a onetime hangout for the American military. The beer makes the boy sleepy, and as he starts to nod off, his case is stolen, thus propelling him on a search parallel to that of the Viet vet for his daughter.

In telling these tales, Bui reveals that while war has come and gone and an entire and different form of government has been established, a grinding poverty remains the lot for many, many Vietnamese, cutting them off from the new modern society emerging, except at the most menial levels. At the same time, he affirms the redemptive power of a selfless love, especially in the instance of Hai and Kien An.

"Three Seasons" is a film of gestures, physical and spiritual, and this spirit is expressed in both Richard Horowitz's stirring score and Lisa Rinzler's glorious, flowing camera work, with its rich muted hues and sensual glow. "Three Seasons," a movie for any and all seasons, gazes with a sense of beauty and compassion at hard realities without glossing them over.

NEW YORK POST, 4/30/99, p. 62, Rod Dreher

Filmmaker Tony Bui doesn't have much to say in "Three Seasons," but thanks to cinematographer Lisa Rinzler, he says it gorgeously.

The film, the first American movie to be filmed in post-war Vietnam, is a sumptuous banquet for the eyes. The Sundance Film Festival jury and audience prize-winner showcases the ethereal lushness of the Vietnamese countryside and the dowdy, ragged beauty of Ho Chi Minh City's bustling backstreets and boulevards.

Bui, 26, was raised in America, and is obviously bowled over by the exotic look of his native land, but his lyrical images can't make up for the movie's stodgy pacing and lack of story.

"Three Seasons" is a quartet of tales about characters seeking redemption, reconciliation and a place in an emerging capitalist society. In the best of the tales, Hai (Don Duong) is a humble cyclo driver who falls in love with the hard-hearted hooker (Zoe Bui) he pedals to her dates in luxury hotels.

Vietnamese film star Duong's kind, weatherbeaten face hides deep reserves of patience and compassion, which eventually acts like a balm on embittered prostitute Lan. He gives her a gift in a moment of charity and grace so surprising and moving it took my breath away.

In the second tale, a woman (Nguyen Ngoc Hiep) who harvests lotus flowers becomes devoted to her employer, a diseased old recluse who dwells in a stately house in the middle of a lake.

Harvey Keitel, the only actor in the cast familiar to American audiences, plays a sad-faced ex-GI, returned to look for the daughter he fathered on his tour of duty. And a street-vending urchin (Nguyen Huu Doc) spends the movie searching for a valise full of merchandise someone has stolen from him. The last two tales never go beyond empty cliche.

Bui is very generous to the culture he celebrates in "Three Seasons," which is fine, but you can't help wondering if he was so dazzled by the smells, sounds and surfaces of Vietnam that he falls victim to naivete. There's no inkling of the brutality imposed on the nation by communism, how it shaped these people's aspirations, or even that communism is part of the Vietnamese experience. One possible explanation: a government censor was constantly present on the set.

NEWSDAY, 4/30/99, Part II/p. B7, John Anderson

By the time "Three Seasons" boogied out of the Sundance Film Festival this January it had become the only dramatic film to win both top honors (jury prize and Audience Award) and a third for Lisa Rinzler's intoxicating cinematography. There's a chance, too, that before taking home the prizes—and the presumed bacon—it reminded festival audiences of what independent cinema can do. And should do.

By honoring Tony Bui's debut feature—the first American production in Vietnam since the war ended—Sundance honored itself. Not that "Three Seasons" is a perfect film, by any means; its seams are as evident as its heart. But in its simple/serious, elegant/iron-willed manner, it fulfills the presumed Sundance imperative—going where independent films are supposed to go, telling stories more commercially minded films never tell, about people other movies never show.

In the case of "Three Seasons," those people live in current day Saigon (its inhabitants still call it Saigon, too), living the old life in a city whose past is being smothered under traffic and Coke ads, neon, plastic and money. Hai (Don Duong) is a "cyclo" or bicycle-taxi driver of indeterminate age; Kien An (Nguyen Ngoc Hiep) is a young woman who picks lotus blossoms and sings folk songs of an earlier, more countrified country; Woody (Nguyen Huu Duoc) is a small boy who sells gum and cigarette lighters from a wooden box that hangs around his neck. All are immune from westernization, and thus standing on a precipice.

But for all their inconsequence in the larger sense of a resurgent economy, all three are agents of change—and will profoundly affect the people they touch. For Hai, it's Lan (Zoe Bui), the beautiful prostitute with whom he falls in love and who thinks paradise is a permanent room at a western hotel. For Kien An, it's Master Dao (Tran Manh Cuong), the reclusive leper whose lotus blossoms she picks and for whom she will serve as the hands to write his poetry. For Woody, it's an ex-Marine named Hager (Harvey Kietel), a morbid American who's come looking for the daughter he left behind after the war and who spends days sitting on a chair on the street outside his hotel.

Bui's point isn't too obscure—the meek shall inherit the earth might be an untidy recap. But "Three Seasons" isn't just narrative. It's about the dignity of its actors, the way Rinzler's camera ennobles what it finds in the steamy/rainy streets of Saigon and in the profound simplicity of its multiple tales. Most movies use the excuse of motion pictures to sell literature—little goes on visually, you might say, than occurs on the printed page. The rarer film recalls that cinema has a virtually unfathomable potential for marrying our eyesight to a story and for enhancing the potentialities of both. "Three Seasons," in its understated fashion, is a bugle call.

NEWSWEEK, 5/3/99, p. 70, David Ansen

The first American movie to be shot in Vietnam since the war, "Three Seasons" arrives garlanded with prizes from the Sundance Film Festival. The writer-director, 26-year-old Tony Bui, walked off with both the jury's Grand Prize and the Audience Award for his subtitled film. In addition, Lisa Rinzler was honored for her cinematography. This last accolade is the easiest to understand: whether she's filming in the humid, bustling streets of Saigon or among lotus-strewn country landscapes, Rinzler's burnished images give off a lovely glow. The heat, the beauty and the poverty of contemporary Vietnam are made tangible.

Bui, who was raised in California (he left Vietnam when he was 2), interweaves three tales intended to reflect a society in painful transition, torn between Eastern and Western traditions. One tells of a poor cyclo driver's (Don Duong) dogged love for an ambitious Saigon prostitute (Zoe Bui). One involves a lovely young lotus picker (Nguyen Ngoc Hiep) whose singing awakens the poetic urge in a reclusive poet (Tran Manh Cuong), who has hidden from the world since losing his looks to leprosy. In the third, we meet a young boy (Nguyen Huu Duoc) who sells trinkets on the street and an American veteran (Harvey Keitel) searching for the half-Vietnamese daughter he has never known.

There's a thin line between the archetypal and the stereotypical. The film's fans clearly think the movie falls into the former category. To my eyes, the novelty and exoticism of the setting couldn't disguise the hackneyed situations and sentimentalized characters. Bui's talent is evident. He has a keen visual sense and a knack for storytelling. But he's brought nothing but received ideas to Vietnam. While questioning the dubious "progress" represented by plastic lotus flowers, luxury hotels and Coca-Cola, Bui lays on his own set of oppressive Western cliches. If the movie were in English, would anyone buy this romantic, leprosy-ridden tragic poet, and one more beautiful whore with a heart of gold?

SIGHT AND SOUND, 2/00, p. 58, Geoffrey Macnab

Vietnam, the present day. Kien An starts a new job picking white lotuses for Teacher Dao, a reclusive master. While at work, she sings an old song her mother taught her many years ago. After hearing her, Dao invites her to his inner sanctum and asks her to write down his dictated poems since he has lost his fingers through leprosy. Meanwhile, impoverished kid Woody wanders the streets of Ho Chi Minh City in the rain with a suitcase full of cigarettes and lighters to sell to tourists. He comes across ex GI James Hager, who is searching for the daughter he left behind after the US Vietnam war. Woody loses his suitcase and mistakenly thinks Hager stole it. His master won't allow him home until he retrieves it.

Hai, a cyclo driver, becomes obsessed with Lan, a young prostitute. He begins to wait for her every night outside the hotels where she services western clients. He earns a big cash prize for winning a cyclo race and with the winnings pays for a night with Lan in a hotel room. To her surprise, he only wants to watch her sleep. Woody finds his suitcase. Kien An's master dies. Hager is reunited with his daughter. Hai tracks Lan down to her grubby apartment. Ashamed of her profession, she tries to make him leave, but is eventually won over by his protestations of love.

Three Seasons portrays Vietnam as a country of glaring contrasts: beautiful lotus-strewn rivers and ancient temples on the one hand; the squalor of Ho Chi Minh City (formerly Saigon) on the other. Writer-director Tony Bui (now 26) may have grown up in Northern California, but his sympathies here are with the Vietnamese, not the rich Westerners visiting the country. Bui repeatedly contrasts the struggles of the locals with the pampered luxury the tourists enjoy. Early on, we see two tourists sitting in the back of a cyclo, sightseeing, blithely unaware of their driver's agony as he pedals uphill.

Rather than analyse the social conditions in Vietnam, Bui (who left the country as a young child) uses them as the backcloth for a very sentimental folk tale. His characters could have stumbled from the pages of Dickens: there's Woody the waif who roams the streets selling cigarettes, Lan the beautiful but unhappy prostitute, Hai the big-hearted cyclo driver and Kien An the demure lotus picker. There's even a gnarled ex GI (Harvey Keitel at his most lugubrious, also the film's executive producer) who haunts the city in search of the daughter he left behind in the war. ("I just know it's time to find her to make some sort of peace with this place," he mumbles.)

Bui made *Three Seasons* in reaction to US war movies in which the Vietnamese are depicted "as faceless people running through the jungle with guns," but he risks replacing one set of stereotypes with another. Outside Woody's Fagin-like boss, there is hardly an unsympathetic Vietnamese character in the film. Outside Keitel's kind-hearted GI, Westerners (and western influence) are invariably seen as a force for the bad.

It is intriguing to compare Bui's vision of contemporary Vietnam with that offered by Tran Anh Hung in *Cyclo*. Like Bui, Hung was born in Vietnam but educated abroad (in his case, in France). *Cyclo* is also set in Ho Chi Minh City and features rickshaw drivers, vagabonds and prostitutes. Instead of picture-postcard imagery, its city is one where corruption is always festering close to the surface, with vicious turf wars going on between pedicab drivers, gangland killings, and drug abuse. *Cyclo* has a delirious, expressionistic quality to its film making which Bui doesn't come close to matching. Where *Cyclo* is dark and ironic, *Three Seasons* is optimistic and benevolent in tone. But there's a thin line between optimism and mawkishness. Whereas the street kid in Walter Salles' *Central Station* was tough and resilient, Woody is a doe-eyed little boy lost. The story of the prostitute and the driver obsessed with her is uncomfortably close to *Mona Lisa*. As Bui flits between the four main characters, there are lapses in continuity editing. (Whenever Woody is on screen, it is pouring with rain, but as soon as Hai appears, the weather miraculously clears up.)

Three Seasons is exquisitely shot and in its own naive, lyrical way, is also often moving. Bui is an accomplished (if very manipulative) storyteller. Whether through the poetry the leprosy ravaged master dictates to Kien An as he prepares to die, the imagery of Woody asleep beside the little girl in the rain, or the big emotional set-pieces (for instance, the ex-GI finally meeting his daughter), the young writer-director knows how to crank up the pathos and makes the one big action sequence—the cyclos hurtling through the city—almost as dynamic as the chariot race in *Ben Hur*. The portrayal of modern-day Vietnam may sometimes seem as ersatz as the fake lotuses sold on the street corners, but taken as simple melodrama, *Three Seasons* just about stays afloat.

VILLAGE VOICE, 5/4/99, p. 113, J. Hoberman

Touted as the first American feature shot in Vietnam since the war, Tony Bui's *Three Seasons* is a movie of multiple nostalgias. The big story at Sundance, where it won both Grand Jury Prize and Audience Award, the movie evoked the festival's more-innocent past as purveyor of dull but worthy regional product. Bui's respite from neo-new-wave attitude orgies transported the festival back to its origins just as, in another way, it did the 26-year-old filmmaker himself.

Bui, whose family moved from South Vietnam to Southern California in 1975, returned to his ancestral homeland to make his movie, and, to judge from the evidence onscreen, the place must have acted on him like a drug. *Three Seasons* is languorously, almost glacially, picturesque. Motion is always slightly retarded. The simplistic narrative is as cloyed by time-consuming fillips as the lake where one character harvests her lotuses is choked with flowers.

The Sundance audience must have been so impressed Bui got *Three Seasons* made that they didn't care if he had anything to say. Set in the former Saigon, the movie focuses on a handful of recognizable types—the young flower-seller, a romantic cyclo driver, a cute li'l street kid named Woody, a not-so-hard-boiled hooker, and an American veteran of the Vietnam War (Harvey Keitel) searching for his lost shaker of salt—in this case, the daughter he left behind.

Relationships ensue: The innocent flower girl befriends her bitter, leprous employer; the cyclo driver (played by local star Don Duong) gets hung up on the hooker (American-raised Zoë Bui); the Viet vet stares at the big Coca-Cola sign while the Apocalypse Now bar while Woody searches the city for his purloined box of lighters, watches, and Chiclets.

Bui coats the clichéd script with a thick lacquer of improbability. The atmosphere of imposed drama and rampant inauthenticity is complicated by the personal weather systems of the various characters. The kid lives a perpetual monsoon; the hooker enjoys the sultry heat. Perhaps the movie really does take place over three seasons, but if so, they've all been superimposed: The American and the cyclo driver both buy lotuses from the flower girl; the cyclo driver rescues Woody after he disrupts a screening of an old Clint Eastwood movie and runs bewildered outside (into the pouring rain), still looking for the suitcase that he thinks the Keitel character has stolen.

Three Seasons culminates in a sentimental crescendo of wild coincidence during which just about all the characters get their heart's desire (including, ultimately, the bored spectator, if not soon enough). So much for what the press notes call the "new" Vietnam. There's not much trace of communism in this Ho Chi Minh City—but then there's not much evidence of anything beyond cinematographer Lisa Rinzler's capacity to produce a crisp image.

Respectably crafted to familiar standards, *Three Seasons* looks better than it plays. This totally unconvincing travelogue accomplishes something that the longest foreign war in American history never could—it turns Vietnam into a Bennetton ad.

Also reviewed in:
NEW YORK TIMES, 4/30/99, p. E21, Stephen Holden
VARIETY, 2/1-7/99, p. 57, Glenn Lovell
WASHINGTON POST, 5/14/99, p. C1, Stephen Hunter
WASHINGTON POST, 5/14/99, Weekend/p. 49, Desson Howe

THREE TO TANGO

A Warner Bros. release in association with Village Roadshow Pictures and Village-Hoyts Film Partnership of an Outlaw production. *Executive Producer:* Lawrence B. Abramson and Bruce Berman. *Producer:* Bobby Newmyer, Jeffrey Silver, and Bettina Sofia Viviano. *Director:* Damon Santostefano. *Screenplay:* Rodney Vacarro and Aline Brosh McKenna. *Story:* Rodney Vacarro. *Director of Photography:* Walt Lloyd. *Editor:* Stephen Semel. *Music:* Graeme Revell. *Music Editor:* Ashley Revell, John LaSalandra, and E. Gedney Webb. *Sound:* Peter Shewchuk and (music) John Kurlander. *Sound Editor:* Michael Kirchberger. *Casting:* Marion Dougherty. *Production Designer:* David Nichols. *Art Director:* Vlasta Svoboda. *Set Decorator:* Enrico A. Campana. *Special Effects:* Martin Malivoire. *Costumes:* Vicki Graef. *Make-up:* Marilyn Terry. *Stunt Coordinator:* Shane Cardwell. *Running time:* 115 minutes. *MPAA Rating:* PG-13.

CAST: Matthew Perry (Oscar Novak); Neve Campbell (Amy Post); Dylan McDermott (Charles Newman); Oliver Platt (Peter Steinberg); Cylk Cozart (Kevin Cartwright); John C. McGinley (Strauss); Bob Balaban (Decker); Deborah Rush (Lenore); Kelly Rowan (Olivia Newman); Rick Gomez (Rick); Patrick Van Horn (Zack); David Ramsey (Bill); Kent Staines (Gallery Owner); Ho Chow (Cabbie); Michael Proudfoot (Diner Waiter); Shaun Smyth, Robin Brûlé, and Brett Heard (Interns); Les Porter, Andrew Dolha, and Ned Vukovic (Peter's Friends); Keith Kemps and Lowell Conrad (Dinner Guests); Rumina Abadjieva (Reception Guest); Lindsey

Connell (Newspaper Reporter); Katherine Steen (Beautiful Girl); Steve Richard (Weight Lifter); Stephanie Belding (Joanne); Ray Kahnert (Jonas); Sven van de Ven (Meeting Leader); Glen Peloso (Business Man); Barbara Gordon (Jenny Novak); Roger Dunn (Edward Novak); Meredith McGeachie (Megan); Marni Thompson, Deborah Pollitt, and Anais Granofsky (Amy's Girlfriends); Ed Sahely (George); Lindsay Lesse (Sandy); Tom Forrest (Kissed Guy); Barbara Radecki (TV Reporter); Shemekia Copeland (Blues Singer).

LOS ANGELES TIMES, 10/22/99, Calendar/p. 16, Eric Harrison

Hollywood romantic comedies, like horror films, ask of audiences a certain amount of, shall we say, laxity, as a matter of course. The Cute First Encounter, the Horrible Misunderstanding That Threatens to Tear Our Couple Apart, the Closing Sweet Embrace—these all are conventions that must be shoe-horned into plots that the marketplace demands while at the same time carrying at least a hint of freshness. These competing requirements—genre cliches versus the appearance of novelty—aren't easy to reconcile. In the wrong hands, the results can be regrettable.

Take "Three to Tango."

The filmmakers seem to know intellectually what is required and they touch all the proper bases. The movie's basic premise isn't new—24 years ago "Shampoo" turned a similar scenario into a multilayered social critique—but it's enough time so that "Tango's" target audience might think it is watching something inventive. And in Matthew Perry and Neve Campbell the film has leads who have limitations as actors but who are attractive, not to mention familiar to that oh-so-valuable young demographic because of their TV shows, "Friends" and "Party of Five," respectively.

But first-time director Damon Santostefano and screenwriters Rodney Vaccaro and Aline Brosh McKenna trip themselves up constantly. It's hard to tell whether the problem was that they weren't thinking or that they were thinking too hard about all the wrong things.

Oscar (Perry) and Peter (Oliver Pratt) are struggling architects. They're competing for a $90-million contract from rich slimeball Charles Newman (Dylan McDermott, from TV's hot drama "The Practice"), who mistakenly believes Oscar is gay. Thinking him "safe," the married Newman enlists him to spy on his mistress, Amy (Campbell). Need we say Oscar and Amy fall in love?

The Big Complication is that Amy, too, believes Oscar is gay. And so they both are in pain, she because she thinks their love is doomed to go forever unrequited, he because he's afraid of losing the contract and so puts up with being treated like a platonic pal while watching Amy frolic with Newman.

Left unexplained is why Amy, a bohemian artist who cares nothing for money, would look twice at the handsome but obviously heartless Newman. Or why she so immediately pursues a friendship with Oscar, who is extraordinarily tongue-tied and klutzy during their first meeting. Or why, besides the requirements of the plot, she'd want to move into Oscar's apartment when she gets evicted, even though she barely knows him.

Rather than deal with these implausibilities, the filmmakers stuff the movie with mindless slapstick, even though Santostefano shows no particular feel for staging it and none of the lead actors has a facility for it. Typical of this movie's cluelessness is the way it cavalierly traffics in stereotypes. The movie has one speaking part of consequence for a black male. Guess which character is a professional ballplayer renowned for the size of his sexual organ? And the one Asian with a speaking role is a cabdriver who doesn't speak English.

Also, for a movie that deals with issues of sexual identity and contains a couple of speeches about the importance of self-acceptance, the movie is curious in its treatment of gays. Pratt's foppish gay architect—he's essentially assigned the role of sidekick—is an excitable hand-waver. When one macho seemingly straight character is revealed as gay, he suddenly turns prissy in a way we're supposed to think is funny.

Perry's anxious-but-ordinary guy role isn't much of a stretch from Chandler on "Friends"—but what's with that hairstyle"—but Campbell isn't the least bit persuasive as a lonely, unconventional artist. One suspects the fault lies more with the writing and directing than with her. She seems to have been directed, like the other actors, to project adorableness. Despite an annoyingly chirpy voice, she succeeds, especially when she crinkles her eyes and flashes her brilliant, toothy grin. But a little of that goes a long way.

As for McDermott, he must have it in all of his contracts that he gets filmed in frequent close-up, the better to execute his patented McDermott Stare, where he lowers his chin and gazes smolderingly into the camera. It's a bit much, but when he's not striking poses he gets laughs with his character who's so bad that if he had a mustache, he'd spend the entire movie twirling it.

NEW YORK POST, 10/22/99, p. 56, Jonathan Foreman

"Three to Tango" starts badly—with an awful title sequence and a couple of manic opening scenes. But it then falls into the right gear and turns into a cute, often very funny romantic comedy and an effective vehicle for Matthew Perry, who may yet be the first "Friends" cast member to become a movie star.

Oscar (Matthew Perry) and Peter (Oliver Platt) are a two-man architectural team. When arrogant zillionaire Charles Newman (Dylan McDermott) decides to rebuild a Chicago arts center, he selects their firm and another, more established one (run by Bob Balaban and John C. McGinley) to make competing plans for the project.

On the mistaken assumption that Oscar is gay, Charles asks him to befriend his artist-mistress Amy (Neve Campbell) and keep an eye on her. He's afraid that she might be seeing her ex-boyfriend Kevin (Cylk Cozart). Oscar develops a crush on her before realizing that both she and Charles assume that he's homosexual.

The pretense that Oscar is gay and Peter is straight gets taken much further than either of them expects, thanks to a reporter doing a story on the design competition. To his horror—and that of his straight friends—Oscar actually becomes the most famous gay man in the city.

Perry plays a slightly less prissy version of his Chandler Bing character in "Friends," and sports a strange, red-dyed haircut, but he carries the picture with an ease that's surprising after his imitating turn in "Fools Rush In."

His character here is a little too passive, but Perry is just masculine enough for the closeted-heterosexual joke to work.

Campbell isn't enough of a bombshell for her role, but she makes the most of an amazing smile. McDermott is effectively cast against type as Charles. But, as usual, it's Oliver Platt, so good in "Bulworth" and "Lake Placid," who steals the movie.

Light-hearted and fast-paced, "Three to Tango" has one of those "Notting Hill" endings that's just too sweet and too unbelievable, even for this frothy genre.

It also assumes to be true the notion that what women really want is a straight man who is exactly like their gay best friend.

NEWSDAY, 10/22/99, Part II/p. B9, John Anderson

Once it gets past its overproduced credit sequence (bad sign) and opening aerial shot (worse sign), the romantic comedy "Three to Tango" temporarily becomes an homage to Doris Day films of the late '50s-early '60s. With all those arch closeups, overly deliberate dialogue and pop-art sensibility, the movie achieves such a period facetiousness it comes across as a campy antique.

Which is appropriate enough, because once director Damon Santostefano gets over his brief flirtation with cinematic sarcasm, what we're left with is a big-screen sitcom whose premise seems decades out of date. And whose sense of humor is so deliberately indelicate it might even distract you from how stale the movie is.

Oscar Novak (Matthew Perry), struggling architect and partner of Peter Steinberg (Oliver Platt), is mistaken for gay by slithering tycoon Charles (Dylan McDermott), who is about to award a big contract for the design of a Chicago cultural center. First, however, he wants Oscar to watchdog his girlfriend Amy (Neve Campbell), while she's out with friends and he's home with his wife.

Fearful of losing the contract they don't yet have, Oscar agrees to the ruse, which sets up a seemingly inevitable succession of mistaken-for-gay jokes, gags about body parts and a valiant struggle to avoid ending Oscar's masquerade where it feels natural to do so, because the movie wouldn't be long enough.

Perry is likable, Campbell is boyish and smiles brilliantly and their initial encounter is a convincing portrayal of spontaneous love. They meet cute, skip out on a screaming Chinese cab driver (one of the various ethnicities to get hammered here) and end the evening throwing up in tandem after eating tuna melts so disgusting a raccoon wouldn't touch them. Our heroes may be stupid, but they're sweet.

But among the various puzzlements presented by "Three to Tango"—other than why most of the music is '40s swing—is why Amy, a glass-blowing artist of no visible means and at least a modicum of integrity, is hooked up with Charles. While taste isn't necessarily synonymous with character, what does it say that Charles is attracted to Amy? Either she's flawed, or he's not, but as far as "Three to Tango" is concerned, nothing makes much sense.

Toward the end, the inevitable guitar-based alt-rock song kicks in and we get the cliched, alternating shots of our lovers, the camera spinning around them in an effort to evoke both confusion and impending resolution. The lesson, although it's barely allowed to sink in, is that without the threat of sex, Oscar has been able to develop a real friendship with Amy and become a better person.

For her part, Amy never changes, never regrets anything and presents herself to Oscar like she's doing him favor. Believe it, with friends like these, you don't need a tuna melt.

SIGHT AND SOUND, 8/00, p. 57, Kay Dickinson

Chicago, the present. Oscar and Peter are two architects pitching to win a large contract from tycoon Charles. Having been deliberately misled by Oscar and Peter's business rivals, Charles wrongly assumes Oscar is gay. He asks Oscar to attend a private view featuring the work of his mistress Amy and report back on any would-be suitors she might be attracting. There, Amy invites Oscar to a party; they spend the rest of the night together and grow close.

The next day, Charles tells Amy that Oscar is gay. He then asks Oscar to continue spying on Amy, hinting that his refusal to do so will result in his losing the contract. Amy moves in with Oscar, ignorant of his attraction to her. At a party unveiling the bids for Charles' contract, Oscar discovers he's won the title of "Gay Professional Man of the Year." After being introduced to Charles' wife, Amy leaves, distraught. Oscar follows her. They nearly kiss, but she runs away. She resurfaces while Oscar is on stage to receive his award; during his speech, he admits he's straight and confesses his feelings for Amy. She storms out; Charles withdraws his previous offer of the contract. Oscar and Amy resolve their differences and Charles' wife insists that Oscar and Peter get the job back.

Three to Tango is a romantic comedy which revolves around a case of mistaken sexual identity—despite falling for the insufferably kooky Amy, architect Oscar has to pretend he's gay throughout in order to win a big business contract. To their credit, director Damon Santostefano (whose past credits include the horror film *Severed Ties)* and screenwriters Rodney Vacarro and Aline Brosh McKenna use this premise to mock the surface-level liberalism of their straight characters. The supposedly tolerant Oscar, for instance, finds the gayness that has been wrongly thrust upon him too much to handle; tycoon Charles is keen to flaunt his business connection with Oscar to win liberal kudos. But for all its well-meaning attempts at satire, the film's own attitude towards homosexuality proves as muddled as Oscar's. Most obviously, in having to hammer home for less cognisant audience members which men in the story really are gay, the film resorts to some limp-wristed caricatures (notably, the effeminate, gossipy guests who attend Peter's dinner party).

The finale—which sees Oscar out himself as straight, while on stage to collect his "Gay Professional Man of the Year" award—feels like a typical Hollywood fudge. In his acceptance speech, Oscar makes an analogy between being in the closet and his inability to tell Amy that he loves her. But aside from momentary embarrassment, his public declaration of love has no lasting negative side effects. His bravery here is of a far lesser order than that of the gay members of his audience when they came out. The facile nature of Oscar's uncomplicated promotion of sexual honesty is brought home in a particularly obnoxious cutaway to Oscar's father. Having reacted furiously to news that his son was gay, he glows with joy on hearing Oscar is straight once more.

This said, when the film sticks to what romantic comedy does best—wryly prolonging unrequited heterosexual love and bouncing indefatigably between one-liners—it's enormously likeable. For once Matthew Perry—whose performance in *The Whole Nine Yards* seemed to have been delivered by rote—has landed an appropriate film role as the "passionate, sincere goofball" Oscar. With his many cartoonish pratfalls captured by fluid, elasticated camerawork (his character wreaks havoc when left alone in Amy's kitchen with only a champagne bottle to hand; a dodgy sandwich provokes a bout of severe vomiting during his first night out with her), Perry's performance neatly plays on the physical and sexual awkwardness he brought to the role of Chandler in *Friends*. And for all its failure to comment intelligently on the intricacies of sexual identity, *Three to Tango* does at least offer a touch more wish-fulfillment for *Friends* fans who like to imagine that Chandler and Joey share more than just a flat.

Also reviewed in:
CHICAGO TRIBUNE, 10/22/99, Friday/p. M, Barbara Shulgasser
NEW YORK TIMES, 10/22/99, p. E17, Stephen Holden
VARIETY, 10/18-24/99, p. 35, Joe Leydon
WASHINGTON POST, 10/22/99, Weekend/p. 45, Michael O'Sullivan

TIME TO DANCE, A: THE LIFE AND WORK OF NORMA CANNER

Producer: Ian Brownell. *Director:* Ian Brownell. *Director of Photography:* David Dawkins. *Editor:* Ian Brownell and Webb Wilcoxen. *Music:* Susan Robbins. *Running time:* 70 minutes. *MPAA Rating:* Not Rated.

WITH: Norma Canner; Ruby Dee (Narrator).

NEW YORK POST, 8/19/99, p. 44, Jonathan Foreman

Narrated with absurd reverence by Ruby Dee, "A Time to Dance" is a biographical tribute to "dance therapist" Norma Canner, who in the 1950s and '60s pioneered the use of dance and movement to help disabled children.

It's a technically proficient but unremarkable film that bookends moving, black-and-white footage of young Canner bringing joy into handicapped children's lives with stunningly embarrassing scenes of Canner's contemporary practice.

Nowadays, Canner helps not-disabled but New Age-inclined adults "unblock" themselves by encouraging them to roll around the floor making animal noises—in sessions that resemble the exercises actors use to break down self-consciousness.

Canner was an actress in New York in the 1940s who gave up the stage when she had children. A neighbor brought Canner to a "creative movement" class with modern dance teacher Barbara Mettler, and the session changed her life.

Inspired by Mettler's dictum that "everyone has talent," Canner started to work with physically and mentally disabled children, encouraging them to move and express themselves. The '50s and '60s footage of Canner playing with these children is extraordinarily powerful.

Canner went to work for the Boston school system, and her revolutionary approach to engaging with handicapped kids became a model for today's "early intervention."

Quite how her techniques for these children evolved into wacky-quacky "body-oriented psychology" for grown-ups is never made clear. But as you watch otherwise healthy baby boomers howling, jumping up and down like bunny rabbits or weeping in a fetal position, you're torn between laughter and disgust.

The contrast between the blind, retarded and autistic children, who really need the kind of attention someone like Canner can give, and these exhibitionistic, self-pitying professional types makes them and the therapy itself seem all the more decadent.

VILLAGE VOICE, 8/24/99, p. 126, Elizabeth Zimmer

Wilcoxen's *A Time To Dance* a family affair, initiated by a young man whose mother's life was changed by dance therapist Norma Canner. Narrated by Ruby Dee, their collage of old footage, new talking-head interviews, still photographs, and videotapes of workshops is really a Festschrift celebrating Canners life.   Now 80, she gave up a career in "the left-wing theater" and on Broadway to have a family.   After encountering groundbreaking creative-dance teacher Barbara Mettler, she herself began teaching, developing approaches to movement with disabled children. Now in Cambridge, Massachusetts, she works with people like Anne Brownell, adults blocked and miserable who, through Canner's attention, recover lives of function and pleasure.   Mrs. Brownell, the film's executive producer, now assists Canner; her son Ian and his codirector have assembled a leisurely tribute that respects figures rarely noticed in the swirl of metropolitan media.

Also reviewed in:
NEW YORK TIMES, 8/19/99, p. E5, Anita Gates

TITUS

A Fox Searchlight Pictures and Clear Blue Sky Productions release in association with Overseas Filmgroup of a Urania Pictures and NDF International co-production. *Executive Producer:* Paul G. Allen. *Producer:* Jody Patton, Conchita Airoldi, and Julie Taymor. *Director:* Julie Taymor. *Screenplay:* Julie Taymor. *Based on the play "Titus Andronicus" by:* William Shakespeare. *Director of Photography:* Luciano Tovoli. *Editor:* Françoise Bonnot. *Music:* Elliot Goldenthal. *Music Editor:* Michael Connell, Todd Kasow, Daryl Kell, and Curtis Roush. *Choreographer:* Giuseppe Pennese. *Sound:* David Stephenson and (music) Joel Iwataki. *Sound Editor:* Blake Leyh. *Casting:* Irene Lamb and Ellen Lewis. *Production Designer:* Dante Ferretti. *Art Director:* Pier Luigi Basile, Massimo Razzi, and Domenico Sica. *Set Decorator:* Carlo Gervasi. *Special Effects:* Renato Agostini. *Costumes:* Milena Canonero. *Make-up:* Luigi Rocchetti and Gino Tamagnini. *Stunt Coordinator:* Stefano Mioni. *Running time:* 160 minutes. *MPAA Rating:* R.

CAST: Anthony Hopkins (Titus Andronicus);   Jessica Lange (Tamora);   Alan Cumming (Saturninus);   Colm Feore (Marcus);   James Frain (Bassianus);   Laura Fraser (Lavinia);   Harry Lennix (Aaron);   Angus Macfaydyen (Lucius);   Matthew Rhys (Demetrius);   Jonathan Rhys Meyers (Chiron);   Osheen Jones (Young Lucius);   Dario D'Ambrosi (Clown);   Raz Degàn (Alarbus);   Kenny Doughty (Quintus);   Blake Ritson (Mutius);   Colin Wells (Martius);   Ettore Geri (Priest);   Constantine Gregory (Aemilius);   Tresy Taddei (Little Girl);   Geraldine McEwan (Nurse);   Bah Soulemayne (Infant);   Antonio Manzini (Publius);   Leonardo Treviglio (Caius); Giacomo Gonnella (Sempronius);   Carlo Medici (Valentine);   Emanuele Vezzoli (Goth Leader); Herman Weiskopf and Christopher Ahrens (Goth Soldiers);   Vito Fasano (Goth General); Maurizio Rapotec (Goth Lieutenant);   Bruno Bilotta (Roman Captain).

LOS ANGELES TIMES, 12/24/99, Calendar/p. 22, Kevin Thomas

"Titus" is more travesty than tragedy, a dynamic film from Shakespeare's "Titus Andronicus" directed with unflagging energy by Julie Taymor, who brought "The Lion King" to Broadway with much acclaim.   But Taymor, who also won plaudits for her 1995 staging of "Titus," is not remotely content to bring the Bard's bloody first tragedy to vigorous life, which would be no small accomplishment considering that it yields Grand Guignol lots more easily than catharsis. No, Taymor has to jazz it up in style and design, intending it to serve as a tragic reflection of the horrors of the 20th century.   The result is much visual chaos featuring deliberately jarring and incessant anachronisms, reverberating still further to a frequent rock beat.

Too much all too rarely seems too much to Taymor, which is unfortunate, because in her feature debut she proves to be so compelling a screen storyteller you're never tempted to take a peek at your watch during her film's remarkably zippy two-hour, 45-minute running time. Theatrics that wow audiences when presented live onstage, however, can seem way, way over the top on the big screen.

Taymor opens with a young boy going berserk as he plays with his toy Roman soldiers on an kitchen table in an apartment house about to be bombed.   We could be in London during the

Blitz, or in Bosnia or Chechnya, for that matter. In any event, a big strong guy picks the kid up and carries him into the center of the Colosseum just in time for a weary but victorious Roman general Titus Andronicus (Anthony Hopkins) to enter the vast arena with his troops, his fallen soldiers and his captives, namely Tamora, Queen of Goths (Jessica Lange) and her three sons, the eldest of whom Titus orders slain to appease the gods.

The Romans cheer their returning hero and urge him to become their emperor, but as a rigid traditionalist, he supports the leading claimant, Saturninus (Alan Cumming), a skinny, hysterical decadent. And when Saturninus claims Titus' beloved daughter Lavinia (Laura Fraser) as his queen, Titus readily accedes despite Lavinia being in love with Saturninus' brother Bassianus (James Frain). A couple of plot twists later, Bassianus winds up dead and Lavinia suffers a much worse fate, while Saturninus happily claims as his new queen the glamorous Tamora, which puts her in the perfect position to exact revenge for her sacrificed son and defeated people. It also provides ample opportunity for her shrewd, opportunistic lover, Aaron the Moor (Harry J. Lennix), to wreak mayhem as well. By the time "Titus" is over, 14 of its 22 key characters have met grisly deaths—and by then the obtuse Titus has attained in insanity an insight he hitherto lacked.

This "Titus" in effect takes place simultaneously in Roman antiquity, the present and at any comparable dire moment that has occurred in the 20th century. Taymor evokes the fascist grandeur of Mussolini, turns Tamora's surviving sons into layabout Goths in the current sense of the term, and piles on the pop culture motifs with a trowel. Throughout, an undaunted Hopkins gives a towering portrayal of a tragic hero in the robust, straightforward style of the classically trained Shakespearean actor and gives this production whatever dimension and majesty it possesses. (You feel that enduring all the razzmatazz is the price you're having to pay for witnessing a notable portrayal or a Shakespearean hero rarely played on the screen—like watching John Gielgud's splendid Prospero in "Prospero's Books," Peter Greenaway's arty treatment of "The Tempest.")

Lange is not remotely so lucky. First of all, "Titus," for all its mirroring of 20th century chaos and cruelty, is so primitive, so much a gory revenge melodrama of its era, it has been considered by some scholars merely a sketchy rewrite by Shakespeare of someone else's play. Only Titus and Aaron approach tragic dimension, enhanced here by the impassioned playing of Hopkins and Lennix, whose portrayal of the Moor emphasizes his contempt for the hypocritical white man, Goth and Roman alike. Tamora is little more than a soap-opera or old-time serial villainess, and the way Lange, who is photographed relentlessly unflatteringly, is dressed and directed, she seems more like Zsa Zsa Gabor in "The Queen of Outer Space" than the Queen of Goths.

Why waste an actress of the beauty, talent and stature of Lange when a Monique van Vooren or a Mamie Van Doren would not only have sufficed but also been lots more fun. No actress has been so bizarrely gowned (by the gifted Milena Canonero, no less) since Otto Preminger turned Rudi Gernreich loose on Carol Channing in "Skidoo." Shakespeare threatens to lapse into camp, and "Titus," in trying so hard to be relevant, will swiftly seem passe—indeed, it already does.

There are times when "Titus," for all its pretentiousness, actually soars, as in several moments of inspired surreal fantasy. But mainly it functions like a giant meat grinder, making hash of everything it depicts. You watch it with that obscene sense of fascination that a freeway catastrophe and its aftermath generate—but, come to think of it, that may be exactly what Taymor intended.

NEW YORK, 12/20-27/99, p. 161, Peter Rainer

Titus Andronicus, Shakespeare's most Marlovian play, arrives onscreen as *Titus*, directed by Julie Taymor, and it probably won't change the mind of that work's many denigrators, such as Harold Bloom, who described it as "Stephen King turned loose among the Romans and the Goths." Actually, the way it's been done here, the play comes across as the granddaddy of all Hollywood ghoulfests. Anthony Hopkins as Titus wreaks his vengeance on Jessica Lange's Goth Queen Tamora by baking her two sons into a meat pie for her unwitting delectation and, in general, there seems to be some kind of limb-hacking going on every other minute. Taymor probably chose to film this play, which she's also directed Off Broadway, because it gives her the opportunity to set in motion a flurry of *tableaux vivants*. The film is striking and original and, in its clash of the brutal and the delicately poetic, supremely offputting.

NEW YORK POST, 12/24/99, p. 36, Jonathan Foreman

Theatrical wizard Julie Taymor strides into the feature film arena with "Titus" and emerges with a conditional victory.

Gutsily grappling with one of Shakespeare's least performed and most gruesomely melodramatic plays, the lauded director of Broadway's "The Lion King" makes this tale of savage revenge in imperial Rome accessible and vivid.

Distinguished by some outstanding performances and an arresting style that successfully mixes modern and ancient motifs, "Titus" nevertheless seems too rarefied and demanding to become the same kind of hit as other recent Shakespeare adaptations—despite the big names involved and a surfeit of action and slaughter.

But if "Titus" fails to connect with a mass audience, it won't be for lack of trying. It seems Taymor's overriding concern here is to make a connection between the criminal acts of Shakespeare's powerful, privileged characters and the lewd, murderous behavior that is increasingly a part of modern life.

A nocturnal ceremony that mixes chariots with modern motorcycles and tanks marks the return to Rome of the great general Titus Andronicus (Anthony Hopkins), who has spent years in the north fighting the Goths and has triumphantly returned with a prized prisoner, their beautiful Queen Tamora (Jessica Lange).

A proud military man who has lost all but four of his 25 sons in battle, Titus insists on executing one of his prisoners, and sets the bloody ball rolling by selecting Tamora's eldest son for the sacrifice.

Although her present circumstances prevent it, the enraged Tamora vows revenge, and she is soon afforded the opportunity to pursue it when she unexpectedly becomes the wife of Rome's new emperor, the shifty and impetuous Saturninus (Alan Cumming).

Aaron (Harry Lennix), a Moor who is the queen's secret lover, engineers the murder of Saturninus' brother Bassianus (James Frain), then turns the latter's wife, Lavinia (Laura Fraser), who is also Titus' only daughter, over to Tamora's punk sons Chiron and Demetrius (Jonathan Rhys Meyers, Matthew Rhys), who rape her and leave her propped up in a wasteland sans tongue and with twigs sticking out where her hands were.

Taymor pushes through all this twisted scene-setting with a muscular, confident attitude. As fanciful and occasionally lackluster as some of the inventions may be, these are far outweighed by the constant inspirations, big and small, that begin by dazzling the viewer but gradually become part of the arresting fabric of the picture.

NEWSDAY, 12/24/99, Part II/p. B6, John Anderson

Amid the avalanche of movies at this year's Cannes Film Festival, one of the more buzzed-about events was the screening of a trailer: a 20-minute reel of "Titus," the quasi-modernized adaptation of Shakespeare's "Titus Andronicus" directed by the Tony-winner Julie Taymor, of Broadway's box-office-busting "The Lion King." The images we saw were startling, bold, savage; the pacing was electric. And given that the movie was yet unsold, the reel was the hard sales pitch it was supposed to be; if I'd had several million francs in my pocket, I would have bought it, even though I could hear those nettlesome voices around me intoning, "It's only a trailer ... "The nettlesome voices, of course, were right. Taymor's "Titus" was a great 20 minutes and is now a lugubrious and occasionally laughable two hours and 40 minutes, with that same startling imagery belabored to the point of triteness and a disregard for the text that seems adolescently defiant. Attaching fascist connotations to Shakespearean tragedy is as old as Orson Welles' 1937 "Julius Caesar" and as fresh as Richard Loncraine's 1995 "Richard III," but Taymor seems convinced it's novel. (She certainly seems enchanted by all the leather and rivets.) She also seems to feel that her coy use of anachronism is the height of wit—i.e., when her title character chops off his hand, and seals it in a Zip-Loc bag.

Most unhappily, there is little or no organic affinity between the play and Taymor's admittedly inventive visuals. Little of what she does to accessorize this tale of the Roman general Titus Andronicus—whose daughter is raped and mutilated, whose sons are killed and who exacts an equally terrible revenge on all of his enemies—advances the narrative in any way. On the contrary: She breaks away from the play itself on any number of occasions simply to indulge in graphic mischief and then returns to the text—which, fortunately, is graced by an Olympian Anthony Hopkins who, unfortunately, seems to be in another film entirely.

Based on Shakespeare's most bloody, decadent play—as well as his first—"Titus" is the story of Rome's greatest general, who returns from his defeat of the Goths with Queen Tamora (Jessica Lange) and her three sons in chains.

Sacrificing the eldest to the gods of war, Titus incurs the understandable wrath of Tamora, who will become the bride of new emperor Saturninus (Alan Cumming), plot with her Moor lover Aaron (Harry Lennix) to rob Titus of everything and, eventually, pay an awful price.

Taymor takes the liberty of opening her movie with the fire-and-brimstone abduction of a young boy (Osheen Jones) from his '90s kitchen, where he's been playing with toy soldiers and apparently not taking warfare seriously enough.

Transported to the ancient Colosseum, he's given a crash course in murder, rape, torture, forced amputation, cannibalism and suicide. Eventually the kid assumes the play's role of young Lucius, grandson of Titus, but along the way he's one irritating observer. As irritating, perhaps, as the assumption that one of Shakespeare's rarely produced plays has suddenly come into its own, merely because the public is numb enough not to rebel at the excesses of Titus, or of Julie Taymor, either.

SIGHT AND SOUND, 10/00, p. 61, John Wrathall

Ancient Rome. Having captured Tamora, queen of the Goths, general Titus has her eldest son sacrificed in accordance with ritual, ignoring her plea for mercy. Saturninus, newly acclaimed emperor of Rome, decides to marry Titus' daughter Lavinia but she elopes with his brother Bassianus. Saturninus marries Tamora, who as empress can avenge herself on Titus.

Encouraged by Tamora's Moorish slave Aaron, her sons Chiron and Demetrius murder Bassianus and rape Lavinia, cutting off her tongue and hands. Aaron frames Titus' sons Martius and Quintus for Bassianus' murder. They are sentenced to death and Titus' only remaining son Lucius is banished. Tricked into believing that his sons will be pardoned in return, Titus lets Aaron cut off his hand only to have Martius and Quintus' heads delivered to him. Titus vows revenge and sends Lucius to the Goths to raise an army. His appetite for vengeance is strengthened when Lavinia identifies her attackers. Meanwhile Tamora has given birth to a son; Aaron, not Saturninus, is the father. Aaron runs away with the child and is captured by the Goths, now commanded by Lucius. In an effort to save his baby, Aaron confesses his crimes. Titus invites Tamora and her entourage to a feast. He then kills Chiron and Demetrius and bakes them in a pie, which he serves to Saturninus and Tamora at the feast. Titus then kills Tamora. Saturninus kills Titus. Lucius kills Saturninus. Lucius is proclaimed emperor. He condemns Aaron to death, but spares his son.

Julie Taymor first directed Shakespeare's early tragedy *Titus Andronicus* off Broadway in 1994, and her film version—her feature debut—incorporates many visual motifs (and one cast member, Harry Lennix) from that production. But anyone expecting a stodgy dose of filmed theatre is immediately wrong-footed by the surreal opening sequence, in which a little boy enacts scenes of carnage with his toys on a kitchen table, and then—as if he has conjured up the spirit of violence—finds himself thrust into a real-life war. He emerges into the Coliseum in time to see Roman general Titus march in at the head of his victorious troops, terrifying in their mud-caked armour. It's a breathtaking and brilliantly choreographed opening, plunging us straight into Act 1, Scene One of the play.

Titus was released in the US last year, but was beaten to a UK release by the later *Gladiator*. It's interesting to note the plot similarities. Titus, like *Gladiator*'s Maximus, declines the chance to rule Rome, and instead finds himself viciously persecuted by a capricious new emperor. Their subsequent blood-soaked revenge is observed by a little boy, in both cases called Lucius and in both cases a pretty, rather feminine child with a pageboy hairstyle, in striking contrast to the brutal war-like adult Roman males. At the end of both films, young Lucius is destined to inherit the throne, and so embodies the nation's hopes for peace.

Taymor's style, however, couldn't be more different from Ridley Scott's. Instead of creating ancient Rome with CGI, she shoots as far as possible in actual locations, in Rome itself and in the awesome coliseum at Pula in Croatia. But her aim in doing so isn't heightened verisimilitude; these authentic Roman stones are trod by actors dressed in an eclectic blend of classical and 20th-century costumes, an unsettling conflation of imperial and fascist Rome, with more than a dash of Las Vegas glamour.

Eager to allow Shakespeare's words to shine through as clearly as possible, Taymor shoots the dialogue scenes fairly straight, with a minimum of background action. As if in compensation, she punctuates them with moments of stunning spectacle, whether set-piece crowd scenes (armies on the move, a Fellini-esque orgy) or hallucinatory flashback sequences using multilayered video imagery. This alternation between talk and spectacle gives the film a slightly awkward, theatrical rhythm, so that despite the dynamism of individual sequences, the film never quite picks up the momentum to sustain it over 160 minutes. But this is as much to do with the unwieldy structure of the play itself, which—apart from its astonishing lurches in tone between atrocity, poetry and wilful absurdity—seems to offer us serial protagonists to root for: first Tamora, then Aaron the Moor, and only lastly, from Act III onwards, Titus himself.

Taymor's audacious mix of styles may not ultimately gel but if you had to film *Titus Andronicus,* it's hard to imagine doing it in a more challenging, dynamic and faithful—way. And what theatre could rival Taymor's cast—Anthony Hopkins as Titus, for once stretched by a role to the range of his talent; Jessica Lange as Tamora, the revenge-driven empress presented here as a human tigress, swathed in tattoos and sheathed in gold lamé; and Harry Lennix bringing a grace and dignity to the role of her lover and henchman, the villainous Aaron.

TIME, 12/27/99, p. 166, Richard Corliss

Shakespeare has caught a few breaks at the movies lately. *Romeo and Juliet* and *Richard III* became vigorous films that did honor to both the Bard and the medium. Now Julie Taymor, the magician, who on Broadway turned *The Lion King* menagerie into masked enchanters on stilts, takes Shakespeare's goriest play, *Titus Andronicus,* and makes it vivid, relevant and of elevating scariness.

A boy, his face hidden by a paper-bag helmet, plays an improvised war game with toy soldiers on his kitchen table. An explosion startles him. the room bursts into flames, and a giant totes him out of the late 20th century and into the 1st century Rome. Hence, the action will take place in both ages. Imperial warriors, caked with the dust of conquest, tramp through the Colosseum like bulky action figures. Their leader Titus (Hopkins) is a straight-spoken military man of the past; his rival, the emperor Saturninus (Cumming), is pure oil of modern politician, oozing endearments and threats, riding through Rome in an open limo with a bubble top, seizing an betraying Titus' daughter Lavinia (Fraser). Tattoos abound, on the royal Goth captives led by Tamora (Lange) and on the Moor Aaron (Lennix). A big band plays at Saturninus' Saturnalia; heavy metal accompanies the Goths. A tiger stalks the forest.

Taymor keeps the eye as busy as the ear; she embellishes the story without disfiguring it. There's room in her bestiary for fine performances, a pretty collision of histrionic styles. Cumming preens, Lennix schemes, Lange smolders. Then all cede to Hopkins, who, in the suitably grisly finale, serves up Titus as Hannibal Lecter with a noble vengeance. Rare and well done!

Other movies this season have bigger stars, higher budgets, pricier effects, deeper tans. But if you're looking for a complex weave of word and image, and an early clue to where film might go in its second century, your Christmas shopping can begin and end with this towering *Titus*.

VILLAGE VOICE, 12/28/99, p.121, J. Hoberman

A nonstop carnival of murder, rape, and mutilation that begins with a human sacrifice and culminates in a cannibal feast, *Titus Andronicus* is William Shakespeare's contribution to the gross-out horror-comedy. The filmmaker best suited to bring it to the screen would've been Hershel Gordon Lewis or the Brian De Palma of *Carrie.* (The most nightmarish prospect: Oliver Stone.) The much lionized Julie Taymor staged the play in 1994, and while her film version isn't exactly a solemn spectacle, neither is it much fun.

Taymor repeats her stage prologue—a kid making an increasingly combustible mess with a bunch of toy soldiers—before making with the Sturm und Drang herself as victorious General Titus Andronicus (Anthony Hopkins) parades his captive Goths through the Roman Colosseum. Taymor's "Look Ma, I'm filming!" use of creative geography and jazzy camera angles precludes even the most minimal emotional involvement. As the body count mounts, the Romans party—a sub-*Rocky Horror* fashion parade of leather trenchcoats and black lipstick.

Competing with this sodden mise-en-scène, the relatively laid-back Americans come off better than the raging Brits. Where Alan Cumming's fascist fop would have been laughed out of *Cabaret*, Jessica Lange makes a splendid Goth queen. (The nipples on her golden breastplate are a nice touch.) Given the stupidity of the tragedy's nominal hero, Taymor zeroes in on Aaron, the supervillainous Moor, as its most articulate figure: "Aaron will have his soul black like his face," Harry Lennix hisses in his big scene. Hopkins meanwhile cavorts like a herky-jerky puppet. Evidently he didn't need to see the finished movie before informing the press of his decision to give up acting.

Also reviewed in:
CHICAGO TRIBUNE, 1/21/00, Friday/p. J, John Petrakis
NATION, 1/24/00, p. 35, Stuart Klawans
NEW YORK TIMES, 12/24/99, p. E19, Stephen Holden
VARIETY, 1/3-9/00, p. 79, Todd McCarthy
WASHINGTON POST, 2/11/00, Weekend/p. 43, Desson Howe

TOPSY-TURVY

A USA Films/October Films release in association with Thin Man Films/The Greenlight Fund/Newmarket Capital Group of a Simon Channing-Williams production. *Producer:* Simon Channing-Williams. *Director:* Mike Leigh. *Screenplay:* Mike Leigh. *Director of Photography:* Dick Pope. *Editor:* Robin Sales. *Music:* Carl Davis and Gary Yershon. *Music Editor:* Michael Connell. *Choreographer:* Francesca Jaynes. *Sound:* Tim Fraser. *Sound Editor:* Peter Joly. *Casting:* Nina Gold. *Production Designer:* Eve Stewart. *Art Director:* Helen Scott. *Set Decorator:* Eve Stewart and John Bush. *Set Dreser:* Lisa Lloyd and Andrea Coathupe. *Costumes:* Lindy Hemming. *Make-up:* Christine Blundell. *Running time:* 160 minutes. *MPAA Rating:* R.

CAST: Jim Broadbent (William Schwenck Gilbert); Allan Corduner (Arthur Sullivan); Timothy Spall (Richard Temple); Lesley Manville (Lucy "Kitty" Gilbert); Ron Cook (Richard D'Oyly Carte); Wendy Nottingham (Helen Lenoir); Kevin McKidd (Durward Lely); Shirley Henderson (Leonora Braham); Dorothy Atkinson (Jessie Bond); Martin Savage (George Grossmith); Eleanor David (Fanny Ronalds); Alison Steadman (Madame Leon); Dexter Fletcher (Louis); Sukie Smith (Clothilde); Roger Heathcott (Stage Doorkeeper); Stefan Bednarczyk (Frank Cellier); Geoffrey Hutchings (Armourer); Francis Lee (Butt); William Neenan (Cook); Adam Searle (Shrimp); Kate Doherty (Mrs. Judd); Kenneth Hadley (Pidgeon); Keeley Gainey (Maidservant); Gary Yershon (Pianist in Brothel); Katrin Cartlidge (Madame); Julia Rayner (Mademoiselle Fromage); Jenny Pickering (Second Prostitute); Sam Kelly (Richard Barker); Charles Simon (Gilbert's Father); Philippe Constantin (Paris Waiter); David Neville (Dentist); Matthew Mills (Walter Simmonds); Nicholas Woodeson (Mr. Seymour); Nick Bartlett and Gary Dunnington (Stage Hands); Amanda Crossley (Emily); Kimi Shaw (Spinner); Toksan Takahashi (Calligrapher); Akemi Otani (Dancer); Kanako Morishita (Shamisen Player); Theresa Watson (Maude Gilbert); Lavinia Bertram (Florence Gilbert); Togo Igawa and Eiji Kusuhara (Kabuki Actors); Naoko Mori (Miss "Sixpence Please"); Eve Pearce (Gilbert's Mother); Neil Humphries (Boy Actor); Vincent Franklin (Rutland Barrington); Michael Simkins (Frederick Bovill); Cathy Sara (Sibyl Grey); Angela Curran (Miss Morton); Millie Gregory (Alice); Jonathan Aris (Wilhelm); Andy Serkis (John d'Auban); Mia Soteriou (Mrs. Russell); Louise Gold (Rosina Brandram); Shaun Glanville (Mr. Harris); Julian Bleach (Mr. Plank); Neil Salvage (Mr. Hurley); Matt Bardock (Mr. Tripp); Brid Brennan (Mad Woman); LADIES AND GENTLEMAN OF THE CHORUS: Mark Benton (Mr. Price); Heather Craney (Miss Russell); Julie Jupp (Miss Meadows); John Warnaby (Mr. Sanders); Kacey Ainsworth (Miss Fitzherbert); Ashley Artus (Mr. Marchmont); Richard Attlee (Mr. Gordon); Paul Barnhill (Mr. Flagstone);

Nicholas Boulton (Mr. Conyngham); Lorraine Brunning (Miss Jardine); Simon Butteriss (Mr. Lewis); Wayne Cater (Mr. Rhys); Rosie Cavaliero (Miss Moore); Michelle Chadwick (Miss Warren); Debbie Chazen (Miss Kingsley); Richard Coyle (Mr. Hammond); Monica Dolan (Miss Barnes); Sophie Duval (Miss Brown); Anna Francolini (Miss Biddles); Teresa Gallagher (Miss Coleford); Sarah Howe (Miss Woods); Ashley Jensen (Miss Tringham); Gemma Page (Miss Langton-James); Paul Rider (Mr. Bentley); Mary Roscoe (Miss Carlyle); Steven Speirs (Mr. Kent); Nicola Wainwright (Miss Betts); Angie Wallis (Miss Wilkinson); Kevin Walton (Mr. Evans).

CHRISTIAN SCIENCE MONITOR, 12/17/99, p. 15, David Sterritt

Gilbert and Sullivan rank with the most legendary teams in the history of musical theater. But their lives weren't always as smooth as the operettas that flowed from their pens during their glory days in the late 19th century.

Sullivan was especially perplexed by the confines of success. Would he ever be able to escape the world of light, frolicsome entertainment and compose the serious music he dreamed of? How could he renew his artistic freshness when an enthusiastic public kept clamoring for more of the same old thing?

Mike Leigh may have been mulling over the same question. He has written and directed a string of acclaimed movies such as "Naked" and "Secrets & Lies" that explore the harshness of modern working-class life, often with a strong dose of political anger.

But his beautiful new picture, "Topsy-Turvy," takes different tack. It etches a vivid portrait of Gilbert and Sullivan as they enjoy professional acclaim, wrestle with private doubts, quarrel with one another, and manage to create "The Mikado" despite all these distractions.

This departure in subject matter is mirrored by lush camera work by cinematographer Dick Pope, who normally captures an expressive grittiness that suits Leigh's alternately sad and ferocious characters.

In other ways, though, the Leigh technique is very much in evidence. The movie was built from the ground up in his usual manner—starting not with a polished script but with a basic idea, a lot of research, and improvisation by the actors, from which the final plot and dialogue were developed. This helps account for passionate conviction of the acting by the cast.

And what a cast it is. Jim Broadbent ("Bullets Over Broadway." "The Crying Game") gives one of his most perfectly tuned performances as William Schwenk Gilbert, and Allan Corduner is equally adept as Arthur Sullivan, the more discontented member of the team. Excellent support comes from Leigh veterans Timothy Spall and Lesley Manville, among many others.

"Topsy-Turvy" is neither as light nor as G-rated as Gilbert and Sullivan's own works. It's a lengthy film—one of the few recent movies to more than justify it leisurely running time—and it takes quick but graphic glimpses at surprisingly dark secrets in the lives of its heroes and their creative partners, related to matters like sex and drug use.

This is a mark of the movie's seriousness, though. It would have been easy for Leigh and company to cook up a soufflé as airy as "The Mikado" itself—and its somber moments are an essential part of its fidelity to the time, place, and people it depicts. One of the year's very best pictures, it's sure to find a wide audience and a lot of nods at Oscar time.

CINEASTE, Vol. XXV, No. 2, p. 57, Richard Porton

For G K. Chesterton, *Bab Ballads,* William Schwenck Gilbert's playfully astringent collection of verse, exemplified quintessentially English nonsense. Armed with what Chesterton labelled "divine lunacy," Gilbert joined forces with the composer Arthur Sullivan in the 1870s. Their peculiar professional chemistry, frequently undermined by their ongoing antipathy towards each other, inspired some of the most popular comic operas (or, if you prefer, operettas) in the English language. From a contemporary vantage point, the ever-bickering team's work is also fascinating for a number of intriguing contradictions. Gilbert and Sullivan gently mocked some of the most hallowed English institutions—the legal system, the House of Lords, and the Royal Navy were all objects of their satirical scrutiny. Yet Gilbert's witty librettos betray a profoundly conservative bias; the growing Victorian movement to educate women, social reformers of all stripes, and upstart esthetes such as Oscar Wilde were all targets of his venomous disdain. Gilbert may have been the reigning Victorian sovereign of *Topsy-Turvy*dom, but in operas like *Iolanthe* and *H.M.S. Pinafore* the social apple cart is upset only to foster a countervailing effort to affirm the status quo at the end of an evening's entertainment. Nevertheless, the operas' tuneful wordplay looked forward to much that was innovative and even subversive in twentieth-century English humor. It is indeed possible to trace a fairly direct path from Gilbert and Sullivan to the brittle flippancy of Noel Coward, the inspired zaniness of Peter Sellers, and even the anarchic shenanigans of Monty Python's Flying Circus. (Across the pond, Groucho Marx paid his respects to G and S by starring in a television version of *The Mikado* in 1960.)

At first glance, Mike Leigh, whose films have consistently mocked the middle-class audiences who made Gilbert and Sullivan's enormous popularity possible, would seem an unlikely champion of these Tory satirists. Leigh, however, is not particularly interested in their putative political agenda. As a connoisseur of English eccentricity, he is far more interested in Gilbert, the dyspeptic, curmudgeon, and Sullivan, the sanguine epicurean, than in issuing Olympian value judgments. Furthermore, as a director who relishes narrative detours as much as linear exposition, he is equally fascinated by the lives led by the musical duo's professional and romantic partners, the theatrical milieu which gave them sustenance, and broader historical premonitions of a British empire slowly losing its moorings despite the triumphalist ideology embraced by most eminent Victorians.

Gilbert and Sullivan's creative enterprises were often fueled by their feuds, a point that *Topsy-Turvy* wittily reiterates as it chronicles their attempt to emerge from a collaborative slough of despond. During a virtuosic scene in which a two shot slyly captures the pair uneasily plopped down on a couch in Sullivan's parlor, the composer objects to a Gilbert libretto which features another whimsical plot involving magical transformations and benign "topsy-turvy" devices. Fearing creative stagnation, Sullivan laments that his "orchestrations are becoming repetitive," having "rung all the changes possible in the way of variety of rhythm." The cantankerous Gilbert's reply to his partner's objections isn't forthcoming until a complementary scene in which the argument continues in producer Richard D'Oyly Carte's office. Gilbert dismisses Sullivan's pleas for greater realism by sardonically insisting that, "If you wish to write a grand opera about a prostitute dying of consumption in a garret, I suggest you contact Mr. Ibsen in Oslo. I am sure that he will be able to furnish you with something suitably dull." His riposte also includes a statement that might well be considered his, and in some respects, Leigh's esthetic credo: "Every theatrical performance is a contrivance, by its very nature."

What seems for a time like a case of irreconcilable differences eventually culminates in Gilbert's inspiration for one of his most enduringly popular operas, *The Mikado*—a wacky Orientalist fantasy that subtly skewers Victorian shibboleths with barbed humor. Leigh has a field day with the Victorian infatuation for all things Japanese. A presumably authentic Japanese village featured at a crowd-pleasing exhibition in London's posh Knightsbridge section provides a great opportunity for the film to highlight Gilbert's unwitting condescension towards a Japan he yearns to emulate but can only hazily comprehend. This delightfully skewed version of musical history later depicts Gilbert practicing kendo with a sword in the seclusion of his study, while *The Mikado* itself envisions Japan as a fun-house mirror reflection of late nineteenth-century England. The opera's comic hero, Ko-Ko, is nearly executed for inordinate flirting (a reference in the libretto to Knightsbridge is one of Gilbert's many in-jokes), and *Topsy-Turvy* is particularly inventive in evoking the Victorian genius for publicly enforcing moral strictures while shamelessly violating taboos in private.

In fact, a somewhat overschematic tendency to ironically contrast several protagonists' public decorum with their private peccadillos might be considered one of the film's few minor structural lapses. George Grossmith, a fine comic actor and master of the patter song, unwinds with morphine injections in his dressing room, the coquettish actress Leonora Braham has a near-fatal weakness for alcohol, and Sullivan, plagued by weak kidneys, relishes his sojourns to a Parisian brothel. While historically accurate, these biographical details pop up like pesky flags to remind us of the Victorian netherworld (it is useful to recall that Steven Marcus called his study of nineteenth-century pornography *The Other Victorians,* and the "other Victorians" were often proper Victorians on a holiday from propriety) that lurked beneath the surface of a hierarchical society.

Topsy-Turvy's references to the accoutrements of creeping modernity are considerably less heavy-handed. Sullivan is fascinated by an early version of a ballpoint pen, while Gilbert delights in gadgets of all sorts. Gilbert's father, however, a remnant of a previous era, refuses to ring his son's electric doorbell. Perhaps, most importantly, the introduction of electric lighting not only makes the Savoy Theater more salubrious: this technological feat almost single-handedly paves the way for an entirely new realm of mass entertainment suitable for middle-class 'toffs' as well as humble groundlings.

Leigh also acknowledges, however obliquely, the relationship between Britain's imperial aggression and the seemingly innocuous entertainment cooked up by Gilbert and Sullivan. Looking back at the nineteenth-century's zeal for imperial aggression in 1902, the American philosopher William James condemned Anglo-Americans' "unhesitating and unreasoning" tendency to "inflict our civilization upon the 'lower' races." This sort of arrogance of power surfaces briefly in *Topsy-Turvy* when Grossmith and his fellow actor, Rutland Barrington, bemoan the humiliation of General Gordon's defeat by the Mahdi's troops at Khartoum. Absurdly oblivious to what would now be termed cultural difference, Grossmith maintains that the "Hottentot in the desert doesn't play cricket." Barrington chimes in: "We strive to bring them Civilization and this is their gratitude," a smugness also evident in a casual racism intermittently discernible in Gilbert's wordplay. One of Ko-Ko's most famous patter songs (not included in the film), for example, enumerates individuals who "surely won't be missed" and takes a passing swipe at "the nigger serenader, and others of his race." (A recent recording of *The Mikado* recasts the offending line by pointing instead to the odiousness of the "banjo serenader.")

Like Renoir's *The Golden Coach* and Carné's *Children of Paradise, Topsy-Turvy* emphasizes the theater's communitarian ethos, although Gilbert is clearly a martinet—even if his gruff bark is at times more ferocious than his bite. In an almost proto-Hitchcockian manner, he arranges the blocking of every opera in advance with the aid of a miniature stage and markers representing the position of all of the actors. Leigh's overweening fascination with the creation of theatrical illusion comes to the fore in an affectionate recreation of one of *The Mikado*'s most famous set pieces, the "Three Little Maids From School" song. Despite the fact that Bertolt Brecht's ideal of 'the Popular' (a left-populist affirmation of "forms of expression intelligible to the broad masses") couldn't be more diametrically opposed to Gilbert and Sullivan's stolidly middle-class conception of popular art, *Topsy-Turvy*'s comic rendering of the rehearsal of this song demonstrates how Gilbert shares Brecht's conviction that, after rehearsals "what ... comes before the spectator is the most frequently repeated of what has not been rejected." The conservative Gilbert, like the Marxist Brecht, scorned undiluted naturalism, although, paradoxically, the "Three Little Maids" sequence derives its humor from Gilbert's hilariously misguided attempt to infuse this elaborate production number with authentic "Japaneseness." After Gilbert recruits several Japanese women to demonstrate appropriately demure manners to his befuddled dancing master and cast, it becomes obvious that the company's stiff-upper-lip emulation of this display is destined to be ineradicably English. The interlude does not merely undermine Gilbert's own capricious aspirations to realism; it also reiterates Leigh's own belief that his work interweaves the flotsam and jetsam of everyday life with a style of dramaturgy and performance that ironizes and theatricalizes the most mundane gestures and incidents.

After the farcical tone of much of the film, as well as the predominantly male spirit of camaraderie shared by the Savoy actors, one of Leigh's penultimate scenes celebrates the quiet fortitude of Gilbert's wife, Kitty, and, by implication, all Victorian wives. Painfully aware of her status as a marginal woman, the childless Kitty, without any hint of sarcasm, suggests that her husband write an opera with a "young and beautiful heroine who gradually becomes older and older" while plagued with visions of "empty perambulators." The usually obstreperous Gilbert can only mutter that he "shouldn't imagine Sullivan'd much care for that."

Leigh has often acknowledged his indebtedness to Dickens, and *Topsy-Turvy*'s memorable gallery of eccentrics and curmudgeons is a fitting tribute to the novelist's legacy. Jim Broadbent's indelibly crusty Gilbert, Allan Corduner's suavely hedonistic Sullivan, Leigh veteran Timothy Spall's endearing portrait of the legendary Savoyard, Richard Temple, and Lesley Manville's stoic Kitty synthesize pathos and humor with a flair Dickens would probably have admired.

FILM QUARTERLY, Fall 2000, p. 39, Jared Rapfogel

In making *Topsy-Turvy* Mike Leigh, a director famous for ignoring the rules of dramatic moviemaking, has made the strange choice of taking those rules upon himself. A Mike Leigh period piece about Gilbert and Sullivan (Sir William and Sir Arthur, respectively, the librettist and composer of the gently satirical and wildly popular late nineteenth-century comic operas) sounds like something out of a Monty Python sketch. What Leigh has come up with is far from laughable—it's one of his best movies—but the Monty Python comparison isn't so far off the mark in terms of his decision to do it in the first place. After the 1999 New York Film Festival screening of *Topsy-Turvy*, Leigh admitted that the improbability, the absurdity, of the idea is at least part of what appealed to him. His "naughty" (Leigh's word) desire to make a movie that apparently goes against the grain of his career seems to have freed him; the movie is unmistakably his own but with a heft, a breadth, and, perhaps because music is at its center, a lyricism that is new and exciting. It's a democratic, big-hearted, open film, but with Leigh's characteristic sharpness and lack of sentimentality.

Topsy-Turvy is the first of the British director's movies to fit comfortably into an established genre. On the surface anyway, it's a part of the well-worn and even old-fashioned tradition of the backstage picture. This is a particularly strange genre for Leigh to take on. His movies are marked by their insistent, stubborn ordinariness, sometimes shading into ugliness. There's never even a suggestion of a Hollywood sheen to his films—the setting is always drab or grim working-class Britain, the characters are, if not unappealing, certainly unexceptional (other than the exceptionally bitter, angry Johnny in *Naked)*. And, with regard to plot, Leigh has always rejected the conventions of narrative filmmaking—the story in his movies is always secondary to the characters. All of which makes *Topsy-Turvy* the least likely Mike Leigh project imaginable. The backstage drama would seem to conflict with every one of these tendencies. Even if the movie weren't about two of England's most famous theatrical figures, the fact that it is a period piece erases any sense of ordinariness. And far from attempting to make this vanished world familiar, Leigh emphasizes its strangeness, from our retrospective vantage point (the obsolete, unwieldy phones) as well as from the characters' perspective (the novelty of a pen which houses its own ink). *Topsy-Turvy* is the best kind of period movie: it immerses us in a world which is richly detailed and entirely convincing, but also as alien as that of a science fiction movie.

The characters in a backstage drama are always charismatic and appealing. And the plot is, broadly speaking, almost as fixed as in sports movies, with the successful show in the place of the big game. Leigh doesn't let the genre shackle or limit him, though. If anything, it gives him something to work from, something to apply his approach to, and as a result, from our point of view, the genre acts as a sort of experimental control. Setting *Topsy-Turvy* alongside other backstage dramas allows Leigh's style to stand out in bold relief. The familiar elements make it even more distinctively a Mike Leigh movie because of how he chooses to approach and subvert the genre.

The beauty of the movie is that there's no tension in the confrontation between the genre's conventions and Leigh's approach. He transforms the traditional format by slowing it down, expanding it. Leigh's movies have always worked against the conventions of dramatic filmmaking; he rejects the plot mechanics and the rush toward the conclusion of most movies, and *Topsy-Turvy* is different only in that it contains the conventions it contradicts. But there's nothing jarring about this contradiction. Leigh's not trying to deconstruct or explode the form, to expose the artificiality of the movie's Hollywood forebears, so the conventions and the anti-conventions coexist peacefully and even with a kind of harmony. Leigh simply cleanses the conventions of their artificiality—working within them, he makes them natural, full, convincing.

The first step in this process is to shift the emphasis away from what, according to the tradition of the great-man (or men) movie, should be the film's subject. The only easy way to describe *Topsy-Turvy* is to say that it's a movie about the creation of Gilbert and Sullivan's operetta *The Mikado*. It begins with the duo, having already collaborated on several works, on the verge of ending their professional relationship. The movie shows us their growing estrangement, and then the conception and creation of *The Mikado* from Gilbert's visit to a travelling exhibition on Japanese customs—the inspiration for the show—through the writing, casting, rehearsals, and, finally, the production. But it's misleading to say that *Topsy-Turvy* is a film about Gilbert and

Sullivan. They're the most famous and, in some ways, the most charismatic of the movie's characters, and as the creative forces behind the show we see taking shape, they're necessarily at its center. But part of what makes *Topsy-Turvy* such an exhilarating movie is that there's very little distinction between the center and the fringes, between Gilbert and Sullivan and the host of characters—producers, actors, stagehands, and others—surrounding them. Where most movies concentrate on an essential character or story line or concept, with the secondary characters less defined the more tangential they are, *Topsy-Turvy* is written in deep focus. It's not the first movie to pull this off: this is Robert Altman's specialty, and it's been fairly popular lately *(Happiness, Boogie Nights, Magnolia, Cradle Will Rock, Black and White,* etc.). But the approach is more striking here because Leigh is dealing with historical characters—and all the audience expectations, conscious and unconscious, that such a choice entails. And it's one thing to expose us to more than the usual number of characters, but Leigh then goes further by declining to introduce them to us. Whole scenes are devoted to characters who seem to be almost totally irrelevant to the story (to what we see as the story) and whose relationships (to Gilbert and Sullivan, to one another) are not at all clear. The movie seems at first sloppy, unfocused, maybe poorly edited. But eventually Leigh's approach comes into focus. What he has put on the screen is a wealth of detail, and it's only when it becomes clear that there is no single subject, that the subject is broad and organic, expanding and shifting to include anything and everything that passes across the screen, that we begin to orient ourselves. Everything eventually falls into place, and the portrait (of a community) turns out to be all the richer and more convincing for having been, at first, apparently so sloppy and chaotic. It's not messy; it's simply full, abundant.

It's partly Leigh's strategy of creating the script in collaboration with his actors, of farming out each character and each scene, that creates *Topsy-Turvy*'s deep, even focus and wealth of detail. Each character, no matter how ostensibly minor, feels vivid enough to be a full-fledged protagonist because each, in a sense, has its own author. Leigh's approach to filmmaking (or, more to the point, to screenwriting) is even more singular than it sounds. Plenty of directors let their actors improvise, and to some improvisation is an integral part of their filmmaking. For Leigh, however, it's not merely a tool for freeing the actors; for him, improvisation doesn't have anything to do with spontaneity, since by the time the cameras are rolling the actors are sticking to the script. His method is a way of freeing the script from the conventions of dramatic writing and of preventing these conventions from overwhelming the characters, from trapping them in an artificial structure. He uses improvisation to write, not to film; to free the characters, not the actors.

As a result, it's not just the number of characters and wealth of detail that take some getting used to the rhythm of the movie is disorienting at first as well. The movies that *Topsy-Turvy* seems to resemble have a headlong quality to them—they rush us on to the conclusion. But each scene in *Topsy-Turvy* is self-contained; the plot is submerged beneath the events of the moment. It's as if Leigh had frozen each frame of a traditional backstage drama, enlarged it, and made a mini-movie out of each one—each scene has its own stars, its own plot trajectory, its own themes. Each character and each scene has an autonomy that's lacking in most movies, they develop independently from the overall plot, the overriding conception. The movie plays out in two dimensions, so to speak; it moves forward (at its own pace) but also expands outward.

In every backstage drama we watch the rehearsals; we're witness to the behind-the-scenes intrigue; we see, eventually, part of the final performance. But we're rarely allowed to settle in, to appreciate the rehearsal or the intrigue or the performance for its own sake. Watching Gilbert and three of his actors rehearse part of *The Mikado*, we're aware that it's a step in a process and that eventually we'll see their work in its finished form, but we're so engrossed we'd hardly care if the payoff were denied to us. This scene, like almost every other, works on many more levels than we're used to. It's documentarylike in that we can take any number of things away front it. We can choose to observe the creative, theatrical process, with regard to either the writer or the actors; we can watch for insights into the characters, Gilbert or the others; we can appreciate the scene they are practicing and think about how it Should be performed; we can simply appreciate the leisurely, open rhythm and shape of the scene. And on some level we appreciate each of these facets.

The same goes for the performances themselves: it's not necessary, plot-wise, to show us the musical numbers in their entirety, but Leigh isn't afraid that engrossing us in a scene from *The*

Mikado will distract us from the movie. And this particular risk has a big payoff—it would be a poor movie about an artist if it were unwilling to give us a substantive glimpse of the art. The excerpts we see from the operetta entertain us in their own right, as well as adding to the portrait Leigh is painting—of Gilbert and Sullivan certainly, but also (especially in the beautiful, majestic final shot) of the characters performing the piece.

Leigh's greatest weakness can be his tendency towards caricature, his habit (paradoxical, given his method) of assigning one grotesque trait to his characters. In fairness, his overall strategy is usually to create seemingly one-note, simplistic characters who, over the course of the movie, develop into complicated, multi-layered people. It's an effective approach, but a slightly schematic and, by now, predictable one. The characters in *Topsy-Turvy*, though, become more and more complicated without starting out as caricatures. Leigh reveals their layers with more subtlety and delicacy, and above all more quietly, than in his recent films. The last ten minutes of *Topsy-Turvy* are revelatory. Jim Broadbent's Gilbert and Allan Corduner's Sullivan have been convincing and charismatic from the beginning, but in these last moments, Leigh takes a graceful, utterly unsentimental dip far deeper into their personalities. Having entertained us with their creativity and charisma, he adds a bold, unexpected, clear-eyed final stroke to their portraits, giving us a glimpse of another, less public, more serious side of their personalities, and deepening the movie's attitude towards them. And in a beautiful, immensely moving final gesture, he gives the last moment to a character who has played a relatively small role in the movie thus far, transforming her, in a matter of seconds, into a vivid, fascinating character, and at the same time demonstrating eloquently that, though she has not created the music she is performing, her profound identification with it makes it as much *hers* as it is Gilbert and Sullivan's. *Topsy-Turvy* is a rarity—a movie about artists that is genuinely about art, and the artistic process, rather than merely personality and fame.

NEW STATESMAN, 2/21/00, p. 46, Jonathan Romney

As a rule, Mike Leigh doesn't do genre films. Indeed, his portraits of the asperities of British life have effectively created a genre in themselves. But his new film, *Topsy-Turvy*, is at once Victorian costume drama, biopic and backstage comedy. It takes some nerve to tackle three unfamiliar genres in one go, and still more to take Gilbert and Sullivan as your subject. After a century, the popular jury is still out on G&S: anyone who isn't a fully paid-up D'Ovly Cartist will come to *Topsy-Turvy* still uncertain whether the Savoy Operas are archaic fustian or brilliant satiric confections ripe for reappraisal. The only certainty is that, when you see the film, you'll realise that you knew more of the songs by heart than you suspected.

In fact, *Topsy-Turvy* has all the Leigh trademarks: an ensemble of fine-tuned performances, with close mapping of characters' idiosyncracies—the way they use language and move in the world. Everything is so actutely observed—"analysed" might be a better word—that the Leigh eye is always evident, from the eating of oysters to the awkward early uses of the telephone. We tend to imagine that we know exactly how Leigh works with his actors—extended preparation making them "live" in a part for months at a time. Yet he has always been exceptionally guarded about what that method actually entails; so we can only wonder how it might have been applied here. It's one thing for David Thewlis, preparing for *Naked*, to devour several Penguin Modern Classics a day, quite another to imagine that Jim Broadbent spent six months with his moustaches perfectly waxed, or that the entire cast might have lived cooped up together in a larger version of *The 1900 House*.

In a sense, Leigh has always gone in for comic opera. The performances he favours are so far from naturalistic drama or comedy that, with their extraordinary heightened modulations, they are actually closer to opera than to straight acting: Brenda Blethyn practically sings her leitmotif, "Alright darlin", in *Secrets and Lies*. The skills it takes to act for Leigh may actually have most in common with the sort of breathing techniques and deportment required to perform a perfect Lord Chancellor's "Nightmare Song".

The story begins a decade into the partnership of Gilbert and Sullivan, with the lukewarm reception of *Princess Ida*. W.S. Gilbert (Jim Broadbent resembling a weary, even more blimpish Auberon Waugh) grizzles at a review detailing "symptoms of fatigue". Meanwhile, the *bon viveur* Sir Arthur Sullivan (Allan Corduner) is tired of "trivial souffles". You can't help suspecting that the film is Leigh's own response to becoming a national institution with the magisterial *Secrets and Lies*, then hitting an awkward anti-climax with *Career Girls; Topsy-Turvy*'s primary subject is the difficulty of finding new tricks in a sustained career.

G&S—tellingly not seen together until 45 minutes into the film—are saved by *The Mikado*, arrived at by chance when Mrs. Gilbert (Lesley Manville) persuades her husband to visit a Japanese exhibition. This is one of several ways in which the film reworks the conventions of the Hollywood backstage musical. Another is the way that a song from the show is axed, then reprised. It's fated to be the show-stopper, the Mikado's "punishment fits the crime" number.

The film is also good on the routineness of success and its effect on the private life. In a wonderfully poignant scene, Gilbert slouches home with another success under his belt: his ever-solicitous wife starts feeding him an idea for the next opera, but it's really her harshly realistic commentary on their marriage.

The 160-minute running time is more than justified by the way the film sprawls into a chorus of key moments and dazzling turns: among them, Gilbert's aged father (the imposingly rheumy Charles Simon) lapsing into aggrieved dementia; Timothy Spall and Kevin McKidd in a savourous luvvie double act; and Shirley Henderson's sensually etiolated soprano. The music, of course, is not only in the numerous, handsomely staged songs, but also in the dialogue. When Ron Cook's Richard D'Oyly Carte announces "I could murder for a pork chop", it may seem anachronistic, but if Leigh—who tends to research these things—says it's so, then who's to argue?

NEW YORK, 12/20-27/99, p. 159, Peter Rainer

Mike Leigh's *Topsy-Turvy* is a rich tribute to the theater and theater people. It's about how Gilbert and Sullivan's *The Mikado* came to be produced, but one never thinks of it as a stuffy biopic, or even, for all its plush period bric-a-brac, as a costume drama. Leigh and his players have such a tender and sympathetic understanding of this late-Victorian era that the pastness before our eyes shades into the present; we need no interpreter to make emotional sense of what we see. The artists' observations and intuitions bring us very deep into the drama.

The surprise here, of course, is that Leigh attempted this project at all; he's essentially a chronicler of the messiness of the modern-day lower-middle classes. The confinements of historical biography and Victorian décor do not, at first blush, jibe with his self-styled "organic" way of working, in which he brings the cast together for many months to improvise character detail and dialogue before the cameras roll. Leigh is a freestyle martinet: He sets up a long-term way to explore the emotional depths of his material that must be tremendously liberating for performers, and yet all the while he's shaping and beveling everything, and when he's finally filming, he's no friendlier to ad-libbing than, say, Cecil B. DeMille was. Leigh is often overpraised, I think, for his method: plenty of filmmakers have elicited from actors the same high degree of psychological nuance without requiring them to live a commune-like existence in which their characters' biographies from birth are minutely recorded and picked over. There are moments in Mike Leigh's movies—I'm thinking especially of *Naked*—when I'd have been grateful for a lot *less* character analysis. The inherent danger in Leigh's technique is overindulgence. In movies, sometimes—oftentimes—you don't really want to know everything about a person. Just like in real life.

The rigors of making a period film, and of sticking relatively close to the facts, probably helped cauterize some of Leigh's usual excesses. Ironically, what should by all rights be his most reined-in film seems instead one of his freest. The freedom shows up in Leigh's love for this milieu—for what Gilbert and Sullivan conjure up for him. He is, above all else, a man of the theater, and he has the true theater lover's passion for the giddy reaches of drama: not only high emotion but low burlesque. That last term is crucial, because it's what W. S. Gilbert, played extraordinarily well here by Jim Broadbent, rails against and tries to deny as he defends what he does to Allan Corduner's equally extraordinary Arthur Sullivan, who longs to write grand opera, not comic operetta. The *topsy-turvy* of the title, derived from a negative review of *Princess Ida* in the London Times, refers to the upside-down clickety-clack cleverness of Gilbert's plots, and it's both a disparagement and a tribute. The beauty of Gilbert and Sullivan's art, which is also its mystery, is that, gloriously minor, it's more redolent and lasting than many works regarded as major.

Unlike a lot of movies about artists that skimp on their art, *Topsy-Turvy* really gives us an earful and an eyeful. Especially once *The Mikado* is in rehearsal, we're never far away from Gilbert and Sullivan's words and music, and this gives the film a continual lilt. Leigh and his longtime cinematographer, Dick Pope, shoot the Savoyards up close, so we can see their sweat and makeup, and that helps make intimate what might otherwise resemble a series of production numbers. The performers, all of whom do their own singing, are playing characters who both fulfill our need for theatrical caricature and move beyond it. And so, for example, Timothy Spall's Richard Temple, who plays the Mikado, is a glorious stage diva who, when his Mikado's song is cut by Gilbert, reveals beneath the vamping a hurt man's pathos. Gilbert himself is a maze of contrariness, resolutely confident and mortally stung by his limitations. On the occasion of his opening-night Mikado triumph, he confesses to his wife, Kitty (Lesley Manville), that "there is something inherently disappointing about success," and he means it. Leigh doesn't play out the sobbiness of moments like these; he just touches on the sadness and moves on.

Though the film runs nearly three hours, it gets better as it goes along. The quirks and peccadilloes of its people, which may at first seem like cute bits, open into a deeper mood. Kitty may appear to be the archetypal "understanding" wife of a genius-autocrat, but she is pained by her separateness from her husband's emotional life, and when, near the end, she suggests to him a scenario for a new opera, it's something mad and surreal—an encoded way of passing along to her husband her hurt. The drinking problem of one of the Savoyards, Leonora (Shirley Henderson), which initially seems like an affectation, tears into her fresh beauty. (It's like watching a rose petal famish from drought.) Leigh gives her the final scene in the film, alone onstage singing "The Sun Whose Rays Are All Ablaze," and it's like his benediction for her, and for all who are fragile like her.

Sullivan comes across at first like a suave libertine, but he has an overcast look. After *The Mikado* has opened, his mistress, Fanny Ronalds (Eleanor David), tells him, as he lies ill in bed, that he lights up the world, and that he can't help it. Sullivan, who composes some of his sweetest music while plagued by bad kidneys, doesn't fully approve of his airy gift; it lacks the seriousness of high art, and so, for him, his renown is a kind of gentle mockery.

With all this, I've rarely seen a movie that brought out more of the affirming joys of a life in the theater. Sullivan conducting *The Mikado* can't hold back his bliss; it overrides everything that pulls him down. Gilbert, directing the cast, is in his eminent domain: The martinet has become patriarch, wit, father-confessor, God. He lives for nothing higher. The players onstage are transformed, too; their vivacity represents their finest dream of themselves. *Topsy-Turvy* delivers an even larger dream; the theater as life's apotheosis.

NEW YORK POST, 12/17/99, p. 61, Jonathan Foreman

Of all the movies that have depicted backstage theater life or followed the creation of a work of art, few are as much fun as "Topsy-Turvy." Mike Leigh's delightful new film about Gilbert and Sullivan, the writing and composing team who dominated light opera at the end of the last century.

This music-filled costume picture is an extraordinary departure for Leigh. a writer-director best known for politically committed realistic dramas ("Naked." "Secrets & Lies") set in contemporary working-class England.

Yet the discipline of working in period style seems to have brought out the best in Leigh, liberating him both as a writer and a director. And his famous method of working with actors, for months before going into production works at least as well here as it has on smaller canvases.

The story focuses on composer Arthur Sullivan and librettist William Schwenk Gilbert as they recover from the critical and box-office failure of their latest work, "Princess Ida," in 1884.

Sullivan (Allen Corduner), a libertine with a married American mistress (a bizarrely accented Eleanor David), decides that the time has come for him to write serious music, and he threatens to split the partnership and break with the Savoy Theater.

But his contractual obligation to impresario Richard D'Olyly Carte (Ron Cook) forces him to continue working for the company and with Gilbert (Jim Broadbent), a much more staid and formal man.

However, Sullivan announces that he hates Gilbert's latest idea for a plot, considering it more silly "topsy-turvy" of the kind the public rejected in "Princess Ida," and he refuses to write any music until his partner can come up with something better.

Gilbert is at a loss until his wife, Kitty (Lesley Manville), drags him to an exhibition of Japanese art and culture. The experience inspires him to draft "The Mikado," a witty satire on English life disguised by a Japanese setting.

Then the real work begins as Gilbert and Sullivan together choose their performers and begin rehearsals. And by the time the production is ready for its first performance, you're almost as desperate for it to go well as are Gilbert, Sullivan and their cast.

It's a film that revels in the sensual pleasure of music while capturing brilliantly the tension that grips any theater company before the curtain goes up.

And with the exception of one silly scene in which Leigh has some singers discuss the murder of Gen. Gordon in a way that's supposed to make them seem idiotically patriotic, the film treats Victorian folk with the respect they deserve. For once they're not just uptight fools in corsets and topcoats.

Both Corduner and Broadbent are terrific. But the actors who play actors, Martin Savage, Timothy Spall, Kevin McKidd and Shirley Henderson, come close to stealing the show.

The overall result of their collaboration with Leigh is a charming, warm, witty movie, funny one minute and moving the next, which brims with love for the theater in general and for Gilbert and Sullivan's work in particular.

To be sure, it's too long, but it never really loses its grip on you, and it's easy to understand why Leigh couldn't bear to cut out several wonderfully executed songs and scenes from "The Mikado" itself.

NEWSDAY, 12/17/99, Part II/p. B2, John Anderson

It's really a shame that this has been such a mediocre season for movies—not bad, per se, just unremarkable—because it lowers the bar for Mike Leigh's "Topsy-Turvy," unquestionably the best film of this year, but with really no competition. No one likes to watch a rout.

To watch "Topsy-Turvy," on the other hand, is an unparalleled delight, a reinvention of the movie musical as well as a tartly funny exploration of art and its invention. By picking up the story of English musical giants Gilbert & Sullivan at a point where their collaboration is expiring from exhaustion, writer-director Leigh can create one of those fabulous constructs that exists on multiple levels. Musical extravaganza. Thriller. (Will they pull it all together and thrill the Savoy Theatre once again?) And as a meditation on artistic solitude and the sacrifices made on behalf of the muse. "Topsy-Turvy" may be a change of pace for Leigh—director of such gritty blue-collar-Brit dramas as "Naked," "Life Is Sweet" and "Secrets & Lies"—but it never betrays his artistic ethos. What goes on behind the stage is as potent as anything upon it.

Even before he crawls off his sickbed to conduct the premiere of "Princess Ida," Sir Arthur Sullivan (Allan Corduner) has had it. His collaborations with librettist W.S. Gilbert (Jim Broadbent)—the so-called "king of topsy-turvydom" thanks to his plots about magic potions/changed identities—have run dry. Sullivan wants to create "legitimate" music. An extroverted sensualist, he heads off to Paris and cavorts with naked prostitutes who sing Offenbach. Upon returning, he still wants to stop.

Gilbert—the beneficiary of Broadbent's finest performance ever—wants things to remain the same. A dyspeptic creature, Gilbert can't express the love he obviously feels for wife Kitty (Lesley Manville), who suffers in their childless marriage. His own mother's a crone, his father is mad; Gilbert is defined by his career as Sullivan's cohort and haunted by the belief that while Sullivan is a genius, he certainly is not.

One of Leigh's masterstrokes is using music that's not so great—the excerpts from "The Sorcerer" and "Princess Ida" are meant to show that perhaps Sullivan is right: G&S are spinning their wheels. While this makes for some slow going at first, it also makes the film's epiphanies all the more exhilarating—specifically when Gilbert's souvenir samurai sword falls off the wall like Newton's apple and—ta da!—inspires "The Mikado."

Wisely, Leigh cuts from the smiling, inspired Gilbert directly to the stage of the Savoy and a full "Mikado" number: The creative process will follow, but the manifestation of Gilbert's brainstorm must first be seen. Backtracking, Leigh shows us Gilbert hiring Japanese people from the exposition to teach his actors how to move and more or less inventing the role of the director—especially in one wonderful set piece that's full of droll harrumphing and might well have been cut from the film by a less adventurous distributor (and probably over Leigh's dead body).

Leigh employs a cooler hand than usual in cataloging the backstage, offstage vagaries of his characters. An exploded vein on the leg of singer Jessie Bond (Dorothy Atkinson) is bandaged by her dresser pre-performance, with little comment and no explanation. Her fellow company member Leonora Braham (the fabulous Shirley Henderson) drinks a bit, although when the impresario D'Oyly Carte (Ron Cook) brings up her "little problem" during contract negotiations, we're not quite sure whether Leonora's got other skeletons in her closet. The redoubtable singer George Grossmith (Martin Savage) keeps a discrete hypodermic in his dressing room, and Richard Temple (a terrific Timothy Spall) has unresolved issues with his mother. Their problems aren't belabored, but rather are part of the fabric of 1880s theater, things to be overcome or ignored in the effort to make art on stage.

Art is what "Topsy-Turvy" is about, both in its story and its execution and especially at its conclusion, when Leonora, played with exquisite desolation by Henderson, takes the stage alone. Artists are always solitary, Leigh is saying: Gilbert and Sullivan may be synonymous to history but what they created they created alone. Knowing this and watching the ensemble glories of "Topsy-Turvy" is a little like reading Dickens on an island. Or hearing the last strains of a symphony echo through an empty room.

NEWSWEEK, 12/24/98, p. 64, David Ansen

"Topsy-Turvy," a period film so lived-in it makes most historical movies look like costume parties, begins in the humid London summer of 1884, when Gilbert and Sullivan's latest Savoy theater production, "Princess Ida," is wilting on the boards, and the two utterly different collaborators have reached a creative impasse. The composer, Arthur Sullivan (Allan Corduner), is a hedonist and bon vivant who aspires to write more serious music. The grouchy, proper W.S. Gilbert (Jim Broadbent), married to the long-suffering, childless Lucy (Lesley Manville), writes the clever librettos, whose inspired silliness seems an unlikely outgrowth of such an anhedonic man.

Mike Leigh's wonderful, bittersweet film (voted best picture of the year by both the New York Film Critics Circle and the National Society of Film Critics) isn't actually about their collaboration—they work separately, and have surprisingly few scenes together. It's Leigh's loving but tough-minded salute to the creative process itself. The G&S stalemate is broken when Gilbert, inspired by a Japanese exhibition in London, conceives of the idea for "The Mikado." In delightful, knowing detail, "Topsy-Turvy" takes us from first rehearsal to opening night. At the helm is Gilbert, virtually inventing the process we now call "directing." Broadbent brilliantly captures his gruff mix of authority and insecurity. This may seem a far cry from Leigh's usual gritty contemporary turf ("Secrets and Lies," "Naked"), but it shares with his other work an abhorrence of cliché and a crowd of richly idiosyncratic characters.

The notion of art as an organically evolving process is crucial to Leigh. Almost alone among directors, he creates his scripts in the rehearsal period through improvisations. Only when all the pieces have fallen into place is the text set in stone and the cameras begin to roll. This is the first time Leigh has turned his eye on his own theatrical world, and it feels giddily right. Naturally, "Topsy-Turvy" is filled with delicious backstage drama, his superb actors reveling in the opportunity to play their 19th-century counterparts. Among the standouts are Timothy Spall as the leading man sent into a tizzy when Gilbert cuts his best song; Martin Savage as the tremulous, morphine-addicted actor George Grossmith; and Shirley Henderson as the hard-drinking Leonora.

There may be a bit too much "Mikado" for everyone's taste, protracting the already long running time, but the scenes Leigh and Co. have created are dazzling, none more so than the heartbreaking encounter near the end between Gilbert and his wife. In this stunning scene of marital misunderstanding, Broadbent and Manville show us what great acting is all about.

SIGHT AND SOUND, 3/00, p. 55, Andy Medhurst

London, 1884. William Gilbert and Arthur Sullivan's new comic opera *Princess Ida* opens to mixed reviews and struggles to attract large audiences during a summer heatwave. This unexpected failure is the catalyst that makes Sullivan decide he must break away from the partnership and compose more serious music.

He leaves London to travel through Europe. Gilbert continues to monitor the progress of *Princess Ida* receiving disappointing news from both the theatre management and his wife Kitty. The show's cast members lament the show's failure, comparing it unfavourably to Gilbert and Sullivan's previous successes.

D'Oyly Carte, the impresario who produces the operas, visits Sullivan in Paris and is told the composer stands firm on his decision to suspend working with Gilbert. Sullivan returns to London and finally tells Gilbert he wishes to work alone. Gilbert is affronted but nonetheless outlines his ideas for their next collaboration. Sullivan remains unimpressed, saying their work has become too predictable. Carte calls a meeting where his colleague Helen Lenoir tries but fails to persuade Gilbert and Sullivan to put aside their differences. To take his mind off his troubles, Kitty takes Gilbert to see an exhibition of Japanese culture, which so impresses him it inspires an idea for a new opera. He takes the idea to Sullivan, who enthusiastically agrees to recommence their partnership.

During the extensive rehearsals for *The Mikado,* Gilbert brings performers from the Japanese exhibition to help train the English singers on how to seem "more Japanese". After the dress rehearsal he cuts the Mikado's main song, upsetting the company's veteran performer, Richard Temple. A protest by other cast members ensures the song is reinstated. *The Mikado* proves to be an enormous success.

After the triumphant premiere, Kitty reveals to Gilbert how unhappy she is with their marriage, in particular their lack of children, but he evades her accusation.

Imagine how startled you'd be to discover that Krzysztof Kieslowski had secretly made a series of knockabout comedies *(Three Colours: Nurse, Three Colours: Camping* and *Three Colours: Up the Khyber)* or that Martin Scorsese's next picture was to be set in an antique shop in Chipping Sodbury. Multiply that surprise a hundredfold and you'll be half way to grasping the shock value of *Tospy-Turvy.* It's a "Mike Leigh film", but you'll scan the screen in vain for the images and sounds that phrase conjures up. Instead of tragi-comically half articulate people in questionable cardigans, *Topsy-Turvy*—an account of a few key years in the career of the popular English operetta team Gilbert and Sullivan and their circle—offers lavish period costumes and screeds of florid dialogue. Leigh the poet of the underclass seems to have been replaced by Leigh the reveller in middlebrow theatrics. Mike the minimalist has delivered a film which frequently merits the adjective "rollicking". Has the man who I'd insist was Britain's greatest living film maker defected to that most reprehensible of tendencies, heritage mongering?

Mercifully not, though there are a few stretches in this overlong film where he teeters on the brink. Leigh's appetite for the music is evidently immense, resulting in too many indulgent performances of their songs. Yet there's still plenty here to satisfy Leigh devotees, if they can peer past the aspidistras. The staging is as rich and complex as one would expect, there is the typically judicious balance of heartbreak and farce, and there are several diamond sharp moments when an apparently casual observation illuminates a whole architecture of social assumptions.

Nonetheless, the film marks an inarguable departure. Leigh is dealing with real historical figures, flirting with traditional genres (the biopic, the backstage musical, the dreaded heritage movie), and shedding his trademark heightened naturalism for a full-blooded plunge into thespian excess. Theatricality is not just the hallmark of the film's method, it forms one of its principal subjects. This allows Leigh (who is also, let's not forget, a seasoned stage director) and his actors to have great fun recreating a world of backstage bitching and production politics while simultaneously indicating how people's egos, health and relationships suffer in such a hothouse atmosphere. Timothy Spall's performance as the ageing star Richard Temple, for example, is a perfectly judged study of juxtaposed fragility and bombast. Throughout the film, Leigh contrasts on-stage polish with private insecurity, the latter manifesting itself in alcoholism, drug dependency and dangerous levels of vanity.

He's also keen to explore the dynamics of creativity, setting the happily repetitive librettist Gilbert (Jim Broadbent) in conflict with composer Sullivan's loftier ideals. Gilbert finds it both perplexing and hurtful that Sullivan (Allan Corduner) wishes to dispense with a hit formula, while Sullivan, anticipating the Woody Allen of *Stardust Memories,* is terrified of being so seduced by a profitable rut he might never fulfil his true potential. This tension between them is so fundamental Sullivan's abrupt and underexplained change of heart to embrace *The Mikado* strikes one of the film's few false notes. It's tempting to speculate how their dispute relates to Leigh himself. Following the huge success of *Secrets and Lies* (after which *Career Girls,* for all its deft pleasures, did little more than mark time), should he choose a Gilbertian path of more-of-the-same, or follow Sullivan towards ambition and risk? In such a context, *Topsy-Turvy*'s unexpected lurch into costume territory seems a bold move, paradoxically lending a dash of daring to this usually ultra-conservative format.

On the surface, Leigh's script urges us to root for Sullivan, not so much because he is particularly admirable but because Gilbert is such a buffoon. Broadbent, however, is so magnificent as Gilbert we can see beneath the gruff foolishness of the facade to the emotionally stunted man underneath. The son of two clearly deranged parents and the husband in a stilted marriage, Gilbert clings to his formulaic writing because formulas offer certainty, a certainty unattainable in the destabilising realm of emotions.

This fear of feeling provides the film with an emotional climax that's one of the greatest scenes in any Leigh film, as Gilbert's wife Kitty (Lesley Manville, hitherto under-used) finally, if obliquely, confesses her longing for children. Gilbert listens as she hovers on the edge of a breakdown but can offer her nothing but bluff masculine evasion. The English dread of open emotion is one of Leigh's abiding obsessions (it forms the core of his excruciatingly precise first film *Bleak Moments),* and his ability to locate it even here, amid all those galumphingly good humoured songs, is another reason why *Topsy-Turvy* is more than just another costume outing.

It's this attention to the anxious underbelly of Victorian culture that does most to save *Topsy-Turvy* from descending into pictorialism. The film leaves us in no doubt that 19th-century England was a society founded on sexual hypocrisy and funded by imperial exploitation. The first threads through the film in various guises: Sullivan's trips to overseas brothels, the Gilberts' barren marriage, the fine lines actresses must tread between propriety and scandal, the repression and hysteria in the home of Gilbert's mother and unmarried sisters. Imperialism emerges in the unadorned racism prompted by the news of General Gordon's defeat at Khartoum and the greedy appropriation that twists the nuances of Japanese culture into the slant-eyed pantomime of *The Mikado.*

There are other, more tantalising asides which further underline how the gathering momentum of modernity was unsettling the texture of the times. A running joke concerns the impact of newfangled technologies such as the electric doorbell, the fountain pen and the telephone, but it's a joke with darker implications about how older ways of communicating were being sidelined. There is the brief journey Gilbert makes through the poverty-stricken streets that lie just beyond the Savoy Theatre; and there are enough hints of queer undercurrents in the backstage milieu to remind us that the Oscar Wilde trial was only a few years away.

These social comments are never crassly driven home, but they resonate strongly in the mind afterwards. That's how Leigh works best, since when he peddles undisguised propaganda the results can be as thin as the one-dimensional Thatcher-bashing which marred *High Hopes. Topsy-Turvy,* like *Life Is Sweet* or *Meantime*, steeps you in a culture so deeply it's only by looking back and peering closely you can detect how wider forces have cruelly impinged on individual lives. In that sense, despite its initially disorienting costume trappings, It's very much "a Mike Leigh film" after all.

TIME, 12/27/99, p. 181, Richard Schickel

It's 1884, and Gilbert and Sullivan need a hit. *Princess Ida* is just not doing the sort of business they're used to. But Sullivan (Corduner) wants to write something more serious than comic operettas. And Gilbert (Broadbent) keeps trying to recycle stale story lines that his collaborator (and the critics) dismiss.

Their solution to this problem—based on Gilbert's chance encounter with Japanese culture at a London exhibition—turns out to be *The Mikado*. And Mike Leigh's movie about mounting that best of all G. & S. works turns out to be one of the year's more beguiling surprises. It is not at all the sort of thing one expects from Leigh, the very sober creator of films like *Naked* and *Secrets and Lies,* for it is basically the story—somewhat comic, somewhat desperate, very carefully detailed—of rehearsing and putting on the operetta.

What gives *Topsy-Turvy* its heartfelt heft is the way in which it shows how this process takes over everyone's life—eventually driving out all distractions, whether they be Gordon's defeat at Khartoum, the sterilities of Gilbert's marriage or the many anxious neuroses of the acting company. It is show biz as therapy, with all tensions temporarily resolved when the show is a hit. But there is also a sense of real, very Mike Leighish, life in this film that darkens and transforms it. And transfixes us.

VILLAGE VOICE, 12/21/99, p. 143, J. Hoberman

Christmas comes early—at least for this reviewer—with a pair of highly audacious, hugely enjoyable, exceptionally well-written, brilliantly edited, and exuberantly actor-driven extravaganzas. Mike Leigh's *Topsy-Turvy* is the year's least likely, most infectious tour de force, with Paul Thomas Anderson's wildly ambitious, if not entirely successful, *Magnolia* chasing it for second place.

Leigh's open-ended, quasi-improvised comedies of working-class manners haven't lacked for gritty humor. Still, nothing in his oeuvre anticipates *Topsy-Turvy*. The whole idea of this acerbic populist doing Gilbert and Sullivan's late-19th-century la-di-da is a jaw-dropper that only makes sense upon seeing the movie. Showman that he is, Leigh has produced a highly personal statement on the subject of middle-class art—an essay both genially digressive and fiercely intelligent, taking as its motto William Gilbert's remark that "every performance is a contrivance by its nature."

Collaborators for a dozen years, writer Gilbert (Jim Broadbent) and composer Arthur Sullivan (Allan Corduner) are two distinct and forceful personalities whose extremely lucrative creative partnership has reached an impasse. (Their first scene together is a long-take, static-camera two shot that gets its twist from the thrust and parry of baroque pleasantries.) The solution must be imported, literally. Inspiration arrives when gloomy Gilbert's long-suffering wife, Kitty (Lesley Manville), talks him into visiting a Japanese culture exhibit that encompasses everything from teahouse rituals to samurai swords. Gilbert is amazed—Leigh allows a kabuki performance to take over the screen—and, back home with a few souvenirs, goes into his trance. Leigh flashforwards to *The Mikado,* a fully realized vision in red, gold, and pink, and then backs up a bit to show Gilbert reading his new script aloud to the appreciatively giggling Sullivan.

Topsy-Turvy is as analytical as it is entertaining. For all its outlandish Japanoiserie, *The Mikado* is clearly a play about England and, even more, a play about playing. *Topsy-Turvy* is set in 1885, at the height of the empire, and as the pop Orientalist *Mikado* goes into rehearsal, the British army is defeated in the Sudan. (The show, however, must go on: The "shocking news from Khartoum" pales before the real story of the day. Two actors have made themselves sick through a surfeit of oysters.) Leigh fragments the various theatrical productions with cutaways to the wings, pit, and—a key location—the producer's office. Itself thriftily produced, *Topsy-Turvy* is a low-budget period piece that solves one major problem by including only three brief exteriors. The past is represented by a mise-en-scéne of Victorian knickknacks (as well as such newfangled communication contraptions as telephones and fountain pens) to emphasize the theatricality of everyday life.

Enlivened by dressing-room shenanigans, star fits, business negotiations, and bits of naturalized comic-opera shtick—Gilbert drafting three abashed Japanese women to demonstrate authentic Japaneseness to his baffled Cockney dancing-master—the movie's last hour is essentially a backstage musical. Leigh has his cake and eats it too. He deconstructs *The Mikado,* reveling in its artifice, even as he successfully defamiliarizes, reinvents, and rehabilitates the play. (I'm told that *Topsy-Turvy* has been less-than-enthusiastically received in England, where the embarrassing resurrection of fusty G&S may be less a curiosity than a slap in the face of public taste.)

A residual socialist, Leigh even contrives a bit of successful mass action in which the show's chorus mobilizes to petition the boss and effect a change in the show. The premise may be a bit weak but the dramatic confrontation is not—indeed, the whole movie is a tribute to collective endeavor. (Would that the entire cast receive a single acting award—although I would single out Broadbent's forbidding, droll Gilbert, Timothy Spall's ripely theatrical diva, and Shirley Henderson's brittle, kittenish soubrette.) Thanks in part to the organic method by which Leigh and his cast compose a screenplay, *Topsy-Turvy* is in no sense schematic—although the rigor of Leigh's technique provides an object lesson for the far creakier *Cradle Will Rock*. The movie's surface ripples with emotional undercurrents. The action continually suggests messier and more complicated lives than can be shown in even a three-hour film—although a sharp and poignant postscript deepens the overall meditation on success, disappointment, and vanity. (As *Topsy-Turvy* is, more than anything else, a paean to actors, Leigh gives the last word to Henderson's triumphant, shamelessly narcissistic Leonora.)

This is not only Mike Leigh's strongest film since *Naked* but a true show-making epic. *The Mikado* may be second-rate popular art but *Topsy-Turvy* is a terrific popular movie—it can be bracketed with *Nashville* and *Children of Paradise* and, as a celebration of human enterprise, it is richer and more fully realized than either.

Also reviewed in:
CHICAGO TRIBUNE, 1/21/00, Friday/p. B, Michael Wilmington
NATION, 1/3/00, p. 35, Stuart Klawans
NEW REPUBLIC, 1/10/00, p. 26, Stanley Kauffmann
NEW YORK TIMES, 12/17/99, p. E15, Janet Maslin
VARIETY, 9/6-12/99, p. 64, Deborah Young
WASHINGTON POST, 1/21/00, p. C5, Rita Kempley
WASHINGTON POST, 1/21/00, Weekend/p. 43, Desson Howe

TOY STORY 2

A Walt Disney Pictures release of a Pixar Animation Studios production. *Executive Producer:* Sarah McArthur. *Producer:* Helene Plotkin and Karen Robert Jackson. *Director:* John Lasseter, Ash Brannon, and Lee Unkrich. *Screenplay:* Andrew Stanton, Rita Hsiao, Doug Chamberlin, and Chris Webb. *Story:* John Lasseter, Pete Docter, Ash Brannon, and Andrew Stanton. *Director of Photography:* Sharon Calahan. *Editor:* Edie Bleiman, David Ian Salter, and Lee Unkrich. *Music:* Randy Newman. *Music Editor:* Bruno Coon. *Sound:* Gary Rydstrom, Tom Myers, and (music) Frank Wolf. *Sound Editor:* Michael Silvers. *Casting:* Ruth Lambert and Mary Hidalgo. *Production Designer:* William Cone and Jim Pearson. *Art Director:* Bryn Imagire. *Set Dresser:* David Eisenmann. *Special Effects:* Kelly T. Peters. *Animator:* Glenn McQueen. *Running time:* 92 minutes. *MPAA Rating:* G.

VOICES: Tom Hanks (Woody); Tim Allen (Buzz Lightyear); Joan Cusack (Jessie); Kelsey Grammer (Prospector); Don Rickles (Mr. Potato Head); Jim Varney (Slinky Dog); Wallace Shawn (Rex); John Ratzenberger (Hamm); Annie Potts (Bo Peep); Wayne Knight (Al McWhiggin); John Morris (Andy); Laurie Metcalf (Andy's Mom); Estelle Harris (Mrs. Potato Head); R. Lee Ermey (Sarge); Jodi Benson (Barbie); Jonathan Harris (Cleaner); Joe Ranft (Wheezy); Andrew Stanton (Emperor Zurg); Jeff Pidgeon (Aliens).

LOS ANGELES TIMES, 11/19/99, Calendar/p. 1, Kenneth Turan

Thirteen years have elapsed between the first Pixar film, an Oscar-nominated two-minute short about an adventurous lamp called "Luxo Jr.," and the current "Toy Story 2," the elaborate successor to one of the highest grossing animated features of all time. But less has changed than you might think.

For what "Luxo Jr." (newly visible as part of a brief Pixar promo that precedes all "Toy 2" showings) and the new film have in common, aside from the gleeful guiding hand of director John Lasseter, is their pleasingly clever and fiendishly inventive sense of humor. Whether it be the first "Toy Story" or last year's "A Bug's Life," to see a Pixar film is to know that the comedy will be as smart as the visuals are impressive. "Toy Story 2," thankfully, is no exception to that rule.

Lively and good-humored with a great sense of fun, "Toy Story 2" picks up the story where its predecessor left off. Improvements in computer technology have made for advances like. greater use of depth of field, but the characters of frontier sheriff Woody (Tom Hanks), over-motivated spaceman Buzz Lightyear (Tim Allen) and the rest of the toys in young Andy's room are just as we remember them.

It's one of the gifts of the gang at Pixar (which includes screenwriters Andrew Stanton, Rita Hsiao, Doug Chamberlin & Chris Weber and story folks Lasseter, Peter Docter, Ash Brannon and Stanton) that they're able to come up with convincing dilemmas for toys to contend with and us to care about, surely no simple task.

This time, the scenarios intrigue on both a psychological and an adventure level, making light and lively work of unexpected but accessible themes like the mortality of playthings and, believe it or not, the very question of what it means to be a toy. When Lee Unkrich (a co-director along with Brannon) is quoted in the press notes about "plumbing the depths of a toy's psyche," he is not really kidding.

After an amusing "Star Wars" opening focusing on a scary new Buzz Lightyear video game, "Toy 2's" scene shifts to the familiar confines of Andy's bedroom, where Woody is preparing the gang for the few days he will be absent. He's accompanying Andy to one of the boy's favorite activities, a weekend of Cowboy Camp.

But everything changes when a tear in Woody's arm causes him to be unceremoniously left behind, bringing on a toy-sized midlife crisis accompanied by nightmares and whispered repetitions of the fatal words, "Woody's been shelved."

Still wounded, Woody is brought out of himself by the even graver dilemma of Wheezy (Joe Ranft, the German caterpillar Heimlich in "A Bug's Life"), a squeak toy penguin who's lost his squeaker and is about to be consigned to hell on Earth for toys: the garage sale. "We're only a stitch away," he says gravely, pointing to Woody's arm and the sale table, "from here to there."

In an attempt to save Wheezy from that unkind fate, Woody comes to the attention of the rotund Al of Al's Toy Barn (Wayne Knight), an unscrupulous collector who pilfers Woody when he realizes how valuable a toy he is. A bit like current literary star Harry Potter, Woody has never known anything about his own illustrious past.

Back at Al's apartment, he watches tapes of "Woody's Roundup," the super-popular "Howdy Doody"-type TV show he was the centerpiece of, and gets exposed to so much Woody paraphernalia, from lunch boxes to record players, it's all he can do to respond, "I'm officially freaked out here."

Helping in Woody's education are his fellow "Roundup" toys, long-lost collaborators he never knew he had, such as his horse Bullseye, irrepressible cowgirl Jessie (Joan Cusack) and the canny old prospector Stinky Pete (Kelsey Grammer), still, Jessie says in awed tones, "mint in the box."

Woody also learns that Al is planning to sell the "Roundup" gang to a posh Japanese toy museum, a situation that leads to many of "Toy 2's" most engaging dilemmas. What does Woody owe to his "Roundup" compatriots, who will have to experience the horrors of storage if he breaks up the set? What does he owe to Buzz and the rest of his posse, who are even now moving heaven and Earth to try to rescue him? What does he owe to Andy, the owner he loves and who dearly loves him back, given the inevitability that Andy will grow up and abandon him? What the heck is a toy to do?

Even if the existential despair of toys has never previously interested you (that probably covers most of us), "Toy Story 2" makes it all irresistibly comic as well as surprisingly emotional. Fast-moving and busy, piling jeopardy on top of jeopardy but still finding time for an amusing subplot involving a Tour Guide Barbie, "Toy Story 2" may not have the most original title, but everything else about it is, well, mint in the box.

NEW YORK, 12/13/99, p. 72, Peter Rainer

In the marvelous *Toy Story 2*, there's a scene in which Mrs. Potato Head gently counsels Mr. Potato Head as he is about to embark on a dangerous mission that is more observant about how married people act than most of this year's overstuffed live-action "relationship" dramas. In this sequel, Woody and Buzz Lightyear and the rest are joined by a fresh fleet of computer-generated wonders, and the results are so exhilaratingly spry that you leave on a high—a sure sign of an instant classic.

NEW YORK POST, 11/24/99, p. 57, Jonathan Foreman

It's rare for a sequel to be anywhere near as good as the original hit, but "Toy Story 2" gives its terrific 1995 predecessor a run for its money.

For one thing, it's a genuine sequel rather than a thinly disguised rehashing of the first movie.

The original, technically revolutionary "Toy Story" had a simpler, stronger story and the advantage of being the first of its kind. But it's quickly apparent that "TS2" represents a major step forward in computer-animation artistry.

The characters' facial expressions and mouth movements are vastly improved: These are cartoons so well drawn you can actually read their lips.

Perhaps even more impressive, the new film has almost as many good jokes as the first, while giving the main characters more emotional depth.

All the old favorites are back: Slinky Dog (Jim Varney); Mr. Potato Head (Don Rickles), who's now married; Hamm, the piggy bank (John Ratzenberger); and Rex, the fearful green dinosaur (Wallace Shawn).

They're joined by new characters, including Jessie the Cowgirl (Joan Cusack), a bunch of Barbies, Buzz Lightyear's Darth Vader-esque nemesis, Emperor Zurg (Andrew Stanton), and Buster, the new puppy (much more real-looking than Sid's evil dog Scud in the first film).

Again the theme of the film is the fickleness of a child's love and the fragility of a toy's way of life.

Woody is "shelved" when his arm is partly pulled off. Toys that are shelved eventually find themselves in a yard sale. And it's when Woody tries to rescue another toy from the 25-cent box at one such sale that he is kidnapped by an unscrupulous collector of valuable toys who turns out to be none other than Al of Al's Toy Barn.

(Al is not only played by Wayne Knight, he actually looks like Newman from TV's "Seinfeld.")

Al takes Woody to his skyscraper apartment, where he has also gathered Jessie the Cowgirl, Stinky Pete the Prospector (Kelsey Grammer) and Bullseye the horse. They were all were Woody's counterparts on the '50s TV show "Woody's Roundup."

The other toys, led by Buzz Lightyear, immediately launch a rescue expedition. It takes them on a perilous journey through the city streets, first to the vast Toy Barn—where Buzz encounters shelf upon shelf of Buzz Lightyears—and then to the elevator shaft of Al's apartment building.

Al plans to sell his now-complete collection to a Japanese museum. Woody wants to escape and go home, but Jessie—who was rejected and put in storage for years by an owner who grew up to prefer makeup to dolls—and Pete prefer immortality in a museum to the cycle of love and rejection offered by children.

So Woody has to decide whether to go back to Andy's house with his friends—who have risked everything to rescue him—or to throw in his lot with the rest of the collection.

If he goes home, he will ruin Jessie's chance for happiness, condemning the incomplete "Roundup" cast to the oblivion of storage.

In the meantime, Buzz finds himself imprisoned in a box by another Buzz doll—one who doesn't realize that he is, in fact, a toy.

Before the bravura summer-movie-style action climax, there are several terrific scenes in the elevator shaft, an airport baggage-handling area and on a wide boulevard that must be crossed by the convoy of toys.

With this movie (his third after "A Bug's Life," and "Toy Story") director John Lasseter confirms his status as the undisputed leader of pioneering animation.

NEWSDAY, 11/24/99, Part II/p. B3, John Anderson

If there's a unifying precept among movie goers young, old, long or short, it's that Sequels Stink. Except, of course, when they don't. "Godfather II." "Superman II." "The Return of Frank James." "The Empire Strikes Back." All exceptions that prove the rule, which is that anything "2" is only in it for the money.

So recoil, if you will, from the commercial aggressiveness of "T2"—"Toy Story 2," which arrives just in time for T-Day and the advent of holiday shopping hysteria. But rest assured: Disney and Pixar Animation Studios have done it again. The story is richer, the jokes seem funnier, and when you consider that the filmmakers are no longer armed with the element of surprise—we've seen this amazing animation before, after all—the second "Toy Story" is better than the first.

Its story is so sophisticated, in fact, that you'll wonder who its audience is—which will be good news for anyone assigned to dragging (or, rather, being dragged by) multiple minors to the mall this weekend. "Toy Story 2" reassembles a cast of characters whose neuroses and issues make them far more human than the alleged humans of the story (real actors probably wouldn't seem any less stilted, though, given how believable the animated characters are). The result is a cross between a Catskills summer colony and a benign lunatic asylum—but a family nonetheless, one whose diversity and stability is dependent on a certain balance.

That balance, in the first film, was thrown out of kilter by the intrusion of Buzz Lightyear (voice of Tim Allen), the space cadet without a clue. This time around, Woody (Tom Hanks), the even-tempered alpha toy of Andy's playroom (which is decidedly patriarchal) is abducted by toy magnate Al McWhiggen (Wayne Knight, doing the full Newman) while trying to get a lost toy penguin (Joe Ranft) back into the fold. Woody pays for his altruism because Al knows immediately not just that Woody's a rare and valuable toy, but that he's the crucial missing piece in his collection—with Woody, Al will have a full set of "Woody's Round-Up," the toy series spun off the '50s TV show of which Woody was the star.

With Woody kidnaped, the other toys, led by Buzz, launch a full-scale rescue mission that takes them through Al's Toy Barn (a cavernous discount house that resembles the same places that will be selling "Toy Story 2" merchandise), a Barbie dance party and a run-in with a second Buzz Lightyear, who's even more of a meathead than the first. The way the rescue party negotiates the real world makes for some of the funniest stuff in the film. And the film's take on the whole toy world is too self-reflective not to crack one up.

But Woody's got a problem. Al's "Round-Up" dolls—Jesse (Joan Cusack), Bullseye the Horse and Stinky Pete the Prospector (Kelsey Grammer, with more than a touch of "The Simpsons"' Sideshow Bob)—have been out of circulation for years. They want the immortality promised by their planned sale to a Japanese toy museum—especially Stinky, who's never been out of his box. Woody, who misses Andy's room but realizes that, like Jesse, he could be easily cast off by his owner the minute the kid hits puberty, is caught on the longhorns of a dilemma.

So in addition to the relentlessly clever humor to be found in "Toy Story 2" we have the idea not just of nuclear families, but of the family of man. The Round-Up gang can be seen as representing Woody's biological relatives, as well as his tribe, his people, the toys with whom he has a past and an implied investment. The playroom, on the other hand, includes Rex the dinosaur (Wallace Shawn), Mr. Potato Head (Don Rickles), Hamm the pig (John Ratzengberger) and Slinky Dog (Jim Varney). It isn't even single-species! Woody controls the fate of Jesse and Stinky, and feels their pain. At the same time, the toy room, symbolizing adulthood and enlightened self-interest, is based on mutual circumstances and concern—even if that sole concern is the continued amusement of Andy (John Morris).

What will Woody do? The enlightened thing. Villains will be vanquished and communities restored. But this doesn't mitigate the fact that, at least while crises are brewing, "Toy Story 2" is not just a very funny, family-friendly film, but one with a political perspective that swings a lot wider than the playroom.

NEWSWEEK, 11/29/99, p. 94, David Ansen

"Toy Story" will stay in the history books not just because it was the first all-computer-generated animated film, but because it set a story-telling, standard that, four years later, has let to be bested. The Pixar-Disney team gave itself close competition with last year's "A Bug's Life," but the only computer-generated film to equal the story of Woody, the pull-string cowboy, and Buzz Lightyear, the delusional space ranger toy, is ... (you guessed it) "Toy Story 2." Sequels, by definition, are shamelessly commercial enterprises, but when the level of invention is this high you can only be grateful to John Lasseter and his gifted company for giving it their creative all.

A torn and frayed Woody (voice of Tom Hanks) is once again at the endangered center of the story. While his beloved lord and master, is off at camp, Woody is kidnapped by the odious, obese and obsessive toy collector Al (Wayne Knight), owner of Al's Toy Barn. Woody had no idea how valuable he was!   Turns out he was the star of a '50 TV show called "Woody's Roundup" (re-created here in all its black-and-white kinescope glory), which was tendered obsolete by Sputnik. By kidnapping Woody, big Al has completed his highly coveted set of the four original toys who starred in the show: Woody, Stinky Pete the Prospector (Kelsey Grammar)—a tough old coot still confined to his original plastic box—Bullseye the horse and the straight-shootin' little cow-gal Jessie (Joan Cusack). Once Woody is repaired to his original glory, they all be shipped off to a Tokyo museum where their immortality will be guaranteed.

While Woody's frantic pals (Mr. Potato Head, Rex the nervous Nellie dinosaur, Slinky Dog, Sarge and, of course. the self-infatuated Buzz) are desperately trying to save him from the clutches of the greedy Al, Woody himself faces a toy's ultimate moral conundrum. Should he be happy to be reunited with his own kind, or devastated to be separated from his home? Is it a finer thing to preserve himself forever in a museum or fulfill his role as a child's playmate, at the risk of life-ending injury? Who knew how complicated it could be to be a toy?

Lasseter and his codirectors, Lee Unkrich and Ash Brannon, wring this complex dilemma for every laugh, thrill and surprise it has to offer (and manage to work in some hilarious "Star Wars" jokes). As in the original, the super-realist images beguile us with their bold wit, and the story-telling is so tight, urgent and inventive there doesn't seem to be a wasted moment. Which makes you wonder—why can't scripts this clever be written for human beings? Could it be because actors are always rewriting their parts? Something a self-respecting toy wouldn't even *consider.*

SIGHT AND SOUND, 3/00, p. 56, Kim Newman

The Tri-County Area, the US, the present. When his shoulder is injured, the cowboy toy Woody is left behind when his young owner Andy goes off to cowboy camp. While rescuing Wheezy the Penguin from a yard sale, Woody is spotted and stolen by Al, a toy store manager. Woody is actually a merchandising tie-in for *Woody's Roundup,* a television puppet show from the 50s. He will complete a set along with Jessie the cowgirl, Bullseye the horse and the still-boxed Stinky Pete the Prospector, all of whom Al wants to sell for a fortune to a Japanese toy museum.

Buzz Lightyear, another of Andy's toys, organises a rescue party which tracks Al to his store. There Buzz is boxed up and replaced by a new Buzz Lightyear model. Woody is persuaded by Jessie, who was donated to charity when her owner hit puberty, to stay with the collection. But when the first Buzz and rescuers find him, they convince Woody to return to Andy. Stinky Pete, however, is determined to go to the museum and sabotages the rescue. The second Buzz stays behind to forge a relationship with his father. The toys follow Al to the airport and spring the others during baggage handling. Stinky Pete is tucked into the rucksack of a little girl, while Woody saves Jessie from the plane's cargo hold with Buzz and Bullseye's help. Andy returns and Jessie and Bullseye are adopted into his toy family.

Although a triumph of cutting-edge technology, demonstrating fully the possibilities of computer animation, *Toy Story* has become such a much-loved film because of its profound, almost old-fashioned humanity. Woody, Buzz and the toy gang, down to the merest walk-on sight gag, are alive in the way all great cartoon creatures are alive (in no small part thanks to canny voice casting that exactly matches the character design). Like this sequel, the first film has an extremely sophisticated, surprisingly melancholy understanding of the importance, resonance and tragically brief shelf-life of the average plaything.

The follow-up may be inevitably less fresh and misses the freakish presence of Sid's mutant toys (the three-eyed grab-machine aliens from the first film, however, have a nice cameo), but it makes a few minor, effective upgrades. Randy Newman's musical numbers, for example, are integrated so as to serve the plot points. *Toy Story 2* focuses even more tightly than the first film on the plight of creatures who are only 'alive' so long as they can retain the attention of their quixotic owners. Their in-built obsolescence is ultimately as poignant as the tiny lifespans of the *Blade Runner* replicants.

So while the plot sets up Woody's rescue from the loathsome Al, affording the opportunity for all manner of extravagant action scenes—a road-crossing set-piece, with the toys hiding under traffic cones and achieving their end while causing human-level chaos they don't notice, and a splendid, protracted peril ride through the airport at the finale—the script takes care to show the downside of toy life. Jessie, for instance, sings about the loss of her owner's love, signified by the junking of cowgirl ephemera in favour of make-up and pop records. The toy villain, one of those sad but valuable items who remains pristine in his original 50s box, yearns for a life in a museum, but Woody and the film finally recognise that toys have no real value, no life, unless they are played with.

Of course, any film with this message that comes (albeit at one remove) from Walt Disney and with an attendant merchandising blitz, has to cope with an ironic bite. Those in the know, especially exasperated parents, will love the cynical gags about the toy business: Rex the dinosaur discovers a Buzz Lightyear video game can't be won without the purchase of a tie-in manual; in the store Tour Guide Barbie explains an aisle-load of Buzz figures by noting that "in 1995, short-sighted retailers understocked." Barbie's licensees refused to allow her to appear in the original, which means she comes in for some hilarious joshing here and generally comes off as an airhead next to the spunkier Bo Peep and Jessie.

Al, the discount-toy entrepreneur, comes in for a lot of criticism, but the film takes advantage of his obsessions to fill in the backgrounds of its own inventions. Video games and the *Star Wars* franchise are parodied as the film delves into the relationship between Buzz and Zurg, while it also perfectly evokes the ramshackle charm represented by *Howdy Doody* in the US and *Muffin the Mule* here—of vintage 50s puppet television, with an attendant panoply of lunch boxes, toy gramophones, cereal promotions ('Cowboy Crunchies') and snake-in-the-boot jack-in-the-boxes. Like *The Iron Giant* the film revisits the 50s for much of its inspiration, rediscovering in the era the dawn of marketing. But a full measure of *Toy Story 2*'s success can be gauged by its undeniable appeal for children who have never seen a Western television show or played with a cowboy toy.

VILLAGE VOICE, 11/30/99, p. 146, Michael Atkinson

Nostalgia throbs through *Toy Story 2*, but in a stranger, more culturally charged way: [The reference is to *Liberty Heights*; see Atkinson's review.] The cross-marketed wisdom of stocking both films with toys more familiar to parents than kids whiplashes back, as the toys themselves know all too well their inevitable fates as landfill-destined junk discarded by distracted teenagers. As Woody (Tom Hanks) must struggle with the almost spiritual crisis of either enjoying the temporary bliss as a kid's toy or opting for an eternity as a toy museum's prized collectible ("Do you really think Andy's gonna take you to college, or on his honeymoon?" somebody mercilessly asks), so we are thunderstruck with the scalding pathos of mournful collectible cowgirl Jessie (Joan Cusack), long outgrown by her owner; her interlude, scored to a Sarah McLachlan ballad, is Brontë by way of action figures.

Even Buzz Lightyear (Tim Allen) is awash with the pathetic but moving servility the toys hold as a principle of faith; prone in a kid's oblivious grasp is the only way they "feel alive," as Jessie says. Otherwise, the kitsch is back in full bloom—gotta love the grouchy Rock 'Em Sock 'Em Robots, and the discovery of the beach-blanket-bingo Barbie aisle. But look under the bed, where a forgotten Jessie spends years watching her human grow up, and the tragic spectacle of lost time burns brightly.

Also reviewed in:
CHICAGO TRIBUNE, 11/24/99, Tempo/p. 1, Mark Caro
NEW YORK TIMES, 11/24/99, p. E1, Janet Maslin
VARIETY, 11/22-28/99, p. 83, Todd McCarthy

WASHINGTON POST, 11/24/99, p. C1, Rita Kempley
WASHINGTON POST, 22/26/99, Weekend/p. 45, Desson Howe

TRAIN OF LIFE

A Paramount Classics release of an Noe Productions/Le Studio Canal Plus/Raphael Films/71A/Hungry Eye Lowland Pictures co-production. *Producer:* Frederique Dumas, Marc Baschet, Cedomir Kolar, Ludi Boeken, and Eric Dussart. *Director:* Radu Mihaileanu. *Screenplay (French and German with English subtitles):* Radu Mihaileanu. *Director of Photography:* Yorgos Arvanitis and Laurent Dailland. *Editor:* Monique Rysselinck. *Music:* Goran Bregovic. *Sound:* Doninique Dalmasso and Pierre Excoffier. *Casting:* Pierre-Jacques Benichou, Tudor Giurgiu, Catalin Dordea, Gerda Diddens, and Rodica Alkalia. *Art Director:* Cristi Niculescu. *Costumes:* Viorica Petrovici. *Running time:* 103 minutes. *MPAA Rating:* R.

CAST: Lionel Abelanski (Shlomo); Rufus (Mordechai); Clement Harari (Rabbi); Michael Muller (Yossi); Bruno Abraham-Kremer (Yankele); Agathe de La Fontaine (Esther); Johan Leysen (Schmecht); Marie-Jose Nat (Sura); Gad Elmaleh (Manzatou); Mihail Calin (Sami).

CHRISTIAN SCIENCE MONITOR, 11/5/99, p. 15, David Sterritt

A new French comedy called *Train of Life* tells the humor-filled tale of an unusual project: Jewish villagers attempt to save their community from the Holocaust by purchasing a railroad train, putting Nazi uniforms on their most military-looking menfolk, and deporting themselves to another country before German boxcars can carry them to extermination camps.

Told in the broadly droll manner of an ironic folk tale, this story raises the same provocative question posed by the Oscar-winning Italian hit "Life Is Beautiful." Can an event as horrific as the Holocaust be responsibly explored through a movie played mainly for laughs?

American moviegoers said "yes" when they made "Life Is Beautiful" the most profitable foreign-language import of all time. But some critics (including this one) disagree with that verdict, arguing that Roberto Benigni's fast-talking farce—about a father who protects his son in a death camp by convincing him it's all an elaborate game—trivializes the Holocaust and paints a distorted picture of Nazi power that could mislead young viewers.

This doesn't mean comedy is never appropriate for storytellers trying sincerely to grapple with history's most difficult realities. Gifted filmmakers have used humor to examine the World War II era before, from Charles Chaplin in "The Great Dictator" to Lina Wertmuller in "Seven Beauties" and Ernst Lubitsch in "To Be or Not To Be," ingenious movies that use their comic edge to undermine forces of evil instead of dodging or denying them.

"Train of Life," directed by Rumanian-born filmmaker Radu Mihaileanu, doesn't reach the level of those classics. But it avoids the pitfalls of "Life Is Beautiful" by using a clearly allegorical tone to dispel any sense of realism from its impossible story, which is based on a rumored event that could never have actually happened.

It also includes a tough-minded ending that reaffirms sad facts of history with a directness Benigni's comedy lacks. What lingers in the mind after "Train of Life" is the resourcefulness not only of its colorful characters but of the great tradition of Eastern European tale-telling, which has spun such yarns for centuries as a way of confronting and understanding severe hardships.

LOS ANGELES TIMES, 11/5/99, Calendar/p. 13, Kevin Thomas

With "Train of Life," writer-director Radu Mihaileanu came up with a clever premise, but you wish he'd played up its potential more for suspense than for broad ethnic humor. To give him credit, he does end on an unexpected note that casts all that comes before in a different light. But so much of this French-language film is tiresome in its relentless reliance on country-bumpkin humor.

The time is the summer of 1941, somewhere in rural Eastern Europe. A young man, Shlomo (Lionel Abelanksi), is running through the forest as fast as he can to his home village with the news that the Nazis have evacuated all the Jews from a clearly not-too-distant community.

Since Shlomo, a mystic, is considered the village fool, the shtetl elders don't take kindly to his suggestion that the entire community escape via a fake deportation train, heading for the Ukraine in a circuitous route to Palestine.

But the Rabbi (Clement Harari), who knows of Nazi executions and the deportation of Jews to "God knows where," sees that Shlomo's idea may well be his people's only chance to escape. The elders appoint the community's prosperous woodworker Mordechai (Rufus) as the man to play the Nazi commander in charge of the train.

The best approach to "Train of Life" is to take it as a fairy tale from the start—as so much wishful thinking. This lends some credibility to the comparatively leisurely manner in which the exodus gets underway and for the numerous stopovers for rest and relaxation that seem lifted from "Fiddler on the Roof," complete with klezmer music—especially when a group of gypsies join the flight.

Certainly, Mihaileanu is affectionate and inventive, but you wish he had aimed higher, trying for more realism and relying less on shtick. There are serious, tender moments but not enough of them to offset, for example, a labored treatment of an unprepossessing young man who decides that communism is the only answer. (It's not for nothing that Mihaileanu is a refugee from Romania).

The veteran Harari, backed by Abelanski and Rufus, does much to hold this most expansive of pictures together through his ingratiating portrayal of the wise Rabbi. But too much of the film is not inspired enough in its humor to overcome the queasy feeling that comes from watching a comedy-adventure involving Jews during the Holocaust.

We in the audience are aware of the magnitude of the Nazi evil of which its targeted victims being depicted on screen still have only an inkling.

It's therefore awfully tough to find anything very funny in their predicament.

NEW YORK POST, 11/3/99, p. 52, Jonathan Foreman

"Train of Life" is yet another European fable about the Holocaust. It's not quite as awful as Robin Williams' "Jakob the Liar" and it's not as fraudulent as "Life Is Beautiful," but it's still a misguided exercise—a crude merger of "Fiddler on the Roof" and "Schindler's List" that somehow reminds you of "Hogan's Heroes."

It does contain moving and amusing moments, but they are all in the second half of the picture. To get to them, you have to sit through some truly dreadful scenes of comical Orthodox Jews in their East European habitat. The film starts in one of those nameless shtetls where the elders are all idiots and the local fool is a genius given to poetic musings about the relation of God and man. Schlomo the fool (Lionel Abelanski) comes rushing into town one day and warns the wise men that the Nazis are coming.

They shout "Oy vey!" and "ai yi" while running around the village, waving their hands in the air.

At Schlomo's suggestion, the unbelievably unworldly wise men of the village decide that the best way to escape deportation and death is to buy a train and put everybody on it—some of them dressed as German troops. They'll escape to Russia and then go to Palestine.

To make the deportation ruse believable, they hire an Austrian Jew to help teach the faux Nazis to speak German without Yiddish accents. The preparation for their escape is accompanied by lots of shouting, kvetching and hysteria that is supposed to be charming.

The train leaves the village without incident, but once it starts steaming eastward, the villagers have near-disastrous encounters with real Germans, partisan guerrillas and fleeing Gypsies.

Internal strife also threatens to bring catastrophe to what the Germans come to call the "ghost train." A Communist on the train starts a revolution against the village elders, and the villagers who are dressed as Germans become increasingly arrogant and authoritarian.

How hilarious.

NEWSDAY, 11/3/99, Part II/p. B11, John Anderson

A tale told by an idiot (a village idiot), "Train of Life" is in the unfortunate position of following "Life Is Beautiful" and "Jakob the Liar" in the dubious genre of Holocaust comedies, and there's little justice there. A film whose full effect cannot be known until its final frame, "Train of Life" may infuriate some audiences, who may see director Radu Mihaileanu as having his Purim cake and eating it, too. But the more generous will accept it as a film whose occasionally daffy fantasy is imbued with the soul of despair.

Mihaileanu, whose comedic touch suggests Ernst Lubitsch filtered through three fingers of Mel Brooks, sets his story in a remote East European shtetl in 1941 and introduces it via Shlomo (Lionel Abelanski), a slow-witted dreamer who brings news of the Nazis' approach to his fussy Jewish village. While the elders, including the long-suffering, Ur-humanist Rabbi (Clement Harari) wring their hands, Shlomo suggests a solution: Buy a train and stage the village's deportation to the camps—except, of course, with a detour through Russia and a full head of steam for Eretz Israel.

That Shlomo should be the one behind the shtetl's escape route is testimony to the illusory element within "Train of Life," whose cast of characters is a droll pageant of human foible, Yiddish theater and European political polarization. A reluctant Mordechai the Woodcutter (the veteran actor Rufus) is cast, because of his education and bearing, as the Nazi officer in charge of the "deportation train;" several other villagers will play the Nazi soldiers under his command and ride in the well-appointed front cars, while most of the village is herded into boxes at the rear.

This sets up a series of comedic confrontations between Mordechai and the communist faction led by Yossi (Michael Muller), who decide they want equal accommodations for all. It also causes social rifts and cultural tempests; the town beauty, Esther (Agathe de la Fontaine), for instance, loves Mordechai's son Sami (Mihai Calin), but because his father is playing a Nazi, Esther is forbidden to see him.

Which doesn't stop her—there's an end-of-the-world arousal to Esther, which contrasts quite humorously with the irrational worries of the villagers, who are often more concerned with keeping kosher than losing their heads. But Mihaileanu, amidst the wacky, quasi-sitcom quality of his story, is all about such detail from the passing visual joke to the droll portrayal Rufus gives Mordechai, a man whose Nazi regalia gives his otherwise admirable leadership qualities all the wrong connotations.

"Train of Life" may flirt with impropriety in its portrayal of its Jews but it is, in the end, primarily an affectionate portrait of people, with a side order of wishful thinking. It's strength is in its lack of hubris, which is precisely where it goes fight and any remotely similar films have gone entirely wrong.

VILLAGE VOICE, 11/9/99, p. 140, Amy Taubin

Annihilation is the basis for Radu Mihaileanu's *Train of Life,* a fable about an Eastern European shtetl that escapes the Holocaust by faking its own deportation in a train rigged to look like those the Nazis used to transport Jews to concentration camps. This train, however, is bound for the Soviet Union and freedom. A Romanian-French director who worked as an actor in Bucharest's Yiddish theater, Mihaileanu employs a farcical style, leaving no doubt that the film is a fantasy spun in the face of death. Unlike the despicable *Life Is Beautiful,* which turned the horror of the camps into a feel-good comedy, *Train of Life* uses mordant Jewish humor to re-create and celebrate the shtetl life that the Nazis destroyed. It's entertainment that never lets us off the hook.

Train of Life, which won a slew of jury and audience awards on the festival circuit, has intelligence and a boisterous charm (though the combination of Yiddish style and the French language is a bit disorienting). In its satiric treatment of Nazism, the film is not unrelated to Agnieszka Holland's World War II epic, *Europa, Europa.* And although Mihaileanu relies on a theatrical tradition that employs stock characters, the film is most engaging when, like *Europa, Europa,* it delves into the connection between masquerade and identity. Because they will inevitably encounter Germans en route, some of the Jews must impersonate Nazis. While everyone's survival depends on their performances, the more convincing they are in their roles, the more the other Jews resent them and the more they feel as if they should hate themselves.

Thus the shtetl woodworker (Rufus) who plays the Nazi train commander is a more compelling character than the hero, the town fool (Lionel Abelanski) who imagines the story to keep his village alive.

Also reviewed in:
NEW YORK TIMES, 11/5/99, p. E5, Stephen Holden
VARIETY, 9/28-10/4/98, p. 52, Lisa Nesselson

TREKKIES

A Paramount Pictures release of a Neo Art & Logic production. *Executive Producer:* Michael Leahy and Joel Soisson. *Producer:* W.K Border. *Director:* Roger Nygard. *Director of Photography:* Harris Done. *Editor:* Roger Nygard. *Music:* Walter Werzowa, Jimmie Wood, J.J. Holiday, and Billy Sullivan. *Running time:* 87 minutes. *MPAA Rating:* PG.

WITH: Denise Crosby (Narrator); Majel Barrett Roddenberry; James Doohan; Walter Koenig; DeForest Kelley; Nichelle Nichols; Leonard Nimoy; William Shatner; George Takei; Grace Lee Whitney; LeVar Burton; Michael Dorn; Jonathan Frakes; Brent Spiner; Buzz Aldrin; Kate Mulgrew; Ethan Phillips; John de Lancie.

LOS ANGELES TIMES, 5/21/99, Calendar/p. 8, Gene Seymour

[The following review by Gene Seymour appeared in a slightly different form in
NEWSDAY, 5/21/99, Part II/p. B9.]

Where oh where to begin this survey of Planet Trek? Do you start with the mob of Klingons who casually walk into a fast-food restaurant and order almost everything on the menu? Do you begin with the people who wear their Star Fleet regalia and insignia to the supermarket, their workplaces, courtrooms? Do you dare ponder the existence of those who would, if they could, surgically alter their ears to look like Mr. Spock's?

Your reviewer almost lost his composure early in "Trekkies" over the story of the guy who paid $60 for the right to finish the half-empty glass of water that a flu-ridden John de Lancie (who played "Q," the perennial bad guy on "Star Trek: The Next Generation") was nursing while speaking at a "Trek" convention. This maniac, after polishing off the glass, shouted repeatedly before what you hope was a stunned audience: "I've got the 'Q' Virus!"

To the credit of the Trekker telling this tale, he was just as freaked as any earthling would be by such behavior. Which, as much as anything could, typifies the attitude taken by director-editor Roger Nygard and the producers of "Trekkies," a laid-back excursion through the "Star Trek" phenomenon that boldly goes where millions and millions of fans have gone—in and out of costume.

As tour guide through this strange world, Denise Crosby, a co-executive producer of the film and an original cast member of "Star Trek: The Next Generation," is both bemused and solicitous toward her various interview subjects. She, Nygard and the other filmmakers manage to stride a thin line between dismay and affection throughout their odyssey.

You can label such an attitude, at best, calculated ambivalence, if you want. But whether you love or hate "Star Trek" in all its various manifestations on the big and small screen, you'd have to be a total grinch not to kick back and enjoy the ride.

You meet, up close and personal, Barbara ("Call Me Commander") Adams, the Arkansas woman who served on the Whitewater jury until she was excused because she kept coming into the courtroom wearing her Star Fleet uniform. (Never leaves the house, she says, without her "tricorder, phaser and communicator badge.") The camera follows her to her day job at a printing plant, where her bosses and co-workers praise her diligence, competence and smarts. So, see? She has a life. Right?

Denis Bourguignon not only has a life. He has a wife, children and a dental practice. His whole office suite is a shrine to "Trek." (Even the receptionists have to dress as though they're working the Starship Enterprise's sick bay.) There's also a fan who legally changed his name to "James T. Kirk" (same as William Shatner's brawny captain of the original TV series) and another who teaches the Klingon language to fans (it says here) "around the world." (If you have to ask what a Klingon is, this documentary may not be for you.)

At some point, the waves of fan excess reach such a peak that, much like Kirk himself used to do, you want to turn to the First Officer nearest you and shout, "Spock, why?" Well, Spock aka Leonard Nimoy is among the actors interviewed by Crosby, and he hasn't a clue. He and everyone else in the various "Trek" casts have simply submitted to the inexhaustible power of the phenomenon. A power that, in at least one instance, saved a life, as shown by James "Scotty" Doohan's touching story of a fan he saved from suicide by inviting her to conventions across the United States.

Laugh if you want at the Trekkers and their obsession. Many of them have enough sense to laugh along with you. But in the end, you find yourself oddly touched by these folks who share a faith in a future of equality and possibility. If you think there aren't worse things to believe in, you've been skipping the front pages lately.

NEW YORK POST, 5/21/99, p. 45, Jonathan Foreman

"Trekkies" may be the "Roger & Me" of 1999; it is certainly one of the funniest movies so far this year. This is a considerable achievement for a feature-length documentary about people who live through and for a 30-year-old TV program and its progeny.

It's filled with laughs. But it's also touching and sometimes verges on disturbing. In scrupulously non-judgmental fashion, "Trekkies," which opens today in the New York area only on Long Island, introduces you not only to people who know the dialogue from every episode, attend "Star Trek" conventions or trade Spock dolls over the Internet, but also to those who have made "Star Trek" and its lore a lodestone of their everyday lives.

People like Whitewater juror "Commander" Barbara Adams, a print-shop worker who wears a uniform everywhere she goes and says without a trace of irony that she's a Starfleet officer 24 hours a day.

These Trekkies aren't fans so much as adherents to a spontaneously generated folk religion. Fortunately, it's a sprawling, diverse and benevolent cult whose most negative manifestation seems to be dressing poodles in nylon space garb.

The film is hosted by actress Denise Crosby (who played Tasha Yar in the first season of "Star Trek—The Next Generation"). She goes to the conventions, interviews fans and follows folk dressed as Klingons into fast-food joints. She also talks to cast members from the various "Star Trek" series about the fans.

In awed tones, cast members tell stories of frenzied autograph signings. Nichelle Nichols (Lt. Uhura in the original series) talks about a young black girl living in the projects who saw her on the show and excitedly called to her mother, "There's a black lady on television who isn't a maid!" The girl grew up to be Whoopi Goldberg.

Some of these hard-core fans reject the term "Trekkie," preferring "Trekker" or "Trekan." One otherwise normal and attractive young woman who moons over scrapbooks filled with photographs of Brent Spiner (who plays Data in "The Next Generation") says that she and her fellow worshipers of the actor call themselves "Spiner-femmes."

But whatever they call themselves, they come in an amazing variety of shapes, colors and sizes. There are transsexual Trekkies, German Trekkies, Trekkies in wheelchairs. There's even a Florida dentist whose family and employees wear full Starfleet garb.

We also meet a middle-aged fellow who's considering having his ears surgically transformed to resemble those of Mr. Spock. My favorite was Gabriel Komer, a brilliant, overenunciating 14-year-old semi-nerd straight out of "Spinal Tap," who's writing a screenplay for his own "Star Trek" movie.

Sure, some of this obsessive stuff seems pathetic, even crazy. You can understand someone making up a Klingon language for a lark; actually attending Klingon language camp crosses the sanity line.

Still, for the most part, these are eccentric but fundamentally decent folk who just happen to have taken a benign hobby to an extreme. Just about everyone interviewed by filmmaker Roger

Nygard takes the humanitarian, progressive values of Gene Roddenberry's original show very seriously indeed.

Their belief in the benevolent, inclusive, diverse future promised by "Star Trek" is inseparable from their need to belong, so it is not surprising they have in common a kind of open, uncynical sweetness.

Even the ones who dress up as Klingons.

VILLAGE VOICE, 5/25/99, p. 125, Gary Daupin

There's a great deal of love in *Trekkies*, Roger Nygard's warm and good-naturedly funny documentary about the world of *Star Trek* fandom. Interviewed by onetime *Next Generation* cast member Denise "Tasha Yar" Crosby, the fans that parade through the frame exude a genuine joy that's all the more infectious for being hard-won. Everyone onscreen has clearly walked the shadowy valley of geek shame but thankfully lived to tell their curious, life-changing tales.

Edited by Nygard with an unpretentiously light touch, *Trekkies* makes all the requisite stops with the true believers who think *Star Trek*'s "philosophy" can bring world peace, pausing in such subcult reflecting pools as slash fan-fiction (sexually explicit Kirk/Spock love stories) and Klingon language courses, and also hangs out with some very likable, quite regular folks. In the first group there's Barbara Adams, the commander of the Little Rock fan club, who wears her Starfleet uniform everywhere, and then there are the fans from Vulcan, Canada, who giddily announce that their yearly *Trek* fest is really picking up. ("Last year, a girl came!") There's a dentist who's turned his office into a memorabilia-crammed Starbase Dental, and a precocious 14-year-old with a prodigious talent for whipping up broadcast-quality special effects. (He, of course, wants to make a movie.) *Trekkies* also offers interviews with four sets of Trek cast members (with an emphasis on the original series), all obviously having given a lot of thought to what Gene Roddenberry spawned in 1969. The eye-mist quotient rises to a crescendo with a *Trek* star's recollection of the quadriplegic who is able to forget her broken body only during the hour *Trek* is on her TV. Her story is a staple of fandom and just a tad manipulative when you realize Paramount released *Trekkies* now to counterprogram in some small way against that other sci-fi franchise. But still, you'd have to be a hard-hearted bastard not to be moved by such a moment, and *Trekkies* is chock-full of them.

Also reviewed in:
CHICAGO TRIBUNE, 5/21/99, Friday/p. C, Mark Caro
NEW REPUBLIC, 6/14/99, p. 30, Stanley Kauffmann
NEW YORK TIMES, 5/21/99, p. E16, Lawrence Van Gelder
VARIETY, 10/27-11/2/97, p. 48, Leonard Klady
WASHINGTON POST, 5/21/99, Weekend/p. 17, Michael O'Sullivan

TRICK

A Fine Line Features release of a Roadside Attractions/Good Machine production. *Executive Producer:* Anthony Bregman and Mary Jane Skalski. *Producer:* Eric d'Arbeloff, Jim Fall, and Ross Katz. *Director:* Jim Fall. *Screenplay:* Jason Schafer. *Director of Photography:* Terry Stacey. *Editor:* Brian A. Kates. *Music:* David Friedman. *Music Editor:* Brian A. Kates. *Choreographer:* Robin Carrigan. *Sound:* Antonio L. Arroyo and (music) Robert Fernandez. *Sound Editor:* Stephen Altobello. *Casting:* Susan Shopmaker. *Production Designer:* Jody Asnes. *Art Director:* Gonzalo Córdoba. *Set Decorator:* Brian Elwell. *Costumes:* Mary Gasser. *Make-up:* Joseph Trapani. *Running time:* 90 minutes. *MPAA Rating:* R.

CAST: Christian Campbell (Gabriel); John Paul Pitoc (Mark); Tori Spelling (Katherine); Steve Hayes (Perry); Brad Beyer (Rich); Lorri Bagley (Judy); Kevin Chamberlin (Perry's Ex); Clinton Leupp (Miss Coco Peru); Eric Bernat (Funky Stage Manager); Joey Dedio (Ex Go-go Boy); Jamie Gustis (Dino); Helen Hanft (Greasy Spoon Waitress); Will Keenan (Dude);

TRICK   1457

Michele Brilliant (Little Dyke); Scottie Epstein (Muscley Chest Guy); Abbey Hope (Business Woman); Lacey Kohl (Genvieve); Missi Pile (Actress with Flowers); Debbie Troché (Actress with Videotape); Becky Caldwell (Yolanda); Kate Flannery (Ridiculous Writer); Ricky Ritzel (Scary Man); Lissette Gutierrez (Woman on the Subway); Kevin Andrew (Stoop Cruiser); Bobby Peaco (Lester Sinclair); Nat Dewolfe (Gay Reveler).

LOS ANGELES TIMES, 7/23/99, Calendar/p. 21, Kenneth Turan

A light and amusing item with a lively sense of humor, "trick" doesn't sound like the kind of film that's going to make a difference. But then again, it just might.

For though its romantic comedy setups are classic, "trick's" protagonists are not Cary Grant and Katharine Hepburn wannabes but two young and attractive gay men. And while the film, a surprise hit at Sundance, was clearly made with a gay audience in mind, it has enough sweetness and humanity, enough ability to involve, that it could cross over into a mainstream independent audience as well.

Unlike mainstream films running the gamut from "Philadelphia" to "Birdcage," "trick" doesn't compromise to attract a straight audience and doesn't need to. Though we're shown nothing more explicit than passionate kisses and lingering glances at attractive bodies, Jason Schafer's charming script has no compunctions about being verbally explicit.

While gay films with serious issues on their minds can be painful or edgy or both, "trick" is simply a boy-meets-boy farce. It's not that this hasn't been attempted before—"Billy's Hollywood Screen Kiss" was a recent example—its that an engaging cast and director Jim Fall, a veteran of Manhattan theater making his feature debut, simply do a more appealing job than the competition.

A story of how complicated things can get when your fantasy threatens to turn real, "trick" begins with a decidedly non-fantasy situation for Gabriel (Christian Campbell, Neve's brother). He's sleeping in the doorway outside his one-room New York apartment, while his straight roommate Rich (Brad Beyer) cavorts with one in an endless string of one-night-stands who fill up his dance card while his fiancee is off in Paris.

Fresh-faced with an appealing boyish smile, but easily flummoxed, Gabriel works as a receptionist in a law office, but his real passion is musical theater. An aspiring songwriter, his latest creation, a musical called "Enter You" (as in "I thought my story line was through, but enter you"), gets a decidedly mixed reception at a Broadway songwriters workshop.

Maybe his friend Perry (actor and cabaret singer Steve Hayes) is right—maybe the problem is that Gabe has never had a really great kiss. Or maybe it's that his old friend Katherine performed the song at the workshop.

A pal since high school, brassy and bossy Katherine (Tori Spelling, alternately effective and excessive) is a hopeless actress oblivious to her lack of talent. A minor league diva currently in a production of "Salome" set in a women's prison, Katherine is as indefatigable as she is impossible to discourage.

To cheer himself up and pass the time, Gabe makes a visit to a gay bar, where he can't take his eyes off a really attractive go-go boy who has the distant, self-absorbed quality of all unattainable fantasies.

But because New York is really nothing more than a big small town, who should he run into on the subway but that very same stunning Mark (J.P. Pitoc). The physical attraction between them is strong enough that when Gabe bemoans the fact that he has to turn his apartment over to his roommate in two hours, Mark immediately replies, "You can do a lot in two hours."

Gabe can't believe his good luck, but that luck is about to change, for everything in the universe soon conspires to create an endless series of obstacles to the two would-be lovers.

First, Katherine is camped out in Gabe's apartment, asking, "What are you guys up to?" with an obliviousness even Grandma Moses wouldn't have been able to match. Then Rich shows up early with girlfriend Judy (Lorri Bagley), newly back from Paris. Then the boys get involved with Perry's romantic woes, and finally an ill-advised trip to a hot dance club involves Greg with some of Mark's old flames, including been-around drag queen Miss Coco Peru (Clinton Leupp).

During the course of these diverting misadventures, something happens to Gabe and Mark. They start to reveal themselves to each other and feelings more complicated than lust threaten to come into play. It's the oldest story in the book, but with actors this appealing, we're happy to see it all over again.

After "trick" was shown at Sundance, screenwriter Schafer told Premier magazine he was besieged by agents who asked, "Have you written anything that isn't gay?," a question that ought to be turned on its head. For what would be really exciting is more films like "trick" that refuse to be limited by their characters' sexuality.

NEW YORK POST, 7/23/99, p. 58, Jonathan Foreman

The badly written and relentlessly overacted "Trick" is supposed to be a romantic comedy about two young men who find something like love as they desperately search for a place to have sex.

Gabriel (Christian Campbell) is a shy writer of musical comedies, who lacks the experience to write about love with any conviction. After a poorly received performance of one of his songs—sung by his best friend, Katherine (Tori Spelling)—he goes out to a "cruise" bar. There Gabriel stares at Mark (John Paul Pitoc) a hunky go-go boy. He also deals with the advances of men who think he's cute with a combination of surprise and ineptitude that becomes increasingly tiresome.

Later Gabe finds himself in the same subway car as the go-go boy, who picks him up with practiced ease. They head back to the tiny West Village apartment Gabe shares with his promiscuous straight roommate. But they find it impossible to consummate the relationship, because, although Gabe's roommate is out, Katherine is there printing out 150 copies of her resume on an old daisy-wheel printer.

Even if you discount the improbability of such a scene in the age of Kinko's copy shops and cheap laser printers, you find yourself asking why she needs to watch the machine churn out each copy when she could just as easily come back later to pick them up.

But then it's hard to care about whether or not the two guys actually manage to get it on. You can see why Gabriel is attracted to Mark, but not the other way around; he's a wimpy, whiny pain in the neck.

With exception of Mark, who has a physique rather than a personality, all of writer Jason Schafer's characters here are unlikable caricatures—the worst being Spelling's Katherine and a mean drag queen (Clinton Leupp) who looks amazingly like her.

NEWSDAY, 7/23/99, Part II/p. B11, Gene Seymour

It's worth noting that when movies featuring gay characters reach the mainstream these days, they tend to be less about "coming out" than "going out." Progress of a sort. But in whatever package, in whatever setting, does the world need another "going out" movie, especially if they're as paint-by-the-numbers as "Trick"? Granted, both Jim Fall's direction and Jason Schafer's script go out of their way to make you feel cozy and warm throughout this long night in lower Manhattan with Gabriel (Christian Campbell), an aspiring musical-comedy writer who shares an apartment with another cute young guy named Rich (Brad Beyer), who unlike Gabriel is a) heterosexual and b) so lucky in love that Gabriel is frequently asked to wait in the hallway all night until his roomie's dates go home.

Both Gabriel's romantic life and artistic yearnings suffer from the fact he's skittish and distant toward everyone except, perhaps, his high-strung best friend Katherine (Tori Spelling), a struggling actress who helps Gabriel with his showcases as Gabriel in turn goes over her lines with her.

One night on the subway, Gabriel finds himself on the same car with Mark (John Paul Pitoc), an exotic dancer whose eyes briefly locked with his a short time before in a gay bar. Typically, he can't make a move, but they end up at the same stop anyway. Somehow they meet and agree to find an intimate place together which proves to be an almost insurmountable task.

From here on, "Trick" becomes one of those episodic, long-night's-journey-into-day romances whose situations become more outlandish (or contrived) as you're kept in suspense over whether this couple will, in some way, couple. Among the many obstacles: Katherine, who spends an inordinate amount of time in Gabriel's otherwise unoccupied (for the moment) apartment.

Soon, Rich returns with another conquest, forcing Mark and Gabriel into the streets, going from bar to restaurant, even a bathroom, for a chance to steal even a kiss.

It isn't "Trick's" formula that puts you off so much as the stock characters that surround Gabe and Mark—who are, thanks to Campbell and Pitoc, more interesting than the story they're trapped in.   Spelling does what she can with a thinly drawn, broadly defined role.   But the hysteria she's forced to adopt conspires against her.

The gay supporting characters fare no better than the straights.   Though Steve Hayes is charming as Perry, the songwriter who sings his campy tunes at piano bars, he sounds too much like what Gabriel calls, in another context, "just another old queen." Then there's Clinton Leupp's drag queen, Miss Coco Peru, who looks eerily like an off-kilter clone of Spelling and seems to be around for outrageous set design.   That is until he delivers what may be the movie's funniest sequence, a men's room monologue about "quickie love" gained and lost that's so scorchingly detailed that Gabriel can't relieve himself. When Leupp goes, he takes a lot of the movie's energy with him.

SIGHT AND SOUND, 5/00, p. 63, Andy Medhurst

New York City, the present. Gabriel is a gay man in his twenties who dreams of writing a hit Broadway musical.   He and his best friend, actress Katherine, audition one of his songs at a writers' workshop where Gabriel's older friend Perry tells Gabriel he needs to take more risks in both his life and work.   Stung, Gabriel visits a bar where he's besotted by attractive dancer Mark. Meeting on the subway, they flirt and Mark follows Gabriel home. Their attempts at sex are frustrated first by Katherine, who has dropped by, and then by Rich, Gabriel's straight room-mate, who returns home early with his girlfriend Judy.

Gabriel tries to borrow Perry's apartment, but that plan falls through. Mark takes Gabriel to a club, when Gabriel becomes uneasy as Mark's popularity leaves him sidelined. He leaves after Miss Coco Peru, an acidic drag queen, recounts a story of how Mark mistreated her during a previous sexual encounter. Mark follows Gabriel and they argue, both unsettled by how quickly they are falling for each other. Gabriel persuades Mark to go for a meal, where they bump into Katherine and her theatrical cronies. Gabriel and Katherine argue over her insensitivity, but are reconciled. Mark goes home, giving Gabriel his phone number. Remembering Miss Coco Peru had warned him Mark always gives a false number, Gabriel calls Mark and is relieved to hear Mark's voice on the answering machine.

The charm of first-time director Jim Fall's *Trick* lies in its good-natured unpretentiousness. It has no cutting edge, vanguard statements about sexuality to make, and it spares both its protagonists and its audience from worthy let's-confront-homophobia scenes (the only anti-gay frame in the film is a disapproving glance from a mute subway passenger). Homosexuality here is as normal and delicious as apple pie.   Consequently some might see the film as evading social issues, but surely the days when every film about gay men had to crusade before it could entertain are long gone. Besides, in a British climate where noxious campaigns to preserve Section 28 are rife, this US picture's view that homosexual love is just as everyday and just as magical as every other kind is vitally important, especially with its 15 certificate. A film doesn't have to trumpet an agenda aloud to be political.

Trick's lack of explicit sexual images (the only bed action we see is heterosexual) could dismay the type of gay audience which drearily evaluates films on their quantity of humping, but such a critique would miss the story's entire point. It's an old fashioned romantic farce about would-be lovers who can never get to be alone, and the narrative twists that conspire to frustrate them are deftly orchestrated. The scene where Mark's level-headed kindness sacrifices another chance of bedding Gabriel in favour of bringing Perry and his ex-lover back together is typical of the film's likeable warmth and emotional generosity. It also forces Gabriel to reassess the situation and confront the scary possibility that what started out as a wet-dream pick—up a fantasy along the lines of 'preppy meets stud, stud screws preppy, preppy seeks solace in Ethel Merman albums'— may be developing into an actual grown-up relationship.

Both Christian Campbell and John Paul Pitoc excel in the central roles, and the fact that both are unfamiliar faces (Campbell was in the Canadian teen series *Degrassi Junior High*, Pitoc has done stage work in New York and Edinburgh) greatly enhances the film's believability. In a few early scenes, Campbell can be too gauchely wholesome, looking and behaving like the lost gay Walton sibling, but his performance grows more complex as Gabriel matures. One of the film's neater touches has Gabriel trying to disavow his queeny, show-tune leanings in order to impress and arouse the seemingly hyper-butch Mark, only to find Mark is perfectly content with the camper aspects of gay culture. Pitoc is a definite find, cleverly catching the nuances of how a man used to being revered for his muscles and penis-size ("My nickname," he proudly informs Katherine, "is Beer Can") learns to contend with deeper feelings.

Tori Spelling, presumably cast for kitsch value, gets a little wearisome as the volatile fag-hag Katherine, although this may be a tribute to her ability to get inside such an irritating character. Her limitations point to *Trick*'s failure to sidestep that familiar minefield for films about gay men, their tendency to offer only short changed and predictable roles for women. It's hardly the worst example of that tendency, however, as it does at least have the ideological gumption to pour most scorn on its solitary heterosexual male—the selfish, priapic Rich. *Trick* is not flawless, but crisp, astute and witty films where gay men get to wallow in the joys of a romantic happy ending aren't so thick on the ground they can be lightly dismissed. It may be a little sugary here and there, but anyone who can own up to a sweet tooth will find it a welcome change from those more astringent gay pictures that make a virtue out of sourness.

VILLAGE VOICE, 7/24/99, p. 54, Dennis Lim

Post-Sundance raves have claimed that *Trick* represents a new, agenda-free brand of gay film (call it the Gay Gay Cinema), "revolutionary" (as more than one reviewer has frothed) precisely for its lack of revolutionary qualities. Setting aside for now the obtuseness and condescension of such a stance, it should be pointed out that, taken *purely* as fluff (which one can safely assume to be "its own terms"), *Trick* is a failure. Jason Schafer's screenplay—about a would-be one-night stand miraculously transformed into something more—is a ragged, witless patchwork of subsitcom scenarios; the godawful acting compounds the torture.

Trick's protagonist, Gabriel (Christian Campbell), is a model of bland, lowest-common-denominator appeal—a musical composer but not a drama queen, dorky but kinda cute, shy but kinky in an unthreatening way (his fantasy is to be serviced while he plays the piano). On the subway one night, he encounters Mark (John Paul Pitoc), a go-go boy whose seeming blockheadedness masks a soft side and a journalism degree. The two spend all night looking for a place to fuck—they're repeatedly thwarted and, owing to the fatuous contingencies of romantic comedy, fall in love.

Trick draws on audience empathy for Gabe—alienated Everygay—and revels in the reassuring accessibility of an idealized object of desire. Or at least in theory it does. The film is so insecure about its own premise—the idea that these two should get together—that it reflexively surrounds them with grotesques. Everyone else is obnoxious, idiotic, or pathetic. Directed in anonymous fashion by Jim Fall, Trick (working title: *Gay Boy)* plays like a neutered dicktease. Sex is the nominal driving force, but the film couldn't be any less sexy. Or any more misogynist. Tori Spelling, shrill and horsey, plays a monstrous fag hag; Gabe's roommate's girlfriend is essentially a breathy, dumb, one-note joke. This film is so retrogressive that it would, in a sane world, inspire not drooling praise but a revolt—in that sense, *Trick* may have some revolutionary worth after all.

Also reviewed in:
CHICAGO TRIBUNE, 8/6/99, Friday/p. P, Michael Wilmington
NEW YORK TIMES, 7/23/99, p. E23, Janet Maslin
VARIETY, 2/1-7/99, p. 59, Emanuel Levy

TRIO, THE

An Attitude Films release of a Next Film production in asociation with NDR, ORF and Arte. *Producer:* Laurens Straub and Pia Frankenberg. *Director:* Hermine Huntgeburth. *Screenplay (German with English subtitles):* Horst Sczerba, Volker Einrauch, and Hermine Huntgeburth. *Director of Photography:* Martin Kukula. *Editor:* Ingrid Martell. *Music:* Niki Reiser. *Art Director:* Katharina Woepperman. *Sound:* Dirk Jacob. *Casting:* Risa Kes. *Costumes:* Peri de Braganca. *Running time:* 97 minutes. *MPAA Rating:* Not Rated.

CAST: Götz George (Zobel);   Christian Redl (Karl);   Jeanette Hain (Lizzie);   Felix Eitner (Rudolf); Angelica Bartsch (Dorothee).

LOS ANGELES TIMES, 8/6/99, Calendar/p. 14, Kevin Thomas

Hermine Huntgeburth's "The Trio" is a zesty, sexy, knockabout German comedy in the irreverent tradition of Doris Dorrie's "Men ... " and Sonke Wortmann's "Maybe ... Maybe Not." It affords a terrific role for Gotz George, one of his country's most durable and versatile stars.

George, son of Heinrich George, a screen icon of the '20s through the '40s, is a burly man of 60 known for his macho roles and has been in films for 45 years. With "The Trio" he adds an extra dimension to that image by playing a gay man, Zobel, in a long-term relationship with the increasingly dissatisfied Karl (Christian Redl).   What Ugo Tognazzi and Michel Serrault's characters were to the world of cabaret in "La Cage aux Folles," Zobel and Karl are to that of professional pickpocketing.

Based in Hamburg, the lovers live in a large van with Zobel's teenage daughter Lizzie (Jeanette Hain), offspring of a youthful heterosexual indiscretion and a full-fledged partner in Zobel and Karl's pickpocketing routine. Zobel is a completely happy man, his ardor for Karl undiminished, but Karl is getting bored and would literally like to kick up his heels. More seriously, Karl is beginning to slip up on the job, eventually winding up in the hospital when he's struck by a car.

Lizzie immediately suggests as a replacement for Karl a young guy hanging about her uncle's carnival, Rudolf (Felix Eitner), whom we first met when he was foolish enough to think he could get away with lifting Karl's wallet.

Rudolf, who is scruffy but not unattractive, proves a quick learner, but in taking Karl's place in the thieving operation so long perfected by Zobel, he creates complications predicted by neither father nor daughter.   Huntgeburth and her co-writers match their imaginative plotting and sharp wit with considerable psychological insight.   "The Trio" is expertly constructed, moving briskly from broad humor to unexpected pathos to all-out farce and culminating in a mellow self-knowledge and acceptance on the part of one and all—if only for the moment.

None of the actors misses a nuance, but it is George who is the commanding presence and rightly so.   His Zobel is a warm, engaging scoundrel of a man, still attractive though he feels compelled to go for an overly obvious dye job on his hair and beard—and is not above relying upon some cosmetics to hold on to the illusion of youth. ("The Trio" is ripe for a Hollywood remake, provided the light, deft touch of the original is preserved—and the role of Zobel is reserved for Burt Reynolds; John Malkovich would be a nifty Karl.) Lizzie and Rudolf brim over with youthful, risk-taking spirits and are played with skill and ease by Hain and Eitner.

This wry, stylish film was co-produced by veteran distributor and producer Laurens Straub, and it completes an informal trilogy of gay-themed films made under Straub's auspices. First was Frank Ripploh's loopy, autobiographical "Taxi zum Klo" (1980), in which a philandering Ripploh struggled to work out a stable relationship with his monogamous stay-at-home lover Bernd, and "A Man Called Eva" (1982), in which esteemed stage and screen actress Eva Mattes managed to pull off the challenging task of playing her own complex and destructive mentor, R.W. Fassbinder. "The Trio" is a noteworthy, if more mainstream, successor to the earlier films.

NEW YORK POST, 2/12/99, p. 52, Rod Dreher

"The Trio" is disappointing, but not for the usual reasons. The promotional material promised a German sex comedy and hey, right there you know it's going to be about as felicitous as pigs dancing the tarantella.

Anyway, the film is directed by someone named Hermine Huntgeburth, and it's about an amateur pickpocket gang in which the gay father and his straight daughter compete for the affections of their cute new partner—all while trying to observe the gang's rule against "the spilling of bodily fluids" within the team.

In the event, "The Trio" proves not to be the entertainingly pretentious, inept travesty one might have enjoyed for its hoot value. It's just garden-variety German dullardry: leaden, earnest and altogether boring.

Beefy, middle-aged Zobel (Goetz George), his lover Karl (Christian Redl) and Zobel's teen-age daughter Lizzie (Jeanette Hain) grift their way around Germany in a battered RV, pulling scams on pedestrians and lifting their wallets. When an accident forces Karl to drop out, Lizzie recruits Rudolf (Felix Eitner), a green, young sticky fingers who once tried to steal a wallet from Zobel and Karl.

Turns out Rudolf swings both ways. There's a brief buzz of excitement in the picture as father and daughter spar over his affections, but if the distastefulness of this plotting doesn't put you off, the tired execution of it will. Unsexy, uninteresting, and free of anything resembling wit, lightness or piquancy, the competently acted "The Trio" slogs dutifully along toward a cloying but unsurprising conclusion. Ho-hum.

NEWSDAY, 2/12/99, Part II/p. B9, John Anderson

Raised the daughter of a conservative Catholic gynecologist, German filmmaker Hermine Huntgeburth has no problems synthesizing the proper and the louche, or accomplishing the sexual boundary-jumping of "The Trio."

Nor, for that matter, does she have any problem exploring a seemingly oxymoronic milieu, in this case German trailer trash. Zobel (film veteran Gotz George) and his daughter, Lizzie (Jeanette Hain), and his lover, Karl (Christian Redl) are fringe carnies and petty pickpockets who exist within their own peculiar brand of bourgeoise domesticity. They pull jobs together (although Lizzie occasionally freelances by picking up men and emptying their pockets), sharing a trailer and what seems like a desperately stifled existence.

Unlike the child's balloon in Fritz Lang's "M" or, better, the insane carousel of Hitchcock's "Strangers on a Train," Huntgeburth's use of carnival atmosphere doesn't portend masked evil, just banality and pointlessness. There's no direction to the criminality of the trio until Karl—who, in sequined gown and feather boa and finishing a mock-tragic rendition of "My Girl"—sighs that life has hit a rut. Zobel disagrees, and then makes the fatal mistake that has derailed more criminals in movies than all the kops in Keystone: He defies nature and lets Karl—uncharacteristically and fatally—play the blind decoy in a department store rip-off. Karl rises to the occasion by being hit by a truck.

Their family unit shattered, Zobel and Lizzie fill their human-resource gap by taking on Rudolf (Felix Eitner), who may be inept but expands the gang's possibilities: He becomes the lover of both father and daughter—unbeknownst to Lizzie—making for a nuclear family with a volatile payload.

"The Trio" is most charming when trying to be funny: Stuck on a roadside in need of help, their internal jealousies can't let the three decide who should go for help and who should stay. So they all go. The absurdity of their situation masks its understated pathos, but "The Trio" is ultimately, albeit oddly, about the resilient nature of family—what it can abide and how it survives when the choice is mutation or atrophy.

VILLAGE VOICE, 2/16/99, p. 152, Elliott Stein

This seems to be pickpocket season. First, a revival of Bresson's transcendental film in the MOMA retro, and now Hermine Huntgeburth's wholly down-to-earth The Trio, whose titular characters, a group of petty thieves, live in a trailer and bounce around Germany pilfering wallets while undergoing emotional crises.

At the outset the gang consists of the testy Zobel (Goetz George) and his lover Karl (Christian Redl), both nudging past middle age, and Zobel's tomboy daughter (Jeanette Hain). When Karl is killed in an accident, his place is taken by young Rudy (Felix Eitner), the amiable town misfit who writes dreadful poetry and keeps pet snakes. Father and daughter promptly fall in love with him; eventually, he obliges both. The movie takes its merry time getting into gear, but does fully come to life once it gets around to the libidinal circumnavigation of these three well-defined characters.

Trio is ex-cinematographer Huntgeburth's second feature. She sets most of the activities of her marginal tricksters against a Fassbinder-ish background of new urban dreariness—tacky carnivals, sterile hotel rooms, and oppressive shopping malls. This dramatic comedy of cohabiting sexualities is an extremely sophisticated little juggling act, unencumbered by the usual pieties—we're spared any expense of pathos or moral penalties for its gay or straight cutpurses. Barely 10 minutes after the opening credits, there's an extraordinary in-your-face sex sequence, with Karl doing his best to arouse Zobel by getting up in drag, strutting his stuff in a form-fitting evening gown while singing along to a Temptations tune. When the men then get around to making it, we're treated to one of the screen's rare depictions of beefy middle-aged gays doing the old rumpy-pumpy.

The performances feel natural and lived-in. Hain is a feisty, strong-minded Lizzie. Eitner is charming as the replacement thief who becomes the bisexual cutie pie in the middle. But the trio is dominated by the veteran George; he looks startlingly like a Burt Reynolds who's been left out in the rain for a week. George (the son of famed character actor Heinrich George, one of the pillars of Weimar and Nazi cinema) is the star of Germany's most popular TV cop show. His bravura performance as the tough-yet-tender queen in *Trio* should now win him a following on this side of the Atlantic.

Also reviewed in:
CHICAGO TRIBUNE, 8/13/99, Friday/p. G, Michael Wilmington
NEW YORK TIMES, 2/12/99, p. E26, Stephen Holden
VARIETY, 6/8-14/98, p. 72, Derek Elley

TRIPPIN'

A Rogue Pictures release of a Beacon Communications production. *Executive Producer:* Thomas A. Bliss. *Producer:* Marc Abraham and Caitlin Scanlon. *Director:* David Raynr. *Screenplay:* Gary Hardwick. *Director of Photography:* John Aronson. *Editor:* Earl Watson. *Music:* Michel Columbier. *Sound:* Philip Seretti. *Production Designer:* Aaron Osborne. *Art Director:* Eric Cochran. *Costumes:* Jennifer L. Bryant. *Running time:* 100 minutes. *MPAA Rating:* R.

CAST: Deon Richmond (Gregory Reed); Donald Adeosun Faison (June); Maia Campbell (Cinny Hawkins); Guy Torry (Fish); Aloma Wright (Louise Reed); Harold Sylvester (Willie Reed); Cleavon McClendon (Jamal); Bill Henderson (Gramps); Michael Warren (Shapic); Countess Vaughn (Anetta); Stoney Jackson (Kenyatta).

LOS ANGELES TIMES, 5/14/99, Calendar/p. 12, Gene Seymour

[The following review by Gene Seymour appeared in a slightly different form in **NEWSDAY, 5/12/99, Part II/p. B6.]**

There's no sense in wishing that a movie be something it isn't. But "Trippin,'" in applying an African American spin to that stale, old subgenre of teenagers-with-overactive-imaginations, could have done something new with it by resisting the temptation to uplift its audience and using the device to pound pop cliches into the ground.

Instead, "Trippin'" settles for "chillin'" its audience, offering puffed-up platitudes to wayward teens about "focus," even as it lacks its own comic focus.

Not to say there's nothing to laugh at in this story of Greg (Deon Richmond), a high school senior who's far more concerned about whom he's taking to the prom than where he's going to college next year.

G, as his friends call him, keeps distracting himself from the urgent business of filling out applications, by daydreaming himself into various scenarios of glory. One morning may find him dreaming of being a "major playa" on an island paradise. That afternoon, he may drift off in the middle of class into a future in which he is a superstar poet. (One poem in particular, with a title that can't be repeated here, is a comic peak for the film.) Always in these dreams, there are women, women and more women, enraptured by G's awkward brashness.

There is one woman in particular who figures prominently in his dreams: bright, beautiful Cinny (Maia Campbell), who, like G, is a senior. Unlike G, she gets good grades and has a sure sense of her future. Nevertheless, G's determined to make her his prom date, even if it means fibbing about his college prospects.

As it is, "Trippin'" is serviceable as an undemanding date movie. It's not too dissimilar from the teen movies that have proliferated this season; "Trippin'" looks a lot like an "Afterschool Special" goosed with dirty words and R-rated sex. With its energetic young cast and flashes of insolence, you wish for more coherence and less meandering in the script. You also wish it would goof on its own didactic impulses. That way, even if it didn't make sense, you wouldn't care.

NEW YORK POST, 5/12/99, p. 56, Rod Dreher

The best parts of "Trippin'" are in its terrific trailer, which, with its daydreaming high-school protagonist given to lurid flights of playa fancy, promises a delirious hip-hop spin on the Walter Mitty fable. What it actually delivers is an after-school special posing as "Booty Call," stumbling badly over its clunky message-movie scripting.

Greg Reed (Deon Richmond) is a so-so student at Dubois High, a likable senior who can't keep his mind on his schoolwork. Greg or as his friends call him, "G"—keeps losing himself in ribald fantasies, nearly all involving some permutation of bosomy babes, butt-kissing cronies, fancy clothes and assorted luxuries.

Trouble is, he keeps waking up in the real world. In one daydream, he buries his face in a bimbo's bare breasts, only to wake up with his head down in his two fried-egg breakfast, and his mom and dad yelling at him to get his act together and start applying to colleges.

Worse, the absolute knockout he falls for, Cinny Hawkins (Maia Campbell), is a smarty who only has time for guys who have a future. Unless Greg can quit trippin' on his schoolboy reveries and act like a college-bound man, he doesn't stand a chance with her.

Screenwriter Gary Hardwick says he wrote "Trippin'" in two weeks, which sounds about right. The movie is none too subtle in pushing its moral, which is that kids should wise up and quit living solely for the pleasures of today. What's more, says the movie, they need to commit themselves to study and work, not a life of crime, to secure a prosperous future and, improbably, date Naomi Campbell, who makes a cameo appearance on the arm of Montel Williams-like schoolteacher Mr. Shapic (Michael Warren).

Can't argue with that, though this eat-your-peas stuff would go down a lot more smoothly if "Trippin'" were actually surprising, or funny for more than five minutes.

Greg's fantasies are amusing at first, but they don't show much variation or imagination. They're supposed to satirize the tastes and ambitions of an urban black teen-age male, but Hardwick can't touch the Wayanses as senders-up of black pop culture. Scenes around the Reed family dinner table, complete with amusingly irascible Gramps (Bill Henderson), play like cheap imitations of Eddie Murphy's inimitable work in "The Nutty Professor."

Though "Trippin'" is not the raucous comedy you expect, it is watchable, and its charismatic cast is a treat, particularly Richmond and Donald Adeosun Faison, who plays Greg's buddy June. Keep an eye on these fresh talents, who could break big with better material.

Also reviewed in:
CHICAGO TRIBUNE, 5/12/99, Tempo/p. 2, Allan Johnson
NEW YORK TIMES, 5/12/99, p. E5, Lawrence Van Gelder
VARIETY, 5/17-23/99, p. 54, Dennis Harvey

TRUE CRIME

A Warner Bros. release of a Zanuck Company/Malpaso production. *Executive Producer:* Tom Rooker. *Producer:* Clint Eastwood, Richard D. Zanuck, and Lili Fini Zanuck. *Director:* Clint Eastwood. *Screenplay:* Larry Gross, Paul Brickman, and Stephen Schiff. *Based on the novel by:* Andrew Klavan. *Director of Photography:* Jack N. Green. *Editor:* Joel Cox. *Music:* Lennie Niehaus. *Music Editor:* Don Harris. *Sound:* Walt Martin and (music) Bobby Fernandez. *Sound Editor:* Alan Robert Murray and Bub Asman. *Casting:* Phyllis Huffman. *Production Designer:* Henry Bumstead. *Art Director:* Jack G. Taylor, Jr. *Set Designer:* Joe Pacelli. *Set Decorator:* Richard Goddard. *Special Effects:* John Frazier. *Costumes:* Deborah Hopper. *Make-up:* Tania

McComas-Campanelli. *Stunt Coordinator:* Buddy Van Horn. *Running time:* 127 minutes. *MPAA Rating:* R.

CAST: Clint Eastwood (Steve Everett); Isaiah Washington (Frank Louis Beachum); Denis Leary (Bob Findley); Lisa Gay Hamilton (Bonnie Beachum); Diane Venora (Barbara Everett); Bernard Hill (Warden Luther Plunkitt); James Woods (Alan Mann); Michael McKean (Reverend Shillerman); Michael Jeter (Dale Porterhouse); Mary McCormack (Michelle Ziegler); Hattie Winston (Mrs. Russel); Penny Bae Bridges (Gail Beachum); Francesca Fisher-Eastwood (Kate Everett); John Finn (Reedy); Laila Robins (Patricia Findley); Sydney Poiter (Jane March); Erik King (Pussy Man, the Tramp); Graham Beckel (Arnold McCardle); Frances Fisher (Cecilia Nussbaum); Marissa Ribisi (Amy Wilson); Christine Ebersole (Bridget Rossiter); Anthony Zerbe (Governor Henry Lowenstein); Nancy Giles (Leesha Mitchell, Frank's Lawyer); Tom McGowan (Tom Donaldson); William Windom (Neil, the Bartender); Don West (Dr. Roger Waters); Lucy Alexis Liu (Toy Store Girl); Dina Eastwood (Wilma Francis); Leslie Griffith and Dennis Richmond (TV Anchors); Frank Somerville (Afternoon News Anchor); Dan Green (Field Producer); Nicolas Bearde (Reuben Skycock); Frances Lee McCain (Mrs. Lowenstein); Cecil Williams (Reverend Williams); Casey Lee (Warren Russel); Jack Kehler (Mr. Ziegler); Colman Domingo (Wally Cartwright); Linda Hoy (Counter Woman); Danny Kovacs (Atkins); Kelvin Han Yee (Zachary Platt); Kathryn Howell (Nurse); Beaulah Stanley (Female Guard); George Maguire (Fredrick Robertson); Bill Wattenburg (Radio Announcer); Cathy Fithian (Nancy Larson); Roland Abasolo (Guard, First Night); Michael Halton (Guard, Execution Day); Jade Marx-Berti (Waitress); Velica Marie Davis (Purse Whacker); John B. Scott (Colonel Drummond); Edward Silva (Colonel Hernandez); Jordan Sax (Colonel Badger); Rob Reece (Executioner); Walter Brown (Beechum Family Member).

LOS ANGELES TIMES, 3/19/99, Calendar/p. 1, Kenneth Turan

There's only one Clint Eastwood (more's the pity) but two kinds of Clint Eastwood movies. Alongside steely-eyed, hard-bitten items like "The Outlaw Josey Wales" and "Unforgiven," Eastwood has periodically directed softer, more sweet-natured ruminations like "Honkytonk Man" and the underappreciated "Bronco Billy." His latest, "True Crime," has elements of both. It's a gritty story made in the director's more elegiacal mode, a confusion of style and content that is not in the film's best interests.

At its heart, "True Crime," based on a novel by Andrew Klavan, is a time-is-running-out thriller in which a weary old warhorse of a reporter (guess who) has to fight the clock to determine if a man waiting on death row is in fact the person who committed the crime he's about to be executed for.

Sounds exciting, and at moments it is. But Eastwood, who produced and directed as well as starred, has put "True Crime" together in a languid, leisurely manner that tends to emphasize character moments over tension. It's a scheme that results in some strong scenes, but overall what's on the screen ends up caught between two stools, not involving enough emotionally to make up for its lack of overriding tension.

Eastwood plays Steve Everett, an investigative reporter with a celebrated nose for the truth and a well-defined upper body despite an equally legendary appetite for womanizing and alcohol. Recently sober, he's at the Oakland Tribune because Alan Mann (James Woods), the paper's editor in chief, thinks he's one of the best.

City editor Bob Findley (Denis Leary) is not interested in the past, he wants to know what Everett has done lately, which unfortunately includes going on a misguided crusade to free a guilty rapist. Having a "real dyed-in-the-wool son of a bitch" who drives a battered red junker on his staff is not to this editor's liking.

"True Crime" intercuts introductory scenes of Everett with scenes at San Quentin, where convicted murderer Frank Beachum (Isaiah Washington) is being prepared for the death house. Though about to die for the murder of a young college student in a botched convenience store robbery, Beachum insists he did not do the crime.

Ordinarily, a situation like this would never involve a hard news guy like Everett, but a quirk of fate has him pinch-hitting for another reporter and interviewing Beachum for a "human interest" sidebar to the main execution story.

Almost as a reflex, Everett starts to pull the case apart, playing hunches and following leads. He checks out the crime scene, interrogates eyewitnesses and subjects everyone to his nonpareil steely gaze. When Everett visits San Quentin to interview the condemned man, he's impressed both by Beachum and his supportive wife, Bonnie ("Beloved's" Lisa Gay Hamilton).

When it comes to his own family, Everett is in serious arrears. His wife, Barbara (Diane Venora), has lost patience with him, and he's been so neglectful of his little daughter Kate that he has to take her to the zoo right in the middle of trying to solve this crime with the execution mere hours away.

Just as the zoo visit intrudes on Everett's investigative time, so that sequence, like many of the film's softer ones, stops "True Crime" in its tracks. Viewers who are not Eastwood loyalists may have trouble appreciating the director's fascination with these kinds of diversions.

"True Crime's" inability to settle on a single direction is reflected in a writing credit that is shared by three screenwriters with widely different resumes: Larry Gross ("48 HRS."), Paul Brickman ("Risky Business") and Steven Schiff ("Lolita"). Similarly unfocused is the film's acting, with Gay Hamilton doing "True Crime's" best work as an anguished wife and Washington, as her husband, not far behind.

Though it's impossible to do anything more than speculate about how much Eastwood may or may not have connected with his character's unstable romantic life and lack of time for his children, "True Crime" nevertheless feels like a very personal film for its producer-director-star.

Not only did Eastwood shift the novel's St. Louis setting to Oakland, the city he grew up in, but he cast his wife, Dina, as a television newswoman; his daughter Francesa Fisher-Eastwood as his on-screen daughter Kate; and Francesa's mother, Francis Fisher, as a tough city attorney. Given all that, it's not to be wondered at that Eastwood is in no particular hurry with "True Crime." It's his family album, after all.

NEW YORK, 3/29/99, p. 69, Peter Rainer

Clint Eastwood is playing a good guy in his new movie, *True Crime*, but he looks leaner and hungrier than ever. His voice has a midnight-caller raspiness, and his smile is a sneer. No matter what the role, there's always something a bit deranged and wolfish about Eastwood. Even as Mr. Sensitive in *The Bridges of Madison County*, he had that unhinged gleam in the eye, especially near the end, when he was standing out in the rain, jilted. He seemed close to Dirty Harry meltdown in that moment, and it made me wish he'd played the whole thing as Harry Callahan gone undercover. (It would have been more fun to watch.) Eastwood is unquestionably a movie star, but he doesn't have much range as an actor, and whenever he ventures into the drippier realms of feeling, as in *True Crime*, his hard-bitterness intrudes. Decency doesn't animate him; snarling does.

He's playing Steve Everett here, a recovering alcoholic hacking out stories on the metro beat for the *Oakland Tribune*. Since the role is almost entirely in Eastwood's good-guy zone, he gets to indulge his penchant for bluesy blahness. He spends lots of time in dank places, feeling down on his luck. But not *too* down. Steve's libido is still in mint condition. Fired from the *New York Times*, where he screwed around with the publisher's daughter, he's pulling a similar stunt in Oakland with his assignment editor's wife. Besides this, he's married; his own wife (Diane Venora) might as well have LONG-SUFFERING stamped on her forehead. Despite the hurt he causes others, we're supposed to see Steve as a superannuated scamp; in the *Tribune* office, the female staff takes turns giving him the eye. There's a pasha quality to all this googliness—it's a bit like Dean Martin on his old TV show being vamped by every babe in sight. Except Eastwood isn't exactly playing it for laughs; it's more like self-congratulation. For Eastwood, being autumnal means showing off your foliage.

The film is engineered to be about Steve's redemption. When a comely reporter—whom he, natch, nuzzled—is killed in a car accident, he inherits her assignment: a human-interest piece on convicted murderer Frank Beachum (Isaiah Washington), who is less than a day away from death by lethal injection. Steve plods dutifully through the paces, but his nose for news leads him to conclude Frank is innocent. How to prove it in time?

Eastwood, who also directed, from a script credited to Larry Gross, Paul Brickman, and Stephen Schiff, doesn't lock in the suspense until close to the zero hour. Then he goes in for the kind of creaky crosscutting we haven't seen since *The Perils of Pauline*. There's something antediluvian about *True Crime;* it resurrects ploys and crotchets you never thought you'd see again. Eastwood wants to be a classic. His entire approach to film is no-nonsense. But sometimes there's a lot of nonsense in his no-nonsense. In *True Crime*, Eastwood shifts tones, and you're never quite sure why. In one sequence near the end, he cuts back and forth between Frank in the death chamber and Steve careering goofily in his car en route to the governor's mansion; all that's missing to make the scene complete is the orangutan Eastwood once co-starred with. In a more ambitious movie, these kinds of mood flip-flops might signify something, but here it just looks like Eastwood couldn't resist going for the easy yuks.

Maybe this explains why the newsroom atmosphere in this film seems so phony. As the editor of the *Tribune,* James Woods carries on like a cackling banshee; he's about as believable as Perry White in the old *Superman* TV series. Don't the people who make newspaper movies bother to check out newsrooms anymore? The equally specious *Message in a Bottle* also featured a newsroom that looked as counterfeit as a Potemkin village.

In the great era of newspaper films—the thirties and early forties—the screenwriters often came out of journalism, and you could tell. Films as diverse as *His Girl Friday*, and *Citizen Kane* had the zing and velocity of the real thing; the office lingo clicked. I spent almost twenty years working on several newspapers, and I never encountered anything like the burlesqued bonhomie on display in *True Crime*. It's a raffish actor's dumbo notion of what a newsroom should be.

All this clunky newspaper stuff wouldn't seem so bizarre if elsewhere Eastwood wasn't trying to score heavy-duty points. Steve, for example, is showcased as an old-fashioned anti-hero—in other words, a softie. He tells Frank that he just wants a good story; that he doesn't care about right and wrong, which, of course, tips us off that he cares about right and wrong. The film puts Steve and Frank on parallel tracks: Both have doting daughters; both have had to live down their past; both are looking for salvation. Is there any doubt these glory guys will pull into the station at the same time? Since Steve's redemption is essentially a foregone conclusion, his ascension has the air of a coronation about it. And since Frank is black and all his accusers were white, there's even a race angle: Steve, by implication, becomes the liberal righter of historic wrongs. I guess we should be grateful. In political terms. *True Crime* is a far cry from *Dirty Harry*—it actually stands up for due process of law. In Hollywood, I believe this is known as mellowing.

NEW YORK POST, 3/19/99, p. 38, Rod Dreher

Clint Eastwood's would-be thriller "True Crime" is a carefully calibrated cadaver of a picture, and I'm afraid it's all his fault.

Based on a novel by Andrew Klavan, "True Crime" is about Steve Everett, a grizzled newspaper reporter who has half a day to save a condemned prisoner, who may be innocent, from a midnight execution.

You expect a race-against-time film to steadily ratchet up the suspense. Doesn't happen.

Twelve hours drag out like 12 weeks as we are asked to meditate on the interesting cracks in Everett's character (to say nothing of his craggy face).

Eastwood, whose directorial style is stately bordering on staid, gets the pacing all wrong. Only in the last half hour (the movie's more than two hours long) does the film bother to break a sweat.

Eastwood is more interested in exploring Everett's identity as a broken-down, filterless-cigarette-smoking, ex-alcoholic, self-destructive, womanizing burnout of a reporter.

A hell of a guy, in other words, but the petrified Eastwood is exactly the wrong actor to play him.

Everett was a hotshot New York Times reporter who messed up on the job and got booted across the country and down the corporate ladder to the Oakland Tribune, where his drinking and reckless reporting have hardly endeared him to his editors.

We first meet "Ev" sharing a drink with a fetching young female colleague at a bar. She's young enough to be Eastwood's granddaughter, understand, but this is Movieland, where full-blown coothood is hardly a barrier to winning a nubile's affections.

He next turns up, shirtless (he's 69!), in a post-coital scene with the city editor's wife. Phone rings. It's the city editor, who knows he's there. Caught red-handed cuckolding the boss! A slight grimace crosses Eastwood's face, the kind of minor gesture most people make when they have a gas cramp.

Something's preventing the gamine lovely Ev was chatting up the night before from fulfilling her assignment that day, which was to interview convicted murderer Frank Beachum (Isaiah Washington) on the afternoon before his execution.

City editor Bob Findley (Denis Leary) orders the unreliable Ev to go to San Quentin, do the interview, and come back with a straight human-interest story.

But Ev has a hunch Frank is innocent, even though the investigation and trial took six years, and everybody thinks Beachum did it. Ev revisits the crime scene, talks to a key witness and, thanks to the kind of fortuitous coincidences that only happen in movies—look, that absolutely crucial piece of evidence that could be anywhere in the stacks of papers in this room happens to be right on top!—puts together a strong case for reasonable doubt.

How he does this while stopping to do things like take his neglected little girl (Eastwood's actual daughter, Francesa Fisher-Eastwood) to the zoo, and having an anguished heart-to-heart with his estranged wife, must make more sense to the three screenwriters who worked on "True Crime" than it does to me.

As the death-row inmate, Isaiah Washington conveys dignity and calm; and his wife (Lisa Gay Hamilton) is a picture of stiff-upper-lip heartbreak. But by far the liveliest performance belongs to James Woods, a live wire as Ev's profane editor in chief. In fact, "True Crime" would have been a much better film with Woods in the lead.

He's the kind of volatile wack job who could have played a brilliant screw-up like Ev to perfection.

Eastwood has done great work before, and is always a magnificent monument to gaze upon, but in this picture his performance is as dry as his rasp. His Ev is a dead man walking.

NEWSDAY, 3/19/99, Part II/p. B7, John Anderson

To explore the paradox of Clint Eastwood—yes, behind that hard-boiled exterior and squinting grimace, the guy is complex—you have to look at what he is, as well as what he's not.

What he is is the nearest thing to a deity currently occupying the pantheon of Hollywood—no one exercises his control as a director; few can command the loyalty of his fans as a box-office draw. He's never really pretended to be an actor, because he has seldom strayed from the basic specs of his chosen role—the loner-outsider with a set of principles and a self-destructive streak. In an industry that gets all fired up by conformity, he's made money, but also attained his godhead through a large capacity for defiance.

That defiance has manifested itself in increasingly interesting ways. In his Oscar-winning "Unforgiven," he challenged almost every presumption of the western—the genre that made him—and played a hero who was essentially a heartless killer. "In the Line of Fire" (which he didn't direct) cast mortality as his costar. And in "A Perfect World," perhaps his best film as a director, he demolished cliched precept after cliched precept and left us wondering what to make either of a character whose entire ethos had been proved impotent, or of a man who'd become a star playing just that character.

If one presumes Eastwood is trying to pop the bubble of his own celebrity, then Steve Everett—the ex-drinker, ex-husband and ex-New York Times reporter of "True Crime"—makes perfect sense. He's basically a louse, a thoroughly unsympathetic character who's under the protection of Eastwood's charisma. A member of the media—and a broken-down one at that—he loses jobs, neglects his little daughter, sabotages any chance he has with his estranged wife (Diane Venora), drives drunk, pooh-poohs seat-belt laws and smokes. Yikes. But every time Eastwood defies us not to like him, we like him better—precisely because he has invited us into his process, and shared his view of celebrity as absurdity.

This is a reflection on his contemporaries as much as it is on him. When Everett tries to pick up a much younger woman, for example, he is turned down cold—unlike recent characters played by, oh, I don't know, let's say Woody Allen or Warren Beatty. When he's phoned by his prickly boss Bob Findley (Denis Leary) while in bed with Findley's wife, Everett's naked, wrinkled torso is a flipping-of-the-bird to anyone who wants to say the actor is either not aging gracefully (which he is) or aging at all—unlike, oh, let's say Robert Redford, whose handsome wrinkled face is gradually disappearing behind lenses covered in Vaseline.

Eastwood isn't averse to the heroic saga, in this case White Savior-Black Convict: Everett, busy alienating everyone around him, gets the story of Frank Beachum (Isaiah Washington) dumped in his lap. (Remember that young woman he tried to pick up? She happened to be his colleague on the Tribune, who was working the story before she ran her car into a tree; Eastwood may be complex, but when you're the director there are ways to avenge rejection.) Beachum is on Death Row for a 6-year-old murder. Something smells about the case, and Everett's going to find out what it is.

OK, the story is full of gaping holes, unlikely occurrences, weird epiphanies; strangers talk to Everett the way they never talk to reporters and there are several elements—a comical homeless man, a crude joke from a fellow reporter that hangs in the air like the Hindenburg—that indicate Eastwood wasn't always on his game here.

But for a reputed conservative, he makes a strong case against capital punishment; as the born-again Death Row family, Washington and Lisa Gay Hamilton are heartbreaking. The frivolous nature of Everett's entire life, juxtaposed with the urgency and devoutness of Beachum's, gives the movie a dimension that's unexpected and profound. And when Everett tells Hamilton's Bonnie Beachum that he believes them, and she responds despairingly "Where were you all this time?" his answer constitutes as morally unnerving a moment as you're likely to see on film all year. "It wasn't my story."

And while the virtually unspoken subtext of the Beachum story is race, race and race, Eastwood is deft with the comedy relief, he and James Woods, who plays the paper's editor-in-chief, have a scene that's pure hysteria and Everett's feeble attempts at attentive fatherhood are hopeless and funny. Ultimately, however, "True Crime" succeeds because of what it's not—a redemption tale. Everett is after a story, not his soul, and how easy it is to perceive otherwise is another one of Clint Eastwood's sly little jokes.

SIGHT AND SOUND, 6/99, p. 53, John Wrathall

Following the death of Michelle, his young colleague on the *Oakland Tribune*, journalist Steve Everett inherits her assignment: interviewing Frank Beachum eight hours before his execution for the murder of a checkout girl. The paper only wants a "human-interest" story, but Everett decides to follow his hunch that Beachum is innocent.

After realising that a chief prosecution witness' testimony is flawed, Everett goes to San Quentin to interview Beachum, who reveals his version of events: he came out of the restroom to find the checkout girl already dead. Now convinced of Beachum's innocence, Everett confronts the prosecutor, who mentions that an unidentified witness left the store moments before the killing. Breaking into Michelle's apartment, Everett finds the name of the witness "Warren" in her notes. He locates Warren's grandmother, only to learn that Warren is dead. Giving up hope, Everett gets drunk. On a news bulletin half an hour before the execution, he sees a picture of the checkout girl wearing the locket he just saw on Warren's grandmother's neck. Still drunk, Everett races round to the grandmother's house and convinces her to testify. There's no time to get her to San Quentin, so he drives to the home of the Tribune's proprietor, who calls the prison governor in the nick of time. The following Christmas, Everett sees Beachum with his family in the street.

Clint Eastwood's deal with Warner Bros, through his production company Malpaso, allows him to turn out a film a year, but only, it appears, on condition that he alternates his artier, more upmarket projects with straight-down-the line—or, frankly, run of-the-mill—thrillers. Thus *True Crime* follows last year's *Midnight in the Garden of Good and Evil*, just as *Absolute Power* followed *The Bridges of Madison County*, and *The Rookie* followed *White Hunter Black Heart*.

On paper, *True Crime* is achingly formulaic: the premise—cynical reporter races against time to save innocent man from execution—has already served multiple screen versions of *The Front Page*. The film never really bothers with *how* Everett establishes Beachum's innocence. Although Everett, we discover in the epilogue, wins the Pulitzer Prize for his story, it's surely not for his investigative skills: all he has to do is chance upon the name of a suspect in his colleague's notes and then spot the crucial piece of evidence on the news. The requisite action climax, a car chase with Everett racing through the streets in a last minute bid to avert the execution, is similarly slapdash. Why on earth didn't he use a telephone? To maintain any momentum while Everett stumbles towards the truth, the film has to keep cutting away to scenes of Beachum's final hours on Death Row, the prison staff's preparations for the execution, and rivalry between Everett and his boss.

With Eastwood's advancing age (he turned 69 in May) limiting his capacity for action, he now has to pay more attention to character than he did in the days of *Dirty Harry* (1971). And since his apotheosis at the Oscars with *Unforgiven*, he has been able to attract the necessary talent even to his most routine assignments. *True Crime* boasts three name screenwriters, including Larry Gross *(48 HRS.)* and Stephen Schiff, whose years as a staff writer at the *New Yorker* guarantee a level of authenticity to the film's newspaper background.

Everett is certainly a memorably downbeat creation: a washed-up, womanising hack with a failing marriage and a skeleton in his professional closet (he campaigned to free a rapist who turned out to be guilty). But while Eastwood is prepared to take risks with his screen persona, he will only go so far. In *Unforgiven* he lost his stomach for gunfighting, only to be miraculously transformed into a lethal avenger in the final reel. Similarly, in the opening scene of *True Crime*, the haggard Everett makes a pass at his 23-year old colleague Michelle and, is mercifully rebuffed. But within minutes Michelle is dead (whereas if she'd stayed with him she would have survived), and Everett is baring his chest in bed with his boss' wife—not 45 years' age difference, granted, but a good 30.

The script sets up an interesting contrast between Beachum and Everett: both have a wife and infant daughter, but Everett, who has the freedom to enjoy his family life, is bent on destroying it. The prison scenes, with Beachum clinging to his family as they visit him for the last time, are extremely powerful, thanks to Isaiah Washington's resolute performance as the condemned man. But Everett's domestic scenes are perfunctory in the extreme: a bizarre comic interlude in which he races his daughter round the zoo, and a belated and tired scene in which his wife throws him out. As director, Eastwood's attention seems to wander from scene to scene: if a scene doesn't grab him, he just knocks it out and moves on to the next. Where the film really sparks, however, is in Everett's sparring matches with his editor-in-chief—a gleeful, cigar-chomping performance from James Woods, who relishes such hard-boiled lines as: "Issues are shit which we make up as an excuse to run good stories." Suddenly we're watching *The Front Page* again—but all too briefly.

VILLAGE VOICE, 3/30/99, p. 126, J. Hoberman

A ridiculous deus-ex-machina "wrong man" story, Clint Eastwood's *True Crime* begins as though it might be *Escape From Alcatraz II,* a sequel to the star's 1979 vehicle. But Eastwood is here only a metaphoric prisoner. On one hand, the venerable director-star imagines himself back in his hometown of Oakland as an aging scamp saddled with a demanding wife (Diane Venora) and an annoying three-year-old (unfortunately played by Eastwood's own daughter). On the other, he is pondering that fate from which there is no escape.

Casting himself as a much-traveled crime reporter at *The Oakland Tribune,* Eastwood plays a compulsively antiauthoritarian type who smokes in the newsroom, drinks and drives (a moldering heap), sasses his superiors, and defiantly hits on his female coworkers. Thanks to one rejected pass (combined with an act of God), this ink-stained, one-man rat pack inherits the assignment to cover the last hours of a convicted killer (played by Isaiah Washington with preternatural dignity), who shot a pregnant convenience store counter girl for $96—at least according to circumstantial evidence and two white witnesses—and is scheduled for lethal injection at midnight.

The movie makes elaborate use of match-cut parallel action. The near-slapstick chaos of Eastwood's personal and professional escapades is juxtaposed with solemn death-row overhead shots of the presumably innocent Washington's last day on earth, establishing a certain stringent urgency that's rendered all the more overdetermined by the carefully doubled wife-and-small-daughter setups shared by the reporter and the condemned man.

Hired for what looks like a day and a half of shooting, James Woods idles in and out of the movie as a well-oiled riff machine, portraying a cynical editor-in-chief who plays mind games with his underlings while supplying the requisite snickering bromides: All "people want to read about [are] sex organs and blood." Indeed, the movie's mixture of extravagantly hard-boiled professionalism, lurid issue-mongering, and clock-ticking narrative structure sometimes suggests a throwback to the Warner Bros. crime flicks of the early 1930s. For perhaps 70 minutes (which was as long as those old Warners movies ran), *True Crime* has more formal integrity than any movie Eastwood has directed since his 1990 masterpiece *White Hunter, Black Heart.* There are even subliminal traces of Errol Morris's *The Thin Blue Line* in the use of flashbacks and playfully frozen moments, not to mention in the crime's ultimate solution. Then, around the time it becomes oppressively apparent that saving Washington's life will be the Clint character's redemption, *True Crime* falls apart.

Despite three credited writers, none of whom apparently worked together, the final script contains several dreadfully written breakup scenes between Eastwood and Venora and, unless a Ouija-board flashback to an interview with a dead man has been left on the cutting room floor, one flagrant inconsistency. Meanwhile, the movie's unavoidable anti-capital punishment message and self-congratulatory racial correctness allow for (or perhaps demand) placating the action audience with a constant discharge of sour antifeminism.

A respite from the weird and wrenching farewells ("Why can't you just kill all the people and come home?" Washington's little girl wants to know), the set-piece death-house interview is a small classic of *Front Page* attitudinizing. Doodling in shorthand while Washington spouts Bible clichés, Eastwood suddenly hisses that, although he personally doesn't "give a rat's ass for Jesus Christ," his nose for news tells him that something stinks. Or, to put it another way, there's only room for one deity in this particular universe.

Now at the Rooster Cogburn stage of his career, Eastwood has gazed into the abyss and backed off. Whatever his character's lovingly etched flaws, suffice to say that the filmmaker ultimately affirms that old Hollywood religion. Death be not proud. There is no problem so great that it cannot be resolved by movie-star charisma.

Also reviewed in:
CHICAGO TRIBUNE, 3/19/99, Friday/p. A, Michael Wilmington
NATION, 4/19/99, p. 43, Stuart Klawans
NEW REPUBLIC, 4/19/99, p. 28, Stanley Kauffmann
NEW YORK TIMES, 3/19/99, p. E13, Janet Maslin
NEW YORKER, 3/29/99, p. 116, David Denby
VARIETY, 3/15-21/99, p. 37, Todd McCarthy
WASHINGTON POST, 3/19/99, p. C1, Stephen Hunter
WASHINGTON POST, 3/19/99, Weekend/p. 42, Desson Howe

TUMBLEWEEDS

A Fine Line Features release in association with Spanky Pictures of a Solaris production in association with River One Films. *Executive Producer:* Ted Demme, Joel Stillerman, Jerry McFadden, Angela Shelton, Gregory O'Connor, Gavin O'Connor, and Thomas J. Mangan IV. *Producer:* Gregory O'Connor. *Director:* Gavin O'Connor. *Screenplay:* Gavin O'Connor and Angela Shelton. *Story:* Angela Shelton. *Director of Photography:* Daniel Stoloff. *Editor:* John Gilroy. *Music:* David Mansfield and Brian Ross. *Music Editor:* Shari Schwartz Johanson. *Sound:* Lee Alexander. *Sound Editor:* Chen Harpaz. *Casting:* Tod Thaler. *Production Designer:* Bruce Eric Holtshousen. *Art Director:* Wayne Acton. *Costumes:* Mimi Maxmen. *Make-up:* Jennifer Turchi. *Running time:* 100 minutes. *MPAA Rating:* PG-13.

CAST: Janet McTeer (Mary Jo Walker); Jay O. Sanders (Dan Miller); Kimberly J. Brown (Ava Walker); Gavin O'Connor (Jack Ranson); Laurel Holloman (Laurie Pendleton); Lois Smith (Ginger); Michael J. Pollard (Mr. Cummings); Ashley Buccille (Zoe Broussard); Cody McMains (Adam Riley); Linda Porter (Mrs. Boman); Brian Tahash (Winston Jackson); Josh Carmichael (Billy Jo); Dennis Ford (Check-out Clerk); Sara Downing (Rachel Riley); Joel Polis (Vice Principal); Christian Payne (Rachel's Boyfriend); Harry Gradzhyan (Gas Attendant); Renelouise Smith (Captain Nemo's Waitress); Kelly Rogers (Zoe's Man at Cast Party);

Stephanie Zajac (Lady Capulet); Jennifer Page (Nurse); Lisa Persky (Diner Waitress); Noah Emmerich (Vertis Dewey).

LOS ANGELES TIMES, 11/24/99, Calendar/p. 9, Kevin Thomas

"Tumbleweeds" is one of those wonderful, deeply personal pictures that pop up every now and then to lift your spirits.

British actress Janet McTeer, who won a Tony for her Nora in Ibsen's "A Doll's House," persuades you instantly that to the core she is Mary Jo Walker, a working-class native North Carolinian.

McTeer is superlative in every way, and her performance ranks among the year's best—but it's in the kind of low-budget film that usually doesn't receive the big, expensive push needed to cop the top annual film awards. McTeer in turn is well matched by resourceful Kimberly J. Brown as her 12-year-old daughter, Ava.

Mary Jo is one of those women who could never be described as beautiful but she has lots of personality and an appealing figure. A bottle-blond with her share of bad hair days, Mary Jo is a hearty, free-spirited good-time gal who is beginning to show some mileage, but who long ago decided that life was to be enjoyed. She hasn't her daughter's high level of intelligence but is a most loving and devoted mother, no matter how reckless she may otherwise be.

When we meet her, she's in a pitched battle with a seedy, T-shirted drunk in a trailer. He turns out to be her current boyfriend—and we may be somewhere in West Virginia. In an instant, she's gathered up Ava and their belongings and hits the road in an old car, heading eventually, at Ava's insistence, for California to begin a new life.

In time we learn this is an old pattern for Mary Jo, who first married at 17. Three husbands later and who knows how many lovers, she has in fact become like a tumbleweed, moving from man to man and place to place when things don't work out.

Ava, however, has grown weary of rootlessness and soon has reason to believe she was right to hold out for California, where she and her mother settle in a suburban San Diego coastal community. Ava loves the ocean, makes friends at school and even tries out for a student production of "Romeo and Juliet."

Mary Jo, meanwhile, lands a job in a security company office run by the eccentric Mr. Cummings—how could he not be weird since he's played by the always bizarre Michael J. Pollard? Most important, she finds shelter and a hot romance with a big, warm-natured truck driver, Jack (Gavin O'Connor, who also directed the film, which he wrote with Angela Shelton, inspired by her experiences with her own restless mother).

O'Connor is as skilled a director as he is an actor, and he also draws fine portrayals from Jay O. Sanders as a withdrawn but kindly co-worker to Mary Jo; Laurel Holloman as the fun-loving but caring co-worker who befriends Mary Jo; and Lois Smith as an older woman, a kindred spirit with Mary Jo who also befriends her.

Like lots of us, Mary Jo can be foolishly obtuse. Clearly, she has scant financial resources—in fact, if this were real life and not a movie, she would surely have even less—but she is not about to take that into consideration for very long. Jack seems like your stereotypical good old boy, but he is in fact far more sensitive than Mary Jo, and he is a caring and responsible man who wants to be a good mate and father.

But Mary Jo is so oblivious and Ava so innocent and their mother-and-daughter bond so strong that they tend thoughtlessly to leave Jack out. Mary Jo, who is arguably less mature at the core than her daughter, isn't smart or focused enough to make any substantial effort to see the need to encourage Ava to respect the overly conventional Jack or his earnest attempts to do the right thing.

But then Mary Jo is the kind of woman who'll move in with a man and start changing things around without any discussion with him—she even moves Jack's beloved Lazy Boy away from his TV set. You can see where this relationship is headed for sure, unless Mary Jo wises up fast. But this time there is a difference: Ava may not understand the need to share her mother with Jack but she definitely doesn't want to hit the road again.

What sets "Tumbleweeds" apart from many similar pictures, beyond the high quality of its performances, is O'Connor and Shelton's perspective on Mary Jo. It would seem that they wisely don't expect her to be capable of a shattering self-discovery and transformation.

It's quite enough for her to be confronted with herself to the degree that she acknowledges that she has spent her whole life running away from her problems and that it might be a smart thing to stop and deal with them. They don't expect her to see that it is she—and not Jack—who has messed up or that she's not always going to find it possible to land a man or a job with ease.

The major accomplishment of McTeer and therefore the film itself is that Mary Jo is in so many ways endearing and so authentic in her foolhardiness and lack of appreciation of how lucky she is that it is possible to see in ourselves these very same tendencies. "Tumbleweeds," which is suffused with the love with which it was made, seems like a fairy tale yet it reminds us how easy it is to evade reflection and simply to trust in fate.

NEW YORK POST, 11/24/99, p. 60, Lou Lumenick

"Tumbleweeds" is the poor woman's "Anywhere but Here"—a little indie movie showcasing a terrific performance by Janet McTeer as a narcissistic mother whose whims drive her adolescent daughter crazy.

McTeer, a British actress who won raves for her Broadway debut in "A Doll's House" two years ago, is utterly convincing as Mary Jo Walker, a much-married North Carolinian in her 30s who forcibly uproots her long-suffering daughter Ava (Kimberly J. Brown) when her latest relationship doesn't work out.

Like Susan Sarandon's character in the eerily similar "Anywhere but Here" (whose catering budget may have exceeded the total cost of "Tumbleweeds"), the self-absorbed Mary Jo heads for California—in this case, a hard-scrabble existence near San Diego.

Ava, who's on the cusp of adolescence, is enough of a wise child to expect the worst when Mary Jo moves them in with Jack Ranson (Gavin O'Connor, who also directed and co-wrote the script with his ex-wife, Angela Shelton).

Ranson is a long-haul trucker who doesn't have much patience with Ava's free-spirited mother, who's hilariously ill-suited to a new job as a filing clerk.

"Tumbleweeds" is most worthwhile for its mother-daughter scenes, which ring truer than those in "Anywhere but Here" but aren't as flashy or as deftly staged. (Nor are they as likely to grab Oscar nominations as those by Sarandon and her co-star, Natalie Portman.)

The endearing Brown holds her own with McTeer. Her feisty Ava wins the part of Romeo in a school production—and resists her mother's impulse to cut and run when things get dicey with the man she contemptuously refers to as "the future ex-husband."

The supporting performers aren't great. O'Connor's lackluster acting nearly sinks the movie—his character is even duller than that of the boring-but-nice guy (Jay O. Sanders) who worships Mary Jo from afar.

And Michael J. Pollard is twitchily dreadful as Mary Jo's boss, deflating what could have been a hilarious resignation scene.

Slight and predictable, "Tumbleweeds" is worth seeing for McTeer's touching, funny and richly detailed performance, which should put her on the map in Hollywood.

NEWSDAY, 11/24/99, Part II/p. B7, Gene Seymour

At one point in "Tumbleweeds," 12-year-old Ava Walker (Kimberly J. Brown) is seen struggling through her lines as she prepares for a school production of Shakespeare's "Romeo and Juliet." Dan (Jay O. Sanders), who works in an office with Ava's mom, Mary Jo (Janet McTeer), suggests that Ava read the lines in time with the beating of her heart. To Ava's surprise, it works.

There are times when one feels as if "Tumbleweeds," the vibrant and engaging first feature by director Gavin O'Connor, is similarly propelled by the human heart; not its pulse so much as its impulses. That the movie works as well as it does is almost as surprising as Ava's stumble through the doorway of Shakespeare's diction.

Stumbling through life is what Ava's mom does best of all. Mary Jo Walker is a hopeless—and hapless—romantic from North Carolina, who from age 17 has gone through three marriages and several boyfriends. If Mary Jo threw touchdown passes with the same consistency that she picks short-tempered, lowlife losers, the Giants would be pounding at her door. Whenever a relationship goes sour, she and Ava pack their things and head for the nearest Interstate in search of something newer and better.

Ava, however, is getting tired of her mother's itchy feet. She wants the next stop to be semipermanent and it looks as if that stop will come at the continent's southwestern edge. San Diego's bucolic Starlight Beach is airy, hospitable and seemingly devoid of lowlife losers. But wouldn't you know? Mary Jo happens to bump into the "cute" trucker (O'Connor) who helped them out of a jam a few weeks and several miles ago. Here, Ava thinks with exasperation and dread, we go again.

Comparisons to "Anywhere but Here" are unavoidable. Although that film and "Tumbleweeds" share the trope of mother-and-daughter-on-the-road-to-sunny-California, the latter film has a richer, subtler connection with its characters. No one, not even Mary Jo or O'Connor's grouchy trucker, comes across as an extreme monster, except perhaps for Michael J. Pollard's slimy, annoying Mr. Cummings, who hires Mary Jo to work in his security office.

And though "Tumbleweeds" may not have big-name stars, it is a star-making vehicle, beginning with its director (who grew up on Long Island with his brother Greg, who is one of this film's producers). Gavin O'Connor's narrative control is as steady and assured as Brown's portrayal of Ava, a fresh-faced jumble of jittery intelligence and moody intensity.

But it's the British-born McTeer's performance that makes "Tumbleweeds" potentially historic for what it forebodes for her movie career. Her rangy physical presence—seemingly all long limbs and blond hair—can't help but dominate your field of vision whenever she's on camera. Yet the temptation to characterize Mary Jo as the prototype for Elvis' "Hunk o'Burnin' Love" is both mitigated and enhanced by the avidity of her desires and the uncertainty of her identity. She's bigger, physically and otherwise, than the men she falls for. But she doesn't know her own strength, except when her daughter's around to reinforce it. McTeer brilliantly orchestrates these tensions. Her impeccable Carolina accent is enough to nail down the Oscar nomination that just about everyone, including your reviewer, is predicting.

SIGHT AND SOUND, 3/00, p. 57, Demetrios Matheou

The Walkers are a two-unit family: mother Mary Jo is a spirited Southerner and serial spouse who flees town whenever a relationship breaks down; Ava is her 12-year-old daughter, an intelligent child buffeted by her mother's erratic love life.

Following the failure of her last relationship, Mary Jo again uproots herself and Ava and moves to Starlight Beach, near San Diego. There she gets a job as a secretary and Ava enrols in the local school. Mary Jo soon hooks up with Jack, a trucker. Despite a promising beginning, the relationship soon crumbles and Mary Jo decides to leave Starlight Beach. This time Ava, who has developed strong friendships at school, refuses to go with her. She runs away, hiding out at the home of Dan, a work colleague of Mary Jo. Mary Jo finally realises that it is time to put down roots with her child. The two are reconciled. Only then does Mary Jo notice the sensitive Dan, who has been attracted to her all along. Together, they go to see Ava's successful performance as Romeo in a school production of *Romeo and Juliet*.

Sandwiched between the visceral New York films which established his career, *Mean Streets* (1973) and *Taxi Driver* (1976), Martin Scorsese made *Alice Doesn't Live Here Anymore*. A road movie about a newly widowed woman who sets out to find a new life with a young son in tow, the 1974 film very much comes to mind when watching *Tumbleweeds,* although the allusion doesn't necessarily favour first-time director Gavin O'Connor.

While Alice tries her hardest to avoid men, Mary Jo's compulsive behaviour towards them is the driving force of *Tumbleweeds*—responsible both for mother and daughter's nomadic lifestyle, and for the tensions between them. In exploring this, the script is often funny, and insightful. In particular, O'Connor and his co-screenwriter Angela Shelton (on whose memoir this film was based) avoid the usual overwrought rationalisations for Mary Jo's insecurities: hers is simply a banal life story, in which one mistake leads to another, until misadventure becomes a habit.

The depiction of the parent/child relationship is also well observed, less in the dialogue, perhaps, than in its palpable physicality: frequent meals, food fights, farting displays; Ava's first period; a trip to the beach wearing matching (and ill-fitting) bathing costumes. Rather than the saccharine show one might find in a more mainstream movie, Janet McTeer and young Kimberly J. Brown's tactile rapport offers something infinitely more believable. Indeed, it's the rich, febrile performance of the British actress, bringing just the right blend of charisma and chaos to her characterisation, that lifts this essentially modest film. Driving her Mustang as if dressed for Ascot, Mary Jo comes across as a raunchier version of Blanche Du Bois, still reckless before tragedy has taken its indelible hold.

The affinities with Scorsese's film are everywhere: in the scenario; the rather naive view of men—as either nice guys or irredeemable brutes—that one sometimes finds in female-centred films made by male directors; and the naturalistic performances. But O'Connor's handling of the *mise en scenè* pales in comparison, exposing the ordinariness of his direction.

This is epitomised by his misguided use of the jarring naturalism—the skittish, arbitrary camerawork—of US television police dramas. Even a quiet dinner scene between mother and child is shot as if the cameraman needs a detox. The result is as intrusive as the writing is subtle. O'Connor also appears in the film, as the trucker Jack; ironically, it is when he's on the road that the director, like his character, seems most at ease.

TIME, 11/22/99, p. 104, Richard Schickel

A flaky mom, restless with unrealized dreams. A wise child, stubbornly asserting the reality principle. An old car and an open road at the end of which all the problems they're running away from reassert themselves, largely in the form of feckless males.

It is one of feminism's Ur-legends, the stuff of countless contemporary novels and films. The question is, How do you color outside its lines, give the story a little waywardness, while at the same time imparting to it the honest weight of felt experience?

The answer to that question may be: Keep it authentic, keep it modest, keep it hopping. That's what happens in *Tumbleweeds*; that's what doesn't happen in *Anywhere but Here*. If you follow the form charts, it should have been otherwise. The latter film has the big stars (Susan Sarandon and Natalie Portman), the name creators (director Wayne Wang of *The Joy Luck Club;* writer Alvin Sargent, adapting the best-selling novel by Mona Simpson), a capacious budget. What it doesn't have is a central figure you can give a hoot about.

Sarandon's Adele August is running away from nothing very much—a boring small-town life and boyfriend—and she's not running toward much either—a dopey dream that life in Beverly Hills is bound to be more exciting. She is one of those irritating people who cover wrongheadedness with eccentric excess. This is supposed to be charming, but it is merely tiresome. Portman pouts prettily at Adele's all too predictable capers—naturally she forgets to pay the utility bills, misreads her daughter's dreams and that handsome orthodontist's intentions. But you can feel these beats coming—thump, thump—a mile off, and Wang's inert direction does nothing to enliven their inevitable arrival.

Meantime, down the coast, near San Diego, Mary Jo Walker (Janet McTeer) and her daughter Ava (Kimberly J. Brown), having survived a more problematical journey west, struggle much more realistically for survival in Tumbleweeds. Mary Jo is fleeing an abusive marriage (her fourth), but can't quite escape her taste for sexy, damaged guys. In a film that moves with an easy, unforced pace, she settles in with a truck driver (played by director and co-writer Gavin O'Connor) who's good in bed but damply insistent on clockwork routine outside it. She has a job that matches her relationship—too much filing—and a daughter who fills her good-to-bursting heart.

Ava keeps mice, plays Romeo (that's not a misprint) in the school play, and though occasionally exasperated by her mother, adores her funky, spunky spirit. As do we, for McTeer, the English actress who stunned Broadway in *A Doll's House* two seasons back, is a wonder—sweet and fierce, a creature of good instincts and bad (but reparable) judgments. She's probably never going to get anywhere very grand, but she's going to get there intact. You suspect her child—her only true love—may do better than that. Meantime, we have this movie—full of acceptant, sidelong glances at human quirkiness—to delight us.

VILLAGE VOICE, 11/30/99, p. 142, Jessica Winter

Just on the stiletto heels of Susan Sarandon comes another dramedy about a flighty, rudderless small-town mom hitting the road for California with her reluctant, precocious daughter in tow. Unlike Natalie Portman's wise, restless late-teen in *Anywhere but Here,* however, *Tumbleweeds'*

13-year-old Ava (Kimberly J. Brown) is still young enough that her mother, Mary Jo, seems like the center of the world. Mary Jo (pitch-perfect Janet McTeer), meanwhile, might not be the most practical woman in western North Carolina, but she's not the childish, reckless loon Sarandon has to interpret. That is, McTeer gets to play a person, not a type, and one of the refreshing aspects of the slight, flawed *Tumbleweeds* is that it creates a world inhabited by recognizable people—they might have extra meat on their bones, their faces might be what a casting director would call "interesting," and their personalities elude tidy summary.

Once arriving in tacky, cheerful Starlight Beach, the four-times-married Mary Jo continues a pattern familiar to sarcastic, adaptable Ava: Mom moves in, meets lout, shacks up, things go wrong, so mother and daughter move again—in one telling vignette, Ava introduces Mom to her "new best friend." First-time director and cowriter Gavin O'Connor (who also plays Mary Jo's new boyfriend) shoots his picture documentary-style every scene seems happened upon, no one gets caught acting, and there's almost no exposition. *Tumbleweeds* is a slender novella of a film, but it's closely observed and honestly presented, and makes an implicit promise for what O'Connor—not to mention McTeer—will offer in the future.

Also reviewed in:
CHICAGO TRIBUNE, 12/10/99, Friday/p. A, Michael Wilmington
NEW YORK TIMES, 11/24/99, p. E5, Stephen Holden
VARIETY, 2/1-7/99, p. 57, Glenn Lovell
WASHINGTON POST, 12/10/99, p. C1, Stephen Hunter
WASHINGTON POST, 12/10/99, Weekend/p. 45, Desson Howe

20 DATES

A Fox Searchlight Pictures release of a Phoenician Films production. *Executive Producer:* Tia Carrere. *Producer:* Elie Samaha, Mark McGarry, and Jason Villard. *Director:* Myles Berkowitz. *Screenplay:* Myles Berkowitz. *Director of Photography:* Adam Biggs. *Editor:* Michael Elliot and Lisa Cheek. *Music:* Steve Tyrell and Bob Mann. *Music Editor:* Jonathan Karp. *Sound:* Greg Kita. *Sound Editor:* Andrew DeCristofaro. *Running time:* 88 minutes. *MPAA Rating:* R.

WITH: Myles Berkowitz; Elisabeth Wagner; Richard Arlook; Robert McKee; Tia Carrere.

CHRISTIAN SCIENCE MONITOR, 2/26/99, p. 15, David Sterritt

A few scenes into *20 Dates*, Myles Berkowitz sits down with his favorite guru, Robert McKee, a screenwriting expert who has strongly influenced the shape of recent filmmaking. Pointing to "Sleepless in Seattle" as evidence, McKee tells Berkowitz, who is the film's director and star, that today's romantic movies aren't about love but about the longing for love, which is quite a different thing.

He could be right. Current attractions as varied as the sentimental "Message in a Bottle" and the antic "Rushmore" are less about full-blown romance than about the desire for desire. One focus of their subjects is the contrast between everyday life and the wish for love affairs like the ones we used to see in movies all the time.

The same goes for "20 Dates," suggesting that McKee's formula applies to a wide range of current films. Yet a new romantic picture with a bigger budget and a more famous cast, *The Other Sister*, only follows his description until about the halfway point, reminding us that Hollywood pictures—like love itself—often break away from the categories that are supposed to explain them.

"The Other Sister" focuses on an unusual love-story heroine. Her name is Carla Tate, a twentysomething woman who has spent most of her early years in a boarding school for mildly retarded youngsters. Now she's back home with her wealthy parents, who hope she'll settle down to a quiet life.

But she has bigger plans: computer courses, a job in the outside world, and enough independence to find contentment on her own terms. Her parents react to these ambitions with a mixture of anxiety and acceptance. What nobody expects is the arrival of Danny McCann, who resembles Carla in both his mental condition and his unquenchable high spirits.

Are they a perfect match or a disaster waiting to happen? That's the question Carla's parents and the movie's audience are given to ponder.

The first hour of "The Other Sister" introduces Carla and her family, including her very different siblings, and eases Danny onto the scene through a "cute meet" at the computer school.

This portion neatly fits McKee's recipe for contemporary romance, since Carla and Danny are attracted by the idea of love, but don't fall automatically into conventional girlfriend-boyfriend patterns. The second half of the story takes romance from theory to practice, though, suggesting that everyone has a right to amorous pleasures regardless of social or cultural labels. McKee's formula bites the dust as Carla and Danny pursue their affection wherever it may lead, including the sexual intimacy that earns the picture its PG-13 rating.

"The Other Sister" was directed by Garry Marshall with the same glossy touch he's brought to earlier movie and TV work. There's not much depth to the tale, but the offbeat characters have a reasonable amount of dignity. And it's impossible not to care about the outcome of the couple's relationship.

Juliette Lewis and Giovanni Ribisi play Carla and Danny with full-throttle commitment, supported by Diane Keaton and Tom Skerritt as Carla's often-befuddled parents. Dante Spinotti provides the glistening camera work.

Little is glossy or glistening in "20 Dates," made on a shoestring by a director with a romantic ambition of his own: to capture on film the magical moment when two real-life people fall in love. Calculating the odds at about 1 in 20, he decides to videotape his own dates with that number of eligible women. If all goes well, the experiment will give him a steady girlfriend and the first movie of his budding career. If it doesn't, he won't be any worse off than he was, unless an angry companion finds out about his hidden camera and decides to clunk him over the head with it.

In pursuing this project, Berkowitz runs the risk of turning himself into an obnoxious on-screen cad. Fortunately for all concerned, his voyeurism isn't as flagrant as it first appears, and he eventually learns that leveling with his dates is a more effective policy than sneaking up on them.

The movie can't be called a clear-cut documentary since Berkowitz has manipulated his material as well as his "performers," going more for candid-camera laughs than sociological views of the dating game. In the end, "20 Dates" is as entertaining and irksome as an evening with Berkowitz must have seemed to most of the women he went out with.

LOS ANGELES TIMES, 2/26/99, Calendar/p. 22, Eric Harrison

[The following review by Eric Harrison appeared in a slightly different form in **NEWSDAY, 2/26/99, Part II/p. B7.]**

Myles Berkowitz needs you to like his movie. As writer, director, narrator and star of "20 Dates," his offbeat, kinda-sorta documentary about dating, he's in our faces like a desperate suitor. He's scared to death we won't find him funny or charming or exciting enough. It made me want to slap him. You're funny, Myles. You're charming. But why do you have to be so annoying?

Ingeniously conceived, "20 Dates" is a laugh-out-loud chronicle of the struggling filmmaker's hunt for a girlfriend (and, not incidentally, a cool Hollywood job). It's nothing less than Berkowitz's blunt celluloid advertisement for himself, a calling card for producers and a dynamite way to meet chicks.

Much of it plays like a longer big-screen merger of "Love Connection" and "Candid Camera"—you get to see the dates instead of just hearing about them. And in a couple of deliciously uncomfortable sequences, you watch the storm clouds gather about the head of some unsuspecting woman as she learns halfway through a meal that the evening is being filmed.

The interesting thing is that, even though two women sued to keep Berkowitz from including footage of them, most of the dates agreed to appear, even some who seemed hurt or angered by his deception. It's hard to resist being in a movie, I guess.

This is part of the fascination about "20 Dates"—the way it manifests the current phenomenon of ordinary people offering themselves up naked for public display. Fifteen minutes of fame aren't enough anymore; now everyone wants a movie deal, his or her own home Web cam or—at the very least—a Web site featuring photos of the family. ("Hi, I'm Ted. This is my dog Shirley. Here's a picture of where I work.")

The movie feeds on a kind of me-centered energy that may not be restricted to Los Angeles, where it was filmed, but is certainly endemic here. Like "Love Connection," a show I confess to having once found addictive, the film tells us things Berkowitz never intended about our lives and culture today.

The movie exuberantly jumbles real life, staged scenes, interviews and a few supposedly true-to-life characters and encounters that seem too wacky or well-formed to be true.

Example: Over dinner, Berkowitz points out the camera to a date, a "feminist ballerina," as she holds a fork in her hand. In the next scene he's sporting bandages. He tells us in a voice-over that he needed 20 stitches, but the more cynical among us—and perhaps some of his other dates—might want to see the injury afflicted.

Then there is the matter of Elie Samaha, the ill-tempered, profane and never-seen investor who hovers over this story like a Mafia don. He repeatedly clashes with Berkowitz over how to make the movie, going so far as to fix him up with an attractive and, shall we say, sexually accessible model in hopes of spicing up the story line. (Shamelessly, Berkowitz cuts from their sexual banter over lunch to a shot of himself in underwear closing the curtains in the model's apartment.)

Samaha doesn't want to be filmed, so Berkowitz sneaks a tape recorder into their meetings. It's a good thing, because his rants are among the movie's best lines. "If this expletive movie doesn't make five times my investment, you're going to expletive wish you'd never been born," he yells at one point, threatening to break Berkowitz's legs.

There are undeniable pleasures in eavesdropping on someone's unedited life. But for all of its documentary trappings, "20 Dates" has the arc of a feature narrative with rising and modulated tension, a powerful villain, the requisite bits of sex and violence and the all-important happy ending: Berkowitz is engaged to the woman he pursued most ardently in the film.

All of this gives the movie verve—it should have way more mainstream appeal than the usual documentary—but it causes some unease. Because he's winking at us throughout, it feels peevish to get steamed over the way Berkowitz trumps up and manipulates reality. But boundaries get blurry. Should he really call this a documentary?

And it's annoying the way he works within scenes, putting people on the spot or goading them in hopes of juicing things up. At times like these he comes across as a user, and his treatment of people seems cruel.

It made me question a time or two whether this cinematic date with Berkowitz was a good idea. Then I'd start laughing and forget to be annoyed.

NEW YORK POST, 2/26/99, p. 49, Thelma Adams

Myles Berkowitz dreamed an impossible dream: He vowed to find love and direct his first feature within "20 Dates."

The crackpot documentary, with cameos from Tia Carrere and script guru Robert McKee, delivers on both fronts. Berkowitz finds love with a linen saleswoman and plays the dating game 20 times, all on camera.

The movie turns on Berkowitz, the last of the lukewarm lovers. His inner circle critiques his social skills in talking-head shots; his pregnant ex-wife accuses him of walking out on their marriage long before she left him.

The thirtysomething resembles a high-waisted, Semitic John Kennedy Jr., so his prospects aren't as dim as he portrays them. While he passes himself off as a schlemiel, the writer, director and star has calculated every move.

Berkowitz practices a form of Michael ("Roger & Me") Moore ambush, with himself as the target. He and his camera crew—who alternate between laughing at Berkowitz's humiliations and stumbling over fireplugs—cruise eligible Hollywood bachelorettes. This leads to fits of bungee-jumping, a near arrest and two lawsuits.

As the lovelorn filmmaker struggles to realize his artistic vision, a crassly funny subplot finds his shady producer urging him to prostitute his talent in increasingly profane ways. Berkowitz defends his vision but makes the ultimate "sacrifice": He dates "Wayne's World" beauty Carrere, and she gets credit as an executive producer.

While the film's technical quality would command a refund on the Leonard's of Great Neck wedding circuit, Berkowitz's self-deprecating comedy makes "20 Dates" a funny, belated valentine.

VILLAGE VOICE, 3/2/99, p. 139, Justine Elias

Like an obnoxious four-year-old who believes everything he does is fascinating and adorable, filmmaker Myles Berkowitz likes to announce, at the very start of a first date, that certain foods cause him to suffer from diarrhea or constipation. Later, he asks his browbeaten dinner companion if she thinks he is cute. "Do you like me?" he simpers, in his fingernails-on-a-blackboard voice. "How much?"

In a better world, we wouldn't have to know this. Berkowitz's knack for annoying everyone he meets would be familiar only to a small circle of unfortunate acquaintances in Los Angeles, where he labors, none too successfully, as a writer-director. But Berkowitz is a man with a movie camera, and a financial backer, and he had the grandiose idea of filming himself and 20 luckless women—but mostly himself—as they embark on a series of first dates. Though a few victims consent up front to being filmed, others are shot with a hidden camera and ambushed at the conclusion of dinner. One woman appears to be hurt almost beyond tears by this deception. Another stabs him in the hand, but sadly this scene is not included.

20 Dates is also padded with clips from popular romantic movies—*Singin' in the Rain, Titanic*—and interviews with screenwriting guru Robert McKee, who gently points out that Berkowitz isn't capable of making a movie about love, or longing, since he doesn't know how to feel either emotion. The movie's best observations come from its sinister, unseen producer, who sneers at Berkowitz, "You're making a cartoon piece of shit ... that ends with you jerking off by yourself." Begins and ends, actually.

Also reviewed in:
CHICAGO TRIBUNE, 3/12/99, Friday/p. O, Mark Caro
NEW YORK TIMES, 2/26/99, p. E26, Janet Maslin
VARIETY, 1/26-2/1/98, p. 72, Leonard Klady

24 HOUR WOMAN, THE

A Shooting Gallery release of a Redeemable Features/Exile Films production in association with Dirt Road Productions. *Executive Producer:* Stephen Carlis, Donald C. Carter, and Daniel J. Victor. *Producer:* Richard Guay, Larry Meistrich, and Peter Newman. *Director:* Nancy Savoca. *Screenplay:* Nancy Savoca and Richard Guay. *Director of Photography:* Teresa Medina. *Editor:* Camilla Toniolo. *Music:* Louis Vega, Kenny Gonzalez, Barry Cole, and Christopher Colbert. *Sound:* Joe White and (music) Rosa Howell-Thornhill. *Casting:* Sheila Jaffe and Georgianne Walken. *Production Designer:* Bob Shaw. *Art Director:* Sarah Frank. *Set Decorator:* Caroline Ghertler. *Costumes:* Kathleen Mobley. *Running time:* 95 minutes. *MPAA Rating:* R.

CAST: Rosie Perez (Grace Santos); Marianne Jean-Baptiste (Madeline Labelle); Patti LuPone (Joan Marshall); Karen Duffy (Margo Lynn); Diego Serrano (Eddie Diaz); Wendell Pierce (Roy Labelle); Melissa Leo (Dr. Suzanne Pincus); Aida Turturro (Brenda); Rosana Desoto (Linda); Alicia Renee Washington (Patty); Reno (Crystal); Wally Dun (Ray).

CHRISTIAN SCIENCE MONITOR, 1/29/99, p. 15, David Sterritt

A growing number of American women are making their mark as movie directors, and none has shown a livelier commitment to exploring the complexity of women's lives than Nancy Savoca, whose boldly independent films include the wryly amusing "True Love" and the deeply moving "Household Saints," which gave actresses Annabella Sciorra and Lili Taylor two of their most fascinating roles.

Savoca teams with Rosie Perez for her new picture, "The 24 Hour Woman," which makes up in energy and dedication what it lacks in polish and finesse. As the title hints, it looks at challenges faced by "jugglers" who try to balance the demands of home and family with the requirements of an outside career.

Perez plays a married TV producer who's eager for the rewards of motherhood. Combining the personal with the professional, she goes public with her pregnancy, making it a part of her program, which focuses on women's issues. This turns the show into a top-rated hit, raising the pressure on everyone connected with it and creating more tension during the baby's first year. "The 24 Hour Woman" is frequently ragged around the edges—low budgets and rushed schedules are common in non-Hollywood filmmaking—and it doesn't quite resolve the questions it raises, wishing them away in a feel-good finale that's less convincing than it ought to be.

Yet the movie still ranks with the most entertaining releases of this young year, tackling rich material with a stimulating blend of high seriousness and spirited humor. Praise also goes to the energetic cast, including Patti LuPone as an edgy executive, Wendell Pierce and Diego Serrano as frequently confused husbands, and Marianne Jean-Baptiste as an assistant who may also be a rival. Savoca wrote the screenplay with longtime collaborator Richard Guay, and Teresa Medina did the colorful camera work.

LOS ANGELES TIMES, 2/12/99, Calendar/p. 6, Jack Mathews

[The following review by Jack Mathews appeared in a slightly different form in **NEWSDAY, 2/12/99, Part II/p. B11.]**

For her latest film, a comedy about working mothers in the '90s, Nancy Savoca must have chosen the title "The 24 Hour Woman" because "Scream" was already taken. This is a movie of ear-busting, wall-to-wall, rock-concert-level screaming. Married couples scream, their children scream, and on the set of the New York morning television show where the two wives work, screaming is an occupational necessity practiced as high-decibel art.

As I write this review, 12 hours after enduring "24 Hour," I still cannot hear the keys clicking under my fingers.

Somewhere in the din of Savoca's unruly fourth feature is the story of Grace (Rosie Perez) and Madeline (Marianne Jean-Baptiste, the black daughter who confronts her white mother in "Secrets & Lies") and their attempts to balance the obligations of marriage, motherhood and careers. It's a balancing act that never quite gets its feet under it.

Grace is a high-energy producer for "The 24 Hour Woman," a fluff morning show blasted out of the Nielsen cellar when her hunky actor-husband Eddie (Diego Serrano), the program's co-host, reveals on air that his wife is pregnant and calls her out of the control booth to take a bow. Somehow, this translates as high television drama for the show's opportunistic boss (Karen Duffy), who immediately reformats "24 Hour Woman" as a hit baby-in-progress chronicle.

To keep up with the demands of her new role on the program, Grace hires as her assistant Madeline, an accomplished TV producer in her own right, who's coming off a four-year maternal hiatus, and entrusting the daily child-rearing of her three sons to her unemployed husband, Ray (Wally Dunn). He's not thrilled.

Once Eddie's daughter arrives and Grace begins making parenting demands on him, he's not thrilled, either. In fact, nobody's thrilled. Grace, buffeted by career concerns and maternal guilt, is moving toward a nervous breakdown. She screams, he screams, their baby screams, they all scream for ... well, about 95 minutes.

"24 Hour Woman," co-written by Savoca and Richard Guay, her collaborator on "True Love" and "Household Saints," must have looked much better on paper. There is some sharp dialogue scattered throughout, and a couple of scenes—one in which a gun-wielding Grace attacks Eddie during a live broadcast—that might have seemed inspired, if they had been well-executed.

But there's an awkwardness, partially intended, about the film that undermines its farcical comedy. For one thing, the morning show that dominates the background of the story is about as slick as public access television. And it's not funny bad, just plain bad.

Savoca clearly means to underpin the nonsense with serious commentary on the difficulty of being a career woman with young children, and ultimately argues for the sanctity and compatibility of both. But all this is wrapped in such siren-testing shrillness that even the occasional insert of a smiling baby can't make the pain go away.

NEW YORK, 2/8/99, p. 58, Peter Rainer

It's a good thing Rosie Perez is such a one-woman show, because she doesn't get much support in her new film, *The 24 Hour Woman*. As Grace, a workaholic producer for the frenetic morning TV chat show that gives the film its title, she always seems to be boogying to an inner beat. The actors surrounding her—including Marianne Jean-Baptiste and Diego Serrano, playing the co-host of the show and Grace's blow-dried actor hubby—seem blah by comparison. Co-written and directed by Nancy Savoca, the film is about what happens when Grace unhappily discovers she's pregnant. The show's executive producer (Patti LuPone), sensing a ratings bonanza, wastes no time hauling Grace on camera at every opportunity—she's even due during sweeps week. But Grace isn't cut out to be superwoman, and that's glum news on the feminist front: After all, if somebody as full-throttle as Perez can't manage career and kids, what hope is there for all us iron-depleted types?

Perez is a pint-size dynamo, but she can wear you out. She always seems to be having a tantrum, or working up to one. Listening to her rhythmic rinky-dink squeal for an entire movie can be harmful to your nerve endings. And yet there's nobody else like her in the movies. She has a gift for effrontery that turns all her encounters into mini-dramas; her scenes with other actors never quite play out the way you expect because she's always lobbing grenades into the patter. She comes across best when her directors just sit back and accept her as a force of nature—notably in Ron Shelton's *White Men Can't Jump,* where her scene as a quizshow contestant was like Preston Sturges on salsa.

The problem with *The 24 Hour Woman* is that Savoca is trying to turn this Latin jabberqueen into a conventional heroine. Grace must choose between being with her baby or remaining on the job, but the film doesn't play fair. Her TV show is depicted as a barrage of nudnick segments aimed at dopey housewives and presided over by a ratings-crazed shrew. Suppose, for instance, Grace were doing something she really cared about? Movies about the career/family dilemma usually come down on the side of family by implying that the career is valueless anyway. The old fiction that we owe everything to our jobs has been replaced by the new fiction that we owe them nothing. Savoca makes fun of the gobbets of self-actualization unloaded on women by the morning TV shows, but her film is part of the same syndrome. It juices us with real-life problems only to dispel them in a fairy-tale finale. It's fitting that Jerry Springer puts in an appearance. The movie has all the weight of one of Jerry's Final Thoughts.

NEW YORK POST, 1/29/99, p. 52, Jonathan Foreman

"The 24 Hour Woman" is an original, smart, funny and moving New York film by Nancy Savoca, the maker of "True Love." It takes an honest, unsentimental look at contemporary family life and at how hard it can be for all but the wealthy to balance work and parenthood. Refreshingly, it pays no heed to modern orthodoxy about having it all.

Grace (Rosie Perez) is the producer of a daytime TV talk show ("The 24 Hour Woman") co-hosted by her husband, Eddie (Diego Serrano). When she becomes pregnant, her shark-eyed boss, Joan (Patti LuPone), decides to grab ratings by making Grace's condition part of the show. After all, the baby is expected during the November "sweeps" ratings period!

In order to cope, Grace hires Madeline (Marianne Jean-Baptiste) as an assistant. She's an experienced producer desperate to get back into the business after six years raising her two children. Madeline's husband, the unemployed Roy (Wendell Pierce), is now staying home looking after the kids—and not finding it easy.

Grace finds it increasingly difficult to stay on top of the job she adores. After she gives birth, the conflict between her priorities becomes almost unbearable. Grace is high-strung and difficult, but she wants to do the best thing for herself as well as for her baby. Unfortunately, it's just not possible. And it doesn't help that Eddie's acting career is beginning to take off, taking him away to L.A. Something's gotta give ... and it does.

The scenes in which the 6-week-old baby is screaming, and the sleepless couple confront all the havoc that parenthood has wrought on their life together, pull no punches: They could be used as advertisements for contraceptive products.

But the grimness is punctuated by humor, much of it with a warm, Latin flavor. And there's something extraordinarily real and intimate about the way we see the characters interact, thanks largely to Savoca's knack for evoking superb performances.

Perez, always underrated, is simply terrific as Grace. And the rest of the cast, including LuPone, Karen Duffy and Wendell Pierce, is excellent. Playing Eddie, the handsome Serrano has almost certainly kick-started a big screen career.

"The 24 Hour Woman" has one major flaw: a plot diversion in the last quarter involving an improbably loaded gun. The scene is intended to illustrate just how crazy the demands of motherhood and work have driven Grace. But it is so jarringly unrealistic that it almost could have come from another movie (and is indeed powerfully reminiscent of 1976's "Network").

The film also feels as if it were edited down by someone who amputated a little too much. The story of Madeline and Roy—so important for the first two thirds—just disappears. And we never see enough of the changing relationship between Grace and Madeline, as the latter gradually supplants Grace's position at the office.

That said, "The 24 Hour Woman" is a film about growing up that is itself grown-up. It raises important questions without supplying easy answers.

At the same time, in a cool, quiet way, it daringly flouts movieland conventions, notably in the area of casting. It was about a third of the way through the movie before I noticed that of the two couples, one is Hispanic and the other is black. Even more outrageously, Savoca breaks the "pretty people sex rule" by showing a plump, middle-aged couple getting it on—and she makes it erotic rather than comic.

VILLAGE VOICE, 2/2/99, p. 60, Amy Taubin

Nancy Savoca is one of a kind—a female director who carved a niche for herself in the Amerindie boys' club by making four theatrical features in 10 years. True, Allison Anders has made five (her fifth debuts at Sundance this week), but numbers are not the whole story. Anders is not nearly as subtle and assured a filmmaker as Savoca.

Savoca's first feature, *True Love,* won the grand prize at Sundance in 1989. The glory, however, went to another film in competition that year, Steven Soderbergh's *sex, lies and videotape,* credited in almost every inventory as the film that put Amerindies on the mass-culture map. And while Soderbergh's movie has more flash and perversity (meaning that it's sexier) than Savoca's, *True Love* depicts a specifically female experience that had never before been quite so sharply limned in an American feature film. It's the experience of a young woman raised in a conservative community who behaves as she's expected to until she realizes that the deck is overwhelmingly stacked in men's favor and that the desires she acts on are not her own. That lightning flash of recognition is what connects Annabella Sciorra's bride in *True Love,* Lili Taylor's wallflower in *Dogfight* (Savoca's only studio film), Tracey Ullman's sheltered wife and mother in the remarkably magic-realist *Household Saints,* and Rosie Perez's workaholic in *The 24 Hour Woman,* Savoca's latest film.

But unlike Savoca's earlier bittersweet films (which all screen at AMMI this weekend), The *24 Hour Woman* is a flat-out comedy of jackhammer speed and decibel level. And nothing testifies so well to Savoca's dexterity as her ability to find variety and modulation within this hyper and seemingly chaotic mise-en-scène.

Perez plays Grace Santos, the producer of a tacky cable morning show titled *The 24 Hour Woman.* When Eddie (Diego Serrano), the host of the show who's also Grace's husband, casually announces on air that his wife is pregnant, the ratings skyrocket. By the time Grace is lying in a hospital bed trying to figure out why she's supposed to be ecstatic that a yappy newborn daughter is gumming her breast, the show has gone network. It's Grace's big break, but does she want it, or does she want to stay at home with her kid? And if she quits work to stay at home, how will she be able to afford to feed the kid organic applesauce rather than supermarket garbage? Unlike her assistant (Marianne Jean-Baptiste), who has to persuade her husband to stay home with their three children, Grace can afford a full-time baby-sitter. But leaving her daughter with a stranger, however highly recommended, just adds another layer to Grace's guilt.

Of course, Grace tries to do it all, which leads to terminal exhaustion and the constant feeling that whatever she's doing she should be doing something else. And Eddie's no help even though he thinks he's the perfect working parent. "You get to have everything, Eddie. You get to have a kid. You get to have a career. It's unfair. It's fucking unfair," Grace shrieks, as she barges onto the set of her own show, firing real bullets in her husband's general direction.

Unlike the disingenuous and hideously sexist *Stepmom,* where no one even considers the possibility of Ed Harris taking a time-out from his law practice to care for his children, The *24 Hour Woman* zeroes in on the fact that, even in seemingly equitable households, it's still the mother who feels most responsible for the kids (and most guilty about the time she spends away from them). Savoca finds half a dozen ways to show that Grace is always being pulled in at least two directions at once (it's not just Perez's lurching, yo-yo moves, but the way the camera and the editing mime the internal and external forces that jerk her around). *The 24 Hour Woman* is a tour de force of barely controlled hysteria that's as funny as it's insightful. The only pity is that the audience that might enjoy it most won't have the time to see it until it's out on video.

Also reviewed in:
CHICAGO TRIBUNE, 2/19/99, Friday/p. B, Mark Caro
NEW YORK TIMES, 1/29/99, p. E10, Janet Maslin
VARIETY, 1/25-31/99, p. 75, Dennis Harvey

TWICE UPON A YESTERDAY

A Trimark Pictures and Paragon Entertainment Corporation & Handmade Films release in association with CLT-UFA International, Mandarin Films and Wild Rose Productions, of an Esicma production. *Executive Producer:* Jon Slan and Gareth Jones. *Producer:* Juan Gordon. *Director:* María Ripoll. *Screenplay:* Rafa Russo. *Director of Photography:* Javier Salmones. *Editor:* Nacho Ruiz-Capillas. *Music:* Luis Mendo, Bernardo Fuster, and Angel Illarramendi. *Sound:* Mark Trevis. *Sound Editor:* Goldstein & Steinberg. *Casting:* Liora Reich. *Production Designer:* Grant Hicks. *Art Director:* Eddy Andres. *Set Decorator:* Neesh Ruben. *Special Effects:* Stuart Brisdon. *Costumes:* John Krausa. *Make-up:* Alex Volpe. *Stunt Coordinator:* Helen Caldwell. *Running time:* 96 minutes. *MPAA Rating:* R.

CAST: Lena Headey (Sylvia Weld); Douglas Henshall (Victor Bukowski); Penélope Cruz (Louise); Gustavo Salmerón (Rafael); Mark Strong (Dave Summers); Eusebio Lázaro (Don Miguel); Charlotte Coleman (Alison Hayes); Neil Stuke (Freddy); Elizabeth McGovern (Diane); Antonio Gil Martínez (Director); Heather Weeks (Carol); Inday Ba (Janice); Paul Popplewell (Simon); Dave Spinxs (Vendor); Dave Fishley (Pianist); Robert Oates (Driver); Toby Davies (James); Emily Hillier (Young Girl); Rafa Russo (Shoplifter); Tim Griggs (Bar Manager); Max Gold (Young Customer/Usher); Emma Freud (MC); Simon Meacock (Young Actor); Caprice Bourett (Presenter).

LOS ANGELES TIMES, 6/4/99, Calendar/p. 8, Kevin Thomas

Love stories with supernatural elements are a dime a dozen, but "Twice Upon a Yesterday," which marks the feature debuts of director Maria Ripoll and writer Rafa Russo, brings an element of fantasy to bear upon real-life emotional predicaments with notable insight and imagination. The result is a picture of charm and substance.

Had the Hugh Grant-Julia Roberts movie not already taken it, "Notting Hill" could just as easily have been the title of this engaging picture, as it also takes place in that charming section of London that recalls Greenwich Village. Douglas Henshall's Victor, a shaggy, struggling stage actor and bookstore clerk, lives there with his lover of six years, Sylvia (Lena Headey), a beautiful psychologist.

While rehearsing a play Victor falls hard and unexpectedly for a young actress (Heather Weeks) also in the cast. In a burst of honesty Victor not only confesses his infidelity but also his love for the actress, destroying in an instant his relationship with the devastated Sylvia. Victor's life swiftly spins into a downward spiral as he realizes too late that Sylvia is his true love.

Literally ending up in a trash heap, he encounters a pair of otherworldly garbage collectors (Gustavo Salmeron, Eusebio Lazaro), who may incarnate the souls of Don Quixote and Sancho Panza and who offer him that magical opportunity we have all craved for one reason or another: to turn back the clock and do things differently. "Twice" so far is autobiographical, with Spanish novelist-songwriter Russo drawing upon his own romantic mistake made while living in London. At this point he begins to speculate what might happen if his hero were given a second chance.

Armed with foreknowledge, Victor believes that by not confessing to Sylvia and by bringing his affair to an abrupt halt that he can continue his relationship with her on an even more solid basis, now that he's in a unique position of appreciating her all the more for having lived through losing her. But what will that great unknown, the future, bring? And what of Sylvia's encounter with the attractive Dave (Mark Strong)? Or of Victor's with the lovely Louise (Penelope Cruz)?

There is an undeniable evening-the-score quality to Russo's script, yet it takes the larger view: Since lovers can scarcely count on falling out of love simultaneously, they might well consider the wisdom of Cervantes expressed in "Don Quixote": "Don't look for this year's birds in last year's nest."

So assured is Ripoll's direction you would never suspect that this film is a first feature. A veteran of Spanish TV, Ripoll trained at AFI and USC. There is an effortlessness to both the polished "Twice" and its performances, all of which have considerable wit and charm. Headey and Cruz are radiant, and although Henshall is no Hugh Grant when it comes to looks, he has considerable charisma and intensity.

Charlotte Coleman is featured as Sylvia's best friend, an outspoken, even interfering type, who has never thought Victor was remotely good enough for Sylvia. Elizabeth McGovern is a sympathetic bartender who seems to possess the same special powers as those garbage collectors. For all the seriousness "Twice Upon a Yesterday" takes with romantic love it has plenty of humor and a consistent light touch.

NEW YORK POST, 5/28/99, p. 58, Hannah Brown

"Twice Upon a Yesterday" has a feeling of deja vu about it.

It tells an age-old story about going back in time to undo romantic mistakes, and it brings to mind dozens of other movies, most recently the Gwyneth Paltrow vehicle "Sliding Doors."

"Twice" tells a similar story, but from a male perspective.

Victor (Douglas Henshall), a struggling actor in London, is trying to win back Sylvia (Lena Headey), the girlfriend who broke up with him when she learned of his affair with an actress.

Now the too-good-to-be-true Sylvia (she's bright, patient, beautiful and a psychologist) is about to marry an engineer. Desperate to stop her wedding, Victor manages to travel back in time, via an excruciating sequence in which two Cervantes-quoting garbage men take him to a metaphysical junkyard.

He is sent back to the Notting Hill neighborhood where he once lived with Sylvia (Notting Hill has definitely replaced SoHo as the trendiest address in recent movies)—to the moment just before he admitted he was having an affair.

But things don't go as smoothly as he planned—do they ever, in these kinds of movies?

Sylvia ends up meeting the engineer in spite of Victor's efforts to keep them apart, and has an affair with him.

She breaks up with Victor, who then takes up with Spanish barmaid and aspiring novelist Louise (Penelope Cruz). Cruz is both charming and sexy in her underwritten role, and the movie comes to life whenever she's onscreen.

Thanks partly to Cruz, long stretches of the film are enjoyable and funny.

The actors are all good, although Henshall can't seem to make the infantile Victor as cuddly as the moviemakers want him to be. The London backdrop is fun, and everyone is attractive and stylishly dressed down.

But the film is marred by a certain lack of urgency. The engineer seems much better suited to the serious Sylvia than Victor does, while Victor obviously will have much more fun with Louise.

Although the predictable story plays itself out agreeably, this slight film may actually be more fun on the small screen, once it comes out on video.

NEWSDAY, 5/28/99, Part II/p. B6, Gene Seymour

What the world needs now is love, sweet love. On that matter, we can call a vote and get a simple majority with no filibuster. But does the world really need yet another version of "Groundhog Day's" premise? You know. The one that offers a ne'er-do-well another chance to make things right through a temporal shift.

"Twice Upon a Yesterday," like its clumsy eager-to-please hero, is asking a lot of its audience when it tries to make this idea seem fresh and interesting. Yet there's such an engaging earnestness to this British romantic comedy, written and directed, respectively, by Spanish natives Rafa Russo and Maria Ripoll, that you don't mind hearing this old song filtered through a different channel.

The aforementioned hero is Victor (Douglas Henshall), an aspiring actor whose cluttered life becomes even more of a mess after his breakup with Sylvia (Lena Headey), who's about to marry someone else less a year after Victor blurts his confession of infidelity.

Grieving and drunk, he is consoled by a bewitching bartender (Elizabeth McGovern), who sends him out into the rain where he encounters two Spanish garbage collectors endowed with mystic powers. They blindfold Victor, spin him around and before you can say, "Punxsutawney Phil!" he's back in time to the point when he was about to spill the beans to Sylvia.

The "If-I-Had-the-Chance-to-Do-All-Over-Again..." pipe dream has universal appeal, but not much legs—especially if you grow to realize, as Victor eventually does, that if you really *did* get the chance all over again, you either end up in the same place you were before or don't quite get what you wanted in the first place. Both happen to Victor. Yet he finds true enchantment in the form of another bartender (Penelope Cruz), whose life is almost as messy as his.

Screenwriter Russo writes songs as well as novels and scripts. And there are times when the conventions he uses are so hackneyed that you swear that the song you're listening to is "Feelings."

Still, the film's attractive and capable cast makes up for a lot. Though it's easy to see how Victor can get on your nerves, Henshall, a gifted comic actor, blends frenzied self-absorption and puppyish melancholy into a well-rounded portrayal. Headey brings subtlety and beguiling serenity to what could have easily been a thankless role. All the magnetic Cruz has to do is simply materialize on screen to deliver the magic the rest of the movie frantically seeks.

SIGHT AND SOUND, 12/98, p. 45, Melanie McGrath

Failing actor Victor Bukowski is in love with his ex-girlfriend Sylvia, a psychologist, who is marrying his friend Dave tomorrow. Sylvia and Victor broke up because he told her he was having an affair. A last-ditch campaign to win her back fails. Victor pours his heart out to nubile barmaid Diane, then stumbles out drunk into the night, intending to kill himself. As he leaves, Diane gives him an umbrella.

Two eccentric dustmen, Rafael and Don Miguel, take him to their trash-filled hangar and by some magic take him back in time to the August Bank Holiday when be told Sylvia about his affair. He now has the opportunity to replay his life from that moment. Anxious not to make the same mistake, Victor keeps mum. He makes efforts to be less selfish and tidies up his act. Sylvia's best friend Alison starts going out with Dave. Despite Victor's efforts to keep Sylvia away from Dave, she embarks on an affair with him and falls in love. Distraught, Victor returns to Diane's bar, only to discover her predecessor, aspiring novelist Louise.

His work picks up when he lands a role in a sitcom. Gradually his friendship with Louise develops into love. When Victor wins a BAFTA award, Sylvia turns up at the ceremony to see if there is any hope of resurrecting their relationship, but Victor explains he has moved on and is happy with Louise. As Sylvia leaves, Victor gives her the umbrella.

If Only/Lluvia en los zapatos could have been called *Zen and the Art Of Don Quixote*. Protagonist Victor—trying to win back his girlfriend after he is sent back in time by a magic umbrella and a pair of dustmen—is cast as a contemporary knight errant, a chaotic, delusional dreamer to Dave's dependable, pragmatic Sancho Panza. The lesson Victor learns is Quixote *dharma:* to move on, one has to live with one's mistakes, compromise and learn to let go. The point is life replayed may not repeat the same mistakes, but most likely others will take their place.

There is a lack of cynicism to this softly charming romantic comedy that makes one almost overlook its patchiness. Realism and magic realism make uneasy bedfellows, and they don't gel together here. While director Maria Ripoll (*El dominio de los sentidos*) follows Victor's plight in realist style, the magical intrusion of the eccentric dustmen lends the film an air both of wonderment and absurdity which tests our willing naïvety too far. This reviewer was left longing for a *Performance*-style narcotics trip to explain (or even blow) the whole dustmen ploy away.

If Only announces itself as a film about Everyman in Anytown, yet the setting is so characteristically Notting Hill it is hard not to compare the film with other romantic comedies of the New British Revival, such as *Four Weddings and a Funeral* or—most particularly *Sliding Doors,* which offers a similar parallel narrative.

Star charisma is crucial to this kind of fluff and Douglas Henshall gives a bravado performance as Victor, Charlotte Coleman is perfecting cast as Sylvia's feisty friend Alison and Lena Headey is convincing as the whiny, passive Sylvia. The woman Victor falls for, Louise, on the other hand, is little more than camera-fodder. Casting such a beautiful woman as clumsily inept may appear subversive, but the camera lingers too much on Penelope Cruz's doe eyes for the characterisation to appear anything but hollow.

Just as *Don Quixote* is both a model and satire of the courtly code, *If Only* sets itself up not simply as a romantic comedy but as a satire of the genre. Victor is thus both a convincing hero (bold, idealistic, fundamentally decent) and an equally convincing anti-hero (chaotic, self obsessed and childish), as Louise is both a idealised love object and a klutz. So this is a film in which the men get to be (in Victor's case) shambolic and self absorbed and (in Dave's case) moralistic and smug, but the leading women remain essentially old-fashioned hearth side angels equipped with minor decorative neuroses.

VILLAGE VOICE, 6/1/99, p. 126, Michael Atkinson

Cringingly titled and lumpily assembled, this stew of Brit romance and banal magical realism is conceptually lame in hot-diggity ways we haven't seen since 1995's *Destiny Turns on the Radio.* A philandering London bloke (Douglas Henshall) loses his girlfriend (Lena Headey) and then, thanks to the intervention of a mystical bartender (Elizabeth McGovern, you read right) and two magical Spanish garbagemen, gets to relive a chunk of his life and try to set things straight. The fateful appearance of new-girl-in-town Penelope Cruz tosses a wrench into his gears. *Groundhog Day* put this sort of fanciful sheep wash to rest some time ago, and spell-spinning junkyard workers only make what already seems tired seem infantile, too. Thankfully, the actors are energetic: Henshall is earnestly frantic and Headey is Irish-setter-puppy cute, but the movie is thieved by Cruz, for whom movie theft has become a career. (Do you remember anything else from *The Hi-Lo Country?*) She needn't do more than offhandedly struggle with an oversized sweater to make the rest of the film instantly fade in the mind.

Also reviewed in:
CHICAGO TRIBUNE, 6/25/99, Friday/p. B, Mark Caro
NEW YORK TIMES, 5/28/99, p. E10, Stephen Holden

TWIN DRAGONS

A Dimension Films release of a Distant Horizon and Media Asia Distribution presentation of a Hong Kong Film Director's Guild production. *Executive Producer:* Ng Sze Yeun. *Producer:* Teddy Robin. *Director:* Tsui Hark and Ringo Lam. *Screenplay:* Barry Wong, Tsui Hark, Cheung Tung Jo, and Wong Yik. *Director of Photography:* Wong Wing Hang and Wong Ngor Tai. *Editor:* Mak Che Sin. *Music:* Phe Loung. *Sound:* Val Kuklowsky and (music) Dan Wallin. *Sound Editor:* Erick Jolley-Clark, Sam Hinckley, and Scott Koue. *Art Director:* Lun Chon Hung and Lam Chun Fai. *Costumes:* Chong Che Leung. *Make-up:* Lam Che Chung. *Stunt Choreographer:* Jackie Chan, Yuan Wo Ping, Ching Siu Tung, Tung Wai, and Tsui Siu Ming. *Running time:* 88 minutes. *MPAA Rating:* PG-13.

CAST: Jackie Chan (Boomer/John Ma); Maggie Cheung (Barbara); Teddy Robin (Tyson); Anthony Chan (Hotel Staffer); Philip Chan (Hotel Manager); Sylvia Chang (Twins' Mother); Alfred Cheung (Boss Wing); Jacob Cheung (Cashier); Cheung Tung Jo (Orchestra Member); Chor Yuen (Tammy's Father); John Keung (Hotel Security); Ringo Lam (Car Mechanic); Lau Ka Leung (Doctor); Lai Ying Chow (Gang Leader); Nina Li Chi (Tammy); Jamie Luk (Rocky); Pa Shan (Thug); Ng Sze Yuen (Car Mechanic); John Wu (Priest); Eric Tsang (Man on Phone); Tsui Siu Ming (Car Mechanic); James Wong (Twins' Father); Kirk Wong (Crazy Kung); Wong Lung Wai (Thug); David Wu (Waiter).

LOS ANGELES TIMES, 4/12/99, Calendar/p. 4, Gene Seymour

[The following review by Gene Seymour appeared in a slightly different form in **NEWSDAY, 4/9/99, Part II/p. B6.]**

Mark Twain had his "Prince and the Pauper." Elvis Presley had his "Double Trouble." Patty Duke had her sitcom. Jackie Chan has "Twin Dragons." Who'd have guessed that what Patty Lane would no doubt have dubbed "the doppelganger bit" still has legs?

And legs, comprising a principal implement in the Jackie Chan universe, fly, slash and scissor-kick all over this tongue-in-cheek meringue of mistaken identity and whimsical mayhem. It's a standard-issue Jackie Chan product—which means that you won't have time to cringe at the corny jokes and campy acting before some snazzy physical exertion comes along to sustain your interest.

The setup is, as noted, tried and true. Twin brothers are barely out of the womb before they're split apart by a firefight between the whole Hong Kong police force and a vicious gangster. One brother, lost in the battle, is raised on the streets while the other becomes an internationally renowned classical musician.

Fate (of course) brings them together 30 years later as John Ma (Chan) returns to Hong Kong to conduct a prestigious concert while Boomer (Chan), a garage mechanic who grabs extra money racing cars, is forced to save his friend from gangsters by driving the car that will help spring the same gangster who caused their separation.

Through wacky complications orchestrated just shy of banality by co-directors Tsui Hark and Ringo Lam, the brothers end up switching roles, with the shy, refined Ma smashing through police barricades and the swaggering, unpolished Boomer conducting a full symphony orchestra as if he were performing aerobics.

Grimace at the deus ex machina all you want. It's all an excuse for Chan to do what he does best: perform all manner of prestidigitation with whatever his body or his environment will allow. Some of the sight gags drag too long (the hotel bathtub, for example) and bang too hard (the whole concert sequence). But for the most part, he keeps things moving too fast for you to let the limitations sink in.

In the tradition of the movies' great circus performers, Chan gives people what they want and throws in a few unexpected curves when he feels the freshness fading. The climactic sequence, set in a car-testing facility, would be useful to any movie-maker of any cultural or commercial aspiration who wants to know how to make creative use of every object on the set. (Even the wrenches and the trunk doors take on personalities!) That this stuff is done on a more modest scale than America's noisier, gaudier action machines only increases its efficiency as mindless escape.

NEW YORK POST, 4/9/99, p. 59, Jonathan Foreman

"Twin Dragons" is a 1992 action-comedy re-released to capitalize on Jackie Chan's success with last year's "Rush Hour."

"Dragons" is not Chan's best movie, but it does showcase the extraordinary physical talents and self-deprecating charm that have made Chan the world's most popular movie actor.

Here Chan plays twins separated at birth. John Ma (Jackie Chan) becomes a pianist and orchestral conductor; Boomer (Jackie Chan) grows up to be a street fighter.

Boomer gets caught up in some gangland affairs just as John Ma comes to Hong Kong to perform, and coincidental encounters cause one man to be mistaken for the other.

The emphasis here is on farce rather than action, to an extent that may disappoint hard-core martial arts fanatics.

SIGHT AND SOUND, 6/99, p. 54, Kim Newman

Hong Kong, 1965. Newborn twin brothers are separated when a fleeing crook barges through a hospital room, taking one baby as hostage. Although the criminal is captured, the child becomes a foundling. Raised by a good-natured but alcoholic floozy, he grows up to be Boomer, a mechanic and racing driver. He has a knack for martial arts and is often dragged into trouble by his friend Tyson. Meanwhile, John Ma, Boomer's brother, grows up in wealthy surroundings and becomes a concert pianist and conductor. The brothers share a psychic link and tune into each other's sneezes and sensations at odd moments.

John arrives in Hong Kong for a concert and hooks up with Tammy. Her father, eager for an advantageous marriage, has provided her as an assistant, although Tammy has a violent boyfriend. Thanks to Tyson, Boomer has to rescue Barbara, a singer, from a nightclub and, after losing a bet on a car race, is forced to flee from gangsters by boat. When the chase winds up with the crooks' best driver in traction and Tyson in the care of a gangster-run hospital, Boomer is forced to help rescue a gang boss from police custody. John and Boomer get mixed up, each falling in with the other's girl. They are forced to blunder through each other's special tasks. Boomer conducting a concert and John driving the getaway car on the rescue attempt. John escapes with a valise full of money and the crooks threaten to kill Tyson unless it is returned, which prompts the brothers to collaborate on a rescue mission.

After the villains are defeated and Tyson is saved, everyone realises they are twins. At a double wedding, Barbara and Tammy are unable to tell which brother is which but opt to marry the ones they have hold of.

Given a fresh dub in English, with Jackie Chan speaking his own lines on the voice-track, this 1992 effort has been slightly trimmed to trot out smartly on the coat-tails of his long-delayed English-language breakthrough *Rush Hour*. (He has been making the odd American film since *The Cannonball Run* in 1980.) An obvious twist on the 1991 Jean-Claude Van Damme video perennial *Double Impact, Twin Dragons* is pretty much a ramshackle affair. It blends knockabout comedy with the regulation incredible stuntwork, and tries for a freewheeling, farcical tone that falls flat as often as it soars gracefully. It is perhaps unfair to judge the movie by the standards even of its genre since it was undertaken as a fund-raiser for the Directors Guild of Hong Kong. Unusually, it pairs directors Tsui Hark and Ringo Lam ling-Tung (splitting the job between the Boomer and John scenes), while every role in the film (apart from the two female leads) is taken by a director, the ultimate evolution of a casting style John Landis developed in *Into the Night*. Though Hark and Lam (who can be spotted playing cards just before the final set-piece fight in a garage) get away with their in-joke, the procession of bit parts for astonished waiters, passers by and hotel functionaries becomes wearying. You suspect even Hong Kong audiences would be hard-pressed to identify all of the wannabe scene-stealers, and few of the distinguished participants show much skill with double-take comedy.

Taken on its own merits, this is very much the Chan mixture in its most unambitious form, with a lot of action but no danger. There are comic skits (Boomer's manic attempt at conducting), chases (with speedboats and cars) and many, many fights, plus rather too much of that overfamiliar mixing-up-the twins plotting and the psychic-link gambit. Some of the double exposures are ropey, and the ponytail Boomer wears to distinguish him from John doesn't help much. The girls, especially the kittenish Nina Li Chi wriggling in sheath dresses, are great fun, but Teddy Robin Kwan's pigeon-chested bantamweight big-mouth Tyson wins on points as the most obnoxious sidekick in movie history and since Chan can be his own sidekick here, the most superfluous. As is often the case, Chan is at his most impressive in the tiniest stunts: flicking away each of the tools arrayed on a bench in turn as a villain reaches for weapons and walking over a careening car.

Also reviewed in:
CHICAGO TRIBUNE, 4/9/99, Friday/p. F, Mark Caro
NEW YORK TIMES, 4/10/99, p. B9, Lawrence Van Gelder
VARIETY, 4/12-18/99, p. 65, Joe Leydon

TWIN FALLS IDAHO

A Sony Pictures Classics release of a Seattle Pacific Investments and The Fresh Produce Company production in association with Steven J. Wolfe and Sneak Preview Entertainment. *Executive Producer:* Joyce Schweickert. *Producer:* Marshall Persinger, Rena Ronson, and Steven J. Wolfe. *Director:* Michael Polish. *Screenplay:* Mark Polish and Michael Polish. *Director of Photography:* M. David Mullen. *Editor:* Leo Trombetta. *Music:* Stuart Matthewman. *Sound:* Matthew Nicolay and (music) Stuart Matthewman. *Sound Editor:* Jay Nierenberg. *Casting:* Heather Nunn. *Production Designer:* Warren Alan Young. *Art Director:* Grace Li. *Set Decorator:* Alysia D. Allen. *Costumes:* Bic Owen. *Make-up:* Jo Strettell. *"Twin" Make-up Effects:* Gary J. Tunnicliffe. *Running time:* 110 minutes. *MPAA Rating:* R.

CAST: Mark Polish (Blake Falls); Michael Polish (Francis Falls); Michele Hicks (Penny); Jon Gries (Jay Harrison); Patrick Bauchau (Miles); Garrett Morris (Jesus); William Katt (Surgeon); Lesley Ann Warren (Francine); Teresa Hill (Sissy); Robert Beecher (D'Walt); Jill Andre (Waitress); Ant (Tre).   Holly Woodlawn (Flamboyant at Party); Sasha Alexander (Miss America); Socorra Mora (Guadelupe); Mary-Pat Green (Nurse); Patty Maloney (June).

CHRISTIAN SCIENCE MONITOR, 7/30/99, p. 15, David Sterritt

Movies about twins can't be called a major genre, but there's a long tradition of pictures on this multifaceted subject, stretching from little-known curiosities—like the 1935 thriller "Murder by Television," starring Bela Lugosi—through modern-day treatments as different as "The Parent Trap", and "Dead Ringers."

As varied as these movies are, they have something in common. None were actually made by twins who knew this territory from personal experience.

In recent years, however, there's been a growing tendency for siblings to work on films together—the Coen Brothers and the Farrelly Brothers are well-known examples—and twins are also on this bandwagon, led by the Hughes Brothers, the Brothers Quay, and now the Polish Brothers.

The appropriately titled "Twin Falls Idaho" was directed by Michael Polish from a screenplay he wrote with Mark Polish, his identical twin. They also play the main characters: two brothers who, unlike the Polish Brothers themselves, were born with conjoined bodies.

Their names are Blake and Francis Falls, and they've lived as an inseparable couple for every day of their 25-year-old lives. While they have their share of eccentricities—they're quiet, reclusive, and wary of strangers—their relationship with each other is loving and comfortable. But can it last forever? What would happen if unexpected events disrupted the only way of living they've ever known?

These questions arise when an outsider enters the brothers' lives. She's a restless young woman named Penny, and she's drawn to Blake and Francis first by curiosity and then by the emotional neediness she senses in their personalities.

Although she befriends both of them, she and Blake bond together more closely This poses a romantic challenge for all three, and it's complicated by another hard problem. Blake is very healthy, but there are signs that Francis's life may not be as long as his.

Their future is unclear in many ways, and nobody is certain what the course of action should be.

In some respects, "Twin Falls Idaho" presents an old-fashioned love triangle, using twin-movie twists to dress up the ancient two-guys-and-a-girl formula. The film has a distinctive style, though, with understated images that counteract any possibility of exploitation or sensationalism. Equally impressive is the sincerity of its feelings.

The filmmakers obviously care about their characters—not just the twins, but Penny, too—and by the end of the story most viewers are likely to feel poignantly swept up in its emotional currents.

Blake and Francis are sensitively played by the Polish Brothers, and Michele Hicks is similarly strong as Penny, whose investigation into the past of the Falls family provides another of the movie's important threads.

Lesley Ann Warren and Garrett Morris also make solid impressions in a movie as compelling and unusual as its subject.

LOS ANGELES TIMES, 7/30/99, Calendar/p. 16, Kevin Thomas

At the beginning of the sensitive and decidedly offbeat love story "Twin Falls Idaho," a beautiful young call girl, Penny (Michele Hicks), enters a Victorian-era skid row hotel—it looks to be the 103-year-old Barclay at 4th and Main in downtown L.A.—in an unnamed city. She knocks on a door at the end of a hall and announces as she goes in, "This place is full of freaks!," to a thin, nice-looking young man, Francis Falls (Michael Polish) as he emerges from the bathroom.

She comments on how normal he looks but swiftly realizes that she's made an embarrassing faux pas, for Francis turns out to be conjoined to his identical twin Blake (Mark Polish).

The twins, in town on a special mission, are celebrating their 25th birthday, complete with chocolate cake and candles, and Francis intends that Penny be his present to Blake. Penny is, of course, taken aback at what she has encountered; still, she is no hardened hooker but a kind, intelligent young woman struggling to get her life together and not succeeding very well. Perhaps the sweet, shy personalities of the Falls brothers bring out the maternal in her, perhaps she identifies with them as outsiders. In any event, she responds to them as human beings and not as monsters.

Suddenly, Francis is hit with intestinal flu, deflecting any sexual moment of truth and allowing for a friendship between Penny and the brothers to develop after she insists on sending for one of her johns named Miles (Patrick Bauchau), a middle-aged doctor, to treat Francis. Mutual attraction develops between Penny and Blake, who says wistfully, as Francis sleeps, "Maybe I'll call you when I'm single."

That could actually happen sooner rather than later, for Francis has a serious heart condition and believes, accurately or otherwise, that it's blood pumped from Blake's heart that keeps him alive. But should Francis start dying, Blake himself might not be able to undergo separation if it should turn out that their systems are hopelessly intertwined. (Francis has the left arm, Blake the right; Francis has two good legs, but Blake's left leg is severely stunted.)

As identical twins, the Polish brothers—Michael directed and he and Mark co-wrote the script—have been fascinated since grade school with the legend of Chang and Eng Bunker, the "Siamese" twins, who actually were born in Siam and became circus sideshow attractions in 19th century America, marrying sisters and fathering 22 children. In the Bunkers' literal bond—a thick band of tissue that in their case probably could have easily been severed today—the Polish brothers perceived the psychic bond that often exists between identical twins. What the Polish twins explore in their film in such illuminating fashion is the paradox that conjoined twins represent: the eternally alternating impulse for dependence and independence within human relationships.

Miles suggests to Penny that she finds the brothers' dependency upon each other for survival threatening; Blake yearns to be free as the physically weaker Francis seems not to, yet he concludes that he and Francis never really wanted to be separated for any other reason than to avoid being gawked at as freaks. You get the feeling that Penny and the Falls twins just might have it in them to work out something romantically between them, but you can't actually guess where the film is ultimately taking us.

In their first feature, Mark, a full-time actor, and Michael, a filmmaker who studied at Cal Arts, eschew the bizarre and sensational entirely and go instead for a sensitive, poignant tone that is underlined by Stuart Matthewman's gentle score. The Polish brothers give us a respite from the dark humor that has become de rigueur these days and, in doing so, have created a graceful mood piece that is infinitely moving. "Twin Falls Idaho" takes its title not from the city of that name but from the brothers' relationship and name; Idaho is the name of the street where their hotel is.

The brothers are as persuasive behind the camera as in front of it, and Michael's careful direction of Hicks yields from her a most promising debut performance. Lesley Ann Warren playing a key figure in the twins' lives, Jon Gries as Penny's crass pimp who sees the Falls brothers as a million-dollar property ripe for exploitation, Garrett Morris as an ebullient preacher and William Katt as a conscientious medico are all on target.

Warren Alan Young's production design and color scheme subtly suggest that the twins and their mother have, in a sense, been stuck in a kind of limbo since their birth. Photographed by M. David Mullen to give the film considerable scope and elegance, "Twin Falls Idaho" is a lot closer to Tod Browning's compassionate classic "Freaks" (1932) than to Brian De Palma's memorably Grand Guignol-ish "Sisters" (1973) with Margot Kidder, and, given its story, is all the better for it. Now, if we could just see the late Violet and Daisy Hilton, real-life conjoined twins, in their rarely seen 1940s low-budget "Chained for Life." ...

NEW YORK POST, 7/30/99, p. 57, Jonathan Foreman

"Twin Falls Idaho" has nothing to do with the potato state. This strange, at times compelling cross between a David Lynch film and one of those disease-of-the-week TV movies is actually about a pair of twentysomething conjoined ("Siamese") twins, last name of Falls, who are staying on Idaho Avenue in a nameless American city.

Joined at the shoulder and torso, they have two arms and three legs between them, and are played by Michael and Mark Polish, identical but not conjoined twins who also wrote and directed the movie.

Penny (Michele Hicks), a beautiful, trampily dressed girl wearing gothic eyeshadow, turns up at the twins' rooms in a honky-tonk hotel. They put her up for the night, and in the morning she finds them in the bathroom Blake (Mark Polish) cradling Francis (Michael Polish) as Francis throws up.

Penny calls her avuncular doctor (Patrick Bachau from TV's "The Pretender"), who examines the pair. He notes how strange it is that one twin should be sick and not the other, given that they share the same blood.

Francis recovers. Penny befriends the twins and takes them to a Halloween costume party. "It's the one night of the whole year that they can be normal," she explains to a friend. Afterward, they crash at her place, and she begins a romance with Blake, (the healthier, stronger twin) while Francis sleeps.

Although the brothers—abandoned as babies by mother Lesley Ann Warren—had resolved never to separate, Blake's feelings for Penny upset the twins' amazingly close, almost marital relationship just as Francis' already feeble heart begins to weaken.

Former fashion model Hicks gives an assured performance as Penny—though she looks more like someone in a hooker costume than an actual call girl, which is what she turns out to be. And the Polish brothers pull off the physical imitation of conjoined twins with fluid ease.

Unfortunately, both tend to mumble their lines. It's one of a number of irritating indie ticks that tend to undermine the film's believability, including heavy-handed symbolism (Penny is given a $2 bill by a cab driver) and scenes that are ludicrously short on dialogue.

Generally speaking, the whole film could use a jolt of caffeine, and a lugubrious woodwind score doesn't help. It's a shame, because "Twin Falls Idaho" has some wryly funny and moving moments (there's also a remarkably sexy scene in which Penny paints Blake's toenails).

And the Polish brothers are obviously talented filmmakers with interesting things to say about brotherhood and intimacy.

NEWSDAY, 7/30/99, Part II/p. B2, John Anderson

"They're just two brothers. They got three legs. They got two arms. What's the problem?" No, Penny (Michele Hicks), you enlightened hooker you. The question should be: Who's got the problem? There's certainly no question that Blake and Francis Falls (Mark and Michael Polish), who share one leg and one heart and are the inseparable duo of "Twin Falls Idaho" have a big one: the world at large. But, as we've seen in "The Elephant Man," "Freaks," "The

Hunchback of Notre Dame" or any work that probes the humanity of the physical outcast, it's really the world that has the problem and is too blind to see.

We know this, don't we? The message has been delivered—it may never have been heard, but it's been delivered. So the only question is the manner of delivery.

A film by the Polish brothers—which may sound like a "Saturday Night Live" skit, but who are identical, moviemaking twins—"Twin Falls Idaho" may not offer any revelatory exploration of man's inhumanity toward the congenitally maimed. And it's a bit too clever for it's own good: Penny, arriving at the hotel where she's to meet the brothers for the first time, is handed a $2 bill in change from a cab driver with a prosthetic hand; a hotel guest is watching "A Tale of Two Cities" on the lobby TV. (There's also one gratuitous Utah joke that seems to have been calculated to tickle audiences at Sundance, where the film got all its initial attention.)

But the tone, especially once the brothers themselves appear and woo us with their monkish serenity and their whispering fraternal intimacy, has the austere richness of a Penelope Fitzgerald novel crossed with the rarified hysteria of "Black Narcissus." The brothers are not spectacularly odd. On the contrary. They seem quite normal, considering they've been ostracized from birth, abandoned by their mother (Lesley Ann Warren) and considered by most people best intended as circus attractions.

Would their appearance on the street (in director Michael Polish's purposely anonymous city) actually attract a photo-snapping mob of gawkers? Maybe, but it seems unlikely people would so flagrantly flaunt their morbid curiosity. And that's where the Polish boys go astray, by not exhibiting the reserve of their own, very precise characters.

The story is about Blake—the stronger of the two twins, the one who could survive alone—and Francis' realization that he's doomed and how it might be better considering Blake's budding romance with Penny. The totally affected Hicks, a fashion model making her screen debut, doesn't necessarily give a performance, but it rings true enough: Her world-weary cool is apt counterpoint to the brothers' naivete and guilelessness. And despite what happens to the brothers, it's Penny's character that develops over the course of the film.

There's a fantasy sequence, shot home-movie style, that's probably the most moving in all of "Twin Falls": Francis and Blake, separate of each other, riding bicycles across the edge of a seaside cliff. You want the film to end there. But, then again, you'd also have preferred that Penny, thinking about the brothers, not absentmindedly snap apart a fresh pair of chopsticks. You can't have everything, of course, and while "Twin Falls Idaho" hardly gives it to you, it does offer quite a bit.

Maybe even twice what you'd expect.

SIGHT AND SOUND, 10/00, p. 62, Philip Kemp

US, the present. A hooker, Penny, is called to the Imperial Hotel on Idaho Avenue. Her client, Francis Falls, is a conjoined twin with brother Blake. She runs away, leaving her handbag behind. Returning for it, she starts to feel sympathy for the twins; when Francis gets sick, she stays overnight and gets her doctor, Miles, to help. She learns that the twins were abandoned at birth by their mother and were adopted.

Penny invites the twins to a Halloween party. Back at her apartment she and Blake start to make love, but stop when Francis wakes up. In Penny's absence her pimp, Jay Harrison, shows up and enthuses over the twins' showbiz potential. They flee, attracting a crowd in the street, and lock themselves in their apartment, refusing to let Penny in. Blake and Francis fight. Francis is fatally weakened. They're discovered by their neighbour, preacher Jesus; he takes them to hospital, where Penny visits them. She tracks down their mother and begs her to see her sons. The twins are separated as the only way of saving Blake, and Francis dies. Later Penny visits Blake, now a disabled recluse, and they duet on the guitar the twins used to play.

There's a touching moment in Tod Browning's classic *Freaks* (1932) when one of a pair of conjoined twins is kissed by her fiancé. Her sister, who has been tactfully reading, ignoring their love talk, looks up with an involuntary shiver of pleasure. *Twin Falls Idaho,* the exceptional first feature from the Polish Brothers explores the implications of that moment to their fullest and darkest extent. And, like Browning's film (or like David Lynch's *The Elephant Man,* 1980), it reaches a bitter if predictable conclusion as to who the real freaks are—most trenchantly in the scene where Siamese twins Blake and Francis, fleeing from Penny's salivatingly venal pimp, huddle protectively together in a scruffy downtown recreation ground as a gawking crowd collects. "We didn't have a problem," Blake tells Penny, recalling the twins' years as circus artistes. "The audience who came to see us did."

There are echoes of Lynch, too, in the texture of the film, especially the early scenes in the terminally cruddy Imperial Hotel with its gurgling faucets, sputtering bathroom lights and consciously wacky denizens. ("Fifty-Two years—and I have yet to guess the desired floor," laments the wizened old lift operator.) But the film soon establishes a tone, and vision, of its own, thanks to the subdued intensity and utter conviction of its twin lead performances. That Mark and Michael Polish are in fact identical (though not conjoined) twins obviously helped those qualities no end. But that isn't in any way to diminish their achievement: not only scripting and starring in the film, but creating it while strapped into what sounds like a horrendously uncomfortable double harness throughout the 17-day shoot. What makes it all the more impressive is that the central illusion (the Falls twins share three legs and two arms between them) is effected purely with old-fashioned camera wizardry and carefully worked-out angles; not a single element has been computer-generated.

Twin Falls Idaho treads a sure-footed path between poignancy and ironic humour. "Maybe I'll call you when I'm single," Blake tells Penny, and there's a diverting episode when the twins, liberated for once into a world where they can fit in, go trick-or-treating at Halloween. "Why, you look quite real," gasps a startled nun. "You look real too," they respond politely.

It's largely through Blake that we gain insights into the brothers' condition, since he's the one who talks more to Penny, our surrogate (a warm, appealingly tentative performance from Michele Hicks). Vividly expressing the mixture of tenderness and resentment the twins feel towards each other, he talks of "the two minutes a day when I feel alone: the minute when I wake up and the minute when I fall asleep. Two minutes to remind me of who I am." But "who he is" is inextricable from his dual identity with his brother. "Blake will live a normal life when I go," says Francis wistfully; but the film's melancholy coda, after Francis' death, shows this to be no more than wishful thinking. Blake's incomplete body (he lacks a left arm, and his left leg is vestigial) mirrors his spiritual state: without his twin Blake will always be less than whole, and even Penny's comforting presence can be no substitute. it's a bleak, honest ending to a courageous film.

VILLAGE VOICE, 8/3/99, p. 59, Dennis Lim

In *Twin Falls Idaho*, their somber, fablelike first feature, identical twins Michael and Mark Polish try to milk resonance from novelty value—the execution is surefooted, but it's a futile endeavor, and a laborious one to watch. The brothers, who share a writing credit, play conjoined twins Blake and Francis Falls. The title is indeed a feeble pun: when we first meet the twin Falls, they're living in a nameless city on "Idaho Avenue"—in a spooky *Barton Fink* hotel, complete with flickering fluorescent lights and Lynchian elevator guy. Salvation of sorts arrives in the form of Penny (Michele Hicks), a trashily made-up, good-hearted—oh yes—hooker.

The film's slapped-on eeriness peels away to reveal little more than simplistic dramatic ploys. Francis (Michael) is seriously ill, and even though the twins share vital organs and a bloodstream, Blake (Mark) remains fit—"Who'd take care of Francis otherwise?" Add to this metaphysical medical drama a romantic complication: Penny and Blake fall in love. The two subplots dovetail into a tidy, fussy delineation of a love triangle—an offbeat one, we're constantly reminded. The Polish brothers also factor in a leisurely examination of fraternal bonds and an illustration of separation anxiety at its most profound. By the end, though, the film is content to play out simply as a conventional tearjerker—with a tasteful freak-show aspect.

Twin Falls—which was featured in the last New Directors alongside a vastly more haunting and suggestive Siamese-twin tale, Alexei Balabanov's exquisite, still distributor-less *Of Freaks and Men*—leaves far too little to the imagination. The screenplay, for all its minimalist airs and pregnant pauses, is dependent on the odd declamatory outburst and crashing symbolism—in particular, a recurring $2 bill (as in, you don't get two singles if you tear it in half. The gauntly handsome leads are decent enough actors, but they're hardly immune to the sedate tone and pace—a measure of the self-importance of a film that's neither as weighty nor as weird as it would like to think.

Also reviewed in:
CHICAGO TRIBUNE, 9/17/99, Friday/p. D, Michael Wilmington
NEW YORK TIMES, 7/30/99, p. E24, Janet Maslin
VARIETY, 2/15/-21/99, p. 62, Todd McCarthy
WASHINGTON POST, 8/27/99, p. C1, Rita Kempley
WASHINGTON POST, 8/27/99, Weekend/p. 37, Desson Howe

2 BY 4

A Strand Releasing and Red Horse Films release of an Electric Head production. *Executive Producer:* Darren Davy. *Producer:* John Hall and Virginia Biddle. *Director:* Jimmy Smallhorne. *Screenplay:* Jimmy Smallborne, Terrence McGoff, and Fergus Tighe. *Based on an original story by:* Jimmy Smallborne and Terrence McGoff. *Director of Photography:* Declan Quinn. *Editor:* Laure Sullivan and Scott Balcerek. *Music:* Productions HuncaMunca Music. *Sound:* Rick Dior. *Production Designer:* Hazel Mailloux. *Costumes:* Ivan Ingermann. *Running time:* 90 minutes. *MPAA Rating:* Not Rated.

CAST: Jimmy Smallhorne (Johnnie); Chris O'Neill (Trump); Bradley Fitts (Christian); Joe Holyoake (Joe); Terrence McGoff (Billy); Michael Liebmann (Eddie); Ronan Carr (Brains); Leo Hamill (Paddy); Seamus McDonagh (Conor); Kimberly Topper (Maria); Conor Foran (Paul); James Hanrahan (Taigh); Marian Quinn (Bibi).

NEW YORK POST, 11/26/99, p. 44, Lou Lumenick

Yet another gay coming-of-age movie—this one set in a community of Irish immigrants in the west Bronx—"2 by 4" is about as subtle as a whack over the head with a plank.

Johnny Maher (Jimmy Smallhorne) is a foreman for a construction company run by his sleazy Uncle Trump (the late Chris O'Neill), a fast-talking con man who's ripping off both his employees and his latest employers, a group of Hasidic businessmen.

Plagued by nightmares, Johnny keeps his mystified girlfriend (Kimberly Topper) at a distance while seeking solace in booze, cocaine and anonymous sexual encounters with other men.

After a pathetic, crack-addicted hustler (Bradley Fitts) tracks him down at home, Johnny is forced to confront a dark "secret"—but the secret is something that most audience members will have figured out long before.

The acting is fresher and less predictable than the storyline, but the main virtue of "2 by 4" is evocative cinematography by Declan Quinn ("Leaving Las Vegas").

VILLAGE VOICE, 11/30/99, p. 142, Dennis Lim

Though twice the macho man of De Niro's Walt [The reference is to *Flawless*; see Lim's review of that film.], *2 by 4*'s Johnnie dabbles in drag with as much flair as the flaming Rusty. After a hard day's work at the construction site, Johnnie kicks back by donning mascara and feather boa, and heading down to the local pub for karaoke night (his "20th Century Boy" strut-and-pout would do Jonathan Rhys-Meyers proud. From the outset, a meltdown is in the cards—a Bronx-residing Irish émigré with a patient girlfriend and a taste for boy hustlers, Johnnie suffers recurring nightmares that hint loudly at past trauma.

In the lead role, director-cowriter Jimmy Smallhorne gives a forceful, concentrated performance. The film also benefits from expressive photography by Declan Quinn (who, coincidentally, also shot *Flawless,* and seems to have been a marginally calming influence on Schumacher). *2 by 4*'s main strength is its raw, weathered feel, but the film's glib framing psychology—with intimations of abuse and talk of absent fathers—is like sandpaper on its rough naturalism.

Also reviewed in:
NEW YORK TIMES, 11/26/99, p. E30, Anita Gates
VARIETY, 2/2-8/98, p. 33, Glenn Lovell

200 CIGARETTES

A Paramount Pictures and Lakeshore Entertainment release in association with MTV Films and Dogstar Films. *Executive Producer:* Tom Rosenberg, Mike Newell, Alan Greenspan, Ted Tannebaum, and Sigurjon Sightvatsson. *Producer:* Betsy Beers, David Gale, and Van Toffler. *Director:* Risa Bramon Garcia. *Screenplay:* Shana Larsen. *Director of Photography:* Frank Prinzi. *Editor:* Lisa Zeno Churgin. *Music:* Bob Mothersbaugh, Mark Mothersbaugh, Randall Poster, and Elvis Costello. *Sound:* Scott Breindel. *Casting:* Deborah Aquila and Sarah Halley Finn. *Production Designer:* Ina Mayhew. *Art Director:* Judy Rhee. *Set Decorator:* Paul Weathered. *Costume Designer:* Susan Lyall. *Running time:* 102 minutes. *MPAA Rating:* R.

CAST: Ben Affleck (Bartender); Casey Affleck (Tom); David Chappelle (Disco Cabbie); Guillermo Diaz (Dave); Angela Featherstone (Caitlyn); Janeane Garofalo (Ellie); Gaby Hoffmann (Stephie); Kate Hudson (Cindy); Catherine Kellner (Hilary); Courtney Love (Lucy); Brian McCardie (Eric); Jay Mohr (Jack); Nicole Parker (Bridget); Matha Plimpton (Monica); Christina Ricci (Val); Paul Rudd (Kevin); Elvis Costello (Himself).

LOS ANGELES TIMES, 2/26/99, Calendar/p. 10, Kevin Thomas

When people celebrate New Year's Eve, they feel they've just got to have fun—and that of course means having someone important in your life to enjoy it with. Director Risa Bramon Garcia and writer Shana Larsen, in their ruefully breezy "200 Cigarettes," zero in on a large group of young New Yorkers out to have a good time on New Year's Eve, 1981, yet because it is this particular holiday—a time for taking stock of one's life—it means that many of them are looking for love more than they realize.

Why the filmmakers pick 1981 rather than a more recent year is not all that clear on the screen, but the flowering of the self-absorbed Me Decade is surely part of their point. And it does allow them to work in lots of potent vintage music, epitomized by Elvis Costello, on the soundtrack (and in a cameo).

The film's title refers to a carton of cigarettes bought by Lucy (Courtney Love) for her friend Kevin (Paul Rudd) for his birthday, who late in the film observes that smoking cigarettes can be a way of keeping people from having "meaningful interaction" with one another. What goes on in the film seems no different from what goes on now, except that most everyone smokes lots more than they do today.

Lucy and Kevin are arguably the film's key among many couples. Friends for five years, they are dateless—but as the evening progresses they begin to wonder whether they can be more than friends. Kevin is down in the dumps because he's just lost his girlfriend Ellie (Janeane Garofalo), while Lucy, having set her sights on a sexy bartender (Ben Affleck), is determined to get a kick out of the evening. This same bartender also has attracted two friends, Caitlyn (Angela Featherstone) and Bridget (Nicole Parker), who breaks it off with her boyfriend Eric (Brian McCardie). (Amusingly, the bartender sabotages his charisma when he finally opens his mouth with such off-putting lines as "Well, girls, would you like your eggs scrambled or fertilized?")

Eric goes on alone to a party at the East Village apartment of his former girlfriend Monica (Martha Plimpton), who is coming apart in fear that nobody will show up besides her best friend Hilary (Catherine Kellner), who takes off, promising to return. That leaves Eric and Monica alone—and Eric inadvertently forces Monica to admit he is the worst lover she ever had—"including high school."

Then there are Christina Ricci's adventuresome Val and her reluctant, complaining and scared pal Stephie (Gaby Hoffmann), a couple of garish girls from Long Island lost in the East Village and winding up in a rock club, where they meet punk types Tom (Casey Affleck) and orange-haired Dave (Guillermo Diaz). In a glossier section of Manhattan, Cindy (Kate Hudson), a pretty klutz, is professing love to womanizer Jack (Jay Mohr), to whom she lost her virginity the night before. Weaving through the film's intersecting plots is irrepressible, advice-giving Disco Cabbie (Dave Chappelle).

The filmmakers strike a deft balance between humor and sentiment, and their movie's large cast reminds you of the abundance of talented and attractive young people on the screen these days. Performances are remarkably even, but some roles are a tad bigger than others, which may be the reason why Love, Rudd, Plimpton, Hudson and Chappelle have been able to make perhaps the strongest impressions. Love clearly can play comedy as effectively as she did drama ("The People vs. Larry Flynt"). As for Hudson, this film marks the Hollywood film debut of this lovely and poised actress, the daughter of Goldie Hawn and singer Bill Hudson.

"200 Cigarettes" is a light comedy, pure and simple (and hardly unfamiliar), but its makers sustain its energy through the unraveling of an intricate plot and bring to it a certain edge through a witty, sharp sense of observation.

NEW YORK, 3/8/99, p. 97, Peter Rainer

As if *Playing By Heart* weren't enough, here's another multi-character, multi-plot movie that once again gives the term *Altman-esque* a bad name. *200 Cigarettes* is about partygoers in the East Village on New Year's Eve, 1981, and as we bop back and forth among the many converging story lines, a troubling thought arises: *None* of these episodes merits our time.

The film is filled with actors you want to see—just not in this thing. Ben Affleck plays a yuppie bartender with an Adam Ant coif; Courtney Love looks world-weary smoking up a storm while trying to keep her dress on; Christina Ricci, as a Long Island teenybopper out for thrills, teeters on high heels. Janeane Garofalo, who seems to be making a career out of being far better than her movies, has the film's sole good line: Unable to light a cigarette, she proclaims, "These matches are disappointing." First-time director Risa Bramon Garcia is also a renowned casting director, but except for Dave Chappelle's disco cabbie, who has a slithery rap, she lets her actors get away from her. Everybody vamps and preens as if it were amateur night in SoHo, and a few of the performers, such as Kate Hudson, appear ill-used—in several scenes, she is required to walk around in a jacket smeared with dog poop. This sort of stunt might work in a John Waters movie, but *200 Cigarettes*, for all its punk trappings, is squeaky-clean. It's all about finding love with the right partner, and there are no gender-benders, no hard-core druggies in sight. Just poop.

NEW YORK POST, 2/26/99, p. 49, Jonathan Foreman

The folks behind this lousy, amateurish movie are clearly hoping that its early-'80s soundtrack—an all-too-predictable collection of greatest hits—will seduce a nostalgic Gen X audience. But as a Gen X friend who endured this movie put it, "200 Cigarettes" is "a bad student film with famous people in it."

Based on the idea that New Year's Eve can be a comically depressing and desperate affair, the film follows several twentysomething couples around East Village bars and restaurants before they all turn up at a party given by sad sack Monica (Martha Plimpton).

They are all downtown types of one sort or another—except for two Ronkonkoma girls (Christina Ricci and Gaby Hoffman, with awful Lorn-Guyland accents), and an Upper West Side princess in pink (Kate Hudson).

Essentially, everyone's priority is to find someone to wake up with in 1982. It's all frantic, antic and utterly unbelievable thanks to dreadful dialogue and direction.

The saddest thing about "200 Cigarettes," besides its waste of good music, is Christina Ricci giving a truly terrible performance for the first time. Unfortunately, she's not alone: Plimpton is unwatchably bad, and the rest of the cast flounder in a sea of bad lines.

The only members of the ensemble who manage to keep their heads above water are Ben Affleck and Janeane Garofalo in small roles, and singer-turned-actress Courtney Love.

Newcomer Kate Hudson at least has a lovely smile. (She looks like Cameron Diaz with a severe nose job, but sounds just like her mother, Goldie Hawn.)

Anachronisms abound. The Checker cab driven by Dave Chappelle, in which everyone ends up riding at one point, is surrounded by very '90s-looking traffic. And white guys in 1981 did not use the phrase "skanky 'ho." The filmmakers shot various Alphabet City locations as they are today, apparently unaware that the neighborhood has been massively gentrified since the early '80s.

"200 Cigarettes" pulls off a few good jokes, but it strains so hard to be funny that it injures itself in the process, and the movie's 102 minutes feel like three hours.

The film also contains one of the most obvious and shameless instances of product placement in recent years: Expensive Veuve Cliquot champagne is prominently displayed at a supposedly bohemian East Village party.

NEWSDAY, 2/26/99, Part II/p. B3, Gene Seymour

The sight of Courtney Love's rangy frame draped over a jukebox as she wails along with "Through the Eyes of Love" (aka "Theme from Ice Castles") is one of the fleeting moments of sneaky fun and incongruous wonder that gives "200 Cigarettes" its justification for being. This is the kind of movie that's so overly crowded with people, plot complications, color and noise that your brain feels as if it's riding the Lexington Avenue subway at rush hour. All the more reason to be grateful for the little things you catch out of the corner of your eye that distract you from the blur and din.

This frenzied romantic roundelay takes place on New Year's Eve 1981 in Manhattan's Lower East Side, which serves as a pinball machine for several high-strung 20-somethings bouncing all over the neighborhood in search of love, thrills, fabulous prizes of some sort.

No one wants to go home empty-handed—or—bedded. Least of all, Caitlyn (Angela Featherstone) and Bridget (Nicole Parker), who believe a horrific 1982 awaits them if they don't score by midnight. They have their eyes on a hunky bartender (Ben Affleck), who's also being scoped by Lucy (Love), who's out with bitter, broken-hearted Kevin (Paul Rudd), who's just been dumped by a sourpuss artist (Janeane Garofalo).

Got that? Now while all this is going on, teen pals Val (Christina Ricci) and Stephie (Gaby Hoffman) have come into the city from Ronkonkoma, all rouged up and not at all sure of where they're going, except to a party staged by Val's cousin Monica (Martha Plimpton), who's having serious panic attacks over whether anyone at all will show up. Not too far away, an actor (Jay Mohr) and a pretty-in-pink blonde (Kate Hudson) fumble and stumble their way through their first real date. (Actually, it's their second, but, see ... ah, skip it!)

A cabbie (Dave Chappelle) serves as a disco-playing Greek chorus for all this stuff. But not even he can keep track of all the mess without a scorecard.

Director Risa Bramon Garcia, working from a script by Shana Larsen, does a decent job of traffic control, and she makes the cusp of the '80s as gauzy and ideal a dreamworld as the late '50s. The pitfalls of drugs and promiscuity are, more or less, bleached out. And one of the scariest-looking of the leather punks (Casey Affleck) turns out to be the most romantic guy in Alphabet City. For all its retro-boho hauteur, "200 Cigarettes" is as conventional as a date movie can get.

There are so many missed connections, sitcom-style misunderstandings and pratfalls in "200 Cigarettes" that it often seems like "The Last Days of Disco" trying to be a cooler, sleeker "Caddyshack."

It's a lot more sweet-natured than that. But don't expect anything more than empty calories.

VILLAGE VOICE, 3/9/99, p. 124, Jessica Winter

Millennial angst and mounting Y2K panic indicate that 1999's New Year's Eve festivities will be more than the usual debauchery. Otherwise, New Year's is just another Saturday night: lots of anxious thumb-twiddling before the "fun" starts, drinking to kill the time until it does, and idle speculation about where—and in what condition—you'll be waking up tomorrow.

200 Cigarettes, which takes place on the evening of December 31, 1981, is as loud and garish and silly as the holiday it celebrates. In this *Waiting for Godot*-like scenario, a loosely connected ensemble of New Yorkers bides away hours before attending a party the audience never sees, while party thrower Monica (Martha Plimpton) frets about guests who never arrive—at least as far as she knows, since poor soused Monica passes out before they show up. These aimless legions pounding pavement and hopping bars include freshly dumped, whiny Kevin (Paul Rudd) and his wry, patient best friend Lucy (Courtney Love); freshly deflowered, accident-prone Cindy (Kate Hudson) and her blandly insincere actor beau Jack (Jay Mohr); and fresh-off-the-LIRR high-school adventurers Val (Christina Ricci) and Stephie (Gaby Hoffmann).

Nothing much happens, and that's the point, but all this wheel spinning could have used more grease: Ricci and Hoffmann's roles exist simply to poke fun at Long Islandese ("Aw moy gawd," indeed), and Hudson's pratfalls and blubbering tend to stall the film's momentum.   Most compelling of the bunch is Lucy, a party girl a little past her prime who's willing to push a none-too-burning crush on Kevin beyond the hypothetical stage.   Lucy is no doubt the supplicant of the pair, but Love plays her as a rational, self-respecting supplicant, turning ridiculous lines like "I dare you to fuck me" into a parody of the sexual gamesmanship Lucy wants to abandon.   Love and walk-on players Janeane Garofalo and Elvis Costello seem outsiders to the frenzied inertia; these three are the witty, familiar sparks that make all the waiting around somewhat worthwhile. It's no coincidence that Lucy is the first character in *200 Cigarettes* to get soundly drunk and curse New Year's Eve: she's a sensible girl with honorable expectations, and she's only having fun.

Also reviewed in:
CHICAGO TRIBUNE, 2/26/99, Friday/p. D, Michael Wilmington
NATION, 3/29/99, p. 35, Stuart Klawans
NEW YORK TIMES, 2/26/99, p. E20, Janet Maslin
NEW YORKER, 3/15/99, p. 99, David Denby
VARIETY, 3/1-7/99, p. 78, Todd McCarthy
WASHINGTON POST, 2/26/99, Weekend/p. 41, Desson Howe

UNCOMMON FRIENDS OF THE 20TH CENTURY

Producer: John Biffar. *Director:* John Biffar. *Running time:* 63 minutes. *MPAA Rating:* Not Rated.

WITH: Walter Cronkite (Narrator); James D. Newton; Ellie Newton.

NEW YORK POST, 10/1/99, p. 62, Lou Lumenick

"Uncommon Friends of the 20th Century" is an alternately fascinating and exasperating documentary about a Forrest Gump-like Florida man who forged close relationships with such icons as Thomas Edison, Henry Ford and Charles Lindbergh.

The movie is based on the 1994 biography of one Jim Newton, who met the elderly Edison when Newton was a 20-year-old real-estate developer building homes across from Ford's estate in Fort Myers, Fla.

Newton, now 94 and still living in Fort Myers, recalls how Edison introduced him to Ford, and a decade later, how he met Lindbergh, who became best man at Newton's 1943 wedding to Newton's wife, Ellie, who is now 99.

Some of Newton's recollections are terrific, but more often he and Ellie offer vague, second-hand accounts of events they haven't witnessed.   And the overblown narration (delivered by Walter Cronkite) too often confuses rather than clarifies.

VILLAGE VOICE, 10/5/99, p. 206, Nico Baumbach

James Newton's life, the occasion for the not uncommon documentary *Uncommon Friends of the 20th Century,* plays like a stodgier, real-life Forrest Gump.   Always the other guy in the famous photograph, Newton's claim to fame is a list of late friends: Thomas Edison, Henry Ford, Harvey Firestone, Dr. Alexis Carrel, and Charles Lindbergh.   Narrated by the ur-avuncular Walter Cronkite, Newton's story purports to take us "beyond the history books" to reveal the private life of the men who "invented the 20th century."

Unfortunately, in John Biffar's documentary—composed of talking-head interviews, archival footage, and sepia-toned re-creations—Newton merely provides the human-interest entry point for a nostalgic, reverent gloss on the lives of these men.

We do meet Newton—at 94 he and his wife still live in idyllic Fort Meyers, Florida, a hometown he once shared with Edison, Ford, and Firestone—but his anecdotes are so unspecific that his ostensible authority, the premise of the film, feels like a put-on. Perhaps going "beyond the history books" means only that we should ignore the limited and slipshod use of facts (no, Edison did not "make the first 1000 movies") in favor of the film's interest in instilling values. Key qualities intoned by Cronkite and shared by Newton and his friends include genius, character, integrity, and especially faith. (Newton's genius, incidentally, is a "genius for friendship.") Given that the film is intended as a timely look at men who represent a conservative and unquestioning notion of American values, even on its wholesome textbook level, it falls flat.

Also reviewed in:
NEW YORK TIMES, 10/1/99, p. E8, Lawrence Van Gelder

UNDERGROUND COMEDY MOVIE, THE

A Phaedra Cinema release of a Best Offer Productions film. *Producer:* Jeffrey Jaeger. *Director:* Vince Offer. *Screenplay:* Vince Offer. *Director of Photography:* Michael Hofstein. *Editor:* Luis Ruiz. *Music:* David Rotter and Danny Rotter. *Sound:* Gallen Walker. *Running time:* 87 minutes. *MPAA Rating:* Not Rated.

CAST: Gena Lee Nolin (Marilyn); Slash (Himself); Michael Clarke Duncan (Gay Virgin); Joey Buttafuoco (Sonny); Lightfield Lewis (Virgin Hunter/Juror); Karen Black (Mother); Rebecca Chaney (Supermodel/Pregnant Girl); Jerry Mongo Brownlee (Juror); Michael Parisi (Godmother/Psychologist); Gloria Sperling (Granny); Bobby Lee (Sushi Papa).

NEW YORK POST, 5/28/99, p. 58, Rod Dreher

"The Underground Comedy Movie" starts with a portentous cautionary statement: "Warning! Guaranteed to offend!" Which would be okay if only it were guaranteed to make you laugh. This abysmal "Kentucky Fried Movie" clone may be the least amusing comedy ever made.

It's a pathetic collection of sketches based on a public-access TV show the film's witless writer-director-star Vince Offer did years ago. The humor level here is so scuzzy and dumb it makes Andrew Dice Clay look like Preston Sturges. To wit: He shows supermodels grunting while defecating. That's it. That's the joke.

In another bit, Joey "the Pride of Massapequa" Buttafuoco plays consigliere to the Godmother, a fat guy in hideous drag. It is suggested to the Godmother that her crime family's restaurant could benefit by substituting aborted fetuses for ground beef in the spaghetti, and that unborn Jewish children should be used to keep things kosher. A real laff riot, this.

Offer, a mop-headed imbecile, sued Peter and Bobby Farrelly, claiming they stole "There's Something About Mary" from him. Talk about delusions of grandeur! Even if the Farrellys were blind hermits, they couldn't hope to make a movie this bad. "The Underground Comedy Movie" makes one wonder: How can the War Crimes Tribunal indict Slobodan Milosevic but let Vince Offer still walk the streets?

VILLAGE VOICE, 6/1/99, p. 124, Rob Davis

The only discernible reason to sit through *The Underground Comedy Movie* is to admire writer-director-star Vince Offer's marketing hustle. By filing a copyright-infringement lawsuit against the makers of *There's Something About Mary*, Offer was able to drum up enough publicity to get his lunkheaded, amateurish movie released. Based on some public-access TV shows he shot years ago, Offer's film is a listless, laughless attempt at a *Kentucky Fried Movie*-esque sketch comedy, one that—with its rampant racism, sexism, ageism, anti-Semitism, and homophobia—would be wildly offensive if it weren't so obvious Offer doesn't know any better. Some sample humor: In a parody skit called "Flirty Harry," Offer-as-Eastwood points his gun and growls, "Go ahead. Make me gay." Is that even, technically, a joke? That bit is emblematic: Offer takes an obvious, out-of-date target, witlessly plugs in some curse words and crude scatological references that might appeal to particularly boorish junior high school students, and makes it into an overly long scene with the technical sophistication of a worse-than-average home movie. For masochists only.

Also reviewed in:
NEW YORK TIMES, 5/28/99, p. E23, Lawrence Van Gelder

UNDERGROUND ORCHESTRA, THE

A First Run/Icarus Films release of a Pieter van Huystee Film & TV production in coproduction with VPRO Television. *Producer:* Pieter van Huystee. *Director:* Heddy Honigmann. *Screenplay (French and Spanish with English subtitles):* Nosh van der Lely and Heddy Honigmann. *Director of Photography:* Eric Guichard. *Editor:* Mario Steenbergen. *Sound:* Piotr van Dijk. *Running time:* 108 minutes. *MPAA Rating:* Not Rated.

NEW YORK POST, 3/31/99, p. 73, Jonathan Foreman

One of the lessons of this warm, easygoing documentary "The Underground Orchestra" is that the Paris police come down much harder on people who use video cameras in subway stations than they do on people who play music for 10-franc coins.

(Indeed it seems that you can barely point a camera anywhere near a train before tough plainclothes officers appear and make you rewind your film.)

And if the street musicians filmed here are at all representative, it would also seem that Parisian buskers are of a much, much higher quality than most of those to be found in New York.

Dutch documentarian Heddy Honigmann has fashioned a gentle, unhurried ride through a fascinating, musically diverse world. Her initial focus on foreign street musicians working in and around the Paris Metro expands to cover other exiled musicians who have made the French capital their home.

The result is part concert, part meditation on exile. It is also a low-key, but no less effective celebration of Paris in all its cosmopolitan glory.

We meet a Venezuelan harpist, a two-thirds African-one third French blues trio, a Bosnian army deserter/violinist who once played in his national orchestra and a Romanian family who take turns on the zither, violin and accordion.

Then, as the movie widens its focus, we encounter musical refugees from all over the French-speaking world: a beautiful singer from Mali, a wonderful guitarist from Algeria, and other singers from Vietnam and Zaire.

There's also an Argentine pianist who doesn't play in the streets, but tells the story of his imprisonment and torture (naturally, they broke his hands) back home.

Sure these people miss their homelands and several of them have immigration and housing problems, but Paris seems to welcome them and their music. And a series of traveling shots of Parisian streets and rooftops at dusk, with various exotic kinds of music in the background makes it easy to understand why any refugee would want to stay.

Despite an apparently mistaken presumption that her non-white interviewees must suffer grievously from the racism of the French police, Honigmann's questioning successfully evokes the uniqueness of each of these lives—and the good humor that all of them seem to share. The result is a kind of sweetness that all but makes up for the film's shapelessness and its lack of any pounding revelations.

NEWSDAY, 3/31/99, Part II/p. B11, John Anderson

Virtually devoid of an organizing structure but rich in naivete, Heddy Honigmann's "The Underground Orchestra" uses the Third World-exported musical denizens of the Paris Metro and the city's streets to "j'accuse" the rest of Europe (and the United States, too). Which is fine. But thanks to a nonexistent political context and her own gosh-almighty response to the plight of the emigres she's filmed, Honigmann's movie will likely sit as well with the rightist National Front as with Amnesty International.

Following her ears into the subway—where post-Metro-bombing security sends her scurrying out again—Honigmann finds some really fascinating people, and occasionally some fascinating exchanges: an Armenian emigre violinist-singer, whose playing of the Iranian kamancha, a lute, attracts refugees from that country as well as a clarinetist from Algeria (who appreciates the synthesis). An almost saintly Venezuelan harpist loses his apartment to craven landlords; a family of Romanian street musicians works the Metro in shifts. A Bosnian cellist reveals the heartbreak of life without a country and of fatherhood in exile.

Paris has been the repository of the world's justly disgruntled since Victor Hugo was l'enfant, but it's precisely this rootless immigration that has rightist Europe enflamed; many of the musicians, if they can, are making money to spend at "home." (Let's not even get into the current examples of refugee-overrun Greece and Italy.) Honigmann (of the poetic "O Amor Natural") is an example of the documentarian who goes into a project assuming she has right and good on her side, and she probably does, but she offers little to convince the opposition of her arguments—other than, perhaps, that the Pinochet regime was evil and malignant.

The Peruvian, Netherlands-based filmmaker also seems to be showing us every inch of footage she shot (she's certainly convinced that every inch is revelatory). Not until the final scenes is there a real sense of either emotion or momentum, where we're reunited with the various musicians she's profiled and hear the stirring Algerian music of Fateh Benlala and the Orchestre National de Barbes. (I think that's who it is, anyway; no one is identified until the end credits.) The people who inhabit "The Underground Orchestra" are an inspiration largely, and a reminder that for some nations—Mali, Zaire, Bosnia, Algeria, Romania, Argentina—the greatest export is people.

Honigmann, however, might have taken a deep breath before trying to tell their story.

VILLAGE VOICE, 4/6/99, p, 121, J. Hoberman

There's a free-form, Altman-esque quality to the latest documentary feature by Peruvian-born Dutch filmmaker Heddy Honigmann. Likably eccentric, often touching, and somewhat self-indulgent, The *Underground Orchestra* concerns a number of street musicians eking out a living in the crevices of a very diverse (and exceedingly springlike) Paris.

The *Underground Orchestra*, begins with a handheld descent into the Paris Metro. Soon learning that it is forbidden to film in the subway (a legacy, perhaps, of the 1996 bombings), Honigmann returns with her camera concealed to document a Venezuelan harpist and several combos—one of which takes over an entire subway car to perform an elaborate version of "Try a Little Tenderness" seemingly between stops.

In the best tradition of stolen locations and I-spy cinematography, Honigmann observes not only the musicians but their underground audience—the curious kids, grouchy elders, self-involved lovers. But when the music ends and the filmmaker attempts to interview the artists, they are immediately spotted by a squadron of plainclothes cops. The police demand that everyone produce passports, serving to introduce the movie's real themes—insecurity, marginality, and exile.

Now banished from the Metro herself, Honigmann finds even more radically displaced musicians above ground—singers from West Africa and Vietnam, a denim-clad street violinist who turns out to have deserted the Bosnian army (which drafted him from the Sarajevo symphony orchestra), and a Romanian family who work in shifts, handing off their *cymbalo* the way an independent cab driver might sublease his hack. The interactions are varied and surprising. Even as Honigmann discovers an Iranian master of the Armenian stand-up fiddle, demonstrating his exotic skill in an outdoor market, his performance attracts the fraternal attention of an Algerian classical clarinetist.

Suffused with music and punctuated by recurring shots of the Paris rooftops, *The Underground Orchestra* is a world-beat city symphony. It conjures up a free-floating internationale of refugee musicians. Most of Hohigmarin's subjects have left their homelands—Argentina and Zaire, as well as the Balkans—for political reasons. Paris offers what one Romanian cellist wryly calls a "kind of freedom." His son—a more contemporary musician with the Guns N' Roses T-shirt to prove it—demonstrates this by comparing Jimi Hendrix to Beethoven, Jim Morrison to Schubert, and AC/DC to J.S. Bach.

Also reviewed in:
NEW YORK TIMES, 3/31/99, p. E5, Stephen Holden
VARIETY, 3/9-15/98, p. 47, David Rooney

UNIVERSAL SOLDIER: THE RETURN

A TriStar Pictures release of a Baumgarten Prophet Entertainment/IndieprodCompany/LongRoad production. *Executive Producer:* Michael Rachmil and Daniel Melnick. *Producer:* Craig Baumgarten, Allen Shapiro, and Jean-Claude Van Damme. *Director:* Mic Rodgers. *Screenplay:* William Malone and John Fasano. *Based on characters created by:* Richard Rothstein, Christopher Leitch, and Dean Devlin. *Director of Photography:* Michael A. Benson. *Editor:* Peck Prior. *Music:* Don Davis, Jason Alexander, and Micki Stern. *Music Editor:* Robert Garrett. *Sound:* Pud Cusack and (music) Kathleen Cusack. *Sound Editor:* Greg Hedgepath. *Casting:* Rachel Abroms and Jory Weitz. *Production Designer:* David Chapman. *Art Director:* John Frick. *Set Designer:* Thomas H. Paul. *Set Decorator:* Donnasu Sealy. *Special Effects:* Joey DiGaetano and Bobby Vazquez. *Costumes:* Jennifer L. Bryan. *Make-up:* Keith Sayer. *Stunt Coordinator:* Michael Runyard. *Running time:* 82 minutes. *MPAA Rating:* R.

CAST: Jean-Claude Van Damme (Luc Deveraux); Michael Jai White (Seth); Heidi Schanz (Erin); Xander Berkeley (Dylan Cotner); Justin Lazard (Captain Blackburn); Kiana Tom (Maggie); Daniel von Bargen (General Radford); James Black (Sergeant Morrow); Karis Paige Bryant (Hillary); Bill Goldberg (Romeo); Brent Anderson (2nd Technician); Brent Hinkley (Squid); Woody Watson (RL Gate Guard); Jacqueline Klein (Betty Wilson); Maria Artita (Kitty Anderson); Sam Williamson (Hillary's Doctor); Dion Culberson (Drag Queen); Pam Dougherty (60 Year Old Woman); Heidi Franz (Erin's Stripper); Barbara Petricini Buxton (Female News Anchor); Molly Moroney (Pediatric Nurse); Josh Berry (Radio Man); Mic Rodgers (Big Hiker); Mark Dalton (Lead RL Guard); Gino Crognale (Puppeteer).

LOS ANGELES TIMES, 8/23/99, Calendar/p. 3, Kevin Thomas

The sleek and exciting action-filled "Universal Soldier: The Return" stars Jean-Claude Van Damme in a satisfying sequel to one of his biggest hits. The filmmakers shrewdly use the seven years that have gone by since the first film to suggest that in that period Van Damme's cyborg Luc has fully evolved into a human being. He in fact is a widower still grieving and raising his young daughter (Karis Paige Bryant) on his own.

When we catch up with Luc he has become a technical expert on a special government project dedicated to breeding super-soldiers, recycling battlefield casualties into warriors of superior intellect and strength. The army captain (Xander Berkeley) in charge of the project, however, has bad news for Luc and his key aide, Maggie (Kiana Tom of the ESPN 2 workout show "Kiana's Flex Appeal"). Cutbacks in military spending dictate canceling the project.

As it turns out, the captain's words have actually come too late, for catastrophe strikes before we even get a chance to wonder what will be done with a passel of Unisols who are more than robots but not quite human and in the process of being trained. It seems that the project has done its work too well, relying upon a computer called Seth, whose artificial intelligence has evolved to the level that he has been able to assume human form with the help of a crazed renegade (Brent Hinkley).

In human form Seth (martial arts superstar-actor Michael Jai White) is possessed of a magnificent physique and an even more impressive mind. As if Seth weren't enough for Luc to tackle, he's got another formidable nemesis in the Unisol named Romeo, who is played by wrestling legend Bill Goldberg. Seth naturally intends to lead the other Unisols (who all look to have been recruited from a World Gym) in a conquest of the world.

Writers William Malone and John Fasano take it from here in clever fashion, never overlooking opportunities to inject humor to leaven the action, so expertly staged by Mic Rodgers, a veteran second unit director in a most assured feature debut. (Rodgers did the second unit on "Braveheart," doubled for Mel Gibson on "Lethal Weapon" and coordinated the stunts on its sequels.) The filmmakers are fortunate that in this post-Columbine era that their film, hard-hitting as it is in the literal sense, does point up the dangers of a cyborg future in which humans could find themselves at the mercy of heavily armed supermen. The easy, amused personality of Goldberg, a natural screen presence if ever there was one, brings a welcome tongue-in-cheek quality to the entire film.

Van Damme easily dominates, suggesting that in the crunch heart and courage might still be able to win over pure strength and intellect untempered by emotion, but teaming him with White and especially Goldberg keeps him plugged into contemporary audiences. Van Damme's leading lady, a determined TV reporter, is well-played by Heidi Schanz, whose Erin is every bit as smart, resourceful and determined as Luc. Bryant is pretty and poised as Luc's daughter.

"Sleek" is the word for "Universal Soldier: The Return," which moves with such swiftness and ease, its story blending seamlessly into its sci-fi technology and special effects. This is one "return" that's surely welcome.

SIGHT AND SOUND, 11/99, p. 59, Jamie Graham

A military complex in the US. Luc Deveraux, sole survivor of a band of military cyborgs called UniSols (short for "Universal Soldiers"), is overseeing a government initiative to design a new, superior breed of UniSols. Panic breaks out when the soldiers' central-intelligence computer, the Self-Evolving Thought Helix (SETH), develops an independent intelligence. Knowing it is at risk of being shut down, SETH relocates itself into a moveable host by commandeering the body of an elite UniSol. Supported by his fellow UniSols, SM sets out to kill Deveraux.

Deveraux escapes the compound but not the unwelcome company of Erin, an assertive television reporter. Together they search for SETH, a quest that leads them to the home of Squid, the former technical genius of the UniSol operation. Squid, who was fired for harbouring dangerously radical ideas, helped to relocate SETH into his cyborg body. Deveraux tortures Squid for information, but SETH appears and kills his now redundant helper. SETH then departs only to up the stakes when he kidnaps Deveraux's young daughter and returns to the military complex. Deveraux and Erin enter the compound and fight off several UniSols before Deveraux and SETH match up for a final showdown. Deveraux gains a small advantage and flees the building with Erin and his daughter. The military forces blow up the compound and destroy SETH.

There is a wonderful moment in *Stand by Me* when one of the quartet of young friends turns to another and asks "Do you think Mighty Mouse could beat up Superman?" This childish delight at pitting two seemingly indestructible forces against each other be they monsters *(King Kong vs Godzilla* (1962), cyborgs *(Terminator 2 Judgment Day,* 1991) or real-life legends (Bruce Lee squaring up to Chuck Norris in *The Way of the Dragon* (1972)—forms the basis of Jean-Claude Van Damme's first ever sequel, just as it did of the original *Universal Soldier* picture (1992) in which Van Damme took on fellow muscled import Dolph Lundgren. Not only were they two of Hollywood's leading action heroes of the time, but in their pre-Hollywood incarnations Van Damme and Lundgren were both European karate champions and rivals off as well as on screen.

Universal Soldier The Return may not be able to match its predecessor in terms of casting savvy—although one of the UniSol villains is played by the mountainous WCW wrestling champion Bill Goldberg but it does boast a fearsome screen foe in the form of SETH, a parent computer that monitors the thoughts and "emotions" of the UniSol army. SETH not only parades a preternatural intellect to rival *2001*'s HAL, but soon after orchestrating a cyborg uprising against their human creators finds itself a body worthy of such a brain. Subsequently, Van Damme's Luc Deveraux is confronted by a vastly superior opponent, a state-of the-art android capable of outwitting, outmanoeuvring and outfighting him at every turn.

With the solid if unoriginal set-up bolted firmly in place, however, first time director Mic Rodgers fails to deliver. Despite his vast experience as a stunt coordinator (on the *Lethal Weapon* series) and a second unit director *(Braveheart)*, his action sequences are filmed with little flair or imagination, and actually come off second best to those in *Universal Soldier*'s other unofficial sequel *Brothers in Arms*, which went straight to video this year. Matters aren't helped any by a plodding script. The refusal to shape characters or develop relationships is endemic to the genre, perhaps, but a fatal lack of humour ensures that *Universal Soldier The Return* is a disappointing entry to the sci-fi/action movie canon.

Also reviewed in:
CHICAGO TRIBUNE, 8/25/99, Tempo/p. 2, Barbara Shulgasser
NEW YORK TIMES, 8/21/99, p. B12, Lawrence Van Gelder
VARIETY, 8/23-29/99, p. 108, Joe Leydon

VARSITY BLUES

A Paramount Pictures release in association with MTV Films of a Marquee Tollin/Robbins production in association with Tova Laiter Productions. *Executive Producer:* David Gale and Van Toffler. *Producer:* Tova Laiter, Mike Tollin, and Brian Robbins. *Director:* Brian Robbins. *Screenplay:* W. Peter Iliff. *Director of Photography:* Charles Cohen. *Editor:* Ned Bastille. *Music:* Mark Isham, Ken Kugler, and G. Marq Roswell. *Music Editor:* Helena Lea. *Sound:* Jennifer Murphy and (music) Stephen Krause. *Sound Editor:* Beth Sterner. *Casting:* Bob Krakower and Sarah Halley Finn. *Production Designer:* Jaymes Hinkle. *Art Director:* Keith Donnelly. *Set Decorator:* Tad Smalley. *Costumes:* Wendy Chuck. *Make-up:* Catherine Conrad. *Stunt Coordinator:* Russell Towery. *Football Coordinator:* Mark Ellis. *Running time:* 106 minutes. *MPAA Rating:* R.

CAST: James Van Der Beek (Jonathan "Mox" Moxon); Jon Voight (Coach Bud Kilmer); Paul Walker (Lance Harbor); Ron Lester (Billy Bob); Scott Caan (Tweeter); Amy Smart (Julie Harbor); Thomas F. Duffy (Sam Moxon); Ali Larter (Darcy); Joe Pichler (Kyle Moxon); Eliel Swinton (Wendell); Richard Lineback (Joe Harbor); Tiffany C. Love (Collette Harbor); Jill Parker Jones (Mo Moxon); Mark Walters (Chet McNurry); Brady Coleman (Sheriff Bigelow); James Harrell (Murray); Tonie Perensky (Miss Davis); Jesse Plemmons (Tommy Harbor); Sam Pleasant (Cashier); Tim Crowley (Coach Bates); Joe Stevens (Young Deputy 1); Don Cass (Young Deputy 2); James Michael O'Brien (Brett); Robert Ellis (Referee); Robert S. Lott (Middle-aged Fan); Barry Switzer (Bronco Coach); Mona Lee (Old Miss Logan); Kevin Reid (Wilkes); Eric Jungmann (Elliot); Laura Olsen and Ryan Allen (Teen Babes); Bristi Havins (Cute Naked Girl); John Hyrns (Bald Guy); Rome Azzaro (Young Father); Marco Perella (Doctor Benton); Doyle Carter (Doctor/Field); Tony Frank (Clerk); Sue Rock (Minnie); Olin Buchanan (Reporter); David Williams (Coyote Player); John Gatins (Smiling Man).

LOS ANGELES TIMES, 1/15/99, Calendar/p. 6, John Anderson

[*The following review by John Anderson appeared in a slightly different form in* **NEWSDAY, 11/15/99, Part II/p. B7.**]

Call it the Extraterrestrial Movie. You know, the kind in which an entire region of the country is trashed, the flaws of its characters are pretty much blamed on geography and the hero seems never to have met anyone else in the movie, much less grown up among them.

"Varsity Blues," a trashy little movie about drinking, football and drinking, is also one of those films that pretends to moralize about the very behavior it milks for every giggle it can get. "In

America we have laws," says second-string quarterback Jonathan "Mox" Moxon (James Van Der Beek of TV's "Dawson's Creek"). "In West Canaan, Texas, there's a society that has its own laws."

Yup. And that society is bounded by the rules and scoreboard of high school football, a pangenerational obsession that leads fathers to act like idiots, young women to throw themselves at the nearest quarterback and the audience to believe that there's very little else to do down there in the Lone Star State.

People's entire lives are dictated by whether they were starting quarterback or sat on the bench, which is pathetic, but apparently true. At the same time, the attitude of the film—in which the West Canaan Coyotes eventually rebel against tyrannical coach Bud Kilmer (Jon Voight)—kind of makes you wonder: If Texans are really so rabid about their high school football, how are they going to see this movie? As a documentary?

Likewise, the take on high school sociology (almost everyone in the movie seems destined for AA meetings or the morgue) may not be far from the mark, but the movie's blithe acceptance of aberrant behavior makes you wonder if the watchdogs of decency aren't right.

Among the things the movie frowns on are Coach Kilmer's freewheeling way with painkillers, and the way foxy Darcy (Ali Larter) gives herself a whipped-cream bikini to seduce Mox, once her old boyfriend Lance (Paul Walker) gets his knee, and his future, totaled. Mox, who's waiting to hear from Brown University (a full academic scholarship is on the line, just in case you thought the movie was harboring any actual reverence for athletics), is above sleeping with his best friend's girl, or cheating on his true love Julie (Amy Smart). But then again, Mox, his Texas drawl ebbing and flowing, seems to be from a planet other than the one on which West Canaan is situated.

What the movie seems to accept happily are drunkenness, promiscuity and debauchery. And frankly, if it were actually successful and didn't seem to be striving quite so desperately for gross-out laughs and adolescent titillation, we probably wouldn't care. But the sociopathic deportment of the Coyotes isn't treated as irresponsible, or as a result of a community's misguided indulgence toward its football stars, It's just there for laughs, so the more sophomoric element of its audience can say, "Isn't that cool?"

Voight, who these days seems to be working like a madman (his performance in "The General" is his best in years), is thoroughly convincing as Coach Kilmer, a guy who has had things his own way so long he can't quite fathom that a snotty little brat like Mox wouldn't kiss his feet. Mox is right, of course, Kilmer is a fiend. But what we can't quite fathom is why Mox isn't like anyone else in the movie, devoted to football, adoring of Kilmer. It's not in the script. It's certainly not in Van Der Beek's performance.

But heck: Beer, sex and football. It doesn't get any better than that. Not in West Canaan, Texas, anyway.

NEW YORK POST, 1/15/99, p. 47, Jonathan Foreman

Predictable, shameless and uneven "Varsity Blues" still somehow manages to be great fun. And despite its flaws, it's one of the best football movies in years. It's no "North Dallas Forty," but even at its corniest it is superior to "Wildcats" and "Necessary Roughness".

The latest in the post-"Scream" caravan of knowing teen pics—and a star vehicle for James Van Der Beek of TV's "Dawson's Creek"—this particular take on coming of age in high school differs from the rest by being set in the alternate universe of rural Texas.

This is that part of the United States where high school football is not only King, but an all-encompassing combination of politics, religion and theater. Coach Bud Kilmer (Jon Voight), who has taken the team to the division title 22 times, has a big bronze statue of himself outside the stadium—which is named after him.

Mox (Van Der Beek) and his girlfriend, Julie (Amy Smart), are rebels against the football cult that grips the town. Unlike their pathetic parents, they can see that it's all nonsense, even though Mox is the back-up quarterback and Julie's brother Lance (Paul Walker) is the star of the team.

But when Lance wrecks his knee with five games to go in a winning season, Mox has to lead the team. Unfortunately, the tyrannical coach hates his guts, Julie won't go out with a football hero, and Mox himself becomes the unwilling target of a babe who sees herself as the quarterback's official consort.

Mox and the Coach clash over the latter's tendency to force injured guys to play, his refusal to let black players get any glory, and most important, his preference for a cautious running game. But the Coach is by far the most powerful man in town, and Mox doesn't want anything to sabotage his chances of a scholarship to Brown.

Mox is an absurd paragon, one of those sensitive, well-read, thoughtful football studs—with unnatural restraint when it comes to refusing the advances of all-but-naked cheerleaders. But Van Der Beek, less bland here than on TV, charms his way through the role. Amy Smart does her best with a grossly underwritten part. And Voight, on top bad-guy form again, is terrific as the bullying Coach Kilmer.

Laced though it is with raunchy comedy (the only likable adult is a stripper!), "Varsity Blues" has its heart in the right place. And director Brian Robbins has the sense to make fun of an excessive football culture rather than parody the game itself, which is made to look breathtakingly exciting.

SIGHT AND SOUND, 8/99, p. 54, Mark Morris

West Canaan, Texas, the mid 90s. Jonathan Moxon is the reserve quarterback on the high-school football team. The bookish Moxon, however, is on the margins of the team, preferring to spend time with his girlfriend Julie. Even so, he comes into conflict with Bud Kilmer, the coach who has bullied his teams into success for 30 years.

Kilmer forces blocker Billy Bob to keep playing after a severe concussion. Kilmer then blames him for the career-threatening injury to the team's star, Lance Harbor, even though Kilmer had been keeping Harbor on the field with injections of pain killers. Moxon proves a more than adequate replacement for Harbor and the team seems headed for the championship, although Kilmer resents Moxon's attempts to make the team play more imaginatively. After being briefly intoxicated by his success—and alienating Julie—Moxon is reminded of his responsibilities by Kilmer's treatment of African-American running back Wendell and the headache-prone Billy Bob. At half-time in the championship game, Moxon leads a rebellion that drives Kilmer out. The team pull off a dramatic victory.

Recent US films aimed at the teen market have traded heavily on being knowingly self-referential ever since the Kevin Wllliamson-scripted *Scream*. As *Varsity Blue*'s star James Van Der Beek made his name in the Williamson-conceived television series *Dawson's Creek* more of the same might be expected. *Varsity Blues,* however, plays it resolutely straight. Although momentarily tempted by egotism and a sexy cheerleader, Jonathan Moxon is a character with Gary Cooperish moral resolve. Most of the problems raised in the story are settled by the short, inspirational chats he gives the other characters: he builds up Billy Bob's sense of self-esteem and reassures Wendell that all whites are not racist. Coach Kilmer, memorably incarnated by Jon Voight, is by contrast a grotesque monster, whose position in the town is indicated by a Stalinist statue that towers over the football field.

But Kilmer is the film's only villain: the other characters are only occasionally misguided, too caught up in the desire to win—as Moxon says, "You never question the sanctity of football." The reverence to the game displayed here runs throughout *Varsity Blues:* nowhere in the film is there either a truly incisive examination of the pressures of the US school sports system as in *Hoop Dreams* or the hedonistic rejection of it that occurs in Richard Linklater's *Dazed and Confused*.

Instead, director Brian Robbins and writer W. Peter Iliff have fashioned a liberal-conservative fantasy which suggests that there would be nothing wrong with the American South's bull-headedly macho culture as long as this system was (somehow) handed over to the literate, non-racist young. The film's confused values are demonstrated by the way the sensitive, chaste Moxon still leads his fellow players on a night of drunken debauchery at a local strip club.

Stylistically, Robbins—whose background lies in teen TV (he was a regular cast member of the US sitcom *Head of the Class* before directing *Good Burger)*—never deviates from the mainstream. Despite the involvement of MTV in the production, *Varsity Blues* is an old-fashioned film: even its more modern elements—some semi-nudity, a hard-rock soundtrack could have come from any time in the last 30 years. The climactic scenes of the championship game and the team's spirited locker-room rebellion against Kilmer, for instance, are traditionally, almost blatantly, manipulative. Robbins' cast do well enough, although the immense popularity among teenagers of Van Der Beek (who has great trouble here with the Texan accent) remains a mystery. Voight's tyrannical Kilmer is a treat, but the only way to enjoy this film is to surrender to its well-orchestrated, swelling clichés.

Also reviewed in:
CHICAGO TRIBUNE, 1/15/99, Friday/p. D, John Petrakis
NEW YORK TIMES, 1/15/99, p. E14, Stephen Holden
VARIETY, 1/18-24/99, p. 43, Joe Leydon

VELOCITY OF GARY, THE (NOT HIS REAL NAME)

A Next Millenium Entertainment release of a Cineville presentation of a Dan Lupovitz/Joe Simon production in association with Ventana Rosa Films. *Executive Producer:* Carl-Jan Colpaert, Kathryn Arnold, Ellen Wonder, Joe Simon, Vincent D'Onofrio, and Dan Ireland. *Producer:* Dan Lupovitz. *Director:* Dan Ireland. *Screenplay (based on his play):* James Still. *Director of Photography:* Claudio Rocha. *Editor:* Louis Colina. *Sound:* David Chornow. *Casting:* Laurel Smith. *Production Designer:* Amy Ancona. *Art Director:* Rachel Kamerman. *Set Decorator:* Melissa Levander. *Costumes:* Tim Chappel. *Running time:* 100 minutes. *MPAA Rating:* R.

CAST: Salma Hayek (Mary Carmen); Vincent D'Onfrio (Valentino); Thomas Jane (Gary); Olivia d'Abo (Veronica); Chad Lindberg (Kid Joey); Luckuy Luciano (The King); Shawn Michael Howard (Coco); Khalil Kain (Venus); Elizabeth D'Onofrio (Dorothy).

LOS ANGELES TIMES, 7/16/99, Calendar/p. 11, Kevin Thomas

The best thing that can be said about a picture as misfired as "The Velocity of Gary* (*Not His Real Name)" is that it's not likely to damage the careers of the talented people involved in its making. Relative newcomer Thomas Jane soon will be seen in the action thriller "Deep Blue Sea", Salma Hayek is in this summer's "Wild Wild West," and Vincent D'Onofrio is firmly established as a versatile risk-taker. (There's also a cameo by Ethan Hawke.)

Even director Dan Ireland, a film industry veteran, who made his directorial debut with the well-received 1995 "The Whole Wide World," which starred D'Onofrio as pulp novelist Robert E. Howard, already has a new project. So the big question is: How did these people get caught up in first-time writer James Still's wretched script? The story, said to be true, has real possibilities: a menage-a-trois among three young street people. The trouble is that it doesn't seem to be unfolding in the real world, no matter that it was shot largely on downtown L.A. streets, passing as Manhattan, which is seen in establishing shots. The gritty locales serve only to make the material seem all the more artificial.

There is almost nothing going on to anchor these people to everyday existence. Jane's handsome Gary, for example, is a hustler who never seems to have to work at it. Anyway, the attraction between D'Onofrio's Valentino and Gary is instant and strong. We know that Valentino (D'Onofrio) made at least one porn film, but we don't know if he is actually a porn film regular. In the meantime Hayek's tempestuous—really, that's too mild a word here—waitress Mary Carmen has a grand passion for Valentino.

There is no sense of how these people manage to survive from day to day. Mary, in fact, quits her job at an all-night doughnut shop early on. Therefore, most of the film finds these three sitting around indulging in their all-consuming feelings for each other with Mary somewhat less than thrilled to share Valentino with Gary. Then AIDS and pregnancy enter the picture.

Very little is demanded of D'Onofrio and Jane as actors, which may be fortunate for them, because Hayek has been asked to throw hysterics almost continually. In committing herself to her role and in trusting her director she gives a screeching, over-the-top performance that is just plain awful. As it nears its conclusion, "Velocity" starts working up some involvement with these three, but it's way too late to matter.

NEW YORK POST, 7/16/99, p. 46, Rod Dreher

"The Velocity of Gary (Not His Real Name)" is a ludicrous title for an even more ludicrous movie.

The velocity of "Gary" is positively glacial compared with the speed at which patrons will flee theaters after half an hour of this indie stink bomb.

It's another affected navel-gazer trying to wring Art and Meaning out of the pointless lives of boring, pretentious, downtown freaks in this case, a porn star carrying on a bisexual menage a trois with a gay hustler and a mouthy diner waitress.

But "Gary" has superior production values, thanks to the participation of director Dan Ireland and actor Vincent D'Onofrio, whose last collaboration was the exceedingly fine 1996 romantic tragedy "The Whole Wide World."

"Everything's wrong with everything that used to be right," one character tritely observes, offering an inadvertent commentary on the Ireland-D'Onofrio collaboration this time around.

D'Onofrio dons a stringy black fright wig to play Valentino, an allegedly charismatic porn thesp carrying on an affair with Mary Carmen (Salma Hayek, badly overdone), a sassy waitress of the sort that only gets hired at movie diners. "You can't fire me, I quit!" she snaps, revealing scripter James Still's special flair for dialogue.

As woefully cliched as she is, Mary Carmen has nothing on Kid Joey (Chad Lindberg), a skinny baby drag queen who minces through a Patsy Cline lip-synch number. Obviously, originality is not this movie's strong suit.

Valentino is also involved with gay hustler Gary (the very blond, very blank Thomas Jane), with whom he shares laughably unconvincing kisses. Mary Carmen and Gary know about each other, but they're united in their love for Valentino.

There's a screamingly awful scene in a disco, where Mary Carmen and Gary trade off "sexy" dances with the hulking Valentino. They look like they're rubbing up against a smoldering sasquatch in Alanis Morissette drag.

Speaking of bad drag, the movie's centerpiece is a musical number set amid the Village's Halloween parade. Hayek plays Diana Ross, with transvestites Jane and D'Onofrio as broad-shouldered Supremes, in an homage to "Ain't No Mountain High Enough."

A friend of mine theorizes that the mere existence of pseudo-gay material this hideous may have put Alan Carr in a premature grave. Avoid, avoid.

NEWSDAY, 7/16/99, Part II/. B6, Gene Seymour

With a promising director like Dan Ireland, a very good cast and material that probes a sordid environment in search of human values, "The Velocity of Gary" should be a sure thing. But it isn't. And it's hard to figure out what went wrong.

Part of it may be that we've seen some of this before. A beautiful blond young man (Thomas Jane) comes to New York and literally stumbles into the evil city's sexual underworld. Even more predictably, life for this guy, who adopts the name Gary, is no more or less banal than it would be if his bus had taken the wrong turn to Danbury or Glens Falls.

To some extent, Valentino (Vincent D'Onofrio) the swaggering force-of-nature porn actor who picks up Gary off the street and becomes his lover-mentor, is someone we haven't seen before. But that may be because D'Onofrio, who helped produce this film and all but dominated Ireland's 1995 breakthrough "The Whole Wide World," is an actor whose instincts with a role like this are always interesting to follow.

Then there's Mary Cannen (Salma Hayek), a fiery, short-fused waitress who's also in love with Valentino and thus can't stand Gary. Yet, as you'd expect, a curious, contentious bond develops between these three lost souls; a bond that is, of course, tested when Valentino is dying of AIDS.

It sounds as if we're supposed to care deeply about these folks and the other losers in their orbit, including another porn player (Olivia d'Abo) whose presence is neither understandable or wanted and a deaf transvestite (Chad Lindberg), who, like the extra crewman in a "Star Trek" landing party, has "doom" written all over him.

Yet we don't care, and the conception of the characters doesn't help. Despite his earnest compassion, Jane's Gary comes across as a prig while the pathos of Hayek's Mary Carmen is offset by her shrill brattiness.

VILLAGE VOICE, 7/20/99, p. 142, Jessica Winter

Calculating Gary's said velocity might give occasion to a new definition of *warp speed:* lumbering and misshapen, apparently stitched together from the discarded limbs of unrelated scripts. Take the film's first 20 minutes, in which deaf transsexual Kid Joey (Chad Lindberg), just off the bus to the big city, gets viciously gay-bashed a few blocks from Port Authority. Brooding beauty Gary (Thomas Jane) comes to the rescue, but following a pointless musical interlude lip-synched to Patsy Cline's "Walkin' After Midnight," Kid Joey is hit and killed by a car. And that's it—we never hear about Joey again, as the film U-turns back to concentrate (however fitfully) on the fractious love triangle formed by Gary, Gary's lover Valentino (Vincent D'Onofrio), and Val's high-strung girlfriend Mary Carmen (Salma Hayek). Two end up with AIDS and a baby enters the picture, as we're informed through a back-and-forth narrative that would confuse even if the film weren't so atrociously directed and edited. The paper-doll characters exist solely to evoke our pity. For a cut-and-paste job this sloppy, they could at least have given the actors messier roles to play.

Also reviewed in:
CHICAGO TRIBUNE, 7/30/99, Friday/p. L, John Petrakis
NEW YORK TIMES, 7/16/99, p. E24, Stephen Holden
VARIETY, 10/5-11/98, p. 70, David Rooney

VERY THOUGHT OF YOU, THE

A Miramax Films release of a Channel Four Films presentation of a Banshee production. *Producer:* Grainne Marmion. *Director:* Nick Hamm. *Screenplay:* Peter Morgan. *Director of Photography:* David Johnson. *Editor:* Michael Bradsell. *Music:* Ed Shearmur. *Sound:* Tim Fraser and Matthew Quast. *Sound Editor:* Colin Miller. *Casting:* Mary Selway. *Production Designer:* Max Gottlieb. *Art Director:* Mark Raggett. *Set Dresser:* Stuart Skrien and Cindy Skrien. *Costumes:* Anna Sheppard. *Make-up:* Chris Blundell. *Stunt Coordinator:* Terry Forrestal. *Running time:* 88 minutes. *MPAA Rating:* PG-13.

CAST: Monica Potter (Martha); Rufus Sewell (Frank); Tom Hollander (Daniel); Joseph Fiennes (Laurence); Ray Winstone (Pedersen); Debora Weston (First Class Passenger); Jan Pearson (Senior Partner); Steven O'Donnell (Male Information Official); Rebecca Craig (Female Information Official); Paul Bigley (Hotel Employee); Geoffrey McGivern (Travel Agent); Hamish Clarke (Icelandair Official); Lorelei King (US Ground Stewardess); Steven Speirs (Taxi Driver); Robert Brydon (Bus Driver); Luke De Lacey (Actor 1); Sam Rumbelow (Actor 2); Stephen Mangan (Actor 3).

LOS ANGELES TIMES, 8/27/99, Calendar/p. 16, Kevin Thomas

"The Very Thought of You" is yet another blithe yet engaging romantic comedy from Britain distinguished by the ingenuity of its intricate plot and the appeal of its four stars. If you can't get enough of films like "Notting Hill" and "Sliding Doors," this picture is for you. Light and breezy, made with feeling, finesse and a sure sense of humor, writer Peter Morgan and director Nick Hamm have come up with a delightful late-summer diversion.

Much of the film unfolds in flashback as a distraught young man, Laurence (Joseph Fiennes), pours out his heart to an admirably attentive and constructive therapist (Ray Winstone). Laurence, who teaches bridge to London matrons, is lifelong friends with Frank (Rufus Sewell), a onetime child star on the skids, and Daniel (Tom Hollander), an immensely successful pop music industry executive.

Ready to board a flight from Minneapolis to London, Daniel is swept off his feet by a beautiful young blond, Martha (Monica Potter). Turning on all his considerable charm Daniel successfully conspires to get Martha, London-bound but on another airline, shifted to his flight—at a cost of $5,000.

Discovering that Martha is fleeing a bad relationship and a dull job with only $35 to her name, Daniel persuades her to let him put her up at a posh hotel, where he's to meet her for lunch the next day. Understandably, Daniel is stunned when she stands him up, but when he tells his sad story over lunch to his two oldest friends, Frank, jealous of Daniel and his success, makes no attempt to disguise his glee.

Right away we can see that a lifetime spent in the midst of his friends' unending rivalry has left the gentle Laurence chronically distraught and quick to freeze up. And when in Hyde Park Frank encounters none other than Martha, despondent and all set to return home, he quickly figures out who she is and is overcome with joy at the prospect of finding a way to trump Daniel resoundingly. But why did Martha, clearly a lovely and kindly young woman, stand up her rescuer and what has made her so despondent?

Morgan and Hamm make the unfolding of the film a significant part of the pleasure in watching it. One vignette keys the next with a consistent lack of predictability, with each development dovetailing precisely, if unexpectedly, with all that has gone before. Yet there is nothing mechanical about the movie, which is driven by the nature and temperament of its characters, in collision with one another and fate itself.

Soon we're caught up in their destinies and start rooting for Martha to find some happiness somewhere and for Laurence to get away from his bickering pals long enough to develop some self-confidence. And I when you find yourself caring for people in a film it generates suspense as to what their ultimate fates will be.

Since "The Very Thought of You" is a romantic comedy this means that the immature, self-defeating Frank and the glib Daniel have to come across as appealing despite their drawbacks, which in Frank's case are considerable. (Daniel is actually quite likable but has let his career consume him.) Rufus Sewell is just the actor to play Frank. He's a chameleon in his ability to inhabit a wide range of characters no matter what kind of individual they may be.

Potter and Fiennes are at once quirky and captivating, and there's an ensemble feel to the entire cast of this glowing, amusing movie that's a good bet to lift your spirits.

NEW YORK POST, 8/27/99, p. 56, Rod Dreher

We've grown so accustomed to romantic comedies attempting to sweep us off our feet that it's easy to undervalue the slight but thoroughly enjoyable pleasures offered by movies with no greater ambition than to flirt coquettishly and sweetly.

I'm thinking of movies such as "Sliding Doors," "Next Stop Wonderland," and this weekend's Miramax confection, "The Very Thought of You."

It's a minor but delightful ensemble comedy in which a beautiful, sad American girl runs off to London on a desperate lark and excites the interest of three Englishmen—one of whom is destined to be her true love.

There's something about Martha (Monica Potter), the lemony-fresh, Julia Roberts-y blonde who inadvertently wows smooth-talking English record exec Daniel (Tom Hollander) at the Minneapolis airport.

Martha, frustrated with her going-nowhere life, hopes something exciting will turn up in London. Daniel is determined to be that something. He cheesily woos Martha by offering her a room at a posh hotel, and only asks that she agree to have lunch with him.

She wanly accepts, though clearly believes this sideburned player is more hot air than hip.

Meanwhile, Daniel's drunken failed-actor friend Frank (Rufus Sewell) runs across Martha in the park. Seeing an opportunity to twit his pal, rascally Frank makes his best case to win the standoffish Yank's affections.

Finally, Laurence (Joseph Fiennes), Daniel and Frank's buddy, becomes mixed up in the farcical affair when he crosses paths with Martha in an only-in-the-movies twist that's as giddily fun as it is implausible.

She's only going to end up with one of these guys, and it's a fair bet it'll be the one with the doe eyes and the decent heart.

"The Very Thought of You" is about aging Gen-Xers stuck in comfortable ruts they lack the courage to leap out of. Hollander and Sewell could hardly be more entertaining as a pair of self-absorbed ninnies too sidelined by their self-absorption to capture the heart of a princess.

The movie could have used more of their edgy, appalling antics, because Fiennes is agonizingly soft and dewy and right-minded as the male lead. His shy Laurence is the sort of sallow-chested sensitive who, if he ever gets around to seizing the day, will drown it in clammy-palmed perspiration.

OK, so it's not "Shakespeare in Love." Still, "The Very Thought of You" is too pleasingly cluttered with fabulous shots of London, appealing performances and sardonic English sensibility to be dismissed. It's as light as a feather yet tickles all the same.

NEWSDAY, 8/27/99, Part II/p. B10, John Anderson

A ragingly adequate romance, "The Very Thought of You" demands unconditional surrender to some very dubious circumstances. Chief among them: Could three Englishmen—friends since childhood—fall for the same American tourist within, oh, say, 12 hours of each other? If you think so, here's your movie.

Some of us may need further convincing; in which case, good luck. If this movie is anything, it isn't convincing—except regarding the comedic talents of Rufus Sewell, who has usually taken rather serious parts (as Fortinbras in Kenneth Branagh's "Hamlet," for instance, or the hero of "Dark City"), but is a very funny actor, something he's currently proving in John Turturro's "Illuminata." Alas, the Murphy's Law of the '90s Romantic Comedy states that the most interesting part of a movie gets the least amount of screen time. In accordance, Sewell's character, Frank, is relegated to playing third fiddle.

Who's on first? Laurence ("Shakespeare in Love's" Joseph Fiennes), a bridge instructor with some indistinct issues who plays middle man for his two lifelong and rather narcissistic buddies: Daniel (Tom Hollander), a high-powered music promoter, and Frank, a child-star-turned-unemployed-actor. When Daniel and Frank aren't warring with each other, they're using the selfless Laurence as a sounding board for their romantic adventures, etc.

Director Nick Hamm, a British TV-theater director best known here for the film "Talk of Angels," interweaves with competent skill the three friends' encounters with Martha (Monica Potter), a beautiful, footloose American whom 1) Daniel meets in the Minneapolis airport, 2) Laurence literally runs into at Heathrow and 3) Frank meets by chance during their individual but equal drinking binges in a public London park.

Frank is unhappy about his life and work and Martha about having just fallen in love. But with whom?

Follow Murphy's Law, and it'll be immediately clear.

Fiennes, whose appeal has always been a mystery to its, seems overwrought. Potter, whose physical similarity to Julia Roberts is pronounced enough, but whose vocal resemblance is uncanny, plays it all very cute. Ray Winstone ("Nil By Mouth," "The War Zone") is, after Sewell, the most interesting thing in the picture, as a neighbor Laurence goes to for advice. He's also part of the movie's biggest gag, a total cheat that's as unconvincing as the rest of the film. But as we said, if you surrender immediately to the dubious qualities of "The Very Thought of You," you stand a much better chance of survival,

SIGHT AND SOUND, 5/98, p. 52, Charlotte O'Sullivan

Frank (an acerbic, unemployed actor), Daniel (a flashy music executive) and Laurence (a sensitive painter) are London-based friends. When Daniel espies American Martha as he's boarding a plane to London, he has her ticket upgraded so she'll have to sit next to him in first class, but she simply sells the ticket. He then offers to put her up in a hotel suite if she'll meet him the following day for lunch. She fails to appear.

Frank is wandering through Hyde Park when he stumbles into Martha. He and Martha go to an art exhibition, where she disappears. It is revealed that Laurence met Martha at the airport. She brought him to her hotel suite but, realising her connection with Daniel, he left without saying goodbye. Now the two meet again and return to Laurence's flat. There, Martha works out that the three men are friends and rejects them all. A miserable Laurence decides to leave the country and Martha joins him on the plane, where they declare their love.

Martha—Meet Frank, Daniel and Laurence, a 90s tale of 'friendship, love and deceit' according to its tagline—is the latest British hope from Channel Four Films. Its city bound, cross-cultural romance is heavily indebted to Richard Linklater's *Before Sunrise,* its dense flashbacks and three-pursuers-after-one-love-interest plot recall the labyrinthine structure of Gilles Mimouni's recent confection, *L'Appartement.* Unfortunately, where those films allow perverse, tenderly awkward details to worm their way into the otherwise formulaic handling of slackers and young professionals, almost everything about Peter Morgan's script for *Martha—Meet Frank, Daniel and Laurence* feels stale and over-used.

Rufus Sewell (wisely) refuses to take his part as Frank the unemployed actor seriously—and with that Mantegna-coloured, pudding-perfect face, he hardly needs to try. By contrast, Joseph Fiennes as Laurence lunges at cuteness like a wolf, forever widening his little-boy-lost eyes and rubbing his hand helplessly through his hair. He buffs and puffs to seduce us but (perhaps because we're so aware of the effort) never manages to blow the house down.

Newcomer Monica Potter, perhaps chosen for her not-quite Julia Roberts looks, can't make sense of a character transfixed from masochistic mule into spunky fairy-tale princess by the simple decision to 'pack up and clear out'. We hear of poverty, abuse from boyfriends and employers, but there's not a hint of gloom in Martha's chocolate-cheesecake eyes. Nor does she ever seem in danger of slipping back into her dysfunctional old ways.

Such comely blandness pervades the film as a whole: deprivation can be discussed, for example, but it must never be seen. To the warblings of the band Texas (the perfect MOR accompaniment) the characters flitter through London's luxurious, tourist-friendly hotels, parks, theatres and galleries. Desperate not to depress, director Nick Hamm (whose credits include episodes of *The Bill* and *Rik Mayall Presents* and several documentaries) presents us with images of the city so familiar and yet so anonymous they barely register.

There's a careless malice at work, too. Early on, music executive Daniel finds that instead of Martha as a plane companion, he'll be sitting next to a middle-aged woman, complete with Pat Phoenix cleavage. Cue laughter: her size and age make her a visual joke. Later, Martha and Laurence discuss the nightmare of 'sagging, surgically altered faces'. So they despise the aged for having ruined bodies and for trying to hide such ruin. *Martha—Meet Frank, Daniel and Laurence* is more like an advert than a movie: what it's selling is youth, beauty and first-class travel, as cynical and as empty an exercise as one could wish to see.

Also reviewed in:
NEW YORK TIMES, 8/27/99, p. E14, Stephen Holden
VARIETY, 5/11-17/98, p. 64, Derek Elley

VIOLENT COP

A Winstar Cinema release. *Producer:* Hisao Nabeshima, Takio Yoshida, and Shozo Ichiyama. *Director:* Takeshi Kitano. *Screenplay (Japanese with English subtitles):* Hisashi Nozawa. *Director of Photography:* Yasushi Sakakibara. *Editor:* Nobutake Kamiya. *Music:* Daisaku Kumé. *Running time:* 103 minutes. *MPAA Rating:* Not Rated.

CAST: Takeshi Kitano (Azuma); Hakuryu (Nindo's Henchman); Maiko Kawakami (Akari); Shiro Sano (Police Chief Yoshinari); Shigeru Hiraizumi (Iwaki); Mikiko Otonashi (Iwaki's Wife); Ittoku Kishibe (Nindo).

NEW YORK POST, 7/16/99, p. 46, Jonathan Foreman

Unlike some of the later work of Takeshi Kitano (nicknamed "Beat" Takeshi), "Violent Cop,"—the first film directed by the cult Japanese actor-director—is quite amazingly slow and boring.

It's exceptionally well-photographed and has pretty theme music, but the plot is vague and crude (something about corrupt cops and drug-smuggling businessmen) and the occasional scenes of bloody violence are brutal but not especially interesting.

Half of the film is taken up with the main character walking up corridors or down streets. By the 10th corridor you are ready to scream with boredom.

You first encounter Azuma using some well-placed kicks to persuade a teen-age hooligan who has taken part in the murder of a homeless man to give himself up. Nothing much happens for the next 35 minutes.

Eventually, Azuma and his partner turn up at a drug bust, where three other cops get beaten up by a single very-tough suspect. Azuma chases the guy down the street for miles and eventually rams the suspect with his car. He gets in trouble with his superiors for being "violently wild and stupid."

Then Azuma discovers that the drug dealer is working for a conspiracy and goes after it, if it means his getting fired from the force.

Both Azuma and the main bad guy—a gangland enforcer—are able to absorb a remarkable number of in-and-out gunshot wounds, and they keep on coming.

VILLAGE VOICE, 7/20/99, p. 135, J. Hoberman

Another paragon of B-movie virtue, Takeshi Kitano's first feature, *Violent Cop*, has finally gone into U.S. distribution a decade after it was released in Japan. With *Fireworks* and *Sonatine* both shown theatrically last year, local audiences should be more than prepared for this oddball, brutal *policier*, although it's intriguing to wonder what Kitano's Japanese fans initially made of his jolting screen debut—the popular stand-up comedian upped his aggression quotient drastically here by casting himself as a deadpan Dirty Harry.

No less eccentric than its successors, *Violent Cop* features Kitano beating drug-dealer butt and stepping on authority's toes to the accompaniment of an infectious theme that reconfigures a melancholy Eric Satie refrain into something more appropriate to the video game Tetris. Impassive, slightly quizzical, smiling no more than once or twice during the whole movie, the star is most expressive when socking someone. Kitano's put-upon police officer never misses an opportunity to stomp a suspect-even kicking his own partner when he gets in the way. "You're violently wild and stupid," the cop's superior explains, but departmental discipline has no effect; the movie's Japanese title translates as *Warning: This Man Is Dangerous.*

Not unlike Toshiro Mifune (the last Japanese action star to intrude on American consciousness), Kitano uses a distinctive body language to telegraph his emotions. But where the young Mifune was eloquently hyperkinetic, middle-aged Kitano is a rock of concentration in a treacherous world. *Violent Cop*, which features no guns in its first half, is a film of pummeling physicality—it's been suggested that it recreates the distinctive rhythm of Kitano's heavy, hunched-over, off-kilter stride, as well as his surprise eruptions.

The central set piece is a botched drug bust in which the suspect takes out three detectives, decks a fourth in a slo-mo punch-out, then (to the accompaniment of some unlikely cocktail jazz) sprints through an unheeding workaday neighborhood, lethal baseball bat in hand. The prolonged, naturalistically grueling pursuit ends with Kitano ramming the perp with his squad car. Still, Kitano—who even in his first film is a wonderfully classical director—more typically uses long shots to muffle or defamiliarize mayhem. What's blatant is the sense of his "honest" rage at having to live amid cowardice and corruption.

Also reviewed in:
NEW YORK TIMES, 7/16/99, p. 18, Lawrence Van Gelder

VIRTUAL SEXUALITY

A TriStar Pictures release of a Bridge presentation of a Noel Gay Motion Picture Company production. *Executive Producer:* Kevin Loader, Jonathan Darby, and Charles Armitage. *Producer:* Christopher Figg. *Director:* Nick Hurran. *Screenplay:* Nick Fisher. *Based on the novel by:* Chloe Rayban. *Director of Photography:* Brian Tufano. *Editor:* John Richards. *Music:* Rupert Gregson Williams and Elliot Johnson. *Sound:* Andy Kennedy and (music) Cameron McBride. *Casting:* Janey Fothergill and Jane Davies. *Production Designer:* Chris Edwards. *Art Director:* Humphrey Bangham. *Costumes:* Joanna Freedman. *Make-up:* Juliana Mendes-Ebden. *Stunt Coordinator:* Terry Forrestal. *Running time:* 90 minutes. *MPAA Rating:* R.

CAST: Laura Fraser (Justine); Rupert Penry-Jones (Jake); Luke De Lacey (Chas); Kieran O'Brien (Alex); Marcelle Duprey (Fran); Natasha Bell (Hoover); Steve John Shepherd (Jason); Laura Macaulay (Monica); Roger Frost (Frank); Ruth Sheen (Jackie); Laura Aikman (Lucy); Ram John Holder (Declan); Amanda Holden (Shoe Shop Assistant); Alan Westaway (Geoff); William Osborne (Sex Shop Assistant); Philip Bird (Justine's Dad); Judith Scott (Sharon); Stewart Harwood and Nicolas Pry (Laborers); Alison Garland (Scary Nurse); Robert Oates (Cabbie); Caroline Chikezie (Gushy Assistant); Trish Bertram (Reporter); Toby Cockerell (Wiry Lad); Keeley Gainey (Receptionist); Melinda Messenger (Superbra Girl); THE BOYS: Jake Curran (Nick); James Daley (Margot); Monty Fromant (Taylor); Martin Hutson (Rory); Joseph Kpobie (Knobhead); Peter McCabe (Spriggs); Ozdemir Mamodeally (Rex); Carl Pizzie (Floyd); Del Synott (Carter); Freddie White (Giblet); James D. White (Matt); THE GIRLS: Zoe Hodges (Lily); Preeya Kalidas (Charlotte); Samantha Levelle (Louise); Tracey Murphy (Helen); Emma Jane Pierson (Fiona); Ania Sowinski (Vicky); Ebony Thomas (Rachel); Lynne Wilmot (Laura).

NEW YORK POST, 12/4/99, p. 26, Lou Lumenick

There's no sex—real or even computer-generated—in "Virtual Sexuality," a clueless British teen comedy that's unaccountably stopping briefly in theaters en route to the video racks.

Justine (Laura Fraser, who resembles a younger, prettier Kristin Scott Thomas) is a London high school girl eager to lose her virginity to a "Mr. Right Bloke."

An accident in a makeover booth at a computer fair turns her into her dream guy (Rupert Penry-Jones), a blond airhead. Justine's new male persona, Jake, and the movie in general share an obsession with a certain part of the male anatomy, which goes on view in the boys' locker room thanks to a few quick full-frontal shots.

This barely tolerable comic conceit turns ridiculous when Justine turns up in female form as well—and develops a roaring crush on Jake. He's understandably skittish about deflowering his female self, not to mention being confused by his feelings for a man-trap named Hoover.

Mightily baffled by this all—an emotion audiences will no doubt share—is Justine/Jake's nerdy best friend, Chas (Luke De Lacy), whose parents cheerfully tolerate his bunking with a teenage boy who minces around in a pink bathrobe and keeps asking to see his "willie" to compare sizes.

Will Justine give it up (off screen, of course) to Jake, Chas or a hunky but boorish soccer player? The answer is a no-brainer, just like this movie.

In addition to a cast that appears to be a decade too old for their roles, "Virtual Sexuality" presents such a thicket of accents and British slang that subtitles wouldn't hurt.

SIGHT AND SOUND, 8/99, p. 55, Melanie McGrath

West London, the present. Seventeen-year-old Justine is desperate to lose her virginity and hopes Alex, the school stud, will assist. But Alex's attentions are focused on Hoover, the school vamp. Helped by her friends Fran and Chas, Justine sets up a date with Alex at a computer exposition but at the last moment Alex backs out to see Hoover. Justine goes to the expo anyway where she is talked into trying out a new makeover machine called Narcissus by its inventors Jason and Monica. Once inside the machine, Justine designs her perfect man on screen. During a sudden power cut the machine malfunctions and Justine is transmogrified into two people: herself with amnesia and her perfect man, who has her mind and memories. He names himself Jake.

Jake heads over to Chas' house to explain what has happened and moves in. Chas gives him advice on how to act like a man. Unaware that Jake is part of herself, Justine develops a crush on him. Hoover is also interested in the sexy new boy on the block. Monica and Jason are keen to track him down for scientific purposes.

Deflated by Jake's apparent lack of interest, Justine plots to sleep with Alex, hoping that it would make her more desirable to Jake. Appalled, Jake explains what happened in the Narcissus but minutes later Monica and Jason kidnap him. Justine and Chas rescue him and using the Narcissus, morph Jake back into Justine's body. Justine and Chas start dating and eventually have sex with each other.

Despite its misleadingly cerebral title, this fresh teen flick treads lightly while retaining a seriousness of purpose, a considerable triumph for a genre which so often devolves into grainy, self-important cool *(kids)* or vacuous crudity *(Porky's)*, Telling the story of a girl whose perfect man (with her mind) comes to life via computer technology, *Virtual Sexuality* steers a visual course somewhere between the boldly coloured, cartoonish two-dimensionality of a John Waters enterprise—complete with self-reflexive asides and graphics—and the sassy realism of such recent American teen products as *Clueless* and *She's All That*.

At the head of the film, protagonist Justine defines herself entirely in terms of her consumer choices, but the story goes on to explore her struggles to engage with a deeper identity. "Be the Justine you want to be, not the Justine you think you need to be," exhorts her friend. Our heroine's perfect man is her own *animus* but the gender switch allows for some unexpected comic twists as well as the more routine teen-pleasing knob and tit jokes. In one very funny scene, Jake disturbs Chas' sleep with his rhythmic hand action. Both the audience (at first) and Chas assume Jake is masturbating for the first time as a man until the camera tilts to reveal he's frantically polishing Chas' silver picture frame. Very solid performances from the cast keep the film buoyant throughout—Rupert Penry-Jones' camp, prancing, androgynous Adonis Jake deserves special mention.

There is a sexual playfulness and candour in *Virtual Sexuality* that is rare in British films which tend either to overplay sex or reduce it to a series of embarrassed and embarrassing jokes about body size. In going against this grain, what we have here is a very adult film, putting an ironic twist on the usual create-the-perfect-partner rubric by reversing the genders, marking this film out as truly of its time. That said, *Virtual Sexuality* doesn't shy away from more traditional equations. Egghead Monica is meant to be ugly as sin while Natasha Bell's alluring vamp Hoover (so called because she sucks all men towards her) is extremely dumb and very, very blonde.

Tradition also creeps into *Virtual Sexuality*'s rather absurd depiction of technology as a dangerous and magical zone of enormous and unpredictable transformative power. Perhaps the generational gap between Hurran and screenwriter Nick Fisher (working from Chloe Rayban's novel) and their characters is too wide since the depiction of what is to most teenagers a fully integrated and unquestioned environment saturated with technology as something wild and dangerous will ring few bells for them. This is the 90s. Teens don't expect a literal *deus ex machina* to emerge magically from their gadgets. They just expect them to work.

Still, *Virtual Sexuality* is an ambitious project which treats such heavy duty themes as narcissism, identity, sexual enfranchisement and fidelity without resorting to a heavy-duty harangue.

Also reviewed in:
NEW YORK TIMES, 12/4/99, p. B19, Anita Gates
VARIETY, 7/12-18/99, p. 39, Derek Elley

VIRUS

A Universal Pictures and Mutual Film Company release of a Dark Horse Entertainment/Valhalla Motion Pictures production. *Executive Producer:* Mike Richardson, Chuck Pfarrer, Gary Levinsohn, and Mark Gordon. *Producer:* Gale Anne Hurd. *Director:* John Bruno. *Screenplay:* Chuck Pfarrer and Dennis Feldman. *Based on The Dark Horse comic book series "Virus" created by:* Chuck Pfarrer. *Director of Photography:* David Eggby. *Editor:* Scott Smith. *Music:* Joel McNeely. *Music Editor:* Johnny Caruso and Craig Pettigrew. *Sound:* Jay Meagher and (music) Shawn Murphy. *Sound Editor:* Richard L. Anderson and George Simpson. *Casting:* Amy Gerber. *Production Designer:* Mayling Cheng. *Art Director:* Donald B. Woodruff, Jay Hinkle, and Robert J. Quinn. *Set Designer:* Daniel Jennings, Dale Allan Pelton, Geoffrey S. Grimsman, Domenic Silvestri, Bill Taliaferro, Patte Strong, Charlie Vassar, Alan Au, Allan Hook, and William Davis. *Set Decorator:* Donald Krafft. *Set Dresser:* John T. Bromell, Jay Meyer, Michael A. Shapiro, George Harding, Hal Gardner, Lee Hendersen, E. Lawrence Brew, Andrea Sywanyk, David Lyons, Kip Bartlett, Eric W. Skipper, Bruce Seymour, Joseph R. McGuire, Jr.,

William F. Alford, and William Lindsey, Jr. *Special Effects:* Chuck Gaspar. *Robotics Effects:* Steve Johnson and Eric Allard. *Robot Animation:* Phil Tippett. *Costumes:* Frank Perry Rose. *Make-up:* Jeff Goodwin. *Stunt Coordinator:* Joel Kramer. *Running time:* 110 minutes. *MPAA Rating:* R.

CAST: Jamie Lee Curtis (Kit Foster); William Baldwin (Steve Baker); Donald Sutherland (Captain Everton); Joanna Pacula (Nadia); Marshall Bell (J.W. Woods, Jr.); Julio Oscar Mechoso (Squeaky); Sherman Augustus (Richie); Cliff Curtis (Hiko); Yuri Chervotkin (Colonel Kominski); Keith Flippen (Captain Lonya Rostov); Olga Rzhepetskaya-Retchin (Female Cosmonaut); Levani (Captain Alexi); David Eggby (Norfolk Captain).

LOS ANGELES TIMES, 1/18/99, Calendar/p. 3, Kevin Thomas

Imagine an alien life force that is electrical rather than protoplasmic in nature, and you've got the gimmick that energizes "Virus," an unpretentious, amusing thrill-a-minute sci-fi horror thriller/monster movie that plugs night into fears of a Y2K crisis.

Inspired by Chuck Pfarrer's comic book series of the same name, this imaginatively designed (by Mayling Cheng) Universal release marks an authoritative, vigorous directorial debut for special effects Oscar winner John Bruno, who understands the need to balance technical wizardry with solid storytelling and strong characterizations. Amid outsized mechanical arachnids and Terminator-like mutants, Jamie Lee Curtis, William Baldwin and Donald Sutherland more than hold their own and carry the day.

When a Russian missile satellite tracking ship trolling the South Seas connects with space station MIR it gets such a jolt it's transformed into a ghost vessel. When a salvage ship owned by Sutherland's Captain Everton comes upon the seemingly abandoned Akademic Vadislav Volkov, Everton and his men smell millions in profit. Navigator Kit Foster (Curtis), a no-nonsense admiral's daughter, prophetically counters that "There's no such thing as easy money."

From the moment Sutherland and his crew step aboard the Russian ship they encounter evidence of strange and violent occurrences. And whatever happened to the Russians? Helpfully, the Russian chief science officer, Nadia (Joanna Pacula), has survived. Fighting back shock and fear, Nadia has a story to tell that makes "The Rime of the Ancient Mariner" sound like a fairy tale.

The stars are all coming off career highs: Curtis with "Halloween: H20," Sutherland with "Without Limits" and Baldwin with the dazzling and venturesome "Shattered Image." In "Virus" Sutherland supplies the greed and stupidity, Curtis the brains and guts and Baldwin the staunch backup. As for Pacula, "Virus" represents one of the best opportunities she has had since her debut in "Gorky Park," playing a beautiful woman of superior intelligence and selfless courage.

Cheng's stunning production design is equaled by the contributions of the various special effects crews, and cinematographer David Eggby's fluid, shadowy camera work and Joel McNeely's brooding score. For all of this lively and entertaining film's considerable artistry and craftsmanship, "Virus" opened Friday without benefit of press previews. It may not be, in studio parlance, a "critic-driven" kind of film, but the many people who contributed to its success deserved more respect than that.

NEW YORK POST, 1/16/99, p. 21, Rod Dreher

"Virus" comes off as completely predictable and largely fright-free, but not as bad as you might expect from the fact that Universal refused to screen it in advance for critics.

It's a formulaic creature feature pitting the indefatigable Jamie Lee Curtis (yeah!) against a hideous malefactor (boo!) that has lodged itself on a ship. Yep, it's "Alien" on a boat, and there's nothing new here, but director John Bruno keeps things moving deftly, and the players—especially Donald Sutherland as a corrupt sea captain—are hammily entertaining.

"Virus," which is based on a comic-book series, will play much better on the VCR than on the big screen, certainly, but if you're bound and determined to see a horror thriller this weekend, better this efficient, by-the-numbers exercise than the loony "In Dreams."

The action begins in outer space and in the South Pacific, where the Mir space station is trading data with a Russian scientific research vessel. Suddenly the cosmonauts see a mysterious cloud barreling toward them. The cloud overtakes the orbiter and zaps itself down to the ship in a blinding flash.

Cut to a deep-sea tugboat pulling a barge in a typhoon. Greedy Captain Everton (Sutherland) has all his savings riding on getting the barge to shore. When it breaks loose and sinks, he's devastated. The crew, which includes Jamie Lee as the brainy navigator and William Baldwin as Sutherland's chief antagonist, pilots the tug to the eye of the storm, hoping to repair leaks in the engine in calm waters.

There they discover the Russian vessel, dead in the water and looking pretty banged up. Upon boarding, they find the ship abandoned. Dollar signs flashing in his eyes, salty old Everton nearly drools on the deck thinking of the salvage money he can make if he can drag the tub to shore.

Trouble is, something—or someone—aboard drops the big boat's anchor through the deck of the tug, sinking it. Then they find the sole Russian survivor, Nadia (Joanna Pacula), the babelicious chief science officer, who informs them that they are all going to die. "Russian rubbish!" spits Everton, which tells us that "Virus" has big things in store for this old salt.

Nadia explains that the thing is "a life form, electrical in nature," that has taken over the ship's mechanical systems. What we have here, then, is a demonic Reddi Kilowaft that has learned how to use the research ship's convenient robotics lab, and is building misanthropic deathbots. There's even a cannibalistic zombie element to this nasty business, which provides for several exemplary gross-out sequences.

As if all this weren't enough, the typhoon returns, plunging the whole lot of them into the throes of a dark and stormy night. Though the seas are dreadfully rough, this is one of those movie hurricanes that only makes the ship pitch and roll when it serves the plot.

The only questions are how Jamie Lee will smite the alien, and which of the crew will survive. For a formless entity composed of electricity, that alien S.O.B. sure can work with its hands. It's got the soul of Charles Manson, the brains of an MIT grad student, and the make-do inventiveness you'd expect from the love child of MacGyver and Martha Stewart.

What "Virus" doesn't have much of is scariness, but look, it's January, so whaddaya expect?

NEWSDAY, 1/16/99, Part II/p. B8, Bob Heisler

Getting to work during last week's ice storm was scarier than "Virus," a clattering collection of clunker "Alien" cliches that abandons hope when it switches languages from Russian to English in its fourth minute.

No, sci-fi fans, the movie neither asks nor answers the promise of its promotion: What if human beings were considered as pathological to the universal organism as, say, an out-of-control virus, and therefore required elimination?

Instead, on its way to the midnight show on cable movie stations around the world, "Virus" pits a small group of pathetic Earthlings against an electronic life-form advanced enough to travel through space and transmit itself from the Russian space station Mir to a space-tracking ship in the Pacific. Of course, at that point the alien energy, which should simply use the same process to move across and dominate the globe, decides to hang out in the ship's computer and take a break to play with its cache of human and mechanical parts.

By the time the crew of the salvage tug Sea Star arrives aboard the nearly lifeless Russian vessel, the electronic pulsemeister is happily creating little erector-set monsters (think "Toy Story") and trying to figure out what to do with the human threat.

Now, you may ask, why did this advanced life-form travel across space to destroy humankind? What led it to conclude that the species was a threat to the whole? Interesting questions. Too good to be answered in what passes for a script.

What's left is a shipboard chase along darkened hallways and through dangling wires, waiting for the odd confrontation with increasingly powerful and angry beings made from computer chips, body parts and metal rods. It's tempting to call these beings monsters, but perhaps they are aware they're in a January movie and their anger is justified.

Certainly there is no reason for the monster-builder to change its consciousness given the contents of the Sea Star from central casting: a dangerously violent captain, a Cuban engine-room assistant, an African-American weapons expert, crew who represent stoic courage and selfish cowardice, and Jamie Lee Curtis. Also William Baldwin, engineer, nice guy.

You know who will die. You know that they will appear again, looking like freshly made Borgs. You know they will die again, only with less emotional involvement. This does not encourage fright. It does encourage flight to another movie in the multiplex.

Say this for Jamie Lee Curtis: She's a Hall of Fame actress among mouth-breathers. You know the moment when the car door/ship's latch/attic trap slams shut and the only noise you hear just before the killer/machine/alien crashes through the wall/floor/bulkhead is the deep breathing of the survivors? And she can recuperate faster than you can say, "Hey, wait a minute, shouldn't she be dead—or at least tired?"

Say this for Donald Sutherland: He's game for the role of crusty sea dog captain, even borrowing a cup of Sean Connery's accent and remembering to roll his R's most of the time. And he has enough respect for the audience to break character and just grin foolishly when the plot breaks down completely.

Say this for William Baldwin: He survives. He's too noble to want to, but he does. One of the monster-chase movie rules is that more than one person survives to confirm the harrowing tale.

And, one hopes, to prevent the other from creating a sequel.

SIGHT AND SOUND, 6/99, p. 56, Philip Strick

As the *Mir* space station prepares an alignment with the satellite-tracking research ship *Volkov,* a vast energy mass approaches suddenly from outer space. Enveloping *Mir,* the entity flashes down to the data receptors on the *Volkov* engulfing the ship's electrical systems. A week later, as a typhoon rages in the area, the tugboat *Sea Star* finds the *Volkov* drifting lifelessly. Boarding her, the *Sea Star's* Captain Everton realises that a possible $30 million salvage fee awaits him and his crew.

When the *Sea Star* is sunk in an accident the crew begin to explore their derelict discovery. They soon find a survivor, Nadia, who claims that a malevolent force has taken over the ship; she warns them, too late, not to turn on the power system. Reactivated, the ship's workshops resume a host of mysterious projects, assimilating components of human captives in a fusion of flesh and metal. Nadia recognises the remains of her husband among the new lifeforms. Through the ship's computer the alien presence announces that the humans are a virus that will be eliminated and used for spare parts.

While Everton tries to bargain for his own survival, *Sea Star* navigator Kit Foster realises that the *Volkov* is being steered towards a satellite monitoring centre with a global linkup. Kit and Nadia prepare to blow up the ship with the help of engineer Steve Baker. They are attacked by Everton, now a biomechanoid, but blow him apart. Kit is trapped by the entity but released by fellow crewman Richie who has been developing an escape rocket. Sole survivors, Kit and Steve cling to the rocket as its take-off detonates the destruction of the *Volkov.* A helicopter rescues them.

Adapted by Chuck Pfarrer from his own four part Dark Horse comic book series, *Virus* is a haphazard collection of emergencies ranging from typhoons to zombie attacks, from would-be suicide to first-aid surgery, from computerised sadism to last minute just-for-the-hell-of-it hallucination. Negotiating the risks is the usual handful of expendables, gamely portrayed by players hoping to impress in the brief moments before something more memorable chops them down. But this erratic adventure is not really about them: it's about the concerted skills of a special-effects team that has dominated fantasy film making for more than a decade.

The assembled production talent for *Virus* could hardly be bettered, headed by Mike Richardson, owner of Dark Horse Comics and producer of *The Mask,* by the Levinsohn Gordon partnership responsible for *Saving Private Ryan* and by Gale Anne Hurd, launcher of James Cameron and *The Terminator.* At the sharp end of design and animation for the film's delirious array of mechanoid killers are specialists like Eric Allard *(Short Circuit),* Steve Johnson *(Species)* and near-legendary Oscar-winner Phil Tippett (the *Star Wars* trilogy, *RoboCop*). And although John Bruno at last makes his debut as feature director here, his 30-year career seems to have involved every possible role in the visual effects business from Disney animation to co-direction with James Cameron of the *Terminator* 2-3D theme park. Awarded an Oscar for *The Abyss,* followed by five subsequent nominations, he was immersed in preproduction for *Titanic* when *Virus* staked its claim.

Given that Bruno's experiences when working on *Titanic* included two hurricanes endured aboard a Russian research vessel, events which became integrated into the *Virus* script, it is tempting to glimpse in his film a private subtext something about the traps and tortures of inventing fresh technology in a desperate struggle to meet the extravagant demands of James Cameron.

In parallel, *Virus* is also a seafaring yarn, not too many leagues away from *Titanic* itself or from *The Abyss* with its vulnerable cargo of lost souls: setting aside such distractions as alien invasion and berserk equipment, the film offers a series of maritime contests from the effort to control one salvaged ship to the race to destroy another. At the epicentre is the discovery of the derelict ship, approached in wonder by the tugboat crew. Savouring a classic moment, Bruno floats his camera above as the search party gingerly makes its way across the decks.

Plunging from this pinnacle into a formulaic series of duels, *Virus* either sinks or swims according to one's taste for ingenuity The skills at work are enthralling but the concepts familiar, from the scuttling insectoid emissaries *(Runaway,* 1984) to the giant Proteus-voiced computer that once, similarly, had its way with Julie Christie in *Demon Seed* (1977).

The part-flesh, part-transistor phenomenon, at its cleanest in *RoboCop,* its most brutal in *Hardware,* its most disgusting in *Tetsuo,* reaches its apotheosis in the well-wired form of Donald Sutherland wandering in as if recruited by the Borg in *Star Trek* and looking irremediably silly. Having hewn out for himself a fair chunk of the film's early exchanges in which, with a sea-doggish gleefully accent, he establishes the tugboat captain as a raving nutter, he plainly finds the rest of his role ridiculous but enjoys it to the full. Alongside, Jamie Lee Curtis and Joanna Pacula form a macho team with enough spirit to fight off all contenders, metallic or otherwise. While never entirely explaining why a lifeform of pure energy needs to encumber itself with bits of flesh and scrap metal, *Virus* makes another loud and colourful case for the special-effects epidemic.

Also reviewed in:
CHICAGO TRIBUNE, 1/17/99, Metro/p. 8, Michael Wilmington
NEW YORK TIMES, 1/16/99, p. B14, Lawrence Van Gelder
WASHINGTON POST, 1/16/99, p. C1, Stephen Hunter

WALK ON THE MOON, A

A Miramax Films release of a Punch production in association with Village Roadshow Pictures-Groucho Film Partnership. *Executive Producer:* Graham Burke and Greg Coote. *Producer:* Neil Koenigsberg, Lee Gottsegen, Murray Schisgal, Dustin Hoffman, Tony Goldwyn, and Jay Cohen. *Director:* Tony Goldwyn. *Screenplay:* Pamela Gray. *Director of Photography:* Anthony Richmond. *Editor:* Dana Congdon. *Music:* Mason Daring and Stephan R. Goldman. *Music Editor:* Patrick Mullins. *Sound:* Claude La Haye and (music) Dave Shacter. *Sound Editor:* Jeffrey Stern. *Casting:* Billy Hopkins, Suzanne Smith, Kerry Barden, and Ann Goulder. *Production Designer:* Dan Leigh. *Art Director:* Gilles Aird. *Set Dresser:* Francine Danis and Paul Hotte. *Costumes:* Jess Goldstein. *Make-up:* Lizane Lasalle. *Stunt Coordinator:* Minor Mustain and Dave McKeown. *Running time:* 107 minutes. *MPAA Rating:* R.

CAST: Bobby Boriello (Daniel Kantrowitz); Diane Lane (Pearl Kantrowitz); Anna Paquin (Alison Kantrowitz); Tovah Feldshuh (Lilian Kantrowitz); Liev Schreiber (Marty Kantrowitz); Stewart Bick (Neil Leiberman); Jess Platt (Herb Fogler); Mahee Paiment (Mrs. Dymbort); Star Jasper (Rhoda Leiberman); Ellen David (Eleanor Gelfand); Lisa Bronwyn Moore (Norma Fogler); Viggo Mortensen (Walker Jerome); Vicky Barkoff (Selma Levitsky); Tamar Kozlov (Wendy Green); Lisa Jakub (Myra Naidell); Joseph Perrino (Ross Epstein); Jesse Lavendel (Carl Applebaum); James Liboiron (Jeffrey Fogler); Howard Rosenstein (Sheldon Dymbort); Mal Z. Lawrence (Comedian); Joel Miller (Sid Shapiro); Bill Brownstein (Customer #1); Sam Gesser (Customer #2).

LOS ANGELES TIMES, 3/26/99, Calendar/p. 17, Kevin Thomas

"A Walk on the Moon," a film of exceptional emotional honesty, takes place at a pivotal time in American life, the summer of 1969, when the Apollo II mission and Woodstock approach while the Vietnam War, with its divisive impact on the home front, rages on. Yet life goes on as usual at Dr. Fogler's Bungalows, an old Catskills summer resort, where the Kantrowitz family traditionally spends its vacations.

The Kantrowitzes take a cottage for the summer, with Marty (Liev Schreiber) coming up on the weekends from the city, where he works long hours as a TV repairman. Sharing the cottage are Marty's wife, Pearl (Diane Lane); her 14-year-old daughter Alison (Anna Paquin); her young son Daniel (Bobby Boriello); and her mother-in-law, Lilian (Tovah Feldshuh). With the moon landing imminent, Woodstock only a stone's throw away and her daughter on the brink of womanhood, Pearl is feeling unusually restless, suspecting that life is passing her by.

She questions her friends as to whether they ever feel trapped by their lives and even admits to wishing sometimes that she were a "whole other person." Marty, who is regarded as a lovable square by his daughter, is a devoted, dutiful husband, but the excitement has faded from his marriage, as he and Pearl are both weighed down by responsibilities and hemmed in by working-class economic realities.

Daily routine at the resort is punctuated by loudspeaker announcements, uttered by an unseen Julie Kavner, heralding the arrival of "the knish man," "the ice cream man" and "the blouse man." The last sells women's clothing out of a specially equipped van.

The new "blouse man" is a sexy free spirit named Walker (a low-key Viggo Mortensen). A spark ignites instantly between Pearl and Walker, and it's only a matter of time before it catches fire. Pearl, a beautiful woman who's only 31—she was only a teenager when she had Alison—longs for the sexual ecstasy and freedom Walker represents, but their torrid affair inevitably will provoke a major crisis in the Kantrowitz family.

How the Kantrowitzes cope is the heart of the matter. Having succumbed to temptation, Pearl must now deal with the consequences to herself and her family as each one's capacity for understanding and forgiveness is tested. The way things are thrashed out presents challenging roles for Lane, Paquin and especially Schreiber, who fulfills the promise he has demonstrated in smaller roles in films like "Daytrippers."

Schreiber gives us a good man, hurt to the quick, but who must nevertheless find within himself the resources to rise to the painful occasion if his marriage is to have a prayer of survival. Pearl is in turn faced with inescapably hard choices—provided her husband proves to be even willing to take her back; Lane does such a good job of illuminating Pearl in all her frustrations and longing that we never lose sympathy for her.

In the meantime, Paquin, as Alison, reveals a joy at coming of age cruelly dashed by the wracking pain and fear that her parents may separate.

One of the most refreshing aspects of the film is that Lilian, played with effective understatement by Feldshuh, is not a stereotypical Jewish mother. She senses early what's going on between Pearl and Walker, but in her attempt to cut short the affair she appeals to Pearl's sense of responsibility rather than merely condemning her daughter-in-law. She reminds Pearl that she's not the only person whose dreams didn't come true.

"A Walk on the Moon" represents a double debut: for actor Tony Goldwyn as a feature director and Pamela Gray as a screenwriter, and they show both courage and judgment in dealing straight on with so much naked emotion. Their film goes right up to the edge, inviting compassion rather than uneasy laughter at the spectacle of people behaving foolishly in the grip of heart-wrenching pain and overpowering emotion. It is a happy coincidence that Goldwyn should be directing a script that as a UCLA thesis won the Samuel Goldwyn Award, a prize established by Goldwyn's legendary grandfather.

NEW YORK POST, 3/26/99, p. 63, Jonathan Foreman

Unfortunately for the believability of "A Walk on the Moon"—an otherwise affecting and well-made movie—screenwriter Pamela Gray is one of those folks who have swallowed the myth that no one had a clue about sex—least of all married people—until the hippies taught everyone how to do it in the late '60s. But fine performances elevate this film above such cliches—and make up for its too-easy mocking of the lower-middle-class world of a Jewish Catskills resort.

Pearl (Diane Lane) and Marty (Liev Schreiber) are a thirtysomething couple with a small boy and a 14-year-old girl (Anna Paquin) on the cusp on womanhood. Neither of them have had any part of the countercultural revolution. As Pearl says, the only important decision she's made during the entire decade is which market to shop at. And square Marty, who never got to go to college because he impregnated Pearl, has been too busy supporting the family as a TV repairman to do anything far out or groovy.

It all gets to be too much for Pearl when Marty has to spend more time back in the city fixing TVs so his customers can watch the moon landing. So when hippie-ish, WASP blouse salesman Walker (Viggo Mortensen) visits the resort and comes on to her, she gives in to a liberating hedonism, and, before you know, the two of them are cavorting in waterfalls.

Marty's superstitious mother Lilian (Tovah Feldshuh), who's staying in the bungalow, figures out there's something going on. But things only really come to a head when rebellious daughter Alison (a terrific Anna Paquin), who has sneaked off to the Woodstock festival, is horrified to see her body-painted mother writhing around in the crowd. The movie deals with what follows with remarkable sense and sensitivity. Although there are hints that letting it all hang out and getting down to rock'n' roll might be the solution to life's problems, the outraged, betrayed but responsible Marty is far too sympathetic a figure for there to be any easy answers.

Actor-turned-(first-time)-director Tony Goldwyn shows a real mastery of tone here. He allows his actors to strut their stuff without letting them going over the top. And, with the exception of a laid-back Mortensen playing a sketchily drawn character, all of them—especially the ravishing Lane—respond with some of their best work.

NEWSDAY, 3/26/99, Part II/p. B11, John Anderson

If a family is a universe and a country is a family, is there a Big Bang theory, too? Is every body in motion subject to forces that are pulling them apart? Or, to paraphrase Swinging '60s icon Dick Nixon, do we simply get going when the going gets tough?

In "A Walk on the Moon"—actor Tony Goldwyn's directing debut from an extraordinary script by Pamela Gray—the forces include all the social upheavals of an era that seems somehow quaint right now. The perspective, however, is that of a '60s element that the movies have never explored, nor felt compelled to explore: the people on the sidelines of the sexual revolution who never stormed the barricades of protest or bra-lessness, but felt the impact as keenly as anyone—be it on their self-image, concept of family or sense of security in the world they'd made.

The family in question is Brooklyn Jewish and subject to the annual call of the Catskills. "Why do we do this every summer?" asks pubescent activist Alison Kantrowitz (Anna Paquin) as the family Studebaker wheels by the Red Apple Rest. "Because we do," chirps the patiently maternal Pearl Kantrowitz (Diane Lane), who can barely keep her restlessness in check. Married to the hardworking Marty (Liev Schreiber) since she was a teenager, Pearl looks longingly at the hippie hitchhikers along Route 17, who—unbeknownst to any Kantrowitz—are heading north to something called Woodstock.

Goldwyn directs with great sensitivity and sophistication, but it's Lane—an actress who sparks with sexual awareness like no one since Natalie Wood—who makes much of the movie work. The adulterous affair Pearl has with the hipster clothes salesman played by Viggo Mortensen would seem completely contrived if Lane wasn't making Pearl's longing and conflicted impulses so tangible. And while "A Walk on the Moon" might be part portrait of a traditionalist community under assault by Jimi Hendrix and the tragedy of tie-dyed T-shirts, it's the personal crises that make the movie so warm, and lift it far beyond ethnic fable.

Produced by Goldwyn, Dustin Hoffman and Jay Cohen, the movie is likely to have the same effect on audiences as "The Joy Luck Club," another film that was ethnically specific but struck a chord among many because its depiction of traditional family transcended any particular culture. In other words, you don't need the background to appreciate the sentiments.

Or the humor: The Kantrowitzes' bungalow colony—where Marty's mother Lilian (a scene-stealing Tovah Feldshuh) reads Tarot cards and the voice of Julie Kavner echoes across the lake with "M*A*S*H"-like announcements ("Attention: The knish man is on the premises ...")—is affectionately droll.   The sound track makes better use than most of the period's music (Janis Joplin's shredding of "Summertime" makes nice counterpoint to Pearl's erotic Waterloo).   And the performances are uniformly outstanding: Liev Schreiber, one of the best young actors around, imbues the unglamorous Marty with such dignity and sorrow that you have a real dilemma on your hands.   You sympathize with Pearl, you sympathize with Marty.   Oy.   "A Walk on the Moon" doesn't make it easy.   For many, it'll be like the '60s all over again.

SIGHT AND SOUND, 12/99, p. 61, Nina Caplan

New York, 1969.   Pearl and Marty Kantrowitz, with Marty's mother Lilian, take their kids—teenage Alison and young son Daniel—up to the Catskills resort where they spend every summer.   Marty returns to his job as television repairman during the week, leaving Pearl to get on with the rebellious Alison and simmer over the 60s excitements she has missed because of her early marriage.   When Marty gets stuck in the city, Pearl starts an affair with free-spirited resort employee Walker Jerome.   Meanwhile, a boy called Ross becomes Alison's first boyfriend.

Lilian challenges Pearl about her infidelity and reminds her of Marty's sacrifices—he jettisoned science studies when she got pregnant—so she breaks with Walker.   But when Marty can't bypass the Woodstock festival blockades, she goes to Woodstock with Walker, where Alison—there with Ross—spots her.   Summoned by his mother, Marty confronts Pearl.   She confesses her infidelity and Marty drives off enraged, returning unsuccessfully to snatch Daniel.   An upset Alison suggests sex to Ross, running off in tearful rage when he counsels against it.   She fights with her mother.   Pearl visits Walker, who asks her to come away with him.   They return to camp to find Daniel covered in wasp stings which Walker soothes.   A bitter Marty arrives.   When he leaves, Pearl bids goodbye to Walker.   Alison makes up with Ross.   Marty returns again, charmed by Pearl's present of a microscope, and they move towards a tentative reconciliation.

Just as the mock quotidian title suggests, this affectionate comedy examines seemingly banal actions (infidelity, teenage rebellion) taking place in extraordinary times whose consequences, like the moon landing itself, are more significant than the actions themselves.   60s housewife Pearl is desperate to launch into the sexual experimentation of the times while her television-repairman husband Marty has sublimated his intellectual curiosity to the immediate needs of a family with two children to feed.   While his career and her life have both fossilised, hippies occupy a parallel world: hitching on the highway as the luggage-laden Kantrowitzes drive out to their Catskills resort; wading naked into the resort's lake to the ineffectual, uncomprehending hostility of the residents.   Resort employee Walker Jerome has a backwards name suggestive of freedom despite the unglamorous trappings of his campervan.   He offers Pearl liberation in a tight tie-dye t-shirt, his wooden face and vacant smile making him a perfect recipient for her fantasies.

Teen actor cum debut director Tony Goldwyn (grandson of Sam Goldwyn) resists the temptation to mock Pearl's stolid, well-intentioned husband.   Marty hides his feelings behind a jokey exterior but, unlike Walker, he has feelings to hide.   Like the New York Jewish community summering in time-honoured fashion in the Catskills, his deceptively easy-going ethos is enclosed in moral barbed wire.   He'll accept anything that doesn't threaten the family, but he sees his wife's infidelity as a reversal of the natural order.

It isn't just Marty who is marked by Pearl's discontent.   Their mannered, graceless daughter Alison (prevented, by Anna Paquin's sensitive performance from degenerating into a caricatured adolescent) bears the brunt of her mother's hopes, but also of her envy, enjoying the liberating adolescence Pearl was deprived of.   Pearl and Walker's affair parallels Alison and Ross' more innocent relations, but the competition between mother and daughter sizzles: Pearl's *moués* and mannerisms are a prettier, leaner version of Alison's, who is equally desperate to escape the passivity that comes with obedience.   We voyeuristically watch the community watching the moonlandings and Pearl and Walker having colourful sex in the grey lunar light; Goldwyn slyly intercuts the enthusiastic applause for the astronauts with the couple's rather different performance.   From this washed-out beginning, everything brightens progressively, peaking in the slow-motion hedonism and sunlit bodypaint of Woodstock.   This time, the nominal voyeur is Alison, whose reaction suggesting sex to Ross—only narrowly escapes repeating history after the shock of watching her mother try to escape it.   The film is better at groups than at individuals: the Catskills community is lovingly drawn, the family unit convincing, but the personal dramas don't always bypass cliché.   There are too many heartfelt sentences beginning with

"Sometimes..." and the excellent 60s soundtrack is drowned out by the clunk of set-pieces slotting into place.

TIME, 4/12/99, p. 90, Richard Corliss

Perhaps you remember the episode of *The Honeymooners* where the Kramdens take a break from their marital fractiousness to go out dancing. When they get home, they warmly recall the sweet savor of their romantic prime. Ralph and Alice were, what—33, 35? Yet they saw their good old days as past; the greatest thrill they could have at their advanced age was to reminisce. *A Walk on the Moon*, set in the summer of 1969, raises similar issues: How young can you get old? And can you get young again? Pearl Kantrowitz (Diane Lane), who is maybe 32, thinks she's an old lady because she has a tepid husband Marty (Liev Schreiber) and a daughter Alison (Anna Paquin) who at 14 is revving up for the sexual adventures Pearl never enjoyed. She says of Alison, "I just hope she doesn't end up like us." Poor Pearl. In a Catskills bungalow not far from Woodstock, she feels she's already come to a dead end in her undramatic life story.

Enter romantic possibility—or, in a coming-of-middle-age tale like this, inevitability—in the lank person of Walker Jerome (Viggo Mortensen), a peddler they call "the blouse man." While the others watch Neil Armstrong walk on the moon, Pearl is in the back of the blouse man's truck becoming a giddy, blossoming girl again. A few weeks later, she goes with him to Woodstock, gets baptized in Day-Glo body paint and is spotted by a horrified Alison. My mother—the hippie whore!

The movie, written by Pamela Gray and directed by Tony Goldwyn, stretches plausibility to the snapping point. (In Woodstock, an impromptu city of 300,000 people that weekend, what are the odds you'd spot your mom with the blouse man? And, at the time of the moon landing, wasn't everyone talking about another little event that happened that weekend—Chappaquiddick?) It also lays on the Kantrowitzes' ethnicity too heavily; they are like chicken soup that's all schmaltz.

So you look past the gaffes and cliches into the heart of the performances. Here you find Paquin lending a tough intelligence to Alison's confusions; and Lane so all-American gorgeous she needn't act to be the center of every shot. She does act, though, and nicely. She locates Pearl's yearning in vagrant sighs and in sidelong glances at the big world exploding, outside her small one, into sex, drugs and eternal adolescence.

VILLAGE VOICE, 3/30/99, p. 130, Abby McGanney Nolan

Taking a provocative culture clash (hippies versus Catskills vacationers during 1969's Woodstock summer) and turning it into a fairly conventional sexual-awakening story, *A Walk on the Moon* gets a bit of a lift from the appealing choice (Viggo Mortensen or Liev Schreiber) faced by its protagonist. Diane Lane plays Pearl, a not-so-young married looking for a little liberation of her own—it's another in the quiet-life-upturned-by-turbulent-times series. With her husband (Schreiber) repairing TVs in New York during the week and her two kids watched over by her mother-in-law (Tovah Feldshuh), Pearl has some spare time for a flirtation that soon evolves into sex under a waterfall. Mortensen—these days the actor most likely to seduce willing wives—plays the free spirit she can't resist.

Actor Tony Goldwyn, making his directorial debut, lets his cast do the work for him, and they hold up well, with Schreiber nicely revealing the efforts that go into being a mensch. Lane is a bit more opaque, sympathetic in an underwritten role. Pamela Gray's screenplay, chockablock with the requisite period details and rounded out with all the music you'd expect, turns slightly ridiculous when the parallel mother-daughter romances run smack into each other at Woodstock, but, hey, I guess those were wild times. (As the daughter, Anna Paquin is suitably petulant, with some distracting down under inflections.) The film's title refers to that eventful summer's lunar landing, and a curious question is unintentionally posed about the close connection between Pearl's sex drive and outer-space events. Star power indeed.

Also reviewed in:
CHICAGO TRIBUNE, 4/2/99, Friday/p. A, Michael Wilmington
NEW YORK TIMES, 3/26/99, p. E24, Janet Maslin
NEW YORKER, 4/12/99, p. 111, David Denby

VARIETY, 3/8-14/99, p. 62, Glenn Lovell
WASHINGTON POST, 4/2/99, p. C1, Stephen Hunter
WASHINGTON POST, 4/2/99, Weekend/p. 42, Desson Howe

WALLOWITCH & ROSS: THIS MOMENT

A First Run Features release of a Karmic Release Ltd. production. *Executive Producer:* Nathan Purdee. *Producer:* Roberta Morris-Purdee. *Director:* Richard Morris. *Director of Photography:* Don Lenzer. *Editor:* Marsha Moore and Richard Morris. *Music:* John Wallowitch. *Sound:* Eddie L. O'Connor. *Running time:* 77 minutes. *MPAA Rating:* Not Rated.

WITH: John Wallowitch; Bertram Ross.

NEW YORK POST, 12/10/99, p. 54, Hannah Brown

A documentary focused on the New York cabaret scene runs the risk of being too in love with its subject, a little smug and insular.

But "Wallowitch & Ross: This Moment" manages to present an endearing portrait of a cabaret duo who formed an artistic and romantic partnership that has lasted over 30 years.

While they perform a nightclub act together, the two are better known for their solo careers.

John Wallowitch, a pianist and composer, is the author of many ballads and witty songs that have been recorded by performers such as Tony Bennett, including "Come a Little Closer."

Bertram Ross was a dancer and Martha Graham's muse for years.

Watching their act and hearing the story of their lives is like spending an evening in a sophisticated '40s musical comedy.

NEWSDAY, 12/10/99, Part II/p. B8, John Anderson

For the uninitiated the opening of "Wallowitch & Ross: This Moment" could be enough to curl the hair: Against a backdrop of newsclippings, posters, personal photos and pencil sketches we get two aging, tuxedoed musicians, more or less croaking their way through a quip-rich comedic cabaret number. Where can this possibly be going?

Straight to the heart, it turns out. The twosome, John Wallowitch and Bertram Ross, now in their 70s, have been together 30 years, performed together for less than that but have established themselves as more or less an institution on the Manhattan cabaret scene. But their personal histories are fascinating. And director Richard Morris has a well-founded confidence in his two subjects, allowing the men to tell their own story (while seducing the viewer) with stories, impromptu songs and anecdotes that range from their strained relationships with their mothers to their longtime Christmas Eve tradition of serenading Irving Berlin at his East Side home (which they still do, even though Berlin is dead).

Ross spent 30 years as the principal male dancer in the Martha Graham Dance Co., introducing countless roles until he resigned from the company in 1973. Wallowitch is a Juilliard-trained (or, as he'd put it, mis-trained) pianist who made his classical debut at Carnegie Hall but found his real calling writing the kind of smart sophisticated numbers that recall Noel Coward or, often, Berlin himself. In addition to the standards "This Moment" and "My Lover Went to London" (written for Ross) Wallowitch's more acerbic songs include "If You Don't Love Me I'll Kill Myself—or Maybe I'll Kill You" and his O.J. Simpson tribute, "I'm Stalking Behind You."

Together, they make ... well, not beautiful music, exactly. But certainly a beautiful love story.

VILLAGE VOICE, 12/14/99, p. 188, Nico Baumbach

John Wallowitch has made a career of composing highly credible, if perhaps less than distinctive, would-be pop standards. Now in his seventies and an old pro on the cabaret circuit, he expresses disappointment at never being offered his own Broadway show, but no matter, he's clearly in it for the love of the game. Watching Robert Morris's warm tribute of simply edited interviews and performance clips, one is inclined to give an old dog his day and make some excessive claim, painting him as, say, the unsung Cole Porter. Bertram Ross, Wallowitch's reticent partner, gets less airtime. Ross has less to do onstage as well, but he was once a remarkable dancer, Martha Graham's leading man. The romance between the two men, assumed though never stated as such, is the subtext that sustains both the film and the act. The pleasure of watching them perform has much to do with their own enjoyment, which, in turn, clearly owes much to the fact that they are performing together. Cole Porter or not, it's hard not to be moved by Wallowitch's "My Love Went to London" after watching the tears well up in his eyes as he recalls Ross's trip to London, which separated the two soon after they had met.

Also reviewed in:
NEW YORK TIMES, 12/10/99, p. E40, Stephen Holden
VARIETY, 1/25-31/99, p. 76, Lael Loewenstein

WAR ZONE, THE

A Lot 47 Films release of a Sarah Radclyffe Productions/Portobello Pictures production in association with Fandango and Mikado. *Executive Producer:* Eric Abraham. *Producer:* Sarah Radclyffe and Dixie Linder. *Director:* Tim Roth. *Screenplay (based in his novel):* Alexander Stuart. *Director of Photography:* Seamus McGarvey. *Editor:* Trevor Waite. *Music:* Simon Boswell. *Sound:* Robert Farr and (music) Geoff Foster. *Sound Editor:* Ian Wilson. *Casting:* Jina Jay and Sharon Howard-Field. *Production Designer:* Michael Carlin. *Art Director:* Karen Wakefield. *Special Effects:* Dave Beavis. *Costumes:* Mary Jane Reyner. *Make-up:* Ivana Primorac. *Stunt Coordinator:* Jim Dowall. *Running time:* 99 minutes. *MPAA Rating:* Not Rated.

CAST: Ray Winstone (Dad); Lara Belmont (Jessie); Freddie Cunliffe (Tom); Tilda Swinton (Mum); Annabelle Apsion (Nurse); Kate Ashfield (Lucy); Colin J. Farrell (Nick); Aisling O'Sullivan (Carol); Megan Thorp (Baby Alice); Kim Wall (Barman).

CHRISTIAN SCIENCE MONITOR, 12/10/99, p. 15, David Sterritt

Families and households have been at the heart of many recent movies, but that doesn't mean filmmakers are generally upbeat about the subject. Two of this week's releases present gloomy views of domestic life in two different centuries.

The War Zone is newsworthy because it marks the directorial debut of Tim Roth, one of today's most respected screen actors. Like some other actors-turned-directors in recent years, including Sean Penn and Gary Oldman, he has launched the new phase of his career with a drama about family life at its most emotionally harrowing.

The main characters are a married couple, their two teenage children, and a newborn daughter. They've recently moved from London to northern England and their adjustments to this change have been complicated by simmering hostilities between the generations. These escalate when 15-year-old Tom begins to suspect his 17-year-old sister is being sexually abused by their father. Tom tries to investigate the situation without causing additional pain, but tensions increase to a point where some kind of an explosion is inevitable.

The brilliant acting in "The War Zone" comes as little surprise, given Roth's expertise in this department. More unexpected is the cinematic skill he displays in telling this relentlessly bleak story without lapsing into either sensationalism or sentimentality.

This doesn't mean "The War Zone" is easy to watch—quite the opposite, since some scenes are unflinchingly graphic—but it does mean Roth has established himself as a very promising new director.

LOS ANGELES TIMES, 12/10/99, Calendar/p. 8, Eric Harrison

The jagged and starkly beautiful coastline of North Devon provides an evocative setting for "The War Zone," British actor Tim Roth's small-scale directing debut. The film is as severe and compelling—and, yes, in its harrowing way, as beautiful—as anything Roth trained his gaze upon in that rocky landscape.

The "war" to which the title alludes is waged, for the most part, internally, on bleak and emotionally craggy terrain. This makes it no less hellish or deadly, particularly when the conflict spills out into the larger arena of a seemingly contented middle-class home.

The film deals with incest. If the subject seems better suited to television, it's because that medium has staked an unwarranted claim on intimate stories. But television tepefies such material in the process of turning it into melodrama. "The War Zone" is decidedly unmelodramatic. Much of its strength resides in the way it eschews narrative contrivance. The movie observes behavior without explaining or judging it.

The family at the heart of this impressively acted drama has moved from London to Devon, where the father (Ray Winstone, best known here for "Nil by Mouth") struggles to reestablish a business. A sexually active 18-year-old daughter (Lara Belmont, in her first acting role) is looking forward to moving back to London to attend college. Her watchful younger brother (Freddie Cunliffe, also in his first role) wrestles with loneliness, his emerging sexuality and a troubling family secret. The mother (Tilda Swinton) gives birth to a third child early in the film. No more than this should be said about the plot.

Roth (a fine actor who has appeared in two Quentin Tarantino films and other movies, including "Rob Roy") and his cinematographer, Seamus McGarvey, and production designer, Michael Carlin, have done superlative work here. Not one shot escaped the filmmakers' exacting attention to detail. The chilly blue and green-tinged hues; the drab, cramped interiors; the empty outdoor spaces; the bare, grasping branches on gnarled and lonely trees—the images all conspire to tell us, even without words, that we've passed into a wintry wasteland of the soul.

The story is told largely through such painterly images and through behavior photographed in lingering shots. Like in real life, the reasons behind the characters' actions are not always immediately apparent. The effect is of watching lives unspool before an unobtrusive camera, the way truth may be revealed before the documentarian's gaze.

Alexander Stuart wrote the screenplay from his own novel, which was published in 1989 to immediate controversy and acclaim. Selected to receive the Whitbread Prize, the judges reportedly had the award withdrawn because of the subject matter. Perhaps to counter expected controversy over the movie, Roth talks in the film's production notes about its social significance, but such talk inevitably is reductive. The movie stands on its own.

The family is the story's obsessive focus, and because of this, characters on the periphery tend to blur. The script's reticence may be faulted for causing more confusion than is necessary about how one or two characters are related to the others. This is a minor quibble. Somewhat more serious is the way, when one looks back on the film, one bloody and shocking scene near the beginning juts out. In another type of movie, the scene's power might serve as its own justification. But in this film, which makes so few marketplace concessions, one struggles to find a valid reason for violating the movie's general atmosphere of restraint.

NEW YORK POST, 12/10/99, p. 54, Jonathan Foreman

In the fashion of directorial debuts by serious, talented English actors (think Gary Oldman's "Nil by Mouth"), Tim Roth's "The War Zone" is a relentlessly grim, rather heavy-handed drama of family dysfunction. In this case, the horror is father-daughter incest.

The film is weighed down by art-house mannerisms, including excessive, ludicrously unrealistic silences, under-lit scenes and pointless shots of people staring into space or walking through incessantly gloomy weather.

But it also includes some painterly photography and a simply outstanding performance by first-time actress Lara Belmont.

Tom (Freddie Cunliffe) is a sullen, pimply kid who has moved from London to the rocky coast of Devon with Dad (Ray Winstone), heavily pregnant Mum (Tilda Swinton) and sister Jessie

(Lara Belmont). He's taciturn and alienated even before he witnesses Dad doing something inappropriate with Jessie.

He breaks out of his glum silence to confront Jessie, but she points out that he's a virgin himself and has an unhealthy fascination with her sex life. Still, when Tom sees a weeping Jessie being sodomized by Dad in a old bunker on a cliff, it's clear he's eventually going to do something about it—even though he blames his sister for what's happening.

Somehow the film is both bleaker and yet less disturbing than Alexander Stuart's 1989 novel of the same title, even though the author himself adapted it for the screen. You're a witness to terrible things, but thanks to the minimalist, needlessly obscure writing you know so little about the people involved that it's hard to care about them.

The alienation born of this lack of information increases as the film rubs your face in incest as if anyone really needed to know how gross, cruel and vicious it is. It's all supposed to be unsparing, uncompromising, and so forth. But it comes perilously close to exploitation. While much in the story is hidden from you, you do get to see a great deal of Belmont's naked body.

Still, this film is saved from being merely a well-intentioned test of endurance by her extraordinary raw and heartfelt performance.

NEWSDAY, 12/10/99, Part II/p. B9, Jan Stuart

When some British actors take to film directing for the first time, it becomes an occasion for ruffling feathers and rattling cages. Two years back, Gary Oldman charged into the mire of domestic violence with alarming candor in "Nil By Mouth." And now Tim Roth tackles the subject of incest in "The War Zone" with a similarly unflinching gaze that will assuredly have many moviegoers shifting in their seats.

Where Oldman chose a gritty, cinema-verite style for his tale of spousal abuse, Roth employs an austerely beautiful wide screen canvas on which to paint a scalding portrait of a seemingly normal family with something seriously awry.

Sparingly scripted by Alexander Stuart from his controversial novel, "The War Zone" presents an unremarkable family that has just moved from London to a remote oceanside perch: a gentle businessman (Ray Winstone), his very pregnant wife (Tilda Swinton), their 17-year-old daughter, Jessie (Lara Belmont), and their 15-year-old son, Tom (Freddie Cunliffe). After a muted domestic prelude, the film takes off on a stunningly metaphoric note as Dad races Mum to the hospital and crashes the car, turning it upside down and forcing an on-the- spot delivery.

It won't be long before the family's life is turned topsy turvy as well. As if Tom doesn't have enough on his mind with acne and other pubescent disturbances, he suspects his sister is carrying on with his tirelessly nurturing dad. Polaroid photos offer the incriminating evidence and, in a gut-busting moment of final revelation, Tom catches Dad and a tearful Jessie in the confines of an abandoned bunker.

As Tom, Cunliffe's dour mask offers a mirror for our own sense of outrage and helplessness. Where movies such as "The Celebration" and "Happiness" pay lip service to the shocking phenomenon of community pillars abusing their children, "The War Zone" shoves the bad news in our faces, unfettered by peripheral characters or narrative window dressing. If anything, "The War Zone" is single-minded to a fault: We get no sense of these family members as being grounded to any other reality beyond each other.

But this is a formidable directing debut for Roth and a courageous feat on the part of his four leads. As the deluded father, Winstone is devastating. Previously the punch-drunk patriarch of "Nil by Mouth," he is no less frightening here for grafting a lamb's face onto a shark's body.

SIGHT AND SOUND, 9/99, p. 59, Xan Brooks

Mum, Dad and their teenaged children Tom and Jessie relocate from their native London to a cottage on the coast of Devon. Mum gives birth to a baby girl, Alice. Returning home one day, Tom looks through the window and sees Jessie taking a bath with Dad. Tom questions Jessie. Despite her assurances that the bath was innocent, Tom's suspicions are aroused. He hunts through Jessie's art-college portfolio and finds a photograph of his sister naked with Dad. Tom tracks Jessie to a concrete shelter on the cliff top. There he videotapes her unwillingly submitting to sex with Dad. Sickened, he tosses the camera into the sea. Again, Tom confronts Jessie. She invites him to punish her by holding a cigarette lighter to her bare breast. Dad travels up to London on business and a takes Tom and Jessie along with him. There, Jessie escorts Tom to meet her college friend Carol who attempts to seduce him.

Back in Devon, baby Alice falls ill and Mum stays with her at the hospital. During a visit, Tom warns Mum about Dad. Returning home, he finds Dad has already spoken to Mum on the phone and is panicked and angry. Even when Jessie confirms Tom's accusations, Dad denies he has done anything wrong. Tom stabs Dad and leaves him for dead. He and Jessie hide out in the shelter.

There is a key shot near the start of *The War Zone* where the camera dollies in towards the hunched form of Ray Winstone, crawls up close behind him as he chats into the telephone and scrutinises the back of his meaty neck. It is a *Peeping Tom* moment: the viewer cast simultaneously in the role of voyeur and potential threat. It both mimics the movements of the tale's adolescent onlooker and foreshadows his eventual knife-thrust denouement. The whole film seems to reside in that lone, lingering point in time. Adapted from the 1989 novel by Alexander Stuart, *The War Zone* can perhaps best be read as a kind of nightmare of adolescence. Fifteen-year old Tom is at once defined by his close-knit family and alienated from it his fledgling independence has repositioned him as an outsider looking in but, as yet, he lacks the experience to interpret confidently what he sees.

So while Tom effectively serves as our guide through *The War Zone,* his vision is dotted with blind spots. Significantly the audience is never allowed to witness the sight which first triggers his suspicions of incest (Dad and Jessie bathing), suggesting that the boy's initial conclusions could be misguided, coloured by his own charged and complex feelings for his sister. Even when the mystery is cleared away, the film's landscape stays foggy, its inhabitants oblique and unreadable. We are never certain, for example, if Jessie's London pal is also her lesbian lover, or if Mum is entirely unaware of Dad's doings. The film's *Play School*-style house is home to all manner of secrets. In *The War Zone*, what we aren't shown is often as important as what we are.

In making his directorial debut, Tim Roth has cited Alan Clarke as a primary influence. But unlike fellow Clarke graduate Gary Oldman (whose *Nil by Mouth* bore obvious Clarke hallmarks), Roth proves surprisingly free of the great man's coarse-grained, edgy style. Instead, his film feels more indebted to Russian or European art-house (Roth claims Tarkovsky and Bergman as other influences). Because despite its hothouse environment, there is a chill beauty to *The War Zone*. Its narrative is framed in elegant long shots and nudged along by spartan editing. Its characters—frequently naked—are posed like figures in a Lucien Freud canvas; all purplish breasts and dangling cock and balls.

Like Andrew Birkin's similarly themed 1993 *The Cement Garden, The War Zone* trades in a kind of trancey naturalism. Throughout it all Roth keeps the acting down-played, the dialogue murmurous, the atmosphere an ongoing ennui. Fittingly the cast come together as a study in neutrals. Newcomer Lara Belmont provides a magnificently restrained and unsettling performance as Jessie. Tilda Swinton makes a still and inscrutable Mum, while Ray Winstone's past pedigree in films such as *Nil by Mouth* ensures that his Dad fairly crackles with the implied threat of violence.

Only Freddie Cunliffe hits a false note at times in the taxing central role. His endless thousand-yard stare finally grows overdone. In the film's dying minutes you start to spot the mechanics behind his performance, and those behind *The War Zone* as a whole. Because what Roth has done is to garnish a fairly stock domestic drama (seemingly nice dad, deep, dark secret) with so much artful window-dressing, rearranging familiar furnishings in a minimalist *feng shui* styling. This becomes apparent only at the finish, with an explosive dramatic showdown that is the scene with the least impact in the entire picture. It is the moment when *The War Zone* tumbles back to earth; as though Roth felt that his perfectly maintained stasis had to pay off somehow. If so, he needn't have worried, because *The War Zone* is at its best in its most seemingly idle moments. This is where the real drama resides, where the real spell is cast, where the picture comes alive, those quiet times before the storm.

VILLAGE VOICE, 12/14/99, p. 180, Amy Taubin

Though movies trade in sex and violence, it's a rare film that faces up to the body as flesh—to its mottled colors, smothering weight, and all-too-evident mortality. In fetishizing the body, movies repress the signs of corporeality. The body was made virtual by the movies long before anyone conceived of cyberspace. On the other hand, the flesh, and the ambivalence we feel about it, is one of the great subjects in the history of painting.

In Tim Roth's *The War Zone,* bodies look the way they do in old master paintings, and they inspire as much repulsion as attraction. The bodies in question belong to the members of a seemingly ordinary nuclear family: a dad (Ray Winstone), a mum (Tilda Swinton), and their teenage children, Tom (Freddie Cunliffe) and Jessie (Lara Belmont). For reasons having to do with Dad's work, the family has recently relocated from London to a lonely house on the harsh Devon coast. No one except Dad is happy with the move, but no one except Dad has any power. Roth makes that evident with the first scene of the family in their small but comfy living room. Dad is the last to make an appearance. We hear him offscreen before we see him. His voice is like a magnet; it causes a barely visible shift in the arrangement of the three bodies already settled in the room.

Roth shapes his first feature like the most subtle of horror films. Something is amiss about this family, but we don't know what it is. Dad is an affable guy. He and Mum, who's hugely pregnant, seem to have a loving relationship. When Mum sponges down Dad's burly back in the kitchen sink, the kids shrink away from the unselfconscious spectacle of intimacy, but that might simply be a matter of unresolved Oedipal feelings. Later that night, Mum goes into labor and everyone bundles into the car. Driving like mad, Dad loses control of the wheel and the car flips upside down into a ditch where Mum, screaming in pain and terror, gives birth. The next morning in the hospital, everyone smiles at the new baby, but their faces are covered with purple bruises, red gashes, and black sutures. And now that we're focused on the flesh, we notice that 15-year-old Tom has a terrible case of acne.

It's Tom who guides us through the film. Tortured by adolescent sexual longings, Tom spies on Dad and Mum in bed (fat, middle-aged Dad caressing Mum's saggy, postpartum belly is not a pretty picture, but Rembrandt would have cherished it). And he can't take his eyes off his sulky sister Jessie's big boobs. Roth implicates us in Tom's confused incestuous longings and in his compulsive voyeurism. It makes us feel bad to look.

Films that deal with sexuality always risk an element of exploitation. Roth would have been in as much trouble if he'd never shown Jessie naked. Given his predilections as an actor, it was inevitable that he'd take a confrontational approach. It's the strategy of confrontation that's surprising. With its static, wide-screen compositions and its measured pace, the film keeps us at a distance. Because we can't lose ourselves in it, we become extremely aware of our own relationship to the horrific story unfolding before our eyes. And no matter what that relationship is, it's a harrowing experience. The style of The *War Zone* has been compared to Tarkovsky and Bergman. And while it's true that the expressive, painterly quality of both the harsh, forbidding landscapes and the deceptively warm, closeted interiors have an art-film patina, the strongest influence on Roth is the late British television director Alan Clarke, who employed a similarly cool, distanced perspective in such hot-topic films as *Christine* (about teenage junkies) and *Elephant* (about assassination in Northern Ireland).

The ensemble of accomplished and untried actors come together as if they were indeed a real family. Winstone gives his most nuanced performance as the Dad in denial and Swinton, in a less demanding role, is just as subtle and brave. But it's the kids who are the revelation. Though Cunliffe and Belmont had never acted before, they bring a level of concentration, intensity, and openness that would be remarkable in old pros. Roth knows how to get what he wants from his actors but he also respects their freedom and trusts what they bring.

The horror at the heart of the film is incest. Peering through the slit in a disused World War II bunker perched high on a cliff overlooking the shore, Tom sees his father anally rape his sister. The sight more than fulfills his—and our—worst expectations. But there's more unraveling to come. *The War Zone* is a brutal, unsparing, high-risk film. It forces us to look at things we'd prefer not to examine closely. We may not want another film about incest, but there's a necessity about this one that won't be denied.

Also reviewed in:
CHICAGO TRIBUNE, 1/14/00, Friday/p. A, Barbara Shulgasser
NEW YORK TIMES, 12/10/99, p. E10, Janet Maslin
VARIETY, 2/8-14/99, p. 77, Emanuel Levy

WELCOME BACK, MR. McDONALD

A Viz Films/Tidepoint Pictures release of a Fuji Television Network/Toho Company production. *Producer:* Chiaki Matsushita, Hisao Masuda, Takashi Ishihara, and Kanjiro Sakura. *Director:* Koki Mitani. *Screenplay (Japanese with English subtitles):* Koki Mitani. *Based on the play "Radio no jikan" by:* Koki Mitani and Tokyo Sunshine Boys. *Director of Photography:* Kenji Takama and Junichi Tozawa. *Editor:* Hirohide Abe. *Music:* Takayuki Hattori. *Sound:* Tetsuo Segawa. *Art Director:* Tomio Ogawa. *Running time:* 103 minutes. *MPAA Rating:* Not Rated.

CAST: Toshiaki Karasawa (Kudo); Kyoka Suzuki (Miyako Suzuki); Masahiko Nishimura (Ushijima); Keiko Toda (Nokko Senbon); Takehiko Ono (Ben Noda); Shiro Namiki (Suguru Hosaka); Yasukiyo Umeno (Furukawa); Jun Inoue (Hiromitsu); Yoshimasa Kondo (Miyako's Husband); Hiromasa Taguchi (Tatsumi); Moro Morooka (Bucky); Akira Fuse (Horinouchi); Toshiyuki Hosokawa (Hamamura Jo); Ken Watanabe (Truck Driver); Shunji Fujimura (Security Guard).

LOS ANGELES TIMES, 9/17/99, Calendar/p. 14, Kenneth Turan

"Welcome Back, Mr. McDonald" is an unexpected name for a Japanese film, but on the other hand there's never been a Japanese film exactly like this one. A classic screwball farce graced with high energy and wonderful comic timing, "Mr. McDonald" is as genuinely funny as it is surprising, and that is saying a lot.

"Welcome Back, Mr. McDonald" (it's not until the film's over that you appreciate or even understand the title) is the directing debut for its screenwriter, Koki Mitani. He was the founder of Tokyo Sunshine Boys, described as an avant-garde theater troupe, and this film is based on a play called "Radio Time" that he wrote and directed for his actors' gang.

Though almost every event in it takes place on one large set, the studio of a Tokyo radio station, "Mr. McDonald" doesn't feel hampered by its surroundings. Traditional screwball comedies like "The Front Page" also had a limited number of physical settings, and the clever work of the film's ensemble diverts our attention from the location.

The film begins just as the final rehearsal of a contest-winning radio drama, "Woman of Destiny," is winding down. It's a silly and soap romantic triangle, with lines like "This is not the beginning of the end, just the end of the beginning," and at precisely midnight it will be broadcast live over the network. "Unusual, isn't it?" says producer Ushijima (Masahiko Nishimura) of the live transmission. "But life demands adventure." Little does he know ...

Aside from this obsequious character, "McDonald" is peopled by a number of other expertly realized types. These include Nokko Senbon (Keiko Toda), a temperamental diva of a leading lady; Hiromitsu (Jun Inoue), her self-absorbed co-star; Kudo (Toshiaki Karasawa), the otherwise sensible director with a weakness for expensive sweaters; Horinouchi (Akira Fuse), the spineless executive producer; and, finally, Miyako Suzuki (Kyoka Suzuki), the earnest writer.

A housewife in sensible shoes, she only won the contest because no one else entered. "I'll surely remember this night as long as I live," Miyako says early on, not dreaming exactly why that will be true.

It's Nokko, probably just looking to be difficult, who starts the trouble. Her character's name, Ritsuko, troubles her: Why can't she be called Mary Jane? Her co-star, not to be outdone, wants an American name, too, and, with the help of a handy hamburger bag, he eventually becomes Donald McDonald.

Changes of the kind poor Miyako never dreamed possible overwhelm her simple script. Soon the setting is changed from the humble Japanese village of Atami to Manhattan, Mary Jane goes from being the hostess of a pachinko parlor to a high-powered defense attorney, Donald from a simple fisherman to a dashing pilot, and the sweet love story soon involves machine guns, bursting dams, rocket launches and characters named Heinrich and Giuseppi. No sooner does the eager-to-please Ushijima say, "Nothing else has to change," than something else does.

Though this situation may sound too flimsy to sustain an entire feature, it's one of writer-director Mitani's gifts that he knows how to let the comic momentum build. He also periodically brings in new and amusing characters, like the Hawaiian shirt-wearing Bucky (Moro Morooka), the show's demon rewrite man, and an ancient security guard (Shunji Fujimura) who turns out to be an expert at producing radio special effects. There's even an amusing cameo for veteran Japanese star Ken Watanabe as, a long-distance truck driver who may be the drama's only listener and biggest fan.

Periodically, one or another of these characters makes a speech about how much radio drama means to him or her, and though those are played for laughs, filmmaker Mitani's obvious fondness for the genre is what sustains the comic edifice he's built. And while the screwball form is quite Western, it's how stereotypically Japanese the characters are—concerned with apologizing, accommodating and saving face—that adds a final twist to this completely delightful situation.

NEW YORK POST, 9/8/99, p. 42, Jonathan Foreman

Moviegoers generally don't associate Japanese films with comedy (of the intentional kind), but "Welcome Back, Mr. McDonald" could change all that.

It's a farcical sitcom set in a Tokyo radio station and it really is funny. In a gentle—and fascinating—way it also takes some well-aimed shots at Japan's rigid social codes.

Miyako (Kyoka Suzuki), a mousy, deferential housewife, is thrilled when the sappy romantic play she has written—"woman of destiny" wins a radio-station contest and is scheduled to be broadcast live.

But just before the show is to begin, the spoiled lead actress Nokko (Keiko Toda) insists that the script be changed.

Mr. Ushijima (Masahiko Nishimura), the craven producer of the show, gives in to her first demand: that her character be renamed Mary Jane; then a second demand, that Mary Jane be a trial lawyer rather than a fisherman's wife; and then a third, that the whole play be set in New York instead of a tiny Japanese fishing village.

The male lead then demands that his character also be given a Western name. Other actors also demand huge changes to their roles.

Some of the broadcast crew are as outraged as poor Miyako at the violence being done to her play, while others don't care, as long as the show goes on. But with each commercial break the actors demand more changes and each change forces further alterations in the basic story until the crew has to find a way to simulate sounds for machine-gun fire, a dam collapse and a rocket ship launch.

Eventually, Miyako cannot take any more rewriting of her script and commits a desperate act of defiance, setting off a chain of rebellions and throwing everything into chaos.

Writer-director Koki Mitani gets perfectly pitched performances from his cast and moves the action along so quickly that you barely notice how familiar the basic plot is.

There are moments when the humor feels a little over the top, but for the most part it translates just fine for American tastes. And you can easily imagine "Welcome Back, Mr. McDonald" being remade by Hollywood.

VILLAGE VOICE, 9/14/99, p. 133, J. Hoberman

Koki Mitani's *Welcome Back, Mr. McDonald,* the wacky backstage radio-drama drama currently at Film Forum, is a more genteel sideshow than *Black Cat, White Cat*—as well as more self-reflexive in its musings.

Having won first prize as the only contestant to enter an amateur script-writing competition, a timorous housewife is having her play performed on the air. But, due to circumstances beyond her control (star egos, sponsor sensitivities, and a series of escalating, irreversible blunders), *A Woman of Fate* is subjected to numerous last-minute revisions-mutating, in the course of its broadcast, from sappy romance melodrama to outlandish extraterrestrial disaster epic.

The comedy is broad but self-contained, mainly because virtually the entire movie is played out within the confines of the radio station—every so often, Mitani cuts away to the Stetson-wearing trucker who represents the radio audience. As the show's imagined locations fluctuate and its protagonists change their occupations or even identities (the title comes from one actor's postprandial inspiration to rename his character "Donald McDonald"), the producers race to solve the various problems—stalling for time with extra news breaks or prolonged ad-libbing, as they rush to improvise, for example, the sound of one dam breaking.

Mitani likes to move his camera and the film's visual choreography is considerably better than the jokes. The overall cuteness is further accentuated by a syrupy score and the cast's relentlessly overacted overacting. Even more than *Black Cat, White Cat,* each frame is crammed with a crew of face-pulling hambones playing easily reducible types—the pompous announcer, flighty diva, doltish husband, perky secretary, vain actor, cynical director, flaky assistant, mousy hausfrau.

Here, too, momentum peaks well before the closer—a deus ex machina reinforced by the arrival of the overwrought audience-surrogate in his giant rig. Throughout, Mitani has made much of the radio performers' overidentification with their roles. This is nothing compared to how he imagines their listeners. *Welcome Back, Mr. McDonald's* happy ending is a paean less to the power of make-believe than to the presumed idiocy of the audience.

Also reviewed in:
CHICAGO TRIBUNE, 10/29/99, Friday/p. H, Michael Wilmington
NEW YORK TIMES, 9/8/99, p. E1, Stephen Holden
VARIETY, 3/9-15/98, p. 42, Derek Elley

WEST BEIRUT

A Cowboy Booking International release of a La Sept Art3, 3B Production. *Producer:* Rachid Bouchareb and Jean Bréhat. *Director:* Ziad Doueiri. *Screenplay (Arabic and French with English subtitles):* Ziad Doueiri. *Director of Photography:* Richard Jacques Gale. *Editor:* Dominique Marocombe. *Music:* Stewart Copeland. *Sound:* Nicolas Cantin, Thierry Sabatier, and (music) Jeff Seitz. *Sound Editor:* Ulrike Laub. *Costumes:* Pierre Matard. *Make-up:* Heidi Baumberger. *Running time:* 105 minutes. *MPAA Rating:* Not Rated.

CAST: Rami Doueiri (Tarek Noueiri); Mohammad Chamas (Omar); Rola Al Amin (May); Carmen Lebbos (Hala Noueiri); Joseph Bou Nassar (Riad Noueiri); Liliane Nemry (Nahida); Leila Karam (Oum Walid); Mahmoud Mabsout (Hassan); Hassan Farhat (Milicien Zeytouni); Fadi Abou Khalil (Darwiche).

LOS ANGELES TIMES, 9/3/99, Calendar/p. 4, Kenneth Turan

"West Beirut" is, literally, another country heard from. It's not only that Lebanon, all but destroyed by more than a decade of civil war, has sent hardly any films to the wider world, but that the entirety of Arabic-speaking cultures rarely appears on American screens. This new film, honest, authentic and heartfelt, gives us a sense of what we've been missing.

"West Beirut" is written and directed by Ziad Doueiri, a 36-year-old filmmaker who studied at UCLA and has been part of the camera crew on all of Quentin Tarantino's films. His is an autobiographical film based on his coming-of-age years in Beirut, but in both setting and, more important, attitude, it couldn't be further away from the kind of self-indulgent moroseness that similar American films project.

Teenage Tarek (effectively played by Rami Doueiri, the filmmaker's brother) is that instantly recognizable type, the class clown, the kind of guy who can't help but smirk when his teacher, in this case a humorless disciplinarian at the city's French-speaking high school, bawls him out for his insubordinate nature.

But while Tarek is exiled in the hall for being a troublemaker, he sees something out the window that will change his life: A group of hooded gunmen inexplicably massacres the passengers on a local bus. It is April 13, 1975, the start of Lebanon's civil war.

For Tarek's lawyer mother, Hala (Carmen Lebbos), and father Riad (Joseph Bou Nassar), this conflict, even in a city that had known many, is hard to understand. "They'll send some Americans to do a little negotiating and it's over," Riad says, but it turns out to be hardly that simple. In fact, the city is soon divided into warring halves, Christian East Beirut and Muslim West Beirut, and passage between them occurs only at very real risk to your life.

At first Tarek and his best friend, the short but high-energy Omar (Mohammad Chamas), can't focus on these adult concerns. All they know is that school is closed for the duration, leaving them more time to indulge in their joint passion for Super-8 filmmaking.

"West Beirut" is especially good at providing an affectionate portrait of these guys just hanging out, smoking, listening to American music, spinning sexual fantasies and trying to figure out life. What sets this apart from similar autobiographical forays is that writer-director Doueiri is able to remain noticeably cleareyed, not indulgent, in looking backward, presenting characters for exactly who they are, irritations and all.

Slowly, partly because he becomes infatuated with the beautiful Catholic refugee girl May (Rola Al Amin), who moves into his building—an irked and slightly displaced Omar calls her "the Virgin Mary"—Tarek comes to an understanding of what is happening to his city and his family. Though still spaced-out enough at times to have people yell at him, "What planet are you from?," Tarek reluctantly grasps that nothing will ever be simple again.

Given that "West Beirut" is essentially an episodic film, a series of loosely connected incidents, it's fortunate that Doueiri has both a gift for creating vivid, eccentric characters and enabling his actors, who range from children cast from orphanages to some of Lebanon's most respected professionals, to realize his words.

There's the celebrated madam Oum Walid (Leila Karam), a manic neighborhood baker (Mahmoud Mabsout) and a hefty, sharp-tongued neighbor (Liliane Nemry) who has command of a variety of memorable curses like "May Allah spread pain all over you" and the always popular "Your son is a blood clot in my vein."

This verbal expressiveness ("You're shish-kabobing me on a small flame," someone complains) is part of the reason Doueiri is able to accomplish so much with "West Beirut." He conveys a sense of what his city was like during the turmoil and how it was for teenagers finding their way in a world where gunfire can be counted on to punctuate everything.

As always, it's a grounding in specific reality that makes something ring universally true.

NEW STATESMAN, 7/26/99, p. 38, Jonathan Romney

In some respects, Ziad Doueiri's first feature is the sort of male coming-of-age film that could have been made anywhere in the world. The adolescent hero hangs out with his best buddy, listens to 1970s soul, gets the hots for the new girl in his block and has the thrill of his life when he accidentally finds himself in the legendary local brothel. But we're more than one step away from *Porky's* territory here: Doueiri's spirited sentimental education is set in Beirut in 1975, at the start of the Lebanese civil war. *West Beirut* is a classic example of the "first film" genre, if there is such a thing—one of those stories in which film-makers reveal, expressly or incidentally, how they came to be film-makers. According to Doueiri, his film is 90 per cent autobiographical, and you wonder whether that's an underestimate: his protagonist's surname is Noueiri and he is played by the director's own younger brother.

The film begins in April 1975, as two Muslim boys, Tarek (Rami Doueiri) and his best friend Omar (Mohammad Chamas), stand in the playground of Beirut's French high school and point their Super-8 camera at the fighter planes above. By the next morning, the city has been divided into Christian and Muslim zones, with militia patrolling every corner. For the boys it's all a lark, and life goes on—there are comic neighbours to be spied on, classmates to be taunted and Omar's glamorous young aunt to be ogled. It's teenage lust that provides their initiation into the new hell they live in: they are trying to get their film of the aunt's cleavage developed when they encounter their first menacing patrol.

Doueiri, who has lived in the States since 1983, put in several years working on Quentin Tarantino's crews before making his first feature. But if the visual confidence and pacing suggest an American education, there's also a strong French influence (the film is in fact a French co-production), as befits a film that addresses the aftermath of French colonialism. In the opening school scenes, Tarek cheerfully sabotages the "Marseillaise", then twits his French teacher, who could have walked straight out of Truffaut's *Les Quatre Cent Coups;* she responds with a stiff lecture about how Lebanon owes everything to France. As if on cue, the first gunshots are heard. French colonialist pride is later lampooned in the form of a crowing rooster. Tarek grumbles about having to learn his Corneille, but Doueiri airs his French influences with pride: there's a strong hint of Vigo's *Zéro de Conduite* in Tarek's opening salvo on school decorum, while the Truffaut echoes extend to a bike ride *à trois* that's pure *Jules et Jim.*

Doueiri's film is acute in its observations of the way that people, especially the young, resist changes imposed by history and imperviously go on pursuing their usual occupations. For Tarek and Omar, the collapse of the recognised order is a liberating rush that allows them to devote further energies to their prime obsessions. Their lives are ruled by American disaster movies, girls and an adolescent homoeroticism that Doueiri handles beautifully.

In one scene, Omar winds Tarek up with a hot story about his aunt: the powerful frisson between the boys vanishes only when Omar deflates the tension right at the last minute. It's awkward that the third corner of the triangle—the Christian girl called May (Rola Al Amin), whose crucifix pendant proves a liability in the Muslim side of town—has little to do. But then, that rather fits with the way the boys sideline her as they cultivate their burgeoning machismo: Tarek, out with May for the first time, insists on greeting every local character they pass, like a Scorsese wiseguy glad-handing the neighbourhood.

The sense of collapse, when it finally dawns on them, is heralded by ominous domestic signs: suddenly Omar's father insists that his easy-going Muslim family start reading the Koran and even condemns rock'n'roll as evil ("is Paul Anka the work of Satan?" the boys worry). Tarek's intellectual liberal parents are left stranded and confused and helpless: tenderly played by Carmen Lebbos and Joseph Bou Nassar, they get more space for intimacy than parents are usually allotted in such memoirs, and Doueiri is careful not to over-milk the irony of the father's insistence that everything will soon return to normal. Where other directors would make these scenes pay off with a tragic shock, Doueiri orchestrates the film's emotional climax around a subtle and understated *coup de cinéma* at the very end.

Rami Doueiri as Tarek is a natural, swaggering along in his flares or launching into barrages of sly face-pulling; he must have cheeked his director brother something rotten throughout the shoot. Mohammad Chamas as his mouthy, dimunitive sidekick is even better, an abrasive Joe Pesci to Tarek's De Niro. They're a terrific double act, especially considering how tough it must be for teenage actors to cast the machismo aside and suggest a vulnerable, equivocal intimacy.

More memoir than history lesson, the film doesn't spell out a great deal about the forces that transform Beirut, but it gives you a strong sense of the city (or, at least, half of it) as a lived in place. Mixing its intimate good humour with something of the urgency of Pontecorvo's *The Battle of Algiers, West Beirut* conveys the feel of life as usual in a war zone.

NEW YORK POST, 9/3/99, p. 51, Rod Dreher

Beirut, 1975. For teenager Tarek Noueiri, coming of age as Lebanese society is coming apart, the Talking Heads song got it all wrong: Life during wartime is a party, it is a disco, it is about fooling around.

That's the surprising insight that writer-director Ziad Doueiri brings to "West Beirut," his debut film and autobiography of his younger years growing up in the city's Muslim sector.

As John Boorman revealed in "Hope and Glory," the violence and chaos of war can be fun for kids, for whom its most salient fact might be: School's out forever!

The often humorous "West Beirut" limns the political conflicts that inspired the savagery, but it doesn't have an agenda—or, for that matter, a plot.

Doueiri is more interested in pasting together a collage of images and experiences that suggest what it's like to be a teenage boy, dealing with normal teenage-boy issues (girls, pop music, overbearing parents), as your city is being shot to hell.

Tarek (Rami Doueiri, the director's brother) is a smarty-pants rebel who shares a flat with his parents, both professionals. He pals around with classmate Omar (Mohammad Chamas), with whom he ogles babes, smokes cigarettes, dances to cheesy Western pop and makes Super-8 movies.

When the war begins, Tarek and Omar gallivant all over town, getting into dangerous scrapes with militiamen, hilariously stumbling into a brothel and marching in street protests for lack of anything more exciting to do. The boys don't seem to grasp what's happening to their society.

But when Tarek falls for a new neighbor, a Christian girl named May (Rola Al Amin, the Winnie Cooper of the Levant), the sectarian hatred that has partitioned Beirut into the Muslim East and the Christian West comes home.

"West Beirut" rambles, but Doueiri's scenes linger long after you've left the theater. In the film's most poignant scene, Tarek's father (Joseph Bou Nassar) softly reminds his son that the Arabs were once a great and learned people.

Now they're destroying themselves with hatred, and are dismissed as barbaric trash by Westerners.

It's a heartbreaking moment. And it makes you wonder why we never see Muslims like this in the movies.

NEW YORK POST, 3/27/99, p. 21, Thelma Adams

In fourth grade, I saw snow for the first time. We ran to the school windows, curious, excited. We climbed over each other to see the rare San Diego snow.

In Ziad Doueiri's lively, episodic "West Beirut," a bored class of Lebanese middle-schoolers run to the windows. They have heard gunshots. Curious, excited, the students jockey for position. In the street below, masked gunmen slaughter a busload of passengers.

That day in 1975 signals the beginning of war's long winter. Gunfire splits the cosmopolitan capital between Muslim-controlled West Beirut and Christian East.

For Muslim teens Tarek (the director's brother Rami), his filmmaking pal Omar (Mohammad Chamas) and their Christian friend May (Rola Al Amin), school's out for war. Their lives continue in coming-of-age cliches; they smoke and make super-8mm movies while their hormones rage, relishing their newfound freedom.

Writer-director Doueiri makes the experience of these class cut-ups both universal and specific. In one funny image, the boys strut down their bomb-shredded streets in bell-bottoms, in a nod to "Saturday Night Fever." Later, as the war lengthens, Omar's increasingly fundamentalist father cuts his son off from movies and Western music. Omar asks Tarek: "Is Paul Anka the work of Satan?"

While the boys adjust to war's awkward rhythms, Tarek's mom Hala (Carmen Lebbos) crumbles like their neighborhood. The vivid redhead conveys the fear of a cosmopolitan adult who sees her world and her family caught in the crossfire of a religious conflict in which she has no stake.

By trying to preserve life as it was, Hala has the most at risk. It's the mother's plight that clings to us like gunpowder, long after we've left "West Beirut."

NEWSDAY, 9/3/99, Part II/p. B3, John Anderson

What planet are you from?" an astonished brothel owner (Leila Karam) asks the audacious Tarek (Rami Doueiri), after the teenager somehow sneaks into her place of business. "West Beirut," the smiling Tarek tells her, as if from across the universe, or several states of mind.

The creation of East and West sectors of the city during the Syrian-Israeli war in 1975—East for Christians, West for Muslims—was, aside from being lethal, repugnant to the more westernized inhabitants of that Lebanese port; it destroyed ways of life, relationships, traditions.

And it gives the title of Ziad Doueiri's "West Beirut" more than a little irony. What, it asks, would have become of anyone had the war never come, most essentially Tarek—who at one point interrupts the singing of "La Marseillaise" at his French high school to sing the Lebanese anthem instead (a clever riposte to Paul Henreid's similar scene in "Casablanca")?

What if, by some miracle, the nonwarring inhabitants of Beirut had known what was to come? Like the Jews who refused to leave Germany because they believed they lived in a country where a Holocaust could never happen—or, more mistakenly, believed that it was their country—the intellectual and cultural elite of Lebanon refuse to go on principles that no longer have a foundation in society, because there is no society. And they get sucked into the irreversible vortex of religious hate and bloodlust.

Director-writer Doueiri, who was born in Lebanon in 1963—and whose central character, Tarek Noueiri, is played by his brother, Rami—is not in pursuit of angry catharses. His is a movie about the people whose lives are changed because they are too few and too removed.

Stereotypes are few: Tarek's family falls far wide of the teenage movie model. His father Riad (Joseph Bou Nassar) is a farming intellectual; his mother, Hala (Carmen Lebbos) is a lawyer. Although both their livelihoods are destroyed as the city is destroyed, their love—and sexual hunger—for each other remains.

Tarek's friend Omar (Mohammad Chamas), with whom he roams the city taking Super-8 movies and jive-dancing to American pop music, is a sawed-off dynamo whose diatribes about Tarek's death-defying incursions into East Beirut sound hysterical, but are simply rooted in fact—as is his initial resistance to Tarek's girlfriend, May (Rola Al Amin), a Christian whose crucifix might as well be a sign around her neck saying "shoot me."

It's not really personal with Omar. It's just survival.

"West Beirut," which begins with schoolboys watching an air fight between Syrian and Israeli pilots and ends with the war invading the living room, is an often frisky, always adventurous film that unfolds flawlessly, with characters and characterizations you never question, points that are made without bombast or bile and that may sincerely make you believe you're watching a teenager coming of age amid a city coming apart.

The effect is enhanced by the fact that Rami Doueiri visibly matures throughout the course of the film. But then there's also his performance, which is both rebelliously free and ultimately heartbreaking.

SIGHT AND SOUND, 8/99, p. 56, Geoffrey Macnab

Beirut, Lebanon, 1975. As fighting breaks out between the Lebanese Muslims and the Christian militias, the city is split in two: East Beirut is Christian-controlled and West Beirut is Muslim. The social and political upheaval has a dramatic effect on the life of Tarek, a teenager at school, and his parents. His mother wants to leave Beirut but his father is determined to stay.

At first, Tarek relishes the disruption since it means he can escape school. He runs amok in the bombed-out streets with his friend Omar and May, a beautiful young Christian girl. Tarek and Omar have a Super-8 camera, but the store which develops their films is on the other side of town. Tarek ventures across no-man's land, a dangerous zone. On one of his missions, he comes across a famous brothel where Christians and Muslims alike are welcome and where he meets Madam Oum Walid, who is amazed by his audacity and treats him with kindness. The months pass and the war shows no sign of ending.

Bombed-out cities make wonderful playgrounds, and it's this paradox which writer-director Ziad Doueiri (who himself grew up in the war-torn Beirut of the mid 70s) explores to such rich effect in his debut feature. While their parents are tearing their hair out in grief and fear, the children run amok, relishing the anarchy which war brings. Doueiri's background as Quentin Tarantino's assistant cameraman has been much hyped by the publicists, but *West Beirut* owes less to *Reservoir Dogs* than to the kind of naturalistic, street-level cinema patented by the neorealists in the 50s. Doueiri is equally adept at showing the tensions between neighbours living on top of one another as the divisions within the city as a whole.

There is also conflict between generations—while Christians battle against Muslims, adolescents are pitted against their elders. In one of the very first scenes, the teenage protagonist Tarek refuses to sing the French anthem at his school assembly. Robustly played by the director's younger brother Rami Doueiri, Tarek is a renegade with the same disdain for authority that Truffaut's Antoine Doinel showed in *The 400 Blows* (1959). For all his bravado, he is sensitive enough to understand the strains the war is placing on his parents' marriage. Doueiri never lets us forget what a calamity the war is. Tarek's long-suffering but philosophical father insists it is just another episode in the chequered history of Beirut, a city riven by violence many times before. He seems to believe that if the family endures long enough, the violence will go away—but, of course, that's not going to happen.

Without going into exhaustive detail about why the fighting between Beirut's Muslims and Christians broke out, Doueiri shows its effects. Militia men mount roadblocks at street corners. We see a massacre of bus passengers. As bread supplies become short, crowds swell outside the bakery. Rows break out for almost no reason. The war zone has its own conventions, some of them painfully absurd. In no-man's land, bras stand in for white flags and no sniper will shoot at anybody brandishing one, which fascinates Tarek, his curiosity about sex quickly mounting.

West Beirut is not only a chronicle of a city at war but also a rites-of-passage story and a study of young friendship. Tarek and his friend Omar roam around the city in search of adventure, sometimes with a young Christian girl in tow. This is very much an insider's vision of Beirut. The director knows the city as intimately as the people who inhabit it. The storytelling isn't exactly impressionistic, but we're given little sense of time passing or of a narrative building up to a conventional ending. Instead, Doueiri offers us a series of lyrical snapshots of the world of his childhood. The film finishes in oblique fashion, with the implication that one of Tarek's family died in the civil war. Doueiri doesn't need to spell matters out—the sense of loss and yearning felt by those caught in this divided city is always apparent.

VILLAGE VOICE, 9/7/99, p. 118, Dennis Lim

The freshest aspect of Ziad Doueiri's largely autobiographical first feature, *West Beirut*, is its offhand acknowledgment that war zones can be perversely fun—not least if you're a hormonal teen with a Super-8 camera. Like its close antecedent, John Boorman's Blitz-time *Hope and Glory*, *West Beirut* gets across this deceptively slight point without seeming glib or irresponsible. Set during the Lebanese civil war, Doueiri's film captures the initial liberating thrill of anarchy and chaos but also, no less acutely, the creeping onset of fear, helplessness, and claustrophobia.

The 15-year-old protagonist, Tarek (Rami Doueiri, the director's brother), is established in the opening moments as a wiseass prankster, interrupting the singing of the "Marseillaise" at school with a megaphone rendition of the Lebanese national anthem. Dismissed from class for insolence one day, he witnesses the massacre of a busload of Muslims by masked militia—it's April 1975, the start of the war between Muslims and Christians that leaves Beirut torn in two.

For the first hour or so, *West Beirut* revels in a peculiar kind of idyll. School's out—indefinitely—so Tarek and his friend Omar (Mohammad Chamas) get right to the business of living dangerously. They strut about in their bell-bottoms, turn Omar's camera on what's happening around them, risk their lives in an attempt to reach the only lab in Beirut that processes Super-8 film. The boys, both Muslim, are sometimes accompanied by May, a Christian girl from the Muslim west, whom Tarek plainly worships. Indeed, sexual curiosity often serves as a prime motivation for Tarek's adventures, one of which leads him to a legendary brothel, situated in a no-man's-land where items of women's underwear double as white flags.

As the war drags on, religion impinges for the first time on the consciousness of these pop-culture-raised teens, who'd rather live in a world of movie posters and disco 45s. (Tarek mockingly wonders, "Is Paul Anka the work of Satan?") The most resonant scenes in *West Beirut* deal with such day-to-day microshifts, in particular the ones that depict Tarek's home life, as the only son of devoted, intellectual parents. His mother is a lawyer, tormented by the thought of losing her family, his father is an academic who refuses to leave his homeland.

Sketchy and scruffy, *West Beirut* does lose focus occasionally. Many of its rites-of-passage setups are conventional, and some of the attempts at humor are botched (comic relief too often consists of high-volume neighborhood arguments), but on the whole, Doueiri demonstrates surefootedness as a storyteller. He's also not lacking in formal ideas. Time is elided, chronology suggested only obliquely with inserts of news footage (the movie apparently spans eight years, but the characters never seem to age). The structure is episodic, though not typically so—each vignette, far from self-contained, is a little ragged on the edges, and all the more vivid for it. Rich in incidental detail, short on political context, *West Beirut* plays more like a memory piece than a historical document, its rough-hewn urgency in the service of impressionistic intimacy as much as harsh realism.

Also reviewed in:
CHICAGO TRIBUNE, 3/31/00, Friday/p. J, Michael Wilmington
NATION, 9/27/99, p. 34, Stuart Klawans
NEW REPUBLIC, 9/27/99, p. 30, Stanley Kauffmann
NEW YORK TIMES, 9/3/99, p. E25, Janet Maslin
NEW YORKER, 9/6/99, p. 88, Anthony Lane

VARIETY, 6/1-7/98, p. 37, Lisa Nesselson
WASHINGTON POST, 8/25/00, p. C12, Stephen Hunter
WASHINGTON POST, 8/25/00, Weekend/p. 37, Michael O'Sullivan

WHEN LOVE COMES

A Jour de Fête Films release of an MF Films production in association with the New Zealand Film Commission. *Producer:* Michele Fantl and Jonathan Dowling. *Director:* Garth Maxwell. *Screenplay:* Garth Maxwell, Rex Pilgrim, and Peter Wells. *Director of Photography:* Darryl Ward. *Editor:* Cushla Dillon. *Music:* Chris Anderson. *Sound:* Michael Hedges. *Sound Editor:* Dick Reade and Colleen Brennan. *Production Designer:* Grace Mok. *Art Director:* Anthony Sumich and Charles McGuiness. *Costumes:* Kirsty Cameron. *Make-up:* Rita Lynch. *Running time:* 94 minutes. *MPAA Rating:* Not Rated.

CAST: Rena Owen (Katie Keen); Dean O'Gorman (Mark); Simon Prast (Stephen); Nancy Brunning (Fig); Sophia Hawthorne (Sally); Simon Westaway (Eddie); Judith Gibson (Magazine Reporter); Barret Irwin (Dreadlock Guy); Yolan Moodley (Boy at Club); Jon Brazier (Recording Engineer); Celia Nicholson (Drunk Woman); Grant Triplow (Waiter); Lulu Alach (Lounge Bar Waitress); John Dybvig and Irene Drake (Lounge Bar Couple); Paul Adams, Bill Fitzgerald, and Gary Sullivan (Lounge Bar Band); Phoebe Falconer (Cindy the Zombie); Nic Smith (Cindy's Boyfriend); Nikolas Beachman (Slasher Zombie); Alex Jarman (Gridiron Player).

LOS ANGELES TIMES, 8/20/99, Calendar/p. 18, Kevin Thomas

Garth Maxwell's "When Love Comes" is an edgy, multi-character love story whose central figure, a fading pop singer, is played by the compelling New Zealand actress Rena Owen, who won international acclaim as the weary, abused wife in Lee Tamahori's 1994 "Once Were Warriors."

Owen's Katie Keen is a country girl whose natural singing talent took her to America in the late '70s, where she scored a No. 1 hit. She's been living off that renown ever since with increasingly diminishing returns. Reduced to playing rowdy clubs whose youthful audiences don't know who she is and couldn't care less, Katie can no longer hold an audience's attention.

Realizing that she's hit rock bottom, she sees her only salvation in returning home to her native New Zealand in an attempt to rebuild her life and hopefully reinvent herself as a performer. Her parents have died, and she looks for refuge in her best friend, Stephen (Simon Prast), who is a waiter at a posh Auckland restaurant. Somewhere in her 40s, Katie combines majestic poise, a sometimes ravaged beauty with an earthy, unpretentious personality and an uncommon capacity for self-reflection. Beneath her star's poise and glamour look, however, lies a highly vulnerable woman.

Katie and Stephen have one of those deep bonds that transcends time and distance. They are completely open with each other, and if either should upset the other, they get over it with a forthrightness and forgiveness that's enviable. Katie is thinking of making a comeback via a one-woman show, and her manager-lover, Eddie (Simon Westaway), back in the U.S. even has a taping set that could lead to a TV variety series. Eddie sees in the eloquence and detachment with which she is able to speak of herself and her career the perfect material with which to frame a revival performance.

In the meantime, Stephen himself is at a crossroads. Whether through inheritance or investments, Stephen has acquired a comfortable, tasteful lifestyle. He has fallen in love with a classic golden boy, Mark (Dean O'Gorman), who was a male hustler when they first met. Mark has moved on to become a gifted pop lyricist, and his pals, Fig (Nancy Brunning), a drummer, and her lover and performing partner, Sally (Sophia Hawthorne), a singer, are trying to break through as rock performers. They have enough drive, energy and talent to have a chance of making it.

Fig and Sally, in their youth, are blessedly uncomplicated and resilient, but Mark is steeped in confusion and uncertainty about every aspect of his life. He seems to care for Stephen but isn't ready to settle down. Having moved beyond a commercial relationship with the older man, he's unsure of whether he's up to the responsibilities of being Stephen's lover. "When Love Comes" culminates with this group, later joined by Eddie, taking off to the beautiful seaside region where Katie grew up.

All of this is, thankfully, not as neat and tidy as it sounds. Maxwell, who has directed episodes on both the "Xena" and "Hercules" series and has one well-received feature, "Jack Be Nimble," behind him, plays against the send-'em-home-happy trajectory of his story with an aura of tentativeness. Stephen and Mark may well reach a moment of rapport, but there's no telling whether they will be able to build a relationship upon it, let alone one that will endure, and while Katie and Eddie may be heading off into the sunset together, there's no certainty that Katie will be able to revive her career and take it in a new direction. Only Fig and Sally, without having any conflict in the first place, continuing bobbing along a bit wiser from all the emotional fireworks around them.

Although "When Love Comes" is traditional in structure, it is nonetheless risky; it allows its characters plenty of time and space to be insufferable, as most people can be in real life. Yet Maxwell has the kind of compassion and detachment to keep his picture from becoming insufferable.

Beyond that, Maxwell displays a talent for dialogue and direction—and also for apt song lyrics—to make these people engaging and worth caring about. Owen and Prast, both of whom are well-seasoned actors, possess a wit and depth that lend gravity to a film intent on capturing the skittishness and tentativeness that so often accompany matters of the heart.

NEW YORK POST, 6/25/99, p. 56, Jonathan Foreman

Shot in New Zealand, "When Love Comes" stands out from the recent crop of bad independent movies featuring gay and/or lesbian couples by virtue of its unusually fine lighting and photography.

Unfortunately, its visual appeal cannot make up for an incoherent yet predictable plot, by-the-numbers characterization, endemic overacting and a screenplay so cliche-ridden you almost wish the whole thing were some kind of spoof.

It starts with Sally (Sophia Hawthorne) and Fig (Nancy Brunning) talking to the camera. They're two rock chicks who are a couple, though Sally sometimes has sex with guys, especially Mark (Dean O'Gorman), a long-haired songwriter-current-boy who's a dead-ringer for Matthew McConaughey.

Mark has a troubled relationship with his older boyfriend Stephen (Simon Prast). Stephen is reasonable, cultured and in love. But abusive Mark gets drunk and stoned a lot, fools around with other guys, and breaks things in Stephen's nice apartment for no apparent reason.

His I'm-a-difficult-young-handsome-genius behavior worsens when Stephen's old friend Katie Keen turns up in Auckland.

Katie (Rena Owen from "Once Were Warriors") was once New Zealand's most famous singer and had a No. 1 hit in America in the '70s before washing up in a Vegas lounge act. Her talents may be just what Fig and Sally need to make a decent record using Mark's lyrics ("Suck the hand that hits you/Kiss the boot that kicks you"), but Katie is hung up about her loss of fame, not to mention her married American lover Eddie.

After various amazingly cliche-packed arguments, everyone ends up at Katie's family's empty beach house—even Eddie, who suddenly arrives from the United States. And after various tearful scenes and confessions, it looks like all the couples, even the hetero pair, might get to work out their soap-operatic problems.

The funniest thing about "When Loves Come" is its provinciality. It's as if writer-director Garth Maxwell were desperate to let the rest of the world know that New Zealand may be far off and small, with a reputation for colonial civility, but hey, "We're actually pretty dam wild. We've got rock bands, and clubs and drugs and everything..."

SIGHT AND SOUND, 8/01, p. 57, Amanda Lipman

New Zealand, the present. Two young women, Fig and Sally, lovers and co-musicians in a band, meet Mark, a songwriter. Mark is seeing Stephen, an older man who is besotted with him. An old friend of Stephen, Katie Keen, a pop star who made it big in the 70s, visits. Katie, at a low point in her career, needs to reinvent herself, she also needs time away from her married lover Eddie in the US. Stephen and Mark have a row, and Mark goes off on a sex-and-drugs binge with Fig and Sally. Driving around, Stephen finds Mark with the girls.

Later, Mark takes Katie to a club where she meets Fig and Sally, who persuade her to sing backing vocals on a single they're recording. Katie decides to go back to her home by the sea, and drives there with Stephen. Mark, Sally and Fig arrive. So too, unexpectedly, does Eddie. While the girls carouse on the beach, Mark decides to leave Stephen. Fig is upset. Later that night, Katie tells them all that she is still recovering from the grief of a miscarriage. Stephen persuades her to go to Eddie, who confesses that he has only been pretending to be married because she claimed to like married men. Mark returns and tells Stephen that he loves him. Fig and Sally report to camera that they have asked Katie to be their manager.

Garth Maxwell's film begins as a winsome look at the sub-culture of urban New Zealand, with a mock amateur video in which Fig and Sally, the members of a wannabe band, tell their story to camera. There's something to be said for the way the film, initially at least, introduces us to the lives and mores of its characters without passing judgement: Mark is a talented, somewhat enigmatic young man with a penchant for writing lyrics about death, and no idea what he wants from life; his lack of direction contrasts with the ambitions of Fig and Sally, who are apparently equally talented but more self-assured. Gay sex, straight sex, sex and drugs, drugs without sex—they're all charted here with equal candour and enthusiasm. None of this is unengaging, although it does put one in mind of the Australian-punks-on-heroin film, *Dogs in Space* which featured Michael Hutchence.

But then *When Love Comes* goes its own way, attempting to pit Fig and Sally's modern sensibilities against those of a bygone age, the 70s disco diva who visits Mark's lover Stephen after a long time in the US, represents the other side of showbiz, swooshing around in evening wear, perched on high heels, hidden under layers of make-up. The contrast between Katie, an ageing woman wondering what is left of herself beneath the image, and the blithely optimistic younger women Fig and Sally is a potentially interesting one. But Maxwell struggles to make much of his material. Katie remains a camp cliché throughout; lumbered with terrible lines such as "I know that place; I can smell it from here; it's called Rock Bottom." Rena Owen, playing Katie, is allowed to indulge in the kind of quivering overacting that veers closer to comedy than drama.

While the younger actors just about get away with the mundane dialogue, the older ones sound either hammy or stilted. Maxwell's attempts at sketching a convincing emotional backstory for his characters are just as misguided. We hear a lot about pain—Katie's pain, Stephen's pain, Mark's pain—but never get a true sense of the emotional hurt the characters are suffering. And as if overworking every clichéd line is not enough, the film engages in a number of unnecessary visual antics. In any one scene Mark is seen from numerous different angles—a favourite being his profile as foreground to the rest of the scene. The film constantly cuts and focus pulls—a stylistic device that was presumably intended to suggest the sense of disjunction the characters experience, but ends up looking more like a toy in the hand's of an over-eager film student (this is in fact Maxwell's second feature; his first, the 1994 *Jack Be Nimble*, was a bleak family drama). And the endless foregrounding of objects—a large wine glass at the front of the picture, for instance, with the characters hamming their way through the scene in the background—is reminiscent of the gag in the 1984 comedy *Top Secret!*, where a telephone, similarly placed in the foreground, is revealed to be hugely oversized in reality.

In fact the film's only unpredictable note comes as it suddenly ditches all the pain and problems and slips into a facile happy ending, by which time we've given up caring.

VILLAGE VOICE, 6/29/99, p. 152, Jessica Winter

The title of this New Zealand-bred film derives from its fictional singers late-'70s disco smash, "When Love Comes Along," but Katie Keen (Rena Owen) never managed to parlay resultant guest spots on *The Love Boat* into a lasting career. Twenty years later, married to shlumpy, loyal

Eddie, the aging diva returns to her native New Zealand to pause and reflect. She soul-searches with old friend Stephen, who pines for a barter-free relationship with rent boy Mark, who writes angst-riddled lyrics ("Suck the hand that hits you/Kiss the boot that kicks you") for would-be rocker girls who could make a pretty good Cycle Sluts From Hell cover band if they didn't take themselves so seriously. The movie itself grapples with the importance of being earnest: witness our Mark scrunching that pensive surfer-boy face and declaring, "The love thing, it's weirder than you think." Not weird enough, in this case-despite Katie's late-inning forays into performance art (don't ask), in *When Love Comes,* solemnity breeds somnolence.

Also reviewed in:
CHICAGO TRIBUNE, 6/30/99, Tempo/p. 1, Michael Wilmington
NEW YORK TIMES, 6/25/99, p. E13, Stephen Holden
VARIETY, 11/28/98, p. 55, Glenn Lovell

WHERE'S MARLOWE?

A Paramount Classics release in association with Western Sandpast Project. *Executive Producer:* Aaron Lipstadt, John Mankiewicz, and Daniel Pyne. *Producer:* Clayton Townsend. *Director:* Daniel Pyne. *Screenplay:* Daniel Pyne and John Mankiewicz. *Director of Photography:* Greg Gardiner. *Editor:* Lee Butler. *Music:* Michael Convertino. *Sound:* Bob Jackson and Marc Steinbeck. *Casting:* Rick Pagano. *Production Designer:* Garreth Stover. *Art Director:* Chris Cornwell. *Costumes:* Mary Zophres. *Running time:* 97 minutes. *MPAA Rating:* R.

CAST: Miguel Ferrer (Joe Boone); Mos Def (Wilton Crawley); John Livingston (A.J. Edison); Allison Dean (Angela); John Slattery (Murphy); Elizabeth Schofield (Monica Collins); Barbara Howard (Emma Huffington); Clayton Rohner (Beep Collins).

LOS ANGELES TIMES, 11/12/99, Calendar/p. 20, Gene Seymour

[The following review by Gene Seymour appeared in a slightly different form in
NEWSDAY, 11/12/99, Part II/p. B6.]

People keep kicking at the prone form of the private-eye movie genre, but it's often hard to tell why. Are they trying to wake it up? Finish it off? Or do they just want to make sure that it's just unconscious and not already dead?

Given that Daniel Pyne, the director of "Where's Marlowe?," has in his previous television and movie work shown a warm affinity for crime melodrama, you assume that his movie comes primarily to praise and not to bury the P.I. iconography. But despite its hip "mockumentary" trappings, "Where's Marlowe?" won't convince too many people that this once-proud genre has enough get-up-and-go for the new millennium.

The setup, at least, has potential. It starts with "footage" from an epic three-hour documentary on the New York City water system by independent filmmakers Wilt Crawley (Mos Def) and A.J. Edison (John Livingston). The movie goes over like a fat boulder at a festival screening, making the pair believe that there's probably a better subject waiting for them on the left coast.

Hence "Where's Marlowe?," which Wilt and A.J. bill as an inquiry into the so-called real life of the Southern California private investigator. Their subject couldn't be more perfectly suited for their purposes: a self-styled romantic, prosaically named Boone (Miguel Ferrer), who spends most of his time finding runaway teenage girls, shadowing cheating spouses and strong-arming owners of obnoxious pets. He clings to the dream of finding his own Black Dahlia case.

It's hard to tell why Boone's cynical partner, Murphy (John Slattery), is involved with what he calls this "Hardy Boys crap." But before Wilt and A.J. can get that angle resolved on camera, Murphy gets caught up in a bizarre case of sex and murder. Boone can't handle a case of such complex and potentially dangerous dimension by himself So it's not long before "Where's Marlowe?" turns, as A.J. puts it, into a "documentary about two documentary guys who are making a documentary about a private eye."

Pyne, who co-wrote the script with John Mankiewicz, manages to sustain this conceit for a little while it isn't long, however, before there's irreconcilable tension between the satire of "indie" movie pretensions and the muddled mystery plot. Neither of these strains is carried out to a satisfying end, which may have been the point. Still, the droll cast—especially Ferrer, who's exquisite as a tough-talking dunce—deserved something more fully realized than this.

NEW YORK POST, 11/12/99, p. 55, Lou Lumenick

"Where's Marlowe?" You don't want to know. As one of the heroes of this headache-inducing mess describes it, "Where's Marlowe?" is "a documentary about two documentary makers making a documentary about a private detective, except now we're the detectives."

The title of this mock documentary is, of course, meant to evoke Raymond Chandler's Philip Marlowe. But the plot is an updated (and incoherent) mishmash of Sam Spade's adventures in Dashiell Hammett's "The Maltese Falcon," and it features an actor who evokes Jack Webb's Sgt. Joe Friday of "Dragnet" at his most monotonous.

That would be Miguel Ferrer as down-and-out Los Angeles private eye Joe Boone, who welcomes filmmakers A.J. Edison (John Livingston) and Wilton Crawley (Mos Def) to film his work, despite the fact that their previous effort was a three-hour flick on New York City's public water system.

Boone's partner Murphy (John Slattery) is a decidedly less-willing participant, quite possibly because he's shagging a woman whose boyfriend has hired Joe to follow her. When Murphy turns up dead, A.J. and Wilton decide it would help their plotline even more if they offered their services to help Joe solve the case—taking turns behind the camera.

At one point, Joe picks up the camera himself and lets the boys run the case.

Though there are a handful of scattered laughs (such as when a blind man's help is enlisted so all three can appear in the same shot), director Daniel Pyne and his co-writer, John Mankiewicz, don't have the lightness of touch to pull off a mockumentary.

The kind of jittery hand-held camerawork that lent verisimilitude to "The Blair Witch Project" merely seems annoying here.

"Where's Marlowe?" was expanded from a TV pilot produced for ABC. Small wonder it never found its way on the air.

Also reviewed in:
CHICAGO TRIBUNE, 11/12/99, Friday/p. N, Barbara Shulgasser
NEW YORK TIMES, 11/13/99, p. B16, Anita Gates
VARIETY, 10/26-11/1/98, p. 54, Dennis Harvey

WHITEBOYS

A Fox Searchlight Pictures release in association with BAC Films and Le Studio Canal+ of an Offline Entertainment Group production. *Executive Producer:* David Peipers and John Sloss. *Producer:* Henri Kessler, Richard Stratton, and Ezra Swerdlow. *Director:* Marc Levin. *Screenplay:* Garth Belcon, Danny Hoch, Marc Levin, and Richard Stratton. *Story:* Garth Belcon and Danny Hoch. *Director of Photography:* Mark Benjamin. *Editor:* Emir Lewis. *Music:* Steve Gottlieb and Che Guevara. *Music Editor:* Joe Lisanti. *Sound:* Felix Andrew. *Sound Editor:* Bitty O'Sullivan. *Casting:* Kathleen Chopin and Sue Crystal. *Production Designer:* David Doernberg. *Art Director:* Amy Silver. *Set Decorator:* Dewey Ambrosino. *Special Effects:* Danny Sokolowski. *Costumes:* Carolyn Greco. *Makeup:* James Lacey. *Stunt Coordinator:* Tom Lowell. *Running time:* 89 minutes. *MPAA Rating:* R.

CAST: Danny Hoch (Flip); Dash Mihok (James); Mark Webber (Trevor); Piper Perabo (Sara); Eugene Byrd (Khalid); Bonz Malone (Darius); Dr. Dre (Don Flip Crew #1); Rich Komenich (Flip's Dad); Annabel Armour (Flip's Mom); Lisa Jane Todd (Trevor's Mom); Brooke Byam (Country Western Singer); Diane Rinehart (Sara's Sister); Rick Snyder (Sara's Dad); Jacqueline Williams (Khalid's Mom); Reno Wilson (Mace); Fat Joe (Don Flip Crew #2); Dead Prez

(Cornfield Rappers); Mic Geronimo (Friend of Mace); Slick Rick (Parking Lot Rapper #2); Doug E. Fresh (Parking Lot Rapper #1); Snoop Dogg (Himself).

LOS ANGELES TIMES, 10/8/99, Calendar/p. 10, Gene Seymour

[The following review by Gene Seymour appeared in a slightly different form in
NEWSDAY, 10/8/99, Part II/p. B8.]

To those with a fervent belief in the positive energy of cultural crossover, "Whiteboys" offers a stern test—if not a hesitant leap—of faith. The movie documents accurately the capacity of pop culture to make mongrels of its consumers. But it doesn't quite know (or want to know) what to make of it.

"Whiteboys" is basically a travelogue of a glandular state of mind; belonging, in this case, to Flip (co-writer Danny Hoch), a gawky white kid from Iowa's corn country transfigured by the signals he picks up from MTV and the mall's record rack into a gold-chain-wearing, slow-walking, quick-rhyming, self-styled "B-boy." He's so deep into "blackness" that the mother of Flip's only African American friend (Eugene Byrd) wonders if he's Creole.

Flip's generation of white kids isn't the first to be galvanized by the seeming "freedom" of African American culture. Nor is he the first to believe that internalizing some of the broad aspects of this culture entitles him to the assumed "privileges" of outlaw life. His ideas of "being white" and "being black" are informed solely by media images that contrast with the seeming blandness of his daily life.

It never once occurs to Flip that having a bitter, unemployed father and a mother forced to buy groceries with food stamps links him more authentically to the urban street life he finds so glamorous. Nor does it occur to him that the aforementioned black friend, given the choice between being "down" with the street action and opting for upward mobility, will choose the latter in a heartbeat. At some point, Flip heads on a road trip to Chicago with his "posse" to score some drugs. When he comes to the forbidding Cabrini Green housing project, Flip points as if it were the Lincoln Memorial. Does it turn out bad? Hey-yo, do bullets hurt?

Director Marc Levin, whose critically acclaimed "Slam" showed a far more assured grasp of the Washington, D.C., street subculture it documented, tries to bring some of the same stylistic invention to Flip's crossover dreams. One amusing morsel of surrealism takes place in Flip's conception of prison life as one fat power trip, complete with buffet.

But despite the presence of such rap eminences as Snoop Dogg, Slick Rick and Doug E. Fresh, there's something about "Whiteboys" that makes one wonder whether what's proclaimed as "hip-hop nation" really has the goods to transcend as much as it dominates pop culture. Because when all is said and done, Flip doesn't come across as cultural avatar so much as a new subspecies of clueless hick.

NEW YORK POST, 10/11/99, p. 50, Jonathan Foreman

"Whiteboys" is an attempt to make a whole movie out of a single joke: the incongruous sight of a white teenager doing his best to look and sound like a down-with-the-'hood black rapper in the middle of an Iowa cornfield.

It's very funny to begin with—and in spots throughout—but without a real story to go with the notion of Farm Belt "wiggas," the humor wears thinner and thinner until it disappears.

It's a shame because hip-hop culture—and gangsta rap in particular—has a powerful appeal for millions of white teenagers, a phenomenon that's fascinating.

"Whiteboys" is also a disappointment because it's the film debut of Danny Hoch, who stars but also co-wrote the film based on a sketch from his solo stage show "Jails, Hospitals and Hip-Hop."

Hoch plays Flip, a character we first encounter as he covers a barn with graffiti. Unemployed, Flip and his friends Trevor and James make money selling fake cocaine to mall rats in the nearest town.

The rest of the time the boys craft rap songs, listen to Flip talking about his plans to relocate to a Chicago housing project, and dream about making fortunes as rappers and/or drug dealers.

Flip happens to be an irritatingly dumb and selfish jerk for whom its impossible to feel any sympathy. Most of the movie is taken up with Flip doing his astonishingly seamless black act and explaining that his white skin is just a kind of birthmark.

Unrealistically, Flip's facade never cracks, perhaps because Hoch is so anxious to show off his perfect ear for dialect.

But two-thirds of the way through there's a perfunctory road trip, in which the boys go to Chicago with their only black friend, Khalid an upper-middle-class kid bound for college so that Flip can meet some real drug dealers and form some kind of multi-state cartel. (Khalid knows somebody who knows somebody who deals drugs at the Cabrini Green projects).

The expedition is, of course, a disaster and ends in a ridiculous firefight between real gangsters and some cops.

But the real problem with the film is that its four screenwriters, including director Mark Levin, cannot seem to decide what they think about the phenomenon they're dealing with.

Is the whole thug-life aesthetic harmless and amusing, or is it something that's going to get naive kids into a world of trouble? Are these kids rebels bucking an insipid white-bread culture or victims of a mass-marketing pop-culture machine—or both?

VILLAGE VOICE, 10/12/99, p. 150, Jessica Winter

Despite the ascendancy of hick-hop stars like Eminem and Kid Rock, despite the ongoing Hilfiger-underwritten experiment in selling black culture to conspicuously white consumers, despite the disenfranchisement of the invisible white underclass, *Whiteboys* is not a movie that can afford to take itself seriously. The sight of heartland farm teens in baggy B-boy drag, freestyling in their rec rooms and twanging ghetto slang they picked up from MTV, is too absurdly funny and pathetic to withstand the leakage of any weighty issues into the frame. Based on a character created for the stage by Danny Hoch, *Whiteboys* concerns the Iowa Gangsta Blood Thugs—working-class Flip (Hoch, who cowrote the script), middle-class Trevor, and straight-out-the-RV James, who eschew walking the local mail in favor of Philly blunts and daydreams of success on Death Row (these fantasies feature cameos from Slick Rick, Doug E. Fresh, and Snoop Dogg). Flip claims that his skin color is an accident, an obstacle he has to surmount so he can keep keepin' it real. He presses this point hard with one of the few black kids at school, Khalid, who has cousins in Chicago Flip hopes can introduce him to the thug life; a subsequent episode in which a black drug dealer dies in a firefight with cops seems contrived only so that Flip can learn a valuable lesson about what it really means to "represent." It's a lesson lost on Hoch, who never decides what view to take of his subjects—should he wax those chumps like candles or let them rock the mic like vandals? Where's Marty DiBergi when you need him?

Also reviewed in:
NEW YORK TIMES, 10/8/99, p. E22, Anita Gates
VARIETY, 9/27-10/3/99, p. 44, Lisa Nesselson

WILD WILD WEST

A Warner Bros. release of a Peters Entertainment/Sonnenfeld-Josephson production in association with Todman, Simon, LeMasters Productions. *Executive Producer:* Bill Todman, Jr., Joel Simon, Kim LeMasters, Tracy Glaser, and Barry Josephson. *Producer:* Jon Peters and Barry Sonnenfeld. *Director:* Barry Sonnefeld. *Screenplay:* S.S. Wilson, Brent Maddock, Jeffrey Price, and Peter S. Seaman. *Story:* Jim Thomas and John Thomas. *Director of Photography:* Michael Ballhaus. *Editor:* Jim Miller. *Music:* Elmer Bernstein. *Music Editor:* Kathy Durning and Patricia Carlin. *Choreographer:* Lynne Hockney and Monica Guy. *Sound:* Peter Kurland and (music) Dan Wallin. *Sound Editor:* Skip Lievsay and Bobby Mackston. *Casting:* David Rubin and Ronna Kress. *Production Designer:* Bo Welch. *Art Director:* Tom Duffield. *Set Designer:* Patrick Sullivan, Maya Shimoguchi, Gerald Sullivan, and Mariko Braswell. *Set Decorator:* Cheryl Carasik. *Special Effects:* Michael Lantieri. *Costumes:* Deborah L. Scott. *Make-up:* Whitney L.

James. *Special Effects Make-up:* Rick Baker. *Stunt Coordinator:* Terry J. Leonard, Artie Malesci, and Philip Tan. *Running time:* 107 minutes. *MPAA Rating:* PG.

CAST: Will Smith (James West); Kevin Kline (Artemus Gordon/President Ulysses S. Grant); Kenneth Branagh (Dr. Arliss Loveless); Salma Hayek (Rita Escobar); M. Emmet Walsh (Coleman); Ted Levine (General McGrath); Frederique Van Der Wal (Amazonia); Musetta Vander (Munitia); Sofia Eng (Miss Lippenreider); Bai Ling (Miss East); Garcelle Beauvais (Girl in Water Tower); Mike McGaughy (Big Reb); Jerry Wills (Other Reb); Rodney A. Grant (Hudson); Buck Taylor (Eye-crossed Reb); E.J. Callahan (Mr. Pinkerton); Debra Christofferson (Dora Lookalike); James Lashly (Reb 1); Dean Rader-Duval (Reb 2); Christian Aubert (French Dignitary); Orestes Matacena (Spanish Dignitary); Ian Abercrombie (British Dignitary); Ismael Carlo (Mexican Dignitary); Bob Rumnock (Whitehouse Aide); Carlos Cervantes (Rita's Husband); Jerry Potter (George Washington); Mik Scriba (Guard); Michael Sims (Morton).

CHRISTIAN SCIENCE MONITOR, 7/2/99, p. 15, David Sterritt

Hoping to grab a big brass ring at the Fourth of July box office, Hollywood has turned to television for inspiration.

Wild Wild West takes its cue from a mid-'60s TV series that brought James Bond's aura—action, gadgetry, womanizing—to the then-popular western format.

South Park: Bigger, Longer & Uncut is an expanded edition of the cartoon show on Comedy Central that's been titillating youngsters and irritating parents for the past several seasons.

Regrettably, both pictures deliver less entertainment value than their well-tested formulas promise. They'll earn quick dollars from audiences seeking light holiday fare, but neither is likely to have much staying power—which means the field may be wide open for the next set of would-be blockbusters lined up at the midsummer gate.

"Wild Wild West" is another of Hollywood's intermittent attempts to reinvent the western genre for a new generation. On paper, it looks great: two of today's liveliest stars (Will Smith and Kevin Kline) directed by the maker of "Men in Black" and the "Addams Family" pictures (Barry Sonnenfeld) in a story blending western heroics with high-tech adventure and pitch-dark comedy. Smith and Kline have admirable energy as the heroes, government agents who squabble with each other while chasing a mad scientist (Kenneth Branagh) bent on conquering America with weapons as surrealistic as they are scary.

But their skills are no match for the triteness of the action scenes—haven't we seen enough fiery explosions and headbutting fistfights by now?—and the flatness of the dialogue, which sinks into racial slurs and disability jokes every time it runs out of better ideas. That happens constantly, even though no fewer than six writers cooked up the screenplay. Ace cinematographer Michael Ballhaus makes the picture look better than it deserves to.

"South Park" has the advantage of being childish and offensive by design instead of by accident. It's about a bunch of grade-school kids who sneak into an NC-17 movie that teaches them even more obscenities than they already know, outraging their parents and sparking (among other things) a journey to Hades, a visit with Saddam Hussein, and a full-scale war with Canada.

As immature and obnoxious as much of "South Park" is, it pauses occasionally to make a serious point—suggesting that violence is a greater social scourge than cuss words, for instance—and parts of it are wildly inventive in an idiotic sort of way. Traditional moviegoers may despise it, but worse fare can be found slouching through multiplexes in the age of Austin Powers.

LOS ANGELES TIMES, 6/30/99, Calendar/p. 3, Kenneth Turan

Like the curious children they often resemble, filmmakers can be fatally distracted by toys. Big, expensive toys that are no doubt enormous fun to play with in person but don't register quite the same way on screen. Toys like the ones that dominate and finally destroy "Wild Wild West."

Few things are potentially more dangerous to the health of a studio picture than giving a director and a star enough rope to hang themselves. With the hugely (and deservedly) successful "Men in Black" behind them, Barry Sonnenfeld and Will Smith were granted carte blanche this time around, not to mention a $100-million-plus budget, considerably larger than what the entire four years of the '60s TV series everything is based on originally cost.

The result is that "Wild Wild West" gets its proportions wrong. As clumsy and top-heavy as the 80-foot-high mechanical tarantula that is its prize special effect, the film sacrifices playfulness and humor to concentrate on a relentless display of elaborate but ho-hum gadgets and gizmos. The subversive sense of fun that's marked almost all of Sonnenfeld's work, not to mention Smith's, is just about buried under the output of obsessive inventors run amok.

Television origins notwithstanding, "Wild Wild West" plays more like a pinball machine than something made for a screen of any size. It's loud and busy, with frequent explosions and brawls standing in for blinking lights and ringing bells. And not even the ministrations of six credited writers (story by Jim Thomas & John Thomas, screenplay by S.S. Wilson & Brent Maddock and Jeffrey Price & Peter S. Seaman) can give it a story or dialogue worth paying more than sporadic attention to.

That is especially unfortunate because in Smith as Capt. James West and Kevin Kline as Artemus Gordon, "Wild Wild West" has co-stars who are capable of much better. Neither one, however, gets to play to his strength long enough to make a difference.

While the TV show had West and Gordon as collaborating Secret Service agents, the movie functions as kind of a prequel, showing how the two men, one in the U.S. Army and the other a U.S. Marshal, came to work together.

That idea originated with President Ulysses S. Grant (played here by Kline as well), understandably perturbed by a letter announcing he'll be called upon to hand over the country to an unknown party in a week. Sensing a connection between the note and a run of disappearances of key American scientists, Grant orders West and Gordon to collaborate in solving the mystery.

Naturally, these two prima donnas don't get along. West is Mr. Action, described as someone who will "shoot first, shoot later, shoot some more and when everyone's dead ask a few questions." Gordon, by contrast, is the cerebral type, a believer in disguise and the kind of inventor who hides knives in the soles of people's boots. "I think," West truly tells him, "you underestimate the convenience of a pocket."

Just because "Wild Wild West" is the disappointment it is doesn't mean you come out with anything against Smith. As innately likable an actor as today's Hollywood has, he is simply not playing to his strength here, concentrating on being steely and resilient when the film is dying on the vine for want of genuine humor. Similarly, Kline, a marvelous farceur, has one or two amusing moments but is often called on to play things so blandly that he almost disappears from the screen.

Joining this pair on the hunt is Rita Escobar (Salma Hayek), who wins the boys' sympathy by telling them her father is one of the kidnapped scientists. A popular ingenue these days, Hayek is capable enough in what may be an abbreviated role (a scene involving a horde of spiders that appeared prominently in reports from the set is not in the film), but her character is used mainly as an excuse for tired double-entendre jokes and peek-a-boo glimpses of her body.

The trail to what's menacing the country leads through former Confederate Gen. "Bloodbath" McGrath (Ted Levine) to the evil genius himself, Dr. Arliss Loveless, an unrepentant son of the South who gave half his body to "The Cause" and now tools around in a kind of electric cart. As strenuously overplayed by Kenneth Branagh in an insufferable accent, Loveless likes nothing better than to trade mild racial and disability insults with West. It's about as funny as it sounds.

Like West's partner Gordon, Loveless is also a mad inventor (his inspirations look like they were constructed from a malevolent Erector set), and between the two of them they litter the screen with all manner of misbegotten inspirations. Fewer of these would have gone a much longer way, but, like a headstrong runaway train, "Wild Wild West" is determined to hurtle down the wrong track, full speed ahead.

NEW YORK POST, 6/30/99, p. 49, Rod Dreher

"Wild Wild West" is the movie that stole Will Smith's mojo! Heaven knows he gives it his best, but not even the smart, sexy and immensely likable Smith can save this awful Barry Sonnenfeld picture from the oblivion it surely deserves.

Nothing goes right in this empty-headed, extraordinarily dull and pointless exercise in throwing Warner Bros. money down a rat hole. It's a wild, wild waste of time.

The film is based on the 1960s television show, which paired Robert Conrad and Ross Martin as secret-agent men snooping around cowboy country with Jules Verne-style gadgetry at their disposal. The movie version casts Smith as James West, a gunslinging man of action, and Kevin Kline as the eggheaded master of disguise Artemus Gordon.

The year is 1869, and West teams with Gordon to stop evil ex-Confederate inventor Arliss Loveless (Kenneth Branagh) from taking over the U.S. government. They track Loveless and his associates through a whorehouse, a New Orleans society ball, and finally to his desert lair, where they grapple with a lethal do-hickey that looks like a giant steam-driven spider.

Along the way, they get into various uninteresting scrapes and run into Salma Hayek, whose role is so bland she appears to have been hired only as a bosom-delivery device.

The screenplay has no rhythm, arc, rhyme or reason (the racial-justice angle is a gratuitous groaner). The action sequences are joyless, lifeless and utterly perfunctory, as if everyone involved were just fulfilling the terms of a contract they wish they hadn't signed.

Cross-breeding sci-fi fantasy with an old-style Western worked on TV 30 years ago (the show was on for five seasons), but it's hard to see the appeal now.

The quirky gadgets might have been fun to discover, if the trailer and TV commercials hadn't revealed most of them already. Still, in the summer of "The Phantom Menace," the gears, pulleys, and frippery on display here look dorky.

Strangely enough for a film marketed to children, "Wild Wild West" has a lot of crude sexual innuendo, including quick asides referencing a giant dildo and whorehouse bestiality. Maybe the filmmakers hope their stupid sex jokes will fly over children's heads, but not a few moms and dads will dread being asked to explain the whips, handcuffs and leather gear over the pretty lady's bed.

If NATO had dropped prints of this $160 million boondoggle on the Serbs, Slobodan Milosevic would have given up on the first day of the war.

SIGHT AND SOUND, 9/99, p. 60, Andrew O'Hehir

The American West, 1869. James West, a black US army special officer is pursuing a former Confederate general named McGrath, whom he believes is stockpiling weapons and kidnapping scientists. West encounters Artemus Gordon who is also after McGrath. When McGrath escapes to New West and Gordon return to Washington where President Ulysses S. Grant orders them to work together.

In New Orleans, the duo learn that the real mastermind behind McGrath is Dr. Arliss Loveless, an evil genius who was crippled fighting for the South in the Civil War and who still hopes to bring down the US government. During the war, Loveless built a tank that massacred many people in an Illinois town of freed slaves, including West's family. After testing his new weapon by killing McGrath and his men, Loveless flees west, planning to capture Grant in Utah. Loveless is pursued by West, Gordon and a beautiful woman Rita, who says her father is one of the kidnapped scientists. West and Gordon are twice captured by Loveless, and must work together to escape and do battle with flying steel discs, robots and a mechanical spider. Finally they defeat Loveless, thwarting his plan to divide the US between Britain, Spain, Mexico and himself. Rita is reunited with the missing scientist, actually her husband. President Grant names West and Gordon the first two agents in the US Secret Service.

Crammed full of outrageous visual effects and the careening camerawork that has made Barry Sonnenfeld justly famous, Wild Wild West gets by on sheer style, as well as the irrepressible likeability of its star Will Smith. But it's reasonable to ask why a film that exists solely to have fun should seem so laboured. Counting the story and screenplay credits, six writers have their names attached to this film. None of them, apparently, could improve on the embarrassing faux-homoerotic banter between West and Gordon, or the even more witless exchanges of insults between West and the legless Loveless ("It's a dark day," drawls the latter; "Well, I'm stumped," sneers the former). As is typical of Sonnenfeld's films, the best jokes are visual, and even then there's often no point to them. When a pup approaches the dead McGrath's ear trumpet and strikes the familiar "His Master's Voice" pose, it only makes you feel that the director is bored.

Smith breezes through the film with customary aplomb. Nonetheless, the role and Smith's casting are something of a missed opportunity. Wild Wild West never tries to explain how a black man has become a prominent federal agent less than four years after the abolition of slavery.

West recounts the story of his own flight from bondage with the air of a man reading aloud a tiresome history lesson. While Sonnenfeld and his numerous screenwriters aren't obliged to be instructive, they evidently don't give a damn about the character's plausibility or motivation—even when these seem potentially so powerful—and it doesn't occur to them that the audience might.

Kevin Kline's fussy, unfocused performance as Gordon is still more disappointing. Although he's a talented actor, Kline is not the natural physical comedian a chaotic spectacle like this demands. (He's far better in his secondary role as the gruff President Grant.) At least Kenneth Branagh, with his outlandish Blanche DuBois accent and his elaborate moustache, seems to enjoy himself as the preening, scene-hogging Loveless and understand that any efforts at subtlety would be wasted. Salma Hayek certainly has the proportions for the bustier she wears in most of her scenes, and that's just as well, since the screenwriters give Rita no better reason for being in the movie.

But then, all this highfalutin talk about writing and acting is beside the point. For the most part, Sonnenfeld and his production team have translated the quirky, Jules Verne sci-fi aesthetic of the 1965-68 US television series to the big screen with smashing success. From the green and gold wallpaper of a New Orleans mansion to the gorgeous wrought iron railings on the bridge of Loveless' enormous steam-driven spider, all the wit and verve missing from the screenplay are present in Bo Welch's opulent production design. Sonnenfeld can now be relied on for imaginative credit sequences (this one's a mix of Sergio Leone and the early Bond films) and crowd-pleasing, gizmo-driven action climaxes. These qualities have made him one of the most successful Hollywood film-makers of the 90s. But in a sense his roots are still showing. As he gets further away from his apprentice years as the Coen brothers' cinematographer, it's increasingly clear that Sonnenfeld shares their fascination with technique and genre, but has none of their genius for characterisation and little interest in human beings except as design elements.

TIME, 7/12/99, p. 68, Richard Schickel

Wild, Wild West poses this not very pressing question: Can a comedy—we use that term in the broadest possible sense—costing something north of $100 million hope to succeed solely on the basis of special effects, cross-dressing and a vertically challenged villain? The depressing answer, given the apparently endless supply of adolescents with nothing better to do in the summer, is probably yes.

But for adults with fond recall of the retro James Bond TV show on which the movie is based, and with more recent memories of the sharp yet genial bite of director Barry Sonnenfeld's *Men in Black* and *Get Shorty*, the film is an unmitigated disaster. That's especially so considering that hotheaded Jim West is played by the coolly calculating Will Smith, his epicurean colleague Artemus Gordon by the subtly self-regarding Kevin Kline and Dr. Arliss Loveless by Kenneth Branagh, who seems more amused by Loveless' absolute evil than any audience will be.

You can't really blame the actors for the failure of a raft of screenwriters to provide them with even vaguely funny lines. They were doubtless too busy helping invent the film's visual effects, which most prominently include the gigantic mechanical tarantula with which Loveless hopes to induce a post-Civil War U.S. to surrender its sovereignty to him. But like men in frocks or the doctor's steam-driven wheelchair, it is just a sight gag—a one-shot deal out of which you cannot build intricately sustained comedy. The movie is loaded with this junk, but it has no authentic momentum or satirical viewpoint—and is finally lost to its own desperate, unavailing search for a laugh.

VILLAGE VOICE, 7/19/99, p. 60, Amy Taubin

When I was about eight years old, a boy in my class requested my company after school to play with his erection set. Oblivious to the snickering of his friends, I responded with the smugness of a budding intellectual, "You mean erector set, don't you?" Scarcely had the words left my lips when I realized that I had walked into some sexual minefield, although of what nature I was unclear. I blushed, panicked, and fled. When I recall the incident today, I feel as horribly confused and as embarrassed by my naiveté as I was then.

I make this disclosure, dear reader, so that you will understand why I'm unable to be completely impartial in my assessment of *Wild Wild West*, a movie that plays the erection/erector set association to the hilt. Given the tangle of my psyche, I even considered refusing this assignment entirely. But since *Wild Wild West* is so extremely stupid and incompetent, I doubt that even the most impartial critic could find much to praise. Unless, of course, they themselves are fixated at the erection-set stage of development. And by the way, are erector sets still popular with young boys? I haven't seen them featured in toy store windows in a long time. And if not, for whom did the powers behind this picture imagine they were making it?

Actually, the answer should be obvious to anyone who knows how studio movies come into being. *Wild Wild West* was created to please the audience whose Fourth of July weekend would be incomplete without seeing Will Smith save the Republic from aliens. But since Smith had already gone mano a mano with standard-issue extraterrestrials in *Independence Day* and *Men in Black,* some higher concept was needed. We may never know who among the four credited screenwriters and the two writers who share the ambiguous "story by" credit arrived at the inspired notion of sending Smith back into the post-Civil War era (great possibilities for costumes, not to mention quips about slavery) and making him a federal marshal on the trail of a renegade Confederate veteran—a half-flesh, half-metal creature bent on overthrowing the government and selling the U.S. piecemeal to the highest foreign bidders.

It's awesome to think that a mere mortal, or even a half-dozen mere mortals, could have arrived at a concept so ripe with genre possibilities, every one of which seems to have been brought into play for at least a minute or two in the pricey ($100 million plus) hodgepodge that is *Wild Wild West.* There's a James Bond secret-service gadgetry adventure crossed with a Jules Verne sci-fi gadgetry adventure; a mad-scientist horror flick crossed with a kickboxing cowboy shoot-'em-up. There are, in fact, so many genres competing for attention that there's no time to develop any semblance of plot or characters.

Ham-fisted even in his most stylish efforts (*Men in Black* and *Get Shorty*), Barry Sonnenfeld lacks the directorial abandon to pull off delirious Monty Python-esque undoings of time and space, which would have been the only way to handle the every-which-way anachronisms of the script. There are hints that he tried. An early scene involving a decapitation is strangely recalled much later in the film in a scene where Smith cross-dresses as Salome and shakes his booty in lieu of removing his seven veils. More notably, our hero, who is introduced in a scene where the enemy is struck dumb by a full-frontal view of his naked bod (a view that we, unhappily, do not share), soon confronts the film's archvillain who blew his lower body to bits during an experiment and now relies on various erector set-like metal machines to make him into a whole man. The largest of these is an 80-foot-high, eight-legged contraption dubbed the Tarantula, which rattles across Monument Valley as monstrously as Godzilla thuds around Midtown.

Played by Kenneth Branagh and Ted Levine the Grand Guignol-style bad guys of *Wild Wild West* are so massively disfigured as to suggest that someone got an early peek at Thomas Harris's *Hannibal.* Levine has the to understand that when you have a rheumy eye and a guck-spewing trumpet affixed to the side of your head in lieu of an ear, the less acting you do the better, Branagh, however, is his usual insufferable mix of flat affect and hammy vocalization. As the putative love interest, Salma Hayek is only around to inspire an endless stream of "boobie" jokes. Same goes for the gun-toting Rhine Maidens in Branagh's personal guard (Since the film lacks even the suggestion of characters, I think it's a fairer indication of what takes place on the screen to refer to actors by their own names.)

As Smith's sidekick, Kevin Kline, a witty and inventive comic actor (whose much-lauded Hamlet, however, was nearly as dull as Branagh's), tries to make himself as inconspicuous as possible, which, under the circumstances, is a wise choice. But it leaves Smith to carry the whole misbegotten enterprise on his graceful shoulders. Smith has terrific presence and charm to spare, and he moves as well as any actor around excepting Jeff Bridges and Tommy Lee Jones. It doesn't help him here, however, that his rhythms are undermined by Elmer Bernstein's plodding score or that he's required to deliver some of the worst one-liners ever written. Still, there's no doubt that he has the charisma of a star, a distinction that may doom him to a career of movies as dumb and pointless as this one.

Also reviewed in:
NEW YORK TIMES, 6/30/99, p. E6, Janet Maslin
NEW YORKER, 7/12/99, p. 88, David Denby
VARIETY, 7/12-18/99, p. 38, Todd McCarthy
WASHINGTON POST, 6/30/99, p. C1, Stephen Hunter
WASHINGTON POST, 7/2/99, Weekend/p. 39, Michael O'Sullivan

WILLIAM SHAKESPEARE'S A MIDSUMMER NIGHT'S DREAM

A Fox Searchlight Pictures and Regency Enterprises release of a Taurus Films production. *Executive Producer:* Arnon Milchan. *Producer:* Leslie Urdang and Michael Hoffman. *Screenplay:* Michael Hoffman. *Based on the play by:* William Shakespeare. *Director of Photography:* Oliver Stapleton. *Editor:* Garth Craven. *Music:* Simon Boswell and Robin Urdang. *Music Editor:* Paul Rabjohns and Robert Randles. *Sound:* Petur Hliddal. *Sound Editor:* Frank Eulner. *Casting:* Lora Kennedy. *Production Designer:* Luciana Arrighi. *Art Director:* Gianni Giovagnoni. *Set Decorator:* Ian Whittaker. *Special Effects:* Antonio Corridori. *Costumes:* Gabriella Pescucci. *Make-up:* Paul Engelen. *Stunt Coordiantor:* Riccardo Mioni. *Running time:* 115 minutes. *MPAA Rating:* PG-13.

CAST: Kevin Kline (Nick Bottom); Michelle Pfeiffer (Titania); Rupert Everett (Oberon); Stanley Tucci (Puck); Calista Flockhart (Helena); Anna Friel (Hermia); Christian Bale (Demetrius); Dominic West (Lysander); David Strathairn (Theseus); Sophie Marceau (Hippolyta); Roger Rees (Peter Quince); Max Wright (Robin Starveling); Gregory Jbara (Snug); Bill Irwin (Tom Snout); Sam Rockwell (Francis Flute); Bernard Hill (Egeus); John Sessions (Philostrate); Deirdre A. Harrison (Hard-eyed Fairy); Heather Elizabeth Parisi (Bottom's Wife); Annalisa Cordone (Cobweb); Paola Pessot (Mustardseed); Solena Nocentini (Moth); Flaminia Fegarotti (Peaseblossom); Valerio Isidori (Master Antonio); Daniele Finizio and Damiano Salvatori (Dangerous Boys); Chomoke Bhuiyan (Changling Boy); Roberta Galli and Anna Burt (Furies); Victoria Eugenia Martinez (Female Monster); Luisa Nardelli and Lucia Nardelli (Janus Figures); Paola Murgia and Alba Tiberi (Sphinxes); Francesco Caruso and Giuseppe Gambino (Winged Men); Tommaso Accardo (Forge Man); Cristina Mantis (Medusa); Filippo Fugazzotto (Goat-headed Creature); Isabella Rita Gallinelli (Soprano/Aida); Mauro Marino (Egyptian Pharaoh); Endrius Colombaioni (Fire Eater); Giancarlo Colombaioni and Angela Bonello (Jugglers); Vincenzo Moretti (Othello); Manuela Metri (Desdemona); Laura Maltoni, Ester Salis, and Donato Fierro-Perez (Commedia Dell'Arte Troupe); Lilliana Vitale (Storyteller).

LOS ANGELES TIMES, 5/14/99, Calendar/p. 6, Kenneth Turan

Starring everyone from Michelle Pfeiffer and Calista Flockhart to Kevin Kline and Stanley Tucci, "William Shakespeare's A Midsummer Night's Dream" is presenting itself as "a 400-year-old whimsical romantic comedy as it's never been seen before." In other words, this is a chance to see Shakespeare with mud wrestling, something the Bard surely would have put in if only he'd thought of it himself.

As written and directed by Michael Hoffman ("One Fine Day," "Restoration"), "Midsummer" tries to be as many things to as many people as possible. It sticks close to Shakespeare's language and the original plot while making liberal use of movie and TV stars and tossing in over-insistent moments of slapstick farce to entertain those whose tastes run more toward "Ace Ventura."

If there is a model for how to do this kind of modernized yet traditional production well, it's Kenneth Branagh's excellent 1993 "Much Ado About Nothing," which possessed an energy, brio and high spirits that this production does not match. There's nothing wrong with what this frantic

"Midsummer" is attempting, but in trying too hard to be funny, it ends up being almost no fun at all.

What's left of the fun quotient is largely the result of Kline, a prince among modern farceurs, who plays Nick Bottom, the hammiest of nonprofessional actors. One of "Midsummer's" subplots involves an extremely amateur production of a mock-tragedy called "The Most Lamentable Comedy, and Cruel Death of Pyramus and Thisby"; Kline's portrayal of the lovelorn Pyramus, though it comes too late in the film to make a major difference, is the closest thing to genuine comedy on offer.

Though the original play is nominally set in ancient Athens, Hoffman's version is changed to a Tuscan hill town named Mt. Athena, which gives the film the kind of lush setting "Much Ado" benefited from and allows for a key plot element concerning characters who wear "Athenian dress."

The time is also updated, to the turn of the century and its craze for bicycles. These machines figure overly much in the film's cumbersome slapstick but fondly recall A.J. Antoon's landmark 1972 New York Shakespeare Festival production of "Much Ado About Nothing," set in a similar time period and broadcast with great success on CBS.

Theseus (the protean David Strathaim), duke of Mt. Athena, is about to be married to the lovely Hippolyta (a barely visible Sophie Marceau). His final and least appealing prenuptial duty is an audience with an angry father named Egeus (Bernard Hill, last seen captaining the sinking "Titanic").

Egeus wants daughter Hermia (Anna Friel) to marry Demetrius (Christian Bale), but she is intent on wedding Lysander (Dominic West). Complicating things further, Hermia's close friend Helena (Flockhart, TV's "Ally McBeal") is mad about indifferent Demetrius.

If this sounds initially confusing, it may well be to those unfamiliar with the play, but things do get clearer as these four young people end up headed for a nearby wood. Also retiring there is the theatrical troupe that includes Bottom, its members intent on rehearsing "Pyramus and Thisby" and then putting it on for the duke and perhaps getting some financial reward on his wedding day.

This turns out to be not just any wood but the home of a legion of fairies ruled by Titania and Oberon (Pfeiffer and Rupert Everett, an appropriately regal pair). On this of all nights, however, the king and queen are having a tiff, and when Oberon enlists Tucci as the playful Puck to administer a powerful love potion, all kinds of unforeseen nonsense takes place.

Shakespeare's play, the source of celebrated lines like "The path of true love never did run smooth" and "Lord, what fools these mortals be," is a glistening examination of the interlinked foolishness and magic of romantic love, but though the language remains the same on film, the essence of the play seems to have eluded this production.

A good chunk of the problem is that the performers playing the two pairs of Athenian lovers are too blandly undifferentiated to hold our interest during the increasingly tedious confusion that unfolds in the forest: They look and act alike even before they start rolling in the mud.

The smooth Kline, who as the hapless Bottom ends up with an ass-like head and a weakness for braying his lines, fares better. When he and his ragtag troupe, including Bill Irwin as Tom Snout and Gregory Jbara as Snug the joiner, work up their peculiar "Pyramus," that is something to smile at.

This "Midsummer Night's" is handsomely outfitted visually and has the advantage of both Felix Mendelssohn's lush music and chunks of classic Italian opera. Though the actors have no major problems handling the language, the whole venture is listless when it should be sparkling. Shakespeare, even with mud wrestling, needn't be quite so much of a slog.

NEW YORK, 5/17/99, p. 58, Peter Rainer

Years ago I got into trouble while participating in a daylong panel discussion on Shakespeare and the movies by suggesting that if the Bard were alive today, he'd be writing film scripts. The point I was trying to make was not about the noxious effect of Hollywood on artists: That argument has already been made, in another context, by Paul Mazursky, who said that if Alexander Solzhenitsyn had moved to Beverly Hills instead of Vermont he'd be writing episodes of *Police Story* from his hot tub. No, my point was simply that Shakespeare, in addition to everything else, had the most "cinematic" of imaginations. Reading his plays is a far greater visual experience than watching most movies. Inevitably, the films derived from his dramas are diminutions. Who can hope to compete with the imagery conjured up by his language? And yet there have been directors—such as Orson Welles in *Othello* and *Chimes at Midnight,* and Kurosawa in his *Macbeth* adaptation *Throne of Blood*—who have brought their own voluptuous rage and passion to the Shakespearean panorama and, in so doing, honor both the playwright and the movie medium. And, of course, the greatest Shakespearean screen actors are always *better* than we could ever have imagined on our own. When Laurence Olivier is Othello, he's Shakespeare's collaborator; he's not merely acting the part but *realizing it.*

A *Midsummer Night's Dream*—with its fairy king and queen and sprites, its oafish players and star-crossed, cross-eyed lovers, its pomp and slapstick and filigree—is one of the most opulent and movie-ish of Shakespeare's plays. (It's been filmed often, most memorably in the 1935 Max Reinhardt production with Jimmy Cagney as Bottom and Mickey Rooney as Puck.) The best thing about the new movie version of *A Midsummer Night's Dream,* which stars Kevin Kline as Bottom and a radiantly gauzy Michelle Pfeiffer as Titania, is that it doesn't try to set itself up as some radical reinterpretation. Neither does it punch up Shakespeare with a lot of galumphing calisthenics designed to show us how danged *enjoyable* the old guy can be. (This was the *Shakespeare in Love* approach, and may have been the key to its success; the filmmakers treated us all like precocious groundlings.) This new *Midsummer Night's Dream* is, thankfully, not a work of genius; it's captivatingly modest. The director, Michael Hoffman, who transposes the play's setting from Athens to late-1800s Tuscany while keeping most everything else intact, is content to treat the play as a showcase for his superb performers, who also include Rupert Everett as Oberon, Calista Flockhart as Helena, Anna Friel as Hermia, and Stanley Tucci as the horned Puck. Hoffman isn't much of a conjurer; his poetic effects—lots of arboreal dew and fairy dust and golden light—are a sugar-dipped mélange of Pre-Raphaelite and faux Etruscan and Maxfield Parrish. But there's a sly knowingness to his method that redeems it. *A Midsummer Night's Dream,* after all, is about how the base is transformed into the blessed. Hoffman transmutes the heavy syrup of kitsch into Shakespearean nectar.

As it's performed here, *A Midsummer Night's Dream* is a supremely joyous play. No Jan Kott broodings for this bunch. Inevitably, the comical catastrophe of love sorts itself out—whether that love be unrequited, like Helena's for Hermia's suitor Demetrius (Christian Bale), or blind, like the fairy queen Titania's for Bottom, with his ass's ears and furry cheeks. Just about everybody ends up paired off in the best of ways. The sprites and nymphs of the forest are naughty jesters, but they're romantics as well; they know they have to undo their whammies and make things right. Only one of the lovers is left lovelorn: the lowly, princely Bottom, whose transcendent tryst with Titania gives him a glimpse of the ethereal he can't dispel. For most of the way, Kevin Kline is marvelously robust and hammy, but ultimately his Bottom has a touch of the forlorn about him. Whose dream is being dreamt in *A Midsummer Night's Dream?* That's always been one of the play's resonant mysteries. In Hoffman's movie, the dream belongs to Bottom, and he's sad in the end for having woken up.

NEW YORK POST, 5/14/99, p. 41, Jonathan Foreman

Michael Hoffman's version of "A Midsummer Night's Dream" is a funny and sexy movie, at least as enjoyable and accessible as Kenneth Branagh's "Much Ado About Nothing." But it's also vastly inferior as Shakespeare adaptation.

It misses out on many of the play's delights, thanks to savage cuts in the text, a wrong-headed setting in late Victorian Italy, rhythms of speech and scene that are far too slow, and an inappropriate operatic score.

On the plus side, the acting is mostly of a high order and Shakespeare's verse is spoken surprisingly well, even by the non-British actors.

And wisely, Hoffman keeps intact the complex plot of this play about love versus reason. Duke Theseus (a subdued David Strathairn) is about to marry Hippolyta (Sophie Marceau). During the wedding preparations he is approached by old Egeus (Bernard Hill from "Titanic") whose daughter Hermia is refusing to go through with an arranged marriage to Demetrius (Christian Bale) because she and Lysander (Dominic West), another eligible young man, are in love.

Unfortunately, as Theseus points out, the law says that daughters must obey their fathers in such matters or face either death or the nunnery. Hermia and Lysander therefore resolve to elope.

But Hermia's best friend, Helena (Calista Flockhart), who unrequitedly loves Demetrius, warns him that his betrothed is about to split, and they all run off into a magical forest.

In the same wood, five local workmen including Bottom the weaver (Kevin Kline) are rehearsing a ridiculous play to be performed in a competition at the duke's wedding.

Unknown to actors and lovers, there is a marital squabble going on in the forest between Oberon, King of the Fairies (a diffident Rupert Everett) and Titania, his queen (Michelle Pfeiffer).

Oberon has the fairy trickster Puck (Stanley Tucci) mix up a powerful love potion as part of a plot to humiliate Titania (by making her fall for someone or something hideous), but decides to help out the four young humans chasing each other through the forest. Puck, however, gives the potion to the wrong lovers at the wrong time.

Kline and Tucci are terrific (although Kline looks too dashing for the part and is burdened with a back story invented by Hoffman about a difficult wife). Flockhart shows she can go mano a mano with a stage actress as accomplished as Anna Friel.

And Pfeiffer performs Titania as if she were born to play a naked pagan goddess of erotic perfection—which she arguably was.

It's a shame that Hoffman substitutes romantic music for Shakespeare's verse. There's also no rational explanation for his relocation of a play set in ancient Greece to Tuscany, except the fact that the countryside there is a lovely place to spend six months making a movie.

This is also a play that could benefit from modern special effects. Yet Hoffman renders the fairies as Tinkerbell-style flying light bulbs or long-haired babes wearing too much glitter. There is also an unforgivable mud-wrestling bout between Hermia and Helena.

Such slapstick misses the play's point that when love makes us lose our dignity, it does so in ways that are as liberating as they are frightening and confusing.

Still, it's joyful, lively stuff, and it's Shakespeare.

NEWSDAY, 5/14/99, Part II/p. B3, Gene Seymour

Beyond the sun-dappled beauty of the Tuscan landscape in daylight, there's not much about this adaptation of "A Midsummer Night's Dream" that will make you transported. This is a problem since, as the title implies, everything consequential and magical, in this story happens at night.

Director Michael Hoffman's decision to transplant William Shakespeare's Arcadian frolic from Hellenic Greece to 1890s Italy seems intended to give it some grounding. (And to offer audiences the pleasure of watching pretty people crashing about on bicycles.) But the production feels too earthbound by half. Clutter and tumult may be desirable in a knockabout farce like Hoffman's underrated "Soapdish" (1991). But they cramp Willie the Shake's ethereal mischief here.

Moreover, Hoffman's approach seems less like a fully realized vision of "Midsummer Night's Dream" and more like an extended, patchwork improvisation. There's a let's-try-this air to the proceedings that makes them resemble a fancy dress rehearsal—much like the one that almost comes off in the woods among the play's rep company of bumbling locals.

With all that said, it isn't every dress rehearsal that can boast the star power summoned for this project. From David Straithairn and Sophie Marceau as betrothed nobles Theseus and Hippolyta to Roger Rees and Bill Irwin as members of the aforementioned troupe, the magnetism of Hoffman's cast more than makes up for the lapses in production, giving it a buoyancy that keeps you involved even when the frantic pacing hits a dead spot.

Perhaps the biggest gamble taken in this production was enhancing the presence of Nick Bottom, self-styled leading man among the amateur actors. It's a risk that pays off, thanks to the quicksilver inventiveness of Kevin Kline, who frames the buffoonish Bottom with a melancholy knowledge of his own limits. The clown-with-a-broken-heart can be wearying as an archtype and Hoffman lays on the pathos a little thick at times. But Kline applies just enough delicacy to even the broadest of Bottom's dimensions to make it work.

The engine that drives the play remains the confusion among the four young lovers. Hermia (Anna Friel) loves Lysander (Dominic West) but is compelled to marry Demetrius (Christian Bale), who is longed for by Helena (Calista Flockhart).

The latter, a ubiquitous cover girl this month, is getting the most attention for her stepping from small-screen hipness to big-screen prestige. It's no surprise to those who know Flockhart from her stage work that she can ride the Bard at any speed. But if she thought playing the frenzied, obsessed Helena would make anyone overlook her "Ally McBeal" persona, she'd better think again. Despite/because of the resemblances, she remains compulsively watchable.

So does Michelle Pfeiffer, who is radiant and sensuous as fairy queen Titania, especially in those scenes when she is bewitched into falling for Kline's Bottom after he's transformed into a ... let's say donkey and we shall trouble you no more.

Such trickery, as you'll recall from the play, comes from the collaboration of fairy king Oberon (Rupert Everett) and his messenger Puck (Stanley Tucci). Everett plays the king with gimlet-dry suaveness well-matched with Tucci, who plays the traditional sprite's role as if he were a Marx brother, or rather a coolly modulated amalgam of Groucho and Harpo.

Because it's "William Shakespeare's 'A Midsummer Night's Dream,'" you expect things to be missing and added throughout, especially given Hoffman's willingness to toss curveballs at the oddest places. One of his sneakiest throws comes in the climactic "play within a play," when Irwin, the one true professional clown in the bunch, suddenly shifts away from the manic bumptiousness and plays things straight.

Why there? Why then? Why doesn't it matter more? Whatever the reasons, the moment neatly encompasses what's both disquieting and appealing about this midsummer night.

NEWSWEEK, 4/24/99, p. 74, Jack Kroll

Having written the ultimate tragic love story in "Romeo and Juliet," that irrepressible know-it-all Shakespeare next turned out the ultimate play about love as pure nuttiness. Michael Hoffman's uneven but spunkily energetic movie "William Shakespeare's A Midsummer Night's Dream" transfers the setting to 1900 Tuscany. This allows him to use the newly invented bicycle as the mode of transportation for his quartet of loony lovers chasing each other through a magic forest. Oberon, the fairy king, dispatches his hit man, Puck, with a potion to scramble the desires of the four. He also causes his estranged queen, Titania, to fall for Bottom, the weaver, whom he has transformed with an ass's head. Result: total erotic chaos.

Hoffman ("One Fine Day") makes some dubious moves. He miscegenates chunks of Mendelssohn's celebrated music with gobbets of Italian opera. His forest, built on a sound stage, looks stagy and airless. But much of this magical, wise, sardonic, sexy play comes through. Michelle Pfeiffer's Titania is radioactively beautiful. Stanley Tucci's Puck is amusingly jaded after centuries of playing tricks on hapless mortals. Calista Flockhart de-McBeals herself and cuts loose as Helena, the girl nobody wants. Kevin Kline is a brilliant Bottom, ecstatically hammy in his amateur acting group, wallowing in Titania's bewitched embrace, poignant as he muses on his dream of asinine metamorphosis.

SIGHT AND SOUND, 10/99, p. 51, Leslie Felperin

Monte Athena, Italy, the 1890s. Duke Theseus is asked to adjudicate a complaint brought by Egeus: his daughter Helena refuses to marry Demetrius, Egeus' preferred suitor, and insists on marrying Lysander. Theseus tells Helena she must either obey or become a nun by his own wedding day. Helena and Lysander decide to elope. They are pursued into the woods by Helena's friend Hermia, who is in love with Demetrius despite his indifference, and Demetrius himself. Meanwhile, some amateur actors rehearse *Pyramus and Thisbe*. The weaver Bottom will play Pyramus.

In the woods, Oberon, the king of the fairies, is having an argument with his queen, Titania. To humiliate Titania, Oberon charges his minion Puck to anoint her eyes with a love potion that will cause her to fall in love with the first creature she sees when she wakes up; this turns out to be Bottom, whom Puck also turns into an ass. Chancing upon the mortal foursome in the woods, Oberon instructs Puck to use the same love juice on Demetrius, but Puck mistakenly bewitches Lysander instead who awakes and falls in love with Hermia. Trying to correct the problem, Demetrius is also made to fall in love with Hermia. Eventually Puck sorts things out so that Lysander is in love with Helena and Demetrius with Hermia. Bottom awakes returned to mortal form after his night of passion with Titania. Back in Monte Athena, Egeus relents and lets Helena choose her mate. *Pyramus and Thisbe* is performed before the Duke and his bride Hippolyta, the four lovers and the court.

Decrying the deployment of operatic spectacle in Georgian productions of *A Midsummer Night's Dream*, William Hazlitt once wrote, "That which is merely an airy shape, a dream, a passing thought, immediately becomes an unmanageable reality." And indeed, this play above all of Shakespeare's others, for all its fey charm and the witty delicacy of its verse, lends itself to pageantry and tricks. All those fairy costumes to make! Peter Brook's famous 1970 staging of the play, with its bare, white set and caftan-clad cast, attempted to strip the text back to the bone. The patrician Hazlitt would have approved. He'd probably have been suspicious of this latest film version's use of twinkling digital effects and lurex-and-lamé encrusted production design, although its frothy, nineteenth-century *jeu d'esprit* would probably seem more familiar to him than Brook's cerebral, Beckettian, Age of Aquarius workout.

Sporting a shamelessly commercial all-star cast and textually shorn to make a comfortable, diverting two-hour flick, it's the lack of intellectual pretensions that finally makes this version so endearing. Director Michael Hoffman is best known for the playful period film *Restoration,* based on the novel by Rose Tremain, and the romantic comedy *One Fine Day*—a perfect track record for juggling *Midsummer*'s upscale literary pedigree with its screwball knockabout. just to drive home the source material's relevance to the quixotic, irrational perils of single life, Hoffman has cast Calista Flockhart as Hermia, one of the hapless, foolish lovers. Clad here as 1890s 'modern woman' with daring pantaloons and a (scandalously anachronistic) bicycle, her neurotic persona from *Ally McBeal* dovetails nicely with Hermia's whiny, desperate pursuit of Demetrius, and her verse delivery is impeccable. Sadly, the same can't be said for Michelle Pfeiffer (supposedly Ally McBeal's real-life model), whose Titania is more wood than wood sprite.

With such a well known play, viewers familiar with the work are invited to assess the production on how well cast and executed the performances are. Hoffman's quartet of bickering lovers, eventually reduced to ungainly mud-wrestling, are all cohesive and excellent, though Kevin Kline's Bottom (indeed most of his anatomy) is annoyingly preening here, smug in its blithe competence and straining too hard for sympathy.

An ambitious and logical crack is taken at playing the story's two realms—real world 'Monte Athena' (the version's no-good reason substitute for the original's Athens) versus the fairy grove —in two different registers, the first grounded in Italian real locations, the second shot on the Cinecitta's sound stages, enhancing it's theatrical quality and making it likeably reminiscent of Wilhelm Dieterle's beguiling, nitrate-rich monochrome 1935 film version (famous for starring James Cagney, Mickey Rooney and, in a tiny part, Kenneth Anger). Despite Hazlitt, the artificial glamour of the set makes this *Midsummer*'s reality all the more manageable.

TIME, 5/10/99, p. 82, Richard Schickel

It's the fate of Anna Friel's character, Hermia, to get rather lost in so-so productions of *A Midsummer Night's Dream*, and sure enough, that's what happens in Michael Hoffman's adaptation, which oxymoronically manages to seem both leaden and hasty. Reset for no discernible reason from ancient Athens to 19th century Tuscany, it focuses on the fun stuff—the fairies who inhabit the damp but enchanted wood, the rude mechanicals (led by Kevin Kline's hammy but well-cured Bottom) and their awful-wonderful production of Pyramus and Thisbe.

Hoffman stages their play-within-a-play with energetic conviction, and Bottom's misalliance with Titania, the fairy queen (Michelle Pfeiffer), is played with a certain sexy intensity. But the human lovers (who include Calista Flockhart as the comically obsessed Helena, muddled by the carelessness of Stanley Tucci's smug Puck with his love potions, don't achieve firm definition. Lacking the center of concern they might provide, this version of the play becomes a collection of well-loved scenes: dutiful but mostly unmagical.

VILLAGE VOICE, 5/18/99, p. 121, Jessica Winter

The sole apparent reason for relocating the latest adaptation of *A Midsummer Night's Dream* to turn-of-the-century Tuscany is so that the fairy-dazed lovers can putter around the enchanted forest on their newfangled, unwieldy bicycles. It's a charming conceit—the sacred Bard comes wheeling and crashing into the 20th century—but the film's temporal suspension between its source and the present day typifies the way in which this *Midsummer* dangles uncertainly between mannerly devotion to Big Will and susceptibility to a recent cinematic pandemic, the update.

Too bad, because the early scenes whir and buzz along to create quite a pleasing clamor. Thwarted lovers Hermia (Anna Friel) and Lysander (Dominic West) make effortless complements, Hermia's intended match, Demetrius (Christian Bale), exudes just the right smug stiffness, and Calista Flockhart evokes empathy for that articulate train wreck, Helena. Director Michael Hoffman hangs back at medium range, making cuts at longish intervals to maintain the integrity of the action. The pace should accelerate all the more once the youngsters escape into the woods, but the transition to the spirit level is abrupt and clumsy—the ornate forest is lit like a Little League night game—and the film never quite regains its footing. The script isn't sure if Stanley Tucci's Puck is a dullard or a nihilist; neither version leaves room for Tucci to sell us his closing "if we shadows have offended" speech.

What Kevin Kline has to hawk as Bottom, however, downright stinks. The movie saddles Shakespeare's holy fool with a maudlin back story and a self-pitying streak; its rendering of his absurdly inept play-within-a-play is funny enough, but Hoffman's fervor to showcase Bottom's "redemption" (via unwitting humiliation, no less) reaches Branaghian levels of bathos. Not content merely to strain Shakespeare's meaning, Hoffman tacks on his own as well. 'Tis a weak and idle theme.

Also reviewed in:
CHICAGO TRIBUNE, 5/14/99, Friday/p. A, Michael Wilmington
NEW REPUBLIC, 5/31/99, p. 32, Stanley Kauffmann
NEW YORK TIMES, 5/14/99, p. E1, Janet Maslin
NEW YORKER, 5/17/99, p. 96, David Denby
VARIETY, 5/10-16/99, p. 49, Emanuel Levy
WASHINGTON POST, 5/14/99, p. C1, Jane Horwitz
WASHINGTON POST, 5/14/99, Weekend/p. 47, Desson Howe

WINDHORSE

A Shadow Distribution release of a High Plateau LLC/Paul Wagner Productions production. *Executive Producer:* Ellen Casey Wagner. *Producer:* Paul Wagner. *Director:* Paul Wagner. *Screenplay (Tibetan and Mandarin with English subtitles):* Julia Elliott, Thupten Tsering and Paul Wagner. *Director of Photography:* Steven Schecter. *Editor:* Paul Wagner and Tony Black. *Music:* Tommy Hayes, Sam Chapin, and John Dana. *Sound:* Sam Chapin, Skip SoRelle, and Jim Kreidler. *Running time:* 97 minutes. *MPAA Rating:* Not Rated.

CAST: Dadon (Dolkar); Jampa Kelsang (Dorjee); Richard Chang (Duan-ping); Taije Silverman (Amy); Lu Yu (Du Han-shen); Thupten Sherab (Samden); Lodoe Nangyal (Tashi); Tenzin Pema (Young Dolkar); Pasang Dolma (Young Pema); Deepak Tserin (Young Dorjee).

LOS ANGELES TIMES, 2/26/99, Calendar/p. 8, Kevin Thomas

Paul Wagner's stunning and courageous "Windhorse" opens in a remote mountain village in western Tibet in 1979 as two girls and a boy are jumping rope. As the children Dolkar, her brother Dorjee and their cousin Pema watch, two Chinese soldiers appear and gun down their praying grandfather, who had dared to put up a poster declaring, "Chinese go back to China!" Wagner, a prizewinning documentarian making his feature debut, shot key establishing sequences inside Tibet, where many of his collaborators must remain anonymous for fear of Chinese reprisal, and finished the film in Nepal.

Eighteen years hence, the three children have taken very different paths. Pema (name withheld) has become a Buddhist nun in an isolated convent while the rest of the family has moved to Lhasa, where Dolkar (Dadon) and Dorjee (Jampa Kelsang) live with their parents and grandmother, a feisty, old lady who protests a new edict banning the display of photos of the Dalai Lama, even in private homes. Dolkar has become a beautiful and popular singing star, willing to cooperate with the Chinese bureaucracy, which aims to turn her into a kind of poster girl for the "New Tibet."

Dolkar is excited by the prospect of becoming a star all over China and sees it as the only way she and her family can escape poverty. She has fallen in love with a kind and caring young Chinese, Duan-ping (Richard Chang), an assistant producer at the Lhasa radio and TV station, who also is eager to further her career.

Handsome and moody, Dorjee has become a hard-drinking, chain-smoking pool hall habitue, cynical and embittered by Chinese oppression yet convinced that any resistance is futile.

The trio's lives intersect again and are disrupted when Pema rallies to the support of a fellow nun, who confesses during a police raid of the convent that she has continued to display a photo of the Dalai Lama.

Wagner, who wrote his script with his niece and co-producer Julia Elliott and her Tibetan boyfriend Thupten Tsering, who also co-directed, has the right idea about how to make an effective protest film: Frame the message in a well-developed plot with three-dimensional characters. Clearly, a commitment to revealing the dire plight of the Tibetan people under Chinese rule has fueled this project, and Wagner has pulled off the not inconsiderable feat of eliciting natural and effective portrayals from nonprofessionals acting in languages foreign to him. "Windhorse" takes its title from bits of paper, inscribed with prayers for hope and freedom, that Tibetans set aloft in the winds. The film is remarkably accomplished, virtually free of self-consciousness and awkwardness and buoyed by Tommy Hayes' plaintive score, which incorporates traditional Tibetan music.

NEW YORK POST, 4/30/99, p. 63, Jonathan Foreman

"Windhorse" wears its consciousness-raising aims so high on its sleeve, it could be a co-production of Amnesty International and Richard Gere.

Set in Chinese-occupied Tibet using some Tibetan actors, much of "Windhorse" was actually shot in secret in Lhasa, the Tibetan capital. The filmmakers posed as tourists.

Unfortunately, this footage looks as though it had been recorded by a tourist who didn't really know how to use his camcorder.

The film opens in a small village in western Tibet. Three little kids are playing when their grandfather is murdered by Chinese police.

Twenty years later, sister Dolkar is a singer about to make it in the Chinese-controlled pop industry, thanks to the help of her Chinese boyfriend, Duan-ping.

Brother Dorjee is an unemployed no-goodnik who lacks the courage to join the anti-Chinese resistance. And cousin Pema is a Buddhist nun.

At the same time that Dorjee meets a Tibetan-speaking American tourist, a Chinese crackdown on banned pictures of the Dalai Lama provokes Pema into shouting "Free Tibet" during a visit to Lhasa. She is arrested, imprisoned and tortured.

Chinese authorities summon Dolkar, Dorjee and their parents to pick up her near-lifeless body.

Seeing what has happened to her cousin forces Dolkar to re-evaluate her music career and the way the Chinese are manipulating it for propagandistic ends. Dorjee, too, realizes that he must do something to bring Chinese brutality to the attention of the outside world.

The filmmakers clearly thought that by focusing on the experiences of a single family they might bring home the cruelty of the occupation. But they came up with a crude, predictable plot peopled by crudely, thinly drawn characters.

It's also a film that conspicuously fails to make the most of the extraordinary beauty of the Tibetan landscape.

In the end, you cannot help but wonder why Oscar-winning documentarist Paul Wagner bothered with this earnest but lame tale instead of making a killer documentary about the occupation.

NEWSDAY, 4/30/99, Part II/p. B6, Gene Seymour

That "Windhorse" exists at all is reason enough for admiration. Paul Wagner, best known for making documentaries about subjects ranging from Pullman porters to polio, filmed parts of this blunt-edged thriller about life in occupied Tibet beneath the attentive radar of that country's

Chinese overseers, who almost surely would have confiscated the cameras—and, likely, most of its cast and crew.

The film has run through a gauntlet of festivals on its way to limited release and at each stop, voices of condemnation have been heard from Chinese authorites seeking its removal. At one festival in Hawaii, according to the filmmakers, "Windhorse" was screened, but removed from competition.

The closing credits display enough "Name Withhelds" to demonstrate Wagner's courage and, especially, that of the Tibetans who helped him make this project carry on this project. In fact, the story behind the cameras sounds much more interesting than the one placed before them, despite its basis on "true events."

Written by Wagner, this melodrama focuses on three members of the same Tibetan family struggling to survive in contemporary Lhasa. Dolkar, an aspiring pop singer played by real-life Tibetan songstress Dadon, makes nice with the Chinese government to land a nationwide TV gig while her brother Dorjee (Jampa Kelsang), smolders with bitterness that can only be soothed by indolence and alcohol.

Meanwhile, their cousin, a Buddhist nun named Pema (one of those whose name is withheld) is jailed and tortured for daring to proclaim, in a public marketplace, devotion to the Dalai Lama. When Pema is sent home to die, Dadon and Dorjee are galvanized away from their respective holding patterns and towards government opposition. They, along with their parents and their openly defiant grandmother, are further endangered by the confiscation of incriminating videotape taken by a sympathetic American tourist (Taije Silverman).

Wagner's "J'Accuse" has the force, if not the texture, of a Roosevelt-era Warner Brothers romance about struggle in the streets. No one who sees "Windhorse" will be left cold towards the ongoing tragedy being depicted, but many might wish for subtlety or complexity. Under the circumstances, there probably wasn't the time for either attribute to take root.

VILLAGE VOICE, 5/4/99, p. 116, Amy Taubin

Slighter and certainly more conventional than Scorsese's epic struggle to give expression to a culture in which aesthetics are inseparable from spirituality is Paul Wagner's no-budget melodrama, *Windhorse,* set in present-day Tibet. [The reference is to *In Search of Kundun*; see Taubin's review.] The most fascinating aspect of *Windhorse* is the footage shot on hidden video cameras inside Tibet and smuggled out of the country. Wagner gives serious meaning to the self-styled guerrilla filmmaker's notion of "stealing a shot."

The audience likely to be most appreciative of the film are Tibetans in exile, who might have wished for more documentary and less fiction. *Windhorse* tells the story of a Tibetan family living in Lhasa and trying to survive under Chinese rule. The grandmother, whose husband was murdered by the Chinese, is openly defiant; the parents try to keep a low profile while putting food on the table; the son is a dropout who stops short of joining the underground; and the daughter, a nightclub singer, tries to win favor with the Chinese masters with songs about the glory of Chairman Mao. When their young cousin, a nun who was arrested and tortured by the Chinese, is sent home to die, the brother and sister are forced to reassess their choices. Wagner executes this familiar narrative competently enough, but the effect is to turn the Tibetan tragedy into a pale imitation of a 1940s studio movie about resistance and collaboration.

Also reviewed in:
NATION, 5/24/99, p. 36, Stuart Klawans
NEW REPUBLIC, 5/10/99, p. 36, Stanley Kauffmann
NEW YORK TIMES, 4/30/99, p. E12, Lawrence Van Gelder
VARIETY, 1/4-10/99, p. 100, Derek Elley
WASHINGTON POST, 10/15/99, Weekend/p. 44, Desson Howe

WING COMMANDER

A Twentieth Century Fox release of a No Prisoners Productions and Digital Anvil presentation in association with Origin Systems, Inc. and The Carousel Picture Company. *Executive Producer:* Jean-Martial LeFranc and Romain Schroeder. *Producer:* Todd Moyer. *Director:* Chris Roberts. *Screenplay:* Kevin Droney. *Based on a story and characters created by:* Chris Roberts. *Director of Photography:* Thierry Arbogast. *Editor:* Peter Davies. *Music:* Kevin Kiner and David Arnold. *Production Designer:* Peter Lamont. *Visual Effects:* Chris Brown. *Costumes:* Magali Guidasci. *Music:* David Arnold. *Running time:* 105 minutes. *MPAA Rating:* PG-13.

CAST: Freddie Prinze, Jr. (Blair); Saffron Burrows (Deveraux); Matthew Lillard (Maniac); Tchéky Karyo (Paladin); Jürgen Prochnow (Gerald); David Suchet (Sansky); David Warner (Tolwyn); Ginny Holden (Rosie).

LOS ANGELES TIMES, 3/12/99, Calendar/p. 10, Gene Seymour

[The following review by Gene Seymour appeared in a slightly different form in **NEWSDAY, 3/12/99, Part II/p. B7.]**

Among the few differences between "Wing Commander" the movie and a high-concept thrill ride is that nobody tells you to keep your hands inside a moving vehicle. You won't feel dizzy or shaken up either. You won't feel anything. Period.

Oh, maybe bored or disoriented by the inside jargon and alien references that will be comprehensible only if you happen to have played the computer game on which "Wing Commander" is based.

For the uninitiated, the movie and the game are set in the 26th century, by which time mankind has colonized more than a few solar systems, through all manner of wormholes and time-space jumps, and now finds itself at war with (what else?) a bloodthirsty alien race named the Kilrathi.

In this particular round, the Kilrathi—who are seen only intermittently and look like (what else?) green wart hogs in suits of armor—have figured out the coordinates to bust through some space wormholes and come within miles of Earth. The only thing standing in their way is a star-spanning version of an aircraft carrier that ferries the best darned fighter squadron in the universe.

The leader is sultry, steel-nerved Jeannette "Angel" Devereaux (Saffron Burrows), who takes no guff from anyone, especially the two renegade pilots who become part of the squadron after delivering orders from Adm. Geoffery Tolwyn (David Warner).

One of the pilots, Todd "Maniac" Marshall (Matthew Lillard), is a hot dog with no inner voice telling him to be careful. The other, Christopher "Maverick" Blair (Freddie Prinze Jr.), is a brooding navigational genius haunted by the death of his parents in another galactic war.

Only a romantic would call any of these types characters and, though there is talk among these freedom fighters and by the enigmatic Paladin (Tcheky Karyo) about feelings and emotions, what you get instead are stock sentiments in spacesuits.

Though its military bravado has echoes of "Starship Troopers," "Wing Commander" is pretty much a gentler, kinder variation on the intergalactic war subgenre. Fans of "Troopers" may wish for grander, grosser effects than the ones displayed here.

Despite some racy moments between Maniac and a pretty, but doomed, pilot, this is a kid-friendly project with dialogue that's several kernels below "Star Trek" in corn content.

And it succeeds in making you at least curious about what the game is like. But that may be because you feel so uninvolved in what's on the screen that a joy stick or a mouse would be the only thing that would arouse your interest.

NEW YORK POST, 3/12/99, p. 46, Jonathan Foreman

Based on the science-fiction computer game, "Wing Commander" cheerfully borrows scenes, characters and storylines from World War II movies and resets them in outer space. For the most part—except for a couple of embarrassingly corny or crudely written scenes—this cherry-picked mixture of "Midway" "Run Silent, Run Deep" "The Battle of Britain" and a host of other films works well.

"Wing Commander" is set in a 26th century when humans have expanded deep into space—but still use projectile weapons and speak using late 20th-century slang. Before the present conflict with the lion-faced Kilrathi aliens, the Earth Confederation fought a successful civil war against "The Pilgrims": human space colonists who evolved into genetically superior pilots over centuries of space exploration. As this predictable but no less watchable movie begins, hot-shot pilots Freddie Prinze Jr. and Matthew Lillard are on a freighter captained by a mysterious Frenchman called Taggart (the excellent Tcheky Karyo from "Addicted to Love"), on their way to join the carrier Tiger Claw.

But the aliens have just wiped out an Earth fleet, and it will fall to the boys, Taggart and the crew of their new vessel to save the planet. Fortunately, the boys' new wing commander turns out to be the tough but gorgeous Capt. Deveraux (Saffron Burrows), their messmates are a bunch of good-looking men and women with Australian and British accents, and the senior officers—mostly veteran British character actors like David Warner and David Suchet—are wise and sympathetic, with the exception of the bigoted Gerald (Jurgen Prochnow).

For those who like their sci-fi properly naval, "Wing Commander" includes a healthy variety of engagements: There's lots of Pacific-style carrier combat (the starfighters even look like World War II Corsairs), as well as a raid by a marine boarding party and a submarine scene in which a silent spaceship hides in a crater while depth-charging destroyers pass overhead. There's even an 18th-century style broadside.

Unlike "Starship Troopers," this genial B movie never makes a joke of the genre or its war-movie roots, and is competently acted throughout. Actress Ginny Holden stands out among the young pilots. Prinze is appealing within his limited range, and even Lillard manages to soften his persona to a tolerable level. The whole film is buoyed by the professionalism of the supporting cast, and the computer-generated special effects include some surprisingly beautiful space shots.

To its credit, the movie daringly but casually includes an attractive interracial pairing that features a black woman and a white man, rather than the other way around.

VILLAGE VOICE, 3/23/99, p. 130, Athima Chansanchai

The latest in a long line of video games making the jump from cyberspace into a theater near you, *Wing Commander* falls far short of its legacy and gets sucked into a gravitational cesspool of sci-fi clichés. Introduced in 1990, the interactive game was a pioneer in space combat-flight simulations. Featuring stellar special effects, it allowed players to determine their own fate and mold the main character by making tactical decisions. Creator Chris Roberts, in his directing debut, seems to have lost sight of his successful formula.

In *Wing Commander* the movie, the fate of the Earth rests on the shoulders of a blankly earnest rookie pilot, Lieutenant Christopher Blair (Freddie Prinze Jr.), who was born with the ability to navigate through space and time. Blair comes from troubled stock, a superhuman race called the Pilgrims imbued with something akin to the Force. They are ostracized by humans as potential betrayers even though the real enemy would seem to be the Kilrathi alien invaders. The wing commander (Saffron Burrows) and her squadron are called upon to deliver secret intelligence past enemy lines. Though this could be the meat of a good space story, the combat scenes are weak variations of the game's. The props are sadly antiquated by 27th-century standards—torpedos, bullets, and huge headphone sets that make the original *Star Trek* series look light years ahead by comparison. And Matthew Lillard, as Blair's fly-boy buddy, keeps his manic side in check, which is unfortunate since what this film needs is more of what made *Starship Troopers* so enjoyable—campy comic-book fervor.

Also reviewed in:
CHICAGO TRIBUNE, 3/12/99, Friday/p. L, Maureen Ryan
NEW YORK TIMES, 3/12/99, p. E24, Anita Gates
VARIETY, 3/15-21/99, p. 39, Godfrey Cheshire

WINNERS, THE

A First Run Features release of a VPRO/BRTN production. *Producer:* Nellie Kamer. *Director:* Paul Cohen. *Screenplay (English, French, Russian and Flemish with English subtitles):* Paul Cohen and David van Tijn. *Director of Photography:* Paul Cohen. *Editor:* Ian Overweg. *Sound:* Hugo Helmond and Menno Euwe. *Running time:* 85 minutes. *MPAA Rating:* Not Rated.

WITH: Philipp Hirschhorn; Berl Senofsky; Yevgeny Mogilevsky; Mikhail Bezverkhny; Gidon Kremer; Mischa Maisky.

LOS ANGELES TIMES, 4/9/99, Calendar/p. 12, Chris Pasles

Juxtaposing historical footage with contemporary interviews, Paul Cohen's documentary "The Winners" works like a great Dostoevsky novel, plunging us into the hearts, minds and souls of four first-prize winners of the prestigious Queen Elisabeth International Music Competition in Brussels, none of whom, for various reasons, made major careers.

This is fairly straightforward documentary making—its great strength lies in Cohen's ability to get the musicians to talk honestly about themselves and their lives.

American violinist Berl Senofsky, who took top prize in 1955, may be the most content today. After winning his medal, Senofsky says that he realized he really didn't have good technique after all, or the stomach for making a career.

He abruptly withdrew from concert life to work on his playing. He is supremely resigned and philosophical about the way his life worked out, but still makes us understand the high standard he set and the price he's paid for it. He now teaches at Baltimore's Peabody Conservatory.

Russian pianist Yevgeny Mogilevsky was not supposed to be the winner in 1964. Communist Party bosses already had designated another musician in the Soviet delegation as their choice that year. When Mogilevsky returned to the Soviet Union, he was not allowed out again, though he was able to play in that country.

Since the fall of the Iron Curtain he has begun to make a career in the West, but he is noticeably uncomfortable with the marketing requirements set by his New York agent, who talks about his having lost nearly 30 precious years of exposure.

Violinist Mikhail Bezverkhny, the 1976 winner, was a devoted communist. But he abandoned the ideology and his country after years of fruitless efforts to convince the party powers that an international career would benefit the Soviet Union as well as himself. He, too, was not allowed out.

Now living in Brussels, he is surrounded by neighbors who hate classical music, and has to practice in an old van. He is shown becoming increasingly frustrated as he rehearses with his wife, pianist Olga Bezverkhnaya.

Most tragic and probably most talented of the four is the once broodingly handsome violinist Philipp Hirschhorn, who beat former classmate and friend Gidon Kremer to win first prize in 1967.

Kremer (who also appears in the film and talks about his friend) won third prize that year, but his career soared. Hirschhorn's was ended suddenly by the onset of a disease that he doesn't name, but which he suggests was cancer. (He died in 1996, just after this documentary was made.)

"Tragedy," Hirschhorn says, looking at a photo of himself and the other winners that year. "That guy knows that there is no happy end, no grand finale. Despair on a couple of faces. Really, a despair."

His playing of staggering beauty and his pithy, insightful remarks suggest the loss of a mind and talent that we can scarcely comprehend. The loss is close to unbearable.

NEW YORK, 1/25/99, p. 47, Peter Rainer

The Winners is a documentary about what became of a handful of violinists and pianists who at various times copped first prize at Belgium's prestigious Queen Elisabeth Competition. The Dutch director, Paul Cohen, limits his lineup to artists who won back in the fifties through the seventies and went on to middling performing careers—or less. It's a fascinating subject, and even though in many ways Cohen's approach is wrongheaded, you're still left with something resonant. So few movies convey the almost transcendental exhilaration of great classical concert performing that here, where we see that exhilaration dampened and bollixed and thwarted, it seems more heartbreakingly beautiful than ever. The sheer fragility of the performer's life has rarely been so manifest onscreen.

Where the film goes awry is in romanticizing that fragility—or, worse, implying that artistic sensibility and self-destruction are linked. It's a pop-cult cliché that continues to have tremendous high-art currency, and nowhere more so than in the movies. Audience members who consider themselves too elevated of brow to accept Paul Henreid cracking apart as Schumann in *Song of Love* have no trouble buying into essentially the same thing, tricked up in art-house duds in such movies as *Thirty-Two Short Films About Glenn Gould* and *Shine* and *Hilary and Jackie*. Geniuses like Gould and Jacqueline Du Pré are held up as sacrificial martyrs; there's something unseemly in the way they are brought down. Emily Watson's Jackie, in particular, is portrayed as such a mass of madness that the film doesn't even clearly make the point that much of her psychological turmoil was brought on by her multiple sclerosis. Her physical affliction is made to seem merely the outer manifestation of an innate warp of character. This is a disservice to a great artist.

There's a mad-artist type in *The Winners*—the Russian violinist Philipp Hirschhorn, whom we see winning the Queen Elisabeth in 1967 in a startling black-and-white movie clip where he seems, for that one moment, the equal of any violinist on the planet. Then we watch him being interviewed as he was in 1996 (he died shortly after the film was shot). The Byronic smolder of his youth has given way to a pudgy formlessness; and he can barely stand to watch himself in that old clip. "I did something tricky to fool the jury," he says finally. Hirschhorn is an unfortunate case, but Cohen makes too much of his fall. His demise is presented as the flameout of an angel whose wings got too close to the sun. Meanwhile, the debilitating illness that held up Hirschhorn's concert career is never even described. The *Winners* is about the tragedy of artistry denied, but Cohen's view of the artist's predicament is too winner-oriented. Berl Senofsky, who is featured in the film, gave up his pressure-cooker concert career decades ago and now teaches violin at Baltimore's Peabody Conservatory; he is shown there teaching a gifted young violinist, and even though Cohen gives the scene short shrift, it's an ecstatic moment—for us, and for teacher and pupil. How can we feel this man has wasted his life? When Senofsky is asked by the interviewer at one point to produce his Queen Elisabeth medal, he rummages around without finding it, and we're meant to think, *How sad*. But it's not, really. It's a sign of life. He's moved on.

NEW YORK POST, 1/20/99, p. 44, Rod Dreher

Do you have to be crazy to be a musical virtuoso? The art-house hit "Hilary and Jackie" dramatizes the connection between artistic genius and madness, a subject given nonfiction treatment in "The Winners," a Dutch documentary tracking the careers of four musicians who did not live up to the promise of their early years.

Director Paul Cohen went in search of three violinists and a pianist, each of whom had once won the prestigious Queen Elisabeth Competition in Brussels, Belgium, usually a certain steppingstone to success. But for the four men profiled in "The Winners," their dazzling debuts proved the high point of their careers.

The film's pianist, Yevgeny Mogilevsky, was a surprise 1964 winner. The Soviets, who had expected a more politically malleable pet to win, were so outraged that they refused to send anyone to meet the young man on what should have been a triumphal return home. And the government frequently refused Mogilevsky, a surprisingly passive individual, permission to perform abroad—effectively breaking his career.

Violinist Mikhail Bezverkhny, a 1976 Queen Elisabeth winner, is as wild-eyed as Mogilevsky is sedate. He emigrated from Russia in 1990 and currently teaches music in Brussels. Cohen shows Bezverkhny tyrannizing his accompanist wife, and railing against record companies, who, in his view, refuse to make room for eccentrics such as himself.

The most interesting of the quartet is Philipp Hirschhorn ('67), who was widely expected to be one of the great violinists of the century. We see the Russia-born Hirschhorn at the competition in black-and-white footage, an intense, fiery countenance glowing like a white-hot ember.

In 1996, when he was interviewed (he has since died), Hirschhorn looks addled, a sparking nest of frazzled wires.

Why did Hirschhorn fail? It remains a mystery. Hirschhorn's oblique self-analysis doesn't clear things up. Cohen portrays him as an exceptionally fragile wunderkind whose hothouse emotional state allowed him to play with a rarely paralleled expressiveness, but which hobbled attempts to build a career and a life.

Yet, as in "Hilary and Jackie," the onset of a medical condition is unsatisfactorily downplayed as a motivation for self-destructive behavior.

All of the men are depicted as tragic cases, except one: Berl Senofsky ('56), a gentle violinist who teaches at a Baltimore conservatory. Senofsky is tragic only if you think he should have been Isaac Stern or Itzhak Perlman; he seems happy to have been modest little Berl Senofsky.

Astute, absorbing and at times quite moving, "The Winners" suggests that the road to fame and fortune in the classical-music world is fraught with psychological peril. It's an old story, but a cautionary tale no less compelling for its familiarity.

VILLAGE VOICE, 1/26/99, p. 64, Jessica Winter

A stark irony underpins the title of this Dutch-produced documentary about the often unbridgeable gap between the promise and fulfillment of prodigy. Cohen's subjects—two Russian violinists, an American violinist, and a Russian pianist—are past winners of Brussels's Queen Elisabeth Competition; a first-place prize is widely considered the most prestigious accolade in classical music but does not, apparently, guarantee a stellar career. All four of these champions went on to middling-at-best success, variously hampered by illness, depression, bad luck, sheer indifference, and, for the Russians, the vagaries of the Soviet regime. Soon after winning the 1964 competition (even though another member of the Soviet delegation had been "planned" for the prize), pianist Yevgeny Mogilevsky was officially branded "politically unreliable" and prohibited from leaving his country for 10 years despite invitations from orchestras around the world.

The disappointments met by the other men are less readily explicable. Violinist Philipp Hirschhorn, who won in 1967 and now exudes stultified self-contempt, simply collapsed under the weight of expectation once he'd emigrated to the West. He now likens his winning performance to artistic deceit: "It seems I did something tricky to convince the jury, like a successful lie." Scenes in which the bitter, slightly daffy Hirshhorn (who died in 1996) watches 30-year-old footage of his Queen Elisabeth win, scoffing at his broodingly handsome former self, are painful to watch.

The dark, melancholy air of *The Winners* unfortunately carries with it a distinct whiff of condescension toward its subjects. I'm not sure what Cohen is out to prove when his camera gawks at paunchy, elderly Berl Senofsky while he lumbers about his apartment, knocking over plants as he searches in vain for his Queen Elisabeth medal, or when it stares at Hirshhorn for long intervals between Cohen's questions. Cohen feels sorry for these men whose lives never matched their brilliance, but offers little insight into the slow leaking process by which their gifts went to waste. The simplicity and straightforwardness of his approach is too pseudo-objective for such a murky, elusive topic as genius and its betrayals. At times, Cohen comes off as little more than a pitying voyeur; his subjects have always deserved a better audience.

Also reviewed in:
NEW YORK TIMES, 1/20/99, p. E3, Stephen Holden
VARIETY, 11/17-23/97, p. 65, Ken Eisner

WINSLOW BOY, THE

A Sony Pictures Classics release of a David Mamet film. *Producer:* Sarah Green. *Director:* David Mamet. *Screenplay:* David Mamet. *Based on the play by:* Terence Rattigan. *Director of Photography:* Benoît Delhomme. *Editor:* Barbara Tulliver. *Music:* Alaric Jans and Sunnie Hikawa. *Music Editor:* David Carbonara. *Sound:* Clive Winter and (music) Alan Silverman. *Sound Editor:* Maurice Schell. *Casting:* Ros Hubbard and John Hubbard. *Production Designer:* Gemma Jackson. *Art Director:* Andrew Munro. *Set Decorator:* Trisha Edwards. *Costumes:* Consolata Boyle. *Make-up:* Peter Robb-King. *Running time:* 110 minutes. *MPAA Rating:* G.

CAST: Nigel Hawthorne (Arthur Winslow); Jeremy Northam (Sir Robert Morton); Rebecca Pidgeon (Catherine Winslow); Gemma Jones (Grace Winslow); Matthew Pidgeon (Dickie Winslow); Lana Blizerian (Undermaid); Sarah Flind (Violet); Aden Gillett (John Watherstone); Guy Edwards (Ronnie Winslow); Colin Stinton (Desmond Curry); Eve Bland (Suffragette); Sara Stewart (Miss Barnes); Perry Fenwick (Fred); Alan Polonsky (Mr. Michaels); Neil North (First Lord of the Admiralty); Chris Porter (MP); Jim Dunk (Colleague); Duncan Gould (Commons Reporter); Ian Soundy (Local Reporter).

LOS ANGELES TIMES, 4/30/99, Calendar/p. 4, Kenneth Turan

David Mamet has raised profanity to an art form in many of his plays, but don't think his tastes are profane. Mamet did the adaptation of Chekov's "Uncle Vanya" that ended up as "Vanya on 42nd Street," and, says his wife, actress Rebecca Pidgeon, he's fond of playing Victorian songs on the piano. So there.

Still, it's a bit of a surprise to find that Mamet's sixth film as a director, "The Winslow Boy," is a remarkably faithful adaptation of a half-century-old theatrical warhorse by Terence Rattigan ("The Browning Version"), the master of the well-made British play. Set in England just before the Great War, when men still dressed for dinner and grumbled about old cricket injuries, it's an unlooked-for venture into Merchant Ivory country for Mamet, but not any less welcome for that.

While the writer-director must have been bemused at being associated with a G-rated venture in which "what utter rot" is the strongest imprecation going, Mamet has not taken "The Winslow Boy" on because of some misguided reverence for the theatrical past.

Rather Mamet has recognized the dramatic tension still inherent in the original. And, though it was previously filmed more than 50 years ago, he's seen how relevant to the issues of the day the play's managed to remain. For "The Winslow Boy," a pointed examination of the price of seeking justice, also deals with concepts like the power of the media and private rights versus the public good and raises issues whose echoes are as up-to-the-minute as the impeachment imbroglio.

The Winslow family seems the unlikeliest incubator for such a fuss in 1912's England. Father Arthur (Nigel Hawthorne) is a banker so proper he grouses at older son Dickie (Matthew Pidgeon, Rebecca's brother), a wastrel-in-training at Oxford, that a gramophone is out of place in a civilized home.

Most of the obvious spunk in the family resides in daughter Catherine (Rebecca Pidgeon). Though the piece opens with her about to be officially engaged to military man John Watherstone (Aden Gillett), Catherine is a committed suffragist and is sympathetic to trade-union radicals as well.

Fourteen-year-old Ronnie (Guy Edwards) is nominally away at school, but he shows up unexpectedly with a letter announcing he's been summarily dismissed from the Royal Naval College at Osborne, accused of stealing a five-shilling postal order. After a stern examination ("If you tell me a lie, I shall know it, because a lie between you and me can't be hidden"), Arthur accepts his son's protestations of innocence and embarks on a campaign to get him a proper trial.

Because of the complexities of British law and tradition, this is a tricky business to pull off, and Arthur, in addition to using the media to further his cause, asks family lawyer Desmond Curry (Colin Stinton) for help in seeking the services of Britain's top solicitor, Sir Robert Morton (Jeremy Northam).

A model of icy decorum, Sir Robert is suavity itself, but Catherine thinks he is too heartless for a case like this. Catherine is also disturbed by Sir Robert's establishment views: "He always speaks out against what is right," she says, not a little angry.

One of the main thrusts of "The Winslow Boy" is the terrible human costs of this attempt to do the right thing, the life-changing stresses borne by wife and mother Grace (Gemma Jones) and by each member of the family. When Arthur asks his daughter at one point, "Kate, are we both mad, you and I?," it's a much more difficult question to answer than anyone anticipated.

Playwright Rattigan based "The Winslow Boy" on a celebrated real case, though he moved the date up from 1912 to put his story under the shadow of World War I, and he made the family's conservative older sister into a suffragist. As for the changes Mamet made in Rattigan's work, they are surprisingly few, the main one being the expected one of opening the play from its exclusive setting in the Winslows' Kensington drawing room.

Quite a precise writer on his own turf, Mamet has warmed to that aspect of Rattigan and gotten consistently good performances from his well-cast actors. Hawthorne, Oscar-nominated for his role in "The Madness of King George," brings a humanity and a caring to his role that "Winslow" would be lost without. The theater-trained Northam is ideal as the exacting Sir Robert, and Rebecca Pidgeon deftly handles the slight hint of a flirtation between her and the solicitor that the play doesn't have.

Genteel moviemaking with modern overtones, "The Winslow Boy" is especially good at the visual re-creation of its time. Production designer Gemma Jackson and Mamet clearly had a great deal of fun creating so many Winslow-mania objects, from pins to umbrellas to political cartoons, that the case seems as real, and as much of a public furor, as the O.J. Simpson trial.

And when people say that the Winslow case was terrible for the country but also a good thing because "it could only happen in England," statements made during President Clinton's impeachment trial come immediately to mind. There is a difference, Sir Robert says in the play, between doing justice and doing right, and their joint understanding of this is where Terence Rattigan and David Mamet, nominally so different, have no difficulty joining hands.

NEW YORK, 5/10/99, p. 63, Peter Rainer

A lot of people are mystified that David Mamet chose to adapt and direct for the screen Terence Rattigan's 1946 play *The Winslow Boy* (which was filmed once before, in 1948, starring Robert Donat). On the face of it, this *does* seem an odd choice: Rattigan, that minor master of the British "well-made play," is not the first—or even the fiftieth—name that springs to mind in connection with the playwright who wrote *American Buffalo* and *Glengarry Glen Ross*. In theory, Anton Chekhov wouldn't spring to mind, either, and yet Mamet has adapted or translated *The Cherry Orchard, Three Sisters*, and *Uncle Vanya*. The question isn't so much why Mamet would choose to adapt a project so ostensibly far from his temperament; the real head-scratcher is why, for his first film directing someone else's material, he would give himself over to a play that is less than great—less than, say, something by Chekhov.

The answer may be that Rattigan's play is just good enough to appeal to the Victorian gentleman lurking inside Mamet. Rattigan's *Winslow Boy* has a very pleasing formality, with each character's psychological dimensions calibrated to the millimeter. As you watch the movie, it doesn't seem so strange anymore that Mamet decided to do it: His plays, beneath their surface unruliness, have a great formality, too. As a dramatist, he may indulge in bad manners, but they still are manners. The brittle cadences of Rattigan's upper-crusters are continuous with the jabbing syncopations of Mamet's lowlifes and tricksters. He's obsessed by the ways in which speech camouflages our secret selves. For him, it's the subtext, the pause, that resonates—even when, as in Rattigan's play, there isn't much inside the characters to resound.

Set in 1912, *The Winslow Boy* is about how a well-to-do family dedicates itself to the defense of their young and presumably innocent son (Guy Edwards) after he is expelled from the Royal Naval Academy for allegedly stealing a five-shilling postal note. Arthur Winslow (Nigel Hawthorne, who is especially fine), the ailing family patriarch, goes up against the Crown to achieve justice; he hires a famous attorney and member of Parliament, Sir Robert Morton (Jeremy Northam), whose dashing conservatism both attracts and repels Winslow's suffragette daughter, Catherine (Rebecca Pidgeon).

The final verdict comes at great personal cost to the family, and yet Mamet, who streamlines Rattigan's play and makes it less pontifical, doesn't take the material as far as it can go; he doesn't bring out the arrogance in Arthur's mania. Victory here is shown to be debilitating but not all-consuming, and so we're left with a pleasing fable about the battle of the sexes and the virtues of persistence in a just cause. The neatness of it all is both appealing and appalling, and perhaps this combo is what finally hooked Mamet.

NEW YORK POST, 4/30/99, p. 55, Rod Dreher

The only thing more surprising than the fact that David Mamet has made a talky social drama set in Edwardian England is how exceptionally well he pulls it off. This absorbing, splendidly acted film is based on Terence Rattigan's popular 1946 play, which was itself loosely based on a true story that gripped England earlier this century.

The movie opens with its title character, Ronnie Winslow (Guy Edwards), turning up unexpectedly at his family's London town house. The dapper 14-year-old has been dismissed from a naval academy for having stolen a petty amount from a classmate—a charge he vehemently denies.

Arthur, the fearsomely proper Winslow patriarch (Nigel Hawthorne), is scandalized, but his youngest son looks at him with brave eyes and a clear gaze and insists he did not steal the postal order.

That decides it: The elder Winslow puts his family's reputation and fortune on the line in a quixotic attempt to clear his son's name, and restore the honor that has been stripped from the lad by the Admiralty.

But the Admiralty can't be sued under British law unless the monarch agrees to it. To secure this result and to press the case, the Winslows hire the country's leading lawyer, Sir Robert Morton (Jeremy Northam).

A quintessential establishmentarian, Sir Robert seems to be made of leather and mahogany paneling, and there's the sharp crack of the headmaster's paddle in his voice. When he interrogates the Winslow boy, you wince at the cruelty of his questioning.

But Sir Robert is a slyboots, and his advocacy helps turn the Winslow family's cause into a national sensation. Alas, the act of pressing the Winslow cause nearly bankrupts the well-off family, and the notoriety that comes with attacking a revered institution like the Royal Navy takes its toll on their private lives.

Until the very last, there's no assurance that young Winslow is indeed innocent, or that victory, if it comes at all, will be anything but Pyrrhic.

The film is concerned with the crusade's effects on the Winslow family, which suffers progressively for Ronnie's honor. An increasingly ashen Arthur Winslow slowly unravels as his family's financial security slips through his fingers. The elder son (Matthew Pidgeon) has to withdraw from Oxford, which his father can no longer afford. Grace, the mother (Gemma Jones), finds her forbearance sorely tried.

And suffragette daughter Catherine (Rebecca Pidgeon) is torn between loyalty to her family and devotion not only to her political cause, but to her fiance (Aden Gillett), a military man who threatens to break off their engagement if her family doesn't cease its attack upon the Admiralty.

Catherine is the key figure in "The Winslow Boy," poised between obligations demanded by an older social order that no longer seems just, and a new, more democratic era about to emerge from the catastrophe of the approaching war.

What a pity that Pidgeon, Mamet's wife, gives another of her competent but stiff performances, rendering a character that should embody the roiling emotions at the heart of the plot distressingly flat and empty.

You expect a major courtroom showdown in "The Winslow Boy," but Mamet doesn't supply it. We only hear Sir Robert's barn-burning speeches in Parliament and before the jury spoken of after the fact. Creating these scenes would have given us greater dramatic intensity and emotional satisfaction, as well as more of Jeremy Northam's stunning performance.

Mamet is so good with this material that maybe even he is getting tired of his trademark staccato, profane style.

NEWSDAY, 4/30/99, Part II/p. B6, John Anderson

Sturdy, stirring and balanced somewhere between the stiff upper lip and ironic underbelly of imperial Britain, "The Winslow Boy" hasn't exactly been stamping his feet for a new hearing. Not recently, anyway. Written by Terence Rattigan in 1946, it's unquestionably a post-war play—the kind meant to reassure a nation that what it suffered had preserved something worth preserving.

That was certainly the thrust of the 1950 adaptation directed by Anthony Asquith, in which Robert Donat was the lordly attorney Sir Robert Morton and Cedric Hardwicke was Arthur Winslow, both battling the expulsion of Winslow's son's from naval college over the theft of a five-shilling postal order. Neither that movie nor David Mamet's new one explains the nature of said postal order, but what's clear enough is that honor, not currency, propelled the original, celebrated Winslow case.

What's driving Mamet's film is another matter. It's generally impertinent, as well as irrelevant, to compare one film version to another, but in the case of the revisited "Winslow Boy" such tactics seem to illuminate at least a something of what its screenwriter-director is about.

One is compression. Mamet not only reduces the action, he takes the Rattigan play, which in Asquith's film wandered all over London, and brings it more or less back indoors—not quite to its original one-drawing-room set, but certainly into a far more static atmosphere. Why? For the same reasons, it seems, that he pares away the larger ramifications of the case itself, distilling the play to its root mechanics, which are the individual self-interests of the Winslow family.

The case itself (which actually began in 1908 and which Rattigan moved to 1911 for its pre-World War echoes) was about challenging the assumption of regal infallibility in English law. By demanding due process for a naval cadet, in other words, Arthur Winslow was challenging the king. The question that split British society was whether the rights of an individual—in this case a barely adolescent naval cadet—was worth tying up an entire political system, especially one warming up for war.

Mamet's doesn't care about this. He leaps from the bitterwsweet Christmas homecoming of Ronnie (Guy Edwards) and his insistent pleas of innocence, to a point where his father Arthur (Nigel Hawthorne) has already exhausted much of himself and his monies pursuing a seemingly lost legal cause. Mamet eschews a larger social canvas for domestic banalities—the engagement of Catherine Winslow (Rebecca Pidgeon) to her army beau John Watherstone (Aden Gillett), whose father will eventually break them up over the Winslow "scandal," or the sorrow of Grace Winslow (Gemma Jones), because her husband's expensive crusade is eroding their middle-class lifestyle. The question ever-present in Rattigan's play is "What price honor?" Mamet adds something like "What is honor?" Because he de-empasizes to such a degree the magnitude of the Winslow case in British jurisprudence, we concentrate by default on what's left—the actions and motivations of players caught up in something that can only hurt them, and which they can't resist.

Hawthorne offers vague complexities as Arthur; Jones' Grace is exactly what a woman of her age and times would have been—superfluous to the critical matters at hand. Pidgeon (who is Mamet's wife) displays the same insistent postmodernity that she did in her husband's "The Spanish Prisoner," which was funny there and off-putting here. This is not to say that her Catherine Winslow fails to meet the movie's oft-repeated motto of "Let right be done:" As a suffragette and thereby champion of another "lost cause," Catherine presents herself as more reserved than her nature and less susceptible to the emotions of the case—lest she seem weak and thus betray that cause. When her fiance leaves her, or she feels herself drawn to Morton, she resists—much as Arthur resists his natural inclination to cut his losses and quit the case.

Northam, as the story's one-man Edwardian Dream Team, gives a polished, nuanced performance, even if he never makes you forget Donat, or Asquith's electrifying scene between Morton and Ronnie that assures the barrister of the boy's innocence and makes him take the case. But Mamet ignores virtually all the opportunities for grandeur in his "Winslow." There are no courtroom scenes at all, in fact—a rare thing among legal dramas. Instead, Mamet seems to be asking at what point the internal structure of such a story can still bear the weight of theater. Most audiences will probably agree that Mamet reaches his destination with some distance to spare, although "The Winslow Boy" does remain a very interesting experiment.

SIGHT AND SOUND, 11/99, p. 60, Geoffrey Macnab

London, 1912. Arthur Winslow's daughter Catherine, an ardent suffragette, becomes engaged to a young soldier, John Watherstone. The family celebrate. Arthur discovers his youngest son Ronnie is back home early from naval college. Ronnie is carrying a letter which explains he has been expelled for stealing a postal order. Arthur asks him if he is guilty, and Ronnie insists he is not. Arthur resolves to fight to clear Ronnie's name.

Many months pass. An independent inquiry is called but Ronnie is not represented and is again found guilty. The family suffer financially. Arthur's health is broken. His oldest son Dickie is forced to leave university without completing his studies. Arthur hires brilliant attorney and politician Sir Robert Morton to represent Ronnie. After prolonged debate in the House of Lords, Sir Robert succeeds in bringing the case to court. Catherine, initially suspicious of Sir Robert, learns that he has made his own sacrifices to prove Ronnie's innocence. Embarrassed about the publicity the Winslow case is generating and aware that Arthur can no longer provide a dowry, John breaks off his engagement to Catherine. Arthur learns that the case is won. Sir Robert drops by to offer his congratulations. Catherine shows him out of the house.

When Mike Figgis adapted *The Browning Version* in 1994 he updated Terence Rattigan's original play to the present. David Mamet resists such tampering in his surprisingly faithful adaptation of Rattigan's *The Winslow Boy* (first filmed by Anthony Asquith in 1948). The drama remains firmly rooted in the Edwardian era. Apart from a few outside excursions, we rarely venture from the Winslows' home. At times the domesticity can become claustrophobic. Characters are invariably shot in medium close-up and Mamet doesn't skimp on the period detail. Everything—from little Ronnie's naval-cadet costume and Arthur's whiskers to Catherine's starched blouses and the dark, heavy furnishings which (along with Benoît Delhomme's cinematography) make the Winslow drawing room seem so sombre—is as fussily rendered as in any Merchant-Ivory E. M. Forster adaptation.

Given the multiple deceptions of Mamet's last film *The Spanish Prisoner*, audiences are likely to approach *The Winslow Boy* with suspicion. Early on, the very air of normality in the Winslow household puts us on our guard. With its euphemisms, irony and understatement, the language used by the family and their associates isn't so far removed from the sly vernacular found in Mamet's own work. There are even moments when the characters echo one another's sentences, Mamet-style. ("You don't behave as if you were in love," the mother Grace tells her daughter Catherine. "How does one behave as if one is in love?" she replies.) Rebecca Pidgeon plays Catherine in precisely the same coquettish way as she did the siren who led Campbell Scott astray in *The Spanish Prisoner*. We wonder when Mamet will pull the carpet from beneath us, but there is no sinister subtext here. Mamet, who describes *The Winslow Boy* as "one of the most immaculately crafted plays I've read," was loath to tinker with its structure. He has edited, compressed, and even written new speeches for some characters, but they're barely detectable.

The pleasures of his version of *The Winslow Boy* are predictable ones. This is a consummately crafted costume drama galvanised by a handful of excellent, if very stagy, performances. Nigel Hawthorne's Arthur starts off as a robust Edwardian patriarch, but as the film progresses his beard whitens and his health deteriorates. Hawthorne brings an unlikely tragic grandeur to the character, conveying in scowls and mutters Arthur's extreme stubbornness as well as his uncertainty.

The fact that neither he nor anybody else betrays any emotion serves, if anything, to heighten the pathos. The characters all speak in coded language and treat one another with exaggerated courtesy. Sir Robert seems incapable of expressing his interest in Catherine in any other way than by paying her anodyne compliments about her hat. The solicitor Desmond proposes to her as if he's a bailiff delivering a summons. For all their polish and wit, both come across as forlorn and lonely figures.

Mamet claims that the themes of *The Winslow Boy* are universal, but he seems as fascinated by the nuances of English society as by any abstract ideas about justice, rights and victimhood Rattigan's text may illustrate. The drama is set at a very specific moment—on the eve of World War I. As Mamet clearly realised, if he had taken away the historical context his film would have lost the sense of time and place which make the original play so distinct.

VILLAGE VOICE, 5/4/99, p. 116, Jessica Winter

The Winslow Boy is the unexpectedly suitable marriage of Terence Rattigan's 1946 play and David Mamet's more nettlesome tendencies as a dramatist and filmmaker. Rattigan fictionalized the 1910 trial of an English military cadet wrongfully dismissed for stealing a postal order—this tiny incident becomes an issue of national import as young Ronnie Winslow's father, Arthur (Nigel Hawthorne), and suffragette sister, Catherine (Rebecca Pidgeon), petition the crown to clear the boy's name.

The Winslow Boy is a scrupulous play, but a static one: by mostly staying outside the courtroom and within the Winslow household—stoical, reticent Edwardian types all—the play is deliberately claustrophobic. And *claustrophobic* is this mellowing Mr. Tough Guy's middle name—Mamet's films create stagnant worlds seemingly inhabited only by their pertinent characters, and this irreality suits a story about people living in a bubble, obsessed with their pursuit of a small share of justice. The play's need for secret-keeping flatters Mamet's similar fondness for concealment: the revelation of the alleged crime is dangled too long, and even the delivery of the verdict is attenuated to frustrate dramatic payoff.

Rattigan's mannered, unmistakably *written* speech is readily translatable into Mametese, in which dialogue always seems disembodied and actors affectless. Adapting *The Winslow Boy* to the screen allows the former potty-mouthed paranoiac to graduate to stiff-upper-lipped costume fare (rated G!) without altering his own entrenched sensibilities. Since the drama stays in the drawing room, even Mamet's inert, point-and-shoot directing style can slide by with impunity.

Of course Mamet would feel affinity for any playwright who employs the stage direction *"in a flat voice"* as often as Rattigan, but still one wonders why Mamet made this unlikely choice for adaptation to the screen. Rattigan's play suggested that the British press and judicial system will right any wrong if a citizen presents his suit with conviction, though he took care to portray the damage sustained by each Winslow as the matter dragged on: Arthur's health deteriorates, Catherine's marriage prospects collapse, and so on. *The Winslow Boy* demonstrates the simple truth that justice is often hard-won, and Mamet's impassive interpretation of the play remains nicely ambivalent about whether the cost was too high in this case. The Winslow family's head-strong refusal to yield, however, holds up a mirror to Mamet's stubborn rigidity as a director. This film is solidly built, faithful to its material, and utterly lacking in pretense, but its maker is still running in place.

Also reviewed in:
NATION, 5/10/99, p. 34, Stuart Klawans
NEW REPUBLIC, 5/24/99, p. 32, Stanley Kauffmann
NEW YORK TIMES, 4/30/99, p. E15, Janet Maslin
NEW YORKER, 5/17/99, p. 99, David Denby
VARIETY, 4/26-5/2/99, p. 44, Dennis Harvey
WASHINGTON POST, 5/14/99, p. C5, Rita Kempley
WASHINGTON POST, 5/14/99, Weekend/p. 47, Desson Howe

WISCONSIN DEATH TRIP

A Cinemax Reel Life and BBC Arena release. *Producer:* Maureen A. Ryan and James Marsh. *Director:* James Marsh. *Screenplay:* James Marsh. *Based on the book by:* Michael Lesy. *Director of Photography:* Eigil Bryld. *Editor:* Jinx Godfrey. *Running time:* 76 minutes. *MPAA Rating:* Not Rated.

CAST: Ian Holm (Narrator); Jo Vukelich (Mary Sweeney); Marilyn White (Pauline L'Allemand); Jeff Golden (Newspaper Editor); Marcus Monroe (Young Anderson); John Schneider (Asylum Clerk).

NEW YORK POST, 12/1/99, p. 59, Jonathan Foreman

Part documentary, part re-enactment, "Wisconsin Death Trip" is a gorgeously photographed, highly original film based on the well-known (but out-of-print) 1973 book by Michael Lesy.

"Trip" is used in its 1960s metaphorical sense: No one in this film actually goes anywhere, but you do get taken on a kind of morbid, tour-by-vignette of a terrible decade in the life of Black River Falls, Wis.

During the 1890s, this community of German and Scandinavian immigrant farmers and merchants experienced a severe economic depression, along with a bizarre plague of suicides, murders and madness.

The film's narration is constructed mostly out of actual reports from the local newspaper, (whose English editor is voiced by Ian Holm) and excerpts from the records of the nearby Mendota insane asylum (whispered by John Schneider).

A teenage girl drowns herself over unrequited love, an unemployed farmer lies down in front of a train in the snow, a grown woman finds a mole on her back and sets herself on fire with kerosene to get rid of it.

Then there's the 74-year-old German who kills himself at the house of his friend when the friend's 77-year-old wife refuses his advances. You also have Mary Sweeney, a schoolteacher who tours the state snorting cocaine and smashing windows until she's finally locked up.

At first, it's tempting to attribute all the drownings, self-immolations and self-inflicted gunshot wounds to the fabled North European gloominess familiar from Bergman films.

But when those accounts are combined with the un-Victorian stories of children killing children—including a 9-year-old deaf and dumb boy you see murdering his sister—you realize you're witnessing something different, though the film never posits any explanation for all the mayhem.

The original photographs are often haunting, and the black-and-white re-enactments have none of the cheesiness of reality-TV programs like "Unsolved Mysteries" and "America's Most Wanted."

Indeed, they're shot in such a way as to make acts of violence truly shocking.

Purists may dislike how difficult it is to tell the difference between the original photographs and stills from the newly shot material. But the main problem with "Wisconsin Death Trip" is the way the format distances you from the subject matter, so that stories may shock, but they never move you.

And, occasionally, a touch of Euro condescension creeps into the film, especially in the scenes of contemporary life in Black River Falls (baton twirlers on parade, and the like), which English writer-director James Marsh intercuts with stories from the past.

Although he's not as snotty as, say, Louis Theroux, Marsh simply cannot resist cheap ironic shots at the supposed crassness of modern American life. One example is the scene in an old people's home that shows the assembled elderly staring vacantly into space while a singing group performs the national anthem.

It's a shame, because Marsh has no problem treating the troubled Wisconsinites of the 1890s with dignity and respect.

NEWSDAY, 12/1/99, Part II/p. B3, Gene Seymour

Sometime in the last decade of the 19th Century, a plague hunkered down among the citizens of Black River Falls, Wis. This was not your garden-variety infestation of locusts or your basic swarm of diseased rats. If only things were that simple.

This plague—if the stories from the local paper, the Badger State Banner, are to be believed—was an invisible yet overpowering cloud of insanity that descended upon this small community of farmers and merchants, many of whom had just come from Germany and Scandinavia to settle and make money. This may have been harder to do in 1890s America than at other times, given a bad economic depression whose severity would be exceeded 40 years later.

"Wisconsin Death Trip," a dramatization of Michael Lesy's 1973 mutant coffee-table book of archival photos and news accounts from that sad, mad decade in Black River Falls, alludes to this economic depression as a possible cause of the town's peculiarly widespread clinical depression.

Root causes, however, get lost in the unrelenting strangeness that writer-director James Marsh parades before our eyes in beautiful black and white.

Mixing some of the same photos unearthed by Lesy with some dramatized footage of his own, Marsh presents his own version of "You Can't Make This Stuff Up." His stars include Young Anderson (Marcus Monroe), a 13-year-old boy playing with guns in a farmer's backyard, then killing the farmer just for fun and leading a posse on a merry and murderous chase.

Then, there's the coke-sniffing schoolmarm named Mary Sweeney (Jo Vukelich), who frequently goes off on window-breaking rampages. Also a man named Henry Johnson, who for no apparent reason cut the heads off all his chickens and set them on fire. He then threw his best clothes—and himself—into the fire. And then there's the opera singer (Marilyn White), who just shows up in town, stays for a while and goes quietly crazy before being sent off to the nearby Mendota Asylum for the Insane—which, you imagine, must have been as crowded as a trendy restaurant on a weekend.

Young lovers making suicide-murder pacts, teenaged girls committing arson because they're bored, vagrants killing people who give them bread, lonely old people who shoot themselves because they can't stand themselves any longer ...

Oddly enough, the more such stories you hear, the less removed from the present day they sound. Though actor Jeffrey Golden is shown portraying the newspaper editor who keeps tabs on this shocking stuff, it is the soft voice of Ian Holm that you hear reading the editor's stories as if he were calmly delivering a coroner's report to a dumbfounded jury.

VILLAGE VOICE, 12/7/99, p. 144, Amy Taubin

James Marsh's *Wisconsin Death Trip* is a tricky, empty film adaptation of Michael Lesy's overrated 1973 book of the same name. Lesy discovered a treasure trove of photographs taken during the 1890s in the small town of Black Falls, Wisconsin. The photos and the newspaper clippings that accompanied them suggested that the violence of rural America in the 19th century was more than a match for anything on the evening news in the year that the U.S. admitted defeat in Vietnam. Lesy was no purist and not much of a photo historian. He collaged the photos, cropping them and blowing up details, revealing as much about his own taste for freak-show gothic as he did about the madness inherent in the American psyche.

Marsh, a British documentary filmmaker for the stylish Arena series, uses the original photos and newspaper texts, fleshing them out, as it were, with film reenactments and also adding documentary footage of Black Falls today—the highlights of which include an interview with the homecoming queen, some people in a bar discussing who else but that Wisconsin celebrity Ed Gein, and a woman getting drunk on church wine. Am I being selective? You bet, but not half as much as Marsh, whose contempt for weirdo Americans and for the German and Scandinavian immigrants who settled Black Falls leaks all over the film.

Also reviewed in:
NEW YORK TIMES, 12/1/99, p. E1, Stephen Holden

WOMEN ("ELLES")

A Winstar Cinema release of a Samsa Film production in association with Canal Plus/Esicma. *Producer:* Jani Thiltges and Claude Waringo. *Director:* Luís Galvão Teles. *Screenplay (French with English subtitles):* Luis Gälväo Teles and Don Bohlinger. *Director of Photography:* Alfredo Mayo. *Editor:* Regina Bartschi. *Music:* Alejandro Massó. *Art Director:* Veronique Scarez. *Costumes:* Evelyne Correard. *Running time:* 97 minutes. *MPAA Rating:* Not Rated.

CAST: Miou-Miou (Eva); Carmen Maura (Linda); Marthe Keller (Barbara); Marisa Berenson (Chloé); Guesch Patti (Branca); Joaquim de Almeida (Gigi); Morgan Perez (Luís); Didier Flamand (Edgar); Mapi Galan (Raquel); Florence Loiret (Tiago).

LOS ANGELES TIMES, 9/17/99, Calendar/p. 10, Kevin Thomas

Luis Galvao Teles' "Women" ("Elles") is a woman's film of the old-fashioned variety, affording good roles for five internationally renowned actresses who portray middle-aged women, longtime friends who sustain one another throughout life's inevitable changes and losses.

The film offers nothing new whatsoever, yet there is much pleasure to be derived in the uniformly impressive portrayals of the actresses and in the level of sophistication of the film's perspective and tone, and in its simplicity of style. The stars of the film, written by Galvao Teles with Don Bohlinger, are elegant and beautiful—yet again the European cinema reminds us how desirable a woman past 40 can be. The timeless splendor of Lisbon provides a stunning setting.

Carmen Maura's Linda is a renowned television personality and commentator who sets the film in motion when, for one of her programs, she decides to turn the camera on her own friends to ask them the eternal question: "What do women want?" The answers emerge from what each woman is facing in her life at present. As for Linda herself, her dedication to her high-pressure job is threatening her relationship with her handsome co-worker and lover (Joaquim de Almeida, a mainstay of Spanish and Portuguese films and a familiar face in international cinema), making him vulnerable to the advances of an aggressive younger staffer at the TV station.

Miou-Miou is Eva, a widowed professor of literature ardently pursued by one of her pupils (Morgan Perez). Eva might not have succumbed to her student if she had known he was the son of Barbara (Marthe Keller), who belongs to her circle of friends. Of the five women, Barbara faces the greatest challenge. Not only has she lost her beloved husband (Didier Flamand), an ophthalmologist, to a much younger woman, but when she goes to him for some tests prompted by dizzy spells, his news is not encouraging. The discovery of her son's affair pales in comparison to this grim diagnosis—which comes just as she's losing the man she loves.

The radiant Keller is the movie's mainstay, and her intuitive, commanding portrayal epitomizes the filmmaker's ability to avert soap-operatics with in-depth characterization.

Meanwhile, the gamin Branca (Guesch Patti, a noted European dancer and singer in her film debut), a cabaret performer and stage actress, clutches at youth through a succession of affairs with younger men. She's so distracted that she fails to realize that the teenage daughter she is raising alone has begun using hard drugs. She is grateful that her friend Chloe (Marisa Berenson), a fashionable hairstylist—having overcome addiction herself—can come to her rescue. But Branca is thrown into a dilemma when the bisexual Chloe comes on to her.

"Women" is as lustrous as its stars and wisely resists neat resolutions, opting instead to leave us with the mature recognition that life goes on relentlessly, whether we're prepared to deal with it or not.

NEWSDAY, 10/29/99, Part II/p. B7, Jan Stuart

Intelligent movies about friendships between older women are such four-leaf clovers that, when more than a couple turn up in any given year, it feels like a dam break. A first-rate soap opera out of Luxembourg—Luis Galvao Teles'"Women"—is several leagues ahead of Franco Zefferelli's "Tea With Mussolini," if not half as audacious as Pedro Almodovar's upcoming "All About My Mother." As with women's clothing designed by men, these films reflect the male reveries of their creators as much as the female desires of their audience. The five middle-aged women who compose Teles' circle of friends are idealizations of what we would all like to be after we hurdle 40: employed in interesting jobs, surrounded by family and desirable to men and women of all ages.

Ah, but they have yearnings! Hairdresser Chloe (Marisa Berenson) pines for actress Branca (Guesch Patti, the soul of vivacity), who in turn longs for tranquility with her heroin-addict daughter. Eva, widow, mother and schoolteacher (Miou-Miou) burns for a handsome student (Morgan Perez), who happens to be the son of her friend Barbara. Faced with a terminal illness, gourmet chef Barbara (Marthe Keller) wants life. TV journalist Linda (Carmen Maura, whose billiard ball eyes seem to take in everything) wants the answers to life, if not a stable relationship with her man, Gigi (Joaquim de Almeida).

In her quest for these answers, Linda corrals all of her friends to do a TV segment on the wishes of her peer group. Through a cunning alternation between Linda's videotape results and her friends' personal dramas, we hear their desires expressed twice: first over the opening credits, and again toward the end, when the wishes take on greater emotional weight.   Linda is the greatest enigma of the lot, and the angst-ridden fervor with which she dances toward self-knowledge is also the film's weakest element.

If we have to have daytime TV at the movies—and why not, after all?—we couldn't ask for a more luminous gathering of actresses to live out our Sturm und Drang.

Somehow, Teles manages to give his divas equal time.   Miou-Miou is arguably the most poised and gracefully beautiful actress in Western civilization since Audrey Hepburn.   Marthe Keller is one of those women who, like Ann-Margret and the late Romy Schneider, only become more interesting with time.   And that incomparable woman-on-the-verge, Carmen Maura, proves that there is, indeed, life after Pedro Almodovar, as well as after 40.

VILLAGE VOICE, 11/9/99, p. 140, Yael Schacher

Women is the soppy French-language version of *Steel Magnolias*, featuring five middle-aged femmes—one dying, all longing—and a beauty parlor.   With a bouquet of lascivious lilies standing in for their slower southern sisters, Luis Galvao Teles's film is another foolhardy, albeit sexier, attempt to capture the "essential feminine" plagued by waning looks, painful loss, and desperate desire.   Carmen Maura (of Almodóvar fame) plays Linda, a TV journalist who interviews her four best friends, Branca (Guesch Patti), Eva (Miou-Miou), Chloe (Marisa Berenson), and Barbara (Marthe Keller), for a feature about what women want.   Teles answers this question in the film's theme song, a cabaret number about pleasure and useless men sung by Branca, the group's prodigal mom.   Pleasure is depicted as sex that simultaneously transcends and sanctifies traditional taboos: a quasi-incestuous fling between Barbara's son and Eva (his literature professor) is blessed by everyone including Barbara.   Excepting Branca's strung-out daughter, Teles's vision of youth is unbearably light—women under 30 appear in roller skates or braids. Men in the movie likewise carry little weight.   Linda's broken clocks and a cat named Kafka remind us that *Women* is about time and identity, issues Teles seems to think apply to just the female half of humanity.

Also reviewed in:
CHICAGO TRIBUNE, 1/14/00, Friday/p. G, Michael Wilmington
NEW REPUBLIC, 11/15/99, p. 28, Stanley Kauffmann
NEW YORK TIMES, 10/29/99, p. E24, Stephen Holden
VARIETY, 3/30-4/5/98, p. 65, Emanuel Levy

WOOD, THE

A Paramount Pictures release of an MTV Films production in association with Bona Fide Productions. *Executive Producer:* Van Toffler. *Producer:* Albert Berger, Ron Yerxa, and David Gale. *Director:* Rick Famuyiwa. *Screenplay:* Rick Famuyiwa. *Story:* Rick Famuyiwa and Todd Boyd. *Director of Photography:* Steven Bernstein. *Editor:* John Carter. *Music:* Robert Hurst and Pilar McCurry. *Music Editor:* Jay Bolton and Michael T. Ryan. *Choreographer:* Jossie Harris Thacker. *Sound:* Walter P. Anderson. *Sound Editor:* Gregory Hedgepath. *Casting:* Mali Finn and Emily Schweber. *Production Designer:* Roger Fortune and Maxine Shepard. *Art Director:* Richard Haase. *Set Designer:* Masako Masuda. *Set Decorator:* David Smith and F. Beauchamp Hebb. *Special Effects:* Bruce Steinheimer. *Costumes:* Darryle Johnson. *Make-up:* Laini Thompson. *Stunt Coordinator:* Eddie Watkins. *Running time:* 106 minutes. *MPAA Rating:* R.

CAST: Taye Diggs (Roland);   Omar Epps (Mike);   Richard T. Jones (Slim);   Sean Nelson (Young Mike);   Trent Cameron (Young Roland);   Duane Finley (Young Slim);   Malinda Williams (Young Alicia);   De'Aundre Bonds (Stacey);   Sanaa Lathan (Alicia);   LisaRaye (Lisa);   Tamaia Jones (Tanya);   Elayn Taylor (Roland's Mother);   Patricia Belcher (Mrs. Hughes);   Cynthia Martells (Mike's Mother);   Wyking Jones and Geoffrey Blackshire (Cashiers in Mini Mart);

Jascha Washington (Mike's Brother); Alysha Sinclair (Tracey); Melvin Lyons (Gang Member); Samuel Hiona (Cashier in Mini Mart 1986); Antwon Tanner (Boo); John Wesley and Oscar Dillon (Police Officers); Tia Gainer (Girl at Dance); Howard Thompson (DJ at Dance); Douglas Shamburger (DJ on Radio); Brandi Wilson and Christina Milian (Girls at Dance); Dawnn Lewis (Woman in Cleaners); Crystal Grant (Girl with Slim); La'Myia Good (Monica); Alecia Smith (Girl with Roland); Kongit Farrell (Girl with Slim); Stacey Arnell (Woman with Stacey); Telma Hopkins (Slim's Mother); Basil Wallace (Lisa's Father); Todd Boyd (Reverend Parker).

LOS ANGELES TIMES, 7/16/99, Calendar/p. 14, Kevin Thomas

[The following review by Kevin Thomas appeared in a slightly different form in **NEWSDAY, 7/16/99, Part II/p. B7.]**

When several years ago a friend told aspiring filmmaker Rick Famuyiwa that he was getting married, the two of them started reminiscing about growing up in the African American middle-class neighborhood of Inglewood (now becoming increasingly Latino).

Famuyiwa, a 1996 USC film school graduate, came away hours later with the idea for his fresh and funny first feature, "The Wood," which he adapted from a story he wrote with one of his former USC professors, Todd Boyd. "The Wood" is an across-the-board delight featuring a spot-on ensemble cast that treats the most awkward and embarrassing moments in the rites of passage with affectionate hilarity.

"The Wood" begins in the present, roughly 2½ hours before Taye Diggs' Roland is to get married at a fancy backyard wedding. In the grip of prenuptial jitters, Roland has gotten drunk and taken refuge at the home of his tart but stalwart high school sweetheart (Tamaia Jones), where he is retrieved by his best pals, Mike (Omar Epps) and Slim (Richard T. Jones). In the process of sobering up Roland and getting him to his wedding on time, the three start reminiscing, looking back to 1986 when 14-year-old Mike (Sean Nelson), fresh from North Carolina, met Slim (Duane Finley) and Roland (Trent Cameron) in junior high. The film unfolds from the point of view of Mike, the film's narrator.

Music, the latest styles and, way above all else, girls, are on the boys' minds. Roland and Slim present themselves as the ultimate in cool to the uncertain newcomer even though they are faking it at least part of the time. They put Mike up to making a grab at the most beautiful girl in their class—the whole school, really—the lovely and intelligent Alicia (Malinda Williams), failing to mention that her older brother, Stacey (De'Aundre Bonds), is one very protective and very bad dude. Yet both Alicia and Stacey are ultimately smart enough to see that Mike is a good guy who had been set up as a patsy, and Mike and Alicia begin a long and complicated relationship in which they become such good friends it impedes romance.

Indeed, "The Wood" is a film that honors women in their wisdom and patience for putting up with stubborn male reluctance in growing up. It suggests that even the smoothest, best-looking young men, the ones who have no trouble getting girls' phone numbers, can be achingly, hilariously clumsy in their initial forays into romance. As we move back and forth in time, we discover that the three friends are achievers, but Famuyiwa celebrates the value of friends just hanging out and having fun, something that's easy to lose sight of in this era that puts so much emphasis on competition.

Famuyiwa shrewdly makes no point of the fact that his heroes are black, but that they are implicitly underlines how solid their middle-class environment really is. This is the kind of black world that is not nearly so frequently portrayed in films as are poverty-stricken, drug-ridden ghettos. The strong pull of the security of their community upon the three friends, and the strength they derive from their firm bond, also says something about their wariness of the outside world.

The very large cast is a seamless pleasure, with the six actors playing the three friends in their early teens and late 20s standing out in their ability to range from high humor to dead seriousness. Bonds is a sly, dexterous comedian as Stacey, but the film's special joy is Williams, whose talent easily equals her beauty. "The Wood" is a winner.

NEW YORK, 7/26/99, p. 50, Peter Rainer

In the otherwise inane coming-of-age comedy *The Wood*, there's a sequence that's more upsetting—without trying to be—than anything in *Eyes Wide Shut*. We've been following, in flashback, the horny-guy exploits of a trio of African-American high-school buddies in the L.A. neighborhood of Inglewood. Stopping off at a local convenience store to stock up on breath mints before a big dance, they find themselves caught in the middle of a holdup. Guns are drawn; the terrified store owner, probably Korean, doesn't resist; the robbery is short-circuited when one of the buddies recognizes the gang-member leader as the brother of a girl he's sweet on, and everybody piles into the getaway car. This is all played for laughs, and there are no repercussions. It's one thing when one of the Tarantinoids pulls off this kind of conscienceless jamboree; at least the pop-nihilist context has been set. But seeing this sort of stuff in a movie that's about as trenchant as *Booty Call* is unsettling: Have we arrived at the point in our movies when an inner-city convenience-store holdup is viewed as simple slapstick? The people who made this movie have either seen too much mayhem—or they haven't seen any.

NEW YORK POST, 7/16/99, p. 47, Jonathan Foreman

"The Wood" (the title refers to the Southern California town of Inglewood) is a sentimental, occasionally very funny, coming-of-age comedy about a trio of middle class African-American guys.

Given that movies featuring black characters who are neither ghetto-dwellers nor Cosby-esque yuppies are as common as snow in August, the mere existence of "The Wood" is remarkable.

Which makes it a shame that "The Wood" doesn't really work. Instead of telling a straightforward comic-nostalgic story about growing up in the 1980s, first-time writer-director Rick Famuyiwa mixes long flashbacks to his underwritten characters' teen years with an artificial, tension-free, pre-wedding scenario: Will Roland (Taye Diggs) bug out and fall to meet his bride at the altar?

The story starts three hours before the ceremony, with Roland drunk and hiding out at an ex-girlfriend's apartment, and his two best friends, Mike (Epps) and Slim (Jones), already in their formal wear, desperately searching for him.

Mike, who also narrates the film, is reminded of the day he first met his homies, when he had just arrived in town from North Carolina, and we see the first of many flashbacks accompanied by a period soundtrack.

Famuyiwa takes a commendable risk by having different, younger actors play the trio during their high-school years. But not only do Sean Nelson (who is excellent), Duane Finlay and Trent Cameron bear no resemblance to Epps, Jones and Diggs, they are so much less handsome that the contrast is jarring.

You also never get a sense as to what brings the three boys together. Nor is there any sign of the tension that tends to afflict trios of friends in real life.

It's a sweet-natured film. But in both the present day and (more interesting) '80s scenes, the film exhibits a "culturally specific," in-your-face frankness about bodily functions, erections, bad breath and vomit.

On the other hand, aficionados of bawdy black movies should be warned that "The Wood," with its slow stretches and almost sickly sentimentality, is no "Booty Call."

SIGHT AND SOUND, 2/00, p. 59, Leslie Felperin

Inglewood (nicknamed the "Wood") in Los Angeles, the present. On the day of his wedding, a drunken Roland summons his friends since childhood Slim and Mike to come and meet him at his ex-girlfriend Tanya's house. He's panicking about getting married. Slim and Mike sober him up, revisit some of their childhood haunts and remember their teenage years.

In 1986, the three met at middle school. Mike developed a crush on Alicia, the prettiest girl in their class, and was beaten up by her brother Stacey for daring to touch her backside in a bet with Slim and Roland. Later that year, he and Alicia danced together. Mike won Stacey's respect for withstanding the beating and distracting a cop's attention away from a gun in Stacey's car. When they were in their junior year at high school, the three friends had a bet on who would lose his virginity first. Mike was the first to have sex, with Alicia, though he concealed the fact from his friends. In the present, after being ribbed by Mike and Slim for agreeing to move for the sake of his bride-to-be Lisa's job, Roland convinces the furious Lisa to go through with the wedding. The day is a success. Alicia, now a successful lawyer in New York, and Mike have a dance. He asks about the weather in New York.

Focusing on three friends growing up in the middle-class black community of Inglewood in Los Angeles during the 80s, *The Wood* was released late last summer, coasting the last breaking wave of the teen comedies that so dominated 1999. Although its makers stress its 'universal' themes, the best things about it are its culturally specific details rather than its male-bonding and friendship homilies and stabs at gross-out burnout, including a copious-vomiting sequence.

The film-makers, including debut feature writer-director Rick Famuyiwa, have taken exacting pains to include enough jheri curls, K-Swiss trainers and posters for De La Soul in the *mise en scène* to induce terminal nostalgia in a finely calibrated section of the target audience. And, as seems befitting for a film financed by MTV's new film-production arm, key hip-hop, soul and R&B tunes are lined up to bring sense memories flooding back on cue. Each flashback is presaged by a spinning LP, and Luther Vandross' cover of 'If This World Were Mine' plays a key role in helping Mike win over Alicia at the dance.

The fact that it works, making Alicia a kind of Pavlov's dog in a party dress, only shows up how programmatic the characterisation is. *The Wood* never delves much deeper into the three friends' psychology than a sitcom pilot would, though the cast try their best. Sean Nelson as young Mike particularly shines, and ultimately carries the film since the present-time-frame device feels like it lost a few segments somewhere between the preview cinemas and here. Some viewers may find the casual sexism of the three protagonists offensive, but (as with *American Pie)* they are more often than not shown to be ineffectual in their efforts to get "booty" and fairly hopeless at it when they do get it. Even the bizarre debate about whether it's acceptable for a guy to follow his wife when her job requires it rather than the other way round is shown up to be hollow, macho posturing by the film's conclusion.

VILLAGE VOICE, 7/27/99, p. 70, Gary Dauphin

Walking a gauzy zigzag from *Soul Food* to *The Wedding Singer* and back again, *The Wood* is a diverting but uneven nostalgia trip, a black male-centric hug fest culled from writer-director Rick Famuyiwa's memories of late-'80s junior high days. *The Wood* (shorthand for Inglewood, California) opens present-tense with two well-adjusted, grown-up buds, Mike (Omar Epps) and Slim (Richard T. Jones), trying to get Roland (Taye Diggs) to the church on time. Cracking wise and overcoming a number of vomit- and tuxedo-related obstacles, the trio valiantly fight their way to the altar, all the while shaking their heads and knee-slapping each other over "the good old days."

All that shaking and slapping unlooses a string of flashbacks to the days of old-school hip hop and shell-top Adidas, when Mike *(Fresh's* Sean Nelson, who gives the film's most layered performance) was a clean-cut country boy from North Carolina, Slim (Duane Finely) was a Jheri Curl-wearing wannabe ballplayer, and Roland (Trent Cameron) was, as he repeatedly assures everyone, just getting better looking every week. *The Wood's* kid stuff is suffused throughout with unexpected humor and intelligence—from the ill-advised schoolyard ass grab that will forge the trio's bond, to Mike's near-apoplectic crisis over his first dance, to the technical difficulties with condoms that will attend their first lays. But, unfortunately, most of *The Wood* involves bickering and high jinks passing between Epps, et al. *The Wood* is a nice enough movie in its predictable, haphazard way, but it would have been much nicer to actually meet the men Famuyiwa's fondly remembered boys grew up to be.

Also reviewed in:
NEW YORK TIMES, 7/16/99, p. E22, Stephen Holden
VARIETY, 7/12-18/99, p. 37, Robert Koehler

WORLD IS NOT ENOUGH, THE

A Metro-Goldwyn-Mayer release of Albert R. Broccoli's Eon Pproductions Ltd. presentation. *Producer:* Michael G. Wilson and Barbara Broccoli. *Director:* Michael Apted. *Screenplay:* Neal Purvis, Robert Wade, and Bruce Feirstein. *Story:* Neal Purvis and Robert Wade. *Director of Photography:* Adrian Biddle. *Editor:* Jim Clark. *Music:* David Arnold. *Music Editor:* Dina Eaton. *Sound:* Chris Munro and (music) Geoff Foster. *Sound Editor:* Martin Evans. *Casting:* Debbie McWilliams. *Production Designer:* Peter Lamont. *Art Director:* Neil Lamont. *Set Decorator:* Simon Wakefield. *Special Effects:* Chris Corbould. *Visual Effects:* Mara Bryan. *Costumes:* Lindy Hemming. *Make-up:* Linda De Vetta. *Stunt Coordinator:* Simon Crane. *Running time:* 128 minutes. *MPAA Rating:* PG-13.

CAST: Pierce Brosnan (James Bond); Sophie Marceau (Elektra); Robert Carlyle (Renard); Denise Richards (Christmas Jones); Robbie Coltrane (Valentin Zukovsky); Judi Dench (M); Desmond Llewelyn (Q); John Cleese (R); Maria Grazia Cucinotta (Cigar Girl); Samantha Bond (Moneypenny); Michael Kitchen (Tanner); Colin Salmon (Robinson); Goldie (Bull); David Calder (Sir Robert King); Serena Scott Thomas (Dr. Molly Warmflash); Ulrich Thomsen (Davidov); John Seru (Gabor); Claude-Oliver Rudolph (Colonel Akakievich); Patrick Malahide (Lachaise); Omid Djalili (Foreman); Jeff Nuttall (Dr. Arkov); Diran Meghreblian (Coptic Priest); John Albasiny (Helicopter Pilot); Patrick Romer (Pilot); Jimmy Roussounis (Pipeline Technician); Justus von Dohnanyi (Captain Nikoli); Hassani Shapi (Doctor); Carl McCrystal (Trukhin); Martyn Lewis (Newscaster); Kouroush Asad (Russian Radio Operator); Daisy Beaumont (Nina); Nina Muschallik (Verushka); Daz Crawford (Casino Thug); Peter Mehtab (Casino Dealer).

LOS ANGELES TIMES, 11/19/99, Calendar/p. 4, Kevin Thomas

"The World Is Not Enough," the 19th James Bond movie, is in the "Mission: Impossible" tradition: It presents action, adventure and romance with maximum sophistication and spectacle and minimal clarity.

Director Michael Apted and his writers admirably maintain a balance between complexity of character and in special effects, only to undercut their impact with a murky narrative. This sleek, fast-paced entertainment is further evidence of a steady erosion of confidence in the power of storytelling for its own sake on the part of contemporary blockbuster filmmakers, and truth to tell, that audiences may have trouble following the plot probably won't make a dent at the box office.

A pre-credit jaw-dropping sequence is de rigueur for the Bonds, and "World" delivers big time with Pierce Brosnan's Agent 007 in a terrific speedboat chase down the River Thames that culminates with the suspect attempting to escape via balloon and Bond landing on top of London's Millennium Dome. Through a series of sequences, each one a triumph of production design and technical bravura, we gather that Bond has been sent by M (Judi Dench) to Bilbao, Spain, to retrieve a ransom payment paid by an oil tycoon, Sir Robert King (David Calder), to rescue his kidnapped daughter Elektra (Sophie Marceau) from the arch anarchist Renard (Robert Carlyle), whose only goal, it seems, is to create chaos.

But when Sir Robert comes to M16 headquarters in London to collect his money a fiendish device blows him to bits. Bond is off to Baku, Azerbaijan, to keep a protective eye on Elektra, who is carrying on her father's ambitious and perilous task of building an oil pipeline across Western Asia to Istanbul so that, in the words of M, "the West can count on oil reserves for the next century."

As a survivor of a kidnapping, Elektra is seemingly as fearless as she is gorgeous, not welcoming Bond's presence as a protector but eager to have him as a bedmate. He tries to resist but is beguiled by this beauty who soon proves to be complicated indeed. Bond begins suspecting that she may be a victim of the "Stockholm syndrome," secretly remaining in the thrall of Renard. But what if Renard in turn has fallen in love with her? Apted is adroit in suggesting the contradictions that riddle Elektra and others that render their behavior ambiguous at best.

Similarly, he's good at evoking an aura of complicity that governs interplay between the pursuer and the pursued, revealing vulnerability in all of the film's key players, a quality that has become a must in screen heroes and villains alike. All this is to the good; Brosnan, Marceau (whose 15 movies include "Braveheart" and some prestigious French pictures) and Britain's ever-versatile Carlyle and Dench all have the talent and experience necessary in creating three-dimensional characters. But too often the filmmakers allow a concern for complexity of motivation to lapse into needless confusion.

All the elements that audiences have come to expect of Bond pictures are securely in place: fabulous gadgetry, superbly photographed exotic locales, stupendous production values, inspired action sequences, gorgeous women, considerable zingy double-entendres, a driving score that incorporates the familiar Bond theme and an overall feeling of tremendous-scale, no-expenses-spared film-making.

Robbie Coltrane reprises vividly bad-guy-turned-good-guy Valentin Zukovsky and John Cleese is on hand for some comic relief as R, aide to series veteran Desmond Llewelyn's Q, M16's inventor extraordinaire. But beautiful Denise Richards draws unintended laughs for her singularly callow portrayal of a nuclear weapons whiz. "The World Is Not Enough" in fact offers not enough to add up to a fully satisfying movie.

NEW STATESMAN, 11/29/99, p. 71, Jonathan Romney

One of the great axioms of cinema's that there's no point in parodying the James Bond films because they already parody themselves. In fact, that's not quite true: it's more as if the films parodied themselves only in order to counter the weight of parody from elsewhere. The spoofs have been coming thick and fast at least since Kenneth Williams wore a fez with his tux in *Carry On Spying* (1965); the most recent is Mike Myers's toothy Lothario in the Austin Powers films. But Myers's jovialty priapic swinger is really a third-generation Bond, a parody less of 007 than of his semi-parodic imitators of the 1960s smirking Lotharios like Dean Martin's Matt Helm and James Coburn's Flint.

Such parody has now moved so far away from it's original target that Bond is almost immune from barbs. The series may, in its imperturbable fashion, carry on making the same dry jokes about itself, but if Bond still flirts with Moneypenny, still arches an eyebrow while ordering his Martini, these old habits are rituals to ensure the smooth functioning of the status quo—like Masonic handshakes or barristers invoking "my learned friend". The series in the 1990s has acquired a new sleek dignity and reestablished itself as a classic. I use that word in the way you'd call a car a classic—one you'd never think of driving but that looks sublime in a showroom window. In the same way, the classiness of 1990s Bond seems designed to reassure more than to entertain.

The World Is Not Enough—directed by Michael Apted, a more prestigious journeyman than most—is the 19th Bond film and pretty much offers business as usual. Yet Bond business is never quite as usual. Each film's structure may be unfailingly regular, barely changed since *Dr. No*—from initial tentative skirmishes to showdown at the villain's over-designed HQ --and yet little things change from year to year. The series is a self-repairing organism, constantly modifying its parts but retaining the same shape and meaning. There's a wonderfully, explicit moment of such system-regeneration in *The World Is Not Enough*, when venerable boffin Q (the ever-dependable Desmond Llewellyn) introduces his new assistant (none other than John Cleese—codename R, naturally. Cleese's irascible pratfalls serve no other purpose than to imply that he's been booked in for the next ten films. Meanwhile Q announces his retirement by gently sinking into the floor—the single most graceful moment in the entire series.

The organism mutates in other ways. The music still has the urgent fanfares of the old John Barry scores, but it's now composed by David Arnold, with a discreet bass 'n' drum rattle. And the film discreetly asserts its up-to-scratch cosmopolitanism by recruiting faces from recent European art films—Ulrich Thomsen, the doleful hero of *Festen,* and Maria Grazia Cucinotta from *Il Postino.* Most cosmopolitan of all is Sophie Marceau, whose heiress, Elektra is the classiest thing here—a true sophisticate who, you imagine, is no stranger to Ferrero Rocher.

What never changes is the peculiar political bubble that the series inhabits. The films may look superficially, like the most ideologically overloaded cinema made, yet their codes became fixed so long ago that they now appear to have no political meaning whatsoever. In effect, the films' politics were always really of a 19th-century Napoleonic variety, imagining history as made not by political forces but by two duelling individuals, Bond and the villain of the moment. This film is slightly less Manichaean than the rest—Marceau's character is intriguingly ambivalent, and M16 ethical duplicity is implied. But the Bonds offer a reassuring antidote to conspiracy theory: in their world, real power belongs to any person who can afford a private fleet of killer 'copters.

For all this vagueness, the film works hard to persuade us that it has some purchase on reality, which figures mainly as architecture: a gleaming flash of the Guggenheim in Bilbao, and the Millennium Dome as scene of an air-balloon struggle. It's a fair exchange: the Dome gets its certificate of mythic status, while Bond gets a grounding in the here and now. And the film's use of old-fashioned special effects, rather than digitals, seems almost a matter of moral probity. The credits read like a roll of Renaissance artisanship: parachute pilots, boat engineers, ski rig specialists.

What does strike an odd note is that, for all his supposed sophistication, Pierce Brosnan's rather tight-arsed, tetchy Bond seems to have been implanted with the sexual maturity of a *Viz* character. His innuendo addiction always gets the better of him: Denise Richards' nuclear expert Christmas Jones, apparently Lara Croft's callow kid sister, is there purely for the sake of an excruciating closing gag bout her name. And when Bond dons his X-ray glasses in a casino, he can barely suppress a Benny Hill smirk on realising that they reveal both guns and lingerie. As straight as the film plays itself, there's one respect in which the self-parody has looped round on itself so that, at times, Bond could almost be parodying Austin Powers. But then, it's a safe bet that the series will still be going on in another 30 years, when Austin Powers is long forgotten. Bond is film's equivalent to the Queen Mother, really—expensive to maintain, and doesn't necessarily afford anyone much pleasure, but terribly reassuring in a *plus ça change* way.

NEW YORK, 11/29/99, p. 131, Peter Rainer

The World Is Not Enough, starring Pierce Brosnan, is the twentieth James Bond film in 37 years, and the formula has never been more formulaic. It doesn't seem to matter who makes these movies anymore: The work of a journeyman director like John Glen (*For Your Eyes Only* through *License to Kill*) wasn't much different from what the extravagantly gifted Roger Spottiswoode (*Tomorrow Never Dies*) and the current film's capable Michael Apted have come up with. For all concerned, it's become a job of work in which all the bases must be touched: the pre-credit smash-grab sequence (in this case a speedboat chase on the Thames); the requisite sinister villain (Robert Carlyle, playing a baddie with a bullet embedded in his brain); the shaken-not-stirred repartee the glossy Bond babes (Sophie Marceau and Denise Richards, whose performance as a nuclear-weapons expert is a Golden Turkey shoo-in). It's all so ... so *fetishistic*. The only bright spot is John Cleese's brief appearance as Q's associate, R. Could we pretty please have Cleese play Bond in the next one? (*The Spy Who Walked Funny? Fawltyfinger?*)

NEW YORK POST, 11/19/99, p. 50, Jonathan Foreman

Too many of the recent Bond movies seem to have been made by people who don't really "get" the whole Bond mystique; fortunately, "The World Is Not Enough," (No. 19) comes closer to what a Bond movie should be and once was.

Its terrific opening sequence—including a spectacular chase along the river Thames—is up there with the best Bond scenes.

Apart from that, the most gratifying thing about the film is that director Michael Apted and his writing team understand that James Bond isn't just another action hero to be squandered in the long shootouts that took up so much of the last two films, "Goldeneye" and "Tomorrow Never Dies."

There's also less of the tiresome political correctness that came into the series with the charmless and humorless Timothy Dalton. Once again, agent 007 is a properly promiscuous womanizer and, when necessary, a ruthless killer.

On the other hand, the punning, lubricious humor that is a key part of the formula is weaker than it has been for years.

Robert Carlyle (the psychopathic Begby in "Trainspotting") makes a surprisingly weak villain, and the gadgetry provided by Q (Desmond Llewelyn, who has been in the series for 40 years) and his heir, John Cleese, is mostly unimpressive. (Again, Bond's auto isn't some wonderful British sports car but a BMW coupe).

After British Intelligence fails to protect a powerful businessman from the vengeance of the terrorist Renard (Carlyle), Bond is sent to the Caspian oil town of Baku by M (Judi Dench) to make sure that the tycoon's gorgeous daughter Elektra (Sophie Marceau) doesn't become his next victim.

Elektra is building a pipeline across Central Asia to Turkey, a pipeline that many people would prefer remained unfinished. Assassins in motorized paragliders duly try to kill her when she and Bond are surveying the route on skis.

Bond suspects one of Elektra's employees of disloyalty and after shadowing him ends up at a Russian nuclear missile base in Kazakhstan. There he falls to prevent the theft of a nuclear warhead by Renard but meets Dr. Christmas Jones, embodied by Denise Richards as one of those nubile scientists (Nicole Kidman "The Peacemaker," Elizabeth Shue in "The Saint") who look terrific in a tank top and short shorts.

The warhead then ends up in Istanbul as part of an evil scheme to destroy the city and the West's access to oil from the East.

There are some big, jagged gaps in the complicated and often confusing story—as if a whole subplot involving Judi Dench's M has been cut out.

But it could just be bad writing that makes the film feel mutilated, despite its length and complexity. The three screenwriters are, after all, responsible for some terrible lines that make Marceau and, especially, Richards seem even more bimbonic than necessary.

It's a shame that director Apted (whose documentary "42 Up" opened this week) doesn't allow Brosnan the tough unflappability of Sean Connery's Bond—perhaps out of a misguided desire to make the spy a more well-rounded character—because Brosnan is growing more comfortable in the role.

As his boyish face ages and his frame fills out, he's becoming more appealing as a leading man and more convincing as the quietly tough superagent who's seen it all.

The locations are as exotic as ever (although an Orthodox church turns up in a key scene in Muslim Azerbaijan), and well-photographed. The action scenes are top-notch, even when they don't make much sense.

NEWSDAY, 11/19/99, Part II/p. B3, Gene Seymour

Even with all the expensive toys and brand names scattered throughout "The World Is Not Enough," the 19th "official" feature film installment of James Bond's adventures, the movie's most conspicuously advertised product is the Bond franchise itself. There's a serene, self-congratulatory air pervading the film that's similar to what you find in the annual report of a flush, well-established international corporation. Nice to know, for instance, that the company is easing Q (Desmond Llewelyn) out and bringing in a new weapons whiz (John Cleese), but not too fast, don't you know? Wouldn't want to upset the stockholders, right? Yes, we're still around, aren't we?, the franchise insinuates in what you imagine to be a smooth, clipped British accent. And we do what we do so much better than anyone else, don't we? There's plenty of room to argue that last point—though it's true that while other action-movie franchises have foundered, the Bonds have hung on if for no other reason than their brand-name familiarity. People know, more or less, what they're getting in a James Bond movie and, after 36 years, the mule-headed doggedness of the franchise has qualified as a saving grace even its critics can't dispute.

The franchise is so mule-headed that it still refuses to acknowledge the existence of 1967's cotton-candy spoof "Casino Royale" or 1983's sentimental journey with Sean Connery, "Never Say Never Again." The public, however, does include those movies as part of the canon, which only proves that the Bond persona is in many ways bigger than the franchise—and more resilient than the shaky geopolitical order that Agent 007 is pledged to defend with life, limb and license to kill.

For three films now, Pierce Brosnan has carried that persona, and the best news to be found in "The World Is Not Enough" is that he's getting even better at the job. Brosnan may never entirely convey that hard cruel streak that made Connery's portrayal so inimitable. But he compensates admirably with an incisive reserve, a dark-edged insouciance and a cagier-than-usual adroitness with those smirky double-entendres. Somewhere in the wide space separating Connery's Bond from Roger Moore's glib, toon-town version, Brosnan occupies a comfortable, well- deserved niche.

So what's the second-best thing to be said about "The World Is Not Enough"?

Probably that it's not nearly as obnoxious with product placement as the previous Bond flick, "Tomorrow Never Dies" (1997). And if you buy into the notion that following through on the standard Bond-movie conventions with blithe efficiency constitutes aesthetic achievement, then you might even raise "World Is Not Enough" to the dizzying heights of, say, "Thunderball" (1965) or "The Spy Who Loved Me" (1977).

In other words, director Michael Apted does just enough not to make a mess of things; not even with the elaborate set-pieces, which are, after all, what attracts the crowds. Not one, but two such set-pieces are shown before the opening credits, including a wild hydrofoil chase along the Thames River that ends with a hot-air balloon blowing up in mid-air. (Lots of stuff gets blowed up real good for those of you who like that sort of thing.) The plot, such as it is, acts as filler between the set-pieces. The life of Elektra King (Sophie Marceau), daughter of a murdered oil magnate, is threatened by a notorious freelance terrorist named (how perfect is this?) Renard (Robert Carlyle), who's carrying a bullet in his brain that makes him even more cold-blooded than your average notorious freelance terrorist.

Bond, nursing a busted collarbone throughout (nice touch, that), is called upon by his boss, M (Judi Dench), to protect Elektra from dangers coming from above (killers on skis, again?) and below (H-bombs in her family's oil pipeline).

Just when he gets cozy with Elektra, Bond finds himself forced to join forces with his old KGB enemy Valentin (Robbie Coltrane), who's now another post-Cold War hustler out to stop Renard. Improbable, you say? No more improbable than Denise Richards being cast as a nuclear physicist named (how perfect is this?) Christmas Jones.

It's only after you get off the roller coaster that you're bothered by the many ways "World Is Not Enough" panders to its audience's expectations. (The trademark "Bond... James Bond" introduction is given three jokey references, where one-or none-would have been sufficient.) It's also apparent that the acting, beyond Brosnan, is erratic. Carlyle and Dench do OK with the little they're given to do and you wish there were more of Coltrane and less of Marceau and Richards, both of whom lose your interest as soon as they open their mouths.

But more than anything, you wonder just how long the franchise can keep running on automatic pilot. With Brosnan firmly in place, the franchise has a chance to recapture some of that cheeky mix of dark humor and sadism that gave the first Bonds that gin-and-vermouth kick. If things stay status quo, then sooner or later there may be a Bond movie with a title like "Everything Eventually Dies."

SIGHT AND SOUND, 1/00, p. 62, José Arroyo

Superspy James Bond retrieves a suitcase of money for oil magnate Sir Robert King in Bilbao and returns it to him at M16 headquarters in London. A remote-controlled booby trap hidden in King's lapel pin explodes, killing King. At King's funeral in Scotland, Bond meets the deceased's daughter Elektra, who was once kidnapped by Renard, a terrorist. Renard has a bullet lodged in his skull that's slowly killing him, but which renders him impervious to pain. Bond's boss M sends Bond to the Caucasus to protect Elektra and discover who killed King. After escaping an attack while skiing, Elektra and Bond visit a local casino run by Valentin Zukovsky, a Russian mafioso, and then make love. Soon after, Bond is led to an atomic test facility in Kazakhstan.

There Bond meets scientist Christmas Jones and discovers Renard stealing an atomic missile, but Bond is unable to stop him. Bond follows Renard to Istanbul and discovers the missile has been inserted into Elektra's pipeline. Realising it's not atomic, Bond and Christmas let it explode so the culprit might think them dead. Bond discovers Renard and Elektra are lovers, working together; she is the real mastermind and her father's murderer. Her targets are rival pipelines. They have kidnapped M and intend to kill her. Bond kills Elektra, saves M, and with Christmas follows Renard to a submarine where they finally defeat him.

Inherent in the notion of a film sequel is the lure of an intensified repetition of previous pleasures. After close to four decades of changing socio-sexual mores, competition from satires and rip offs such as the *Austin Powers* and *Matt Helm* films, and the obvious difficulty of engaging the public with five different incarnations of an iconic character, the very existence of *The World Is Not Enough,* the nineteenth official Bond movie, is proof that Bond's makers have mostly been delivering the goods.

James Bond is the icon other icons look up to.   When Arnold Schwarzenegger thought his cyborg turn needed uplift, he merged Bond with his Terminator persona for *True Lies.*   Singer Robbie Williams says he wants to be Bond in the new millennium, as does openly gay actor Rupert Everett.   Yet although Bond obviously represents an enduring masculine ideal, on the evidence of *The World Is Not Enough* the filmmakers don't seem to understand why this might be so, and seem to feel licensed to kill off what made Bond iconic.

Bond films are formula film-making, and the production machinery behind them is so extensive and expert the movies are almost director-proof.   *The World Is Not Enough* duly follows the traditional blueprint with nifty gadgets and cars, beautiful and available women and a couple of superb set pieces (the precredit sequence and the skiing scene).   However, an equally important part of the Bond formula is cartoonish style, a light tone and two-dimensional characterisation.   Many of us like it that way—we care more about what Bond wears and drives than what he feels.

The makers of *The World Is Not Enough* of whom director Michael Apted should be singled out for blame, have attempted to depict all-too fleshy characters who desire, lack and feel.   It's what is valued in a Ken Loach film, but it acts as an explosive and unsettling expulsion from the fantasies Bond films invite us to.   One can't name a patricidal character Elektra and then expect the audience not to giggle at the film's attempts to psychologise her; one can't have Denise Richards play a nuclear physicist and make any claims to conventional believability.   Robert Carlyle striving to imbue a character with truth and depth is almost always a good thing, but when that character is a Bond villain who wants to conquer the world, one has to ask what the director was thinking of.   Worst of all they've done the same to Bond, not understanding that deep feelings don't go easily with nonchalance, suavity, elegance or cool, much less with killing people as a profession.

Intending to turn Bond and his world into what they can't be, these attempts to create emotional depth reveal an underlying contempt for what the Bond movies actually are.   They imply realism is not just one mode among many but the superior, most culturally worthy and difficult mode.   By that logic, of course, to make Bond films better is to make them more 'realistic', like Apted's *Nell,* presumably.   Thank God for action, production values and the second unit.   They're what make *The World Is Not Enough* still worth watching.

VILLAGE VOICE, 11/30/99, p. 142, Dennis Lim

That Bond guy still seems to elicit an enormous amount of goodwill—a readiness to gloss over the movies' brazen irrelevance, and reflexive chatter about the supposedly comforting familiarity of on-cue explosions, antiquated politics, and atrocious puns.   The turgid hysteria of Bond 19, *The World Is Not Enough,* makes the strongest case for retirement since late-period Roger Moore.   The quaintly elaborate (yet strangely unexciting) precredit sequence catapults Pierce Brosnan's 007 from Bilbao (he strolls past Frank Gehry's new Guggenheim Museum, just because it's there) to a high-speed boat chase along the Thames (not a good idea so soon after *Face/Off*) that sends him crashing onto the barely completed Millennium Dome in Greenwich.   More blandly extravagant set pieces follow, involving paragliders, a helicopter with attached buzzsaw, and a nuclear sub.

Character-actor Brits abound: Robert Carlyle as the villain (vaguely superhuman as the result of a nerve-severing bullet in the brain), Judi Dench as M (acting up a storm—for what?), and an amusing John Cleese as R, presumed successor to gadget freak Q.   Sophie Marceau, as an imperiled oil heiress, may seem smart and tough by Bond-babe standards, but the film is more interested in portraying her as a disturbed bitch.   Denise Richards is, at least, an entertaining running joke, playing a pert and toothy nuclear physicist.   (She's also named Christmas, and you can bet your life on the eventual appearance of a pun about Christmas coming.)   What's most disappointing about *The World Is Not Enough* is that the famously adaptable Michael Apted—the man behind the *7 Up* series—adapts all too easily.   Far too reverent in its winking irreverence, the film treats a ragged formula as if it were sacred.

Also reviewed in:
CHICAGO TRIBUNE, 11/19/99, Friday/p. A, Michael Wilmington
NEW YORK TIMES, 11/19/99, p. E20, Janet Maslin
NEW YORKER, 11/29, p. 138, Anthony Lane
VARIETY, 11/15-21/99, p. 88, Todd McCarthy
WASHINGTON POST, 11/19/99, p. C1, Stephen Hunter
WASHINGTON POST, 11/19/99, Weekend/p. 49, Desson Howe

WOUNDS, THE

A Leisure Time Features release of a Cobra Film production. *Producer:* Dragan Bjelogrlic. *Director:* Srdjan Dragojevic. *Screenplay (Serbo-Croatian with English subtitles):* Srdjan Dragojevic. *Director of Photography:* Dusan Joksimovic. *Editor:* Petar Markovic. *Music:* Aleksandar Sasa Habic. *Production Designer:* Aleksandar Denic. *Running time:* 103 minutes. *MPAA Rating:* Not Rated.

CAST: Dusan Pekic (Pinki); Milan Maric (Kraut); Dragan Bjelogrlic (Dickie); Branka Katic (Suki); Predrag Miki Manojlovic (Stojan); Vesna Trivalic (Lidija); Andreja Jovanovic (Dijabola); WITH: Nikola Kojo; Gorica Popovic; Bata Stojkovic.

CHRISTIAN SCIENCE MONITOR, 8/27/99, p. 15, David Sterritt

The Wounds was written and directed by Srdjan Dragojevic, who hails from Belgrade, where this movie set box-office records despite a ban on publicity issued by the Serbian government, which was displeased by its highly critical content.

Like the somewhat similar "Cabaret Balkan," which opened recently in American theaters, "The Wounds" focuses less on political or governmental issues than on the personal failings and everyday miseries that affect ordinary people who are simply trying to live their lives despite the chaos that surrounds them.

Dragojevic aims tragicomic barbs at everything from teenage violence to television trash. His message is as cynical as it is sardonic, but it etches a harrowing portrait of social dysfunction in a land that has been experiencing more than its share of sorrows.

NEW YORK POST, 4/1/99, p. 97, Thelma Adams

Interesting timing: As NATO continues to attack Serb forces, New Yorkers attending the New Directors/New Films festival will get a chance to see "The Wounds," a kinetic, visceral glimpse of Serbian life in the '90s. Call it "Serbz N the Hood."

From 1991 to 1996, teens Kraut (Milan Maric) and Pinki (Dusan Pekic) come of age in war-shredded Bosnia. While the boys' families reel from atrocities past and present, rampant inflation, and ethnic violence, Pinki and Kraut find an outlet for their testosterone-charged aggressive impulses in the external chaos.

The pair apprentice to a maniacal gangster with a thing for Cagney, Clint and a .357 Magnum. As their peach fuzz turns to stubble, the teens eclipse their mentor, packing pistols, peddling and using drugs, and moving from the slums to a high-rise.

Pinki and Kraut become outlaws, Bosnan war profiteers with no recollection of peace and no fear of justice.

The teens have 15 minutes of fame when they appear on their favorite reality TV show, "Asphalt Pulse"—a "Larry King Live" with felonious guests. The seductive hostess asks them to show their wounds, a regular part of the broadcast. The youthful criminals don't have any bullet scars, so Kraut shoots himself on live TV.

Director Srdjan Dragojevic, working from his own script based on actual events, probes the wounds of war with a hot poker. Nihilistic, engaging, riding the wild surf of economic and political instability, Pinki and Kraut are compelling and repulsive, gangstas in a global ghetto.

NEW YORK POST, 8/27/99, p. 56, Rod Dreher

Whatever else might be said of the vile Slobodan Milosevic, he has been good for the film industry in the former Yugoslavia.

Two of the decade's best films—Emir Kusturica's "Underground" and Goran Paskeljevic's "Cabaret Balkan"—attacked the regime with grim humor and bitter realism.

Now comes another exiled filmmaker's lacerating anti-Milosevic broadside, Srdjan Dragojevic's "The Wounds." It's not as coherent and accomplished as the others, but it still packs a powerful wallop, depicting the chaos, violence and moral collapse of Serbian society through the live-fast, die-young careers of two teenage gangsters.

It's Belgrade in 1991, the war with Croatia rages, and Belgraders suffer under economic sanctions. Bored adolescent buddies Pinki and Kraut (newcomers Dusan Pekic and Milan Maric) find themselves drawn to scuzzy gangster Dickie (Dragan Bjelogrlic), who impresses them with his gun, his Versace suit and his cheap moll.

The vulgar and sadistic Dickie takes them under his wing as apprentice thugs. And why shouldn't the boys join him? Writer-director Dragojevic has said he believes young people in Serbia have a right to commit crimes, even to murder, in response to the hopeless world the older generations have given them.

Pinki's father (Miki Manojlovic) is a career army vet who believed the nationalist-communist lies he was raised on; now he's a pathetic figure.

The boys mature into vicious drug dealers in a macho culture that idolizes strong men. Ultimately, their insane, coke-fueled rampages lead to a reckoning that highlights how suicidal this culture's inability to forgive is.

"The Wounds" is harsh and unremittingly bleak, though despair like this is rarely so slickly filmed. But the film is more interesting as a sociopolitical testament than an emotionally involving drama.

NEWSDAY, 8/27/99, Part II/p. B7, John Anderson

The only American equivalent to Srdjan Dragojevic's "The Wounds," which autopsies the corpse of postwar Belgrade, might be the Hughes Brothers' "Menace II Society," a film in which moral disequilibrium was ingrained in the celluloid and where the execution of the story itself was possessed by a kind of societal bankruptcy.

The Serbian director, however, isn't portraying a cancerous element in an otherwise healthy society. He's performing exploratory cinema about a country that's terminally ill. Picking up in 1996 and flashing back to 1991, he shows us the disintegration of Belgrade through two boys who come of age knowing nothing else but war's material destruction and moral decay. Neither forgiving them their sins nor making high-minded pronouncements about their guilt—or propagandizing, except as regards pure evil—Dragojevic does ask the loaded question about what else his boys might be expected to do.

Pinki (Dusan Pekic) and Kraut (Milan Maric) idolize older criminals like Dickie (Dragan Bjelogrlic), who have the women, the money and drugs to not only make life livable in decrepit Serbia, but maintain some dignity, too. Men like Pinki's father (the terrific Yugoslav actor Miki Manojlovic of "Underground" and "Cabaret Balkan") meanwhile, storm around impotently, complaining about the state of the nation while blaming the ethnic Other. Pinki and Kraut's fondest dream is to become guests on "Asphalt Pulse," a TV talk show featuring the most ruthless of Belgrade's criminals (a type of show that actually existed), hosted by the sultry Lidja (Vesna Trivalic), the talk-show host from hell. By the time they get their big shot at stardom, however, their sense of anarchy has outgrown the small screen.

Dragojevic, whose "Pretty Village, Pretty Flame" was a self-described "tragicomedy" about the war in Bosnia, promised himself he wouldn't make another war film, but has—one full of rich symbolism, magic realism and venom. "The Wounds" also stars two young former Yugoslavs who've never acted before and are the embodiment of futureless youth.

Both Pekic and Maric could become real stars of European cinema—if they can manage to live through the present.

VILLAGE VOICE, 8/31/99, p. 120, Amy Taubin

When Pinki, the teenage killer and governing conscience of Srdjan Dragojevic's harrowing *The Wounds*, arrives at a hospital, shot nearly dead by his best friend, he identifies himself to the operating-room nurse hovering over him as "Bond, James Bond." As he sinks under the anesthetic, he confides to us that it's better to die as Bond than as himself.

Dusan Pekic, a scrawny, feral-faced 15-year-old with rotting teeth and no prior acting experience, plays Pinki with ferocious and disarming wit. Dragojevic, who also has practiced transactional psychotherapy, says he picked Pekic out of 5000 kids who auditioned for the film; he notes that the fledgling actor's background has a certain similarity to the character he embodies. Pekic could become an Eastern European Tim Roth if he survives into adulthood in the former Yugoslavia.

Dragojevic makes Pinki the spokeschild for a generation that reached adolescence in the '90s under the insanity of the Milosevic regime. The Serb director's position is that kids are justified in taking revenge on adults in a society that took away their childhood. That the children also wind up dead in the process seems less problematic than inevitable. From the first image of a red crucifix to the final shot of kids lying dead in the rubble-strewn lot where they used to hurl stones at one another, *The Wounds* is a bit too invested in martyrdom. It's a politicized and catholicized version of live fast, die young, leave a beautiful (or, in this case, not so beautiful) corpse. But that's an easy critique for an outsider to make.

Based on the true story of two teenaged Serb killers, *The Wounds* follows Pinki and his buddy Kraut (Milan Maric, in a restrained debut performance) as they come of age in Belgrade when Serb nationalism is running amok and the economic embargo has brought the middle-class to starvation. By the time the boys are 17-year-olds, they've realized almost all their youthful ambitions and destroyed each other in the process.

Apprenticing themselves to the neighborhood smuggler and drug dealer, they take over his business and his girlfriend when he gets strung out on his own dope. Their first killing wins them a guest slot on The Street Pulse, a celebrity-gangster TV talk show hosted by Lidja (Vesna Trivalic), a schoolmarmish dominatrix who's also the mother of a boy Pinki and Kraut love to scapegoat.

Determined to give the audience something it has never seen before, the excited Kraut whips out his semi-automatic, and while Lidja signals the camera to keep rolling, shoots himself in the thigh. (Dragojevic says that The Street Pulse is based on *Black Pearls,* a show that ran on Yugoslavian TV for five years.)

Their brains fried by coke and fame, the boys kill anyone who gets in their way or on their frazzled nerves. Pinki explains that killing mutes the pain of his father's suicide. A former army officer, Pinki's dad impulsively blew his brains out with one foot stuck in a toilet bowl. There's a touch of Holden Caulfield in Pinki's voiceover narration, which, I suspect, loses some of its subtlety in the English subtitled version.

Constructed as a series of flashbacks, *The Wounds* moves at an erratic, frequently frantic pace until the closing scene, which has a relentless, demented logic of its own. Dragojevic uses jagged cuts, oblique angles, and shaky camera moves, but there's nothing gratuitous about the violence of his cinematic language. *Catcher in the Rye* aside, the film plays like a cross between *Los Olvidados* and *Dead Presidents;* it achieves its most surreal moment in the closing credits, where the McDonald's and Fruit of the Loom logos are prominently displayed on the list of "sponsors." Whoever thought *The Wounds* would be a promo vehicle for the youth market must have been disappointed when the Milosevic government banned all advertisements for the film.

Also reviewed in:
CHICAGO TRIBUNE, 1/14/00, Friday/p. K, John Petrakis
NEW YORK TIMES, 8/27/99, p. E18, Janet Maslin
VARIETY, 10/12-18/98, p. 43, Derek Elley

XIU XIU: THE SENT DOWN GIRL

A Stratosphere Entertainment and Whispering Steppes release of a Whispering Steppes production. *Executive Producer:* Joan Chen, Allison Liu, and Cecile Shah Tsuei. *Producer:* Joan Chen and Alice Chan. *Director:* Joan Chen. *Screenplay (Mandarin with English subtitles):* Yan Geling and Joan Chen. *Based on the novella "Tian yu" by:* Yan Geling. *Director of Photography:* Lu Yue. *Editor:* Ruby Yang. *Music:* Johnny Chen. *Sound:* Jay Boekelheide, Yang Zhanshan, and David Parker. *Production Designer:* Pan Lai. *Art Director:* Liu Shiyun. *Costumes:* Pan Lai. *Running time:* 99 minutes. *MPAA Rating:* R.

CAST: Lu Lu (Xiu Xiu); Lopsang (Lao Jin); Qian Zheng (Li Chuanbei); Gao Jie (Mother); Li Zhizhen (Headquarters Chief); Gao Qiang (Peddler); Qin Wenyuan (Motorcycle Man); Cao Jiang (Three Toes); Wang Luoyang (Narrator).

CINEASTE, Vol. XXIV, No. 4, 1999, p. 40, Pauline Chen

After the release of her recent film, *Xiu-Xiu: The Sent Down Girl,* director Joan Chen was banned from working in China for one year and fined $50,000 by the Chinese authorities. Aside from Chen's failure to submit to the Chinese Film Bureau's censorship procedures when shooting the film on the Sichuan-Tibet border, some aspects of *Xiu Xiu*'s content may have been especially galling to the Chinese government. The film chronicles the fate of a teenage girl Xiu Xiu (Lu Lu), who along with millions of other youths, was 'sent down' during the Cultural Revolution to perform manual labor in the countryside. She is assigned to live with Lao Jin (Lopsang), a middle-aged Tibetan herder, to learn horsemanship. Believing that they will help her return to her home in the city, Xiu Xiu sleeps with a series of men from the local Communist headquarters, only to find that her efforts are to no avail.

While the Chinese government has always been sensitive about negative portrayals of the Cultural Revolution, banning Chen Kaige's *Farewell My Concubine,* Tian Zhuangzhuang's *The Blue Kite,* and Zhang Yimou's *To Live* in recent years, it has reason to find *Xiu Xiu*'s account particularly troubling. These other films have depicted the violence and discord of this period as erupting from a social and political atmosphere of escalating hysteria, fanaticism, and fear. Chen, in contrast, treating a slightly later period of the Cultural Revolution, gives little space to tensions in the broader social context, portraying Chengdu, Xiu Xiu's hometown, as curiously peaceful and idyllic at the time of her departure in 1974. Instead, in Chen's account, once Xiu Xiu has been sent down, most of her suffering stems from the widespread corruption and abuse of power by local Communist officials in their implementation of central policies. The local bureaucrats' sexual exploitation of the sent-down girls is openly tolerated by the nearby Communist headquarters, and is even treated as a routine occurrence; a nurse at the infirmary there notes that Xiu Xiu is the fifth girl who has come in pregnant that week.

In a blistering indictment of the Cultural Revolution, Chen seems to suggest that such corruption and abuses of power were so rampant as to define the movement itself. *Xiu Xiu*'s provocative and ambiguous portrayal of racial relations between the Han majority and the Tibetan 'ethnic minority' may also disquiet Chinese authorities. On the one hand, the film seems to lend support to their party line of 'harmonious racial integration under Communism,' by presenting a seamlessly assimilated Lao Jin, speaking flawless Mandarin Chinese and winning awards for his faithful service to the government. The 'backwardness' of traditional Tibetan culture is suggested by the fact that Lao Jin was castrated in a Tibetan 'tribal war' twenty years earlier, before the civilizing influence of Han culture tamed the region.

On the other hand, the film seems to critique Han ethnocentrism by unflatteringly depicting the faintly dismissive attitude that infects the Han characters' interactions with Lao Jin. Xiu Xiu herself, revealing a less endearing side, is wont to marvel at the infrequency of his bathing, and, in moments of irritation, to call him an animal. In defiance of prevailing stereotypes, by the end of the film it is the Tibetan Lao Jin who emerges as the upholder of honor and enemy of oppression, furiously defending Xiu Xiu's virtue against the depredations of Han men. This configuration, in which a representative of a 'less civilized' race defends a Han woman against her own kind, seems a pointed reversal of the plots of some of the 'ethnic minority' films of the

1950s, which typically depicted Han Communists liberating the lower-class members of ethnic groups from oppressors of their own race, and defending minority women from the assaults of their own swarthy compatriots.

Despite its thought-provoking treatments of the Cultural Revolution and Chinese racial relations, *Xiu Xiu* on the whole does not fulfill the dramatic promise held out by its compelling plot and subject matter. While skillfully shot and well-acted, the film is flawed by its one-dimensional and static portrayal of the title character. Joan Chen has characterized Xiu Xiu as a "sacrifice," a "symbol for innocence lost and regained." In Chen's eagerness to create an appropriately pathetic victim, she does not allow Xiu Xiu any psychological complexity in responding to the new and difficult circumstances in which she finds herself. Besides her artless winsomeness, Xiu Xiu's characterization seems to consist of two features: an acute and unabating longing to return home, and her purity and innocence, for which her love of bathing serves as a heavy-handed metaphor. (The film's crisis occurs when she sacrifices the second of these for the first.)

In what is surely an atypical experience for a sent-down youth, she manages to learn few new skills living with Lao Jin in the grasslands, and prefers to gaze through a kaleidoscope given her by her hometown admirer, rather than interacting with the magnificent scenery that surrounds her. The film's depiction of Xiu Xiu's failure to adapt to her new environment contrasts strongly with the portrayals of sent down youths in earlier films such as Chen Kaige's *King of the Children* and Zhang Nuanxin's *Sacrificed Youth,* in which the protagonists gain insight into their own culture from their sojourns in a remote village and Dai ethnic minority community, respectively.

Moreover, the film's persistent and disturbing emphasis on Xiu Xiu as an object of sexual desire leaves little room for the exploration of other dimensions of her character and experience. Towards the end of the film, when Xiu Xiu becomes the passive participant in increasingly brutal sexual acts, this emphasis is to some extent justified. However, even earlier in the film, she is repeatedly shown naked or partially undressed, when such shots are not necessitated by plot or character development. When she is first introduced at the beginning of the film, her hometown admirer, who narrates the story, is shown gazing earnestly at her, as he states that he has just realized that Xiu Xiu has become a woman. The following scene reveals her nude in a bathtub; her mother instructs her on the use of sanitary pads as her admirer looks up at her through the window.

Later in the film, the camera angles frequently approximate Lao Jin's gaze, as he looks at (or tries not to look at) her nubile body, often only partially clothed, sometimes silhouetted naked through a sheet. Xiu Xiu's own point of view remains largely unexplored throughout the film. It seems to be Chen's intention to suggest through the film's tragic denouement that in China men sexually exploit women while disregarding their emotional states. Ironically, *Xiu Xiu's* camerawork and structure have been engaged in the very same practice all along.

Using the perspective of Xiu Xiu's admirer, rather than her own, to narrate her story, is another blatant example of how the film accentuates Xiu Xiu's desirability from a male perspective at the expense of conveying her own subjective vision. His character appears on screen for the first ten minutes of the film, as his voice introduces himself as a neighbor and schoolmate smitten by Xiu Xiu's charms. However, as he has managed to avoid being sent down himself thanks to family connections, he never sees her again. His voice-over first-person narration recurs at several points, telling us how he has tried to piece together and envision Xiu Xiu's fate from scattered rumors. It is his soft-focus and romanticized remembrance and imaginings of her that end the film. The adoption of his unconnected and distant viewpoint only detracts from the impact and immediacy of Xiu Xiu's story.

Finally, the panoramic shots of the landscape interspersed through the film, as lovely as they are, actually undermine the film's attempts to build up emotional intensity. These lush shots express neither Xiu Xiu's nor Lao Jin's appreciation of their natural surroundings, and are, moreover, inconsonant with the film's mood. One can only suppose that they are inserted to give the audience an opportunity to pause to admire the beauty of Western China. To intercut Xiu Xiu's story with these picturesquely shot, travelog-worthy images may ultimately allow the audience to view her harrowing experience with the same esthetic distance with which they view the landscape, as something dramatic and striking, but at a great remove from themselves.

Joan Chen seems to share the assumption, common to a number of other Chinese filmmakers and perhaps justified, that they can only attract international audiences by depicting China as a breathtakingly exotic and photogenic spectacle for the eyes and ears. Thus, in the last fifteen years, few Chinese imports have done without titillating sex scenes (Zhang Yimou's *Ju Dou,* Chen Kaige's *Temptress Moon*), performances of excitingly unfamiliar 'ethnic' arts (this year's *King of Masks* by Wu Tianming, Zhang's *To Live, Farewell My Concubine),* or exotic customs (Zhang's *Raise the Red Lantern)* and locales (Xie Fei's *Mongolian Tale).* United with strong characters and a well-developed plot, these elements need not detract from a film. It's when they overwhelm the stories they embellish, as in *Xiu Xiu,* that Chinese cinema loses its heart.

FILM QUARTERLY, Spring 2000, p. 49, Wena Poon

At first glance, veteran actress Joan Chen seems to have done what every enterprising Chinese dissident would have loved to do: pack a bus full of cast and crew, trundle off to a forbidden border of Tibet and China, and shoot a film worthy enough of arousing the rancour of an arrogant government—all on a shoestring budget.   Like Martin Scorsese's *Kundun* and Jean-Jacques Annaud's *Seven Years in Tibet,* her film uses the beauty of the Tibetan landscape as a template for exposing China's dismal human rights record.

The message behind the film, however, is anything but straightforward. *Xiu Xiu: The Sent Down Girl* shown as *Tian Yu (Heavenly Pond)* in Asia—stands alone amid the pageant of China-bashing films as a political conundrum. Joan Chen's perplexing take on China renders the earnest indignation of Hollywood films about "the Tibet question" hopelessly one-dimensional. A simple film with two Chinese actors unknown outside of their own country, *Xiu Xiu* is a gorgeously filmed, harrowing tale of a government's idealism gone wrong. Yet, for all its cinematic glory on screen, nothing teases the cinema-goer's imagination more than the perplexing dissonance between what the film's makers and advertisers claim the film to be, and what unfolds on the screen.

A love story between a man and a woman. A haunting raw landscape of wildflowers and sky. A tale of compassion, lost love, martyrdom, innocence. That's apparently how the film's marketers—including Chen herself—wanted the American cinemagoer to interpret the film. Chen says in her director's statement to the press that the landscape of the Tibetan border was "haunting yet beautiful," that Xiu Xiu was a "martyr ... born under the silver moonlight." She describes how she and screenwriter Yan Geling finished writing the script "during the most beautiful month of the year on the high plateau." Chen gets high marks for waxing lyrical about her story, but her film is at odds with her marketing intent. It's just as well that much of the film takes place in a cheerless, icy wasteland without a name—it is a story about the termination of hope and life, a bone-chilling indictment of a political system that victimizes its own offspring, then blames them for their failures.

Xiu Xiu traces a bizarre program run by Communist China in the 1960s-70s of "sending down" urban prepubescents to the remote Chinese countryside in order to seal the ideological gulf between the city bourgeois and the illiterate sons of the soil.   The children, each wearing a military-issue coat, wave flags and sing patriotic jingles as they are packed off into military trucks.

Typical of ideological governments whose social agendas are far loftier than the morals of the people who execute them, the Cultural Youth Revolution ended up mass-mailing children like Xiu Xiu into the outermost regions of the steppes, where they were stranded for years because the people who crafted their leadership programs had changed their minds, moved on, and forgotten about them. Disoriented, lonely, and desperate, these urban teens became easy prey for the packs of petty village officials and corrupted peasantry who harbored little cultural or social empathy for them.

Strangely, for all the razor-sharp political observations in her film, Chen claims she is no dissident. Seemingly apologetic about offending the Chinese government, she paid up the fine for shooting on the Tibetan border without permission. She has explained her act without any indignation, rancor, or even slight irritation at her government for restricting artistic enterprise in a manner unfamiliar to many other countries. Her attitude suggests that perhaps not all who criticize authoritarian regimes do so without deference to their awful power, and that "dissent" and "nationalistic pride" may sometimes be the most natural of bedfellows. American moviegoers who are titillated by film's advertisements (bearing the gleeful marketing stamp "Banned in China for Political and Sexual Content") and who come away thinking they have seen another sad, beautiful film about the "awful Tibet situation" may not be truly appreciating the pedigree and psychological ambivalence of its makers.

It is no secret that Joan Chen grew up in Mao China and was personally handpicked by Mao's infamous wife, the ambitious and ruthless Jiang Qing, to be a model young actress. Yan Geling, who wrote the novella upon which *Xiu Xiu* is based and scripted the film with Chen, belonged to Chen's generation. For both Yan and Chen, the experience of being "sent down" by the Communist government was a prevalent threat in their youth. Both female artists are no stranger to "The System": its cold calculation of human life, its sorting of human talents, its casting of individual destinies. They saw it happen to fathers, friends, neighbors. They narrowly escaped: the system, recognizing their artistic talents, had a better plan for them. Chen was drafted into an acting program in the Shanghai Film Studio in 1975; Yan was trained as professional ballerina at age 12 to perform for the People's Liberation Army.

That these two extraordinary young prodigies could come out of the Communist system two decades later and make a film about the system that sorted their own fortunes testifies to the human intellect's irrepressible and admirable capacity for self-reflection. *Xiu Xiu* is a bittersweet memory of two Chinese artistic superstars about their own loss of innocence. It seems that both women, who have married and settled in the United States, have come together to make an elegiac tribute from afar to those from their generation who didn't make it. Because of the tension between marketing and political intent, it is easier to read *Xiu Xiu* as not so much a dissident's film as a cathartic work of art (precipitating perhaps from its makers' own tremors of survivor guilt?). "*Xiu Xiu* commemorates the last generation that came of age during the Chinese Cultural Revolution," says the director in her press statement. Chen, Yan, and the rest of their distinguished cast and crew are genuine children of the very system that they depict, and they have come together to look back with mixed feelings at their cultural history. Precisely because the State has its hand in every domain of intellectual life in China, the film's cast and crew were hand-picked, raised, accoladed, and primed by the Chinese Government. Thus, if one comes away thinking how brave and controversial these "dissidents" were in making a banned film, one perhaps underestimates the greater psychological complexity—and intellectual beauty—of what Chen and Yan have wrought.

Consideration of the filmmaker's background is important for another reason. It is almost too easy to forget, since Chen herself is so famous in Hollywood, that *Xiu Xiu* is directed by a China-born woman. Viewers are so used to Chen's sex-siren charm that one might have expected a pretty little film rather than the political bombshell that it is (flowers, sunsets, and all). *Xiu Xiu* brings home the point that before she was a pretty face, Chen was an artistic product of the second largest Communist regime in the world. It is refreshing to see Chen articulate in her own cultural medium and in her own gendered vision.

The imprint of a female directorial vision asserts itself in piercingly sad ways throughout the film, and Chen's narrative willingly embraces all these aspects of her heroine's body (one of the first scenes shows Xiu Xiu's mother carefully packing rough-hewn "fancy-grade" toilet paper and a handsewn cotton garter for her daughter's period before Xiu Xiu leaves for the barren countryside). In doing so, she reminds us in heartbreaking ways of the quotidian and human aspects of girlhood, so that we will later feel even more keenly the physical pain that Xiu Xiu undergoes in the film. The mother's tender worry for her daughter's intimate needs will contrast sharply with the chauvinist brutality of the system that invades and desecrates her daughter's person.

Lee Xiaolu (Lu Lu) plays Wen Xiu ("refined and exquisite"), the perfect flower of Chinese girlhood around whom this sad operetta of youth corrupted revolves. The 15-year old actress discovered by Chen reminds us of young Chen herself in her early film, *Little Flower* (1979), when she smiles her sharp-chinned, poster-perfect smile. Xiu Xiu is the very incarnation of Communist Youth posters, complete with cheap nylon taffeta scarf, striped sweater, and symmetrical pigtails. A nubile Lolita, Xiu Xiu romps around the film flashing her child-like nudity at men with gullible ease. Almost from the very beginning, Chen films her little protégée with adoring close-ups, making us fall in love with her babyish sweetness even as we shudder in the anticipation of some horrible fate.

True enough, Chen then brings us down a roller-coaster track of child sexual exploitation and innocence gnawed to the raw as Xiu Xiu is repeatedly and brutally raped by small-time peddlers and petty officials in the countryside. Her physical corruption, however, is not as depressing as the mental corruption that she inherits from her sexual abusers. As if to illustrate how a mind can be rendered soft and facile when habitually force-fed with government propaganda, Xiu Xiu easily believes everything that comes forth from the lips of adult men. They tell her that the way pretty girls like her can get home quickly is to offer her body to them. They can get her the relevant paperwork to escape. After all, no child can see her parents again unless she convinces a government official to give her a return permit. Any child caught in the city without a permit would be sent back into the countryside in a trice. That's right. Think about it. Here's some "candy." She takes it, and the game begins.

Desperate to see her parents and her beloved urban environment again, Xiu Xiu numbly consents to being pummeled and sodomized at all hours of the night. Typical of desperate civilians under a Communist regime, Xiu Xiu would do anything to survive. This was the only "education" that Xiu Xiu ever received from her government. Imbibing their lies as easily as she had imbibed party indoctrination, she says with child-like simplicity, "How else can a girl get by? After all, I have nothing: no money, no connections ... I only have myself." As word gets round that a pretty city child out in the steppes can be had for a song, more and more anonymous men from the village headquarters casually drive by to have sex with her, each deluding her with lies.

Heroism, like hope, never has a chance to rear its head in Chen's bleak tale. Tibetan actor Lopsang plays the male lead, Lao Jin, a Tibetan herdsman into whose tent Xiu Xiu is unceremoniously dumped by program staff as part of her "training" in the art of peasant life. Joan Chen wrote that she thought of Lopsang as the perfect "fairytale hero," but her romantic assertion is belied by the testimony of her own film. Swarthy, muscular, and perennially armed with a rifle, Lao Jin does carve a heroic figure in the film as the gruff Caliban who adores Xiu Xiu. Yet the protector-princess romance fails to develop. Lao Jin was brutally castrated by his enemies during a Tibetan war; as a result, he has chosen to lead a solitary existence with a flock of wild horses, turning away from life and opportunity in order to live out his own enigma.

That Chen chose as her main subjects a young Chinese girl and a castrated Tibetan pauper is no coincidence. These are by far the most telling archetypes of politically oppressed peoples in China. Chen excruciatingly illustrates what such disenfranchised groups have lost by emphasizing Lao Jin's mental impotence. The vacuum of heroism hums deafeningly in her film: Lao Jin cannot fill the heroic niche in the story. When petty tradesmen saunter into his own tent to rape Xiu Xiu before his very eyes, Lao Jin can only lower his gaze in regret. Even though he is armed to the teeth, and has no problems firing at people who come near his livestock, he does not dare to raise his rifle against Xiu Xiu's rapists. So powerful and entrenched is the exploitative system that Lao Jin did not even think of challenging it. In a blinding moment of suppressed rage, all Lao Jin can do is to pluck the rapist's shoe surreptitiously from under the bed and burn it in the fire as the merest whisper of civil disobedience.

Chen rather duplicitously writes that she thought of Lao Jin as the personification of the "nobleness of the human emotion called love." Yet throughout the entire film, Lao Jin displays a powerfully wretched passivity that is quite compatible with Xiu Xiu's own infantile vulnerability. Their final decision, which leads to the tragic conclusion of the film, resembles more the cul-de-sac desperation of a people who have lost all hope and who have nothing to live for. Passivity and the implicit acceptance of evil robs Lao Jin of the heroism of the archetypal tragic hero. His every act—and omission—in the film can be seen as a politically resonant moment that reverberates within the history of Chinese oppression. His behavior speaks volumes about how the Chinese Communist regime destroys people's regard of their own self-worth and possibilities.

Chen claims that her urge to direct her first film came from sitting through too many "end-of-the-millennium." "nihilistic" pictures at the 1996 Berlin Film Festival. She was inspired to make a "more hopeful, more poetic" tale. If Chen really means what she says, *Xiu Xiu* is a classic demonstration of how the poem may be larger than the poet. Chen may dress up her film with flowers, soaring melodies, and pink-cheeked grins, but she also deals with death, rape, and loss with a heavy hand. Besides, today's audiences, numbed by media coverage of daily atrocities in the international arena, can hardly be expected to ignore the politics of exploitation in *Xiu Xiu*.

Yet the director and her film marketers are keen to sell *Xiu Xiu* to American audiences as a beautiful love story set in sumptuous National Geographic landscape—"a fable that redeemed the innocence of a lost generation." gushes the press kit "[about] the timeless imagination of love." And, based on the pedigree of the film's creators and Chen's press statements and payment of the fine to the Chinese authorities, it is hard to believe that Chen intended her product as an indictment of the government that gave her the shot at stardom at an early age.

Nonetheless, Art asserts itself in curious ways. Yan Geling tells us that *Xiu Xiu* was based on the true life story of a woman she herself had known as a child and met after the Cultural Youth Revolution. All that happened to the screen Xiu Xiu happened to her friend—except that the *real* Xiu Xiu lived. "She told me how she suffered psychologically and physically," says Yan in her press statement. "But she managed not to lose herself, or to lose her hope."

Interestingly, Chen and Yan chose not to make a film about the triumph of human hope over circumstances. They preferred a very different ending. Their coda is a sharp, well-aimed stab of political criticism—a singular gesture, but a powerful one.

Joan Chen's public attitude about her film, which jars so interestingly with the message of the film itself, perhaps reflects her generation's own schizophrenic uncertainty about the system that has sculpted their careers and run their lives. She frames an interesting question: Can someone made successful by her own political system publicly turn against it? The director's reaction to her country proves that despite the Western press's ceaseless commentary on how China chooses to handle its domestic affairs, there are no clear-cut answers as to who is in the right. The Cultural Youth Movement was a horrific enterprise, but Chen and Yan claim they can see beauty in it—a kind of beauty paired with regret and a latent anger at what had to happen.

But those of us who didn't share their upbringing and can't see much "sweet" in their bittersweet tale, may find it difficult to be distracted from the bleak conclusions prompted by the film. One may speculate about the filmmakers' intent in dressing up a brutal tragedy in the colors of romance; one may incline to blame the distorting forces of film marketing, yet the film's final moments leave little doubt about Chen and Yan's intentions. The tragedy that both Xiu Xiu and Lao Jin share as exploited peoples on the lowest rung of a gigantic bureaucracy form a tidy and chilling parable of the horrors of absolutism. Despite yards of film dedicated to breathtaking landscapes and dimpled smiles, Chen's creation is just about as sweet as cyanide.

"Power kills, and absolute power kills absolutely," quotes Iris Chang in her 1997 work, *The Rape of Nanking,* when discussing the dynamics of war and oppression. The phrase came from R.J. Rummel's book, *Death by Government,* a study of genocide and government-motivated mass murder, and could easily have served as a sound bite for *Xiu Xiu.* Like *The Rape of Nanking,* Joan Chen's film testifies to the effects of absolute power when pursued to its logical conclusion. Chang, however, was writing about the genocidal horrors that Japanese troops had visited upon the Chinese during World War II. The fact that postwar China could revisit such rapes upon its own children during peace time makes Chen's indictment all the more scorching.

LOS ANGELES TIMES, 6/25/99, Calendar/p. 9, Kevin Thomas

During the Cultural Revolution (1967-76), some 7.5 million urban Chinese teens were "sent down" for "re-education," working alongside peasants often in the remotest regions of a vast country. These young people, often from educated, middle-class families, were to return home eventually, having been indoctrinated in the government's dream of creating a communist utopia—but just if or when became increasingly uncertain as time passed.

Joan Chen's prize-laden "Xiu Xiu: The Sent Down Girl" is intended to honor that last generation who came of age during that brutal period. Adapted by Chen and Yan Geling from Yan's novella "Heavenly Bath," the beautiful but devastating "Xiu Xiu" tells the story of the daughter of a clothing factory worker in the city of Chengdu. Xiu Xiu (Lu Lu) is a pretty, vivacious girl, nourished in a poor but loving family. When she is taken away, as part of a large group, she feels as if she is off to an exciting adventure.

After a year of service at a camp in the country, where the young people undergo tedious indoctrination in communism and work the fields, she is eager to return to her family. It is a cruel irony that her commander rewards her diligence with six months of "private training" to prepare her for the prestigious White River Iron Girls Cavalry. What this means is that Xiu Xiu is to be transported to the plains of Tibet, where she will learn how to train horses and yak herding from a Tibetan, Lao Jin (Lopsang), renowned as a rifleman as well as for his skill with horses.

Lao Jin, however, is even better known for having been emasculated by the Chinese. A stocky, kindly middle-aged man with an earthy sense of humor, Lao Jin has come to terms with his fate by living a simple, nomadic existence. He's used to being jeered at over his fate, and he can take in stride Xiu Xiu's contempt for him as she settles in the much-patched army tent she is to share with him. As Xiu Xiu grows increasingly unhappy and restless over her fate, Lao Jin falls ever more deeply, if silently, in love with her, caring for and protecting her in ways she lacks the capacity to appreciate.

When six months pass and no one comes to take her home, she becomes increasing overcome with despair, propelling her into a downward spiral. The fate that awaits her, which on one level embodies Tibetan legend, is scarcely less dire than the one accorded to "The Last Emperor's" beautiful empress, played so memorably by Chen herself.

The connection between what happened to Lao Jin and what happens to Xiu Xiu is unmistakable and constitutes a condemnation of the terrible savagery of the Cultural Revolution and of China's longtime oppression of Tibet. (Chen was fined heavily by the government for having made this film and was further barred from filmmaking in China.) The ability to express the utmost suffering and degradation with detachment and beautiful imagery is a major constant of Asian cinema. In its impassioned concerns and in the lyrical simplicity of its style, "Xiu Xiu" is, in fact, in the classic manner, and Lu Yue's glorious camera work and Johnny Chen's soaring score contribute strongly to this effect.

"Xiu Xiu" is remarkably mature for a first work, and Chen, accomplished actress that she is, displays an assured, understated skill in inspiring so young a talent as Lu Lu (she was 15 at the time of filming) in expressing so faultlessly Xiu Xiu's wrenching transformations. At the same time, she knows how to draw upon Lopsang's experience and solid presence to anchor her film. There's no denying that "Xiu Xiu" gets tougher and tougher to take, but it leaves you rewarded with the lingering intensity of its impact.

NEW YORK, 5/16/99, p. 59, Peter Rainer

Joan Chen's directing debut, *Xiu Xiu: The Sent Down Girl*, is an uneven, sometimes affecting coming-of-age story about a 15-year-old city girl (Lu Lu) during China's Cultural Revolution who is removed from her family and assigned to live on the remote plains of Tibet with Lao Jin (Lopsang), a middle-aged Tibetan horse trainer. The relationship between the maidenly Xiu Xiu and Lao Jin, who was emasculated in a war and secretly loves her, is a shade too Chaplinesque. Chen wants us to appreciate her film as a bittersweet fable, but what we see is too grotesquely unsettling for that.

NEW YORK POST, 5/7/99, p. 52, Hannah Brown

"Xie Xiu: The Sent Down Girl," the accomplished directorial debut of actress Joan Chen, has the power and sweep of a Chinese "Tess."

Set during the Cultural Revolution, "Xiu Xiu" tells the story of a 16-year-old city girl who is forcibly "sent down" to the countryside, as were millions of urban youth.

Excited by the chance to serve the government, Xiu Xiu (pronounced "Show Show") is chosen to learn horse-herding so she can join the Girls' Iron Cavalry.

She is sent to a remote, rural area to be trained by Lao Jin (Lopsang), a Tibetan who was castrated years ago when he was a prisoner of war. Xiu Xiu is dismayed that the two of them must share a tent.

But although Lao Jin's country-bumpkin habits annoy her, he never harms her and is actually quite considerate, in his strange way.

After her apprenticeship is over, she waits for a party official to arrive and escort her home. But no one comes. A peddler shows up, telling her that the Iron Cavalry has been disbanded and most "educated youth" have gone back home.

Without the necessary permits, she can't return to her family. Convinced that the peddler has connections that will help her secure the documents she needs, Xiu Xiu sleeps with him—and all the cronies he sends to see her.

Isolated and abandoned by the authorities, Xiu Xiu falls into a downward spiral. Only Lao Jin tries to save her.

Set against the stark beauty of the Tibetan plains (masterfully photographed by Lu Yue), the tragic story—like "Tess"—shows the gradual corruption and victimization of a docile young woman.

It's also clearly a metaphor for the government's betrayal and manipulation of its own people, but the characters are so compelling, it doesn't feel heavy-handed.

Based on a novella by Yan Geling, the movie so angered the Chinese government that Chen (best known for her role as the empress in Bertolucci's "The Last Emperor") has been banned from working in her native China. The film itself has been banned there as well.

Lu Lu is beautiful but unfortunately inexpressive as the heroine. Still, there's real urgency and lyricism in "Xiu Xiu."

NEWSDAY, 5/7/99, Part II/p. B6, John Anderson

The mass relocation of China's urban youth during Mao's 10-year Cultural Revolution left an indelible mark on the country—and, of course, its movies. Many of the more prominent directors were "sent down" to the countryside in the late '60s and '70s, to become more rounded members of society (and get the corruption of the city out of their systems). That phenomenon and the way it scarred a generation is inseparable from what we've come to know as the best of contemporary Chinese cinema.

Joan Chen, the Shanghai-born actress best known for "The Last Emperor" and the TV series "Twin Peaks," was almost too young to have been a "sent down;" her acceptance by the Shanghai Film Studio's training program in 1975 made it a moot point (the Cultural Revolution ended in 1976). Still, for her debut as a director, Chen has been drawn to the story that reflects her generation's crisis, albeit in an almost apocryphal manner.

"Xiu Xiu: The Sent Down Girl," from the novella by Chen's co-screenwriter, Yan Geling, is about one young girl, who is sent to the grasslands along the Tibetan-Sichuan border and in her efforts to return home destroys herself. It's never quite clear that what happens to Xiu Xiu (Lu Lu) isn't a work of imagination: Narration—the last refuge of an uncertain director, unfortunately —comes from a neighbor boy (voice of Wang Luoyong) who's in love with Xiu Xiu, watches her board the trucks for the country and is ashamed because he lacks the courage to join her and has the right family connections to keep him exempt. He tells us that what follows is the story he's pieced together from second-hand reports and his own imagination—which, perhaps subconsciously, creates utter tragedy for his departing love.

"Xiu Xiu" is best at the beginning, more alive, with patriotic music crackling out of steel speakers and Chinese students giddy with the expectations of what they'll find. What Xiu Xiu (Lu Lu) expects is to go home after a year. But she's such an excellent worker she's sent to learn horse herding, so she can return and join an elite women's cavalry unit.

She's already crushed, but once she reaches the remote campsite of the mysterious Tibetan Lao Jin (Lopsang)—who becomes her teacher if not her protector—she's thoroughly defeated. Her friends have all started going home, through money or connections. All Xiu Xiu has are her looks, through which she incompetently tries to secure her freedom by sleeping with supposedly influential men, all of who treat her like less than a comrade.

You're born, you suffer, you die and Beijing doesn't care. That, basically, is the lesson of "Xiu Xiu: The Sent Down Girl." Xiu Xiu is beautiful—but so what? It has very little to do with the story, even cheapening it a bit. Would anything have occurred differently if she'd been homely? No, so the implication is that the waste of a beautiful young woman is even more tragic than that of a plain one. What matters far more is how we feel about Xiu Xiu—a social revolutionary Marxist princess if ever there's been one. To say she's unsympathetic is to put it mildly. As the noble, love-struck Lao Jin—renowned for having lost his male equipment in a tribal war—watches various men invade their tent, his misery is what really matters.

Chen has a decent eye for detail, but a heavy hand with the symbolism. When the first of Xiu Xiu's many lovers visit her at the tent, he offers her an apple, her trembling hand reaching out tentatively to receive it. The next thing we see are those hands, but now they're knitting a small sweater—and you know what that means. Running to meet her faithless seducer at the Saturday movies, she finds herself lost in a rainstorm of biblical proportions. And during a moment of truth that confounds all expectations and reason, Xiu Xiu knots a red kerchief tightly around her throat, thereby signifying the brutalities of both communism tyranny and clumsy allusion.

Xiu Xiu is all but sainted by the end of the film, and it's hard to fathom just why. She throws away her supposed virtue at the first opportunity and treats the noble Lao Jin like a servant. Xiu Xiu may have been sent down, but she should have been sent packing.

VILLAGE VOICE, 5/11/99, p. 72, Dennis Lim

Joan Chen's first movie as director, *Xiu Xiu: The Sent Down Girl,* is set in the mid '70s and concerns the Cultural Revolution practice of packing Chinese youngsters off to the countryside to work and be indoctrinated. Xiu Xiu (Lu Lu), one such "sent down" teenager, is assigned to the remote plains of Tibet, where she is stranded with a castrated herdsman (Lopsang). Still, he turns out to be a decent fellow (and, of course, no sexual threat); they bond, hesitantly and quite poignantly—until government officials show up, and Xiu Xiu accedes to their sexual advances in the hope that she will finally be allowed to return home.

Adapted from a novella, *Xiu Xiu* plays like an exploitative melodrama. The movie is competently filmed (the steppe landscapes and night skies are in fact gorgeous), but it's fundamentally misconceived. For a vastly more scrupulous and moving examination of Cultural Revolution fuckups on a young psyche, see *The Blue Kite*. Chen's film, which is methodically devastating and yet barely cognizant of the complicated psychology of the situations it hurls its characters into, has one main point to make—"This is tragic"—and knows precisely one way of making it: rub the viewer's face in the tragedy.

Also reviewed in:
CHICAGO TRIBUNE, 7/30/99, Friday/p. A, Monica Eng
NEW YORK TIMES, 5/7/99, p. E21, Stephen Holden
VARIETY, 3/2-8/98, p. 86, Derek Elley
WASHINGTON POST, 6/4/99, Weekend/p. 54, Desson Howe

AWARDS

ACADEMY OF MOTION PICTURE ARTS AND SCIENCES
72th Annual Academy Awards — March 26, 1999

BEST PICTURE — *American Beauty*
Other Nominees: *The Cider House Rules; The Green Mile; The Insider; The Sixth Sense*

BEST ACTOR — Kevin Spacey in *American Beauty*
Other Nominees: Russell Crowe in *The Insider*; Richard Farnsworth in *The Straight Story*; Sean Penn in *Sweet and Lowdown*; Denzel Washington in *The Hurricane*

BEST ACTRESS — Hilary Swank in *Boys Don't Cry*
Other Nominees: Annette Bening in *American Beauty*; Janet McTeer in *Tumbleweeds*; Julianne Moore in *The End of the Affair*; Meryl Streep in *Music of the Heart*

BEST SUPPORTING ACTOR — Michael Caine in *The Cider House Rules*
Other Nominees: Tom Cruise in *Magnolia*; Michael Clarke Duncan in *The Green Mile*; Jude Law in *The Talented Mr. Ripley*; Haley Joel Osment in *The Sixth Sense*

BEST SUPPORTING ACTRESS — Angelina Jolie in *Girl, Interrupted*
Other Nominees: Toni Collette in *The Sixth Sense*; Catherine Keener in *Being John Malkovich*; Samantha Morton in *Sweet and Lowdown*; Chloë Sevigny in *Boys Don't Cry*

BEST DIRECTOR — Sam Mendes for *American Beauty*
Other Nominees: Spike Jonze for *Being John Malkovich*; Lasse Hallstrom for *The Cider House Rules*; Michael Mann for *The Insider*; M. Night Shyamalan for *The Sixth Sense*

BEST FOREIGN-LANGUAGE FILM — *All About My Mother* (Spain)
Other Nominees: *Caravan* (Nepal); *East-West* (France); *Solomon and Gaenor* (U.K.); *Under the Sun* (Sweden)

BEST ORIGINAL SCREENPLAY — Alan Ball for *American Beauty*
Other Nominees: Charlie Kaufman for *Being John Malkovich*; Paul
Thomas Anderson for *Magnolia*; M. Night Shyamalan for *The Sixth
Sense*; Mike Leigh for *Topsy-Turvy*

BEST ADAPTED SCREENPLAY — John Irving for *The Cider House
Rules*
Other nominees: Alexander Payne and Jim Taylor for *Election*; Frank
Darabont for *The Green Mile*; Eric Roth and Michael Mann for *The
Insider*; Anthony Minghella for *The Talented Mr. Ripley*

BEST CINEMATOGRAPHY — Conrad L. Hall for *American Beauty*
Other Nominees: Roger Pratt for *The End of the Affair*; Dante Spinotti
for *The Insider*; Emmanuel Lubezki for *Sleepy Hollow*; Robert
Richardson for *Snow Falling on Cedars*

BEST FILM EDITING — Zach Staenberg for *The Matrix*
Other Nominees: Tariq Anwar and Christopher Greenbury for *American
Beauty*; Lisa Zeno Churgin for *The Cider House Rules*; William
Goldenberg, Paul Rubeil, and David Rosenbloom for *The Insider*;
Andrew Mondshein for *The Sixth Sense*

BEST ART DIRECTION — Rick Heinrichs with set decoration by Peter
Young for *Sleepy Hollow*
Other Nominees: Luciana Arrighi with set decoration by Ian Whittaker
for *Anna and the King*; David Gropman with set decoration by Beth
Rubino for *The Cider House Rules*; Roy Walker with set decoration by
Bruno Cesari for *The Talented Mr. Ripley*; Eve Stewart with set
decoration by John Bush for *Topsy-Turvy*

BEST COSTUME DESIGN — Linda Hemming for *Topsy-Turvy*
Other Nominees: Jenny Beavan for *Anna and the King*; Coleen Atwood
for *Sleepy Hollow*; Ann Roth and Gary Jones for *The Talented Mr.
Ripley*; Milena Canonero for *Titus*

BEST MAKE-UP — Christine Blundell and Trefor Proud for *Topsy-
Turvy*
Other Nominees: Michele Burke and Mike Smithson for *Austin Powers:
The Spy Who Shagged Me;* Greg Cannom for *Bicentennial Man*; Rick
Baker for *Life*

BEST ORIGINAL SCORE — John Corigliano for *The Red Violin*
Other Nominees: Thomas Newman for *American Beauty*; John Williams
for *Angela's Ashes*; Rachel Portman for *The Cider House Rules*; Gabriel
Yared for *The Talented Mr. Ripley*

BEST ORIGINAL SONG — "You'll Be in My Heart" from *Tarzan*, music and lyric by Phil Collins
Other Nominees: "Blame Canada" from *South Park: Bigger, Longer & Uncut*, music and lyric by Trey Parker and Marc Shaiman; "Music of My Heart" from *Music of the Heart*, music and lyric by Diane Warren; "Save Me" from *Magnolia*, music and lyric by Aimee Mann; "When She Loved Me" from *Toy Story 2*, music and lyric by Randy Newman

BEST SOUND — John Reitz, Gregg Rudloff, David Campbell, and David Lee for *The Matrix*
Other Nominees: Robert J. Litt, Elliot Tyson, Michael Herbick, and Willie D. Burton for *The Green Mile*; Andy Nelson, Doug Hemphill, and Lee Orloff for *The Insider*; Leslie Shatz, Chris Carpenter, Rick Kline, and Chris Munro for *The Mummy*; Gary Rydstrom, Tom Johnson, Shawn Murphy, John Midgley for *Star Wars: Episode One — The Phantom Menace*

BEST SOUND EFFECTS EDITING — Dane A. Davis for *The Matrix*
Other Nominees: Ren Klyce and Richard Hymns for *Fight Club*; Ben Burtt and Tom Bellfort for *Star Wars: Episode One — The Phantom Menace*

BEST VISUAL EFFECTS — John Gaeta, Janek Sirrs, Steve Courtley, and Jon Thum for *The Matrix*
Other Nominees: John Knoll, Dennis Muren, Scott Squires, and Rob Coleman for *Star Wars: Episode One — The Phantom Menace*; John Dykstra, Jerome Chen, Henry F. Anderson III, and Eric Ailard for *Stuart Little*

BEST DOCUMENTARY FEATURE — *One Day in September*
Other Nominees: *Buena Vista Social Club; Genghis Blues; On the Ropes; Speaking in Strings*

BEST DOCUMENTARY SHORT — *King Gimp*
Other Nominees: *Eyewitness; The Wildest Show in the South: The Angola Prison Rodeo*

BEST ANIMATED SHORT — *The Old Man and the Sea*
Other Nominees: *Humdrum; My Grandmother Ironed the King's Shirts; 3 Misses; When the Day Breaks*

BEST LIVE ACTION SHORT — *My Mother Dreams the Satan's Disciples in New York*
Other Nominees: *Bror, Min Bror* (Ties and Nico); *Killing Joe; Kleingeld (Small Change); Major and Minor Miracles*

HONORARY AWARD

Andrzej Wajda

IRVING THALBERG MEMORIAL AWARD

Warren Beatty

GORDON E. SAWYER AWARD

Roderick T. Ryan "for creating a film processor for use in special effects and whose technological contributions have brought credit to the industry."

JOHN A. BONNER MEDAL OF COMMENDATION

Edmund M. Di Giulio and Takuo Miyagashima "for outstanding service and dedication in upholding the high standards of the Academy of Motion Picture Arts and Sciences."

AWARD OF COMMENDATION

Barry M. Stultz and Milton Jan Friedman "for the development and implementation of an environmentally responsible program to recycle or destroy discarded motion picture prints."

SCIENTIFIC AND ENGINEERING AWARDS

Fritz Gabriel Bauer "for the concept, design and engineering of the Moviecam Superlight 35mm Motion Picture Camera."

Iain Neil, Rick Gelbard and Panavision, Inc. "For the optical design, mechanical design, and for the development of the Millennium Camera System viewfinder."

James Moultrie, Mike Salter and Mark Craig Gerchman "for the mechanical design and optical design of the Cooke S4 Range of Fixed Focal Length Lenses for 35mm motion picture photography."

Nat Tiffen "for the production of high-quality, durable laminated color filters for motion picture photography."

Marlowe A. Pichel "for development of the process for manufacturing Electro-Formed Metal Reflectors which, when combined with the DC Short Arc Xenon Lamp, became the worldwide standard for motion picture projection systems."

L. Ron Schmidt "for the concept, design and engineering of the Linear Loop Film Projectors."

Huw Gwilym, Karl Lynch and Mark Crabtree "for the design and development of the AMS/Neve-Logic Digital Film console for motion picture sound mixing."

Leslie Drever "for the design and development of the Light Wave microphone windscreens and isolation mounts from Light Wave Systems."

Vivienne Dyer and Chris Woolf "for the design and development of the Rycote Microphone Windshield Modular System."

Nick Phillips "for the design and development of the three-axis Libra III remote control camera head."

TECHNICAL ACHIEVEMENT AWARDS

Hoyt H. Yeatman, Jr. and John C. Brewer "for the identification and diagnosis leading to the elimination of the "red fringe" artifact in traveling matte composite photography."

Richard C. Sehlin, Dr. Mitchell J. Bogdanowicz and Mary L. Schmoeger "for the concept, design and development of the Eastman Lamphouse Modification Filters."

NATIONAL SOCIETY OF FILM CRITICS
January 8, 2000

BEST PICTURE (tie) — *Being John Malkovich* and *Topsy-Turvy*

BEST ACTOR — Russell Crowe in *The Insider*

BEST ACTRESS — Reese Witherspoon in *Election*

BEST SUPPORTING ACTOR — Christopher Plummer in *The Insider*

BEST SUPPORTING ACTRESS — Chloe Sevigny in *Boys Don't Cry*

BEST DIRECTOR — Mike Leigh for *Topsy-Turvy*

BEST SCREENPLAY — Charlie Kaufman for *Being John Malkovich*

BEST FOREIGN-LANGUAGE FILM — *Autumn Tales* (France)

BEST DOCUMENTARY — *Buena Vista Social Club*

BEST CINEMATOGRAPHY — Conrad L. Hall for *American Beauty*

NEW YORK FILM CRITICS CIRCLE
January 9, 2000

BEST PICTURE — *Topsy-Turvy*

BEST ACTOR — Richard Farnsworth in *The Straight Story*

BEST ACTRESS — Hilary Swank in *Boys Don't Cry*

BEST SUPPORTING ACTOR — John Malkovich in *Being John Malkovich*

BEST SUPPORTING ACTRESS — Catherine Keener in *Being John Malkovich*

BEST DIRECTOR — Mike Leigh for *Topsy-Turvy*

BEST SCREENPLAY — Jim Taylor and Alexander Payne for *Election*

BEST CINEMATOGRAPHER — Freddie Francis for *The Straight Story*

BEST FOREIGN-LANGUAGE FILM — *All About My Mother* (Spain)

BEST DOCUMENTARY — *Buena Vista Social Club*

BEST ANIMATED FILM — *South Park: Bigger, Longer and Uncut*

BEST FIRST FEATURE — Spike Jonze for *Being John Malkovich*

SPECIAL AWARD — Manny Farber "for his distinguished contribution to film criticism."

GOLDEN GLOBE
57th Annual Awards — January 23, 2000

BEST PICTURE (drama) — *American Beauty*

BEST PICTURE (musical or comedy) — *Toy Story 2*

BEST ACTOR (drama) — Denzel Washington in *The Hurricane*

BEST ACTOR (musical or comedy) — Jim Carrey in *Man on the Moon*

BEST ACTRESS (drama) — Hilary Swank in *Boys Don't Cry*

BEST ACTRESS (musical or comedy) — Janet McTeer in *Tumbleweeds*

BEST SUPPORTING ACTOR — Tom Cruise in *Magnolia*

BEST SUPPORTING ACTRESS — Angelina Jolie in *Girl, Interrupted*

BEST DIRECTOR — Sam Mendes for *American Beauty*

BEST SCREENPLAY — Alan Ball for *American Beauty*

BEST ORIGINAL SCORE — Ennio Morricone for *The Legend of 1900*

BEST ORIGINAL SONG — "You'll Be in My Heart" from *Tarzan*, music and lyrics by Phil Collins

BEST FOREIGN-LANGUAGE FILM — *All About My Mother* (Spain)

CECIL B. DeMILLE AWARD FOR LIFETIME ACHIEVEMENT — Barbra Streisand

LOS ANGELES FILM CRITICS ASSOCIATION
January 19, 2000

BEST PICTURE — *The Insider*

BEST ANIMATED FILM — *The Iron Giant*

BEST ACTOR — Russell Crowe in *The Insider*

BEST ACTRESS — Hilary Swank in *Boys Don't Cry*

BEST SUPPORTING ACTOR — Christopher Plummer in *The Insider*

BEST SUPPORTING ACTRESS — Chloe Sevigny in *Boys Don't Cry*

BEST DIRECTOR — Sam Mendes for *American Beauty*

BEST SCREENPLAY — Charlie Kaufman for *Being John Malkovich*

BEST CINEMATOGRAPHY — Dante Spinotti for *The Insider*

BEST SCORE — Trey Parker and Marc Shaiman for *South Park: Bigger, Longer and Uncut*

BEST PRODUCTION DESIGN — Rich Heinrichs for *Sleepy Hollow*

BEST FOREIGN-LANGUAGE FILM — *All About My Mother* (Spain)

BEST DOCUMENTARY FILM — *The Buena Vista Social Club*

DOUGLAS EDWARDS/INDEPENDENT/EXPERIMENTAL FILM/ VIDEO AWARD — Owen Land

NEW GENERATION AWARD — Alexander Payne and Jim Taylor for *Citizen Ruth* and *Election*

SPECIAL CITATION — Rick Schmidlin and Roger Mayer of Turner Classic Movies for their work on the re-creation and presentation of Erich Von Stroheim's *Greed*

NATIONAL BOARD OF REVIEW
January 18, 2000

BEST PICTURE — *American Beauty*

BEST ACTOR — Russell Crowe in *The Insider*

BEST ACTRESS — Janet McTeer in *Tumbleweeds*

BEST SUPPORTING ACTOR — Philip Seymour Hoffman in *The Talented Mr. Ripley*

BEST SUPPORTING ACTRESS — Julianne Moore in *A Map of the World, An Ideal Husband,* and *Cookie's Fortune*

BEST DIRECTOR — Anthony Minghella for *The Talented Mr. Ripley*

CAREER ACHIEVEMENT AWARD — Clint Eastwood

BEST FOREIGN-LANGUAGE FILM — *All About My Mother* (Spain)

BEST DOCUMENTARY — *The Buena Vista Social Club*

BEST SCREENPLAY — John Irving for *The Cider House Rules*

ENSEMBLE ACTING AWARD — The cast of *Magnolia*

BREAKTHROUGH PERFORMER (tie) — Hilary Swank in *Boys Don't Cry* and Wes Bentley in *American Beauty*

SPECIAL FILMMAKING AWARD — Tim Robbins for writing and directing *The Cradle Will Rock*

FREEDOM OF EXPRESSION AWARD — Michael Mann for *The Insider*

INTERNATIONAL FREEDOM OF EXPRESSION AWARD — Joan Chen for *Xiu Xiu*

BILLY WILDER AWARD — John Frankenheimer

CANNES FILM FESTIVAL
52nd Annual Awards — May 16, 1999

BEST PICTURE (Golden Palm Award) — *Rosetta* (Belgium-France)

BEST DIRECTOR — Pedro Almodovar for *All About My Mother*

BEST ACTOR — Emmanuel Schotte in *Humanity*

BEST ACTRESS (tie) — Séverine Caneele in *Humanity* and *Emilie* Dequennne in *Rosetta*

GRAND PRIX — *Humanity* (France)

JURY PRIZE — *The Letter* (Spain)

BEST SCREENPLAY — Yuri Arabov and Marina Koreneve for *Moloch*

TECHNICAL PRIZE — Tu Juhua for *The Emperor and The Assassin*

CAMERA D'OR (Best First Film) — *Throne of Death*

PALME D'OR (Short Film) — *When the Day Breaks* (Canada)

JURY PRIZE (Short Film)— (tie) *So-Pojong* (South Korea) and *Stop* (France)

FIPRESCI (INTERNATIONAL FILM CRITICS) — *New Dawn* (France)

INDEX

CAST

PRODUCERS

Stewart, Annie, 833, 935
Stillerman, Joel, 1471
Stillman, Matthew, 1089
Stipe, Michael, 152
Stipetic, Lucki, 974
Stoff, Erwin, 120, 898
Stone, Ed, 637
Stone, Matt, 1255
Stone, Oliver, 84, 309
Stott, Jeffrey, 1298
Stover, Susan, 1280
Stratton, Richard, 1542
Straub, Laurens, 1480
Stroh, Etchie, 304, 935
Stroller, Louis A., 220
Styler, Trudie, 825
Sudzin, Jeffrey, 697
Sughand, Jhamu, 416
Suzuki, Toshio, 1101
Sweeney, Mary, 1302
Swerdlow, Ezra, 1542
Swofford, Scott, 1042

Tadross, Michael, 1395
Tannebaum, Ted, 106, 1185, 1495
Tarantino, Quentin, 613
Taylor, Jennifer Maytorena, 1069
Taylor, Michael, 730
Taylor, Stephen, 592
Taymor, Julie, 1426
Tchalgadjieff, Stephane, 178
Teitler, William, 677
Teper, Meir, 321
Theobald, Jeremy, 544
Thiltges, Jani, 1571
Thomas, Emma, 544
Thomas, Jeremy, 28

Thomas, Mark, 392
Thomas, Philip E., 1059
Thompson, Barnaby, 691
Thompson, David M., 881
Thompson, John, 631
Thomson, Peggy, 175
Threadgill, Walter L., 1261
Tianming, Wu, 769
Ticotin, Marcus, 1068
Tinchant, Maurice, 1201
Tisch, Steve, 825
Toberoff, Marc, 978
Todd, Jennifer, 120, 697
Todd, Suzanne, 120, 697
Todman, Bill, Jr., 1544
Toffler, Van, 440, 1495, 1504, 1573
Toga, Yutaka, 1077
Tokuma, Yasuyoshi, 1101
Tollefson, Rhonda, 470
Tollin, Mike, 1504
Tornatore, Francesco, 790
Tornell, Lisa, 747
Townsend, Clayton, 84, 1541
Townsend, Pete, 735
Tozzi, Riccardo, 1362
Tsai, Fabienne, 1197
Tsuei, Cecile Shah, 1586
Tsurmi, Yuichi, 1077
Tucker, Paul, 516
Tucker, Ryan, 350
Turturro, John, 700
Tyrer, William, 1265

Ufland, Harry J., 1245

Urbanski, Douglas, 1089
Urdang, Leslie, 1550
Usborne, Alex, 1

Vachon, Christine, 236, 703
Vaines, Colin, 134
Vajna, Andrew G., 1387
Valdes, David, 623
Van Damme, Jean-Claude, 1502
van Huystee, Pieter, 1500
Van Rellim, Tim, 1126
Vasconcelos, José Luis, 1374
Vaughn, Matthew, 825
Vicente, Joana, 1416
Victor, Daniel J., 571, 1479
Vignet, Dominique, 676
Villard, Jason, 1476
Vilsmaier, Joseph, 643
Viviano, Bettina Sofia, 1421
Vlessing, Marc, 577
Voeten, Peter J., 824
von Fürstenberg, Molly, 142
Vonier, 1197

Wachowski, Andy, 898
Wachowski, Larry, 898
Wachsberger, Patrick, 833
Wagner, Ellen Casey, 1550
Wagner, Paul, 1550
Ward, Peter, 1235

Waringo, Claude, 1571
Warren, Harold, 1142
Waterman, Steve, 1315
Weber, Eric, 1324
Weber, Marco, 1384
Webster, Paul, 982
Weiner, Jane, 673
Weinstein, Bob, 134, 292, 631, 667, 713, 734, 881, 970, 982, 1063, 1084, 1101, 1203, 1366
Weinstein, Harvey, 134, 292, 631, 667, 713, 734, 881, 970, 982, 1063, 1084, 1101, 1203
Weinstein, Paula, 59, 800
Weisler, Michele, 1294
Weiss, Robert K., 1331
Weitz, Chris, 50
West, Howard, 871
Weston, Brad, 631
Whitten, Brian, 113
Wick, Douglas, 597, 1315
Wilhite, Tom, 1084
Willenson, Seth, 1206
Williams, Bernie, 225
Williams, Lona, 405
Williams, Marsha Garces, 741
Williams, Michael, 939
Williams, Robin, 741
Willis, David, 243
Wilson, Chapin John, 634
Wilson, Colin, 648
Wilson, Hugh, 204, 413
Wilson, Jim, 906
Wilson, Michael G., 1577
Wilson, Michael Henry, 712

Windom, William, 1486
Winkler, Irwin, 116
Winspeare, Edoardo, 1082
Winter, Ralph, 727
Witt, Paul Junger, 1407
Witten, Brian, 352
Woertz, Greg, 1011
Wolf, Wallace, 468
Wolfe, Steven J., 1142, 1489
Wonder, Ellen, 1507
Woods, Cary, 756
Woods, James, 80
Woolley, Stephen, 134, 455, 523, 706
Workman, Chuck, 1250
Wright, Kevin P., 350

Yamagata, Hiro, 1250
Yasuda, Masahiro, 9
Yerxa, Ron, 440, 557, 1573
Yoshida, Takio, 1512
Yoshikawa, Choji, 1093

Zal, Roxana, 262
Zane, Billy, 690
Zannoni, Giovannella, 1362
Zanuck, Lili Fini, 1464
Zanuck, Richard D., 1464
Zarrin, Ali Reza, 299
Zemeckis, Robert, 674
Zickler, Thomas, 772
Zide, Warren, 50
Ziehl, Scott, 262
Zimbert, Jonathan A., 289
Zock, Joseph A., 1250
Zweibel, Alan, 1298

DIRECTORS

Abdykalykov, Aktan, 161
Abraham, Adam, 868
Abugov, Jeff, 896
Algar, James, 510
Allen, Woody, 1332
Allouache, Merzak, 848
Almodóvar, Pedro, 19
Altman, Robert, 304
Amenábar, Alejandro, 1049
Amiel, Jon, 470
Anders, Allison, 1321
Anderson, Paul Thomas, 859
Angelopoulos, Theo, 462, 474
Antonioni, Michelangelo, 178
Apted, Michael, 562, 1577
Araki, Gregg, 1265
Asher, John, 362
Assayas, Olivier, 787
Ataman, Kutlug, 831

Baichwal, Jennifer, 799
Banderas, Antonio, 321
Barker, Mike, 168
Barney, Matthew, 324
Belic, Roko, 588
Beresford, Bruce, 387
Bergman, Ingmar, 711
Berkowitz, Myles, 1476
Bernstein, Adam, 1224
Berri, Claude, 855
Bertolucci, Bernardo, 163
Besson, Luc, 912
Biffar, John, 1498
Bindler, S.R., 634
Bird, Antonia, 1126
Bird, Brad, 735
Blake, Tessa, 539
Block, Doug, 673
Bolotin, Craig, 810
Brannon, Ash, 1445
Breillat, Catherine, 1154
Brizzi, Gaëtan, 510

Brodie, Kevin, 375
Brooks, Albert, 963
Brougher, Hilary, 1280
Brownell, Ian, 1425
Bruno, John, 1515
Buck, Chris, 1354
Buck, Jeanette L., 1059
Bui, Tony, 1416
Burnett, Robert Meyer, 566
Burstein, Nanette, 1043
Burton, Tim, 1238
Butoy, Hendel, 510

Campion, Jane, 667
Carnahan, Joe, 210
Carroll, Willard, 1084
Castellaneta, P.J., 1142
Chen, Joan, 1586
Chéreau, Patrice, 1402
Chiten, Laurel, 752
Cinciripini, Tony, 659
Clark, Bob, 136

Clark, Larry, 80
Cohen, Paul, 1561
Columbus, Chris, 181
Corrente, Michael, 1063
Craven, Wes, 970
Cristofer, Michael, 216
Cronenberg, David, 479

Darabont, Frank, 623
Dardenne, Jean-Pierre, 1162
Dardenne, Luc, 1162
De Bont, Jan, 648
Decaux-Thomlet, Françoise, 848
de la Iglesia, Alex, 333
Demme, Ted, 807
Diamond, Matthew, 330
Dickerson, Ernest, 209
di Florio, Paola, 1264
Doueiri, Ziad, 1532
Dragojevic, Srdjan, 1583

Ducastel, Olivier, 750
Dudgan, Dennis, 1315
Dugowson, Martine, 1100
Duigan, John, 947
Duncan, Peter, 824
Dupeyron, François, 848
Dvortsevoy, Sergeï, 666

Eastwood, Clint, 1464
Egoyan, Atom, 516
Eichinger, Bernd, 596
Elders, Kevin, 1215
Elliott, Scott, 888
Erdevicki-Charap, Mira, 198
Evan, David, 523

Fall, Jim, 1456
Famuyiwa, Rick, 1573
Fancher, Hampton, 931
Faucon, Philippe, 848
Fellini, Federico, 1013

SCREENWRITERS

CINEMATOGRAPHERS

EDITORS

MUSIC

PRODUCTION CREW